Peterson's
How to Get Money for College
Financing Your Future Beyond Federal Aid

2011

$$E = MC^2$$

PETERSON'S
A nelnet COMPANY

About Peterson's

To succeed on your lifelong educational journey, you will need accurate, dependable, and practical tools and resources. That is why Peterson's is everywhere education happens. Because whenever and however you need education content delivered, you can rely on Peterson's to provide the information, know-how, and guidance to help you reach your goals. Tools to match the right students with the right school. It's here. Personalized resources and expert guidance. It's here. Comprehensive and dependable education content—delivered whenever and however you need it. It's all here.

For more information, contact Peterson's, 2000 Lenox Drive, Lawrenceville, NJ 08648; 800-338-3282 Ext. 54229.

© 2010 Peterson's, a Nelnet company

Previous editions published as *Peterson's College Money Handbook* © 1983, 1984, 1985, 1986, 1987, 1988, 1989, 1990, 1991, 1996, 1997, 1998, 1999, 2000, 2001 2002, 2003, 2004, 2005, 2006, 2007, 2008, 2009 and as *Paying Less for College* © 1992, 1993, 1994, 1995

Facebook® and Facebook logos are registered trademarks of Facebook, Inc. Twitter™ and Twitter logos are registered trademarks of Twitter, Inc. Neither Facebook, Inc. nor Twitter, Inc. were involved in the production of this book and make no endorsement of this product.

Stephen Clemente, Managing Director, Publishing and Institutional Research; Bernadette Webster, Director of Publishing; Jill C. Schwartz, Editor; Ken Britschge, Research Project Manager; Jim Ranish, Research Associate; Phyllis Johnson, Programmer; Ray Golaszewski, Publishing Operations Manager; Linda M. Williams, Composition Manager

ISSN 1089-831X
ISBN-13: 978-0-7689-2886-0
ISBN-10: 0-7689-2886-9

Printed in the United States of America

10 9 8 7 6 5 4 3 2 1   12 11 10

Twenty-eighth Edition

By producing this book on recycled paper (40% post consumer waste) 250 trees were saved.

Other Recommended Titles

Peterson's Scholarships, Grants & Prizes
Peterson's Best Scholarships for the Best Students (available December 2010)

Contents

A Note from the Peterson's Editors

The news media seem to constantly remind us that a college education is expensive. It certainly appears to be beyond the means of many Americans. The sticker price for four years at state-supported colleges can be more than $45,000, and private colleges and universities can cost more than $150,000. And these numbers continue to rise.

But there is good news. The system operates to provide the needed money so that most families and students are able to afford a college education while making only a reasonable financial sacrifice. However, because the college financial aid system is complex, finding the money is often easier said than done. That is why the process demands study, planning, calculation, flexibility, filling out forms, and meeting deadlines. Fortunately, for most people, it can produce positive results. There are many ways to manage college costs and many channels through which you can receive help. Be sure to take full advantage of the opportunities that have been opened up to students and their families by the many organizations, foundations, and businesses that have organized to help you with the burden of college expenses.

For nearly forty years, Peterson's has given students and parents the most comprehensive, up-to-date information on how to get their fair share of the financial aid pie. *Peterson's How to Get Money for College* is both a quick reference and a comprehensive resource that puts valuable information about college costs and financial aid opportunities at your fingertips.

■ **The ABCs of Paying for College** provides insight into federal financial aid programs that are available, offers an overview of the financial aid landscape, walks you through the process of filing for aid, and provides proven tips on how to successfully navigate the financial aid process to obtain the federal, state, and institutional aid you deserve.

■ The **Quick-Reference Chart** offers a snapshot comparison of the financial aid programs available at more than 2,100 four-year institutions across the country.

■ The **Profiles of College Financial Aid Programs** provide unbiased financial aid data for each of the more than 2,100 four-year institutions listed.

■ The **Appendix** lists the state scholarship and grant programs offered by all fifty states and the District of Columbia.

■ The six **Indexes** included in the back of the book allow you to search for specific award programs based on a variety of criteria, including merit-based awards, athletic grants, ROTC programs, and much more.

Join Peterson's financial aid conversation on Facebook® and Twitter™ at www.facebook.com/pay4undergrad and www.twitter.com/pay4undergrad. Peterson's resources are available to help you find your slice of the financial aid pie.

Peterson's publishes a full line of books—financial aid, education exploration, test prep, and career preparation. Peterson's publications can be found at high school guidance offices, college libraries and career centers, and your local bookstore and library. Peterson's books are now also available as eBooks.

We welcome any comments or suggestions you may have about this publication. Your feedback will help us make educational dreams possible for you—and others like you.

The ABCs of Paying for College

A Guide to Financing Your Child's College Education

Don Betterton

Given the lifelong benefit of a college degree (college graduates are projected to earn in a lifetime $1 million more than those with only a high school diploma), higher education is a worthwhile investment. However, it is also an expensive one made even more difficult to manage by cost increases that have outpaced both inflation and gains in family income. This reality of higher education economics is that paying for a child's college education is a dilemma that shows no sign of getting easier.

Because of the high cost involved (even the most inexpensive four-year education at a public institution costs about $10,000 a year), good information about college budgets and strategies for reducing the "sticker price" is essential. You have made a good start by taking the time to read *Peterson's How to Get Money for College*. In the pages that follow, you will find valuable information about the four main sources of aid—federal, state, institutional, and private. Before you learn about the various programs, however, it will be helpful if you have an overview of how the college financial aid system operates and what long-range financing strategies are available.

Financial Aid

Financial aid refers to money that is awarded to a student, usually in a "package" that consists of gift aid (commonly called a scholarship or grant), a student loan, and a campus job.

College Costs

The starting point for organizing a plan to pay for your child's college education is to make a good estimate of the yearly cost of attendance. You can use the **College Cost Worksheet** on the next page to do this.

To estimate your college costs for 2011–12, refer to the tuition and fees and room and board figures shown in the **College Costs At-a-Glance** chart. If your child will commute from your home, use $2500 instead of the college's room and board charges and $900 for transportation. We have used $800 for books and $1500 for personal expenses. Finally, estimate the cost of two round

trips if your home is more than a few hundred miles from the college. Add the items to calculate the total budget. You should now have a reasonably good estimate of college costs for 2011–12. (To determine the costs for later years, adding 4 percent per year will probably give you a fairly accurate estimate.)

Do You Qualify for Need-Based Aid?

The next step is to evaluate whether or not you are likely to qualify for financial aid based on need. This step is critical, since more than 90 percent of the yearly total of $128 billion in student aid is awarded only after a determination is made that the family lacks sufficient financial resources to pay the full cost of college on its own. To judge your chance of receiving need-based aid, it is necessary to estimate an Expected Family Contribution (EFC) according to a government formula known as the Federal Methodology (FM). You can estimate how much you will be expected to contribute by referring to the EFC Calculator at http://www.finaid.org/calculators/quickefc.phtml.

Applying for Need-Based Aid

Because the federal government provides about 67 percent of all aid awarded, the application and need evaluation process is controlled by Congress and the U.S. Department of Education. The application is the Free Application for Federal Student Aid, or FAFSA. In addition, nearly every state that offers student assistance uses the federal government's system to award its own aid. Furthermore, in addition to arranging for the payment of federal and state aid, many colleges use the FAFSA to award their own funds to eligible students. (Note: In addition to the FAFSA, some colleges also ask the family to complete the CSS/Financial Aid PROFILE® application.)

The FAFSA is your "passport" to receiving your share of the billions of dollars awarded annually in need-based aid. Even if you're uncertain as to whether or not you qualify for need-based aid, everyone who might need assistance in financing an

College Cost Worksheet

	College 1	College 2	College 3	Commuter College
Tuition and Fees	_____	_____	_____	_____
Room and Board	_____	_____	_____	$2,500
Books	$ 800	$ 800	$ 800	$ 750
Personal Expenses	$1,500	$1,500	$1,500	$1,500
Travel	_____	_____	_____	$ 900
Total Budget	_____	_____	_____	_____

education should pick up a FAFSA from the high school guidance office after mid-November 2010. This form will ask for 2010 financial data, and it should be filed after January 1, 2011, in time to meet the earliest college or state scholarship deadline. Within two to four weeks after you submit the form, you will receive a summary of the FAFSA information, called the Student Aid Report, or SAR. The SAR will give you the EFC and also allow you to make corrections to the data you submitted.

You can also apply for federal student aid via the Internet using FAFSA on the Web. FAFSA on the Web can be accessed at www.fafsa.ed.gov. Both the student and at least one parent should apply for a federal PIN number at www.pin.ed.gov. The PIN number serves as your electronic signature when applying for aid on the Web. (Note: Many colleges provide the option to apply for early decision or early action admission. If you apply for this before January 1, 2011, which is prior to when the FAFSA can be used, follow the college's instructions. Many colleges use either PROFILE or their own application form for early admission candidates.)

Awarding Aid

About the same time you receive the SAR, the colleges you list will receive your FAFSA information so they can calculate a financial aid award in a package that typically includes aid from at least one of the major sources—federal, state, college, or private. In addition, the award will probably consist of a combination of a scholarship or a grant, a loan, and a campus job. These last two pieces—loan and job—are called self-help aid because they require effort on your child's part (that is, the aid must be either earned through work or paid back later). Scholarships or grants are outright gifts that have no such obligation.

How Need Is Calculated and Aid Is Awarded

	College 1	College 2
Total Cost of Attendance	$10,000	$ 24,000
− Expected Family Contribution	− 5,500	− 5,500
= Financial Need	$ 4,500	$ 18,500
− Grant Aid Awarded	− 675	−14,575
− Campus Job (Work-Study) Awarded	− 1,400	− 1,300
− Student Loan Awarded	− 2,425	− 2,625
= Unmet Need	0	0

Note: Sometimes an institution is unable to meet all need. The amount of unmet need is called "the gap."

Comparing Financial Aid Awards and Family Contribution Worksheet

	College 1	College 2	College 3
Cost of Attendance	_____	_____	_____
Aid Awarded	_____	_____	_____
Grant/Scholarship	_____	_____	_____
Loan	_____	_____	_____
Job	_____	_____	_____
Total Aid	_____	_____	_____
Expected Family Contribution	_____	_____	_____
Student Contribution	_____	_____	_____
Parent Contribution	_____	_____	_____

It is important that you understand each part of the package. You'll want to know, for example, how much does gift aid provide, the interest rate and repayment terms of the student loan, and how many hours per week the campus job requires. There should be an enclosure with the award letter that answers these questions. If not, make a list of your questions and call or visit the financial aid office.

Once you understand the terms of each item in the award letter, you should turn your attention to the "bottom line"—how much you will have to pay at each college where your child was accepted. In addition to understanding the aid award, this means having a good estimate of the college budget so you can accurately calculate how much you and your child will have to contribute. (Often, an aid package does not cover the entire need.) Colleges differ in how much detail they include in their award notifications. Many colleges provide full information—types and amounts of aid, yearly costs, and the EFC for the parent and student shares. If these important items are missing or incomplete, you can do the work on your own. (See the **Comparing Financial Aid Awards and Family Contribution Worksheet** on this page.) For example, if only the college's direct charges for tuition, room, and board are shown on the award letter, make your own estimate of indirect costs like books, personal expenses, and travel. Then subtract the total aid awarded from the yearly cost to get the EFC. A portion of that amount may be your child's contribution (35 percent of student assets and 50 percent of student earnings over $2200) and the remainder is the parental share. If you can afford this amount at your child's first-choice college, the financial aid system has worked well for you, and your child's college enrollment plans can go forward.

But if you think your EFC is too high, you should contact the college's financial aid office and ask whether additional aid is available. Many colleges, private high-cost colleges in particular, are enrollment-oriented—they are willing to work with families to help make attendance at their institutions possible. Most colleges also allow applicants to appeal their financial aid awards, the budget used for you, or any of the elements used to determine the family contribution, especially if there are extenuating circumstances or if the information has changed since the application was submitted. Some colleges may also reconsider an award based on a "competitive appeal," the submission of a more favorable award letter from another college.

If your appeal is unsuccessful and there is still a gap between the expected family contribution and what you feel you can pay from income and savings, you are left with two choices. One option is for your child to attend a college where paying your share of the bill will not be a problem. (This assumes that an affordable option was included on your child's original list of colleges, a wise admission application strategy.) The second is to look into alternate methods of financing. At this stage, parental loans and tuition payment plans are the best financing options. A parental loan can bring the yearly cost down to a manageable level by spreading payments over a number of years. This is the type of financing that families use when purchasing a home or automobile. A tuition payment plan is essentially a short-term loan and allows you to pay the costs over ten to twelve months. It is an option for families who have the resources available but need help with managing their cash flow.

Non-Need-Based Aid

Regardless of whether you might qualify for a need-based award, it is always worthwhile to look into merit, or non-need, scholarships from sources such as foundations, agencies, religious groups, and service organizations. For a family that isn't eligible for need-based aid, merit scholarships are the only form of gift aid available. If your child later qualifies for a need-based award, a merit scholarship can be quite helpful in providing additional resources if the aid does not fully cover the costs. Even if the college meets 100 percent of need, a merit scholarship reduces the self-help (loan and job) portion of an award.

In searching for merit-based scholarships, keep in mind that there are relatively few awards (compared to those that are need-based), and most of them are highly competitive. Use the following checklist when investigating merit scholarships.

- Take advantage of any scholarships for which your child is automatically eligible based on parents' employer benefits, military service, association or church membership, other affiliations, or student or parent attributes (ethnic background, nationality, etc.). Company or union tuition remissions are the most common examples of these awards.

- Look for other awards for which your child might be eligible based on the previous characteristics and affiliations but where there is a selection process and an application is required. Free computerized searches are available on the Internet. (You should not pay a fee for a scholarship search.) Peterson's free scholarship search can be accessed by logging on to www.petersons.com/finaid. Scholarship directories, such as *Peterson's Scholarships, Grants & Prizes*, which details more than 4,000 scholarship programs, are useful resources and can be found in bookstores, high school guidance offices, or public libraries.

- See if your state has a merit scholarship program.

- Look into national scholarship competitions. High school guidance counselors usually know about these scholarships. Examples of these awards are the National Merit® Scholarship Program, the Coca-Cola Scholarship, Gates Millennium Scholars, Intel Science Talent Search, and the U.S. Senate Youth Program.

- ROTC (Reserve Officers' Training Corps) scholarships are offered by the Army, Navy, Air Force, and Marine Corps. A full ROTC scholarship covers tuition, fees, textbook costs and, in some cases, a stipend. Acceptance of an ROTC scholarship entails a commitment to take military science courses and to serve for a specific number of years as an officer in the sponsoring branch of the service. Competition is heavy, and preference may be given to students in certain fields of study, such as engineering, languages, science, and health professions. Application procedures vary by service. Contact an armed services recruiter or high school guidance counselor for further information.

- Investigate community scholarships. High school guidance counselors usually have a list of these awards, and announcements are published in local newspapers. Most common are awards given by service organizations like the American Legion, Rotary International, and the local women's club.

- If your child is strong academically (for example, a National Merit Commended Student or better) or is very talented in fields such as athletics or performing/creative arts, you may want to consider colleges that offer their own merit awards to gifted students they wish to enroll. Refer to the Non-Need Scholarships for Undergraduates index.

In addition to merit scholarships, there are loan and job opportunities for students who do not qualify for need-based aid. Some

Note

A point of clarification about whether to put college savings in your name or your child's: If you are certain that your child will not be a candidate for need-based aid, there may be a tax advantage to accumulating money in his or her name. However, when it comes to maximizing aid eligibility, it is important to understand that student assets are assessed at a 20 percent rate and parental assets at about 5 percent. Therefore, if your college savings are in your child's name, it may be wise to reestablish title to these funds before applying for financial aid. You should contact your financial planner or accountant before making any modifications to your asset structure.

What Is CSS/Financial Aid PROFILE®?

There are many complexities in the financial aid process: knowing which aid is merit-based and which aid is need-based; understanding the difference between grants, loans, and work-study; and determining whether funds are from federal, state, institutional, or private sources.

In addition, the aid application process itself can be confusing. It can involve more than the Free Application for Federal Student Aid (FAFSA) and the Federal Methodology (FM). Many colleges feel that the federal aid system (FAFSA and FM) does not collect or evaluate information thoroughly enough for them to award their own institutional funds. These colleges have made an arrangement with the College Scholarship Service, a branch of the College Board, to establish a separate application system.

The application is called the CSS/Financial Aid PROFILE®, and the need-analysis formula is referred to as the Institutional Methodology (IM). If you apply for financial aid at one of the colleges that uses PROFILE, the admission material will state that PROFILE is required in addition to the FAFSA. You should read the information carefully and file PROFILE to meet the earliest college deadline. Before you can receive PROFILE, however, you must register, either by phone or through the Web (https://profileonline.collegeboard.com/index.jsp), providing enough basic information so the PROFILE package can be designed specifically for you. The FAFSA is free, but there is a charge for PROFILE. As with the FAFSA, PROFILE can be submitted via the Internet.

In addition to the requirement by certain colleges that you submit both the FAFSA and PROFILE (when used, PROFILE is always in addition to the FAFSA; it does not replace it), you should understand that each system has its own method for analyzing a family's ability to pay for college. The main differences between PROFILE's Institutional Methodology and the FAFSA's Federal Methodology are:

- PROFILE includes equity in the family home as an asset; the FAFSA doesn't.

- PROFILE takes a broader look at assets not included on the FAFSA.

- PROFILE expects a minimum student contribution, usually in the form of summer earnings; the FAFSA has no such minimum.

- PROFILE may collect information on the noncustodial parent; the FAFSA does not.

- PROFILE allows for more professional judgment than the FAFSA. Medical expenses, private secondary school costs, and a variety of special circumstances are considered under PROFILE, subject to the discretion of the aid counselor on campus.

- PROFILE includes information on assets not reported on the FAFSA, including life insurance, annuities, retirement plans, etc.

To summarize: PROFILE's Institutional Methodology tends to be both more complete in its data collection and more rigorous in its analysis than the FAFSA's Federal Methodology. When IM results are compared to FM results for thousands of applicants, IM will usually come up with a somewhat higher expected parental contribution than FM.

Creditworthiness

If you will be borrowing to pay for your child's college education, making sure you qualify for a loan is critical. For the most part, that means your credit record must be free of default or delinquency. You can check your credit history with one or more of the following three major credit bureaus and clean up any adverse information that appears. The numbers below will offer specific information on what you need to provide to obtain a report. All of the credit bureaus accept credit report requests over their Web sites. You will usually be asked to provide your full name, phone number, social security number, birth date, and addresses for the last five years. You are entitled to a free report from each bureau.

Equifax Credit Information
P.O. Box 740241
Atlanta, GA 30374
800-685-1111
http://www.equifax.com

Trans Union
800-888-4213
http://www.transunion.com

Experian
888-397-3742
http://www.experian.com

of the organizations that sponsor scholarships—for example, the Air Force Aid Society—also provide loans.

Work opportunities during the academic year are another type of assistance that is not restricted to aid recipients. Many colleges will, after assigning jobs to students on aid, open campus positions to all students looking for work. In addition, there are usually off-campus employment opportunities available to everyone.

Financing Your Child's College Education

"Financing" means putting together resources to pay the balance due the college over and above payments from the primary sources of aid—grants, scholarships, student loans, and jobs. Financing strategies are important because the high cost of a college education today often requires a family, whether or not it receives aid, to think about stretching its college payment beyond the four-year period of enrollment. For high-cost colleges, it is not unreasonable to think about a 10-4-10 plan: ten years of saving; four years of paying college bills out of current income, savings, and borrowing; and ten years to repay a parental loan.

Savings

Although saving for college is always a good idea, many families are unclear about its advantages. Some families do not save because after normal living expenses have been covered, they do not have much money to set aside. An affordable but regular savings plan through a payroll deduction is usually the answer to the problem of spending your entire paycheck every month.

The second reason why saving for college is not a high priority is the belief that the financial aid system penalizes a family by lowering aid eligibility. The Federal Methodology of

need determination is very kind to families that save. In fact, savings are ignored completely for most families that earn less than $50,000. Savings in the form of home equity, retirement plans, and most annuities are excluded from the calculation. And even when savings are counted, a maximum of 5 percent of the total is expected each year. In other words, if a family has $40,000 in savings after an asset protection allowance is considered, the contribution is no greater than $2000. Given the impact of compound interest it is easy to see that a long-term savings plan can make paying for college much easier.

A sensible savings plan is important because of the financial advantage of saving compared to borrowing. The amount of money students borrow for college is now greater than the amount they receive in grants and scholarships. With loans becoming so widespread, savings should be carefully considered as an alternative to borrowing. Your incentive for saving is that a dollar saved is a dollar not borrowed.

Borrowing

Once you've calculated your "bottom-line" parental contribution and determined that the amount is not affordable out of your current income and assets, the most likely alternative is borrowing. Beginning July 1, 2010, as a result of the Health Care and Education Reconciliation Act, federal student loans will no longer be made by private lenders under the Federal Family Education Loan (FFEL) Program. Instead, all new federal student loans will come directly from the U.S. Department of Education under the Direct Loan Program, which offers subsidized and unsubsidized (Stafford) loans for students, PLUS loans for parents and graduate/professional students, and consolidation loans for both students and parents. For additional information, go online to https://studentloans.gov/myDirectLoan/index.action or call 800-4-FED-AID (toll-free).

For the Direct PLUS Loan, parents must complete a Direct PLUS Loan application and promissory note, contained in a single form that can be obtained from a school's financial aid office. The yearly limit on a PLUS Loan is equal to the student's cost of attendance minus any other financial aid the student receives. For example, if your cost of attendance is $6000, and you receive $4,500 in other financial aid, your parents can borrow up to $1500. For 2010–11, the variable rate for PLUS Loans (in both the Direct and FFEL programs) is 3.27 percent. Interest is charged on a PLUS Loan from the date of the first disbursement until the loan is paid in full. A PLUS Loan made to the parent cannot be transferred to the student. The parent is responsible for repaying the PLUS Loan. For more details about PLUS Loans, visit www.direct.ed.gov/about.html.

Make Financial Aid Work for You

If you are like millions of families that benefit from financial aid, it is likely that your child's college plans can go forward without undue worry about the costs involved. The key is to understand the financial aid system and to follow the best path for your family. The result of good information and good planning should be that you will receive your fair share of the billions of dollars available each year and that the cost of college will not prevent your child from attending.

———————

Don Betterton is a former Director of Undergraduate Financial Aid at Princeton University.

Federal Financial Aid Programs

There are a number of sources of financial aid available to students: federal and state governments, private agencies, and the colleges themselves. In addition, there are three different forms of aid: grants, earnings, and loans.

The federal government is the single largest source of financial aid for students. In recent years, the U.S. Department of Education's student financial aid programs made more than $80 billion available in loans, grants, and other aid to 14 million students. At present, there are four federal grant programs—Federal Pell Grant, Federal Supplemental Educational Opportunity Grant (FSEOG), Academic Competitiveness Grant (ACG), and National Smart Grant (SMART). There are two federal loan programs: Federal Perkins Loan Program and the Direct Loan Program. The federal government also has a job program, Federal Work-Study Program (FWS), which helps colleges provide employment for students. In addition to the student aid programs, there are also tuition tax credits and deductions. They are the Hope Credit for freshmen and sophomores, the Lifetime Learning Credit for undergraduate students after their second year, the Tuition and Fees Tax Deduction, and the Student Loan Interest Tax Deduction. Also, there is AmeriCorps. AmeriCorps will pay the interest that is accrued on qualified student loans for members who complete the service program.

The majority of federal higher education loans are made in the Direct Loan Program, which makes available two kinds of loans: loans to students and PLUS loans to parents or to graduate or professional students. These loans are either subsidized or unsubsidized. Subsidized loans are made on the basis of demonstrated student need, and the interest is paid by the government during the time the student is in school. For the unsubsidized (non-need-based) loans and PLUS loans, interest begins to accrue as funds are disbursed.

As a result of the Health Care and Education Reconciliation Act, beginning July 1, 2010, federal student loans will no longer be made by private lenders under the Federal Family Education Loan (FFEL) Program. Instead, all new federal student loans will come directly from the U.S. Department of Education under the Direct Loan Program. This change does not impact the process of applying for federal grants, loans, and work-study opportunities or the amount of federal aid that students are eligible to receive. Students interested in receiving federal student aid should continue to complete a Free Application for Federal Student Aid (FAFSASM) for each school year that they wish to be considered for aid. For more information about applying for federal student aid, call 800-4-FED-AID (toll-free).

Federal Pell Grant

The Federal Pell Grant is the largest grant program; more than 6 million students receive Pell Grants annually. This grant is intended to be the starting point of assistance for lower-income families. Eligibility for a Pell Grant is based on the Expected Family Contribution. The amount you receive will depend on your EFC and the cost of education at the college you will attend. The highest award depends on how much funding the program receives from the government. The maximum for 2010–11 is $5550.

To give you some idea of your possible eligibility for a Pell Grant, the following table may be helpful. The amounts shown are based on a family of four, with one student in college, no emergency expenses, no contribution from student income or assets, and college costs of at least $4050 per year. Pell Grants range from $555 to $5550.

Federal Supplemental Educational Opportunity Grant (FSEOG)

As its name implies, Federal Supplemental Educational Opportunity Grants provide additional need-based federal grant money to supplement the Federal Pell Grant Program. Each participating college is given funds to award to especially needy students. The maximum award is $4000 per year, but the amount you receive depends on the college's awarding policy, the availability of FSEOG funds, the total cost of education, and the amount of other aid awarded.

Federal Financial Aid Programs

Name of Program	Type of Program	Maximum Award Per Year
Federal Pell Grant	need-based grant	$5550
Federal Supplemental Educational Opportunity Grant (FSEOG)	need-based grant	$4000
Academic Competitiveness Grant (ACG)	need/merit	$750 (first year) $1300 (second year)
National Smart Grant (SMART)	need/merit/program	up to $4000 (third- and fourth-year undergraduate)
Federal Work-Study Program (FWS)	need-based part-time job	no maximum
Federal Perkins Loan Program	need-based loan	$5000
Subsidized Federal Direct Loan	need-based student loan	$3500 (first year)
Unsubsidized Federal Direct Loan	non-need-based student loan	$5500 (first year, dependent student)

Academic Competitiveness Grant (ACG)

U.S. citizens who are Pell Grant–eligible and who attended a "rigorous" high school program, as defined by the U.S. Secretary of Education, can receive up to $750 in their first year and $1300 in their second year if they have a minimum 3.0 GPA. More information about this program is available from the high school or college financial aid office.

National Smart Grant (SMART)

Third- and fourth-year undergraduates who are Pell Grant–eligible and major in math, science, technology, or certain foreign languages and have a minimum 3.0 in their major can qualify for a grant of up to $4000. More information about this program is available from the high school or college financial aid office.

Federal Work-Study Program (FWS)

This program provides jobs for students who demonstrate need. Salaries are paid by funds from the federal government as well as the college. Students work on an hourly basis on or off campus and must be paid at least the federal minimum wage. Students may earn only up to the amount awarded in the financial aid package.

Federal Perkins Loan Program

This is a low-interest loan for students with exceptional financial need. Perkins Loans are made through the college's financial aid office with the college as the lender. Students can borrow a maximum of $4500 per year for up to five years of undergraduate study. Borrowers may take up to ten years to repay the loan, beginning nine months after they graduate, leave school, or drop below half-time status. No interest accrues while they are in school, and, under certain conditions (e.g., they teach in low-income areas, work in law enforcement, are full-time nurses or medical technicians, serve as Peace Corps or VISTA volunteers, etc.), some or all of the loan can be cancelled. In addition, payments can be deferred under certain conditions such as unemployment.

Federal Direct Loans

A Direct Loan is borrowed directly from the U.S. Department of Education through the college's financial aid office.

The unsubsidized Direct Loan Program carries a fixed 6.8 percent interest rate. The interest rate for subsidized Federal Direct Loans first dispursed between July 1, 2010, and June 30, 2011, is 4.5 percent. If a student qualifies for a need-based subsidized Federal Direct Loan, the interest is paid by the federal government while he or she is enrolled in college, during grace, and during periods of deferment. Over a four-year period beginning July 1, 2008, the fixed interest rate on subsidized Direct Student Loans made to undergraduate students who purchased a loan made before July 1, 2006, will be reduced in phases. For loans first disbursed on or after

- July 1, 2010, and before July 1, 2011, the interest rate will be fixed at 4.50 percent;
- July 1, 2011, and before July 1, 2012, the interest rate will be fixed at 3.40 percent.

The maximum amount dependent students may borrow in any one year is $5500 for freshmen, $6500 for sophomores, and $7500 for juniors and seniors, with a maximum of $31,000 for the total undergraduate program (of which not more than $23,000 can be subsidized). The maximum amount independent students can borrow is $9500 for freshmen (of which no more than $3500 can be subsidized), $10,500 for sophomores (of which no more than $4500 can be subsidized), and $12,500 for juniors and seniors (of which no more than $5500 can be subsidized). Independent students can borrow up to $57,500 (of which no more than $23,000 can be subsidized) for the total undergraduate program. Borrowers may be charged a small origination fee, which is deducted from the loan proceeds.

To apply for a Federal Student Loan, you must first complete the FAFSA to determine eligibility for a subsidized loan and then complete a separate loan application that is submitted to the Department of Education. The Department of Education will send a master promissory for completion. The proceeds of the loan, less the origination fee, will be sent to the college to be either credited to your account or released to you directly. Direct loans are processed by the financial aid office as part of the overall financial aid package.

Once the repayment period starts, borrowers of both subsidized and unsubsidized Federal Direct Loans have to pay a combination of interest and principal monthly for up to a ten-year period. There are a number of repayment options as well as opportunities to consolidate federal loans. There are also provisions for extended repayments, deferments, and repayment forbearance, if needed.

Direct PLUS Loans

PLUS loans are for parents of dependent students to help families with the cost of education. There is no needs test to qualify. A Direct PLUS Loan has a fixed interest rate of 7.9 percent. There is no yearly limit; you can borrow up to the cost of your child's education, less other financial aid received. Repayment begins sixty days after the funds are disbursed. The origination fee is 4 percent and may be subtracted from the proceeds. Parent borrowers must generally have a good credit record to qualify.

Hope Credit and Lifetime Learning Credit

Tuition tax credits allow families to reduce their tax bill by the out-of-pocket college tuition expense. Unlike a tax deduction, which is modified according to your tax bracket, a tax credit is a dollar-for-dollar reduction in taxes paid.

There are two programs: the Hope Credit and the Lifetime Learning Credit. As is true of many federal programs, there are numerous rules and restrictions that apply. You should check with your tax preparer, financial adviser, or IRS Publication 970 for information about your own particular situation.

Hope Credit

The Hope Credit offsets some of the expense for the first two years of college or vocational school. Students or the parents of dependent students can claim an annual income tax credit of up to $1800—100 percent of the first $1200 of tuition and required fees and 50 percent of the second $1200. Grants, scholarships, and other tax-free educational assistance must be deducted from the total tuition and fee payments.

This credit can be claimed for students who are in their first two years of college and who are enrolled on at least a half-time basis in a degree or certificate program for any portion of the year. This credit phases out for joint filers who have an income between $96,000 and $116,000 and for single filers who have between $48,000 and $58,000 of income. Parents may claim credits for more than one qualifying student. (The income figures are subject to change and can be found in each year's IRS Publication 970.)

Lifetime Learning Credit

The Lifetime Learning Credit is the counterpart of the Hope Credit; it is for college juniors, seniors, graduate students, and part-time students pursuing lifelong learning to improve or upgrade their job skills. The qualifying taxpayer can claim an annual tax credit of up to $2000—20 percent of the first $10,000 of tuition. The credit is available for net tuition and fees, less grant aid. The total credit available is limited to $2000 per year per taxpayer (or joint-filing couple), and is phased out at the same income levels as the Hope Credit. (The income figures are subject to change and can be found in each year's IRS Publication 970.)

Tuition and Fees Tax Deduction

The Tuition and Fees Tax Deduction could reduce taxable income by as much as $4000. This deduction is taken as an adjustment to income, which means you can claim this deduction even if you do not itemize deductions on Schedule A of Form 1040. This deduction may benefit taxpayers who do not qualify for either the Hope Credit or Lifetime Learning Credit.

Up to $4000 may be deducted for tuition and fees required for enrollment or attendance at an eligible postsecondary institution. Personal living and family expenses, including room and board, insurance, medical, and transportation, are not deductible expenses.

The exact amount of the Tuition and Fees Tax Deduction depends on the amount of qualified tuition and related expenses paid for one's self, spouse, or dependents, and your Adjusted Gross Income. Consult the IRS or your tax preparer for more information.

Student Loan Interest Tax Deduction

If you made student loan interest payments in 2010, you may be able to reduce your taxable income by up to $2500. You should check with your lender with regards to the amount of interest you paid if you did not receive an IRS Form 1098-E and your tax preparer or IRS Publication 970 for additional information.

AmeriCorps

AmeriCorps is a national umbrella group of service programs for students. Participants work in a public or private nonprofit agency and provide service to the community in one of four priority areas: education, human services, the environment, and public safety. In exchange, they earn a stipend (for living expenses), health insurance coverage, and $4725 per year for up to two years to apply toward college expenses. Many student-loan lenders will postpone the repayment of student loans during service in AmeriCorps, and AmeriCorps will pay the interest that is accrued on qualified student loans for members who complete the service program. Participants can work before, during, or after college and can use the funds to either pay current educational expenses or repay federal student loans. For more information, visit www.americorps.org.

Analyzing Financial Aid Award Letters

Richard Woodland

You have just received the financial aid award letters. Now what? This is the time to do a detailed analysis of each college's offer to help you pay for your child's education. Remember, accepting financial aid is a family matter. More often than not, parents need to borrow money to send their dependent children to college. You need to clearly understand the types of aid you and your child are being offered. How much is "free" money in the form of grants and/or scholarships that does not have to be repaid? If your financial aid award package includes loans, what are the terms and conditions for these loans? A good tool to have with you is the federal government's most recent issue of *Funding Education Beyond High School: The Guide to Federal Student Aid*, available from the school's financial aid office or at http://studentaid.ed.gov/students/publications/student_guide/index.html. This publication is very helpful in explaining the federal grant and loan programs that are usually a part of the aid package.

Let's take a minute to explain what is meant by "financial aid award package." A college will offer an aid applicant a combination of aid types, "packaged" in the form of grants and scholarships, loans, and a work-study job, based on the information provided on the FAFSA and/or another application. Many schools use a priority filing date, which guarantees that all applications received by this date will be considered for the full range of institutional aid programs available. Late applicants (by even one day!) often are only awarded the basic aid programs from state and federal sources. *It is important to apply on time.*

Evaluate Each Letter

As each award letter comes in, read it through carefully. The following are some critical points to consider:

- **Does the Cost of Attendance (COA) include all projected costs?** Each award letter should state the school's academic year COA. Tuition, fees, room, board, books, transportation, and personal expenses are what normally make up the COA. Does the award letter itemize all these components? Or does it omit some? This is crucial because this is what you will need to budget for. If you need additional information, be sure to contact the financial aid office. They will be glad to provide you with information or answer any questions you may have about their costs.

- **What is your Expected Family Contribution (EFC)?** Is the school's—not just the federal government's—EFC listed on the award letter? Some schools may require a higher EFC than you expected. Be aware that the EFC may increase or decrease each year depending on the information you provide on the renewal FAFSA or other financial aid application.

- **Is there unmet need?** Does the aid package cover the difference between the COA and the EFC? Not every school can cover your full need. If the aid package does not cover your full need, does the information with the award letter provide you with alternative loan options? If not, contact the financial aid office for more information.

- **Is the scholarship renewable for four years?** If your child is awarded a scholarship based on scholastic achievement or talent, you need to ask these questions: Is there a minimum grade point average he has to maintain? Can he switch majors but keep the scholarship? Does he need to participate in an "honors college" program to maintain the scholarship? If he needs to change to part-time status, will the award amount be prorated, or does he need to maintain full-time status? If it is an athletic or "special talent" scholarship, will he continue to receive the award if for some reason he cannot continue with the specific program? Renewal of scholarship funds is often the biggest misunderstanding between families and colleges. Be sure you clearly understand the terms and conditions of all grants and scholarships.

- **What will the college do to your child's award if she receives outside, noninstitutional scholarships?** Will the award be used to cover unmet need or reduce her student loans? Will the college reduce her institutional grants or scholarships? Or will they reduce her work-study award? (This is a good time to compare each school's policy on this matter.) Remember, your overall aid cannot total more than the COA, and many programs cannot exceed your financial need.

- **What are the interest rates of the loans that are offered?** Did another school offer you more than one loan and why? *Do not* sign the award letter until you understand your loan obligations.

Again, *Funding Education Beyond High School: The Guide to Federal Student Aid* can be very helpful with this part of the analysis.

■ **Is the school likely to cover the same expenses every year?** In particular, ask if grant or scholarship funds are normally reduced or increased after the freshman year, even if family income and EFC remain the same. Some colleges will *increase* the self-help (loan, job) percentage every year but not necessarily the free money.

■ **If work-study was awarded, how many hours a week will your child be expected to work?** If you feel working that many hours will have a negative impact on your child's academic performance, you may want to request that the awarded job funds be changed to a loan. You must ask immediately because funds are limited. Many schools are flexible with these funds early in the process.

■ **What happens if (or more likely, when) tuition increases?** Check with the financial aid office to find out what its policy is for renewing an aid package. If, for example, tuition increases by 5 percent each of the next three years and your EFC remains the same, what will happen to your scholarships, grants, and loans?

You can always appeal your award letter if you feel that your needs are not being met, if your family situation has changed, or if you have received a better award from a competitive school. You have the right to ask for a reconsideration of your award. (Do not use the word *negotiate*.) When asking for reconsideration, be sure to provide the aid officer with all relevant information.

Compare Letters

After you have received and reviewed all the award letters from the schools your child is considering, the next step is to compare them and determine which schools are offering the best aid packages. Following are three sample award letters and a sample spreadsheet that shows you how to analyze and compare each school's awards.

(Note: These award letters are simply for discussion purposes. They should not be considered to be representative award letters with an EFC of $9550.)

UNIVERSITY A
FINANCIAL AID AWARD LETTER
2010–2011

Date: 4/21/10
ID#: 000000009

Dear Jane Smith,

We are pleased to inform you that you are eligible to receive the financial assistance indicated in the area labeled "Your Financial Aid." We estimated your budget based on the following assumptions:

In-state resident and living on campus.

	FALL	SPRING	TOTAL
Tuition and Fees	$3849	$3849	$ 7698
Room & Board	3769	3770	7539
Books	420	420	840
Transportation	973	974	1947
Personal Expenses	369	369	738
Estimated Cost of Attendance	**$9380**	**$9382**	**$18,762**

Your Financial Aid

	FALL	SPRING	TOTAL
Federal Pell Grant	$1950	$1950	$ 3900
Federal Direct Subsidized Loan	1750	1750	3500
State Grant	432	432	864
Total Financial Aid	**$4132**	**$4132**	**$ 8264**
Unmet Need	**$5248**	**$5250**	**$10,498**

What to Do Next:

- Verify that accurate assumptions have been used to determine your awards.
- Carefully review and follow the instructions on the Data Changes Form.
- To reduce or decline all or part of your loans, you must complete and return the Data Changes Form.
- We will assume you fully accept the awards above unless you submit changes to us immediately.
- Return corrections and required documents promptly.
- Retain this letter for your records.

UNIVERSITY B
FINANCIAL AID AWARD LETTER
2010–2011

Date: 4/21/10
ID#: 000000009

Dear Jane Smith,

We are pleased to inform you that you are eligible to receive the financial assistance indicated in the area labeled "Your Financial Aid." We estimated your budget based on the following assumptions:

Nonresident and living on campus.

	FALL	SPRING	TOTAL
Tuition and Fees	$ 9085	$ 9085	$18,170
Room & Board	2835	2835	5670
Books	410	410	820
Transportation	875	875	1750
Personal Expenses	378	377	755
Estimated Cost of Attendance	**$13,583**	**$13,582**	**$27,165**

Your Financial Aid

	FALL	SPRING	TOTAL
Federal Pell Grant	$ 1950	$ 1950	$ 3900
Federal SEOG Grant	225	225	450
Academic Excellence Scholarship	500	500	1000
Federal Work-Study Program	1050	1050	2100
Federal Perkins Loan Program	1250	1250	2500
Subsidized Federal Stafford Student Loan	1750	1750	3500
University Student Loan	2000	2000	4000
Total Financial Aid	**$ 8725**	**$ 8725**	**$17,450**
Unmet Need	**$ 4858**	**$ 4857**	**$ 9715**

What to Do Next:

- Verify that accurate assumptions have been used to determine your awards.
- Carefully review and follow the instructions on the Data Changes Form.
- To reduce or decline all or part of your loans, you must complete and return the Data Changes Form.
- We will assume you fully accept the awards above unless you submit changes to us immediately.
- Return corrections and required documents promptly.
- Retain this letter for your records.

UNIVERSITY C
FINANCIAL AID AWARD LETTER
2010–2011

Date: 4/21/10
ID#: 000000009

Dear Jane Smith,

We are pleased to inform you that you are eligible to receive the financial assistance indicated in the area labeled "Your Financial Aid." We estimated your budget based on the following assumptions:

Living on campus.

	FALL	SPRING	TOTAL
Tuition and Fees	$14,955	$14,955	$29,910
Room & Board	4194	4193	8387
Books	450	450	900
Transportation	350	350	700
Personal Expenses	1295	1293	2588
Estimated Cost of Attendance	**$21,244**	**$21,241**	**$42,485**

Your Financial Aid

	FALL	SPRING	TOTAL
Institutional Grant	$10,805	$10,805	$21,610
Federal Pell Grant	1950	1950	3900
Federal SEOG Grant	2000	2000	4000
Federal Work-Study Program	1713	1712	3425
Total Financial Aid	**$16,468**	**$16,467**	**$32,935**
Unmet Need	**$ 4776**	**$ 4774**	**$ 9550**

What to Do Next:

- Verify that accurate assumptions have been used to determine your awards.
- Carefully review and follow the instructions on the Data Changes Form.
- To reduce or decline all or part of your loans, you must complete and return the Data Changes Form.
- We will assume you fully accept the awards above unless you submit changes to us immediately.
- Return corrections and required documents promptly.
- Retain this letter for your records.

Comparison Grid

	University A (State University)	University B (Nonresident State University)	University C (Private College)
Cost of Attendance	**$18,762**	**$27,165**	**$42,485**
Tuition and Fees	7698	18,170	29,910
Room & Board	7539	5670	8367
Books	840	820	900
Transportation	1947	1750	700
Personal Expenses	738	755	2558
Grants and Scholarships	**4764**	**5350**	**29,510**
Loans	**3500**	**10,000**	**0**
Work-Study	**0**	**2100**	**3425**
Expected Family Contribution	**9550**	**9550**	**9550**
Balance	**$ 948**	**$ 165**	**$ 0**

Some things to notice:

- At all schools, the Federal Pell Grant remains the same.
- The loan amounts varied greatly among these schools.
- Even though University C (a private college) has the highest "sticker price," the net cost is less than the state schools.
- University B is a state university, but are classified as an out-of-state resident (or nonresident). Many students in this situation find that the higher out-of-state costs combined with lower grant aid make this a costly decision.
- All schools assume that you will be residing in on-campus housing. But if you choose to commute to University A, you would save a substantial amount because you would not have the $7539 room and board cost.

Once you have entered all the information into a spreadsheet of your own and come up with the balances, here are some things to consider for each school:

- **How much is the balance?** Ideally, your balance should be $0, but look to see which school has the lowest balance amount.
- **What part of the aid package comes in the form of grants and scholarships?** It is important to note this because these awards (gift aid) do not have to be paid back.
- **Look at the loans.** Usually, the best financial deal contains more money in scholarships and less in loan dollars. Based on expected freshman-year borrowing, determine the debt burden at each school once your child graduates. You have to multiply the amount of your loan by four or five years, depending on

how long it will take for your child to graduate. And remember that the loan amounts will probably increase each year. You also should take into consideration that you will have to borrow even more as the COA increases each year. To determine the best loan deal, consider:

—What are the terms of the loans?

—What are interest rates?

—Do you pay the yearly interest rate during enrollment or is the interest subsidized or paid by the government?

—Is any money due during enrollment or is it deferred until after graduation? Figuring out how much you will owe at each school at graduation will give you a clear picture of what your financial situation will be *after* graduation.

However, unless cost is your only concern, you shouldn't simply choose the school offering the lowest loan amounts.

Many other factors need to be considered, such as academic and social environment. And you should never reject a school based solely on insufficient financial aid. Consult with an aid administrator to discuss possible alternatives.

Finally, if the college that costs the most is still the one your child wants to attend, there are a number of ways to find money to cover the gap between the aid package and your actual cost,

including paying more than the EFC figure, increasing student borrowing, working more hours, and taking out a PLUS loan.

Richard Woodland is the former Director of Financial Aid at Rutgers University–Camden and the current Director of Student Services and Financial Aid at the Curtis Institute of Music in Philadelphia, Pennsylvania.

Online Filing of FAFSA and CSS/Financial Aid PROFILE® Applications

Richard Woodland

Over the past few years, there have been major advancements in the way students apply both for admission to college and for financial aid. The two primary financial aid applications, the Free Application for Federal Student Aid (FAFSA) and the CSS/Financial Aid PROFILE® application from the College Scholarship Service offer direct, online applications. FAFSA on the Web and PROFILE are available in both English and Spanish.

Why File Online?

There are two reasons why it is a good idea to file online. First, the online environment prevents you from making many mistakes. For example, if there is a question that is required of all applicants, you cannot inadvertently skip it. If the application software thinks your answer may not be accurate, it will prompt you to check it before proceeding. The financial aid process can be complicated, and applying online greatly reduces the chance for error. The second reason is turnaround time. The online applications are processed in a matter of days, not weeks. Since time is an important factor when applying for financial aid, it is prudent to have your application processed as quickly as possible.

Some Common Concerns About Online Filing

Both the FASFA and PROFILE online applications have become much more user-friendly. You do not have to be a computer expert to use these programs. Both applications allow you to save your completed data and return later if you are interrupted or need to gather additional information. Both systems use secure encryption technology to protect your privacy. FASFA information is shared with other federal agencies as required as part of the application process, online or paper. FAFSA information is also sent to your state of legal residence for state aid purposes and to any college or program your child lists on the application. The information on the application is highly personal, and every precaution is taken to safeguard your privacy.

Now, let's discuss some specific issues related to each application.

The FAFSA

The FAFSA is the universal application for all federal financial aid programs. It is the primary application used for most state and college financial aid programs. Before using the FAFSA online application, you need to secure an electronic signature, or Personal Identification Number (PIN). This is similar to the access codes used at ATM machines, online banking, etc. It is easy to obtain a PIN number. Simply go to www.pin.ed.gov and apply online. You will receive a reply via e-mail in about 48 hours. If your child is under 24 years of age, he or she and one parent will need a PIN number. If there is more than one child in college, a parent only needs one PIN number. However, each college applicant will need to have his or her own PIN.

The FASFA online application is not presented in the same format as the paper FAFSA. Although all of the questions are exactly the same, the order of some of the items on the online application has been rearranged to make it easier to complete and allow for some built-in skip-logic. You can easily obtain a copy of the electronic FAFSA by logging on to www.fafsa.ed.gov. Just click on "FAFSA on the Web Worksheet." Completing this first will make the online entry that much easier. There are a number of other worksheets available that can also make the process easier. You should print them out and decide which are applicable to your situation. Everyone should review Worksheets A, B, and C. If you have not completed your federal tax return, the Income Estimator worksheets are easy to use and can reduce much of the guesswork.

After completing the online FASFA, be sure to print a copy of the pages at the end of the process so that you have a copy of your answers and the confirmation number. Although lost applications are extremely rare, having this information will give you peace of mind. You can go online as often as you wish to check the status of your application.

The CSS/Financial Aid PROFILE®

The CSS/Financial Aid PROFILE® is a more comprehensive financial aid application that is used primarily at private, higher-cost colleges and universities to award nonfederal student aid funds. Many private scholarship programs also use the PROFILE. A complete list of colleges and programs that use the PROFILE can be found at https://profileonline.collegeboard.com/index.jsp.

The PROFILE application has a $9 registration fee and an additional $16 for each school or program you select to receive your information. You must have a credit card, debit card, or checking account to use this service. (Note: A limited number of fee waivers are available for families with incomes below the poverty line. See the high school guidance officer for more information on the fee waiver program.)

Complete information on the online PROFILE application is available at www.collegeboard.com/profile. Although the customized PROFILE application is processed in about one week, you should allow for enough processing time (usually two to three weeks) to meet the earliest deadline established by the school or program.

What Happens Next?

Both the FAFSA and PROFILE processors want more applicants to use the online environment. Not only is the process easier for them, but it is faster and more accurate. Once you decide to apply online, the processors will only respond to you electronically. You will not receive any paper acknowledgments—all confirmations will be sent via e-mail. When it is time to reapply for aid in subsequent years (usually quite easy as most of the data are carried over from the previous application), all reminders will be sent to the e-mail address that is on file, so it is important to report any changes in your e-mail address.

It is easy to update the FAFSA following your initial application. For example, if you used estimated income information and now you have your federal tax return completed, you can simply return to www.fafsa.ed.gov and change your income figures. But be sure to go through the entire process and print out the updated confirmation page. In general, the PROFILE is a one-time application, filed well before tax season. Any updates are usually done directly through the schools.

Both processors offer helpful information, both in print and online. Check with your high school guidance office or local college financial aid office for additional assistance. If you need to call the FAFSA processor, the phone number is 800-4-FED-AID (toll-free). You can contact PROFILE customer service via e-mail at help@cssprofile.org or by phone at 305-829-9793 or 800-915-9990 (toll-free).

_____

Richard Woodland is the former Director of Financial Aid at Rutgers University–Camden and the current Director of Student Services and Financial Aid at the Curtis Institute of Music in Philadelphia, Pennsylvania.

Middle-Income Families: Making the Financial Aid Process Work

Richard Woodland

A report from the U.S. Department of Education's National Center for Education Statistics took a close look at how middle-income families finance a college education. The report, *Middle Income Undergraduates: Where They Enroll and How They Pay for Their Education,* was one of the first detailed studies of these families. Even though 31 percent of middle-income families have the entire cost of attendance covered by financial aid, there is widespread angst among middle-income families that, while they earn too much to qualify for grant assistance, they are financially unable to pay the spiraling costs of higher education.

First, we have to agree on what constitutes a "middle-income" family. For the purposes of the federal study, middle income is defined as those families with incomes between $35,000 and $70,000. The good news is that 52 percent of these families received grants, while the balance received loans. Other sources of aid, including work-study, also helped close the gap.

So how do these families do it? Is there a magic key that will open the door to significant amounts of grants and scholarships?

The report found some interesting trends. One way families can make college more affordable is by choosing a less expensive college. In fact, in this income group, 29 percent choose to enroll in low- to moderate-cost schools. These include schools where the total cost is less than $8500 per year. In this sector, we find the community colleges and lower-priced state colleges and universities. But almost half of these middle-income families choose schools in the upper-level tier, with costs ranging from $8500 to $16,000. The remaining 23 percent enrolled at the highest-tier schools, with costs above $16,000. Clearly, while cost is a factor, middle-income families are not limiting their choices based on costs alone.

The report shows that families pay these higher costs with a combination of family assets, current income, and long-term borrowing. This is often referred to as the "past-present-future"

model of financing. In fact, just by looking at the Expected Family Contributions, it is clear that there is a significant gap in what families need and what the financial aid process can provide. Families are closing this gap by making the financial sacrifices necessary to pay the price at higher-cost schools, especially if they think their child is academically strong. The report concludes that parents are more likely to pay for a higher-priced education if their child scores high on the SAT.

The best place for middle-income families to start is with the high school guidance office. This office has information on financial aid and valuable leads on local scholarships. Most guidance officers report that there are far fewer applicants for these locally based scholarships than one would expect. So read the information they send home and check on the application process. A few of those $500–$1000 scholarships can add up!

Plan to attend a financial aid awareness program. If your school does not offer one, contact your local college financial aid office and see when and where they will be speaking. You can get a lot of "inside" information on how the financial aid process works.

Next, be sure to file the correct applications for aid. Remember, each school can have a different set of requirements. For example, many higher-cost private colleges will require the CSS/Financial Aid PROFILE® application, filed in September or October of the senior year. Other schools may have their own institutional aid application. All schools will require the Free Application for Federal Student Aid (FAFSA). Watch the deadlines! It is imperative that you meet the school's published application deadline. Generally, schools are not flexible about this, so be sure to double-check the due date of all applications.

Finally, become a smart educational consumer. Peterson's has a wide range of resources available to help you understand the process. Be sure to also check your local library, bookstore, and of course, the Internet. Two great Web sites to check are www.petersons.com and www.finaid.org.

Once admitted to the various colleges and universities, you will receive an award notice outlining the aid you are eligible to receive. If you feel the offer is not sufficient, or if you have some unique financial circumstances, call the school's financial aid office to see if you can have your application reviewed again. The financial aid office is your best source for putting the pieces together and finding financial solutions.

The financial aid office will help you determine the "net price." This is the actual out-of-pocket cost that you will need to cover. Through a combination of student and parent loans, most families are able to meet these expenses with other forms of financial aid and family resources.

Many students help meet their educational expenses by working while in school. While this works for many students, research shows that too many hours spent away from your studies will negatively impact your academic success. Most experts feel that working 10 to 15 hours a week is optimal.

An overlooked source of aid is the tax credits given to middle-income families. Rather than extending eligibility for traditional sources of grant assistance to middle-income families, the federal tax system has built in a number of significant tax benefits, known as the Hope Scholarship and Lifetime Learning tax credit, for middle-income families. While it may be seven or eight months before you see the tax credit, most families in this income group can count on this benefit, usually between $1500 to $2000 per student. This is real money in your pocket. You do not need to itemize your deductions to qualify for this tax credit.

A tool to help families get a handle on the ever-rising costs of college is to assume that you can pay one third of the "net charges" from savings, another third from available (non-retirement) assets, and the rest from parent borrowing. If any one of these "thirds" is not available, shift that amount to one of the other resources. However, if it looks like you will be financing most or all of the costs from future income (borrowing), it may be wise to consider a lower-cost college.

Millions of middle-income families send their children to colleges and universities every year. Only 8 percent attend the lowest-priced schools. By using the concept of past-present-future financing, institutional assistance, federal and state aid, meaningful targeted tax relief, and student earnings, you can afford even the highest-cost schools.

_____

Richard Woodland is the former Director of Financial Aid at Rutgers University–Camden and the current Director of Student Services and Financial Aid at the Curtis Institute of Music in Philadelphia, Pennsylvania.

Parents' and Students' Common Questions Answered

Q *Are a student's chances of being admitted to a college reduced if the student applies for financial aid?*

A Generally no. Nearly all colleges have a policy of "need-blind" admissions, which means that a student's financial need is not taken into account in the admission decision. There are a few selective colleges, however, that do consider ability to pay before deciding whether or not to admit a student. Some colleges will mention this in their literature; others may not. The best advice is to apply for financial aid if the student needs assistance to attend college.

Q *Are parents penalized for saving money for college?*

A No. As a matter of fact, families that have made a concerted effort to save money for college are in a much better position than those that have not. For example, a student from a family that has saved money may not have to borrow as much. Furthermore, the "taxing rate" on savings is quite low—only about 5 percent of the parents' assets are assessed and neither the home equity nor retirement savings are included. For example, a single 40-year-old parent who saved $40,000 for college expenses will have about $1900 counted as part of the parental contribution. Two parents, if the older one is 40 years old (a parent's age factors into the formulation), would have about $300 counted. (Note: The "taxing rate" for student assets is much higher—20 percent—compared to 5 percent for parents.)

Q *How does the financial aid system work in cases of divorce or separation? How are stepparents treated?*

A In cases of divorce or separation, the financial aid application(s) should be completed by the parent with whom the student lived for the longest period of time in the past twelve months (custodial parent). If the custodial parent has remarried, the stepparent is considered a family member and must complete the application along with the biological parent. If your family has any special circumstances, you should discuss these directly with the financial aid office. (Note: Colleges that award their own aid may ask the noncustodial biological parent to complete a separate aid application and a contribution will be calculated.)

Q *When are students considered independent of parental support in applying for financial aid?*

A The student must be at least 24 years of age in order to be considered independent. If younger than 24, the student must be married, be a graduate or professional student, have legal dependents other than a spouse, be an orphan or ward of the court, or be a veteran of the armed forces or on active military duty. However, in very unusual situations, students who can clearly document estrangement from their parents can appeal to the financial aid office for additional consideration.

Q *What can a family do if a job loss occurs?*

A Financial aid eligibility is based on the previous year's income. So the family's 2010 income would be reported to determine eligibility for the 2011–12 academic year. In that way, the family's income can be verified with an income tax return. But the previous year's income may not accurately reflect the current financial situation, particularly if a parent lost a job or retired. In these instances, the projected income for the coming year can be used instead. Families should discuss the situation directly with the financial aid office and be prepared to provide appropriate documentation.

Q *When my daughter first went to college, we applied for financial aid and were denied because our Expected Family Contribution was too high. Now, my* son is a high school senior, and we will soon have two in college. Will we get the same results?

A The results will definitely be different. Both your son and your daughter should apply. As described earlier, need-based financial aid is based on your Expected Family Contribution, or EFC. When you have two children in college, this amount is divided in half for each child.

Q *I've heard about the "middle-income squeeze" in regard to financial aid. What is it?*

A The so-called "middle-income squeeze" is the idea that low-income families qualify for aid, high-income families have adequate resources to pay for education, and those in the middle are not eligible for aid but do not have the ability to pay full college costs. There is no provision in the Federal Methodology that treats middle-income students differently than others (such as an income cutoff for eligibility). The Expected Family Contribution rises proportionately as income and assets increase. If a middle-income family does not qualify for aid, it is because the need analysis formula yields a contribution that exceeds college costs. But keep in mind that if a $65,000-income family does not qualify for grant aid at a public university with a $16,000 cost, the same family will likely be eligible for aid at a private college with a cost of $25,000 or more. Also, there are loan programs available to parents and students that are not based on need. Middle-income families should realize, however, that many of the grant programs funded by federal and state governments are directed at lower-income families. It is therefore likely that a larger share of an aid package for a middle-income student will consist of loans rather than grants.

Q *Given our financial condition, my daughter will be receiving financial aid. We will help out as much as we can, and, in fact, we ourselves will be borrowing. But I am concerned that she will have to take on a lot of loans in order to go to the college of her choice. Does she have any options?*

A She does. If offered a loan, she can decline all or part of it. One option is for her to ask in the financial aid office to have some of the loan changed to a work-study job. If this is not possible, she can find her own part-time work. Often there is an employment office on campus that can help her locate a job. In most cases, the more she works, the less she has to borrow. It is important to remember that the education loans offered to students have very attractive terms and conditions, with flexible repayment options. Students should look upon these loans as a long-term investment that will reap significant rewards.

Q *What are some easy ways to improve my chances of receiving aid?*

A When filling out your scholarship or financial aid application, it's important to remember that the smallest mistake could hurt your chances for landing free money, or even worse, it could disqualify you completely from an awards contest. Grants and scholarships are highly competitive, so it's a good idea to make a list of what's needed and make sure you have everything before submitting your application. If you are submitting an essay, have another pair of eyes look at it for any spelling and grammar errors. Keep a file on everything you're applying for so that you don't miss any elements of an application. Make sure you're using reputable sites to conduct your free scholarship searches. If you have to pay to apply for an award or look for scholarships, chances are you're being scammed. In a nutshell, the best advice is to follow all directions, and make sure that you meet all deadlines.

In addition, when filling out the FAFSA, it's important to pay close attention to the details, since any errors may delay the application process. These days, it's preferable to fill out the FAFSA online, since mailed forms can take weeks to process. If you're confused or concerned about something on the application, contact the Federal Student Aid Information Center at 1-800-4-FED-AID; questions can also be asked through the FAFSA Web site. Your college's financial aid office should also be able to assist you. The FAFSA is available each year starting Jan. 1, and it's essential that you don't miss the deadline to apply. The sooner you apply, the sooner you'll know the kind of funding package you are likely to receive, and this will help you determine if you need to apply for any additional aid.

Q *Is it possible to change your financial aid package?*

A Yes. Most colleges have an appeal process. A request to change a need-based loan to a work-study job is usually approved if funds are available. A request to consider special financial circumstances may also be granted. At most colleges, a request for more grant money is rarely approved unless it is based on a change in the information reported. Applicants should speak with the financial aid office if they have concerns about their financial package. Some colleges may even respond to a competitive appeal, that is, a request to match another college's offer.

Q *The cost of attending college seems to be going up so much faster than the Consumer Price Index. Why is that, and how can I plan for my child's four years?*

A The cost of higher education cannot be compared to the Consumer Price Index (CPI). The CPI does not take into account most of the costs faced by colleges. For example, the dollars that universities spend on grants and scholarships have risen rapidly. Many universities have increased enrollment of

Parents' and Students' Common Questions Answered

students from less affluent families, further increasing the need for institutional financial aid. Colleges are expected to be on the cutting edge of technology, not only in research but also in the classroom and in the library. Many colleges have deferred needed maintenance and repairs that can now no longer be put off. In addition, there is market pressure to provide many expensive lifestyle amenities that were not expected ten years ago. In general, you can expect that college costs will rise at least 2 to 3 percent faster than inflation.

Q *I'm struggling with the idea that all students should apply to the college of their choice, regardless of cost, because financial aid will level the playing field. I feel I will be penalized because I have saved for college. My son has been required to save half of his allowance since age six for his college education. Will that count against him when he applies for financial aid? It's difficult to explain to him that his college choices may be limited because of the responsible choices and sacrifices we have made as a family. What can we do to make the most of our situation?*

A In general, it is always better to have planned ahead for college by saving. Families that have put away sufficient funds to pay for college will quickly realize that they have made the burden easier for themselves and their children. In today's college financing world, schools assume that paying for the cost of attendance is a ten-year commitment. So by saving when your child is young, you reap significant advantages from compound interest on the assets and reduce the need to borrow as much while in school. This should reduce the number of years after college that you will be burdened with loans. Families should spend the student's assets first, since the financial aid formulas count these more heavily than parental assets. Then, after the first year, you can explain to the college how you spent these assets, and why you might now need assistance. When looking at parental information, the income of the family is by far the most important component. Contrary to popular belief, parental assets play a minor role in the calculation of need. With this strategy, you have done the right thing, and in the long run, it should prove to be a wise financial plan.

Picking the right college also involves other factors. Students should select the colleges to which they are going to apply in two ways. First, and most important, is to look at colleges that meet your son's academic and lifestyle interests. Most experts will tell him to pick a few "reach" schools (i.e., schools where he is not sure he has the grades and scores required) and at least one or two academically "safe" schools. He should also select one or two financially "safe" schools that you are sure you can afford with either moderate or little financial aid. Most students do not get into all of their first-choice schools, and not everyone can afford the schools to which they are admitted. By working closely with the guidance office in high school and the admissions and financial aid offices at the college, you can maximize your options.

Q *My son was awarded a $2500 scholarship. This can be split and used for two years. When filling out the FAFSA, do we have to claim the full amount, or just the $1250 he plans to use the first year?*

A Congratulations to your son on the scholarship. Nowhere on the FAFSA should you report this scholarship. It is not considered income or an asset. However, once you choose a school to attend, you must notify the financial aid office for its advice on how to take the funds. But remember, do NOT report it on the FAFSA.

Q *I will be receiving a scholarship from my local high school. How will this scholarship be treated in my financial aid award?*

A Federal student aid regulations specify that all forms of aid must be included within the defined level of need. This means that additional aid, such as outside scholarships, must be combined with any need-based aid you receive; it may not be kept separate and used to reduce your family's contribution. If the college has not filled 100 percent of your need, it will usually allow outside scholarships to close the gap. Once your total need has been met, the college must reduce other aid and replace it with the outside award. Most colleges will allow you to use some, if not all, of an outside scholarship to replace self-help aid (loans and Federal Work-Study Program awards) rather than grant aid.

Q *I know we're supposed to apply for financial aid as soon as possible after January 1. What if I don't have my W-2s yet and my tax return isn't done?*

A The first financial aid application deadlines usually fall in early February. Most colleges use either March 1 or March 15 as their "priority filing date." Chances are you'll have your W-2 forms by then, but you won't have a completed tax return. If that is the case, complete the financial aid application using your best estimates. Then, when you receive the Student Aid Report (SAR), you can use your tax return to make corrections. Just be sure to check with each college for its deadline.

Q *Is there enough aid available to make it worthwhile for me to consider colleges that are more expensive than I can afford?*

A Definitely. More than $100 billion in aid is awarded to undergraduates every year. With more than half of all enrolled students qualifying for some type of assistance, this totals more than $5500 per student. You should view financial aid as a large, national system of tuition discounts, some given according to a student's ability and talent, others based on what a student's family can afford to pay. If you qualify for need-based financial aid, you will essentially pay only your calculated family contribution, regardless of the cost of the college. You will not pay the "sticker price" (the cost of attendance listed in the college catalog) but a lower rate that is reduced by the amount of aid you receive. No college should be ruled out until after financial aid is considered. In addition, when deciding which college to attend, consider that the short-term cost of a college education is only one criterion. If the college meets your educational needs and you are convinced it can launch you on an exciting career, a significant up-front investment may turn out to be a bargain over the long run.

Q *If I don't qualify for need-based aid, what options are available?*

A You should try to put together your own aid package to help reduce your parents' share. There are three sources to look into. First, search for merit scholarships. Second, seek employment, during both the summer and the academic year. The student employment office should be able to help you find a campus job. Third, look into borrowing. Even if you don't qualify for the need-based loan programs, the unsubsidized Federal Direct Loan is available to all students. The terms and conditions are the same as the subsidized loan programs except that interest accrues while you are in college.

After you have contributed what you can through scholarships, employment, and loans, your parents will be faced with their share of the college bill. Many colleges have monthly payment plans that allow families to spread their payments over the academic year. If these monthly payments turn out to be more than your parents can afford, they can take out a parent loan. By borrowing from the college itself, from a commercial agency or lender, or through PLUS, your parents can extend the payments over a ten-year period or longer. Borrowing reduces the monthly obligation to its lowest level, but the total amount paid will be the highest due to principal and interest payments. Before making a decision on where to borrow parental loan funds, be sure to first check with the financial aid office to determine what is the best source of alternative funds.

Searching for Scholarships Online

Today's students need all the help they can get when looking for ways to pay for their college education. Skyrocketing tuition costs, state budget cuts, and diminished personal savings have combined to make financing a college education perhaps the number-one concern for parents. College sticker shock is driving many families away from college. No wonder: The "purchasing power" of all aid programs from federal, state, and institutional sources has declined over the past two decades. And it's not only lower-income families who are affected. Some fear they make *too much* money to qualify for financial aid. Regardless of their situations, most families struggle to make sense of the college financial aid process and to decide which aid package is the right one for them.

Despite the confusion, students and parents can and should research as many sources as they can to find the money they need. The Internet can be a great source of information. Many worthwhile sites are ready to help you search and apply for your fair share of awards, including Peterson's comprehensive financial aid site at www.petersons.com/finaid.

Peterson's "Pay For School"

Peterson's Pay for School financial aid Web site at www.petersons.com/finaid provides families with a wealth of information on college funding for every step of their college admission process.

Expert Advice

By logging on to www.petersons.com/finaid, you gain access to comprehensive articles that describe the ins and outs of federal and state funding, tips for filing the FAFSA and the CSS/Financial Aid PROFILE®, step-by-step advice on what you should be doing during junior and senior years of high school, and an audio clip of an interview with a real financial aid expert. Links to state programs and agencies help you connect directly to those resources. You can also access articles on specific topics, such as advice on 529 Plans, loans and payment plans, scholarship scams, the military, and international students. A section called "Financial Aid This Month" contains the latest news on government programs and other college funding topics.

Scholarship Search

Peterson's free **Scholarship Search** connects you to information on millions of scholarships, grants, and prizes totaling more than $8 billion, and lets you do an individualized search for awards that match your financial and educational needs. In just three easy steps you can register; complete a customized profile indicating your scholastic and personal background, intended major, work experience, and a host of other criteria; and access a list of scholarships that match your needs. Each scholarship is described in detail, including eligibility and application requirements and contact information, with links to the program's e-mail address and Web site. Finding money for college couldn't be easier!

Interactive Tools

When it's time to get to the nuts and bolts of your college financial planning, Peterson's has the tools to help. You can access a calculator to find your Estimated Family Contribution (EFC) and a **College Financial Planning Calculator** that lets you calculate your personal savings plan. After you have received award letters from the colleges you've applied to, you can use the **Award Analyzer**. If you click on the "Pay for School" tab and scroll down to "College-Based Awards," you will find the **Award Analyzer** under the "Have Your Award Letters?" box. The **Award Analyzer** helps you compare award letters to determine which school is prepared to give you the most aid. You simply enter the information from each award letter you receive, click on the Calculate button, and discover which school has offered you the best package.

Searching and applying for financial aid is a complicated process. The resources and tools available to you on www.petersons.com/finaid can help you get your fair share of the financial aid pie. So, what are you waiting for? Log on! Free money for college may be just a mouse click away.

How to Use This Guide

Quick-Reference Chart

The amount of aid available at colleges can vary greatly. "College Costs At-a-Glance" lists the percent of freshmen who applied for and received need-based gift aid and the percent of those whose need was fully met. Also listed are the average freshman financial aid package, the average cost after aid, and the average indebtedness upon graduation.

Profiles of College Financial Aid Programs

After the federal government, colleges provide the largest amount of financial aid to students. In addition, they control most of the money channeled to students from the federal government. The amount and makeup of your financial aid package will depend on the institution's particular circumstances and its decisions concerning your application. The main section of this book shows you the pattern and extent of each college's current awards. The profiles present detailed factual and statistical data for each school in a uniform format to enable easy, quick references and comparisons. Items that could not be collected in time for publication for specific institutions do not appear in those institutions' profiles. Colleges that supplied no data are listed by name and address only so that you do not overlook them in your search for colleges.

There is much anecdotal evidence that students and their families fail to apply for financial aid under the misconception that student aid goes only to poor families. Financial need in the context of college expenses is not the same as being needy in the broad social context. Middle-class families typically qualify for need-based financial aid; at expensive schools, even upper-middle-income families can qualify for need-based financial aid. Peterson's encourages you to apply for financial aid whether or not you think that you will qualify.

To help you understand the definition and significance of each item, the following outline of the profile format explains what is covered in each section. The term college or colleges is frequently used throughout to refer to any institution of higher education, regardless of its official definition.

The College

The name of the college is the official name as it appears on the institution's charter. The city and state listed are the official location of the school. The subhead line shows tuition and required fees, as they were charged to the majority of full-time undergraduate students in the 2009–10 academic year. Any exceptions to the 2009–10 academic year are so noted. For a public institution, the tuition and fees shown are for state residents, and this is noted. If a college's annual expenses are expressed as a comprehensive fee (including full-time tuition, mandatory fees, and college room and board), this is noted, as are any unusual definitions, such as tuition only. The average undergraduate aid package is the average total package of grant, loan, and work-study aid that was awarded to meet the officially defined financial need of full-time undergraduates enrolled in fall 2009 (or fall 2008) who applied for financial aid, were determined to have need, and then actually received financial aid. This information appears in more detail in each profile.

About the Institution

This paragraph gives the reader a brief introduction to a college. It contains the following elements:

Institutional Control

Private institutions are designated as *independent* (nonprofit), *independent/religious* (sponsored by or affiliated with a religious group or having a nondenominational or interdenominational religious orientation), or *proprietary* (profit-making). Public institutions are designated by their primary source of support, such as *federal*, *state*, *commonwealth* (Puerto Rico), *territory* (U.S. territories), *county, district* (an administrative unit of public education, often having boundaries different from those of units of local government), *state- and locally-supported* ("locally" refers to county, district, or city), *state-supported* (funded by the state), or *state-related* (funded primarily by the state but administered autonomously).

Type of Student Body

The categories are *men* (100 percent of student body), *coed-primarily men*, *women* (100 percent of student body), *coed-primarily women*, and *coed*. A few schools are designated as *undergraduate: women only, graduate: coed* or *undergraduate: men only, graduate: coed*.

How to Use This Guide

Degrees Awarded
Associate, bachelor's (baccalaureate), *master's, doctoral* (doctorate), and *first professional* (in such fields as law and medicine). There are no institutions in this book that award the associate degree only. Many award the bachelor's as their highest degree.

Number of Undergraduate Majors
This shows the number of academic fields in which the institution offers associate and/or bachelor's degrees. The purpose of this is to give you an indication of the range of subjects available.

Enrollment
These figures are based on the actual number of full-time and part-time students enrolled in degree programs as of fall 2009. In most instances, they are designated as *total enrollment* (for the specific college or university) and *freshmen*. If the institution is a university and its total enrollment figure includes graduate students, a separate figure for *undergraduates* may be provided. If the profiled institution is a subunit of a university, the figures may be designated *total university enrollment* for the entire university and *total unit enrollment* for the specific subunit.

Methodology Used for Determining Need
Private colleges usually have larger financial aid programs, but public colleges usually have lower sticker prices, especially for in-state or local students. At a public college, your financial need will be less, and you will receive a smaller financial aid package. This note on whether a college uses federal (FAFSA) or institutional methodology (usually CSS/Financial Aid PRO-FILE®) will let you know whether you will have to complete one or two kinds of financial aid application forms. Federal Methodology is the needs-analysis formula used by the U.S. Department of Education to determine the Expected Family Contribution (EFC), which, when subtracted from the cost of attendance at an institution, determines the financial need of a student. There is no relative advantage or disadvantage to using one methodology over the other.

Undergraduate Expenses
If provided by the institution, the one-time application fee is listed. Costs are given for the 2010–11 academic year or for the 2009–10 academic year if 2010–11 figures were not yet available. (Peterson's collects information for freshmen specifically.) Annual expenses may be expressed as a comprehensive fee (including full-time tuition, mandatory fees, and college room and board) or may be given as separate figures for full-time tuition, fees, room and board, or room only. For public institutions where tuition differs according to state residence, separate figures are given for area or state residents and for nonresidents. Part-time tuition is expressed in terms of a per-unit rate (per credit, per semester hour, etc.), as specified by the institution.

The tuition structure at some institutions is complex. Freshmen and sophomores may be charged a different rate from that charged juniors and seniors, a professional or vocational division may have a different fee structure from the liberal arts division of the same institution, or part-time tuition may be prorated on a sliding scale according to the number of credit hours taken. Tuition and fees may vary according to academic program, campus/location, class time (day, evening, weekend), course/credit load, course level, degree level, reciprocity agreements, and student level. If tuition and fees differ for international students, the rate charged is listed.

Room and board charges are reported as a double occupancy and nineteen meals per week plan or the equivalent and may vary according to board plan selected, campus/location, gender, type of housing facility, or student level. If no college-owned or -operated housing facilities are offered, the phrase *college housing not available* will appear.

If a college offers a *guaranteed tuition* plan, it promises that the tuition rate of an entering student will not increase for the entire term of enrollment, from entrance to graduation. Other payment plans might include *tuition prepayment*, which allows an entering student to lock in the current tuition rate for the entire term of enrollment by paying the full amount in advance rather than year by year, and *installment* and *deferred payment* plans, which allow students to delay the payment of the full tuition.

Guaranteed tuition and tuition prepayment help you to plan the total cost of education and can save you from the financial distress sometimes caused by tuition hikes. Colleges that offer such plans may also help you to arrange financing, which in the long run can cost less than the total of four years of increasing tuition rates. Deferred payment or installment payments may better fit your personal financial situation, especially if you do not qualify for financial aid and, due to other financial commitments, find that obtaining the entire amount due is burdensome. Carefully investigate these plans, however, to see what premium you may pay at the end to allow you to defer immediate payment.

Freshman Financial Aid
Usually, these are actual figures for the 2008–09 term, beginning in fall 2008; figures may also be estimated for the 2009–10 term. The particular term for which these data apply is indicated. The figures are for degree-seeking full-time freshman students. The first figure is the number of freshmen who applied for any kind of financial aid. The next figure is the percentage of those freshmen financial aid applicants who were determined to have financial need—that is, through the formal needs-assessment

process, had a calculated expected family contribution that was less than the total college cost. The next figure is the percentage of this group of eligible freshmen who received any financial aid. The next figure is the percentage of this preceding group of eligible aid recipients whose need was fully met by financial aid. The *Average percent of need met* is the average percentage of financial need met for freshmen who received any need-based aid. The *Average financial aid package* is the average dollar amount awarded (need-based or non-need-based) to freshmen who applied for aid, were deemed eligible, and received any aid; awards used to reduce the expected family contribution are excluded from this average. The final line in most profiles is the percentage of freshmen who had no financial need but who received non-need-based aid other than athletic scholarships or special-group tuition benefits.

What do these data mean to you? If financial aid is important in your comparison of colleges, the relative percentage of students who received any aid, whose need was fully met, and the average percentage of need met have the most weight. These figures reflect the relative abundance of student aid available to the average eligible applicant. The average dollar amount of the aid package has real meaning, but only in relation to the college's expense; you will be especially interested in the difference between this figure and the costs figure, which is what the average student (in any given statistical group, there actually may be no average individual) will have to pay. Of course, if the financial aid package is largely loans rather than grants, you will have to pay this amount eventually. Relative differences in the figures of the number of students who apply for aid and who are deemed eligible can hinge on any number of factors: the relative sticker price of the college, the relative level of wealth of the students' families, the proportion of only children in college and students with siblings in college (families with two or more children in college are more likely to apply for aid and be considered eligible), or the relative sophistication in financial aid matters (or quality of college counseling they may have received) of the students and their families. While these may be interesting, they will not mean too much to most students and families. If you are among the unlucky (or, perhaps, lucky) families who do not qualify for need-based financial aid, the final sentence of this paragraph in the profile will be of interest because it reveals the relative policies that the college has in distributing merit-based aid to students who cannot demonstrate need.

Undergraduate Financial Aid

This is the parallel paragraph to the Freshman Financial Aid paragraph. The same definitions apply, except that the group being considered is degree-seeking full-time undergraduate students (including freshmen).

There are cases of students who chose a particular college because they received a really generous financial aid package in their freshman year and then had to scramble to pay the tuition bill in their later years. If a financial aid package is a key factor in the decision to attend a particular college, you want to be certain that the package offered to all undergraduates is not too far from that offered to freshmen. The key figures are those for the percentage of students who received any aid, the percentage of financial aid recipients whose need was fully met, the average percentage of need met, and the dollar figure of the average financial aid package. Generally, colleges assume that after the freshman year, students develop study habits and time-management skills that will allow them to take on part-time and summer employment without hurting their academic performance. So, the proportion of self-help aid (work-study and student loans) in the financial aid package tends to increase after the freshman year. This pattern, which is true of most colleges, can be verified in the freshman-undergraduate figures in the paragraph on Gift Aid (Need-Based).

Gift Aid (Need-Based)

Total amount is the total dollar figure in 2009–10 (estimated) or 2008–09 (actual) of need-based scholarships and grant (gift) aid awarded to degree-seeking full-time and part-time students that was used to meet financial need. The percentages of this aid from federal, state, institutional (college or university), and external (e.g., foundations, civic organizations, etc.) sources are shown. *Receiving aid* shows the percentages (and number, in parentheses) of freshmen and of all undergraduates who applied for aid, were considered eligible, and received any need-based gift aid. *Average award* is the average dollar amount of awards to freshmen and all undergraduates who applied for aid, were considered eligible, and received any need-based gift aid. *Scholarships, grants, and awards* cites major categories of need-based gift aid provided by the college; these include Federal Pell Grants, Federal Supplemental Educational Opportunity Grants (FSEOG), state scholarships, private scholarships, college/university gift aid from institutional funds, United Negro College Fund aid, Federal Nursing Scholarships, and others.

Scholarships and grants are gifts awarded to students that do not need to be repaid. These are preferable to loans, which have to be repaid, or work-study wages, which may take time away from studies and personal pursuits. The total amount of need-based gift aid has to be placed into the context of the total number of undergraduate students (shown in the About the Institution paragraph) and the relative expense of the institution. Filing the FAFSA automatically puts you in line to receive any available federal grants for which you may qualify. However, if the college being considered has a higher than usual proportion of gift aid coming from state, institutional, or external sources, be sure to check with the financial aid office to find out what these sources may be and how to apply for them. For almost all colleges, the percentage of freshmen receiving need-based gift aid will be higher than the percentage of all undergraduates receiving need-based gift aid. However, if you are dependent on need-based gift aid and the particular college under consideration shows a sharper drop from the freshman to undergraduate years than other colleges of a similar type, you might want to think about how this change will affect your ability to pay for later years at this college.

Gift Aid (Non-Need-Based)

Total amount is the total dollar figure in 2009–10 (estimated) or 2008–09 (actual) of non-need-based scholarships and grant (gift) aid awarded to degree-seeking full-time and part-time students. Non-need-based aid that was used to meet financial need is not included in this total. The percentages of this aid from federal, state, institutional (college or university), and external (e.g., National Merit Scholarships, civic, religious, fraternal organizations, etc.) sources are shown. *Receiving aid* shows the percentages (and number, in parentheses) of freshmen and of all undergraduates who were determined to have need and received non-need-based gift aid. *Average award* is the average dollar amount of awards to freshmen and all undergraduates determined to have no need but received non-need-based awards. *Scholarships, grants, and awards by category* cites the major categories in which non-need-based awards are available and the number of awards made in that category (in parentheses, the total dollar value of these awards). The categories listed are *Academic interests/achievement*, *Creative arts/performance*, *Special achievements/activities*, and *Special characteristics*. *Tuition waivers* indicate special categories of students (minority students, children of alumni, college employees or children of employees, adult students, and senior citizens) who may qualify for a full or partial waiver of tuition. *ROTC* indicates Army, Naval, and Air Force ROTC programs that are offered on campus; a program offered by arrangement on another campus is indicated by the word *cooperative*.

This section covers college-administered scholarships awarded to undergraduates on the basis of merit or personal attributes without regard to need. If you do not qualify for financial aid but nevertheless lack the resources to pay for college, non-need-based awards will be of special interest to you. Some personal characteristics are completely beyond an individual's control, and talents and achievements take a number of years to develop or attain. However, certain criteria for these awards, such as religious involvement, community service, and special academic interests can be attained in a relatively brief period of time. ROTC programs offer such benefits as tuition, the cost of textbooks, and living allowances. In return, you must fulfill a

service obligation after graduating from college. Because they can be a significant help in paying for college, these programs have become quite competitive. Certain subject areas, such as nursing, health care, or the technical fields, are in stronger demand than others. Among the obligations to consider about ROTC are that you must spend a regular portion of your available time in military training programs and that ROTC entails a multiyear commitment after your graduation to serve as an officer in the armed services branch sponsoring the program.

Loans

The figures here represent loans that are part of the financial aid award package. *Student loans* represents the total dollar amount of loans from all sources to full-time and part-time degree-seeking undergraduates or their parents. *Average need-based loan* represents the percentage of these loans that goes to meet financial need, and the percentage that goes to pay the non-need portion (the expected family contribution) are indicated. The percentage of a past graduating class who borrowed through any loan program (except parent loans) while enrolled at the college is shown, as is the average dollar figure per-borrower of cumulative undergraduate indebtedness (this does not include loans from other institutions). *Parent loans* shows the total amount borrowed through parent loan programs as well as the percentages that were applied to the need-based and non-need-based portions of financial need. *Programs* indicates the major loan programs available to undergraduates. These include Direct and Federal Stafford Student Loans (subsidized and unsubsidized and PLUS), Perkins Loans, Federal Nursing Loans, state loans, college/university loans, and other types.

Note: As a result of the Health Care and Education Reconciliation Act, beginning July 1, 2010, federal student loans will no longer be made by private lenders under the Federal Family Education Loan (FFEL) Program. Instead, all new federal student loans will come directly from the U.S. Department of Education under the Direct Loan Program. Any FFEL loans noted in this section of an institution's profile will no longer be available.

Loans are forms of aid that must be repaid with interest. Most people will borrow money to pay college costs. The loans available through financial aid programs are offered at very favorable interest rates. Student loans are preferable to parent loans because the payoff is deferred. In comparing colleges, the dollar amount of total indebtedness of the last class is a factor to be considered. Typically, this amount would increase proportionate to the tuition. However, if it does not, this could mean that the college provides relatively generous grant or work-study aid rather than loans in its financial aid package.

Work-Study

The total dollar amounts, number, and average dollar amount of *Federal work-study* (FWS) jobs appear first. The total dollar figure of *State or other work-study/employment*, if available, is shown, as is the percentage of those dollars that go to meet financial need. The number of part-time jobs available on campus to undergraduates, other than work-study, is shown last.

FWS is a federally funded program that enables students with demonstrated need to earn money by working on or off campus, usually in a nonprofit organization. FWS jobs are a special category of jobs that are open to students only through the financial aid office. Other kinds of part-time jobs are routinely available at most colleges and may vary widely. In comparing colleges, you may find characteristic differences in how the "self-help" amounts (loans and work-study) are apportioned.

Athletic Awards

The total dollar amount of athletic scholarships given by the college to undergraduate students, including percentages that are need-based and non-need-based, is indicated.

Applying for Financial Aid

Required financial aid forms include the FAFSA (Free Application for Federal Student Aid), the institution's own form, CSS/Financial Aid PROFILE, a state aid form, a noncustodial (divorced/separated) parent's statement, a business/farm supplement, and others. The college's financial aid application deadline is noted as the *Financial aid deadline* and is shown in one of three ways: as a specific date if it is an absolute deadline; noted as *continuous*, which means processing goes on without a deadline or until all available aid has been awarded; or as a date with the note *(priority)*, meaning that you are encouraged to apply before that date in order to have the best chance of obtaining aid. *Notification date* is listed as either a specific date or *continuous*. The date by which a reply to the college with the decision to accept or decline its financial aid package is listed as either a specific date or as a number of weeks from the date of notification.

Be prepared to check early with the colleges as to exactly which forms will be required. All colleges require the FAFSA for students applying for federal aid. In most cases, colleges have a limited amount of funds set aside to use as financial aid. It is possible that the first eligible students will get a larger share of what is available.

Contact

The name, title, address, telephone and fax numbers, and e-mail address of the person to contact for further information (student financial aid contact) are given at the end of the profile. You should feel free to write or call for any materials you need or if you have questions.

Appendix

This section lists more than 400 state-specific grants and loans. Award amounts, number of awards, eligibility requirements, application requirements, and deadlines are given for all programs.

Indexes

Six indexes in the back of the book allow you to search for particular award programs based on the following criteria:

Non-Need Scholarships for Undergraduates

This index lists the colleges that report that they offer scholarships based on academic interests, abilities, achievements, or personal characteristics other than financial need. Specific categories appear in alphabetical order under the following broad groups:

- Academic Interests/Achievements
- Creative Arts/Performance
- Special Achievements/Activities
- Special Characteristics

See the index for specific categories in each group.

Athletic Grants for Undergraduates

This index lists the colleges that report offering scholarships on the basis of athletic abilities.

Co-op Programs

This index lists colleges that report offering cooperative education programs. These are formal arrangements with off-campus employers that are designed to allow students to combine study and work, often in a position related to the student's field of study. Salaries typically are set at regular marketplace levels, and academic credit is often given.

ROTC Programs

This index lists colleges that offer Reserve Officers' Training Corps programs. The index is arranged by the branch of service that sponsors the program.

Tuition Waivers

This index lists colleges that report offering full or partial tuition waivers for certain categories of students. A majority of colleges offer tuition waivers to employees or children of employees.

How to Use This Guide

Because this benefit is so common and the affected employees usually are aware of it, no separate index of schools offering this option is provided. However, this information is included in the individual college profiles.

Tuition Payment Alternatives

This index lists colleges that report offering tuition payment alternatives. These payment alternatives include deferred payment plans, guaranteed tuition plans, installment payment plans, and prepayment plans.

Data Collection Procedures

The data contained in the college chart, profiles, and indexes were collected in winter and spring 2010 through *Peterson's Annual Survey of Undergraduate Financial Aid* and *Peterson's Annual Survey of Undergraduate Institutions*. Questionnaires were sent to the more than 2,100 institutions of higher education that are accredited in the U.S. and U.S. territories and offer full four- or five-year baccalaureate degrees via full-time on-campus programs of study. Officials at the colleges—usually financial aid or admission officers but sometimes registrars or institutional research staff members—completed and returned the forms. Peterson's has every reason to believe that the data presented in this book are accurate. However, students should always confirm costs and other facts with a specific school at the time of application, since colleges can and do change policies and fees whenever necessary.

The state aid data presented in *Peterson's How to Get Money for College* was submitted by state officials (usually the director of the state scholarship commission) to Peterson's in spring 2010. Because regulations for any government-sponsored program may be changed at any time, you should request written descriptive materials from the office administering a program in which you are interested.

Criteria for Inclusion in This Book

To be included in this guide, an institution must have full accreditation or be a candidate for accreditation (preaccreditation) status by an institutional or specialized accrediting body recognized by the U.S. Department of Education or the Council for Higher Education Accreditation (CHEA). Institutional accrediting bodies, which review each institution as a whole, include the six regional associations of schools and colleges (Middle States, New England, North Central, Northwest, Southern, and Western), each of which is responsible for a specified portion of the United States and its territories. Other institutional accrediting bodies are national in scope and accredit specific kinds of institutions (e.g., Bible colleges, independent colleges, and rabbinical and Talmudic schools). Program registration by the New York State Board of Regents is considered to be the equivalent of institutional accreditation, since the board requires that all programs offered by an institution meet its standards before recognition is granted. There are recognized specialized or professional accrediting bodies in more than forty different fields, each of which is authorized to accredit institutions or specific programs in its particular field. For specialized institutions that offer programs in one field only, we designate this to be the equivalent of institutional accreditation. A full explanation of the accrediting process and complete information on recognized, institutional (regional and national) and specialized accrediting bodies can be found online at www.chea.org or at www.ed.gov/admins/finaid/accred/index.html.

Quick-Reference Chart

College Costs At-a-Glance

Michael Steidel

To help shed some light on the typical patterns of financial aid offered by colleges, we have prepared the following chart. This chart can help you to better understand financial aid practices in general, form realistic expectations about the amounts of aid that might be provided by specific colleges or universities, and prepare for meaningful discussions with the financial aid officers at colleges being considered. The data appearing in the chart have been supplied by the schools themselves and are also shown in the individual college profiles.

Tuition and fees are based on the total of full-time tuition and mandatory fees for the 2010–11 academic year or for the 2009–10 academic year if 2010–11 figures are not available. More information about these costs, as well as the costs of room and board and the year for which they are current, can be found in the individual college profiles. For institutions that have two or more tuition rates for different categories of students or types of programs, the lowest rate is used in figuring the cost.

The colleges are listed alphabetically by state. An "NR" in any individual column indicates that the applicable data element was "Not Reported."

The chart is divided into eight columns of information for each college:

1. Institutional Control

Whether the school is independent (ind.), including independent, independent–religious, and proprietary, or public (pub.), including federal, state, commonwealth, territory, county, district, city, state, local, and state-related.

2. Tuition and Fees

Based on the total of full-time tuition and mandatory fees. An asterisk indicates that the school includes room and board in their mandatory fees.

3. Room and Board

If a school has room and board costs that vary according to the type of accommodation and meal plan, either the lowest figures are represented or the figures are for the most common room arrangement and a full meal plan. If a school has only housing arrangements, a dagger appears to the right of the number. An "NA" will appear in this column if no college-owned or -operated housing facilities are offered.

4. Percent of Eligible Freshmen Receiving Need-Based Gift Awards

Calculated by dividing the number of freshman students determined to have need who received need-based gift aid by the number of full-time freshmen.

5. Percent of Freshmen Whose Need Was Fully Met

Calculated by dividing the number of freshman students whose financial need was fully met by the number of freshmen with need.

6. Average Financial Aid Package for Freshmen

The average dollar amount from all sources, including *gift aid* (scholarships and grants) and *self-help* (jobs and loans), awarded to freshmen receiving aid. Note that this aid package may exceed tuition and fees if the average aid package included coverage of room and board expenses.

7. Average Net Cost After Aid

Average aid package subtracted from published costs (tuition, fees, room, and board) to produce what the average student will have to pay.

8. Average Indebtedness Upon Graduation

Average per-student indebtedness of graduating seniors.

Because personal situations vary widely, it is very important to note that an individual's aid package can be quite different from the averages. Moreover, the data shown for each school can fluctuate widely from year to year, depending on the number of applicants, the amount of need to be met, and the financial resources and policies of the college. Peterson's intent in presenting this chart is to provide you with useful facts and figures that can serve as general guidelines in the pursuit of financial aid. We caution you to use the data only as a jumping-off point for further investigation and analysis, not as a means to rank or select colleges.

After you have narrowed down the choice of colleges based on academic and personal criteria, we recommend that you carefully study this chart. From it, you can develop a list of questions for financial aid officers at the colleges under serious consideration. Here are just a few questions you might want to ask:

■ What are the specific types and sources of aid provided to freshmen at this school?

College Costs At-a-Glance

- What factors does this college consider in determining whether a financial aid applicant is qualified for its need-based aid programs?

- How does the college determine the combination of types of aid that make up an individual's package?

- How are non-need-based awards treated: as a part of the aid package or as a part of the parental/family contribution?

- Does this school "guarantee" financial aid and, if so, how is its policy implemented? Guaranteed aid means that, by policy, 100 percent of need is met for all students judged to have need. Implementation determines *how* need is met and varies widely from school to school. For example, grade point average may determine the apportioning of scholarship, loan, and work-study aid. Rules for freshmen may be different from those for upperclass students.

- To what degree is the admission process "need-blind"? Need-blind means that admission decisions are made without regard to the student's need for financial aid.

- What are the norms and practices for upperclass students? Peterson's chart presents information on *freshmen* financial aid only; however, the financial aid office should be able and willing to provide you with comparable figures for upperclass students. A college might offer a wonderful package for the freshman year, then leave students mostly on their own to fund the remaining three years. Or the school may provide a higher proportion of scholarship money for freshmen, then rebalance its aid packages to contain more self-help aid (loans and work-study) in upperclass years. There is an assumption that, all other factors being equal, students who have settled into the pattern of college time management can handle more work-study hours than freshmen. Grade point average, tuition increases, changes in parental financial circumstances, and other factors may also affect the redistribution.

Michael Steidel is Director of Admission at Carnegie Mellon University.

College Costs At-a-Glance

	Institutional Control ind.=independent; pub.=public	Tuition and Fees	Room and Board	Percent of Eligible Freshmen Receiving Need-Based Gift Awards	Percent of Freshmen Whose Need Was Fully Met	Average Financial Aid Package for Freshmen	Average Net Cost After Aid	Average Indebtedness Upon Graduation
Alabama								
Alabama State University	pub.	$ 6468	$ 4600	86%	12%	$14,192	—	$31,317
Amridge University	ind.	$ 7700	NA	NR	NR	NR	NR	$18,000
Athens State University	pub.	$ 4350	NA	NR	NR	NR	NR	NR
Auburn University	pub.	$ 6972	$ 8972	81%	22%	$ 9182	$ 6762	$22,232
Auburn University Montgomery	pub.	$ 6300	$ 3720†	75%	47%	NR	NR	NR
Faulkner University	ind.	$14,810	$ 6570	NR	NR	NR	NR	NR
Heritage Christian University	ind.	$11,840	$ 5425	NR	NR	NR	NR	NR
Huntingdon College	ind.	$20,990	$ 8000	100%	15%	$16,904	$12,086	$14,034
Jacksonville State University	pub.	$ 6240	$ 5254	52%	NR	$ 5378	$ 6116	NR
Judson College	ind.	$13,535	$ 8300	100%	17%	$12,572	$ 9263	$17,563
Samford University	ind.	$20,420	$ 6624	95%	16%	$17,144	$ 9900	$15,702
Southeastern Bible College	ind.	$11,150	$ 2450†	NR	NR	NR	NR	NR
Spring Hill College	ind.	$25,450	$ 9730	97%	29%	$25,251	$ 9929	$21,823
Stillman College	ind.	$13,462	$ 6336	91%	42%	$19,798	—	$32,188
Troy University	pub.	$ 7016	$ 6042	67%	NR	$ 3854	$ 9204	NR
Tuskegee University	ind.	$16,750	$ 7570	85%	68%	$13,824	$10,496	$31,000
The University of Alabama	pub.	$ 7000	$ 7796	73%	14%	$ 9094	$ 5702	$23,964
The University of Alabama at Birmingham	pub.	$ 5096	$ 8142	56%	21%	$ 9201	$ 4037	$21,670
The University of Alabama in Huntsville	pub.	$ 6510	$ 7208	90%	17%	$ 8925	$ 4793	$24,938
University of Mobile	ind.	$14,850	$ 7570	100%	NR	$14,543	$ 7877	$18,840
University of Montevallo	pub.	$ 7750	$ 4924	91%	24%	$ 8777	$ 3897	$16,581
University of North Alabama	pub.	$ 6042	$ 4784	67%	48%	$ 4230	$ 6596	$24,500
University of South Alabama	pub.	$ 5962	$ 5344	72%	57%	$ 2722	$ 8584	NR
The University of West Alabama	pub.	$ 5420	$ 3748	93%	77%	NR	NR	$17,406
Alaska								
Alaska Pacific University	ind.	$26,360	$ 9300	47%	5%	$10,900	$24,760	$43,392
University of Alaska Anchorage	pub.	$ 4580	$ 7962	76%	18%	$ 9427	$ 3115	$22,043
University of Alaska Fairbanks	pub.	$ 5668	$ 6800	70%	42%	$ 9655	$ 2813	$29,485
Arizona								
Arizona State University	pub.	$ 8132	$ 9706	91%	31%	$10,808	$ 7030	$17,008
College of the Humanities and Sciences, Harrison Middleton University	ind.	$27,200	NR	NR	NR	NR	NR	NR
Embry-Riddle Aeronautical University	ind.	$29,380	$ 8530	100%	NR	$19,633	$18,277	NR
Northern Arizona University	pub.	$ 6632	$ 7872	61%	20%	$ 8623	$ 5881	$16,703
Prescott College	ind.	$23,643	$ 3630†	98%	14%	$15,439	$11,834	$14,947
University of Advancing Technology	ind.	$18,900	$11,034	NR	NR	NR	NR	NR
Western International University	ind.	$11,250	NA	NR	NR	$ 2617	$ 8633	$ 5285
Arkansas								
Arkansas State University—Jonesboro	pub.	$ 6370	$ 5856	98%	33%	$ 9500	$ 2726	$18,900
Arkansas Tech University	pub.	$ 5610	$ 5156	87%	24%	$ 7582	$ 3184	$12,562
Harding University	ind.	$13,580	$ 5814	97%	28%	$11,543	$ 7851	$31,043
Henderson State University	pub.	$ 6204	$ 5034	68%	4%	$11,380	—	$16,529
Hendrix College	ind.	$30,270	$ 8664	100%	43%	$24,108	$14,826	$17,641

NA = not applicable; NR = not reported; * = includes room and board; † = room only; — = not available.

College Costs At-a-Glance

	Institutional Control ind.=independent; pub=public	Tuition and Fees	Room and Board	Percent of Eligible Freshmen Receiving Need-Based Gift Awards	Percent of Freshmen Whose Need Was Fully Met	Average Financial Aid Package for Freshmen	Average Net Cost After Aid	Average Indebtedness Upon Graduation
Arkansas—*continued*								
John Brown University	ind.	$18,880	$ 6876	87%	8%	$15,761	$ 9995	$19,991
Lyon College	ind.	$19,968	$ 7340	100%	25%	$17,086	$10,222	$18,428
Ouachita Baptist University	ind.	$19,820	$ 5840	98%	43%	$16,975	$ 8685	$14,156
Southern Arkansas University–Magnolia	pub.	$ 6066	$ 4400	93%	81%	$ 7486	$ 2980	$15,672
University of Arkansas	pub.	$ 6400	$ 7422	82%	25%	$ 9074	$ 4748	$20,171
University of Central Arkansas	pub.	$ 6699	$ 4880	NR	NR	NR	NR	NR
University of the Ozarks	ind.	$20,530	$ 6300	97%	22%	$19,491	$ 7339	$18,425
Williams Baptist College	ind.	$11,400	$ 5200	100%	NR	$13,676	$ 2924	$16,826
California								
Academy of Art University	ind.	$22,490	$13,400	52%	NR	$ 7005	$28,885	$ 8112
Alliant International University	ind.	$15,220	NR	NR	NR	NR	NR	NR
American Jewish University	ind.	$22,352	$11,216	43%	96%	$24,000	$ 9568	$28,000
Azusa Pacific University	ind.	$27,750	$ 8314	100%	24%	$20,918	$15,146	NR
Biola University	ind.	$28,044	$ 8367	77%	100%	$27,937	$ 8474	$26,555
California Baptist University	ind.	$23,266	$ 8170	87%	88%	$ 8954	$22,482	$34,650
California Christian College	ind.	$ 6840	$ 3850	50%	NR	$ 8003	$ 2687	$ 4500
California College of the Arts	ind.	$33,264	$ 6600†	94%	2%	$25,033	$14,831	$29,508
California Institute of the Arts	ind.	$36,742	$ 9293	94%	5%	$27,722	$18,313	$38,349
California Lutheran University	ind.	$31,000	$10,580	100%	25%	$24,700	$16,880	$23,920
California Maritime Academy	pub.	$ 4400	$ 9750	NR	NR	NR	NR	NR
California Polytechnic State University, San Luis Obispo	pub.	$ 6198	$ 9623	81%	16%	$ 8544	$ 7277	NR
California State Polytechnic University, Pomona	pub.	$ 4551	$ 9570	80%	20%	$ 9932	$ 4189	$14,117
California State University, Chico	pub.	$ 5336	$ 9404	68%	15%	$13,803	$ 937	NR
California State University, Dominguez Hills	pub.	$ 4645	$10,085	85%	1%	$ 4705	$10,025	$ 7946
California State University, East Bay	pub.	$ 4872	$10,029	86%	3%	$10,378	$ 4523	$14,643
California State University, Fresno	pub.	$ 3687	$ 8590	80%	15%	$10,192	$ 2085	$10,406
California State University, Fullerton	pub.	$ 4662	$ 9242	100%	50%	$11,435	$ 2469	$14,706
California State University, Long Beach	pub.	$ 4606	$11,038	86%	72%	$11,917	$ 3727	$10,927
California State University, Los Angeles	pub.	$ 4640	$ 9105	81%	24%	$ 8893	$ 4852	NR
California State University, Monterey Bay	pub.	$ 4517	$ 8290	52%	24%	$ 9438	$ 3369	$15,254
California State University, San Bernardino	pub.	$ 5373	NR	85%	8%	$10,448	—	NR
California State University, Stanislaus	pub.	$ 4840	$ 8880	78%	16%	$ 9879	$ 3841	$16,500
Chapman University	ind.	$38,524	$12,957	98%	100%	$28,920	$22,561	$23,917
Claremont McKenna College	ind.	$38,745	$12,525	98%	100%	$34,428	$16,842	$ 9259
The Colburn School Conservatory of Music	ind.	$ 0	$ 0	NR	NR	NR	NR	NR
Concordia University	ind.	$26,000	$ 8380	93%	19%	$25,589	$ 8791	$23,113
Dominican University of California	ind.	$35,587	$13,560	100%	12%	$22,237	$26,910	$26,176
Golden Gate University	ind.	$15,120	NA	NR	NR	NR	NR	$17,522
Harvey Mudd College	ind.	$40,390	$13,198	98%	100%	$31,455	$22,133	$16,384
Hope International University	ind.	$23,565	$ 7400	100%	NR	$17,152	$13,813	$27,000
Humboldt State University	pub.	$ 5166	$ 9510	76%	4%	$11,048	$ 3628	$17,668
The Master's College and Seminary	ind.	$24,650	$ 8000	100%	25%	$18,617	$14,033	$30,003

NA = not applicable; NR = not reported; * = includes room and board; † = room only; — = not available.

College Costs At-a-Glance

	Institutional Control ind.=independent; pub.=public	Tuition and Fees	Room and Board	Percent of Eligible Freshmen Receiving Need-Based Gift Awards	Percent of Freshmen Whose Need Was Fully Met	Average Financial Aid Package for Freshmen	Average Net Cost After Aid	Average Indebtedness Upon Graduation
California—*continued*								
Menlo College	ind.	$33,550	$11,330	93%	12%	$26,596	$18,284	$25,696
Mills College	ind.	$37,605	$11,644	100%	42%	$34,128	$15,121	$24,255
Mount St. Mary's College	ind.	$30,132	$ 9830	92%	7%	$28,975	$10,987	$33,030
National University	ind.	$10,788	NA	56%	1%	$ 8332	$ 2456	$18,468
Notre Dame de Namur University	ind.	$28,500	$11,600	100%	5%	$25,188	$14,912	$21,758
Occidental College	ind.	$40,903	$11,360	99%	100%	$33,612	$18,651	$17,561
Otis College of Art and Design	ind.	$31,360	NR	96%	4%	$19,616	$11,744	$27,903
Pacific Union College	ind.	$23,979	$ 6750	100%	17%	$18,530	$12,199	$19,000
Pepperdine University (Malibu)	ind.	$37,850	$10,900	86%	32%	$34,936	$13,814	$28,299
Pitzer College	ind.	$39,330	$11,440	100%	100%	$37,361	$13,409	$20,448
Point Loma Nazarene University	ind.	$25,840	$ 8100	86%	9%	$17,046	$16,894	$29,491
Pomona College	ind.	$38,394	$12,936	100%	100%	$37,045	$14,285	$11,700
Saint Mary's College of California	ind.	$33,910	$11,940	85%	2%	$29,442	$16,408	$31,330
Samuel Merritt University	ind.	$34,148	NA	NR	NR	NR	NR	NR
San Diego Christian College	ind.	$22,692	$ 8260	62%	31%	$13,222	$17,730	$24,722
San Diego State University	pub.	$ 4902	$11,485	70%	20%	$ 7700	$ 8687	$14,700
San Francisco Conservatory of Music	ind.	$35,180	NR	100%	17%	$23,064	$12,116	$15,454
San Francisco State University	pub.	$ 4740	$10,904	66%	8%	$10,042	$ 5602	$15,684
San Jose State University	pub.	$ 3992	$ 8663	92%	46%	$12,124	$ 531	$12,313
Santa Clara University	ind.	$36,000	$11,400	78%	42%	$26,456	$20,944	$23,909
Scripps College	ind.	$39,060	$11,850	97%	100%	$36,163	$14,747	$11,270
Simpson University	ind.	$21,000	$ 7000	100%	23%	$ 9912	$18,088	$17,940
Sonoma State University	pub.	$ 5290	$10,086	53%	14%	$ 8841	$ 6535	$15,954
Stanford University	ind.	$37,881	$11,463	98%	96%	$40,204	$ 9140	$16,219
Thomas Aquinas College	ind.	$22,400	$ 7400	91%	100%	$19,716	$10,084	$14,303
University of California, Berkeley	pub.	$ 9817	$15,308	94%	51%	$20,400	$ 4725	$14,493
University of California, Davis	pub.	$ 9364	$12,361	96%	15%	$17,676	$ 4049	$16,222
University of California, Irvine	pub.	$11,913	$10,655	92%	38%	$16,321	$ 6247	$15,529
University of California, Los Angeles	pub.	$ 9151	$13,314	95%	23%	$17,905	$ 4560	$16,824
University of California, Riverside	pub.	$ 8507	$10,900	95%	49%	$18,067	$ 1340	$16,398
University of California, San Diego	pub.	$ 9698	$11,057	97%	38%	$19,318	$ 1437	$17,679
University of California, Santa Barbara	pub.	$ 9055	$12,765	92%	35%	$18,878	$ 2942	$17,768
University of California, Santa Cruz	pub.	$10,095	$13,641	92%	51%	$19,228	$ 4508	$16,024
University of La Verne	ind.	$29,800	$10,440	68%	9%	$26,195	$14,045	$25,491
University of Redlands	ind.	$33,894	$10,472	100%	19%	$29,994	$14,372	$24,218
University of San Diego	ind.	$36,292	$12,602	96%	28%	$33,076	$15,818	$27,999
University of Southern California	ind.	$39,184	$11,458	85%	97%	$35,653	$14,989	$30,097
University of the Pacific	ind.	$32,230	$10,616	96%	37%	$29,490	$13,356	NR
Vanguard University of Southern California	ind.	$26,342	$ 8274	84%	13%	$19,528	$15,088	$26,435
Westmont College	ind.	$34,460	$10,960	100%	10%	$24,160	$21,260	$25,565
Whittier College	ind.	$34,388	$ 9758	82%	25%	$31,833	$12,313	$40,862
William Jessup University	ind.	$19,980	$ 7840	41%	20%	$16,789	$11,031	$15,802
Woodbury University	ind.	$28,855	$ 9293	98%	5%	$18,655	$19,493	$47,059

NA = not applicable; NR = not reported; * = includes room and board; † = room only; — = not available.

College Costs At-a-Glance

	Institutional Control ind.=independent; pub.=public	Tuition and Fees	Room and Board	Percent of Eligible Freshmen Receiving Need-Based Gift Awards	Percent of Freshmen Whose Need Was Fully Met	Average Financial Aid Package for Freshmen	Average Net Cost After Aid	Average Indebtedness Upon Graduation
Colorado								
Adams State College	pub.	$ 4454	$ 7020	92%	1%	$ 8649	$ 2825	$21,211
The Colorado College	ind.	$37,478	$ 9624	95%	55%	$29,359	$17,743	$16,172
Colorado School of Mines	pub.	$12,244	$ 8120	73%	37%	$13,830	$ 6534	$22,500
Colorado State University	pub.	$ 6318	$ 8378	94%	44%	$ 9564	$ 5132	$20,432
Colorado State University–Pueblo	pub.	$ 5210	$ 6750	88%	9%	$ 7980	$ 3980	$16,981
Fort Lewis College	pub.	$ 7632	$ 8304	72%	22%	$ 7154	$ 8782	$15,962
Johnson & Wales University	ind.	$24,141	$ 8904	86%	15%	$15,748	$17,297	NR
Jones International University	ind.	$11,400	NR	86%	NR	$ 7175	$ 4225	NR
Metropolitan State College of Denver	pub.	$ 3639	NA	96%	4%	$ 6018	—	$20,620
Naropa University	ind.	$23,520	$ 8478	97%	10%	$24,300	$ 7698	$23,717
Nazarene Bible College	ind.	$ 8640	NA	67%	NR	$ 4506	$ 4134	$28,448
Rocky Mountain College of Art + Design	ind.	$26,832	NA	41%	3%	$14,687	$12,145	$28,872
University of Colorado at Boulder	pub.	$ 7932	$10,378	90%	73%	$13,445	$ 4865	$19,211
University of Colorado at Colorado Springs	pub.	$ 5693	$ 7490	82%	10%	$ 7176	$ 6007	$20,923
University of Colorado Denver	pub.	$ 6657	$11,374	96%	10%	$ 8129	$ 9902	$21,264
University of Denver	ind.	$36,501	$10,224	99%	30%	$29,211	$17,514	$26,986
University of Northern Colorado	pub.	$ 5116	$ 8370	81%	62%	$14,785	—	NR
Western State College of Colorado	pub.	$ 4064	$ 8324	50%	15%	$ 7500	$ 4888	$17,750
Connecticut								
Albertus Magnus College	ind.	$23,126	$ 9914	48%	4%	$11,098	$21,942	$26,404
Central Connecticut State University	pub.	$ 7414	$ 9122	92%	13%	$ 7770	$ 8766	$19,200
Connecticut College	ind.	*$51,115	NR	90%	100%	$30,502	$20,613	$22,038
Fairfield University	ind.	$37,490	$11,270	86%	22%	$29,123	$19,637	$35,161
Lyme Academy College of Fine Arts	ind.	$24,860	NA	71%	NR	$14,405	$10,455	$18,460
Post University	ind.	$25,050	$ 9700	95%	1%	$16,087	$18,663	$18,000
Quinnipiac University	ind.	$34,250	$12,730	98%	13%	$20,351	$26,629	$34,621
Sacred Heart University	ind.	$30,298	$11,684	99%	13%	$19,074	$22,908	$27,000
Saint Joseph College	ind.	$27,202	$12,437	100%	10%	$23,828	$15,811	$39,743
Southern Connecticut State University	pub.	$ 8050	$ 9983	80%	31%	$ 8291	$ 9742	$17,374
Trinity College	ind.	$42,370	$10,960	95%	100%	$36,504	$16,826	$20,174
University of Bridgeport	ind.	$25,465	$11,080	94%	11%	$25,307	$11,238	NR
University of Connecticut	pub.	$10,416	$10,782	80%	19%	$12,930	$ 8268	$21,257
University of Hartford	ind.	$29,852	$11,572	30%	15%	$21,105	$20,319	$29,869
University of New Haven	ind.	$29,470	$12,204	100%	15%	$20,193	$21,481	$36,272
Wesleyan University	ind.	$40,092	$11,040	91%	100%	$34,382	$16,750	$29,174
Western Connecticut State University	pub.	$ 7909	$ 5858†	31%	41%	$ 4662	$ 9105	$26,024
Yale University	ind.	$36,500	$11,000	100%	100%	$39,282	$ 8218	$10,717
Delaware								
Goldey-Beacom College	ind.	$18,660	$ 5021†	96%	23%	$13,799	$ 9882	NR
University of Delaware	pub.	$ 9486	$ 9066	75%	56%	$12,610	$ 5942	$17,200
District of Columbia								
American University	ind.	$36,697	$13,468	56%	30%	$33,429	$16,736	$40,966

NA = not applicable; NR = not reported; * = includes room and board; † = room only; — = not available.

College Costs At-a-Glance

	Institutional Control ind.=independent; pub.=public	Tuition and Fees	Room and Board	Percent of Eligible Freshmen Receiving Need-Based Gift Awards	Percent of Freshmen Whose Need Was Fully Met	Average Financial Aid Package for Freshmen	Average Net Cost After Aid	Average Indebtedness Upon Graduation
District of Columbia—_continued_								
The Catholic University of America	ind.	$31,890	$12,134	99%	49%	$21,198	$22,826	NR
Gallaudet University	ind.	$11,226	$ 9660	99%	39%	$16,894	$ 3992	$13,484
The George Washington University	ind.	$41,655	$10,120	97%	88%	$36,215	$15,560	$31,299
Howard University	ind.	$16,075	$ 7966	45%	36%	$16,889	$ 7152	$16,473
University of the District of Columbia	pub.	$ 5370	NA	88%	32%	$ 5250	$ 120	$17,547
Florida								
Ave Maria University	ind.	$17,745	$ 7980	99%	18%	$14,730	$10,995	NR
The Baptist College of Florida	ind.	$ 8500	$ 4066	92%	7%	$ 5830	$ 6736	$ 5316
Barry University	ind.	$25,500	$ 8486	79%	11%	$24,934	$ 9052	NR
Bethune-Cookman University	ind.	$12,936	$ 7672	97%	4%	$12,204	$ 8404	$27,103
Clearwater Christian College	ind.	$14,710	$ 6740	100%	16%	$10,913	$10,537	$18,000
Eckerd College	ind.	$33,228	$ 9326	100%	50%	$26,761	$15,793	$30,494
Embry-Riddle Aeronautical University	ind.	$29,724	$ 8840	99%	NR	$12,906	$25,658	NR
Embry-Riddle Aeronautical University Worldwide	ind.	$ 5520	NA	59%	NR	$ 5834	—	NR
Flagler College	ind.	$13,330	$ 7190	85%	8%	$12,302	$ 8218	$18,190
Florida Atlantic University	pub.	$ 4187	$ 9582	95%	13%	$ 8847	$ 4922	$17,338
Florida College	ind.	$12,150	$ 6440	66%	6%	$11,126	$ 7464	NR
Florida Gulf Coast University	pub.	$ 5724	$ 7642	52%	10%	$ 6852	$ 6514	$21,247
Florida Institute of Technology	ind.	$31,520	$10,630	100%	24%	$29,134	$13,016	$40,630
Florida International University	pub.	$ 4580	$11,946	55%	13%	$ 6369	$10,157	$14,912
Florida Southern College	ind.	$24,662	$ 8310	69%	31%	$19,543	$13,429	$22,910
Florida State University	pub.	$ 4566	$ 8000	57%	81%	$10,263	$ 2303	$19,364
Hodges University	ind.	$16,940	NA	94%	31%	$ 8500	$ 8440	$17,600
Jacksonville University	ind.	$25,300	$ 9060	81%	20%	$20,744	$13,616	NR
Johnson & Wales University	ind.	$24,429	$ 8904	95%	10%	$18,957	$14,376	NR
Lynn University	ind.	$30,100	$10,900	87%	99%	$22,852	$18,148	$34,075
New College of Florida	pub.	$ 4784	$ 7783	100%	67%	$13,471	—	$14,794
Northwood University, Florida Campus	ind.	$18,408	$ 8562	88%	12%	$17,741	$ 9229	$29,264
Nova Southeastern University	ind.	$21,100	$ 8360	58%	12%	$18,542	$10,918	$36,908
Palm Beach Atlantic University	ind.	$22,700	$ 8220	87%	33%	$19,644	$11,276	$22,443
Ringling College of Art and Design	ind.	$28,470	$10,470	94%	4%	$15,103	$23,837	$52,173
Rollins College	ind.	$36,220	$11,320	99%	26%	$33,073	$14,467	$22,255
Saint Leo University	ind.	$17,646	$ 8724	100%	26%	$18,200	$ 8170	$23,787
St. Thomas University	ind.	$21,690	$ 6516	74%	19%	NR	NR	NR
Southeastern University	ind.	$15,000	$ 7566	98%	15%	$10,088	$12,478	$23,613
Stetson University	ind.	$33,424	$ 9805	99%	25%	$29,858	$13,371	$30,914
Trinity College of Florida	ind.	$11,824	$ 6656	100%	15%	$ 4371	$14,109	$15,233
University of Central Florida	pub.	$ 4526	$ 8540	58%	19%	$ 7956	$ 5110	$17,044
University of Florida	pub.	$ 4373	$ 7500	60%	41%	$12,792	—	$15,932
University of Miami	ind.	$37,836	$11,062	97%	35%	$31,230	$17,668	$24,396
University of North Florida	pub.	$ 4193	$ 9982	70%	15%	$ 1635	$12,540	$15,619
The University of Tampa	ind.	$22,482	$ 8296	78%	22%	$15,900	$14,878	$28,129

NA = not applicable; NR = not reported; * = includes room and board; † = room only; — = not available.

College Costs At-a-Glance

	Institutional Control ind.=independent; pub.=public	Tuition and Fees	Room and Board	Percent of Eligible Freshmen Receiving Need-Based Gift Awards	Percent of Freshmen Whose Need Was Fully Met	Average Financial Aid Package for Freshmen	Average Net Cost After Aid	Average Indebtedness Upon Graduation
Florida—*continued*								
University of West Florida	pub.	$ 4210	$ 6900	NR	NR	NR	NR	NR
Webber International University	ind.	$17,850	$ 6972	100%	18%	$17,870	$ 6952	$25,962
Georgia								
Agnes Scott College	ind.	$31,283	$ 9850	100%	30%	$30,031	$11,102	$23,176
Armstrong Atlantic State University	pub.	$ 4048	$ 5398	80%	82%	$ 6500	$ 2946	$19,000
Berry College	ind.	$23,360	$ 8340	100%	23%	$20,971	$10,729	$17,502
Brenau University	ind.	$20,130	$10,065	100%	24%	$21,146	$ 9049	$17,999
Brewton-Parker College	ind.	$15,290	$ 6253	100%	19%	$11,647	$ 9896	$28,231
Columbus State University	pub.	$ 5024	$ 7090	66%	17%	$ 8238	$ 3876	$21,538
Covenant College	ind.	$25,270	$ 7170	97%	35%	$19,717	$12,723	$17,824
Dalton State College	pub.	$ 2292	NR	79%	20%	$ 6566	—	$11,953
Emmanuel College	ind.	$12,880	$ 5520	98%	15%	$13,988	$ 4412	$23,880
Emory University	ind.	$38,600	$12,300	97%	97%	$33,262	$17,638	$25,865
Georgia College & State University	pub.	$ 6902	$ 8228	43%	NR	$ 8197	$ 6933	$15,800
Georgia Institute of Technology	pub.	$ 7506	$ 8384	94%	44%	$11,216	$ 4674	$21,239
Georgia Southern University	pub.	$ 5440	$ 7900	86%	17%	$ 7646	$ 5694	$18,618
Georgia State University	pub.	$ 7498	$10,140	64%	7%	$10,157	$ 7481	$13,166
Kennesaw State University	pub.	$ 5144	$ 6593	50%	13%	$ 4068	$ 7669	$ 2845
LaGrange College	ind.	$21,169	$ 8576	NR	NR	NR	NR	NR
Life University	ind.	$ 8352	$12,480	80%	NR	$ 9800	$11,032	$17,600
Medical College of Georgia	pub.	$ 6782	NR	NR	NR	NR	NR	NR
Mercer University	ind.	$29,540	$ 8788	100%	52%	$31,648	$ 6680	$29,065
Morehouse College	ind.	$21,376	$10,946	50%	9%	$10,925	$21,397	$32,125
North Georgia College & State University	pub.	$ 5036	$ 5248	NR	NR	NR	NR	$ 9885
Oglethorpe University	ind.	$26,700	$ 9990	100%	38%	$26,585	$10,105	$18,650
Piedmont College	ind.	$18,000	NR	29%	34%	$18,230	—	$16,910
Reinhardt University	ind.	$16,670	$ 6272	99%	10%	$ 8071	$14,871	$21,095
Savannah College of Art and Design	ind.	$29,570	$11,750	61%	8%	$13,771	$27,549	NR
Southern Polytechnic State University	pub.	$ 4498	$ 6350	56%	37%	$ 3101	$ 7747	$16,280
Truett-McConnell College	ind.	$14,000	$ 5700	99%	16%	$11,888	$ 7812	$16,742
University of Georgia	pub.	$ 7530	$ 8046	97%	29%	$11,122	$ 4454	$14,766
University of West Georgia	pub.	$ 4582	$ 6254	88%	22%	$ 8427	$ 2409	$14,347
Valdosta State University	pub.	$ 4488	$ 6480	79%	53%	$11,142	—	$18,221
Wesleyan College	ind.	$17,500	$ 8000	100%	37%	$14,567	$10,933	$20,983
Guam								
University of Guam	pub.	$ 5770	$ 9102	93%	NR	NR	NR	NR
Hawaii								
Chaminade University of Honolulu	ind.	$17,740	$10,420	NR	NR	NR	NR	$22,263
Hawai'i Pacific University	ind.	$14,960	$11,094	77%	NR	$14,414	$11,640	$22,802
University of Hawaii–West Oahu	pub.	$ 4666	NA	100%	NR	$ 2470	$ 2196	NR
Idaho								
Boise State University	pub.	$ 4864	$ 5602	78%	21%	$ 7401	$ 3065	$38,056

NA = not applicable; NR = not reported; * = includes room and board; † = room only; — = not available.

College Costs At-a-Glance	Institutional Control ind.=independent; pub.=public	Tuition and Fees	Room and Board	Percent of Eligible Freshmen Receiving Need-Based Gift Awards	Percent of Freshmen Whose Need Was Fully Met	Average Financial Aid Package for Freshmen	Average Net Cost After Aid	Average Indebtedness Upon Graduation
Idaho—continued								
The College of Idaho	ind.	$21,050	$ 7700	69%	20%	$17,364	$11,386	$24,919
Idaho State University	pub.	$ 4968	$ 5050	NR	NR	NR	NR	NR
Northwest Nazarene University	ind.	$23,090	$ 6020	81%	25%	$16,586	$12,524	$25,758
University of Idaho	pub.	$ 4932	$ 7242	60%	30%	$11,284	$ 890	$21,702
Illinois								
Augustana College	ind.	$31,326	$ 7950	100%	42%	$26,748	$12,528	NR
Aurora University	ind.	$18,700	$ 8800	75%	37%	$17,761	$ 9739	$23,935
Benedictine University	ind.	$22,310	$ 7360	66%	NR	$19,182	$10,488	$25,781
Blessing-Rieman College of Nursing	ind.	$22,290	$ 7890	NR	NR	NR	NR	$20,000
Bradley University	ind.	$24,224	$ 7650	99%	34%	$17,449	$14,425	$17,067
Columbia College Chicago	ind.	$19,850	$10,780†	2%	73%	$ 8383	$22,247	NR
Concordia University Chicago	ind.	$24,581	$ 8000	100%	22%	$21,902	$10,679	$21,086
DePaul University	ind.	$27,342	$10,617	85%	12%	$22,449	$15,510	$19,072
Dominican University	ind.	$24,700	$ 7620	100%	13%	$20,477	$11,843	$21,392
Eastern Illinois University	pub.	$ 9540	$ 8078	53%	10%	$ 8624	$ 8994	$14,233
East-West University	ind.	$15,750	NA	100%	NR	$10,318	$ 5432	$ 3500
Elmhurst College	ind.	$28,660	$ 8216	98%	35%	$22,312	$14,564	$18,329
Greenville College	ind.	$20,924	$ 7034	100%	11%	$16,727	$11,231	NR
Illinois College	ind.	$21,300	$ 7600	100%	30%	$18,322	$10,578	$21,258
Illinois Institute of Technology	ind.	$32,443	$10,094	99%	27%	$27,509	$15,028	NR
Illinois State University	pub.	$10,471	$ 8093	64%	41%	$11,528	$ 7036	$20,105
Illinois Wesleyan University	ind.	$33,982	$ 7776	100%	37%	$25,359	$16,399	$26,458
Knox College	ind.	$31,911	$ 7164	100%	32%	$26,016	$13,059	$24,018
Lake Forest College	ind.	$34,206	$ 8006	100%	100%	$28,600	$13,612	$29,279
Lakeview College of Nursing	ind.	$12,800	NA	NR	NR	NR	NR	NR
Lewis University	ind.	$22,990	$ 8350	72%	47%	$16,414	$14,926	$20,413
Lexington College	ind.	$23,800	NA	NR	NR	NR	NR	NR
Loyola University Chicago	ind.	$32,114	$11,220	99%	10%	$27,357	$15,977	$35,526
MacMurray College	ind.	$18,165	$ 7538	98%	53%	$23,423	$ 2280	$27,524
McKendree University	ind.	$22,070	$ 7850	100%	19%	$20,472	$ 9448	$19,445
Millikin University	ind.	$26,345	$ 7866	97%	43%	$22,656	$11,555	$28,449
Monmouth College	ind.	$24,950	$ 7300	100%	22%	$22,388	$ 9862	$24,476
Moody Bible Institute	ind.	$ 1275	$ 8240	NR	NR	NR	NR	NR
North Central College	ind.	$26,916	$ 8565	100%	32%	$21,663	$13,818	$27,285
Northeastern Illinois University	pub.	$ 8508	NA	92%	3%	$ 8042	$ 466	$10,903
Northern Illinois University	pub.	$ 9079	$ 9588	71%	9%	$11,877	$ 6790	$24,154
North Park University	ind.	$18,800	$ 7580	97%	7%	$11,550	$14,830	NR
Northwestern University	ind.	$38,461	$11,703	94%	100%	$30,424	$19,740	$20,802
Principia College	ind.	$23,625	$ 9000	78%	88%	$23,837	$ 8788	$14,963
Quincy University	ind.	$22,030	$ 8380	100%	24%	$22,199	$ 8211	$21,785
Robert Morris University Illinois	ind.	$20,100	$ 9945	81%	4%	$11,980	$18,065	$26,752
Rockford College	ind.	$24,750	$ 6950	99%	14%	$17,362	$14,338	$25,845

NA = not applicable; NR = not reported; * = includes room and board; † = room only; — = not available.

College Costs At-a-Glance

	Institutional Control ind.=independent; pub.=public	Tuition and Fees	Room and Board	Percent of Eligible Freshmen Receiving Need-Based Gift Awards	Percent of Freshmen Whose Need Was Fully Met	Average Financial Aid Package for Freshmen	Average Net Cost After Aid	Average Indebtedness Upon Graduation
Illinois—continued								
Saint Anthony College of Nursing	ind.	$19,250	NA	NR	NR	NR	NR	$26,000
Saint Francis Medical Center College of Nursing	ind.	$15,436	$ 2400†	NR	NR	NR	NR	NR
Saint Xavier University	ind.	$24,340	$ 8408	100%	19%	$22,370	$10,378	$26,939
School of the Art Institute of Chicago	ind.	$35,950	$ 9800†	99%	3%	$24,480	$21,270	$34,578
Shimer College	ind.	$27,810	$12,850	100%	NR	$17,911	$22,749	NR
Southern Illinois University Carbondale	pub.	$10,411	$ 7673	75%	88%	$11,811	$ 6273	$21,359
Southern Illinois University Edwardsville	pub.	$ 8336	$ 7461	53%	20%	$16,090	—	$20,603
Trinity Christian College	ind.	$21,335	$ 8125	97%	7%	$15,134	$14,326	$33,133
Trinity College of Nursing and Health Sciences	ind.	$ 5186	NA	NR	NR	NR	NR	NR
Trinity International University	ind.	$21,980	$ 7430	75%	11%	$20,998	$ 8412	$23,864
University of Chicago	ind.	$39,432	$11,697	99%	100%	$39,153	$11,976	$24,238
University of Illinois at Chicago	pub.	$12,034	$ 9435	80%	22%	$12,813	$ 8656	$17,276
University of Illinois at Springfield	pub.	$ 9532	$ 9200	95%	14%	$11,499	$ 7233	$14,717
University of Illinois at Urbana–Champaign	pub.	$12,660	$ 9284	81%	50%	$13,146	$ 8798	$19,378
University of St. Francis	ind.	$22,698	$ 7938	61%	63%	$20,943	$ 9693	$21,594
Western Illinois University	pub.	$ 8958	$ 7642	72%	37%	$ 9087	$ 7513	$20,550
West Suburban College of Nursing	ind.	$21,536	NA	NR	NR	NR	NR	NR
Wheaton College	ind.	$27,580	$ 8050	93%	25%	$24,042	$11,588	$20,455
Indiana								
Anderson University	ind.	$23,970	$ 8350	99%	20%	$20,170	$12,150	$25,401
Ball State University	pub.	$ 7830	$ 7932	56%	26%	$ 9489	$ 6273	$22,598
Bethel College	ind.	$20,978	$ 6250	68%	NR	NR	NR	$17,800
Butler University	ind.	$29,246	$ 9740	99%	20%	$22,592	$16,394	$30,470
Calumet College of Saint Joseph	ind.	$13,220	NA	84%	5%	$11,579	$ 1641	$22,534
Crossroads Bible College	ind.	$ 9850	$ 3000†	NR	NR	NR	NR	NR
DePauw University	ind.	$33,250	$ 8740	100%	33%	$29,279	$12,711	$24,210
Earlham College	ind.	$36,494	$ 7400	90%	32%	$28,502	$15,392	$23,752
Franklin College	ind.	$23,275	$ 6885	100%	18%	$17,652	$12,508	$26,903
Grace College	ind.	$21,100	$ 6880	NR	NR	NR	NR	NR
Hanover College	ind.	$26,350	$ 7900	100%	33%	$23,593	$10,657	$27,807
Holy Cross College	ind.	$18,700	$ 8000	NR	NR	NR	NR	NR
Huntington University	ind.	$22,330	$ 7430	98%	9%	$17,010	$12,750	$27,541
Indiana State University	pub.	$ 7426	$ 7463	66%	15%	$ 8938	$ 5951	$23,963
Indiana University Bloomington	pub.	$ 8613	$ 7546	84%	20%	$10,799	$ 5360	$25,522
Indiana University East	pub.	$ 5801	NA	89%	11%	$ 7254	—	$27,300
Indiana University Kokomo	pub.	$ 5838	NA	76%	6%	$ 6696	—	$24,788
Indiana University Northwest	pub.	$ 5919	NA	81%	4%	$ 7480	—	$28,403
Indiana University–Purdue University Fort Wayne	pub.	$ 6233	$ 5620†	55%	1%	$ 8190	$ 3663	$22,092
Indiana University–Purdue University Indianapolis	pub.	$ 7523	$ 3370†	81%	6%	$ 9083	$ 1810	$27,062
Indiana University South Bend	pub.	$ 6015	NA	83%	4%	$ 7018	—	$25,384
Indiana University Southeast	pub.	$ 5890	$ 5630†	83%	6%	$ 6904	$ 4616	$22,649
Indiana Wesleyan University	ind.	$21,213	$ 7008	91%	10%	$19,867	$ 8354	$26,610

NA = not applicable; NR = not reported; * = includes room and board; † = room only; — = not available.

College Costs At-a-Glance

	Institutional Control ind.=independent; pub.=public	Tuition and Fees	Room and Board	Percent of Eligible Freshmen Receiving Need-Based Gift Awards	Percent of Freshmen Whose Need Was Fully Met	Average Financial Aid Package for Freshmen	Average Net Cost After Aid	Average Indebtedness Upon Graduation
Indiana—*continued*								
Manchester College	ind.	$23,790	$ 8550	90%	10%	$20,391	$11,949	$16,235
Marian University	ind.	$24,960	$ 7810	59%	29%	$22,298	$10,472	$23,467
Martin University	ind.	$13,520	NA	15%	7%	$ 8231	$ 5289	$28,600
Purdue University	pub.	$ 8638	$ 8710	72%	57%	$10,950	$ 6398	$23,924
Purdue University Calumet	pub.	$ 6337	$ 6653	67%	43%	$ 3960	$ 9030	$19,706
Purdue University North Central	pub.	$ 6704	NA	52%	12%	$ 5783	$ 921	$20,859
Rose-Hulman Institute of Technology	ind.	$34,560	$ 9441	100%	19%	$26,184	$17,817	$35,261
Saint Joseph's College	ind.	$24,530	$ 7420	97%	35%	$22,827	$ 9123	$28,135
Saint Mary's College	ind.	$29,616	$ 9206	95%	23%	$25,163	$13,659	$25,531
Taylor University	ind.	$25,396	$ 6708	98%	19%	$17,990	$14,114	$22,971
Trine University	ind.	$25,400	$ 8500	58%	100%	$19,118	$14,782	$19,334
University of Evansville	ind.	$26,756	$ 8670	100%	30%	$25,222	$10,204	$25,598
University of Indianapolis	ind.	$21,170	$ 8040	75%	20%	$18,127	$11,083	$27,070
University of Notre Dame	ind.	$38,477	$10,368	97%	98%	$34,802	$14,043	$28,371
University of Saint Francis	ind.	$21,760	$ 6750	99%	19%	$18,231	$10,279	$28,428
University of Southern Indiana	pub.	$ 5474	$ 6700	75%	17%	$ 8172	$ 4002	NR
Valparaiso University	ind.	$28,320	$ 7960	99%	24%	$21,739	$14,541	$31,783
Wabash College	ind.	$29,750	$ 7600	100%	94%	$28,136	$ 9214	$28,383
Iowa								
Allen College	ind.	$14,995	NR	100%	NR	$ 9491	$ 5504	$29,010
Briar Cliff University	ind.	$22,536	$ 6978	100%	69%	$ 6500	$23,014	$31,853
Buena Vista University	ind.	$25,540	$ 7292	90%	56%	$26,306	$ 6526	$40,569
Central College	ind.	$25,010	$ 8368	100%	26%	$23,302	$10,076	$36,068
Clarke College	ind.	$23,520	$ 6840	100%	27%	$20,370	$ 9990	$34,386
Coe College	ind.	$29,270	$ 7150	100%	27%	$24,679	$11,741	$30,665
Cornell College	ind.	$29,400	$ 7500	100%	44%	$30,205	$ 6695	$27,990
Dordt College	ind.	$22,080	$ 6010	100%	16%	$21,991	$ 6099	$19,988
Drake University	ind.	$25,622	$ 7800	99%	34%	$20,921	$12,501	$34,919
Graceland University	ind.	$20,980	$ 7040	100%	21%	$20,874	$ 7146	$29,934
Grand View University	ind.	$19,324	$ 6442	91%	26%	$17,732	$ 8034	$28,041
Grinnell College	ind.	$36,476	$ 8536	100%	100%	$34,463	$10,549	$19,540
Iowa State University of Science and Technology	pub.	$ 6997	NR	99%	46%	$10,780	—	$30,411
Iowa Wesleyan College	ind.	$21,000	$ 6654	NR	NR	NR	NR	NR
Loras College	ind.	$26,234	$ 7271	90%	45%	$20,546	$12,959	$30,100
Luther College	ind.	$33,480	$ 5800	100%	37%	$26,727	$12,553	$34,101
Morningside College	ind.	$22,980	$ 7040	82%	30%	$19,430	$10,590	$37,479
Mount Mercy College	ind.	$22,100	$ 6984	100%	22%	$18,647	$10,437	$30,233
St. Ambrose University	ind.	$23,910	$ 8585	100%	49%	$17,785	$14,710	$33,216
Simpson College	ind.	$25,733	$ 7261	100%	25%	$25,779	$ 7215	$34,354
University of Dubuque	ind.	$21,590	$ 7370	100%	29%	$19,471	$ 9489	$41,399
The University of Iowa	pub.	$ 7417	$ 8331	60%	54%	$ 7344	$ 8404	$22,684
University of Northern Iowa	pub.	$ 7008	$ 7189	51%	27%	$ 7911	$ 6286	$24,123

NA = not applicable; NR = not reported; * = includes room and board; † = room only; — = not available.

College Costs At-a-Glance

	Institutional Control ind.=independent; pub.=public	Tuition and Fees	Room and Board	Percent of Eligible Freshmen Receiving Need-Based Gift Awards	Percent of Freshmen Whose Need Was Fully Met	Average Financial Aid Package for Freshmen	Average Net Cost After Aid	Average Indebtedness Upon Graduation
Iowa—_continued_								
Waldorf College	ind.	$18,760	$5954	100%	18%	$16,104	$ 8610	$30,348
Wartburg College	ind.	$29,020	$7975	100%	21%	$21,441	$15,554	$27,225
Kansas								
Baker University	ind.	$21,050	$6800	NR	NR	$11,453	$16,397	$26,869
Benedictine College	ind.	$19,500	$6575	100%	24%	$22,120	$ 3955	$25,749
Bethany College	ind.	$20,026	$6174	87%	47%	$20,763	$ 5437	$22,699
Bethel College	ind.	$19,990	$6770	79%	47%	$21,053	$ 5707	$24,241
Emporia State University	pub.	$ 4374	$6146	94%	15%	$ 5472	$ 5048	$21,158
Kansas State University	pub.	$ 6870	$6752	64%	23%	$ 9488	$ 4134	$19,281
McPherson College	ind.	$18,400	$6910	86%	36%	$19,181	$ 6129	$25,787
MidAmerica Nazarene University	ind.	$20,250	$6750	100%	17%	$15,258	$11,742	$28,859
Newman University	ind.	$20,712	$6938	80%	29%	$16,017	$11,633	$23,996
Pittsburg State University	pub.	$ 4592	$5744	71%	69%	$ 9820	$ 516	$18,516
Southwestern College	ind.	$19,630	$5750	100%	20%	$20,328	$ 5052	$27,973
Tabor College	ind.	$19,660	$6870	81%	15%	$19,133	$ 7397	$20,500
The University of Kansas	pub.	$ 8206	$6802	69%	20%	$ 8437	$ 6571	$22,478
Washburn University	pub.	$ 6116	$5792	61%	14%	$ 7670	$ 4238	$17,031
Wichita State University	pub.	$ 5450	$6700	64%	73%	$ 6676	$ 5474	$15,769
Kentucky								
Alice Lloyd College	ind.	$ 1400	$4450	100%	17%	$ 9736	—	$ 6500
Asbury University	ind.	$23,303	$5566	100%	32%	$19,835	$ 9034	$26,150
Bellarmine University	ind.	$30,310	$8550	100%	24%	$25,373	$13,487	$21,639
Berea College	ind.	$ 876	$5768	100%	NR	$33,840	—	$ 8133
Brescia University	ind.	$17,390	$8000	NR	NR	NR	NR	$18,638
Campbellsville University	ind.	$19,710	$6740	100%	22%	$16,321	$10,129	$18,100
Clear Creek Baptist Bible College	ind.	$ 8700	NR	100%	NR	$ 6314	$ 2386	NR
Eastern Kentucky University	pub.	$ 6312	$6020	67%	14%	$10,719	$ 1613	$12,588
Georgetown College	ind.	$26,080	$7030	100%	38%	$24,384	$ 8726	$24,462
Kentucky State University	pub.	$ 5920	$6480	81%	19%	$ 8370	$ 4030	$24,826
Kentucky Wesleyan College	ind.	$16,870	$6440	100%	25%	$16,819	$ 6491	$20,906
Lindsey Wilson College	ind.	$18,950	$7645	100%	33%	$15,063	$11,532	$24,741
Mid-Continent University	ind.	$13,700	$6500	95%	3%	$ 7718	$12,482	$10,782
Morehead State University	pub.	$ 6036	$6192	65%	33%	$ 9432	$ 2796	$24,045
Murray State University	pub.	$ 5976	$6562	90%	91%	$ 5110	$ 7428	$18,000
Northern Kentucky University	pub.	$ 6792	NR	46%	18%	$ 6886	—	$23,129
Pikeville College	ind.	$14,535	$6000	97%	74%	$15,558	$ 4977	$18,103
Thomas More College	ind.	$24,720	$6530	98%	28%	$18,249	$13,001	$26,862
Transylvania University	ind.	$25,280	$7770	100%	22%	$22,378	$10,672	$19,893
Union College	ind.	$18,860	$5950	100%	21%	$18,884	$ 5926	$22,388
University of Kentucky	pub.	$ 8123	$9125	40%	20%	$13,180	$ 4068	$22,943
University of Louisville	pub.	$ 7944	$5437	97%	26%	$10,465	$ 2916	$17,651
University of the Cumberlands	ind.	$17,000	$6826	100%	31%	$17,384	$ 6442	$19,339

NA = not applicable; NR = not reported; * = includes room and board; † = room only; — = not available.

College Costs At-a-Glance

	Institutional Control ind.=independent; pub.=public	Tuition and Fees	Room and Board	Percent of Eligible Freshmen Receiving Need-Based Gift Awards	Percent of Freshmen Whose Need Was Fully Met	Average Financial Aid Package for Freshmen	Average Net Cost After Aid	Average Indebtedness Upon Graduation
Kentucky—*continued*								
Western Kentucky University	pub.	$ 7200	$ 6351	69%	32%	$11,180	$ 2371	$17,436
Louisiana								
Centenary College of Louisiana	ind.	$23,280	$ 7940	100%	36%	$20,292	$10,928	$18,100
Dillard University	ind.	$13,880	$ 8386	100%	7%	$16,148	$ 6118	$27,500
Louisiana State University and Agricultural and Mechanical College	pub.	$ 5233	$ 7738	97%	25%	$10,976	$ 1995	$18,118
Louisiana Tech University	pub.	$ 5220	$ 5055	94%	27%	$ 9278	$ 997	$12,408
Loyola University New Orleans	ind.	$31,504	$10,388	100%	25%	$26,836	$15,056	$22,320
Nicholls State University	pub.	$ 3965	$ 7310	94%	82%	$ 8124	$ 3151	$18,822
Northwestern State University of Louisiana	pub.	$ 3786	$ 6682	71%	52%	$ 6459	$ 4009	$21,773
Our Lady of Holy Cross College	ind.	$ 4035	NA	63%	NR	$ 7550	—	$48,000
Saint Joseph Seminary College	ind.	$12,882	$11,168	100%	100%	$ 5350	$18,700	$ 5000
Southeastern Louisiana University	pub.	$ 3932	$ 6450	57%	36%	$ 6118	$ 4264	$18,947
Tulane University	ind.	$40,584	$ 9606	98%	69%	$34,265	$15,925	$27,461
University of New Orleans	pub.	$ 4372	$ 6700	65%	21%	$ 8799	$ 2273	$13,623
Xavier University of Louisiana	ind.	$15,300	$ 7000	73%	1%	$15,114	$ 7186	$32,872
Maine								
Bates College	ind.	*$51,300	NR	98%	93%	$35,342	$15,958	$17,945
Bowdoin College	ind.	$40,020	$10,880	100%	100%	$35,470	$15,430	$18,382
Colby College	ind.	*$50,320	NR	98%	100%	$34,919	$15,401	$21,697
College of the Atlantic	ind.	$34,380	$ 8250	100%	70%	$35,406	$ 7224	$20,170
Husson University	ind.	$13,450	$ 7239	88%	6%	$12,187	$ 8502	$33,010
Maine College of Art	ind.	$30,115	$ 9800	100%	3%	$13,152	$26,763	$33,350
Maine Maritime Academy	pub.	$10,105	$ 8450	63%	11%	$ 7299	$11,256	$39,237
New England School of Communications	ind.	$11,500	$ 6994	76%	71%	NR	NR	$33,000
Saint Joseph's College of Maine	ind.	$26,050	$10,350	100%	9%	$21,499	$14,901	$36,071
University of Maine	pub.	$ 9626	$ 8008	89%	31%	$10,342	$ 7292	$30,824
University of Maine at Augusta	pub.	$ 6855	NA	91%	13%	$ 6538	$ 317	$15,842
University of Maine at Fort Kent	pub.	$ 6803	$ 7080	61%	47%	$ 6089	$ 7794	NR
University of Maine at Presque Isle	pub.	$ 6875	$ 7300	100%	52%	$ 9268	$ 4907	NR
University of New England	ind.	$27,920	$10,870	100%	15%	$23,854	$14,936	$44,325
Maryland								
Bowie State University	pub.	$ 6040	$ 7536	73%	57%	$ 7913	$ 5663	$17,108
College of Notre Dame of Maryland	ind.	$28,350	$ 9500	100%	24%	$22,926	$14,924	$33,882
Coppin State University	pub.	$ 5276	$ 7496	80%	15%	$ 8859	$ 3913	$ 9005
Frostburg State University	pub.	$ 6684	$ 7304	75%	28%	$ 9783	$ 4205	$18,255
Goucher College	ind.	$35,142	$10,756	96%	18%	$26,553	$19,345	$18,465
Hood College	ind.	$29,860	$ 9901	99%	26%	$23,557	$16,204	$17,382
The Johns Hopkins University	ind.	$39,150	$12,040	81%	94%	$29,322	$21,868	$21,859
Loyola University Maryland	ind.	$37,610	$11,280	90%	100%	$26,345	$22,545	$26,855
McDaniel College	ind.	$32,000	$ 6820	99%	30%	$25,979	$12,841	$25,325
Mount St. Mary's University	ind.	$30,350	$10,308	100%	26%	$20,278	$20,380	$26,160
Peabody Conservatory of The Johns Hopkins University	ind.	$34,675	$11,100	95%	29%	$19,838	$25,937	$39,482

NA = not applicable; NR = not reported; * = includes room and board; † = room only; — = not available.

College Costs At-a-Glance	Institutional Control ind.=independent; pub.=public	Tuition and Fees	Room and Board	Percent of Eligible Freshmen Receiving Need-Based Gift Awards	Percent of Freshmen Whose Need Was Fully Met	Average Financial Aid Package for Freshmen	Average Net Cost After Aid	Average Indebtedness Upon Graduation
Maryland—continued								
St. John's College	ind.	$42,192	$ 9984	79%	75%	$28,282	$23,894	$24,216
St. Mary's College of Maryland	pub.	$13,630	$10,245	38%	NR	$ 7500	$16,375	$17,125
Salisbury University	pub.	$ 6618	$ 8070	88%	23%	$ 6850	$ 7838	$17,521
Stevenson University	ind.	$20,644	$10,296	97%	26%	$15,294	$15,646	$20,779
Towson University	pub.	$ 7418	$ 8670	63%	18%	$ 8910	$ 7178	$13,245
University of Maryland, Baltimore County	pub.	$ 8872	$ 9303	88%	33%	$12,294	$ 5881	$19,353
University of Maryland, College Park	pub.	$ 8053	$ 9377	58%	15%	$ 9920	$ 7510	$20,256
University of Maryland Eastern Shore	pub.	$ 6082	$ 7230	95%	54%	$14,879	—	$ 8500
University of Maryland University College	pub.	$ 5760	NA	71%	NR	$ 5214	$ 546	NR
Washington College	ind.	$35,350	$ 7460	100%	50%	$22,987	$19,823	$20,611
Massachusetts								
Amherst College	ind.	$38,928	$10,150	98%	100%	$40,107	$ 8971	$11,347
Anna Maria College	ind.	$26,620	$ 9630	99%	8%	$18,507	$17,743	$35,575
The Art Institute of Boston at Lesley University	ind.	$27,600	$12,800	NR	NR	$17,174	$23,226	$17,000
Assumption College	ind.	$30,171	$ 6340	100%	18%	$18,975	$17,536	$24,382
Atlantic Union College	ind.	$17,066	$ 5150	100%	11%	$12,991	$ 9225	$39,013
Babson College	ind.	$37,824	$13,500	91%	24%	$29,408	$21,916	$28,164
Bard College at Simon's Rock	ind.	$40,170	$10,960	81%	14%	$33,119	$18,011	$20,000
Becker College	ind.	$27,748	$ 9760	92%	3%	$13,959	$23,549	$31,800
Bentley University	ind.	$35,828	$11,740	84%	43%	$29,106	$18,462	$33,073
Berklee College of Music	ind.	$30,650	$15,080	51%	5%	$12,207	$33,523	NR
Boston Architectural College	ind.	$11,468	NA	64%	NR	$ 7102	$ 4366	$52,300
Boston College	ind.	$39,130	$12,909	90%	100%	$31,591	$20,448	$19,514
The Boston Conservatory	ind.	$33,700	$15,880	88%	8%	$13,972	$35,608	$34,931
Boston University	ind.	$39,864	$12,260	94%	57%	$35,431	$16,693	$30,998
Brandeis University	ind.	$38,762	$10,792	93%	13%	$30,398	$19,156	$26,078
Bridgewater State College	pub.	$ 6604	$ 9670	85%	NR	$ 7660	$ 8614	$22,093
Cambridge College	ind.	$10,950	NA	81%	NR	$ 3478	$ 7472	NR
Clark University	ind.	$36,420	$ 6950	99%	63%	$25,904	$17,466	$21,925
College of the Holy Cross	ind.	$39,892	$10,940	82%	100%	$30,760	$20,072	$23,785
Eastern Nazarene College	ind.	$23,772	$ 8000	98%	32%	$23,129	$ 8643	$47,815
Emerson College	ind.	$29,918	$12,280	88%	69%	$18,553	$23,645	$15,262
Emmanuel College	ind.	$29,365	$11,950	94%	45%	$24,212	$17,103	NR
Endicott College	ind.	$25,376	$11,836	75%	12%	$16,920	$20,292	$33,783
Fitchburg State College	pub.	$ 6900	$ 7632	81%	93%	$ 8402	$ 6130	$18,177
Framingham State College	pub.	$ 6540	$ 8148	81%	73%	$ 6802	$ 7886	$19,000
Franklin W. Olin College of Engineering	ind.	$38,045	$13,230	100%	100%	$42,275	$ 9000	NR
Gordon College	ind.	$29,458	$ 8100	100%	18%	$19,624	$17,934	$32,405
Hampshire College	ind.	$39,912	$10,433	100%	76%	$35,840	$14,505	$20,669
Harvard University	ind.	$36,828	$11,856	100%	100%	$41,157	$ 7527	$10,871
Hellenic College	ind.	$18,850	$11,780	100%	NR	$10,100	$20,530	$15,000
Lasell College	ind.	$25,300	$10,500	100%	14%	$21,181	$14,619	$38,428

NA = not applicable; NR = not reported; * = includes room and board; † = room only; — = not available.

College Costs At-a-Glance

	Institutional Control ind.=independent; pub.=public	Tuition and Fees	Room and Board	Percent of Eligible Freshmen Receiving Need-Based Gift Awards	Percent of Freshmen Whose Need Was Fully Met	Average Financial Aid Package for Freshmen	Average Net Cost After Aid	Average Indebtedness Upon Graduation
Massachusetts—*continued*								
Lesley University	ind.	$29,400	$12,800	97%	13%	$19,753	$22,447	$17,000
Massachusetts College of Art and Design	pub.	$ 8400	$11,288	55%	NR	$ 8088	$11,600	NR
Massachusetts College of Liberal Arts	pub.	$ 6875	$ 7868	81%	NR	$10,392	$ 4351	$17,297
Massachusetts College of Pharmacy and Health Sciences	ind.	$24,550	$11,900	85%	52%	$14,986	$21,464	NR
Massachusetts Institute of Technology	ind.	$37,782	$11,360	99%	100%	$35,919	$13,223	$15,043
Massachusetts Maritime Academy	pub.	$ 6509	$ 8917	NR	NR	NR	NR	$26,037
Merrimack College	ind.	$29,810	$10,190	75%	90%	$16,727	$23,273	$24,000
Mount Holyoke College	ind.	$39,126	$11,450	99%	100%	$35,797	$14,779	$23,008
Mount Ida College	ind.	$24,500	$12,000	98%	7%	$16,446	$20,054	$43,911
New England Conservatory of Music	ind.	$34,950	$12,100	100%	22%	$20,626	$26,424	$38,509
Nichols College	ind.	$28,870	$ 9330	95%	9%	$22,773	$15,427	$27,112
Northeastern University	ind.	$35,362	$12,350	97%	18%	$23,155	$24,557	NR
Regis College	ind.	$28,900	$12,190	95%	13%	$23,757	$17,333	$24,178
Salem State College	pub.	$ 6790	$ 6625†	NR	NR	NR	NR	NR
School of the Museum of Fine Arts, Boston	ind.	$30,660	$13,046†	86%	16%	$19,081	$24,625	$ 8179
Simmons College	ind.	$31,450	$12,050	100%	7%	$21,704	$21,796	$45,237
Smith College	ind.	$37,758	$12,622	93%	100%	$33,269	$17,111	$21,573
Stonehill College	ind.	$31,210	$12,240	99%	22%	$22,152	$21,298	$29,163
Suffolk University	ind.	$27,208	$14,544	95%	11%	$20,415	$21,337	NR
Tufts University	ind.	$40,342	$10,746	92%	100%	$29,559	$21,529	$23,731
University of Massachusetts Amherst	pub.	$11,917	$ 8276	84%	21%	$12,256	$ 7937	$23,614
University of Massachusetts Boston	pub.	$10,611	NA	93%	63%	$11,660	—	$19,327
University of Massachusetts Dartmouth	pub.	$10,358	$ 8950	99%	45%	$13,643	$ 5665	$21,905
University of Massachusetts Lowell	pub.	$10,681	$ 8635	91%	71%	$10,614	$ 8702	$21,542
Wellesley College	ind.	$38,062	$11,732	98%	100%	$36,064	$13,730	$13,324
Western New England College	ind.	$28,816	$10,980	100%	13%	$20,409	$19,387	NR
Westfield State College	pub.	$ 7016	$ 7728	69%	17%	$ 7853	$ 6891	$18,648
Wheaton College	ind.	$41,084	$10,180	97%	51%	$31,605	$19,659	$25,540
Wheelock College	ind.	$28,160	$11,200	100%	18%	$22,857	$16,503	$43,319
Williams College	ind.	$39,490	$10,390	100%	100%	$38,531	$11,349	$ 7960
Worcester Polytechnic Institute	ind.	$38,920	$11,610	99%	47%	$26,408	$24,122	$44,340
Worcester State College	pub.	$ 6605	$ 9067	87%	44%	$ 9591	$ 6081	$17,819
Michigan								
Adrian College	ind.	$24,440	$ 7460	84%	14%	$20,848	$11,052	$17,160
Albion College	ind.	$30,002	$ 8510	100%	30%	$26,214	$12,298	$30,149
Alma College	ind.	$26,068	$ 8518	99%	24%	$24,671	$ 9915	$31,476
Andrews University	ind.	$21,170	$ 6860	72%	17%	$22,079	$ 5951	$33,931
Calvin College	ind.	$24,035	$ 8275	100%	20%	$18,792	$13,518	$28,500
Central Michigan University	pub.	$10,170	$ 7896	88%	57%	$11,026	$ 7040	$26,615
Cleary University	ind.	$15,600	NA	78%	2%	$13,214	$ 2386	$20,528
College for Creative Studies	ind.	$31,275	$ 8500	NR	NR	NR	NR	$47,604
Concordia University	ind.	$20,390	$ 7606	100%	24%	$17,664	$10,332	$25,789

NA = not applicable; NR = not reported; * = includes room and board; † = room only; — = not available.

College Costs At-a-Glance

College Costs At-a-Glance	Institutional Control ind.=independent; pub.=public	Tuition and Fees	Room and Board	Percent of Eligible Freshmen Receiving Need-Based Gift Awards	Percent of Freshmen Whose Need Was Fully Met	Average Financial Aid Package for Freshmen	Average Net Cost After Aid	Average Indebtedness Upon Graduation
Michigan—*continued*								
Cornerstone University	ind.	$20,520	$ 6510	100%	19%	$20,252	$ 6778	$26,025
Davenport University (Grand Rapids)	ind.	$11,241	$ 9500	NR	NR	NR	NR	NR
Eastern Michigan University	pub.	$ 8378	$ 7785	79%	15%	$ 8930	$ 7233	$22,370
Finlandia University	ind.	$18,436	$ 5974	91%	2%	$16,000	$ 8410	$17,500
Grace Bible College	ind.	$11,400	$ 6250	73%	8%	$10,264	$ 7386	$20,802
Grand Valley State University	pub.	$ 8630	$ 7478	86%	9%	$ 9597	$ 6511	$24,030
Hope College	ind.	$26,510	$ 8110	84%	35%	$22,978	$11,642	$28,682
Kalamazoo College	ind.	$32,643	$ 7776	97%	66%	$26,616	$13,803	NR
Kettering University	ind.	$29,120	$ 6390	88%	19%	$21,719	$13,791	$41,485
Kuyper College	ind.	$16,416	$ 6280	100%	9%	$11,857	$10,839	$21,618
Lake Superior State University	pub.	$ 8384	$ 7994	66%	62%	$12,129	$ 4249	$21,573
Lawrence Technological University	ind.	$23,008	$ 9353	93%	23%	$18,343	$14,018	$42,723
Michigan State University	pub.	$10,880	$ 7394	57%	24%	$11,357	$ 6917	$19,696
Michigan Technological University	pub.	$11,348	$ 8121	83%	13%	$11,961	$ 7508	$26,764
Northern Michigan University	pub.	$ 7454	$ 7846	53%	22%	$ 7596	$ 7704	$24,074
Northwood University	ind.	$18,408	NR	88%	21%	$16,516	$ 1892	$28,634
Oakland University	pub.	$ 8783	$ 7350	73%	19%	$10,510	$ 5623	$19,967
Olivet College	ind.	$19,928	$ 6872	100%	30%	$15,440	$11,360	$21,820
Sacred Heart Major Seminary	ind.	$14,390	$ 7800	NR	NR	NR	NR	NR
Saginaw Valley State University	pub.	$ 6890	$ 7270	62%	22%	$ 7136	$ 7024	$23,555
Spring Arbor University	ind.	$19,790	$ 6950	100%	48%	$22,450	$ 4290	$26,052
University of Michigan	pub.	$12,589	$ 8924	52%	90%	$ 8615	$12,898	$26,819
University of Michigan–Dearborn	pub.	$ 9100	NA	59%	10%	$ 5196	$ 3904	$29,564
University of Michigan–Flint	pub.	$ 8279	$ 6874	NR	NR	NR	NR	NR
Wayne State University	pub.	$ 8643	$ 7210	78%	22%	$11,934	$ 3919	$19,781
Minnesota								
Augsburg College	ind.	$28,864	$ 7760	98%	24%	$23,896	$12,728	$28,988
Bemidji State University	pub.	$ 7510	$ 6425	69%	21%	$ 8223	$ 5712	$24,474
Bethany Lutheran College	ind.	$20,650	$ 6500	100%	21%	$15,621	$11,529	$22,410
Bethel University	ind.	$28,080	$ 8220	100%	22%	$22,343	$13,957	$30,496
Carleton College	ind.	$41,304	$10,806	100%	100%	$31,789	$20,321	$18,601
College of Saint Benedict	ind.	$30,186	$ 8358	99%	55%	$24,818	$13,726	NR
The College of St. Scholastica	ind.	$28,370	$ 7498	84%	15%	$22,896	$12,972	$40,401
College of Visual Arts	ind.	$23,988	NA	100%	3%	$15,906	$ 8082	$38,402
Concordia College	ind.	$27,160	$ 6510	100%	28%	$18,599	$15,071	$29,885
Concordia University, St. Paul	ind.	$27,400	$ 7500	99%	18%	$21,176	$13,724	$32,444
Crown College	ind.	$20,870	$ 7580	76%	14%	$16,722	$11,728	$31,804
Gustavus Adolphus College	ind.	$33,400	$ 8400	100%	45%	$25,665	$16,135	$24,297
Hamline University	ind.	$30,503	$ 8396	100%	24%	$25,046	$13,853	$34,598
Macalester College	ind.	$40,046	$ 9078	99%	100%	$32,533	$16,591	$17,275
Martin Luther College	ind.	$10,990	$ 4260	83%	31%	$ 9294	$ 5956	$15,600
McNally Smith College of Music	ind.	$23,770	NA	NR	NR	NR	NR	NR

NA = not applicable; NR = not reported; * = includes room and board; † = room only; — = not available.

College Costs At-a-Glance

College Costs At-a-Glance	Institutional Control ind.=independent; pub.=public	Tuition and Fees	Room and Board	Percent of Eligible Freshmen Receiving Need-Based Gift Awards	Percent of Freshmen Whose Need Was Fully Met	Average Financial Aid Package for Freshmen	Average Net Cost After Aid	Average Indebtedness Upon Graduation
Minnesota—*continued*								
Metropolitan State University	pub.	$ 5627	NA	NR	NR	NR	NR	NR
Minneapolis College of Art and Design	ind.	$29,700	NR	95%	10%	$15,131	$14,569	$42,346
Minnesota State University Mankato	pub.	$ 6429	$6019	80%	38%	$ 7969	$ 4479	$25,667
Minnesota State University Moorhead	pub.	$ 6918	$6468	65%	100%	$ 7754	$ 5632	$27,918
Northwestern College	ind.	$24,570	$7720	99%	11%	$17,247	$15,043	$26,259
St. Catherine University	ind.	$28,758	$7330	93%	10%	$28,870	$ 7218	$24,400
St. Cloud State University	pub.	$ 6300	$5984	78%	65%	$10,612	$ 1672	$24,484
Saint John's University	ind.	$29,936	$7714	98%	60%	$25,930	$11,720	NR
Saint Mary's University of Minnesota	ind.	$26,090	$6940	100%	19%	$20,617	$12,413	$32,166
St. Olaf College	ind.	$35,500	$8200	100%	100%	$28,081	$15,619	$25,853
Southwest Minnesota State University	pub.	$ 7229	$6846	72%	15%	$ 8615	$ 5460	$18,830
University of Minnesota, Crookston	pub.	$10,647	$6563	96%	35%	$11,188	$ 6022	$26,199
University of Minnesota, Duluth	pub.	$11,004	$6176	100%	33%	$10,805	$ 6375	$27,931
University of Minnesota, Morris	pub.	$10,716	$7050	100%	52%	$14,707	$ 3059	$25,855
University of Minnesota, Twin Cities Campus	pub.	$11,017	$7534	99%	52%	$12,948	$ 5603	$26,516
University of St. Thomas	ind.	$29,467	$8042	99%	82%	$25,400	$12,109	$32,132
Winona State University	pub.	$ 7916	$6556	49%	5%	$ 6028	$ 8444	$27,190
Mississippi								
Alcorn State University	pub.	$ 4488	$5384	88%	55%	$ 9798	$ 74	$18,123
Belhaven University	ind.	$17,700	$6500	100%	12%	$14,628	$ 9572	$32,728
Blue Mountain College	ind.	$ 8570	$3850	91%	69%	$ 9725	$ 2695	NR
Delta State University	pub.	$ 4450	$5714	83%	NR	$ 5495	$ 4669	$19,840
Millsaps College	ind.	$26,240	$9252	99%	48%	$27,574	$ 7918	$31,304
Mississippi College	ind.	$13,550	$6150	73%	37%	$15,070	$ 4630	$26,323
Mississippi State University	pub.	$ 5151	$7520	96%	28%	$ 9743	$ 2928	$23,413
Mississippi University for Women	pub.	$ 4423	$5164	77%	50%	$ 9132	$ 455	$18,363
University of Southern Mississippi	pub.	$ 5096	$6200	65%	27%	$ 9433	$ 1863	$19,915
William Carey University	ind.	$ 9750	$4815	100%	94%	$15,000	—	$17,500
Missouri								
Avila University	ind.	$21,800	$6350	98%	96%	$11,847	$16,303	$16,508
Calvary Bible College and Theological Seminary	ind.	$ 8328	$4400	NR	NR	NR	NR	NR
Central Methodist University	ind.	$18,670	$6240	89%	17%	$15,778	$ 9132	$26,487
College of the Ozarks	ind.	$ 410	$5300	100%	18%	$14,217	—	$ 6029
Columbia College	ind.	$15,596	$6074	83%	6%	$11,270	$10,400	$13,948
Culver-Stockton College	ind.	$22,550	$7400	100%	20%	$20,994	$ 8956	$23,761
Drury University	ind.	$19,854	$6971	94%	87%	$ 7600	$19,225	$20,500
Evangel University	ind.	$15,950	$6000	86%	NR	$10,651	$11,299	$30,506
Hannibal-LaGrange College	ind.	$15,380	$6000	99%	16%	$ 9285	$12,095	NR
Harris-Stowe State University	pub.	$ 5320	$7861	100%	75%	$ 8000	$ 5181	$16,000
Kansas City Art Institute	ind.	$28,580	$8710	100%	20%	$20,773	$16,517	$23,375
Lincoln University	pub.	$ 5685	NR	89%	6%	$ 9258	—	$26,114
Lindenwood University	ind.	$13,600	$7210	63%	35%	$ 7175	$13,635	NR

NA = not applicable; NR = not reported; * = includes room and board; † = room only; — = not available.

College Costs At-a-Glance

	Institutional Control ind.=independent; pub.=public	Tuition and Fees	Room and Board	Percent of Eligible Freshmen Receiving Need-Based Gift Awards	Percent of Freshmen Whose Need Was Fully Met	Average Financial Aid Package for Freshmen	Average Net Cost After Aid	Average Indebtedness Upon Graduation
Missouri—*continued*								
Maryville University of Saint Louis	ind.	$20,994	$ 8210	99%	20%	$18,408	$10,796	$ 18,341
Missouri Baptist University	ind.	$17,860	$ 7090	NR	NR	NR	NR	NR
Missouri Southern State University	pub.	$ 4290	$ 5500	80%	16%	$ 7066	$ 2724	$ 10,006
Missouri State University	pub.	$ 6972	$ 5925	92%	28%	$ 7664	$ 5233	$ 19,813
Missouri University of Science and Technology	pub.	$ 8488	$ 7595	59%	60%	$14,282	$ 1801	$ 24,235
Missouri Western State University	pub.	$ 5560	$ 6600	97%	16%	$ 7556	$ 4604	NR
Rockhurst University	ind.	$25,890	$ 7080	81%	21%	$26,952	$ 6018	$ 21,950
St. Louis Christian College	ind.	$11,000	$ 3600	100%	22%	$15,520	—	$ 11,654
St. Louis College of Pharmacy	ind.	$23,010	$ 8560	100%	9%	$14,172	$17,398	$107,649
Saint Louis University	ind.	$31,342	$ 8900	97%	20%	$24,100	$16,142	$ 33,747
Saint Luke's College	ind.	$ 9520	NA	NR	NR	NR	NR	NR
Southeast Missouri State University	pub.	$ 6255	$ 6358	95%	25%	$ 8660	$ 3953	$ 19,613
Southwest Baptist University	ind.	$17,280	$ 5720	65%	28%	$15,610	$ 7390	NR
Stephens College	ind.	$25,400	$ 7170	100%	22%	$21,020	$11,550	$ 22,942
Truman State University	pub.	$ 6692	$ 6854	73%	70%	$ 8875	$ 4671	$ 21,858
University of Central Missouri	pub.	$ 7311	$ 6320	43%	21%	$ 9024	$ 4607	$ 18,272
University of Missouri	pub.	$ 8501	$ 8100	89%	19%	$14,346	$ 2255	$ 20,689
University of Missouri–Kansas City	pub.	$ 8273	$10,467	95%	10%	$10,758	$ 7982	$ 20,512
University of Missouri–St. Louis	pub.	$ 8595	$ 8164	95%	11%	$ 9205	$ 7554	$ 25,776
Washington University in St. Louis	ind.	$40,374	$12,941	97%	100%	$31,489	$21,826	NR
Webster University	ind.	$21,056	$ 9070	79%	NR	$23,852	$ 6274	$ 26,184
Westminster College	ind.	$17,990	$ 7120	100%	59%	$18,906	$ 6204	$ 20,018
William Jewell College	ind.	$28,750	$ 7200	100%	28%	$23,595	$12,355	$ 24,102
Montana								
Carroll College	ind.	$22,592	$ 7118	83%	23%	$17,292	$12,418	$ 25,246
Montana State University	pub.	$ 5988	NR	75%	8%	$10,635	—	$ 21,571
Montana State University Billings	pub.	$ 5207	$ 5460	79%	4%	$ 8055	$ 2612	$ 23,189
Montana Tech of The University of Montana	pub.	$ 6007	$ 6602	92%	28%	$ 8100	$ 4509	$ 23,000
Rocky Mountain College	ind.	$21,100	$ 6580	98%	18%	$23,280	$ 4400	$ 24,361
University of Great Falls	ind.	$18,856	$ 6712	58%	4%	$15,452	$10,116	NR
The University of Montana	pub.	$ 5533	$ 6611	68%	16%	$ 7871	$ 4273	$ 20,223
The University of Montana Western	pub.	$ 4279	$ 6420	82%	6%	$ 2757	$ 7942	$ 21,969
Nebraska								
College of Saint Mary	ind.	$23,130	$ 6400	99%	10%	$19,481	$10,049	$ 3408
Concordia University, Nebraska	ind.	$22,115	$ 5820	100%	31%	$17,983	$ 9952	$ 21,941
Creighton University	ind.	$22,118	$ 8814	100%	58%	$25,628	$ 5304	$ 32,888
Dana College	ind.	$21,100	$ 6220	76%	23%	$19,085	$ 8235	$ 21,170
Doane College	ind.	$21,040	$ 5970	100%	40%	$18,049	$ 8961	$ 19,196
Grace University	ind.	$14,290	$ 5740	100%	22%	$12,027	$ 8003	$ 17,820
Nebraska Methodist College	ind.	$12,740	$ 5770†	100%	26%	$10,367	$ 8143	$ 34,264
Nebraska Wesleyan University	ind.	$22,432	$ 6230	99%	17%	$16,854	$11,808	$ 21,931
University of Nebraska at Kearney	pub.	$ 5634	$ 6830	66%	33%	$10,019	$ 2445	$ 19,160

NA = not applicable; NR = not reported; * = includes room and board; † = room only; — = not available.

College Costs At-a-Glance

	Institutional Control ind.=independent; pub.=public	Tuition and Fees	Room and Board	Percent of Eligible Freshmen Receiving Need-Based Gift Awards	Percent of Freshmen Whose Need Was Fully Met	Average Financial Aid Package for Freshmen	Average Net Cost After Aid	Average Indebtedness Upon Graduation
Nebraska—continued								
University of Nebraska at Omaha	pub.	$ 6229	$ 7230	66%	NR	$ 2215	$11,244	$19,500
University of Nebraska–Lincoln	pub.	$ 6857	$ 7260	86%	30%	$10,708	$ 3409	$19,128
Wayne State College	pub.	$ 4805	$ 5280	77%	49%	$ 6787	$ 3298	NR
York College	ind.	$14,998	$ 5680	100%	27%	$13,531	$ 7147	$22,020
Nevada								
University of Nevada, Las Vegas	pub.	$ 5525	$10,454	68%	19%	$ 9291	$ 6688	$17,256
University of Nevada, Reno	pub.	$ 5051	$10,595	86%	15%	$ 5860	$ 9786	$15,854
New Hampshire								
Dartmouth College	ind.	$38,679	$11,295	98%	100%	$40,531	$ 9443	$19,081
Franklin Pierce University	ind.	$28,700	$ 9800	89%	15%	$19,282	$19,218	$38,148
Keene State College	pub.	$ 9334	$ 8444	60%	16%	$ 8103	$ 9675	$27,785
New England College	ind.	$27,450	$ 9626	98%	14%	$25,105	$11,971	$33,466
Plymouth State University	pub.	$ 8944	$ 8594	82%	23%	$ 9285	$ 8253	$29,709
Rivier College	ind.	$25,050	$ 9428	99%	6%	$16,773	$17,705	$36,389
Saint Anselm College	ind.	$30,515	$11,550	100%	17%	$24,243	$17,822	$36,823
University of New Hampshire	pub.	$12,743	$ 8874	64%	25%	$18,633	$ 2984	$30,760
University of New Hampshire at Manchester	pub.	$11,126	NA	40%	12%	$ 8959	$ 2167	$23,786
New Jersey								
Bloomfield College	ind.	$21,000	$10,300	96%	2%	$17,893	$13,407	$28,310
The College of New Jersey	pub.	$12,722	$ 9996	44%	15%	$10,442	$12,276	$24,801
College of Saint Elizabeth	ind.	$25,058	$10,904	83%	NR	NR	NR	NR
Drew University	ind.	$38,017	$10,368	100%	22%	$27,846	$20,539	$17,444
Felician College	ind.	$25,050	$ 9700	78%	8%	$21,609	$13,141	$17,026
Georgian Court University	ind.	$24,490	$ 9386	100%	11%	$22,045	$11,831	$33,729
Kean University	pub.	$ 9446	$12,264	99%	9%	$ 9818	$11,892	$19,698
Monmouth University	ind.	$25,013	$ 9554	42%	5%	$18,930	$15,637	$25,000
Montclair State University	pub.	$ 7042	NR	54%	24%	$ 8988	—	$24,226
New Jersey City University	pub.	$ 8988	$ 9043	85%	4%	$ 9098	$ 8933	$11,337
New Jersey Institute of Technology	pub.	$12,856	$ 9806	78%	17%	$13,500	$ 9162	$20,000
Princeton University	ind.	$36,640	$11,940	100%	100%	$34,804	$13,776	$ 4957
Ramapo College of New Jersey	pub.	$11,416	$11,290	44%	19%	$11,783	$10,923	$19,789
The Richard Stockton College of New Jersey	pub.	$11,041	$10,189	49%	30%	$16,224	$ 5006	$27,847
Rider University	ind.	$29,060	$10,720	99%	22%	$22,721	$17,059	$35,042
Rowan University	pub.	$11,234	$ 9958	38%	13%	$ 6977	$14,215	$26,379
Rutgers, The State University of New Jersey, Camden	pub.	$11,698	$ 9788	67%	51%	$11,915	$ 9571	$22,552
Rutgers, The State University of New Jersey, Newark	pub.	$11,414	$11,155	75%	35%	$12,579	$ 9990	$19,500
Rutgers, The State University of New Jersey, New Brunswick	pub.	$11,886	$10,676	57%	48%	$14,625	$ 7937	$19,760
Thomas Edison State College	pub.	$ 4695	NA	NR	NR	NR	NR	NR
William Paterson University of New Jersey	pub.	$10,838	$10,280	55%	38%	$14,180	$ 6938	$25,893
New Mexico								
Eastern New Mexico University	pub.	$ 3552	$ 5374	92%	100%	$ 9379	—	$11,769
New Mexico Institute of Mining and Technology	pub.	$ 4607	$ 5702	52%	36%	$ 9886	$ 423	$ 7894

NA = not applicable; NR = not reported; * = includes room and board; † = room only; — = not available.

College Costs At-a-Glance

	Institutional Control ind.=independent; pub.=public	Tuition and Fees	Room and Board	Percent of Eligible Freshmen Receiving Need-Based Gift Awards	Percent of Freshmen Whose Need Was Fully Met	Average Financial Aid Package for Freshmen	Average Net Cost After Aid	Average Indebtedness Upon Graduation
New Mexico—*continued*								
New Mexico State University	pub.	$ 4998	$ 6338	93%	8%	$ 6783	$ 4553	$23,262
St. John's College	ind.	$40,392	$ 9562	95%	94%	$28,791	$21,163	$27,235
University of the Southwest	ind.	$12,964	$ 9385	54%	10%	$ 1216	$21,133	$32,200
Western New Mexico University	pub.	$ 3589	$ 5200	86%	6%	$ 7297	$ 1492	$ 5500
New York								
Alfred University	ind.	$25,976	$11,364	99%	16%	$24,067	$13,273	$30,731
Bard College	ind.	$39,880	$11,300	94%	60%	$31,959	$19,221	$26,131
Barnard College	ind.	$38,650	$12,319	95%	100%	$35,689	$15,280	$14,706
Bernard M. Baruch College of the City University of New York	pub.	$ 4600	NA	94%	18%	$ 6750	—	$14,265
Brooklyn College of the City University of New York	pub.	$ 5051	NA	93%	98%	$ 5500	—	$16,600
Canisius College	ind.	$29,512	$10,556	99%	37%	$26,843	$13,225	$33,645
Cazenovia College	ind.	$24,152	$10,222	100%	21%	$20,721	$13,653	NR
City College of the City University of New York	pub.	$ 4929	NR	99%	75%	$ 8754	—	$15,100
Clarkson University	ind.	$34,760	$11,564	99%	27%	$32,449	$13,875	$32,125
Colgate University	ind.	$40,970	$ 9970	100%	100%	$39,758	$11,182	$19,202
The College at Brockport, State University of New York	pub.	$ 6108	$ 9200	85%	25%	$ 9345	$ 5963	$26,095
The College of New Rochelle	ind.	$26,426	$ 9600	88%	6%	$25,043	$10,983	$30,052
The College of Saint Rose	ind.	$24,135	$ 9880	90%	3%	$ 9949	$24,066	$29,391
College of Staten Island of the City University of New York	pub.	$ 4978	NA	99%	6%	$ 7264	—	$ 5079
Columbia University	ind.	$39,296	$10,228	99%	100%	$38,196	$11,328	NR
Columbia University, School of General Studies	ind.	$39,910	$12,020	NR	NR	NR	NR	NR
Cooper Union for the Advancement of Science and Art	ind.	$36,650	$13,700	100%	61%	$35,000	$15,350	$13,037
Cornell University	ind.	$37,954	$12,160	98%	100%	$36,062	$14,052	$21,549
The Culinary Institute of America	ind.	$24,550	$ 8110	NR	NR	NR	NR	$29,351
Daemen College	ind.	$20,720	$ 9450	75%	NR	$15,319	$14,851	$18,910
Dominican College	ind.	$21,120	$10,150	85%	19%	$17,002	$14,268	$18,398
Dowling College	ind.	$22,850	$10,200	96%	2%	$18,136	$14,914	$31,000
D'Youville College	ind.	$20,030	$ 9800	100%	30%	$16,190	$13,640	NR
Elmira College	ind.	$34,800	$10,800	100%	19%	$26,911	$18,689	$26,874
Eugene Lang College The New School for Liberal Arts	ind.	$34,550	$15,260	95%	3%	$31,585	$18,225	$25,348
Fashion Institute of Technology	pub.	$ 5618	$11,248	71%	18%	$10,135	$ 6731	$24,554
Five Towns College	ind.	$17,750	$12,300	90%	70%	$ 5400	$24,650	$19,000
Hamilton College	ind.	$39,760	$10,100	100%	100%	$36,931	$12,929	$19,466
Hartwick College	ind.	$33,330	$ 9075	100%	12%	$25,720	$16,685	$32,800
Hofstra University	ind.	$30,130	$11,330	92%	22%	$20,000	$21,460	NR
Houghton College	ind.	$24,440	$ 7000	100%	20%	$21,138	$10,302	$28,334
Hunter College of the City University of New York	pub.	$ 4999	$ 5500†	100%	23%	$ 5241	$ 5258	$ 7500
Iona College	ind.	$28,850	$11,800	84%	20%	$20,002	$20,648	$24,213
Ithaca College	ind.	$32,060	$11,780	98%	63%	$29,600	$14,240	NR
John Jay College of Criminal Justice of the City University of New York	pub.	$ 4600	NA	86%	NR	$10,150	—	$45,000
The Juilliard School	ind.	$30,500	$11,810	88%	24%	$24,656	$17,654	$26,780
Keuka College	ind.	$22,680	$ 9160	100%	8%	$18,666	$13,174	$23,379

NA = not applicable; NR = not reported; * = includes room and board; † = room only; — = not available.

College Costs At-a-Glance

College Costs At-a-Glance	Institutional Control ind.=independent; pub.=public	Tuition and Fees	Room and Board	Percent of Eligible Freshmen Receiving Need-Based Gift Awards	Percent of Freshmen Whose Need Was Fully Met	Average Financial Aid Package for Freshmen	Average Net Cost After Aid	Average Indebtedness Upon Graduation
New York—*continued*								
The King's College	ind.	$27,350	$10,500†	100%	13%	$20,914	$16,936	$15,434
Lehman College of the City University of New York	pub.	$ 4770	$12,569	99%	4%	$ 3889	$13,450	$11,100
Le Moyne College	ind.	$25,830	$ 9990	91%	29%	$20,230	$15,590	$27,483
Manhattan College	ind.	$27,455	$10,670	93%	13%	$17,122	$21,003	$31,076
Manhattanville College	ind.	$34,350	$13,920	96%	10%	$29,687	$18,583	NR
Mannes College The New School for Music	ind.	$33,600	$15,260	91%	NR	$21,033	$27,827	$30,942
Marist College	ind.	$26,604	$11,225	98%	20%	$15,558	$22,271	$35,993
Marymount Manhattan College	ind.	$22,656	$12,874	99%	7%	$14,025	$21,505	$15,988
Medaille College	ind.	$19,590	$ 9288	100%	8%	$24,000	$ 4878	$21,000
Medgar Evers College of the City University of New York	pub.	$ 4902	NA	99%	NR	$ 3865	$ 1037	NR
Molloy College	ind.	$20,960	NA	97%	15%	$14,447	$ 6513	$29,823
Monroe College (New Rochelle)	ind.	$11,744	$ 7940	97%	60%	$11,256	$ 8428	$25,913
Mount Saint Mary College	ind.	$23,300	$11,900	99%	23%	$15,196	$20,004	$32,729
Nazareth College of Rochester	ind.	$26,140	$10,716	100%	23%	$19,324	$17,532	$35,010
The New School for General Studies	ind.	$24,288	$15,260	NR	NR	NR	NR	NR
The New School for Jazz and Contemporary Music	ind.	$33,600	$15,260	87%	NR	$24,582	$24,278	$27,582
New York City College of Technology of the City University of New York	pub.	$ 4939	$ 1500	100%	8%	$ 7839	—	NR
New York Institute of Technology	ind.	$24,140	$10,520	66%	NR	$14,352	$20,308	NR
New York School of Interior Design	ind.	$22,895	$15,600†	72%	11%	$ 8441	$30,054	$21,000
New York University	ind.	$38,765	$13,228	98%	NR	$26,287	$25,706	$33,487
Niagara University	ind.	$24,700	$10,250	99%	55%	$20,592	$14,358	$27,215
Nyack College	ind.	$20,500	$ 8200	100%	13%	$16,493	$12,207	$29,081
Pace University	ind.	$33,542	$12,240	100%	12%	$27,786	$17,996	$34,115
Parsons The New School for Design	ind.	$36,010	$15,260	98%	5%	$30,776	$20,494	$33,576
Polytechnic Institute of NYU	ind.	$34,420	$ 9000	92%	77%	$30,099	$13,321	$31,035
Pratt Institute	ind.	$36,790	$10,020	88%	NR	$12,926	$33,884	NR
Purchase College, State University of New York	pub.	$ 6431	$ 9908	77%	7%	$ 8175	$ 8164	$26,275
Queens College of the City University of New York	pub.	$ 5047	$11,125	79%	NR	$ 7500	$ 8672	$14,000
Rensselaer Polytechnic Institute	ind.	$39,165	$11,145	100%	44%	$33,062	$17,248	$30,838
Roberts Wesleyan College	ind.	$23,780	$ 8520	100%	10%	$21,741	$10,559	$30,329
Rochester Institute of Technology	ind.	$29,283	$ 9642	94%	82%	$22,600	$16,325	NR
Russell Sage College	ind.	$27,790	$ 9670	100%	67%	$32,416	$ 5044	$29,000
Sage College of Albany	ind.	$27,790	$ 9830	82%	73%	$32,500	$ 5120	$24,000
St. Bonaventure University	ind.	$26,895	$ 9071	100%	24%	$24,153	$11,813	$36,832
St. John Fisher College	ind.	$24,320	$10,090	100%	40%	$19,670	$14,740	$30,281
St. John's University	ind.	$30,040	$13,140	90%	9%	$24,228	$18,952	$30,692
St. Joseph's College, Long Island Campus	ind.	$16,765	NA	100%	33%	$10,769	$ 5996	$21,023
St. Joseph's College, New York	ind.	$16,765	NA	100%	27%	$12,314	$ 4451	$20,616
St. Lawrence University	ind.	$39,765	$10,160	100%	41%	$30,029	$19,896	$31,653
Siena College	ind.	$25,285	$ 9930	96%	13%	$17,117	$18,098	$28,200
Skidmore College	ind.	$40,420	$10,776	100%	100%	$33,054	$18,142	$18,303
State University of New York at Binghamton	pub.	$ 6761	$10,614	80%	18%	$11,083	$ 6292	$14,560

NA = not applicable; NR = not reported; * = includes room and board; † = room only; — = not available.

College Costs At-a-Glance

	Institutional Control ind.=independent; pub.=public	Tuition and Fees	Room and Board	Percent of Eligible Freshmen Receiving Need-Based Gift Awards	Percent of Freshmen Whose Need Was Fully Met	Average Financial Aid Package for Freshmen	Average Net Cost After Aid	Average Indebtedness Upon Graduation
New York—*continued*								
State University of New York at Fredonia	pub.	$ 6308	$ 9330	82%	22%	$ 7783	$ 7855	$34,935
State University of New York at New Paltz	pub.	$ 6081	$ 9202	52%	15%	$ 9748	$ 5535	$16,823
State University of New York at Oswego	pub.	$ 6256	$10,870	89%	48%	$10,847	$ 6279	$25,351
State University of New York at Plattsburgh	pub.	$ 6100	$ 8600	91%	37%	$11,182	$ 3518	$21,010
State University of New York College at Geneseo	pub.	$ 6326	$ 9550	47%	70%	$ 4213	$11,663	$21,000
State University of New York College at Old Westbury	pub.	$ 5797	$ 9390	100%	100%	$ 7402	$ 7785	$17,104
State University of New York College at Oneonta	pub.	$ 6185	$ 8900	83%	15%	$10,804	$ 4281	$16,490
State University of New York College at Potsdam	pub.	$ 6124	$ 9270	93%	87%	$14,853	$ 541	$19,220
State University of New York College of Environmental Science and Forestry	pub.	$ 5891	$12,460	100%	100%	$12,500	$ 5851	$27,000
State University of New York College of Technology at Canton	pub.	$ 6279	$ 9320	NR	NR	NR	NR	NR
State University of New York College of Technology at Delhi	pub.	$ 6360	$ 9300	NR	NR	NR	NR	NR
State University of New York Upstate Medical University	pub.	$ 5550	$10,422	NR	NR	NR	NR	NR
Stony Brook University, State University of New York	pub.	$ 6489	$ 9590	92%	20%	$10,904	$ 5175	$17,528
Syracuse University	ind.	$34,926	$12,374	93%	84%	$32,500	$14,800	$28,358
Union College	ind.	*$50,439	NR	96%	99%	$35,815	$14,624	$24,739
University at Albany, State University of New York	pub.	$ 6748	$10,238	89%	13%	$10,008	$ 6978	$22,092
University at Buffalo, the State University of New York	pub.	$ 7013	$ 9648	53%	25%	$ 2386	$14,275	$39,191
University of Rochester	ind.	$38,690	$11,200	100%	100%	$33,413	$16,477	$27,121
Utica College	ind.	$27,284	$10,850	100%	8%	$22,824	$15,310	$35,534
Vassar College	ind.	$41,930	$ 9370	100%	100%	$39,069	$12,231	$18,876
Vaughn College of Aeronautics and Technology	ind.	$16,700	$11,280	NR	35%	$18,000	$ 9980	$17,125
Villa Maria College of Buffalo	ind.	$14,380	NA	83%	NR	$ 5335	$ 9045	NR
Wagner College	ind.	$32,580	$ 9700	99%	25%	$21,102	$21,178	$36,988
Webb Institute	ind.	$ 0	$10,200	NR	NR	$ 3500	$ 6700	$ 8545
Wells College	ind.	$29,680	$ 9000	99%	13%	$24,878	$13,802	$24,180
York College of the City University of New York	pub.	$ 4912	NA	100%	NR	$ 3586	$ 1326	$ 9351
North Carolina								
Appalachian State University	pub.	$ 4425	$ 6400	90%	52%	$ 9369	$ 1456	$16,153
Barton College	ind.	$20,648	$ 7012	76%	15%	$21,177	$ 6483	$28,343
Belmont Abbey College	ind.	$21,506	$ 9948	100%	19%	$17,598	$13,856	$21,000
Brevard College	ind.	$20,900	$ 7850	100%	27%	$19,400	$ 9350	$20,700
Carolina Christian College	ind.	$ 6200	$12,108	NR	NR	NR	NR	NR
Catawba College	ind.	$23,740	$ 8200	72%	25%	$21,067	$10,873	$25,506
Chowan University	ind.	$18,850	$ 7310	100%	18%	$19,792	$ 6368	$25,168
Davidson College	ind.	$35,124	$ 9906	91%	100%	$24,899	$20,131	$20,858
Duke University	ind.	$40,243	$11,622	98%	100%	$37,956	$13,909	$23,059
East Carolina University	pub.	$ 4477	$ 7480	78%	29%	$ 8874	$ 3083	NR
Elon University	ind.	$25,489	$ 8236	90%	NR	$19,487	$14,238	$22,939
Gardner-Webb University	ind.	$22,440	$ 6810	94%	23%	$17,717	$11,533	NR
Guilford College	ind.	$27,450	$ 7560	100%	13%	$23,989	$11,021	$24,580
High Point University	ind.	*$35,900	NR	86%	52%	$10,875	$25,025	$ 9437
Johnson & Wales University—Charlotte Campus	ind.	$24,429	$ 9918	92%	14%	$18,673	$15,674	NR

NA = not applicable; NR = not reported; * = includes room and board; † = room only; — = not available.

College Costs At-a-Glance

	Institutional Control ind.=independent; pub.=public	Tuition and Fees	Room and Board	Percent of Eligible Freshmen Receiving Need-Based Gift Awards	Percent of Freshmen Whose Need Was Fully Met	Average Financial Aid Package for Freshmen	Average Net Cost After Aid	Average Indebtedness Upon Graduation
North Carolina—_continued_								
Johnson C. Smith University	ind.	$15,754	$ 6132	91%	4%	$12,865	$ 9021	$19,000
Mars Hill College	ind.	$20,849	$ 7285	100%	26%	$16,885	$11,249	$16,025
Methodist University	ind.	$24,220	$ 8400	89%	19%	$17,546	$15,074	$38,820
Mid-Atlantic Christian University	ind.	$10,320	$ 6790	92%	30%	$11,010	$ 6100	$26,953
Mount Olive College	ind.	$13,776	$ 5540	100%	15%	$11,324	$ 7992	$16,117
North Carolina Agricultural and Technical State University	pub.	$ 3899	$ 5839	70%	13%	$12,389	—	$16,289
North Carolina State University	pub.	$ 5474	$ 7966	98%	57%	$10,943	$ 2497	$19,011
Peace College	ind.	$24,308	$ 8250	100%	7%	$22,522	$10,036	$22,428
Pfeiffer University	ind.	$19,040	$ 7798	100%	16%	$17,163	$ 9675	$23,000
Piedmont Baptist College and Graduate School	ind.	$11,170	$ 5760	NR	NR	NR	NR	NR
St. Andrews Presbyterian College	ind.	$21,190	$ 8672	100%	20%	$16,117	$13,745	$19,366
Salem College	ind.	$21,965	$11,520	95%	100%	$24,045	$ 9440	$19,000
The University of North Carolina at Asheville	pub.	$ 4411	$ 6890	96%	61%	$ 9967	$ 1334	$14,596
The University of North Carolina at Chapel Hill	pub.	$ 5626	$ 8670	99%	98%	$12,755	$ 1541	NR
The University of North Carolina at Charlotte	pub.	$ 4427	$ 6796	94%	28%	$ 8765	$ 2458	$17,964
The University of North Carolina at Greensboro	pub.	$ 4234	$ 6506	51%	33%	$ 9173	$ 1567	$18,604
The University of North Carolina at Pembroke	pub.	$ 3890	$ 5990	96%	21%	$ 9666	$ 214	NR
University of North Carolina School of the Arts	pub.	$ 5299	$ 7256	NR	NR	NR	NR	$26,616
The University of North Carolina Wilmington	pub.	$ 4873	$ 7798	88%	46%	$ 9038	$ 3633	$16,115
Wake Forest University	ind.	$39,970	$11,010	96%	93%	$33,285	$17,695	$24,561
Warren Wilson College	ind.	$24,196	$ 7770	96%	18%	$21,716	$10,250	$20,441
Western Carolina University	pub.	$ 4330	$ 5912	98%	33%	$ 8865	$ 1377	$11,609
Wingate University	ind.	$21,140	$ 8350	79%	23%	$19,420	$10,070	$23,279
North Dakota								
Dickinson State University	pub.	$ 5249	$ 4262	91%	99%	$ 7863	$ 1648	$18,852
Jamestown College	ind.	$16,780	$ 5536	100%	25%	$12,428	$ 9888	$25,717
Mayville State University	pub.	$ 5793	$ 4488	87%	51%	$ 4958	$ 5323	$19,338
Medcenter One College of Nursing	ind.	$10,012	NA	NR	NR	NR	NR	NR
Minot State University	pub.	$ 5389	$ 4602	65%	27%	$ 4354	$ *5637	$15,193
University of Mary	ind.	$13,126	$ 5150	64%	NR	$10,972	$ 7304	NR
University of North Dakota	pub.	$ 6727	$ 5702	56%	43%	$ 4932	$ 7497	$22,137
Valley City State University	pub.	$ 6075	$ 4528	94%	99%	$ 8770	$ 1833	$25,929
Ohio								
Antioch University McGregor	ind.	$20,760	NA	NR	NR	NR	NR	$23,000
Ashland University	ind.	$25,640	$ 9352	100%	NR	$24,727	$10,265	$36,545
Baldwin-Wallace College	ind.	$24,230	$ 7960	100%	35%	$20,860	$11,330	$17,716
Bluffton University	ind.	$24,930	$ 8348	100%	37%	$22,683	$10,595	$26,896
Bowling Green State University	pub.	$ 9060	$ 7670	85%	15%	$11,920	$ 4810	$28,542
Case Western Reserve University	ind.	$36,238	$10,890	96%	89%	$33,515	$13,613	$37,496
Cedarville University	ind.	$23,500	$ 5086	70%	16%	$12,699	$15,887	$26,672
Central State University	pub.	$ 5294	$ 7920	86%	NR	NR	NR	NR
Cincinnati Christian University	ind.	$12,580	$ 6470	94%	10%	$ 9277	$ 9773	NR

NA = not applicable; NR = not reported; * = includes room and board; † = room only; — = not available.

College Costs At-a-Glance

	Institutional Control ind.=independent; pub.=public	Tuition and Fees	Room and Board	Percent of Eligible Freshmen Receiving Need-Based Gift Awards	Percent of Freshmen Whose Need Was Fully Met	Average Financial Aid Package for Freshmen	Average Net Cost After Aid	Average Indebtedness Upon Graduation
Ohio—*continued*								
The Cleveland Institute of Art	ind.	$31,904	$10,536	100%	13%	$23,309	$19,131	$61,270
Cleveland Institute of Music	ind.	$36,590	$ 9052	100%	52%	$21,222	$24,420	$26,355
Cleveland State University	pub.	$ 8196	$10,250	87%	6%	$ 9016	$ 9430	NR
College of Mount St. Joseph	ind.	$22,800	$ 7000	98%	20%	$18,275	$11,525	$33,648
The College of Wooster	ind.	$36,598	$ 9070	97%	46%	$28,225	$17,443	$25,140
Columbus College of Art & Design	ind.	$24,648	$ 8630	100%	13%	$16,499	$16,779	$39,023
Defiance College	ind.	$24,330	$ 8120	85%	9%	$18,904	$13,546	$25,388
Denison University	ind.	$36,560	$ 8930	100%	39%	$32,758	$12,732	NR
Franciscan University of Steubenville	ind.	$20,320	$ 6900	98%	16%	$12,510	$14,710	$30,180
Heidelberg University	ind.	$22,962	$ 8635	100%	14%	$19,780	$11,817	$35,397
John Carroll University	ind.	$30,250	$ 8750	100%	22%	$25,065	$13,935	$28,830
Kent State University	pub.	$ 8726	$ 7940	79%	44%	$ 8479	$ 8187	$26,698
Kent State University at Stark	pub.	$ 4938	NA	76%	35%	$ 6449	—	NR
Kenyon College	ind.	$40,900	$ 9500	95%	51%	$30,190	$20,210	$19,934
Lake Erie College	ind.	$25,674	$ 8192	100%	14%	$21,291	$12,575	NR
Lourdes College	ind.	$15,300	NA	78%	NR	$12,086	$ 3214	NR
Malone University	ind.	$22,444	$ 7548	100%	18%	$19,314	$10,678	$25,655
Marietta College	ind.	$27,066	$ 8046	97%	52%	$25,970	$ 9142	$27,455
Mercy College of Northwest Ohio	ind.	$10,090	NR	49%	4%	$ 6470	$ 3620	$19,620
Miami University	pub.	$11,910	$ 9458	88%	30%	$14,052	$ 7316	$26,582
Mount Vernon Nazarene University	ind.	$21,330	$ 6180	97%	12%	$17,380	$10,130	$29,761
Notre Dame College	ind.	$22,742	$ 7592	NR	NR	NR	NR	NR
Oberlin College	ind.	$40,004	$10,480	98%	100%	$30,403	$20,081	$18,604
Ohio Northern University	ind.	$31,866	$ 8280	95%	18%	$27,073	$13,073	$45,902
The Ohio State University	pub.	$ 8706	$ 8409	65%	26%	$10,575	$ 6540	$18,426
Ohio University	pub.	$ 8973	$ 9408	96%	15%	$ 8272	$10,109	$22,095
Ohio University–Zanesville	pub.	$ 4662	NR	91%	16%	$ 6315	—	$22,095
Ohio Wesleyan University	ind.	$35,030	$ 9224	98%	32%	$30,406	$13,848	$30,954
Tiffin University	ind.	$18,390	$ 8340	71%	8%	$14,652	$12,078	$26,345
The University of Akron	pub.	$ 8752	$ 8697	58%	7%	$ 7593	$ 9856	$19,000
University of Cincinnati	pub.	$ 9399	$ 9702	46%	4%	$ 7650	$11,451	$25,878
University of Dayton	ind.	$29,930	$ 9400	69%	47%	$19,992	$19,338	$35,865
The University of Findlay	ind.	$25,774	$ 8554	89%	10%	$19,022	$15,306	$32,800
University of Mount Union	ind.	$23,880	$ 7420	100%	8%	$19,130	$12,170	$25,804
The University of Toledo	pub.	$ 8066	$ 9478	99%	20%	$14,094	$ 3450	$27,066
Ursuline College	ind.	$23,000	$ 7664	100%	24%	$20,296	$10,368	$25,830
Wilmington College	ind.	$24,286	$ 8272	96%	25%	$21,700	$10,858	NR
Wittenberg University	ind.	$34,190	$ 8772	99%	32%	$30,966	$11,996	$28,729
Wright State University	pub.	$ 7797	NR	80%	11%	$ 8785	—	$25,357
Xavier University	ind.	$28,570	$ 9530	96%	22%	$19,215	$18,885	$27,098
Youngstown State University	pub.	$ 6956	$ 7400	75%	12%	$ 7949	$ 6407	NR

NA = not applicable; NR = not reported; * = includes room and board; † = room only; — = not available.

College Costs At-a-Glance

	Institutional Control ind.=independent; pub.=public	Tuition and Fees	Room and Board	Percent of Eligible Freshmen Receiving Need-Based Gift Awards	Percent of Freshmen Whose Need Was Fully Met	Average Financial Aid Package for Freshmen	Average Net Cost After Aid	Average Indebtedness Upon Graduation
Oklahoma								
Cameron University	pub.	$ 5415	$ 3589	94%	83%	$12,100	—	$ 7000
Hillsdale Free Will Baptist College	ind.	$ 9650	$ 5200	73%	13%	$ 8510	$ 6340	$23,822
Northeastern State University	pub.	$ 4155	$ 4826	72%	68%	$ 8752	$ 229	$ 2143
Oklahoma Baptist University	ind.	$18,670	$ 5630	75%	17%	$14,897	$ 9403	$21,554
Oklahoma Christian University	ind.	$17,456	$ 5850	56%	20%	$15,612	$ 7694	$26,612
Oklahoma City University	ind.	$22,250	$ 8350	99%	59%	$21,998	$ 8602	$26,844
Oklahoma Panhandle State University	pub.	$ 4242	$ 3320	82%	NR	$ 7418	$ 144	NR
Oklahoma State University	pub.	$ 6202	$ 6402	77%	18%	$11,477	$ 1127	$19,468
Oklahoma Wesleyan University	ind.	$17,970	$ 6288	96%	22%	$12,947	$11,311	$20,852
Oral Roberts University	ind.	$18,916	$ 7916	99%	37%	$15,320	$11,512	$34,555
Rogers State University	pub.	$ 4277	$ 4505†	75%	8%	$ 7529	$ 1253	$11,880
Southeastern Oklahoma State University	pub.	$ 4316	$ 4290	74%	12%	$ 1266	$ 7340	$ 4967
Southern Nazarene University	ind.	$17,664	$ 6490	NR	NR	NR	NR	NR
University of Central Oklahoma	pub.	$ 4223	$ 7776	97%	9%	$ 6917	$ 5082	NR
University of Oklahoma	pub.	$ 5245	$ 7598	8%	53%	$11,348	$ 1495	$15,659
University of Science and Arts of Oklahoma	pub.	$ 4440	$ 4850	98%	22%	$ 9208	$ 82	$15,598
University of Tulsa	ind.	$25,144	$ 8544	39%	53%	$28,783	$ 4905	$35,816
Oregon								
Corban University	ind.	$24,230	$ 7642	100%	13%	$19,888	$11,984	$28,537
Eastern Oregon University	pub.	$ 6456	$ 7870	70%	40%	$ 9381	$ 4945	$19,881
George Fox University	ind.	$26,180	$ 8320	94%	43%	$25,545	$ 8955	$24,624
Lewis & Clark College	ind.	$35,233	$ 9006	96%	17%	$27,150	$17,089	$17,084
Linfield College	ind.	$29,034	$ 8280	85%	35%	$19,474	$17,840	$27,750
Marylhurst University	ind.	$16,920	NA	78%	NR	$ 8699	$ 8221	$27,846
Northwest Christian University	ind.	$22,900	$ 6800	100%	22%	$18,806	$10,894	$21,633
Oregon College of Art & Craft	ind.	$22,608	$ 6210	100%	NR	$ 9000	$19,818	$37,000
Oregon Health & Science University	pub.	$16,051	NA	NR	NR	NR	NR	NR
Oregon Institute of Technology	pub.	$ 6765	$ 8615	39%	27%	$ 3725	$11,655	$27,266
Oregon State University	pub.	$ 6727	$ 8352	78%	19%	$ 9646	$ 5433	NR
Pacific University	ind.	$29,966	$ 8118	98%	32%	$26,379	$11,705	$27,770
Portland State University	pub.	$ 6764	$ 9774	70%	9%	$ 8640	$ 7898	$22,440
Reed College	ind.	$39,700	$10,250	85%	97%	$33,161	$16,789	$20,750
University of Oregon	pub.	$ 7428	$ 8620	53%	15%	$ 9071	$ 6977	$19,336
University of Portland	ind.	$31,996	$ 9135	75%	10%	$23,598	$17,533	$ 9046
Warner Pacific College	ind.	$17,110	$ 6646	89%	11%	$13,992	$ 9764	$22,433
Western Oregon University	pub.	$ 7458	$ 8208	85%	20%	$ 8944	$ 6722	$25,063
Willamette University	ind.	$35,610	$ 8350	99%	15%	$29,353	$14,607	$23,643
Pennsylvania								
Albright College	ind.	$32,740	$ 8858	100%	14%	$27,252	$14,346	$31,845
Allegheny College	ind.	$34,810	$ 8790	100%	40%	$27,731	$15,869	NR
Arcadia University	ind.	$31,260	$10,680	99%	14%	$22,416	$19,524	$35,975
Bloomsburg University of Pennsylvania	pub.	$ 7110	$ 6488	54%	90%	$11,880	$ 1718	$21,322

NA = not applicable; NR = not reported; * = includes room and board; † = room only; — = not available.

College Costs At-a-Glance

College Costs At-a-Glance	Institutional Control ind.=independent; pub.=public	Tuition and Fees	Room and Board	Percent of Eligible Freshmen Receiving Need-Based Gift Awards	Percent of Freshmen Whose Need Was Fully Met	Average Financial Aid Package for Freshmen	Average Net Cost After Aid	Average Indebtedness Upon Graduation
Pennsylvania—*continued*								
Bryn Athyn College of the New Church	ind.	$15,000	$ 8541	100%	35%	$11,104	$12,437	$ 8299
Bryn Mawr College	ind.	$39,360	$12,420	100%	100%	$36,562	$15,218	$20,156
Bucknell University	ind.	$42,342	$ 9938	100%	94%	$26,900	$25,380	$18,800
Cabrini College	ind.	$31,030	$11,400	87%	14%	$22,851	$19,579	$30,633
Carnegie Mellon University	ind.	$40,728	$10,840	96%	31%	$28,678	$22,890	$29,456
Cedar Crest College	ind.	$28,135	$ 9321	100%	11%	$23,552	$13,904	$24,641
Chestnut Hill College	ind.	$27,100	$ 8800	100%	22%	$19,274	$16,626	NR
Clarion University of Pennsylvania	pub.	$ 7381	$ 6884	80%	18%	$ 7440	$ 6825	NR
Delaware Valley College	ind.	$29,284	$10,326	99%	14%	$19,957	$19,653	$26,350
DeSales University	ind.	$27,200	$ 9750	99%	17%	$19,654	$17,296	$31,077
Dickinson College	ind.	$40,114	$10,080	98%	78%	$34,568	$15,626	$23,224
Drexel University	ind.	$33,005	$13,125	99%	40%	$22,769	$23,361	NR
Duquesne University	ind.	$26,468	$ 9200	99%	30%	$21,127	$14,541	NR
East Stroudsburg University of Pennsylvania	pub.	$ 7394	$ 6418	62%	70%	$ 5402	$ 8410	$25,887
Edinboro University of Pennsylvania	pub.	$ 7316	$ 7430	92%	5%	$ 7146	$ 7600	$28,392
Elizabethtown College	ind.	$33,250	$ 8500	100%	22%	$23,278	$18,472	NR
Franklin & Marshall College	ind.	$39,990	$10,430	97%	100%	$32,885	$17,535	$27,162
Gannon University	ind.	$23,574	$ 9330	99%	25%	$20,797	$12,107	$31,234
Geneva College	ind.	$22,236	$ 8000	100%	16%	$18,382	$11,854	$22,680
Grove City College	ind.	$12,590	$ 6824	100%	12%	$ 6024	$13,390	$24,895
Gwynedd-Mercy College	ind.	$25,610	$ 9760	97%	25%	$14,625	$20,745	$29,380
Harrisburg University of Science and Technology	ind.	$19,500	NA	NR	NR	NR	NR	$21,500
Haverford College	ind.	$39,085	$11,890	97%	100%	$34,976	$15,999	$16,500
Holy Family University	ind.	$23,520	$10,400	99%	12%	$18,752	$15,168	$31,855
Indiana University of Pennsylvania	pub.	$ 7209	$ 8558	69%	12%	$10,032	$ 5735	$25,224
Juniata College	ind.	$32,820	$ 8980	100%	20%	$26,119	$15,681	$23,618
Keystone College	ind.	$19,120	$ 9250	100%	34%	$23,718	$ 4652	$24,750
King's College	ind.	$25,644	$ 9838	100%	19%	$20,209	$15,273	$30,843
Kutztown University of Pennsylvania	pub.	$ 7397	$ 7698	71%	77%	$ 6713	$ 8382	$20,707
Lafayette College	ind.	$37,815	$11,799	97%	49%	$35,727	$13,887	$20,745
Lancaster Bible College & Graduate School	ind.	$15,840	$ 6780	94%	16%	$12,106	$10,514	$21,611
La Roche College	ind.	$21,638	$ 8756	74%	33%	$23,466	$ 6928	$69,494
Lebanon Valley College	ind.	$30,490	$ 8080	100%	24%	$23,790	$14,780	$33,348
Lehigh University	ind.	$38,630	$10,200	97%	56%	$32,081	$16,749	$31,123
Lincoln University	pub.	$ 8222	$ 7770	77%	NR	$ 5302	$10,690	$30,818
Lock Haven University of Pennsylvania	pub.	$ 7201	$ 6736	66%	45%	$ 8394	$ 5543	$22,585
Lycoming College	ind.	$29,894	$ 8134	100%	15%	$24,693	$13,335	$29,478
Marywood University	ind.	$26,270	$11,498	85%	19%	$23,580	$14,188	$31,471
Mercyhurst College	ind.	$26,346	$ 9195	80%	50%	$23,226	$12,315	$22,630
Messiah College	ind.	$27,480	$ 8160	99%	21%	$18,939	$16,701	$33,867
Millersville University of Pennsylvania	pub.	$ 7147	$ 7766	76%	15%	$ 8390	$ 6523	$22,479
Misericordia University	ind.	$24,050	$10,050	100%	15%	$16,852	$17,248	$33,641
Moravian College	ind.	$32,177	$ 9164	100%	12%	$25,954	$15,387	NR

NA = not applicable; NR = not reported; * = includes room and board; † = room only; — = not available.

College Costs At-a-Glance

	Institutional Control ind.=independent; pub.=public	Tuition and Fees	Room and Board	Percent of Eligible Freshmen Receiving Need-Based Gift Awards	Percent of Freshmen Whose Need Was Fully Met	Average Financial Aid Package for Freshmen	Average Net Cost After Aid	Average Indebtedness Upon Graduation
Pennsylvania—*continued*								
Mount Aloysius College	ind.	$17,280	$ 7300	100%	NR	$14,980	$ 9600	$29,802
Muhlenberg College	ind.	$36,990	$ 8440	97%	93%	$23,182	$22,248	$18,542
Neumann University	ind.	$21,360	$ 9718	100%	66%	$19,000	$12,078	$30,000
Peirce College	ind.	$14,850	NA	93%	NR	$ 8470	$ 6380	$19,748
Penn State Abington	pub.	$12,250	NA	77%	4%	$ 9306	$ 2944	$28,680
Penn State Altoona	pub.	$12,750	$ 8170	63%	6%	$ 8103	$12,817	$28,680
Penn State Berks	pub.	$12,750	$ 8940	62%	4%	$ 7675	$14,015	$28,680
Penn State Erie, The Behrend College	pub.	$12,750	$ 8170	67%	5%	$ 8318	$12,602	$28,680
Penn State Harrisburg	pub.	$12,750	$ 9350	62%	8%	$ 8208	$13,892	$28,680
Penn State University Park	pub.	$14,416	$ 8170	47%	8%	$ 8531	$14,055	$28,680
Pennsylvania College of Technology	pub.	$12,480	$ 8350	100%	NR	NR	NR	NR
Philadelphia Biblical University	ind.	$19,997	$ 8050	99%	16%	$13,544	$14,503	$28,214
Philadelphia University	ind.	$27,498	$ 9182	99%	12%	$22,240	$14,440	$32,037
Point Park University	ind.	$21,334	$ 9020	100%	16%	$18,939	$11,415	$31,656
Robert Morris University	ind.	$20,560	$10,370	99%	13%	$18,482	$12,448	$35,055
Rosemont College	ind.	$26,250	$10,580	100%	9%	$24,399	$12,431	$21,338
St. Charles Borromeo Seminary, Overbrook	ind.	$15,190	$ 9560	40%	80%	$15,795	$ 8955	$19,000
Saint Francis University	ind.	$25,554	$ 8716	100%	31%	$19,174	$15,096	$10,632
Saint Joseph's University	ind.	$34,090	$11,575	98%	25%	$19,574	$26,091	NR
Saint Vincent College	ind.	$27,190	$ 9048	100%	26%	$23,489	$12,749	NR
Seton Hill University	ind.	$26,622	$ 8810	100%	19%	$23,712	$11,720	$25,807
Shippensburg University of Pennsylvania	pub.	$ 7444	$ 7086	74%	16%	$ 7701	$ 6829	$21,163
Slippery Rock University of Pennsylvania	pub.	$ 7235	$ 8454	69%	42%	$ 8254	$ 7435	$23,879
Susquehanna University	ind.	$32,850	$ 8800	99%	20%	$23,903	$17,747	$20,915
Swarthmore College	ind.	$37,860	$11,740	100%	100%	$36,008	$13,592	$15,737
Temple University	pub.	$11,764	$ 9198	100%	36%	$15,722	$ 5240	$29,886
Thiel College	ind.	$20,998	$ 8790	100%	10%	$19,698	$10,090	$37,783
University of Pennsylvania	ind.	$40,514	$11,430	95%	100%	$33,773	$18,171	$17,787
University of Pittsburgh	pub.	$14,154	$ 8900	74%	39%	$10,530	$12,524	NR
University of Pittsburgh at Bradford	pub.	$11,722	$ 7480	65%	98%	$13,628	$ 5574	$21,683
University of Pittsburgh at Greensburg	pub.	$11,852	$ 7840	40%	21%	$ 9900	$ 9792	$24,707
University of Pittsburgh at Johnstown	pub.	$11,754	$ 7290	76%	5%	$10,185	$ 8859	$23,243
The University of Scranton	ind.	$34,536	$11,862	98%	11%	$23,357	$23,041	$30,920
University of the Sciences in Philadelphia	ind.	$29,630	$11,582	93%	52%	$ 8764	$32,448	$34,019
Ursinus College	ind.	$40,120	$ 9750	100%	24%	$29,053	$20,817	$25,875
Valley Forge Christian College	ind.	$16,250	$ 7556	88%	5%	$10,205	$13,601	$42,894
Villanova University	ind.	$38,305	$10,320	93%	27%	$30,122	$18,503	$31,048
Washington & Jefferson College	ind.	$32,895	$ 8925	82%	20%	$24,661	$17,159	$23,000
Waynesburg University	ind.	$17,760	$ 7370	99%	18%	$14,316	$10,814	$22,000
West Chester University of Pennsylvania	pub.	$ 7211	$ 7032	68%	46%	$ 6962	$ 7281	$19,820
Westminster College	ind.	$29,150	$ 8840	99%	26%	$23,090	$14,900	$28,262
Widener University	ind.	$31,840	$11,270	84%	14%	$25,475	$17,635	$38,372
Wilkes University	ind.	$26,010	$11,100	100%	15%	$21,111	$15,999	$34,775

NA = not applicable; NR = not reported; * = includes room and board; † = room only; — = not available.

College Costs At-a-Glance

	Institutional Control ind.=independent; pub.=public	Tuition and Fees	Room and Board	Percent of Eligible Freshmen Receiving Need-Based Gift Awards	Percent of Freshmen Whose Need Was Fully Met	Average Financial Aid Package for Freshmen	Average Net Cost After Aid	Average Indebtedness Upon Graduation
Pennsylvania—_continued_								
Wilson College	ind.	$28,220	$ 9430	100%	22%	$23,512	$14,138	$33,673
York College of Pennsylvania	ind.	$15,140	$ 8530	79%	24%	$11,110	$12,560	$27,583
Puerto Rico								
Carlos Albizu University	ind.	$ 6739	NA	NR	NR	NR	NR	NR
Columbia College (Caguas)	ind.	$ 9100	NA	NR	NR	$ 4035	$ 5065	NR
Inter American University of Puerto Rico, Bayamón Campus	ind.	$ 5136	NA	88%	NR	$ 144	$ 4992	NR
Inter American University of Puerto Rico, Guayama Campus	ind.	$ 5368	NA	69%	NR	NR	NR	NR
Inter American University of Puerto Rico, Ponce Campus	ind.	$ 4428	NA	88%	NR	$ 494	$ 3934	NR
Polytechnic University of Puerto Rico	ind.	$ 6837	$11,704	100%	1%	$ 4503	$14,038	NR
Universidad Adventista de las Antillas	ind.	$ 6170	$ 2900	100%	NR	NR	NR	$ 4400
University of Puerto Rico at Bayamón	pub.	$ 2076	NA	NR	NR	NR	NR	NR
University of Puerto Rico, Río Piedras	pub.	$ 1320	$ 8280	NR	NR	NR	NR	NR
Rhode Island								
Bryant University	ind.	$32,106	$11,757	88%	67%	$21,005	$22,858	$38,270
Johnson & Wales University	ind.	$24,141	NR	88%	13%	$16,857	$ 7284	NR
Providence College	ind.	$39,435	$11,690	85%	55%	$22,050	$29,075	$34,927
Rhode Island College	pub.	$ 6976	$ 9270	86%	25%	$ 8837	$ 7409	$18,352
Salve Regina University	ind.	$30,000	$10,950	96%	7%	$22,822	$18,128	$35,553
University of Rhode Island	pub.	$ 9528	$ 9892	100%	97%	$12,463	$ 6957	$23,000
South Carolina								
Anderson University	ind.	$19,212	$ 7250	NR	NR	NR	NR	NR
Bob Jones University	ind.	$11,920	$ 5100	NR	NR	NR	NR	NR
The Citadel, The Military College of South Carolina	pub.	$ 9824	$ 5965	82%	26%	$14,900	$ 889	$25,817
Clemson University	pub.	$11,609	$ 6774	35%	26%	$11,462	$ 6921	$18,463
Coastal Carolina University	pub.	$ 8950	$ 7200	41%	12%	$ 8311	$ 7839	$26,646
Coker College	ind.	$19,858	$ 6240	91%	40%	$20,414	$ 5684	$24,601
College of Charleston	pub.	$ 8988	$ 9411	72%	29%	$12,690	$ 5709	$19,875
Columbia International University	ind.	$17,395	$ 6410	NR	NR	$ 5200	$18,605	$16,500
Converse College	ind.	$26,138	$ 8032	100%	30%	$23,261	$10,909	$20,739
Erskine College	ind.	$24,645	$ 8325	100%	43%	$21,557	$11,413	$24,058
Francis Marion University	pub.	$ 7960	$ 6024	84%	NR	NR	NR	$24,347
Furman University	ind.	$36,656	$ 9170	100%	43%	$28,945	$16,881	$27,373
Limestone College	ind.	$19,200	$ 7000	100%	16%	$12,863	$13,337	NR
Medical University of South Carolina	pub.	$13,768	NA	NR	NR	NR	NR	NR
Newberry College	ind.	$22,470	$ 7750	100%	20%	$21,205	$ 9015	$30,693
North Greenville University	ind.	$12,264	$ 7056	61%	90%	NR	NR	$18,200
Presbyterian College	ind.	$28,880	$ 8345	100%	53%	$31,409	$ 5816	$23,391
University of South Carolina	pub.	$ 9156	$ 7328	41%	29%	$10,987	$ 5497	$21,755
University of South Carolina Beaufort	pub.	$ 7330	$ 6100	NR	NR	NR	NR	NR
University of South Carolina Upstate	pub.	$ 8862	$ 6300	62%	21%	$ 9744	$ 5418	$18,762
Winthrop University	pub.	$11,606	$ 6530	98%	19%	$11,228	$ 6908	$24,463
Wofford College	ind.	$30,280	$ 8480	92%	49%	$29,406	$ 9354	$22,199

NA = not applicable; NR = not reported; * = includes room and board; † = room only; — = not available.

College Costs At-a-Glance

	Institutional Control ind.=independent; pub.=public	Tuition and Fees	Room and Board	Percent of Eligible Freshmen Receiving Need-Based Gift Awards	Percent of Freshmen Whose Need Was Fully Met	Average Financial Aid Package for Freshmen	Average Net Cost After Aid	Average Indebtedness Upon Graduation
South Dakota								
Augustana College	ind.	$23,550	$ 6188	100%	23%	$20,991	$ 8747	$29,531
Black Hills State University	pub.	$ 6227	$ 5523	NR	NR	NR	NR	$21,069
Dakota State University	pub.	$ 6872	$ 4818	48%	13%	$ 6902	$ 4788	$21,189
Dakota Wesleyan University	ind.	$19,850	NR	100%	20%	$19,200	$ 650	$30,000
Mount Marty College	ind.	$18,908	$ 5366	100%	47%	$21,223	$ 3051	$22,699
Northern State University	pub.	$ 6063	$ 4874	94%	19%	$ 6003	$ 4934	NR
South Dakota School of Mines and Technology	pub.	$ 6830	$ 5080	77%	21%	$ 9006	$ 2904	$20,165
South Dakota State University	pub.	$ 6155	$ 5668	58%	81%	$ 8114	$ 3709	$22,914
The University of South Dakota	pub.	$ 6468	$ 5787	44%	23%	$ 5136	$ 7119	$23,676
Tennessee								
American Baptist College of American Baptist Theological Seminary	ind.	$ 4800	$ 2600	NR	NR	$ 2675	$ 4725	NR
Aquinas College	ind.	$17,180	NA	NR	NR	$ 5600	$11,580	$17,875
Austin Peay State University	pub.	$ 5808	$ 6120	51%	NR	$ 8962	$ 2966	$20,158
Belmont University	ind.	$22,360	$10,000	39%	27%	$13,032	$19,328	$19,268
Bryan College	ind.	$18,740	$ 5454	94%	66%	$17,870	$ 6324	$14,976
Carson-Newman College	ind.	$20,562	$ 5918	100%	27%	$16,493	$ 9987	$14,164
Christian Brothers University	ind.	$23,730	$ 6140	57%	29%	$22,450	$ 7420	$28,259
East Tennessee State University	pub.	$ 5533	$ 5500	87%	35%	$ 7617	$ 3416	$16,635
Fisk University	ind.	$18,345	$ 8585	100%	20%	$15,576	$11,354	$27,345
Freed-Hardeman University	ind.	$14,998	$ 7090	98%	24%	$15,107	$ 6981	$33,659
Free Will Baptist Bible College	ind.	$13,534	$ 5700	74%	NR	$ 8556	$10,678	$18,487
Johnson Bible College	ind.	$ 9100	$ 5100	100%	NR	$ 7785	$ 6415	$18,661
King College	ind.	$21,880	$ 7418	100%	19%	$19,789	$ 9509	$15,757
Lambuth University	ind.	$18,570	$ 8015	99%	52%	$16,295	$10,290	$19,000
Lane College	ind.	$ 8000	$ 5520	18%	49%	$ 3272	$10,248	$ 8769
Lee University	ind.	$11,610	$ 5650	91%	31%	$10,688	$ 6572	$27,549
LeMoyne-Owen College	ind.	$10,318	$ 4852	95%	9%	$10,235	$ 4935	$22,733
Lincoln Memorial University	ind.	$15,700	$ 5680	99%	12%	$17,483	$ 3897	$10,623
Lipscomb University	ind.	$20,390	$ 7850	46%	21%	$15,500	$12,740	$19,523
Maryville College	ind.	$29,473	$ 9032	100%	33%	$27,839	$10,666	$22,268
Memphis College of Art	ind.	$23,950	$ 8000	58%	23%	$10,424	$21,526	$34,360
Milligan College	ind.	$23,460	$ 5650	100%	29%	$18,213	$10,897	$19,803
Rhodes College	ind.	$33,710	$ 8314	98%	48%	$31,290	$10,734	$26,071
Southern Adventist University	ind.	$17,712	$ 5174	100%	97%	$20,130	$ 2756	$22,977
Tennessee Technological University	pub.	$ 5498	$ 7124	55%	31%	$ 8342	$ 4280	$14,691
Tennessee Wesleyan College	ind.	$18,600	$ 6100	100%	30%	$14,731	$ 9969	$16,304
Trevecca Nazarene University	ind.	$18,318	$ 7734	NR	NR	NR	NR	NR
Tusculum College	ind.	$19,530	$ 7735	100%	NR	$ 9845	$17,420	$ 8632
Union University	ind.	$20,940	$ 6930	76%	22%	$17,752	$10,118	$24,253
University of Memphis	pub.	$ 7058	$ 5950	96%	17%	$ 9539	$ 3469	$23,342
The University of Tennessee	pub.	$ 6850	$ 7254	97%	38%	$11,408	$ 2696	$24,593
The University of Tennessee at Chattanooga	pub.	$ 5656	$ 8056	93%	65%	$ 9220	$ 4492	$19,456

NA = not applicable; NR = not reported; * = includes room and board; † = room only; — = not available.

College Costs At-a-Glance

	Institutional Control ind.=independent; pub.=public	Tuition and Fees	Room and Board	Percent of Eligible Freshmen Receiving Need-Based Gift Awards	Percent of Freshmen Whose Need Was Fully Met	Average Financial Aid Package for Freshmen	Average Net Cost After Aid	Average Indebtedness Upon Graduation
Tennessee—continued								
The University of Tennessee at Martin	pub.	$ 5769	$ 4914	66%	42%	$11,877	—	$20,997
Vanderbilt University	ind.	$38,578	$12,650	91%	100%	$41,002	$10,226	$19,563
Victory University	ind.	$10,320	NA	88%	NR	$ 4212	$ 6108	$21,505
Watkins College of Art, Design, & Film	ind.	$18,600	$ 6000†	33%	13%	$ 9327	$15,273	$15,000
Texas								
Abilene Christian University	ind.	$20,290	$ 7510	100%	18%	$14,046	$13,754	$35,453
Angelo State University	pub.	$ 6138	$ 6612	82%	33%	$ 6604	$ 6146	$16,372
Austin College	ind.	$29,235	$ 9549	100%	95%	$27,388	$11,396	NR
Austin Graduate School of Theology	ind.	$ 7100	NA	NR	NR	NR	NR	NR
Baylor University	ind.	$29,754	$ 8331	100%	13%	$22,045	$16,040	NR
Concordia University Texas	ind.	$21,200	$ 8000	78%	56%	$20,298	$ 8902	$22,095
The Criswell College	ind.	$ 6532	NA	NR	NR	$ 725	$ 5807	NR
Dallas Baptist University	ind.	$17,490	$ 5636	64%	66%	$14,752	$ 8374	$17,214
East Texas Baptist University	ind.	$19,550	$ 5436	79%	21%	$14,783	$10,203	$21,380
Hardin-Simmons University	ind.	$20,990	$ 6282	74%	32%	$24,841	$ 2431	$35,429
Houston Baptist University	ind.	$23,180	$ 6975	85%	34%	$23,016	$ 7139	NR
Howard Payne University	ind.	$19,950	$ 5694	100%	38%	$16,982	$ 8662	$28,400
Huston-Tillotson University	ind.	$11,434	$ 6690	56%	30%	$15,162	$ 2962	NR
Jarvis Christian College	ind.	$ 9600	$ 6715	75%	4%	$12,709	$ 3606	$18,550
Lamar University	pub.	$ 6944	$ 6900	63%	19%	$10,723	$ 3121	$ 7856
LeTourneau University	ind.	$21,980	$ 8390	97%	17%	$16,301	$14,069	NR
Lubbock Christian University	ind.	$15,120	$ 6182	98%	10%	$13,169	$ 8133	$26,320
McMurry University	ind.	$19,205	$ 6757	97%	17%	$19,120	$ 6842	$27,935
Midland College	pub.	$ 2192	$ 3900	NR	NR	NR	NR	NR
Midwestern State University	pub.	$ 6226	$ 5560	91%	29%	$ 9140	$ 2646	$19,049
Northwood University, Texas Campus	ind.	$18,408	$ 7590	87%	14%	$18,128	$ 7870	$23,182
Our Lady of the Lake University of San Antonio	ind.	$21,900	$ 6838	NR	NR	NR	NR	NR
Rice University	ind.	$32,105	$11,230	100%	100%	$31,863	$11,472	$11,108
St. Edward's University	ind.	$26,484	$ 9036	92%	12%	$22,340	$13,180	$29,810
St. Mary's University	ind.	$22,556	$ 7550	99%	31%	$22,432	$ 7674	$22,592
Sam Houston State University	pub.	$ 7000	$ 7022	57%	NR	$ 5832	$ 8190	$ 6196
Schreiner University	ind.	$18,731	$ 8726	100%	19%	$14,469	$12,988	$27,986
Southern Methodist University	ind.	$35,160	$12,445	82%	44%	$33,921	$13,684	$20,180
Southwestern University	ind.	$30,220	$ 9130	100%	41%	$26,804	$12,546	$24,036
Stephen F. Austin State University	pub.	$ 6732	$ 7377	77%	65%	$ 9059	$ 5050	$20,547
Sul Ross State University	pub.	$ 2928	$ 6370	87%	NR	$11,428	—	NR
Tarleton State University	pub.	$ 7150	$ 6591	NR	NR	$10,022	$ 3719	$18,223
Texas A&M University	pub.	$ 8176	$ 8039	98%	61%	$16,119	$ 96	$21,276
Texas A&M University–Commerce	pub.	$ 5500	$ 7090	94%	44%	$11,581	$ 1009	$21,918
Texas A&M University–Corpus Christi	pub.	$ 6221	$ 9528	87%	13%	$10,137	$ 5612	$13,335
Texas Christian University	ind.	$30,048	$10,112	98%	30%	$19,821	$20,339	$32,357
Texas College	ind.	$ 9490	$ 6600	98%	5%	$ 8905	$ 7185	$18,735

NA = not applicable; NR = not reported; * = includes room and board; † = room only; — = not available.

College Costs At-a-Glance	Institutional Control ind.=independent; pub.=public	Tuition and Fees	Room and Board	Percent of Eligible Freshmen Receiving Need-Based Gift Awards	Percent of Freshmen Whose Need Was Fully Met	Average Financial Aid Package for Freshmen	Average Net Cost After Aid	Average Indebtedness Upon Graduation
Texas—*continued*								
Texas Lutheran University	ind.	$21,910	$ 6400	100%	42%	$20,591	$ 7719	$29,200
Texas State University–San Marcos	pub.	$ 7482	$ 6392	74%	8%	$14,974	—	$19,670
Texas Tech University	pub.	$ 7485	$ 7527	62%	8%	$ 7362	$ 7650	$21,001
Texas Woman's University	pub.	$ 6660	$ 5967	100%	64%	$ 9151	$ 3476	$22,293
Trinity University	ind.	$29,317	$ 8895	99%	51%	$26,181	$12,031	NR
University of Dallas	ind.	$27,815	$ 8650	100%	28%	$21,054	$15,411	$24,650
University of Houston	pub.	$ 8496	$ 7164	92%	39%	$12,752	$ 2908	$22,573
University of Houston–Clear Lake	pub.	$ 5708	$ 7896†	NR	NR	NR	NR	NR
University of Houston–Downtown	pub.	$ 5232	NA	94%	5%	$ 9330	—	$13,204
University of Mary Hardin-Baylor	ind.	$20,650	$ 5350	86%	30%	$15,844	$10,156	$17,500
University of North Texas	pub.	$ 7301	$ 6534	86%	45%	$12,122	$ 1713	NR
University of St. Thomas	ind.	$21,830	$ 7400	99%	12%	$16,133	$13,097	$22,857
The University of Texas at Arlington	pub.	$ 8186	$ 6658	78%	24%	$10,858	$ 3986	$18,749
The University of Texas at Austin	pub.	$ 8930	$ 9602	93%	34%	$13,378	$ 5154	$22,102
The University of Texas at Brownsville	pub.	$ 4547	$ 5742	93%	NR	$ 8431	$ 1858	NR
The University of Texas at Dallas	pub.	$10,340	$ 7733	94%	8%	$14,509	$ 3564	$17,483
The University of Texas at San Antonio	pub.	$ 7527	$ 8937	83%	26%	$ 9137	$ 7327	$23,152
The University of Texas at Tyler	pub.	$ 6042	$ 8016	87%	24%	$ 8342	$ 5716	$18,041
The University of Texas Medical Branch	pub.	$ 5502	$ 4620†	NR	NR	NR	NR	NR
The University of Texas of the Permian Basin	pub.	$ 5378	$ 6445	65%	26%	$ 8021	$ 3802	$18,507
The University of Texas–Pan American	pub.	$ 4304	$ 5294	97%	6%	$ 9560	$ 38	$13,088
The University of Texas Southwestern Medical Center at Dallas	pub.	$ 4878	$11,353	NR	NR	NR	NR	NR
University of the Incarnate Word	ind.	$21,890	$ 9220	99%	29%	$18,080	$13,030	NR
Wayland Baptist University	ind.	$12,470	$ 3864	100%	23%	$11,447	$ 4887	$25,387
Utah								
Brigham Young University	ind.	$ 4420	$ 7120	58%	3%	$ 5610	$ 5930	$10,730
Dixie State College of Utah	pub.	$ 3146	$ 3948	NR	NR	NR	NR	NR
Southern Utah University	pub.	$ 4269	$ 1950†	100%	14%	$ 5986	$ 233	$10,485
University of Utah	pub.	$ 5746	$ 6240	79%	21%	$ 9295	$ 2691	$11,749
Utah State University	pub.	$ 4828	$ 4900	55%	16%	$ 7974	$ 1754	NR
Utah Valley University	pub.	$ 4258	$ 8670	76%	6%	$ 6243	$ 6685	$17,274
Westminster College	ind.	$24,996	$ 7006	100%	35%	$20,571	$11,431	$20,251
Vermont								
Bennington College	ind.	$39,760	$11,100	98%	17%	$32,427	$18,433	$22,402
Burlington College	ind.	$20,424	$ 6750†	92%	NR	$13,335	$13,839	$38,198
Green Mountain College	ind.	$26,910	$ 9670	99%	10%	$18,198	$18,382	$39,862
Marlboro College	ind.	$33,660	$ 9220	85%	NR	$21,326	$21,554	$ 6713
Middlebury College	ind.	*$50,780	NR	100%	100%	$35,197	$15,583	$21,458
Saint Michael's College	ind.	$34,845	$ 8685	98%	27%	$28,393	$15,137	$30,742
Sterling College	ind.	$23,621	$ 7554	100%	5%	$20,313	$10,862	$31,867
University of Vermont	pub.	$13,524	$ 9026	97%	18%	$20,894	$ 1656	$27,696
Vermont Technical College	pub.	$10,892	$ 7808	84%	15%	$ 8194	$10,506	$26,000

NA = not applicable; NR = not reported; * = includes room and board; † = room only; — = not available.

College Costs At-a-Glance

	Institutional Control ind.=independent; pub.=public	Tuition and Fees	Room and Board	Percent of Eligible Freshmen Receiving Need-Based Gift Awards	Percent of Freshmen Whose Need Was Fully Met	Average Financial Aid Package for Freshmen	Average Net Cost After Aid	Average Indebtedness Upon Graduation
Virginia								
Averett University	ind.	$22,112	$ 7800	99%	16%	$15,272	$14,640	$30,943
Bluefield College	ind.	$18,800	$ 7350	100%	24%	$16,171	$ 9979	$ 6403
Bridgewater College	ind.	$25,500	$10,350	100%	19%	$21,959	$13,891	$29,331
Christendom College	ind.	$19,668	$ 7506	92%	100%	$13,024	$14,150	$24,000
Christopher Newport University	pub.	$11,720	$ 9240	86%	8%	$ 8102	$12,858	$18,285
The College of William and Mary	pub.	$10,800	$ 8382	74%	41%	$13,219	$ 5963	$18,410
Emory & Henry College	ind.	$24,880	$ 8300	72%	31%	$23,469	$ 9711	$19,168
Ferrum College	ind.	$23,565	$ 7630	100%	NR	$20,634	$10,561	$29,040
George Mason University	pub.	$ 8024	$ 7700	82%	12%	$11,991	$ 3733	$19,528
Hampden-Sydney College	ind.	$32,364	$10,126	100%	26%	$23,957	$18,533	$23,822
Hampton University	ind.	$17,212	$ 7664	97%	38%	$ 3725	$21,151	$ 4783
Hollins University	ind.	$28,115	$10,040	100%	13%	$23,508	$14,647	$24,002
James Madison University	pub.	$ 7860	$ 8020	53%	94%	$ 8389	$ 7491	$18,183
Jefferson College of Health Sciences	ind.	$17,740	$ 7010	99%	5%	$10,201	$14,549	$17,327
Liberty University	ind.	$17,202	$ 5996	NR	NR	NR	NR	$31,418
Longwood University	pub.	$ 8925	$ 7596	98%	53%	$ 9813	$ 6708	$20,855
Lynchburg College	ind.	$28,925	$ 6970	100%	20%	$22,027	$13,868	$30,954
Mary Baldwin College	ind.	$24,585	$ 7070	95%	18%	$20,319	$11,336	$25,665
Marymount University	ind.	$22,620	$ 9745	65%	21%	$17,362	$15,003	$22,946
Norfolk State University	pub.	$ 5138	NR	86%	36%	$14,617	—	$19,371
Old Dominion University	pub.	$ 7318	$ 7868	50%	58%	$ 7742	$ 7444	$17,250
Patrick Henry College	ind.	$21,770	$ 8530	NR	NR	NR	NR	NR
Potomac College	ind.	$16,020	NR	NR	NR	NR	NR	NR
Radford University	pub.	$ 6904	$ 6970	63%	21%	$ 8887	$ 4987	$18,817
Randolph College	ind.	$29,254	$ 9995	100%	25%	$22,341	$16,908	$26,395
Randolph-Macon College	ind.	$29,182	$ 8891	100%	22%	$22,871	$15,202	$26,763
Regent University	ind.	$14,200	$ 5175†	NR	NR	NR	NR	NR
Roanoke College	ind.	$31,214	$10,308	98%	35%	$24,994	$16,528	$25,932
Saint Paul's College	ind.	$13,210	$ 6640	76%	3%	$ 8233	$11,617	$21,917
Shenandoah University	ind.	$25,080	$ 8870	86%	26%	$16,250	$17,700	$20,000
Sweet Briar College	ind.	$30,195	$10,780	94%	82%	$15,051	$25,924	$20,118
University of Mary Washington	pub.	$ 3900	$ 8200	60%	12%	$ 8380	$ 3720	$16,000
University of Richmond	ind.	$41,610	$ 8810	99%	91%	$37,759	$12,661	$21,555
University of Virginia	pub.	$ 9672	$ 8290	91%	58%	$19,578	—	$19,939
The University of Virginia's College at Wise	pub.	$ 6748	$ 7323	86%	79%	$13,128	$ 943	$12,120
Valley Forge Christian College Woodbridge Campus	ind.	$ 7150	NR	NR	NR	NR	NR	NR
Virginia Commonwealth University	pub.	$ 7117	$ 8335	69%	11%	$ 8381	$ 7071	$22,864
Virginia Intermont College	ind.	$23,373	$ 7324	52%	11%	$18,862	$11,835	$16,337
Virginia Military Institute	pub.	$11,190	$ 6792	97%	65%	$17,634	$ 348	$19,046
Virginia Union University	ind.	$14,630	$ 6830	82%	NR	$ 9816	$11,644	NR
Virginia University of Lynchburg	ind.	$ 5300	$ 3600	100%	100%	$ 4013	$ 4887	$ 9500
Virginia Wesleyan College	ind.	$27,476	$ 7384	100%	13%	$22,996	$11,864	$27,658
Washington and Lee University	ind.	$38,877	$ 8410	96%	100%	$38,620	$ 8667	$23,615

NA = not applicable; NR = not reported; * = includes room and board; † = room only; — = not available.

College Costs At-a-Glance	Institutional Control ind.=independent; pub.=public	Tuition and Fees	Room and Board	Percent of Eligible Freshmen Receiving Need-Based Gift Awards	Percent of Freshmen Whose Need Was Fully Met	Average Financial Aid Package for Freshmen	Average Net Cost After Aid	Average Indebtedness Upon Graduation
Washington								
Bastyr University	ind.	$19,050	NR	NR	NR	NR	NR	$32,500
Cornish College of the Arts	ind.	$28,297	$8500	100%	8%	$16,102	$20,695	$36,026
DigiPen Institute of Technology	ind.	$20,760	NA	NR	NR	NR	NR	$89,000
Eastern Washington University	pub.	$ 5872	$7080	79%	36%	$10,332	$ 2620	$18,435
The Evergreen State College	pub.	$ 5959	$8052	70%	41%	$ 9330	$ 4681	$14,310
Northwest University	ind.	$22,650	$6724	99%	18%	$15,462	$13,912	$23,965
Pacific Lutheran University	ind.	$28,100	$8600	100%	35%	$28,330	$ 8370	$24,639
Saint Martin's University	ind.	$26,402	$8660	100%	29%	$20,109	$14,953	$27,807
Seattle Pacific University	ind.	$27,810	$8544	99%	9%	$26,110	$10,244	$25,800
Seattle University	ind.	$29,340	$8805	98%	18%	$26,748	$11,397	$26,665
University of Puget Sound	ind.	$37,225	$9650	98%	29%	$28,277	$18,598	$29,514
University of Washington	pub.	$ 7692	$7800	79%	39%	$10,580	$ 4912	$16,800
University of Washington, Tacoma	pub.	$ 7653	$8949†	77%	23%	$11,200	$ 5402	$17,900
Washington State University	pub.	$ 8489	$8886	62%	32%	$10,887	$ 6488	NR
Western Washington University	pub.	$ 6159	$8393	82%	25%	$11,233	$ 3319	$15,929
Whitman College	ind.	$38,770	$9720	98%	84%	$28,133	$20,357	$16,782
West Virginia								
Alderson-Broaddus College	ind.	$21,654	$7002	100%	33%	$21,963	$ 6693	$29,613
Appalachian Bible College	ind.	$10,290	$5400	97%	7%	$ 5452	$10,238	NR
Bethany College	ind.	$21,465	$8700	97%	NR	NR	NR	NR
Bluefield State College	pub.	$ 4596	NA	100%	57%	$ 6200	—	$22,000
Concord University	pub.	$ 4974	$6766	81%	40%	$ 9823	$ 1917	$14,210
Fairmont State University	pub.	$ 5372	$6900	76%	20%	$ 7459	$ 4813	NR
Glenville State College	pub.	$ 4888	$6460	81%	22%	$11,112	$ 236	$19,722
Marshall University	pub.	$ 5236	$7556	68%	30%	$ 9688	$ 3104	$18,146
Mountain State University	ind.	$ 8700	$6116	76%	100%	$ 5651	$ 9165	$33,218
Ohio Valley University	ind.	$17,200	$6676	95%	18%	$12,980	$10,896	$14,976
Shepherd University	pub.	$ 5234	$7228	68%	25%	$ 9881	$ 2581	$20,053
University of Charleston	ind.	$24,000	$8700	97%	29%	$23,280	$ 9420	$23,250
West Liberty University	pub.	$ 4880	$6870	67%	NR	$ 6357	$ 5393	NR
West Virginia University	pub.	$ 5304	$7770	73%	30%	$ 4124	$ 8950	NR
West Virginia Wesleyan College	ind.	$23,980	$7140	100%	22%	$24,424	$ 6696	$21,502
Wheeling Jesuit University	ind.	$24,390	NR	71%	35%	$23,733	$ 657	$26,334
Wisconsin								
Beloit College	ind.	$33,368	$6830	100%	48%	$28,126	$12,072	$17,909
Carroll University	ind.	$22,937	$7668	100%	70%	$17,723	$12,882	$27,066
Carthage College	ind.	$28,250	$7750	100%	15%	$18,778	$17,222	$29,075
Concordia University Wisconsin	ind.	$20,996	$7990	95%	30%	$22,911	$ 6075	$25,169
Edgewood College	ind.	$21,042	$7234	100%	17%	$17,820	$10,456	$31,327
Lakeland College	ind.	$19,640	$7016	96%	10%	$15,512	$11,144	NR
Lawrence University	ind.	$34,596	$7053	97%	78%	$27,875	$13,774	$25,049
Maranatha Baptist Bible College	ind.	$11,550	$6290	24%	6%	$ 4993	$12,847	$15,191

NA = not applicable; NR = not reported; * = includes room and board; † = room only; — = not available.

College Costs At-a-Glance

	Institutional Control ind.=independent; pub.=public	Tuition and Fees	Room and Board	Percent of Eligible Freshmen Receiving Need-Based Gift Awards	Percent of Freshmen Whose Need Was Fully Met	Average Financial Aid Package for Freshmen	Average Net Cost After Aid	Average Indebtedness Upon Graduation
Wisconsin—*continued*								
Marian University	ind.	$20,900	$5640	100%	40%	$19,855	$ 6685	$23,625
Marquette University	ind.	$30,462	NR	99%	27%	$21,961	$ 8501	$31,469
Milwaukee School of Engineering	ind.	$29,520	$7431	100%	14%	$17,868	$19,083	$35,722
Mount Mary College	ind.	$22,118	$7498	100%	6%	$19,419	$10,197	$21,414
Northland College	ind.	$25,241	$6930	100%	28%	$19,843	$12,328	$23,630
Ripon College	ind.	$25,445	$7270	100%	21%	$23,714	$ 9001	$26,073
St. Norbert College	ind.	$26,972	$7052	97%	42%	$24,838	$ 9186	$30,001
Silver Lake College	ind.	$21,180	$6700	100%	28%	$18,013	$ 9867	$18,706
University of Wisconsin–Eau Claire	pub.	$ 6633	$5730	65%	64%	$ 7731	$ 4632	$19,687
University of Wisconsin–Green Bay	pub.	$ 6909	$6500	62%	43%	$10,053	$ 3356	$19,636
University of Wisconsin–La Crosse	pub.	$ 7509	$5630	40%	29%	$ 5931	$ 7208	$21,998
University of Wisconsin–Madison	pub.	$ 8314	$7157	60%	22%	$11,050	$ 4421	$21,552
University of Wisconsin–Milwaukee	pub.	$ 8522	$4290†	39%	27%	$ 6470	$ 6342	$15,772
University of Wisconsin–Parkside	pub.	$ 7196	$6252	58%	31%	$ 8160	$ 5288	$18,254
University of Wisconsin–River Falls	pub.	$ 6460	$5372	49%	NR	$ 2326	$ 9506	$ 8000
University of Wisconsin–Stevens Point	pub.	$ 6530	$5612	51%	70%	$ 6446	$ 5696	$19,738
University of Wisconsin–Stout	pub.	$ 7821	$5336	52%	54%	$ 8805	$ 4352	$27,478
University of Wisconsin–Superior	pub.	$ 6736	$5485	61%	26%	NR	NR	$22,516
University of Wisconsin–Whitewater	pub.	$ 7439	$5028	58%	57%	$ 7408	$ 5059	$20,715
Wisconsin Lutheran College	ind.	$21,180	$7450	100%	20%	$17,272	$11,358	$17,596
Wyoming								
University of Wyoming	pub.	$ 3927	$8360	53%	36%	$ 9535	$ 2752	$17,084

NA = not applicable; NR = not reported; * = includes room and board; † = room only; — = not available.

Profiles of College Financial Aid Programs

ABILENE CHRISTIAN UNIVERSITY
Abilene, TX

Tuition & fees: $20,290	Average undergraduate aid package: $13,841

ABOUT THE INSTITUTION Independent religious, coed. 72 undergraduate majors. Federal methodology is used as a basis for awarding need-based institutional aid.

UNDERGRADUATE EXPENSES for 2009–10 *Comprehensive fee:* $27,800 includes full-time tuition ($19,200), mandatory fees ($1090), and room and board ($7510). *College room only:* $3260. Full-time tuition and fees vary according to course load. Room and board charges vary according to board plan and student level. *Part-time tuition:* $640 per semester hour. *Part-time fees:* $53.50 per semester hour; $10 per term. Part-time tuition and fees vary according to course load. *Payment plans:* Tuition prepayment, installment.

FRESHMAN FINANCIAL AID (Fall 2009, est.) 876 applied for aid; of those 77% were deemed to have need. 100% of freshmen with need received aid; of those 18% had need fully met. *Average percent of need met:* 67% (excluding resources awarded to replace EFC). *Average financial aid package:* $14,046 (excluding resources awarded to replace EFC). 21% of all full-time freshmen had no need and received non-need-based gift aid.

UNDERGRADUATE FINANCIAL AID (Fall 2009, est.) 2,990 applied for aid; of those 80% were deemed to have need. 100% of undergraduates with need received aid; of those 18% had need fully met. *Average percent of need met:* 67% (excluding resources awarded to replace EFC). *Average financial aid package:* $13,841 (excluding resources awarded to replace EFC). 14% of all full-time undergraduates had no need and received non-need-based gift aid.

GIFT AID (NEED-BASED) *Total amount:* $21,579,860 (18% federal, 20% state, 56% institutional, 6% external sources). *Receiving aid:* Freshmen: 68% (669); all full-time undergraduates: 65% (2,348). *Average award:* Freshmen: $10,633; Undergraduates: $10,152. *Scholarships, grants, and awards:* Federal Pell, FSEOG, state, private, college/university gift aid from institutional funds, United Negro College Fund.

GIFT AID (NON-NEED-BASED) *Total amount:* $6,804,901 (1% state, 93% institutional, 6% external sources). *Receiving aid:* Freshmen: 59% (581). Undergraduates: 57% (2,033). *Average award:* Freshmen: $7738. Undergraduates: $6690. *Scholarships, grants, and awards by category: Academic interests/achievement:* agriculture, biological sciences, business, communication, education, English, foreign languages, general academic interests/achievements, mathematics, physical sciences, religion/biblical studies, social sciences. *Creative arts/performance:* art/fine arts, debating, journalism/publications, music, theater/drama. *Special achievements/activities:* cheerleading/drum major, leadership. *Special characteristics:* children of faculty/staff, ethnic background, first-generation college students, local/state students, members of minority groups, out-of-state students, previous college experience, relatives of clergy, religious affiliation. *Tuition waivers:* Full or partial for employees or children of employees.

LOANS *Student loans:* $24,845,655 (31% need-based, 69% non-need-based). 71% of past graduating class borrowed through all loan programs. *Average indebtedness per student:* $35,453. *Average need-based loan:* Freshmen: $3208. Undergraduates: $4228. *Parent loans:* $3,863,596 (100% non-need-based). *Programs:* FFEL (Subsidized and Unsubsidized Stafford, PLUS), Perkins, state, college/university.

WORK-STUDY *Federal work-study:* Total amount: $1,743,092; 540 jobs averaging $3393. *State or other work-study/employment:* Total amount: $89,988 (43% need-based, 57% non-need-based). Part-time jobs available.

ATHLETIC AWARDS Total amount: $3,107,507 (54% need-based, 46% non-need-based).

APPLYING FOR FINANCIAL AID *Required financial aid forms:* FAFSA, institution's own form. *Financial aid deadline (priority):* 3/1. *Notification date:* Continuous beginning 4/1. Students must reply within 3 weeks of notification.

CONTACT Barrett Bell, Director of Student Financial Services, Abilene Christian University, ACU Box 29007, Abilene, TX 79699-9007, 325-674-2643. *E-mail:* bxb10a@acu.edu.

ABRAHAM BALDWIN AGRICULTURAL COLLEGE
Tifton, GA

Tuition & fees: N/R	Average undergraduate aid package: N/A

ABOUT THE INSTITUTION State-supported, coed. 48 undergraduate majors.

GIFT AID (NEED-BASED) *Scholarships, grants, and awards:* Federal Pell, FSEOG, state, private, college/university gift aid from institutional funds, HOPE Scholarships.

GIFT AID (NON-NEED-BASED) *Tuition waivers:* Full or partial for employees or children of employees, senior citizens.

LOANS *Programs:* FFEL (Subsidized and Unsubsidized Stafford, PLUS), Perkins, state.

APPLYING FOR FINANCIAL AID *Required financial aid forms:* FAFSA, institution's own form. *Financial aid deadline:* 7/15. *Notification date:* Continuous beginning 5/15.

CONTACT Jenelle L. Handcox, Director of Financial Aid, Abraham Baldwin Agricultural College, 2802 Moore Highway, ABAC 23, Tifton, GA 31793-2601, 229-391-4910 or toll-free 800-733-3653. *Fax:* 229-391-4911. *E-mail:* finaid@abac.edu.

ACADEMY COLLEGE
Minneapolis, MN

CONTACT Ms. Mary Erickson, Director of Administration, Academy College, 3050 Metro Drive #200, Minneapolis, MN 55425, 612-851-0066 or toll-free 800-292-9149. *Fax:* 612-851-0094. *E-mail:* email@academyeducation.com.

ACADEMY OF ART UNIVERSITY
San Francisco, CA

Tuition & fees: $22,490	Average undergraduate aid package: $7037

ABOUT THE INSTITUTION Proprietary, coed. 19 undergraduate majors. Federal methodology is used as a basis for awarding need-based institutional aid.

UNDERGRADUATE EXPENSES for 2010–11 *Comprehensive fee:* $35,890 includes full-time tuition ($22,200), mandatory fees ($290), and room and board ($13,400). Full-time tuition and fees vary according to course load. Room and board charges vary according to housing facility. *Part-time tuition:* $740 per credit. Part-time tuition and fees vary according to course load. *Payment plan:* Installment.

FRESHMAN FINANCIAL AID (Fall 2008) 605 applied for aid; of those 83% were deemed to have need. 98% of freshmen with need received aid. *Average financial aid package:* $7005 (excluding resources awarded to replace EFC).

UNDERGRADUATE FINANCIAL AID (Fall 2008) 3,558 applied for aid; of those 88% were deemed to have need. 98% of undergraduates with need received aid. *Average financial aid package:* $7037 (excluding resources awarded to replace EFC).

GIFT AID (NEED-BASED) *Total amount:* $14,257,825 (73% federal, 27% state). *Receiving aid:* Freshmen: 31% (260); all full-time undergraduates: 30% (1,773). *Average award:* Freshmen: $4649; Undergraduates: $5787. *Scholarships, grants, and awards:* Federal Pell, FSEOG, state, private.

GIFT AID (NON-NEED-BASED) *Total amount:* $936,364 (100% institutional). *Receiving aid:* Freshmen: 3% (29). Undergraduates: 2% (103).

LOANS *Student loans:* $94,999,448 (45% need-based, 55% non-need-based). 54% of past graduating class borrowed through all loan programs. *Average indebtedness per student:* $8112. *Average need-based loan:* Freshmen: $2647. Undergraduates: $3930. *Parent loans:* $30,537,714 (100% non-need-based). *Programs:* Federal Direct (Subsidized and Unsubsidized Stafford, PLUS), alternative loans.

WORK-STUDY *Federal work-study:* Total amount: $285,310; 105 jobs averaging $2717.

ATHLETIC AWARDS Total amount: $1,846,046 (100% non-need-based).

APPLYING FOR FINANCIAL AID *Required financial aid forms:* FAFSA, institution's own form. *Financial aid deadline (priority):* 3/2. *Notification date:* Continuous. Students must reply within 3 weeks of notification.

CONTACT Mr. Joe Vollaro, Executive Vice President of Financial Aid and Compliance, Academy of Art University, 79 New Montgomery Street, San Francisco, CA 94105-3410, 415-618-6528 or toll-free 800-544-ARTS. *Fax:* 415-618-6273. *E-mail:* jvollaro@academyart.edu.

ADAMS STATE COLLEGE
Alamosa, CO

Tuition & fees (CO res): $4454	Average undergraduate aid package: $8662

ABOUT THE INSTITUTION State-supported, coed. 78 undergraduate majors. Federal methodology is used as a basis for awarding need-based institutional aid.

UNDERGRADUATE EXPENSES for 2009–10 *Tuition, state resident:* full-time $2712; part-time $113 per credit hour. *Tuition, nonresident:* full-time $11,856; part-time $494 per credit hour. *Required fees:* full-time $1742; $73 per credit hour. Full-time tuition and fees vary according to course load. Part-time tuition and fees vary according to course load. *College room and board:* $7020; *Room only:* $3560. Room and board charges vary according to board plan and housing facility. *Payment plans:* Installment, deferred payment.

FRESHMAN FINANCIAL AID (Fall 2008) 436 applied for aid; of those 79% were deemed to have need. 99% of freshmen with need received aid; of those 1% had need fully met. *Average percent of need met:* 51% (excluding resources awarded to replace EFC). *Average financial aid package:* $8649 (excluding resources awarded to replace EFC). 4% of all full-time freshmen had no need and received non-need-based gift aid.

UNDERGRADUATE FINANCIAL AID (Fall 2008) 1,562 applied for aid; of those 84% were deemed to have need. 98% of undergraduates with need received aid; of those .3% had need fully met. *Average percent of need met:* 50% (excluding resources awarded to replace EFC). *Average financial aid package:* $8662 (excluding resources awarded to replace EFC). 2% of all full-time undergraduates had no need and received non-need-based gift aid.

GIFT AID (NEED-BASED) *Total amount:* $6,416,639 (67% federal, 30% state, 1% institutional, 2% external sources). *Receiving aid:* Freshmen: 68% (315); all full-time undergraduates: 72% (1,191). *Average award:* Freshmen: $5084; Undergraduates: $5084. *Scholarships, grants, and awards:* Federal Pell, FSEOG, state, private, college/university gift aid from institutional funds.

GIFT AID (NON-NEED-BASED) *Total amount:* $2,663,636 (1% state, 76% institutional, 23% external sources). *Receiving aid:* Freshmen: 41% (189). Undergraduates: 29% (477). *Average award:* Freshmen: $2377. Undergraduates: $2712. *Tuition waivers:* Full or partial for employees or children of employees, senior citizens.

LOANS *Student loans:* $7,940,563 (49% need-based, 51% non-need-based). 65% of past graduating class borrowed through all loan programs. *Average indebtedness per student:* $21,211. *Average need-based loan:* Freshmen: $2841. Undergraduates: $3537. *Parent loans:* $480,890 (100% non-need-based). *Programs:* FFEL (Subsidized and Unsubsidized Stafford, PLUS), Perkins, alternative loans.

WORK-STUDY *Federal work-study:* Total amount: $244,304; 230 jobs averaging $1062. *State or other work-study/employment:* Total amount: $450,537 (62% need-based, 38% non-need-based). 397 part-time jobs averaging $1024.

ATHLETIC AWARDS Total amount: $1,008,029 (87% need-based, 13% non-need-based).

APPLYING FOR FINANCIAL AID *Required financial aid form:* FAFSA. *Financial aid deadline:* Continuous. *Notification date:* Continuous.

CONTACT Phil Schroeder, Student Financial Aid Director, Adams State College, 208 Edgemont Boulevard, Alamosa, CO 81102, 719-587-7306 or toll-free 800-824-6494. *Fax:* 719-587-7366.

ADELPHI UNIVERSITY
Garden City, NY

Tuition & fees: N/R	Average undergraduate aid package: $17,850

ABOUT THE INSTITUTION Independent, coed. 46 undergraduate majors. Federal methodology is used as a basis for awarding need-based institutional aid.

UNDERGRADUATE EXPENSES for 2010–11 *Tuition:* part-time $780 per credit hour. Full-time tuition and fees vary according to course level, location, and program. Part-time tuition and fees vary according to course level, location, and program. Room and board charges vary according to board plan and housing facility. *Payment plans:* Installment, deferred payment.

FRESHMAN FINANCIAL AID (Fall 2009, est.) 864 applied for aid; of those 83% were deemed to have need. 87% of freshmen with need received aid; of those 2% had need fully met. *Average percent of need met:* 38% (excluding resources awarded to replace EFC). *Average financial aid package:* $17,850 (excluding resources awarded to replace EFC). 58% of all full-time freshmen had no need and received non-need-based gift aid.

UNDERGRADUATE FINANCIAL AID (Fall 2009, est.) 3,444 applied for aid; of those 86% were deemed to have need. 88% of undergraduates with need received aid; of those 2% had need fully met. *Average percent of need met:* 38% (excluding resources awarded to replace EFC). *Average financial aid package:* $17,850 (excluding resources awarded to replace EFC). 64% of all full-time undergraduates had no need and received non-need-based gift aid.

GIFT AID (NEED-BASED) *Total amount:* $28,376,548 (19% federal, 18% state, 63% institutional). *Receiving aid:* Freshmen: 54% (527); all full-time undergraduates: 45% (1,949). *Average award:* Freshmen: $6340; Undergraduates: $6469. *Scholarships, grants, and awards:* Federal Pell, FSEOG, state, private, college/university gift aid from institutional funds, United Negro College Fund, endowed-donor scholarships.

GIFT AID (NON-NEED-BASED) *Total amount:* $10,297,701 (91% institutional, 9% external sources). *Receiving aid:* Freshmen: 47% (466). Undergraduates: 43% (1,830). *Average award:* Freshmen: $8994. Undergraduates: $8353. *Scholarships, grants, and awards by category:* Academic interests/achievement: 2,579 awards ($21,282,513 total): communication, foreign languages, general academic interests/achievements. *Creative arts/performance:* 132 awards ($831,700 total): art/fine arts, dance, music, performing arts, theater/drama. *Special achievements/activities:* 759 awards ($580,750 total): community service, general special achievements/activities, memberships. *Special characteristics:* 355 awards ($2,651,685 total): children and siblings of alumni, children of faculty/staff. *Tuition waivers:* Full or partial for employees or children of employees.

LOANS *Student loans:* $27,669,543 (49% need-based, 51% non-need-based). 69% of past graduating class borrowed through all loan programs. *Average indebtedness per student:* $28,307. *Average need-based loan:* Freshmen: $3979. Undergraduates: $4509. *Parent loans:* $19,961,186 (56% need-based, 44% non-need-based). *Programs:* FFEL (Subsidized and Unsubsidized Stafford, PLUS), Perkins, Federal Nursing, New York HELP Program (private alternative loans).

WORK-STUDY *Federal work-study:* Total amount: $2,388,370; 2,813 jobs averaging $2214. *State or other work-study/employment:* Total amount: $1,774,280 (100% non-need-based). 828 part-time jobs averaging $2143.

ATHLETIC AWARDS Total amount: $3,137,920 (58% need-based, 42% non-need-based).

APPLYING FOR FINANCIAL AID *Required financial aid forms:* FAFSA, state aid form. *Financial aid deadline (priority):* 3/1. *Notification date:* Continuous.

CONTACT Ms. Sheryl Mihopulos, Director of Student Financial Services, Adelphi University, 1 South Avenue, PO Box 701, Garden City, NY 11530, 516-877-3365 or toll-free 800-ADELPHI. *Fax:* 516-877-3380. *E-mail:* mihopulos@adelphi.edu.

ADRIAN COLLEGE
Adrian, MI

Tuition & fees: $24,440	Average undergraduate aid package: $21,057

ABOUT THE INSTITUTION Independent religious, coed. *Awards:* associate and bachelor's degrees. 46 undergraduate majors. *Total enrollment:* 1,469. Undergraduates: 1,469. Freshmen: 500. Both federal and institutional methodology are used as a basis for awarding need-based institutional aid.

UNDERGRADUATE EXPENSES for 2009–10 *Comprehensive fee:* $31,900 includes full-time tuition ($24,140), mandatory fees ($300), and room and board ($7460). *College room only:* $3610. *Part-time tuition:* $685 per credit hour. *Part-time fees:* $75 per term.

FRESHMAN FINANCIAL AID (Fall 2009, est.) 423 applied for aid; of those 91% were deemed to have need. 100% of freshmen with need received aid; of those 14% had need fully met. *Average percent of need met:* 81% (excluding resources awarded to replace EFC). *Average financial aid package:* $20,848 (excluding resources awarded to replace EFC). 9% of all full-time freshmen had no need and received non-need-based gift aid.

UNDERGRADUATE FINANCIAL AID (Fall 2009, est.) 1,362 applied for aid; of those 93% were deemed to have need. 100% of undergraduates with need received aid; of those 12% had need fully met. *Average percent of need met:* 79% (excluding resources awarded to replace EFC). *Average financial aid package:* $21,057 (excluding resources awarded to replace EFC). 11% of all full-time undergraduates had no need and received non-need-based gift aid.

GIFT AID (NEED-BASED) *Total amount:* $22,077,735 (11% federal, 6% state, 82% institutional, 1% external sources). *Receiving aid:* Freshmen: 69% (325);

all full-time undergraduates: 69% (1,077). *Average award:* Freshmen: $10,241; Undergraduates: $9754. *Scholarships, grants, and awards:* Federal Pell, FSEOG, state, private, college/university gift aid from institutional funds.

GIFT AID (NON-NEED-BASED) *Receiving aid:* Freshmen: 72% (339). Undergraduates: 69% (1,072). *Average award:* Freshmen: $11,217. Undergraduates: $10,885. *Scholarships, grants, and awards by category:* Academic interests/achievement: 1,036 awards ($8,338,518 total): business, general academic interests/achievements. *Creative arts/performance:* 908 awards ($1,430,603 total): art/fine arts, music, theater/drama. *Special achievements/activities:* 81 awards ($116,250 total): religious involvement. *Special characteristics:* 193 awards ($1,398,752 total): children and siblings of alumni, children of faculty/staff, children of union members/company employees, ethnic background, general special characteristics, international students, religious affiliation.

LOANS *Student loans:* $9,448,394 (100% need-based). 81% of past graduating class borrowed through all loan programs. *Average indebtedness per student:* $17,160. *Average need-based loan:* Freshmen: $3189. Undergraduates: $4243. *Parent loans:* $11,244,708 (100% need-based). *Programs:* FFEL (Subsidized and Unsubsidized Stafford, PLUS), Perkins.

WORK-STUDY *Federal work-study:* Total amount: $1,724,400; 1,006 jobs averaging $1800. *State or other work-study/employment:* Total amount: $113,700 (100% need-based). 65 part-time jobs averaging $1800.

APPLYING FOR FINANCIAL AID *Required financial aid form:* FAFSA. *Financial aid deadline (priority):* 3/1. *Notification date:* Continuous beginning 3/15. Students must reply by 5/1 or within 2 weeks of notification.

CONTACT Mr. Andrew Spohn, Director of Financial Aid, Adrian College, 110 South Madison Street, Adrian, MI 49221-2575, 517-265-5161 Ext. 4306 or toll-free 800-877-2246. *Fax:* 517-264-3153. *E-mail:* aspohn@adrian.edu.

AGNES SCOTT COLLEGE
Decatur, GA

Tuition & fees: $31,283	Average undergraduate aid package: $28,845

ABOUT THE INSTITUTION Independent religious, undergraduate: women only; graduate: coed. 35 undergraduate majors. Both federal and institutional methodology are used as a basis for awarding need-based institutional aid.

UNDERGRADUATE EXPENSES for 2010–11 *Comprehensive fee:* $41,133 includes full-time tuition ($31,068), mandatory fees ($215), and room and board ($9850). *College room only:* $4925. Full-time tuition and fees vary according to course load. Room and board charges vary according to board plan and housing facility. *Part-time tuition:* $1294 per hour. Part-time tuition and fees vary according to course load. *Payment plan:* Installment.

FRESHMAN FINANCIAL AID (Fall 2009, est.) 200 applied for aid; of those 91% were deemed to have need. 100% of freshmen with need received aid; of those 30% had need fully met. *Average percent of need met:* 91% (excluding resources awarded to replace EFC). *Average financial aid package:* $30,031 (excluding resources awarded to replace EFC). 23% of all full-time freshmen had no need and received non-need-based gift aid.

UNDERGRADUATE FINANCIAL AID (Fall 2009, est.) 619 applied for aid; of those 93% were deemed to have need. 100% of undergraduates with need received aid; of those 34% had need fully met. *Average percent of need met:* 91% (excluding resources awarded to replace EFC). *Average financial aid package:* $28,845 (excluding resources awarded to replace EFC). 24% of all full-time undergraduates had no need and received non-need-based gift aid.

GIFT AID (NEED-BASED) *Total amount:* $13,491,755 (12% federal, 6% state, 81% institutional, 1% external sources). *Receiving aid:* Freshmen: 77% (182); all full-time undergraduates: 73% (571). *Average award:* Freshmen: $24,448; Undergraduates: $23,525. *Scholarships, grants, and awards:* Federal Pell, FSEOG, state, private, college/university gift aid from institutional funds.

GIFT AID (NON-NEED-BASED) *Total amount:* $3,661,600 (10% state, 88% institutional, 2% external sources). *Receiving aid:* Freshmen: 23% (54). Undergraduates: 19% (148). *Average award:* Freshmen: $15,821. Undergraduates: $15,195. *Scholarships, grants, and awards by category:* Academic interests/achievement: general academic interests/achievements. *Creative arts/performance:* music. *Special achievements/activities:* community service, leadership. *Special characteristics:* adult students, children of educators, children of faculty/staff, international students, local/state students, religious affiliation, veterans, veterans' children. *Tuition waivers:* Full or partial for employees or children of employees.

LOANS *Student loans:* $4,385,057 (50% need-based, 50% non-need-based). 69% of past graduating class borrowed through all loan programs. *Average indebtedness per student:* $23,176. *Average need-based loan:* Freshmen: $3293. Undergraduates: $3767. *Parent loans:* $1,187,924 (16% need-based, 84% non-need-based). *Programs:* FFEL (Subsidized and Unsubsidized Stafford, PLUS), college/university.

WORK-STUDY *Federal work-study:* Total amount: $975,282; 495 jobs averaging $1970. *State or other work-study/employment:* Total amount: $205,000 (15% need-based, 85% non-need-based). 103 part-time jobs averaging $1990.

APPLYING FOR FINANCIAL AID *Required financial aid forms:* FAFSA, copy of previous year's tax returns. *Financial aid deadline:* 5/1 (priority: 2/15). *Notification date:* Continuous beginning 3/1. Students must reply within 2 weeks of notification.

CONTACT Patrick Bonones, Director of Financial Aid, Agnes Scott College, 141 East College Avenue, Decatur, GA 30030-3797, 404-471-6395 or toll-free 800-868-8602. *Fax:* 404-471-6159. *E-mail:* finaid@agnesscott.edu.

AIB COLLEGE OF BUSINESS
Des Moines, IA

CONTACT Connie Loven, Financial Aid Director, AIB College of Business, 2500 Fleur Drive, Des Moines, IA 50321, 515-244-4221 Ext. 4145 or toll-free 800-444-1921. *Fax:* 515-244-6773. *E-mail:* jensenc@aib.edu.

ALABAMA AGRICULTURAL AND MECHANICAL UNIVERSITY
Huntsville, AL

Tuition & fees: N/R	Average undergraduate aid package: $8642

ABOUT THE INSTITUTION State-supported, coed. 36 undergraduate majors. Federal methodology is used as a basis for awarding need-based institutional aid.

FRESHMAN FINANCIAL AID (Fall 2009, est.) 982 applied for aid; of those 88% were deemed to have need. 99% of freshmen with need received aid; of those 18% had need fully met. *Average percent of need met:* 18% (excluding resources awarded to replace EFC). *Average financial aid package:* $8875 (excluding resources awarded to replace EFC). 1% of all full-time freshmen had no need and received non-need-based gift aid.

UNDERGRADUATE FINANCIAL AID (Fall 2009, est.) 3,566 applied for aid; of those 89% were deemed to have need. 99% of undergraduates with need received aid; of those 14% had need fully met. *Average percent of need met:* 14% (excluding resources awarded to replace EFC). *Average financial aid package:* $8642 (excluding resources awarded to replace EFC). 1% of all full-time undergraduates had no need and received non-need-based gift aid.

GIFT AID (NEED-BASED) *Total amount:* $16,480,764 (59% federal, 2% state, 33% institutional, 6% external sources). *Receiving aid:* Freshmen: 73% (762); all full-time undergraduates: 66% (2,639). *Average award:* Freshmen: $6795; Undergraduates: $6243. *Scholarships, grants, and awards:* Federal Pell, FSEOG, state, private, college/university gift aid from institutional funds.

GIFT AID (NON-NEED-BASED) *Total amount:* $1,813,159 (2% state, 88% institutional, 10% external sources). *Receiving aid:* Freshmen: 4% (38). Undergraduates: 2% (93). *Average award:* Freshmen: $2038. Undergraduates: $3665. *Scholarships, grants, and awards by category:* Academic interests/achievement: general academic interests/achievements. *Creative arts/performance:* art/fine arts, music. *Special characteristics:* parents of current students. *Tuition waivers:* Full or partial for employees or children of employees.

LOANS *Student loans:* $26,002,757 (98% need-based, 2% non-need-based). 82% of past graduating class borrowed through all loan programs. *Average indebtedness per student:* $32,024. *Average need-based loan:* Freshmen: $3614. Undergraduates: $4265. *Parent loans:* $1,930,608 (98% need-based, 2% non-need-based). *Programs:* FFEL (Subsidized and Unsubsidized Stafford, PLUS), Perkins.

WORK-STUDY *Federal work-study:* Total amount: $352,764; jobs available.

ATHLETIC AWARDS Total amount: $1,578,847 (80% need-based, 20% non-need-based).

APPLYING FOR FINANCIAL AID *Required financial aid form:* FAFSA. *Financial aid deadline (priority):* 3/1. *Notification date:* Continuous beginning 4/15. Students must reply within 2 weeks of notification.

CONTACT Ms. Kai CampBell, Financial Aid Officer, Alabama Agricultural and Mechanical University, 4900 Meridian Street, Normal, AL 35762, 256-851-5400 or toll-free 800-553-0816. *Fax:* 256-851-5407.

ALABAMA STATE UNIVERSITY
Montgomery, AL

Tuition & fees (AL res): $6468	Average undergraduate aid package: $14,148

ABOUT THE INSTITUTION State-supported, coed. 49 undergraduate majors. Federal methodology is used as a basis for awarding need-based institutional aid.

UNDERGRADUATE EXPENSES for 2009–10 *One-time required fee:* $150. *Tuition, state resident:* full-time $5616;. part-time $234 per credit hour. *Tuition, nonresident:* full-time $11,232; part-time $468 per credit hour. *Required fees:* full-time $852; $213 per term. *College room and board:* $4600; *Room only:* $2630. Room and board charges vary according to board plan and housing facility. *Payment plan:* Deferred payment.

FRESHMAN FINANCIAL AID (Fall 2009, est.) 1,159 applied for aid; of those 98% were deemed to have need. 96% of freshmen with need received aid; of those 12% had need fully met. *Average percent of need met:* 60% (excluding resources awarded to replace EFC). *Average financial aid package:* $14,192 (excluding resources awarded to replace EFC). 1% of all full-time freshmen had no need and received non-need-based gift aid.

UNDERGRADUATE FINANCIAL AID (Fall 2009, est.) 4,467 applied for aid; of those 90% were deemed to have need. 95% of undergraduates with need received aid; of those 14% had need fully met. *Average percent of need met:* 68% (excluding resources awarded to replace EFC). *Average financial aid package:* $14,148 (excluding resources awarded to replace EFC). 1% of all full-time undergraduates had no need and received non-need-based gift aid.

GIFT AID (NEED-BASED) *Total amount:* $23,873,280 (73% federal, 5% state, 18% institutional, 4% external sources). *Receiving aid:* Freshmen: 77% (939); all full-time undergraduates: 72% (3,230). *Average award:* Freshmen: $5011; Undergraduates: $14,148. *Scholarships, grants, and awards:* Federal Pell, FSEOG, state, private, college/university gift aid from institutional funds, United Negro College Fund.

GIFT AID (NON-NEED-BASED) *Total amount:* $920,480 (8% federal, 3% state, 82% institutional, 7% external sources). *Receiving aid:* Freshmen: 36% (445). Undergraduates: 32% (1,443). *Average award:* Freshmen: $10,726. Undergraduates: $7280. *Scholarships, grants, and awards by category: Academic interests/achievement:* general academic interests/achievements. *Creative arts/performance:* general creative arts/performance, music, theater/drama. *Special achievements/activities:* leadership. *Special characteristics:* general special characteristics, members of minority groups. *Tuition waivers:* Full or partial for employees or children of employees.

LOANS *Student loans:* $30,127,352 (91% need-based, 9% non-need-based). 90% of past graduating class borrowed through all loan programs. *Average indebtedness per student:* $31,317. *Average need-based loan:* Freshmen: $3263. Undergraduates: $3782. *Parent loans:* $3,481,284 (84% need-based, 16% non-need-based). *Programs:* FFEL (Subsidized and Unsubsidized Stafford, PLUS), Perkins, state.

WORK-STUDY *Federal work-study:* Total amount: $1,264,660; jobs available. *State or other work-study/employment:* Total amount: $154,360 (100% non-need-based). Part-time jobs available.

ATHLETIC AWARDS Total amount: $1,528,006 (87% need-based, 13% non-need-based).

APPLYING FOR FINANCIAL AID *Required financial aid form:* FAFSA. *Financial aid deadline (priority):* 4/1. *Notification date:* Continuous beginning 5/15.

CONTACT Mrs. Dorenda A. Adams, Director of Financial Aid, Alabama State University, PO Box 271, Montgomery, AL 36101-0271, 334-229-4323 or toll-free 800-253-5037. *Fax:* 334-299-4924. *E-mail:* dadams@alasu.edu.

ALASKA BIBLE COLLEGE
Glennallen, AK

Tuition & fees: N/R	Average undergraduate aid package: N/A

ABOUT THE INSTITUTION Independent nondenominational, coed. 1 undergraduate major. Institutional methodology is used as a basis for awarding need-based institutional aid.

FRESHMAN FINANCIAL AID (Fall 2009, est.) 3 applied for aid; of those 100% were deemed to have need. 100% of freshmen with need received aid.

UNDERGRADUATE FINANCIAL AID (Fall 2009, est.) 8 applied for aid; of those 100% were deemed to have need. 100% of undergraduates with need received aid.

GIFT AID (NEED-BASED) *Total amount:* $11,250 (100% institutional). *Receiving aid:* Freshmen: 30% (3); all full-time undergraduates: 27% (8). *Average award:* Freshmen: $850; Undergraduates: $850. *Scholarships, grants, and awards:* private, college/university gift aid from institutional funds.

GIFT AID (NON-NEED-BASED) *Total amount:* $5800 (100% external sources). *Scholarships, grants, and awards by category: Academic interests/achievement:* 3 awards ($1150 total): general academic interests/achievements, religion/biblical studies. *Creative arts/performance:* 1 award ($100 total): music. *Special achievements/activities:* 3 awards ($450 total): religious involvement. *Special characteristics:* 5 awards ($10,650 total): children of faculty/staff, local/state students, married students, religious affiliation, spouses of current students. *Tuition waivers:* Full or partial for employees or children of employees.

LOANS *Student loans:* $56,525 (100% non-need-based). 23% of past graduating class borrowed through all loan programs. *Average indebtedness per student:* $8075. *Programs:* state.

WORK-STUDY *State or other work-study/employment:* Total amount: $17,128 (100% non-need-based). 20 part-time jobs averaging $842.

APPLYING FOR FINANCIAL AID *Required financial aid form:* institution's own form. *Financial aid deadline:* 7/1. *Notification date:* 8/1. Students must reply within 2 weeks of notification.

CONTACT Jared Palmer, Financial Aid Officer, Alaska Bible College, PO Box 289, Glennallen, AK 99588-0289, 907-822-3201 Ext. 225 or toll-free 800-478-7884. *Fax:* 907-822-5027. *E-mail:* jpalmer@akbible.edu.

ALASKA PACIFIC UNIVERSITY
Anchorage, AK

Tuition & fees: $26,360	Average undergraduate aid package: $15,100

ABOUT THE INSTITUTION Independent, coed. 16 undergraduate majors. Federal methodology is used as a basis for awarding need-based institutional aid.

UNDERGRADUATE EXPENSES for 2010–11 *Comprehensive fee:* $35,660 includes full-time tuition ($26,250), mandatory fees ($110), and room and board ($9300). *College room only:* $4400. Full-time tuition and fees vary according to class time, degree level, location, and program. Room and board charges vary according to board plan and housing facility. *Part-time tuition:* $1100 per semester hour. *Part-time fees:* $55 per term. Part-time tuition and fees vary according to class time, course load, degree level, location, and program. *Payment plans:* Guaranteed tuition, installment, deferred payment.

FRESHMAN FINANCIAL AID (Fall 2009, est.) 22 applied for aid; of those 86% were deemed to have need. 100% of freshmen with need received aid; of those 5% had need fully met. *Average percent of need met:* 89% (excluding resources awarded to replace EFC). *Average financial aid package:* $10,900 (excluding resources awarded to replace EFC).

UNDERGRADUATE FINANCIAL AID (Fall 2009, est.) 213 applied for aid; of those 92% were deemed to have need. 99% of undergraduates with need received aid; of those 2% had need fully met. *Average percent of need met:* 92% (excluding resources awarded to replace EFC). *Average financial aid package:* $15,100 (excluding resources awarded to replace EFC). 3% of all full-time undergraduates had no need and received non-need-based gift aid.

GIFT AID (NEED-BASED) *Total amount:* $1,472,143 (43% federal, 35% institutional, 22% external sources). *Receiving aid:* Freshmen: 32% (9); all full-time undergraduates: 43% (108). *Average award:* Freshmen: $7500; Undergraduates: $7900. *Scholarships, grants, and awards:* Federal Pell, FSEOG, state, private, college/university gift aid from institutional funds, Bureau of Indian Affairs Grants, Yellow Ribbon Program.

GIFT AID (NON-NEED-BASED) *Total amount:* $1,828,638 (95% institutional, 5% external sources). *Receiving aid:* Freshmen: 68% (19). Undergraduates: 37% (94). *Average award:* Freshmen: $5198. Undergraduates: $9570. *Scholarships, grants, and awards by category: Academic interests/achievement:* biological sciences, business, education, general academic interests/achievements, humanities, physical sciences, social sciences. *Creative arts/performance:* art/fine arts, music, theater/drama. *Special achievements/activities:* community service, general special achievements/activities, leadership, religious involvement. *Special characteristics:* children and siblings of alumni, children of faculty/staff, ethnic background, general special characteristics, international students, local/

state students, members of minority groups, out-of-state students, religious affiliation. *Tuition waivers:* Full or partial for employees or children of employees, adult students.

LOANS *Student loans:* $2,745,322 (36% need-based, 64% non-need-based). 94% of past graduating class borrowed through all loan programs. *Average indebtedness per student:* $43,392. *Average need-based loan:* Freshmen: $3375. Undergraduates: $4570. *Parent loans:* $477,840 (100% non-need-based). *Programs:* Federal Direct (Subsidized and Unsubsidized Stafford, PLUS), state, alternative loans.

WORK-STUDY *Federal work-study:* Total amount: $81,344; jobs available. *State or other work-study/employment:* Total amount: $148,500 (100% non-need-based). Part-time jobs available.

APPLYING FOR FINANCIAL AID *Required financial aid form:* FAFSA. *Financial aid deadline (priority):* 4/15. *Notification date:* Continuous beginning 2/1. Students must reply by 2/1 or within 4 weeks of notification.

CONTACT Jo Holland, Director of Student Financial Services, Alaska Pacific University, 4101 University Drive, Anchorage, AK 99508-4672, 907-564-8342 or toll-free 800-252-7528. *Fax:* 907-564-8372. *E-mail:* sfs@alaskapacific.edu.

ALBANY COLLEGE OF PHARMACY AND HEALTH SCIENCES
Albany, NY

CONTACT Tiffany M. Gutierrez, Director of Financial Aid, Albany College of Pharmacy and Health Sciences, 106 New Scotland Avenue, Albany, NY 12208-3425, 518-445-7256 or toll-free 888-203-8010. *Fax:* 518-445-7322. *E-mail:* gutierrt@mail.acp.edu.

ALBANY STATE UNIVERSITY
Albany, GA

CONTACT Ms. Kathleen J. Caldwell, Director of Financial Aid, Albany State University, 504 College Drive, Albany, GA 31705-2717, 912-430-4650 or toll-free 800-822-RAMS (in-state). *Fax:* 912-430-3936. *E-mail:* finaid@asurams. edu.

ALBERTUS MAGNUS COLLEGE
New Haven, CT

ABOUT THE INSTITUTION Independent Roman Catholic, coed. 45 undergraduate majors.

GIFT AID (NEED-BASED) *Scholarships, grants, and awards:* Federal Pell, FSEOG, state, college/university gift aid from institutional funds.

GIFT AID (NON-NEED-BASED) *Scholarships, grants, and awards by category: Academic interests/achievement:* biological sciences, business, communication, computer science, education, English, foreign languages, general academic interests/achievements, humanities, international studies, mathematics, physical sciences, premedicine, religion/biblical studies, social sciences. *Creative arts/performance:* art/fine arts, performing arts, theater/drama. *Special achievements/ activities:* community service, leadership. *Special characteristics:* local/state students, religious affiliation.

LOANS *Programs:* FFEL (Subsidized and Unsubsidized Stafford, PLUS), Perkins.

WORK-STUDY *Federal work-study:* Total amount: $171,846; 78 jobs averaging $1583. *State or other work-study/employment:* 34 part-time jobs averaging $3400.

APPLYING FOR FINANCIAL AID *Required financial aid form:* FAFSA.

CONTACT Andrew Foster, Director of Financial Aid, Albertus Magnus College, 700 Prospect Street, New Haven, CT 06511-1189, 203-773-8508 or toll-free 800-578-9160. *Fax:* 203-773-8972. *E-mail:* financial_aid@albertus.edu.

ALBION COLLEGE
Albion, MI

Tuition & fees: $30,002   **Average undergraduate aid package: $24,776**

ABOUT THE INSTITUTION Independent Methodist, coed. 37 undergraduate majors. Federal methodology is used as a basis for awarding need-based institutional aid.

UNDERGRADUATE EXPENSES for 2009–10 *Comprehensive fee:* $38,512 includes full-time tuition ($29,488), mandatory fees ($514), and room and board ($8510). *College room only:* $4162. Room and board charges vary according to housing facility.

FRESHMAN FINANCIAL AID (Fall 2009, est.) 362 applied for aid; of those 86% were deemed to have need. 100% of freshmen with need received aid; of those 30% had need fully met. *Average percent of need met:* 89% (excluding resources awarded to replace EFC). *Average financial aid package:* $26,214 (excluding resources awarded to replace EFC). 28% of all full-time freshmen had no need and received non-need-based gift aid.

UNDERGRADUATE FINANCIAL AID (Fall 2009, est.) 1,267 applied for aid; of those 89% were deemed to have need. 100% of undergraduates with need received aid; of those 31% had need fully met. *Average percent of need met:* 88% (excluding resources awarded to replace EFC). *Average financial aid package:* $24,776 (excluding resources awarded to replace EFC). 33% of all full-time undergraduates had no need and received non-need-based gift aid.

GIFT AID (NEED-BASED) *Total amount:* $22,474,073 (9% federal, 11% state, 79% institutional, 1% external sources). *Receiving aid:* Freshmen: 71% (312); all full-time undergraduates: 65% (1,128). *Average award:* Freshmen: $21,528; Undergraduates: $19,748. *Scholarships, grants, and awards:* Federal Pell, FSEOG, state, private, college/university gift aid from institutional funds.

GIFT AID (NON-NEED-BASED) *Total amount:* $7,887,115 (3% state, 96% institutional, 1% external sources). *Receiving aid:* Freshmen: 70% (304). Undergraduates: 62% (1,068). *Average award:* Freshmen: $14,655. Undergraduates: $13,179. *Scholarships, grants, and awards by category: Academic interests/achievement:* 1,474 awards ($18,832,659 total): business, communication, general academic interests/achievements, mathematics. *Creative arts/ performance:* 140 awards ($139,000 total): art/fine arts, dance, music, performing arts, theater/drama. *Special characteristics:* 231 awards ($346,500 total): children and siblings of alumni, relatives of clergy.

LOANS *Student loans:* $10,819,626 (40% need-based, 60% non-need-based). 55% of past graduating class borrowed through all loan programs. *Average indebtedness per student:* $30,149. *Average need-based loan:* Freshmen: $4429. Undergraduates: $4912. *Parent loans:* $2,218,008 (100% non-need-based). *Programs:* Federal Direct (Subsidized and Unsubsidized Stafford, PLUS), FFEL (Subsidized and Unsubsidized Stafford, PLUS), Perkins.

WORK-STUDY *Federal work-study:* Total amount: $921,724; 664 jobs averaging $1388.

APPLYING FOR FINANCIAL AID *Required financial aid form:* FAFSA. *Financial aid deadline (priority):* 3/1. *Notification date:* Continuous beginning 3/15.

CONTACT Ms. Ann Whitmer, Director of Financial Aid, Albion College, Kellogg Center Box 4670, Albion, MI 49224-1831, 517-629-0440 or toll-free 800-858-6770. *Fax:* 517-629-0581. *E-mail:* awhitmer@albion.edu.

ALBRIGHT COLLEGE
Reading, PA

Tuition & fees: $32,740   **Average undergraduate aid package: $25,053**

ABOUT THE INSTITUTION Independent religious, coed. 44 undergraduate majors. Federal methodology is used as a basis for awarding need-based institutional aid.

UNDERGRADUATE EXPENSES for 2010–11 *Comprehensive fee:* $41,598 includes full-time tuition ($31,940), mandatory fees ($800), and room and board ($8858). *College room only:* $4919. Full-time tuition and fees vary according to course load. Room and board charges vary according to board plan and housing facility. Part-time tuition and fees vary according to course load. *Payment plan:* Installment.

FRESHMAN FINANCIAL AID (Fall 2008) 490 applied for aid; of those 93% were deemed to have need. 99% of freshmen with need received aid; of those 14% had need fully met. *Average percent of need met:* 81% (excluding resources awarded to replace EFC). *Average financial aid package:* $27,252 (excluding resources awarded to replace EFC). 9% of all full-time freshmen had no need and received non-need-based gift aid.

UNDERGRADUATE FINANCIAL AID (Fall 2008) 1,431 applied for aid; of those 92% were deemed to have need. 98% of undergraduates with need received aid; of those 17% had need fully met. *Average percent of need met:* 78% (excluding resources awarded to replace EFC). *Average financial aid package:* $25,053 (excluding resources awarded to replace EFC). 12% of all full-time undergraduates had no need and received non-need-based gift aid.

GIFT AID (NEED-BASED) *Total amount:* $25,016,081 (13% federal, 8% state, 74% institutional, 5% external sources). *Receiving aid:* Freshmen: 88% (451); all full-time undergraduates: 82% (1,289). *Average award:* Freshmen: $21,335; Undergraduates: $19,406. *Scholarships, grants, and awards:* Federal Pell, FSEOG, state, private, college/university gift aid from institutional funds, Academic Competitiveness Grants, National SMART Grants.

GIFT AID (NON-NEED-BASED) *Total amount:* $3,473,583 (85% institutional, 15% external sources). *Receiving aid:* Freshmen: 7% (35). Undergraduates: 8% (132). *Average award:* Freshmen: $11,748. Undergraduates: $12,235. *Scholarships, grants, and awards by category: Creative arts/performance:* art/fine arts, journalism/publications, music, theater/drama. *Special achievements/ activities:* general special achievements/activities, leadership, memberships, religious involvement. *Special characteristics:* children and siblings of alumni, ethnic background, siblings of current students. *Tuition waivers:* Full or partial for children of alumni, employees or children of employees, adult students, senior citizens.

LOANS *Student loans:* $12,605,678 (72% need-based, 28% non-need-based). 83% of past graduating class borrowed through all loan programs. *Average indebtedness per student:* $31,845. *Average need-based loan:* Freshmen: $4849. Undergraduates: $4935. *Parent loans:* $2,860,490 (32% need-based, 68% non-need-based). *Programs:* Federal Direct (Subsidized and Unsubsidized Stafford, PLUS), Perkins, private loans.

WORK-STUDY *Federal work-study:* Total amount: $1,700,600; 341 jobs averaging $1800. *State or other work-study/employment:* Total amount: $634,300 (4% need-based, 96% non-need-based). 106 part-time jobs averaging $1860.

APPLYING FOR FINANCIAL AID *Required financial aid form:* FAFSA. *Financial aid deadline:* Continuous. *Notification date:* Continuous beginning 2/15. Students must reply by 5/1 or within 2 weeks of notification.

CONTACT Mary Ellen Duffy, Director of Financial Aid, Albright College, PO Box 15234, Reading, PA 19612-5234, 610-921-7515 or toll-free 800-252-1856. *Fax:* 610-921-7729. *E-mail:* mduffy@alb.edu.

ALCORN STATE UNIVERSITY
Alcorn State, MS

ABOUT THE INSTITUTION State-supported, coed. 31 undergraduate majors.

GIFT AID (NEED-BASED) *Scholarships, grants, and awards:* Federal Pell, FSEOG, state, private, college/university gift aid from institutional funds.

GIFT AID (NON-NEED-BASED) *Scholarships, grants, and awards by category: Academic interests/achievement:* general academic interests/achievements. *Creative arts/performance:* music. *Special characteristics:* children of faculty/ staff, local/state students, members of minority groups.

LOANS *Programs:* Federal Direct (Subsidized and Unsubsidized Stafford, PLUS).

WORK-STUDY *Federal work-study:* Total amount: $177,770; 213 jobs averaging $964.

APPLYING FOR FINANCIAL AID *Required financial aid forms:* FAFSA, institution's own form.

CONTACT Juanita M. Russell, Director of Financial Aid, Alcorn State University, 1000 ASU Drive #28, Alcorn State, MS 39096-7500, 601-877-6190 or toll-free 800-222-6790. *Fax:* 601-877-6110. *E-mail:* juanita@lorman.alcorn.edu.

ALDERSON-BROADDUS COLLEGE
Philippi, WV

Tuition & fees: $21,654	Average undergraduate aid package: $20,942

ABOUT THE INSTITUTION Independent religious, coed. 41 undergraduate majors. Federal methodology is used as a basis for awarding need-based institutional aid.

UNDERGRADUATE EXPENSES for 2009–10 *Comprehensive fee:* $28,656 includes full-time tuition ($21,444), mandatory fees ($210), and room and board ($7002). *College room only:* $3408. Full-time tuition and fees vary according to program and student level. Room and board charges vary according to housing facility. *Part-time tuition:* $715 per credit hour. *Part-time fees:* $52.50 per term. Part-time tuition and fees vary according to program and student level. *Payment plan:* Installment.

FRESHMAN FINANCIAL AID (Fall 2009, est.) 161 applied for aid; of those 95% were deemed to have need. 99% of freshmen with need received aid; of those 33% had need fully met. *Average percent of need met:* 85% (excluding

resources awarded to replace EFC). *Average financial aid package:* $21,963 (excluding resources awarded to replace EFC). 6% of all full-time freshmen had no need and received non-need-based gift aid.

UNDERGRADUATE FINANCIAL AID (Fall 2009, est.) 556 applied for aid; of those 93% were deemed to have need. 100% of undergraduates with need received aid; of those 27% had need fully met. *Average percent of need met:* 81% (excluding resources awarded to replace EFC). *Average financial aid package:* $20,942 (excluding resources awarded to replace EFC). 7% of all full-time undergraduates had no need and received non-need-based gift aid.

GIFT AID (NEED-BASED) *Total amount:* $7,194,543 (23% federal, 15% state, 60% institutional, 2% external sources). *Receiving aid:* Freshmen: 94% (152); all full-time undergraduates: 91% (513). *Average award:* Freshmen: $17,914; Undergraduates: $16,092. *Scholarships, grants, and awards:* Federal Pell, FSEOG, state, private, college/university gift aid from institutional funds, Federal Nursing, National Health Service Corps Scholarships, Scholarships for Disadvantaged Students.

GIFT AID (NON-NEED-BASED) *Total amount:* $453,056 (5% state, 94% institutional, 1% external sources). *Receiving aid:* Freshmen: 20% (32). Undergraduates: 13% (72). *Average award:* Freshmen: $11,039. Undergraduates: $8196. *Scholarships, grants, and awards by category: Academic interests/ achievement:* 493 awards ($3,372,148 total): biological sciences, business, communication, computer science, education, general academic interests/ achievements, health fields, humanities, mathematics, physical sciences, premedicine, religion/biblical studies, social sciences. *Creative arts/performance:* 69 awards ($705,037 total): art/fine arts, creative writing, debating, journalism/ publications, music, performing arts, theater/drama. *Special achievements/ activities:* general special achievements/activities, leadership. *Special characteristics:* 15 awards ($227,970 total): children of faculty/staff, ethnic background, general special characteristics, international students, religious affiliation. *Tuition waivers:* Full or partial for employees or children of employees.

LOANS *Student loans:* $4,327,160 (92% need-based, 8% non-need-based). 98% of past graduating class borrowed through all loan programs. *Average indebtedness per student:* $29,613. *Average need-based loan:* Freshmen: $4450. Undergraduates: $4981. *Parent loans:* $451,732 (73% need-based, 27% non-need-based). *Programs:* FFEL (Subsidized and Unsubsidized Stafford, PLUS), Perkins, Federal Nursing.

WORK-STUDY *Federal work-study:* Total amount: $320,600; 193 jobs averaging $1409. *State or other work-study/employment:* Total amount: $263,931 (100% non-need-based). 134 part-time jobs averaging $1970.

ATHLETIC AWARDS Total amount: $1,235,177 (85% need-based, 15% non-need-based).

APPLYING FOR FINANCIAL AID *Required financial aid form:* FAFSA. *Financial aid deadline (priority):* 3/1. *Notification date:* Continuous beginning 3/1. Students must reply within 2 weeks of notification.

CONTACT Brian Weingart, Director of Financial Aid, Alderson-Broaddus College, College Hill Road, Philippi, WV 26416, 304-457-6354 or toll-free 800-263-1549. *Fax:* 304-457-6391.

ALFRED UNIVERSITY
Alfred, NY

Tuition & fees: $25,976	Average undergraduate aid package: $22,557

ABOUT THE INSTITUTION Independent, coed. 44 undergraduate majors. Both federal and institutional methodology are used as a basis for awarding need-based institutional aid.

UNDERGRADUATE EXPENSES for 2010–11 *Comprehensive fee:* $37,340 includes full-time tuition ($25,096), mandatory fees ($880), and room and board ($11,364). *College room only:* $5766. Full-time tuition and fees vary according to program. Room and board charges vary according to board plan and housing facility. *Part-time tuition:* $814 per credit hour. *Part-time fees:* $72 per term. Part-time tuition and fees vary according to course load. *Payment plans:* Tuition prepayment, installment, deferred payment.

FRESHMAN FINANCIAL AID (Fall 2009, est.) 426 applied for aid; of those 86% were deemed to have need. 100% of freshmen with need received aid; of those 16% had need fully met. *Average percent of need met:* 89% (excluding resources awarded to replace EFC). *Average financial aid package:* $24,067 (excluding resources awarded to replace EFC). 5% of all full-time freshmen had no need and received non-need-based gift aid.

UNDERGRADUATE FINANCIAL AID (Fall 2009, est.) 1,606 applied for aid; of those 88% were deemed to have need. 100% of undergraduates with need

Alfred University

received aid; of those 18% had need fully met. **Average percent of need met:** 85% (excluding resources awarded to replace EFC). **Average financial aid package:** $22,557 (excluding resources awarded to replace EFC). 7% of all full-time undergraduates had no need and received non-need-based gift aid.

GIFT AID (NEED-BASED) Total amount: $23,433,354 (15% federal, 9% state, 76% institutional). **Receiving aid:** Freshmen: 78% (362); all full-time undergraduates: 76% (1,394). **Average award:** Freshmen: $17,882; Undergraduates: $16,137. **Scholarships, grants, and awards:** Federal Pell, FSEOG, state, private, college/university gift aid from institutional funds.

GIFT AID (NON-NEED-BASED) Total amount: $2,541,317 (10% federal, 4% state, 70% institutional, 16% external sources). **Receiving aid:** Freshmen: 50% (231). Undergraduates: 43% (789). **Average award:** Freshmen: $8755. Undergraduates: $8976. **Scholarships, grants, and awards by category:** Academic interests/achievement: biological sciences, business, communication, education, engineering/technologies, English, foreign languages, general academic interests/achievements, humanities, international studies, mathematics, military science, physical sciences, premedicine, social sciences. Creative arts/performance: art/fine arts, general creative arts/performance, performing arts. Special achievements/activities: leadership. Special characteristics: children of educators, children of faculty/staff, international students. **Tuition waivers:** Full or partial for employees or children of employees.

LOANS Student loans: $13,962,797 (51% need-based, 49% non-need-based). 80% of past graduating class borrowed through all loan programs. Average indebtedness per student: $30,731. **Average need-based loan:** Freshmen: $4904. Undergraduates: $5563. **Parent loans:** $2,868,204 (100% non-need-based). **Programs:** Federal Direct (Subsidized and Unsubsidized Stafford, PLUS), Perkins, college/university, alternative loans.

WORK-STUDY Federal work-study: Total amount: $1,705,174; jobs available.

APPLYING FOR FINANCIAL AID Required financial aid forms: FAFSA, institution's own form, state aid form, noncustodial (divorced/separated) parent's statement, business/farm supplement. **Financial aid deadline:** 3/15. **Notification date:** Continuous beginning 2/15. Students must reply by 5/1 or within 2 weeks of notification.

CONTACT Mr. Earl Pierce, Director of Student Financial Aid, Alfred University, Alumni Hall, One Saxon Drive, Alfred, NY 14802-1205, 607-871-2159 or toll-free 800-541-9229. Fax: 607-871-2252. E-mail: pierce@alfred.edu.

ALICE LLOYD COLLEGE
Pippa Passes, KY

Tuition & fees: $1400   **Average undergraduate aid package: $10,124**

ABOUT THE INSTITUTION Independent, coed. **Awards:** bachelor's degrees. 17 undergraduate majors. **Total enrollment:** 609. Undergraduates: 609. Freshmen: 187. Federal methodology is used as a basis for awarding need-based institutional aid.

UNDERGRADUATE EXPENSES for 2009–10 One-time required fee: $50. includes mandatory fees ($1400) and room and board ($4450). **College room only:** $2070. Full-time tuition and fees vary according to course load and location. Room and board charges vary according to location. **Part-time tuition:** $212 per credit hour. full-time students in the 108-county service area are granted guaranteed tuition. **Payment plan:** Deferred payment.

FRESHMAN FINANCIAL AID (Fall 2009, est.) 168 applied for aid; of those 85% were deemed to have need. 99% of freshmen with need received aid; of those 17% had need fully met. **Average percent of need met:** 71% (excluding resources awarded to replace EFC). **Average financial aid package:** $9736 (excluding resources awarded to replace EFC). 14% of all full-time freshmen had no need and received non-need-based gift aid.

UNDERGRADUATE FINANCIAL AID (Fall 2009, est.) 599 applied for aid; of those 83% were deemed to have need. 100% of undergraduates with need received aid; of those 23% had need fully met. **Average percent of need met:** 76% (excluding resources awarded to replace EFC). **Average financial aid package:** $10,124 (excluding resources awarded to replace EFC). 17% of all full-time undergraduates had no need and received non-need-based gift aid.

GIFT AID (NEED-BASED) Total amount: $3,009,736 (53% federal, 37% state, 10% institutional). **Receiving aid:** Freshmen: 83% (141); all full-time undergraduates: 81% (488). **Average award:** Freshmen: $7470; Undergraduates: $7635. **Scholarships, grants, and awards:** Federal Pell, FSEOG, state, private, college/university gift aid from institutional funds.

GIFT AID (NON-NEED-BASED) Total amount: $1,698,091 (32% state, 66% institutional, 2% external sources). **Receiving aid:** Freshmen: 11% (18).

Undergraduates: 11% (68). **Average award:** Freshmen: $4095. Undergraduates: $4482. **Scholarships, grants, and awards by category:** Special achievements/activities: 43 awards ($280,860 total): general special achievements/activities. Special characteristics: 8 awards ($36,029 total): members of minority groups. **Tuition waivers:** Full or partial for employees or children of employees.

LOANS Student loans: $837,523 (44% need-based, 56% non-need-based). 42% of past graduating class borrowed through all loan programs. Average indebtedness per student: $6500. **Average need-based loan:** Freshmen: $702. Undergraduates: $886. **Parent loans:** $35,419 (100% non-need-based). **Programs:** Federal Direct (Subsidized and Unsubsidized Stafford, PLUS), college/university, Bagby Loans (for freshmen).

WORK-STUDY Federal work-study: Total amount: $814,350; 359 jobs averaging $2320. **State or other work-study/employment:** Total amount: $557,581 (100% non-need-based). 250 part-time jobs averaging $2320.

ATHLETIC AWARDS Total amount: $196,850 (100% non-need-based).

APPLYING FOR FINANCIAL AID Required financial aid form: FAFSA. **Financial aid deadline (priority):** 3/15. **Notification date:** Continuous beginning 4/15.

CONTACT Ms. Jacqueline Stewart, Director of Financial Aid, Alice Lloyd College, 100 Purpose Road, Pippa Passes, KY 41844, 606-368-6058. E-mail: jacquelinestewart@alc.edu.

ALLEGHENY COLLEGE
Meadville, PA

Tuition & fees: $34,810   **Average undergraduate aid package: $27,087**

ABOUT THE INSTITUTION Independent, coed. 46 undergraduate majors. Federal methodology is used as a basis for awarding need-based institutional aid.

UNDERGRADUATE EXPENSES for 2010–11 Comprehensive fee: $43,600 includes full-time tuition ($34,490), mandatory fees ($320), and room and board ($8790). **College room only:** $4620. Room and board charges vary according to board plan and housing facility. **Part-time tuition:** $1437 per credit hour. **Part-time fees:** $160 per term. Part-time tuition and fees vary according to course load. **Payment plans:** Tuition prepayment, installment.

FRESHMAN FINANCIAL AID (Fall 2009, est.) 498 applied for aid; of those 81% were deemed to have need. 100% of freshmen with need received aid; of those 40% had need fully met. **Average percent of need met:** 92% (excluding resources awarded to replace EFC). **Average financial aid package:** $27,731 (excluding resources awarded to replace EFC). 30% of all full-time freshmen had no need and received non-need-based gift aid.

UNDERGRADUATE FINANCIAL AID (Fall 2009, est.) 1,655 applied for aid; of those 87% were deemed to have need. 100% of undergraduates with need received aid; of those 33% had need fully met. **Average percent of need met:** 89% (excluding resources awarded to replace EFC). **Average financial aid package:** $27,087 (excluding resources awarded to replace EFC). 28% of all full-time undergraduates had no need and received non-need-based gift aid.

GIFT AID (NEED-BASED) Total amount: $28,439,304 (9% federal, 6% state, 81% institutional, 4% external sources). **Receiving aid:** Freshmen: 69% (402); all full-time undergraduates: 69% (1,443). **Average award:** Freshmen: $21,029; Undergraduates: $20,179. **Scholarships, grants, and awards:** Federal Pell, FSEOG, state, private, college/university gift aid from institutional funds, Academic Competitiveness Grants, National SMART Grants, Veterans Educational Benefits.

GIFT AID (NON-NEED-BASED) Total amount: $8,139,643 (93% institutional, 7% external sources). **Receiving aid:** Freshmen: 12% (71). Undergraduates: 9% (186). **Average award:** Freshmen: $13,523. Undergraduates: $11,621. **Scholarships, grants, and awards by category:** Academic interests/achievement: 1,743 awards ($20,641,500 total): general academic interests/achievements. Special characteristics: 76 awards ($1,790,335 total): adult students, children of educators, children of faculty/staff, international students. **Tuition waivers:** Full or partial for employees or children of employees.

LOANS Student loans: $12,916,102 (46% need-based, 54% non-need-based). **Average need-based loan:** Freshmen: $4761. Undergraduates: $5023. **Parent loans:** $3,240,258 (100% non-need-based). **Programs:** Federal Direct (Subsidized and Unsubsidized Stafford, PLUS), Perkins, private loans.

WORK-STUDY Federal work-study: Total amount: $2,450,566; 1,189 jobs averaging $2100. **State or other work-study/employment:** Total amount: $381,130 (100% non-need-based). 84 part-time jobs averaging $4550.

APPLYING FOR FINANCIAL AID Required financial aid form: FAFSA. **Financial aid deadline (priority):** 2/15. **Notification date:** Continuous beginning 3/1. Students must reply by 5/1 or within 4 weeks of notification.

CONTACT Ms. Sheryle Proper, Director of Financial Aid, Allegheny College, 520 North Main Street, Meadville, PA 16335, 800-835-7780 or toll-free 800-521-5293. *Fax:* 814-332-2837. *E-mail:* fao@allegheny.edu.

ALLEGHENY WESLEYAN COLLEGE
Salem, OH

Tuition & fees: N/R	Average undergraduate aid package: N/A

ABOUT THE INSTITUTION Independent religious, coed. *Awards:* bachelor's degrees. 2 undergraduate majors. *Total enrollment:* 54. Undergraduates: 54.
CONTACT Esther Phelps, Financial Aid Director, Allegheny Wesleyan College, 2161 Woodsdale Road, Salem, OH 44460, 330-337-6403 Ext. 15 or toll-free 800-292-3153. *Fax:* 330-337-6255.

ALLEN COLLEGE
Waterloo, IA

ABOUT THE INSTITUTION Independent, coed, primarily women. 4 undergraduate majors.
GIFT AID (NEED-BASED) *Scholarships, grants, and awards:* Federal Pell, FSEOG, state, private, college/university gift aid from institutional funds, Federal Nursing, Federal Scholarships for Disadvantaged Students.
GIFT AID (NON-NEED-BASED) *Scholarships, grants, and awards by category:* *Academic interests/achievement:* health fields. *Special achievements/activities:* community service, general special achievements/activities, leadership. *Special characteristics:* children of faculty/staff, general special characteristics, local/state students, members of minority groups, out-of-state students.
LOANS *Programs:* Federal Direct (Subsidized and Unsubsidized Stafford, PLUS), Perkins, Federal Nursing, state, college/university.
WORK-STUDY *Federal work-study:* Total amount: $25,188; 18 jobs averaging $2500. *State or other work-study/employment:* Part-time jobs available.
APPLYING FOR FINANCIAL AID *Required financial aid forms:* FAFSA, institution's own form.
CONTACT Kathie S. Walters, Financial Aid Director, Allen College, Barrett Forum, Waterloo, IA 50703, 319-226-2003. *Fax:* 319-226-2051. *E-mail:* walterks@ihs.org.

ALLEN UNIVERSITY
Columbia, SC

CONTACT Ms. Donna Foster, Director of Financial Aid, Allen University, 1530 Harden Street, Columbia, SC 29204-1085, 803-376-5736 or toll-free 877-625-5368 (in-state). *E-mail:* donnaf@allenuniversity.edu.

ALLIANT INTERNATIONAL UNIVERSITY
San Diego, CA

Tuition & fees: $15,220	Average undergraduate aid package: $13,550

ABOUT THE INSTITUTION Independent, coed. 9 undergraduate majors. Federal methodology is used as a basis for awarding need-based institutional aid.
UNDERGRADUATE EXPENSES for 2009–10 *Tuition:* full-time $15,000; part-time $550 per unit.
UNDERGRADUATE FINANCIAL AID (Fall 2009, est.) 75 applied for aid; of those 100% were deemed to have need. 100% of undergraduates with need received aid. *Average percent of need met:* 62% (excluding resources awarded to replace EFC). *Average financial aid package:* $13,550 (excluding resources awarded to replace EFC). 26% of all full-time undergraduates had no need and received non-need-based gift aid.
GIFT AID (NEED-BASED) *Total amount:* $582,440 (82% federal, 18% state). *Receiving aid:* All full-time undergraduates: 54% (70). *Average award:* Undergraduates: $6350. *Scholarships, grants, and awards:* Federal Pell, FSEOG, state, private, college/university gift aid from institutional funds.
GIFT AID (NON-NEED-BASED) *Total amount:* $166,176 (96% institutional, 4% external sources). *Receiving aid:* Undergraduates: 37% (48). *Average award:* Undergraduates: $1700. *Scholarships, grants, and awards by category:* *Academic interests/achievement:* business, communication, computer science, education, English, foreign languages, general academic interests/achievements,

humanities, international studies, social sciences. *Special achievements/activities:* community service, general special achievements/activities, leadership. *Special characteristics:* children and siblings of alumni, children of current students, children of faculty/staff, ethnic background, international students, local/state students, members of minority groups, veterans.
LOANS *Student loans:* $1,134,573 (47% need-based, 53% non-need-based). *Average need-based loan:* Undergraduates: $5500. *Parent loans:* $24,845 (100% non-need-based). *Programs:* Federal Direct (Subsidized and Unsubsidized Stafford, PLUS), FFEL (Subsidized and Unsubsidized Stafford, PLUS), Perkins, alternative loans.
WORK-STUDY *Federal work-study:* Total amount: $50,965; 25 jobs averaging $2000. *State or other work-study/employment:* Total amount: $29,958 (100% non-need-based). 15 part-time jobs averaging $2000.
APPLYING FOR FINANCIAL AID *Required financial aid form:* FAFSA. *Financial aid deadline (priority):* 3/2. *Notification date:* Continuous beginning 3/15. Students must reply within 3 weeks of notification.
CONTACT Deborah Spindler, Director of Financial Aid, Alliant International University, 10455 Pomerado Road, San Diego, CA 92131-1799, 858-635-4559 Ext. 4700 or toll-free 866-825-5426. *Fax:* 858-635-4848.

ALLIED AMERICAN UNIVERSITY
Laguna Hills, CA

CONTACT Financial Aid Office, Allied American University, 22952 Alcade Drive, Laguna Hills, CA 92653, 888-384-0849.

ALMA COLLEGE
Alma, MI

Tuition & fees: $26,068	Average undergraduate aid package: $23,085

ABOUT THE INSTITUTION Independent Presbyterian, coed. 69 undergraduate majors. Federal methodology is used as a basis for awarding need-based institutional aid.
UNDERGRADUATE EXPENSES for 2009–10 *Comprehensive fee:* $34,586 includes full-time tuition ($25,838), mandatory fees ($230), and room and board ($8518). *College room only:* $4196. Room and board charges vary according to board plan and housing facility. *Part-time tuition:* $1000 per credit hour. Part-time tuition and fees vary according to course load. *Payment plans:* Installment, deferred payment.
FRESHMAN FINANCIAL AID (Fall 2009, est.) 386 applied for aid; of those 88% were deemed to have need. 100% of freshmen with need received aid; of those 24% had need fully met. *Average percent of need met:* 87% (excluding resources awarded to replace EFC). *Average financial aid package:* $24,671 (excluding resources awarded to replace EFC). 15% of all full-time freshmen had no need and received non-need-based gift aid.
UNDERGRADUATE FINANCIAL AID (Fall 2009, est.) 1,259 applied for aid; of those 89% were deemed to have need. 100% of undergraduates with need received aid; of those 19% had need fully met. *Average percent of need met:* 84% (excluding resources awarded to replace EFC). *Average financial aid package:* $23,085 (excluding resources awarded to replace EFC). 19% of all full-time undergraduates had no need and received non-need-based gift aid.
GIFT AID (NEED-BASED) *Total amount:* $20,196,358 (10% federal, 13% state, 76% institutional, 1% external sources). *Receiving aid:* Freshmen: 84% (333); all full-time undergraduates: 81% (1,113). *Average award:* Freshmen: $19,894; Undergraduates: $18,926. *Scholarships, grants, and awards:* Federal Pell, FSEOG, state, private, college/university gift aid from institutional funds.
GIFT AID (NON-NEED-BASED) *Total amount:* $4,485,625 (9% state, 89% institutional, 2% external sources). *Receiving aid:* Freshmen: 17% (67). Undergraduates: 13% (181). *Average award:* Freshmen: $14,565. Undergraduates: $11,882. *Scholarships, grants, and awards by category:* *Academic interests/achievement:* 1,327 awards ($13,560,858 total): general academic interests/achievements. *Creative arts/performance:* 241 awards ($297,538 total): art/fine arts, dance, music, performing arts, theater/drama. *Special achievements/activities:* 12 awards ($11,500 total): religious involvement. *Special characteristics:* 204 awards ($193,950 total): children and siblings of alumni, children of current students. *Tuition waivers:* Full or partial for employees or children of employees.
LOANS *Student loans:* $9,059,754 (71% need-based, 29% non-need-based). 74% of past graduating class borrowed through all loan programs. *Average*

indebtedness per student: $31,476. **Average need-based loan:** Freshmen: $4156. Undergraduates: $4829. **Parent loans:** $2,957,868 (26% need-based, 74% non-need-based). **Programs:** Federal Direct (Subsidized and Unsubsidized Stafford, PLUS), Perkins, state, college/university, alternative loans.
WORK-STUDY **Federal work-study:** Total amount: $188,628; 140 jobs averaging $950. **State or other work-study/employment:** Total amount: $17,000 (100% need-based). 30 part-time jobs averaging $700.
APPLYING FOR FINANCIAL AID **Required financial aid form:** FAFSA. **Financial aid deadline (priority):** 3/1. **Notification date:** Continuous beginning 3/1. Students must reply within 3 weeks of notification.
CONTACT Mr. Christopher A. Brown, Director of Student Financial Assistance, Alma College, 614 West Superior Street, Alma, MI 48801-1599, 989-463-7347 or toll-free 800-321-ALMA. Fax: 989-463-7993. E-mail: cabrown@alma.edu.

ALVERNIA UNIVERSITY
Reading, PA

CONTACT Rachel Gordon, Director of Student Financial Planning, Alvernia University, 400 St. Bernardine Street, Reading, PA 19607-1799, 610-796-8275 or toll-free 888-ALVERNIA (in-state). Fax: 610-796-8336. E-mail: rachel.gordon@alvernia.edu.

ALVERNO COLLEGE
Milwaukee, WI

Tuition & fees: N/R	Average undergraduate aid package: $14,191

ABOUT THE INSTITUTION Independent Roman Catholic, undergraduate: women only; graduate: coed. 43 undergraduate majors. Federal methodology is used as a basis for awarding need-based institutional aid.
FRESHMAN FINANCIAL AID (Fall 2009, est.) 224 applied for aid; of those 90% were deemed to have need. 100% of freshmen with need received aid. **Average financial aid package:** $15,716 (excluding resources awarded to replace EFC). 9% of all full-time freshmen had no need and received non-need-based gift aid.
UNDERGRADUATE FINANCIAL AID (Fall 2009, est.) 1,562 applied for aid; of those 90% were deemed to have need. 100% of undergraduates with need received aid. **Average financial aid package:** $14,191 (excluding resources awarded to replace EFC). 12% of all full-time undergraduates had no need and received non-need-based gift aid.
GIFT AID (NEED-BASED) **Total amount:** $16,835,933 (35% federal, 17% state, 48% institutional). **Receiving aid:** Freshmen: 78% (180); all full-time undergraduates: 71% (1,218). **Average award:** Freshmen: $13,044; Undergraduates: $10,651. **Scholarships, grants, and awards:** Federal Pell, FSEOG, state, private, college/university gift aid from institutional funds, Federal Nursing.
GIFT AID (NON-NEED-BASED) **Total amount:** $1,485,711 (83% institutional, 17% external sources). **Receiving aid:** Freshmen: 81% (187). Undergraduates: 66% (1,123). **Average award:** Freshmen: $7664. Undergraduates: $5195. **Scholarships, grants, and awards by category:** Academic interests/achievement: 1,401 awards ($6,623,406 total): general academic interests/achievements. Creative arts/performance: 16 awards ($29,200 total): art/fine arts, music. Special achievements/activities: 4 awards ($76,710 total): community service. Special characteristics: 21 awards ($255,884 total): children of faculty/staff, international students. **Tuition waivers:** Full or partial for employees or children of employees.
LOANS **Student loans:** $17,817,870 (43% need-based, 57% non-need-based). 83% of past graduating class borrowed through all loan programs. Average indebtedness per student: $32,142. **Average need-based loan:** Freshmen: $2903. Undergraduates: $4088. **Parent loans:** $744,204 (100% non-need-based). **Programs:** FFEL (Subsidized and Unsubsidized Stafford, PLUS), Perkins, state.
WORK-STUDY **Federal work-study:** Total amount: $225,405; 222 jobs averaging $2184. **State or other work-study/employment:** Total amount: $508,495 (100% non-need-based). Part-time jobs available.
APPLYING FOR FINANCIAL AID **Required financial aid forms:** FAFSA, institution's own form. **Financial aid deadline (priority):** 3/15. **Notification date:** Continuous beginning 3/15. Students must reply within 2 weeks of notification.
CONTACT Dan Goyette, Director of Financial Aid, Alverno College, 3400 South 43rd Street, PO Box 343922, Milwaukee, WI 53234-3922, 414-382-6046 or toll-free 800-933-3401. Fax: 414-382-6354. E-mail: dan.goyette@alverno.edu.

AMERICAN ACADEMY OF ART
Chicago, IL

CONTACT Ms. Ione Fitzgerald, Director of Financial Aid, American Academy of Art, 332 South Michigan Avenue, Suite 300, Chicago, IL 60604, 312-461-0600. Fax: 312-294-9570.

AMERICAN BAPTIST COLLEGE OF AMERICAN BAPTIST THEOLOGICAL SEMINARY
Nashville, TN

Tuition & fees: $4800	Average undergraduate aid package: $2675

ABOUT THE INSTITUTION Independent Baptist, coed. 1 undergraduate major. Federal methodology is used as a basis for awarding need-based institutional aid.
UNDERGRADUATE EXPENSES for 2010–11 **Comprehensive fee:** $7400 includes full-time tuition ($4560), mandatory fees ($240), and room and board ($2600). **College room only:** $1800. Room and board charges vary according to board plan and housing facility. **Part-time tuition:** $190 per credit hour. **Part-time fees:** $240 per term. **Payment plan:** Deferred payment.
FRESHMAN FINANCIAL AID (Fall 2009, est.) 6 applied for aid; of those 100% were deemed to have need. 100% of freshmen with need received aid. **Average percent of need met:** 75% (excluding resources awarded to replace EFC). **Average financial aid package:** $2675 (excluding resources awarded to replace EFC).
UNDERGRADUATE FINANCIAL AID (Fall 2009, est.) 60 applied for aid; of those 100% were deemed to have need. 100% of undergraduates with need received aid. **Average percent of need met:** 75% (excluding resources awarded to replace EFC). **Average financial aid package:** $2675 (excluding resources awarded to replace EFC).
GIFT AID (NEED-BASED) **Total amount:** $376,064 (82% federal, 9% state, 9% external sources). **Average award:** Freshmen: $1161; Undergraduates: $1161. **Scholarships, grants, and awards:** Federal Pell, FSEOG, state.
GIFT AID (NON-NEED-BASED) **Scholarships, grants, and awards by category:** Academic interests/achievement: 1 award ($7660 total): religion/biblical studies. Special characteristics: religious affiliation.
WORK-STUDY **Federal work-study:** Total amount: $6741; 1 job averaging $6741.
APPLYING FOR FINANCIAL AID **Required financial aid form:** FAFSA. **Financial aid deadline:** 7/23 (priority: 1/2). **Notification date:** Continuous beginning 7/30. Students must reply by 8/1 or within 2 weeks of notification.
CONTACT Marcella Lockhart, Director of Enrollment Management, American Baptist College of American Baptist Theological Seminary, 1800 Baptist World Center Drive, Nashville, TN 37207, 615-687-6896 Ext. 6896. Fax: 615-226-7855. E-mail: mlockhart@abcnash.edu.

AMERICAN INDIAN COLLEGE OF THE ASSEMBLIES OF GOD, INC.
Phoenix, AZ

ABOUT THE INSTITUTION Independent religious, coed. **Awards:** associate and bachelor's degrees. 3 undergraduate majors. **Total enrollment:** 68. Undergraduates: 68.
GIFT AID (NEED-BASED) **Scholarships, grants, and awards:** Federal Pell, FSEOG, state, private, college/university gift aid from institutional funds.
GIFT AID (NON-NEED-BASED) **Scholarships, grants, and awards by category:** Academic interests/achievement: general academic interests/achievements.
LOANS **Programs:** FFEL (Subsidized and Unsubsidized Stafford, PLUS).
APPLYING FOR FINANCIAL AID **Required financial aid form:** FAFSA.
CONTACT Nadine Waldrop, Office of Student Financial Aid, American Indian College of the Assemblies of God, Inc., 10020 North Fifteenth Avenue, Phoenix, AZ 85021-2199, 602-944-3335 or toll-free 800-933-3828. Fax: 602-944-1952. E-mail: financialaid@aicag.edu.

AMERICAN INTERCONTINENTAL UNIVERSITY
Houston, TX

CONTACT Financial Aid Office, American InterContinental University, 9999 Richmond Avenue, Houston, TX 77042, 832-242-5788 or toll-free 888-607-9888.

AMERICAN INTERCONTINENTAL UNIVERSITY BUCKHEAD CAMPUS
Atlanta, GA

CONTACT Sherry Rizzi, Financial Aid Director, American InterContinental University Buckhead Campus, 3330 Peachtree Road NE, Atlanta, GA 30326, 404-965-5796 or toll-free 888-591-7888. *Fax:* 404-965-5704.

AMERICAN INTERCONTINENTAL UNIVERSITY DUNWOODY CAMPUS
Atlanta, GA

CONTACT Financial Aid Office, American InterContinental University Dunwoody Campus, 6600 Peachtree-Dunwoody Road, 500 Embassy Row, Atlanta, GA 30328, 404-965-6500 or toll-free 800-353-1744.

AMERICAN INTERCONTINENTAL UNIVERSITY ONLINE
Hoffman Estates, IL

CONTACT Financial Aid Office, American InterContinental University Online, 5550 Prairie Stone Parkway, Suite 400, Hoffman Estates, IL 60192, 847-851-5000 or toll-free 877-701-3800.

AMERICAN INTERCONTINENTAL UNIVERSITY SOUTH FLORIDA
Weston, FL

CONTACT Financial Aid Office, American InterContinental University South Florida, 2250 North Commerce Parkway, Suite 100, Weston, FL 33326, 954-446-6100 or toll-free 888-603-4888.

AMERICAN INTERNATIONAL COLLEGE
Springfield, MA

Tuition & fees: N/R	Average undergraduate aid package: $21,229

ABOUT THE INSTITUTION Independent, coed. 42 undergraduate majors. Federal methodology is used as a basis for awarding need-based institutional aid.

FRESHMAN FINANCIAL AID (Fall 2009, est.) 334 applied for aid; of those 96% were deemed to have need. 99% of freshmen with need received aid; of those 11% had need fully met. *Average percent of need met:* 71% (excluding resources awarded to replace EFC). *Average financial aid package:* $22,751 (excluding resources awarded to replace EFC). 12% of all full-time freshmen had no need and received non-need-based gift aid.

UNDERGRADUATE FINANCIAL AID (Fall 2009, est.) 1,403 applied for aid; of those 96% were deemed to have need. 99% of undergraduates with need received aid; of those 12% had need fully met. *Average percent of need met:* 68% (excluding resources awarded to replace EFC). *Average financial aid package:* $21,229 (excluding resources awarded to replace EFC). 10% of all full-time undergraduates had no need and received non-need-based gift aid.

GIFT AID (NEED-BASED) *Total amount:* $21,030,398 (17% federal, 4% state, 77% institutional, 2% external sources). *Receiving aid:* Freshmen: 85% (318); all full-time undergraduates: 88% (1,327). *Average award:* Freshmen: $19,266; Undergraduates: $17,033. *Scholarships, grants, and awards:* Federal Pell, FSEOG, state, private, college/university gift aid from institutional funds, Federal Nursing.

GIFT AID (NON-NEED-BASED) *Total amount:* $2,122,249 (95% institutional, 5% external sources). *Receiving aid:* Freshmen: 8% (29). Undergraduates: 8%

(119). *Average award:* Freshmen: $10,859. Undergraduates: $10,928. *Scholarships, grants, and awards by category:* Academic interests/achievement: general academic interests/achievements. Special achievements/activities: general special achievements/activities. Special characteristics: children and siblings of alumni, children of faculty/staff, children of public servants, first-generation college students, previous college experience. *Tuition waivers:* Full or partial for employees or children of employees, senior citizens.

LOANS *Student loans:* $13,410,775 (83% need-based, 17% non-need-based). 100% of past graduating class borrowed through all loan programs. *Average indebtedness per student:* $25,693. *Average need-based loan:* Freshmen: $3159. Undergraduates: $4178. *Parent loans:* $2,389,736 (50% need-based, 50% non-need-based). *Programs:* FFEL (Subsidized and Unsubsidized Stafford, PLUS), Perkins, college/university, alternative loans.

WORK-STUDY *Federal work-study:* Total amount: $532,723; jobs available.

ATHLETIC AWARDS Total amount: $3,573,593 (51% need-based, 49% non-need-based).

APPLYING FOR FINANCIAL AID *Required financial aid forms:* FAFSA, state aid form. *Financial aid deadline (priority):* 5/1. *Notification date:* Continuous beginning 3/15. Students must reply within 2 weeks of notification.

CONTACT Mr. Douglas E. Fish, Associate Vice President for Financial Services, American International College, 1000 State Street, Springfield, MA 01109-3189, 413-205-3259. *Fax:* 413-205-3912. *E-mail:* douglas.fish@aic.edu.

AMERICAN JEWISH UNIVERSITY
Bel Air, CA

Tuition & fees: $22,352	Average undergraduate aid package: $24,500

ABOUT THE INSTITUTION Independent Jewish, coed. 11 undergraduate majors. Both federal and institutional methodology are used as a basis for awarding need-based institutional aid.

UNDERGRADUATE EXPENSES for 2009–10 *One-time required fee:* $200. *Comprehensive fee:* $33,568 includes full-time tuition ($21,408), mandatory fees ($944), and room and board ($11,216). *College room only:* $5982. Full-time tuition and fees vary according to course load and degree level. Room and board charges vary according to board plan and housing facility. *Part-time tuition:* $892 per unit. Part-time tuition and fees vary according to course load and degree level. *Payment plan:* Installment.

FRESHMAN FINANCIAL AID (Fall 2009, est.) 23 applied for aid; of those 100% were deemed to have need. 100% of freshmen with need received aid; of those 96% had need fully met. *Average percent of need met:* 100% (excluding resources awarded to replace EFC). *Average financial aid package:* $24,000 (excluding resources awarded to replace EFC). 61% of all full-time freshmen had no need and received non-need-based gift aid.

UNDERGRADUATE FINANCIAL AID (Fall 2009, est.) 125 applied for aid; of those 100% were deemed to have need. 100% of undergraduates with need received aid; of those 96% had need fully met. *Average percent of need met:* 96% (excluding resources awarded to replace EFC). *Average financial aid package:* $24,500 (excluding resources awarded to replace EFC). 42% of all full-time undergraduates had no need and received non-need-based gift aid.

GIFT AID (NEED-BASED) *Total amount:* $757,507 (26% federal, 11% state, 63% institutional). *Receiving aid:* Freshmen: 43% (10); all full-time undergraduates: 38% (50). *Average award:* Freshmen: $12,995; Undergraduates: $9809. *Scholarships, grants, and awards:* Federal Pell, FSEOG, state, private, college/university gift aid from institutional funds.

GIFT AID (NON-NEED-BASED) *Total amount:* $766,431 (100% institutional). *Receiving aid:* Freshmen: 52% (12). Undergraduates: 59% (78). *Average award:* Freshmen: $2000. Undergraduates: $2000. *Scholarships, grants, and awards by category:* Academic interests/achievement: 24 awards ($298,880 total): general academic interests/achievements, premedicine. Special achievements/activities: 29 awards ($170,000 total): leadership. *Tuition waivers:* Full or partial for employees or children of employees.

LOANS *Student loans:* $524,880 (38% need-based, 62% non-need-based). 75% of past graduating class borrowed through all loan programs. *Average indebtedness per student:* $28,000. *Average need-based loan:* Freshmen: $3500. Undergraduates: $4500. *Parent loans:* $58,933 (100% non-need-based). *Programs:* FFEL (Subsidized and Unsubsidized Stafford, PLUS), alternative loans.

WORK-STUDY *Federal work-study:* Total amount: $50,211; 46 jobs averaging $1092.

APPLYING FOR FINANCIAL AID *Required financial aid forms:* FAFSA, institution's own form, parent and student income tax returns. *Financial aid deadline (priority):* 3/2. *Notification date:* Continuous beginning 3/15. Students must reply within 3 weeks of notification.

CONTACT Larisa Zadoyen, Director of Financial Aid, American Jewish University, 15600 Mulholland Drive, Bel Air, CA 90077-1599, 310-476-9777 Ext. 252 or toll-free 888-853-6763. *Fax:* 310-476-4613. *E-mail:* lzadoyen@ajula.edu.

AMERICAN MUSICAL AND DRAMATIC ACADEMY, LOS ANGELES
Los Angeles, CA

CONTACT Financial Aid Office, American Musical and Dramatic Academy, Los Angeles, 6305 Yucca Street, Los Angeles, CA 90028, 323-469-3300 or toll-free 866-374-5300.

AMERICAN SENTINEL UNIVERSITY
Englewood, CO

CONTACT Financial Aid Office, American Sentinel University, 385 Inverness Parkway, Englewood, CO 80112, toll-free 800-729-2427 (out-of-state).

AMERICAN UNIVERSITY
Washington, DC

Tuition & fees: $36,697	Average undergraduate aid package: $31,258

ABOUT THE INSTITUTION Independent Methodist, coed. 68 undergraduate majors. Both federal and institutional methodology are used as a basis for awarding need-based institutional aid.

UNDERGRADUATE EXPENSES for 2010–11 *Comprehensive fee:* $50,165 includes full-time tuition ($36,180), mandatory fees ($517), and room and board ($13,468). Full-time tuition and fees vary according to degree level. Room and board charges vary according to board plan, housing facility, and location. *Part-time tuition:* $1205 per credit hour. Part-time tuition and fees vary according to course load. *Payment plan:* Installment.

FRESHMAN FINANCIAL AID (Fall 2009, est.) 1,144 applied for aid; of those 74% were deemed to have need. 100% of freshmen with need received aid; of those 30% had need fully met. *Average percent of need met:* 93% (excluding resources awarded to replace EFC). *Average financial aid package:* $33,429 (excluding resources awarded to replace EFC). 18% of all full-time freshmen had no need and received non-need-based gift aid.

UNDERGRADUATE FINANCIAL AID (Fall 2009, est.) 3,910 applied for aid; of those 82% were deemed to have need. 99% of undergraduates with need received aid; of those 78% had need fully met. *Average percent of need met:* 87% (excluding resources awarded to replace EFC). *Average financial aid package:* $31,258 (excluding resources awarded to replace EFC). 17% of all full-time undergraduates had no need and received non-need-based gift aid.

GIFT AID (NEED-BASED) *Total amount:* $27,522,194 (13% federal, 1% state, 77% institutional, 9% external sources). *Receiving aid:* Freshmen: 31% (473); all full-time undergraduates: 24% (1,530). *Average award:* Freshmen: $17,325; Undergraduates: $13,290. *Scholarships, grants, and awards:* Federal Pell, FSEOG, state, private, college/university gift aid from institutional funds.

GIFT AID (NON-NEED-BASED) *Receiving aid:* Freshmen: 25% (379). Undergraduates: 22% (1,372). *Average award:* Freshmen: $20,235. Undergraduates: $18,412. *Scholarships, grants, and awards by category:* Academic interests/achievement: general academic interests/achievements. *Creative arts/performance:* general creative arts/performance. *Special achievements/activities:* general special achievements/activities, leadership, memberships. *Special characteristics:* adult students, children and siblings of alumni, children of faculty/staff, ethnic background, first-generation college students, local/state students, members of minority groups, previous college experience, relatives of clergy, spouses of current students.

LOANS *Student loans:* $39,467,081 (34% need-based, 66% non-need-based). 54% of past graduating class borrowed through all loan programs. *Average indebtedness per student:* $40,966. *Average need-based loan:* Freshmen: $4180. Undergraduates: $4838. *Parent loans:* $16,520,560 (100% non-need-based). *Programs:* Federal Direct (Subsidized and Unsubsidized Stafford, PLUS), Perkins, college/university.

WORK-STUDY *Federal work-study:* Total amount: $4,506,970; jobs available.

ATHLETIC AWARDS Total amount: $3,544,011 (100% non-need-based).

APPLYING FOR FINANCIAL AID *Required financial aid forms:* FAFSA, institution's own form. *Financial aid deadline:* 2/15. *Notification date:* 4/1. Students must reply by 5/1 or within 4 weeks of notification.

CONTACT Brian Lee Sang, Director of Financial Aid, American University, 4400 Massachusetts Avenue, NW, Washington, DC 20016-8001, 202-885-6100. *Fax:* 202-885-1129. *E-mail:* financialaid@american.edu.

AMERICAN UNIVERSITY OF PUERTO RICO
Bayamón, PR

CONTACT Mr. Yahaira Melendez, Financial Aid Director, American University of Puerto Rico, PO Box 2037, Bayamón, PR 00960-2037, 787-620-2040 Ext. 2031. *Fax:* 787-785-7377. *E-mail:* melendezy@aupr.edu.

AMHERST COLLEGE
Amherst, MA

Tuition & fees: $38,928	Average undergraduate aid package: $41,124

ABOUT THE INSTITUTION Independent, coed. 37 undergraduate majors. Institutional methodology is used as a basis for awarding need-based institutional aid.

UNDERGRADUATE EXPENSES for 2010–11 *Comprehensive fee:* $49,078 includes full-time tuition ($38,250), mandatory fees ($678), and room and board ($10,150). *College room only:* $5500. *Payment plans:* Installment, deferred payment.

FRESHMAN FINANCIAL AID (Fall 2009, est.) 319 applied for aid; of those 81% were deemed to have need. 100% of freshmen with need received aid; of those 100% had need fully met. *Average percent of need met:* 100% (excluding resources awarded to replace EFC). *Average financial aid package:* $40,107 (excluding resources awarded to replace EFC).

UNDERGRADUATE FINANCIAL AID (Fall 2009, est.) 1,124 applied for aid; of those 90% were deemed to have need. 100% of undergraduates with need received aid; of those 100% had need fully met. *Average percent of need met:* 100% (excluding resources awarded to replace EFC). *Average financial aid package:* $41,124 (excluding resources awarded to replace EFC).

GIFT AID (NEED-BASED) *Total amount:* $37,581,144 (6% federal, 93% institutional, 1% external sources). *Receiving aid:* Freshmen: 54% (253); all full-time undergraduates: 57% (989). *Average award:* Freshmen: $39,881; Undergraduates: $39,451. *Scholarships, grants, and awards:* Federal Pell, FSEOG, state, private, college/university gift aid from institutional funds, United Negro College Fund.

GIFT AID (NON-NEED-BASED) *Total amount:* $342,668 (30% federal, 70% external sources).

LOANS *Student loans:* $2,137,797 (30% need-based, 70% non-need-based). 41% of past graduating class borrowed through all loan programs. *Average indebtedness per student:* $11,347. *Average need-based loan:* Freshmen: $2392. Undergraduates: $2941. *Parent loans:* $2,672,966 (100% non-need-based). *Programs:* Federal Direct (Subsidized and Unsubsidized Stafford, PLUS), Perkins, college/university.

WORK-STUDY *Federal work-study:* Total amount: $907,652; 551 jobs averaging $1607. *State or other work-study/employment:* Total amount: $396,881 (100% need-based). 240 part-time jobs averaging $1654.

APPLYING FOR FINANCIAL AID *Required financial aid forms:* FAFSA, CSS Financial Aid PROFILE, income tax form(s), W-2 forms. *Financial aid deadline (priority):* 2/15. *Notification date:* 4/1. Students must reply by 5/1.

CONTACT Joe Paul Case, Dean of Financial Aid, Amherst College, B-5 Converse Hall, PO Box 5000, Amherst, MA 01002-5000, 413-542-2296. *Fax:* 413-542-2628. *E-mail:* finaid@amherst.edu.

AMRIDGE UNIVERSITY
Montgomery, AL

ABOUT THE INSTITUTION Independent religious, coed. 12 undergraduate majors.

GIFT AID (NEED-BASED) *Scholarships, grants, and awards:* Federal Pell, FSEOG, state, private, college/university gift aid from institutional funds.

GIFT AID (NON-NEED-BASED) *Scholarships, grants, and awards by category:* Special achievements/activities: religious involvement. Special characteristics: children of faculty/staff, veterans.

LOANS *Programs:* FFEL (Subsidized and Unsubsidized Stafford, PLUS).
WORK-STUDY *Federal work-study:* Total amount: $5000; jobs available.
APPLYING FOR FINANCIAL AID *Required financial aid forms:* FAFSA, institution's own form.
CONTACT Louise Hicks, Financial Aid Director, Amridge University, 1200 Taylor Road, Montgomery, AL 36117, 334-387-3877 Ext. 7525 or toll-free 800-351-4040 Ext. 213. *Fax:* 334-387-3878. *E-mail:* financialaid@amridgeuniversity.edu.

ANDERSON UNIVERSITY
Anderson, IN

Tuition & fees: $23,970	Average undergraduate aid package: $20,553

ABOUT THE INSTITUTION Independent religious, coed. 62 undergraduate majors. Federal methodology is used as a basis for awarding need-based institutional aid.

UNDERGRADUATE EXPENSES for 2010–11 *Comprehensive fee:* $32,320 includes full-time tuition ($23,940), mandatory fees ($30), and room and board ($8350). *College room only:* $5350. Room and board charges vary according to board plan and housing facility. *Part-time tuition:* $998 per semester hour. Part-time tuition and fees vary according to course load. *Payment plan:* Installment.

FRESHMAN FINANCIAL AID (Fall 2008) 563 applied for aid; of those 89% were deemed to have need. 100% of freshmen with need received aid; of those 20% had need fully met. *Average percent of need met:* 98% (excluding resources awarded to replace EFC). *Average financial aid package:* $20,170 (excluding resources awarded to replace EFC). 17% of all full-time freshmen had no need and received non-need-based gift aid.

UNDERGRADUATE FINANCIAL AID (Fall 2008) 1,740 applied for aid; of those 90% were deemed to have need. 100% of undergraduates with need received aid; of those 22% had need fully met. *Average percent of need met:* 93% (excluding resources awarded to replace EFC). *Average financial aid package:* $20,553 (excluding resources awarded to replace EFC). 18% of all full-time undergraduates had no need and received non-need-based gift aid.

GIFT AID (NEED-BASED) *Total amount:* $20,318,290 (16% federal, 12% state, 68% institutional, 4% external sources). *Receiving aid:* Freshmen: 82% (495); all full-time undergraduates: 80% (1,540). *Average award:* Freshmen: $14,115; Undergraduates: $13,414. *Scholarships, grants, and awards:* Federal Pell, FSEOG, state, private, college/university gift aid from institutional funds.

GIFT AID (NON-NEED-BASED) *Total amount:* $4,522,258 (91% institutional, 9% external sources). *Receiving aid:* Freshmen: 25% (150). Undergraduates: 21% (401). *Average award:* Freshmen: $13,000. Undergraduates: $9500. *Scholarships, grants, and awards by category: Academic interests/achievement:* 1,850 awards ($8,500,000 total): general academic interests/achievements. *Creative arts/performance:* 60 awards ($80,000 total): art/fine arts, music. *Special achievements/activities:* 30 awards ($75,000 total): leadership. *Special characteristics:* 350 awards ($2,000,000 total): adult students, children of faculty/staff, international students, relatives of clergy. *Tuition waivers:* Full or partial for employees or children of employees.

LOANS *Student loans:* $14,350,238 (77% need-based, 23% non-need-based). 84% of past graduating class borrowed through all loan programs. *Average indebtedness per student:* $25,401. *Average need-based loan:* Freshmen: $364. Undergraduates: $1651. *Parent loans:* $3,977,858 (37% need-based, 63% non-need-based). *Programs:* FFEL (Subsidized and Unsubsidized Stafford, PLUS), Perkins.

WORK-STUDY *Federal work-study:* Total amount: $510,516; 1,500 jobs averaging $2200. *State or other work-study/employment:* Total amount: $854,501 (26% need-based, 74% non-need-based). Part-time jobs available.

APPLYING FOR FINANCIAL AID *Required financial aid form:* FAFSA. *Financial aid deadline (priority):* 3/1. *Notification date:* Continuous beginning 3/1.

CONTACT Mr. Kenneth Nieman, Director of Student Financial Services, Anderson University, 1100 East Fifth Street, Anderson, IN 46012-3495, 765-641-4180 or toll-free 800-421-3014 (in-state), 800-428-6414 (out-of-state). *Fax:* 765-641-3831. *E-mail:* kfnieman@anderson.edu.

ANDERSON UNIVERSITY
Anderson, SC

Tuition & fees: $19,212	Average undergraduate aid package: N/A

ABOUT THE INSTITUTION Independent Baptist, coed. *Awards:* bachelor's and master's degrees. 32 undergraduate majors. *Total enrollment:* 2,064. Undergraduates: 1,977. Freshmen: 418. Federal methodology is used as a basis for awarding need-based institutional aid.

UNDERGRADUATE EXPENSES for 2009–10 *Application fee:* $25. *Comprehensive fee:* $26,462 includes full-time tuition ($17,876), mandatory fees ($1336), and room and board ($7250). *College room only:* $3700. Full-time tuition and fees vary according to course load and program. Room and board charges vary according to board plan and housing facility. *Part-time tuition:* $450 per credit hour. Part-time tuition and fees vary according to program. *Payment plan:* Installment.

GIFT AID (NEED-BASED) *Scholarships, grants, and awards:* Federal Pell, FSEOG, state, college/university gift aid from institutional funds.

GIFT AID (NON-NEED-BASED) *Tuition waivers:* Full or partial for employees or children of employees. *ROTC:* Army cooperative, Air Force cooperative.

LOANS *Programs:* FFEL (Subsidized and Unsubsidized Stafford, PLUS), Perkins.

APPLYING FOR FINANCIAL AID *Required financial aid form:* FAFSA. *Financial aid deadline:* 7/30 (priority: 3/1). *Notification date:* Continuous beginning 3/15. Students must reply within 2 weeks of notification.

CONTACT Becky Pressley, Director of Financial Aid, Anderson University, 316 Boulevard, Anderson, SC 29621-4035, 864-231-2070 or toll-free 800-542-3594. *Fax:* 864-231-2008. *E-mail:* bpressley@andersonuniversity.edu.

ANDREWS UNIVERSITY
Berrien Springs, MI

Tuition & fees: $21,170	Average undergraduate aid package: $23,932

ABOUT THE INSTITUTION Independent Seventh-day Adventist, coed. 64 undergraduate majors. Federal methodology is used as a basis for awarding need-based institutional aid.

UNDERGRADUATE EXPENSES for 2009–10 *Comprehensive fee:* $28,030 includes full-time tuition ($20,520), mandatory fees ($650), and room and board ($6860). *College room only:* $3510. Full-time tuition and fees vary according to course load. Room and board charges vary according to board plan. *Part-time tuition:* $855 per credit hour. Part-time tuition and fees vary according to course load. *Payment plan:* Installment.

FRESHMAN FINANCIAL AID (Fall 2009, est.) 297 applied for aid; of those 87% were deemed to have need. 100% of freshmen with need received aid; of those 17% had need fully met. *Average percent of need met:* 87% (excluding resources awarded to replace EFC). *Average financial aid package:* $22,079 (excluding resources awarded to replace EFC). 31% of all full-time freshmen had no need and received non-need-based gift aid.

UNDERGRADUATE FINANCIAL AID (Fall 2009, est.) 1,287 applied for aid; of those 91% were deemed to have need. 100% of undergraduates with need received aid; of those 12% had need fully met. *Average percent of need met:* 86% (excluding resources awarded to replace EFC). *Average financial aid package:* $23,932 (excluding resources awarded to replace EFC). 31% of all full-time undergraduates had no need and received non-need-based gift aid.

GIFT AID (NEED-BASED) *Total amount:* $19,923,828 (17% federal, 2% state, 65% institutional, 16% external sources). *Receiving aid:* Freshmen: 49% (186); all full-time undergraduates: 52% (916). *Average award:* Freshmen: $7271; Undergraduates: $8350. *Scholarships, grants, and awards:* Federal Pell, FSEOG, state, private, college/university gift aid from institutional funds.

GIFT AID (NON-NEED-BASED) *Receiving aid:* Freshmen: 69% (259). Undergraduates: 63% (1,105). *Average award:* Freshmen: $6004. Undergraduates: $5853. *Scholarships, grants, and awards by category: Academic interests/achievement:* 1,622 awards ($7,728,696 total): general academic interests/achievements. *Creative arts/performance:* 46 awards ($58,195 total): music. *Special achievements/activities:* 225 awards ($274,801 total): leadership, religious involvement. *Special characteristics:* 122 awards ($1,106,441 total): children of faculty/staff, general special characteristics, international students. *Tuition waivers:* Full or partial for employees or children of employees, senior citizens.

LOANS *Student loans:* $19,439,304 (32% need-based, 68% non-need-based). 73% of past graduating class borrowed through all loan programs. *Average indebtedness per student:* $33,931. *Average need-based loan:* Freshmen: $3408. Undergraduates: $4633. *Parent loans:* $3,844,264 (100% non-need-based). *Programs:* Federal Direct (Subsidized and Unsubsidized Stafford, PLUS), Perkins.

WORK-STUDY *Federal work-study:* Total amount: $589,428; 281 jobs averaging $759. *State or other work-study/employment:* Total amount: $257,553 (100% need-based). 1,121 part-time jobs averaging $2464.

APPLYING FOR FINANCIAL AID *Required financial aid forms:* FAFSA, institution's own form. *Financial aid deadline:* Continuous.

CONTACT Cynthia Gammon, Assistant Director of Student Financial Services, Andrews University, Student Financial Services Administration Building, Berrien Springs, MI 49104, 800-253-2874. *Fax:* 269-471-3228. *E-mail:* sfs@andrews.edu.

ANGELO STATE UNIVERSITY
San Angelo, TX

Tuition & fees (TX res): $6138	Average undergraduate aid package: $7016

ABOUT THE INSTITUTION State-supported, coed. 43 undergraduate majors. Federal methodology is used as a basis for awarding need-based institutional aid.

UNDERGRADUATE EXPENSES for 2010–11 *Tuition, state resident:* full-time $4245; part-time $141.50 per hour. *Tuition, nonresident:* full-time $12,675; part-time $422.50 per hour. *Required fees:* full-time $1893; $366 per term. *College room and board:* $6612; *Room only:* $4112. Room and board charges vary according to board plan and housing facility. *Payment plan:* Installment.

FRESHMAN FINANCIAL AID (Fall 2009, est.) 1,209 applied for aid; of those 77% were deemed to have need. 99% of freshmen with need received aid; of those 33% had need fully met. *Average percent of need met:* 46% (excluding resources awarded to replace EFC). *Average financial aid package:* $6604 (excluding resources awarded to replace EFC). 17% of all full-time freshmen had no need and received non-need-based gift aid.

UNDERGRADUATE FINANCIAL AID (Fall 2009, est.) 3,632 applied for aid; of those 82% were deemed to have need. 99% of undergraduates with need received aid; of those 30% had need fully met. *Average percent of need met:* 45% (excluding resources awarded to replace EFC). *Average financial aid package:* $7016 (excluding resources awarded to replace EFC). 14% of all full-time undergraduates had no need and received non-need-based gift aid.

GIFT AID (NEED-BASED) *Total amount:* $12,272,109 (58% federal, 41% state, 1% institutional). *Receiving aid:* Freshmen: 53% (745); all full-time undergraduates: 50% (2,407). *Average award:* Freshmen: $4966; Undergraduates: $4534. *Scholarships, grants, and awards:* Federal Pell, FSEOG, state, private, college/university gift aid from institutional funds, Federal Nursing.

GIFT AID (NON-NEED-BASED) *Total amount:* $7,542,403 (79% institutional, 21% external sources). *Receiving aid:* Freshmen: 32% (455). Undergraduates: 25% (1,172). *Average award:* Freshmen: $2958. Undergraduates: $3648. *Scholarships, grants, and awards by category: Academic interests/achievement:* agriculture, biological sciences, business, communication, computer science, education, English, foreign languages, general academic interests/achievements, international studies, mathematics, military science, physical sciences, premedicine, social sciences. *Creative arts/performance:* art/fine arts, dance, journalism/publications, music, performing arts, theater/drama. *Special achievements/activities:* cheerleading/drum major, general special achievements/activities, hobbies/interests, leadership, memberships, rodeo. *Special characteristics:* first-generation college students, local/state students. *Tuition waivers:* Full or partial for employees or children of employees, senior citizens.

LOANS *Student loans:* $20,015,816 (42% need-based, 58% non-need-based). 37% of past graduating class borrowed through all loan programs. *Average indebtedness per student:* $16,372. *Average need-based loan:* Freshmen: $2891. Undergraduates: $3655. *Parent loans:* $1,908,186 (100% non-need-based). *Programs:* FFEL (Subsidized and Unsubsidized Stafford, PLUS), Perkins, Federal Nursing, state, college/university, alternative loans.

WORK-STUDY *Federal work-study:* Total amount: $240,350; jobs available. *State or other work-study/employment:* Total amount: $50,907 (100% need-based). Part-time jobs available.

ATHLETIC AWARDS Total amount: $1,006,693 (100% non-need-based).

APPLYING FOR FINANCIAL AID *Required financial aid forms:* FAFSA, institution's own form. *Financial aid deadline (priority):* 4/1. *Notification date:* Continuous.

CONTACT Ms. Michelle Bennett, Director of Financial Aid, Angelo State University, ASU Station #11015, San Angelo, TX 76909-1015, 325-942-2246 or toll-free 800-946-8627 (in-state). *Fax:* 325-942-2082. *E-mail:* michelle.bennett@angelo.edu.

ANNA MARIA COLLEGE
Paxton, MA

ABOUT THE INSTITUTION Independent Roman Catholic, coed. *Awards:* associate, bachelor's, and master's degrees and post-bachelor's and post-master's certificates. 34 undergraduate majors. *Total enrollment:* 1,333. Undergraduates: 1,001. Freshmen: 245.

GIFT AID (NEED-BASED) *Scholarships, grants, and awards:* Federal Pell, FSEOG, state, private, college/university gift aid from institutional funds.

GIFT AID (NON-NEED-BASED) *Scholarships, grants, and awards by category: Academic interests/achievement:* general academic interests/achievements. *Creative arts/performance:* music. *Special achievements/activities:* religious involvement. *Special characteristics:* children and siblings of alumni, children of faculty/staff, children with a deceased or disabled parent, general special characteristics, local/state students, previous college experience, siblings of current students.

LOANS *Programs:* FFEL (Subsidized and Unsubsidized Stafford, PLUS), Perkins, college/university.

WORK-STUDY *Federal work-study:* Total amount: $220,878; 129 jobs averaging $1254.

APPLYING FOR FINANCIAL AID *Required financial aid forms:* FAFSA, state aid form.

CONTACT Colleen King, Director of Financial Aid, Anna Maria College, 50 Sunset Lane, Paxton, MA 01612-1198, 508-849-3363 or toll-free 800-344-4586 Ext. 360. *Fax:* 508-849-3229. *E-mail:* cking@annamaria.edu.

ANTIOCH UNIVERSITY McGREGOR
Yellow Springs, OH

Tuition & fees: $20,760	Average undergraduate aid package: $7200

ABOUT THE INSTITUTION Independent, coed. 9 undergraduate majors. Federal methodology is used as a basis for awarding need-based institutional aid.

UNDERGRADUATE EXPENSES for 2010–11 *Tuition:* full-time $20,160; part-time $315 per credit hour.

UNDERGRADUATE FINANCIAL AID (Fall 2009, est.) 169 applied for aid; of those 81% were deemed to have need. 100% of undergraduates with need received aid. *Average percent of need met:* 25% (excluding resources awarded to replace EFC). *Average financial aid package:* $7200 (excluding resources awarded to replace EFC).

GIFT AID (NEED-BASED) *Total amount:* $518,970 (76% federal, 21% state, 3% external sources). *Receiving aid:* All full-time undergraduates: 55% (96). *Average award:* Undergraduates: $3500. *Scholarships, grants, and awards:* Federal Pell, FSEOG, state.

GIFT AID (NON-NEED-BASED) *Total amount:* $16,000 (100% federal). *Receiving aid:* Undergraduates: 60% (105). *Tuition waivers:* Full or partial for employees or children of employees.

LOANS *Student loans:* $1,791,422 (44% need-based, 56% non-need-based). 67% of past graduating class borrowed through all loan programs. *Average indebtedness per student:* $23,000. *Average need-based loan:* Undergraduates: $5000. *Parent loans:* $8300 (100% non-need-based). *Programs:* Federal Direct (Subsidized and Unsubsidized Stafford, PLUS), Perkins.

WORK-STUDY *Federal work-study:* Total amount: $81,589; 14 jobs averaging $1434.

APPLYING FOR FINANCIAL AID *Required financial aid forms:* FAFSA, institution's own form. *Financial aid deadline:* Continuous. *Notification date:* Continuous beginning 4/1.

CONTACT Kathy John, Director of Financial Aid, Antioch University McGregor, 900 Dayton Street, Yellow Springs, OH 45387, 937-769-1840. *Fax:* 937-769-1804. *E-mail:* kjohn@antioch.edu.

ANTIOCH UNIVERSITY SANTA BARBARA
Santa Barbara, CA

CONTACT Cecilia Schneider, Financial Aid Director, Antioch University Santa Barbara, 801 Garden Street, Santa Barbara, CA 93101-1580, 805-962-8179 Ext. 108. *Fax:* 805-962-4786.

ANTIOCH UNIVERSITY SEATTLE
Seattle, WA

CONTACT Katy Stahl, Director of Financial Aid, Antioch University Seattle, 2326 Sixth Avenue, Seattle, WA 98121-1814, 206-268-4004. *Fax:* 206-268-4242. *E-mail:* kstahl@antiochseattle.edu.

APEX SCHOOL OF THEOLOGY
Durham, NC

CONTACT Financial Aid Office, Apex School of Theology, 2945 South Miami Boulevard, Suite 114, Durham, NC 27703, 919-572-1625.

APPALACHIAN BIBLE COLLEGE
Bradley, WV

Tuition & fees: $10,290	Average undergraduate aid package: $7293

ABOUT THE INSTITUTION Independent nondenominational, coed. 2 undergraduate majors. Both federal and institutional methodology are used as a basis for awarding need-based institutional aid.

UNDERGRADUATE EXPENSES for 2009–10 *Comprehensive fee:* $15,690 includes full-time tuition ($8770), mandatory fees ($1520), and room and board ($5400). Full-time tuition and fees vary according to program. Room and board charges vary according to housing facility. *Part-time tuition:* $365 per credit hour. *Part-time fees:* $550 per term. Part-time tuition and fees vary according to program. *Payment plan:* Installment.

FRESHMAN FINANCIAL AID (Fall 2009, est.) 113 applied for aid; of those 93% were deemed to have need. 68% of freshmen with need received aid; of those 7% had need fully met. *Average percent of need met:* 26% (excluding resources awarded to replace EFC). *Average financial aid package:* $5452 (excluding resources awarded to replace EFC). 8% of all full-time freshmen had no need and received non-need-based gift aid.

UNDERGRADUATE FINANCIAL AID (Fall 2009, est.) 352 applied for aid; of those 91% were deemed to have need. 77% of undergraduates with need received aid; of those 5% had need fully met. *Average percent of need met:* 38% (excluding resources awarded to replace EFC). *Average financial aid package:* $7293 (excluding resources awarded to replace EFC). 7% of all full-time undergraduates had no need and received non-need-based gift aid.

GIFT AID (NEED-BASED) *Total amount:* $1,395,403 (49% federal, 11% state, 30% institutional, 10% external sources). *Receiving aid:* Freshmen: 45% (69); all full-time undergraduates: 58% (240). *Average award:* Freshmen: $4654; Undergraduates: $5799. *Scholarships, grants, and awards:* Federal Pell, FSEOG, state, private, college/university gift aid from institutional funds.

GIFT AID (NON-NEED-BASED) *Total amount:* $110,884 (10% state, 74% institutional, 16% external sources). *Receiving aid:* Freshmen: 2% (3). Undergraduates: 2% (10). *Average award:* Freshmen: $938. Undergraduates: $1919. *Scholarships, grants, and awards by category:* Academic interests/achievement: general academic interests/achievements, religion/biblical studies. Special achievements/activities: general special achievements/activities, religious involvement. Special characteristics: children and siblings of alumni, children of educators, children of faculty/staff, general special characteristics, international students, married students, relatives of clergy, religious affiliation, spouses of current students, veterans. *Tuition waivers:* Full or partial for children of alumni, employees or children of employees, adult students, senior citizens.

LOANS *Student loans:* $524,346 (88% need-based, 12% non-need-based). *Average need-based loan:* Freshmen: $3653. Undergraduates: $3359. *Parent loans:* $57,300 (67% need-based, 33% non-need-based). *Programs:* FFEL (Subsidized and Unsubsidized Stafford, PLUS).

WORK-STUDY *Federal work-study:* Total amount: $20,299; 44 jobs averaging $461. *State or other work-study/employment:* Total amount: $15,435 (67% need-based, 33% non-need-based). Part-time jobs available.

APPLYING FOR FINANCIAL AID *Required financial aid forms:* FAFSA, institution's own form. *Financial aid deadline:* 6/15 (priority: 3/1). *Notification date:* Continuous. Students must reply by 7/30 or within 4 weeks of notification.

CONTACT Cindi Turner, Director of Financial Aid, Appalachian Bible College, 161 College Drive, Mount Hope, WV 25880, 304-877-6428 Ext. 3247 or toll-free 800-678-9ABC Ext. 3213. *Fax:* 304-877-5082. *E-mail:* cindi.turner@abc.edu.

APPALACHIAN STATE UNIVERSITY
Boone, NC

Tuition & fees (NC res): $4425	Average undergraduate aid package: $9991

ABOUT THE INSTITUTION State-supported, coed. 83 undergraduate majors. Federal methodology is used as a basis for awarding need-based institutional aid.

UNDERGRADUATE EXPENSES for 2009–10 *Tuition, state resident:* full-time $2341; part-time $79 per semester hour. *Tuition, nonresident:* full-time $12,962; part-time $437.75 per semester hour. *Required fees:* full-time $2084; $12.25 per semester hour. Part-time tuition and fees vary according to course load. *College room and board:* $6400; *Room only:* $3500. Room and board charges vary according to board plan and housing facility. *Payment plan:* Installment.

FRESHMAN FINANCIAL AID (Fall 2009, est.) 1,537 applied for aid; of those 71% were deemed to have need. 97% of freshmen with need received aid; of those 52% had need fully met. *Average percent of need met:* 86% (excluding resources awarded to replace EFC). *Average financial aid package:* $9369 (excluding resources awarded to replace EFC). 12% of all full-time freshmen had no need and received non-need-based gift aid.

UNDERGRADUATE FINANCIAL AID (Fall 2009, est.) 7,573 applied for aid; of those 78% were deemed to have need. 98% of undergraduates with need received aid; of those 58% had need fully met. *Average percent of need met:* 88% (excluding resources awarded to replace EFC). *Average financial aid package:* $9991 (excluding resources awarded to replace EFC). 8% of all full-time undergraduates had no need and received non-need-based gift aid.

GIFT AID (NEED-BASED) *Total amount:* $33,421,119 (40% federal, 44% state, 11% institutional, 5% external sources). *Receiving aid:* Freshmen: 35% (950); all full-time undergraduates: 37% (5,160). *Average award:* Freshmen: $7288; Undergraduates: $6611. *Scholarships, grants, and awards:* Federal Pell, FSEOG, state, private, college/university gift aid from institutional funds.

GIFT AID (NON-NEED-BASED) *Total amount:* $3,149,991 (3% federal, 23% state, 36% institutional, 38% external sources). *Receiving aid:* Freshmen: 26% (701). Undergraduates: 18% (2,578). *Average award:* Freshmen: $2612. Undergraduates: $2837. *Scholarships, grants, and awards by category:* Academic interests/achievement: 1,612 awards ($3,407,596 total): general academic interests/achievements. Creative arts/performance: general creative arts/performance. Special achievements/activities: general special achievements/activities. Special characteristics: first-generation college students, general special characteristics, handicapped students, members of minority groups, out-of-state students, veterans, veterans' children. *Tuition waivers:* Full or partial for employees or children of employees.

LOANS *Student loans:* $41,680,179 (64% need-based, 36% non-need-based). 55% of past graduating class borrowed through all loan programs. *Average indebtedness per student:* $16,153. *Average need-based loan:* Freshmen: $4553. Undergraduates: $5494. *Parent loans:* $14,476,219 (43% need-based, 57% non-need-based). *Programs:* FFEL (Subsidized and Unsubsidized Stafford, PLUS), Perkins.

WORK-STUDY *Federal work-study:* Total amount: $546,960; 317 jobs averaging $1677.

ATHLETIC AWARDS Total amount: $2,357,402 (40% need-based, 60% non-need-based).

APPLYING FOR FINANCIAL AID *Required financial aid form:* FAFSA. *Financial aid deadline (priority):* 3/1. *Notification date:* 4/1. Students must reply within 3 weeks of notification.

CONTACT Esther Manogin, Director of Student Financial Aid, Appalachian State University, Boone, NC 28608, 828-262-2190. *Fax:* 828-262-2585. *E-mail:* manoginem@appstate.edu.

AQUINAS COLLEGE
Grand Rapids, MI

CONTACT David J. Steffee, Director, Financial Aid, Aquinas College, 1607 Robinson Road, Grand Rapids, MI 49506-1799, 616-459-8281 Ext. 5127 or toll-free 800-678-9593. *Fax:* 616-732-4547. *E-mail:* steffdav@aquinas.edu.

AQUINAS COLLEGE
Nashville, TN

Tuition & fees: $17,180	Average undergraduate aid package: $6100

ABOUT THE INSTITUTION Independent Roman Catholic, coed. 8 undergraduate majors. Federal methodology is used as a basis for awarding need-based institutional aid.

UNDERGRADUATE EXPENSES for 2010–11 *Tuition:* full-time $17,180. Full-time tuition and fees vary according to course load and program. Part-time tuition and fees vary according to course load and program. *Payment plan:* Installment.

FRESHMAN FINANCIAL AID (Fall 2009, est.) *Average percent of need met:* 83% (excluding resources awarded to replace EFC). *Average financial aid package:* $5600 (excluding resources awarded to replace EFC).

UNDERGRADUATE FINANCIAL AID (Fall 2009, est.) *Average percent of need met:* 85% (excluding resources awarded to replace EFC). *Average financial aid package:* $6100 (excluding resources awarded to replace EFC).

GIFT AID (NEED-BASED) *Total amount:* $1,227,989 (64% federal, 32% state, 4% institutional). *Average award:* Freshmen: $3525; Undergraduates: $2025. *Scholarships, grants, and awards:* Federal Pell, FSEOG, state, private, college/university gift aid from institutional funds.

GIFT AID (NON-NEED-BASED) *Total amount:* $665,541 (30% state, 50% institutional, 20% external sources). *Average award:* Freshmen: $1625. Undergraduates: $1700. *Scholarships, grants, and awards by category:* Academic interests/achievement: business, education, general academic interests/achievements, health fields. *Special achievements/activities:* leadership. *Special characteristics:* general special characteristics. *Tuition waivers:* Full or partial for employees or children of employees.

LOANS *Student loans:* $6,135,749 (37% need-based, 63% non-need-based). 70% of past graduating class borrowed through all loan programs. *Average indebtedness per student:* $17,875. *Parent loans:* $117,380 (100% non-need-based). *Programs:* FFEL (Subsidized and Unsubsidized Stafford, PLUS), state, alternative loans.

WORK-STUDY *Federal work-study:* Total amount: $91,791; 48 jobs averaging $1912.

APPLYING FOR FINANCIAL AID *Required financial aid form:* FAFSA. *Financial aid deadline (priority):* 2/15. *Notification date:* Continuous beginning 3/1. Students must reply within 2 weeks of notification.

CONTACT Mrs. Kylie Pruitt, Director of Financial Aid, Aquinas College, 4210 Harding Road, Nashville, TN 37205-2005, 615-297-7545 Ext. 431 or toll-free 800-649-9956. *Fax:* 615-279-3891. *E-mail:* pruittk@aquinascollege.edu.

ARCADIA UNIVERSITY
Glenside, PA

Tuition & fees: $31,260	Average undergraduate aid package: $21,411

ABOUT THE INSTITUTION Independent religious, coed. 66 undergraduate majors. Federal methodology is used as a basis for awarding need-based institutional aid.

UNDERGRADUATE EXPENSES for 2009–10 *One-time required fee:* $100. *Comprehensive fee:* $41,940 includes full-time tuition ($30,780), mandatory fees ($480), and room and board ($10,680). *College room only:* $7620. Full-time tuition and fees vary according to course load, degree level, and program. Room and board charges vary according to board plan. *Part-time tuition:* $515 per credit. *Payment plans:* Installment, deferred payment.

FRESHMAN FINANCIAL AID (Fall 2009, est.) 493 applied for aid; of those 98% were deemed to have need. 99% of freshmen with need received aid; of those 14% had need fully met. *Average percent of need met:* 72% (excluding resources awarded to replace EFC). *Average financial aid package:* $22,416 (excluding resources awarded to replace EFC). 7% of all full-time freshmen had no need and received non-need-based gift aid.

UNDERGRADUATE FINANCIAL AID (Fall 2009, est.) 2,005 applied for aid; of those 94% were deemed to have need. 97% of undergraduates with need received aid; of those 23% had need fully met. *Average percent of need met:* 74% (excluding resources awarded to replace EFC). *Average financial aid package:* $21,411 (excluding resources awarded to replace EFC). 7% of all full-time undergraduates had no need and received non-need-based gift aid.

GIFT AID (NEED-BASED) *Total amount:* $29,837,248 (11% federal, 7% state, 79% institutional, 3% external sources). *Receiving aid:* Freshmen: 90% (474); all full-time undergraduates: 86% (1,815). *Average award:* Freshmen: $19,154; Undergraduates: $17,923. *Scholarships, grants, and awards:* Federal Pell, FSEOG, state, private, college/university gift aid from institutional funds, National SMART Grants, TEACH Grants, Academic Competitiveness Grants.

GIFT AID (NON-NEED-BASED) *Total amount:* $5,042,571 (100% institutional). *Receiving aid:* Freshmen: 11% (60). Undergraduates: 12% (255). *Average award:* Freshmen: $15,002. Undergraduates: $12,735. *Scholarships, grants, and awards by category:* Academic interests/achievement: 1,493 awards ($18,791,906 total): general academic interests/achievements. *Creative arts/performance:* 6 awards ($17,000 total): applied art and design, art/fine arts, theater/drama. *Special achievements/activities:* 668 awards ($4,229,970 total): community service, general special achievements/activities, leadership, memberships. *Special characteristics:* 22 awards ($66,000 total): children and siblings of alumni, relatives of clergy, religious affiliation. *Tuition waivers:* Full or partial for children of alumni, employees or children of employees.

LOANS *Student loans:* $19,632,996 (67% need-based, 33% non-need-based). 88% of past graduating class borrowed through all loan programs. *Average indebtedness per student:* $35,975. *Average need-based loan:* Freshmen: $3422. Undergraduates: $4409. *Parent loans:* $5,009,497 (58% need-based, 42% non-need-based). *Programs:* Federal Direct (Subsidized and Unsubsidized Stafford, PLUS), FFEL (Subsidized and Unsubsidized Stafford, PLUS), Perkins.

WORK-STUDY *Federal work-study:* Total amount: $1,847,232; 1,120 jobs averaging $1620. *State or other work-study/employment:* Total amount: $394,020 (100% non-need-based). 246 part-time jobs averaging $1555.

APPLYING FOR FINANCIAL AID *Required financial aid forms:* FAFSA, institution's own form. *Financial aid deadline (priority):* 3/1. *Notification date:* Continuous beginning 3/1. Students must reply by 5/1.

CONTACT Holly Kirkpatrick, Director of Financial Aid, Arcadia University, 450 South Easton Road, Glenside, PA 19038, 215-572-4475 or toll-free 877-ARCADIA. *Fax:* 215-572-4049. *E-mail:* kirkpath@arcadia.edu.

ARGOSY UNIVERSITY, ATLANTA
Atlanta, GA

UNDERGRADUATE EXPENSES Tuition varies by program. Students should contact Argosy University for tuition information.

CONTACT Financial Aid Office, Argosy University, Atlanta, 980 Hammond Drive, Suite 100, Atlanta, GA 30328, 770-671-1200 or toll-free 888-671-4777.

ARGOSY UNIVERSITY, CHICAGO
Chicago, IL

UNDERGRADUATE EXPENSES Tuition varies by program. Students should contact Argosy University for tuition information.

CONTACT Financial Aid Office, Argosy University, Chicago, 225 North Michigan Avenue, Suite 1300, Chicago, IL 60601, 312-777-7600 or toll-free 800-626-4123.

ARGOSY UNIVERSITY, DALLAS
Farmers Branch, TX

UNDERGRADUATE EXPENSES Tuition varies by program. Students should contact Argosy University for tuition information.

CONTACT Financial Aid Office, Argosy University, Dallas, 5001 Lyndon B. Johnson Freeway, Heritage Square, Farmers Branch, TX 75244, 214-890-9900 or toll-free 866-954-9900.

ARGOSY UNIVERSITY, DENVER
Denver, CO

UNDERGRADUATE EXPENSES Tuition varies by program. Students should contact Argosy University for tuition information.

CONTACT Financial Aid Office, Argosy University, Denver, 1200 Lincoln Street, Denver, CO 80203, 303-248-2700 or toll-free 866-431-5981.

ARGOSY UNIVERSITY, HAWAI'I
Honolulu, HI
UNDERGRADUATE EXPENSES Tuition varies by program. Students should contact Argosy University for tuition information.
CONTACT Financial Aid Office, Argosy University, Hawai'i, 400 ASBTower, 1001 Bishop Street, Honolulu, HI 96813, 808-536-5555 or toll-free 888-323-2777.

ARGOSY UNIVERSITY, INLAND EMPIRE
San Bernardino, CA
UNDERGRADUATE EXPENSES Tuition varies by program. Students should contact Argosy University for tuition information.
CONTACT Financial Aid Office, Argosy University, Inland Empire, 636 East Brier Drive, Suite 120, San Bernardino, CA 92408, 909-915-3800 or toll-free 866-217-9075.

ARGOSY UNIVERSITY, NASHVILLE
Nashville, TN
UNDERGRADUATE EXPENSES Tuition varies by program. Students should contact Argosy University for tuition information.
CONTACT Financial Aid Office, Argosy University, Nashville, 100 Centerview Drive, Suite 225, Nashville, TN 37214, 615-525-2800 or toll-free 866-833-6598 (out-of-state).

ARGOSY UNIVERSITY, ORANGE COUNTY
Orange, CA
UNDERGRADUATE EXPENSES Tuition varies by program. Students should contact Argosy University for tuition information.
CONTACT Financial Aid Office, Argosy University, Orange County, 601 South Lewis Street, Orange, CA 92868, 714-338-6200 or toll-free 800-716-9598.

ARGOSY UNIVERSITY, PHOENIX
Phoenix, AZ
UNDERGRADUATE EXPENSES Tuition varies by program. Students should contact Argosy University for tuition information.
CONTACT Financial Aid Office, Argosy University, Phoenix, 2233 West Dunlap Avenue, Phoenix, AZ 85021, 602-216-2600 or toll-free 866-216-2777.

ARGOSY UNIVERSITY, SALT LAKE CITY
Draper, UT
UNDERGRADUATE EXPENSES Tuition varies by program. Students should contact Argosy University for tuition information.
CONTACT Financial Aid Office, Argosy University, Salt Lake City, 121 West Election Road, Suite 300, Draper, UT 84020, toll-free 888-639-4756.

ARGOSY UNIVERSITY, SAN DIEGO
San Diego, CA
UNDERGRADUATE EXPENSES Tuition varies by program. Students should contact Argosy University for tuition information.
CONTACT Financial Aid Office, Argosy University, San Diego, 1615 Murray Canyon Road, Suite 100, San Diego, CA 92108, 619-321-3000 or toll-free 866-505-0333.

ARGOSY UNIVERSITY, SAN FRANCISCO BAY AREA
Alameda, CA
UNDERGRADUATE EXPENSES Tuition varies by program. Students should contact Argosy University for tuition information.
CONTACT Financial Aid Office, Argosy University, San Francisco Bay Area, 1005 Atlantic Avenue, Alameda, CA 94501, 510-217-4700 or toll-free 866-215-2777.

ARGOSY UNIVERSITY, SARASOTA
Sarasota, FL
UNDERGRADUATE EXPENSES Tuition varies by program. Students should contact Argosy University for tuition information.
CONTACT Financial Aid Office, Argosy University, Sarasota, 5250 17th Street, Sarasota, FL 34235, 941-379-0404 or toll-free 800-331-5995.

ARGOSY UNIVERSITY, SCHAUMBURG
Schaumburg, IL
UNDERGRADUATE EXPENSES Tuition varies by program. Students should contact Argosy University for tuition information.
CONTACT Financial Aid Office, Argosy University, Schaumburg, 999 North Plaza Drive, Suite 111, Schaumburg, IL 60173-5403, 847-969-4900 or toll-free 866-290-2777.

ARGOSY UNIVERSITY, SEATTLE
Seattle, WA
UNDERGRADUATE EXPENSES Tuition varies by program. Students should contact Argosy University for tuition information.
CONTACT Financial Aid Office, Argosy University, Seattle, 2601-A Elliott Avenue, Seattle, WA 98121, 206-283-4500 or toll-free 866-283-2777.

ARGOSY UNIVERSITY, TAMPA
Tampa, FL
UNDERGRADUATE EXPENSES Tuition varies by program. Students should contact Argosy University for tuition information.
CONTACT Financial Aid Office, Argosy University, Tampa, 1403 North Howard Avenue, Tampa, FL 33607, 813-393-5290 or toll-free 800-850-6488.

ARGOSY UNIVERSITY, TWIN CITIES
Eagan, MN
UNDERGRADUATE EXPENSES Tuition varies by program. Students should contact Argosy University for tuition information.
CONTACT Financial Aid Office, Argosy University, Twin Cities, 1515 Central Parkway, Eagan, MN 55121, 651-846-2882 or toll-free 888-844-2004.

ARGOSY UNIVERSITY, WASHINGTON DC
Arlington, VA
UNDERGRADUATE EXPENSES Tuition varies by program. Students should contact Argosy University for tuition information.
CONTACT Financial Aid Office, Argosy University, Washington DC, 1550 Wilson Boulevard, Suite 600, Arlington, VA 22209, 703-526-5800 or toll-free 866-703-2777.

ARIZONA STATE UNIVERSITY
Tempe, AZ
Tuition & fees (AZ res): $8132   **Average undergraduate aid package: $10,290**

ABOUT THE INSTITUTION State-supported, coed. 125 undergraduate majors. Federal methodology is used as a basis for awarding need-based institutional aid.
UNDERGRADUATE EXPENSES for 2010–11 *Tuition, state resident:* full-time $7793; part-time $557 per credit hour. *Tuition, nonresident:* full-time $20,257; part-time $844 per credit hour. *Required fees:* full-time $339. *College room and board:* $9706; *Room only:* $5640.
FRESHMAN FINANCIAL AID (Fall 2008) 5,710 applied for aid; of those 72% were deemed to have need. 100% of freshmen with need received aid; of those 31% had need fully met. *Average percent of need met:* 68% (excluding resources awarded to replace EFC). *Average financial aid package:* $10,808 (excluding resources awarded to replace EFC). 25% of all full-time freshmen had no need and received non-need-based gift aid.

UNDERGRADUATE FINANCIAL AID (Fall 2008) 24,944 applied for aid; of those 81% were deemed to have need. 100% of undergraduates with need received aid; of those 22% had need fully met. *Average percent of need met:* 60% (excluding resources awarded to replace EFC). *Average financial aid package:* $10,290 (excluding resources awarded to replace EFC). 16% of all full-time undergraduates had no need and received non-need-based gift aid.

GIFT AID (NEED-BASED) *Total amount:* $121,246,377 (38% federal, 1% state, 51% institutional, 10% external sources). *Receiving aid:* Freshmen: 44% (3,707); all full-time undergraduates: 39% (16,875). *Average award:* Freshmen: $7965; Undergraduates: $6474. *Scholarships, grants, and awards:* Federal Pell, FSEOG, state, private, college/university gift aid from institutional funds.

GIFT AID (NON-NEED-BASED) *Total amount:* $70,790,183 (1% federal, 78% institutional, 21% external sources). *Receiving aid:* Freshmen: 9% (771). Undergraduates: 4% (1,594). *Average award:* Freshmen: $7571. Undergraduates: $7326. *Scholarships, grants, and awards by category: Academic interests/achievement:* architecture, area/ethnic studies, biological sciences, business, communication, computer science, education, engineering/technologies, English, foreign languages, general academic interests/achievements, health fields, home economics, humanities, mathematics, military science, physical sciences, premedicine, social sciences. *Creative arts/performance:* applied art and design, art/fine arts, cinema/film/broadcasting, creative writing, dance, debating, general creative arts/performance, journalism/publications, music, performing arts, theater/drama. *Special achievements/activities:* general special achievements/activities.

LOANS *Student loans:* $152,584,083 (73% need-based, 27% non-need-based). 45% of past graduating class borrowed through all loan programs. *Average indebtedness per student:* $17,008. *Average need-based loan:* Freshmen: $2852. Undergraduates: $4058. *Parent loans:* $47,255,591 (36% need-based, 64% non-need-based). *Programs:* Federal Direct (Subsidized and Unsubsidized Stafford, PLUS), FFEL (PLUS), Perkins.

WORK-STUDY *Federal work-study:* Total amount: $2,716,672; 843 jobs averaging $3223. *State or other work-study/employment:* Total amount: $19,912,618 (23% need-based, 77% non-need-based). 6,227 part-time jobs averaging $3198.

ATHLETIC AWARDS Total amount: $5,446,937 (34% need-based, 66% non-need-based).

APPLYING FOR FINANCIAL AID *Required financial aid form:* FAFSA. *Financial aid deadline (priority):* 3/1.

CONTACT Craig Fennell, Director of Student Financial Assistance, Arizona State University, Box 870412, Tempe, AZ 85287-0412, 480-965-3355. *Fax:* 480-965-9484. *E-mail:* financialaid@asu.edu.

ARKANSAS BAPTIST COLLEGE
Little Rock, AR

CONTACT Director of Financial Aid, Arkansas Baptist College, 1600 Bishop Street, Little Rock, AR 72202-6067, 501-374-7856.

ARKANSAS STATE UNIVERSITY— JONESBORO
Jonesboro, AR

Tuition & fees (AR res): $6370	Average undergraduate aid package: $9950

ABOUT THE INSTITUTION State-supported, coed. 73 undergraduate majors. Both federal and institutional methodology are used as a basis for awarding need-based institutional aid.

UNDERGRADUATE EXPENSES for 2009–10 *Tuition, state resident:* full-time $4890; part-time $163 per credit hour. *Tuition, nonresident:* full-time $12,810; part-time $427 per credit hour. *Required fees:* full-time $1480; $47 per credit hour or $25 per term. Full-time tuition and fees vary according to course load, location, and program. Part-time tuition and fees vary according to course load, location, and program. *College room and board:* $5856. Room and board charges vary according to board plan, housing facility, and student level. *Payment plan:* Installment.

FRESHMAN FINANCIAL AID (Fall 2009, est.) 1,444 applied for aid; of those 86% were deemed to have need. 100% of freshmen with need received aid; of those 33% had need fully met. *Average percent of need met:* 61% (excluding resources awarded to replace EFC). *Average financial aid package:* $9500 (excluding resources awarded to replace EFC). 7% of all full-time freshmen had no need and received non-need-based gift aid.

UNDERGRADUATE FINANCIAL AID (Fall 2009, est.) 7,245 applied for aid; of those 80% were deemed to have need. 97% of undergraduates with need received aid; of those 25% had need fully met. *Average percent of need met:* 50% (excluding resources awarded to replace EFC). *Average financial aid package:* $9950 (excluding resources awarded to replace EFC). 6% of all full-time undergraduates had no need and received non-need-based gift aid.

GIFT AID (NEED-BASED) *Total amount:* $35,450,000 (57% federal, 9% state, 28% institutional, 6% external sources). *Receiving aid:* Freshmen: 73% (1,210); all full-time undergraduates: 62% (4,801). *Average award:* Freshmen: $6850; Undergraduates: $5875. *Scholarships, grants, and awards:* Federal Pell, FSEOG, state, private, college/university gift aid from institutional funds.

GIFT AID (NON-NEED-BASED) *Receiving aid:* Freshmen: 31% (509). Undergraduates: 30% (2,342). *Average award:* Freshmen: $5200. Undergraduates: $5650. *Scholarships, grants, and awards by category: Academic interests/achievement:* agriculture, area/ethnic studies, biological sciences, business, communication, computer science, education, engineering/technologies, English, general academic interests/achievements, health fields, humanities, library science, mathematics, military science, physical sciences, premedicine, social sciences. *Creative arts/performance:* art/fine arts, cinema/film/broadcasting, debating, journalism/publications, music, performing arts, theater/drama. *Special achievements/activities:* cheerleading/drum major, community service, general special achievements/activities, leadership. *Special characteristics:* adult students, children and siblings of alumni, children of faculty/staff, ethnic background, first-generation college students, general special characteristics, handicapped students, local/state students, members of minority groups, out-of-state students, veterans, veterans' children. *Tuition waivers:* Full or partial for employees or children of employees, senior citizens.

LOANS *Student loans:* $41,300,000 (69% need-based, 31% non-need-based). 68% of past graduating class borrowed through all loan programs. *Average indebtedness per student:* $18,900. *Average need-based loan:* Freshmen: $3500. Undergraduates: $4600. *Programs:* FFEL (Subsidized and Unsubsidized Stafford, PLUS), Perkins.

WORK-STUDY *Federal work-study:* Total amount: $780,600; jobs available. *State or other work-study/employment:* Total amount: $2,200,000 (100% non-need-based). Part-time jobs available.

ATHLETIC AWARDS Total amount: $3,480,000 (71% need-based, 29% non-need-based).

APPLYING FOR FINANCIAL AID *Required financial aid forms:* FAFSA, institution's own form. *Financial aid deadline:* 7/1 (priority: 2/15). *Notification date:* Continuous beginning 6/1. Students must reply within 2 weeks of notification.

CONTACT Mr. Terry Finney, Director of Financial Aid, Arkansas State University—Jonesboro, PO Box 1620, State University, AR 72467, 870-972-2310 or toll-free 800-382-3030 (in-state). *Fax:* 870-972-2794. *E-mail:* tfinney@astate.edu.

ARKANSAS TECH UNIVERSITY
Russellville, AR

Tuition & fees (AR res): $5610	Average undergraduate aid package: $7638

ABOUT THE INSTITUTION State-supported, coed. 57 undergraduate majors. Federal methodology is used as a basis for awarding need-based institutional aid.

UNDERGRADUATE EXPENSES for 2010–11 *Tuition, state resident:* full-time $5010; part-time $167 per credit hour. *Tuition, nonresident:* full-time $10,020; part-time $334 per credit hour. *Required fees:* full-time $600; $9 per credit hour or $140 per term. Full-time tuition and fees vary according to course load and location. Part-time tuition and fees vary according to course load and location. *College room and board:* $5156; *Room only:* $3076. Room and board charges vary according to board plan, housing facility, and location. *Payment plans:* Installment, deferred payment.

FRESHMAN FINANCIAL AID (Fall 2008) 1,170 applied for aid; of those 77% were deemed to have need. 97% of freshmen with need received aid; of those 24% had need fully met. *Average percent of need met:* 73% (excluding resources awarded to replace EFC). *Average financial aid package:* $7582 (excluding resources awarded to replace EFC). 24% of all full-time freshmen had no need and received non-need-based gift aid.

UNDERGRADUATE FINANCIAL AID (Fall 2008) 4,209 applied for aid; of those 82% were deemed to have need. 97% of undergraduates with need received aid; of those 28% had need fully met. *Average percent of need met:* 75% (excluding resources awarded to replace EFC). *Average financial aid package:*

$7638 (excluding resources awarded to replace EFC). 17% of all full-time undergraduates had no need and received non-need-based gift aid.
GIFT AID (NEED-BASED) *Total amount:* $12,832,338 (80% federal, 20% state). *Receiving aid:* Freshmen: 52% (753); all full-time undergraduates: 48% (2,720). *Average award:* Freshmen: $4064; Undergraduates: $3983. *Scholarships, grants, and awards:* Federal Pell, FSEOG, state, private.
GIFT AID (NON-NEED-BASED) *Total amount:* $13,522,306 (6% state, 86% institutional, 8% external sources). *Receiving aid:* Freshmen: 31% (452). Undergraduates: 19% (1,083). *Average award:* Freshmen: $6916. Undergraduates: $6920. *Scholarships, grants, and awards by category: Academic interests/achievement:* agriculture, biological sciences, business, computer science, education, engineering/technologies, English, general academic interests/achievements, health fields, mathematics, military science, physical sciences, social sciences. *Creative arts/performance:* art/fine arts, cinema/film/broadcasting, creative writing, music. *Special achievements/activities:* cheerleading/drum major, community service, general special achievements/activities, hobbies/interests, leadership. *Tuition waivers:* Full or partial for employees or children of employees, senior citizens.
LOANS *Student loans:* $24,770,714 (48% need-based, 52% non-need-based). 51% of past graduating class borrowed through all loan programs. *Average indebtedness per student:* $12,562. *Average need-based loan:* Freshmen: $2835. Undergraduates: $3743. *Parent loans:* $1,025,760 (100% non-need-based). *Programs:* FFEL (Subsidized and Unsubsidized Stafford, PLUS), Perkins.
WORK-STUDY *Federal work-study:* Total amount: $353,641; jobs available. *State or other work-study/employment:* Total amount: $1,142,609 (100% non-need-based). Part-time jobs available.
ATHLETIC AWARDS Total amount: $997,557 (100% non-need-based).
APPLYING FOR FINANCIAL AID *Required financial aid forms:* FAFSA, institution's own form. *Financial aid deadline (priority):* 4/15. *Notification date:* Continuous beginning 5/1. Students must reply within 2 weeks of notification.
CONTACT Financial Aid Office, Arkansas Tech University, 1605 Coliseum Drive, Suite 117, Russellville, AR 72801, 479-968-0399 or toll-free 800-582-6953. *Fax:* 479-964-0857. *E-mail:* fa.help@atu.edu.

ARLINGTON BAPTIST COLLEGE
Arlington, TX

CONTACT Mr. David B. Clogston Jr., Business Manager, Arlington Baptist College, 3001 West Division Street, Arlington, TX 76012-3425, 817-461-8741 Ext. 110. *Fax:* 817-274-1138.

ARMSTRONG ATLANTIC STATE UNIVERSITY
Savannah, GA

Tuition & fees (GA res): $4048	Average undergraduate aid package: $7750

ABOUT THE INSTITUTION State-supported, coed. 33 undergraduate majors. Federal methodology is used as a basis for awarding need-based institutional aid.
UNDERGRADUATE EXPENSES for 2010–11 *Tuition, state resident:* full-time $3120; part-time $130 per credit hour. *Tuition, nonresident:* full-time $12,408; part-time $517 per credit hour. *Required fees:* full-time $928; $464 per term. Full-time tuition and fees vary according to program and student level. Part-time tuition and fees vary according to course load and program. *College room and board:* $5398; *Room only:* $4998. Room and board charges vary according to board plan and housing facility.
FRESHMAN FINANCIAL AID (Fall 2008) 872 applied for aid; of those 75% were deemed to have need. 75% of freshmen with need received aid; of those 82% had need fully met. *Average percent of need met:* 82% (excluding resources awarded to replace EFC). *Average financial aid package:* $6500 (excluding resources awarded to replace EFC). 18% of all full-time freshmen had no need and received non-need-based gift aid.
UNDERGRADUATE FINANCIAL AID (Fall 2008) 3,745 applied for aid; of those 66% were deemed to have need. 65% of undergraduates with need received aid; of those 41% had need fully met. *Average percent of need met:* 82% (excluding resources awarded to replace EFC). *Average financial aid package:* $7750 (excluding resources awarded to replace EFC). 2% of all full-time undergraduates had no need and received non-need-based gift aid.

GIFT AID (NEED-BASED) *Total amount:* $7,123,173 (100% federal). *Receiving aid:* Freshmen: 40% (392); all full-time undergraduates: 3% (1,259). *Average award:* Freshmen: $4000; Undergraduates: $4000. *Scholarships, grants, and awards:* Federal Pell, FSEOG, state, private, college/university gift aid from institutional funds, Federal Nursing.
GIFT AID (NON-NEED-BASED) *Total amount:* $7,394,432 (77% state, 5% institutional, 18% external sources). *Receiving aid:* Freshmen: 49% (474). Undergraduates: 2% (1,084). *Average award:* Freshmen: $3000. Undergraduates: $3000. *Scholarships, grants, and awards by category: Academic interests/achievement:* 588 awards ($1,320,674 total): biological sciences, computer science, education, engineering/technologies, English, foreign languages, general academic interests/achievements, health fields, humanities, international studies, mathematics, military science, physical sciences. *Creative arts/performance:* 66 awards ($43,950 total): art/fine arts, general creative arts/performance, music. *Special achievements/activities:* community service. *Special characteristics:* 41 awards ($199,537 total): ethnic background, international students, religious affiliation. *Tuition waivers:* Full or partial for employees or children of employees, senior citizens.
LOANS *Student loans:* $25,136,902 (55% need-based, 45% non-need-based). 49% of past graduating class borrowed through all loan programs. *Average indebtedness per student:* $19,000. *Average need-based loan:* Freshmen: $4500. Undergraduates: $4500. *Parent loans:* $663,305 (100% non-need-based). *Programs:* Federal Direct (Subsidized and Unsubsidized Stafford, PLUS), FFEL (Subsidized and Unsubsidized Stafford, PLUS), college/university, alternative loans.
WORK-STUDY *Federal work-study:* Total amount: $262,890; 96 jobs averaging $5000. *State or other work-study/employment:* Part-time jobs available.
ATHLETIC AWARDS Total amount: $732,863 (100% non-need-based).
APPLYING FOR FINANCIAL AID *Required financial aid form:* FAFSA. *Financial aid deadline (priority):* 3/15. *Notification date:* Continuous beginning 4/1. Students must reply within 6 weeks of notification.
CONTACT Lee Ann Kirkland, Director of Financial Aid, Armstrong Atlantic State University, 11935 Abercorn Street, Savannah, GA 31419-1997, 912-344-2614 or toll-free 800-633-2349. *Fax:* 912-344-3448: *E-mail:* finaid@armstrong.edu.

ART ACADEMY OF CINCINNATI
Cincinnati, OH

ABOUT THE INSTITUTION Independent, coed. *Awards:* associate, bachelor's, and master's degrees. 11 undergraduate majors. *Total enrollment:* 165. Undergraduates: 164. Freshmen: 47.
GIFT AID (NEED-BASED) *Scholarships, grants, and awards:* Federal Pell, FSEOG, state, private, college/university gift aid from institutional funds.
GIFT AID (NON-NEED-BASED) *Scholarships, grants, and awards by category: Creative arts/performance:* applied art and design, art/fine arts.
LOANS *Programs:* FFEL (Subsidized and Unsubsidized Stafford, PLUS), college/university, alternative loans.
APPLYING FOR FINANCIAL AID *Required financial aid form:* FAFSA.
CONTACT Ms. Karen Geiger, Director of Financial Aid, Art Academy of Cincinnati, 1212 Jackson Street, Cincinnati, OH 45202, 513-562-8773 or toll-free 800-323-5692 (in-state). *Fax:* 513-562-8778. *E-mail:* financialaid@artacademy.edu.

ART CENTER COLLEGE OF DESIGN
Pasadena, CA

CONTACT Clema McKenzie, Director of Financial Aid, Art Center College of Design, 1700 Lida Street, Pasadena, CA 91103-1999, 626-396-2215. *Fax:* 626-683-8684.

THE ART CENTER DESIGN COLLEGE
Tucson, AZ

CONTACT Ms. Margarita Carey, Education Finance Director, The Art Center Design College, 2525 North Country Club Road, Tucson, AZ 85716-2505, 520-325-0123 or toll-free 800-825-8753. *Fax:* 520-325-5535.

THE ART INSTITUTE OF ATLANTA
Atlanta, GA

UNDERGRADUATE EXPENSES Tuition cost varies by program. Prospective students should contact the school for current tuition costs. Other charges include a starting kit for all first-quarter students. Kits vary in price, depending on the program of study.
CONTACT Financial Aid Office, The Art Institute of Atlanta, 6600 Peachtree Dunwoody Road, NE, 100 Embassy Row, Atlanta, GA 30328, 770-394-8300 or toll-free 800-275-4242.

THE ART INSTITUTE OF ATLANTA–DECATUR
Decatur, GA

UNDERGRADUATE EXPENSES Tuition cost varies by program. Prospective students should contact the school for current tuition costs. Other charges include a starting kit for all first-quarter students. Kits vary in price, depending on the program of study.
CONTACT Financial Aid Office, The Art Institute of Atlanta–Decatur, One West Court Square, Suite 110, Decatur, GA 30030, toll-free 866-856-6203.

THE ART INSTITUTE OF AUSTIN
Austin, TX

UNDERGRADUATE EXPENSES Tuition cost varies by program. Prospective students should contact the school for current tuition costs. Other charges include a starting kit for all first-quarter students. Kits vary in price, depending on the program of study.
CONTACT Financial Aid Office, The Art Institute of Austin, 101 W. Louis Henna Boulevard, Suite 100, Austin, TX 78728, 512-691-1707 or toll-free 866-583-7952.

THE ART INSTITUTE OF BOSTON AT LESLEY UNIVERSITY
Boston, MA

ABOUT THE INSTITUTION Independent, coed. 4 undergraduate majors.
GIFT AID (NEED-BASED) *Scholarships, grants, and awards:* Federal Pell, FSEOG, state, private, college/university gift aid from institutional funds.
GIFT AID (NON-NEED-BASED) *Scholarships, grants, and awards by category: Academic interests/achievement:* general academic interests/achievements. *Creative arts/performance:* applied art and design, art/fine arts. *Special achievements/activities:* community service, general special achievements/activities, memberships. *Special characteristics:* ethnic background, local/state students, members of minority groups.
LOANS *Programs:* FFEL (Subsidized and Unsubsidized Stafford, PLUS), Perkins, state.
WORK-STUDY *Federal work-study:* Total amount: $300,000; 225 jobs averaging $1800. *State or other work-study/employment:* 150 part-time jobs averaging $1500.
APPLYING FOR FINANCIAL AID *Required financial aid forms:* FAFSA, institution's own form, parent and student federal income tax forms.
CONTACT Scott Jewell, Director of Financial Aid, The Art Institute of Boston at Lesley University, 29 Everett Street, Cambridge, MA 02138, 617-349-8714 or toll-free 800-773-0494 (in-state).

THE ART INSTITUTE OF CALIFORNIA–HOLLYWOOD
North Hollywood, CA

UNDERGRADUATE EXPENSES Tuition cost varies by program. Prospective students should contact the school for current tuition costs. Other charges include a starting kit for all first-quarter students. Kits vary in price, depending on the program of study.

CONTACT Financial Aid Office, The Art Institute of California–Hollywood, 3440 Wilshire Boulevard, Seventh Floor, Los Angeles, CA 90010, 213-251-3636 Ext. 209 or toll-free 877-468-6232. *Fax:* 213-385-3545. *E-mail:* jason@cdc.edu.

THE ART INSTITUTE OF CALIFORNIA–INLAND EMPIRE
San Bernardino, CA

UNDERGRADUATE EXPENSES Tuition cost varies by program. Prospective students should contact the school for current tuition costs. Other charges include a starting kit for all first-quarter students. Kits vary in price, depending on the program of study.
CONTACT Financial Aid Office, The Art Institute of California–Inland Empire, 674 East Brier Drive, San Bernardino, CA 92408, 909-915-2100 or toll-free 800-353-0812.

THE ART INSTITUTE OF CALIFORNIA–LOS ANGELES
Santa Monica, CA

UNDERGRADUATE EXPENSES Tuition cost varies by program. Prospective students should contact the school for current tuition costs. Other charges include a starting kit for all first-quarter students. Kits vary in price, depending on the program of study.
CONTACT Financial Aid Office, The Art Institute of California–Los Angeles, 2900 31st Street, Santa Monica, CA 90405-3035, 310-752-4700 or toll-free 888-646-4610.

THE ART INSTITUTE OF CALIFORNIA–ORANGE COUNTY
Santa Ana, CA

UNDERGRADUATE EXPENSES Tuition cost varies by program. Prospective students should contact the school for current tuition costs. Other charges include a starting kit for all first-quarter students. Kits vary in price, depending on the program of study.
CONTACT Financial Aid Office, The Art Institute of California–Orange County, 3601 West Sunflower Avenue, Santa Ana, CA 92704, 714-830-0200 or toll-free 888-549-3055.

THE ART INSTITUTE OF CALIFORNIA–SACRAMENTO
Sacramento, CA

UNDERGRADUATE EXPENSES Tuition cost varies by program. Prospective students should contact the school for current tuition costs. Other charges include a starting kit for all first-quarter students. Kits vary in price, depending on the program of study.
CONTACT Financial Aid Office, The Art Institute of California–Sacramento, 2850 Gateway Oaks Drive, Suite 100, Sacramento, CA 95833, toll-free 800-477-1957.

THE ART INSTITUTE OF CALIFORNIA–SAN DIEGO
San Diego, CA

UNDERGRADUATE EXPENSES Tuition cost varies by program. Prospective students should contact the school for current tuition costs. Other charges include a starting kit for all first-quarter students. Kits vary in price, depending on the program of study.
CONTACT Financial Aid Office, The Art Institute of California–San Diego, 10025 Mesa Rim Road, San Diego, CA 92121, 619-546-0602 or toll-free 866-275-2422.

THE ART INSTITUTE OF CALIFORNIA–SAN FRANCISCO
San Francisco, CA
UNDERGRADUATE EXPENSES Tuition cost varies by program. Prospective students should contact the school for current tuition costs. Other charges include a starting kit for all first-quarter students. Kits vary in price, depending on the program of study.
CONTACT Financial Aid Office, The Art Institute of California–San Francisco, 1170 Market Street, San Francisco, CA 94102-4908, 415-865-0198 or toll-free 888-493-3261. *Fax:* 415-863-5831.

THE ART INSTITUTE OF CALIFORNIA–SUNNYVALE
Sunnyvale, CA
UNDERGRADUATE EXPENSES Tuition cost varies by program. Prospective students should contact the school for current tuition costs. Other charges include a starting kit for all first-quarter students. Kits vary in price, depending on the program of study.
CONTACT Financial Aid Office, The Art Institute of California–Sunnyvale, 1120 Kifer Road, Sunnyvale, CA 94086, 408-962-6400 or toll-free 866-583-7961.

THE ART INSTITUTE OF CHARLESTON
Charleston, SC
UNDERGRADUATE EXPENSES Tuition cost varies by program. Prospective students should contact the school for current tuition costs. Other charges include a starting kit for all first-quarter students. Kits vary in price, depending on the program of study.
CONTACT Financial Aid Office, The Art Institute of Charleston, 24 North Market Street, Charleston, SC 29401, 843-727-3500 or toll-free 866-211-0107.

THE ART INSTITUTE OF CHARLOTTE
Charlotte, NC
UNDERGRADUATE EXPENSES Tuition cost varies by program. Prospective students should contact the school for current tuition costs. Other charges include a starting kit for all first-quarter students. Kits vary in price, depending on the program of study.
CONTACT Financial Aid Office, The Art Institute of Charlotte, Three LakePointe Plaza, 2110 Water Ridge Parkway, Charlotte, NC 28217, 704-357-8020 or toll-free 800-872-4417.

THE ART INSTITUTE OF COLORADO
Denver, CO
UNDERGRADUATE EXPENSES Tuition cost varies by program. Prospective students should contact the school for current tuition costs. Other charges include a starting kit for all first-quarter students. Kits vary in price, depending on the program of study.
CONTACT Financial Aid Office, The Art Institute of Colorado, 1200 Lincoln Street, Denver, CO 80203, 303-837-0825 or toll-free 800-275-2420.

THE ART INSTITUTE OF DALLAS
Dallas, TX
UNDERGRADUATE EXPENSES Tuition cost varies by program. Prospective students should contact the school for current tuition costs. Other charges include a starting kit for all first-quarter students. Kits vary in price, depending on the program of study.
CONTACT Financial Aid Office, The Art Institute of Dallas, 8080 Park Lane, Suite 100, Dallas, TX 75231-5993, 214-692-8080 or toll-free 800-275-4243.

THE ART INSTITUTE OF FORT LAUDERDALE
Fort Lauderdale, FL
UNDERGRADUATE EXPENSES Tuition cost varies by program. Prospective students should contact the school for current tuition costs. Other charges include a starting kit for all first-quarter students. Kits vary in price, depending on the program of study.
CONTACT Financial Aid Office, The Art Institute of Fort Lauderdale, 1799 Southeast 17th Street Causeway, Fort Lauderdale, FL 33316-3000, 954-527-1799 or toll-free 800-275-7603.

THE ART INSTITUTE OF FORT WORTH
Fort Worth, TX
UNDERGRADUATE EXPENSES Tuition cost varies by program. Prospective students should contact the school for current tuition costs. Other charges include a starting kit for all first-quarter students. Kits vary in price, depending on the program of study.
CONTACT Financial Aid Office, The Art Institute of Fort Worth, 7000 Calmont Avenue, Suite 150, Fort Worth, TX 76116, 817-210-0808 or toll-free 888-422-9686.

THE ART INSTITUTE OF HOUSTON
Houston, TX
UNDERGRADUATE EXPENSES Tuition cost varies by program. Prospective students should contact the school for current tuition costs. Other charges include a starting kit for all first-quarter students. Kits vary in price, depending on the program of study.
CONTACT Financial Aid Office, The Art Institute of Houston, 1900 Yorktown, Houston, TX 77056, 713-623-2040 Ext. 780 or toll-free 800-275-4244. *Fax:* 713-966-2700. *E-mail:* bensons@aii.edu.

THE ART INSTITUTE OF HOUSTON—NORTH
Houston, TX
UNDERGRADUATE EXPENSES Tuition cost varies by program. Prospective students should contact the school for current tuition costs. Other charges include a starting kit for all first-quarter students. Kits vary in price, depending on the program of study.
CONTACT Financial Aid Office, The Art Institute of Houston—North, 10740 North Gessner Drive, Suite 190, Houston, TX 77064, toll-free 866-830-4450 (out-of-state).

THE ART INSTITUTE OF INDIANAPOLIS
Indianapolis, IN
UNDERGRADUATE EXPENSES Tuition cost varies by program. Prospective students should contact the school for current tuition costs. Other charges include a starting kit for all first-quarter students. Kits vary in price, depending on the program of study.
CONTACT Financial Aid Office, The Art Institute of Indianapolis, 3500 Depauw Boulevard, Suite 1010, Indianapolis, IN 46268, 317-613-4800.

THE ART INSTITUTE OF JACKSONVILLE
Jacksonville, FL
UNDERGRADUATE EXPENSES Tuition cost varies by program. Prospective students should contact the school for current tuition costs. Other charges include a starting kit for all first-quarter students. Kits vary in price, depending on the program of study.
CONTACT Financial Aid Office, The Art Institute of Jacksonville, 8775 Baypine Road, Jacksonville, FL 32256, 904-732-9393 or toll-free 800-924-1589.

THE ART INSTITUTE OF LAS VEGAS
Henderson, NV

UNDERGRADUATE EXPENSES Tuition cost varies by program. Prospective students should contact the school for current tuition costs. Other charges include a starting kit for all first-quarter students. Kits vary in price, depending on the program of study.
CONTACT Financial Aid Office, The Art Institute of Las Vegas, 2350 Corporate Circle Drive, Henderson, NV 89074, 702-369-9944.

THE ART INSTITUTE OF MICHIGAN
Novi, MI

UNDERGRADUATE EXPENSES Tuition cost varies by program. Prospective students should contact the school for current tuition costs. Other charges include a starting kit for all first-quarter students. Kits vary in price, depending on the program of study.
CONTACT Financial Aid Office, The Art Institute of Michigan, 28125 Cabot Drive, Suite 120, Novi, MI 48377, 248-675-3800 or toll-free 800-479-0087.

THE ART INSTITUTE OF PHILADELPHIA
Philadelphia, PA

UNDERGRADUATE EXPENSES Tuition cost varies by program. Prospective students should contact the school for current tuition costs. Other charges include a starting kit for all first-quarter students. Kits vary in price, depending on the program of study.
CONTACT Financial Aid Office, The Art Institute of Philadelphia, 1622 Chestnut Street, Philadelphia, PA 19103-5198, 215-246-3311 or toll-free 800-275-2474. *Fax:* 215-246-3339.

THE ART INSTITUTE OF PHOENIX
Phoenix, AZ

UNDERGRADUATE EXPENSES Tuition cost varies by program. Prospective students should contact the school for current tuition costs. Other charges include a starting kit for all first-quarter students. Kits vary in price, depending on the program of study.
CONTACT Financial Aid Office, The Art Institute of Phoenix, 2233 West Dunlap Avenue, Phoenix, AZ 85021-2859, 602-331-7500 or toll-free 800-474-2479.

THE ART INSTITUTE OF PITTSBURGH
Pittsburgh, PA

UNDERGRADUATE EXPENSES Tuition cost varies by program. Prospective students should contact the school for current tuition costs. Other charges include a starting kit for all first-quarter students. Kits vary in price, depending on the program of study.
CONTACT Financial Aid Office, The Art Institute of Pittsburgh, 526 Penn Avenue, Pittsburgh, PA 15222-3269, 412-263-6600 or toll-free 800-275-2470.

THE ART INSTITUTE OF PORTLAND
Portland, OR

UNDERGRADUATE EXPENSES Tuition cost varies by program. Prospective students should contact the school for current tuition costs. Other charges include a starting kit for all first-quarter students. Kits vary in price, depending on the program of study.
CONTACT Financial Aid Office, The Art Institute of Portland, 1122 NW Davis Street, Portland, OR 97209, 503-228-6528 or toll-free 888-228-6528.

THE ART INSTITUTE OF RALEIGH-DURHAM
Durham, NC

UNDERGRADUATE EXPENSES Tuition cost varies by program. Prospective students should contact the school for current tuition costs. Other charges include a starting kit for all first-quarter students. Kits vary in price, depending on the program of study.
CONTACT Financial Aid Office, The Art Institute of Raleigh-Durham, 410 Blackwell Street, Suite 200, Durham, NC 27701, toll-free 888-245-9593.

THE ART INSTITUTE OF SALT LAKE CITY
Draper, UT

UNDERGRADUATE EXPENSES Tuition cost varies by program. Prospective students should contact the school for current tuition costs. Other charges include a starting kit for all first-quarter students. Kits vary in price, depending on the program of study.
CONTACT Financial Aid Office, The Art Institute of Salt Lake City, 121 West Election Road, Suite 100, Draper, UT 84020-9492, toll-free 800-978-0096.

THE ART INSTITUTE OF SAN ANTONIO
San Antonio, TX

UNDERGRADUATE EXPENSES Tuition cost varies by program. Prospective students should contact the school for current tuition costs. Other charges include a starting kit for all first-quarter students. Kits vary in price, depending on the program of study.
CONTACT Financial Aid Office, The Art Institute of San Antonio, 1000 IH-10 West, Suite 200, San Antonio, TX 78230, 210-338-7320 or toll-free 888-222-0040.

THE ART INSTITUTE OF TAMPA
Tampa, FL

UNDERGRADUATE EXPENSES Tuition cost varies by program. Prospective students should contact the school for current tuition costs. Other charges include a starting kit for all first-quarter students. Kits vary in price, depending on the program of study.
CONTACT Financial Aid Office, The Art Institute of Tampa, Parkside at Tampa Bay Park, 4401 North Himes Avenue, Suite 150, Tampa, FL 33614, 813-873-2112 or toll-free 866-703-3277.

THE ART INSTITUTE OF TENNESSEE–NASHVILLE
Nashville, TN

UNDERGRADUATE EXPENSES Tuition cost varies by program. Prospective students should contact the school for current tuition costs. Other charges include a starting kit for all first-quarter students. Kits vary in price, depending on the program of study.
CONTACT Financial Aid Office, The Art Institute of Tennessee–Nashville, 100 Centerview Drive, Suite 250, Nashville, TN 37214, 615-874-1067 or toll-free 866-747-5770.

THE ART INSTITUTE OF TUCSON
Tucson, AZ

UNDERGRADUATE EXPENSES Tuition cost varies by program. Prospective students should contact the school for current tuition costs. Other charges include a starting kit for all first-quarter students. Kits vary in price, depending on the program of study.
CONTACT Financial Aid Office, The Art Institute of Tucson, 5099 East Grant Road, Suite 100, Tucson, AZ 85712, 520-881-2900 or toll-free 866-690-8850.

THE ART INSTITUTE OF VIRGINIA BEACH
Virginia Beach, VA

UNDERGRADUATE EXPENSES Tuition cost varies by program. Prospective students should contact the school for current tuition costs. Other charges include a starting kit for all first-quarter students. Kits vary in price, depending on the program of study.
CONTACT Financial Aid Office, The Art Institute of Virginia Beach, Two Columbus Center, 4500 Main Street, Suite 100, Virginia Beach, VA 23462, 757-493-6700 or toll-free 877-437-4428.

THE ART INSTITUTE OF WASHINGTON
Arlington, VA

UNDERGRADUATE EXPENSES Tuition cost varies by program. Prospective students should contact the school for current tuition costs. Other charges include a starting kit for all first-quarter students. Kits vary in price, depending on the program of study.

CONTACT Financial Aid Office, The Art Institute of Washington, 1820 North Fort Myer Drive, Arlington, VA 22209, 703-247-6849 or toll-free 877-303-3771. *Fax:* 703-247-6829.

THE ART INSTITUTE OF WASHINGTON–NORTHERN VIRGINIA
Sterling, VA

UNDERGRADUATE EXPENSES Tuition cost varies by program. Prospective students should contact the school for current tuition costs. Other charges include a starting kit for all first-quarter students. Kits vary in price, depending on the program of study.

CONTACT Financial Aid Office, The Art Institute of Washington–Northern Virginia, The Corporate Office Park at Dulles Town Center, 21000 Atlantic Boulevard, Suite 100, Sterling, VA 20166, 571-449-4400 or toll-free 888-627-5008.

THE ART INSTITUTES INTERNATIONAL–KANSAS CITY
Lenexa, KS

UNDERGRADUATE EXPENSES Tuition cost varies by program. Prospective students should contact the school for current tuition costs. Other charges include a starting kit for all first-quarter students. Kits vary in price, depending on the program of study.

CONTACT Financial Aid Office, The Art Institutes International–Kansas City, 8208 Melrose Drive, Lenexa, KS 66214, toll-free 866-530-8508.

THE ART INSTITUTES INTERNATIONAL MINNESOTA
Minneapolis, MN

UNDERGRADUATE EXPENSES Tuition cost varies by program. Prospective students should contact the school for current tuition costs. Other charges include a starting kit for all first-quarter students. Kits vary in price, depending on the program of study.

CONTACT Financial Aid Office, The Art Institutes International Minnesota, 825 2nd Avenue South, Minneapolis, MN 55402, 612-332-3361 Ext. 110 or toll-free 800-777-3643. *Fax:* 612-332-3934. *E-mail:* robbt@aii.edu.

ASBURY UNIVERSITY
Wilmore, KY

Tuition & fees: $23,303	Average undergraduate aid package: $17,794

ABOUT THE INSTITUTION Independent nondenominational, coed. 44 undergraduate majors. Federal methodology is used as a basis for awarding need-based institutional aid.

UNDERGRADUATE EXPENSES for 2010–11 *Comprehensive fee:* $28,869 includes full-time tuition ($23,132), mandatory fees ($171), and room and board ($5566). *College room only:* $3270. Full-time tuition and fees vary according to course load and program. Room and board charges vary according to board plan, housing facility, and location. *Part-time tuition:* $889 per credit hour. Part-time tuition and fees vary according to course load and program. *Payment plan:* Installment.

FRESHMAN FINANCIAL AID (Fall 2009, est.) 289 applied for aid; of those 85% were deemed to have need. 100% of freshmen with need received aid; of those 32% had need fully met. *Average percent of need met:* 89% (excluding resources awarded to replace EFC). *Average financial aid package:* $19,835 (excluding resources awarded to replace EFC). 14% of all full-time freshmen had no need and received non-need-based gift aid.

UNDERGRADUATE FINANCIAL AID (Fall 2009, est.) 1,053 applied for aid; of those 87% were deemed to have need. 100% of undergraduates with need received aid; of those 25% had need fully met. *Average percent of need met:* 81% (excluding resources awarded to replace EFC). *Average financial aid package:* $17,794 (excluding resources awarded to replace EFC). 10% of all full-time undergraduates had no need and received non-need-based gift aid.

GIFT AID (NEED-BASED) *Total amount:* $10,426,551 (18% federal, 17% state, 61% institutional, 4% external sources). *Receiving aid:* Freshmen: 78% (245); all full-time undergraduates: 73% (903). *Average award:* Freshmen: $13,646; Undergraduates: $11,682. *Scholarships, grants, and awards:* Federal Pell, FSEOG, state, private, college/university gift aid from institutional funds.

GIFT AID (NON-NEED-BASED) *Total amount:* $2,420,349 (1% federal, 7% state, 87% institutional, 5% external sources). *Receiving aid:* Freshmen: 29% (90). Undergraduates: 23% (281). *Average award:* Freshmen: $10,501. Undergraduates: $9343. *Scholarships, grants, and awards by category:* Academic interests/achievement: general academic interests/achievements. Creative arts/performance: music. Special achievements/activities: leadership. Special characteristics: children and siblings of alumni, children of faculty/staff, ethnic background, international students, siblings of current students. *Tuition waivers:* Full or partial for employees or children of employees, senior citizens.

LOANS *Student loans:* $9,225,752 (59% need-based, 41% non-need-based). 85% of past graduating class borrowed through all loan programs. *Average indebtedness per student:* $26,150. *Average need-based loan:* Freshmen: $3226. Undergraduates: $3907. *Parent loans:* $1,250,618 (75% need-based, 25% non-need-based). *Programs:* Federal Direct (Subsidized and Unsubsidized Stafford, PLUS), FFEL (Subsidized and Unsubsidized Stafford, PLUS), Perkins, college/university, private loans.

WORK-STUDY *Federal work-study:* Total amount: $845,984; jobs available.

ATHLETIC AWARDS Total amount: $1,146,446 (70% need-based, 30% non-need-based).

APPLYING FOR FINANCIAL AID *Required financial aid forms:* FAFSA, institution's own form. *Financial aid deadline (priority):* 3/1. *Notification date:* Continuous. Students must reply within 4 weeks of notification.

CONTACT Mr. Ronald Anderson, Director of Financial Aid, Asbury University, One Macklem Drive, Wilmore, KY 40390, 859-858-3511 Ext. 2195 or toll-free 800-888-1818. *Fax:* 859-858-3921. *E-mail:* ron.anderson@asbury.edu.

ASHFORD UNIVERSITY
Clinton, IA

CONTACT Lisa Kramer, Director of Financial Aid, Ashford University, 400 North Bluff Boulevard, PO Box 2967, Clinton, IA 52733-2967, 563-242-4023 Ext. 1243 or toll-free 800-242-4153. *Fax:* 563-242-8684.

ASHLAND UNIVERSITY
Ashland, OH

Tuition & fees: $25,640	Average undergraduate aid package: $23,254

ABOUT THE INSTITUTION Independent religious, coed. 67 undergraduate majors. Federal methodology is used as a basis for awarding need-based institutional aid.

UNDERGRADUATE EXPENSES for 2009–10 *Comprehensive fee:* $34,992 includes full-time tuition ($24,828), mandatory fees ($812), and room and board ($9352). *College room only:* $5022. Full-time tuition and fees vary according to degree level, location, and reciprocity agreements. Room and board charges vary according to board plan and housing facility. *Part-time tuition:* $762 per credit. *Part-time fees:* $18 per credit. Part-time tuition and fees vary according to course load, degree level, location, and program. *Payment plan:* Installment.

FRESHMAN FINANCIAL AID (Fall 2009, est.) 605 applied for aid; of those 86% were deemed to have need. 100% of freshmen with need received aid. *Average percent of need met:* 90% (excluding resources awarded to replace EFC). *Average financial aid package:* $24,727 (excluding resources awarded to replace EFC). 9% of all full-time freshmen had no need and received non-need-based gift aid.

UNDERGRADUATE FINANCIAL AID (Fall 2009, est.) 2,136 applied for aid; of those 83% were deemed to have need. 100% of undergraduates with need received aid. *Average percent of need met:* 90% (excluding resources awarded to replace EFC). *Average financial aid package:* $23,254 (excluding resources awarded to replace EFC). 10% of all full-time undergraduates had no need and received non-need-based gift aid.

GIFT AID (NEED-BASED) *Total amount:* $23,027,587 (15% federal, 5% state, 78% institutional, 2% external sources). *Receiving aid:* Freshmen: 86% (521); all full-time undergraduates: 82% (1,769). *Average award:* Freshmen: $16,963; Undergraduates: $15,366. *Scholarships, grants, and awards:* Federal Pell, FSEOG, state, private, college/university gift aid from institutional funds.

GIFT AID (NON-NEED-BASED) *Total amount:* $2,400,448 (1% federal, 1% state, 97% institutional, 1% external sources). *Receiving aid:* Freshmen: 86% (521). Undergraduates: 82% (1,769). *Average award:* Freshmen: $10,490. Undergraduates: $8168. *Scholarships, grants, and awards by category:* Academic interests/achievement: 1,347 awards ($10,116,144 total): general academic interests/achievements, mathematics, physical sciences, social sciences. Creative arts/performance: 134 awards ($317,480 total): art/fine arts, music, theater/drama. Special achievements/activities: 15 awards ($7250 total): cheerleading/drum major. Special characteristics: 131 awards ($2,330,269 total): children and siblings of alumni, children of faculty/staff, international students, relatives of clergy, religious affiliation. *Tuition waivers:* Full or partial for children of alumni, employees or children of employees, senior citizens.

LOANS *Student loans:* $18,188,264 (91% need-based, 9% non-need-based). 82% of past graduating class borrowed through all loan programs. *Average indebtedness per student:* $36,545. *Average need-based loan:* Freshmen: $4044. Undergraduates: $4717. *Parent loans:* $3,282,779 (91% need-based, 9% non-need-based). *Programs:* Federal Direct (Subsidized and Unsubsidized Stafford, PLUS), Perkins, college/university.

WORK-STUDY *Federal work-study:* Total amount: $2,992,511; 1,249 jobs averaging $2396.

ATHLETIC AWARDS Total amount: $4,261,403 (76% need-based, 24% non-need-based).

APPLYING FOR FINANCIAL AID *Required financial aid form:* FAFSA. *Financial aid deadline (priority):* 3/15. *Notification date:* Continuous beginning 3/15. Students must reply within 3 weeks of notification.

CONTACT Mr. Stephen C. Howell, Director of Financial Aid, Ashland University, 401 College Avenue, Ashland, OH 44805-3702, 419-289-5944 or toll-free 800-882-1548. *Fax:* 419-289-5976. *E-mail:* showell@ashland.edu.

ASHWORTH COLLEGE
Norcross, GA

CONTACT Financial Aid Office, Ashworth College, 430 Technology Parkway, Norcross, GA 30092, 770-729-8400 or toll-free 800-957-5412.

ASPEN UNIVERSITY
Denver, CO

ABOUT THE INSTITUTION Independent, coed. 3 undergraduate majors.

CONTACT Jennifer Quinn, Director of Financial Aid, Aspen University, 720 South Colorado Bouleavrd #1150N, Denver, CO 80246, 800-441-4746. *Fax:* 303-336-1144. *E-mail:* jquinn@aspen.edu.

ASSUMPTION COLLEGE
Worcester, MA

Tuition & fees: $30,171	Average undergraduate aid package: $19,557

ABOUT THE INSTITUTION Independent Roman Catholic, coed. 43 undergraduate majors. Federal methodology is used as a basis for awarding need-based institutional aid.

UNDERGRADUATE EXPENSES for 2009–10 *Comprehensive fee:* $36,511 includes full-time tuition ($29,806), mandatory fees ($365), and room and board ($6340). *College room only:* $3730. Full-time tuition and fees vary according to course load and reciprocity agreements. Room and board charges vary according to housing facility. *Part-time tuition:* $993.53 per credit hour. *Part-time fees:* $365 per year. Part-time tuition and fees vary according to course load.

FRESHMAN FINANCIAL AID (Fall 2009, est.) 468 applied for aid; of those 85% were deemed to have need. 100% of freshmen with need received aid; of those 18% had need fully met. *Average percent of need met:* 70% (excluding

resources awarded to replace EFC). *Average financial aid package:* $18,975 (excluding resources awarded to replace EFC). 16% of all full-time freshmen had no need and received non-need-based gift aid.

UNDERGRADUATE FINANCIAL AID (Fall 2009, est.) 1,846 applied for aid; of those 87% were deemed to have need. 99% of undergraduates with need received aid; of those 18% had need fully met. *Average percent of need met:* 71% (excluding resources awarded to replace EFC). *Average financial aid package:* $19,557 (excluding resources awarded to replace EFC). 19% of all full-time undergraduates had no need and received non-need-based gift aid.

GIFT AID (NEED-BASED) *Total amount:* $23,439,269 (7% federal, 4% state, 87% institutional, 2% external sources). *Receiving aid:* Freshmen: 78% (400); all full-time undergraduates: 75% (1,589). *Average award:* Freshmen: $16,000; Undergraduates: $15,334. *Scholarships, grants, and awards:* Federal Pell, FSEOG, state, private, college/university gift aid from institutional funds.

GIFT AID (NON-NEED-BASED) *Total amount:* $4,526,323 (95% institutional, 5% external sources). *Receiving aid:* Freshmen: 10% (49). Undergraduates: 6% (136). *Average award:* Freshmen: $9064. Undergraduates: $9517. *Scholarships, grants, and awards by category:* Academic interests/achievement: 158 awards ($1,573,875 total): general academic interests/achievements. Special characteristics: members of minority groups. *Tuition waivers:* Full or partial for employees or children of employees.

LOANS *Student loans:* $16,021,089 (66% need-based, 34% non-need-based). 83% of past graduating class borrowed through all loan programs. *Average indebtedness per student:* $24,382. *Average need-based loan:* Freshmen: $3430. Undergraduates: $4723. *Parent loans:* $7,016,669 (31% need-based, 69% non-need-based). *Programs:* Federal Direct (Subsidized and Unsubsidized Stafford, PLUS), FFEL (Subsidized and Unsubsidized Stafford), Perkins, state, college/university.

WORK-STUDY *Federal work-study:* Total amount: $393,194; 372 jobs averaging $1663.

ATHLETIC AWARDS Total amount: $1,179,164 (29% need-based, 71% non-need-based).

APPLYING FOR FINANCIAL AID *Required financial aid form:* FAFSA. *Financial aid deadline:* 2/15. *Notification date:* Continuous beginning 2/16. Students must reply by 5/1.

CONTACT Linda Mularczyk, Director of Financial Aid, Assumption College, 500 Salisbury Street, Worcester, MA 01609-1296, 508-767-7157 or toll-free 888-882-7786. *Fax:* 508-767-7376. *E-mail:* fa@assumption.edu.

ATHENS STATE UNIVERSITY
Athens, AL

Tuition & fees (AL res): $4350	Average undergraduate aid package: N/A

ABOUT THE INSTITUTION State-supported, coed. *Awards:* bachelor's degrees. 29 undergraduate majors. *Total enrollment:* 3,114. Undergraduates: 3,114. Federal methodology is used as a basis for awarding need-based institutional aid.

UNDERGRADUATE EXPENSES for 2009–10 *Application fee:* $30. *Tuition, area resident:* part-time $120 per credit hour. *Tuition, state resident:* full-time $3600; part-time $240 per credit hour. *Tuition, nonresident:* full-time $7200. *Required fees:* full-time $750; $25 per credit hour.

UNDERGRADUATE FINANCIAL AID (Fall 2009, est.) 1,058 applied for aid; of those 62% were deemed to have need. 1% of all full-time undergraduates had no need and received non-need-based gift aid.

GIFT AID (NEED-BASED) *Total amount:* $4,819,892 (95% federal, 1% state, 4% institutional). *Receiving aid:* All full-time undergraduates: 13% (201). *Scholarships, grants, and awards:* Federal Pell, FSEOG, state, private, college/university gift aid from institutional funds.

GIFT AID (NON-NEED-BASED) *Total amount:* $607,187 (78% institutional, 22% external sources). *Receiving aid:* Undergraduates: 33% (526).

LOANS *Student loans:* $9,883,395 (45% need-based, 55% non-need-based). *Parent loans:* $56,234 (100% need-based). *Programs:* Federal Direct (Subsidized and Unsubsidized Stafford, PLUS), college/university.

WORK-STUDY *Federal work-study:* Total amount: $92,194; 15 jobs averaging $6100.

APPLYING FOR FINANCIAL AID *Required financial aid form:* FAFSA. *Financial aid deadline:* Continuous. *Notification date:* Continuous beginning 5/1. Students must reply within 2 weeks of notification.

CONTACT Renee Stanford, Financial Aid Officer, Athens State University, 300 North Beaty Street, Athens, AL 35611, 256-233-8122 or toll-free 800-522-0272. *Fax:* 256-233-8178. *E-mail:* renee.stanford@athens.edu.

ATLANTA CHRISTIAN COLLEGE
East Point, GA

CONTACT Blair Walker, Director of Financial Aid, Atlanta Christian College, 2605 Ben Hill Road, East Point, GA 30344, 404-761-8861 or toll-free 800-776-1ACC. *Fax:* 404-669-2024. *E-mail:* blairw@acc.edu.

ATLANTIC COLLEGE
Guaynabo, PR

CONTACT Mrs. Velma Aponte, Financial Aid Coordinator, Atlantic College, Calle Colton #9, Guaynabo, PR 00970, 787-720-1092. *E-mail:* atlaneco@coqui.net.

ATLANTIC UNION COLLEGE
South Lancaster, MA

Tuition & fees: $17,066	Average undergraduate aid package: $12,049

ABOUT THE INSTITUTION Independent Seventh-day Adventist, coed. 21 undergraduate majors. Federal methodology is used as a basis for awarding need-based institutional aid.

UNDERGRADUATE EXPENSES for 2010–11 *Comprehensive fee:* $22,216 includes full-time tuition ($15,408), mandatory fees ($1658), and room and board ($5150). Full-time tuition and fees vary according to course load and program. Room and board charges vary according to board plan and housing facility. Part-time tuition and fees vary according to class time, course load, and program. *Payment plan:* Guaranteed tuition.

FRESHMAN FINANCIAL AID (Fall 2009, est.) 72 applied for aid; of those 93% were deemed to have need. 99% of freshmen with need received aid; of those 11% had need fully met. *Average percent of need met:* 63% (excluding resources awarded to replace EFC). *Average financial aid package:* $12,991 (excluding resources awarded to replace EFC). 20% of all full-time freshmen had no need and received non-need-based gift aid.

UNDERGRADUATE FINANCIAL AID (Fall 2009, est.) 407 applied for aid; of those 93% were deemed to have need. 99% of undergraduates with need received aid; of those 11% had need fully met. *Average percent of need met:* 64% (excluding resources awarded to replace EFC). *Average financial aid package:* $12,049 (excluding resources awarded to replace EFC). 10% of all full-time undergraduates had no need and received non-need-based gift aid.

GIFT AID (NEED-BASED) *Total amount:* $2,469,529 (48% federal, 4% state, 30% institutional, 18% external sources). *Receiving aid:* Freshmen: 63% (66); all full-time undergraduates: 74% (343). *Average award:* Freshmen: $7665; Undergraduates: $6876. *Scholarships, grants, and awards:* Federal Pell, FSEOG, state, private, college/university gift aid from institutional funds.

GIFT AID (NON-NEED-BASED) *Total amount:* $392,591 (1% state, 39% institutional, 60% external sources). *Receiving aid:* Freshmen: 1% (1). Undergraduates: 2% (11). *Average award:* Freshmen: $3069. Undergraduates: $2963. *Scholarships, grants, and awards by category: Academic interests/ achievement:* 77 awards ($153,179 total): business, computer science, education, English, general academic interests/achievements, health fields, mathematics, premedicine, religion/biblical studies. *Creative arts/performance:* 6 awards ($8981 total): music. *Special achievements/activities:* 23 awards ($61,897 total): leadership. *Special characteristics:* 66 awards ($115,653 total): adult students, children of faculty/staff, international students, siblings of current students. *Tuition waivers:* Full or partial for employees or children of employees, senior citizens.

LOANS *Student loans:* $3,854,987 (85% need-based, 15% non-need-based). 82% of past graduating class borrowed through all loan programs. *Average indebtedness per student:* $39,013. *Average need-based loan:* Freshmen: $3691. Undergraduates: $4384. *Parent loans:* $268,260 (80% need-based, 20% non-need-based). *Programs:* FFEL (Subsidized and Unsubsidized Stafford, PLUS), Perkins, TERI Loans, Signature Loans, Campus Door Loans.

WORK-STUDY *Federal work-study:* Total amount: $149,416; 221 jobs averaging $686. *State or other work-study/employment:* Total amount: $497,406 (100% need-based). 240 part-time jobs averaging $1989.

APPLYING FOR FINANCIAL AID *Required financial aid forms:* FAFSA, institution's own form. *Financial aid deadline (priority):* 4/15. *Notification date:* Continuous beginning 4/5. Students must reply within 2 weeks of notification.

CONTACT Sandra Pereira, Director of Financial Aid, Atlantic Union College, PO Box 1000, South Lancaster, MA 01561-1000, 978-368-2284 or toll-free 800-282-2030. *Fax:* 978-368-2283. *E-mail:* sandra.pereira@auc.edu.

AUBURN UNIVERSITY
Auburn University, AL

Tuition & fees (AL res): $6972	Average undergraduate aid package: $8740

ABOUT THE INSTITUTION State-supported, coed. 131 undergraduate majors. Federal methodology is used as a basis for awarding need-based institutional aid.

UNDERGRADUATE EXPENSES for 2009–10 *Tuition, state resident:* full-time $6240; part-time $258 per credit hour. *Tuition, nonresident:* full-time $18,720; part-time $774 per credit hour. *Required fees:* full-time $732. Full-time tuition and fees vary according to course load, program, and reciprocity agreements. Part-time tuition and fees vary according to course load, program, and reciprocity agreements. *College room and board:* $8972; *Room only:* $4038. Room and board charges vary according to board plan and housing facility. *Payment plans:* Tuition prepayment, installment.

FRESHMAN FINANCIAL AID (Fall 2009, est.) 2,097 applied for aid; of those 52% were deemed to have need. 100% of freshmen with need received aid; of those 22% had need fully met. *Average percent of need met:* 56% (excluding resources awarded to replace EFC). *Average financial aid package:* $9182 (excluding resources awarded to replace EFC). 24% of all full-time freshmen had no need and received non-need-based gift aid.

UNDERGRADUATE FINANCIAL AID (Fall 2009, est.) 9,590 applied for aid; of those 57% were deemed to have need. 100% of undergraduates with need received aid; of those 17% had need fully met. *Average percent of need met:* 54% (excluding resources awarded to replace EFC). *Average financial aid package:* $8740 (excluding resources awarded to replace EFC). 13% of all full-time undergraduates had no need and received non-need-based gift aid.

GIFT AID (NEED-BASED) *Total amount:* $20,786,578 (51% federal, 5% state, 33% institutional, 11% external sources). *Receiving aid:* Freshmen: 22% (886); all full-time undergraduates: 20% (3,647). *Average award:* Freshmen: $6195; Undergraduates: $5419. *Scholarships, grants, and awards:* Federal Pell, FSEOG, state, private, college/university gift aid from institutional funds.

GIFT AID (NON-NEED-BASED) *Total amount:* $30,359,908 (8% state, 52% institutional, 40% external sources). *Receiving aid:* Freshmen: 4% (154). Undergraduates: 3% (484). *Average award:* Freshmen: $4474. Undergraduates: $4600. *Scholarships, grants, and awards by category: Academic interests/ achievement:* agriculture, architecture, biological sciences, business, communication, computer science, education, engineering/technologies, English, foreign languages, general academic interests/achievements, health fields, home economics, humanities, mathematics, physical sciences, premedicine, social sciences. *Creative arts/performance:* applied art and design, art/fine arts, cinema/film/ broadcasting, creative writing, journalism/publications, music, performing arts, theater/drama. *Special achievements/activities:* cheerleading/drum major, leadership, memberships. *Special characteristics:* children and siblings of alumni, children of faculty/staff, children of union members/company employees, ethnic background, local/state students, married students, out-of-state students. *Tuition waivers:* Full or partial for employees or children of employees.

LOANS *Student loans:* $59,615,531 (63% need-based, 37% non-need-based). 40% of past graduating class borrowed through all loan programs. *Average indebtedness per student:* $22,232. *Average need-based loan:* Freshmen: $3254. Undergraduates: $4373. *Parent loans:* $15,276,785 (31% need-based, 69% non-need-based). *Programs:* Federal Direct (Subsidized and Unsubsidized Stafford, PLUS), Perkins, Federal Nursing, college/university.

WORK-STUDY *Federal work-study:* Total amount: $1,081,335; 346 jobs averaging $2521.

ATHLETIC AWARDS Total amount: $8,073,870 (2% need-based, 98% non-need-based).

APPLYING FOR FINANCIAL AID *Required financial aid form:* FAFSA. *Financial aid deadline (priority):* 3/1. *Notification date:* Continuous beginning 10/2. Students must reply by 5/1.

CONTACT Mr. Mike Reynolds, Director of Student Financial Services, Auburn University, 203 Mary Martin Hall, Auburn University, AL 36849, 334-844-4634 or toll-free 800-AUBURN9 (in-state). *Fax:* 334-844-6085. *E-mail:* finaid7@auburn.edu.

AUBURN UNIVERSITY MONTGOMERY
Montgomery, AL

Tuition & fees (AL res): $6300	Average undergraduate aid package: N/A

ABOUT THE INSTITUTION State-supported, coed. 24 undergraduate majors. Federal methodology is used as a basis for awarding need-based institutional aid.

UNDERGRADUATE EXPENSES for 2009–10 *Tuition, state resident:* full-time $5970; part-time $188 per credit hour. *Tuition, nonresident:* full-time $17,250; part-time $564 per credit hour. *Required fees:* full-time $330; $8 per semester hour or $45 per term. Full-time tuition and fees vary according to course load. Part-time tuition and fees vary according to course load. *College room and board: Room only:* $3720. Room and board charges vary according to housing facility.

FRESHMAN FINANCIAL AID (Fall 2009, est.) 371 applied for aid; of those 72% were deemed to have need. 100% of freshmen with need received aid; of those 47% had need fully met.

UNDERGRADUATE FINANCIAL AID (Fall 2009, est.) 2,113 applied for aid; of those 78% were deemed to have need. 100% of undergraduates with need received aid; of those 33% had need fully met.

GIFT AID (NEED-BASED) *Total amount:* $9,915,409 (79% federal, 1% state, 14% institutional, 6% external sources). *Receiving aid:* Freshmen: 23% (200); all full-time undergraduates: 26% (1,213). *Average award:* Freshmen: $4732; Undergraduates: $4610. *Scholarships, grants, and awards:* Federal Pell, state, college/university gift aid from institutional funds.

GIFT AID (NON-NEED-BASED) *Scholarships, grants, and awards by category: Academic interests/achievement:* general academic interests/achievements. *Tuition waivers:* Full or partial for employees or children of employees.

LOANS *Student loans:* $28,687,521 (100% need-based). *Average need-based loan:* Freshmen: $3420. Undergraduates: $4241. *Parent loans:* $584,272 (100% need-based). *Programs:* FFEL (Subsidized and Unsubsidized Stafford, PLUS), Perkins.

WORK-STUDY *Federal work-study:* Total amount: $278,011; 58 jobs averaging $3379.

APPLYING FOR FINANCIAL AID *Required financial aid form:* FAFSA. *Financial aid deadline (priority):* 3/1. *Notification date:* 6/1. Students must reply within 2 weeks of notification.

CONTACT Anthony Richey, Senior Director of Financial Aid, Auburn University Montgomery, PO Box 244023, Montgomery, AL 36124-4023, 334-244-3571 or toll-free 800-227-2649 (in-state). *Fax:* 334-244-3913. *E-mail:* arichey@aum.edu.

AUGSBURG COLLEGE
Minneapolis, MN

Tuition & fees: $28,864	Average undergraduate aid package: $18,744

ABOUT THE INSTITUTION Independent Lutheran, coed. 64 undergraduate majors. Federal methodology is used as a basis for awarding need-based institutional aid.

UNDERGRADUATE EXPENSES for 2010–11 *Comprehensive fee:* $36,624 includes full-time tuition ($28,240), mandatory fees ($624), and room and board ($7760). *College room only:* $3920. Full-time tuition and fees vary according to location. Room and board charges vary according to board plan and housing facility. *Part-time tuition:* $3457 per course. Part-time tuition and fees vary according to course load and location. *Payment plan:* Installment.

FRESHMAN FINANCIAL AID (Fall 2009, est.) 452 applied for aid; of those 92% were deemed to have need. 100% of freshmen with need received aid; of those 24% had need fully met. *Average percent of need met:* 75% (excluding resources awarded to replace EFC). *Average financial aid package:* $23,896 (excluding resources awarded to replace EFC). 8% of all full-time freshmen had no need and received non-need-based gift aid.

UNDERGRADUATE FINANCIAL AID (Fall 2009, est.) 2,491 applied for aid; of those 82% were deemed to have need. 100% of undergraduates with need

received aid; of those 12% had need fully met. *Average percent of need met:* 63% (excluding resources awarded to replace EFC). *Average financial aid package:* $18,744 (excluding resources awarded to replace EFC). 5% of all full-time undergraduates had no need and received non-need-based gift aid.

GIFT AID (NEED-BASED) *Total amount:* $28,201,432 (17% federal, 14% state, 64% institutional, 5% external sources). *Receiving aid:* Freshmen: 89% (410); all full-time undergraduates: 74% (1,859). *Average award:* Freshmen: $19,290; Undergraduates: $14,459. *Scholarships, grants, and awards:* Federal Pell, FSEOG, state, private, college/university gift aid from institutional funds, Federal Nursing.

GIFT AID (NON-NEED-BASED) *Total amount:* $2,304,851 (87% institutional, 13% external sources). *Receiving aid:* Freshmen: 13% (61). Undergraduates: 11% (286). *Average award:* Freshmen: $9460. Undergraduates: $7532. *Scholarships, grants, and awards by category: Academic interests/achievement:* biological sciences, business, communication, computer science, education, English, foreign languages, general academic interests/achievements, health fields, international studies, mathematics, physical sciences, religion/biblical studies, social sciences. *Creative arts/performance:* art/fine arts, music, performing arts, theater/drama. *Special achievements/activities:* community service, general special achievements/activities, junior miss, leadership, religious involvement. *Special characteristics:* children and siblings of alumni, international students, members of minority groups, relatives of clergy, siblings of current students. *Tuition waivers:* Full or partial for children of alumni, employees or children of employees, senior citizens.

LOANS *Student loans:* $20,899,338 (71% need-based, 29% non-need-based). 93% of past graduating class borrowed through all loan programs. *Average indebtedness per student:* $28,988. *Average need-based loan:* Freshmen: $3419. Undergraduates: $4695. *Parent loans:* $2,616,351 (11% need-based, 89% non-need-based). *Programs:* Federal Direct (Subsidized and Unsubsidized Stafford, PLUS), FFEL (Subsidized and Unsubsidized Stafford, PLUS), Perkins, Federal Nursing, state.

WORK-STUDY *Federal work-study:* Total amount: $1,306,172; 466 jobs averaging $2741. *State or other work-study/employment:* Total amount: $1,640,001 (99% need-based, 1% non-need-based). 571 part-time jobs averaging $2841.

APPLYING FOR FINANCIAL AID *Required financial aid form:* FAFSA. *Financial aid deadline:* 8/15 (priority: 5/1). *Notification date:* Continuous beginning 3/1. Students must reply within 3 weeks of notification.

CONTACT Mr. Paul L. Terrio, Director of Student Financial Services, Augsburg College, 2211 Riverside Avenue, Minneapolis, MN 55454-1351, 612-330-1049 or toll-free 800-788-5678. *Fax:* 612-330-1308. *E-mail:* terriop@augsburg.edu.

AUGUSTANA COLLEGE
Rock Island, IL

Tuition & fees: $31,326	Average undergraduate aid package: $25,819

ABOUT THE INSTITUTION Independent religious, coed. 69 undergraduate majors. Federal methodology is used as a basis for awarding need-based institutional aid.

UNDERGRADUATE EXPENSES for 2009–10 *Comprehensive fee:* $39,276 includes full-time tuition ($31,326) and room and board ($7950). Full-time tuition and fees vary according to student level. Room and board charges vary according to board plan and housing facility. *Part-time tuition:* $1350 per credit hour. Part-time tuition and fees vary according to course load. *Payment plans:* Tuition prepayment, installment.

FRESHMAN FINANCIAL AID (Fall 2009, est.) 551 applied for aid; of those 80% were deemed to have need. 100% of freshmen with need received aid; of those 42% had need fully met. *Average percent of need met:* 88% (excluding resources awarded to replace EFC). *Average financial aid package:* $26,748 (excluding resources awarded to replace EFC). 27% of all full-time freshmen had no need and received non-need-based gift aid.

UNDERGRADUATE FINANCIAL AID (Fall 2009, est.) 2,046 applied for aid; of those 84% were deemed to have need. 99% of undergraduates with need received aid; of those 42% had need fully met. *Average percent of need met:* 85% (excluding resources awarded to replace EFC). *Average financial aid package:* $25,819 (excluding resources awarded to replace EFC). 29% of all full-time undergraduates had no need and received non-need-based gift aid.

GIFT AID (NEED-BASED) *Total amount:* $25,783,109 (7% federal, 11% state, 80% institutional, 2% external sources). *Receiving aid:* Freshmen: 71% (439); all full-time undergraduates: 69% (1,689). *Average award:* Freshmen: $17,907;

Undergraduates: $15,738. *Scholarships, grants, and awards:* Federal Pell, FSEOG, state, private, college/university gift aid from institutional funds.
GIFT AID (NON-NEED-BASED) *Total amount:* $10,041,649 (98% institutional, 2% external sources). *Receiving aid:* Freshmen: 14% (85). Undergraduates: 10% (256). *Average award:* Freshmen: $13,232. Undergraduates: $11,868. *Scholarships, grants, and awards by category: Academic interests/achievement:* 2,154 awards ($19,393,713 total): biological sciences, business, communication, computer science, education, English, foreign languages, general academic interests/achievements, humanities, mathematics, physical sciences, religion/biblical studies, social sciences. *Creative arts/performance:* 471 awards ($881,385 total): art/fine arts, creative writing, debating, music, theater/drama. *Special characteristics:* 423 awards ($2,516,970 total): children and siblings of alumni, children of faculty/staff, ethnic background, international students, members of minority groups, religious affiliation, siblings of current students. *Tuition waivers:* Full or partial for employees or children of employees.
LOANS *Student loans:* $14,898,892 (63% need-based, 37% non-need-based). *Average need-based loan:* Freshmen: $5856. Undergraduates: $7306. *Parent loans:* $5,207,695 (33% need-based, 67% non-need-based). *Programs:* Federal Direct (Subsidized and Unsubsidized Stafford, PLUS), Perkins.
WORK-STUDY *Federal work-study:* Total amount: $2,351,756; 1,132 jobs averaging $2058.
APPLYING FOR FINANCIAL AID *Required financial aid forms:* FAFSA, institution's own form. *Financial aid deadline (priority):* 4/1. *Notification date:* Continuous. Students must reply by 5/1.
CONTACT Sue Standley, Director of Financial Aid, Augustana College, 639 38th Street, Rock Island, IL 61201-2296, 309-794-7207 or toll-free 800-798-8100. *Fax:* 309-794-7174. *E-mail:* suestandley@augustana.edu.

AUGUSTANA COLLEGE
Sioux Falls, SD

Tuition & fees: $23,550	Average undergraduate aid package: $19,740

ABOUT THE INSTITUTION Independent religious, coed. 58 undergraduate majors. Federal methodology is used as a basis for awarding need-based institutional aid.
UNDERGRADUATE EXPENSES for 2009–10 *Comprehensive fee:* $29,738 includes full-time tuition ($23,276), mandatory fees ($274), and room and board ($6188). *College room only:* $2976. Full-time tuition and fees vary according to course load and degree level. Room and board charges vary according to board plan and housing facility. *Part-time tuition:* $352 per credit hour. Part-time tuition and fees vary according to course load and degree level. *Payment plan:* Installment.
FRESHMAN FINANCIAL AID (Fall 2009, est.) 389 applied for aid; of those 82% were deemed to have need. 100% of freshmen with need received aid; of those 23% had need fully met. *Average percent of need met:* 96% (excluding resources awarded to replace EFC). *Average financial aid package:* $20,991 (excluding resources awarded to replace EFC). 25% of all full-time freshmen had no need and received non-need-based gift aid.
UNDERGRADUATE FINANCIAL AID (Fall 2009, est.) 1,367 applied for aid; of those 84% were deemed to have need. 100% of undergraduates with need received aid; of those 18% had need fully met. *Average percent of need met:* 89% (excluding resources awarded to replace EFC). *Average financial aid package:* $19,740 (excluding resources awarded to replace EFC). 29% of all full-time undergraduates had no need and received non-need-based gift aid.
GIFT AID (NEED-BASED) *Total amount:* $14,448,216 (17% federal, 78% institutional, 5% external sources). *Receiving aid:* Freshmen: 74% (319); all full-time undergraduates: 69% (1,155). *Average award:* Freshmen: $16,594; Undergraduates: $14,921. *Scholarships, grants, and awards:* Federal Pell, FSEOG, state, private, college/university gift aid from institutional funds, need-linked special talent scholarships, minority scholarships.
GIFT AID (NON-NEED-BASED) *Total amount:* $5,882,036 (1% federal, 6% state, 88% institutional, 5% external sources). *Receiving aid:* Freshmen: 73% (316). Undergraduates: 68% (1,131). *Average award:* Freshmen: $11,911. Undergraduates: $10,019. *Scholarships, grants, and awards by category: Academic interests/achievement:* biological sciences, business, communication, computer science, education, English, foreign languages, general academic interests/achievements, health fields, humanities, international studies, mathematics, physical sciences, premedicine, religion/biblical studies, social sciences. *Creative arts/performance:* art/fine arts, creative writing, music, performing arts, theater/drama. *Special achievements/activities:* general special achievements/

activities, leadership. *Special characteristics:* children and siblings of alumni, children of current students, children of faculty/staff, ethnic background, international students, local/state students, members of minority groups, religious affiliation, siblings of current students, spouses of current students, veterans. *Tuition waivers:* Full or partial for employees or children of employees.
LOANS *Student loans:* $11,313,704 (62% need-based, 38% non-need-based). 76% of past graduating class borrowed through all loan programs. *Average indebtedness per student:* $29,531. *Average need-based loan:* Freshmen: $4944. Undergraduates: $5461. *Parent loans:* $942,412 (13% need-based, 87% non-need-based). *Programs:* Federal Direct (Subsidized and Unsubsidized Stafford, PLUS), FFEL (Subsidized and Unsubsidized Stafford, PLUS), Perkins, Federal Nursing, college/university, Minnesota SELF Loans, private alternative loans.
WORK-STUDY *Federal work-study:* Total amount: $641,242; 334 jobs averaging $1595. *State or other work-study/employment:* Total amount: $205,912 (8% need-based, 92% non-need-based). 227 part-time jobs averaging $1275.
ATHLETIC AWARDS Total amount: $2,218,413 (43% need-based, 57% non-need-based).
APPLYING FOR FINANCIAL AID *Required financial aid form:* FAFSA. *Financial aid deadline (priority):* 3/1. *Notification date:* Continuous beginning 4/1. Students must reply by 5/1 or within 3 weeks of notification.
CONTACT Ms. Brenda L. Murtha, Director of Financial Aid, Augustana College, 2001 South Summit Avenue, Sioux Falls, SD 57197, 605-274-5216 or toll-free 800-727-2844 Ext. 5516 (in-state), 800-727-2844 (out-of-state). *Fax:* 605-274-5295. *E-mail:* brenda.murtha@augie.edu.

AUGUSTA STATE UNIVERSITY
Augusta, GA

ABOUT THE INSTITUTION State-supported, coed. *Awards:* associate, bachelor's, and master's degrees and post-master's certificates. 32 undergraduate majors. *Total enrollment:* 6,689. Undergraduates: 5,525. Freshmen: 941.
GIFT AID (NEED-BASED) *Scholarships, grants, and awards:* Federal Pell, FSEOG, state, private, college/university gift aid from institutional funds.
GIFT AID (NON-NEED-BASED) *Scholarships, grants, and awards by category: Academic interests/achievement:* biological sciences, business, communication, computer science, education, English, general academic interests/achievements, health fields, mathematics, military science, physical sciences, social sciences. *Creative arts/performance:* art/fine arts, creative writing, general creative arts/performance, music, performing arts, theater/drama. *Special achievements/activities:* community service, general special achievements/activities, hobbies/interests, leadership. *Special characteristics:* general special characteristics, handicapped students, local/state students.
LOANS *Programs:* FFEL (Subsidized and Unsubsidized Stafford, PLUS), Perkins, state.
APPLYING FOR FINANCIAL AID *Required financial aid form:* FAFSA.
CONTACT Ms. Roxanne Padgett, Assistant Director of Financial Aid, Augusta State University, 2500 Walton Way, Augusta, GA 30904-2200, 706-737-1431 or toll-free 800-341-4373. *Fax:* 706-737-1777. *E-mail:* bpadgett@aug.edu.

AURORA UNIVERSITY
Aurora, IL

Tuition & fees: $18,700	Average undergraduate aid package: $16,334

ABOUT THE INSTITUTION Independent, coed. 28 undergraduate majors. Federal methodology is used as a basis for awarding need-based institutional aid.
UNDERGRADUATE EXPENSES for 2010–11 *Comprehensive fee:* $27,500 includes full-time tuition ($18,600), mandatory fees ($100), and room and board ($8800). Full-time tuition and fees vary according to location. Room and board charges vary according to board plan, housing facility, and location. *Part-time tuition:* $550 per semester hour. Part-time tuition and fees vary according to course load, location, and program. *Payment plans:* Installment, deferred payment.
FRESHMAN FINANCIAL AID (Fall 2009, est.) 395 applied for aid; of those 89% were deemed to have need. 100% of freshmen with need received aid; of those 37% had need fully met. *Average percent of need met:* 90% (excluding resources awarded to replace EFC). *Average financial aid package:* $17,761 (excluding resources awarded to replace EFC). 15% of all full-time freshmen had no need and received non-need-based gift aid.

UNDERGRADUATE FINANCIAL AID (Fall 2009, est.) 1,812 applied for aid; of those 90% were deemed to have need. 100% of undergraduates with need received aid; of those 40% had need fully met. *Average percent of need met:* 92% (excluding resources awarded to replace EFC). *Average financial aid package:* $16,334 (excluding resources awarded to replace EFC). 19% of all full-time undergraduates had no need and received non-need-based gift aid.
GIFT AID (NEED-BASED) *Total amount:* $8,595,588 (42% federal, 39% state, 19% institutional). *Receiving aid:* Freshmen: 63% (264); all full-time undergraduates: 60% (1,242). *Average award:* Freshmen: $7450; Undergraduates: $6587. *Scholarships, grants, and awards:* Federal Pell, FSEOG, state, private, college/university gift aid from institutional funds.
GIFT AID (NON-NEED-BASED) *Total amount:* $13,926,486 (1% federal, 97% institutional, 2% external sources). *Receiving aid:* Freshmen: 83% (344). Undergraduates: 74% (1,527). *Average award:* Freshmen: $9238. Undergraduates: $7301. *Scholarships, grants, and awards by category: Academic interests/achievement:* 1,912 awards ($12,803,369 total): education, general academic interests/achievements, mathematics. *Creative arts/performance:* 56 awards ($87,350 total): music, theater/drama. *Special achievements/activities:* 144 awards ($313,376 total): general special achievements/activities. *Special characteristics:* 290 awards ($769,050 total): children and siblings of alumni, children of educators, children of faculty/staff, members of minority groups, out-of-state students, parents of current students, siblings of current students, spouses of current students. *Tuition waivers:* Full or partial for employees or children of employees, senior citizens.
LOANS *Student loans:* $13,203,662 (43% need-based, 57% non-need-based). 75% of past graduating class borrowed through all loan programs. *Average indebtedness per student:* $23,935. *Average need-based loan:* Freshmen: $3301. Undergraduates: $4364. *Parent loans:* $1,238,873 (100% non-need-based). *Programs:* FFEL (Subsidized and Unsubsidized Stafford, PLUS), Perkins, college/university.
WORK-STUDY *Federal work-study:* Total amount: $1,482,723; 871 jobs averaging $1621. *State or other work-study/employment:* Total amount: $224,120 (100% non-need-based). Part-time jobs available.
APPLYING FOR FINANCIAL AID *Required financial aid form:* FAFSA. *Financial aid deadline (priority):* 4/15. *Notification date:* Continuous beginning 3/1. Students must reply by 5/1 or within 3 weeks of notification.
CONTACT Mrs. Heather McKane, Dean of Student Financial Services, Aurora University, 347 South Gladstone Avenue, Aurora, IL 60506-4892, 630-844-6190 or toll-free 800-742-5281. *Fax:* 630-844-6191. *E-mail:* finaid@aurora.edu.

AUSTIN COLLEGE
Sherman, TX

Tuition & fees: $29,235	Average undergraduate aid package: $26,331

ABOUT THE INSTITUTION Independent Presbyterian, coed. 27 undergraduate majors. Federal methodology is used as a basis for awarding need-based institutional aid.
UNDERGRADUATE EXPENSES for 2010–11 *Comprehensive fee:* $38,784 includes full-time tuition ($29,075), mandatory fees ($160), and room and board ($9549). Full-time tuition and fees vary according to student level. Room and board charges vary according to board plan. *Part-time tuition:* $4216 per course. *Payment plan:* Installment.
FRESHMAN FINANCIAL AID (Fall 2009, est.) 341 applied for aid; of those 83% were deemed to have need. 100% of freshmen with need received aid; of those 95% had need fully met. *Average percent of need met:* 95% (excluding resources awarded to replace EFC). *Average financial aid package:* $27,388 (excluding resources awarded to replace EFC). 15% of all full-time freshmen had no need and received non-need-based gift aid.
UNDERGRADUATE FINANCIAL AID (Fall 2009, est.) 980 applied for aid; of those 83% were deemed to have need. 100% of undergraduates with need received aid; of those 95% had need fully met. *Average percent of need met:* 95% (excluding resources awarded to replace EFC). *Average financial aid package:* $26,331 (excluding resources awarded to replace EFC). 22% of all full-time undergraduates had no need and received non-need-based gift aid.
GIFT AID (NEED-BASED) *Total amount:* $15,239,293 (11% federal, 12% state, 75% institutional, 2% external sources). *Receiving aid:* Freshmen: 68% (282); all full-time undergraduates: 61% (813). *Average award:* Freshmen: $21,036; Undergraduates: $19,001. *Scholarships, grants, and awards:* Federal Pell, FSEOG, state, private, college/university gift aid from institutional funds.

GIFT AID (NON-NEED-BASED) *Total amount:* $7,157,713 (96% institutional, 4% external sources). *Receiving aid:* Freshmen: 41% (168). Undergraduates: 30% (394). *Average award:* Freshmen: $16,020. Undergraduates: $12,949. *Scholarships, grants, and awards by category: Academic interests/achievement:* 910 awards ($9,811,621 total): biological sciences, business, communication, education, engineering/technologies, English, foreign languages, general academic interests/achievements, health fields, humanities, international studies, physical sciences, premedicine, religion/biblical studies, social sciences. *Creative arts/performance:* 50 awards ($228,075 total): art/fine arts, music, theater/drama. *Special achievements/activities:* 232 awards ($1,294,656 total): community service, general special achievements/activities, leadership, religious involvement. *Special characteristics:* 478 awards ($4,392,347 total): children of faculty/staff, ethnic background, first-generation college students, handicapped students, international students, local/state students, relatives of clergy. *Tuition waivers:* Full or partial for employees or children of employees.
LOANS *Student loans:* $10,709,273 (50% need-based, 50% non-need-based). *Average need-based loan:* Freshmen: $4074. Undergraduates: $6200. *Parent loans:* $8,297,472 (8% need-based, 92% non-need-based). *Programs:* FFEL (Subsidized and Unsubsidized Stafford, PLUS), Perkins, state, college/university, alternative loan options through various lenders.
WORK-STUDY *Federal work-study:* Total amount: $620,708; 297 jobs averaging $1628. *State or other work-study/employment:* Total amount: $301,493 (7% need-based, 93% non-need-based). 217 part-time jobs averaging $1469.
APPLYING FOR FINANCIAL AID *Required financial aid form:* FAFSA. *Financial aid deadline (priority):* 4/1. *Notification date:* Continuous beginning 3/1. Students must reply by 5/1.
CONTACT Mrs. Laurie Coulter, Assistant Vice President for Institutional Enrollment and Executive Director of Financial Aid, Austin College, 900 North Grand Avenue, Sherman, TX 75090, 903-813-2900 or toll-free 800-442-5363. *Fax:* 903-813-3198. *E-mail:* finaid@austincollege.edu.

AUSTIN GRADUATE SCHOOL OF THEOLOGY
Austin, TX

Tuition & fees: $7100	Average undergraduate aid package: N/A

ABOUT THE INSTITUTION Independent religious, coed. 1 undergraduate major. Both federal and institutional methodology are used as a basis for awarding need-based institutional aid.
UNDERGRADUATE EXPENSES for 2009–10 *Tuition:* full-time $7000; part-time $275 per semester hour. *Required fees:* full-time $100; $50 per term. Full-time tuition and fees vary according to course load. Part-time tuition and fees vary according to course load. *Payment plan:* Installment.
GIFT AID (NEED-BASED) *Total amount:* $47,625 (74% federal, 26% institutional). *Scholarships, grants, and awards:* Federal Pell, FSEOG, college/university gift aid from institutional funds.
GIFT AID (NON-NEED-BASED) *Scholarships, grants, and awards by category: Academic interests/achievement:* religion/biblical studies. *Special achievements/activities:* religious involvement. *Tuition waivers:* Full or partial for employees or children of employees.
LOANS *Student loans:* $82,200 (100% need-based). *Programs:* Federal Direct (Subsidized and Unsubsidized Stafford, PLUS).
WORK-STUDY *Federal work-study:* Total amount: $3590; 4 jobs averaging $900.
APPLYING FOR FINANCIAL AID *Required financial aid forms:* FAFSA, institution's own form. *Financial aid deadline:* Continuous.
CONTACT David Arthur, Financial Aid Officer, Austin Graduate School of Theology, 7640 Guadalupe Street, Austin, TX 78752, 512-476-2772 Ext. 105 or toll-free 866-AUS-GRAD. *Fax:* 512-476-3919. *E-mail:* darthur@austingrad.edu.

AUSTIN PEAY STATE UNIVERSITY
Clarksville, TN

Tuition & fees (TN res): $5808	Average undergraduate aid package: $8513

ABOUT THE INSTITUTION State-supported, coed. 35 undergraduate majors. Federal methodology is used as a basis for awarding need-based institutional aid.

UNDERGRADUATE EXPENSES for 2009–10 *Tuition, state resident:* full-time $4584; part-time $191 per credit hour. *Tuition, nonresident:* full-time $16,512; part-time $688 per credit hour. *Required fees:* full-time $1224; $61.20 per credit hour. Full-time tuition and fees vary according to location and program. Part-time tuition and fees vary according to location and program. *College room and board:* $6120; *Room only:* $3750. Room and board charges vary according to board plan and housing facility. *Payment plan:* Installment.

FRESHMAN FINANCIAL AID (Fall 2008) 1,254 applied for aid; of those 78% were deemed to have need. 100% of freshmen with need received aid. *Average financial aid package:* $8962 (excluding resources awarded to replace EFC). 18% of all full-time freshmen had no need and received non-need-based gift aid.

UNDERGRADUATE FINANCIAL AID (Fall 2008) 5,721 applied for aid; of those 82% were deemed to have need. 99% of undergraduates with need received aid. *Average financial aid package:* $8513 (excluding resources awarded to replace EFC). 10% of all full-time undergraduates had no need and received non-need-based gift aid.

GIFT AID (NEED-BASED) *Total amount:* $15,453,300 (80% federal, 20% state). *Receiving aid:* Freshmen: 37% (495); all full-time undergraduates: 41% (2,626). *Average award:* Freshmen: $5319; Undergraduates: $4782. *Scholarships, grants, and awards:* Federal Pell, FSEOG, state, private, college/university gift aid from institutional funds.

GIFT AID (NON-NEED-BASED) *Total amount:* $13,830,181 (57% state, 14% institutional, 29% external sources). *Receiving aid:* Freshmen: 53% (706). Undergraduates: 31% (1,985). *Average award:* Freshmen: $4694. Undergraduates: $4655. *Scholarships, grants, and awards by category:* Academic interests/achievement: 466 awards ($1,103,946 total): agriculture, biological sciences, business, communication, computer science, education, English, foreign languages, general academic interests/achievements, health fields, humanities, international studies, mathematics, military science, physical sciences, social sciences. *Creative arts/performance:* 367 awards ($410,568 total): art/fine arts, creative writing, debating, journalism/publications, music, theater/drama. *Special achievements/activities:* 128 awards ($98,931 total): general special achievements/activities, leadership. *Special characteristics:* 128 awards ($237,896 total): children of educators, children of faculty/staff, ethnic background, general special characteristics, members of minority groups, veterans. *Tuition waivers:* Full or partial for employees or children of employees, senior citizens.

LOANS *Student loans:* $34,441,723 (46% need-based, 54% non-need-based). 56% of past graduating class borrowed through all loan programs. *Average indebtedness per student:* $20,158. *Average need-based loan:* Freshmen: $3383. Undergraduates: $4422. *Parent loans:* $1,833,715 (100% non-need-based). *Programs:* FFEL (Subsidized and Unsubsidized Stafford, PLUS), Perkins.

WORK-STUDY *Federal work-study:* Total amount: $456,544; 158 jobs averaging $1701. *State or other work-study/employment:* Total amount: $654,431 (100% non-need-based). 444 part-time jobs averaging $1474.

ATHLETIC AWARDS Total amount: $2,022,084 (100% non-need-based).

APPLYING FOR FINANCIAL AID *Required financial aid form:* FAFSA. *Financial aid deadline (priority):* 4/1. *Notification date:* Continuous beginning 5/1.

CONTACT Donna Price, Director of Student Financial Aid, Austin Peay State University, PO Box 4546, Clarksville, TN 37044, 931-221-7907 or toll-free 800-844-2778 (out-of-state). *Fax:* 931-221-6329. *E-mail:* priced@apsu.edu.

AVE MARIA UNIVERSITY
Ave Maria, FL

Tuition & fees: $17,745	Average undergraduate aid package: $17,162

ABOUT THE INSTITUTION Independent Roman Catholic, coed. *Awards:* bachelor's and master's degrees. 13 undergraduate majors. *Total enrollment:* 672. Undergraduates: 532. Freshmen: 228. Federal methodology is used as a basis for awarding need-based institutional aid.

UNDERGRADUATE EXPENSES for 2009–10 *Comprehensive fee:* $25,725 includes full-time tuition ($17,165), mandatory fees ($580), and room and board ($7980). *College room only:* $4355. *Part-time tuition:* $536.40 per credit hour.

FRESHMAN FINANCIAL AID (Fall 2009, est.) 216 applied for aid; of those 89% were deemed to have need. 100% of freshmen with need received aid; of those 18% had need fully met. *Average percent of need met:* 66% (excluding resources awarded to replace EFC). *Average financial aid package:* $14,730 (excluding resources awarded to replace EFC). 11% of all full-time freshmen had no need and received non-need-based gift aid.

UNDERGRADUATE FINANCIAL AID (Fall 2009, est.) 485 applied for aid; of those 87% were deemed to have need. 100% of undergraduates with need received aid; of those 21% had need fully met. *Average percent of need met:* 75% (excluding resources awarded to replace EFC). *Average financial aid package:* $17,162 (excluding resources awarded to replace EFC). 31% of all full-time undergraduates had no need and received non-need-based gift aid.

GIFT AID (NEED-BASED) *Total amount:* $8,015,689 (12% federal, 3% state, 81% institutional, 4% external sources). *Receiving aid:* Freshmen: 88% (191); all full-time undergraduates: 62% (418). *Average award:* Freshmen: $12,180; Undergraduates: $13,415. *Scholarships, grants, and awards:* Federal Pell, state, private, college/university gift aid from institutional funds.

GIFT AID (NON-NEED-BASED) *Total amount:* $1,098,028 (3% state, 93% institutional, 4% external sources). *Receiving aid:* Freshmen: 12% (27). Undergraduates: 10% (64). *Average award:* Freshmen: $10,697. Undergraduates: $13,459. *Scholarships, grants, and awards by category:* Special achievements/activities: leadership.

LOANS *Student loans:* $2,628,132 (73% need-based, 27% non-need-based). *Average need-based loan:* Freshmen: $3348. Undergraduates: $4025. *Parent loans:* $1,025,670 (37% need-based, 63% non-need-based). *Programs:* college/university.

WORK-STUDY *Federal work-study:* Total amount: $93,454; jobs available. *State or other work-study/employment:* Part-time jobs available.

APPLYING FOR FINANCIAL AID *Required financial aid forms:* FAFSA, state aid form. *Financial aid deadline (priority):* 4/1. *Notification date:* Continuous.

CONTACT Anne Hart, Financial Aid Director, Ave Maria University, 5050 Ave Maria Boulevard, Ave Maria, FL 34142, 239-280-1669 or toll-free 877-283-8648. *Fax:* 239-280-2566. *E-mail:* amufinancialaid@avemaria.edu.

AVERETT UNIVERSITY
Danville, VA

Tuition & fees: $22,112	Average undergraduate aid package: $15,682

ABOUT THE INSTITUTION Independent religious, coed. 54 undergraduate majors. Federal methodology is used as a basis for awarding need-based institutional aid.

UNDERGRADUATE EXPENSES for 2009–10 *Comprehensive fee:* $29,912 includes full-time tuition ($21,112), mandatory fees ($1000), and room and board ($7800). *College room only:* $5280. Full-time tuition and fees vary according to course load, degree level, location, and program. Room and board charges vary according to board plan and housing facility. *Part-time tuition:* $360 per credit hour. Part-time tuition and fees vary according to course load, degree level, location, and program. *Payment plan:* Installment.

FRESHMAN FINANCIAL AID (Fall 2009, est.) 199 applied for aid; of those 91% were deemed to have need. 100% of freshmen with need received aid; of those 16% had need fully met. *Average percent of need met:* 68% (excluding resources awarded to replace EFC). *Average financial aid package:* $15,272 (excluding resources awarded to replace EFC). 19% of all full-time freshmen had no need and received non-need-based gift aid.

UNDERGRADUATE FINANCIAL AID (Fall 2009, est.) 737 applied for aid; of those 91% were deemed to have need. 100% of undergraduates with need received aid; of those 21% had need fully met. *Average percent of need met:* 75% (excluding resources awarded to replace EFC). *Average financial aid package:* $15,682 (excluding resources awarded to replace EFC). 14% of all full-time undergraduates had no need and received non-need-based gift aid.

GIFT AID (NEED-BASED) *Total amount:* $8,285,246 (21% federal, 14% state, 58% institutional, 7% external sources). *Receiving aid:* Freshmen: 77% (179); all full-time undergraduates: 84% (659). *Average award:* Freshmen: $12,590; Undergraduates: $12,492. *Scholarships, grants, and awards:* Federal Pell, FSEOG, state, private, college/university gift aid from institutional funds.

GIFT AID (NON-NEED-BASED) *Total amount:* $1,466,707 (21% state, 65% institutional, 14% external sources). *Receiving aid:* Freshmen: 10% (23). Undergraduates: 10% (80). *Average award:* Freshmen: $8806. Undergraduates: $7934. *Scholarships, grants, and awards by category:* Academic interests/achievement: 110 awards ($236,814 total): biological sciences, business, education, engineering/technologies, English, foreign languages, general academic interests/achievements, health fields, home economics, humanities, mathematics, physical sciences, premedicine, religion/biblical studies. *Creative arts/performance:* 9 awards ($9287 total): art/fine arts, journalism/publications, music, theater/drama. *Special achievements/activities:* 13 awards ($42,376 total): general special achievements/activities, leadership, memberships, religious involvement. *Special characteristics:* 115 awards ($136,443 total): adult students, children and siblings of alumni, children of union members/company employees, first-generation college students, general special characteristics, international students, local/state students, out-of-state students, relatives of clergy, religious affiliation. *Tuition waivers:* Full or partial for employees or children of employees, senior citizens.

LOANS *Student loans:* $5,444,731 (73% need-based, 27% non-need-based). 67% of past graduating class borrowed through all loan programs. *Average indebtedness per student:* $30,943. *Average need-based loan:* Freshmen: $3131. Undergraduates: $3747. *Parent loans:* $1,861,707 (21% need-based, 79% non-need-based). *Programs:* Federal Direct (Subsidized and Unsubsidized Stafford, PLUS), FFEL (Subsidized and Unsubsidized Stafford, PLUS), Perkins, alternative loans.

WORK-STUDY *Federal work-study:* Total amount: $105,750; 152 jobs averaging $953.

APPLYING FOR FINANCIAL AID *Required financial aid forms:* FAFSA, state aid form. *Financial aid deadline (priority):* 4/1. *Notification date:* Continuous. Students must reply within 2 weeks of notification.

CONTACT Carl Bradsher, Dean of Financial Assistance, Averett University, 420 West Main Street, Danville, VA 24541-3692, 434-791-5646 or toll-free 800-AVERETT. *Fax:* 434-791-5647. *E-mail:* carl.bradsher@averett.edu.

AVILA UNIVERSITY
Kansas City, MO

ABOUT THE INSTITUTION Independent Roman Catholic, coed. 35 undergraduate majors.

GIFT AID (NEED-BASED) *Scholarships, grants, and awards:* Federal Pell, FSEOG, state, private, college/university gift aid from institutional funds, Federal Nursing.

GIFT AID (NON-NEED-BASED) *Scholarships, grants, and awards by category: Academic interests/achievement:* biological sciences, communication, general academic interests/achievements, humanities, premedicine. *Creative arts/performance:* art/fine arts, music, performing arts, theater/drama. *Special achievements/activities:* cheerleading/drum major, religious involvement. *Special characteristics:* children and siblings of alumni, children of current students, children of faculty/staff, relatives of clergy, religious affiliation, siblings of current students, spouses of current students.

LOANS *Programs:* FFEL (Subsidized and Unsubsidized Stafford, PLUS), Perkins.

WORK-STUDY *Federal work-study:* Total amount: $145,486; 161 jobs averaging $903. *State or other work-study/employment:* Total amount: $48,682 (100% need-based). 55 part-time jobs averaging $885.

APPLYING FOR FINANCIAL AID *Required financial aid forms:* FAFSA, institution's own form.

CONTACT Nancy Merz, Director of Financial Aid, Avila University, 11901 Wornall Road, Kansas City, MO 64145, 816-501-3782 or toll-free 800-GO-AVILA. *Fax:* 816-501-2462. *E-mail:* nancy.merz@avila.edu.

AZUSA PACIFIC UNIVERSITY
Azusa, CA

Tuition & fees: $27,750	Average undergraduate aid package: $21,269

ABOUT THE INSTITUTION Independent nondenominational, coed. 36 undergraduate majors.

UNDERGRADUATE EXPENSES for 2009–10 *Comprehensive fee:* $36,064 includes full-time tuition ($26,950), mandatory fees ($800), and room and board ($8314). *College room only:* $4840.

FRESHMAN FINANCIAL AID (Fall 2008) 1,020 applied for aid; of those 70% were deemed to have need. 100% of freshmen with need received aid; of those 24% had need fully met. *Average percent of need met:* 67% (excluding resources awarded to replace EFC). *Average financial aid package:* $20,918 (excluding resources awarded to replace EFC). 25% of all full-time freshmen had no need and received non-need-based gift aid.

UNDERGRADUATE FINANCIAL AID (Fall 2008) 3,793 applied for aid; of those 68% were deemed to have need. 100% of undergraduates with need received aid; of those 25% had need fully met. *Average percent of need met:* 64% (excluding resources awarded to replace EFC). *Average financial aid package:* $21,269 (excluding resources awarded to replace EFC). 26% of all full-time undergraduates had no need and received non-need-based gift aid.

GIFT AID (NEED-BASED) *Total amount:* $34,876,765 (27% federal, 20% state, 48% institutional, 5% external sources). *Receiving aid:* Freshmen: 66% (714); all full-time undergraduates: 61% (2,513). *Average award:* Freshmen: $15,616; Undergraduates: $13,386. *Scholarships, grants, and awards:* Federal Pell, FSEOG, state, private, college/university gift aid from institutional funds, Federal Nursing.

GIFT AID (NON-NEED-BASED) *Total amount:* $10,261,731 (18% federal, 71% institutional, 11% external sources). *Receiving aid:* Freshmen: 57% (623). Undergraduates: 57% (2,349). *Average award:* Freshmen: $8103. Undergraduates: $5755. *Scholarships, grants, and awards by category: Academic interests/achievement:* general academic interests/achievements. *Creative arts/performance:* general creative arts/performance. *Special achievements/activities:* leadership. *Special characteristics:* members of minority groups, religious affiliation.

LOANS *Student loans:* $20,906,165 (77% need-based, 23% non-need-based). *Average need-based loan:* Freshmen: $4068. Undergraduates: $6235. *Parent loans:* $15,770,438 (48% need-based, 52% non-need-based). *Programs:* FFEL (Subsidized and Unsubsidized Stafford, PLUS), Perkins, Federal Nursing.

WORK-STUDY *Federal work-study:* Total amount: $1,005,226; jobs available.

ATHLETIC AWARDS Total amount: $2,872,433 (38% need-based, 62% non-need-based).

APPLYING FOR FINANCIAL AID *Required financial aid forms:* FAFSA, institution's own form. *Financial aid deadline:* 7/1 (priority: 3/2). *Notification date:* Continuous beginning 3/1. Students must reply within 3 weeks of notification.

CONTACT Todd Ross, Interim Director, Student Financial Services, Azusa Pacific University, 901 East Alosta Avenue, PO Box 7000, Azusa, CA 91702-7000, 626-812-3009 or toll-free 800-TALK-APU. *E-mail:* tross@apu.edu.

BABSON COLLEGE
Wellesley, MA

Tuition & fees: $37,824	Average undergraduate aid package: $31,719

ABOUT THE INSTITUTION Independent, coed. 24 undergraduate majors. Both federal and institutional methodology are used as a basis for awarding need-based institutional aid.

UNDERGRADUATE EXPENSES for 2009–10 *Comprehensive fee:* $51,324 includes full-time tuition ($37,824) and room and board ($13,500). *College room only:* $8066. Room and board charges vary according to board plan and housing facility. *Payment plan:* Installment.

FRESHMAN FINANCIAL AID (Fall 2009, est.) 265 applied for aid; of those 80% were deemed to have need. 100% of freshmen with need received aid; of those 24% had need fully met. *Average percent of need met:* 92% (excluding resources awarded to replace EFC). *Average financial aid package:* $29,408 (excluding resources awarded to replace EFC). 6% of all full-time freshmen had no need and received non-need-based gift aid.

UNDERGRADUATE FINANCIAL AID (Fall 2009, est.) 893 applied for aid; of those 93% were deemed to have need. 100% of undergraduates with need received aid; of those 68% had need fully met. *Average percent of need met:* 95% (excluding resources awarded to replace EFC). *Average financial aid package:* $31,719 (excluding resources awarded to replace EFC). 7% of all full-time undergraduates had no need and received non-need-based gift aid.

GIFT AID (NEED-BASED) *Total amount:* $21,774,000 (8% federal, 2% state, 90% institutional). *Receiving aid:* Freshmen: 41% (194); all full-time undergraduates: 41% (774). *Average award:* Freshmen: $24,739; Undergraduates: $26,193. *Scholarships, grants, and awards:* Federal Pell, FSEOG, state, college/university gift aid from institutional funds.

GIFT AID (NON-NEED-BASED) *Total amount:* $2,797,000 (86% institutional, 14% external sources). *Receiving aid:* Freshmen: 5% (22). Undergraduates: 5% (102). *Average award:* Freshmen: $21,847. Undergraduates: $17,764. *Scholarships, grants, and awards by category: Academic interests/achievement:* general academic interests/achievements. *Special achievements/activities:* leadership. *Tuition waivers:* Full or partial for employees or children of employees.

LOANS *Student loans:* $7,561,000 (45% need-based, 55% non-need-based). 49% of past graduating class borrowed through all loan programs. *Average indebtedness per student:* $28,164. *Average need-based loan:* Freshmen: $2862. Undergraduates: $4020. *Parent loans:* $4,220,000 (100% non-need-based). *Programs:* Federal Direct (Subsidized and Unsubsidized Stafford, PLUS), Perkins, state.

WORK-STUDY *Federal work-study:* Total amount: $1,253,000; 230 jobs averaging $1242. *State or other work-study/employment:* Total amount: $188,000 (100% non-need-based). Part-time jobs available.
APPLYING FOR FINANCIAL AID *Required financial aid forms:* FAFSA, CSS Financial Aid PROFILE, noncustodial (divorced/separated) parent's statement, business/farm supplement, federal income tax form(s), W-2 forms, verification worksheet. *Financial aid deadline:* 2/15. *Notification date:* 4/1. Students must reply by 5/1.
CONTACT Ms. Melissa Shaak, Director of Financial Aid, Babson College, Hollister Hall, 3rd Floor, Babson Park, MA 02457-0310, 781-239-4219 or toll-free 800-488-3696. *Fax:* 781-239-5510. *E-mail:* shaak@babson.edu.

BACONE COLLEGE
Muskogee, OK

Tuition & fees: N/R	Average undergraduate aid package: N/A

ABOUT THE INSTITUTION Independent religious, coed. *Awards:* associate and bachelor's degrees. 26 undergraduate majors. *Total enrollment:* 884. Undergraduates: 884. Both federal and institutional methodology are used as a basis for awarding need-based institutional aid.
GIFT AID (NEED-BASED) *Scholarships, grants, and awards:* Federal Pell, FSEOG, state, private, college/university gift aid from institutional funds.
LOANS *Programs:* FFEL (Subsidized and Unsubsidized Stafford, PLUS).
WORK-STUDY Federal work-study jobs available.
APPLYING FOR FINANCIAL AID *Required financial aid forms:* FAFSA, institution's own form. *Financial aid deadline (priority):* 3/31. *Notification date:* Continuous beginning 4/1.
CONTACT Mrs. Kathye Watson, Office of Financial Aid, Bacone College, 2299 Old Bacone Road, Muskogee, OK 74403-1597, 918-781-7294 or toll-free 888-682-5514 Ext. 7340. *Fax:* 918-781-7416. *E-mail:* financialaid@bacone.edu.

BAIS BINYOMIN ACADEMY
Stamford, CT
CONTACT Financial Aid Office, Bais Binyomin Academy, 132 Prospect Street, Stamford, CT 06901-1202, 203-325-4351.

BAKER COLLEGE OF ALLEN PARK
Allen Park, MI
CONTACT Financial Aid Office, Baker College of Allen Park, 4500 Enterprise Drive, Allen Park, MI 48101, 313-425-3700 or toll-free 800-767-4120 (in-state).

BAKER COLLEGE OF AUBURN HILLS
Auburn Hills, MI
CONTACT Financial Aid Office, Baker College of Auburn Hills, 1500 University Drive, Auburn Hills, MI 48326-1586, 248-340-0600 or toll-free 888-429-0410 (in-state).

BAKER COLLEGE OF CADILLAC
Cadillac, MI
CONTACT Mr. Maynard Thompson, Director of Financial Aid, Baker College of Cadillac, 9600 East 13th Street, Cadillac, MI 49601-9169, 616-775-8458 or toll-free 888-313-3463 (in-state). *E-mail:* thomps_m@cadillac.baker.edu.

BAKER COLLEGE OF CLINTON TOWNSHIP
Clinton Township, MI
CONTACT Financial Aid Office, Baker College of Clinton Township, 34950 Little Mack Avenue, Clinton Township, MI 48035-4701, 586-791-6610 or toll-free 888-272-2842.

BAKER COLLEGE OF FLINT
Flint, MI
CONTACT Mr. Gerald McCarty II, Director of Student Financial Aid, Baker College of Flint, 1050 Bristol Road, Flint, MI 48507-5508, 810-766-4202 or toll-free 800-964-4299.

BAKER COLLEGE OF JACKSON
Jackson, MI
CONTACT Financial Aid Office, Baker College of Jackson, 2800 Springport Road, Jackson, MI 49202, 517-789-6123 or toll-free 888-343-3683.

BAKER COLLEGE OF MUSKEGON
Muskegon, MI
CONTACT Mr. Thomas R. Jewell, Financial Aid Director, Baker College of Muskegon, 123 East Apple Avenue, Muskegon, MI 49442-3497, 616-726-4904 or toll-free 800-937-0337 (in-state). *E-mail:* jewell_t@muskegon.baker.edu.

BAKER COLLEGE OF OWOSSO
Owosso, MI
CONTACT Mr. David Lewis, Director of Student Services, Baker College of Owosso, 1020 South Washington Street, Owosso, MI 48867-4400, 517-723-5251 or toll-free 800-879-3797. *E-mail:* lewis-d@owosso.baker.edu.

BAKER COLLEGE OF PORT HURON
Port Huron, MI
CONTACT Mrs. Susan Porrett, Director of Financial Aid, Baker College of Port Huron, 3403 Lapeer Road, Port Huron, MI 48060-2597, 810-985-7000 or toll-free 888-262-2442.

BAKER UNIVERSITY
Baldwin City, KS
ABOUT THE INSTITUTION Independent United Methodist, coed. 38 undergraduate majors.
GIFT AID (NEED-BASED) *Scholarships, grants, and awards:* Federal Pell, FSEOG, state, private, college/university gift aid from institutional funds.
GIFT AID (NON-NEED-BASED) *Scholarships, grants, and awards by category:* Academic *interests/achievement:* general academic interests/achievements. *Creative arts/performance:* art/fine arts, cinema/film/broadcasting, dance, debating, journalism/publications, music; theater/drama. *Special achievements/activities:* cheerleading/drum major, leadership, religious involvement. *Special characteristics:* children and siblings of alumni, children of faculty/staff, ethnic background, international students, members of minority groups, out-of-state students, relatives of clergy, religious affiliation.
LOANS *Programs:* FFEL (Subsidized and Unsubsidized Stafford, PLUS), Perkins, alternative loans.
WORK-STUDY *Federal work-study:* Total amount: $466,974; jobs available (averaging $1000). *State or other work-study/employment:* Total amount: $296,541 (100% non-need-based). Part-time jobs available (averaging $1000).
APPLYING FOR FINANCIAL AID *Required financial aid forms:* FAFSA, institution's own form.
CONTACT Mrs. Jeanne Mott, Financial Aid Director, Baker University, Box 65, Baldwin City, KS 66006-0065, 785-594-4595 or toll-free 800-873-4282. *Fax:* 785-594-8358.

BALDWIN-WALLACE COLLEGE
Berea, OH

Tuition & fees: $24,230	Average undergraduate aid package: $19,838

ABOUT THE INSTITUTION Independent Methodist, coed. 65 undergraduate majors. Federal methodology is used as a basis for awarding need-based institutional aid.

Baldwin-Wallace College

UNDERGRADUATE EXPENSES for 2009–10 *Comprehensive fee:* $32,190 includes full-time tuition ($24,230) and room and board ($7960). *College room only:* $3888. Full-time tuition and fees vary according to class time and course load. *Part-time tuition:* $770 per semester hour. Part-time tuition and fees vary according to class time and course load. *Payment plans:* Installment, deferred payment.

FRESHMAN FINANCIAL AID (Fall 2009, est.) 681 applied for aid; of those 89% were deemed to have need. 100% of freshmen with need received aid; of those 35% had need fully met. *Average percent of need met:* 86% (excluding resources awarded to replace EFC). *Average financial aid package:* $20,860 (excluding resources awarded to replace EFC). 17% of all full-time freshmen had no need and received non-need-based gift aid.

UNDERGRADUATE FINANCIAL AID (Fall 2009, est.) 2,859 applied for aid; of those 89% were deemed to have need. 100% of undergraduates with need received aid; of those 48% had need fully met. *Average percent of need met:* 85% (excluding resources awarded to replace EFC). *Average financial aid package:* $19,838 (excluding resources awarded to replace EFC). 17% of all full-time undergraduates had no need and received non-need-based gift aid.

GIFT AID (NEED-BASED) *Total amount:* $32,367,106 (17% federal, 5% state, 77% institutional, 1% external sources). *Receiving aid:* Freshmen: 80% (603); all full-time undergraduates: 80% (2,532). *Average award:* Freshmen: $14,542; Undergraduates: $13,687. *Scholarships, grants, and awards:* Federal Pell, FSEOG, state, private, college/university gift aid from institutional funds.

GIFT AID (NON-NEED-BASED) *Total amount:* $6,643,901 (1% state, 94% institutional, 5% external sources). *Receiving aid:* Freshmen: 10% (74). Undergraduates: 13% (401). *Average award:* Freshmen: $8454. Undergraduates: $10,050. *Scholarships, grants, and awards by category: Academic interests/achievement:* 2,009 awards ($16,162,000 total): general academic interests/achievements. *Creative arts/performance:* 178 awards ($407,000 total): music. *Special achievements/activities:* 108 awards ($248,000 total): leadership. *Special characteristics:* 701 awards ($1,784,000 total): children and siblings of alumni, members of minority groups, religious affiliation, siblings of current students. *Tuition waivers:* Full or partial for children of alumni, employees or children of employees.

LOANS *Student loans:* $24,576,000 (56% need-based, 44% non-need-based). 67% of past graduating class borrowed through all loan programs. *Average indebtedness per student:* $17,716. *Average need-based loan:* Freshmen: $3891. Undergraduates: $4827. *Parent loans:* $7,427,000 (20% need-based, 80% non-need-based). *Programs:* FFEL (Subsidized and Unsubsidized Stafford, PLUS), Perkins, college/university.

WORK-STUDY *Federal work-study:* Total amount: $466,000; 915 jobs averaging $874. *State or other work-study/employment:* Total amount: $1,350,000 (27% need-based, 73% non-need-based). 519 part-time jobs averaging $323.

APPLYING FOR FINANCIAL AID *Required financial aid form:* FAFSA. *Financial aid deadline:* 9/1 (priority: 5/1). *Notification date:* Continuous beginning 2/14.
CONTACT Dr. George L. Rolleston, Director of Financial Aid, Baldwin-Wallace College, 275 Eastland Road, Berea, OH 44017-2088, 440-826-2108 or toll-free 877-BWAPPLY (in-state). *Fax:* 440-826-8048. *E-mail:* grollest@bw.edu.

BALL STATE UNIVERSITY
Muncie, IN

Tuition & fees (IN res): $7830	Average undergraduate aid package: $9450

ABOUT THE INSTITUTION State-supported, coed. 85 undergraduate majors. Federal methodology is used as a basis for awarding need-based institutional aid.

UNDERGRADUATE EXPENSES for 2009–10 *Tuition, state resident:* full-time $7228; part-time $278 per credit hour. *Tuition, nonresident:* full-time $19,796; part-time $728 per credit hour. *Required fees:* full-time $602. Full-time tuition and fees vary according to course level and reciprocity agreements. Part-time tuition and fees vary according to course level and course load. *College room and board:* $7932. Room and board charges vary according to board plan and housing facility. *Payment plan:* Installment.

FRESHMAN FINANCIAL AID (Fall 2009, est.) 3,759 applied for aid; of those 73% were deemed to have need. 99% of freshmen with need received aid; of those 26% had need fully met. *Average percent of need met:* 56% (excluding resources awarded to replace EFC). *Average financial aid package:* $9489 (excluding resources awarded to replace EFC). 10% of all full-time freshmen had no need and received non-need-based gift aid.

UNDERGRADUATE FINANCIAL AID (Fall 2009, est.) 13,484 applied for aid; of those 77% were deemed to have need. 99% of undergraduates with need received aid; of those 25% had need fully met. *Average percent of need met:* 60% (excluding resources awarded to replace EFC). *Average financial aid package:* $9450 (excluding resources awarded to replace EFC). 6% of all full-time undergraduates had no need and received non-need-based gift aid.

GIFT AID (NEED-BASED) *Total amount:* $41,588,322 (52% federal, 38% state, 10% institutional). *Receiving aid:* Freshmen: 37% (1,529); all full-time undergraduates: 38% (6,252). *Average award:* Freshmen: $7145; Undergraduates: $6145. *Scholarships, grants, and awards:* Federal Pell, FSEOG, state, private, college/university gift aid from institutional funds.

GIFT AID (NON-NEED-BASED) *Total amount:* $29,173,584 (7% federal, 23% state, 54% institutional, 16% external sources). *Receiving aid:* Freshmen: 30% (1,243). Undergraduates: 22% (3,600). *Average award:* Freshmen: $4226. Undergraduates: $5062. *Scholarships, grants, and awards by category: Academic interests/achievement:* 2,618 awards ($14,249,339 total): architecture, business, communication, education, engineering/technologies, English, foreign languages, general academic interests/achievements, health fields, humanities, international studies, mathematics, military science, physical sciences, social sciences. *Creative arts/performance:* 90 awards ($127,892 total): art/fine arts, cinema/film/broadcasting, dance, debating, general creative arts/performance, journalism/publications, music, performing arts, theater/drama. *Special achievements/activities:* 156 awards ($1,019,616 total): community service, general special achievements/activities, leadership. *Special characteristics:* 693 awards ($7,126,393 total): adult students, children and siblings of alumni, children of faculty/staff, general special characteristics, international students, local/state students, members of minority groups, veterans. *Tuition waivers:* Full or partial for employees or children of employees.

LOANS *Student loans:* $97,415,046 (38% need-based, 62% non-need-based). 67% of past graduating class borrowed through all loan programs. *Average indebtedness per student:* $22,598. *Average need-based loan:* Freshmen: $3543. Undergraduates: $4170. *Parent loans:* $94,095,488 (100% non-need-based). *Programs:* Federal Direct (Subsidized and Unsubsidized Stafford, PLUS), Perkins.

WORK-STUDY *Federal work-study:* Total amount: $2,793,827; 1,185 jobs averaging $2070. *State or other work-study/employment:* Total amount: $7,800,408 (8% need-based, 92% non-need-based). Part-time jobs available.

ATHLETIC AWARDS Total amount: $4,972,904 (100% non-need-based).

APPLYING FOR FINANCIAL AID *Required financial aid form:* FAFSA. *Financial aid deadline (priority):* 3/10. *Notification date:* Continuous beginning 4/1.
CONTACT John McPherson, Director of Scholarships and Financial Aid, Ball State University, Lucina Hall, Muncie, IN 47306-1099, 800-227-4017 or toll-free 800-482-4BSU. *Fax:* 765-285-4247. *E-mail:* finaid@bsu.edu.

BAPTIST BIBLE COLLEGE
Springfield, MO

CONTACT Bob Kotulski, Director of Financial Aid, Baptist Bible College, 628 East Kearney, Springfield, MO 65803-3498, 417-268-6036. *Fax:* 417-268-6694.

BAPTIST BIBLE COLLEGE OF PENNSYLVANIA
Clarks Summit, PA

ABOUT THE INSTITUTION Independent Baptist, coed. 28 undergraduate majors.

GIFT AID (NEED-BASED) *Scholarships, grants, and awards:* Federal Pell, state, private, college/university gift aid from institutional funds.

GIFT AID (NON-NEED-BASED) *Scholarships, grants, and awards by category: Academic interests/achievement:* education, general academic interests/achievements, religion/biblical studies. *Creative arts/performance:* general creative arts/performance, music. *Special achievements/activities:* general special achievements/activities, leadership, religious involvement. *Special characteristics:* children and siblings of alumni, children of faculty/staff, general special characteristics, married students, relatives of clergy, siblings of current students.

LOANS *Programs:* FFEL (Subsidized and Unsubsidized Stafford, PLUS), alternative loans.

APPLYING FOR FINANCIAL AID *Required financial aid form:* FAFSA.

CONTACT Mrs. Charis Henson, Acting Director of Student Financial Services, Baptist Bible College of Pennsylvania, 538 Venard Road, Clarks Summit, PA 18411, 570-586-2400 Ext. 9272 or toll-free 800-451-7664. *Fax:* 570-587-8045. *E-mail:* chenson@bbc.edu.

THE BAPTIST COLLEGE OF FLORIDA
Graceville, FL

Tuition & fees: $8500   **Average undergraduate aid package: $7075**

ABOUT THE INSTITUTION Independent Southern Baptist, coed. 8 undergraduate majors. Federal methodology is used as a basis for awarding need-based institutional aid.

UNDERGRADUATE EXPENSES for 2009–10 *Comprehensive fee:* $12,566 includes full-time tuition ($8100), mandatory fees ($400), and room and board ($4066). Full-time tuition and fees vary according to course load and location. Room and board charges vary according to board plan and housing facility. *Part-time tuition:* $270 per semester hour. Part-time tuition and fees vary according to course load and location. *Payment plan:* Installment.

FRESHMAN FINANCIAL AID (Fall 2009, est.) 127 applied for aid; of those 86% were deemed to have need. 56% of freshmen with need received aid; of those 7% had need fully met. *Average percent of need met:* 33% (excluding resources awarded to replace EFC). *Average financial aid package:* $5830 (excluding resources awarded to replace EFC). 2% of all full-time freshmen had no need and received non-need-based gift aid.

UNDERGRADUATE FINANCIAL AID (Fall 2009, est.) 554 applied for aid; of those 90% were deemed to have need. 74% of undergraduates with need received aid; of those 7% had need fully met. *Average percent of need met:* 44% (excluding resources awarded to replace EFC). *Average financial aid package:* $7075 (excluding resources awarded to replace EFC). 2% of all full-time undergraduates had no need and received non-need-based gift aid.

GIFT AID (NEED-BASED) *Total amount:* $1,768,119 (57% federal, 25% state, 2% institutional, 16% external sources). *Receiving aid:* Freshmen: 37% (56); all full-time undergraduates: 53% (349). *Average award:* Freshmen: $4296; Undergraduates: $4803. *Scholarships, grants, and awards:* Federal Pell, FSEOG, state, private, college/university gift aid from institutional funds.

GIFT AID (NON-NEED-BASED) *Total amount:* $279,441 (50% state, 7% institutional, 43% external sources). *Receiving aid:* Freshmen: 3% (4). Undergraduates: 4% (24). *Average award:* Freshmen: $1166. Undergraduates: $1409. *Scholarships, grants, and awards by category: Academic interests/achievement:* 268 awards ($244,816 total): education, religion/biblical studies. *Creative arts/performance:* 9 awards ($3323 total): music. *Special characteristics:* 272 awards ($254,464 total): children with a deceased or disabled parent, religious affiliation, spouses of current students. *Tuition waivers:* Full or partial for employees or children of employees.

LOANS *Student loans:* $1,718,701 (82% need-based, 18% non-need-based). 1% of past graduating class borrowed through all loan programs. *Average indebtedness per student:* $5316. *Average need-based loan:* Freshmen: $2805. Undergraduates: $3247. *Parent loans:* $62,855 (45% need-based, 55% non-need-based). *Programs:* FFEL (Subsidized and Unsubsidized Stafford, PLUS).

WORK-STUDY *Federal work-study:* Total amount: $46,853; 20 jobs averaging $2466.

APPLYING FOR FINANCIAL AID *Required financial aid forms:* FAFSA, institution's own form, state aid form, business/farm supplement, student authorization form. *Financial aid deadline:* 4/15 (priority: 4/1). *Notification date:* Continuous beginning 6/15. Students must reply within 4 weeks of notification.

CONTACT Angela Rathel, Director of Financial Aid, The Baptist College of Florida, 5400 College Drive, Graceville, FL 32440-3306, 850-263-3261 Ext. 461 or toll-free 800-328-2660 Ext. 460. *Fax:* 850-263-2141. *E-mail:* finaid@baptistcollege.edu.

BAPTIST COLLEGE OF HEALTH SCIENCES
Memphis, TN

CONTACT Leanne Smith, Financial Aid Officer, Baptist College of Health Sciences, 1003 Monroe Avenue, Memphis, TN 38104, 901-227-6805 or toll-free 866-575-2247. *Fax:* 901-227-4311. *E-mail:* leanne.smith@bchs.edu.

BAPTIST MISSIONARY ASSOCIATION THEOLOGICAL SEMINARY
Jacksonville, TX

CONTACT Dr. Philip Attebery, Dean/Registrar, Baptist Missionary Association Theological Seminary, 1530 East Pine Street, Jacksonville, TX 75766-5407, 903-586-2501. *Fax:* 903-586-0378. *E-mail:* bmatsem@bmats.edu.

BAPTIST UNIVERSITY OF THE AMERICAS
San Antonio, TX

Tuition & fees: N/R   **Average undergraduate aid package: N/A**

ABOUT THE INSTITUTION Independent Baptist, coed. 1 undergraduate major. Both federal and institutional methodology are used as a basis for awarding need-based institutional aid.

GIFT AID (NEED-BASED) *Scholarships, grants, and awards:* Federal Pell, FSEOG, private, college/university gift aid from institutional funds.

GIFT AID (NON-NEED-BASED) *Scholarships, grants, and awards by category: Academic interests/achievement:* 158 awards ($210,900 total): religion/biblical studies.

LOANS *Programs:* Federal Direct (Subsidized and Unsubsidized Stafford).

WORK-STUDY *Federal work-study:* 4 jobs averaging $1875. *State or other work-study/employment:* 103 part-time jobs averaging $2688.

APPLYING FOR FINANCIAL AID *Required financial aid form:* FAFSA.

CONTACT Mrs. Araceli G. Acosta, Financial Aid Administrator, Baptist University of the Americas, 8019 South Pan Am Expressway, San Antonio, TX 78224, 210-924-4338 Ext. 214 or toll-free 800-721-1396. *Fax:* 210-924-2701. *E-mail:* aacosta@bua.edu.

BARCLAY COLLEGE
Haviland, KS

CONTACT Christina Foster, Financial Aid Coordinator, Barclay College, 607 North Kingman, Haviland, KS 67059, 800-862-0226. *Fax:* 620-862-5403. *E-mail:* financialaid@barclaycollege.edu.

BARD COLLEGE
Annandale-on-Hudson, NY

Tuition & fees: $39,880   **Average undergraduate aid package: $34,643**

ABOUT THE INSTITUTION Independent, coed. 78 undergraduate majors. Both federal and institutional methodology are used as a basis for awarding need-based institutional aid.

UNDERGRADUATE EXPENSES for 2009–10 *One-time required fee:* $890. *Comprehensive fee:* $51,180 includes full-time tuition ($39,080), mandatory fees ($800), and room and board ($11,300). *Part-time tuition:* $1222 per credit. *Payment plans:* Tuition prepayment, installment.

FRESHMAN FINANCIAL AID (Fall 2009, est.) 362 applied for aid; of those 93% were deemed to have need. 100% of freshmen with need received aid; of those 60% had need fully met. *Average percent of need met:* 90% (excluding resources awarded to replace EFC). *Average financial aid package:* $31,959 (excluding resources awarded to replace EFC). 1% of all full-time freshmen had no need and received non-need-based gift aid.

UNDERGRADUATE FINANCIAL AID (Fall 2009, est.) 1,270 applied for aid; of those 92% were deemed to have need. 100% of undergraduates with need received aid; of those 51% had need fully met. *Average percent of need met:* 92% (excluding resources awarded to replace EFC). *Average financial aid package:* $34,643 (excluding resources awarded to replace EFC). 2% of all full-time undergraduates had no need and received non-need-based gift aid.

GIFT AID (NEED-BASED) *Total amount:* $29,983,910 (5% federal, 2% state, 91% institutional, 2% external sources). *Receiving aid:* Freshmen: 62% (315); all full-time undergraduates: 56% (1,058). *Average award:* Freshmen: $31,540; Undergraduates: $28,319. *Scholarships, grants, and awards:* Federal Pell, FSEOG, state, private, college/university gift aid from institutional funds.

GIFT AID (NON-NEED-BASED) *Total amount:* $508,970 (3% state, 90% institutional, 7% external sources). *Average award:* Freshmen: $20,594. Undergraduates: $13,098. *Scholarships, grants, and awards by category: Academic interests/achievement:* 1 award ($5000 total): biological sciences, computer science, mathematics, physical sciences. *Special achievements/activities:* leadership. *Special characteristics:* 4 awards ($126,080 total): children of educators, children of faculty/staff. *Tuition waivers:* Full or partial for employees or children of employees.

LOANS *Student loans:* $6,457,562 (83% need-based, 17% non-need-based). 52% of past graduating class borrowed through all loan programs. *Average indebtedness per student:* $26,131. *Average need-based loan:* Freshmen: $3547.

Undergraduates: $4501. *Parent loans:* $3,987,302 (76% need-based, 24% non-need-based). *Programs:* FFEL (Subsidized and Unsubsidized Stafford, PLUS), Perkins, college/university loans from institutional funds (for international students only).

WORK-STUDY *Federal work-study:* Total amount: $1,113,120; 699 jobs averaging $1583. *State or other work-study/employment:* Total amount: $183,975 (100% need-based). 112 part-time jobs averaging $1613.

APPLYING FOR FINANCIAL AID *Required financial aid forms:* FAFSA, CSS Financial Aid PROFILE, state aid form, noncustodial (divorced/separated) parent's statement, business/farm supplement. *Financial aid deadline:* 2/15 (priority: 2/1). *Notification date:* 4/1. Students must reply by 5/1 or within 2 weeks of notification.

CONTACT Denise Ann Ackerman, Director of Financial Aid, Bard College, Annandale Road, Annandale-on-Hudson, NY 12504, 845-758-7525. *Fax:* 845-758-7336. *E-mail:* finaid@bard.edu.

BARD COLLEGE AT SIMON'S ROCK
Great Barrington, MA

Tuition & fees: $40,170	Average undergraduate aid package: $33,639

ABOUT THE INSTITUTION Independent, coed. 45 undergraduate majors. Both federal and institutional methodology are used as a basis for awarding need-based institutional aid.

UNDERGRADUATE EXPENSES for 2009–10 *Comprehensive fee:* $51,130 includes full-time tuition ($39,380), mandatory fees ($790), and room and board ($10,960). Full-time tuition and fees vary according to course load. *Part-time tuition:* $1550 per credit hour. Part-time tuition and fees vary according to course load. *Payment plan:* Installment.

FRESHMAN FINANCIAL AID (Fall 2009, est.) 139 applied for aid; of those 86% were deemed to have need. 100% of freshmen with need received aid; of those 14% had need fully met. *Average percent of need met:* 68% (excluding resources awarded to replace EFC). *Average financial aid package:* $33,119 (excluding resources awarded to replace EFC). 16% of all full-time freshmen had no need and received non-need-based gift aid.

UNDERGRADUATE FINANCIAL AID (Fall 2009, est.) 290 applied for aid; of those 90% were deemed to have need. 100% of undergraduates with need received aid; of those 15% had need fully met. *Average percent of need met:* 68% (excluding resources awarded to replace EFC). *Average financial aid package:* $33,639 (excluding resources awarded to replace EFC). 15% of all full-time undergraduates had no need and received non-need-based gift aid.

GIFT AID (NEED-BASED) *Total amount:* $4,484,284 (12% federal, 1% state, 87% institutional). *Receiving aid:* Freshmen: 54% (97); all full-time undergraduates: 53% (224). *Average award:* Freshmen: $19,144; Undergraduates: $17,567. *Scholarships, grants, and awards:* Federal Pell, FSEOG, state, private, college/university gift aid from institutional funds.

GIFT AID (NON-NEED-BASED) *Total amount:* $4,254,306 (94% institutional, 6% external sources). *Receiving aid:* Freshmen: 48% (85). Undergraduates: 45% (191). *Average award:* Freshmen: $13,268. Undergraduates: $14,929. *Scholarships, grants, and awards by category:* Academic interests/achievement: 166 awards ($2,645,010 total): general academic interests/achievements. *Special characteristics:* 114 awards ($2,488,589 total): children of faculty/staff, local/state students, members of minority groups. *Tuition waivers:* Full or partial for employees or children of employees.

LOANS *Student loans:* $1,945,596 (100% need-based). 38% of past graduating class borrowed through all loan programs. *Average indebtedness per student:* $20,000. *Average need-based loan:* Freshmen: $4412. Undergraduates: $4644. *Parent loans:* $1,154,941 (100% need-based). *Programs:* FFEL (Subsidized and Unsubsidized Stafford, PLUS), Perkins, alternative loans.

WORK-STUDY *Federal work-study:* Total amount: $190,000; 170 jobs averaging $1200.

APPLYING FOR FINANCIAL AID *Required financial aid forms:* FAFSA, CSS Financial Aid PROFILE, noncustodial (divorced/separated) parent's statement, business/farm supplement, federal income tax form(s), federal verification worksheet. *Financial aid deadline (priority):* 4/15. *Notification date:* Continuous beginning 3/15. Students must reply within 2 weeks of notification.

CONTACT Ms. Ann Murtagh Gitto, Director of Financial Aid, Bard College at Simon's Rock, 84 Alford Road, Great Barrington, MA 01230-9702, 413-528-7297 or toll-free 800-235-7186. *Fax:* 413-528-7339. *E-mail:* agitto@simons-rock.edu.

BARNARD COLLEGE
New York, NY

Tuition & fees: $38,650	Average undergraduate aid package: $35,365

ABOUT THE INSTITUTION Independent, women only. 48 undergraduate majors. Both federal and institutional methodology are used as a basis for awarding need-based institutional aid.

UNDERGRADUATE EXPENSES for 2009–10 *Comprehensive fee:* $50,969 includes full-time tuition ($37,051), mandatory fees ($1599), and room and board ($12,319). *College room only:* $7577. Room and board charges vary according to board plan and housing facility. *Part-time tuition:* $1235 per credit. *Payment plans:* Tuition prepayment, installment, deferred payment.

FRESHMAN FINANCIAL AID (Fall 2009, est.) 308 applied for aid; of those 75% were deemed to have need. 100% of freshmen with need received aid; of those 100% had need fully met. *Average percent of need met:* 100% (excluding resources awarded to replace EFC). *Average financial aid package:* $35,689 (excluding resources awarded to replace EFC).

UNDERGRADUATE FINANCIAL AID (Fall 2009, est.) 1,195 applied for aid; of those 84% were deemed to have need. 100% of undergraduates with need received aid; of those 100% had need fully met. *Average percent of need met:* 100% (excluding resources awarded to replace EFC). *Average financial aid package:* $35,365 (excluding resources awarded to replace EFC).

GIFT AID (NEED-BASED) *Total amount:* $29,614,491 (9% federal, 5% state, 84% institutional, 2% external sources). *Receiving aid:* Freshmen: 38% (219); all full-time undergraduates: 42% (973). *Average award:* Freshmen: $33,153; Undergraduates: $30,538. *Scholarships, grants, and awards:* Federal Pell, FSEOG, state, private, college/university gift aid from institutional funds, Academic Competitiveness Grants, National SMART Grants.

GIFT AID (NON-NEED-BASED) *Total amount:* $440,402 (11% federal, 89% external sources). *Tuition waivers:* Full or partial for employees or children of employees.

LOANS *Student loans:* $5,020,641 (74% need-based, 26% non-need-based). 44% of past graduating class borrowed through all loan programs. *Average indebtedness per student:* $14,706. *Average need-based loan:* Freshmen: $3257. Undergraduates: $4692. *Parent loans:* $5,048,469 (100% non-need-based). *Programs:* Federal Direct (Subsidized and Unsubsidized Stafford, PLUS), Perkins, state, college/university, alternative loans.

WORK-STUDY *Federal work-study:* Total amount: $804,747; 422 jobs averaging $1880. *State or other work-study/employment:* Total amount: $718,377 (80% need-based, 20% non-need-based). 341 part-time jobs averaging $2011.

APPLYING FOR FINANCIAL AID *Required financial aid forms:* FAFSA, institution's own form, CSS Financial Aid PROFILE, state aid form, noncustodial (divorced/separated) parent's statement, business/farm supplement, federal income tax returns. *Financial aid deadline:* 2/1. *Notification date:* 3/31. Students must reply by 5/1.

CONTACT Nanette DiLauro, Director of Financial Aid, Barnard College, 3009 Broadway, New York, NY 10027-6598, 212-854-2154. *Fax:* 212-854-2902. *E-mail:* finaid@barnard.edu.

BARRY UNIVERSITY
Miami Shores, FL

Tuition & fees: $25,500	Average undergraduate aid package: $17,576

ABOUT THE INSTITUTION Independent Roman Catholic, coed. 58 undergraduate majors.

UNDERGRADUATE EXPENSES for 2010–11 *Comprehensive fee:* $33,986 includes full-time tuition ($25,500) and room and board ($8486).

FRESHMAN FINANCIAL AID (Fall 2008) 503 applied for aid; of those 91% were deemed to have need. 100% of freshmen with need received aid; of those 11% had need fully met. *Average percent of need met:* 74% (excluding resources awarded to replace EFC). *Average financial aid package:* $24,934 (excluding resources awarded to replace EFC). 11% of all full-time freshmen had no need and received non-need-based gift aid.

UNDERGRADUATE FINANCIAL AID (Fall 2008) 3,307 applied for aid; of those 94% were deemed to have need. 100% of undergraduates with need received aid; of those 6% had need fully met. *Average percent of need met:* 55% (excluding resources awarded to replace EFC). *Average financial aid package:*

$17,576 (excluding resources awarded to replace EFC). 10% of all full-time undergraduates had no need and received non-need-based gift aid. **GIFT AID (NEED-BASED)** *Total amount:* $13,579,213 (54% federal, 12% state, 34% institutional). *Receiving aid:* Freshmen: 61% (359); all full-time undergraduates: 53% (2,164). *Average award:* Freshmen: $7985; Undergraduates: $6596. *Scholarships, grants, and awards:* Federal Pell, FSEOG, state, private, college/university gift aid from institutional funds, Federal Nursing.

GIFT AID (NON-NEED-BASED) *Total amount:* $28,815,635 (1% federal, 29% state, 70% institutional). *Receiving aid:* Freshmen: 78% (455). Undergraduates: 74% (3,044). *Average award:* Freshmen: $8868. Undergraduates: $8090. **LOANS** *Student loans:* $34,312,466 (42% need-based, 58% non-need-based). *Average need-based loan:* Freshmen: $3507. Undergraduates: $5159. *Parent loans:* $2,022,980 (100% non-need-based). *Programs:* FFEL (Subsidized and Unsubsidized Stafford, PLUS), Perkins, Federal Nursing, college/university, alternative loans.

WORK-STUDY *Federal work-study:* Total amount: $3,588,493; jobs available. *State or other work-study/employment:* Total amount: $258,797 (100% non-need-based). Part-time jobs available.

ATHLETIC AWARDS Total amount: $2,211,463 (100% non-need-based).

APPLYING FOR FINANCIAL AID *Required financial aid form:* FAFSA. *Financial aid deadline:* Continuous. *Notification date:* Continuous beginning 1/25.

CONTACT Mr. Dart Humeston, Assistant Dean of Enrollment Services/Director of Financial Aid, Barry University, 11300 Northeast Second Avenue, Miami Shores, FL 33161-6695, 305-899-3673 or toll-free 800-695-2279. *E-mail:* finaid@mail.barry.edu.

BARTON COLLEGE
Wilson, NC

Tuition & fees: $20,648	Average undergraduate aid package: $19,289

ABOUT THE INSTITUTION Independent religious, coed. 32 undergraduate majors. Federal methodology is used as a basis for awarding need-based institutional aid.

UNDERGRADUATE EXPENSES for 2009–10 *Comprehensive fee:* $27,660 includes full-time tuition ($19,100), mandatory fees ($1548), and room and board ($7012). *College room only:* $3782. Full-time tuition and fees vary according to class time, course load, and program. Room and board charges vary according to housing facility. *Part-time tuition:* $810 per credit hour. Part-time tuition and fees vary according to class time, course load, and program. *Payment plan:* Installment.

FRESHMAN FINANCIAL AID (Fall 2009, est.) 217 applied for aid; of those 94% were deemed to have need. 100% of freshmen with need received aid; of those 15% had need fully met. *Average percent of need met:* 76% (excluding resources awarded to replace EFC). *Average financial aid package:* $21,177 (excluding resources awarded to replace EFC). 10% of all full-time freshmen had no need and received non-need-based gift aid.

UNDERGRADUATE FINANCIAL AID (Fall 2009, est.) 791 applied for aid; of those 94% were deemed to have need. 100% of undergraduates with need received aid; of those 10% had need fully met. *Average percent of need met:* 67% (excluding resources awarded to replace EFC). *Average financial aid package:* $19,289 (excluding resources awarded to replace EFC). 13% of all full-time undergraduates had no need and received non-need-based gift aid.

GIFT AID (NEED-BASED) *Total amount:* $3,674,886 (62% federal, 34% state, 1% institutional, 3% external sources). *Receiving aid:* Freshmen: 67% (155); all full-time undergraduates: 64% (562). *Average award:* Freshmen: $6347; Undergraduates: $6134. *Scholarships, grants, and awards:* Federal Pell, FSEOG, state, private, college/university gift aid from institutional funds.

GIFT AID (NON-NEED-BASED) *Total amount:* $4,580,526 (30% state, 64% institutional, 6% external sources). *Receiving aid:* Freshmen: 87% (200). Undergraduates: 82% (723). *Average award:* Freshmen: $4510. Undergraduates: $4837. *Scholarships, grants, and awards by category: Academic interests/achievement:* biological sciences, business, communication, computer science, education, English, general academic interests/achievements, health fields, humanities, international studies, mathematics, physical sciences, religion/biblical studies, social sciences. *Creative arts/performance:* art/fine arts, music, theater/drama. *Special achievements/activities:* general special achievements/activities, leadership, religious involvement. *Special characteristics:* adult students, children and siblings of alumni, children of faculty/staff, international students, local/state students, relatives of clergy, religious affiliation, siblings of current students, veterans. *Tuition waivers:* Full or partial for children of alumni, employees or children of employees, adult students, senior citizens.

LOANS *Student loans:* $7,748,996 (48% need-based, 52% non-need-based). 66% of past graduating class borrowed through all loan programs. *Average indebtedness per student:* $28,343. *Average need-based loan:* Freshmen: $4927. Undergraduates: $5318. *Parent loans:* $792,752 (100% non-need-based). *Programs:* FFEL (Subsidized and Unsubsidized Stafford, PLUS), Perkins, alternative loans.

WORK-STUDY *Federal work-study:* Total amount: $492,600; jobs available.

ATHLETIC AWARDS Total amount: $1,049,554 (100% non-need-based).

APPLYING FOR FINANCIAL AID *Required financial aid form:* FAFSA. *Financial aid deadline (priority):* 4/1. *Notification date:* Continuous. Students must reply by 5/1 or within 2 weeks of notification.

CONTACT Mrs. Bridget Ellis, Director of Financial Aid, Barton College, Box 5000, Wilson, NC 27893, 252-399-6371 or toll-free 800-345-4973. *Fax:* 252-399-6572. *E-mail:* aid@barton.edu.

BASTYR UNIVERSITY
Kenmore, WA

Tuition & fees: $19,050	Average undergraduate aid package: $17,600

ABOUT THE INSTITUTION Independent, coed. 6 undergraduate majors. Federal methodology is used as a basis for awarding need-based institutional aid.

UNDERGRADUATE EXPENSES for 2010–11 *Tuition:* full-time $19,050. Full-time tuition and fees vary according to course load and program. Part-time tuition and fees vary according to course load and program. Room and board charges vary according to housing facility.

UNDERGRADUATE FINANCIAL AID (Fall 2008) 189 applied for aid; of those 94% were deemed to have need. 100% of undergraduates with need received aid. *Average percent of need met:* 50% (excluding resources awarded to replace EFC). *Average financial aid package:* $17,600 (excluding resources awarded to replace EFC). 5% of all full-time undergraduates had no need and received non-need-based gift aid.

GIFT AID (NEED-BASED) *Total amount:* $858,070 (43% federal, 43% state, 11% institutional, 3% external sources). *Receiving aid:* All full-time undergraduates: 75% (157). *Average award:* Undergraduates: $8750. *Scholarships, grants, and awards:* Federal Pell, FSEOG, state, private, college/university gift aid from institutional funds.

GIFT AID (NON-NEED-BASED) *Average award:* Undergraduates: $500. *Scholarships, grants, and awards by category: Academic interests/achievement:* health fields. *Tuition waivers:* Full or partial for employees or children of employees.

LOANS *Student loans:* $2,521,300 (100% need-based). 90% of past graduating class borrowed through all loan programs. *Average indebtedness per student:* $32,500. *Average need-based loan:* Undergraduates: $5500. *Parent loans:* $29,400 (100% need-based). *Programs:* FFEL (Subsidized and Unsubsidized Stafford, PLUS), Perkins.

WORK-STUDY *Federal work-study:* Total amount: $67,321; 40 jobs averaging $3000. *State or other work-study/employment:* Total amount: $40,017 (100% need-based). 31 part-time jobs averaging $3000.

APPLYING FOR FINANCIAL AID *Required financial aid forms:* FAFSA, institution's own form. *Financial aid deadline (priority):* 5/1. *Notification date:* Continuous beginning 5/15. Students must reply within 3 weeks of notification.

CONTACT Sheila Arisa, Financial Aid Advisor, Bastyr University, 14500 Juanita Drive NE, Kenmore, WA 98028-4966, 425-602-3407. *Fax:* 425-602-3094. *E-mail:* finaid@bastyr.edu.

BATES COLLEGE
Lewiston, ME

Comprehensive fee: $51,300	Average undergraduate aid package: $33,852

ABOUT THE INSTITUTION Independent, coed. 34 undergraduate majors. Institutional methodology is used as a basis for awarding need-based institutional aid.

UNDERGRADUATE EXPENSES for 2010–11 *Comprehensive fee:* $51,300. *Payment plans:* Tuition prepayment, installment.

FRESHMAN FINANCIAL AID (Fall 2009, est.) 229 applied for aid; of those 86% were deemed to have need. 95% of freshmen with need received aid; of those

93% had need fully met. *Average percent of need met:* 100% (excluding resources awarded to replace EFC). *Average financial aid package:* $35,342 (excluding resources awarded to replace EFC).

UNDERGRADUATE FINANCIAL AID (Fall 2009, est.) 850 applied for aid; of those 91% were deemed to have need. 96% of undergraduates with need received aid; of those 94% had need fully met. *Average percent of need met:* 100% (excluding resources awarded to replace EFC). *Average financial aid package:* $33,852 (excluding resources awarded to replace EFC).

GIFT AID (NEED-BASED) *Total amount:* $21,975,613 (5% federal, 93% institutional, 2% external sources). *Receiving aid:* Freshmen: 39% (185); all full-time undergraduates: 41% (707). *Average award:* Freshmen: $32,732; Undergraduates: $31,083. *Scholarships, grants, and awards:* Federal Pell, FSEOG, state, private, college/university gift aid from institutional funds.

GIFT AID (NON-NEED-BASED) *Total amount:* $52,890 (100% external sources). *Tuition waivers:* Full or partial for employees or children of employees.

LOANS *Student loans:* $3,898,306 (49% need-based, 51% non-need-based). 38% of past graduating class borrowed through all loan programs. *Average indebtedness per student:* $17,945. *Average need-based loan:* Freshmen: $3956. Undergraduates: $4371. *Parent loans:* $2,590,756 (100% non-need-based). *Programs:* Federal Direct (Subsidized and Unsubsidized Stafford, PLUS), Perkins, state.

WORK-STUDY *Federal work-study:* Total amount: $931,782; 544 jobs averaging $1713. *State or other work-study/employment:* Total amount: $190,150 (100% need-based). 110 part-time jobs averaging $1729.

APPLYING FOR FINANCIAL AID *Required financial aid forms:* FAFSA, CSS Financial Aid PROFILE, noncustodial (divorced/separated) parent's statement. *Financial aid deadline:* 2/1. *Notification date:* 4/1. Students must reply by 5/1.

CONTACT Wendy G. Glass, Director of Student Financial Services, Bates College, 44 Mountain Avenue, Lewiston, ME 04240, 207-786-6096. *Fax:* 207-786-8350. *E-mail:* wglass@bates.edu.

BAUDER COLLEGE
Atlanta, GA

CONTACT Rhonda Staines, Director of Financial Aid, Bauder College, Phipps Plaza, 3500 Peachtree Road NE, Atlanta, GA 30326, 404-237-7573 or toll-free 800-241-3797. *Fax:* 404-261-3087. *E-mail:* finaid@bauder.edu.

BAYAMÓN CENTRAL UNIVERSITY
Bayamón, PR

CONTACT Financial Aid Director, Bayamón Central University, PO Box 1725, Bayamón, PR 00960-1725, 787-786-3030 Ext. 2115. *Fax:* 787-785-4365.

BAYLOR UNIVERSITY
Waco, TX

Tuition & fees: $29,754	Average undergraduate aid package: $20,452

ABOUT THE INSTITUTION Independent Baptist, coed. 126 undergraduate majors. Federal methodology is used as a basis for awarding need-based institutional aid.

UNDERGRADUATE EXPENSES for 2010–11 *Comprehensive fee:* $38,085 includes full-time tuition ($26,996), mandatory fees ($2758), and room and board ($8331). *College room only:* $4494. Room and board charges vary according to board plan and housing facility. *Part-time tuition:* $1124 per semester hour. *Payment plan:* Installment.

FRESHMAN FINANCIAL AID (Fall 2009, est.) 2,410 applied for aid; of those 83% were deemed to have need. 100% of freshmen with need received aid; of those 13% had need fully met. *Average percent of need met:* 69% (excluding resources awarded to replace EFC). *Average financial aid package:* $22,045 (excluding resources awarded to replace EFC). 29% of all full-time freshmen had no need and received non-need-based gift aid.

UNDERGRADUATE FINANCIAL AID (Fall 2009, est.) 7,585 applied for aid; of those 86% were deemed to have need. 100% of undergraduates with need received aid; of those 17% had need fully met. *Average percent of need met:* 67% (excluding resources awarded to replace EFC). *Average financial aid package:* $20,452 (excluding resources awarded to replace EFC). 31% of all full-time undergraduates had no need and received non-need-based gift aid.

GIFT AID (NEED-BASED) *Total amount:* $94,008,344 (14% federal, 14% state, 68% institutional, 4% external sources). *Receiving aid:* Freshmen: 64% (1,983); all full-time undergraduates: 52% (6,212). *Average award:* Freshmen: $16,768; Undergraduates: $15,180. *Scholarships, grants, and awards:* Federal Pell, FSEOG, state, college/university gift aid from institutional funds.

GIFT AID (NON-NEED-BASED) *Total amount:* $34,944,348 (95% institutional, 5% external sources). *Receiving aid:* Freshmen: 63% (1,938). Undergraduates: 47% (5,552). *Average award:* Freshmen: $9270. Undergraduates: $8805. *Scholarships, grants, and awards by category: Academic interests/achievement:* 10,611 awards ($63,826,663 total): business, communication, computer science, education, engineering/technologies, English, foreign languages, general academic interests/achievements, health fields, home economics, humanities, international studies, mathematics, military science, physical sciences, premedicine, religion/biblical studies, social sciences. *Creative arts/performance:* 520 awards ($2,278,702 total): art/fine arts, cinema/film/broadcasting, debating, journalism/publications, music, theater/drama. *Special achievements/activities:* 303 awards ($532,695 total): community service, leadership, religious involvement. *Special characteristics:* 226 awards ($4,414,383 total): children of faculty/staff. *Tuition waivers:* Full or partial for employees or children of employees.

LOANS *Student loans:* $65,440,720 (70% need-based, 30% non-need-based). *Average need-based loan:* Freshmen: $2753. Undergraduates: $3169. *Parent loans:* $14,594,571 (31% need-based, 69% non-need-based). *Programs:* Federal Direct (Subsidized and Unsubsidized Stafford, PLUS), Perkins, Federal Nursing, state, private loans.

WORK-STUDY *Federal work-study:* Total amount: $11,985,954; 4,340 jobs averaging $2762. *State or other work-study/employment:* Part-time jobs available.

ATHLETIC AWARDS Total amount: $8,319,126 (24% need-based, 76% non-need-based).

APPLYING FOR FINANCIAL AID *Required financial aid forms:* FAFSA, state residency affirmation (for Texas residents to receive state grant or loan). *Financial aid deadline (priority):* 3/1. *Notification date:* Continuous beginning 3/15. Students must reply by 5/1 or within 2 weeks of notification.

CONTACT Office of Admission Services, Baylor University, PO Box 97056, Waco, TX 76798-7056, 254-710-3435 or toll-free 800-BAYLORU. *Fax:* 254-710-3436. *E-mail:* admissions@baylor.edu.

BAY PATH COLLEGE
Longmeadow, MA

CONTACT Phyllis Brand, Financial Aid Assistant, Bay Path College, 588 Longmeadow Street, Longmeadow, MA 01106-2292, 413-565-1261 or toll-free 800-782-7284 Ext. 1331. *Fax:* 413-565-1101. *E-mail:* pbrand@baypath.edu.

BEACON COLLEGE
Leesburg, FL

CONTACT Financial Aid Office, Beacon College, 105 East Main Street, Leesburg, FL 34748, 352-787-7660.

BECKER COLLEGE
Worcester, MA

Tuition & fees: $27,748	Average undergraduate aid package: $14,056

ABOUT THE INSTITUTION Independent, coed. *Awards:* associate and bachelor's degrees (also includes Leicester, MA small town campus). 27 undergraduate majors. *Total enrollment:* 1,752. Undergraduates: 1,752. Freshmen: 347. Federal methodology is used as a basis for awarding need-based institutional aid.

UNDERGRADUATE EXPENSES for 2009–10 *Application fee:* $30. *Comprehensive fee:* $37,508 includes full-time tuition ($24,780), mandatory fees ($2968), and room and board ($9760). Full-time tuition and fees vary according to course load. Room and board charges vary according to board plan and housing facility. *Part-time tuition:* $1025 per credit hour. Part-time tuition and fees vary according to course load and program. *Payment plan:* Installment.

FRESHMAN FINANCIAL AID (Fall 2009, est.) 282 applied for aid; of those 77% were deemed to have need. 84% of freshmen with need received aid; of those 3% had need fully met. *Average percent of need met:* 76% (excluding resources awarded to replace EFC). *Average financial aid package:* $13,959 (excluding resources awarded to replace EFC). 98% of all full-time freshmen had no need and received non-need-based gift aid.

UNDERGRADUATE FINANCIAL AID (Fall 2009, est.) 1,679 applied for aid; of those 91% were deemed to have need. 97% of undergraduates with need received aid; of those 2% had need fully met. *Average percent of need met:* 74% (excluding resources awarded to replace EFC). *Average financial aid package:* $14,056 (excluding resources awarded to replace EFC). 24% of all full-time undergraduates had no need and received non-need-based gift aid.
GIFT AID (NEED-BASED) *Total amount:* $10,455,544 (30% federal, 12% state, 57% institutional, 1% external sources). *Receiving aid:* Freshmen: 56% (168); all full-time undergraduates: 15% (301). *Average award:* Freshmen: $14,992; Undergraduates: $12,854. *Scholarships, grants, and awards:* Federal Pell, FSEOG, state, private, college/university gift aid from institutional funds.
GIFT AID (NON-NEED-BASED) *Total amount:* $5,864,788 (3% state, 97% institutional). *Receiving aid:* Freshmen: 58% (173). Undergraduates: 4% (89). *Average award:* Freshmen: $14,722. Undergraduates: $14,032. *Scholarships, grants, and awards by category:* Academic interests/achievement: general academic interests/achievements. Special achievements/activities: general special achievements/activities, leadership. Special characteristics: children of faculty/staff, siblings of current students, twins. *Tuition waivers:* Full or partial for employees or children of employees, senior citizens. *ROTC:* Army cooperative, Naval cooperative, Air Force cooperative.
LOANS *Student loans:* $14,756,330 (37% need-based, 63% non-need-based). 98% of past graduating class borrowed through all loan programs. *Average indebtedness per student:* $31,800. *Average need-based loan:* Freshmen: $2745. Undergraduates: $4031. *Parent loans:* $5,007,740 (100% non-need-based). *Programs:* Federal Direct (Subsidized and Unsubsidized Stafford, PLUS), state, alternative loans.
WORK-STUDY *Federal work-study:* Total amount: $474,560; 338 jobs averaging $1404.
APPLYING FOR FINANCIAL AID *Required financial aid form:* FAFSA. *Financial aid deadline (priority):* 3/1. *Notification date:* Continuous beginning 3/15. Students must reply within 2 weeks of notification.
CONTACT Mr. Russ Romandini, Director of Student Administrative Services, Becker College, 61 Sever Street, Worcester, MA 01615-0071, 508-373-9440 or toll-free 877-5BECKER Ext. 245. *Fax:* 508-890-1511. *E-mail:* financialaid@becker.edu.

BEIS MEDRASH HEICHAL DOVID
Far Rockaway, NY

CONTACT Financial Aid Office, Beis Medrash Heichal Dovid, 257 Beach 17th Street, Far Rockaway, NY 11691, 718-868-2300.

BELHAVEN UNIVERSITY
Jackson, MS

Tuition & fees: $17,700	Average undergraduate aid package: $14,653

ABOUT THE INSTITUTION Independent Presbyterian, coed. 28 undergraduate majors. Federal methodology is used as a basis for awarding need-based institutional aid.
UNDERGRADUATE EXPENSES for 2010–11 *Comprehensive fee:* $24,200 includes full-time tuition ($17,700) and room and board ($6500). *Part-time tuition:* $350 per semester hour. *Payment plan:* Installment.
FRESHMAN FINANCIAL AID (Fall 2009, est.) 165 applied for aid; of those 84% were deemed to have need. 99% of freshmen with need received aid; of those 12% had need fully met. *Average percent of need met:* 62% (excluding resources awarded to replace EFC). *Average financial aid package:* $14,628 (excluding resources awarded to replace EFC). 14% of all full-time freshmen had no need and received non-need-based gift aid.
UNDERGRADUATE FINANCIAL AID (Fall 2009, est.) 742 applied for aid; of those 90% were deemed to have need. 99% of undergraduates with need received aid; of those 12% had need fully met. *Average percent of need met:* 61% (excluding resources awarded to replace EFC). *Average financial aid package:* $14,653 (excluding resources awarded to replace EFC). 10% of all full-time undergraduates had no need and received non-need-based gift aid.
GIFT AID (NEED-BASED) *Total amount:* $3,890,885 (48% federal, 5% state, 39% institutional, 8% external sources). *Receiving aid:* Freshmen: 72% (138); all full-time undergraduates: 72% (654). *Average award:* Freshmen: $11,499; Undergraduates: $10,710. *Scholarships, grants, and awards:* Federal Pell, FSEOG, state, private, college/university gift aid from institutional funds.

GIFT AID (NON-NEED-BASED) *Total amount:* $855,670 (6% state, 74% institutional, 20% external sources). *Receiving aid:* Freshmen: 6% (12). Undergraduates: 5% (46). *Average award:* Freshmen: $7162. Undergraduates: $6318. *Scholarships, grants, and awards by category:* Academic interests/achievement: 310 awards ($2,451,977 total): biological sciences, business, communication, education, English, foreign languages, general academic interests/achievements, humanities, international studies, mathematics, premedicine, religion/biblical studies, social sciences. Creative arts/performance: 279 awards ($2,121,696 total): applied art and design, art/fine arts, creative writing, dance, journalism/publications, music, performing arts, theater/drama. Special achievements/activities: 120 awards ($138,150 total): cheerleading/drum major, general special achievements/activities, junior miss, leadership. Special characteristics: 268 awards ($652,000 total): children of faculty/staff, general special characteristics, international students, local/state students. *Tuition waivers:* Full or partial for employees or children of employees.
LOANS *Student loans:* $5,158,547 (85% need-based, 15% non-need-based). 92% of past graduating class borrowed through all loan programs. *Average indebtedness per student:* $32,728. *Average need-based loan:* Freshmen: $3260. Undergraduates: $4342. *Parent loans:* $673,924 (48% need-based, 52% non-need-based). *Programs:* Federal Direct (Subsidized and Unsubsidized Stafford, PLUS), FFEL (Subsidized and Unsubsidized Stafford, PLUS), Perkins.
WORK-STUDY *Federal work-study:* Total amount: $278,193; 148 jobs averaging $1743.
ATHLETIC AWARDS Total amount: $2,464,684 (78% need-based, 22% non-need-based).
APPLYING FOR FINANCIAL AID *Required financial aid form:* FAFSA. *Financial aid deadline (priority):* 2/1. *Notification date:* Continuous.
CONTACT Ms. Linda Phillips, Assistant Vice President for Institutional Advancement, Belhaven University, 1500 Peachtree Street, Jackson, MS 39202-1789, 601-968-5933 or toll-free 800-960-5940. *Fax:* 601-353-0701. *E-mail:* lphillips@belhaven.edu.

BELLARMINE UNIVERSITY
Louisville, KY

Tuition & fees: $30,310	Average undergraduate aid package: $23,927

ABOUT THE INSTITUTION Independent Roman Catholic, coed. 31 undergraduate majors. Both federal and institutional methodology are used as a basis for awarding need-based institutional aid.
UNDERGRADUATE EXPENSES for 2010–11 *One-time required fee:* $300. *Comprehensive fee:* $38,860 includes full-time tuition ($29,160), mandatory fees ($1150), and room and board ($8550). *College room only:* $4960. Room and board charges vary according to board plan and housing facility. *Part-time tuition:* $690 per credit hour. *Part-time fees:* $45 per course. *Payment plan:* Installment.
FRESHMAN FINANCIAL AID (Fall 2009, est.) 536 applied for aid; of those 89% were deemed to have need. 100% of freshmen with need received aid; of those 24% had need fully met. *Average percent of need met:* 79% (excluding resources awarded to replace EFC). *Average financial aid package:* $25,373 (excluding resources awarded to replace EFC). 21% of all full-time freshmen had no need and received non-need-based gift aid.
UNDERGRADUATE FINANCIAL AID (Fall 2009, est.) 1,677 applied for aid; of those 91% were deemed to have need. 98% of undergraduates with need received aid; of those 25% had need fully met. *Average percent of need met:* 77% (excluding resources awarded to replace EFC). *Average financial aid package:* $23,927 (excluding resources awarded to replace EFC). 24% of all full-time undergraduates had no need and received non-need-based gift aid.
GIFT AID (NEED-BASED) *Total amount:* $28,561,662 (9% federal, 14% state, 74% institutional, 3% external sources). *Receiving aid:* Freshmen: 79% (474); all full-time undergraduates: 74% (1,493). *Average award:* Freshmen: $17,171; Undergraduates: $15,752. *Scholarships, grants, and awards:* Federal Pell, FSEOG, state, private, college/university gift aid from institutional funds.
GIFT AID (NON-NEED-BASED) *Total amount:* $9,379,108 (7% state, 88% institutional, 5% external sources). *Receiving aid:* Freshmen: 27% (160). Undergraduates: 26% (518). *Average award:* Freshmen: $17,840. Undergraduates: $16,198. *Scholarships, grants, and awards by category:* Academic interests/achievement: biological sciences, business, education, general academic interests/achievements, health fields. Creative arts/performance: art/fine arts, music. Special achievements/activities: cheerleading/drum major, community service, general special achievements/activities, leadership, religious involvement.

Bellarmine University

Special characteristics: adult students, children and siblings of alumni, children of faculty/staff, ethnic background, international students, local/state students, members of minority groups, out-of-state students, previous college experience, religious affiliation. *Tuition waivers:* Full or partial for employees or children of employees, senior citizens.

LOANS *Student loans:* $10,368,612 (73% need-based, 27% non-need-based). 69% of past graduating class borrowed through all loan programs. *Average indebtedness per student:* $21,639. *Average need-based loan:* Freshmen: $3303. Undergraduates: $4112. *Parent loans:* $1,909,671 (39% need-based, 61% non-need-based). *Programs:* FFEL (Subsidized and Unsubsidized Stafford, PLUS), Perkins, college/university.

WORK-STUDY *Federal work-study:* Total amount: $400,308; 241 jobs averaging $1661. *State or other work-study/employment:* Total amount: $50,000 (100% non-need-based). Part-time jobs available.

ATHLETIC AWARDS Total amount: $2,300,856 (47% need-based, 53% non-need-based).

APPLYING FOR FINANCIAL AID *Required financial aid form:* FAFSA. *Financial aid deadline (priority):* 3/1. *Notification date:* Continuous beginning 3/15. Students must reply by 5/1.

CONTACT Ms. Heather Boutell, Director of Financial Aid, Bellarmine University, 2001 Newburg Road, Louisville, KY 40205-0671, 502-452-8124 or toll-free 800-274-4723 Ext. 8131. *Fax:* 502-452-8002. *E-mail:* hboutell@bellarmine.edu.

BELLEVUE UNIVERSITY
Bellevue, NE

CONTACT Mr. Jon Dotterer, Director of Financial Aid, Bellevue University, 1000 Galvin Road South, Bellevue, NE 68005, 402-293-3762 or toll-free 800-756-7920. *Fax:* 402-293-2062.

BELLIN COLLEGE
Green Bay, WI

Tuition & fees: N/R	Average undergraduate aid package: $18,429

ABOUT THE INSTITUTION Independent, coed, primarily women. *Awards:* bachelor's and master's degrees. 1 undergraduate major. *Total enrollment:* 304. Undergraduates: 259. Federal methodology is used as a basis for awarding need-based institutional aid.

UNDERGRADUATE FINANCIAL AID (Fall 2008) 119 applied for aid; of those 92% were deemed to have need. 100% of undergraduates with need received aid; of those 13% had need fully met. *Average percent of need met:* 80% (excluding resources awarded to replace EFC). *Average financial aid package:* $18,429 (excluding resources awarded to replace EFC). 1% of all full-time undergraduates had no need and received non-need-based gift aid.

GIFT AID (NEED-BASED) *Total amount:* $578,254 (21% federal, 20% state, 41% institutional, 18% external sources). *Receiving aid:* All full-time undergraduates: 48% (108). *Average award:* Undergraduates: $5314. *Scholarships, grants, and awards:* Federal Pell, FSEOG, state, private, college/university gift aid from institutional funds.

GIFT AID (NON-NEED-BASED) *Total amount:* $36,791 (18% institutional, 82% external sources). *Receiving aid:* Undergraduates: 2% (5). *Average award:* Undergraduates: $1000. *Scholarships, grants, and awards by category:* Academic interests/achievement: 22 awards ($50,492 total): general academic interests/achievements. *ROTC:* Army cooperative.

LOANS *Student loans:* $1,819,380 (75% need-based, 25% non-need-based). 86% of past graduating class borrowed through all loan programs. *Average indebtedness per student:* $38,434. *Average need-based loan:* Undergraduates: $4704. *Parent loans:* $246,707 (50% need-based, 50% non-need-based). *Programs:* Federal Direct (Subsidized and Unsubsidized Stafford, PLUS), state.

WORK-STUDY *Federal work-study:* Total amount: $2500; 2 jobs averaging $1250.

APPLYING FOR FINANCIAL AID *Required financial aid form:* FAFSA. *Financial aid deadline (priority):* 3/1. *Notification date:* 4/1. Students must reply within 2 weeks of notification.

CONTACT Mrs. Lena C. Goodman, Director of Financial Aid, Bellin College, 3201 Eaton Road, Green Bay, WI 54311, 920-433-6638 or toll-free 800-236-8707. *Fax:* 920-433-1922. *E-mail:* lena.goodman@bellincollege.edu.

BELMONT ABBEY COLLEGE
Belmont, NC

Tuition & fees: $21,506	Average undergraduate aid package: $13,151

ABOUT THE INSTITUTION Independent Roman Catholic, coed. 19 undergraduate majors. Federal methodology is used as a basis for awarding need-based institutional aid.

UNDERGRADUATE EXPENSES for 2009–10 *One-time required fee:* $1006. *Comprehensive fee:* $31,454 includes full-time tuition ($20,356), mandatory fees ($1150), and room and board ($9948). *College room only:* $5766. Full-time tuition and fees vary according to class time, course level, course load, location, program, and reciprocity agreements. Room and board charges vary according to board plan, housing facility, and location. *Part-time tuition:* $678 per credit hour. *Part-time fees:* $38 per credit hour. Part-time tuition and fees vary according to class time, course level, course load, location, and reciprocity agreements. *Payment plans:* Installment, deferred payment.

FRESHMAN FINANCIAL AID (Fall 2009, est.) 293 applied for aid; of those 86% were deemed to have need. 100% of freshmen with need received aid; of those 19% had need fully met. *Average percent of need met:* 70% (excluding resources awarded to replace EFC). *Average financial aid package:* $17,598 (excluding resources awarded to replace EFC). 28% of all full-time freshmen had no need and received non-need-based gift aid.

UNDERGRADUATE FINANCIAL AID (Fall 2009, est.) 1,463 applied for aid; of those 92% were deemed to have need. 99% of undergraduates with need received aid; of those 11% had need fully met. *Average percent of need met:* 56% (excluding resources awarded to replace EFC). *Average financial aid package:* $13,151 (excluding resources awarded to replace EFC). 17% of all full-time undergraduates had no need and received non-need-based gift aid.

GIFT AID (NEED-BASED) *Total amount:* $8,854,540 (1% federal, 36% state, 55% institutional, 8% external sources). *Receiving aid:* Freshmen: 70% (251); all full-time undergraduates: 78% (1,318). *Average award:* Freshmen: $15,059; Undergraduates: $9398. *Scholarships, grants, and awards:* Federal Pell, FSEOG, state, private, college/university gift aid from institutional funds.

GIFT AID (NON-NEED-BASED) *Total amount:* $3,877,978 (6% state, 86% institutional, 8% external sources). *Receiving aid:* Freshmen: 12% (43). Undergraduates: 7% (111). *Average award:* Freshmen: $11,642. Undergraduates: $10,008. *Scholarships, grants, and awards by category:* Academic interests/achievement: 681 awards ($5,549,463 total): general academic interests/achievements. *Creative arts/performance:* 31 awards ($60,000 total): theater/drama. *Special achievements/activities:* 20 awards ($298,766 total): religious involvement. *Special characteristics:* 31 awards ($188,286 total): children of faculty/staff. *Tuition waivers:* Full or partial for employees or children of employees, senior citizens.

LOANS *Student loans:* $9,355,216 (81% need-based, 19% non-need-based). 73% of past graduating class borrowed through all loan programs. *Average indebtedness per student:* $21,000. *Average need-based loan:* Freshmen: $3033. Undergraduates: $4073. *Parent loans:* $6,692,158 (30% need-based, 70% non-need-based). *Programs:* Federal Direct (Subsidized and Unsubsidized Stafford, PLUS), Perkins.

WORK-STUDY *Federal work-study:* Total amount: $111,888; 114 jobs averaging $1255.

ATHLETIC AWARDS Total amount: $1,263,745 (46% need-based, 54% non-need-based).

APPLYING FOR FINANCIAL AID *Required financial aid form:* FAFSA. *Financial aid deadline (priority):* 4/1. *Notification date:* Continuous. Students must reply within 2 weeks of notification.

CONTACT Ms. Julie Hodge, Associate Director of Financial Aid, Belmont Abbey College, 100 Belmont Mt. Holly Road, Belmont, NC 28012-1802, 704-461-6718 or toll-free 888-BAC-0110. *Fax:* 704-461-6882. *E-mail:* juliehodge@bac.edu.

BELMONT UNIVERSITY
Nashville, TN

Tuition & fees: $22,360	Average undergraduate aid package: $11,966

ABOUT THE INSTITUTION Independent Christian, coed. 66 undergraduate majors. Federal methodology is used as a basis for awarding need-based institutional aid.

UNDERGRADUATE EXPENSES for 2009–10 *Comprehensive fee:* $32,360 includes full-time tuition ($21,270), mandatory fees ($1090), and room and board ($10,000). *College room only:* $6300. Full-time tuition and fees vary according to class time and course load. Room and board charges vary according to board plan, housing facility, and location. *Part-time tuition:* $820 per credit hour. *Part-time fees:* $365 per term. Part-time tuition and fees vary according to course load. *Payment plans:* Installment, deferred payment.

FRESHMAN FINANCIAL AID (Fall 2009, est.) 938 applied for aid; of those 58% were deemed to have need. 97% of freshmen with need received aid; of those 27% had need fully met. *Average percent of need met:* 87% (excluding resources awarded to replace EFC). *Average financial aid package:* $13,032 (excluding resources awarded to replace EFC). 28% of all full-time freshmen had no need and received non-need-based gift aid.

UNDERGRADUATE FINANCIAL AID (Fall 2009, est.) 3,683 applied for aid; of those 59% were deemed to have need. 97% of undergraduates with need received aid; of those 22% had need fully met. *Average percent of need met:* 80% (excluding resources awarded to replace EFC). *Average financial aid package:* $11,966 (excluding resources awarded to replace EFC). 13% of all full-time undergraduates had no need and received non-need-based gift aid.

GIFT AID (NEED-BASED) *Total amount:* $8,436,038 (37% federal, 7% state, 45% institutional, 11% external sources). *Receiving aid:* Freshmen: 21% (207); all full-time undergraduates: 24% (965). *Average award:* Freshmen: $5563; Undergraduates: $5881. *Scholarships, grants, and awards:* Federal Pell, FSEOG, state, private, college/university gift aid from institutional funds.

GIFT AID (NON-NEED-BASED) *Total amount:* $16,595,179 (26% state, 74% institutional). *Receiving aid:* Freshmen: 49% (481). Undergraduates: 40% (1,602). *Average award:* Freshmen: $6471. Undergraduates: $6326. *Scholarships, grants, and awards by category:* Academic interests/achievement: 1,536 awards ($7,325,766 total): general academic interests/achievements, religion/biblical studies. Creative arts/performance: 207 awards ($475,690 total): music. Special characteristics: 56 awards ($987,895 total): children of faculty/staff. *Tuition waivers:* Full or partial for employees or children of employees, senior citizens.

LOANS *Student loans:* $39,281,532 (50% need-based, 50% non-need-based). 57% of past graduating class borrowed through all loan programs. *Average indebtedness per student:* $19,268. *Average need-based loan:* Freshmen: $3524. Undergraduates: $4394. *Parent loans:* $12,831,749 (100% non-need-based). *Programs:* Federal Direct (PLUS), FFEL (Subsidized and Unsubsidized Stafford, PLUS), Perkins, college/university.

WORK-STUDY *Federal work-study:* Total amount: $435,503; 371 jobs averaging $829.

ATHLETIC AWARDS Total amount: $3,577,717 (1% need-based, 99% non-need-based).

APPLYING FOR FINANCIAL AID *Required financial aid form:* FAFSA. *Financial aid deadline (priority):* 3/1. *Notification date:* Continuous beginning 3/15. Students must reply by 5/1 or within 2 weeks of notification.

CONTACT Mrs. Pat Smedley, Director, Student Financial Services, Belmont University, 1900 Belmont Boulevard, Nashville, TN 37212-3757, 615-460-6403 or toll-free 800-56E-NROL. *E-mail:* pat.smedley@belmont.edu.

BELOIT COLLEGE
Beloit, WI

Tuition & fees: $33,368	Average undergraduate aid package: $28,203

ABOUT THE INSTITUTION Independent, coed. 55 undergraduate majors. Both federal and institutional methodology are used as a basis for awarding need-based institutional aid.

UNDERGRADUATE EXPENSES for 2009–10 *Comprehensive fee:* $40,198 includes full-time tuition ($33,138), mandatory fees ($230), and room and board ($6830). *College room only:* $3348. Room and board charges vary according to board plan. *Part-time tuition:* $4142 per course. *Payment plan:* Installment.

FRESHMAN FINANCIAL AID (Fall 2009, est.) 258 applied for aid; of those 83% were deemed to have need. 100% of freshmen with need received aid; of those 48% had need fully met. *Average percent of need met:* 95% (excluding resources awarded to replace EFC). *Average financial aid package:* $28,126 (excluding resources awarded to replace EFC). 30% of all full-time freshmen had no need and received non-need-based gift aid.

UNDERGRADUATE FINANCIAL AID (Fall 2009, est.) 981 applied for aid; of those 85% were deemed to have need. 100% of undergraduates with need

received aid; of those 39% had need fully met. *Average percent of need met:* 94% (excluding resources awarded to replace EFC). *Average financial aid package:* $28,203 (excluding resources awarded to replace EFC). 27% of all full-time undergraduates had no need and received non-need-based gift aid.

GIFT AID (NEED-BASED) *Total amount:* $17,772,680 (9% federal, 2% state, 86% institutional, 3% external sources). *Receiving aid:* Freshmen: 64% (214); all full-time undergraduates: 63% (828). *Average award:* Freshmen: $23,727; Undergraduates: $21,235. *Scholarships, grants, and awards:* Federal Pell, FSEOG, state, private, college/university gift aid from institutional funds.

GIFT AID (NON-NEED-BASED) *Total amount:* $1,582,088 (95% institutional, 5% external sources). *Average award:* Freshmen: $14,291. Undergraduates: $13,583. *Scholarships, grants, and awards by category:* Academic interests/achievement: 552 awards ($6,178,080 total): general academic interests/achievements. Creative arts/performance: 45 awards ($175,000 total): music. Special achievements/activities: 24 awards ($94,000 total): community service, general special achievements/activities. Special characteristics: 78 awards ($1,172,791 total): members of minority groups, siblings of current students. *Tuition waivers:* Full or partial for employees or children of employees.

LOANS *Student loans:* $7,679,816 (89% need-based, 11% non-need-based). 69% of past graduating class borrowed through all loan programs. *Average indebtedness per student:* $17,909. *Average need-based loan:* Freshmen: $2833. Undergraduates: $5101. *Parent loans:* $1,321,238 (79% need-based, 21% non-need-based). *Programs:* FFEL (Subsidized and Unsubsidized Stafford, PLUS), Perkins, college/university.

WORK-STUDY *Federal work-study:* Total amount: $1,002,953; 572 jobs averaging $1752. *State or other work-study/employment:* Total amount: $429,106 (68% need-based, 32% non-need-based). 470 part-time jobs averaging $1288.

APPLYING FOR FINANCIAL AID *Required financial aid forms:* FAFSA, institution's own form, state aid form. *Financial aid deadline (priority):* 3/1. *Notification date:* Continuous beginning 4/1. Students must reply by 5/1 or within 2 weeks of notification.

CONTACT Mr. Jon Urish, Senior Associate Director of Admissions and Financial Aid, Beloit College, 700 College Street, Beloit, WI 53511-5596, 800-356-0751 or toll-free 800-9-BELOIT. *Fax:* 608-363-2075. *E-mail:* urishj@beloit.edu.

BEMIDJI STATE UNIVERSITY
Bemidji, MN

Tuition & fees (MN res): $7510	Average undergraduate aid package: $9118

ABOUT THE INSTITUTION State-supported, coed. 72 undergraduate majors. Federal methodology is used as a basis for awarding need-based institutional aid.

UNDERGRADUATE EXPENSES for 2010–11 *Tuition, state resident:* full-time $6575; part-time $229 per credit hour. *Tuition, nonresident:* full-time $6575; part-time $229 per credit hour. *Required fees:* full-time $935; $22 per credit hour. Full-time tuition and fees vary according to course load, location, program, and reciprocity agreements. Part-time tuition and fees vary according to course load, location, program, and reciprocity agreements. *College room and board:* $6425. Room and board charges vary according to board plan and housing facility. *Payment plan:* Installment.

FRESHMAN FINANCIAL AID (Fall 2009, est.) 568 applied for aid; of those 69% were deemed to have need. 100% of freshmen with need received aid; of those 21% had need fully met. *Average percent of need met:* 70% (excluding resources awarded to replace EFC). *Average financial aid package:* $8223 (excluding resources awarded to replace EFC). 25% of all full-time freshmen had no need and received non-need-based gift aid.

UNDERGRADUATE FINANCIAL AID (Fall 2009, est.) 2,858 applied for aid; of those 79% were deemed to have need. 100% of undergraduates with need received aid; of those 34% had need fully met. *Average percent of need met:* 72% (excluding resources awarded to replace EFC). *Average financial aid package:* $9118 (excluding resources awarded to replace EFC). 16% of all full-time undergraduates had no need and received non-need-based gift aid.

GIFT AID (NEED-BASED) *Total amount:* $10,205,215 (66% federal, 33% state, 1% external sources). *Receiving aid:* Freshmen: 40% (270); all full-time undergraduates: 48% (1,696). *Average award:* Freshmen: $5557; Undergraduates: $5408. *Scholarships, grants, and awards:* Federal Pell, FSEOG, state, private, college/university gift aid from institutional funds.

GIFT AID (NON-NEED-BASED) *Total amount:* $5,502,305 (25% federal, 17% state, 42% institutional, 16% external sources). *Receiving aid:* Freshmen: 46% (313). Undergraduates: 47% (1,661). *Average award:* Freshmen: $8393.

Undergraduates: $9121. *Scholarships, grants, and awards by category: Academic interests/achievement:* 653 awards ($618,607 total): general academic interests/achievements. *Creative arts/performance:* 44 awards ($98,600 total): general creative arts/performance. *Special characteristics:* 197 awards ($400,715 total): children and siblings of alumni, children of faculty/staff, international students, out-of-state students. *Tuition waivers:* Full or partial for employees or children of employees, senior citizens.

LOANS *Student loans:* $22,823,418 (37% need-based, 63% non-need-based). 80% of past graduating class borrowed through all loan programs. *Average indebtedness per student:* $24,474. *Average need-based loan:* Freshmen: $3201. Undergraduates: $3726. *Parent loans:* $450,821 (100% non-need-based). *Programs:* Federal Direct (Subsidized and Unsubsidized Stafford, PLUS), Perkins, state, Alaska Loans, Canada Student Loans, Norwest Collegiate Loans, CitiAssist Loans, alternative loans.

WORK-STUDY *Federal work-study:* Total amount: $379,251; 251 jobs averaging $1704. *State or other work-study/employment:* Total amount: $1,668,251 (16% need-based, 84% non-need-based). 193 part-time jobs averaging $1542.

ATHLETIC AWARDS Total amount: $913,583 (100% non-need-based).

APPLYING FOR FINANCIAL AID *Required financial aid forms:* FAFSA, institution's own form. *Financial aid deadline (priority):* 4/15. *Notification date:* Continuous beginning 6/15.

CONTACT Financial Aid Office, Bemidji State University, 1500 Birchmont Drive, NE, Bemidji, MN 56601-2699, 218-755-2034 or toll-free 800-475-2001 (in-state), 800-652-9747 (out-of-state). *Fax:* 218-755-4361. *E-mail:* financialaid@ bemidjistate.edu.

BENEDICT COLLEGE
Columbia, SC

Tuition & fees: N/R	Average undergraduate aid package: N/A

ABOUT THE INSTITUTION Independent Baptist, coed. *Awards:* bachelor's degrees. 32 undergraduate majors. *Total enrollment:* 2,641. Undergraduates: 2,641. Both federal and institutional methodology are used as a basis for awarding need-based institutional aid.

GIFT AID (NEED-BASED) *Scholarships, grants, and awards:* Federal Pell, FSEOG, state, private.

GIFT AID (NON-NEED-BASED) *Scholarships, grants, and awards by category: Academic interests/achievement:* general academic interests/achievements. *Creative arts/performance:* general creative arts/performance, music. *ROTC:* Army, Air Force cooperative.

LOANS *Programs:* Federal Direct (Subsidized and Unsubsidized Stafford, PLUS), Perkins, state, college/university.

WORK-STUDY Federal work-study jobs available.

APPLYING FOR FINANCIAL AID *Required financial aid form:* FAFSA. *Financial aid deadline (priority):* 4/15. *Notification date:* Continuous.

CONTACT Mrs. Bichevia Green, Associate Director of Financial Aid, Benedict College, 1600 Harden Street, Columbia, SC 29204, 803-705-4418 or toll-free 800-868-6598 (in-state). *Fax:* 803-705-6629. *E-mail:* greenb@benedict.edu.

BENEDICTINE COLLEGE
Atchison, KS

Tuition & fees: $19,500	Average undergraduate aid package: $22,755

ABOUT THE INSTITUTION Independent Roman Catholic, coed. 34 undergraduate majors. Federal methodology is used as a basis for awarding need-based institutional aid.

UNDERGRADUATE EXPENSES for 2009–10 *Comprehensive fee:* $26,075 includes full-time tuition ($19,500) and room and board ($6575). *College room only:* $3480. Full-time tuition and fees vary according to course load and degree level. Room and board charges vary according to board plan and housing facility. *Part-time tuition:* $540 per credit hour. Part-time tuition and fees vary according to course load and degree level. *Payment plan:* Installment.

FRESHMAN FINANCIAL AID (Fall 2009, est.) 368 applied for aid; of those 81% were deemed to have need. 100% of freshmen with need received aid; of those 24% had need fully met. *Average percent of need met:* 76% (excluding resources awarded to replace EFC). *Average financial aid package:* $22,120 (excluding resources awarded to replace EFC). 16% of all full-time freshmen had no need and received non-need-based gift aid.

UNDERGRADUATE FINANCIAL AID (Fall 2009, est.) 1,209 applied for aid; of those 86% were deemed to have need. 100% of undergraduates with need received aid; of those 21% had need fully met. *Average percent of need met:* 75% (excluding resources awarded to replace EFC). *Average financial aid package:* $22,755 (excluding resources awarded to replace EFC). 12% of all full-time undergraduates had no need and received non-need-based gift aid.

GIFT AID (NEED-BASED) *Total amount:* $11,388,570 (16% federal, 6% state, 75% institutional, 3% external sources). *Receiving aid:* Freshmen: 70% (299); all full-time undergraduates: 73% (1,040). *Average award:* Freshmen: $13,106; Undergraduates: $12,418. *Scholarships, grants, and awards:* Federal Pell, FSEOG, state, private, college/university gift aid from institutional funds.

GIFT AID (NON-NEED-BASED) *Total amount:* $1,899,771 (89% institutional, 11% external sources). *Receiving aid:* Freshmen: 11% (47). Undergraduates: 9% (128). *Average award:* Freshmen: $8253. Undergraduates: $7981. *Scholarships, grants, and awards by category: Academic interests/achievement:* general academic interests/achievements. *Creative arts/performance:* music, theater/ drama. *Special achievements/activities:* general special achievements/activities. *Special characteristics:* children of educators, ethnic background, general special characteristics, international students, local/state students, members of minority groups, out-of-state students, religious affiliation, veterans' children. *Tuition waivers:* Full or partial for employees or children of employees, senior citizens.

LOANS *Student loans:* $7,540,803 (67% need-based, 33% non-need-based). 75% of past graduating class borrowed through all loan programs. *Average indebtedness per student:* $25,749. *Average need-based loan:* Freshmen: $2412. Undergraduates: $3335. *Parent loans:* $1,991,807 (50% need-based, 50% non-need-based). *Programs:* FFEL (Subsidized and Unsubsidized Stafford, PLUS), Perkins, alternative loans.

WORK-STUDY *Federal work-study:* Total amount: $1,016,623; jobs available. *State or other work-study/employment:* Total amount: $171,654 (44% need-based, 56% non-need-based). Part-time jobs available.

ATHLETIC AWARDS Total amount: $2,159,535 (70% need-based, 30% non-need-based).

APPLYING FOR FINANCIAL AID *Required financial aid form:* FAFSA. *Financial aid deadline (priority):* 3/15. *Notification date:* Continuous. Students must reply within 2 weeks of notification.

CONTACT Mr. Tony Tanking, Director of Financial Aid, Benedictine College, 1020 North Second Street, Atchison, KS 66002-1499, 913-360-7484 or toll-free 800-467-5340. *Fax:* 913-367-5462. *E-mail:* ttanking@benedictine.edu.

BENEDICTINE UNIVERSITY
Lisle, IL

Tuition & fees: $22,310	Average undergraduate aid package: $16,602

ABOUT THE INSTITUTION Independent Roman Catholic, coed. 48 undergraduate majors. Federal methodology is used as a basis for awarding need-based institutional aid.

UNDERGRADUATE EXPENSES for 2009–10 *Comprehensive fee:* $29,670 includes full-time tuition ($21,600), mandatory fees ($710), and room and board ($7360). Full-time tuition and fees vary according to class time, degree level, and location. Room and board charges vary according to board plan and housing facility. *Part-time tuition:* $720 per credit hour. *Part-time fees:* $15 per credit hour. Part-time tuition and fees vary according to class time and degree level. *Payment plans:* Installment, deferred payment.

FRESHMAN FINANCIAL AID (Fall 2009, est.) 399 applied for aid; of those 86% were deemed to have need. 100% of freshmen with need received aid. *Average financial aid package:* $19,182 (excluding resources awarded to replace EFC). 68% of all full-time freshmen had no need and received non-need-based gift aid.

UNDERGRADUATE FINANCIAL AID (Fall 2009, est.) 1,791 applied for aid; of those 89% were deemed to have need. 97% of undergraduates with need received aid. *Average financial aid package:* $16,602 (excluding resources awarded to replace EFC). 44% of all full-time undergraduates had no need and received non-need-based gift aid.

GIFT AID (NEED-BASED) *Total amount:* $9,521,661 (50% federal, 46% state, 4% institutional). *Receiving aid:* Freshmen: 50% (226); all full-time undergraduates: 44% (1,009). *Average award:* Freshmen: $8117; Undergraduates: $7641. *Scholarships, grants, and awards:* Federal Pell, FSEOG, state, private, college/ university gift aid from institutional funds.

GIFT AID (NON-NEED-BASED) *Total amount:* $14,275,623 (98% institutional, 2% external sources). *Receiving aid:* Freshmen: 73% (331). Undergraduates:

56% (1,280). *Average award:* Freshmen: $8949. Undergraduates: $8536. *Scholarships, grants, and awards by category: Academic interests/achievement:* 1,952 awards ($14,300,256 total): general academic interests/achievements. *Creative arts/performance:* 13 awards ($38,750 total): music. *Special achievements/activities:* 125 awards ($249,350 total): community service, leadership. *Special characteristics:* 248 awards ($597,211 total): children and siblings of alumni, international students, out-of-state students, relatives of clergy, siblings of current students, veterans, veterans' children. *Tuition waivers:* Full or partial for employees or children of employees.

LOANS *Student loans:* $16,056,104 (43% need-based, 57% non-need-based). 65% of past graduating class borrowed through all loan programs. *Average indebtedness per student:* $25,781. *Average need-based loan:* Freshmen: $3622. Undergraduates: $4394. *Parent loans:* $2,751,860 (100% non-need-based). *Programs:* Federal Direct (Subsidized and Unsubsidized Stafford, PLUS), Perkins, alternative loans.

WORK-STUDY *Federal work-study:* Total amount: $196,333; 174 jobs averaging $1128.

APPLYING FOR FINANCIAL AID *Required financial aid form:* FAFSA. *Financial aid deadline:* Continuous. *Notification date:* Continuous beginning 2/15. Students must reply within 2 weeks of notification.

CONTACT Diane Battistella, Associate Dean, Financial Aid, Benedictine University, 5700 College Road, Lisle, IL 60532, 630-829-6415 or toll-free 888-829-6363 (out-of-state). *Fax:* 630-829-6456. *E-mail:* dbattistella@ben.edu.

BENNETT COLLEGE FOR WOMEN
Greensboro, NC

CONTACT Monty K. Hickman, Financial Aid Director, Bennett College for Women, 900 East Washington Street, Greensboro, NC 27401, 336-370-8677. *Fax:* 336-517-2204. *E-mail:* mhickman@bennett.edu.

BENNINGTON COLLEGE
Bennington, VT

Tuition & fees: $39,760	Average undergraduate aid package: $32,970

ABOUT THE INSTITUTION Independent, coed. 98 undergraduate majors. Both federal and institutional methodology are used as a basis for awarding need-based institutional aid.

UNDERGRADUATE EXPENSES for 2009–10 *Comprehensive fee:* $50,860 includes full-time tuition ($38,730), mandatory fees ($1030), and room and board ($11,100). *College room only:* $5950. *Part-time tuition:* $1290 per credit hour. *Payment plan:* Installment.

FRESHMAN FINANCIAL AID (Fall 2009, est.) 154 applied for aid; of those 92% were deemed to have need. 98% of freshmen with need received aid; of those 17% had need fully met. *Average percent of need met:* 81% (excluding resources awarded to replace EFC). *Average financial aid package:* $32,427 (excluding resources awarded to replace EFC). 11% of all full-time freshmen had no need and received non-need-based gift aid.

UNDERGRADUATE FINANCIAL AID (Fall 2009, est.) 495 applied for aid; of those 93% were deemed to have need. 99% of undergraduates with need received aid; of those 13% had need fully met. *Average percent of need met:* 81% (excluding resources awarded to replace EFC). *Average financial aid package:* $32,970 (excluding resources awarded to replace EFC). 9% of all full-time undergraduates had no need and received non-need-based gift aid.

GIFT AID (NEED-BASED) *Total amount:* $12,747,665 (8% federal, 90% institutional, 2% external sources). *Receiving aid:* Freshmen: 69% (136); all full-time undergraduates: 67% (445). *Average award:* Freshmen: $29,549; Undergraduates: $28,738. *Scholarships, grants, and awards:* Federal Pell, FSEOG, state, private, college/university gift aid from institutional funds.

GIFT AID (NON-NEED-BASED) *Total amount:* $1,212,501 (85% institutional, 15% external sources). *Receiving aid:* Freshmen: 10% (20). Undergraduates: 5% (32). *Average award:* Freshmen: $10,166. Undergraduates: $13,744. *Scholarships, grants, and awards by category: Academic interests/achievement:* general academic interests/achievements. *Creative arts/performance:* general creative arts/performance. *Special achievements/activities:* general special achievements/activities. *Special characteristics:* children of educators, children of faculty/staff, general special characteristics. *Tuition waivers:* Full or partial for employees or children of employees.

LOANS *Student loans:* $2,997,962 (78% need-based, 22% non-need-based). 70% of past graduating class borrowed through all loan programs. *Average indebtedness per student:* $22,402. *Average need-based loan:* Freshmen: $2797. Undergraduates: $3977. *Parent loans:* $1,632,883 (32% need-based, 68% non-need-based). *Programs:* Federal Direct (Subsidized and Unsubsidized Stafford, PLUS); college/university.

WORK-STUDY *Federal work-study:* Total amount: $513,688; 377 jobs averaging $2000. *State or other work-study/employment:* Total amount: $58,000 (93% need-based, 7% non-need-based). 30 part-time jobs averaging $2000.

APPLYING FOR FINANCIAL AID *Required financial aid forms:* FAFSA, institution's own form, CSS Financial Aid PROFILE, noncustodial (divorced/separated) parent's statement, student and parent federal tax returns and W-2 forms. *Financial aid deadline:* 2/15 (priority: 2/1). *Notification date:* 4/1. Students must reply by 5/1 or within 2 weeks of notification.

CONTACT Meg Woolmington, Director of Financial Aid, Bennington College, One College Drive, Bennington, VT 05201, 802-440-4325 or toll-free 800-833-6845. *Fax:* 802-440-4880. *E-mail:* finaid@bennington.edu.

BENTLEY UNIVERSITY
Waltham, MA

Tuition & fees: $35,828	Average undergraduate aid package: $29,415

ABOUT THE INSTITUTION Independent, coed. 16 undergraduate majors. Both federal and institutional methodology are used as a basis for awarding need-based institutional aid.

UNDERGRADUATE EXPENSES for 2009–10 *Comprehensive fee:* $47,568 includes full-time tuition ($34,360), mandatory fees ($1468), and room and board ($11,740). *College room only:* $7010. Room and board charges vary according to board plan and housing facility. *Part-time tuition:* $1642 per course. *Part-time fees:* $45 per term. *Payment plan:* Installment.

FRESHMAN FINANCIAL AID (Fall 2008) 752 applied for aid; of those 64% were deemed to have need. 100% of freshmen with need received aid; of those 43% had need fully met. *Average percent of need met:* 94% (excluding resources awarded to replace EFC). *Average financial aid package:* $29,106 (excluding resources awarded to replace EFC). 18% of all full-time freshmen had no need and received non-need-based gift aid.

UNDERGRADUATE FINANCIAL AID (Fall 2008) 2,987 applied for aid; of those 68% were deemed to have need. 100% of undergraduates with need received aid; of those 40% had need fully met. *Average percent of need met:* 92% (excluding resources awarded to replace EFC). *Average financial aid package:* $29,415 (excluding resources awarded to replace EFC). 14% of all full-time undergraduates had no need and received non-need-based gift aid.

GIFT AID (NEED-BASED) *Total amount:* $33,998,164 (8% federal, 5% state, 87% institutional). *Receiving aid:* Freshmen: 40% (400); all full-time undergraduates: 40% (1,708). *Average award:* Freshmen: $20,801; Undergraduates: $21,991. *Scholarships, grants, and awards:* Federal Pell, FSEOG, state, private, college/university gift aid from institutional funds.

GIFT AID (NON-NEED-BASED) *Total amount:* $18,420,805 (94% institutional, 6% external sources). *Receiving aid:* Freshmen: 18% (179). Undergraduates: 15% (623). *Average award:* Freshmen: $17,052. Undergraduates: $15,729. *Scholarships, grants, and awards by category: Academic interests/achievement:* 1,039 awards ($15,024,923 total): general academic interests/achievements. *Special achievements/activities:* 13 awards ($100,000 total): community service. *Special characteristics:* 10 awards ($187,888 total): international students, members of minority groups. *Tuition waivers:* Full or partial for employees or children of employees.

LOANS *Student loans:* $24,190,611 (41% need-based, 59% non-need-based). 64% of past graduating class borrowed through all loan programs. *Average indebtedness per student:* $33,073. *Average need-based loan:* Freshmen: $4498. Undergraduates: $5324. *Parent loans:* $8,146,458 (100% non-need-based). *Programs:* FFEL (Subsidized and Unsubsidized Stafford, PLUS), Perkins, state.

WORK-STUDY *Federal work-study:* Total amount: $1,771,837; 1,080 jobs averaging $1482. *State or other work-study/employment:* Total amount: $1,606,806 (100% non-need-based). 776 part-time jobs averaging $1078.

ATHLETIC AWARDS Total amount: $1,998,456 (42% need-based, 58% non-need-based).

APPLYING FOR FINANCIAL AID *Required financial aid forms:* FAFSA, CSS Financial Aid PROFILE, noncustodial (divorced/separated) parent's statement, business/farm supplement, federal tax returns, including all schedules for parents and student. *Financial aid deadline:* 4/15. *Notification date:* Continuous beginning 3/25.

CONTACT Ms. Donna Kendall, Executive Director of Financial Assistance, Bentley University, 175 Forest Street, Waltham, MA 02452-4705, 781-891-3441 or toll-free 800-523-2354. *Fax:* 781-891-2448. *E-mail:* finaid@bentley.edu.

BEREA COLLEGE
Berea, KY

Tuition & fees: $876	Average undergraduate aid package: $32,141

ABOUT THE INSTITUTION Independent, coed. 38 undergraduate majors. Federal methodology is used as a basis for awarding need-based institutional aid.

UNDERGRADUATE EXPENSES for 2009–10 includes mandatory fees ($876) and room and board ($5768). financial aid is provided to all students for tuition costs.

FRESHMAN FINANCIAL AID (Fall 2009, est.) 392 applied for aid; of those 100% were deemed to have need. 100% of freshmen with need received aid. *Average percent of need met:* 98% (excluding resources awarded to replace EFC). *Average financial aid package:* $33,840 (excluding resources awarded to replace EFC).

UNDERGRADUATE FINANCIAL AID (Fall 2009, est.) 1,495 applied for aid; of those 100% were deemed to have need. 100% of undergraduates with need received aid. *Average percent of need met:* 93% (excluding resources awarded to replace EFC). *Average financial aid package:* $32,141 (excluding resources awarded to replace EFC).

GIFT AID (NEED-BASED) *Total amount:* $44,951,059 (15% federal, 7% state, 78% institutional). *Receiving aid:* Freshmen: 100% (392); all full-time undergraduates: 100% (1,495). *Average award:* Freshmen: $31,341; Undergraduates: $29,964. *Scholarships, grants, and awards:* Federal Pell, FSEOG, state, private, college/university gift aid from institutional funds.

LOANS *Student loans:* $812,529 (39% need-based, 61% non-need-based). 79% of past graduating class borrowed through all loan programs. *Average indebtedness per student:* $8133. *Average need-based loan:* Freshmen: $25. Undergraduates: $213. *Programs:* FFEL (Subsidized and Unsubsidized Stafford, PLUS), Perkins, college/university.

WORK-STUDY *Federal work-study:* Total amount: $2,549,875; jobs available. *State or other work-study/employment:* Total amount: $425,650 (100% need-based). Part-time jobs available.

APPLYING FOR FINANCIAL AID *Required financial aid form:* FAFSA. *Financial aid deadline (priority):* 3/15. *Notification date:* Continuous beginning 4/1.

CONTACT Nancy Melton, Director, Student Financial Aid Services, Berea College, CPO 2172, Berea, KY 40404, 859-985-3313 or toll-free 800-326-5948. *Fax:* 859-985-3914. *E-mail:* nancy_melton@berea.edu.

BERKLEE COLLEGE OF MUSIC
Boston, MA

Tuition & fees: $30,650	Average undergraduate aid package: $13,303

ABOUT THE INSTITUTION Independent, coed. 12 undergraduate majors. Federal methodology is used as a basis for awarding need-based institutional aid.

UNDERGRADUATE EXPENSES for 2009–10 *Comprehensive fee:* $45,730 includes full-time tuition ($29,700), mandatory fees ($950), and room and board ($15,080). *Part-time tuition:* $1053 per credit hour. there is a one-time $2,950 charge for laptop purchase required of all entering students.

FRESHMAN FINANCIAL AID (Fall 2009, est.) 531 applied for aid; of those 85% were deemed to have need. 99% of freshmen with need received aid; of those 5% had need fully met. *Average percent of need met:* 31% (excluding resources awarded to replace EFC). *Average financial aid package:* $12,207 (excluding resources awarded to replace EFC). 18% of all full-time freshmen had no need and received non-need-based gift aid.

UNDERGRADUATE FINANCIAL AID (Fall 2009, est.) 2,019 applied for aid; of those 88% were deemed to have need. 98% of undergraduates with need received aid; of those 7% had need fully met. *Average percent of need met:* 36% (excluding resources awarded to replace EFC). *Average financial aid package:* $13,303 (excluding resources awarded to replace EFC). 23% of all full-time undergraduates had no need and received non-need-based gift aid.

GIFT AID (NEED-BASED) *Total amount:* $9,829,898 (44% federal, 2% state, 54% institutional). *Receiving aid:* Freshmen: 27% (225); all full-time undergraduates: 24% (898). *Average award:* Freshmen: $5979; Undergraduates: $5530. *Scholarships, grants, and awards:* Federal Pell, FSEOG, state, private, college/university gift aid from institutional funds, Academic Competitiveness Grants.

GIFT AID (NON-NEED-BASED) *Total amount:* $26,107,337 (96% institutional, 4% external sources). *Receiving aid:* Freshmen: 26% (214). Undergraduates: 23% (869). *Average award:* Freshmen: $12,105. Undergraduates: $10,667. *Scholarships, grants, and awards by category:* Academic interests/achievement: education, engineering/technologies. *Creative arts/performance:* music. *Special characteristics:* children of faculty/staff.

LOANS *Student loans:* $29,992,113 (43% need-based, 57% non-need-based). *Average need-based loan:* Freshmen: $4647. Undergraduates: $5406. *Parent loans:* $18,589,510 (100% non-need-based). *Programs:* Federal Direct (Subsidized and Unsubsidized Stafford, PLUS), Perkins, state.

WORK-STUDY *Federal work-study:* Total amount: $519,382; jobs available. *State or other work-study/employment:* Total amount: $2,767,688 (100% non-need-based). Part-time jobs available.

APPLYING FOR FINANCIAL AID *Required financial aid form:* FAFSA. *Financial aid deadline:* 5/1. *Notification date:* Continuous. Students must reply within 2 weeks of notification.

CONTACT Frank Mullen, Director of Financial Aid, Berklee College of Music, 1140 Boylston Street, Boston, MA 02215-3693, 617-747-2274 or toll-free 800-BERKLEE. *Fax:* 617-747-2073. *E-mail:* financialaid@berklee.edu.

BERNARD M. BARUCH COLLEGE OF THE CITY UNIVERSITY OF NEW YORK
New York, NY

Tuition & fees (NY res): $4600	Average undergraduate aid package: $6598

ABOUT THE INSTITUTION State and locally supported, coed. 41 undergraduate majors. Federal methodology is used as a basis for awarding need-based institutional aid.

UNDERGRADUATE EXPENSES for 2010–11 *Tuition, state resident:* full-time $4600. *Tuition, nonresident:* full-time $12,450. Full-time tuition and fees vary according to course load. Part-time tuition and fees vary according to course load. *Payment plans:* Installment, deferred payment.

FRESHMAN FINANCIAL AID (Fall 2009, est.) 3,498 applied for aid; of those 76% were deemed to have need. 93% of freshmen with need received aid; of those 18% had need fully met. *Average percent of need met:* 81% (excluding resources awarded to replace EFC). *Average financial aid package:* $6750 (excluding resources awarded to replace EFC). 1% of all full-time freshmen had no need and received non-need-based gift aid.

UNDERGRADUATE FINANCIAL AID (Fall 2009, est.) 8,812 applied for aid; of those 91% were deemed to have need. 90% of undergraduates with need received aid; of those 16% had need fully met. *Average percent of need met:* 76% (excluding resources awarded to replace EFC). *Average financial aid package:* $6598 (excluding resources awarded to replace EFC). 1% of all full-time undergraduates had no need and received non-need-based gift aid.

GIFT AID (NEED-BASED) *Total amount:* $41,654,966 (57% federal, 43% state). *Receiving aid:* Freshmen: 64% (2,354); all full-time undergraduates: 65% (7,189). *Average award:* Freshmen: $5260; Undergraduates: $4958. *Scholarships, grants, and awards:* Federal Pell, FSEOG, state, college/university gift aid from institutional funds.

GIFT AID (NON-NEED-BASED) *Total amount:* $5,043,218 (29% institutional, 71% external sources). *Receiving aid:* Freshmen: 16% (576). Undergraduates: 12% (1,278). *Average award:* Freshmen: $4600. Undergraduates: $4600. *Scholarships, grants, and awards by category:* Academic interests/achievement: general academic interests/achievements. *Tuition waivers:* Full or partial for employees or children of employees, senior citizens.

LOANS *Student loans:* $17,223,209 (50% need-based, 50% non-need-based). 29% of past graduating class borrowed through all loan programs. *Average indebtedness per student:* $14,265. *Average need-based loan:* Freshmen: $3500. Undergraduates: $5000. *Parent loans:* $413,566 (100% non-need-based). *Programs:* Federal Direct (Subsidized and Unsubsidized Stafford, PLUS), Perkins.

WORK-STUDY *Federal work-study:* Total amount: $475,126; 675 jobs averaging $800. *State or other work-study/employment:* Total amount: $325,900 (100% need-based). 755 part-time jobs averaging $1200.

APPLYING FOR FINANCIAL AID *Required financial aid forms:* FAFSA, state aid form. *Financial aid deadline (priority):* 3/15. *Notification date:* Continuous beginning 4/21. Students must reply by 6/1 or within 6 weeks of notification.
CONTACT Financial Aid Office, Bernard M. Baruch College of the City University of New York, 151 East 25th Street, Room 720, New York, NY 10010-5585, 646-312-1360. *Fax:* 646-312-1361. *E-mail:* financial_aid@baruch.cuny.edu.

BERRY COLLEGE
Mount Berry, GA

Tuition & fees: $23,360	Average undergraduate aid package: $20,606

ABOUT THE INSTITUTION Independent interdenominational, coed. 35 undergraduate majors. Federal methodology is used as a basis for awarding need-based institutional aid.
UNDERGRADUATE EXPENSES for 2009–10 *Comprehensive fee:* $31,700 includes full-time tuition ($23,160), mandatory fees ($200), and room and board ($8340). *College room only:* $4660. Room and board charges vary according to board plan and housing facility. *Part-time tuition:* $772 per credit hour. *Payment plan:* Installment.
FRESHMAN FINANCIAL AID (Fall 2009, est.) 526 applied for aid; of those 79% were deemed to have need. 100% of freshmen with need received aid; of those 23% had need fully met. *Average percent of need met:* 85% (excluding resources awarded to replace EFC). *Average financial aid package:* $20,971 (excluding resources awarded to replace EFC). 27% of all full-time freshmen had no need and received non-need-based gift aid.
UNDERGRADUATE FINANCIAL AID (Fall 2009, est.) 1,454 applied for aid; of those 82% were deemed to have need. 100% of undergraduates with need received aid; of those 21% had need fully met. *Average percent of need met:* 83% (excluding resources awarded to replace EFC). *Average financial aid package:* $20,606 (excluding resources awarded to replace EFC). 28% of all full-time undergraduates had no need and received non-need-based gift aid.
GIFT AID (NEED-BASED) *Total amount:* $17,667,608 (15% federal, 15% state, 68% institutional, 2% external sources). *Receiving aid:* Freshmen: 73% (416); all full-time undergraduates: 68% (1,193). *Average award:* Freshmen: $16,818; Undergraduates: $15,281. *Scholarships, grants, and awards:* Federal Pell, FSEOG, state, private, college/university gift aid from institutional funds.
GIFT AID (NON-NEED-BASED) *Total amount:* $7,449,041 (24% state, 71% institutional, 5% external sources). *Receiving aid:* Freshmen: 15% (86). Undergraduates: 12% (206). *Average award:* Freshmen: $10,453. Undergraduates: $9206. *Scholarships, grants, and awards by category: Academic interests/achievement:* agriculture, education, English, general academic interests/achievements, humanities, religion/biblical studies. *Creative arts/performance:* art/fine arts, debating, journalism/publications, music, theater/drama. *Special achievements/activities:* community service, religious involvement. *Special characteristics:* adult students, children of faculty/staff, ethnic background, local/state students, members of minority groups. *Tuition waivers:* Full or partial for employees or children of employees, senior citizens.
LOANS *Student loans:* $9,311,602 (64% need-based, 36% non-need-based). 82% of past graduating class borrowed through all loan programs. *Average indebtedness per student:* $17,502. *Average need-based loan:* Freshmen: $2968. Undergraduates: $3833. *Parent loans:* $2,756,152 (34% need-based, 66% non-need-based). *Programs:* FFEL (Subsidized and Unsubsidized Stafford, PLUS), Perkins, college/university.
WORK-STUDY *Federal work-study:* Total amount: $739,221; jobs available. *State or other work-study/employment:* Total amount: $6,283,753 (30% need-based, 70% non-need-based). Part-time jobs available.
ATHLETIC AWARDS Total amount: $1,792,688 (31% need-based, 69% non-need-based).
APPLYING FOR FINANCIAL AID *Required financial aid form:* FAFSA. *Financial aid deadline (priority):* 4/1. *Notification date:* Continuous beginning 2/1.
CONTACT Mrs. Marcia McConnell, Director of Financial Aid, Berry College, 2277 Martha Berry Highway, NW, Mount Berry, GA 30149-5007, 706-236-1714 or toll-free 800-237-7942. *Fax:* 706-290-2160. *E-mail:* financialaid@berry.edu.

BETHANY COLLEGE
Lindsborg, KS

Tuition & fees: $20,026	Average undergraduate aid package: $20,638

ABOUT THE INSTITUTION Independent Lutheran, coed. 41 undergraduate majors. Federal methodology is used as a basis for awarding need-based institutional aid.
UNDERGRADUATE EXPENSES for 2010–11 *Comprehensive fee:* $26,200 includes full-time tuition ($19,426), mandatory fees ($600), and room and board ($6174). *College room only:* $3309. Room and board charges vary according to board plan and housing facility. *Part-time tuition:* $405 per credit hour. *Part-time fees:* $75 per term. Part-time tuition and fees vary according to course load. *Payment plan:* Installment.
FRESHMAN FINANCIAL AID (Fall 2009, est.) 167 applied for aid; of those 82% were deemed to have need. 100% of freshmen with need received aid; of those 47% had need fully met. *Average percent of need met:* 99% (excluding resources awarded to replace EFC). *Average financial aid package:* $20,763 (excluding resources awarded to replace EFC). 8% of all full-time freshmen had no need and received non-need-based gift aid.
UNDERGRADUATE FINANCIAL AID (Fall 2009, est.) 551 applied for aid; of those 81% were deemed to have need. 100% of undergraduates with need received aid; of those 42% had need fully met. *Average percent of need met:* 94% (excluding resources awarded to replace EFC). *Average financial aid package:* $20,638 (excluding resources awarded to replace EFC). 7% of all full-time undergraduates had no need and received non-need-based gift aid.
GIFT AID (NEED-BASED) *Total amount:* $2,989,304 (37% federal, 16% state, 47% institutional). *Receiving aid:* Freshmen: 65% (119); all full-time undergraduates: 67% (385). *Average award:* Freshmen: $8026; Undergraduates: $7389. *Scholarships, grants, and awards:* Federal Pell, FSEOG, state, private, college/university gift aid from institutional funds, Academic Competitiveness Grants, National SMART Grants, TEACH Grants.
GIFT AID (NON-NEED-BASED) *Total amount:* $832,160 (100% institutional). *Receiving aid:* Freshmen: 34% (62). Undergraduates: 28% (161). *Average award:* Freshmen: $5683. Undergraduates: $6948. *Scholarships, grants, and awards by category: Academic interests/achievement:* 416 awards ($3,192,065 total): general academic interests/achievements. *Creative arts/performance:* 126 awards ($418,410 total): art/fine arts, music, theater/drama. *Special achievements/activities:* 16 awards ($35,808 total): cheerleading/drum major. *Special characteristics:* 87 awards ($138,680 total): children and siblings of alumni, international students, relatives of clergy, religious affiliation. *Tuition waivers:* Full or partial for employees or children of employees.
LOANS *Student loans:* $3,562,070 (50% need-based, 50% non-need-based). 84% of past graduating class borrowed through all loan programs. *Average indebtedness per student:* $22,699. *Average need-based loan:* Freshmen: $4218. Undergraduates: $4784. *Parent loans:* $353,826 (100% non-need-based). *Programs:* FFEL (Subsidized and Unsubsidized Stafford, PLUS), Perkins, college/university.
WORK-STUDY *Federal work-study:* Total amount: $419,008; 97 jobs averaging $1500. *State or other work-study/employment:* Part-time jobs available.
ATHLETIC AWARDS Total amount: $519,973 (74% need-based, 26% non-need-based).
APPLYING FOR FINANCIAL AID *Required financial aid form:* FAFSA. *Financial aid deadline:* Continuous. *Notification date:* Continuous beginning 3/1. Students must reply within 3 weeks of notification.
CONTACT Ms. Amber Maneth, Director of Financial Aid, Bethany College, 335 East Swensson, Lindsborg, KS 67456-1897, 785-227-3311 Ext. 8248 or toll-free 800-826-2281. *Fax:* 785-227-2004. *E-mail:* meagherb@bethanylb.edu.

BETHANY COLLEGE
Bethany, WV

Tuition & fees: $21,465	Average undergraduate aid package: N/A

ABOUT THE INSTITUTION Independent religious, coed. 33 undergraduate majors. Institutional methodology is used as a basis for awarding need-based institutional aid.
UNDERGRADUATE EXPENSES for 2009–10 *Comprehensive fee:* $30,165 includes full-time tuition ($20,565), mandatory fees ($900), and room and board ($8700). Room and board charges vary according to housing facility. *Part-time tuition:* $650 per credit hour. *Payment plan:* Installment.
FRESHMAN FINANCIAL AID (Fall 2009, est.) 274 applied for aid; of those 92% were deemed to have need. 100% of freshmen with need received aid. *Average percent of need met:* 51% (excluding resources awarded to replace EFC). 8% of all full-time freshmen had no need and received non-need-based gift aid.

UNDERGRADUATE FINANCIAL AID (Fall 2009, est.) 777 applied for aid; of those 90% were deemed to have need. 100% of undergraduates with need received aid. *Average percent of need met:* 49% (excluding resources awarded to replace EFC). 7% of all full-time undergraduates had no need and received non-need-based gift aid.
GIFT AID (NEED-BASED) *Total amount:* $7,811,046 (29% federal, 7% state, 60% institutional, 4% external sources). *Receiving aid:* Freshmen: 86% (243); all full-time undergraduates: 77% (628). *Average award:* Freshmen: $10,988; Undergraduates: $9824. *Scholarships, grants, and awards:* Federal Pell, FSEOG, state, private, college/university gift aid from institutional funds.
GIFT AID (NON-NEED-BASED) *Average award:* Freshmen: $8886. Undergraduates: $7189. *Scholarships, grants, and awards by category: Academic interests/achievement:* general academic interests/achievements. *Creative arts/performance:* music. *Special achievements/activities:* leadership. *Special characteristics:* children and siblings of alumni, children of faculty/staff, international students, relatives of clergy, religious affiliation. *Tuition waivers:* Full or partial for children of alumni, employees or children of employees.
LOANS *Student loans:* $6,867,796 (100% need-based). *Average need-based loan:* Freshmen: $4342. Undergraduates: $7258. *Parent loans:* $5,111,346 (100% need-based). *Programs:* FFEL (Subsidized and Unsubsidized Stafford, PLUS), Perkins, alternative loans.
WORK-STUDY *Federal work-study:* Total amount: $831,854; jobs available. *State or other work-study/employment:* Total amount: $282,623 (100% need-based). Part-time jobs available.
APPLYING FOR FINANCIAL AID *Required financial aid forms:* FAFSA, state aid form, Master Promissory Notes and Entrance Counseling (for federal loans). *Financial aid deadline:* Continuous. *Notification date:* Continuous. Students must reply within 2 weeks of notification.
CONTACT Karina Dayich, Financial Aid Office, Bethany College, PO Box 488, Bethany, WV 26032, 304-829-7141 or toll-free 800-922-7611 (out-of-state). *Fax:* 304-829-7142. *E-mail:* kdayich@bethanywv.edu.

BETHANY LUTHERAN COLLEGE
Mankato, MN

Tuition & fees: $20,650	Average undergraduate aid package: $15,670

ABOUT THE INSTITUTION Independent Lutheran, coed. 19 undergraduate majors. Federal methodology is used as a basis for awarding need-based institutional aid.
UNDERGRADUATE EXPENSES for 2010–11 *Comprehensive fee:* $27,150 includes full-time tuition ($20,650) and room and board ($6500). *College room only:* $2890. Room and board charges vary according to board plan and housing facility. *Payment plan:* Installment.
FRESHMAN FINANCIAL AID (Fall 2009, est.) 167 applied for aid; of those 91% were deemed to have need. 99% of freshmen with need received aid; of those 21% had need fully met. *Average percent of need met:* 86% (excluding resources awarded to replace EFC). *Average financial aid package:* $15,621 (excluding resources awarded to replace EFC). 13% of all full-time freshmen had no need and received non-need-based gift aid.
UNDERGRADUATE FINANCIAL AID (Fall 2009, est.) 535 applied for aid; of those 90% were deemed to have need. 100% of undergraduates with need received aid; of those 21% had need fully met. *Average percent of need met:* 85% (excluding resources awarded to replace EFC). *Average financial aid package:* $15,670 (excluding resources awarded to replace EFC). 16% of all full-time undergraduates had no need and received non-need-based gift aid.
GIFT AID (NEED-BASED) *Total amount:* $4,941,593 (14% federal, 17% state, 66% institutional, 3% external sources). *Receiving aid:* Freshmen: 83% (151); all full-time undergraduates: 80% (481). *Average award:* Freshmen: $11,909; Undergraduates: $11,217. *Scholarships, grants, and awards:* Federal Pell, FSEOG, state, private, college/university gift aid from institutional funds.
GIFT AID (NON-NEED-BASED) *Total amount:* $598,599 (1% state, 95% institutional, 4% external sources). *Receiving aid:* Freshmen: 8% (15). Undergraduates: 7% (43). *Average award:* Freshmen: $5350. Undergraduates: $5278. *Scholarships, grants, and awards by category: Creative arts/performance:* 78 awards ($144,000 total): art/fine arts, debating, journalism/publications, music, theater/drama. *Special characteristics:* 22 awards ($330,987 total): children of faculty/staff. *Tuition waivers:* Full or partial for employees or children of employees.
LOANS *Student loans:* $3,804,938 (65% need-based, 35% non-need-based). 79% of past graduating class borrowed through all loan programs. *Average*

indebtedness per student: $22,410. *Average need-based loan:* Freshmen: $3952. Undergraduates: $4702. *Parent loans:* $316,680 (14% need-based, 86% non-need-based). *Programs:* Federal Direct (Subsidized and Unsubsidized Stafford, PLUS), Perkins, state, alternative loans.
WORK-STUDY *Federal work-study:* Total amount: $36,807; 31 jobs averaging $1187. *State or other work-study/employment:* Total amount: $235,891 (50% need-based, 50% non-need-based). 302 part-time jobs averaging $781.
APPLYING FOR FINANCIAL AID *Required financial aid forms:* FAFSA, institution's own form, business/farm supplement, federal income tax form(s), W-2 forms. *Financial aid deadline (priority):* 4/15. *Notification date:* Continuous beginning 3/1. Students must reply within 4 weeks of notification.
CONTACT Financial Aid Office, Bethany Lutheran College, 700 Luther Drive, Mankato, MN 56001-6163, 507-344-7328 or toll-free 800-944-3066 Ext. 331. *Fax:* 507-344-7376. *E-mail:* finaid@blc.edu.

BETHANY UNIVERSITY
Scotts Valley, CA

CONTACT Deborah Snow, Financial Aid Director, Bethany University, 800 Bethany Drive, Scotts Valley, CA 95066-2820, 831-438-3800 Ext. 1477 or toll-free 800-843-9410. *Fax:* 831-461-1533.

BETHEL COLLEGE
Mishawaka, IN

Tuition & fees: $20,978	Average undergraduate aid package: $18,230

ABOUT THE INSTITUTION Independent religious, coed. 54 undergraduate majors. Federal methodology is used as a basis for awarding need-based institutional aid.
UNDERGRADUATE EXPENSES for 2009–10 *One-time required fee:* $600. *Comprehensive fee:* $27,228 includes full-time tuition ($20,978) and room and board ($6250). *College room only:* $3150. Full-time tuition and fees vary according to program. Room and board charges vary according to board plan and housing facility. *Part-time tuition:* $450 per credit hour. Part-time tuition and fees vary according to course load and program. *Payment plan:* Installment.
FRESHMAN FINANCIAL AID (Fall 2009, est.) 279 applied for aid; of those 86% were deemed to have need. 100% of freshmen with need received aid. 18% of all full-time freshmen had no need and received non-need-based gift aid.
UNDERGRADUATE FINANCIAL AID (Fall 2009, est.) 1,347 applied for aid; of those 88% were deemed to have need. 100% of undergraduates with need received aid. *Average financial aid package:* $18,230 (excluding resources awarded to replace EFC). 12% of all full-time undergraduates had no need and received non-need-based gift aid.
GIFT AID (NEED-BASED) *Total amount:* $6,530,700 (64% federal, 36% state). *Receiving aid:* Freshmen: 55% (163); all full-time undergraduates: 54% (802). *Average award:* Freshmen: $8330; Undergraduates: $8140. *Scholarships, grants, and awards:* Federal Pell, FSEOG, state, private, college/university gift aid from institutional funds, Federal Nursing.
GIFT AID (NON-NEED-BASED) *Total amount:* $7,428,800 (91% institutional, 9% external sources). *Receiving aid:* Freshmen: 80% (235). Undergraduates: 66% (980). *Average award:* Freshmen: $5660. Undergraduates: $6240. *Scholarships, grants, and awards by category: Academic interests/achievement:* 769 awards ($3,619,600 total): biological sciences, business, communication, computer science, education, English, general academic interests/achievements, health fields, mathematics, physical sciences, premedicine, religion/biblical studies, social sciences. *Creative arts/performance:* 69 awards ($148,800 total): art/fine arts, journalism/publications, music, theater/drama. *Special achievements/activities:* 63 awards ($67,500 total): cheerleading/drum major, general special achievements/activities, leadership, religious involvement. *Special characteristics:* 670 awards ($1,892,300 total): adult students, children of faculty/staff, international students, members of minority groups, relatives of clergy, religious affiliation, siblings of current students, spouses of current students. *Tuition waivers:* Full or partial for employees or children of employees.
LOANS *Student loans:* $14,762,500 (87% need-based, 13% non-need-based). 83% of past graduating class borrowed through all loan programs. *Average indebtedness per student:* $17,800. *Average need-based loan:* Undergraduates: $5330. *Parent loans:* $6,805,900 (100% non-need-based). *Programs:* FFEL (Subsidized and Unsubsidized Stafford, PLUS), Perkins, Federal Nursing, college/university, GATE Loans.

WORK-STUDY *Federal work-study:* Total amount: $1,453,900; 674 jobs averaging $2160. *State or other work-study/employment:* Total amount: $669,100 (100% non-need-based). 304 part-time jobs averaging $2200.

ATHLETIC AWARDS Total amount: $1,661,100 (100% non-need-based).

APPLYING FOR FINANCIAL AID *Required financial aid forms:* FAFSA, institution's own form. *Financial aid deadline (priority):* 3/1. *Notification date:* Continuous beginning 4/1.

CONTACT Mr. Guy A. Fisher, Director of Financial Aid, Bethel College, 1001 West McKinley Avenue, Mishawaka, IN 46545-5591, 574-257-3316 or toll-free 800-422-4101. *Fax:* 574-807-7122. *E-mail:* fisherg@bethelcollege.edu.

BETHEL COLLEGE
North Newton, KS

Tuition & fees: $19,990	Average undergraduate aid package: $21,033

ABOUT THE INSTITUTION Independent religious, coed. 17 undergraduate majors. Federal methodology is used as a basis for awarding need-based institutional aid.

UNDERGRADUATE EXPENSES for 2009–10 *Comprehensive fee:* $26,760 includes full-time tuition ($19,990) and room and board ($6770). *College room only:* $3620. Full-time tuition and fees vary according to course load. Room and board charges vary according to board plan and housing facility. *Part-time tuition:* $720 per credit hour. Part-time tuition and fees vary according to course load. *Payment plans:* Installment, deferred payment.

FRESHMAN FINANCIAL AID (Fall 2008) 108 applied for aid; of those 88% were deemed to have need. 100% of freshmen with need received aid; of those 47% had need fully met. *Average percent of need met:* 96% (excluding resources awarded to replace EFC). *Average financial aid package:* $21,053 (excluding resources awarded to replace EFC). 19% of all full-time freshmen had no need and received non-need-based gift aid.

UNDERGRADUATE FINANCIAL AID (Fall 2008) 397 applied for aid; of those 91% were deemed to have need. 100% of undergraduates with need received aid; of those 45% had need fully met. *Average percent of need met:* 94% (excluding resources awarded to replace EFC). *Average financial aid package:* $21,033 (excluding resources awarded to replace EFC). 21% of all full-time undergraduates had no need and received non-need-based gift aid.

GIFT AID (NEED-BASED) *Total amount:* $1,224,607 (58% federal, 42% state). *Receiving aid:* Freshmen: 64% (75); all full-time undergraduates: 55% (261). *Average award:* Freshmen: $4793; Undergraduates: $4978. *Scholarships, grants, and awards:* Federal Pell, FSEOG, state, college/university gift aid from institutional funds.

GIFT AID (NON-NEED-BASED) *Total amount:* $3,172,585 (95% institutional, 5% external sources). *Receiving aid:* Freshmen: 79% (93). Undergraduates: 72% (341). *Average award:* Freshmen: $10,251. Undergraduates: $8852. *Scholarships, grants, and awards by category: Academic interests/achievement:* biological sciences, general academic interests/achievements. *Creative arts/performance:* art/fine arts, debating, music, theater/drama. *Special characteristics:* $1,911,278 total: children and siblings of alumni, children of current students, children of faculty/staff, ethnic background, general special characteristics, international students, local/state students, previous college experience, relatives of clergy, religious affiliation, siblings of current students, spouses of current students. *Tuition waivers:* Full or partial for children of alumni, employees or children of employees, senior citizens.

LOANS *Student loans:* $3,175,220 (60% need-based, 40% non-need-based). 77% of past graduating class borrowed through all loan programs. *Average indebtedness per student:* $24,241. *Average need-based loan:* Freshmen: $5079. Undergraduates: $6905. *Parent loans:* $426,259 (100% non-need-based). *Programs:* Federal Direct (Subsidized and Unsubsidized Stafford, PLUS), Perkins.

WORK-STUDY *Federal work-study:* Total amount: $368,303; 204 jobs averaging $1805. *State or other work-study/employment:* 217 part-time jobs averaging $776.

ATHLETIC AWARDS Total amount: $666,938 (100% non-need-based).

APPLYING FOR FINANCIAL AID *Required financial aid form:* FAFSA. *Financial aid deadline (priority):* 4/1. *Notification date:* Continuous. Students must reply by 5/1 or within 2 weeks of notification.

CONTACT Mr. Tony Graber, Financial Aid Director, Bethel College, 300 East 27th Street, North Newton, KS 67117, 316-284-5232 or toll-free 800-522-1887 Ext. 230. *Fax:* 316-284-5845. *E-mail:* tgraber@bethelks.edu.

BETHEL UNIVERSITY
St. Paul, MN

Tuition & fees: $28,080	Average undergraduate aid package: $20,421

ABOUT THE INSTITUTION Independent religious, coed. 58 undergraduate majors. Federal methodology is used as a basis for awarding need-based institutional aid.

UNDERGRADUATE EXPENSES for 2010–11 *Comprehensive fee:* $36,300 includes full-time tuition ($27,950), mandatory fees ($130), and room and board ($8220). *College room only:* $4900. Room and board charges vary according to board plan. *Part-time tuition:* $1165 per credit. Part-time tuition and fees vary according to course load. *Payment plans:* Tuition prepayment, installment.

FRESHMAN FINANCIAL AID (Fall 2009, est.) 578 applied for aid; of those 85% were deemed to have need. 100% of freshmen with need received aid; of those 22% had need fully met. *Average percent of need met:* 84% (excluding resources awarded to replace EFC). *Average financial aid package:* $22,343 (excluding resources awarded to replace EFC). 23% of all full-time freshmen had no need and received non-need-based gift aid.

UNDERGRADUATE FINANCIAL AID (Fall 2009, est.) 2,225 applied for aid; of those 87% were deemed to have need. 100% of undergraduates with need received aid; of those 19% had need fully met. *Average percent of need met:* 79% (excluding resources awarded to replace EFC). *Average financial aid package:* $20,421 (excluding resources awarded to replace EFC). 23% of all full-time undergraduates had no need and received non-need-based gift aid.

GIFT AID (NEED-BASED) *Total amount:* $26,976,000 (13% federal, 14% state, 70% institutional, 3% external sources). *Receiving aid:* Freshmen: 76% (491); all full-time undergraduates: 73% (1,930). *Average award:* Freshmen: $16,848; Undergraduates: $14,570. *Scholarships, grants, and awards:* Federal Pell, FSEOG, state, private, college/university gift aid from institutional funds.

GIFT AID (NON-NEED-BASED) *Total amount:* $4,101,000 (5% federal, 88% institutional, 7% external sources). *Receiving aid:* Freshmen: 8% (53). Undergraduates: 6% (170). *Average award:* Freshmen: $7477. Undergraduates: $5888. *Scholarships, grants, and awards by category: Academic interests/achievement:* 1,680 awards ($7,515,000 total): general academic interests/achievements. *Creative arts/performance:* 109 awards ($223,000 total): art/fine arts, debating, music, theater/drama. *Special achievements/activities:* 720 awards ($1,060,000 total): community service, junior miss, leadership, religious involvement. *Special characteristics:* 1,350 awards ($5,120,000 total): children and siblings of alumni, children of faculty/staff, ethnic background, international students, members of minority groups, out-of-state students, relatives of clergy, religious affiliation. *Tuition waivers:* Full or partial for employees or children of employees.

LOANS *Student loans:* $22,647,000 (65% need-based, 35% non-need-based). 80% of past graduating class borrowed through all loan programs. *Average indebtedness per student:* $30,496. *Average need-based loan:* Freshmen: $3978. Undergraduates: $4601. *Parent loans:* $4,563,000 (31% need-based, 69% non-need-based). *Programs:* Federal Direct (Subsidized and Unsubsidized Stafford, PLUS), Perkins, state, alternative loans.

WORK-STUDY *Federal work-study:* Total amount: $528,000; 250 jobs averaging $2200. *State or other work-study/employment:* Total amount: $2,505,000 (53% need-based, 47% non-need-based). 1,250 part-time jobs averaging $2200.

APPLYING FOR FINANCIAL AID *Required financial aid forms:* FAFSA, institution's own form. *Financial aid deadline (priority):* 4/15. *Notification date:* Continuous beginning 3/1. Students must reply by 5/1 or within 3 weeks of notification.

CONTACT Mr. Jeffrey D. Olson, Director of Financial Aid, Bethel University, 3900 Bethel Drive, St. Paul, MN 55112-6999, 651-638-6241 or toll-free 800-255-8706 Ext. 6242. *Fax:* 651-635-1491. *E-mail:* jeff-olson@bethel.edu.

BETHEL UNIVERSITY
McKenzie, TN

CONTACT Laura Bateman, Office of Financial Aid, Bethel University, 325 Cherry Avenue, McKenzie, TN 38201, 901-352-4007. *Fax:* 901-352-4069.

BETHESDA CHRISTIAN UNIVERSITY
Anaheim, CA

Tuition & fees: N/R	Average undergraduate aid package: $7000

ABOUT THE INSTITUTION Independent religious, coed. *Awards:* bachelor's and master's degrees. 10 undergraduate majors. *Total enrollment:* 345. Undergraduates: 232. Federal methodology is used as a basis for awarding need-based institutional aid.

FRESHMAN FINANCIAL AID (Fall 2009, est.) 10 applied for aid; of those 100% were deemed to have need. 100% of freshmen with need received aid; of those 80% had need fully met. *Average percent of need met:* 90% (excluding resources awarded to replace EFC). *Average financial aid package:* $5000 (excluding resources awarded to replace EFC). 12% of all full-time freshmen had no need and received non-need-based gift aid.

UNDERGRADUATE FINANCIAL AID (Fall 2009, est.) 35 applied for aid; of those 86% were deemed to have need. 100% of undergraduates with need received aid; of those 83% had need fully met. *Average percent of need met:* 70% (excluding resources awarded to replace EFC). *Average financial aid package:* $7000 (excluding resources awarded to replace EFC). 4% of all full-time undergraduates had no need and received non-need-based gift aid.

GIFT AID (NEED-BASED) *Total amount:* $124,000 (76% federal, 24% institutional). *Receiving aid:* Freshmen: 40% (10); all full-time undergraduates: 16% (20). *Average award:* Freshmen: $3000; Undergraduates: $3000. *Scholarships, grants, and awards:* Federal Pell, FSEOG, college/university gift aid from institutional funds.

GIFT AID (NON-NEED-BASED) *Receiving aid:* Freshmen: 8% (2). Undergraduates: 5% (6). *Average award:* Freshmen: $500. Undergraduates: $500. *Scholarships, grants, and awards by category: Academic interests/achievement:* education, religion/biblical studies. *Creative arts/performance:* applied art and design, music. *Special achievements/activities:* religious involvement. *Special characteristics:* children of faculty/staff, relatives of clergy, siblings of current students, spouses of current students.

LOANS *Student loans:* $85,000 (100% need-based). 5% of past graduating class borrowed through all loan programs. *Average indebtedness per student:* $4000. *Average need-based loan:* Freshmen: $3000. Undergraduates: $3500. *Programs:* Federal Direct (Subsidized and Unsubsidized Stafford).

ATHLETIC AWARDS Total amount: $20,000 (100% non-need-based).

APPLYING FOR FINANCIAL AID *Required financial aid forms:* FAFSA, institution's own form. *Financial aid deadline:* Continuous. *Notification date:* Continuous beginning 9/15. Students must reply within 2 weeks of notification.

CONTACT Ms. Grace Choi, Financial Aid Administrator, Bethesda Christian University, 730 North Euclid Street, Anaheim, CA 92801, 714-683-1413. *Fax:* 714-517-1948. *E-mail:* financialaid@bcu.edu.

BETH HAMEDRASH SHAAREI YOSHER INSTITUTE
Brooklyn, NY

CONTACT Financial Aid Office, Beth HaMedrash Shaarei Yosher Institute, 4102-10 16th Avenue, Brooklyn, NY 11204, 718-854-2290.

BETH HATALMUD RABBINICAL COLLEGE
Brooklyn, NY

CONTACT Financial Aid Office, Beth Hatalmud Rabbinical College, 2127 82nd Street, Brooklyn, NY 11204, 718-259-2525.

BETH MEDRASH GOVOHA
Lakewood, NJ

CONTACT Financial Aid Office, Beth Medrash Govoha, 617 Sixth Street, Lakewood, NJ 08701-2797, 732-367-1060.

BETHUNE-COOKMAN UNIVERSITY
Daytona Beach, FL

Tuition & fees: $12,936	Average undergraduate aid package: $13,046

ABOUT THE INSTITUTION Independent Methodist, coed. 35 undergraduate majors. Federal methodology is used as a basis for awarding need-based institutional aid.

UNDERGRADUATE EXPENSES for 2010–11 *Comprehensive fee:* $20,608 includes full-time tuition ($12,936) and room and board ($7672). Full-time tuition and fees vary according to course load. Part-time tuition and fees vary according to course load. *Payment plan:* Installment.

FRESHMAN FINANCIAL AID (Fall 2009, est.) 968 applied for aid; of those 97% were deemed to have need. 100% of freshmen with need received aid; of those 4% had need fully met. *Average percent of need met:* 52% (excluding resources awarded to replace EFC). *Average financial aid package:* $12,204 (excluding resources awarded to replace EFC). 3% of all full-time freshmen had no need and received non-need-based gift aid.

UNDERGRADUATE FINANCIAL AID (Fall 2009, est.) 3,342 applied for aid; of those 96% were deemed to have need. 100% of undergraduates with need received aid; of those 6% had need fully met. *Average percent of need met:* 52% (excluding resources awarded to replace EFC). *Average financial aid package:* $13,046 (excluding resources awarded to replace EFC). 3% of all full-time undergraduates had no need and received non-need-based gift aid.

GIFT AID (NEED-BASED) *Total amount:* $25,870,048 (52% federal, 26% state, 19% institutional, 3% external sources). *Receiving aid:* Freshmen: 92% (910); all full-time undergraduates: 90% (3,075). *Average award:* Freshmen: $9215; Undergraduates: $9245. *Scholarships, grants, and awards:* Federal Pell, FSEOG, state, private, college/university gift aid from institutional funds, United Negro College Fund.

GIFT AID (NON-NEED-BASED) *Total amount:* $1,494,076 (23% state, 75% institutional, 2% external sources). *Receiving aid:* Freshmen: 3% (25). Undergraduates: 3% (111). *Average award:* Freshmen: $6988. Undergraduates: $8636. *Scholarships, grants, and awards by category: Academic interests/achievement:* 270 awards ($1,836,000 total): general academic interests/achievements. *Tuition waivers:* Full or partial for employees or children of employees.

LOANS *Student loans:* $29,093,977 (93% need-based, 7% non-need-based). 96% of past graduating class borrowed through all loan programs. *Average indebtedness per student:* $27,103. *Average need-based loan:* Freshmen: $3545. Undergraduates: $4659. *Parent loans:* $5,611,765 (67% need-based, 33% non-need-based). *Programs:* Federal Direct (Subsidized and Unsubsidized Stafford, PLUS), FFEL (Subsidized and Unsubsidized Stafford, PLUS).

WORK-STUDY *Federal work-study:* Total amount: $502,820; 230 jobs averaging $2200. *State or other work-study/employment:* 120 part-time jobs averaging $2000.

ATHLETIC AWARDS Total amount: $3,631,891 (75% need-based, 25% non-need-based).

APPLYING FOR FINANCIAL AID *Required financial aid form:* FAFSA. *Financial aid deadline (priority):* 4/1. *Notification date:* Continuous beginning 4/1. Students must reply within 3 weeks of notification.

CONTACT Mr. Joseph Coleman, Director of Financial Aid, Bethune-Cookman University, 640 Mary McLeod Bethune Boulevard, Daytona Beach, FL 32114-3099, 386-481-2626 or toll-free 800-448-0228. *Fax:* 386-481-2621. *E-mail:* colemanj@cookman.edu.

BEULAH HEIGHTS UNIVERSITY
Atlanta, GA

CONTACT Ms. Patricia Banks, Financial Aid Director, Beulah Heights University, 892 Berne Street, SE, Atlanta, GA 30316, 404-627-2681 or toll-free 888-777-BHBC. *Fax:* 404-627-0702. *E-mail:* pat.banks@beulah.org.

BIOLA UNIVERSITY
La Mirada, CA

Tuition & fees: $28,044	Average undergraduate aid package: $28,105

ABOUT THE INSTITUTION Independent interdenominational, coed. *Awards:* bachelor's and master's degrees and post-master's certificates. 32 undergraduate majors. *Total enrollment:* 5,893. Undergraduates: 4,002. Freshmen: 838. Both federal and institutional methodology are used as a basis for awarding need-based institutional aid.

UNDERGRADUATE EXPENSES for 2009–10 *Application fee:* $45. *Comprehensive fee:* $36,411 includes full-time tuition ($27,744), mandatory fees ($300), and room and board ($8367). *College room only:* $4487. Room and board charges vary according to board plan and housing facility. *Part-time tuition:* $1156 per unit. Part-time tuition and fees vary according to course load. *Payment plan:* Installment.

FRESHMAN FINANCIAL AID (Fall 2008) 644 applied for aid; of those 85% were deemed to have need. 100% of freshmen with need received aid; of those 100%· had need fully met. *Average percent of need met:* 69% (excluding resources awarded to replace EFC). *Average financial aid package:* $27,937 (excluding resources awarded to replace EFC). 14% of all full-time freshmen had no need and received non-need-based gift aid.

UNDERGRADUATE FINANCIAL AID (Fall 2008) 2,517 applied for aid; of those 87% were deemed to have need. 100% of undergraduates with need received aid; of those 100% had need fully met. *Average percent of need met:* 68% (excluding resources awarded to replace EFC). *Average financial aid package:* $28,105 (excluding resources awarded to replace EFC). 10% of all full-time undergraduates had no need and received non-need-based gift aid.

GIFT AID (NEED-BASED) *Total amount:* $43,543,124 (9% federal, 14% state, 72% institutional, 5% external sources). *Receiving aid:* Freshmen: 54% (422); all full-time undergraduates: 50% (1,720). *Average award:* Freshmen: $12,247; Undergraduates: $11,426. *Scholarships, grants, and awards:* Federal Pell, FSEOG, state, private, college/university gift aid from institutional funds.

GIFT AID (NON-NEED-BASED) *Receiving aid:* Freshmen: 59% (461). Undergraduates: 51% (1,731). *Average award:* Freshmen: $11,905. Undergraduates: $13,443. *Scholarships, grants, and awards by category: Academic interests/achievement:* 1,291 awards ($7,030,074 total): biological sciences, communication, general academic interests/achievements. *Creative arts/performance:* 242 awards ($683,832 total): art/fine arts, cinema/film/broadcasting, journalism/publications, music, theater/drama. *Special achievements/activities:* 346 awards ($896,819 total): community service, leadership. *Special characteristics:* 875 awards ($3,722,128 total): adult students, children and siblings of alumni, children of faculty/staff, ethnic background, international students, relatives of clergy. *Tuition waivers:* Full or partial for employees or children of employees. *ROTC:* Army cooperative, Air Force cooperative.

LOANS *Student loans:* $39,518,082 (24% need-based, 76% non-need-based). 76% of past graduating class borrowed through all loan programs. *Average indebtedness per student:* $26,555. *Average need-based loan:* Freshmen: $1473. Undergraduates: $1244. *Parent loans:* $7,259,191 (100% non-need-based). *Programs:* Federal Direct (Subsidized and Unsubsidized Stafford, PLUS), Perkins, Federal Nursing, college/university, alternative loans.

WORK-STUDY *Federal work-study:* Total amount: $612,176; 647 jobs averaging $946. *State or other work-study/employment:* Total amount: $552,890 (100% need-based). Part-time jobs available.

ATHLETIC AWARDS Total amount: $1,541,030 (100% non-need-based).

APPLYING FOR FINANCIAL AID *Required financial aid forms:* FAFSA, state aid form. *Financial aid deadline:* Continuous. *Notification date:* Continuous beginning 3/1.

CONTACT Jonathan Choy, Financial Aid Office, Biola University, 13800 Biola Avenue, La Mirada, CA 90639-0001, 562-903-4742 or toll-free 800-652-4652. *Fax:* 562-906-4541. *E-mail:* finaid@biola.edu.

BIRMINGHAM-SOUTHERN COLLEGE
Birmingham, AL

Tuition & fees: N/R	Average undergraduate aid package: **$31,807**

ABOUT THE INSTITUTION Independent Methodist, coed. 47 undergraduate majors. Federal methodology is used as a basis for awarding need-based institutional aid.

FRESHMAN FINANCIAL AID (Fall 2009, est.) 328 applied for aid; of those 80% were deemed to have need. 100% of freshmen with need received aid; of those 49% had need fully met. *Average percent of need met:* 98% (excluding resources awarded to replace EFC). *Average financial aid package:* $31,781 (excluding resources awarded to replace EFC). 36% of all full-time freshmen had no need and received non-need-based gift aid.

UNDERGRADUATE FINANCIAL AID (Fall 2009, est.) 943 applied for aid; of those 83% were deemed to have need. 100% of undergraduates with need received aid; of those 47% had need fully met. *Average percent of need met:* 95% (excluding resources awarded to replace EFC). *Average financial aid package:* $31,807 (excluding resources awarded to replace EFC). 42% of all full-time undergraduates had no need and received non-need-based gift aid.

GIFT AID (NEED-BASED) *Total amount:* $2,644,516 (58% federal, 3% state, 39% institutional). *Receiving aid:* Freshmen: 55% (232); all full-time undergraduates: 44% (650). *Average award:* Freshmen: $8792; Undergraduates: $9137. *Scholarships, grants, and awards:* Federal Pell, FSEOG, state, private, college/university gift aid from institutional funds, United Negro College Fund.

GIFT AID (NON-NEED-BASED) *Total amount:* $21,137,220 (2% state, 92% institutional, 6% external sources). *Receiving aid:* Freshmen: 62% (263). Undergraduates: 53% (775). *Average award:* Freshmen: $13,573. Undergraduates: $13,639. *Scholarships, grants, and awards by category: Academic interests/achievement:* area/ethnic studies, biological sciences, business, communication, computer science, education, engineering/technologies, English, foreign languages, general academic interests/achievements, health fields, humanities, international studies, mathematics, physical sciences, premedicine, religion/biblical studies, social sciences. *Creative arts/performance:* art/fine arts, dance, music, performing arts, theater/drama. *Special achievements/activities:* junior miss, memberships, religious involvement. *Special characteristics:* adult students, children and siblings of alumni, children of faculty/staff, ethnic background, first-generation college students, previous college experience, relatives of clergy, religious affiliation.

LOANS *Student loans:* $4,718,020 (49% need-based, 51% non-need-based). 41% of past graduating class borrowed through all loan programs. *Average indebtedness per student:* $30,907. *Average need-based loan:* Freshmen: $3866. Undergraduates: $4687. *Parent loans:* $1,773,387 (100% non-need-based). *Programs:* Federal Direct (Subsidized and Unsubsidized Stafford, PLUS), Perkins, college/university.

WORK-STUDY *Federal work-study:* Total amount: $263,563; 202 jobs averaging $1305. *State or other work-study/employment:* Total amount: $816,062 (100% non-need-based). 558 part-time jobs averaging $1546.

ATHLETIC AWARDS Total amount: $393,438 (100% non-need-based).

APPLYING FOR FINANCIAL AID *Required financial aid forms:* FAFSA, state aid form. *Financial aid deadline (priority):* 3/1. *Notification date:* Continuous beginning 3/1. Students must reply by 5/30 or within 2 weeks of notification. **CONTACT** Financial Aid Office, Birmingham-Southern College, 900 Arkadelphia Road, Birmingham, AL 35254, 205-226-4688 or toll-free 800-523-5793. *Fax:* 205-226-3082. *E-mail:* finaid@bsc.edu.

BIRTHINGWAY COLLEGE OF MIDWIFERY
Portland, OR

CONTACT Financial Aid Office, Birthingway College of Midwifery, 12113 SE Foster Road, Portland, OR 97299, 503-760-3131.

BLACKBURN COLLEGE
Carlinville, IL

Tuition & fees: N/R	Average undergraduate aid package: **$13,873**

ABOUT THE INSTITUTION Independent Presbyterian, coed. 29 undergraduate majors. Federal methodology is used as a basis for awarding need-based institutional aid.

FRESHMAN FINANCIAL AID (Fall 2009, est.) 139 applied for aid; of those 88% were deemed to have need. 100% of freshmen with need received aid; of those 47% had need fully met. *Average percent of need met:* 78% (excluding resources awarded to replace EFC). *Average financial aid package:* $11,673 (excluding resources awarded to replace EFC). 10% of all full-time freshmen had no need and received non-need-based gift aid.

UNDERGRADUATE FINANCIAL AID (Fall 2009, est.) 581 applied for aid; of those 86% were deemed to have need. 100% of undergraduates with need received aid; of those 39% had need fully met. *Average percent of need met:* 80% (excluding resources awarded to replace EFC). *Average financial aid package:* $13,873 (excluding resources awarded to replace EFC). 10% of all full-time undergraduates had no need and received non-need-based gift aid.

GIFT AID (NEED-BASED) *Total amount:* $3,885,354 (34% federal, 33% state, 31% institutional, 2% external sources). *Receiving aid:* Freshmen: 83% (121); all full-time undergraduates: 81% (492). *Average award:* Freshmen: $10,561; Undergraduates: $11,209. *Scholarships, grants, and awards:* Federal Pell, FSEOG, state, private, college/university gift aid from institutional funds.

GIFT AID (NON-NEED-BASED) *Total amount:* $597,204 (98% institutional, 2% external sources). *Receiving aid:* Freshmen: 21% (31). Undergraduates: 18% (110). *Average award:* Freshmen: $4209. Undergraduates: $5163. *Scholar-*

ships, grants, and awards by category: Academic interests/achievement: $582,629 total: general academic interests/achievements. Special achievements/ activities: general special achievements/activities. Special characteristics: 42 awards ($18,750 total): siblings of current students.

LOANS Student loans: $3,228,354 (45% need-based, 55% non-need-based). 85% of past graduating class borrowed through all loan programs. Average indebtedness per student: $20,077. **Average need-based loan:** Freshmen: $3014. Undergraduates: $4107. **Parent loans:** $347,809 (100% non-need-based). Programs: Federal Direct (Subsidized and Unsubsidized Stafford, PLUS).

WORK-STUDY Federal work-study: Total amount: $1,029,554; 388 jobs averaging $2653. **State or other work-study/employment:** Total amount: $264,106 (100% non-need-based). 113 part-time jobs averaging $2337.

APPLYING FOR FINANCIAL AID Required financial aid form: FAFSA. Financial aid deadline (priority): 4/1. **Notification date:** Continuous. Students must reply within 4 weeks of notification.

CONTACT Mrs. Jane Kelsey, Financial Aid Administrator, Blackburn College, 700 College Avenue, Carlinville, IL 62626-1498, 217-854-3231 Ext. 4227 or toll-free 800-233-3550. Fax: 217-854-3731.

BLACK HILLS STATE UNIVERSITY
Spearfish, SD

Tuition & fees (SD res): $6227	Average undergraduate aid package: N/A

ABOUT THE INSTITUTION State-supported, coed. 47 undergraduate majors. Federal methodology is used as a basis for awarding need-based institutional aid.

UNDERGRADUATE EXPENSES for 2010–11 Tuition, state resident: full-time $2751; part-time $91.70 per credit hour. **Tuition, nonresident:** full-time $4124; part-time $137.45 per credit hour. **Required fees:** full-time $3476. Full-time tuition and fees vary according to course load and reciprocity agreements. Part-time tuition and fees vary according to course load and reciprocity agreements. **College room and board:** $5523; Room only: $2701. Room and board charges vary according to board plan and housing facility. **Payment plans:** Installment, deferred payment.

GIFT AID (NEED-BASED) Total amount: $4,571,673 (96% federal, 4% external sources). Scholarships, grants, and awards: Federal Pell, FSEOG, state, private, college/university gift aid from institutional funds, Academic Competitiveness Grants, National SMART Grants, TEACH Grants.

GIFT AID (NON-NEED-BASED) Total amount: $1,309,105 (6% federal, 13% state, 39% institutional, 42% external sources). **Scholarships, grants, and awards by category:** Academic interests/achievement: biological sciences, business, communication, computer science, education, English, foreign languages, general academic interests/achievements, health fields, humanities, mathematics, military science, physical sciences, social sciences. Creative arts/performance: art/fine arts, music, theater/drama. **Tuition waivers:** Full or partial for employees or children of employees, senior citizens.

LOANS Student loans: $16,689,874 (44% need-based, 56% non-need-based). Average indebtedness per student: $21,069. **Parent loans:** $551,540 (100% non-need-based). **Programs:** FFEL (Subsidized and Unsubsidized Stafford, PLUS), Perkins.

WORK-STUDY Federal work-study: Total amount: $386,220; 242 jobs averaging $1596. **State or other work-study/employment:** Total amount: $635,741 (100% non-need-based). 369 part-time jobs averaging $1723.

ATHLETIC AWARDS Total amount: $406,700 (100% non-need-based).

APPLYING FOR FINANCIAL AID Required financial aid form: FAFSA. Financial aid deadline (priority): 3/1. **Notification date:** Continuous beginning 5/1. Students must reply within 3 weeks of notification.

CONTACT Ms. Deb Henriksen, Director of Financial Aid, Black Hills State University, 1200 University Street, Spearfish, SD 57799-9670, 605-642-6581 or toll-free 800-255-2478. Fax: 605-642-6913. E-mail: debhenriksen@bhsu.edu.

BLESSING-RIEMAN COLLEGE OF NURSING
Quincy, IL

Tuition & fees: $22,290	Average undergraduate aid package: N/A

ABOUT THE INSTITUTION Independent, coed, primarily women. 1 undergraduate major. Federal methodology is used as a basis for awarding need-based institutional aid.

UNDERGRADUATE EXPENSES for 2009–10 Comprehensive fee: $30,180 includes full-time tuition ($21,775), mandatory fees ($515), and room and board ($7890). **College room only:** $3910. Full-time tuition and fees vary according to course load, location, and student level. Room and board charges vary according to board plan, location, and student level. **Part-time tuition:** $498 per credit hour. Part-time tuition and fees vary according to course load, location, and student level. **Payment plan:** Installment.

UNDERGRADUATE FINANCIAL AID (Fall 2009, est.) 186 applied for aid; of those 100% were deemed to have need. 100% of undergraduates with need received aid; of those 100% had need fully met. **Average percent of need met:** 100% (excluding resources awarded to replace EFC).

GIFT AID (NEED-BASED) Total amount: $682,000 (26% federal, 16% state, 58% institutional). **Receiving aid:** All full-time undergraduates: 56% (104). **Average award:** Undergraduates: $7902. **Scholarships, grants, and awards:** Federal Pell, state, private, college/university gift aid from institutional funds.

GIFT AID (NON-NEED-BASED) Total amount: $190,450 (80% institutional, 20% external sources). **Receiving aid:** Undergraduates: 22% (41). **Scholarships, grants, and awards by category:** Academic interests/achievement: $99,773 total: general academic interests/achievements. **Tuition waivers:** Full or partial for employees or children of employees.

LOANS Student loans: $907,700 (100% need-based). 70% of past graduating class borrowed through all loan programs. Average indebtedness per student: $20,000. **Average need-based loan:** Undergraduates: $2394. **Parent loans:** $25,000 (100% need-based). **Programs:** Federal Direct (Subsidized and Unsubsidized Stafford, PLUS), Federal Nursing, college/university.

APPLYING FOR FINANCIAL AID Required financial aid form: FAFSA. Financial aid deadline: Continuous. **Notification date:** Continuous beginning 4/1.

CONTACT Mrs. Misty McBee, Financial Aid Coordinator, Blessing-Rieman College of Nursing, Broadway at 11th Street, PO Box 7005, Quincy, IL 62301, 217-223-8400 Ext. 6993 or toll-free 800-877-9140 Ext. 6964. Fax: 217-223-1781. E-mail: mmcbee@brcn.edu.

BLOOMFIELD COLLEGE
Bloomfield, NJ

Tuition & fees: $21,000	Average undergraduate aid package: $16,521

ABOUT THE INSTITUTION Independent religious, coed. 21 undergraduate majors. Federal methodology is used as a basis for awarding need-based institutional aid.

UNDERGRADUATE EXPENSES for 2009–10 Comprehensive fee: $31,300 includes full-time tuition ($20,000), mandatory fees ($1000), and room and board ($10,300). **College room only:** $5150. Full-time tuition and fees vary according to class time. Room and board charges vary according to housing facility. **Part-time tuition:** $2040 per course. **Part-time fees:** $125 per term. Part-time tuition and fees vary according to class time and course load. **Payment plans:** Installment, deferred payment.

FRESHMAN FINANCIAL AID (Fall 2009, est.) 452 applied for aid; of those 91% were deemed to have need. 98% of freshmen with need received aid; of those 2% had need fully met. **Average percent of need met:** 60% (excluding resources awarded to replace EFC). **Average financial aid package:** $17,893 (excluding resources awarded to replace EFC). 7% of all full-time freshmen had no need and received non-need-based gift aid.

UNDERGRADUATE FINANCIAL AID (Fall 2009, est.) 1,631 applied for aid; of those 90% were deemed to have need. 99% of undergraduates with need received aid; of those 2% had need fully met. **Average percent of need met:** 56% (excluding resources awarded to replace EFC). **Average financial aid package:** $16,521 (excluding resources awarded to replace EFC). 8% of all full-time undergraduates had no need and received non-need-based gift aid.

GIFT AID (NEED-BASED) Total amount: $21,078,504 (27% federal, 47% state, 26% institutional). **Receiving aid:** Freshmen: 85% (389); all full-time undergraduates: 83% (1,379). **Average award:** Freshmen: $15,246; Undergraduates: $13,844. **Scholarships, grants, and awards:** Federal Pell, FSEOG, state, private, college/university gift aid from institutional funds.

GIFT AID (NON-NEED-BASED) Total amount: $2,899,217 (11% federal, 2% state, 83% institutional, 4% external sources). **Receiving aid:** Freshmen: 50% (229). Undergraduates: 39% (652). **Average award:** Freshmen: $8551. Undergraduates: $9828. **Scholarships, grants, and awards by category:** Academic interests/achievement: 239 awards ($1,176,834 total): biological sciences, business, computer science, education, English, general academic interests/achievements, health fields, humanities, mathematics, physical sciences, religion/biblical studies, social sciences. *Creative arts/performance:* 17 awards ($8700 total): applied art and design, art/fine arts, cinema/film/broadcasting, general creative arts/performance, performing arts, theater/drama. *Special achievements/activities:* 320 awards ($2,477,065 total): community service, general special achievements/activities, leadership. *Special characteristics:* 69 awards ($233,953 total): adult students, children and siblings of alumni, children of current students, general special characteristics, international students, out-of-state students, parents of current students, siblings of current students, spouses of current students. *Tuition waivers:* Full or partial for employees or children of employees, senior citizens.

LOANS *Student loans:* $13,454,234 (41% need-based, 59% non-need-based). 87% of past graduating class borrowed through all loan programs. *Average indebtedness per student:* $28,310. *Average need-based loan:* Freshmen: $3306. Undergraduates: $3926. *Programs:* FFEL (Subsidized and Unsubsidized Stafford, PLUS).

WORK-STUDY *Federal work-study:* Total amount: $1,001,285; 454 jobs averaging $2205. *State or other work-study/employment:* Part-time jobs available.

ATHLETIC AWARDS Total amount: $1,543,176 (100% non-need-based).

APPLYING FOR FINANCIAL AID *Required financial aid form:* FAFSA. *Financial aid deadline:* 6/1 (priority: 3/15). *Notification date:* Continuous beginning 3/15. Students must reply within 2 weeks of notification.

CONTACT Ms. Stacy Salinas, Director of Financial Aid, Bloomfield College, 467 Franklin Street, Bloomfield, NJ 07003-9981, 973-748-9000 Ext. 213 or toll-free 800-848-4555 Ext. 230. *Fax:* 973-748-9735. *E-mail:* stacy_salinas@bloomfield.edu.

BLOOMSBURG UNIVERSITY OF PENNSYLVANIA
Bloomsburg, PA

Tuition & fees (PA res): $7110   **Average undergraduate aid package:** $11,899

ABOUT THE INSTITUTION State-supported, coed. 44 undergraduate majors. Federal methodology is used as a basis for awarding need-based institutional aid.

UNDERGRADUATE EXPENSES for 2009–10 *Tuition, state resident:* full-time $5554; part-time $231 per credit. *Tuition, nonresident:* full-time $13,886; part-time $579 per credit. *Required fees:* full-time $1556; $44.50 per credit or $100 per term. Full-time tuition and fees vary according to course load. Part-time tuition and fees vary according to course load. *College room and board:* $6488; *Room only:* $3882. Room and board charges vary according to board plan and housing facility. *Payment plan:* Installment.

FRESHMAN FINANCIAL AID (Fall 2009, est.) 1,882 applied for aid; of those 95% were deemed to have need. 93% of freshmen with need received aid; of those 90% had need fully met. *Average percent of need met:* 74% (excluding resources awarded to replace EFC). *Average financial aid package:* $11,880 (excluding resources awarded to replace EFC). 2% of all full-time freshmen had no need and received non-need-based gift aid.

UNDERGRADUATE FINANCIAL AID (Fall 2009, est.) 7,046 applied for aid; of those 95% were deemed to have need. 97% of undergraduates with need received aid; of those 90% had need fully met. *Average percent of need met:* 72% (excluding resources awarded to replace EFC). *Average financial aid package:* $11,899 (excluding resources awarded to replace EFC). 2% of all full-time undergraduates had no need and received non-need-based gift aid.

GIFT AID (NEED-BASED) *Total amount:* $19,093,085 (59% federal, 38% state, 2% institutional, 1% external sources). *Receiving aid:* Freshmen: 44% (899); all full-time undergraduates: 40% (3,207). *Average award:* Freshmen: $6609; Undergraduates: $5822. *Scholarships, grants, and awards:* Federal Pell, FSEOG, state, private, college/university gift aid from institutional funds, Academic Competitiveness Grants, National SMART Grants.

GIFT AID (NON-NEED-BASED) *Total amount:* $2,856,122 (8% state, 44% institutional, 48% external sources). *Receiving aid:* Freshmen: 21% (420). Undergraduates: 15% (1,186). *Average award:* Freshmen: $2025. Undergraduates: $1971. *Scholarships, grants, and awards by category:* Academic interests/achievement: 451 awards ($701,910 total): biological sciences, business, communication, computer science, education, English, foreign languages, general academic interests/achievements, health fields, humanities, international studies, mathematics, physical sciences, religion/biblical studies, social sciences.

Special characteristics: 249 awards ($1,071,438 total): children of faculty/staff, international students. *Tuition waivers:* Full or partial for minority students, employees or children of employees, senior citizens.

LOANS *Student loans:* $39,284,534 (43% need-based, 57% non-need-based). 71% of past graduating class borrowed through all loan programs. *Average indebtedness per student:* $21,322. *Average need-based loan:* Freshmen: $3395. Undergraduates: $4162. *Parent loans:* $7,017,608 (100% non-need-based). *Programs:* FFEL (Subsidized and Unsubsidized Stafford, PLUS), Perkins, state, alternative loans.

WORK-STUDY *Federal work-study:* Total amount: $3,550,572; 976 jobs averaging $3638. *State or other work-study/employment:* Total amount: $4,360,123 (100% non-need-based). 1,042 part-time jobs averaging $4184.

ATHLETIC AWARDS Total amount: $554,370 (100% non-need-based).

APPLYING FOR FINANCIAL AID *Required financial aid form:* FAFSA. *Financial aid deadline (priority):* 3/15. *Notification date:* Continuous beginning 4/1.

CONTACT Mr. Thomas M. Lyons, Director of Financial Aid, Bloomsburg University of Pennsylvania, 119 Warren Student Services Center, 400 East 2nd Street, Bloomsburg, PA 17815-1301, 570-389-4279. *Fax:* 570-389-4795. *E-mail:* stfinaid@bloomu.edu.

BLUEFIELD COLLEGE
Bluefield, VA

Tuition & fees: $18,800   **Average undergraduate aid package:** $13,338

ABOUT THE INSTITUTION Independent Southern Baptist, coed. 40 undergraduate majors. Federal methodology is used as a basis for awarding need-based institutional aid.

UNDERGRADUATE EXPENSES for 2010–11 *Comprehensive fee:* $26,150 includes full-time tuition ($17,990), mandatory fees ($810), and room and board ($7350). Full-time tuition and fees vary according to program. Room and board charges vary according to housing facility. *Part-time tuition:* $750 per credit hour. *Part-time fees:* $240 per term. Part-time tuition and fees vary according to program. *Payment plan:* Installment.

FRESHMAN FINANCIAL AID (Fall 2009, est.) 111 applied for aid; of those 91% were deemed to have need. 100% of freshmen with need received aid; of those 24% had need fully met. *Average percent of need met:* 79% (excluding resources awarded to replace EFC). *Average financial aid package:* $16,171 (excluding resources awarded to replace EFC). 11% of all full-time freshmen had no need and received non-need-based gift aid.

UNDERGRADUATE FINANCIAL AID (Fall 2009, est.) 668 applied for aid; of those 92% were deemed to have need. 100% of undergraduates with need received aid; of those 17% had need fully met. *Average percent of need met:* 63% (excluding resources awarded to replace EFC). *Average financial aid package:* $13,338 (excluding resources awarded to replace EFC). 10% of all full-time undergraduates had no need and received non-need-based gift aid.

GIFT AID (NEED-BASED) *Total amount:* $4,738,589 (29% federal, 22% state, 35% institutional, 14% external sources). *Receiving aid:* Freshmen: 88% (101); all full-time undergraduates: 82% (591). *Average award:* Freshmen: $13,141; Undergraduates: $9042. *Scholarships, grants, and awards:* Federal Pell, FSEOG, state, private, college/university gift aid from institutional funds.

GIFT AID (NON-NEED-BASED) *Total amount:* $616,401 (33% state, 56% institutional, 11% external sources). *Receiving aid:* Freshmen: 17% (19). Undergraduates: 8% (58). *Average award:* Freshmen: $6518. Undergraduates: $3788. *Scholarships, grants, and awards by category:* Creative arts/performance: 56 awards ($114,330 total): art/fine arts, music, performing arts, theater/drama. *Special characteristics:* children of faculty/staff, ethnic background, first-generation college students, general special characteristics, members of minority groups, religious affiliation, veterans. *Tuition waivers:* Full or partial for employees or children of employees, senior citizens.

LOANS *Student loans:* $5,879,528 (82% need-based, 18% non-need-based). 84% of past graduating class borrowed through all loan programs. *Average indebtedness per student:* $6403. *Average need-based loan:* Freshmen: $3607. Undergraduates: $5151. *Parent loans:* $583,946 (19% need-based, 81% non-need-based). *Programs:* Federal Direct (Subsidized and Unsubsidized Stafford, PLUS), alternative loans.

WORK-STUDY *Federal work-study:* Total amount: $91,359; 82 jobs averaging $1200.

ATHLETIC AWARDS Total amount: $812,845 (70% need-based, 30% non-need-based).

APPLYING FOR FINANCIAL AID *Required financial aid forms:* FAFSA, state aid form. *Financial aid deadline (priority):* 3/15. *Notification date:* Continuous.

CONTACT Mrs. Sheila Nelson-Hensley, Director of Financial Aid, Bluefield College, 3000 College Drive, Bluefield, VA 24605, 276-326-4215 or toll-free 800-872-0175. *Fax:* 276-326-4356. *E-mail:* shensley@bluefield.edu.

BLUEFIELD STATE COLLEGE
Bluefield, WV

Tuition & fees (WV res): $4596	Average undergraduate aid package: $6200

ABOUT THE INSTITUTION State-supported, coed. 18 undergraduate majors. Federal methodology is used as a basis for awarding need-based institutional aid.

UNDERGRADUATE EXPENSES for 2009–10 *Tuition, state resident:* full-time $4596; part-time $192 per credit hour. *Tuition, nonresident:* full-time $9000; part-time $375 per credit hour. *Payment plan:* Installment.

FRESHMAN FINANCIAL AID (Fall 2009, est.) 265 applied for aid; of those 87% were deemed to have need. 100% of freshmen with need received aid; of those 57% had need fully met. *Average percent of need met:* 70% (excluding resources awarded to replace EFC). *Average financial aid package:* $6200 (excluding resources awarded to replace EFC). 18% of all full-time freshmen had no need and received non-need-based gift aid.

UNDERGRADUATE FINANCIAL AID (Fall 2009, est.) 1,270 applied for aid; of those 86% were deemed to have need. 100% of undergraduates with need received aid; of those 40% had need fully met. *Average percent of need met:* 70% (excluding resources awarded to replace EFC). *Average financial aid package:* $6200 (excluding resources awarded to replace EFC). 26% of all full-time undergraduates had no need and received non-need-based gift aid.

GIFT AID (NEED-BASED) *Total amount:* $5,361,434 (74% federal, 26% state). *Receiving aid:* Freshmen: 73% (230); all full-time undergraduates: 67% (1,090). *Average award:* Freshmen: $3500; Undergraduates: $3500. *Scholarships, grants, and awards:* Federal Pell, FSEOG, state.

GIFT AID (NON-NEED-BASED) *Total amount:* $1,906,906 (24% state, 16% institutional, 60% external sources). *Receiving aid:* Freshmen: 27% (85). Undergraduates: 3% (43). *Average award:* Freshmen: $1400. Undergraduates: $1400. *Scholarships, grants, and awards by category:* Academic interests/achievement: 380 awards ($330,000 total): engineering/technologies, general academic interests/achievements. Special achievements/activities: 10 awards ($4300 total): cheerleading/drum major, general special achievements/activities, junior miss, leadership. Special characteristics: 3 awards ($1500 total): general special characteristics. *Tuition waivers:* Full or partial for adult students, senior citizens.

LOANS *Student loans:* $7,576,280 (50% need-based, 50% non-need-based). 65% of past graduating class borrowed through all loan programs. *Average indebtedness per student:* $22,000. *Average need-based loan:* Freshmen: $3600. Undergraduates: $3600. *Parent loans:* $47,196 (100% non-need-based). *Programs:* Federal Direct (Subsidized and Unsubsidized Stafford, PLUS), Perkins.

WORK-STUDY *Federal work-study:* Total amount: $125,000; 63 jobs averaging $2900. *State or other work-study/employment:* Total amount: $214,334 (100% non-need-based). 100 part-time jobs averaging $3000.

ATHLETIC AWARDS Total amount: $273,975 (100% non-need-based).

APPLYING FOR FINANCIAL AID *Required financial aid forms:* FAFSA, institution's own form. *Financial aid deadline (priority):* 3/1. *Notification date:* 6/1.

CONTACT Mr. Tom Ilse, Director of Financial Aid, Bluefield State College, 219 Rock Street, Bluefield, WV 24701-2198, 304-327-4020 or toll-free 800-344-8892 Ext. 4065 (in-state), 800-654-7798 Ext. 4065 (out-of-state). *Fax:* 304-325-7747. *E-mail:* tilse@bluefieldstate.edu.

BLUE MOUNTAIN COLLEGE
Blue Mountain, MS

Tuition & fees: $8570	Average undergraduate aid package: $8899

ABOUT THE INSTITUTION Independent Southern Baptist, coed. 23 undergraduate majors. Federal methodology is used as a basis for awarding need-based institutional aid.

UNDERGRADUATE EXPENSES for 2009–10 *Comprehensive fee:* $12,420 includes full-time tuition ($7650), mandatory fees ($920), and room and board ($3850). Full-time tuition and fees vary according to course load and degree level. Room and board charges vary according to board plan. *Part-time tuition:* $255 per credit hour. Part-time tuition and fees vary according to course load and degree level. *Payment plan:* Installment.

FRESHMAN FINANCIAL AID (Fall 2008) 75 applied for aid; of those 100% were deemed to have need. 100% of freshmen with need received aid; of those 69% had need fully met. *Average percent of need met:* 133% (excluding resources awarded to replace EFC). *Average financial aid package:* $9725 (excluding resources awarded to replace EFC). 4% of all full-time freshmen had no need and received non-need-based gift aid.

UNDERGRADUATE FINANCIAL AID (Fall 2008) 431 applied for aid; of those 61% were deemed to have need. 100% of undergraduates with need received aid; of those 76% had need fully met. *Average percent of need met:* 117% (excluding resources awarded to replace EFC). *Average financial aid package:* $8899 (excluding resources awarded to replace EFC). 57% of all full-time undergraduates had no need and received non-need-based gift aid.

GIFT AID (NEED-BASED) *Receiving aid:* Freshmen: 87% (68); all full-time undergraduates: 43% (198). *Average award:* Freshmen: $2908; Undergraduates: $3551. *Scholarships, grants, and awards:* Federal Pell, FSEOG, state, private, college/university gift aid from institutional funds.

GIFT AID (NON-NEED-BASED) *Receiving aid:* Freshmen: 94% (73). Undergraduates: 57% (261). *Average award:* Freshmen: $4082. *Scholarships, grants, and awards by category:* Academic interests/achievement: biological sciences, business, education, English, general academic interests/achievements, health fields, humanities, library science, mathematics, physical sciences, premedicine, religion/biblical studies, social sciences. Creative arts/performance: art/fine arts, music, theater/drama. Special achievements/activities: general special achievements/activities, leadership, memberships, religious involvement. Special characteristics: children and siblings of alumni, children of current students, children of faculty/staff, married students, parents of current students, religious affiliation, siblings of current students, spouses of current students, twins. *Tuition waivers:* Full or partial for employees or children of employees.

LOANS *Average need-based loan:* Freshmen: $2749. Undergraduates: $4488. *Programs:* Federal Direct (Subsidized and Unsubsidized Stafford, PLUS), Perkins.

WORK-STUDY Federal work-study jobs available (averaging $1200). *State or other work-study/employment:* Part-time jobs available (averaging $1200).

APPLYING FOR FINANCIAL AID *Required financial aid forms:* FAFSA, state aid form. *Financial aid deadline (priority):* 3/1. *Notification date:* Continuous beginning 4/1. Students must reply within 2 weeks of notification.

CONTACT Mrs. Michelle L. Hall, Financial Aid Director, Blue Mountain College, PO Box 160, Blue Mountain, MS 38610-0160, 662-685-4771 Ext. 141 or toll-free 800-235-0136. *Fax:* 662-685-4776. *E-mail:* financialaid@bmc.edu.

BLUFFTON UNIVERSITY
Bluffton, OH

Tuition & fees: $24,930	Average undergraduate aid package: $21,413

ABOUT THE INSTITUTION Independent Mennonite, coed. 39 undergraduate majors. Both federal and institutional methodology are used as a basis for awarding need-based institutional aid.

UNDERGRADUATE EXPENSES for 2010–11 *Comprehensive fee:* $33,278 includes full-time tuition ($24,480), mandatory fees ($450), and room and board ($8348). *College room only:* $4102. Full-time tuition and fees vary according to course load. Room and board charges vary according to board plan and housing facility. *Part-time tuition:* $1020 per credit hour. *Part-time fees:* $113 per term. Part-time tuition and fees vary according to course load. *Payment plan:* Installment.

FRESHMAN FINANCIAL AID (Fall 2009, est.) 250 applied for aid; of those 94% were deemed to have need. 100% of freshmen with need received aid; of those 37% had need fully met. *Average percent of need met:* 91% (excluding resources awarded to replace EFC). *Average financial aid package:* $22,683 (excluding resources awarded to replace EFC). 8% of all full-time freshmen had no need and received non-need-based gift aid.

UNDERGRADUATE FINANCIAL AID (Fall 2009, est.) 842 applied for aid; of those 95% were deemed to have need. 100% of undergraduates with need received aid; of those 43% had need fully met. *Average percent of need met:* 89% (excluding resources awarded to replace EFC). *Average financial aid package:* $21,413 (excluding resources awarded to replace EFC). 11% of all full-time undergraduates had no need and received non-need-based gift aid.

GIFT AID (NEED-BASED) *Total amount:* $10,773,682 (17% federal, 5% state, 72% institutional, 6% external sources). *Receiving aid:* Freshmen: 91% (235);

all full-time undergraduates: 86% (778). *Average award:* Freshmen: $16,684; Undergraduates: $15,092. *Scholarships, grants, and awards:* Federal Pell, FSEOG, state, private, college/university gift aid from institutional funds.

GIFT AID (NON-NEED-BASED) *Total amount:* $1,432,455 (91% institutional, 9% external sources). *Receiving aid:* Freshmen: 1% (3). Undergraduates: 4% (40). *Average award:* Freshmen: $10,043. Undergraduates: $8315. *Scholarships, grants, and awards by category: Academic interests/achievement:* 405 awards ($3,621,550 total): general academic interests/achievements. *Creative arts/performance:* 35 awards ($35,000 total): art/fine arts, music. *Special achievements/activities:* 101 awards ($397,502 total): leadership. *Special characteristics:* 304 awards ($1,301,131 total): children of faculty/staff, international students, members of minority groups, out-of-state students, relatives of clergy, religious affiliation. *Tuition waivers:* Full or partial for employees or children of employees.

LOANS *Student loans:* $7,928,082 (94% need-based, 6% non-need-based). 88% of past graduating class borrowed through all loan programs. *Average indebtedness per student:* $26,896. *Average need-based loan:* Freshmen: $4443. Undergraduates: $4878. *Parent loans:* $1,682,710 (69% need-based, 31% non-need-based). *Programs:* Federal Direct (Subsidized and Unsubsidized Stafford, PLUS), Perkins, alternative loans.

WORK-STUDY *Federal work-study:* Total amount: $1,435,987; 635 jobs averaging $2267. *State or other work-study/employment:* Total amount: $438,100 (50% need-based, 50% non-need-based). 181 part-time jobs averaging $2417.

APPLYING FOR FINANCIAL AID *Required financial aid form:* FAFSA. *Financial aid deadline:* 10/1 (priority: 5/1). *Notification date:* Continuous beginning 3/1. Students must reply within 3 weeks of notification.

CONTACT Lawrence Matthews, Director of Financial Aid, Bluffton University, 1 University Drive, Bluffton, OH 45817-2104, 419-358-3266 or toll-free 800-488-3257. *Fax:* 419-358-3073. *E-mail:* matthewsl@bluffton.edu.

BOB JONES UNIVERSITY
Greenville, SC

Tuition & fees: $11,920	Average undergraduate aid package: N/A

ABOUT THE INSTITUTION Independent religious, coed. 84 undergraduate majors. Both federal and institutional methodology are used as a basis for awarding need-based institutional aid.

UNDERGRADUATE EXPENSES for 2010–11 *One-time required fee:* $610. *Comprehensive fee:* $17,020 includes full-time tuition ($11,920) and room and board ($5100). *Part-time tuition:* $576 per unit. *Payment plan:* Installment.

GIFT AID (NEED-BASED) *Total amount:* $7,372,864 (39% federal, 24% state, 25% institutional, 12% external sources). *Scholarships, grants, and awards:* Federal Pell, FSEOG, state, private, college/university gift aid from institutional funds.

GIFT AID (NON-NEED-BASED) *Total amount:* $4,058,827 (59% state, 41% institutional). *Tuition waivers:* Full or partial for employees or children of employees, senior citizens.

LOANS *Student loans:* $7,706,046 (100% need-based). *Parent loans:* $852,153 (100% need-based). *Programs:* FFEL (Subsidized and Unsubsidized Stafford, PLUS).

WORK-STUDY *Federal work-study:* Total amount: $130,906; jobs available.

APPLYING FOR FINANCIAL AID *Required financial aid form:* FAFSA. *Financial aid deadline:* Continuous. *Notification date:* Continuous.

CONTACT Director of Financial Aid, Bob Jones University, 1700 Wade Hampton Boulevard, Greenville, SC 29614, 864-242-5100 Ext. 3040 or toll-free 800-BJANDME. *E-mail:* finaid@bju.edu.

BOISE BIBLE COLLEGE
Boise, ID

CONTACT Beth Turner, Financial Aid Counselor, Boise Bible College, 8695 West Marigold Street, Boise, ID 83714-1220, 208-376-7731 Ext. 12 or toll-free 800-893-7755. *Fax:* 208-376-7743. *E-mail:* betht@boisebible.edu.

BOISE STATE UNIVERSITY
Boise, ID

Tuition & fees (ID res): $4864	Average undergraduate aid package: $8282

ABOUT THE INSTITUTION State-supported, coed. 73 undergraduate majors. Federal methodology is used as a basis for awarding need-based institutional aid.

UNDERGRADUATE EXPENSES for 2009–10 *One-time required fee:* $75. *Tuition, state resident:* full-time $3106; part-time $168.52 per credit hour. *Tuition, nonresident:* full-time $12,110; part-time $248.52 per credit hour. *Required fees:* full-time $1758; $83.48 per credit hour. Full-time tuition and fees vary according to reciprocity agreements. Part-time tuition and fees vary according to course load. *College room and board:* $5602; *Room only:* $2650. Room and board charges vary according to board plan and housing facility. *Payment plan:* Installment.

FRESHMAN FINANCIAL AID (Fall 2009, est.) 1,576 applied for aid; of those 100% were deemed to have need. 100% of freshmen with need received aid; of those 21% had need fully met. *Average percent of need met:* 19% (excluding resources awarded to replace EFC). *Average financial aid package:* $7401 (excluding resources awarded to replace EFC). 15% of all full-time freshmen had no need and received non-need-based gift aid.

UNDERGRADUATE FINANCIAL AID (Fall 2009, est.) 8,210 applied for aid; of those 100% were deemed to have need. 100% of undergraduates with need received aid; of those 13% had need fully met. *Average percent of need met:* 23% (excluding resources awarded to replace EFC). *Average financial aid package:* $8282 (excluding resources awarded to replace EFC). 5% of all full-time undergraduates had no need and received non-need-based gift aid.

GIFT AID (NEED-BASED) *Total amount:* $30,321,680 (85% federal, 3% state, 8% institutional, 4% external sources). *Receiving aid:* Freshmen: 56% (1,234); all full-time undergraduates: 50% (6,020). *Average award:* Freshmen: $3807; Undergraduates: $4453. *Scholarships, grants, and awards:* Federal Pell, FSEOG, state, private, college/university gift aid from institutional funds, Leveraging Educational Assistance Program (LEAP).

GIFT AID (NON-NEED-BASED) *Total amount:* $923,362 (7% federal, 25% state, 51% institutional, 17% external sources). *Receiving aid:* Freshmen: 8% (174). Undergraduates: 3% (367). *Average award:* Freshmen: $823. Undergraduates: $1071. *Scholarships, grants, and awards by category: Academic interests/achievement:* 2,031 awards ($4,081,205 total): biological sciences, business, communication, computer science, education, engineering/technologies, English, foreign languages, general academic interests/achievements, health fields, humanities, international studies, mathematics, military science, physical sciences, premedicine, social sciences. *Creative arts/performance:* 212 awards ($248,373 total): art/fine arts, dance, debating, general creative arts/performance, journalism/publications, music, performing arts, theater/drama. *Special achievements/activities:* 50 awards ($173,196 total): cheerleading/drum major, community service, leadership, rodeo. *Special characteristics:* 2,668 awards ($2,232,719 total): ethnic background, first-generation college students, general special characteristics, handicapped students, international students, local/state students, members of minority groups, out-of-state students, previous college experience, spouses of current students, veterans, veterans' children. *Tuition waivers:* Full or partial for employees or children of employees, senior citizens.

LOANS *Student loans:* $60,143,383 (78% need-based, 22% non-need-based). 70% of past graduating class borrowed through all loan programs. *Average indebtedness per student:* $38,056. *Average need-based loan:* Freshmen: $4902. Undergraduates: $6599. *Parent loans:* $1,315,628 (25% need-based, 75% non-need-based). *Programs:* Federal Direct (Subsidized and Unsubsidized Stafford, PLUS), Perkins, state, college/university, Alaska Loans.

WORK-STUDY *Federal work-study:* Total amount: $3,668,878; 424 jobs averaging $3410. *State or other work-study/employment:* Total amount: $2,974,819 (100% need-based). 295 part-time jobs averaging $3323.

ATHLETIC AWARDS Total amount: $4,502,988 (92% need-based, 8% non-need-based).

APPLYING FOR FINANCIAL AID *Required financial aid form:* FAFSA. *Financial aid deadline:* 6/1 (priority: 2/15). *Notification date:* Continuous beginning 3/17. Students must reply by 6/1 or within 4 weeks of notification.

CONTACT Office of Financial Aid and Scholarships, Boise State University, Administration Building, Room 123, Boise, ID 83725-1315, 208-426-1664 or toll-free 800-632-6586 (in-state), 800-824-7017 (out-of-state). *Fax:* 208-426-1305. *E-mail:* faquest@boisestate.edu.

BORICUA COLLEGE
New York, NY

CONTACT Ms. Rosalia Cruz, Financial Aid Administrator, Boricua College, 3755 Broadway, New York, NY 10032-1560, 212-694-1000 Ext. 611. *Fax:* 212-694-1015. *E-mail:* rcruz@boricuacollege.edu.

BOSTON ARCHITECTURAL COLLEGE
Boston, MA

Tuition & fees: $11,468	Average undergraduate aid package: $5149

ABOUT THE INSTITUTION Independent, coed. 4 undergraduate majors. Federal methodology is used as a basis for awarding need-based institutional aid.
UNDERGRADUATE EXPENSES for 2009–10 *Tuition:* full-time $11,448; part-time $954 per credit hour. *Required fees:* full-time $20; $10 per term. Full-time tuition and fees vary according to course load, degree level, program, and reciprocity agreements. Part-time tuition and fees vary according to course load, degree level, program, and reciprocity agreements. *Payment plan:* Installment.
FRESHMAN FINANCIAL AID (Fall 2009, est.) 72 applied for aid; of those 90% were deemed to have need. 98% of freshmen with need received aid. *Average percent of need met:* 31% (excluding resources awarded to replace EFC). *Average financial aid package:* $7102 (excluding resources awarded to replace EFC).
UNDERGRADUATE FINANCIAL AID (Fall 2009, est.) 616 applied for aid; of those 90% were deemed to have need. 91% of undergraduates with need received aid; of those 3% had need fully met. *Average percent of need met:* 30% (excluding resources awarded to replace EFC). *Average financial aid package:* $5149 (excluding resources awarded to replace EFC). 1% of all full-time undergraduates had no need and received non-need-based gift aid.
GIFT AID (NEED-BASED) *Total amount:* $901,128 (85% federal, 3% state, 4% institutional, 8% external sources). *Receiving aid:* Freshmen: 55% (41); all full-time undergraduates: 40% (246). *Average award:* Freshmen: $4767; Undergraduates: $2900. *Scholarships, grants, and awards:* Federal Pell, FSEOG, state, college/university gift aid from institutional funds.
GIFT AID (NON-NEED-BASED) *Total amount:* $5920 (37% institutional, 63% external sources). *Receiving aid:* Undergraduates: 2. *Average award:* Undergraduates: $1534. *Scholarships, grants, and awards by category: Academic interests/achievement:* architecture. *Creative arts/performance:* 3 awards ($1629 total): general creative arts/performance. *Tuition waivers:* Full or partial for employees or children of employees.
LOANS *Student loans:* $4,577,797 (88% need-based, 12% non-need-based). 77% of past graduating class borrowed through all loan programs. *Average indebtedness per student:* $52,300. *Average need-based loan:* Freshmen: $3926. Undergraduates: $3662. *Parent loans:* $1,032,477 (59% need-based, 41% non-need-based). *Programs:* Federal Direct (Subsidized and Unsubsidized Stafford, PLUS), state.
WORK-STUDY *Federal work-study:* Total amount: $176,000; 44 jobs averaging $4000.
APPLYING FOR FINANCIAL AID *Required financial aid form:* FAFSA. *Financial aid deadline (priority):* 4/15. *Notification date:* Continuous beginning 4/1. Students must reply within 2 weeks of notification.
CONTACT Anne Downey, Director of Financial Aid, Boston Architectural College, 320 Newbury Street, Boston, MA 02115, 617-585-0125 or toll-free 877-585-0100. *Fax:* 617-585-0131. *E-mail:* anne.downey@the-bac.edu.

BOSTON BAPTIST COLLEGE
Boston, MA

CONTACT Curt A. Wiedenroth, Financial Aid Director, Boston Baptist College, 950 Metropolitan Avenue, Boston, MA 02136, 617-364-3510 or toll-free 888-235-2014 (out-of-state). *Fax:* 617-364-0723. *E-mail:* cw9083@aol.com.

BOSTON COLLEGE
Chestnut Hill, MA

Tuition & fees: $39,130	Average undergraduate aid package: $30,968

ABOUT THE INSTITUTION Independent Roman Catholic (Jesuit), coed. 48 undergraduate majors. Institutional methodology is used as a basis for awarding need-based institutional aid.
UNDERGRADUATE EXPENSES for 2009–10 *One-time required fee:* $438. *Comprehensive fee:* $52,039 includes full-time tuition ($38,530), mandatory fees ($600), and room and board ($12,909). *College room only:* $8369. Room and board charges vary according to housing facility. *Payment plan:* Installment.
FRESHMAN FINANCIAL AID (Fall 2009, est.) 1,091 applied for aid; of those 85% were deemed to have need. 100% of freshmen with need received aid; of those 100% had need fully met. *Average percent of need met:* 100% (excluding resources awarded to replace EFC). *Average financial aid package:* $31,591 (excluding resources awarded to replace EFC). 1% of all full-time freshmen had no need and received non-need-based gift aid.
UNDERGRADUATE FINANCIAL AID (Fall 2009, est.) 4,411 applied for aid; of those 88% were deemed to have need. 100% of undergraduates with need received aid; of those 100% had need fully met. *Average percent of need met:* 100% (excluding resources awarded to replace EFC). *Average financial aid package:* $30,968 (excluding resources awarded to replace EFC). 2% of all full-time undergraduates had no need and received non-need-based gift aid.
GIFT AID (NEED-BASED) *Total amount:* $88,879,757 (8% federal, 1% state, 87% institutional, 4% external sources). *Receiving aid:* Freshmen: 39% (841); all full-time undergraduates: 37% (3,354). *Average award:* Freshmen: $27,532; Undergraduates: $26,500. *Scholarships, grants, and awards:* Federal Pell, FSEOG, state, private, college/university gift aid from institutional funds.
GIFT AID (NON-NEED-BASED) *Total amount:* $6,140,710 (27% federal, 54% institutional, 19% external sources). *Receiving aid:* Freshmen: 1% (29). Undergraduates: 1% (65). *Average award:* Freshmen: $10,656. Undergraduates: $16,443. *Scholarships, grants, and awards by category: Academic interests/achievement:* 99 awards ($2,617,790 total): general academic interests/achievements, military science. *Tuition waivers:* Full or partial for employees or children of employees.
LOANS *Student loans:* $21,192,394 (79% need-based, 21% non-need-based). 49% of past graduating class borrowed through all loan programs. *Average indebtedness per student:* $19,514. *Average need-based loan:* Freshmen: $3512. Undergraduates: $4708. *Parent loans:* $42,421,292 (100% non-need-based). *Programs:* FFEL (Subsidized and Unsubsidized Stafford, PLUS), Perkins, Federal Nursing, state.
WORK-STUDY *Federal work-study:* Total amount: $6,762,213; 3,156 jobs averaging $2143.
ATHLETIC AWARDS Total amount: $13,326,086 (10% need-based, 90% non-need-based).
APPLYING FOR FINANCIAL AID *Required financial aid forms:* FAFSA, CSS Financial Aid PROFILE, business/farm supplement, federal income tax form(s), W-2 forms. *Financial aid deadline (priority):* 2/1. *Notification date:* 4/1. Students must reply by 5/1.
CONTACT Office of Student Services, Boston College, Lyons Hall, 140 Commonwealth Avenue, Chestnut Hill, MA 02467, 617-552-3300 or toll-free 800-360-2522. *Fax:* 617-552-4889. *E-mail:* studentservices@bc.edu.

THE BOSTON CONSERVATORY
Boston, MA

ABOUT THE INSTITUTION Independent, coed. 9 undergraduate majors.
GIFT AID (NEED-BASED) *Scholarships, grants, and awards:* Federal Pell, FSEOG, state, private, college/university gift aid from institutional funds.
GIFT AID (NON-NEED-BASED) *Scholarships, grants, and awards by category: Creative arts/performance:* dance, music, performing arts, theater/drama.
LOANS *Programs:* FFEL (Subsidized and Unsubsidized Stafford, PLUS), state, college/university.
WORK-STUDY *Federal work-study:* Total amount: $134,400; jobs available. *State or other work-study/employment:* Part-time jobs available (averaging $1335).
APPLYING FOR FINANCIAL AID *Required financial aid form:* FAFSA.
CONTACT Jessica Raine, Financial Aid Assistant, The Boston Conservatory, 8 The Fenway, Boston, MA 02215, 617-912-9147. *Fax:* 617-536-1496. *E-mail:* jraine@bostonconservatory.edu.

BOSTON UNIVERSITY
Boston, MA

Tuition & fees: $39,864	Average undergraduate aid package: $34,896

ABOUT THE INSTITUTION Independent, coed. 121 undergraduate majors. Both federal and institutional methodology are used as a basis for awarding need-based institutional aid.

UNDERGRADUATE EXPENSES for 2010–11 *Comprehensive fee:* $52,124 includes full-time tuition ($39,314), mandatory fees ($550), and room and board ($12,260). *College room only:* $7980. Full-time tuition and fees vary according to class time and degree level. Room and board charges vary according to board plan and housing facility. *Part-time tuition:* $1228 per credit. *Part-time fees:* $40 per term. Part-time tuition and fees vary according to class time, course load, and degree level. *Payment plans:* Tuition prepayment, installment.

FRESHMAN FINANCIAL AID (Fall 2009, est.) 2,497 applied for aid; of those 83% were deemed to have need. 100% of freshmen with need received aid; of those 57% had need fully met. *Average percent of need met:* 91% (excluding resources awarded to replace EFC). *Average financial aid package:* $35,431 (excluding resources awarded to replace EFC). 7% of all full-time freshmen had no need and received non-need-based gift aid.

UNDERGRADUATE FINANCIAL AID (Fall 2009, est.) 7,721 applied for aid; of those 91% were deemed to have need. 100% of undergraduates with need received aid; of those 51% had need fully met. *Average percent of need met:* 90% (excluding resources awarded to replace EFC). *Average financial aid package:* $34,896 (excluding resources awarded to replace EFC). 9% of all full-time undergraduates had no need and received non-need-based gift aid.

GIFT AID (NEED-BASED) *Total amount:* $172,027,870 (10% federal, 1% state, 85% institutional, 4% external sources). *Receiving aid:* Freshmen: 47% (1,936); all full-time undergraduates: 42% (6,672). *Average award:* Freshmen: $24,183; Undergraduates: $22,942. *Scholarships, grants, and awards:* Federal Pell, FSEOG, state, private, college/university gift aid from institutional funds, Academic Competitiveness Grants, National SMART Grants.

GIFT AID (NON-NEED-BASED) *Total amount:* $28,411,284 (12% federal, 69% institutional, 19% external sources). *Receiving aid:* Freshmen: 19% (786). Undergraduates: 12% (1,830). *Average award:* Freshmen: $18,862. Undergraduates: $18,898. *Scholarships, grants, and awards by category: Academic interests/achievement:* 1,722 awards ($23,836,048 total): education, engineering/technologies, foreign languages, general academic interests/achievements. *Creative arts/performance:* 183 awards ($1,378,650 total): art/fine arts, music, theater/drama. *Special achievements/activities:* 62 awards ($1,339,717 total): general special achievements/activities, leadership, memberships. *Special characteristics:* 737 awards ($7,533,576 total): children and siblings of alumni, local/state students, relatives of clergy, religious affiliation. *Tuition waivers:* Full or partial for employees or children of employees, senior citizens.

LOANS *Student loans:* $88,086,646 (65% need-based, 35% non-need-based). 57% of past graduating class borrowed through all loan programs. *Average indebtedness per student:* $30,998. *Average need-based loan:* Freshmen: $6331. Undergraduates: $7087. *Parent loans:* $41,368,889 (32% need-based, 68% non-need-based). *Programs:* Federal Direct (Subsidized and Unsubsidized Stafford, PLUS), Perkins, state, alternative loans.

WORK-STUDY *Federal work-study:* Total amount: $7,509,921; 3,187 jobs averaging $2179. *State or other work-study/employment:* Total amount: $2,282,244 (43% need-based, 57% non-need-based). 97 part-time jobs averaging $11,506.

ATHLETIC AWARDS Total amount: $11,485,798 (21% need-based, 79% non-need-based).

APPLYING FOR FINANCIAL AID *Required financial aid forms:* FAFSA, CSS Financial Aid PROFILE. *Financial aid deadline:* 2/15. *Notification date:* Continuous beginning 3/15. Students must reply by 5/1 or within 2 weeks of notification.

CONTACT Christine McGuire, Director of Financial Assistance, Boston University, 881 Commonwealth Avenue, Boston, MA 02215, 617-353-4176. *Fax:* 617-353-8200. *E-mail:* finaid@bu.edu.

BOWDOIN COLLEGE
Brunswick, ME

Tuition & fees: $40,020	Average undergraduate aid package: $34,960

ABOUT THE INSTITUTION Independent, coed. 43 undergraduate majors. Institutional methodology is used as a basis for awarding need-based institutional aid.

UNDERGRADUATE EXPENSES for 2009–10 *One-time required fee:* $100. *Comprehensive fee:* $50,900 includes full-time tuition ($39,605), mandatory fees ($415), and room and board ($10,880). *College room only:* $5085. Room and board charges vary according to board plan. *Payment plans:* Installment, deferred payment.

FRESHMAN FINANCIAL AID (Fall 2009, est.) 274 applied for aid; of those 73% were deemed to have need. 100% of freshmen with need received aid; of those 100% had need fully met. *Average percent of need met:* 100% (excluding resources awarded to replace EFC). *Average financial aid package:* $35,470 (excluding resources awarded to replace EFC). 4% of all full-time freshmen had no need and received non-need-based gift aid.

UNDERGRADUATE FINANCIAL AID (Fall 2009, est.) 928 applied for aid; of those 82% were deemed to have need. 100% of undergraduates with need received aid; of those 100% had need fully met. *Average percent of need met:* 100% (excluding resources awarded to replace EFC). *Average financial aid package:* $34,960 (excluding resources awarded to replace EFC). 4% of all full-time undergraduates had no need and received non-need-based gift aid.

GIFT AID (NEED-BASED) *Total amount:* $25,814,160 (6% federal, 91% institutional, 3% external sources). *Receiving aid:* Freshmen: 40% (199); all full-time undergraduates: 43% (763). *Average award:* Freshmen: $35,007; Undergraduates: $33,832. *Scholarships, grants, and awards:* Federal Pell, FSEOG, state, private, college/university gift aid from institutional funds.

GIFT AID (NON-NEED-BASED) *Total amount:* $857,090 (9% institutional, 91% external sources). *Average award:* Freshmen: $1000. Undergraduates: $1000. *Scholarships, grants, and awards by category: Academic interests/achievement:* 77 awards ($77,000 total): general academic interests/achievements. *Special achievements/activities:* leadership. *Special characteristics:* children of faculty/staff. *Tuition waivers:* Full or partial for employees or children of employees.

LOANS *Student loans:* 45% of past graduating class borrowed through all loan programs. *Average indebtedness per student:* $18,382. *Programs:* FFEL (Subsidized and Unsubsidized Stafford, PLUS), Perkins, state.

WORK-STUDY *Federal work-study:* Total amount: $233,950; 132 jobs averaging $1772. *State or other work-study/employment:* Total amount: $770,618 (100% need-based). 428 part-time jobs averaging $1800.

APPLYING FOR FINANCIAL AID *Required financial aid forms:* FAFSA, CSS Financial Aid PROFILE, noncustodial (divorced/separated) parent's statement, business/farm supplement. *Financial aid deadline:* 2/15. *Notification date:* 4/5. Students must reply by 5/1 or within 1 week of notification.

CONTACT Mr. Stephen H. Joyce, Director of Student Aid, Bowdoin College, 5300 College Station, Brunswick, ME 04011-8444, 207-725-3273. *Fax:* 207-725-3864. *E-mail:* sjoyce@bowdoin.edu.

BOWIE STATE UNIVERSITY
Bowie, MD

Tuition & fees (MD res): $6040	Average undergraduate aid package: $8359

ABOUT THE INSTITUTION State-supported, coed. 29 undergraduate majors. Both federal and institutional methodology are used as a basis for awarding need-based institutional aid.

UNDERGRADUATE EXPENSES for 2009–10 *Tuition, state resident:* full-time $4286; part-time $189 per credit hour. *Tuition, nonresident:* full-time $14,725; part-time $620 per credit hour. *Required fees:* full-time $1754; $88.30 per credit hour. Part-time tuition and fees vary according to course load. *College room and board:* $7536. Room and board charges vary according to board plan and housing facility. *Payment plans:* Installment, deferred payment.

FRESHMAN FINANCIAL AID (Fall 2008) 496 applied for aid; of those 100% were deemed to have need. 100% of freshmen with need received aid; of those 57% had need fully met. *Average percent of need met:* 47% (excluding resources awarded to replace EFC). *Average financial aid package:* $7913 (excluding resources awarded to replace EFC). 2% of all full-time freshmen had no need and received non-need-based gift aid.

UNDERGRADUATE FINANCIAL AID (Fall 2008) 2,507 applied for aid; of those 99% were deemed to have need. 100% of undergraduates with need received aid; of those 46% had need fully met. *Average percent of need met:* 49% (excluding resources awarded to replace EFC). *Average financial aid package:* $8359 (excluding resources awarded to replace EFC). 1% of all full-time undergraduates had no need and received non-need-based gift aid.

GIFT AID (NEED-BASED) *Total amount:* $16,739,649 (50% federal, 30% state, 19% institutional, 1% external sources). *Receiving aid:* Freshmen: 59% (363); all full-time undergraduates: 60% (1,891). *Average award:* Freshmen: $6730; Undergraduates: $6569. *Scholarships, grants, and awards:* Federal Pell, FSEOG, state, private, college/university gift aid from institutional funds, United Negro College Fund, Federal Nursing.

GIFT AID (NON-NEED-BASED) *Total amount:* $763,972 (20% state, 76% institutional, 4% external sources). *Receiving aid:* Freshmen: 65% (403). Undergraduates: 61% (1,906). *Average award:* Freshmen: $162. Undergraduates: $151. *Scholarships, grants, and awards by category: Academic interests/ achievement:* biological sciences, business, communication, computer science, engineering/technologies, mathematics, military science. *Creative arts/ performance:* applied art and design, art/fine arts, general creative arts/ performance, music. *Special characteristics:* first-generation college students. *Tuition waivers:* Full or partial for employees or children of employees, senior citizens.

LOANS *Student loans:* $20,206,374 (78% need-based, 22% non-need-based). 66% of past graduating class borrowed through all loan programs. *Average indebtedness per student:* $17,108. *Average need-based loan:* Freshmen: $3413. Undergraduates: $4145. *Parent loans:* $18,857,482 (85% need-based, 15% non-need-based). *Programs:* Federal Direct (Subsidized and Unsubsidized Stafford, PLUS), Perkins, Federal Nursing, state, college/university.

WORK-STUDY *Federal work-study:* Total amount: $233,224; jobs available.

ATHLETIC AWARDS Total amount: $717,208 (64% need-based, 36% non-need-based).

APPLYING FOR FINANCIAL AID *Required financial aid forms:* FAFSA, institution's own form. *Financial aid deadline (priority):* 3/1. *Notification date:* Continuous beginning 4/1. Students must reply within 2 weeks of notification.

CONTACT Deborah Stanley, Financial Aid Director, Bowie State University, 14000 Jericho Park Road, Bowie, MD 20715, 301-860-3543 or toll-free 877-772-6943 (out-of-state). *Fax:* 301-860-3549. *E-mail:* dstanley@bowiestate.edu.

BOWLING GREEN STATE UNIVERSITY
Bowling Green, OH

Tuition & fees (OH res): $9060   **Average undergraduate aid package: $12,886**

ABOUT THE INSTITUTION State-supported, coed. 202 undergraduate majors. Federal methodology is used as a basis for awarding need-based institutional aid.

UNDERGRADUATE EXPENSES for 2009–10 *Tuition, state resident:* full-time $7778; part-time $324 per credit hour. *Tuition, nonresident:* full-time $15,086; part-time $629 per credit hour. *Required fees:* full-time $1282; $53 per credit hour. Full-time tuition and fees vary according to course load and location. Part-time tuition and fees vary according to course load and location. *College room and board:* $7670. Room and board charges vary according to board plan and housing facility. *Payment plan:* Installment.

FRESHMAN FINANCIAL AID (Fall 2008) 2,659 applied for aid; of those 79% were deemed to have need. 99% of freshmen with need received aid; of those 15% had need fully met. *Average percent of need met:* 77% (excluding resources awarded to replace EFC). *Average financial aid package:* $11,920 (excluding resources awarded to replace EFC). 19% of all full-time freshmen had no need and received non-need-based gift aid.

UNDERGRADUATE FINANCIAL AID (Fall 2008) 10,157 applied for aid; of those 84% were deemed to have need. 99% of undergraduates with need received aid; of those 14% had need fully met. *Average percent of need met:* 76% (excluding resources awarded to replace EFC). *Average financial aid package:* $12,886 (excluding resources awarded to replace EFC). 15% of all full-time undergraduates had no need and received non-need-based gift aid.

GIFT AID (NEED-BASED) *Total amount:* $40,284,421 (36% federal, 11% state, 48% institutional, 5% external sources). *Receiving aid:* Freshmen: 58% (1,772); all full-time undergraduates: 45% (6,155). *Average award:* Freshmen: $6058; Undergraduates: $6327. *Scholarships, grants, and awards:* Federal Pell, FSEOG, state, private, college/university gift aid from institutional funds.

GIFT AID (NON-NEED-BASED) *Total amount:* $12,625,630 (1% federal, 5% state, 84% institutional, 10% external sources). *Receiving aid:* Freshmen: 6% (171). Undergraduates: 4% (501). *Average award:* Freshmen: $2712. Undergraduates: $4727. *Scholarships, grants, and awards by category: Academic interests/ achievement:* biological sciences, business, communication, computer science, education, engineering/technologies, English, foreign languages, general academic interests/achievements, health fields, home economics, humanities, inter-

national studies, mathematics, military science, physical sciences, social sciences. *Creative arts/performance:* art/fine arts, cinema/film/broadcasting, creative writing, dance, debating, journalism/publications, music, performing arts, theater/ drama. *Special achievements/activities:* general special achievements/activities, leadership. *Special characteristics:* children and siblings of alumni, children of faculty/staff, general special characteristics, international students, members of minority groups. *Tuition waivers:* Full or partial for employees or children of employees, senior citizens.

LOANS *Student loans:* $94,631,989 (73% need-based, 27% non-need-based). 72% of past graduating class borrowed through all loan programs. *Average indebtedness per student:* $28,542. *Average need-based loan:* Freshmen: $5924. Undergraduates: $7674. *Parent loans:* $11,907,906 (44% need-based, 56% non-need-based). *Programs:* Federal Direct (Subsidized and Unsubsidized Stafford, PLUS), Perkins, Federal Nursing, state, college/university, alternative loans.

WORK-STUDY *Federal work-study:* Total amount: $988,794; 900 jobs averaging $1145.

ATHLETIC AWARDS Total amount: $5,085,091 (30% need-based, 70% non-need-based).

APPLYING FOR FINANCIAL AID *Required financial aid form:* FAFSA. *Financial aid deadline:* Continuous. *Notification date:* Continuous beginning 4/15. Students must reply within 3 weeks of notification.

CONTACT Eric Bucks, Associate Director, Office of Student Financial Aid, Bowling Green State University, 231 Administration Building, Bowling Green, OH 43403, 419-372-2651. *Fax:* 419-372-0404.

BRADLEY UNIVERSITY
Peoria, IL

Tuition & fees: $24,224   **Average undergraduate aid package: $16,201**

ABOUT THE INSTITUTION Independent, coed. 102 undergraduate majors. Federal methodology is used as a basis for awarding need-based institutional aid.

UNDERGRADUATE EXPENSES for 2009–10 *Comprehensive fee:* $31,874 includes full-time tuition ($23,950), mandatory fees ($274), and room and board ($7650). *Part-time tuition:* $650 per credit hour. Part-time tuition and fees vary according to course load.

FRESHMAN FINANCIAL AID (Fall 2009, est.) 976 applied for aid; of those 80% were deemed to have need. 99% of freshmen with need received aid; of those 34% had need fully met. *Average percent of need met:* 73% (excluding resources awarded to replace EFC). *Average financial aid package:* $17,449 (excluding resources awarded to replace EFC). 25% of all full-time freshmen had no need and received non-need-based gift aid.

UNDERGRADUATE FINANCIAL AID (Fall 2009, est.) 4,050 applied for aid; of those 85% were deemed to have need. 99% of undergraduates with need received aid; of those 18% had need fully met. *Average percent of need met:* 69% (excluding resources awarded to replace EFC). *Average financial aid package:* $16,201 (excluding resources awarded to replace EFC). 28% of all full-time undergraduates had no need and received non-need-based gift aid.

GIFT AID (NEED-BASED) *Total amount:* $42,500,632 (13% federal, 16% state, 68% institutional, 3% external sources). *Receiving aid:* Freshmen: 69% (769); all full-time undergraduates: 68% (3,285). *Average award:* Freshmen: $14,312; Undergraduates: $12,618. *Scholarships, grants, and awards:* Federal Pell, FSEOG, state, private, college/university gift aid from institutional funds.

GIFT AID (NON-NEED-BASED) *Total amount:* $9,238,454 (91% institutional, 9% external sources). *Receiving aid:* Freshmen: 8% (94). Undergraduates: 7% (356). *Average award:* Freshmen: $7325. Undergraduates: $7764. *Scholarships, grants, and awards by category: Academic interests/achievement:* 3,687 awards ($19,447,212 total): general academic interests/achievements. *Creative arts/performance:* 237 awards ($291,900 total): art/fine arts, music, theater/ drama. *Special achievements/activities:* 47 awards ($43,000 total): community service, leadership. *Special characteristics:* 1,183 awards ($4,299,100 total): children and siblings of alumni, children of faculty/staff.

LOANS *Student loans:* $29,871,980 (57% need-based, 43% non-need-based). 85% of past graduating class borrowed through all loan programs. *Average indebtedness per student:* $17,067. *Average need-based loan:* Freshmen: $3676. Undergraduates: $4608. *Parent loans:* $8,948,946 (31% need-based, 69% non-need-based). *Programs:* Federal Direct (Subsidized and Unsubsidized Stafford, PLUS), Perkins, Federal Nursing.

WORK-STUDY *Federal work-study:* Total amount: $584,493; 390 jobs averaging $1790.

ATHLETIC AWARDS Total amount: $1,773,416 (54% need-based, 46% non-need-based).

APPLYING FOR FINANCIAL AID *Required financial aid form:* FAFSA. *Financial aid deadline (priority):* 3/1. *Notification date:* Continuous beginning 3/1.

CONTACT Mr. David L. Pardieck, Director of Financial Assistance, Bradley University, 1501 West Bradley Avenue, Peoria, IL 61625-0002, 309-677-3089 or toll-free 800-447-6460. *E-mail:* dlp@bradley.edu.

BRANDEIS UNIVERSITY
Waltham, MA

Tuition & fees: $38,762	Average undergraduate aid package: $30,397

ABOUT THE INSTITUTION Independent, coed. 42 undergraduate majors. Institutional methodology is used as a basis for awarding need-based institutional aid.

UNDERGRADUATE EXPENSES for 2009–10 *Comprehensive fee:* $49,554 includes full-time tuition ($37,530), mandatory fees ($1232), and room and board ($10,792). Room and board charges vary according to board plan and housing facility. Part-time tuition and fees vary according to course load. *Payment plans:* Tuition prepayment, installment.

FRESHMAN FINANCIAL AID (Fall 2009, est.) 546 applied for aid; of those 83% were deemed to have need. 99% of freshmen with need received aid; of those 13% had need fully met. *Average percent of need met:* 82% (excluding resources awarded to replace EFC). *Average financial aid package:* $30,398 (excluding resources awarded to replace EFC). 5% of all full-time freshmen had no need and received non-need-based gift aid.

UNDERGRADUATE FINANCIAL AID (Fall 2009, est.) 1,928 applied for aid; of those 88% were deemed to have need. 99% of undergraduates with need received aid; of those 15% had need fully met. *Average percent of need met:* 81% (excluding resources awarded to replace EFC). *Average financial aid package:* $30,397 (excluding resources awarded to replace EFC). 12% of all full-time undergraduates had no need and received non-need-based gift aid.

GIFT AID (NEED-BASED) *Total amount:* $41,011,686 (9% federal, 1% state, 87% institutional, 3% external sources). *Receiving aid:* Freshmen: 53% (415); all full-time undergraduates: 48% (1,590). *Average award:* Freshmen: $27,392; Undergraduates: $25,790. *Scholarships, grants, and awards:* Federal Pell, FSEOG, state, private, college/university gift aid from institutional funds.

GIFT AID (NON-NEED-BASED) *Total amount:* $11,573,826 (89% institutional, 11% external sources). *Receiving aid:* Freshmen: 4% (31). Undergraduates: 4% (129). *Average award:* Freshmen: $23,479. Undergraduates: $23,564. *Scholarships, grants, and awards by category:* Academic interests/achievement: general academic interests/achievements. *Tuition waivers:* Full or partial for employees or children of employees.

LOANS *Student loans:* $14,080,736 (70% need-based, 30% non-need-based). 58% of past graduating class borrowed through all loan programs. *Average indebtedness per student:* $26,078. *Average need-based loan:* Freshmen: $3696. Undergraduates: $5085. *Parent loans:* $6,064,776 (37% need-based, 63% non-need-based). *Programs:* Federal Direct (Subsidized and Unsubsidized Stafford, PLUS), Perkins, state, college/university.

WORK-STUDY *Federal work-study:* Total amount: $2,252,967; jobs available. *State or other work-study/employment:* Total amount: $679,384 (27% need-based, 73% non-need-based). Part-time jobs available.

APPLYING FOR FINANCIAL AID *Required financial aid forms:* FAFSA, CSS Financial Aid PROFILE, noncustodial (divorced/separated) parent's statement, business/farm supplement. *Financial aid deadline (priority):* 2/1.

CONTACT Peter Giumette, Student Financial Services, Brandeis University, 415 South Street, Usdan Student Center, Waltham, MA 02454-9110, 781-736-3700 or toll-free 800-622-0622 (out-of-state). *Fax:* 781-736-3719. *E-mail:* sfs@brandeis.edu.

BRENAU UNIVERSITY
Gainesville, GA

Tuition & fees: $20,130	Average undergraduate aid package: $18,874

ABOUT THE INSTITUTION Independent, women only. 29 undergraduate majors. Federal methodology is used as a basis for awarding need-based institutional aid.

UNDERGRADUATE EXPENSES for 2010–11 *Comprehensive fee:* $30,195 includes full-time tuition ($19,870), mandatory fees ($260), and room and board ($10,065). Full-time tuition and fees vary according to location and program. *Part-time tuition:* $662 per credit hour. *Part-time fees:* $130 per term. Part-time tuition and fees vary according to course load, location, and program. *Payment plan:* Installment.

FRESHMAN FINANCIAL AID (Fall 2009, est.) 146 applied for aid; of those 88% were deemed to have need. 99% of freshmen with need received aid; of those 24% had need fully met. *Average percent of need met:* 79% (excluding resources awarded to replace EFC). *Average financial aid package:* $21,146 (excluding resources awarded to replace EFC). 13% of all full-time freshmen had no need and received non-need-based gift aid.

UNDERGRADUATE FINANCIAL AID (Fall 2009, est.) 634 applied for aid; of those 89% were deemed to have need. 99% of undergraduates with need received aid; of those 14% had need fully met. *Average percent of need met:* 73% (excluding resources awarded to replace EFC). *Average financial aid package:* $18,874 (excluding resources awarded to replace EFC). 18% of all full-time undergraduates had no need and received non-need-based gift aid.

GIFT AID (NEED-BASED) *Total amount:* $9,490,593 (18% federal, 10% state, 71% institutional, 1% external sources). *Receiving aid:* Freshmen: 82% (128); all full-time undergraduates: 73% (560). *Average award:* Freshmen: $16,666; Undergraduates: $14,244. *Scholarships, grants, and awards:* Federal Pell, FSEOG, state, private, college/university gift aid from institutional funds, Academic Competitiveness Grants, National SMART Grants.

GIFT AID (NON-NEED-BASED) *Total amount:* $2,600,112 (28% state, 71% institutional, 1% external sources). *Receiving aid:* Freshmen: 14% (22). Undergraduates: 11% (82). *Average award:* Freshmen: $10,924. Undergraduates: $10,492. *Scholarships, grants, and awards by category:* Academic interests/achievement: biological sciences, business, communication, education, general academic interests/achievements, health fields, humanities. Creative arts/performance: applied art and design, art/fine arts, cinema/film/broadcasting, creative writing, dance, journalism/publications, music, performing arts, theater/drama. Special achievements/activities: general special achievements/activities, leadership. Special characteristics: children of faculty/staff, first-generation college students, general special characteristics, international students. *Tuition waivers:* Full or partial for employees or children of employees.

LOANS *Student loans:* $4,358,865 (50% need-based, 50% non-need-based). 64% of past graduating class borrowed through all loan programs. *Average indebtedness per student:* $17,999. *Average need-based loan:* Freshmen: $3257. *Parent loans:* $328,237 (60% need-based, 40% non-need-based). *Programs:* FFEL (Subsidized and Unsubsidized Stafford, PLUS), Perkins, state.

WORK-STUDY *Federal work-study:* Total amount: $245,410; 131 jobs averaging $1897.

ATHLETIC AWARDS Total amount: $1,193,827 (42% need-based, 58% non-need-based).

APPLYING FOR FINANCIAL AID *Required financial aid forms:* FAFSA, state aid form. *Financial aid deadline (priority):* 3/15. *Notification date:* Continuous beginning 2/1.

CONTACT Pam Barrett, Associate Vice President and Director of Financial Aid, Brenau University, 500 Washington Street, SE, Gainesville, GA 30501-3697, 770-534-6176 or toll-free 800-252-5119. *Fax:* 770-538-4306. *E-mail:* pbarrett@brenau.edu.

BRESCIA UNIVERSITY
Owensboro, KY

Tuition & fees: $17,390	Average undergraduate aid package: N/A

ABOUT THE INSTITUTION Independent Roman Catholic, coed. 32 undergraduate majors. Federal methodology is used as a basis for awarding need-based institutional aid.

UNDERGRADUATE EXPENSES for 2010–11 *One-time required fee:* $120. *Comprehensive fee:* $25,390 includes full-time tuition ($16,950), mandatory fees ($440), and room and board ($8000). Full-time tuition and fees vary according to class time. Room and board charges vary according to board plan and housing facility. *Part-time tuition:* $495 per credit hour. Part-time tuition and fees vary according to class time. *Payment plan:* Installment.

UNDERGRADUATE FINANCIAL AID (Fall 2009, est.) 609 applied for aid; of those 95% were deemed to have need. 100% of undergraduates with need received aid.

GIFT AID (NEED-BASED) *Total amount:* $2,939,747 (43% federal, 40% state, 12% institutional, 5% external sources). *Scholarships, grants, and awards:* Federal Pell, FSEOG, state, private, college/university gift aid from institutional funds.

GIFT AID (NON-NEED-BASED) *Total amount:* $2,086,993 (2% federal, 17% state, 75% institutional, 6% external sources). *Scholarships, grants, and awards by category: Academic interests/achievement:* 12 awards ($14,100 total): biological sciences, business, education, English, general academic interests/achievements, health fields, physical sciences, premedicine, religion/biblical studies, social sciences. *Creative arts/performance:* 18 awards ($18,383 total): art/fine arts, creative writing, music. *Special achievements/activities:* 16 awards ($106,550 total): leadership. *Special characteristics:* 22 awards ($120,506 total): children and siblings of alumni, children of faculty/staff, ethnic background, international students, members of minority groups. *Tuition waivers:* Full or partial for employees or children of employees.

LOANS *Student loans:* $3,095,782 (47% need-based, 53% non-need-based). 93% of past graduating class borrowed through all loan programs. *Average indebtedness per student:* $18,638. *Parent loans:* $343,489 (100% non-need-based). *Programs:* Federal Direct (Subsidized and Unsubsidized Stafford, PLUS), FFEL (Subsidized and Unsubsidized Stafford, PLUS), Perkins, college/university.

WORK-STUDY *Federal work-study:* Total amount: $64,426; 64 jobs averaging $1200. *State or other work-study/employment:* Total amount: $71,236 (100% non-need-based). 15 part-time jobs averaging $2500.

ATHLETIC AWARDS Total amount: $1,083,823 (100% non-need-based).

APPLYING FOR FINANCIAL AID *Required financial aid form:* FAFSA. *Financial aid deadline (priority):* 3/15. *Notification date:* Continuous beginning 2/15. Students must reply by 8/1 or within 2 weeks of notification.

CONTACT Mr. Britton Hibbitt, Administrative Assistant to Financial Aid, Brescia University, 717 Frederica Street, Owensboro, KY 42301-3023, 270-686-4253 or toll-free 877-273-7242. *Fax:* 270-686-4253. *E-mail:* financial.aid@brescia.edu.

BREVARD COLLEGE
Brevard, NC

Tuition & fees: $20,900	Average undergraduate aid package: $20,500

ABOUT THE INSTITUTION Independent United Methodist, coed. 18 undergraduate majors. Federal methodology is used as a basis for awarding need-based institutional aid.

UNDERGRADUATE EXPENSES for 2009–10 *Comprehensive fee:* $28,750 includes full-time tuition ($20,900) and room and board ($7850). Full-time tuition and fees vary according to course load. Room and board charges vary according to board plan and housing facility. *Part-time tuition:* $770 per contact hour. Part-time tuition and fees vary according to course load. *Payment plan:* Installment.

FRESHMAN FINANCIAL AID (Fall 2009, est.) 150 applied for aid; of those 88% were deemed to have need. 100% of freshmen with need received aid; of those 27% had need fully met. *Average percent of need met:* 81% (excluding resources awarded to replace EFC). *Average financial aid package:* $19,400 (excluding resources awarded to replace EFC). 18% of all full-time freshmen had no need and received non-need-based gift aid.

UNDERGRADUATE FINANCIAL AID (Fall 2009, est.) 512 applied for aid; of those 90% were deemed to have need. 100% of undergraduates with need received aid; of those 28% had need fully met. *Average percent of need met:* 83% (excluding resources awarded to replace EFC). *Average financial aid package:* $20,500 (excluding resources awarded to replace EFC). 20% of all full-time undergraduates had no need and received non-need-based gift aid.

GIFT AID (NEED-BASED) *Total amount:* $5,610,000 (20% federal, 16% state, 61% institutional, 3% external sources). *Receiving aid:* Freshmen: 69% (132); all full-time undergraduates: 72% (460). *Average award:* Freshmen: $13,500; Undergraduates: $14,200. *Scholarships, grants, and awards:* Federal Pell, FSEOG, state, private, college/university gift aid from institutional funds.

GIFT AID (NON-NEED-BASED) *Total amount:* $2,631,000 (9% state, 87% institutional, 4% external sources). *Receiving aid:* Freshmen: 8% (15). Undergraduates: 9% (55). *Average award:* Freshmen: $3500. Undergraduates: $2600. *Scholarships, grants, and awards by category: Academic interests/achievement:* $1,750,000 total: biological sciences, business, education, English, general academic interests/achievements, health fields, mathematics, physical sciences, premedicine, religion/biblical studies, social sciences. *Creative arts/performance:* $235,000 total: art/fine arts, journalism/publications, music, theater/drama. *Special achievements/activities:* $450,000 total: cheerleading/drum major,

community service, general special achievements/activities, hobbies/interests, leadership. *Special characteristics:* $2,125,000 total: children of faculty/staff, international students, local/state students, previous college experience, relatives of clergy, religious affiliation, siblings of current students, veterans' children. *Tuition waivers:* Full or partial for employees or children of employees, senior citizens.

LOANS *Student loans:* $3,500,000 (71% need-based, 29% non-need-based). 59% of past graduating class borrowed through all loan programs. *Average indebtedness per student:* $20,700. *Average need-based loan:* Freshmen: $3850. Undergraduates: $4260. *Parent loans:* $680,000 (40% need-based, 60% non-need-based). *Programs:* FFEL (Subsidized and Unsubsidized Stafford, PLUS), Perkins, state.

WORK-STUDY *Federal work-study:* Total amount: $75,000; 50 jobs averaging $1550. *State or other work-study/employment:* Total amount: $100,000 (70% need-based, 30% non-need-based). 80 part-time jobs averaging $1500.

ATHLETIC AWARDS Total amount: $1,795,000 (61% need-based, 39% non-need-based).

APPLYING FOR FINANCIAL AID *Required financial aid forms:* FAFSA, state aid form. *Financial aid deadline (priority):* 4/15. *Notification date:* Continuous beginning 2/1. Students must reply within 4 weeks of notification.

CONTACT Ms. Lisanne J. Masterson, Director of Financial Aid, Brevard College, 1 Brevard College Drive, Brevard, NC 28712, 828-884-8287 or toll-free 800-527-9090. *Fax:* 828-884-3790. *E-mail:* finaid@brevard.edu.

BREWTON-PARKER COLLEGE
Mt. Vernon, GA

Tuition & fees: $15,290	Average undergraduate aid package: $11,736

ABOUT THE INSTITUTION Independent Southern Baptist, coed. 31 undergraduate majors. Federal methodology is used as a basis for awarding need-based institutional aid.

UNDERGRADUATE EXPENSES for 2009–10 *Comprehensive fee:* $21,543 includes full-time tuition ($13,920), mandatory fees ($1370), and room and board ($6253). *College room only:* $2620. Room and board charges vary according to board plan and housing facility. *Part-time tuition:* $435 per credit hour. *Payment plan:* Installment.

FRESHMAN FINANCIAL AID (Fall 2009, est.) 191 applied for aid; of those 90% were deemed to have need. 99% of freshmen with need received aid; of those 19% had need fully met. *Average percent of need met:* 73% (excluding resources awarded to replace EFC). *Average financial aid package:* $11,647 (excluding resources awarded to replace EFC). 12% of all full-time freshmen had no need and received non-need-based gift aid.

UNDERGRADUATE FINANCIAL AID (Fall 2009, est.) 819 applied for aid; of those 90% were deemed to have need. 98% of undergraduates with need received aid; of those 16% had need fully met. *Average percent of need met:* 71% (excluding resources awarded to replace EFC). *Average financial aid package:* $11,736 (excluding resources awarded to replace EFC). 11% of all full-time undergraduates had no need and received non-need-based gift aid.

GIFT AID (NEED-BASED) *Total amount:* $6,203,565 (29% federal, 20% state, 42% institutional, 9% external sources). *Receiving aid:* Freshmen: 70% (170); all full-time undergraduates: 80% (710). *Average award:* Freshmen: $9501; Undergraduates: $9011. *Scholarships, grants, and awards:* Federal Pell, FSEOG, state, private, college/university gift aid from institutional funds, United Negro College Fund.

GIFT AID (NON-NEED-BASED) *Total amount:* $1,096,367 (44% state, 46% institutional, 10% external sources). *Receiving aid:* Freshmen: 9% (21). Undergraduates: 9% (79). *Average award:* Freshmen: $3887. Undergraduates: $3915. *Scholarships, grants, and awards by category: Academic interests/achievement:* 288 awards ($1,037,348 total): general academic interests/achievements. *Creative arts/performance:* 30 awards ($103,386 total): music. *Special achievements/activities:* 55 awards ($33,373 total): cheerleading/drum major, religious involvement. *Special characteristics:* 306 awards ($184,612 total): children of faculty/staff, international students, out-of-state students, relatives of clergy, religious affiliation. *Tuition waivers:* Full or partial for employees or children of employees, senior citizens.

LOANS *Student loans:* $5,656,658 (75% need-based, 25% non-need-based). 89% of past graduating class borrowed through all loan programs. *Average indebtedness per student:* $28,231. *Average need-based loan:* Freshmen: $2782.

Undergraduates: $3436. *Parent loans:* $230,279 (23% need-based, 77% non-need-based). *Programs:* FFEL (Subsidized and Unsubsidized Stafford, PLUS), Perkins, state, college/university.

WORK-STUDY *Federal work-study:* Total amount: $92,982; 170 jobs averaging $676. *State or other work-study/employment:* Total amount: $54,786 (17% need-based, 83% non-need-based). 114 part-time jobs averaging $466.

ATHLETIC AWARDS Total amount: $874,281 (69% need-based, 31% non-need-based).

APPLYING FOR FINANCIAL AID *Required financial aid forms:* FAFSA, state aid form, individual grant forms. *Financial aid deadline:* 5/1. *Notification date:* Continuous. Students must reply within 2 weeks of notification.

CONTACT Mrs. Shannon Mullins, Executive Director of Financial Aid, Brewton-Parker College, PO Box 197, Mt. Vernon, GA 30445-0197, 800-342-1087 Ext. 213 or toll-free 800-342-1087 Ext. 245. *Fax:* 912-583-3598. *E-mail:* smullins@bpc.edu.

BRIARCLIFFE COLLEGE
Bethpage, NY

CONTACT Johanna Kelly, Financial Aid Director, Briarcliffe College, 1055 Stewart Avenue, Bethpage, NY 11714, 516-918-3600 or toll-free 888-333-1150 (in-state).

BRIAR CLIFF UNIVERSITY
Sioux City, IA

Tuition & fees: $22,536	Average undergraduate aid package: $6300

ABOUT THE INSTITUTION Independent Roman Catholic, coed. 30 undergraduate majors. Federal methodology is used as a basis for awarding need-based institutional aid.

UNDERGRADUATE EXPENSES for 2010–11 *Comprehensive fee:* $29,514 includes full-time tuition ($21,867), mandatory fees ($669), and room and board ($6978). *College room only:* $3357. Room and board charges vary according to board plan and housing facility. *Part-time tuition:* $729 per credit hour. *Part-time fees:* $22 per credit hour. Part-time tuition and fees vary according to class time and course load. *Payment plans:* Installment, deferred payment.

FRESHMAN FINANCIAL AID (Fall 2009, est.) 220 applied for aid; of those 81% were deemed to have need. 100% of freshmen with need received aid; of those 69% had need fully met. *Average percent of need met:* 87% (excluding resources awarded to replace EFC). *Average financial aid package:* $6500 (excluding resources awarded to replace EFC). 20% of all full-time freshmen had no need and received non-need-based gift aid.

UNDERGRADUATE FINANCIAL AID (Fall 2009, est.) 875 applied for aid; of those 71% were deemed to have need. 100% of undergraduates with need received aid; of those 68% had need fully met. *Average percent of need met:* 78% (excluding resources awarded to replace EFC). *Average financial aid package:* $6300 (excluding resources awarded to replace EFC). 30% of all full-time undergraduates had no need and received non-need-based gift aid.

GIFT AID (NEED-BASED) *Total amount:* $4,668,466 (29% federal, 34% state, 31% institutional, 6% external sources). *Receiving aid:* Freshmen: 80% (178); all full-time undergraduates: 70% (625). *Average award:* Freshmen: $6300; Undergraduates: $6200. *Scholarships, grants, and awards:* Federal Pell, FSEOG, state, private, college/university gift aid from institutional funds.

GIFT AID (NON-NEED-BASED) *Total amount:* $5,044,421 (100% institutional). *Receiving aid:* Freshmen: 80% (178). Undergraduates: 70% (625). *Average award:* Freshmen: $12,250. Undergraduates: $11,550. *Scholarships, grants, and awards by category:* Academic interests/achievement: 650 awards ($3,131,864 total): biological sciences, business, communication, computer science, education, English, foreign languages, general academic interests/achievements, health fields, humanities, mathematics, physical sciences, religion/biblical studies, social sciences. *Creative arts/performance:* 76 awards ($170,351 total): art/fine arts, music, theater/drama. *Special achievements/activities:* 257 awards ($250,662 total): leadership, religious involvement. *Special characteristics:* 319 awards ($181,710 total): children and siblings of alumni, international students, members of minority groups. *Tuition waivers:* Full or partial for employees or children of employees, adult students, senior citizens.

LOANS *Student loans:* $7,501,424 (68% need-based, 32% non-need-based). 88% of past graduating class borrowed through all loan programs. *Average*

indebtedness per student: $31,853. *Average need-based loan:* Freshmen: $3900. Undergraduates: $4775. *Parent loans:* $650,540 (100% non-need-based). *Programs:* Federal Direct (Subsidized and Unsubsidized Stafford, PLUS), FFEL (Subsidized Stafford), Perkins, alternative loans, partnership loans, Minnesota SELF Loans.

WORK-STUDY *Federal work-study:* Total amount: $225,391; 240 jobs averaging $1500. *State or other work-study/employment:* Total amount: $345,000 (100% non-need-based). 115 part-time jobs averaging $1500.

ATHLETIC AWARDS Total amount: $2,101,183 (100% non-need-based).

APPLYING FOR FINANCIAL AID *Required financial aid forms:* FAFSA, income tax form(s). *Financial aid deadline:* 3/15. *Notification date:* Continuous beginning 3/20. Students must reply within 4 weeks of notification.

CONTACT Financial Aid Office, Briar Cliff University, 3303 Rebecca Street, PO Box 2100, Sioux City, IA 51104-2100, 712-279-5239 or toll-free 800-662-3303 Ext. 5200. *Fax:* 712-279-1632.

BRIDGEWATER COLLEGE
Bridgewater, VA

Tuition & fees: $25,500	Average undergraduate aid package: $21,596

ABOUT THE INSTITUTION Independent religious, coed. 45 undergraduate majors. Federal methodology is used as a basis for awarding need-based institutional aid.

UNDERGRADUATE EXPENSES for 2010–11 *Comprehensive fee:* $35,850 includes full-time tuition ($25,500) and room and board ($10,350). *College room only:* $5260. Room and board charges vary according to board plan and housing facility. *Part-time tuition:* $850 per credit hour. *Part-time fees:* $30 per term. *Payment plan:* Installment.

FRESHMAN FINANCIAL AID (Fall 2009, est.) 461 applied for aid; of those 89% were deemed to have need. 100% of freshmen with need received aid; of those 19% had need fully met. *Average percent of need met:* 79% (excluding resources awarded to replace EFC). *Average financial aid package:* $21,959 (excluding resources awarded to replace EFC). 18% of all full-time freshmen had no need and received non-need-based gift aid.

UNDERGRADUATE FINANCIAL AID (Fall 2009, est.) 1,345 applied for aid; of those 88% were deemed to have need. 100% of undergraduates with need received aid; of those 14% had need fully met. *Average percent of need met:* 79% (excluding resources awarded to replace EFC). *Average financial aid package:* $21,596 (excluding resources awarded to replace EFC). 24% of all full-time undergraduates had no need and received non-need-based gift aid.

GIFT AID (NEED-BASED) *Total amount:* $20,364,709 (10% federal, 14% state, 73% institutional, 3% external sources). *Receiving aid:* Freshmen: 82% (407); all full-time undergraduates: 76% (1,187). *Average award:* Freshmen: $17,512; Undergraduates: $17,183. *Scholarships, grants, and awards:* Federal Pell, FSEOG, state, private, college/university gift aid from institutional funds.

GIFT AID (NON-NEED-BASED) *Total amount:* $4,708,153 (1% federal, 17% state, 81% institutional, 1% external sources). *Receiving aid:* Freshmen: 80% (399). Undergraduates: 73% (1,149). *Average award:* Freshmen: $10,876. Undergraduates: $9887. *Scholarships, grants, and awards by category:* Academic interests/achievement: general academic interests/achievements. Creative arts/performance: music. Special characteristics: international students, religious affiliation, siblings of current students. *Tuition waivers:* Full or partial for employees or children of employees, senior citizens.

LOANS *Student loans:* $9,842,138 (73% need-based, 27% non-need-based). 74% of past graduating class borrowed through all loan programs. *Average indebtedness per student:* $29,331. *Average need-based loan:* Freshmen: $4315. Undergraduates: $4923. *Parent loans:* $3,018,272 (76% need-based, 24% non-need-based). *Programs:* FFEL (Subsidized and Unsubsidized Stafford, PLUS), Perkins.

WORK-STUDY *Federal work-study:* Total amount: $361,440; jobs available.

APPLYING FOR FINANCIAL AID *Required financial aid forms:* FAFSA, state aid form. *Financial aid deadline (priority):* 3/1. *Notification date:* Continuous beginning 3/16. Students must reply within 2 weeks of notification.

CONTACT Mr. Scott Morrison, Director of Financial Aid, Bridgewater College, 402 East College Street, Bridgewater, VA 22812-1599, 540-828-5376 or toll-free 800-759-8328. *Fax:* 540-828-5671. *E-mail:* smorriso@bridgewater.edu.

BRIDGEWATER STATE COLLEGE
Bridgewater, MA

Tuition & fees (MA res): $6604 **Average undergraduate aid package: $7345**

ABOUT THE INSTITUTION State-supported, coed. 75 undergraduate majors. Federal methodology is used as a basis for awarding need-based institutional aid.

UNDERGRADUATE EXPENSES for 2010–11 *Tuition, state resident:* full-time $910; part-time $38 per credit hour. *Tuition, nonresident:* full-time $7050; part-time $294 per credit hour. *Required fees:* full-time $5694; $231.80 per credit hour. *College room and board:* $9670; *Room only:* $6420. Room and board charges vary according to board plan and housing facility. *Payment plan:* Installment.

FRESHMAN FINANCIAL AID (Fall 2008) 1,251 applied for aid; of those 70% were deemed to have need. 99% of freshmen with need received aid. *Average percent of need met:* 75% (excluding resources awarded to replace EFC). *Average financial aid package:* $7660 (excluding resources awarded to replace EFC). 1% of all full-time freshmen had no need and received non-need-based gift aid.

UNDERGRADUATE FINANCIAL AID (Fall 2008) 5,109 applied for aid; of those 78% were deemed to have need. 98% of undergraduates with need received aid. *Average percent of need met:* 75% (excluding resources awarded to replace EFC). *Average financial aid package:* $7345 (excluding resources awarded to replace EFC). 1% of all full-time undergraduates had no need and received non-need-based gift aid.

GIFT AID (NEED-BASED) *Total amount:* $10,808,610 (53% federal, 30% state, 17% institutional). *Receiving aid:* Freshmen: 51% (738); all full-time undergraduates: 40% (3,014). *Average award:* Freshmen: $4184; Undergraduates: $3679. *Scholarships, grants, and awards:* Federal Pell, FSEOG, state, private, college/university gift aid from institutional funds.

GIFT AID (NON-NEED-BASED) *Total amount:* $764,499 (3% federal, 50% state, 47% institutional). *Receiving aid:* Freshmen: 17% (240). Undergraduates: 7% (490). *Average award:* Freshmen: $6230. Undergraduates: $5710. *Scholarships, grants, and awards by category: Academic interests/achievement:* general academic interests/achievements. *Special achievements/activities:* leadership. *Special characteristics:* local/state students, members of minority groups. *Tuition waivers:* Full or partial for employees or children of employees.

LOANS *Student loans:* $38,451,963 (41% need-based, 59% non-need-based). 80% of past graduating class borrowed through all loan programs. *Average indebtedness per student:* $22,093. *Average need-based loan:* Freshmen: $3442. Undergraduates: $3913. *Parent loans:* $3,649,149 (100% non-need-based). *Programs:* Federal Direct (Subsidized and Unsubsidized Stafford, PLUS), Perkins, state.

WORK-STUDY *Federal work-study:* Total amount: $700,876; jobs available.

APPLYING FOR FINANCIAL AID *Required financial aid form:* FAFSA. *Financial aid deadline (priority):* 3/1. *Notification date:* 4/1.

CONTACT Office of Financial Aid, Bridgewater State College, Tillinghast Hall, Room 100, 45 School Street, Bridgewater, MA 02325-0001, 508-531-1341. *Fax:* 508-531-1728. *E-mail:* finaid@bridgew.edu.

BRIGHAM YOUNG UNIVERSITY
Provo, UT

Tuition & fees: $4420 **Average undergraduate aid package: $6656**

ABOUT THE INSTITUTION Independent religious, coed. 102 undergraduate majors. Both federal and institutional methodology are used as a basis for awarding need-based institutional aid.

UNDERGRADUATE EXPENSES for 2010–11 *Comprehensive fee:* $11,540 includes full-time tuition ($4420) and room and board ($7120). *Part-time tuition:* $227 per credit hour. Part-time tuition and fees vary according to course load. Latter Day Saints full-time student $4,420 per year, non-LDS full-time student $8,840.

FRESHMAN FINANCIAL AID (Fall 2009, est.) 1,988 applied for aid; of those 61% were deemed to have need. 87% of freshmen with need received aid; of those 3% had need fully met. *Average percent of need met:* 40% (excluding resources awarded to replace EFC). *Average financial aid package:* $5610 (excluding resources awarded to replace EFC). 38% of all full-time freshmen had no need and received non-need-based gift aid.

UNDERGRADUATE FINANCIAL AID (Fall 2009, est.) 14,361 applied for aid; of those 83% were deemed to have need. 92% of undergraduates with need received aid; of those 3% had need fully met. *Average percent of need met:* 44% (excluding resources awarded to replace EFC). *Average financial aid package:* $6656 (excluding resources awarded to replace EFC). 27% of all full-time undergraduates had no need and received non-need-based gift aid.

GIFT AID (NEED-BASED) *Total amount:* $40,114,693 (83% federal, 17% institutional). *Receiving aid:* Freshmen: 12% (612); all full-time undergraduates: 29% (8,921). *Average award:* Freshmen: $3922; Undergraduates: $4252. *Scholarships, grants, and awards:* Federal Pell, state, private, college/university gift aid from institutional funds.

GIFT AID (NON-NEED-BASED) *Total amount:* $44,276,890 (80% institutional, 20% external sources). *Receiving aid:* Freshmen: 13% (681). Undergraduates: 16% (4,912). *Average award:* Freshmen: $3326. Undergraduates: $3188.

LOANS *Student loans:* $43,196,139 (52% need-based, 48% non-need-based). 24% of past graduating class borrowed through all loan programs. *Average indebtedness per student:* $10,730. *Average need-based loan:* Freshmen: $3269. Undergraduates: $4374. *Parent loans:* $2,295,357 (100% non-need-based). *Programs:* FFEL (Subsidized and Unsubsidized Stafford, PLUS).

WORK-STUDY *State or other work-study/employment:* Total amount: $106,278 (100% need-based). Part-time jobs available.

ATHLETIC AWARDS Total amount: $4,084,665 (100% non-need-based).

APPLYING FOR FINANCIAL AID *Required financial aid forms:* FAFSA, institution's own form. *Financial aid deadline (priority):* 4/15. *Notification date:* Continuous beginning 5/1.

CONTACT Paul R. Conrad, Director of Financial Aid, Brigham Young University, A-41 ASB, Provo, UT 84602, 801-422-7355. *Fax:* 801-422-0234. *E-mail:* paul_conrad@byu.edu.

BRIGHAM YOUNG UNIVERSITY–HAWAII
Laie, HI

CONTACT Mr. Wes Duke, Director of Financial Aid, Brigham Young University–Hawaii, BYUH #1980, 55-220 Kulanui Street, Laie, HI 96762, 808-293-3530. *Fax:* 808-293-3349. *E-mail:* duekw@byuh.edu.

BROOKLINE COLLEGE
Phoenix, AZ

CONTACT Financial Aid Office, Brookline College, 2445 West Dunlap Avenue, Suite 100, Phoenix, AZ 85021, 602-242-6265 or toll-free 800-793-2428.

BROOKLINE COLLEGE
Tempe, AZ

CONTACT Financial Aid Office, Brookline College, 1140-1150 South Priest Drive, Tempe, AZ 85281, 480-545-8755 or toll-free 888-886-2428.

BROOKLINE COLLEGE
Tucson, AZ

CONTACT Financial Aid Office, Brookline College, 5441 East 22nd Street, Suite 125, Tucson, AZ 85711, 520-748-9799 or toll-free 888-292-2428.

BROOKLINE COLLEGE
Albuquerque, NM

CONTACT Financial Aid Office, Brookline College, 4201 Central Avenue NW, Suite J, Albuquerque, NM 87105-1649, 505-880-2877 or toll-free 888-660-2428.

BROOKLYN COLLEGE OF THE CITY UNIVERSITY OF NEW YORK
Brooklyn, NY

ABOUT THE INSTITUTION State and locally supported, coed. 76 undergraduate majors.

GIFT AID (NEED-BASED) *Scholarships, grants, and awards:* Federal Pell, FSEOG, state, private, college/university gift aid from institutional funds.

GIFT AID (NON-NEED-BASED) *Scholarships, grants, and awards by category: Academic interests/achievement:* general academic interests/achievements. *Creative arts/performance:* general creative arts/performance. *Special achievements/activities:* general special achievements/activities. *Special characteristics:* general special characteristics.

LOANS *Programs:* Federal Direct (Subsidized and Unsubsidized Stafford, PLUS), Perkins.

WORK-STUDY *Federal work-study:* Total amount: $670,000; 1,100 jobs averaging $1200.

APPLYING FOR FINANCIAL AID *Required financial aid forms:* FAFSA, state aid form.

CONTACT Sherwood Johnson, Director of Financial Aid, Brooklyn College of the City University of New York, 2900 Bedford Avenue, Brooklyn, NY 11210-2889, 718-951-5045. *Fax:* 718-951-4778. *E-mail:* sjohnson@brooklyn.cuny.edu.

BROOKS INSTITUTE
Santa Barbara, CA

Tuition & fees: N/R	Average undergraduate aid package: N/A

ABOUT THE INSTITUTION Proprietary, coed. 4 undergraduate majors. Federal methodology is used as a basis for awarding need-based institutional aid.

GIFT AID (NEED-BASED) *Scholarships, grants, and awards:* Federal Pell, FSEOG, state, private, college/university gift aid from institutional funds.

LOANS *Programs:* Federal Direct (Subsidized and Unsubsidized Stafford, PLUS), alternative loans.

WORK-STUDY Federal work-study jobs available.

APPLYING FOR FINANCIAL AID *Required financial aid forms:* FAFSA, institution's own form. *Financial aid deadline:* Continuous. *Notification date:* Continuous. Students must reply within 4 weeks of notification.

CONTACT Stacey Eymann, Director of Financial Aid, Brooks Institute, 27 East Cota Street, Santa Barbara, CA 93101, 888-304-3456 or toll-free 888-276-4999 (out-of-state). *Fax:* 805-966-2909. *E-mail:* seymann@brooks.edu.

BROWN UNIVERSITY
Providence, RI

Tuition & fees: N/R	Average undergraduate aid package: $34,586

ABOUT THE INSTITUTION Independent, coed. *Awards:* bachelor's and master's degrees. 76 undergraduate majors. *Total enrollment:* 8,131. Undergraduates: 6,095. Freshmen: 1,548. Both federal and institutional methodology are used as a basis for awarding need-based institutional aid.

FRESHMAN FINANCIAL AID (Fall 2009, est.) 880 applied for aid; of those 72% were deemed to have need. 100% of freshmen with need received aid; of those 100% had need fully met. *Average percent of need met:* 100% (excluding resources awarded to replace EFC). *Average financial aid package:* $33,802 (excluding resources awarded to replace EFC). 1% of all full-time freshmen had no need and received non-need-based gift aid.

UNDERGRADUATE FINANCIAL AID (Fall 2009, est.) 3,096 applied for aid; of those 84% were deemed to have need. 100% of undergraduates with need received aid; of those 100% had need fully met. *Average percent of need met:* 100% (excluding resources awarded to replace EFC). *Average financial aid package:* $34,586 (excluding resources awarded to replace EFC). 1% of all full-time undergraduates had no need and received non-need-based gift aid.

GIFT AID (NEED-BASED) *Total amount:* $78,308,932 (6% federal, 90% institutional, 4% external sources). *Receiving aid:* Freshmen: 41% (610); all full-time undergraduates: 39% (2,338). *Average award:* Freshmen: $32,100; Undergraduates: $31,474. *Scholarships, grants, and awards:* Federal Pell, FSEOG, state, private, college/university gift aid from institutional funds.

GIFT AID (NON-NEED-BASED) *Total amount:* $3,694,809 (12% federal, 3% institutional, 85% external sources). *Receiving aid:* Freshmen: 2. Undergraduates: 4. *Average award:* Freshmen: $14,000. Undergraduates: $14,000. *Scholarships, grants, and awards by category: Special characteristics:* 7 awards ($98,000 total): veterans, veterans' children. *Tuition waivers:* Full or partial for employees or children of employees. *ROTC:* Army cooperative.

LOANS *Student loans:* $12,050,462 (61% need-based, 39% non-need-based). 41% of past graduating class borrowed through all loan programs. *Average*

indebtedness per student: $21,858. *Average need-based loan:* Freshmen: $4659. Undergraduates: $5208. *Parent loans:* $9,461,876 (2% need-based, 98% non-need-based). *Programs:* Federal Direct (Subsidized and Unsubsidized Stafford, PLUS), Perkins, college/university.

WORK-STUDY *Federal work-study:* Total amount: $3,020,870; 1,441 jobs averaging $2147. *State or other work-study/employment:* Total amount: $689,132 (100% need-based). 313 part-time jobs averaging $2263.

APPLYING FOR FINANCIAL AID *Required financial aid forms:* FAFSA, CSS Financial Aid PROFILE, noncustodial (divorced/separated) parent's statement. *Financial aid deadline:* 2/1. *Notification date:* 4/1. Students must reply by 5/1.

CONTACT Office of Financial Aid, Brown University, Box 1827, Providence, RI 02912, 401-863-2721. *Fax:* 401-863-7575. *E-mail:* financial_aid@brown.edu.

BRYAN COLLEGE
Dayton, TN

Tuition & fees: $18,740	Average undergraduate aid package: $14,768

ABOUT THE INSTITUTION Independent interdenominational, coed. 28 undergraduate majors. Both federal and institutional methodology are used as a basis for awarding need-based institutional aid.

UNDERGRADUATE EXPENSES for 2010–11 *Comprehensive fee:* $24,194 includes full-time tuition ($18,620), mandatory fees ($120), and room and board ($5454). Room and board charges vary according to board plan and housing facility. *Part-time tuition:* $775 per credit. *Payment plan:* Installment.

FRESHMAN FINANCIAL AID (Fall 2009, est.) 174 applied for aid; of those 87% were deemed to have need. 99% of freshmen with need received aid; of those 66% had need fully met. *Average percent of need met:* 81% (excluding resources awarded to replace EFC). *Average financial aid package:* $17,870 (excluding resources awarded to replace EFC). 18% of all full-time freshmen had no need and received non-need-based gift aid.

UNDERGRADUATE FINANCIAL AID (Fall 2009, est.) 832 applied for aid; of those 88% were deemed to have need. 99% of undergraduates with need received aid; of those 51% had need fully met. *Average percent of need met:* 76% (excluding resources awarded to replace EFC). *Average financial aid package:* $14,768 (excluding resources awarded to replace EFC). 10% of all full-time undergraduates had no need and received non-need-based gift aid.

GIFT AID (NEED-BASED) *Total amount:* $5,074,252 (33% federal, 26% state, 4% institutional, 37% external sources). *Receiving aid:* Freshmen: 74% (141); all full-time undergraduates: 66% (648). *Average award:* Freshmen: $11,374; Undergraduates: $8587. *Scholarships, grants, and awards:* Federal Pell, FSEOG, state, private, college/university gift aid from institutional funds.

GIFT AID (NON-NEED-BASED) *Total amount:* $1,156,260 (21% state, 4% institutional, 75% external sources). *Receiving aid:* Freshmen: 43% (81). Undergraduates: 26% (250). *Average award:* Freshmen: $5307. Undergraduates: $4703. *Scholarships, grants, and awards by category: Academic interests/achievement:* biological sciences, business, communication, computer science, education, English, foreign languages, general academic interests/achievements, humanities, mathematics, physical sciences, premedicine, religion/biblical studies, social sciences. *Creative arts/performance:* journalism/publications, music, performing arts, theater/drama. *Special achievements/activities:* community service, general special achievements/activities, leadership, religious involvement. *Special characteristics:* children and siblings of alumni, children of current students, children of educators, children of faculty/staff, general special characteristics, handicapped students, international students, local/state students, members of minority groups, relatives of clergy, spouses of current students. *Tuition waivers:* Full or partial for employees or children of employees.

LOANS *Student loans:* $3,571,791 (65% need-based, 35% non-need-based). 74% of past graduating class borrowed through all loan programs. *Average indebtedness per student:* $14,976. *Average need-based loan:* Freshmen: $2919. Undergraduates: $3678. *Parent loans:* $827,983 (20% need-based, 80% non-need-based). *Programs:* Federal Direct (Subsidized and Unsubsidized Stafford, PLUS), FFEL (Subsidized and Unsubsidized Stafford, PLUS), Perkins, college/university.

WORK-STUDY *Federal work-study:* Total amount: $624,531; jobs available.

ATHLETIC AWARDS Total amount: $1,462,552 (65% need-based, 35% non-need-based).

APPLYING FOR FINANCIAL AID *Required financial aid form:* FAFSA. *Financial aid deadline (priority):* 2/15. *Notification date:* Continuous beginning 2/15.

CONTACT Rick Taphorn, Director of Financial Aid, Bryan College, PO Box 7000, Dayton, TN 37321-7000, 423-775-7339 or toll-free 800-277-9522. *Fax:* 423-775-7300. *E-mail:* finaid@bryan.edu.

BRYANT & STRATTON COLLEGE
Cleveland, OH

CONTACT Bill Davenport, Financial Aid Supervisor, Bryant & Stratton College, 1700 East 13th Street, Cleveland, OH 44114-3203, 216-771-1700. *Fax:* 216-771-7787.

BRYANT & STRATTON COLLEGE—WAUWATOSA CAMPUS
Wauwatosa, WI

CONTACT Financial Aid Office, Bryant & Stratton College—Wauwatosa Campus, 10950 W. Potter Road, Wauwatosa, WI 53226, 414-302-7000.

BRYANT UNIVERSITY
Smithfield, RI

Tuition & fees: $32,106	Average undergraduate aid package: $20,116

ABOUT THE INSTITUTION Independent, coed. 25 undergraduate majors. Federal methodology is used as a basis for awarding need-based institutional aid.

UNDERGRADUATE EXPENSES for 2009–10 *Comprehensive fee:* $43,863 includes full-time tuition ($31,794), mandatory fees ($312), and room and board ($11,757). *College room only:* $7038. Room and board charges vary according to board plan and housing facility. *Part-time tuition:* $1347 per course. Part-time tuition and fees vary according to course load. *Payment plan:* Installment.

FRESHMAN FINANCIAL AID (Fall 2009, est.) 573 applied for aid; of those 83% were deemed to have need. 100% of freshmen with need received aid; of those 67% had need fully met. *Average percent of need met:* 67% (excluding resources awarded to replace EFC). *Average financial aid package:* $21,005 (excluding resources awarded to replace EFC). 12% of all full-time freshmen had no need and received non-need-based gift aid.

UNDERGRADUATE FINANCIAL AID (Fall 2009, est.) 2,462 applied for aid; of those 88% were deemed to have need. 100% of undergraduates with need received aid; of those 66% had need fully met. *Average percent of need met:* 66% (excluding resources awarded to replace EFC). *Average financial aid package:* $20,116 (excluding resources awarded to replace EFC). 12% of all full-time undergraduates had no need and received non-need-based gift aid.

GIFT AID (NEED-BASED) *Total amount:* $22,104,193 (10% federal, 2% state, 86% institutional, 2% external sources). *Receiving aid:* Freshmen: 56% (423); all full-time undergraduates: 57% (1,856). *Average award:* Freshmen: $13,850; Undergraduates: $12,555. *Scholarships, grants, and awards:* Federal Pell, FSEOG, state, private, college/university gift aid from institutional funds.

GIFT AID (NON-NEED-BASED) *Total amount:* $14,135,622 (98% institutional, 2% external sources). *Receiving aid:* Freshmen: 35% (262). Undergraduates: 33% (1,067). *Average award:* Freshmen: $13,174. Undergraduates: $12,455. *Scholarships, grants, and awards by category: Academic interests/achievement:* engineering/technologies, general academic interests/achievements. *Special characteristics:* children and siblings of alumni, local/state students, members of minority groups, siblings of current students. *Tuition waivers:* Full or partial for employees or children of employees.

LOANS *Student loans:* $24,829,232 (38% need-based, 62% non-need-based). 75% of past graduating class borrowed through all loan programs. *Average indebtedness per student:* $38,270. *Average need-based loan:* Freshmen: $3360. Undergraduates: $4521. *Parent loans:* $9,904,198 (15% need-based, 85% non-need-based). *Programs:* Federal Direct (Subsidized and Unsubsidized Stafford, PLUS), Perkins, privately funded education loans.

WORK-STUDY *Federal work-study:* Total amount: $580,099; jobs available. *State or other work-study/employment:* Total amount: $723,658 (37% need-based, 63% non-need-based). Part-time jobs available.

ATHLETIC AWARDS Total amount: $3,451,360 (30% need-based, 70% non-need-based).

APPLYING FOR FINANCIAL AID *Required financial aid form:* FAFSA. *Financial aid deadline (priority):* 2/15. *Notification date:* 3/24. Students must reply by 5/1.

CONTACT Mr. John B. Canning, Director of Financial Aid, Bryant University, 1150 Douglas Pike, Smithfield, RI 02917-1284, 401-232-6020 or toll-free 800-622-7001. *Fax:* 401-232-6293. *E-mail:* jcanning@bryant.edu.

BRYN ATHYN COLLEGE OF THE NEW CHURCH
Bryn Athyn, PA

ABOUT THE INSTITUTION Independent religious, coed. 7 undergraduate majors.

GIFT AID (NEED-BASED) *Scholarships, grants, and awards:* Federal Pell, FSEOG, state, private, college/university gift aid from institutional funds.

GIFT AID (NON-NEED-BASED) *Scholarships, grants, and awards by category: Academic interests/achievement:* general academic interests/achievements. *Special characteristics:* general special characteristics.

LOANS *Programs:* Federal Direct (Subsidized and Unsubsidized Stafford, PLUS), FFEL (Subsidized and Unsubsidized Stafford, PLUS), state, college/university, private alternative loans.

WORK-STUDY *State or other work-study/employment:* Total amount: $62,345 (15% need-based, 85% non-need-based). Part-time jobs available.

APPLYING FOR FINANCIAL AID *Required financial aid forms:* FAFSA, institution's own form, income tax form(s).

CONTACT Wendy Cooper, Associate Director of Financial Aid, Bryn Athyn College of the New Church, Box 717, Bryn Athyn, PA 19009, 267-502-2630. *Fax:* 267-502-4866. *E-mail:* financialaid@brynathyn.edu.

BRYN MAWR COLLEGE
Bryn Mawr, PA

Tuition & fees: $39,360	Average undergraduate aid package: $35,351

ABOUT THE INSTITUTION Independent, undergraduate: women only; graduate: coed. 33 undergraduate majors. Both federal and institutional methodology are used as a basis for awarding need-based institutional aid.

UNDERGRADUATE EXPENSES for 2010–11 *Comprehensive fee:* $51,780 includes full-time tuition ($38,420), mandatory fees ($940), and room and board ($12,420). *College room only:* $7100. *Part-time tuition:* $4800 per course. *Payment plans:* Tuition prepayment, installment.

FRESHMAN FINANCIAL AID (Fall 2009, est.) 278 applied for aid; of those 90% were deemed to have need. 100% of freshmen with need received aid; of those 100% had need fully met. *Average percent of need met:* 100% (excluding resources awarded to replace EFC). *Average financial aid package:* $36,562 (excluding resources awarded to replace EFC).

UNDERGRADUATE FINANCIAL AID (Fall 2009, est.) 807 applied for aid; of those 91% were deemed to have need. 100% of undergraduates with need received aid; of those 100% had need fully met. *Average percent of need met:* 100% (excluding resources awarded to replace EFC). *Average financial aid package:* $35,351 (excluding resources awarded to replace EFC). 2% of all full-time undergraduates had no need and received non-need-based gift aid.

GIFT AID (NEED-BASED) *Total amount:* $21,893,227 (6% federal, 1% state, 92% institutional, 1% external sources). *Receiving aid:* Freshmen: 69% (249); all full-time undergraduates: 57% (730). *Average award:* Freshmen: $33,108; Undergraduates: $29,927. *Scholarships, grants, and awards:* Federal Pell, FSEOG, state, college/university gift aid from institutional funds.

GIFT AID (NON-NEED-BASED) *Total amount:* $633,901 (1% federal, 1% state, 82% institutional, 16% external sources). *Receiving aid:* Freshmen: 3% (12). Undergraduates: 3% (38). *Average award:* Undergraduates: $15,438.

LOANS *Student loans:* $4,637,439 (62% need-based, 38% non-need-based). 52% of past graduating class borrowed through all loan programs. *Average indebtedness per student:* $20,156. *Average need-based loan:* Freshmen: $3330. Undergraduates: $5018. *Parent loans:* $2,220,864 (100% non-need-based). *Programs:* Federal Direct (Subsidized and Unsubsidized Stafford, PLUS), Perkins.

WORK-STUDY *Federal work-study:* Total amount: $1,123,940; 528 jobs averaging $1992. *State or other work-study/employment:* Total amount: $189,500 (100% need-based). Part-time jobs available.

APPLYING FOR FINANCIAL AID *Required financial aid forms:* FAFSA, CSS Financial Aid PROFILE, business/farm supplement. *Financial aid deadline:* 3/1. *Notification date:* 3/23. Students must reply by 5/1.

CONTACT Ethel M. Desmarais, Director of Financial Aid, Bryn Mawr College, 101 North Merion Avenue, Bryn Mawr, PA 19010-2899, 610-526-7922 or toll-free 800-BMC-1885 (out-of-state). *Fax:* 610-526-5249. *E-mail:* edesmara@brynmawr.edu.

BUCKNELL UNIVERSITY
Lewisburg, PA

Tuition & fees: $42,342	Average undergraduate aid package: $25,500

ABOUT THE INSTITUTION Independent, coed. 60 undergraduate majors. Both federal and institutional methodology are used as a basis for awarding need-based institutional aid.

UNDERGRADUATE EXPENSES for 2010–11 *Comprehensive fee:* $52,280 includes full-time tuition ($42,112), mandatory fees ($230), and room and board ($9938). *College room only:* $5768. Room and board charges vary according to board plan and housing facility. *Payment plans:* Tuition prepayment, installment.

FRESHMAN FINANCIAL AID (Fall 2009, est.) 527 applied for aid; of those 82% were deemed to have need. 100% of freshmen with need received aid; of those 94% had need fully met. *Average percent of need met:* 95% (excluding resources awarded to replace EFC). *Average financial aid package:* $26,900 (excluding resources awarded to replace EFC). 5% of all full-time freshmen had no need and received non-need-based gift aid.

UNDERGRADUATE FINANCIAL AID (Fall 2009, est.) 1,851 applied for aid; of those 87% were deemed to have need. 100% of undergraduates with need received aid; of those 95% had need fully met. *Average percent of need met:* 95% (excluding resources awarded to replace EFC). *Average financial aid package:* $25,500 (excluding resources awarded to replace EFC). 4% of all full-time undergraduates had no need and received non-need-based gift aid.

GIFT AID (NEED-BASED) *Total amount:* $40,993,492 (6% federal, 2% state, 90% institutional, 2% external sources). *Receiving aid:* Freshmen: 47% (434); all full-time undergraduates: 42% (1,474). *Average award:* Freshmen: $22,500; Undergraduates:. $21,300. *Scholarships, grants, and awards:* Federal Pell, FSEOG, state, private, college/university gift aid from institutional funds, Academic Competitiveness Grants, National SMART Grants.

GIFT AID (NON-NEED-BASED) *Total amount:* $1,965,154 (100% institutional). *Receiving aid:* Freshmen: 6% (58). Undergraduates: 5% (181). *Average award:* Freshmen: $10,325. Undergraduates: $11,907. *Scholarships, grants, and awards by category: Academic interests/achievement:* 48 awards ($553,000 total): business, engineering/technologies, general academic interests/achievements, mathematics, physical sciences. *Creative arts/performance:* 128 awards ($790,500 total): art/fine arts, creative writing, dance, music, performing arts, theater/drama. *Special achievements/activities:* general special achievements/activities, leadership. *Tuition waivers:* Full or partial for employees or children of employees.

LOANS *Student loans:* $11,900,000 (100% need-based). 61% of past graduating class borrowed through all loan programs. *Average indebtedness per student:* $18,800. *Average need-based loan:* Freshmen: $4400. Undergraduates: $5400. *Parent loans:* $8,000,000 (100% non-need-based). *Programs:* FFEL (Subsidized and Unsubsidized Stafford, PLUS), Perkins.

WORK-STUDY *Federal work-study:* Total amount: $800,000; 700 jobs averaging $1500. *State or other work-study/employment:* Total amount: $60,000 (100% need-based). 50 part-time jobs averaging $1500.

ATHLETIC AWARDS Total amount: $449,000 (100% non-need-based).

APPLYING FOR FINANCIAL AID *Required financial aid forms:* FAFSA, CSS Financial Aid PROFILE, noncustodial (divorced/separated) parent's statement. *Financial aid deadline:* 1/1. *Notification date:* 4/1. Students must reply by 5/1.

CONTACT Andrea Leithner Stauffer, Director of Financial Aid, Bucknell University, 701 Moore Avenue, Lewisburg, PA 17837, 570-577-1331. *Fax:* 570-577-1481. *E-mail:* finaid@bucknell.edu.

BUENA VISTA UNIVERSITY
Storm Lake, IA

Tuition & fees: $25,540	Average undergraduate aid package: $24,136

ABOUT THE INSTITUTION Independent religious, coed. 59 undergraduate majors. Federal methodology is used as a basis for awarding need-based institutional aid.

UNDERGRADUATE EXPENSES for 2009–10 *Comprehensive fee:* $32,832 includes full-time tuition ($25,540) and room and board ($7292). Full-time tuition and fees vary according to location. Room and board charges vary according to board plan. *Part-time tuition:* $858 per credit hour. Part-time tuition and fees vary according to location. *Payment plans:* Guaranteed tuition, installment.

FRESHMAN FINANCIAL AID (Fall 2009, est.) 256 applied for aid; of those 96% were deemed to have need. 100% of freshmen with need received aid; of those 56% had need fully met. *Average percent of need met:* 59% (excluding resources awarded to replace EFC). *Average financial aid package:* $26,306 (excluding resources awarded to replace EFC). 4% of all full-time freshmen had no need and received non-need-based gift aid.

UNDERGRADUATE FINANCIAL AID (Fall 2009, est.) 871 applied for aid; of those 93% were deemed to have need. 100% of undergraduates with need received aid; of those 52% had need fully met. *Average percent of need met:* 50% (excluding resources awarded to replace EFC). *Average financial aid package:* $24,136 (excluding resources awarded to replace EFC). 7% of all full-time undergraduates had no need and received non-need-based gift aid.

GIFT AID (NEED-BASED) *Total amount:* $6,620,617 (31% federal, 29% state, 40% institutional). *Receiving aid:* Freshmen: 81% (221); all full-time undergraduates: 74% (690). *Average award:* Freshmen: $12,031; Undergraduates: $9415. *Scholarships, grants, and awards:* Federal Pell, FSEOG, state, private, college/university gift aid from institutional funds.

GIFT AID (NON-NEED-BASED) *Total amount:* $9,403,382 (97% institutional, 3% external sources). *Receiving aid:* Freshmen: 88% (239). Undergraduates: 86% (797). *Average award:* Freshmen: $11,632. Undergraduates: $11,139. *Scholarships, grants, and awards by category: Academic interests/achievement:* biological sciences, business, computer science, education, general academic interests/achievements, humanities, international studies, mathematics. *Creative arts/performance:* art/fine arts, music, theater/drama. *Special achievements/activities:* general special achievements/activities, leadership. *Special characteristics:* children of faculty/staff, ethnic background, international students, out-of-state students, religious affiliation, siblings of current students. *Tuition waivers:* Full or partial for employees or children of employees.

LOANS *Student loans:* $6,635,166 (55% need-based, 45% non-need-based). 91% of past graduating class borrowed through all loan programs. *Average indebtedness per student:* $40,569. *Average need-based loan:* Freshmen: $5291. Undergraduates: $5120. *Parent loans:* $435,974 (100% non-need-based). *Programs:* FFEL (Subsidized and Unsubsidized Stafford, PLUS), Perkins, college/university.

WORK-STUDY *Federal work-study:* Total amount: $521,050; jobs available. *State or other work-study/employment:* Total amount: $121,175 (100% non-need-based). Part-time jobs available.

APPLYING FOR FINANCIAL AID *Required financial aid form:* FAFSA. *Financial aid deadline (priority):* 6/1. *Notification date:* Continuous.

CONTACT Mrs. Leanne Valentine, Director of Financial Assistance, Buena Vista University, 610 West Fourth Street, Storm Lake, IA 50588, 712-749-2164 or toll-free 800-383-9600. *Fax:* 712-749-1451. *E-mail:* valentinel@bvu.edu.

BUFFALO STATE COLLEGE, STATE UNIVERSITY OF NEW YORK
Buffalo, NY

ABOUT THE INSTITUTION State-supported, coed. 80 undergraduate majors.

GIFT AID (NEED-BASED) *Scholarships, grants, and awards:* Federal Pell, FSEOG, state.

GIFT AID (NON-NEED-BASED) *Scholarships, grants, and awards by category: Academic interests/achievement:* general academic interests/achievements. *Creative arts/performance:* general creative arts/performance. *Special achievements/activities:* general special achievements/activities.

LOANS *Programs:* FFEL (Subsidized and Unsubsidized Stafford, PLUS), Perkins.

APPLYING FOR FINANCIAL AID *Required financial aid form:* FAFSA.

CONTACT Mr. Kent McGowan, Director of Financial Aid, Buffalo State College, State University of New York, 1300 Elmwood Avenue, Buffalo, NY 14222-1095, 716-878-4902. *Fax:* 716-878-4903. *E-mail:* mcgowakm@buffalostate.edu.

BURLINGTON COLLEGE
Burlington, VT

Tuition & fees: $20,424	Average undergraduate aid package: $12,910

ABOUT THE INSTITUTION Independent, coed. 15 undergraduate majors. Federal methodology is used as a basis for awarding need-based institutional aid.

UNDERGRADUATE EXPENSES for 2010–11 *One-time required fee:* $200. *Tuition:* full-time $20,424; part-time $675 per credit hour. Full-time tuition and fees vary according to course load, program, and reciprocity agreements. Part-time tuition and fees vary according to course load, program, and reciprocity agreements. Room and board charges vary according to housing facility. *Payment plan:* Installment.

FRESHMAN FINANCIAL AID (Fall 2009, est.) 15 applied for aid; of those 87% were deemed to have need. 100% of freshmen with need received aid. *Average percent of need met:* 49% (excluding resources awarded to replace EFC). *Average financial aid package:* $13,335 (excluding resources awarded to replace EFC).

UNDERGRADUATE FINANCIAL AID (Fall 2009, est.) 93 applied for aid; of those 88% were deemed to have need. 100% of undergraduates with need received aid; of those 1% had need fully met. *Average percent of need met:* 52% (excluding resources awarded to replace EFC). *Average financial aid package:* $12,910 (excluding resources awarded to replace EFC).

GIFT AID (NEED-BASED) *Total amount:* $598,221 (47% federal, 28% state, 23% institutional, 2% external sources). *Receiving aid:* Freshmen: 60% (12); all full-time undergraduates: 61% (73). *Average award:* Freshmen: $9321; Undergraduates: $7443. *Scholarships, grants, and awards:* Federal Pell, FSEOG, state, private, college/university gift aid from institutional funds.

GIFT AID (NON-NEED-BASED) *Total amount:* $1750 (57% institutional, 43% external sources). *Scholarships, grants, and awards by category: Special achievements/activities:* 63 awards ($139,105 total): community service, general special achievements/activities, leadership. *Tuition waivers:* Full or partial for employees or children of employees.

LOANS *Student loans:* $1,166,085 (83% need-based, 17% non-need-based). 80% of past graduating class borrowed through all loan programs. *Average indebtedness per student:* $38,198. *Average need-based loan:* Freshmen: $3730. Undergraduates: $5518. *Parent loans:* $204,561 (62% need-based, 38% non-need-based). *Programs:* FFEL (Subsidized and Unsubsidized Stafford, PLUS), Perkins.

WORK-STUDY *Federal work-study:* Total amount: $69,750; 77 jobs averaging $1114.

APPLYING FOR FINANCIAL AID *Required financial aid form:* FAFSA. *Financial aid deadline:* Continuous. *Notification date:* Continuous beginning 3/1. Students must reply within 4 weeks of notification.

CONTACT Ms. Lindy Walsh, Director of Financial Aid, Burlington College, 95 North Avenue, Burlington, VT 05401, 802-862-9616 or toll-free 800-862-9616. *Fax:* 802-846-3072. *E-mail:* lwalsh@burlington.edu.

BUTLER UNIVERSITY
Indianapolis, IN

Tuition & fees: $29,246	Average undergraduate aid package: $20,922

ABOUT THE INSTITUTION Independent, coed. 61 undergraduate majors. Federal methodology is used as a basis for awarding need-based institutional aid.

UNDERGRADUATE EXPENSES for 2009–10 *Comprehensive fee:* $38,986 includes full-time tuition ($28,460), mandatory fees ($786), and room and board ($9740). *College room only:* $4770. Full-time tuition and fees vary according to course load, degree level, and program. Room and board charges vary according to housing facility. *Part-time tuition:* $1200 per credit hour. Part-time tuition and fees vary according to course load, degree level, and program. *Payment plan:* Installment.

FRESHMAN FINANCIAL AID (Fall 2009, est.) 895 applied for aid; of those 74% were deemed to have need. 100% of freshmen with need received aid; of those 20% had need fully met. *Average percent of need met:* 79% (excluding resources awarded to replace EFC). *Average financial aid package:* $22,592 (excluding resources awarded to replace EFC). 21% of all full-time freshmen had no need and received non-need-based gift aid.

UNDERGRADUATE FINANCIAL AID (Fall 2009, est.) 3,581 applied for aid; of those 72% were deemed to have need. 100% of undergraduates with need

received aid; of those 19% had need fully met. *Average percent of need met:* 75% (excluding resources awarded to replace EFC). *Average financial aid package:* $20,922 (excluding resources awarded to replace EFC). 22% of all full-time undergraduates had no need and received non-need-based gift aid.

GIFT AID (NEED-BASED) *Total amount:* $37,728,981 (8% federal, 6% state, 76% institutional, 10% external sources). *Receiving aid:* Freshmen: 69% (655); all full-time undergraduates: 63% (2,457). *Average award:* Freshmen: $17,486; Undergraduates: $15,800. *Scholarships, grants, and awards:* Federal Pell, FSEOG, state, private, college/university gift aid from institutional funds.

GIFT AID (NON-NEED-BASED) *Total amount:* $12,489,318 (82% institutional, 18% external sources). *Receiving aid:* Freshmen: 13% (122). Undergraduates: 11% (414). *Average award:* Freshmen: $9278. Undergraduates: $11,674. *Scholarships, grants, and awards by category: Academic interests/achievement:* biological sciences, business, communication, computer science, education, engineering/technologies, English, foreign languages, general academic interests/achievements, humanities, international studies, mathematics, physical sciences, social sciences. *Creative arts/performance:* art/fine arts, cinema/film/broadcasting, dance, music, theater/drama. *Tuition waivers:* Full or partial for employees or children of employees.

LOANS *Student loans:* $30,980,343 (66% need-based, 34% non-need-based). 64% of past graduating class borrowed through all loan programs. *Average indebtedness per student:* $30,470. *Average need-based loan:* Freshmen: $4512. Undergraduates: $5387. *Parent loans:* $4,566,967 (24% need-based, 76% non-need-based). *Programs:* FFEL (Subsidized and Unsubsidized Stafford, PLUS), Perkins.

WORK-STUDY *Federal work-study:* Total amount: $400,000; jobs available. *State or other work-study/employment:* Part-time jobs available.

ATHLETIC AWARDS Total amount: $3,556,650 (34% need-based, 66% non-need-based).

APPLYING FOR FINANCIAL AID *Required financial aid form:* FAFSA. *Financial aid deadline (priority):* 3/1. *Notification date:* 3/15. Students must reply within 3 weeks of notification.

CONTACT Ms. Kristine Butz, Associate Director of Financial Aid, Butler University, 4600 Sunset Avenue, Indianapolis, IN 46208-3485, 317-940-8200 or toll-free 888-940-8100. *Fax:* 317-940-8250. *E-mail:* kbutz@butler.edu..

CABARRUS COLLEGE OF HEALTH SCIENCES
Concord, NC

ABOUT THE INSTITUTION Independent, coed. *Awards:* associate and bachelor's degrees. 6 undergraduate majors. *Total enrollment:* 372. Undergraduates: 372. Freshmen: 25.

GIFT AID (NEED-BASED) *Scholarships, grants, and awards:* Federal Pell, FSEOG, state, private, college/university gift aid from institutional funds.

GIFT AID (NON-NEED-BASED) *Scholarships, grants, and awards by category: Special characteristics:* first-generation college students.

LOANS *Programs:* FFEL (Subsidized and Unsubsidized Stafford, PLUS), state.

APPLYING FOR FINANCIAL AID *Required financial aid form:* FAFSA.

CONTACT Valerie Richard, Director of Financial Aid, Cabarrus College of Health Sciences, 401 Medical Park Drive, Concord, NC 28025, 704-403-3507. *Fax:* 704-403-2077. *E-mail:* valerie.richard@carolinashealthcare.org.

CABRINI COLLEGE
Radnor, PA

Tuition & fees: $31,030	Average undergraduate aid package: $21,251

ABOUT THE INSTITUTION Independent Roman Catholic, coed. 35 undergraduate majors. Federal methodology is used as a basis for awarding need-based institutional aid.

UNDERGRADUATE EXPENSES for 2009–10 *Comprehensive fee:* $42,430 includes full-time tuition ($30,120), mandatory fees ($910), and room and board ($11,400). Room and board charges vary according to board plan and housing facility. *Part-time tuition:* $455 per credit hour. *Part-time fees:* $45 per term. Part-time tuition and fees vary according to course load. *Payment plan:* Installment.

FRESHMAN FINANCIAL AID (Fall 2009, est.) 315 applied for aid; of those 89% were deemed to have need. 100% of freshmen with need received aid; of those

14% had need fully met. *Average percent of need met:* 71% (excluding resources awarded to replace EFC). *Average financial aid package:* $22,851 (excluding resources awarded to replace EFC). 19% of all full-time freshmen had no need and received non-need-based gift aid.

UNDERGRADUATE FINANCIAL AID (Fall 2009, est.) 1,165 applied for aid; of those 92% were deemed to have need. 100% of undergraduates with need received aid; of those 16% had need fully met. *Average percent of need met:* 71% (excluding resources awarded to replace EFC). *Average financial aid package:* $21,251 (excluding resources awarded to replace EFC). 24% of all full-time undergraduates had no need and received non-need-based gift aid.

GIFT AID (NEED-BASED) *Total amount:* $17,796,260 (10% federal, 7% state, 81% institutional, 2% external sources). *Receiving aid:* Freshmen: 68% (244); all full-time undergraduates: 60% (871). *Average award:* Freshmen: $9890; Undergraduates: $8116. *Scholarships, grants, and awards:* Federal Pell, FSEOG, state, private, college/university gift aid from institutional funds.

GIFT AID (NON-NEED-BASED) *Total amount:* $3,747,260 (98% institutional, 2% external sources). *Receiving aid:* Freshmen: 70% (251). Undergraduates: 68% (992). *Average award:* Freshmen: $10,079. Undergraduates: $10,454. *Scholarships, grants, and awards by category: Academic interests/achievement:* general academic interests/achievements. *Special characteristics:* children of faculty/staff, ethnic background. *Tuition waivers:* Full or partial for children of alumni, employees or children of employees, senior citizens.

LOANS *Student loans:* $11,668,968 (63% need-based, 37% non-need-based). 81% of past graduating class borrowed through all loan programs. *Average indebtedness per student:* $30,633. *Average need-based loan:* Freshmen: $3696. Undergraduates: $4657. *Parent loans:* $3,881,647 (89% need-based, 11% non-need-based). *Programs:* FFEL (Subsidized and Unsubsidized Stafford, PLUS), Perkins.

WORK-STUDY *Federal work-study:* Total amount: $370,583; jobs available.

APPLYING FOR FINANCIAL AID *Required financial aid form:* FAFSA. *Financial aid deadline:* Continuous. *Notification date:* Continuous beginning 2/15.

CONTACT Mike Colahan, Director of Financial Aid, Cabrini College, 610 King of Prussia Road, Grace Hall, First Floor, Radnor, PA 19087-3698, 610-902-8420 or toll-free 800-848-1003. *Fax:* 610-902-8426.

CALDWELL COLLEGE
Caldwell, NJ

Tuition & fees: N/R	Average undergraduate aid package: $17,182

ABOUT THE INSTITUTION Independent Roman Catholic, coed. 26 undergraduate majors. Both federal and institutional methodology are used as a basis for awarding need-based institutional aid.

FRESHMAN FINANCIAL AID (Fall 2009, est.) 258 applied for aid; of those 92% were deemed to have need. 100% of freshmen with need received aid; of those 19% had need fully met. *Average percent of need met:* 76% (excluding resources awarded to replace EFC). *Average financial aid package:* $19,142 (excluding resources awarded to replace EFC). 23% of all full-time freshmen had no need and received non-need-based gift aid.

UNDERGRADUATE FINANCIAL AID (Fall 2009, est.) 1,001 applied for aid; of those 89% were deemed to have need. 99% of undergraduates with need received aid; of those 16% had need fully met. *Average percent of need met:* 74% (excluding resources awarded to replace EFC). *Average financial aid package:* $17,182 (excluding resources awarded to replace EFC). 19% of all full-time undergraduates had no need and received non-need-based gift aid.

GIFT AID (NEED-BASED) *Total amount:* $12,051,436 (20% federal, 30% state, 49% institutional, 1% external sources). *Receiving aid:* Freshmen: 71% (230); all full-time undergraduates: 70% (834). *Average award:* Freshmen: $15,965; Undergraduates: $14,002. *Scholarships, grants, and awards:* Federal Pell, FSEOG, state, private, college/university gift aid from institutional funds.

GIFT AID (NON-NEED-BASED) *Total amount:* $4,216,894 (96% institutional, 4% external sources). *Receiving aid:* Freshmen: 12% (38). Undergraduates: 9% (109). *Average award:* Freshmen: $13,569. Undergraduates: $14,703. *Scholarships, grants, and awards by category: Academic interests/achievement:* 788 awards ($6,631,992 total): general academic interests/achievements. *Creative arts/performance:* 32 awards ($84,700 total): art/fine arts, music. *Special achievements/activities:* 6 awards ($9500 total): religious involvement. *Tuition waivers:* Full or partial for children of alumni, employees or children of employees, senior citizens.

LOANS *Student loans:* $9,154,665 (66% need-based, 34% non-need-based). 84% of past graduating class borrowed through all loan programs. *Average*

indebtedness per student: $8165. *Average need-based loan:* Freshmen: $3637. Undergraduates: $4452. *Parent loans:* $1,928,906 (38% need-based, 62% non-need-based). *Programs:* Federal Direct (Subsidized and Unsubsidized Stafford, PLUS), state.

WORK-STUDY *Federal work-study:* Total amount: $127,458; 183 jobs averaging $1000.

ATHLETIC AWARDS Total amount: $778,110 (100% non-need-based).

APPLYING FOR FINANCIAL AID *Required financial aid forms:* FAFSA, state aid form. *Financial aid deadline:* Continuous. *Notification date:* Continuous beginning 2/15. Students must reply within 4 weeks of notification.

CONTACT Mr. Vincent Zelizo, Financial Aid Counselor, Caldwell College, 120 Bloomfield Avenue, Caldwell, NJ 07006, 973-618-3261 or toll-free 888-864-9516 (out-of-state). *Fax:* 973-618-3650. *E-mail:* financialaid@caldwell.edu.

CALIFORNIA BAPTIST UNIVERSITY
Riverside, CA

Tuition & fees: $23,266	Average undergraduate aid package: $8651

ABOUT THE INSTITUTION Independent Southern Baptist, coed. 46 undergraduate majors. Federal methodology is used as a basis for awarding need-based institutional aid.

UNDERGRADUATE EXPENSES for 2009–10 *Comprehensive fee:* $31,436 includes full-time tuition ($21,866), mandatory fees ($1400), and room and board ($8170). *College room only:* $3960. Full-time tuition and fees vary according to class time and program. Room and board charges vary according to board plan and housing facility. *Part-time tuition:* $841 per semester hour. *Part-time fees:* $235 per term. Part-time tuition and fees vary according to class time and program. *Payment plan:* Installment.

FRESHMAN FINANCIAL AID (Fall 2009, est.) 426 applied for aid; of those 69% were deemed to have need. 100% of freshmen with need received aid; of those 88% had need fully met. *Average percent of need met:* 59% (excluding resources awarded to replace EFC). *Average financial aid package:* $8954 (excluding resources awarded to replace EFC). 17% of all full-time freshmen had no need and received non-need-based gift aid.

UNDERGRADUATE FINANCIAL AID (Fall 2009, est.) 2,576 applied for aid; of those 74% were deemed to have need. 100% of undergraduates with need received aid; of those 85% had need fully met. *Average percent of need met:* 58% (excluding resources awarded to replace EFC). *Average financial aid package:* $8651 (excluding resources awarded to replace EFC). 16% of all full-time undergraduates had no need and received non-need-based gift aid.

GIFT AID (NEED-BASED) *Total amount:* $19,010,084 (28% federal, 34% state, 37% institutional, 1% external sources). *Receiving aid:* Freshmen: 54% (256); all full-time undergraduates: 57% (1,552). *Average award:* Freshmen: $4503; Undergraduates: $4677. *Scholarships, grants, and awards:* Federal Pell, FSEOG, state, private, college/university gift aid from institutional funds.

GIFT AID (NON-NEED-BASED) *Total amount:* $5,340,914 (96% institutional, 4% external sources). *Receiving aid:* Freshmen: 40% (187). Undergraduates: 42% (1,139). *Average award:* Freshmen: $3514. Undergraduates: $3656. *Scholarships, grants, and awards by category: Academic interests/achievement:* 914 awards ($3,155,328 total): general academic interests/achievements, religion/biblical studies. *Creative arts/performance:* 480 awards ($1,611,400 total): art/fine arts, music, theater/drama. *Special achievements/activities:* 31 awards ($119,500 total): cheerleading/drum major. *Special characteristics:* 798 awards ($4,003,742 total): adult students, children and siblings of alumni, children of faculty/staff, international students, relatives of clergy, siblings of current students, veterans. *Tuition waivers:* Full or partial for employees or children of employees.

LOANS *Student loans:* $25,846,301 (58% need-based, 42% non-need-based). 89% of past graduating class borrowed through all loan programs. *Average indebtedness per student:* $34,650. *Average need-based loan:* Freshmen: $1726. Undergraduates: $2298. *Parent loans:* $4,788,167 (58% need-based, 42% non-need-based). *Programs:* FFEL (Subsidized and Unsubsidized Stafford, PLUS), Perkins, alternative loans.

WORK-STUDY *Federal work-study:* Total amount: $142,195; 178 jobs averaging $888.

ATHLETIC AWARDS Total amount: $3,607,947 (58% need-based, 42% non-need-based).

APPLYING FOR FINANCIAL AID *Required financial aid forms:* FAFSA, state aid form. *Financial aid deadline (priority):* 3/2. *Notification date:* Continuous beginning 3/1. Students must reply by 4/1 or within 3 weeks of notification.

California Baptist University

CONTACT Ms. Rebecca Sanchez, Financial Aid Director, California Baptist University, 8432 Magnolia Avenue, Riverside, CA 92504-3297, 951-343-4236 or toll-free 877-228-8866. *Fax:* 951-343-4518. *E-mail:* rsanchez@calbaptist.edu.

CALIFORNIA CHRISTIAN COLLEGE
Fresno, CA

Tuition & fees: $6840	Average undergraduate aid package: $12,030

ABOUT THE INSTITUTION Independent religious, coed. **Awards:** associate and bachelor's degrees. 1 undergraduate major. **Total enrollment:** 28. Undergraduates: 28. Freshmen: 10. Federal methodology is used as a basis for awarding need-based institutional aid.

UNDERGRADUATE EXPENSES for 2009–10 *Application fee:* $40. *Comprehensive fee:* $10,690 includes full-time tuition ($6840) and room and board ($3850). *Part-time tuition:* $285 per unit.

FRESHMAN FINANCIAL AID (Fall 2008) 2 applied for aid; of those 100% were deemed to have need. 100% of freshmen with need received aid. *Average percent of need met:* 51% (excluding resources awarded to replace EFC). *Average financial aid package:* $8003 (excluding resources awarded to replace EFC).

UNDERGRADUATE FINANCIAL AID (Fall 2008) 22 applied for aid; of those 91% were deemed to have need. 100% of undergraduates with need received aid. *Average percent of need met:* 62% (excluding resources awarded to replace EFC). *Average financial aid package:* $12,030 (excluding resources awarded to replace EFC).

GIFT AID (NEED-BASED) *Total amount:* $106,263 (62% federal, 38% state). *Receiving aid:* Freshmen: 20% (1); all full-time undergraduates: 64% (16). *Average award:* Freshmen: $3181; Undergraduates: $6641. **Scholarships, grants, and awards:** Federal Pell, FSEOG, state, private, college/university gift aid from institutional funds.

LOANS *Student loans:* $156,549 (82% need-based, 18% non-need-based). 100% of past graduating class borrowed through all loan programs. *Average indebtedness per student:* $4500. *Average need-based loan:* Freshmen: $3500. Undergraduates: $6797. *Programs:* Federal Direct (Subsidized and Unsubsidized Stafford, PLUS).

WORK-STUDY *Federal work-study:* Total amount: $7046; jobs available.

APPLYING FOR FINANCIAL AID *Required financial aid forms:* FAFSA, institution's own form, GPA verification form (for CA residents). *Financial aid deadline (priority):* 3/2. *Notification date:* 8/15.

CONTACT Mindy Scroggins, Financial Aid Coordinator, California Christian College, 4881 East University Avenue, Fresno, CA 93703, 559-251-4215 Ext. 5580. *Fax:* 559-251-4231. *E-mail:* cccfindir@sbcglobal.net.

CALIFORNIA COAST UNIVERSITY
Santa Ana, CA

CONTACT Financial Aid Office, California Coast University, 700 North Main Street, Santa Ana, CA 92701, 714-547-9625 or toll-free 888-CCU-UNIV (out-of-state).

CALIFORNIA COLLEGE
San Diego, CA

CONTACT Financial Aid Office, California College, 2820 Camino del Rio South, Suite 300, San Diego, CA 92108, 619-295-5785 or toll-free 800-622-3188 (out-of-state).

CALIFORNIA COLLEGE OF THE ARTS
San Francisco, CA

Tuition & fees: $33,264	Average undergraduate aid package: $22,702

ABOUT THE INSTITUTION Independent, coed. 18 undergraduate majors. Federal methodology is used as a basis for awarding need-based institutional aid.

UNDERGRADUATE EXPENSES for 2009–10 *Tuition:* full-time $32,904; part-time $1371 per unit. Full-time tuition and fees vary according to course load and degree level. Part-time tuition and fees vary according to course load and degree level. Room and board charges vary according to housing facility. *Payment plans:* Installment, deferred payment.

FRESHMAN FINANCIAL AID (Fall 2009, est.) 146 applied for aid; of those 88% were deemed to have need. 100% of freshmen with need received aid; of those 2% had need fully met. *Average percent of need met:* 66% (excluding resources awarded to replace EFC). *Average financial aid package:* $25,033 (excluding resources awarded to replace EFC). 26% of all full-time freshmen had no need and received non-need-based gift aid.

UNDERGRADUATE FINANCIAL AID (Fall 2009, est.) 918 applied for aid; of those 93% were deemed to have need. 100% of undergraduates with need received aid; of those 5% had need fully met. *Average percent of need met:* 58% (excluding resources awarded to replace EFC). *Average financial aid package:* $22,702 (excluding resources awarded to replace EFC). 13% of all full-time undergraduates had no need and received non-need-based gift aid.

GIFT AID (NEED-BASED) *Total amount:* $15,285,863 (16% federal, 8% state, 75% institutional, 1% external sources). *Receiving aid:* Freshmen: 59% (121); all full-time undergraduates: 64% (804). *Average award:* Freshmen: $21,856; Undergraduates: $17,858. *Scholarships, grants, and awards:* Federal Pell, FSEOG, state, private, college/university gift aid from institutional funds, Academic Competitiveness Grants.

GIFT AID (NON-NEED-BASED) *Total amount:* $1,369,393 (96% institutional, 4% external sources). *Receiving aid:* Freshmen: 52% (108). Undergraduates: 33% (415). *Average award:* Freshmen: $7704. Undergraduates: $7212. *Scholarships, grants, and awards by category:* Academic interests/achievement: architecture, general academic interests/achievements. Creative arts/performance: applied art and design, art/fine arts, creative writing, general creative arts/performance. *Tuition waivers:* Full or partial for employees or children of employees.

LOANS *Student loans:* $9,032,262 (91% need-based, 9% non-need-based). 69% of past graduating class borrowed through all loan programs. *Average indebtedness per student:* $29,508. *Average need-based loan:* Freshmen: $3517. Undergraduates: $4632. *Parent loans:* $2,624,147 (61% need-based, 39% non-need-based). *Programs:* Federal Direct (Subsidized and Unsubsidized Stafford, PLUS), Perkins, private loans.

WORK-STUDY *Federal work-study:* Total amount: $676,479; 776 jobs averaging $2912. *State or other work-study/employment:* Total amount: $275,000 (100% non-need-based). 101 part-time jobs averaging $2875.

APPLYING FOR FINANCIAL AID *Required financial aid form:* FAFSA. *Financial aid deadline (priority):* 3/1. *Notification date:* Continuous beginning 4/1. Students must reply by 5/1 or within 3 weeks of notification.

CONTACT Financial Aid Office, California College of the Arts, 1111 Eighth Street, San Francisco, CA 94107, 415-703-9528 or toll-free 800-447-1ART. *Fax:* 415-551-9261. *E-mail:* finaid@cca.edu.

CALIFORNIA INSTITUTE OF INTEGRAL STUDIES
San Francisco, CA

CONTACT Financial Aid Office, California Institute of Integral Studies, 1453 Mission Street, San Francisco, CA 94103, 415-575-6122. *Fax:* 415-575-1268. *E-mail:* finaid@ciis.edu.

CALIFORNIA INSTITUTE OF TECHNOLOGY
Pasadena, CA

Tuition & fees: N/R	Average undergraduate aid package: $33,902

ABOUT THE INSTITUTION Independent, coed. 25 undergraduate majors. Federal methodology is used as a basis for awarding need-based institutional aid.

FRESHMAN FINANCIAL AID (Fall 2009, est.) 176 applied for aid; of those 82% were deemed to have need. 100% of freshmen with need received aid; of those 100% had need fully met. *Average percent of need met:* 100% (excluding resources awarded to replace EFC). *Average financial aid package:* $30,960 (excluding resources awarded to replace EFC). 1% of all full-time freshmen had no need and received non-need-based gift aid.

UNDERGRADUATE FINANCIAL AID (Fall 2009, est.) 565 applied for aid; of those 92% were deemed to have need. 100% of undergraduates with need received aid; of those 100% had need fully met. *Average percent of need met:* 100% (excluding resources awarded to replace EFC). *Average financial aid*

package: $33,902 (excluding resources awarded to replace EFC). 4% of all full-time undergraduates had no need and received non-need-based gift aid.

GIFT AID (NEED-BASED) *Total amount:* $14,848,530 (6% federal, 3% state, 87% institutional, 4% external sources). *Receiving aid:* Freshmen: 57% (144); all full-time undergraduates: 55% (519). *Average award:* Freshmen: $28,991; Undergraduates: $30,069. *Scholarships, grants, and awards:* Federal Pell, FSEOG, state, private, college/university gift aid from institutional funds.

GIFT AID (NON-NEED-BASED) *Total amount:* $1,506,694 (4% state, 81% institutional, 15% external sources). *Receiving aid:* Freshmen: 10% (26). Undergraduates: 4% (35). *Average award:* Freshmen: $16,849. Undergraduates: $34,967. *Scholarships, grants, and awards by category:* Academic interests/achievement: 35 awards ($1,223,830 total): general academic interests/achievements. *Tuition waivers:* Full or partial for employees or children of employees.

LOANS *Student loans:* $1,305,771 (74% need-based, 26% non-need-based). 42% of past graduating class borrowed through all loan programs. *Average indebtedness per student:* $8218. *Average need-based loan:* Freshmen: $2900. Undergraduates: $2502. *Parent loans:* $508,652 (4% need-based, 96% non-need-based). *Programs:* Federal Direct (Subsidized and Unsubsidized Stafford, PLUS), Perkins, college/university.

WORK-STUDY *Federal work-study:* Total amount: $920,176; 297 jobs averaging $3098. *State or other work-study/employment:* Total amount: $95,390 (100% need-based). 53 part-time jobs averaging $1800.

APPLYING FOR FINANCIAL AID *Required financial aid forms:* FAFSA, CSS Financial Aid PROFILE, state aid form, noncustodial (divorced/separated) parent's statement, business/farm supplement. *Financial aid deadline (priority):* 2/1. *Notification date:* Continuous beginning 3/20. Students must reply by 5/1 or within 2 weeks of notification.

CONTACT Don Crewell, Director of Financial Aid, California Institute of Technology, 1200 East California Boulevard, MC 110-87, Pasadena, CA 91125-8700, 626-395-6280. *Fax:* 626-564-8136. *E-mail:* dcrewell@caltech.edu.

CALIFORNIA INSTITUTE OF THE ARTS
Valencia, CA

Tuition & fees: $36,742	Average undergraduate aid package: $30,252

ABOUT THE INSTITUTION Independent, coed. 10 undergraduate majors. Federal methodology is used as a basis for awarding need-based institutional aid.

UNDERGRADUATE EXPENSES for 2010–11 *Comprehensive fee:* $46,035 includes full-time tuition ($36,166), mandatory fees ($576), and room and board ($9293). *College room only:* $5236. Room and board charges vary according to board plan, housing facility, and location. Part-time tuition and fees vary according to course load. *Payment plan:* Installment.

FRESHMAN FINANCIAL AID (Fall 2009, est.) 132 applied for aid; of those 82% were deemed to have need. 97% of freshmen with need received aid; of those 5% had need fully met. *Average percent of need met:* 71% (excluding resources awarded to replace EFC). *Average financial aid package:* $27,722 (excluding resources awarded to replace EFC). 8% of all full-time freshmen had no need and received non-need-based gift aid.

UNDERGRADUATE FINANCIAL AID (Fall 2009, est.) 717 applied for aid; of those 84% were deemed to have need. 98% of undergraduates with need received aid; of those 5% had need fully met. *Average percent of need met:* 77% (excluding resources awarded to replace EFC). *Average financial aid package:* $30,252 (excluding resources awarded to replace EFC). 9% of all full-time undergraduates had no need and received non-need-based gift aid.

GIFT AID (NEED-BASED) *Total amount:* $8,496,487 (19% federal, 10% state, 70% institutional, 1% external sources). *Receiving aid:* Freshmen: 62% (99); all full-time undergraduates: 64% (563). *Average award:* Freshmen: $14,771; Undergraduates: $15,035. *Scholarships, grants, and awards:* Federal Pell, FSEOG, state, private, college/university gift aid from institutional funds.

GIFT AID (NON-NEED-BASED) *Total amount:* $406,772 (96% institutional, 4% external sources). *Average award:* Freshmen: $4554. Undergraduates: $5085. *Scholarships, grants, and awards by category:* Creative arts/performance: 80 awards ($406,772 total): applied art and design, art/fine arts, cinema/film/broadcasting, creative writing, dance, music, performing arts, theater/drama. *Tuition waivers:* Full or partial for employees or children of employees.

LOANS *Student loans:* $7,680,210 (94% need-based, 6% non-need-based). 67% of past graduating class borrowed through all loan programs. *Average indebtedness per student:* $38,349. *Average need-based loan:* Freshmen: $4502. Undergraduates: $5249. *Parent loans:* $2,305,582 (77% need-based, 23%

non-need-based). *Programs:* FFEL (Subsidized and Unsubsidized Stafford, PLUS), Perkins, college/university, private alternative loans.

WORK-STUDY *Federal work-study:* Total amount: $508,500; 295 jobs averaging $1724. *State or other work-study/employment:* Total amount: $24,250 (100% need-based). 17 part-time jobs averaging $1426.

APPLYING FOR FINANCIAL AID *Required financial aid form:* FAFSA. *Financial aid deadline (priority):* 3/2. *Notification date:* Continuous beginning 4/1. Students must reply by 5/1 or within 3 weeks of notification.

CONTACT Ms. Bobbi Heuer, Director, Financial Aid, California Institute of the Arts, 24700 McBean Parkway, Valencia, CA 91355-2340, 661-253-7869 or toll-free 800-545-2787. *Fax:* 661-287-3816. *E-mail:* bheuer@calarts.edu.

CALIFORNIA INTERCONTINENTAL UNIVERSITY
Diamond Bar, CA

CONTACT Financial Aid Office, California Intercontinental University, 1470 Valley Vista Drive, Suite 150, Diamond Bar, CA 91765, 909-396-6090 or toll-free 866-687-2258.

CALIFORNIA LUTHERAN UNIVERSITY
Thousand Oaks, CA

Tuition & fees: $31,000	Average undergraduate aid package: $22,500

ABOUT THE INSTITUTION Independent Lutheran, coed. 55 undergraduate majors. Both federal and institutional methodology are used as a basis for awarding need-based institutional aid.

UNDERGRADUATE EXPENSES for 2010–11 *Comprehensive fee:* $41,580 includes full-time tuition ($30,750), mandatory fees ($250), and room and board ($10,580). *College room only:* $5690. Room and board charges vary according to board plan. *Part-time tuition:* $990 per unit. *Part-time fees:* $250 per year. *Payment plan:* Installment.

FRESHMAN FINANCIAL AID (Fall 2009, est.) 455 applied for aid; of those 71% were deemed to have need. 100% of freshmen with need received aid; of those 25% had need fully met. *Average percent of need met:* 88% (excluding resources awarded to replace EFC). *Average financial aid package:* $24,700 (excluding resources awarded to replace EFC). 30% of all full-time freshmen had no need and received non-need-based gift aid.

UNDERGRADUATE FINANCIAL AID (Fall 2009, est.) 2,053 applied for aid; of those 66% were deemed to have need. 99% of undergraduates with need received aid; of those 20% had need fully met. *Average percent of need met:* 84% (excluding resources awarded to replace EFC). *Average financial aid package:* $22,500 (excluding resources awarded to replace EFC). 35% of all full-time undergraduates had no need and received non-need-based gift aid.

GIFT AID (NEED-BASED) *Total amount:* $24,039,400 (11% federal, 13% state, 74% institutional, 2% external sources). *Receiving aid:* Freshmen: 69% (322); all full-time undergraduates: 61% (1,292). *Average award:* Freshmen: $17,600; Undergraduates: $16,300. *Scholarships, grants, and awards:* Federal Pell, FSEOG, state, private, college/university gift aid from institutional funds.

GIFT AID (NON-NEED-BASED) *Total amount:* $6,515,897 (99% institutional, 1% external sources). *Receiving aid:* Freshmen: 17% (81). Undergraduates: 13% (268). *Average award:* Freshmen: $12,400. Undergraduates: $10,900. *Scholarships, grants, and awards by category:* Academic interests/achievement: 480 awards ($3,120,000 total): biological sciences, business, communication, computer science, education, English, foreign languages, general academic interests/achievements, humanities, international studies, mathematics, physical sciences, religion/biblical studies, social sciences. Creative arts/performance: 80 awards ($160,000 total): art/fine arts, creative writing, journalism/publications, music, performing arts, theater/drama. Special achievements/activities: 30 awards ($37,500 total): community service, general special achievements/activities, leadership, religious involvement. Special characteristics: 140 awards ($224,000 total): adult students, children and siblings of alumni, children of faculty/staff, ethnic background, first-generation college students, international students, relatives of clergy, religious affiliation. *Tuition waivers:* Full or partial for employees or children of employees.

LOANS *Student loans:* $14,170,841 (87% need-based, 13% non-need-based). 68% of past graduating class borrowed through all loan programs. *Average indebtedness per student:* $23,920. *Average need-based loan:* Freshmen: $3400.

Undergraduates: $3700. *Parent loans:* $7,851,800 (81% need-based, 19% non-need-based). *Programs:* Federal Direct (Subsidized and Unsubsidized Stafford, PLUS), Perkins.

WORK-STUDY *Federal work-study:* Total amount: $1,462,740; 636 jobs averaging $2300. *State or other work-study/employment:* Total amount: $174,700 (56% need-based, 44% non-need-based). 85 part-time jobs averaging $2000.

APPLYING FOR FINANCIAL AID *Required financial aid forms:* FAFSA, state aid form. *Financial aid deadline (priority):* 3/1. *Notification date:* Continuous beginning 3/15. Students must reply by 5/1 or within 2 weeks of notification.

CONTACT Rebecca Kennan, Associate Director of Financial Aid and Scholarships, California Lutheran University, 60 West Olsen Road, Thousand Oaks, CA 91360-2787, 805-493-3115 or toll-free 877-258-3678. *Fax:* 805-493-3114. *E-mail:* rkeenan@callutheran.edu.

CALIFORNIA MARITIME ACADEMY
Vallejo, CA

Tuition & fees (CA res): $4400	Average undergraduate aid package: N/A

ABOUT THE INSTITUTION State-supported, coed. 4 undergraduate majors. Federal methodology is used as a basis for awarding need-based institutional aid.

UNDERGRADUATE EXPENSES for 2010–11 *Tuition, state resident:* full-time $0. *Tuition, nonresident:* full-time $10,170. *Required fees:* full-time $4400. *College room and board:* $9750. *Payment plan:* Installment.

GIFT AID (NEED-BASED) *Total amount:* $1,865,069 (70% federal, 16% state, 5% institutional, 9% external sources). *Scholarships, grants, and awards:* Federal Pell, FSEOG, state, private, college/university gift aid from institutional funds.

GIFT AID (NON-NEED-BASED) *Total amount:* $101,000 (100% institutional). *Scholarships, grants, and awards by category:* Academic interests/achievement: general academic interests/achievements. *Special achievements/activities:* community service, leadership. *Special characteristics:* first-generation college students, general special characteristics, local/state students, out-of-state students.

LOANS *Student loans:* $3,784,134 (53% need-based, 47% non-need-based). *Parent loans:* $1,937,325 (100% non-need-based). *Programs:* FFEL (Subsidized and Unsubsidized Stafford, PLUS), Perkins.

WORK-STUDY *Federal work-study:* Total amount: $57,724; jobs available.

ATHLETIC AWARDS Total amount: $40,750 (100% non-need-based).

APPLYING FOR FINANCIAL AID *Required financial aid form:* FAFSA. *Financial aid deadline (priority):* 3/3. *Notification date:* Continuous beginning 4/15. Students must reply by 6/30.

CONTACT Ken Walsh, Director of Financial Aid, California Maritime Academy, 200 Maritime Academy Drive, Vallejo, CA 94590-0644, 707-654-1275 or toll-free 800-561-1945. *Fax:* 707-654-1007. *E-mail:* finaid@csum.edu.

CALIFORNIA MIRAMAR UNIVERSITY
San Diego, CA

CONTACT Financial Aid Office, California Miramar University, 9750 Miramar Road, Suite 180, San Diego, CA 92126, 858-653-3000 or toll-free 877-570-5678 (out-of-state).

CALIFORNIA NATIONAL UNIVERSITY FOR ADVANCED STUDIES
Northridge, CA

CONTACT Office of Academic Affairs, California National University for Advanced Studies, 16909 Parthenia Street, North Hills, CA 91343, 800-782-2422 or toll-free 800-744-2822 (in-state).

CALIFORNIA POLYTECHNIC STATE UNIVERSITY, SAN LUIS OBISPO
San Luis Obispo, CA

Tuition & fees (CA res): $6198	Average undergraduate aid package: $8687

ABOUT THE INSTITUTION State-supported, coed. 65 undergraduate majors. Federal methodology is used as a basis for awarding need-based institutional aid.

UNDERGRADUATE EXPENSES for 2009–10 *Tuition, state resident:* full-time $0. *Tuition, nonresident:* full-time $11,160; part-time $248 per unit. *Required fees:* full-time $6198; $1371 per term. Full-time tuition and fees vary according to course load, degree level, and program. Part-time tuition and fees vary according to course load, degree level, and program. *College room and board:* $9623; *Room only:* $5383. Room and board charges vary according to board plan and housing facility. *Payment plan:* Installment.

FRESHMAN FINANCIAL AID (Fall 2009, est.) 2,401 applied for aid; of those 49% were deemed to have need. 90% of freshmen with need received aid; of those 16% had need fully met. *Average percent of need met:* 66% (excluding resources awarded to replace EFC). *Average financial aid package:* $8544 (excluding resources awarded to replace EFC). 6% of all full-time freshmen had no need and received non-need-based gift aid.

UNDERGRADUATE FINANCIAL AID (Fall 2009, est.) 8,863 applied for aid; of those 65% were deemed to have need. 93% of undergraduates with need received aid; of those 13% had need fully met. *Average percent of need met:* 63% (excluding resources awarded to replace EFC). *Average financial aid package:* $8687 (excluding resources awarded to replace EFC). 4% of all full-time undergraduates had no need and received non-need-based gift aid.

GIFT AID (NEED-BASED) *Total amount:* $27,964,201 (41% federal, 43% state, 7% institutional, 9% external sources). *Receiving aid:* Freshmen: 25% (855); all full-time undergraduates: 24% (4,152). *Average award:* Freshmen: $2050; Undergraduates: $2390. *Scholarships, grants, and awards:* Federal Pell, FSEOG, state, private, college/university gift aid from institutional funds, TEACH Grants.

GIFT AID (NON-NEED-BASED) *Total amount:* $4,487,085 (43% institutional, 57% external sources). *Receiving aid:* Freshmen: 2% (54). Undergraduates: 1% (123). *Average award:* Freshmen: $2018. Undergraduates: $2498. *Scholarships, grants, and awards by category:* Academic interests/achievement: agriculture, architecture, biological sciences, business, communication, computer science, education, engineering/technologies, English, foreign languages, general academic interests/achievements, health fields, home economics, humanities, international studies, library science, mathematics, military science, physical sciences, social sciences. *Creative arts/performance:* applied art and design, art/fine arts, cinema/film/broadcasting, creative writing, dance, debating, general creative arts/performance, journalism/publications, music, performing arts, theater/drama. *Special achievements/activities:* community service, leadership, rodeo. *Special characteristics:* children and siblings of alumni, general special characteristics, local/state students. *Tuition waivers:* Full or partial for employees or children of employees.

LOANS *Student loans:* $35,546,943 (63% need-based, 37% non-need-based). *Average need-based loan:* Freshmen: $3149. Undergraduates: $3696. *Parent loans:* $17,889,794 (19% need-based, 81% non-need-based). *Programs:* Federal Direct (Subsidized and Unsubsidized Stafford, PLUS), Perkins, college/university, alternative loans.

WORK-STUDY *Federal work-study:* Total amount: $665,782; jobs available.

ATHLETIC AWARDS Total amount: $2,868,903 (27% need-based, 73% non-need-based).

APPLYING FOR FINANCIAL AID *Required financial aid form:* FAFSA. *Financial aid deadline (priority):* 3/2. *Notification date:* Continuous beginning 4/1.

CONTACT Lois Kelly, Director, Financial Aid, California Polytechnic State University, San Luis Obispo, 1 Grand Avenue, San Luis Obispo, CA 93407, 805-756-5893. *Fax:* 805-756-7243. *E-mail:* lkelly@calpoly.edu.

CALIFORNIA STATE POLYTECHNIC UNIVERSITY, POMONA
Pomona, CA

Tuition & fees (CA res): $4551	Average undergraduate aid package: $10,970

ABOUT THE INSTITUTION State-supported, coed. 58 undergraduate majors. Federal methodology is used as a basis for awarding need-based institutional aid.

UNDERGRADUATE EXPENSES for 2010–11 *Tuition, state resident:* full-time $0. *Tuition, nonresident:* full-time $11,160; part-time $248 per unit. *Required fees:* full-time $4551; $2859 per year. Full-time tuition and fees vary according to degree level and program. Part-time tuition and fees vary according to course load, degree level, and program. *College room and board:* $9570;

Room only: $6027. Room and board charges vary according to board plan and housing facility. *Payment plans:* Installment, deferred payment.

FRESHMAN FINANCIAL AID (Fall 2009, est.) 2,143 applied for aid; of those 70% were deemed to have need. 93% of freshmen with need received aid; of those 20% had need fully met. *Average percent of need met:* 79% (excluding resources awarded to replace EFC). *Average financial aid package:* $9932 (excluding resources awarded to replace EFC). 1% of all full-time freshmen had no need and received non-need-based gift aid.

UNDERGRADUATE FINANCIAL AID (Fall 2009, est.) 11,832 applied for aid; of those 85% were deemed to have need. 96% of undergraduates with need received aid; of those 24% had need fully met. *Average percent of need met:* 72% (excluding resources awarded to replace EFC). *Average financial aid package:* $10,970 (excluding resources awarded to replace EFC). 1% of all full-time undergraduates had no need and received non-need-based gift aid.

GIFT AID (NEED-BASED) *Total amount:* $79,586,951 (48% federal, 52% state). *Receiving aid:* Freshmen: 41% (1,122); all full-time undergraduates: 44% (7,904). *Average award:* Freshmen: $9241; Undergraduates: $8931. *Scholarships, grants, and awards:* Federal Pell, FSEOG, state, private, college/university gift aid from institutional funds.

GIFT AID (NON-NEED-BASED) *Total amount:* $1,889,105 (9% state, 20% institutional, 71% external sources). *Receiving aid:* Freshmen: 5% (147). Undergraduates: 4% (656). *Average award:* Freshmen: $5544. Undergraduates: $2640. *Scholarships, grants, and awards by category:* Academic interests/achievement: agriculture, architecture, biological sciences, business, computer science, education, engineering/technologies, general academic interests/achievements, humanities, mathematics, physical sciences, social sciences. Special achievements/activities: hobbies/interests, leadership. Special characteristics: children and siblings of alumni, children of current students, members of minority groups. *Tuition waivers:* Full or partial for employees or children of employees.

LOANS *Student loans:* $80,798,848 (49% need-based, 51% non-need-based). 37% of past graduating class borrowed through all loan programs. *Average indebtedness per student:* $14,117. *Average need-based loan:* Freshmen: $2994. Undergraduates: $4049. *Parent loans:* $1,607,331 (100% non-need-based). *Programs:* FFEL (Subsidized and Unsubsidized Stafford, PLUS), Perkins, college/university, alternative loans.

WORK-STUDY *Federal work-study:* Total amount: $838,678; 375 jobs averaging $2261.

ATHLETIC AWARDS Total amount: $513,176 (100% non-need-based).

APPLYING FOR FINANCIAL AID *Required financial aid form:* FAFSA. *Financial aid deadline:* Continuous. *Notification date:* Continuous beginning 4/1. Students must reply within 6 weeks of notification.

CONTACT Diana Minor, Director of Financial Aid and Scholarships, California State Polytechnic University, Pomona, 3801 West Temple Avenue, Pomona, CA 91768-2557, 909-869-3704. *Fax:* 909-869-4757. *E-mail:* dyminor@csupomona.edu.

CALIFORNIA STATE UNIVERSITY, BAKERSFIELD
Bakersfield, CA

ABOUT THE INSTITUTION State-supported, coed. 30 undergraduate majors.

GIFT AID (NEED-BASED) *Scholarships, grants, and awards:* Federal Pell, FSEOG, state, private, college/university gift aid from institutional funds, Federal Nursing.

GIFT AID (NON-NEED-BASED) *Scholarships, grants, and awards by category:* Academic interests/achievement: agriculture, architecture, biological sciences, business, communication, education, foreign languages, general academic interests/achievements, health fields, humanities, mathematics, physical sciences, premedicine, religion/biblical studies, social sciences. Creative arts/performance: art/fine arts, dance, music, theater/drama. Special achievements/activities: community service, general special achievements/activities. Special characteristics: children of faculty/staff, children of union members/company employees, ethnic background, first-generation college students, veterans.

LOANS *Programs:* Federal Direct (Subsidized and Unsubsidized Stafford, PLUS), Perkins, Federal Nursing.

APPLYING FOR FINANCIAL AID *Required financial aid form:* FAFSA.

CONTACT Mr. Ron Radney, Interim Director of Financial Aid, California State University, Bakersfield, 9001 Stockdale Highway, Bakersfield, CA 93311-1099, 661-654-3271 or toll-free 800-788-2782 (in-state). *Fax:* 661-654-6800. *E-mail:* rradney@csub.edu.

CALIFORNIA STATE UNIVERSITY CHANNEL ISLANDS
Camarillo, CA

CONTACT Financial Aid Office, California State University Channel Islands, One University Drive, Camarillo, CA 93012, 805-437-8400.

CALIFORNIA STATE UNIVERSITY, CHICO
Chico, CA

Tuition & fees (CA res): $5336	Average undergraduate aid package: $12,447

ABOUT THE INSTITUTION State-supported, coed. 114 undergraduate majors. Federal methodology is used as a basis for awarding need-based institutional aid.

UNDERGRADUATE EXPENSES for 2010–11 *Tuition, state resident:* full-time $0. *Tuition, nonresident:* full-time $11,160; part-time $372 per unit. *Required fees:* full-time $5336. Full-time tuition and fees vary according to degree level. Part-time tuition and fees vary according to course load and degree level. *College room and board:* $9404; *Room only:* $6692. Room and board charges vary according to board plan and housing facility. *Payment plans:* Installment, deferred payment.

FRESHMAN FINANCIAL AID (Fall 2009, est.) 1,382 applied for aid; of those 85% were deemed to have need. 96% of freshmen with need received aid; of those 15% had need fully met. *Average percent of need met:* 89% (excluding resources awarded to replace EFC). *Average financial aid package:* $13,803 (excluding resources awarded to replace EFC). 4% of all full-time freshmen had no need and received non-need-based gift aid.

UNDERGRADUATE FINANCIAL AID (Fall 2009, est.) 8,352 applied for aid; of those 81% were deemed to have need. 97% of undergraduates with need received aid; of those 15% had need fully met. *Average percent of need met:* 90% (excluding resources awarded to replace EFC). *Average financial aid package:* $12,447 (excluding resources awarded to replace EFC). 4% of all full-time undergraduates had no need and received non-need-based gift aid.

GIFT AID (NEED-BASED) *Total amount:* $46,007,227 (53% federal, 47% state). *Receiving aid:* Freshmen: 31% (772); all full-time undergraduates: 36% (5,170). *Average award:* Freshmen: $9376; Undergraduates: $8292. *Scholarships, grants, and awards:* Federal Pell, FSEOG, state, private, college/university gift aid from institutional funds, United Negro College Fund.

GIFT AID (NON-NEED-BASED) *Total amount:* $2,396,583 (3% state, 47% institutional, 50% external sources). *Receiving aid:* Freshmen: 12% (298). Undergraduates: 8% (1,088). *Average award:* Freshmen: $1467. Undergraduates: $1978. *Scholarships, grants, and awards by category:* Academic interests/achievement: agriculture, area/ethnic studies, biological sciences, business, communication, computer science, education, engineering/technologies, English, foreign languages, general academic interests/achievements, health fields, humanities, international studies, mathematics, physical sciences, social sciences. Creative arts/performance: applied art and design, art/fine arts, cinema/film/broadcasting, creative writing, dance, debating, general creative arts/performance, journalism/publications, music, performing arts, theater/drama. Special achievements/activities: community service, general special achievements/activities, hobbies/interests, leadership, memberships. Special characteristics: adult students, children of faculty/staff, ethnic background, first-generation college students, handicapped students, international students, local/state students, married students, members of minority groups, out-of-state students. *Tuition waivers:* Full or partial for employees or children of employees, senior citizens.

LOANS *Student loans:* $37,587,317 (60% need-based, 40% non-need-based). *Average need-based loan:* Freshmen: $3420. Undergraduates: $4475. *Parent loans:* $3,970,483 (100% non-need-based). *Programs:* Federal Direct (Subsidized and Unsubsidized Stafford, PLUS), Perkins, college/university.

WORK-STUDY *Federal work-study:* Total amount: $8,924,581; jobs available.

ATHLETIC AWARDS Total amount: $635,736 (65% need-based, 35% non-need-based).

APPLYING FOR FINANCIAL AID *Required financial aid forms:* FAFSA, institution's own form. *Financial aid deadline:* Continuous. *Notification date:* Continuous beginning 3/2.

CONTACT Dan Reed, Director, Financial Aid and Scholarship Office, California State University, Chico, 400 West First Street, Student Services Center, Room 250, Chico, CA 95929-0705, 530-898-6451 or toll-free 800-542-4426. *Fax:* 530-898-6883. *E-mail:* finaid@csuchico.edu.

CALIFORNIA STATE UNIVERSITY, DOMINGUEZ HILLS
Carson, CA

Tuition & fees (CA res): $4645	Average undergraduate aid package: $5457

ABOUT THE INSTITUTION State-supported, coed. 69 undergraduate majors. Federal methodology is used as a basis for awarding need-based institutional aid.

UNDERGRADUATE EXPENSES for 2010–11 *Tuition, state resident:* full-time $0. *Tuition, nonresident:* full-time $11,160; part-time $372 per unit. *Required fees:* full-time $4645; $1479 per term. *College room and board:* $10,085; *Room only:* $5693. Room and board charges vary according to housing facility. *Payment plan:* Installment.

FRESHMAN FINANCIAL AID (Fall 2009, est.) 984 applied for aid; of those 92% were deemed to have need. 96% of freshmen with need received aid; of those 1% had need fully met. *Average percent of need met:* 34% (excluding resources awarded to replace EFC). *Average financial aid package:* $4705 (excluding resources awarded to replace EFC). 4% of all full-time freshmen had no need and received non-need-based gift aid.

UNDERGRADUATE FINANCIAL AID (Fall 2009, est.) 4,684 applied for aid; of those 95% were deemed to have need. 96% of undergraduates with need received aid; of those 2% had need fully met. *Average percent of need met:* 34% (excluding resources awarded to replace EFC). *Average financial aid package:* $5457 (excluding resources awarded to replace EFC). 2% of all full-time undergraduates had no need and received non-need-based gift aid.

GIFT AID (NEED-BASED) *Total amount:* $22,339,397 (49% federal, 49% state, 1% institutional, 1% external sources). *Receiving aid:* Freshmen: 69% (741); all full-time undergraduates: 52% (3,494). *Average award:* Freshmen: $4454; Undergraduates: $4310. *Scholarships, grants, and awards:* Federal Pell, FSEOG, state, private, college/university gift aid from institutional funds.

GIFT AID (NON-NEED-BASED) *Total amount:* $25,338 (8% state, 82% institutional, 10% external sources). *Receiving aid:* Freshmen: 12% (126). Undergraduates: 14% (953). *Average award:* Freshmen: $2629. Undergraduates: $3165. *Tuition waivers:* Full or partial for employees or children of employees, senior citizens.

LOANS *Student loans:* $10,916,378 (92% need-based, 8% non-need-based). 56% of past graduating class borrowed through all loan programs. *Average indebtedness per student:* $7946. *Average need-based loan:* Freshmen: $1637. Undergraduates: $2401. *Parent loans:* $70,221 (34% need-based, 66% non-need-based). *Programs:* Federal Direct (Subsidized and Unsubsidized Stafford, PLUS), Perkins, college/university.

WORK-STUDY *Federal work-study:* Total amount: $362,804; 189 jobs averaging $1920.

ATHLETIC AWARDS Total amount: $205,695 (92% need-based, 8% non-need-based).

APPLYING FOR FINANCIAL AID *Required financial aid form:* FAFSA. *Financial aid deadline (priority):* 3/2. *Notification date:* Continuous beginning 3/15. Students must reply within 2 weeks of notification.

CONTACT Mrs. Delores S. Lee, Director of Financial Aid, California State University, Dominguez Hills, 1000 East Victoria Street, Carson, CA 90747-0001, 310-243-3189. *Fax:* 310-516-4498. *E-mail:* dslee@csudh.edu.

CALIFORNIA STATE UNIVERSITY, EAST BAY
Hayward, CA

Tuition & fees (CA res): $4872	Average undergraduate aid package: $10,000

ABOUT THE INSTITUTION State-supported, coed. 90 undergraduate majors. Federal methodology is used as a basis for awarding need-based institutional aid.

UNDERGRADUATE EXPENSES for 2010–11 *Tuition, state resident:* full-time $0. *Tuition, nonresident:* full-time $13,800. *Required fees:* full-time $4872. *College room and board:* $10,029. *Payment plan:* Installment.

FRESHMAN FINANCIAL AID (Fall 2009, est.) 924 applied for aid; of those 92% were deemed to have need. 98% of freshmen with need received aid; of those 3% had need fully met. *Average percent of need met:* 57% (excluding resources awarded to replace EFC). *Average financial aid package:* $10,378 (excluding resources awarded to replace EFC).

UNDERGRADUATE FINANCIAL AID (Fall 2009, est.) 5,017 applied for aid; of those 96% were deemed to have need. 98% of undergraduates with need received aid; of those 2% had need fully met. *Average percent of need met:* 53% (excluding resources awarded to replace EFC). *Average financial aid package:* $10,000 (excluding resources awarded to replace EFC).

GIFT AID (NEED-BASED) *Total amount:* $36,396,142 (52% federal, 45% state, 2% institutional, 1% external sources). *Receiving aid:* Freshmen: 50% (718); all full-time undergraduates: 40% (3,819). *Average award:* Freshmen: $8900; Undergraduates: $8594. *Scholarships, grants, and awards:* Federal Pell, FSEOG, state, private, college/university gift aid from institutional funds.

GIFT AID (NON-NEED-BASED) *Scholarships, grants, and awards by category:* *Academic interests/achievement:* general academic interests/achievements. *Creative arts/performance:* music. *Tuition waivers:* Full or partial for employees or children of employees, senior citizens.

LOANS *Student loans:* $27,424,942 (86% need-based, 14% non-need-based). 34% of past graduating class borrowed through all loan programs. *Average indebtedness per student:* $14,643. *Average need-based loan:* Freshmen: $4906. Undergraduates: $7120. *Parent loans:* $2,457,953 (32% need-based, 68% non-need-based). *Programs:* Federal Direct (Subsidized and Unsubsidized Stafford, PLUS), Perkins, college/university.

WORK-STUDY *Federal work-study:* Total amount: $829,922; 493 jobs averaging $2400.

ATHLETIC AWARDS Total amount: $282,889 (100% need-based).

APPLYING FOR FINANCIAL AID *Required financial aid form:* FAFSA. *Financial aid deadline (priority):* 3/2. *Notification date:* Continuous beginning 3/31. Students must reply within 4 weeks of notification.

CONTACT Office of Financial Aid, California State University, East Bay, 25800 Carlos Bee Boulevard, Hayward, CA 94542-3028, 510-885-2784. *Fax:* 510-885-2161. *E-mail:* finaid@csueastbay.edu.

CALIFORNIA STATE UNIVERSITY, FRESNO
Fresno, CA

Tuition & fees (CA res): $3687	Average undergraduate aid package: $10,984

ABOUT THE INSTITUTION State-supported, coed. 88 undergraduate majors. Federal methodology is used as a basis for awarding need-based institutional aid.

UNDERGRADUATE EXPENSES for 2009–10 *Tuition, state resident:* full-time $0. *Tuition, nonresident:* full-time $10,170. *Required fees:* full-time $3687. *College room and board:* $8590; *Room only:* $4100. Room and board charges vary according to board plan. *Payment plan:* Installment.

FRESHMAN FINANCIAL AID (Fall 2009, est.) 2,153 applied for aid; of those 82% were deemed to have need. 96% of freshmen with need received aid; of those 15% had need fully met. *Average percent of need met:* 74% (excluding resources awarded to replace EFC). *Average financial aid package:* $10,192 (excluding resources awarded to replace EFC). 3% of all full-time freshmen had no need and received non-need-based gift aid.

UNDERGRADUATE FINANCIAL AID (Fall 2009, est.) 11,086 applied for aid; of those 90% were deemed to have need. 97% of undergraduates with need received aid; of those 15% had need fully met. *Average percent of need met:* 72% (excluding resources awarded to replace EFC). *Average financial aid package:* $10,984 (excluding resources awarded to replace EFC). 1% of all full-time undergraduates had no need and received non-need-based gift aid.

GIFT AID (NEED-BASED) *Total amount:* $78,901,293 (51% federal, 49% state). *Receiving aid:* Freshmen: 52% (1,361); all full-time undergraduates: 51% (7,924). *Average award:* Freshmen: $9888; Undergraduates: $9209. *Scholarships, grants, and awards:* Federal Pell, FSEOG, state, private, college/university gift aid from institutional funds.

GIFT AID (NON-NEED-BASED) *Total amount:* $4,729,312 (54% institutional, 46% external sources). *Receiving aid:* Freshmen: 12% (303). Undergraduates: 7% (1,046). *Average award:* Freshmen: $2609. Undergraduates: $3310. *Scholarships, grants, and awards by category: Academic interests/achievement:* 1,061 awards ($2,446,691 total): agriculture, area/ethnic studies, biological sciences, business, communication, education, engineering/technologies, English, foreign languages, general academic interests/achievements, health fields, humanities, mathematics, physical sciences, social sciences. *Creative arts/performance:* 232 awards ($224,467 total): art/fine arts, journalism/publications, music, theater/drama. *Special achievements/activities:* 23 awards ($39,000 total): community service, leadership. *Special characteristics:* 4 awards ($5192 total): handicapped students, local/state students.

LOANS *Student loans:* $67,485,417 (56% need-based, 44% non-need-based). 65% of past graduating class borrowed through all loan programs. *Average indebtedness per student:* $10,406. *Average need-based loan:* Freshmen: $2944. Undergraduates: $4086. *Parent loans:* $1,728,715 (100% non-need-based). *Programs:* FFEL (Subsidized and Unsubsidized Stafford, PLUS), Perkins, Federal Nursing, college/university, alternative loans.

WORK-STUDY *Federal work-study:* Total amount: $877,391; 285 jobs averaging $3040.

ATHLETIC AWARDS Total amount: $4,023,675 (100% non-need-based).

APPLYING FOR FINANCIAL AID *Required financial aid form:* FAFSA. *Financial aid deadline (priority):* 3/2. *Notification date:* Continuous beginning 4/1. Students must reply within 3 weeks of notification.

CONTACT Maria Hernandez, Director of Financial Aid, California State University, Fresno, 5150 North Maple Avenue, Fresno, CA 93740, 559-278-2182. *Fax:* 559-278-4833. *E-mail:* mariah@csufresno.edu.

CALIFORNIA STATE UNIVERSITY, FULLERTON
Fullerton, CA

Tuition & fees (CA res): $4662	Average undergraduate aid package: $12,421

ABOUT THE INSTITUTION State-supported, coed. 74 undergraduate majors. Federal methodology is used as a basis for awarding need-based institutional aid.

UNDERGRADUATE EXPENSES for 2010–11 *Tuition, state resident:* full-time $0. *Tuition, nonresident:* full-time $15,822; part-time $3717 per term. *Required fees:* full-time $4662; $1485 per term. Full-time tuition and fees vary according to course load. Part-time tuition and fees vary according to course load. *College room and board:* $9242; *Room only:* $5775. *Payment plans:* Installment, deferred payment.

FRESHMAN FINANCIAL AID (Fall 2009, est.) 2,997 applied for aid; of those 74% were deemed to have need. 85% of freshmen with need received aid; of those 50% had need fully met. *Average percent of need met:* 52% (excluding resources awarded to replace EFC). *Average financial aid package:* $11,435 (excluding resources awarded to replace EFC). 19% of all full-time freshmen had no need and received non-need-based gift aid.

UNDERGRADUATE FINANCIAL AID (Fall 2009, est.) 14,650 applied for aid; of those 84% were deemed to have need. 96% of undergraduates with need received aid; of those 5% had need fully met. *Average percent of need met:* 51% (excluding resources awarded to replace EFC). *Average financial aid package:* $12,421 (excluding resources awarded to replace EFC). 8% of all full-time undergraduates had no need and received non-need-based gift aid.

GIFT AID (NEED-BASED) *Total amount:* $86,665,289 (44% federal, 53% state, 1% institutional, 2% external sources). *Receiving aid:* Freshmen: 49% (1,873); all full-time undergraduates: 48% (11,027). *Average award:* Freshmen: $6463; Undergraduates: $7123. *Scholarships, grants, and awards:* Federal Pell, FSEOG, state, private, college/university gift aid from institutional funds, Federal Nursing.

GIFT AID (NON-NEED-BASED) *Total amount:* $2,197,649 (42% institutional, 58% external sources). *Receiving aid:* Freshmen: 1% (29). Undergraduates: 44. *Average award:* Freshmen: $5781. Undergraduates: $6277. *Scholarships, grants, and awards by category: Academic interests/achievement:* 1,698 awards ($2,830,932 total): business, communication, engineering/technologies, general academic interests/achievements, humanities, mathematics, military science, social sciences. *Creative arts/performance:* 85 awards ($52,275 total): art/fine arts, dance, music, performing arts, theater/drama. *Special achievements/activities:* 60 awards ($202,918 total): general special achievements/activities,

leadership. *Special characteristics:* 38 awards ($213,479 total): general special characteristics. *Tuition waivers:* Full or partial for employees or children of employees, senior citizens.

LOANS *Student loans:* $44,781,685 (64% need-based, 36% non-need-based). 39% of past graduating class borrowed through all loan programs. *Average indebtedness per student:* $14,706. *Average need-based loan:* Freshmen: $2879. Undergraduates: $4124. *Parent loans:* $714,539 (100% non-need-based). *Programs:* Federal Direct (Subsidized and Unsubsidized Stafford, PLUS), Perkins, college/university, private alternative loans.

WORK-STUDY *Federal work-study:* Total amount: $1,075,788; 531 jobs averaging $2825.

ATHLETIC AWARDS Total amount: $2,381,417 (32% need-based, 68% non-need-based).

APPLYING FOR FINANCIAL AID *Required financial aid form:* FAFSA. *Financial aid deadline (priority):* 3/2. *Notification date:* Continuous beginning 4/22. Students must reply within 4 weeks of notification.

CONTACT Ms. Jessica Schutte, Acting Director of Financial Aid, California State University, Fullerton, 800 North State College Boulevard, Fullerton, CA 92831-3599, 657-278-3128. *Fax:* 657-278-7090. *E-mail:* jschutte@fullerton.edu.

CALIFORNIA STATE UNIVERSITY, LONG BEACH
Long Beach, CA

Tuition & fees (CA res): $4606	Average undergraduate aid package: $12,627

ABOUT THE INSTITUTION State-supported, coed. 148 undergraduate majors. Federal methodology is used as a basis for awarding need-based institutional aid.

UNDERGRADUATE EXPENSES for 2010–11 *Tuition, state resident:* full-time $0. *Tuition, nonresident:* full-time $11,160. *Required fees:* full-time $4606. Full-time tuition and fees vary according to program. Part-time tuition and fees vary according to course load and program. *College room and board:* $11,038. Room and board charges vary according to board plan. *Payment plan:* Installment.

FRESHMAN FINANCIAL AID (Fall 2009, est.) 2,831 applied for aid; of those 77% were deemed to have need. 91% of freshmen with need received aid; of those 72% had need fully met. *Average percent of need met:* 81% (excluding resources awarded to replace EFC). *Average financial aid package:* $11,917 (excluding resources awarded to replace EFC). 4% of all full-time freshmen had no need and received non-need-based gift aid.

UNDERGRADUATE FINANCIAL AID (Fall 2009, est.) 17,167 applied for aid; of those 94% were deemed to have need. 86% of undergraduates with need received aid; of those 58% had need fully met. *Average percent of need met:* 83% (excluding resources awarded to replace EFC). *Average financial aid package:* $12,627 (excluding resources awarded to replace EFC). 6% of all full-time undergraduates had no need and received non-need-based gift aid.

GIFT AID (NEED-BASED) *Total amount:* $110,894,849 (45% federal, 52% state, 2% institutional, 1% external sources). *Receiving aid:* Freshmen: 49% (1,688); all full-time undergraduates: 49% (10,888). *Average award:* Freshmen: $5755; Undergraduates: $5697. *Scholarships, grants, and awards:* Federal Pell, FSEOG, state, private, college/university gift aid from institutional funds.

GIFT AID (NON-NEED-BASED) *Total amount:* $63,358 (64% federal, 36% state). *Receiving aid:* Freshmen: 7% (250). Undergraduates: 9% (2,066). *Average award:* Freshmen: $2164. Undergraduates: $2247. *Tuition waivers:* Full or partial for employees or children of employees, senior citizens.

LOANS *Student loans:* $81,630,486 (54% need-based, 46% non-need-based). 43% of past graduating class borrowed through all loan programs. *Average indebtedness per student:* $10,927. *Average need-based loan:* Freshmen: $3065. Undergraduates: $3455. *Parent loans:* $2,404,882 (100% non-need-based). *Programs:* Federal Direct (Subsidized and Unsubsidized Stafford, PLUS), Perkins.

WORK-STUDY *Federal work-study:* Total amount: $1,575,000; jobs available.

ATHLETIC AWARDS Total amount: $1,585,399 (100% non-need-based).

APPLYING FOR FINANCIAL AID *Required financial aid form:* FAFSA. *Financial aid deadline (priority):* 3/2. *Notification date:* Continuous beginning 3/30. Students must reply within 3 weeks of notification.

CONTACT Nicolas Valdivia, Office of Financial Aid, California State University, Long Beach, 1250 Bellflower Boulevard, Long Beach, CA 90840, 562-985-8403.

CALIFORNIA STATE UNIVERSITY, LOS ANGELES
Los Angeles, CA

ABOUT THE INSTITUTION State-supported, coed. 62 undergraduate majors.

GIFT AID (NEED-BASED) *Scholarships, grants, and awards:* Federal Pell, FSEOG, state, private, college/university gift aid from institutional funds.

GIFT AID (NON-NEED-BASED) *Scholarships, grants, and awards by category: Academic interests/achievement:* biological sciences, business, communication, computer science, education, engineering/technologies, English, foreign languages, general academic interests/achievements, health fields, mathematics, physical sciences, social sciences. *Creative arts/performance:* art/fine arts, general creative arts/performance, journalism/publications, music, theater/drama. *Special achievements/activities:* community service, general special achievements/activities. *Special characteristics:* general special characteristics.

LOANS *Programs:* Federal Direct (Subsidized and Unsubsidized Stafford, PLUS), FFEL (PLUS), Perkins, Federal Nursing.

WORK-STUDY *Federal work-study:* Total amount: $478,101; jobs available.

APPLYING FOR FINANCIAL AID *Required financial aid form:* FAFSA.

CONTACT Tamie L. Nguyen, Director of Financial Aid, California State University, Los Angeles, 5151 State University Drive, Los Angeles, CA 90032, 323-343-6260. *Fax:* 323-343-3166. *E-mail:* tnguyen10@cslanet.calstatela.edu.

CALIFORNIA STATE UNIVERSITY, MONTEREY BAY
Seaside, CA

Tuition & fees (CA res): $4517   **Average undergraduate aid package: $9181**

ABOUT THE INSTITUTION State-supported, coed. 20 undergraduate majors. Federal methodology is used as a basis for awarding need-based institutional aid.

UNDERGRADUATE EXPENSES for 2009–10 *Tuition, state resident:* full-time $0. *Tuition, nonresident:* full-time $11,160; part-time $372 per unit. *Required fees:* full-time $4517; $1167 per term. Full-time tuition and fees vary according to degree level. Part-time tuition and fees vary according to degree level. *College room and board:* $8290; *Room only:* $5340. Room and board charges vary according to board plan and housing facility. *Payment plans:* Installment, deferred payment.

FRESHMAN FINANCIAL AID (Fall 2009, est.) 763 applied for aid; of those 66% were deemed to have need. 93% of freshmen with need received aid; of those 24% had need fully met. *Average percent of need met:* 70% (excluding resources awarded to replace EFC). *Average financial aid package:* $9438 (excluding resources awarded to replace EFC).

UNDERGRADUATE FINANCIAL AID (Fall 2009, est.) 2,814 applied for aid; of those 79% were deemed to have need. 91% of undergraduates with need received aid; of those 18% had need fully met. *Average percent of need met:* 74% (excluding resources awarded to replace EFC). *Average financial aid package:* $9181 (excluding resources awarded to replace EFC).

GIFT AID (NEED-BASED) *Total amount:* $12,985,355 (54% federal, 45% state, 1% institutional). *Receiving aid:* Freshmen: 26% (246); all full-time undergraduates: 40% (1,584). *Average award:* Freshmen: $9244; Undergraduates: $7782. *Scholarships, grants, and awards:* Federal Pell, FSEOG, state, private, college/university gift aid from institutional funds.

GIFT AID (NON-NEED-BASED) *Total amount:* $247,964 (100% external sources). *Receiving aid:* Freshmen: 6% (60). Undergraduates: 4% (171). *Scholarships, grants, and awards by category: Academic interests/achievement:* business, general academic interests/achievements. *Special achievements/activities:* leadership. *Special characteristics:* children and siblings of alumni, general special characteristics, local/state students. *Tuition waivers:* Full or partial for employees or children of employees, senior citizens.

LOANS *Student loans:* $10,683,211 (56% need-based, 44% non-need-based). 63% of past graduating class borrowed through all loan programs. *Average indebtedness per student:* $15,254. *Average need-based loan:* Freshmen: $3288. Undergraduates: $4138. *Parent loans:* $2,374,283 (100% non-need-based). *Programs:* Federal Direct (Subsidized and Unsubsidized Stafford, PLUS), Perkins.

WORK-STUDY *Federal work-study:* Total amount: $149,445; jobs available. *State or other work-study/employment:* Part-time jobs available.

ATHLETIC AWARDS Total amount: $292,050 (100% non-need-based).

APPLYING FOR FINANCIAL AID *Required financial aid forms:* FAFSA, state aid form. *Financial aid deadline (priority):* 3/2.

CONTACT Financial Aid Office, California State University, Monterey Bay, 100 Campus Center, Building 47, Seaside, CA 93955-8001, 831-582-5100. *Fax:* 831-582-3782.

CALIFORNIA STATE UNIVERSITY, NORTHRIDGE
Northridge, CA

Tuition & fees: N/R   **Average undergraduate aid package: $12,547**

ABOUT THE INSTITUTION State-supported, coed. 47 undergraduate majors. Federal methodology is used as a basis for awarding need-based institutional aid.

FRESHMAN FINANCIAL AID (Fall 2008) 3,472 applied for aid; of those 86% were deemed to have need. 100% of freshmen with need received aid. *Average financial aid package:* $8447 (excluding resources awarded to replace EFC). 2% of all full-time freshmen had no need and received non-need-based gift aid.

UNDERGRADUATE FINANCIAL AID (Fall 2008) 15,508 applied for aid; of those 93% were deemed to have need. 100% of undergraduates with need received aid. *Average financial aid package:* $12,547 (excluding resources awarded to replace EFC). 4% of all full-time undergraduates had no need and received non-need-based gift aid.

GIFT AID (NEED-BASED) *Total amount:* $89,103,114 (48% federal, 52% state). *Receiving aid:* Freshmen: 54% (2,433); all full-time undergraduates: 50% (11,630). *Average award:* Freshmen: $7804; Undergraduates: $9690. *Scholarships, grants, and awards:* Federal Pell, FSEOG, state, private, college/university gift aid from institutional funds.

GIFT AID (NON-NEED-BASED) *Total amount:* $2,187,889 (54% institutional, 46% external sources). *Receiving aid:* Freshmen: 2% (86). Undergraduates: 22% (5,146). *Average award:* Freshmen: $1462. Undergraduates: $1615. *Scholarships, grants, and awards by category: Academic interests/achievement:* business, communication, computer science, education, engineering/technologies, English, general academic interests/achievements, mathematics, social sciences. *Creative arts/performance:* journalism/publications, music. *Special achievements/activities:* leadership. *Tuition waivers:* Full or partial for employees or children of employees, senior citizens.

LOANS *Student loans:* $60,941,165 (59% need-based, 41% non-need-based). 39% of past graduating class borrowed through all loan programs. *Average indebtedness per student:* $14,691. *Average need-based loan:* Freshmen: $3565. Undergraduates: $6000. *Parent loans:* $1,841,909 (100% non-need-based). *Programs:* FFEL (Subsidized and Unsubsidized Stafford, PLUS), Perkins.

WORK-STUDY *Federal work-study:* Total amount: $1,731,991; 501 jobs averaging $2726.

ATHLETIC AWARDS Total amount: $1,581,663 (100% non-need-based).

APPLYING FOR FINANCIAL AID *Required financial aid forms:* FAFSA, state aid form. *Financial aid deadline (priority):* 3/2. *Notification date:* Continuous beginning 4/1.

CONTACT Lili Vidal, Director of Financial Aid and Scholarships, California State University, Northridge, 18111 Nordhoff Street, Northridge, CA 91330-8307, 818-677-4085. *Fax:* 818-677-3047. *E-mail:* financial.aid@csun.edu.

CALIFORNIA STATE UNIVERSITY, SACRAMENTO
Sacramento, CA

Tuition & fees: N/R   **Average undergraduate aid package: $7030**

ABOUT THE INSTITUTION State-supported, coed. 55 undergraduate majors. Federal methodology is used as a basis for awarding need-based institutional aid.

FRESHMAN FINANCIAL AID (Fall 2008) 2,608 applied for aid; of those 87% were deemed to have need. 68% of freshmen with need received aid; of those 11% had need fully met. *Average percent of need met:* 53% (excluding resources awarded to replace EFC). *Average financial aid package:* $7030 (excluding resources awarded to replace EFC). 1% of all full-time freshmen had no need and received non-need-based gift aid.

UNDERGRADUATE FINANCIAL AID (Fall 2008) 15,970 applied for aid; of those 93% were deemed to have need. 90% of undergraduates with need received aid; of those 12% had need fully met. *Average percent of need met:* 90% (excluding resources awarded to replace EFC). *Average financial aid package:* $7030 (excluding resources awarded to replace EFC). 1% of all full-time undergraduates had no need and received non-need-based gift aid.

GIFT AID (NEED-BASED) *Total amount:* $64,245,914 (48% federal, 49% state, 1% institutional, 2% external sources). *Receiving aid:* Freshmen: 38% (1,032); all full-time undergraduates: 52% (9,130). *Average award:* Freshmen: $3871; Undergraduates: $5716. *Scholarships, grants, and awards:* Federal Pell, FSEOG, state, private, college/university gift aid from institutional funds, Federal Nursing.

GIFT AID (NON-NEED-BASED) *Total amount:* $34,314 (100% external sources). *Receiving aid:* Freshmen: 8% (227). Undergraduates: 6% (1,044). *Average award:* Freshmen: $646. Undergraduates: $1250. *Tuition waivers:* Full or partial for employees or children of employees, senior citizens.

LOANS *Student loans:* $57,248,143 (56% need-based, 44% non-need-based). 35% of past graduating class borrowed through all loan programs. *Average indebtedness per student:* $12,473. *Average need-based loan:* Freshmen: $1716. Undergraduates: $4072. *Parent loans:* $5,561,065 (100% non-need-based). *Programs:* FFEL (Subsidized and Unsubsidized Stafford, PLUS), Perkins, Federal Nursing.

WORK-STUDY *Federal work-study:* Total amount: $873,629; jobs available. *State or other work-study/employment:* Total amount: $171,727 (100% need-based). Part-time jobs available.

ATHLETIC AWARDS Total amount: $2,705,017 (100% need-based).

APPLYING FOR FINANCIAL AID *Required financial aid form:* FAFSA. *Financial aid deadline:* Continuous. *Notification date:* Continuous.

CONTACT Financial Aid Office, California State University, Sacramento, 6000 J Street, Sacramento, CA 95819-6044, 916-278-6554. *Fax:* 916-278-6082.

CALIFORNIA STATE UNIVERSITY, SAN BERNARDINO
San Bernardino, CA

Tuition & fees (CA res): $5373   **Average undergraduate aid package: $10,373**

ABOUT THE INSTITUTION State-supported, coed. 52 undergraduate majors. Federal methodology is used as a basis for awarding need-based institutional aid.

UNDERGRADUATE EXPENSES for 2010–11 *Tuition, state resident:* full-time $0. *Tuition, nonresident:* full-time $11,445; part-time $226 per unit. *Required fees:* full-time $5373. Part-time tuition and fees vary according to course load. Room and board charges vary according to board plan and housing facility.

FRESHMAN FINANCIAL AID (Fall 2009, est.) 1,610 applied for aid; of those 87% were deemed to have need. 98% of freshmen with need received aid; of those 8% had need fully met. *Average percent of need met:* 68% (excluding resources awarded to replace EFC). *Average financial aid package:* $10,448 (excluding resources awarded to replace EFC). 1% of all full-time freshmen had no need and received non-need-based gift aid.

UNDERGRADUATE FINANCIAL AID (Fall 2009, est.) 9,691 applied for aid; of those 91% were deemed to have need. 98% of undergraduates with need received aid; of those 7% had need fully met. *Average percent of need met:* 64% (excluding resources awarded to replace EFC). *Average financial aid package:* $10,373 (excluding resources awarded to replace EFC). 1% of all full-time undergraduates had no need and received non-need-based gift aid.

GIFT AID (NEED-BASED) *Total amount:* $67,126,801 (50% federal, 47% state, 2% institutional, 1% external sources). *Receiving aid:* Freshmen: 61% (1,169); all full-time undergraduates: 59% (7,237). *Average award:* Freshmen: $8602; Undergraduates: $7810. *Scholarships, grants, and awards:* Federal Pell, FSEOG, state, private, college/university gift aid from institutional funds, Academic Competitiveness Grants, National SMART Grants.

GIFT AID (NON-NEED-BASED) *Total amount:* $308,118 (100% institutional). *Receiving aid:* Freshmen: 8% (144). Undergraduates: 6% (757). *Average award:* Freshmen: $2900. Undergraduates: $3188. *Scholarships, grants, and awards by category: Academic interests/achievement:* biological sciences, business, computer science, education, foreign languages, general academic interests/achievements, health fields, mathematics, physical sciences, social sciences. *Creative arts/performance:* art/fine arts, general creative arts/performance, journalism/publications, music, theater/drama. *Special achievements/activities:* community service, general special achievements/activities, hobbies/interests,

memberships. *Special characteristics:* children of public servants, children with a deceased or disabled parent, first-generation college students, handicapped students. *Tuition waivers:* Full or partial for employees or children of employees.

LOANS *Student loans:* $42,721,294 (92% need-based, 8% non-need-based). *Average need-based loan:* Freshmen: $2879. Undergraduates: $3569. *Parent loans:* $37,933,252 (100% non-need-based). *Programs:* Federal Direct (Subsidized and Unsubsidized Stafford, PLUS), Perkins.

WORK-STUDY *Federal work-study:* Total amount: $1,306,468; 348 jobs averaging $4051.

ATHLETIC AWARDS Total amount: $569,169 (100% non-need-based).

APPLYING FOR FINANCIAL AID *Required financial aid forms:* FAFSA, state aid form. *Financial aid deadline (priority):* 3/2. *Notification date:* Continuous beginning 4/1.

CONTACT Ms. Roseanna Ruiz, Director of Financial Aid, California State University, San Bernardino, 5500 University Parkway, San Bernardino, CA 92407-2397, 909-537-5227. *Fax:* 909-537-4024.

CALIFORNIA STATE UNIVERSITY, SAN MARCOS
San Marcos, CA

CONTACT Addalou Davis, Director of Financial Aid, California State University, San Marcos, 333 South Twin Oaks Valley Road, San Marcos, CA 92096-0001, 760-750-4852. *Fax:* 760-750-3047. *E-mail:* finaid@csusm.edu.

CALIFORNIA STATE UNIVERSITY, STANISLAUS
Turlock, CA

Tuition & fees (CA res): $4840   **Average undergraduate aid package: $10,247**

ABOUT THE INSTITUTION State-supported, coed. 38 undergraduate majors. Federal methodology is used as a basis for awarding need-based institutional aid.

UNDERGRADUATE EXPENSES for 2010–11 *Tuition, state resident:* full-time $0. *Tuition, nonresident:* full-time $11,160; part-time $372 per unit. *Required fees:* full-time $4840. Full-time tuition and fees vary according to course load, degree level, reciprocity agreements, and student level. Part-time tuition and fees vary according to course load, degree level, reciprocity agreements, and student level. *College room and board:* $8880; *Room only:* $6038. Room and board charges vary according to board plan and housing facility. *Payment plans:* Installment, deferred payment.

FRESHMAN FINANCIAL AID (Fall 2009, est.) 602 applied for aid; of those 83% were deemed to have need. 98% of freshmen with need received aid; of those 16% had need fully met. *Average percent of need met:* 63% (excluding resources awarded to replace EFC). *Average financial aid package:* $9879 (excluding resources awarded to replace EFC). 1% of all full-time freshmen had no need and received non-need-based gift aid.

UNDERGRADUATE FINANCIAL AID (Fall 2009, est.) 4,431 applied for aid; of those 92% were deemed to have need. 98% of undergraduates with need received aid; of those 4% had need fully met. *Average percent of need met:* 56% (excluding resources awarded to replace EFC). *Average financial aid package:* $10,247 (excluding resources awarded to replace EFC). 1% of all full-time undergraduates had no need and received non-need-based gift aid.

GIFT AID (NEED-BASED) *Total amount:* $29,227,440 (48% federal, 51% state, 1% institutional). *Receiving aid:* Freshmen: 47% (379); all full-time undergraduates: 65% (3,183). *Average award:* Freshmen: $5586; Undergraduates: $6103. *Scholarships, grants, and awards:* Federal Pell, FSEOG, state, private, college/university gift aid from institutional funds.

GIFT AID (NON-NEED-BASED) *Total amount:* $1,260,783 (60% institutional, 40% external sources). *Receiving aid:* Freshmen: 3% (21). Undergraduates: 4% (205). *Average award:* Freshmen: $4833. Undergraduates: $4238. *Scholarships, grants, and awards by category: Academic interests/achievement:* 127 awards ($228,600 total): agriculture, area/ethnic studies, biological sciences, business, communication, computer science, education, English, foreign languages, general academic interests/achievements, health fields, humanities, international studies, mathematics, physical sciences, premedicine, social sciences. *Creative arts/performance:* 45 awards ($52,520 total): art/fine arts, music. *Special achievements/activities:* 128 awards ($429,775 total): com-

munity service, general special achievements/activities, leadership, memberships. *Special characteristics:* 40 awards ($37,240 total): children of faculty/staff, ethnic background, first-generation college students, general special characteristics, local/state students, members of minority groups. *Tuition waivers:* Full or partial for employees or children of employees, adult students, senior citizens. **LOANS** *Student loans:* $17,545,085 (56% need-based, 44% non-need-based). 25% of past graduating class borrowed through all loan programs. *Average indebtedness per student:* $16,500. *Average need-based loan:* Freshmen: $4939. Undergraduates: $5402. *Parent loans:* $1,237,289 (100% non-need-based). *Programs:* FFEL (Subsidized and Unsubsidized Stafford, PLUS), Perkins, college/university, private alternative loans.
WORK-STUDY *Federal work-study:* Total amount: $541,172; 168 jobs averaging $3478. *State or other work-study/employment:* Part-time jobs available.
ATHLETIC AWARDS Total amount: $417,100 (100% non-need-based). ·
APPLYING FOR FINANCIAL AID *Required financial aid forms:* FAFSA, state aid form. *Financial aid deadline (priority):* 3/2. *Notification date:* Continuous beginning 3/15. Students must reply within 3 weeks of notification.
CONTACT Ms. Noelia Gonzalez, Director, Financial Aid/Scholarships Department, California State University, Stanislaus, One University Circle, Turlock, CA 95382, 209-664-6583 or toll-free 800-300-7420 (in-state). *Fax:* 209-667-3337. *E-mail:* ngonzalez4@csustan.edu.

CALIFORNIA UNIVERSITY OF PENNSYLVANIA
California, PA

CONTACT Financial Aid Office, California University of Pennsylvania, 250 University Avenue, California, PA 15419-1394, 724-938-4415.

CALUMET COLLEGE OF SAINT JOSEPH
Whiting, IN

Tuition & fees: $13,220	Average undergraduate aid package: $11,510

ABOUT THE INSTITUTION Independent Roman Catholic, coed. 28 undergraduate majors. Federal methodology is used as a basis for awarding need-based institutional aid.
UNDERGRADUATE EXPENSES for 2009–10 *Tuition:* full-time $13,050; part-time $410 per credit hour. *Required fees:* full-time $170; $80 per term. *Payment plan:* Installment.
FRESHMAN FINANCIAL AID (Fall 2009, est.) 147 applied for aid; of those 76% were deemed to have need. 98% of freshmen with need received aid; of those 5% had need fully met. *Average percent of need met:* 78% (excluding resources awarded to replace EFC). *Average financial aid package:* $11,579 (excluding resources awarded to replace EFC). 1% of all full-time freshmen had no need and received non-need-based gift aid.
UNDERGRADUATE FINANCIAL AID (Fall 2009, est.) 588 applied for aid; of those 84% were deemed to have need. 99% of undergraduates with need received aid; of those 4% had need fully met. *Average percent of need met:* 72% (excluding resources awarded to replace EFC). *Average financial aid package:* $11,510 (excluding resources awarded to replace EFC). 1% of all full-time undergraduates had no need and received non-need-based gift aid.
GIFT AID (NEED-BASED) *Total amount:* $3,405,090 (56% federal, 25% state, 15% institutional, 4% external sources). *Receiving aid:* Freshmen: 59% (92); all full-time undergraduates: 61% (378). *Average award:* Freshmen: $6702; Undergraduates: $7300. *Scholarships, grants, and awards:* Federal Pell, FSEOG, state, private, college/university gift aid from institutional funds, United Negro College Fund.
GIFT AID (NON-NEED-BASED) *Total amount:* $222,027 (83% institutional, 17% external sources). *Receiving aid:* Freshmen: 52% (81). Undergraduates: 57% (356). *Average award:* Freshmen: $3000. Undergraduates: $2400. *Scholarships, grants, and awards by category:* Academic interests/achievement: 8 awards ($13,000 total). *Special characteristics:* children and siblings of alumni. *Tuition waivers:* Full or partial for children of alumni, employees or children of employees, senior citizens.
LOANS *Student loans:* $6,532,481 (87% need-based, 13% non-need-based). 80% of past graduating class borrowed through all loan programs. *Average indebtedness per student:* $22,534. *Average need-based loan:* Freshmen: $2857.

Undergraduates: $3591. *Parent loans:* $135,553 (56% need-based, 44% non-need-based). *Programs:* Federal Direct (Subsidized and Unsubsidized Stafford, PLUS).
WORK-STUDY *Federal work-study:* Total amount: $17,558; 16 jobs averaging $1097. *State or other work-study/employment:* 1 part-time job averaging $1365.
ATHLETIC AWARDS Total amount: $1,384,637 (84% need-based, 16% non-need-based).
APPLYING FOR FINANCIAL AID *Required financial aid form:* FAFSA. *Financial aid deadline (priority):* 3/1. *Notification date:* Continuous.
CONTACT Gina Pirtle, Director of Admissions and Financial Aid, Calumet College of Saint Joseph, 2400 New York Avenue, Whiting, IN 46394, 219-473-4379 or toll-free 877-700-9100. *E-mail:* gpirtle@ccsj.edu.

CALVARY BIBLE COLLEGE AND THEOLOGICAL SEMINARY
Kansas City, MO

Tuition & fees: $8328	Average undergraduate aid package: N/A

ABOUT THE INSTITUTION Independent nondenominational, coed. 17 undergraduate majors. Both federal and institutional methodology are used as a basis for awarding need-based institutional aid.
UNDERGRADUATE EXPENSES for 2010–11 *Comprehensive fee:* $12,728 includes full-time tuition ($7560), mandatory fees ($768), and room and board ($4400). *College room only:* $2200. Room and board charges vary according to housing facility. *Part-time tuition:* $280 per credit hour. *Payment plan:* Guaranteed tuition.
GIFT AID (NEED-BASED) *Total amount:* $550,057 (65% federal, 17% institutional, 18% external sources). *Scholarships, grants, and awards:* Federal Pell, FSEOG, private, college/university gift aid from institutional funds.
GIFT AID (NON-NEED-BASED) *Scholarships, grants, and awards by category:* Academic interests/achievement: general academic interests/achievements. Creative arts/performance: general creative arts/performance. Special achievements/activities: general special achievements/activities, religious involvement. Special characteristics: children and siblings of alumni, children of educators, children of faculty/staff, relatives of clergy, religious affiliation, siblings of current students, spouses of current students. *Tuition waivers:* Full or partial for employees or children of employees.
LOANS *Student loans:* $943,386 (100% need-based). *Parent loans:* $16,387 (100% need-based). *Programs:* FFEL (Subsidized and Unsubsidized Stafford, PLUS).
APPLYING FOR FINANCIAL AID *Required financial aid forms:* FAFSA, institution's own form. *Financial aid deadline:* 4/1 (priority: 3/1). *Notification date:* Continuous beginning 5/1.
CONTACT Financial Aid Administrator, Calvary Bible College and Theological Seminary, 15800 Calvary Road, Kansas City, MO 64147-1341, 816-322-0110 Ext. 1323 or toll-free 800-326-3960. *Fax:* 816-331-4474. *E-mail:* finaid@calvary.edu.

CALVIN COLLEGE
Grand Rapids, MI

Tuition & fees: $24,035	Average undergraduate aid package: $17,931

ABOUT THE INSTITUTION Independent Christian Reformed, coed. 85 undergraduate majors. Both federal and institutional methodology are used as a basis for awarding need-based institutional aid.
UNDERGRADUATE EXPENSES for 2009–10 *Comprehensive fee:* $32,310 includes full-time tuition ($23,810), mandatory fees ($225), and room and board ($8275). Full-time tuition and fees vary according to degree level and program. Room and board charges vary according to board plan. *Part-time tuition:* $570 per credit hour. Part-time tuition and fees vary according to course load and degree level. *Payment plans:* Tuition prepayment, installment.
FRESHMAN FINANCIAL AID (Fall 2009, est.) 843 applied for aid; of those 78% were deemed to have need. 100% of freshmen with need received aid; of those 20% had need fully met. *Average percent of need met:* 79% (excluding resources awarded to replace EFC). *Average financial aid package:* $18,792 (excluding resources awarded to replace EFC). 27% of all full-time freshmen had no need and received non-need-based gift aid.

UNDERGRADUATE FINANCIAL AID (Fall 2009, est.) 3,093 applied for aid; of those 81% were deemed to have need. 100% of undergraduates with need received aid; of those 22% had need fully met. *Average percent of need met:* 78% (excluding resources awarded to replace EFC). *Average financial aid package:* $17,931 (excluding resources awarded to replace EFC). 29% of all full-time undergraduates had no need and received non-need-based gift aid.

GIFT AID (NEED-BASED) *Total amount:* $29,228,214 (17% federal, 6% state, 75% institutional, 2% external sources). *Receiving aid:* Freshmen: 69% (655); all full-time undergraduates: 65% (2,505). *Average award:* Freshmen: $13,132; Undergraduates: $11,375. *Scholarships, grants, and awards:* Federal Pell, FSEOG, state, private, college/university gift aid from institutional funds.

GIFT AID (NON-NEED-BASED) *Total amount:* $8,438,899 (1% federal, 90% institutional, 9% external sources). *Receiving aid:* Freshmen: 11% (108). Undergraduates: 11% (427). *Average award:* Freshmen: $5565. Undergraduates: $4509. *Scholarships, grants, and awards by category: Academic interests/ achievement:* $10,500,000 total: biological sciences, business, communication, computer science, education, engineering/technologies, English, foreign languages, general academic interests/achievements, health fields, humanities, international studies, mathematics, physical sciences, premedicine, religion/ biblical studies, social sciences. *Creative arts/performance:* $200,000 total: art/fine arts, music, performing arts, theater/drama. *Special achievements/ activities:* $50,000 total: community service, religious involvement. *Special characteristics:* $6,400,000 total: adult students, children and siblings of alumni, children of faculty/staff, children of union members/company employees, ethnic background, first-generation college students, handicapped students, international students, members of minority groups, religious affiliation, twins. *Tuition waivers:* Full or partial for employees or children of employees.

LOANS *Student loans:* $24,144,987 (67% need-based, 33% non-need-based). 68% of past graduating class borrowed through all loan programs. *Average indebtedness per student:* $28,500. *Average need-based loan:* Freshmen: $3905. Undergraduates: $6270. *Parent loans:* $2,342,264 (29% need-based, 71% non-need-based). *Programs:* Federal Direct (Subsidized and Unsubsidized Stafford, PLUS), Perkins, state, college/university, alternative loans.

WORK-STUDY *Federal work-study:* Total amount: $2,224,000; 1,061 jobs averaging $1331. *State or other work-study/employment:* Total amount: $2,048,000 (5% need-based, 95% non-need-based). 1,062 part-time jobs averaging $1390.

APPLYING FOR FINANCIAL AID *Required financial aid form:* FAFSA. *Financial aid deadline (priority):* 2/15. *Notification date:* Continuous beginning 3/15.

CONTACT Mr. Craig Heerema, Financial Aid Administrator, Calvin College, Spoelhof Center 263, Grand Rapids, MI 49546, 616-526-6134 or toll-free 800-688-0122. *Fax:* 616-526-6883. *E-mail:* cheerema@calvin.edu.

CAMBRIDGE COLLEGE
Cambridge, MA

Tuition & fees: $10,950	Average undergraduate aid package: $4328

ABOUT THE INSTITUTION Independent, coed. 7 undergraduate majors. Federal methodology is used as a basis for awarding need-based institutional aid.

UNDERGRADUATE EXPENSES for 2009–10 *Tuition:* full-time $10,950; part-time $365 per credit. *Payment plan:* Installment.

FRESHMAN FINANCIAL AID (Fall 2009, est.) 35 applied for aid; of those 97% were deemed to have need. 94% of freshmen with need received aid. *Average percent of need met:* 26% (excluding resources awarded to replace EFC). *Average financial aid package:* $3478 (excluding resources awarded to replace EFC).

UNDERGRADUATE FINANCIAL AID (Fall 2009, est.) 230 applied for aid; of those 97% were deemed to have need. 100% of undergraduates with need received aid. *Average percent of need met:* 31% (excluding resources awarded to replace EFC). *Average financial aid package:* $4328 (excluding resources awarded to replace EFC).

GIFT AID (NEED-BASED) *Total amount:* $1,895,512 (76% federal, 19% state, 2% institutional, 3% external sources). *Receiving aid:* Freshmen: 50% (26); all full-time undergraduates: 53% (163). *Average award:* Freshmen: $5092; Undergraduates: $5277. *Scholarships, grants, and awards:* Federal Pell, FSEOG, state, private, college/university gift aid from institutional funds.

GIFT AID (NON-NEED-BASED) *Scholarships, grants, and awards by category: Academic interests/achievement:* education. *Tuition waivers:* Full or partial for employees or children of employees.

LOANS *Student loans:* $6,584,195 (100% need-based). *Average need-based loan:* Freshmen: $3478. Undergraduates: $4328. *Parent loans:* $6000 (100% need-based). *Programs:* FFEL (Subsidized and Unsubsidized Stafford, PLUS), Perkins.

WORK-STUDY *Federal work-study:* Total amount: $57,925; jobs available.

APPLYING FOR FINANCIAL AID *Required financial aid forms:* FAFSA, institution's own form. *Financial aid deadline (priority):* 9/1. *Notification date:* Continuous beginning 6/1.

CONTACT Dr. Frank Lauder, Director of Financial Aid, Cambridge College, 1000 Massachusetts Avenue, Cambridge, MA 02138, 617-868-1000 Ext. 1440 or toll-free 800-877-4723. *Fax:* 617-349-3561. *E-mail:* francis.lauder@cambridgecollege.edu.

CAMERON UNIVERSITY
Lawton, OK

Tuition & fees (OK res): $5415	Average undergraduate aid package: $12,100

ABOUT THE INSTITUTION State-supported, coed. 41 undergraduate majors. Federal methodology is used as a basis for awarding need-based institutional aid.

UNDERGRADUATE EXPENSES for 2010–11 *Tuition, state resident:* full-time $4110; part-time $93.50 per credit hour. *Tuition, nonresident:* full-time $9974; part-time $289 per credit hour. *Required fees:* full-time $1305; $43.50 per credit hour. Full-time tuition and fees vary according to course load. Part-time tuition and fees vary according to course load. *College room and board:* $3589; *Room only:* $2586. Room and board charges vary according to board plan. *Payment plan:* Installment.

FRESHMAN FINANCIAL AID (Fall 2008) 688 applied for aid; of those 88% were deemed to have need. 88% of freshmen with need received aid; of those 83% had need fully met. *Average percent of need met:* 92% (excluding resources awarded to replace EFC). *Average financial aid package:* $12,100 (excluding resources awarded to replace EFC). 38% of all full-time freshmen had no need and received non-need-based gift aid.

UNDERGRADUATE FINANCIAL AID (Fall 2008) 2,532 applied for aid; of those 86% were deemed to have need. 93% of undergraduates with need received aid; of those 92% had need fully met. *Average percent of need met:* 89% (excluding resources awarded to replace EFC). *Average financial aid package:* $12,100 (excluding resources awarded to replace EFC). 42% of all full-time undergraduates had no need and received non-need-based gift aid.

GIFT AID (NEED-BASED) *Total amount:* $9,227,512 (68% federal, 24% state, 4% institutional, 4% external sources). *Receiving aid:* Freshmen: 52% (500); all full-time undergraduates: 51% (1,920). *Average award:* Freshmen: $4000; Undergraduates: $3500. *Scholarships, grants, and awards:* Federal Pell, FSEOG, state, private, college/university gift aid from institutional funds.

GIFT AID (NON-NEED-BASED) *Total amount:* $1,167,341 (8% state, 24% institutional, 68% external sources). *Receiving aid:* Freshmen: 48% (462). Undergraduates: 32% (1,205). *Average award:* Freshmen: $750. Undergraduates: $500. *Scholarships, grants, and awards by category: Academic interests/ achievement:* agriculture, biological sciences, business, communication, computer science, education, engineering/technologies, English, foreign languages, general academic interests/achievements, mathematics, military science, social sciences. *Creative arts/performance:* art/fine arts, creative writing, debating, journalism/ publications, music, theater/drama. *Special achievements/activities:* leadership. *Special characteristics:* members of minority groups. *Tuition waivers:* Full or partial for employees or children of employees, senior citizens.

LOANS *Student loans:* $9,601,746 (55% need-based, 45% non-need-based). 30% of past graduating class borrowed through all loan programs. *Average indebtedness per student:* $7000. *Average need-based loan:* Freshmen: $1200. Undergraduates: $5000. *Parent loans:* $52,293 (100% non-need-based). *Programs:* FFEL (Subsidized and Unsubsidized Stafford, PLUS).

WORK-STUDY *Federal work-study:* Total amount: $178,505; jobs available. *State or other work-study/employment:* Total amount: $749,593 (100% non-need-based). Part-time jobs available.

ATHLETIC AWARDS Total amount: $526,833 (100% non-need-based).

APPLYING FOR FINANCIAL AID *Required financial aid form:* FAFSA. *Financial aid deadline:* Continuous. *Notification date:* Continuous beginning 4/1. Students must reply by 8/7 or within 2 weeks of notification.

CONTACT Carol Claiborne, Interim Financial Aid Director, Cameron University, 2800 West Gore Boulevard, Lawton, OK 73505-6377, 580-581-2292 or toll-free 888-454-7600. *Fax:* 580-581-2556.

CAMPBELLSVILLE UNIVERSITY
Campbellsville, KY

Tuition & fees: $19,710	Average undergraduate aid package: $14,521

ABOUT THE INSTITUTION Independent religious, coed. 55 undergraduate majors. Federal methodology is used as a basis for awarding need-based institutional aid.

UNDERGRADUATE EXPENSES for 2010–11 *Comprehensive fee:* $26,450 includes full-time tuition ($19,310), mandatory fees ($400), and room and board ($6740). Room and board charges vary according to housing facility. *Part-time tuition:* $805 per credit hour. *Payment plan:* Installment.

FRESHMAN FINANCIAL AID (Fall 2008) 371 applied for aid; of those 95% were deemed to have need. 100% of freshmen with need received aid; of those 22% had need fully met. *Average percent of need met:* 78% (excluding resources awarded to replace EFC). *Average financial aid package:* $16,321 (excluding resources awarded to replace EFC). 5% of all full-time freshmen had no need and received non-need-based gift aid.

UNDERGRADUATE FINANCIAL AID (Fall 2008) 1,557 applied for aid; of those 94% were deemed to have need. 99% of undergraduates with need received aid; of those 17% had need fully met. *Average percent of need met:* 74% (excluding resources awarded to replace EFC). *Average financial aid package:* $14,521 (excluding resources awarded to replace EFC). 5% of all full-time undergraduates had no need and received non-need-based gift aid.

GIFT AID (NEED-BASED) *Total amount:* $14,773,437 (21% federal, 33% state, 41% institutional, 5% external sources). *Receiving aid:* Freshmen: 79% (350); all full-time undergraduates: 83% (1,418). *Average award:* Freshmen: $13,510; Undergraduates: $11,351. *Scholarships, grants, and awards:* Federal Pell, FSEOG, state, college/university gift aid from institutional funds.

GIFT AID (NON-NEED-BASED) *Total amount:* $1,640,395 (19% state, 69% institutional, 12% external sources). *Receiving aid:* Freshmen: 11% (50). Undergraduates: 9% (152). *Average award:* Freshmen: $6763. Undergraduates: $5340. *Scholarships, grants, and awards by category: Academic interests/achievement:* 495 awards ($2,852,361 total): biological sciences, business, communication, computer science, education, English, general academic interests/achievements, humanities, mathematics, physical sciences, premedicine, religion/biblical studies, social sciences. *Creative arts/performance:* 160 awards ($483,720 total): art/fine arts, journalism/publications, music, theater/drama. *Special achievements/activities:* 275 awards ($635,235 total): cheerleading/drum major, junior miss, leadership, religious involvement. *Special characteristics:* 142 awards ($775,465 total): adult students, children of educators, children of faculty/staff, international students, relatives of clergy, religious affiliation, veterans. *Tuition waivers:* Full or partial for employees or children of employees, senior citizens.

LOANS *Student loans:* $8,407,165 (80% need-based, 20% non-need-based). 81% of past graduating class borrowed through all loan programs. *Average indebtedness per student:* $18,100. *Average need-based loan:* Freshmen: $2859. Undergraduates: $3785. *Parent loans:* $871,810 (40% need-based, 60% non-need-based). *Programs:* Federal Direct (Subsidized and Unsubsidized Stafford, PLUS), Perkins, college/university.

WORK-STUDY *Federal work-study:* Total amount: $611,826; 360 jobs averaging $1695. *State or other work-study/employment:* Total amount: $69,735 (28% need-based, 72% non-need-based). 36 part-time jobs averaging $1950.

ATHLETIC AWARDS Total amount: $2,302,239 (53% need-based, 47% non-need-based).

APPLYING FOR FINANCIAL AID *Required financial aid form:* FAFSA. *Financial aid deadline (priority):* 3/1. *Notification date:* Continuous beginning 3/15. Students must reply within 3 weeks of notification.

CONTACT Mr. Aaron Gabehart, Financial Aid Counselor, Campbellsville University, 1 University Drive, Campbellsville, KY 42718, 270-789-5305 or toll-free 800-264-6014. *Fax:* 270-789-5060. *E-mail:* finaid@campbellsville.edu.

CAMPBELL UNIVERSITY
Buies Creek, NC

Tuition & fees: N/R	Average undergraduate aid package: $31,629

ABOUT THE INSTITUTION Independent religious, coed. *Awards:* associate, bachelor's, and master's degrees. 85 undergraduate majors. *Total enrollment:* 4,743. Undergraduates: 2,934. Freshmen: 899. Federal methodology is used as a basis for awarding need-based institutional aid.

FRESHMAN FINANCIAL AID (Fall 2009, est.) 654 applied for aid; of those 89% were deemed to have need. 100% of freshmen with need received aid; of those 95% had need fully met. *Average percent of need met:* 80% (excluding resources awarded to replace EFC). *Average financial aid package:* $32,293 (excluding resources awarded to replace EFC). 28% of all full-time freshmen had no need and received non-need-based gift aid.

UNDERGRADUATE FINANCIAL AID (Fall 2009, est.) 3,746 applied for aid; of those 89% were deemed to have need. 100% of undergraduates with need received aid; of those 90% had need fully met. *Average percent of need met:* 80% (excluding resources awarded to replace EFC). *Average financial aid package:* $31,629 (excluding resources awarded to replace EFC). 25% of all full-time undergraduates had no need and received non-need-based gift aid.

GIFT AID (NEED-BASED) *Total amount:* $29,746,001 (17% federal, 26% state, 54% institutional, 3% external sources). *Receiving aid:* Freshmen: 62% (453); all full-time undergraduates: 69% (2,904). *Average award:* Freshmen: $7923; Undergraduates: $6504. *Scholarships, grants, and awards:* Federal Pell, FSEOG, state, private, college/university gift aid from institutional funds.

GIFT AID (NON-NEED-BASED) *Total amount:* $2,545,779 (1% federal, 15% state, 69% institutional, 15% external sources). *Receiving aid:* Freshmen: 77% (561). Undergraduates: 68% (2,859). *Average award:* Freshmen: $5203. Undergraduates: $4961. *Scholarships, grants, and awards by category: Academic interests/achievement:* 1,747 awards ($13,977,560 total): general academic interests/achievements. *Creative arts/performance:* 76 awards ($75,000 total): art/fine arts, creative writing, journalism/publications, music, theater/drama. *Special achievements/activities:* 27 awards ($85,000 total): cheerleading/drum major, religious involvement. *Special characteristics:* 84 awards ($859,947 total): children of faculty/staff. *ROTC:* Army.

LOANS *Student loans:* $26,554,247 (37% need-based, 63% non-need-based). 75% of past graduating class borrowed through all loan programs. *Average indebtedness per student:* $38,696. *Average need-based loan:* Freshmen: $3011. Undergraduates: $3998. *Parent loans:* $21,197,811 (98% need-based, 2% non-need-based). *Programs:* Federal Direct (Subsidized and Unsubsidized Stafford, PLUS), Perkins, state.

WORK-STUDY *Federal work-study:* Total amount: $734,581; 1,186 jobs averaging $619. *State or other work-study/employment:* Total amount: $618,861 (100% non-need-based). 604 part-time jobs averaging $773.

ATHLETIC AWARDS Total amount: $3,273,958 (91% need-based, 9% non-need-based).

APPLYING FOR FINANCIAL AID *Required financial aid form:* FAFSA. *Financial aid deadline (priority):* 2/15. *Notification date:* Continuous. Students must reply within 2 weeks of notification.

CONTACT Financial Aid Office, Campbell University, PO Box 36, Buies Creek, NC 27506, 910-893-1310 or toll-free 800-334-4111. *Fax:* 910-814-5788.

CANISIUS COLLEGE
Buffalo, NY

Tuition & fees: $29,512	Average undergraduate aid package: $24,558

ABOUT THE INSTITUTION Independent Roman Catholic (Jesuit), coed. 42 undergraduate majors. Federal methodology is used as a basis for awarding need-based institutional aid.

UNDERGRADUATE EXPENSES for 2009–10 *Comprehensive fee:* $40,068 includes full-time tuition ($28,455), mandatory fees ($1057), and room and board ($10,556). *College room only:* $6230. Full-time tuition and fees vary according to course load. Room and board charges vary according to board plan and housing facility. *Part-time tuition:* $812 per credit hour. *Part-time fees:* $20.50 per credit hour; $33 per term. Part-time tuition and fees vary according to course load. *Payment plans:* Installment, deferred payment.

FRESHMAN FINANCIAL AID (Fall 2009, est.) 641 applied for aid; of those 91% were deemed to have need. 100% of freshmen with need received aid; of those 37% had need fully met. *Average percent of need met:* 86% (excluding resources awarded to replace EFC). *Average financial aid package:* $26,843 (excluding resources awarded to replace EFC). 21% of all full-time freshmen had no need and received non-need-based gift aid.

UNDERGRADUATE FINANCIAL AID (Fall 2009, est.) 2,510 applied for aid; of those 93% were deemed to have need. 100% of undergraduates with need

received aid; of those 28% had need fully met. *Average percent of need met:* 81% (excluding resources awarded to replace EFC). *Average financial aid package:* $24,558 (excluding resources awarded to replace EFC). 20% of all full-time undergraduates had no need and received non-need-based gift aid.

GIFT AID (NEED-BASED) *Total amount:* $40,297,437 (13% federal, 10% state, 77% institutional). *Receiving aid:* Freshmen: 82% (579); all full-time undergraduates: 75% (2,303). *Average award:* Freshmen: $20,026; Undergraduates: $18,092. *Scholarships, grants, and awards:* Federal Pell, FSEOG, state, private, college/university gift aid from institutional funds.

GIFT AID (NON-NEED-BASED) *Total amount:* $3,566,933 (1% federal, 1% state, 97% institutional, 1% external sources). *Receiving aid:* Freshmen: 19% (134). Undergraduates: 14% (436). *Average award:* Freshmen: $11,145. Undergraduates: $13,797. *Scholarships, grants, and awards by category:* Academic interests/achievement: 2,376 awards ($25,147,740 total): general academic interests/achievements. *Creative arts/performance:* 60 awards ($117,500 total): art/fine arts, music. *Special achievements/activities:* 2 awards ($9898 total): religious involvement. *Special characteristics:* 477 awards ($3,535,042 total): children and siblings of alumni, children of educators, children of faculty/staff, international students, religious affiliation. *Tuition waivers:* Full or partial for employees or children of employees.

LOANS *Student loans:* $20,278,447 (71% need-based, 29% non-need-based). 77% of past graduating class borrowed through all loan programs. *Average indebtedness per student:* $33,645. *Average need-based loan:* Freshmen: $3294. Undergraduates: $4228. *Parent loans:* $8,287,535 (25% need-based, 75% non-need-based). *Programs:* FFEL (Subsidized and Unsubsidized Stafford, PLUS), Perkins, college/university.

WORK-STUDY *Federal work-study:* Total amount: $22,956; 558 jobs averaging $1703. *State or other work-study/employment:* Total amount: $40,716 (56% need-based, 44% non-need-based). Part-time jobs available.

ATHLETIC AWARDS Total amount: $1,792,585 (65% need-based, 35% non-need-based).

APPLYING FOR FINANCIAL AID *Required financial aid forms:* FAFSA, state aid form. *Financial aid deadline (priority):* 2/15. *Notification date:* Continuous beginning 3/1. Students must reply by 5/1.

CONTACT Mr. Curtis Gaume, Director of Student Financial Aid, Canisius College, 2001 Main Street, Buffalo, NY 14208-1098, 716-888-2300 or toll-free 800-843-1517. *Fax:* 716-888-2377. *E-mail:* gaume@canisius.edu.

CAPELLA UNIVERSITY
Minneapolis, MN

CONTACT University Services, Capella University, 222 South Ninth Street, Minneapolis, MN 55402, 888-227-3552 or toll-free 888-CAPELLA.

CAPITAL UNIVERSITY
Columbus, OH

CONTACT Pamela Varda, Office of Financial Aid, Capital University, 1 College and Main Street, Columbus, OH 43209-2394, 614-236-6511 or toll-free 800-289-6289. *Fax:* 614-236-6926. *E-mail:* finaid@capital.edu.

CAPITOL COLLEGE
Laurel, MD

Tuition & fees: N/R	Average undergraduate aid package: N/A

ABOUT THE INSTITUTION Independent, coed. *Awards:* associate, bachelor's, and master's degrees and post-bachelor's certificates. 13 undergraduate majors. *Total enrollment:* 699. Undergraduates: 309. Federal methodology is used as a basis for awarding need-based institutional aid.

UNDERGRADUATE EXPENSES for 2009–10 *Application fee:* $25. *Tuition:* part-time $619 per credit. *Required fees:* $25 per credit.

FRESHMAN FINANCIAL AID (Fall 2009, est.) 66 applied for aid; of those 98% were deemed to have need. 100% of freshmen with need received aid.

GIFT AID (NEED-BASED) *Total amount:* $2,116,754 (31% federal, 18% state, 48% institutional, 3% external sources). *Scholarships, grants, and awards:* Federal Pell, FSEOG, state, private, college/university gift aid from institutional funds.

GIFT AID (NON-NEED-BASED) *Total amount:* $78,450 (100% institutional). *Scholarships, grants, and awards by category:* Academic interests/achievement: general academic interests/achievements. *ROTC:* Army cooperative.

LOANS *Student loans:* $2,659,778 (100% need-based). *Parent loans:* $329,534 (100% need-based). *Programs:* Federal Direct (Subsidized and Unsubsidized Stafford, PLUS), FFEL (Subsidized and Unsubsidized Stafford, PLUS), Perkins.

WORK-STUDY *Federal work-study:* Total amount: $69,597; jobs available.

APPLYING FOR FINANCIAL AID *Required financial aid form:* FAFSA. *Financial aid deadline:* Continuous. *Notification date:* Continuous. Students must reply within 3 weeks of notification.

CONTACT Suzanne Thompson, Director of Financial Aid, Capitol College, 11301 Springfield Road, Laurel, MD 20708-9759, 301-369-2800 Ext. 3037 or toll-free 800-950-1992. *Fax:* 301-369-2328. *E-mail:* sthompson@capitol-college.edu.

CARDINAL STRITCH UNIVERSITY
Milwaukee, WI

CONTACT Financial Aid Director, Cardinal Stritch University, 6801 North Yates Road, Milwaukee, WI 53217-3985, 414-410-4000 or toll-free 800-347-8822 Ext. 4040.

CARIBBEAN UNIVERSITY
Bayamón, PR

CONTACT Financial Aid Office, Caribbean University, Box 493, Bayamón, PR 00960-0493, 787-780-0070.

CARLETON COLLEGE
Northfield, MN

Tuition & fees: $41,304	Average undergraduate aid package: $34,141

ABOUT THE INSTITUTION Independent, coed. 38 undergraduate majors. Both federal and institutional methodology are used as a basis for awarding need-based institutional aid.

UNDERGRADUATE EXPENSES for 2010–11 *Comprehensive fee:* $52,110 includes full-time tuition ($41,076), mandatory fees ($228), and room and board ($10,806). *College room only:* $5676. Room and board charges vary according to board plan. *Payment plan:* Installment.

FRESHMAN FINANCIAL AID (Fall 2009, est.) 406 applied for aid; of those 77% were deemed to have need. 100% of freshmen with need received aid; of those 100% had need fully met. *Average percent of need met:* 100% (excluding resources awarded to replace EFC). *Average financial aid package:* $31,789 (excluding resources awarded to replace EFC). 5% of all full-time freshmen had no need and received non-need-based gift aid.

UNDERGRADUATE FINANCIAL AID (Fall 2009, est.) 1,725 applied for aid; of those 64% were deemed to have need. 100% of undergraduates with need received aid; of those 100% had need fully met. *Average percent of need met:* 100% (excluding resources awarded to replace EFC). *Average financial aid package:* $34,141 (excluding resources awarded to replace EFC). 7% of all full-time undergraduates had no need and received non-need-based gift aid.

GIFT AID (NEED-BASED) *Total amount:* $28,646,103 (3% federal, 2% state, 91% institutional, 4% external sources). *Receiving aid:* Freshmen: 59% (311); all full-time undergraduates: 56% (1,111). *Average award:* Freshmen: $28,868; Undergraduates: $27,989. *Scholarships, grants, and awards:* Federal Pell, FSEOG, state, private, college/university gift aid from institutional funds.

GIFT AID (NON-NEED-BASED) *Total amount:* $1,263,673 (4% federal, 36% institutional, 60% external sources). *Receiving aid:* Freshmen: 10% (53). Undergraduates: 11% (217). *Average award:* Freshmen: $1962. Undergraduates: $2644. *Scholarships, grants, and awards by category:* Academic interests/achievement: 265 awards ($337,516 total): general academic interests/achievements. *Creative arts/performance:* 3 awards ($1470 total): music. *Tuition waivers:* Full or partial for employees or children of employees.

LOANS *Student loans:* $5,654,855 (94% need-based, 6% non-need-based). 54% of past graduating class borrowed through all loan programs. *Average indebtedness per student:* $18,601. *Average need-based loan:* Freshmen: $3979. Undergraduates: $4802. *Parent loans:* $1,351,886 (77% need-based, 23% non-need-based). *Programs:* FFEL (Subsidized and Unsubsidized Stafford, PLUS), Perkins, state, college/university.

WORK-STUDY *Federal work-study:* Total amount: $875,781; 435 jobs averaging $2013. *State or other work-study/employment:* Total amount: $3,289,763 (57% need-based, 43% non-need-based). 1,305 part-time jobs averaging $2509.

APPLYING FOR FINANCIAL AID *Required financial aid forms:* FAFSA, CSS Financial Aid PROFILE, noncustodial (divorced/separated) parent's statement. *Financial aid deadline:* 2/15. *Notification date:* 4/1. Students must reply by 5/1 or within 2 weeks of notification.

CONTACT Mr. Rodney M. Oto, Director of Student Financial Services, Carleton College, One North College Street, Northfield, MN 55057-4001, 507-222-4138 or toll-free 800-995-2275. *Fax:* 507-222-4269.

CARLOS ALBIZU UNIVERSITY
San Juan, PR

Tuition & fees: $6739	Average undergraduate aid package: $6537

ABOUT THE INSTITUTION Independent, coed, primarily women. 2 undergraduate majors. Federal methodology is used as a basis for awarding need-based institutional aid.

UNDERGRADUATE EXPENSES for 2010–11 *Tuition:* full-time $5760; part-time $160 per credit. *Required fees:* full-time $979; $323 per term.

UNDERGRADUATE FINANCIAL AID (Fall 2008) 86 applied for aid; of those 100% were deemed to have need. 97% of undergraduates with need received aid. *Average percent of need met:* 26% (excluding resources awarded to replace EFC). *Average financial aid package:* $6537 (excluding resources awarded to replace EFC).

GIFT AID (NEED-BASED) *Total amount:* $393,277 (92% federal, 6% state, 1% institutional, 1% external sources). *Receiving aid:* All full-time undergraduates: 63% (62). *Average award:* Undergraduates: $4853. *Scholarships, grants, and awards:* Federal Pell, FSEOG, state, college/university gift aid from institutional funds.

GIFT AID (NON-NEED-BASED) *Scholarships, grants, and awards by category: Academic interests/achievement:* 34 awards ($108,753 total): social sciences. *Tuition waivers:* Full or partial for employees or children of employees.

LOANS *Student loans:* $490,620 (78% need-based, 22% non-need-based). *Average need-based loan:* Undergraduates: $3897. *Programs:* FFEL (Subsidized and Unsubsidized Stafford, PLUS).

WORK-STUDY *Federal work-study:* Total amount: $18,587; 8 jobs averaging $2323.

CONTACT Mrs. Doris J. Quero, Director, Carlos Albizu University, PO Box 9023711, San Juan, PR 00901, 787-725-6500 Ext. 1529. *Fax:* 787-721-4008. *E-mail:* dquero@albizu.edu.

CARLOS ALBIZU UNIVERSITY, MIAMI CAMPUS
Miami, FL

CONTACT Maria V. Chavez, Senior Financial Aid Officer, Carlos Albizu University, Miami Campus, 2173 Northwest 99th Avenue, Miami, FL 33172, 305-593-1223 Ext. 153 or toll-free 888-672-3246. *Fax:* 305-593-8902. *E-mail:* mchavez@albizu.edu.

CARLOW UNIVERSITY
Pittsburgh, PA

CONTACT Ms. Natalie Wilson, Director of Financial Aid, Carlow University, 3333 Fifth Avenue, Pittsburgh, PA 15213-3165, 412-578-6171 or toll-free 800-333-CARLOW.

CARNEGIE MELLON UNIVERSITY
Pittsburgh, PA

Tuition & fees: $40,728	Average undergraduate aid package: $28,013

ABOUT THE INSTITUTION Independent, coed. 79 undergraduate majors. Both federal and institutional methodology are used as a basis for awarding need-based institutional aid.

UNDERGRADUATE EXPENSES for 2009–10 *One-time required fee:* $192. *Comprehensive fee:* $51,568 includes full-time tuition ($40,300), mandatory fees ($428), and room and board ($10,840). *College room only:* $6060. Room and board charges vary according to board plan and housing facility. *Part-time tuition:* $547 per unit. *Payment plan:* Installment.

FRESHMAN FINANCIAL AID (Fall 2009, est.) 1,014 applied for aid; of those 78% were deemed to have need. 99% of freshmen with need received aid; of those 31% had need fully met. *Average percent of need met:* 82% (excluding resources awarded to replace EFC). *Average financial aid package:* $28,678 (excluding resources awarded to replace EFC). 9% of all full-time freshmen had no need and received non-need-based gift aid.

UNDERGRADUATE FINANCIAL AID (Fall 2009, est.) 3,433 applied for aid; of those 85% were deemed to have need. 99% of undergraduates with need received aid; of those 31% had need fully met. *Average percent of need met:* 80% (excluding resources awarded to replace EFC). *Average financial aid package:* $28,013 (excluding resources awarded to replace EFC). 8% of all full-time undergraduates had no need and received non-need-based gift aid.

GIFT AID (NEED-BASED) *Total amount:* $63,397,962 (10% federal, 1% state, 85% institutional, 4% external sources). *Receiving aid:* Freshmen: 53% (754); all full-time undergraduates: 47% (2,770). *Average award:* Freshmen: $24,707; Undergraduates: $22,789. *Scholarships, grants, and awards:* Federal Pell, FSEOG, state, private, college/university gift aid from institutional funds.

GIFT AID (NON-NEED-BASED) *Total amount:* $13,128,912 (84% institutional, 16% external sources). *Receiving aid:* Freshmen: 21% (295). Undergraduates: 18% (1,037). *Average award:* Freshmen: $10,643. Undergraduates: $12,083. *Scholarships, grants, and awards by category: Academic interests/achievement:* general academic interests/achievements. *Creative arts/performance:* art/fine arts, music. *Special achievements/activities:* leadership. *Special characteristics:* members of minority groups, out-of-state students. *Tuition waivers:* Full or partial for employees or children of employees.

LOANS *Student loans:* $19,297,272 (91% need-based, 9% non-need-based). 50% of past graduating class borrowed through all loan programs. *Average indebtedness per student:* $29,456. *Average need-based loan:* Freshmen: $3657. Undergraduates: $4661. *Parent loans:* $8,738,589 (22% need-based, 78% non-need-based). *Programs:* FFEL (Subsidized and Unsubsidized Stafford, PLUS), Perkins.

WORK-STUDY *Federal work-study:* Total amount: $5,405,607; 2,047 jobs averaging $2600. *State or other work-study/employment:* 7 part-time jobs averaging $3174.

APPLYING FOR FINANCIAL AID *Required financial aid forms:* FAFSA, institution's own form, parent and student federal tax returns and parent W-2 forms. *Financial aid deadline:* 5/1 (priority: 2/15). *Notification date:* 3/15.

CONTACT Linda M. Anderson, Director, Enrollment Services, Carnegie Mellon University, 5000 Forbes Avenue, Pittsburgh, PA 15213-3890, 412-268-8186. *Fax:* 412-268-8084. *E-mail:* thehub@andrew.cmu.edu.

CAROLINA CHRISTIAN COLLEGE
Winston-Salem, NC

Tuition & fees: $6200	Average undergraduate aid package: N/A

ABOUT THE INSTITUTION Independent nondenominational, coed. 1 undergraduate major. Federal methodology is used as a basis for awarding need-based institutional aid.

UNDERGRADUATE EXPENSES for 2010–11 *Comprehensive fee:* $18,308 includes full-time tuition ($6200) and room and board ($12,108). *Part-time tuition:* $875 per course. *Payment plan:* Installment.

UNDERGRADUATE FINANCIAL AID (Fall 2008) 35 applied for aid; of those 100% were deemed to have need. 100% of undergraduates with need received aid.

GIFT AID (NEED-BASED) *Total amount:* $5000 (100% federal). *Receiving aid:* All full-time undergraduates: 15% (6). *Average award:* Undergraduates: $1500. *Scholarships, grants, and awards:* Federal Pell, FSEOG.

LOANS *Student loans:* $140,000 (100% need-based). *Programs:* FFEL (Subsidized and Unsubsidized Stafford).

CONTACT LaTanya V. Lucas, Academic Dean, Carolina Christian College, 4209 Indiana Avenue, Winston Salem, NC 27105, 336-744-0900 Ext. 106. *E-mail:* latanya@carolina.edu.

CARROLL COLLEGE
Helena, MT

ABOUT THE INSTITUTION Independent Roman Catholic, coed. *Awards:* associate and bachelor's degrees. 43 undergraduate majors. *Total enrollment:* 1,409. Undergraduates: 1,409. Freshmen: 345.

GIFT AID (NEED-BASED) *Scholarships, grants, and awards:* Federal Pell, FSEOG, state, private, college/university gift aid from institutional funds.

GIFT AID (NON-NEED-BASED) *Scholarships, grants, and awards by category: Academic interests/achievement:* general academic interests/achievements. *Creative arts/performance:* debating, theater/drama. *Special achievements/activities:* general special achievements/activities, religious involvement. *Special characteristics:* children of faculty/staff, children of union members/company employees, international students, siblings of current students, spouses of current students, veterans.

LOANS *Programs:* FFEL (Subsidized and Unsubsidized Stafford, PLUS), Perkins, private loans.

WORK-STUDY *Federal work-study:* Total amount: $337,136; jobs available. *State or other work-study/employment:* Total amount: $7712 (50% need-based, 50% non-need-based). Part-time jobs available.

APPLYING FOR FINANCIAL AID *Required financial aid form:* FAFSA.

CONTACT Ms. Janet Riis, Director of Financial Aid, Carroll College, 1601 North Benton Avenue, Helena, MT 59625-0002, 406-447-5423 or toll-free 800-992-3648. *Fax:* 406-447-4533. *E-mail:* jriis@carroll.edu.

CARROLL UNIVERSITY
Waukesha, WI

Tuition & fees: $22,937	Average undergraduate aid package: $17,231

ABOUT THE INSTITUTION Independent Presbyterian, coed. 77 undergraduate majors. Both federal and institutional methodology are used as a basis for awarding need-based institutional aid.

UNDERGRADUATE EXPENSES for 2009–10 *Comprehensive fee:* $30,605 includes full-time tuition ($22,470), mandatory fees ($467), and room and board ($7668). *College room only:* $3833. Full-time tuition and fees vary according to program. Room and board charges vary according to board plan and housing facility. *Part-time tuition:* $270 per credit. Part-time tuition and fees vary according to course load and program. *Payment plan:* Installment.

FRESHMAN FINANCIAL AID (Fall 2009, est.) 675 applied for aid; of those 85% were deemed to have need. 100% of freshmen with need received aid; of those 70% had need fully met. *Average percent of need met:* 97% (excluding resources awarded to replace EFC). *Average financial aid package:* $17,723 (excluding resources awarded to replace EFC). 22% of all full-time freshmen had no need and received non-need-based gift aid.

UNDERGRADUATE FINANCIAL AID (Fall 2009, est.) 2,342 applied for aid; of those 90% were deemed to have need. 100% of undergraduates with need received aid; of those 29% had need fully met. *Average percent of need met:* 80% (excluding resources awarded to replace EFC). *Average financial aid package:* $17,231 (excluding resources awarded to replace EFC). 22% of all full-time undergraduates had no need and received non-need-based gift aid.

GIFT AID (NEED-BASED) *Total amount:* $22,538,562 (14% federal, 10% state, 76% institutional). *Receiving aid:* Freshmen: 79% (576); all full-time undergraduates: 80% (2,108). *Average award:* Freshmen: $14,608; Undergraduates: $12,726. *Scholarships, grants, and awards:* Federal Pell, FSEOG, state, private, college/university gift aid from institutional funds.

GIFT AID (NON-NEED-BASED) *Total amount:* $8,911,175 (90% institutional, 10% external sources). *Average award:* Freshmen: $11,043. Undergraduates: $9370. *Scholarships, grants, and awards by category: Academic interests/achievement:* $17,205,992 total: biological sciences, business, computer science, education, general academic interests/achievements, health fields, humanities, international studies, mathematics, physical sciences, premedicine, social sciences. *Creative arts/performance:* $167,250 total: art/fine arts, journalism/publications, music, performing arts, theater/drama. *Special achievements/activities:* $343,913 total: general special achievements/activities, junior miss, leadership, memberships, religious involvement. *Special characteristics:* $1,414,175 total: adult students, children and siblings of alumni, children of current students, children of faculty/staff, general special characteristics, international students, siblings of current students, spouses of current students. *Tuition waivers:* Full or partial for employees or children of employees.

LOANS *Student loans:* $21,155,190 (39% need-based, 61% non-need-based). 78% of past graduating class borrowed through all loan programs. *Average indebtedness per student:* $27,066. *Average need-based loan:* Freshmen: $2282. Undergraduates: $3170. *Parent loans:* $2,758,284 (75% need-based, 25% non-need-based). *Programs:* FFEL (Subsidized and Unsubsidized Stafford, PLUS), Perkins, state, college/university.

WORK-STUDY *Federal work-study:* Total amount: $1,535,908; 774 jobs averaging $1986. *State or other work-study/employment:* Total amount: $1,631,563 (100% non-need-based). 858 part-time jobs averaging $1926.

APPLYING FOR FINANCIAL AID *Required financial aid form:* FAFSA. *Financial aid deadline:* Continuous. *Notification date:* Continuous beginning 2/15. Students must reply by 5/1 or within 2 weeks of notification.

CONTACT Dawn Scott, Director of Financial Aid, Carroll University, 100 North East Avenue, Waukesha, WI 53186-5593, 262-524-7297 or toll-free 800-CARROLL. *Fax:* 262-951-3037. *E-mail:* dscott@carrollu.edu.

CARSON-NEWMAN COLLEGE
Jefferson City, TN

Tuition & fees: $20,562	Average undergraduate aid package: $15,747

ABOUT THE INSTITUTION Independent Southern Baptist, coed. 71 undergraduate majors. Federal methodology is used as a basis for awarding need-based institutional aid.

UNDERGRADUATE EXPENSES for 2010–11 *Comprehensive fee:* $26,480 includes full-time tuition ($19,628), mandatory fees ($934), and room and board ($5918). Full-time tuition and fees vary according to class time and course load. Room and board charges vary according to board plan, gender, and housing facility. *Part-time tuition:* $818 per semester hour. *Payment plans:* Installment, deferred payment.

FRESHMAN FINANCIAL AID (Fall 2009, est.) 499 applied for aid; of those 88% were deemed to have need. 100% of freshmen with need received aid; of those 27% had need fully met. *Average percent of need met:* 78% (excluding resources awarded to replace EFC). *Average financial aid package:* $16,493 (excluding resources awarded to replace EFC). 14% of all full-time freshmen had no need and received non-need-based gift aid.

UNDERGRADUATE FINANCIAL AID (Fall 2009, est.) 1,642 applied for aid; of those 85% were deemed to have need. 100% of undergraduates with need received aid; of those 25% had need fully met. *Average percent of need met:* 74% (excluding resources awarded to replace EFC). *Average financial aid package:* $15,747 (excluding resources awarded to replace EFC). 17% of all full-time undergraduates had no need and received non-need-based gift aid.

GIFT AID (NEED-BASED) *Total amount:* $16,300,371 (20% federal, 26% state, 50% institutional, 4% external sources). *Receiving aid:* Freshmen: 85% (436); all full-time undergraduates: 78% (1,384). *Average award:* Freshmen: $13,460; Undergraduates: $11,740. *Scholarships, grants, and awards:* Federal Pell, FSEOG, state, private, college/university gift aid from institutional funds.

GIFT AID (NON-NEED-BASED) *Total amount:* $2,400,649 (27% state, 69% institutional, 4% external sources). *Receiving aid:* Freshmen: 83% (428). Undergraduates: 76% (1,340). *Average award:* Freshmen: $7516. Undergraduates: $6853. *Scholarships, grants, and awards by category: Academic interests/achievement:* biological sciences, business, education, general academic interests/achievements, home economics, mathematics, military science, religion/biblical studies. *Creative arts/performance:* art/fine arts, debating, journalism/publications, music. *Special achievements/activities:* leadership, memberships. *Special characteristics:* children and siblings of alumni, members of minority groups, relatives of clergy, siblings of current students. *Tuition waivers:* Full or partial for employees or children of employees, senior citizens.

LOANS *Student loans:* $8,383,403 (93% need-based, 7% non-need-based). 67% of past graduating class borrowed through all loan programs. *Average indebtedness per student:* $14,164. *Average need-based loan:* Freshmen: $2690. Undergraduates: $3517. *Parent loans:* $1,403,629 (87% need-based, 13% non-need-based). *Programs:* FFEL (Subsidized and Unsubsidized Stafford, PLUS), Perkins, state, college/university, alternative loans.

WORK-STUDY *Federal work-study:* Total amount: $161,215; 110 jobs averaging $1466. *State or other work-study/employment:* Total amount: $10,875 (76% need-based, 24% non-need-based). 11 part-time jobs averaging $988.

ATHLETIC AWARDS Total amount: $1,693,069 (68% need-based, 32% non-need-based).

APPLYING FOR FINANCIAL AID *Required financial aid forms:* FAFSA, institution's own form. *Financial aid deadline (priority):* 4/1. *Notification date:* Continuous. Students must reply within 2 weeks of notification.

CONTACT Danette Seale, Director of Financial Aid, Carson-Newman College, 1646 Russell Avenue, Jefferson City, TN 37760, 865-471-3247 or toll-free 800-678-9061. *Fax:* 865-471-3502. *E-mail:* dseale@cn.edu.

CARTHAGE COLLEGE
Kenosha, WI

Tuition & fees: $28,250	Average undergraduate aid package: $18,268

ABOUT THE INSTITUTION Independent religious, coed. *Awards:* bachelor's and master's degrees. 50 undergraduate majors. *Total enrollment:* 2,778. Undergraduates: 2,660. Freshmen: 686. Federal methodology is used as a basis for awarding need-based institutional aid.

UNDERGRADUATE EXPENSES for 2009–10 *Application fee:* $25. *Comprehensive fee:* $36,000 includes full-time tuition ($28,250) and room and board ($7750). Full-time tuition and fees vary according to reciprocity agreements. Room and board charges vary according to board plan and housing facility. *Part-time tuition:* $400 per credit hour. Part-time tuition and fees vary according to class time. *Payment plan:* Installment.

FRESHMAN FINANCIAL AID (Fall 2009, est.) 671 applied for aid; of those 84% were deemed to have need. 100% of freshmen with need received aid; of those 15% had need fully met. *Average percent of need met:* 65% (excluding resources awarded to replace EFC). *Average financial aid package:* $18,778 (excluding resources awarded to replace EFC). 22% of all full-time freshmen had no need and received non-need-based gift aid.

UNDERGRADUATE FINANCIAL AID (Fall 2009, est.) 2,172 applied for aid; of those 85% were deemed to have need. 100% of undergraduates with need received aid; of those 14% had need fully met. *Average percent of need met:* 65% (excluding resources awarded to replace EFC). *Average financial aid package:* $18,268 (excluding resources awarded to replace EFC). 23% of all full-time undergraduates had no need and received non-need-based gift aid.

GIFT AID (NEED-BASED) *Total amount:* $24,772,813 (13% federal, 4% state, 76% institutional, 7% external sources). *Receiving aid:* Freshmen: 78% (564); all full-time undergraduates: 75% (1,854). *Average award:* Freshmen: $14,223; Undergraduates: $13,416. *Scholarships, grants, and awards:* Federal Pell, FSEOG, state, private, college/university gift aid from institutional funds.

GIFT AID (NON-NEED-BASED) *Total amount:* $7,132,153 (1% federal, 90% institutional, 9% external sources). *Receiving aid:* Freshmen: 10% (75). Undergraduates: 9% (219). *Average award:* Freshmen: $10,343. Undergraduates: $9564. *Scholarships, grants, and awards by category: Academic interests/ achievement:* biological sciences, business, computer science, engineering/ technologies, foreign languages, general academic interests/achievements, health fields, mathematics, physical sciences, premedicine, religion/biblical studies. *Creative arts/performance:* applied art and design, art/fine arts, music, theater/ drama. *Special achievements/activities:* general special achievements/activities, leadership, religious involvement. *Special characteristics:* children and siblings of alumni, children of educators, children of faculty/staff, children of public servants, local/state students, members of minority groups, previous college experience, relatives of clergy, religious affiliation, siblings of current students. *Tuition waivers:* Full or partial for children of alumni, employees or children of employees. *ROTC:* Army cooperative, Air Force cooperative.

LOANS *Student loans:* $19,247,230 (72% need-based, 28% non-need-based). 80% of past graduating class borrowed through all loan programs. *Average indebtedness per student:* $29,075. *Average need-based loan:* Freshmen: $3737. Undergraduates: $4266. *Parent loans:* $7,258,469 (48% need-based, 52% non-need-based). *Programs:* Federal Direct (Subsidized and Unsubsidized Stafford, PLUS), FFEL (Subsidized and Unsubsidized Stafford, PLUS), Perkins, state, college/university.

WORK-STUDY *Federal work-study:* Total amount: $358,859; 843 jobs averaging $4000. *State or other work-study/employment:* Total amount: $7000 (100% non-need-based). Part-time jobs available.

APPLYING FOR FINANCIAL AID *Required financial aid form:* FAFSA. *Financial aid deadline (priority):* 2/15. *Notification date:* Continuous beginning 3/1.

CONTACT Vatistas Vatistas, Director of Financial Aid, Carthage College, 2001 Alford Park Drive, Kenosha, WI 53140, 262-551-6001 or toll-free 800-351-4058. *Fax:* 262-551-5762. *E-mail:* vvatistas@carthage.edu.

CASE WESTERN RESERVE UNIVERSITY
Cleveland, OH

Tuition & fees: $36,238	Average undergraduate aid package: $33,478

ABOUT THE INSTITUTION Independent, coed. 64 undergraduate majors. Federal methodology is used as a basis for awarding need-based institutional aid.

UNDERGRADUATE EXPENSES for 2009–10 *One-time required fee:* $370. *Comprehensive fee:* $47,128 includes full-time tuition ($35,900), mandatory fees ($338), and room and board ($10,890). *College room only:* $6270. Room and board charges vary according to board plan, housing facility, and student level. *Part-time tuition:* $1496 per credit hour. Part-time tuition and fees vary according to course load. *Payment plan:* Installment.

FRESHMAN FINANCIAL AID (Fall 2009, est.) 748 applied for aid; of those 83% were deemed to have need. 100% of freshmen with need received aid; of those 89% had need fully met. *Average percent of need met:* 90% (excluding resources awarded to replace EFC). *Average financial aid package:* $33,515 (excluding resources awarded to replace EFC). 19% of all full-time freshmen had no need and received non-need-based gift aid.

UNDERGRADUATE FINANCIAL AID (Fall 2009, est.) 2,934 applied for aid; of those 89% were deemed to have need. 100% of undergraduates with need received aid; of those 92% had need fully met. *Average percent of need met:* 87% (excluding resources awarded to replace EFC). *Average financial aid package:* $33,478 (excluding resources awarded to replace EFC). 20% of all full-time undergraduates had no need and received non-need-based gift aid.

GIFT AID (NEED-BASED) *Total amount:* $61,742,767 (10% federal, 2% state, 84% institutional, 4% external sources). *Receiving aid:* Freshmen: 61% (594); all full-time undergraduates: 63% (2,522). *Average award:* Freshmen: $24,926; Undergraduates: $22,793. *Scholarships, grants, and awards:* Federal Pell, FSEOG, state, private, college/university gift aid from institutional funds.

GIFT AID (NON-NEED-BASED) *Total amount:* $15,471,989 (1% state, 96% institutional, 3% external sources). *Receiving aid:* Freshmen: 62% (598). Undergraduates: 63% (2,505). *Average award:* Freshmen: $18,931. Undergraduates: $18,930. *Scholarships, grants, and awards by category: Academic interests/achievement:* 2,237 awards ($40,326,487 total): biological sciences, business, communication, computer science, education, engineering/technologies, English, foreign languages, general academic interests/achievements, health fields, humanities, international studies, mathematics, physical sciences, premedicine, religion/biblical studies, social sciences. *Creative arts/performance:* 35 awards ($448,000 total): art/fine arts, creative writing, dance, general creative arts/performance, music, performing arts, theater/drama. *Special achievements/ activities:* 55 awards ($164,250 total): leadership. *Special characteristics:* 169 awards ($5,873,154 total): children of faculty/staff. *Tuition waivers:* Full or partial for employees or children of employees.

LOANS *Student loans:* $36,546,256 (69% need-based, 31% non-need-based). 64% of past graduating class borrowed through all loan programs. *Average indebtedness per student:* $37,496. *Average need-based loan:* Freshmen: $6728. Undergraduates: $7474. *Parent loans:* $8,354,810 (95% need-based, 5% non-need-based). *Programs:* FFEL (Subsidized and Unsubsidized Stafford, PLUS), Perkins, Federal Nursing, state, college/university, alternative loans.

WORK-STUDY *Federal work-study:* Total amount: $5,204,407; 1,796 jobs averaging $2812.

APPLYING FOR FINANCIAL AID *Required financial aid forms:* FAFSA, institution's own form. *Financial aid deadline (priority):* 2/15. *Notification date:* Continuous beginning 3/15. Students must reply by 5/1 or within 2 weeks of notification.

CONTACT Mrs. Venus M. Puliafico, Director, University Financial Aid, Case Western Reserve University, 10900 Euclid Avenue, Cleveland, OH 44106-7049, 216-368-4530. *Fax:* 216-368-5054. *E-mail:* vxp4@case.edu.

CASTLETON STATE COLLEGE
Castleton, VT

CONTACT Kathleen O'Meara, Director of Financial Aid, Castleton State College, Castleton, VT 05735, 802-468-1292 or toll-free 800-639-8521. *Fax:* 802-468-5237. *E-mail:* kathy.omeara@castleton.edu.

CATAWBA COLLEGE
Salisbury, NC

Tuition & fees: $23,740 **Average undergraduate aid package: $18,422**

ABOUT THE INSTITUTION Independent religious, coed. 42 undergraduate majors. Federal methodology is used as a basis for awarding need-based institutional aid.

UNDERGRADUATE EXPENSES for 2009–10 *Comprehensive fee:* $31,940 includes full-time tuition ($23,740) and room and board ($8200). *Part-time tuition:* $620 per credit hour. *Payment plan:* Installment.

FRESHMAN FINANCIAL AID (Fall 2009, est.) 279 applied for aid; of those 85% were deemed to have need. 100% of freshmen with need received aid; of those 25% had need fully met. *Average percent of need met:* 71% (excluding resources awarded to replace EFC). *Average financial aid package:* $21,067 (excluding resources awarded to replace EFC). 10% of all full-time freshmen had no need and received non-need-based gift aid.

UNDERGRADUATE FINANCIAL AID (Fall 2009, est.) 1,074 applied for aid; of those 88% were deemed to have need. 100% of undergraduates with need received aid; of those 23% had need fully met. *Average percent of need met:* 70% (excluding resources awarded to replace EFC). *Average financial aid package:* $18,422 (excluding resources awarded to replace EFC). 9% of all full-time undergraduates had no need and received non-need-based gift aid.

GIFT AID (NEED-BASED) *Total amount:* $14,179,969 (17% federal, 23% state, 58% institutional, 2% external sources). *Receiving aid:* Freshmen: 56% (171); all full-time undergraduates: 51% (643). *Average award:* Freshmen: $6797; Undergraduates: $5861. *Scholarships, grants, and awards:* Federal Pell, FSEOG, state, private, college/university gift aid from institutional funds.

GIFT AID (NON-NEED-BASED) *Receiving aid:* Freshmen: 77% (238). Undergraduates: 74% (939). *Average award:* Undergraduates: $5405. *Scholarships, grants, and awards by category:* Academic interests/achievement: education, general academic interests/achievements. Creative arts/performance: music, theater/drama. Special achievements/activities: general special achievements/activities. *Tuition waivers:* Full or partial for employees or children of employees.

LOANS *Student loans:* $6,801,148 (55% need-based, 45% non-need-based). 72% of past graduating class borrowed through all loan programs. *Average indebtedness per student:* $25,506. *Average need-based loan:* Freshmen: $2977. Undergraduates: $4026. *Parent loans:* $1,537,228 (100% non-need-based). *Programs:* Federal Direct (Subsidized and Unsubsidized Stafford, PLUS), Perkins, college/university, TERI Loans, Nellie Mae Loans, Advantage Loans, alternative loans, CitiAssist Loans, "Extra" loans.

WORK-STUDY *Federal work-study:* Total amount: $349,752; 199 jobs averaging $1757. *State or other work-study/employment:* Total amount: $456,441 (100% need-based). 268 part-time jobs averaging $1703.

ATHLETIC AWARDS Total amount: $2,704,713 (100% need-based).

APPLYING FOR FINANCIAL AID *Required financial aid forms:* FAFSA, state aid form. *Financial aid deadline (priority):* 3/15. *Notification date:* Continuous beginning 2/15. Students must reply within 2 weeks of notification.

CONTACT Mrs. Melanie McCulloh, Director of Scholarships and Financial Aid, Catawba College, 2300 West Innes Street, Salisbury, NC 28144-2488, 704-637-4416 or toll-free 800-CATAWBA. *Fax:* 704-637-4252. *E-mail:* mcmccull@catawba.edu.

THE CATHOLIC UNIVERSITY OF AMERICA
Washington, DC

Tuition & fees: $31,890 **Average undergraduate aid package: $20,209**

ABOUT THE INSTITUTION Independent religious, coed. 62 undergraduate majors. Federal methodology is used as a basis for awarding need-based institutional aid.

UNDERGRADUATE EXPENSES for 2009–10 *One-time required fee:* $425. *Comprehensive fee:* $44,024 includes full-time tuition ($31,740), mandatory fees ($150), and room and board ($12,134). *College room only:* $7340. Full-time tuition and fees vary according to program. Room and board charges vary according to board plan and housing facility. *Part-time tuition:* $1170 per credit hour. *Part-time fees:* $75 per year. Part-time tuition and fees vary according to course load. *Payment plans:* Tuition prepayment, installment.

FRESHMAN FINANCIAL AID (Fall 2009, est.) 659 applied for aid; of those 80% were deemed to have need. 100% of freshmen with need received aid; of those 49% had need fully met. *Average percent of need met:* 86% (excluding resources awarded to replace EFC). *Average financial aid package:* $21,198 (excluding resources awarded to replace EFC). 28% of all full-time freshmen had no need and received non-need-based gift aid.

UNDERGRADUATE FINANCIAL AID (Fall 2009, est.) 2,221 applied for aid; of those 84% were deemed to have need. 100% of undergraduates with need received aid; of those 46% had need fully met. *Average percent of need met:* 81% (excluding resources awarded to replace EFC). *Average financial aid package:* $20,209 (excluding resources awarded to replace EFC). 31% of all full-time undergraduates had no need and received non-need-based gift aid.

GIFT AID (NEED-BASED) *Total amount:* $28,449,956 (8% federal, 90% institutional, 2% external sources). *Receiving aid:* Freshmen: 64% (521); all full-time undergraduates: 56% (1,818). *Average award:* Freshmen: $16,752; Undergraduates: $15,576. *Scholarships, grants, and awards:* Federal Pell, FSEOG, state, private, college/university gift aid from institutional funds.

GIFT AID (NON-NEED-BASED) *Total amount:* $10,570,490 (99% institutional, 1% external sources). *Average award:* Freshmen: $10,317. Undergraduates: $10,449. *Scholarships, grants, and awards by category:* Academic interests/achievement: general academic interests/achievements. Creative arts/performance: music, theater/drama. Special achievements/activities: general special achievements/activities. Special characteristics: children and siblings of alumni, children of faculty/staff, religious affiliation, siblings of current students, twins, veterans, veterans' children. *Tuition waivers:* Full or partial for children of alumni, employees or children of employees, adult students.

LOANS *Student loans:* $20,142,869 (85% need-based, 15% non-need-based). *Average need-based loan:* Freshmen: $3416. Undergraduates: $4377. *Parent loans:* $10,001,217 (83% need-based, 17% non-need-based). *Programs:* Federal Direct (Subsidized and Unsubsidized Stafford, PLUS), commercial loans.

WORK-STUDY *Federal work-study:* Total amount: $2,497,500; 966 jobs averaging $2370.

APPLYING FOR FINANCIAL AID *Required financial aid forms:* FAFSA, alumni and parish scholarship application (if appropriate). *Financial aid deadline:* 4/10 (priority: 2/15). *Notification date:* Continuous beginning 4/1. Students must reply by 5/1 or within 2 weeks of notification.

CONTACT Mr. Donald Bosse, Director of Financial Aid, The Catholic University of America, 620 Michigan Avenue, NE, Washington, DC 20064, 202-319-5307 or toll-free 800-673-2772 (out-of-state). *Fax:* 202-319-5573. *E-mail:* bosse@cua.edu.

CAZENOVIA COLLEGE
Cazenovia, NY

Tuition & fees: $24,152 **Average undergraduate aid package: $20,838**

ABOUT THE INSTITUTION Independent, coed. 21 undergraduate majors. Federal methodology is used as a basis for awarding need-based institutional aid.

UNDERGRADUATE EXPENSES for 2009–10 *Comprehensive fee:* $34,374 includes full-time tuition ($23,752), mandatory fees ($400), and room and board ($10,222). Full-time tuition and fees vary according to class time, course load, and program. Room and board charges vary according to board plan and housing facility. *Part-time tuition:* $504 per credit hour. Part-time tuition and fees vary according to class time and course load. *Payment plan:* Installment.

FRESHMAN FINANCIAL AID (Fall 2009, est.) 265 applied for aid; of those 88% were deemed to have need. 100% of freshmen with need received aid; of those 21% had need fully met. *Average percent of need met:* 77% (excluding resources awarded to replace EFC). *Average financial aid package:* $20,721 (excluding resources awarded to replace EFC). 10% of all full-time freshmen had no need and received non-need-based gift aid.

UNDERGRADUATE FINANCIAL AID (Fall 2009, est.) 892 applied for aid; of those 92% were deemed to have need. 100% of undergraduates with need received aid; of those 18% had need fully met. *Average percent of need met:* 77% (excluding resources awarded to replace EFC). *Average financial aid package:* $20,838 (excluding resources awarded to replace EFC). 11% of all full-time undergraduates had no need and received non-need-based gift aid.

GIFT AID (NEED-BASED) *Total amount:* $14,730,376 (14% federal, 12% state, 72% institutional, 2% external sources). *Receiving aid:* Freshmen: 83% (234); all full-time undergraduates: 85% (819). *Average award:* Freshmen: $14,711; Undergraduates: $16,422. *Scholarships, grants, and awards:* Federal Pell, FSEOG, state, private, college/university gift aid from institutional funds.

GIFT AID (NON-NEED-BASED) *Total amount:* $1,314,997 (1% federal, 98% institutional, 1% external sources). *Receiving aid:* Freshmen: 9% (26).

Undergraduates: 8% (75). *Average award:* Freshmen: $9034. Undergraduates: $11,444. *Scholarships, grants, and awards by category: Academic interests/achievement:* general academic interests/achievements. *Tuition waivers:* Full or partial for employees or children of employees.

LOANS *Student loans:* $7,749,744 (93% need-based, 7% non-need-based). 85% of past graduating class borrowed through all loan programs. *Average need-based loan:* Freshmen: $3067. Undergraduates: $4068. *Parent loans:* $2,579,854 (88% need-based, 12% non-need-based). *Programs:* Federal Direct (Subsidized and Unsubsidized Stafford, PLUS).

WORK-STUDY *Federal work-study:* Total amount: $290,000; jobs available.

APPLYING FOR FINANCIAL AID *Required financial aid forms:* FAFSA, state aid form. *Financial aid deadline (priority):* 3/1. *Notification date:* Continuous. Students must reply by 5/1 or within 2 weeks of notification.

CONTACT Christine L. Mandel, Director of Financial Aid, Cazenovia College, 3 Sullivan Street, Cazenovia, NY 13035, 315-655-7887 or toll-free 800-654-3210. *Fax:* 315-655-7219. *E-mail:* finaid@cazenovia.edu.

CEDAR CREST COLLEGE
Allentown, PA

Tuition & fees: $28,135	Average undergraduate aid package: $21,570

ABOUT THE INSTITUTION Independent religious, women only. 35 undergraduate majors. Federal methodology is used as a basis for awarding need-based institutional aid.

UNDERGRADUATE EXPENSES for 2009–10 *Comprehensive fee:* $37,456 includes full-time tuition ($27,735), mandatory fees ($400), and room and board ($9321). *College room only:* $4912. Full-time tuition and fees vary according to class time, course load, degree level, and program. Room and board charges vary according to board plan and housing facility. *Part-time tuition:* $772 per credit hour. *Part-time fees:* $125 per term. Part-time tuition and fees vary according to class time, course load, degree level, and program. *Payment plans:* Installment, deferred payment.

FRESHMAN FINANCIAL AID (Fall 2009, est.) 191 applied for aid; of those 96% were deemed to have need. 100% of freshmen with need received aid; of those 11% had need fully met. *Average percent of need met:* 79% (excluding resources awarded to replace EFC). *Average financial aid package:* $23,552 (excluding resources awarded to replace EFC). 8% of all full-time freshmen had no need and received non-need-based gift aid.

UNDERGRADUATE FINANCIAL AID (Fall 2009, est.) 796 applied for aid; of those 93% were deemed to have need. 100% of undergraduates with need received aid; of those 12% had need fully met. *Average percent of need met:* 76% (excluding resources awarded to replace EFC). *Average financial aid package:* $21,570 (excluding resources awarded to replace EFC). 10% of all full-time undergraduates had no need and received non-need-based gift aid.

GIFT AID (NEED-BASED) *Total amount:* $12,636,650 (15% federal, 9% state, 70% institutional, 6% external sources). *Receiving aid:* Freshmen: 93% (183); all full-time undergraduates: 90% (737). *Average award:* Freshmen: $19,347; Undergraduates: $16,975. *Scholarships, grants, and awards:* Federal Pell, FSEOG, state, private, college/university gift aid from institutional funds, Federal Nursing.

GIFT AID (NON-NEED-BASED) *Total amount:* $1,128,365 (1% state, 80% institutional, 19% external sources). *Receiving aid:* Freshmen: 8% (15). Undergraduates: 8% (63). *Average award:* Freshmen: $6915. Undergraduates: $8626. *Scholarships, grants, and awards by category: Academic interests/achievement:* 293 awards ($3,197,340 total): business, communication, English, general academic interests/achievements. *Creative arts/performance:* 134 awards ($199,500 total): art/fine arts, dance, performing arts, theater/drama. *Special achievements/activities:* 63 awards ($74,360 total): community service, general special achievements/activities, junior miss, leadership, memberships, religious involvement. *Special characteristics:* 104 awards ($403,000 total): adult students, children and siblings of alumni, general special characteristics, previous college experience, relatives of clergy, religious affiliation, siblings of current students. *Tuition waivers:* Full or partial for children of alumni, employees or children of employees.

LOANS *Student loans:* $7,496,235 (75% need-based, 25% non-need-based). 92% of past graduating class borrowed through all loan programs. *Average indebtedness per student:* $24,641. *Average need-based loan:* Freshmen: $3552. Undergraduates: $4628. *Parent loans:* $2,481,273 (36% need-based, 64% non-need-based). *Programs:* Federal Direct (Subsidized and Unsubsidized Stafford, PLUS), Perkins, Federal Nursing.

WORK-STUDY *Federal work-study:* Total amount: $190,029; 86 jobs averaging $2200. *State or other work-study/employment:* Total amount: $410,971 (80% need-based, 20% non-need-based). 300 part-time jobs averaging $2200.

APPLYING FOR FINANCIAL AID *Required financial aid forms:* FAFSA, state aid form. *Financial aid deadline:* 5/1 (priority: 3/15). *Notification date:* Continuous beginning 11/1. Students must reply by 5/15.

CONTACT Ms. Lori Williams, Director, Student Financial Services, Cedar Crest College, 100 College Drive, Allentown, PA 18104-6196, 610-606-4602 or toll-free 800-360-1222. *Fax:* 610-606-4653. *E-mail:* financialservices@cedarcrest.edu.

CEDARVILLE UNIVERSITY
Cedarville, OH

Tuition & fees: $23,500	Average undergraduate aid package: $12,685

ABOUT THE INSTITUTION Independent Baptist, coed. 84 undergraduate majors. Federal methodology is used as a basis for awarding need-based institutional aid.

UNDERGRADUATE EXPENSES for 2010–11 *One-time required fee:* $130. *Comprehensive fee:* $28,586 includes full-time tuition ($23,500) and room and board ($5086). *College room only:* $2820. Room and board charges vary according to board plan. Part-time tuition and fees vary according to course load. *Payment plan:* Installment.

FRESHMAN FINANCIAL AID (Fall 2008) 684 applied for aid; of those 80% were deemed to have need. 100% of freshmen with need received aid; of those 16% had need fully met. *Average percent of need met:* 38% (excluding resources awarded to replace EFC). *Average financial aid package:* $12,699 (excluding resources awarded to replace EFC). 20% of all full-time freshmen had no need and received non-need-based gift aid.

UNDERGRADUATE FINANCIAL AID (Fall 2008) 2,133 applied for aid; of those 83% were deemed to have need. 100% of undergraduates with need received aid; of those 15% had need fully met. *Average percent of need met:* 42% (excluding resources awarded to replace EFC). *Average financial aid package:* $12,685 (excluding resources awarded to replace EFC). 18% of all full-time undergraduates had no need and received non-need-based gift aid.

GIFT AID (NEED-BASED) *Total amount:* $7,001,988 (31% federal, 8% state, 60% institutional, 1% external sources). *Receiving aid:* Freshmen: 45% (381); all full-time undergraduates: 47% (1,333). *Average award:* Freshmen: $3316; Undergraduates: $3663. *Scholarships, grants, and awards:* Federal Pell, FSEOG, state, private, college/university gift aid from institutional funds.

GIFT AID (NON-NEED-BASED) *Total amount:* $13,307,685 (6% state, 70% institutional, 24% external sources). *Receiving aid:* Freshmen: 59% (497). Undergraduates: 53% (1,511). *Average award:* Freshmen: $14,083. Undergraduates: $14,310. *Scholarships, grants, and awards by category: Academic interests/achievement:* 1,429 awards ($3,777,294 total): general academic interests/achievements. *Creative arts/performance:* 68 awards ($153,840 total): debating, music. *Special achievements/activities:* 501 awards ($1,148,291 total): leadership. *Special characteristics:* 183 awards ($2,153,373 total): children and siblings of alumni, children of faculty/staff, ethnic background, general special characteristics, religious affiliation, veterans. *Tuition waivers:* Full or partial for employees or children of employees, senior citizens.

LOANS *Student loans:* $11,984,801 (59% need-based, 41% non-need-based). 67% of past graduating class borrowed through all loan programs. *Average indebtedness per student:* $26,672. *Average need-based loan:* Freshmen: $4761. Undergraduates: $5898. *Parent loans:* $12,743,449 (100% non-need-based). *Programs:* FFEL (Subsidized and Unsubsidized Stafford, PLUS), Perkins, Federal Nursing, college/university.

WORK-STUDY *Federal work-study:* Total amount: $119,475; 175 jobs averaging $683. *State or other work-study/employment:* Total amount: $1,874,752 (100% non-need-based). 1,557 part-time jobs averaging $1204.

ATHLETIC AWARDS Total amount: $772,901 (100% non-need-based).

APPLYING FOR FINANCIAL AID *Required financial aid form:* FAFSA. *Financial aid deadline (priority):* 3/1. *Notification date:* Continuous beginning 3/1. Students must reply within 4 weeks of notification.

CONTACT Mr. Fred Merritt, Director of Financial Aid, Cedarville University, 251 North Main Street, Cedarville, OH 45314-0601, 937-766-7866 or toll-free 800-CEDARVILLE. *E-mail:* merrittf@cedarville.edu.

CENTENARY COLLEGE
Hackettstown, NJ

Tuition & fees: N/R   **Average undergraduate aid package: $17,741**

ABOUT THE INSTITUTION Independent religious, coed. 27 undergraduate majors. Federal methodology is used as a basis for awarding need-based institutional aid.

UNDERGRADUATE EXPENSES for 2009–10 *Tuition:* part-time $490 per credit. *Required fees:* $30 per term. Full-time tuition and fees vary according to program. Part-time tuition and fees vary according to program. Room and board charges vary according to board plan. *Payment plan:* Installment.

FRESHMAN FINANCIAL AID (Fall 2008) 264 applied for aid; of those 85% were deemed to have need. 100% of freshmen with need received aid; of those 22% had need fully met. *Average percent of need met:* 75% (excluding resources awarded to replace EFC). *Average financial aid package:* $19,100 (excluding resources awarded to replace EFC). 35% of all full-time freshmen had no need and received non-need-based gift aid.

UNDERGRADUATE FINANCIAL AID (Fall 2008) 1,165 applied for aid; of those 88% were deemed to have need. 100% of undergraduates with need received aid; of those 19% had need fully met. *Average percent of need met:* 67% (excluding resources awarded to replace EFC). *Average financial aid package:* $17,741 (excluding resources awarded to replace EFC). 26% of all full-time undergraduates had no need and received non-need-based gift aid.

GIFT AID (NEED-BASED) *Total amount:* $13,115,999 (10% federal, 24% state, 62% institutional, 4% external sources). *Receiving aid:* Freshmen: 57% (223); all full-time undergraduates: 67% (1,003). *Average award:* Freshmen: $14,806; Undergraduates: $13,066. *Scholarships, grants, and awards:* Federal Pell, FSEOG, state, private, college/university gift aid from institutional funds.

GIFT AID (NON-NEED-BASED) *Total amount:* $3,920,008 (1% state, 81% institutional, 18% external sources). *Receiving aid:* Freshmen: 7% (26). Undergraduates: 6% (84). *Average award:* Freshmen: $8206. Undergraduates: $7453. *Scholarships, grants, and awards by category: Academic interests/ achievement:* general academic interests/achievements. *Special achievements/ activities:* leadership. *Special characteristics:* 920 awards ($3,694,255 total): children and siblings of alumni, children of faculty/staff, ethnic background, general special characteristics, local/state students, out-of-state students, previous college experience, religious affiliation, siblings of current students.

LOANS *Student loans:* $11,614,475 (64% need-based, 36% non-need-based). 88% of past graduating class borrowed through all loan programs. *Average indebtedness per student:* $20,649. *Average need-based loan:* Freshmen: $5143. Undergraduates: $5625. *Parent loans:* $1,558,116 (43% need-based, 57% non-need-based). *Programs:* FFEL (Subsidized and Unsubsidized Stafford, PLUS), Perkins, state, NJ Class Loans.

WORK-STUDY *Federal work-study:* Total amount: $154,269; 239 jobs averaging $645. *State or other work-study/employment:* Total amount: $261,796 (100% non-need-based). 276 part-time jobs averaging $480.

APPLYING FOR FINANCIAL AID *Required financial aid form:* FAFSA. *Financial aid deadline (priority):* 4/1. *Notification date:* Continuous. Students must reply within 2 weeks of notification.

CONTACT Michelle Burwell, Associate Director of Financial Aid, Centenary College, 400 Jefferson Street, Hackettstown, NJ 07840-2100, 908-852-1400 Ext. 2207 or toll-free 800-236-8679. *Fax:* 908-813-2632. *E-mail:* burwellm@ centenarycollege.edu.

CENTENARY COLLEGE OF LOUISIANA
Shreveport, LA

Tuition & fees: $23,280   **Average undergraduate aid package: $19,140**

ABOUT THE INSTITUTION Independent United Methodist, coed. 29 undergraduate majors. Federal methodology is used as a basis for awarding need-based institutional aid.

UNDERGRADUATE EXPENSES for 2010–11 *Comprehensive fee:* $31,220 includes full-time tuition ($22,080), mandatory fees ($1200), and room and board ($7940). *College room only:* $4020. Room and board charges vary according to board plan and housing facility. Part-time tuition and fees vary according to course load and program. *Payment plans:* Installment, deferred payment.

FRESHMAN FINANCIAL AID (Fall 2009, est.) 251 applied for aid; of those 76% were deemed to have need. 100% of freshmen with need received aid; of those 36% had need fully met. *Average percent of need met:* 83% (excluding resources awarded to replace EFC). *Average financial aid package:* $20,292 (excluding resources awarded to replace EFC). 25% of all full-time freshmen had no need and received non-need-based gift aid.

UNDERGRADUATE FINANCIAL AID (Fall 2009, est.) 723 applied for aid; of those 76% were deemed to have need. 100% of undergraduates with need received aid; of those 29% had need fully met. *Average percent of need met:* 81% (excluding resources awarded to replace EFC). *Average financial aid package:* $19,140 (excluding resources awarded to replace EFC). 26% of all full-time undergraduates had no need and received non-need-based gift aid.

GIFT AID (NEED-BASED) *Total amount:* $7,602,449 (14% federal, 13% state, 72% institutional, 1% external sources). *Receiving aid:* Freshmen: 69% (191); all full-time undergraduates: 63% (550). *Average award:* Freshmen: $17,639; Undergraduates: $16,330. *Scholarships, grants, and awards:* Federal Pell, FSEOG, state, private, college/university gift aid from institutional funds.

GIFT AID (NON-NEED-BASED) *Total amount:* $3,769,602 (11% state, 88% institutional, 1% external sources). *Receiving aid:* Freshmen: 21% (58). Undergraduates: 14% (122). *Average award:* Freshmen: $11,159. Undergraduates: $10,442. *Scholarships, grants, and awards by category: Academic interests/achievement:* 738 awards ($5,735,318 total): biological sciences, business, communication, education, engineering/technologies, English, foreign languages, general academic interests/achievements, health fields, humanities, mathematics, physical sciences, premedicine, religion/biblical studies, social sciences. *Creative arts/performance:* 205 awards ($772,675 total): art/fine arts, dance, general creative arts/performance, music, performing arts, theater/ drama. *Special achievements/activities:* 73 awards ($130,500 total): community service, general special achievements/activities, hobbies/interests, religious involvement. *Special characteristics:* 120 awards ($584,426 total): children of educators, children of faculty/staff, ethnic background, general special characteristics, international students, local/state students, members of minority groups, out-of-state students, relatives of clergy, religious affiliation. *Tuition waivers:* Full or partial for employees or children of employees.

LOANS *Student loans:* $2,635,279 (46% need-based, 54% non-need-based). 58% of past graduating class borrowed through all loan programs. *Average indebtedness per student:* $18,100. *Average need-based loan:* Freshmen: $3353. Undergraduates: $3998. *Parent loans:* $2,332,475 (55% need-based, 45% non-need-based). *Programs:* FFEL (Subsidized and Unsubsidized Stafford, PLUS), Perkins.

WORK-STUDY *Federal work-study:* Total amount: $386,325; 201 jobs averaging $1922. *State or other work-study/employment:* Total amount: $57,583 (100% non-need-based). 62 part-time jobs averaging $929.

ATHLETIC AWARDS Total amount: $2,822,146 (46% need-based, 54% non-need-based).

APPLYING FOR FINANCIAL AID *Required financial aid form:* FAFSA. *Financial aid deadline (priority):* 2/15. *Notification date:* 3/15. Students must reply by 5/1.

CONTACT Ms. Mary Sue Rix, Director of Financial Aid, Centenary College of Louisiana, PO Box 41188, Shreveport, LA 71134-1188, 318-869-5137 or toll-free 800-234-4448. *Fax:* 318-841-7266. *E-mail:* msrix@centenary.edu.

CENTRAL BAPTIST COLLEGE
Conway, AR

CONTACT Christi Bell, Financial Aid Director, Central Baptist College, 1501 College Avenue, Conway, AR 72032-6470, 800-205-6872 Ext. 185 or toll-free 800-205-6872. *Fax:* 501-329-2941. *E-mail:* financialaid@cbc.edu.

CENTRAL BIBLE COLLEGE
Springfield, MO

CONTACT Rick Woolverton, Director of Financial Aid, Central Bible College, 3000 North Grant, Springfield, MO 65803-1096, 417-833-2551 or toll-free 800-831-4222 Ext. 1184. *Fax:* 417-833-2168.

CENTRAL CHRISTIAN COLLEGE OF KANSAS
McPherson, KS

CONTACT Mike Reimer, Financial Aid Director, Central Christian College of Kansas, 1200 South Main, PO Box 1403, McPherson, KS 67460, 620-241-0723 Ext. 333 or toll-free 800-835-0078 Ext. 337. *Fax:* 620-241-6032. *E-mail:* miker@ centralchristian.edu.

CENTRAL CHRISTIAN COLLEGE OF THE BIBLE
Moberly, MO

ABOUT THE INSTITUTION Independent religious, coed. 7 undergraduate majors.
GIFT AID (NEED-BASED) *Scholarships, grants, and awards:* Federal Pell, FSEOG, private, college/university gift aid from institutional funds.
GIFT AID (NON-NEED-BASED) *Scholarships, grants, and awards by category:* Academic interests/achievement: religion/biblical studies.
LOANS *Programs:* FFEL (Subsidized and Unsubsidized Stafford, PLUS), alternative loans.
WORK-STUDY *Federal work-study:* Total amount: $25,000; 9 jobs averaging $2741.
APPLYING FOR FINANCIAL AID *Required financial aid form:* FAFSA.
CONTACT Rhonda J. Dunham, Financial Aid Director, Central Christian College of the Bible, 911 East Urbandale Drive, Moberly, MO 65270-1997, 660-263-3900 Ext. 121 or toll-free 888-263-3900 (in-state). *Fax:* 660-263-3936. *E-mail:* rdunham@cccb.edu.

CENTRAL COLLEGE
Pella, IA

Tuition & fees: $25,010	Average undergraduate aid package: $22,115

ABOUT THE INSTITUTION Independent religious, coed. 37 undergraduate majors. Federal methodology is used as a basis for awarding need-based institutional aid.
UNDERGRADUATE EXPENSES for 2009–10 *Comprehensive fee:* $33,378 includes full-time tuition ($24,630), mandatory fees ($380), and room and board ($8368). *College room only:* $4104. Room and board charges vary according to board plan. *Part-time tuition:* $855 per semester hour. Part-time tuition and fees vary according to course load. *Payment plan:* Installment.
FRESHMAN FINANCIAL AID (Fall 2009, est.) 443 applied for aid; of those 89% were deemed to have need. 100% of freshmen with need received aid; of those 26% had need fully met. *Average percent of need met:* 87% (excluding resources awarded to replace EFC). *Average financial aid package:* $23,302 (excluding resources awarded to replace EFC). 11% of all full-time freshmen had no need and received non-need-based gift aid.
UNDERGRADUATE FINANCIAL AID (Fall 2009, est.) 1,508 applied for aid; of those 82% were deemed to have need. 100% of undergraduates with need received aid; of those 20% had need fully met. *Average percent of need met:* 84% (excluding resources awarded to replace EFC). *Average financial aid package:* $22,115 (excluding resources awarded to replace EFC). 18% of all full-time undergraduates had no need and received non-need-based gift aid.
GIFT AID (NEED-BASED) *Total amount:* $19,577,052 (13% federal, 14% state, 71% institutional, 2% external sources). *Receiving aid:* Freshmen: 89% (393); all full-time undergraduates: 82% (1,238). *Average award:* Freshmen: $17,824; Undergraduates: $16,141. *Scholarships, grants, and awards:* Federal Pell, FSEOG, state, private, college/university gift aid from institutional funds.
GIFT AID (NON-NEED-BASED) *Total amount:* $3,862,768 (1% federal, 95% institutional, 4% external sources). *Receiving aid:* Freshmen: 16% (72). Undergraduates: 11% (172). *Average award:* Freshmen: $12,169. Undergraduates: $10,799. *Scholarships, grants, and awards by category:* Academic interests/achievement: biological sciences, business, communication, computer science, education, foreign languages, general academic interests/achievements, health fields, humanities, international studies, mathematics, physical sciences, premedicine, religion/biblical studies, social sciences. Creative arts/performance: art/fine arts, creative writing, music, theater/drama. Special achievements/ activities: community service, religious involvement. Special characteristics: children and siblings of alumni, children of current students, children of faculty/

staff, general special characteristics, handicapped students, international students, local/state students, members of minority groups, out-of-state students, previous college experience, religious affiliation, siblings of current students, twins, veterans, veterans' children. *Tuition waivers:* Full or partial for employees or children of employees.
LOANS *Student loans:* $10,634,006 (69% need-based, 31% non-need-based). 86% of past graduating class borrowed through all loan programs. *Average indebtedness per student:* $36,068. *Average need-based loan:* Freshmen: $3928. Undergraduates: $4643. *Parent loans:* $3,650,196 (27% need-based, 73% non-need-based). *Programs:* Federal Direct (Subsidized and Unsubsidized Stafford, PLUS), Perkins, college/university, alternative loans.
WORK-STUDY *Federal work-study:* Total amount: $1,243,541; 916 jobs averaging $1365. *State or other work-study/employment:* Total amount: $474,370 (17% need-based, 83% non-need-based). 351 part-time jobs averaging $1316.
APPLYING FOR FINANCIAL AID *Required financial aid form:* FAFSA. *Financial aid deadline (priority):* 3/15. *Notification date:* Continuous beginning 3/15. Students must reply by 5/1 or within 2 weeks of notification.
CONTACT Ms. Jean L. Vander Wert, Director of Financial Aid, Central College, 812 University Street, Campus Box 5800, Pella, IA 50219-1999, 641-628-5336 or toll-free 877-462-3687 (in-state), 877-462-3689 (out-of-state). *Fax:* 641-628-7199. *E-mail:* vanderwertj@central.edu.

CENTRAL CONNECTICUT STATE UNIVERSITY
New Britain, CT

Tuition & fees (CT res): $7414	Average undergraduate aid package: $7913

ABOUT THE INSTITUTION State-supported, coed. 53 undergraduate majors. Federal methodology is used as a basis for awarding need-based institutional aid.
UNDERGRADUATE EXPENSES for 2009–10 *Tuition, state resident:* full-time $3742; part-time $350 per credit. *Tuition, nonresident:* full-time $12,112; part-time $350 per credit. *Required fees:* full-time $3672; $55 per term. Full-time tuition and fees vary according to course level, course load, program, and reciprocity agreements. Part-time tuition and fees vary according to course level, course load, and program. *College room and board:* $9122; *Room only:* $5308. Room and board charges vary according to board plan. *Payment plan:* Installment.
FRESHMAN FINANCIAL AID (Fall 2009, est.) 1,168 applied for aid; of those 69% were deemed to have need. 91% of freshmen with need received aid; of those 13% had need fully met. *Average percent of need met:* 66% (excluding resources awarded to replace EFC). *Average financial aid package:* $7770 (excluding resources awarded to replace EFC). 2% of all full-time freshmen had no need and received non-need-based gift aid.
UNDERGRADUATE FINANCIAL AID (Fall 2009, est.) 6,475 applied for aid; of those 75% were deemed to have need. 91% of undergraduates with need received aid; of those 12% had need fully met. *Average percent of need met:* 66% (excluding resources awarded to replace EFC). *Average financial aid package:* $7913 (excluding resources awarded to replace EFC). 1% of all full-time undergraduates had no need and received non-need-based gift aid.
GIFT AID (NEED-BASED) *Total amount:* $18,691,415 (52% federal, 22% state, 26% institutional). *Receiving aid:* Freshmen: 52% (669); all full-time undergraduates: 56% (4,430). *Average award:* Freshmen: $4133; Undergraduates: $4306. *Scholarships, grants, and awards:* Federal Pell, FSEOG, state, private, college/ university gift aid from institutional funds.
GIFT AID (NON-NEED-BASED) *Total amount:* $2,399,520 (67% institutional, 33% external sources). *Receiving aid:* Freshmen: 13% (165). Undergraduates: 5% (402). *Average award:* Freshmen: $2581. Undergraduates: $2416. *Scholarships, grants, and awards by category:* Academic interests/achievement: general academic interests/achievements. Special characteristics: members of minority groups. *Tuition waivers:* Full or partial for employees or children of employees, senior citizens.
LOANS *Student loans:* $46,853,800 (47% need-based, 53% non-need-based). 48% of past graduating class borrowed through all loan programs. *Average indebtedness per student:* $19,200. *Average need-based loan:* Freshmen: $3383. Undergraduates: $4128. *Parent loans:* $8,465,905 (100% non-need-based). *Programs:* Federal Direct (Subsidized and Unsubsidized Stafford, PLUS), FFEL (Subsidized and Unsubsidized Stafford, PLUS), Perkins.

WORK-STUDY *Federal work-study:* Total amount: $246,748; jobs available. *State or other work-study/employment:* Part-time jobs available.

ATHLETIC AWARDS Total amount: $2,576,408 (100% non-need-based).

APPLYING FOR FINANCIAL AID *Required financial aid forms:* FAFSA, institution's own form. *Financial aid deadline (priority):* 3/1. *Notification date:* Continuous. Students must reply within 3 weeks of notification.

CONTACT Mr. Dennis Williams, Associate Director of Financial Aid, Central Connecticut State University, Memorial Hall, Room 103, New Britain, CT 06050-4010, 860-832-2200 or toll-free 888-733-2278 (in-state). *Fax:* 860-832-1105. *E-mail:* lupachinok@ccsu.edu.

CENTRAL METHODIST UNIVERSITY
Fayette, MO

ABOUT THE INSTITUTION Independent Methodist, coed. *Awards:* associate, bachelor's, and master's degrees. 47 undergraduate majors. *Total enrollment:* 1,031. Undergraduates: 1,031. Freshmen: 300.

GIFT AID (NEED-BASED) *Scholarships, grants, and awards:* Federal Pell, FSEOG, state, private, college/university gift aid from institutional funds.

GIFT AID (NON-NEED-BASED) *Scholarships, grants, and awards by category:* *Academic interests/achievement:* biological sciences, business, communication, computer science, education, English, foreign languages, general academic interests/achievements, health fields, humanities, mathematics, physical sciences, premedicine, religion/biblical studies, social sciences. *Creative arts/performance:* music, theater/drama. *Special achievements/activities:* cheerleading/drum major, leadership, religious involvement. *Special characteristics:* children and siblings of alumni, children of faculty/staff, general special characteristics, international students, relatives of clergy, religious affiliation, siblings of current students, spouses of current students.

LOANS *Programs:* FFEL (Subsidized and Unsubsidized Stafford, PLUS), Perkins, college/university.

WORK-STUDY *Federal work-study:* Total amount: $124,017; 145 jobs averaging $1000. *State or other work-study/employment:* Total amount: $140,800 (100% non-need-based). 90 part-time jobs averaging $1619.

APPLYING FOR FINANCIAL AID *Required financial aid form:* FAFSA.

CONTACT Linda Mackey, Director of Financial Assistance, Central Methodist University, 411 Central Methodist Square, Fayette, MO 65248-1198, 660-248-6244 or toll-free 888-CMU-1854 (in-state). *Fax:* 660-248-6288. *E-mail:* lmackey@centralmethodist.edu.

CENTRAL MICHIGAN UNIVERSITY
Mount Pleasant, MI

Tuition & fees (MI res): $10,170	Average undergraduate aid package: $10,428

ABOUT THE INSTITUTION State-supported, coed. 133 undergraduate majors. Federal methodology is used as a basis for awarding need-based institutional aid.

UNDERGRADUATE EXPENSES for 2009-10 *Tuition, state resident:* full-time $10,170; part-time $339 per credit hour. *Tuition, nonresident:* full-time $23,670; part-time $789 per credit hour. Full-time tuition and fees vary according to student level. Part-time tuition and fees vary according to student level. *College room and board:* $7896; *Room only:* $3948. Room and board charges vary according to board plan, housing facility, location, and student level. *Payment plan:* Installment.

FRESHMAN FINANCIAL AID (Fall 2008) 3,139 applied for aid; of those 70% were deemed to have need. 98% of freshmen with need received aid; of those 57% had need fully met. *Average percent of need met:* 83% (excluding resources awarded to replace EFC). *Average financial aid package:* $11,026 (excluding resources awarded to replace EFC). 12% of all full-time freshmen had no need and received non-need-based gift aid.

UNDERGRADUATE FINANCIAL AID (Fall 2008) 13,216 applied for aid; of those 74% were deemed to have need. 99% of undergraduates with need received aid; of those 57% had need fully met. *Average percent of need met:* 83% (excluding resources awarded to replace EFC). *Average financial aid package:* $10,428 (excluding resources awarded to replace EFC). 9% of all full-time undergraduates had no need and received non-need-based gift aid.

GIFT AID (NEED-BASED) *Total amount:* $36,331,625 (49% federal, 13% state, 34% institutional, 4% external sources). *Receiving aid:* Freshmen: 49% (1,884); all full-time undergraduates: 43% (7,653). *Average award:* Freshmen: $5822;

Undergraduates: $4768. *Scholarships, grants, and awards:* Federal Pell, FSEOG, state, private, college/university gift aid from institutional funds.

GIFT AID (NON-NEED-BASED) *Total amount:* $11,212,644 (8% federal, 20% state, 53% institutional, 19% external sources). *Receiving aid:* Freshmen: 6% (219). Undergraduates: 3% (584). *Average award:* Freshmen: $3160. Undergraduates: $3467. *Scholarships, grants, and awards by category:* *Academic interests/achievement:* biological sciences, business, communication, computer science, education, engineering/technologies, English, foreign languages, general academic interests/achievements, health fields, humanities, international studies, mathematics, military science, physical sciences, social sciences. *Creative arts/performance:* applied art and design, art/fine arts, cinema/film/broadcasting, creative writing, dance, journalism/publications, music, performing arts, theater/drama. *Special achievements/activities:* leadership. *Special characteristics:* children and siblings of alumni, children of faculty/staff, children of union members/company employees, first-generation college students, international students, local/state students, members of minority groups, out-of-state students, veterans, veterans' children. *Tuition waivers:* Full or partial for children of alumni, employees or children of employees, senior citizens.

LOANS *Student loans:* $105,113,236 (59% need-based, 41% non-need-based). 71% of past graduating class borrowed through all loan programs. *Average indebtedness per student:* $26,615. *Average need-based loan:* Freshmen: $5410. Undergraduates: $6481. *Parent loans:* $18,979,945 (20% need-based, 80% non-need-based). *Programs:* Federal Direct (Subsidized and Unsubsidized Stafford, PLUS), alternative loans.

WORK-STUDY *Federal work-study:* Total amount: $1,256,597; jobs available. *State or other work-study/employment:* Total amount: $9,494,278 (22% need-based, 78% non-need-based). Part-time jobs available.

ATHLETIC AWARDS Total amount: $4,172,301 (37% need-based, 63% non-need-based).

APPLYING FOR FINANCIAL AID *Required financial aid form:* FAFSA. *Financial aid deadline (priority):* 3/1. *Notification date:* Continuous beginning 4/1.

CONTACT Mr. Kirk Yats, Associate Director/Operations, Scholarships and Financial Aid, Central Michigan University, WA 202, Mount Pleasant, MI 48859, 989-774-7428 or toll-free 888-292-5366. *Fax:* 989-774-3634. *E-mail:* yats1km@cmich.edu.

CENTRAL PENNSYLVANIA COLLEGE
Summerdale, PA

CONTACT Kathy Shepard, Financial Aid Director, Central Pennsylvania College, College Hill and Valley Roads, Summerdale, PA 17093, 717-728-2261 or toll-free 800-759-2727 Ext. 2201. *Fax:* 717-728-2350. *E-mail:* financial-aid@centralpenn.edu.

CENTRAL STATE UNIVERSITY
Wilberforce, OH

ABOUT THE INSTITUTION State-supported, coed. 30 undergraduate majors.

GIFT AID (NEED-BASED) *Scholarships, grants, and awards:* Federal Pell, FSEOG, state, private, college/university gift aid from institutional funds.

GIFT AID (NON-NEED-BASED) *Scholarships, grants, and awards by category:* *Academic interests/achievement:* business, computer science, education, engineering/technologies, general academic interests/achievements, physical sciences. *Creative arts/performance:* music. *Special characteristics:* children of faculty/staff, veterans, veterans' children.

LOANS *Programs:* FFEL (Subsidized and Unsubsidized Stafford, PLUS).

WORK-STUDY *Federal work-study:* Total amount: $701,884; 408 jobs averaging $1720.

APPLYING FOR FINANCIAL AID *Required financial aid form:* FAFSA.

CONTACT Jean Hurst, Interim Director of Student Financial Aid, Central State University, PO Box 1004, Wilberforce, OH 45384, 937-376-6579 or toll-free 800-388-CSU1 (in-state). *Fax:* 937-376-6519. *E-mail:* jhurst@centralstate.edu.

CENTRAL WASHINGTON UNIVERSITY
Ellensburg, WA

CONTACT Ms. Agnes Canedo, Director of Financial Aid, Central Washington University, 400 East University Way, Ellensburg, WA 98926-7495, 509-963-3049 or toll-free 866-298-4968. *Fax:* 509-963-1788. *E-mail:* canedoa@cwu.edu.

CENTRAL YESHIVA TOMCHEI TMIMIM-LUBAVITCH
Brooklyn, NY

CONTACT Rabbi Moshe M. Gluckowsky, Director of Financial Aid, Central Yeshiva Tomchei Tmimim-Lubavitch, 841-853 Ocean Parkway, Brooklyn, NY 11230, 718-859-2277.

CENTRE COLLEGE
Danville, KY

Tuition & fees: N/R	Average undergraduate aid package: $25,091

ABOUT THE INSTITUTION Independent religious, coed. *Awards:* bachelor's degrees. 27 undergraduate majors. *Total enrollment:* 1,197. Undergraduates: 1,197. Freshmen: 336. Institutional methodology is used as a basis for awarding need-based institutional aid.

FRESHMAN FINANCIAL AID (Fall 2009, est.) 272 applied for aid; of those 79% were deemed to have need. 100% of freshmen with need received aid; of those 46% had need fully met. *Average percent of need met:* 92% (excluding resources awarded to replace EFC). *Average financial aid package:* $26,221 (excluding resources awarded to replace EFC). 33% of all full-time freshmen had no need and received non-need-based gift aid.

UNDERGRADUATE FINANCIAL AID (Fall 2009, est.) 866 applied for aid; of those 83% were deemed to have need. 100% of undergraduates with need received aid; of those 30% had need fully met. *Average percent of need met:* 85% (excluding resources awarded to replace EFC). *Average financial aid package:* $25,091 (excluding resources awarded to replace EFC). 36% of all full-time undergraduates had no need and received non-need-based gift aid.

GIFT AID (NEED-BASED) *Total amount:* $15,610,982 (7% federal, 14% state, 76% institutional, 3% external sources). *Receiving aid:* Freshmen: 64% (214); all full-time undergraduates: 59% (721). *Average award:* Freshmen: $23,827; Undergraduates: $21,641. *Scholarships, grants, and awards:* Federal Pell, FSEOG, state, private, college/university gift aid from institutional funds, Academic Competitiveness Grants, National SMART Grants.

GIFT AID (NON-NEED-BASED) *Total amount:* $6,235,243 (8% state, 87% institutional, 5% external sources). *Average award:* Freshmen: $17,038. Undergraduates: $14,106. *Scholarships, grants, and awards by category: Academic interests/achievement:* 885 awards ($10,586,600 total): general academic interests/achievements. *Creative arts/performance:* 104 awards ($358,000 total): music, theater/drama. *Special achievements/activities:* 20 awards ($47,500 total): community service. *Special characteristics:* 187 awards ($1,686,598 total): children and siblings of alumni, children of faculty/staff, ethnic background, first-generation college students. *Tuition waivers:* Full or partial for employees or children of employees. *ROTC:* Army cooperative, Air Force cooperative.

LOANS *Student loans:* $3,785,948 (61% need-based, 39% non-need-based). 53% of past graduating class borrowed through all loan programs. *Average indebtedness per student:* $17,190. *Average need-based loan:* Freshmen: $3618. Undergraduates: $4803. *Parent loans:* $1,582,189 (100% non-need-based). *Programs:* FFEL (Subsidized and Unsubsidized Stafford, PLUS), Perkins, college/university.

WORK-STUDY *Federal work-study:* Total amount: $485,610; 305 jobs averaging $1570. *State or other work-study/employment:* Total amount: $10,900 (100% non-need-based). 6 part-time jobs averaging $1810.

APPLYING FOR FINANCIAL AID *Required financial aid forms:* FAFSA, institution's own form. *Financial aid deadline:* 3/1. *Notification date:* 4/1. Students must reply by 5/1.

CONTACT Ms. Elaine Larson, Director of Student Financial Planning, Centre College, 600 West Walnut Street, Danville, KY 40422-1394, 859-238-5365 or toll-free 800-423-6236. *Fax:* 859-238-8719. *E-mail:* finaid@centre.edu.

CHADRON STATE COLLEGE
Chadron, NE

CONTACT Ms. Sherry Douglas, Director of Financial Aid, Chadron State College, 1000 Main Street, Chadron, NE 69337, 308-432-6230 or toll-free 800-242-3766 (in-state). *Fax:* 308-432-6229. *E-mail:* finaid@csc.edu.

CHAMBERLAIN COLLEGE OF NURSING
St. Louis, MO

Tuition & fees: N/R	Average undergraduate aid package: N/A

ABOUT THE INSTITUTION Proprietary, coed. *Awards:* associate and bachelor's degrees. 1 undergraduate major. *Total enrollment:* 1,452. Undergraduates: 1,452. Both federal and institutional methodology are used as a basis for awarding need-based institutional aid.

GIFT AID (NEED-BASED) *Scholarships, grants, and awards:* Federal Pell, FSEOG, private, college/university gift aid from institutional funds.

GIFT AID (NON-NEED-BASED) *Scholarships, grants, and awards by category: Academic interests/achievement:* general academic interests/achievements, health fields. *Special achievements/activities:* leadership. *ROTC:* Army cooperative.

LOANS *Programs:* FFEL (Subsidized and Unsubsidized Stafford, PLUS), state.

APPLYING FOR FINANCIAL AID *Required financial aid forms:* FAFSA, institution's own form. *Financial aid deadline (priority):* 4/1. *Notification date:* Continuous. Students must reply within 2 weeks of notification.

CONTACT Financial Aid Counselor, Chamberlain College of Nursing, 6150 Oakland Avenue, St. Louis, MO 63139-3215, 314-768-5604 or toll-free 800-942-4310.

CHAMINADE UNIVERSITY OF HONOLULU
Honolulu, HI

Tuition & fees: $17,740	Average undergraduate aid package: $12,846

ABOUT THE INSTITUTION Independent Roman Catholic, coed. 22 undergraduate majors. Federal methodology is used as a basis for awarding need-based institutional aid.

UNDERGRADUATE EXPENSES for 2010–11 *Comprehensive fee:* $28,160 includes full-time tuition ($17,600), mandatory fees ($140), and room and board ($10,420). *College room only:* $5170. Full-time tuition and fees vary according to course load. Room and board charges vary according to board plan and housing facility. *Part-time tuition:* $587 per credit hour. Part-time tuition and fees vary according to course load. *Payment plan:* Installment.

UNDERGRADUATE FINANCIAL AID (Fall 2008) *Average percent of need met:* 66% (excluding resources awarded to replace EFC). *Average financial aid package:* $12,846 (excluding resources awarded to replace EFC).

GIFT AID (NEED-BASED) *Average award:* Undergraduates: $8257. *Scholarships, grants, and awards:* Federal Pell, FSEOG, state, private, college/university gift aid from institutional funds.

GIFT AID (NON-NEED-BASED) *Average award:* Undergraduates: $4565. *Scholarships, grants, and awards by category: Academic interests/achievement:* general academic interests/achievements.

LOANS *Student loans:* 56% of past graduating class borrowed through all loan programs. *Average indebtedness per student:* $22,263. *Programs:* FFEL (Subsidized and Unsubsidized Stafford, PLUS), Perkins, alternative loans.

WORK-STUDY Federal work-study jobs available.

APPLYING FOR FINANCIAL AID *Required financial aid form:* FAFSA. *Financial aid deadline (priority):* 3/1. *Notification date:* Continuous beginning 3/1. Students must reply within 4 weeks of notification.

CONTACT Mr. Eric Nemoto, Director of Financial Aid, Chaminade University of Honolulu, 3140 Waialae Avenue, Honolulu, HI 96816-1578, 808-735-4780 or toll-free 800-735-3733 (out-of-state). *Fax:* 808-739-8362. *E-mail:* finaid@chaminade.edu.

CHAMPLAIN COLLEGE
Burlington, VT

CONTACT David B. Myette, Director of Financial Aid, Champlain College, 163 South Willard Street, Burlington, VT 05401, 802-865-6430 or toll-free 800-570-5858. *Fax:* 802-860-2775. *E-mail:* myette@champlain.edu.

CHANCELLOR UNIVERSITY
Cleveland, OH

CONTACT Eric Damon, Director of Financial Aid, Chancellor University, 3921 Chester Avenue, Cleveland, OH 44114, 216-361-2734 or toll-free 877-366-9377. *Fax:* 216-361-9096.

CHAPMAN UNIVERSITY
Orange, CA

Tuition & fees: $38,524	Average undergraduate aid package: $27,771

ABOUT THE INSTITUTION Independent religious, coed. 51 undergraduate majors. Both federal and institutional methodology are used as a basis for awarding need-based institutional aid.

UNDERGRADUATE EXPENSES for 2010–11 *Comprehensive fee:* $51,481 includes full-time tuition ($37,500), mandatory fees ($1024), and room and board ($12,957). *College room only:* $9255. Room and board charges vary according to board plan and housing facility. *Part-time tuition:* $1170 per credit. Part-time tuition and fees vary according to course load. *Payment plans:* Tuition prepayment, installment, deferred payment.

FRESHMAN FINANCIAL AID (Fall 2009, est.) 783 applied for aid; of those 73% were deemed to have need. 100% of freshmen with need received aid; of those 100% had need fully met. *Average percent of need met:* 100% (excluding resources awarded to replace EFC). *Average financial aid package:* $28,920 (excluding resources awarded to replace EFC). 10% of all full-time freshmen had no need and received non-need-based gift aid.

UNDERGRADUATE FINANCIAL AID (Fall 2009, est.) 3,778 applied for aid; of those 70% were deemed to have need. 100% of undergraduates with need received aid; of those 100% had need fully met. *Average percent of need met:* 100% (excluding resources awarded to replace EFC). *Average financial aid package:* $27,771 (excluding resources awarded to replace EFC). 17% of all full-time undergraduates had no need and received non-need-based gift aid.

GIFT AID (NEED-BASED) *Total amount:* $57,899,688 (9% federal, 8% state, 82% institutional, 1% external sources). *Receiving aid:* Freshmen: 55% (563); all full-time undergraduates: 61% (2,612). *Average award:* Freshmen: $26,497; Undergraduates: $24,076. *Scholarships, grants, and awards:* Federal Pell, FSEOG, state, private, college/university gift aid from institutional funds.

GIFT AID (NON-NEED-BASED) *Total amount:* $13,009,914 (99% institutional, 1% external sources). *Average award:* Freshmen: $21,261. Undergraduates: $17,256. *Scholarships, grants, and awards by category: Academic interests/achievement:* 931 awards ($11,089,514 total): biological sciences, general academic interests/achievements, physical sciences. *Creative arts/performance:* 146 awards ($596,702 total): art/fine arts, cinema/film/broadcasting, creative writing, dance, music, performing arts, theater/drama. *Special characteristics:* 29 awards ($29,000 total): children and siblings of alumni. *Tuition waivers:* Full or partial for employees or children of employees.

LOANS *Student loans:* $18,267,850 (91% need-based, 9% non-need-based). 64% of past graduating class borrowed through all loan programs. *Average indebtedness per student:* $23,917. *Average need-based loan:* Freshmen: $3330. Undergraduates: $4511. *Parent loans:* $11,105,693 (81% need-based, 19% non-need-based). *Programs:* Federal Direct (Subsidized and Unsubsidized Stafford), Perkins.

WORK-STUDY *Federal work-study:* Total amount: $1,856,517; 828 jobs averaging $2186.

APPLYING FOR FINANCIAL AID *Required financial aid forms:* FAFSA, state aid form. *Financial aid deadline (priority):* 3/2. *Notification date:* Continuous beginning 3/15. Students must reply within 3 weeks of notification.

CONTACT Mr. Gregory L. Ball, Director of Financial Aid, Chapman University, One University Drive, Orange, CA 92866, 714-997-6740 or toll-free 888-CUAPPLY. *Fax:* 714-997-6743. *E-mail:* gball@chapman.edu.

CHARLES DREW UNIVERSITY OF MEDICINE AND SCIENCE
Los Angeles, CA

CONTACT Financial Aid Office, Charles Drew University of Medicine and Science, 1731 East 120th Street, Los Angeles, CA 90059, 323-563-4824. *Fax:* 323-569-0597.

CHARLESTON SOUTHERN UNIVERSITY
Charleston, SC

CONTACT Mr. Jim Rhoden, Director of Admissions, Charleston Southern University, PO Box 118087, 9200 University Boulevard, Charleston, SC 29423-8087, 843-863-7050 or toll-free 800-947-7474. *Fax:* 843-863-7070.

CHARTER OAK STATE COLLEGE
New Britain, CT

CONTACT Velma Walters, Director, Financial Aid, Charter Oak State College, 55 Paul J. Manafort Drive, New Britain, CT 06053-2142, 860-832-3872. *Fax:* 860-832-3999. *E-mail:* sfa@charteroak.edu.

CHATHAM UNIVERSITY
Pittsburgh, PA

Tuition & fees: N/R	Average undergraduate aid package: $15,515

ABOUT THE INSTITUTION Independent, undergraduate: women only; graduate: coed. 44 undergraduate majors. Both federal and institutional methodology are used as a basis for awarding need-based institutional aid.

UNDERGRADUATE EXPENSES for 2010–11 *Tuition:* part-time $662 per credit hour. Full-time tuition and fees vary according to degree level and student level. Part-time tuition and fees vary according to course load. Room and board charges vary according to board plan and housing facility. *Payment plan:* Installment.

FRESHMAN FINANCIAL AID (Fall 2009, est.) 110 applied for aid; of those 95% were deemed to have need. 100% of freshmen with need received aid; of those 24% had need fully met. *Average percent of need met:* 78% (excluding resources awarded to replace EFC). *Average financial aid package:* $26,715 (excluding resources awarded to replace EFC). 5% of all full-time freshmen had no need and received non-need-based gift aid.

UNDERGRADUATE FINANCIAL AID (Fall 2009, est.) 552 applied for aid; of those 94% were deemed to have need. 100% of undergraduates with need received aid; of those 15% had need fully met. *Average percent of need met:* 66% (excluding resources awarded to replace EFC). *Average financial aid package:* $15,515 (excluding resources awarded to replace EFC). 4% of all full-time undergraduates had no need and received non-need-based gift aid.

GIFT AID (NEED-BASED) *Total amount:* $3,458,152 (34% federal, 25% state, 40% institutional, 1% external sources). *Receiving aid:* Freshmen: 67% (88); all full-time undergraduates: 64% (436). *Average award:* Freshmen: $8021; Undergraduates: $8645. *Scholarships, grants, and awards:* Federal Pell, FSEOG, state, private, college/university gift aid from institutional funds, United Negro College Fund.

GIFT AID (NON-NEED-BASED) *Total amount:* $6,679,645 (98% institutional, 2% external sources). *Receiving aid:* Freshmen: 80% (105). Undergraduates: 75% (507). *Average award:* Freshmen: $17,000. Undergraduates: $13,107. *Scholarships, grants, and awards by category: Academic interests/achievement:* biological sciences, business, communication, education, English, general academic interests/achievements, international studies, mathematics, physical sciences, premedicine, social sciences. *Creative arts/performance:* theater/drama. *Special characteristics:* children and siblings of alumni, children of faculty/staff, siblings of current students. *Tuition waivers:* Full or partial for employees or children of employees.

LOANS *Student loans:* $5,406,208 (41% need-based, 59% non-need-based). *Average need-based loan:* Freshmen: $4586. Undergraduates: $9265. *Parent loans:* $1,364,672 (22% need-based, 78% non-need-based). *Programs:* FFEL (Subsidized and Unsubsidized Stafford, PLUS), Perkins.

WORK-STUDY *Federal work-study:* Total amount: $443,558; jobs available. *State or other work-study/employment:* Part-time jobs available.

APPLYING FOR FINANCIAL AID *Required financial aid form:* FAFSA. *Financial aid deadline (priority):* 5/1. *Notification date:* Continuous beginning 2/15. Students must reply by 5/1 or within 2 weeks of notification.

CONTACT Jennifer Burns, Director of Financial Aid, Chatham University, Woodland Road, Pittsburgh, PA 15232-2826, 800-837-1610 or toll-free 800-837-1290. *Fax:* 412-365-1643. *E-mail:* jburns@chatham.edu.

CHESTER COLLEGE OF NEW ENGLAND
Chester, NH

CONTACT Jason Graves, Director of Financial Aid, Chester College of New England, 40 Chester Street, Chester, NH 03036-4331, 603-887-4401 Ext. 7404 or toll-free 800-974-6372. *Fax:* 603-887-1777. *E-mail:* financialaid@chestercollege.edu.

CHESTNUT HILL COLLEGE
Philadelphia, PA

Tuition & fees: $27,100 **Average undergraduate aid package:** $17,839

ABOUT THE INSTITUTION Independent Roman Catholic, coed. *Awards:* associate, bachelor's, and master's degrees and post-bachelor's and post-master's certificates (profile includes figures from both traditional and accelerated (part-time) programs). 37 undergraduate majors. *Total enrollment:* 2,085. Undergraduates: 1,329. Freshmen: 201. Federal methodology is used as a basis for awarding need-based institutional aid.

UNDERGRADUATE EXPENSES for 2009–10 *Application fee:* $35. *Comprehensive fee:* $35,900 includes full-time tuition ($27,000), mandatory fees ($100), and room and board ($8800). Room and board charges vary according to housing facility. *Part-time tuition:* $575 per credit. *Payment plans:* Installment, deferred payment.

FRESHMAN FINANCIAL AID (Fall 2009, est.) 268 applied for aid; of those 84% were deemed to have need. 99% of freshmen with need received aid; of those 22% had need fully met. *Average percent of need met:* 75% (excluding resources awarded to replace EFC). *Average financial aid package:* $19,274 (excluding resources awarded to replace EFC). 1% of all full-time freshmen had no need and received non-need-based gift aid.

UNDERGRADUATE FINANCIAL AID (Fall 2009, est.) 976 applied for aid; of those 91% were deemed to have need. 99% of undergraduates with need received aid; of those 18% had need fully met. *Average percent of need met:* 71% (excluding resources awarded to replace EFC). *Average financial aid package:* $17,839 (excluding resources awarded to replace EFC). 1% of all full-time undergraduates had no need and received non-need-based gift aid.

GIFT AID (NEED-BASED) *Total amount:* $12,102,391 (21% federal, 11% state, 66% institutional, 2% external sources). *Receiving aid:* Freshmen: 82% (223); all full-time undergraduates: 77% (879). *Average award:* Freshmen: $15,577; Undergraduates: $13,510. *Scholarships, grants, and awards:* Federal Pell, FSEOG, state, private, college/university gift aid from institutional funds.

GIFT AID (NON-NEED-BASED) *Total amount:* $2,157,976 (98% institutional, 2% external sources). *Receiving aid:* Freshmen: 14% (38). Undergraduates: 8% (94). *Average award:* Freshmen: $1000. Undergraduates: $5837. *Scholarships, grants, and awards by category: Academic interests/achievement:* general academic interests/achievements. *Creative arts/performance:* music, theater/drama. *Special characteristics:* children and siblings of alumni, children of faculty/staff, relatives of clergy. *Tuition waivers:* Full or partial for employees or children of employees, senior citizens.

LOANS *Student loans:* $10,453,860 (75% need-based, 25% non-need-based). *Average need-based loan:* Freshmen: $3836. Undergraduates: $4528. *Parent loans:* $1,593,701 (26% need-based, 74% non-need-based). *Programs:* FFEL (Subsidized and Unsubsidized Stafford, PLUS), Perkins.

WORK-STUDY *Federal work-study:* Total amount: $142,398; jobs available. *State or other work-study/employment:* Part-time jobs available.

ATHLETIC AWARDS Total amount: $638,250 (59% need-based, 41% non-need-based).

APPLYING FOR FINANCIAL AID *Required financial aid form:* FAFSA. *Financial aid deadline:* 4/15 (priority: 1/31). *Notification date:* Continuous beginning 2/15.

CONTACT Mr. Nicholas Flocco, Director of Financial Aid, Chestnut Hill College, 9601 Germantown Avenue, Philadelphia, PA 19118-2693, 215-248-7192 or toll-free 800-248-0052 (out-of-state). *Fax:* 215-248-7217. *E-mail:* nfloccon@chc.edu.

CHEYNEY UNIVERSITY OF PENNSYLVANIA
Cheyney, PA

CONTACT Mr. James Brown, Director of Financial Aid, Cheyney University of Pennsylvania, 1837 University Circle, Cheyney, PA 19319, 610-399-2302 or toll-free 800-CHEYNEY. *Fax:* 610-399-2411. *E-mail:* jbrown@cheyney.edu.

CHICAGO STATE UNIVERSITY
Chicago, IL

CONTACT Director of Student Financial Aid, Chicago State University, 9501 South Martin Luther King Drive, Chicago, IL 60628, 773-995-2304.

CHOWAN UNIVERSITY
Murfreesboro, NC

Tuition & fees: $18,850 **Average undergraduate aid package:** $17,453

ABOUT THE INSTITUTION Independent Baptist, coed. 50 undergraduate majors. Federal methodology is used as a basis for awarding need-based institutional aid.

UNDERGRADUATE EXPENSES for 2010–11 *One-time required fee:* $145. *Comprehensive fee:* $26,160 includes full-time tuition ($18,850) and room and board ($7310). *College room only:* $3460. Room and board charges vary according to board plan. *Part-time tuition:* $325 per credit hour. *Payment plans:* Installment, deferred payment.

FRESHMAN FINANCIAL AID (Fall 2009, est.) 465 applied for aid; of those 95% were deemed to have need. 99% of freshmen with need received aid; of those 18% had need fully met. *Average percent of need met:* 80% (excluding resources awarded to replace EFC). *Average financial aid package:* $19,792 (excluding resources awarded to replace EFC). 5% of all full-time freshmen had no need and received non-need-based gift aid.

UNDERGRADUATE FINANCIAL AID (Fall 2009, est.) 1,065 applied for aid; of those 98% were deemed to have need. 100% of undergraduates with need received aid; of those 15% had need fully met. *Average percent of need met:* 75% (excluding resources awarded to replace EFC). *Average financial aid package:* $17,453 (excluding resources awarded to replace EFC). 9% of all full-time undergraduates had no need and received non-need-based gift aid.

GIFT AID (NEED-BASED) *Total amount:* $13,420,883 (36% federal, 8% state, 48% institutional, 8% external sources). *Receiving aid:* Freshmen: 90% (439); all full-time undergraduates: 92% (1,019). *Average award:* Freshmen: $14,508; Undergraduates: $13,105. *Scholarships, grants, and awards:* Federal Pell, FSEOG, state, private, college/university gift aid from institutional funds.

GIFT AID (NON-NEED-BASED) *Total amount:* $1,120,595 (13% state, 80% institutional, 7% external sources). *Receiving aid:* Freshmen: 9% (43). Undergraduates: 8% (83). *Average award:* Freshmen: $10,966. Undergraduates: $9175. *Scholarships, grants, and awards by category: Academic interests/achievement:* 733 awards ($4,066,574 total): general academic interests/achievements. *Creative arts/performance:* 26 awards ($48,112 total): music. *Special achievements/activities:* 299 awards ($823,851 total): leadership. *Special characteristics:* 233 awards ($400,692 total): children of educators, children of faculty/staff, first-generation college students, international students, local/state students, relatives of clergy, religious affiliation. *Tuition waivers:* Full or partial for employees or children of employees, senior citizens.

LOANS *Student loans:* $8,037,430 (73% need-based, 27% non-need-based). 95% of past graduating class borrowed through all loan programs. *Average indebtedness per student:* $25,168. *Average need-based loan:* Freshmen: $3317. Undergraduates: $3105. *Parent loans:* $1,315,595 (55% need-based, 45% non-need-based). *Programs:* FFEL (Subsidized and Unsubsidized Stafford, PLUS), Perkins, state, alternative loans.

WORK-STUDY *Federal work-study:* Total amount: $200,399; 486 jobs averaging $1288. *State or other work-study/employment:* Total amount: $205,350 (100% non-need-based). 169 part-time jobs averaging $1215.

ATHLETIC AWARDS Total amount: $1,137,493 (70% need-based, 30% non-need-based).

APPLYING FOR FINANCIAL AID *Required financial aid form:* FAFSA. *Financial aid deadline (priority):* 5/1. *Notification date:* Continuous. Students must reply within 2 weeks of notification.

CONTACT Mrs. Sharon W. Rose, Director of Financial Aid, Chowan University, One University Place, Murfreesboro, NC 27855, 252-398-1229 or toll-free 888-4-Chowan. *Fax:* 252-398-6513. *E-mail:* roses1@chowan.edu.

CHRISTENDOM COLLEGE
Front Royal, VA

Tuition & fees: $19,668 **Average undergraduate aid package:** $13,500

ABOUT THE INSTITUTION Independent Roman Catholic, coed. 7 undergraduate majors. Institutional methodology is used as a basis for awarding need-based institutional aid.

UNDERGRADUATE EXPENSES for 2010–11 *Comprehensive fee:* $27,174 includes full-time tuition ($19,118), mandatory fees ($550), and room and board ($7506). *Payment plan:* Installment.

FRESHMAN FINANCIAL AID (Fall 2009, est.) 57 applied for aid; of those 68% were deemed to have need. 100% of freshmen with need received aid; of those 100% had need fully met. *Average percent of need met:* 90% (excluding resources awarded to replace EFC). *Average financial aid package:* $13,024 (excluding resources awarded to replace EFC). 26% of all full-time freshmen had no need and received non-need-based gift aid.

UNDERGRADUATE FINANCIAL AID (Fall 2009, est.) 225 applied for aid; of those 81% were deemed to have need. 100% of undergraduates with need received aid; of those 100% had need fully met. *Average percent of need met:* 90% (excluding resources awarded to replace EFC). *Average financial aid package:* $13,500 (excluding resources awarded to replace EFC). 25% of all full-time undergraduates had no need and received non-need-based gift aid.

GIFT AID (NEED-BASED) *Total amount:* $1,357,698 (100% institutional). *Receiving aid:* Freshmen: 40% (36); all full-time undergraduates: 46% (178). *Average award:* Freshmen: $6505; Undergraduates: $7675. *Scholarships, grants, and awards:* private, college/university gift aid from institutional funds.

GIFT AID (NON-NEED-BASED) *Total amount:* $715,298 (89% institutional, 11% external sources). *Receiving aid:* Freshmen: 15% (14). Undergraduates: 14% (53). *Average award:* Freshmen: $6735. Undergraduates: $6530. *Scholarships, grants, and awards by category:* Academic interests/achievement: 150 awards ($871,784 total): general academic interests/achievements. *Tuition waivers:* Full or partial for employees or children of employees.

LOANS *Student loans:* $1,391,502 (73% need-based, 27% non-need-based). 61% of past graduating class borrowed through all loan programs. *Average indebtedness per student:* $24,000. *Average need-based loan:* Freshmen: $5465. Undergraduates: $5695. *Programs:* college/university.

WORK-STUDY *State or other work-study/employment:* Total amount: $287,100 (100% need-based). 145 part-time jobs averaging $1980.

APPLYING FOR FINANCIAL AID *Required financial aid form:* institution's own form. *Financial aid deadline (priority):* 4/1. *Notification date:* Continuous beginning 3/1. Students must reply within 4 weeks of notification.

CONTACT Mrs. Alisa Polk, Financial Aid Officer, Christendom College, 134 Christendom Drive, Front Royal, VA 22630-5103, 800-877-5456 Ext. 1214 or toll-free 800-877-5456 Ext. 290. *Fax:* 540-636-1655. *E-mail:* apolk@christendom. edu.

CHRISTIAN BROTHERS UNIVERSITY
Memphis, TN

Tuition & fees: $23,730	Average undergraduate aid package: $19,826

ABOUT THE INSTITUTION Independent Roman Catholic, coed. 32 undergraduate majors. Federal methodology is used as a basis for awarding need-based institutional aid.

UNDERGRADUATE EXPENSES for 2009–10 *Comprehensive fee:* $29,870 includes full-time tuition ($23,180), mandatory fees ($550), and room and board ($6140). *College room only:* $2800. Full-time tuition and fees vary according to class time and course load. Room and board charges vary according to board plan and housing facility. *Part-time tuition:* $740 per credit hour. Part-time tuition and fees vary according to class time. *Payment plans:* Installment, deferred payment.

FRESHMAN FINANCIAL AID (Fall 2009, est.) 280 applied for aid; of those 84% were deemed to have need. 100% of freshmen with need received aid; of those 29% had need fully met. *Average percent of need met:* 89% (excluding resources awarded to replace EFC). *Average financial aid package:* $22,450 (excluding resources awarded to replace EFC). 15% of all full-time freshmen had no need and received non-need-based gift aid.

UNDERGRADUATE FINANCIAL AID (Fall 2009, est.) 1,130 applied for aid; of those 83% were deemed to have need. 100% of undergraduates with need received aid; of those 27% had need fully met. *Average percent of need met:* 85% (excluding resources awarded to replace EFC). *Average financial aid package:* $19,826 (excluding resources awarded to replace EFC). 19% of all full-time undergraduates had no need and received non-need-based gift aid.

GIFT AID (NEED-BASED) *Total amount:* $4,195,061 (67% federal, 33% state). *Receiving aid:* Freshmen: 45% (133); all full-time undergraduates: 44% (553). *Average award:* Freshmen: $7388; Undergraduates: $7004. *Scholarships, grants, and awards:* Federal Pell, FSEOG, state, private, college/university gift aid from institutional funds.

GIFT AID (NON-NEED-BASED) *Total amount:* $14,065,039 (17% state, 79% institutional, 4% external sources). *Receiving aid:* Freshmen: 77% (228). Undergraduates: 63% (793). *Average award:* Freshmen: $10,162. Undergradu-

ates: $10,240. *Scholarships, grants, and awards by category:* Academic interests/achievement: 856 awards ($8,626,719 total): engineering/technologies, general academic interests/achievements. *Creative arts/performance:* 24 awards ($15,250 total): general creative arts/performance. *Special achievements/activities:* 131 awards ($629,800 total): general special achievements/activities, leadership. *Special characteristics:* 575 awards ($1,859,671 total): children and siblings of alumni, general special characteristics, religious affiliation. *Tuition waivers:* Full or partial for children of alumni, employees or children of employees.

LOANS *Student loans:* $7,303,660 (40% need-based, 60% non-need-based). 69% of past graduating class borrowed through all loan programs. *Average indebtedness per student:* $28,259. *Average need-based loan:* Freshmen: $3285. Undergraduates: $4404. *Parent loans:* $380,505 (100% non-need-based). *Programs:* FFEL (Subsidized and Unsubsidized Stafford, PLUS), Perkins, college/university, alternative loans.

WORK-STUDY *Federal work-study:* Total amount: $270,910; 226 jobs averaging $1199. *State or other work-study/employment:* Total amount: $203,620 (100% non-need-based). 194 part-time jobs averaging $1050.

ATHLETIC AWARDS Total amount: $1,322,037 (100% non-need-based).

APPLYING FOR FINANCIAL AID *Required financial aid form:* FAFSA. *Financial aid deadline (priority):* 2/15. *Notification date:* Continuous beginning 2/28. Students must reply by 5/1 or within 2 weeks of notification.

CONTACT Mr. Jim Shannon, Dean, Student Financial Assistance, Christian Brothers University, 650 East Parkway South, Memphis, TN 38104, 901-321-3305 or toll-free 800-288-7576. *Fax:* 901-321-3327. *E-mail:* jshannon@cbu. edu.

CHRISTIAN LIFE COLLEGE
Mount Prospect, IL

CONTACT Jeanna Wilson, Office of Financial Aid, Christian Life College, 400 East Gregory Street, Mt. Prospect, IL 60056, 847-259-1840. *Fax:* 847-259-3888.

CHRISTOPHER NEWPORT UNIVERSITY
Newport News, VA

Tuition & fees (VA res): $11,720	Average undergraduate aid package: $7937

ABOUT THE INSTITUTION State-supported, coed. 38 undergraduate majors. Federal methodology is used as a basis for awarding need-based institutional aid.

UNDERGRADUATE EXPENSES for 2009–10 *Tuition, state resident:* full-time $8050; part-time $335 per credit hour. *Tuition, nonresident:* full-time $15,992; part-time $665 per credit hour. *Required fees:* full-time $3670; $152 per credit hour. Full-time tuition and fees vary according to course load and degree level. Part-time tuition and fees vary according to course load and degree level. *College room and board:* $9240. Room and board charges vary according to board plan and housing facility. *Payment plan:* Installment.

FRESHMAN FINANCIAL AID (Fall 2009, est.) 913 applied for aid; of those 56% were deemed to have need. 96% of freshmen with need received aid; of those 8% had need fully met. *Average percent of need met:* 72% (excluding resources awarded to replace EFC). *Average financial aid package:* $8102 (excluding resources awarded to replace EFC). 9% of all full-time freshmen had no need and received non-need-based gift aid.

UNDERGRADUATE FINANCIAL AID (Fall 2009, est.) 2,982 applied for aid; of those 65% were deemed to have need. 96% of undergraduates with need received aid; of those 11% had need fully met. *Average percent of need met:* 72% (excluding resources awarded to replace EFC). *Average financial aid package:* $7937 (excluding resources awarded to replace EFC). 6% of all full-time undergraduates had no need and received non-need-based gift aid.

GIFT AID (NEED-BASED) *Total amount:* $7,545,550 (39% federal, 53% state, 8% institutional). *Receiving aid:* Freshmen: 35% (420); all full-time undergraduates: 33% (1,537). *Average award:* Freshmen: $5081; Undergraduates: $4719. *Scholarships, grants, and awards:* Federal Pell, FSEOG, state, private, college/university gift aid from institutional funds.

GIFT AID (NON-NEED-BASED) *Total amount:* $2,062,383 (2% state, 60% institutional, 38% external sources). *Receiving aid:* Freshmen: 19% (227). Undergraduates: 10% (448). *Average award:* Freshmen: $843. Undergraduates: $961. *Scholarships, grants, and awards by category:* Academic interests/achievement: 107 awards ($142,000 total): biological sciences, business, communication, computer science, education, engineering/technologies, English, foreign languages, general academic interests/achievements, humanities, mathematics, military science, religion/biblical studies. *Creative arts/performance:* 49 awards ($64,421 total): art/fine arts, music, theater/drama. *Special achievements/activities:* 563 awards ($1,030,353 total): general special achievements/activities, leadership. *Tuition waivers:* Full or partial for employees or children of employees, senior citizens.

LOANS *Student loans:* $18,836,758 (36% need-based, 64% non-need-based). 55% of past graduating class borrowed through all loan programs. *Average indebtedness per student:* $18,285. *Average need-based loan:* Freshmen: $3129. Undergraduates: $3849. *Parent loans:* $4,108,619 (100% non-need-based). *Programs:* FFEL (Subsidized and Unsubsidized Stafford, PLUS), state, college/university, alternative loans.

WORK-STUDY *Federal work-study:* Total amount: $95,382; 124 jobs averaging $769. *State or other work-study/employment:* Total amount: $1,538,584 (100% non-need-based). 975 part-time jobs averaging $1578.

APPLYING FOR FINANCIAL AID *Required financial aid form:* FAFSA. *Financial aid deadline (priority):* 3/1. *Notification date:* Continuous. Students must reply within 3 weeks of notification.

CONTACT Mary L. Wigginton, Director of Financial Aid, Christopher Newport University, 1 University Place, Newport News, VA 23606, 757-594-7170 or toll-free 800-333-4268. *Fax:* 757-594-7113. *E-mail:* finaid@cnu.edu.

CINCINNATI CHRISTIAN UNIVERSITY
Cincinnati, OH

Tuition & fees: $12,580	Average undergraduate aid package: $8830

ABOUT THE INSTITUTION Independent religious, coed. 12 undergraduate majors. Federal methodology is used as a basis for awarding need-based institutional aid.

UNDERGRADUATE EXPENSES for 2009–10 *Comprehensive fee:* $19,050 includes full-time tuition ($12,380), mandatory fees ($200), and room and board ($6470). *College room only:* $3210. Full-time tuition and fees vary according to course load and student level. Room and board charges vary according to board plan, housing facility, and student level. *Part-time tuition:* $399 per credit hour. Part-time tuition and fees vary according to course load and student level. *Payment plan:* Installment.

FRESHMAN FINANCIAL AID (Fall 2008) 123 applied for aid; of those 93% were deemed to have need. 100% of freshmen with need received aid; of those 10% had need fully met. *Average percent of need met:* 54% (excluding resources awarded to replace EFC). *Average financial aid package:* $9277 (excluding resources awarded to replace EFC). 7% of all full-time freshmen had no need and received non-need-based gift aid.

UNDERGRADUATE FINANCIAL AID (Fall 2008) 478 applied for aid; of those 95% were deemed to have need. 100% of undergraduates with need received aid. *Average percent of need met:* 48% (excluding resources awarded to replace EFC). *Average financial aid package:* $8830 (excluding resources awarded to replace EFC). 5% of all full-time undergraduates had no need and received non-need-based gift aid.

GIFT AID (NEED-BASED) *Total amount:* $2,605,519 (35% federal, 18% state, 37% institutional, 10% external sources). *Receiving aid:* Freshmen: 87% (107); all full-time undergraduates: 50% (405). *Average award:* Freshmen: $6033; Undergraduates: $5000. *Scholarships, grants, and awards:* Federal Pell, FSEOG, state, private, college/university gift aid from institutional funds.

GIFT AID (NON-NEED-BASED) *Total amount:* $334,005 (11% state, 60% institutional, 29% external sources). *Receiving aid:* Freshmen: 9% (11). *Average award:* Freshmen: $2986. Undergraduates: $3390. *Scholarships, grants, and awards by category:* Academic interests/achievement: religion/biblical studies. *Creative arts/performance:* music. *Special achievements/activities:* general special achievements/activities, leadership, religious involvement. *Special characteristics:* children of current students, children of faculty/staff, international students, married students, members of minority groups, parents of current students, siblings of current students, spouses of current students, twins. *Tuition waivers:* Full or partial for employees or children of employees.

LOANS *Student loans:* $5,487,866 (80% need-based, 20% non-need-based). 100% of past graduating class borrowed through all loan programs. *Average need-based loan:* Freshmen: $3846. Undergraduates: $4492. *Parent loans:* $649,437 (41% need-based, 59% non-need-based). *Programs:* Federal Direct (Subsidized and Unsubsidized Stafford, PLUS), college/university, alternative loans.

WORK-STUDY *Federal work-study:* Total amount: $75,192; jobs available.
ATHLETIC AWARDS Total amount: $106,750 (68% need-based, 32% non-need-based).
APPLYING FOR FINANCIAL AID *Required financial aid forms:* FAFSA, state aid form. *Financial aid deadline (priority):* 3/15. *Notification date:* Continuous beginning 4/1. Students must reply within 2 weeks of notification.
CONTACT Michael R. Gibboney Jr., Financial Aid Coordinator, Cincinnati Christian University, 2700 Glenway Avenue, Cincinnati, OH 45204-1799, 513-244-8450 or toll-free 800-949-4228 (in-state). *Fax:* 513-244-8140. *E-mail:* financialaid@ccuniversity.edu.

CINCINNATI COLLEGE OF MORTUARY SCIENCE
Cincinnati, OH

CONTACT Ms. Pat Leon, Financial Aid Officer, Cincinnati College of Mortuary Science, 645 West North Bend Road, Cincinnati, OH 45224-1428, 513-761-2020.

THE CITADEL, THE MILITARY COLLEGE OF SOUTH CAROLINA
Charleston, SC

Tuition & fees (SC res): $9824	Average undergraduate aid package: $14,910

ABOUT THE INSTITUTION State-supported, coed. 16 undergraduate majors. Federal methodology is used as a basis for awarding need-based institutional aid.

UNDERGRADUATE EXPENSES for 2009–10 *Tuition, state resident:* full-time $8735; part-time $341 per credit. *Tuition, nonresident:* full-time $22,545; part-time $598 per credit. *Required fees:* full-time $1089; $15 per term. *College room and board:* $5965.

FRESHMAN FINANCIAL AID (Fall 2009, est.) 497 applied for aid; of those 75% were deemed to have need. 97% of freshmen with need received aid; of those 26% had need fully met. *Average percent of need met:* 69% (excluding resources awarded to replace EFC). *Average financial aid package:* $14,900 (excluding resources awarded to replace EFC). 6% of all full-time freshmen had no need and received non-need-based gift aid.

UNDERGRADUATE FINANCIAL AID (Fall 2009, est.) 1,581 applied for aid; of those 75% were deemed to have need. 97% of undergraduates with need received aid; of those 31% had need fully met. *Average percent of need met:* 71% (excluding resources awarded to replace EFC). *Average financial aid package:* $14,910 (excluding resources awarded to replace EFC). 10% of all full-time undergraduates had no need and received non-need-based gift aid.

GIFT AID (NEED-BASED) *Total amount:* $11,250,067 (18% federal, 12% state, 22% institutional, 48% external sources). *Receiving aid:* Freshmen: 50% (293); all full-time undergraduates: 41% (927). *Average award:* Freshmen: $12,229; Undergraduates: $10,908. *Scholarships, grants, and awards:* Federal Pell, FSEOG, state, private, college/university gift aid from institutional funds.

GIFT AID (NON-NEED-BASED) *Total amount:* $7,788,942 (13% state, 27% institutional, 60% external sources). *Receiving aid:* Freshmen: 22% (132). Undergraduates: 18% (410). *Average award:* Freshmen: $11,857. Undergraduates: $9626. *Scholarships, grants, and awards by category:* Academic interests/achievement: 127 awards ($1,484,547 total): biological sciences, business, engineering/technologies, general academic interests/achievements, humanities, military science, religion/biblical studies. *Creative arts/performance:* 6 awards ($30,000 total): journalism/publications, music. *Special achievements/activities:* 58 awards ($382,674 total): community service, leadership, religious involvement. *Special characteristics:* 50 awards ($150,000 total): children and siblings of alumni, children with a deceased or disabled parent, local/state students, out-of-state students. *Tuition waivers:* Full or partial for employees or children of employees, senior citizens.

LOANS *Student loans:* $7,431,650 (80% need-based, 20% non-need-based). 73% of past graduating class borrowed through all loan programs. *Average indebtedness per student:* $25,817. *Average need-based loan:* Freshmen: $3537. Undergraduates: $4361. *Parent loans:* $7,568,729 (75% need-based, 25% non-need-based). *Programs:* Federal Direct (Subsidized and Unsubsidized Stafford, PLUS), Perkins, state, college/university.

WORK-STUDY *Federal work-study:* Total amount: $40,000; 34 jobs averaging $1250.

ATHLETIC AWARDS Total amount: $4,147,526 (44% need-based, 56% non-need-based).

APPLYING FOR FINANCIAL AID *Required financial aid form:* FAFSA. *Financial aid deadline (priority):* 2/28. *Notification date:* 3/15. Students must reply within 2 weeks of notification.

CONTACT Lt. Col. Hank M. Fuller, Director of Financial Aid and Scholarships, The Citadel, The Military College of South Carolina, 171 Moultrie Street, Charleston, SC 29409, 843-953-5187 or toll-free 800-868-1842. *Fax:* 843-953-6759. *E-mail:* fullerh@citadel.edu.

CITY COLLEGE OF THE CITY UNIVERSITY OF NEW YORK
New York, NY

Tuition & fees (NY res): $4929	Average undergraduate aid package: $10,166

ABOUT THE INSTITUTION State and locally supported, coed. 67 undergraduate majors. Federal methodology is used as a basis for awarding need-based institutional aid.

UNDERGRADUATE EXPENSES for 2010–11 *Tuition, state resident:* full-time $4600. *Tuition, nonresident:* full-time $9960. *Required fees:* full-time $329. Full-time tuition and fees vary according to course load and program. Part-time tuition and fees vary according to course load and program. Room and board charges vary according to housing facility. *Payment plan:* Deferred payment.

FRESHMAN FINANCIAL AID (Fall 2009, est.) 1,596 applied for aid; of those 98% were deemed to have need. 98% of freshmen with need received aid; of those 75% had need fully met. *Average percent of need met:* 80% (excluding resources awarded to replace EFC). *Average financial aid package:* $8754 (excluding resources awarded to replace EFC). 22% of all full-time freshmen had no need and received non-need-based gift aid.

UNDERGRADUATE FINANCIAL AID (Fall 2009, est.) 9,202 applied for aid; of those 96% were deemed to have need. 96% of undergraduates with need received aid; of those 61% had need fully met. *Average percent of need met:* 81% (excluding resources awarded to replace EFC). *Average financial aid package:* $10,166 (excluding resources awarded to replace EFC). 15% of all full-time undergraduates had no need and received non-need-based gift aid.

GIFT AID (NEED-BASED) *Total amount:* $42,404,000 (43% federal, 52% state, 4% institutional, 1% external sources). *Receiving aid:* Freshmen: 86% (1,512); all full-time undergraduates: 77% (7,464). *Average award:* Freshmen: $6103; Undergraduates: $6846. *Scholarships, grants, and awards:* Federal Pell, FSEOG, state, private, college/university gift aid from institutional funds.

GIFT AID (NON-NEED-BASED) *Total amount:* $2,909,000 (13% state, 77% institutional, 10% external sources). *Receiving aid:* Freshmen: 35% (605). Undergraduates: 14% (1,380). *Average award:* Freshmen: $2098. Undergraduates: $2153. *Scholarships, grants, and awards by category: Academic interests/achievement:* architecture, area/ethnic studies, biological sciences, communication, computer science, education, engineering/technologies, English, foreign languages, general academic interests/achievements, humanities, international studies, mathematics, premedicine, social sciences. *Creative arts/performance:* applied art and design, art/fine arts, cinema/film/broadcasting, creative writing, general creative arts/performance, music, performing arts. *Special achievements/activities:* community service, general special achievements/activities, leadership. *Tuition waivers:* Full or partial for senior citizens.

LOANS *Student loans:* $18,173,000 (95% need-based, 5% non-need-based). 24% of past graduating class borrowed through all loan programs. *Average indebtedness per student:* $15,100. *Average need-based loan:* Freshmen: $1859. Undergraduates: $4103. *Parent loans:* $675,000 (100% non-need-based). *Programs:* Federal Direct (Subsidized and Unsubsidized Stafford, PLUS), Perkins.

WORK-STUDY *Federal work-study:* Total amount: $3,100,000; 2,070 jobs averaging $1820. *State or other work-study/employment:* Total amount: $115,000 (100% need-based). Part-time jobs available.

APPLYING FOR FINANCIAL AID *Required financial aid forms:* FAFSA, state aid form. *Financial aid deadline (priority):* 4/1. *Notification date:* Continuous.

CONTACT Thelma Mason, Director of Financial Aid, City College of the City University of New York, 160 Convent Avenue, Administration Building, Room 104, New York, NY 10031, 212-650-6656. *Fax:* 212-650-5829. *E-mail:* thelma@finance.ccny.cuny.edu.

CITY UNIVERSITY OF SEATTLE
Bellevue, WA

CONTACT Ms. Jean L. Roberts, Director of Student Financial Services, City University of Seattle, 11900 Northeast 1st Street, Bellevue, WA 98005, 425-709-5251 or toll-free 888-42-CITYU. *Fax:* 425-709-5263. *E-mail:* jroberts@cityu.edu.

CITY VISION COLLEGE
Kansas City, MO

CONTACT Financial Aid Office, City Vision College, PO Box 413188, Kansas City, MO 64141-3188, 816-960-2008.

CLAFLIN UNIVERSITY
Orangeburg, SC

CONTACT Ms. Yolanda Frazier, Interim Director of Financial Aid, Claflin University, Tingly Hall, Suite 12, 400 Magnolia Street, Orangeburg, SC 29115, 803-535-5720 or toll-free 800-922-1276 (in-state). *Fax:* 803-535-5383. *E-mail:* yfrazier@claflin.edu.

CLAREMONT McKENNA COLLEGE
Claremont, CA

Tuition & fees: $38,745	Average undergraduate aid package: $35,177

ABOUT THE INSTITUTION Independent, coed. 83 undergraduate majors. Institutional methodology is used as a basis for awarding need-based institutional aid.

UNDERGRADUATE EXPENSES for 2009–10 *One-time required fee:* $235. *Comprehensive fee:* $51,270 includes full-time tuition ($38,510), mandatory fees ($235), and room and board ($12,525). *College room only:* $6470. Full-time tuition and fees vary according to reciprocity agreements. Room and board charges vary according to board plan and housing facility. *Part-time tuition:* $6379.17 per course. Part-time tuition and fees vary according to reciprocity agreements. *Payment plans:* Tuition prepayment, installment.

FRESHMAN FINANCIAL AID (Fall 2009, est.) 178 applied for aid; of those 65% were deemed to have need. 100% of freshmen with need received aid; of those 100% had need fully met. *Average percent of need met:* 100% (excluding resources awarded to replace EFC). *Average financial aid package:* $34,428 (excluding resources awarded to replace EFC). 1% of all full-time freshmen had no need and received non-need-based gift aid.

UNDERGRADUATE FINANCIAL AID (Fall 2009, est.) 607 applied for aid; of those 88% were deemed to have need. 100% of undergraduates with need received aid; of those 100% had need fully met. *Average percent of need met:* 100% (excluding resources awarded to replace EFC). *Average financial aid package:* $35,177 (excluding resources awarded to replace EFC). 7% of all full-time undergraduates had no need and received non-need-based gift aid.

GIFT AID (NEED-BASED) *Total amount:* $17,832,178 (6% federal, 5% state, 87% institutional, 2% external sources). *Receiving aid:* Freshmen: 40% (113); all full-time undergraduates: 44% (529). *Average award:* Freshmen: $33,966; Undergraduates: $34,276. *Scholarships, grants, and awards:* Federal Pell, FSEOG, state, college/university gift aid from institutional funds.

GIFT AID (NON-NEED-BASED) *Total amount:* $1,195,838 (91% institutional, 9% external sources). *Receiving aid:* Freshmen: 1. Undergraduates: 7% (86). *Average award:* Freshmen: $38,275. Undergraduates: $12,591. *Scholarships, grants, and awards by category: Academic interests/achievement:* general academic interests/achievements. *Special achievements/activities:* 86 awards ($1,082,827 total): leadership. *Tuition waivers:* Full or partial for employees or children of employees.

LOANS *Student loans:* $924,048 (86% need-based, 14% non-need-based). 30% of past graduating class borrowed through all loan programs. *Average indebtedness per student:* $9259. *Parent loans:* $2,274,980 (60% need-based, 40% non-need-based). *Programs:* Federal Direct (Subsidized and Unsubsidized Stafford, PLUS), FFEL (Subsidized and Unsubsidized Stafford, PLUS), Perkins, college/university.

WORK-STUDY *Federal work-study:* Total amount: $250,000; 280 jobs averaging $1850. *State or other work-study/employment:* Part-time jobs available.

APPLYING FOR FINANCIAL AID *Required financial aid forms:* FAFSA, CSS Financial Aid PROFILE, business/farm supplement. *Notification date:* 4/1. Students must reply by 5/1.

CONTACT Ms. Georgette R. DeVeres, Associate Vice President of Admission and Director of Financial Aid, Claremont McKenna College, 890 Columbia Avenue, Claremont, CA 91711, 909-621-8356. *Fax:* 909-607-0661. *E-mail:* gdeveres@cmc.edu.

CLARION UNIVERSITY OF PENNSYLVANIA
Clarion, PA

Tuition & fees (PA res): $7381	Average undergraduate aid package: $7743

ABOUT THE INSTITUTION State-supported, coed. 55 undergraduate majors. Federal methodology is used as a basis for awarding need-based institutional aid.

UNDERGRADUATE EXPENSES for 2010–11 *One-time required fee:* $30. *Tuition, state resident:* full-time $5554; part-time $231 per credit hour. *Tuition, nonresident:* full-time $11,108; part-time $463 per credit hour. *Required fees:* full-time $1827; $54 per credit hour or $54 per credit hour. Full-time tuition and fees vary according to course load. Part-time tuition and fees vary according to course load. *College room and board:* $6884; *Room only:* $4348. Room and board charges vary according to board plan. *Payment plan:* Installment.

FRESHMAN FINANCIAL AID (Fall 2008) 1,209 applied for aid; of those 79% were deemed to have need. 96% of freshmen with need received aid; of those 18% had need fully met. *Average percent of need met:* 69% (excluding resources awarded to replace EFC). *Average financial aid package:* $7440 (excluding resources awarded to replace EFC). 8% of all full-time freshmen had no need and received non-need-based gift aid.

UNDERGRADUATE FINANCIAL AID (Fall 2008) 4,401 applied for aid; of those 83% were deemed to have need. 97% of undergraduates with need received aid; of those 18% had need fully met. *Average percent of need met:* 72% (excluding resources awarded to replace EFC). *Average financial aid package:* $7743 (excluding resources awarded to replace EFC). 6% of all full-time undergraduates had no need and received non-need-based gift aid.

GIFT AID (NEED-BASED) *Total amount:* $14,526,077 (43% federal, 43% state, 6% institutional, 8% external sources). *Receiving aid:* Freshmen: 56% (732); all full-time undergraduates: 52% (2,634). *Average award:* Freshmen: $5735; Undergraduates: $5348. *Scholarships, grants, and awards:* Federal Pell, FSEOG, state, private, college/university gift aid from institutional funds, Federal Nursing.

GIFT AID (NON-NEED-BASED) *Receiving aid:* Freshmen: 20% (258). Undergraduates: 19% (961). *Average award:* Freshmen: $2571. Undergraduates: $3058. *Tuition waivers:* Full or partial for employees or children of employees, senior citizens.

LOANS *Student loans:* $28,492,392 (53% need-based, 47% non-need-based). *Average need-based loan:* Freshmen: $3164. Undergraduates: $3897. *Parent loans:* $2,859,793 (100% non-need-based). *Programs:* FFEL (Subsidized and Unsubsidized Stafford, PLUS), Perkins.

WORK-STUDY *Federal work-study:* Total amount: $489,704; jobs available. *State or other work-study/employment:* Total amount: $1,626,974 (100% non-need-based). Part-time jobs available.

ATHLETIC AWARDS Total amount: $604,757 (100% need-based).

APPLYING FOR FINANCIAL AID *Required financial aid form:* FAFSA. *Financial aid deadline:* 4/15. *Notification date:* Continuous.

CONTACT Dr. Kenneth Grugel, Director of Financial Aid, Clarion University of Pennsylvania, 104 Egbert Hall, Clarion, PA 16214, 814-393-2315 or toll-free 800-672-7171. *Fax:* 814-393-2520. *E-mail:* maphillips@clarion.edu.

CLARK ATLANTA UNIVERSITY
Atlanta, GA

CONTACT Office of Financial Aid, Clark Atlanta University, 223 James P. Brawley Drive, Atlanta, GA 30314, 404-880-8992 or toll-free 800-688-3228. *Fax:* 404-880-8070. *E-mail:* studentfinancialaid@cau.edu.

CLARKE COLLEGE
Dubuque, IA

Tuition & fees: $23,520	Average undergraduate aid package: $19,614

ABOUT THE INSTITUTION Independent Roman Catholic, coed. 34 undergraduate majors. Federal methodology is used as a basis for awarding need-based institutional aid.

UNDERGRADUATE EXPENSES for 2009–10 *Comprehensive fee:* $30,360 includes full-time tuition ($22,800), mandatory fees ($720), and room and board ($6840). *College room only:* $3360. Room and board charges vary according to board plan and housing facility. *Part-time tuition:* $578 per credit hour. *Payment plans:* Installment, deferred payment.

FRESHMAN FINANCIAL AID (Fall 2009, est.) 140 applied for aid; of those 90% were deemed to have need. 100% of freshmen with need received aid; of those 27% had need fully met. *Average percent of need met:* 87% (excluding resources awarded to replace EFC). *Average financial aid package:* $20,370 (excluding resources awarded to replace EFC). 11% of all full-time freshmen had no need and received non-need-based gift aid.

UNDERGRADUATE FINANCIAL AID (Fall 2009, est.) 734 applied for aid; of those 90% were deemed to have need. 100% of undergraduates with need received aid; of those 24% had need fully met. *Average percent of need met:* 88% (excluding resources awarded to replace EFC). *Average financial aid package:* $19,614 (excluding resources awarded to replace EFC). 11% of all full-time undergraduates had no need and received non-need-based gift aid.

GIFT AID (NEED-BASED) *Total amount:* $8,015,314 (18% federal, 14% state, 66% institutional, 2% external sources). *Receiving aid:* Freshmen: 86% (126); all full-time undergraduates: 86% (658). *Average award:* Freshmen: $17,053; Undergraduates: $15,231. *Scholarships, grants, and awards:* Federal Pell, FSEOG, state, private, college/university gift aid from institutional funds.

GIFT AID (NON-NEED-BASED) *Total amount:* $666,017 (98% institutional, 2% external sources). *Receiving aid:* Freshmen: 81% (119). Undergraduates: 78% (595). *Average award:* Freshmen: $13,069. Undergraduates: $15,566. *Scholarships, grants, and awards by category:* Academic interests/achievement: computer science, foreign languages, general academic interests/achievements. Creative arts/performance: art/fine arts, music, theater/drama. Special achievements/activities: leadership. Special characteristics: $699,472 total: children and siblings of alumni, children of faculty/staff, children with a deceased or disabled parent, general special characteristics, international students, local/state students, members of minority groups, relatives of clergy, religious affiliation, siblings of current students. *Tuition waivers:* Full or partial for children of alumni, employees or children of employees, adult students, senior citizens.

LOANS *Student loans:* $7,178,544 (46% need-based, 54% non-need-based). 90% of past graduating class borrowed through all loan programs. *Average indebtedness per student:* $34,386. *Average need-based loan:* Freshmen: $3281. Undergraduates: $4670. *Parent loans:* $771,789 (97% need-based, 3% non-need-based). *Programs:* FFEL (Subsidized and Unsubsidized Stafford, PLUS), Perkins, Federal Nursing, state, college/university, private loans.

WORK-STUDY *Federal work-study:* Total amount: $236,171; 154 jobs averaging $1500. *State or other work-study/employment:* Part-time jobs available.

ATHLETIC AWARDS Total amount: $1,157,831 (100% non-need-based).

APPLYING FOR FINANCIAL AID *Financial aid deadline (priority):* 4/15. *Notification date:* Continuous beginning 3/15. Students must reply by 5/1 or within 2 weeks of notification.

CONTACT Sharon Willenborg, Director of Financial Aid, Clarke College, 1550 Clarke Drive, Dubuque, IA 52001-3198, 563-588-6327 or toll-free 800-383-2345. *Fax:* 563-584-8605. *E-mail:* sharon.willenborg@clarke.edu.

CLARKSON COLLEGE
Omaha, NE

CONTACT Pam Shelton, Director of Financial Aid, Clarkson College, 101 South 42nd Street, Omaha, NE 68131-2739, 402-552-2749 or toll-free 800-647-5500. *Fax:* 402-552-6165. *E-mail:* shelton@clarksoncollege.edu.

CLARKSON UNIVERSITY
Potsdam, NY

Tuition & fees: $34,760	Average undergraduate aid package: $31,447

ABOUT THE INSTITUTION Independent, coed. 35 undergraduate majors. Federal methodology is used as a basis for awarding need-based institutional aid.

UNDERGRADUATE EXPENSES for 2010–11 *Comprehensive fee:* $46,324 includes full-time tuition ($34,070), mandatory fees ($690), and room and board ($11,564). *College room only:* $6126. Full-time tuition and fees vary according to course load. Room and board charges vary according to board plan and housing facility. *Part-time tuition:* $1136 per credit. Part-time tuition and fees vary according to course load. *Payment plans:* Tuition prepayment, installment.

FRESHMAN FINANCIAL AID (Fall 2009, est.) 733 applied for aid; of those 87% were deemed to have need. 100% of freshmen with need received aid; of those 27% had need fully met. *Average percent of need met:* 85% (excluding resources awarded to replace EFC). *Average financial aid package:* $32,449 (excluding resources awarded to replace EFC). 12% of all full-time freshmen had no need and received non-need-based gift aid.

UNDERGRADUATE FINANCIAL AID (Fall 2009, est.) 2,474 applied for aid; of those 89% were deemed to have need. 100% of undergraduates with need received aid; of those 22% had need fully met. *Average percent of need met:* 87% (excluding resources awarded to replace EFC). *Average financial aid package:* $31,447 (excluding resources awarded to replace EFC). 10% of all full-time undergraduates had no need and received non-need-based gift aid.

GIFT AID (NEED-BASED) *Total amount:* $47,417,046 (8% federal, 6% state, 82% institutional, 4% external sources). *Receiving aid:* Freshmen: 82% (636); all full-time undergraduates: 79% (2,174). *Average award:* Freshmen: $24,862; Undergraduates: $21,803. *Scholarships, grants, and awards:* Federal Pell, FSEOG, state, private, college/university gift aid from institutional funds.

GIFT AID (NON-NEED-BASED) *Total amount:* $6,215,130 (2% state, 92% institutional, 6% external sources). *Receiving aid:* Freshmen: 22% (170). Undergraduates: 17% (455). *Average award:* Freshmen: $16,595. Undergraduates: $14,547. *Scholarships, grants, and awards by category: Academic interests/achievement:* 1,635 awards ($12,411,743 total): biological sciences, business, communication, computer science, engineering/technologies, general academic interests/achievements, humanities, mathematics, military science, physical sciences, social sciences. *Special achievements/activities:* 852 awards ($6,330,750 total): general special achievements/activities, leadership. *Special characteristics:* 693 awards ($1,999,695 total): children and siblings of alumni, children of faculty/staff, general special characteristics, international students, local/state students, members of minority groups, veterans. *Tuition waivers:* Full or partial for employees or children of employees.

LOANS *Student loans:* $20,602,422 (69% need-based, 31% non-need-based). 85% of past graduating class borrowed through all loan programs. *Average indebtedness per student:* $32,125. *Average need-based loan:* Freshmen: $4066. Undergraduates: $5218. *Parent loans:* $5,455,708 (36% need-based, 64% non-need-based). *Programs:* Federal Direct (Subsidized and Unsubsidized Stafford, PLUS), FFEL (Subsidized and Unsubsidized Stafford, PLUS), Perkins, college/university, alternative loans.

WORK-STUDY *Federal work-study:* Total amount: $634,313; 1,480 jobs averaging $1643. *State or other work-study/employment:* Total amount: $32,000 (19% need-based, 81% non-need-based). 26 part-time jobs averaging $942.

ATHLETIC AWARDS Total amount: $1,529,211 (7% need-based, 93% non-need-based).

APPLYING FOR FINANCIAL AID *Required financial aid forms:* FAFSA, state aid form. *Financial aid deadline (priority):* 2/15. *Notification date:* Continuous beginning 3/19. Students must reply by 5/1 or within 2 weeks of notification.

CONTACT Mrs. Pamela A. Nichols, Director of Financial Aid, Clarkson University, PO Box 5615, Potsdam, NY 13699, 315-268-6413 or toll-free 800-527-6577. *Fax:* 315-268-3899. *E-mail:* pnichols@clarkson.edu.

CLARK UNIVERSITY
Worcester, MA

Tuition & fees: $36,420	Average undergraduate aid package: $25,904

ABOUT THE INSTITUTION Independent, coed. 48 undergraduate majors. Institutional methodology is used as a basis for awarding need-based institutional aid.

UNDERGRADUATE EXPENSES for 2010–11 *Comprehensive fee:* $43,370 includes full-time tuition ($36,100), mandatory fees ($320), and room and board ($6950). *College room only:* $4000. Room and board charges vary according to board plan and housing facility. *Part-time tuition:* $1128 per course. *Part-time fees:* $1128 per credit hour. *Payment plans:* Tuition prepayment, installment.

FRESHMAN FINANCIAL AID (Fall 2009, est.) 404 applied for aid; of those 76% were deemed to have need. 99% of freshmen with need received aid; of those 63% had need fully met. *Average percent of need met:* 94% (excluding

resources awarded to replace EFC). *Average financial aid package:* $25,904 (excluding resources awarded to replace EFC). 34% of all full-time freshmen had no need and received non-need-based gift aid.

UNDERGRADUATE FINANCIAL AID (Fall 2009, est.) 1,620 applied for aid; of those 76% were deemed to have need. 99% of undergraduates with need received aid; of those 63% had need fully met. *Average percent of need met:* 94% (excluding resources awarded to replace EFC). *Average financial aid package:* $25,904 (excluding resources awarded to replace EFC). 34% of all full-time undergraduates had no need and received non-need-based gift aid.

GIFT AID (NEED-BASED) *Total amount:* $23,364,940 (12% federal, 2% state, 84% institutional, 2% external sources). *Receiving aid:* Freshmen: 55% (300); all full-time undergraduates: 55% (1,203). *Average award:* Freshmen: $20,705; Undergraduates: $20,705. *Scholarships, grants, and awards:* Federal Pell, FSEOG, state, college/university gift aid from institutional funds.

GIFT AID (NON-NEED-BASED) *Total amount:* $10,180,292 (100% institutional). *Receiving aid:* Freshmen: 24% (129). Undergraduates: 24% (517). *Average award:* Freshmen: $13,013. Undergraduates: $13,013. *Scholarships, grants, and awards by category: Academic interests/achievement:* general academic interests/achievements. *Special achievements/activities:* community service, general special achievements/activities. *Tuition waivers:* Full or partial for employees or children of employees.

LOANS *Student loans:* $9,932,044 (55% need-based, 45% non-need-based). 86% of past graduating class borrowed through all loan programs. *Average indebtedness per student:* $21,925. *Average need-based loan:* Freshmen: $3288. Undergraduates: $3288. *Parent loans:* $3,915,320 (6% need-based, 94% non-need-based). *Programs:* Federal Direct (Subsidized and Unsubsidized Stafford, PLUS), Perkins, state.

WORK-STUDY *Federal work-study:* Total amount: $1,722,259; 1,000 jobs averaging $2000.

APPLYING FOR FINANCIAL AID *Required financial aid forms:* FAFSA, CSS Financial Aid PROFILE, noncustodial (divorced/separated) parent's statement. *Financial aid deadline:* 2/1. *Notification date:* 3/31. Students must reply by 5/1.

CONTACT Ms. Mary Ellen Severance, Director, Office of Financial Assistance, Clark University, 950 Main Street, Worcester, MA 01610-1477, 508-793-7478 or toll-free 800-GO-CLARK. *Fax:* 508-793-8802. *E-mail:* finaid@clarku.edu.

CLAYTON STATE UNIVERSITY
Morrow, GA

ABOUT THE INSTITUTION State-supported, coed. 39 undergraduate majors.

GIFT AID (NEED-BASED) *Scholarships, grants, and awards:* Federal Pell, FSEOG, state, college/university gift aid from institutional funds, Federal Nursing.

GIFT AID (NON-NEED-BASED) *Scholarships, grants, and awards by category: Special characteristics:* general special characteristics.

LOANS *Programs:* FFEL (Subsidized and Unsubsidized Stafford, PLUS), Federal Nursing, state.

APPLYING FOR FINANCIAL AID *Required financial aid forms:* FAFSA, institution's own form, state aid form.

CONTACT Pat Barton, Director of Financial Aid, Clayton State University, 2000 Clayton State Boulevard, Morrow, GA 30260, 678-466-4185. *Fax:* 678-466-4189. *E-mail:* financialaid@mail.clayton.edu.

CLEAR CREEK BAPTIST BIBLE COLLEGE
Pineville, KY

Tuition & fees: $8700	Average undergraduate aid package: $6876

ABOUT THE INSTITUTION Independent Southern Baptist, coed, primarily men. 2 undergraduate majors. Institutional methodology is used as a basis for awarding need-based institutional aid.

UNDERGRADUATE EXPENSES for 2010–11 *Tuition:* full-time $8700.

FRESHMAN FINANCIAL AID (Fall 2009, est.) 12 applied for aid; of those 75% were deemed to have need. 100% of freshmen with need received aid. *Average percent of need met:* 66% (excluding resources awarded to replace EFC). *Average financial aid package:* $6314 (excluding resources awarded to replace EFC). 25% of all full-time freshmen had no need and received non-need-based gift aid.

UNDERGRADUATE FINANCIAL AID (Fall 2009, est.) 134 applied for aid; of those 83% were deemed to have need. 100% of undergraduates with need received aid. *Average percent of need met:* 71% (excluding resources awarded to replace EFC). *Average financial aid package:* $6876 (excluding resources awarded to replace EFC). 17% of all full-time undergraduates had no need and received non-need-based gift aid.

GIFT AID (NEED-BASED) *Total amount:* $742,334 (74% federal, 2% state, 18% institutional, 6% external sources). *Receiving aid:* Freshmen: 75% (9); all full-time undergraduates: 78% (111). *Average award:* Freshmen: $6314; Undergraduates: $6876. *Scholarships, grants, and awards:* Federal Pell, FSEOG, state, private, college/university gift aid from institutional funds.

GIFT AID (NON-NEED-BASED) *Total amount:* $66,557 (83% federal, 17% institutional). *Receiving aid:* Freshmen: 67% (8). Undergraduates: 26% (37). *Average award:* Freshmen: $700. Undergraduates: $1674. *Scholarships, grants, and awards by category:* Academic interests/achievement: 8 awards ($1743 total): general academic interests/achievements. *Creative arts/performance:* 6 awards ($1200 total): music. *Special characteristics:* 2 awards ($646 total): handicapped students, international students.

LOANS *Student loans:* $17,000 (100% non-need-based).

WORK-STUDY *Federal work-study:* Total amount: $38,082; 30 jobs averaging $1269.

APPLYING FOR FINANCIAL AID *Required financial aid forms:* FAFSA, institution's own form. *Financial aid deadline (priority):* 6/30. *Notification date:* 7/1.

CONTACT Mr. Sam Risner, Director of Financial Aid, Clear Creek Baptist Bible College, 300 Clear Creek Road, Pineville, KY 40977-9754, 606-337-3196 Ext. 142. *Fax:* 606-337-1631. *E-mail:* srisner@ccbbc.edu.

CLEARWATER CHRISTIAN COLLEGE
Clearwater, FL

Tuition & fees: $14,710	Average undergraduate aid package: $10,353

ABOUT THE INSTITUTION Independent nondenominational, coed. 24 undergraduate majors. Federal methodology is used as a basis for awarding need-based institutional aid.

UNDERGRADUATE EXPENSES for 2009–10 *Comprehensive fee:* $21,450 includes full-time tuition ($14,710) and room and board ($6740). *College room only:* $4140. Room and board charges vary according to board plan. *Part-time tuition:* $580 per credit hour. *Payment plans:* Guaranteed tuition, installment.

FRESHMAN FINANCIAL AID (Fall 2009, est.) 132 applied for aid; of those 83% were deemed to have need. 99% of freshmen with need received aid; of those 16% had need fully met. *Average percent of need met:* 64% (excluding resources awarded to replace EFC). *Average financial aid package:* $10,913 (excluding resources awarded to replace EFC). 24% of all full-time freshmen had no need and received non-need-based gift aid.

UNDERGRADUATE FINANCIAL AID (Fall 2009, est.) 543 applied for aid; of those 80% were deemed to have need. 100% of undergraduates with need received aid; of those 15% had need fully met. *Average percent of need met:* 60% (excluding resources awarded to replace EFC). *Average financial aid package:* $10,353 (excluding resources awarded to replace EFC). 22% of all full-time undergraduates had no need and received non-need-based gift aid.

GIFT AID (NEED-BASED) *Total amount:* $3,432,692 (23% federal, 26% state, 42% institutional, 9% external sources). *Receiving aid:* Freshmen: 74% (108); all full-time undergraduates: 72% (427). *Average award:* Freshmen: $8422; Undergraduates: $7918. *Scholarships, grants, and awards:* Federal Pell, FSEOG, state, private, college/university gift aid from institutional funds.

GIFT AID (NON-NEED-BASED) *Total amount:* $860,643 (33% state, 47% institutional, 20% external sources). *Receiving aid:* Freshmen: 8% (11). Undergraduates: 8% (46). *Average award:* Freshmen: $2871. Undergraduates: $2848. *Scholarships, grants, and awards by category:* Academic interests/achievement: 134 awards ($350,000 total): business, education, general academic interests/achievements, premedicine, religion/biblical studies. *Creative arts/performance:* 45 awards ($84,000 total): music. *Special achievements/activities:* 151 awards ($75,000 total): leadership. *Special characteristics:* 145 awards ($310,000 total): children and siblings of alumni, ethnic background, religious affiliation, siblings of current students. *Tuition waivers:* Full or partial for employees or children of employees.

LOANS *Student loans:* $2,041,141 (75% need-based, 25% non-need-based). 54% of past graduating class borrowed through all loan programs. *Average indebtedness per student:* $18,000. *Average need-based loan:* Freshmen: $3789. Undergraduates: $4324. *Parent loans:* $564,856 (39% need-based, 61% non-need-based). *Programs:* FFEL (Subsidized and Unsubsidized Stafford, PLUS), state, alternative loans.

WORK-STUDY *Federal work-study:* Total amount: $27,000; 50 jobs averaging $670. *State or other work-study/employment:* Total amount: $15,000 (100% need-based). 20 part-time jobs averaging $612.

APPLYING FOR FINANCIAL AID *Required financial aid forms:* FAFSA, institution's own form, state aid form. *Financial aid deadline:* Continuous. *Notification date:* Continuous beginning 1/1.

CONTACT Mrs. Ruth Strum, Director of Financial Aid, Clearwater Christian College, 3400 Gulf-to-Bay Boulevard, Clearwater, FL 33759-4595, 727-726-1153 Ext. 214 or toll-free 800-348-4463. *Fax:* 727-791-1347. *E-mail:* ruthstrum@ clearwater.edu.

CLEARY UNIVERSITY
Ann Arbor, MI

Tuition & fees: $15,600	Average undergraduate aid package: $12,044

ABOUT THE INSTITUTION Independent, coed. 10 undergraduate majors. Federal methodology is used as a basis for awarding need-based institutional aid.

UNDERGRADUATE EXPENSES for 2009–10 *Tuition:* full-time $15,600; part-time $325 per quarter hour. Full-time tuition and fees vary according to degree level. *Payment plans:* Guaranteed tuition, installment, deferred payment.

FRESHMAN FINANCIAL AID (Fall 2009, est.) 54 applied for aid; of those 100% were deemed to have need. 100% of freshmen with need received aid; of those 2% had need fully met. *Average percent of need met:* 41% (excluding resources awarded to replace EFC). *Average financial aid package:* $13,214 (excluding resources awarded to replace EFC). 20% of all full-time freshmen had no need and received non-need-based gift aid.

UNDERGRADUATE FINANCIAL AID (Fall 2009, est.) 366 applied for aid; of those 100% were deemed to have need. 100% of undergraduates with need received aid; of those 4% had need fully met. *Average percent of need met:* 35% (excluding resources awarded to replace EFC). *Average financial aid package:* $12,044 (excluding resources awarded to replace EFC). 15% of all full-time undergraduates had no need and received non-need-based gift aid.

GIFT AID (NEED-BASED) *Total amount:* $941,094 (62% federal, 37% state, 1% institutional). *Receiving aid:* Freshmen: 43% (42); all full-time undergraduates: 46% (264). *Average award:* Freshmen: $1293; Undergraduates: $1142. *Scholarships, grants, and awards:* Federal Pell, FSEOG, state, private, college/university gift aid from institutional funds.

GIFT AID (NON-NEED-BASED) *Total amount:* $22,708 (99% state, 1% institutional). *Receiving aid:* Freshmen: 7% (7). Undergraduates: 2% (13). *Average award:* Freshmen: $2303. Undergraduates: $2698. *Scholarships, grants, and awards by category:* Academic interests/achievement: 69 awards ($126,894 total): business, computer science, general academic interests/achievements. *Special characteristics:* 49 awards ($287,989 total): children of faculty/staff, veterans. *Tuition waivers:* Full or partial for employees or children of employees, senior citizens.

LOANS *Student loans:* $4,203,030 (40% need-based, 60% non-need-based). 78% of past graduating class borrowed through all loan programs. *Average indebtedness per student:* $20,528. *Average need-based loan:* Freshmen: $1172. Undergraduates: $1291. *Parent loans:* $147,171 (100% non-need-based). *Programs:* Federal Direct (Subsidized and Unsubsidized Stafford, PLUS).

WORK-STUDY *Federal work-study:* Total amount: $43,362; 25 jobs averaging $1734. *State or other work-study/employment:* Total amount: $6589 (100% need-based). Part-time jobs available.

APPLYING FOR FINANCIAL AID *Required financial aid form:* FAFSA. *Financial aid deadline:* 7/1 (priority: 4/1). *Notification date:* Continuous beginning 4/1. Students must reply by 7/1 or within 2 weeks of notification.

CONTACT Vesta Smith-Campbell, Director of Financial Aid, Cleary University, 3750 Cleary Drive, Howell, MI 48843, 800-589-1979 Ext. 2234 or toll-free 888-5-CLEARY Ext. 2249. *Fax:* 517-552-8022. *E-mail:* vscampbell@cleary.edu.

CLEMSON UNIVERSITY
Clemson, SC

Tuition & fees (SC res): $11,609	Average undergraduate aid package: $10,911

ABOUT THE INSTITUTION State-supported, coed. 76 undergraduate majors. Federal methodology is used as a basis for awarding need-based institutional aid.

UNDERGRADUATE EXPENSES for 2009–10 *One-time required fee:* $1250. *Tuition, state resident:* full-time $11,487. *Tuition, nonresident:* full-time $25,788. *Required fees:* full-time $122. Full-time tuition and fees vary according to course load, location, and program. Part-time tuition and fees vary according to program. *College room and board:* $6774; *Room only:* $4132. Room and board charges vary according to board plan, housing facility, and location. *Payment plan:* Installment.

FRESHMAN FINANCIAL AID (Fall 2009, est.) 2,454 applied for aid; of those 65% were deemed to have need. 95% of freshmen with need received aid; of those 26% had need fully met. *Average percent of need met:* 71% (excluding resources awarded to replace EFC). *Average financial aid package:* $11,462 (excluding resources awarded to replace EFC). 18% of all full-time freshmen had no need and received non-need-based gift aid.

UNDERGRADUATE FINANCIAL AID (Fall 2009, est.) 8,403 applied for aid; of those 74% were deemed to have need. 96% of undergraduates with need received aid; of those 24% had need fully met. *Average percent of need met:* 61% (excluding resources awarded to replace EFC). *Average financial aid package:* $10,911 (excluding resources awarded to replace EFC). 18% of all full-time undergraduates had no need and received non-need-based gift aid.

GIFT AID (NEED-BASED) *Total amount:* $17,486,797 (64% federal, 12% state, 11% institutional, 13% external sources). *Receiving aid:* Freshmen: 16% (539); all full-time undergraduates: 19% (2,553). *Average award:* Freshmen: $5178; Undergraduates: $4714. *Scholarships, grants, and awards:* Federal Pell, FSEOG, state, private, college/university gift aid from institutional funds.

GIFT AID (NON-NEED-BASED) *Total amount:* $57,677,290 (72% state, 16% institutional, 12% external sources). *Receiving aid:* Freshmen: 40% (1,326). Undergraduates: 28% (3,814). *Average award:* Freshmen: $1789. Undergraduates: $2489. *Scholarships, grants, and awards by category: Academic interests/ achievement:* agriculture, architecture, biological sciences, business, communication, computer science, education, engineering/technologies, English, foreign languages, general academic interests/achievements, health fields, humanities, international studies, mathematics, military science, physical sciences, premedicine, social sciences. *Creative arts/performance:* applied art and design, art/fine arts, performing arts, theater/drama. *Special achievements/activities:* community service, general special achievements/activities, leadership. *Special characteristics:* children of faculty/staff, ethnic background, local/state students, members of minority groups. *Tuition waivers:* Full or partial for senior citizens.

LOANS *Student loans:* $73,889,406 (36% need-based, 64% non-need-based). 49% of past graduating class borrowed through all loan programs. *Average indebtedness per student:* $18,463. *Average need-based loan:* Freshmen: $3462. Undergraduates: $4196. *Parent loans:* $15,698,342 (100% non-need-based). *Programs:* Federal Direct (Subsidized and Unsubsidized Stafford, PLUS), Perkins, state, college/university, private loans.

WORK-STUDY *Federal work-study:* Total amount: $1,966,130; 916 jobs averaging $2146. *State or other work-study/employment:* Total amount: $6,000,000 (100% non-need-based). 3,000 part-time jobs averaging $1700.

ATHLETIC AWARDS Total amount: $6,047,395 (100% non-need-based).

APPLYING FOR FINANCIAL AID *Required financial aid form:* FAFSA. *Financial aid deadline (priority):* 4/1. *Notification date:* Continuous beginning 4/16. Students must reply within 3 weeks of notification.

CONTACT Mr. Marvin G. Carmichael, Director of Financial Aid, Clemson University, G01 Sikes Hall, Clemson, SC 29634-5123, 864-656-2280. *Fax:* 864-656-1831. *E-mail:* finaid@clemson.edu.

THE CLEVELAND INSTITUTE OF ART
Cleveland, OH

Tuition & fees: $31,904	Average undergraduate aid package: $21,225

ABOUT THE INSTITUTION Independent, coed. 17 undergraduate majors. Federal methodology is used as a basis for awarding need-based institutional aid.

UNDERGRADUATE EXPENSES for 2009–10 *Comprehensive fee:* $42,440 includes full-time tuition ($29,870), mandatory fees ($2034), and room and board ($10,536). *College room only:* $6126. Full-time tuition and fees vary according to program. Room and board charges vary according to board plan. *Part-time tuition:* $1250 per credit hour. *Part-time fees:* $140 per credit hour. Part-time tuition and fees vary according to course load and program. *Payment plan:* Installment.

FRESHMAN FINANCIAL AID (Fall 2009, est.) 111 applied for aid; of those 95% were deemed to have need. 100% of freshmen with need received aid; of those 13% had need fully met. *Average percent of need met:* 63% (excluding

resources awarded to replace EFC). *Average financial aid package:* $23,309 (excluding resources awarded to replace EFC). 6% of all full-time freshmen had no need and received non-need-based gift aid.

UNDERGRADUATE FINANCIAL AID (Fall 2009, est.) 486 applied for aid; of those 94% were deemed to have need. 100% of undergraduates with need received aid; of those 9% had need fully met. *Average percent of need met:* 57% (excluding resources awarded to replace EFC). *Average financial aid package:* $21,225 (excluding resources awarded to replace EFC). 12% of all full-time undergraduates had no need and received non-need-based gift aid.

GIFT AID (NEED-BASED) *Total amount:* $6,958,933 (15% federal, 3% state, 80% institutional, 2% external sources). *Receiving aid:* Freshmen: 93% (105); all full-time undergraduates: 88% (457). *Average award:* Freshmen: $17,672; Undergraduates: $15,205. *Scholarships, grants, and awards:* Federal Pell, FSEOG, state, private, college/university gift aid from institutional funds.

GIFT AID (NON-NEED-BASED) *Total amount:* $747,134 (1% state, 99% institutional). *Receiving aid:* Freshmen: 11% (12). Undergraduates: 6% (29). *Average award:* Freshmen: $12,838. Undergraduates: $9654. *Scholarships, grants, and awards by category: Creative arts/performance:* 457 awards ($5,586,013 total): art/fine arts. *Tuition waivers:* Full or partial for employees or children of employees.

LOANS *Student loans:* $5,932,639 (81% need-based, 19% non-need-based). 81% of past graduating class borrowed through all loan programs. *Average indebtedness per student:* $61,270. *Average need-based loan:* Freshmen: $4453. Undergraduates: $4818. *Parent loans:* $1,656,683 (60% need-based, 40% non-need-based). *Programs:* FFEL (Subsidized and Unsubsidized Stafford, PLUS), Perkins.

WORK-STUDY *Federal work-study:* Total amount: $710,787; 358 jobs averaging $2222.

APPLYING FOR FINANCIAL AID *Required financial aid forms:* FAFSA, institution's own form. *Financial aid deadline (priority):* 3/15. *Notification date:* Continuous beginning 3/1. Students must reply by 5/1 or within 3 weeks of notification.

CONTACT Karen Kopp, Director of Financial Aid, The Cleveland Institute of Art, 11141 East Boulevard, Cleveland, OH 44106-1700, 216-421-7425 or toll-free 800-223-4700. *Fax:* 216-754-3634. *E-mail:* financialaid@cia.edu.

CLEVELAND INSTITUTE OF MUSIC
Cleveland, OH

Tuition & fees: $36,590	Average undergraduate aid package: $21,389

ABOUT THE INSTITUTION Independent, coed. 6 undergraduate majors. Federal methodology is used as a basis for awarding need-based institutional aid.

UNDERGRADUATE EXPENSES for 2009–10 *Comprehensive fee:* $45,642 includes full-time tuition ($33,750), mandatory fees ($2840), and room and board ($9052). Room and board charges vary according to board plan. *Part-time tuition:* $1406 per credit hour. *Payment plan:* Installment.

FRESHMAN FINANCIAL AID (Fall 2009, est.) 31 applied for aid; of those 87% were deemed to have need. 100% of freshmen with need received aid; of those 52% had need fully met. *Average percent of need met:* 81% (excluding resources awarded to replace EFC). *Average financial aid package:* $21,222 (excluding resources awarded to replace EFC). 33% of all full-time freshmen had no need and received non-need-based gift aid.

UNDERGRADUATE FINANCIAL AID (Fall 2009, est.) 164 applied for aid; of those 85% were deemed to have need. 100% of undergraduates with need received aid; of those 35% had need fully met. *Average percent of need met:* 77% (excluding resources awarded to replace EFC). *Average financial aid package:* $21,389 (excluding resources awarded to replace EFC). 35% of all full-time undergraduates had no need and received non-need-based gift aid.

GIFT AID (NEED-BASED) *Total amount:* $2,165,283 (7% federal, 2% state, 87% institutional, 4% external sources). *Receiving aid:* Freshmen: 60% (27); all full-time undergraduates: 62% (140). *Average award:* Freshmen: $16,870; Undergraduates: $15,427. *Scholarships, grants, and awards:* Federal Pell, FSEOG, state, private, college/university gift aid from institutional funds.

GIFT AID (NON-NEED-BASED) *Total amount:* $1,305,779 (2% state, 92% institutional, 6% external sources). *Receiving aid:* Freshmen: 22% (10). Undergraduates: 16% (35). *Average award:* Freshmen: $12,833. Undergraduates: $12,686. *Scholarships, grants, and awards by category: Creative arts/ performance:* music. *Tuition waivers:* Full or partial for employees or children of employees.

LOANS *Student loans:* $1,411,780 (65% need-based, 35% non-need-based). 68% of past graduating class borrowed through all loan programs. *Average indebtedness per student:* $26,355. *Average need-based loan:* Freshmen: $5126. Undergraduates: $6812. *Parent loans:* $549,224 (29% need-based, 71% non-need-based). *Programs:* Federal Direct (Subsidized and Unsubsidized Stafford, PLUS), Perkins, college/university, private alternative loans.

WORK-STUDY *Federal work-study:* Total amount: $141,267; 76 jobs averaging $1859. *State or other work-study/employment:* Total amount: $45,000 (100% non-need-based). 21 part-time jobs averaging $2143.

APPLYING FOR FINANCIAL AID *Required financial aid form:* FAFSA. *Financial aid deadline:* 2/15. *Notification date:* 4/1. Students must reply by 5/1.

CONTACT Ms. Kristie Gripp, Director of Financial Aid, Cleveland Institute of Music, 11021 East Boulevard, Cleveland, OH 44106-1776, 216-795-3192. *Fax:* 216-707-4519. *E-mail:* kxg26@case.edu.

CLEVELAND STATE UNIVERSITY
Cleveland, OH

Tuition & fees (OH res): $8196	Average undergraduate aid package: $8565

ABOUT THE INSTITUTION State-supported, coed. 82 undergraduate majors. Federal methodology is used as a basis for awarding need-based institutional aid.

UNDERGRADUATE EXPENSES for 2010–11 *Tuition, state resident:* full-time $8196; part-time $341.50 per credit hour. *Tuition, nonresident:* full-time $11,026; part-time $459.40 per credit hour. Full-time tuition and fees vary according to course load and program. Part-time tuition and fees vary according to course load and program. *College room and board:* $10,250; *Room only:* $6700. Room and board charges vary according to board plan and housing facility. *Payment plan:* Installment.

FRESHMAN FINANCIAL AID (Fall 2009, est.) 811 applied for aid; of those 92% were deemed to have need. 98% of freshmen with need received aid; of those 6% had need fully met. *Average percent of need met:* 52% (excluding resources awarded to replace EFC). *Average financial aid package:* $9016 (excluding resources awarded to replace EFC). 4% of all full-time freshmen had no need and received non-need-based gift aid.

UNDERGRADUATE FINANCIAL AID (Fall 2009, est.) 6,443 applied for aid; of those 91% were deemed to have need. 97% of undergraduates with need received aid; of those 8% had need fully met. *Average percent of need met:* 49% (excluding resources awarded to replace EFC). *Average financial aid package:* $8565 (excluding resources awarded to replace EFC). 5% of all full-time undergraduates had no need and received non-need-based gift aid.

GIFT AID (NEED-BASED) *Total amount:* $28,204,381 (71% federal, 12% state, 12% institutional, 5% external sources). *Receiving aid:* Freshmen: 56% (632); all full-time undergraduates: 59% (4,374). *Average award:* Freshmen: $7106; Undergraduates: $6172. *Scholarships, grants, and awards:* Federal Pell, FSEOG, state, private, college/university gift aid from institutional funds.

GIFT AID (NON-NEED-BASED) *Total amount:* $2,223,563 (1% federal, 7% state, 81% institutional, 11% external sources). *Receiving aid:* Freshmen: 2% (21). Undergraduates: 3% (190). *Average award:* Freshmen: $2036. Undergraduates: $4242. *Scholarships, grants, and awards by category: Academic interests/achievement:* biological sciences, business, communication, computer science, education, engineering/technologies, English, general academic interests/achievements, health fields, humanities, mathematics, physical sciences, premedicine, social sciences. *Creative arts/performance:* art/fine arts, creative writing, dance, music, performing arts, theater/drama. *Special achievements/activities:* cheerleading/drum major. *Special characteristics:* children and siblings of alumni, children of faculty/staff, general special characteristics, out-of-state students. *Tuition waivers:* Full or partial for employees or children of employees, senior citizens.

LOANS *Student loans:* $55,707,418 (85% need-based, 15% non-need-based). *Average need-based loan:* Freshmen: $3286. Undergraduates: $4157. *Parent loans:* $1,335,060 (36% need-based, 64% non-need-based). *Programs:* FFEL (Subsidized and Unsubsidized Stafford, PLUS), Perkins, state, alternative loans.

WORK-STUDY *Federal work-study:* Total amount: $1,180,555; jobs available. *State or other work-study/employment:* Total amount: $8067 (100% non-need-based). Part-time jobs available.

ATHLETIC AWARDS Total amount: $2,104,185 (40% need-based, 60% non-need-based).

APPLYING FOR FINANCIAL AID *Required financial aid form:* FAFSA. *Financial aid deadline (priority):* 2/15. *Notification date:* Continuous beginning 3/15. Students must reply within 4 weeks of notification.

CONTACT Director of Financial Aid, Cleveland State University, 1621 Euclid Avenue, Cleveland, OH 44115, 216-687-5594 or toll-free 888-CSU-OHIO.

COASTAL CAROLINA UNIVERSITY
Conway, SC

Tuition & fees (SC res): $8950	Average undergraduate aid package: $8461

ABOUT THE INSTITUTION State-supported, coed. 36 undergraduate majors. Federal methodology is used as a basis for awarding need-based institutional aid.

UNDERGRADUATE EXPENSES for 2009–10 *Tuition, state resident:* full-time $8870; part-time $373 per credit hour. *Tuition, nonresident:* full-time $18,690; part-time $782 per credit hour. *Required fees:* full-time $80. Full-time tuition and fees vary according to course load. Part-time tuition and fees vary according to course load. *College room and board:* $7200; *Room only:* $4650. Room and board charges vary according to board plan and housing facility. *Payment plan:* Installment.

FRESHMAN FINANCIAL AID (Fall 2008) 1,419 applied for aid; of those 73% were deemed to have need. 97% of freshmen with need received aid; of those 12% had need fully met. *Average percent of need met:* 53% (excluding resources awarded to replace EFC). *Average financial aid package:* $8311 (excluding resources awarded to replace EFC). 21% of all full-time freshmen had no need and received non-need-based gift aid.

UNDERGRADUATE FINANCIAL AID (Fall 2008) 5,331 applied for aid; of those 77% were deemed to have need. 97% of undergraduates with need received aid; of those 11% had need fully met. *Average percent of need met:* 51% (excluding resources awarded to replace EFC). *Average financial aid package:* $8461 (excluding resources awarded to replace EFC). 19% of all full-time undergraduates had no need and received non-need-based gift aid.

GIFT AID (NEED-BASED) *Total amount:* $8,080,723 (87% federal, 13% state). *Receiving aid:* Freshmen: 25% (411); all full-time undergraduates: 26% (1,754). *Average award:* Freshmen: $4664; Undergraduates: $4412. *Scholarships, grants, and awards:* Federal Pell, FSEOG, state, private, college/university gift aid from institutional funds, Academic Competitiveness Grants, National SMART Grants.

GIFT AID (NON-NEED-BASED) *Total amount:* $11,192,035 (66% state, 16% institutional, 18% external sources). *Receiving aid:* Freshmen: 29% (478). Undergraduates: 16% (1,073). *Average award:* Freshmen: $9526. Undergraduates: $10,228. *Scholarships, grants, and awards by category: Academic interests/achievement:* 1,336 awards ($2,753,988 total): biological sciences, business, education, general academic interests/achievements, humanities, mathematics. *Creative arts/performance:* 40 awards ($31,735 total): art/fine arts, music, theater/drama. *Special achievements/activities:* 33 awards ($30,250 total): cheerleading/drum major. *Special characteristics:* 1,198 awards ($3,032,708 total): general special characteristics, international students, local/state students, out-of-state students, veterans' children. *Tuition waivers:* Full or partial for employees or children of employees, senior citizens.

LOANS *Student loans:* $42,018,477 (33% need-based, 67% non-need-based). 71% of past graduating class borrowed through all loan programs. *Average indebtedness per student:* $26,646. *Average need-based loan:* Freshmen: $7279. Undergraduates: $7744. *Parent loans:* $7,738,436 (100% non-need-based). *Programs:* FFEL (Subsidized and Unsubsidized Stafford, PLUS), Perkins, state.

WORK-STUDY *Federal work-study:* Total amount: $250,920; 261 jobs averaging $955. *State or other work-study/employment:* Total amount: $1,228,429 (19% need-based, 81% non-need-based). 1,070 part-time jobs averaging $2377.

ATHLETIC AWARDS Total amount: $3,244,785 (100% non-need-based).

APPLYING FOR FINANCIAL AID *Required financial aid form:* FAFSA. *Financial aid deadline (priority):* 3/1. *Notification date:* Continuous beginning 3/1. Students must reply by 5/15.

CONTACT Dawn Hitchcock, Director of Financial Aid, Coastal Carolina University, PO Box 261954, Conway, SC 29528-6054, 843-349-2190 or toll-free 800-277-7000. *Fax:* 843-349-2347. *E-mail:* dawn@coastal.edu.

COE COLLEGE
Cedar Rapids, IA

Tuition & fees: $29,270	Average undergraduate aid package: $23,085

ABOUT THE INSTITUTION Independent religious, coed. *Awards:* bachelor's and master's degrees. 64 undergraduate majors. *Total enrollment:* 1,326. Undergraduates: 1,310. Freshmen: 342. Federal methodology is used as a basis for awarding need-based institutional aid.

UNDERGRADUATE EXPENSES for 2009–10 *Application fee:* $30. *Comprehensive fee:* $36,420 includes full-time tuition ($28,950), mandatory fees ($320), and room and board ($7150). *College room only:* $3210. Room and board charges vary according to board plan and housing facility. *Part-time tuition:* $3620 per course. *Payment plan:* Installment.

FRESHMAN FINANCIAL AID (Fall 2009, est.) 297 applied for aid; of those 89% were deemed to have need. 100% of freshmen with need received aid; of those 27% had need fully met. *Average percent of need met:* 86% (excluding resources awarded to replace EFC). *Average financial aid package:* $24,679 (excluding resources awarded to replace EFC). 15% of all full-time freshmen had no need and received non-need-based gift aid.

UNDERGRADUATE FINANCIAL AID (Fall 2009, est.) 1,039 applied for aid; of those 91% were deemed to have need. 100% of undergraduates with need received aid; of those 23% had need fully met. *Average percent of need met:* 82% (excluding resources awarded to replace EFC). *Average financial aid package:* $23,085 (excluding resources awarded to replace EFC). 21% of all full-time undergraduates had no need and received non-need-based gift aid.

GIFT AID (NEED-BASED) *Total amount:* $16,912,674 (10% federal, 11% state, 77% institutional, 2% external sources). *Receiving aid:* Freshmen: 79% (263); all full-time undergraduates: 77% (939). *Average award:* Freshmen: $20,446; Undergraduates: $18,611. *Scholarships, grants, and awards:* Federal Pell, FSEOG, state, private, college/university gift aid from institutional funds, Federal Nursing, ROTC scholarships.

GIFT AID (NON-NEED-BASED) *Total amount:* $5,480,757 (3% federal, 94% institutional, 3% external sources). *Receiving aid:* Freshmen: 15% (51). Undergraduates: 12% (152). *Average award:* Freshmen: $16,822. Undergraduates: $16,112. *Scholarships, grants, and awards by category: Academic interests/achievement:* 1,191 awards ($12,510,021 total): biological sciences, business, English, foreign languages, general academic interests/achievements, mathematics, physical sciences, premedicine. *Creative arts/performance:* 239 awards ($579,015 total): art/fine arts, creative writing, music, performing arts, theater/drama. *Special characteristics:* 341 awards ($2,164,769 total): adult students, children and siblings of alumni, children of educators, children of faculty/staff, international students, members of minority groups, siblings of current students, veterans. *Tuition waivers:* Full or partial for children of alumni, employees or children of employees, adult students, senior citizens. *ROTC:* Army cooperative, Air Force cooperative.

LOANS *Student loans:* $7,614,919 (73% need-based, 27% non-need-based). 83% of past graduating class borrowed through all loan programs. *Average indebtedness per student:* $30,665. *Average need-based loan:* Freshmen: $4632. Undergraduates: $5054. *Parent loans:* $2,277,139 (33% need-based, 67% non-need-based). *Programs:* Federal Direct (Subsidized and Unsubsidized Stafford, PLUS), Perkins, college/university.

WORK-STUDY *Federal work-study:* Total amount: $465,493; 373 jobs averaging $1400. *State or other work-study/employment:* Total amount: $281,700 (9% need-based, 91% non-need-based). 187 part-time jobs averaging $1300.

APPLYING FOR FINANCIAL AID *Required financial aid form:* FAFSA. *Financial aid deadline (priority):* 3/1. *Notification date:* Continuous beginning 3/15. Students must reply by 5/1 or within 2 weeks of notification.

CONTACT Ms. Barbara Hoffman, Director of Financial Aid, Coe College, 1220 1st Avenue, NE, Cedar Rapids, IA 52402-5070, 319-399-8540 or toll-free 877-225-5263. *Fax:* 319-399-8886.

COGSWELL POLYTECHNICAL COLLEGE
Sunnyvale, CA

ABOUT THE INSTITUTION Independent, coed, primarily men. 6 undergraduate majors.

GIFT AID (NEED-BASED) *Scholarships, grants, and awards:* Federal Pell, FSEOG, state, private, college/university gift aid from institutional funds.

LOANS *Programs:* FFEL (Subsidized and Unsubsidized Stafford, PLUS).

APPLYING FOR FINANCIAL AID *Required financial aid forms:* FAFSA, state aid form.

CONTACT Andrew Hagedorn, Financial Aid Director, Cogswell Polytechnical College, 1175 Bordeaux Drive, Sunnyvale, CA 94089, 408-541-0100 Ext. 107 or toll-free 800-264-7955. *Fax:* 408-747-0766. *E-mail:* ahagedorn@cogswell.edu.

COKER COLLEGE
Hartsville, SC

Tuition & fees: $19,858	Average undergraduate aid package: $19,956

ABOUT THE INSTITUTION Independent, coed. 46 undergraduate majors. Both federal and institutional methodology are used as a basis for awarding need-based institutional aid.

UNDERGRADUATE EXPENSES for 2009–10 *Comprehensive fee:* $26,098 includes full-time tuition ($19,368), mandatory fees ($490), and room and board ($6240). *College room only:* $3070. *Part-time tuition:* $807 per semester hour.

FRESHMAN FINANCIAL AID (Fall 2009, est.) 186 applied for aid; of those 92% were deemed to have need. 100% of freshmen with need received aid; of those 40% had need fully met. *Average percent of need met:* 91% (excluding resources awarded to replace EFC). *Average financial aid package:* $20,414 (excluding resources awarded to replace EFC). 10% of all full-time freshmen had no need and received non-need-based gift aid.

UNDERGRADUATE FINANCIAL AID (Fall 2009, est.) 597 applied for aid; of those 92% were deemed to have need. 100% of undergraduates with need received aid; of those 39% had need fully met. *Average percent of need met:* 89% (excluding resources awarded to replace EFC). *Average financial aid package:* $19,956 (excluding resources awarded to replace EFC). 13% of all full-time undergraduates had no need and received non-need-based gift aid.

GIFT AID (NEED-BASED) *Total amount:* $3,808,860 (41% federal, 36% state, 20% institutional, 3% external sources). *Receiving aid:* Freshmen: 82% (156); all full-time undergraduates: 81% (521). *Average award:* Freshmen: $6986; Undergraduates: $7208. *Scholarships, grants, and awards:* Federal Pell, FSEOG, state, private, college/university gift aid from institutional funds.

GIFT AID (NON-NEED-BASED) *Total amount:* $6,169,620 (1% federal, 22% state, 76% institutional, 1% external sources). *Receiving aid:* Freshmen: 90% (171). Undergraduates: 82% (523). *Average award:* Freshmen: $7717. Undergraduates: $7228. *Scholarships, grants, and awards by category: Academic interests/achievement:* general academic interests/achievements. *Creative arts/performance:* art/fine arts, creative writing, dance, general creative arts/performance, music, theater/drama. *Special characteristics:* children and siblings of alumni, children of faculty/staff, international students, previous college experience.

LOANS *Student loans:* $3,998,577 (94% need-based, 6% non-need-based). 81% of past graduating class borrowed through all loan programs. *Average indebtedness per student:* $24,601. *Average need-based loan:* Freshmen: $3424. Undergraduates: $4258. *Parent loans:* $286,351 (100% non-need-based). *Programs:* Federal Direct (Subsidized and Unsubsidized Stafford, PLUS), Perkins, state, private loans.

WORK-STUDY *Federal work-study:* Total amount: $165,218; 144 jobs averaging $1147. *State or other work-study/employment:* Total amount: $500 (100% need-based). Part-time jobs available.

ATHLETIC AWARDS Total amount: $753,948 (100% non-need-based).

APPLYING FOR FINANCIAL AID *Required financial aid form:* FAFSA. *Financial aid deadline:* 6/1 (priority: 4/1). *Notification date:* Continuous beginning 3/1. Students must reply by 5/1 or within 3 weeks of notification.

CONTACT Betty Williams, Director of Financial Aid, Coker College, 300 East College Avenue, Hartsville, SC 29550, 843-383-8055 or toll-free 800-950-1908. *Fax:* 843-383-8056. *E-mail:* bwilliams@coker.edu.

THE COLBURN SCHOOL CONSERVATORY OF MUSIC
Los Angeles, CA

ABOUT THE INSTITUTION Independent, coed. 4 undergraduate majors.

UNDERGRADUATE EXPENSES for 2010–11 *One-time required fee:* $500. The Colburn School does not charge its Conservatory students for tuition, room or board.

The Colburn School Conservatory of Music

CONTACT Ms. Kathleen Tesar, Associate Dean, The Colburn School Conservatory of Music, 200 South Grand Avenue, Los Angeles, CA 90012, 213-621-4534. *Fax:* 213-625-0371. *E-mail:* admissions@colburnschool.edu.

COLBY COLLEGE
Waterville, ME

Comprehensive fee: $50,320	Average undergraduate aid package: $32,252

ABOUT THE INSTITUTION Independent, coed. 41 undergraduate majors. Both federal and institutional methodology are used as a basis for awarding need-based institutional aid.

UNDERGRADUATE EXPENSES for 2009–10 *Comprehensive fee:* $50,320. Full-time tuition and fees vary according to course load. Room and board charges vary according to housing facility. Part-time tuition and fees vary according to course load. *Payment plan:* Installment.

FRESHMAN FINANCIAL AID (Fall 2009, est.) 255 applied for aid; of those 78% were deemed to have need. 100% of freshmen with need received aid; of those 100% had need fully met. *Average percent of need met:* 100% (excluding resources awarded to replace EFC). *Average financial aid package:* $34,919 (excluding resources awarded to replace EFC). 1% of all full-time freshmen had no need and received non-need-based gift aid.

UNDERGRADUATE FINANCIAL AID (Fall 2009, est.) 816 applied for aid; of those 86% were deemed to have need. 100% of undergraduates with need received aid; of those 100% had need fully met. *Average percent of need met:* 100% (excluding resources awarded to replace EFC). *Average financial aid package:* $32,252 (excluding resources awarded to replace EFC). 3% of all full-time undergraduates had no need and received non-need-based gift aid.

GIFT AID (NEED-BASED) *Total amount:* $21,723,897 (6% federal, 92% institutional, 2% external sources). *Receiving aid:* Freshmen: 41% (195); all full-time undergraduates: 38% (694). *Average award:* Freshmen: $34,092; Undergraduates: $31,423. *Scholarships, grants, and awards:* Federal Pell, FSEOG, state, private, college/university gift aid from institutional funds, Academic Competitiveness Grants, National SMART Grants, Colby National Merit Scholarships.

GIFT AID (NON-NEED-BASED) *Total amount:* $385,372 (2% federal, 75% institutional, 23% external sources). *Receiving aid:* Freshmen: 1% (3). Undergraduates: 1% (14). *Average award:* Freshmen: $1000. Undergraduates: $337. *Scholarships, grants, and awards by category:* Academic interests/achievement: 49 awards ($16,500 total): general academic interests/achievements. *Special characteristics:* 16 awards ($272,660 total): ethnic background. *Tuition waivers:* Full or partial for employees or children of employees.

LOANS *Student loans:* $4,264,866 (100% non-need-based). 41% of past graduating class borrowed through all loan programs. *Average indebtedness per student:* $21,697. *Average need-based loan:* Freshmen: $1500. Undergraduates: $22,340. *Parent loans:* $2,621,080 (100% non-need-based). *Programs:* Federal Direct (Subsidized and Unsubsidized Stafford, PLUS), FFEL (Subsidized and Unsubsidized Stafford, PLUS), Perkins, state, alternative loans.

WORK-STUDY *Federal work-study:* Total amount: $739,685; 458 jobs averaging $1615. *State or other work-study/employment:* Total amount: $211,180 (100% need-based). 119 part-time jobs averaging $1745.

APPLYING FOR FINANCIAL AID *Required financial aid forms:* FAFSA, CSS Financial Aid PROFILE, federal tax returns for student and parents. *Financial aid deadline:* 2/1. *Notification date:* 4/1. Students must reply by 5/1.

CONTACT Ms. Lucia Whittelsey, Director of Financial Aid, Colby College, 4850 Mayflower Hill, Waterville, ME 04901-8848, 207-859-4832 or toll-free 800-723-3032. *Fax:* 207-859-4828. *E-mail:* finaid@colby.edu.

COLBY-SAWYER COLLEGE
New London, NH

CONTACT Office of Financial Aid, Colby-Sawyer College, 541 Main Street, New London, NH 03257-7835, 603-526-3717 or toll-free 800-272-1015. *Fax:* 603-526-3452. *E-mail:* cscfinaid@colby-sawyer.edu.

COLEGIO PENTECOSTAL MIZPA
Río Piedras, PR

CONTACT Financial Aid Office, Colegio Pentecostal Mizpa, Bo Caimito Road 199, Apartado 20966, Río Piedras, PR 00928-0966, 787-720-4476.

COLEMAN UNIVERSITY
San Diego, CA

Tuition & fees: N/R	Average undergraduate aid package: N/A

ABOUT THE INSTITUTION Independent, coed. *Awards:* associate, bachelor's, and master's degrees. 4 undergraduate majors. *Total enrollment:* 488. Undergraduates: 477. Federal methodology is used as a basis for awarding need-based institutional aid.

GIFT AID (NEED-BASED) *Scholarships, grants, and awards:* Federal Pell, FSEOG, state.

GIFT AID (NON-NEED-BASED) *Scholarships, grants, and awards by category:* Academic interests/achievement: general academic interests/achievements. *Special characteristics:* children and siblings of alumni.

LOANS *Programs:* Federal Direct (Subsidized and Unsubsidized Stafford, PLUS), FFEL (Subsidized and Unsubsidized Stafford, PLUS).

WORK-STUDY Federal work-study jobs available.

APPLYING FOR FINANCIAL AID *Required financial aid forms:* FAFSA, institution's own form, state aid form. *Financial aid deadline:* Continuous. *Notification date:* Continuous.

CONTACT Financial Aid Office, Coleman University, 8888 Balboa Avenue, San Diego, CA 92123, 858-499-0202. *Fax:* 858-499-0233. *E-mail:* faoffice@coleman.edu.

COLGATE UNIVERSITY
Hamilton, NY

Tuition & fees: $40,970	Average undergraduate aid package: $37,738

ABOUT THE INSTITUTION Independent, coed. 51 undergraduate majors. Institutional methodology is used as a basis for awarding need-based institutional aid.

UNDERGRADUATE EXPENSES for 2009–10 *One-time required fee:* $50. *Comprehensive fee:* $50,940 includes full-time tuition ($40,690), mandatory fees ($280), and room and board ($9970). *College room only:* $4815. Full-time tuition and fees vary according to course load. Room and board charges vary according to board plan and housing facility. *Part-time tuition:* $5086.25 per course. Part-time tuition and fees vary according to course load. *Payment plans:* Tuition prepayment, installment, deferred payment.

FRESHMAN FINANCIAL AID (Fall 2009, est.) 318 applied for aid; of those 79% were deemed to have need. 100% of freshmen with need received aid; of those 100% had need fully met. *Average percent of need met:* 100% (excluding resources awarded to replace EFC). *Average financial aid package:* $39,758 (excluding resources awarded to replace EFC).

UNDERGRADUATE FINANCIAL AID (Fall 2009, est.) 1,022 applied for aid; of those 96% were deemed to have need. 100% of undergraduates with need received aid; of those 100% had need fully met. *Average percent of need met:* 100% (excluding resources awarded to replace EFC). *Average financial aid package:* $37,738 (excluding resources awarded to replace EFC).

GIFT AID (NEED-BASED) *Total amount:* $32,575,571 (5% federal, 2% state, 92% institutional, 1% external sources). *Receiving aid:* Freshmen: 34% (252); all full-time undergraduates: 35% (968). *Average award:* Freshmen: $35,526; Undergraduates: $33,211. *Scholarships, grants, and awards:* Federal Pell, FSEOG, state, college/university gift aid from institutional funds.

GIFT AID (NON-NEED-BASED) *Tuition waivers:* Full or partial for employees or children of employees.

LOANS *Student loans:* $4,492,812 (56% need-based, 44% non-need-based). 30% of past graduating class borrowed through all loan programs. *Average indebtedness per student:* $19,202. *Average need-based loan:* Freshmen: $2107. Undergraduates: $4505. *Parent loans:* $4,978,374 (100% non-need-based). *Programs:* Federal Direct (Subsidized and Unsubsidized Stafford, PLUS), Perkins.

WORK-STUDY *Federal work-study:* Total amount: $1,069,299; 486 jobs averaging $2137. *State or other work-study/employment:* Total amount: $521,346 (100% need-based). 273 part-time jobs averaging $1985.

ATHLETIC AWARDS Total amount: $6,157,558 (100% non-need-based).

APPLYING FOR FINANCIAL AID *Required financial aid forms:* CSS Financial Aid PROFILE, noncustodial (divorced/separated) parent's statement. *Financial aid deadline:* 1/15. *Notification date:* 4/1. Students must reply by 5/1 or within 2 weeks of notification.

CONTACT Financial Aid Office, Colgate University, 13 Oak Drive, Hamilton, NY 13346, 315-228-7431. *Fax:* 315-228-7050. *E-mail:* financialaid@colgate.edu.

THE COLLEGE AT BROCKPORT, STATE UNIVERSITY OF NEW YORK
Brockport, NY

Tuition & fees (NY res): $6108   **Average undergraduate aid package: $9606**

ABOUT THE INSTITUTION State-supported, coed. 107 undergraduate majors. Federal methodology is used as a basis for awarding need-based institutional aid.

UNDERGRADUATE EXPENSES for 2010–11 *Tuition, state resident:* full-time $4970. *Tuition, nonresident:* full-time $12,870. *Required fees:* full-time $1138. Part-time tuition and fees vary according to course load. *College room and board:* $9200; *Room only:* $6040. Room and board charges vary according to board plan and housing facility. *Payment plans:* Installment, deferred payment.

FRESHMAN FINANCIAL AID (Fall 2009, est.) 949 applied for aid; of those 74% were deemed to have need. 100% of freshmen with need received aid; of those 25% had need fully met. *Average percent of need met:* 76% (excluding resources awarded to replace EFC). *Average financial aid package:* $9345 (excluding resources awarded to replace EFC). 7% of all full-time freshmen had no need and received non-need-based gift aid.

UNDERGRADUATE FINANCIAL AID (Fall 2009, est.) 4,887 applied for aid; of those 79% were deemed to have need. 99% of undergraduates with need received aid; of those 29% had need fully met. *Average percent of need met:* 74% (excluding resources awarded to replace EFC). *Average financial aid package:* $9606 (excluding resources awarded to replace EFC). 3% of all full-time undergraduates had no need and received non-need-based gift aid.

GIFT AID (NEED-BASED) *Total amount:* $19,596,478 (59% federal, 41% state). *Receiving aid:* Freshmen: 59% (598); all full-time undergraduates: 61% (3,350). *Average award:* Freshmen: $5439; Undergraduates: $5045. *Scholarships, grants, and awards:* Federal Pell, FSEOG, state, private, college/university gift aid from institutional funds.

GIFT AID (NON-NEED-BASED) *Total amount:* $5,008,047 (6% federal, 10% state, 62% institutional, 22% external sources). *Receiving aid:* Freshmen: 26% (265). Undergraduates: 15% (823). *Average award:* Freshmen: $3171. Undergraduates: $4245. *Scholarships, grants, and awards by category:* Academic interests/achievement: 425 awards ($1,100,000 total): biological sciences, business, communication, computer science, education, English, foreign languages, general academic interests/achievements, health fields, humanities, international studies, mathematics, military science, physical sciences, premedicine, social sciences. *Creative arts/performance:* 50 awards ($80,000 total): art/fine arts, cinema/film/broadcasting, creative writing, dance, general creative arts/performance, journalism/publications, music, performing arts, theater/drama. *Special achievements/activities:* 25 awards ($25,000 total): community service, general special achievements/activities, hobbies/interests, leadership, religious involvement. *Special characteristics:* 45 awards ($43,000 total): children and siblings of alumni, ethnic background, first-generation college students, general special characteristics, international students, local/state students, married students, members of minority groups, out-of-state students, previous college experience, religious affiliation, veterans. *Tuition waivers:* Full or partial for employees or children of employees, senior citizens.

LOANS *Student loans:* $41,276,943 (45% need-based, 55% non-need-based). 81% of past graduating class borrowed through all loan programs. *Average indebtedness per student:* $26,095. *Average need-based loan:* Freshmen: $3623. Undergraduates: $4605. *Parent loans:* $4,324,684 (100% non-need-based). *Programs:* Federal Direct (Subsidized and Unsubsidized Stafford, PLUS), Perkins, Federal Nursing, alternative loans.

WORK-STUDY *Federal work-study:* Total amount: $1,176,809; 654 jobs averaging $1799. *State or other work-study/employment:* Total amount: $2,256,321 (100% non-need-based). 1,664 part-time jobs averaging $1356.

APPLYING FOR FINANCIAL AID *Required financial aid forms:* FAFSA, state aid form. *Financial aid deadline (priority):* 2/15. *Notification date:* Continuous beginning 3/15. Students must reply by 5/1.

CONTACT Mr. J. Scott Atkinson, Interim Assistant Vice President for Enrollment Management, The College at Brockport, State University of New York, 350 New Campus Drive, Brockport, NY 14420-2937, 585-395-2501. *Fax:* 585-395-5445. *E-mail:* satkinso@brockport.edu.

COLLEGE FOR CREATIVE STUDIES
Detroit, MI

Tuition & fees: $31,275   **Average undergraduate aid package: N/A**

ABOUT THE INSTITUTION Independent, coed. 10 undergraduate majors. Federal methodology is used as a basis for awarding need-based institutional aid.

UNDERGRADUATE EXPENSES for 2010–11 *Comprehensive fee:* $39,775 includes full-time tuition ($29,940), mandatory fees ($1335), and room and board ($8500). *College room only:* $4900. Full-time tuition and fees vary according to course load. Room and board charges vary according to board plan and housing facility. *Part-time tuition:* $998 per credit hour. Part-time tuition and fees vary according to course load. *Payment plan:* Installment.

GIFT AID (NEED-BASED) *Total amount:* $4,115,999 (37% federal, 28% state, 34% institutional, 1% external sources). *Scholarships, grants, and awards:* Federal Pell, FSEOG, state, private, college/university gift aid from institutional funds.

GIFT AID (NON-NEED-BASED) *Total amount:* $7,299,007 (2% state, 95% institutional, 3% external sources). *Scholarships, grants, and awards by category:* Academic interests/achievement: general academic interests/achievements. Creative arts/performance: applied art and design, art/fine arts. *Special characteristics:* members of minority groups. *Tuition waivers:* Full or partial for employees or children of employees.

LOANS *Student loans:* $12,466,214 (30% need-based, 70% non-need-based). 79% of past graduating class borrowed through all loan programs. *Average indebtedness per student:* $47,604. *Parent loans:* $1,943,656 (100% non-need-based). *Programs:* Federal Direct (Subsidized and Unsubsidized Stafford, PLUS), private loans.

WORK-STUDY *Federal work-study:* Total amount: $101,391; jobs available. *State or other work-study/employment:* Total amount: $197,428 (14% need-based, 86% non-need-based). Part-time jobs available.

APPLYING FOR FINANCIAL AID *Required financial aid form:* FAFSA. *Financial aid deadline:* Continuous. *Notification date:* Continuous beginning 3/15. Students must reply within 3 weeks of notification.

CONTACT Financial Aid Office, College for Creative Studies, 201 East Kirby, Detroit, MI 48202-4034, 313-664-7495 or toll-free 800-872-2739. *Fax:* 313-872-1521. *E-mail:* finaid@collegeforcreativestudies.edu.

COLLEGE OF BIBLICAL STUDIES–HOUSTON
Houston, TX

CONTACT Financial Aid Office, College of Biblical Studies–Houston, 7000 Regency Square Boulevard, Houston, TX 77036, 713-785-5995.

COLLEGE OF CHARLESTON
Charleston, SC

Tuition & fees (SC res): $8988   **Average undergraduate aid package: $12,882**

ABOUT THE INSTITUTION State-supported, coed. 44 undergraduate majors. Federal methodology is used as a basis for awarding need-based institutional aid.

UNDERGRADUATE EXPENSES for 2009–10 *Tuition, state resident:* full-time $8988; part-time $375 per semester hour. *Tuition, nonresident:* full-time $21,846; part-time $910 per semester hour. Full-time tuition and fees vary according to degree level. Part-time tuition and fees vary according to course load and degree level. *College room and board:* $9411; *Room only:* $6421. Room and board charges vary according to board plan and housing facility. *Payment plan:* Installment.

FRESHMAN FINANCIAL AID (Fall 2009, est.) 1,449 applied for aid; of those 66% were deemed to have need. 96% of freshmen with need received aid; of those 29% had need fully met. *Average percent of need met:* 64% (excluding resources awarded to replace EFC). *Average financial aid package:* $12,690 (excluding resources awarded to replace EFC). 13% of all full-time freshmen had no need and received non-need-based gift aid.

UNDERGRADUATE FINANCIAL AID (Fall 2009, est.) 5,407 applied for aid; of those 75% were deemed to have need. 96% of undergraduates with need received aid; of those 28% had need fully met. *Average percent of need met:* 63% (excluding resources awarded to replace EFC). *Average financial aid*

package: $12,882 (excluding resources awarded to replace EFC). 12% of all full-time undergraduates had no need and received non-need-based gift aid.

GIFT AID (NEED-BASED) *Total amount:* $20,574,311 (42% federal, 34% state, 18% institutional, 6% external sources). *Receiving aid:* Freshmen: 31% (669); all full-time undergraduates: 28% (2,578). *Average award:* Freshmen: $3073; Undergraduates: $3173. *Scholarships, grants, and awards:* Federal Pell, FSEOG, state, private, college/university gift aid from institutional funds.

GIFT AID (NON-NEED-BASED) *Total amount:* $20,006,664 (55% state, 33% institutional, 12% external sources). *Receiving aid:* Freshmen: 33% (701). Undergraduates: 19% (1,753). *Average award:* Freshmen: $11,412. Undergraduates: $11,423. *Scholarships, grants, and awards by category: Academic interests/achievement:* biological sciences, business, communication, computer science, education, engineering/technologies, English, foreign languages, general academic interests/achievements, health fields, humanities, mathematics, physical sciences, premedicine, social sciences. *Creative arts/performance:* art/fine arts, music, performing arts, theater/drama. *Special characteristics:* general special characteristics. *Tuition waivers:* Full or partial for senior citizens.

LOANS *Student loans:* $31,798,211 (64% need-based, 36% non-need-based). 46% of past graduating class borrowed through all loan programs. *Average indebtedness per student:* $19,875. *Average need-based loan:* Freshmen: $3199. Undergraduates: $4008. *Parent loans:* $22,648,232 (53% need-based, 47% non-need-based). *Programs:* Federal Direct (Subsidized and Unsubsidized Stafford, PLUS), Perkins.

WORK-STUDY *Federal work-study:* Total amount: $291,211; jobs available. *State or other work-study/employment:* Total amount: $13,200 (18% need-based, 82% non-need-based). Part-time jobs available.

ATHLETIC AWARDS Total amount: $3,272,212 (31% need-based, 69% non-need-based).

APPLYING FOR FINANCIAL AID *Required financial aid form:* FAFSA. *Financial aid deadline (priority):* 4/15. *Notification date:* Continuous beginning 4/10. Students must reply within 8 weeks of notification.

CONTACT Mr. Don Griggs, Financial Aid Director, College of Charleston, 66 George Street, Charleston, SC 29424, 843-953-5540 or toll-free 843-953-5670 (in-state). *Fax:* 843-953-7192.

COLLEGE OF COASTAL GEORGIA
Brunswick, GA

CONTACT Betty F. Coen, Director of Financial Aid, College of Coastal Georgia, 3700 Altama Avenue, Financial Aid Office, Brunswick, GA 31520, 912-264-7262 or toll-free 800-675-7235. *Fax:* 912-262-3073. *E-mail:* bcoen@bc9000.bc.peachnet.edu.

THE COLLEGE OF IDAHO
Caldwell, ID

ABOUT THE INSTITUTION Independent, coed. 36 undergraduate majors.

GIFT AID (NEED-BASED) *Scholarships, grants, and awards:* Federal Pell, FSEOG, state, private, college/university gift aid from institutional funds.

GIFT AID (NON-NEED-BASED) *Scholarships, grants, and awards by category: Academic interests/achievement:* biological sciences, business, education, English, foreign languages, humanities, mathematics, physical sciences, premedicine, religion/biblical studies, social sciences. *Creative arts/performance:* art/fine arts, debating, music, performing arts, theater/drama. *Special achievements/activities:* leadership. *Special characteristics:* children and siblings of alumni, children of educators, children of faculty/staff, first-generation college students, international students, members of minority groups.

LOANS *Programs:* FFEL (Subsidized and Unsubsidized Stafford, PLUS), Perkins, alternative private loans.

WORK-STUDY *Federal work-study:* Total amount: $145,010; 19 jobs averaging $830. *State or other work-study/employment:* Total amount: $42,830 (84% need-based, 16% non-need-based). 24 part-time jobs averaging $908.

APPLYING FOR FINANCIAL AID *Required financial aid forms:* FAFSA, institution's own form.

CONTACT Merna Davis, Data Coordinator, The College of Idaho, 2112 Cleveland Boulevard, Caldwell, ID 83605-4432, 208-459-5380 or toll-free 800-244-3246. *Fax:* 208-459-5844. *E-mail:* mdavis@collegeofidaho.edu.

COLLEGE OF MOUNT ST. JOSEPH
Cincinnati, OH

Tuition & fees: $22,800	Average undergraduate aid package: $16,176

ABOUT THE INSTITUTION Independent Roman Catholic, coed. 35 undergraduate majors. Federal methodology is used as a basis for awarding need-based institutional aid.

UNDERGRADUATE EXPENSES for 2009–10 *One-time required fee:* $150. *Comprehensive fee:* $29,800 includes full-time tuition ($22,000), mandatory fees ($800), and room and board ($7000). *College room only:* $3500. Full-time tuition and fees vary according to course load, program, and reciprocity agreements. Room and board charges vary according to board plan and housing facility. *Part-time tuition:* $465 per credit hour. *Part-time fees:* $400 per year. Part-time tuition and fees vary according to course load, location, program, and reciprocity agreements. *Payment plans:* Installment, deferred payment.

FRESHMAN FINANCIAL AID (Fall 2008) 343 applied for aid; of those 90% were deemed to have need. 100% of freshmen with need received aid; of those 20% had need fully met. *Average percent of need met:* 81% (excluding resources awarded to replace EFC). *Average financial aid package:* $18,275 (excluding resources awarded to replace EFC). 13% of all full-time freshmen had no need and received non-need-based gift aid.

UNDERGRADUATE FINANCIAL AID (Fall 2008) 1,237 applied for aid; of those 89% were deemed to have need. 100% of undergraduates with need received aid; of those 20% had need fully met. *Average percent of need met:* 75% (excluding resources awarded to replace EFC). *Average financial aid package:* $16,176 (excluding resources awarded to replace EFC). 13% of all full-time undergraduates had no need and received non-need-based gift aid.

GIFT AID (NEED-BASED) *Total amount:* $14,047,506 (22% federal, 6% state, 70% institutional, 2% external sources). *Receiving aid:* Freshmen: 84% (301); all full-time undergraduates: 80% (1,073). *Average award:* Freshmen: $14,456; Undergraduates: $12,251. *Scholarships, grants, and awards:* Federal Pell, FSEOG, state, private, college/university gift aid from institutional funds.

GIFT AID (NON-NEED-BASED) *Total amount:* $1,404,366 (6% federal, 93% institutional, 1% external sources). *Receiving aid:* Freshmen: 9% (31). Undergraduates: 8% (104). *Average award:* Freshmen: $10,361. Undergraduates: $8166. *Scholarships, grants, and awards by category: Academic interests/achievement:* 896 awards ($6,877,260 total): general academic interests/achievements. *Creative arts/performance:* 62 awards ($144,040 total): art/fine arts, music. *Special achievements/activities:* 20 awards ($51,800 total): community service, leadership. *Special characteristics:* 37 awards ($686,551 total): adult students, children and siblings of alumni, children of faculty/staff. *Tuition waivers:* Full or partial for employees or children of employees, senior citizens.

LOANS *Student loans:* $12,991,690 (92% need-based, 8% non-need-based). 84% of past graduating class borrowed through all loan programs. *Average indebtedness per student:* $33,648. *Average need-based loan:* Freshmen: $4035. Undergraduates: $4518. *Parent loans:* $1,951,798 (86% need-based, 14% non-need-based). *Programs:* FFEL (Subsidized and Unsubsidized Stafford, PLUS), Perkins, Federal Nursing, state.

WORK-STUDY *Federal work-study:* Total amount: $320,561; 218 jobs averaging $1470. *State or other work-study/employment:* Total amount: $161,025 (96% need-based, 4% non-need-based). 113 part-time jobs averaging $1425.

APPLYING FOR FINANCIAL AID *Required financial aid form:* FAFSA. *Financial aid deadline (priority):* 3/1. *Notification date:* Continuous beginning 1/31. Students must reply by 5/1 or within 4 weeks of notification.

CONTACT Ms. Kathryn Kelly, Director of Student Administrative Services, College of Mount St. Joseph, 5701 Delhi Road, Cincinnati, OH 45233-1670, 513-244-4418 or toll-free 800-654-9314. *Fax:* 513-244-4201. *E-mail:* kathy_kelly@mail.msj.edu.

COLLEGE OF MOUNT SAINT VINCENT
Riverdale, NY

CONTACT Ms. Monica Simotas, Director of Financial Aid, College of Mount Saint Vincent, 6301 Riverdale Avenue, Riverdale, NY 10471, 718-405-3290 or toll-free 800-665-CMSV. *Fax:* 718-405-3490. *E-mail:* msimotas@mountsaintvincent.edu.

THE COLLEGE OF NEW JERSEY
Ewing, NJ

Tuition & fees (NJ res): $12,722   Average undergraduate aid package: $10,088

ABOUT THE INSTITUTION State-supported, coed. 48 undergraduate majors. Federal methodology is used as a basis for awarding need-based institutional aid.

UNDERGRADUATE EXPENSES for 2009–10 *Tuition, state resident:* full-time $8980; part-time $318.25 per credit hour. *Tuition, nonresident:* full-time $17,666; part-time $625.25 per credit hour. *Required fees:* full-time $3742; $149.60 per credit hour. Part-time tuition and fees vary according to course load. *College room and board:* $9996; *Room only:* $7238. Room and board charges vary according to board plan. *Payment plan:* Installment.

FRESHMAN FINANCIAL AID (Fall 2009, est.) 1,107 applied for aid; of those 59% were deemed to have need. 98% of freshmen with need received aid; of those 15% had need fully met. *Average percent of need met:* 48% (excluding resources awarded to replace EFC). *Average financial aid package:* $10,442 (excluding resources awarded to replace EFC). 25% of all full-time freshmen had no need and received non-need-based gift aid.

UNDERGRADUATE FINANCIAL AID (Fall 2009, est.) 4,364 applied for aid; of those 68% were deemed to have need. 97% of undergraduates with need received aid; of those 20% had need fully met. *Average percent of need met:* 52% (excluding resources awarded to replace EFC). *Average financial aid package:* $10,088 (excluding resources awarded to replace EFC). 18% of all full-time undergraduates had no need and received non-need-based gift aid.

GIFT AID (NEED-BASED) *Total amount:* $19,183,222 (22% federal, 38% state, 33% institutional, 7% external sources). *Receiving aid:* Freshmen: 22% (283); all full-time undergraduates: 19% (1,132). *Average award:* Freshmen: $11,280; Undergraduates: $10,974. *Scholarships, grants, and awards:* Federal Pell, FSEOG, state, private, college/university gift aid from institutional funds.

GIFT AID (NON-NEED-BASED) *Total amount:* $7,097,170 (9% state, 80% institutional, 11% external sources). *Receiving aid:* Freshmen: 33% (422). Undergraduates: 19% (1,160). *Average award:* Freshmen: $3470. Undergraduates: $4777. *Scholarships, grants, and awards by category:* Academic interests/achievement: general academic interests/achievements. Creative arts/performance: music. Special characteristics: children with a deceased or disabled parent, members of minority groups. *Tuition waivers:* Full or partial for employees or children of employees, senior citizens.

LOANS *Student loans:* $31,013,638 (73% need-based, 27% non-need-based). 58% of past graduating class borrowed through all loan programs. *Average indebtedness per student:* $24,801. *Average need-based loan:* Freshmen: $3599. Undergraduates: $4326. *Parent loans:* $3,844,240 (63% need-based, 37% non-need-based). *Programs:* Federal Direct (Subsidized and Unsubsidized Stafford, PLUS), Perkins, Federal Nursing.

WORK-STUDY *Federal work-study:* Total amount: $277,839; jobs available.

APPLYING FOR FINANCIAL AID *Required financial aid form:* FAFSA. *Financial aid deadline (priority):* 3/1. *Notification date:* Continuous beginning 6/1. Students must reply within 2 weeks of notification.

CONTACT Jamie Hightower, Director of Student Financial Services, The College of New Jersey, PO Box 7718, Ewing, NJ 08628, 609-771-2211 or toll-free 800-624-0967. *Fax:* 609-637-5154. *E-mail:* hightowe@tcnj.edu.

THE COLLEGE OF NEW ROCHELLE
New Rochelle, NY

Tuition & fees: $26,426   Average undergraduate aid package: $20,856

ABOUT THE INSTITUTION Independent, coed, primarily women. 36 undergraduate majors. Federal methodology is used as a basis for awarding need-based institutional aid.

UNDERGRADUATE EXPENSES for 2009–10 *Comprehensive fee:* $36,026 includes full-time tuition ($25,576), mandatory fees ($850), and room and board ($9600). Full-time tuition and fees vary according to course load and program. Room and board charges vary according to housing facility. *Part-time tuition:* $861 per credit. *Part-time fees:* $225 per term. Part-time tuition and fees vary according to course load. *Payment plan:* Installment.

FRESHMAN FINANCIAL AID (Fall 2008) 101 applied for aid; of those 94% were deemed to have need. 100% of freshmen with need received aid; of those 6% had need fully met. *Average percent of need met:* 92% (excluding resources

awarded to replace EFC). *Average financial aid package:* $25,043 (excluding resources awarded to replace EFC). 8% of all full-time freshmen had no need and received non-need-based gift aid.

UNDERGRADUATE FINANCIAL AID (Fall 2008) 549 applied for aid; of those 94% were deemed to have need. 100% of undergraduates with need received aid; of those 4% had need fully met. *Average percent of need met:* 68% (excluding resources awarded to replace EFC). *Average financial aid package:* $20,856 (excluding resources awarded to replace EFC). 7% of all full-time undergraduates had no need and received non-need-based gift aid.

GIFT AID (NEED-BASED) *Total amount:* $8,263,359 (21% federal, 14% state, 64% institutional, 1% external sources). *Receiving aid:* Freshmen: 80% (84); all full-time undergraduates: 79% (455). *Average award:* Freshmen: $18,061; Undergraduates: $11,743. *Scholarships, grants, and awards:* Federal Pell, FSEOG, state, private, college/university gift aid from institutional funds.

GIFT AID (NON-NEED-BASED) *Total amount:* $573,108 (1% state, 99% institutional). *Receiving aid:* Freshmen: 38% (40). Undergraduates: 45% (258). *Average award:* Freshmen: $12,787. Undergraduates: $12,764. *Scholarships, grants, and awards by category:* Academic interests/achievement: 250 awards ($3,010,000 total): area/ethnic studies, biological sciences, business, communication, education, English, foreign languages, general academic interests/achievements, health fields, humanities, mathematics, physical sciences, premedicine, religion/biblical studies, social sciences. Creative arts/performance: 55 awards ($390,000 total): applied art and design, art/fine arts, cinema/film/broadcasting, creative writing, dance, debating, general creative arts/performance, journalism/publications, music, performing arts, theater/drama. Special achievements/activities: 110 awards ($1,125,000 total): community service, general special achievements/activities, hobbies/interests, junior miss, leadership, memberships, religious involvement. Special characteristics: 76 awards ($300,000 total): children of current students, children of faculty/staff, general special characteristics, out-of-state students, parents of current students, previous college experience, siblings of current students, spouses of current students. *Tuition waivers:* Full or partial for employees or children of employees, senior citizens.

LOANS *Student loans:* $6,905,083 (48% need-based, 52% non-need-based). 88% of past graduating class borrowed through all loan programs. *Average indebtedness per student:* $30,052. *Average need-based loan:* Freshmen: $4470. Undergraduates: $6075. *Parent loans:* $504,178 (81% need-based, 19% non-need-based). *Programs:* Federal Direct (Subsidized and Unsubsidized Stafford, PLUS), Perkins, Federal Nursing.

WORK-STUDY *Federal work-study:* Total amount: $1,126,968; 425 jobs averaging $2651. *State or other work-study/employment:* Part-time jobs available.

APPLYING FOR FINANCIAL AID *Required financial aid forms:* FAFSA, institution's own form, federal income tax form(s). *Financial aid deadline:* Continuous. *Notification date:* Continuous beginning 1/1. Students must reply within 2 weeks of notification.

CONTACT Anne Pelak, Director of Financial Aid, The College of New Rochelle, 29 Castle Place, New Rochelle, NY 10805-2339, 914-654-5225 or toll-free 800-933-5923. *Fax:* 914-654-5420. *E-mail:* apelak@cnr.edu.

COLLEGE OF NOTRE DAME OF MARYLAND
Baltimore, MD

Tuition & fees: $28,350   Average undergraduate aid package: $19,708

ABOUT THE INSTITUTION Independent Roman Catholic, undergraduate: women only; graduate: coed. 38 undergraduate majors. Federal methodology is used as a basis for awarding need-based institutional aid.

UNDERGRADUATE EXPENSES for 2010–11 *Comprehensive fee:* $37,850 includes full-time tuition ($27,600), mandatory fees ($750), and room and board ($9500). Room and board charges vary according to board plan. *Part-time tuition:* $425 per credit hour.

FRESHMAN FINANCIAL AID (Fall 2009, est.) 100 applied for aid; of those 94% were deemed to have need. 100% of freshmen with need received aid; of those 24% had need fully met. *Average percent of need met:* 77% (excluding resources awarded to replace EFC). *Average financial aid package:* $22,926 (excluding resources awarded to replace EFC). 8% of all full-time freshmen had no need and received non-need-based gift aid.

UNDERGRADUATE FINANCIAL AID (Fall 2009, est.) 445 applied for aid; of those 93% were deemed to have need. 100% of undergraduates with need received aid; of those 18% had need fully met. *Average percent of need met:* 69% (excluding resources awarded to replace EFC). *Average financial aid*

package: $19,708 (excluding resources awarded to replace EFC). 9% of all full-time undergraduates had no need and received non-need-based gift aid.
GIFT AID (NEED-BASED) *Total amount:* $6,573,991 (20% federal, 13% state, 66% institutional, 1% external sources). *Receiving aid:* Freshmen: 91% (94); all full-time undergraduates: 81% (399). *Average award:* Freshmen: $18,995; Undergraduates: $15,921. *Scholarships, grants, and awards:* Federal Pell, FSEOG, state, private, college/university gift aid from institutional funds, Academic Competitiveness Grants, National SMART Grants, TEACH Grants.
GIFT AID (NON-NEED-BASED) *Total amount:* $1,040,280 (1% state, 98% institutional, 1% external sources). *Receiving aid:* Freshmen: 16% (16). Undergraduates: 11% (52). *Average award:* Freshmen: $19,044. Undergraduates: $14,732. *Scholarships, grants, and awards by category:* Academic interests/achievement: 142 awards ($1,759,066 total): general academic interests/achievements. *Creative arts/performance:* 32 awards ($191,500 total): art/fine arts, general creative arts/performance. *Special achievements/activities:* 287 awards ($1,353,387 total): community service, general special achievements/activities, leadership, memberships, religious involvement. *Special characteristics:* 2 awards ($13,625 total): international students.
LOANS *Student loans:* $6,402,134 (76% need-based, 24% non-need-based). 72% of past graduating class borrowed through all loan programs. *Average indebtedness per student:* $33,882. *Average need-based loan:* Freshmen: $3526. Undergraduates: $4079. *Parent loans:* $971,599 (62% need-based, 38% non-need-based). *Programs:* Federal Direct (Subsidized and Unsubsidized Stafford, PLUS), Perkins.
WORK-STUDY *Federal work-study:* Total amount: $107,192; 102 jobs averaging $1026.
APPLYING FOR FINANCIAL AID *Required financial aid form:* FAFSA. *Financial aid deadline (priority):* 2/15. *Notification date:* Continuous beginning 3/1. Students must reply by 5/1.
CONTACT Zhanna Goltser, Director of Financial Aid, College of Notre Dame of Maryland, 4701 North Charles Street, Baltimore, MD 21210-2404, 410-532-5369 or toll-free 800-435-0200 (in-state), 800-435-0300 (out-of-state). *Fax:* 410-532-6287. *E-mail:* finaid@ndm.edu.

COLLEGE OF SAINT BENEDICT
Saint Joseph, MN

Tuition & fees: $30,186	Average undergraduate aid package: $23,152

ABOUT THE INSTITUTION Independent Roman Catholic, coed, primarily women. 50 undergraduate majors. Federal methodology is used as a basis for awarding need-based institutional aid.
UNDERGRADUATE EXPENSES for 2009–10 *Comprehensive fee:* $38,544 includes full-time tuition ($29,388), mandatory fees ($798), and room and board ($8358). *College room only:* $4025. Room and board charges vary according to board plan and housing facility. *Part-time tuition:* $1225 per credit hour. Part-time tuition and fees vary according to course load. *Payment plan:* Installment.
FRESHMAN FINANCIAL AID (Fall 2009, est.) 447 applied for aid; of those 84% were deemed to have need. 100% of freshmen with need received aid; of those 55% had need fully met. *Average percent of need met:* 94% (excluding resources awarded to replace EFC). *Average financial aid package:* $24,818 (excluding resources awarded to replace EFC). 26% of all full-time freshmen had no need and received non-need-based gift aid.
UNDERGRADUATE FINANCIAL AID (Fall 2009, est.) 1,541 applied for aid; of those 87% were deemed to have need. 100% of undergraduates with need received aid; of those 39% had need fully met. *Average percent of need met:* 88% (excluding resources awarded to replace EFC). *Average financial aid package:* $23,152 (excluding resources awarded to replace EFC). 29% of all full-time undergraduates had no need and received non-need-based gift aid.
GIFT AID (NEED-BASED) *Total amount:* $24,591,616 (9% federal, 11% state, 76% institutional, 4% external sources). *Receiving aid:* Freshmen: 68% (373); all full-time undergraduates: 65% (1,327). *Average award:* Freshmen: $20,316; Undergraduates: $17,595. *Scholarships, grants, and awards:* Federal Pell, FSEOG, state, private, college/university gift aid from institutional funds.
GIFT AID (NON-NEED-BASED) *Total amount:* $8,747,035 (96% institutional, 4% external sources). *Receiving aid:* Freshmen: 67% (371). Undergraduates: 62% (1,276). *Average award:* Freshmen: $11,985. Undergraduates: $10,821. *Scholarships, grants, and awards by category:* Academic interests/achievement: general academic interests/achievements, military science. *Creative arts/*

performance: art/fine arts, music, theater/drama. *Special achievements/activities:* junior miss. *Special characteristics:* ethnic background, international students.
LOANS *Student loans:* $15,069,291 (88% need-based, 12% non-need-based). *Average need-based loan:* Freshmen: $3422. Undergraduates: $4405. *Parent loans:* $1,306,160 (78% need-based, 22% non-need-based). *Programs:* Federal Direct (Subsidized and Unsubsidized Stafford, PLUS), Perkins, state, private alternative loans.
WORK-STUDY *Federal work-study:* Total amount: $1,226,992; 600 jobs averaging $2050. *State or other work-study/employment:* Total amount: $1,879,477 (66% need-based, 34% non-need-based). 300 part-time jobs averaging $2050.
APPLYING FOR FINANCIAL AID *Required financial aid forms:* FAFSA, institution's own form. *Financial aid deadline (priority):* 3/15. *Notification date:* Continuous beginning 3/1. Students must reply by 5/1.
CONTACT Ms. Jane Haugen, Executive Director of Financial Aid, College of Saint Benedict, 37 South College Avenue, Saint Joseph, MN 56374-2099, 320-363-5388 or toll-free 800-544-1489. *Fax:* 320-363-6099. *E-mail:* jhaugen@csbsju.edu.

COLLEGE OF SAINT ELIZABETH
Morristown, NJ

Tuition & fees: $25,058	Average undergraduate aid package: N/A

ABOUT THE INSTITUTION Independent Roman Catholic, undergraduate: women only; graduate: coed. 28 undergraduate majors. Both federal and institutional methodology are used as a basis for awarding need-based institutional aid.
UNDERGRADUATE EXPENSES for 2009–10 *Comprehensive fee:* $35,962 includes full-time tuition ($23,642), mandatory fees ($1416), and room and board ($10,904). *Part-time tuition:* $623 per credit. *Part-time fees:* $65 per credit. Part-time tuition and fees vary according to course load and location. *Payment plan:* Installment.
FRESHMAN FINANCIAL AID (Fall 2008) 156 applied for aid; of those 81% were deemed to have need. 100% of freshmen with need received aid. 19% of all full-time freshmen had no need and received non-need-based gift aid.
UNDERGRADUATE FINANCIAL AID (Fall 2008) 631 applied for aid; of those 80% were deemed to have need. 100% of undergraduates with need received aid. 16% of all full-time undergraduates had no need and received non-need-based gift aid.
GIFT AID (NEED-BASED) *Total amount:* $3,075,474 (41% federal, 59% institutional). *Receiving aid:* Freshmen: 66% (105); all full-time undergraduates: 58% (392). *Average award:* Freshmen: $17,149; Undergraduates: $14,148. *Scholarships, grants, and awards:* Federal Pell, FSEOG, state, private, college/university gift aid from institutional funds.
GIFT AID (NON-NEED-BASED) *Total amount:* $4,357,518 (1% state, 99% institutional). *Receiving aid:* Freshmen: 70% (111). Undergraduates: 63% (422). *Average award:* Freshmen: $13,440. Undergraduates: $12,471. *Tuition waivers:* Full or partial for children of alumni, employees or children of employees, senior citizens.
LOANS *Student loans:* $5,250,741 (48% need-based, 52% non-need-based). *Average need-based loan:* Freshmen: $4291. Undergraduates: $5315. *Programs:* FFEL (Subsidized and Unsubsidized Stafford, PLUS), Perkins.
WORK-STUDY *Federal work-study:* Total amount: $68,913; jobs available.
APPLYING FOR FINANCIAL AID *Required financial aid form:* FAFSA. *Financial aid deadline:* Continuous. *Notification date:* Continuous beginning 11/15. Students must reply by 5/1 or within 2 weeks of notification.
CONTACT Debra Wulff, Director of Financial Aid, College of Saint Elizabeth, 2 Convent Road, Morristown, NJ 07960-6989, 973-290-4492 or toll-free 800-210-7900. *E-mail:* dwulff@cse.edu.

COLLEGE OF ST. JOSEPH
Rutland, VT

ABOUT THE INSTITUTION Independent Roman Catholic, coed. 14 undergraduate majors.
GIFT AID (NEED-BASED) *Scholarships, grants, and awards:* Federal Pell, FSEOG, state, private, college/university gift aid from institutional funds.
GIFT AID (NON-NEED-BASED) *Scholarships, grants, and awards by category:* Academic interests/achievement: general academic interests/achievements. *Special*

achievements/activities: leadership. *Special characteristics:* general special characteristics, local/state students, previous college experience, religious affiliation.

LOANS *Programs:* FFEL (Subsidized and Unsubsidized Stafford, PLUS), Perkins.

APPLYING FOR FINANCIAL AID *Required financial aid forms:* FAFSA, institution's own form.

CONTACT Julie Rosmus, Director of Financial Aid, College of St. Joseph, 71 Clement Road, Rutland, VT 05701-3899, 802-773-5900 Ext. 3274 or toll-free 877-270-9998 (in-state). *Fax:* 802-776-5275. *E-mail:* jrosmus@csj.edu.

COLLEGE OF SAINT MARY
Omaha, NE

Tuition & fees: $23,130	Average undergraduate aid package: $15,316

ABOUT THE INSTITUTION Independent Roman Catholic, women only. 28 undergraduate majors. Federal methodology is used as a basis for awarding need-based institutional aid.

UNDERGRADUATE EXPENSES for 2010–11 *Comprehensive fee:* $29,530 includes full-time tuition ($22,650), mandatory fees ($480), and room and board ($6400). Full-time tuition and fees vary according to location. *Part-time tuition:* $750 per credit. *Part-time fees:* $16 per credit. Part-time tuition and fees vary according to class time and location. *Payment plans:* Installment, deferred payment.

FRESHMAN FINANCIAL AID (Fall 2009, est.) 94 applied for aid; of those 95% were deemed to have need. 100% of freshmen with need received aid; of those 10% had need fully met. *Average percent of need met:* 71% (excluding resources awarded to replace EFC). *Average financial aid package:* $19,481 (excluding resources awarded to replace EFC). 4% of all full-time freshmen had no need and received non-need-based gift aid.

UNDERGRADUATE FINANCIAL AID (Fall 2009, est.) 689 applied for aid; of those 93% were deemed to have need. 100% of undergraduates with need received aid; of those 6% had need fully met. *Average percent of need met:* 58% (excluding resources awarded to replace EFC). *Average financial aid package:* $15,316 (excluding resources awarded to replace EFC). 5% of all full-time undergraduates had no need and received non-need-based gift aid.

GIFT AID (NEED-BASED) *Total amount:* $6,299,422 (30% federal, 4% state, 59% institutional, 7% external sources). *Receiving aid:* Freshmen: 94% (88); all full-time undergraduates: 88% (607). *Average award:* Freshmen: $16,064; Undergraduates: $10,534. *Scholarships, grants, and awards:* Federal Pell, FSEOG, state, college/university gift aid from institutional funds.

GIFT AID (NON-NEED-BASED) *Total amount:* $253,275 (87% institutional, 13% external sources). *Receiving aid:* Freshmen: 7% (7). Undergraduates: 3% (23). *Average award:* Freshmen: $10,436. Undergraduates: $5187. *Scholarships, grants, and awards by category: Academic interests/achievement:* 549 awards ($2,196,266 total): biological sciences, education, general academic interests/achievements, mathematics. *Creative arts/performance:* 9 awards ($11,250 total): art/fine arts, music. *Special achievements/activities:* 101 awards ($171,750 total): community service, general special achievements/activities, leadership. *Special characteristics:* 53 awards ($49,500 total): first-generation college students. *Tuition waivers:* Full or partial for employees or children of employees, senior citizens.

LOANS *Student loans:* $6,927,042 (87% need-based, 13% non-need-based). 75% of past graduating class borrowed through all loan programs. *Average indebtedness per student:* $3408. *Average need-based loan:* Freshmen: $3247. Undergraduates: $5158. *Parent loans:* $1,089,825 (43% need-based, 57% non-need-based). *Programs:* Federal Direct (Subsidized and Unsubsidized Stafford, PLUS), Perkins, Federal Nursing.

WORK-STUDY *Federal work-study:* Total amount: $122,299; 173 jobs averaging $1200. *State or other work-study/employment:* Total amount: $28,746 (100% need-based). 10 part-time jobs averaging $6400.

ATHLETIC AWARDS Total amount: $375,283 (75% need-based, 25% non-need-based).

APPLYING FOR FINANCIAL AID *Required financial aid form:* FAFSA. *Financial aid deadline (priority):* 3/15. *Notification date:* Continuous beginning 3/15. Students must reply within 2 weeks of notification.

CONTACT Beth Sisk, Director of Financial Aid, College of Saint Mary, 7000 Mercy Road, Omaha, NE 68106, 402-399-2415 or toll-free 800-926-5534. *Fax:* 402-399-2480. *E-mail:* bsisk@csm.edu.

THE COLLEGE OF SAINT ROSE
Albany, NY

Tuition & fees: $24,135	Average undergraduate aid package: $8897

ABOUT THE INSTITUTION Independent, coed. 49 undergraduate majors. Federal methodology is used as a basis for awarding need-based institutional aid.

UNDERGRADUATE EXPENSES for 2010–11 *Comprehensive fee:* $34,015 includes full-time tuition ($23,329), mandatory fees ($806), and room and board ($9880). *College room only:* $4859. Full-time tuition and fees vary according to class time and course load. Room and board charges vary according to board plan and housing facility. *Part-time tuition:* $776 per credit. Part-time tuition and fees vary according to class time and course load. *Payment plan:* Deferred payment.

FRESHMAN FINANCIAL AID (Fall 2008) 540 applied for aid; of those 99% were deemed to have need. 100% of freshmen with need received aid; of those 3% had need fully met. *Average percent of need met:* 11% (excluding resources awarded to replace EFC). *Average financial aid package:* $9949 (excluding resources awarded to replace EFC). 10% of all full-time freshmen had no need and received non-need-based gift aid.

UNDERGRADUATE FINANCIAL AID (Fall 2008) 2,808 applied for aid; of those 99% were deemed to have need. 99% of undergraduates with need received aid; of those 2% had need fully met. *Average percent of need met:* 8% (excluding resources awarded to replace EFC). *Average financial aid package:* $8897 (excluding resources awarded to replace EFC). 9% of all full-time undergraduates had no need and received non-need-based gift aid.

GIFT AID (NEED-BASED) *Total amount:* $25,912,154 (12% federal, 12% state, 75% institutional, 1% external sources). *Receiving aid:* Freshmen: 84% (484); all full-time undergraduates: 81% (2,294). *Average award:* Freshmen: $4098; Undergraduates: $3453. *Scholarships, grants, and awards:* Federal Pell, FSEOG, state, private, college/university gift aid from institutional funds.

GIFT AID (NON-NEED-BASED) *Total amount:* $1,431,571 (99% institutional, 1% external sources). *Average award:* Freshmen: $2451. Undergraduates: $2104. *Scholarships, grants, and awards by category: Academic interests/achievement:* 10 awards ($6654 total): business, education, engineering/technologies, English, foreign languages, general academic interests/achievements, mathematics, premedicine, social sciences. *Creative arts/performance:* 101 awards ($11,109 total): art/fine arts, music. *Special achievements/activities:* community service. *Special characteristics:* 500 awards ($3312 total): adult students, children and siblings of alumni, children of faculty/staff, children of union members/company employees, ethnic background, general special characteristics, members of minority groups, out-of-state students, siblings of current students, twins. *Tuition waivers:* Full or partial for employees or children of employees.

LOANS *Student loans:* $18,746,104 (97% need-based, 3% non-need-based). 84% of past graduating class borrowed through all loan programs. *Average indebtedness per student:* $29,391. *Average need-based loan:* Freshmen: $1638. Undergraduates: $2346. *Parent loans:* $4,326,013 (98% need-based, 2% non-need-based). *Programs:* FFEL (Subsidized and Unsubsidized Stafford, PLUS), Perkins.

WORK-STUDY *Federal work-study:* Total amount: $421,352; 405 jobs averaging $760. *State or other work-study/employment:* Total amount: $334,034 (90% need-based, 10% non-need-based). 8 part-time jobs averaging $796.

ATHLETIC AWARDS Total amount: $2,021,689 (92% need-based, 8% non-need-based).

APPLYING FOR FINANCIAL AID *Required financial aid form:* FAFSA. *Financial aid deadline (priority):* 3/1. *Notification date:* 3/15. Students must reply by 5/1 or within 2 weeks of notification.

CONTACT Steven Dwire, Director of Financial Aid, The College of Saint Rose, 432 Western Avenue, Albertus Hall, Room 206, Albany, NY 12203-1419, 518-458-4915 or toll-free 800-637-8556. *Fax:* 518-454-2802. *E-mail:* finaid@strose.edu.

THE COLLEGE OF ST. SCHOLASTICA
Duluth, MN

Tuition & fees: $28,370	Average undergraduate aid package: $21,625

The College of St. Scholastica

ABOUT THE INSTITUTION Independent religious, coed. 38 undergraduate majors. Federal methodology is used as a basis for awarding need-based institutional aid.

UNDERGRADUATE EXPENSES for 2010–11 *Comprehensive fee:* $35,868 includes full-time tuition ($28,200), mandatory fees ($170), and room and board ($7498). *College room only:* $4248. Full-time tuition and fees vary according to class time. Room and board charges vary according to board plan and housing facility. *Part-time tuition:* $881 per credit hour. Part-time tuition and fees vary according to class time and course load. *Payment plan:* Installment.

FRESHMAN FINANCIAL AID (Fall 2009, est.) 484 applied for aid; of those 87% were deemed to have need. 100% of freshmen with need received aid; of those 15% had need fully met. *Average percent of need met:* 82% (excluding resources awarded to replace EFC). *Average financial aid package:* $22,896 (excluding resources awarded to replace EFC). 11% of all full-time freshmen had no need and received non-need-based gift aid.

UNDERGRADUATE FINANCIAL AID (Fall 2009, est.) 1,838 applied for aid; of those 90% were deemed to have need. 100% of undergraduates with need received aid; of those 14% had need fully met. *Average percent of need met:* 77% (excluding resources awarded to replace EFC). *Average financial aid package:* $21,625 (excluding resources awarded to replace EFC). 8% of all full-time undergraduates had no need and received non-need-based gift aid.

GIFT AID (NEED-BASED) *Total amount:* $9,712,473 (30% federal, 34% state, 36% institutional). *Receiving aid:* Freshmen: 66% (356); all full-time undergraduates: 65% (1,365). *Average award:* Freshmen: $8043; Undergraduates: $7011. *Scholarships, grants, and awards:* Federal Pell, FSEOG, state, private, college/university gift aid from institutional funds.

GIFT AID (NON-NEED-BASED) *Total amount:* $23,236,888 (2% federal, 94% institutional, 4% external sources). *Receiving aid:* Freshmen: 76% (409). Undergraduates: 74% (1,564). *Average award:* Freshmen: $11,691. Undergraduates: $10,496. *Scholarships, grants, and awards by category: Academic interests/achievement:* $17,899,125 total: general academic interests/achievements. *Creative arts/performance:* $51,250 total: music. *Special characteristics:* $3,880,399 total: children and siblings of alumni, children of faculty/staff, ethnic background, handicapped students, international students, members of minority groups, previous college experience, religious affiliation, siblings of current students, spouses of current students. *Tuition waivers:* Full or partial for employees or children of employees, senior citizens.

LOANS *Student loans:* $19,710,482 (29% need-based, 71% non-need-based). 81% of past graduating class borrowed through all loan programs. *Average indebtedness per student:* $40,401. *Average need-based loan:* Freshmen: $3434. Undergraduates: $4381. *Parent loans:* $2,255,541 (100% non-need-based). *Programs:* Federal Direct (Subsidized and Unsubsidized Stafford, PLUS), Perkins, Federal Nursing, state, private loans.

WORK-STUDY *Federal work-study:* Total amount: $439,480; 321 jobs averaging $2703. *State or other work-study/employment:* Total amount: $898,682 (24% need-based, 76% non-need-based). 478 part-time jobs averaging $1087.

APPLYING FOR FINANCIAL AID *Required financial aid form:* FAFSA. *Financial aid deadline (priority):* 3/1. *Notification date:* Continuous beginning 3/1. Students must reply by 5/1 or within 2 weeks of notification.

CONTACT Mr. Jon P. Erickson, Director of Financial Aid, The College of St. Scholastica, 1200 Kenwood Avenue, Duluth, MN 55811-4199, 218-723-6725 or toll-free 800-249-6412. *Fax:* 218-733-2229. *E-mail:* jerickso@css.edu.

THE COLLEGE OF SAINT THOMAS MORE
Fort Worth, TX

Tuition & fees: N/R	Average undergraduate aid package: $7675

ABOUT THE INSTITUTION Independent religious, coed. 1 undergraduate major. Federal methodology is used as a basis for awarding need-based institutional aid.

FRESHMAN FINANCIAL AID (Fall 2009, est.) 5 applied for aid; of those 80% were deemed to have need. 100% of freshmen with need received aid; of those 75% had need fully met. *Average percent of need met:* 85% (excluding resources awarded to replace EFC). *Average financial aid package:* $7987 (excluding resources awarded to replace EFC). 17% of all full-time freshmen had no need and received non-need-based gift aid.

UNDERGRADUATE FINANCIAL AID (Fall 2009, est.) 22 applied for aid; of those 77% were deemed to have need. 100% of undergraduates with need received aid; of those 71% had need fully met. *Average percent of need met:* 85% (excluding resources awarded to replace EFC). *Average financial aid package:*

$7675 (excluding resources awarded to replace EFC). 7% of all full-time undergraduates had no need and received non-need-based gift aid.

GIFT AID (NEED-BASED) *Total amount:* $84,926 (28% federal, 41% state, 27% institutional, 4% external sources). *Receiving aid:* Freshmen: 67% (4); all full-time undergraduates: 63% (17). *Average award:* Freshmen: $3920; Undergraduates: $3813. *Scholarships, grants, and awards:* Federal Pell, state, private, college/university gift aid from institutional funds.

GIFT AID (NON-NEED-BASED) *Receiving aid:* Freshmen: 33% (2). Undergraduates: 59% (16). *Average award:* Freshmen: $2000. Undergraduates: $3000. *Scholarships, grants, and awards by category: Academic interests/achievement:* 9 awards ($23,000 total): general academic interests/achievements.

LOANS *Student loans:* $99,960 (100% need-based). 58% of past graduating class borrowed through all loan programs. *Average indebtedness per student:* $9670. *Average need-based loan:* Freshmen: $3500. Undergraduates: $3738. *Parent loans:* $8000 (100% need-based). *Programs:* FFEL (Subsidized and Unsubsidized Stafford, PLUS).

WORK-STUDY *State or other work-study/employment:* Total amount: $2000 (100% need-based). 5 part-time jobs averaging $625.

APPLYING FOR FINANCIAL AID *Required financial aid form:* FAFSA. *Financial aid deadline (priority):* 4/15. *Notification date:* 6/1. Students must reply within 2 weeks of notification.

CONTACT Mrs. Mary E. Swanson, Director of Financial Aid, The College of Saint Thomas More, 1463 Beechwood Lane, Abilene, TX 79603, 325-673-1934 or toll-free 800-583-6489 (out-of-state). *Fax:* 325-673-1934. *E-mail:* corkyswanson@suddenlink.net.

COLLEGE OF SANTA FE
Santa Fe, NM

CONTACT Ms. Jill Robertson, Director, Student Financial Services, College of Santa Fe, 1600 St. Michael's Drive, Santa Fe, NM 87505-7634, 505-473-6454 or toll-free 800-456-2673. *Fax:* 505-473-6464. *E-mail:* sfs@csf.edu.

COLLEGE OF STATEN ISLAND OF THE CITY UNIVERSITY OF NEW YORK
Staten Island, NY

Tuition & fees (NY res): $4978	Average undergraduate aid package: $7520

ABOUT THE INSTITUTION State and locally supported, coed. 34 undergraduate majors. Federal methodology is used as a basis for awarding need-based institutional aid.

UNDERGRADUATE EXPENSES for 2009–10 *Tuition, state resident:* full-time $4600; part-time $195 per credit. *Tuition, nonresident:* full-time $9960; part-time $415 per credit. *Required fees:* full-time $378; $113 per term. Full-time tuition and fees vary according to course load. Part-time tuition and fees vary according to course load. *Payment plan:* Installment.

FRESHMAN FINANCIAL AID (Fall 2009, est.) 2,035 applied for aid; of those 73% were deemed to have need. 96% of freshmen with need received aid; of those 6% had need fully met. *Average percent of need met:* 62% (excluding resources awarded to replace EFC). *Average financial aid package:* $7264 (excluding resources awarded to replace EFC). 10% of all full-time freshmen had no need and received non-need-based gift aid.

UNDERGRADUATE FINANCIAL AID (Fall 2009, est.) 7,066 applied for aid; of those 77% were deemed to have need. 97% of undergraduates with need received aid; of those 6% had need fully met. *Average percent of need met:* 60% (excluding resources awarded to replace EFC). *Average financial aid package:* $7520 (excluding resources awarded to replace EFC). 5% of all full-time undergraduates had no need and received non-need-based gift aid.

GIFT AID (NEED-BASED) *Total amount:* $38,019,029 (59% federal, 39% state, 2% external sources). *Receiving aid:* Freshmen: 59% (1,413); all full-time undergraduates: 56% (5,113). *Average award:* Freshmen: $6765; Undergraduates: $6695. *Scholarships, grants, and awards:* Federal Pell, FSEOG, state, private, college/university gift aid from institutional funds.

GIFT AID (NON-NEED-BASED) *Total amount:* $1,542,924 (6% federal, 42% state, 52% external sources). *Receiving aid:* Freshmen: 16% (387). Undergraduates: 8% (715). *Average award:* Freshmen: $1039. Undergraduates: $1545. *Scholarships, grants, and awards by category: Academic interests/achievement:* 144 awards ($198,000 total): biological sciences, business, computer science, education, engineering/technologies, general academic interests/achievements, health fields, humanities, international studies, mathematics, physical sciences, premedicine, social sciences. *Creative arts/performance:* 3 awards ($2900 total): art/fine arts, music, theater/drama. *Special achievements/activities:* 5 awards ($6000 total): community service, general special achievements/activities. *Special characteristics:* 6 awards ($6500 total): children of public servants, children with a deceased or disabled parent, general special characteristics, handicapped students, international students, members of minority groups, public servants, spouses of deceased or disabled public servants, veterans' children. *Tuition waivers:* Full or partial for employees or children of employees, senior citizens.

LOANS *Student loans:* $7,730,015 (100% need-based). 17% of past graduating class borrowed through all loan programs. *Average indebtedness per student:* $5079. *Average need-based loan:* Freshmen: $3129. Undergraduates: $4143. *Programs:* Federal Direct (Subsidized and Unsubsidized Stafford, PLUS), Perkins.

WORK-STUDY *Federal work-study:* Total amount: $1,027,475; 1,091 jobs averaging $1188. *State or other work-study/employment:* Total amount: $1200 (100% non-need-based). Part-time jobs available.

APPLYING FOR FINANCIAL AID *Required financial aid forms:* FAFSA, state aid form. *Financial aid deadline (priority):* 3/31. *Notification date:* Continuous beginning 6/1.

CONTACT Mr. Philippe Marius, Director of Financial Aid, College of Staten Island of the City University of New York, 2800 Victory Boulevard, 2A-401A, Staten Island, NY 10314-6600, 718-982-2030. *Fax:* 718-982-2037. *E-mail:* philippe.marius@csi.cuny.edu.

COLLEGE OF THE ATLANTIC
Bar Harbor, ME

Tuition & fees: $34,380	Average undergraduate aid package: $30,646

ABOUT THE INSTITUTION Independent, coed. 42 undergraduate majors. Both federal and institutional methodology are used as a basis for awarding need-based institutional aid.

UNDERGRADUATE EXPENSES for 2010–11 *Comprehensive fee:* $42,630 includes full-time tuition ($33,885), mandatory fees ($495), and room and board ($8250). *College room only:* $5400. Room and board charges vary according to board plan. *Part-time tuition:* $3765 per credit. *Payment plan:* Installment.

FRESHMAN FINANCIAL AID (Fall 2009, est.) 69 applied for aid; of those 99% were deemed to have need. 99% of freshmen with need received aid; of those 70% had need fully met. *Average percent of need met:* 96% (excluding resources awarded to replace EFC). *Average financial aid package:* $35,406 (excluding resources awarded to replace EFC).

UNDERGRADUATE FINANCIAL AID (Fall 2009, est.) 264 applied for aid; of those 99% were deemed to have need. 99% of undergraduates with need received aid; of those 72% had need fully met. *Average percent of need met:* 96% (excluding resources awarded to replace EFC). *Average financial aid package:* $30,646 (excluding resources awarded to replace EFC).

GIFT AID (NEED-BASED) *Total amount:* $6,718,955 (8% federal, 1% state, 89% institutional, 2% external sources). *Receiving aid:* Freshmen: 88% (67); all full-time undergraduates: 81% (247). *Average award:* Undergraduates: $26,366. *Scholarships, grants, and awards:* Federal Pell, FSEOG, state, private, college/university gift aid from institutional funds.

GIFT AID (NON-NEED-BASED) *Tuition waivers:* Full or partial for employees or children of employees, adult students, senior citizens.

LOANS *Student loans:* $1,304,465 (66% need-based, 34% non-need-based). 54% of past graduating class borrowed through all loan programs. *Average indebtedness per student:* $20,170. *Average need-based loan:* Freshmen: $4132. Undergraduates: $4830. *Parent loans:* $296,259 (100% non-need-based). *Programs:* FFEL (Subsidized and Unsubsidized Stafford, PLUS), Perkins.

WORK-STUDY *Federal work-study:* Total amount: $495,390; 218 jobs averaging $2249. *State or other work-study/employment:* Total amount: $69,300 (100% need-based). 41 part-time jobs averaging $1561.

APPLYING FOR FINANCIAL AID *Required financial aid forms:* FAFSA, institution's own form, noncustodial (divorced/separated) parent's statement. *Financial aid deadline (priority):* 2/15. *Notification date:* 4/1. Students must reply by 5/1 or within 2 weeks of notification.

CONTACT Bruce Hazam, Director of Financial Aid, College of the Atlantic, 105 Eden Street, Bar Harbor, ME 04609-1198, 207-801-5645 or toll-free 800-528-0025. *Fax:* 207-288-4126. *E-mail:* bhazam@coa.edu.

COLLEGE OF THE HOLY CROSS
Worcester, MA

Tuition & fees: $39,892	Average undergraduate aid package: $29,393

ABOUT THE INSTITUTION Independent Roman Catholic (Jesuit), coed. 34 undergraduate majors. Both federal and institutional methodology are used as a basis for awarding need-based institutional aid.

UNDERGRADUATE EXPENSES for 2010–11 *Comprehensive fee:* $50,832 includes full-time tuition ($39,330), mandatory fees ($562), and room and board ($10,940). *College room only:* $5700. Room and board charges vary according to board plan and housing facility. *Payment plans:* Tuition prepayment, installment.

FRESHMAN FINANCIAL AID (Fall 2009, est.) 522 applied for aid; of those 84% were deemed to have need. 94% of freshmen with need received aid; of those 100% had need fully met. *Average percent of need met:* 100% (excluding resources awarded to replace EFC). *Average financial aid package:* $30,760 (excluding resources awarded to replace EFC). 1% of all full-time freshmen had no need and received non-need-based gift aid.

UNDERGRADUATE FINANCIAL AID (Fall 2009, est.) 1,822 applied for aid; of those 90% were deemed to have need. 95% of undergraduates with need received aid; of those 100% had need fully met. *Average percent of need met:* 100% (excluding resources awarded to replace EFC). *Average financial aid package:* $29,393 (excluding resources awarded to replace EFC). 1% of all full-time undergraduates had no need and received non-need-based gift aid.

GIFT AID (NEED-BASED) *Total amount:* $30,279,482 (7% federal, 1% state, 87% institutional, 5% external sources). *Receiving aid:* Freshmen: 45% (339); all full-time undergraduates: 43% (1,244). *Average award:* Freshmen: $26,977; Undergraduates: $27,089. *Scholarships, grants, and awards:* Federal Pell, FSEOG, state, private, college/university gift aid from institutional funds.

GIFT AID (NON-NEED-BASED) *Total amount:* $1,718,507 (100% institutional). *Receiving aid:* Freshmen: 2% (14). Undergraduates: 1% (39). *Average award:* Freshmen: $21,207. Undergraduates: $24,997. *Scholarships, grants, and awards by category: Academic interests/achievement:* 43 awards ($1,097,788 total): general academic interests/achievements, humanities, military science. *Creative arts/performance:* 5 awards ($190,900 total): music. *Special characteristics:* 34 awards ($1,240,850 total): children of faculty/staff. *Tuition waivers:* Full or partial for employees or children of employees.

LOANS *Student loans:* $11,463,503 (88% need-based, 12% non-need-based). 57% of past graduating class borrowed through all loan programs. *Average indebtedness per student:* $23,785. *Average need-based loan:* Freshmen: $5262. Undergraduates: $5320. *Parent loans:* $11,675,020 (100% non-need-based). *Programs:* Federal Direct (Subsidized and Unsubsidized Stafford, PLUS), Perkins, MEFA Loans.

WORK-STUDY *Federal work-study:* Total amount: $1,647,369; 1,027 jobs averaging $1604.

ATHLETIC AWARDS Total amount: $6,837,058 (70% need-based, 30% non-need-based).

APPLYING FOR FINANCIAL AID *Required financial aid forms:* FAFSA, CSS Financial Aid PROFILE, noncustodial (divorced/separated) parent's statement, business/farm supplement, parent and student federal income tax forms. *Financial aid deadline:* 2/1. *Notification date:* 4/1. Students must reply by 5/1. **CONTACT** Lynne Myers, Director of Financial Aid, College of the Holy Cross, One College Street, Worcester, MA 01610-2395, 508-793-2265 or toll-free 800-442-2421. *Fax:* 508-793-2527.

COLLEGE OF THE HUMANITIES AND SCIENCES, HARRISON MIDDLETON UNIVERSITY
Tempe, AZ

Tuition & fees: $27,200	Average undergraduate aid package: N/A

ABOUT THE INSTITUTION Independent, coed. 6 undergraduate majors.

UNDERGRADUATE EXPENSES for 2010–11 *Tuition:* full-time $27,200. *Payment plan:* Installment.

CONTACT Ms. Susan Chiaramonte, Registrar, College of the Humanities and Sciences, Harrison Middleton University, 1105 East Broadway Road, Tempe, AZ 85282, 877-248-6724. *Fax:* 800-762-0010. *E-mail:* information@hmu.edu.

COLLEGE OF THE OZARKS
Point Lookout, MO

Tuition & fees: $410 **Average undergraduate aid package: $15,783**

ABOUT THE INSTITUTION Independent Presbyterian, coed. 65 undergraduate majors. Federal methodology is used as a basis for awarding need-based institutional aid.

UNDERGRADUATE EXPENSES for 2010–11 includes mandatory fees ($410) and room and board ($5300). *College room only:* $2600. *Part-time tuition:* $295 per credit hour. Part-time tuition and fees vary according to course load. the college guarantees to meet all of the tuition cost for each full-time student by using earnings from its endowment, operation of its own mandatory student work program, accepting student aid grants, gifts and other sources. In effect, each full-time student's Cost of Education (tuition) is met 100 percent by participating in the work program and a combination of private, institutional and federal/state student aid. *Payment plan:* Installment.

FRESHMAN FINANCIAL AID (Fall 2008) 363 applied for aid; of those 95% were deemed to have need. 100% of freshmen with need received aid; of those 18% had need fully met. *Average percent of need met:* 80% (excluding resources awarded to replace EFC). *Average financial aid package:* $14,217 (excluding resources awarded to replace EFC). 18% of all full-time freshmen had no need and received non-need-based gift aid.

UNDERGRADUATE FINANCIAL AID (Fall 2008) 1,432 applied for aid; of those 94% were deemed to have need. 100% of undergraduates with need received aid; of those 31% had need fully met. *Average percent of need met:* 82% (excluding resources awarded to replace EFC). *Average financial aid package:* $15,783 (excluding resources awarded to replace EFC). 8% of all full-time undergraduates had no need and received non-need-based gift aid.

GIFT AID (NEED-BASED) *Total amount:* $16,917,005 (15% federal, 12% state, 71% institutional, 2% external sources). *Receiving aid:* Freshmen: 82% (346); all full-time undergraduates: 90% (1,346). *Average award:* Freshmen: $11,067; Undergraduates: $12,613. *Scholarships, grants, and awards:* Federal Pell, FSEOG, state, private, college/university gift aid from institutional funds.

GIFT AID (NON-NEED-BASED) *Total amount:* $2,642,917 (98% institutional, 2% external sources). *Receiving aid:* Freshmen: 9% (39). Undergraduates: 16% (242). *Average award:* Freshmen: $8857. Undergraduates: $10,299. *Tuition waivers:* Full or partial for employees or children of employees.

LOANS *Student loans:* $344,144 (96% need-based, 4% non-need-based). 7% of past graduating class borrowed through all loan programs. *Average indebtedness per student:* $6029. *Programs:* alternative loans.

WORK-STUDY *Federal work-study:* Total amount: $3,652,887; 835 jobs averaging $4379. *State or other work-study/employment:* Total amount: $2,233,271 (29% need-based, 71% non-need-based). 700 part-time jobs averaging $3193.

ATHLETIC AWARDS Total amount: $227,745 (36% need-based, 64% non-need-based).

APPLYING FOR FINANCIAL AID *Required financial aid form:* FAFSA. *Financial aid deadline (priority):* 2/15. *Notification date:* 7/1.

CONTACT Mrs. Kyla R. McCarty, Director of Financial Aid, College of the Ozarks, PO Box 17, Point Lookout, MO 65726, 417-690-3290 or toll-free 800-222-0525. *Fax:* 417-690-3286.

COLLEGE OF VISUAL ARTS
St. Paul, MN

Tuition & fees: $23,988 **Average undergraduate aid package: $14,826**

ABOUT THE INSTITUTION Independent, coed. 7 undergraduate majors. Federal methodology is used as a basis for awarding need-based institutional aid.

UNDERGRADUATE EXPENSES for 2010–11 *Tuition:* full-time $23,488; part-time $1174 per credit. *Required fees:* full-time $500; $50 per course. Full-time tuition and fees vary according to course load. Part-time tuition and fees vary according to course load. *Payment plan:* Installment.

FRESHMAN FINANCIAL AID (Fall 2009, est.) 36 applied for aid; of those 94% were deemed to have need. 100% of freshmen with need received aid; of those 3% had need fully met. *Average percent of need met:* 58% (excluding resources awarded to replace EFC). *Average financial aid package:* $15,906 (excluding resources awarded to replace EFC). 6% of all full-time freshmen had no need and received non-need-based gift aid.

UNDERGRADUATE FINANCIAL AID (Fall 2009, est.) 166 applied for aid; of those 92% were deemed to have need. 100% of undergraduates with need received aid; of those 2% had need fully met. *Average percent of need met:* 53% (excluding resources awarded to replace EFC). *Average financial aid package:* $14,826 (excluding resources awarded to replace EFC). 7% of all full-time undergraduates had no need and received non-need-based gift aid.

GIFT AID (NEED-BASED) *Total amount:* $1,511,129 (19% federal, 27% state, 54% institutional). *Receiving aid:* Freshmen: 94% (34); all full-time undergraduates: 87% (153). *Average award:* Freshmen: $12,507; Undergraduates: $9863. *Scholarships, grants, and awards:* Federal Pell, FSEOG, state, private, college/university gift aid from institutional funds, Academic Competitiveness Grants.

GIFT AID (NON-NEED-BASED) *Total amount:* $141,772 (25% institutional, 75% external sources). *Receiving aid:* Freshmen: 8% (3). Undergraduates: 16% (29). *Average award:* Freshmen: $5000. Undergraduates: $2431. *Scholarships, grants, and awards by category: Academic interests/achievement:* general academic interests/achievements. *Creative arts/performance:* art/fine arts. *Special characteristics:* children of faculty/staff. *Tuition waivers:* Full or partial for employees or children of employees.

LOANS *Student loans:* $1,707,848 (63% need-based, 37% non-need-based). 29% of past graduating class borrowed through all loan programs. *Average indebtedness per student:* $38,402. *Average need-based loan:* Freshmen: $3328. Undergraduates: $4488. *Parent loans:* $173,798 (72% need-based, 28% non-need-based). *Programs:* Federal Direct (Subsidized and Unsubsidized Stafford, PLUS), state, alternative loans.

WORK-STUDY *Federal work-study:* Total amount: $27,096; 22 jobs averaging $2000. *State or other work-study/employment:* Total amount: $73,679 (86% need-based, 14% non-need-based). 65 part-time jobs averaging $2000.

APPLYING FOR FINANCIAL AID *Required financial aid forms:* FAFSA, institution's own form. *Financial aid deadline:* 6/1 (priority: 4/1). *Notification date:* Continuous beginning 2/15. Students must reply within 4 weeks of notification.

CONTACT David Woodward, Director of Financial Aid, College of Visual Arts, 344 Summit Avenue, St. Paul, MN 55102-2124, 651-757-4020 or toll-free 800-224-1536. *Fax:* 651-224-0090. *E-mail:* financialaid@cva.edu.

THE COLLEGE OF WILLIAM AND MARY
Williamsburg, VA

Tuition & fees (VA res): $10,800 **Average undergraduate aid package: $13,789**

ABOUT THE INSTITUTION State-supported, coed. 41 undergraduate majors. Federal methodology is used as a basis for awarding need-based institutional aid.

UNDERGRADUATE EXPENSES for 2009–10 *One-time required fee:* $153. *Tuition, state resident:* full-time $6388; part-time $240 per credit hour. *Tuition, nonresident:* full-time $26,180; part-time $880 per credit hour. *Required fees:* full-time $4412. *College room and board:* $8382; *Room only:* $4930. Room and board charges vary according to board plan and housing facility. *Payment plan:* Installment.

FRESHMAN FINANCIAL AID (Fall 2008) 815 applied for aid; of those 49% were deemed to have need. 100% of freshmen with need received aid; of those 41% had need fully met. *Average percent of need met:* 80% (excluding resources awarded to replace EFC). *Average financial aid package:* $13,219 (excluding resources awarded to replace EFC). 3% of all full-time freshmen had no need and received non-need-based gift aid.

UNDERGRADUATE FINANCIAL AID (Fall 2008) 2,751 applied for aid; of those 62% were deemed to have need. 100% of undergraduates with need received aid; of those 32% had need fully met. *Average percent of need met:* 80% (excluding resources awarded to replace EFC). *Average financial aid package:* $13,789 (excluding resources awarded to replace EFC). 5% of all full-time undergraduates had no need and received non-need-based gift aid.

GIFT AID (NEED-BASED) *Total amount:* $13,674,166 (17% federal, 20% state, 63% institutional). *Receiving aid:* Freshmen: 21% (295); all full-time undergraduates: 23% (1,329). *Average award:* Freshmen: $12,219; Undergraduates: $13,486. *Scholarships, grants, and awards:* Federal Pell, FSEOG, state, private, college/university gift aid from institutional funds.

GIFT AID (NON-NEED-BASED) *Total amount:* $5,885,506 (8% federal, 49% institutional, 43% external sources). *Receiving aid:* Freshmen: 14% (196). Undergraduates: 11% (619). *Average award:* Freshmen: $6246. Undergraduates: $5625. *Scholarships, grants, and awards by category: Academic interests/achievement:* 17 awards ($310,692 total): general academic interests/achievements. *Creative arts/performance:* 79 awards ($59,821 total): music, theater/drama. *Special characteristics:* 168 awards ($1,656,035 total): general special characteristics. *Tuition waivers:* Full or partial for employees or children of employees, senior citizens.

LOANS *Student loans:* $14,775,919 (33% need-based, 67% non-need-based). 40% of past graduating class borrowed through all loan programs. *Average indebtedness per student:* $18,410. *Average need-based loan:* Freshmen: $2704. Undergraduates: $3307. *Parent loans:* $5,363,379 (100% non-need-based). *Programs:* FFEL (Subsidized and Unsubsidized Stafford, PLUS), Perkins.

WORK-STUDY *Federal work-study:* Total amount: $29,292; 37 jobs averaging $808.

ATHLETIC AWARDS Total amount: $5,367,354 (8% need-based, 92% non-need-based).

APPLYING FOR FINANCIAL AID *Required financial aid form:* FAFSA. *Financial aid deadline (priority):* 3/15. *Notification date:* Continuous beginning 3/15. Students must reply by 5/1 or within 2 weeks of notification.

CONTACT Mr. Edward P. Irish, Director of Financial Aid, The College of William and Mary, PO Box 8795, Williamsburg, VA 23187, 757-221-2425. *Fax:* 757-221-2515. *E-mail:* epiris@wm.edu.

THE COLLEGE OF WOOSTER
Wooster, OH

Tuition & fees: $36,598	Average undergraduate aid package: $27,955

ABOUT THE INSTITUTION Independent religious, coed. 46 undergraduate majors. Both federal and institutional methodology are used as a basis for awarding need-based institutional aid.

UNDERGRADUATE EXPENSES for 2010–11 *Comprehensive fee:* $45,668 includes full-time tuition ($36,320), mandatory fees ($278), and room and board ($9070). *College room only:* $4110. Full-time tuition and fees vary according to course load. Room and board charges vary according to board plan and housing facility. Part-time tuition and fees vary according to course load. *Payment plan:* Installment.

FRESHMAN FINANCIAL AID (Fall 2009, est.) 385 applied for aid; of those 81% were deemed to have need. 100% of freshmen with need received aid; of those 46% had need fully met. *Average percent of need met:* 89% (excluding resources awarded to replace EFC). *Average financial aid package:* $28,225 (excluding resources awarded to replace EFC). 28% of all full-time freshmen had no need and received non-need-based gift aid.

UNDERGRADUATE FINANCIAL AID (Fall 2009, est.) 1,239 applied for aid; of those 87% were deemed to have need. 100% of undergraduates with need received aid; of those 40% had need fully met. *Average percent of need met:* 86% (excluding resources awarded to replace EFC). *Average financial aid package:* $27,955 (excluding resources awarded to replace EFC). 35% of all full-time undergraduates had no need and received non-need-based gift aid.

GIFT AID (NEED-BASED) *Total amount:* $23,933,925 (8% federal, 1% state, 90% institutional, 1% external sources). *Receiving aid:* Freshmen: 63% (304); all full-time undergraduates: 59% (1,059). *Average award:* Freshmen: $23,066; Undergraduates: $22,600. *Scholarships, grants, and awards:* Federal Pell, FSEOG, state, private, college/university gift aid from institutional funds.

GIFT AID (NON-NEED-BASED) *Total amount:* $10,886,540 (99% institutional, 1% external sources). *Receiving aid:* Freshmen: 12% (56). Undergraduates: 8% (139). *Average award:* Freshmen: $15,650. Undergraduates: $15,642. *Scholarships, grants, and awards by category:* Academic interests/achievement: 1,481 awards ($18,766,289 total): general academic interests/achievements. Creative arts/performance: 71 awards ($297,500 total): dance, music, theater/drama. Special achievements/activities: 98 awards ($638,350 total): community service, religious involvement. Special characteristics: 41 awards ($847,516 total): members of minority groups. *Tuition waivers:* Full or partial for employees or children of employees.

LOANS *Student loans:* $6,682,312 (72% need-based, 28% non-need-based). 58% of past graduating class borrowed through all loan programs. *Average indebtedness per student:* $25,140. *Average need-based loan:* Freshmen: $3511. Undergraduates: $4550. *Parent loans:* $4,108,021 (26% need-based, 74% non-need-based). *Programs:* Federal Direct (Subsidized and Unsubsidized Stafford, PLUS), Perkins, college/university.

WORK-STUDY *Federal work-study:* Total amount: $917,503; 651 jobs averaging $1371. *State or other work-study/employment:* Total amount: $161,100 (1% need-based, 99% non-need-based). 82 part-time jobs averaging $1928.

APPLYING FOR FINANCIAL AID *Required financial aid forms:* FAFSA, institution's own form. *Financial aid deadline:* 9/1 (priority: 2/15). *Notification date:* 4/1. Students must reply by 5/1.

CONTACT Dr. David Miller, Director of Financial Aid, The College of Wooster, 1189 Beall Avenue, Wooster, OH 44691-2363, 800-877-3688 or toll-free 800-877-9905. *Fax:* 330-263-2634. *E-mail:* financialaid@wooster.edu.

COLLINS COLLEGE: A SCHOOL OF DESIGN AND TECHNOLOGY
Tempe, AZ

ABOUT THE INSTITUTION Proprietary, coed. 7 undergraduate majors.

GIFT AID (NEED-BASED) *Scholarships, grants, and awards:* Federal Pell, FSEOG, state, private, college/university gift aid from institutional funds.

LOANS *Programs:* Federal Direct (Subsidized and Unsubsidized Stafford, PLUS), FFEL (Subsidized and Unsubsidized Stafford, PLUS), college/university.

APPLYING FOR FINANCIAL AID *Required financial aid forms:* FAFSA, institution's own form.

CONTACT Kari Yearwood, Director of Financial Aid, Collins College: A School of Design and Technology, 4750 South 44th Place, Phoenix, AZ 85040, 800-876-7070. *Fax:* 866-553-6597. *E-mail:* fa@collinscollege.edu.

COLORADO CHRISTIAN UNIVERSITY
Lakewood, CO

CONTACT Mr. Steve Woodburn, Director of Financial Aid, Colorado Christian University, 180 South Garrison Street, Lakewood, CO 80226-7499, 303-963-3230 or toll-free 800-44-FAITH. *Fax:* 303-963-3231. *E-mail:* sfs@ccu.edu.

THE COLORADO COLLEGE
Colorado Springs, CO

Tuition & fees: $37,478	Average undergraduate aid package: $30,203

ABOUT THE INSTITUTION Independent, coed. 48 undergraduate majors. Both federal and institutional methodology are used as a basis for awarding need-based institutional aid.

UNDERGRADUATE EXPENSES for 2009–10 *One-time required fee:* $150. *Comprehensive fee:* $47,102 includes full-time tuition ($37,278), mandatory fees ($200), and room and board ($9624). *College room only:* $5184. Full-time tuition and fees vary according to degree level. Room and board charges vary according to board plan and housing facility. *Part-time tuition:* $6213 per course. Part-time tuition and fees vary according to course load and degree level. *Payment plan:* Installment.

FRESHMAN FINANCIAL AID (Fall 2009, est.) 233 applied for aid; of those 79% were deemed to have need. 100% of freshmen with need received aid; of those 55% had need fully met. *Average percent of need met:* 92% (excluding resources awarded to replace EFC). *Average financial aid package:* $29,359 (excluding resources awarded to replace EFC). 8% of all full-time freshmen had no need and received non-need-based gift aid.

UNDERGRADUATE FINANCIAL AID (Fall 2009, est.) 870 applied for aid; of those 83% were deemed to have need. 100% of undergraduates with need received aid; of those 48% had need fully met. *Average percent of need met:* 92% (excluding resources awarded to replace EFC). *Average financial aid package:* $30,203 (excluding resources awarded to replace EFC). 10% of all full-time undergraduates had no need and received non-need-based gift aid.

GIFT AID (NEED-BASED) *Total amount:* $19,358,350 (6% federal, 1% state, 91% institutional, 2% external sources). *Receiving aid:* Freshmen: 33% (174); all full-time undergraduates: 36% (698). *Average award:* Freshmen: $28,241; Undergraduates: $28,207. *Scholarships, grants, and awards:* Federal Pell, FSEOG, state, private, college/university gift aid from institutional funds.

GIFT AID (NON-NEED-BASED) *Total amount:* $5,626,917 (85% institutional, 15% external sources). *Receiving aid:* Freshmen: 10% (55). Undergraduates: 11% (208). *Average award:* Freshmen: $10,276. Undergraduates: $17,773. *Scholarships, grants, and awards by category:* Academic interests/achievement: 155 awards ($1,700,000 total): biological sciences, general academic interests/achievements, mathematics, physical sciences. *Tuition waivers:* Full or partial for employees or children of employees.

LOANS *Student loans:* $3,953,071 (47% need-based, 53% non-need-based). 35% of past graduating class borrowed through all loan programs. *Average indebtedness per student:* $16,172. *Average need-based loan:* Freshmen: $2444. Undergraduates: $3284. *Parent loans:* $2,236,958 (9% need-based, 91% non-need-based). *Programs:* Federal Direct (Subsidized and Unsubsidized Stafford, PLUS), Perkins.

WORK-STUDY *Federal work-study:* Total amount: $351,112; 274 jobs averaging $1688. *State or other work-study/employment:* Total amount: $313,036 (64% need-based, 36% non-need-based). 165 part-time jobs averaging $1674.

ATHLETIC AWARDS Total amount: $1,393,212 (10% need-based, 90% non-need-based).

APPLYING FOR FINANCIAL AID *Required financial aid forms:* FAFSA, CSS Financial Aid PROFILE, noncustodial (divorced/separated) parent's statement, federal income tax form(s) for parents and student. *Financial aid deadline:* 2/15. *Notification date:* 3/20. Students must reply by 5/1.

CONTACT Mr. James M. Swanson, Director of Financial Aid, The Colorado College, 14 East Cache La Poudre Street, Colorado Springs, CO 80903-3294, 719-389-6651 or toll-free 800-542-7214. *Fax:* 719-389-6173. *E-mail:* financialaid@coloradocollege.edu.

COLORADO HEIGHTS UNIVERSITY
Denver, CO

CONTACT Financial Aid Office, Colorado Heights University, 3001 South Federal Boulevard, Denver, CO 80236, 303-936-4200.

COLORADO SCHOOL OF MINES
Golden, CO

Tuition & fees (CO res): $12,244   Average undergraduate aid package: $11,927

ABOUT THE INSTITUTION State-supported, coed. 12 undergraduate majors. Federal methodology is used as a basis for awarding need-based institutional aid.

UNDERGRADUATE EXPENSES for 2009–10 *Tuition, state resident:* full-time $10,590; part-time $353 per credit hour. *Tuition, nonresident:* full-time $24,750; part-time $825 per credit hour. *Required fees:* full-time $1654. Part-time tuition and fees vary according to course load. *College room and board:* $8120. Room and board charges vary according to board plan and housing facility. *Payment plan:* Installment.

FRESHMAN FINANCIAL AID (Fall 2008) 689 applied for aid; of those 64% were deemed to have need. 100% of freshmen with need received aid; of those 37% had need fully met. *Average percent of need met:* 84% (excluding resources awarded to replace EFC). *Average financial aid package:* $13,830 (excluding resources awarded to replace EFC). 16% of all full-time freshmen had no need and received non-need-based gift aid.

UNDERGRADUATE FINANCIAL AID (Fall 2008) 2,053 applied for aid; of those 71% were deemed to have need. 96% of undergraduates with need received aid; of those 23% had need fully met. *Average percent of need met:* 68% (excluding resources awarded to replace EFC). *Average financial aid package:* $11,927 (excluding resources awarded to replace EFC). 21% of all full-time undergraduates had no need and received non-need-based gift aid.

GIFT AID (NEED-BASED) *Total amount:* $8,981,282 (23% federal, 12% state, 53% institutional, 12% external sources). *Receiving aid:* Freshmen: 38% (323); all full-time undergraduates: 30% (988). *Average award:* Freshmen: $7357; Undergraduates: $6586. *Scholarships, grants, and awards:* Federal Pell, FSEOG, state, private, college/university gift aid from institutional funds.

GIFT AID (NON-NEED-BASED) *Total amount:* $4,177,049 (1% federal, 1% state, 75% institutional, 23% external sources). *Receiving aid:* Freshmen: 23% (192). Undergraduates: 8% (270). *Average award:* Freshmen: $4408. Undergraduates: $4633. *Scholarships, grants, and awards by category: Academic interests/achievement:* business, computer science, engineering/technologies, general academic interests/achievements, mathematics, military science, physical sciences. *Tuition waivers:* Full or partial for employees or children of employees.

LOANS *Student loans:* $13,720,664 (80% need-based, 20% non-need-based). 62% of past graduating class borrowed through all loan programs. *Average indebtedness per student:* $22,500. *Average need-based loan:* Freshmen: $4471. Undergraduates: $5041. *Parent loans:* $3,831,393 (55% need-based, 45% non-need-based). *Programs:* FFEL (Subsidized and Unsubsidized Stafford, PLUS), Perkins, college/university.

WORK-STUDY *Federal work-study:* Total amount: $165,324; jobs available. *State or other work-study/employment:* Total amount: $1,828,574 (62% need-based, 38% non-need-based). Part-time jobs available.

ATHLETIC AWARDS Total amount: $1,819,072 (30% need-based, 70% non-need-based).

APPLYING FOR FINANCIAL AID *Required financial aid forms:* FAFSA, institution's own form. *Financial aid deadline (priority):* 2/1. *Notification date:* Continuous beginning 3/1.

CONTACT Jill Robertson, Director of Financial Aid, Colorado School of Mines, 1600 Maple Street, Golden, CO 80401-1887, 303-273-3220 or toll-free 800-446-9488 Ext. 3220 (out-of-state). *Fax:* 303-384-2252. *E-mail:* finaid@mines.edu.

COLORADO STATE UNIVERSITY
Fort Collins, CO

Tuition & fees (CO res): $6318   Average undergraduate aid package: $10,051

ABOUT THE INSTITUTION State-supported, coed. 111 undergraduate majors. Federal methodology is used as a basis for awarding need-based institutional aid.

UNDERGRADUATE EXPENSES for 2009–10 *Tuition, state resident:* full-time $4822; part-time $241.10 per credit hour. *Tuition, nonresident:* full-time $20,744; part-time $1037 per credit hour. *Required fees:* full-time $1496; $24.60 per credit hour or $123 per term. Full-time tuition and fees vary according to course load. Part-time tuition and fees vary according to course load. *College room and board:* $8378; *Room only:* $4238. Room and board charges vary according to board plan and housing facility. *Payment plan:* Installment.

FRESHMAN FINANCIAL AID (Fall 2008) 3,152 applied for aid; of those 55% were deemed to have need. 100% of freshmen with need received aid; of those 44% had need fully met. *Average percent of need met:* 73% (excluding resources awarded to replace EFC). *Average financial aid package:* $9564 (excluding resources awarded to replace EFC). 11% of all full-time freshmen had no need and received non-need-based gift aid.

UNDERGRADUATE FINANCIAL AID (Fall 2008) 12,223 applied for aid; of those 66% were deemed to have need. 100% of undergraduates with need received aid; of those 42% had need fully met. *Average percent of need met:* 74% (excluding resources awarded to replace EFC). *Average financial aid package:* $10,051 (excluding resources awarded to replace EFC). 9% of all full-time undergraduates had no need and received non-need-based gift aid.

GIFT AID (NEED-BASED) *Total amount:* $37,369,201 (40% federal, 18% state, 32% institutional, 10% external sources). *Receiving aid:* Freshmen: 37% (1,615); all full-time undergraduates: 37% (7,221). *Average award:* Freshmen: $6728; Undergraduates: $5170. *Scholarships, grants, and awards:* Federal Pell, FSEOG, state, private, college/university gift aid from institutional funds.

GIFT AID (NON-NEED-BASED) *Total amount:* $10,261,814 (20% federal, 1% state, 55% institutional, 24% external sources). *Average award:* Freshmen: $2970. Undergraduates: $3371. *Scholarships, grants, and awards by category: Academic interests/achievement:* 11,621 awards ($15,830,717 total): general academic interests/achievements. *Creative arts/performance:* 207 awards ($350,000 total): art/fine arts, creative writing, dance, music, theater/drama. *Special achievements/activities:* 233 awards ($590,527 total): general special achievements/activities. *Special characteristics:* 417 awards ($946,902 total): children of faculty/staff, first-generation college students. *Tuition waivers:* Full or partial for employees or children of employees.

LOANS *Student loans:* $67,297,655 (72% need-based, 28% non-need-based). 57% of past graduating class borrowed through all loan programs. *Average indebtedness per student:* $20,432. *Average need-based loan:* Freshmen: $4595. Undergraduates: $6525. *Parent loans:* $30,865,912 (58% need-based, 42% non-need-based). *Programs:* Federal Direct (Subsidized and Unsubsidized Stafford, PLUS), Perkins, alternative loans.

WORK-STUDY *Federal work-study:* Total amount: $743,839; 346 jobs averaging $2071. *State or other work-study/employment:* Total amount: $2,170,575 (71% need-based, 29% non-need-based). 1,172 part-time jobs averaging $1831.

ATHLETIC AWARDS Total amount: $5,482,215 (19% need-based, 81% non-need-based).

APPLYING FOR FINANCIAL AID *Required financial aid form:* FAFSA. *Financial aid deadline (priority):* 3/1. *Notification date:* Continuous beginning 3/1.

CONTACT Office of Student Financial Services, Colorado State University, Room 103, Centennial Hall, Fort Collins, CO 80523-8024, 970-491-6321. *E-mail:* sfs@colostate.edu.

CONTACT Ms. Natalie Dietsch, Financial Aid Manager, Colorado Technical University Denver, 5775 Denver Tech Center Boulevard, Suite 100, Greenwood Village, CO 80111, 303-694-6600. *Fax:* 303-694-6673.

COLORADO STATE UNIVERSITY–PUEBLO
Pueblo, CO

ABOUT THE INSTITUTION State-supported, coed. 26 undergraduate majors.
GIFT AID (NEED-BASED) *Scholarships, grants, and awards:* Federal Pell, FSEOG, state, private, college/university gift aid from institutional funds, Academic Competitiveness Grants, National SMART Grants, TEACH Grants.
GIFT AID (NON-NEED-BASED) *Scholarships, grants, and awards by category: Academic interests/achievement:* biological sciences, business, communication, computer science, education, engineering/technologies, English, foreign languages, general academic interests/achievements, health fields, mathematics, physical sciences, premedicine, social sciences. *Creative arts/performance:* applied art and design, art/fine arts, cinema/film/broadcasting, journalism/publications, music. *Special achievements/activities:* community service, general special achievements/activities, leadership. *Special characteristics:* children and siblings of alumni, children of faculty/staff, ethnic background, first-generation college students, general special characteristics, handicapped students, international students, out-of-state students.
LOANS *Programs:* Federal Direct (Subsidized and Unsubsidized Stafford, PLUS), FFEL (Subsidized and Unsubsidized Stafford, PLUS), Perkins.
WORK-STUDY *Federal work-study:* Total amount: $485,234; 225 jobs averaging $2095. *State or other work-study/employment:* Total amount: $916,994 (70% need-based, 30% non-need-based). 337 part-time jobs averaging $2472.
APPLYING FOR FINANCIAL AID *Required financial aid forms:* FAFSA, institution's own form.
CONTACT Sean McGivney, Director of Student Financial Services, Colorado State University–Pueblo, 2200 Bonforte Boulevard, Pueblo, CO 81001-4901, 719-549-2753. *Fax:* 719-549-2088.

COLORADO TECHNICAL UNIVERSITY COLORADO SPRINGS
Colorado Springs, CO

ABOUT THE INSTITUTION Proprietary, coed. *Awards:* associate, bachelor's, and master's degrees. 14 undergraduate majors. *Total enrollment:* 2,359. Undergraduates: 1,896.
GIFT AID (NEED-BASED) *Scholarships, grants, and awards:* Federal Pell, FSEOG, state, college/university gift aid from institutional funds.
GIFT AID (NON-NEED-BASED) *Scholarships, grants, and awards by category: Academic interests/achievement:* business, computer science, engineering/technologies, general academic interests/achievements.
LOANS *Programs:* FFEL (Subsidized and Unsubsidized Stafford, PLUS), Perkins.
APPLYING FOR FINANCIAL AID *Required financial aid forms:* FAFSA, state aid form.
CONTACT Jacqueline Harris, Senior Director of Student Finance Services, Colorado Technical University Colorado Springs, 4435 North Chestnut Street, Colorado Springs, CO 80907-3896, 719-598-0200. *Fax:* 719-598-3740.

COLORADO TECHNICAL UNIVERSITY DENVER
Greenwood Village, CO

ABOUT THE INSTITUTION Proprietary, coed. *Awards:* associate, bachelor's, and master's degrees. 9 undergraduate majors. *Total enrollment:* 733. Undergraduates: 573. Freshmen: 52.
GIFT AID (NEED-BASED) *Scholarships, grants, and awards:* Federal Pell, FSEOG, state.
GIFT AID (NON-NEED-BASED) *Scholarships, grants, and awards by category: Academic interests/achievement:* business, computer science, engineering/technologies, general academic interests/achievements.
LOANS *Programs:* FFEL (Subsidized and Unsubsidized Stafford, PLUS), Perkins.
APPLYING FOR FINANCIAL AID *Required financial aid forms:* FAFSA, state aid form.

COLORADO TECHNICAL UNIVERSITY NORTH KANSAS CITY
North Kansas City, MO

CONTACT Ms. Judy Richman, Director of Financial Assistance, Colorado Technical University North Kansas City, 520 East 19th Avenue, North Kansas City, MO 64116, 816-472-7400.

COLORADO TECHNICAL UNIVERSITY SIOUX FALLS
Sioux Falls, SD

ABOUT THE INSTITUTION Proprietary, coed. *Awards:* associate, bachelor's, and master's degrees. 15 undergraduate majors. *Total enrollment:* 912. Undergraduates: 816. Freshmen: 105.
GIFT AID (NEED-BASED) *Scholarships, grants, and awards:* Federal Pell, FSEOG.
LOANS *Programs:* FFEL (Subsidized and Unsubsidized Stafford, PLUS), Perkins.
APPLYING FOR FINANCIAL AID *Required financial aid forms:* FAFSA, institution's own form.
CONTACT Vikki Van Hull, Financial Aid Officer, Colorado Technical University Sioux Falls, 3901 West 59th Street, Sioux Falls, SD 57108, 605-361-0200 Ext. 140. *Fax:* 605-361-5954. *E-mail:* vvanhull@sf.coloradotech.edu.

COLUMBIA COLLEGE
Columbia, MO

Tuition & fees: $15,596	Average undergraduate aid package: $11,935

ABOUT THE INSTITUTION Independent religious, coed. 37 undergraduate majors. Federal methodology is used as a basis for awarding need-based institutional aid.
UNDERGRADUATE EXPENSES for 2010–11 *Comprehensive fee:* $21,670 includes full-time tuition ($15,596) and room and board ($6074). *College room only:* $3780. Full-time tuition and fees vary according to class time and course load. Room and board charges vary according to board plan. *Part-time tuition:* $312 per semester hour. Part-time tuition and fees vary according to class time, course load, and location. *Payment plans:* Installment, deferred payment.
FRESHMAN FINANCIAL AID (Fall 2008) 114 applied for aid; of those 97% were deemed to have need. 100% of freshmen with need received aid; of those 6% had need fully met. *Average percent of need met:* 53% (excluding resources awarded to replace EFC). *Average financial aid package:* $11,270 (excluding resources awarded to replace EFC). 14% of all full-time freshmen had no need and received non-need-based gift aid.
UNDERGRADUATE FINANCIAL AID (Fall 2008) 502 applied for aid; of those 98% were deemed to have need. 100% of undergraduates with need received aid; of those 7% had need fully met. *Average percent of need met:* 54% (excluding resources awarded to replace EFC). *Average financial aid package:* $11,935 (excluding resources awarded to replace EFC). 12% of all full-time undergraduates had no need and received non-need-based gift aid.
GIFT AID (NEED-BASED) *Total amount:* $2,117,418 (50% federal, 47% state, 3% institutional). *Receiving aid:* Freshmen: 44% (92); all full-time undergraduates: 42% (376). *Average award:* Freshmen: $5299; Undergraduates: $5213. *Scholarships, grants, and awards:* Federal Pell, FSEOG, state, private, college/university gift aid from institutional funds.
GIFT AID (NON-NEED-BASED) *Total amount:* $3,025,334 (1% state, 92% institutional, 7% external sources). *Receiving aid:* Freshmen: 35% (72). Undergraduates: 31% (276). *Average award:* Freshmen: $6793. Undergraduates: $7566. *Scholarships, grants, and awards by category: Academic interests/achievement:* 428 awards ($3,914,207 total): biological sciences, business, education, English, general academic interests/achievements, humanities, mathematics, physical sciences, religion/biblical studies, social sciences. *Creative arts/performance:* 17 awards ($12,000 total): art/fine arts, creative writing, music. *Special achievements/activities:* 39 awards ($37,750 total): leadership. *Special characteristics:* 175 awards ($806,627 total): children and siblings of

alumni, children of current students, children of educators, children of faculty/staff, first-generation college students, international students, local/state students, parents of current students, previous college experience, religious affiliation, siblings of current students, spouses of current students, veterans. *Tuition waivers:* Full or partial for children of alumni, employees or children of employees, senior citizens.

LOANS *Student loans:* $4,528,618 (39% need-based, 61% non-need-based). 63% of past graduating class borrowed through all loan programs. *Average indebtedness per student:* $13,948. *Average need-based loan:* Freshmen: $3166. Undergraduates: $3956. *Parent loans:* $666,914 (100% non-need-based). *Programs:* Federal Direct (Subsidized and Unsubsidized Stafford, PLUS).

WORK-STUDY *Federal work-study:* Total amount: $220,917; 149 jobs averaging $1620. *State or other work-study/employment:* Total amount: $209,773 (100% non-need-based). 157 part-time jobs averaging $1206.

ATHLETIC AWARDS Total amount: $1,034,452 (100% non-need-based).

APPLYING FOR FINANCIAL AID *Required financial aid form:* FAFSA. *Financial aid deadline (priority):* 3/1. *Notification date:* Continuous beginning 3/1.

CONTACT Sharon Abernathy, Director of Financial Aid, Columbia College, 1001 Rogers Street, Columbia, MO 65216-0002, 573-875-7390 or toll-free 800-231-2391 Ext. 7366. *Fax:* 573-875-7452. *E-mail:* saabernathy@ccis.edu.

COLUMBIA COLLEGE
Caguas, PR

Tuition & fees: $9100	Average undergraduate aid package: $4035

ABOUT THE INSTITUTION Proprietary, coed. 7 undergraduate majors. Federal methodology is used as a basis for awarding need-based institutional aid.

UNDERGRADUATE EXPENSES for 2010–11 *Tuition:* full-time $9000. *Required fees:* full-time $100; $100 per credit. Full-time tuition and fees vary according to program. Part-time tuition and fees vary according to program. *Payment plan:* Installment.

FRESHMAN FINANCIAL AID (Fall 2008) 119 applied for aid; of those 86% were deemed to have need. 100% of freshmen with need received aid. *Average percent of need met:* 11% (excluding resources awarded to replace EFC). *Average financial aid package:* $4035 (excluding resources awarded to replace EFC).

UNDERGRADUATE FINANCIAL AID (Fall 2008) 974 applied for aid; of those 84% were deemed to have need. 100% of undergraduates with need received aid. *Average percent of need met:* 11% (excluding resources awarded to replace EFC). *Average financial aid package:* $4035 (excluding resources awarded to replace EFC).

GIFT AID (NEED-BASED) *Total amount:* $3,300,814 (97% federal, 3% state). *Scholarships, grants, and awards:* Federal Pell, FSEOG, state, college/university gift aid from institutional funds.

GIFT AID (NON-NEED-BASED) *Scholarships, grants, and awards by category:* Academic interests/achievement: general academic interests/achievements. *Tuition waivers:* Full or partial for employees or children of employees.

WORK-STUDY *Federal work-study:* Total amount: $59,906; 61 jobs averaging $982.

APPLYING FOR FINANCIAL AID *Required financial aid forms:* FAFSA, institution's own form. *Financial aid deadline:* Continuous. *Notification date:* 9/1. Students must reply by 9/15 or within 2 weeks of notification.

CONTACT Financial Aid Officer, Columbia College, Carr 183, Km 1.7, PO Box 8517, Caguas, PR 00726, 787-743-4041 Ext. 244 or toll-free 800-981-4877 Ext. 239 (in-state). *Fax:* 787-744-7031.

COLUMBIA COLLEGE
Yauco, PR

CONTACT Financial Aid Office, Columbia College, Box 3062, Yauco, PR 00698, 787-856-0945.

COLUMBIA COLLEGE
Columbia, SC

CONTACT Anita Kaminer Elliott, Director of Financial Aid, Columbia College, 1301 Columbia College Drive, Columbia, SC 29203-5998, 803-786-3612 or toll-free 800-277-1301. *Fax:* 803-786-3560.

COLUMBIA COLLEGE CHICAGO
Chicago, IL

Tuition & fees: $19,850	Average undergraduate aid package: $8922

ABOUT THE INSTITUTION Independent, coed. 41 undergraduate majors. Federal methodology is used as a basis for awarding need-based institutional aid.

UNDERGRADUATE EXPENSES for 2010–11 *Tuition:* full-time $19,140; part-time $661 per credit hour. *Required fees:* full-time $710; $300 per semester hour. Full-time tuition and fees vary according to course load. Part-time tuition and fees vary according to course load. Room and board charges vary according to housing facility. *Payment plan:* Installment.

FRESHMAN FINANCIAL AID (Fall 2009, est.) 1,837 applied for aid; of those 84% were deemed to have need. 99% of freshmen with need received aid; of those 73% had need fully met. *Average percent of need met:* 23% (excluding resources awarded to replace EFC). *Average financial aid package:* $8383 (excluding resources awarded to replace EFC).

UNDERGRADUATE FINANCIAL AID (Fall 2009, est.) 7,243 applied for aid; of those 89% were deemed to have need. 96% of undergraduates with need received aid; of those 93% had need fully met. *Average percent of need met:* 29% (excluding resources awarded to replace EFC). *Average financial aid package:* $8922 (excluding resources awarded to replace EFC).

GIFT AID (NEED-BASED) *Total amount:* $23,228,751 (50% federal, 47% state, 3% institutional). *Receiving aid:* Freshmen: 2% (37); all full-time undergraduates: 2% (226). *Average award:* Freshmen: $1834; Undergraduates: $2347. *Scholarships, grants, and awards:* Federal Pell, FSEOG, state, private, college/university gift aid from institutional funds.

GIFT AID (NON-NEED-BASED) *Total amount:* $9,267,430 (82% institutional, 18% external sources). *Receiving aid:* Freshmen: 61% (1,430). Undergraduates: 57% (5,976). *Scholarships, grants, and awards by category:* Academic interests/achievement: business, communication, education, general academic interests/achievements. *Creative arts/performance:* applied art and design, art/fine arts, cinema/film/broadcasting, creative writing, dance, journalism/publications, music, performing arts, theater/drama. *Special achievements/activities:* leadership. *Special characteristics:* children of faculty/staff, handicapped students. *Tuition waivers:* Full or partial for employees or children of employees.

LOANS *Student loans:* $100,066,949 (100% need-based). *Average need-based loan:* Freshmen: $3408. Undergraduates: $4337. *Parent loans:* $46,325,225 (100% need-based). *Programs:* Federal Direct (Subsidized and Unsubsidized Stafford, PLUS).

WORK-STUDY Federal work-study jobs available. *State or other work-study/employment:* Part-time jobs available.

APPLYING FOR FINANCIAL AID *Required financial aid forms:* FAFSA, institution's own form. *Financial aid deadline (priority):* 8/15. *Notification date:* Continuous.

CONTACT Ms. Jennifer Waters, Executive Director of Student Financial Services, Columbia College Chicago, 600 South Michigan Avenue, Chicago, IL 60605-1996, 312-369-7831. *Fax:* 312-986-7008. *E-mail:* jwaters@colum.edu.

COLUMBIA COLLEGE HOLLYWOOD
Tarzana, CA

Tuition & fees: N/R	Average undergraduate aid package: $6119

ABOUT THE INSTITUTION Independent, coed. *Awards:* associate and bachelor's degrees. 5 undergraduate majors. *Total enrollment:* 301. Undergraduates: 301. Federal methodology is used as a basis for awarding need-based institutional aid.

UNDERGRADUATE FINANCIAL AID (Fall 2009, est.) 259 applied for aid; of those 92% were deemed to have need. 100% of undergraduates with need received aid. *Average financial aid package:* $6119 (excluding resources awarded to replace EFC).

GIFT AID (NEED-BASED) *Total amount:* $990,092 (65% federal, 29% state, 6% external sources). *Receiving aid:* All full-time undergraduates: 40% (142). *Average award:* Undergraduates: $2063. *Scholarships, grants, and awards:* Federal Pell, FSEOG, state, private.

GIFT AID (NON-NEED-BASED) *Tuition waivers:* Full or partial for employees or children of employees.

LOANS *Student loans:* $4,165,708 (100% need-based). 75% of past graduating class borrowed through all loan programs. *Average need-based loan:*

Undergraduates: $1362. *Parent loans:* $1,075,384 (100% need-based). *Programs:* Federal Direct (Subsidized and Unsubsidized Stafford, PLUS), private loans.

WORK-STUDY *Federal work-study:* Total amount: $20,000; 10 jobs averaging $2000.

APPLYING FOR FINANCIAL AID *Required financial aid forms:* FAFSA, institution's own form. *Financial aid deadline:* Continuous. *Notification date:* Continuous. Students must reply within 2 weeks of notification.

CONTACT Mr. Jan Hastings, Financial Aid Administrator, Columbia College Hollywood, 18618 Oxnard Street, Tarzana, CA 91356, 818-401-1030 or toll-free 800-785-0585 (in-state). *Fax:* 818-345-8660. *E-mail:* finaid@columbiacollege.edu.

COLUMBIA INTERNATIONAL UNIVERSITY
Columbia, SC

ABOUT THE INSTITUTION Independent nondenominational, coed. 15 undergraduate majors.

GIFT AID (NEED-BASED) *Scholarships, grants, and awards:* Federal Pell, FSEOG, state, private, college/university gift aid from institutional funds.

GIFT AID (NON-NEED-BASED) *Scholarships, grants, and awards by category: Academic interests/achievement:* business, communication, education, English, general academic interests/achievements, international studies, religion/biblical studies. *Creative arts/performance:* music, performing arts. *Special achievements/activities:* general special achievements/activities, leadership. *Special characteristics:* children and siblings of alumni, ethnic background, international students, married students, relatives of clergy, religious affiliation, spouses of current students, veterans, veterans' children.

LOANS *Programs:* FFEL (Subsidized and Unsubsidized Stafford, PLUS).

WORK-STUDY *Federal work-study:* Total amount: $177,500; 68 jobs averaging $2500.

APPLYING FOR FINANCIAL AID *Required financial aid forms:* FAFSA, institution's own form.

CONTACT Nicole Mathison, Office Manager, Columbia International University, 7435 Monticello Road, Columbia, SC 29203, 800-777-2227 Ext. 5036 or toll-free 800-777-2227 Ext. 3024. *Fax:* 803-223-2505. *E-mail:* nmathison@ciu.edu.

COLUMBIA UNIVERSITY
New York, NY

Tuition & fees: $39,296	Average undergraduate aid package: $37,490

ABOUT THE INSTITUTION Independent, coed. 78 undergraduate majors. Both federal and institutional methodology are used as a basis for awarding need-based institutional aid.

UNDERGRADUATE EXPENSES for 2009–10 *Comprehensive fee:* $49,524 includes full-time tuition ($39,296) and room and board ($10,228).

FRESHMAN FINANCIAL AID (Fall 2009, est.) 908 applied for aid; of those 85% were deemed to have need. 100% of freshmen with need received aid; of those 100% had need fully met. *Average percent of need met:* 100% (excluding resources awarded to replace EFC). *Average financial aid package:* $38,196 (excluding resources awarded to replace EFC).

UNDERGRADUATE FINANCIAL AID (Fall 2009, est.) 3,269 applied for aid; of those 89% were deemed to have need. 100% of undergraduates with need received aid; of those 100% had need fully met. *Average percent of need met:* 100% (excluding resources awarded to replace EFC). *Average financial aid package:* $37,490 (excluding resources awarded to replace EFC).

GIFT AID (NEED-BASED) *Total amount:* $104,055,854 (6% federal, 2% state, 90% institutional, 2% external sources). *Receiving aid:* Freshmen: 54% (766); all full-time undergraduates: 49% (2,839). *Average award:* Freshmen: $36,464; Undergraduates: $35,705. *Scholarships, grants, and awards:* Federal Pell, FSEOG, state, private, college/university gift aid from institutional funds.

GIFT AID (NON-NEED-BASED) *Total amount:* $463,893 (6% federal, 6% state, 88% external sources).

LOANS *Student loans:* $4,994,882 (33% need-based, 67% non-need-based). *Average need-based loan:* Freshmen: $2698. Undergraduates: $2541. *Parent loans:* $9,126,532 (5% need-based, 95% non-need-based). *Programs:* FFEL (Subsidized and Unsubsidized Stafford, PLUS), Perkins, alternative loans.

WORK-STUDY *Federal work-study:* Total amount: $3,551,364; jobs available. *State or other work-study/employment:* Total amount: $1,908,648 (31% need-based, 69% non-need-based). Part-time jobs available.

APPLYING FOR FINANCIAL AID *Required financial aid forms:* FAFSA, CSS Financial Aid PROFILE, noncustodial (divorced/separated) parent's statement, parent and student income tax forms. *Financial aid deadline:* 3/1. *Notification date:* 4/1. Students must reply by 5/1.

CONTACT Daniel T. Barkowitz, Dean of Financial Aid/Associate Dean of Student Affairs, Columbia University, 100 Hamilton Hall, MC 2802, 1130 Amsterdam Avenue, New York, NY 10027, 212-854-3711. *Fax:* 212-854-5353. *E-mail:* db2660@columbia.edu.

COLUMBIA UNIVERSITY, SCHOOL OF GENERAL STUDIES
New York, NY

Tuition & fees: $39,910	Average undergraduate aid package: N/A

ABOUT THE INSTITUTION Independent, coed. 77 undergraduate majors. Both federal and institutional methodology are used as a basis for awarding need-based institutional aid.

UNDERGRADUATE EXPENSES for 2009–10 *Comprehensive fee:* $51,930 includes full-time tuition ($38,100), mandatory fees ($1810), and room and board ($12,020). *College room only:* $8550. Full-time tuition and fees vary according to course load. Room and board charges vary according to board plan and housing facility. *Part-time tuition:* $1270 per credit hour. Part-time tuition and fees vary according to course load. *Payment plans:* Tuition prepayment, installment.

GIFT AID (NEED-BASED) *Total amount:* $10,666,447 (30% federal, 6% state, 63% institutional, 1% external sources). *Scholarships, grants, and awards:* Federal Pell, FSEOG, state, private, college/university gift aid from institutional funds.

GIFT AID (NON-NEED-BASED) *Total amount:* $2,673,883 (18% federal, 81% institutional, 1% external sources). *Scholarships, grants, and awards by category: Academic interests/achievement:* general academic interests/achievements. *Tuition waivers:* Full or partial for employees or children of employees.

LOANS *Student loans:* $12,731,837 (43% need-based, 57% non-need-based). *Parent loans:* $1,101,983 (100% non-need-based). *Programs:* FFEL (Subsidized and Unsubsidized Stafford, PLUS), Perkins, college/university.

WORK-STUDY *Federal work-study:* Total amount: $840,706; jobs available.

APPLYING FOR FINANCIAL AID *Required financial aid forms:* FAFSA, institution's own form. *Financial aid deadline:* 6/1. *Notification date:* Continuous. Students must reply within 3 weeks of notification.

CONTACT Mr. Skip Bailey, Director of Educational Financing, Columbia University, School of General Studies, 408 Lewisohn Hall, 2970 Broadway, New York, NY 10027, 212-854-2772 or toll-free 800-895-1169 (out-of-state).

COLUMBUS COLLEGE OF ART & DESIGN
Columbus, OH

Tuition & fees: $24,648	Average undergraduate aid package: $16,439

ABOUT THE INSTITUTION Independent, coed. 7 undergraduate majors. Federal methodology is used as a basis for awarding need-based institutional aid.

UNDERGRADUATE EXPENSES for 2009–10 *Comprehensive fee:* $33,278 includes full-time tuition ($23,688), mandatory fees ($960), and room and board ($8630). Full-time tuition and fees vary according to course load. Room and board charges vary according to housing facility and student level. *Part-time tuition:* $987 per credit hour. *Part-time fees:* $180 per term. Part-time tuition and fees vary according to course load. *Payment plans:* Installment, deferred payment.

FRESHMAN FINANCIAL AID (Fall 2009, est.) 290 applied for aid; of those 89% were deemed to have need. 97% of freshmen with need received aid; of those 13% had need fully met. *Average percent of need met:* 59% (excluding resources awarded to replace EFC). *Average financial aid package:* $16,499 (excluding resources awarded to replace EFC). 14% of all full-time freshmen had no need and received non-need-based gift aid.

UNDERGRADUATE FINANCIAL AID (Fall 2009, est.) 1,253 applied for aid; of those 89% were deemed to have need. 98% of undergraduates with need

received aid; of those 15% had need fully met. *Average percent of need met:* 60% (excluding resources awarded to replace EFC). *Average financial aid package:* $16,439 (excluding resources awarded to replace EFC). 15% of all full-time undergraduates had no need and received non-need-based gift aid.
GIFT AID (NEED-BASED) *Total amount:* $11,910,031 (19% federal, 6% state, 72% institutional, 3% external sources). *Receiving aid:* Freshmen: 86% (252); all full-time undergraduates: 80% (1,068). *Average award:* Freshmen: $13,168; Undergraduates: $11,043. *Scholarships, grants, and awards:* Federal Pell, FSEOG, state, private, college/university gift aid from institutional funds.
GIFT AID (NON-NEED-BASED) *Total amount:* $1,869,805 (1% state, 95% institutional, 4% external sources). *Receiving aid:* Freshmen: 5% (14). Undergraduates: 4% (57). *Average award:* Freshmen: $7321. Undergraduates: $7552. *Scholarships, grants, and awards by category: Creative arts/performance:* art/fine arts. *Special characteristics:* children of educators, children of faculty/staff, local/state students. *Tuition waivers:* Full or partial for employees or children of employees.
LOANS *Student loans:* $10,719,573 (76% need-based, 24% non-need-based). 71% of past graduating class borrowed through all loan programs. *Average indebtedness per student:* $39,023. *Average need-based loan:* Freshmen: $3859. Undergraduates: $5991. *Parent loans:* $3,747,834 (70% need-based, 30% non-need-based). *Programs:* Federal Direct (Subsidized and Unsubsidized Stafford, PLUS), Perkins, state.
WORK-STUDY *Federal work-study:* Total amount: $426,779; 150 jobs averaging $3500. *State or other work-study/employment:* 340 part-time jobs averaging $3000.
APPLYING FOR FINANCIAL AID *Required financial aid forms:* FAFSA, institution's own form, income tax forms, verification statement. *Financial aid deadline (priority):* 3/1. *Notification date:* 3/15. Students must reply within 2 weeks of notification.
CONTACT Mrs. Anna Marie Schofield, Director of Financial Aid, Columbus College of Art & Design, 107 North Ninth Street, Columbus, OH 43215-1758, 614-224-9101 Ext. 3274 or toll-free 877-997-2223. *Fax:* 614-222-4034. *E-mail:* aschofield@ccad.edu.

COLUMBUS STATE UNIVERSITY
Columbus, GA

Tuition & fees (GA res): $5024	Average undergraduate aid package: $8161

ABOUT THE INSTITUTION State-supported, coed. 38 undergraduate majors. Federal methodology is used as a basis for awarding need-based institutional aid.
UNDERGRADUATE EXPENSES for 2009–10 *Tuition, state resident:* full-time $3874; part-time $130 per semester hour. *Tuition, nonresident:* full-time $15,488; part-time $517 per semester hour. *Required fees:* full-time $1150. Full-time tuition and fees vary according to course level and student level. Part-time tuition and fees vary according to course level and student level. *College room and board:* $7090. Room and board charges vary according to board plan and location.
FRESHMAN FINANCIAL AID (Fall 2009, est.) 1,023 applied for aid; of those 78% were deemed to have need. 98% of freshmen with need received aid; of those 17% had need fully met. *Average percent of need met:* 72% (excluding resources awarded to replace EFC). *Average financial aid package:* $8238 (excluding resources awarded to replace EFC). 3% of all full-time freshmen had no need and received non-need-based gift aid.
UNDERGRADUATE FINANCIAL AID (Fall 2009, est.) 3,828 applied for aid; of those 79% were deemed to have need. 98% of undergraduates with need received aid; of those 22% had need fully met. *Average percent of need met:* 72% (excluding resources awarded to replace EFC). *Average financial aid package:* $8161 (excluding resources awarded to replace EFC). 3% of all full-time undergraduates had no need and received non-need-based gift aid.
GIFT AID (NEED-BASED) *Total amount:* $12,052,454 (99% federal, 1% external sources). *Receiving aid:* Freshmen: 44% (516); all full-time undergraduates: 41% (1,994). *Average award:* Freshmen: $4984; Undergraduates: $4804. *Scholarships, grants, and awards:* Federal Pell, FSEOG, state, private, college/university gift aid from institutional funds.
GIFT AID (NON-NEED-BASED) *Total amount:* $10,361,110 (89% state, 6% institutional, 5% external sources). *Receiving aid:* Freshmen: 36% (421). Undergraduates: 21% (1,008). *Average award:* Freshmen: $1721. Undergraduates: $1514. *Scholarships, grants, and awards by category: Academic interests/achievement:* 54 awards ($80,568 total): biological sciences, business, com-

munication, computer science, education, English, general academic interests/achievements, health fields, humanities, international studies, mathematics, military science, physical sciences. *Creative arts/performance:* 164 awards ($317,996 total): art/fine arts, dance, music, performing arts, theater/drama. *Special achievements/activities:* 92 awards ($110,216 total): cheerleading/drum major, community service, general special achievements/activities, leadership. *Tuition waivers:* Full or partial for employees or children of employees, senior citizens.
LOANS *Student loans:* $25,871,943 (44% need-based, 56% non-need-based). 64% of past graduating class borrowed through all loan programs. *Average indebtedness per student:* $21,538. *Average need-based loan:* Freshmen: $3214. Undergraduates: $3993. *Parent loans:* $831,169 (100% non-need-based). *Programs:* Federal Direct (Subsidized and Unsubsidized Stafford, PLUS), Perkins, state, college/university.
WORK-STUDY *Federal work-study:* Total amount: $295,743; 76 jobs averaging $1996.
ATHLETIC AWARDS Total amount: $884,568 (100% non-need-based).
APPLYING FOR FINANCIAL AID *Required financial aid form:* FAFSA. *Financial aid deadline (priority):* 5/1. *Notification date:* Continuous beginning 5/1.
CONTACT Ms. Janis Bowles, Director of Financial Aid, Columbus State University, 4225 University Avenue, Columbus, GA 31907-5645, 706-507-8800 or toll-free 866-264-2035. *Fax:* 706-568-2230. *E-mail:* bowles_janis@colstate.edu.

CONCEPTION SEMINARY COLLEGE
Conception, MO

CONTACT Br. Justin Hernandez, PhD, Financial Aid Director, Conception Seminary College, PO Box 502, Conception, MO 64433-0502, 660-944-2851. *Fax:* 660-944-2829. *E-mail:* justin@conception.edu.

CONCORDIA COLLEGE
Selma, AL

ABOUT THE INSTITUTION Independent Lutheran, coed. *Awards:* associate and bachelor's degrees. 4 undergraduate majors. *Total enrollment:* 555. Undergraduates: 555.
GIFT AID (NEED-BASED) *Scholarships, grants, and awards:* Federal Pell, FSEOG, state, private, college/university gift aid from institutional funds.
GIFT AID (NON-NEED-BASED) *Scholarships, grants, and awards by category: Academic interests/achievement:* business, computer science, education, general academic interests/achievements, religion/biblical studies. *Creative arts/performance:* music. *Special achievements/activities:* cheerleading/drum major.
LOANS *Programs:* FFEL (Subsidized Stafford).
WORK-STUDY *Federal work-study:* Total amount: $60,947; 86 jobs averaging $600. *State or other work-study/employment:* Part-time jobs available.
APPLYING FOR FINANCIAL AID *Required financial aid forms:* FAFSA, institution's own form, state aid form.
CONTACT Mrs. T. H. Bridges, Financial Aid Office, Concordia College, 1804 Green Street, Selma, AL 36701, 334-874-5700. *Fax:* 334-874-3728. *E-mail:* tbridges@concordiaselma.edu.

CONCORDIA COLLEGE
Moorhead, MN

Tuition & fees: $27,160	Average undergraduate aid package: $18,090

ABOUT THE INSTITUTION Independent religious, coed. 77 undergraduate majors. Federal methodology is used as a basis for awarding need-based institutional aid.
UNDERGRADUATE EXPENSES for 2010–11 *Comprehensive fee:* $33,670 includes full-time tuition ($26,950), mandatory fees ($210), and room and board ($6510). *College room only:* $2890. Full-time tuition and fees vary according to course load and degree level. Room and board charges vary according to board plan and housing facility. *Part-time tuition:* $1060 per credit hour. *Part-time fees:* $105 per term. Part-time tuition and fees vary according to course load and degree level. *Payment plan:* Installment.
FRESHMAN FINANCIAL AID (Fall 2009, est.) 674 applied for aid; of those 83% were deemed to have need. 100% of freshmen with need received aid; of those 28% had need fully met. *Average percent of need met:* 88% (excluding

resources awarded to replace EFC). *Average financial aid package:* $18,599 (excluding resources awarded to replace EFC). 26% of all full-time freshmen had no need and received non-need-based gift aid.

UNDERGRADUATE FINANCIAL AID (Fall 2009, est.) 2,310 applied for aid; of those 84% were deemed to have need. 100% of undergraduates with need received aid; of those 24% had need fully met. *Average percent of need met:* 83% (excluding resources awarded to replace EFC). *Average financial aid package:* $18,090 (excluding resources awarded to replace EFC). 27% of all full-time undergraduates had no need and received non-need-based gift aid.

GIFT AID (NEED-BASED) *Total amount:* $24,894,909 (11% federal, 11% state, 70% institutional, 8% external sources). *Receiving aid:* Freshmen: 73% (556); all full-time undergraduates: 69% (1,932). *Average award:* Freshmen: $14,140; Undergraduates: $12,808. *Scholarships, grants, and awards:* Federal Pell, FSEOG, state, private, college/university gift aid from institutional funds.

GIFT AID (NON-NEED-BASED) *Total amount:* $9,061,931 (1% federal, 80% institutional, 19% external sources). *Receiving aid:* Freshmen: 12% (94). Undergraduates: 9% (262). *Average award:* Freshmen: $9075. Undergraduates: $8580. *Scholarships, grants, and awards by category: Academic interests/ achievement:* 2,402 awards ($16,719,401 total): general academic interests/ achievements. *Creative arts/performance:* 241 awards ($509,386 total): art/fine arts, debating, music, theater/drama. *Special characteristics:* 200 awards ($3,220,792 total): children of faculty/staff, international students. *Tuition waivers:* Full or partial for minority students, employees or children of employees.

LOANS *Student loans:* $20,286,440 (57% need-based, 43% non-need-based). 87% of past graduating class borrowed through all loan programs. *Average indebtedness per student:* $29,885. *Average need-based loan:* Freshmen: $3791. Undergraduates: $4492. *Parent loans:* $2,979,048 (18% need-based, 82% non-need-based). *Programs:* Federal Direct (Subsidized and Unsubsidized Stafford, PLUS), Perkins, state, college/university, private loans.

WORK-STUDY *Federal work-study:* Total amount: $1,172,040; 691 jobs averaging $1684. *State or other work-study/employment:* Total amount: $3,740,591 (41% need-based, 59% non-need-based). 2,059 part-time jobs averaging $1689.

APPLYING FOR FINANCIAL AID *Required financial aid form:* FAFSA. *Financial aid deadline:* Continuous. *Notification date:* Continuous beginning 3/1.

CONTACT Mrs. Jane Williams, Financial Aid Director, Concordia College, 901 South 8th Street, Moorhead, MN 56562, 218-299-3010 or toll-free 800-699-9897. *Fax:* 218-299-3025. *E-mail:* jwilliam@cord.edu.

CONCORDIA COLLEGE–NEW YORK
Bronxville, NY

ABOUT THE INSTITUTION Independent Lutheran, coed. *Awards:* associate and bachelor's degrees. 21 undergraduate majors. *Total enrollment:* 748. Undergraduates: 748. Freshmen: 128.

GIFT AID (NEED-BASED) *Scholarships, grants, and awards:* Federal Pell, FSEOG, state, college/university gift aid from institutional funds.

GIFT AID (NON-NEED-BASED) *Scholarships, grants, and awards by category: Academic interests/achievement:* education, general academic interests/ achievements, religion/biblical studies, social sciences. *Creative arts/performance:* music. *Special achievements/activities:* community service. *Special characteristics:* children of faculty/staff, relatives of clergy, religious affiliation.

LOANS *Programs:* Federal Direct (Subsidized and Unsubsidized Stafford, PLUS), FFEL (Subsidized and Unsubsidized Stafford, PLUS).

WORK-STUDY *Federal work-study:* Total amount: $39,398; jobs available.

APPLYING FOR FINANCIAL AID *Required financial aid form:* FAFSA.

CONTACT Janice Spikereit, Director of Financial Aid, Concordia College–New York, 171 White Plains Road, Bronxville, NY 10708, 914-337-9300 Ext. 2146 or toll-free 800-YES-COLLEGE. *Fax:* 914-395-4500. *E-mail:* financialaid@concordia-ny.edu.

CONCORDIA UNIVERSITY
Irvine, CA

Tuition & fees: $26,000	Average undergraduate aid package: $24,529

ABOUT THE INSTITUTION Independent religious, coed. 27 undergraduate majors. Federal methodology is used as a basis for awarding need-based institutional aid.

UNDERGRADUATE EXPENSES for 2010–11 *Comprehensive fee:* $34,380 includes full-time tuition ($25,400), mandatory fees ($600), and room and board ($8380). *College room only:* $4800. Full-time tuition and fees vary according to course load. Room and board charges vary according to board plan and housing facility. *Part-time tuition:* $775 per semester hour. Part-time tuition and fees vary according to course load. *Payment plan:* Installment.

FRESHMAN FINANCIAL AID (Fall 2009, est.) 267 applied for aid; of those 79% were deemed to have need. 100% of freshmen with need received aid; of those 19% had need fully met. *Average percent of need met:* 67% (excluding resources awarded to replace EFC). *Average financial aid package:* $25,589 (excluding resources awarded to replace EFC). 22% of all full-time freshmen had no need and received non-need-based gift aid.

UNDERGRADUATE FINANCIAL AID (Fall 2009, est.) 1,160 applied for aid; of those 78% were deemed to have need. 100% of undergraduates with need received aid; of those 19% had need fully met. *Average percent of need met:* 62% (excluding resources awarded to replace EFC). *Average financial aid package:* $24,529 (excluding resources awarded to replace EFC). 20% of all full-time undergraduates had no need and received non-need-based gift aid.

GIFT AID (NEED-BASED) *Total amount:* $9,465,393 (15% federal, 22% state, 63% institutional). *Receiving aid:* Freshmen: 66% (197); all full-time undergraduates: 57% (760). *Average award:* Freshmen: $13,074; Undergraduates: $12,705. *Scholarships, grants, and awards:* Federal Pell, FSEOG, state, private, college/university gift aid from institutional funds.

GIFT AID (NON-NEED-BASED) *Total amount:* $2,325,808 (100% institutional). *Receiving aid:* Freshmen: 9% (28). Undergraduates: 7% (93). *Average award:* Freshmen: $6894. Undergraduates: $7043. *Scholarships, grants, and awards by category: Academic interests/achievement:* 808 awards ($4,529,626 total): general academic interests/achievements. *Creative arts/performance:* 150 awards ($396,800 total): applied art and design, debating, music, theater/drama. *Special characteristics:* 243 awards ($1,274,857 total): children of faculty/staff, first-generation college students, religious affiliation, siblings of current students. *Tuition waivers:* Full or partial for employees or children of employees.

LOANS *Student loans:* $8,883,188 (33% need-based, 67% non-need-based). 67% of past graduating class borrowed through all loan programs. *Average indebtedness per student:* $23,113. *Average need-based loan:* Freshmen: $3355. Undergraduates: $4382. *Parent loans:* $2,874,246 (100% non-need-based). *Programs:* Federal Direct (Subsidized and Unsubsidized Stafford, PLUS), FFEL (Subsidized and Unsubsidized Stafford, PLUS), alternative loans.

WORK-STUDY *Federal work-study:* Total amount: $92,500; 41 jobs averaging $2250. *State or other work-study/employment:* Total amount: $56,248 (100% need-based). 30 part-time jobs averaging $1875.

ATHLETIC AWARDS Total amount: $4,086,845 (50% need-based, 50% non-need-based).

APPLYING FOR FINANCIAL AID *Required financial aid forms:* FAFSA, state aid form. *Financial aid deadline:* 2/1. *Notification date:* Continuous beginning 2/15. Students must reply within 4 weeks of notification.

CONTACT Lori McDonald, Director of Financial Aid, Concordia University, 1530 Concordia West, Irvine, CA 92612-3299, 949-854-8002 Ext. 1170 or toll-free 800-229-1200. *Fax:* 949-854-6709. *E-mail:* lori.mcdonald@cui.edu.

CONCORDIA UNIVERSITY
Ann Arbor, MI

Tuition & fees: $20,390	Average undergraduate aid package: $15,916

ABOUT THE INSTITUTION Independent religious, coed. *Awards:* associate, bachelor's, and master's degrees and post-bachelor's certificates. 47 undergraduate majors. *Total enrollment:* 1,075. Undergraduates: 521. Freshmen: 94. Federal methodology is used as a basis for awarding need-based institutional aid.

UNDERGRADUATE EXPENSES for 2009–10 *Application fee:* $25. *One-time required fee:* $125. *Comprehensive fee:* $27,996 includes full-time tuition ($20,390) and room and board ($7606). Full-time tuition and fees vary according to location and program. Room and board charges vary according to housing facility. *Part-time tuition:* $673 per credit hour. Part-time tuition and fees vary according to course load, location, and program. *Payment plan:* Installment.

FRESHMAN FINANCIAL AID (Fall 2008) 97 applied for aid; of those 86% were deemed to have need. 99% of freshmen with need received aid; of those 24% had need fully met. *Average percent of need met:* 83% (excluding resources awarded to replace EFC). *Average financial aid package:* $17,664 (excluding resources awarded to replace EFC). 20% of all full-time freshmen had no need and received non-need-based gift aid.

UNDERGRADUATE FINANCIAL AID (Fall 2008) 392 applied for aid; of those 88% were deemed to have need. 99% of undergraduates with need received aid; of those 27% had need fully met. *Average percent of need met:* 82% (excluding resources awarded to replace EFC). *Average financial aid package:* $15,916 (excluding resources awarded to replace EFC). 16% of all full-time undergraduates had no need and received non-need-based gift aid.

GIFT AID (NEED-BASED) *Total amount:* $3,270,105 (16% federal, 12% state, 62% institutional, 10% external sources). *Receiving aid:* Freshmen: 68% (82); all full-time undergraduates: 77% (338). *Average award:* Freshmen: $13,223; Undergraduates: $11,436. *Scholarships, grants, and awards:* Federal Pell, FSEOG, state, private, college/university gift aid from institutional funds.

GIFT AID (NON-NEED-BASED) *Total amount:* $640,317 (4% state, 76% institutional, 20% external sources). *Receiving aid:* Freshmen: 9% (11). Undergraduates: 13% (58). *Average award:* Freshmen: $5474. Undergraduates: $5417. *Scholarships, grants, and awards by category: Academic interests/achievement:* 324 awards ($980,525 total): business, education, general academic interests/achievements, religion/biblical studies. *Creative arts/performance:* 90 awards ($244,836 total): art/fine arts, music, performing arts, theater/drama. *Special characteristics:* 221 awards ($491,590 total): children and siblings of alumni, children of faculty/staff, ethnic background, general special characteristics, out-of-state students, religious affiliation, siblings of current students. *Tuition waivers:* Full or partial for employees or children of employees. *ROTC:* Army cooperative, Air Force cooperative.

LOANS *Student loans:* $2,928,772 (67% need-based, 33% non-need-based). 69% of past graduating class borrowed through all loan programs. *Average indebtedness per student:* $25,789. *Average need-based loan:* Freshmen: $4941. Undergraduates: $5818. *Parent loans:* $503,887 (26% need-based, 74% non-need-based). *Programs:* Federal Direct (Subsidized and Unsubsidized Stafford, PLUS), FFEL (Subsidized and Unsubsidized Stafford, PLUS), Perkins.

WORK-STUDY *Federal work-study:* Total amount: $51,306; 55 jobs averaging $1393. *State or other work-study/employment:* Total amount: $106,161 (35% need-based, 65% non-need-based). 5 part-time jobs averaging $1362.

ATHLETIC AWARDS Total amount: $861,711 (59% need-based, 41% non-need-based).

APPLYING FOR FINANCIAL AID *Required financial aid form:* FAFSA. *Financial aid deadline:* Continuous. *Notification date:* Continuous beginning 3/1. Students must reply by 5/1 or within 4 weeks of notification.

CONTACT Karen Neuendorf, Financial Aid Office, Concordia University, 4090 Geddes Road, Ann Arbor, MI 48105-2797, 734-995-7439 or toll-free 800-253-0680. *Fax:* 734-995-4610. *E-mail:* acosta@cuaa.edu.

CONCORDIA UNIVERSITY
Portland, OR

ABOUT THE INSTITUTION Independent religious, coed. *Awards:* associate, bachelor's, and master's degrees and post-bachelor's certificates. 32 undergraduate majors. *Total enrollment:* 1,709. Undergraduates: 1,065. Freshmen: 164.

GIFT AID (NEED-BASED) *Scholarships, grants, and awards:* Federal Pell, FSEOG, state, private, college/university gift aid from institutional funds.

GIFT AID (NON-NEED-BASED) *Scholarships, grants, and awards by category: Academic interests/achievement:* general academic interests/achievements, religion/biblical studies. *Creative arts/performance:* music. *Special achievements/activities:* leadership, religious involvement. *Special characteristics:* children of faculty/staff, relatives of clergy, religious affiliation.

LOANS *Programs:* FFEL (Subsidized and Unsubsidized Stafford, PLUS), Perkins, alternative loans.

APPLYING FOR FINANCIAL AID *Required financial aid form:* FAFSA.

CONTACT Mr. James W. Cullen, Director of Financial Aid, Concordia University, 2811 Northeast Holman Street, Portland, OR 97211-6099, 503-493-6508 or toll-free 800-321-9371. *Fax:* 503-280-8661. *E-mail:* jcullen@cu-portland.edu.

CONCORDIA UNIVERSITY CHICAGO
River Forest, IL

Tuition & fees: $24,581	Average undergraduate aid package: $21,338

ABOUT THE INSTITUTION Independent religious, coed. 54 undergraduate majors. Federal methodology is used as a basis for awarding need-based institutional aid.

UNDERGRADUATE EXPENSES for 2010–11 *Comprehensive fee:* $32,581 includes full-time tuition ($23,918), mandatory fees ($663), and room and board ($8000). Full-time tuition and fees vary according to program. *Part-time tuition:* $747 per semester hour. Part-time tuition and fees vary according to program. *Payment plan:* Installment.

FRESHMAN FINANCIAL AID (Fall 2009, est.) 235 applied for aid; of those 87% were deemed to have need. 100% of freshmen with need received aid; of those 22% had need fully met. *Average percent of need met:* 77% (excluding resources awarded to replace EFC). *Average financial aid package:* $21,902 (excluding resources awarded to replace EFC). 18% of all full-time freshmen had no need and received non-need-based gift aid.

UNDERGRADUATE FINANCIAL AID (Fall 2009, est.) 931 applied for aid; of those 87% were deemed to have need. 100% of undergraduates with need received aid; of those 26% had need fully met. *Average percent of need met:* 76% (excluding resources awarded to replace EFC). *Average financial aid package:* $21,338 (excluding resources awarded to replace EFC). 19% of all full-time undergraduates had no need and received non-need-based gift aid.

GIFT AID (NEED-BASED) *Total amount:* $9,090,062 (14% federal, 15% state, 71% institutional). *Receiving aid:* Freshmen: 82% (203); all full-time undergraduates: 77% (786). *Average award:* Freshmen: $13,670; Undergraduates: $11,506. *Scholarships, grants, and awards:* Federal Pell, FSEOG, state, private, college/university gift aid from institutional funds.

GIFT AID (NON-NEED-BASED) *Total amount:* $2,426,422 (100% institutional). *Receiving aid:* Freshmen: 15% (37). Undergraduates: 17% (171). *Average award:* Freshmen: $9634. Undergraduates: $9037. *Scholarships, grants, and awards by category: Academic interests/achievement:* biological sciences, business, communication, computer science, education, English, foreign languages, general academic interests/achievements, mathematics, religion/biblical studies. *Creative arts/performance:* art/fine arts, music. *Special characteristics:* children and siblings of alumni, children of faculty/staff, international students, religious affiliation. *Tuition waivers:* Full or partial for minority students, children of alumni, employees or children of employees, senior citizens.

LOANS *Student loans:* $6,897,917 (39% need-based, 61% non-need-based). 82% of past graduating class borrowed through all loan programs. *Average indebtedness per student:* $21,086. *Average need-based loan:* Freshmen: $3644. Undergraduates: $4189. *Parent loans:* $795,405 (100% non-need-based). *Programs:* FFEL (Subsidized and Unsubsidized Stafford, PLUS), Perkins.

WORK-STUDY *Federal work-study:* Total amount: $333,072; 89 jobs averaging $1593. *State or other work-study/employment:* Total amount: $408,371 (100% non-need-based). 351 part-time jobs averaging $1710.

APPLYING FOR FINANCIAL AID *Required financial aid form:* FAFSA. *Financial aid deadline:* 8/15 (priority: 4/1). *Notification date:* Continuous. Students must reply within 4 weeks of notification.

CONTACT Aida Asencio-Pinto, Director of Student Financial Planning, Concordia University Chicago, 7400 Augusta Street, River Forest, IL 60305-1499, 708-209-3113 or toll-free 800-285-2668. *Fax:* 708-209-3176. *E-mail:* patricia.williamson@cuchicago.edu.

CONCORDIA UNIVERSITY, NEBRASKA
Seward, NE

Tuition & fees: $22,115	Average undergraduate aid package: $17,208

ABOUT THE INSTITUTION Independent religious, coed. 73 undergraduate majors. Federal methodology is used as a basis for awarding need-based institutional aid.

UNDERGRADUATE EXPENSES for 2010–11 *Comprehensive fee:* $27,935 includes full-time tuition ($21,940), mandatory fees ($175), and room and board ($5820). *College room only:* $2470. Room and board charges vary according to board plan and housing facility. *Part-time tuition:* $685 per credit hour. *Payment plan:* Installment.

FRESHMAN FINANCIAL AID (Fall 2009, est.) 268 applied for aid; of those 84% were deemed to have need. 100% of freshmen with need received aid; of those 31% had need fully met. *Average percent of need met:* 79% (excluding resources awarded to replace EFC). *Average financial aid package:* $17,983 (excluding resources awarded to replace EFC). 11% of all full-time freshmen had no need and received non-need-based gift aid.

UNDERGRADUATE FINANCIAL AID (Fall 2009, est.) 962 applied for aid; of those 85% were deemed to have need. 100% of undergraduates with need received aid; of those 29% had need fully met. *Average percent of need met:* 79% (excluding resources awarded to replace EFC). *Average financial aid*

package: $17,208 (excluding resources awarded to replace EFC). 11% of all full-time undergraduates had no need and received non-need-based gift aid.

GIFT AID (NEED-BASED) *Total amount:* $9,417,903 (18% federal, 1% state, 66% institutional, 15% external sources). *Receiving aid:* Freshmen: 77% (223); all full-time undergraduates: 77% (816). *Average award:* Freshmen: $14,260; Undergraduates: $13,086. *Scholarships, grants, and awards:* Federal Pell, FSEOG, state, private, college/university gift aid from institutional funds.

GIFT AID (NON-NEED-BASED) *Total amount:* $2,509,056 (100% institutional). *Receiving aid:* Freshmen: 19% (54). Undergraduates: 13% (142). *Average award:* Freshmen: $10,225. Undergraduates: $8914. *Scholarships, grants, and awards by category: Academic interests/achievement:* biological sciences, business, communication, computer science, education, English, general academic interests/achievements, health fields, humanities, mathematics, physical sciences, premedicine, religion/biblical studies, social sciences. *Creative arts/performance:* applied art and design, art/fine arts, dance, debating, music, theater/drama. *Special characteristics:* children and siblings of alumni, children of educators, children of faculty/staff, international students, local/state students, members of minority groups, religious affiliation, veterans, veterans' children. *Tuition waivers:* Full or partial for employees or children of employees.

LOANS *Student loans:* $5,809,594 (44% need-based, 56% non-need-based). 79% of past graduating class borrowed through all loan programs. *Average indebtedness per student:* $21,941. *Average need-based loan:* Freshmen: $3659. Undergraduates: $4374. *Parent loans:* $2,122,978 (100% non-need-based). *Programs:* Federal Direct (Subsidized and Unsubsidized Stafford, PLUS), Perkins.

WORK-STUDY *Federal work-study:* Total amount: $111,326; 116 jobs averaging $960.

ATHLETIC AWARDS Total amount: $2,023,245 (76% need-based, 24% non-need-based).

APPLYING FOR FINANCIAL AID *Required financial aid form:* FAFSA. *Financial aid deadline (priority):* 3/1. *Notification date:* Continuous beginning 3/1. Students must reply within 4 weeks of notification.

CONTACT Mr. Aaron W. Roberts, Director of Undergraduate Recruitment, Concordia University, Nebraska, 800 North Columbia Avenue, Seward, NE 68434-1556, 800-535-5494. *Fax:* 402-643-4073. *E-mail:* admiss@cune.edu.

CONCORDIA UNIVERSITY, ST. PAUL
St. Paul, MN

Tuition & fees: $27,400	Average undergraduate aid package: $17,022

ABOUT THE INSTITUTION Independent religious, coed. 41 undergraduate majors. Federal methodology is used as a basis for awarding need-based institutional aid.

UNDERGRADUATE EXPENSES for 2010–11 *Comprehensive fee:* $34,900 includes full-time tuition ($27,400) and room and board ($7500). Full-time tuition and fees vary according to program. Room and board charges vary according to housing facility. *Part-time tuition:* $580 per credit. Part-time tuition and fees vary according to course load and program. *Payment plan:* Installment.

FRESHMAN FINANCIAL AID (Fall 2009, est.) 183 applied for aid; of those 89% were deemed to have need. 100% of freshmen with need received aid; of those 18% had need fully met. *Average percent of need met:* 80% (excluding resources awarded to replace EFC). *Average financial aid package:* $21,176 (excluding resources awarded to replace EFC). 11% of all full-time freshmen had no need and received non-need-based gift aid.

UNDERGRADUATE FINANCIAL AID (Fall 2009, est.) 1,125 applied for aid; of those 84% were deemed to have need. 100% of undergraduates with need received aid; of those 14% had need fully met. *Average percent of need met:* 67% (excluding resources awarded to replace EFC). *Average financial aid package:* $17,022 (excluding resources awarded to replace EFC). 9% of all full-time undergraduates had no need and received non-need-based gift aid.

GIFT AID (NEED-BASED) *Total amount:* $10,514,022 (24% federal, 17% state, 56% institutional, 3% external sources). *Receiving aid:* Freshmen: 88% (161); all full-time undergraduates: 61% (821). *Average award:* Freshmen: $16,705; Undergraduates: $13,962. *Scholarships, grants, and awards:* Federal Pell, FSEOG, state, private, college/university gift aid from institutional funds.

GIFT AID (NON-NEED-BASED) *Total amount:* $1,098,076 (15% federal, 2% state, 77% institutional, 6% external sources). *Average award:* Freshmen: $8462. Undergraduates: $6867. *Scholarships, grants, and awards by category: Academic interests/achievement:* 889 awards ($4,196,120 total): general academic interests/achievements, mathematics, physical sciences, religion/biblical studies.

Creative arts/performance: 93 awards ($139,750 total): art/fine arts, music, theater/drama. *Special characteristics:* 222 awards ($421,428 total): children of faculty/staff, religious affiliation, veterans, veterans' children. *Tuition waivers:* Full or partial for employees or children of employees.

LOANS *Student loans:* $9,631,715 (90% need-based, 10% non-need-based). 85% of past graduating class borrowed through all loan programs. *Average indebtedness per student:* $32,444. *Average need-based loan:* Freshmen: $4320. Undergraduates: $4888. *Parent loans:* $1,193,382 (86% need-based, 14% non-need-based). *Programs:* FFEL (Subsidized and Unsubsidized Stafford, PLUS), Perkins, state, college/university, private alternative loans.

WORK-STUDY *Federal work-study:* Total amount: $270,502; 122 jobs averaging $2217. *State or other work-study/employment:* Total amount: $785,369 (99% need-based, 1% non-need-based). 352 part-time jobs averaging $2231.

ATHLETIC AWARDS Total amount: $2,127,795 (82% need-based, 18% non-need-based).

APPLYING FOR FINANCIAL AID *Required financial aid form:* FAFSA. *Financial aid deadline (priority):* 5/1. *Notification date:* Continuous.

CONTACT Carolyn Chesebrough, Financial Aid Director, Concordia University, St. Paul, 275 North Syndicate Street, St. Paul, MN 55104-5494, 651-603-6300 or toll-free 800-333-4705. *Fax:* 651-603-6298. *E-mail:* bearcenter@csp.edu.

CONCORDIA UNIVERSITY TEXAS
Austin, TX

Tuition & fees: $21,200	Average undergraduate aid package: $17,507

ABOUT THE INSTITUTION Independent religious, coed. 21 undergraduate majors. Federal methodology is used as a basis for awarding need-based institutional aid.

UNDERGRADUATE EXPENSES for 2009–10 *Comprehensive fee:* $29,200 includes full-time tuition ($20,800), mandatory fees ($400), and room and board ($8000). *College room only:* $4700. Full-time tuition and fees vary according to course load, degree level, location, and program. Room and board charges vary according to board plan. *Part-time tuition:* $700 per hour. *Part-time fees:* $18 per credit hour; $200 per term. Part-time tuition and fees vary according to course load, degree level, location, and program. *Payment plan:* Installment.

FRESHMAN FINANCIAL AID (Fall 2008) 60 applied for aid; of those 78% were deemed to have need. 96% of freshmen with need received aid; of those 56% had need fully met. *Average percent of need met:* 89% (excluding resources awarded to replace EFC). *Average financial aid package:* $20,298 (excluding resources awarded to replace EFC). 9% of all full-time freshmen had no need and received non-need-based gift aid.

UNDERGRADUATE FINANCIAL AID (Fall 2008) 210 applied for aid; of those 74% were deemed to have need. 97% of undergraduates with need received aid; of those 63% had need fully met. *Average percent of need met:* 90% (excluding resources awarded to replace EFC). *Average financial aid package:* $17,507 (excluding resources awarded to replace EFC). 7% of all full-time undergraduates had no need and received non-need-based gift aid.

GIFT AID (NEED-BASED) *Total amount:* $4,137,834 (27% federal, 37% state, 14% institutional, 22% external sources). *Receiving aid:* Freshmen: 25% (35); all full-time undergraduates: 19% (117). *Average award:* Freshmen: $11,481; Undergraduates: $9126. *Scholarships, grants, and awards:* Federal Pell, FSEOG, state, private, college/university gift aid from institutional funds.

GIFT AID (NON-NEED-BASED) *Total amount:* $3,787,627 (100% institutional). *Receiving aid:* Freshmen: 20% (27). Undergraduates: 13% (82). *Average award:* Freshmen: $7512. Undergraduates: $6936. *Scholarships, grants, and awards by category: Academic interests/achievement:* 350 awards ($2,821,289 total): biological sciences, business, computer science, education, foreign languages, general academic interests/achievements, health fields, international studies, mathematics, physical sciences, religion/biblical studies, social sciences. *Creative arts/performance:* 8 awards ($23,900 total): music. *Special achievements/activities:* 100 awards ($679,575 total): junior miss, leadership, religious involvement. *Special characteristics:* 21 awards ($144,910 total): adult students, children and siblings of alumni, children of faculty/staff, religious affiliation, veterans, veterans' children. *Tuition waivers:* Full or partial for employees or children of employees.

LOANS *Student loans:* $7,363,332 (33% need-based, 67% non-need-based). 66% of past graduating class borrowed through all loan programs. *Average indebtedness per student:* $22,095. *Average need-based loan:* Freshmen: $8926.

Undergraduates: $8900. *Parent loans:* $657,438 (100% non-need-based). *Programs:* Federal Direct (Subsidized and Unsubsidized Stafford, PLUS), FFEL (Subsidized and Unsubsidized Stafford, PLUS), state.

WORK-STUDY *Federal work-study:* Total amount: $102,067; 77 jobs averaging $1326. *State or other work-study/employment:* Total amount: $12,655 (100% need-based). 4 part-time jobs averaging $3164.

APPLYING FOR FINANCIAL AID *Required financial aid forms:* FAFSA, institution's own form. *Financial aid deadline:* Continuous. *Notification date:* Continuous beginning 2/15. Students must reply within 2 weeks of notification.

CONTACT Mrs. Cathy L. Schryer, Director of Student Financial Services, Concordia University Texas, 11400 Concordia University Drive, Austin, TX 78726, 512-313-4671 or toll-free 800-865-4282. *Fax:* 888-828-5120. *E-mail:* cathy.schryer@concordia.edu.

CONCORDIA UNIVERSITY WISCONSIN
Mequon, WI

Tuition & fees: $20,996	Average undergraduate aid package: $21,364

ABOUT THE INSTITUTION Independent religious, coed. 62 undergraduate majors. Federal methodology is used as a basis for awarding need-based institutional aid.

UNDERGRADUATE EXPENSES for 2009–10 *Comprehensive fee:* $28,986 includes full-time tuition ($20,896), mandatory fees ($100), and room and board ($7990). Full-time tuition and fees vary according to program. Room and board charges vary according to board plan. *Part-time tuition:* $870 per credit hour. Part-time tuition and fees vary according to program. *Payment plans:* Guaranteed tuition, installment, deferred payment.

FRESHMAN FINANCIAL AID (Fall 2009, est.) 444 applied for aid; of those 85% were deemed to have need. 100% of freshmen with need received aid; of those 30% had need fully met. *Average percent of need met:* 77% (excluding resources awarded to replace EFC). *Average financial aid package:* $22,911 (excluding resources awarded to replace EFC). 18% of all full-time freshmen had no need and received non-need-based gift aid.

UNDERGRADUATE FINANCIAL AID (Fall 2009, est.) 1,879 applied for aid; of those 87% were deemed to have need. 100% of undergraduates with need received aid; of those 29% had need fully met. *Average percent of need met:* 73% (excluding resources awarded to replace EFC). *Average financial aid package:* $21,364 (excluding resources awarded to replace EFC). 15% of all full-time undergraduates had no need and received non-need-based gift aid.

GIFT AID (NEED-BASED) *Total amount:* $18,966,048 (26% federal, 8% state, 60% institutional, 6% external sources). *Receiving aid:* Freshmen: 78% (359); all full-time undergraduates: 75% (1,513). *Average award:* Freshmen: $12,889; Undergraduates: $10,948. *Scholarships, grants, and awards:* Federal Pell, FSEOG, state, private, college/university gift aid from institutional funds.

GIFT AID (NON-NEED-BASED) *Total amount:* $4,958,053 (100% institutional). *Receiving aid:* Freshmen: 24% (111). Undergraduates: 22% (439). *Average award:* Freshmen: $9716. Undergraduates: $8303. *Scholarships, grants, and awards by category:* Academic interests/achievement: 346 awards ($4,256,153 total): religion/biblical studies. Creative arts/performance: 60 awards ($76,000 total): music. Special characteristics: 242 awards ($240,275 total): out-of-state students. *Tuition waivers:* Full or partial for employees or children of employees.

LOANS *Student loans:* $23,822,216 (54% need-based, 46% non-need-based). 75% of past graduating class borrowed through all loan programs. *Average indebtedness per student:* $25,169. *Average need-based loan:* Freshmen: $4855. Undergraduates: $5939. *Parent loans:* $2,439,142 (100% non-need-based). *Programs:* Federal Direct (Subsidized and Unsubsidized Stafford, PLUS), state.

WORK-STUDY *Federal work-study:* Total amount: $590,896; 223 jobs averaging $1731.

APPLYING FOR FINANCIAL AID *Required financial aid form:* FAFSA. *Financial aid deadline (priority):* 4/1. *Notification date:* Continuous beginning 2/1. Students must reply within 3 weeks of notification.

CONTACT Mr. Steven P. Taylor, Director of Financial Aid, Concordia University Wisconsin, 12800 North Lake Shore Drive, Mequon, WI 53097-2402, 262-243-4392 or toll-free 888-628-9472. *Fax:* 262-243-2992. *E-mail:* steve.taylor@cuw.edu.

CONCORD UNIVERSITY
Athens, WV

Tuition & fees (WV res): $4974	Average undergraduate aid package: $9562

ABOUT THE INSTITUTION State-supported, coed. 36 undergraduate majors. Federal methodology is used as a basis for awarding need-based institutional aid.

UNDERGRADUATE EXPENSES for 2010–11 *Tuition, state resident:* full-time $4974; part-time $207 per credit hour. *Tuition, nonresident:* full-time $11,050; part-time $460 per credit hour. Full-time tuition and fees vary according to course load. Part-time tuition and fees vary according to course load. *College room and board:* $6766; *Room only:* $3446. *Payment plan:* Installment.

FRESHMAN FINANCIAL AID (Fall 2009, est.) 556 applied for aid; of those 73% were deemed to have need. 100% of freshmen with need received aid; of those 40% had need fully met. *Average percent of need met:* 100% (excluding resources awarded to replace EFC). *Average financial aid package:* $9823 (excluding resources awarded to replace EFC). 20% of all full-time freshmen had no need and received non-need-based gift aid.

UNDERGRADUATE FINANCIAL AID (Fall 2009, est.) 2,081 applied for aid; of those 78% were deemed to have need. 100% of undergraduates with need received aid; of those 39% had need fully met. *Average percent of need met:* 99% (excluding resources awarded to replace EFC). *Average financial aid package:* $9562 (excluding resources awarded to replace EFC). 8% of all full-time undergraduates had no need and received non-need-based gift aid.

GIFT AID (NEED-BASED) *Total amount:* $7,028,309 (73% federal, 27% state). *Receiving aid:* Freshmen: 54% (325); all full-time undergraduates: 55% (1,292). *Average award:* Freshmen: $5453; Undergraduates: $5604. *Scholarships, grants, and awards:* Federal Pell, FSEOG, state, college/university gift aid from institutional funds.

GIFT AID (NON-NEED-BASED) *Total amount:* $4,609,725 (45% state, 43% institutional, 12% external sources). *Receiving aid:* Freshmen: 44% (267). Undergraduates: 28% (653). *Average award:* Freshmen: $1704. Undergraduates: $3345. *Scholarships, grants, and awards by category:* Academic interests/achievement: 715 awards ($1,339,360 total): business, communication, education, English, general academic interests/achievements, social sciences. Creative arts/performance: 28 awards ($64,327 total): art/fine arts, journalism/publications, music, theater/drama. Special achievements/activities: 222 awards ($75,375 total): community service, general special achievements/activities, leadership. *Tuition waivers:* Full or partial for employees or children of employees, adult students, senior citizens.

LOANS *Student loans:* $8,089,607 (96% need-based, 4% non-need-based). 87% of past graduating class borrowed through all loan programs. *Average indebtedness per student:* $14,210. *Average need-based loan:* Freshmen: $2754. Undergraduates: $3604. *Parent loans:* $526,923 (100% non-need-based). *Programs:* FFEL (Subsidized and Unsubsidized Stafford, PLUS), Perkins.

WORK-STUDY *Federal work-study:* Total amount: $625,888; 461 jobs averaging $1329. *State or other work-study/employment:* Total amount: $353,664 (100% non-need-based). 352 part-time jobs averaging $972.

ATHLETIC AWARDS Total amount: $1,173,405 (100% non-need-based).

APPLYING FOR FINANCIAL AID *Required financial aid forms:* FAFSA, institution's own form, verification worksheet. *Financial aid deadline (priority):* 4/15. *Notification date:* Continuous. Students must reply within 2 weeks of notification.

CONTACT Lisa Spencer, Concord University, PO Box 1000, Athens, WV 24712-1000, 304-384-6069 or toll-free 888-384-5249. *Fax:* 304-384-9044.

CONNECTICUT COLLEGE
New London, CT

Comprehensive fee: $51,115	Average undergraduate aid package: $31,101

ABOUT THE INSTITUTION Independent, coed. 52 undergraduate majors. Both federal and institutional methodology are used as a basis for awarding need-based institutional aid.

UNDERGRADUATE EXPENSES for 2009–10 *Comprehensive fee:* $51,115. *Part-time tuition:* $1186 per credit hour. *Payment plan:* Installment.

FRESHMAN FINANCIAL AID (Fall 2009, est.) 300 applied for aid; of those 80% were deemed to have need. 100% of freshmen with need received aid; of those

100% had need fully met. *Average percent of need met:* 100% (excluding resources awarded to replace EFC). *Average financial aid package:* $30,502 (excluding resources awarded to replace EFC).

UNDERGRADUATE FINANCIAL AID (Fall 2009, est.) 997 applied for aid; of those 86% were deemed to have need. 100% of undergraduates with need received aid; of those 100% had need fully met. *Average percent of need met:* 100% (excluding resources awarded to replace EFC). *Average financial aid package:* $31,101 (excluding resources awarded to replace EFC).

GIFT AID (NEED-BASED) *Total amount:* $23,440,332 (5% federal, 2% state, 89% institutional, 4% external sources). *Receiving aid:* Freshmen: 42% (214); all full-time undergraduates: 41% (777). *Average award:* Freshmen: $30,739; Undergraduates: $29,616. *Scholarships, grants, and awards:* Federal Pell, FSEOG, state, college/university gift aid from institutional funds.

GIFT AID (NON-NEED-BASED) *Total amount:* $441,790 (2% institutional, 98% external sources). *Tuition waivers:* Full or partial for employees or children of employees, senior citizens.

LOANS *Student loans:* $6,792,297 (46% need-based, 54% non-need-based). 34% of past graduating class borrowed through all loan programs. *Average indebtedness per student:* $22,038. *Average need-based loan:* Freshmen: $3022. Undergraduates: $4389. *Parent loans:* $4,269,219 (100% non-need-based). *Programs:* Federal Direct (Subsidized and Unsubsidized Stafford, PLUS), Perkins, college/university.

WORK-STUDY *Federal work-study:* Total amount: $984,468; 719 jobs averaging $1386. *State or other work-study/employment:* Total amount: $17,703 (100% need-based). 18 part-time jobs averaging $992.

APPLYING FOR FINANCIAL AID *Required financial aid forms:* FAFSA, CSS Financial Aid PROFILE, noncustodial (divorced/separated) parent's statement, business/farm supplement. *Financial aid deadline:* 2/1. *Notification date:* 4/1. Students must reply by 5/1 or within 2 weeks of notification.

CONTACT Ms. Elaine Solinga, Director of Financial Aid Services, Connecticut College, 270 Mohegan Avenue, New London, CT 06320-4196, 860-439-2058. *Fax:* 860-439-2159. *E-mail:* finaid@conncoll.edu.

CONSERVATORY OF MUSIC OF PUERTO RICO
San Juan, PR

CONTACT Mr. Jorge Medina, Director of Financial Aid, Conservatory of Music of Puerto Rico, 350 Rafael Lamar Street at FDR Avenue, San Juan, PR 00918, 787-751-0160 Ext. 230. *Fax:* 787-758-8268. *E-mail:* jmedina@cmpr.gobierno.pr.

CONVERSE COLLEGE
Spartanburg, SC

Tuition & fees: $26,138	Average undergraduate aid package: $22,193

ABOUT THE INSTITUTION Independent, undergraduate: women only; graduate: coed. 45 undergraduate majors. Federal methodology is used as a basis for awarding need-based institutional aid.

UNDERGRADUATE EXPENSES for 2010–11 *One-time required fee:* $100. *Comprehensive fee:* $34,170 includes full-time tuition ($26,138) and room and board ($8032). Full-time tuition and fees vary according to reciprocity agreements. Room and board charges vary according to housing facility. *Payment plan:* Installment.

FRESHMAN FINANCIAL AID (Fall 2009, est.) 156 applied for aid; of those 91% were deemed to have need. 100% of freshmen with need received aid; of those 30% had need fully met. *Average percent of need met:* 86% (excluding resources awarded to replace EFC). *Average financial aid package:* $23,261 (excluding resources awarded to replace EFC). 12% of all full-time freshmen had no need and received non-need-based gift aid.

UNDERGRADUATE FINANCIAL AID (Fall 2009, est.) 529 applied for aid; of those 92% were deemed to have need. 100% of undergraduates with need received aid; of those 30% had need fully met. *Average percent of need met:* 82% (excluding resources awarded to replace EFC). *Average financial aid package:* $22,193 (excluding resources awarded to replace EFC). 16% of all full-time undergraduates had no need and received non-need-based gift aid.

GIFT AID (NEED-BASED) *Total amount:* $8,717,569 (16% federal, 21% state, 61% institutional, 2% external sources). *Receiving aid:* Freshmen: 91% (142); all full-time undergraduates: 13% (78). *Average award:* Freshmen: $19,848;

Undergraduates: $18,754. *Scholarships, grants, and awards:* Federal Pell, FSEOG, state, private, college/university gift aid from institutional funds.

GIFT AID (NON-NEED-BASED) *Total amount:* $2,300,320 (33% state, 64% institutional, 3% external sources). *Receiving aid:* Freshmen: 22% (34). Undergraduates: 18% (106). *Average award:* Freshmen: $14,313. Undergraduates: $13,251. *Scholarships, grants, and awards by category:* Academic interests/achievement: 457 awards ($4,391,151 total): general academic interests/achievements. Creative arts/performance: 219 awards ($1,230,877 total): applied art and design, general creative arts/performance, music, theater/drama. Special achievements/activities: 31 awards ($215,600 total): leadership. Special characteristics: 52 awards ($73,860 total): children and siblings of alumni, children of faculty/staff. *Tuition waivers:* Full or partial for employees or children of employees, adult students.

LOANS *Student loans:* $4,579,427 (77% need-based, 23% non-need-based). 61% of past graduating class borrowed through all loan programs. *Average indebtedness per student:* $20,739. *Average need-based loan:* Freshmen: $4526. Undergraduates: $4989. *Parent loans:* $858,693 (24% need-based, 76% non-need-based). *Programs:* FFEL (Subsidized and Unsubsidized Stafford, PLUS), Perkins, state.

WORK-STUDY *Federal work-study:* Total amount: $156,720; 97 jobs averaging $1589. *State or other work-study/employment:* 60 part-time jobs averaging $1000.

ATHLETIC AWARDS Total amount: $604,850 (61% need-based, 39% non-need-based).

APPLYING FOR FINANCIAL AID *Required financial aid form:* FAFSA. *Financial aid deadline (priority):* 3/15. *Notification date:* Continuous beginning 3/15. Students must reply by 5/1 or within 2 weeks of notification.

CONTACT Ms. Margaret P. Collins, Director of Financial Assistance, Converse College, 580 East Main Street, Spartanburg, SC 29302-0006, 864-596-9019 or toll-free 800-766-1125. *Fax:* 864-596-9749. *E-mail:* peggy.collins@converse.edu.

COOPER UNION FOR THE ADVANCEMENT OF SCIENCE AND ART
New York, NY

Tuition & fees: $36,650	Average undergraduate aid package: $35,000

ABOUT THE INSTITUTION Independent, coed. 8 undergraduate majors. Both federal and institutional methodology are used as a basis for awarding need-based institutional aid.

UNDERGRADUATE EXPENSES for 2010–11 *Comprehensive fee:* $50,350 includes full-time tuition ($35,000), mandatory fees ($1650), and room and board ($13,700). *College room only:* $9700. Room and board charges vary according to board plan and housing facility.

FRESHMAN FINANCIAL AID (Fall 2008) 112 applied for aid; of those 62% were deemed to have need. 100% of freshmen with need received aid; of those 61% had need fully met. *Average percent of need met:* 91% (excluding resources awarded to replace EFC). *Average financial aid package:* $35,000 (excluding resources awarded to replace EFC). 66% of all full-time freshmen had no need and received non-need-based gift aid.

UNDERGRADUATE FINANCIAL AID (Fall 2008) 365 applied for aid; of those 71% were deemed to have need. 100% of undergraduates with need received aid; of those 60% had need fully met. *Average percent of need met:* 92% (excluding resources awarded to replace EFC). *Average financial aid package:* $35,000 (excluding resources awarded to replace EFC). 72% of all full-time undergraduates had no need and received non-need-based gift aid.

GIFT AID (NEED-BASED) *Total amount:* $1,807,669 (33% federal, 20% state, 33% institutional, 14% external sources). *Receiving aid:* Freshmen: 34% (69); all full-time undergraduates: 28% (260). *Average award:* Freshmen: $4937; Undergraduates: $5535. *Scholarships, grants, and awards:* Federal Pell, FSEOG, state, private, college/university gift aid from institutional funds.

GIFT AID (NON-NEED-BASED) *Total amount:* $28,277,237 (100% institutional). *Receiving aid:* Freshmen: 34% (69). Undergraduates: 28% (260). *Average award:* Freshmen: $35,000. Undergraduates: $35,000. *Scholarships, grants, and awards by category:* Academic interests/achievement: 602 awards ($21,070,000 total): architecture, engineering/technologies. Creative arts/performance: 278 awards ($9,730,000 total): art/fine arts.

LOANS *Student loans:* $641,757 (73% need-based, 27% non-need-based). 33% of past graduating class borrowed through all loan programs. *Average* *indebtedness per student:* $13,037. *Average need-based loan:* Freshmen: $2057. Undergraduates: $2664. *Parent loans:* $99,216 (40% need-based, 60% non-need-based). *Programs:* FFEL (Subsidized and Unsubsidized Stafford, PLUS), Perkins, college/university.

WORK-STUDY *Federal work-study:* Total amount: $53,783; 50 jobs averaging $1000. *State or other work-study/employment:* Total amount: $793,527 (25% need-based, 75% non-need-based). 527 part-time jobs averaging $1505.

APPLYING FOR FINANCIAL AID *Required financial aid forms:* FAFSA, CSS Financial Aid PROFILE. *Financial aid deadline:* 6/1 (priority: 4/15). *Notification date:* 6/1. Students must reply by 6/30 or within 2 weeks of notification.

CONTACT Ms. Mary Ruokonen, Director of Financial Aid, Cooper Union for the Advancement of Science and Art, 30 Cooper Square, New York, NY 10003-7120, 212-353-4130. *Fax:* 212-353-4343. *E-mail:* ruokon@cooper.edu.

COPPIN STATE UNIVERSITY
Baltimore, MD

Tuition & fees (MD res): $5276	Average undergraduate aid package: $9359

ABOUT THE INSTITUTION State-supported, coed. 20 undergraduate majors. Federal methodology is used as a basis for awarding need-based institutional aid.

UNDERGRADUATE EXPENSES for 2009–10 *Tuition, state resident:* full-time $3527; part-time $151 per credit hour. *Tuition, nonresident:* full-time $12,222; part-time $420 per credit hour. *Required fees:* full-time $1749; $27.18 per credit hour. Full-time tuition and fees vary according to course load. Part-time tuition and fees vary according to course load. *College room and board:* $7496; *Room only:* $4686. Room and board charges vary according to board plan. *Payment plan:* Deferred payment.

FRESHMAN FINANCIAL AID (Fall 2009, est.) 508 applied for aid; of those 90% were deemed to have need. 91% of freshmen with need received aid; of those 15% had need fully met. *Average percent of need met:* 65% (excluding resources awarded to replace EFC). *Average financial aid package:* $8859 (excluding resources awarded to replace EFC). 3% of all full-time freshmen had no need and received non-need-based gift aid.

UNDERGRADUATE FINANCIAL AID (Fall 2009, est.) 2,314 applied for aid; of those 92% were deemed to have need. 94% of undergraduates with need received aid; of those 29% had need fully met. *Average percent of need met:* 79% (excluding resources awarded to replace EFC). *Average financial aid package:* $9359 (excluding resources awarded to replace EFC). 1% of all full-time undergraduates had no need and received non-need-based gift aid.

GIFT AID (NEED-BASED) *Total amount:* $42,973,511 (72% federal, 5% state, 23% institutional). *Receiving aid:* Freshmen: 62% (330); all full-time undergraduates: 66% (1,674). *Average award:* Freshmen: $5836; Undergraduates: $6086. *Scholarships, grants, and awards:* Federal Pell, FSEOG, state, private, college/university gift aid from institutional funds, Federal Nursing.

GIFT AID (NON-NEED-BASED) *Total amount:* $5,556,961 (33% state, 41% institutional, 26% external sources). *Receiving aid:* Freshmen: 18% (98). Undergraduates: 14% (359). *Average award:* Freshmen: $2284. Undergraduates: $2540. *Scholarships, grants, and awards by category: Academic interests/achievement:* general academic interests/achievements. *Tuition waivers:* Full or partial for minority students, children of alumni, employees or children of employees, adult students, senior citizens.

LOANS *Student loans:* $28,094,069 (68% need-based, 32% non-need-based). 98% of past graduating class borrowed through all loan programs. *Average indebtedness per student:* $9005. *Average need-based loan:* Freshmen: $3237. Undergraduates: $3784. *Parent loans:* $664,586 (100% non-need-based). *Programs:* Federal Direct (Subsidized and Unsubsidized Stafford, PLUS), Perkins, alternative loans.

WORK-STUDY *Federal work-study:* Total amount: $2,378,727; 180 jobs averaging $2030.

ATHLETIC AWARDS Total amount: $9,500,511 (100% non-need-based).

APPLYING FOR FINANCIAL AID *Required financial aid form:* FAFSA. *Financial aid deadline (priority):* 3/1. *Notification date:* 4/15. Students must reply within 4 weeks of notification.

CONTACT Fay Tayree, Associate Director of Financial Aid, Coppin State University, 2500 West North Avenue, Baltimore, MD 21216-3698, 410-951-3636 or toll-free 800-635-3674. *Fax:* 410-951-3637. *E-mail:* ftayree@coppin.edu.

CORBAN UNIVERSITY
Salem, OR

Tuition & fees: $24,230	Average undergraduate aid package: $17,364

ABOUT THE INSTITUTION Independent religious, coed. 45 undergraduate majors. Federal methodology is used as a basis for awarding need-based institutional aid.

UNDERGRADUATE EXPENSES for 2010–11 *One-time required fee:* $100. *Comprehensive fee:* $31,872 includes full-time tuition ($23,950), mandatory fees ($280), and room and board ($7642). Room and board charges vary according to board plan. *Part-time tuition:* $997.92 per credit hour. Part-time tuition and fees vary according to course load. *Payment plan:* Installment.

FRESHMAN FINANCIAL AID (Fall 2009, est.) 187 applied for aid; of those 94% were deemed to have need. 100% of freshmen with need received aid; of those 13% had need fully met. *Average percent of need met:* 72% (excluding resources awarded to replace EFC). *Average financial aid package:* $19,888 (excluding resources awarded to replace EFC). 16% of all full-time freshmen had no need and received non-need-based gift aid.

UNDERGRADUATE FINANCIAL AID (Fall 2009, est.) 650 applied for aid; of those 91% were deemed to have need. 100% of undergraduates with need received aid; of those 13% had need fully met. *Average percent of need met:* 65% (excluding resources awarded to replace EFC). *Average financial aid package:* $17,364 (excluding resources awarded to replace EFC). 14% of all full-time undergraduates had no need and received non-need-based gift aid.

GIFT AID (NEED-BASED) *Total amount:* $6,603,482 (22% federal, 4% state, 66% institutional, 8% external sources). *Receiving aid:* Freshmen: 83% (175); all full-time undergraduates: 83% (594). *Average award:* Freshmen: $17,115; Undergraduates: $13,897. *Scholarships, grants, and awards:* Federal Pell, FSEOG, state, private, college/university gift aid from institutional funds.

GIFT AID (NON-NEED-BASED) *Total amount:* $739,561 (8% federal, 81% institutional, 11% external sources). *Receiving aid:* Freshmen: 7% (14). Undergraduates: 7% (50). *Average award:* Freshmen: $6327. Undergraduates: $5336. *Scholarships, grants, and awards by category: Academic interests/achievement:* general academic interests/achievements. *Creative arts/performance:* music, performing arts. *Special achievements/activities:* general special achievements/activities, hobbies/interests, leadership, memberships, religious involvement. *Special characteristics:* children and siblings of alumni, children of faculty/staff, international students, relatives of clergy, siblings of current students. *Tuition waivers:* Full or partial for employees or children of employees.

LOANS *Student loans:* $4,322,179 (81% need-based, 19% non-need-based). 91% of past graduating class borrowed through all loan programs. *Average indebtedness per student:* $28,537. *Average need-based loan:* Freshmen: $3881. Undergraduates: $4505. *Parent loans:* $863,396 (65% need-based, 35% non-need-based). *Programs:* Federal Direct (Subsidized and Unsubsidized Stafford, PLUS), Perkins, state.

WORK-STUDY Federal work-study jobs available.

ATHLETIC AWARDS Total amount: $1,209,019 (73% need-based, 27% non-need-based).

APPLYING FOR FINANCIAL AID *Required financial aid form:* FAFSA. *Financial aid deadline (priority):* 2/15. *Notification date:* Continuous beginning 3/1.

CONTACT Nathan Warthan, Director of Financial Aid, Corban University, 5000 Deer Park Drive, SE, Salem, OR 97301-9392, 503-375-7006 or toll-free 800-845-3005 (out-of-state). *Fax:* 503-585-4316. *E-mail:* nwarthan@corban.edu.

CORCORAN COLLEGE OF ART AND DESIGN
Washington, DC

Tuition & fees: N/R	Average undergraduate aid package: $15,591

ABOUT THE INSTITUTION Independent, coed. 8 undergraduate majors. Federal methodology is used as a basis for awarding need-based institutional aid.

FRESHMAN FINANCIAL AID (Fall 2009, est.) 50 applied for aid; of those 100% were deemed to have need. 100% of freshmen with need received aid. *Average percent of need met:* 24% (excluding resources awarded to replace EFC). *Average financial aid package:* $22,507 (excluding resources awarded to replace EFC). 10% of all full-time freshmen had no need and received non-need-based gift aid.

UNDERGRADUATE FINANCIAL AID (Fall 2009, est.) 240 applied for aid; of those 96% were deemed to have need. 100% of undergraduates with need received aid. *Average percent of need met:* 28% (excluding resources awarded to replace EFC). *Average financial aid package:* $15,591 (excluding resources awarded to replace EFC). 20% of all full-time undergraduates had no need and received non-need-based gift aid.

GIFT AID (NEED-BASED) *Total amount:* $1,847,721 (33% federal, 2% state, 65% institutional). *Receiving aid:* Freshmen: 73% (46); all full-time undergraduates: 63% (205). *Average award:* Freshmen: $8678; Undergraduates: $8949. *Scholarships, grants, and awards:* Federal Pell, FSEOG, state, college/university gift aid from institutional funds.

GIFT AID (NON-NEED-BASED) *Total amount:* $1,813,108 (98% institutional, 2% external sources). *Receiving aid:* Freshmen: 79% (50). Undergraduates: 71% (230). *Average award:* Freshmen: $8000. Undergraduates: $6313. *Scholarships, grants, and awards by category: Academic interests/achievement:* 247 awards ($1,663,936 total): general academic interests/achievements. *Creative arts/performance:* 39 awards ($236,992 total): applied art and design.

LOANS *Student loans:* $17,358,609 (5% need-based, 95% non-need-based). 64% of past graduating class borrowed through all loan programs. *Average indebtedness per student:* $42,355. *Average need-based loan:* Freshmen: $3460. Undergraduates: $4234. *Parent loans:* $16,406,054 (100% non-need-based). *Programs:* FFEL (Subsidized and Unsubsidized Stafford, PLUS), Perkins.

WORK-STUDY *Federal work-study:* Total amount: $125,493; 72 jobs averaging $1743.

APPLYING FOR FINANCIAL AID *Required financial aid forms:* FAFSA, institution's own form. *Financial aid deadline (priority):* 3/1. *Notification date:* Continuous beginning 4/1. Students must reply within 2 weeks of notification.

CONTACT Diane Morris, Financial Aid Director, Corcoran College of Art and Design, 500 17th Street, NW, Washington, DC 20006-4804, 202-639-1816 or toll-free 888-CORCORAN (out-of-state). *Fax:* 202-737-6921. *E-mail:* dmorris@corcoran.org.

CORNELL COLLEGE
Mount Vernon, IA

Tuition & fees: $29,400	Average undergraduate aid package: $25,535

ABOUT THE INSTITUTION Independent Methodist, coed. 49 undergraduate majors. Both federal and institutional methodology are used as a basis for awarding need-based institutional aid.

UNDERGRADUATE EXPENSES for 2009–10 *Comprehensive fee:* $36,900 includes full-time tuition ($29,400) and room and board ($7500). *College room only:* $3500. Room and board charges vary according to board plan and housing facility. Part-time tuition and fees vary according to course load and reciprocity agreements. *Payment plan:* Deferred payment.

FRESHMAN FINANCIAL AID (Fall 2009, est.) 277 applied for aid; of those 87% were deemed to have need. 100% of freshmen with need received aid; of those 44% had need fully met. *Average percent of need met:* 95% (excluding resources awarded to replace EFC). *Average financial aid package:* $30,205 (excluding resources awarded to replace EFC). 22% of all full-time freshmen had no need and received non-need-based gift aid.

UNDERGRADUATE FINANCIAL AID (Fall 2009, est.) 913 applied for aid; of those 90% were deemed to have need. 100% of undergraduates with need received aid; of those 38% had need fully met. *Average percent of need met:* 93% (excluding resources awarded to replace EFC). *Average financial aid package:* $25,535 (excluding resources awarded to replace EFC). 19% of all full-time undergraduates had no need and received non-need-based gift aid.

GIFT AID (NEED-BASED) *Total amount:* $16,801,967 (11% federal, 3% state, 84% institutional, 2% external sources). *Receiving aid:* Freshmen: 72% (242); all full-time undergraduates: 74% (824). *Average award:* Freshmen: $22,730; Undergraduates: $20,545. *Scholarships, grants, and awards:* Federal Pell, FSEOG, state, private, college/university gift aid from institutional funds, Academic Competitiveness Grants, National SMART Grants, TEACH Grants.

GIFT AID (NON-NEED-BASED) *Total amount:* $3,341,726 (96% institutional, 4% external sources). *Receiving aid:* Freshmen: 69% (231). Undergraduates: 62% (684). *Average award:* Freshmen: $13,570. Undergraduates: $13,250. *Scholarships, grants, and awards by category: Academic interests/achievement:* 365 awards ($4,803,520 total): general academic interests/achievements. *Creative arts/performance:* 115 awards ($647,156 total): art/fine arts, music, performing arts, theater/drama. *Special achievements/activities:* 269 awards ($1,895,256 total): community service, leadership, religious involvement. *Special characteristics:* 189 awards ($2,347,101 total): children of educators, children of faculty/staff,

---

ethnic background, international students, local/state students, members of minority groups, relatives of clergy, religious affiliation. *Tuition waivers:* Full or partial for employees or children of employees.

LOANS *Student loans:* $6,343,023 (69% need-based, 31% non-need-based). 72% of past graduating class borrowed through all loan programs. *Average indebtedness per student:* $27,990. *Average need-based loan:* Freshmen: $3517. Undergraduates: $4755. *Parent loans:* $1,610,321 (100% non-need-based). *Programs:* Federal Direct (Subsidized and Unsubsidized Stafford, PLUS), Perkins, state, college/university.

WORK-STUDY *Federal work-study:* Total amount: $838,387; 590 jobs averaging $1420. *State or other work-study/employment:* Part-time jobs available.

APPLYING FOR FINANCIAL AID *Required financial aid forms:* FAFSA, institution's own form, noncustodial (divorced/separated) parent's statement. *Financial aid deadline:* 3/1. *Notification date:* Continuous beginning 3/1. Students must reply by 5/1 or within 2 weeks of notification.

CONTACT Ms. Cindi P. Reints, Director of Financial Assistance, Cornell College, Wade House, 600 1st Street West, Mount Vernon, IA 52314-1098, 319-895-4216 or toll-free 800-747-1112. *Fax:* 319-895-4106. *E-mail:* creints@cornellcollege.edu.

CORNELL UNIVERSITY
Ithaca, NY

Tuition & fees: $37,954	Average undergraduate aid package: $34,538

ABOUT THE INSTITUTION Independent, coed. 109 undergraduate majors. Institutional methodology is used as a basis for awarding need-based institutional aid.

UNDERGRADUATE EXPENSES for 2009–10 *Comprehensive fee:* $50,114 includes full-time tuition ($37,750), mandatory fees ($204), and room and board ($12,160). *College room only:* $7210. Full-time tuition and fees vary according to degree level and program. Room and board charges vary according to board plan and housing facility. *Payment plan:* Installment.

FRESHMAN FINANCIAL AID (Fall 2009, est.) 2,223 applied for aid; of those 74% were deemed to have need. 100% of freshmen with need received aid; of those 100% had need fully met. *Average percent of need met:* 100% (excluding resources awarded to replace EFC). *Average financial aid package:* $36,062 (excluding resources awarded to replace EFC).

UNDERGRADUATE FINANCIAL AID (Fall 2009, est.) 8,302 applied for aid; of those 78% were deemed to have need. 100% of undergraduates with need received aid; of those 100% had need fully met. *Average percent of need met:* 100% (excluding resources awarded to replace EFC). *Average financial aid package:* $34,538 (excluding resources awarded to replace EFC).

GIFT AID (NEED-BASED) *Total amount:* $191,021,886 (8% federal, 3% state, 86% institutional, 3% external sources). *Receiving aid:* Freshmen: 51% (1,622); all full-time undergraduates: 46% (6,324). *Average award:* Freshmen: $32,614; Undergraduates: $30,197. *Scholarships, grants, and awards:* Federal Pell, FSEOG, state, private, college/university gift aid from institutional funds.

GIFT AID (NON-NEED-BASED) *Tuition waivers:* Full or partial for employees or children of employees.

LOANS *Student loans:* $21,693,519 (100% need-based). 53% of past graduating class borrowed through all loan programs. *Average indebtedness per student:* $21,549. *Average need-based loan:* Freshmen: $2944. Undergraduates: $3611. *Parent loans:* $9,662,233 (100% need-based). *Programs:* Federal Direct (Subsidized and Unsubsidized Stafford, PLUS), FFEL (Subsidized and Unsubsidized Stafford, PLUS), Perkins, college/university.

WORK-STUDY *Federal work-study:* Total amount: $8,055,376; 4,598 jobs averaging $1663. *State or other work-study/employment:* Total amount: $1,879,858 (100% need-based). 1,333 part-time jobs averaging $1442.

APPLYING FOR FINANCIAL AID *Required financial aid forms:* FAFSA, institution's own form, CSS Financial Aid PROFILE, noncustodial (divorced/separated) parent's statement, business/farm supplement, prior year tax forms. *Financial aid deadline:* 1/2. *Notification date:* 4/1. Students must reply by 5/1.

CONTACT Mr. Thomas Keane, Director of Financial Aid and Student Employment, Cornell University, 410 Thurston Avenue, Ithaca, NY 14853-2488, 607-255-5147.

CORNERSTONE UNIVERSITY
Grand Rapids, MI

Tuition & fees: $20,520   **Average undergraduate aid package: $18,623**

ABOUT THE INSTITUTION Independent nondenominational, coed. 39 undergraduate majors. Federal methodology is used as a basis for awarding need-based institutional aid.

UNDERGRADUATE EXPENSES for 2009–10 *Comprehensive fee:* $27,030 includes full-time tuition ($19,960), mandatory fees ($560), and room and board ($6510). Full-time tuition and fees vary according to course load and reciprocity agreements. Room and board charges vary according to board plan. *Part-time tuition:* $765 per credit hour. Part-time tuition and fees vary according to course load. *Payment plan:* Installment.

FRESHMAN FINANCIAL AID (Fall 2008) 301 applied for aid; of those 90% were deemed to have need. 100% of freshmen with need received aid; of those 19% had need fully met. *Average percent of need met:* 89% (excluding resources awarded to replace EFC). *Average financial aid package:* $20,252 (excluding resources awarded to replace EFC). 16% of all full-time freshmen had no need and received non-need-based gift aid.

UNDERGRADUATE FINANCIAL AID (Fall 2008) 948 applied for aid; of those 92% were deemed to have need. 100% of undergraduates with need received aid; of those 15% had need fully met. *Average percent of need met:* 85% (excluding resources awarded to replace EFC). *Average financial aid package:* $18,623 (excluding resources awarded to replace EFC). 15% of all full-time undergraduates had no need and received non-need-based gift aid.

GIFT AID (NEED-BASED) *Total amount:* $8,920,848 (19% federal, 14% state, 65% institutional, 2% external sources). *Receiving aid:* Freshmen: 84% (270); all full-time undergraduates: 84% (865). *Average award:* Freshmen: $15,398; Undergraduates: $11,526. *Scholarships, grants, and awards:* Federal Pell, FSEOG, state, private, college/university gift aid from institutional funds.

GIFT AID (NON-NEED-BASED) *Total amount:* $1,189,266 (97% institutional, 3% external sources). *Receiving aid:* Freshmen: 84% (270). Undergraduates: 80% (824). *Average award:* Freshmen: $8038. Undergraduates: $6113. *Scholarships, grants, and awards by category: Academic interests/achievement:* 980 awards ($3,988,280 total): business, education, general academic interests/ achievements, religion/biblical studies. *Creative arts/performance:* 61 awards ($156,325 total): music. *Special achievements/activities:* 69 awards ($95,879 total): leadership, religious involvement. *Special characteristics:* 155 awards ($169,040 total): children and siblings of alumni, children of faculty/staff, children of union members/company employees, ethnic background, general special characteristics, international students, members of minority groups, out-of-state students. *Tuition waivers:* Full or partial for employees or children of employees.

LOANS *Student loans:* $7,024,031 (90% need-based, 10% non-need-based). 83% of past graduating class borrowed through all loan programs. *Average indebtedness per student:* $26,025. *Average need-based loan:* Freshmen: $3394. Undergraduates: $4352. *Parent loans:* $572,804 (68% need-based, 32% non-need-based). *Programs:* FFEL (Subsidized and Unsubsidized Stafford, PLUS), Perkins, college/university.

WORK-STUDY *Federal work-study:* Total amount: $215,084; 172 jobs averaging $921. *State or other work-study/employment:* Part-time jobs available.

ATHLETIC AWARDS Total amount: $883,413 (74% need-based, 26% non-need-based).

APPLYING FOR FINANCIAL AID *Required financial aid form:* FAFSA. *Financial aid deadline:* Continuous. *Notification date:* Continuous beginning 3/1. Students must reply within 2 weeks of notification.

CONTACT Mr. Scott W. Stewart, Director of Student Financial Services, Cornerstone University, 1001 East Beltline Avenue, NE, Grand Rapids, MI 49525-5897, 616-222-1424 or toll-free 800-787-9778. *Fax:* 616-222-1400. *E-mail:* scott_w_stewart@cornerstone.edu.

CORNISH COLLEGE OF THE ARTS
Seattle, WA

ABOUT THE INSTITUTION Independent, coed. 16 undergraduate majors.

GIFT AID (NEED-BASED) *Scholarships, grants, and awards:* Federal Pell, FSEOG, state, private, college/university gift aid from institutional funds.

GIFT AID (NON-NEED-BASED) *Scholarships, grants, and awards by category: Academic interests/achievement:* general academic interests/achievements. *Creative arts/performance:* art/fine arts, dance, music, theater/drama.

LOANS *Programs:* Federal Direct (Subsidized and Unsubsidized Stafford, PLUS).

WORK-STUDY *Federal work-study:* Total amount: $1,370,094; jobs available (averaging $3000). *State or other work-study/employment:* Part-time jobs available (averaging $3000).

APPLYING FOR FINANCIAL AID *Required financial aid form:* FAFSA.

CONTACT Sharron Starling, Office of Admissions, Cornish College of the Arts, 1000 Lenora Street, Seattle, WA 98121, 206-726-5017 or toll-free 800-726-ARTS. *Fax:* 206-720-1011. *E-mail:* admissions@cornish.edu.

COVENANT COLLEGE
Lookout Mountain, GA

Tuition & fees: $25,270   **Average undergraduate aid package: $18,057**

ABOUT THE INSTITUTION Independent religious, coed. 27 undergraduate majors. Federal methodology is used as a basis for awarding need-based institutional aid.

UNDERGRADUATE EXPENSES for 2009–10 *Comprehensive fee:* $32,440 includes full-time tuition ($24,520), mandatory fees ($750), and room and board ($7170). Full-time tuition and fees vary according to course load. *Part-time tuition:* $1025 per credit hour. Part-time tuition and fees vary according to course load. *Payment plan:* Installment.

FRESHMAN FINANCIAL AID (Fall 2008) 226 applied for aid; of those 79% were deemed to have need. 100% of freshmen with need received aid; of those 35% had need fully met. *Average percent of need met:* 83% (excluding resources awarded to replace EFC). *Average financial aid package:* $19,717 (excluding resources awarded to replace EFC). 17% of all full-time freshmen had no need and received non-need-based gift aid.

UNDERGRADUATE FINANCIAL AID (Fall 2008) 718 applied for aid; of those 82% were deemed to have need. 100% of undergraduates with need received aid; of those 31% had need fully met. *Average percent of need met:* 78% (excluding resources awarded to replace EFC). *Average financial aid package:* $18,057 (excluding resources awarded to replace EFC). 22% of all full-time undergraduates had no need and received non-need-based gift aid.

GIFT AID (NEED-BASED) *Total amount:* $8,000,645 (11% federal, 6% state, 77% institutional, 6% external sources). *Receiving aid:* Freshmen: 64% (172); all full-time undergraduates: 60% (574). *Average award:* Freshmen: $12,928; Undergraduates: $12,385. *Scholarships, grants, and awards:* Federal Pell, FSEOG, state, private, college/university gift aid from institutional funds.

GIFT AID (NON-NEED-BASED) *Total amount:* $2,719,773 (11% state, 72% institutional, 17% external sources). *Average award:* Freshmen: $6980. Undergraduates: $7607. *Scholarships, grants, and awards by category: Academic interests/achievement:* general academic interests/achievements. *Creative arts/performance:* music. *Special achievements/activities:* leadership. *Special characteristics:* children of faculty/staff, international students, members of minority groups, religious affiliation. *Tuition waivers:* Full or partial for employees or children of employees, senior citizens.

LOANS *Student loans:* $3,927,574 (90% need-based, 10% non-need-based). 64% of past graduating class borrowed through all loan programs. *Average indebtedness per student:* $17,824. *Average need-based loan:* Freshmen: $4830. Undergraduates: $4869. *Parent loans:* $1,605,472 (76% need-based, 24% non-need-based). *Programs:* FFEL (Subsidized and Unsubsidized Stafford, PLUS), Perkins, state, college/university.

WORK-STUDY *Federal work-study:* Total amount: $299,657; jobs available. *State or other work-study/employment:* Total amount: $517,537 (83% need-based, 17% non-need-based). Part-time jobs available.

ATHLETIC AWARDS Total amount: $1,324,926 (66% need-based, 34% non-need-based).

APPLYING FOR FINANCIAL AID *Required financial aid forms:* FAFSA, institution's own form, state aid form. *Financial aid deadline:* Continuous. *Notification date:* Continuous beginning 2/1. Students must reply within 3 weeks of notification.

CONTACT Mrs. Margaret Stewart, Assistant Director of Student Financial Planning, Covenant College, 14049 Scenic Highway, Lookout Mountain, GA 30750, 706-419-1152 or toll-free 888-451-2683. *Fax:* 706-820-2820. *E-mail:* margaret.stewart@covenant.edu.

COX COLLEGE OF NURSING AND HEALTH SCIENCES
Springfield, MO

Tuition & fees: N/R   **Average undergraduate aid package:** N/A

ABOUT THE INSTITUTION Independent, coed, primarily women. 1 undergraduate major. Federal methodology is used as a basis for awarding need-based institutional aid.

GIFT AID (NEED-BASED) *Total amount:* $1,442,186 (68% federal, 15% state, 13% institutional, 4% external sources). *Scholarships, grants, and awards:* Federal Pell, FSEOG, state, private, college/university gift aid from institutional funds, United Negro College Fund, Federal Nursing.

LOANS *Student loans:* $3,561,004 (100% need-based). *Parent loans:* $76,540 (100% need-based). *Programs:* Federal Direct (Subsidized and Unsubsidized Stafford, PLUS), Perkins, Federal Nursing, state, college/university.

WORK-STUDY *Federal work-study:* Total amount: $26,231; 16 jobs averaging $1639.

APPLYING FOR FINANCIAL AID *Required financial aid form:* FAFSA. *Financial aid deadline (priority):* 4/1.

CONTACT Leesa Taylor, Financial Aid Counselor, Cox College of Nursing and Health Sciences, 1423 North Jefferson Avenue, Springfield, MO 65802, 417-269-3160 or toll-free 866-898-5355 (in-state). *Fax:* 417-269-3586. *E-mail:* ltaylo@coxcollege.edu.

CREIGHTON UNIVERSITY
Omaha, NE

Tuition & fees: $22,118   **Average undergraduate aid package:** $25,003

ABOUT THE INSTITUTION Independent Roman Catholic (Jesuit), coed. 46 undergraduate majors. Federal methodology is used as a basis for awarding need-based institutional aid.

UNDERGRADUATE EXPENSES for 2009–10 *Comprehensive fee:* $30,932 includes full-time tuition ($20,812), mandatory fees ($1306), and room and board ($8814). *College room only:* $4984. Full-time tuition and fees vary according to degree level and location. Room and board charges vary according to board plan and housing facility. *Part-time tuition:* $882 per semester hour. *Part-time fees:* $252 per year. Part-time tuition and fees vary according to degree level. *Payment plan:* Installment.

FRESHMAN FINANCIAL AID (Fall 2009, est.) 840 applied for aid; of those 78% were deemed to have need. 100% of freshmen with need received aid; of those 58% had need fully met. *Average percent of need met:* 93% (excluding resources awarded to replace EFC). *Average financial aid package:* $25,628 (excluding resources awarded to replace EFC). 32% of all full-time freshmen had no need and received non-need-based gift aid.

UNDERGRADUATE FINANCIAL AID (Fall 2009, est.) 2,498 applied for aid; of those 83% were deemed to have need. 100% of undergraduates with need received aid; of those 51% had need fully met. *Average percent of need met:* 91% (excluding resources awarded to replace EFC). *Average financial aid package:* $25,003 (excluding resources awarded to replace EFC). 27% of all full-time undergraduates had no need and received non-need-based gift aid.

GIFT AID (NEED-BASED) *Total amount:* $34,760,994 (10% federal, 1% state, 83% institutional, 6% external sources). *Receiving aid:* Freshmen: 62% (649); all full-time undergraduates: 49% (2,015). *Average award:* Freshmen: $20,675; Undergraduates: $19,497. *Scholarships, grants, and awards:* Federal Pell, FSEOG, state, private, college/university gift aid from institutional funds, Federal Nursing.

GIFT AID (NON-NEED-BASED) *Total amount:* $13,387,995 (97% institutional, 3% external sources). *Receiving aid:* Freshmen: 47% (491). Undergraduates: 38% (1,573). *Average award:* Freshmen: $13,614. Undergraduates: $11,594. *Scholarships, grants, and awards by category: Academic interests/achievement:* business, education, general academic interests/achievements, military science. *Creative arts/performance:* art/fine arts, creative writing, dance, debating, journalism/publications, music, performing arts, theater/drama. *Special achievements/activities:* leadership. *Special characteristics:* children of faculty/staff, first-generation college students, handicapped students, local/state students, members of minority groups, religious affiliation, siblings of current students. *Tuition waivers:* Full or partial for employees or children of employees, adult students.

LOANS *Student loans:* $24,146,027 (48% need-based, 52% non-need-based). 70% of past graduating class borrowed through all loan programs. *Average indebtedness per student:* $32,888. *Average need-based loan:* Freshmen: $5755. Undergraduates: $6649. *Parent loans:* $4,674,758 (100% non-need-based). *Programs:* Federal Direct (Subsidized and Unsubsidized Stafford, PLUS), Perkins, Federal Nursing, college/university.

WORK-STUDY *Federal work-study:* Total amount: $1,678,865; 836 jobs averaging $2008.

ATHLETIC AWARDS Total amount: $3,229,277 (36% need-based, 64% non-need-based).

APPLYING FOR FINANCIAL AID *Required financial aid forms:* FAFSA, institution's own form. *Financial aid deadline (priority):* 3/1. *Notification date:* Continuous beginning 3/15. Students must reply by 5/1 or within 4 weeks of notification.

CONTACT Sarah Sell, Assistant Director of Financial Aid, Creighton University, 2500 California Plaza, Omaha, NE 68178, 402-280-2731 or toll-free 800-282-5835. *Fax:* 402-280-2895. *E-mail:* sarahsell@creighton.edu.

THE CRISWELL COLLEGE
Dallas, TX

ABOUT THE INSTITUTION Independent religious, coed. 2 undergraduate majors.

GIFT AID (NEED-BASED) *Scholarships, grants, and awards:* private, college/university gift aid from institutional funds.

GIFT AID (NON-NEED-BASED) *Scholarships, grants, and awards by category: Academic interests/achievement:* general academic interests/achievements. *Special achievements/activities:* religious involvement. *Special characteristics:* children and siblings of alumni, children of faculty/staff, religious affiliation.

LOANS *Programs:* college/university.

WORK-STUDY *State or other work-study/employment:* Total amount: $50,547 (100% need-based). 24 part-time jobs averaging $2089.

APPLYING FOR FINANCIAL AID *Required financial aid form:* institution's own form.

CONTACT Ester Waggoner, Financial Aid Director, The Criswell College, 4010 Gaston Avenue, Dallas, TX 75246, 800-899-0012. *Fax:* 214-818-1310. *E-mail:* ewaggoner@criswell.edu.

CROSSROADS BIBLE COLLEGE
Indianapolis, IN

Tuition & fees: $9850   **Average undergraduate aid package:** N/A

ABOUT THE INSTITUTION Independent Baptist, coed. 1 undergraduate major. Institutional methodology is used as a basis for awarding need-based institutional aid.

UNDERGRADUATE EXPENSES for 2009–10 *Tuition:* full-time $9480. *Payment plan:* Installment.

GIFT AID (NEED-BASED) *Total amount:* $657,729 (55% federal, 39% state, 6% institutional). *Scholarships, grants, and awards:* Federal Pell, FSEOG, state, college/university gift aid from institutional funds.

GIFT AID (NON-NEED-BASED) *Scholarships, grants, and awards by category: Special characteristics:* children of faculty/staff, married students, siblings of current students, spouses of current students. *Tuition waivers:* Full or partial for employees or children of employees.

LOANS *Student loans:* $1,478,985 (100% need-based). *Parent loans:* $15,987 (100% need-based). *Programs:* Federal Direct (Subsidized and Unsubsidized Stafford, PLUS).

WORK-STUDY *Federal work-study:* Total amount: $34,262; jobs available. *State or other work-study/employment:* Part-time jobs available.

APPLYING FOR FINANCIAL AID *Required financial aid forms:* FAFSA, institution's own form. *Financial aid deadline:* 6/30 (priority: 5/31). *Notification date:* 7/31. Students must reply within 2 weeks of notification.

CONTACT Mrs. Phyllis Dodson, Director of Financial Aid, Crossroads Bible College, 601 North Shortridge Road, Indianapolis, IN 46219, 317-352-8736 Ext. 228 or toll-free 800-273-2224 Ext. 230. *Fax:* 317-352-9145.

CROSSROADS COLLEGE
Rochester, MN

Tuition & fees: N/R	Average undergraduate aid package: N/A

ABOUT THE INSTITUTION Independent religious, coed. *Awards:* associate and bachelor's degrees. 13 undergraduate majors. *Total enrollment:* 160. Undergraduates: 160. Freshmen: 24. Federal methodology is used as a basis for awarding need-based institutional aid.

GIFT AID (NEED-BASED) *Scholarships, grants, and awards:* Federal Pell, FSEOG, state, private, college/university gift aid from institutional funds.

GIFT AID (NON-NEED-BASED) *Scholarships, grants, and awards by category: Academic interests/achievement:* general academic interests/achievements, religion/biblical studies. *Creative arts/performance:* music. *Special achievements/ activities:* general special achievements/activities, religious involvement. *Special characteristics:* children of faculty/staff, general special characteristics, international students, parents of current students, religious affiliation, siblings of current students, spouses of current students.

LOANS *Programs:* FFEL (Subsidized and Unsubsidized Stafford, PLUS), state, college/university, alternative loans.

WORK-STUDY Federal work-study jobs available. *State or other work-study/ employment:* Part-time jobs available.

APPLYING FOR FINANCIAL AID *Required financial aid forms:* FAFSA, institution's own form. *Financial aid deadline (priority):* 5/1. *Notification date:* Continuous. Students must reply within 2 weeks of notification.

CONTACT Polly Kellogg-Bradley, Director of Financial Aid, Crossroads College, 920 Mayowood Road SW, Rochester, MN 55902, 507-288-4563 or toll-free 800-456-7651. *Fax:* 507-288-9046. *E-mail:* financialaid@crossroadscollege. edu.

CROWN COLLEGE
St. Bonifacius, MN

Tuition & fees: $20,870	Average undergraduate aid package: $15,394

ABOUT THE INSTITUTION Independent religious, coed. 26 undergraduate majors. Both federal and institutional methodology are used as a basis for awarding need-based institutional aid.

UNDERGRADUATE EXPENSES for 2010–11 *Comprehensive fee:* $28,450 includes full-time tuition ($20,870) and room and board ($7580). *Part-time tuition:* $870 per credit.

FRESHMAN FINANCIAL AID (Fall 2009, est.) 143 applied for aid; of those 87% were deemed to have need. 100% of freshmen with need received aid; of those 14% had need fully met. *Average percent of need met:* 66% (excluding resources awarded to replace EFC). *Average financial aid package:* $16,722 (excluding resources awarded to replace EFC). 11% of all full-time freshmen had no need and received non-need-based gift aid.

UNDERGRADUATE FINANCIAL AID (Fall 2009, est.) 596 applied for aid; of those 86% were deemed to have need. 100% of undergraduates with need received aid; of those 13% had need fully met. *Average percent of need met:* 61% (excluding resources awarded to replace EFC). *Average financial aid package:* $15,394 (excluding resources awarded to replace EFC). 7% of all full-time undergraduates had no need and received non-need-based gift aid.

GIFT AID (NEED-BASED) *Total amount:* $2,313,688 (50% federal, 33% state, 17% institutional). *Receiving aid:* Freshmen: 64% (95); all full-time undergraduates: 35% (369). *Average award:* Freshmen: $6547; Undergraduates: $6232. *Scholarships, grants, and awards:* Federal Pell, FSEOG, state, private, college/ university gift aid from institutional funds.

GIFT AID (NON-NEED-BASED) *Total amount:* $3,854,656 (95% institutional, 5% external sources). *Receiving aid:* Freshmen: 82% (122). Undergraduates: 45% (473). *Average award:* Freshmen: $6354. Undergraduates: $7375. *Scholarships, grants, and awards by category: Academic interests/achievement:* general academic interests/achievements. *Creative arts/performance:* music. *Special achievements/activities:* leadership. *Special characteristics:* children and siblings of alumni, children of faculty/staff, international students, members of minority groups, relatives of clergy, siblings of current students.

LOANS *Student loans:* $4,188,135 (42% need-based, 58% non-need-based). 88% of past graduating class borrowed through all loan programs. *Average indebtedness per student:* $31,804. *Average need-based loan:* Freshmen: $3693. Undergraduates: $4364. *Parent loans:* $706,153 (100% non-need-based).

Programs: FFEL (Subsidized and Unsubsidized Stafford, PLUS), Perkins, state, SELF Loans, CitiAssist Loans, Signature Loans, U.S. Bank No Fee Educational Loans, Wells Fargo Collegiate Loans.

WORK-STUDY *Federal work-study:* Total amount: $291,938; jobs available. *State or other work-study/employment:* Total amount: $4226 (100% need-based). Part-time jobs available.

APPLYING FOR FINANCIAL AID *Required financial aid forms:* FAFSA, institution's own form. *Financial aid deadline:* 8/1 (priority: 4/5). *Notification date:* Continuous. Students must reply within 3 weeks of notification.

CONTACT Marla Rupp, Director of Financial Aid, Crown College, 8700 College View Drive, St. Bonifacius, MN 55375-9001, 952-446-4175 or toll-free 800-68-CROWN. *Fax:* 952-446-4178. *E-mail:* finaid@crown.edu.

THE CULINARY INSTITUTE OF AMERICA
Hyde Park, NY

ABOUT THE INSTITUTION Independent, coed. 3 undergraduate majors.

GIFT AID (NEED-BASED) *Scholarships, grants, and awards:* Federal Pell, FSEOG, state, private, college/university gift aid from institutional funds.

GIFT AID (NON-NEED-BASED) *Scholarships, grants, and awards by category: Academic interests/achievement:* general academic interests/achievements. *Creative arts/performance:* general creative arts/performance. *Special achievements/ activities:* general special achievements/activities. *Special characteristics:* adult students, children and siblings of alumni, children of faculty/staff, general special characteristics, handicapped students, international students, veterans.

LOANS *Programs:* FFEL (Subsidized and Unsubsidized Stafford, PLUS), Perkins, alternative loans.

WORK-STUDY *Federal work-study:* Total amount: $559,961; 900 jobs averaging $435.

APPLYING FOR FINANCIAL AID *Required financial aid form:* FAFSA.

CONTACT Patricia A. Arcuri, Director of Financial Aid, The Culinary Institute of America, 1946 Campus Drive, Hyde Park, NY 12538-1499, 845-451-1243 or toll-free 800-CULINARY. *Fax:* 845-905-4030. *E-mail:* p_arcuri@culinary.edu.

CULINARY INSTITUTE OF VIRGINIA
Norfolk, VA

CONTACT Ms. Lynn Robinson, Director of Financial Aid, Culinary Institute of Virginia, 8 Abbott Park Place, Providence, RI 02903, 401-598-4648 or toll-free 866-619-CHEF. *Fax:* 401-598-1040. *E-mail:* fp@jwu.edu.

CULVER-STOCKTON COLLEGE
Canton, MO

Tuition & fees: $22,550	Average undergraduate aid package: $20,481

ABOUT THE INSTITUTION Independent religious, coed. 30 undergraduate majors. Federal methodology is used as a basis for awarding need-based institutional aid.

UNDERGRADUATE EXPENSES for 2010–11 *One-time required fee:* $200. *Comprehensive fee:* $29,950 includes full-time tuition ($22,250), mandatory fees ($300), and room and board ($7400). *College room only:* $3300. Full-time tuition and fees vary according to course level. Room and board charges vary according to board plan. *Part-time tuition:* $515 per credit hour. *Part-time fees:* $12.50 per credit hour. Part-time tuition and fees vary according to course level. *Payment plan:* Installment.

FRESHMAN FINANCIAL AID (Fall 2009, est.) 141 applied for aid; of those 94% were deemed to have need. 100% of freshmen with need received aid; of those 20% had need fully met. *Average percent of need met:* 78% (excluding resources awarded to replace EFC). *Average financial aid package:* $20,994 (excluding resources awarded to replace EFC). 11% of all full-time freshmen had no need and received non-need-based gift aid.

UNDERGRADUATE FINANCIAL AID (Fall 2009, est.) 612 applied for aid; of those 94% were deemed to have need. 100% of undergraduates with need received aid; of those 19% had need fully met. *Average percent of need met:* 79% (excluding resources awarded to replace EFC). *Average financial aid package:* $20,481 (excluding resources awarded to replace EFC). 13% of all full-time undergraduates had no need and received non-need-based gift aid.

GIFT AID (NEED-BASED) *Total amount:* $8,396,202 (18% federal, 9% state, 71% institutional, 2% external sources). *Receiving aid:* Freshmen: 89% (132); all full-time undergraduates: 87% (575). *Average award:* Freshmen: $17,385; Undergraduates: $15,634. *Scholarships, grants, and awards:* Federal Pell, FSEOG, state, private, college/university gift aid from institutional funds.

GIFT AID (NON-NEED-BASED) *Total amount:* $1,413,686 (1% state, 95% institutional, 4% external sources). *Receiving aid:* Freshmen: 16% (23). Undergraduates: 13% (85). *Average award:* Freshmen: $13,953. Undergraduates: $11,829. *Scholarships, grants, and awards by category: Academic interests/achievement:* 668 awards ($5,703,396 total): general academic interests/ achievements, international studies. *Creative arts/performance:* 102 awards ($213,325 total): art/fine arts, debating, music, theater/drama. *Special achievements/ activities:* 13 awards ($24,300 total): cheerleading/drum major, general special achievements/activities, leadership. *Special characteristics:* 102 awards ($547,090 total): children and siblings of alumni, children of faculty/staff, international students, local/state students, religious affiliation, veterans, veterans' children. *Tuition waivers:* Full or partial for employees or children of employees, senior citizens.

LOANS *Student loans:* $5,320,667 (76% need-based, 24% non-need-based). 90% of past graduating class borrowed through all loan programs. *Average indebtedness per student:* $23,761. *Average need-based loan:* Freshmen: $3916. Undergraduates: $4939. *Parent loans:* $1,484,809 (37% need-based, 63% non-need-based). *Programs:* Federal Direct (Subsidized and Unsubsidized Stafford, PLUS), Perkins, Federal Nursing, state, college/university.

WORK-STUDY *Federal work-study:* Total amount: $55,938; 42 jobs averaging $1619. *State or other work-study/employment:* Total amount: $340,871 (67% need-based, 33% non-need-based). 232 part-time jobs averaging $1534.

ATHLETIC AWARDS Total amount: $901,468 (80% need-based, 20% non-need-based).

APPLYING FOR FINANCIAL AID *Required financial aid form:* FAFSA. *Financial aid deadline:* 6/1 (priority: 3/1). *Notification date:* Continuous. Students must reply within 2 weeks of notification.

CONTACT Ms. Tina M. Wiseman, Director of Financial Aid, Culver-Stockton College, One College Hill, Canton,. MO 63435, 573-288-6307 Ext. 6306 or toll-free 800-537-1883. *Fax:* 573-288-6308. *E-mail:* twiseman@culver.edu.

CUMBERLAND UNIVERSITY
Lebanon, TN

CONTACT Ms. Beatrice LaChance, Director of Student Financial Services, Cumberland University, One Cumberland Square, Lebanon, TN 37087-3554, 615-444-2562 Ext. 1244 or toll-free 800-467-0562. *Fax:* 615-443-8424. *E-mail:* lvaughan@ cumberland.edu.

CURRY COLLEGE
Milton, MA

Tuition & fees: N/R	Average undergraduate aid package: $18,475

ABOUT THE INSTITUTION Independent, coed. 28 undergraduate majors. Federal methodology is used as a basis for awarding need-based institutional aid.

UNDERGRADUATE EXPENSES for 2010–11 *Tuition:* part-time $933 per credit hour. Part-time tuition and fees vary according to course load. Room and board charges vary according to board plan and housing facility. *Payment plan:* Installment.

FRESHMAN FINANCIAL AID (Fall 2009, est.) 469 applied for aid; of those 96% were deemed to have need. 100% of freshmen with need received aid; of those 5% had need fully met. *Average percent of need met:* 64% (excluding resources awarded to replace EFC). *Average financial aid package:* $19,206 (excluding resources awarded to replace EFC). 5% of all full-time freshmen had no need and received non-need-based gift aid.

UNDERGRADUATE FINANCIAL AID (Fall 2009, est.) 1,407 applied for aid; of those 99% were deemed to have need. 100% of undergraduates with need received aid; of those 6% had need fully met. *Average percent of need met:* 66% (excluding resources awarded to replace EFC). *Average financial aid package:* $18,475 (excluding resources awarded to replace EFC). 4% of all full-time undergraduates had no need and received non-need-based gift aid.

GIFT AID (NEED-BASED) *Total amount:* $18,114,116 (14% federal, 5% state, 78% institutional, 3% external sources). *Receiving aid:* Freshmen: 72% (436); all full-time undergraduates: 63% (1,265). *Average award:* Freshmen: $12,979;

Undergraduates: $12,322. *Scholarships, grants, and awards:* Federal Pell, FSEOG, state, private, college/university gift aid from institutional funds, Academic Competitiveness Grants, National SMART Grants.

GIFT AID (NON-NEED-BASED) *Total amount:* $590,205 (81% institutional, 19% external sources). *Receiving aid:* Freshmen: 1% (7). Undergraduates: 1% (20). *Average award:* Freshmen: $4810. Undergraduates: $5293. *Scholarships, grants, and awards by category: Academic interests/achievement:* 299 awards ($1,698,575 total): general academic interests/achievements. *Tuition waivers:* Full or partial for children of alumni, employees or children of employees.

LOANS *Student loans:* $18,225,127 (35% need-based, 65% non-need-based). 78% of past graduating class borrowed through all loan programs. *Average indebtedness per student:* $38,374. *Average need-based loan:* Freshmen: $3485. Undergraduates: $4360. *Parent loans:* $9,635,568 (100% non-need-based). *Programs:* FFEL (Subsidized and Unsubsidized Stafford, PLUS), Perkins, state.

WORK-STUDY *Federal work-study:* Total amount: $1,391,045; 763 jobs averaging $1858.

APPLYING FOR FINANCIAL AID *Required financial aid form:* FAFSA. *Financial aid deadline (priority):* 3/1. *Notification date:* Continuous beginning 3/1.

CONTACT Dyan Teehan, Director of Financial Aid/Assistant Director of Student Financial Services, Curry College, 1071 Blue Hill Avenue, Milton, MA 02186-2395, 617-333-2354 or toll-free 800-669-0686. *Fax:* 617-333-2915. *E-mail:* dteehan0107@curry.edu.

CURTIS INSTITUTE OF MUSIC
Philadelphia, PA

ABOUT THE INSTITUTION Independent, coed. *Awards:* bachelor's and master's degrees and post-bachelor's certificates. 3 undergraduate majors. *Total enrollment:* 164. Undergraduates: 135.

GIFT AID (NEED-BASED) *Scholarships, grants, and awards:* Federal Pell, college/university gift aid from institutional funds.

LOANS *Programs:* FFEL (Subsidized and Unsubsidized Stafford, PLUS).

APPLYING FOR FINANCIAL AID *Required financial aid forms:* FAFSA, institution's own form, bank statements, tax returns.

CONTACT Richard Woodland, Director of Student Financial Assistance, Curtis Institute of Music, 1726 Locust Street, Philadelphia, PA 19103-6107, 215-717-3143. *E-mail:* richard.woodland@curtis.edu.

DAEMEN COLLEGE
Amherst, NY

Tuition & fees: $20,720	Average undergraduate aid package: $14,529

ABOUT THE INSTITUTION Independent, coed. 31 undergraduate majors. Federal methodology is used as a basis for awarding need-based institutional aid.

UNDERGRADUATE EXPENSES for 2009–10 *Comprehensive fee:* $30,170 includes full-time tuition ($20,250), mandatory fees ($470), and room and board ($9450). Full-time tuition and fees vary according to course load. Room and board charges vary according to board plan and housing facility. *Part-time tuition:* $675 per credit hour. *Part-time fees:* $4 per credit hour; $70 per term. Part-time tuition and fees vary according to course load. *Payment plans:* Installment, deferred payment.

FRESHMAN FINANCIAL AID (Fall 2008) 366 applied for aid; of those 98% were deemed to have need. 100% of freshmen with need received aid. *Average financial aid package:* $15,319 (excluding resources awarded to replace EFC). 15% of all full-time freshmen had no need and received non-need-based gift aid.

UNDERGRADUATE FINANCIAL AID (Fall 2008) 1,302 applied for aid; of those 98% were deemed to have need. 100% of undergraduates with need received aid. *Average financial aid package:* $14,529 (excluding resources awarded to replace EFC). 15% of all full-time undergraduates had no need and received non-need-based gift aid.

GIFT AID (NEED-BASED) *Total amount:* $6,461,063 (29% federal, 32% state, 39% institutional). *Receiving aid:* Freshmen: 67% (270); all full-time undergraduates: 67% (948). *Average award:* Freshmen: $7130; Undergraduates: $6229. *Scholarships, grants, and awards:* Federal Pell, FSEOG, state, private, college/ university gift aid from institutional funds.

GIFT AID (NON-NEED-BASED) *Total amount:* $8,369,674 (1% federal, 1% state, 98% institutional). *Receiving aid:* Freshmen: 61% (246). Undergraduates: 59% (833). *Average award:* Freshmen: $6290. Undergraduates: $5805.

Scholarships, grants, and awards by category: *Academic interests/achievement:* 1,113 awards ($6,453,895 total): general academic interests/achievements. *Creative arts/performance:* 7 awards ($31,000 total): art/fine arts. *Special characteristics:* 80 awards ($897,809 total): children and siblings of alumni, children of faculty/staff, general special characteristics, siblings of current students. **Tuition waivers:** Full or partial for employees or children of employees, senior citizens.

LOANS Student loans: $10,950,465 (41% need-based, 59% non-need-based). 90% of past graduating class borrowed through all loan programs. *Average indebtedness per student:* $18,910. **Average need-based loan:** Freshmen: $3789. Undergraduates: $4370. **Parent loans:** $704,124 (44% need-based, 56% non-need-based). **Programs:** FFEL (Subsidized and Unsubsidized Stafford, PLUS), Perkins, college/university, alternative loans.

WORK-STUDY Federal work-study: Total amount: $340,686; 256 jobs averaging $1328. **State or other work-study/employment:** Total amount: $624,128 (30% need-based, 70% non-need-based). 242 part-time jobs averaging $1059.

ATHLETIC AWARDS Total amount: $621,788 (68% need-based, 32% non-need-based).

APPLYING FOR FINANCIAL AID Required financial aid forms: FAFSA, state aid form. **Financial aid deadline (priority):** 2/15. **Notification date:** Continuous. Students must reply within 2 weeks of notification.

CONTACT Jeffrey Pagano, Director of Financial Aid, Daemen College, 4380 Main Street, Amherst, NY 14226-3592, 716-839-8254 or toll-free 800-462-7652. *Fax:* 716-839-8378. *E-mail:* jpagano@daemen.edu.

DAKOTA STATE UNIVERSITY
Madison, SD

Tuition & fees (SD res): $6872	Average undergraduate aid package: $7269

ABOUT THE INSTITUTION State-supported, coed. 31 undergraduate majors. Federal methodology is used as a basis for awarding need-based institutional aid.

UNDERGRADUATE EXPENSES for 2009–10 Tuition, state resident: full-time $2751; part-time $92 per credit hour. **Tuition, nonresident:** full-time $4124; part-time $137 per credit hour. **Required fees:** full-time $4121; $114 per credit hour. Full-time tuition and fees vary according to location and reciprocity agreements. Part-time tuition and fees vary according to location and reciprocity agreements. **College room and board:** $4818; **Room only:** $2640. Room and board charges vary according to board plan and housing facility. **Payment plans:** Installment, deferred payment.

FRESHMAN FINANCIAL AID (Fall 2008) 228 applied for aid; of those 74% were deemed to have need. 100% of freshmen with need received aid; of those 13% had need fully met. **Average percent of need met:** 80% (excluding resources awarded to replace EFC). **Average financial aid package:** $6902 (excluding resources awarded to replace EFC). 11% of all full-time freshmen had no need and received non-need-based gift aid.

UNDERGRADUATE FINANCIAL AID (Fall 2008) 930 applied for aid; of those 76% were deemed to have need. 100% of undergraduates with need received aid; of those 18% had need fully met. **Average percent of need met:** 82% (excluding resources awarded to replace EFC). **Average financial aid package:** $7269 (excluding resources awarded to replace EFC). 9% of all full-time undergraduates had no need and received non-need-based gift aid.

GIFT AID (NEED-BASED) Total amount: $2,044,169 (70% federal, 4% state, 16% institutional, 10% external sources). **Receiving aid:** Freshmen: 31% (81); all full-time undergraduates: 31% (340). **Average award:** Freshmen: $3957; Undergraduates: $4106. **Scholarships, grants, and awards:** Federal Pell, FSEOG, state, private, college/university gift aid from institutional funds, Agency Assistance (Veteran Benefits/Department of Labor), National SMART Grants.

GIFT AID (NON-NEED-BASED) Total amount: $406,597 (39% federal, 9% state, 32% institutional, 20% external sources). **Receiving aid:** Freshmen: 43% (112). Undergraduates: 27% (300). **Average award:** Freshmen: $3268. Undergraduates: $3652. **Scholarships, grants, and awards by category:** *Academic interests/achievement:* business, communication, computer science, education, English, general academic interests/achievements, mathematics. *Creative arts/performance:* music. *Special achievements/activities:* general special achievements/activities. *Special characteristics:* children and siblings of alumni, ethnic background, local/state students, members of minority groups. **Tuition waivers:** Full or partial for employees or children of employees, senior citizens.

LOANS Student loans: $7,593,841 (71% need-based, 29% non-need-based). 92% of past graduating class borrowed through all loan programs. *Average indebtedness per student:* $21,189. **Average need-based loan:** Freshmen: $3283. Undergraduates: $3752. **Parent loans:** $580,043 (71% need-based, 29% non-need-based). **Programs:** Federal Direct (Subsidized and Unsubsidized Stafford, PLUS), FFEL (Subsidized and Unsubsidized Stafford, PLUS), Perkins, alternative commercial loans.

WORK-STUDY Federal work-study: Total amount: $261,779; jobs available. **State or other work-study/employment:** Total amount: $99,729 (100% non-need-based). Part-time jobs available.

ATHLETIC AWARDS Total amount: $211,467 (71% need-based, 29% non-need-based).

APPLYING FOR FINANCIAL AID Required financial aid form: FAFSA. **Financial aid deadline (priority):** 3/1. **Notification date:** Continuous beginning 4/1. Students must reply within 2 weeks of notification.

CONTACT Denise Grayson, Financial Aid Director, Dakota State University, 103 Heston Hall, 820 North Washington Avenue, Madison, SD 57042-1799, 605-256-5158 or toll-free 888-DSU-9988. *Fax:* 605-256-5020. *E-mail:* fa@dsu.edu.

DAKOTA WESLEYAN UNIVERSITY
Mitchell, SD

Tuition & fees: $19,850	Average undergraduate aid package: $19,000

ABOUT THE INSTITUTION Independent United Methodist, coed. 45 undergraduate majors. Federal methodology is used as a basis for awarding need-based institutional aid.

UNDERGRADUATE EXPENSES for 2010–11 Tuition: full-time $19,850. Room and board charges vary according to board plan and housing facility.

FRESHMAN FINANCIAL AID (Fall 2009, est.) 159 applied for aid; of those 89% were deemed to have need. 100% of freshmen with need received aid; of those 20% had need fully met. **Average percent of need met:** 66% (excluding resources awarded to replace EFC). **Average financial aid package:** $19,200 (excluding resources awarded to replace EFC). 7% of all full-time freshmen had no need and received non-need-based gift aid.

UNDERGRADUATE FINANCIAL AID (Fall 2009, est.) 633 applied for aid; of those 93% were deemed to have need. 100% of undergraduates with need received aid; of those 14% had need fully met. **Average percent of need met:** 70% (excluding resources awarded to replace EFC). **Average financial aid package:** $19,000 (excluding resources awarded to replace EFC). 8% of all full-time undergraduates had no need and received non-need-based gift aid.

GIFT AID (NEED-BASED) Total amount: $5,991,162 (29% federal, 1% state, 68% institutional, 2% external sources). **Receiving aid:** Freshmen: 84% (141); all full-time undergraduates: 85% (574). **Average award:** Freshmen: $10,600; Undergraduates: $9812. **Scholarships, grants, and awards:** Federal Pell, FSEOG, state, college/university gift aid from institutional funds.

GIFT AID (NON-NEED-BASED) Total amount: $1,035,586 (1% federal, 4% state, 90% institutional, 5% external sources). **Receiving aid:** Freshmen: 14% (24). Undergraduates: 10% (70). **Average award:** Freshmen: $8200. Undergraduates: $11,000. **Tuition waivers:** Full or partial for senior citizens.

LOANS Student loans: $5,832,459 (76% need-based, 24% non-need-based). 67% of past graduating class borrowed through all loan programs. *Average indebtedness per student:* $30,000. **Average need-based loan:** Freshmen: $3300. Undergraduates: $4300. **Parent loans:** $363,638 (37% need-based, 63% non-need-based). **Programs:** Federal Direct (Subsidized and Unsubsidized Stafford, PLUS), Perkins, private alternative loans, United Methodist Student Loans (for members of Methodist Church).

WORK-STUDY Federal work-study: Total amount: $104,099; 107 jobs averaging $1400. **State or other work-study/employment:** Total amount: $7700 (100% non-need-based). 5 part-time jobs averaging $1400.

ATHLETIC AWARDS Total amount: $1,351,198 (69% need-based, 31% non-need-based).

APPLYING FOR FINANCIAL AID Financial aid deadline (priority): 4/1. **Notification date:** Continuous beginning 3/1. Students must reply within 2 weeks of notification.

CONTACT Kristy O'Kief, Director of Financial Aid, Dakota Wesleyan University, 1200 West University Avenue, Mitchell, SD 57301, 605-995-2656 or toll-free 800-333-8506. *Fax:* 605-995-2638. *E-mail:* krokief@dwu.edu.

DALLAS BAPTIST UNIVERSITY
Dallas, TX

Tuition & fees: $17,490 | **Average undergraduate aid package:** $13,557

ABOUT THE INSTITUTION Independent religious, coed. 45 undergraduate majors. Federal methodology is used as a basis for awarding need-based institutional aid.

UNDERGRADUATE EXPENSES for 2009–10 *Comprehensive fee:* $23,126 includes full-time tuition ($17,490) and room and board ($5636). *College room only:* $2236. Room and board charges vary according to board plan and housing facility. *Part-time tuition:* $583 per credit hour. *Payment plans:* Installment, deferred payment.

FRESHMAN FINANCIAL AID (Fall 2009, est.) 335 applied for aid; of those 71% were deemed to have need. 100% of freshmen with need received aid; of those 66% had need fully met. *Average percent of need met:* 75% (excluding resources awarded to replace EFC). *Average financial aid package:* $14,752 (excluding resources awarded to replace EFC). 22% of all full-time freshmen had no need and received non-need-based gift aid.

UNDERGRADUATE FINANCIAL AID (Fall 2009, est.) 1,916 applied for aid; of those 72% were deemed to have need. 98% of undergraduates with need received aid; of those 47% had need fully met. *Average percent of need met:* 64% (excluding resources awarded to replace EFC). *Average financial aid package:* $13,557 (excluding resources awarded to replace EFC). 18% of all full-time undergraduates had no need and received non-need-based gift aid.

GIFT AID (NEED-BASED) *Total amount:* $6,540,890 (56% federal, 44% state). *Receiving aid:* Freshmen: 43% (152); all full-time undergraduates: 42% (929). *Average award:* Freshmen: $3384; Undergraduates: $3624. *Scholarships, grants, and awards:* Federal Pell, FSEOG, state, private, college/university gift aid from institutional funds.

GIFT AID (NON-NEED-BASED) *Total amount:* $12,008,453 (84% institutional, 16% external sources). *Receiving aid:* Freshmen: 64% (225). Undergraduates: 50% (1,106). *Average award:* Freshmen: $7739. Undergraduates: $7088. *Scholarships, grants, and awards by category: Academic interests/achievement:* 1,499 awards ($2,915,753 total): business, communication, computer science, education, general academic interests/achievements, humanities, mathematics, premedicine, religion/biblical studies. *Creative arts/performance:* 83 awards ($247,398 total): music. *Special achievements/activities:* 1,384 awards ($4,865,349 total): community service, general special achievements/activities, leadership, memberships, religious involvement. *Special characteristics:* 197 awards ($748,685 total): children of faculty/staff, general special characteristics, relatives of clergy, religious affiliation. *Tuition waivers:* Full or partial for employees or children of employees.

LOANS *Student loans:* $17,543,982 (36% need-based, 64% non-need-based). 79% of past graduating class borrowed through all loan programs. *Average indebtedness per student:* $17,214. *Average need-based loan:* Freshmen: $3247. Undergraduates: $3991. *Parent loans:* $9,596,273 (68% need-based, 32% non-need-based). *Programs:* Federal Direct (Subsidized and Unsubsidized Stafford, PLUS), FFEL (Subsidized and Unsubsidized Stafford, PLUS), Perkins, state, college/university.

WORK-STUDY *Federal work-study:* Total amount: $183,119; 117 jobs averaging $2872. *State or other work-study/employment:* Total amount: $20,140 (100% need-based). 48 part-time jobs averaging $577.

ATHLETIC AWARDS Total amount: $1,311,335 (100% non-need-based).

APPLYING FOR FINANCIAL AID *Required financial aid forms:* FAFSA, institution's own form. *Financial aid deadline:* Continuous. *Notification date:* Continuous beginning 2/1.

CONTACT Mr. Donald G. Zackary, Director of Financial Aid, Dallas Baptist University, 3000 Mountain Creek Parkway, Dallas, TX 75211-9299, 214-333-5363 or toll-free 800-460-1328. *Fax:* 214-333-5586. *E-mail:* donz@dbu.edu.

DALLAS CHRISTIAN COLLEGE
Dallas, TX

CONTACT Robin L. Walker, Director of Student Financial Aid, Dallas Christian College, 2700 Christian Parkway, Dallas, TX 75234-7299, 972-241-3371 Ext. 105. *Fax:* 972-241-8021. *E-mail:* finaid@dallas.edu.

DALTON STATE COLLEGE
Dalton, GA

Tuition & fees (GA res): $2292 | **Average undergraduate aid package:** $8985

ABOUT THE INSTITUTION State-supported, coed. 64 undergraduate majors. Federal methodology is used as a basis for awarding need-based institutional aid.

UNDERGRADUATE EXPENSES for 2009–10 *Tuition, state resident:* full-time $2016; part-time $84 per credit hour. *Tuition, nonresident:* full-time $7992; part-time $333 per credit hour. *Required fees:* full-time $276; $7.33 per credit hour or $50 per term.

FRESHMAN FINANCIAL AID (Fall 2008) 708 applied for aid; of those 76% were deemed to have need. 95% of freshmen with need received aid; of those 20% had need fully met. *Average percent of need met:* 68% (excluding resources awarded to replace EFC). *Average financial aid package:* $6566 (excluding resources awarded to replace EFC). 1% of all full-time freshmen had no need and received non-need-based gift aid.

UNDERGRADUATE FINANCIAL AID (Fall 2008) 2,064 applied for aid; of those 74% were deemed to have need. 96% of undergraduates with need received aid; of those 49% had need fully met. *Average percent of need met:* 76% (excluding resources awarded to replace EFC). *Average financial aid package:* $8985 (excluding resources awarded to replace EFC). 1% of all full-time undergraduates had no need and received non-need-based gift aid.

GIFT AID (NEED-BASED) *Total amount:* $6,536,589 (100% federal). *Receiving aid:* Freshmen: 42% (402); all full-time undergraduates: 46% (1,187). *Average award:* Freshmen: $3568; Undergraduates: $3636. *Scholarships, grants, and awards:* Federal Pell, FSEOG, state, private.

GIFT AID (NON-NEED-BASED) *Total amount:* $1,938,099 (82% state, 8% institutional, 10% external sources). *Receiving aid:* Freshmen: 40% (384). Undergraduates: 52% (1,326). *Average award:* Freshmen: $1000. Undergraduates: $1345. *Scholarships, grants, and awards by category: Academic interests/achievement:* biological sciences, business, computer science, education, engineering/technologies, English, general academic interests/achievements, health fields, humanities, social sciences. *Special achievements/activities:* community service, hobbies/interests, leadership, memberships. *Special characteristics:* adult students, children of faculty/staff, local/state students, members of minority groups, out-of-state students.

LOANS *Student loans:* $5,675,415 (53% need-based, 47% non-need-based). 44% of past graduating class borrowed through all loan programs. *Average indebtedness per student:* $11,953. *Average need-based loan:* Freshmen: $2650. Undergraduates: $3476. *Parent loans:* $24,356 (100% non-need-based). *Programs:* FFEL (Subsidized and Unsubsidized Stafford, PLUS), state.

WORK-STUDY *Federal work-study:* Total amount: $104,563; jobs available. *State or other work-study/employment:* Total amount: $259,044 (100% non-need-based). Part-time jobs available.

APPLYING FOR FINANCIAL AID *Required financial aid form:* FAFSA. *Financial aid deadline:* 7/1 (priority: 6/1). *Notification date:* Continuous beginning 4/1.

CONTACT Holly Woods, Interim Director of Student Financial Aid, Dalton State College, 650 College Drive, Dalton, GA 30720, 706-272-4545 or toll-free 800-829-4436. *Fax:* 706-272-2458. *E-mail:* hwoods@daltonstate.edu.

DANA COLLEGE
Blair, NE

ABOUT THE INSTITUTION Independent religious, coed. 47 undergraduate majors.

GIFT AID (NEED-BASED) *Scholarships, grants, and awards:* Federal Pell, FSEOG, state, private, college/university gift aid from institutional funds.

GIFT AID (NON-NEED-BASED) *Scholarships, grants, and awards by category: Academic interests/achievement:* biological sciences, business, communication, education, English, foreign languages, general academic interests/achievements, health fields, international studies, mathematics, military science, premedicine, religion/biblical studies, social sciences. *Creative arts/performance:* applied art and design, art/fine arts, music, theater/drama. *Special achievements/activities:* general special achievements/activities, leadership, religious involvement. *Special characteristics:* ethnic background, international students, local/state students, members of minority groups, out-of-state students, religious affiliation.

LOANS *Programs:* FFEL (Subsidized and Unsubsidized Stafford, PLUS), Perkins.

WORK-STUDY *Federal work-study:* Total amount: $285,860; jobs available (averaging $1000). *State or other work-study/employment:* Part-time jobs available.

APPLYING FOR FINANCIAL AID *Required financial aid forms:* FAFSA, institution's own form.

CONTACT Rita McManigal, Director of Financial Aid, Dana College, 2848 College Drive, Blair, NE 68008-1099, 402-426-7227 or toll-free 800-444-3262. *Fax:* 402-426-7225. *E-mail:* rmcmanig@dana.edu.

DANIEL WEBSTER COLLEGE
Nashua, NH

CONTACT Office of Financial Aid, Daniel Webster College, 20 University Drive, Nashua, NH 03063-1300, 603-577-6590 or toll-free 800-325-6876. *Fax:* 603-577-6593.

DANIEL WEBSTER COLLEGE–PORTSMOUTH CAMPUS
Portsmouth, NH

CONTACT Financial Aid Office, Daniel Webster College–Portsmouth Campus, 119 International Drive, Pease International Tradeport, Portsmouth, NH 03801, 603-430-4077 or toll-free 800-794-6188.

DARKEI NOAM RABBINICAL COLLEGE
Brooklyn, NY

CONTACT Ms. Rivi Horowitz, Director of Financial Aid, Darkei Noam Rabbinical College, 2822 Avenue J, Brooklyn, NY 11219, 718-338-6464.

DARTMOUTH COLLEGE
Hanover, NH

Tuition & fees: $38,679	Average undergraduate aid package: $38,449

ABOUT THE INSTITUTION Independent, coed. 60 undergraduate majors. Both federal and institutional methodology are used as a basis for awarding need-based institutional aid.

UNDERGRADUATE EXPENSES for 2010–11 *Comprehensive fee:* $49,974 includes full-time tuition ($38,445), mandatory fees ($234), and room and board ($11,295). *College room only:* $6750. Room and board charges vary according to board plan. *Part-time tuition:* $5126 per credit hour. *Payment plans:* Tuition prepayment, installment.

FRESHMAN FINANCIAL AID (Fall 2009, est.) 708 applied for aid; of those 83% were deemed to have need. 100% of freshmen with need received aid; of those 100% had need fully met. *Average percent of need met:* 100% (excluding resources awarded to replace EFC). *Average financial aid package:* $40,531 (excluding resources awarded to replace EFC). 1% of all full-time freshmen had no need and received non-need-based gift aid.

UNDERGRADUATE FINANCIAL AID (Fall 2009, est.) 2,623 applied for aid; of those 86% were deemed to have need. 100% of undergraduates with need received aid; of those 100% had need fully met. *Average percent of need met:* 100% (excluding resources awarded to replace EFC). *Average financial aid package:* $38,449 (excluding resources awarded to replace EFC). 1% of all full-time undergraduates had no need and received non-need-based gift aid.

GIFT AID (NEED-BASED) *Total amount:* $77,287,023 (7% federal, 90% institutional, 3% external sources). *Receiving aid:* Freshmen: 53% (579); all full-time undergraduates: 53% (2,195). *Average award:* Freshmen: $36,866; Undergraduates: $35,209. *Scholarships, grants, and awards:* Federal Pell, FSEOG, state, private, college/university gift aid from institutional funds.

GIFT AID (NON-NEED-BASED) *Total amount:* $1,059,431 (36% federal, 64% external sources). *Average award:* Freshmen: $450. Undergraduates: $450.

LOANS *Student loans:* $10,177,761 (58% need-based, 42% non-need-based). 48% of past graduating class borrowed through all loan programs. *Average indebtedness per student:* $19,081. *Average need-based loan:* Freshmen: $3102. Undergraduates: $3340. *Parent loans:* $4,972,060 (100% non-need-based). *Programs:* FFEL (Subsidized and Unsubsidized Stafford, PLUS), Perkins, college/university.

WORK-STUDY *Federal work-study:* Total amount: $2,809,686; 1,399 jobs averaging $1983. *State or other work-study/employment:* Total amount: $946,075 (100% need-based). 582 part-time jobs averaging $1594.

APPLYING FOR FINANCIAL AID *Required financial aid forms:* FAFSA, CSS Financial Aid PROFILE, noncustodial (divorced/separated) parent's statement, business/farm supplement, federal income tax form(s), W-2 forms. *Financial aid deadline:* 2/1. *Notification date:* 3/31. Students must reply by 5/1.

CONTACT Ms. Virginia S. Hazen, Director of Financial Aid, Dartmouth College, 6024 McNutt Hall, Hanover, NH 03755, 603-646-2451. *Fax:* 603-646-1414. *E-mail:* virginia.s.hazen@dartmouth.edu.

DAVENPORT UNIVERSITY
Grand Rapids, MI

Tuition & fees: $11,241	Average undergraduate aid package: N/A

ABOUT THE INSTITUTION Independent, coed. 24 undergraduate majors. Federal methodology is used as a basis for awarding need-based institutional aid.

UNDERGRADUATE EXPENSES for 2009–10 *Comprehensive fee:* $20,741 includes full-time tuition ($11,016), mandatory fees ($225), and room and board ($9500). Full-time tuition and fees vary according to location. Room and board charges vary according to board plan and housing facility. *Part-time tuition:* $459 per credit hour. Part-time tuition and fees vary according to location. *Payment plan:* Installment.

GIFT AID (NEED-BASED) *Total amount:* $22,481,224 (87% federal, 13% state). *Scholarships, grants, and awards:* Federal Pell, FSEOG, state, private, college/university gift aid from institutional funds.

GIFT AID (NON-NEED-BASED) *Total amount:* $9,214,703 (3% state, 97% institutional). *Scholarships, grants, and awards by category: Academic interests/achievement:* general academic interests/achievements. *Special achievements/activities:* memberships. *Tuition waivers:* Full or partial for employees or children of employees.

LOANS *Student loans:* $73,404,523 (100% need-based). *Parent loans:* $3,211,498 (100% need-based). *Programs:* FFEL (Subsidized and Unsubsidized Stafford, PLUS), private alternative loans.

WORK-STUDY *Federal work-study:* Total amount: $922,857; jobs available. *State or other work-study/employment:* Part-time jobs available.

ATHLETIC AWARDS Total amount: $1,861,517 (100% non-need-based).

APPLYING FOR FINANCIAL AID *Required financial aid form:* FAFSA. *Financial aid deadline (priority):* 3/1. *Notification date:* 3/1.

CONTACT David DeBoer, Executive Director of Financial Aid, Davenport University, 6191 Kraft Avenue SE, Grand Rapids, MI 49512, 616-732-1132 or toll-free 800-632-9569. *Fax:* 616-732-1167. *E-mail:* david.debore@davenport.edu.

DAVIDSON COLLEGE
Davidson, NC

Tuition & fees: $35,124	Average undergraduate aid package: $24,121

ABOUT THE INSTITUTION Independent Presbyterian, coed. 21 undergraduate majors. Both federal and institutional methodology are used as a basis for awarding need-based institutional aid.

UNDERGRADUATE EXPENSES for 2009–10 *Comprehensive fee:* $45,030 includes full-time tuition ($34,776), mandatory fees ($348), and room and board ($9906). *College room only:* $5231.

FRESHMAN FINANCIAL AID (Fall 2008) 306 applied for aid; of those 69% were deemed to have need. 96% of freshmen with need received aid; of those 100% had need fully met. *Average percent of need met:* 100% (excluding resources awarded to replace EFC). *Average financial aid package:* $24,899 (excluding resources awarded to replace EFC). 12% of all full-time freshmen had no need and received non-need-based gift aid.

UNDERGRADUATE FINANCIAL AID (Fall 2008) 867 applied for aid; of those 85% were deemed to have need. 97% of undergraduates with need received aid; of those 100% had need fully met. *Average percent of need met:* 100% (excluding resources awarded to replace EFC). *Average financial aid package:* $24,121 (excluding resources awarded to replace EFC). 14% of all full-time undergraduates had no need and received non-need-based gift aid.

GIFT AID (NEED-BASED) *Total amount:* $13,550,141 (5% federal, 3% state, 92% institutional). *Receiving aid:* Freshmen: 38% (184); all full-time undergraduates: 37% (617). *Average award:* Freshmen: $23,853; Undergraduates: $21,962.

Scholarships, grants, and awards: Federal Pell, FSEOG, state, private, college/university gift aid from institutional funds, need-linked special talent scholarships.
GIFT AID (NON-NEED-BASED) *Total amount:* $8,423,980 (6% federal, 8% state, 78% institutional, 8% external sources). *Receiving aid:* Freshmen: 19% (93). Undergraduates: 23% (376). *Average award:* Freshmen: $19,079. Undergraduates: $17,182. *Scholarships, grants, and awards by category:* *Academic interests/achievement:* 136 awards ($2,557,589 total): biological sciences, business, education, foreign languages, general academic interests/achievements, mathematics, physical sciences, premedicine, religion/biblical studies, social sciences. *Creative arts/performance:* 36 awards ($276,000 total): art/fine arts, creative writing, music, performing arts, theater/drama. *Special achievements/activities:* 100 awards ($1,589,996 total): community service, general special achievements/activities, leadership, religious involvement. *Special characteristics:* 122 awards ($1,411,910 total): first-generation college students, general special characteristics, local/state students, out-of-state students, relatives of clergy. *Tuition waivers:* Full or partial for employees or children of employees.
LOANS *Student loans:* $3,027,406 (14% need-based, 86% non-need-based). 38% of past graduating class borrowed through all loan programs. *Average indebtedness per student:* $20,858. *Average need-based loan:* Freshmen: $2313. Undergraduates: $3250. *Parent loans:* $1,858,212 (100% non-need-based). *Programs:* Federal Direct (Subsidized and Unsubsidized Stafford, PLUS), alternative loans.
WORK-STUDY *Federal work-study:* Total amount: $245,827; 190 jobs averaging $1294. *State or other work-study/employment:* Total amount: $142,758 (100% need-based). 102 part-time jobs averaging $1400.
ATHLETIC AWARDS Total amount: $2,721,708 (100% non-need-based).
APPLYING FOR FINANCIAL AID *Required financial aid forms:* FAFSA, CSS Financial Aid PROFILE, noncustodial (divorced/separated) parent's statement, business/farm supplement, parent and student tax returns and W-2 forms, corporate tax returns (if applicable). *Financial aid deadline:* 2/15. *Notification date:* 4/5. Students must reply by 5/1.
CONTACT Mr. David R. Gelinas, Director of Financial Aid, Davidson College, 413 North Main Street, Box 7157, Davidson, NC 28035-7157, 704-894-2232 or toll-free 800-768-0380. *Fax:* 704-894-2845. *E-mail:* dagelinas@davidson.edu.

DAVIS & ELKINS COLLEGE
Elkins, WV

CONTACT Susan M. George, Director of Financial Planning, Davis & Elkins College, 100 Campus Drive, Elkins, WV 26241-3996, 304-637-1373 or toll-free 800-624-3157 Ext. 1230. *Fax:* 304-637-1986. *E-mail:* ssw@davisandelkins.edu.

DAVIS COLLEGE
Johnson City, NY

ABOUT THE INSTITUTION Independent nondenominational, coed. 8 undergraduate majors.
GIFT AID (NEED-BASED) *Scholarships, grants, and awards:* Federal Pell, FSEOG, state, private, college/university gift aid from institutional funds.
GIFT AID (NON-NEED-BASED) *Scholarships, grants, and awards by category:* *Academic interests/achievement:* general academic interests/achievements, religion/biblical studies. *Creative arts/performance:* music. *Special achievements/activities:* leadership. *Special characteristics:* children and siblings of alumni, children of educators, children of faculty/staff, general special characteristics, international students, married students, out-of-state students, relatives of clergy, siblings of current students, spouses of current students.
LOANS *Programs:* FFEL (Subsidized and Unsubsidized Stafford, PLUS), college/university.
APPLYING FOR FINANCIAL AID *Required financial aid forms:* FAFSA, institution's own form, state aid form.
CONTACT Stephanie D. Baker, Financial Aid Director, Davis College, 400 Riverside Drive, Johnson City, NY 13790, 607-729-1581 Ext. 401 or toll-free 800-331-4137 Ext. 406. *Fax:* 607-770-6886. *E-mail:* financialaid@davisny.edu.

DAYMAR INSTITUTE
Clarksville, TN

CONTACT Ms. Angie Sanford, Financial Aid Officer, Daymar Institute, 1860 Wilma Rudolph Boulevard, Clarksville, TN 37040, 931-552-7600.

DEFIANCE COLLEGE
Defiance, OH

Tuition & fees: $24,330 | **Average undergraduate aid package: $18,433**

ABOUT THE INSTITUTION Independent religious, coed. 33 undergraduate majors. Federal methodology is used as a basis for awarding need-based institutional aid.
UNDERGRADUATE EXPENSES for 2010–11 *One-time required fee:* $75. *Comprehensive fee:* $32,450 includes full-time tuition ($23,800), mandatory fees ($530), and room and board ($8120). *College room only:* $4460. Full-time tuition and fees vary according to program. Room and board charges vary according to board plan and housing facility. *Part-time tuition:* $385 per credit hour. *Part-time fees:* $75 per term. Part-time tuition and fees vary according to course load. *Payment plan:* Installment.
FRESHMAN FINANCIAL AID (Fall 2009, est.) 212 applied for aid; of those 96% were deemed to have need. 100% of freshmen with need received aid; of those 9% had need fully met. *Average percent of need met:* 79% (excluding resources awarded to replace EFC). *Average financial aid package:* $18,904 (excluding resources awarded to replace EFC). 5% of all full-time freshmen had no need and received non-need-based gift aid.
UNDERGRADUATE FINANCIAL AID (Fall 2009, est.) 729 applied for aid; of those 96% were deemed to have need. 100% of undergraduates with need received aid; of those 13% had need fully met. *Average percent of need met:* 75% (excluding resources awarded to replace EFC). *Average financial aid package:* $18,433 (excluding resources awarded to replace EFC). 7% of all full-time undergraduates had no need and received non-need-based gift aid.
GIFT AID (NEED-BASED) *Total amount:* $7,789,201 (23% federal, 6% state, 69% institutional, 2% external sources). *Receiving aid:* Freshmen: 80% (172); all full-time undergraduates: 71% (538). *Average award:* Freshmen: $6636; Undergraduates: $6007. *Scholarships, grants, and awards:* Federal Pell, FSEOG, state, private, college/university gift aid from institutional funds.
GIFT AID (NON-NEED-BASED) *Total amount:* $1,979,315 (91% institutional, 9% external sources). *Receiving aid:* Freshmen: 92% (198). Undergraduates: 90% (679). *Average award:* Freshmen: $10,364. Undergraduates: $9308. *Scholarships, grants, and awards by category:* *Academic interests/achievement:* biological sciences, business, communication, computer science, education, English, general academic interests/achievements, health fields, humanities, international studies, mathematics, physical sciences, premedicine, religion/biblical studies, social sciences. *Special achievements/activities:* community service, general special achievements/activities, leadership, religious involvement. *Special characteristics:* children of faculty/staff, international students, members of minority groups, out-of-state students, previous college experience, religious affiliation. *Tuition waivers:* Full or partial for employees or children of employees, senior citizens.
LOANS *Student loans:* $7,597,361 (62% need-based, 38% non-need-based). 90% of past graduating class borrowed through all loan programs. *Average indebtedness per student:* $25,388. *Average need-based loan:* Freshmen: $3523. Undergraduates: $4544. *Parent loans:* $838,822 (24% need-based, 76% non-need-based). *Programs:* Federal Direct (Subsidized and Unsubsidized Stafford, PLUS), Perkins, alternative education loans.
WORK-STUDY *Federal work-study:* Total amount: $895,513; 465 jobs averaging $1915. *State or other work-study/employment:* Total amount: $110,495 (100% non-need-based). 63 part-time jobs averaging $1243.
APPLYING FOR FINANCIAL AID *Required financial aid form:* FAFSA. *Financial aid deadline (priority):* 4/1. *Notification date:* Continuous beginning 2/1. Students must reply by 5/1 or within 2 weeks of notification.
CONTACT Amy Francis, Director of Financial Aid, Defiance College, 701 North Clinton Street, Defiance, OH 43512-1610, 419-783-2376 or toll-free 800-520-4632 Ext. 2359. *Fax:* 419-783-2579. *E-mail:* afrancis@defiance.edu.

DELAWARE STATE UNIVERSITY
Dover, DE

CONTACT Associate Director of Financial Aid, Delaware State University, 1200 North DuPont Highway, Dover, DE 19901-2277, 302-857-6250 or toll-free 800-845-2544.

DELAWARE VALLEY COLLEGE
Doylestown, PA

Tuition & fees: $29,284   **Average undergraduate aid package: $19,249**

ABOUT THE INSTITUTION Independent, coed. 29 undergraduate majors. Federal methodology is used as a basis for awarding need-based institutional aid.

UNDERGRADUATE EXPENSES for 2010–11 Comprehensive fee: $39,610 includes full-time tuition ($27,234), mandatory fees ($2050), and room and board ($10,326). **College room only:** $4682. **Part-time tuition:** $750 per credit.

FRESHMAN FINANCIAL AID (Fall 2009, est.) 416 applied for aid; of those 90% were deemed to have need. 100% of freshmen with need received aid; of those 14% had need fully met. **Average percent of need met:** 70% (excluding resources awarded to replace EFC). **Average financial aid package:** $19,957 (excluding resources awarded to replace EFC). 17% of all full-time freshmen had no need and received non-need-based gift aid.

UNDERGRADUATE FINANCIAL AID (Fall 2009, est.) 1,434 applied for aid; of those 91% were deemed to have need. 100% of undergraduates with need received aid; of those 11% had need fully met. **Average percent of need met:** 68% (excluding resources awarded to replace EFC). **Average financial aid package:** $19,249 (excluding resources awarded to replace EFC). 20% of all full-time undergraduates had no need and received non-need-based gift aid.

GIFT AID (NEED-BASED) Total amount: $18,838,016 (12% federal, 8% state, 78% institutional, 2% external sources). **Receiving aid:** Freshmen: 82% (369); all full-time undergraduates: 78% (1,300). **Average award:** Freshmen: $15,780; Undergraduates: $14,435. **Scholarships, grants, and awards:** Federal Pell, FSEOG, state, private, college/university gift aid from institutional funds.

GIFT AID (NON-NEED-BASED) Total amount: $3,914,617 (1% federal, 98% institutional, 1% external sources). **Receiving aid:** Freshmen: 10% (47). Undergraduates: 8% (128). **Average award:** Freshmen: $11,847. Undergraduates: $10,096. **Scholarships, grants, and awards by category:** Academic interests/achievement: general academic interests/achievements. Creative arts/performance: general creative arts/performance. Special characteristics: children and siblings of alumni.

LOANS Student loans: $13,572,040 (72% need-based, 28% non-need-based). 63% of past graduating class borrowed through all loan programs. Average indebtedness per student: $26,350. **Average need-based loan:** Freshmen: $3570. Undergraduates: $4371. **Parent loans:** $4,866,726 (41% need-based, 59% non-need-based). **Programs:** Federal Direct (Subsidized and Unsubsidized Stafford, PLUS), FFEL (Subsidized and Unsubsidized Stafford, PLUS), Perkins, alternative loans.

WORK-STUDY Federal work-study: Total amount: $247,446; jobs available. **State or other work-study/employment:** Total amount: $443,753 (52% need-based, 48% non-need-based). Part-time jobs available.

APPLYING FOR FINANCIAL AID Required financial aid forms: FAFSA, state aid form. **Financial aid deadline:** 4/1. **Notification date:** Continuous beginning 2/1. Students must reply by 5/1 or within 2 weeks of notification.

CONTACT Ms. Joan Hock, Interim Director of Student Financial Aid, Delaware Valley College, 700 East Butler Avenue, Doylestown, PA 18901-2697, 215-489-2975 or toll-free 800-2DELVAL (in-state). E-mail: finaid@devalcol.edu.

DELTA STATE UNIVERSITY
Cleveland, MS

Tuition & fees (MS res): $4450   **Average undergraduate aid package: $7213**

ABOUT THE INSTITUTION State-supported, coed. 37 undergraduate majors. Federal methodology is used as a basis for awarding need-based institutional aid.

UNDERGRADUATE EXPENSES for 2009–10 Tuition, state resident: full-time $4450; part-time $185 per credit hour. **Tuition, nonresident:** full-time $11,520; part-time $480 per credit hour. Part-time tuition and fees vary according to course load. **College room and board:** $5714. Room and board charges vary according to housing facility. **Payment plan:** Installment.

FRESHMAN FINANCIAL AID (Fall 2008) 295 applied for aid; of those 84% were deemed to have need. 100% of freshmen with need received aid. **Average financial aid package:** $5495 (excluding resources awarded to replace EFC).

UNDERGRADUATE FINANCIAL AID (Fall 2008) 2,122 applied for aid; of those 77% were deemed to have need. 100% of undergraduates with need received aid. **Average financial aid package:** $7213 (excluding resources awarded to replace EFC).

GIFT AID (NEED-BASED) Total amount: $5,557,679 (90% federal, 1% state, 9% institutional). **Receiving aid:** Freshmen: 53% (206); all full-time undergraduates: 48% (1,274). **Average award:** Freshmen: $3574; Undergraduates: $3931. **Scholarships, grants, and awards:** Federal Pell, FSEOG, state, private, college/university gift aid from institutional funds.

GIFT AID (NON-NEED-BASED) Total amount: $4,907,000 (18% state, 54% institutional, 28% external sources). **Scholarships, grants, and awards by category:** Academic interests/achievement: 280 awards ($485,073 total): biological sciences, business, computer science, education, English, foreign languages, general academic interests/achievements, health fields, humanities, mathematics, physical sciences, premedicine, social sciences. Creative arts/performance: 132 awards ($355,100 total): art/fine arts, creative writing, journalism/publications, music, performing arts. Special achievements/activities: 465 awards ($537,074 total): cheerleading/drum major, general special achievements/activities, leadership, memberships. Special characteristics: 333 awards ($1,750,194 total): children and siblings of alumni, children of faculty/staff, general special characteristics, out-of-state students. **Tuition waivers:** Full or partial for children of alumni, employees or children of employees, senior citizens.

LOANS Student loans: $18,377,000 (53% need-based, 47% non-need-based). 65% of past graduating class borrowed through all loan programs. Average indebtedness per student: $19,840. **Parent loans:** $466,000 (100% non-need-based). **Programs:** Federal Direct (Subsidized and Unsubsidized Stafford, PLUS), FFEL (Subsidized and Unsubsidized Stafford, PLUS), Perkins.

WORK-STUDY Federal work-study: Total amount: $467,000; 237 jobs averaging $1850. **State or other work-study/employment:** Total amount: $218,000 (100% non-need-based). 50 part-time jobs averaging $1200.

ATHLETIC AWARDS Total amount: $1,660,000 (100% non-need-based).

APPLYING FOR FINANCIAL AID Required financial aid forms: FAFSA, institution's own form. **Financial aid deadline (priority):** 3/1. **Notification date:** Continuous beginning 5/1.

CONTACT Ms. Ann Margaret Mullins, Director of Student Financial Assistance, Delta State University, Kent Wyatt Hall 144, Highway 8 West, Cleveland, MS 38733-0001, 662-846-4670 or toll-free 800-468-6378. Fax: 662-846-4683. E-mail: amullins@deltastate.edu.

DENISON UNIVERSITY
Granville, OH

Tuition & fees: $36,560   **Average undergraduate aid package: $32,040**

ABOUT THE INSTITUTION Independent, coed. 38 undergraduate majors. Federal methodology is used as a basis for awarding need-based institutional aid.

UNDERGRADUATE EXPENSES for 2009–10 Comprehensive fee: $45,490 includes full-time tuition ($35,650), mandatory fees ($910), and room and board ($8930). **College room only:** $5040. Room and board charges vary according to housing facility. **Part-time tuition:** $1115 per semester hour. **Part-time fees:** $1115 per semester hour; $455 per term. Part-time tuition and fees vary according to course load. **Payment plan:** Installment.

FRESHMAN FINANCIAL AID (Fall 2009, est.) 434 applied for aid; of those 79% were deemed to have need. 100% of freshmen with need received aid; of those 39% had need fully met. **Average percent of need met:** 94% (excluding resources awarded to replace EFC). **Average financial aid package:** $32,758 (excluding resources awarded to replace EFC). 39% of all full-time freshmen had no need and received non-need-based gift aid.

UNDERGRADUATE FINANCIAL AID (Fall 2009, est.) 1,228 applied for aid; of those 84% were deemed to have need. 100% of undergraduates with need received aid; of those 30% had need fully met. **Average percent of need met:** 96% (excluding resources awarded to replace EFC). **Average financial aid package:** $32,040 (excluding resources awarded to replace EFC). 47% of all full-time undergraduates had no need and received non-need-based gift aid.

GIFT AID (NEED-BASED) Total amount: $15,340,390 (12% federal, 1% state, 83% institutional, 4% external sources). **Receiving aid:** Freshmen: 53% (344); all full-time undergraduates: 46% (1,020). **Average award:** Freshmen: $27,128; Undergraduates: $26,112. **Scholarships, grants, and awards:** Federal Pell, FSEOG, state, private, college/university gift aid from institutional funds.

GIFT AID (NON-NEED-BASED) Total amount: $28,700,783 (100% institutional). **Receiving aid:** Freshmen: 45% (290). Undergraduates: 40% (890). **Average**

award: Freshmen: $16,959. Undergraduates: $15,282. *Tuition waivers:* Full or partial for employees or children of employees.

LOANS *Student loans:* $6,546,535 (100% need-based). *Average need-based loan:* Freshmen: $3954. Undergraduates: $4387. *Parent loans:* $3,836,707 (100% non-need-based). *Programs:* Federal Direct (Subsidized and Unsubsidized Stafford, PLUS), Perkins, college/university.

WORK-STUDY *Federal work-study:* Total amount: $1,056,862; 537 jobs averaging $2000. *State or other work-study/employment:* Total amount: $3,028,106 (100% non-need-based). Part-time jobs available.

APPLYING FOR FINANCIAL AID *Required financial aid form:* FAFSA. *Financial aid deadline (priority):* 2/15. *Notification date:* 3/30. Students must reply within 2 weeks of notification.

CONTACT Ms. Nancy Hoover, Director of Financial Aid, Denison University, PO Box M, Granville, OH 43023-0613, 740-587-6279 or toll-free 800-DENISON. *Fax:* 740-587-5706. *E-mail:* hoover@denison.edu.

DePAUL UNIVERSITY
Chicago, IL

Tuition & fees: $27,342	Average undergraduate aid package: $20,459

ABOUT THE INSTITUTION Independent Roman Catholic, coed. 113 undergraduate majors. Federal methodology is used as a basis for awarding need-based institutional aid.

UNDERGRADUATE EXPENSES for 2009–10 *Comprehensive fee:* $37,959 includes full-time tuition ($26,765), mandatory fees ($577), and room and board ($10,617). *College room only:* $7827. Full-time tuition and fees vary according to program. Room and board charges vary according to board plan, housing facility, and location. *Part-time tuition:* $475 per quarter hour. Part-time tuition and fees vary according to program. *Payment plans:* Installment, deferred payment.

FRESHMAN FINANCIAL AID (Fall 2009, est.) 2,291 applied for aid; of those 80% were deemed to have need. 98% of freshmen with need received aid; of those 12% had need fully met. *Average percent of need met:* 72% (excluding resources awarded to replace EFC). *Average financial aid package:* $22,449 (excluding resources awarded to replace EFC). 7% of all full-time freshmen had no need and received non-need-based gift aid.

UNDERGRADUATE FINANCIAL AID (Fall 2009, est.) 10,763 applied for aid; of those 80% were deemed to have need. 97% of undergraduates with need received aid; of those 11% had need fully met. *Average percent of need met:* 67% (excluding resources awarded to replace EFC). *Average financial aid package:* $20,459 (excluding resources awarded to replace EFC). 4% of all full-time undergraduates had no need and received non-need-based gift aid.

GIFT AID (NEED-BASED) *Total amount:* $97,580,000 (16% federal, 19% state, 65% institutional). *Receiving aid:* Freshmen: 60% (1,505); all full-time undergraduates: 52% (6,805). *Average award:* Freshmen: $16,124; Undergraduates: $14,428. *Scholarships, grants, and awards:* Federal Pell, FSEOG, state, private, college/university gift aid from institutional funds, Academic Competitiveness Grants, National SMART Grants, TEACH Grants.

GIFT AID (NON-NEED-BASED) *Total amount:* $29,220,000 (94% institutional, 6% external sources). *Receiving aid:* Freshmen: 36% (910). Undergraduates: 22% (2,934). *Average award:* Freshmen: $9314. Undergraduates: $9128. *Scholarships, grants, and awards by category: Academic interests/achievement:* general academic interests/achievements. *Creative arts/performance:* art/fine arts, debating, music, performing arts, theater/drama. *Special achievements/ activities:* community service, leadership. *Special characteristics:* children of faculty/staff, local/state students. *Tuition waivers:* Full or partial for employees or children of employees.

LOANS *Student loans:* $122,000,000 (72% need-based, 28% non-need-based). 64% of past graduating class borrowed through all loan programs. *Average indebtedness per student:* $19,072. *Average need-based loan:* Freshmen: $3457. Undergraduates: $4732. *Parent loans:* $40,000,000 (100% non-need-based). *Programs:* Federal Direct (Subsidized and Unsubsidized Stafford, PLUS), Perkins, private loans.

WORK-STUDY *Federal work-study:* Total amount: $2,300,000; jobs available. *State or other work-study/employment:* Total amount: $6,800,000 (31% need-based, 69% non-need-based). Part-time jobs available.

ATHLETIC AWARDS Total amount: $4,800,000 (100% non-need-based).

APPLYING FOR FINANCIAL AID *Required financial aid form:* FAFSA. *Financial aid deadline (priority):* 3/1. *Notification date:* Continuous beginning 3/15. Students must reply by 5/1 or within 4 weeks of notification.

CONTACT Christopher Rone, Associate Director of Financial Aid, DePaul University, 1 East Jackson Boulevard, Chicago, IL 60604-2287, 773-325-7815. *Fax:* 773-325-7746.

DePAUW UNIVERSITY
Greencastle, IN

Tuition & fees: $33,250	Average undergraduate aid package: $28,224

ABOUT THE INSTITUTION Independent religious, coed. 45 undergraduate majors. Federal methodology is used as a basis for awarding need-based institutional aid.

UNDERGRADUATE EXPENSES for 2009–10 *Comprehensive fee:* $41,990 includes full-time tuition ($32,800), mandatory fees ($450), and room and board ($8740).

FRESHMAN FINANCIAL AID (Fall 2009, est.) 518 applied for aid; of those 79% were deemed to have need. 100% of freshmen with need received aid; of those 33% had need fully met. *Average percent of need met:* 90% (excluding resources awarded to replace EFC). *Average financial aid package:* $29,279 (excluding resources awarded to replace EFC). 42% of all full-time freshmen had no need and received non-need-based gift aid.

UNDERGRADUATE FINANCIAL AID (Fall 2009, est.) 1,474 applied for aid; of those 84% were deemed to have need. 100% of undergraduates with need received aid; of those 33% had need fully met. *Average percent of need met:* 90% (excluding resources awarded to replace EFC). *Average financial aid package:* $28,224 (excluding resources awarded to replace EFC). 45% of all full-time undergraduates had no need and received non-need-based gift aid.

GIFT AID (NEED-BASED) *Total amount:* $29,825,861 (9% federal, 3% state, 80% institutional, 8% external sources). *Receiving aid:* Freshmen: 57% (408); all full-time undergraduates: 53% (1,235). *Average award:* Freshmen: $25,918; Undergraduates: $24,150. *Scholarships, grants, and awards:* Federal Pell, FSEOG, state, private, college/university gift aid from institutional funds, United Negro College Fund.

GIFT AID (NON-NEED-BASED) *Total amount:* $19,790,999 (92% institutional, 8% external sources). *Receiving aid:* Freshmen: 13% (92). Undergraduates: 11% (251). *Average award:* Freshmen: $17,134. Undergraduates: $15,637. *Scholarships, grants, and awards by category: Academic interests/achievement:* biological sciences, business, communication, computer science, English, foreign languages, general academic interests/achievements, health fields, international studies, mathematics, physical sciences. *Creative arts/performance:* art/fine arts, journalism/publications, music, performing arts. *Special achievements/ activities:* community service, leadership. *Special characteristics:* children and siblings of alumni, children of faculty/staff, first-generation college students, international students, local/state students, members of minority groups, relatives of clergy, religious affiliation.

LOANS *Student loans:* $10,219,100 (56% need-based, 44% non-need-based). 48% of past graduating class borrowed through all loan programs. *Average indebtedness per student:* $24,210. *Average need-based loan:* Freshmen: $2905. Undergraduates: $3870. *Parent loans:* $3,415,798 (19% need-based, 81% non-need-based). *Programs:* Federal Direct (Subsidized and Unsubsidized Stafford, PLUS), FFEL (Subsidized and Unsubsidized Stafford, PLUS), Perkins, state, college/university.

WORK-STUDY *Federal work-study:* Total amount: $1,164,883; jobs available. *State or other work-study/employment:* Total amount: $376,273 (58% need-based, 42% non-need-based). Part-time jobs available.

APPLYING FOR FINANCIAL AID *Required financial aid forms:* FAFSA, institution's own form. *Financial aid deadline:* Continuous. *Notification date:* 4/1. Students must reply by 5/1.

CONTACT Craig Slaughter, Financial Aid Director, DePauw University, PO Box 37, Greencastle, IN 46135-0037, 765-658-4030 or toll-free 800-447-2495. *Fax:* 765-658-4137. *E-mail:* craigslaughter@depauw.edu.

DeSALES UNIVERSITY
Center Valley, PA

Tuition & fees: $27,200	Average undergraduate aid package: $17,336

DeSales University

ABOUT THE INSTITUTION Independent Roman Catholic, coed. 32 undergraduate majors. Federal methodology is used as a basis for awarding need-based institutional aid.

UNDERGRADUATE EXPENSES for 2009–10 *One-time required fee:* $200. *Comprehensive fee:* $36,950 includes full-time tuition ($26,000), mandatory fees ($1200), and room and board ($9750). Full-time tuition and fees vary according to class time and degree level. Room and board charges vary according to board plan. *Part-time tuition:* $1085 per credit hour. Part-time tuition and fees vary according to class time and degree level. *Payment plan:* Installment.

FRESHMAN FINANCIAL AID (Fall 2009, est.) 347 applied for aid; of those 85% were deemed to have need. 100% of freshmen with need received aid; of those 17% had need fully met. *Average percent of need met:* 70% (excluding resources awarded to replace EFC). *Average financial aid package:* $19,654 (excluding resources awarded to replace EFC). 19% of all full-time freshmen had no need and received non-need-based gift aid.

UNDERGRADUATE FINANCIAL AID (Fall 2009, est.) 1,472 applied for aid; of those 88% were deemed to have need. 99% of undergraduates with need received aid; of those 15% had need fully met. *Average percent of need met:* 68% (excluding resources awarded to replace EFC). *Average financial aid package:* $17,336 (excluding resources awarded to replace EFC). 15% of all full-time undergraduates had no need and received non-need-based gift aid.

GIFT AID (NEED-BASED) *Total amount:* $15,678,571 (10% federal, 8% state, 81% institutional, 1% external sources). *Receiving aid:* Freshmen: 77% (291); all full-time undergraduates: 68% (1,177). *Average award:* Freshmen: $15,482; Undergraduates: $13,352. *Scholarships, grants, and awards:* Federal Pell, FSEOG, state, private, college/university gift aid from institutional funds.

GIFT AID (NON-NEED-BASED) *Total amount:* $2,538,745 (5% federal, 94% institutional, 1% external sources). *Receiving aid:* Freshmen: 61% (232). Undergraduates: 50% (856). *Average award:* Freshmen: $8464. Undergraduates: $8494. *Scholarships, grants, and awards by category: Academic interests/achievement:* 174 awards ($980,600 total): biological sciences, business, communication, computer science, education, English, foreign languages, general academic interests/achievements, health fields, humanities, mathematics, physical sciences, premedicine, religion/biblical studies, social sciences. *Creative arts/performance:* 24 awards ($42,250 total): cinema/film/broadcasting, dance, performing arts, theater/drama. *Tuition waivers:* Full or partial for employees or children of employees, adult students, senior citizens.

LOANS *Student loans:* $12,871,350 (90% need-based, 10% non-need-based). 76% of past graduating class borrowed through all loan programs. *Average indebtedness per student:* $31,077. *Average need-based loan:* Freshmen: $3352. Undergraduates: $4287. *Parent loans:* $3,196,316 (84% need-based, 16% non-need-based). *Programs:* FFEL (Subsidized and Unsubsidized Stafford, PLUS).

WORK-STUDY *Federal work-study:* Total amount: $745,717; 400 jobs averaging $2000. *State or other work-study/employment:* Total amount: $565,145 (57% need-based, 43% non-need-based). 314 part-time jobs averaging $2000.

APPLYING FOR FINANCIAL AID *Required financial aid forms:* FAFSA, state aid form. *Financial aid deadline (priority):* 2/1. *Notification date:* Continuous beginning 2/15. Students must reply by 5/1.

CONTACT Mrs. Joyce Farmer, Director of Financial Aid, DeSales University, 2755 Station Avenue, Center Valley, PA 18034-9568, 610-282-1100 Ext. 1208 or toll-free 877-4DESALES. *Fax:* 610-282-0131. *E-mail:* joyce.farmer@desales.edu.

DESIGN INSTITUTE OF SAN DIEGO
San Diego, CA

CONTACT Financial Aid Office, Design Institute of San Diego, 8555 Commerce Avenue, San Diego, CA 92121, 858-566-1200 or toll-free 800-619-4337.

DeVRY COLLEGE OF NEW YORK
Long Island City, NY

ABOUT THE INSTITUTION Proprietary, coed. 7 undergraduate majors.

GIFT AID (NEED-BASED) *Scholarships, grants, and awards:* Federal Pell, FSEOG, state, private, college/university gift aid from institutional funds.

LOANS *Programs:* FFEL (Subsidized and Unsubsidized Stafford, PLUS), Perkins.

APPLYING FOR FINANCIAL AID *Required financial aid form:* FAFSA.

CONTACT Elvira Senese, Dean of Student Finance, DeVry College of New York, 30-20 Thomson Avenue, Long Island City, NY 11101, 718-472-2728. *Fax:* 718-269-4284.

DeVRY UNIVERSITY
Mesa, AZ

CONTACT Financial Aid Office, DeVry University, 1201 South Alma School Road, Mesa, AZ 85210-2011, 480-827-1511.

DeVRY UNIVERSITY
Phoenix, AZ

ABOUT THE INSTITUTION Proprietary, coed. 10 undergraduate majors.

GIFT AID (NEED-BASED) *Scholarships, grants, and awards:* Federal Pell, FSEOG, state, private, college/university gift aid from institutional funds.

LOANS *Programs:* FFEL (Subsidized and Unsubsidized Stafford, PLUS), Perkins.

APPLYING FOR FINANCIAL AID *Required financial aid form:* FAFSA.

CONTACT Kathy Wyse, Dean of Student Finance, DeVry University, 2149 West Dunlap Avenue, Phoenix, AZ 85021-2995, 602-870-9222. *Fax:* 602-870-1209.

DeVRY UNIVERSITY
Alhambra, CA

CONTACT Financial Aid Office, DeVry University, Unit 100, Building A-11, First Floor, 1000 South Fremont Avenue, Alhambra, CA 91803, 626-293-4300.

DeVRY UNIVERSITY
Anaheim, CA

CONTACT Financial Aid Office, DeVry University, 1900 South State College Boulevard, Suite 150, Anaheim, CA 92806-6136, 714-935-3200.

DeVRY UNIVERSITY
Bakersfield, CA

CONTACT Financial Aid Office, DeVry University, 3000 Ming Avenue, Bakersfield, CA 93304-4136, 661-833-7120.

DeVRY UNIVERSITY
Daly City, CA

CONTACT Financial Aid Office, DeVry University, 2001 Junipero Serra Boulevard, Suite 161, Daly City, CA 94014-3899, 650-991-3520.

DeVRY UNIVERSITY
Elk Grove, CA

CONTACT Financial Aid Office, DeVry University, Sacramento Center, 2216 Kausen Drive, Elk Grove, CA 95758, 916-478-2847 or toll-free 866-573-3879.

DeVRY UNIVERSITY
Fremont, CA

ABOUT THE INSTITUTION Proprietary, coed. 10 undergraduate majors.

GIFT AID (NEED-BASED) *Scholarships, grants, and awards:* Federal Pell, FSEOG, state, private, college/university gift aid from institutional funds.

LOANS *Programs:* FFEL (Subsidized and Unsubsidized Stafford, PLUS), Perkins.

APPLYING FOR FINANCIAL AID *Required financial aid form:* FAFSA.

CONTACT Kim Kane, Director of Student Finance, DeVry University, 6600 Dumbarton Circle, Fremont, CA 94555, 510-574-1100. *Fax:* 510-742-0868.

DeVRY UNIVERSITY
Irvine, CA

CONTACT Financial Aid Office, DeVry University, 430 Exchange, Suite 250, Irvine, CA 92602-1303, 949-752-5631.

DeVRY UNIVERSITY
Long Beach, CA

ABOUT THE INSTITUTION Proprietary, coed. 9 undergraduate majors.
GIFT AID (NEED-BASED) *Scholarships, grants, and awards:* Federal Pell, FSEOG, state, private, college/university gift aid from institutional funds.
LOANS *Programs:* FFEL (Subsidized and Unsubsidized Stafford, PLUS), Perkins.
APPLYING FOR FINANCIAL AID *Required financial aid form:* FAFSA.
CONTACT Kathy Odom, Director of Financial Aid, DeVry University, 3880 Kilroy Airport Way, Long Beach, CA 90806, 562-427-0861. *Fax:* 562-989-1578.

DeVRY UNIVERSITY
Oakland, CA

CONTACT Financial Aid Office, DeVry University, 505 14th Street, Oakland, CA 94612, 866-473-3879.

DeVRY UNIVERSITY
Palmdale, CA

CONTACT Ann Logan, Dean of Student Finance, DeVry University, 22801 Roscoe Boulevard, West Hills, CA 91304, 818-932-3001 or toll-free 866-986-9388. *Fax:* 818-932-3131.

DeVRY UNIVERSITY
Pomona, CA

ABOUT THE INSTITUTION Proprietary, coed. 11 undergraduate majors.
GIFT AID (NEED-BASED) *Scholarships, grants, and awards:* Federal Pell, FSEOG, state, private, college/university gift aid from institutional funds.
LOANS *Programs:* FFEL (Subsidized and Unsubsidized Stafford, PLUS), Perkins.
APPLYING FOR FINANCIAL AID *Required financial aid form:* FAFSA.
CONTACT Kathy Odom, Director of Financial Aid, DeVry University, 901 Corporate Center Drive, Pomona, CA 91768-2642, 909-622-8866. *Fax:* 909-623-5666.

DeVRY UNIVERSITY
San Diego, CA

CONTACT Financial Aid Office, DeVry University, 2655 Camino Del Rio North, Suite 201, San Diego, CA 92108-1633, 619-683-2446.

DeVRY UNIVERSITY
Sherman Oaks, CA

ABOUT THE INSTITUTION Proprietary, coed. 9 undergraduate majors.
GIFT AID (NEED-BASED) *Scholarships, grants, and awards:* Federal Pell, FSEOG, state, private, college/university gift aid from institutional funds.
LOANS *Programs:* FFEL (Subsidized and Unsubsidized Stafford, PLUS), Perkins.
APPLYING FOR FINANCIAL AID *Required financial aid form:* FAFSA.
CONTACT Financial Aid Office, DeVry University, 15301 Ventura Boulevard, D-100, Sherman Oaks, CA 91403, 888-610-0800.

DeVRY UNIVERSITY
Colorado Springs, CO

CONTACT Carol Oppman, Director of Financial Aid, DeVry University, 225 South Union Boulevard, Colorado Springs, CO 80910, 719-632-3000 or toll-free 866-338-7934. *Fax:* 719-632-1909.

DeVRY UNIVERSITY
Westminster, CO

ABOUT THE INSTITUTION Proprietary, coed. 9 undergraduate majors.
GIFT AID (NEED-BASED) *Scholarships, grants, and awards:* Federal Pell, FSEOG, state, private, college/university gift aid from institutional funds.
LOANS *Programs:* FFEL (Subsidized and Unsubsidized Stafford, PLUS), Perkins.
APPLYING FOR FINANCIAL AID *Required financial aid form:* FAFSA.
CONTACT Office of Financial Aid, DeVry University, 1870 West 122nd Avenue, Westminster, CO 80234-2010, 303-280-7400.

DeVRY UNIVERSITY
Jacksonville, FL

CONTACT Financial Aid Office, DeVry University, 5200 Belfort Road, Jacksonville, FL 32256-6040.

DeVRY UNIVERSITY
Miami, FL

CONTACT Financial Aid Office, DeVry University, 8700 West Flagler Street, Suite 100, Miami, FL 33174-2535, 305-229-4833.

DeVRY UNIVERSITY
Miramar, FL

ABOUT THE INSTITUTION Proprietary, coed. 9 undergraduate majors.
GIFT AID (NEED-BASED) *Scholarships, grants, and awards:* Federal Pell, FSEOG, state, private, college/university gift aid from institutional funds.
LOANS *Programs:* FFEL (Subsidized and Unsubsidized Stafford, PLUS), Perkins.
APPLYING FOR FINANCIAL AID *Required financial aid form:* FAFSA.
CONTACT Office of Financial Aid, DeVry University, 2300 Southwest 145th Avenue, Miramar, FL 33027, 954-499-9700.

DeVRY UNIVERSITY
Orlando, FL

ABOUT THE INSTITUTION Proprietary, coed. 10 undergraduate majors.
GIFT AID (NEED-BASED) *Scholarships, grants, and awards:* Federal Pell, FSEOG, state, private, college/university gift aid from institutional funds.
LOANS *Programs:* FFEL (Subsidized and Unsubsidized Stafford, PLUS), Perkins.
APPLYING FOR FINANCIAL AID *Required financial aid form:* FAFSA.
CONTACT Estrella Velazquez-Domenech, Director of Student Finance, DeVry University, 4000 Millenia Boulevard, Orlando, FL 32839, 407-345-2816. *Fax:* 407-355-4855.

DeVRY UNIVERSITY
Tampa, FL

CONTACT Financial Aid Office, DeVry University, 3030 North Rocky Point Drive West, Suite 100, Tampa, FL 33607-5901, 813-288-8994.

DeVRY UNIVERSITY
Alpharetta, GA

ABOUT THE INSTITUTION Proprietary, coed. 9 undergraduate majors.
GIFT AID (NEED-BASED) *Scholarships, grants, and awards:* Federal Pell, FSEOG, state, private, college/university gift aid from institutional funds.
LOANS *Programs:* FFEL (Subsidized and Unsubsidized Stafford, PLUS), Perkins.
APPLYING FOR FINANCIAL AID *Required financial aid form:* FAFSA.
CONTACT David Pickett, Assistant Director of Financial Aid, DeVry University, 2555 Northwinds Parkway, Alpharetta, GA 30004, 770-521-4900 or toll-free 800-346-5420. *Fax:* 770-664-8024.

DeVRY UNIVERSITY
Decatur, GA

ABOUT THE INSTITUTION Proprietary, coed. 11 undergraduate majors.
GIFT AID (NEED-BASED) *Scholarships, grants, and awards:* Federal Pell, FSEOG, state, private, college/university gift aid from institutional funds.
LOANS *Programs:* FFEL (Subsidized and Unsubsidized Stafford, PLUS), Perkins.
APPLYING FOR FINANCIAL AID *Required financial aid form:* FAFSA.
CONTACT Robin Winston, Director of Financial Aid, DeVry University, 250 North Arcadia Avenue, Decatur, GA 30030-2198, 404-292-7900. *Fax:* 404-292-2321.

DEVRY UNIVERSITY
Duluth, GA

CONTACT Financial Aid Office, DeVry University, 3505 Koger Boulevard, Suite 170, Duluth, GA 30096-7671, 678-380-9780.

DEVRY UNIVERSITY
Addison, IL

ABOUT THE INSTITUTION Proprietary, coed. 9 undergraduate majors.

GIFT AID (NEED-BASED) *Scholarships, grants, and awards:* Federal Pell, FSEOG, state, private, college/university gift aid from institutional funds.

LOANS *Programs:* FFEL (Subsidized and Unsubsidized Stafford, PLUS), Perkins.

APPLYING FOR FINANCIAL AID *Required financial aid form:* FAFSA.

CONTACT Sejal Amin, Director of Student Finance, DeVry University, 1221 North Swift Road, Addison, IL 60101-6106, 630-953-1300 or toll-free 800-346-5420.

DEVRY UNIVERSITY
Chicago, IL

ABOUT THE INSTITUTION Proprietary, coed. 9 undergraduate majors.

GIFT AID (NEED-BASED) *Scholarships, grants, and awards:* Federal Pell, FSEOG, state, private, college/university gift aid from institutional funds.

LOANS *Programs:* FFEL (Subsidized and Unsubsidized Stafford, PLUS), Perkins.

APPLYING FOR FINANCIAL AID *Required financial aid form:* FAFSA.

CONTACT Milena Dobrina, Director of Financial Aid, DeVry University, 3300 North Campbell Avenue, Chicago, IL 60618-5994, 773-929-8500. *Fax:* 773-348-1780.

DEVRY UNIVERSITY
Downers Grove, IL

CONTACT Financial Aid Office, DeVry University, 3005 Highland Parkway, Downers Grove, IL 60515, 630-515-3000.

DEVRY UNIVERSITY
Elgin, IL

CONTACT Financial Aid Office, DeVry University, Randall Point, 2250 Point Boulevard, Suite 250, Elgin, IL 60123, 847-649-3980.

DEVRY UNIVERSITY
Gurnee, IL

CONTACT Financial Aid Office, DeVry University, 1075 Tri-State Parkway, Suite 800, Gurnee, IL 60031-9126, 847-855-2649 or toll-free 866-563-3879.

DEVRY UNIVERSITY
Naperville, IL

CONTACT Financial Aid Office, DeVry University, 2056 Westings Avenue, Suite 40, Naperville, IL 60563-2361, 630-428-9086 or toll-free 877-496-9050.

DEVRY UNIVERSITY
Tinley Park, IL

ABOUT THE INSTITUTION Proprietary, coed. 9 undergraduate majors.

GIFT AID (NEED-BASED) *Scholarships, grants, and awards:* Federal Pell, FSEOG, state, private, college/university gift aid from institutional funds.

LOANS *Programs:* FFEL (Subsidized and Unsubsidized Stafford, PLUS), Perkins.

APPLYING FOR FINANCIAL AID *Required financial aid form:* FAFSA.

CONTACT Director of Student Finance, DeVry University, 18624 West Creek Drive, Tinley Park, IL 60477, 708-342-3300. *Fax:* 708-342-3120.

DEVRY UNIVERSITY
Indianapolis, IN

ABOUT THE INSTITUTION Proprietary, coed. 6 undergraduate majors.

GIFT AID (NEED-BASED) *Scholarships, grants, and awards:* state, college/university gift aid from institutional funds.

CONTACT Financial Aid Office, DeVry University, 9100 Keystone Crossing, Suite 350, Indianapolis, IN 46240-2158, 317-581-8854.

DEVRY UNIVERSITY
Merrillville, IN

CONTACT Financial Aid Office, DeVry University, Twin Towers, 1000 East 80th Place, Suite 222 Mall, Merrillville, IN 46410-5673, 219-736-7440.

DEVRY UNIVERSITY
Louisville, KY

ABOUT THE INSTITUTION Proprietary, coed. 5 undergraduate majors.

GIFT AID (NEED-BASED) *Scholarships, grants, and awards:* Federal Pell, FSEOG, state, private, college/university gift aid from institutional funds.

LOANS *Programs:* FFEL (Subsidized and Unsubsidized Stafford, PLUS), Perkins.

APPLYING FOR FINANCIAL AID *Required financial aid form:* FAFSA.

CONTACT Financial Aid Office, DeVry University, 10172 Linn Station Road, Suite 300, Louisville, KY 40223, toll-free 866-906-9388.

DEVRY UNIVERSITY
Bethesda, MD

ABOUT THE INSTITUTION Proprietary, coed. 3 undergraduate majors.

GIFT AID (NEED-BASED) *Scholarships, grants, and awards:* Federal Pell, FSEOG, state, private, college/university gift aid from institutional funds.

LOANS *Programs:* FFEL (Subsidized and Unsubsidized Stafford, PLUS), Perkins.

APPLYING FOR FINANCIAL AID *Required financial aid form:* FAFSA.

CONTACT Financial Aid Office, DeVry University, 4550 Montgomery Avenue. Suite 100 North, Bethesda, MD 20814-3304, 301-652-8477.

DEVRY UNIVERSITY
Southfield, MI

ABOUT THE INSTITUTION Proprietary, coed. 4 undergraduate majors.

GIFT AID (NEED-BASED) *Scholarships, grants, and awards:* Federal Pell, FSEOG, state, private, college/university gift aid from institutional funds.

LOANS *Programs:* FFEL (Subsidized and Unsubsidized Stafford, PLUS), Perkins.

APPLYING FOR FINANCIAL AID *Required financial aid form:* FAFSA.

CONTACT Mr. Stephen Haworth, Regulatory Compliance Specialist, DeVry University, 26999 Central Park Boulevard, Suite 125, Southfield, MI 48076, 630-706-3172. *Fax:* 630-574-1991. *E-mail:* shaworth@devry.com.

DEVRY UNIVERSITY
Edina, MN

ABOUT THE INSTITUTION Proprietary, coed. 8 undergraduate majors.

GIFT AID (NEED-BASED) *Scholarships, grants, and awards:* Federal Pell, FSEOG, state, private, college/university gift aid from institutional funds.

LOANS *Programs:* FFEL (Subsidized and Unsubsidized Stafford, PLUS), Perkins.

APPLYING FOR FINANCIAL AID *Required financial aid form:* FAFSA.

CONTACT Financial Aid Office, DeVry University, 7700 France Avenue South, Suite 575, Edina, MN 55435, 952-838-1860.

DEVRY UNIVERSITY
Kansas City, MO

ABOUT THE INSTITUTION Proprietary, coed. 8 undergraduate majors.

GIFT AID (NEED-BASED) *Scholarships, grants, and awards:* Federal Pell, FSEOG, state, private, college/university gift aid from institutional funds.

LOANS *Programs:* FFEL (Subsidized and Unsubsidized Stafford, PLUS), Perkins.

APPLYING FOR FINANCIAL AID *Required financial aid form:* FAFSA.
CONTACT Maureen Kelly, Senior Associate Director of Financial Aid, DeVry University, 11224 Holmes Street, Kansas City, MO 64131-3698, 816-941-0430.

DeVRY UNIVERSITY
Kansas City, MO

CONTACT Financial Aid Office, DeVry University, City Center Square, 1100 Main Street, Suite 118, Kansas City, MO 64105-2112, 816-221-1300.

DeVRY UNIVERSITY
St. Louis, MO

CONTACT Financial Aid Office, DeVry University, 1801 Park 270 Drive, Suite 260, St. Louis, MO 63146-4020, 314-542-4222.

DeVRY UNIVERSITY
Henderson, NV

ABOUT THE INSTITUTION Proprietary, coed. 6 undergraduate majors.
GIFT AID (NEED-BASED) *Scholarships, grants, and awards:* Federal Pell, FSEOG, state, private, college/university gift aid from institutional funds.
LOANS *Programs:* FFEL (Subsidized and Unsubsidized Stafford, PLUS), Perkins.
APPLYING FOR FINANCIAL AID *Required financial aid form:* FAFSA.
CONTACT Financial Aid Office, DeVry University, 2490 Paseo Verde Parkway, Henderson, NV 89074-7120, 702-933-9700.

DeVRY UNIVERSITY
North Brunswick, NJ

ABOUT THE INSTITUTION Proprietary, coed. 8 undergraduate majors.
GIFT AID (NEED-BASED) *Scholarships, grants, and awards:* state, college/university gift aid from institutional funds.
CONTACT Albert Cama, Director of Financial Aid, DeVry University, 630 US Highway 1, North Brunswick, NJ 08902, 732-435-4880. *Fax:* 732-435-4867.

DeVRY UNIVERSITY
Paramus, NJ

CONTACT Financial Aid Office, DeVry University, 35 Plaza, 81 East State Route 4, Suite 102, Paramus, NJ 07652, 201-556-2840.

DeVRY UNIVERSITY
Charlotte, NC

ABOUT THE INSTITUTION Proprietary, coed. 5 undergraduate majors.
GIFT AID (NEED-BASED) *Scholarships, grants, and awards:* Federal Pell, FSEOG, state, private, college/university gift aid from institutional funds.
LOANS *Programs:* FFEL (Subsidized and Unsubsidized Stafford, PLUS), Perkins.
APPLYING FOR FINANCIAL AID *Required financial aid form:* FAFSA.
CONTACT Financial Aid Office, DeVry University, 2015 Ayrsley Town Boulevard, Suite 109, Charlotte, NC 28273-4068, 704-362-2345.

DeVRY UNIVERSITY
Columbus, OH

ABOUT THE INSTITUTION Proprietary, coed. 9 undergraduate majors.
GIFT AID (NEED-BASED) *Scholarships, grants, and awards:* Federal Pell, FSEOG, state, private, college/university gift aid from institutional funds.
LOANS *Programs:* FFEL (Subsidized and Unsubsidized Stafford, PLUS), Perkins.
APPLYING FOR FINANCIAL AID *Required financial aid form:* FAFSA.
CONTACT Cynthia Price, Director of Financial Aid, DeVry University, 1350 Alum Creek Drive, Columbus, OH 43209-2705, 614-253-7291. *Fax:* 614-252-4108.

DeVRY UNIVERSITY
Columbus, OH

CONTACT Financial Aid Office, DeVry University, 8800 Lyra Drive, Columbus, OH 43240, 614-854-7500.

DeVRY UNIVERSITY
Seven Hills, OH

CONTACT Financial Aid Office, DeVry University, The Genesis Building, 6000 Lombardo Center, Suite 200, Seven Hills, OH 44131, 216-328-8754 or toll-free 866-453-3879.

DeVRY UNIVERSITY
Oklahoma City, OK

ABOUT THE INSTITUTION Proprietary, coed. 5 undergraduate majors.
GIFT AID (NEED-BASED) *Scholarships, grants, and awards:* Federal Pell, FSEOG, state, private, college/university gift aid from institutional funds.
LOANS *Programs:* FFEL (Subsidized and Unsubsidized Stafford, PLUS), Perkins.
APPLYING FOR FINANCIAL AID *Required financial aid form:* FAFSA.
CONTACT Financial Aid Office, DeVry University, Lakepointe Towers, 4013 Northwest Expressway Street, Suite 100, Oklahoma City, OK 73116, 405-767-9516.

DeVRY UNIVERSITY
Portland, OR

ABOUT THE INSTITUTION Proprietary, coed. 5 undergraduate majors.
GIFT AID (NEED-BASED) *Scholarships, grants, and awards:* Federal Pell, FSEOG, state, private, college/university gift aid from institutional funds.
LOANS *Programs:* FFEL (Subsidized and Unsubsidized Stafford, PLUS), Perkins.
APPLYING FOR FINANCIAL AID *Required financial aid form:* FAFSA.
CONTACT Financial Aid Office, DeVry University, 9755 Southwest Barnes Road, Suite 150, Portland, OR 97225-6651, 503-296-7468.

DeVRY UNIVERSITY
Fort Washington, PA

ABOUT THE INSTITUTION Proprietary, coed. 10 undergraduate majors.
GIFT AID (NEED-BASED) *Scholarships, grants, and awards:* Federal Pell, FSEOG, state, private, college/university gift aid from institutional funds.
LOANS *Programs:* FFEL (Subsidized and Unsubsidized Stafford, PLUS), Perkins.
APPLYING FOR FINANCIAL AID *Required financial aid form:* FAFSA.
CONTACT Financial Aid Office, DeVry University, 1140 Virginia Drive, Fort Washington, PA 19034, 215-591-5700.

DeVRY UNIVERSITY
King of Prussia, PA

CONTACT Financial Aid Office, DeVry University, 150 Allendale Road, Buillding 3, Suite 3201, King of Prussia, PA 19406-2926, 610-205-3130.

DeVRY UNIVERSITY
Philadelphia, PA

CONTACT Financial Aid Office, DeVry University, Philadelphia Downtown Center, 1800 JFK Boulevard, Suite 104, Philadelphia, PA 19103-7421.

DeVRY UNIVERSITY
Pittsburgh, PA

CONTACT Financial Aid Office, DeVry University, FreeMarkets Center, 210 Sixth Avenue, Suite 200, Pittsburgh, PA 15222-2606, 412-642-9072 or toll-free 866-77DEVRY.

DeVRY UNIVERSITY
Memphis, TN

ABOUT THE INSTITUTION Proprietary, coed. 3 undergraduate majors.

GIFT AID (NEED-BASED) *Scholarships, grants, and awards:* Federal Pell, FSEOG, state, private, college/university gift aid from institutional funds.

LOANS *Programs:* FFEL (Subsidized and Unsubsidized Stafford, PLUS), Perkins.

APPLYING FOR FINANCIAL AID *Required financial aid form:* FAFSA.

CONTACT Financial Aid Office, DeVry University, 6401 Poplar Avenue, Suite 600, Memphis, TN 38119, 901-537-2560 or toll-free 888-563-3879.

DeVRY UNIVERSITY
Nashville, TN

CONTACT Financial Aid Office, DeVry University, 3343 Perimeter Hill Drive, Suite 200, Nashville, TN 37211-4147, 615-445-3456.

DeVRY UNIVERSITY
Houston, TX

ABOUT THE INSTITUTION Proprietary, coed. 8 undergraduate majors.

GIFT AID (NEED-BASED) *Scholarships, grants, and awards:* Federal Pell, FSEOG, state, private, college/university gift aid from institutional funds.

LOANS *Programs:* FFEL (Subsidized and Unsubsidized Stafford, PLUS), Perkins.

APPLYING FOR FINANCIAL AID *Required financial aid form:* FAFSA.

CONTACT Financial Aid Office, DeVry University, 11125 Equity Drive, Houston, TX 77041, 713-850-0888 or toll-free 866-703-3879.

DeVRY UNIVERSITY
Irving, TX

ABOUT THE INSTITUTION Proprietary, coed. 10 undergraduate majors.

GIFT AID (NEED-BASED) *Scholarships, grants, and awards:* Federal Pell, FSEOG, state, private, college/university gift aid from institutional funds.

LOANS *Programs:* FFEL (Subsidized and Unsubsidized Stafford, PLUS), Perkins.

APPLYING FOR FINANCIAL AID *Required financial aid form:* FAFSA.

CONTACT Tommy Sims, Financial Aid Officer, DeVry University, 4800 Regent Boulevard, Irving, TX 75063-2440, 972-929-6777.

DeVRY UNIVERSITY
Richardson, TX

CONTACT Financial Aid Office, DeVry University, Richardson Center, 2201 North Central Expressway, Richardson, TX 75080, 972-792-7450.

DeVRY UNIVERSITY
Sandy, UT

ABOUT THE INSTITUTION Proprietary, coed. 5 undergraduate majors.

GIFT AID (NEED-BASED) *Scholarships, grants, and awards:* Federal Pell, FSEOG, state, private, college/university gift aid from institutional funds.

LOANS *Programs:* FFEL (Subsidized and Unsubsidized Stafford, PLUS), Perkins.

APPLYING FOR FINANCIAL AID *Required financial aid form:* FAFSA.

CONTACT Financial Aid Office, DeVry University, 9350 South 150 E, Suite 420, Sandy, UT 84070, 801-565-5110.

DeVRY UNIVERSITY
Arlington, VA

ABOUT THE INSTITUTION Proprietary, coed. 8 undergraduate majors.

GIFT AID (NEED-BASED) *Scholarships, grants, and awards:* Federal Pell, FSEOG, state, private, college/university gift aid from institutional funds.

LOANS *Programs:* FFEL (Subsidized and Unsubsidized Stafford, PLUS), Perkins.

APPLYING FOR FINANCIAL AID *Required financial aid form:* FAFSA.

CONTACT Roberta McDevitt, Director of Student Finance, DeVry University, 2341 Jefferson Davis Highway, Arlington, VA 22202, 866-338-7932. *Fax:* 703-414-4040.

DeVRY UNIVERSITY
Chesapeake, VA

CONTACT Financial Aid Office, DeVry University, 1317 Executive Boulevard, Suite 100, Chesapeake, VA 23320-3671, 757-382-5680.

DeVRY UNIVERSITY
Manassas, VA

CONTACT Financial Aid Office, DeVry University, 10432 Balls Ford Road, Suite 130, Manassas, VA 20109-3173, 703-396-6611.

DeVRY UNIVERSITY
Bellevue, WA

CONTACT Financial Aid Office, DeVry University, 600 108th Avenue NE, Suite 230, Bellevue, WA 98004-5110, 425-455-2242.

DeVRY UNIVERSITY
Federal Way, WA

ABOUT THE INSTITUTION Proprietary, coed. 9 undergraduate majors.

GIFT AID (NEED-BASED) *Scholarships, grants, and awards:* Federal Pell, FSEOG, state, private, college/university gift aid from institutional funds.

LOANS *Programs:* FFEL (Subsidized and Unsubsidized Stafford, PLUS), Perkins.

APPLYING FOR FINANCIAL AID *Required financial aid form:* FAFSA.

CONTACT Diane Rooney, Assistant Director of Student Finance, DeVry University, 3600 South 344th Way, Federal Way, WA 98001, 253-943-2800. *Fax:* 253-943-5503.

DeVRY UNIVERSITY
Milwaukee, WI

ABOUT THE INSTITUTION Proprietary, coed. 3 undergraduate majors.

GIFT AID (NEED-BASED) *Scholarships, grants, and awards:* Federal Pell, FSEOG, state, private, college/university gift aid from institutional funds.

LOANS *Programs:* FFEL (Subsidized and Unsubsidized Stafford, PLUS), Perkins.

APPLYING FOR FINANCIAL AID *Required financial aid form:* FAFSA.

CONTACT Financial Aid Office, DeVry University, 411 East Wisconsin Avenue, Suite 300, Milwaukee, WI 53202, 414-278-7677.

DeVRY UNIVERSITY
Waukesha, WI

CONTACT Financial Aid Office, DeVry University, N14 W23833 Stone Ridge Drive, Suite 450, Waukesha, WI 53188-1157, 262-347-2911.

DeVRY UNIVERSITY ONLINE
Addison, IL

CONTACT Financial Aid Office, DeVry University Online, 1221 North Swift Road, Addison, IL 60101-6106, 877-496-9050.

DICKINSON COLLEGE
Carlisle, PA

Tuition & fees: $40,114	Average undergraduate aid package: $33,332

ABOUT THE INSTITUTION Independent, coed. 42 undergraduate majors. Both federal and institutional methodology are used as a basis for awarding need-based institutional aid.

UNDERGRADUATE EXPENSES for 2009–10 *One-time required fee:* $25. *Comprehensive fee:* $50,194 includes full-time tuition ($39,780), mandatory fees ($334), and room and board ($10,080). *College room only:* $5200. Room and board charges vary according to board plan and housing facility. *Part-time tuition:* $4975 per course. *Part-time fees:* $42 per course. *Payment plan:* Installment.

FRESHMAN FINANCIAL AID (Fall 2009, est.) 393 applied for aid; of those 82% were deemed to have need. 99% of freshmen with need received aid; of those 78% had need fully met. *Average percent of need met:* 97% (excluding resources awarded to replace EFC). *Average financial aid package:* $34,568 (excluding resources awarded to replace EFC). 7% of all full-time freshmen had no need and received non-need-based gift aid.

UNDERGRADUATE FINANCIAL AID (Fall 2009, est.) 1,375 applied for aid; of those 89% were deemed to have need. 99% of undergraduates with need received aid; of those 67% had need fully met. *Average percent of need met:* 94% (excluding resources awarded to replace EFC). *Average financial aid package:* $33,832 (excluding resources awarded to replace EFC). 8% of all full-time undergraduates had no need and received non-need-based gift aid.

GIFT AID (NEED-BASED) *Total amount:* $31,994,870 (5% federal, 1% state, 92% institutional, 2% external sources). *Receiving aid:* Freshmen: 54% (313); all full-time undergraduates: 50% (1,160). *Average award:* Freshmen: $28,583; Undergraduates: $27,318. *Scholarships, grants, and awards:* Federal Pell, FSEOG, state, private, college/university gift aid from institutional funds.

GIFT AID (NON-NEED-BASED) *Total amount:* $3,809,645 (26% federal, 65% institutional, 9% external sources). *Receiving aid:* Freshmen: 5% (30). Undergraduates: 3% (75). *Average award:* Freshmen: $10,177. Undergraduates: $11,709. *Scholarships, grants, and awards by category:* Academic interests/achievement: 444 awards ($5,251,727 total): general academic interests/achievements, military science. *Special characteristics:* 26 awards ($492,813 total): children and siblings of alumni, children of faculty/staff. *Tuition waivers:* Full or partial for employees or children of employees, senior citizens.

LOANS *Student loans:* $8,612,612 (66% need-based, 34% non-need-based). 55% of past graduating class borrowed through all loan programs. *Average indebtedness per student:* $23,224. *Average need-based loan:* Freshmen: $4026. Undergraduates: $4716. *Parent loans:* $4,594,728 (20% need-based, 80% non-need-based). *Programs:* Federal Direct (Subsidized and Unsubsidized Stafford, PLUS), Perkins, college/university.

WORK-STUDY *Federal work-study:* Total amount: $1,820,110; 889 jobs averaging $2047. *State or other work-study/employment:* Total amount: $577,919 (64% need-based, 36% non-need-based). 169 part-time jobs averaging $3420.

APPLYING FOR FINANCIAL AID *Required financial aid forms:* FAFSA, CSS Financial Aid PROFILE, state aid form, noncustodial (divorced/separated) parent's statement. *Financial aid deadline:* 2/1 (priority: 11/15). *Notification date:* 3/20. Students must reply by 5/1 or within 2 weeks of notification.

CONTACT Judith B. Carter, Director of Financial Aid, Dickinson College, PO Box 1773, Carlisle, PA 17013-2896, 717-245-1308 or toll-free 800-644-1773. *Fax:* 717-245-1972. *E-mail:* finaid@dickinson.edu.

DICKINSON STATE UNIVERSITY
Dickinson, ND

Tuition & fees (ND res): $5249   **Average undergraduate aid package: $7914**

ABOUT THE INSTITUTION State-supported, coed. 43 undergraduate majors. Federal methodology is used as a basis for awarding need-based institutional aid.

UNDERGRADUATE EXPENSES for 2010–11 *Tuition, state resident:* full-time $4160. *Tuition, nonresident:* full-time $11,106. *Required fees:* full-time $1089. *College room and board:* $4262; *Room only:* $1610. Room and board charges vary according to board plan. *Payment plan:* Installment.

FRESHMAN FINANCIAL AID (Fall 2009, est.) 227 applied for aid; of those 78% were deemed to have need. 96% of freshmen with need received aid; of those 99% had need fully met. *Average percent of need met:* 39% (excluding resources awarded to replace EFC). *Average financial aid package:* $7863 (excluding resources awarded to replace EFC). 39% of all full-time freshmen had no need and received non-need-based gift aid.

UNDERGRADUATE FINANCIAL AID (Fall 2009, est.) 1,110 applied for aid; of those 73% were deemed to have need. 97% of undergraduates with need received aid; of those 99% had need fully met. *Average percent of need met:* 32% (excluding resources awarded to replace EFC). *Average financial aid package:* $7914 (excluding resources awarded to replace EFC). 30% of all full-time undergraduates had no need and received non-need-based gift aid.

GIFT AID (NEED-BASED) *Total amount:* $3,407,174 (73% federal, 10% state, 10% institutional, 7% external sources). *Receiving aid:* Freshmen: 47% (154); all full-time undergraduates: 40% (689). *Average award:* Freshmen: $4568;

Undergraduates: $4257. *Scholarships, grants, and awards:* Federal Pell, FSEOG, state, college/university gift aid from institutional funds, National Guard tuition waivers, staff waivers.

GIFT AID (NON-NEED-BASED) *Total amount:* $60,710 (7% federal, 32% institutional, 61% external sources). *Receiving aid:* Freshmen: 2% (5). Undergraduates: 1% (15). *Average award:* Freshmen: $1162. Undergraduates: $1290. *Scholarships, grants, and awards by category:* Academic interests/achievement: agriculture, biological sciences, business, communication, computer science, education, English, foreign languages, general academic interests/achievements, health fields, humanities, mathematics, physical sciences, premedicine, social sciences. Creative arts/performance: art/fine arts, creative writing, journalism/publications, music, theater/drama. Special achievements/activities: cheerleading/drum major, leadership, rodeo. Special characteristics: children of faculty/staff, children with a deceased or disabled parent, ethnic background, general special characteristics, international students, members of minority groups, veterans, veterans' children. *Tuition waivers:* Full or partial for minority students, children of alumni, employees or children of employees, adult students, senior citizens.

LOANS *Student loans:* $5,350,393 (76% need-based, 24% non-need-based). 78% of past graduating class borrowed through all loan programs. *Average indebtedness per student:* $18,852. *Average need-based loan:* Freshmen: $3240. Undergraduates: $3726. *Parent loans:* $45,346 (15% need-based, 85% non-need-based). *Programs:* FFEL (Subsidized and Unsubsidized Stafford, PLUS), Perkins, Federal Nursing, state, college/university, Alaska Loans, alternative loans.

WORK-STUDY *Federal work-study:* Total amount: $216,911; 89 jobs averaging $2437. *State or other work-study/employment:* Part-time jobs available.

ATHLETIC AWARDS Total amount: $92,001 (64% need-based, 36% non-need-based).

APPLYING FOR FINANCIAL AID *Required financial aid form:* FAFSA. *Financial aid deadline (priority):* 3/15. *Notification date:* Continuous beginning 6/15. Students must reply by 7/31 or within 4 weeks of notification.

CONTACT Ms. Sandy Klein, Director of Financial Aid, Dickinson State University, 291 Campus Drive, Dickinson, ND 58601-4896, 701-483-2371 or toll-free 800-279-4295. *Fax:* 701-483-2720. *E-mail:* sandy.klein@dsu.nodak.edu.

DIGIPEN INSTITUTE OF TECHNOLOGY
Redmond, WA

Tuition & fees: $20,760   **Average undergraduate aid package: $6500**

ABOUT THE INSTITUTION Proprietary, coed. 7 undergraduate majors. Federal methodology is used as a basis for awarding need-based institutional aid.

UNDERGRADUATE EXPENSES for 2010–11 *One-time required fee:* $150. *Tuition:* full-time $20,600; part-time $515 per semester hour. *Required fees:* full-time $160; $80 per term. Full-time tuition and fees vary according to course load, location, and program. Part-time tuition and fees vary according to course load, location, and program. Room and board charges vary according to housing facility. *Payment plan:* Installment.

UNDERGRADUATE FINANCIAL AID (Fall 2009, est.) *Average percent of need met:* 67% (excluding resources awarded to replace EFC). *Average financial aid package:* $6500 (excluding resources awarded to replace EFC).

GIFT AID (NEED-BASED) *Total amount:* $1,847,774 (50% federal, 25% state, 22% institutional, 3% external sources). *Average award:* Undergraduates: $2300. *Scholarships, grants, and awards:* Federal Pell, state, private, college/university gift aid from institutional funds.

GIFT AID (NON-NEED-BASED) *Total amount:* $294,000 (68% federal, 20% institutional, 12% external sources). *Scholarships, grants, and awards by category:* Special achievements/activities: 46 awards ($225,000 total): community service, general special achievements/activities. Special characteristics: 32 awards ($32,000 total): ethnic background, local/state students, members of minority groups, spouses of current students, veterans, veterans' children. *Tuition waivers:* Full or partial for employees or children of employees.

LOANS *Student loans:* $4,900,000 (51% need-based, 49% non-need-based). 72% of past graduating class borrowed through all loan programs. *Average indebtedness per student:* $89,000. *Parent loans:* $3,600,000 (100% non-need-based). *Programs:* Federal Direct (Subsidized and Unsubsidized Stafford, PLUS).

WORK-STUDY Federal work-study jobs available. *State or other work-study/employment:* Part-time jobs available.

DigiPen Institute of Technology

DILLARD UNIVERSITY
New Orleans, LA

Tuition & fees: $13,880	Average undergraduate aid package: $14,443

ABOUT THE INSTITUTION Independent interdenominational, coed. 28 undergraduate majors. Federal methodology is used as a basis for awarding need-based institutional aid.
UNDERGRADUATE EXPENSES for 2010–11 *Comprehensive fee:* $22,266 includes full-time tuition ($13,000), mandatory fees ($880), and room and board ($8386). *College room only:* $5360. Room and board charges vary according to housing facility. *Part-time tuition:* $542 per credit hour. Part-time tuition and fees vary according to course load. *Payment plan:* Installment.
FRESHMAN FINANCIAL AID (Fall 2009, est.) 324 applied for aid; of those 96% were deemed to have need. 100% of freshmen with need received aid; of those 7% had need fully met. *Average percent of need met:* 69% (excluding resources awarded to replace EFC). *Average financial aid package:* $16,148 (excluding resources awarded to replace EFC). 6% of all full-time freshmen had no need and received non-need-based gift aid.
UNDERGRADUATE FINANCIAL AID (Fall 2009, est.) 946 applied for aid; of those 96% were deemed to have need. 99% of undergraduates with need received aid; of those 8% had need fully met. *Average percent of need met:* 63% (excluding resources awarded to replace EFC). *Average financial aid package:* $14,443 (excluding resources awarded to replace EFC). 3% of all full-time undergraduates had no need and received non-need-based gift aid.
GIFT AID (NEED-BASED) *Total amount:* $9,190,377 (42% federal, 6% state, 35% institutional, 17% external sources). *Receiving aid:* Freshmen: 92% (310); all full-time undergraduates: 90% (859). *Average award:* Freshmen: $12,226; Undergraduates: $10,525. *Scholarships, grants, and awards:* Federal Pell, FSEOG, state, private, college/university gift aid from institutional funds, United Negro College Fund, Federal Nursing.
GIFT AID (NON-NEED-BASED) *Total amount:* $602,103 (7% state, 59% institutional, 34% external sources). *Receiving aid:* Freshmen: 5% (16). Undergraduates: 4% (41). *Average award:* Freshmen: $10,012. Undergraduates: $8434. *Scholarships, grants, and awards by category:* Academic interests/achievement: general academic interests/achievements. Creative arts/performance: 29 awards ($83,500 total): art/fine arts, music, theater/drama. Special characteristics: children of faculty/staff, religious affiliation. *Tuition waivers:* Full or partial for employees or children of employees.
LOANS *Student loans:* $8,109,666 (89% need-based, 11% non-need-based). *Average indebtedness per student:* $27,500. *Average need-based loan:* Freshmen: $3691. Undergraduates: $4365. *Parent loans:* $913,955 (62% need-based, 38% non-need-based). *Programs:* Federal Direct (Subsidized and Unsubsidized Stafford, PLUS), FFEL (Subsidized and Unsubsidized Stafford, PLUS), Perkins, Federal Nursing, alternative loans.
WORK-STUDY *Federal work-study:* Total amount: $362,433; 234 jobs averaging $1496. *State or other work-study/employment:* Part-time jobs available.
ATHLETIC AWARDS Total amount: $512,778 (100% need-based).

DIXIE STATE COLLEGE OF UTAH
St. George, UT

Tuition & fees (UT res): $3146	Average undergraduate aid package: N/A

ABOUT THE INSTITUTION State-supported, coed. 25 undergraduate majors. Federal methodology is used as a basis for awarding need-based institutional aid.
UNDERGRADUATE EXPENSES for 2009–10 *Tuition, state resident:* full-time $2640; part-time $110 per credit. *Tuition, nonresident:* full-time $10,392; part-time $433 per credit. *Required fees:* full-time $506. Full-time tuition and fees vary according to course load and program. Part-time tuition and fees vary according to course load and program. *College room and board:* $3948; *Room only:* $1450. Room and board charges vary according to board plan and housing facility. *Payment plan:* Installment.
GIFT AID (NEED-BASED) *Total amount:* $9,621,195 (73% federal, 2% state, 19% institutional, 6% external sources). *Scholarships, grants, and awards:* Federal Pell, FSEOG, state, private, college/university gift aid from institutional funds.
GIFT AID (NON-NEED-BASED) *Tuition waivers:* Full or partial for children of alumni, employees or children of employees, senior citizens.
LOANS *Student loans:* $12,847,580 (56% need-based, 44% non-need-based). *Parent loans:* $263,458 (100% non-need-based). *Programs:* FFEL (Subsidized and Unsubsidized Stafford, PLUS), Perkins.
WORK-STUDY *Federal work-study:* Total amount: $213,858; jobs available. *State or other work-study/employment:* Total amount: $112,817 (100% need-based). Part-time jobs available.
ATHLETIC AWARDS Total amount: $821,756 (100% need-based).

DOANE COLLEGE
Crete, NE

Tuition & fees: $21,040	Average undergraduate aid package: $17,462

ABOUT THE INSTITUTION Independent religious, coed. 41 undergraduate majors. Federal methodology is used as a basis for awarding need-based institutional aid.
UNDERGRADUATE EXPENSES for 2009–10 *Comprehensive fee:* $27,010 includes full-time tuition ($20,540), mandatory fees ($500), and room and board ($5970). *College room only:* $2270. Full-time tuition and fees vary according to location. Room and board charges vary according to board plan, housing facility, and location. *Part-time tuition:* $680 per credit hour. Part-time tuition and fees vary according to course load and location. *Payment plan:* Installment.
FRESHMAN FINANCIAL AID (Fall 2009, est.) 305 applied for aid; of those 87% were deemed to have need. 100% of freshmen with need received aid; of those 40% had need fully met. *Average percent of need met:* 92% (excluding resources awarded to replace EFC). *Average financial aid package:* $18,049 (excluding resources awarded to replace EFC). 5% of all full-time freshmen had no need and received non-need-based gift aid.
UNDERGRADUATE FINANCIAL AID (Fall 2009, est.) 865 applied for aid; of those 88% were deemed to have need. 100% of undergraduates with need received aid; of those 40% had need fully met. *Average percent of need met:* 91% (excluding resources awarded to replace EFC). *Average financial aid package:* $17,462 (excluding resources awarded to replace EFC). 8% of all full-time undergraduates had no need and received non-need-based gift aid.
GIFT AID (NEED-BASED) *Total amount:* $5,279,351 (32% federal, 6% state, 51% institutional, 11% external sources). *Receiving aid:* Freshmen: 85% (264); all full-time undergraduates: 78% (753). *Average award:* Freshmen: $14,211; Undergraduates: $13,506. *Scholarships, grants, and awards:* Federal Pell, FSEOG, state, private, college/university gift aid from institutional funds.
GIFT AID (NON-NEED-BASED) *Total amount:* $3,609,845 (100% institutional). *Receiving aid:* Freshmen: 16% (49). *Average award:* Freshmen: $8118. Undergraduates: $10,924. *Scholarships, grants, and awards by category:* Academic interests/achievement: general academic interests/achievements. Creative arts/performance: art/fine arts, debating, music, performing arts, theater/drama. Special characteristics: children and siblings of alumni, children of faculty/staff, religious affiliation, siblings of current students. *Tuition waivers:* Full or partial for employees or children of employees, senior citizens.

LOANS *Student loans:* $5,601,578 (47% need-based, 53% non-need-based). 82% of past graduating class borrowed through all loan programs. *Average indebtedness per student:* $19,196. *Average need-based loan:* Freshmen: $3887. Undergraduates: $4464. *Parent loans:* $1,762,540 (100% non-need-based). *Programs:* Federal Direct (Subsidized and Unsubsidized Stafford, PLUS), Perkins.

WORK-STUDY *Federal work-study:* Total amount: $158,056; jobs available. *State or other work-study/employment:* Total amount: $330,660 (100% non-need-based). Part-time jobs available.

ATHLETIC AWARDS Total amount: $3,192,551 (61% need-based, 39% non-need-based).

APPLYING FOR FINANCIAL AID *Required financial aid form:* FAFSA. *Financial aid deadline:* Continuous. *Notification date:* Continuous beginning 3/1. Students must reply within 2 weeks of notification.

CONTACT Peggy Tvrdy, Director of Financial Aid, Doane College, 1014 Boswell Avenue, Crete, NE 68333-2430, 402-826-8260 or toll-free 800-333-6263. *Fax:* 402-826-8600. *E-mail:* peggy.tvrdy@doane.edu.

DOMINICAN COLLEGE
Orangeburg, NY

| Tuition & fees: $21,120 | Average undergraduate aid package: $15,918 |

ABOUT THE INSTITUTION Independent, coed. 36 undergraduate majors. Federal methodology is used as a basis for awarding need-based institutional aid.

UNDERGRADUATE EXPENSES for 2009–10 *One-time required fee:* $35. *Comprehensive fee:* $31,270 includes full-time tuition ($20,420), mandatory fees ($700), and room and board ($10,150). Room and board charges vary according to board plan and housing facility. *Part-time tuition:* $615 per credit hour. *Part-time fees:* $175 per term. Part-time tuition and fees vary according to program. *Payment plans:* Installment, deferred payment.

FRESHMAN FINANCIAL AID (Fall 2009, est.) 350 applied for aid; of those 96% were deemed to have need. 100% of freshmen with need received aid; of those 19% had need fully met. *Average percent of need met:* 78% (excluding resources awarded to replace EFC). *Average financial aid package:* $17,002 (excluding resources awarded to replace EFC). 12% of all full-time freshmen had no need and received non-need-based gift aid.

UNDERGRADUATE FINANCIAL AID (Fall 2009, est.) 1,288 applied for aid; of those 96% were deemed to have need. 100% of undergraduates with need received aid; of those 12% had need fully met. *Average percent of need met:* 75% (excluding resources awarded to replace EFC). *Average financial aid package:* $15,918 (excluding resources awarded to replace EFC). 7% of all full-time undergraduates had no need and received non-need-based gift aid.

GIFT AID (NEED-BASED) *Total amount:* $11,800,443 (29% federal, 12% state, 58% institutional, 1% external sources). *Receiving aid:* Freshmen: 76% (285); all full-time undergraduates: 80% (1,092). *Average award:* Freshmen: $11,829; Undergraduates: $10,619. *Scholarships, grants, and awards:* Federal Pell, FSEOG, state, private, college/university gift aid from institutional funds.

GIFT AID (NON-NEED-BASED) *Total amount:* $1,710,789 (3% state, 85% institutional, 12% external sources). *Receiving aid:* Freshmen: 13% (50). Undergraduates: 8% (112). *Average award:* Freshmen: $8050. Undergraduates: $6147. *Scholarships, grants, and awards by category:* Academic interests/ achievement: 105 awards ($645,435 total): education, general academic interests/ achievements, health fields. *Special characteristics:* 18 awards ($178,200 total): children of faculty/staff, general special characteristics, relatives of clergy. *Tuition waivers:* Full or partial for employees or children of employees, senior citizens.

LOANS *Student loans:* $11,180,301 (87% need-based, 13% non-need-based). 97% of past graduating class borrowed through all loan programs. *Average indebtedness per student:* $18,398. *Average need-based loan:* Freshmen: $3270. Undergraduates: $4360. *Parent loans:* $2,524,117 (33% need-based, 67% non-need-based). *Programs:* FFEL (Subsidized and Unsubsidized Stafford, PLUS), Perkins, Federal Nursing.

WORK-STUDY *Federal work-study:* Total amount: $243,556; 203 jobs averaging $1200. *State or other work-study/employment:* Total amount: $279,210 (71% need-based, 29% non-need-based). 69 part-time jobs averaging $3000.

ATHLETIC AWARDS Total amount: $1,666,493 (57% need-based, 43% non-need-based).

APPLYING FOR FINANCIAL AID *Required financial aid forms:* FAFSA, state aid form. *Financial aid deadline (priority):* 2/15. *Notification date:* Continuous beginning 2/15. Students must reply within 4 weeks of notification.

CONTACT Ms. Eileen Felske, Director of Financial Aid, Dominican College, 470 Western Highway, Orangeburg, NY 10962-1210, 845-848-7818 or toll-free 866-432-4636. *Fax:* 845-359-4317. *E-mail:* eileen.felske@dc.edu.

DOMINICAN UNIVERSITY
River Forest, IL

| Tuition & fees: $24,700 | Average undergraduate aid package: $18,277 |

ABOUT THE INSTITUTION Independent Roman Catholic, coed. 50 undergraduate majors. Federal methodology is used as a basis for awarding need-based institutional aid.

UNDERGRADUATE EXPENSES for 2009–10 *One-time required fee:* $150. *Comprehensive fee:* $32,320 includes full-time tuition ($24,600), mandatory fees ($100), and room and board ($7620). Full-time tuition and fees vary according to program. Room and board charges vary according to board plan and housing facility. *Part-time tuition:* $820 per semester hour. *Part-time fees:* $10 per course. Part-time tuition and fees vary according to location and program. *Payment plan:* Installment.

FRESHMAN FINANCIAL AID (Fall 2009, est.) 380 applied for aid; of those 91% were deemed to have need. 100% of freshmen with need received aid; of those 13% had need fully met. *Average percent of need met:* 81% (excluding resources awarded to replace EFC). *Average financial aid package:* $20,477 (excluding resources awarded to replace EFC). 10% of all full-time freshmen had no need and received non-need-based gift aid.

UNDERGRADUATE FINANCIAL AID (Fall 2009, est.) 1,494 applied for aid; of those 93% were deemed to have need. 100% of undergraduates with need received aid; of those 14% had need fully met. *Average percent of need met:* 74% (excluding resources awarded to replace EFC). *Average financial aid package:* $18,277 (excluding resources awarded to replace EFC). 12% of all full-time undergraduates had no need and received non-need-based gift aid.

GIFT AID (NEED-BASED) *Total amount:* $17,263,792 (18% federal, 20% state, 61% institutional, 1% external sources). *Receiving aid:* Freshmen: 86% (347); all full-time undergraduates: 81% (1,348). *Average award:* Freshmen: $16,452; Undergraduates: $14,403. *Scholarships, grants, and awards:* Federal Pell, FSEOG, state, private, college/university gift aid from institutional funds.

GIFT AID (NON-NEED-BASED) *Total amount:* $1,900,770 (97% institutional, 3% external sources). *Receiving aid:* Freshmen: 10% (40). Undergraduates: 8% (130). *Average award:* Freshmen: $9016. Undergraduates: $7912. *Scholarships, grants, and awards by category:* Academic interests/achievement: general academic interests/achievements, physical sciences. *Special achievements/ activities:* leadership. *Special characteristics:* children and siblings of alumni, international students, religious affiliation, siblings of current students, twins. *Tuition waivers:* Full or partial for children of alumni, employees or children of employees.

LOANS *Student loans:* $11,437,584 (75% need-based, 25% non-need-based). 89% of past graduating class borrowed through all loan programs. *Average indebtedness per student:* $21,392. *Average need-based loan:* Freshmen: $2916. Undergraduates: $4132. *Parent loans:* $1,303,903 (21% need-based, 79% non-need-based). *Programs:* Federal Direct (Subsidized and Unsubsidized Stafford, PLUS), Perkins.

WORK-STUDY *Federal work-study:* Total amount: $279,600; jobs available. *State or other work-study/employment:* Total amount: $429,078 (100% non-need-based). Part-time jobs available.

APPLYING FOR FINANCIAL AID *Required financial aid form:* FAFSA. *Financial aid deadline (priority):* 4/15. *Notification date:* Continuous. Students must reply within 2 weeks of notification.

CONTACT Michael Shields, Director of Financial Aid, Dominican University, 7900 West Division Street, River Forest, IL 60305-1099, 708-524-6807 or toll-free 800-828-8475. *Fax:* 708-366-6478. *E-mail:* mshields@dom.edu.

DOMINICAN UNIVERSITY OF CALIFORNIA
San Rafael, CA

| Tuition & fees: $35,587 | Average undergraduate aid package: $20,065 |

ABOUT THE INSTITUTION Independent religious, coed. 24 undergraduate majors. Federal methodology is used as a basis for awarding need-based institutional aid.

UNDERGRADUATE EXPENSES for 2010–11 *Comprehensive fee:* $49,147 includes full-time tuition ($35,220), mandatory fees ($367), and room and board ($13,560). *College room only:* $7720. Full-time tuition and fees vary according to course load, degree level, and program. Room and board charges vary according to board plan. *Part-time tuition:* $1470 per unit. *Part-time fees:* $300 per term. Part-time tuition and fees vary according to degree level and program. *Payment plan:* Installment.

FRESHMAN FINANCIAL AID (Fall 2008) 246 applied for aid; of those 88% were deemed to have need. 100% of freshmen with need received aid; of those 12% had need fully met. *Average percent of need met:* 67% (excluding resources awarded to replace EFC). *Average financial aid package:* $22,237 (excluding resources awarded to replace EFC). 16% of all full-time freshmen had no need and received non-need-based gift aid.

UNDERGRADUATE FINANCIAL AID (Fall 2008) 931 applied for aid; of those 91% were deemed to have need. 100% of undergraduates with need received aid; of those 8% had need fully met. *Average percent of need met:* 58% (excluding resources awarded to replace EFC). *Average financial aid package:* $20,065 (excluding resources awarded to replace EFC). 19% of all full-time undergraduates had no need and received non-need-based gift aid.

GIFT AID (NEED-BASED) *Total amount:* $13,047,314 (12% federal, 15% state, 71% institutional, 2% external sources). *Receiving aid:* Freshmen: 81% (217); all full-time undergraduates: 73% (837). *Average award:* Freshmen: $20,065; Undergraduates: $16,347. *Scholarships, grants, and awards:* Federal Pell, FSEOG, state, private, college/university gift aid from institutional funds, Scholarships for Disadvantaged Students (SDS).

GIFT AID (NON-NEED-BASED) *Total amount:* $2,931,344 (98% institutional, 2% external sources). *Receiving aid:* Freshmen: 18% (48). Undergraduates: 12% (142). *Average award:* Freshmen: $11,767. Undergraduates: $10,057. *Scholarships, grants, and awards by category:* Academic interests/achievement: general academic interests/achievements. *Creative arts/performance:* music. *Special achievements/activities:* community service, general special achievements/activities, leadership. *Special characteristics:* adult students, children and siblings of alumni, children of faculty/staff, ethnic background, first-generation college students, international students, members of minority groups. *Tuition waivers:* Full or partial for employees or children of employees, senior citizens.

LOANS *Student loans:* $12,903,937 (73% need-based, 27% non-need-based). 84% of past graduating class borrowed through all loan programs. *Average indebtedness per student:* $26,176. *Average need-based loan:* Freshmen: $3837. Undergraduates: $4857. *Parent loans:* $2,932,920 (20% need-based, 80% non-need-based). *Programs:* FFEL (Subsidized and Unsubsidized Stafford, PLUS), Perkins, college/university, private loans.

WORK-STUDY *Federal work-study:* Total amount: $294,313; jobs available. *State or other work-study/employment:* Total amount: $203,396 (43% need-based, 57% non-need-based). Part-time jobs available.

ATHLETIC AWARDS Total amount: $405,920 (64% need-based, 36% non-need-based).

APPLYING FOR FINANCIAL AID *Required financial aid forms:* FAFSA, institution's own form. *Financial aid deadline (priority):* 3/2. *Notification date:* Continuous beginning 3/15. Students must reply within 2 weeks of notification.

CONTACT Ms. Shanon Little, Director of Financial Aid, Dominican University of California, 50 Acacia Avenue, San Rafael, CA 94901-2298, 415-257-1302 or toll-free 888-323-6763. *Fax:* 415-485-3294. *E-mail:* shanon.little@dominican.edu.

DORDT COLLEGE
Sioux Center, IA

Tuition & fees: $22,080	Average undergraduate aid package: $20,705

ABOUT THE INSTITUTION Independent Christian Reformed, coed. 84 undergraduate majors. Federal methodology is used as a basis for awarding need-based institutional aid.

UNDERGRADUATE EXPENSES for 2009–10 *Comprehensive fee:* $28,090 includes full-time tuition ($21,720), mandatory fees ($360), and room and board ($6010). *College room only:* $3170. Full-time tuition and fees vary according to course load. Room and board charges vary according to board plan and housing facility. *Part-time tuition:* $880 per semester hour. *Part-time fees:* $160 per term. *Payment plan:* Installment.

FRESHMAN FINANCIAL AID (Fall 2009, est.) 317 applied for aid; of those 86% were deemed to have need. 100% of freshmen with need received aid; of those 16% had need fully met. *Average percent of need met:* 90% (excluding

resources awarded to replace EFC). *Average financial aid package:* $21,991 (excluding resources awarded to replace EFC). 18% of all full-time freshmen had no need and received non-need-based gift aid.

UNDERGRADUATE FINANCIAL AID (Fall 2009, est.) 1,110 applied for aid; of those 86% were deemed to have need. 100% of undergraduates with need received aid; of those 16% had need fully met. *Average percent of need met:* 88% (excluding resources awarded to replace EFC). *Average financial aid package:* $20,705 (excluding resources awarded to replace EFC). 20% of all full-time undergraduates had no need and received non-need-based gift aid.

GIFT AID (NEED-BASED) *Total amount:* $12,208,643 (14% federal, 10% state, 68% institutional, 8% external sources). *Receiving aid:* Freshmen: 76% (274); all full-time undergraduates: 74% (954). *Average award:* Freshmen: $13,246; Undergraduates: $11,515. *Scholarships, grants, and awards:* Federal Pell, FSEOG, state, private, college/university gift aid from institutional funds.

GIFT AID (NON-NEED-BASED) *Total amount:* $1,679,767 (92% institutional, 8% external sources). *Average award:* Freshmen: $13,389. Undergraduates: $11,435. *Scholarships, grants, and awards by category:* Academic interests/achievement: agriculture, biological sciences, business, communication, computer science, education, engineering/technologies, English, foreign languages, general academic interests/achievements, humanities, mathematics, physical sciences, premedicine, religion/biblical studies, social sciences. *Creative arts/performance:* journalism/publications, music, theater/drama. *Special achievements/activities:* general special achievements/activities, leadership. *Special characteristics:* children and siblings of alumni, children of faculty/staff, general special characteristics, handicapped students, international students, local/state students, members of minority groups, out-of-state students, religious affiliation. *Tuition waivers:* Full or partial for employees or children of employees, senior citizens.

LOANS *Student loans:* $9,153,990 (89% need-based, 11% non-need-based). 84% of past graduating class borrowed through all loan programs. *Average indebtedness per student:* $19,988. *Average need-based loan:* Freshmen: $5266. Undergraduates: $5437. *Parent loans:* $3,786,735 (87% need-based, 13% non-need-based). *Programs:* Federal Direct (Subsidized and Unsubsidized Stafford, PLUS), FFEL (Subsidized and Unsubsidized Stafford, PLUS), Perkins, state, college/university, alternative loans.

WORK-STUDY *Federal work-study:* Total amount: $899,795; 480 jobs averaging $1500. *State or other work-study/employment:* Total amount: $885,310 (69% need-based, 31% non-need-based). 590 part-time jobs averaging $1500.

ATHLETIC AWARDS Total amount: $1,319,250 (75% need-based, 25% non-need-based).

APPLYING FOR FINANCIAL AID *Required financial aid forms:* FAFSA, institution's own form. *Financial aid deadline (priority):* 4/1. *Notification date:* Continuous beginning 3/1. Students must reply within 3 weeks of notification.

CONTACT Michael Epema, Director of Financial Aid, Dordt College, 498 4th Avenue NE, Sioux Center, IA 51250-1697, 712-722-6087 Ext. 6082 or toll-free 800-343-6738. *Fax:* 712-722-6035. *E-mail:* epema@dordt.edu.

DOWLING COLLEGE
Oakdale, NY

Tuition & fees: $22,850	Average undergraduate aid package: $16,426

ABOUT THE INSTITUTION Independent, coed. 47 undergraduate majors. Federal methodology is used as a basis for awarding need-based institutional aid.

UNDERGRADUATE EXPENSES for 2010–11 *Comprehensive fee:* $33,050 includes full-time tuition ($20,860), mandatory fees ($1990), and room and board ($10,200). Full-time tuition and fees vary according to course load and degree level. Room and board charges vary according to housing facility and location. *Part-time tuition:* $698 per credit. *Part-time fees:* $500 per term. Part-time tuition and fees vary according to course load and degree level. *Payment plans:* Installment, deferred payment.

FRESHMAN FINANCIAL AID (Fall 2009, est.) 368 applied for aid; of those 98% were deemed to have need. 100% of freshmen with need received aid; of those 2% had need fully met. *Average percent of need met:* 95% (excluding resources awarded to replace EFC). *Average financial aid package:* $18,136 (excluding resources awarded to replace EFC). 8% of all full-time freshmen had no need and received non-need-based gift aid.

UNDERGRADUATE FINANCIAL AID (Fall 2009, est.) 1,535 applied for aid; of those 100% were deemed to have need. 100% of undergraduates with need received aid; of those 2% had need fully met. *Average percent of need met:* 94% (excluding resources awarded to replace EFC). *Average financial aid*

package: $16,426 (excluding resources awarded to replace EFC). 7% of all full-time undergraduates had no need and received non-need-based gift aid.

GIFT AID (NEED-BASED) *Total amount:* $12,362,144 (33% federal, 25% state, 42% institutional). *Receiving aid:* Freshmen: 66% (347); all full-time undergraduates: 69% (1,461). *Average award:* Freshmen $3261; Undergraduates: $9144. *Scholarships, grants, and awards:* Federal Pell, FSEOG, state, private, college/university gift aid from institutional funds.

GIFT AID (NON-NEED-BASED) *Total amount:* $7,722,156 (2% federal, 1% state, 94% institutional, 3% external sources). *Receiving aid:* Freshmen: 56% (295). Undergraduates: 38% (815). *Average award:* Freshmen: $7875. Undergraduates: $5478. *Scholarships, grants, and awards by category:* Academic interests/achievement: 719 awards ($3,614,714 total): business, education, general academic interests/achievements, mathematics, social sciences. *Special achievements/activities:* 212 awards ($11,000 total): general special achievements/activities. *Special characteristics:* 422 awards ($2,584,194 total): adult students, children and siblings of alumni, children of educators, children of faculty/staff, children of public servants, children of union members/company employees, children of workers in trades, ethnic background, first-generation college students, general special characteristics, local/state students, members of minority groups, previous college experience, public servants, siblings of current students, twins, veterans. *Tuition waivers:* Full or partial for minority students, children of alumni, employees or children of employees, adult students, senior citizens.

LOANS *Student loans:* $6,409,388 (100% need-based). 75% of past graduating class borrowed through all loan programs. *Average indebtedness per student:* $31,000. *Average need-based loan:* Freshmen: $3241. Undergraduates: $4406. *Parent loans:* $4,568,155 (100% non-need-based). *Programs:* Federal Direct (Subsidized and Unsubsidized Stafford, PLUS), FFEL (Subsidized and Unsubsidized Stafford, PLUS), Perkins, state.

WORK-STUDY *Federal work-study:* Total amount: $1,872,842; 289 jobs averaging $1400. *State or other work-study/employment:* Total amount: $263,785 (76% need-based, 24% non-need-based). 60 part-time jobs averaging $3700.

ATHLETIC AWARDS Total amount: $2,424,637 (100% non-need-based).

APPLYING FOR FINANCIAL AID *Required financial aid forms:* FAFSA, state aid form. *Financial aid deadline (priority):* 3/1. *Notification date:* Continuous beginning 3/15.

CONTACT Ms. Patricia Noren, Director of Student Financial Services, Dowling College, 150 Idle Hour Boulevard, Oakdale, NY 11769-1999, 631-244-3368 or toll-free 800-DOWLING. *E-mail:* norenp@dowling.edu.

DRAKE UNIVERSITY
Des Moines, IA

Tuition & fees: $25,622	Average undergraduate aid package: $20,813

ABOUT THE INSTITUTION Independent, coed. 66 undergraduate majors. Federal methodology is used as a basis for awarding need-based institutional aid.

UNDERGRADUATE EXPENSES for 2009–10 *Comprehensive fee:* $33,422 includes full-time tuition ($25,160), mandatory fees ($462), and room and board ($7800). *College room only:* $4100. Full-time tuition and fees vary according to course load, program, and student level. Room and board charges vary according to board plan. *Part-time tuition:* $520 per hour. *Part-time fees:* $44 per term. Part-time tuition and fees vary according to class time and program. *Payment plan:* Installment.

FRESHMAN FINANCIAL AID (Fall 2009, est.) 726 applied for aid; of those 75% were deemed to have need. 100% of freshmen with need received aid; of those 34% had need fully met. *Average percent of need met:* 83% (excluding resources awarded to replace EFC). *Average financial aid package:* $20,921 (excluding resources awarded to replace EFC). 32% of all full-time freshmen had no need and received non-need-based gift aid.

UNDERGRADUATE FINANCIAL AID (Fall 2009, est.) 2,349 applied for aid; of those 80% were deemed to have need. 100% of undergraduates with need received aid; of those 32% had need fully met. *Average percent of need met:* 82% (excluding resources awarded to replace EFC). *Average financial aid package:* $20,813 (excluding resources awarded to replace EFC). 36% of all full-time undergraduates had no need and received non-need-based gift aid.

GIFT AID (NEED-BASED) *Total amount:* $26,112,507 (13% federal, 8% state, 76% institutional, 3% external sources). *Receiving aid:* Freshmen: 63% (538); all full-time undergraduates: 56% (1,823). *Average award:* Freshmen: $14,496; Undergraduates: $13,960. *Scholarships, grants, and awards:* Federal Pell, FSEOG, state, private, college/university gift aid from institutional funds.

GIFT AID (NON-NEED-BASED) *Total amount:* $15,426,687 (2% federal, 95% institutional, 3% external sources). *Receiving aid:* Freshmen: 15% (133). Undergraduates: 11% (374). *Average award:* Freshmen: $11,324. Undergraduates: $10,664. *Scholarships, grants, and awards by category:* Academic interests/achievement: 2,523 awards ($25,130,907 total): general academic interests/achievements. Creative arts/performance: 272 awards ($1,143,932 total): art/fine arts, music, theater/drama. Special characteristics: 264 awards ($405,000 total): children and siblings of alumni, international students. *Tuition waivers:* Full or partial for children of alumni, employees or children of employees, senior citizens.

LOANS *Student loans:* $26,743,547 (47% need-based, 53% non-need-based). 71% of past graduating class borrowed through all loan programs. *Average indebtedness per student:* $34,919. *Average need-based loan:* Freshmen: $4499. Undergraduates: $4951. *Parent loans:* $31,149,767 (16% need-based, 84% non-need-based). *Programs:* FFEL (Subsidized and Unsubsidized Stafford, PLUS), Perkins, college/university.

WORK-STUDY *Federal work-study:* Total amount: $3,000,850; 1,574 jobs averaging $1907. *State or other work-study/employment:* Part-time jobs available.

ATHLETIC AWARDS Total amount: $3,374,854 (26% need-based, 74% non-need-based).

APPLYING FOR FINANCIAL AID *Required financial aid form:* FAFSA. *Financial aid deadline (priority):* 3/1. *Notification date:* Continuous beginning 3/1. Students must reply by 5/1 or within 3 weeks of notification.

CONTACT Office of Student Financial Planning, Drake University, 2507 University Avenue, Des Moines, IA 50311-4516, 800-44-DRAKE Ext. 2905 or toll-free 800-44DRAKE Ext. 3181. *Fax:* 515-271-4042.

DREW UNIVERSITY
Madison, NJ

Tuition & fees: $38,017	Average undergraduate aid package: $29,480

ABOUT THE INSTITUTION Independent religious, coed. 30 undergraduate majors. Institutional methodology is used as a basis for awarding need-based institutional aid.

UNDERGRADUATE EXPENSES for 2009–10 *Comprehensive fee:* $48,385 includes full-time tuition ($37,310), mandatory fees ($707), and room and board ($10,368). *College room only:* $6702. Full-time tuition and fees vary according to course load. Room and board charges vary according to board plan and housing facility. *Part-time tuition:* $1554 per credit. Part-time tuition and fees vary according to course load. *Payment plans:* Tuition prepayment, installment, deferred payment.

FRESHMAN FINANCIAL AID (Fall 2008) 282 applied for aid; of those 74% were deemed to have need. 100% of freshmen with need received aid; of those 22% had need fully met. *Average percent of need met:* 77% (excluding resources awarded to replace EFC). *Average financial aid package:* $27,846 (excluding resources awarded to replace EFC). 43% of all full-time freshmen had no need and received non-need-based gift aid.

UNDERGRADUATE FINANCIAL AID (Fall 2008) 1,015 applied for aid; of those 80% were deemed to have need. 100% of undergraduates with need received aid; of those 27% had need fully met. *Average percent of need met:* 81% (excluding resources awarded to replace EFC). *Average financial aid package:* $29,480 (excluding resources awarded to replace EFC). 39% of all full-time undergraduates had no need and received non-need-based gift aid.

GIFT AID (NEED-BASED) *Total amount:* $19,123,042 (8% federal, 13% state, 77% institutional, 2% external sources). *Receiving aid:* Freshmen: 53% (207); all full-time undergraduates: 52% (805). *Average award:* Freshmen: $23,175; Undergraduates: $23,755. *Scholarships, grants, and awards:* Federal Pell, FSEOG, state, private, college/university gift aid from institutional funds.

GIFT AID (NON-NEED-BASED) *Total amount:* $8,174,133 (2% state, 94% institutional, 4% external sources). *Receiving aid:* Freshmen: 8% (33). Undergraduates: 7% (105). *Average award:* Freshmen: $10,432. Undergraduates: $11,707. *Scholarships, grants, and awards by category:* Academic interests/achievement: general academic interests/achievements. Creative arts/performance: general creative arts/performance. Special characteristics: members of minority groups. *Tuition waivers:* Full or partial for employees or children of employees, senior citizens.

LOANS *Student loans:* $5,050,444 (69% need-based, 31% non-need-based). 61% of past graduating class borrowed through all loan programs. *Average indebtedness per student:* $17,444. *Average need-based loan:* Freshmen: $4517.

Undergraduates: $5386. *Parent loans:* $10,569,956 (22% need-based, 78% non-need-based). *Programs:* FFEL (Subsidized and Unsubsidized Stafford, PLUS), Perkins, state.

WORK-STUDY *Federal work-study:* Total amount: $315,479; 266 jobs averaging $1186. *State or other work-study/employment:* Total amount: $342,985 (74% need-based, 26% non-need-based). Part-time jobs available.

APPLYING FOR FINANCIAL AID *Required financial aid forms:* FAFSA, CSS Financial Aid PROFILE. *Financial aid deadline:* 2/15. *Notification date:* 3/30. Students must reply by 5/1.

CONTACT Renee Volak, Director of Financial Assistance, Drew University, 36 Madison Avenue, Madison, NJ 07940-1493, 973-408-3112. *Fax:* 973-408-3188. *E-mail:* finaid@drew.edu.

DREXEL UNIVERSITY
Philadelphia, PA

ABOUT THE INSTITUTION Independent, coed. 55 undergraduate majors.

GIFT AID (NEED-BASED) *Scholarships, grants, and awards:* Federal Pell, FSEOG, state, private, college/university gift aid from institutional funds, United Negro College Fund.

GIFT AID (NON-NEED-BASED) *Scholarships, grants, and awards by category:* Academic interests/achievement: general academic interests/achievements. *Creative arts/performance:* dance, music, performing arts, theater/drama. *Special achievements/activities:* cheerleading/drum major. *Special characteristics:* children and siblings of alumni, siblings of current students, twins.

LOANS *Programs:* FFEL (Subsidized and Unsubsidized Stafford, PLUS), Perkins, Federal Nursing, college/university.

WORK-STUDY *Federal work-study:* Total amount: $4,891,861; jobs available.

APPLYING FOR FINANCIAL AID *Required financial aid form:* FAFSA.

CONTACT Helen Gourousis, Director of Financial Aid, Drexel University, 3141 Chestnut Street, Philadelphia, PA 19104-2875, 215-895-5928 or toll-free 800-2-DREXEL. *Fax:* 215-895-6903. *E-mail:* gouroush@drexel.edu.

DRURY UNIVERSITY
Springfield, MO

Tuition & fees: $19,854	Average undergraduate aid package: $7985

ABOUT THE INSTITUTION Independent, coed. 61 undergraduate majors. Federal methodology is used as a basis for awarding need-based institutional aid.

UNDERGRADUATE EXPENSES for 2010–11 *One-time required fee:* $145. *Comprehensive fee:* $26,825 includes full-time tuition ($19,325), mandatory fees ($529), and room and board ($6971). Full-time tuition and fees vary according to class time. Room and board charges vary according to board plan and housing facility. Part-time tuition and fees vary according to class time. *Payment plans:* Tuition prepayment, installment, deferred payment.

FRESHMAN FINANCIAL AID (Fall 2009, est.) 338 applied for aid; of those 91% were deemed to have need. 100% of freshmen with need received aid; of those 87% had need fully met. *Average percent of need met:* 84% (excluding resources awarded to replace EFC). *Average financial aid package:* $7600 (excluding resources awarded to replace EFC). 16% of all full-time freshmen had no need and received non-need-based gift aid.

UNDERGRADUATE FINANCIAL AID (Fall 2009, est.) 1,483 applied for aid; of those 99% were deemed to have need. 100% of undergraduates with need received aid; of those 86% had need fully met. *Average percent of need met:* 86% (excluding resources awarded to replace EFC). *Average financial aid package:* $7985 (excluding resources awarded to replace EFC). 14% of all full-time undergraduates had no need and received non-need-based gift aid.

GIFT AID (NEED-BASED) *Total amount:* $9,142,403 (10% federal, 14% state, 66% institutional, 10% external sources). *Receiving aid:* Freshmen: 81% (289); all full-time undergraduates: 88% (1,362). *Average award:* Freshmen: $5680; Undergraduates: $6990. *Scholarships, grants, and awards:* Federal Pell, FSEOG, state, private, college/university gift aid from institutional funds.

GIFT AID (NON-NEED-BASED) *Total amount:* $3,297,349 (10% state, 86% institutional, 4% external sources). *Receiving aid:* Freshmen: 76% (273). Undergraduates: 95% (1,471). *Average award:* Freshmen: $4250. Undergraduates: $3585. *Scholarships, grants, and awards by category:* Academic interests/ achievement: architecture, biological sciences, business, communication, computer science, education, English, foreign languages, general academic interests/achievements, health fields, humanities, mathematics, physical sci-

ences, premedicine, social sciences. *Creative arts/performance:* art/fine arts, creative writing, debating, music, theater/drama. *Special achievements/activities:* cheerleading/drum major, leadership, religious involvement. *Special characteristics:* children and siblings of alumni, children of faculty/staff, relatives of clergy, religious affiliation. *Tuition waivers:* Full or partial for minority students, children of alumni, employees or children of employees.

LOANS *Student loans:* $24,002,635 (94% need-based, 6% non-need-based). 67% of past graduating class borrowed through all loan programs. *Average indebtedness per student:* $20,500. *Average need-based loan:* Freshmen: $4500. Undergraduates: $5500. *Parent loans:* $1,429,845 (100% need-based). *Programs:* FFEL (Subsidized and Unsubsidized Stafford, PLUS), Perkins.

WORK-STUDY *Federal work-study:* Total amount: $387,856; 793 jobs averaging $3000. *State or other work-study/employment:* Total amount: $169,887 (100% non-need-based). 229 part-time jobs averaging $3000.

ATHLETIC AWARDS Total amount: $2,593,359 (19% need-based, 81% non-need-based).

APPLYING FOR FINANCIAL AID *Required financial aid forms:* FAFSA, institution's own form. *Financial aid deadline (priority):* 3/15. *Notification date:* Continuous beginning 3/15. Students must reply within 2 weeks of notification.

CONTACT Ms. Annette Avery, Director of Financial Aid, Drury University, 900 North Benton Avenue, Springfield, MO 65802-3791, 417-873-7312 or toll-free 800-922-2274. *Fax:* 417-873-6906. *E-mail:* aavery@drury.edu.

DUKE UNIVERSITY
Durham, NC

Tuition & fees: $40,243	Average undergraduate aid package: $36,576

ABOUT THE INSTITUTION Independent religious, coed. 45 undergraduate majors. Both federal and institutional methodology are used as a basis for awarding need-based institutional aid.

UNDERGRADUATE EXPENSES for 2010–11 *Comprehensive fee:* $51,865 includes full-time tuition ($38,985), mandatory fees ($1258), and room and board ($11,622). *College room only:* $6502. Room and board charges vary according to board plan and housing facility. *Part-time tuition:* $4872 per course. Part-time tuition and fees vary according to course load. *Payment plans:* Tuition prepayment, installment, deferred payment.

FRESHMAN FINANCIAL AID (Fall 2009, est.) 899 applied for aid; of those 85% were deemed to have need. 100% of freshmen with need received aid; of those 100% had need fully met. *Average percent of need met:* 100% (excluding resources awarded to replace EFC). *Average financial aid package:* $37,956 (excluding resources awarded to replace EFC). 4% of all full-time freshmen had no need and received non-need-based gift aid.

UNDERGRADUATE FINANCIAL AID (Fall 2009, est.) 3,076 applied for aid; of those 91% were deemed to have need. 100% of undergraduates with need received aid; of those 100% had need fully met. *Average percent of need met:* 100% (excluding resources awarded to replace EFC). *Average financial aid package:* $36,576 (excluding resources awarded to replace EFC). 6% of all full-time undergraduates had no need and received non-need-based gift aid.

GIFT AID (NEED-BASED) *Total amount:* $89,987,939 (7% federal, 2% state, 85% institutional, 6% external sources). *Receiving aid:* Freshmen: 43% (748); all full-time undergraduates: 41% (2,714). *Average award:* Freshmen: $35,440; Undergraduates: $33,810. *Scholarships, grants, and awards:* Federal Pell, FSEOG, state, private, college/university gift aid from institutional funds.

GIFT AID (NON-NEED-BASED) *Total amount:* $12,043,075 (6% state, 74% institutional, 20% external sources). *Receiving aid:* Freshmen: 5% (85). Undergraduates: 3% (214). *Average award:* Freshmen: $22,049. Undergraduates: $23,185. *Scholarships, grants, and awards by category:* Academic interests/achievement: 119 awards ($5,769,040 total): general academic interests/ achievements, mathematics. *Creative arts/performance:* creative writing. *Special achievements/activities:* 74 awards ($3,545,399 total): general special achievements/ activities, leadership. *Special characteristics:* 35 awards ($1,622,614 total): children and siblings of alumni, ethnic background, local/state students. *Tuition waivers:* Full or partial for employees or children of employees.

LOANS *Student loans:* $8,563,834 (70% need-based, 30% non-need-based). 40% of past graduating class borrowed through all loan programs. *Average indebtedness per student:* $23,059. *Average need-based loan:* Freshmen: $2399. Undergraduates: $2666. *Parent loans:* $7,889,268 (65% need-based, 35% non-need-based). *Programs:* Federal Direct (Subsidized and Unsubsidized Stafford, PLUS), Perkins, college/university, alternative loans.

WORK-STUDY *Federal work-study:* Total amount: $2,736,230; 1,735 jobs averaging $1789. *State or other work-study/employment:* Total amount: $969,043 (79% need-based, 21% non-need-based). 685 part-time jobs averaging $1548.
ATHLETIC AWARDS Total amount: $13,251,211 (22% need-based, 78% non-need-based).
APPLYING FOR FINANCIAL AID *Required financial aid forms:* FAFSA, CSS Financial Aid PROFILE, noncustodial (divorced/separated) parent's statement, business/farm supplement, income tax form(s), W-2 forms. *Financial aid deadline:* 3/1. *Notification date:* 4/1. Students must reply by 5/1.
CONTACT Alison Rabil, Director, Duke University, 2122 Campus Drive, Durham, NC 27708-0397, 919-684-6225. *Fax:* 919-660-9811. *E-mail:* finaid@duke.edu.

DUNLAP-STONE UNIVERSITY
Phoenix, AZ

CONTACT Financial Aid Office, Dunlap-Stone University, 11225 North 28th Drive, Suite B-201, Phoenix, AZ 85029, 602-648-5750 or toll-free 800-474-8013.

DUQUESNE UNIVERSITY
Pittsburgh, PA

Tuition & fees: $26,468	Average undergraduate aid package: $20,187

ABOUT THE INSTITUTION Independent Roman Catholic, coed. 70 undergraduate majors. Federal methodology is used as a basis for awarding need-based institutional aid.
UNDERGRADUATE EXPENSES for 2009–10 *Comprehensive fee:* $35,668 includes full-time tuition ($24,385), mandatory fees ($2083), and room and board ($9200). *College room only:* $5018. Full-time tuition and fees vary according to program. Room and board charges vary according to board plan and housing facility. *Part-time tuition:* $795 per credit. *Part-time fees:* $81 per credit. Part-time tuition and fees vary according to program. *Payment plans:* Installment, deferred payment.
FRESHMAN FINANCIAL AID (Fall 2008) 1,278 applied for aid; of those 76% were deemed to have need. 100% of freshmen with need received aid; of those 30% had need fully met. *Average percent of need met:* 91% (excluding resources awarded to replace EFC). *Average financial aid package:* $21,127 (excluding resources awarded to replace EFC). 30% of all full-time freshmen had no need and received non-need-based gift aid.
UNDERGRADUATE FINANCIAL AID (Fall 2008) 4,418 applied for aid; of those 83% were deemed to have need. 100% of undergraduates with need received aid; of those 28% had need fully met. *Average percent of need met:* 91% (excluding resources awarded to replace EFC). *Average financial aid package:* $20,187 (excluding resources awarded to replace EFC). 25% of all full-time undergraduates had no need and received non-need-based gift aid.
GIFT AID (NEED-BASED) *Total amount:* $44,632,240 (8% federal, 13% state, 72% institutional, 7% external sources). *Receiving aid:* Freshmen: 67% (967); all full-time undergraduates: 67% (3,616). *Average award:* Freshmen: $14,011; Undergraduates: $11,967. *Scholarships, grants, and awards:* Federal Pell, FSEOG, state, private, college/university gift aid from institutional funds, United Negro College Fund.
GIFT AID (NON-NEED-BASED) *Total amount:* $10,785,516 (93% institutional, 7% external sources). *Receiving aid:* Freshmen: 66% (951). Undergraduates: 59% (3,176). *Average award:* Freshmen: $8228. Undergraduates: $7479. *Scholarships, grants, and awards by category:* Academic interests/achievement: 4,183 awards ($27,224,540 total): general academic interests/achievements. Creative arts/performance: 209 awards ($1,615,290 total): dance, music. *Special characteristics:* 865 awards ($8,129,262 total): children and siblings of alumni, children of faculty/staff, ethnic background, general special characteristics, international students, members of minority groups, relatives of clergy, religious affiliation. *Tuition waivers:* Full or partial for employees or children of employees, senior citizens.
LOANS *Student loans:* $49,262,683 (87% need-based, 13% non-need-based). *Average need-based loan:* Freshmen: $4160. Undergraduates: $4839. *Parent loans:* $10,049,359 (84% need-based, 16% non-need-based). *Programs:* FFEL (Subsidized and Unsubsidized Stafford, PLUS), Perkins, Federal Nursing, private alternative loans.
WORK-STUDY *Federal work-study:* Total amount: $7,755,445; 2,723 jobs averaging $2848.

ATHLETIC AWARDS Total amount: $4,932,434 (55% need-based, 45% non-need-based).
APPLYING FOR FINANCIAL AID *Required financial aid forms:* FAFSA, institution's own form. *Financial aid deadline:* 5/1. *Notification date:* Continuous beginning 3/1. Students must reply by 5/1 or within 3 weeks of notification.
CONTACT Mr. Richard C. Esposito, Director of Financial Aid, Duquesne University, 600 Forbes Avenue, Pittsburgh, PA 15282-0299, 412-396-6607 or toll-free 800-456-0590. *Fax:* 412-396-5284. *E-mail:* esposito@duq.edu.

D'YOUVILLE COLLEGE
Buffalo, NY

Tuition & fees: $20,030	Average undergraduate aid package: $14,972

ABOUT THE INSTITUTION Independent, coed. 25 undergraduate majors. Federal methodology is used as a basis for awarding need-based institutional aid.
UNDERGRADUATE EXPENSES for 2009–10 *Comprehensive fee:* $29,830 includes full-time tuition ($19,800), mandatory fees ($230), and room and board ($9800). Full-time tuition and fees vary according to course load, degree level, and program. Room and board charges vary according to board plan and housing facility. *Part-time tuition:* $575 per credit hour. *Part-time fees:* $2 per credit hour; $40 per term. Part-time tuition and fees vary according to course load, degree level, and program. *Payment plans:* Tuition prepayment, installment, deferred payment.
FRESHMAN FINANCIAL AID (Fall 2009, est.) 190 applied for aid; of those 88% were deemed to have need. 100% of freshmen with need received aid; of those 30% had need fully met. *Average percent of need met:* 79% (excluding resources awarded to replace EFC). *Average financial aid package:* $16,190 (excluding resources awarded to replace EFC). 12% of all full-time freshmen had no need and received non-need-based gift aid.
UNDERGRADUATE FINANCIAL AID (Fall 2009, est.) 1,332 applied for aid; of those 91% were deemed to have need. 99% of undergraduates with need received aid; of those 18% had need fully met. *Average percent of need met:* 64% (excluding resources awarded to replace EFC). *Average financial aid package:* $14,972 (excluding resources awarded to replace EFC). 10% of all full-time undergraduates had no need and received non-need-based gift aid.
GIFT AID (NEED-BASED) *Total amount:* $11,339,322 (28% federal, 17% state, 51% institutional, 4% external sources). *Receiving aid:* Freshmen: 85% (168); all full-time undergraduates: 79% (1,152). *Average award:* Freshmen: $12,792; Undergraduates: $9957. *Scholarships, grants, and awards:* Federal Pell, FSEOG, state, private, college/university gift aid from institutional funds.
GIFT AID (NON-NEED-BASED) *Total amount:* $1,026,506 (4% state, 91% institutional, 5% external sources). *Receiving aid:* Freshmen: 13% (25). Undergraduates: 6% (90). *Average award:* Freshmen: $8101. Undergraduates: $5731. *Scholarships, grants, and awards by category:* Academic interests/achievement: 994 awards ($4,847,216 total): biological sciences, business, education, English, general academic interests/achievements, health fields, humanities, international studies, mathematics, premedicine, social sciences. *Special characteristics:* 111 awards ($706,912 total): children and siblings of alumni, children of faculty/staff. *Tuition waivers:* Full or partial for children of alumni, employees or children of employees, senior citizens.
LOANS *Student loans:* $16,255,742 (80% need-based, 20% non-need-based). 91% of past graduating class borrowed through all loan programs. *Average need-based loan:* Freshmen: $3580. Undergraduates: $5784. *Parent loans:* $859,419 (42% need-based, 58% non-need-based). *Programs:* Federal Direct (Subsidized and Unsubsidized Stafford, PLUS), Perkins, Federal Nursing, college/university.
WORK-STUDY *Federal work-study:* Total amount: $300,000; 269 jobs averaging $1115. *State or other work-study/employment:* Total amount: $132,000 (100% non-need-based). 90 part-time jobs averaging $1467.
APPLYING FOR FINANCIAL AID *Required financial aid forms:* FAFSA, state aid form. *Financial aid deadline (priority):* 2/15. *Notification date:* Continuous beginning 3/15. Students must reply within 2 weeks of notification.
CONTACT Ms. Lorraine A. Metz, Director of Financial Aid, D'Youville College, 320 Porter Avenue, Buffalo, NY 14201-1084, 716-829-7500 or toll-free 800-777-3921. *Fax:* 716-829-7779. *E-mail:* metzla@dyc.edu.

EARLHAM COLLEGE
Richmond, IN

Tuition & fees: $36,494	Average undergraduate aid package: $27,660

ABOUT THE INSTITUTION Independent religious, coed. 37 undergraduate majors. Federal methodology is used as a basis for awarding need-based institutional aid.

UNDERGRADUATE EXPENSES for 2010–11 *Comprehensive fee:* $43,894 includes full-time tuition ($35,720), mandatory fees ($774), and room and board ($7400). *College room only:* $3750. *Part-time tuition:* $1194 per credit.

FRESHMAN FINANCIAL AID (Fall 2009, est.) 200 applied for aid; of those 88% were deemed to have need. 99% of freshmen with need received aid; of those 32% had need fully met. *Average percent of need met:* 92% (excluding resources awarded to replace EFC). *Average financial aid package:* $28,502 (excluding resources awarded to replace EFC). 14% of all full-time freshmen had no need and received non-need-based gift aid.

UNDERGRADUATE FINANCIAL AID (Fall 2009, est.) 719 applied for aid; of those 91% were deemed to have need. 100% of undergraduates with need received aid; of those 32% had need fully met. *Average percent of need met:* 90% (excluding resources awarded to replace EFC). *Average financial aid package:* $27,660 (excluding resources awarded to replace EFC). 26% of all full-time undergraduates had no need and received non-need-based gift aid.

GIFT AID (NEED-BASED) *Total amount:* $17,013,930 (9% federal, 3% state, 88% institutional). *Receiving aid:* Freshmen: 54% (157); all full-time undergraduates: 50% (560). *Average award:* Freshmen: $21,441; Undergraduates: $19,870. *Scholarships, grants, and awards:* Federal Pell, FSEOG, state, private, college/university gift aid from institutional funds.

GIFT AID (NON-NEED-BASED) *Total amount:* $4,672,962 (91% institutional, 9% external sources). *Receiving aid:* Freshmen: 32% (93). Undergraduates: 30% (337). *Average award:* Freshmen: $8310. Undergraduates: $10,413. *Scholarships, grants, and awards by category:* Academic interests/achievement: general academic interests/achievements.

LOANS *Student loans:* $5,144,270 (63% need-based, 37% non-need-based). 55% of past graduating class borrowed through all loan programs. *Average indebtedness per student:* $23,752. *Average need-based loan:* Freshmen: $3727. Undergraduates: $4832. *Parent loans:* $1,559,874 (100% non-need-based). *Programs:* Federal Direct (Subsidized and Unsubsidized Stafford, PLUS), Perkins, college/university.

WORK-STUDY *Federal work-study:* Total amount: $400,000; 375 jobs averaging $2058. *State or other work-study/employment:* Total amount: $405,000 (48% need-based, 52% non-need-based). 112 part-time jobs averaging $2250.

APPLYING FOR FINANCIAL AID *Required financial aid forms:* FAFSA, institution's own form. *Financial aid deadline (priority):* 3/1. *Notification date:* Continuous beginning 2/15. Students must reply by 5/1 or within 3 weeks of notification.

CONTACT Mr. Robert W. Arnold, Director of Financial Aid, Earlham College, National Road West, Richmond, IN 47374-4095, 765-983-1217 or toll-free 800-327-5426. *Fax:* 765-983-1299. *E-mail:* boba@earlham.edu.

EAST CAROLINA UNIVERSITY
Greenville, NC

Tuition & fees (NC res): $4477	Average undergraduate aid package: $8964

ABOUT THE INSTITUTION State-supported, coed. 86 undergraduate majors. Federal methodology is used as a basis for awarding need-based institutional aid.

UNDERGRADUATE EXPENSES for 2009–10 *Tuition, state resident:* full-time $2491. *Tuition, nonresident:* full-time $13,325. *Required fees:* full-time $1986. Part-time tuition and fees vary according to course load. *College room and board:* $7480; *Room only:* $4350. Room and board charges vary according to board plan and housing facility. *Payment plans:* Installment, deferred payment.

FRESHMAN FINANCIAL AID (Fall 2009, est.) 3,008 applied for aid; of those 64% were deemed to have need. 97% of freshmen with need received aid; of those 29% had need fully met. *Average percent of need met:* 78% (excluding resources awarded to replace EFC). *Average financial aid package:* $8874 (excluding resources awarded to replace EFC). 1% of all full-time freshmen had no need and received non-need-based gift aid.

UNDERGRADUATE FINANCIAL AID (Fall 2009, est.) 12,473 applied for aid; of those 75% were deemed to have need. 98% of undergraduates with need received aid; of those 24% had need fully met. *Average percent of need met:* 77% (excluding resources awarded to replace EFC). *Average financial aid package:* $8964 (excluding resources awarded to replace EFC). 2% of all full-time undergraduates had no need and received non-need-based gift aid.

GIFT AID (NEED-BASED) *Total amount:* $55,407,873 (48% federal, 37% state, 14% institutional, 1% external sources). *Receiving aid:* Freshmen: 37% (1,441); all full-time undergraduates: 40% (7,248). *Average award:* Freshmen: $7943; Undergraduates: $6637. *Scholarships, grants, and awards:* Federal Pell, FSEOG, state, private, college/university gift aid from institutional funds, Federal Nursing.

GIFT AID (NON-NEED-BASED) *Total amount:* $5,414,054 (25% state, 15% institutional, 60% external sources). *Receiving aid:* Freshmen: 4% (172). Undergraduates: 7% (1,174). *Average award:* Freshmen: $2155. Undergraduates: $2473. *Scholarships, grants, and awards by category:* Academic interests/achievement: biological sciences, business, communication, education, engineering/technologies, English, foreign languages, general academic interests/achievements, health fields, home economics, humanities, mathematics, military science, physical sciences. Creative arts/performance: applied art and design, art/fine arts, music. Special characteristics: adult students, children and siblings of alumni, children of faculty/staff, ethnic background, handicapped students. *Tuition waivers:* Full or partial for employees or children of employees, senior citizens.

LOANS *Student loans:* $77,559,693 (75% need-based, 25% non-need-based). 55% of past graduating class borrowed through all loan programs. *Average need-based loan:* Freshmen: $2833. Undergraduates: $3731. *Parent loans:* $12,329,997 (51% need-based, 49% non-need-based). *Programs:* FFEL (Subsidized and Unsubsidized Stafford, PLUS), Perkins, Federal Nursing, state.

WORK-STUDY *Federal work-study:* Total amount: $940,410; jobs available. *State or other work-study/employment:* Part-time jobs available.

ATHLETIC AWARDS Total amount: $3,161,290 (44% need-based, 56% non-need-based).

APPLYING FOR FINANCIAL AID *Required financial aid forms:* FAFSA, institution's own form. *Financial aid deadline (priority):* 3/1. *Notification date:* 4/1. Students must reply within 3 weeks of notification.

CONTACT Julie Poorman, Director, Financial Aid, East Carolina University, East 5th Street, Greenville, NC 27858-4353, 252-328-6610. *Fax:* 252-328-4347. *E-mail:* poormanj@ecu.edu.

EAST CENTRAL UNIVERSITY
Ada, OK

CONTACT Marcia Carter, Director of Financial Aid, East Central University, 1100 East 14th, Ada, OK 74820-6899, 580-332-8000 Ext. 242. *Fax:* 580-436-5612.

EASTERN CONNECTICUT STATE UNIVERSITY
Willimantic, CT

CONTACT Assistant to the Director of Financial Aid, Eastern Connecticut State University, 83 Windham Street, Willimantic, CT 06226-2295, 860-465-5205 or toll-free 877-353-3278. *Fax:* 860-465-2811. *E-mail:* financialaid@easternct.edu.

EASTERN ILLINOIS UNIVERSITY
Charleston, IL

ABOUT THE INSTITUTION State-supported, coed. 45 undergraduate majors.

GIFT AID (NEED-BASED) *Scholarships, grants, and awards:* Federal Pell, FSEOG, state, private, college/university gift aid from institutional funds.

LOANS *Programs:* Federal Direct (Subsidized and Unsubsidized Stafford, PLUS), Perkins, college/university.

WORK-STUDY *Federal work-study:* Total amount: $770,304; 466 jobs averaging $1056. *State or other work-study/employment:* Total amount: $6693 (7% need-based, 93% non-need-based). 2,547 part-time jobs averaging $1221.

APPLYING FOR FINANCIAL AID *Required financial aid form:* FAFSA.

CONTACT Tracy L. Hall, Assistant Director of Financial Aid, Eastern Illinois University, 600 Lincoln Avenue, Charleston, IL 61920-3099, 217-581-7511 or toll-free 800-252-5711. *Fax:* 217-581-6422. *E-mail:* tlhall@eiu.edu.

EASTERN KENTUCKY UNIVERSITY
Richmond, KY

Tuition & fees (KY res): $6312   **Average undergraduate aid package: $10,183**

ABOUT THE INSTITUTION State-supported, coed. *Awards:* associate, bachelor's, and master's degrees and post-bachelor's and post-master's certificates. 112 undergraduate majors. *Total enrollment:* 15,839. Undergraduates: 13,659. Freshmen: 2,493. Federal methodology is used as a basis for awarding need-based institutional aid.

UNDERGRADUATE EXPENSES for 2009–10 *Application fee:* $30. *Tuition, state resident:* full-time $6312; part-time $263 per credit hour. *Tuition, nonresident:* full-time $17,280; part-time $720 per credit hour. Part-time tuition and fees vary according to course load. *College room and board:* $6020; *Room only:* $3074. Room and board charges vary according to board plan and housing facility. *Payment plan:* Deferred payment.

FRESHMAN FINANCIAL AID (Fall 2009, est.) 2,318 applied for aid; of those 77% were deemed to have need. 99% of freshmen with need received aid; of those 14% had need fully met. *Average percent of need met:* 84% (excluding resources awarded to replace EFC). *Average financial aid package:* $10,719 (excluding resources awarded to replace EFC). 13% of all full-time freshmen had no need and received non-need-based gift aid.

UNDERGRADUATE FINANCIAL AID (Fall 2009, est.) 9,259 applied for aid; of those 81% were deemed to have need. 98% of undergraduates with need received aid; of those 9% had need fully met. *Average percent of need met:* 83% (excluding resources awarded to replace EFC). *Average financial aid package:* $10,183 (excluding resources awarded to replace EFC). 12% of all full-time undergraduates had no need and received non-need-based gift aid.

GIFT AID (NEED-BASED) *Total amount:* $40,097,731 (59% federal, 25% state, 14% institutional, 2% external sources). *Receiving aid:* Freshmen: 45% (1,174); all full-time undergraduates: 41% (4,848). *Average award:* Freshmen: $6517; Undergraduates: $5949. *Scholarships, grants, and awards:* Federal Pell, FSEOG, state, private, college/university gift aid from institutional funds.

GIFT AID (NON-NEED-BASED) *Total amount:* $6,151,144 (53% state, 38% institutional, 9% external sources). *Receiving aid:* Freshmen: 55% (1,437). Undergraduates: 33% (3,845). *Average award:* Freshmen: $5797. Undergraduates: $5126. *Scholarships, grants, and awards by category:* Academic interests/achievement: 1,734 awards ($8,229,412 total): general academic interests/achievements. Creative arts/performance: 128 awards ($332,184 total): music. Special achievements/activities: 21 awards ($18,930 total): cheerleading/drum major. Special characteristics: 488 awards ($1,446,356 total): children and siblings of alumni, children of faculty/staff, members of minority groups. *Tuition waivers:* Full or partial for employees or children of employees, senior citizens. *ROTC:* Army, Air Force cooperative.

LOANS *Student loans:* $74,197,900 (84% need-based, 16% non-need-based). 66% of past graduating class borrowed through all loan programs. *Average indebtedness per student:* $12,588. *Average need-based loan:* Freshmen: $2405. Undergraduates: $3652. *Parent loans:* $15,632,230 (61% need-based, 39% non-need-based). *Programs:* Federal Direct (Subsidized and Unsubsidized Stafford, PLUS), Perkins, college/university.

WORK-STUDY *Federal work-study:* Total amount: $3,210,833; 1,000 jobs averaging $1800. *State or other work-study/employment:* Total amount: $4,216,957 (100% non-need-based). 1,000 part-time jobs averaging $1800.

ATHLETIC AWARDS Total amount: $3,720,820 (40% need-based, 60% non-need-based).

APPLYING FOR FINANCIAL AID *Required financial aid form:* FAFSA. *Financial aid deadline (priority):* 3/15. *Notification date:* Continuous beginning 4/1.

CONTACT Financial Aid Office Staff, Eastern Kentucky University, 521 Lancaster Avenue, SSB CPO 59, Richmond, KY 40475-3102, 859-622-2361 or toll-free 800-465-9191 (in-state). *Fax:* 859-622-2019. *E-mail:* finaid@eku.edu.

EASTERN MENNONITE UNIVERSITY
Harrisonburg, VA

CONTACT Ms. Renee Leap, Assistant Director of Financial Assistance, Eastern Mennonite University, 1200 Park Road, Harrisonburg, VA 22802-2462, 540-432-4138 or toll-free 800-368-2665. *Fax:* 540-432-4081. *E-mail:* leapr@emu.edu.

EASTERN MICHIGAN UNIVERSITY
Ypsilanti, MI

Tuition & fees (MI res): $8378   **Average undergraduate aid package: $7844**

ABOUT THE INSTITUTION State-supported, coed. 132 undergraduate majors. Federal methodology is used as a basis for awarding need-based institutional aid.

UNDERGRADUATE EXPENSES for 2009–10 *One-time required fee:* $300. *Tuition, state resident:* full-time $7148; part-time $238 per credit hour. *Tuition, nonresident:* full-time $21,053; part-time $701.75 per credit hour. *Required fees:* full-time $1230; $38 per credit hour or $44.75 per term. Full-time tuition and fees vary according to course level and reciprocity agreements. Part-time tuition and fees vary according to course level and reciprocity agreements. *College room and board:* $7785; *Room only:* $3656. Room and board charges vary according to board plan, housing facility, and location. *Payment plan:* Installment.

FRESHMAN FINANCIAL AID (Fall 2008) 1,839 applied for aid; of those 81% were deemed to have need. 98% of freshmen with need received aid; of those 15% had need fully met. *Average percent of need met:* 62% (excluding resources awarded to replace EFC). *Average financial aid package:* $8930 (excluding resources awarded to replace EFC). 19% of all full-time freshmen had no need and received non-need-based gift aid.

UNDERGRADUATE FINANCIAL AID (Fall 2008) 7,084 applied for aid; of those 84% were deemed to have need. 98% of undergraduates with need received aid; of those 2% had need fully met. *Average percent of need met:* 56% (excluding resources awarded to replace EFC). *Average financial aid package:* $7844 (excluding resources awarded to replace EFC). 10% of all full-time undergraduates had no need and received non-need-based gift aid.

GIFT AID (NEED-BASED) *Total amount:* $22,716,727 (83% federal, 5% state, 12% institutional). *Receiving aid:* Freshmen: 53% (1,153); all full-time undergraduates: 29% (3,589). *Average award:* Freshmen: $4231; Undergraduates: $3886. *Scholarships, grants, and awards:* Federal Pell, FSEOG, state, private, college/university gift aid from institutional funds.

GIFT AID (NON-NEED-BASED) *Total amount:* $14,683,331 (2% state, 89% institutional, 9% external sources). *Receiving aid:* Freshmen: 40% (877). Undergraduates: 16% (1,988). *Average award:* Freshmen: $3943. Undergraduates: $3549. *Scholarships, grants, and awards by category:* Academic interests/achievement: 2,122 awards ($5,619,471 total): agriculture, architecture, biological sciences, business, communication, computer science, education, engineering/technologies, English, foreign languages, general academic interests/achievements, health fields, home economics, humanities, mathematics, physical sciences, religion/biblical studies, social sciences. Creative arts/performance: 143 awards ($118,770 total): applied art and design, art/fine arts, cinema/film/broadcasting, creative writing, dance, debating, general creative arts/performance, music, performing arts, theater/drama. Special achievements/activities: 288 awards ($316,850 total): general special achievements/activities, leadership, memberships, religious involvement. Special characteristics: 267 awards ($2,511,482 total): children and siblings of alumni, ethnic background, international students, members of minority groups, out-of-state students, previous college experience, religious affiliation. *Tuition waivers:* Full or partial for employees or children of employees.

LOANS *Student loans:* $126,585,955 (39% need-based, 61% non-need-based). 63% of past graduating class borrowed through all loan programs. *Average indebtedness per student:* $22,370. *Average need-based loan:* Freshmen: $3700. Undergraduates: $4436. *Parent loans:* $8,560,461 (100% non-need-based). *Programs:* Federal Direct (Subsidized and Unsubsidized Stafford), FFEL (PLUS), Perkins, college/university, alternative private loans.

WORK-STUDY *Federal work-study:* Total amount: $1,203,008; 609 jobs averaging $1753. *State or other work-study/employment:* Total amount: $340,800 (100% need-based). 322 part-time jobs averaging $1058.

ATHLETIC AWARDS Total amount: $5,651,156 (100% non-need-based).

APPLYING FOR FINANCIAL AID *Required financial aid form:* FAFSA. *Financial aid deadline:* Continuous. *Notification date:* Continuous beginning 3/1.

CONTACT Cynthia Van Pelt, Director, Eastern Michigan University, 403 Pierce Hall, Ypsilanti, MI 48197, 734-487-1048 or toll-free 800-GO TO EMU. *Fax:* 734-487-0174. *E-mail:* cvanpelt@emich.edu.

EASTERN NAZARENE COLLEGE
Quincy, MA

Tuition & fees: $23,772	Average undergraduate aid package: $20,974

ABOUT THE INSTITUTION Independent religious, coed. 106 undergraduate majors. Federal methodology is used as a basis for awarding need-based institutional aid.

UNDERGRADUATE EXPENSES for 2010–11 *Comprehensive fee:* $31,772 includes full-time tuition ($22,982), mandatory fees ($790), and room and board ($8000). Full-time tuition and fees vary according to course load, degree level, program, reciprocity agreements, and student level. Room and board charges vary according to board plan and housing facility. *Part-time tuition:* $901 per credit hour. *Part-time fees:* $102 per term. Part-time tuition and fees vary according to degree level, program, reciprocity agreements, and student level. *Payment plan:* Installment.

FRESHMAN FINANCIAL AID (Fall 2008) 175 applied for aid; of those 90% were deemed to have need. 100% of freshmen with need received aid; of those 32% had need fully met. *Average percent of need met:* 76% (excluding resources awarded to replace EFC). *Average financial aid package:* $23,129 (excluding resources awarded to replace EFC). 12% of all full-time freshmen had no need and received non-need-based gift aid.

UNDERGRADUATE FINANCIAL AID (Fall 2008) 500 applied for aid; of those 83% were deemed to have need. 100% of undergraduates with need received aid; of those 31% had need fully met. *Average percent of need met:* 72% (excluding resources awarded to replace EFC). *Average financial aid package:* $20,974 (excluding resources awarded to replace EFC). 11% of all full-time undergraduates had no need and received non-need-based gift aid.

GIFT AID (NEED-BASED) *Total amount:* $5,120,368 (27% federal, 2% state, 69% institutional, 2% external sources). *Receiving aid:* Freshmen: 83% (155); all full-time undergraduates: 58% (368). *Average award:* Freshmen: $12,667; Undergraduates: $8326. *Scholarships, grants, and awards:* Federal Pell, FSEOG, state, private, college/university gift aid from institutional funds, United Negro College Fund.

GIFT AID (NON-NEED-BASED) *Total amount:* $1,001,879 (1% federal, 89% institutional, 10% external sources). *Receiving aid:* Freshmen: 10% (19). Undergraduates: 6% (35). *Average award:* Freshmen: $9446. Undergraduates: $7848. *Tuition waivers:* Full or partial for children of alumni, employees or children of employees.

LOANS *Student loans:* $5,653,453 (80% need-based, 20% non-need-based). 83% of past graduating class borrowed through all loan programs. *Average indebtedness per student:* $47,815. *Average need-based loan:* Freshmen: $7813. Undergraduates: $9166. *Parent loans:* $1,742,403 (64% need-based, 36% non-need-based). *Programs:* Federal Direct (Subsidized and Unsubsidized Stafford, PLUS), FFEL (Subsidized and Unsubsidized Stafford, PLUS), Perkins, state, alternative loans.

WORK-STUDY *Federal work-study:* Total amount: $84,203; 245 jobs averaging $1750. *State or other work-study/employment:* Total amount: $4,616,021 (100% need-based). Part-time jobs available.

APPLYING FOR FINANCIAL AID *Required financial aid forms:* FAFSA, institution's own form. *Financial aid deadline (priority):* 7/1. *Notification date:* Continuous beginning 3/15. Students must reply within 2 weeks of notification.

CONTACT Mr. Dana LeRoy Parker, Director of Financial Aid, Eastern Nazarene College, 23 East Elm Avenue, Quincy, MA 02170, 617-745-3712 or toll-free 800-88-ENC88. *Fax:* 617-745-3992. *E-mail:* financialaid@enc.edu.

EASTERN NEW MEXICO UNIVERSITY
Portales, NM

Tuition & fees (NM res): $3552	Average undergraduate aid package: $8869

ABOUT THE INSTITUTION State-supported, coed. 54 undergraduate majors. Federal methodology is used as a basis for awarding need-based institutional aid.

UNDERGRADUATE EXPENSES for 2009–10 *Tuition, state resident:* full-time $2514; part-time $104.75 per credit hour. *Tuition, nonresident:* full-time $8064; part-time $336 per credit hour. *Required fees:* full-time $1038; $43.25 per credit hour. Full-time tuition and fees vary according to course load and

reciprocity agreements. *College room and board:* $5374; *Room only:* $2542. Room and board charges vary according to housing facility. *Payment plan:* Installment.

FRESHMAN FINANCIAL AID (Fall 2009, est.) 390 applied for aid; of those 100% were deemed to have need. 100% of freshmen with need received aid; of those 100% had need fully met. *Average percent of need met:* 40% (excluding resources awarded to replace EFC). *Average financial aid package:* $9379 (excluding resources awarded to replace EFC). 1% of all full-time freshmen had no need and received non-need-based gift aid.

UNDERGRADUATE FINANCIAL AID (Fall 2009, est.) 1,540 applied for aid; of those 100% were deemed to have need. 100% of undergraduates with need received aid; of those 100% had need fully met. *Average percent of need met:* 47% (excluding resources awarded to replace EFC). *Average financial aid package:* $8869 (excluding resources awarded to replace EFC). 1% of all full-time undergraduates had no need and received non-need-based gift aid.

GIFT AID (NEED-BASED) *Total amount:* $12,515,968 (77% federal, 23% state). *Receiving aid:* Freshmen: 58% (359); all full-time undergraduates: 56% (1,404). *Average award:* Freshmen: $4191; Undergraduates: $4442. *Scholarships, grants, and awards:* Federal Pell, FSEOG, state, private, college/university gift aid from institutional funds.

GIFT AID (NON-NEED-BASED) *Total amount:* $2,152,073 (54% institutional, 46% external sources). *Receiving aid:* Freshmen: 57% (355). Undergraduates: 36% (904). *Average award:* Freshmen: $2589. Undergraduates: $2293. *Scholarships, grants, and awards by category: Academic interests/achievement:* agriculture, biological sciences, business, communication, computer science, education, engineering/technologies, English, foreign languages, general academic interests/achievements, health fields, home economics, humanities, mathematics, military science, physical sciences, premedicine, religion/biblical studies, social sciences. *Creative arts/performance:* applied art and design, art/fine arts, cinema/film/broadcasting, creative writing, dance, debating, general creative arts/performance, journalism/publications, music, performing arts, theater/drama. *Special achievements/activities:* community service, general special achievements/activities, hobbies/interests, leadership, memberships, rodeo. *Special characteristics:* children and siblings of alumni, ethnic background, first-generation college students, general special characteristics, international students, members of minority groups, out-of-state students, veterans. *Tuition waivers:* Full or partial for employees or children of employees, senior citizens.

LOANS *Student loans:* $17,580,060 (67% need-based, 33% non-need-based). 1% of past graduating class borrowed through all loan programs. *Average indebtedness per student:* $11,769. *Average need-based loan:* Freshmen: $3243. Undergraduates: $4082. *Parent loans:* $92,475 (100% non-need-based). *Programs:* Federal Direct (Subsidized and Unsubsidized Stafford, PLUS), FFEL (Subsidized and Unsubsidized Stafford, PLUS), Perkins, state, college/university.

WORK-STUDY *Federal work-study:* Total amount: $1,585,910; jobs available. *State or other work-study/employment:* Total amount: $370,345 (100% need-based). Part-time jobs available.

ATHLETIC AWARDS Total amount: $891,732 (100% non-need-based).

APPLYING FOR FINANCIAL AID *Required financial aid form:* FAFSA. *Financial aid deadline:* Continuous. *Notification date:* Continuous beginning 3/1.

CONTACT Mr. Brent Small, Director, Financial Aid, Eastern New Mexico University, Station 20, 1500 S. Ave K, Portales, NM 88130, 575-562-2194 or toll-free 800-367-3668. *Fax:* 575-562-2198. *E-mail:* brent.small@enmu.edu.

EASTERN OREGON UNIVERSITY
La Grande, OR

Tuition & fees (OR res): $6456	Average undergraduate aid package: $9776

ABOUT THE INSTITUTION State-supported, coed. *Awards:* bachelor's and master's degrees. 22 undergraduate majors. *Total enrollment:* 3,666. Undergraduates: 3,127. Freshmen: 350. Federal methodology is used as a basis for awarding need-based institutional aid.

UNDERGRADUATE EXPENSES for 2009–10 *Application fee:* $50. *Tuition, state resident:* full-time $5109; part-time $115 per credit hour. *Tuition, nonresident:* full-time $5109; part-time $115 per credit hour. *Required fees:* full-time $1347. Full-time tuition and fees vary according to course load. Part-time tuition and fees vary according to course load. *College room and board:* $7870; *Room only:* $4335. Room and board charges vary according to board plan and housing facility. *Payment plan:* Installment.

FRESHMAN FINANCIAL AID (Fall 2009, est.) 406 applied for aid; of those 80% were deemed to have need. 100% of freshmen with need received aid; of those

40% had need fully met. *Average percent of need met:* 53% (excluding resources awarded to replace EFC). *Average financial aid package:* $9381 (excluding resources awarded to replace EFC). 1% of all full-time freshmen had no need and received non-need-based gift aid.

UNDERGRADUATE FINANCIAL AID (Fall 2009, est.) 1,785 applied for aid; of those 88% were deemed to have need. 98% of undergraduates with need received aid; of those 26% had need fully met. *Average percent of need met:* 57% (excluding resources awarded to replace EFC). *Average financial aid package:* $9776 (excluding resources awarded to replace EFC). 1% of all full-time undergraduates had no need and received non-need-based gift aid.

GIFT AID (NEED-BASED) *Total amount:* $9,037,276 (83% federal, 17% state). *Receiving aid:* Freshmen: 52% (227); all full-time undergraduates: 54% (1,137). *Average award:* Freshmen: $5901; Undergraduates: $6065. *Scholarships, grants, and awards:* Federal Pell, FSEOG, state, private, college/university gift aid from institutional funds.

GIFT AID (NON-NEED-BASED) *Total amount:* $639,887 (25% institutional, 75% external sources). *Receiving aid:* Freshmen: 32% (138). Undergraduates: 21% (446). *Average award:* Freshmen: $875. Undergraduates: $852. *Scholarships, grants, and awards by category:* Academic interests/achievement: general academic interests/achievements. Creative arts/performance: general creative arts/performance. Special achievements/activities: leadership. Special characteristics: local/state students, members of minority groups. *Tuition waivers:* Full or partial for employees or children of employees, senior citizens. *ROTC:* Army.

LOANS *Student loans:* $19,060,531 (44% need-based, 56% non-need-based). 77% of past graduating class borrowed through all loan programs. *Average indebtedness per student:* $19,881. *Average need-based loan:* Freshmen: $2570. Undergraduates: $3443. *Parent loans:* $3,361,840 (100% non-need-based). *Programs:* FFEL (Subsidized and Unsubsidized Stafford, PLUS), Perkins.

WORK-STUDY *Federal work-study:* Total amount: $181,658; jobs available.

ATHLETIC AWARDS Total amount: $377,024 (100% non-need-based).

APPLYING FOR FINANCIAL AID *Required financial aid form:* FAFSA. *Financial aid deadline (priority):* 3/1. *Notification date:* Continuous beginning 4/1. Students must reply within 4 weeks of notification.

CONTACT Mr. Sam Collie, Interim Director of Financial Aid, Eastern Oregon University, One University Boulevard, La Grande, OR 97850-2899, 541-962-3121 or toll-free 800-452-8639 (in-state), 800-452-3393 (out-of-state). *Fax:* 541-962-3661. *E-mail:* scollie@eou.edu.

EASTERN UNIVERSITY
St. Davids, PA

CONTACT Financial Aid Office, Eastern University, 1300 Eagle Road, St. Davids, PA 19087-3696, 610-341-5842 or toll-free 800-452-0996. *Fax:* 610-341-1492. *E-mail:* finaid@eastern.edu.

EASTERN WASHINGTON UNIVERSITY
Cheney, WA

Tuition & fees (WA res): $5872   **Average undergraduate aid package: $11,043**

ABOUT THE INSTITUTION State-supported, coed. 76 undergraduate majors. Federal methodology is used as a basis for awarding need-based institutional aid.

UNDERGRADUATE EXPENSES for 2009–10 *Tuition, state resident:* full-time $5340; part-time $160 per credit hour. *Tuition, nonresident:* full-time $14,058; part-time $451 per credit hour. *Required fees:* full-time $532; $532.14 per year. Full-time tuition and fees vary according to course load and program. Part-time tuition and fees vary according to course load and program. *College room and board:* $7080. Room and board charges vary according to board plan and housing facility. *Payment plan:* Installment.

FRESHMAN FINANCIAL AID (Fall 2008) 1,203 applied for aid; of those 69% were deemed to have need. 98% of freshmen with need received aid; of those 36% had need fully met. *Average percent of need met:* 91% (excluding resources awarded to replace EFC). *Average financial aid package:* $10,332 (excluding resources awarded to replace EFC). 8% of all full-time freshmen had no need and received non-need-based gift aid.

UNDERGRADUATE FINANCIAL AID (Fall 2008) 6,028 applied for aid; of those 78% were deemed to have need. 98% of undergraduates with need received aid; of those 33% had need fully met. *Average percent of need met:* 71% (excluding resources awarded to replace EFC). *Average financial aid package:*

$11,043 (excluding resources awarded to replace EFC). 5% of all full-time undergraduates had no need and received non-need-based gift aid.

GIFT AID (NEED-BASED) *Total amount:* $25,396,640 (42% federal, 42% state, 7% institutional, 9% external sources). *Receiving aid:* Freshmen: 43% (645); all full-time undergraduates: 45% (3,744). *Average award:* Freshmen: $6041; Undergraduates: $5875. *Scholarships, grants, and awards:* Federal Pell, FSEOG, state, private, college/university gift aid from institutional funds.

GIFT AID (NON-NEED-BASED) *Total amount:* $694,196 (20% institutional, 80% external sources). *Receiving aid:* Freshmen: 18% (262). Undergraduates: 9% (766). *Average award:* Freshmen: $2864. Undergraduates: $2908. *Scholarships, grants, and awards by category:* Academic interests/achievement: 454 awards ($622,382 total): area/ethnic studies, biological sciences, business, communication, computer science, education, engineering/technologies, English, foreign languages, general academic interests/achievements, health fields, mathematics, military science, physical sciences, social sciences. Creative arts/performance: 60 awards ($75,000 total): art/fine arts, cinema/film/broadcasting, creative writing, journalism/publications, music, theater/drama. Special characteristics: 318 awards ($685,535 total): children of union members/company employees, ethnic background, first-generation college students, handicapped students, local/state students, spouses of deceased or disabled public servants, veterans, veterans' children.

LOANS *Student loans:* $32,812,758 (79% need-based, 21% non-need-based). 68% of past graduating class borrowed through all loan programs. *Average indebtedness per student:* $18,435. *Average need-based loan:* Freshmen: $2266. Undergraduates: $3217. *Parent loans:* $5,194,811 (54% need-based, 46% non-need-based). *Programs:* Federal Direct (Subsidized and Unsubsidized Stafford, PLUS), Perkins.

WORK-STUDY *Federal work-study:* Total amount: $441,048; 193 jobs averaging $2237. *State or other work-study/employment:* Total amount: $878,695 (100% need-based). 266 part-time jobs averaging $3002.

ATHLETIC AWARDS Total amount: $1,570,948 (47% need-based, 53% non-need-based).

APPLYING FOR FINANCIAL AID *Required financial aid form:* FAFSA. *Financial aid deadline (priority):* 2/15. *Notification date:* Continuous beginning 4/1. Students must reply within 4 weeks of notification.

CONTACT Mr. Bruce DeFrates, Director of Financial Aid and Scholarships, Eastern Washington University, 102 Sutton Hall, Cheney, WA 99004-2447, 509-359-2314. *Fax:* 509-359-4330. *E-mail:* bdefrates@ewu.edu.

EAST STROUDSBURG UNIVERSITY OF PENNSYLVANIA
East Stroudsburg, PA

Tuition & fees (PA res): $7394   **Average undergraduate aid package: $5933**

ABOUT THE INSTITUTION State-supported, coed. 50 undergraduate majors. Federal methodology is used as a basis for awarding need-based institutional aid.

UNDERGRADUATE EXPENSES for 2010–11 *Tuition, state resident:* full-time $5554; part-time $231 per credit. *Tuition, nonresident:* full-time $13,886; part-time $579 per credit. *Required fees:* full-time $1840; $66 per credit hour. Full-time tuition and fees vary according to course load. Part-time tuition and fees vary according to course load. *College room and board:* $6418; *Room only:* $4272. Room and board charges vary according to board plan and housing facility. *Payment plan:* Installment.

FRESHMAN FINANCIAL AID (Fall 2008) 1,045 applied for aid; of those 69% were deemed to have need. 83% of freshmen with need received aid; of those 70% had need fully met. *Average percent of need met:* 80% (excluding resources awarded to replace EFC). *Average financial aid package:* $5402 (excluding resources awarded to replace EFC). 23% of all full-time freshmen had no need and received non-need-based gift aid.

UNDERGRADUATE FINANCIAL AID (Fall 2008) 4,144 applied for aid; of those 73% were deemed to have need. 82% of undergraduates with need received aid; of those 71% had need fully met. *Average percent of need met:* 83% (excluding resources awarded to replace EFC). *Average financial aid package:* $5933 (excluding resources awarded to replace EFC). 18% of all full-time undergraduates had no need and received non-need-based gift aid.

GIFT AID (NEED-BASED) *Total amount:* $9,646,587 (48% federal, 35% state, 12% institutional, 5% external sources). *Receiving aid:* Freshmen: 27% (371); all full-time undergraduates: 27% (1,596). *Average award:* Freshmen: $4497;

East Stroudsburg University of Pennsylvania

Undergraduates: $4312. *Scholarships, grants, and awards:* Federal Pell, FSEOG, state, private, college/university gift aid from institutional funds.
GIFT AID (NON-NEED-BASED) *Receiving aid:* Freshmen: 3% (39). Undergraduates: 2% (136). *Average award:* Freshmen: $9613. Undergraduates: $10,063. *Scholarships, grants, and awards by category: Academic interests/achievement:* biological sciences, business, communication, computer science, education, English, foreign languages, general academic interests/achievements, health fields, mathematics, physical sciences, social sciences. *Creative arts/performance:* applied art and design, music, theater/drama. *Special achievements/activities:* general special achievements/activities, leadership. *Special characteristics:* adult students, children and siblings of alumni, handicapped students, international students, local/state students, members of minority groups, religious affiliation. *Tuition waivers:* Full or partial for employees or children of employees, senior citizens.
LOANS *Student loans:* $39,570,797 (34% need-based, 66% non-need-based). 73% of past graduating class borrowed through all loan programs. *Average indebtedness per student:* $25,887. *Average need-based loan:* Freshmen: $3334. Undergraduates: $4106. *Parent loans:* $4,667,356 (100% non-need-based). *Programs:* FFEL (Subsidized and Unsubsidized Stafford, PLUS), Perkins.
WORK-STUDY *Federal work-study:* Total amount: $367,832; jobs available. *State or other work-study/employment:* Total amount: $1,226,790 (100% non-need-based). Part-time jobs available.
ATHLETIC AWARDS Total amount: $510,650 (100% need-based).
APPLYING FOR FINANCIAL AID *Required financial aid form:* FAFSA. *Financial aid deadline:* 3/1. *Notification date:* 4/1. Students must reply by 5/1.
CONTACT Kizzy Morris, Registrar/Director of Enrollment Services, East Stroudsburg University of Pennsylvania, 200 Prospect Street, East Stroudsburg, PA 18301-2999, 570-422-2820 or toll-free 877-230-5547. *Fax:* 570-422-2849.

EAST TENNESSEE STATE UNIVERSITY
Johnson City, TN

ABOUT THE INSTITUTION State-supported, coed. 49 undergraduate majors.
GIFT AID (NEED-BASED) *Scholarships, grants, and awards:* Federal Pell, FSEOG, state, private, college/university gift aid from institutional funds, Federal Nursing.
GIFT AID (NON-NEED-BASED) *Scholarships, grants, and awards by category: Academic interests/achievement:* biological sciences, business, computer science, education, engineering/technologies, English, general academic interests/achievements, health fields, mathematics, military science, social sciences. *Creative arts/performance:* art/fine arts, journalism/publications, music, theater/drama. *Special achievements/activities:* leadership, memberships. *Special characteristics:* children of union members/company employees, members of minority groups.
LOANS *Programs:* Federal Direct (Subsidized and Unsubsidized Stafford, PLUS), Perkins, Federal Nursing, college/university.
WORK-STUDY *Federal work-study:* Total amount: $2,279,946; 1,019 jobs averaging $1525. *State or other work-study/employment:* Total amount: $616,781 (100% non-need-based). 379 part-time jobs averaging $1161.
APPLYING FOR FINANCIAL AID *Required financial aid form:* FAFSA.
CONTACT Cindy A. Johnson, Assistant Director of Financial Aid, East Tennessee State University, PO Box 70722, Johnson City, TN 37614, 423-439-4300 or toll-free 800-462-3878.

EAST TEXAS BAPTIST UNIVERSITY
Marshall, TX

Tuition & fees: $19,550	Average undergraduate aid package: $13,484

ABOUT THE INSTITUTION Independent Baptist, coed. 45 undergraduate majors. Federal methodology is used as a basis for awarding need-based institutional aid.
UNDERGRADUATE EXPENSES for 2010–11 *Comprehensive fee:* $24,986 includes full-time tuition ($18,750), mandatory fees ($800), and room and board ($5436). *College room only:* $2340. Room and board charges vary according to board plan and housing facility. *Part-time tuition:* $625 per credit hour. *Part-time fees:* $20 per credit hour. *Payment plan:* Installment.
FRESHMAN FINANCIAL AID (Fall 2009, est.) 282 applied for aid; of those 88% were deemed to have need. 100% of freshmen with need received aid; of those 21% had need fully met. *Average percent of need met:* 46% (excluding

resources awarded to replace EFC). *Average financial aid package:* $14,783 (excluding resources awarded to replace EFC). 16% of all full-time freshmen had no need and received non-need-based gift aid.
UNDERGRADUATE FINANCIAL AID (Fall 2009, est.) 1,028 applied for aid; of those 85% were deemed to have need. 100% of undergraduates with need received aid; of those 19% had need fully met. *Average percent of need met:* 54% (excluding resources awarded to replace EFC). *Average financial aid package:* $13,484 (excluding resources awarded to replace EFC). 14% of all full-time undergraduates had no need and received non-need-based gift aid.
GIFT AID (NEED-BASED) *Total amount:* $3,735,982 (47% federal, 53% state). *Receiving aid:* Freshmen: 66% (194); all full-time undergraduates: 66% (720). *Average award:* Freshmen: $6538; Undergraduates: $6316. *Scholarships, grants, and awards:* Federal Pell, FSEOG, state, private, college/university gift aid from institutional funds, Federal Nursing.
GIFT AID (NON-NEED-BASED) *Total amount:* $7,172,139 (1% state, 94% institutional, 5% external sources). *Receiving aid:* Freshmen: 82% (241). Undergraduates: 69% (756). *Average award:* Freshmen: $8412. Undergraduates: $7025. *Scholarships, grants, and awards by category: Academic interests/achievement:* $1,418,534 total: biological sciences, business, communication, education, English, general academic interests/achievements, health fields, humanities, mathematics, physical sciences, religion/biblical studies, social sciences. *Creative arts/performance:* $207,235 total: music, theater/drama. *Special achievements/activities:* $1,180,329 total: cheerleading/drum major, general special achievements/activities, leadership, religious involvement. *Special characteristics:* $1,120,797 total: children and siblings of alumni, children of educators, children of faculty/staff, general special characteristics, international students, local/state students, previous college experience, religious affiliation, siblings of current students, twins. *Tuition waivers:* Full or partial for employees or children of employees.
LOANS *Student loans:* $5,598,105 (44% need-based, 56% non-need-based). 77% of past graduating class borrowed through all loan programs. *Average indebtedness per student:* $21,380. *Average need-based loan:* Freshmen: $3044. Undergraduates: $3693. *Parent loans:* $325,674 (100% non-need-based). *Programs:* FFEL (Subsidized and Unsubsidized Stafford, PLUS), Perkins, state.
WORK-STUDY *Federal work-study:* Total amount: $99,326; 105 jobs averaging $1189. *State or other work-study/employment:* Total amount: $280,026 (6% need-based, 94% non-need-based). 191 part-time jobs averaging $1262.
APPLYING FOR FINANCIAL AID *Required financial aid forms:* FAFSA, institution's own form. *Financial aid deadline (priority):* 6/1. *Notification date:* Continuous beginning 1/1. Students must reply within 3 weeks of notification.
CONTACT Tommy Young, Director of Financial Aid, East Texas Baptist University, 1209 North Grove Street, Marshall, TX 75670-1498, 903-923-2137 or toll-free 800-804-ETBU. *Fax:* 903-934-8120. *E-mail:* tyoung@etbu.edu.

EAST-WEST UNIVERSITY
Chicago, IL

Tuition & fees: $15,750	Average undergraduate aid package: $10,318

ABOUT THE INSTITUTION Independent, coed. 7 undergraduate majors. Federal methodology is used as a basis for awarding need-based institutional aid.
UNDERGRADUATE EXPENSES for 2010–11 *One-time required fee:* $45. *Tuition:* full-time $15,000; part-time $500 per credit hour. Full-time tuition and fees vary according to degree level and program. *Payment plan:* Installment.
FRESHMAN FINANCIAL AID (Fall 2009, est.) 686 applied for aid; of those 100% were deemed to have need. 100% of freshmen with need received aid. *Average percent of need met:* 90% (excluding resources awarded to replace EFC). *Average financial aid package:* $10,318 (excluding resources awarded to replace EFC).
UNDERGRADUATE FINANCIAL AID (Fall 2009, est.) 1,286 applied for aid; of those 100% were deemed to have need. 100% of undergraduates with need received aid. *Average percent of need met:* 90% (excluding resources awarded to replace EFC). *Average financial aid package:* $10,318 (excluding resources awarded to replace EFC).
GIFT AID (NEED-BASED) *Total amount:* $5,771,018 (57% federal, 41% state, 2% institutional). *Receiving aid:* Freshmen: 100% (686); all full-time undergraduates: 100% (1,286). *Average award:* Freshmen: $4500; Undergraduates: $4500. *Scholarships, grants, and awards:* Federal Pell, FSEOG, state, college/university gift aid from institutional funds.

GIFT AID (NON-NEED-BASED) *Scholarships, grants, and awards by category:* *Academic interests/achievement:* general academic interests/achievements. *Tuition waivers:* Full or partial for employees or children of employees.

LOANS *Student loans:* $2,249,234 (100% need-based). 35% of past graduating class borrowed through all loan programs. *Average indebtedness per student:* $3500. *Parent loans:* $63,717 (100% need-based). *Programs:* Federal Direct (Subsidized and Unsubsidized Stafford, PLUS).

WORK-STUDY *Federal work-study:* Total amount: $155,340; 45 jobs averaging $4200.

APPLYING FOR FINANCIAL AID *Required financial aid form:* FAFSA. *Financial aid deadline (priority):* 3/30. *Notification date:* Continuous beginning 1/31. Students must reply by 5/28 or within 4 weeks of notification.

CONTACT Elizabeth Guzman, Financial Aid Office, East-West University, 816 South Michigan Avenue, Chicago, IL 60605-2103, 312-939-0111 Ext. 1801. *Fax:* 312-939-0083. *E-mail:* elizabth@eastwest.edu.

ECCLESIA COLLEGE
Springdale, AR

CONTACT Financial Aid Office, Ecclesia College, 9653 Nations Drive, Springdale, AR 72762, 479-248-7236 or toll-free 800-735-9926 (out-of-state).

ECKERD COLLEGE
St. Petersburg, FL

Tuition & fees: $33,228	Average undergraduate aid package: $27,743

ABOUT THE INSTITUTION Independent Presbyterian, coed. 37 undergraduate majors. Federal methodology is used as a basis for awarding need-based institutional aid.

UNDERGRADUATE EXPENSES for 2010–11 *Comprehensive fee:* $42,554 includes full-time tuition ($32,932), mandatory fees ($296), and room and board ($9326). *College room only:* $4716. Room and board charges vary according to board plan and housing facility. *Payment plan:* Installment.

FRESHMAN FINANCIAL AID (Fall 2009, est.) 369 applied for aid; of those 75% were deemed to have need. 100% of freshmen with need received aid; of those 50% had need fully met. *Average percent of need met:* 88% (excluding resources awarded to replace EFC). *Average financial aid package:* $26,761 (excluding resources awarded to replace EFC).

UNDERGRADUATE FINANCIAL AID (Fall 2009, est.) 1,253 applied for aid; of those 84% were deemed to have need. 100% of undergraduates with need received aid; of those 23% had need fully met. *Average percent of need met:* 87% (excluding resources awarded to replace EFC). *Average financial aid package:* $27,743 (excluding resources awarded to replace EFC).

GIFT AID (NEED-BASED) *Total amount:* $18,228,621 (11% federal, 8% state, 79% institutional, 2% external sources). *Receiving aid:* Freshmen: 277; all full-time undergraduates: 1,048. *Average award:* Freshmen: $18,322; Undergraduates: $18,255. *Scholarships, grants, and awards:* Federal Pell, FSEOG, state, private, college/university gift aid from institutional funds.

GIFT AID (NON-NEED-BASED) *Total amount:* $8,186,536 (7% state, 90% institutional, 3% external sources). *Average award:* Freshmen: $12,191. Undergraduates: $10,777. *Scholarships, grants, and awards by category:* *Academic interests/achievement:* 500 awards ($5,000,000 total): general academic interests/achievements. *Creative arts/performance:* 40 awards ($200,000 total): art/fine arts, creative writing, music, theater/drama. *Special achievements/ activities:* 100 awards ($500,000 total): community service, leadership. *Special characteristics:* 233 awards ($1,116,402 total): children of faculty/staff, international students, local/state students, religious affiliation. *Tuition waivers:* Full or partial for employees or children of employees.

LOANS *Student loans:* $11,291,990 (65% need-based, 35% non-need-based). 63% of past graduating class borrowed through all loan programs. *Average indebtedness per student:* $30,494. *Average need-based loan:* Freshmen: $4173. Undergraduates: $4807. *Parent loans:* $3,477,356 (53% need-based, 47% non-need-based). *Programs:* FFEL (Subsidized and Unsubsidized Stafford, PLUS), Perkins, college/university.

WORK-STUDY *Federal work-study:* Total amount: $1,550,874; 600 jobs averaging $2000. *State or other work-study/employment:* Total amount: $78,750 (100% non-need-based). Part-time jobs available.

ATHLETIC AWARDS Total amount: $1,157,941 (48% need-based, 52% non-need-based).

APPLYING FOR FINANCIAL AID *Required financial aid form:* FAFSA. *Financial aid deadline (priority):* 3/1. *Notification date:* Continuous. Students must reply by 5/1.

CONTACT Dr. Pat Garrett Watkins, Director of Financial Aid, Eckerd College, 4200 54th Avenue, South, St. Petersburg, FL 33711, 727-864-8334 or toll-free 800-456-9009. *Fax:* 727-866-2304. *E-mail:* watkinpe@eckerd.edu.

ECPI COLLEGE OF TECHNOLOGY
Virginia Beach, VA

Tuition & fees: N/R	Average undergraduate aid package: N/A

ABOUT THE INSTITUTION Proprietary, coed. 27 undergraduate majors. Federal methodology is used as a basis for awarding need-based institutional aid.

FRESHMAN FINANCIAL AID (Fall 2009, est.) 1,810 applied for aid.

UNDERGRADUATE FINANCIAL AID (Fall 2009, est.) 8,775 applied for aid.

GIFT AID (NEED-BASED) *Total amount:* $56,842,290 (89% federal, 1% state, 10% institutional). *Scholarships, grants, and awards:* Federal Pell, FSEOG, state, private, college/university gift aid from institutional funds.

GIFT AID (NON-NEED-BASED) *Total amount:* $16,578,121 (86% federal, 11% institutional, 3% external sources). *Scholarships, grants, and awards by category:* *Academic interests/achievement:* business, computer science, engineering/technologies, health fields. *Special achievements/activities:* community service, general special achievements/activities. *Special characteristics:* adult students, children and siblings of alumni, children of current students, children of faculty/staff, general special characteristics, parents of current students, veterans, veterans' children.

LOANS *Student loans:* $110,124,402 (98% need-based, 2% non-need-based). 93% of past graduating class borrowed through all loan programs. *Parent loans:* $4,224,289 (100% non-need-based). *Programs:* Federal Direct (Subsidized and Unsubsidized Stafford, PLUS), Perkins, college/university, private loans.

WORK-STUDY *Federal work-study:* Total amount: $350,000; jobs available.

APPLYING FOR FINANCIAL AID *Required financial aid forms:* FAFSA, institution's own form. *Financial aid deadline:* Continuous. *Notification date:* Continuous beginning 3/1. Students must reply within 12 weeks of notification.

CONTACT Mrs. Kathi Turner, Financial Aid Director, ECPI College of Technology, 5555 Greenwich Road, Suite 300, Virginia Beach, VA 23462, 757-490-9090 or toll-free 800-986-1200. *Fax:* 757-671-8661. *E-mail:* kturner@ecpi.edu.

ECPI TECHNICAL COLLEGE
Roanoke, VA

Tuition & fees: N/R	Average undergraduate aid package: N/A

ABOUT THE INSTITUTION Proprietary, coed. 21 undergraduate majors. Federal methodology is used as a basis for awarding need-based institutional aid.

FRESHMAN FINANCIAL AID (Fall 2008) 63 applied for aid; of those 97% were deemed to have need.

UNDERGRADUATE FINANCIAL AID (Fall 2008) 425 applied for aid; of those 96% were deemed to have need.

GIFT AID (NEED-BASED) *Total amount:* $1,748,917 (89% federal, 11% institutional). *Scholarships, grants, and awards:* Federal Pell, FSEOG, state, private, college/university gift aid from institutional funds.

GIFT AID (NON-NEED-BASED) *Total amount:* $16,550 (95% institutional, 5% external sources). *Scholarships, grants, and awards by category:* *Academic interests/achievement:* business, computer science, engineering/technologies, health fields. *Special achievements/activities:* community service, general special achievements/activities. *Special characteristics:* adult students, children of faculty/staff, general special characteristics, previous college experience, veterans, veterans' children.

LOANS *Student loans:* $4,379,636 (97% need-based, 3% non-need-based). *Parent loans:* $134,602 (100% non-need-based). *Programs:* Federal Direct (Subsidized and Unsubsidized Stafford, PLUS), Perkins, college/university, private loans.

WORK-STUDY *Federal work-study:* Total amount: $30,000; jobs available. *State or other work-study/employment:* Part-time jobs available.

APPLYING FOR FINANCIAL AID *Required financial aid form:* FAFSA. *Financial aid deadline:* Continuous. *Notification date:* Continuous beginning 3/1. Students must reply within 12 weeks of notification.

CONTACT Ms. Amanda Little, Financial Aid Director, ECPI Technical College, 5234 Airport Road, Roanoke, VA 24012, 540-563-8080 or toll-free 800-986-1200. *E-mail:* alittle@ecpi.edu.

EDGEWOOD COLLEGE
Madison, WI

Tuition & fees: $21,042	Average undergraduate aid package: $16,399

ABOUT THE INSTITUTION Independent Roman Catholic, coed, primarily women. 47 undergraduate majors. Federal methodology is used as a basis for awarding need-based institutional aid.

UNDERGRADUATE EXPENSES for 2009–10 *Comprehensive fee:* $28,276 includes full-time tuition ($21,042) and room and board ($7234). *College room only:* $3606. Full-time tuition and fees vary according to degree level. Room and board charges vary according to housing facility. *Part-time tuition:* $662 per credit. Part-time tuition and fees vary according to course load and degree level. *Payment plan:* Installment.

FRESHMAN FINANCIAL AID (Fall 2009, est.) 250 applied for aid; of those 90% were deemed to have need. 100% of freshmen with need received aid; of those 17% had need fully met. *Average percent of need met:* 81% (excluding resources awarded to replace EFC). *Average financial aid package:* $17,820 (excluding resources awarded to replace EFC). 16% of all full-time freshmen had no need and received non-need-based gift aid.

UNDERGRADUATE FINANCIAL AID (Fall 2009, est.) 1,318 applied for aid; of those 90% were deemed to have need. 100% of undergraduates with need received aid; of those 13% had need fully met. *Average percent of need met:* 53% (excluding resources awarded to replace EFC). *Average financial aid package:* $16,399 (excluding resources awarded to replace EFC). 15% of all full-time undergraduates had no need and received non-need-based gift aid.

GIFT AID (NEED-BASED) *Total amount:* $11,788,783 (21% federal, 13% state, 56% institutional, 10% external sources). *Receiving aid:* Freshmen: 79% (223); all full-time undergraduates: 69% (1,081). *Average award:* Freshmen: $13,458; Undergraduates: $10,575. *Scholarships, grants, and awards:* Federal Pell, FSEOG, state, private, college/university gift aid from institutional funds.

GIFT AID (NON-NEED-BASED) *Total amount:* $1,623,116 (2% federal, 65% institutional, 33% external sources). *Receiving aid:* Freshmen: 8% (23). Undergraduates: 4% (62). *Average award:* Freshmen: $5665. Undergraduates: $3910. *Scholarships, grants, and awards by category: Academic interests/ achievement:* 943 awards ($3,288,698 total): foreign languages, general academic interests/achievements. *Creative arts/performance:* 91 awards ($100,750 total): art/fine arts, creative writing, music, performing arts, theater/drama. *Special achievements/activities:* 6 awards ($120,135 total): community service. *Special characteristics:* 38 awards ($559,888 total): children of faculty/staff, local/state students. *Tuition waivers:* Full or partial for employees or children of employees.

LOANS *Student loans:* $14,064,247 (73% need-based, 27% non-need-based). 70% of past graduating class borrowed through all loan programs. *Average indebtedness per student:* $31,327. *Average need-based loan:* Freshmen: $3651. Undergraduates: $5296. *Parent loans:* $1,794,923 (37% need-based, 63% non-need-based). *Programs:* FFEL (Subsidized and Unsubsidized Stafford, PLUS), Perkins, state, college/university.

WORK-STUDY *Federal work-study:* Total amount: $684,950; jobs available (averaging $1944). *State or other work-study/employment:* Total amount: $1,899,311 (47% need-based, 53% non-need-based). Part-time jobs available (averaging $1963).

APPLYING FOR FINANCIAL AID *Required financial aid forms:* FAFSA, institution's own form. *Financial aid deadline (priority):* 3/1. *Notification date:* Continuous beginning 3/15. Students must reply within 2 weeks of notification.

CONTACT Kari Gribble, Director for Financial Aid, Edgewood College, 1000 Edgewood College Drive, Madison, WI 53711-1997, 608-663-4300 or toll-free 800-444-4861 Ext. 2294. *E-mail:* kgribble@edgewood.edu.

EDINBORO UNIVERSITY OF PENNSYLVANIA
Edinboro, PA

Tuition & fees (PA res): $7316	Average undergraduate aid package: $7473

ABOUT THE INSTITUTION State-supported, coed. 55 undergraduate majors. Federal methodology is used as a basis for awarding need-based institutional aid.

UNDERGRADUATE EXPENSES for 2009–10 *Tuition, state resident:* full-time $5554; part-time $231 per credit hour. *Tuition, nonresident:* full-time $8332; part-time $347 per credit hour. *Required fees:* full-time $1762; $65.03 per credit hour. Part-time tuition and fees vary according to course load. *College room and board:* $7430; *Room only:* $4780. Room and board charges vary according to board plan. *Payment plan:* Installment.

FRESHMAN FINANCIAL AID (Fall 2008) 1,174 applied for aid; of those 82% were deemed to have need. 97% of freshmen with need received aid; of those 5% had need fully met. *Average percent of need met:* 59% (excluding resources awarded to replace EFC). *Average financial aid package:* $7146 (excluding resources awarded to replace EFC). 5% of all full-time freshmen had no need and received non-need-based gift aid.

UNDERGRADUATE FINANCIAL AID (Fall 2008) 4,952 applied for aid; of those 84% were deemed to have need. 97% of undergraduates with need received aid; of those 8% had need fully met. *Average percent of need met:* 63% (excluding resources awarded to replace EFC). *Average financial aid package:* $7473 (excluding resources awarded to replace EFC). 6% of all full-time undergraduates had no need and received non-need-based gift aid.

GIFT AID (NEED-BASED) *Total amount:* $14,753,927 (58% federal, 41% state, 1% institutional). *Receiving aid:* Freshmen: 70% (864); all full-time undergraduates: 70% (3,799). *Average award:* Freshmen: $2586; Undergraduates: $3080. *Scholarships, grants, and awards:* Federal Pell, FSEOG, state, private, college/university gift aid from institutional funds.

GIFT AID (NON-NEED-BASED) *Total amount:* $2,882,642 (3% federal, 11% state, 63% institutional, 23% external sources). *Receiving aid:* Freshmen: 74% (907). Undergraduates: 72% (3,907). *Average award:* Freshmen: $3000. Undergraduates: $2100. *Scholarships, grants, and awards by category: Academic interests/achievement:* 225 awards ($252,582 total): biological sciences, business, communication, computer science, education, engineering/technologies, English, foreign languages, general academic interests/achievements, health fields, humanities, mathematics, military science, physical sciences, premedicine, religion/biblical studies, social sciences. *Creative arts/performance:* 27 awards ($12,418 total): art/fine arts, cinema/film/broadcasting, journalism/publications, music. *Special achievements/activities:* 4 awards ($3080 total): general special achievements/activities. *Special characteristics:* 745 awards ($2,104,852 total): adult students, children and siblings of alumni, children of faculty/staff, children of union members/company employees, children with a deceased or disabled parent, first-generation college students, general special characteristics, handicapped students, international students, local/state students, members of minority groups, out-of-state students, religious affiliation, veterans, veterans' children. *Tuition waivers:* Full or partial for minority students, employees or children of employees.

LOANS *Student loans:* $35,776,863 (42% need-based, 58% non-need-based). 85% of past graduating class borrowed through all loan programs. *Average indebtedness per student:* $28,392. *Average need-based loan:* Freshmen: $2924. Undergraduates: $3622. *Parent loans:* $3,279,382 (100% non-need-based). *Programs:* Federal Direct (Subsidized and Unsubsidized Stafford), FFEL (Subsidized and Unsubsidized Stafford, PLUS), Perkins, Federal Nursing, college/university.

WORK-STUDY *Federal work-study:* Total amount: $651,611; 442 jobs averaging $1474. *State or other work-study/employment:* Total amount: $1,042,816 (8% need-based, 92% non-need-based). 689 part-time jobs averaging $1515.

ATHLETIC AWARDS Total amount: $810,780 (100% non-need-based).

APPLYING FOR FINANCIAL AID *Required financial aid form:* FAFSA. *Financial aid deadline (priority):* 3/15. *Notification date:* 3/31. Students must reply within 2 weeks of notification.

CONTACT Ms. Dorothy Body, Assistant Vice President for Financial Aid, Edinboro University of Pennsylvania, Hamilton Hall, Edinboro, PA 16444, 814-732-5555 Ext. 474 or toll-free 888-846-2676 (in-state), 800-626-2203 (out-of-state). *Fax:* 814-732-2129. *E-mail:* dbody@edinboro.edu.

EDP COLLEGE OF PUERTO RICO, INC.
Hato Rey, PR

ABOUT THE INSTITUTION Proprietary, coed. 12 undergraduate majors.
GIFT AID (NEED-BASED) *Scholarships, grants, and awards:* Federal Pell, FSEOG, state.

GIFT AID (NON-NEED-BASED) *Scholarships, grants, and awards by category:* *Special characteristics:* veterans, veterans' children.
LOANS *Programs:* FFEL (Subsidized and Unsubsidized Stafford, PLUS).
APPLYING FOR FINANCIAL AID *Required financial aid form:* FAFSA.
CONTACT Marie Luz Pastrana Muriel, Associate Dean of Financial Aid, EDP College of Puerto Rico, Inc., PO Box 192303, San Juan, PR 00919-2303, 787-765-3560 Ext. 249. *Fax:* 787-765-2650. *E-mail:* marieuz@edpcollege.edu.

EDP COLLEGE OF PUERTO RICO– SAN SEBASTIAN
San Sebastian, PR

CONTACT Financial Aid Office, EDP College of Puerto Rico–San Sebastian, Avenue Betances #49, San Sebastian, PR 00685, 787-896-2137.

EDWARD WATERS COLLEGE
Jacksonville, FL

CONTACT Gabriel Mbomeh, Director of Financial Aid, Edward Waters College, 1658 Kings Road, Jacksonville, FL 32209-6199, 904-366-2528 or toll-free 888-898-3191.

ELIZABETH CITY STATE UNIVERSITY
Elizabeth City, NC

CONTACT Assistant Director of Financial Aid, Elizabeth City State University, 1704 Weeksville Road, Campus Box 914, Elizabeth City, NC 27909-7806, 252-335-3285 or toll-free 800-347-3278. *Fax:* 252-335-3716.

ELIZABETHTOWN COLLEGE
Elizabethtown, PA

Tuition & fees: $33,250	Average undergraduate aid package: $22,582

ABOUT THE INSTITUTION Independent religious, coed. 51 undergraduate majors. Both federal and institutional methodology are used as a basis for awarding need-based institutional aid.
UNDERGRADUATE EXPENSES for 2010–11 *Comprehensive fee:* $41,750 includes full-time tuition ($33,250) and room and board ($8500). *College room only:* $4250. Full-time tuition and fees vary according to course load. Room and board charges vary according to board plan and housing facility. *Part-time tuition:* $805 per credit hour. Part-time tuition and fees vary according to class time and course load. *Payment plan:* Installment.
FRESHMAN FINANCIAL AID (Fall 2009, est.) 479 applied for aid; of those 85% were deemed to have need. 100% of freshmen with need received aid; of those 22% had need fully met. *Average percent of need met:* 84% (excluding resources awarded to replace EFC). *Average financial aid package:* $23,278 (excluding resources awarded to replace EFC). 24% of all full-time freshmen had no need and received non-need-based gift aid.
UNDERGRADUATE FINANCIAL AID (Fall 2009, est.) 1,557 applied for aid; of those 88% were deemed to have need. 100% of undergraduates with need received aid; of those 19% had need fully met. *Average percent of need met:* 82% (excluding resources awarded to replace EFC). *Average financial aid package:* $22,582 (excluding resources awarded to replace EFC). 21% of all full-time undergraduates had no need and received non-need-based gift aid.
GIFT AID (NEED-BASED) *Total amount:* $25,106,391 (8% federal, 8% state, 76% institutional, 8% external sources). *Receiving aid:* Freshmen: 74% (409); all full-time undergraduates: 72% (1,356). *Average award:* Freshmen: $19,243; Undergraduates: $17,947. *Scholarships, grants, and awards:* Federal Pell, FSEOG, state, private, college/university gift aid from institutional funds.
GIFT AID (NON-NEED-BASED) *Total amount:* $7,086,375 (76% institutional, 24% external sources). *Receiving aid:* Freshmen: 13% (74). Undergraduates: 9% (170). *Average award:* Freshmen: $14,357. Undergraduates: $11,974. *Scholarships, grants, and awards by category:* Academic interests/achievement: biological sciences, business, communication, computer science, education, engineering/technologies, English, foreign languages, general academic interests/achievements, health fields, humanities, international studies, mathematics, physical sciences, premedicine, religion/biblical studies, social sciences. *Creative arts/performance:* art/fine arts, music, performing arts, theater/drama. *Special*

achievements/activities: religious involvement. *Special characteristics:* children of faculty/staff, international students, local/state students, members of minority groups, religious affiliation, siblings of current students. *Tuition waivers:* Full or partial for employees or children of employees.
LOANS *Student loans:* $14,782,314 (63% need-based, 37% non-need-based). *Average need-based loan:* Freshmen: $3733. Undergraduates: $4438. *Parent loans:* $5,171,250 (21% need-based, 79% non-need-based). *Programs:* Federal Direct (Subsidized and Unsubsidized Stafford, PLUS), Perkins, state.
WORK-STUDY *Federal work-study:* Total amount: $1,287,686; 974 jobs averaging $1375.
APPLYING FOR FINANCIAL AID *Required financial aid forms:* FAFSA, institution's own form, state aid form, federal income tax form(s), W-2 forms. *Financial aid deadline (priority):* 3/15. *Notification date:* Continuous beginning 3/15. Students must reply by 5/1 or within 2 weeks of notification.
CONTACT Ms. Elizabeth K. McCloud, Director of Financial Aid, Elizabethtown College, 1 Alpha Drive, Elizabethtown, PA 17022-2298, 717-361-1404. *Fax:* 717-361-1514. *E-mail:* mcclouek@etown.edu.

ELLIS UNIVERSITY
Chicago, IL

CONTACT Financial Aid Office, Ellis University, 111 North Canal Street, Suite 380, Chicago, IL 60606-7204, toll-free 877-355-4762 (out-of-state).

ELMHURST COLLEGE
Elmhurst, IL

Tuition & fees: $28,660	Average undergraduate aid package: $21,073

ABOUT THE INSTITUTION Independent religious, coed. 68 undergraduate majors. Federal methodology is used as a basis for awarding need-based institutional aid.
UNDERGRADUATE EXPENSES for 2010–11 *Comprehensive fee:* $36,876 includes full-time tuition ($28,600), mandatory fees ($60), and room and board ($8216). *College room only:* $4956. Room and board charges vary according to board plan and housing facility. Part-time tuition and fees vary according to course load. *Payment plan:* Installment.
FRESHMAN FINANCIAL AID (Fall 2009, est.) 488 applied for aid; of those 88% were deemed to have need. 100% of freshmen with need received aid; of those 35% had need fully met. *Average percent of need met:* 83% (excluding resources awarded to replace EFC). *Average financial aid package:* $22,312 (excluding resources awarded to replace EFC). 9% of all full-time freshmen had no need and received non-need-based gift aid.
UNDERGRADUATE FINANCIAL AID (Fall 2009, est.) 2,140 applied for aid; of those 92% were deemed to have need. 100% of undergraduates with need received aid; of those 31% had need fully met. *Average percent of need met:* 78% (excluding resources awarded to replace EFC). *Average financial aid package:* $21,073 (excluding resources awarded to replace EFC). 6% of all full-time undergraduates had no need and received non-need-based gift aid.
GIFT AID (NEED-BASED) *Total amount:* $33,615,705 (11% federal, 12% state, 76% institutional, 1% external sources). *Receiving aid:* Freshmen: 72% (419); all full-time undergraduates: 67% (1,923). *Average award:* Freshmen: $17,499; Undergraduates: $17,050. *Scholarships, grants, and awards:* Federal Pell, FSEOG, state, private, college/university gift aid from institutional funds.
GIFT AID (NON-NEED-BASED) *Total amount:* $7,352,273 (98% institutional, 2% external sources). *Receiving aid:* Freshmen: 10% (60). Undergraduates: 10% (277). *Average award:* Freshmen: $11,587. Undergraduates: $10,816. *Scholarships, grants, and awards by category:* Academic interests/achievement: 2,087 awards ($20,847,035 total): biological sciences, business, communication, computer science, education, English, foreign languages, general academic interests/achievements, health fields, humanities, international studies, mathematics, physical sciences, premedicine, religion/biblical studies, social sciences. *Creative arts/performance:* 189 awards ($1,316,670 total): art/fine arts, music, theater/drama. *Special characteristics:* 607 awards ($1,932,550 total): children and siblings of alumni, children of current students, ethnic background, members of minority groups, religious affiliation, siblings of current students, spouses of current students. *Tuition waivers:* Full or partial for employees or children of employees, senior citizens.
LOANS *Student loans:* $18,504,958 (44% need-based, 56% non-need-based). 90% of past graduating class borrowed through all loan programs. *Average*

indebtedness per student: $18,329. **Average need-based loan:** Freshmen: $3962. Undergraduates: $4575. **Parent loans:** $4,662,595 (33% need-based, 67% non-need-based). **Programs:** Federal Direct (Subsidized and Unsubsidized Stafford, PLUS), Perkins, alternative loans.

WORK-STUDY *Federal work-study:* Total amount: $486,347; 442 jobs averaging $1100. *State or other work-study/employment:* Total amount: $324,231 (100% non-need-based). 304 part-time jobs averaging $1067.

APPLYING FOR FINANCIAL AID *Required financial aid form:* FAFSA. *Financial aid deadline (priority):* 4/15. *Notification date:* Continuous beginning 2/20. Students must reply within 3 weeks of notification.

CONTACT Ruth A. Pusich, Director of Financial Aid, Elmhurst College, Goebel Hall 106A, 190 Prospect Avenue, Elmhurst, IL 60126-3296, 630-617-3080 or toll-free 800-697-1871 (out-of-state). *Fax:* 630-617-5188. *E-mail:* ruthp@elmhurst.edu.

ELMIRA COLLEGE
Elmira, NY

Tuition & fees: $34,800	Average undergraduate aid package: $26,317

ABOUT THE INSTITUTION Independent, coed. 61 undergraduate majors. Federal methodology is used as a basis for awarding need-based institutional aid.

UNDERGRADUATE EXPENSES for 2009–10 *Comprehensive fee:* $45,600 includes full-time tuition ($33,500), mandatory fees ($1300), and room and board ($10,800). Room and board charges vary according to housing facility. *Payment plans:* Tuition prepayment, installment.

FRESHMAN FINANCIAL AID (Fall 2009, est.) 277 applied for aid; of those 91% were deemed to have need. 100% of freshmen with need received aid; of those 19% had need fully met. *Average percent of need met:* 80% (excluding resources awarded to replace EFC). *Average financial aid package:* $26,911 (excluding resources awarded to replace EFC). 16% of all full-time freshmen had no need and received non-need-based gift aid.

UNDERGRADUATE FINANCIAL AID (Fall 2009, est.) 940 applied for aid; of those 93% were deemed to have need. 100% of undergraduates with need received aid; of those 16% had need fully met. *Average percent of need met:* 80% (excluding resources awarded to replace EFC). *Average financial aid package:* $26,317 (excluding resources awarded to replace EFC). 19% of all full-time undergraduates had no need and received non-need-based gift aid.

GIFT AID (NEED-BASED) *Total amount:* $18,671,100 (8% federal, 5% state, 82% institutional, 5% external sources). *Receiving aid:* Freshmen: 83% (252); all full-time undergraduates: 78% (873). *Average award:* Freshmen: $23,653; Undergraduates: $22,110. *Scholarships, grants, and awards:* Federal Pell, FSEOG, state, private, college/university gift aid from institutional funds.

GIFT AID (NON-NEED-BASED) *Total amount:* $4,961,050 (1% state, 87% institutional, 12% external sources). *Receiving aid:* Freshmen: 12% (38). Undergraduates: 9% (100). *Average award:* Freshmen: $19,134. Undergraduates: $17,653. *Scholarships, grants, and awards by category: Academic interests/achievement:* 680 awards ($10,646,171 total): general academic interests/achievements. *Special achievements/activities:* 110 awards ($581,000 total): leadership. *Special characteristics:* 129 awards ($1,620,432 total): children of faculty/staff, international students, local/state students, previous college experience, siblings of current students. *Tuition waivers:* Full or partial for employees or children of employees.

LOANS *Student loans:* $8,471,805 (71% need-based, 29% non-need-based). 81% of past graduating class borrowed through all loan programs. *Average indebtedness per student:* $26,874. *Average need-based loan:* Freshmen: $3266. Undergraduates: $4354. *Parent loans:* $3,479,737 (40% need-based, 60% non-need-based). *Programs:* Federal Direct (Subsidized and Unsubsidized Stafford, PLUS), Perkins, college/university.

WORK-STUDY *Federal work-study:* Total amount: $425,541; 327 jobs averaging $1300. *State or other work-study/employment:* Total amount: $246,100 (34% need-based, 66% non-need-based). 224 part-time jobs averaging $1100.

APPLYING FOR FINANCIAL AID *Required financial aid forms:* FAFSA, state aid form. *Financial aid deadline (priority):* 2/1. *Notification date:* Continuous beginning 2/1. Students must reply by 5/1 or within 3 weeks of notification.

CONTACT Kathleen L. Cohen, Dean of Financial Aid, Elmira College, One Park Place, Elmira, NY 14901-2099, 607-735-1728 or toll-free 800-935-6472. *Fax:* 607-735-1718. *E-mail:* kcohen@elmira.edu.

ELMS COLLEGE
Chicopee, MA

CONTACT Ms. April Arcouette, Assistant Director of Student Financial Aid Services, Elms College, 291 Springfield Street, Chicopee, MA 01013-2839, 413-265-2249 or toll-free 800-255-ELMS. *Fax:* 413-265-2671. *E-mail:* arcouettea@elms.edu.

ELON UNIVERSITY
Elon, NC

Tuition & fees: $25,489	Average undergraduate aid package: $18,939

ABOUT THE INSTITUTION Independent religious, coed. 54 undergraduate majors. Institutional methodology is used as a basis for awarding need-based institutional aid.

UNDERGRADUATE EXPENSES for 2009–10 *Comprehensive fee:* $33,725 includes full-time tuition ($25,159), mandatory fees ($330), and room and board ($8236). *College room only:* $3992. Room and board charges vary according to board plan and housing facility. *Part-time tuition:* $790 per hour. Part-time tuition and fees vary according to course load. *Payment plan:* Installment.

FRESHMAN FINANCIAL AID (Fall 2009, est.) 776 applied for aid; of those 59% were deemed to have need. 99% of freshmen with need received aid. *Average percent of need met:* 86% (excluding resources awarded to replace EFC). *Average financial aid package:* $19,487 (excluding resources awarded to replace EFC). 22% of all full-time freshmen had no need and received non-need-based gift aid.

UNDERGRADUATE FINANCIAL AID (Fall 2009, est.) 2,368 applied for aid; of those 70% were deemed to have need. 100% of undergraduates with need received aid. *Average percent of need met:* 82% (excluding resources awarded to replace EFC). *Average financial aid package:* $18,939 (excluding resources awarded to replace EFC). 23% of all full-time undergraduates had no need and received non-need-based gift aid.

GIFT AID (NEED-BASED) *Total amount:* $19,020,146 (11% federal, 35% state, 51% institutional, 3% external sources). *Receiving aid:* Freshmen: 32% (407); all full-time undergraduates: 31% (1,490). *Average award:* Freshmen: $13,887; Undergraduates: $12,840. *Scholarships, grants, and awards:* Federal Pell, FSEOG, state, private, college/university gift aid from institutional funds.

GIFT AID (NON-NEED-BASED) *Total amount:* $9,306,302 (34% state, 61% institutional, 5% external sources). *Receiving aid:* Freshmen: 5% (60). Undergraduates: 3% (170). *Average award:* Freshmen: $5670. Undergraduates: $5442. *Scholarships, grants, and awards by category: Academic interests/achievement:* 1,761 awards ($7,739,729 total): biological sciences, business, communication, computer science, education, engineering/technologies, general academic interests/achievements, mathematics, military science, physical sciences, premedicine, religion/biblical studies, social sciences. *Creative arts/performance:* 59 awards ($134,200 total): art/fine arts, journalism/publications, music, performing arts, theater/drama. *Special achievements/activities:* 28 awards ($51,000 total): community service, general special achievements/activities, leadership, religious involvement. *Special characteristics:* 81 awards ($981,884 total): adult students, children of faculty/staff, ethnic background, first-generation college students, international students, members of minority groups, relatives of clergy. *Tuition waivers:* Full or partial for employees or children of employees.

LOANS *Student loans:* $16,640,609 (37% need-based, 63% non-need-based). 45% of past graduating class borrowed through all loan programs. *Average indebtedness per student:* $22,939. *Average need-based loan:* Freshmen: $4100. Undergraduates: $4907. *Parent loans:* $8,210,745 (35% need-based, 65% non-need-based). *Programs:* FFEL (Subsidized and Unsubsidized Stafford, PLUS), Perkins, state, college/university, alternative loans.

WORK-STUDY *Federal work-study:* Total amount: $2,280,441; 946 jobs averaging $2344.

ATHLETIC AWARDS Total amount: $5,859,959 (45% need-based, 55% non-need-based).

APPLYING FOR FINANCIAL AID *Required financial aid forms:* FAFSA, institution's own form, CSS Financial Aid PROFILE. *Financial aid deadline (priority):* 3/15. *Notification date:* 3/30.

CONTACT Patrick Murphy, Director of Financial Planning, Elon University, 2725 Campus Box, Elon, NC 27244, 336-278-7640 or toll-free 800-334-8448. *Fax:* 336-278-7639. *E-mail:* finaid@elon.edu.

EMBRY-RIDDLE AERONAUTICAL UNIVERSITY
Prescott, AZ

Tuition & fees: $29,380	Average undergraduate aid package: $20,161

ABOUT THE INSTITUTION Independent, coed. 14 undergraduate majors. Federal methodology is used as a basis for awarding need-based institutional aid.

UNDERGRADUATE EXPENSES for 2010–11 *Comprehensive fee:* $37,910 includes full-time tuition ($28,560), mandatory fees ($820), and room and board ($8530). *College room only:* $4780. Room and board charges vary according to board plan and housing facility. *Part-time tuition:* $1190 per credit hour. *Payment plans:* Installment, deferred payment.

FRESHMAN FINANCIAL AID (Fall 2009, est.) 288 applied for aid; of those 86% were deemed to have need. 99% of freshmen with need received aid. *Average financial aid package:* $19,633 (excluding resources awarded to replace EFC).

UNDERGRADUATE FINANCIAL AID (Fall 2009, est.) 1,143 applied for aid; of those 89% were deemed to have need. 99% of undergraduates with need received aid. *Average financial aid package:* $20,161 (excluding resources awarded to replace EFC).

GIFT AID (NEED-BASED) *Total amount:* $20,082,614 (12% federal, 62% institutional, 26% external sources). *Receiving aid:* Freshmen: 77% (245); all full-time undergraduates: 64% (962). *Average award:* Freshmen: $13,944; Undergraduates: $11,989. *Scholarships, grants, and awards:* Federal Pell, FSEOG, state, private, college/university gift aid from institutional funds.

GIFT AID (NON-NEED-BASED) *Scholarships, grants, and awards by category:* Academic interests/achievement: 713 awards ($4,934,940 total): general academic interests/achievements. Special achievements/activities: 21 awards ($107,563 total): leadership. Special characteristics: 79 awards ($772,850 total): children and siblings of alumni, children of faculty/staff. *Tuition waivers:* Full or partial for employees or children of employees.

LOANS *Student loans:* $12,318,855 (100% need-based). 74% of past graduating class borrowed through all loan programs. *Average need-based loan:* Freshmen: $3457. Undergraduates: $4970. *Parent loans:* $6,600,044 (100% need-based). *Programs:* FFEL (Subsidized and Unsubsidized Stafford, PLUS), Perkins.

WORK-STUDY *Federal work-study:* Total amount: $79,239; 69 jobs averaging $1077. *State or other work-study/employment:* Total amount: $1,130,053 (100% need-based). 448 part-time jobs averaging $1378.

ATHLETIC AWARDS Total amount: $798,602 (100% need-based).

APPLYING FOR FINANCIAL AID *Required financial aid form:* FAFSA. *Financial aid deadline (priority):* 3/1. *Notification date:* Continuous beginning 3/1. Students must reply within 4 weeks of notification.

CONTACT Mr. Dan Lupin, Director of Financial Aid, Embry-Riddle Aeronautical University, 3700 Willow Creek Road, Prescott, AZ 86301-3720, 800-888-3728. *Fax:* 928-777-3893. *E-mail:* prfinaid@erau.edu.

EMBRY-RIDDLE AERONAUTICAL UNIVERSITY
Daytona Beach, FL

Tuition & fees: $29,724	Average undergraduate aid package: $15,246

ABOUT THE INSTITUTION Independent, coed. 22 undergraduate majors. Federal methodology is used as a basis for awarding need-based institutional aid.

UNDERGRADUATE EXPENSES for 2010–11 *Comprehensive fee:* $38,564 includes full-time tuition ($28,560), mandatory fees ($1164), and room and board ($8840). *College room only:* $5300. Room and board charges vary according to board plan and housing facility. *Part-time tuition:* $1190 per credit hour. *Payment plans:* Installment, deferred payment.

FRESHMAN FINANCIAL AID (Fall 2009, est.) 699 applied for aid; of those 86% were deemed to have need. 100% of freshmen with need received aid. *Average financial aid package:* $12,906 (excluding resources awarded to replace EFC).

UNDERGRADUATE FINANCIAL AID (Fall 2009, est.) 2,917 applied for aid; of those 88% were deemed to have need. 99% of undergraduates with need received aid. *Average financial aid package:* $15,246 (excluding resources awarded to replace EFC).

GIFT AID (NEED-BASED) *Total amount:* $40,003,794 (12% federal, 8% state, 52% institutional, 28% external sources). *Receiving aid:* Freshmen: 69% (592); all full-time undergraduates: 59% (2,463). *Average award:* Freshmen: $9119; Undergraduates: $9085. *Scholarships, grants, and awards:* Federal Pell, FSEOG, state, private, college/university gift aid from institutional funds.

GIFT AID (NON-NEED-BASED) *Scholarships, grants, and awards by category:* Academic interests/achievement: 1,525 awards ($7,583,867 total): general academic interests/achievements. Special achievements/activities: 66 awards ($218,633 total): leadership. Special characteristics: 188 awards ($2,267,300 total): children of faculty/staff. *Tuition waivers:* Full or partial for employees or children of employees.

LOANS *Student loans:* $34,192,935 (100% need-based). 66% of past graduating class borrowed through all loan programs. *Average need-based loan:* Freshmen: $3432. Undergraduates: $4672. *Parent loans:* $17,871,872 (100% need-based). *Programs:* FFEL (Subsidized and Unsubsidized Stafford, PLUS), Perkins.

WORK-STUDY *Federal work-study:* Total amount: $308,367; 193 jobs averaging $1425. *State or other work-study/employment:* Total amount: $3,817,639 (100% need-based). 1,133 part-time jobs averaging $1838.

ATHLETIC AWARDS Total amount: $2,025,511 (100% need-based).

APPLYING FOR FINANCIAL AID *Required financial aid form:* FAFSA. *Financial aid deadline (priority):* 3/1. *Notification date:* Continuous beginning 3/1. Students must reply within 4 weeks of notification.

CONTACT Barbara Dryden, Director of Financial Aid, Embry-Riddle Aeronautical University, 600 South Clyde Morris Boulevard, Daytona Beach, FL 32114-3900, 800-943-6279 or toll-free 800-862-2416. *Fax:* 386-226-6307. *E-mail:* dbfinaid@erau.edu.

EMBRY-RIDDLE AERONAUTICAL UNIVERSITY WORLDWIDE
Daytona Beach, FL

Tuition & fees: $5520	Average undergraduate aid package: $6753

ABOUT THE INSTITUTION Independent, coed. 4 undergraduate majors. Federal methodology is used as a basis for awarding need-based institutional aid.

UNDERGRADUATE EXPENSES for 2010–11 *Tuition:* full-time $5520. Room and board charges vary according to location. *Payment plan:* Deferred payment.

FRESHMAN FINANCIAL AID (Fall 2009, est.) 20 applied for aid; of those 85% were deemed to have need. 100% of freshmen with need received aid. *Average financial aid package:* $5834 (excluding resources awarded to replace EFC).

UNDERGRADUATE FINANCIAL AID (Fall 2009, est.) 631 applied for aid; of those 85% were deemed to have need. 99% of undergraduates with need received aid. *Average financial aid package:* $6753 (excluding resources awarded to replace EFC).

GIFT AID (NEED-BASED) *Total amount:* $2,189,220 (50% federal, 46% state, 1% institutional, 3% external sources). *Receiving aid:* Freshmen: 12% (10); all full-time undergraduates: 17% (354). *Average award:* Freshmen: $5310; Undergraduates: $4469. *Scholarships, grants, and awards:* Federal Pell, state, private, college/university gift aid from institutional funds.

GIFT AID (NON-NEED-BASED) *Scholarships, grants, and awards by category:* Academic interests/achievement: general academic interests/achievements. Special achievements/activities: leadership. Special characteristics: children of faculty/staff. *Tuition waivers:* Full or partial for employees or children of employees.

LOANS *Student loans:* $14,221,696 (100% need-based). 14% of past graduating class borrowed through all loan programs. *Average need-based loan:* Freshmen: $3291. Undergraduates: $4304. *Parent loans:* $87,441 (100% need-based). *Programs:* FFEL (Subsidized and Unsubsidized Stafford, PLUS).

APPLYING FOR FINANCIAL AID *Required financial aid form:* FAFSA. *Financial aid deadline:* Continuous. *Notification date:* Continuous beginning 3/1. Students must reply within 4 weeks of notification.

CONTACT Frederic Ndiaye, Director of Financial Aid, Embry-Riddle Aeronautical University Worldwide, 600 South Clyde Morris Boulevard, Daytona Beach, FL 32114-3900, 866-567-7202 or toll-free 800-522-6787. *Fax:* 386-226-6915. *E-mail:* wwfinaid@erau.edu.

EMERSON COLLEGE
Boston, MA

Tuition & fees: $29,918	Average undergraduate aid package: $17,364

ABOUT THE INSTITUTION Independent, coed. 28 undergraduate majors. Institutional methodology is used as a basis for awarding need-based institutional aid.

UNDERGRADUATE EXPENSES for 2009–10 *Comprehensive fee:* $42,198 includes full-time tuition ($29,408), mandatory fees ($510), and room and board ($12,280). *Part-time tuition:* $919 per credit hour. *Payment plan:* Installment.

FRESHMAN FINANCIAL AID (Fall 2009, est.) 536 applied for aid; of those 82% were deemed to have need. 99% of freshmen with need received aid; of those 69% had need fully met. *Average percent of need met:* 76% (excluding resources awarded to replace EFC). *Average financial aid package:* $18,553 (excluding resources awarded to replace EFC). 6% of all full-time freshmen had no need and received non-need-based gift aid.

UNDERGRADUATE FINANCIAL AID (Fall 2009, est.) 2,249 applied for aid; of those 86% were deemed to have need. 100% of undergraduates with need received aid; of those 61% had need fully met. *Average percent of need met:* 73% (excluding resources awarded to replace EFC). *Average financial aid package:* $17,364 (excluding resources awarded to replace EFC). 5% of all full-time undergraduates had no need and received non-need-based gift aid.

GIFT AID (NEED-BASED) *Total amount:* $23,964,330 (11% federal, 2% state, 80% institutional, 7% external sources). *Receiving aid:* Freshmen: 50% (381); all full-time undergraduates: 47% (1,609). *Average award:* Freshmen: $16,756; Undergraduates: $15,028. *Scholarships, grants, and awards:* Federal Pell, FSEOG, state, private, college/university gift aid from institutional funds.

GIFT AID (NON-NEED-BASED) *Total amount:* $2,600,103 (89% institutional, 11% external sources). *Receiving aid:* Freshmen: 4% (27). Undergraduates: 2% (69). *Average award:* Freshmen: $13,833. Undergraduates: $12,327. *Scholarships, grants, and awards by category: Academic interests/achievement:* general academic interests/achievements. *Creative arts/performance:* performing arts. *Special characteristics:* general special characteristics. *Tuition waivers:* Full or partial for employees or children of employees.

LOANS *Student loans:* $24,546,684 (68% need-based, 32% non-need-based). 59% of past graduating class borrowed through all loan programs. *Average indebtedness per student:* $15,262. *Average need-based loan:* Freshmen: $3593. Undergraduates: $4509. *Parent loans:* $10,884,608 (37% need-based, 63% non-need-based). *Programs:* FFEL (Subsidized and Unsubsidized Stafford, PLUS), Perkins, state.

WORK-STUDY *Federal work-study:* Total amount: $792,586; 591 jobs averaging $1900. *State or other work-study/employment:* Total amount: $593,847 (41% need-based, 59% non-need-based). 67 part-time jobs averaging $11,200.

APPLYING FOR FINANCIAL AID *Required financial aid forms:* FAFSA, CSS Financial Aid PROFILE, noncustodial (divorced/separated) parent's statement, business/farm supplement. *Financial aid deadline (priority):* 3/1. *Notification date:* 4/1. Students must reply by 5/1 or within 3 weeks of notification.

CONTACT Michelle Smith, Director, Office of Student Financial Services, Emerson College, 120 Boylston Street, Boston, MA 02116-4624, 617-824-8655. *Fax:* 617-824-8619. *E-mail:* finaid@emerson.edu.

EMMANUEL COLLEGE
Franklin Springs, GA

ABOUT THE INSTITUTION Independent religious, coed. 23 undergraduate majors.

GIFT AID (NEED-BASED) *Scholarships, grants, and awards:* Federal Pell, FSEOG, state, college/university gift aid from institutional funds.

GIFT AID (NON-NEED-BASED) *Scholarships, grants, and awards by category: Academic interests/achievement:* business, communication, education, English, general academic interests/achievements, health fields, religion/biblical studies. *Creative arts/performance:* applied art and design, art/fine arts, creative writing, dance, general creative arts/performance, music, performing arts, theater/drama. *Special achievements/activities:* general special achievements/activities, leadership, memberships, religious involvement. *Special characteristics:* adult students, children of current students, children of faculty/staff, first-generation college students, general special characteristics, international students, married students, parents of current students, relatives of clergy, religious affiliation, siblings of current students, spouses of current students, twins.

LOANS *Programs:* FFEL (Subsidized and Unsubsidized Stafford, PLUS).

WORK-STUDY *Federal work-study:* Total amount: $430,163; 219 jobs averaging $1964. *State or other work-study/employment:* Total amount: $156,654 (100% non-need-based). 100 part-time jobs averaging $1567.

APPLYING FOR FINANCIAL AID *Required financial aid forms:* FAFSA, institution's own form, state aid form.

CONTACT Gloria Hambrick, Director of Financial Aid, Emmanuel College, PO Box 129, Franklin Springs, GA 30639-0129, 706-245-2844 or toll-free 800-860-8800 (in-state). *Fax:* 706-245-2846. *E-mail:* ghambrick@ec.edu.

EMMANUEL COLLEGE
Boston, MA

Tuition & fees: $29,365	Average undergraduate aid package: $21,994

ABOUT THE INSTITUTION Independent Roman Catholic, coed. 36 undergraduate majors. Federal methodology is used as a basis for awarding need-based institutional aid.

UNDERGRADUATE EXPENSES for 2009–10 *Comprehensive fee:* $41,315 includes full-time tuition ($29,200), mandatory fees ($165), and room and board ($11,950). Full-time tuition and fees vary according to course load, degree level, and program. Room and board charges vary according to housing facility. *Part-time tuition:* $912.50 per credit. Part-time tuition and fees vary according to program. *Payment plan:* Installment.

FRESHMAN FINANCIAL AID (Fall 2009, est.) 385 applied for aid; of those 89% were deemed to have need. 100% of freshmen with need received aid; of those 45% had need fully met. *Average percent of need met:* 75% (excluding resources awarded to replace EFC). *Average financial aid package:* $24,212 (excluding resources awarded to replace EFC). 13% of all full-time freshmen had no need and received non-need-based gift aid.

UNDERGRADUATE FINANCIAL AID (Fall 2009, est.) 1,414 applied for aid; of those 92% were deemed to have need. 100% of undergraduates with need received aid; of those 42% had need fully met. *Average percent of need met:* 69% (excluding resources awarded to replace EFC). *Average financial aid package:* $21,994 (excluding resources awarded to replace EFC). 10% of all full-time undergraduates had no need and received non-need-based gift aid.

GIFT AID (NEED-BASED) *Total amount:* $21,624,289 (12% federal, 4% state, 82% institutional, 2% external sources). *Receiving aid:* Freshmen: 76% (322); all full-time undergraduates: 77% (1,275). *Average award:* Freshmen: $20,527; Undergraduates: $15,747. *Scholarships, grants, and awards:* Federal Pell, FSEOG, state, private, college/university gift aid from institutional funds.

GIFT AID (NON-NEED-BASED) *Total amount:* $2,216,201 (10% federal, 85% institutional, 5% external sources). *Receiving aid:* Freshmen: 70% (298). Undergraduates: 42% (685). *Average award:* Freshmen: $9890. Undergraduates: $11,671. *Scholarships, grants, and awards by category: Academic interests/achievement:* biological sciences, education, engineering/technologies, foreign languages, general academic interests/achievements, health fields, humanities, mathematics, physical sciences, religion/biblical studies, social sciences. *Creative arts/performance:* general creative arts/performance. *Special achievements/activities:* community service, leadership. *Special characteristics:* children and siblings of alumni, children of educators, children of faculty/staff, children of union members/company employees, ethnic background, general special characteristics, handicapped students, international students, local/state students, religious affiliation, siblings of current students. *Tuition waivers:* Full or partial for employees or children of employees.

LOANS *Student loans:* $14,747,251 (92% need-based, 8% non-need-based). *Average need-based loan:* Freshmen: $3688. Undergraduates: $4975. *Parent loans:* $6,776,198 (100% non-need-based). *Programs:* Federal Direct (Subsidized and Unsubsidized Stafford, PLUS), Perkins, state, alternative loans.

WORK-STUDY *Federal work-study:* Total amount: $1,517,353; jobs available. *State or other work-study/employment:* Total amount: $350,000 (100% non-need-based). Part-time jobs available.

APPLYING FOR FINANCIAL AID *Required financial aid forms:* FAFSA, institution's own form. *Financial aid deadline (priority):* 4/1. *Notification date:* Continuous beginning 3/15.

CONTACT Jennifer Porter, Associate Vice President for Student Financial Services, Emmanuel College, 400 The Fenway, Boston, MA 02115, 617-735-9938. *Fax:* 617-735-9939. *E-mail:* financialservices@emmanuel.edu.

EMMAUS BIBLE COLLEGE
Dubuque, IA

CONTACT Steve Seeman, Financial Aid Director, Emmaus Bible College, 2570 Asbury Road, Dubuque, IA 52001-3097, 800-397-2425 Ext. 1309 or toll-free 800-397-2425. *Fax:* 563-588-1216. *E-mail:* financialaid@emmaus.edu.

EMORY & HENRY COLLEGE
Emory, VA

Tuition & fees: $24,880	Average undergraduate aid package: $23,244

ABOUT THE INSTITUTION Independent United Methodist, coed. 37 undergraduate majors. Federal methodology is used as a basis for awarding need-based institutional aid.

UNDERGRADUATE EXPENSES for 2009–10 *Comprehensive fee:* $33,180 includes full-time tuition ($24,880) and room and board ($8300). *College room only:* $4250. Full-time tuition and fees vary according to course load and degree level. Room and board charges vary according to board plan. *Part-time tuition:* $995 per credit hour. Part-time tuition and fees vary according to course load and degree level. *Payment plan:* Installment.

FRESHMAN FINANCIAL AID (Fall 2009, est.) 265 applied for aid; of those 87% were deemed to have need. 100% of freshmen with need received aid; of those 31% had need fully met. *Average percent of need met:* 90% (excluding resources awarded to replace EFC). *Average financial aid package:* $23,469 (excluding resources awarded to replace EFC). 20% of all full-time freshmen had no need and received non-need-based gift aid.

UNDERGRADUATE FINANCIAL AID (Fall 2009, est.) 806 applied for aid; of those 90% were deemed to have need. 100% of undergraduates with need received aid; of those 27% had need fully met. *Average percent of need met:* 86% (excluding resources awarded to replace EFC). *Average financial aid package:* $23,244 (excluding resources awarded to replace EFC). 19% of all full-time undergraduates had no need and received non-need-based gift aid.

GIFT AID (NEED-BASED) *Total amount:* $13,182,135 (15% federal, 10% state, 73% institutional, 2% external sources). *Receiving aid:* Freshmen: 57% (166); all full-time undergraduates: 64% (575). *Average award:* Freshmen: $22,287; Undergraduates: $20,989. *Scholarships, grants, and awards:* Federal Pell, FSEOG, state, private, college/university gift aid from institutional funds.

GIFT AID (NON-NEED-BASED) *Total amount:* $2,610,306 (13% state, 86% institutional, 1% external sources). *Receiving aid:* Freshmen: 23% (66). Undergraduates: 17% (151). *Average award:* Freshmen: $12,813. Undergraduates: $11,497. *Scholarships, grants, and awards by category:* Academic interests/achievement: 747 awards ($6,218,173 total): general academic interests/achievements, premedicine, religion/biblical studies. *Creative arts/performance:* 22 awards ($28,196 total): art/fine arts, journalism/publications, music, theater/drama. *Special characteristics:* 238 awards ($985,895 total): children of educators, children of faculty/staff, out-of-state students. *Tuition waivers:* Full or partial for employees or children of employees.

LOANS *Student loans:* $4,656,417 (75% need-based, 25% non-need-based). 65% of past graduating class borrowed through all loan programs. *Average indebtedness per student:* $19,168. *Average need-based loan:* Freshmen: $3375. Undergraduates: $4283. *Parent loans:* $2,282,579 (32% need-based, 68% non-need-based). *Programs:* FFEL (Subsidized and Unsubsidized Stafford, PLUS), Perkins.

WORK-STUDY *Federal work-study:* Total amount: $184,315; 150 jobs averaging $1091.

APPLYING FOR FINANCIAL AID *Required financial aid forms:* FAFSA, state aid form. *Financial aid deadline (priority):* 4/15. *Notification date:* Continuous. Students must reply within 2 weeks of notification.

CONTACT Margaret L. Murphy, Director of Student Financial Planning, Emory & Henry College, PO Box 947, Emory, VA 24327-0010, 276-944-6115 or toll-free 800-848-5493. *Fax:* 276-944-6884. *E-mail:* mmurphy@ehc.edu.

EMORY UNIVERSITY
Atlanta, GA

Tuition & fees: $38,600	Average undergraduate aid package: $32,415

ABOUT THE INSTITUTION Independent Methodist, coed. 58 undergraduate majors. Both federal and institutional methodology are used as a basis for awarding need-based institutional aid.

UNDERGRADUATE EXPENSES for 2010–11 *Comprehensive fee:* $50,900 includes full-time tuition ($38,064), mandatory fees ($536), and room and board ($12,300). *College room only:* $7503. Full-time tuition and fees vary according to location. Room and board charges vary according to board plan, housing facility, location, and student level. *Payment plan:* Installment.

FRESHMAN FINANCIAL AID (Fall 2009, est.) 937 applied for aid; of those 85% were deemed to have need. 100% of freshmen with need received aid; of those 97% had need fully met. *Average percent of need met:* 100% (excluding resources awarded to replace EFC). *Average financial aid package:* $33,262 (excluding resources awarded to replace EFC). 4% of all full-time freshmen had no need and received non-need-based gift aid.

UNDERGRADUATE FINANCIAL AID (Fall 2009, est.) 3,433 applied for aid; of those 88% were deemed to have need. 100% of undergraduates with need received aid; of those 95% had need fully met. *Average percent of need met:* 100% (excluding resources awarded to replace EFC). *Average financial aid package:* $32,415 (excluding resources awarded to replace EFC). 6% of all full-time undergraduates had no need and received non-need-based gift aid.

GIFT AID (NEED-BASED) *Total amount:* $85,088,934 (9% federal, 4% state, 85% institutional, 2% external sources). *Receiving aid:* Freshmen: 46% (771); all full-time undergraduates: 43% (2,885). *Average award:* Freshmen: $30,448; Undergraduates: $28,053. *Scholarships, grants, and awards:* Federal Pell, FSEOG, state, private, college/university gift aid from institutional funds.

GIFT AID (NON-NEED-BASED) *Total amount:* $12,858,044 (17% state, 77% institutional, 6% external sources). *Receiving aid:* Freshmen: 7% (116). Undergraduates: 4% (262). *Average award:* Freshmen: $19,439. Undergraduates: $21,345. *Scholarships, grants, and awards by category:* Academic interests/achievement: general academic interests/achievements. *Creative arts/performance:* art/fine arts, music, theater/drama. *Special achievements/activities:* leadership. *Special characteristics:* religious affiliation. *Tuition waivers:* Full or partial for employees or children of employees.

LOANS *Student loans:* $20,660,335 (41% need-based, 59% non-need-based). 42% of past graduating class borrowed through all loan programs. *Average indebtedness per student:* $25,865. *Average need-based loan:* Freshmen: $3288. Undergraduates: $4333. *Parent loans:* $7,695,343 (100% non-need-based). *Programs:* FFEL (Subsidized and Unsubsidized Stafford, PLUS), Perkins, Federal Nursing, state, college/university.

WORK-STUDY *Federal work-study:* Total amount: $4,383,434; jobs available. *State or other work-study/employment:* Total amount: $514,674 (70% need-based, 30% non-need-based). Part-time jobs available.

APPLYING FOR FINANCIAL AID *Required financial aid forms:* FAFSA, CSS Financial Aid PROFILE, noncustodial (divorced/separated) parent's statement. *Financial aid deadline:* 3/1 (priority: 2/15). *Notification date:* 4/1. Students must reply by 5/1.

CONTACT Dean Bentley, Director of Financial Aid, Emory University, 200 Dowman Drive, Atlanta, GA 30322-1960, 404-727-6039 or toll-free 800-727-6036. *Fax:* 404-727-6709. *E-mail:* finaid1@emory.edu.

EMPORIA STATE UNIVERSITY
Emporia, KS

Tuition & fees (KS res): $4374	Average undergraduate aid package: $4968

ABOUT THE INSTITUTION State-supported, coed. 35 undergraduate majors. Federal methodology is used as a basis for awarding need-based institutional aid.

UNDERGRADUATE EXPENSES for 2009–10 *Tuition, state resident:* full-time $3426; part-time $114 per credit hour. *Tuition, nonresident:* full-time $12,630; part-time $421 per credit hour. *Required fees:* full-time $948; $58 per credit hour. Full-time tuition and fees vary according to course load, degree level, and location. Part-time tuition and fees vary according to course load, degree level, and location. *College room and board:* $6146; *Room only:* $3146. Room and board charges vary according to board plan and housing facility. *Payment plans:* Installment, deferred payment.

FRESHMAN FINANCIAL AID (Fall 2009, est.) 589 applied for aid; of those 74% were deemed to have need. 99% of freshmen with need received aid; of those 15% had need fully met. *Average percent of need met:* 88% (excluding

resources awarded to replace EFC). *Average financial aid package:* $5472 (excluding resources awarded to replace EFC). 18% of all full-time freshmen had no need and received non-need-based gift aid.

UNDERGRADUATE FINANCIAL AID (Fall 2009, est.) 2,811 applied for aid; of those 78% were deemed to have need. 99% of undergraduates with need received aid; of those 17% had need fully met. *Average percent of need met:* 88% (excluding resources awarded to replace EFC). *Average financial aid package:* $4968 (excluding resources awarded to replace EFC). 14% of all full-time undergraduates had no need and received non-need-based gift aid.

GIFT AID (NEED-BASED) *Total amount:* $9,403,731 (72% federal, 8% state, 10% institutional, 10% external sources). *Receiving aid:* Freshmen: 62% (406); all full-time undergraduates: 50% (1,820). *Average award:* Freshmen: $5232; Undergraduates: $5258. *Scholarships, grants, and awards:* Federal Pell, FSEOG, state, private, college/university gift aid from institutional funds, Jones Foundation Grants, grants from outside sources.

GIFT AID (NON-NEED-BASED) *Total amount:* $2,004,934 (2% federal, 4% state, 38% institutional, 56% external sources). *Receiving aid:* Freshmen: 22% (147). Undergraduates: 11% (398). *Average award:* Freshmen: $1598. Undergraduates: $1335. *Scholarships, grants, and awards by category: Academic interests/achievement:* 1,888 awards ($1,897,297 total): biological sciences, business, communication, computer science, education, engineering/technologies, English, foreign languages, general academic interests/achievements, health fields, humanities, library science, mathematics, physical sciences, premedicine, social sciences. *Creative arts/performance:* 104 awards ($88,040 total): art/fine arts, creative writing, debating, music, theater/drama. *Special achievements/activities:* 20 awards ($8750 total): memberships. *Special characteristics:* 35 awards ($20,226 total): children and siblings of alumni, children of faculty/staff, children of union members/company employees, handicapped students, international students, members of minority groups, religious affiliation, veterans, veterans' children. *Tuition waivers:* Full or partial for employees or children of employees, senior citizens.

LOANS *Student loans:* $16,107,203 (67% need-based, 33% non-need-based). 68% of past graduating class borrowed through all loan programs. *Average indebtedness per student:* $21,158. *Average need-based loan:* Freshmen: $4829. Undergraduates: $5765. *Parent loans:* $2,554,264 (13% need-based, 87% non-need-based). *Programs:* FFEL (Subsidized and Unsubsidized Stafford, PLUS), Perkins, Alaska Loans, alternative loans.

WORK-STUDY *Federal work-study:* Total amount: $555,643; 289 jobs averaging $1904. *State or other work-study/employment:* Total amount: $34,665 (68% need-based, 32% non-need-based). 18 part-time jobs averaging $1814.

ATHLETIC AWARDS Total amount: $1,107,054 (46% need-based, 54% non-need-based).

APPLYING FOR FINANCIAL AID *Required financial aid forms:* FAFSA, state aid form. *Financial aid deadline (priority):* 3/15. *Notification date:* Continuous. Students must reply within 2 weeks of notification.

CONTACT Elaine Henrie, Director of Financial Aid, Emporia State University, 1200 Commercial Street, Emporia, KS 66801-5087, 620-341-5457 or toll-free 877-GOTOESU (in-state), 877-468-6378 (out-of-state). *Fax:* 620-341-6088. *E-mail:* ehenrie@emporia.edu.

ENDICOTT COLLEGE
Beverly, MA

Tuition & fees: $25,376	Average undergraduate aid package: $16,827

ABOUT THE INSTITUTION Independent, coed. 24 undergraduate majors. Federal methodology is used as a basis for awarding need-based institutional aid.

UNDERGRADUATE EXPENSES for 2009–10 *Comprehensive fee:* $37,212 includes full-time tuition ($24,976), mandatory fees ($400), and room and board ($11,836). *College room only:* $8248. Room and board charges vary according to board plan and housing facility. *Part-time tuition:* $766 per credit hour. *Part-time fees:* $150 per term. *Payment plan:* Installment.

FRESHMAN FINANCIAL AID (Fall 2009, est.) 503 applied for aid; of those 74% were deemed to have need. 99% of freshmen with need received aid; of those 12% had need fully met. *Average percent of need met:* 60% (excluding resources awarded to replace EFC). *Average financial aid package:* $16,920 (excluding resources awarded to replace EFC). 16% of all full-time freshmen had no need and received non-need-based gift aid.

UNDERGRADUATE FINANCIAL AID (Fall 2009, est.) 1,757 applied for aid; of those 72% were deemed to have need. 99% of undergraduates with need received aid; of those 12% had need fully met. *Average percent of need met:*

61% (excluding resources awarded to replace EFC). *Average financial aid package:* $16,827 (excluding resources awarded to replace EFC). 17% of all full-time undergraduates had no need and received non-need-based gift aid.

GIFT AID (NEED-BASED) *Total amount:* $12,660,120 (11% federal, 3% state, 86% institutional). *Receiving aid:* Freshmen: 49% (276); all full-time undergraduates: 45% (959). *Average award:* Freshmen: $9439; Undergraduates: $9103. *Scholarships, grants, and awards:* Federal Pell, FSEOG, state, private, college/university gift aid from institutional funds.

GIFT AID (NON-NEED-BASED) *Total amount:* $3,089,393 (86% institutional, 14% external sources). *Receiving aid:* Freshmen: 44% (246). Undergraduates: 35% (739). *Average award:* Freshmen: $6306. Undergraduates: $7007. *Scholarships, grants, and awards by category: Academic interests/achievement:* 943 awards ($6,094,768 total): business, education, general academic interests/achievements, health fields. *Creative arts/performance:* art/fine arts. *Special achievements/activities:* 12 awards ($7100 total): community service, general special achievements/activities, leadership, religious involvement. *Special characteristics:* 132 awards ($505,489 total): children and siblings of alumni; children of educators, general special characteristics, international students, local/state students, religious affiliation. *Tuition waivers:* Full or partial for employees or children of employees.

LOANS *Student loans:* $15,748,935 (35% need-based, 65% non-need-based). 69% of past graduating class borrowed through all loan programs. *Average indebtedness per student:* $33,783. *Average need-based loan:* Freshmen: $3803. Undergraduates: $4594. *Parent loans:* $5,338,749 (100% non-need-based). *Programs:* FFEL (Subsidized and Unsubsidized Stafford, PLUS), Perkins, college/university.

WORK-STUDY *Federal work-study:* Total amount: $773,470; 403 jobs averaging $2000.

APPLYING FOR FINANCIAL AID *Required financial aid forms:* FAFSA, institution's own form. *Financial aid deadline (priority):* 3/15. *Notification date:* Continuous beginning 3/15. Students must reply within 2 weeks of notification.

CONTACT Ms. Marcia Toomey, Director of Financial Aid, Endicott College, 376 Hale Street, Beverly, MA 01915-2096, 978-232-2060 or toll-free 800-325-1114 (out-of-state). *Fax:* 978-232-2085. *E-mail:* mtoomey@endicott.edu.

EPIC BIBLE COLLEGE
Sacramento, CA

CONTACT Financial Aid Office, Epic Bible College, 5225 Hillsdale Boulevard, Sacramento, CA 95842, 916-348-4689.

ERSKINE COLLEGE
Due West, SC

Tuition & fees: $24,645	Average undergraduate aid package: $20,694

ABOUT THE INSTITUTION Independent religious, coed. 23 undergraduate majors. Federal methodology is used as a basis for awarding need-based institutional aid.

UNDERGRADUATE EXPENSES for 2009–10 *Comprehensive fee:* $32,970 includes full-time tuition ($23,000), mandatory fees ($1645), and room and board ($8325). *Part-time tuition:* $852 per semester hour. *Payment plan:* Installment.

FRESHMAN FINANCIAL AID (Fall 2009, est.) 158 applied for aid; of those 80% were deemed to have need. 100% of freshmen with need received aid; of those 43% had need fully met. *Average percent of need met:* 83% (excluding resources awarded to replace EFC). *Average financial aid package:* $21,557 (excluding resources awarded to replace EFC). 20% of all full-time freshmen had no need and received non-need-based gift aid.

UNDERGRADUATE FINANCIAL AID (Fall 2009, est.) 492 applied for aid; of those 80% were deemed to have need. 100% of undergraduates with need received aid; of those 38% had need fully met. *Average percent of need met:* 83% (excluding resources awarded to replace EFC). *Average financial aid package:* $20,694 (excluding resources awarded to replace EFC). 20% of all full-time undergraduates had no need and received non-need-based gift aid.

GIFT AID (NEED-BASED) *Total amount:* $2,052,121 (43% federal, 46% state, 11% institutional). *Receiving aid:* Freshmen: 70% (127); all full-time undergraduates: 69% (394). *Average award:* Freshmen: $16,158; Undergraduates: $16,158.

Scholarships, grants, and awards: Federal Pell, FSEOG, state, private, college/university gift aid from institutional funds, Academic Competitiveness Grants, National SMART Grants, TEACH Grants.

GIFT AID (NON-NEED-BASED) *Total amount:* $6,772,274 (25% state, 73% institutional, 2% external sources). *Receiving aid:* Freshmen: 70% (127). Undergraduates: 69% (394). *Average award:* Freshmen: $10,000. Undergraduates: $10,645. *Scholarships, grants, and awards by category: Academic interests/achievement:* biological sciences, business, education, English, foreign languages, general academic interests/achievements, mathematics, premedicine, religion/biblical studies, social sciences. *Creative arts/performance:* music, theater/drama. *Special achievements/activities:* general special achievements/activities, leadership, memberships. *Special characteristics:* children and siblings of alumni, children of faculty/staff, children with a deceased or disabled parent, ethnic background, first-generation college students, members of minority groups, out-of-state students, relatives of clergy, religious affiliation, siblings of current students. *Tuition waivers:* Full or partial for children of alumni, employees or children of employees.

LOANS *Student loans:* $2,913,225 (36% need-based, 64% non-need-based). 66% of past graduating class borrowed through all loan programs. *Average indebtedness per student:* $24,058. *Average need-based loan:* Freshmen: $3500. Undergraduates: $4750. *Parent loans:* $347,775 (100% non-need-based). *Programs:* Federal Direct (Subsidized and Unsubsidized Stafford, PLUS), FFEL (Subsidized and Unsubsidized Stafford, PLUS), Perkins, state, college/university, alternative loans.

WORK-STUDY *Federal work-study:* Total amount: $94,580; jobs available. *State or other work-study/employment:* Total amount: $15,375 (100% non-need-based). Part-time jobs available.

ATHLETIC AWARDS Total amount: $3,199,173 (100% non-need-based).

APPLYING FOR FINANCIAL AID *Required financial aid forms:* FAFSA, institution's own form, state aid form. *Financial aid deadline (priority):* 4/1. *Notification date:* Continuous beginning 12/15. Students must reply within 2 weeks of notification.

CONTACT Becky Pressley, Director of Financial Aid, Erskine College, PO Box 337, Due West, SC 29639, 864-379-8832 or toll-free 800-241-8721. *Fax:* 864-379-2172. *E-mail:* pressley@erskine.edu.

ESCUELA DE ARTES PLASTICAS DE PUERTO RICO
San Juan, PR

ABOUT THE INSTITUTION Commonwealth-supported, coed. 7 undergraduate majors.

GIFT AID (NEED-BASED) *Scholarships, grants, and awards:* Federal Pell, FSEOG, state, private, college/university gift aid from institutional funds.

APPLYING FOR FINANCIAL AID *Required financial aid form:* FAFSA.

CONTACT Mr. Alfred Diaz Melendez, Financial Aid Administrator, Escuela de Artes Plasticas de Puerto Rico, PO Box 9021112, San Juan, PR 00902-1112, 787-725-8120 Ext. 317. *Fax:* 787-725-3798. *E-mail:* adiaz@eap.edu.

EUGENE BIBLE COLLEGE
Eugene, OR

CONTACT Mrs. Rulena Mellor, Financial Aid Director, Eugene Bible College, 2155 Bailey Hill Road, Eugene, OR 97405-1194, 541-485-1780 Ext. 125 or toll-free 800-322-2638. *Fax:* 541-343-5801. *E-mail:* finaid@ebc.edu.

EUGENE LANG COLLEGE THE NEW SCHOOL FOR LIBERAL ARTS
New York, NY

Tuition & fees: $34,550	Average undergraduate aid package: $30,365

ABOUT THE INSTITUTION Independent, coed. 23 undergraduate majors. Federal methodology is used as a basis for awarding need-based institutional aid.

UNDERGRADUATE EXPENSES for 2009–10 *Comprehensive fee:* $49,810 includes full-time tuition ($33,810), mandatory fees ($740), and room and board ($15,260). *College room only:* $12,260. Room and board charges vary according to board plan and housing facility. *Part-time tuition:* $1150 per credit. Part-time tuition and fees vary according to course load. *Payment plan:* Installment.

FRESHMAN FINANCIAL AID (Fall 2009, est.) 201 applied for aid; of those 86% were deemed to have need. 100% of freshmen with need received aid; of those 3% had need fully met. *Average percent of need met:* 75% (excluding resources awarded to replace EFC). *Average financial aid package:* $31,585 (excluding resources awarded to replace EFC). 8% of all full-time freshmen had no need and received non-need-based gift aid.

UNDERGRADUATE FINANCIAL AID (Fall 2009, est.) 829 applied for aid; of those 90% were deemed to have need. 100% of undergraduates with need received aid; of those 7% had need fully met. *Average percent of need met:* 74% (excluding resources awarded to replace EFC). *Average financial aid package:* $30,365 (excluding resources awarded to replace EFC). 5% of all full-time undergraduates had no need and received non-need-based gift aid.

GIFT AID (NEED-BASED) *Total amount:* $16,230,994 (11% federal, 3% state, 84% institutional, 2% external sources). *Receiving aid:* Freshmen: 56% (164); all full-time undergraduates: 54% (724). *Average award:* Freshmen: $23,130; Undergraduates: $20,637. *Scholarships, grants, and awards:* Federal Pell, FSEOG, state, private, college/university gift aid from institutional funds.

GIFT AID (NON-NEED-BASED) *Total amount:* $1,183,086 (100% institutional). *Receiving aid:* Freshmen: 7% (20). Undergraduates: 1% (17). *Average award:* Freshmen: $2600. Undergraduates: $1280. *Scholarships, grants, and awards by category: Academic interests/achievement:* general academic interests/achievements. *Special achievements/activities:* general special achievements/activities, leadership. *Tuition waivers:* Full or partial for employees or children of employees.

LOANS *Student loans:* $5,146,827 (100% need-based). 70% of past graduating class borrowed through all loan programs. *Average indebtedness per student:* $25,348. *Average need-based loan:* Freshmen: $9913. Undergraduates: $9394. *Parent loans:* $2,152,525 (89% need-based, 11% non-need-based). *Programs:* FFEL (Subsidized and Unsubsidized Stafford, PLUS), Perkins.

WORK-STUDY *Federal work-study:* Total amount: $266,060; jobs available. *State or other work-study/employment:* Part-time jobs available.

APPLYING FOR FINANCIAL AID *Required financial aid forms:* FAFSA, state aid form. *Financial aid deadline:* Continuous. *Notification date:* 3/1. Students must reply within 4 weeks of notification.

CONTACT Financial Aid Counselor, Eugene Lang College The New School for Liberal Arts, 65 West 11th Street, New York, NY 10011, 212-229-5665 or toll-free 877-528-3321.

EUREKA COLLEGE
Eureka, IL

Tuition & fees: N/R	Average undergraduate aid package: $11,105

ABOUT THE INSTITUTION Independent religious, coed. *Awards:* bachelor's degrees. 35 undergraduate majors. *Total enrollment:* 672. Undergraduates: 672. Both federal and institutional methodology are used as a basis for awarding need-based institutional aid.

FRESHMAN FINANCIAL AID (Fall 2009, est.) 130 applied for aid; of those 62% were deemed to have need. 100% of freshmen with need received aid; of those 8% had need fully met. *Average percent of need met:* 60% (excluding resources awarded to replace EFC). *Average financial aid package:* $11,449 (excluding resources awarded to replace EFC). 16% of all full-time freshmen had no need and received non-need-based gift aid.

UNDERGRADUATE FINANCIAL AID (Fall 2009, est.) 617 applied for aid; of those 83% were deemed to have need. 100% of undergraduates with need received aid; of those 13% had need fully met. *Average percent of need met:* 61% (excluding resources awarded to replace EFC). *Average financial aid package:* $11,105 (excluding resources awarded to replace EFC). 15% of all full-time undergraduates had no need and received non-need-based gift aid.

GIFT AID (NEED-BASED) *Total amount:* $4,148,440 (26% federal, 35% state, 37% institutional, 2% external sources). *Receiving aid:* Freshmen: 56% (80); all full-time undergraduates: 72% (510). *Average award:* Freshmen: $7518; Undergraduates: $7062. *Scholarships, grants, and awards:* Federal Pell, FSEOG, state, private, college/university gift aid from institutional funds.

GIFT AID (NON-NEED-BASED) *Total amount:* $983,551 (100% institutional). *Average award:* Freshmen: $3845. Undergraduates: $3232. *Scholarships, grants, and awards by category: Academic interests/achievement:* 590 awards ($2,518,080 total): general academic interests/achievements. *Creative arts/*

performance: 87 awards ($81,293 total): art/fine arts, music, performing arts, theater/drama. *Special achievements/activities:* 20 awards ($293,637 total): leadership. *Special characteristics:* 111 awards ($371,654 total): children and siblings of alumni, children of faculty/staff, religious affiliation, siblings of current students.

LOANS *Student loans:* $4,329,131 (47% need-based, 53% non-need-based). 79% of past graduating class borrowed through all loan programs. *Average indebtedness per student:* $15,390. *Average need-based loan:* Freshmen: $4932. Undergraduates: $3486. *Parent loans:* $936,913 (100% non-need-based). *Programs:* Federal Direct (Subsidized and Unsubsidized Stafford, PLUS), FFEL (Subsidized and Unsubsidized Stafford, PLUS), Perkins, college/university, alternative loans.

WORK-STUDY *Federal work-study:* Total amount: $73,907; 115 jobs averaging $642. *State or other work-study/employment:* Total amount: $221,325 (100% non-need-based). 116 part-time jobs averaging $1908.

APPLYING FOR FINANCIAL AID *Required financial aid form:* FAFSA. *Financial aid deadline (priority):* 4/1. *Notification date:* 5/1. Students must reply within 2 weeks of notification.

CONTACT Ms. Ellen Rigsby, Assistant Dean and Director of Financial Aid, Eureka College, 300 East College Avenue, Eureka, IL 61530, 309-467-6311 or toll-free 888-4-EUREKA. *Fax:* 309-467-6897. *E-mail:* eraid@eureka.edu.

EVANGEL UNIVERSITY
Springfield, MO

Tuition & fees: $15,950	Average undergraduate aid package: $10,564

ABOUT THE INSTITUTION Independent religious, coed. 48 undergraduate majors. Federal methodology is used as a basis for awarding need-based institutional aid.

UNDERGRADUATE EXPENSES for 2010–11 *Comprehensive fee:* $21,950 includes full-time tuition ($15,950) and room and board ($6000). *College room only:* $3100. Full-time tuition and fees vary according to course load. Room and board charges vary according to board plan. *Payment plan:* Installment.

FRESHMAN FINANCIAL AID (Fall 2008) 303 applied for aid; of those 81% were deemed to have need. 99% of freshmen with need received aid; of those .4% had need fully met. *Average percent of need met:* 60% (excluding resources awarded to replace EFC). *Average financial aid package:* $10,651 (excluding resources awarded to replace EFC).

UNDERGRADUATE FINANCIAL AID (Fall 2008) 1,510 applied for aid; of those 87% were deemed to have need. 98% of undergraduates with need received aid; of those 1% had need fully met. *Average percent of need met:* 53% (excluding resources awarded to replace EFC). *Average financial aid package:* $10,564 (excluding resources awarded to replace EFC).

GIFT AID (NEED-BASED) *Total amount:* $6,175,070 (36% federal, 2% state, 49% institutional, 13% external sources). *Receiving aid:* Freshmen: 65% (211); all full-time undergraduates: 66% (1,018). *Average award:* Freshmen: $6347; Undergraduates: $6109. *Scholarships, grants, and awards:* Federal Pell, FSEOG, state, private, college/university gift aid from institutional funds.

GIFT AID (NON-NEED-BASED) *Scholarships, grants, and awards by category: Academic interests/achievement:* 697 awards ($1,746,828 total): business, communication, computer science, education, engineering/technologies, English, foreign languages, general academic interests/achievements, humanities, mathematics, physical sciences, religion/biblical studies, social sciences. *Creative arts/performance:* 132 awards ($270,300 total): art/fine arts, music, theater/drama. *Special achievements/activities:* 223 awards ($131,422 total): cheerleading/drum major, general special achievements/activities, leadership, religious involvement. *Special characteristics:* 334 awards ($1,776,581 total): adult students, children and siblings of alumni, children of educators, children of faculty/staff, general special characteristics, relatives of clergy, religious affiliation. *Tuition waivers:* Full or partial for employees or children of employees.

LOANS *Student loans:* $13,328,476 (65% need-based, 35% non-need-based). 77% of past graduating class borrowed through all loan programs. *Average indebtedness per student:* $30,506. *Average need-based loan:* Freshmen: $3593. Undergraduates: $4572. *Parent loans:* $2,170,702 (100% non-need-based). *Programs:* FFEL (Subsidized and Unsubsidized Stafford, PLUS), Perkins, college/university.

WORK-STUDY *Federal work-study:* Total amount: $396,912; 888 jobs averaging $553. *State or other work-study/employment:* Total amount: $124,390 (100% need-based). 69 part-time jobs averaging $288.

ATHLETIC AWARDS Total amount: $1,607,091 (99% need-based, 1% non-need-based).

APPLYING FOR FINANCIAL AID *Required financial aid form:* FAFSA. *Financial aid deadline:* Continuous. *Notification date:* Continuous beginning 3/15. Students must reply within 3 weeks of notification.

CONTACT Mrs. Dorynda Carpenter, Director of Student Financial Services, Evangel University, 1111 North Glenstone Avenue, Springfield, MO 65802-2191, 417-865-2811 Ext. 7302 or toll-free 800-382-6435 (in-state). *Fax:* 417-575-5478. *E-mail:* carpenterd@evangel.edu.

EVEREST UNIVERSITY
Clearwater, FL

ABOUT THE INSTITUTION Proprietary, coed. *Awards:* associate, bachelor's, and master's degrees. 7 undergraduate majors. *Total enrollment:* 261. Undergraduates: 243.

GIFT AID (NEED-BASED) *Scholarships, grants, and awards:* Federal Pell, FSEOG, state, private, college/university gift aid from institutional funds.

GIFT AID (NON-NEED-BASED) *Scholarships, grants, and awards by category: Academic interests/achievement:* business, computer science, general academic interests/achievements, health fields.

LOANS *Programs:* Federal Direct (Subsidized and Unsubsidized Stafford, PLUS), FFEL (Subsidized and Unsubsidized Stafford, PLUS), Signature Loans.

WORK-STUDY *Federal work-study:* Total amount: $52,395; 8 jobs averaging $6500.

APPLYING FOR FINANCIAL AID *Required financial aid form:* FAFSA.

CONTACT Mr. Will Scott, Director of Student Finance, Everest University, 1199 East Bay Drive, Largo, FL 33770, 727-725-2688 Ext. 166 or toll-free 800-353-FMUS. *Fax:* 727-373-4408. *E-mail:* wscott@cci.edu.

EVEREST UNIVERSITY
Jacksonville, FL

CONTACT Financial Aid Office, Everest University, 8226 Phillips Highway, Jacksonville, FL 32256, 904-731-4949 or toll-free 888-741-4270.

EVEREST UNIVERSITY
Lakeland, FL

CONTACT Brian Jones, Senior Finance Officer, Everest University, Office of Financial Aid, 995 East Memorial Boulevard, Lakeland, FL 33801, 863-686-1444 Ext. 118 or toll-free 877-225-0014 (in-state). *Fax:* 863-682-1077.

EVEREST UNIVERSITY
Melbourne, FL

Tuition & fees: N/R	Average undergraduate aid package: N/A

ABOUT THE INSTITUTION Proprietary, coed. *Awards:* associate, bachelor's, and master's degrees. 10 undergraduate majors. *Total enrollment:* 291. Undergraduates: 287. Federal methodology is used as a basis for awarding need-based institutional aid.

GIFT AID (NEED-BASED) *Scholarships, grants, and awards:* Federal Pell, FSEOG, state, private, college/university gift aid from institutional funds.

GIFT AID (NON-NEED-BASED) *Scholarships, grants, and awards by category: Academic interests/achievement:* business, computer science, health fields. *Creative arts/performance:* cinema/film/broadcasting. *Special characteristics:* children of faculty/staff, children of union members/company employees.

LOANS *Programs:* Federal Direct (Subsidized and Unsubsidized Stafford, PLUS), FFEL (Subsidized and Unsubsidized Stafford, PLUS), college/university.

WORK-STUDY Federal work-study jobs available.

APPLYING FOR FINANCIAL AID *Required financial aid form:* FAFSA. *Financial aid deadline:* Continuous. *Notification date:* Continuous.

CONTACT Ida C. Liska, Director of Student Finance, Everest University, 2401 North Harbor City Boulevard, Melbourne, FL 32935-6657, 321-253-2929 Ext. 142. *E-mail:* iliska@cci.edu.

EVEREST UNIVERSITY
Orlando, FL

CONTACT Ms. Linda Kaisrlik, Director of Student Finance, Everest University, 5421 Diplomat Circle, Orlando, FL 32810-5674, 407-628-5870 Ext. 118 or toll-free 800-628-5870.

EVEREST UNIVERSITY
Orlando, FL

CONTACT Sherri Williams, Director of Financial Aid, Everest University, 2411 Sand Lake Road, Orlando, FL 32809, 407-851-2525 or toll-free 888-471-4270 (out-of-state).

EVEREST UNIVERSITY
Pompano Beach, FL

CONTACT Sharon Scheible, Director of Student Financial Aid, Everest University, 1040 Bayview Drive, Fort Lauderdale, FL 33304-2522, 954-568-1600 Ext. 52 or toll-free 800-468-0168. *Fax:* 954-564-5283. *E-mail:* scheible@cci.edu.

EVEREST UNIVERSITY
Tampa, FL

CONTACT Mr. Rod Kirkwood, Financial Aid Director, Everest University, 3319 West Hillsborough Avenue, Tampa, FL 33614, 813-879-6000 Ext. 145. *Fax:* 813-871-2483. *E-mail:* rkirkwoo@cci.edu.

EVEREST UNIVERSITY
Tampa, FL

CONTACT Ms. Ginger Waymire, Director of Financial Aid, Everest University, 3924 Coconut Palm Drive, Tampa, FL 33619, 813-621-0041 Ext. 118 or toll-free 877-338-0068. *Fax:* 813-621-6283. *E-mail:* gwaymire@cci.edu.

EVERGLADES UNIVERSITY
Altamonte Springs, FL

CONTACT Financial Aid Office, Everglades University, 887 East Altamonte Drive, Altamonte Springs, FL 32701, 407-277-0311 or toll-free 866-289-1078 (out-of-state).

EVERGLADES UNIVERSITY
Boca Raton, FL

ABOUT THE INSTITUTION Independent, coed. 6 undergraduate majors.
GIFT AID (NEED-BASED) *Scholarships, grants, and awards:* Federal Pell, FSEOG, state, private, college/university gift aid from institutional funds.
LOANS *Programs:* Federal Direct (Subsidized and Unsubsidized Stafford, PLUS), FFEL (Subsidized and Unsubsidized Stafford, PLUS), Perkins.
APPLYING FOR FINANCIAL AID *Required financial aid forms:* FAFSA, institution's own form.
CONTACT Seeta Singh Moonilal, Financial Aid Director, Everglades University, 5002 T Rex Avenue, Suite 100, Boca Raton, FL 33431, 561-912-1211 or toll-free 888-772-6077 (out-of-state). *Fax:* 561-912-1191. *E-mail:* seetasm@evergladesuniversity.edu.

EVERGLADES UNIVERSITY
Sarasota, FL

CONTACT Financial Aid Office, Everglades University, 6151 Lake Osprey Drive, Sarasota, FL 34240, 941-907-2262 or toll-free 866-907-2262.

THE EVERGREEN STATE COLLEGE
Olympia, WA

Tuition & fees (WA res): $5959	Average undergraduate aid package: $10,554

ABOUT THE INSTITUTION State-supported, coed. 44 undergraduate majors. Federal methodology is used as a basis for awarding need-based institutional aid.
UNDERGRADUATE EXPENSES for 2009–10 *Tuition, state resident:* full-time $5412; part-time $180.40 per credit hour. *Tuition, nonresident:* full-time $16,440; part-time $547.60 per credit hour. *Required fees:* full-time $547; $7.85 per credit hour or $61 per term. Full-time tuition and fees vary according to location. Part-time tuition and fees vary according to course load and location. *College room and board:* $8052; *Room only:* $5454. Room and board charges vary according to board plan, housing facility, location, and student level. *Payment plan:* Installment.
FRESHMAN FINANCIAL AID (Fall 2009, est.) 416 applied for aid; of those 72% were deemed to have need. 95% of freshmen with need received aid; of those 41% had need fully met. *Average percent of need met:* 78% (excluding resources awarded to replace EFC). *Average financial aid package:* $9330 (excluding resources awarded to replace EFC). 4% of all full-time freshmen had no need and received non-need-based gift aid.
UNDERGRADUATE FINANCIAL AID (Fall 2009, est.) 2,912 applied for aid; of those 85% were deemed to have need. 94% of undergraduates with need received aid; of those 39% had need fully met. *Average percent of need met:* 79% (excluding resources awarded to replace EFC). *Average financial aid package:* $10,554 (excluding resources awarded to replace EFC). 1% of all full-time undergraduates had no need and received non-need-based gift aid.
GIFT AID (NEED-BASED) *Total amount:* $14,535,631 (51% federal, 39% state, 8% institutional, 2% external sources). *Receiving aid:* Freshmen: 34% (199); all full-time undergraduates: 44% (1,827). *Average award:* Freshmen: $8161; Undergraduates: $7978. *Scholarships, grants, and awards:* Federal Pell, FSEOG, state, private, college/university gift aid from institutional funds.
GIFT AID (NON-NEED-BASED) *Total amount:* $1,641,410 (7% state, 31% institutional, 62% external sources). *Receiving aid:* Freshmen: 29% (168). Undergraduates: 13% (515). *Average award:* Freshmen: $4118. Undergraduates: $4128. *Scholarships, grants, and awards by category: Academic interests/achievement:* general academic interests/achievements. *Creative arts/performance:* applied art and design, art/fine arts, creative writing. *Special achievements/activities:* community service, general special achievements/activities. *Special characteristics:* adult students, first-generation college students, members of minority groups, veterans, veterans' children. *Tuition waivers:* Full or partial for employees or children of employees.
LOANS *Student loans:* $12,757,389 (52% need-based, 48% non-need-based). 51% of past graduating class borrowed through all loan programs. *Average indebtedness per student:* $14,310. *Average need-based loan:* Freshmen: $3091. Undergraduates: $3952. *Parent loans:* $2,907,435 (40% need-based, 60% non-need-based). *Programs:* FFEL (Subsidized and Unsubsidized Stafford, PLUS), Perkins, college/university.
WORK-STUDY *Federal work-study:* Total amount: $327,578; jobs available. *State or other work-study/employment:* Total amount: $417,879 (100% need-based). Part-time jobs available.
ATHLETIC AWARDS Total amount: $95,465 (66% need-based, 34% non-need-based).
APPLYING FOR FINANCIAL AID *Required financial aid forms:* FAFSA, institution's own form. *Financial aid deadline (priority):* 3/15. *Notification date:* Continuous beginning 4/1. Students must reply within 6 weeks of notification.
CONTACT Financial Aid Office, The Evergreen State College, 2700 Evergreen Parkway NW, Olympia, WA 98505, 360-867-6205. *Fax:* 360-866-6576. *E-mail:* financialaid@evergreen.edu.

EXCELSIOR COLLEGE
Albany, NY

Tuition & fees: N/R	Average undergraduate aid package: $5237

ABOUT THE INSTITUTION Independent, coed. 40 undergraduate majors. Federal methodology is used as a basis for awarding need-based institutional aid.
UNDERGRADUATE EXPENSES for 2010–11 *Tuition:* part-time $315 per credit hour. *Required fees:* $440 per year. *Payment plan:* Installment.
UNDERGRADUATE FINANCIAL AID (Fall 2008) 85% of undergraduates with need received aid; of those 93% had need fully met. *Average percent of need met:* 90% (excluding resources awarded to replace EFC). *Average financial aid package:* $5237 (excluding resources awarded to replace EFC).

GIFT AID (NEED-BASED) *Total amount:* $1,709,338 (47% federal, 14% state, 24% institutional, 15% external sources). *Receiving aid:* All full-time undergraduates: 352. *Average award:* Undergraduates: $2235. *Scholarships, grants, and awards:* Federal Pell, FSEOG, state, private, college/university gift aid from institutional funds.

GIFT AID (NON-NEED-BASED) *Tuition waivers:* Full or partial for employees or children of employees.

LOANS *Student loans:* $7,344,816 (29% need-based, 71% non-need-based). *Average need-based loan:* Undergraduates: $3501. *Programs:* Federal Direct (Subsidized and Unsubsidized Stafford, PLUS), FFEL (Subsidized and Unsubsidized Stafford), Federal Nursing, college/university, private bank loans.

CONTACT Donna L. Cooper, Director of Financial Aid, Excelsior College, 7 Columbia Circle, Albany, NY 12203-5159, 518-464-8500 or toll-free 888-647-2388. *Fax:* 518-464-8777.

FAIRFIELD UNIVERSITY
Fairfield, CT

Tuition & fees: $37,490	Average undergraduate aid package: $27,082

ABOUT THE INSTITUTION Independent Roman Catholic (Jesuit), coed. 45 undergraduate majors. Both federal and institutional methodology are used as a basis for awarding need-based institutional aid.

UNDERGRADUATE EXPENSES for 2009–10 *One-time required fee:* $60. *Comprehensive fee:* $48,760 includes full-time tuition ($36,900), mandatory fees ($590), and room and board ($11,270). *College room only:* $6730. Room and board charges vary according to board plan and housing facility. *Part-time tuition:* $495 per credit hour. *Part-time fees:* $25 per term. Part-time tuition and fees vary according to course load. *Payment plan:* Installment.

FRESHMAN FINANCIAL AID (Fall 2009, est.) 624 applied for aid; of those 79% were deemed to have need. 98% of freshmen with need received aid; of those 22% had need fully met. *Average percent of need met:* 92% (excluding resources awarded to replace EFC). *Average financial aid package:* $29,123 (excluding resources awarded to replace EFC). 7% of all full-time freshmen had no need and received non-need-based gift aid.

UNDERGRADUATE FINANCIAL AID (Fall 2009, est.) 2,157 applied for aid; of those 84% were deemed to have need. 99% of undergraduates with need received aid; of those 21% had need fully met. *Average percent of need met:* 85% (excluding resources awarded to replace EFC). *Average financial aid package:* $27,082 (excluding resources awarded to replace EFC). 6% of all full-time undergraduates had no need and received non-need-based gift aid.

GIFT AID (NEED-BASED) *Total amount:* $35,781,527 (7% federal, 6% state, 87% institutional). *Receiving aid:* Freshmen: 49% (414); all full-time undergraduates: 49% (1,616). *Average award:* Freshmen: $24,000; Undergraduates: $20,623. *Scholarships, grants, and awards:* Federal Pell, FSEOG, state, private, college/university gift aid from institutional funds, United Negro College Fund.

GIFT AID (NON-NEED-BASED) *Total amount:* $7,943,125 (93% institutional, 7% external sources). *Receiving aid:* Freshmen: 17% (145). Undergraduates: 15% (482). *Average award:* Freshmen: $17,000. Undergraduates: $13,813. *Scholarships, grants, and awards by category: Academic interests/achievement:* 554 awards ($6,707,915 total): biological sciences, business, education, engineering/technologies, foreign languages, general academic interests/achievements, physical sciences. *Creative arts/performance:* 17 awards ($19,929 total): art/fine arts, music, performing arts. *Special achievements/activities:* 20 awards ($101,500 total): religious involvement. *Special characteristics:* 58 awards ($1,443,716 total): children and siblings of alumni, ethnic background, first-generation college students, members of minority groups, parents of current students, religious affiliation. *Tuition waivers:* Full or partial for employees or children of employees.

LOANS *Student loans:* $23,868,148 (41% need-based, 59% non-need-based). 60% of past graduating class borrowed through all loan programs. *Average indebtedness per student:* $35,161. *Average need-based loan:* Freshmen: $4012. Undergraduates: $4671. *Parent loans:* $6,081,517 (100% non-need-based). *Programs:* Federal Direct (Subsidized and Unsubsidized Stafford, PLUS), Perkins, Federal Nursing, alternative loans.

WORK-STUDY *Federal work-study:* Total amount: $1,319,390; 530 jobs averaging $1518.

ATHLETIC AWARDS Total amount: $4,952,320 (100% non-need-based).

APPLYING FOR FINANCIAL AID *Required financial aid forms:* FAFSA, CSS Financial Aid PROFILE, noncustodial (divorced/separated) parent's statement, business/farm supplement. *Financial aid deadline:* 2/15. *Notification date:* 4/1. Students must reply by 5/1.

CONTACT Erin Chiaro, Director of Financial Aid, Fairfield University, 1073 North Benson Road, Fairfield, CT 06824-5195, 203-254-4125. *Fax:* 203-254-4008. *E-mail:* echiaro@fairfield.edu.

FAIRLEIGH DICKINSON UNIVERSITY, COLLEGE AT FLORHAM
Madison, NJ

ABOUT THE INSTITUTION Independent, coed. 32 undergraduate majors.

GIFT AID (NEED-BASED) *Scholarships, grants, and awards:* Federal Pell, FSEOG, state, private, college/university gift aid from institutional funds, Federal Nursing.

LOANS *Programs:* FFEL (Subsidized and Unsubsidized Stafford, PLUS), Perkins, Federal Nursing, state.

APPLYING FOR FINANCIAL AID *Required financial aid form:* FAFSA.

CONTACT Financial Aid Office, Fairleigh Dickinson University, College at Florham, 285 Madison Avenue, Madison, NJ 07940-1099, 973-443-8700 or toll-free 800-338-8803.

FAIRLEIGH DICKINSON UNIVERSITY, METROPOLITAN CAMPUS
Teaneck, NJ

ABOUT THE INSTITUTION Independent, coed. 42 undergraduate majors.

GIFT AID (NEED-BASED) *Scholarships, grants, and awards:* Federal Pell, FSEOG, state, private, college/university gift aid from institutional funds, Federal Nursing.

LOANS *Programs:* FFEL (Subsidized and Unsubsidized Stafford, PLUS), Perkins, Federal Nursing, state.

APPLYING FOR FINANCIAL AID *Required financial aid form:* FAFSA.

CONTACT Financial Aid Office, Fairleigh Dickinson University, Metropolitan Campus, 100 River Road, Teaneck, NJ 07666-1914, 201-692-2363 or toll-free 800-338-8803.

FAIRMONT STATE UNIVERSITY
Fairmont, WV

Tuition & fees (WV res): $5372	Average undergraduate aid package: $7654

ABOUT THE INSTITUTION State-supported, coed. 60 undergraduate majors. Federal methodology is used as a basis for awarding need-based institutional aid.

UNDERGRADUATE EXPENSES for 2009–10 *Tuition, state resident:* full-time $5172; part-time $210 per credit hour. *Tuition, nonresident:* full-time $10,904; part-time $442 per credit hour. *Required fees:* full-time $200. Full-time tuition and fees vary according to degree level and location. Part-time tuition and fees vary according to course load, degree level, and location. *College room and board:* $6900; *Room only:* $3300. Room and board charges vary according to board plan and housing facility. *Payment plan:* Installment.

FRESHMAN FINANCIAL AID (Fall 2008) 643 applied for aid; of those 77% were deemed to have need. 100% of freshmen with need received aid; of those 20% had need fully met. *Average financial aid package:* $7459 (excluding resources awarded to replace EFC). 21% of all full-time freshmen had no need and received non-need-based gift aid.

UNDERGRADUATE FINANCIAL AID (Fall 2008) 2,896 applied for aid; of those 81% were deemed to have need. 100% of undergraduates with need received aid; of those 14% had need fully met. *Average financial aid package:* $7654 (excluding resources awarded to replace EFC). 11% of all full-time undergraduates had no need and received non-need-based gift aid.

GIFT AID (NEED-BASED) *Total amount:* $7,915,441 (72% federal, 20% state, 4% institutional, 4% external sources). *Receiving aid:* Freshmen: 47% (377); all full-time undergraduates: 52% (1,825). *Average award:* Freshmen: $9886; Undergraduates: $11,064. *Scholarships, grants, and awards:* Federal Pell, FSEOG, state, private, college/university gift aid from institutional funds, Academic Competitiveness Grants, National SMART Grants.

GIFT AID (NON-NEED-BASED) *Total amount:* $1,145,091 (74% state, 12% institutional, 14% external sources). *Receiving aid:* Freshmen: 13% (101). Undergraduates: 9% (302). *Average award:* Freshmen: $1136. Undergraduates: $1109. *Tuition waivers:* Full or partial for employees or children of employees.

LOANS *Student loans:* $17,252,978 (42% need-based, 58% non-need-based). *Average need-based loan:* Freshmen: $2694. Undergraduates: $3635. *Parent loans:* $793,854 (70% need-based, 30% non-need-based). *Programs:* Federal Direct (Subsidized and Unsubsidized Stafford, PLUS), Perkins.

WORK-STUDY *Federal work-study:* Total amount: $295,356; jobs available. *State or other work-study/employment:* Part-time jobs available.

ATHLETIC AWARDS Total amount: $398,519 (53% need-based, 47% non-need-based).

APPLYING FOR FINANCIAL AID *Required financial aid form:* FAFSA. *Financial aid deadline (priority):* 3/1. *Notification date:* Continuous beginning 4/1. Students must reply within 2 weeks of notification.

CONTACT Cynthia K. Hudok, Director of Financial Aid and Scholarships, Fairmont State University, 1201 Locust Avenue, Fairmont, WV 26554, 304-367-4213 or toll-free 800-641-5678. *Fax:* 304-367-4584. *E-mail:* financialaid@fairmontstate.edu.

FAITH BAPTIST BIBLE COLLEGE AND THEOLOGICAL SEMINARY
Ankeny, IA

CONTACT Mr. Breck Appell, Director of Financial Assistance, Faith Baptist Bible College and Theological Seminary, 1900 Northwest 4th Street, Ankeny, IA 50021-2152, 515-964-0601 or toll-free 888-FAITH 4U. *Fax:* 515-964-1638.

FAITH THEOLOGICAL SEMINARY
Baltimore, MD

CONTACT Financial Aid Office, Faith Theological Seminary, 529 Walker Avenue, Baltimore, MD 21212, 410-323-6211.

FARMINGDALE STATE COLLEGE
Farmingdale, NY

CONTACT Dionne Walker-Belgrave, Assistant Director of Financial Aid, Farmingdale State College, 2350 Broadhollow Road, Route 110, Farmingdale, NY 11735, 631-420-2328 or toll-free 877-4-FARMINGDALE. *Fax:* 631-420-3662.

FASHION INSTITUTE OF TECHNOLOGY
New York, NY

Tuition & fees (NY res): $5618	Average undergraduate aid package: $11,288

ABOUT THE INSTITUTION State and locally supported, coed, primarily women. 21 undergraduate majors. Federal methodology is used as a basis for awarding need-based institutional aid.

UNDERGRADUATE EXPENSES for 2009–10 *Tuition, state resident:* full-time $5168; part-time $215 per credit hour. *Tuition, nonresident:* full-time $12,604; part-time $525 per credit hour. *Required fees:* full-time $450; $70 per year. Full-time tuition and fees vary according to degree level. Part-time tuition and fees vary according to degree level. *College room and board:* $11,248. Room and board charges vary according to board plan and housing facility. *Payment plan:* Installment.

FRESHMAN FINANCIAL AID (Fall 2009, est.) 829 applied for aid; of those 67% were deemed to have need. 99% of freshmen with need received aid; of those 18% had need fully met. *Average percent of need met:* 70% (excluding resources awarded to replace EFC). *Average financial aid package:* $10,135 (excluding resources awarded to replace EFC). 5% of all full-time freshmen had no need and received non-need-based gift aid.

UNDERGRADUATE FINANCIAL AID (Fall 2009, est.) 4,507 applied for aid; of those 78% were deemed to have need. 99% of undergraduates with need received aid; of those 13% had need fully met. *Average percent of need met:* 66% (excluding resources awarded to replace EFC). *Average financial aid package:* $11,288 (excluding resources awarded to replace EFC). 2% of all full-time undergraduates had no need and received non-need-based gift aid.

GIFT AID (NEED-BASED) *Total amount:* $14,705,933 (64% federal, 31% state, 5% institutional). *Receiving aid:* Freshmen: 37% (394); all full-time undergraduates: 35% (2,534). *Average award:* Freshmen: $5260; Undergraduates: $5327. *Scholarships, grants, and awards:* Federal Pell, FSEOG, state, private, college/university gift aid from institutional funds.

GIFT AID (NON-NEED-BASED) *Total amount:* $1,248,736 (6% institutional, 94% external sources). *Receiving aid:* Freshmen: 14% (143). Undergraduates: 5% (354). *Average award:* Freshmen: $1236. Undergraduates: $1641. *Scholarships, grants, and awards by category:* Creative arts/performance: 160 awards ($77,500 total): applied art and design. *Tuition waivers:* Full or partial for employees or children of employees.

LOANS *Student loans:* $34,548,508 (36% need-based, 64% non-need-based). 57% of past graduating class borrowed through all loan programs. *Average indebtedness per student:* $24,554. *Average need-based loan:* Freshmen: $3384. Undergraduates: $4292. *Parent loans:* $6,500,016 (100% non-need-based). *Programs:* Federal Direct (Subsidized and Unsubsidized Stafford, PLUS), Perkins, alternative loans.

WORK-STUDY *Federal work-study:* Total amount: $813,843; jobs available.

APPLYING FOR FINANCIAL AID *Required financial aid forms:* FAFSA, state aid form. *Financial aid deadline (priority):* 2/15. *Notification date:* Continuous beginning 4/15. Students must reply within 2 weeks of notification.

CONTACT Financial Aid Office, Fashion Institute of Technology, Seventh Avenue at 27th Street, New York, NY 10001-5992, 212-217-3560 or toll-free 800-GOTOFIT (out-of-state).

FAULKNER UNIVERSITY
Montgomery, AL

Tuition & fees: $14,810	Average undergraduate aid package: N/A

ABOUT THE INSTITUTION Independent religious, coed. 30 undergraduate majors. Federal methodology is used as a basis for awarding need-based institutional aid.

UNDERGRADUATE EXPENSES for 2010–11 *Comprehensive fee:* $21,380 includes full-time tuition ($13,740), mandatory fees ($1070), and room and board ($6570). Full-time tuition and fees vary according to program. Room and board charges vary according to board plan and housing facility. *Part-time tuition:* $480 per semester hour. *Part-time fees:* $270 per semester hour; $60 per term. *Payment plan:* Installment.

GIFT AID (NEED-BASED) *Scholarships, grants, and awards:* Federal Pell, FSEOG, state, private, college/university gift aid from institutional funds.

GIFT AID (NON-NEED-BASED) *Scholarships, grants, and awards by category:* Academic interests/achievement: general academic interests/achievements, religion/biblical studies. *Creative arts/performance:* journalism/publications, music, theater/drama. *Special achievements/activities:* cheerleading/drum major, leadership, religious involvement. *Special characteristics:* adult students, children and siblings of alumni, children of faculty/staff, local/state students, relatives of clergy, religious affiliation, siblings of current students. *Tuition waivers:* Full or partial for employees or children of employees, adult students, senior citizens.

LOANS *Programs:* FFEL (Subsidized and Unsubsidized Stafford, PLUS), Perkins.

WORK-STUDY Federal work-study jobs available. *State or other work-study/employment:* Part-time jobs available.

APPLYING FOR FINANCIAL AID *Required financial aid forms:* FAFSA, institution's own form, state aid form. *Financial aid deadline (priority):* 5/1. *Notification date:* 4/1. Students must reply by 8/1.

CONTACT Mr. William G. Jackson II, Director of Financial Aid, Faulkner University, 5345 Atlanta Highway, Montgomery, AL 36109-3398, 334-386-7195 or toll-free 800-879-9816. *Fax:* 334-386-7201. *E-mail:* faid@faulkner.edu.

FAYETTEVILLE STATE UNIVERSITY
Fayetteville, NC

Tuition & fees: N/R	Average undergraduate aid package: N/A

ABOUT THE INSTITUTION State-supported, coed. 39 undergraduate majors. Federal methodology is used as a basis for awarding need-based institutional aid.

FRESHMAN FINANCIAL AID (Fall 2009, est.) 553 applied for aid; of those 92% were deemed to have need. 99% of freshmen with need received aid; of those 8% had need fully met.

UNDERGRADUATE FINANCIAL AID (Fall 2009, est.) 3,901 applied for aid; of those 92% were deemed to have need. 99% of undergraduates with need received aid; of those 6% had need fully met.

GIFT AID (NEED-BASED) *Total amount:* $27,057,104 (56% federal, 27% state, 13% institutional, 4% external sources). *Receiving aid:* Freshmen: 88% (497); all full-time undergraduates: 77% (3,281). *Scholarships, grants, and awards:* Federal Pell, FSEOG, state, private, college/university gift aid from institutional funds, United Negro College Fund, Federal Nursing.

GIFT AID (NON-NEED-BASED) *Total amount:* $278,910 (4% state, 44% institutional, 52% external sources). *Receiving aid:* Freshmen: 64% (363). Undergraduates: 57% (2,413). *Scholarships, grants, and awards by category:* Academic interests/achievement: general academic interests/achievements. Creative arts/performance: music. Special characteristics: local/state students. *Tuition waivers:* Full or partial for employees or children of employees, senior citizens.

LOANS *Student loans:* $32,630,583 (93% need-based, 7% non-need-based). 63% of past graduating class borrowed through all loan programs. *Average indebtedness per student:* $20,185. *Parent loans:* $410,453 (76% need-based, 24% non-need-based). *Programs:* Federal Direct (Subsidized and Unsubsidized Stafford, PLUS), Perkins.

WORK-STUDY *Federal work-study:* Total amount: $312,270; jobs available. *State or other work-study/employment:* Part-time jobs available.

ATHLETIC AWARDS Total amount: $393,117 (81% need-based, 19% non-need-based).

APPLYING FOR FINANCIAL AID *Required financial aid forms:* FAFSA, federal income tax returns, W-2 forms. *Financial aid deadline:* 3/1.

CONTACT Lois L. McKoy, Director of Financial Aid, Fayetteville State University, 1200 Murchison Road, Fayetteville, NC 28301-4298, 910-672-1325 or toll-free 800-222-2594. *Fax:* 910-672-1423. *E-mail:* lmckoy@uncfsu.edu.

FELICIAN COLLEGE
Lodi, NJ

Tuition & fees: $25,050	Average undergraduate aid package: $18,560

ABOUT THE INSTITUTION Independent Roman Catholic, coed. 39 undergraduate majors. Federal methodology is used as a basis for awarding need-based institutional aid.

UNDERGRADUATE EXPENSES for 2009–10 *Comprehensive fee:* $34,750 includes full-time tuition ($23,650), mandatory fees ($1400), and room and board ($9700). *Part-time tuition:* $780 per credit. *Payment plan:* Installment.

FRESHMAN FINANCIAL AID (Fall 2009, est.) 232 applied for aid; of those 91% were deemed to have need. 99% of freshmen with need received aid; of those 8% had need fully met. *Average percent of need met:* 59% (excluding resources awarded to replace EFC). *Average financial aid package:* $21,609 (excluding resources awarded to replace EFC). 8% of all full-time freshmen had no need and received non-need-based gift aid.

UNDERGRADUATE FINANCIAL AID (Fall 2009, est.) 1,177 applied for aid; of those 93% were deemed to have need. 97% of undergraduates with need received aid; of those 11% had need fully met. *Average percent of need met:* 56% (excluding resources awarded to replace EFC). *Average financial aid package:* $18,560 (excluding resources awarded to replace EFC). 6% of all full-time undergraduates had no need and received non-need-based gift aid.

GIFT AID (NEED-BASED) *Total amount:* $9,310,739 (36% federal, 60% state, 4% institutional). *Receiving aid:* Freshmen: 65% (162); all full-time undergraduates: 52% (699). *Average award:* Freshmen: $13,497; Undergraduates: $12,359. *Scholarships, grants, and awards:* Federal Pell, FSEOG, state, private, college/university gift aid from institutional funds.

GIFT AID (NON-NEED-BASED) *Total amount:* $5,108,434 (6% federal, 92% institutional, 2% external sources). *Receiving aid:* Freshmen: 60% (150). Undergraduates: 40% (542). *Average award:* Freshmen: $11,531. Undergraduates: $10,963. *Scholarships, grants, and awards by category:* Academic interests/achievement: 525 awards ($3,560,184 total): business, education, English, general academic interests/achievements, health fields, religion/biblical studies. Special characteristics: 10 awards ($197,208 total): children of faculty/staff, siblings of current students.

LOANS *Student loans:* $15,635,920 (34% need-based, 66% non-need-based). 62% of past graduating class borrowed through all loan programs. *Average indebtedness per student:* $17,026. *Average need-based loan:* Freshmen: $3279.

Undergraduates: $4246. *Parent loans:* $2,439,136 (100% non-need-based). *Programs:* FFEL (Subsidized and Unsubsidized Stafford, PLUS), state.

WORK-STUDY *Federal work-study:* Total amount: $206,888; 93 jobs averaging $2065. *State or other work-study/employment:* 90 part-time jobs averaging $2652.

ATHLETIC AWARDS Total amount: $1,637,572 (100% non-need-based).

APPLYING FOR FINANCIAL AID *Required financial aid form:* FAFSA. *Financial aid deadline:* Continuous. *Notification date:* Continuous beginning 4/1.

CONTACT Janet Mariano Merli, Financial Aid Director, Felician College, 262 South Main Street, Lodi, NJ 07644, 201-559-6040. *Fax:* 201-559-6025. *E-mail:* merlij@felician.edu.

FERRIS STATE UNIVERSITY
Big Rapids, MI

Tuition & fees: N/R	Average undergraduate aid package: $15,531

ABOUT THE INSTITUTION State-supported, coed. 119 undergraduate majors. Federal methodology is used as a basis for awarding need-based institutional aid.

FRESHMAN FINANCIAL AID (Fall 2009, est.) 1,502 applied for aid; of those 82% were deemed to have need. 99% of freshmen with need received aid; of those 16% had need fully met. *Average percent of need met:* 88% (excluding resources awarded to replace EFC). *Average financial aid package:* $16,355 (excluding resources awarded to replace EFC). 14% of all full-time freshmen had no need and received non-need-based gift aid.

UNDERGRADUATE FINANCIAL AID (Fall 2009, est.) 6,843 applied for aid; of those 79% were deemed to have need. 99% of undergraduates with need received aid; of those 15% had need fully met. *Average percent of need met:* 84% (excluding resources awarded to replace EFC). *Average financial aid package:* $15,531 (excluding resources awarded to replace EFC). 10% of all full-time undergraduates had no need and received non-need-based gift aid.

GIFT AID (NEED-BASED) *Total amount:* $25,426,126 (82% federal, 2% state, 16% institutional). *Receiving aid:* Freshmen: 55% (888); all full-time undergraduates: 50% (3,748). *Average award:* Freshmen: $5154; Undergraduates: $4830. *Scholarships, grants, and awards:* Federal Pell, FSEOG, state, private, college/university gift aid from institutional funds.

GIFT AID (NON-NEED-BASED) *Total amount:* $13,499,764 (33% state, 59% institutional, 8% external sources). *Receiving aid:* Freshmen: 52% (844). Undergraduates: 36% (2,721). *Average award:* Freshmen: $4374. Undergraduates: $3690. *Scholarships, grants, and awards by category:* Academic interests/achievement: 2,551 awards ($7,733,169 total): agriculture, architecture, biological sciences, business, communication, computer science, education, engineering/technologies, general academic interests/achievements, health fields, mathematics. Creative arts/performance: 12 awards ($6440 total): applied art and design, art/fine arts, debating, general creative arts/performance, journalism/publications, music, theater/drama. Special achievements/activities: 221 awards ($92,010 total): general special achievements/activities, memberships. Special characteristics: 161 awards ($143,825 total): adult students, children and siblings of alumni, ethnic background, general special characteristics, international students, local/state students, members of minority groups, previous college experience, veterans. *Tuition waivers:* Full or partial for employees or children of employees.

LOANS *Student loans:* $76,345,957 (40% need-based, 60% non-need-based). 76% of past graduating class borrowed through all loan programs. *Average indebtedness per student:* $34,767. *Average need-based loan:* Freshmen: $3313. Undergraduates: $4292. *Parent loans:* $9,314,534 (100% non-need-based). *Programs:* Federal Direct (Subsidized and Unsubsidized Stafford, PLUS), Perkins, Federal Nursing, college/university, alternative loans.

WORK-STUDY *Federal work-study:* Total amount: $1,430,729; 675 jobs averaging $2150. *State or other work-study/employment:* 27 part-time jobs averaging $1166.

ATHLETIC AWARDS Total amount: $1,899,299 (100% non-need-based).

APPLYING FOR FINANCIAL AID *Required financial aid form:* FAFSA. *Financial aid deadline (priority):* 3/1. *Notification date:* Continuous beginning 4/1. Students must reply within 3 weeks of notification.

CONTACT Nancy Wencl, Coordinator of Federal Aid Programs, Ferris State University, 1201 South State Street, Big Rapids, MI 49307-2020, 231-591-2100 or toll-free 800-433-7747. *Fax:* 231-591-2950. *E-mail:* wencln@ferris.edu.

FERRUM COLLEGE
Ferrum, VA

Tuition & fees: $23,565	Average undergraduate aid package: $19,884

ABOUT THE INSTITUTION Independent United Methodist, coed. 33 undergraduate majors. Both federal and institutional methodology are used as a basis for awarding need-based institutional aid.

UNDERGRADUATE EXPENSES for 2009–10 *Comprehensive fee:* $31,195 includes full-time tuition ($23,520), mandatory fees ($45), and room and board ($7630). *College room only:* $3880. Full-time tuition and fees vary according to course load. Room and board charges vary according to housing facility. *Part-time tuition:* $470 per credit hour. Part-time tuition and fees vary according to course load. *Payment plan:* Installment.

FRESHMAN FINANCIAL AID (Fall 2009, est.) 540 applied for aid; of those 91% were deemed to have need. 100% of freshmen with need received aid. *Average percent of need met:* 87% (excluding resources awarded to replace EFC). *Average financial aid package:* $20,634 (excluding resources awarded to replace EFC). 11% of all full-time freshmen had no need and received non-need-based gift aid.

UNDERGRADUATE FINANCIAL AID (Fall 2009, est.) 1,362 applied for aid; of those 92% were deemed to have need. 100% of undergraduates with need received aid. *Average percent of need met:* 88% (excluding resources awarded to replace EFC). *Average financial aid package:* $19,884 (excluding resources awarded to replace EFC). 12% of all full-time undergraduates had no need and received non-need-based gift aid.

GIFT AID (NEED-BASED) *Total amount:* $18,627,076 (18% federal, 16% state, 63% institutional, 3% external sources). *Receiving aid:* Freshmen: 89% (490); all full-time undergraduates: 88% (1,252). *Average award:* Freshmen: $15,957; Undergraduates: $14,425. *Scholarships, grants, and awards:* Federal Pell, FSEOG, state, private, college/university gift aid from institutional funds.

GIFT AID (NON-NEED-BASED) *Total amount:* $1,326,911 (27% state, 68% institutional, 5% external sources). *Receiving aid:* Freshmen: 84% (466). Undergraduates: 81% (1,158). *Average award:* Freshmen: $9618. Undergraduates: $7151. *Scholarships, grants, and awards by category: Academic interests/achievement:* $6,931,594 total: general academic interests/achievements. *Special achievements/activities:* $45,600 total: general special achievements/activities, religious involvement. *Special characteristics:* $4,190,740 total: children of faculty/staff, international students, local/state students, relatives of clergy, religious affiliation. *Tuition waivers:* Full or partial for employees or children of employees, senior citizens.

LOANS *Student loans:* $9,763,303 (95% need-based, 5% non-need-based). 82% of past graduating class borrowed through all loan programs. *Average indebtedness per student:* $29,040. *Average need-based loan:* Freshmen: $2833. Undergraduates: $3674. *Parent loans:* $3,242,403 (84% need-based, 16% non-need-based). *Programs:* Federal Direct (Subsidized and Unsubsidized Stafford, PLUS), FFEL (Subsidized and Unsubsidized Stafford, PLUS), Perkins.

WORK-STUDY *Federal work-study:* Total amount: $1,464,520; 866 jobs averaging $1692.

APPLYING FOR FINANCIAL AID *Required financial aid forms:* FAFSA, state aid form. *Financial aid deadline (priority):* 3/1. *Notification date:* Continuous.

CONTACT Heather Hollandsworth, Director of Financial Aid, Ferrum College, PO Box 1000, Ferrum, VA 24088-9001, 540-365-4282 or toll-free 800-868-9797. *Fax:* 540-365-4266. *E-mail:* hhollandsworth@ferrum.edu.

FINLANDIA UNIVERSITY
Hancock, MI

ABOUT THE INSTITUTION Independent religious, coed. *Awards:* associate and bachelor's degrees. 15 undergraduate majors. *Total enrollment:* 545. Undergraduates: 545. Freshmen: 82.

GIFT AID (NEED-BASED) *Scholarships, grants, and awards:* Federal Pell, FSEOG, state, private, college/university gift aid from institutional funds.

GIFT AID (NON-NEED-BASED) *Scholarships, grants, and awards by category: Academic interests/achievement:* general academic interests/achievements. *Creative arts/performance:* art/fine arts, general creative arts/performance. *Special achievements/activities:* community service, general special achievements/activities, leadership, religious involvement. *Special characteristics:* children of

current students, children of faculty/staff, first-generation college students, international students, religious affiliation, siblings of current students, spouses of current students, twins.

LOANS *Programs:* FFEL (Subsidized and Unsubsidized Stafford, PLUS), state, private loans.

WORK-STUDY *Federal work-study:* Total amount: $240,000; 154 jobs averaging $1600. *State or other work-study/employment:* Total amount: $21,000 (100% need-based). 25 part-time jobs averaging $1200.

APPLYING FOR FINANCIAL AID *Required financial aid forms:* FAFSA, institution's own form.

CONTACT Sandra Turnquist, Director of Financial Aid, Finlandia University, 601 Quincy Street, Hancock, MI 49930, 906-487-7240 or toll-free 877-202-5491. *Fax:* 906-487-7509. *E-mail:* sandy.turnquist@finlandia.edu.

FISHER COLLEGE
Boston, MA

CONTACT Jacqueline Johnson, Associate Director of Financial Aid, Fisher College, 118 Beacon Street, Boston, MA 02116, 617-236-8800 Ext. 424 or toll-free 800-821-3050 (in-state), 800-446-1226 (out-of-state). *Fax:* 617-236-8858. *E-mail:* jjohnson@fisher.edu.

FISK UNIVERSITY
Nashville, TN

Tuition & fees: $18,345	Average undergraduate aid package: $14,957

ABOUT THE INSTITUTION Independent religious, coed. 20 undergraduate majors. Both federal and institutional methodology are used as a basis for awarding need-based institutional aid.

UNDERGRADUATE EXPENSES for 2010–11 *Comprehensive fee:* $26,930 includes full-time tuition ($16,835), mandatory fees ($1510), and room and board ($8585). *College room only:* $4975. Full-time tuition and fees vary according to course load. Room and board charges vary according to board plan. Part-time tuition and fees vary according to course load. *Payment plan:* Installment.

FRESHMAN FINANCIAL AID (Fall 2009, est.) 86 applied for aid; of those 100% were deemed to have need. 100% of freshmen with need received aid; of those 20% had need fully met. *Average percent of need met:* 65% (excluding resources awarded to replace EFC). *Average financial aid package:* $15,576 (excluding resources awarded to replace EFC).

UNDERGRADUATE FINANCIAL AID (Fall 2009, est.) 541 applied for aid; of those 100% were deemed to have need. 100% of undergraduates with need received aid; of those 27% had need fully met. *Average percent of need met:* 71% (excluding resources awarded to replace EFC). *Average financial aid package:* $14,957 (excluding resources awarded to replace EFC).

GIFT AID (NEED-BASED) *Total amount:* $5,922,355 (30% federal, 7% state, 57% institutional, 6% external sources). *Receiving aid:* Freshmen: 93% (86); all full-time undergraduates: 88% (503). *Average award:* Freshmen: $12,661; Undergraduates: $12,028. *Scholarships, grants, and awards:* Federal Pell, FSEOG, state, private, college/university gift aid from institutional funds, United Negro College Fund.

GIFT AID (NON-NEED-BASED) *Tuition waivers:* Full or partial for employees or children of employees.

LOANS *Student loans:* $3,390,434 (100% need-based). 77% of past graduating class borrowed through all loan programs. *Average indebtedness per student:* $27,345. *Average need-based loan:* Freshmen: $3202. Undergraduates: $4387. *Parent loans:* $1,819,218 (100% need-based). *Programs:* Federal Direct (Subsidized and Unsubsidized Stafford, PLUS), Perkins.

WORK-STUDY *Federal work-study:* Total amount: $282,902; 181 jobs averaging $1573.

APPLYING FOR FINANCIAL AID *Required financial aid form:* FAFSA. *Financial aid deadline:* 6/1 (priority: 3/1). *Notification date:* Continuous beginning 4/1. Students must reply within 2 weeks of notification.

CONTACT Russelle Keese, Director of Financial Aid, Fisk University, 1000 17th Avenue North, Nashville, TN 37208-3051, 615-329-8735 or toll-free 800-443-FISK. *E-mail:* finaid@fisk.edu.

FITCHBURG STATE COLLEGE
Fitchburg, MA

Tuition & fees (MA res): $6900   **Average undergraduate aid package: $8238**

ABOUT THE INSTITUTION State-supported, coed. 56 undergraduate majors. Federal methodology is used as a basis for awarding need-based institutional aid.

UNDERGRADUATE EXPENSES for 2009–10 *Tuition, state resident:* full-time $970; part-time $40.42 per credit. *Tuition, nonresident:* full-time $7050; part-time $293.75 per credit. *Required fees:* full-time $5930; $247.08 per credit. Full-time tuition and fees vary according to reciprocity agreements. Part-time tuition and fees vary according to class time and reciprocity agreements. *College room and board:* $7632. Room and board charges vary according to board plan and housing facility. *Payment plan:* Installment.

FRESHMAN FINANCIAL AID (Fall 2008) 727 applied for aid; of those 61% were deemed to have need. 98% of freshmen with need received aid; of those 93% had need fully met. *Average percent of need met:* 93% (excluding resources awarded to replace EFC). *Average financial aid package:* $8402 (excluding resources awarded to replace EFC). 7% of all full-time freshmen had no need and received non-need-based gift aid.

UNDERGRADUATE FINANCIAL AID (Fall 2008) 2,844 applied for aid; of those 60% were deemed to have need. 97% of undergraduates with need received aid; of those 93% had need fully met. *Average percent of need met:* 93% (excluding resources awarded to replace EFC). *Average financial aid package:* $8238 (excluding resources awarded to replace EFC). 2% of all full-time undergraduates had no need and received non-need-based gift aid.

GIFT AID (NEED-BASED) *Total amount:* $6,513,105 (47% federal, 22% state, 31% institutional). *Receiving aid:* Freshmen: 45% (351); all full-time undergraduates: 39% (1,263). *Average award:* Freshmen: $4391; Undergraduates: $3947. *Scholarships, grants, and awards:* Federal Pell, FSEOG, state, private, college/university gift aid from institutional funds.

GIFT AID (NON-NEED-BASED) *Total amount:* $1,557,867 (13% state, 22% institutional, 65% external sources). *Receiving aid:* Freshmen: 10% (81). Undergraduates: 4% (136). *Average award:* Freshmen: $1431. Undergraduates: $1338. *Scholarships, grants, and awards by category: Academic interests/achievement:* 154 awards ($198,511 total): biological sciences, business, communication, computer science, education, English, general academic interests/achievements, health fields, mathematics, social sciences. *Creative arts/performance:* 1 award ($250 total): general creative arts/performance. *Special achievements/activities:* 56 awards ($94,075 total): general special achievements/activities, leadership. *Special characteristics:* 39 awards ($17,726 total): adult students, children and siblings of alumni, local/state students. *Tuition waivers:* Full or partial for employees or children of employees, senior citizens.

LOANS *Student loans:* $15,767,394 (39% need-based, 61% non-need-based). 68% of past graduating class borrowed through all loan programs. *Average indebtedness per student:* $18,177. *Average need-based loan:* Freshmen: $2463. Undergraduates: $3286. *Parent loans:* $1,097,560 (100% non-need-based). *Programs:* Federal Direct (Subsidized and Unsubsidized Stafford, PLUS), Perkins, Federal Nursing, state.

WORK-STUDY *Federal work-study:* Total amount: $375,000; 231 jobs averaging $1680.

APPLYING FOR FINANCIAL AID *Required financial aid form:* FAFSA. *Financial aid deadline (priority):* 3/1. *Notification date:* Continuous beginning 3/15.

CONTACT Lynn Beauregard, Director of Financial Aid and Student Accounts, Fitchburg State College, 160 Pearl Street, Fitchburg, MA 01420-2697, 978-665-3156 or toll-free 800-705-9692. *Fax:* 978-665-3559. *E-mail:* finaid@fsc.edu.

FIVE TOWNS COLLEGE
Dix Hills, NY

Tuition & fees: $17,750   **Average undergraduate aid package: $8100**

ABOUT THE INSTITUTION Independent, coed. 17 undergraduate majors. Federal methodology is used as a basis for awarding need-based institutional aid.

UNDERGRADUATE EXPENSES for 2010–11 *One-time required fee:* $500. *Comprehensive fee:* $30,050 includes full-time tuition ($17,400), mandatory fees ($350), and room and board ($12,300). *College room only:* $7800. Full-time tuition and fees vary according to course load, degree level, and program. Room and board charges vary according to board plan. *Part-time*

tuition: $725 per credit hour. *Part-time fees:* $60 per term. Part-time tuition and fees vary according to course load, degree level, and program. *Payment plan:* Installment.

FRESHMAN FINANCIAL AID (Fall 2009, est.) 301 applied for aid; of those 85% were deemed to have need. 100% of freshmen with need received aid; of those 70% had need fully met. *Average percent of need met:* 48% (excluding resources awarded to replace EFC). *Average financial aid package:* $5400 (excluding resources awarded to replace EFC). 9% of all full-time freshmen had no need and received non-need-based gift aid.

UNDERGRADUATE FINANCIAL AID (Fall 2009, est.) 939 applied for aid; of those 84% were deemed to have need. 100% of undergraduates with need received aid; of those 59% had need fully met. *Average percent of need met:* 48% (excluding resources awarded to replace EFC). *Average financial aid package:* $8100 (excluding resources awarded to replace EFC). 6% of all full-time undergraduates had no need and received non-need-based gift aid.

GIFT AID (NEED-BASED) *Total amount:* $5,724,000 (24% federal, 29% state, 44% institutional, 3% external sources). *Receiving aid:* Freshmen: 65% (231); all full-time undergraduates: 66% (711). *Average award:* Freshmen: $7800; Undergraduates: $5500. *Scholarships, grants, and awards:* Federal Pell, FSEOG, state, private, college/university gift aid from institutional funds.

GIFT AID (NON-NEED-BASED) *Total amount:* $46,000 (87% federal, 13% institutional). *Receiving aid:* Freshmen: 41% (143). Undergraduates: 41% (442). *Average award:* Freshmen: $2170. Undergraduates: $2400. *Scholarships, grants, and awards by category: Academic interests/achievement:* 253 awards ($1,172,532 total): business, education, general academic interests/achievements. *Creative arts/performance:* 242 awards ($823,514 total): cinema/film/broadcasting, music, theater/drama. *Special characteristics:* 11 awards ($17,000 total): siblings of current students. *Tuition waivers:* Full or partial for employees or children of employees.

LOANS *Student loans:* $7,605,200 (39% need-based, 61% non-need-based). 80% of past graduating class borrowed through all loan programs. *Average indebtedness per student:* $19,000. *Average need-based loan:* Freshmen: $3500. Undergraduates: $3700. *Parent loans:* $3,966,000 (100% non-need-based). *Programs:* Federal Direct (Subsidized and Unsubsidized Stafford, PLUS).

WORK-STUDY *Federal work-study:* Total amount: $131,758; 95 jobs averaging $1387. *State or other work-study/employment:* Total amount: $80,000 (100% non-need-based). Part-time jobs available.

APPLYING FOR FINANCIAL AID *Required financial aid forms:* FAFSA, institution's own form, state aid form. *Financial aid deadline (priority):* 3/31. *Notification date:* Continuous beginning 5/1. Students must reply within 4 weeks of notification.

CONTACT Ms. Mary Venezia, Financial Aid Director, Five Towns College, 305 North Service Road, Dix Hills, NY 11746-6055, 631-656-2113. *Fax:* 631-656-2191. *E-mail:* mvenezia@ftc.edu.

FLAGLER COLLEGE
St. Augustine, FL

Tuition & fees: $13,330   **Average undergraduate aid package: $17,705**

ABOUT THE INSTITUTION Independent, coed. 24 undergraduate majors. Federal methodology is used as a basis for awarding need-based institutional aid.

UNDERGRADUATE EXPENSES for 2009–10 *Comprehensive fee:* $20,520 includes full-time tuition ($13,330) and room and board ($7190). Room and board charges vary according to board plan. *Part-time tuition:* $445 per credit hour.

FRESHMAN FINANCIAL AID (Fall 2009, est.) 460 applied for aid; of those 72% were deemed to have need. 100% of freshmen with need received aid; of those 8% had need fully met. *Average percent of need met:* 61% (excluding resources awarded to replace EFC). *Average financial aid package:* $12,302 (excluding resources awarded to replace EFC). 2% of all full-time freshmen had no need and received non-need-based gift aid.

UNDERGRADUATE FINANCIAL AID (Fall 2009, est.) 1,845 applied for aid; of those 77% were deemed to have need. 99% of undergraduates with need received aid; of those 12% had need fully met. *Average percent of need met:* 91% (excluding resources awarded to replace EFC). *Average financial aid package:* $17,705 (excluding resources awarded to replace EFC). 7% of all full-time undergraduates had no need and received non-need-based gift aid.

GIFT AID (NEED-BASED) *Total amount:* $9,136,649 (30% federal, 46% state, 22% institutional, 2% external sources). *Receiving aid:* Freshmen: 50% (282); all full-time undergraduates: 39% (1,048). *Average award:* Freshmen: $5378;

Undergraduates: $4664. *Scholarships, grants, and awards:* Federal Pell, FSEOG, state, private, college/university gift aid from institutional funds.

GIFT AID (NON-NEED-BASED) *Total amount:* $3,833,774 (82% state, 14% institutional, 4% external sources). *Receiving aid:* Freshmen: 43% (244). Undergraduates: 38% (1,039). *Average award:* Freshmen: $4000. Undergraduates: $1731. *Scholarships, grants, and awards by category: Academic interests/achievement:* 134 awards ($192,600 total): business, communication, education, English, foreign languages, general academic interests/achievements, humanities, religion/biblical studies, social sciences. *Creative arts/performance:* 13 awards ($13,400 total): applied art and design, art/fine arts, cinema/film/broadcasting, performing arts, theater/drama. *Special achievements/activities:* 67 awards ($143,600 total): general special achievements/activities, leadership, memberships, religious involvement. *Special characteristics:* 304 awards ($677,742 total): children of educators, children of faculty/staff, ethnic background, first-generation college students, general special characteristics, local/state students, members of minority groups, out-of-state students. *Tuition waivers:* Full or partial for employees or children of employees.

LOANS *Student loans:* $10,597,938 (74% need-based, 26% non-need-based). 55% of past graduating class borrowed through all loan programs. *Average indebtedness per student:* $18,190. *Average need-based loan:* Freshmen: $3203. Undergraduates: $4151. *Parent loans:* $1,997,527 (62% need-based, 38% non-need-based). *Programs:* Federal Direct (Subsidized and Unsubsidized Stafford, PLUS), Perkins.

WORK-STUDY *Federal work-study:* Total amount: $230,900; 193 jobs averaging $1321. *State or other work-study/employment:* Total amount: $80,900 (12% need-based, 88% non-need-based). 58 part-time jobs averaging $1320.

ATHLETIC AWARDS Total amount: $1,021,010 (37% need-based, 63% non-need-based).

APPLYING FOR FINANCIAL AID *Required financial aid forms:* FAFSA, institution's own form. *Financial aid deadline (priority):* 4/1. *Notification date:* Continuous. Students must reply within 2 weeks of notification.

CONTACT Ms. Sheia Pleasant, Assistant Director of Financial Aid, Flagler College, PO Box 1027, St. Augustine, FL 32085-1027, 904-819-6225 or toll-free 800-304-4208. *Fax:* 904-819-6453. *E-mail:* spleasant@flagler.edu.

FLORIDA AGRICULTURAL AND MECHANICAL UNIVERSITY
Tallahassee, FL

Tuition & fees: N/R	Average undergraduate aid package: $12,216

ABOUT THE INSTITUTION State-supported, coed. 79 undergraduate majors. Federal methodology is used as a basis for awarding need-based institutional aid.

FRESHMAN FINANCIAL AID (Fall 2008) 1,705 applied for aid; of those 97% were deemed to have need. 99% of freshmen with need received aid; of those 24% had need fully met. *Average percent of need met:* 75% (excluding resources awarded to replace EFC). *Average financial aid package:* $12,409 (excluding resources awarded to replace EFC). 6% of all full-time freshmen had no need and received non-need-based gift aid.

UNDERGRADUATE FINANCIAL AID (Fall 2008) 6,899 applied for aid; of those 97% were deemed to have need. 99% of undergraduates with need received aid; of those 30% had need fully met. *Average percent of need met:* 80% (excluding resources awarded to replace EFC). *Average financial aid package:* $12,216 (excluding resources awarded to replace EFC). 4% of all full-time undergraduates had no need and received non-need-based gift aid.

GIFT AID (NEED-BASED) *Total amount:* $26,587,036 (81% federal, 17% state, 1% institutional, 1% external sources). *Receiving aid:* Freshmen: 58% (1,222); all full-time undergraduates: 58% (5,079). *Average award:* Freshmen: $5821; Undergraduates: $5077. *Scholarships, grants, and awards:* Federal Pell, FSEOG, state, private, college/university gift aid from institutional funds, United Negro College Fund, Federal Nursing.

GIFT AID (NON-NEED-BASED) *Total amount:* $13,772,386 (32% state, 65% institutional, 3% external sources). *Receiving aid:* Freshmen: 36% (745). Undergraduates: 25% (2,178). *Average award:* Freshmen: $5479. Undergraduates: $5285. *Scholarships, grants, and awards by category: Academic interests/achievement:* agriculture, business, engineering/technologies, general academic interests/achievements, health fields. *Tuition waivers:* Full or partial for employees or children of employees, senior citizens.

LOANS *Student loans:* $48,382,791 (47% need-based, 53% non-need-based). 81% of past graduating class borrowed through all loan programs. *Average indebtedness per student:* $27,253. *Average need-based loan:* Freshmen: $3161. Undergraduates: $3982. *Parent loans:* $5,511,123 (100% non-need-based). *Programs:* Federal Direct (Subsidized and Unsubsidized Stafford, PLUS), Perkins.

WORK-STUDY *Federal work-study:* Total amount: $631,304; 304 jobs averaging $2077.

ATHLETIC AWARDS Total amount: $1,544,219 (100% non-need-based).

APPLYING FOR FINANCIAL AID *Required financial aid form:* FAFSA. *Financial aid deadline:* 6/30 (priority: 3/1). *Notification date:* Continuous. Students must reply within 2 weeks of notification.

CONTACT Dr. Marcia D. Boyd, Director of Student Financial Aid, Florida Agricultural and Mechanical University, 101 Foote-Hilyer Administration Center, Tallahassee, FL 32307, 850-599-3730. *E-mail:* marcia.boyd@famu.edu.

FLORIDA ATLANTIC UNIVERSITY
Boca Raton, FL

Tuition & fees (FL res): $4187	Average undergraduate aid package: $8271

ABOUT THE INSTITUTION State-supported, coed. 65 undergraduate majors. Federal methodology is used as a basis for awarding need-based institutional aid.

UNDERGRADUATE EXPENSES for 2009–10 *Tuition, state resident:* full-time $4187; part-time $139.55 per credit hour. *Tuition, nonresident:* full-time $17,532; part-time $584.41 per credit hour. Full-time tuition and fees vary according to course load. Part-time tuition and fees vary according to course load. *College room and board:* $9582. Room and board charges vary according to board plan and housing facility. *Payment plans:* Tuition prepayment, installment, deferred payment.

FRESHMAN FINANCIAL AID (Fall 2009, est.) 1,717 applied for aid; of those 70% were deemed to have need. 99% of freshmen with need received aid; of those 13% had need fully met. *Average percent of need met:* 72% (excluding resources awarded to replace EFC). *Average financial aid package:* $8847 (excluding resources awarded to replace EFC).

UNDERGRADUATE FINANCIAL AID (Fall 2009, est.) 8,376 applied for aid; of those 82% were deemed to have need. 98% of undergraduates with need received aid; of those 11% had need fully met. *Average percent of need met:* 69% (excluding resources awarded to replace EFC). *Average financial aid package:* $8271 (excluding resources awarded to replace EFC).

GIFT AID (NEED-BASED) *Total amount:* $57,153,316 (50% federal, 33% state, 13% institutional, 4% external sources). *Receiving aid:* Freshmen: 47% (1,134); all full-time undergraduates: 44% (5,657). *Average award:* Freshmen: $7158; Undergraduates: $6358. *Scholarships, grants, and awards:* Federal Pell, FSEOG, state, private, college/university gift aid from institutional funds, Federal Nursing.

GIFT AID (NON-NEED-BASED) *Scholarships, grants, and awards by category: Academic interests/achievement:* business, engineering/technologies, general academic interests/achievements, physical sciences, social sciences. *Creative arts/performance:* music, performing arts. *Tuition waivers:* Full or partial for employees or children of employees, senior citizens.

LOANS *Student loans:* $61,261,624 (43% need-based, 57% non-need-based). 47% of past graduating class borrowed through all loan programs. *Average indebtedness per student:* $17,338. *Average need-based loan:* Freshmen: $2919. Undergraduates: $3972. *Parent loans:* $1,928,004 (100% non-need-based). *Programs:* FFEL (Subsidized and Unsubsidized Stafford, PLUS), Perkins, college/university.

WORK-STUDY *Federal work-study:* Total amount: $646,234; 171 jobs averaging $3163. *State or other work-study/employment:* Total amount: $11,925 (100% need-based). 4 part-time jobs averaging $3023.

ATHLETIC AWARDS Total amount: $2,589,051 (100% need-based).

APPLYING FOR FINANCIAL AID *Required financial aid form:* FAFSA. *Financial aid deadline (priority):* 3/1. *Notification date:* Continuous beginning 5/1. Students must reply within 3 weeks of notification.

CONTACT Carole Pfeilsticker, Director of Student Financial Aid, Florida Atlantic University, 777 Glades Road, Boca Raton, FL 33431-0991, 561-297-3528 or toll-free 800-299-4FAU. *E-mail:* pfeilsti@fau.edu.

FLORIDA CHRISTIAN COLLEGE
Kissimmee, FL

CONTACT Ms. Sandra Peppard, Director of Student Financial Aid, Florida Christian College, 1011 Bill Beck Boulevard, Kissimmee, FL 34744-5301, 407-847-8966 Ext. 365 or toll-free 888-GO-TO-FCC (in-state). *Fax:* 407-847-3925. *E-mail:* sandi.peppard@fcc.edu.

FLORIDA COLLEGE
Temple Terrace, FL

Tuition & fees: $12,150	Average undergraduate aid package: $11,396

ABOUT THE INSTITUTION Independent, coed. 5 undergraduate majors. Both federal and institutional methodology are used as a basis for awarding need-based institutional aid.

UNDERGRADUATE EXPENSES for 2010–11 *One-time required fee:* $150. *Comprehensive fee:* $18,590 includes full-time tuition ($11,400), mandatory fees ($750), and room and board ($6440). Room and board charges vary according to board plan and housing facility. *Part-time tuition:* $450 per credit hour. Part-time tuition and fees vary according to course load. *Payment plan:* Installment.

FRESHMAN FINANCIAL AID (Fall 2009, est.) 97 applied for aid; of those 99% were deemed to have need. 100% of freshmen with need received aid; of those 6% had need fully met. *Average percent of need met:* 29% (excluding resources awarded to replace EFC). *Average financial aid package:* $11,126 (excluding resources awarded to replace EFC). 33% of all full-time freshmen had no need and received non-need-based gift aid.

UNDERGRADUATE FINANCIAL AID (Fall 2009, est.) 267 applied for aid; of those 95% were deemed to have need. 100% of undergraduates with need received aid; of those 11% had need fully met. *Average percent of need met:* 30% (excluding resources awarded to replace EFC). *Average financial aid package:* $11,396 (excluding resources awarded to replace EFC). 28% of all full-time undergraduates had no need and received non-need-based gift aid.

GIFT AID (NEED-BASED) *Total amount:* $1,077,107 (42% federal, 3% state, 54% institutional, 1% external sources). *Receiving aid:* Freshmen: 36% (63); all full-time undergraduates: 38% (179). *Average award:* Freshmen: $6224; Undergraduates: $7457. *Scholarships, grants, and awards:* Federal Pell, FSEOG, state, private, college/university gift aid from institutional funds.

GIFT AID (NON-NEED-BASED) *Total amount:* $1,643,714 (34% state, 40% institutional, 26% external sources). *Receiving aid:* Freshmen: 48% (84). Undergraduates: 49% (230). *Average award:* Freshmen: $2149. Undergraduates: $2222. *Scholarships, grants, and awards by category: Academic interests/achievement:* general academic interests/achievements. *Creative arts/performance:* debating, journalism/publications, music, theater/drama. *Special characteristics:* children of educators, children of faculty/staff. *Tuition waivers:* Full or partial for employees or children of employees.

LOANS *Student loans:* $1,953,385 (46% need-based, 54% non-need-based). *Average need-based loan:* Freshmen: $3607. Undergraduates: $3888. *Parent loans:* $742,107 (100% non-need-based). *Programs:* Federal Direct (Subsidized and Unsubsidized Stafford, PLUS), Perkins.

WORK-STUDY *Federal work-study:* Total amount: $23,279; jobs available. *State or other work-study/employment:* Part-time jobs available.

ATHLETIC AWARDS Total amount: $144,250 (100% non-need-based).

APPLYING FOR FINANCIAL AID *Required financial aid form:* FAFSA. *Financial aid deadline (priority):* 4/1. *Notification date:* Continuous. Students must reply within 2 weeks of notification.

CONTACT Lisa McClister, Director of Financial Aid, Florida College, 119 North Glen Arven Avenue, Temple Terrace, FL 33617, 813-849-6720 or toll-free 800-326-7655. *Fax:* 813-899-6772. *E-mail:* mcclisterl@floridacollege.edu.

FLORIDA CULINARY INSTITUTE
West Palm Beach, FL

CONTACT Financial Aid Office, Florida Culinary Institute, 2400 Metrocenter Boulevard, West Palm Beach, FL 33407, 561-688-2001 or toll-free 800-826-9986 (in-state).

FLORIDA GULF COAST UNIVERSITY
Fort Myers, FL

Tuition & fees (FL res): $5724	Average undergraduate aid package: $7231

ABOUT THE INSTITUTION State-supported, coed. 48 undergraduate majors. Federal methodology is used as a basis for awarding need-based institutional aid.

UNDERGRADUATE EXPENSES for 2009–10 *Tuition, state resident:* full-time $4191. *Tuition, nonresident:* full-time $19,450. *Required fees:* full-time $1533. Full-time tuition and fees vary according to course load. Part-time tuition and fees vary according to course load. *College room and board:* $7642. Room and board charges vary according to board plan.

FRESHMAN FINANCIAL AID (Fall 2009, est.) 1,579 applied for aid; of those 37% were deemed to have need. 100% of freshmen with need received aid; of those 10% had need fully met. *Average percent of need met:* 63% (excluding resources awarded to replace EFC). *Average financial aid package:* $6852 (excluding resources awarded to replace EFC).

UNDERGRADUATE FINANCIAL AID (Fall 2009, est.) 5,281 applied for aid; of those 43% were deemed to have need. 100% of undergraduates with need received aid; of those 9% had need fully met. *Average percent of need met:* 62% (excluding resources awarded to replace EFC). *Average financial aid package:* $7231 (excluding resources awarded to replace EFC).

GIFT AID (NEED-BASED) *Total amount:* $11,274,997 (41% federal, 36% state, 18% institutional, 5% external sources). *Receiving aid:* Freshmen: 17% (305); all full-time undergraduates: 19% (1,304). *Average award:* Freshmen: $4456; Undergraduates: $4430. *Scholarships, grants, and awards:* Federal Pell, FSEOG, state, private, college/university gift aid from institutional funds.

GIFT AID (NON-NEED-BASED) *Total amount:* $9,484,680 (70% state, 25% institutional, 5% external sources). *Receiving aid:* Freshmen: 25% (465). Undergraduates: 31% (2,166). *Average award:* Freshmen: $85. Undergraduates: $304. *Scholarships, grants, and awards by category: Academic interests/achievement:* biological sciences, business, education, engineering/technologies, general academic interests/achievements, health fields, humanities, mathematics, physical sciences, religion/biblical studies, social sciences. *Creative arts/performance:* art/fine arts, music. *Special achievements/activities:* community service, leadership. *Special characteristics:* adult students, ethnic background, handicapped students, international students, local/state students, members of minority groups, out-of-state students. *Tuition waivers:* Full or partial for employees or children of employees, senior citizens.

LOANS *Student loans:* $17,855,604 (72% need-based, 28% non-need-based). 35% of past graduating class borrowed through all loan programs. *Average indebtedness per student:* $21,247. *Average need-based loan:* Freshmen: $3912. Undergraduates: $5272. *Programs:* FFEL (Subsidized and Unsubsidized Stafford, PLUS).

WORK-STUDY *Federal work-study:* Total amount: $251,494; jobs available. *State or other work-study/employment:* Total amount: $1,959,918 (100% need-based). Part-time jobs available.

ATHLETIC AWARDS Total amount: $494,209 (100% non-need-based).

APPLYING FOR FINANCIAL AID *Required financial aid form:* FAFSA. *Financial aid deadline:* 6/30 (priority: 3/1). *Notification date:* Continuous.

CONTACT Jorge Lopez-Rosado, Director, Student Financial Services, Florida Gulf Coast University, 10501 FGCU Boulevard South, Fort Myers, FL 33965, 239-590-1210 or toll-free 888-889-1095. *Fax:* 239-590-7923. *E-mail:* faso@fgcu.edu.

FLORIDA HOSPITAL COLLEGE OF HEALTH SCIENCES
Orlando, FL

Tuition & fees: N/R	Average undergraduate aid package: N/A

ABOUT THE INSTITUTION Independent, coed. *Awards:* associate, bachelor's, and master's degrees. 6 undergraduate majors. *Total enrollment:* 2,207. Undergraduates: 2,207. Federal methodology is used as a basis for awarding need-based institutional aid.

GIFT AID (NEED-BASED) *Total amount:* $1,636,153 (84% federal, 13% state, 3% institutional). *Scholarships, grants, and awards:* Federal Pell, FSEOG, state, private, college/university gift aid from institutional funds.

GIFT AID (NON-NEED-BASED) *Total amount:* $2,381,111 (67% state, 9% institutional, 24% external sources). *Tuition waivers:* Full or partial for employees or children of employees. *ROTC:* Air Force cooperative.

LOANS *Student loans:* $10,952,756 (31% need-based, 69% non-need-based). *Parent loans:* $210,971 (100% non-need-based). *Programs:* Federal Direct (Subsidized and Unsubsidized Stafford, PLUS), FFEL (Subsidized and Unsubsidized Stafford, PLUS), private alternative loans.

APPLYING FOR FINANCIAL AID *Required financial aid forms:* FAFSA, institution's own form. *Financial aid deadline:* 7/22 (priority: 4/10). *Notification date:* Continuous. Students must reply within 2 weeks of notification.

CONTACT Starr Bender, Financial Aid Director, Florida Hospital College of Health Sciences, 671 Winyah Drive, Orlando, FL 32803, 407-303-6963 or toll-free 800-500-7747 (out-of-state). *Fax:* 407-303-7680. *E-mail:* starr.bender@fhchs.edu.

FLORIDA INSTITUTE OF TECHNOLOGY
Melbourne, FL

Tuition & fees: $31,520	Average undergraduate aid package: $27,868

ABOUT THE INSTITUTION Independent, coed. 63 undergraduate majors. Federal methodology is used as a basis for awarding need-based institutional aid.

UNDERGRADUATE EXPENSES for 2009–10 *Comprehensive fee:* $42,150 includes full-time tuition ($31,020), mandatory fees ($500), and room and board ($10,630). *College room only:* $6220. Full-time tuition and fees vary according to course load, location, and program. Room and board charges vary according to board plan and housing facility. *Part-time tuition:* $930 per credit hour. Part-time tuition and fees vary according to course load, location, and program. *Payment plan:* Installment.

FRESHMAN FINANCIAL AID (Fall 2009, est.) 417 applied for aid; of those 90% were deemed to have need. 100% of freshmen with need received aid; of those 24% had need fully met. *Average percent of need met:* 83% (excluding resources awarded to replace EFC). *Average financial aid package:* $29,134 (excluding resources awarded to replace EFC). 28% of all full-time freshmen had no need and received non-need-based gift aid.

UNDERGRADUATE FINANCIAL AID (Fall 2009, est.) 1,650 applied for aid; of those 89% were deemed to have need. 100% of undergraduates with need received aid; of those 25% had need fully met. *Average percent of need met:* 81% (excluding resources awarded to replace EFC). *Average financial aid package:* $27,868 (excluding resources awarded to replace EFC). 26% of all full-time undergraduates had no need and received non-need-based gift aid.

GIFT AID (NEED-BASED) *Total amount:* $27,291,308 (16% federal, 12% state, 70% institutional, 2% external sources). *Receiving aid:* Freshmen: 69% (374); all full-time undergraduates: 60% (1,459). *Average award:* Freshmen: $20,802; Undergraduates: $19,004. *Scholarships, grants, and awards:* Federal Pell, FSEOG, state, private, college/university gift aid from institutional funds.

GIFT AID (NON-NEED-BASED) *Total amount:* $8,572,235 (16% federal, 7% state, 76% institutional, 1% external sources). *Receiving aid:* Freshmen: 69% (374). Undergraduates: 55% (1,337). *Average award:* Freshmen: $11,189. Undergraduates: $10,155. *Scholarships, grants, and awards by category:* Academic interests/achievement: 1,615 awards ($11,746,478 total): general academic interests/achievements, military science. Special achievements/activities: 40 awards ($206,500 total): cheerleading/drum major, hobbies/interests. Special characteristics: 801 awards ($1,987,322 total): children and siblings of alumni, children of faculty/staff, general special characteristics, previous college experience, siblings of current students. *Tuition waivers:* Full or partial for employees or children of employees, senior citizens.

LOANS *Student loans:* $14,200,442 (94% need-based, 6% non-need-based). 69% of past graduating class borrowed through all loan programs. *Average indebtedness per student:* $40,630. *Average need-based loan:* Freshmen: $3501. Undergraduates: $4704. *Parent loans:* $4,174,935 (92% need-based, 8% non-need-based). *Programs:* FFEL (Subsidized and Unsubsidized Stafford, PLUS), Perkins, state, college/university.

WORK-STUDY *Federal work-study:* Total amount: $1,336,617; 903 jobs averaging $1480. *State or other work-study/employment:* Total amount: $10,660 (100% need-based). 4 part-time jobs averaging $2665.

ATHLETIC AWARDS Total amount: $3,071,401 (54% need-based, 46% non-need-based).

APPLYING FOR FINANCIAL AID *Required financial aid forms:* FAFSA, state aid form. *Financial aid deadline (priority):* 3/1. *Notification date:* Continuous beginning 2/15. Students must reply by 5/1 or within 4 weeks of notification.

CONTACT Melissa Todd, Financial Aid Administrator, Florida Institute of Technology, 150 West University Boulevard, Melbourne, FL 32901-6975, 321-674-8070 or toll-free 800-888-4348. *Fax:* 321-724-2778. *E-mail:* toddm@fit.edu.

FLORIDA INTERNATIONAL UNIVERSITY
Miami, FL

Tuition & fees (FL res): $4580	Average undergraduate aid package: $7341

ABOUT THE INSTITUTION State-supported, coed. 64 undergraduate majors. Federal methodology is used as a basis for awarding need-based institutional aid.

UNDERGRADUATE EXPENSES for 2009–10 *Tuition, state resident:* full-time $4261; part-time $142.04 per credit hour. *Tuition, nonresident:* full-time $16,660; part-time $555.34 per credit hour. *Required fees:* full-time $319; $319 per credit hour. Full-time tuition and fees vary according to course load. Part-time tuition and fees vary according to course load. *College room and board:* $11,946; *Room only:* $7536. Room and board charges vary according to housing facility.

FRESHMAN FINANCIAL AID (Fall 2008) 2,156 applied for aid; of those 98% were deemed to have need. 97% of freshmen with need received aid; of those 13% had need fully met. *Average percent of need met:* 28% (excluding resources awarded to replace EFC). *Average financial aid package:* $6369 (excluding resources awarded to replace EFC). 32% of all full-time freshmen had no need and received non-need-based gift aid.

UNDERGRADUATE FINANCIAL AID (Fall 2008) 11,248 applied for aid; of those 98% were deemed to have need. 97% of undergraduates with need received aid; of those 13% had need fully met. *Average percent of need met:* 25% (excluding resources awarded to replace EFC). *Average financial aid package:* $7341 (excluding resources awarded to replace EFC). 5% of all full-time undergraduates had no need and received non-need-based gift aid.

GIFT AID (NEED-BASED) *Total amount:* $50,679,463 (70% federal, 15% state, 15% institutional). *Receiving aid:* Freshmen: 39% (1,138); all full-time undergraduates: 38% (7,365). *Average award:* Freshmen: $5043; Undergraduates: $4868. *Scholarships, grants, and awards:* Federal Pell, FSEOG, state, private, college/university gift aid from institutional funds.

GIFT AID (NON-NEED-BASED) *Total amount:* $34,874,001 (6% federal, 65% state, 20% institutional, 9% external sources). *Receiving aid:* Freshmen: 61% (1,766). Undergraduates: 27% (5,293). *Average award:* Freshmen: $739. Undergraduates: $662. *Scholarships, grants, and awards by category:* Academic interests/achievement: biological sciences, business, communication, computer science, education, engineering/technologies, English, foreign languages, general academic interests/achievements, health fields, humanities, mathematics, physical sciences, social sciences. Creative arts/performance: dance, journalism/publications, music, performing arts, theater/drama. Special characteristics: children and siblings of alumni, members of minority groups. *Tuition waivers:* Full or partial for employees or children of employees, senior citizens.

LOANS *Student loans:* $134,042,625 (52% need-based, 48% non-need-based). 39% of past graduating class borrowed through all loan programs. *Average indebtedness per student:* $14,912. *Average need-based loan:* Freshmen: $6516. Undergraduates: $7674. *Parent loans:* $1,601,723 (100% non-need-based). *Programs:* Federal Direct (Subsidized and Unsubsidized Stafford, PLUS), FFEL (Subsidized and Unsubsidized Stafford, PLUS), Perkins, college/university.

WORK-STUDY *Federal work-study:* Total amount: $1,516,012; jobs available. *State or other work-study/employment:* Total amount: $78,371 (100% need-based). Part-time jobs available.

ATHLETIC AWARDS Total amount: $4,541,768 (2% need-based, 98% non-need-based).

APPLYING FOR FINANCIAL AID *Required financial aid form:* FAFSA. *Financial aid deadline:* 5/15 (priority: 3/1). *Notification date:* Continuous. Students must reply within 4 weeks of notification.

CONTACT Francisco Valines, Director, Financial Aid, Florida International University, 12200 SW 8th Street, PC 125, Miami, FL 33199, 305-348-7272. *Fax:* 305-348-2346. *E-mail:* finaid@fiu.edu.

FLORIDA MEMORIAL UNIVERSITY
Miami-Dade, FL

CONTACT Brian Phillip, Director of Financial Aid, Florida Memorial University, 15800 Northwest 42nd Avenue, Miami, FL 33054, 305-626-3745 or toll-free 800-822-1362. *Fax:* 305-626-3106.

FLORIDA NATIONAL COLLEGE
Hialeah, FL

CONTACT Mr. Omar Sanchez, Vice President for Planning and Evaluation/ Director of Financial Aid, Florida National College, 4206 West 12th Avenue, Hialeah, FL 33012, 305-821-3333 Ext. 1003. *Fax:* 305-362-0595. *E-mail:* hialeah@ icanect.net.

FLORIDA SOUTHERN COLLEGE
Lakeland, FL

Tuition & fees: $24,662	Average undergraduate aid package: $19,093

ABOUT THE INSTITUTION Independent religious, coed. 54 undergraduate majors. Federal methodology is used as a basis for awarding need-based institutional aid.

UNDERGRADUATE EXPENSES for 2010–11 *Comprehensive fee:* $32,972 includes full-time tuition ($24,112), mandatory fees ($550), and room and board ($8310). *College room only:* $4700. Room and board charges vary according to board plan and housing facility. *Part-time tuition:* $700 per credit hour. *Part-time fees:* $50 per term. Part-time tuition and fees vary according to class time. *Payment plan:* Installment.

FRESHMAN FINANCIAL AID (Fall 2009, est.) 489 applied for aid; of those 87% were deemed to have need. 100% of freshmen with need received aid; of those 31% had need fully met. *Average percent of need met:* 68% (excluding resources awarded to replace EFC). *Average financial aid package:* $19,543 (excluding resources awarded to replace EFC). 12% of all full-time freshmen had no need and received non-need-based gift aid.

UNDERGRADUATE FINANCIAL AID (Fall 2009, est.) 1,406 applied for aid; of those 88% were deemed to have need. 100% of undergraduates with need received aid; of those 28% had need fully met. *Average percent of need met:* 71% (excluding resources awarded to replace EFC). *Average financial aid package:* $19,093 (excluding resources awarded to replace EFC). 11% of all full-time undergraduates had no need and received non-need-based gift aid.

GIFT AID (NEED-BASED) *Total amount:* $22,100,682 (12% federal, 22% state, 50% institutional, 16% external sources). *Receiving aid:* Freshmen: 53% (292); all full-time undergraduates: 47% (855). *Average award:* Freshmen: $6470; Undergraduates: $6615. *Scholarships, grants, and awards:* Federal Pell, FSEOG, state, private, college/university gift aid from institutional funds.

GIFT AID (NON-NEED-BASED) *Total amount:* $2,055,450 (23% state, 60% institutional, 17% external sources). *Receiving aid:* Freshmen: 74% (411). Undergraduates: 63% (1,149). *Average award:* Freshmen: $9590. Undergraduates: $9903. *Scholarships, grants, and awards by category: Academic interests/ achievement:* agriculture, biological sciences, business, communication, education, general academic interests/achievements, health fields, physical sciences, religion/biblical studies, social sciences. *Creative arts/performance:* art/fine arts, music, theater/drama. *Special achievements/activities:* community service, general special achievements/activities, leadership. *Special characteristics:* children and siblings of alumni, children of faculty/staff, general special characteristics, local/state students, out-of-state students, relatives of clergy, siblings of current students. *Tuition waivers:* Full or partial for children of alumni, employees or children of employees.

LOANS *Student loans:* $3,632,845 (98% need-based, 2% non-need-based). 63% of past graduating class borrowed through all loan programs. *Average indebtedness per student:* $22,910. *Average need-based loan:* Freshmen: $3325. Undergraduates: $4228. *Programs:* FFEL (Subsidized and Unsubsidized Stafford, PLUS), Perkins.

WORK-STUDY *Federal work-study:* Total amount: $503,401; jobs available (averaging $1500). *State or other work-study/employment:* Total amount: $406,099 (86% need-based, 14% non-need-based). Part-time jobs available.

ATHLETIC AWARDS Total amount: $2,086,901 (88% need-based, 12% non-need-based).

APPLYING FOR FINANCIAL AID *Required financial aid forms:* FAFSA, institution's own form. *Financial aid deadline:* 7/1 (priority: 3/1). *Notification date:* Continuous beginning 3/1. Students must reply within 3 weeks of notification.

CONTACT William L. Healy, Financial Aid Director, Florida Southern College, 111 Lake Hollingsworth Drive, Lakeland, FL 33801-5698, 863-680-4140 or toll-free 800-274-4131. *Fax:* 863-680-4567. *E-mail:* whealy@flsouthern.edu.

FLORIDA STATE UNIVERSITY
Tallahassee, FL

Tuition & fees (FL res): $4566	Average undergraduate aid package: $10,419

ABOUT THE INSTITUTION State-supported, coed. 91 undergraduate majors. Federal methodology is used as a basis for awarding need-based institutional aid.

UNDERGRADUATE EXPENSES for 2009–10 *Tuition, state resident:* full-time $2933; part-time $97.77 per credit hour. *Tuition, nonresident:* full-time $17,171; part-time $579.25 per credit hour. *Required fees:* full-time $1633; $53.10 per credit hour or $20 per term. *College room and board:* $8000; *Room only:* $4800. Room and board charges vary according to board plan and housing facility. *Payment plans:* Tuition prepayment, installment.

FRESHMAN FINANCIAL AID (Fall 2009, est.) 4,359 applied for aid; of those 47% were deemed to have need. 100% of freshmen with need received aid; of those 81% had need fully met. *Average percent of need met:* 74% (excluding resources awarded to replace EFC). *Average financial aid package:* $10,263 (excluding resources awarded to replace EFC). 10% of all full-time freshmen had no need and received non-need-based gift aid.

UNDERGRADUATE FINANCIAL AID (Fall 2009, est.) 16,943 applied for aid; of those 50% were deemed to have need. 100% of undergraduates with need received aid; of those 77% had need fully met. *Average percent of need met:* 76% (excluding resources awarded to replace EFC). *Average financial aid package:* $10,419 (excluding resources awarded to replace EFC). 6% of all full-time undergraduates had no need and received non-need-based gift aid.

GIFT AID (NEED-BASED) *Total amount:* $70,726,325 (51% federal, 31% state, 16% institutional, 2% external sources). *Receiving aid:* Freshmen: 20% (1,166); all full-time undergraduates: 20% (4,922). *Average award:* Freshmen: $4231; Undergraduates: $4071. *Scholarships, grants, and awards:* Federal Pell, FSEOG, state, private, college/university gift aid from institutional funds, Academic Competitiveness Grants, National SMART Grants.

GIFT AID (NON-NEED-BASED) *Total amount:* $52,704,030 (78% state, 16% institutional, 6% external sources). *Receiving aid:* Freshmen: 34% (1,937). Undergraduates: 26% (6,423). *Average award:* Freshmen: $2353. Undergraduates: $2254. *Scholarships, grants, and awards by category: Academic interests/ achievement:* general academic interests/achievements. *Creative arts/performance:* cinema/film/broadcasting, dance, music, theater/drama. *Special characteristics:* local/state students. *Tuition waivers:* Full or partial for employees or children of employees, senior citizens.

LOANS *Student loans:* $87,759,246 (53% need-based, 47% non-need-based). 48% of past graduating class borrowed through all loan programs. *Average indebtedness per student:* $19,364. *Average need-based loan:* Freshmen: $2825. Undergraduates: $3648. *Parent loans:* $6,740,203 (22% need-based, 78% non-need-based). *Programs:* Federal Direct (Subsidized and Unsubsidized Stafford, PLUS), Perkins, college/university.

WORK-STUDY *Federal work-study:* Total amount: $1,626,350; 762 jobs averaging $1200. *State or other work-study/employment:* Total amount: $40,876 (100% need-based). 40 part-time jobs averaging $641.

ATHLETIC AWARDS Total amount: $2,040,115 (6% need-based, 94% non-need-based).

APPLYING FOR FINANCIAL AID *Required financial aid form:* FAFSA. *Financial aid deadline:* Continuous. *Notification date:* Continuous beginning 3/1.

CONTACT Darryl Marshall, Director of Financial Aid, Florida State University, University Center A4400, Tallahassee, FL 32306-2430, 850-644-5716. *Fax:* 850-644-6404. *E-mail:* ofacs@admin.fsu.edu.

FONTBONNE UNIVERSITY
St. Louis, MO

CONTACT Financial Aid Office, Fontbonne University, 6800 Wydown Boulevard, St. Louis, MO 63105-3098, 314-889-1414. *Fax:* 314-889-1451.

FORDHAM UNIVERSITY
New York, NY

Tuition & fees: N/R	Average undergraduate aid package: $23,597

ABOUT THE INSTITUTION Independent Roman Catholic (Jesuit), coed. 93 undergraduate majors. Both federal and institutional methodology are used as a basis for awarding need-based institutional aid.

FRESHMAN FINANCIAL AID (Fall 2008) 1,696 applied for aid; of those 66% were deemed to have need. 100% of freshmen with need received aid; of those 30% had need fully met. *Average percent of need met:* 77% (excluding resources awarded to replace EFC). *Average financial aid package:* $23,809 (excluding resources awarded to replace EFC). 34% of all full-time freshmen had no need and received non-need-based gift aid.

UNDERGRADUATE FINANCIAL AID (Fall 2008) 6,112 applied for aid; of those 76% were deemed to have need. 100% of undergraduates with need received aid; of those 26% had need fully met. *Average percent of need met:* 74% (excluding resources awarded to replace EFC). *Average financial aid package:* $23,597 (excluding resources awarded to replace EFC). 21% of all full-time undergraduates had no need and received non-need-based gift aid.

GIFT AID (NEED-BASED) *Total amount:* $67,398,888 (11% federal, 10% state, 75% institutional, 4% external sources). *Receiving aid:* Freshmen: 59% (1,095); all full-time undergraduates: 61% (4,466). *Average award:* Freshmen: $17,210; Undergraduates: $16,236. *Scholarships, grants, and awards:* Federal Pell, FSEOG, state, private, college/university gift aid from institutional funds.

GIFT AID (NON-NEED-BASED) *Total amount:* $19,285,338 (3% state, 86% institutional, 11% external sources). *Receiving aid:* Freshmen: 13% (247). Undergraduates: 11% (793). *Average award:* Freshmen: $9405. Undergraduates: $9448. *Scholarships, grants, and awards by category:* Academic interests/achievement: biological sciences, business, communication, foreign languages, general academic interests/achievements. Creative arts/performance: dance, music. Special achievements/activities: general special achievements/activities. Special characteristics: adult students, children and siblings of alumni, children of faculty/staff, children with a deceased or disabled parent, handicapped students.

LOANS *Student loans:* $47,025,736 (65% need-based, 35% non-need-based). 62% of past graduating class borrowed through all loan programs. *Average indebtedness per student:* $31,300. *Average need-based loan:* Freshmen: $5065. Undergraduates: $6310. *Parent loans:* $15,722,373 (32% need-based, 68% non-need-based). *Programs:* FFEL (Subsidized and Unsubsidized Stafford, PLUS), Perkins.

WORK-STUDY *Federal work-study:* Total amount: $3,372,322; 1,232 jobs averaging $2731. *State or other work-study/employment:* Total amount: $1,307,068 (52% need-based, 48% non-need-based). 114 part-time jobs averaging $11,466.

ATHLETIC AWARDS Total amount: $8,965,158 (67% need-based, 33% non-need-based).

APPLYING FOR FINANCIAL AID *Required financial aid forms:* FAFSA, CSS Financial Aid PROFILE, noncustodial (divorced/separated) parent's statement, business/farm supplement. *Financial aid deadline:* 2/1. *Notification date:* Continuous beginning 4/1. Students must reply by 5/1 or within 2 weeks of notification.

CONTACT Angela Van Dekker, Assistant Vice President, Student Financial Services, Fordham University, 441 East Fordham Road, Thebaud Hall, Room 208, New York, NY 10458, 718-817-3804 or toll-free 800-FORDHAM. *Fax:* 718-817-3817. *E-mail:* avandekker@fordham.edu.

FORT HAYS STATE UNIVERSITY
Hays, KS

ABOUT THE INSTITUTION State-supported, coed. 67 undergraduate majors.

GIFT AID (NEED-BASED) *Scholarships, grants, and awards:* Federal Pell, FSEOG, state, private, college/university gift aid from institutional funds.

LOANS *Programs:* FFEL (Subsidized and Unsubsidized Stafford, PLUS), Perkins, college/university.

APPLYING FOR FINANCIAL AID *Required financial aid forms:* FAFSA, state aid form.

CONTACT Craig Karlin, Director of Financial Assistance, Fort Hays State University, Custer Hall, Room 306, 600 Park Street, Hays, KS 67601, 785-628-4408 or toll-free 800-628-FHSU. *Fax:* 785-628-4014. *E-mail:* finaid@fhsu.edu.

FORT LEWIS COLLEGE
Durango, CO

Tuition & fees (CO res): $7632	Average undergraduate aid package: $8042

ABOUT THE INSTITUTION State-supported, coed. 62 undergraduate majors. Federal methodology is used as a basis for awarding need-based institutional aid.

UNDERGRADUATE EXPENSES for 2009–10 *One-time required fee:* $135. *Tuition, state resident:* full-time $6204; part-time $155 per credit hour. *Tuition, nonresident:* full-time $16,072; part-time $803 per credit hour. *Required fees:* full-time $1428; $51.45 per credit hour. Full-time tuition and fees vary according to reciprocity agreements. Part-time tuition and fees vary according to course load and reciprocity agreements. *College room and board:* $8304; *Room only:* $4800. Room and board charges vary according to board plan and housing facility. *Payment plan:* Installment.

FRESHMAN FINANCIAL AID (Fall 2009, est.) 548 applied for aid; of those 69% were deemed to have need. 99% of freshmen with need received aid; of those 22% had need fully met. *Average percent of need met:* 66% (excluding resources awarded to replace EFC). *Average financial aid package:* $7154 (excluding resources awarded to replace EFC). 30% of all full-time freshmen had no need and received non-need-based gift aid.

UNDERGRADUATE FINANCIAL AID (Fall 2009, est.) 2,213 applied for aid; of those 78% were deemed to have need. 98% of undergraduates with need received aid; of those 24% had need fully met. *Average percent of need met:* 71% (excluding resources awarded to replace EFC). *Average financial aid package:* $8042 (excluding resources awarded to replace EFC). 12% of all full-time undergraduates had no need and received non-need-based gift aid.

GIFT AID (NEED-BASED) *Total amount:* $7,731,960 (60% federal, 15% state, 20% institutional, 5% external sources). *Receiving aid:* Freshmen: 34% (269); all full-time undergraduates: 41% (1,373). *Average award:* Freshmen: $3315; Undergraduates: $3660. *Scholarships, grants, and awards:* Federal Pell, FSEOG, state, private, college/university gift aid from institutional funds.

GIFT AID (NON-NEED-BASED) *Total amount:* $1,470,333 (2% federal, 2% state, 65% institutional, 31% external sources). *Receiving aid:* Freshmen: 38% (298). Undergraduates: 25% (845). *Average award:* Freshmen: $1034. Undergraduates: $1241. *Scholarships, grants, and awards by category:* Academic interests/achievement: agriculture, area/ethnic studies, biological sciences, business, communication, computer science, education, English, general academic interests/achievements, humanities, mathematics, physical sciences, social sciences. Creative arts/performance: art/fine arts, music, performing arts, theater/drama. Special achievements/activities: general special achievements/activities, leadership. Special characteristics: children and siblings of alumni, children of faculty/staff, ethnic background, first-generation college students, general special characteristics, handicapped students, international students, local/state students, members of minority groups, out-of-state students, veterans' children. *Tuition waivers:* Full or partial for minority students, employees or children of employees.

LOANS *Student loans:* $9,762,368 (72% need-based, 28% non-need-based). 54% of past graduating class borrowed through all loan programs. *Average indebtedness per student:* $15,962. *Average need-based loan:* Freshmen: $3062. Undergraduates: $3835. *Parent loans:* $1,241,301 (46% need-based, 54% non-need-based). *Programs:* FFEL (Subsidized and Unsubsidized Stafford, PLUS), Perkins, college/university.

WORK-STUDY *Federal work-study:* Total amount: $259,412; jobs available. *State or other work-study/employment:* Total amount: $1,155,999 (79% need-based, 21% non-need-based). Part-time jobs available.

ATHLETIC AWARDS Total amount: $1,485,049 (37% need-based, 63% non-need-based).

APPLYING FOR FINANCIAL AID *Required financial aid form:* FAFSA. *Financial aid deadline (priority):* 2/15. *Notification date:* Continuous beginning 3/15. Students must reply within 2 weeks of notification.

CONTACT Ms. Elaine Redwine, Director of Financial Aid, Fort Lewis College, 1000 Rim Drive, 101 Miller Student Services Building, Durango, CO 81301, 970-247-7464. *Fax:* 970-247-7108. *E-mail:* redwine_e@fortlewis.edu.

FORT VALLEY STATE UNIVERSITY
Fort Valley, GA

Tuition & fees: N/R	Average undergraduate aid package: $4400

ABOUT THE INSTITUTION State-supported, coed. 35 undergraduate majors. Federal methodology is used as a basis for awarding need-based institutional aid.

FRESHMAN FINANCIAL AID (Fall 2009, est.) 980 applied for aid; of those 100% were deemed to have need. 87% of freshmen with need received aid.

Average percent of need met: 96% (excluding resources awarded to replace EFC). *Average financial aid package:* $4400 (excluding resources awarded to replace EFC). 1% of all full-time freshmen had no need and received non-need-based gift aid.

UNDERGRADUATE FINANCIAL AID (Fall 2009, est.) 2,671 applied for aid; of those 92% were deemed to have need. 94% of undergraduates with need received aid. *Average percent of need met:* 82% (excluding resources awarded to replace EFC). *Average financial aid package:* $4400 (excluding resources awarded to replace EFC). 1% of all full-time undergraduates had no need and received non-need-based gift aid.

GIFT AID (NEED-BASED) *Total amount:* $4,986,893 (100% federal). *Receiving aid:* Freshmen: 65% (652); all full-time undergraduates: 72% (1,985). *Average award:* Freshmen: $1717; Undergraduates: $3798. *Scholarships, grants, and awards:* Federal Pell, FSEOG, state, private, college/university gift aid from institutional funds, United Negro College Fund, Academic Competitiveness Grants, TEACH Grants.

GIFT AID (NON-NEED-BASED) *Total amount:* $1,889,476 (1% federal, 57% state, 41% institutional, 1% external sources). *Receiving aid:* Freshmen: 80% (798). Undergraduates: 47% (1,297). *Average award:* Freshmen: $4234. Undergraduates: $1776. *Scholarships, grants, and awards by category: Academic interests/achievement:* agriculture, business, general academic interests/achievements, home economics, military science, premedicine, social sciences. *Creative arts/performance:* journalism/publications, music. *Special achievements/activities:* general special achievements/activities. *Special characteristics:* handicapped students, international students, local/state students, members of minority groups, out-of-state students. *Tuition waivers:* Full or partial for employees or children of employees, senior citizens.

LOANS *Student loans:* $9,711,429 (43% need-based, 57% non-need-based). 97% of past graduating class borrowed through all loan programs. *Average indebtedness per student:* $37,000. *Average need-based loan:* Freshmen: $1704. Undergraduates: $1990. *Programs:* Federal Direct (Subsidized and Unsubsidized Stafford, PLUS), Perkins, state, college/university.

WORK-STUDY *Federal work-study:* Total amount: $169,959; jobs available.

ATHLETIC AWARDS Total amount: $315,994 (100% non-need-based).

APPLYING FOR FINANCIAL AID *Required financial aid forms:* FAFSA, state aid form. *Financial aid deadline:* 6/30 (priority: 4/15). *Notification date:* Continuous beginning 7/1. Students must reply by 8/15.

CONTACT Financial Aid Director, Fort Valley State University, PO Box 4129, Fort Valley, GA 31030-3298, 478-825-6182 or toll-free 877-462-3878. *Fax:* 478-825-6976.

FRAMINGHAM STATE COLLEGE
Framingham, MA

Tuition & fees (MA res): $6540   **Average undergraduate aid package: $6934**

ABOUT THE INSTITUTION State-supported, coed. 23 undergraduate majors. Federal methodology is used as a basis for awarding need-based institutional aid.

UNDERGRADUATE EXPENSES for 2009–10 *Tuition, state resident:* full-time $970; part-time $162 per course. *Tuition, nonresident:* full-time $7050; part-time $1175 per course. *Required fees:* full-time $5570; $993.50 per course. Full-time tuition and fees vary according to class time. Part-time tuition and fees vary according to class time and course load. *College room and board:* $8148; *Room only:* $5248. Room and board charges vary according to board plan and housing facility. *Payment plans:* Tuition prepayment, installment.

FRESHMAN FINANCIAL AID (Fall 2008) 526 applied for aid; of those 70% were deemed to have need. 100% of freshmen with need received aid; of those 73% had need fully met. *Average percent of need met:* 76% (excluding resources awarded to replace EFC). *Average financial aid package:* $6802 (excluding resources awarded to replace EFC). 3% of all full-time freshmen had no need and received non-need-based gift aid.

UNDERGRADUATE FINANCIAL AID (Fall 2008) 2,151 applied for aid; of those 71% were deemed to have need. 100% of undergraduates with need received aid; of those 79% had need fully met. *Average percent of need met:* 79% (excluding resources awarded to replace EFC). *Average financial aid package:* $6934 (excluding resources awarded to replace EFC). 2% of all full-time undergraduates had no need and received non-need-based gift aid.

GIFT AID (NEED-BASED) *Total amount:* $5,071,294 (42% federal, 34% state, 20% institutional, 4% external sources). *Receiving aid:* Freshmen: 41% (299); all full-time undergraduates: 32% (1,233). *Average award:* Freshmen: $4060;

Undergraduates: $4142. *Scholarships, grants, and awards:* Federal Pell, FSEOG, state, private, college/university gift aid from institutional funds.

GIFT AID (NON-NEED-BASED) *Total amount:* $414,940 (21% state, 63% institutional, 16% external sources). *Receiving aid:* Freshmen: 11% (78). Undergraduates: 6% (225). *Average award:* Freshmen: $2174. Undergraduates: $2278. *Scholarships, grants, and awards by category: Academic interests/achievement:* biological sciences, education, general academic interests/achievements, home economics, physical sciences. *Special characteristics:* children of faculty/staff, children of public servants, children of union members/company employees, veterans. *Tuition waivers:* Full or partial for employees or children of employees, senior citizens.

LOANS *Student loans:* $13,270,727 (71% need-based, 29% non-need-based). 65% of past graduating class borrowed through all loan programs. *Average indebtedness per student:* $19,000. *Average need-based loan:* Freshmen: $4525. Undergraduates: $4988. *Parent loans:* $1,606,149 (62% need-based, 38% non-need-based). *Programs:* Federal Direct (Subsidized and Unsubsidized Stafford, PLUS), FFEL (Subsidized and Unsubsidized Stafford, PLUS), Perkins, state.

WORK-STUDY *Federal work-study:* Total amount: $130,000; jobs available. *State or other work-study/employment:* Total amount: $84,112 (100% need-based). Part-time jobs available.

APPLYING FOR FINANCIAL AID *Required financial aid form:* FAFSA. *Financial aid deadline (priority):* 3/1. *Notification date:* Continuous beginning 4/15. Students must reply by 5/1 or within 2 weeks of notification.

CONTACT Financial Aid Office, Framingham State College, 100 State Street, PO Box 9101, Framingham, MA 01701-9101, 508-626-4534. *Fax:* 508-626-4598.

FRANCISCAN UNIVERSITY OF STEUBENVILLE
Steubenville, OH

Tuition & fees: $20,320   **Average undergraduate aid package: $12,549**

ABOUT THE INSTITUTION Independent Roman Catholic, coed. 32 undergraduate majors. Federal methodology is used as a basis for awarding need-based institutional aid.

UNDERGRADUATE EXPENSES for 2010–11 *One-time required fee:* $150. *Comprehensive fee:* $27,220 includes full-time tuition ($19,900), mandatory fees ($420), and room and board ($6900). Full-time tuition and fees vary according to degree level. Room and board charges vary according to board plan. *Part-time tuition:* $665 per credit hour. *Part-time fees:* $15 per credit hour. Part-time tuition and fees vary according to class time, course load, and degree level. *Payment plan:* Installment.

FRESHMAN FINANCIAL AID (Fall 2009, est.) 370 applied for aid; of those 83% were deemed to have need. 100% of freshmen with need received aid; of those 16% had need fully met. *Average percent of need met:* 63% (excluding resources awarded to replace EFC). *Average financial aid package:* $12,510 (excluding resources awarded to replace EFC). 11% of all full-time freshmen had no need and received non-need-based gift aid.

UNDERGRADUATE FINANCIAL AID (Fall 2009, est.) 1,577 applied for aid; of those 84% were deemed to have need. 100% of undergraduates with need received aid; of those 14% had need fully met. *Average percent of need met:* 60% (excluding resources awarded to replace EFC). *Average financial aid package:* $12,549 (excluding resources awarded to replace EFC). 12% of all full-time undergraduates had no need and received non-need-based gift aid.

GIFT AID (NEED-BASED) *Total amount:* $9,581,456 (26% federal, 2% state, 61% institutional, 11% external sources). *Receiving aid:* Freshmen: 68% (302); all full-time undergraduates: 65% (1,270). *Average award:* Freshmen: $9006; Undergraduates: $8177. *Scholarships, grants, and awards:* Federal Pell, FSEOG, state, private, college/university gift aid from institutional funds.

GIFT AID (NON-NEED-BASED) *Total amount:* $1,432,598 (4% federal, 76% institutional, 20% external sources). *Receiving aid:* Freshmen: 6% (25). Undergraduates: 4% (70). *Average award:* Freshmen: $4961. Undergraduates: $4094. *Scholarships, grants, and awards by category: Academic interests/achievement:* general academic interests/achievements. *Special achievements/activities:* religious involvement. *Special characteristics:* children of faculty/staff, international students, local/state students, religious affiliation, siblings of current students. *Tuition waivers:* Full or partial for employees or children of employees.

LOANS *Student loans:* $15,695,860 (67% need-based, 33% non-need-based). 79% of past graduating class borrowed through all loan programs. *Average indebtedness per student:* $30,180. *Average need-based loan:* Freshmen: $3326. Undergraduates: $4311. *Parent loans:* $3,057,856 (41% need-based, 59% non-need-based). *Programs:* FFEL (Subsidized and Unsubsidized Stafford, PLUS), Perkins, Federal Nursing.

WORK-STUDY *Federal work-study:* Total amount: $143,290; jobs available. *State or other work-study/employment:* Total amount: $971,486 (85% need-based, 15% non-need-based). Part-time jobs available.

APPLYING FOR FINANCIAL AID *Required financial aid form:* FAFSA. *Financial aid deadline (priority):* 4/1. *Notification date:* Continuous beginning 3/1. Students must reply within 3 weeks of notification.

CONTACT John Herrmann, Director of Student Financial Services, Franciscan University of Steubenville, 1235 University Boulevard, Steubenville, OH 43952-1763, 740-284-5215 or toll-free 800-783-6220. *Fax:* 740-284-5469. *E-mail:* jherrmann@franciscan.edu.

FRANCIS MARION UNIVERSITY
Florence, SC

Tuition & fees (SC res): $7960	Average undergraduate aid package: N/A

ABOUT THE INSTITUTION State-supported, coed. 31 undergraduate majors. Federal methodology is used as a basis for awarding need-based institutional aid.

UNDERGRADUATE EXPENSES for 2009–10 *Tuition, state resident:* full-time $7625; part-time $381.25 per credit hour. *Tuition, nonresident:* full-time $15,250; part-time $762.50 per credit hour. *Required fees:* full-time $335; $12.25 per credit hour. Part-time tuition and fees vary according to course load. *College room and board:* $6024; *Room only:* $3424. Room and board charges vary according to board plan and housing facility. *Payment plan:* Installment.

FRESHMAN FINANCIAL AID (Fall 2009, est.) 761 applied for aid; of those 91% were deemed to have need. 90% of freshmen with need received aid. 2% of all full-time freshmen had no need and received non-need-based gift aid.

UNDERGRADUATE FINANCIAL AID (Fall 2009, est.) 2,618 applied for aid; of those 93% were deemed to have need. 100% of undergraduates with need received aid. 1% of all full-time undergraduates had no need and received non-need-based gift aid.

GIFT AID (NEED-BASED) *Total amount:* $10,196,735 (90% federal, 10% state). *Receiving aid:* Freshmen: 65% (518); all full-time undergraduates: 58% (1,877). *Average award:* Freshmen: $5236; Undergraduates: $4873. *Scholarships, grants, and awards:* Federal Pell, FSEOG, state, private, Academic Competitiveness Grants, National SMART Grants.

GIFT AID (NON-NEED-BASED) *Total amount:* $7,596,128 (79% state, 13% institutional, 8% external sources). *Receiving aid:* Freshmen: 66% (523). Undergraduates: 33% (1,069). *Average award:* Freshmen: $2456. Undergraduates: $3134. *Scholarships, grants, and awards by category:* Academic interests/achievement: biological sciences, business, computer science, education, English, general academic interests/achievements, health fields, humanities, mathematics, premedicine, social sciences. Creative arts/performance: art/fine arts, music, theater/drama. Special achievements/activities: cheerleading/drum major. Special characteristics: adult students, children and siblings of alumni, children of faculty/staff, children of union members/company employees, handicapped students, international students, out-of-state students, spouses of deceased or disabled public servants, veterans, veterans' children. Tuition waivers: Full or partial for employees or children of employees, senior citizens.

LOANS *Student loans:* $24,378,297 (45% need-based, 55% non-need-based). 76% of past graduating class borrowed through all loan programs. *Average indebtedness per student:* $24,347. *Average need-based loan:* Freshmen: $3440. Undergraduates: $4349. *Parent loans:* $776,594 (100% non-need-based). *Programs:* Federal Direct (Subsidized and Unsubsidized Stafford, PLUS), Perkins, state.

WORK-STUDY *Federal work-study:* Total amount: $136,000; jobs available. *State or other work-study/employment:* Total amount: $500,000 (100% non-need-based). Part-time jobs available.

ATHLETIC AWARDS Total amount: $715,280 (100% non-need-based).

APPLYING FOR FINANCIAL AID *Required financial aid form:* FAFSA. *Financial aid deadline (priority):* 3/1. *Notification date:* Continuous beginning 1/30.

CONTACT Kim Ellisor, Director of Financial Assistance, Francis Marion University, PO Box 100547, Florence, SC 29502-0547, 843-661-1190 or toll-free 800-368-7551.

FRANKLIN & MARSHALL COLLEGE
Lancaster, PA

Tuition & fees: $39,990	Average undergraduate aid package: $29,613

ABOUT THE INSTITUTION Independent, coed. 38 undergraduate majors. Both federal and institutional methodology are used as a basis for awarding need-based institutional aid.

UNDERGRADUATE EXPENSES for 2010–11 *Comprehensive fee:* $50,420 includes full-time tuition ($39,930), mandatory fees ($60), and room and board ($10,430). *College room only:* $6575. Room and board charges vary according to board plan and housing facility. *Part-time tuition:* $4991 per course. *Payment plans:* Installment, deferred payment.

FRESHMAN FINANCIAL AID (Fall 2009, est.) 407 applied for aid; of those 71% were deemed to have need. 100% of freshmen with need received aid; of those 100% had need fully met. *Average percent of need met:* 100% (excluding resources awarded to replace EFC). *Average financial aid package:* $32,885 (excluding resources awarded to replace EFC). 10% of all full-time freshmen had no need and received non-need-based gift aid.

UNDERGRADUATE FINANCIAL AID (Fall 2009, est.) 1,232 applied for aid; of those 80% were deemed to have need. 100% of undergraduates with need received aid; of those 48% had need fully met. *Average percent of need met:* 93% (excluding resources awarded to replace EFC). *Average financial aid package:* $29,613 (excluding resources awarded to replace EFC). 12% of all full-time undergraduates had no need and received non-need-based gift aid.

GIFT AID (NEED-BASED) *Total amount:* $23,617,508 (5% federal, 2% state, 90% institutional, 3% external sources). *Receiving aid:* Freshmen: 45% (283); all full-time undergraduates: 41% (922). *Average award:* Freshmen: $28,914; Undergraduates: $25,470. *Scholarships, grants, and awards:* Federal Pell, FSEOG, state, private, college/university gift aid from institutional funds.

GIFT AID (NON-NEED-BASED) *Total amount:* $4,173,485 (80% institutional, 20% external sources). *Receiving aid:* Freshmen: 3% (20). Undergraduates: 2% (49). *Average award:* Freshmen: $11,437. Undergraduates: $10,789. *Scholarships, grants, and awards by category:* Academic interests/achievement: general academic interests/achievements. Creative arts/performance: music. *Tuition waivers:* Full or partial for employees or children of employees.

LOANS *Student loans:* $9,714,091 (62% need-based, 38% non-need-based). 52% of past graduating class borrowed through all loan programs. *Average indebtedness per student:* $27,162. *Average need-based loan:* Freshmen: $3554. Undergraduates: $4569. *Parent loans:* $4,337,440 (18% need-based, 82% non-need-based). *Programs:* Federal Direct (Subsidized and Unsubsidized Stafford, PLUS), Perkins, college/university.

WORK-STUDY *Federal work-study:* Total amount: $1,371,956; jobs available. *State or other work-study/employment:* Total amount: $294,789 (99% need-based, 1% non-need-based). Part-time jobs available.

APPLYING FOR FINANCIAL AID *Required financial aid forms:* FAFSA, CSS Financial Aid PROFILE, noncustodial (divorced/separated) parent's statement, business/farm supplement, federal income tax form(s), W-2 forms. *Financial aid deadline:* 2/15. *Notification date:* 4/1. Students must reply by 5/1.

CONTACT Mr. Clarke Paine, Director of Financial Aid, Franklin & Marshall College, PO Box 3003, Lancaster, PA 17604-3003, 717-291-3991. *Fax:* 717-291-4462. *E-mail:* clarke.paine@fandm.edu.

FRANKLIN COLLEGE
Franklin, IN

Tuition & fees: $23,275	Average undergraduate aid package: $17,703

ABOUT THE INSTITUTION Independent religious, coed. 32 undergraduate majors. Federal methodology is used as a basis for awarding need-based institutional aid.

UNDERGRADUATE EXPENSES for 2009–10 *Comprehensive fee:* $30,160 includes full-time tuition ($23,100), mandatory fees ($175), and room and board ($6885). *College room only:* $4085. Room and board charges vary according to board plan and housing facility. *Part-time tuition:* $325 per credit hour. Part-time tuition and fees vary according to course load. *Payment plan:* Installment.

FRESHMAN FINANCIAL AID (Fall 2009, est.) 312 applied for aid; of those 85% were deemed to have need. 100% of freshmen with need received aid; of those 18% had need fully met. *Average percent of need met:* 82% (excluding resources awarded to replace EFC). *Average financial aid package:* $17,652 (excluding resources awarded to replace EFC). 22% of all full-time freshmen had no need and received non-need-based gift aid.

UNDERGRADUATE FINANCIAL AID (Fall 2009, est.) 980 applied for aid; of those 87% were deemed to have need. 100% of undergraduates with need received aid; of those 15% had need fully met. *Average percent of need met:* 82% (excluding resources awarded to replace EFC). *Average financial aid package:* $17,703 (excluding resources awarded to replace EFC). 19% of all full-time undergraduates had no need and received non-need-based gift aid.

GIFT AID (NEED-BASED) *Total amount:* $11,705,773 (10% federal, 28% state, 58% institutional, 4% external sources). *Receiving aid:* Freshmen: 78% (265); all full-time undergraduates: 80% (845). *Average award:* Freshmen: $14,379; Undergraduates: $13,782. *Scholarships, grants, and awards:* Federal Pell, FSEOG, state, private, college/university gift aid from institutional funds.

GIFT AID (NON-NEED-BASED) *Total amount:* $2,331,152 (2% state, 89% institutional, 9% external sources). *Receiving aid:* Freshmen: 13% (45). Undergraduates: 11% (112). *Average award:* Freshmen: $9968. Undergraduates: $8851. *Scholarships, grants, and awards by category: Academic interests/achievement:* 1,052 awards ($7,988,971 total): general academic interests/achievements. *Creative arts/performance:* 23 awards ($165,961 total): art/fine arts, journalism/publications, music, performing arts, theater/drama. *Special characteristics:* 232 awards ($637,114 total): children and siblings of alumni, children of faculty/staff, ethnic background, members of minority groups, out-of-state students, religious affiliation, siblings of current students. *Tuition waivers:* Full or partial for employees or children of employees, senior citizens.

LOANS *Student loans:* $7,451,327 (66% need-based, 34% non-need-based). 85% of past graduating class borrowed through all loan programs. *Average indebtedness per student:* $26,903. *Average need-based loan:* Freshmen: $4024. Undergraduates: $4665. *Parent loans:* $1,170,215 (15% need-based, 85% non-need-based). *Programs:* Federal Direct (Subsidized and Unsubsidized Stafford, PLUS), Perkins, college/university.

WORK-STUDY *Federal work-study:* Total amount: $69,704; jobs available (averaging $1500). *State or other work-study/employment:* Total amount: $162,981 (61% need-based, 39% non-need-based). Part-time jobs available.

APPLYING FOR FINANCIAL AID *Required financial aid forms:* FAFSA, institution's own form. *Financial aid deadline (priority):* 3/10. *Notification date:* Continuous beginning 3/1. Students must reply by 5/1 or within 4 weeks of notification.

CONTACT Elizabeth Sappenfield, Director of Financial Aid, Franklin College, 101 Branigin Boulevard, Franklin, IN 46131-2598, 317-738-8075 or toll-free 800-852-0232. *Fax:* 317-738-8072. *E-mail:* finaid@franklincollege.edu.

FRANKLIN PIERCE UNIVERSITY
Rindge, NH

ABOUT THE INSTITUTION Independent, coed. 50 undergraduate majors.

GIFT AID (NEED-BASED) *Scholarships, grants, and awards:* Federal Pell, FSEOG, state, private, college/university gift aid from institutional funds.

GIFT AID (NON-NEED-BASED) *Scholarships, grants, and awards by category: Academic interests/achievement:* communication, general academic interests/achievements. *Creative arts/performance:* performing arts, theater/drama. *Special achievements/activities:* general special achievements/activities, leadership. *Special characteristics:* adult students, children and siblings of alumni, children of current students, children of educators, children of faculty/staff, general special characteristics, international students, local/state students, married students, parents of current students, siblings of current students, spouses of current students.

LOANS *Programs:* FFEL (Subsidized and Unsubsidized Stafford, PLUS), Perkins.

WORK-STUDY *Federal work-study:* Total amount: $606,564; jobs available. *State or other work-study/employment:* Part-time jobs available.

APPLYING FOR FINANCIAL AID *Required financial aid form:* FAFSA.

CONTACT Kenneth Ferreira, Executive Director of Student Financial Services, Franklin Pierce University, 20 College Road, Rindge, NH 03461-0060, 603-899-4180 or toll-free 800-437-0048. *Fax:* 603-899-4372. *E-mail:* ferreirak@fpc.edu.

FRANKLIN UNIVERSITY
Columbus, OH

CONTACT Ms. Marlowe Collier, Financial Aid Assistant, Franklin University, 201 South Grant Avenue, Columbus, OH 43215-5399, 614-797-4700 or toll-free 877-341-6300. *Fax:* 614-220-8931. *E-mail:* finaid@franklin.edu.

FRANKLIN W. OLIN COLLEGE OF ENGINEERING
Needham, MA

Tuition & fees: $38,045   **Average undergraduate aid package: $42,275**

ABOUT THE INSTITUTION Independent, coed. 4 undergraduate majors. Federal methodology is used as a basis for awarding need-based institutional aid.

UNDERGRADUATE EXPENSES for 2009–10 *Comprehensive fee:* $51,275 includes full-time tuition ($36,400), mandatory fees ($1645), and room and board ($13,230). *College room only:* $8500. Room and board charges vary according to board plan. all students are awarded full-tuition scholarships. *Payment plan:* Installment.

FRESHMAN FINANCIAL AID (Fall 2009, est.) 51 applied for aid; of those 14% were deemed to have need. 100% of freshmen with need received aid; of those 100% had need fully met. *Average percent of need met:* 100% (excluding resources awarded to replace EFC). *Average financial aid package:* $42,275 (excluding resources awarded to replace EFC). 92% of all full-time freshmen had no need and received non-need-based gift aid.

UNDERGRADUATE FINANCIAL AID (Fall 2009, est.) 111 applied for aid; of those 32% were deemed to have need. 100% of undergraduates with need received aid; of those 100% had need fully met. *Average percent of need met:* 100% (excluding resources awarded to replace EFC). *Average financial aid package:* $42,275 (excluding resources awarded to replace EFC). 89% of all full-time undergraduates had no need and received non-need-based gift aid.

GIFT AID (NEED-BASED) *Total amount:* $615,083 (20% federal, 13% state, 35% institutional, 32% external sources). *Receiving aid:* Freshmen: 8% (7); all full-time undergraduates: 11% (35). *Average award:* Freshmen: $5875; Undergraduates: $5875. *Scholarships, grants, and awards:* Federal Pell, FSEOG, state, private, college/university gift aid from institutional funds, Academic Competitiveness Grants, National SMART Grants, National Merit Scholarships.

GIFT AID (NON-NEED-BASED) *Total amount:* $10,727,500 (100% institutional). *Receiving aid:* Freshmen: 8% (7). Undergraduates: 11% (35). *Average award:* Freshmen: $36,400. Undergraduates: $36,400. *Scholarships, grants, and awards by category: Academic interests/achievement:* 330 awards ($10,727,500 total): general academic interests/achievements.

LOANS *Student loans:* $227,153 (32% need-based, 68% non-need-based). *Parent loans:* $38,246 (100% non-need-based). *Programs:* Federal Direct (Subsidized and Unsubsidized Stafford, PLUS).

APPLYING FOR FINANCIAL AID *Required financial aid form:* FAFSA. *Financial aid deadline:* 2/15. *Notification date:* Continuous beginning 3/31. Students must reply by 5/1.

CONTACT Ms. Jean Ricker, Manager, Financial Aid, Franklin W. Olin College of Engineering, Campus Center 300, Needham, MA 02492, 781-292-2343. *E-mail:* jean.ricker@olin.edu.

FREED-HARDEMAN UNIVERSITY
Henderson, TN

Tuition & fees: $14,998   **Average undergraduate aid package: $13,942**

ABOUT THE INSTITUTION Independent religious, coed. 54 undergraduate majors. Federal methodology is used as a basis for awarding need-based institutional aid.

UNDERGRADUATE EXPENSES for 2009–10 *Comprehensive fee:* $22,088 includes full-time tuition ($12,060), mandatory fees ($2938), and room and board ($7090). *College room only:* $3980. Full-time tuition and fees vary according to course load and degree level. Room and board charges vary according to board plan and housing facility. *Part-time tuition:* $402 per semester hour. Part-time tuition and fees vary according to course load and degree level. *Payment plan:* Installment.

FRESHMAN FINANCIAL AID (Fall 2009, est.) 383 applied for aid; of those 83% were deemed to have need. 100% of freshmen with need received aid; of those 24% had need fully met. *Average percent of need met:* 72% (excluding resources awarded to replace EFC). *Average financial aid package:* $15,107 (excluding resources awarded to replace EFC). 19% of all full-time freshmen had no need and received non-need-based gift aid.

UNDERGRADUATE FINANCIAL AID (Fall 2009, est.) 1,308 applied for aid; of those 85% were deemed to have need. 99% of undergraduates with need received aid; of those 23% had need fully met. *Average percent of need met:* 66% (excluding resources awarded to replace EFC). *Average financial aid package:* $13,942 (excluding resources awarded to replace EFC). 17% of all full-time undergraduates had no need and received non-need-based gift aid.

GIFT AID (NEED-BASED) *Total amount:* $9,748,592 (31% federal, 18% state, 49% institutional, 2% external sources). *Receiving aid:* Freshmen: 77% (313); all full-time undergraduates: 75% (1,053). *Average award:* Freshmen: $11,779; Undergraduates: $10,139. *Scholarships, grants, and awards:* Federal Pell, FSEOG, state, private, college/university gift aid from institutional funds.

GIFT AID (NON-NEED-BASED) *Total amount:* $2,892,414 (5% federal, 27% state, 63% institutional, 5% external sources). *Receiving aid:* Freshmen: 18% (74). Undergraduates: 17% (231). *Average award:* Freshmen: $5685. Undergraduates: $6191. *Tuition waivers:* Full or partial for employees or children of employees, senior citizens.

LOANS *Student loans:* $9,366,080 (76% need-based, 24% non-need-based). 67% of past graduating class borrowed through all loan programs. *Average indebtedness per student:* $33,659. *Average need-based loan:* Freshmen: $3395. Undergraduates: $4188. *Parent loans:* $3,047,011 (38% need-based, 62% non-need-based). *Programs:* FFEL (Subsidized and Unsubsidized Stafford, PLUS), Perkins, alternative loans.

WORK-STUDY *Federal work-study:* Total amount: $1,006,681; jobs available.

ATHLETIC AWARDS Total amount: $1,233,724 (57% need-based, 43% non-need-based).

APPLYING FOR FINANCIAL AID *Required financial aid form:* FAFSA. *Financial aid deadline (priority):* 8/1. *Notification date:* Continuous beginning 3/1. Students must reply within 4 weeks of notification.

CONTACT Ms. Molly Risley, Director of Financial Aid, Freed-Hardeman University, 158 East Main Street, Henderson, TN 38340-2399, 731-989-6662 or toll-free 800-630-3480. *Fax:* 731-989-6775. *E-mail:* mrisley@fhu.edu.

FREE WILL BAPTIST BIBLE COLLEGE
Nashville, TN

ABOUT THE INSTITUTION Independent Free Will Baptist, coed. 30 undergraduate majors.

GIFT AID (NEED-BASED) *Scholarships, grants, and awards:* Federal Pell, FSEOG, state, private, college/university gift aid from institutional funds.

GIFT AID (NON-NEED-BASED) *Scholarships, grants, and awards by category:* Special characteristics: children of faculty/staff, international students, married students, relatives of clergy, veterans, veterans' children.

LOANS *Programs:* FFEL (Subsidized and Unsubsidized Stafford, PLUS), alternative loans.

WORK-STUDY *Federal work-study:* Total amount: $20,602; 6 jobs averaging $3434. *State or other work-study/employment:* 84 part-time jobs averaging $1414.

APPLYING FOR FINANCIAL AID *Required financial aid forms:* FAFSA, institution's own form.

CONTACT Jeff Caudill, Director of Enrollment Services, Free Will Baptist Bible College, 3606 West End Avenue, Nashville, TN 37205, 615-844-5000 or toll-free 800-763-9222. *Fax:* 615-269-6028. *E-mail:* jcaudill@fwbbc.edu.

FRESNO PACIFIC UNIVERSITY
Fresno, CA

Tuition & fees: N/R	Average undergraduate aid package: $15,215

ABOUT THE INSTITUTION Independent religious, coed. *Awards:* associate, bachelor's, and master's degrees. 42 undergraduate majors. *Total enrollment:* 2,353. Undergraduates: 1,539. Freshmen: 170. Federal methodology is used as a basis for awarding need-based institutional aid.

FRESHMAN FINANCIAL AID (Fall 2009, est.) 157 applied for aid; of those 92% were deemed to have need. 99% of freshmen with need received aid; of those

10% had need fully met. *Average percent of need met:* 72% (excluding resources awarded to replace EFC). *Average financial aid package:* $21,525 (excluding resources awarded to replace EFC). 8% of all full-time freshmen had no need and received non-need-based gift aid.

UNDERGRADUATE FINANCIAL AID (Fall 2009, est.) 1,372 applied for aid; of those 93% were deemed to have need. 99% of undergraduates with need received aid; of those 8% had need fully met. *Average percent of need met:* 58% (excluding resources awarded to replace EFC). *Average financial aid package:* $15,215 (excluding resources awarded to replace EFC). 50% of all full-time undergraduates had no need and received non-need-based gift aid.

GIFT AID (NEED-BASED) *Total amount:* $6,667,259 (34% federal, 52% state, 14% institutional). *Receiving aid:* Freshmen: 69% (119); all full-time undergraduates: 62% (954). *Average award:* Freshmen: $12,621; Undergraduates: $8667. *Scholarships, grants, and awards:* Federal Pell, FSEOG, state, private, college/university gift aid from institutional funds.

GIFT AID (NON-NEED-BASED) *Total amount:* $6,387,719 (97% institutional, 3% external sources). *Receiving aid:* Freshmen: 81% (139). Undergraduates: 40% (624). *Average award:* Freshmen: $8332. Undergraduates: $7812. *Scholarships, grants, and awards by category:* Academic interests/achievement: business, general academic interests/achievements, humanities, social sciences. Creative arts/performance: music, performing arts, theater/drama. Special characteristics: children of faculty/staff, members of minority groups, relatives of clergy, religious affiliation, spouses of current students. *Tuition waivers:* Full or partial for employees or children of employees, senior citizens.

LOANS *Student loans:* $6,742,368 (100% need-based). 82% of past graduating class borrowed through all loan programs. *Average indebtedness per student:* $18,929. *Average need-based loan:* Freshmen: $5571. Undergraduates: $4616. *Parent loans:* $629,658 (100% need-based). *Programs:* Federal Direct (Subsidized and Unsubsidized Stafford, PLUS), FFEL (Subsidized and Unsubsidized Stafford, PLUS), Perkins.

WORK-STUDY *Federal work-study:* Total amount: $807,415; jobs available.

ATHLETIC AWARDS Total amount: $2,067,548 (100% non-need-based).

APPLYING FOR FINANCIAL AID *Required financial aid forms:* FAFSA, institution's own form. *Financial aid deadline (priority):* 3/2. *Notification date:* Continuous beginning 3/2. Students must reply by 7/30 or within 3 weeks of notification.

CONTACT April Powell, Associate Director of Financial Aid, Fresno Pacific University, 1717 South Chestnut Avenue, #2004, Fresno, CA 93702, 559-453-2041 or toll-free 800-660-6089 (in-state). *Fax:* 559-453-5595. *E-mail:* sfs@fresno.edu.

FRIENDS UNIVERSITY
Wichita, KS

CONTACT Brandon Pierce, Director of Financial Aid, Friends University, 2100 University Street, Wichita, KS 67213, 316-295-5658 or toll-free 800-577-2233. *Fax:* 316-295-5703. *E-mail:* piercb@friends.edu.

FROSTBURG STATE UNIVERSITY
Frostburg, MD

Tuition & fees (MD res): $6684	Average undergraduate aid package: $8927

ABOUT THE INSTITUTION State-supported, coed. 56 undergraduate majors. Federal methodology is used as a basis for awarding need-based institutional aid.

UNDERGRADUATE EXPENSES for 2010–11 *Tuition, state resident:* full-time $5000; part-time $207 per credit hour. *Tuition, nonresident:* full-time $15,196; part-time $427 per credit hour. *Required fees:* full-time $1684; $82 per credit hour or $11 per term. Full-time tuition and fees vary according to location. Part-time tuition and fees vary according to course load and location. *College room and board:* $7304; *Room only:* $3474. Room and board charges vary according to board plan and housing facility. *Payment plans:* Installment, deferred payment.

FRESHMAN FINANCIAL AID (Fall 2009, est.) 931 applied for aid; of those 65% were deemed to have need. 100% of freshmen with need received aid; of those 28% had need fully met. *Average percent of need met:* 73% (excluding resources awarded to replace EFC). *Average financial aid package:* $9783 (excluding resources awarded to replace EFC). 11% of all full-time freshmen had no need and received non-need-based gift aid.

UNDERGRADUATE FINANCIAL AID (Fall 2009, est.) 3,645 applied for aid; of those 70% were deemed to have need. 100% of undergraduates with need received aid; of those 25% had need fully met. *Average percent of need met:* 71% (excluding resources awarded to replace EFC). *Average financial aid package:* $8927 (excluding resources awarded to replace EFC). 10% of all full-time undergraduates had no need and received non-need-based gift aid.

GIFT AID (NEED-BASED) *Total amount:* $12,988,925 (52% federal, 32% state, 11% institutional, 5% external sources). *Receiving aid:* Freshmen: 42% (450); all full-time undergraduates: 40% (1,864). *Average award:* Freshmen: $7915; Undergraduates: $6538. *Scholarships, grants, and awards:* Federal Pell, FSEOG, state, private, college/university gift aid from institutional funds.

GIFT AID (NON-NEED-BASED) *Total amount:* $3,466,865 (14% state, 74% institutional, 12% external sources). *Receiving aid:* Freshmen: 17% (179). Undergraduates: 15% (713). *Average award:* Freshmen: $3105. Undergraduates: $2995. *Scholarships, grants, and awards by category: Academic interests/achievement:* biological sciences, business, communication, computer science, education, engineering/technologies, English, foreign languages, general academic interests/achievements, health fields, humanities, international studies, mathematics, physical sciences, premedicine, social sciences. *Creative arts/performance:* art/fine arts, creative writing, journalism/publications, music, performing arts, theater/drama. *Special achievements/activities:* community service, leadership. *Special characteristics:* adult students, children of union members/company employees, international students, local/state students, out-of-state students, veterans, veterans' children. *Tuition waivers:* Full or partial for employees or children of employees, senior citizens.

LOANS *Student loans:* $23,571,528 (41% need-based, 59% non-need-based). 64% of past graduating class borrowed through all loan programs. *Average indebtedness per student:* $18,255. *Average need-based loan:* Freshmen: $3308. Undergraduates: $3794. *Parent loans:* $3,714,783 (100% non-need-based). *Programs:* Federal Direct (Subsidized and Unsubsidized Stafford, PLUS), FFEL (Subsidized and Unsubsidized Stafford, PLUS), Perkins.

WORK-STUDY *Federal work-study:* Total amount: $127,227; 209 jobs averaging $608. *State or other work-study/employment:* Part-time jobs available.

APPLYING FOR FINANCIAL AID *Required financial aid form:* FAFSA. *Financial aid deadline (priority):* 3/1. *Notification date:* Continuous beginning 3/15. Students must reply within 3 weeks of notification.

CONTACT Mrs. Angela Hovatter, Director of Financial Aid, Frostburg State University, 114 Pullen Hall, Frostburg, MD 21532-1099, 301-687-4301. *Fax:* 301-687-7074. *E-mail:* ahovatter@frostburg.edu.

FULL SAIL UNIVERSITY
Winter Park, FL

Tuition & fees: N/R	Average undergraduate aid package: $7921

ABOUT THE INSTITUTION Proprietary, coed, primarily men. 20 undergraduate majors. Federal methodology is used as a basis for awarding need-based institutional aid.

UNDERGRADUATE EXPENSES for 2009–10 please contact school for program costs.

FRESHMAN FINANCIAL AID (Fall 2008) 4,496 applied for aid; of those 47% were deemed to have need. 91% of freshmen with need received aid. *Average financial aid package:* $5777 (excluding resources awarded to replace EFC). 10% of all full-time freshmen had no need and received non-need-based gift aid.

UNDERGRADUATE FINANCIAL AID (Fall 2008) 7,337 applied for aid; of those 94% were deemed to have need. 89% of undergraduates with need received aid. *Average financial aid package:* $7921 (excluding resources awarded to replace EFC). 12% of all full-time undergraduates had no need and received non-need-based gift aid.

GIFT AID (NEED-BASED) *Total amount:* $10,453,531 (84% federal, 2% state, 14% institutional). *Receiving aid:* Freshmen: 11% (653); all full-time undergraduates: 20% (2,171). *Average award:* Freshmen: $3422; Undergraduates: $4212. *Scholarships, grants, and awards:* Federal Pell, FSEOG, state, college/university gift aid from institutional funds, Office of Vocational Rehabilitation Awards.

GIFT AID (NON-NEED-BASED) *Total amount:* $6,718,360 (8% federal, 6% state, 86% institutional). *Receiving aid:* Freshmen: 6% (338). Undergraduates: 13% (1,483). *Average award:* Freshmen: $5121. Undergraduates: $3572.

LOANS *Student loans:* $171,723,008 (22% need-based, 78% non-need-based). 85% of past graduating class borrowed through all loan programs. *Average*

indebtedness per student: $63,978. *Parent loans:* $99,539,236 (100% non-need-based). *Programs:* Federal Direct (Subsidized and Unsubsidized Stafford, PLUS).

WORK-STUDY *Federal work-study:* Total amount: $655,500; 475 jobs averaging $1380.

APPLYING FOR FINANCIAL AID *Required financial aid form:* FAFSA. *Financial aid deadline:* Continuous. *Notification date:* Continuous.

CONTACT Financial Aid Office, Full Sail University, 3300 University Boulevard, Winter Park, FL 32792, 800-575-1142 or toll-free 800-226-7625.

FURMAN UNIVERSITY
Greenville, SC

Tuition & fees: $36,656	Average undergraduate aid package: $28,079

ABOUT THE INSTITUTION Independent, coed. 48 undergraduate majors. Both federal and institutional methodology are used as a basis for awarding need-based institutional aid.

UNDERGRADUATE EXPENSES for 2009–10 *Comprehensive fee:* $45,826 includes full-time tuition ($36,296), mandatory fees ($360), and room and board ($9170). *College room only:* $4928. Room and board charges vary according to board plan and housing facility. *Part-time tuition:* $1134 per credit hour. Part-time tuition and fees vary according to course load. *Payment plan:* Installment.

FRESHMAN FINANCIAL AID (Fall 2009, est.) 447 applied for aid; of those 78% were deemed to have need. 100% of freshmen with need received aid; of those 43% had need fully met. *Average percent of need met:* 85% (excluding resources awarded to replace EFC). *Average financial aid package:* $28,945 (excluding resources awarded to replace EFC). 24% of all full-time freshmen had no need and received non-need-based gift aid.

UNDERGRADUATE FINANCIAL AID (Fall 2009, est.) 1,468 applied for aid; of those 84% were deemed to have need. 99% of undergraduates with need received aid; of those 36% had need fully met. *Average percent of need met:* 81% (excluding resources awarded to replace EFC). *Average financial aid package:* $28,079 (excluding resources awarded to replace EFC). 27% of all full-time undergraduates had no need and received non-need-based gift aid.

GIFT AID (NEED-BASED) *Total amount:* $23,935,416 (9% federal, 7% state, 76% institutional, 8% external sources). *Receiving aid:* Freshmen: 53% (348); all full-time undergraduates: 47% (1,223). *Average award:* Freshmen: $26,737; Undergraduates: $24,782. *Scholarships, grants, and awards:* Federal Pell, FSEOG, state, private, college/university gift aid from institutional funds, Academic Competitiveness Grants, National SMART Grants.

GIFT AID (NON-NEED-BASED) *Total amount:* $20,801,927 (21% state, 74% institutional, 5% external sources). *Receiving aid:* Freshmen: 49% (318). Undergraduates: 37% (968). *Average award:* Freshmen: $16,230. Undergraduates: $16,007. *Scholarships, grants, and awards by category: Academic interests/achievement:* area/ethnic studies, biological sciences, business, communication, computer science, education, engineering/technologies, English, foreign languages, general academic interests/achievements, health fields, humanities, international studies, mathematics, military science, physical sciences, premedicine, religion/biblical studies, social sciences. *Creative arts/performance:* art/fine arts, creative writing, music, theater/drama. *Special achievements/activities:* community service, leadership, religious involvement. *Special characteristics:* children of faculty/staff, ethnic background, international students, local/state students, relatives of clergy, religious affiliation, veterans. *Tuition waivers:* Full or partial for employees or children of employees.

LOANS *Student loans:* $8,978,485 (75% need-based, 25% non-need-based). 40% of past graduating class borrowed through all loan programs. *Average indebtedness per student:* $27,373. *Average need-based loan:* Freshmen: $3297. Undergraduates: $4935. *Parent loans:* $3,580,921 (67% need-based, 33% non-need-based). *Programs:* FFEL (Subsidized and Unsubsidized Stafford, PLUS), Perkins, state, alternative loans.

WORK-STUDY *Federal work-study:* Total amount: $844,255; 572 jobs averaging $1489.

ATHLETIC AWARDS Total amount: $7,017,749 (43% need-based, 57% non-need-based).

APPLYING FOR FINANCIAL AID *Required financial aid forms:* FAFSA, CSS Financial Aid PROFILE, state aid form. *Financial aid deadline:* 1/15. *Notification date:* 3/15. Students must reply by 5/1.

CONTACT Forrest Stuart, Director of Financial Aid, Furman University, 3300 Poinsett Highway, Greenville, SC 29613, 864-294-2204. *Fax:* 864-294-3127. *E-mail:* forrest.stuart@furman.edu.

GALLAUDET UNIVERSITY
Washington, DC

Tuition & fees: $11,226	Average undergraduate aid package: $16,918

ABOUT THE INSTITUTION Independent, coed. 52 undergraduate majors. Federal methodology is used as a basis for awarding need-based institutional aid.

UNDERGRADUATE EXPENSES for 2010–11 *Comprehensive fee:* $20,886 includes full-time tuition ($10,850), mandatory fees ($376), and room and board ($9660). *College room only:* $5460. Full-time tuition and fees vary according to degree level. Room and board charges vary according to board plan. *Part-time tuition:* $542.50 per credit hour. Part-time tuition and fees vary according to degree level.

FRESHMAN FINANCIAL AID (Fall 2008) 169 applied for aid; of those 82% were deemed to have need. 100% of freshmen with need received aid; of those 39% had need fully met. *Average percent of need met:* 84% (excluding resources awarded to replace EFC). *Average financial aid package:* $16,894 (excluding resources awarded to replace EFC). 9% of all full-time freshmen had no need and received non-need-based gift aid.

UNDERGRADUATE FINANCIAL AID (Fall 2008) 900 applied for aid; of those 84% were deemed to have need. 99% of undergraduates with need received aid; of those 39% had need fully met. *Average percent of need met:* 84% (excluding resources awarded to replace EFC). *Average financial aid package:* $16,918 (excluding resources awarded to replace EFC). 4% of all full-time undergraduates had no need and received non-need-based gift aid.

GIFT AID (NEED-BASED) *Total amount:* $11,016,880 (13% federal, 62% state, 24% institutional, 1% external sources). *Receiving aid:* Freshmen: 76% (137); all full-time undergraduates: 72% (740). *Average award:* Freshmen: $16,069; Undergraduates: $15,364. *Scholarships, grants, and awards:* Federal Pell, FSEOG, state, private, college/university gift aid from institutional funds.

GIFT AID (NON-NEED-BASED) *Total amount:* $2,150,806 (85% state, 14% institutional, 1% external sources). *Receiving aid:* Freshmen: 27% (48). Undergraduates: 26% (268). *Average award:* Freshmen: $7297. Undergraduates: $6967. *Scholarships, grants, and awards by category:* Academic interests/achievement: general academic interests/achievements. Special achievements/activities: leadership. Special characteristics: members of minority groups. *Tuition waivers:* Full or partial for employees or children of employees.

LOANS *Student loans:* $2,185,870 (91% need-based, 9% non-need-based). 54% of past graduating class borrowed through all loan programs. *Average indebtedness per student:* $13,484. *Average need-based loan:* Freshmen: $2778. Undergraduates: $3574. *Parent loans:* $242,869 (57% need-based, 43% non-need-based). *Programs:* FFEL (Subsidized and Unsubsidized Stafford, PLUS), Perkins.

WORK-STUDY *Federal work-study:* Total amount: $55,044; jobs available.

APPLYING FOR FINANCIAL AID *Required financial aid forms:* FAFSA, institution's own form. *Financial aid deadline:* Continuous. *Notification date:* Continuous beginning 3/1.

CONTACT Mrs. Nancy C. Goodman, Director of Financial Aid, Gallaudet University, 800 Florida Avenue, NE, Washington, DC 20002, 202-651-5290 or toll-free 800-995-0550 (out-of-state). *Fax:* 202-651-5740.

GANNON UNIVERSITY
Erie, PA

Tuition & fees: $23,574	Average undergraduate aid package: $19,802

ABOUT THE INSTITUTION Independent Roman Catholic, coed. 63 undergraduate majors. Federal methodology is used as a basis for awarding need-based institutional aid.

UNDERGRADUATE EXPENSES for 2009–10 *Comprehensive fee:* $32,904 includes full-time tuition ($23,050), mandatory fees ($524), and room and board ($9330). *College room only:* $4850. Full-time tuition and fees vary according to class time and program. Room and board charges vary according to board plan and housing facility. *Part-time tuition:* $715 per credit hour. *Part-time fees:* $17 per credit hour. Part-time tuition and fees vary according to class time and program. *Payment plans:* Installment, deferred payment.

FRESHMAN FINANCIAL AID (Fall 2009, est.) 620 applied for aid; of those 92% were deemed to have need. 100% of freshmen with need received aid; of those 25% had need fully met. *Average percent of need met:* 83% (excluding resources awarded to replace EFC). *Average financial aid package:* $20,797 (excluding resources awarded to replace EFC). 7% of all full-time freshmen had no need and received non-need-based gift aid.

UNDERGRADUATE FINANCIAL AID (Fall 2009, est.) 2,281 applied for aid; of those 92% were deemed to have need. 100% of undergraduates with need received aid; of those 24% had need fully met. *Average percent of need met:* 79% (excluding resources awarded to replace EFC). *Average financial aid package:* $19,802 (excluding resources awarded to replace EFC). 9% of all full-time undergraduates had no need and received non-need-based gift aid.

GIFT AID (NEED-BASED) *Total amount:* $29,454,471 (16% federal, 11% state, 68% institutional, 5% external sources). *Receiving aid:* Freshmen: 87% (567); all full-time undergraduates: 84% (2,056). *Average award:* Freshmen: $17,012; Undergraduates: $15,398. *Scholarships, grants, and awards:* Federal Pell, FSEOG, state, private, college/university gift aid from institutional funds.

GIFT AID (NON-NEED-BASED) *Total amount:* $6,141,553 (51% institutional, 49% external sources). *Receiving aid:* Freshmen: 12% (79). Undergraduates: 11% (269). *Average award:* Freshmen: $10,158. Undergraduates: $8170. *Scholarships, grants, and awards by category:* Academic interests/achievement: $9,028,287 total: biological sciences, business, education, engineering/technologies, English, foreign languages, general academic interests/achievements, humanities, international studies, mathematics, premedicine, religion/biblical studies, social sciences. Creative arts/performance: $127,250 total: music, performing arts, theater/drama. Special achievements/activities: $2,177,564 total: community service, leadership. Special characteristics: $1,196,729 total: adult students, ethnic background, international students, members of minority groups, religious affiliation, veterans. *Tuition waivers:* Full or partial for employees or children of employees, senior citizens.

LOANS *Student loans:* $18,849,046 (57% need-based, 43% non-need-based). 86% of past graduating class borrowed through all loan programs. *Average indebtedness per student:* $31,234. *Average need-based loan:* Freshmen: $3390. Undergraduates: $4180. *Parent loans:* $3,103,382 (91% need-based, 9% non-need-based). *Programs:* Federal Direct (Subsidized and Unsubsidized Stafford, PLUS), FFEL (Subsidized and Unsubsidized Stafford, PLUS), Perkins, Federal Nursing.

WORK-STUDY *Federal work-study:* Total amount: $798,458; 582 jobs averaging $2300. *State or other work-study/employment:* Total amount: $262,200 (100% non-need-based). 150 part-time jobs averaging $2300.

ATHLETIC AWARDS Total amount: $3,017,309 (73% need-based, 27% non-need-based).

APPLYING FOR FINANCIAL AID *Required financial aid forms:* FAFSA, institution's own form. *Financial aid deadline (priority):* 3/15. *Notification date:* Continuous beginning 11/1. Students must reply by 5/1 or within 4 weeks of notification.

CONTACT Ms. Sharon Krahe, Director of Financial Aid, Gannon University, 109 University Square, Erie, PA 16541, 814-871-7670 or toll-free 800-GANNONU. *Fax:* 814-871-5826. *E-mail:* krahe001@gannon.edu.

GARDNER-WEBB UNIVERSITY
Boiling Springs, NC

Tuition & fees: $22,440	Average undergraduate aid package: $17,438

ABOUT THE INSTITUTION Independent Baptist, coed. 65 undergraduate majors. Federal methodology is used as a basis for awarding need-based institutional aid.

UNDERGRADUATE EXPENSES for 2010–11 *One-time required fee:* $100. *Comprehensive fee:* $29,250 includes full-time tuition ($22,050), mandatory fees ($390), and room and board ($6810). *College room only:* $3490. Full-time tuition and fees vary according to degree level and program. Room and board charges vary according to board plan and housing facility. *Part-time tuition:* $345 per credit hour. Part-time tuition and fees vary according to course load. *Payment plan:* Installment.

FRESHMAN FINANCIAL AID (Fall 2009, est.) 407 applied for aid; of those 84% were deemed to have need. 100% of freshmen with need received aid; of those 23% had need fully met. *Average percent of need met:* 71% (excluding resources awarded to replace EFC). *Average financial aid package:* $17,717 (excluding resources awarded to replace EFC). 18% of all full-time freshmen had no need and received non-need-based gift aid.

UNDERGRADUATE FINANCIAL AID (Fall 2009, est.) 1,318 applied for aid; of those 88% were deemed to have need. 100% of undergraduates with need received aid; of those 19% had need fully met. *Average percent of need met:* 71% (excluding resources awarded to replace EFC). *Average financial aid package:* $17,438 (excluding resources awarded to replace EFC). 12% of all full-time undergraduates had no need and received non-need-based gift aid.

GIFT AID (NEED-BASED) *Total amount:* $12,653,739 (23% federal, 32% state, 41% institutional, 4% external sources). *Receiving aid:* Freshmen: 72% (322); all full-time undergraduates: 45% (1,021). *Average award:* Freshmen: $9602; Undergraduates: $8412. *Scholarships, grants, and awards:* Federal Pell, FSEOG, state, private, college/university gift aid from institutional funds.

GIFT AID (NON-NEED-BASED) *Total amount:* $2,582,259 (13% state, 85% institutional, 2% external sources). *Receiving aid:* Freshmen: 56% (250). Undergraduates: 36% (810). *Average award:* Freshmen: $6958. Undergraduates: $6860. *Scholarships, grants, and awards by category: Academic interests/achievement:* biological sciences, business, communication, computer science, education, English, foreign languages, general academic interests/achievements, health fields, humanities, mathematics, physical sciences, premedicine, religion/biblical studies, social sciences. *Creative arts/performance:* art/fine arts, music, theater/drama. *Special achievements/activities:* cheerleading/drum major, religious involvement. *Special characteristics:* children of faculty/staff, handicapped students, local/state students, members of minority groups, out-of-state students, previous college experience, relatives of clergy. *Tuition waivers:* Full or partial for employees or children of employees, senior citizens.

LOANS *Student loans:* $8,542,714 (93% need-based, 7% non-need-based). *Average need-based loan:* Freshmen: $3517. Undergraduates: $4266. *Parent loans:* $1,802,674 (88% need-based, 12% non-need-based). *Programs:* Federal Direct (Subsidized and Unsubsidized Stafford, PLUS), Perkins, state, alternative loans.

WORK-STUDY *Federal work-study:* Total amount: $325,575; jobs available. *State or other work-study/employment:* Total amount: $108,501 (66% need-based, 34% non-need-based). Part-time jobs available.

ATHLETIC AWARDS Total amount: $5,039,687 (54% need-based, 46% non-need-based).

APPLYING FOR FINANCIAL AID *Required financial aid forms:* FAFSA, state aid form. *Financial aid deadline (priority):* 3/15. *Notification date:* 3/1. Students must reply within 2 weeks of notification.

CONTACT Summer Nance, Director of Financial Planning, Gardner-Webb University, PO Box 955, Boiling Springs, NC 28017, 704-406-4243 or toll-free 800-253-6472. *Fax:* 704-406-4102.

GENEVA COLLEGE
Beaver Falls, PA

Tuition & fees: $22,236	Average undergraduate aid package: $17,681

ABOUT THE INSTITUTION Independent religious, coed. 29 undergraduate majors. Federal methodology is used as a basis for awarding need-based institutional aid.

UNDERGRADUATE EXPENSES for 2010–11 *Comprehensive fee:* $30,236 includes full-time tuition ($22,236) and room and board ($8000). Full-time tuition and fees vary according to course load. Room and board charges vary according to board plan. *Part-time tuition:* $745 per credit. Part-time tuition and fees vary according to course load. *Payment plan:* Installment.

FRESHMAN FINANCIAL AID (Fall 2009, est.) 317 applied for aid; of those 92% were deemed to have need. 100% of freshmen with need received aid; of those 16% had need fully met. *Average percent of need met:* 81% (excluding resources awarded to replace EFC). *Average financial aid package:* $18,382 (excluding resources awarded to replace EFC). 9% of all full-time freshmen had no need and received non-need-based gift aid.

UNDERGRADUATE FINANCIAL AID (Fall 2009, est.) 1,240 applied for aid; of those 92% were deemed to have need. 100% of undergraduates with need received aid; of those 18% had need fully met. *Average percent of need met:* 80% (excluding resources awarded to replace EFC). *Average financial aid package:* $17,681 (excluding resources awarded to replace EFC). 13% of all full-time undergraduates had no need and received non-need-based gift aid.

GIFT AID (NEED-BASED) *Total amount:* $14,428,252 (17% federal, 14% state, 65% institutional, 4% external sources). *Receiving aid:* Freshmen: 90% (293); all full-time undergraduates: 84% (1,128). *Average award:* Freshmen: $14,377; Undergraduates: $13,388. *Scholarships, grants, and awards:* Federal Pell, FSEOG, state, private, college/university gift aid from institutional funds.

GIFT AID (NON-NEED-BASED) *Total amount:* $1,582,584 (3% state, 91% institutional, 6% external sources). *Receiving aid:* Freshmen: 7% (22). Undergraduates: 8% (106). *Average award:* Freshmen: $6076. Undergraduates: $6711. *Scholarships, grants, and awards by category: Academic interests/achievement:* engineering/technologies, general academic interests/achievements, religion/biblical studies. *Creative arts/performance:* music. *Special characteristics:* children of faculty/staff, religious affiliation. *Tuition waivers:* Full or partial for minority students, employees or children of employees.

LOANS *Student loans:* $8,456,049 (73% need-based, 27% non-need-based). 94% of past graduating class borrowed through all loan programs. *Average indebtedness per student:* $22,680. *Average need-based loan:* Freshmen: $3657. Undergraduates: $4109. *Parent loans:* $1,419,007 (32% need-based, 68% non-need-based). *Programs:* Federal Direct (Subsidized and Unsubsidized Stafford, PLUS), Perkins.

WORK-STUDY *Federal work-study:* Total amount: $920,370; 250 jobs averaging $2000.

ATHLETIC AWARDS Total amount: $1000 (100% need-based).

APPLYING FOR FINANCIAL AID *Required financial aid form:* FAFSA. *Financial aid deadline (priority):* 3/15. *Notification date:* Continuous beginning 3/1. Students must reply within 4 weeks of notification.

CONTACT Mr. Steve Bell, Director of Financial Aid, Geneva College, 3200 College Avenue, Beaver Falls, PA 15010-3599, 800-847-8255. *Fax:* 724-847-6776. *E-mail:* financialaid@geneva.edu.

GEORGE FOX UNIVERSITY
Newberg, OR

Tuition & fees: $26,180	Average undergraduate aid package: $23,840

ABOUT THE INSTITUTION Independent Friends, coed. 42 undergraduate majors. Federal methodology is used as a basis for awarding need-based institutional aid.

UNDERGRADUATE EXPENSES for 2009–10 *Comprehensive fee:* $34,500 includes full-time tuition ($25,860), mandatory fees ($320), and room and board ($8320). *College room only:* $4680. Room and board charges vary according to board plan. *Part-time tuition:* $780 per semester hour. Part-time tuition and fees vary according to course load. *Payment plan:* Installment.

FRESHMAN FINANCIAL AID (Fall 2009, est.) 360 applied for aid; of those 89% were deemed to have need. 100% of freshmen with need received aid; of those 43% had need fully met. *Average percent of need met:* 90% (excluding resources awarded to replace EFC). *Average financial aid package:* $25,545 (excluding resources awarded to replace EFC). 8% of all full-time freshmen had no need and received non-need-based gift aid.

UNDERGRADUATE FINANCIAL AID (Fall 2009, est.) 1,376 applied for aid; of those 90% were deemed to have need. 100% of undergraduates with need received aid; of those 43% had need fully met. *Average percent of need met:* 89% (excluding resources awarded to replace EFC). *Average financial aid package:* $23,840 (excluding resources awarded to replace EFC). 6% of all full-time undergraduates had no need and received non-need-based gift aid.

GIFT AID (NEED-BASED) *Total amount:* $18,839,703 (10% federal, 3% state, 81% institutional, 6% external sources). *Receiving aid:* Freshmen: 74% (301); all full-time undergraduates: 68% (1,138). *Average award:* Freshmen: $10,215; Undergraduates: $9057. *Scholarships, grants, and awards:* Federal Pell, FSEOG, state, private, college/university gift aid from institutional funds, Academic Competitiveness Grants, National SMART Grants, TEACH Grants.

GIFT AID (NON-NEED-BASED) *Total amount:* $1,315,183 (92% institutional, 8% external sources). *Receiving aid:* Freshmen: 67% (273). Undergraduates: 60% (1,002). *Average award:* Freshmen: $6740. Undergraduates: $7163. *Scholarships, grants, and awards by category: Academic interests/achievement:* biological sciences, computer science, education, engineering/technologies, general academic interests/achievements, mathematics, physical sciences, religion/biblical studies. *Creative arts/performance:* art/fine arts, debating, music, theater/drama. *Special achievements/activities:* leadership, religious involvement. *Special characteristics:* children and siblings of alumni, children of faculty/staff, ethnic background, international students, members of minority groups, out-of-state students, relatives of clergy, religious affiliation. *Tuition waivers:* Full or partial for employees or children of employees, senior citizens.

LOANS *Student loans:* $9,488,326 (84% need-based, 16% non-need-based). 83% of past graduating class borrowed through all loan programs. *Average indebtedness per student:* $24,624. *Average need-based loan:* Freshmen: $3155.

Undergraduates: $3633. *Parent loans:* $725,541 (51% need-based, 49% non-need-based). *Programs:* Federal Direct (Subsidized and Unsubsidized Stafford, PLUS), Perkins, alternative loans.

WORK-STUDY *Federal work-study:* Total amount: $379,009; jobs available. *State or other work-study/employment:* Total amount: $1,813,289 (90% need-based, 10% non-need-based). Part-time jobs available.

APPLYING FOR FINANCIAL AID *Required financial aid forms:* FAFSA, state aid form. *Financial aid deadline (priority):* 2/1. *Notification date:* Continuous beginning 3/1. Students must reply by 5/1 or within 6 weeks of notification.

CONTACT James Oshiro, Associate Director of Financial Services, George Fox University, 414 North Meridian Street, Newberg, OR 97132-2697, 503-554-2290 or toll-free 800-765-4369. *Fax:* 503-554-3880. *E-mail:* sfs@georgefox.edu.

GEORGE MASON UNIVERSITY
Fairfax, VA

Tuition & fees (VA res): $8024	Average undergraduate aid package: $11,449

ABOUT THE INSTITUTION State-supported, coed. 56 undergraduate majors. Federal methodology is used as a basis for awarding need-based institutional aid.

UNDERGRADUATE EXPENSES for 2009–10 *Tuition, state resident:* full-time $5640; part-time $235 per credit hour. *Tuition, nonresident:* full-time $21,624; part-time $901 per credit hour. *Required fees:* full-time $2384; $91 per credit hour. Full-time tuition and fees vary according to course load. Part-time tuition and fees vary according to course load. *College room and board:* $7700; *Room only:* $4500. Room and board charges vary according to board plan and housing facility. *Payment plans:* Installment, deferred payment.

FRESHMAN FINANCIAL AID (Fall 2009, est.) 1,948 applied for aid; of those 63% were deemed to have need. 97% of freshmen with need received aid; of those 12% had need fully met. *Average percent of need met:* 74% (excluding resources awarded to replace EFC). *Average financial aid package:* $11,991 (excluding resources awarded to replace EFC). 4% of all full-time freshmen had no need and received non-need-based gift aid.

UNDERGRADUATE FINANCIAL AID (Fall 2009, est.) 9,425 applied for aid; of those 75% were deemed to have need. 97% of undergraduates with need received aid; of those 11% had need fully met. *Average percent of need met:* 71% (excluding resources awarded to replace EFC). *Average financial aid package:* $11,449 (excluding resources awarded to replace EFC). 2% of all full-time undergraduates had no need and received non-need-based gift aid.

GIFT AID (NEED-BASED) *Total amount:* $39,546,906 (52% federal, 40% state, 8% institutional). *Receiving aid:* Freshmen: 37% (979); all full-time undergraduates: 36% (5,427). *Average award:* Freshmen: $7157; Undergraduates: $6685. *Scholarships, grants, and awards:* Federal Pell, FSEOG, state, private, college/university gift aid from institutional funds.

GIFT AID (NON-NEED-BASED) *Total amount:* $6,598,597 (71% institutional, 29% external sources). *Receiving aid:* Freshmen: 14% (362). Undergraduates: 7% (1,057). *Average award:* Freshmen: $7329. Undergraduates: $6171. *Scholarships, grants, and awards by category:* Academic interests/achievement: 1,152 awards ($4,727,726 total): general academic interests/achievements. Creative arts/performance: general creative arts/performance. Special characteristics: general special characteristics. *Tuition waivers:* Full or partial for employees or children of employees, senior citizens.

LOANS *Student loans:* $66,666,132 (67% need-based, 33% non-need-based). 52% of past graduating class borrowed through all loan programs. Average indebtedness per student: $19,528. *Average need-based loan:* Freshmen: $3528. Undergraduates: $4454. *Parent loans:* $10,729,112 (34% need-based, 66% non-need-based). *Programs:* Federal Direct (Subsidized and Unsubsidized Stafford, PLUS), FFEL (Subsidized and Unsubsidized Stafford, PLUS), Perkins, Federal Nursing.

WORK-STUDY *Federal work-study:* Total amount: $604,166; 323 jobs averaging $1518.

ATHLETIC AWARDS Total amount: $3,802,202 (100% non-need-based).

APPLYING FOR FINANCIAL AID *Required financial aid form:* FAFSA. *Financial aid deadline (priority):* 3/1. *Notification date:* Continuous beginning 4/1. Students must reply within 3 weeks of notification.

CONTACT Office of Student Financial Aid, George Mason University, Mail Stop 3B5, Fairfax, VA 22030-4444, 703-993-2353. *Fax:* 703-993-2350. *E-mail:* finaid@gmu.edu.

GEORGETOWN COLLEGE
Georgetown, KY

Tuition & fees: $26,080	Average undergraduate aid package: $22,830

ABOUT THE INSTITUTION Independent religious, coed. 35 undergraduate majors. Federal methodology is used as a basis for awarding need-based institutional aid.

UNDERGRADUATE EXPENSES for 2009–10 *Comprehensive fee:* $33,110 includes full-time tuition ($26,080) and room and board ($7030). *College room only:* $3390. Full-time tuition and fees vary according to course load. Room and board charges vary according to board plan and housing facility. *Part-time tuition:* $1080 per credit hour. *Payment plan:* Deferred payment.

FRESHMAN FINANCIAL AID (Fall 2009, est.) 345 applied for aid; of those 90% were deemed to have need. 100% of freshmen with need received aid; of those 38% had need fully met. *Average percent of need met:* 87% (excluding resources awarded to replace EFC). *Average financial aid package:* $24,384 (excluding resources awarded to replace EFC). 18% of all full-time freshmen had no need and received non-need-based gift aid.

UNDERGRADUATE FINANCIAL AID (Fall 2009, est.) 1,079 applied for aid; of those 92% were deemed to have need. 100% of undergraduates with need received aid; of those 31% had need fully met. *Average percent of need met:* 83% (excluding resources awarded to replace EFC). *Average financial aid package:* $22,830 (excluding resources awarded to replace EFC). 22% of all full-time undergraduates had no need and received non-need-based gift aid.

GIFT AID (NEED-BASED) *Total amount:* $17,639,946 (12% federal, 13% state, 72% institutional, 3% external sources). *Receiving aid:* Freshmen: 82% (311); all full-time undergraduates: 77% (984). *Average award:* Freshmen: $21,622; Undergraduates: $19,189. *Scholarships, grants, and awards:* Federal Pell, FSEOG, state, private, college/university gift aid from institutional funds.

GIFT AID (NON-NEED-BASED) *Total amount:* $6,071,748 (2% federal, 27% state, 68% institutional, 3% external sources). *Receiving aid:* Freshmen: 17% (64). Undergraduates: 12% (160). *Average award:* Freshmen: $14,127. Undergraduates: $13,990. *Scholarships, grants, and awards by category:* Academic interests/achievement: 725 awards ($7,085,545 total): general academic interests/achievements. Creative arts/performance: 104 awards ($231,445 total): art/fine arts, music, performing arts, theater/drama. Special achievements/activities: 251 awards ($358,110 total): junior miss, leadership, religious involvement. Special characteristics: 404 awards ($1,004,014 total): children and siblings of alumni, children of faculty/staff, local/state students, out-of-state students, relatives of clergy, religious affiliation. *Tuition waivers:* Full or partial for employees or children of employees.

LOANS *Student loans:* $6,938,570 (43% need-based, 57% non-need-based). 76% of past graduating class borrowed through all loan programs. *Average indebtedness per student:* $24,462. *Average need-based loan:* Freshmen: $3229. Undergraduates: $4622. *Parent loans:* $1,818,891 (100% non-need-based). *Programs:* FFEL (Subsidized and Unsubsidized Stafford, PLUS), Perkins, college/university.

WORK-STUDY *Federal work-study:* Total amount: $638,421; 557 jobs averaging $1097.

ATHLETIC AWARDS Total amount: $2,616,316 (68% need-based, 32% non-need-based).

APPLYING FOR FINANCIAL AID *Required financial aid forms:* FAFSA, institution's own form. *Financial aid deadline:* 3/15 (priority: 2/15). *Notification date:* 3/15. Students must reply by 5/1.

CONTACT Rhyan Conyers, Assistant Vice President for Enrollment and Student Financial Planning, Georgetown College, 400 East College Street, Georgetown, KY 40324-1696, 502-863-8027 or toll-free 800-788-9985. *Fax:* 502-868-7733. *E-mail:* financialaid@georgetowncollege.edu.

GEORGETOWN UNIVERSITY
Washington, DC

Tuition & fees: N/R	Average undergraduate aid package: $31,181

ABOUT THE INSTITUTION Independent Roman Catholic (Jesuit), coed. 48 undergraduate majors. Both federal and institutional methodology are used as a basis for awarding need-based institutional aid.

FRESHMAN FINANCIAL AID (Fall 2009, est.) 1,051 applied for aid; of those 67% were deemed to have need. 98% of freshmen with need received aid; of those 100% had need fully met. *Average percent of need met:* 100% (excluding resources awarded to replace EFC). *Average financial aid package:* $31,102 (excluding resources awarded to replace EFC).

UNDERGRADUATE FINANCIAL AID (Fall 2009, est.) 3,582 applied for aid; of those 83% were deemed to have need. 100% of undergraduates with need received aid; of those 100% had need fully met. *Average percent of need met:* 100% (excluding resources awarded to replace EFC). *Average financial aid package:* $31,181 (excluding resources awarded to replace EFC).

GIFT AID (NEED-BASED) *Total amount:* $77,400,000 (7% federal, 89% institutional, 4% external sources). *Receiving aid:* Freshmen: 43% (666); all full-time undergraduates: 37% (2,568). *Average award:* Freshmen: $28,295; Undergraduates: $30,140. *Scholarships, grants, and awards:* Federal Pell, FSEOG, state, private, college/university gift aid from institutional funds.

GIFT AID (NON-NEED-BASED) *Total amount:* $3,825,000 (39% federal, 6% institutional, 55% external sources). *Receiving aid:* Freshmen: 17% (266). Undergraduates: 11% (769). *Scholarships, grants, and awards by category: Special characteristics:* 129 awards ($3,040,477 total): children of faculty/staff.

LOANS *Student loans:* $21,900,000 (45% need-based, 55% non-need-based). 45% of past graduating class borrowed through all loan programs. *Average indebtedness per student:* $25,085. *Average need-based loan:* Freshmen: $3036. Undergraduates: $4492. *Parent loans:* $10,500,000 (100% non-need-based). *Programs:* FFEL (Subsidized and Unsubsidized Stafford, PLUS), Perkins, Federal Nursing, alternative loans.

WORK-STUDY *Federal work-study:* Total amount: $5,400,000; 2,000 jobs averaging $3300.

ATHLETIC AWARDS Total amount: $6,200,000 (25% need-based, 75% non-need-based).

APPLYING FOR FINANCIAL AID *Required financial aid forms:* FAFSA, CSS Financial Aid PROFILE, business/farm supplement. *Financial aid deadline:* 2/1. *Notification date:* 4/1. Students must reply by 5/1 or within 2 weeks of notification.

CONTACT Ms. Patricia A. McWade, Dean of Student Financial Services, Georgetown University, 37th and O Street, NW, Box 1252, Washington, DC 20057, 202-687-4547. *Fax:* 202-687-6542. *E-mail:* mcwadep@georgetown.edu.

THE GEORGE WASHINGTON UNIVERSITY
Washington, DC

Tuition & fees: $41,655	Average undergraduate aid package: $37,252

ABOUT THE INSTITUTION Independent, coed. 81 undergraduate majors. Federal methodology is used as a basis for awarding need-based institutional aid.

UNDERGRADUATE EXPENSES for 2009–10 *Comprehensive fee:* $51,775 includes full-time tuition ($41,610), mandatory fees ($45), and room and board ($10,120). *College room only:* $6720. Full-time tuition and fees vary according to student level. Room and board charges vary according to housing facility. *Part-time tuition:* $1157 per credit hour. *Part-time fees:* $1.50 per credit hour; $22.50 per term. Part-time tuition and fees vary according to course load. *Payment plans:* Guaranteed tuition, installment.

FRESHMAN FINANCIAL AID (Fall 2008) 1,356 applied for aid; of those 75% were deemed to have need. 95% of freshmen with need received aid; of those 88% had need fully met. *Average percent of need met:* 94% (excluding resources awarded to replace EFC). *Average financial aid package:* $36,215 (excluding resources awarded to replace EFC). 18% of all full-time freshmen had no need and received non-need-based gift aid.

UNDERGRADUATE FINANCIAL AID (Fall 2008) 4,663 applied for aid; of those 84% were deemed to have need. 97% of undergraduates with need received aid; of those 84% had need fully met. *Average percent of need met:* 93% (excluding resources awarded to replace EFC). *Average financial aid package:* $37,252 (excluding resources awarded to replace EFC). 22% of all full-time undergraduates had no need and received non-need-based gift aid.

GIFT AID (NEED-BASED) *Total amount:* $100,784,376 (6% federal, 94% institutional). *Receiving aid:* Freshmen: 38% (940); all full-time undergraduates: 38% (3,637). *Average award:* Freshmen: $25,467; Undergraduates: $24,075. *Scholarships, grants, and awards:* Federal Pell, FSEOG, state, college/university gift aid from institutional funds.

GIFT AID (NON-NEED-BASED) *Total amount:* $21,670,704 (100% institutional). *Receiving aid:* Freshmen: 11% (262). Undergraduates: 9% (897). *Average award:* Freshmen: $21,083. Undergraduates: $19,616. *Scholarships, grants, and awards by category: Academic interests/achievement:* general academic

interests/achievements. *Creative arts/performance:* general creative arts/performance. *Tuition waivers:* Full or partial for employees or children of employees.

LOANS *Student loans:* $37,223,572 (87% need-based, 13% non-need-based). 47% of past graduating class borrowed through all loan programs. *Average indebtedness per student:* $31,299. *Average need-based loan:* Freshmen: $4649. Undergraduates: $6892. *Parent loans:* $22,700,610 (13% need-based, 87% non-need-based). *Programs:* FFEL (Subsidized and Unsubsidized Stafford, PLUS), Perkins.

WORK-STUDY *Federal work-study:* Total amount: $3,414,684; jobs available.

ATHLETIC AWARDS Total amount: $5,385,655 (25% need-based, 75% non-need-based).

APPLYING FOR FINANCIAL AID *Required financial aid forms:* FAFSA, CSS Financial Aid PROFILE. *Financial aid deadline:* 2/1. *Notification date:* Continuous beginning 3/24. Students must reply by 5/1.

CONTACT Dan Small, Executive Director of Student Financial Assistance, The George Washington University, 2121 I Street, NW, Rice Hall, Suite 301, Washington, DC 21044, 202-994-6620 or toll-free 800-447-3765 (in-state). *Fax:* 202-994-0906. *E-mail:* finaid@gwu.edu.

GEORGIA COLLEGE & STATE UNIVERSITY
Milledgeville, GA

Tuition & fees (GA res): $6902	Average undergraduate aid package: $7514

ABOUT THE INSTITUTION State-supported, coed. 36 undergraduate majors. Federal methodology is used as a basis for awarding need-based institutional aid.

UNDERGRADUATE EXPENSES for 2009–10 *Tuition, state resident:* full-time $5684; part-time $190 per credit hour. *Tuition, nonresident:* full-time $22,722; part-time $758 per credit hour. *Required fees:* full-time $1218; $609 per term. Full-time tuition and fees vary according to location and student level. Part-time tuition and fees vary according to course load and location. *College room and board:* $8228; *Room only:* $4568. Room and board charges vary according to board plan and housing facility. *Payment plan:* Installment.

FRESHMAN FINANCIAL AID (Fall 2009, est.) 1,092 applied for aid; of those 44% were deemed to have need. 98% of freshmen with need received aid; of those .2% had need fully met. *Average percent of need met:* 33% (excluding resources awarded to replace EFC). *Average financial aid package:* $8197 (excluding resources awarded to replace EFC). 1% of all full-time freshmen had no need and received non-need-based gift aid.

UNDERGRADUATE FINANCIAL AID (Fall 2009, est.) 4,678 applied for aid; of those 49% were deemed to have need. 97% of undergraduates with need received aid. *Average percent of need met:* 37% (excluding resources awarded to replace EFC). *Average financial aid package:* $7514 (excluding resources awarded to replace EFC). 1% of all full-time undergraduates had no need and received non-need-based gift aid.

GIFT AID (NEED-BASED) *Total amount:* $4,829,834 (100% federal). *Receiving aid:* Freshmen: 18% (204); all full-time undergraduates: 20% (1,013). *Average award:* Freshmen: $4009; Undergraduates: $4104. *Scholarships, grants, and awards:* Federal Pell, FSEOG, state, college/university gift aid from institutional funds.

GIFT AID (NON-NEED-BASED) *Total amount:* $18,633,868 (94% state, 3% institutional, 3% external sources). *Receiving aid:* Freshmen: 41% (464). Undergraduates: 42% (2,119). *Average award:* Freshmen: $761. Undergraduates: $1197. *Scholarships, grants, and awards by category: Academic interests/achievement:* business, computer science, education, English, foreign languages, general academic interests/achievements, health fields, humanities, international studies, mathematics, physical sciences, social sciences. *Creative arts/performance:* applied art and design, art/fine arts, creative writing, journalism/publications, music, performing arts, theater/drama. *Special achievements/activities:* community service, general special achievements/activities, leadership. *Special characteristics:* adult students, children of faculty/staff, children with a deceased or disabled parent, handicapped students, international students, local/state students, members of minority groups, out-of-state students, religious affiliation. *Tuition waivers:* Full or partial for employees or children of employees, senior citizens.

LOANS *Student loans:* $18,982,915 (50% need-based, 50% non-need-based). 52% of past graduating class borrowed through all loan programs. *Average indebtedness per student:* $15,800. *Average need-based loan:* Freshmen: $3087.

Undergraduates: $4057. *Parent loans:* $1,333,340 (100% non-need-based). *Programs:* Federal Direct (PLUS), FFEL (Subsidized and Unsubsidized Stafford, PLUS), Perkins, state, college/university.
WORK-STUDY *Federal work-study:* Total amount: $200,000; 75 jobs averaging $2800.
ATHLETIC AWARDS Total amount: $761,775 (100% non-need-based).
APPLYING FOR FINANCIAL AID *Required financial aid form:* FAFSA. *Financial aid deadline (priority):* 3/1. *Notification date:* Continuous beginning 3/1. Students must reply within 2 weeks of notification.
CONTACT Mrs. Cathy Crawley, Director of Financial Aid, Georgia College & State University, Campus Box 30, Milledgeville, GA 31061, 478-445-5149 or toll-free 800-342-0471 (in-state). *Fax:* 478-445-0729. *E-mail:* cathy.crawley@gcsu.edu.

GEORGIA GWINNETT COLLEGE
Lawrenceville, GA
CONTACT Financial Aid Office, Georgia Gwinnett College, 1000 University Center Lane, Lawrenceville, GA 60043, 678-407-5000.

GEORGIA INSTITUTE OF TECHNOLOGY
Atlanta, GA

Tuition & fees (GA res): $7506	Average undergraduate aid package: $9941

ABOUT THE INSTITUTION State-supported, coed, primarily men. 35 undergraduate majors. Federal methodology is used as a basis for awarding need-based institutional aid.
UNDERGRADUATE EXPENSES for 2009–10 *Tuition, state resident:* full-time $6070; part-time $300 per credit hour. *Tuition, nonresident:* full-time $24,480; part-time $1200 per credit hour. *Required fees:* full-time $1436; $275 per course or $718 per term. Full-time tuition and fees vary according to course load and reciprocity agreements. Part-time tuition and fees vary according to course load and reciprocity agreements. *College room and board:* $8384; *Room only:* $5054. Room and board charges vary according to board plan and housing facility.
FRESHMAN FINANCIAL AID (Fall 2008) 1,974 applied for aid; of those 45% were deemed to have need. 97% of freshmen with need received aid; of those 44% had need fully met. *Average percent of need met:* 74% (excluding resources awarded to replace EFC). *Average financial aid package:* $11,216 (excluding resources awarded to replace EFC). 9% of all full-time freshmen had no need and received non-need-based gift aid.
UNDERGRADUATE FINANCIAL AID (Fall 2008) 7,123 applied for aid; of those 59% were deemed to have need. 97% of undergraduates with need received aid; of those 38% had need fully met. *Average percent of need met:* 64% (excluding resources awarded to replace EFC). *Average financial aid package:* $9941 (excluding resources awarded to replace EFC). 6% of all full-time undergraduates had no need and received non-need-based gift aid.
GIFT AID (NEED-BASED) *Total amount:* $26,504,736 (25% federal, 37% state, 34% institutional, 4% external sources). *Receiving aid:* Freshmen: 31% (824); all full-time undergraduates: 28% (3,389). *Average award:* Freshmen: $9512; Undergraduates: $8138. *Scholarships, grants, and awards:* Federal Pell, FSEOG, state, private, college/university gift aid from institutional funds, Academic Competitiveness Grants, National SMART Grants, Wayne Clough Georgia Tech Promise Program.
GIFT AID (NON-NEED-BASED) *Total amount:* $23,024,180 (80% state, 14% institutional, 6% external sources). *Receiving aid:* Freshmen: 26% (677). Undergraduates: 19% (2,337). *Average award:* Freshmen: $4025. Undergraduates: $3845. *Scholarships, grants, and awards by category:* Academic interests/achievement: 2,002 awards ($7,646,011 total): architecture, biological sciences, computer science, engineering/technologies, general academic interests/achievements, physical sciences. Special achievements/activities: 5,455 awards ($33,277,121 total): cheerleading/drum major, general special achievements/activities, leadership. *Tuition waivers:* Full or partial for employees or children of employees.
LOANS *Student loans:* $34,827,559 (71% need-based, 29% non-need-based). 57% of past graduating class borrowed through all loan programs. *Average indebtedness per student:* $21,239. *Average need-based loan:* Freshmen: $3526. Undergraduates: $4061. *Parent loans:* $13,815,113 (64% need-based, 36% non-need-based). *Programs:* Federal Direct (Subsidized and Unsubsidized Stafford, PLUS), Perkins, college/university.

WORK-STUDY *Federal work-study:* Total amount: $592,837; 354 jobs averaging $2412.
ATHLETIC AWARDS Total amount: $4,959,158 (38% need-based, 62% non-need-based).
APPLYING FOR FINANCIAL AID *Required financial aid forms:* FAFSA, institution's own form. *Financial aid deadline:* 3/1. *Notification date:* 4/1. Students must reply by 5/1.
CONTACT Ms. Marie Mons, Director of Student Financial Planning and Services, Georgia Institute of Technology, 225 North Avenue, NW, Atlanta, GA 30332-0460, 404-894-4160. *Fax:* 404-894-7412. *E-mail:* marie.mons@finaid.gatech.edu.

GEORGIAN COURT UNIVERSITY
Lakewood, NJ

Tuition & fees: $24,490	Average undergraduate aid package: $17,906

ABOUT THE INSTITUTION Independent Roman Catholic, coed, primarily women. 29 undergraduate majors. Federal methodology is used as a basis for awarding need-based institutional aid.
UNDERGRADUATE EXPENSES for 2009–10 *Comprehensive fee:* $33,876 includes full-time tuition ($23,246), mandatory fees ($1244), and room and board ($9386). *Part-time tuition:* $570 per credit. *Part-time fees:* $311 per term. Part-time tuition and fees vary according to location. *Payment plan:* Installment.
FRESHMAN FINANCIAL AID (Fall 2009, est.) 250 applied for aid; of those 90% were deemed to have need. 100% of freshmen with need received aid; of those 11% had need fully met. *Average percent of need met:* 73% (excluding resources awarded to replace EFC). *Average financial aid package:* $22,045 (excluding resources awarded to replace EFC). 11% of all full-time freshmen had no need and received non-need-based gift aid.
UNDERGRADUATE FINANCIAL AID (Fall 2009, est.) 1,419 applied for aid; of those 92% were deemed to have need. 100% of undergraduates with need received aid; of those 11% had need fully met. *Average percent of need met:* 67% (excluding resources awarded to replace EFC). *Average financial aid package:* $17,906 (excluding resources awarded to replace EFC). 7% of all full-time undergraduates had no need and received non-need-based gift aid.
GIFT AID (NEED-BASED) *Total amount:* $16,879,055 (18% federal, 31% state, 50% institutional, 1% external sources). *Receiving aid:* Freshmen: 89% (224); all full-time undergraduates: 82% (1,242). *Average award:* Freshmen: $18,731; Undergraduates: $14,262. *Scholarships, grants, and awards:* Federal Pell, FSEOG, state, private, college/university gift aid from institutional funds.
GIFT AID (NON-NEED-BASED) *Total amount:* $1,198,971 (1% state, 88% institutional, 11% external sources). *Receiving aid:* Freshmen: 7% (17). Undergraduates: 7% (101). *Average award:* Freshmen: $9538. Undergraduates: $7232. *Scholarships, grants, and awards by category:* Academic interests/achievement: biological sciences, business, English, foreign languages, general academic interests/achievements, mathematics, physical sciences. Creative arts/performance: art/fine arts, creative writing, music. Special achievements/activities: general special achievements/activities. Special characteristics: children of faculty/staff, religious affiliation, spouses of current students, veterans. *Tuition waivers:* Full or partial for employees or children of employees.
LOANS *Student loans:* $11,298,829 (73% need-based, 27% non-need-based). 85% of past graduating class borrowed through all loan programs. *Average indebtedness per student:* $33,729. *Average need-based loan:* Freshmen: $3656. Undergraduates: $4667. *Parent loans:* $806,977 (37% need-based, 63% non-need-based). *Programs:* FFEL (Subsidized and Unsubsidized Stafford, PLUS), state.
WORK-STUDY *Federal work-study:* Total amount: $377,000; 209 jobs averaging $1760. *State or other work-study/employment:* Total amount: $80,000 (16% need-based, 84% non-need-based). 40 part-time jobs averaging $1950.
ATHLETIC AWARDS Total amount: $970,900 (77% need-based, 23% non-need-based).
APPLYING FOR FINANCIAL AID *Required financial aid form:* FAFSA. *Financial aid deadline:* 8/1 (priority: 4/15). *Notification date:* Continuous beginning 2/1. Students must reply within 2 weeks of notification.
CONTACT Larry Sharp, Director of Financial Aid, Georgian Court University, 900 Lakewood Avenue, Lakewood, NJ 08701-2697, 732-987-2258 or toll-free 800-458-8422. *Fax:* 732-987-2012. *E-mail:* financialaid@georgian.edu.

GEORGIA SOUTHERN UNIVERSITY
Statesboro, GA

Tuition & fees (GA res): $5440 | **Average undergraduate aid package:** $7587

ABOUT THE INSTITUTION State-supported, coed. 75 undergraduate majors. Federal methodology is used as a basis for awarding need-based institutional aid.

UNDERGRADUATE EXPENSES for 2009–10 *Tuition, state resident:* full-time $3996; part-time $134 per semester hour. *Tuition, nonresident:* full-time $15,972; part-time $533 per semester hour. *Required fees:* full-time $1444; $722 per term. Full-time tuition and fees vary according to degree level, location, and program. Part-time tuition and fees vary according to course load, degree level, location, and program. *College room and board:* $7900; *Room only:* $5070. Room and board charges vary according to board plan and housing facility.

FRESHMAN FINANCIAL AID (Fall 2008) 2,842 applied for aid; of those 58% were deemed to have need. 98% of freshmen with need received aid; of those 17% had need fully met. *Average percent of need met:* 60% (excluding resources awarded to replace EFC). *Average financial aid package:* $7646 (excluding resources awarded to replace EFC). 5% of all full-time freshmen had no need and received non-need-based gift aid.

UNDERGRADUATE FINANCIAL AID (Fall 2008) 11,779 applied for aid; of those 64% were deemed to have need. 97% of undergraduates with need received aid; of those 13% had need fully met. *Average percent of need met:* 56% (excluding resources awarded to replace EFC). *Average financial aid package:* $7587 (excluding resources awarded to replace EFC). 3% of all full-time undergraduates had no need and received non-need-based gift aid.

GIFT AID (NEED-BASED) *Total amount:* $30,407,597 (52% federal, 43% state, 2% institutional, 3% external sources). *Receiving aid:* Freshmen: 44% (1,369); all full-time undergraduates: 42% (5,729). *Average award:* Freshmen: $6145; Undergraduates: $5353. *Scholarships, grants, and awards:* Federal Pell, FSEOG, state, private, college/university gift aid from institutional funds, Academic Competitiveness Grants, National SMART Grants, TEACH Grants, HOPE Scholarships.

GIFT AID (NON-NEED-BASED) *Total amount:* $12,665,981 (90% state, 6% institutional, 4% external sources). *Receiving aid:* Freshmen: 5% (143). Undergraduates: 3% (419). *Average award:* Freshmen: $2049. Undergraduates: $1766. *Scholarships, grants, and awards by category: Academic interests/ achievement:* 751 awards ($1,097,897 total): biological sciences, business, communication, computer science, education, engineering/technologies, English, foreign languages, general academic interests/achievements, health fields, humanities, international studies, mathematics, military science, social sciences. *Creative arts/performance:* 49 awards ($60,750 total): art/fine arts, cinema/film/ broadcasting, general creative arts/performance, music, theater/drama. *Special achievements/activities:* 204 awards ($190,699 total): cheerleading/drum major, community service, junior miss, leadership, memberships, religious involvement. *Special characteristics:* 15 awards ($38,450 total): children and siblings of alumni, children of public servants, first-generation college students, handicapped students, married students, members of minority groups. *Tuition waivers:* Full or partial for employees or children of employees, senior citizens.

LOANS *Student loans:* $48,955,820 (75% need-based, 25% non-need-based). 65% of past graduating class borrowed through all loan programs. *Average indebtedness per student:* $18,618. *Average need-based loan:* Freshmen: $3287. Undergraduates: $4154. *Parent loans:* $7,917,531 (60% need-based, 40% non-need-based). *Programs:* Federal Direct (Subsidized and Unsubsidized Stafford, PLUS), Perkins, state, Service-Cancelable State Direct Student Loans, private alternative loans.

WORK-STUDY *Federal work-study:* Total amount: $341,572; 231 jobs averaging $1479.

ATHLETIC AWARDS Total amount: $2,076,218 (49% need-based, 51% non-need-based).

APPLYING FOR FINANCIAL AID *Required financial aid form:* FAFSA. *Financial aid deadline (priority):* 4/20. *Notification date:* Continuous beginning 4/20.

CONTACT Mrs. Elise Boyett, Associate Director of Financial Aid, Georgia Southern University, Box 8065, Statesboro, GA 30460-8065, 912-478-5413. *Fax:* 912-478-0573. *E-mail:* eboyett@georgiasouthern.edu.

GEORGIA SOUTHWESTERN STATE UNIVERSITY
Americus, GA

Tuition & fees: N/R | **Average undergraduate aid package:** $7655

ABOUT THE INSTITUTION State-supported, coed. *Awards:* bachelor's and master's degrees and post-bachelor's and post-master's certificates. 29 undergraduate majors. *Total enrollment:* 2,405. Undergraduates: 2,221. Freshmen: 426. Federal methodology is used as a basis for awarding need-based institutional aid.

FRESHMAN FINANCIAL AID (Fall 2009, est.) 383 applied for aid; of those 78% were deemed to have need. 100% of freshmen with need received aid; of those 13% had need fully met. *Average percent of need met:* 61% (excluding resources awarded to replace EFC). *Average financial aid package:* $8335 (excluding resources awarded to replace EFC). 8% of all full-time freshmen had no need and received non-need-based gift aid.

UNDERGRADUATE FINANCIAL AID (Fall 2009, est.) 1,563 applied for aid; of those 83% were deemed to have need. 100% of undergraduates with need received aid; of those 21% had need fully met. *Average percent of need met:* 56% (excluding resources awarded to replace EFC). *Average financial aid package:* $7655 (excluding resources awarded to replace EFC). 6% of all full-time undergraduates had no need and received non-need-based gift aid.

GIFT AID (NEED-BASED) *Total amount:* $4,654,316 (100% federal). *Receiving aid:* Freshmen: 47% (206); all full-time undergraduates: 45% (865). *Average award:* Freshmen: $4912; Undergraduates: $4475. *Scholarships, grants, and awards:* Federal Pell, FSEOG, state, private, college/university gift aid from institutional funds.

GIFT AID (NON-NEED-BASED) *Total amount:* $3,439,768 (79% state, 14% institutional, 7% external sources). *Receiving aid:* Freshmen: 42% (181). Undergraduates: 30% (580). *Average award:* Freshmen: $1726. Undergraduates: $1886. *Scholarships, grants, and awards by category: Academic interests/ achievement:* general academic interests/achievements. *Creative arts/performance:* art/fine arts, music. *Special achievements/activities:* leadership.

LOANS *Student loans:* $9,518,210 (47% need-based, 53% non-need-based). 62% of past graduating class borrowed through all loan programs. *Average indebtedness per student:* $20,505. *Average need-based loan:* Freshmen: $4081. Undergraduates: $3914. *Parent loans:* $187,111 (100% non-need-based). *Programs:* FFEL (Subsidized and Unsubsidized Stafford, PLUS), Perkins, state, college/university.

WORK-STUDY *Federal work-study:* Total amount: $86,607; 58 jobs averaging $1493. *State or other work-study/employment:* Part-time jobs available.

ATHLETIC AWARDS Total amount: $381,140 (100% non-need-based).

APPLYING FOR FINANCIAL AID *Required financial aid forms:* FAFSA, institution's own form. *Financial aid deadline (priority):* 4/1. *Notification date:* Continuous beginning 5/1. Students must reply within 8 weeks of notification.

CONTACT Angela Bryant, Director of Financial Aid, Georgia Southwestern State University, 800 Georgia Southwestern State University Drive, Americus, GA 31709-4693, 229-928-1378 or toll-free 800-338-0082. *Fax:* 229-931-2061.

GEORGIA STATE UNIVERSITY
Atlanta, GA

Tuition & fees (GA res): $7498 | **Average undergraduate aid package:** $8393

ABOUT THE INSTITUTION State-supported, coed. 57 undergraduate majors. Federal methodology is used as a basis for awarding need-based institutional aid.

UNDERGRADUATE EXPENSES for 2009–10 *Tuition, state resident:* full-time $6070; part-time $203 per credit hour. *Tuition, nonresident:* full-time $24,280; part-time $810 per credit hour. *Required fees:* full-time $1428; $714 per term. Part-time tuition and fees vary according to course load. *College room and board:* $10,140; *Room only:* $6950. Room and board charges vary according to housing facility.

FRESHMAN FINANCIAL AID (Fall 2009, est.) 2,565 applied for aid; of those 79% were deemed to have need. 98% of freshmen with need received aid; of those 7% had need fully met. *Average percent of need met:* 11% (excluding resources awarded to replace EFC). *Average financial aid package:* $10,157 (excluding resources awarded to replace EFC). 1% of all full-time freshmen had no need and received non-need-based gift aid.

UNDERGRADUATE FINANCIAL AID (Fall 2009, est.) 13,418 applied for aid; of those 83% were deemed to have need. 96% of undergraduates with need received aid; of those 8% had need fully met. *Average percent of need met:* 12% (excluding resources awarded to replace EFC). *Average financial aid package:* $8393 (excluding resources awarded to replace EFC). 1% of all full-time undergraduates had no need and received non-need-based gift aid.

GIFT AID (NEED-BASED) *Total amount:* $38,403,645 (100% federal). *Receiving aid:* Freshmen: 44% (1,270); all full-time undergraduates: 42% (7,218). *Average award:* Freshmen: $4978; Undergraduates: $4443. *Scholarships, grants, and awards:* Federal Pell, FSEOG, state, private, college/university gift aid from institutional funds.

GIFT AID (NON-NEED-BASED) *Total amount:* $29,232,738 (95% state, 3% institutional, 2% external sources). *Receiving aid:* Freshmen: 55% (1,592). Undergraduates: 30% (5,146). *Average award:* Freshmen: $1400. Undergraduates: $3503. *Tuition waivers:* Full or partial for employees or children of employees, senior citizens.

LOANS *Student loans:* $132,683,358 (44% need-based, 56% non-need-based). 58% of past graduating class borrowed through all loan programs. *Average indebtedness per student:* $13,166. *Average need-based loan:* Freshmen: $1984. Undergraduates: $5341. *Parent loans:* $6,432,262 (100% non-need-based). *Programs:* Federal Direct (Subsidized and Unsubsidized Stafford, PLUS), FFEL (PLUS), Perkins, state.

WORK-STUDY *Federal work-study:* Total amount: $462,667; 210 jobs averaging $2300.

ATHLETIC AWARDS Total amount: $645,639 (100% non-need-based).

APPLYING FOR FINANCIAL AID *Required financial aid form:* FAFSA. *Financial aid deadline:* 11/1 (priority: 4/1). *Notification date:* Continuous beginning 3/30.

CONTACT Louis Scott, Financial Aid Office, Georgia State University, PO Box 4040, Atlanta, GA 30302, 404-413-2102.

GETTYSBURG COLLEGE
Gettysburg, PA

Tuition & fees: N/R	Average undergraduate aid package: $31,030

ABOUT THE INSTITUTION Independent religious, coed. 82 undergraduate majors. Both federal and institutional methodology are used as a basis for awarding need-based institutional aid.

FRESHMAN FINANCIAL AID (Fall 2009, est.) 574 applied for aid; of those 76% were deemed to have need. 99% of freshmen with need received aid; of those 98% had need fully met. *Average percent of need met:* 100% (excluding resources awarded to replace EFC). *Average financial aid package:* $31,946 (excluding resources awarded to replace EFC). 17% of all full-time freshmen had no need and received non-need-based gift aid.

UNDERGRADUATE FINANCIAL AID (Fall 2009, est.) 1,764 applied for aid; of those 83% were deemed to have need. 98% of undergraduates with need received aid; of those 98% had need fully met. *Average percent of need met:* 100% (excluding resources awarded to replace EFC). *Average financial aid package:* $31,030 (excluding resources awarded to replace EFC). 14% of all full-time undergraduates had no need and received non-need-based gift aid.

GIFT AID (NEED-BASED) *Total amount:* $37,745,071 (4% federal, 2% state, 92% institutional, 2% external sources). *Receiving aid:* Freshmen: 58% (425); all full-time undergraduates: 52% (1,392). *Average award:* Freshmen: $24,791; Undergraduates: $23,781. *Scholarships, grants, and awards:* Federal Pell, FSEOG, state, private, college/university gift aid from institutional funds, Academic Competitiveness Grants, National SMART Grants.

GIFT AID (NON-NEED-BASED) *Total amount:* $4,588,743 (94% institutional, 6% external sources). *Receiving aid:* Freshmen: 31% (231). Undergraduates: 26% (696). *Average award:* Freshmen: $9983. Undergraduates: $10,713. *Scholarships, grants, and awards by category:* Academic interests/achievement: 1,025 awards ($11,002,000 total): general academic interests/achievements. Creative arts/performance: 29 awards ($270,500 total): music. *Tuition waivers:* Full or partial for employees or children of employees.

LOANS *Student loans:* $9,712,996 (58% need-based, 42% non-need-based). 61% of past graduating class borrowed through all loan programs. *Average indebtedness per student:* $23,258. *Average need-based loan:* Freshmen: $3701. Undergraduates: $5051. *Parent loans:* $7,161,124 (100% non-need-based). *Programs:* FFEL (Subsidized and Unsubsidized Stafford, PLUS), Perkins, college/university.

WORK-STUDY *Federal work-study:* Total amount: $525,603; 520 jobs averaging $1010. *State or other work-study/employment:* Total amount: $22,807 (100% need-based). 650 part-time jobs averaging $1000.

APPLYING FOR FINANCIAL AID *Required financial aid forms:* FAFSA, CSS Financial Aid PROFILE, business/farm supplement, income tax form(s), verification worksheet. *Financial aid deadline:* 2/15. *Notification date:* 3/27. Students must reply by 5/1.

CONTACT Christina Gormley, Director of Financial Aid, Gettysburg College, 300 North Washington Street, Gettysburg, PA 17325, 717-337-6620 or toll-free 800-431-0803. *Fax:* 717-337-8555. *E-mail:* finaid@gettysburg.edu.

GLENVILLE STATE COLLEGE
Glenville, WV

Tuition & fees (WV res): $4888	Average undergraduate aid package: $11,448

ABOUT THE INSTITUTION State-supported, coed. 32 undergraduate majors. Federal methodology is used as a basis for awarding need-based institutional aid.

UNDERGRADUATE EXPENSES for 2009–10 *Tuition, state resident:* full-time $4888; part-time $203.67 per credit hour. *Tuition, nonresident:* full-time $11,702; part-time $487.58 per credit hour. Part-time tuition and fees vary according to course load. *College room and board:* $6460; *Room only:* $3210. Room and board charges vary according to housing facility. *Payment plan:* Installment.

FRESHMAN FINANCIAL AID (Fall 2009, est.) 323 applied for aid; of those 89% were deemed to have need. 99% of freshmen with need received aid; of those 22% had need fully met. *Average percent of need met:* 74% (excluding resources awarded to replace EFC). *Average financial aid package:* $11,112 (excluding resources awarded to replace EFC). 4% of all full-time freshmen had no need and received non-need-based gift aid.

UNDERGRADUATE FINANCIAL AID (Fall 2009, est.) 1,065 applied for aid; of those 90% were deemed to have need. 99% of undergraduates with need received aid; of those 26% had need fully met. *Average percent of need met:* 76% (excluding resources awarded to replace EFC). *Average financial aid package:* $11,448 (excluding resources awarded to replace EFC). 4% of all full-time undergraduates had no need and received non-need-based gift aid.

GIFT AID (NEED-BASED) *Total amount:* $4,571,789 (72% federal, 27% state, 1% institutional). *Receiving aid:* Freshmen: 70% (229); all full-time undergraduates: 63% (730). *Average award:* Freshmen: $5856; Undergraduates: $5650. *Scholarships, grants, and awards:* Federal Pell, FSEOG, state, private, college/university gift aid from institutional funds.

GIFT AID (NON-NEED-BASED) *Total amount:* $1,243,536 (60% state, 23% institutional, 17% external sources). *Receiving aid:* Freshmen: 53% (173). Undergraduates: 42% (488). *Average award:* Freshmen: $1507. Undergraduates: $2089. *Scholarships, grants, and awards by category:* Academic interests/achievement: 154 awards ($283,311 total): biological sciences, business, education, English, general academic interests/achievements, mathematics, social sciences. Creative arts/performance: 27 awards ($34,427 total): journalism/publications, music. Special achievements/activities: 4 awards ($2000 total): cheerleading/drum major. Special characteristics: 53 awards ($45,500 total): first-generation college students, veterans' children. *Tuition waivers:* Full or partial for senior citizens.

LOANS *Student loans:* $6,220,115 (47% need-based, 53% non-need-based). 77% of past graduating class borrowed through all loan programs. *Average indebtedness per student:* $19,722. *Average need-based loan:* Freshmen: $3014. Undergraduates: $3663. *Parent loans:* $385,707 (100% non-need-based). *Programs:* Federal Direct (Subsidized and Unsubsidized Stafford, PLUS).

WORK-STUDY *Federal work-study:* Total amount: $141,328; 88 jobs averaging $1600. *State or other work-study/employment:* Total amount: $420,196 (100% non-need-based). 200 part-time jobs averaging $1500.

ATHLETIC AWARDS Total amount: $603,786 (100% non-need-based).

APPLYING FOR FINANCIAL AID *Required financial aid forms:* FAFSA, application for admissions and related documents. *Financial aid deadline (priority):* 2/1. *Notification date:* Continuous beginning 3/1. Students must reply within 3 weeks of notification.

CONTACT Ms. Karen Lay, Director of Financial Aid, Glenville State College, 200 High Street, Glenville, WV 26351-1200, 304-462-4103 Ext. 5 or toll-free 800-924-2010 (in-state). *Fax:* 304-462-4407. *E-mail:* karen.lay@glenville.edu.

GLOBAL COLLEGE OF LONG ISLAND UNIVERSITY
Brooklyn, NY

CONTACT Mr. Richard D. Mallett, Director of Financial Aid, Global College of Long Island University, 9 Hanover Place, 4th Floor, Brooklyn, NY 11201, 516-549-5000.

GLOBE INSTITUTE OF TECHNOLOGY
New York, NY

CONTACT Office of Admissions, Globe Institute of Technology, 291 Broadway, 2nd Floor, New York, NY 10007, 212-349-4330 or toll-free 877-394-5623. *Fax:* 212-227-5920. *E-mail:* admission@globe.edu.

GLOBE UNIVERSITY
Woodbury, MN

CONTACT Financial Aid Office, Globe University, 8089 Globe Drive, Woodbury, MN 55125, 651-730-5100.

GLOBE UNIVERSITY
Sioux Falls, SD

CONTACT Financial Aid Office, Globe University, 5101 South Broadband Lane, Sioux Falls, SD 57108-2208, 605-977-0705 or toll-free 866-437-0705 (out-of-state).

GODDARD COLLEGE
Plainfield, VT

ABOUT THE INSTITUTION Independent, coed. 14 undergraduate majors.
GIFT AID (NEED-BASED) *Scholarships, grants, and awards:* Federal Pell, FSEOG, state, private, college/university gift aid from institutional funds.
LOANS *Programs:* FFEL (Subsidized and Unsubsidized Stafford, PLUS), Perkins, college/university.
APPLYING FOR FINANCIAL AID *Required financial aid form:* FAFSA.
CONTACT Beverly Jene, Director of Financial Aid, Goddard College, 123 Pitkin Road, Plainfield, VT 05667, 802-454-8311 Ext. 324 or toll-free 800-906-8312 Ext. 243. *Fax:* 802-454-1029. *E-mail:* beverly.jene@goddard.edu.

GOD'S BIBLE SCHOOL AND COLLEGE
Cincinnati, OH

Tuition & fees: N/R	Average undergraduate aid package: N/A

ABOUT THE INSTITUTION Independent interdenominational, coed. 13 undergraduate majors. Both federal and institutional methodology are used as a basis for awarding need-based institutional aid.
GIFT AID (NEED-BASED) *Total amount:* $705,775 (85% federal, 1% state, 11% institutional, 3% external sources). *Scholarships, grants, and awards:* Federal Pell, state, college/university gift aid from institutional funds.
GIFT AID (NON-NEED-BASED) *Total amount:* $4000 (100% state). *Scholarships, grants, and awards by category: Academic interests/achievement:* general academic interests/achievements. *Creative arts/performance:* music. *Special characteristics:* international students. *Tuition waivers:* Full or partial for employees or children of employees.
LOANS *Student loans:* $188,917 (100% need-based). *Parent loans:* $4608 (100% need-based). *Programs:* Federal Direct (Subsidized and Unsubsidized Stafford, PLUS).
APPLYING FOR FINANCIAL AID *Required financial aid form:* FAFSA. *Financial aid deadline:* Continuous. *Notification date:* Continuous.
CONTACT Mrs. Lori Waggoner, Financial Aid Director, God's Bible School and College, 1810 Young Street, Cincinnati, OH 45202-6899, 513-721-7944 Ext. 205 or toll-free 800-486-4637. *Fax:* 513-721-1357. *E-mail:* lwaggoner@gbs.edu.

GOLDEN GATE UNIVERSITY
San Francisco, CA

ABOUT THE INSTITUTION Independent, coed. *Awards:* bachelor's and master's degrees and post-bachelor's certificates. 8 undergraduate majors. *Total enrollment:* 3,528. Undergraduates: 414.
GIFT AID (NEED-BASED) *Scholarships, grants, and awards:* Federal Pell, FSEOG, state, private, college/university gift aid from institutional funds.
GIFT AID (NON-NEED-BASED) *Scholarships, grants, and awards by category: Academic interests/achievement:* business, computer science, general academic interests/achievements. *Special achievements/activities:* leadership. *Special characteristics:* adult students, general special characteristics, members of minority groups, previous college experience.
LOANS *Programs:* FFEL (Subsidized and Unsubsidized Stafford, PLUS), Perkins.
WORK-STUDY *Federal work-study:* Total amount: $10,000; 2 jobs averaging $5000.
APPLYING FOR FINANCIAL AID *Required financial aid forms:* FAFSA, institution's own form.
CONTACT Ken Walsh, Associate Director of Financial Services, Golden Gate University, 536 Mission Street, San Francisco, CA 94105-2968, 415-442-7262 or toll-free 800-448-3381. *Fax:* 415-442-7819. *E-mail:* kwalsh@ggu.edu.

GOLDEY-BEACOM COLLEGE
Wilmington, DE

Tuition & fees: $18,660	Average undergraduate aid package: N/A

ABOUT THE INSTITUTION Independent, coed. 18 undergraduate majors. Federal methodology is used as a basis for awarding need-based institutional aid.
UNDERGRADUATE EXPENSES for 2010–11 *Tuition:* full-time $18,360; part-time $612 per credit hour. *Required fees:* full-time $300; $10 per credit hour. Full-time tuition and fees vary according to course load. Part-time tuition and fees vary according to course load. Room and board charges vary according to housing facility. *Payment plans:* Installment, deferred payment.
FRESHMAN FINANCIAL AID (Fall 2008) 88 applied for aid; of those 90% were deemed to have need. 100% of freshmen with need received aid; of those 23% had need fully met. *Average percent of need met:* 61% (excluding resources awarded to replace EFC). *Average financial aid package:* $13,799 (excluding resources awarded to replace EFC). 11% of all full-time freshmen had no need and received non-need-based gift aid.
GIFT AID (NEED-BASED) *Receiving aid:* Freshmen: 82% (76). *Average award:* Freshmen: $10,667. *Scholarships, grants, and awards:* Federal Pell, FSEOG, state, private, college/university gift aid from institutional funds.
GIFT AID (NON-NEED-BASED) *Receiving aid:* Freshmen: 18% (17). *Average award:* Freshmen: $9863. *Scholarships, grants, and awards by category: Academic interests/achievement:* business. *Tuition waivers:* Full or partial for employees or children of employees.
LOANS *Student loans:* 53% of past graduating class borrowed through all loan programs. *Average need-based loan:* Freshmen: $3947. *Programs:* Federal Direct (Subsidized and Unsubsidized Stafford, PLUS), Perkins.
WORK-STUDY Federal work-study jobs available.
APPLYING FOR FINANCIAL AID *Required financial aid form:* FAFSA. *Financial aid deadline (priority):* 4/1. *Notification date:* Continuous beginning 10/1. Students must reply within 2 weeks of notification.
CONTACT Jane H. Lysle, Dean of Enrollment Management, Goldey-Beacom College, 4701 Limestone Road, Wilmington, DE 19808-1999, 302-225-6274 or toll-free 800-833-4877. *Fax:* 302-998-8631. *E-mail:* lyslej@goldey.gbc.edu.

GOLDFARB SCHOOL OF NURSING AT BARNES-JEWISH COLLEGE
St. Louis, MO

CONTACT Regina Blackshear, Chief Financial Aid Officer, Goldfarb School of Nursing at Barnes-Jewish College, 306 South Kingshighway, St. Louis, MO 63110-1091, 314-454-7770 or toll-free 800-832-9009 (in-state).

GONZAGA UNIVERSITY
Spokane, WA

Tuition & fees: N/R	Average undergraduate aid package: $22,921

ABOUT THE INSTITUTION Independent Roman Catholic, coed. 51 undergraduate majors. Federal methodology is used as a basis for awarding need-based institutional aid.

FRESHMAN FINANCIAL AID (Fall 2009, est.) 1,031 applied for aid; of those 69% were deemed to have need. 100% of freshmen with need received aid; of those 32% had need fully met. *Average percent of need met:* 85% (excluding resources awarded to replace EFC). *Average financial aid package:* $23,680 (excluding resources awarded to replace EFC). 38% of all full-time freshmen had no need and received non-need-based gift aid.

UNDERGRADUATE FINANCIAL AID (Fall 2009, est.) 3,370 applied for aid; of those 76% were deemed to have need. 100% of undergraduates with need received aid; of those 29% had need fully met. *Average percent of need met:* 83% (excluding resources awarded to replace EFC). *Average financial aid package:* $22,921 (excluding resources awarded to replace EFC). 37% of all full-time undergraduates had no need and received non-need-based gift aid.

GIFT AID (NEED-BASED) *Total amount:* $39,786,668 (10% federal, 6% state, 80% institutional, 4% external sources). *Receiving aid:* Freshmen: 59% (706); all full-time undergraduates: 57% (2,552). *Average award:* Freshmen: $17,764; Undergraduates: $16,521. *Scholarships, grants, and awards:* Federal Pell, FSEOG, state, private, college/university gift aid from institutional funds, United Negro College Fund, Federal Nursing, Academic Competitiveness Grants, National SMART Grants, TEACH Grants.

GIFT AID (NON-NEED-BASED) *Total amount:* $20,951,394 (89% institutional, 11% external sources). *Receiving aid:* Freshmen: 15% (180). Undergraduates: 11% (501). *Average award:* Freshmen: $11,539. Undergraduates: $10,028. *Scholarships, grants, and awards by category:* Academic interests/achievement: 122 awards ($288,175 total): business, engineering/technologies, military science. Creative arts/performance: 78 awards ($160,200 total): debating, music. Special achievements/activities: 146 awards ($455,000 total): leadership, memberships. Special characteristics: 426 awards ($3,401,520 total): children and siblings of alumni, children of faculty/staff, international students, members of minority groups, siblings of current students.

LOANS *Student loans:* $21,938,730 (56% need-based, 44% non-need-based). 70% of past graduating class borrowed through all loan programs. *Average indebtedness per student:* $24,883. *Average need-based loan:* Freshmen: $4349. Undergraduates: $5312. *Parent loans:* $5,268,917 (63% need-based, 37% non-need-based). *Programs:* FFEL (Subsidized and Unsubsidized Stafford, PLUS), Perkins, Federal Nursing, state, college/university.

WORK-STUDY *Federal work-study:* Total amount: $1,895,716; 538 jobs averaging $3032. *State or other work-study/employment:* Total amount: $2,260,113 (100% need-based). 553 part-time jobs averaging $4118.

ATHLETIC AWARDS Total amount: $3,172,031 (18% need-based, 82% non-need-based).

APPLYING FOR FINANCIAL AID *Required financial aid form:* FAFSA. *Financial aid deadline (priority):* 2/1. *Notification date:* Continuous beginning 3/1. Students must reply by 5/1 or within 3 weeks of notification.

CONTACT James White, Director of Operations for Financial Aid, Gonzaga University, 502 East Boone Avenue, Spokane, WA 99258-0072, 509-313-6568 or toll-free 800-322-2584 Ext. 6572. *Fax:* 509-313-5816. *E-mail:* whitej@gonzaga.edu.

GORDON COLLEGE
Wenham, MA

Tuition & fees: $29,458	Average undergraduate aid package: $19,311

ABOUT THE INSTITUTION Independent nondenominational, coed. 32 undergraduate majors. Both federal and institutional methodology are used as a basis for awarding need-based institutional aid.

UNDERGRADUATE EXPENSES for 2010–11 *Comprehensive fee:* $37,558 includes full-time tuition ($28,210), mandatory fees ($1248), and room and board ($8100). *College room only:* $5400. Full-time tuition and fees vary according to course load. Room and board charges vary according to board plan and housing facility. Part-time tuition and fees vary according to course load. *Payment plan:* Installment.

FRESHMAN FINANCIAL AID (Fall 2009, est.) 327 applied for aid; of those 84% were deemed to have need. 100% of freshmen with need received aid; of those 18% had need fully met. *Average percent of need met:* 74% (excluding resources awarded to replace EFC). *Average financial aid package:* $19,624 (excluding resources awarded to replace EFC). 26% of all full-time freshmen had no need and received non-need-based gift aid.

UNDERGRADUATE FINANCIAL AID (Fall 2009, est.) 1,197 applied for aid; of those 87% were deemed to have need. 100% of undergraduates with need received aid; of those 17% had need fully met. *Average percent of need met:* 75% (excluding resources awarded to replace EFC). *Average financial aid package:* $19,311 (excluding resources awarded to replace EFC). 24% of all full-time undergraduates had no need and received non-need-based gift aid.

GIFT AID (NEED-BASED) *Total amount:* $13,037,905 (12% federal, 3% state, 74% institutional, 11% external sources). *Receiving aid:* Freshmen: 71% (274); all full-time undergraduates: 67% (1,027). *Average award:* Freshmen: $13,957; Undergraduates: $12,579. *Scholarships, grants, and awards:* Federal Pell, FSEOG, state, private, college/university gift aid from institutional funds.

GIFT AID (NON-NEED-BASED) *Total amount:* $5,030,548 (78% institutional, 22% external sources). *Receiving aid:* Freshmen: 60% (233). Undergraduates: 59% (915). *Average award:* Freshmen: $10,343. Undergraduates: $9343. *Scholarships, grants, and awards by category:* Academic interests/achievement: 923 awards ($6,901,839 total): general academic interests/achievements. Creative arts/performance: 85 awards ($185,136 total): art/fine arts, music, theater/drama. Special achievements/activities: 101 awards ($1,175,490 total): leadership. Special characteristics: 213 awards ($145,623 total): children and siblings of alumni, relatives of clergy. *Tuition waivers:* Full or partial for employees or children of employees.

LOANS *Student loans:* $12,300,836 (68% need-based, 32% non-need-based). 81% of past graduating class borrowed through all loan programs. *Average indebtedness per student:* $32,405. *Average need-based loan:* Freshmen: $5725. Undergraduates: $7043. *Parent loans:* $3,018,165 (44% need-based, 56% non-need-based). *Programs:* Federal Direct (Subsidized and Unsubsidized Stafford, PLUS), Perkins, state.

WORK-STUDY *Federal work-study:* Total amount: $746,304; 731 jobs averaging $1509.

APPLYING FOR FINANCIAL AID *Required financial aid forms:* FAFSA, institution's own form, state aid form. *Financial aid deadline (priority):* 3/1. *Notification date:* Continuous beginning 3/1. Students must reply by 5/1 or within 2 weeks of notification.

CONTACT Daniel O'Connell, Director of Student Financial Services, Gordon College, 255 Grapevine Road, Wenham, MA 01984-1899, 978-867-4246 or toll-free 866-464-6736. *Fax:* 978-867-4657. *E-mail:* daniel.oconnell@gordon.edu.

GOSHEN COLLEGE
Goshen, IN

CONTACT Mr. Galen Graber, Director of Enrollment, Goshen College, 1700 South Main Street, Goshen, IN 46526-4794, 574-535-7525 or toll-free 800-348-7422. *Fax:* 574-535-7654.

GOUCHER COLLEGE
Baltimore, MD

Tuition & fees: $35,142	Average undergraduate aid package: $25,518

ABOUT THE INSTITUTION Independent, coed. 29 undergraduate majors. Both federal and institutional methodology are used as a basis for awarding need-based institutional aid.

UNDERGRADUATE EXPENSES for 2010–11 *Comprehensive fee:* $45,898 includes full-time tuition ($34,626), mandatory fees ($516), and room and board ($10,756). Room and board charges vary according to board plan and housing facility. *Part-time tuition:* $1154 per credit hour. *Payment plans:* Tuition prepayment, installment.

FRESHMAN FINANCIAL AID (Fall 2009, est.) 314 applied for aid; of those 79% were deemed to have need. 100% of freshmen with need received aid; of those 18% had need fully met. *Average percent of need met:* 82% (excluding resources awarded to replace EFC). *Average financial aid package:* $26,553 (excluding resources awarded to replace EFC). 15% of all full-time freshmen had no need and received non-need-based gift aid.

UNDERGRADUATE FINANCIAL AID (Fall 2009, est.) 975 applied for aid; of those 86% were deemed to have need. 100% of undergraduates with need received aid; of those 25% had need fully met. *Average percent of need met:* 80% (excluding resources awarded to replace EFC). *Average financial aid package:* $25,518 (excluding resources awarded to replace EFC). 20% of all full-time undergraduates had no need and received non-need-based gift aid.

GIFT AID (NEED-BASED) *Total amount:* $17,670,119 (9% federal, 4% state, 83% institutional, 4% external sources). *Receiving aid:* Freshmen: 60% (240); all full-time undergraduates: 55% (791). *Average award:* Freshmen: $23,816; Undergraduates: $22,271. *Scholarships, grants, and awards:* Federal Pell, FSEOG, state, private, college/university gift aid from institutional funds.

GIFT AID (NON-NEED-BASED) *Total amount:* $4,910,562 (1% state, 80% institutional, 19% external sources). *Receiving aid:* Freshmen: 5% (20). Undergraduates: 6% (83). *Average award:* Freshmen: $13,046. Undergraduates: $12,129. *Scholarships, grants, and awards by category: Creative arts/ performance:* 11 awards ($55,000 total): art/fine arts, dance, music, performing arts, theater/drama. *Tuition waivers:* Full or partial for employees or children of employees, adult students, senior citizens.

LOANS *Student loans:* $7,733,866 (63% need-based, 37% non-need-based). 65% of past graduating class borrowed through all loan programs. *Average indebtedness per student:* $18,465. *Average need-based loan:* Freshmen: $3182. Undergraduates: $4250. *Parent loans:* $3,413,186 (20% need-based, 80% non-need-based). *Programs:* Federal Direct (Subsidized and Unsubsidized Stafford, PLUS), Perkins, college/university.

WORK-STUDY *Federal work-study:* Total amount: $555,877; 385 jobs averaging $986. *State or other work-study/employment:* Part-time jobs available.

APPLYING FOR FINANCIAL AID *Required financial aid forms:* FAFSA, CSS Financial Aid PROFILE. *Financial aid deadline (priority):* 2/1. *Notification date:* 4/1. Students must reply by 5/1 or within 2 weeks of notification.

CONTACT Sharon Hassan, Director of Student Financial Aid, Goucher College, 1021 Dulaney Valley Road, Baltimore, MD 21204-2794, 410-337-6141 or toll-free 800-468-2437. *Fax:* 410-337-6504.

GOVERNORS STATE UNIVERSITY
University Park, IL

CONTACT Financial Aid Office, Governors State University, One University Parkway, University Park, IL 60466-0975, 708-534-4480.

GRACE BIBLE COLLEGE
Grand Rapids, MI

Tuition & fees: $11,400	Average undergraduate aid package: $9165

ABOUT THE INSTITUTION Independent religious, coed. 19 undergraduate majors. Federal methodology is used as a basis for awarding need-based institutional aid.

UNDERGRADUATE EXPENSES for 2010–11 *Comprehensive fee:* $17,650 includes full-time tuition ($11,400) and room and board ($6250). *College room only:* $3150. Room and board charges vary according to housing facility. Part-time tuition and fees vary according to course load. *Payment plan:* Installment.

FRESHMAN FINANCIAL AID (Fall 2008) 49 applied for aid; of those 98% were deemed to have need. 100% of freshmen with need received aid; of those 8% had need fully met. *Average percent of need met:* 64% (excluding resources awarded to replace EFC). *Average financial aid package:* $10,264 (excluding resources awarded to replace EFC). 8% of all full-time freshmen had no need and received non-need-based gift aid.

UNDERGRADUATE FINANCIAL AID (Fall 2008) 153 applied for aid; of those 96% were deemed to have need. 100% of undergraduates with need received aid; of those 5% had need fully met. *Average percent of need met:* 59% (excluding resources awarded to replace EFC). *Average financial aid package:* $9165 (excluding resources awarded to replace EFC). 11% of all full-time undergraduates had no need and received non-need-based gift aid.

GIFT AID (NEED-BASED) *Total amount:* $505,904 (59% federal, 41% state). *Receiving aid:* Freshmen: 67% (35); all full-time undergraduates: 69% (116). *Average award:* Freshmen: $4599; Undergraduates: $4255. *Scholarships, grants, and awards:* Federal Pell, FSEOG, state, private, college/university gift aid from institutional funds.

GIFT AID (NON-NEED-BASED) *Total amount:* $435,485 (1% federal, 2% state, 90% institutional, 7% external sources). *Receiving aid:* Freshmen: 90% (47). Undergraduates: 70% (119). *Average award:* Freshmen: $3675. Undergraduates: $2797. *Scholarships, grants, and awards by category: Academic interests/ achievement:* 126 awards ($228,050 total): general academic interests/ achievements. *Creative arts/performance:* 10 awards ($9500 total): music. *Special characteristics:* 74 awards ($145,436 total): children of faculty/staff, general special characteristics, relatives of clergy. *Tuition waivers:* Full or partial for employees or children of employees.

LOANS *Student loans:* $1,177,013 (43% need-based, 57% non-need-based). 93% of past graduating class borrowed through all loan programs. *Average indebtedness per student:* $20,802. *Average need-based loan:* Freshmen: $3254. Undergraduates: $4065. *Parent loans:* $95,356 (100% non-need-based). *Programs:* Federal Direct (Subsidized and Unsubsidized Stafford, PLUS).

WORK-STUDY *Federal work-study:* Total amount: $24,581; 39 jobs averaging $525. *State or other work-study/employment:* Total amount: $7045 (100% need-based). 24 part-time jobs averaging $235.

APPLYING FOR FINANCIAL AID *Required financial aid form:* FAFSA. *Financial aid deadline (priority):* 2/28. *Notification date:* Continuous beginning 5/15. Students must reply within 2 weeks of notification.

CONTACT Mr. Kurt Postma, Director of Financial Aid, Grace Bible College, 1011 Aldon Street, SW, Grand Rapids, MI 49509-1921, 616-538-2330 or toll-free 800-968-1887. *Fax:* 616-538-0599. *E-mail:* kpostma@gbcol.edu.

GRACE COLLEGE
Winona Lake, IN

Tuition & fees: $21,100	Average undergraduate aid package: N/A

ABOUT THE INSTITUTION Independent religious, coed. 55 undergraduate majors. Federal methodology is used as a basis for awarding need-based institutional aid.

UNDERGRADUATE EXPENSES for 2009–10 *Comprehensive fee:* $27,980 includes full-time tuition ($21,100) and room and board ($6880). Full-time tuition and fees vary according to program. Room and board charges vary according to board plan and housing facility. *Part-time tuition:* $466 per credit hour. Part-time tuition and fees vary according to course load. *Payment plan:* Installment.

GIFT AID (NEED-BASED) *Total amount:* $9,357,979 (19% federal, 27% state, 54% institutional). *Scholarships, grants, and awards:* Federal Pell, FSEOG, state, private, college/university gift aid from institutional funds.

GIFT AID (NON-NEED-BASED) *Total amount:* $3,598,470 (100% institutional). *Scholarships, grants, and awards by category: Academic interests/achievement:* business. *Creative arts/performance:* applied art and design, art/fine arts, music, theater/drama. *Special achievements/activities:* junior miss. *Special characteristics:* children of faculty/staff, ethnic background, relatives of clergy, religious affiliation. *Tuition waivers:* Full or partial for employees or children of employees, senior citizens.

LOANS *Student loans:* $7,062,592 (43% need-based, 57% non-need-based). *Parent loans:* $479,343 (100% non-need-based). *Programs:* FFEL (Subsidized and Unsubsidized Stafford, PLUS), Perkins.

WORK-STUDY *Federal work-study:* Total amount: $460,784; jobs available.

ATHLETIC AWARDS Total amount: $878,102 (21% need-based, 79% non-need-based).

APPLYING FOR FINANCIAL AID *Required financial aid form:* FAFSA. *Financial aid deadline (priority):* 3/10. *Notification date:* Continuous.

CONTACT Charlette Sauders, Director of Financial Aid, Grace College, 200 Seminary Drive, Winona Lake, IN 46590-1294, 574-372-5100 Ext. 6161 or toll-free 800-54-GRACE Ext. 6412 (in-state), 800-54 GRACE Ext. 6412 (out-of-state). *Fax:* 574-372-5144. *E-mail:* charlette.sauders@grace.edu.

GRACELAND UNIVERSITY
Lamoni, IA

Tuition & fees: $20,980	Average undergraduate aid package: $18,566

ABOUT THE INSTITUTION Independent Community of Christ, coed. 50 undergraduate majors. Federal methodology is used as a basis for awarding need-based institutional aid.

UNDERGRADUATE EXPENSES for 2010–11 *Comprehensive fee:* $28,020 includes full-time tuition ($20,680), mandatory fees ($300), and room and board ($7040). *College room only:* $2810. Room and board charges vary according to board plan, housing facility, and location. *Part-time tuition:* $650 per semester hour. *Payment plan:* Installment.

FRESHMAN FINANCIAL AID (Fall 2009, est.) 202 applied for aid; of those 94% were deemed to have need. 98% of freshmen with need received aid; of those 21% had need fully met. *Average percent of need met:* 86% (excluding resources awarded to replace EFC). *Average financial aid package:* $20,874 (excluding resources awarded to replace EFC). 16% of all full-time freshmen had no need and received non-need-based gift aid.

UNDERGRADUATE FINANCIAL AID (Fall 2009, est.) 1,000 applied for aid; of those 92% were deemed to have need. 97% of undergraduates with need received aid; of those 19% had need fully met. *Average percent of need met:* 78% (excluding resources awarded to replace EFC). *Average financial aid package:* $18,566 (excluding resources awarded to replace EFC). 19% of all full-time undergraduates had no need and received non-need-based gift aid.

GIFT AID (NEED-BASED) *Total amount:* $8,537,500 (28% federal, 9% state, 59% institutional, 4% external sources). *Receiving aid:* Freshmen: 81% (185); all full-time undergraduates: 66% (819). *Average award:* Freshmen: $15,432; Undergraduates: $13,960. *Scholarships, grants, and awards:* Federal Pell, FSEOG, state, private, college/university gift aid from institutional funds.

GIFT AID (NON-NEED-BASED) *Total amount:* $2,542,547 (5% federal, 77% institutional, 18% external sources). *Receiving aid:* Freshmen: 44% (101). Undergraduates: 30% (368). *Average award:* Freshmen: $7021. Undergraduates: $10,029. *Scholarships, grants, and awards by category: Academic interests/achievement:* $987,619 total: computer science, engineering/technologies, English, general academic interests/achievements, physical sciences. *Creative arts/performance:* $313,805 total: applied art and design, creative writing, dance, music, theater/drama. *Special achievements/activities:* $196,530 total: cheerleading/drum major, general special achievements/activities, leadership, religious involvement. *Special characteristics:* $6,264,660 total: children and siblings of alumni, children of faculty/staff, first-generation college students, general special characteristics, international students, local/state students, members of minority groups, religious affiliation. *Tuition waivers:* Full or partial for employees or children of employees, senior citizens.

LOANS *Student loans:* $8,784,953 (76% need-based, 24% non-need-based). 89% of past graduating class borrowed through all loan programs. *Average indebtedness per student:* $29,934. *Average need-based loan:* Freshmen: $4790. Undergraduates: $5397. *Parent loans:* $1,075,849 (37% need-based, 63% non-need-based). *Programs:* Federal Direct (Subsidized and Unsubsidized Stafford, PLUS), Perkins, state, college/university.

WORK-STUDY *Federal work-study:* Total amount: $921,052; 383 jobs averaging $1382. *State or other work-study/employment:* Total amount: $569,174 (3% need-based, 97% non-need-based). 303 part-time jobs averaging $1708.

ATHLETIC AWARDS Total amount: $2,783,282 (65% need-based, 35% non-need-based).

APPLYING FOR FINANCIAL AID *Required financial aid form:* FAFSA. *Financial aid deadline:* Continuous. *Notification date:* Continuous beginning 2/1. Students must reply within 2 weeks of notification.

CONTACT Director of Financial Aid, Graceland University, 1 University Place, Lamoni, IA 50140, 641-784-5136 or toll-free 866-GRACELAND. *Fax:* 641-784-5020. *E-mail:* financialaidservices@graceland.edu.

GRACE UNIVERSITY
Omaha, NE

Tuition & fees: $14,290	Average undergraduate aid package: $12,607

ABOUT THE INSTITUTION Independent interdenominational, coed. *Awards:* associate, bachelor's, and master's degrees. 34 undergraduate majors. *Total enrollment:* 434. Undergraduates: 366. Freshmen: 97. Federal methodology is used as a basis for awarding need-based institutional aid.

UNDERGRADUATE EXPENSES for 2009–10 *Application fee:* $20. *Comprehensive fee:* $20,030 includes full-time tuition ($13,900), mandatory fees ($390), and room and board ($5740). *College room only:* $2550. *Part-time tuition:* $390 per credit hour. *Part-time fees:* $165 per term.

FRESHMAN FINANCIAL AID (Fall 2009, est.) 61 applied for aid; of those 84% were deemed to have need. 100% of freshmen with need received aid; of those 22% had need fully met. *Average percent of need met:* 74% (excluding

resources awarded to replace EFC). *Average financial aid package:* $12,027 (excluding resources awarded to replace EFC). 24% of all full-time freshmen had no need and received non-need-based gift aid.

UNDERGRADUATE FINANCIAL AID (Fall 2009, est.) 247 applied for aid; of those 85% were deemed to have need. 100% of undergraduates with need received aid; of those 16% had need fully met. *Average percent of need met:* 72% (excluding resources awarded to replace EFC). *Average financial aid package:* $12,607 (excluding resources awarded to replace EFC). 20% of all full-time undergraduates had no need and received non-need-based gift aid.

GIFT AID (NEED-BASED) *Total amount:* $2,098,585 (28% federal, 3% state, 60% institutional, 9% external sources). *Receiving aid:* Freshmen: 67% (51); all full-time undergraduates: 73% (208). *Average award:* Freshmen: $9186; Undergraduates: $8841. *Scholarships, grants, and awards:* Federal Pell, FSEOG, state, private, college/university gift aid from institutional funds, Academic Competitiveness Grants, TEACH Grants.

GIFT AID (NON-NEED-BASED) *Total amount:* $565,031 (3% federal, 1% state, 78% institutional, 18% external sources). *Receiving aid:* Freshmen: 14% (11). Undergraduates: 9% (27). *Average award:* Freshmen: $6783. Undergraduates: $5924. *Scholarships, grants, and awards by category: Academic interests/achievement:* 239 awards ($1,540,898 total): business, education, general academic interests/achievements, health fields, international studies, religion/biblical studies. *Creative arts/performance:* 13 awards ($18,000 total): cinema/film/broadcasting, music. *Special achievements/activities:* 56 awards ($62,511 total): general special achievements/activities, leadership, religious involvement. *Special characteristics:* 103 awards ($224,476 total): adult students, children and siblings of alumni, children of current students, children of faculty/staff, ethnic background, general special characteristics, international students, local/state students, married students, members of minority groups, out-of-state students, relatives of clergy, siblings of current students, spouses of current students. *ROTC:* Army cooperative, Air Force cooperative.

LOANS *Student loans:* $2,331,166 (80% need-based, 20% non-need-based). 92% of past graduating class borrowed through all loan programs. *Average indebtedness per student:* $17,820. *Average need-based loan:* Freshmen: $3274. Undergraduates: $4089. *Parent loans:* $1,139,637 (34% need-based, 66% non-need-based). *Programs:* FFEL (Subsidized and Unsubsidized Stafford, PLUS).

WORK-STUDY *Federal work-study:* Total amount: $37,000; 37 jobs averaging $1103. *State or other work-study/employment:* Total amount: $50,200 (36% need-based, 64% non-need-based). 45 part-time jobs averaging $1101.

APPLYING FOR FINANCIAL AID *Required financial aid forms:* FAFSA, institution's own form. *Financial aid deadline (priority):* 4/1. *Notification date:* Continuous. Students must reply within 2 weeks of notification.

CONTACT Marcy Pierce, Director of Financial Aid, Grace University, 1311 South Ninth Street, Omaha, NE 68108-3629, 402-449-2810 or toll-free 800-383-1422. *Fax:* 402-449-2921. *E-mail:* gufinaid@graceu.edu.

GRAMBLING STATE UNIVERSITY
Grambling, LA

CONTACT Assistant Director of Student Financial Aid and Scholarships, Grambling State University, PO Box 629, Grambling, LA 71245, 318-274-6415. *Fax:* 318-274-3358.

GRAND CANYON UNIVERSITY
Phoenix, AZ

CONTACT Director of Financial Aid, Grand Canyon University, 3300 West Camelback Road, PO Box 11097, Phoenix, AZ 85017-3030, 800-800-9776 Ext. 2885 or toll-free 800-800-9776 (in-state). *Fax:* 602-589-2044.

GRAND VALLEY STATE UNIVERSITY
Allendale, MI

Tuition & fees (MI res): $8630	Average undergraduate aid package: $8485

ABOUT THE INSTITUTION State-supported, coed. 105 undergraduate majors. Federal methodology is used as a basis for awarding need-based institutional aid.

UNDERGRADUATE EXPENSES for 2009–10 *Tuition, state resident:* full-time $8630; part-time $375 per credit hour. *Tuition, nonresident:* full-time $12,944; part-time $551 per credit hour. Full-time tuition and fees vary according to degree level, program, and student level. Part-time tuition and fees vary according to course load, degree level, program, and student level. *College room and board:* $7478; *Room only:* $5406. Room and board charges vary according to board plan, housing facility, and location. *Payment plans:* Installment, deferred payment.

FRESHMAN FINANCIAL AID (Fall 2009, est.) 3,283 applied for aid; of those 70% were deemed to have need. 99% of freshmen with need received aid; of those 9% had need fully met. *Average percent of need met:* 73% (excluding resources awarded to replace EFC). *Average financial aid package:* $9597 (excluding resources awarded to replace EFC). 13% of all full-time freshmen had no need and received non-need-based gift aid.

UNDERGRADUATE FINANCIAL AID (Fall 2009, est.) 14,812 applied for aid; of those 77% were deemed to have need. 99% of undergraduates with need received aid; of those 10% had need fully met. *Average percent of need met:* 61% (excluding resources awarded to replace EFC). *Average financial aid package:* $8485 (excluding resources awarded to replace EFC). 8% of all full-time undergraduates had no need and received non-need-based gift aid.

GIFT AID (NEED-BASED) *Total amount:* $47,647,891 (62% federal, 4% state, 30% institutional, 4% external sources). *Receiving aid:* Freshmen: 53% (1,952); all full-time undergraduates: 47% (8,594). *Average award:* Freshmen: $6494; Undergraduates: $5572. *Scholarships, grants, and awards:* Federal Pell, FSEOG, state, private, college/university gift aid from institutional funds.

GIFT AID (NON-NEED-BASED) *Total amount:* $7,451,291 (5% federal, 3% state, 79% institutional, 13% external sources). *Receiving aid:* Freshmen: 3% (97). Undergraduates: 2% (300). *Average award:* Freshmen: $2363. Undergraduates: $3384. *Scholarships, grants, and awards by category:* Academic interests/achievement: business, communication, computer science, education, engineering/technologies, English, foreign languages, general academic interests/achievements, health fields, humanities, international studies, mathematics, physical sciences, premedicine, social sciences. Creative arts/performance: applied art and design, art/fine arts, cinema/film/broadcasting, dance, journalism/publications, music, theater/drama. Special characteristics: adult students, children and siblings of alumni, children of faculty/staff, children of union members/company employees, children of workers in trades, general special characteristics, handicapped students, international students, local/state students, out-of-state students, public servants, spouses of deceased or disabled public servants, veterans, veterans' children. *Tuition waivers:* Full or partial for employees or children of employees.

LOANS *Student loans:* $120,348,243 (41% need-based, 59% non-need-based). 70% of past graduating class borrowed through all loan programs. *Average indebtedness per student:* $24,030. *Average need-based loan:* Freshmen: $3895. Undergraduates: $4542. *Parent loans:* $47,529,538 (100% non-need-based). *Programs:* Federal Direct (Subsidized and Unsubsidized Stafford, PLUS), Perkins, Federal Nursing.

WORK-STUDY *Federal work-study:* Total amount: $3,102,905; jobs available. *State or other work-study/employment:* Part-time jobs available.

ATHLETIC AWARDS Total amount: $2,223,893 (51% need-based, 49% non-need-based).

APPLYING FOR FINANCIAL AID *Required financial aid form:* FAFSA. *Financial aid deadline (priority):* 3/1. *Notification date:* 3/10. Students must reply by 5/1 or within 4 weeks of notification.

CONTACT Director of Financial Aid, Grand Valley State University, 100 Student Services Building, Allendale, MI 49401, 616-331-3234 or toll-free 800-748-0246. *Fax:* 616-331-3180. *E-mail:* finaid@gvsu.edu.

GRAND VIEW UNIVERSITY
Des Moines, IA

Tuition & fees: $19,324	Average undergraduate aid package: $14,309

ABOUT THE INSTITUTION Independent religious, coed. 30 undergraduate majors. Federal methodology is used as a basis for awarding need-based institutional aid.

UNDERGRADUATE EXPENSES for 2009–10 *Comprehensive fee:* $25,766 includes full-time tuition ($18,944), mandatory fees ($380), and room and board ($6442). Full-time tuition and fees vary according to class time and course load. Room and board charges vary according to board plan and housing facility. *Part-time tuition:* $485 per hour. Part-time tuition and fees vary according to class time and course load. *Payment plan:* Installment.

FRESHMAN FINANCIAL AID (Fall 2009, est.) 219 applied for aid; of those 87% were deemed to have need. 100% of freshmen with need received aid; of those

26% had need fully met. *Average percent of need met:* 86% (excluding resources awarded to replace EFC). *Average financial aid package:* $17,732 (excluding resources awarded to replace EFC). 17% of all full-time freshmen had no need and received non-need-based gift aid.

UNDERGRADUATE FINANCIAL AID (Fall 2009, est.) 1,468 applied for aid; of those 89% were deemed to have need. 100% of undergraduates with need received aid; of those 20% had need fully met. *Average percent of need met:* 75% (excluding resources awarded to replace EFC). *Average financial aid package:* $14,309 (excluding resources awarded to replace EFC). 15% of all full-time undergraduates had no need and received non-need-based gift aid.

GIFT AID (NEED-BASED) *Total amount:* $13,022,269 (25% federal, 27% state, 47% institutional, 1% external sources). *Receiving aid:* Freshmen: 75% (173); all full-time undergraduates: 74% (1,185). *Average award:* Freshmen: $14,884; Undergraduates: $11,883. *Scholarships, grants, and awards:* Federal Pell, FSEOG, state, private, college/university gift aid from institutional funds, Academic Competitiveness Grants, National SMART Grants.

GIFT AID (NON-NEED-BASED) *Total amount:* $1,767,537 (5% federal, 7% state, 82% institutional, 6% external sources). *Receiving aid:* Freshmen: 14% (33). Undergraduates: 8% (134). *Average award:* Freshmen: $6975. Undergraduates: $5861. *Scholarships, grants, and awards by category:* Academic interests/achievement: 1,545 awards ($6,474,219 total): general academic interests/achievements. Creative arts/performance: 74 awards ($71,047 total): art/fine arts, music, theater/drama. Special achievements/activities: 6 awards ($4750 total): junior miss, religious involvement. Special characteristics: 114 awards ($513,301 total): children and siblings of alumni, children of educators, children of faculty/staff. *Tuition waivers:* Full or partial for children of alumni, employees or children of employees, senior citizens.

LOANS *Student loans:* $15,282,445 (65% need-based, 35% non-need-based). 83% of past graduating class borrowed through all loan programs. *Average indebtedness per student:* $28,041. *Average need-based loan:* Freshmen: $3772. Undergraduates: $4029. *Parent loans:* $1,085,951 (10% need-based, 90% non-need-based). *Programs:* Federal Direct (Subsidized and Unsubsidized Stafford, PLUS), FFEL (Subsidized and Unsubsidized Stafford, PLUS), Perkins, Federal Nursing.

WORK-STUDY *Federal work-study:* Total amount: $676,790; 426 jobs averaging $1336. *State or other work-study/employment:* Part-time jobs available.

ATHLETIC AWARDS Total amount: $1,729,911 (66% need-based, 34% non-need-based).

APPLYING FOR FINANCIAL AID *Required financial aid form:* FAFSA. *Financial aid deadline (priority):* 3/1. *Notification date:* Continuous beginning 3/10. Students must reply by 5/1 or within 3 weeks of notification.

CONTACT Michele Dunne, Director of Financial Aid, Grand View University, 1200 Grandview Avenue, Des Moines, IA 50316-1599, 515-263-2820 or toll-free 800-444-6083 Ext. 2810. *Fax:* 515-263-6191. *E-mail:* mdunne@grandview.edu.

GRATZ COLLEGE
Melrose Park, PA

CONTACT Karen West, Student Financial Services Adviser, Gratz College, 7605 Old York Road, Melrose Park, PA 19027, 215-635-7300 Ext. 163 or toll-free 800-475-4635 Ext. 140 (out-of-state). *Fax:* 215-635-7320.

GREAT LAKES CHRISTIAN COLLEGE
Lansing, MI

CONTACT Financial Aid Officer, Great Lakes Christian College, 6211 West Willow Highway, Lansing, MI 48917-1299, 517-321-0242 or toll-free 800-YES-GLCC.

GREEN MOUNTAIN COLLEGE
Poultney, VT

Tuition & fees: $26,910	Average undergraduate aid package: $19,464

ABOUT THE INSTITUTION Independent, coed. 20 undergraduate majors. Federal methodology is used as a basis for awarding need-based institutional aid.

UNDERGRADUATE EXPENSES for 2009–10 *One-time required fee:* $225. *Comprehensive fee:* $36,580 includes full-time tuition ($25,910), mandatory fees ($1000), and room and board ($9670). *College room only:* $5704. Full-time tuition and fees vary according to course load, location, and program.

Room and board charges vary according to housing facility. *Part-time tuition:* $864 per credit. *Part-time fees:* $990 per credit. Part-time tuition and fees vary according to course load, location, and program. *Payment plan:* Installment.

FRESHMAN FINANCIAL AID (Fall 2009, est.) 192 applied for aid; of those 88% were deemed to have need. 100% of freshmen with need received aid; of those 10% had need fully met. *Average percent of need met:* 63% (excluding resources awarded to replace EFC). *Average financial aid package:* $18,198 (excluding resources awarded to replace EFC). 20% of all full-time freshmen had no need and received non-need-based gift aid.

UNDERGRADUATE FINANCIAL AID (Fall 2009, est.) 661 applied for aid; of those 90% were deemed to have need. 98% of undergraduates with need received aid; of those 13% had need fully met. *Average percent of need met:* 65% (excluding resources awarded to replace EFC). *Average financial aid package:* $19,464 (excluding resources awarded to replace EFC). 16% of all full-time undergraduates had no need and received non-need-based gift aid.

GIFT AID (NEED-BASED) *Total amount:* $8,493,355 (19% federal, 4% state, 75% institutional, 2% external sources). *Receiving aid:* Freshmen: 76% (167); all full-time undergraduates: 78% (575). *Average award:* Freshmen: $15,232; Undergraduates: $15,201. *Scholarships, grants, and awards:* Federal Pell, FSEOG, state, private, college/university gift aid from institutional funds.

GIFT AID (NON-NEED-BASED) *Total amount:* $1,610,264 (95% institutional, 5% external sources). *Receiving aid:* Freshmen: 6% (13). Undergraduates: 6% (41). *Average award:* Freshmen: $11,289. Undergraduates: $11,488. *Scholarships, grants, and awards by category:* Academic interests/achievement: 101 awards ($321,813 total): biological sciences, business, education, English, general academic interests/achievements, physical sciences, social sciences. *Creative arts/performance:* 56 awards ($114,500 total): art/fine arts, creative writing, music, performing arts, theater/drama. *Special achievements/activities:* 248 awards ($1,114,750 total): community service, leadership, religious involvement. *Special characteristics:* 20 awards ($128,935 total): children and siblings of alumni, children of current students, international students, parents of current students, relatives of clergy, religious affiliation, siblings of current students. *Tuition waivers:* Full or partial for employees or children of employees.

LOANS *Student loans:* $5,743,142 (74% need-based, 26% non-need-based). 82% of past graduating class borrowed through all loan programs. *Average indebtedness per student:* $39,862. *Average need-based loan:* Freshmen: $2822. Undergraduates: $4512. *Parent loans:* $1,774,428 (52% need-based, 48% non-need-based). *Programs:* Federal Direct (Subsidized and Unsubsidized Stafford, PLUS), private lending educational loans.

WORK-STUDY *Federal work-study:* Total amount: $236,865; 212 jobs averaging $1700. *State or other work-study/employment:* Total amount: $167,785 (62% need-based, 38% non-need-based). 91 part-time jobs averaging $1700.

APPLYING FOR FINANCIAL AID *Required financial aid form:* FAFSA. *Financial aid deadline (priority):* 3/1. *Notification date:* Continuous. Students must reply by 5/1 or within 4 weeks of notification.

CONTACT Wendy J. Ellis, Director of Financial Aid, Green Mountain College, One Brennan Circle, Poultney, VT 05764-1199, 800-776-6675 Ext. 8209 or toll-free 800-776-6675 (out-of-state). *Fax:* 802-287-8099. *E-mail:* ellisw@greenmtn.edu.

GREENSBORO COLLEGE
Greensboro, NC

ABOUT THE INSTITUTION Independent United Methodist, coed. 48 undergraduate majors.

GIFT AID (NEED-BASED) *Scholarships, grants, and awards:* Federal Pell, FSEOG, state, private, college/university gift aid from institutional funds.

GIFT AID (NON-NEED-BASED) *Scholarships, grants, and awards by category:* Academic interests/achievement: general academic interests/achievements. Creative arts/performance: art/fine arts, music, theater/drama. Special achievements/activities: community service, leadership, religious involvement. Special characteristics: adult students, children and siblings of alumni, children of faculty/staff, international students, relatives of clergy, religious affiliation, siblings of current students, veterans.

LOANS *Programs:* FFEL (Subsidized and Unsubsidized Stafford, PLUS), Perkins, college/university.

APPLYING FOR FINANCIAL AID *Required financial aid forms:* FAFSA, institution's own form, state aid form.

CONTACT Dawn VanArsdale Young, Director of Financial Aid, Greensboro College, 815 West Market Street, Greensboro, NC 27401-1875, 336-272-7102 Ext. 408 or toll-free 800-346-8226. *Fax:* 336-271-6634. *E-mail:* dvanarsdale@reensgborocollege.edu.

GREENVILLE COLLEGE
Greenville, IL

Tuition & fees: $20,924	Average undergraduate aid package: $15,347

ABOUT THE INSTITUTION Independent Free Methodist, coed. 54 undergraduate majors. Federal methodology is used as a basis for awarding need-based institutional aid.

UNDERGRADUATE EXPENSES for 2010–11 *Comprehensive fee:* $27,958 includes full-time tuition ($20,766), mandatory fees ($158), and room and board ($7034). *College room only:* $3374. Room and board charges vary according to housing facility. *Part-time tuition:* $437 per credit hour. Part-time tuition and fees vary according to course load.

FRESHMAN FINANCIAL AID (Fall 2009, est.) 219 applied for aid; of those 94% were deemed to have need. 100% of freshmen with need received aid; of those 11% had need fully met. *Average percent of need met:* 72% (excluding resources awarded to replace EFC). *Average financial aid package:* $16,727 (excluding resources awarded to replace EFC). 14% of all full-time freshmen had no need and received non-need-based gift aid.

UNDERGRADUATE FINANCIAL AID (Fall 2009, est.) 1,188 applied for aid; of those 93% were deemed to have need. 100% of undergraduates with need received aid; of those 11% had need fully met. *Average percent of need met:* 68% (excluding resources awarded to replace EFC). *Average financial aid package:* $15,347 (excluding resources awarded to replace EFC). 11% of all full-time undergraduates had no need and received non-need-based gift aid.

GIFT AID (NEED-BASED) *Total amount:* $12,205,787 (18% federal, 16% state, 61% institutional, 5% external sources). *Receiving aid:* Freshmen: 85% (205); all full-time undergraduates: 82% (1,049). *Average award:* Freshmen: $13,269; Undergraduates: $11,629. *Scholarships, grants, and awards:* Federal Pell, FSEOG, state, private, college/university gift aid from institutional funds.

GIFT AID (NON-NEED-BASED) *Total amount:* $1,309,149 (90% institutional, 10% external sources). *Receiving aid:* Freshmen: 6% (14). Undergraduates: 6% (71). *Average award:* Freshmen: $7848. Undergraduates: $6763. *Scholarships, grants, and awards by category:* Academic interests/achievement: biological sciences, business, education, engineering/technologies, general academic interests/achievements, mathematics, physical sciences, religion/biblical studies. Creative arts/performance: applied art and design, art/fine arts, music, performing arts. Special achievements/activities: leadership, memberships, religious involvement. Special characteristics: children and siblings of alumni, children of faculty/staff, international students, local/state students, out-of-state students, relatives of clergy, religious affiliation, siblings of current students. *Tuition waivers:* Full or partial for employees or children of employees, senior citizens.

LOANS *Student loans:* $8,748,088 (81% need-based, 19% non-need-based). *Average need-based loan:* Freshmen: $3263. Undergraduates: $4158. *Parent loans:* $1,304,642 (34% need-based, 66% non-need-based). *Programs:* Federal Direct (Subsidized and Unsubsidized Stafford, PLUS), Perkins, college/university.

WORK-STUDY *Federal work-study:* Total amount: $615,449; jobs available. *State or other work-study/employment:* Total amount: $6750 (100% non-need-based). Part-time jobs available.

APPLYING FOR FINANCIAL AID *Required financial aid form:* FAFSA. *Financial aid deadline (priority):* 4/15. *Notification date:* Continuous beginning 3/1. Students must reply within 3 weeks of notification.

CONTACT Marilae Latham, Director of Financial Aid, Greenville College, 315 East College Avenue, Greenville, IL 62246-0159, 618-664-7110 or toll-free 800-345-4440. *Fax:* 618-664-7198. *E-mail:* marilae.latham@greenville.edu.

GRINNELL COLLEGE
Grinnell, IA

Tuition & fees: $36,476	Average undergraduate aid package: $32,958

ABOUT THE INSTITUTION Independent, coed. 27 undergraduate majors. Both federal and institutional methodology are used as a basis for awarding need-based institutional aid.

UNDERGRADUATE EXPENSES for 2009–10 *Comprehensive fee:* $45,012 includes full-time tuition ($35,976), mandatory fees ($500), and room and board ($8536). *College room only:* $3968. Full-time tuition and fees vary according to student level. Room and board charges vary according to board plan and housing facility. *Part-time tuition:* $1124 per credit. Part-time tuition and fees vary according to student level. *Payment plans:* Tuition prepayment, installment.

FRESHMAN FINANCIAL AID (Fall 2009, est.) 321 applied for aid; of those 84% were deemed to have need. 100% of freshmen with need received aid; of those 100% had need fully met. *Average percent of need met:* 100% (excluding resources awarded to replace EFC). *Average financial aid package:* $34,463 (excluding resources awarded to replace EFC). 13% of all full-time freshmen had no need and received non-need-based gift aid.

UNDERGRADUATE FINANCIAL AID (Fall 2009, est.) 1,154 applied for aid; of those 90% were deemed to have need. 100% of undergraduates with need received aid; of those 100% had need fully met. *Average percent of need met:* 100% (excluding resources awarded to replace EFC). *Average financial aid package:* $32,958 (excluding resources awarded to replace EFC). 21% of all full-time undergraduates had no need and received non-need-based gift aid.

GIFT AID (NEED-BASED) *Total amount:* $28,752,550 (6% federal, 1% state, 91% institutional, 2% external sources). *Receiving aid:* Freshmen: 71% (269); all full-time undergraduates: 63% (1,027). *Average award:* Freshmen: $28,905; Undergraduates: $27,997. *Scholarships, grants, and awards:* Federal Pell, FSEOG, state, private, college/university gift aid from institutional funds.

GIFT AID (NON-NEED-BASED) *Total amount:* $4,806,163 (1% federal, 82% institutional, 17% external sources). *Receiving aid:* Freshmen: 8% (32). Undergraduates: 6% (90). *Average award:* Freshmen: $9269. Undergraduates: $10,181. *Scholarships, grants, and awards by category:* Academic interests/ achievement: general academic interests/achievements. *Tuition waivers:* Full or partial for employees or children of employees.

LOANS *Student loans:* $2,865,574 (78% need-based, 22% non-need-based). 54% of past graduating class borrowed through all loan programs. *Average indebtedness per student:* $19,540. *Average need-based loan:* Freshmen: $2854. Undergraduates: $3133. *Programs:* FFEL (Subsidized and Unsubsidized Stafford, PLUS), Perkins, college/university.

WORK-STUDY *Federal work-study:* Total amount: $1,092,223; 563 jobs averaging $1938. *State or other work-study/employment:* Total amount: $838,492 (37% need-based, 63% non-need-based). 407 part-time jobs averaging $2060.

APPLYING FOR FINANCIAL AID *Required financial aid forms:* FAFSA, institution's own form, noncustodial (divorced/separated) parent's statement. *Financial aid deadline:* 2/1. *Notification date:* 4/1. Students must reply by 5/1.

CONTACT Mr. Arnold Woods, Director of Student Financial Aid, Grinnell College, 1103 Park Street, Grinnell, IA 50112-1690, 641-269-3250 or toll-free 800-247-0113. *Fax:* 641-269-4937. *E-mail:* woods@grinnell.edu.

GROVE CITY COLLEGE
Grove City, PA

Tuition & fees: $12,590	Average undergraduate aid package: $5726

ABOUT THE INSTITUTION Independent Presbyterian, coed. 44 undergraduate majors. Institutional methodology is used as a basis for awarding need-based institutional aid.

UNDERGRADUATE EXPENSES for 2009–10 *Comprehensive fee:* $19,414 includes full-time tuition ($12,590) and room and board ($6824). Full-time tuition and fees vary according to course load. Room and board charges vary according to housing facility. *Part-time tuition:* $395 per credit. *Payment plan:* Installment.

FRESHMAN FINANCIAL AID (Fall 2009, est.) 373 applied for aid; of those 76% were deemed to have need. 96% of freshmen with need received aid; of those 12% had need fully met. *Average percent of need met:* 53% (excluding resources awarded to replace EFC). *Average financial aid package:* $6024 (excluding resources awarded to replace EFC). 8% of all full-time freshmen had no need and received non-need-based gift aid.

UNDERGRADUATE FINANCIAL AID (Fall 2009, est.) 1,141 applied for aid; of those 84% were deemed to have need. 99% of undergraduates with need received aid; of those 9% had need fully met. *Average percent of need met:* 50% (excluding resources awarded to replace EFC). *Average financial aid package:* $5726 (excluding resources awarded to replace EFC). 13% of all full-time undergraduates had no need and received non-need-based gift aid.

GIFT AID (NEED-BASED) *Total amount:* $5,434,410 (18% state, 72% institutional, 10% external sources). *Receiving aid:* Freshmen: 42% (275); all full-time undergraduates: 36% (906). *Average award:* Freshmen: $6024; Undergraduates: $5942. *Scholarships, grants, and awards:* state, private, college/university gift aid from institutional funds.

GIFT AID (NON-NEED-BASED) *Total amount:* $1,649,871 (52% institutional, 48% external sources). *Receiving aid:* Freshmen: 5% (34). Undergraduates: 3% (78). *Average award:* Freshmen: $2188. Undergraduates: $2369. *Scholarships, grants, and awards by category:* Academic interests/achievement: 480 awards ($863,508 total): biological sciences, business, communication, education, engineering/technologies, English, foreign languages, general academic interests/achievements, physical sciences, religion/biblical studies, social sciences. *Creative arts/performance:* 4 awards ($26,200 total): creative writing, music. *Special achievements/activities:* 21 awards ($75,300 total): general special achievements/activities, leadership, memberships, religious involvement. *Special characteristics:* 10 awards ($36,100 total): ethnic background, general special characteristics, members of minority groups. *Tuition waivers:* Full or partial for employees or children of employees.

LOANS *Student loans:* $9,485,283 (34% need-based, 66% non-need-based). 45% of past graduating class borrowed through all loan programs. *Average indebtedness per student:* $24,895. *Programs:* alternative loans.

WORK-STUDY *State or other work-study/employment:* Part-time jobs available.

APPLYING FOR FINANCIAL AID *Required financial aid forms:* institution's own form, state aid form. *Financial aid deadline:* 4/15. *Notification date:* Continuous beginning 3/18.

CONTACT Thomas G. Ball, Director of Financial Aid, Grove City College, 100 Campus Drive, Grove City, PA 16127-2104, 724-458-3300. *Fax:* 724-450-4040. *E-mail:* financialaid@gcc.edu.

GUILFORD COLLEGE
Greensboro, NC

Tuition & fees: $27,450	Average undergraduate aid package: $21,918

ABOUT THE INSTITUTION Independent religious, coed. 37 undergraduate majors. Federal methodology is used as a basis for awarding need-based institutional aid.

UNDERGRADUATE EXPENSES for 2009–10 *Comprehensive fee:* $35,010 includes full-time tuition ($27,120), mandatory fees ($330), and room and board ($7560). Room and board charges vary according to board plan and housing facility. *Part-time tuition:* $840 per credit hour. *Part-time fees:* $285 per credit hour. Part-time tuition and fees vary according to course load. *Payment plan:* Installment.

FRESHMAN FINANCIAL AID (Fall 2009, est.) 399 applied for aid; of those 86% were deemed to have need. 100% of freshmen with need received aid; of those 13% had need fully met. *Average percent of need met:* 87% (excluding resources awarded to replace EFC). *Average financial aid package:* $23,989 (excluding resources awarded to replace EFC). 11% of all full-time freshmen had no need and received non-need-based gift aid.

UNDERGRADUATE FINANCIAL AID (Fall 2009, est.) 1,994 applied for aid; of those 80% were deemed to have need. 100% of undergraduates with need received aid; of those 18% had need fully met. *Average percent of need met:* 91% (excluding resources awarded to replace EFC). *Average financial aid package:* $21,918 (excluding resources awarded to replace EFC). 6% of all full-time undergraduates had no need and received non-need-based gift aid.

GIFT AID (NEED-BASED) *Total amount:* $20,051,642 (28% federal, 18% state, 47% institutional, 7% external sources). *Receiving aid:* Freshmen: 76% (343); all full-time undergraduates: 53% (1,167). *Average award:* Freshmen: $20,529; Undergraduates: $7857. *Scholarships, grants, and awards:* Federal Pell, FSEOG, state, private, college/university gift aid from institutional funds.

GIFT AID (NON-NEED-BASED) *Total amount:* $6,554,968 (21% state, 76% institutional, 3% external sources). *Receiving aid:* Freshmen: 57% (257). Undergraduates: 48% (1,054). *Average award:* Freshmen: $10,000. Undergraduates: $7307. *Scholarships, grants, and awards by category:* Academic interests/ achievement: biological sciences, general academic interests/achievements. *Creative arts/performance:* 66 awards: music, theater/drama. *Special achievements/activities:* 21 awards: religious involvement. *Special characteristics:* children of faculty/staff, first-generation college students, local/state students. *Tuition waivers:* Full or partial for employees or children of employees.

LOANS *Student loans:* $12,900,065 (86% need-based, 14% non-need-based). 71% of past graduating class borrowed through all loan programs. *Average indebtedness per student:* $24,580. *Average need-based loan:* Freshmen: $7436. Undergraduates: $5126. *Parent loans:* $2,266,763 (92% need-based, 8% non-need-based). *Programs:* FFEL (Subsidized and Unsubsidized Stafford, PLUS), Perkins, college/university.

WORK-STUDY *Federal work-study:* Total amount: $426,250; 213 jobs averaging $1993. *State or other work-study/employment:* Total amount: $241,308 (80% need-based, 20% non-need-based). 121 part-time jobs averaging $1588.
APPLYING FOR FINANCIAL AID *Required financial aid forms:* FAFSA, noncustodial (divorced/separated) parent's statement, business/farm supplement. *Financial aid deadline (priority):* 3/1. *Notification date:* Continuous. Students must reply within 2 weeks of notification.
CONTACT Mr. Paul J. Coscia, Interim Director of Student Financial Services, Guilford College, 5800 West Friendly Avenue, Greensboro, NC 27410, 336-316-2395 or toll-free 800-992-7759. *Fax:* 336-316-2942. *E-mail:* pcoscia@guilford.edu.

GUSTAVUS ADOLPHUS COLLEGE
St. Peter, MN

Tuition & fees: $33,400	Average undergraduate aid package: $23,652

ABOUT THE INSTITUTION Independent religious, coed. 67 undergraduate majors. Both federal and institutional methodology are used as a basis for awarding need-based institutional aid.
UNDERGRADUATE EXPENSES for 2010–11 *One-time required fee:* $400. *Comprehensive fee:* $41,800 includes full-time tuition ($33,100), mandatory fees ($300), and room and board ($8400). *College room only:* $5400.
FRESHMAN FINANCIAL AID (Fall 2009, est.) 526 applied for aid; of those 84% were deemed to have need. 100% of freshmen with need received aid; of those 45% had need fully met. *Average percent of need met:* 94% (excluding resources awarded to replace EFC). *Average financial aid package:* $25,665 (excluding resources awarded to replace EFC). 30% of all full-time freshmen had no need and received non-need-based gift aid.
UNDERGRADUATE FINANCIAL AID (Fall 2009, est.) 1,911 applied for aid; of those 86% were deemed to have need. 100% of undergraduates with need received aid; of those 42% had need fully met. *Average percent of need met:* 90% (excluding resources awarded to replace EFC). *Average financial aid package:* $23,652 (excluding resources awarded to replace EFC). 32% of all full-time undergraduates had no need and received non-need-based gift aid.
GIFT AID (NEED-BASED) *Total amount:* $7,729,161 (8% federal, 10% state, 82% institutional). *Receiving aid:* Freshmen: 70% (440); all full-time undergraduates: 65% (1,642). *Average award:* Undergraduates: $18,834. *Scholarships, grants, and awards:* Federal Pell, FSEOG, state, private, college/university gift aid from institutional funds.
GIFT AID (NON-NEED-BASED) *Total amount:* $2,980,624 (81% institutional, 19% external sources). *Receiving aid:* Freshmen: 35% (221). Undergraduates: 39% (975). *Average award:* Freshmen: $8095. Undergraduates: $7352. *Scholarships, grants, and awards by category: Academic interests/achievement:* general academic interests/achievements. *Creative arts/performance:* art/fine arts, dance, debating, music, theater/drama. *Special achievements/activities:* junior miss. *Special characteristics:* children and siblings of alumni, ethnic background, first-generation college students, international students, members of minority groups, out-of-state students, siblings of current students.
LOANS *Student loans:* $3,611,214 (63% need-based, 37% non-need-based). 70% of past graduating class borrowed through all loan programs. *Average indebtedness per student:* $24,297. *Average need-based loan:* Freshmen: $3352. Undergraduates: $4812. *Parent loans:* $940,193 (100% non-need-based). *Programs:* Federal Direct (Subsidized and Unsubsidized Stafford, PLUS), Perkins, state.
WORK-STUDY *Federal work-study:* Total amount: $384,291; jobs available. *State or other work-study/employment:* Total amount: $390,536 (84% need-based, 16% non-need-based). Part-time jobs available.
APPLYING FOR FINANCIAL AID *Required financial aid form:* FAFSA. *Financial aid deadline:* 4/15 (priority: 2/15). *Notification date:* Continuous beginning 1/20. Students must reply by 5/1 or within 2 weeks of notification.
CONTACT Doug Minter, Director of Financial Aid, Gustavus Adolphus College, 800 West College Avenue, St. Peter, MN 56082-1498, 507-933-7527 or toll-free 800-GUSTAVU(S). *Fax:* 507-933-7727. *E-mail:* finaid@gustavus.edu.

GUTENBERG COLLEGE
Eugene, OR

CONTACT Financial Aid Office, Gutenberg College, 1883 University Street, Eugene, OR 97403, 541-683-5141.

GWYNEDD-MERCY COLLEGE
Gwynedd Valley, PA

Tuition & fees: $25,610	Average undergraduate aid package: $14,187

ABOUT THE INSTITUTION Independent Roman Catholic, coed. 32 undergraduate majors. Federal methodology is used as a basis for awarding need-based institutional aid.
UNDERGRADUATE EXPENSES for 2010–11 *Comprehensive fee:* $35,370 includes full-time tuition ($25,160), mandatory fees ($450), and room and board ($9760). Full-time tuition and fees vary according to program. Room and board charges vary according to board plan and housing facility. *Part-time tuition:* $515 per credit hour. *Part-time fees:* $10 per credit. Part-time tuition and fees vary according to program. *Payment plan:* Installment.
FRESHMAN FINANCIAL AID (Fall 2008) 318 applied for aid; of those 81% were deemed to have need. 100% of freshmen with need received aid; of those 25% had need fully met. *Average percent of need met:* 75% (excluding resources awarded to replace EFC). *Average financial aid package:* $14,625 (excluding resources awarded to replace EFC). 20% of all full-time freshmen had no need and received non-need-based gift aid.
UNDERGRADUATE FINANCIAL AID (Fall 2008) 1,152 applied for aid; of those 84% were deemed to have need. 100% of undergraduates with need received aid; of those 18% had need fully met. *Average percent of need met:* 72% (excluding resources awarded to replace EFC). *Average financial aid package:* $14,187 (excluding resources awarded to replace EFC). 20% of all full-time undergraduates had no need and received non-need-based gift aid.
GIFT AID (NEED-BASED) *Total amount:* $12,175,601 (11% federal, 19% state, 69% institutional, 1% external sources). *Receiving aid:* Freshmen: 71% (249); all full-time undergraduates: 72% (947). *Average award:* Freshmen: $12,479; Undergraduates: $11,605. *Scholarships, grants, and awards:* Federal Pell, FSEOG, state, private, college/university gift aid from institutional funds.
GIFT AID (NON-NEED-BASED) *Total amount:* $4,917,053 (99% institutional, 1% external sources). *Receiving aid:* Freshmen: 57% (199). Undergraduates: 57% (744). *Average award:* Freshmen: $14,710. Undergraduates: $15,592. *Scholarships, grants, and awards by category: Academic interests/achievement:* 630 awards ($4,716,810 total): general academic interests/achievements. *Special achievements/activities:* 347 awards ($1,625,875 total): general special achievements/activities. *Special characteristics:* 78 awards ($143,700 total): children and siblings of alumni, siblings of current students. *Tuition waivers:* Full or partial for employees or children of employees.
LOANS *Student loans:* $11,156,467 (32% need-based, 68% non-need-based). 90% of past graduating class borrowed through all loan programs. *Average indebtedness per student:* $29,380. *Average need-based loan:* Freshmen: $4210. Undergraduates: $6441. *Parent loans:* $809,784 (24% need-based, 76% non-need-based). *Programs:* Federal Direct (Subsidized and Unsubsidized Stafford, PLUS), Perkins, Federal Nursing, alternative loans.
WORK-STUDY *Federal work-study:* Total amount: $113,753; 169 jobs averaging $889. *State or other work-study/employment:* Total amount: $17,885 (100% need-based). 16 part-time jobs averaging $1118.
APPLYING FOR FINANCIAL AID *Required financial aid forms:* FAFSA, institution's own form. *Financial aid deadline (priority):* 3/15. *Notification date:* Continuous beginning 3/1. Students must reply by 5/1 or within 2 weeks of notification.
CONTACT Sr. Barbara A. Kaufmann, Director of Student Financial Aid, Gwynedd-Mercy College, PO Box 901, Gwynedd Valley, PA 19437-0901, 215-641-5570 or toll-free 800-DIAL-GMC (in-state). *Fax:* 215-641-5556.

HAMILTON COLLEGE
Clinton, NY

Tuition & fees: $39,760	Average undergraduate aid package: $36,305

ABOUT THE INSTITUTION Independent, coed. 44 undergraduate majors. Both federal and institutional methodology are used as a basis for awarding need-based institutional aid.
UNDERGRADUATE EXPENSES for 2009–10 *Comprehensive fee:* $49,860 includes full-time tuition ($39,370), mandatory fees ($390), and room and board ($10,100). *College room only:* $5520. Room and board charges vary according to board plan. *Part-time tuition:* $4921 per course. *Payment plan:* Installment.

FRESHMAN FINANCIAL AID (Fall 2009, est.) 269 applied for aid; of those 77% were deemed to have need. 100% of freshmen with need received aid; of those 100% had need fully met. *Average percent of need met:* 100% (excluding resources awarded to replace EFC). *Average financial aid package:* $36,931 (excluding resources awarded to replace EFC). 1% of all full-time freshmen had no need and received non-need-based gift aid.

UNDERGRADUATE FINANCIAL AID (Fall 2009, est.) 913 applied for aid; of those 83% were deemed to have need. 100% of undergraduates with need received aid; of those 100% had need fully met. *Average percent of need met:* 100% (excluding resources awarded to replace EFC). *Average financial aid package:* $36,305 (excluding resources awarded to replace EFC). 2% of all full-time undergraduates had no need and received non-need-based gift aid.

GIFT AID (NEED-BASED) *Total amount:* $23,995,858 (6% federal, 3% state, 89% institutional, 2% external sources). *Receiving aid:* Freshmen: 44% (207); all full-time undergraduates: 41% (755). *Average award:* Freshmen: $34,004; Undergraduates: $35,502. *Scholarships, grants, and awards:* Federal Pell, FSEOG, state, private, college/university gift aid from institutional funds.

GIFT AID (NON-NEED-BASED) *Total amount:* $1,228,694 (5% state, 61% institutional, 34% external sources). *Average award:* Freshmen: $39,370. Undergraduates: $22,205. *Tuition waivers:* Full or partial for employees or children of employees.

LOANS *Student loans:* $2,473,973 (99% need-based, 1% non-need-based). 46% of past graduating class borrowed through all loan programs. *Average indebtedness per student:* $19,466. *Average need-based loan:* Freshmen: $2914. Undergraduates: $3835. *Programs:* Federal Direct (Subsidized and Unsubsidized Stafford, PLUS), Perkins, college/university.

WORK-STUDY *Federal work-study:* Total amount: $706,866; 478 jobs averaging $1479. *State or other work-study/employment:* Total amount: $110,114 (100% need-based). 62 part-time jobs averaging $1776.

APPLYING FOR FINANCIAL AID *Required financial aid forms:* FAFSA, institution's own form, CSS Financial Aid PROFILE, state aid form, noncustodial (divorced/separated) parent's statement, business/farm supplement. *Financial aid deadline:* 2/8. *Notification date:* 4/1. Students must reply by 5/1.

CONTACT Office of Financial Aid, Hamilton College, 198 College Hill Road, Clinton, NY 13323, 315-859-4434 or toll-free 800-843-2655. *Fax:* 315-859-4962. *E-mail:* finaid@hamilton.edu.

HAMILTON TECHNICAL COLLEGE
Davenport, IA

CONTACT Ms. Lisa Boyd, Executive Vice President/Director of Financial Aid, Hamilton Technical College, 1011 East 53rd Street, Davenport, IA 52807-2653, 563-386-3570 Ext. 33. *Fax:* 563-386-6756.

HAMLINE UNIVERSITY
St. Paul, MN

Tuition & fees: $30,503	Average undergraduate aid package: $22,477

ABOUT THE INSTITUTION Independent religious, coed. 62 undergraduate majors. Federal methodology is used as a basis for awarding need-based institutional aid.

UNDERGRADUATE EXPENSES for 2010–11 *One-time required fee:* $260. *Comprehensive fee:* $38,899 includes full-time tuition ($30,016), mandatory fees ($487), and room and board ($8396). *College room only:* $4172. Room and board charges vary according to board plan and housing facility. *Part-time tuition:* $938 per credit hour. *Part-time fees:* $356 per term. Part-time tuition and fees vary according to course load. *Payment plan:* Installment.

FRESHMAN FINANCIAL AID (Fall 2009, est.) 371 applied for aid; of those 88% were deemed to have need. 100% of freshmen with need received aid; of those 24% had need fully met. *Average percent of need met:* 87% (excluding resources awarded to replace EFC). *Average financial aid package:* $25,046 (excluding resources awarded to replace EFC). 13% of all full-time freshmen had no need and received non-need-based gift aid.

UNDERGRADUATE FINANCIAL AID (Fall 2009, est.) 1,568 applied for aid; of those 88% were deemed to have need. 100% of undergraduates with need received aid; of those 19% had need fully met. *Average percent of need met:* 81% (excluding resources awarded to replace EFC). *Average financial aid package:* $22,477 (excluding resources awarded to replace EFC). 15% of all full-time undergraduates had no need and received non-need-based gift aid.

GIFT AID (NEED-BASED) *Total amount:* $22,226,342 (13% federal, 12% state, 73% institutional, 2% external sources). *Receiving aid:* Freshmen: 82% (328); all full-time undergraduates: 78% (1,374). *Average award:* Freshmen: $19,225; Undergraduates: $16,092. *Scholarships, grants, and awards:* Federal Pell, FSEOG, state, private, college/university gift aid from institutional funds, Academic Competitiveness Grants, National SMART Grants, United Methodist scholarships.

GIFT AID (NON-NEED-BASED) *Total amount:* $3,780,856 (1% federal, 1% state, 92% institutional, 6% external sources). *Receiving aid:* Freshmen: 12% (48). Undergraduates: 8% (142). *Average award:* Freshmen: $11,474. Undergraduates: $10,309. *Scholarships, grants, and awards by category:* *Academic interests/achievement:* 1,366 awards ($9,326,993 total): biological sciences, communication, English, foreign languages, general academic interests/achievements, physical sciences, premedicine. *Creative arts/performance:* 36 awards ($107,622 total): art/fine arts, creative writing, general creative arts/performance, music, theater/drama. *Special achievements/activities:* 54 awards ($120,079 total): leadership, memberships. *Special characteristics:* 215 awards ($1,081,648 total): ethnic background, general special characteristics, international students, local/state students, members of minority groups, relatives of clergy, veterans. *Tuition waivers:* Full or partial for employees or children of employees.

LOANS *Student loans:* $13,920,225 (38% need-based, 62% non-need-based). 79% of past graduating class borrowed through all loan programs. *Average indebtedness per student:* $34,598. *Average need-based loan:* Freshmen: $4044. Undergraduates: $4736. *Parent loans:* $2,869,715 (100% non-need-based). *Programs:* Federal Direct (Subsidized and Unsubsidized Stafford, PLUS), Perkins, state, non-federal alternative loans, United Methodist Student Loans.

WORK-STUDY *Federal work-study:* Total amount: $969,549; 407 jobs averaging $2382. *State or other work-study/employment:* Total amount: $2,604,747 (66% need-based, 34% non-need-based). 1,117 part-time jobs averaging $2332.

APPLYING FOR FINANCIAL AID *Required financial aid form:* FAFSA. *Financial aid deadline (priority):* 3/15. *Notification date:* Continuous beginning 3/15. Students must reply by 5/1 or within 2 weeks of notification.

CONTACT Ms. Lynette Wahl, Office of Financial Aid, Hamline University, 1536 Hewitt Avenue, MS C1915, St. Paul, MN 55104, 651-523-3000 or toll-free 800-753-9753. *Fax:* 651-523-2585. *E-mail:* sasmail@hamline.edu.

HAMPDEN-SYDNEY COLLEGE
Hampden-Sydney, VA

Tuition & fees: $32,364	Average undergraduate aid package: $23,772

ABOUT THE INSTITUTION Independent religious, men only. 28 undergraduate majors. Both federal and institutional methodology are used as a basis for awarding need-based institutional aid.

UNDERGRADUATE EXPENSES for 2010–11 *Comprehensive fee:* $42,490 includes full-time tuition ($30,994), mandatory fees ($1370), and room and board ($10,126). Room and board charges vary according to board plan and housing facility. *Payment plan:* Installment.

FRESHMAN FINANCIAL AID (Fall 2009, est.) 232 applied for aid; of those 74% were deemed to have need. 100% of freshmen with need received aid; of those 26% had need fully met. *Average percent of need met:* 81% (excluding resources awarded to replace EFC). *Average financial aid package:* $23,957 (excluding resources awarded to replace EFC). 41% of all full-time freshmen had no need and received non-need-based gift aid.

UNDERGRADUATE FINANCIAL AID (Fall 2009, est.) 680 applied for aid; of those 81% were deemed to have need. 100% of undergraduates with need received aid; of those 26% had need fully met. *Average percent of need met:* 80% (excluding resources awarded to replace EFC). *Average financial aid package:* $23,772 (excluding resources awarded to replace EFC). 44% of all full-time undergraduates had no need and received non-need-based gift aid.

GIFT AID (NEED-BASED) *Total amount:* $10,457,994 (9% federal, 11% state, 77% institutional, 3% external sources). *Receiving aid:* Freshmen: 58% (171); all full-time undergraduates: 52% (552). *Average award:* Freshmen: $19,751; Undergraduates: $18,945. *Scholarships, grants, and awards:* Federal Pell, FSEOG, state, private, college/university gift aid from institutional funds.

GIFT AID (NON-NEED-BASED) *Total amount:* $6,614,153 (16% state, 73% institutional, 11% external sources). *Receiving aid:* Freshmen: 13% (37). Undergraduates: 9% (100). *Average award:* Freshmen: $9033. Undergraduates: $9413. *Scholarships, grants, and awards by category:* *Academic interests/achievement:* 432 awards ($4,769,295 total): biological sciences, education, general academic interests/achievements, health fields, international studies, premedicine, religion/biblical studies. *Creative arts/performance:* music. *Special achievements/activities:* general special achievements/activities, leadership. *Special characteristics:* 93 awards ($1,555,125 total): children of educators, children of faculty/staff, ethnic background, international students, members of minority groups, out-of-state students, religious affiliation. *Tuition waivers:* Full or partial for employees or children of employees.

LOANS *Student loans:* $5,420,936 (58% need-based, 42% non-need-based). 54% of past graduating class borrowed through all loan programs. *Average indebtedness per student:* $23,822. *Average need-based loan:* Freshmen: $3876. Undergraduates: $4725. *Parent loans:* $8,974,151 (19% need-based, 81% non-need-based). *Programs:* FFEL (Subsidized and Unsubsidized Stafford, PLUS), Perkins, college/university.

WORK-STUDY *Federal work-study:* Total amount: $571,282; 264 jobs averaging $1674.

APPLYING FOR FINANCIAL AID *Required financial aid forms:* FAFSA, CSS Financial Aid PROFILE, state aid form. *Financial aid deadline (priority):* 3/1. *Notification date:* Continuous. Students must reply by 5/1 or within 2 weeks of notification.

CONTACT Mrs. Zita Marie Barree, Director of Financial Aid, Hampden-Sydney College, PO Box 726, Hampden-Sydney, VA 23943-0726, 434-223-6119 or toll-free 800-755-0733. *Fax:* 434-223-6075. *E-mail:* hsfinaid@hsc.edu.

HAMPSHIRE COLLEGE
Amherst, MA

Tuition & fees: $39,912	Average undergraduate aid package: $35,310

ABOUT THE INSTITUTION Independent, coed. 55 undergraduate majors. Institutional methodology is used as a basis for awarding need-based institutional aid.

UNDERGRADUATE EXPENSES for 2009–10 *Comprehensive fee:* $50,345 includes full-time tuition ($39,112), mandatory fees ($800), and room and board ($10,433). *College room only:* $6653. Room and board charges vary according to board plan. *Payment plan:* Installment.

FRESHMAN FINANCIAL AID (Fall 2009, est.) 295 applied for aid; of those 89% were deemed to have need. 100% of freshmen with need received aid; of those 76% had need fully met. *Average percent of need met:* 98% (excluding resources awarded to replace EFC). *Average financial aid package:* $35,840 (excluding resources awarded to replace EFC). 17% of all full-time freshmen had no need and received non-need-based gift aid.

UNDERGRADUATE FINANCIAL AID (Fall 2009, est.) 951 applied for aid; of those 91% were deemed to have need. 100% of undergraduates with need received aid; of those 81% had need fully met. *Average percent of need met:* 98% (excluding resources awarded to replace EFC). *Average financial aid package:* $35,310 (excluding resources awarded to replace EFC). 17% of all full-time undergraduates had no need and received non-need-based gift aid.

GIFT AID (NEED-BASED) *Total amount:* $24,331,575 (7% federal, 92% institutional, 1% external sources). *Receiving aid:* Freshmen: 69% (264); all full-time undergraduates: 61% (870). *Average award:* Freshmen: $30,240; Undergraduates: $28,085. *Scholarships, grants, and awards:* Federal Pell, FSEOG, state, private, college/university gift aid from institutional funds.

GIFT AID (NON-NEED-BASED) *Total amount:* $1,545,330 (2% federal, 1% state, 96% institutional, 1% external sources). *Receiving aid:* Freshmen: 63% (243). Undergraduates: 53% (759). *Average award:* Freshmen: $7280. Undergraduates: $6220. *Scholarships, grants, and awards by category:* Academic interests/achievement: 241 awards ($1,437,500 total): general academic interests/achievements, international studies, physical sciences, social sciences. *Creative arts/performance:* creative writing. *Special achievements/activities:* 4 awards ($30,000 total): community service, leadership. *Special characteristics:* 14 awards ($483,627 total): children of faculty/staff. *Tuition waivers:* Full or partial for employees or children of employees.

LOANS *Student loans:* $4,011,280 (91% need-based, 9% non-need-based). 51% of past graduating class borrowed through all loan programs. *Average indebtedness per student:* $20,669. *Average need-based loan:* Freshmen: $3500. Undergraduates: $4750. *Parent loans:* $3,078,955 (69% need-based, 31% non-need-based). *Programs:* Federal Direct (Subsidized and Unsubsidized Stafford, PLUS), FFEL (PLUS), Perkins.

WORK-STUDY *Federal work-study:* Total amount: $1,320,130; 595 jobs averaging $2200. *State or other work-study/employment:* Total amount: $600,890 (80% need-based, 20% non-need-based). 270 part-time jobs averaging $2245.

APPLYING FOR FINANCIAL AID *Required financial aid forms:* FAFSA, CSS Financial Aid PROFILE, noncustodial (divorced/separated) parent's statement. *Financial aid deadline (priority):* 2/1. *Notification date:* 4/1. Students must reply by 5/1 or within 2 weeks of notification.

CONTACT Ms. Kathleen Methot, Director of Financial Aid, Hampshire College, 893 West Street, Amherst, MA 01002, 413-559-5484 or toll-free 877-937-4267 (out-of-state). *Fax:* 413-559-5585. *E-mail:* financialaid@hampshire.edu.

HAMPTON UNIVERSITY
Hampton, VA

Tuition & fees: $17,212	Average undergraduate aid package: $4545

ABOUT THE INSTITUTION Independent, coed. 82 undergraduate majors. Federal methodology is used as a basis for awarding need-based institutional aid.

UNDERGRADUATE EXPENSES for 2009–10 *Comprehensive fee:* $24,876 includes full-time tuition ($15,464), mandatory fees ($1748), and room and board ($7664). *College room only:* $3986. Full-time tuition and fees vary according to course load, degree level, and program. Room and board charges vary according to board plan and housing facility. *Part-time tuition:* $390 per credit hour. *Part-time fees:* $1748 per year. *Payment plan:* Deferred payment.

FRESHMAN FINANCIAL AID (Fall 2009, est.) 687 applied for aid; of those 76% were deemed to have need. 94% of freshmen with need received aid; of those 38% had need fully met. *Average percent of need met:* 40% (excluding resources awarded to replace EFC). *Average financial aid package:* $3725 (excluding resources awarded to replace EFC). 7% of all full-time freshmen had no need and received non-need-based gift aid.

UNDERGRADUATE FINANCIAL AID (Fall 2009, est.) 2,015 applied for aid; of those 83% were deemed to have need. 92% of undergraduates with need received aid; of those 39% had need fully met. *Average percent of need met:* 41% (excluding resources awarded to replace EFC). *Average financial aid package:* $4545 (excluding resources awarded to replace EFC). 3% of all full-time undergraduates had no need and received non-need-based gift aid.

GIFT AID (NEED-BASED) *Total amount:* $12,431,241 (59% federal, 16% state, 1% institutional, 24% external sources). *Receiving aid:* Freshmen: 39% (476); all full-time undergraduates: 38% (1,418). *Average award:* Freshmen: $3136; Undergraduates: $3349. *Scholarships, grants, and awards:* Federal Pell, FSEOG, state, private, college/university gift aid from institutional funds, Federal Nursing.

GIFT AID (NON-NEED-BASED) *Total amount:* $7,088,434 (10% state, 39% institutional, 51% external sources). *Receiving aid:* Freshmen: 9% (112). Undergraduates: 10% (374). *Average award:* Freshmen: $6708. Undergraduates: $8442. *Scholarships, grants, and awards by category:* Academic interests/achievement: 351 awards ($7,998,893 total): architecture, biological sciences, business, communication, computer science, education, engineering/technologies, general academic interests/achievements, health fields, physical sciences. *Creative arts/performance:* 23 awards ($38,800 total): music. *Special achievements/activities:* 97 awards ($237,998 total): leadership. *Special characteristics:* 378 awards ($1,160,602 total): adult students, children of faculty/staff, international students, members of minority groups, veterans, veterans' children. *Tuition waivers:* Full or partial for employees or children of employees.

LOANS *Student loans:* $35,253,625 (67% need-based, 33% non-need-based). 85% of past graduating class borrowed through all loan programs. *Average indebtedness per student:* $4783. *Average need-based loan:* Freshmen: $3728. Undergraduates: $3214. *Parent loans:* $29,378,489 (49% need-based, 51% non-need-based). *Programs:* FFEL (Subsidized and Unsubsidized Stafford, PLUS), Perkins, Federal Nursing, college/university, private loans.

WORK-STUDY *Federal work-study:* Total amount: $490,170; 376 jobs averaging $2150. *State or other work-study/employment:* 78 part-time jobs averaging $2924.

ATHLETIC AWARDS Total amount: $4,055,587 (100% non-need-based).

APPLYING FOR FINANCIAL AID *Required financial aid forms:* FAFSA, Virginia Tuition Assistance Grant forms (VA residents only). *Financial aid deadline:* 4/15 (priority: 3/1). *Notification date:* Continuous beginning 4/15. Students must reply within 2 weeks of notification.

CONTACT Martin Miles, Director, Financial Aid, Hampton University, Hampton, VA 23668, 757-727-5332 or toll-free 800-624-3328. *Fax:* 757-728-6567. *E-mail:* martin.miles@hamptonu.edu.

HANNIBAL-LaGRANGE COLLEGE
Hannibal, MO

Tuition & fees: $15,380 | **Average undergraduate aid package: $9792**

ABOUT THE INSTITUTION Independent Southern Baptist, coed. 42 undergraduate majors. Federal methodology is used as a basis for awarding need-based institutional aid.

UNDERGRADUATE EXPENSES for 2009–10 *One-time required fee:* $100. *Comprehensive fee:* $21,380 includes full-time tuition ($14,820), mandatory fees ($560), and room and board ($6000). Full-time tuition and fees vary according to class time, course load, degree level, program, and reciprocity agreements. Room and board charges vary according to housing facility. *Part-time tuition:* $494 per credit hour. *Part-time fees:* $560 per year; $100 per year. Part-time tuition and fees vary according to class time, course load, degree level, program, and reciprocity agreements. *Payment plan:* Installment.

FRESHMAN FINANCIAL AID (Fall 2008) 429 applied for aid; of those 72% were deemed to have need. 100% of freshmen with need received aid; of those 16% had need fully met. *Average percent of need met:* 59% (excluding resources awarded to replace EFC). *Average financial aid package:* $9285 (excluding resources awarded to replace EFC). 24% of all full-time freshmen had no need and received non-need-based gift aid.

UNDERGRADUATE FINANCIAL AID (Fall 2008) 1,418 applied for aid; of those 87% were deemed to have need. 88% of undergraduates with need received aid; of those 15% had need fully met. *Average percent of need met:* 59% (excluding resources awarded to replace EFC). *Average financial aid package:* $9792 (excluding resources awarded to replace EFC). 13% of all full-time undergraduates had no need and received non-need-based gift aid.

GIFT AID (NEED-BASED) *Total amount:* $6,751,421 (43% federal, 13% state, 40% institutional, 4% external sources). *Receiving aid:* Freshmen: 54% (308); all full-time undergraduates: 63% (1,022). *Average award:* Freshmen: $7694; Undergraduates: $7356. *Scholarships, grants, and awards:* Federal Pell, FSEOG, state, private, college/university gift aid from institutional funds.

GIFT AID (NON-NEED-BASED) *Total amount:* $1,525,904 (1% federal, 2% state, 92% institutional, 5% external sources). *Receiving aid:* Freshmen: 5% (29). Undergraduates: 5% (74). *Average award:* Freshmen: $6337. Undergraduates: $6180. *Scholarships, grants, and awards by category:* Academic interests/achievement: general academic interests/achievements, religion/biblical studies. Creative arts/performance: art/fine arts, journalism/publications, music, performing arts, theater/drama. Special characteristics: children of faculty/staff, public servants, relatives of clergy, religious affiliation. *Tuition waivers:* Full or partial for employees or children of employees.

LOANS *Student loans:* $6,599,868 (77% need-based, 23% non-need-based). *Average need-based loan:* Freshmen: $3059. Undergraduates: $3889. *Parent loans:* $2,643,367 (20% need-based, 80% non-need-based). *Programs:* Federal Direct (Subsidized and Unsubsidized Stafford, PLUS), Perkins.

WORK-STUDY *Federal work-study:* Total amount: $182,739; 80 jobs averaging $575.

ATHLETIC AWARDS Total amount: $1,287,298 (57% need-based, 43% non-need-based).

APPLYING FOR FINANCIAL AID *Required financial aid forms:* FAFSA, institution's own form. *Financial aid deadline:* Continuous.

CONTACT Brice Baumgardner, Director of Financial Aid, Hannibal-LaGrange College, 2800 Palmyra Road, Hannibal, MO 63401-1940, 573-629-3279 Ext. 3279 or toll-free 800-HLG-1119. *Fax:* 573-248-0954. *E-mail:* bbaumgardner@hlg.edu.

HANOVER COLLEGE
Hanover, IN

Tuition & fees: $26,350 | **Average undergraduate aid package: $23,495**

ABOUT THE INSTITUTION Independent Presbyterian, coed. 29 undergraduate majors. Federal methodology is used as a basis for awarding need-based institutional aid.

UNDERGRADUATE EXPENSES for 2009–10 *One-time required fee:* $250. *Comprehensive fee:* $34,250 includes full-time tuition ($25,800), mandatory fees ($550), and room and board ($7900). *College room only:* $3850. Full-time tuition and fees vary according to reciprocity agreements. Room and board charges vary according to housing facility and location. *Part-time tuition:* $2860 per unit. Part-time tuition and fees vary according to course load and reciprocity agreements. *Payment plan:* Installment.

FRESHMAN FINANCIAL AID (Fall 2009, est.) 274 applied for aid; of those 93% were deemed to have need. 100% of freshmen with need received aid; of those 33% had need fully met. *Average percent of need met:* 89% (excluding resources awarded to replace EFC). *Average financial aid package:* $23,593 (excluding resources awarded to replace EFC). 12% of all full-time freshmen had no need and received non-need-based gift aid.

UNDERGRADUATE FINANCIAL AID (Fall 2009, est.) 803 applied for aid; of those 91% were deemed to have need. 100% of undergraduates with need received aid; of those 31% had need fully met. *Average percent of need met:* 88% (excluding resources awarded to replace EFC). *Average financial aid package:* $23,495 (excluding resources awarded to replace EFC). 22% of all full-time undergraduates had no need and received non-need-based gift aid.

GIFT AID (NEED-BASED) *Total amount:* $14,270,762 (8% federal, 8% state, 75% institutional, 9% external sources). *Receiving aid:* Freshmen: 87% (254); all full-time undergraduates: 76% (734). *Average award:* Freshmen: $20,616; Undergraduates: $19,414. *Scholarships, grants, and awards:* Federal Pell, FSEOG, state, private, college/university gift aid from institutional funds.

GIFT AID (NON-NEED-BASED) *Total amount:* $3,786,001 (79% institutional, 21% external sources). *Receiving aid:* Freshmen: 14% (42). Undergraduates: 11% (108). *Average award:* Freshmen: $13,572. Undergraduates: $12,193. *Scholarships, grants, and awards by category:* Academic interests/achievement: general academic interests/achievements. Creative arts/performance: art/fine arts, music, theater/drama. Special characteristics: children and siblings of alumni, children of faculty/staff, international students, members of minority groups, out-of-state students, religious affiliation, siblings of current students. *Tuition waivers:* Full or partial for employees or children of employees, senior citizens.

LOANS *Student loans:* $4,785,383 (64% need-based, 36% non-need-based). 67% of past graduating class borrowed through all loan programs. *Average indebtedness per student:* $27,807. *Average need-based loan:* Freshmen: $2720. Undergraduates: $3530. *Parent loans:* $1,370,211 (23% need-based, 77% non-need-based). *Programs:* FFEL (Subsidized and Unsubsidized Stafford, PLUS), college/university.

WORK-STUDY *Federal work-study:* Total amount: $57,100; 66 jobs averaging $865. *State or other work-study/employment:* Total amount: $1,360,098 (54% need-based, 46% non-need-based). Part-time jobs available.

APPLYING FOR FINANCIAL AID *Required financial aid form:* FAFSA. *Financial aid deadline (priority):* 3/1. *Notification date:* Continuous beginning 3/1. Students must reply by 5/1.

CONTACT Richard A. Nash, Director of Financial Assistance, Hanover College, PO Box 108, Hanover, IN 47243-0108, 800-213-2178 Ext. 7029 or toll-free 800-213-2178. *Fax:* 812-866-7284. *E-mail:* finaid@hanover.edu.

HARDING UNIVERSITY
Searcy, AR

Tuition & fees: $13,580 | **Average undergraduate aid package: $11,146**

ABOUT THE INSTITUTION Independent religious, coed. 91 undergraduate majors. Federal methodology is used as a basis for awarding need-based institutional aid.

UNDERGRADUATE EXPENSES for 2009–10 *Comprehensive fee:* $19,394 includes full-time tuition ($13,140), mandatory fees ($440), and room and board ($5814). *College room only:* $2880. Full-time tuition and fees vary according to course load. Room and board charges vary according to board plan and housing facility. *Part-time tuition:* $438 per credit hour. *Part-time fees:* $22 per credit hour. Part-time tuition and fees vary according to course load. *Payment plans:* Tuition prepayment, installment.

FRESHMAN FINANCIAL AID (Fall 2009, est.) 772 applied for aid; of those 74% were deemed to have need. 99% of freshmen with need received aid; of those 28% had need fully met. *Average percent of need met:* 76% (excluding resources awarded to replace EFC). *Average financial aid package:* $11,543 (excluding resources awarded to replace EFC). 19% of all full-time freshmen had no need and received non-need-based gift aid.

UNDERGRADUATE FINANCIAL AID (Fall 2009, est.) 2,789 applied for aid; of those 79% were deemed to have need. 99% of undergraduates with need received aid; of those 23% had need fully met. *Average percent of need met:* 68% (excluding resources awarded to replace EFC). *Average financial aid*

package: $11,146 (excluding resources awarded to replace EFC). 11% of all full-time undergraduates had no need and received non-need-based gift aid.

GIFT AID (NEED-BASED) *Total amount:* $13,566,052 (36% federal, 5% state, 56% institutional, 3% external sources). *Receiving aid:* Freshmen: 58% (551); all full-time undergraduates: 52% (1,978). *Average award:* Freshmen: $7886; Undergraduates: $7199. *Scholarships, grants, and awards:* Federal Pell, FSEOG, state, private, college/university gift aid from institutional funds.

GIFT AID (NON-NEED-BASED) *Total amount:* $10,311,169 (7% state, 88% institutional, 5% external sources). *Receiving aid:* Freshmen: 13% (125). Undergraduates: 9% (337). *Average award:* Freshmen: $6012. Undergraduates: $5370. *Scholarships, grants, and awards by category: Academic interests/achievement:* 3,323 awards ($1,260,238 total): communication, computer science, engineering/technologies, English, general academic interests/achievements, health fields, religion/biblical studies. *Creative arts/performance:* 167 awards ($174,354 total): art/fine arts, cinema/film/broadcasting, debating, journalism/publications, music. *Special achievements/activities:* 105 awards ($82,732 total): cheerleading/drum major, leadership, religious involvement. *Special characteristics:* 523 awards ($2,509,447 total): children of faculty/staff, children with a deceased or disabled parent, international students, relatives of clergy, siblings of current students. *Tuition waivers:* Full or partial for employees or children of employees, senior citizens.

LOANS *Student loans:* $20,254,674 (64% need-based, 36% non-need-based). 70% of past graduating class borrowed through all loan programs. *Average indebtedness per student:* $31,043. *Average need-based loan:* Freshmen: $3947. Undergraduates: $4520. *Parent loans:* $4,010,444 (27% need-based, 73% non-need-based). *Programs:* FFEL (Subsidized and Unsubsidized Stafford, PLUS), Perkins, Federal Nursing, state, college/university.

WORK-STUDY *Federal work-study:* Total amount: $395,205; 422 jobs averaging $909. *State or other work-study/employment:* Total amount: $1,332,990 (23% need-based, 77% non-need-based). 1,056 part-time jobs averaging $1253.

ATHLETIC AWARDS Total amount: $1,821,684 (28% need-based, 72% non-need-based).

APPLYING FOR FINANCIAL AID *Required financial aid form:* FAFSA. *Financial aid deadline (priority):* 4/15. *Notification date:* Continuous. Students must reply within 2 weeks of notification.

CONTACT Dr. Jonathan C. Roberts, Director of Student Financial Services, Harding University, Box 12282, Searcy, AR 72149-2282, 501-279-4257 or toll-free 800-477-4407. *Fax:* 501-279-4129. *E-mail:* jroberts@harding.edu.

HARDIN-SIMMONS UNIVERSITY
Abilene, TX

Tuition & fees: $20,990	Average undergraduate aid package: $16,930

ABOUT THE INSTITUTION Independent Baptist, coed. 71 undergraduate majors. Federal methodology is used as a basis for awarding need-based institutional aid.

UNDERGRADUATE EXPENSES for 2010–11 *Comprehensive fee:* $27,272 includes full-time tuition ($19,950), mandatory fees ($1040), and room and board ($6282). *College room only:* $3123. Full-time tuition and fees vary according to program. Room and board charges vary according to board plan and housing facility. *Part-time tuition:* $665 per credit hour. *Part-time fees:* $150 per term. Part-time tuition and fees vary according to course load and program. *Payment plans:* Guaranteed tuition, installment.

FRESHMAN FINANCIAL AID (Fall 2009, est.) 401 applied for aid; of those 76% were deemed to have need. 100% of freshmen with need received aid; of those 32% had need fully met. *Average percent of need met:* 81% (excluding resources awarded to replace EFC). *Average financial aid package:* $24,841 (excluding resources awarded to replace EFC). 24% of all full-time freshmen had no need and received non-need-based gift aid.

UNDERGRADUATE FINANCIAL AID (Fall 2009, est.) 1,691 applied for aid; of those 72% were deemed to have need. 100% of undergraduates with need received aid; of those 22% had need fully met. *Average percent of need met:* 69% (excluding resources awarded to replace EFC). *Average financial aid package:* $16,930 (excluding resources awarded to replace EFC). 28% of all full-time undergraduates had no need and received non-need-based gift aid.

GIFT AID (NEED-BASED) *Total amount:* $5,577,152 (47% federal, 53% state). *Receiving aid:* Freshmen: 55% (225); all full-time undergraduates: 51% (879). *Average award:* Freshmen: $7301; Undergraduates: $6349. *Scholarships, grants, and awards:* Federal Pell, FSEOG, state, private, college/university gift aid from institutional funds, Academic Competitiveness Grants, National SMART Grants.

GIFT AID (NON-NEED-BASED) *Total amount:* $11,890,079 (93% institutional, 7% external sources). *Receiving aid:* Freshmen: 66% (271). Undergraduates: 60% (1,035). *Average award:* Freshmen: $9970. Undergraduates: $6983. *Scholarships, grants, and awards by category: Academic interests/achievement:* 1,579 awards ($7,889,949 total): biological sciences, business, communication, computer science, education, English, foreign languages, general academic interests/achievements, health fields, humanities, mathematics, physical sciences, premedicine, religion/biblical studies, social sciences. *Creative arts/performance:* 156 awards ($318,138 total): applied art and design, art/fine arts, creative writing, journalism/publications, music, performing arts, theater/drama. *Special achievements/activities:* 151 awards ($184,640 total): general special achievements/activities, junior miss, leadership. *Special characteristics:* 401 awards ($1,208,780 total): children of educators, children of faculty/staff, ethnic background, general special characteristics, handicapped students, local/state students, members of minority groups, out-of-state students, public servants, relatives of clergy, religious affiliation, siblings of current students. *Tuition waivers:* Full or partial for employees or children of employees.

LOANS *Student loans:* $20,348,275 (33% need-based, 67% non-need-based). 73% of past graduating class borrowed through all loan programs. *Average indebtedness per student:* $35,429. *Average need-based loan:* Freshmen: $2889. Undergraduates: $4113. *Parent loans:* $557,476 (100% non-need-based). *Programs:* FFEL (Subsidized and Unsubsidized Stafford, PLUS), Perkins, state, college/university.

WORK-STUDY *Federal work-study:* Total amount: $152,214; 113 jobs averaging $1700. *State or other work-study/employment:* Total amount: $319,193 (8% need-based, 92% non-need-based). 344 part-time jobs averaging $1700.

APPLYING FOR FINANCIAL AID *Required financial aid form:* FAFSA. *Financial aid deadline (priority):* 3/15. *Notification date:* Continuous beginning 2/1.

CONTACT Jim Jones, Director of Financial Aid, Hardin-Simmons University, PO Box 16050, Abilene, TX 79698-6050, 325-670-5891 or toll-free 877-464-7889. *Fax:* 325-670-5822. *E-mail:* jjones@hsutx.edu.

HARRINGTON COLLEGE OF DESIGN
Chicago, IL

CONTACT Ms. Renee Darosky, Director of Financial Aid, Harrington College of Design, 410 South Michigan Avenue, Chicago, IL 60605-1496, 312-939-4975 or toll-free 877-939-4975. *Fax:* 312-697-8058. *E-mail:* financialaid@interiordesign.edu.

HARRISBURG UNIVERSITY OF SCIENCE AND TECHNOLOGY
Harrisburg, PA

Tuition & fees: $19,500	Average undergraduate aid package: $13,708

ABOUT THE INSTITUTION Independent, coed. 5 undergraduate majors. Federal methodology is used as a basis for awarding need-based institutional aid.

UNDERGRADUATE EXPENSES for 2010–11 *Tuition:* full-time $19,500; part-time $800 per semester hour. Part-time tuition and fees vary according to course load. *Payment plans:* Installment, deferred payment.

UNDERGRADUATE FINANCIAL AID (Fall 2009, est.) *Average percent of need met:* 49% (excluding resources awarded to replace EFC). *Average financial aid package:* $13,708 (excluding resources awarded to replace EFC).

GIFT AID (NEED-BASED) *Total amount:* $1,186,913 (35% federal, 20% state, 45% institutional). *Average award:* Undergraduates: $9894. *Scholarships, grants, and awards:* Federal Pell, FSEOG, state, private, college/university gift aid from institutional funds.

GIFT AID (NON-NEED-BASED) *Total amount:* $6000 (100% external sources). *Average award:* Undergraduates: $2812. *Scholarships, grants, and awards by category: Academic interests/achievement:* biological sciences, business, computer science, physical sciences.

LOANS *Student loans:* $1,184,066 (93% need-based, 7% non-need-based). 100% of past graduating class borrowed through all loan programs. *Average indebtedness per student:* $21,500. *Parent loans:* $70,850 (100% need-based). *Programs:* Federal Direct (Subsidized and Unsubsidized Stafford, PLUS).

WORK-STUDY *Federal work-study:* Total amount: $9636; 10 jobs averaging $1000.

APPLYING FOR FINANCIAL AID *Required financial aid form:* FAFSA. *Financial aid deadline:* Continuous. *Notification date:* Continuous. Students must reply within 2 weeks of notification.

CONTACT Mr. Vince P. Frank, Director of Financial Aid Services, Harrisburg University of Science and Technology, 326 Market Street, Harrisburg, PA 17101, 717-901-5115 or toll-free 866-HBG-UNIV. *Fax:* 717-901-3115. *E-mail:* vfrank@ harrisburgu.edu.

HARRIS-STOWE STATE UNIVERSITY
St. Louis, MO

ABOUT THE INSTITUTION State-supported, coed. 17 undergraduate majors.

GIFT AID (NEED-BASED) *Scholarships, grants, and awards:* Federal Pell, FSEOG, state, private, college/university gift aid from institutional funds.

GIFT AID (NON-NEED-BASED) *Scholarships, grants, and awards by category: Academic interests/achievement:* general academic interests/achievements. *Creative arts/performance:* music, theater/drama.

LOANS *Programs:* FFEL (Subsidized and Unsubsidized Stafford, PLUS), college/ university.

WORK-STUDY *Federal work-study:* Total amount: $123,973; 86 jobs averaging $2000. *State or other work-study/employment:* Total amount: $75,000 (100% non-need-based). 80 part-time jobs averaging $2000.

APPLYING FOR FINANCIAL AID *Required financial aid forms:* FAFSA, institution's own form.

CONTACT Regina Blackshear, Director of Financial Aid, Harris-Stowe State University, 3026 Laclede Avenue, St. Louis, MO 63103-2136, 314-340-3502. *Fax:* 314-340-3503.

HARTWICK COLLEGE
Oneonta, NY

Tuition & fees: $33,330	Average undergraduate aid package: $24,206

ABOUT THE INSTITUTION Independent, coed. 33 undergraduate majors. Federal methodology is used as a basis for awarding need-based institutional aid.

UNDERGRADUATE EXPENSES for 2009–10 *One-time required fee:* $300. *Comprehensive fee:* $42,405 includes full-time tuition ($32,550), mandatory fees ($780), and room and board ($9075). *College room only:* $4700. Full-time tuition and fees vary according to student level. Room and board charges vary according to board plan and housing facility. *Part-time tuition:* $1030 per credit hour. *Payment plan:* Installment.

FRESHMAN FINANCIAL AID (Fall 2009, est.) 342 applied for aid; of those 90% were deemed to have need. 100% of freshmen with need received aid; of those 12% had need fully met. *Average percent of need met:* 81% (excluding resources awarded to replace EFC). *Average financial aid package:* $25,720 (excluding resources awarded to replace EFC). 22% of all full-time freshmen had no need and received non-need-based gift aid.

UNDERGRADUATE FINANCIAL AID (Fall 2009, est.) 1,159 applied for aid; of those 91% were deemed to have need. 100% of undergraduates with need received aid; of those 11% had need fully met. *Average percent of need met:* 78% (excluding resources awarded to replace EFC). *Average financial aid package:* $24,206 (excluding resources awarded to replace EFC). 23% of all full-time undergraduates had no need and received non-need-based gift aid.

GIFT AID (NEED-BASED) *Total amount:* $19,842,283 (10% federal, 7% state, 79% institutional, 4% external sources). *Receiving aid:* Freshmen: 76% (308); all full-time undergraduates: 74% (1,057). *Average award:* Freshmen: $21,721; Undergraduates: $19,972. *Scholarships, grants, and awards:* Federal Pell, FSEOG, state, private, college/university gift aid from institutional funds.

GIFT AID (NON-NEED-BASED) *Total amount:* $4,003,120 (1% state, 94% institutional, 5% external sources). *Receiving aid:* Freshmen: 6% (25). Undergraduates: 5% (72). *Average award:* Freshmen: $10,081. Undergraduates: $10,267. *Scholarships, grants, and awards by category: Special characteristics:* 131 awards ($1,479,651 total): children and siblings of alumni, children of faculty/staff, international students, siblings of current students. *Tuition waivers:* Full or partial for employees or children of employees.

LOANS *Student loans:* $11,448,834 (90% need-based, 10% non-need-based). 74% of past graduating class borrowed through all loan programs. *Average indebtedness per student:* $32,800. *Average need-based loan:* Freshmen: $4414. Undergraduates: $4681. *Parent loans:* $14,096,505 (29% need-based, 71%

non-need-based). *Programs:* FFEL (Subsidized and Unsubsidized Stafford, PLUS), Perkins, Federal Nursing, college/university, alternative loans.

WORK-STUDY *Federal work-study:* Total amount: $1,110,444; 700 jobs averaging $1500.

ATHLETIC AWARDS Total amount: $710,878 (21% need-based, 79% non-need-based).

APPLYING FOR FINANCIAL AID *Required financial aid form:* FAFSA. *Financial aid deadline:* Continuous. *Notification date:* Continuous beginning 10/15. Students must reply by 5/1 or within 2 weeks of notification.

CONTACT Melissa Allen, Director, Financial Aid, Hartwick College, One Hartwick Drive, Oneonta, NY 13820, 607-431-4130 or toll-free 888-HARTWICK (out-of-state). *Fax:* 607-431-4006. *E-mail:* allenm@hartwick.edu.

HARVARD UNIVERSITY
Cambridge, MA

Tuition & fees: $36,828	Average undergraduate aid package: $40,234

ABOUT THE INSTITUTION Independent, coed. 45 undergraduate majors. Institutional methodology is used as a basis for awarding need-based institutional aid.

UNDERGRADUATE EXPENSES for 2010–11 *Comprehensive fee:* $48,684 includes full-time tuition ($33,696), mandatory fees ($3132), and room and board ($11,856). *Payment plans:* Tuition prepayment, installment.

FRESHMAN FINANCIAL AID (Fall 2009, est.) 1,210 applied for aid; of those 89% were deemed to have need. 100% of freshmen with need received aid; of those 100% had need fully met. *Average percent of need met:* 100% (excluding resources awarded to replace EFC). *Average financial aid package:* $41,157 (excluding resources awarded to replace EFC).

UNDERGRADUATE FINANCIAL AID (Fall 2009, est.) 4,399 applied for aid; of those 92% were deemed to have need. 100% of undergraduates with need received aid; of those 100% had need fully met. *Average percent of need met:* 100% (excluding resources awarded to replace EFC). *Average financial aid package:* $40,234 (excluding resources awarded to replace EFC).

GIFT AID (NEED-BASED) *Total amount:* $152,665,039 (6% federal, 90% institutional, 4% external sources). *Receiving aid:* Freshmen: 65% (1,076); all full-time undergraduates: 60% (4,058). *Average award:* Freshmen: $39,536; Undergraduates: $37,620. *Scholarships, grants, and awards:* Federal Pell, FSEOG, state, private, college/university gift aid from institutional funds.

GIFT AID (NON-NEED-BASED) *Total amount:* $5,096,878 (15% federal, 3% institutional, 82% external sources).

LOANS *Student loans:* $4,715,754 (82% need-based, 18% non-need-based). 38% of past graduating class borrowed through all loan programs. *Average indebtedness per student:* $10,871. *Average need-based loan:* Freshmen: $3846. Undergraduates: $4461. *Parent loans:* $9,148,414 (100% non-need-based). *Programs:* Federal Direct (Subsidized and Unsubsidized Stafford, PLUS), Perkins, state, college/university.

WORK-STUDY *Federal work-study:* Total amount: $2,352,329; 984 jobs averaging $2546. *State or other work-study/employment:* Total amount: $5,700,264 (84% need-based, 16% non-need-based). 2,119 part-time jobs averaging $2617.

APPLYING FOR FINANCIAL AID *Required financial aid forms:* FAFSA, CSS Financial Aid PROFILE, noncustodial (divorced/separated) parent's statement, business/farm supplement, income tax form(s). *Financial aid deadline (priority):* 2/1. *Notification date:* 4/1. Students must reply by 5/1 or within 2 weeks of notification.

CONTACT Financial Aid Office, Harvard University, 86 Brattle Street, Cambridge, MA 02138, 617-495-1581. *Fax:* 617-496-0256.

HARVEY MUDD COLLEGE
Claremont, CA

Tuition & fees: $40,390	Average undergraduate aid package: $32,547

ABOUT THE INSTITUTION Independent, coed. 6 undergraduate majors. Both federal and institutional methodology are used as a basis for awarding need-based institutional aid.

UNDERGRADUATE EXPENSES for 2010–11 *Comprehensive fee:* $53,588 includes full-time tuition ($40,133), mandatory fees ($257), and room and

board ($13,198). *College room only:* $6935. Room and board charges vary according to board plan. *Part-time tuition:* $1194 per credit hour. *Payment plan:* Installment.

FRESHMAN FINANCIAL AID (Fall 2009, est.) 150 applied for aid; of those 83% were deemed to have need. 100% of freshmen with need received aid; of those 100% had need fully met. *Average percent of need met:* 100% (excluding resources awarded to replace EFC). *Average financial aid package:* $31,455 (excluding resources awarded to replace EFC). 18% of all full-time freshmen had no need and received non-need-based gift aid.

UNDERGRADUATE FINANCIAL AID (Fall 2009, est.) 468 applied for aid; of those 88% were deemed to have need. 100% of undergraduates with need received aid; of those 100% had need fully met. *Average percent of need met:* 100% (excluding resources awarded to replace EFC). *Average financial aid package:* $32,547 (excluding resources awarded to replace EFC). 23% of all full-time undergraduates had no need and received non-need-based gift aid.

GIFT AID (NEED-BASED) *Total amount:* $11,893,764 (6% federal, 5% state, 85% institutional, 4% external sources). *Receiving aid:* Freshmen: 59% (122); all full-time undergraduates: 54% (408). *Average award:* Freshmen: $29,400; Undergraduates: $28,269. *Scholarships, grants, and awards:* Federal Pell, FSEOG, state, private, college/university gift aid from institutional funds, Academic Competitiveness Grants, National SMART Grants.

GIFT AID (NON-NEED-BASED) *Total amount:* $2,456,271 (86% institutional, 14% external sources). *Receiving aid:* Freshmen: 23% (47). Undergraduates: 26% (196). *Average award:* Freshmen: $9842. Undergraduates: $11,375. *Scholarships, grants, and awards by category:* Academic interests/achievement: 384 awards ($4,308,056 total): general academic interests/achievements. Special characteristics: 7 awards ($272,500 total): international students. *Tuition waivers:* Full or partial for employees or children of employees.

LOANS *Student loans:* $2,755,617 (92% need-based, 8% non-need-based). 59% of past graduating class borrowed through all loan programs. *Average indebtedness per student:* $16,384. *Average need-based loan:* Freshmen: $3587. Undergraduates: $5052. *Parent loans:* $966,091 (70% need-based, 30% non-need-based). *Programs:* Federal Direct (Subsidized and Unsubsidized Stafford), Perkins, college/university, alternative loans.

WORK-STUDY *Federal work-study:* Total amount: $512,235; 228 jobs averaging $2247. *State or other work-study/employment:* Total amount: $107,730 (75% need-based, 25% non-need-based). 18 part-time jobs averaging $5985.

APPLYING FOR FINANCIAL AID *Required financial aid forms:* FAFSA, CSS Financial Aid PROFILE, state aid form, noncustodial (divorced/separated) parent's statement, business/farm supplement. *Financial aid deadline:* 2/1. *Notification date:* 4/1. Students must reply by 5/1 or within 2 weeks of notification.

CONTACT Mrs. Gilma Lopez, Office of Financial Aid, Harvey Mudd College, 301 Platt Boulevard, Claremont, CA 91711-5994, 909-621-8055. *Fax:* 909-607-7046. *E-mail:* financial_aid@hmc.edu.

HASKELL INDIAN NATIONS UNIVERSITY
Lawrence, KS

CONTACT Reta Beaver Brewer, Director of Financial Aid, Haskell Indian Nations University, 155 Indian Avenue, Box 5027, Lawrence, KS 66046-4800, 785-749-8468. *Fax:* 785-832-6617.

HASTINGS COLLEGE
Hastings, NE

ABOUT THE INSTITUTION Independent Presbyterian, coed. *Awards:* bachelor's and master's degrees. 81 undergraduate majors. *Total enrollment:* 1,138. Undergraduates: 1,091. Freshmen: 304.

GIFT AID (NEED-BASED) *Scholarships, grants, and awards:* Federal Pell, FSEOG, state, private, college/university gift aid from institutional funds.

GIFT AID (NON-NEED-BASED) *Scholarships, grants, and awards by category:* Academic interests/achievement: communication, general academic interests/achievements, religion/biblical studies. Creative arts/performance: art/fine arts, dance, debating, journalism/publications, music, performing arts, theater/drama. Special achievements/activities: cheerleading/drum major, rodeo. Special characteristics: adult students, children of educators, children of faculty/staff, relatives of clergy, religious affiliation, siblings of current students.

LOANS *Programs:* FFEL (Subsidized and Unsubsidized Stafford, PLUS), Perkins, college/university.

WORK-STUDY *Federal work-study:* Total amount: $55,000; jobs available (averaging $600). *State or other work-study/employment:* Total amount: $33,498 (35% need-based, 65% non-need-based). Part-time jobs available.

APPLYING FOR FINANCIAL AID *Required financial aid forms:* FAFSA, institution's own form.

CONTACT Mr. Ian Roberts, Associate Vice President-Administration, Hastings College, 7th and Turner, Hastings, NE 68901, 402-461-7455 or toll-free 800-532-7642. *Fax:* 402-461-7714. *E-mail:* iroberts@hastings.edu.

HAVERFORD COLLEGE
Haverford, PA

Tuition & fees: $39,085	Average undergraduate aid package: $34,629

ABOUT THE INSTITUTION Independent, coed. 44 undergraduate majors. Institutional methodology is used as a basis for awarding need-based institutional aid.

UNDERGRADUATE EXPENSES for 2009–10 *One-time required fee:* $190. *Comprehensive fee:* $50,975 includes full-time tuition ($38,735), mandatory fees ($350), and room and board ($11,890). *College room only:* $6750. *Payment plans:* Tuition prepayment, installment.

FRESHMAN FINANCIAL AID (Fall 2009, est.) 206 applied for aid; of those 76% were deemed to have need. 100% of freshmen with need received aid; of those 100% had need fully met. *Average percent of need met:* 100% (excluding resources awarded to replace EFC). *Average financial aid package:* $34,976 (excluding resources awarded to replace EFC).

UNDERGRADUATE FINANCIAL AID (Fall 2009, est.) 663 applied for aid; of those 87% were deemed to have need. 100% of undergraduates with need received aid; of those 100% had need fully met. *Average percent of need met:* 100% (excluding resources awarded to replace EFC). *Average financial aid package:* $34,629 (excluding resources awarded to replace EFC).

GIFT AID (NEED-BASED) *Total amount:* $18,002,440 (4% federal, 1% state, 93% institutional, 2% external sources). *Receiving aid:* Freshmen: 47% (151); all full-time undergraduates: 46% (544). *Average award:* Freshmen: $33,575; Undergraduates: $33,093. *Scholarships, grants, and awards:* Federal Pell, FSEOG, state, college/university gift aid from institutional funds.

GIFT AID (NON-NEED-BASED) *Tuition waivers:* Full or partial for employees or children of employees.

LOANS *Student loans:* $1,628,737 (56% need-based, 44% non-need-based). 38% of past graduating class borrowed through all loan programs. *Average indebtedness per student:* $16,500. *Average need-based loan:* Undergraduates: $17,534. *Parent loans:* $1,924,878 (100% non-need-based). *Programs:* Federal Direct (Subsidized and Unsubsidized Stafford, PLUS), Perkins.

WORK-STUDY *Federal work-study:* Total amount: $271,301; jobs available. *State or other work-study/employment:* Total amount: $570,990 (24% need-based, 76% non-need-based). Part-time jobs available.

APPLYING FOR FINANCIAL AID *Required financial aid forms:* FAFSA, CSS Financial Aid PROFILE, noncustodial (divorced/separated) parent's statement, business/farm supplement. *Financial aid deadline:* 2/1. *Notification date:* 4/1. Students must reply by 5/1.

CONTACT Mr. David J. Hoy, Director of Financial Aid Office, Haverford College, 370 Lancaster Avenue, Haverford, PA 19041-1392, 610-896-1350. *Fax:* 610-896-1338. *E-mail:* finaid@haverford.edu.

HAWAI'I PACIFIC UNIVERSITY
Honolulu, HI

Tuition & fees: $14,960	Average undergraduate aid package: $14,529

ABOUT THE INSTITUTION Independent, coed. 65 undergraduate majors. Federal methodology is used as a basis for awarding need-based institutional aid.

UNDERGRADUATE EXPENSES for 2009–10 *Comprehensive fee:* $26,054 includes full-time tuition ($14,860), mandatory fees ($100), and room and board ($11,094). Full-time tuition and fees vary according to course load, program, and student level. Room and board charges vary according to housing facility. *Part-time tuition:* $300 per credit. Part-time tuition and fees vary according to course load. *Payment plan:* Installment.

FRESHMAN FINANCIAL AID (Fall 2009, est.) 556 applied for aid; of those 62% were deemed to have need. 97% of freshmen with need received aid. *Average percent of need met:* 83% (excluding resources awarded to replace EFC).

Average financial aid package: $14,414 (excluding resources awarded to replace EFC). 56% of all full-time freshmen had no need and received non-need-based gift aid.

UNDERGRADUATE FINANCIAL AID (Fall 2009, est.) 2,832 applied for aid; of those 62% were deemed to have need. 99% of undergraduates with need received aid; of those 11% had need fully met. *Average percent of need met:* 77% (excluding resources awarded to replace EFC). *Average financial aid package:* $14,529 (excluding resources awarded to replace EFC). 52% of all full-time undergraduates had no need and received non-need-based gift aid.

GIFT AID (NEED-BASED) *Total amount:* $5,172,382 (93% federal, 4% state, 3% institutional). *Receiving aid:* Freshmen: 43% (257); all full-time undergraduates: 27% (1,011). *Average award:* Freshmen: $1956; Undergraduates: $2016. *Scholarships, grants, and awards:* Federal Pell, FSEOG, state, private, college/university gift aid from institutional funds, Federal Nursing.

GIFT AID (NON-NEED-BASED) *Total amount:* $11,022,983 (83% institutional, 17% external sources). *Receiving aid:* Freshmen: 21% (125). Undergraduates: 14% (528). *Average award:* Freshmen: $4545. Undergraduates: $4402. *Scholarships, grants, and awards by category: Academic interests/achievement:* biological sciences, business, communication, general academic interests/achievements, health fields, social sciences. *Creative arts/performance:* dance, journalism/publications, music. *Special achievements/activities:* cheerleading/drum major, hobbies/interests, leadership, memberships, religious involvement. *Special characteristics:* ethnic background, international students, local/state students, out-of-state students, previous college experience, relatives of clergy, religious affiliation. *Tuition waivers:* Full or partial for employees or children of employees.

LOANS *Student loans:* $28,834,378 (100% need-based). *Average indebtedness per student:* $22,802. *Average need-based loan:* Freshmen: $4776. Undergraduates: $6501. *Parent loans:* $5,948,974 (100% need-based). *Programs:* FFEL (Subsidized and Unsubsidized Stafford, PLUS), Perkins, Federal Nursing.

WORK-STUDY *Federal work-study:* Total amount: $343,159; 148 jobs averaging $2093.

ATHLETIC AWARDS Total amount: $1,649,128 (100% non-need-based).

APPLYING FOR FINANCIAL AID *Required financial aid form:* FAFSA. *Financial aid deadline (priority):* 3/1. *Notification date:* Continuous beginning 3/15. Students must reply within 3 weeks of notification.

CONTACT Adam Hatch, Director of Financial Aid, Hawai'i Pacific University, 1164 Bishop Street, Suite 201, Honolulu, HI 96813-2785, 808-544-0253 or toll-free 866-225-5478 (out-of-state). *Fax:* 808-544-0884. *E-mail:* financialaid@hpu.edu.

14% had need fully met. *Average percent of need met:* 80% (excluding resources awarded to replace EFC). *Average financial aid package:* $19,780 (excluding resources awarded to replace EFC). 12% of all full-time freshmen had no need and received non-need-based gift aid.

UNDERGRADUATE FINANCIAL AID (Fall 2009, est.) 1,071 applied for aid; of those 79% were deemed to have need. 100% of undergraduates with need received aid; of those 24% had need fully met. *Average percent of need met:* 79% (excluding resources awarded to replace EFC). *Average financial aid package:* $16,911 (excluding resources awarded to replace EFC). 10% of all full-time undergraduates had no need and received non-need-based gift aid.

GIFT AID (NEED-BASED) *Total amount:* $13,491,544 (18% federal, 5% state, 75% institutional, 2% external sources). *Receiving aid:* Freshmen: 90% (327); all full-time undergraduates: 70% (828). *Average award:* Freshmen: $14,695; Undergraduates: $11,834. *Scholarships, grants, and awards:* Federal Pell, FSEOG, state, private, college/university gift aid from institutional funds.

GIFT AID (NON-NEED-BASED) *Total amount:* $1,413,151 (99% institutional, 1% external sources). *Receiving aid:* Freshmen: 81% (296). Undergraduates: 56% (663). *Average award:* Freshmen: $9660. Undergraduates: $8359. *Scholarships, grants, and awards by category: Academic interests/achievement:* 803 awards ($5,473,308 total): general academic interests/achievements. *Creative arts/performance:* 72 awards ($115,800 total): music, performing arts. *Special characteristics:* 280 awards ($1,334,296 total): children of faculty/staff, international students, out-of-state students, relatives of clergy, religious affiliation. *Tuition waivers:* Full or partial for employees or children of employees.

LOANS *Student loans:* $7,776,986 (94% need-based, 6% non-need-based). 90% of past graduating class borrowed through all loan programs. *Average indebtedness per student:* $35,397. *Average need-based loan:* Freshmen: $4143. Undergraduates: $4605. *Parent loans:* $2,707,327 (45% need-based, 55% non-need-based). *Programs:* Federal Direct (Subsidized and Unsubsidized Stafford, PLUS), Perkins.

WORK-STUDY *Federal work-study:* Total amount: $1,260,021; 698 jobs averaging $1700. *State or other work-study/employment:* Total amount: $156,471 (62% need-based, 38% non-need-based). 112 part-time jobs averaging $1558.

APPLYING FOR FINANCIAL AID *Required financial aid form:* FAFSA. *Financial aid deadline (priority):* 3/1. *Notification date:* Continuous beginning 3/1. Students must reply within 2 weeks of notification.

CONTACT Ms. Juli L. Weininger, Director of Financial Aid, Heidelberg University, 310 East Market Street, Tiffin, OH 44883-2462, 419-448-2293 or toll-free 800-434-3352. *Fax:* 419-448-2296.

HEBREW COLLEGE
Newton Centre, MA

CONTACT Marilyn Jaye, Registrar, Hebrew College, 160 Herrick Road, Newton Centre, MA 02459, 617-559-8612 or toll-free 800-866-4814 Ext. 8619. *Fax:* 617-559-8601. *E-mail:* mjaye@hebrewcollege.edu.

HEBREW THEOLOGICAL COLLEGE
Skokie, IL

CONTACT Ms. Rhoda Morris, Financial Aid Administrator, Hebrew Theological College, 7135 Carpenter Road, Skokie, IL 60077-3263, 847-982-2500. *Fax:* 847-674-6381.

HEIDELBERG UNIVERSITY
Tiffin, OH

Tuition & fees: $22,962	Average undergraduate aid package: $16,911

ABOUT THE INSTITUTION Independent religious, coed. 48 undergraduate majors. Federal methodology is used as a basis for awarding need-based institutional aid.

UNDERGRADUATE EXPENSES for 2010–11 *Comprehensive fee:* $31,597 includes full-time tuition ($22,424), mandatory fees ($538), and room and board ($8635). *College room only:* $4087. Full-time tuition and fees vary according to course load, degree level, and location. Room and board charges vary according to housing facility and location. Part-time tuition and fees vary according to course load, degree level, and location. *Payment plan:* Installment.

FRESHMAN FINANCIAL AID (Fall 2009, est.) 356 applied for aid; of those 92% were deemed to have need. 100% of freshmen with need received aid; of those

HELLENIC COLLEGE
Brookline, MA

ABOUT THE INSTITUTION Independent Greek Orthodox, coed. 6 undergraduate majors.

GIFT AID (NEED-BASED) *Scholarships, grants, and awards:* Federal Pell, FSEOG, state, private, college/university gift aid from institutional funds.

GIFT AID (NON-NEED-BASED) *Scholarships, grants, and awards by category: Academic interests/achievement:* religion/biblical studies. *Special achievements/activities:* religious involvement.

LOANS *Programs:* FFEL (Subsidized and Unsubsidized Stafford, PLUS), state.

WORK-STUDY Federal work-study jobs available.

APPLYING FOR FINANCIAL AID *Required financial aid forms:* FAFSA, institution's own form.

CONTACT Gregory Floor, Director of Admissions/Financial Aid, Hellenic College, 50 Goddard Avenue, Brookline, MA 02146-7496, 617-731-3500 Ext. 1285 or toll-free 866-424-2338. *Fax:* 617-850-1465. *E-mail:* gfloor@hchc.edu.

HENDERSON STATE UNIVERSITY
Arkadelphia, AR

Tuition & fees (AR res): $6204	Average undergraduate aid package: $10,648

ABOUT THE INSTITUTION State-supported, coed. 39 undergraduate majors. Federal methodology is used as a basis for awarding need-based institutional aid.

UNDERGRADUATE EXPENSES for 2009–10 *Tuition, state resident:* full-time $5100; part-time $170 per credit hour. *Tuition, nonresident:* full-time $10,200; part-time $340 per credit hour. *Required fees:* full-time $1104. Full-time tuition

and fees vary according to course load. Part-time tuition and fees vary according to course load. **College room and board:** $5034. Room and board charges vary according to board plan and housing facility.
FRESHMAN FINANCIAL AID (Fall 2009, est.) 593 applied for aid; of those 81% were deemed to have need. 99% of freshmen with need received aid; of those 4% had need fully met. **Average percent of need met:** 83% (excluding resources awarded to replace EFC). **Average financial aid package:** $11,380 (excluding resources awarded to replace EFC). 13% of all full-time freshmen had no need and received non-need-based gift aid.
UNDERGRADUATE FINANCIAL AID (Fall 2009, est.) 3,026 applied for aid; of those 84% were deemed to have need. 99% of undergraduates with need received aid; of those 1% had need fully met. **Average percent of need met:** 83% (excluding resources awarded to replace EFC). **Average financial aid package:** $10,648 (excluding resources awarded to replace EFC). 3% of all full-time undergraduates had no need and received non-need-based gift aid.
GIFT AID (NEED-BASED) Total amount: $13,332,787 (50% federal, 11% state, 29% institutional, 10% external sources). **Receiving aid:** Freshmen: 51% (323); all full-time undergraduates: 51% (1,731). **Average award:** Freshmen: $11,558; Undergraduates: $11,908. **Scholarships, grants, and awards:** Federal Pell, FSEOG, state, private, college/university gift aid from institutional funds.
GIFT AID (NON-NEED-BASED) Total amount: $1,883,552 (81% institutional, 19% external sources). **Receiving aid:** Freshmen: 37% (230). Undergraduates: 65% (2,198). **Average award:** Freshmen: $9354. Undergraduates: $9096. **Scholarships, grants, and awards by category:** Academic interests/achievement: biological sciences, education, general academic interests/achievements, international studies, mathematics. Creative arts/performance: art/fine arts, cinema/film/broadcasting, dance, debating, journalism/publications, music, performing arts, theater/drama. Special achievements/activities: cheerleading/drum major, general special achievements/activities, leadership. Special characteristics: children and siblings of alumni, children of faculty/staff, international students, out-of-state students. **Tuition waivers:** Full or partial for children of alumni, employees or children of employees.
LOANS Student loans: $15,012,872 (50% need-based, 50% non-need-based). 56% of past graduating class borrowed through all loan programs. Average indebtedness per student: $16,529. **Average need-based loan:** Freshmen: $3500. Undergraduates: $3984. **Parent loans:** $490,621 (100% non-need-based). **Programs:** FFEL (Subsidized and Unsubsidized Stafford, PLUS), Perkins.
WORK-STUDY Federal work-study: Total amount: $159,111; jobs available. **State or other work-study/employment:** Total amount: $148,188 (100% non-need-based). Part-time jobs available.
ATHLETIC AWARDS Total amount: $190,935 (84% need-based, 16% non-need-based).
APPLYING FOR FINANCIAL AID Required financial aid form: FAFSA. **Financial aid deadline (priority):** 6/1. **Notification date:** Continuous.
CONTACT Ms. Vicki Taylor, Director of Financial Aid, Henderson State University, 1100 Henderson Street, HSU Box 7812, Arkadelphia, AR 71999-0001, 870-230-5138 or toll-free 800-228-7333. Fax: 870-230-5481. E-mail: taylorv@hsu.edu.

HENDRIX COLLEGE
Conway, AR

Tuition & fees: $30,270	Average undergraduate aid package: $22,498

ABOUT THE INSTITUTION Independent United Methodist, coed. 31 undergraduate majors. Federal methodology is used as a basis for awarding need-based institutional aid.
UNDERGRADUATE EXPENSES for 2009–10 Comprehensive fee: $38,934 includes full-time tuition ($29,970), mandatory fees ($300), and room and board ($8664). **College room only:** $4400. Full-time tuition and fees vary according to course load. Room and board charges vary according to board plan and housing facility. **Part-time tuition:** $3470 per course. Part-time tuition and fees vary according to course load. **Payment plan:** Installment.
FRESHMAN FINANCIAL AID (Fall 2009, est.) 338 applied for aid; of those 72% were deemed to have need. 100% of freshmen with need received aid; of those 43% had need fully met. **Average percent of need met:** 87% (excluding resources awarded to replace EFC). **Average financial aid package:** $24,108 (excluding resources awarded to replace EFC). 40% of all full-time freshmen had no need and received non-need-based gift aid.
UNDERGRADUATE FINANCIAL AID (Fall 2009, est.) 1,152 applied for aid; of those 77% were deemed to have need. 100% of undergraduates with need received aid; of those 38% had need fully met. **Average percent of need met:**

83% (excluding resources awarded to replace EFC). **Average financial aid package:** $22,498 (excluding resources awarded to replace EFC). 38% of all full-time undergraduates had no need and received non-need-based gift aid.
GIFT AID (NEED-BASED) Total amount: $15,529,570 (9% federal, 5% state, 84% institutional, 2% external sources). **Receiving aid:** Freshmen: 59% (244); all full-time undergraduates: 61% (885). **Average award:** Freshmen: $20,593; Undergraduates: $18,080. **Scholarships, grants, and awards:** Federal Pell, FSEOG, state, private, college/university gift aid from institutional funds.
GIFT AID (NON-NEED-BASED) Total amount: $10,991,390 (10% state, 87% institutional, 3% external sources). **Receiving aid:** Freshmen: 22% (90). Undergraduates: 17% (247). **Average award:** Freshmen: $17,466. Undergraduates: $14,775. **Scholarships, grants, and awards by category:** Academic interests/achievement: $13,254,299 total: general academic interests/achievements. Creative arts/performance: $191,000 total: art/fine arts, dance, music, theater/drama. Special achievements/activities: $4,104,250 total: community service, general special achievements/activities, leadership, religious involvement. Special characteristics: $1,253,880 total: children of educators, children of faculty/staff, international students, previous college experience, relatives of clergy. **Tuition waivers:** Full or partial for employees or children of employees.
LOANS Student loans: $6,696,947 (60% need-based, 40% non-need-based). 87% of past graduating class borrowed through all loan programs. Average indebtedness per student: $17,641. **Average need-based loan:** Freshmen: $4219. Undergraduates: $4919. **Parent loans:** $4,813,364 (20% need-based, 80% non-need-based). **Programs:** Federal Direct (Subsidized and Unsubsidized Stafford, PLUS), FFEL (Subsidized and Unsubsidized Stafford, PLUS), Perkins, United Methodist Student Loans.
WORK-STUDY Federal work-study: Total amount: $799,731; 561 jobs averaging $1389. **State or other work-study/employment:** Total amount: $245,462 (8% need-based, 92% non-need-based). 254 part-time jobs averaging $1229.
APPLYING FOR FINANCIAL AID Required financial aid forms: FAFSA, state aid form. **Financial aid deadline (priority):** 2/15. **Notification date:** Continuous beginning 2/15. Students must reply by 5/1.
CONTACT Mr. Mark Bandre, Director of Financial Aid, Hendrix College, 1600 Washington Avenue, Conway, AR 72032, 501-450-1368 or toll-free 800-277-9017. Fax: 501-450-3871. E-mail: student_aid@hendrix.edu.

HENLEY-PUTNAM UNIVERSITY
San Jose, CA

CONTACT Financial Aid Office, Henley-Putnam University, 25 Metro Drive, Suite 500, San Jose, CA 95110, 408-453-9900.

HERITAGE BIBLE COLLEGE
Dunn, NC

CONTACT Mrs. Laurie Minard, Director of Financial Aid, Heritage Bible College, Box 1628, Dunn, NC 28335, 800-297-6351 Ext. 226 or toll-free 800-297-6351 Ext. 230. Fax: 910-892-1809. E-mail: lminard@heritagebiblecollege.edu.

HERITAGE CHRISTIAN UNIVERSITY
Florence, AL

Tuition & fees: $11,840	Average undergraduate aid package: N/A

ABOUT THE INSTITUTION Independent religious, coed, primarily men. 1 undergraduate major. Federal methodology is used as a basis for awarding need-based institutional aid.
UNDERGRADUATE EXPENSES for 2010–11 One-time required fee: $300. **Comprehensive fee:** $17,265 includes full-time tuition ($11,360), mandatory fees ($480), and room and board ($5425). **College room only:** $3000. Room and board charges vary according to housing facility. **Part-time tuition:** $355 per credit hour. **Part-time fees:** $20 per credit hour. **Payment plans:** Installment, deferred payment.
GIFT AID (NEED-BASED) Scholarships, grants, and awards: Federal Pell, FSEOG, college/university gift aid from institutional funds.
GIFT AID (NON-NEED-BASED) Scholarships, grants, and awards by category: Academic interests/achievement: general academic interests/achievements. Special

characteristics: children and siblings of alumni, children of educators, children of faculty/staff, spouses of current students. *Tuition waivers:* Full or partial for employees or children of employees.

LOANS *Programs:* FFEL (Subsidized and Unsubsidized Stafford, PLUS).

WORK-STUDY Federal work-study jobs available.

APPLYING FOR FINANCIAL AID *Required financial aid forms:* FAFSA, federal income tax form(s). *Financial aid deadline (priority):* 6/1. *Notification date:* Continuous beginning 7/15. Students must reply within 2 weeks of notification.

CONTACT Mechelle Thompson, Financial Aid Administrator, Heritage Christian University, PO Box HCU, Florence, AL 35630, 800-367-3565 Ext. 224 or toll-free 800-367-3565. *Fax:* 256-766-9289. *E-mail:* mthompson@hcu.edu.

HERITAGE UNIVERSITY
Toppenish, WA

CONTACT Mr. Norberto Espindola, Director of Enrollment Management Services, Heritage University, 3240 Fort Road, Toppenish, WA 98948-9599, 509-865-8500 or toll-free 888-272-6190 (in-state). *Fax:* 509-865-8659. *E-mail:* financial_aid@heritage.edu.

HERZING UNIVERSITY
Atlanta, GA

CONTACT Ms. Amy Myer, Financial Aid Director, Herzing University, 3355 Lenox Road, Suite 100, Atlanta, GA 30326, 404-816-4533 or toll-free 800-573-4533. *Fax:* 404-816-5576. *E-mail:* frankw@atl.herzing.edu.

HERZING UNIVERSITY
Madison, WI

CONTACT Mrs. Beverly A. Faga, Financial Aid Director, Herzing University, 1227 North Sherman Avenue, Madison, WI 53704, 608-663-0811 or toll-free 800-582-1227. *Fax:* 608-249-8593. *E-mail:* bevfaga@msn.herzing.edu.

HICKEY COLLEGE
St. Louis, MO

CONTACT Financial Aid Office, Hickey College, 940 West Port Plaza, Suite 101, St. Louis, MO 63146, 314-434-2212 or toll-free 800-777-1544.

HIGH POINT UNIVERSITY
High Point, NC

Comprehensive fee: $35,900	Average undergraduate aid package: $10,995

ABOUT THE INSTITUTION Independent United Methodist, coed. 49 undergraduate majors. Institutional methodology is used as a basis for awarding need-based institutional aid.

UNDERGRADUATE EXPENSES for 2010–11 *Comprehensive fee:* $35,900. Full-time tuition and fees vary according to class time, course load, and reciprocity agreements. Room and board charges vary according to board plan, housing facility, and location. *Part-time tuition:* $749 per credit hour. Part-time tuition and fees vary according to class time, course load, and reciprocity agreements. *Payment plan:* Installment.

FRESHMAN FINANCIAL AID (Fall 2009, est.) 916 applied for aid; of those 76% were deemed to have need. 100% of freshmen with need received aid; of those 52% had need fully met. *Average percent of need met:* 56% (excluding resources awarded to replace EFC). *Average financial aid package:* $10,875 (excluding resources awarded to replace EFC). 20% of all full-time freshmen had no need and received non-need-based gift aid.

UNDERGRADUATE FINANCIAL AID (Fall 2009, est.) 2,919 applied for aid; of those 71% were deemed to have need. 100% of undergraduates with need received aid; of those 57% had need fully met. *Average percent of need met:* 56% (excluding resources awarded to replace EFC). *Average financial aid package:* $10,995 (excluding resources awarded to replace EFC). 21% of all full-time undergraduates had no need and received non-need-based gift aid.

GIFT AID (NEED-BASED) *Total amount:* $7,801,845 (39% federal, 25% state, 36% institutional). *Receiving aid:* Freshmen: 58% (593); all full-time undergradu-

ates: 47% (1,465). *Average award:* Freshmen: $2555; Undergraduates: $2884. *Scholarships, grants, and awards:* Federal Pell, FSEOG, state, private, college/university gift aid from institutional funds.

GIFT AID (NON-NEED-BASED) *Total amount:* $9,207,100 (23% state, 62% institutional, 15% external sources). *Receiving aid:* Freshmen: 43% (444). Undergraduates: 39% (1,236). *Average award:* Freshmen: $1884. Undergraduates: $2117. *Scholarships, grants, and awards by category: Academic interests/achievement:* biological sciences, business, education, English, foreign languages, general academic interests/achievements, humanities, international studies, mathematics, physical sciences, premedicine, religion/biblical studies. *Creative arts/performance:* art/fine arts, music. *Special achievements/activities:* general special achievements/activities. *Special characteristics:* relatives of clergy. *Tuition waivers:* Full or partial for employees or children of employees.

LOANS *Student loans:* $19,583,897 (39% need-based, 61% non-need-based). 69% of past graduating class borrowed through all loan programs. *Average indebtedness per student:* $9437. *Average need-based loan:* Freshmen: $3500. Undergraduates: $5082. *Parent loans:* $7,859,839 (100% non-need-based). *Programs:* Federal Direct (Subsidized and Unsubsidized Stafford, PLUS), FFEL (Subsidized and Unsubsidized Stafford, PLUS), Perkins.

WORK-STUDY *Federal work-study:* Total amount: $926,484; 633 jobs averaging $1463. *State or other work-study/employment:* Part-time jobs available.

ATHLETIC AWARDS Total amount: $2,911,021 (100% non-need-based).

APPLYING FOR FINANCIAL AID *Required financial aid forms:* FAFSA, state aid form. *Financial aid deadline (priority):* 3/1. *Notification date:* Continuous. Students must reply within 3 weeks of notification.

CONTACT Ms. Julie Setzer, Director of Student Financial Planning, High Point University, Box 3232, University Station, 833 Montlieu Avenue, High Point, NC 27262, 336-841-9128 or toll-free 800-345-6993. *Fax:* 336-884-0221. *E-mail:* jsetzer@highpoint.edu.

HILBERT COLLEGE
Hamburg, NY

CONTACT Beverly Chudy, Director of Financial Aid, Hilbert College, 5200 South Park Avenue, Hamburg, NY 14075-1597, 716-649-7900 Ext. 207. *Fax:* 716-649-1152. *E-mail:* bchudy@hilbert.edu.

HILLSDALE COLLEGE
Hillsdale, MI

CONTACT Mr. Rich Moeggengberg, Director of Student Financial Aid, Hillsdale College, 33 East College Street, Hillsdale, MI 49242-1298, 517-607-2550. *Fax:* 517-607-2298. *E-mail:* rich.moeggenbeng@hillsdale.edu.

HILLSDALE FREE WILL BAPTIST COLLEGE
Moore, OK

Tuition & fees: $9650	Average undergraduate aid package: $9253

ABOUT THE INSTITUTION Independent Free Will Baptist, coed. 22 undergraduate majors. Both federal and institutional methodology are used as a basis for awarding need-based institutional aid.

UNDERGRADUATE EXPENSES for 2009–10 *One-time required fee:* $20. *Comprehensive fee:* $14,850 includes full-time tuition ($8100), mandatory fees ($1550), and room and board ($5200). *College room only:* $2200. Full-time tuition and fees vary according to course load. Room and board charges vary according to board plan and housing facility. *Part-time tuition:* $340 per credit hour. *Part-time fees:* $20 per credit hour; $210 per term. Part-time tuition and fees vary according to course load. *Payment plan:* Installment.

FRESHMAN FINANCIAL AID (Fall 2008) 67 applied for aid; of those 85% were deemed to have need. 96% of freshmen with need received aid; of those 13% had need fully met. *Average percent of need met:* 40% (excluding resources awarded to replace EFC). *Average financial aid package:* $8510 (excluding resources awarded to replace EFC). 29% of all full-time freshmen had no need and received non-need-based gift aid.

UNDERGRADUATE FINANCIAL AID (Fall 2008) 172 applied for aid; of those 83% were deemed to have need. 99% of undergraduates with need received aid; of those 13% had need fully met. *Average percent of need met:* 49% (excluding resources awarded to replace EFC). *Average financial aid package:*

$9253 (excluding resources awarded to replace EFC). 33% of all full-time undergraduates had no need and received non-need-based gift aid. **GIFT AID (NEED-BASED)** *Total amount:* $480,981 (63% federal, 27% state, 10% institutional). *Receiving aid:* Freshmen: 50% (40); all full-time undergraduates: 51% (109). *Average award:* Freshmen: $3257; Undergraduates: $3821. *Scholarships, grants, and awards:* Federal Pell, FSEOG, state, college/university gift aid from institutional funds, Bureau of Indian Affairs Grants. **GIFT AID (NON-NEED-BASED)** *Total amount:* $503,530 (2% federal, 11% state, 65% institutional, 22% external sources). *Receiving aid:* Freshmen: 56% (45). Undergraduates: 49% (105). *Average award:* Freshmen: $3119. Undergraduates: $3113. *Scholarships, grants, and awards by category: Academic interests/ achievement:* 86 awards ($226,050 total): business, education, English, general academic interests/achievements, mathematics, religion/biblical studies. *Creative arts/performance:* 1 award ($1000 total): music, performing arts. *Special achievements/activities:* 13 awards ($8150 total): community service, religious involvement. *Special characteristics:* 95 awards ($80,744 total): adult students, children and siblings of alumni, children of educators, children of faculty/staff, relatives of clergy, religious affiliation, siblings of current students, spouses of current students. *Tuition waivers:* Full or partial for children of alumni, employees or children of employees, senior citizens. **LOANS** *Student loans:* $1,003,027 (47% need-based, 53% non-need-based). 85% of past graduating class borrowed through all loan programs. *Average indebtedness per student:* $23,822. *Average need-based loan:* Freshmen: $2949. Undergraduates: $3017. *Parent loans:* $16,700 (100% non-need-based). *Programs:* Federal Direct (Subsidized and Unsubsidized Stafford, PLUS), Perkins. **WORK-STUDY** *Federal work-study:* Total amount: $47,713; 48 jobs averaging $994. *State or other work-study/employment:* Part-time jobs available. **APPLYING FOR FINANCIAL AID** *Required financial aid forms:* FAFSA, institution's own form. *Financial aid deadline (priority):* 6/30. *Notification date:* Continuous beginning 4/1. Students must reply within 2 weeks of notification. **CONTACT** Denise Conklin, Director of Financial Aid, Hillsdale Free Will Baptist College, PO Box 7208, Moore, OK 73153-1208, 405-912-9012. *Fax:* 405-912-9050. *E-mail:* dconklin@hc.edu.

HIRAM COLLEGE
Hiram, OH

CONTACT Ann Marie Gruber, Associate Director of Financial Aid, Hiram College, Box 67, Hiram, OH 44234-0067, 330-569-5107 or toll-free 800-362-5280. *Fax:* 330-569-5499.

HOBART AND WILLIAM SMITH COLLEGES
Geneva, NY

Tuition & fees: N/R	Average undergraduate aid package: $29,433

ABOUT THE INSTITUTION Independent, coed. *Awards:* bachelor's and master's degrees and post-bachelor's certificates. 54 undergraduate majors. *Total enrollment:* 2,009. Undergraduates: 2,001. Freshmen: 619. Both federal and institutional methodology are used as a basis for awarding need-based institutional aid. **FRESHMAN FINANCIAL AID (Fall 2009, est.)** 435 applied for aid; of those 81% were deemed to have need. 99% of freshmen with need received aid; of those 97% had need fully met. *Average percent of need met:* 82% (excluding resources awarded to replace EFC). *Average financial aid package:* $31,102 (excluding resources awarded to replace EFC). 25% of all full-time freshmen had no need and received non-need-based gift aid. **UNDERGRADUATE FINANCIAL AID (Fall 2009, est.)** 1,581 applied for aid; of those 84% were deemed to have need. 98% of undergraduates with need received aid; of those 85% had need fully met. *Average percent of need met:* 78% (excluding resources awarded to replace EFC). *Average financial aid package:* $29,433 (excluding resources awarded to replace EFC). 23% of all full-time undergraduates had no need and received non-need-based gift aid. **GIFT AID (NEED-BASED)** *Total amount:* $32,354,341 (7% federal, 5% state, 83% institutional, 5% external sources). *Receiving aid:* Freshmen: 74% (348); all full-time undergraduates: 74% (1,295). *Average award:* Freshmen: $27,407; Undergraduates: $24,984. *Scholarships, grants, and awards:* Federal Pell, FSEOG, state, private, college/university gift aid from institutional funds, Academic Competitiveness Grants, National SMART Grants. **GIFT AID (NON-NEED-BASED)** *Total amount:* $7,490,874 (1% state, 89% institutional, 10% external sources). *Receiving aid:* Freshmen: 10% (47).

Undergraduates: 10% (180). *Average award:* Freshmen: $15,029. Undergraduates: $14,177. *Scholarships, grants, and awards by category: Academic interests/achievement:* 137 awards ($1,764,590 total): general academic interests/ achievements. *Creative arts/performance:* 11 awards ($97,000 total): art/fine arts, creative writing, dance, music, performing arts. *Special achievements/ activities:* 49 awards ($551,000 total): leadership. *Tuition waivers:* Full or partial for employees or children of employees. **LOANS** *Student loans:* $11,014,156 (65% need-based, 35% non-need-based). 79% of past graduating class borrowed through all loan programs. *Average indebtedness per student:* $30,970. *Average need-based loan:* Freshmen: $3332. Undergraduates: $4190. *Parent loans:* $4,944,170 (32% need-based, 68% non-need-based). *Programs:* FFEL (Subsidized and Unsubsidized Stafford, PLUS), Perkins. **WORK-STUDY** *Federal work-study:* Total amount: $1,580,525; 900 jobs averaging $1756. *State or other work-study/employment:* Total amount: $1,059,155 (14% need-based, 86% non-need-based). 423 part-time jobs averaging $1909. **APPLYING FOR FINANCIAL AID** *Required financial aid forms:* FAFSA, CSS Financial Aid PROFILE, state aid form, noncustodial (divorced/separated) parent's statement, income tax form(s). *Financial aid deadline:* 3/15 (priority: 2/15). *Notification date:* 4/1. Students must reply by 5/1. **CONTACT** Beth Turner, Director of Financial Aid, Hobart and William Smith Colleges, Geneva, NY 14456-3397, 315-781-3315 or toll-free 800-245-0100. *Fax:* 315-781-3655. *E-mail:* finaid@hws.edu.

HOBE SOUND BIBLE COLLEGE
Hobe Sound, FL

CONTACT Director of Financial Aid, Hobe Sound Bible College, PO Box 1065, Hobe Sound, FL 33475-1065, 561-546-5534 or toll-free 800-881-5534. *Fax:* 561-545-1422.

HODGES UNIVERSITY
Naples, FL

Tuition & fees: $16,940	Average undergraduate aid package: $9200

ABOUT THE INSTITUTION Independent, coed. 8 undergraduate majors. Federal methodology is used as a basis for awarding need-based institutional aid. **UNDERGRADUATE EXPENSES for 2009–10** *Tuition:* full-time $16,560; part-time $460 per semester hour. *Payment plan:* Installment. **FRESHMAN FINANCIAL AID (Fall 2009, est.)** 170 applied for aid; of those 91% were deemed to have need. 100% of freshmen with need received aid; of those 31% had need fully met. *Average percent of need met:* 67% (excluding resources awarded to replace EFC). *Average financial aid package:* $8500 (excluding resources awarded to replace EFC). 19% of all full-time freshmen had no need and received non-need-based gift aid. **UNDERGRADUATE FINANCIAL AID (Fall 2009, est.)** 1,600 applied for aid; of those 83% were deemed to have need. 100% of undergraduates with need received aid; of those 20% had need fully met. *Average percent of need met:* 74% (excluding resources awarded to replace EFC). *Average financial aid package:* $9200 (excluding resources awarded to replace EFC). 4% of all full-time undergraduates had no need and received non-need-based gift aid. **GIFT AID (NEED-BASED)** *Total amount:* $9,166,665 (98% federal, 2% state). *Receiving aid:* Freshmen: 78% (145); all full-time undergraduates: 74% (1,325). *Average award:* Freshmen: $2600; Undergraduates: $4600. *Scholarships, grants, and awards:* Federal Pell, FSEOG, state, private, college/university gift aid from institutional funds. **GIFT AID (NON-NEED-BASED)** *Total amount:* $4,621,643 (78% state, 19% institutional, 3% external sources). *Receiving aid:* Freshmen: 38% (71). Undergraduates: 49% (875). *Average award:* Freshmen: $375. Undergraduates: $260. *Scholarships, grants, and awards by category: Special achievements/ activities:* general special achievements/activities. *Tuition waivers:* Full or partial for employees or children of employees. **LOANS** *Student loans:* $15,000,000 (50% need-based, 50% non-need-based). 78% of past graduating class borrowed through all loan programs. *Average indebtedness per student:* $17,600. *Average need-based loan:* Freshmen: $2800. Undergraduates: $2800. *Parent loans:* $300,000 (100% need-based). *Programs:* FFEL (Subsidized and Unsubsidized Stafford, PLUS). **WORK-STUDY** *Federal work-study:* Total amount: $200,000; 45 jobs averaging $4444.

APPLYING FOR FINANCIAL AID *Required financial aid form:* FAFSA. *Financial aid deadline:* Continuous. *Notification date:* Continuous.

CONTACT Mr. Joe Gilchrist, Vice President of Student Financial Assistance, Hodges University, 2655 Northbrooke Drive, Naples, FL 34119, 239-598-6116 or toll-free 800-466-8017. *Fax:* 239-598-6257. *E-mail:* jgilchrist@hodges.edu.

HOFSTRA UNIVERSITY
Hempstead, NY

Tuition & fees: $30,130	Average undergraduate aid package: $18,000

ABOUT THE INSTITUTION Independent, coed. 125 undergraduate majors. Federal methodology is used as a basis for awarding need-based institutional aid.

UNDERGRADUATE EXPENSES for 2009–10 *Comprehensive fee:* $41,460 includes full-time tuition ($29,080), mandatory fees ($1050), and room and board ($11,330). *College room only:* $7600. Full-time tuition and fees vary according to course load and program. Room and board charges vary according to board plan and housing facility. *Part-time tuition:* $890 per term. *Part-time fees:* $155 per term. Part-time tuition and fees vary according to course load and program. *Payment plans:* Installment, deferred payment.

FRESHMAN FINANCIAL AID (Fall 2009, est.) 1,349 applied for aid; of those 78% were deemed to have need. 99% of freshmen with need received aid; of those 22% had need fully met. *Average percent of need met:* 59% (excluding resources awarded to replace EFC). *Average financial aid package:* $20,000 (excluding resources awarded to replace EFC). 22% of all full-time freshmen had no need and received non-need-based gift aid.

UNDERGRADUATE FINANCIAL AID (Fall 2009, est.) 5,488 applied for aid; of those 82% were deemed to have need. 99% of undergraduates with need received aid; of those 20% had need fully met. *Average percent of need met:* 56% (excluding resources awarded to replace EFC). *Average financial aid package:* $18,000 (excluding resources awarded to replace EFC). 19% of all full-time undergraduates had no need and received non-need-based gift aid.

GIFT AID (NEED-BASED) *Total amount:* $42,080,000 (19% federal, 12% state, 67% institutional, 2% external sources). *Receiving aid:* Freshmen: 61% (958); all full-time undergraduates: 53% (3,829). *Average award:* Freshmen: $13,000; Undergraduates: $11,000. *Scholarships, grants, and awards:* Federal Pell, FSEOG, state, private, college/university gift aid from institutional funds, Academic Competitiveness Grants, National SMART Grants.

GIFT AID (NON-NEED-BASED) *Total amount:* $17,980,000 (1% federal, 2% state, 93% institutional, 4% external sources). *Receiving aid:* Freshmen: 10% (149). Undergraduates: 6% (419). *Average award:* Freshmen: $12,000. Undergraduates: $10,000. *Scholarships, grants, and awards by category:* Academic interests/achievement: 5,106 awards ($39,320,891 total): communication, general academic interests/achievements. Creative arts/performance: 179 awards ($442,708 total): art/fine arts, dance, music, theater/drama. Special achievements/activities: 326 awards ($8,122,755 total): general special achievements/activities, leadership. Special characteristics: 319 awards ($6,026,320 total): children and siblings of alumni, children of union members/company employees, general special characteristics, handicapped students, public servants. *Tuition waivers:* Full or partial for employees or children of employees, senior citizens.

LOANS *Student loans:* $61,200,000 (67% need-based, 33% non-need-based). 64% of past graduating class borrowed through all loan programs. *Average need-based loan:* Freshmen: $3000. Undergraduates: $5000. *Parent loans:* $30,000,000 (45% need-based, 55% non-need-based). *Programs:* FFEL (Subsidized and Unsubsidized Stafford, PLUS), Perkins, college/university.

WORK-STUDY *Federal work-study:* Total amount: $4,000,000; 1,353 jobs averaging $2979. *State or other work-study/employment:* Total amount: $5,300,000 (26% need-based, 74% non-need-based). 1,854 part-time jobs averaging $2403.

ATHLETIC AWARDS Total amount: $8,700,000 (52% need-based, 48% non-need-based).

APPLYING FOR FINANCIAL AID *Required financial aid forms:* FAFSA, state aid form. *Financial aid deadline (priority):* 2/15. *Notification date:* Continuous beginning 3/1. Students must reply by 5/1 or within 2 weeks of notification.

CONTACT Sandra Filbry, Director of Financial Aid Operations and Compliance, Hofstra University, 126 Hofstra University, Hempstead, NY 11549, 516-463-4335 or toll-free 800-HOFSTRA. *Fax:* 516-463-4936. *E-mail:* sandra.a.filbry@hofstra.edu.

HOLLINS UNIVERSITY
Roanoke, VA

Tuition & fees: $28,115	Average undergraduate aid package: $22,059

ABOUT THE INSTITUTION Independent, undergraduate: women only; graduate: coed. 28 undergraduate majors. Federal methodology is used as a basis for awarding need-based institutional aid.

UNDERGRADUATE EXPENSES for 2009–10 *Comprehensive fee:* $38,155 includes full-time tuition ($27,550), mandatory fees ($565), and room and board ($10,040). *Part-time tuition:* $860 per credit. *Part-time fees:* $143.75 per term. *Payment plans:* Tuition prepayment, installment.

FRESHMAN FINANCIAL AID (Fall 2009, est.) 179 applied for aid; of those 87% were deemed to have need. 100% of freshmen with need received aid; of those 13% had need fully met. *Average percent of need met:* 90% (excluding resources awarded to replace EFC). *Average financial aid package:* $23,508 (excluding resources awarded to replace EFC). 14% of all full-time freshmen had no need and received non-need-based gift aid.

UNDERGRADUATE FINANCIAL AID (Fall 2009, est.) 665 applied for aid; of those 89% were deemed to have need. 100% of undergraduates with need received aid; of those 13% had need fully met. *Average percent of need met:* 84% (excluding resources awarded to replace EFC). *Average financial aid package:* $22,059 (excluding resources awarded to replace EFC). 21% of all full-time undergraduates had no need and received non-need-based gift aid.

GIFT AID (NEED-BASED) *Total amount:* $8,961,847 (16% federal, 10% state, 73% institutional, 1% external sources). *Receiving aid:* Freshmen: 76% (156); all full-time undergraduates: 79% (590). *Average award:* Freshmen: $17,236; Undergraduates: $16,471. *Scholarships, grants, and awards:* Federal Pell, FSEOG, state, private, college/university gift aid from institutional funds.

GIFT AID (NON-NEED-BASED) *Total amount:* $3,451,459 (6% state, 94% institutional). *Receiving aid:* Freshmen: 55% (113). Undergraduates: 43% (324). *Average award:* Freshmen: $12,749. Undergraduates: $11,994. *Scholarships, grants, and awards by category:* Academic interests/achievement: 318 awards ($4,174,437 total): general academic interests/achievements. Creative arts/performance: 210 awards ($952,170 total): art/fine arts, creative writing, dance, music. Special achievements/activities: 67 awards ($411,015 total): community service, leadership. Special characteristics: 237 awards ($1,205,280 total): adult students, children and siblings of alumni, children of faculty/staff, international students, local/state students, out-of-state students, previous college experience, veterans. *Tuition waivers:* Full or partial for employees or children of employees.

LOANS *Student loans:* $3,976,967 (100% need-based). 63% of past graduating class borrowed through all loan programs. *Average indebtedness per student:* $24,002. *Average need-based loan:* Freshmen: $6768. Undergraduates: $5240. *Parent loans:* $1,708,659 (35% need-based, 65% non-need-based). *Programs:* Federal Direct (Subsidized and Unsubsidized Stafford, PLUS), Perkins, college/university, alternative loans.

WORK-STUDY *Federal work-study:* Total amount: $728,007; 291 jobs averaging $2388. *State or other work-study/employment:* Total amount: $214,315 (41% need-based, 59% non-need-based). 94 part-time jobs averaging $2218.

APPLYING FOR FINANCIAL AID *Required financial aid forms:* FAFSA, state aid form. *Financial aid deadline:* 2/15 (priority: 2/1). *Notification date:* Continuous beginning 3/1. Students must reply by 5/1.

CONTACT Ms. Amy Moore, Acting Director of Scholarships and Financial Assistance, Hollins University, PO Box 9718, Roanoke, VA 24020-1688, 540-362-6332 or toll-free 800-456-9595. *Fax:* 540-362-6093. *E-mail:* amoore@hollins.edu.

HOLY CROSS COLLEGE
Notre Dame, IN

Tuition & fees: $18,700	Average undergraduate aid package: N/A

ABOUT THE INSTITUTION Independent Roman Catholic, coed. 1 undergraduate major. Federal methodology is used as a basis for awarding need-based institutional aid.

UNDERGRADUATE EXPENSES for 2009–10 *Comprehensive fee:* $26,700 includes full-time tuition ($17,700), mandatory fees ($1000), and room and board ($8000). Room and board charges vary according to housing facility. *Part-time tuition:* $590 per semester hour.

GIFT AID (NEED-BASED) *Scholarships, grants, and awards:* Federal Pell, FSEOG, state, private, college/university gift aid from institutional funds.
LOANS *Programs:* FFEL (Subsidized and Unsubsidized Stafford, PLUS), Perkins, alternative loans.
APPLYING FOR FINANCIAL AID *Required financial aid form:* FAFSA. *Financial aid deadline (priority):* 3/1. *Notification date:* Continuous beginning 3/15.
CONTACT Robert Benjamin, Director of Financial Aid, Holy Cross College, PO Box 308, Notre Dame, IN 46556, 574-239-8362. *E-mail:* rbenjamin@hcc-nd.edu.

HOLY FAMILY UNIVERSITY
Philadelphia, PA

Tuition & fees: $23,520	Average undergraduate aid package: $16,005

ABOUT THE INSTITUTION Independent Roman Catholic, coed, primarily women. 43 undergraduate majors. Federal methodology is used as a basis for awarding need-based institutional aid.
UNDERGRADUATE EXPENSES for 2010–11 *Comprehensive fee:* $33,920 includes full-time tuition ($22,870), mandatory fees ($650), and room and board ($10,400). *College room only:* $6200. Full-time tuition and fees vary according to course load and program. Room and board charges vary according to board plan and housing facility. *Part-time tuition:* $490 per credit hour. *Part-time fees:* $60 per term. Part-time tuition and fees vary according to course load and program. *Payment plans:* Installment, deferred payment.
FRESHMAN FINANCIAL AID (Fall 2009, est.) 363 applied for aid; of those 88% were deemed to have need. 100% of freshmen with need received aid; of those 12% had need fully met. *Average percent of need met:* 77% (excluding resources awarded to replace EFC). *Average financial aid package:* $18,752 (excluding resources awarded to replace EFC). 11% of all full-time freshmen had no need and received non-need-based gift aid.
UNDERGRADUATE FINANCIAL AID (Fall 2009, est.) 1,447 applied for aid; of those 89% were deemed to have need. 99% of undergraduates with need received aid; of those 17% had need fully met. *Average percent of need met:* 71% (excluding resources awarded to replace EFC). *Average financial aid package:* $16,005 (excluding resources awarded to replace EFC). 8% of all full-time undergraduates had no need and received non-need-based gift aid.
GIFT AID (NEED-BASED) *Total amount:* $13,890,011 (21% federal, 18% state, 58% institutional, 3% external sources). *Receiving aid:* Freshmen: 84% (316); all full-time undergraduates: 79% (1,236). *Average award:* Freshmen: $13,978; Undergraduates: $11,705. *Scholarships, grants, and awards:* Federal Pell, FSEOG, state, private, college/university gift aid from institutional funds.
GIFT AID (NON-NEED-BASED) *Total amount:* $1,053,757 (95% institutional, 5% external sources). *Receiving aid:* Freshmen: 29% (109). Undergraduates: 8% (132). *Average award:* Freshmen: $9254. Undergraduates: $8093. *Scholarships, grants, and awards by category:* Academic interests/achievement: general academic interests/achievements. *Tuition waivers:* Full or partial for employees or children of employees, senior citizens.
LOANS *Student loans:* $15,045,324 (90% need-based, 10% non-need-based). 82% of past graduating class borrowed through all loan programs. *Average indebtedness per student:* $31,855. *Average need-based loan:* Freshmen: $4009. Undergraduates: $4351. *Parent loans:* $1,470,498 (89% need-based, 11% non-need-based). *Programs:* FFEL (Subsidized and Unsubsidized Stafford, PLUS), Perkins, Federal Nursing.
WORK-STUDY *Federal work-study:* Total amount: $492,125; 324 jobs averaging $1518.
ATHLETIC AWARDS Total amount: $1,320,068 (81% need-based, 19% non-need-based).
APPLYING FOR FINANCIAL AID *Required financial aid form:* FAFSA. *Financial aid deadline (priority):* 3/15. *Notification date:* Continuous beginning 3/15.
CONTACT Financial Aid Office, Holy Family University, 9801 Frankford Avenue, Philadelphia, PA 19114-2094, 215-637-7700 Ext. 3233 or toll-free 800-637-1191. *Fax:* 215-599-1694. *E-mail:* finaid@holyfamily.edu.

HOLY NAMES UNIVERSITY
Oakland, CA

CONTACT Christina Miller, Director of Financial Aid, Holy Names University, 3500 Mountain Boulevard, Oakland, CA 94619-1699, 510-436-1327 or toll-free 800-430-1321. *Fax:* 510-436-1199. *E-mail:* miller@hnu.edu.

HOOD COLLEGE
Frederick, MD

Tuition & fees: $29,860	Average undergraduate aid package: $21,899

ABOUT THE INSTITUTION Independent, coed. 30 undergraduate majors. Federal methodology is used as a basis for awarding need-based institutional aid.
UNDERGRADUATE EXPENSES for 2010–11 *Comprehensive fee:* $39,761 includes full-time tuition ($29,440), mandatory fees ($420), and room and board ($9901). *College room only:* $5171. Room and board charges vary according to board plan. *Part-time tuition:* $850 per credit hour. *Part-time fees:* $140 per term. *Payment plan:* Installment.
FRESHMAN FINANCIAL AID (Fall 2009, est.) 231 applied for aid; of those 87% were deemed to have need. 96% of freshmen with need received aid; of those 26% had need fully met. *Average percent of need met:* 80% (excluding resources awarded to replace EFC). *Average financial aid package:* $23,557 (excluding resources awarded to replace EFC). 20% of all full-time freshmen had no need and received non-need-based gift aid.
UNDERGRADUATE FINANCIAL AID (Fall 2009, est.) 1,154 applied for aid; of those 90% were deemed to have need. 98% of undergraduates with need received aid; of those 23% had need fully met. *Average percent of need met:* 78% (excluding resources awarded to replace EFC). *Average financial aid package:* $21,899 (excluding resources awarded to replace EFC). 18% of all full-time undergraduates had no need and received non-need-based gift aid.
GIFT AID (NEED-BASED) *Total amount:* $18,640,125 (11% federal, 9% state, 76% institutional, 4% external sources). *Receiving aid:* Freshmen: 76% (192); all full-time undergraduates: 81% (1,009). *Average award:* Freshmen: $20,993; Undergraduates: $18,444. *Scholarships, grants, and awards:* Federal Pell, FSEOG, state, private, college/university gift aid from institutional funds.
GIFT AID (NON-NEED-BASED) *Total amount:* $4,562,176 (1% federal, 2% state, 80% institutional, 17% external sources). *Receiving aid:* Freshmen: 15% (38). Undergraduates: 15% (183). *Average award:* Freshmen: $21,810. Undergraduates: $18,175. *Scholarships, grants, and awards by category:* Academic interests/achievement: general academic interests/achievements. Creative arts/performance: creative writing. Special characteristics: children and siblings of alumni, children of faculty/staff, international students, siblings of current students. *Tuition waivers:* Full or partial for employees or children of employees, senior citizens.
LOANS *Student loans:* $7,675,866 (73% need-based, 27% non-need-based). 64% of past graduating class borrowed through all loan programs. *Average indebtedness per student:* $17,382. *Average need-based loan:* Freshmen: $3153. Undergraduates: $4242. *Parent loans:* $3,067,072 (28% need-based, 72% non-need-based). *Programs:* Federal Direct (Subsidized and Unsubsidized Stafford, PLUS), FFEL (Subsidized and Unsubsidized Stafford, PLUS), Perkins.
WORK-STUDY *Federal work-study:* Total amount: $262,518; 159 jobs averaging $1084. *State or other work-study/employment:* Total amount: $104,400 (22% need-based, 78% non-need-based). 63 part-time jobs averaging $1529.
APPLYING FOR FINANCIAL AID *Required financial aid form:* FAFSA. *Financial aid deadline (priority):* 2/15. *Notification date:* Continuous beginning 3/1. Students must reply by 5/1 or within 3 weeks of notification.
CONTACT Ms. Carol Schroyer, Director of Financial Aid, Hood College, 401 Rosemont Avenue, Frederick, MD 21701-8575, 301-696-3411 or toll-free 800-922-1599. *Fax:* 301-696-3812. *E-mail:* finaid@hood.edu.

HOPE COLLEGE
Holland, MI

Tuition & fees: $26,510	Average undergraduate aid package: $22,419

ABOUT THE INSTITUTION Independent religious, coed. 61 undergraduate majors. Federal methodology is used as a basis for awarding need-based institutional aid.
UNDERGRADUATE EXPENSES for 2010–11 *Comprehensive fee:* $34,620 includes full-time tuition ($26,350), mandatory fees ($160), and room and board ($8110). *College room only:* $3710. Room and board charges vary according to board plan. Part-time tuition and fees vary according to course load. *Payment plan:* Installment.
FRESHMAN FINANCIAL AID (Fall 2009, est.) 673 applied for aid; of those 79% were deemed to have need. 100% of freshmen with need received aid; of those 35% had need fully met. *Average percent of need met:* 84% (excluding

resources awarded to replace EFC). *Average financial aid package:* $22,978 (excluding resources awarded to replace EFC). 25% of all full-time freshmen had no need and received non-need-based gift aid.

UNDERGRADUATE FINANCIAL AID (Fall 2009, est.) 2,261 applied for aid; of those 83% were deemed to have need. 100% of undergraduates with need received aid; of those 35% had need fully met. *Average percent of need met:* 84% (excluding resources awarded to replace EFC). *Average financial aid package:* $22,419 (excluding resources awarded to replace EFC). 26% of all full-time undergraduates had no need and received non-need-based gift aid.

GIFT AID (NEED-BASED) *Total amount:* $23,890,441 (11% federal, 10% state, 79% institutional). *Receiving aid:* Freshmen: 56% (446); all full-time undergraduates: 53% (1,615). *Average award:* Freshmen: $18,368; Undergraduates: $17,144. *Scholarships, grants, and awards:* Federal Pell, FSEOG, state, private, college/university gift aid from institutional funds.

GIFT AID (NON-NEED-BASED) *Total amount:* $9,175,190 (1% federal, 8% state, 80% institutional, 11% external sources). *Receiving aid:* Freshmen: 51% (402). Undergraduates: 44% (1,322). *Average award:* Freshmen: $7579. Undergraduates: $7532. *Scholarships, grants, and awards by category:* Academic interests/achievement: general academic interests/achievements. Creative arts/performance: art/fine arts, creative writing, dance, music, theater/drama. Special characteristics: ethnic background. *Tuition waivers:* Full or partial for employees or children of employees.

LOANS *Student loans:* $11,977,021 (57% need-based, 43% non-need-based). 64% of past graduating class borrowed through all loan programs. *Average indebtedness per student:* $28,682. *Average need-based loan:* Freshmen: $3733. Undergraduates: $4612. *Parent loans:* $3,568,727 (100% non-need-based). *Programs:* Federal Direct (Subsidized and Unsubsidized Stafford, PLUS), Perkins, college/university.

WORK-STUDY *Federal work-study:* Total amount: $438,741; 287 jobs averaging $1121. *State or other work-study/employment:* Total amount: $1,464,414 (62% need-based, 38% non-need-based). 405 part-time jobs averaging $742.

APPLYING FOR FINANCIAL AID *Required financial aid forms:* FAFSA, institution's own form, business/farm supplement. *Financial aid deadline (priority):* 3/1. *Notification date:* Continuous beginning 3/15. Students must reply by 5/1 or within 2 weeks of notification.

CONTACT Ms. Phyllis Hooyman, Director of Financial Aid, Hope College, 141 East 12th Street, Holland, MI 49422-9000, 616-395-7765 or toll-free 800-968-7850. *Fax:* 616-395-7160. *E-mail:* hooyman@hope.edu.

HOPE INTERNATIONAL UNIVERSITY
Fullerton, CA

Tuition & fees: $23,565	Average undergraduate aid package: $14,597

ABOUT THE INSTITUTION Independent religious, coed. *Awards:* associate, bachelor's, and master's degrees and post-bachelor's and post-master's certificates. 19 undergraduate majors. *Total enrollment:* 1,059. Undergraduates: 794. Freshmen: 87. Federal methodology is used as a basis for awarding need-based institutional aid.

UNDERGRADUATE EXPENSES for 2009–10 *Application fee:* $40. *One-time required fee:* $300. *Comprehensive fee:* $30,965 includes full-time tuition ($22,220), mandatory fees ($1345), and room and board ($7400). *College room only:* $4300. Full-time tuition and fees vary according to course load, location, and program. Room and board charges vary according to board plan and student level. *Part-time tuition:* $825 per unit. *Part-time fees:* $825 per unit. Part-time tuition and fees vary according to course load, location, and program. *Payment plan:* Installment.

FRESHMAN FINANCIAL AID (Fall 2009, est.) 68 applied for aid; of those 46% were deemed to have need. 100% of freshmen with need received aid. *Average percent of need met:* 50% (excluding resources awarded to replace EFC). *Average financial aid package:* $17,152 (excluding resources awarded to replace EFC).

UNDERGRADUATE FINANCIAL AID (Fall 2009, est.) 321 applied for aid; of those 45% were deemed to have need. 100% of undergraduates with need received aid; of those 6% had need fully met. *Average percent of need met:* 43% (excluding resources awarded to replace EFC). *Average financial aid package:* $14,597 (excluding resources awarded to replace EFC). 2% of all full-time undergraduates had no need and received non-need-based gift aid.

GIFT AID (NEED-BASED) *Total amount:* $1,607,473 (44% federal, 41% state, 15% institutional). *Receiving aid:* Freshmen: 39% (31); all full-time undergradu-

ates: 37% (144). *Average award:* Freshmen: $10,327; Undergraduates: $9339. *Scholarships, grants, and awards:* Federal Pell, FSEOG, state, private, college/university gift aid from institutional funds.

GIFT AID (NON-NEED-BASED) *Total amount:* $1,919,537 (97% institutional, 3% external sources). *Receiving aid:* Freshmen: 25% (20). Undergraduates: 25% (98). *Average award:* Undergraduates: $5400. *Scholarships, grants, and awards by category:* Academic interests/achievement: 298 awards ($1,464,215 total): general academic interests/achievements. Special achievements/activities: 55 awards ($32,250 total): leadership. Special characteristics: 77 awards ($504,376 total): children of faculty/staff, international students, relatives of clergy, religious affiliation, spouses of current students. *Tuition waivers:* Full or partial for employees or children of employees.

LOANS *Student loans:* $2,743,143 (44% need-based, 56% non-need-based). 97% of past graduating class borrowed through all loan programs. *Average indebtedness per student:* $27,000. *Average need-based loan:* Freshmen: $3583. Undergraduates: $4688. *Parent loans:* $586,287 (100% non-need-based). *Programs:* Federal Direct (Subsidized and Unsubsidized Stafford, PLUS), Perkins.

WORK-STUDY *Federal work-study:* Total amount: $282,842; 50 jobs averaging $2000. *State or other work-study/employment:* Part-time jobs available.

ATHLETIC AWARDS Total amount: $1,670,672 (100% non-need-based).

APPLYING FOR FINANCIAL AID *Required financial aid forms:* FAFSA, institution's own form. *Financial aid deadline (priority):* 3/2. *Notification date:* Continuous beginning 4/1. Students must reply within 2 weeks of notification.

CONTACT Mrs. Shannon O'Shields, Director of Financial Aid, Hope International University, 2500 East Nutwood Avenue, Fullerton, CA 92831, 714-879-3901 or toll-free 800-762-1294. *Fax:* 714-681-7421. *E-mail:* soshields@hiu.edu.

HOUGHTON COLLEGE
Houghton, NY

Tuition & fees: $24,440	Average undergraduate aid package: $20,192

ABOUT THE INSTITUTION Independent Wesleyan, coed. 49 undergraduate majors. Federal methodology is used as a basis for awarding need-based institutional aid.

UNDERGRADUATE EXPENSES for 2009–10 *Comprehensive fee:* $31,440 includes full-time tuition ($24,440) and room and board ($7000). *College room only:* $3780. Room and board charges vary according to board plan and housing facility. *Part-time tuition:* $1025 per credit hour. *Payment plan:* Installment.

FRESHMAN FINANCIAL AID (Fall 2009, est.) 259 applied for aid; of those 89% were deemed to have need. 100% of freshmen with need received aid; of those 20% had need fully met. *Average percent of need met:* 79% (excluding resources awarded to replace EFC). *Average financial aid package:* $21,138 (excluding resources awarded to replace EFC). 19% of all full-time freshmen had no need and received non-need-based gift aid.

UNDERGRADUATE FINANCIAL AID (Fall 2009, est.) 1,109 applied for aid; of those 92% were deemed to have need. 100% of undergraduates with need received aid; of those 18% had need fully met. *Average percent of need met:* 78% (excluding resources awarded to replace EFC). *Average financial aid package:* $20,192 (excluding resources awarded to replace EFC). 15% of all full-time undergraduates had no need and received non-need-based gift aid.

GIFT AID (NEED-BASED) *Total amount:* $12,602,715 (19% federal, 10% state, 66% institutional, 5% external sources). *Receiving aid:* Freshmen: 81% (230); all full-time undergraduates: 81% (1,007). *Average award:* Freshmen: $15,549; Undergraduates: $14,050. *Scholarships, grants, and awards:* Federal Pell, FSEOG, state, private, college/university gift aid from institutional funds, United Negro College Fund.

GIFT AID (NON-NEED-BASED) *Total amount:* $2,250,619 (1% federal, 2% state, 83% institutional, 14% external sources). *Receiving aid:* Freshmen: 12% (35). Undergraduates: 9% (115). *Average award:* Freshmen: $9091. Undergraduates: $8825. *Scholarships, grants, and awards by category:* Academic interests/achievement: 664 awards ($3,181,850 total): general academic interests/achievements. Creative arts/performance: 104 awards ($289,970 total): art/fine arts, music. Special achievements/activities: 333 awards ($254,368 total): religious involvement. Special characteristics: 648 awards ($2,628,740 total): children and siblings of alumni, children of faculty/staff, international students, local/state students, relatives of clergy, religious affiliation, siblings of current students. *Tuition waivers:* Full or partial for employees or children of employees.

LOANS *Student loans:* $9,254,667 (73% need-based, 27% non-need-based). 95% of past graduating class borrowed through all loan programs. *Average*

indebtedness per student: $28,334. **Average need-based loan:** Freshmen: $4482. Undergraduates: $5316. **Parent loans:** $3,395,188 (24% need-based, 76% non-need-based). **Programs:** FFEL (Subsidized and Unsubsidized Stafford, PLUS), Perkins, college/university, alternative loans.

WORK-STUDY Federal work-study: Total amount: $1,528,729; 749 jobs averaging $1978. **State or other work-study/employment:** Total amount: $91,125 (100% non-need-based). 41 part-time jobs averaging $2140.

ATHLETIC AWARDS Total amount: $532,505 (71% need-based, 29% non-need-based).

APPLYING FOR FINANCIAL AID Required financial aid forms: FAFSA, state aid form. **Financial aid deadline (priority):** 3/1. **Notification date:** Continuous beginning 3/15. Students must reply by 5/1 or within 4 weeks of notification.

CONTACT Mr. Troy Martin, Director of Financial Aid, Houghton College, One Willard Avenue, Houghton, NY 14744, 585-567-9328 or toll-free 800-777-2556. Fax: 585-567-9610. E-mail: troy.martin@houghton.edu.

HOUSTON BAPTIST UNIVERSITY
Houston, TX

Tuition & fees: $23,180	Average undergraduate aid package: $17,712

ABOUT THE INSTITUTION Independent Baptist, coed. 65 undergraduate majors. Federal methodology is used as a basis for awarding need-based institutional aid.

UNDERGRADUATE EXPENSES for 2010–11 Comprehensive fee: $30,155 includes full-time tuition ($21,970), mandatory fees ($1210), and room and board ($6975). Room and board charges vary according to board plan and housing facility. **Part-time tuition:** $750 per semester hour. Part-time tuition and fees vary according to course load. **Payment plan:** Installment.

FRESHMAN FINANCIAL AID (Fall 2009, est.) 464 applied for aid; of those 89% were deemed to have need. 100% of freshmen with need received aid; of those 34% had need fully met. **Average percent of need met:** 85% (excluding resources awarded to replace EFC). **Average financial aid package:** $23,016 (excluding resources awarded to replace EFC). 14% of all full-time freshmen had no need and received non-need-based gift aid.

UNDERGRADUATE FINANCIAL AID (Fall 2009, est.) 1,533 applied for aid; of those 90% were deemed to have need. 99% of undergraduates with need received aid; of those 30% had need fully met. **Average percent of need met:** 83% (excluding resources awarded to replace EFC). **Average financial aid package:** $17,712 (excluding resources awarded to replace EFC). 5% of all full-time undergraduates had no need and received non-need-based gift aid.

GIFT AID (NEED-BASED) Total amount: $17,553,448 (32% federal, 21% state, 46% institutional, 1% external sources). **Receiving aid:** Freshmen: 64% (348); all full-time undergraduates: 58% (1,167). **Average award:** Freshmen: $6228; Undergraduates: $7266. **Scholarships, grants, and awards:** Federal Pell, FSEOG, state, private, college/university gift aid from institutional funds.

GIFT AID (NON-NEED-BASED) Total amount: $796,649 (97% institutional, 3% external sources). **Receiving aid:** Freshmen: 63% (346). Undergraduates: 52% (1,048). **Average award:** Freshmen: $3758. Undergraduates: $3749. **Scholarships, grants, and awards by category:** Academic interests/achievement: 1,101 awards ($9,393,874 total): general academic interests/achievements, health fields, religion/biblical studies. Creative arts/performance: 45 awards ($100,500 total): art/fine arts, debating, music. Special achievements/activities: 136 awards ($227,149 total): cheerleading/drum major, community service, leadership, religious involvement. Special characteristics: 37 awards ($510,724 total): children of faculty/staff, relatives of clergy. **Tuition waivers:** Full or partial for employees or children of employees.

LOANS Student loans: $11,133,990 (93% need-based, 7% non-need-based). **Average need-based loan:** Freshmen: $2703. Undergraduates: $1263. **Parent loans:** $5,502,069 (83% need-based, 17% non-need-based). **Programs:** Federal Direct (Subsidized and Unsubsidized Stafford, PLUS), FFEL (Subsidized and Unsubsidized Stafford, PLUS).

WORK-STUDY Federal work-study: Total amount: $2,080,877; 780 jobs available. **State or other work-study/employment:** Part-time jobs available.

ATHLETIC AWARDS Total amount: $4,338,220 (97% need-based, 3% non-need-based).

APPLYING FOR FINANCIAL AID Required financial aid form: FAFSA. **Financial aid deadline:** 4/15 (priority: 3/1). **Notification date:** Continuous beginning 3/10.

CONTACT Sherry Byrd, Director of Student Aid Programs, Houston Baptist University, 7502 Fondren Road, Houston, TX 77074-3298, 281-649-3389 or toll-free 800-696-3210. Fax: 281-649-3298. E-mail: financial_services@hbu.edu.

HOWARD PAYNE UNIVERSITY
Brownwood, TX

Tuition & fees: $19,950	Average undergraduate aid package: $15,273

ABOUT THE INSTITUTION Independent religious, coed. 65 undergraduate majors. Federal methodology is used as a basis for awarding need-based institutional aid.

UNDERGRADUATE EXPENSES for 2010–11 Comprehensive fee: $25,644 includes full-time tuition ($18,850), mandatory fees ($1100), and room and board ($5694). **College room only:** $2280. Full-time tuition and fees vary according to location and program. Room and board charges vary according to board plan and housing facility. **Part-time tuition:** $575 per credit hour. Part-time tuition and fees vary according to location and program. **Payment plans:** Guaranteed tuition, installment.

FRESHMAN FINANCIAL AID (Fall 2009, est.) 199 applied for aid; of those 88% were deemed to have need. 100% of freshmen with need received aid; of those 38% had need fully met. **Average percent of need met:** 88% (excluding resources awarded to replace EFC). **Average financial aid package:** $16,982 (excluding resources awarded to replace EFC). 16% of all full-time freshmen had no need and received non-need-based gift aid.

UNDERGRADUATE FINANCIAL AID (Fall 2009, est.) 823 applied for aid; of those 89% were deemed to have need. 100% of undergraduates with need received aid; of those 35% had need fully met. **Average percent of need met:** 86% (excluding resources awarded to replace EFC). **Average financial aid package:** $15,273 (excluding resources awarded to replace EFC). 18% of all full-time undergraduates had no need and received non-need-based gift aid.

GIFT AID (NEED-BASED) Total amount: $6,727,269 (29% federal, 22% state, 45% institutional, 4% external sources). **Receiving aid:** Freshmen: 84% (175); all full-time undergraduates: 77% (720). **Average award:** Freshmen: $13,181; Undergraduates: $10,858. **Scholarships, grants, and awards:** Federal Pell, FSEOG, state, private, college/university gift aid from institutional funds.

GIFT AID (NON-NEED-BASED) Total amount: $2,730,442 (93% institutional, 7% external sources). **Receiving aid:** Freshmen: 17% (36). Undergraduates: 11% (103). **Average award:** Freshmen: $6896. Undergraduates: $6166. **Scholarships, grants, and awards by category:** Academic interests/achievement: biological sciences, business, communication, education, English, general academic interests/achievements, mathematics, physical sciences, premedicine, religion/biblical studies, social sciences. Creative arts/performance: art/fine arts, music, theater/drama. Special achievements/activities: community service, leadership, religious involvement. Special characteristics: children and siblings of alumni, children of faculty/staff, local/state students, relatives of clergy, religious affiliation. **Tuition waivers:** Full or partial for employees or children of employees, senior citizens.

LOANS Student loans: $5,853,187 (55% need-based, 45% non-need-based). 75% of past graduating class borrowed through all loan programs. Average indebtedness per student: $28,400. **Average need-based loan:** Freshmen: $3022. Undergraduates: $3927. **Parent loans:** $734,053 (24% need-based, 76% non-need-based). **Programs:** Federal Direct (Subsidized and Unsubsidized Stafford, PLUS), Perkins, state.

WORK-STUDY Federal work-study: Total amount: $112,000; 105 jobs averaging $1217. **State or other work-study/employment:** Total amount: $12,500 (100% need-based). 9 part-time jobs averaging $1333.

APPLYING FOR FINANCIAL AID Required financial aid forms: FAFSA, institution's own form. **Financial aid deadline (priority):** 3/15. **Notification date:** Continuous beginning 2/1. Students must reply within 2 weeks of notification.

CONTACT Glenda Huff, Director of Financial Aid, Howard Payne University, 1000 Fisk Avenue, Brownwood, TX 76801, 325-649-8014 or toll-free 800-880-4478. Fax: 325-649-8973. E-mail: ghuff@hputx.edu.

HOWARD UNIVERSITY
Washington, DC

ABOUT THE INSTITUTION Independent, coed. **Awards:** bachelor's and master's degrees and post-master's certificates. 64 undergraduate majors. **Total enrollment:** 10,288. Undergraduates: 6,969.

GIFT AID (NEED-BASED) *Scholarships, grants, and awards:* Federal Pell, FSEOG, state, private, college/university gift aid from institutional funds, Federal Nursing.

GIFT AID (NON-NEED-BASED) *Scholarships, grants, and awards by category:* Creative arts/performance: art/fine arts, dance, music.

LOANS *Programs:* Federal Direct (Subsidized and Unsubsidized Stafford, PLUS), FFEL (Subsidized and Unsubsidized Stafford, PLUS), Perkins, Federal Nursing, district, college/university.

WORK-STUDY *Federal work-study:* Total amount: $269,763; 440 jobs averaging $3559. *State or other work-study/employment:* 230 part-time jobs averaging $2087.

APPLYING FOR FINANCIAL AID *Required financial aid form:* FAFSA.

CONTACT Derek Kindle, Director of Financial Aid and Scholarships, Howard University, 2400 Sixth Street, NW, Washington, DC 20059-0002, 202-806-2850 or toll-free 800-HOWARD-U. *Fax:* 202-806-2818. *E-mail:* dkindle@howard.edu.

HUMBOLDT STATE UNIVERSITY
Arcata, CA

Tuition & fees (CA res): $5166	Average undergraduate aid package: $10,984

ABOUT THE INSTITUTION State-supported, coed. 72 undergraduate majors. Federal methodology is used as a basis for awarding need-based institutional aid.

UNDERGRADUATE EXPENSES for 2009–10 *Tuition, state resident:* full-time $0. *Tuition, nonresident:* full-time $14,094; part-time $372 per unit. *Required fees:* full-time $5166; $247 per unit. Full-time tuition and fees vary according to degree level. Part-time tuition and fees vary according to course load and degree level. *College room and board:* $9510; *Room only:* $4820. Room and board charges vary according to board plan and housing facility. *Payment plan:* Installment.

FRESHMAN FINANCIAL AID (Fall 2009, est.) 1,093 applied for aid; of those 74% were deemed to have need. 93% of freshmen with need received aid; of those 4% had need fully met. *Average percent of need met:* 71% (excluding resources awarded to replace EFC). *Average financial aid package:* $11,048 (excluding resources awarded to replace EFC). 6% of all full-time freshmen had no need and received non-need-based gift aid.

UNDERGRADUATE FINANCIAL AID (Fall 2009, est.) 4,781 applied for aid; of those 83% were deemed to have need. 96% of undergraduates with need received aid; of those 2% had need fully met. *Average percent of need met:* 71% (excluding resources awarded to replace EFC). *Average financial aid package:* $10,984 (excluding resources awarded to replace EFC). 3% of all full-time undergraduates had no need and received non-need-based gift aid.

GIFT AID (NEED-BASED) *Total amount:* $29,000,333 (48% federal, 15% state, 34% institutional, 3% external sources). *Receiving aid:* Freshmen: 44% (568); all full-time undergraduates: 48% (3,129). *Average award:* Freshmen: $9999; Undergraduates: $8560. *Scholarships, grants, and awards:* Federal Pell, FSEOG, state, private, college/university gift aid from institutional funds.

GIFT AID (NON-NEED-BASED) *Total amount:* $137,761 (9% institutional, 91% external sources). *Receiving aid:* Freshmen: 10% (136). Undergraduates: 4% (285). *Average award:* Freshmen: $1648. Undergraduates: $2011. *Scholarships, grants, and awards by category:* Academic interests/achievement: general academic interests/achievements. *Tuition waivers:* Full or partial for employees or children of employees.

LOANS *Student loans:* $28,637,909 (88% need-based, 12% non-need-based). 66% of past graduating class borrowed through all loan programs. *Average indebtedness per student:* $17,668. *Average need-based loan:* Freshmen: $3338. Undergraduates: $4248. *Parent loans:* $3,965,920 (11% need-based, 89% non-need-based). *Programs:* Federal Direct (Subsidized and Unsubsidized Stafford, PLUS), Perkins.

WORK-STUDY *Federal work-study:* Total amount: $1,152,214; 500 jobs averaging $2000.

ATHLETIC AWARDS Total amount: $326,865 (81% need-based, 19% non-need-based).

APPLYING FOR FINANCIAL AID *Required financial aid form:* FAFSA. *Financial aid deadline (priority):* 3/2. *Notification date:* Continuous beginning 3/7.

CONTACT Kim Coughlin-Lamphear, Director of Financial Aid, Humboldt State University, 1 Harpst Street, Arcata, CA 95521-8299, 707-826-4321. *E-mail:* coughlin@humboldt.edu.

HUMPHREYS COLLEGE
Stockton, CA

Tuition & fees: N/R	Average undergraduate aid package: N/A

ABOUT THE INSTITUTION Independent, coed. *Awards:* associate, bachelor's, and master's degrees. 11 undergraduate majors. *Total enrollment:* 756. Undergraduates: 669. Federal methodology is used as a basis for awarding need-based institutional aid.

GIFT AID (NEED-BASED) *Scholarships, grants, and awards:* Federal Pell, FSEOG, state.

GIFT AID (NON-NEED-BASED) *Scholarships, grants, and awards by category:* Academic interests/achievement: business, computer science, general academic interests/achievements. *Special achievements/activities:* community service. *Special characteristics:* ethnic background, members of minority groups.

LOANS *Programs:* FFEL (Subsidized and Unsubsidized Stafford, PLUS).

WORK-STUDY Federal work-study jobs available.

APPLYING FOR FINANCIAL AID *Required financial aid form:* FAFSA. *Financial aid deadline:* Continuous. *Notification date:* Continuous. Students must reply by 6/30.

CONTACT Rita Franco, Director of Financial Aid, Humphreys College, 6650 Inglewood Avenue, Stockton, CA 95207-3896, 209-478-0800. *Fax:* 209-235-2983.

HUNTER COLLEGE OF THE CITY UNIVERSITY OF NEW YORK
New York, NY

Tuition & fees (NY res): $4999	Average undergraduate aid package: $5092

ABOUT THE INSTITUTION State and locally supported, coed. 63 undergraduate majors. Federal methodology is used as a basis for awarding need-based institutional aid.

UNDERGRADUATE EXPENSES for 2009–10 *Tuition, state resident:* full-time $4600; part-time $195 per term. *Tuition, nonresident:* full-time $12,450; part-time $415 per term. *Required fees:* full-time $399; $183.50 per term. Full-time tuition and fees vary according to degree level and program. Part-time tuition and fees vary according to degree level and program. *College room and board:* Room only: $5500. *Payment plan:* Installment.

FRESHMAN FINANCIAL AID (Fall 2009, est.) 1,571 applied for aid; of those 78% were deemed to have need. 100% of freshmen with need received aid; of those 23% had need fully met. *Average percent of need met:* 77% (excluding resources awarded to replace EFC). *Average financial aid package:* $5241 (excluding resources awarded to replace EFC). 16% of all full-time freshmen had no need and received non-need-based gift aid.

UNDERGRADUATE FINANCIAL AID (Fall 2009, est.) 7,634 applied for aid; of those 83% were deemed to have need. 100% of undergraduates with need received aid; of those 16% had need fully met. *Average percent of need met:* 78% (excluding resources awarded to replace EFC). *Average financial aid package:* $5092 (excluding resources awarded to replace EFC). 7% of all full-time undergraduates had no need and received non-need-based gift aid.

GIFT AID (NEED-BASED) *Total amount:* $33,469,767 (50% federal, 47% state, 3% institutional). *Receiving aid:* Freshmen: 62% (1,222); all full-time undergraduates: 57% (6,313). *Average award:* Freshmen: $5599; Undergraduates: $4141. *Scholarships, grants, and awards:* Federal Pell, FSEOG, state, private, college/university gift aid from institutional funds.

GIFT AID (NON-NEED-BASED) *Total amount:* $2,515,188 (55% institutional, 45% external sources). *Receiving aid:* Freshmen: 43% (846). Undergraduates: 20% (2,218). *Average award:* Freshmen: $2110. Undergraduates: $2368. *Scholarships, grants, and awards by category:* Academic interests/achievement: general academic interests/achievements.

LOANS *Student loans:* $4,478,506 (26% need-based, 74% non-need-based). 53% of past graduating class borrowed through all loan programs. *Average indebtedness per student:* $7500. *Average need-based loan:* Freshmen: $2746. Undergraduates: $3179. *Parent loans:* $3,038,020 (100% need-based). *Programs:* Federal Direct (Subsidized and Unsubsidized Stafford, PLUS), Perkins.

WORK-STUDY *Federal work-study:* Total amount: $1,376,919; jobs available.

APPLYING FOR FINANCIAL AID *Required financial aid forms:* FAFSA, state aid form. *Financial aid deadline (priority):* 4/1. *Notification date:* Continuous beginning 5/15.

CONTACT Aristalia Cortorreal Diaz, Director of Financial Aid, Hunter College of the City University of New York, 695 Park Avenue, New York, NY 10065-5085, 212-772-4400. *Fax:* 212-650-3666. *E-mail:* aristalia@hunter.cuny.edu.

HUNTINGDON COLLEGE
Montgomery, AL

Tuition & fees: $20,990   **Average undergraduate aid package: $14,949**

ABOUT THE INSTITUTION Independent United Methodist, coed. 28 undergraduate majors. Both federal and institutional methodology are used as a basis for awarding need-based institutional aid.

UNDERGRADUATE EXPENSES for 2010–11 *Comprehensive fee:* $28,990 includes full-time tuition ($19,990), mandatory fees ($1000), and room and board ($8000). Full-time tuition and fees vary according to course load, program, and student level. Room and board charges vary according to housing facility. *Part-time tuition:* $830 per credit hour. Part-time tuition and fees vary according to course load and program. *Payment plans:* Guaranteed tuition, deferred payment.

FRESHMAN FINANCIAL AID (Fall 2009, est.) 213 applied for aid; of those 90% were deemed to have need. 100% of freshmen with need received aid; of those 15% had need fully met. *Average percent of need met:* 73% (excluding resources awarded to replace EFC). *Average financial aid package:* $16,904 (excluding resources awarded to replace EFC). 19% of all full-time freshmen had no need and received non-need-based gift aid.

UNDERGRADUATE FINANCIAL AID (Fall 2009, est.) 690 applied for aid; of those 87% were deemed to have need. 100% of undergraduates with need received aid; of those 19% had need fully met. *Average percent of need met:* 74% (excluding resources awarded to replace EFC). *Average financial aid package:* $14,949 (excluding resources awarded to replace EFC). 27% of all full-time undergraduates had no need and received non-need-based gift aid.

GIFT AID (NEED-BASED) *Total amount:* $7,260,844 (21% federal, 2% state, 74% institutional, 3% external sources). *Receiving aid:* Freshmen: 81% (191); all full-time undergraduates: 69% (594). *Average award:* Freshmen: $14,071; Undergraduates: $12,025. *Scholarships, grants, and awards:* Federal Pell, FSEOG, state, private, college/university gift aid from institutional funds.

GIFT AID (NON-NEED-BASED) *Total amount:* $2,800,914 (2% state, 88% institutional, 10% external sources). *Receiving aid:* Freshmen: 10% (24). Undergraduates: 10% (84). *Average award:* Freshmen: $11,076. Undergraduates: $9324. *Scholarships, grants, and awards by category:* Academic interests/achievement: 73 awards ($460,294 total): biological sciences, computer science, general academic interests/achievements, mathematics. Creative arts/performance: 16 awards ($47,649 total): music, performing arts. Special achievements/activities: 18 awards ($151,941 total): cheerleading/drum major, community service, junior miss. Special characteristics: 347 awards ($2,933,962 total): children and siblings of alumni, children of faculty/staff, children of workers in trades, international students, local/state students, religious affiliation, spouses of current students, veterans, veterans' children. *Tuition waivers:* Full or partial for children of alumni, employees or children of employees.

LOANS *Student loans:* $4,911,742 (63% need-based, 37% non-need-based). 58% of past graduating class borrowed through all loan programs. *Average indebtedness per student:* $14,034. *Average need-based loan:* Freshmen: $2983. Undergraduates: $3491. *Parent loans:* $1,108,607 (43% need-based, 57% non-need-based). *Programs:* FFEL (Subsidized and Unsubsidized Stafford, PLUS), Perkins.

WORK-STUDY *Federal work-study:* Total amount: $216,759; 221 jobs averaging $934.

APPLYING FOR FINANCIAL AID *Required financial aid form:* institution's own form. *Financial aid deadline (priority):* 4/15. *Notification date:* Continuous beginning 3/1. Students must reply by 5/1 or within 2 weeks of notification.

CONTACT Ms. Belinda Goris Duett, Director of Student Financial Services and Financial Aid, Huntingdon College, 1500 East Fairview Avenue, Montgomery, AL 36106-2148, 334-833-4519 or toll-free 800-763-0313. *Fax:* 334-833-4235. *E-mail:* bduett@huntingdon.edu.

HUNTINGTON UNIVERSITY
Huntington, IN

Tuition & fees: $22,330   **Average undergraduate aid package: $16,098**

ABOUT THE INSTITUTION Independent religious, coed. 57 undergraduate majors. Both federal and institutional methodology are used as a basis for awarding need-based institutional aid.

UNDERGRADUATE EXPENSES for 2010–11 *Comprehensive fee:* $29,760 includes full-time tuition ($21,850), mandatory fees ($480), and room and board ($7430). Full-time tuition and fees vary according to course load, degree level, and program. Room and board charges vary according to board plan. *Part-time tuition:* $650 per credit hour. *Part-time fees:* $240 per term. Part-time tuition and fees vary according to course load, degree level, and program. *Payment plan:* Installment.

FRESHMAN FINANCIAL AID (Fall 2009, est.) 234 applied for aid; of those 90% were deemed to have need. 100% of freshmen with need received aid; of those 9% had need fully met. *Average percent of need met:* 74% (excluding resources awarded to replace EFC). *Average financial aid package:* $17,010 (excluding resources awarded to replace EFC). 18% of all full-time freshmen had no need and received non-need-based gift aid.

UNDERGRADUATE FINANCIAL AID (Fall 2009, est.) 900 applied for aid; of those 86% were deemed to have need. 100% of undergraduates with need received aid; of those 8% had need fully met. *Average percent of need met:* 72% (excluding resources awarded to replace EFC). *Average financial aid package:* $16,098 (excluding resources awarded to replace EFC). 16% of all full-time undergraduates had no need and received non-need-based gift aid.

GIFT AID (NEED-BASED) *Total amount:* $8,855,794 (18% federal, 13% state, 65% institutional, 4% external sources). *Receiving aid:* Freshmen: 83% (206); all full-time undergraduates: 70% (726). *Average award:* Freshmen: $11,888; Undergraduates: $12,852. *Scholarships, grants, and awards:* Federal Pell, FSEOG, state, private, college/university gift aid from institutional funds.

GIFT AID (NON-NEED-BASED) *Total amount:* $663,810 (89% institutional, 11% external sources). *Receiving aid:* Freshmen: 27% (68). Undergraduates: 25% (258). *Average award:* Freshmen: $7115. Undergraduates: $7555. *Scholarships, grants, and awards by category:* Academic interests/achievement: biological sciences, business, communication, computer science, education, general academic interests/achievements, mathematics. Creative arts/performance: applied art and design, art/fine arts, cinema/film/broadcasting, creative writing, journalism/publications, music, theater/drama. Special achievements/activities: cheerleading/drum major, religious involvement. Special characteristics: children and siblings of alumni, children of current students, children of faculty/staff, ethnic background, international students, local/state students, parents of current students, previous college experience, relatives of clergy, religious affiliation, siblings of current students, spouses of current students, veterans, veterans' children. *Tuition waivers:* Full or partial for employees or children of employees.

LOANS *Student loans:* $6,612,595 (75% need-based, 25% non-need-based). 55% of past graduating class borrowed through all loan programs. *Average indebtedness per student:* $27,541. *Average need-based loan:* Freshmen: $3550. Undergraduates: $4495. *Parent loans:* $1,158,440 (40% need-based, 60% non-need-based). *Programs:* FFEL (Subsidized and Unsubsidized Stafford, PLUS), Perkins.

WORK-STUDY *Federal work-study:* Total amount: $327,800; 160 jobs averaging $2051.

ATHLETIC AWARDS Total amount: $805,754 (52% need-based, 48% non-need-based).

APPLYING FOR FINANCIAL AID *Required financial aid form:* FAFSA. *Financial aid deadline (priority):* 3/1. *Notification date:* Continuous beginning 2/15. Students must reply by 5/1 or within 2 weeks of notification.

CONTACT Mrs. Sharon Woods, Director of Financial Aid, Huntington University, 2303 College Avenue, Huntington, IN 46750, 260-359-4014 or toll-free 800-642-6493. *Fax:* 260-358-3699. *E-mail:* swoods@huntington.edu.

HUSSON UNIVERSITY
Bangor, ME

Tuition & fees: $13,450   **Average undergraduate aid package: $11,462**

ABOUT THE INSTITUTION Independent, coed. 31 undergraduate majors. Federal methodology is used as a basis for awarding need-based institutional aid.

UNDERGRADUATE EXPENSES for 2010–11 *Comprehensive fee:* $20,689 includes full-time tuition ($13,140), mandatory fees ($310), and room and board ($7239). Full-time tuition and fees vary according to class time. *Part-time tuition:* $438 per credit hour. Part-time tuition and fees vary according to class time and course load. *Payment plans:* Tuition prepayment, installment.

FRESHMAN FINANCIAL AID (Fall 2009, est.) 522 applied for aid; of those 91% were deemed to have need. 100% of freshmen with need received aid; of those 6% had need fully met. *Average percent of need met:* 75% (excluding resources awarded to replace EFC). *Average financial aid package:* $12,187 (excluding resources awarded to replace EFC). 9% of all full-time freshmen had no need and received non-need-based gift aid.

UNDERGRADUATE FINANCIAL AID (Fall 2009, est.) 1,782 applied for aid; of those 87% were deemed to have need. 99% of undergraduates with need received aid; of those 11% had need fully met. *Average percent of need met:* 73% (excluding resources awarded to replace EFC). *Average financial aid package:* $11,462 (excluding resources awarded to replace EFC). 6% of all full-time undergraduates had no need and received non-need-based gift aid.

GIFT AID (NEED-BASED) *Total amount:* $11,228,688 (46% federal, 9% state, 40% institutional, 5% external sources). *Receiving aid:* Freshmen: 78% (422); all full-time undergraduates: 75% (1,357). *Average award:* Freshmen: $8979; Undergraduates: $7963. *Scholarships, grants, and awards:* Federal Pell, FSEOG, state, private, college/university gift aid from institutional funds.

GIFT AID (NON-NEED-BASED) *Total amount:* $613,850 (84% institutional, 16% external sources). *Receiving aid:* Freshmen: 2% (10). Undergraduates: 3% (50). *Average award:* Freshmen: $3446. Undergraduates: $3687. *Scholarships, grants, and awards by category:* Academic interests/achievement: business, computer science, education, general academic interests/achievements, health fields. Special achievements/activities: general special achievements/activities, leadership. Special characteristics: children of union members/company employees. *Tuition waivers:* Full or partial for employees or children of employees, senior citizens.

LOANS *Student loans:* $14,615,166 (70% need-based, 30% non-need-based). 88% of past graduating class borrowed through all loan programs. *Average indebtedness per student:* $33,010. *Average need-based loan:* Freshmen: $3079. Undergraduates: $4076. *Parent loans:* $1,591,596 (26% need-based, 74% non-need-based). *Programs:* Federal Direct (Subsidized and Unsubsidized Stafford, PLUS), FFEL (Subsidized and Unsubsidized Stafford, PLUS), Perkins, state, alternative loans.

WORK-STUDY *Federal work-study:* Total amount: $937,184; 778 jobs averaging $1490.

APPLYING FOR FINANCIAL AID *Required financial aid form:* FAFSA. *Financial aid deadline (priority):* 4/15. *Notification date:* Continuous. Students must reply by 5/1 or within 2 weeks of notification.

CONTACT Linda B. Conant, Director of Financial Aid, Husson University, One College Circle, Bangor, ME 04401, 207-941-7156 or toll-free 800-4-HUSSON. *Fax:* 207-973-1038. *E-mail:* conantl@husson.edu.

HUSTON-TILLOTSON UNIVERSITY
Austin, TX

Tuition & fees: $11,434	Average undergraduate aid package: $14,885

ABOUT THE INSTITUTION Independent interdenominational, coed. 20 undergraduate majors. Federal methodology is used as a basis for awarding need-based institutional aid.

UNDERGRADUATE EXPENSES for 2009–10 *Comprehensive fee:* $18,124 includes full-time tuition ($9450), mandatory fees ($1984), and room and board ($6690). *College room only:* $2880. Full-time tuition and fees vary according to course load. Room and board charges vary according to housing facility. *Part-time tuition:* $315 per credit hour. *Part-time fees:* $138 per credit hour. Part-time tuition and fees vary according to course load. *Payment plan:* Deferred payment.

FRESHMAN FINANCIAL AID (Fall 2009, est.) 229 applied for aid; of those 91% were deemed to have need. 100% of freshmen with need received aid; of those 30% had need fully met. *Average percent of need met:* 82% (excluding resources awarded to replace EFC). *Average financial aid package:* $15,162 (excluding resources awarded to replace EFC).

UNDERGRADUATE FINANCIAL AID (Fall 2009, est.) 775 applied for aid; of those 99% were deemed to have need. 100% of undergraduates with need received aid; of those 21% had need fully met. *Average percent of need met:* 78% (excluding resources awarded to replace EFC). *Average financial aid package:* $14,885 (excluding resources awarded to replace EFC). 1% of all full-time undergraduates had no need and received non-need-based gift aid.

GIFT AID (NEED-BASED) *Total amount:* $4,222,542 (71% federal, 28% state, 1% institutional). *Receiving aid:* Freshmen: 45% (117); all full-time undergraduates: 52% (460). *Average award:* Freshmen: $10,025; Undergraduates: $9772. *Scholarships, grants, and awards:* Federal Pell, FSEOG, state, private, college/university gift aid from institutional funds.

GIFT AID (NON-NEED-BASED) *Total amount:* $408,000 (100% external sources). *Receiving aid:* Freshmen: 27% (71). Undergraduates: 20% (175). *Scholarships, grants, and awards by category:* Academic interests/achievement: general academic interests/achievements. Creative arts/performance: music. Special characteristics: general special characteristics. *Tuition waivers:* Full or partial for employees or children of employees.

LOANS *Student loans:* $5,848,730 (45% need-based, 55% non-need-based). *Average need-based loan:* Freshmen: $3331. Undergraduates: $4875. *Parent loans:* $249,076 (100% non-need-based). *Programs:* FFEL (Subsidized and Unsubsidized Stafford, PLUS), alternative loans.

WORK-STUDY *Federal work-study:* Total amount: $122,312; jobs available. *State or other work-study/employment:* Total amount: $6411 (100% need-based). Part-time jobs available.

ATHLETIC AWARDS Total amount: $600,000 (100% non-need-based).

APPLYING FOR FINANCIAL AID *Required financial aid forms:* FAFSA, institution's own form. *Financial aid deadline (priority):* 3/15. *Notification date:* Continuous. Students must reply within 2 weeks of notification.

CONTACT Antonio Holloway, Director of Financial Aid, Huston-Tillotson University, 900 Chicon Street, Austin, TX 78702, 512-505-3031. *Fax:* 512-505-3192. *E-mail:* aholloway@htu.edu.

IDAHO STATE UNIVERSITY
Pocatello, ID

Tuition & fees (ID res): $4968	Average undergraduate aid package: N/A

ABOUT THE INSTITUTION State-supported, coed. 106 undergraduate majors. Federal methodology is used as a basis for awarding need-based institutional aid.

UNDERGRADUATE EXPENSES for 2009–10 *One-time required fee:* $40. *Tuition, state resident:* full-time $3318; part-time $253 per credit hour. *Tuition, nonresident:* full-time $13,120; part-time $393 per credit hour. *Required fees:* full-time $1650. Full-time tuition and fees vary according to course load, program, and reciprocity agreements. Part-time tuition and fees vary according to course load and reciprocity agreements. *College room and board:* $5050; *Room only:* $2350. Room and board charges vary according to board plan and housing facility. *Payment plan:* Deferred payment.

GIFT AID (NEED-BASED) *Scholarships, grants, and awards:* Federal Pell, FSEOG, state, private, college/university gift aid from institutional funds, Federal Nursing.

GIFT AID (NON-NEED-BASED) *Scholarships, grants, and awards by category:* Academic interests/achievement: 1,554 awards ($4,071,315 total): biological sciences, business, communication, computer science, education, engineering/technologies, English, foreign languages, general academic interests/achievements, health fields, home economics, humanities, international studies, mathematics, military science, physical sciences, premedicine, religion/biblical studies, social sciences. Creative arts/performance: 203 awards ($124,340 total): art/fine arts, dance, debating, music, performing arts, theater/drama. Special achievements/activities: 46 awards ($86,822 total): cheerleading/drum major, general special achievements/activities, junior miss, leadership, memberships, rodeo. Special characteristics: 901 awards ($453,536 total): children and siblings of alumni, children of faculty/staff, ethnic background, first-generation college students, general special characteristics, handicapped students, international students, local/state students, members of minority groups, out-of-state students, previous college experience. *Tuition waivers:* Full or partial for employees or children of employees, senior citizens.

LOANS *Programs:* Federal Direct (Subsidized and Unsubsidized Stafford, PLUS), Perkins, Federal Nursing.

WORK-STUDY Federal work-study jobs available. *State or other work-study/employment:* Part-time jobs available.

APPLYING FOR FINANCIAL AID *Required financial aid forms:* FAFSA, university application for admission. *Financial aid deadline:* 3/1. *Notification date:* Continuous beginning 4/1.

CONTACT Mr. Kent Larson, Director of Financial Aid, Idaho State University, 921 South 8th Avenue, Stop 8077, Pocatello, ID 83209, 208-282-2981. *Fax:* 208-282-4755. *E-mail:* larskent@isu.edu.

ILLINOIS COLLEGE
Jacksonville, IL

Tuition & fees: $21,300	Average undergraduate aid package: $18,014

ABOUT THE INSTITUTION Independent interdenominational, coed. 44 undergraduate majors. Federal methodology is used as a basis for awarding need-based institutional aid.

UNDERGRADUATE EXPENSES for 2009–10 *Comprehensive fee:* $28,900 includes full-time tuition ($20,900), mandatory fees ($400), and room and board ($7600). *College room only:* $3800. Full-time tuition and fees vary according to student level. Room and board charges vary according to board plan and housing facility. *Part-time tuition:* $700 per semester hour. *Part-time fees:* $200 per year. *Payment plan:* Installment.

FRESHMAN FINANCIAL AID (Fall 2009, est.) 200 applied for aid; of those 87% were deemed to have need. 100% of freshmen with need received aid; of those 30% had need fully met. *Average percent of need met:* 88% (excluding resources awarded to replace EFC). *Average financial aid package:* $18,322 (excluding resources awarded to replace EFC). 19% of all full-time freshmen had no need and received non-need-based gift aid.

UNDERGRADUATE FINANCIAL AID (Fall 2009, est.) 789 applied for aid; of those 89% were deemed to have need. 100% of undergraduates with need received aid; of those 29% had need fully met. *Average percent of need met:* 89% (excluding resources awarded to replace EFC). *Average financial aid package:* $18,014 (excluding resources awarded to replace EFC). 17% of all full-time undergraduates had no need and received non-need-based gift aid.

GIFT AID (NEED-BASED) *Total amount:* $9,361,013 (13% federal, 17% state, 67% institutional, 3% external sources). *Receiving aid:* Freshmen: 80% (174); all full-time undergraduates: 81% (696). *Average award:* Freshmen: $14,346; Undergraduates: $13,434. *Scholarships, grants, and awards:* Federal Pell, FSEOG, state, private, college/university gift aid from institutional funds.

GIFT AID (NON-NEED-BASED) *Total amount:* $1,930,464 (1% state, 95% institutional, 4% external sources). *Receiving aid:* Freshmen: 14% (30). Undergraduates: 12% (103). *Average award:* Freshmen: $9852. Undergraduates: $8805. *Scholarships, grants, and awards by category: Academic interests/ achievement:* general academic interests/achievements. *Creative arts/performance:* music, theater/drama. *Special characteristics:* 120 awards ($919,305 total): children of faculty/staff, international students, previous college experience. *Tuition waivers:* Full or partial for employees or children of employees.

LOANS *Student loans:* $6,073,645 (61% need-based, 39% non-need-based). 76% of past graduating class borrowed through all loan programs. *Average indebtedness per student:* $21,258. *Average need-based loan:* Freshmen: $3864. Undergraduates: $4660. *Parent loans:* $1,137,558 (20% need-based, 80% non-need-based). *Programs:* Federal Direct (Subsidized and Unsubsidized Stafford, PLUS), Perkins.

WORK-STUDY *Federal work-study:* Total amount: $536,656; 427 jobs averaging $1792. *State or other work-study/employment:* Part-time jobs available.

APPLYING FOR FINANCIAL AID *Required financial aid form:* FAFSA. *Financial aid deadline (priority):* 3/1. *Notification date:* Continuous beginning 3/7. Students must reply within 2 weeks of notification.

CONTACT Kate Taylor, Director of Financial Aid, Illinois College, 1101 West College Avenue, Jacksonville, IL 62650-2299, 217-245-3035 or toll-free 866-464-5265. *Fax:* 217-245-3274. *E-mail:* finaid@hilltop.ic.edu.

THE ILLINOIS INSTITUTE OF ART–CHICAGO
Chicago, IL

UNDERGRADUATE EXPENSES Tuition cost varies by program. Prospective students should contact the school for current tuition costs. Other charges include a starting kit for all first-quarter students. Kits vary in price, depending on the program of study.

CONTACT Financial Aid Office, The Illinois Institute of Art–Chicago, 350 North Orleans Street, Suite 136, Chicago, IL 60654-1593, 800-351-3450.

THE ILLINOIS INSTITUTE OF ART–SCHAUMBURG
Schaumburg, IL

UNDERGRADUATE EXPENSES Tuition cost varies by program. Prospective students should contact the school for current tuition costs. Other charges include a starting kit for all first-quarter students. Kits vary in price, depending on the program of study.

CONTACT Financial Aid Office, The Illinois Institute of Art–Schaumburg, 1000 North Plaza Drive, Suite 100, Schaumburg, IL 60173, 847-619-3450 or toll-free 800-314-3450.

ILLINOIS INSTITUTE OF TECHNOLOGY
Chicago, IL

Tuition & fees: $32,443	Average undergraduate aid package: $24,602

ABOUT THE INSTITUTION Independent, coed. 28 undergraduate majors. Federal methodology is used as a basis for awarding need-based institutional aid.

UNDERGRADUATE EXPENSES for 2010–11 *Comprehensive fee:* $42,537 includes full-time tuition ($31,363), mandatory fees ($1080), and room and board ($10,094). *College room only:* $5384. Full-time tuition and fees vary according to student level. Room and board charges vary according to board plan and housing facility. *Part-time tuition:* $975 per credit hour. *Part-time fees:* $8.50 per credit hour; $100 per term. Part-time tuition and fees vary according to student level. *Payment plan:* Installment.

FRESHMAN FINANCIAL AID (Fall 2009, est.) 370 applied for aid; of those 89% were deemed to have need. 100% of freshmen with need received aid; of those 27% had need fully met. *Average percent of need met:* 84% (excluding resources awarded to replace EFC). *Average financial aid package:* $27,509 (excluding resources awarded to replace EFC). 27% of all full-time freshmen had no need and received non-need-based gift aid.

UNDERGRADUATE FINANCIAL AID (Fall 2009, est.) 1,677 applied for aid; of those 93% were deemed to have need. 100% of undergraduates with need received aid; of those 18% had need fully met. *Average percent of need met:* 75% (excluding resources awarded to replace EFC). *Average financial aid package:* $24,602 (excluding resources awarded to replace EFC). 36% of all full-time undergraduates had no need and received non-need-based gift aid.

GIFT AID (NEED-BASED) *Total amount:* $28,647,765 (17% federal, 9% state, 73% institutional, 1% external sources). *Receiving aid:* Freshmen: 72% (328); all full-time undergraduates: 62% (1,545). *Average award:* Freshmen: $21,652; Undergraduates: $18,411. *Scholarships, grants, and awards:* Federal Pell, FSEOG, state, private, college/university gift aid from institutional funds.

GIFT AID (NON-NEED-BASED) *Total amount:* $14,095,277 (5% federal, 94% institutional, 1% external sources). *Receiving aid:* Freshmen: 14% (64). Undergraduates: 7% (175). *Average award:* Freshmen: $13,058. Undergraduates: $12,584. *Scholarships, grants, and awards by category: Academic interests/achievement:* 1,855 awards ($23,426,681 total): architecture, business, engineering/technologies, foreign languages, general academic interests/achievements, health fields. *Special achievements/activities:* 455 awards ($2,903,923 total): community service, general special achievements/activities, hobbies/interests, leadership, memberships. *Special characteristics:* 489 awards ($5,225,491 total): children and siblings of alumni, children of faculty/staff, children of public servants, ethnic background, general special characteristics, international students, members of minority groups, previous college experience, veterans, veterans' children. *Tuition waivers:* Full or partial for employees or children of employees.

LOANS *Student loans:* $12,833,355 (78% need-based, 22% non-need-based). *Average need-based loan:* Freshmen: $3511. Undergraduates: $4555. *Parent loans:* $3,984,015 (41% need-based, 59% non-need-based). *Programs:* FFEL (Subsidized and Unsubsidized Stafford, PLUS), Perkins, college/university.

WORK-STUDY *Federal work-study:* Total amount: $2,004,718; 847 jobs averaging $2367. *State or other work-study/employment:* Part-time jobs available.

ATHLETIC AWARDS Total amount: $876,090 (39% need-based, 61% non-need-based).

APPLYING FOR FINANCIAL AID *Required financial aid form:* FAFSA. *Financial aid deadline (priority):* 4/15. *Notification date:* Continuous beginning 3/5.

CONTACT Nareth Phin, Assistant Director of Financial Aid, Illinois Institute of Technology, 3300 South Federal Street, Chicago, IL 60616, 312-567-5730 or toll-free 800-448-2329 (out-of-state). *Fax:* 312-567-3982. *E-mail:* finaid@iit.edu.

CONTACT Mr. David Krueger, Assistant Director of Financial Aid, Illinois State University, Campus Box 2320, Normal, IL 61790-2320, 309-438-2231 or toll-free 800-366-2478 (in-state). *Fax:* 309-438-3755. *E-mail:* financialaid@illinoisitate.edu.

ILLINOIS STATE UNIVERSITY
Normal, IL

Tuition & fees (IL res): $10,471   **Average undergraduate aid package:** $11,678

ABOUT THE INSTITUTION State-supported, coed. 68 undergraduate majors. Federal methodology is used as a basis for awarding need-based institutional aid.

UNDERGRADUATE EXPENSES for 2009–10 *Tuition, state resident:* full-time $8220; part-time $276 per credit hour. *Tuition, nonresident:* full-time $14,310; part-time $477 per credit hour. *Required fees:* full-time $2251; $64.30 per credit hour or $964.50 per term. Full-time tuition and fees vary according to course load and degree level. Part-time tuition and fees vary according to course load and degree level. *College room and board:* $8093; *Room only:* $4190. Room and board charges vary according to board plan, housing facility, and location. *Payment plans:* Guaranteed tuition, installment.

FRESHMAN FINANCIAL AID (Fall 2009, est.) 2,535 applied for aid; of those 68% were deemed to have need. 93% of freshmen with need received aid; of those 41% had need fully met. *Average percent of need met:* 78% (excluding resources awarded to replace EFC). *Average financial aid package:* $11,528 (excluding resources awarded to replace EFC). 2% of all full-time freshmen had no need and received non-need-based gift aid.

UNDERGRADUATE FINANCIAL AID (Fall 2009, est.) 12,398 applied for aid; of those 77% were deemed to have need. 94% of undergraduates with need received aid; of those 40% had need fully met. *Average percent of need met:* 79% (excluding resources awarded to replace EFC). *Average financial aid package:* $11,678 (excluding resources awarded to replace EFC). 2% of all full-time undergraduates had no need and received non-need-based gift aid.

GIFT AID (NEED-BASED) *Total amount:* $46,288,919 (37% federal, 44% state, 17% institutional, 2% external sources). *Receiving aid:* Freshmen: 34% (1,029); all full-time undergraduates: 31% (5,268). *Average award:* Freshmen: $9134; Undergraduates: $8857. *Scholarships, grants, and awards:* Federal Pell, FSEOG, state, private, college/university gift aid from institutional funds, Federal Nursing.

GIFT AID (NON-NEED-BASED) *Total amount:* $7,107,649 (4% federal, 65% state, 20% institutional, 11% external sources). *Receiving aid:* Freshmen: 31% (939). Undergraduates: 16% (2,703). *Average award:* Freshmen: $2062. Undergraduates: $3231. *Scholarships, grants, and awards by category: Academic interests/achievement:* 351 awards ($1,352,226 total): agriculture, biological sciences, business, communication, computer science, education, engineering/technologies, English, foreign languages, general academic interests/achievements, health fields, home economics, humanities, international studies, library science, mathematics, military science, physical sciences, premedicine, social sciences. *Creative arts/performance:* 116 awards ($270,588 total): applied art and design, art/fine arts, cinema/film/broadcasting, creative writing, debating, general creative arts/performance, music, performing arts, theater/drama. *Special achievements/activities:* 1 award ($1500 total): community service, leadership. *Special characteristics:* 333 awards ($1,609,404 total): children of faculty/staff, children of union members/company employees, children with a deceased or disabled parent, first-generation college students, general special characteristics, members of minority groups, previous college experience. *Tuition waivers:* Full or partial for minority students, employees or children of employees, senior citizens.

LOANS *Student loans:* $84,822,703 (62% need-based, 38% non-need-based). 61% of past graduating class borrowed through all loan programs. *Average indebtedness per student:* $20,105. *Average need-based loan:* Freshmen: $6349. Undergraduates: $7103. *Parent loans:* $23,425,336 (23% need-based, 77% non-need-based). *Programs:* Federal Direct (Subsidized and Unsubsidized Stafford, PLUS), Perkins, Federal Nursing.

WORK-STUDY *Federal work-study:* Total amount: $1,489,658; 430 jobs averaging $2641. *State or other work-study/employment:* Total amount: $109,791 (66% need-based, 34% non-need-based). 26 part-time jobs averaging $1935.

ATHLETIC AWARDS Total amount: $4,249,888 (31% need-based, 69% non-need-based).

APPLYING FOR FINANCIAL AID *Required financial aid form:* FAFSA. *Financial aid deadline (priority):* 3/1. *Notification date:* Continuous beginning 4/1.

ILLINOIS WESLEYAN UNIVERSITY
Bloomington, IL

Tuition & fees: $33,982   **Average undergraduate aid package:** $25,753

ABOUT THE INSTITUTION Independent, coed. 48 undergraduate majors. Both federal and institutional methodology are used as a basis for awarding need-based institutional aid.

UNDERGRADUATE EXPENSES for 2009–10 *Comprehensive fee:* $41,758 includes full-time tuition ($33,808), mandatory fees ($174), and room and board ($7776). *College room only:* $4800. Room and board charges vary according to board plan and housing facility. *Part-time tuition:* $1057 per credit hour.

FRESHMAN FINANCIAL AID (Fall 2009, est.) 417 applied for aid; of those 83% were deemed to have need. 100% of freshmen with need received aid; of those 37% had need fully met. *Average percent of need met:* 92% (excluding resources awarded to replace EFC). *Average financial aid package:* $25,359 (excluding resources awarded to replace EFC). 28% of all full-time freshmen had no need and received non-need-based gift aid.

UNDERGRADUATE FINANCIAL AID (Fall 2009, est.) 1,365 applied for aid; of those 88% were deemed to have need. 100% of undergraduates with need received aid; of those 67% had need fully met. *Average percent of need met:* 97% (excluding resources awarded to replace EFC). *Average financial aid package:* $25,753 (excluding resources awarded to replace EFC). 30% of all full-time undergraduates had no need and received non-need-based gift aid.

GIFT AID (NEED-BASED) *Total amount:* $22,924,260 (8% federal, 9% state, 82% institutional, 1% external sources). *Receiving aid:* Freshmen: 67% (347); all full-time undergraduates: 59% (1,206). *Average award:* Freshmen: $19,231; Undergraduates: $18,340. *Scholarships, grants, and awards:* Federal Pell, FSEOG, state, private, college/university gift aid from institutional funds.

GIFT AID (NON-NEED-BASED) *Total amount:* $8,084,716 (99% institutional, 1% external sources). *Receiving aid:* Freshmen: 14% (70). Undergraduates: 8% (164). *Average award:* Freshmen: $13,460. Undergraduates: $11,861. *Scholarships, grants, and awards by category: Academic interests/achievement:* general academic interests/achievements. *Creative arts/performance:* general creative arts/performance, music, theater/drama. *Special characteristics:* children of faculty/staff, general special characteristics, international students.

LOANS *Student loans:* $9,172,437 (61% need-based, 39% non-need-based). 56% of past graduating class borrowed through all loan programs. *Average indebtedness per student:* $26,458. *Average need-based loan:* Freshmen: $3951. Undergraduates: $5313. *Parent loans:* $2,439,948 (100% non-need-based). *Programs:* FFEL (Subsidized and Unsubsidized Stafford, PLUS), Perkins, Federal Nursing, college/university.

WORK-STUDY *Federal work-study:* Total amount: $380,871; jobs available. *State or other work-study/employment:* Total amount: $2,130,217 (78% need-based, 22% non-need-based). Part-time jobs available.

APPLYING FOR FINANCIAL AID *Required financial aid form:* FAFSA, institution's own financial aid form, or CSS/Financial Aid PROFILE. *Financial aid deadline:* 3/1. *Notification date:* Continuous beginning 2/15. Students must reply by 5/1.

CONTACT Mr. Scott Seibring, Director of Financial Aid, Illinois Wesleyan University, 1312 North Park Street, PO Box 2900, Bloomington, IL 61702-2900, 309-556-3393 or toll-free 800-332-2498. *Fax:* 309-556-3833. *E-mail:* seibring@iwu.edu.

IMMACULATA UNIVERSITY
Immaculata, PA

CONTACT Mr. Peter Lysionek, Director of Student Financial Aid, Immaculata University, 1145 King Road, Box 500, Immaculata, PA 19345, 610-647-4400 Ext. 3026 or toll-free 877-428-6329. *Fax:* 610-640-0836. *E-mail:* plysionek@immaculata.edu.

INDEPENDENCE UNIVERSITY
Salt Lake City, UT

CONTACT Financial Aid Director, Independence University, 2423 Hoover Avenue, National City, CA 91950-6605, 619-477-4800 or toll-free 800-791-7353. *Fax:* 619-477-5202.

INDIANA STATE UNIVERSITY
Terre Haute, IN

Tuition & fees (IN res): $7426   **Average undergraduate aid package:** $9198

ABOUT THE INSTITUTION State-supported, coed. 65 undergraduate majors. Federal methodology is used as a basis for awarding need-based institutional aid.

UNDERGRADUATE EXPENSES for 2009–10 *Tuition, state resident:* full-time $7226; part-time $262 per credit hour. *Tuition, nonresident:* full-time $15,802; part-time $558 per credit hour. *Required fees:* full-time $200; $100 per term. Part-time tuition and fees vary according to course load. *College room and board:* $7463; *Room only:* $4254. Room and board charges vary according to board plan, housing facility, and student level. *Payment plans:* Installment, deferred payment.

FRESHMAN FINANCIAL AID (Fall 2009, est.) 1,827 applied for aid; of those 82% were deemed to have need. 97% of freshmen with need received aid; of those 15% had need fully met. *Average percent of need met:* 78% (excluding resources awarded to replace EFC). *Average financial aid package:* $8938 (excluding resources awarded to replace EFC). 12% of all full-time freshmen had no need and received non-need-based gift aid.

UNDERGRADUATE FINANCIAL AID (Fall 2009, est.) 6,161 applied for aid; of those 82% were deemed to have need. 97% of undergraduates with need received aid; of those 17% had need fully met. *Average percent of need met:* 80% (excluding resources awarded to replace EFC). *Average financial aid package:* $9198 (excluding resources awarded to replace EFC). 10% of all full-time undergraduates had no need and received non-need-based gift aid.

GIFT AID (NEED-BASED) *Total amount:* $20,622,653 (64% federal, 32% state, 2% institutional, 2% external sources). *Receiving aid:* Freshmen: 49% (965); all full-time undergraduates: 44% (3,201). *Average award:* Freshmen: $6425; Undergraduates: $6110. *Scholarships, grants, and awards:* Federal Pell, FSEOG, state, private, college/university gift aid from institutional funds.

GIFT AID (NON-NEED-BASED) *Total amount:* $13,585,753 (31% state, 54% institutional, 15% external sources). *Receiving aid:* Freshmen: 43% (843). Undergraduates: 28% (2,067). *Average award:* Freshmen: $3949. Undergraduates: $4820. *Scholarships, grants, and awards by category:* Academic interests/ achievement: 1,721 awards ($3,897,140 total): general academic interests/ achievements, premedicine. *Creative arts/performance:* 95 awards ($222,400 total): art/fine arts, performing arts. *Special characteristics:* 246 awards ($703,985 total): children and siblings of alumni, children of faculty/staff, members of minority groups, previous college experience, veterans. *Tuition waivers:* Full or partial for employees or children of employees, senior citizens.

LOANS *Student loans:* $32,278,227 (42% need-based, 58% non-need-based). 65% of past graduating class borrowed through all loan programs. *Average indebtedness per student:* $23,963. *Average need-based loan:* Freshmen: $3045. Undergraduates: $3755. *Parent loans:* $6,621,001 (100% non-need-based). *Programs:* Federal Direct (Subsidized and Unsubsidized Stafford, PLUS), Perkins, alternative loans.

WORK-STUDY *Federal work-study:* Total amount: $509,352; 441 jobs averaging $1247. *State or other work-study/employment:* Part-time jobs available.

ATHLETIC AWARDS Total amount: $3,136,626 (100% non-need-based).

APPLYING FOR FINANCIAL AID *Required financial aid form:* FAFSA. *Financial aid deadline (priority):* 3/1. *Notification date:* Continuous beginning 4/1.

CONTACT Kim Donat, Director of Student Financial Aid, Indiana State University, 150 Tirey Hall, Terre Haute, IN 47809-1401, 812-237-2215 or toll-free 800-742-0891. *Fax:* 812-237-4330. *E-mail:* finaid@indstate.edu.

INDIANA TECH
Fort Wayne, IN

CONTACT Financial Aid Office, Indiana Tech, 1600 East Washington Boulevard, Fort Wayne, IN 46803-1297, 800-937-2448 or toll-free 888-666-TECH (out-of-state). *Fax:* 219-422-1578.

INDIANA UNIVERSITY BLOOMINGTON
Bloomington, IN

Tuition & fees (IN res): $8613   **Average undergraduate aid package:** $10,440

ABOUT THE INSTITUTION State-supported, coed. 122 undergraduate majors. Federal methodology is used as a basis for awarding need-based institutional aid.

UNDERGRADUATE EXPENSES for 2009–10 *Tuition, state resident:* full-time $7722; part-time $241.10 per credit hour. *Tuition, nonresident:* full-time $25,269; part-time $789.80 per credit hour. *Required fees:* full-time $891. Full-time tuition and fees vary according to location and program. Part-time tuition and fees vary according to course load, location, and program. *College room and board:* $7546; *Room only:* $4646. Room and board charges vary according to board plan and housing facility. *Payment plan:* Deferred payment.

FRESHMAN FINANCIAL AID (Fall 2009, est.) 5,272 applied for aid; of those 64% were deemed to have need. 97% of freshmen with need received aid; of those 20% had need fully met. *Average percent of need met:* 90% (excluding resources awarded to replace EFC). *Average financial aid package:* $10,799 (excluding resources awarded to replace EFC). 24% of all full-time freshmen had no need and received non-need-based gift aid.

UNDERGRADUATE FINANCIAL AID (Fall 2009, est.) 18,740 applied for aid; of those 71% were deemed to have need. 97% of undergraduates with need received aid; of those 15% had need fully met. *Average percent of need met:* 89% (excluding resources awarded to replace EFC). *Average financial aid package:* $10,440 (excluding resources awarded to replace EFC). 22% of all full-time undergraduates had no need and received non-need-based gift aid.

GIFT AID (NEED-BASED) *Total amount:* $84,980,146 (31% federal, 26% state, 37% institutional, 6% external sources). *Receiving aid:* Freshmen: 37% (2,737); all full-time undergraduates: 32% (9,987). *Average award:* Freshmen: $9761; Undergraduates: $8677. *Scholarships, grants, and awards:* Federal Pell, FSEOG, state, private, college/university gift aid from institutional funds.

GIFT AID (NON-NEED-BASED) *Total amount:* $53,393,969 (3% state, 81% institutional, 16% external sources). *Receiving aid:* Freshmen: 7% (518). Undergraduates: 4% (1,354). *Average award:* Freshmen: $6651. Undergraduates: $5708. *Tuition waivers:* Full or partial for employees or children of employees.

LOANS *Student loans:* $120,047,264 (55% need-based, 45% non-need-based). 54% of past graduating class borrowed through all loan programs. *Average indebtedness per student:* $25,522. *Average need-based loan:* Freshmen: $3106. Undergraduates: $4322. *Parent loans:* $40,059,623 (29% need-based, 71% non-need-based). *Programs:* Federal Direct (Subsidized and Unsubsidized Stafford, PLUS), Perkins, college/university.

WORK-STUDY Federal work-study jobs available. *State or other work-study/ employment:* Total amount: $30,679 (43% need-based, 57% non-need-based). Part-time jobs available.

ATHLETIC AWARDS Total amount: $9,076,374 (28% need-based, 72% non-need-based).

APPLYING FOR FINANCIAL AID *Required financial aid form:* FAFSA. *Financial aid deadline (priority):* 3/1. *Notification date:* Continuous beginning 4/1.

CONTACT Susan Pugh, Director of the Office of Student Financial Assistance, Indiana University Bloomington, Franklin Hall, Bloomington, IN 47405, 812-855-0321. *Fax:* 812-855-7615. *E-mail:* rsvposfa@indiana.edu.

INDIANA UNIVERSITY EAST
Richmond, IN

Tuition & fees (IN res): $5801   **Average undergraduate aid package:** $7943

ABOUT THE INSTITUTION State-supported, coed. 39 undergraduate majors. Federal methodology is used as a basis for awarding need-based institutional aid.

UNDERGRADUATE EXPENSES for 2009–10 *Tuition, state resident:* full-time $5416; part-time $180.54 per credit hour. *Tuition, nonresident:* full-time $14,572; part-time $485.72 per credit hour. *Required fees:* full-time $385. Full-time tuition and fees vary according to course load, program, and reciprocity agreements. Part-time tuition and fees vary according to course load, location, program, and reciprocity agreements. *Payment plan:* Deferred payment.

FRESHMAN FINANCIAL AID (Fall 2009, est.) 340 applied for aid; of those 87% were deemed to have need. 98% of freshmen with need received aid; of those

Indiana University East

11% had need fully met. *Average percent of need met:* 97% (excluding resources awarded to replace EFC). *Average financial aid package:* $7254 (excluding resources awarded to replace EFC). 4% of all full-time freshmen had no need and received non-need-based gift aid.

UNDERGRADUATE FINANCIAL AID (Fall 2009, est.) 1,382 applied for aid; of those 89% were deemed to have need. 98% of undergraduates with need received aid; of those 5% had need fully met. *Average percent of need met:* 95% (excluding resources awarded to replace EFC). *Average financial aid package:* $7943 (excluding resources awarded to replace EFC). 4% of all full-time undergraduates had no need and received non-need-based gift aid.

GIFT AID (NEED-BASED) *Total amount:* $7,303,099 (65% federal, 26% state, 5% institutional, 4% external sources). *Receiving aid:* Freshmen: 72% (257); all full-time undergraduates: 69% (1,039). *Average award:* Freshmen: $6090; Undergraduates: $5769. *Scholarships, grants, and awards:* Federal Pell, FSEOG, state, private, college/university gift aid from institutional funds.

GIFT AID (NON-NEED-BASED) *Total amount:* $246,905 (9% federal, 13% state, 38% institutional, 40% external sources). *Receiving aid:* Freshmen: 6% (22). Undergraduates: 2% (36). *Average award:* Freshmen: $1786. Undergraduates: $1275. *Tuition waivers:* Full or partial for employees or children of employees.

LOANS *Student loans:* $11,206,367 (82% need-based, 18% non-need-based). 78% of past graduating class borrowed through all loan programs. *Average indebtedness per student:* $27,300. *Average need-based loan:* Freshmen: $2813. Undergraduates: $3684. *Parent loans:* $80,304 (35% need-based, 65% non-need-based). *Programs:* Federal Direct (Subsidized and Unsubsidized Stafford, PLUS), Perkins, college/university.

WORK-STUDY Federal work-study jobs available.

ATHLETIC AWARDS Total amount: $60,750 (100% need-based).

APPLYING FOR FINANCIAL AID *Required financial aid forms:* FAFSA, institution's own form. *Financial aid deadline (priority):* 3/1. *Notification date:* Continuous beginning 5/1. Students must reply within 2 weeks of notification.

CONTACT William Gill, Financial Aid Director, Indiana University East, 2325 Chester Boulevard, Richmond, IN 47374-1289, 765-973-8231 or toll-free 800-959-EAST. *Fax:* 765-973-8288.

INDIANA UNIVERSITY KOKOMO
Kokomo, IN

Tuition & fees (IN res): $5838	Average undergraduate aid package: $7733

ABOUT THE INSTITUTION State-supported, coed. 40 undergraduate majors. Federal methodology is used as a basis for awarding need-based institutional aid.

UNDERGRADUATE EXPENSES for 2009–10 *Tuition, state resident:* full-time $5408; part-time $180.25 per credit hour. *Tuition, nonresident:* full-time $14,097; part-time $469.89 per credit hour. *Required fees:* full-time $430. Full-time tuition and fees vary according to course load, location, and program. Part-time tuition and fees vary according to course load, location, and program. Room and board charges vary according to board plan, housing facility, and location. *Payment plan:* Deferred payment.

FRESHMAN FINANCIAL AID (Fall 2009, est.) 372 applied for aid; of those 74% were deemed to have need. 95% of freshmen with need received aid; of those 6% had need fully met. *Average percent of need met:* 91% (excluding resources awarded to replace EFC). *Average financial aid package:* $6696 (excluding resources awarded to replace EFC). 6% of all full-time freshmen had no need and received non-need-based gift aid.

UNDERGRADUATE FINANCIAL AID (Fall 2009, est.) 1,351 applied for aid; of those 81% were deemed to have need. 96% of undergraduates with need received aid; of those 4% had need fully met. *Average percent of need met:* 92% (excluding resources awarded to replace EFC). *Average financial aid package:* $7733 (excluding resources awarded to replace EFC). 4% of all full-time undergraduates had no need and received non-need-based gift aid.

GIFT AID (NEED-BASED) *Total amount:* $6,277,685 (57% federal, 33% state, 6% institutional, 4% external sources). *Receiving aid:* Freshmen: 49% (199); all full-time undergraduates: 53% (816). *Average award:* Freshmen: $6393; Undergraduates: $6231. *Scholarships, grants, and awards:* Federal Pell, FSEOG, state, private, college/university gift aid from institutional funds.

GIFT AID (NON-NEED-BASED) *Total amount:* $569,226 (7% federal, 23% state, 17% institutional, 53% external sources). *Receiving aid:* Freshmen: 3% (11). Undergraduates: 2% (29). *Average award:* Freshmen: $1475. Undergraduates: $1237. *Tuition waivers:* Full or partial for employees or children of employees.

LOANS *Student loans:* $9,615,997 (73% need-based, 27% non-need-based). 65% of past graduating class borrowed through all loan programs. *Average indebtedness per student:* $24,788. *Average need-based loan:* Freshmen: $2854. Undergraduates: $3671. *Parent loans:* $65,654 (14% need-based, 86% non-need-based). *Programs:* Federal Direct (Subsidized and Unsubsidized Stafford, PLUS), Perkins, Federal Nursing, college/university.

WORK-STUDY Federal work-study jobs available. *State or other work-study/employment:* Total amount: $3363 (35% need-based, 65% non-need-based). Part-time jobs available.

APPLYING FOR FINANCIAL AID *Required financial aid forms:* FAFSA, institution's own form. *Financial aid deadline:* 3/1. *Notification date:* Continuous beginning 5/1. Students must reply within 4 weeks of notification.

CONTACT Jolane Rohr, Director of Financial Aid, Indiana University Kokomo, 2300 South Washington Street, PO Box 9003, Kokomo, IN 46904-9003, 765-455-9216 or toll-free 888-875-4485. *Fax:* 765-455-9537.

INDIANA UNIVERSITY NORTHWEST
Gary, IN

Tuition & fees (IN res): $5919	Average undergraduate aid package: $8238

ABOUT THE INSTITUTION State-supported, coed. 39 undergraduate majors. Federal methodology is used as a basis for awarding need-based institutional aid.

UNDERGRADUATE EXPENSES for 2009–10 *Tuition, state resident:* full-time $5478; part-time $182.61 per credit hour. *Tuition, nonresident:* full-time $14,583; part-time $486.11 per credit hour. *Required fees:* full-time $441. Full-time tuition and fees vary according to course load, location, and program. Part-time tuition and fees vary according to course load, location, and program. *Payment plans:* Installment, deferred payment.

FRESHMAN FINANCIAL AID (Fall 2009, est.) 640 applied for aid; of those 82% were deemed to have need. 94% of freshmen with need received aid; of those 4% had need fully met. *Average percent of need met:* 91% (excluding resources awarded to replace EFC). *Average financial aid package:* $7480 (excluding resources awarded to replace EFC). 6% of all full-time freshmen had no need and received non-need-based gift aid.

UNDERGRADUATE FINANCIAL AID (Fall 2009, est.) 2,524 applied for aid; of those 85% were deemed to have need. 96% of undergraduates with need received aid; of those 3% had need fully met. *Average percent of need met:* 90% (excluding resources awarded to replace EFC). *Average financial aid package:* $8238 (excluding resources awarded to replace EFC). 5% of all full-time undergraduates had no need and received non-need-based gift aid.

GIFT AID (NEED-BASED) *Total amount:* $12,494,598 (64% federal, 30% state, 3% institutional, 3% external sources). *Receiving aid:* Freshmen: 51% (398); all full-time undergraduates: 53% (1,625). *Average award:* Freshmen: $6068; Undergraduates: $6334. *Scholarships, grants, and awards:* Federal Pell, FSEOG, state, private, college/university gift aid from institutional funds, Federal Nursing.

GIFT AID (NON-NEED-BASED) *Total amount:* $860,048 (9% federal, 9% state, 65% institutional, 17% external sources). *Receiving aid:* Freshmen: 2% (13). Undergraduates: 1% (25). *Average award:* Freshmen: $3223. Undergraduates: $3260. *Tuition waivers:* Full or partial for employees or children of employees.

LOANS *Student loans:* $21,718,145 (79% need-based, 21% non-need-based). 68% of past graduating class borrowed through all loan programs. *Average indebtedness per student:* $28,403. *Average need-based loan:* Freshmen: $3141. Undergraduates: $3727. *Parent loans:* $179,336 (25% need-based, 75% non-need-based). *Programs:* Federal Direct (Subsidized and Unsubsidized Stafford, PLUS), Perkins, college/university.

WORK-STUDY Federal work-study jobs available.

ATHLETIC AWARDS Total amount: $41,700 (54% need-based, 46% non-need-based).

APPLYING FOR FINANCIAL AID *Required financial aid forms:* FAFSA, institution's own form. *Financial aid deadline (priority):* 3/1. *Notification date:* Continuous beginning 5/1. Students must reply within 2 weeks of notification.

CONTACT Harold Burtley, Director of Scholarships and Financial Aid, Indiana University Northwest, 3400 Broadway, Gary, IN 46408-1197, 877-280-4593 or toll-free 800-968-7486. *Fax:* 219-981-5622.

INDIANA UNIVERSITY OF PENNSYLVANIA
Indiana, PA

Tuition & fees (PA res): $7209   **Average undergraduate aid package: $8991**

ABOUT THE INSTITUTION State-supported, coed. 70 undergraduate majors. Federal methodology is used as a basis for awarding need-based institutional aid.

UNDERGRADUATE EXPENSES for 2009–10 *Tuition, state resident:* full-time $5554; part-time $231 per credit hour. *Tuition, nonresident:* full-time $13,886; part-time $579 per credit hour. *Required fees:* full-time $1655; $23.10 per credit hour or $238.50 per credit hour. Full-time tuition and fees vary according to course load and reciprocity agreements. Part-time tuition and fees vary according to course load and reciprocity agreements. *College room and board:* $8558; *Room only:* $6140. Room and board charges vary according to board plan, housing facility, and location. *Payment plans:* Installment, deferred payment.

FRESHMAN FINANCIAL AID (Fall 2008) 2,787 applied for aid; of those 75% were deemed to have need. 99% of freshmen with need received aid; of those 12% had need fully met. *Average percent of need met:* 77% (excluding resources awarded to replace EFC). *Average financial aid package:* $10,032 (excluding resources awarded to replace EFC). 5% of all full-time freshmen had no need and received non-need-based gift aid.

UNDERGRADUATE FINANCIAL AID (Fall 2008) 9,293 applied for aid; of those 79% were deemed to have need. 99% of undergraduates with need received aid; of those 10% had need fully met. *Average percent of need met:* 70% (excluding resources awarded to replace EFC). *Average financial aid package:* $8991 (excluding resources awarded to replace EFC). 3% of all full-time undergraduates had no need and received non-need-based gift aid.

GIFT AID (NEED-BASED) *Total amount:* $26,068,563 (56% federal, 44% state). *Receiving aid:* Freshmen: 47% (1,433); all full-time undergraduates: 46% (5,029). *Average award:* Freshmen: $5387; Undergraduates: $5035. *Scholarships, grants, and awards:* Federal Pell, FSEOG, state, private, college/university gift aid from institutional funds, United Negro College Fund.

GIFT AID (NON-NEED-BASED) *Total amount:* $5,633,503 (53% institutional, 47% external sources). *Receiving aid:* Freshmen: 25% (766). Undergraduates: 15% (1,680). *Average award:* Freshmen: $2346. Undergraduates: $2705. *Scholarships, grants, and awards by category: Academic interests/achievement:* 1,158 awards ($2,510,567 total): area/ethnic studies, biological sciences, business, communication, computer science, education, engineering/technologies, English, foreign languages, general academic interests/achievements, health fields, home economics, humanities, international studies, mathematics, physical sciences, premedicine, social sciences. *Creative arts/performance:* applied art and design, art/fine arts, dance, general creative arts/performance, journalism/publications, music, performing arts, theater/drama. *Special achievements/activities:* community service, general special achievements/activities, hobbies/interests, leadership. *Special characteristics:* 2,016 awards ($10,503,441 total): adult students, children of faculty/staff, ethnic background, international students. *Tuition waivers:* Full or partial for employees or children of employees, senior citizens.

LOANS *Student loans:* $66,222,332 (42% need-based, 58% non-need-based). 84% of past graduating class borrowed through all loan programs. *Average indebtedness per student:* $25,224. *Average need-based loan:* Freshmen: $3650. Undergraduates: $4093. *Parent loans:* $6,219,320 (100% non-need-based). *Programs:* FFEL (Subsidized and Unsubsidized Stafford, PLUS), Perkins, alternative loans, private loans.

WORK-STUDY *Federal work-study:* Total amount: $7,256,912; 1,158 jobs averaging $1827. *State or other work-study/employment:* 1,767 part-time jobs averaging $2550.

ATHLETIC AWARDS Total amount: $833,814 (100% non-need-based).

APPLYING FOR FINANCIAL AID *Required financial aid form:* FAFSA. *Financial aid deadline:* 4/15. *Notification date:* Continuous.

CONTACT Mrs. Patricia C. McCarthy, Director of Financial Aid, Indiana University of Pennsylvania, 213 Clark Hall, Indiana, PA 15705, 724-357-2218 or toll-free 800-442-6830. *Fax:* 724-357-2094. *E-mail:* mccarthy@iup.edu.

INDIANA UNIVERSITY–PURDUE UNIVERSITY FORT WAYNE
Fort Wayne, IN

Tuition & fees (IN res): $6233   **Average undergraduate aid package: $8981**

ABOUT THE INSTITUTION State-supported, coed. 101 undergraduate majors. Federal methodology is used as a basis for awarding need-based institutional aid.

UNDERGRADUATE EXPENSES for 2009–10 *Tuition, state resident:* full-time $5441; part-time $202 per credit hour. *Tuition, nonresident:* full-time $14,037; part-time $520 per credit hour. *Required fees:* full-time $792; $29.35 per credit hour. Full-time tuition and fees vary according to course load. Part-time tuition and fees vary according to course load. *College room and board: Room only:* $5620. Room and board charges vary according to housing facility. *Payment plans:* Installment, deferred payment.

FRESHMAN FINANCIAL AID (Fall 2008) 1,671 applied for aid; of those 77% were deemed to have need. 95% of freshmen with need received aid; of those 1% had need fully met. *Average percent of need met:* 52% (excluding resources awarded to replace EFC). *Average financial aid package:* $8190 (excluding resources awarded to replace EFC). 1% of all full-time freshmen had no need and received non-need-based gift aid.

UNDERGRADUATE FINANCIAL AID (Fall 2008) 6,218 applied for aid; of those 81% were deemed to have need. 95% of undergraduates with need received aid; of those 1% had need fully met. *Average percent of need met:* 53% (excluding resources awarded to replace EFC). *Average financial aid package:* $8981 (excluding resources awarded to replace EFC). 2% of all full-time undergraduates had no need and received non-need-based gift aid.

GIFT AID (NEED-BASED) *Total amount:* $21,951,710 (50% federal, 43% state, 3% institutional, 4% external sources). *Receiving aid:* Freshmen: 36% (677); all full-time undergraduates: 39% (2,988). *Average award:* Freshmen: $5890; Undergraduates: $5473. *Scholarships, grants, and awards:* Federal Pell, FSEOG, state, private, college/university gift aid from institutional funds.

GIFT AID (NON-NEED-BASED) *Total amount:* $1,373,068 (31% state, 27% institutional, 42% external sources). *Receiving aid:* Freshmen: 25% (479). Undergraduates: 15% (1,159). *Average award:* Freshmen: $3805. Undergraduates: $2011. *Scholarships, grants, and awards by category: Academic interests/achievement:* general academic interests/achievements. *Special characteristics:* local/state students. *Tuition waivers:* Full or partial for employees or children of employees, senior citizens.

LOANS *Student loans:* $44,883,326 (96% need-based, 4% non-need-based). 34% of past graduating class borrowed through all loan programs. *Average indebtedness per student:* $22,092. *Average need-based loan:* Freshmen: $3104. Undergraduates: $3828. *Parent loans:* $1,329,090 (94% need-based, 6% non-need-based). *Programs:* FFEL (Subsidized and Unsubsidized Stafford, PLUS), Perkins.

WORK-STUDY *Federal work-study:* Total amount: $282,841; jobs available.

ATHLETIC AWARDS Total amount: $1,645,312 (24% need-based, 76% non-need-based).

APPLYING FOR FINANCIAL AID *Required financial aid form:* FAFSA. *Financial aid deadline (priority):* 3/10. *Notification date:* Continuous beginning 5/15. Students must reply within 3 weeks of notification.

CONTACT Ms. Judith Cramer, Director of Financial Aid, Indiana University–Purdue University Fort Wayne, 2101 East Coliseum Boulevard, Fort Wayne, IN 46805-1499, 260-481-6130 or toll-free 800-324-4739 (in-state). *E-mail:* cramerj@ipfw.edu.

INDIANA UNIVERSITY–PURDUE UNIVERSITY INDIANAPOLIS
Indianapolis, IN

Tuition & fees (IN res): $7523   **Average undergraduate aid package: $8978**

ABOUT THE INSTITUTION State-supported, coed. 101 undergraduate majors. Federal methodology is used as a basis for awarding need-based institutional aid.

UNDERGRADUATE EXPENSES for 2009–10 *Tuition, state resident:* full-time $6923; part-time $230.76 per credit hour. *Tuition, nonresident:* full-time $21,820; part-time $727.33 per credit hour. *Required fees:* full-time $600. Full-time tuition and fees vary according to course load, location, and program. Part-time tuition and fees vary according to course load, location, and program. *College room and board: Room only:* $3370. Room and board charges vary according to housing facility. *Payment plans:* Installment, deferred payment.

FRESHMAN FINANCIAL AID (Fall 2009, est.) 2,460 applied for aid; of those 79% were deemed to have need. 96% of freshmen with need received aid; of those 6% had need fully met. *Average percent of need met:* 89% (excluding resources awarded to replace EFC). *Average financial aid package:* $9083 (excluding resources awarded to replace EFC). 7% of all full-time freshmen had no need and received non-need-based gift aid.

UNDERGRADUATE FINANCIAL AID (Fall 2009, est.) 12,508 applied for aid; of those 84% were deemed to have need. 97% of undergraduates with need received aid; of those 5% had need fully met. *Average percent of need met:* 90% (excluding resources awarded to replace EFC). *Average financial aid package:* $8978 (excluding resources awarded to replace EFC). 7% of all full-time undergraduates had no need and received non-need-based gift aid.

GIFT AID (NEED-BASED) *Total amount:* $60,309,156 (51% federal, 32% state, 13% institutional, 4% external sources). *Receiving aid:* Freshmen: 54% (1,526); all full-time undergraduates: 52% (8,019). *Average award:* Freshmen: $8144; Undergraduates: $6925. *Scholarships, grants, and awards:* Federal Pell, FSEOG, state, private, college/university gift aid from institutional funds.

GIFT AID (NON-NEED-BASED) *Total amount:* $12,353,006 (5% federal, 10% state, 38% institutional, 47% external sources). *Receiving aid:* Freshmen: 4% (103). Undergraduates: 2% (365). *Average award:* Freshmen: $5043. Undergraduates: $3407. *Tuition waivers:* Full or partial for employees or children of employees.

LOANS *Student loans:* $100,493,979 (77% need-based, 23% non-need-based). 72% of past graduating class borrowed through all loan programs. *Average indebtedness per student:* $27,062. *Average need-based loan:* Freshmen: $3235. Undergraduates: $4127. *Parent loans:* $5,085,243 (29% need-based, 71% non-need-based). *Programs:* Federal Direct (Subsidized and Unsubsidized Stafford, PLUS), Perkins, Federal Nursing, college/university.

WORK-STUDY Federal work-study jobs available. *State or other work-study/ employment:* Total amount: $43,078 (65% need-based, 35% non-need-based). Part-time jobs available.

ATHLETIC AWARDS Total amount: $1,659,503 (46% need-based, 54% non-need-based).

APPLYING FOR FINANCIAL AID *Required financial aid form:* FAFSA. *Financial aid deadline (priority):* 3/1. *Notification date:* Continuous beginning 4/1.

CONTACT Kathy Purris, Director of Financial Aid Services, Indiana University–Purdue University Indianapolis, 425 North University Boulevard, Indianapolis, IN 46202-5145, 317-274-4162. *Fax:* 317-274-5930.

INDIANA UNIVERSITY SOUTH BEND
South Bend, IN

Tuition & fees (IN res): $6015	Average undergraduate aid package: $7902

ABOUT THE INSTITUTION State-supported, coed. 71 undergraduate majors. Federal methodology is used as a basis for awarding need-based institutional aid.

UNDERGRADUATE EXPENSES for 2009–10 *Tuition, state resident:* full-time $5573; part-time $185.75 per credit hour. *Tuition, nonresident:* full-time $15,270; part-time $509 per credit hour. *Required fees:* full-time $442. Full-time tuition and fees vary according to course load, location, and program. Part-time tuition and fees vary according to course load, location, and program. Room and board charges vary according to board plan, housing facility, and location. *Payment plan:* Deferred payment.

FRESHMAN FINANCIAL AID (Fall 2009, est.) 944 applied for aid; of those 83% were deemed to have need. 94% of freshmen with need received aid; of those 4% had need fully met. *Average percent of need met:* 91% (excluding resources awarded to replace EFC). *Average financial aid package:* $7018 (excluding resources awarded to replace EFC). 2% of all full-time freshmen had no need and received non-need-based gift aid.

UNDERGRADUATE FINANCIAL AID (Fall 2009, est.) 3,619 applied for aid; of those 84% were deemed to have need. 96% of undergraduates with need received aid; of those 3% had need fully met. *Average percent of need met:* 93% (excluding resources awarded to replace EFC). *Average financial aid package:* $7902 (excluding resources awarded to replace EFC). 4% of all full-time undergraduates had no need and received non-need-based gift aid.

GIFT AID (NEED-BASED) *Total amount:* $17,539,817 (59% federal, 30% state, 6% institutional, 5% external sources). *Receiving aid:* Freshmen: 58% (603); all full-time undergraduates: 56% (2,386). *Average award:* Freshmen: $6158; Undergraduates: $6266. *Scholarships, grants, and awards:* Federal Pell, FSEOG, state, private, college/university gift aid from institutional funds.

GIFT AID (NON-NEED-BASED) *Total amount:* $1,752,523 (7% federal, 8% state, 36% institutional, 49% external sources). *Receiving aid:* Freshmen: 1% (13). Undergraduates: 1% (59). *Average award:* Freshmen: $2980. Undergraduates: $3361. *Tuition waivers:* Full or partial for employees or children of employees.

LOANS *Student loans:* $24,466,124 (78% need-based, 22% non-need-based). 71% of past graduating class borrowed through all loan programs. *Average indebtedness per student:* $25,384. *Average need-based loan:* Freshmen: $2830. Undergraduates: $3634. *Parent loans:* $564,859 (22% need-based, 78% non-need-based). *Programs:* Federal Direct (Subsidized and Unsubsidized Stafford, PLUS), Perkins, college/university.

WORK-STUDY Federal work-study jobs available. *State or other work-study/ employment:* Total amount: $16,302 (82% need-based, 18% non-need-based). Part-time jobs available.

ATHLETIC AWARDS Total amount: $166,484 (66% need-based, 34% non-need-based).

APPLYING FOR FINANCIAL AID *Required financial aid forms:* FAFSA, institution's own form. *Financial aid deadline:* 3/1. *Notification date:* Continuous beginning 5/1.

CONTACT Bev Cooper, Financial Aid Director, Indiana University South Bend, 1700 Mishawaka Avenue, South Bend, IN 46634-7111, 574-520-4357 or toll-free 877-GO-2-IUSB. *Fax:* 574-520-5561. *E-mail:* beacoope@iusb.edu.

INDIANA UNIVERSITY SOUTHEAST
New Albany, IN

Tuition & fees (IN res): $5890	Average undergraduate aid package: $7611

ABOUT THE INSTITUTION State-supported, coed. 49 undergraduate majors. Federal methodology is used as a basis for awarding need-based institutional aid.

UNDERGRADUATE EXPENSES for 2009–10 *Tuition, state resident:* full-time $5417; part-time $180.58 per credit hour. *Tuition, nonresident:* full-time $14,105; part-time $470.15 per credit hour. *Required fees:* full-time $473. Full-time tuition and fees vary according to course load, location, program, and reciprocity agreements. Part-time tuition and fees vary according to course load, location, program, and reciprocity agreements. *College room and board: Room only:* $5630. Room and board charges vary according to board plan and housing facility. *Payment plan:* Deferred payment.

FRESHMAN FINANCIAL AID (Fall 2009, est.) 864 applied for aid; of those 78% were deemed to have need. 95% of freshmen with need received aid; of those 6% had need fully met. *Average percent of need met:* 92% (excluding resources awarded to replace EFC). *Average financial aid package:* $6904 (excluding resources awarded to replace EFC). 4% of all full-time freshmen had no need and received non-need-based gift aid.

UNDERGRADUATE FINANCIAL AID (Fall 2009, est.) 3,129 applied for aid; of those 80% were deemed to have need. 96% of undergraduates with need received aid; of those 5% had need fully met. *Average percent of need met:* 92% (excluding resources awarded to replace EFC). *Average financial aid package:* $7611 (excluding resources awarded to replace EFC). 5% of all full-time undergraduates had no need and received non-need-based gift aid.

GIFT AID (NEED-BASED) *Total amount:* $13,766,957 (61% federal, 28% state, 6% institutional, 5% external sources). *Receiving aid:* Freshmen: 53% (529); all full-time undergraduates: 51% (1,975). *Average award:* Freshmen: $5962; Undergraduates: $6010. *Scholarships, grants, and awards:* Federal Pell, FSEOG, state, private, college/university gift aid from institutional funds.

GIFT AID (NON-NEED-BASED) *Total amount:* $1,236,005 (16% state, 30% institutional, 54% external sources). *Receiving aid:* Freshmen: 3% (26). Undergraduates: 2% (69). *Average award:* Freshmen: $1781. Undergraduates: $1482. *Tuition waivers:* Full or partial for employees or children of employees.

LOANS *Student loans:* $19,749,558 (74% need-based, 26% non-need-based). 60% of past graduating class borrowed through all loan programs. *Average indebtedness per student:* $22,649. *Average need-based loan:* Freshmen: $3125. Undergraduates: $3793. *Parent loans:* $506,070 (32% need-based, 68% non-need-based). *Programs:* Federal Direct (Subsidized and Unsubsidized Stafford, PLUS), Perkins, Federal Nursing, college/university.

WORK-STUDY Federal work-study jobs available. *State or other work-study/employment:* Total amount: $4588 (100% non-need-based). Part-time jobs available.

ATHLETIC AWARDS Total amount: $90,963 (66% need-based, 34% non-need-based).

APPLYING FOR FINANCIAL AID *Required financial aid form:* FAFSA. *Financial aid deadline (priority):* 3/1. *Notification date:* Continuous beginning 5/1. Students must reply within 3 weeks of notification.

CONTACT Brittany Hubbard, Director of Financial Aid, Indiana University Southeast, University Center, South Room 105, New Albany, IN 47150, 812-941-2246 or toll-free 800-852-8835 (in-state). *Fax:* 812-941-2546. *E-mail:* mibarlow@ius.edu.

INDIANA WESLEYAN UNIVERSITY
Marion, IN

Tuition & fees: $21,213	Average undergraduate aid package: $19,336

ABOUT THE INSTITUTION Independent Wesleyan, coed. 60 undergraduate majors. Federal methodology is used as a basis for awarding need-based institutional aid.

UNDERGRADUATE EXPENSES for 2010–11 *Comprehensive fee:* $28,221 includes full-time tuition ($21,213) and room and board ($7008). *College room only:* $3390. Room and board charges vary according to board plan. Part-time tuition and fees vary according to course load. *Payment plan:* Installment.

FRESHMAN FINANCIAL AID (Fall 2008) 930 applied for aid; of those 83% were deemed to have need. 100% of freshmen with need received aid; of those 10% had need fully met. *Average percent of need met:* 92% (excluding resources awarded to replace EFC). *Average financial aid package:* $19,867 (excluding resources awarded to replace EFC). 16% of all full-time freshmen had no need and received non-need-based gift aid.

UNDERGRADUATE FINANCIAL AID (Fall 2008) 2,863 applied for aid; of those 77% were deemed to have need. 100% of undergraduates with need received aid; of those 15% had need fully met. *Average percent of need met:* 92% (excluding resources awarded to replace EFC). *Average financial aid package:* $19,336 (excluding resources awarded to replace EFC). 11% of all full-time undergraduates had no need and received non-need-based gift aid.

GIFT AID (NEED-BASED) *Total amount:* $15,349,555 (21% federal, 23% state, 56% institutional). *Receiving aid:* Freshmen: 69% (702); all full-time undergraduates: 61% (1,960). *Average award:* Freshmen: $7972; Undergraduates: $7815. *Scholarships, grants, and awards:* Federal Pell, FSEOG, state, private, college/university gift aid from institutional funds.

GIFT AID (NON-NEED-BASED) *Total amount:* $9,803,757 (77% institutional, 23% external sources). *Receiving aid:* Freshmen: 62% (635). Undergraduates: 57% (1,818). *Average award:* Freshmen: $3113. Undergraduates: $3148. *Scholarships, grants, and awards by category:* Academic interests/achievement: 1,177 awards ($5,921,260 total): general academic interests/achievements. Creative arts/performance: 145 awards ($220,526 total): art/fine arts, music, theater/drama. Special achievements/activities: 18 awards ($17,600 total): cheerleading/drum major. Special characteristics: 1,356 awards ($4,981,925 total): children and siblings of alumni, children of faculty/staff, relatives of clergy, religious affiliation, siblings of current students, veterans. *Tuition waivers:* Full or partial for employees or children of employees.

LOANS *Student loans:* $18,185,787 (46% need-based, 54% non-need-based). 75% of past graduating class borrowed through all loan programs. *Average indebtedness per student:* $26,610. *Average need-based loan:* Freshmen: $5699. Undergraduates: $6200. *Parent loans:* $2,610,563 (100% non-need-based). *Programs:* Federal Direct (Subsidized and Unsubsidized Stafford, PLUS), Perkins, college/university.

WORK-STUDY *Federal work-study:* Total amount: $604,372; 449 jobs averaging $1700.

ATHLETIC AWARDS Total amount: $1,244,709 (100% non-need-based).

APPLYING FOR FINANCIAL AID *Required financial aid form:* FAFSA. *Financial aid deadline (priority):* 3/10. *Notification date:* Continuous beginning 2/15.

CONTACT Undergraduate Traditional Financial Aid, Indiana Wesleyan University, 4201 South Washington Street, Marion, IN 46953-4999, 765-677-2116 or toll-free 800-332-6901. *Fax:* 765-677-2809. *E-mail:* finaid@indwes.edu.

INSTE BIBLE COLLEGE
Ankeny, IA

CONTACT Financial Aid Office, INSTE Bible College, 2302 SW 3rd Street, Ankeny, IA 50023, 515-289-9200.

INTER AMERICAN UNIVERSITY OF PUERTO RICO, AGUADILLA CAMPUS
Aguadilla, PR

CONTACT Mr. Juan Gonzalez, Director of Financial Aid, Inter American University of Puerto Rico, Aguadilla Campus, PO Box 20000, Aguadilla, PR 00605, 787-891-0925 Ext. 2108. *Fax:* 787-882-3020.

INTER AMERICAN UNIVERSITY OF PUERTO RICO, ARECIBO CAMPUS
Arecibo, PR

ABOUT THE INSTITUTION Independent, coed. 22 undergraduate majors.

GIFT AID (NEED-BASED) *Scholarships, grants, and awards:* Federal Pell, FSEOG, state, private, college/university gift aid from institutional funds.

LOANS *Programs:* Federal Direct (Subsidized and Unsubsidized Stafford, PLUS), FFEL (Subsidized and Unsubsidized Stafford, PLUS), Perkins.

WORK-STUDY *Federal work-study:* Total amount: $278,780; 238 jobs averaging $1600.

APPLYING FOR FINANCIAL AID *Required financial aid forms:* FAFSA, institution's own form.

CONTACT Ramón O. de Jesús, Financial Aid Director, Inter American University of Puerto Rico, Arecibo Campus, PO Box 4050, Arecibo, PR 00614-4050, 787-878-5475 Ext. 2275. *Fax:* 787-880-1624.

INTER AMERICAN UNIVERSITY OF PUERTO RICO, BARRANQUITAS CAMPUS
Barranquitas, PR

Tuition & fees: N/R	Average undergraduate aid package: N/A

ABOUT THE INSTITUTION Independent, coed. *Awards:* associate, bachelor's, and master's degrees and post-bachelor's certificates. 15 undergraduate majors. *Total enrollment:* 2,329. Undergraduates: 2,106. Federal methodology is used as a basis for awarding need-based institutional aid.

GIFT AID (NEED-BASED) *Scholarships, grants, and awards:* Federal Pell, FSEOG, state, private, college/university gift aid from institutional funds.

GIFT AID (NON-NEED-BASED) *Scholarships, grants, and awards by category: Special characteristics:* adult students, veterans. *ROTC:* Army cooperative.

LOANS *Programs:* Federal Direct (Subsidized Stafford), Perkins.

APPLYING FOR FINANCIAL AID *Required financial aid forms:* FAFSA, institution's own form. *Financial aid deadline (priority):* 4/30.

CONTACT Mr. Eduardo Fontanez Colon, Financial Aid Officer, Inter American University of Puerto Rico, Barranquitas Campus, Box 517, Barranquitas, PR 00794, 787-857-3600 Ext. 2049. *Fax:* 787-857-2244.

INTER AMERICAN UNIVERSITY OF PUERTO RICO, BAYAMÓN CAMPUS
Bayamón, PR

Tuition & fees: $5136	Average undergraduate aid package: $1002

ABOUT THE INSTITUTION Independent, coed. 45 undergraduate majors.

UNDERGRADUATE EXPENSES for 2010–11 *Tuition:* full-time $4620.

FRESHMAN FINANCIAL AID (Fall 2009, est.) 1,111 applied for aid; of those 96% were deemed to have need. 61% of freshmen with need received aid; of those .2% had need fully met. *Average percent of need met:* 1% (excluding resources awarded to replace EFC). *Average financial aid package:* $144 (excluding resources awarded to replace EFC).

UNDERGRADUATE FINANCIAL AID (Fall 2009, est.) 3,122 applied for aid; of those 97% were deemed to have need. 61% of undergraduates with need received aid; of those .2% had need fully met. *Average percent of need met:* 6% (excluding resources awarded to replace EFC). *Average financial aid package:* $1002 (excluding resources awarded to replace EFC).
GIFT AID (NEED-BASED) *Total amount:* $1,033,990 (34% federal, 9% state, 57% institutional). *Receiving aid:* Freshmen: 51% (570); all full-time undergraduates: 41% (1,320). *Average award:* Freshmen: $105; Undergraduates: $338. *Scholarships, grants, and awards:* state, .college/university gift aid from institutional funds.
LOANS *Student loans:* $2,800,941 (100% need-based). *Average need-based loan:* Freshmen: $140. Undergraduates: $1594. *Parent loans:* $1680 (100% need-based).
WORK-STUDY *Federal work-study:* Total amount: $163,254; jobs available.
ATHLETIC AWARDS Total amount: $39,936 (100% need-based).
CONTACT Mr. Carlos N. Alicea, Students Services Director, Inter American University of Puerto Rico, Bayamón Campus, 500 Road Dr. John Will Harris, Bayamon, PR 00957, 787-279-1912 Ext. 2017. *E-mail:* calicea@bc.inter.edu.

INTER AMERICAN UNIVERSITY OF PUERTO RICO, FAJARDO CAMPUS
Fajardo, PR

CONTACT Financial Aid Director, Inter American University of Puerto Rico, Fajardo Campus, Call Box 700003, Fajardo, PR 00738-7003, 787-863-2390 Ext. 2208.

INTER AMERICAN UNIVERSITY OF PUERTO RICO, GUAYAMA CAMPUS
Guayama, PR

ABOUT THE INSTITUTION Independent, coed. 14 undergraduate majors.
GIFT AID (NEED-BASED) *Scholarships, grants, and awards:* Federal Pell, FSEOG, state, college/university gift aid from institutional funds, Federal Nursing.
LOANS *Programs:* Federal Direct (Subsidized and Unsubsidized Stafford, PLUS), Perkins, Federal Nursing.
WORK-STUDY *Federal work-study:* Total amount: $44,163; jobs available. *State or other work-study/employment:* Part-time jobs available.
APPLYING FOR FINANCIAL AID *Required financial aid form:* FAFSA.
CONTACT Senor Jose A. Vechini, Director of Financial Aid Office, Inter American University of Puerto Rico, Guayama Campus, Call Box 10004, Guyama, PR 00785, 787-864-2222 Ext. 2206 or toll-free 787-864-2222 Ext. 2243 (in-state). *Fax:* 787-864-8232. *E-mail:* javechi@inter.edu.

INTER AMERICAN UNIVERSITY OF PUERTO RICO, METROPOLITAN CAMPUS
San Juan, PR

CONTACT Mrs. Luz M. Medina, Acting Director of Financial Aid, Inter American University of Puerto Rico, Metropolitan Campus, PO Box 191293, San Juan, PR 00919-1293, 787-758-2891. *Fax:* 787-250-0782.

INTER AMERICAN UNIVERSITY OF PUERTO RICO, PONCE CAMPUS
Mercedita, PR

Tuition & fees: $4428	Average undergraduate aid package: $1702

ABOUT THE INSTITUTION Independent, coed. 37 undergraduate majors. Both federal and institutional methodology are used as a basis for awarding need-based institutional aid.
UNDERGRADUATE EXPENSES for 2010–11 *Tuition:* full-time $3912; part-time $163 per credit. *Required fees:* full-time $516; $422 per year. Full-time tuition and fees vary according to course load and program. Part-time tuition and fees vary according to course load and program. *Payment plan:* Deferred payment.
FRESHMAN FINANCIAL AID (Fall 2008) 1,305 applied for aid; of those 100% were deemed to have need. 82% of freshmen with need received aid. *Average*

percent of need met: 3% (excluding resources awarded to replace EFC). *Average financial aid package:* $494 (excluding resources awarded to replace EFC).
UNDERGRADUATE FINANCIAL AID (Fall 2008) 3,209 applied for aid; of those 100% were deemed to have need. 83% of undergraduates with need received aid. *Average percent of need met:* 10% (excluding resources awarded to replace EFC). *Average financial aid package:* $1702 (excluding resources awarded to replace EFC).
GIFT AID (NEED-BASED) *Total amount:* $3,717,466 (31% federal, 37% state, 32% institutional). *Receiving aid:* Freshmen: 71% (936); all full-time undergraduates: 69% (2,262). *Average award:* Freshmen: $280; Undergraduates: $537. *Scholarships, grants, and awards:* Federal Pell, FSEOG, state, college/university gift aid from institutional funds, Federal Nursing.
GIFT AID (NON-NEED-BASED) *Receiving aid:* Freshmen: 3. Undergraduates: 1% (23).
LOANS *Student loans:* $9,608,464 (100% need-based). *Average need-based loan:* Freshmen: $464. Undergraduates: $2248. *Parent loans:* $17,728 (100% need-based). *Programs:* Federal Direct (Subsidized and Unsubsidized Stafford, PLUS), FFEL (Subsidized and Unsubsidized Stafford, PLUS), Perkins.
WORK-STUDY *Federal work-study:* Total amount: $526,896; jobs available.
ATHLETIC AWARDS Total amount: $114,034 (100% need-based).
APPLYING FOR FINANCIAL AID *Required financial aid form:* FAFSA. *Financial aid deadline:* Continuous.
CONTACT Juan Portalatin, Financial Aid Officer, Inter American University of Puerto Rico, Ponce Campus, 104 Turpeaux Industrial Park, Mercedita, PR 00715-2201, 787-284-1912 Ext. 2161. *Fax:* 787-841-0103. *E-mail:* japortal@ponce.inter.edu.

INTER AMERICAN UNIVERSITY OF PUERTO RICO, SAN GERMÁN CAMPUS
San Germán, PR

CONTACT Ms. María I. Lugo, Financial Aid Director, Inter American University of Puerto Rico, San Germán Campus, PO Box 5100, San Germán, PR 00683-5008, 787-264-1912 Ext. 7252. *Fax:* 787-892-6350.

INTERIOR DESIGNERS INSTITUTE
Newport Beach, CA

CONTACT Office of Financial Aid, Interior Designers Institute, 1061 Camelback Road, Newport Beach, CA 92660, 949-675-4451.

INTERNATIONAL ACADEMY OF DESIGN & TECHNOLOGY
Tampa, FL

CONTACT Financial Aid Office, International Academy of Design & Technology, 5225 Memorial Highway, Tampa, FL 33634-7350, 813-881-0007 or toll-free 800-ACADEMY. *Fax:* 813-881-3440.

INTERNATIONAL ACADEMY OF DESIGN & TECHNOLOGY
Chicago, IL

CONTACT Barbara Williams, Financial Aid Director, International Academy of Design & Technology, 1 North State Street, Suite 400, Chicago, IL 60602, 312-980-9200 or toll-free 877-ACADEMY (out-of-state). *Fax:* 312-541-3929.

INTERNATIONAL BAPTIST COLLEGE
Chandler, AZ

CONTACT Financial Aid Office, International Baptist College, 2211 West Germann Road, Chandler, AZ 85286, 480-838-7070 Ext. 268 or toll-free 800-422-4858. *Fax:* 480-838-5432. *E-mail:* financialaid@ibconline.edu.

INTERNATIONAL BUSINESS COLLEGE
Fort Wayne, IN

CONTACT Ms. Roxanna Shull, Financial Aid Director, International Business College, 3811 Illinois Road, Fort Wayne, IN 46804-1217, 219-459-4600 or toll-free 800-589-6363.

IONA COLLEGE
New Rochelle, NY

Tuition & fees: $28,850	Average undergraduate aid package: $18,067

ABOUT THE INSTITUTION Independent religious, coed. 58 undergraduate majors. Federal methodology is used as a basis for awarding need-based institutional aid.

UNDERGRADUATE EXPENSES for 2010–11 *Comprehensive fee:* $40,650 includes full-time tuition ($26,850), mandatory fees ($2000), and room and board ($11,800). Full-time tuition and fees vary according to class time. Room and board charges vary according to housing facility. *Part-time tuition:* $892 per credit. Part-time tuition and fees vary according to class time and course load. *Payment plans:* Installment, deferred payment.

FRESHMAN FINANCIAL AID (Fall 2009, est.) 783 applied for aid; of those 80% were deemed to have need. 100% of freshmen with need received aid; of those 20% had need fully met. *Average percent of need met:* 31% (excluding resources awarded to replace EFC). *Average financial aid package:* $20,002 (excluding resources awarded to replace EFC). 18% of all full-time freshmen had no need and received non-need-based gift aid.

UNDERGRADUATE FINANCIAL AID (Fall 2009, est.) 3,152 applied for aid; of those 77% were deemed to have need. 100% of undergraduates with need received aid; of those 24% had need fully met. *Average percent of need met:* 29% (excluding resources awarded to replace EFC). *Average financial aid package:* $18,067 (excluding resources awarded to replace EFC). 21% of all full-time undergraduates had no need and received non-need-based gift aid.

GIFT AID (NEED-BASED) *Total amount:* $11,465,725 (33% federal, 29% state, 37% institutional, 1% external sources). *Receiving aid:* Freshmen: 67% (529); all full-time undergraduates: 49% (1,575). *Average award:* Freshmen: $6039; Undergraduates: $5153. *Scholarships, grants, and awards:* Federal Pell, FSEOG, state, private, college/university gift aid from institutional funds.

GIFT AID (NON-NEED-BASED) *Total amount:* $25,863,929 (98% institutional, 2% external sources). *Receiving aid:* Freshmen: 77% (613). Undergraduates: 72% (2,346). *Average award:* Freshmen: $10,964. Undergraduates: $11,070. *Scholarships, grants, and awards by category: Academic interests/achievement:* 3,049 awards ($24,875,914 total): general academic interests/achievements. *Creative arts/performance:* 28 awards ($85,000 total): music. *Special characteristics:* 376 awards ($1,211,658 total): children and siblings of alumni, children of faculty/staff, religious affiliation, siblings of current students. *Tuition waivers:* Full or partial for employees or children of employees, senior citizens.

LOANS *Student loans:* $18,967,549 (36% need-based, 64% non-need-based). 68% of past graduating class borrowed through all loan programs. *Average indebtedness per student:* $24,213. *Average need-based loan:* Freshmen: $3077. Undergraduates: $2964. *Parent loans:* $6,801,827 (100% non-need-based). *Programs:* FFEL (Subsidized and Unsubsidized Stafford, PLUS), Perkins, alternative loans.

WORK-STUDY *Federal work-study:* Total amount: $808,881; 377 jobs averaging $694. *State or other work-study/employment:* Total amount: $310,000 (100% non-need-based). 251 part-time jobs averaging $871.

ATHLETIC AWARDS Total amount: $3,167,010 (100% non-need-based).

APPLYING FOR FINANCIAL AID *Required financial aid forms:* FAFSA, institution's own form, state aid form. *Financial aid deadline:* 4/15 (priority: 2/15). *Notification date:* Continuous. Students must reply by 5/1 or within 2 weeks of notification.

CONTACT Mary Grant, Director of Financial Aid, Iona College, 715 North Avenue, New Rochelle, NY 10801-1890, 914-633-2676 or toll-free 800-231-IONA (in-state). *Fax:* 914-633-2486.

IOWA STATE UNIVERSITY OF SCIENCE AND TECHNOLOGY
Ames, IA

Tuition & fees (IA res): $6997	Average undergraduate aid package: $10,771

ABOUT THE INSTITUTION State-supported, coed. 115 undergraduate majors. Federal methodology is used as a basis for awarding need-based institutional aid.

UNDERGRADUATE EXPENSES for 2010–11 *Tuition, state resident:* full-time $6102; part-time $255 per semester hour. *Tuition, nonresident:* full-time $17,668; part-time $736 per semester hour. *Required fees:* full-time $895. Full-time tuition and fees vary according to class time, degree level, and program. Part-time tuition and fees vary according to class time, course load, degree level, and program. Room and board charges vary according to board plan and housing facility. *Payment plans:* Installment, deferred payment.

FRESHMAN FINANCIAL AID (Fall 2009, est.) 3,623 applied for aid; of those 65% were deemed to have need. 99% of freshmen with need received aid; of those 46% had need fully met. *Average percent of need met:* 83% (excluding resources awarded to replace EFC). *Average financial aid package:* $10,780 (excluding resources awarded to replace EFC). 34% of all full-time freshmen had no need and received non-need-based gift aid.

UNDERGRADUATE FINANCIAL AID (Fall 2009, est.) 15,139 applied for aid; of those 71% were deemed to have need. 99% of undergraduates with need received aid; of those 40% had need fully met. *Average percent of need met:* 82% (excluding resources awarded to replace EFC). *Average financial aid package:* $10,771 (excluding resources awarded to replace EFC). 31% of all full-time undergraduates had no need and received non-need-based gift aid.

GIFT AID (NEED-BASED) *Total amount:* $51,005,425 (34% federal, 5% state, 54% institutional, 7% external sources). *Receiving aid:* Freshmen: 51% (2,314); all full-time undergraduates: 52% (10,522). *Average award:* Freshmen: $6560; Undergraduates: $5560. *Scholarships, grants, and awards:* Federal Pell, FSEOG, state, college/university gift aid from institutional funds.

GIFT AID (NON-NEED-BASED) *Total amount:* $21,862,509 (5% federal, 3% state, 77% institutional, 15% external sources). *Receiving aid:* Freshmen: 25% (1,130). Undergraduates: 26% (5,242). *Average award:* Freshmen: $2903. Undergraduates: $2285. *Scholarships, grants, and awards by category: Academic interests/achievement:* agriculture, architecture, area/ethnic studies, biological sciences, business, communication, computer science, education, engineering/technologies, English, foreign languages, general academic interests/achievements, health fields, home economics, humanities, international studies, library science, mathematics, military science, physical sciences, premedicine, social sciences. *Creative arts/performance:* applied art and design, art/fine arts, journalism/publications, music, theater/drama. *Special achievements/activities:* community service, general special achievements/activities, leadership, rodeo. *Special characteristics:* adult students, children and siblings of alumni, ethnic background, first-generation college students, general special characteristics, international students, local/state students, members of minority groups, out-of-state students, religious affiliation.

LOANS *Student loans:* $111,216,034 (58% need-based, 42% non-need-based). 71% of past graduating class borrowed through all loan programs. *Average indebtedness per student:* $30,411. *Average need-based loan:* Freshmen: $3780. Undergraduates: $4359. *Parent loans:* $18,644,038 (21% need-based, 79% non-need-based). *Programs:* Federal Direct (Subsidized and Unsubsidized Stafford, PLUS), Perkins, state, college/university, private alternative loans.

WORK-STUDY *Federal work-study:* Total amount: $2,026,330; jobs available. *State or other work-study/employment:* Total amount: $698,672 (100% need-based). Part-time jobs available.

ATHLETIC AWARDS Total amount: $4,777,506 (45% need-based, 55% non-need-based).

APPLYING FOR FINANCIAL AID *Required financial aid form:* FAFSA. *Financial aid deadline (priority):* 3/1. *Notification date:* Continuous beginning 4/1. Students must reply by 5/1.

CONTACT Roberta Johnson, Director of Financial Aid, Iowa State University of Science and Technology, 0210 Beardshear Hall, Ames, IA 50011, 515-294-2223 or toll-free 800-262-3810. *Fax:* 515-294-3622. *E-mail:* rljohns@iastate.edu.

IOWA WESLEYAN COLLEGE
Mount Pleasant, IA

Tuition & fees: $21,000	Average undergraduate aid package: N/A

ABOUT THE INSTITUTION Independent United Methodist, coed. 40 undergraduate majors. Federal methodology is used as a basis for awarding need-based institutional aid.

UNDERGRADUATE EXPENSES for 2009–10 *Comprehensive fee:* $27,654 includes full-time tuition ($21,000) and room and board ($6654). *College room only:* $2710. Room and board charges vary according to board plan and housing facility. *Part-time tuition:* $520 per credit hour. Part-time tuition and fees vary according to class time and course load. *Payment plans:* Installment, deferred payment.

GIFT AID (NEED-BASED) *Total amount:* $3,188,865 (58% federal, 27% state, 15% institutional). *Scholarships, grants, and awards:* Federal Pell, FSEOG, state, private, college/university gift aid from institutional funds.

GIFT AID (NON-NEED-BASED) *Total amount:* $4,049,897 (97% institutional, 3% external sources). *Scholarships, grants, and awards by category: Academic interests/achievement:* general academic interests/achievements. *Creative arts/ performance:* art/fine arts, music. *Special characteristics:* children of faculty/ staff, international students, religious affiliation. *Tuition waivers:* Full or partial for employees or children of employees.

LOANS *Student loans:* $5,399,641 (43% need-based, 57% non-need-based). *Parent loans:* $397,869 (100% non-need-based). *Programs:* Federal Direct (Subsidized and Unsubsidized Stafford, PLUS), Perkins, alternative loans.

WORK-STUDY *Federal work-study:* Total amount: $137,816; jobs available.

ATHLETIC AWARDS Total amount: $1,566,496 (100% non-need-based).

APPLYING FOR FINANCIAL AID *Required financial aid form:* FAFSA.

CONTACT Debra Morrissey, Director of Financial Aid, Iowa Wesleyan College, 601 North Main Street, Mount Pleasant, IA 52641-1398, 319-385-6242 or toll-free 800-582-2383 Ext. 6231. *Fax:* 319-385-6203. *E-mail:* dmorrissey@iwc.edu.

ITHACA COLLEGE
Ithaca, NY

Tuition & fees: $32,060	Average undergraduate aid package: $28,273

ABOUT THE INSTITUTION Independent, coed. 105 undergraduate majors. Institutional methodology is used as a basis for awarding need-based institutional aid.

UNDERGRADUATE EXPENSES for 2009–10 *Comprehensive fee:* $43,840 includes full-time tuition ($32,060) and room and board ($11,780). *College room only:* $6238. Room and board charges vary according to board plan. *Part-time tuition:* $1067 per credit hour. *Payment plan:* Installment.

FRESHMAN FINANCIAL AID (Fall 2009, est.) 1,777 applied for aid; of those 84% were deemed to have need. 100% of freshmen with need received aid; of those 63% had need fully met. *Average percent of need met:* 93% (excluding resources awarded to replace EFC). *Average financial aid package:* $29,600 (excluding resources awarded to replace EFC). 19% of all full-time freshmen had no need and received non-need-based gift aid.

UNDERGRADUATE FINANCIAL AID (Fall 2009, est.) 5,012 applied for aid; of those 87% were deemed to have need. 100% of undergraduates with need received aid; of those 54% had need fully met. *Average percent of need met:* 90% (excluding resources awarded to replace EFC). *Average financial aid package:* $28,273 (excluding resources awarded to replace EFC). 18% of all full-time undergraduates had no need and received non-need-based gift aid.

GIFT AID (NEED-BASED) *Total amount:* $79,566,225 (8% federal, 5% state, 85% institutional, 2% external sources). *Receiving aid:* Freshmen: 73% (1,473); all full-time undergraduates: 67% (4,277). *Average award:* Freshmen: $19,799; Undergraduates: $18,579. *Scholarships, grants, and awards:* Federal Pell, FSEOG, state, private, college/university gift aid from institutional funds.

GIFT AID (NON-NEED-BASED) *Total amount:* $15,697,803 (1% federal, 1% state, 90% institutional, 8% external sources). *Receiving aid:* Freshmen: 23% (468). Undergraduates: 17% (1,071). *Average award:* Freshmen: $8718. Undergraduates: $9551. *Scholarships, grants, and awards by category: Academic interests/achievement:* 2,469 awards ($25,693,266 total): communication, general academic interests/achievements. *Creative arts/performance:* 48 awards ($455,105 total): cinema/film/broadcasting, dance, journalism/publications, music, performing arts, theater/drama. *Special achievements/activities:* 240 awards ($1,342,000 total): leadership. *Special characteristics:* 1,886 awards ($11,091,906 total): children and siblings of alumni, children of faculty/staff, general special characteristics, members of minority groups, siblings of current students. *Tuition waivers:* Full or partial for employees or children of employees.

LOANS *Student loans:* $33,805,021 (74% need-based, 26% non-need-based). *Average need-based loan:* Freshmen: $5746. Undergraduates: $6243. *Parent loans:* $28,229,796 (27% need-based, 73% non-need-based). *Programs:* Federal Direct (Subsidized and Unsubsidized Stafford, PLUS), Perkins, alternative loans.

WORK-STUDY *Federal work-study:* Total amount: $1,500,000; 3,154 jobs averaging $2360. *State or other work-study/employment:* Total amount: $10,363,178 (63% need-based, 37% non-need-based). 1,856 part-time jobs averaging $2400.

APPLYING FOR FINANCIAL AID *Required financial aid forms:* FAFSA, CSS Financial Aid PROFILE. *Financial aid deadline (priority):* 2/1. *Notification date:* Continuous beginning 2/15.

CONTACT Mr. Larry Chambers, Director of Financial Aid, Ithaca College, 953 Danby Road, Ithaca, NY 14850-7000, 800-429-4275 or toll-free 800-429-4274. *Fax:* 607-274-1895. *E-mail:* finaid@ithaca.edu.

ITT TECHNICAL INSTITUTE
Tempe, AZ

CONTACT Financial Aid Office, ITT Technical Institute, 5005 S. Wendler Drive, Tempe, AZ 85282, 602-437-7500 or toll-free 800-879-4881.

ITT TECHNICAL INSTITUTE
Clovis, CA

CONTACT Financial Aid Office, ITT Technical Institute, 362 N. Clovis Avenue, Clovis, CA 93612, 559-325-5400 or toll-free 800-564-9771 (in-state).

ITT TECHNICAL INSTITUTE
Concord, CA

CONTACT Financial Aid Office, ITT Technical Institute, 1140 Galaxy Way, Suite 400, Concord, CA 94520, 925-674-8200 or toll-free 800-211-7062.

ITT TECHNICAL INSTITUTE
Corona, CA

CONTACT Financial Aid Office, ITT Technical Institute, 4160 Temescal Canyon Road, Suite 100, Corona, CA 92883, 951-277-5400 or toll-free 877-764-9661 (out-of-state).

ITT TECHNICAL INSTITUTE
South Bend, IN

CONTACT Financial Aid Office, ITT Technical Institute, 17390 Dugdale Drive, Suite 100, South Bend, IN 46635, 574-247-8300 or toll-free 877-474-1926.

ITT TECHNICAL INSTITUTE
Wichita, KS

CONTACT Financial Aid Office, ITT Technical Institute, One Brittany Place, Suite 100, 2024 North Woodlawn, Wichita, KS 67208, 316-681-8400 or toll-free 877-207-1047.

ITT TECHNICAL INSTITUTE
Lexington, KY

CONTACT Financial Aid Office, ITT Technical Institute, 2473 Fortune Drive, Suite 180, Lexington, KY 40509, 859-246-3300 or toll-free 800-519-8151.

ITT TECHNICAL INSTITUTE
Madison, MS

CONTACT Financial Aid Office, ITT Technical Institute, 382 Galleria Parkway, Suite 100, Madison, MS 39110, 601-607-4500 or toll-free 800-209-2521.

ITT TECHNICAL INSTITUTE
Springfield, MO

CONTACT Financial Aid Office, ITT Technical Institute, 3216 South National Avenue, Springfield, MO 65807, 417-877-4800 or toll-free 877-219-4387.

ITT TECHNICAL INSTITUTE
Charlotte, NC

CONTACT Financial Aid Office, ITT Technical Institute, 10926 David Taylor Drive, Suite 100, Charlotte, NC 28262, 704-548-2300 or toll-free 877-243-7685.

ITT TECHNICAL INSTITUTE
Oklahoma City, OK

CONTACT Financial Aid Office, ITT Technical Institute, 50 Penn Place Office Tower, 1900 Northwest Expressway, Suite 305R, Oklahoma City, OK 73118, 405-810-4100 or toll-free 800-518-1612.

JACKSON STATE UNIVERSITY
Jackson, MS

CONTACT B. J. Moncure, Director of Financial Aid, Jackson State University, 1400 J.R. Lynch Street, PO Box 17065, Jackson, MS 39217, 601-979-2227 or toll-free 800-682-5390 (in-state), 800-848-6817 (out-of-state). *Fax:* 601-979-2237.

JACKSONVILLE STATE UNIVERSITY
Jacksonville, AL

Tuition & fees (AL res): $6240   **Average undergraduate aid package: $6563**

ABOUT THE INSTITUTION State-supported, coed. 58 undergraduate majors. Federal methodology is used as a basis for awarding need-based institutional aid.

UNDERGRADUATE EXPENSES for 2009–10 *Tuition, state resident:* full-time $6240; part-time $208 per credit hour. *Tuition, nonresident:* full-time $12,480; part-time $416 per credit hour. *College room and board:* $5254. Room and board charges vary according to board plan and housing facility. *Payment plan:* Installment.

FRESHMAN FINANCIAL AID (Fall 2008) 1,074 applied for aid. *Average financial aid package:* $5378 (excluding resources awarded to replace EFC).

UNDERGRADUATE FINANCIAL AID (Fall 2008) 4,765 applied for aid. *Average financial aid package:* $6563 (excluding resources awarded to replace EFC).

GIFT AID (NEED-BASED) *Total amount:* $16,424,738 (67% federal, 4% state, 25% institutional, 4% external sources). *Receiving aid:* Freshmen: 44% (538); all full-time undergraduates: 42% (2,522). *Average award:* Freshmen: $4094; Undergraduates: $3878. *Scholarships, grants, and awards:* Federal Pell, FSEOG, state, private, college/university gift aid from institutional funds.

GIFT AID (NON-NEED-BASED) *Receiving aid:* Freshmen: 36% (435). Undergraduates: 25% (1,498). *Scholarships, grants, and awards by category:* Academic interests/achievement: biological sciences, business, communication, computer science, education, English, health fields, home economics, humanities, mathematics, military science, physical sciences, social sciences. *Creative arts/performance:* art/fine arts, journalism/publications, music, theater/drama. *Special achievements/activities:* general special achievements/activities. *Tuition waivers:* Full or partial for employees or children of employees.

LOANS *Student loans:* $43,312,871 (50% need-based, 50% non-need-based). *Average need-based loan:* Freshmen: $3192. Undergraduates: $3889. *Parent loans:* $1,469,994 (100% non-need-based). *Programs:* Federal Direct (Subsidized and Unsubsidized Stafford, PLUS), state, college/university.

WORK-STUDY *Federal work-study:* Total amount: $562,989; 224 jobs averaging $1302. *State or other work-study/employment:* Total amount: $1,266,552 (100% non-need-based). Part-time jobs available.

ATHLETIC AWARDS Total amount: $3,572,455 (100% non-need-based).

APPLYING FOR FINANCIAL AID *Required financial aid forms:* FAFSA, institution's own form. *Financial aid deadline (priority):* 3/15. *Notification date:* Continuous beginning 5/15. Students must reply within 2 weeks of notification.

CONTACT Ms. Vickie Adams, Director of Financial Aid, Jacksonville State University, 700 Pelham Road North, Jacksonville, AL 36265-9982, 256-782-5006 Ext. 8399 or toll-free 800-231-5291. *Fax:* 256-782-5476. *E-mail:* finaid@jsu.edu.

JACKSONVILLE UNIVERSITY
Jacksonville, FL

Tuition & fees: $25,300   **Average undergraduate aid package: $19,580**

ABOUT THE INSTITUTION Independent, coed. 58 undergraduate majors. Federal methodology is used as a basis for awarding need-based institutional aid.

UNDERGRADUATE EXPENSES for 2009–10 *Comprehensive fee:* $34,360 includes full-time tuition ($25,300) and room and board ($9060). *College room only:* $5300. Room and board charges vary according to board plan and housing facility. *Part-time tuition:* $840 per credit hour.

FRESHMAN FINANCIAL AID (Fall 2009, est.) 568 applied for aid; of those 88% were deemed to have need. 100% of freshmen with need received aid; of those 20% had need fully met. *Average percent of need met:* 66% (excluding resources awarded to replace EFC). *Average financial aid package:* $20,744 (excluding resources awarded to replace EFC). 23% of all full-time freshmen had no need and received non-need-based gift aid.

UNDERGRADUATE FINANCIAL AID (Fall 2009, est.) 1,714 applied for aid; of those 89% were deemed to have need. 100% of undergraduates with need received aid; of those 17% had need fully met. *Average percent of need met:* 61% (excluding resources awarded to replace EFC). *Average financial aid package:* $19,580 (excluding resources awarded to replace EFC). 25% of all full-time undergraduates had no need and received non-need-based gift aid.

GIFT AID (NEED-BASED) *Total amount:* $24,847,493 (24% federal, 15% state, 60% institutional, 1% external sources). *Receiving aid:* Freshmen: 61% (405); all full-time undergraduates: 61% (1,312). *Average award:* Freshmen: $17,471; Undergraduates: $15,432. *Scholarships, grants, and awards:* Federal Pell, FSEOG, state, private, college/university gift aid from institutional funds, Academic Competitiveness Grants, National SMART Grants.

GIFT AID (NON-NEED-BASED) *Total amount:* $7,313,787 (21% federal, 12% state, 67% institutional). *Receiving aid:* Freshmen: 14% (92). Undergraduates: 9% (203). *Average award:* Freshmen: $10,361. Undergraduates: $8925. *Scholarships, grants, and awards by category:* Academic interests/achievement: business, general academic interests/achievements. *Creative arts/performance:* general creative arts/performance. *Special achievements/activities:* general special achievements/activities, leadership. *Special characteristics:* children of educators, children of faculty/staff, international students.

LOANS *Student loans:* $14,117,873 (92% need-based, 8% non-need-based). *Average need-based loan:* Freshmen: $3227. Undergraduates: $4433. *Parent loans:* $3,467,087 (86% need-based, 14% non-need-based). *Programs:* FFEL (Subsidized and Unsubsidized Stafford, PLUS), Perkins, college/university, private loans.

WORK-STUDY *Federal work-study:* Total amount: $364,081; jobs available.

ATHLETIC AWARDS Total amount: $3,504,076 (47% need-based, 53% non-need-based).

APPLYING FOR FINANCIAL AID *Required financial aid forms:* FAFSA, institution's own form, state aid form. *Financial aid deadline (priority):* 3/1. *Notification date:* Continuous beginning 2/15.

CONTACT Mrs. Catherine Huntress, Director of Financial Aid, Jacksonville University, 2800 University Boulevard North, Jacksonville, FL 32211, 904-256-7060 or toll-free 800-225-2027. *Fax:* 904-256-7148. *E-mail:* chuntres@ju.edu.

JAMES MADISON UNIVERSITY
Harrisonburg, VA

Tuition & fees (VA res): $7860   **Average undergraduate aid package: $7885**

ABOUT THE INSTITUTION State-supported, coed. 48 undergraduate majors. Federal methodology is used as a basis for awarding need-based institutional aid.

UNDERGRADUATE EXPENSES for 2010–11 *Tuition, state resident:* full-time $4182. *Tuition, nonresident:* full-time $16,946. *Required fees:* full-time $3678. *College room and board:* $8020; *Room only:* $4028.

FRESHMAN FINANCIAL AID (Fall 2009, est.) 3,106 applied for aid; of those 50% were deemed to have need. 83% of freshmen with need received aid; of those 94% had need fully met. *Average percent of need met:* 44% (excluding resources awarded to replace EFC). *Average financial aid package:* $8389 (excluding resources awarded to replace EFC). 1% of all full-time freshmen had no need and received non-need-based gift aid.

UNDERGRADUATE FINANCIAL AID (Fall 2009, est.) 15,194 applied for aid; of those 43% were deemed to have need. 84% of undergraduates with need received aid; of those 74% had need fully met. *Average percent of need met:* 51% (excluding resources awarded to replace EFC). *Average financial aid package:* $7885 (excluding resources awarded to replace EFC). 1% of all full-time undergraduates had no need and received non-need-based gift aid.

GIFT AID (NEED-BASED) *Total amount:* $20,504,844 (40% federal, 32% state, 19% institutional, 9% external sources). *Receiving aid:* Freshmen: 17% (686); all full-time undergraduates: 15% (2,495). *Average award:* Freshmen: $7029; Undergraduates: $7055. *Scholarships, grants, and awards:* Federal Pell, FSEOG, state, private, college/university gift aid from institutional funds.

GIFT AID (NON-NEED-BASED) *Total amount:* $2,387,689 (6% state, 72% institutional, 22% external sources). *Receiving aid:* Freshmen: 2% (77). Undergraduates: 2% (343). *Average award:* Freshmen: $3614. Undergraduates: $3056. *Scholarships, grants, and awards by category: Academic interests/achievement:* 535 awards ($1,246,090 total): architecture, biological sciences, business, computer science, education, engineering/technologies, English, general academic interests/achievements, health fields, humanities, international studies, mathematics, military science, physical sciences, premedicine, religion/biblical studies, social sciences. *Creative arts/performance:* 87 awards ($111,950 total): art/fine arts, cinema/film/broadcasting, dance, journalism/publications, music, theater/drama. *Special achievements/activities:* 88 awards ($49,174 total): cheerleading/drum major, general special achievements/activities, leadership. *Special characteristics:* 82 awards ($97,300 total): children and siblings of alumni, children of faculty/staff, handicapped students, international students, local/state students, members of minority groups, out-of-state students, siblings of current students.

LOANS *Student loans:* $47,068,838 (39% need-based, 61% non-need-based). 51% of past graduating class borrowed through all loan programs. *Average indebtedness per student:* $18,183. *Average need-based loan:* Freshmen: $3673. Undergraduates: $4189. *Parent loans:* $32,077,987 (100% non-need-based). *Programs:* Federal Direct (Subsidized and Unsubsidized Stafford, PLUS), Perkins, Federal Nursing.

WORK-STUDY *Federal work-study:* Total amount: $421,840; 314 jobs averaging $1983. *State or other work-study/employment:* Total amount: $5,075,000 (100% non-need-based). 2,492 part-time jobs averaging $1985.

ATHLETIC AWARDS Total amount: $5,174,300 (100% non-need-based).

APPLYING FOR FINANCIAL AID *Required financial aid form:* FAFSA. *Financial aid deadline (priority):* 3/1. *Notification date:* Continuous beginning 4/1. Students must reply within 4 weeks of notification.

CONTACT Lisa L. Tumer, Director of Financial Aid and Scholarships, James Madison University, 800 South Main Street, MSC 3519, Harrisonburg, VA 22807, 540-568-7820. *Fax:* 540-568-7994. *E-mail:* fin_aid@jmu.edu.

JAMESTOWN COLLEGE
Jamestown, ND

Tuition & fees: $16,780	Average undergraduate aid package: $11,987

ABOUT THE INSTITUTION Independent Presbyterian, coed. 40 undergraduate majors. Both federal and institutional methodology are used as a basis for awarding need-based institutional aid.

UNDERGRADUATE EXPENSES for 2010–11 *Comprehensive fee:* $22,316 includes full-time tuition ($16,360), mandatory fees ($420), and room and board ($5536). *College room only:* $2456. Room and board charges vary according to board plan. *Part-time tuition:* $400 per credit hour. Part-time tuition and fees vary according to course load. *Payment plan:* Installment.

FRESHMAN FINANCIAL AID (Fall 2009, est.) 213 applied for aid; of those 78% were deemed to have need. 100% of freshmen with need received aid; of those 25% had need fully met. *Average percent of need met:* 79% (excluding resources awarded to replace EFC). *Average financial aid package:* $12,428 (excluding resources awarded to replace EFC). 29% of all full-time freshmen had no need and received non-need-based gift aid.

UNDERGRADUATE FINANCIAL AID (Fall 2009, est.) 818 applied for aid; of those 79% were deemed to have need. 100% of undergraduates with need received aid; of those 22% had need fully met. *Average percent of need met:* 78% (excluding resources awarded to replace EFC). *Average financial aid*

package: $11,987 (excluding resources awarded to replace EFC). 29% of all full-time undergraduates had no need and received non-need-based gift aid.

GIFT AID (NEED-BASED) *Total amount:* $4,511,554 (31% federal, 6% state, 57% institutional, 6% external sources). *Receiving aid:* Freshmen: 71% (166); all full-time undergraduates: 66% (641). *Average award:* Freshmen: $9513; Undergraduates: $8297. *Scholarships, grants, and awards:* Federal Pell, FSEOG, state, private, college/university gift aid from institutional funds, Federal Nursing, Academic Competitiveness Grants, National SMART Grants.

GIFT AID (NON-NEED-BASED) *Total amount:* $1,681,210 (2% state, 90% institutional, 8% external sources). *Receiving aid:* Freshmen: 13% (31). Undergraduates: 11% (102). *Average award:* Freshmen: $5392. Undergraduates: $4787. *Scholarships, grants, and awards by category: Academic interests/achievement:* $3,379,973 total: general academic interests/achievements, physical sciences. *Creative arts/performance:* $150,895 total: art/fine arts, music, theater/drama. *Special achievements/activities:* $328,494 total: community service, leadership. *Special characteristics:* $372,586 total: children of faculty/staff, general special characteristics, international students, relatives of clergy, religious affiliation, siblings of current students, spouses of current students, veterans. *Tuition waivers:* Full or partial for employees or children of employees.

LOANS *Student loans:* $5,976,007 (57% need-based, 43% non-need-based). 84% of past graduating class borrowed through all loan programs. *Average indebtedness per student:* $25,717. *Average need-based loan:* Freshmen: $3391. Undergraduates: $4265. *Parent loans:* $278,912 (17% need-based, 83% non-need-based). *Programs:* Federal Direct (Subsidized and Unsubsidized Stafford, PLUS), FFEL (Subsidized and Unsubsidized Stafford, PLUS), Perkins, college/university, alternative loans.

WORK-STUDY *Federal work-study:* Total amount: $214,776; 274 jobs averaging $1085. *State or other work-study/employment:* Total amount: $59,032 (100% non-need-based). 72 part-time jobs averaging $820.

ATHLETIC AWARDS Total amount: $1,335,408 (61% need-based, 39% non-need-based).

APPLYING FOR FINANCIAL AID *Required financial aid form:* FAFSA. *Financial aid deadline (priority):* 3/15. *Notification date:* Continuous beginning 1/15. Students must reply within 3 weeks of notification.

CONTACT Margery Michael, Director of Financial Aid, Jamestown College, 6085 College Lane, Jamestown, ND 58405, 701-252-3467 Ext. 5568 or toll-free 800-336-2554. *Fax:* 701-253-4318. *E-mail:* mmichael@jc.edu.

JARVIS CHRISTIAN COLLEGE
Hawkins, TX

Tuition & fees: $9600	Average undergraduate aid package: $11,020

ABOUT THE INSTITUTION Independent religious, coed. 17 undergraduate majors. Federal methodology is used as a basis for awarding need-based institutional aid.

UNDERGRADUATE EXPENSES for 2009–10 *One-time required fee:* $25. *Comprehensive fee:* $16,315 includes full-time tuition ($8520), mandatory fees ($1080), and room and board ($6715). *College room only:* $2997. Room and board charges vary according to housing facility. *Part-time tuition:* $355 per semester hour. *Part-time fees:* $1080 per term. Part-time tuition and fees vary according to course load. *Payment plans:* Installment, deferred payment.

FRESHMAN FINANCIAL AID (Fall 2009, est.) 119 applied for aid; of those 84% were deemed to have need. 100% of freshmen with need received aid; of those 4% had need fully met. *Average percent of need met:* 83% (excluding resources awarded to replace EFC). *Average financial aid package:* $12,709 (excluding resources awarded to replace EFC). 1% of all full-time freshmen had no need and received non-need-based gift aid.

UNDERGRADUATE FINANCIAL AID (Fall 2009, est.) 614 applied for aid; of those 100% were deemed to have need. 100% of undergraduates with need received aid; of those 11% had need fully met. *Average percent of need met:* 82% (excluding resources awarded to replace EFC). *Average financial aid package:* $11,020 (excluding resources awarded to replace EFC).

GIFT AID (NEED-BASED) *Total amount:* $3,459,332 (72% federal, 27% state, 1% external sources). *Receiving aid:* Freshmen: 63% (75); all full-time undergraduates: 82% (502). *Average award:* Freshmen: $4979; Undergraduates: $6957. *Scholarships, grants, and awards:* Federal Pell, FSEOG, state, private.

GIFT AID (NON-NEED-BASED) *Total amount:* $759,656 (73% institutional, 27% external sources). *Receiving aid:* Freshmen: 8% (9). Undergraduates: 35% (213). *Average award:* Freshmen: $16,323. *Scholarships, grants, and awards* *by category: Academic interests/achievement:* 73 awards ($545,843 total): education, general academic interests/achievements. *Special characteristics:* 7 awards ($52,239 total): religious affiliation.

LOANS *Student loans:* $3,987,401 (49% need-based, 51% non-need-based). 83% of past graduating class borrowed through all loan programs. *Average indebtedness per student:* $18,550. *Average need-based loan:* Freshmen: $3371. Undergraduates: $3604. *Parent loans:* $464,122 (100% non-need-based). *Programs:* Federal Direct (Subsidized and Unsubsidized Stafford, PLUS), FFEL (Subsidized and Unsubsidized Stafford, PLUS), Perkins.

WORK-STUDY *Federal work-study:* Total amount: $221,339; 151 jobs averaging $1472. *State or other work-study/employment:* Total amount: $5000 (100% need-based). 3 part-time jobs averaging $1667.

ATHLETIC AWARDS Total amount: $358,783 (100% non-need-based).

APPLYING FOR FINANCIAL AID *Required financial aid form:* FAFSA. *Financial aid deadline (priority):* 4/15. *Notification date:* Continuous beginning 5/1. Students must reply within 2 weeks of notification.

CONTACT Alice Copeland, Assistant Director of Financial Aid, Jarvis Christian College, PO Box 1470, Hawkins, TX 75765, 903-769-5733. *Fax:* 903-769-1282. *E-mail:* alice.copeland@jarvis.edu.

JEFFERSON COLLEGE OF HEALTH SCIENCES
Roanoke, VA

Tuition & fees: $17,740	Average undergraduate aid package: $11,255

ABOUT THE INSTITUTION Independent, coed. 11 undergraduate majors. Federal methodology is used as a basis for awarding need-based institutional aid.

UNDERGRADUATE EXPENSES for 2009–10 *Comprehensive fee:* $24,750 includes full-time tuition ($17,740) and room and board ($7010). *Part-time tuition:* $515 per credit hour. *Payment plan:* Installment.

FRESHMAN FINANCIAL AID (Fall 2009, est.) 307 applied for aid; of those 79% were deemed to have need. 70% of freshmen with need received aid; of those 5% had need fully met. *Average percent of need met:* 44% (excluding resources awarded to replace EFC). *Average financial aid package:* $10,201 (excluding resources awarded to replace EFC). 1% of all full-time freshmen had no need and received non-need-based gift aid.

UNDERGRADUATE FINANCIAL AID (Fall 2009, est.) 1,281 applied for aid; of those 86% were deemed to have need. 76% of undergraduates with need received aid; of those 6% had need fully met. *Average percent of need met:* 45% (excluding resources awarded to replace EFC). *Average financial aid package:* $11,255 (excluding resources awarded to replace EFC). 3% of all full-time undergraduates had no need and received non-need-based gift aid.

GIFT AID (NEED-BASED) *Total amount:* $7,754,746 (32% federal, 17% state, 27% institutional, 24% external sources). *Receiving aid:* Freshmen: 12% (167); all full-time undergraduates: 32% (828). *Average award:* Freshmen: $8295; Undergraduates: $8482. *Scholarships, grants, and awards:* Federal Pell, FSEOG, state, private, college/university gift aid from institutional funds.

GIFT AID (NON-NEED-BASED) *Total amount:* $1,733,985 (10% state, 14% institutional, 76% external sources). *Receiving aid:* Freshmen: 5. Undergraduates: 1% (25). *Average award:* Freshmen: $4703. Undergraduates: $3148. *Scholarships, grants, and awards by category: Academic interests/achievement:* 737 awards ($2,084,250 total): biological sciences, health fields. *Special characteristics:* 620 awards ($1,544,970 total): local/state students. *Tuition waivers:* Full or partial for employees or children of employees.

LOANS *Student loans:* $5,627,786 (86% need-based, 14% non-need-based). 43% of past graduating class borrowed through all loan programs. *Average indebtedness per student:* $17,327. *Average need-based loan:* Freshmen: $3662. Undergraduates: $4252. *Parent loans:* $929,500 (52% need-based, 48% non-need-based). *Programs:* FFEL (Subsidized and Unsubsidized Stafford, PLUS), alternative loans.

WORK-STUDY *Federal work-study:* Total amount: $78,790; 91 jobs averaging $1050. *State or other work-study/employment:* Total amount: $151,147 (68% need-based, 32% non-need-based). 106 part-time jobs averaging $1552.

APPLYING FOR FINANCIAL AID *Required financial aid forms:* FAFSA, state aid form. *Financial aid deadline (priority):* 5/1. *Notification date:* Continuous beginning 5/1.

CONTACT Debra A. Johnson, Director of Financial Aid, Jefferson College of Health Sciences, 920 South Jefferson Street, PO Box 13186, Roanoke, VA 24031-3186, 540-985-8492 or toll-free 888-985-8483. *Fax:* 540-224-6916. *E-mail:* djohnson@jchs.edu.

THE JEWISH THEOLOGICAL SEMINARY
New York, NY

CONTACT Linda Levine, Registrar/Director of Financial Aid, The Jewish Theological Seminary, 3080 Broadway, New York, NY 10027-4649, 212-678-8007. *Fax:* 212-678-8947. *E-mail:* financialaid@jtsa.edu.

JOHN BROWN UNIVERSITY
Siloam Springs, AR

Tuition & fees: $18,880	Average undergraduate aid package: $15,787

ABOUT THE INSTITUTION Independent interdenominational, coed. 98 undergraduate majors. Federal methodology is used as a basis for awarding need-based institutional aid.

UNDERGRADUATE EXPENSES for 2009–10 *Comprehensive fee:* $25,756 includes full-time tuition ($18,032), mandatory fees ($848), and room and board ($6876). Full-time tuition and fees vary according to course load. Room and board charges vary according to board plan and housing facility. *Part-time tuition:* $720 per credit hour. Part-time tuition and fees vary according to course load. *Payment plan:* Installment.

FRESHMAN FINANCIAL AID (Fall 2009, est.) 245 applied for aid; of those 51% were deemed to have need. 100% of freshmen with need received aid; of those 8% had need fully met. *Average percent of need met:* 50% (excluding resources awarded to replace EFC). *Average financial aid package:* $15,761 (excluding resources awarded to replace EFC). 13% of all full-time freshmen had no need and received non-need-based gift aid.

UNDERGRADUATE FINANCIAL AID (Fall 2009, est.) 1,017 applied for aid; of those 88% were deemed to have need. 100% of undergraduates with need received aid; of those 4% had need fully met. *Average percent of need met:* 50% (excluding resources awarded to replace EFC). *Average financial aid package:* $15,787 (excluding resources awarded to replace EFC). 14% of all full-time undergraduates had no need and received non-need-based gift aid.

GIFT AID (NEED-BASED) *Total amount:* $9,097,537 (21% federal, 4% state, 70% institutional, 5% external sources). *Receiving aid:* Freshmen: 36% (109); all full-time undergraduates: 58% (788). *Average award:* Freshmen: $7061; Undergraduates: $7787. *Scholarships, grants, and awards:* Federal Pell, FSEOG, state, private, college/university gift aid from institutional funds.

GIFT AID (NON-NEED-BASED) *Total amount:* $2,019,216 (7% state, 87% institutional, 6% external sources). *Receiving aid:* Freshmen: 24% (74). Undergraduates: 35% (479). *Average award:* Freshmen: $6269. Undergraduates: $6308. *Scholarships, grants, and awards by category: Academic interests/achievement:* general academic interests/achievements. *Creative arts/performance:* art/fine arts, journalism/publications, music, theater/drama. *Special achievements/activities:* cheerleading/drum major, leadership. *Special characteristics:* children and siblings of alumni, children of educators, children of faculty/staff, ethnic background, international students, members of minority groups, relatives of clergy, siblings of current students. *Tuition waivers:* Full or partial for employees or children of employees.

LOANS *Student loans:* $5,727,342 (92% need-based, 8% non-need-based). 60% of past graduating class borrowed through all loan programs. *Average indebtedness per student:* $19,991. *Average need-based loan:* Freshmen: $3042. Undergraduates: $4330. *Parent loans:* $1,254,419 (84% need-based, 16% non-need-based). *Programs:* Federal Direct (Subsidized and Unsubsidized Stafford, PLUS), FFEL (Subsidized and Unsubsidized Stafford, PLUS), Perkins, college/university.

WORK-STUDY *Federal work-study:* Total amount: $589,190; jobs available. *State or other work-study/employment:* Total amount: $388,330 (65% need-based, 35% non-need-based). Part-time jobs available.

ATHLETIC AWARDS Total amount: $1,299,862 (29% need-based, 71% non-need-based).

APPLYING FOR FINANCIAL AID *Required financial aid form:* FAFSA. *Financial aid deadline (priority):* 3/1. *Notification date:* Continuous beginning 3/1. Students must reply by 6/1 or within 4 weeks of notification.

CONTACT Mr. Kim Eldridge, Director of Student Financial Aid, John Brown University, 2000 West University Street, Siloam Springs, AR 72761-2121, 479-524-7424 or toll-free 877-JBU-INFO. *Fax:* 479-524-7405. *E-mail:* keldridg@jbu.edu.

JOHN CARROLL UNIVERSITY
University Heights, OH

Tuition & fees: $30,250	Average undergraduate aid package: $23,033

ABOUT THE INSTITUTION Independent Roman Catholic (Jesuit), coed. 50 undergraduate majors. Federal methodology is used as a basis for awarding need-based institutional aid.

UNDERGRADUATE EXPENSES for 2010–11 *One-time required fee:* $325. *Comprehensive fee:* $39,000 includes full-time tuition ($29,250), mandatory fees ($1000), and room and board ($8750). *College room only:* $4640. Room and board charges vary according to board plan and housing facility. *Part-time tuition:* $890 per credit hour. Part-time tuition and fees vary according to course load. *Payment plans:* Installment, deferred payment.

FRESHMAN FINANCIAL AID (Fall 2009, est.) 563 applied for aid; of those 87% were deemed to have need. 100% of freshmen with need received aid; of those 22% had need fully met. *Average percent of need met:* 85% (excluding resources awarded to replace EFC). *Average financial aid package:* $25,065 (excluding resources awarded to replace EFC). 22% of all full-time freshmen had no need and received non-need-based gift aid.

UNDERGRADUATE FINANCIAL AID (Fall 2009, est.) 1,854 applied for aid; of those 87% were deemed to have need. 100% of undergraduates with need received aid; of those 19% had need fully met. *Average percent of need met:* 81% (excluding resources awarded to replace EFC). *Average financial aid package:* $23,033 (excluding resources awarded to replace EFC). 18% of all full-time undergraduates had no need and received non-need-based gift aid.

GIFT AID (NEED-BASED) *Total amount:* $21,983,524 (20% federal, 6% state, 73% institutional, 1% external sources). *Receiving aid:* Freshmen: 74% (490); all full-time undergraduates: 55% (1,600). *Average award:* Freshmen: $17,877; Undergraduates: $15,809. *Scholarships, grants, and awards:* Federal Pell, FSEOG, state, private, college/university gift aid from institutional funds.

GIFT AID (NON-NEED-BASED) *Total amount:* $21,916,675 (97% institutional, 3% external sources). *Receiving aid:* Freshmen: 10% (69). Undergraduates: 6% (166). *Average award:* Freshmen: $10,462. Undergraduates: $9983. *Scholarships, grants, and awards by category;* Academic interests/achievement: biological sciences, business, communication, computer science, education, English, foreign languages, health fields, mathematics, military science, physical sciences, premedicine, religion/biblical studies, social sciences. *Special achievements/activities:* community service, leadership, religious involvement. *Special characteristics:* children and siblings of alumni, children of educators, children of faculty/staff, ethnic background, first-generation college students, local/state students, members of minority groups, veterans, veterans' children. *Tuition waivers:* Full or partial for employees or children of employees, senior citizens.

LOANS *Student loans:* $14,943,465 (93% need-based, 7% non-need-based). 74% of past graduating class borrowed through all loan programs. *Average indebtedness per student:* $28,830. *Average need-based loan:* Freshmen: $3975. Undergraduates: $4296. *Parent loans:* $5,094,992 (100% need-based). *Programs:* Federal Direct (Subsidized and Unsubsidized Stafford, PLUS), Perkins.

WORK-STUDY *Federal work-study:* Total amount: $1,233,460; jobs available. *State or other work-study/employment:* Part-time jobs available.

APPLYING FOR FINANCIAL AID *Required financial aid form:* FAFSA. *Financial aid deadline:* 3/15 (priority: 2/15). *Notification date:* Continuous. Students must reply by 5/1.

CONTACT Director of Financial Aid, John Carroll University, 20700 North Park Boulevard, University Heights, OH 44118-4581, 216-397-4248. *Fax:* 216-397-3098. *E-mail:* jcuofa@jcu.edu.

JOHN F. KENNEDY UNIVERSITY
Pleasant Hill, CA

CONTACT Mindy Bergeron, Director of Financial Aid, John F. Kennedy University, 100 Ellinwood Way, Pleasant Hill, CA 94523, 925-969-3385 or toll-free 800-696-JFKU. *Fax:* 925-969-3390. *E-mail:* bergeron@jfku.edu.

JOHN JAY COLLEGE OF CRIMINAL JUSTICE OF THE CITY UNIVERSITY OF NEW YORK
New York, NY

Tuition & fees (NY res): $4600	Average undergraduate aid package: $10,150

ABOUT THE INSTITUTION State and locally supported, coed. 17 undergraduate majors. Federal methodology is used as a basis for awarding need-based institutional aid.

UNDERGRADUATE EXPENSES for 2010–11 *Tuition, state resident:* full-time $4600; part-time $195 per credit. *Tuition, nonresident:* full-time $12,450; part-time $415 per credit. *Required fees:* $139.85 per course. *Payment plan:* Installment.

FRESHMAN FINANCIAL AID (Fall 2009, est.) 2,557 applied for aid; of those 88% were deemed to have need. 86% of freshmen with need received aid. *Average percent of need met:* 85% (excluding resources awarded to replace EFC). *Average financial aid package:* $10,150 (excluding resources awarded to replace EFC).

UNDERGRADUATE FINANCIAL AID (Fall 2009, est.) 9,114 applied for aid; of those 94% were deemed to have need. 93% of undergraduates with need received aid. *Average percent of need met:* 85% (excluding resources awarded to replace EFC). *Average financial aid package:* $10,150 (excluding resources awarded to replace EFC).

GIFT AID (NEED-BASED) *Total amount:* $71,921,089 (70% federal, 28% state, 1% institutional, 1% external sources). *Receiving aid:* Freshmen: 57% (1,651); all full-time undergraduates: 71% (7,394). *Average award:* Freshmen: $3175; Undergraduates: $3175. *Scholarships, grants, and awards:* Federal Pell, FSEOG, state, college/university gift aid from institutional funds.

GIFT AID (NON-NEED-BASED) *Receiving aid:* Freshmen: 7% (212). Undergraduates: 3% (300). *Scholarships, grants, and awards by category:* Academic interests/achievement: general academic interests/achievements. *Tuition waivers:* Full or partial for senior citizens.

LOANS *Student loans:* $20,472,490 (100% need-based). 49% of past graduating class borrowed through all loan programs. *Average indebtedness per student:* $45,000. *Average need-based loan:* Freshmen: $3500. Undergraduates: $3500. *Parent loans:* $485,890 (100% need-based). *Programs:* Federal Direct (Subsidized and Unsubsidized Stafford, PLUS), Perkins.

WORK-STUDY *Federal work-study:* Total amount: $168,677; jobs available. *State or other work-study/employment:* Total amount: $19,971 (100% need-based). Part-time jobs available.

APPLYING FOR FINANCIAL AID *Required financial aid forms:* FAFSA, state aid form. *Financial aid deadline:* Continuous. *Notification date:* 4/1. Students must reply within 2 weeks of notification.

CONTACT Sylvia Lopez-Crespo, Director of Financial Aid, John Jay College of Criminal Justice of the City University of New York, 445 West 59th Street, New York, NY 10019-1093, 212-237-8897 or toll-free 877-JOHNJAY. *Fax:* 212-237-8936. *E-mail:* slopez@jjay.cuny.edu.

THE JOHNS HOPKINS UNIVERSITY
Baltimore, MD

Tuition & fees: $39,150	Average undergraduate aid package: $31,853

ABOUT THE INSTITUTION Independent, coed. 61 undergraduate majors. Institutional methodology is used as a basis for awarding need-based institutional aid.

UNDERGRADUATE EXPENSES for 2009–10 *One-time required fee:* $500. *Comprehensive fee:* $51,190 includes full-time tuition ($39,150) and room and board ($12,040). *College room only:* $6882. Room and board charges vary according to board plan and housing facility. *Part-time tuition:* $1305 per credit hour. *Payment plan:* Installment.

FRESHMAN FINANCIAL AID (Fall 2009, est.) 801 applied for aid; of those 70% were deemed to have need. 100% of freshmen with need received aid; of those 94% had need fully met. *Average percent of need met:* 94% (excluding resources awarded to replace EFC). *Average financial aid package:* $29,322 (excluding resources awarded to replace EFC). 1% of all full-time freshmen had no need and received non-need-based gift aid.

UNDERGRADUATE FINANCIAL AID (Fall 2009, est.) 2,732 applied for aid; of those 84% were deemed to have need. 100% of undergraduates with need

received aid; of those 99% had need fully met. *Average percent of need met:* 98% (excluding resources awarded to replace EFC). *Average financial aid package:* $31,853 (excluding resources awarded to replace EFC). 1% of all full-time undergraduates had no need and received non-need-based gift aid.

GIFT AID (NEED-BASED) *Total amount:* $59,207,410 (7% federal, 1% state, 89% institutional, 3% external sources). *Receiving aid:* Freshmen: 34% (453); all full-time undergraduates: 40% (1,972). *Average award:* Freshmen: $27,706; Undergraduates: $28,380. *Scholarships, grants, and awards:* Federal Pell, FSEOG, state, private, college/university gift aid from institutional funds.

GIFT AID (NON-NEED-BASED) *Total amount:* $4,916,055 (18% federal, 4% state, 56% institutional, 22% external sources). *Receiving aid:* Freshmen: 5% (62). Undergraduates: 5% (266). *Average award:* Freshmen: $31,100. Undergraduates: $27,360. *Scholarships, grants, and awards by category: Academic interests/achievement:* 79 awards ($2,015,600 total): engineering/ technologies, general academic interests/achievements. *Special characteristics:* 115 awards ($3,716,965 total): children of faculty/staff, local/state students. *Tuition waivers:* Full or partial for employees or children of employees.

LOANS *Student loans:* $14,263,755 (60% need-based, 40% non-need-based). 46% of past graduating class borrowed through all loan programs. *Average indebtedness per student:* $21,859. *Average need-based loan:* Freshmen: $3364. Undergraduates: $4530. *Parent loans:* $10,059,367 (12% need-based, 88% non-need-based). *Programs:* Federal Direct (Subsidized and Unsubsidized Stafford, PLUS), Perkins, college/university.

WORK-STUDY *Federal work-study:* Total amount: $4,077,994; 1,723 jobs averaging $2367.

ATHLETIC AWARDS Total amount: $1,295,263 (30% need-based, 70% non-need-based).

APPLYING FOR FINANCIAL AID *Required financial aid forms:* FAFSA, CSS Financial Aid PROFILE, noncustodial (divorced/separated) parent's statement, business/farm supplement, current year federal income tax form(s). *Financial aid deadline:* 3/1. *Notification date:* 4/1. Students must reply by 5/1 or within 2 weeks of notification.

CONTACT Mr. Vincent Amoroso, Director of Student Financial Services, The Johns Hopkins University, 146 Garland Hall, Baltimore, MD 21218, 410-516-8028. *Fax:* 410-516-6015. *E-mail:* vamoros1@jhu.edu.

JOHNSON & WALES UNIVERSITY
Denver, CO

Tuition & fees: $24,141	Average undergraduate aid package: $15,792

ABOUT THE INSTITUTION Independent, coed. 18 undergraduate majors. Federal methodology is used as a basis for awarding need-based institutional aid.

UNDERGRADUATE EXPENSES for 2010–11 *One-time required fee:* $288. *Comprehensive fee:* $33,045 includes full-time tuition ($23,034), mandatory fees ($1107), and room and board ($8904). Room and board charges vary according to board plan, housing facility, and location. *Payment plan:* Installment.

FRESHMAN FINANCIAL AID (Fall 2009, est.) 355 applied for aid; of those 88% were deemed to have need. 99% of freshmen with need received aid; of those 15% had need fully met. *Average percent of need met:* 65% (excluding resources awarded to replace EFC). *Average financial aid package:* $15,748 (excluding resources awarded to replace EFC). 18% of all full-time freshmen had no need and received non-need-based gift aid.

UNDERGRADUATE FINANCIAL AID (Fall 2009, est.) 1,233 applied for aid; of those 87% were deemed to have need. 99% of undergraduates with need received aid; of those 14% had need fully met. *Average percent of need met:* 69% (excluding resources awarded to replace EFC). *Average financial aid package:* $15,792 (excluding resources awarded to replace EFC). 19% of all full-time undergraduates had no need and received non-need-based gift aid.

GIFT AID (NEED-BASED) *Total amount:* $6,004,136 (38% federal, 62% institutional). *Receiving aid:* Freshmen: 67% (267); all full-time undergraduates: 62% (891). *Average award:* Freshmen: $6045; Undergraduates: $6502. *Scholarships, grants, and awards:* Federal Pell, FSEOG, state, private, college/ university gift aid from institutional funds.

GIFT AID (NON-NEED-BASED) *Total amount:* $7,261,897 (90% institutional, 10% external sources). *Receiving aid:* Freshmen: 73% (293). Undergraduates: 61% (875). *Average award:* Freshmen: $6155. Undergraduates: $6141. *Scholarships, grants, and awards by category: Academic interests/achievement:* general academic interests/achievements. *Special achievements/activities:* leadership,

memberships. *Special characteristics:* children and siblings of alumni, children of faculty/staff, local/state students. *Tuition waivers:* Full or partial for employees or children of employees.

LOANS *Student loans:* $11,240,784 (80% need-based, 20% non-need-based). 79% of past graduating class borrowed through all loan programs. *Average need-based loan:* Freshmen: $3356. Undergraduates: $4987. *Parent loans:* $2,721,647 (100% non-need-based). *Programs:* Federal Direct (Subsidized and Unsubsidized Stafford, PLUS), FFEL (Subsidized and Unsubsidized Stafford, PLUS), Perkins.

WORK-STUDY *Federal work-study:* Total amount: $811,220; jobs available.

APPLYING FOR FINANCIAL AID *Required financial aid form:* FAFSA. *Financial aid deadline (priority):* 3/1. *Notification date:* Continuous beginning 3/15.

CONTACT Ms. Lynn Robinson, Executive Director of Student Financial Services, Johnson & Wales University, 8 Abbott Park Place, Providence, RI 02903, 401-598-4648 or toll-free 877-598-3368. *Fax:* 401-598-1040. *E-mail:* fp@jwu.edu.

JOHNSON & WALES UNIVERSITY
North Miami, FL

Tuition & fees: $24,429	Average undergraduate aid package: $18,270

ABOUT THE INSTITUTION Independent, coed. 16 undergraduate majors. Federal methodology is used as a basis for awarding need-based institutional aid.

UNDERGRADUATE EXPENSES for 2010–11 *Comprehensive fee:* $33,333 includes full-time tuition ($23,034), mandatory fees ($1395), and room and board ($8904). Room and board charges vary according to board plan and housing facility. *Payment plan:* Installment.

FRESHMAN FINANCIAL AID (Fall 2009, est.) 538 applied for aid; of those 93% were deemed to have need. 100% of freshmen with need received aid; of those 10% had need fully met. *Average percent of need met:* 67% (excluding resources awarded to replace EFC). *Average financial aid package:* $18,957 (excluding resources awarded to replace EFC). 10% of all full-time freshmen had no need and received non-need-based gift aid.

UNDERGRADUATE FINANCIAL AID (Fall 2009, est.) 1,651 applied for aid; of those 94% were deemed to have need. 99% of undergraduates with need received aid; of those 11% had need fully met. *Average percent of need met:* 70% (excluding resources awarded to replace EFC). *Average financial aid package:* $18,270 (excluding resources awarded to replace EFC). 13% of all full-time undergraduates had no need and received non-need-based gift aid.

GIFT AID (NEED-BASED) *Total amount:* $12,296,275 (43% federal, 6% state, 51% institutional). *Receiving aid:* Freshmen: 81% (476); all full-time undergraduates: 73% (1,450). *Average award:* Freshmen: $8600; Undergraduates: $8337. *Scholarships, grants, and awards:* Federal Pell, FSEOG, state, private, college/ university gift aid from institutional funds.

GIFT AID (NON-NEED-BASED) *Total amount:* $8,206,245 (5% state, 88% institutional, 7% external sources). *Receiving aid:* Freshmen: 77% (453). Undergraduates: 57% (1,126). *Average award:* Freshmen: $5365. Undergraduates: $5009. *Scholarships, grants, and awards by category: Academic interests/ achievement:* general academic interests/achievements. *Special achievements/ activities:* leadership, memberships. *Special characteristics:* children and siblings of alumni, children of faculty/staff, local/state students. *Tuition waivers:* Full or partial for employees or children of employees.

LOANS *Student loans:* $16,190,008 (91% need-based, 9% non-need-based). 86% of past graduating class borrowed through all loan programs. *Average need-based loan:* Freshmen: $3407. Undergraduates: $5378. *Parent loans:* $2,705,364 (100% non-need-based). *Programs:* Federal Direct (Subsidized and Unsubsidized Stafford, PLUS), FFEL (Subsidized and Unsubsidized Stafford, PLUS), Perkins.

WORK-STUDY *Federal work-study:* Total amount: $1,379,497; jobs available. *State or other work-study/employment:* Part-time jobs available.

APPLYING FOR FINANCIAL AID *Required financial aid form:* FAFSA. *Financial aid deadline (priority):* 3/1. *Notification date:* Continuous beginning 3/15.

CONTACT Ms. Lynn Robinson, Executive Director of Student Financial Services, Johnson & Wales University, 8 Abbott Park Place, Providence, RI 02903, 401-598-4648 or toll-free 800-232-2433. *Fax:* 401-598-1040. *E-mail:* fp@jwu.edu.

JOHNSON & WALES UNIVERSITY
Providence, RI

Tuition & fees: $24,141 | **Average undergraduate aid package:** $15,772

ABOUT THE INSTITUTION Independent, coed. 40 undergraduate majors. Federal methodology is used as a basis for awarding need-based institutional aid.

UNDERGRADUATE EXPENSES for 2010–11 *One-time required fee:* $288. *Tuition:* full-time $23,034. Room and board charges vary according to board plan, housing facility, and location. *Payment plan:* Installment.

FRESHMAN FINANCIAL AID (Fall 2009, est.) 1,869 applied for aid; of those 89% were deemed to have need. 100% of freshmen with need received aid; of those 13% had need fully met. *Average percent of need met:* 67% (excluding resources awarded to replace EFC). *Average financial aid package:* $16,857 (excluding resources awarded to replace EFC). 19% of all full-time freshmen had no need and received non-need-based gift aid.

UNDERGRADUATE FINANCIAL AID (Fall 2009, est.) 6,745 applied for aid; of those 88% were deemed to have need. 99% of undergraduates with need received aid; of those 12% had need fully met. *Average percent of need met:* 68% (excluding resources awarded to replace EFC). *Average financial aid package:* $15,772 (excluding resources awarded to replace EFC). 17% of all full-time undergraduates had no need and received non-need-based gift aid.

GIFT AID (NEED-BASED) *Total amount:* $37,625,582 (33% federal, 2% state, 65% institutional). *Receiving aid:* Freshmen: 65% (1,462); all full-time undergraduates: 58% (5,048). *Average award:* Freshmen: $7754; Undergraduates: $7226. *Scholarships, grants, and awards:* Federal Pell, FSEOG, state, private, college/university gift aid from institutional funds.

GIFT AID (NON-NEED-BASED) *Total amount:* $30,571,253 (91% institutional, 9% external sources). *Receiving aid:* Freshmen: 68% (1,543). Undergraduates: 49% (4,225). *Average award:* Freshmen: $5247. Undergraduates: $4618. *Scholarships, grants, and awards by category: Academic interests/achievement:* general academic interests/achievements. *Special achievements/activities:* leadership, memberships. *Special characteristics:* children and siblings of alumni, children of faculty/staff, local/state students. *Tuition waivers:* Full or partial for employees or children of employees.

LOANS *Student loans:* $65,004,476 (81% need-based, 19% non-need-based). 83% of past graduating class borrowed through all loan programs. *Average need-based loan:* Freshmen: $3392. Undergraduates: $5297. *Parent loans:* $19,118,437 (100% non-need-based). *Programs:* Federal Direct (Subsidized and Unsubsidized Stafford, PLUS), FFEL (Subsidized and Unsubsidized Stafford, PLUS), Perkins.

WORK-STUDY *Federal work-study:* Total amount: $4,333,126; jobs available.

APPLYING FOR FINANCIAL AID *Required financial aid form:* FAFSA. *Financial aid deadline (priority):* 3/1. *Notification date:* Continuous beginning 3/15.

CONTACT Ms. Lynn Robinson, Executive Director of Student Financial Services, Johnson & Wales University, 8 Abbott Park Place, Providence, RI 02903, 401-598-4648 or toll-free 800-598-1000 (in-state), 800-342-5598 (out-of-state). *Fax:* 401-598-1040.

JOHNSON & WALES UNIVERSITY— CHARLOTTE CAMPUS
Charlotte, NC

Tuition & fees: $24,429 | **Average undergraduate aid package:** $17,625

ABOUT THE INSTITUTION Independent, coed. 13 undergraduate majors. Federal methodology is used as a basis for awarding need-based institutional aid.

UNDERGRADUATE EXPENSES for 2010–11 *Comprehensive fee:* $34,347 includes full-time tuition ($23,034), mandatory fees ($1395), and room and board ($9918). Room and board charges vary according to board plan, housing facility, and location. *Payment plan:* Installment.

FRESHMAN FINANCIAL AID (Fall 2009, est.) 642 applied for aid; of those 91% were deemed to have need. 100% of freshmen with need received aid; of those 14% had need fully met. *Average percent of need met:* 69% (excluding resources awarded to replace EFC). *Average financial aid package:* $18,673 (excluding resources awarded to replace EFC). 31% of all full-time freshmen had no need and received non-need-based gift aid.

UNDERGRADUATE FINANCIAL AID (Fall 2009, est.) 2,154 applied for aid; of those 91% were deemed to have need. 100% of undergraduates with need

received aid; of those 14% had need fully met. *Average percent of need met:* 71% (excluding resources awarded to replace EFC). *Average financial aid package:* $17,625 (excluding resources awarded to replace EFC). 13% of all full-time undergraduates had no need and received non-need-based gift aid.

GIFT AID (NEED-BASED) *Total amount:* $14,286,936 (36% federal, 8% state, 56% institutional). *Receiving aid:* Freshmen: 79% (537); all full-time undergraduates: 74% (1,784). *Average award:* Freshmen: $8760; Undergraduates: $7894. *Scholarships, grants, and awards:* Federal Pell, FSEOG, state, private, college/university gift aid from institutional funds.

GIFT AID (NON-NEED-BASED) *Total amount:* $11,466,368 (12% state, 80% institutional, 8% external sources). *Receiving aid:* Freshmen: 82% (556). Undergraduates: 69% (1,679). *Average award:* Freshmen: $5966. Undergraduates: $5275. *Scholarships, grants, and awards by category: Academic interests/achievement:* general academic interests/achievements. *Special achievements/activities:* leadership, memberships. *Special characteristics:* children and siblings of alumni, children of faculty/staff, local/state students. *Tuition waivers:* Full or partial for employees or children of employees.

LOANS *Student loans:* $20,185,123 (87% need-based, 13% non-need-based). 87% of past graduating class borrowed through all loan programs. *Average need-based loan:* Freshmen: $3397. Undergraduates: $5205. *Parent loans:* $4,907,799 (100% non-need-based). *Programs:* Federal Direct (Subsidized and Unsubsidized Stafford, PLUS), FFEL (Subsidized and Unsubsidized Stafford, PLUS), Perkins.

WORK-STUDY *Federal work-study:* Total amount: $1,235,629; jobs available.

APPLYING FOR FINANCIAL AID *Required financial aid form:* FAFSA. *Financial aid deadline (priority):* 3/1. *Notification date:* Continuous beginning 3/15.

CONTACT Ms. Lynn Robinson, Executive Director of Student Financial Services, Johnson & Wales University—Charlotte Campus, 8 Abbott Park Place, Providence, RI 02903, 401-598-1648 or toll-free 866-598-2427, *Fax:* 401-598-4751. *E-mail:* fp@jwu.edu.

JOHNSON BIBLE COLLEGE
Knoxville, TN

Tuition & fees: $9100 | **Average undergraduate aid package:** $8399

ABOUT THE INSTITUTION Independent religious, coed. 6 undergraduate majors. Institutional methodology is used as a basis for awarding need-based institutional aid.

UNDERGRADUATE EXPENSES for 2010–11 *Comprehensive fee:* $14,200 includes full-time tuition ($8300), mandatory fees ($800), and room and board ($5100). *College room only:* $2400. Room and board charges vary according to board plan and housing facility. *Part-time tuition:* $332 per credit hour. *Part-time fees:* $35 per credit hour. Part-time tuition and fees vary according to course load. *Payment plan:* Installment.

FRESHMAN FINANCIAL AID (Fall 2009, est.) 127 applied for aid; of those 91% were deemed to have need. 100% of freshmen with need received aid. *Average percent of need met:* 87% (excluding resources awarded to replace EFC). *Average financial aid package:* $7785 (excluding resources awarded to replace EFC).

UNDERGRADUATE FINANCIAL AID (Fall 2009, est.) 602 applied for aid; of those 90% were deemed to have need. 100% of undergraduates with need received aid. *Average percent of need met:* 93% (excluding resources awarded to replace EFC). *Average financial aid package:* $8399 (excluding resources awarded to replace EFC).

GIFT AID (NEED-BASED) *Total amount:* $3,158,950 (42% federal, 13% state, 45% institutional). *Receiving aid:* Freshmen: 91% (115); all full-time undergraduates: 90% (544). *Average award:* Freshmen: $4232; Undergraduates: $4582. *Scholarships, grants, and awards:* Federal Pell, FSEOG, state, private, college/university gift aid from institutional funds, Academic Competitiveness Grants.

GIFT AID (NON-NEED-BASED) *Total amount:* $682,786 (100% external sources). *Receiving aid:* Freshmen: 76% (97). Undergraduates: 76% (458). *Scholarships, grants, and awards by category: Academic interests/achievement:* $654,465 total: business, communication, education, general academic interests/achievements, religion/biblical studies. *Creative arts/performance:* $3500 total: art/fine arts, general creative arts/performance, music. *Special achievements/activities:* $110,017 total: community service, general special achievements/activities, leadership, religious involvement. *Special characteristics:* $289,414 total: children of current students, children of educators, children of faculty/staff, ethnic background, general special characteristics, international students, married students, members of minority groups, parents of current students, relatives of clergy, religious affiliation, siblings of current students, spouses of current students. *Tuition waivers:* Full or partial for employees or children of employees.

LOANS *Student loans:* $2,711,582 (52% need-based, 48% non-need-based). 65% of past graduating class borrowed through all loan programs. *Average indebtedness per student:* $18,661. *Average need-based loan:* Freshmen: $3146. Undergraduates: $4145. *Parent loans:* $376,391 (100% non-need-based). *Programs:* Federal Direct (Subsidized and Unsubsidized Stafford), FFEL (Subsidized and Unsubsidized Stafford, PLUS), college/university, alternative loans.

WORK-STUDY *Federal work-study:* Total amount: $103,483; 126 jobs averaging $1824.

APPLYING FOR FINANCIAL AID *Required financial aid forms:* FAFSA, institution's own form. *Financial aid deadline (priority):* 3/1. *Notification date:* Continuous beginning 4/1. Students must reply within 2 weeks of notification.

CONTACT Mr. Lawrence Rector, CPA, Financial Aid Director, Johnson Bible College, 7900 Johnson Drive, Knoxville, TN 37998, 865-251-2303 Ext. 2316 or toll-free 800-827-2122. *Fax:* 865-251-2337. *E-mail:* lrector@jbc.edu.

JOHNSON C. SMITH UNIVERSITY
Charlotte, NC

Tuition & fees: $15,754	Average undergraduate aid package: $12,940

ABOUT THE INSTITUTION Independent, coed. 28 undergraduate majors. Federal methodology is used as a basis for awarding need-based institutional aid.

UNDERGRADUATE EXPENSES for 2009–10 *Comprehensive fee:* $21,886 includes full-time tuition ($13,361), mandatory fees ($2393), and room and board ($6132). *College room only:* $3529. Full-time tuition and fees vary according to course load. Room and board charges vary according to board plan and housing facility. *Part-time tuition:* $361 per credit hour. *Part-time fees:* $252.50 per term. Part-time tuition and fees vary according to course load. *Payment plan:* Installment.

FRESHMAN FINANCIAL AID (Fall 2009, est.) 269 applied for aid; of those 96% were deemed to have need. 100% of freshmen with need received aid; of those 4% had need fully met. *Average percent of need met:* 51% (excluding resources awarded to replace EFC). *Average financial aid package:* $12,865 (excluding resources awarded to replace EFC). 2% of all full-time freshmen had no need and received non-need-based gift aid.

UNDERGRADUATE FINANCIAL AID (Fall 2009, est.) 1,361 applied for aid; of those 95% were deemed to have need. 100% of undergraduates with need received aid; of those 4% had need fully met. *Average percent of need met:* 51% (excluding resources awarded to replace EFC). *Average financial aid package:* $12,940 (excluding resources awarded to replace EFC). 2% of all full-time undergraduates had no need and received non-need-based gift aid.

GIFT AID (NEED-BASED) *Total amount:* $9,230,477 (56% federal, 16% state, 23% institutional, 5% external sources). *Receiving aid:* Freshmen: 84% (236); all full-time undergraduates: 80% (1,137). *Average award:* Freshmen: $10,086; Undergraduates: $8759. *Scholarships, grants, and awards:* Federal Pell, FSEOG, state, private, college/university gift aid from institutional funds, United Negro College Fund.

GIFT AID (NON-NEED-BASED) *Total amount:* $389,172 (1% federal, 13% state, 70% institutional, 16% external sources). *Receiving aid:* Freshmen: 4% (10). Undergraduates: 3% (45). *Average award:* Freshmen: $7891. Undergraduates: $6654. *Scholarships, grants, and awards by category:* Academic interests/achievement: computer science, general academic interests/achievements, mathematics. *Creative arts/performance:* music. *Special achievements/activities:* community service, general special achievements/activities, leadership. *Special characteristics:* children of faculty/staff, ethnic background, siblings of current students. *Tuition waivers:* Full or partial for employees or children of employees.

LOANS *Student loans:* $12,083,214 (93% need-based, 7% non-need-based). 81% of past graduating class borrowed through all loan programs. *Average indebtedness per student:* $19,000. *Average need-based loan:* Freshmen: $3676. Undergraduates: $5105. *Parent loans:* $5,984,982 (69% need-based, 31% non-need-based). *Programs:* Federal Direct (Subsidized and Unsubsidized Stafford, PLUS), FFEL (PLUS), Perkins, alternative loans.

WORK-STUDY *Federal work-study:* Total amount: $384,415; jobs available. *State or other work-study/employment:* Total amount: $178,280 (78% need-based, 22% non-need-based). Part-time jobs available.

ATHLETIC AWARDS Total amount: $1,352,194 (77% need-based, 23% non-need-based).

APPLYING FOR FINANCIAL AID *Required financial aid form:* FAFSA. *Financial aid deadline (priority):* 3/1. *Notification date:* Continuous beginning 3/1. Students must reply within 2 weeks of notification.

CONTACT Ms. Keisha Ramey, Interim Director of Financial Aid, Johnson C. Smith University, 100 Beatties Ford Road, Charlotte, NC 28216, 704-378-1207 or toll-free 800-782-7303. *Fax:* 704-378-1292. *E-mail:* kramey@jcsu.edu.

JOHNSON STATE COLLEGE
Johnson, VT

CONTACT Ms. Kimberly Goodell, Financial Aid Officer, Johnson State College, 337 College Hill, Johnson, VT 05656-9405, 802-635-2356 or toll-free 800-635-2356. *Fax:* 802-635-1463. *E-mail:* goodellk@badger.jsc.vsc.edu.

JOHN WESLEY COLLEGE
High Point, NC

CONTACT Mrs. Shirley Carter, Director of Financial Aid, John Wesley College, 2314 North Centennial Street, High Point, NC 27265-3197, 336-889-2262. *Fax:* 336-889-2261. *E-mail:* scarter@johnwesley.edu.

JONES COLLEGE
Jacksonville, FL

CONTACT Mrs. Becky Davis, Director of Financial Assistance, Jones College, 5353 Arlington Expressway, Jacksonville, FL 32211-5540, 904-743-1122. *Fax:* 904-743-4446.

JONES INTERNATIONAL UNIVERSITY
Centennial, CO

Tuition & fees: $11,400	Average undergraduate aid package: $8175

ABOUT THE INSTITUTION Proprietary, coed. 12 undergraduate majors. Federal methodology is used as a basis for awarding need-based institutional aid.

UNDERGRADUATE EXPENSES for 2010–11 *Tuition:* full-time $11,400; part-time $475 per credit hour. Full-time tuition and fees vary according to course level, course load, degree level, and program. Part-time tuition and fees vary according to course level, course load, degree level, and program. *Payment plan:* Installment.

FRESHMAN FINANCIAL AID (Fall 2008) 29 applied for aid; of those 100% were deemed to have need. 100% of freshmen with need received aid. *Average percent of need met:* 40% (excluding resources awarded to replace EFC). *Average financial aid package:* $7175 (excluding resources awarded to replace EFC).

UNDERGRADUATE FINANCIAL AID (Fall 2008) 235 applied for aid; of those 74% were deemed to have need. 100% of undergraduates with need received aid. *Average percent of need met:* 46% (excluding resources awarded to replace EFC). *Average financial aid package:* $8175 (excluding resources awarded to replace EFC).

GIFT AID (NEED-BASED) *Total amount:* $1,115,433 (100% federal). *Receiving aid:* Freshmen: 86% (25); all full-time undergraduates: 39% (91). *Average award:* Freshmen: $3608; Undergraduates: $3262. *Scholarships, grants, and awards:* Federal Pell, FSEOG, private.

GIFT AID (NON-NEED-BASED) *Tuition waivers:* Full or partial for employees or children of employees.

LOANS *Student loans:* $8,795,200 (28% need-based, 72% non-need-based). *Average need-based loan:* Freshmen: $4363. Undergraduates: $4979. *Parent loans:* $145,099 (100% non-need-based). *Programs:* Federal Direct (Subsidized and Unsubsidized Stafford, PLUS), Wells Fargo Collegaite Loans, alternative loans.

APPLYING FOR FINANCIAL AID *Required financial aid forms:* FAFSA, Master Promissory Note. *Financial aid deadline:* Continuous. *Notification date:* Continuous.

CONTACT Stacy Broadus, Financial Aid Manager, Jones International University, 9697 East Mineral Avenue, Centennial, CO 80112, 800-811-5663 Ext. 3 or toll-free 800-811-5663. *Fax:* 303-784-8530. *E-mail:* financialaid@international.edu.

JUDSON COLLEGE
Marion, AL

Tuition & fees: $13,535 | **Average undergraduate aid package:** $13,259

ABOUT THE INSTITUTION Independent Baptist, women only. 19 undergraduate majors. Both federal and institutional methodology are used as a basis for awarding need-based institutional aid.

UNDERGRADUATE EXPENSES for 2010–11 *One-time required fee:* $110. *Comprehensive fee:* $21,835 includes full-time tuition ($12,960), mandatory fees ($575), and room and board ($8300). Full-time tuition and fees vary according to course load. *Part-time tuition:* $432 per semester hour. Part-time tuition and fees vary according to course load. *Payment plans:* Installment, deferred payment.

FRESHMAN FINANCIAL AID (Fall 2009, est.) 61 applied for aid; of those 98% were deemed to have need. 100% of freshmen with need received aid; of those 17% had need fully met. *Average percent of need met:* 69% (excluding resources awarded to replace EFC). *Average financial aid package:* $12,572 (excluding resources awarded to replace EFC). 10% of all full-time freshmen had no need and received non-need-based gift aid.

UNDERGRADUATE FINANCIAL AID (Fall 2009, est.) 209 applied for aid; of those 94% were deemed to have need. 100% of undergraduates with need received aid; of those 13% had need fully met. *Average percent of need met:* 76% (excluding resources awarded to replace EFC). *Average financial aid package:* $13,259 (excluding resources awarded to replace EFC). 8% of all full-time undergraduates had no need and received non-need-based gift aid.

GIFT AID (NEED-BASED) *Total amount:* $1,564,319 (32% federal, 6% state, 55% institutional, 7% external sources). *Receiving aid:* Freshmen: 87% (60); all full-time undergraduates: 78% (181). *Average award:* Freshmen: $5835; Undergraduates: $9855. *Scholarships, grants, and awards:* Federal Pell, FSEOG, state, private, college/university gift aid from institutional funds, Academic Competitiveness Grants, National SMART Grants, TEACH Grants.

GIFT AID (NON-NEED-BASED) *Total amount:* $385,307 (5% state, 90% institutional, 5% external sources). *Receiving aid:* Freshmen: 10% (7). Undergraduates: 10% (22). *Average award:* Freshmen: $11,297. Undergraduates: $8859. *Scholarships, grants, and awards by category: Academic interests/achievement:* biological sciences, general academic interests/achievements, premedicine. *Creative arts/performance:* art/fine arts, music. *Special achievements/activities:* general special achievements/activities. *Special characteristics:* children of educators, children of faculty/staff, relatives of clergy, religious affiliation. *Tuition waivers:* Full or partial for employees or children of employees.

LOANS *Student loans:* $1,131,903 (69% need-based, 31% non-need-based). 60% of past graduating class borrowed through all loan programs. *Average indebtedness per student:* $17,563. *Average need-based loan:* Freshmen: $3471. Undergraduates: $3926. *Parent loans:* $178,086 (80% need-based, 20% non-need-based). *Programs:* FFEL (Subsidized and Unsubsidized Stafford, PLUS), Perkins, college/university.

WORK-STUDY *Federal work-study:* Total amount: $117,547; jobs available. *State or other work-study/employment:* Total amount: $47,360 (79% need-based, 21% non-need-based). Part-time jobs available.

ATHLETIC AWARDS Total amount: $249,203 (85% need-based, 15% non-need-based).

APPLYING FOR FINANCIAL AID *Required financial aid forms:* FAFSA, institution's own form, state aid form. *Financial aid deadline (priority):* 3/1. *Notification date:* Continuous beginning 3/15. Students must reply within 2 weeks of notification.

CONTACT Mrs. Doris A. Wilson, Director of Financial Aid, Judson College, 302 Bibb Street, Marion, AL 36756, 334-683-5157 or toll-free 800-447-9472. *Fax:* 334-683-5282. *E-mail:* dwilson@judson.edu.

JUDSON UNIVERSITY
Elgin, IL

CONTACT Michael Davis, Director of Financial Aid, Judson University, 1151 North State Street, Elgin, IL 60123-1498, 847-628-2532 or toll-free 800-879-5376. *Fax:* 847-628-2533. *E-mail:* mdavis@judsoncollege.edu.

THE JUILLIARD SCHOOL
New York, NY

Tuition & fees: $30,500 | **Average undergraduate aid package:** $24,344

ABOUT THE INSTITUTION Independent, coed. 4 undergraduate majors. Federal methodology is used as a basis for awarding need-based institutional aid.

UNDERGRADUATE EXPENSES for 2009–10 *Comprehensive fee:* $42,310 includes full-time tuition ($30,500) and room and board ($11,810). Room and board charges vary according to housing facility. *Payment plan:* Installment.

FRESHMAN FINANCIAL AID (Fall 2009, est.) 101 applied for aid; of those 79% were deemed to have need. 100% of freshmen with need received aid; of those 24% had need fully met. *Average percent of need met:* 75% (excluding resources awarded to replace EFC). *Average financial aid package:* $24,656 (excluding resources awarded to replace EFC). 5% of all full-time freshmen had no need and received non-need-based gift aid.

UNDERGRADUATE FINANCIAL AID (Fall 2009, est.) 449 applied for aid; of those 88% were deemed to have need. 100% of undergraduates with need received aid; of those 24% had need fully met. *Average percent of need met:* 77% (excluding resources awarded to replace EFC). *Average financial aid package:* $24,344 (excluding resources awarded to replace EFC). 6% of all full-time undergraduates had no need and received non-need-based gift aid.

GIFT AID (NEED-BASED) *Total amount:* $8,564,525 (7% federal, 1% state, 90% institutional, 2% external sources). *Receiving aid:* Freshmen: 69% (70); all full-time undergraduates: 75% (365). *Average award:* Freshmen: $22,359; Undergraduates: $23,290. *Scholarships, grants, and awards:* Federal Pell, FSEOG, state, private, college/university gift aid from institutional funds.

GIFT AID (NON-NEED-BASED) *Total amount:* $424,875 (1% state, 92% institutional, 7% external sources). *Average award:* Freshmen: $15,600. Undergraduates: $14,500. *Scholarships, grants, and awards by category: Creative arts/performance:* dance, music, performing arts, theater/drama. *Tuition waivers:* Full or partial for employees or children of employees.

LOANS *Student loans:* $2,115,440 (95% need-based, 5% non-need-based). 64% of past graduating class borrowed through all loan programs. *Average indebtedness per student:* $26,780. *Average need-based loan:* Freshmen: $3333. Undergraduates: $4780. *Parent loans:* $777,344 (92% need-based, 8% non-need-based). *Programs:* Federal Direct (Subsidized and Unsubsidized Stafford, PLUS), FFEL (PLUS), Perkins.

WORK-STUDY *Federal work-study:* Total amount: $581,938; jobs available. *State or other work-study/employment:* Total amount: $711,475 (73% need-based, 27% non-need-based). Part-time jobs available.

APPLYING FOR FINANCIAL AID *Required financial aid forms:* FAFSA, institution's own form. *Financial aid deadline:* 3/1. *Notification date:* 4/1. Students must reply by 5/1.

CONTACT Lee Cioppa, Associate Dean for Admissions, The Juilliard School, 60 Lincoln Center Plaza, New York, NY 10023, 212-799-5000 Ext. 223. *Fax:* 212-769-6420. *E-mail:* admissions@juilliard.edu.

JUNIATA COLLEGE
Huntingdon, PA

Tuition & fees: $32,820 | **Average undergraduate aid package:** $24,152

ABOUT THE INSTITUTION Independent religious, coed. 88 undergraduate majors. Federal methodology is used as a basis for awarding need-based institutional aid.

UNDERGRADUATE EXPENSES for 2010–11 *Comprehensive fee:* $41,800 includes full-time tuition ($32,120), mandatory fees ($700), and room and board ($8980). *College room only:* $4730. Room and board charges vary according to board plan. *Payment plan:* Installment.

FRESHMAN FINANCIAL AID (Fall 2009, est.) 305 applied for aid; of those 86% were deemed to have need. 100% of freshmen with need received aid; of those 20% had need fully met. *Average percent of need met:* 86% (excluding resources awarded to replace EFC). *Average financial aid package:* $26,119 (excluding resources awarded to replace EFC). 28% of all full-time freshmen had no need and received non-need-based gift aid.

UNDERGRADUATE FINANCIAL AID (Fall 2009, est.) 1,136 applied for aid; of those 89% were deemed to have need. 100% of undergraduates with need received aid; of those 23% had need fully met. *Average percent of need met:* 83% (excluding resources awarded to replace EFC). *Average financial aid*

package: $24,152 (excluding resources awarded to replace EFC). 28% of all full-time undergraduates had no need and received non-need-based gift aid.

GIFT AID (NEED-BASED) *Total amount:* $19,046,775 (8% federal, 8% state, 82% institutional, 2% external sources). *Receiving aid:* Freshmen: 72% (262); all full-time undergraduates: 71% (1,004). *Average award:* Freshmen: $21,571; Undergraduates: $18,970. *Scholarships, grants, and awards:* Federal Pell, FSEOG, state, private, college/university gift aid from institutional funds.

GIFT AID (NON-NEED-BASED) *Total amount:* $6,514,809 (1% federal, 97% institutional, 2% external sources). *Receiving aid:* Freshmen: 10% (35). Undergraduates: 10% (145). *Average award:* Freshmen: $13,609. Undergraduates: $13,879. *Scholarships, grants, and awards by category:* Academic interests/achievement: biological sciences, business, communication, computer science, education, English, foreign languages, general academic interests/ achievements, health fields, humanities, international studies, mathematics, physical sciences, premedicine, social sciences. *Creative arts/performance:* art/ fine arts, music, performing arts. *Special achievements/activities:* community service, general special achievements/activities, leadership. *Special characteristics:* adult students, children of faculty/staff, ethnic background, international students, local/state students. *Tuition waivers:* Full or partial for employees or children of employees, adult students, senior citizens.

LOANS *Student loans:* $8,323,316 (63% need-based, 37% non-need-based). 89% of past graduating class borrowed through all loan programs. *Average indebtedness per student:* $23,618. *Average need-based loan:* Freshmen: $3847. Undergraduates: $4865. *Parent loans:* $2,584,996 (35% need-based, 65% non-need-based). *Programs:* FFEL (Subsidized and Unsubsidized Stafford, PLUS), Perkins, college/university.

WORK-STUDY *Federal work-study:* Total amount: $1,021,786; 666 jobs averaging $1540. *State or other work-study/employment:* Total amount: $1,013,350 (9% need-based, 91% non-need-based). 662 part-time jobs averaging $1757.

APPLYING FOR FINANCIAL AID *Required financial aid form:* FAFSA. *Financial aid deadline:* 3/1. *Notification date:* Continuous. Students must reply by 5/1 or within 2 weeks of notification.

CONTACT Valerie Rennell, Director of Student Financial Planning, Juniata College, 1700 Moore Street, Huntingdon, PA 16652-2119, 814-641-3141 or toll-free 877-JUNIATA. *Fax:* 814-641-5311. *E-mail:* rennelv@juniata.edu.

KALAMAZOO COLLEGE
Kalamazoo, MI

Tuition & fees: $32,643	Average undergraduate aid package: N/A

ABOUT THE INSTITUTION Independent religious, coed. 24 undergraduate majors. Both federal and institutional methodology are used as a basis for awarding need-based institutional aid.

UNDERGRADUATE EXPENSES for 2009–10 *One-time required fee:* $100. *Comprehensive fee:* $40,419 includes full-time tuition ($32,643) and room and board ($7776). *College room only:* $3792. Room and board charges vary according to board plan. *Payment plan:* Installment.

FRESHMAN FINANCIAL AID (Fall 2009, est.) 286 applied for aid; of those 74% were deemed to have need. 100% of freshmen with need received aid; of those 66% had need fully met. *Average financial aid package:* $26,616 (excluding resources awarded to replace EFC). 45% of all full-time freshmen had no need and received non-need-based gift aid.

GIFT AID (NEED-BASED) *Total amount:* $11,902,598 (10% federal, 6% state, 84% institutional). *Receiving aid:* Freshmen: 52% (205). *Average award:* Freshmen: $23,090. *Scholarships, grants, and awards:* Federal Pell, FSEOG, state, private, college/university gift aid from institutional funds.

GIFT AID (NON-NEED-BASED) *Total amount:* $10,675,750 (88% institutional, 12% external sources). *Receiving aid:* Freshmen: 54% (211). *Average award:* Freshmen: $12,190. *Tuition waivers:* Full or partial for employees or children of employees.

LOANS *Student loans:* $4,989,035 (56% need-based, 44% non-need-based). *Average need-based loan:* Freshmen: $2125. *Parent loans:* $2,483,864 (100% non-need-based). *Programs:* Federal Direct (Subsidized and Unsubsidized Stafford, PLUS), Perkins.

WORK-STUDY *Federal work-study:* Total amount: $375,000; jobs available. *State or other work-study/employment:* Part-time jobs available.

APPLYING FOR FINANCIAL AID *Required financial aid forms:* FAFSA, CSS Financial Aid PROFILE. *Financial aid deadline (priority):* 2/15. *Notification date:* Continuous beginning 3/21. Students must reply by 5/1.

CONTACT Judy Clark, Associate Director of Financial Aid, Kalamazoo College, 1200 Academy Street, Kalamazoo, MI 49006-3295, 269-337-7192 or toll-free 800-253-3602. *Fax:* 269-337-7390.

KANSAS CITY ART INSTITUTE
Kansas City, MO

Tuition & fees: $28,580	Average undergraduate aid package: $20,854

ABOUT THE INSTITUTION Independent, coed. *Awards:* bachelor's degrees. 12 undergraduate majors. *Total enrollment:* 676. Undergraduates: 676. Freshmen: 152. Federal methodology is used as a basis for awarding need-based institutional aid.

UNDERGRADUATE EXPENSES for 2009–10 *Application fee:* $35. *Comprehensive fee:* $37,290 includes full-time tuition ($28,580) and room and board ($8710). Full-time tuition and fees vary according to program. Room and board charges vary according to board plan and housing facility. *Part-time tuition:* $1190 per credit hour. Part-time tuition and fees vary according to program.

FRESHMAN FINANCIAL AID (Fall 2008) 119 applied for aid; of those 93% were deemed to have need. 100% of freshmen with need received aid; of those 20% had need fully met. *Average percent of need met:* 70% (excluding resources awarded to replace EFC). *Average financial aid package:* $20,773 (excluding resources awarded to replace EFC). 7% of all full-time freshmen had no need and received non-need-based gift aid.

UNDERGRADUATE FINANCIAL AID (Fall 2008) 168 applied for aid; of those 93% were deemed to have need. 100% of undergraduates with need received aid; of those 19% had need fully met. *Average percent of need met:* 71% (excluding resources awarded to replace EFC). *Average financial aid package:* $20,854 (excluding resources awarded to replace EFC). 7% of all full-time undergraduates had no need and received non-need-based gift aid.

GIFT AID (NEED-BASED) *Total amount:* $2,330,577 (11% federal, 6% state, 80% institutional, 3% external sources). *Receiving aid:* Freshmen: 93% (111); all full-time undergraduates: 93% (156). *Average award:* Freshmen: $15,345; Undergraduates: $14,763. *Scholarships, grants, and awards:* Federal Pell, FSEOG, state, private, college/university gift aid from institutional funds.

GIFT AID (NON-NEED-BASED) *Total amount:* $310,071 (1% state, 97% institutional, 2% external sources). *Receiving aid:* Freshmen: 14% (17). Undergraduates: 12% (21). *Average award:* Freshmen: $13,875. Undergraduates: $13,666. *Scholarships, grants, and awards by category:* Creative arts/ performance: $3,254,128 total: art/fine arts. *Tuition waivers:* Full or partial for employees or children of employees.

LOANS *Student loans:* $1,403,278 (81% need-based, 19% non-need-based). 96% of past graduating class borrowed through all loan programs. *Average indebtedness per student:* $23,375. *Average need-based loan:* Freshmen: $6026. Undergraduates: $6580. *Parent loans:* $1,153,784 (47% need-based, 53% non-need-based). *Programs:* FFEL (Subsidized and Unsubsidized Stafford, PLUS), Perkins, alternative loans.

WORK-STUDY *Federal work-study:* Total amount: $140,768; 124 jobs averaging $997. *State or other work-study/employment:* Total amount: $70,967 (100% non-need-based). 30 part-time jobs averaging $1000.

APPLYING FOR FINANCIAL AID *Required financial aid form:* FAFSA. *Financial aid deadline (priority):* 3/1. *Notification date:* Continuous beginning 3/15. Students must reply within 2 weeks of notification.

CONTACT Ms. Kimberly Warren, Director of Financial Aid, Kansas City Art Institute, 4415 Warwick Boulevard, Kansas City, MO 64111-1874, 816-802-3448 or toll-free 800-522-5224. *Fax:* 816-802-3453. *E-mail:* kwarren@kcai.edu.

KANSAS STATE UNIVERSITY
Manhattan, KS

Tuition & fees (KS res): $6870	Average undergraduate aid package: $9490

ABOUT THE INSTITUTION State-supported, coed. 81 undergraduate majors. Federal methodology is used as a basis for awarding need-based institutional aid.

UNDERGRADUATE EXPENSES for 2009–10 *Tuition, state resident:* full-time $6186. *Tuition, nonresident:* full-time $16,893. *Required fees:* full-time $684. Full-time tuition and fees vary according to course load, location, program, and reciprocity agreements. Part-time tuition and fees vary according to course load, location, program, and reciprocity agreements. *College room and board:*

$6752. Room and board charges vary according to board plan, housing facility, and location. *Payment plans:* Installment, deferred payment.

FRESHMAN FINANCIAL AID (Fall 2008) 2,563 applied for aid; of those 67% were deemed to have need. 97% of freshmen with need received aid; of those 23% had need fully met. *Average percent of need met:* 82% (excluding resources awarded to replace EFC). *Average financial aid package:* $9488 (excluding resources awarded to replace EFC). 15% of all full-time freshmen had no need and received non-need-based gift aid.

UNDERGRADUATE FINANCIAL AID (Fall 2008) 11,009 applied for aid; of those 74% were deemed to have need. 98% of undergraduates with need received aid; of those 19% had need fully met. *Average percent of need met:* 80% (excluding resources awarded to replace EFC). *Average financial aid package:* $9490 (excluding resources awarded to replace EFC). 1% of all full-time undergraduates had no need and received non-need-based gift aid.

GIFT AID (NEED-BASED) *Total amount:* $33,517,927 (39% federal, 10% state, 42% institutional, 9% external sources). *Receiving aid:* Freshmen: 30% (1,064); all full-time undergraduates: 28% (4,601). *Average award:* Freshmen: $3822; Undergraduates: $3937. *Scholarships, grants, and awards:* Federal Pell, FSEOG, state, private, college/university gift aid from institutional funds.

GIFT AID (NON-NEED-BASED) *Total amount:* $5,157,157 (1% state, 75% institutional, 24% external sources). *Receiving aid:* Freshmen: 32% (1,138). Undergraduates: 21% (3,411). *Average award:* Freshmen: $3490. Undergraduates: $2930. *Tuition waivers:* Full or partial for employees or children of employees.

LOANS *Student loans:* $61,481,962 (68% need-based, 32% non-need-based). 57% of past graduating class borrowed through all loan programs. *Average indebtedness per student:* $19,281. *Average need-based loan:* Freshmen: $3309. Undergraduates: $4082. *Parent loans:* $22,783,878 (25% need-based, 75% non-need-based). *Programs:* Federal Direct (Subsidized and Unsubsidized Stafford, PLUS), Perkins, college/university.

WORK-STUDY *Federal work-study:* Total amount: $1,185,784; jobs available. *State or other work-study/employment:* Total amount: $114,256 (82% need-based, 18% non-need-based). Part-time jobs available.

ATHLETIC AWARDS Total amount: $4,109,089 (89% need-based, 11% non-need-based).

APPLYING FOR FINANCIAL AID *Required financial aid form:* FAFSA. *Financial aid deadline (priority):* 3/1. *Notification date:* Continuous beginning 4/1. Students must reply within 2 weeks of notification.

CONTACT Mr. Larry Moeder, Director of Admissions and Student Financial Assistance, Kansas State University, 104 Fairchild Hall, Manhattan, KS 66506, 785-532-6420 or toll-free 800-432-8270 (in-state). *E-mail:* larrym@ksu.edu.

KANSAS WESLEYAN UNIVERSITY
Salina, KS

CONTACT Mrs. Glenna Alexander, Director of Financial Assistance, Kansas Wesleyan University, 100 East Claflin, Salina, KS 67401-6196, 785-827-5541 Ext. 1130 or toll-free 800-874-1154 Ext. 1285. *Fax:* 785-827-0927. *E-mail:* kglennaa@acck.edu.

KAPLAN UNIVERSITY, DAVENPORT CAMPUS
Davenport, IA

CONTACT Matt McEnany, Coordinator of School Operations, Kaplan University, Davenport Campus, 1801 East Kimberly Road, Davenport, IA 52806, 319-355-3500 or toll-free 800-747-1035 (in-state). *Fax:* 319-355-1320.

KAPLAN UNIVERSITY, MASON CITY CAMPUS
Mason City, IA

CONTACT Financial Aid Office, Kaplan University, Mason City Campus, 2570 4th Street, SW, Mason City, IA 50401, 641-423-2530.

KEAN UNIVERSITY
Union, NJ

Tuition & fees (NJ res): $9446	Average undergraduate aid package: $9810

ABOUT THE INSTITUTION State-supported, coed. 50 undergraduate majors. Federal methodology is used as a basis for awarding need-based institutional aid.

UNDERGRADUATE EXPENSES for 2009–10 *Tuition, state resident:* full-time $6165; part-time $205.50 per credit hour. *Tuition, nonresident:* full-time $10,800; part-time $360 per credit hour. *Required fees:* full-time $3281; $110.10 per credit hour. Part-time tuition and fees vary according to course load. *College room and board:* $12,264; *Room only:* $9400. Room and board charges vary according to board plan and housing facility. *Payment plan:* Installment.

FRESHMAN FINANCIAL AID (Fall 2009, est.) 1,331 applied for aid; of those 82% were deemed to have need. 92% of freshmen with need received aid; of those 9% had need fully met. *Average percent of need met:* 58% (excluding resources awarded to replace EFC). *Average financial aid package:* $9818 (excluding resources awarded to replace EFC). 1% of all full-time freshmen had no need and received non-need-based gift aid.

UNDERGRADUATE FINANCIAL AID (Fall 2009, est.) 7,132 applied for aid; of those 84% were deemed to have need. 96% of undergraduates with need received aid; of those 16% had need fully met. *Average percent of need met:* 56% (excluding resources awarded to replace EFC). *Average financial aid package:* $9810 (excluding resources awarded to replace EFC). 1% of all full-time undergraduates had no need and received non-need-based gift aid.

GIFT AID (NEED-BASED) *Total amount:* $32,626,314 (54% federal, 40% state, 5% institutional, 1% external sources). *Receiving aid:* Freshmen: 66% (1,003); all full-time undergraduates: 62% (5,706). *Average award:* Freshmen: $8414; Undergraduates: $7731. *Scholarships, grants, and awards:* Federal Pell, FSEOG, state, private, college/university gift aid from institutional funds.

GIFT AID (NON-NEED-BASED) *Total amount:* $586,163 (5% federal, 16% state, 79% institutional). *Receiving aid:* Freshmen: 9% (138). Undergraduates: 8% (749). *Average award:* Freshmen: $5400. Undergraduates: $2703. *Scholarships, grants, and awards by category: Academic interests/achievement:* 920 awards ($1,323,606 total): area/ethnic studies, biological sciences, business, communication, computer science, education, English, foreign languages, general academic interests/achievements, health fields, humanities, international studies, mathematics, physical sciences, social sciences. *Creative arts/performance:* 11 awards ($77,085 total): applied art and design, art/fine arts, cinema/film/broadcasting, general creative arts/performance, music, performing arts, theater/drama. *Special achievements/activities:* 24 awards ($172,398 total): community service, leadership. *Special characteristics:* 113 awards ($668,632 total): general special characteristics. *Tuition waivers:* Full or partial for employees or children of employees, senior citizens.

LOANS *Student loans:* $56,452,366 (42% need-based, 58% non-need-based). 68% of past graduating class borrowed through all loan programs. *Average indebtedness per student:* $19,698. *Average need-based loan:* Freshmen: $3550. Undergraduates: $4454. *Parent loans:* $4,145,353 (100% non-need-based). *Programs:* Federal Direct (Subsidized and Unsubsidized Stafford, PLUS), Perkins.

WORK-STUDY *Federal work-study:* Total amount: $719,251; 267 jobs averaging $2008.

APPLYING FOR FINANCIAL AID *Required financial aid form:* FAFSA. *Financial aid deadline (priority):* 3/15. *Notification date:* Continuous beginning 3/15. Students must reply by 5/1.

CONTACT Ms. Sharon Audet, Associate Director, Office of Financial Aid, Kean University, 1000 Morris Avenue, Union, NJ 07083, 908-737-3190. *Fax:* 908-737-3200. *E-mail:* finaid@kean.edu.

KEENE STATE COLLEGE
Keene, NH

Tuition & fees (NH res): $9334	Average undergraduate aid package: $8603

ABOUT THE INSTITUTION State-supported, coed. 72 undergraduate majors. Federal methodology is used as a basis for awarding need-based institutional aid.

UNDERGRADUATE EXPENSES for 2009–10 *Tuition, state resident:* full-time $7000; part-time $292 per credit. *Tuition, nonresident:* full-time $15,170; part-time $632 per credit. *Required fees:* full-time $2334; $92 per credit.

Part-time tuition and fees vary according to course load. *College room and board:* $8444; *Room only:* $5520. Room and board charges vary according to board plan and housing facility. *Payment plan:* Installment.

FRESHMAN FINANCIAL AID (Fall 2008) 1,103 applied for aid; of those 68% were deemed to have need. 98% of freshmen with need received aid; of those 16% had need fully met. *Average percent of need met:* 65% (excluding resources awarded to replace EFC). *Average financial aid package:* $8103 (excluding resources awarded to replace EFC). 6% of all full-time freshmen had no need and received non-need-based gift aid.

UNDERGRADUATE FINANCIAL AID (Fall 2008) 3,577 applied for aid; of those 70% were deemed to have need. 99% of undergraduates with need received aid; of those 20% had need fully met. *Average percent of need met:* 68% (excluding resources awarded to replace EFC). *Average financial aid package:* $8603 (excluding resources awarded to replace EFC). 7% of all full-time undergraduates had no need and received non-need-based gift aid.

GIFT AID (NEED-BASED) *Total amount:* $8,013,119 (34% federal, 9% state, 47% institutional, 10% external sources). *Receiving aid:* Freshmen: 34% (439); all full-time undergraduates: 32% (1,489). *Average award:* Freshmen: $5512; Undergraduates: $5091. *Scholarships, grants, and awards:* Federal Pell, FSEOG, state, private, college/university gift aid from institutional funds.

GIFT AID (NON-NEED-BASED) *Total amount:* $2,964,248 (1% state, 83% institutional, 16% external sources). *Receiving aid:* Freshmen: 13% (167). Undergraduates: 12% (565). *Average award:* Freshmen: $2624. Undergraduates: $3026. *Scholarships, grants, and awards by category: Academic interests/achievement:* 557 awards ($1,253,375 total): general academic interests/achievements. *Creative arts/performance:* 17 awards ($125,375 total): applied art and design, art/fine arts, cinema/film/broadcasting, dance, general creative arts/performance, music, theater/drama. *Special achievements/activities:* 11 awards ($33,000 total): general special achievements/activities. *Tuition waivers:* Full or partial for employees or children of employees, senior citizens.

LOANS *Student loans:* $30,963,984 (29% need-based, 71% non-need-based). 78% of past graduating class borrowed through all loan programs. *Average indebtedness per student:* $27,785. *Average need-based loan:* Freshmen: $3386. Undergraduates: $4085. *Parent loans:* $6,716,320 (100% non-need-based). *Programs:* FFEL (Subsidized and Unsubsidized Stafford, PLUS), Perkins, college/university.

WORK-STUDY *Federal work-study:* Total amount: $2,588,753; 673 jobs averaging $1078. *State or other work-study/employment:* Total amount: $667,056 (100% non-need-based). 698 part-time jobs averaging $956.

APPLYING FOR FINANCIAL AID *Required financial aid form:* FAFSA. *Financial aid deadline:* 3/1. *Notification date:* Continuous. Students must reply within 4 weeks of notification.

CONTACT Ms. Patricia Blodgett, Director of Student Financial Management, Keene State College, 229 Main Street, Keene, NH 03435-2606, 603-358-2280 or toll-free 800-KSC-1909. *Fax:* 603-358-2794. *E-mail:* pblodget@keene.edu.

KEHILATH YAKOV RABBINICAL SEMINARY
Ossining, NY

CONTACT Financial Aid Office, Kehilath Yakov Rabbinical Seminary, 206 Wilson Street, Brooklyn, NY 11211-7207, 718-963-1212.

KEISER UNIVERSITY
Fort Lauderdale, FL

ABOUT THE INSTITUTION Proprietary, coed. 45 undergraduate majors.

GIFT AID (NEED-BASED) *Scholarships, grants, and awards:* Federal Pell, FSEOG, state, private, college/university gift aid from institutional funds.

LOANS *Programs:* Federal Direct (Subsidized and Unsubsidized Stafford, PLUS), FFEL (Subsidized and Unsubsidized Stafford, PLUS), Perkins.

APPLYING FOR FINANCIAL AID *Required financial aid forms:* FAFSA, institution's own form.

CONTACT Judy Martin, Financial Aid Director, Keiser University, 1500 NW 49 Street, Fort Lauderdale, FL 33309, 954-776-4456 or toll-free 888-KEISER-9 (out-of-state). *Fax:* 954-749-4456. *E-mail:* judym@keiseruniversity.edu.

KENDALL COLLEGE
Chicago, IL

ABOUT THE INSTITUTION Independent United Methodist, coed. 25 undergraduate majors.

GIFT AID (NEED-BASED) *Scholarships, grants, and awards:* Federal Pell, FSEOG, state, private, college/university gift aid from institutional funds.

GIFT AID (NON-NEED-BASED) *Scholarships, grants, and awards by category: Academic interests/achievement:* business, education, general academic interests/achievements. *Special characteristics:* children of faculty/staff, international students, members of minority groups, out-of-state students, veterans, veterans' children.

LOANS *Programs:* FFEL (Subsidized and Unsubsidized Stafford, PLUS), Perkins, alternative loans.

WORK-STUDY *Federal work-study:* Total amount: $75,039; 30 jobs averaging $1100.

APPLYING FOR FINANCIAL AID *Required financial aid forms:* FAFSA, institution's own form.

CONTACT Chris Miller, Director of Financial Aid, Kendall College, 900 N North Branch Street, Chicago, IL 60622, 312-752-2428 or toll-free 866-667-3344 (in-state), 877-588-8860 (out-of-state). *Fax:* 312-752-2267.

KENNESAW STATE UNIVERSITY
Kennesaw, GA

Tuition & fees (GA res): $5144	Average undergraduate aid package: $3970

ABOUT THE INSTITUTION State-supported, coed. 49 undergraduate majors. Federal methodology is used as a basis for awarding need-based institutional aid.

UNDERGRADUATE EXPENSES for 2010–11 *Tuition, state resident:* full-time $4196; part-time $134 per credit hour. *Tuition, nonresident:* full-time $16,172; part-time $533 per credit hour. *Required fees:* full-time $948. Part-time tuition and fees vary according to course load. *College room and board:* $6593. Room and board charges vary according to board plan and housing facility. *Payment plan:* Deferred payment.

FRESHMAN FINANCIAL AID (Fall 2009, est.) 2,240 applied for aid; of those 68% were deemed to have need. 99% of freshmen with need received aid; of those 13% had need fully met. *Average percent of need met:* 20% (excluding resources awarded to replace EFC). *Average financial aid package:* $4068 (excluding resources awarded to replace EFC). 17% of all full-time freshmen had no need and received non-need-based gift aid.

UNDERGRADUATE FINANCIAL AID (Fall 2009, est.) 11,340 applied for aid; of those 76% were deemed to have need. 97% of undergraduates with need received aid; of those 14% had need fully met. *Average percent of need met:* 24% (excluding resources awarded to replace EFC). *Average financial aid package:* $3970 (excluding resources awarded to replace EFC). 19% of all full-time undergraduates had no need and received non-need-based gift aid.

GIFT AID (NEED-BASED) *Total amount:* $11,928,851 (97% federal, 2% state, 1% institutional). *Receiving aid:* Freshmen: 28% (750); all full-time undergraduates: 29% (4,542). *Average award:* Freshmen: $2391; Undergraduates: $2321. *Scholarships, grants, and awards:* Federal Pell, FSEOG, state, private, college/university gift aid from institutional funds.

GIFT AID (NON-NEED-BASED) *Total amount:* $24,594,943 (97% state, 1% institutional, 2% external sources). *Receiving aid:* Freshmen: 37% (996). Undergraduates: 22% (3,390). *Average award:* Freshmen: $1199. Undergraduates: $1087. *Scholarships, grants, and awards by category: Academic interests/achievement:* biological sciences, business, communication, computer science, education, English, foreign languages, general academic interests/achievements, health fields, humanities, international studies, mathematics, physical sciences, premedicine, social sciences. *Creative arts/performance:* music, performing arts, theater/drama. *Special achievements/activities:* community service, leadership, memberships. *Special characteristics:* children and siblings of alumni, children of union members/company employees, children of workers in trades, ethnic background, general special characteristics, handicapped students, international students, local/state students, members of minority groups, religious affiliation, veterans' children. *Tuition waivers:* Full or partial for employees or children of employees, senior citizens.

LOANS *Student loans:* $42,206,022 (42% need-based, 58% non-need-based). 68% of past graduating class borrowed through all loan programs. *Average*

indebtedness per student: $2845. *Average need-based loan:* Freshmen: $1643. Undergraduates: $2115. *Parent loans:* $702,657 (100% non-need-based). *Programs:* FFEL (Subsidized and Unsubsidized Stafford, PLUS), Perkins, Federal Nursing, state.

WORK-STUDY *Federal work-study:* Total amount: $478,657; 213 jobs averaging $2247.

ATHLETIC AWARDS Total amount: $514,797 (100% non-need-based).

APPLYING FOR FINANCIAL AID *Required financial aid form:* FAFSA. *Financial aid deadline (priority):* 4/1. *Notification date:* Continuous beginning 4/1.

CONTACT Mr. Ron H. Day, Director of Student Financial Aid, Kennesaw State University, 1000 Chastain Road, Kennesaw, GA 30144-5591, 770-423-6021. *Fax:* 770-423-6708. *E-mail:* finaid@kennesaw.edu.

KENT STATE UNIVERSITY
Kent, OH

Tuition & fees (OH res): $8726	Average undergraduate aid package: $8820

ABOUT THE INSTITUTION State-supported, coed. 124 undergraduate majors. Federal methodology is used as a basis for awarding need-based institutional aid.

UNDERGRADUATE EXPENSES for 2009–10 *Tuition, state resident:* full-time $8726; part-time $397 per credit hour. *Tuition, nonresident:* full-time $16,418; part-time $747 per credit hour. Full-time tuition and fees vary according to course level, course load, degree level, program, and reciprocity agreements. Part-time tuition and fees vary according to course level, course load, degree level, program, and reciprocity agreements. *College room and board:* $7940; *Room only:* $4850. Room and board charges vary according to board plan and housing facility. *Payment plans:* Tuition prepayment, installment, deferred payment.

FRESHMAN FINANCIAL AID (Fall 2009, est.) 3,347 applied for aid; of those 79% were deemed to have need. 100% of freshmen with need received aid; of those 44% had need fully met. *Average percent of need met:* 56% (excluding resources awarded to replace EFC). *Average financial aid package:* $8479 (excluding resources awarded to replace EFC). 17% of all full-time freshmen had no need and received non-need-based gift aid.

UNDERGRADUATE FINANCIAL AID (Fall 2009, est.) 12,945 applied for aid; of those 84% were deemed to have need. 100% of undergraduates with need received aid; of those 36% had need fully met. *Average percent of need met:* 52% (excluding resources awarded to replace EFC). *Average financial aid package:* $8820 (excluding resources awarded to replace EFC). 12% of all full-time undergraduates had no need and received non-need-based gift aid.

GIFT AID (NEED-BASED) *Total amount:* $51,191,019 (56% federal, 9% state, 31% institutional, 4% external sources). *Receiving aid:* Freshmen: 52% (2,077); all full-time undergraduates: 45% (7,912). *Average award:* Freshmen: $6248; Undergraduates: $6152. *Scholarships, grants, and awards:* Federal Pell, FSEOG, state, private, college/university gift aid from institutional funds.

GIFT AID (NON-NEED-BASED) *Total amount:* $11,317,450 (5% federal, 13% state, 74% institutional, 8% external sources). *Receiving aid:* Freshmen: 16% (645). Undergraduates: 8% (1,442). *Average award:* Freshmen: $3609. Undergraduates: $3815. *Scholarships, grants, and awards by category: Academic interests/achievement:* architecture, area/ethnic studies, biological sciences, business, communication, computer science, education, engineering/technologies, English, general academic interests/achievements, health fields, international studies, library science, mathematics, military science, physical sciences, social sciences. *Creative arts/performance:* art/fine arts, dance, journalism/publications, music, performing arts, theater/drama. *Special achievements/activities:* community service, general special achievements/activities, leadership. *Special characteristics:* adult students, children and siblings of alumni, children of faculty/staff, children of union members/company employees, children with a deceased or disabled parent, ethnic background, first-generation college students, handicapped students, international students, local/state students, members of minority groups, out-of-state students. *Tuition waivers:* Full or partial for employees or children of employees, senior citizens.

LOANS *Student loans:* $105,976,013 (42% need-based, 58% non-need-based). 75% of past graduating class borrowed through all loan programs. *Average indebtedness per student:* $26,698. *Average need-based loan:* Freshmen: $3217. Undergraduates: $3989. *Parent loans:* $25,584,370 (15% need-based, 85% non-need-based). *Programs:* Federal Direct (Subsidized and Unsubsidized Stafford, PLUS), Perkins, Federal Nursing, state, college/university, alternative loans.

WORK-STUDY *Federal work-study:* Total amount: $1,123,719; jobs available.

ATHLETIC AWARDS Total amount: $4,768,913 (50% need-based, 50% non-need-based).

APPLYING FOR FINANCIAL AID *Required financial aid form:* FAFSA. *Financial aid deadline (priority):* 3/1. *Notification date:* 3/15. Students must reply within 2 weeks of notification.

CONTACT Mark A. Evans, Director of Student Financial Aid, Kent State University, 103 Michael Schwartz Center, Kent, OH 44242-0001, 330-672-2972 or toll-free 800-988-KENT. *Fax:* 330-672-4014. *E-mail:* mevans@kent.edu.

KENT STATE UNIVERSITY AT STARK
Canton, OH

Tuition & fees (OH res): $4938	Average undergraduate aid package: $7006

ABOUT THE INSTITUTION State-supported, coed. 9 undergraduate majors. Federal methodology is used as a basis for awarding need-based institutional aid.

UNDERGRADUATE EXPENSES for 2009–10 *Tuition, state resident:* full-time $4938; part-time $225 per credit hour. *Tuition, nonresident:* full-time $12,630; part-time $575 per credit hour. Full-time tuition and fees vary according to course level, course load, and location. Part-time tuition and fees vary according to course level, course load, and location. *Payment plan:* Installment.

FRESHMAN FINANCIAL AID (Fall 2009, est.) 530 applied for aid; of those 86% were deemed to have need. 100% of freshmen with need received aid; of those 35% had need fully met. *Average percent of need met:* 56% (excluding resources awarded to replace EFC). *Average financial aid package:* $6449 (excluding resources awarded to replace EFC). 3% of all full-time freshmen had no need and received non-need-based gift aid.

UNDERGRADUATE FINANCIAL AID (Fall 2009, est.) 2,071 applied for aid; of those 87% were deemed to have need. 99% of undergraduates with need received aid; of those 29% had need fully met. *Average percent of need met:* 49% (excluding resources awarded to replace EFC). *Average financial aid package:* $7006 (excluding resources awarded to replace EFC). 2% of all full-time undergraduates had no need and received non-need-based gift aid.

GIFT AID (NEED-BASED) *Total amount:* $7,723,542 (95% federal, 3% institutional, 2% external sources). *Receiving aid:* Freshmen: 52% (348); all full-time undergraduates: 44% (1,286). *Average award:* Freshmen: $4401; Undergraduates: $4688. *Scholarships, grants, and awards:* Federal Pell, FSEOG, state, private, college/university gift aid from institutional funds.

GIFT AID (NON-NEED-BASED) *Total amount:* $486,112 (23% federal, 21% state, 36% institutional, 20% external sources). *Receiving aid:* Freshmen: 5% (32). Undergraduates: 3% (89). *Average award:* Freshmen: $2080. Undergraduates: $2108. *Scholarships, grants, and awards by category: Academic interests/achievement:* general academic interests/achievements. *Creative arts/performance:* art/fine arts, music, theater/drama. *Special achievements/activities:* leadership. *Special characteristics:* children and siblings of alumni, local/state students, members of minority groups. *Tuition waivers:* Full or partial for employees or children of employees, senior citizens.

LOANS *Student loans:* $18,297,178 (48% need-based, 52% non-need-based). *Average need-based loan:* Freshmen: $2913. Undergraduates: $3587. *Parent loans:* $368,092 (7% need-based, 93% non-need-based). *Programs:* Federal Direct (Subsidized and Unsubsidized Stafford, PLUS), Perkins, Federal Nursing, state, college/university, alternative loans.

WORK-STUDY *Federal work-study:* Total amount: $113,007; jobs available.

APPLYING FOR FINANCIAL AID *Required financial aid form:* FAFSA. *Financial aid deadline (priority):* 3/1. *Notification date:* 3/15. Students must reply within 2 weeks of notification.

CONTACT Gail Pukys, Assistant Director for Enrollment Management for Financial Aid, Kent State University at Stark, Office of Student Services, 134 Main Hall, North Canton, OH 44720, 330-244-3257. *E-mail:* gpukys@kent.edu.

KENTUCKY CHRISTIAN UNIVERSITY
Grayson, KY

ABOUT THE INSTITUTION Independent religious, coed. *Awards:* bachelor's and master's degrees. 17 undergraduate majors. *Total enrollment:* 663. Undergraduates: 630. Freshmen: 191.

- **GIFT AID (NEED-BASED)** *Scholarships, grants, and awards:* Federal Pell, FSEOG, state, private, college/university gift aid from institutional funds, Academic Competitiveness Grants.
GIFT AID (NON-NEED-BASED) *Scholarships, grants, and awards by category:* *Academic interests/achievement:* business, education, general academic interests/achievements, religion/biblical studies. *Creative arts/performance:* debating, music, performing arts, theater/drama. *Special achievements/activities:* community service, general special achievements/activities, leadership, religious involvement. *Special characteristics:* children and siblings of alumni, children of faculty/staff, general special characteristics, international students, members of minority groups, religious affiliation.
LOANS *Programs:* FFEL (Subsidized and Unsubsidized Stafford, PLUS), Perkins.
APPLYING FOR FINANCIAL AID *Required financial aid form:* FAFSA.
CONTACT Mrs. Jennie M. Bender, Director of Financial Aid, Kentucky Christian University, 100 Academic Parkway, Grayson, KY 41143-2205, 606-474-3226 or toll-free 800-522-3181. *Fax:* 606-474-3155. *E-mail:* jbender@kcu.edu.

KENTUCKY MOUNTAIN BIBLE COLLEGE
Vancleve, KY

Tuition & fees: N/R	Average undergraduate aid package: N/A

ABOUT THE INSTITUTION Independent interdenominational, coed. 1 undergraduate major. Both federal and institutional methodology are used as a basis for awarding need-based institutional aid.
GIFT AID (NEED-BASED) *Scholarships, grants, and awards:* Federal Pell, FSEOG, state, private, college/university gift aid from institutional funds.
GIFT AID (NON-NEED-BASED) *Scholarships, grants, and awards by category:* *Academic interests/achievement:* general academic interests/achievements. *Creative arts/performance:* music, theater/drama. *Special characteristics:* children of faculty/staff. *Tuition waivers:* Full or partial for employees or children of employees.
LOANS *Programs:* FFEL (Subsidized and Unsubsidized Stafford, PLUS), college/university.
WORK-STUDY Federal work-study jobs available. *State or other work-study/employment:* Part-time jobs available.
APPLYING FOR FINANCIAL AID *Required financial aid forms:* FAFSA, institution's own form. *Financial aid deadline (priority):* 4/1. *Notification date:* Continuous.
CONTACT Mrs. Rosita Marshall, Director of Financial Aid, Kentucky Mountain Bible College, PO Box 10, Vancleve, KY 41385-0010, 800-879-KMBC Ext. 175 or toll-free 800-879-KMBC Ext. 130 (in-state), 800-879-KMBC Ext. 136 (out-of-state). *Fax:* 800-659-4324. *E-mail:* finaid@kmbc.edu.

KENTUCKY STATE UNIVERSITY
Frankfort, KY

Tuition & fees (KY res): $5920	Average undergraduate aid package: $8529

ABOUT THE INSTITUTION State-related, coed. 23 undergraduate majors. Federal methodology is used as a basis for awarding need-based institutional aid.
UNDERGRADUATE EXPENSES for 2009–10 *Tuition, state resident:* full-time $5170; part-time $172 per credit hour. *Tuition, nonresident:* full-time $13,458; part-time $449 per credit hour. *Required fees:* full-time $750; $25 per credit hour. Part-time tuition and fees vary according to course load. *College room and board:* $6480; *Room only:* $3240. Room and board charges vary according to board plan and housing facility. *Payment plan:* Installment.
FRESHMAN FINANCIAL AID (Fall 2009, est.) 457 applied for aid; of those 100% were deemed to have need. 91% of freshmen with need received aid; of those 19% had need fully met. *Average percent of need met:* 18% (excluding resources awarded to replace EFC). *Average financial aid package:* $8370 (excluding resources awarded to replace EFC). 4% of all full-time freshmen had no need and received non-need-based gift aid.
UNDERGRADUATE FINANCIAL AID (Fall 2009, est.) 1,719 applied for aid; of those 100% were deemed to have need. 94% of undergraduates with need received aid; of those 18% had need fully met. *Average percent of need met:* 20% (excluding resources awarded to replace EFC). *Average financial aid package:* $8529 (excluding resources awarded to replace EFC). 4% of all full-time undergraduates had no need and received non-need-based gift aid.
GIFT AID (NEED-BASED) *Total amount:* $7,301,157 (92% federal, 6% state, 2% institutional). *Receiving aid:* Freshmen: 64% (335); all full-time undergradu-

ates: 62% (1,302). *Average award:* Freshmen: $5739; Undergraduates: $5405. *Scholarships, grants, and awards:* Federal Pell, FSEOG, state, private, college/university gift aid from institutional funds, United Negro College Fund, Federal Nursing.
GIFT AID (NON-NEED-BASED) *Total amount:* $3,415,996 (1% federal, 13% state, 71% institutional, 15% external sources). *Receiving aid:* Freshmen: 40% (212). Undergraduates: 38% (795). *Average award:* Freshmen: $5246. Undergraduates: $4918. *Scholarships, grants, and awards by category:* *Academic interests/achievement:* $1,531,681 total: agriculture, general academic interests/achievements. *Creative arts/performance:* $399,290 total: art/fine arts, journalism/publications, music, performing arts. *Special achievements/activities:* $14,500 total: cheerleading/drum major. *Special characteristics:* $558,785 total: adult students, children with a deceased or disabled parent, ethnic background, general special characteristics, international students, local/state students, public servants, veterans. *Tuition waivers:* Full or partial for employees or children of employees.
LOANS *Student loans:* $14,400,171 (44% need-based, 56% non-need-based). 64% of past graduating class borrowed through all loan programs. *Average indebtedness per student:* $24,826. *Average need-based loan:* Freshmen: $3441. Undergraduates: $3972. *Parent loans:* $2,338,001 (100% non-need-based). *Programs:* Federal Direct (Subsidized and Unsubsidized Stafford, PLUS), Perkins.
WORK-STUDY *Federal work-study:* Total amount: $762,272; 446 jobs averaging $1709. *State or other work-study/employment:* Total amount: $299,390 (100% non-need-based). 103 part-time jobs averaging $894.
ATHLETIC AWARDS Total amount: $912,652 (100% non-need-based).
APPLYING FOR FINANCIAL AID *Required financial aid form:* FAFSA. *Financial aid deadline (priority):* 4/15. *Notification date:* Continuous. Students must reply within 2 weeks of notification.
CONTACT Myrna C. Bryant, Assistant Director of Financial Aid, Kentucky State University, 400 East Main Street, Frankfort, KY 40601, 502-597-5960 or toll-free 800-633-9415 (in-state), 800-325-1716 (out-of-state). *Fax:* 502-597-5950. *E-mail:* myrna.bryant@kysu.edu.

KENTUCKY WESLEYAN COLLEGE
Owensboro, KY

Tuition & fees: $16,870	Average undergraduate aid package: $16,017

ABOUT THE INSTITUTION Independent Methodist, coed. 41 undergraduate majors. Federal methodology is used as a basis for awarding need-based institutional aid.
UNDERGRADUATE EXPENSES for 2009–10 *Comprehensive fee:* $23,310 includes full-time tuition ($16,870) and room and board ($6440). *College room only:* $2920. Full-time tuition and fees vary according to course load. Room and board charges vary according to board plan and housing facility. Part-time tuition and fees vary according to course load. *Payment plans:* Installment, deferred payment.
FRESHMAN FINANCIAL AID (Fall 2009, est.) 210 applied for aid; of those 95% were deemed to have need. 98% of freshmen with need received aid; of those 25% had need fully met. *Average percent of need met:* 80% (excluding resources awarded to replace EFC). *Average financial aid package:* $16,819 (excluding resources awarded to replace EFC). 9% of all full-time freshmen had no need and received non-need-based gift aid.
UNDERGRADUATE FINANCIAL AID (Fall 2009, est.) 775 applied for aid; of those 90% were deemed to have need. 99% of undergraduates with need received aid; of those 30% had need fully met. *Average percent of need met:* 78% (excluding resources awarded to replace EFC). *Average financial aid package:* $16,017 (excluding resources awarded to replace EFC). 16% of all full-time undergraduates had no need and received non-need-based gift aid.
GIFT AID (NEED-BASED) *Total amount:* $8,927,945 (22% federal, 24% state, 51% institutional, 3% external sources). *Receiving aid:* Freshmen: 89% (197); all full-time undergraduates: 82% (690). *Average award:* Freshmen: $14,085; Undergraduates: $12,886. *Scholarships, grants, and awards:* Federal Pell, FSEOG, state, private, college/university gift aid from institutional funds.
GIFT AID (NON-NEED-BASED) *Total amount:* $2,006,988 (12% state, 82% institutional, 6% external sources). *Receiving aid:* Freshmen: 11% (25). Undergraduates: 12% (103). *Average award:* Freshmen: $10,678. Undergraduates: $8955. *Scholarships, grants, and awards by category:* *Academic interests/achievement:* 763 awards ($3,907,405 total): general academic interests/achievements. *Creative arts/performance:* 35 awards ($56,622 total): art/fine arts, creative writing, general creative arts/performance, music, performing

arts. *Special achievements/activities:* 79 awards ($191,584 total): general special achievements/activities, junior miss, leadership. *Special characteristics:* 212 awards ($417,553 total): general special characteristics, out-of-state students, relatives of clergy, religious affiliation, veterans. *Tuition waivers:* Full or partial for children of alumni, employees or children of employees, senior citizens.
LOANS *Student loans:* $3,800,899 (75% need-based, 25% non-need-based). 89% of past graduating class borrowed through all loan programs. *Average indebtedness per student:* $20,906. *Average need-based loan:* Freshmen: $3847. Undergraduates: $4078. *Parent loans:* $346,892 (19% need-based, 81% non-need-based). *Programs:* FFEL (Subsidized and Unsubsidized Stafford, PLUS), Perkins, alternative loans.
WORK-STUDY *Federal work-study:* Total amount: $146,178; 104 jobs averaging $1398. *State or other work-study/employment:* Total amount: $7500 (100% need-based). Part-time jobs available.
ATHLETIC AWARDS Total amount: $1,316,380 (100% non-need-based).
APPLYING FOR FINANCIAL AID *Required financial aid form:* FAFSA. *Financial aid deadline:* 3/15. *Notification date:* Continuous. Students must reply within 2 weeks of notification.
CONTACT Mrs. Samantha Hays, Director of Financial Aid, Kentucky Wesleyan College, 3000 Frederica Street, Owensboro, KY 42301, 270-852-3130 or toll-free 800-999-0592 (in-state), 800-990-0592 (out-of-state). *Fax:* 270-852-3133. *E-mail:* shays@kwc.edu.

KENYON COLLEGE
Gambier, OH

Tuition & fees: $40,900	Average undergraduate aid package: $31,610

ABOUT THE INSTITUTION Independent, coed. 31 undergraduate majors. Both federal and institutional methodology are used as a basis for awarding need-based institutional aid.
UNDERGRADUATE EXPENSES for 2010–11 *Comprehensive fee:* $50,400 includes full-time tuition ($39,420), mandatory fees ($1480), and room and board ($9500). *Payment plan:* Installment.
FRESHMAN FINANCIAL AID (Fall 2009, est.) 281 applied for aid; of those 75% were deemed to have need. 100% of freshmen with need received aid; of those 51% had need fully met. *Average percent of need met:* 98% (excluding resources awarded to replace EFC). *Average financial aid package:* $30,190 (excluding resources awarded to replace EFC). 26% of all full-time freshmen had no need and received non-need-based gift aid.
UNDERGRADUATE FINANCIAL AID (Fall 2009, est.) 892 applied for aid; of those 84% were deemed to have need. 100% of undergraduates with need received aid; of those 48% had need fully met. *Average percent of need met:* 98% (excluding resources awarded to replace EFC). *Average financial aid package:* $31,610 (excluding resources awarded to replace EFC). 21% of all full-time undergraduates had no need and received non-need-based gift aid.
GIFT AID (NEED-BASED) *Total amount:* $20,579,922 (4% federal, 1% state, 87% institutional, 8% external sources). *Receiving aid:* Freshmen: 43% (201); all full-time undergraduates: 41% (720). *Average award:* Freshmen: $28,858; Undergraduates: $28,583. *Scholarships, grants, and awards:* Federal Pell, FSEOG, state, private, college/university gift aid from institutional funds.
GIFT AID (NON-NEED-BASED) *Total amount:* $3,384,660 (77% institutional, 23% external sources). *Receiving aid:* Freshmen: 15% (71). Undergraduates: 10% (175). *Average award:* Freshmen: $9813. Undergraduates: $11,847. *Scholarships, grants, and awards by category: Academic interests/achievement:* 320 awards ($2,935,455 total): general academic interests/achievements. *Creative arts/performance:* 1 award ($1500 total): art/fine arts, creative writing, music. *Special characteristics:* 55 awards ($750,455 total): ethnic background, first-generation college students. *Tuition waivers:* Full or partial for employees or children of employees.
LOANS *Student loans:* $5,274,958 (54% need-based, 46% non-need-based). 58% of past graduating class borrowed through all loan programs. *Average indebtedness per student:* $19,934. *Average need-based loan:* Freshmen: $3389. Undergraduates: $4500. *Parent loans:* $2,572,980 (3% need-based, 97% non-need-based). *Programs:* Federal Direct (Subsidized and Unsubsidized Stafford, PLUS), Perkins, college/university.
WORK-STUDY *Federal work-study:* Total amount: $176,908; 225 jobs averaging $722. *State or other work-study/employment:* Total amount: $505,794 (45% need-based, 55% non-need-based). 176 part-time jobs averaging $687.

APPLYING FOR FINANCIAL AID *Required financial aid forms:* FAFSA, CSS Financial Aid PROFILE, income tax form(s). *Financial aid deadline (priority):* 2/15. *Notification date:* 4/1. Students must reply by 5/1.
CONTACT Mr. Craig Daugherty, Director of Financial Aid, Kenyon College, Stephens Hall, Gambier, OH 43022-9623, 740-427-5430 or toll-free 800-848-2468. *Fax:* 740-427-5240. *E-mail:* daugherty@kenyon.edu.

KETTERING COLLEGE OF MEDICAL ARTS
Kettering, OH

CONTACT Kim Snell, Director of Student Finance, Kettering College of Medical Arts, 3737 Southern Boulevard, Kettering, OH 45429, 937-298-3399 Ext. 5617 or toll-free 800-433-5262. *Fax:* 937-296-4238. *E-mail:* kim_snell@ketthealth.com.

KETTERING UNIVERSITY
Flint, MI

Tuition & fees: $29,120	Average undergraduate aid package: $18,029

ABOUT THE INSTITUTION Independent, coed, primarily men. 13 undergraduate majors. Federal methodology is used as a basis for awarding need-based institutional aid.
UNDERGRADUATE EXPENSES for 2010–11 *One-time required fee:* $310. *Comprehensive fee:* $35,510 includes full-time tuition ($28,672), mandatory fees ($448), and room and board ($6390). *College room only:* $4000. *Part-time tuition:* $896 per credit hour. *Payment plan:* Installment.
FRESHMAN FINANCIAL AID (Fall 2009, est.) 406 applied for aid; of those 89% were deemed to have need. 100% of freshmen with need received aid; of those 19% had need fully met. *Average percent of need met:* 91% (excluding resources awarded to replace EFC). *Average financial aid package:* $21,719 (excluding resources awarded to replace EFC). 17% of all full-time freshmen had no need and received non-need-based gift aid.
UNDERGRADUATE FINANCIAL AID (Fall 2009, est.) 1,501 applied for aid; of those 92% were deemed to have need. 100% of undergraduates with need received aid; of those 17% had need fully met. *Average percent of need met:* 87% (excluding resources awarded to replace EFC). *Average financial aid package:* $18,029 (excluding resources awarded to replace EFC). 20% of all full-time undergraduates had no need and received non-need-based gift aid.
GIFT AID (NEED-BASED) *Total amount:* $16,016,332 (14% federal, 8% state, 77% institutional, 1% external sources). *Receiving aid:* Freshmen: 73% (320); all full-time undergraduates: 62% (1,294). *Average award:* Freshmen: $17,135; Undergraduates: $13,575. *Scholarships, grants, and awards:* Federal Pell, FSEOG, state, private, college/university gift aid from institutional funds.
GIFT AID (NON-NEED-BASED) *Total amount:* $5,572,805 (2% state, 95% institutional, 3% external sources). *Receiving aid:* Freshmen: 10% (42). Undergraduates: 6% (132). *Average award:* Freshmen: $13,130. Undergraduates: $11,477. *Scholarships, grants, and awards by category: Academic interests/achievement:* business, computer science, engineering/technologies, general academic interests/achievements, mathematics, physical sciences. *Special achievements/activities:* general special achievements/activities, leadership, memberships. *Special characteristics:* children of faculty/staff, local/state students, members of minority groups, siblings of current students. *Tuition waivers:* Full or partial for employees or children of employees.
LOANS *Student loans:* $16,377,658 (67% need-based, 33% non-need-based). 84% of past graduating class borrowed through all loan programs. *Average indebtedness per student:* $41,485. *Average need-based loan:* Freshmen: $3402. Undergraduates: $4302. *Parent loans:* $1,786,278 (53% need-based, 47% non-need-based). *Programs:* Federal Direct (Subsidized and Unsubsidized Stafford, PLUS).
WORK-STUDY *Federal work-study:* Total amount: $1,382,655; jobs available. *State or other work-study/employment:* Part-time jobs available.
APPLYING FOR FINANCIAL AID *Required financial aid form:* FAFSA. *Financial aid deadline:* Continuous. *Notification date:* Continuous beginning 1/31.
CONTACT Diane Bice, Director of Financial Aid, Kettering University, 1700 West Third Avenue, Flint, MI 48504-4898, 800-955-4464 Ext. 7859 or toll-free 800-955-4464 Ext. 7865 (in-state), 800-955-4464 (out-of-state). *Fax:* 810-762-9807. *E-mail:* finaid@kettering.edu.

KEUKA COLLEGE
Keuka Park, NY

Tuition & fees: $22,680	Average undergraduate aid package: $16,576

ABOUT THE INSTITUTION Independent religious, coed. 34 undergraduate majors. Federal methodology is used as a basis for awarding need-based institutional aid.

UNDERGRADUATE EXPENSES for 2009–10 *Comprehensive fee:* $31,840 includes full-time tuition ($22,040), mandatory fees ($640), and room and board ($9160). *College room only:* $4350. Full-time tuition and fees vary according to program. Room and board charges vary according to board plan and housing facility. *Part-time tuition:* $735 per credit hour. Part-time tuition and fees vary according to program. *Payment plan:* Installment.

FRESHMAN FINANCIAL AID (Fall 2009, est.) 240 applied for aid; of those 94% were deemed to have need. 100% of freshmen with need received aid; of those 8% had need fully met. *Average percent of need met:* 70% (excluding resources awarded to replace EFC). *Average financial aid package:* $18,666 (excluding resources awarded to replace EFC). 7% of all full-time freshmen had no need and received non-need-based gift aid.

UNDERGRADUATE FINANCIAL AID (Fall 2009, est.) 1,174 applied for aid; of those 91% were deemed to have need. 99% of undergraduates with need received aid; of those 11% had need fully met. *Average percent of need met:* 74% (excluding resources awarded to replace EFC). *Average financial aid package:* $16,576 (excluding resources awarded to replace EFC). 7% of all full-time undergraduates had no need and received non-need-based gift aid.

GIFT AID (NEED-BASED) *Total amount:* $12,017,630 (19% federal, 16% state, 62% institutional, 3% external sources). *Receiving aid:* Freshmen: 91% (225); all full-time undergraduates: 85% (1,008). *Average award:* Freshmen: $14,052; Undergraduates: $11,866. *Scholarships, grants, and awards:* Federal Pell, FSEOG, state, college/university gift aid from institutional funds.

GIFT AID (NON-NEED-BASED) *Total amount:* $1,170,155 (5% federal, 6% state, 84% institutional, 5% external sources). *Receiving aid:* Freshmen: 6% (15). Undergraduates: 7% (82). *Average award:* Freshmen: $8039. Undergraduates: $9185. *Scholarships, grants, and awards by category: Academic interests/ achievement:* general academic interests/achievements, international studies. *Special achievements/activities:* community service, general special achievements/ activities, leadership. *Special characteristics:* children and siblings of alumni, children of faculty/staff, international students, siblings of current students. *Tuition waivers:* Full or partial for employees or children of employees.

LOANS *Student loans:* $14,440,081 (71% need-based, 29% non-need-based). 95% of past graduating class borrowed through all loan programs. *Average indebtedness per student:* $23,379. *Average need-based loan:* Freshmen: $5087. Undergraduates: $5811. *Parent loans:* $1,077,967 (43% need-based, 57% non-need-based). *Programs:* FFEL (Subsidized and Unsubsidized Stafford, PLUS), Perkins.

WORK-STUDY *Federal work-study:* Total amount: $348,238; jobs available. *State or other work-study/employment:* Total amount: $134,358 (11% need-based, 89% non-need-based). Part-time jobs available.

APPLYING FOR FINANCIAL AID *Required financial aid form:* FAFSA. *Financial aid deadline:* Continuous. *Notification date:* Continuous beginning 3/1. Students must reply by 5/1 or within 2 weeks of notification.

CONTACT Jennifer Bates, Director of Financial Aid, Keuka College, 141 Central Avenue, Keuka Park, NY 14478-0098, 315-279-5232 or toll-free 800-33-KEUKA. *Fax:* 315-536-5327. *E-mail:* jbates@keuka.edu.

KEYSTONE COLLEGE
La Plume, PA

Tuition & fees: $19,120	Average undergraduate aid package: $22,554

ABOUT THE INSTITUTION Independent, coed. 63 undergraduate majors. Federal methodology is used as a basis for awarding need-based institutional aid.

UNDERGRADUATE EXPENSES for 2010–11 *One-time required fee:* $200. *Comprehensive fee:* $28,370 includes full-time tuition ($18,170), mandatory fees ($950), and room and board ($9250). *College room only:* $4500. Full-time tuition and fees vary according to course load. Room and board charges vary according to board plan and housing facility. *Part-time tuition:* $390 per credit. *Part-time fees:* $200 per term. Part-time tuition and fees vary according to course load. *Payment plans:* Installment, deferred payment.

FRESHMAN FINANCIAL AID (Fall 2009, est.) 288 applied for aid; of those 93% were deemed to have need. 100% of freshmen with need received aid; of those 34% had need fully met. *Average percent of need met:* 81% (excluding resources awarded to replace EFC). *Average financial aid package:* $23,718 (excluding resources awarded to replace EFC). 3% of all full-time freshmen had no need and received non-need-based gift aid.

UNDERGRADUATE FINANCIAL AID (Fall 2009, est.) 1,095 applied for aid; of those 93% were deemed to have need. 100% of undergraduates with need received aid; of those 35% had need fully met. *Average percent of need met:* 77% (excluding resources awarded to replace EFC). *Average financial aid package:* $22,554 (excluding resources awarded to replace EFC). 3% of all full-time undergraduates had no need and received non-need-based gift aid.

GIFT AID (NEED-BASED) *Total amount:* $7,247,917 (61% federal, 34% state, 3% institutional, 2% external sources). *Receiving aid:* Freshmen: 86% (268); all full-time undergraduates: 86% (1,015). *Average award:* Freshmen: $21,369; Undergraduates: $20,719. *Scholarships, grants, and awards:* Federal Pell, FSEOG, state, private, college/university gift aid from institutional funds.

GIFT AID (NON-NEED-BASED) *Total amount:* $8,436,957 (99% institutional, 1% external sources). *Receiving aid:* Freshmen: 86% (268). Undergraduates: 86% (1,015). *Average award:* Freshmen: $12,074. Undergraduates: $11,868. *Scholarships, grants, and awards by category: Academic interests/achievement:* 32 awards ($71,034 total): computer science, education. *Special characteristics:* 63 awards ($38,568 total): children and siblings of alumni, international students, siblings of current students. *Tuition waivers:* Full or partial for employees or children of employees, senior citizens.

LOANS *Student loans:* $10,358,095 (48% need-based, 52% non-need-based). 88% of past graduating class borrowed through all loan programs. *Average indebtedness per student:* $24,750. *Average need-based loan:* Freshmen: $5500. Undergraduates: $6500. *Parent loans:* $2,310,068 (100% non-need-based). *Programs:* FFEL (Subsidized and Unsubsidized Stafford, PLUS), Perkins, alternative loans, Miller Loan Fund.

WORK-STUDY *Federal work-study:* Total amount: $181,577; jobs available. *State or other work-study/employment:* Total amount: $125,000 (100% non-need-based). Part-time jobs available.

APPLYING FOR FINANCIAL AID *Required financial aid forms:* FAFSA, state aid form. *Financial aid deadline:* Continuous. *Notification date:* Continuous. Students must reply within 2 weeks of notification.

CONTACT Ginger Kline, Director of Financial Assistance and Planning, Keystone College, One College Green, Sabiston Hall, 2nd Floor, La Plume, AB 18440, 570-945-8130 or toll-free 877-4COLLEGE Ext. 1. *Fax:* 570-945-8967. *E-mail:* ginger.kline@keystone.edu.

KING COLLEGE
Bristol, TN

Tuition & fees: $21,880	Average undergraduate aid package: $16,736

ABOUT THE INSTITUTION Independent religious, coed. 58 undergraduate majors. Federal methodology is used as a basis for awarding need-based institutional aid.

UNDERGRADUATE EXPENSES for 2009–10 *Comprehensive fee:* $29,298 includes full-time tuition ($20,592), mandatory fees ($1288), and room and board ($7418). *College room only:* $3726. Full-time tuition and fees vary according to course load and program. Room and board charges vary according to board plan. *Part-time tuition:* $600 per credit hour. *Part-time fees:* $120 per term. Part-time tuition and fees vary according to course load and program. *Payment plan:* Installment.

FRESHMAN FINANCIAL AID (Fall 2009, est.) 222 applied for aid; of those 88% were deemed to have need. 100% of freshmen with need received aid; of those 19% had need fully met. *Average percent of need met:* 78% (excluding resources awarded to replace EFC). *Average financial aid package:* $19,789 (excluding resources awarded to replace EFC). 10% of all full-time freshmen had no need and received non-need-based gift aid.

UNDERGRADUATE FINANCIAL AID (Fall 2009, est.) 768 applied for aid; of those 91% were deemed to have need. 99% of undergraduates with need received aid; of those 10% had need fully met. *Average percent of need met:* 69% (excluding resources awarded to replace EFC). *Average financial aid package:* $16,736 (excluding resources awarded to replace EFC). 5% of all full-time undergraduates had no need and received non-need-based gift aid.

GIFT AID (NEED-BASED) *Total amount:* $8,147,122 (28% federal, 14% state, 53% institutional, 5% external sources). *Receiving aid:* Freshmen: 78% (196);

all full-time undergraduates: 74% (640). *Average award:* Freshmen: $17,190; Undergraduates: $14,125. *Scholarships, grants, and awards:* Federal Pell, FSEOG, state, private, college/university gift aid from institutional funds.

GIFT AID (NON-NEED-BASED) *Total amount:* $824,957 (21% state, 56% institutional, 23% external sources). *Receiving aid:* Freshmen: 15% (37). Undergraduates: 7% (63). *Average award:* Freshmen: $8814. Undergraduates: $8610. *Scholarships, grants, and awards by category: Academic interests/ achievement:* 501 awards ($3,807,521 total): general academic interests/ achievements. *Creative arts/performance:* 59 awards ($134,438 total): music, performing arts, theater/drama. *Special achievements/activities:* 294 awards ($2,050,214 total): general special achievements/activities. *Special characteristics:* 63 awards ($561,378 total): children of faculty/staff, members of minority groups, relatives of clergy. *Tuition waivers:* Full or partial for employees or children of employees, senior citizens.

LOANS *Student loans:* $4,582,333 (86% need-based, 14% non-need-based). 96% of past graduating class borrowed through all loan programs. *Average indebtedness per student:* $15,757. *Average need-based loan:* Freshmen: $3690. Undergraduates: $4773. *Parent loans:* $508,233 (49% need-based, 51% non-need-based). *Programs:* FFEL (Subsidized and Unsubsidized Stafford, PLUS), Perkins, college/university.

WORK-STUDY Federal work-study jobs available. *State or other work-study/ employment:* Part-time jobs available.

ATHLETIC AWARDS Total amount: $1,324,115 (78% need-based, 22% non-need-based).

APPLYING FOR FINANCIAL AID *Required financial aid form:* FAFSA. *Financial aid deadline (priority):* 3/1. *Notification date:* Continuous beginning 3/1. Students must reply within 2 weeks of notification.

CONTACT Nancy M. Beverly, Director of Financial Aid, King College, 1350 King College Road, Bristol, TN 37620-2699, 423-652-4728 or toll-free 800-362-0014. *Fax:* 423-652-6039. *E-mail:* nmbeverly@king.edu.

THE KING'S COLLEGE
New York, NY

Tuition & fees: $27,350	Average undergraduate aid package: $20,902

ABOUT THE INSTITUTION Independent nondenominational, coed. 2 undergraduate majors. Federal methodology is used as a basis for awarding need-based institutional aid.

UNDERGRADUATE EXPENSES for 2010–11 *Tuition:* full-time $27,000; part-time $1125 per credit hour. Full-time tuition and fees vary according to course load. Part-time tuition and fees vary according to course load. *Payment plans:* Installment, deferred payment.

FRESHMAN FINANCIAL AID (Fall 2009, est.) 91 applied for aid; of those 86% were deemed to have need. 100% of freshmen with need received aid; of those 13% had need fully met. *Average percent of need met:* 63% (excluding resources awarded to replace EFC). *Average financial aid package:* $20,914 (excluding resources awarded to replace EFC). 24% of all full-time freshmen had no need and received non-need-based gift aid.

UNDERGRADUATE FINANCIAL AID (Fall 2009, est.) 236 applied for aid; of those 86% were deemed to have need. 100% of undergraduates with need received aid; of those 16% had need fully met. *Average percent of need met:* 71% (excluding resources awarded to replace EFC). *Average financial aid package:* $20,902 (excluding resources awarded to replace EFC). 29% of all full-time undergraduates had no need and received non-need-based gift aid.

GIFT AID (NEED-BASED) *Total amount:* $3,603,101 (10% federal, 1% state, 87% institutional, 2% external sources). *Receiving aid:* Freshmen: 76% (78); all full-time undergraduates: 70% (203). *Average award:* Freshmen: $17,776; Undergraduates: $17,159. *Scholarships, grants, and awards:* Federal Pell, FSEOG, state, private, college/university gift aid from institutional funds.

GIFT AID (NON-NEED-BASED) *Total amount:* $1,004,600 (99% institutional, 1% external sources). *Receiving aid:* Freshmen: 76% (78). Undergraduates: 70% (203). *Average award:* Freshmen: $15,547. Undergraduates: $11,993. *Tuition waivers:* Full or partial for employees or children of employees.

LOANS *Student loans:* $1,826,258 (88% need-based, 12% non-need-based). 79% of past graduating class borrowed through all loan programs. *Average indebtedness per student:* $15,434. *Average need-based loan:* Freshmen: $3500. Undergraduates: $4269. *Parent loans:* $667,024 (77% need-based, 23% non-need-based). *Programs:* FFEL (Subsidized and Unsubsidized Stafford, PLUS).

WORK-STUDY *Federal work-study:* Total amount: $25,705; 14 jobs averaging $750.

APPLYING FOR FINANCIAL AID *Required financial aid form:* FAFSA. *Financial aid deadline:* Continuous. *Notification date:* Continuous beginning 2/15.

CONTACT Anna Peters, Director of Financial Aid, The King's College, 350 Fifth Avenue, Suite 1500, New York, NY 10118, 212-659-7281 or toll-free 888-969-7200 Ext. 3610. *Fax:* 212-659-3611. *E-mail:* apeters@tkc.edu.

KING'S COLLEGE
Wilkes-Barre, PA

Tuition & fees: $25,644	Average undergraduate aid package: $18,300

ABOUT THE INSTITUTION Independent Roman Catholic, coed. 40 undergraduate majors. Federal methodology is used as a basis for awarding need-based institutional aid.

UNDERGRADUATE EXPENSES for 2009–10 *Comprehensive fee:* $35,482 includes full-time tuition ($25,644) and room and board ($9838). *College room only:* $4578. Room and board charges vary according to board plan. *Part-time tuition:* $495 per credit hour. *Payment plans:* Installment, deferred payment.

FRESHMAN FINANCIAL AID (Fall 2009, est.) 474 applied for aid; of those 90% were deemed to have need. 100% of freshmen with need received aid; of those 19% had need fully met. *Average percent of need met:* 73% (excluding resources awarded to replace EFC). *Average financial aid package:* $20,209 (excluding resources awarded to replace EFC). 14% of all full-time freshmen had no need and received non-need-based gift aid.

UNDERGRADUATE FINANCIAL AID (Fall 2009, est.) 1,773 applied for aid; of those 90% were deemed to have need. 99% of undergraduates with need received aid; of those 16% had need fully met. *Average percent of need met:* 69% (excluding resources awarded to replace EFC). *Average financial aid package:* $18,300 (excluding resources awarded to replace EFC). 18% of all full-time undergraduates had no need and received non-need-based gift aid.

GIFT AID (NEED-BASED) *Total amount:* $21,458,019 (13% federal, 13% state, 73% institutional, 1% external sources). *Receiving aid:* Freshmen: 86% (427); all full-time undergraduates: 80% (1,578). *Average award:* Freshmen: $16,246; Undergraduates: $14,278. *Scholarships, grants, and awards:* Federal Pell, FSEOG, state, private, college/university gift aid from institutional funds.

GIFT AID (NON-NEED-BASED) *Total amount:* $4,994,361 (10% federal, 2% state, 86% institutional, 2% external sources). *Receiving aid:* Freshmen: 10% (48). Undergraduates: 8% (165). *Average award:* Freshmen: $12,165. Undergraduates: $11,244. *Scholarships, grants, and awards by category: Academic interests/achievement:* 1,401 awards ($13,803,317 total): biological sciences, business, communication, computer science, education, English, foreign languages, general academic interests/achievements, health fields, humanities, mathematics, physical sciences, premedicine, religion/biblical studies, social sciences. *Special achievements/activities:* 503 awards ($2,761,675 total): community service, general special achievements/activities, leadership. *Special characteristics:* 234 awards ($1,751,452 total): children of educators, children of faculty/staff, international students, members of minority groups, relatives of clergy, siblings of current students. *Tuition waivers:* Full or partial for employees or children of employees, senior citizens.

LOANS *Student loans:* $10,424,050 (75% need-based, 25% non-need-based). 84% of past graduating class borrowed through all loan programs. *Average indebtedness per student:* $30,843. *Average need-based loan:* Freshmen: $4129. Undergraduates: $4830. *Parent loans:* $1,948,323 (88% need-based, 12% non-need-based). *Programs:* FFEL (Subsidized and Unsubsidized Stafford, PLUS), Perkins, private loans.

WORK-STUDY *Federal work-study:* Total amount: $188,182; 306 jobs averaging $1305. *State or other work-study/employment:* Total amount: $392,644 (78% need-based, 22% non-need-based). 339 part-time jobs averaging $997.

APPLYING FOR FINANCIAL AID *Required financial aid forms:* FAFSA, institution's own form. *Financial aid deadline (priority):* 2/15. *Notification date:* Continuous beginning 3/1. Students must reply by 5/1 or within 2 weeks of notification.

CONTACT Ms. Donna Cerza, Director of Financial Aid, King's College, 133 North River Street, Wilkes-Barre, PA 18711-0801, 570-208-5868 or toll-free 888-KINGSPA. *Fax:* 570-208-6015. *E-mail:* finaid@kings.edu.

THE KING'S COLLEGE AND SEMINARY
Van Nuys, CA

CONTACT Financial Aid Office, The King's College and Seminary, 14800 Sherman Way, Van Nuys, CA 91405-8040, 818-779-8040 or toll-free 888-779-8040 (in-state).

KNOX COLLEGE
Galesburg, IL

Tuition & fees: $31,911	Average undergraduate aid package: $25,642

ABOUT THE INSTITUTION Independent, coed. 33 undergraduate majors. Both federal and institutional methodology are used as a basis for awarding need-based institutional aid.

UNDERGRADUATE EXPENSES for 2009–10 *Comprehensive fee:* $39,075 includes full-time tuition ($31,575), mandatory fees ($336), and room and board ($7164). *College room only:* $3603. Room and board charges vary according to board plan. *Part-time tuition:* $3508 per credit. Part-time tuition and fees vary according to course load. *Payment plan:* Installment.

FRESHMAN FINANCIAL AID (Fall 2009, est.) 345 applied for aid; of those 85% were deemed to have need. 100% of freshmen with need received aid; of those 32% had need fully met. *Average percent of need met:* 92% (excluding resources awarded to replace EFC). *Average financial aid package:* $26,016 (excluding resources awarded to replace EFC). 22% of all full-time freshmen had no need and received non-need-based gift aid.

UNDERGRADUATE FINANCIAL AID (Fall 2009, est.) 1,072 applied for aid; of those 90% were deemed to have need. 100% of undergraduates with need received aid; of those 27% had need fully met. *Average percent of need met:* 90% (excluding resources awarded to replace EFC). *Average financial aid package:* $25,642 (excluding resources awarded to replace EFC). 20% of all full-time undergraduates had no need and received non-need-based gift aid.

GIFT AID (NEED-BASED) *Total amount:* $19,102,415 (10% federal, 7% state, 81% institutional, 2% external sources). *Receiving aid:* Freshmen: 74% (293); all full-time undergraduates: 69% (961). *Average award:* Freshmen: $21,625; Undergraduates: $19,765. *Scholarships, grants, and awards:* Federal Pell, FSEOG, state, private, college/university gift aid from institutional funds.

GIFT AID (NON-NEED-BASED) *Receiving aid:* Freshmen: 13% (50). Undergraduates: 8% (114). *Average award:* Freshmen: $11,908. Undergraduates: $10,845. *Scholarships, grants, and awards by category: Academic interests/achievement:* general academic interests/achievements, mathematics. *Creative arts/performance:* art/fine arts, creative writing, dance, music, theater/drama. *Special achievements/activities:* community service. *Tuition waivers:* Full or partial for employees or children of employees.

LOANS *Student loans:* $8,394,299 (49% need-based, 51% non-need-based). 73% of past graduating class borrowed through all loan programs. *Average indebtedness per student:* $24,018. *Average need-based loan:* Freshmen: $4289. Undergraduates: $5062. *Parent loans:* $2,420,561 (100% non-need-based). *Programs:* Federal Direct (Subsidized and Unsubsidized Stafford, PLUS), Perkins, college/university, private loans.

WORK-STUDY *Federal work-study:* Total amount: $1,471,804; 697 jobs averaging $2111. *State or other work-study/employment:* Total amount: $165,925 (100% need-based). 72 part-time jobs averaging $2304.

APPLYING FOR FINANCIAL AID *Required financial aid forms:* FAFSA, institution's own form, income tax form(s), W-2 forms. *Financial aid deadline (priority):* 2/15. *Notification date:* Continuous beginning 3/15. Students must reply by 5/1 or within 2 weeks of notification.

CONTACT Ms. Ann M. Brill, Director of Financial Aid, Knox College, 2 East South Street, Galesburg, IL 61401, 309-341-7130 or toll-free 800-678-KNOX. *Fax:* 309-341-7453. *E-mail:* abrill@knox.edu.

KOL YAAKOV TORAH CENTER
Monsey, NY

CONTACT Office of Financial Aid, Kol Yaakov Torah Center, 29 West Maple Avenue, Monsey, NY 10952-2954, 914-425-3863.

KUTZTOWN UNIVERSITY OF PENNSYLVANIA
Kutztown, PA

Tuition & fees (PA res): $7397	Average undergraduate aid package: $7379

ABOUT THE INSTITUTION State-supported, coed. 59 undergraduate majors. Federal methodology is used as a basis for awarding need-based institutional aid.

UNDERGRADUATE EXPENSES for 2009–10 *Tuition, state resident:* full-time $5554; part-time $231 per credit hour. *Tuition, nonresident:* full-time $13,886; part-time $579 per credit hour. *Required fees:* full-time $1843; $68 per credit hour or $60 per term. *College room and board:* $7698; *Room only:* $4768. Room and board charges vary according to board plan and housing facility. *Payment plans:* Installment, deferred payment.

FRESHMAN FINANCIAL AID (Fall 2009, est.) 1,653 applied for aid; of those 68% were deemed to have need. 97% of freshmen with need received aid; of those 77% had need fully met. *Average percent of need met:* 54% (excluding resources awarded to replace EFC). *Average financial aid package:* $6713 (excluding resources awarded to replace EFC). 4% of all full-time freshmen had no need and received non-need-based gift aid.

UNDERGRADUATE FINANCIAL AID (Fall 2009, est.) 7,291 applied for aid; of those 71% were deemed to have need. 96% of undergraduates with need received aid; of those 87% had need fully met. *Average percent of need met:* 58% (excluding resources awarded to replace EFC). *Average financial aid package:* $7379 (excluding resources awarded to replace EFC). 4% of all full-time undergraduates had no need and received non-need-based gift aid.

GIFT AID (NEED-BASED) *Total amount:* $15,239,408 (46% federal, 45% state, 5% institutional, 4% external sources). *Receiving aid:* Freshmen: 42% (772); all full-time undergraduates: 39% (3,410). *Average award:* Freshmen: $4766; Undergraduates: $4698. *Scholarships, grants, and awards:* Federal Pell, FSEOG, state, private, college/university gift aid from institutional funds.

GIFT AID (NON-NEED-BASED) *Total amount:* $1,142,667 (15% federal, 21% state, 21% institutional, 43% external sources). *Receiving aid:* Freshmen: 2% (31). Undergraduates: 2% (205). *Average award:* Freshmen: $1872. Undergraduates: $2071. *Scholarships, grants, and awards by category: Academic interests/achievement:* 528 awards ($1,249,927 total): biological sciences, business, communication, computer science, education, English, foreign languages, general academic interests/achievements, health fields, humanities, international studies, library science, mathematics, physical sciences. *Creative arts/performance:* 46 awards ($40,338 total): applied art and design, art/fine arts, dance, music. *Special achievements/activities:* 546 awards ($610,281 total): community service, general special achievements/activities, leadership, religious involvement. *Special characteristics:* 157 awards ($582,526 total): children of faculty/staff, children of union members/company employees, first-generation college students, handicapped students, local/state students. *Tuition waivers:* Full or partial for employees or children of employees, senior citizens.

LOANS *Student loans:* $50,494,255 (58% need-based, 42% non-need-based). 86% of past graduating class borrowed through all loan programs. *Average indebtedness per student:* $20,707. *Average need-based loan:* Freshmen: $3269. Undergraduates: $4048. *Parent loans:* $8,958,865 (23% need-based, 77% non-need-based). *Programs:* FFEL (Subsidized and Unsubsidized Stafford, PLUS), Perkins.

WORK-STUDY *Federal work-study:* Total amount: $297,547; 213 jobs averaging $1397.

ATHLETIC AWARDS Total amount: $574,336 (56% need-based, 44% non-need-based).

APPLYING FOR FINANCIAL AID *Required financial aid form:* FAFSA. *Financial aid deadline (priority):* 2/15. *Notification date:* Continuous beginning 3/30. Students must reply by 5/1 or within 4 weeks of notification.

CONTACT Mr. Bernard McCree, Director of Financial Aid, Kutztown University of Pennsylvania, 209 Stratton Administration Center, Kutztown, PA 19530-0730, 610-683-4032 or toll-free 877-628-1915. *Fax:* 610-683-1380. *E-mail:* mccree@kutztown.edu.

KUYPER COLLEGE
Grand Rapids, MI

Tuition & fees: $16,416	Average undergraduate aid package: $11,674

ABOUT THE INSTITUTION Independent religious, coed. 26 undergraduate majors. Federal methodology is used as a basis for awarding need-based institutional aid.

UNDERGRADUATE EXPENSES for 2010–11 *Comprehensive fee:* $22,696 includes full-time tuition ($15,866), mandatory fees ($550), and room and board ($6280). Full-time tuition and fees vary according to course load. Room and board charges vary according to board plan, housing facility, and student level. *Part-time tuition:* $760 per credit hour. Part-time tuition and fees vary according to course load. *Payment plan:* Installment.

FRESHMAN FINANCIAL AID (Fall 2009, est.) 73 applied for aid; of those 92% were deemed to have need. 100% of freshmen with need received aid; of those 9% had need fully met. *Average percent of need met:* 68% (excluding resources awarded to replace EFC). *Average financial aid package:* $11,857 (excluding resources awarded to replace EFC).

UNDERGRADUATE FINANCIAL AID (Fall 2009, est.) 258 applied for aid; of those 100% were deemed to have need. 100% of undergraduates with need received aid; of those 9% had need fully met. *Average percent of need met:* 68% (excluding resources awarded to replace EFC). *Average financial aid package:* $11,674 (excluding resources awarded to replace EFC). 1% of all full-time undergraduates had no need and received non-need-based gift aid.

GIFT AID (NEED-BASED) *Total amount:* $1,906,388 (33% federal, 18% state, 48% institutional, 1% external sources). *Receiving aid:* Freshmen: 88% (67); all full-time undergraduates: 85% (257). *Average award:* Freshmen: $7565; Undergraduates: $7196. *Scholarships, grants, and awards:* Federal Pell, FSEOG, state, private, college/university gift aid from institutional funds.

GIFT AID (NON-NEED-BASED) *Total amount:* $70,351 (3% state, 91% institutional, 6% external sources). *Receiving aid:* Freshmen: 45% (34). Undergraduates: 42% (126). *Average award:* Undergraduates: $2750. *Scholarships, grants, and awards by category:* Academic interests/achievement: 159 awards ($390,965 total): general academic interests/achievements. *Creative arts/performance:* 9 awards ($3475 total): general creative arts/performance. *Special achievements/activities:* 11 awards ($15,375 total): leadership, religious involvement. *Special characteristics:* 55 awards ($293,123 total): children of faculty/staff, international students, members of minority groups. *Tuition waivers:* Full or partial for employees or children of employees.

LOANS *Student loans:* $1,755,302 (92% need-based, 8% non-need-based). 67% of past graduating class borrowed through all loan programs. *Average indebtedness per student:* $21,618. *Average need-based loan:* Freshmen: $4336. Undergraduates: $5754. *Parent loans:* $250,587 (91% need-based, 9% non-need-based). *Programs:* Federal Direct (Subsidized and Unsubsidized Stafford, PLUS), FFEL (Subsidized and Unsubsidized Stafford, PLUS), alternative loans.

WORK-STUDY *Federal work-study:* Total amount: $25,269; 14 jobs averaging $1598. *State or other work-study/employment:* Total amount: $252,000 (100% non-need-based). 88 part-time jobs averaging $1962.

APPLYING FOR FINANCIAL AID *Required financial aid form:* FAFSA. *Financial aid deadline (priority):* 3/1. *Notification date:* Continuous beginning 3/20. Students must reply within 2 weeks of notification.

CONTACT Ms. Agnes Russell, Director of Financial Aid, Kuyper College, 3333 East Beltline NE, Grand Rapids, MI 49525-9749, 616-222-3000 Ext. 656 or toll-free 800-511-3749. *Fax:* 616-222-3045. *E-mail:* arussell@kuyper.edu.

LA COLLEGE INTERNATIONAL
Los Angeles, CA

ABOUT THE INSTITUTION Proprietary, coed. *Awards:* associate and bachelor's degrees. 3 undergraduate majors. *Total enrollment:* 85. Undergraduates: 85. Freshmen: 70.

GIFT AID (NEED-BASED) *Scholarships, grants, and awards:* Federal Pell, FSEOG, state.

GIFT AID (NON-NEED-BASED) *Scholarships, grants, and awards by category:* Academic interests/achievement: general academic interests/achievements.

LOANS *Programs:* FFEL (Subsidized and Unsubsidized Stafford, PLUS), college/university.

APPLYING FOR FINANCIAL AID *Required financial aid forms:* FAFSA, entrance exam, Master Prommisory Note, reference sheet.

CONTACT Office of Financial Aid, LA College International, 3200 Wilshire Boulevard, Los Angeles, CA 90010, 800-218-7274 or toll-free 800-57 GO ICT (in-state). *Fax:* 866-304-7741. *E-mail:* financialaid@lac.edu.

LAFAYETTE COLLEGE
Easton, PA

Tuition & fees: $37,815	Average undergraduate aid package: $34,061

ABOUT THE INSTITUTION Independent religious, coed. 34 undergraduate majors. Institutional methodology is used as a basis for awarding need-based institutional aid.

UNDERGRADUATE EXPENSES for 2009–10 *One-time required fee:* $675. *Comprehensive fee:* $49,614 includes full-time tuition ($37,520), mandatory fees ($295), and room and board ($11,799). *College room only:* $7105. Room and board charges vary according to board plan. *Part-time tuition:* $1682 per course. *Payment plans:* Tuition prepayment, installment.

FRESHMAN FINANCIAL AID (Fall 2009, est.) 395 applied for aid; of those 66% were deemed to have need. 99% of freshmen with need received aid; of those 49% had need fully met. *Average percent of need met:* 98% (excluding resources awarded to replace EFC). *Average financial aid package:* $35,727 (excluding resources awarded to replace EFC). 5% of all full-time freshmen had no need and received non-need-based gift aid.

UNDERGRADUATE FINANCIAL AID (Fall 2009, est.) 1,421 applied for aid; of those 77% were deemed to have need. 100% of undergraduates with need received aid; of those 59% had need fully met. *Average percent of need met:* 98% (excluding resources awarded to replace EFC). *Average financial aid package:* $34,061 (excluding resources awarded to replace EFC). 7% of all full-time undergraduates had no need and received non-need-based gift aid.

GIFT AID (NEED-BASED) *Total amount:* $30,464,416 (5% federal, 1% state, 93% institutional, 1% external sources). *Receiving aid:* Freshmen: 41% (251); all full-time undergraduates: 45% (1,059). *Average award:* Freshmen: $31,097; Undergraduates: $28,697. *Scholarships, grants, and awards:* Federal Pell, FSEOG, state, private, college/university gift aid from institutional funds.

GIFT AID (NON-NEED-BASED) *Total amount:* $4,923,091 (81% institutional, 19% external sources). *Receiving aid:* Freshmen: 11% (69). Undergraduates: 13% (299). *Average award:* Freshmen: $18,968. Undergraduates: $17,090. *Scholarships, grants, and awards by category:* Academic interests/achievement: 455 awards ($4,923,091 total): general academic interests/achievements.

LOANS *Student loans:* $8,349,922 (42% need-based, 58% non-need-based). 47% of past graduating class borrowed through all loan programs. *Average indebtedness per student:* $20,745. *Average need-based loan:* Freshmen: $3579. Undergraduates: $4090. *Parent loans:* $5,912,400 (47% need-based, 53% non-need-based). *Programs:* FFEL (Subsidized and Unsubsidized Stafford, PLUS), Perkins, college/university, HELP Loan to Parents ((Lafayette Loan Program).

WORK-STUDY *Federal work-study:* Total amount: $639,077; jobs available. *State or other work-study/employment:* Total amount: $1,172,422 (48% need-based, 52% non-need-based). Part-time jobs available.

ATHLETIC AWARDS Total amount: $1,617,101 (3% need-based, 97% non-need-based).

APPLYING FOR FINANCIAL AID *Required financial aid forms:* FAFSA, CSS Financial Aid PROFILE, business/farm supplement. *Financial aid deadline:* 1/15. *Notification date:* 4/1. Students must reply by 5/1.

CONTACT Arlinda DeNardo, Director, Financial Aid, Lafayette College, 107 Markle Hall, Easton, PA 18042-1777, 610-330-5055. *Fax:* 610-330-5758. *E-mail:* denardoa@lafayette.edu.

LaGRANGE COLLEGE
LaGrange, GA

Tuition & fees: $21,169	Average undergraduate aid package: N/A

ABOUT THE INSTITUTION Independent United Methodist, coed. 30 undergraduate majors. Federal methodology is used as a basis for awarding need-based institutional aid.

UNDERGRADUATE EXPENSES for 2009–10 *Comprehensive fee:* $29,745 includes full-time tuition ($21,094), mandatory fees ($75), and room and board ($8576). *College room only:* $5022. Full-time tuition and fees vary according to class time, course load, degree level, and program. Room and board charges vary according to board plan and housing facility. *Part-time tuition:* $869 per hour. Part-time tuition and fees vary according to class time, course load, degree level, and program. *Payment plan:* Installment.

GIFT AID (NEED-BASED) *Scholarships, grants, and awards:* Federal Pell, FSEOG, state, private, college/university gift aid from institutional funds.

GIFT AID (NON-NEED-BASED) *Scholarships, grants, and awards by category:* *Academic interests/achievement:* biological sciences, education, English, general academic interests/achievements, health fields, religion/biblical studies, social sciences. *Creative arts/performance:* music, theater/drama. *Special achievements/activities:* leadership. *Special characteristics:* children of faculty/staff, ethnic background, first-generation college students, relatives of clergy, religious affiliation. *Tuition waivers:* Full or partial for employees or children of employees. **LOANS** *Programs:* FFEL (Subsidized and Unsubsidized Stafford, PLUS), Perkins, state.

APPLYING FOR FINANCIAL AID *Required financial aid forms:* FAFSA, state aid form. *Financial aid deadline (priority):* 3/1. *Notification date:* Continuous beginning 3/15. Students must reply within 3 weeks of notification.

CONTACT Michelle Reeves, Assistant Director, LaGrange College, 601 Broad Street, LaGrange, GA 30240-2999, 888-253-9918 or toll-free 800-593-2885. *Fax:* 706-880-8348. *E-mail:* mreeves@lagrange.edu.

LAGUNA COLLEGE OF ART & DESIGN
Laguna Beach, CA

CONTACT Christopher Brown, Director of Student Services, Laguna College of Art & Design, 2222 Laguna Canyon Road, Laguna Beach, CA 92651-1136, 949-376-6000 or toll-free 800-255-0762. *Fax:* 949-497-5220. *E-mail:* cbrown@lagunacollege.edu.

LAKE ERIE COLLEGE
Painesville, OH

Tuition & fees: $25,674	Average undergraduate aid package: $19,991

ABOUT THE INSTITUTION Independent, coed. 31 undergraduate majors. Federal methodology is used as a basis for awarding need-based institutional aid.

UNDERGRADUATE EXPENSES for 2010–11 *One-time required fee:* $200. *Comprehensive fee:* $33,866 includes full-time tuition ($24,308), mandatory fees ($1366), and room and board ($8192). *College room only:* $4057. Full-time tuition and fees vary according to course load and program. Room and board charges vary according to board plan. *Part-time tuition:* $665 per credit hour. *Part-time fees:* $51 per credit hour. Part-time tuition and fees vary according to course load and program. *Payment plan:* Installment.

FRESHMAN FINANCIAL AID (Fall 2009, est.) 246 applied for aid; of those 94% were deemed to have need. 100% of freshmen with need received aid; of those 14% had need fully met. *Average percent of need met:* 72% (excluding resources awarded to replace EFC). *Average financial aid package:* $21,291 (excluding resources awarded to replace EFC). 9% of all full-time freshmen had no need and received non-need-based gift aid.

UNDERGRADUATE FINANCIAL AID (Fall 2009, est.) 804 applied for aid; of those 95% were deemed to have need. 99% of undergraduates with need received aid; of those 13% had need fully met. *Average percent of need met:* 69% (excluding resources awarded to replace EFC). *Average financial aid package:* $19,991 (excluding resources awarded to replace EFC). 8% of all full-time undergraduates had no need and received non-need-based gift aid.

GIFT AID (NEED-BASED) *Total amount:* $10,662,236 (16% federal, 5% state, 78% institutional, 1% external sources). *Receiving aid:* Freshmen: 89% (230); all full-time undergraduates: 91% (753). *Average award:* Freshmen: $18,040; Undergraduates: $16,203. *Scholarships, grants, and awards:* Federal Pell, FSEOG, state, private, college/university gift aid from institutional funds.

GIFT AID (NON-NEED-BASED) *Total amount:* $785,920 (1% federal, 97% institutional, 2% external sources). *Receiving aid:* Freshmen: 8% (21). Undergraduates: 8% (63). *Average award:* Freshmen: $11,757. Undergraduates: $10,714. *Scholarships, grants, and awards by category:* Academic interests/achievement: biological sciences, business, education, English, foreign languages, general academic interests/achievements, humanities, international studies, mathematics, physical sciences, social sciences. *Creative arts/performance:* art/fine arts, dance, general creative arts/performance, music, performing arts, theater/drama. *Special achievements/activities:* community service, general special achievements/activities, hobbies/interests. *Special characteristics:* children of faculty/staff, twins, veterans, veterans' children. *Tuition waivers:* Full or partial for employees or children of employees.

LOANS *Student loans:* $6,971,367 (79% need-based, 21% non-need-based). 83% of past graduating class borrowed through all loan programs. *Average*

need-based loan: Freshmen: $3359. Undergraduates: $4238. *Parent loans:* $1,240,904 (42% need-based, 58% non-need-based). *Programs:* Federal Direct (Subsidized and Unsubsidized Stafford, PLUS), Perkins.

WORK-STUDY *Federal work-study:* Total amount: $126,666; jobs available (averaging $2000).

ATHLETIC AWARDS Total amount: $1,783,139 (76% need-based, 24% non-need-based).

APPLYING FOR FINANCIAL AID *Required financial aid form:* FAFSA. *Financial aid deadline:* Continuous. *Notification date:* Continuous beginning 2/15. Students must reply by 5/1 or within 4 weeks of notification.

CONTACT Patricia Pangonis, Director of Financial Aid, Lake Erie College, 391 West Washington Street, Painesville, OH 44077-3389, 440-375-7100 or toll-free 800-916-0904. *Fax:* 440-375-7103.

LAKE FOREST COLLEGE
Lake Forest, IL

Tuition & fees: $34,206	Average undergraduate aid package: $26,500

ABOUT THE INSTITUTION Independent, coed. 34 undergraduate majors. Both federal and institutional methodology are used as a basis for awarding need-based institutional aid.

UNDERGRADUATE EXPENSES for 2009–10 *Comprehensive fee:* $42,212 includes full-time tuition ($33,576), mandatory fees ($630), and room and board ($8006). *College room only:* $3966. Full-time tuition and fees vary according to course load. Room and board charges vary according to board plan and housing facility. *Part-time tuition:* $4200 per course. Part-time tuition and fees vary according to course load. *Payment plan:* Installment.

FRESHMAN FINANCIAL AID (Fall 2009, est.) 282 applied for aid; of those 100% were deemed to have need. 100% of freshmen with need received aid; of those 100% had need fully met. *Average percent of need met:* 85% (excluding resources awarded to replace EFC). *Average financial aid package:* $28,600 (excluding resources awarded to replace EFC). 16% of all full-time freshmen had no need and received non-need-based gift aid.

UNDERGRADUATE FINANCIAL AID (Fall 2009, est.) 1,050 applied for aid; of those 100% were deemed to have need. 100% of undergraduates with need received aid; of those 100% had need fully met. *Average percent of need met:* 80% (excluding resources awarded to replace EFC). *Average financial aid package:* $26,500 (excluding resources awarded to replace EFC). 17% of all full-time undergraduates had no need and received non-need-based gift aid.

GIFT AID (NEED-BASED) *Total amount:* $25,500,249 (10% federal, 6% state, 80% institutional, 4% external sources). *Receiving aid:* Freshmen: 79% (282); all full-time undergraduates: 76% (1,050). *Average award:* Freshmen: $26,800; Undergraduates: $23,300. *Scholarships, grants, and awards:* Federal Pell, FSEOG, state, private, college/university gift aid from institutional funds.

GIFT AID (NON-NEED-BASED) *Total amount:* $2,811,470 (1% federal, 99% institutional). *Average award:* Freshmen: $13,800. Undergraduates: $12,400. *Scholarships, grants, and awards by category:* Academic interests/achievement: 1,023 awards ($10,302,776 total): biological sciences, computer science, foreign languages, general academic interests/achievements, mathematics, physical sciences. *Creative arts/performance:* 160 awards ($546,800 total): art/fine arts, creative writing, music, theater/drama. *Special achievements/activities:* 112 awards ($387,400 total): leadership. *Special characteristics:* 60 awards ($724,976 total): children and siblings of alumni, previous college experience. *Tuition waivers:* Full or partial for employees or children of employees.

LOANS *Student loans:* $8,208,388 (93% need-based, 7% non-need-based). 74% of past graduating class borrowed through all loan programs. *Average indebtedness per student:* $29,279. *Average need-based loan:* Freshmen: $4300. Undergraduates: $4900. *Parent loans:* $1,701,966 (85% need-based, 15% non-need-based). *Programs:* FFEL (Subsidized and Unsubsidized Stafford, PLUS), Perkins, private loans.

WORK-STUDY *Federal work-study:* Total amount: $1,520,794; jobs available. *State or other work-study/employment:* Part-time jobs available.

APPLYING FOR FINANCIAL AID *Required financial aid forms:* FAFSA, institution's own form. *Financial aid deadline:* 5/1 (priority: 3/1). *Notification date:* Continuous beginning 3/1. Students must reply by 5/1 or within 3 weeks of notification.

CONTACT Mr. Jerry Cebrzynski, Director of Financial Aid, Lake Forest College, 555 North Sheridan Road, Lake Forest, IL 60045-2399, 847-735-5104 or toll-free 800-828-4751. *Fax:* 847-735-6271. *E-mail:* cebrzynski@lakeforest.edu.

LAKELAND COLLEGE
Sheboygan, WI

Tuition & fees: $19,640	Average undergraduate aid package: $11,992

ABOUT THE INSTITUTION Independent religious, coed. 29 undergraduate majors. Federal methodology is used as a basis for awarding need-based institutional aid.

UNDERGRADUATE EXPENSES for 2010–11 *Comprehensive fee:* $26,656 includes full-time tuition ($19,640) and room and board ($7016). *Part-time tuition:* $657 per credit. *Payment plans:* Guaranteed tuition, tuition prepayment, installment, deferred payment.

FRESHMAN FINANCIAL AID (Fall 2009, est.) 171 applied for aid; of those 92% were deemed to have need. 98% of freshmen with need received aid; of those 10% had need fully met. *Average percent of need met:* 73% (excluding resources awarded to replace EFC). *Average financial aid package:* $15,512 (excluding resources awarded to replace EFC). 29% of all full-time freshmen had no need and received non-need-based gift aid.

UNDERGRADUATE FINANCIAL AID (Fall 2009, est.) 1,372 applied for aid; of those 90% were deemed to have need. 99% of undergraduates with need received aid; of those 9% had need fully met. *Average percent of need met:* 65% (excluding resources awarded to replace EFC). *Average financial aid package:* $11,992 (excluding resources awarded to replace EFC). 12% of all full-time undergraduates had no need and received non-need-based gift aid.

GIFT AID (NEED-BASED) *Total amount:* $9,665,154 (31% federal, 10% state, 50% institutional, 9% external sources). *Receiving aid:* Freshmen: 60% (148); all full-time undergraduates: 67% (1,028). *Average award:* Freshmen: $11,608; Undergraduates: $8840. *Scholarships, grants, and awards:* Federal Pell, FSEOG, state, private, college/university gift aid from institutional funds, Academic Competitiveness Grants, National SMART Grants.

GIFT AID (NON-NEED-BASED) *Total amount:* $1,803,388 (1% state, 93% institutional, 6% external sources). *Receiving aid:* Freshmen: 3% (8). Undergraduates: 4% (60). *Average award:* Freshmen: $10,872. Undergraduates: $8075. *Scholarships, grants, and awards by category: Academic interests/achievement:* 512 awards ($3,074,010 total): business, engineering/technologies, English, general academic interests/achievements, religion/biblical studies. *Creative arts/performance:* 44 awards ($90,150 total): art/fine arts, creative writing, journalism/publications, music, performing arts. *Special achievements/activities:* 111 awards ($203,795 total): community service, leadership, religious involvement. *Special characteristics:* 165 awards ($539,534 total): children and siblings of alumni, children of faculty/staff, religious affiliation, siblings of current students. *Tuition waivers:* Full or partial for employees or children of employees, senior citizens.

LOANS *Student loans:* $15,552,586 (79% need-based, 21% non-need-based). *Average need-based loan:* Freshmen: $3557. Undergraduates: $4441. *Parent loans:* $510,528 (40% need-based, 60% non-need-based). *Programs:* Federal Direct (Subsidized and Unsubsidized Stafford, PLUS), FFEL (PLUS), Perkins, alternative loans.

WORK-STUDY *Federal work-study:* Total amount: $564,391; 262 jobs averaging $2500. *State or other work-study/employment:* Total amount: $276,866 (11% need-based, 89% non-need-based). 150 part-time jobs averaging $2500.

APPLYING FOR FINANCIAL AID *Required financial aid forms:* FAFSA, institution's own form. *Financial aid deadline:* 7/1 (priority: 3/31). *Notification date:* Continuous beginning 3/1. Students must reply within 2 weeks of notification.

CONTACT Ms. Patty Taylor, Director of Financial Aid, Lakeland College, PO Box 359, Sheboygan, WI 53082-0359, 920-565-1214 or toll-free 800-242-3347 (in-state). *Fax:* 920-565-1470.

LAKE SUPERIOR STATE UNIVERSITY
Sault Sainte Marie, MI

Tuition & fees (MI res): $8384	Average undergraduate aid package: $11,200

ABOUT THE INSTITUTION State-supported, coed. 63 undergraduate majors. Both federal and institutional methodology are used as a basis for awarding need-based institutional aid.

UNDERGRADUATE EXPENSES for 2010–11 *One-time required fee:* $125. *Tuition, state resident:* full-time $8284; part-time $341 per credit hour. *Tuition, nonresident:* full-time $16,468; part-time $682 per credit hour. *Required fees:* full-time $100. Full-time tuition and fees vary according to reciprocity agreements.

Part-time tuition and fees vary according to course load and reciprocity agreements. *College room and board:* $7994. Room and board charges vary according to board plan and housing facility. *Payment plans:* Installment, deferred payment.

FRESHMAN FINANCIAL AID (Fall 2009, est.) 384 applied for aid; of those 100% were deemed to have need. 100% of freshmen with need received aid; of those 62% had need fully met. *Average percent of need met:* 82% (excluding resources awarded to replace EFC). *Average financial aid package:* $12,129 (excluding resources awarded to replace EFC). 8% of all full-time freshmen had no need and received non-need-based gift aid.

UNDERGRADUATE FINANCIAL AID (Fall 2009, est.) 1,904 applied for aid; of those 100% were deemed to have need. 100% of undergraduates with need received aid; of those 61% had need fully met. *Average percent of need met:* 81% (excluding resources awarded to replace EFC). *Average financial aid package:* $11,200 (excluding resources awarded to replace EFC). 11% of all full-time undergraduates had no need and received non-need-based gift aid.

GIFT AID (NEED-BASED) *Total amount:* $5,759,876 (68% federal, 20% state, 5% institutional, 7% external sources). *Receiving aid:* Freshmen: 63% (255); all full-time undergraduates: 52% (1,099). *Average award:* Freshmen: $4971; Undergraduates: $5244. *Scholarships, grants, and awards:* Federal Pell, FSEOG, state, private, college/university gift aid from institutional funds, Federal Nursing.

GIFT AID (NON-NEED-BASED) *Total amount:* $2,469,890 (1% federal, 1% state, 83% institutional, 15% external sources). *Receiving aid:* Freshmen: 63% (254). Undergraduates: 48% (1,005). *Average award:* Freshmen: $1545. Undergraduates: $2416. *Tuition waivers:* Full or partial for minority students, children of alumni, employees or children of employees, senior citizens.

LOANS *Student loans:* $12,798,499 (100% need-based). 67% of past graduating class borrowed through all loan programs. *Average indebtedness per student:* $21,573. *Average need-based loan:* Freshmen: $5415. Undergraduates: $6647. *Parent loans:* $2,447,240 (100% need-based). *Programs:* Federal Direct (Subsidized and Unsubsidized Stafford, PLUS), Perkins, Federal Nursing, state.

WORK-STUDY *Federal work-study:* Total amount: $177,928; 301 jobs averaging $1363. *State or other work-study/employment:* Total amount: $23,868 (100% need-based). 89 part-time jobs averaging $1161.

ATHLETIC AWARDS Total amount: $1,102,182 (100% non-need-based).

APPLYING FOR FINANCIAL AID *Required financial aid form:* FAFSA. *Financial aid deadline (priority):* 2/21. *Notification date:* Continuous. Students must reply within 3 weeks of notification.

CONTACT Deborah Faust, Director of Financial Aid, Lake Superior State University, 650 West Easterday Avenue, Sault Sainte Marie, MI 49783, 906-635-2678 or toll-free 888-800-LSSU Ext. 2231. *Fax:* 906-635-6669. *E-mail:* finaid@lssu.edu.

LAKEVIEW COLLEGE OF NURSING
Danville, IL

Tuition & fees: $12,800	Average undergraduate aid package: N/A

ABOUT THE INSTITUTION Independent, coed. 1 undergraduate major. Federal methodology is used as a basis for awarding need-based institutional aid.

UNDERGRADUATE EXPENSES for 2009–10 *Tuition:* full-time $10,880; part-time $340 per credit hour. *Required fees:* full-time $1920; $60 per credit hour.

GIFT AID (NEED-BASED) *Total amount:* $2,065,000 (58% federal, 42% state). *Scholarships, grants, and awards:* Federal Pell, state, private, college/university gift aid from institutional funds.

GIFT AID (NON-NEED-BASED) *Total amount:* $220,000 (55% institutional, 45% external sources). *Scholarships, grants, and awards by category: Academic interests/achievement:* health fields.

LOANS *Student loans:* $3,000,000 (100% need-based). *Parent loans:* $150,000 (100% non-need-based). *Programs:* Federal Direct (Subsidized and Unsubsidized Stafford, PLUS).

APPLYING FOR FINANCIAL AID *Required financial aid form:* FAFSA. *Financial aid deadline:* Continuous. *Notification date:* Continuous beginning 4/1. Students must reply within 4 weeks of notification.

CONTACT Ms. Janet Ingargiola, Director of Financial Aid, Lakeview College of Nursing, 903 North Logan Avenue, Danville, IL 61832, 217-554-6887. *Fax:* 217-443-5238. *E-mail:* jingarg@lakeviewcol.edu.

LAMAR UNIVERSITY
Beaumont, TX

Tuition & fees (TX res): $6944 | **Average undergraduate aid package: $10,723**

ABOUT THE INSTITUTION State-supported, coed. 102 undergraduate majors. Federal methodology is used as a basis for awarding need-based institutional aid.

UNDERGRADUATE EXPENSES for 2010–11 *Tuition, state resident:* full-time $4740; part-time $158 per credit hour. *Tuition, nonresident:* full-time $14,040; part-time $468 per credit hour. *Required fees:* full-time $2204. *College room and board:* $6900; *Room only:* $4500.

FRESHMAN FINANCIAL AID (Fall 2009, est.) 1,041 applied for aid; of those 63% were deemed to have need. 100% of freshmen with need received aid; of those 19% had need fully met. *Average percent of need met:* 56% (excluding resources awarded to replace EFC). *Average financial aid package:* $10,723 (excluding resources awarded to replace EFC). 38% of all full-time freshmen had no need and received non-need-based gift aid.

UNDERGRADUATE FINANCIAL AID (Fall 2009, est.) 5,104 applied for aid; of those 73% were deemed to have need. 99% of undergraduates with need received aid; of those 6% had need fully met. *Average percent of need met:* 54% (excluding resources awarded to replace EFC). *Average financial aid package:* $10,723 (excluding resources awarded to replace EFC). 20% of all full-time undergraduates had no need and received non-need-based gift aid.

GIFT AID (NEED-BASED) *Total amount:* $22,607,366 (69% federal, 31% state). *Receiving aid:* Freshmen: 29% (413); all full-time undergraduates: 45% (3,112). *Scholarships, grants, and awards:* Federal Pell, FSEOG, state, college/university gift aid from institutional funds.

GIFT AID (NON-NEED-BASED) *Total amount:* $6,260,475 (78% institutional, 22% external sources). *Receiving aid:* Freshmen: 13% (189). Undergraduates: 7% (513). *Average award:* Freshmen: $1827. Undergraduates: $1476. *Scholarships, grants, and awards by category:* Academic interests/achievement: general academic interests/achievements. Creative arts/performance: general creative arts/performance. Special achievements/activities: general special achievements/activities.

LOANS *Student loans:* $42,208,756 (46% need-based, 54% non-need-based). 41% of past graduating class borrowed through all loan programs. *Average indebtedness per student:* $7856. *Parent loans:* $805,855 (100% non-need-based). *Programs:* FFEL (Subsidized and Unsubsidized Stafford, PLUS), Perkins, state, college/university.

WORK-STUDY *Federal work-study:* Total amount: $309,476; jobs available. *State or other work-study/employment:* Total amount: $74,250 (100% need-based). Part-time jobs available.

ATHLETIC AWARDS Total amount: $273,874 (100% non-need-based).

APPLYING FOR FINANCIAL AID *Required financial aid forms:* FAFSA, institution's own form. *Financial aid deadline (priority):* 4/1. *Notification date:* Continuous beginning 5/1. Students must reply within 2 weeks of notification.

CONTACT Financial Aid Department, Lamar University, PO Box 10042, Beaumont, TX 77710, 409-880-8450. *Fax:* 409-880-8934. *E-mail:* financialaid@lamar.edu.

LAMBUTH UNIVERSITY
Jackson, TN

ABOUT THE INSTITUTION Independent United Methodist, coed. *Awards:* bachelor's degrees. 65 undergraduate majors. *Total enrollment:* 815. Undergraduates: 815. Freshmen: 205.

GIFT AID (NEED-BASED) *Scholarships, grants, and awards:* Federal Pell, FSEOG, state, private, college/university gift aid from institutional funds.

GIFT AID (NON-NEED-BASED) *Scholarships, grants, and awards by category:* Academic interests/achievement: general academic interests/achievements. Creative arts/performance: music, theater/drama. Special achievements/activities: religious involvement. Special characteristics: children and siblings of alumni, children of faculty/staff, relatives of clergy, religious affiliation.

LOANS *Programs:* FFEL (Subsidized and Unsubsidized Stafford, PLUS), Perkins, United Methodist Student Loans.

WORK-STUDY *Federal work-study:* Total amount: $123,077; 93 jobs averaging $1348. *State or other work-study/employment:* Total amount: $26,522 (100% non-need-based). 20 part-time jobs averaging $1238.

APPLYING FOR FINANCIAL AID *Required financial aid form:* FAFSA.

CONTACT Ms. Karen Myers, Director of Scholarships and Financial Aid, Lambuth University, 705 Lambuth Boulevard, Jackson, TN 38301, 731-425-3332 or toll-free 800-526-2884. *Fax:* 731-425-3496. *E-mail:* myers-k@lambuth.edu.

LANCASTER BIBLE COLLEGE & GRADUATE SCHOOL
Lancaster, PA

Tuition & fees: $15,840 | **Average undergraduate aid package: $11,552**

ABOUT THE INSTITUTION Independent nondenominational, coed. 17 undergraduate majors. Federal methodology is used as a basis for awarding need-based institutional aid.

UNDERGRADUATE EXPENSES for 2009–10 *Comprehensive fee:* $22,620 includes full-time tuition ($15,240), mandatory fees ($600), and room and board ($6780). *College room only:* $2990. Room and board charges vary according to board plan. *Part-time tuition:* $513 per credit hour. *Part-time fees:* $25 per credit hour. Part-time tuition and fees vary according to course load. *Payment plan:* Installment.

FRESHMAN FINANCIAL AID (Fall 2009, est.) 121 applied for aid; of those 86% were deemed to have need. 100% of freshmen with need received aid; of those 16% had need fully met. *Average percent of need met:* 67% (excluding resources awarded to replace EFC). *Average financial aid package:* $12,106 (excluding resources awarded to replace EFC). 11% of all full-time freshmen had no need and received non-need-based gift aid.

UNDERGRADUATE FINANCIAL AID (Fall 2009, est.) 577 applied for aid; of those 93% were deemed to have need. 100% of undergraduates with need received aid; of those 15% had need fully met. *Average percent of need met:* 65% (excluding resources awarded to replace EFC). *Average financial aid package:* $11,552 (excluding resources awarded to replace EFC). 11% of all full-time undergraduates had no need and received non-need-based gift aid.

GIFT AID (NEED-BASED) *Total amount:* $4,263,632 (31% federal, 18% state, 47% institutional, 4% external sources). *Receiving aid:* Freshmen: 77% (98); all full-time undergraduates: 83% (489). *Average award:* Freshmen: $10,929; Undergraduates: $8334. *Scholarships, grants, and awards:* Federal Pell, FSEOG, state, private, college/university gift aid from institutional funds, Office of Vocational Rehabilitation, Blindness and Visual Services Awards.

GIFT AID (NON-NEED-BASED) *Total amount:* $409,938 (93% institutional, 7% external sources). *Receiving aid:* Freshmen: 76% (97). Undergraduates: 68% (397). *Average award:* Freshmen: $4800. Undergraduates: $4488. *Scholarships, grants, and awards by category:* Academic interests/achievement: 327 awards ($1,050,298 total): general academic interests/achievements. Creative arts/performance: 34 awards ($40,325 total): general creative arts/performance, music. Special achievements/activities: 82 awards ($121,650 total): general special achievements/activities, leadership, religious involvement. Special characteristics: 327 awards ($1,124,423 total): adult students, children and siblings of alumni, children of current students, children of faculty/staff, international students, married students, previous college experience, relatives of clergy, religious affiliation, siblings of current students, spouses of current students. Tuition waivers: Full or partial for children of alumni, employees or children of employees, senior citizens.

LOANS *Student loans:* $4,211,000 (82% need-based, 18% non-need-based). 41% of past graduating class borrowed through all loan programs. *Average indebtedness per student:* $21,611. *Average need-based loan:* Freshmen: $3412. Undergraduates: $4123. *Parent loans:* $628,117 (45% need-based, 55% non-need-based). *Programs:* Federal Direct (Subsidized and Unsubsidized Stafford, PLUS), FFEL (Subsidized and Unsubsidized Stafford, PLUS), Perkins, state, alternative loans.

WORK-STUDY *Federal work-study:* Total amount: $153,535; 103 jobs averaging $1579.

APPLYING FOR FINANCIAL AID *Required financial aid forms:* FAFSA, state aid form. *Financial aid deadline (priority):* 5/1. *Notification date:* Continuous beginning 3/1. Students must reply within 3 weeks of notification.

CONTACT Karen Fox, Director of Financial Aid, Lancaster Bible College & Graduate School, 901 Eden Road, Lancaster, PA 17601, 717-560-8254 Ext. 5352 or toll-free 866-LBC4YOU. *Fax:* 717-560-8216. *E-mail:* kfox@lbc.edu.

LANDER UNIVERSITY
Greenwood, SC

CONTACT Director of Financial Aid, Lander University, 320 Stanley Avenue, Greenwood, SC 29649, 864-388-8340 or toll-free 888-452-6337. *Fax:* 864-388-8811. *E-mail:* fhardin@lander.edu.

LANE COLLEGE
Jackson, TN

Tuition & fees: $8000	Average undergraduate aid package: $3304

ABOUT THE INSTITUTION Independent religious, coed. 17 undergraduate majors. Federal methodology is used as a basis for awarding need-based institutional aid.

UNDERGRADUATE EXPENSES for 2009–10 *Comprehensive fee:* $13,520 includes full-time tuition ($7330), mandatory fees ($670), and room and board ($5520). Full-time tuition and fees vary according to course load. *Part-time tuition:* $310 per hour. *Part-time fees:* $670 per year. Part-time tuition and fees vary according to course load. *Payment plans:* Installment, deferred payment.

FRESHMAN FINANCIAL AID (Fall 2009, est.) 686 applied for aid; of those 96% were deemed to have need. 100% of freshmen with need received aid; of those 49% had need fully met. *Average percent of need met:* 43% (excluding resources awarded to replace EFC). *Average financial aid package:* $3272 (excluding resources awarded to replace EFC). 1% of all full-time freshmen had no need and received non-need-based gift aid.

UNDERGRADUATE FINANCIAL AID (Fall 2009, est.) 2,102 applied for aid; of those 96% were deemed to have need. 100% of undergraduates with need received aid; of those 45% had need fully met. *Average percent of need met:* 43% (excluding resources awarded to replace EFC). *Average financial aid package:* $3304 (excluding resources awarded to replace EFC). 2% of all full-time undergraduates had no need and received non-need-based gift aid.

GIFT AID (NEED-BASED) *Total amount:* $6,938,897 (73% federal, 22% state, 4% institutional, 1% external sources). *Receiving aid:* Freshmen: 17% (119); all full-time undergraduates: 16% (345). *Average award:* Freshmen: $1727; Undergraduates: $1730. *Scholarships, grants, and awards:* Federal Pell, FSEOG, state, private, college/university gift aid from institutional funds, United Negro College Fund.

GIFT AID (NON-NEED-BASED) *Total amount:* $63,306 (38% state, 53% institutional, 9% external sources). *Receiving aid:* Freshmen: 7% (51). Undergraduates: 6% (118). *Average award:* Freshmen: $2953. Undergraduates: $2713. *Tuition waivers:* Full or partial for employees or children of employees, adult students.

LOANS *Student loans:* $6,037,094 (83% need-based, 17% non-need-based). 88% of past graduating class borrowed through all loan programs. *Average indebtedness per student:* $8769. *Average need-based loan:* Freshmen: $1700. Undergraduates: $1968. *Parent loans:* $702,042 (89% need-based, 11% non-need-based). *Programs:* Federal Direct (Subsidized and Unsubsidized Stafford, PLUS).

WORK-STUDY *Federal work-study:* Total amount: $151,331; jobs available.

ATHLETIC AWARDS Total amount: $101,975 (89% need-based, 11% non-need-based).

APPLYING FOR FINANCIAL AID *Required financial aid form:* FAFSA. *Financial aid deadline (priority):* 4/1. *Notification date:* Continuous beginning 4/15. Students must reply within 2 weeks of notification.

CONTACT Mr. Tony Calhoun, Director of Financial Aid, Lane College, 545 Lane Avenue, Jackson, TN 38301, 731-426-7558 or toll-free 800-960-7533. *Fax:* 731-426-7652. *E-mail:* tcalhoun@lanecollege.edu.

LANGSTON UNIVERSITY
Langston, OK

Tuition & fees: N/R	Average undergraduate aid package: $8855

ABOUT THE INSTITUTION State-supported, coed. 56 undergraduate majors. Federal methodology is used as a basis for awarding need-based institutional aid.

FRESHMAN FINANCIAL AID (Fall 2009, est.) 589 applied for aid; of those 89% were deemed to have need. 98% of freshmen with need received aid; of those 22% had need fully met. *Average percent of need met:* 56% (excluding resources awarded to replace EFC). *Average financial aid package:* $8792 (excluding resources awarded to replace EFC). 14% of all full-time freshmen had no need and received non-need-based gift aid.

UNDERGRADUATE FINANCIAL AID (Fall 2009, est.) 2,599 applied for aid; of those 78% were deemed to have need. 99% of undergraduates with need received aid; of those 32% had need fully met. *Average percent of need met:* 59% (excluding resources awarded to replace EFC). *Average financial aid package:* $8855 (excluding resources awarded to replace EFC). 27% of all full-time undergraduates had no need and received non-need-based gift aid.

GIFT AID (NEED-BASED) *Total amount:* $8,452,702 (94% federal, 6% state). *Receiving aid:* Freshmen: 74% (452); all full-time undergraduates: 63% (1,730). *Average award:* Freshmen: $4433; Undergraduates: $4727. *Scholarships, grants, and awards:* Federal Pell, FSEOG, state.

GIFT AID (NON-NEED-BASED) *Total amount:* $1,375,521 (28% state, 52% institutional, 20% external sources). *Receiving aid:* Freshmen: 39% (236). Undergraduates: 33% (901). *Average award:* Freshmen: $3630. Undergraduates: $1884. *Scholarships, grants, and awards by category: Academic interests/achievement:* 47 awards ($271,280 total): agriculture, business, education, engineering/technologies, general academic interests/achievements, health fields. *Creative arts/performance:* 46 awards ($40,621 total): music. *Special achievements/activities:* 21 awards ($31,500 total): cheerleading/drum major, leadership. *Special characteristics:* 14 awards ($8700 total): ethnic background.

LOANS *Student loans:* $18,500,191 (49% need-based, 51% non-need-based). 84% of past graduating class borrowed through all loan programs. *Average indebtedness per student:* $33,875. *Average need-based loan:* Freshmen: $3338. Undergraduates: $4956. *Parent loans:* $1,570,762 (100% need-based). *Programs:* Federal Direct (Subsidized and Unsubsidized Stafford, PLUS), FFEL (Subsidized and Unsubsidized Stafford, PLUS).

WORK-STUDY *Federal work-study:* Total amount: $307,658; jobs available.

ATHLETIC AWARDS Total amount: $280,880 (100% non-need-based).

APPLYING FOR FINANCIAL AID *Required financial aid forms:* FAFSA, institution's own form. *Financial aid deadline (priority):* 3/15. *Notification date:* 6/30.

CONTACT Linda Morris, Associate Director of Financial Aid, Langston University, Gandy Hall, Langston, OK 73050, 405-466-3287. *Fax:* 405-466-2986. *E-mail:* ifmorris@lunet.edu.

LA ROCHE COLLEGE
Pittsburgh, PA

Tuition & fees: $21,638	Average undergraduate aid package: $21,212

ABOUT THE INSTITUTION Independent religious, coed. 38 undergraduate majors. Federal methodology is used as a basis for awarding need-based institutional aid.

UNDERGRADUATE EXPENSES for 2009–10 *Comprehensive fee:* $30,394 includes full-time tuition ($20,938), mandatory fees ($700), and room and board ($8756). *College room only:* $5484. Full-time tuition and fees vary according to program. Room and board charges vary according to board plan. *Part-time tuition:* $525 per credit hour. Part-time tuition and fees vary according to program. *Payment plan:* Installment.

FRESHMAN FINANCIAL AID (Fall 2009, est.) 164 applied for aid; of those 95% were deemed to have need. 97% of freshmen with need received aid; of those 33% had need fully met. *Average percent of need met:* 93% (excluding resources awarded to replace EFC). *Average financial aid package:* $23,466 (excluding resources awarded to replace EFC). 6% of all full-time freshmen had no need and received non-need-based gift aid.

UNDERGRADUATE FINANCIAL AID (Fall 2009, est.) 765 applied for aid; of those 91% were deemed to have need. 98% of undergraduates with need received aid; of those 50% had need fully met. *Average percent of need met:* 90% (excluding resources awarded to replace EFC). *Average financial aid package:* $21,212 (excluding resources awarded to replace EFC). 7% of all full-time undergraduates had no need and received non-need-based gift aid.

GIFT AID (NEED-BASED) *Total amount:* $3,606,814 (49% federal, 36% state, 15% institutional). *Receiving aid:* Freshmen: 59% (111); all full-time undergraduates: 53% (509). *Average award:* Freshmen: $3586; Undergraduates: $2292. *Scholarships, grants, and awards:* Federal Pell, FSEOG, state, private, college/university gift aid from institutional funds.

GIFT AID (NON-NEED-BASED) *Total amount:* $6,594,660 (96% institutional, 4% external sources). *Receiving aid:* Freshmen: 77% (144). Undergraduates:

70% (680). *Average award:* Freshmen: $4951. Undergraduates: $4803. *Scholarships, grants, and awards by category:* Academic interests/achievement: 789 awards ($4,920,584 total): general academic interests/achievements. *Tuition waivers:* Full or partial for employees or children of employees, senior citizens.
LOANS *Student loans:* $8,527,834 (39% need-based, 61% non-need-based). 78% of past graduating class borrowed through all loan programs. *Average indebtedness per student:* $69,494. *Average need-based loan:* Freshmen: $4955. Undergraduates: $2596. *Parent loans:* $1,017,484 (100% non-need-based). *Programs:* Federal Direct (Subsidized and Unsubsidized Stafford, PLUS), Perkins, state.
WORK-STUDY *Federal work-study:* Total amount: $244,370; 143 jobs averaging $2000.
APPLYING FOR FINANCIAL AID *Required financial aid form:* FAFSA. *Financial aid deadline (priority):* 5/1. *Notification date:* Continuous beginning 3/1. Students must reply within 2 weeks of notification.
CONTACT Mrs. Sharon Platt, Director of Financial Aid, La Roche College, 9000 Babcock Boulevard, Pittsburgh, PA 15237-5898, 412-536-1125 or toll-free 800-838-4LRC. *Fax:* 412-536-1072. *E-mail:* sharon.platt@laroche.edu.

LA SALLE UNIVERSITY
Philadelphia, PA

CONTACT Robert G. Voss, Dean of Admission and Financial Aid, La Salle University, 1900 West Olney Avenue, Philadelphia, PA 19141-1199, 215-951-1500 or toll-free 800-328-1910.

LASELL COLLEGE
Newton, MA

Tuition & fees: $25,300	Average undergraduate aid package: $20,097

ABOUT THE INSTITUTION Independent, coed. 40 undergraduate majors. Both federal and institutional methodology are used as a basis for awarding need-based institutional aid.
UNDERGRADUATE EXPENSES for 2009–10 *Comprehensive fee:* $35,800 includes full-time tuition ($24,300), mandatory fees ($1000), and room and board ($10,500). Room and board charges vary according to housing facility. *Part-time tuition:* $775 per credit. *Part-time fees:* $280 per term. *Payment plan:* Installment.
FRESHMAN FINANCIAL AID (Fall 2009, est.) 480 applied for aid; of those 90% were deemed to have need. 100% of freshmen with need received aid; of those 14% had need fully met. *Average percent of need met:* 89% (excluding resources awarded to replace EFC). *Average financial aid package:* $21,181 (excluding resources awarded to replace EFC). 9% of all full-time freshmen had no need and received non-need-based gift aid.
UNDERGRADUATE FINANCIAL AID (Fall 2009, est.) 1,308 applied for aid; of those 90% were deemed to have need. 100% of undergraduates with need received aid; of those 16% had need fully met. *Average percent of need met:* 89% (excluding resources awarded to replace EFC). *Average financial aid package:* $20,097 (excluding resources awarded to replace EFC). 9% of all full-time undergraduates had no need and received non-need-based gift aid.
GIFT AID (NEED-BASED) *Total amount:* $17,325,871 (12% federal, 4% state, 82% institutional, 2% external sources). *Receiving aid:* Freshmen: 83% (431); all full-time undergraduates: 78% (1,172). *Average award:* Freshmen: $16,546; Undergraduates: $14,766. *Scholarships, grants, and awards:* Federal Pell, FSEOG, state, private, college/university gift aid from institutional funds.
GIFT AID (NON-NEED-BASED) *Total amount:* $2,503,361 (91% institutional, 9% external sources). *Receiving aid:* Freshmen: 8% (41). Undergraduates: 5% (72). *Average award:* Freshmen: $8488. Undergraduates: $7742. *Scholarships, grants, and awards by category:* Academic interests/achievement: 290 awards ($3,804,970 total): general academic interests/achievements. *Special achievements/activities:* 427 awards ($2,538,860 total): community service, general special achievements/activities, leadership. *Special characteristics:* 35 awards ($196,602 total): children and siblings of alumni, children of faculty/staff, siblings of current students, veterans, veterans' children. *Tuition waivers:* Full or partial for employees or children of employees.
LOANS *Student loans:* $11,831,710 (67% need-based, 33% non-need-based). 64% of past graduating class borrowed through all loan programs. *Average indebtedness per student:* $38,428. *Average need-based loan:* Freshmen: $2057.

Undergraduates: $7221. *Parent loans:* $4,098,766 (36% need-based, 64% non-need-based). *Programs:* FFEL (Subsidized and Unsubsidized Stafford, PLUS), Perkins.
WORK-STUDY *Federal work-study:* Total amount: $1,455,200; 919 jobs averaging $1900.
APPLYING FOR FINANCIAL AID *Required financial aid forms:* FAFSA, institution's own form. *Financial aid deadline (priority):* 3/1. *Notification date:* Continuous beginning 2/15.
CONTACT Michele R. Kosboth, Director of Student Financial Planning, Lasell College, 1844 Commonwealth Avenue, Newton, MA 02466-2709, 617-243-2227 or toll-free 888-LASELL-4. *Fax:* 617-243-2326. *E-mail:* finaid@lasell.edu.

LA SIERRA UNIVERSITY
Riverside, CA

CONTACT Financial Aid Office, La Sierra University, 4500 Riverwalk Parkway, Riverside, CA 92515, 951-785-2175 or toll-free 800-874-5587. *Fax:* 951-785-2942. *E-mail:* sfs@lasierra.edu.

LAURA AND ALVIN SIEGAL COLLEGE OF JUDAIC STUDIES
Beachwood, OH

CONTACT Ruth Kronick, Director of Student Services, Laura and Alvin Siegal College of Judaic Studies, 26500 Shaker Boulevard, Cleveland, OH 44122, 216-464-4050 Ext. 101 or toll-free 888-336-2257. *Fax:* 216-464-5278. *E-mail:* rkronick@siegalcollege.edu.

LAWRENCE TECHNOLOGICAL UNIVERSITY
Southfield, MI

Tuition & fees: $23,008	Average undergraduate aid package: $17,563

ABOUT THE INSTITUTION Independent, coed. 42 undergraduate majors. Federal methodology is used as a basis for awarding need-based institutional aid.
UNDERGRADUATE EXPENSES for 2009–10 *Comprehensive fee:* $32,361 includes full-time tuition ($22,638), mandatory fees ($370), and room and board ($9353). *College room only:* $5573. Full-time tuition and fees vary according to course level, degree level, location, program, and student level. Room and board charges vary according to board plan and housing facility. *Part-time tuition:* $755 per credit hour. *Part-time fees:* $185 per term. Part-time tuition and fees vary according to course level, degree level, location, program, and student level. *Payment plan:* Installment.
FRESHMAN FINANCIAL AID (Fall 2008) 262 applied for aid; of those 80% were deemed to have need. 99% of freshmen with need received aid; of those 23% had need fully met. *Average percent of need met:* 69% (excluding resources awarded to replace EFC). *Average financial aid package:* $18,343 (excluding resources awarded to replace EFC). 13% of all full-time freshmen had no need and received non-need-based gift aid.
UNDERGRADUATE FINANCIAL AID (Fall 2008) 1,346 applied for aid; of those 73% were deemed to have need. 99% of undergraduates with need received aid; of those 14% had need fully met. *Average percent of need met:* 66% (excluding resources awarded to replace EFC). *Average financial aid package:* $17,563 (excluding resources awarded to replace EFC). 16% of all full-time undergraduates had no need and received non-need-based gift aid.
GIFT AID (NEED-BASED) *Total amount:* $9,542,260 (22% federal, 19% state, 58% institutional, 1% external sources). *Receiving aid:* Freshmen: 70% (194); all full-time undergraduates: 55% (888). *Average award:* Freshmen: $11,703; Undergraduates: $9383. *Scholarships, grants, and awards:* Federal Pell, FSEOG, state, private, college/university gift aid from institutional funds, Michigan National Guard and ROTC scholarships.
GIFT AID (NON-NEED-BASED) *Total amount:* $2,306,891 (6% state, 90% institutional, 4% external sources). *Receiving aid:* Freshmen: 58% (161). Undergraduates: 39% (635). *Average award:* Freshmen: $8788. Undergraduates: $7067. *Scholarships, grants, and awards by category:* Academic interests/achievement: 1,886 awards ($8,173,033 total): architecture, business, computer science, education, engineering/technologies, general academic interests/achievements, humanities, international studies, mathematics, military science, physical sciences. *Special achievements/activities:* 3 awards ($1000 total): general

special achievements/activities. *Special characteristics:* 67 awards ($680,316 total): children of faculty/staff, members of minority groups. *Tuition waivers:* Full or partial for employees or children of employees.

LOANS *Student loans:* $9,703,987 (95% need-based, 5% non-need-based). 73% of past graduating class borrowed through all loan programs. *Average indebtedness per student:* $42,723. *Average need-based loan:* Freshmen: $6079. Undergraduates: $6581. *Parent loans:* $4,297,914 (87% need-based, 13% non-need-based). *Programs:* Federal Direct (Subsidized and Unsubsidized Stafford, PLUS), Perkins, state, college/university, alternative loans.

WORK-STUDY *Federal work-study:* Total amount: $981,691; 73 jobs averaging $1912. *State or other work-study/employment:* Total amount: $46,000 (100% need-based). 10 part-time jobs averaging $2753.

APPLYING FOR FINANCIAL AID *Required financial aid form:* FAFSA. *Financial aid deadline (priority):* 4/1. *Notification date:* Continuous beginning 4/1. Students must reply within 2 weeks of notification.

CONTACT Mr. Mark Martin, Director of Financial Aid, Lawrence Technological University, 21000 West Ten Mile Road, Southfield, MI 48075-1058, 248-204-2126 or toll-free 800-225-5588. *Fax:* 248-204-2124. *E-mail:* mmartin@ltu.edu.

LAWRENCE UNIVERSITY
Appleton, WI

Tuition & fees: $34,596	Average undergraduate aid package: $26,155

ABOUT THE INSTITUTION Independent, coed. 58 undergraduate majors. Institutional methodology is used as a basis for awarding need-based institutional aid.

UNDERGRADUATE EXPENSES for 2009–10 *Comprehensive fee:* $41,649 includes full-time tuition ($34,326), mandatory fees ($270), and room and board ($7053). Room and board charges vary according to board plan. *Payment plans:* Tuition prepayment, installment.

FRESHMAN FINANCIAL AID (Fall 2009, est.) 284 applied for aid; of those 77% were deemed to have need. 100% of freshmen with need received aid; of those 78% had need fully met. *Average percent of need met:* 94% (excluding resources awarded to replace EFC). *Average financial aid package:* $27,875 (excluding resources awarded to replace EFC). 32% of all full-time freshmen had no need and received non-need-based gift aid.

UNDERGRADUATE FINANCIAL AID (Fall 2009, est.) 1,050 applied for aid; of those 83% were deemed to have need. 100% of undergraduates with need received aid; of those 77% had need fully met. *Average percent of need met:* 92% (excluding resources awarded to replace EFC). *Average financial aid package:* $26,155 (excluding resources awarded to replace EFC). 31% of all full-time undergraduates had no need and received non-need-based gift aid.

GIFT AID (NEED-BASED) *Total amount:* $17,050,691 (9% federal, 4% state, 84% institutional, 3% external sources). *Receiving aid:* Freshmen: 61% (213); all full-time undergraduates: 60% (855). *Average award:* Freshmen: $21,485; Undergraduates: $18,952. *Scholarships, grants, and awards:* Federal Pell, FSEOG, state, private, college/university gift aid from institutional funds.

GIFT AID (NON-NEED-BASED) *Total amount:* $5,643,216 (1% federal, 96% institutional, 3% external sources). *Average award:* Freshmen: $11,811. Undergraduates: $12,417. *Scholarships, grants, and awards by category:* Academic interests/achievement: 642 awards ($6,304,000 total): general academic interests/achievements. Creative arts/performance: 148 awards ($1,179,256 total): music. Special characteristics: 216 awards ($2,551,736 total): children and siblings of alumni, ethnic background, international students. *Tuition waivers:* Full or partial for employees or children of employees.

LOANS *Student loans:* $7,509,052 (54% need-based, 46% non-need-based). 76% of past graduating class borrowed through all loan programs. *Average indebtedness per student:* $25,049. *Average need-based loan:* Freshmen: $4555. Undergraduates: $5540. *Parent loans:* $1,911,898 (100% non-need-based). *Programs:* Federal Direct (Subsidized and Unsubsidized Stafford, PLUS), Perkins, alternative loans.

WORK-STUDY *Federal work-study:* Total amount: $1,524,871; 708 jobs averaging $2370. *State or other work-study/employment:* Total amount: $816,402 (100% non-need-based). 400 part-time jobs averaging $2250.

APPLYING FOR FINANCIAL AID *Required financial aid forms:* FAFSA, institution's own form, noncustodial (divorced/separated) parent's statement, federal tax returns and W-2 forms for parents and students. *Financial aid deadline (priority):* 3/1. *Notification date:* Continuous beginning 3/1. Students must reply by 5/1.

CONTACT Mrs. Sara Beth Holman, Director of Financial Aid, Lawrence University, 711 East Boldt Way, Appleton, WI 54911, 920-832-6583 or toll-free 800-227-0982. *Fax:* 920-832-6582. *E-mail:* sara.b.holman@lawrence.edu.

LEBANON VALLEY COLLEGE
Annville, PA

Tuition & fees: $30,490	Average undergraduate aid package: $22,686

ABOUT THE INSTITUTION Independent United Methodist, coed. 37 undergraduate majors. Federal methodology is used as a basis for awarding need-based institutional aid.

UNDERGRADUATE EXPENSES for 2009–10 *Comprehensive fee:* $38,570 includes full-time tuition ($29,780), mandatory fees ($710), and room and board ($8080). *College room only:* $3960. Room and board charges vary according to board plan and housing facility. *Part-time tuition:* $500 per credit. Part-time tuition and fees vary according to class time and degree level. *Payment plans:* Tuition prepayment, installment.

FRESHMAN FINANCIAL AID (Fall 2009, est.) 364 applied for aid; of those 88% were deemed to have need. 100% of freshmen with need received aid; of those 24% had need fully met. *Average percent of need met:* 85% (excluding resources awarded to replace EFC). *Average financial aid package:* $23,790 (excluding resources awarded to replace EFC). 13% of all full-time freshmen had no need and received non-need-based gift aid.

UNDERGRADUATE FINANCIAL AID (Fall 2009, est.) 1,402 applied for aid; of those 91% were deemed to have need. 99% of undergraduates with need received aid; of those 25% had need fully met. *Average percent of need met:* 82% (excluding resources awarded to replace EFC). *Average financial aid package:* $22,686 (excluding resources awarded to replace EFC). 15% of all full-time undergraduates had no need and received non-need-based gift aid.

GIFT AID (NEED-BASED) *Total amount:* $20,265,495 (8% federal, 9% state, 83% institutional). *Receiving aid:* Freshmen: 85% (321); all full-time undergraduates: 80% (1,254). *Average award:* Freshmen: $20,015; Undergraduates: $18,957. *Scholarships, grants, and awards:* Federal Pell, FSEOG, state, private, college/university gift aid from institutional funds, Academic Competitiveness Grants, National SMART Grants, TEACH Grants.

GIFT AID (NON-NEED-BASED) *Total amount:* $4,765,828 (1% federal, 2% state, 82% institutional, 15% external sources). *Receiving aid:* Freshmen: 10% (38). Undergraduates: 8% (127). *Average award:* Freshmen: $12,684. Undergraduates: $12,717. *Scholarships, grants, and awards by category:* Academic interests/achievement: 1,281 awards ($15,569,872 total): biological sciences, general academic interests/achievements, religion/biblical studies. Creative arts/performance: 46 awards ($81,800 total): music. Special achievements/activities: 85 awards ($42,250 total): general special achievements/activities. Special characteristics: 186 awards ($1,381,189 total): children and siblings of alumni, children of faculty/staff, ethnic background, international students, veterans. *Tuition waivers:* Full or partial for employees or children of employees, senior citizens.

LOANS *Student loans:* $13,055,464 (39% need-based, 61% non-need-based). 82% of past graduating class borrowed through all loan programs. *Average indebtedness per student:* $33,348. *Average need-based loan:* Freshmen: $4318. Undergraduates: $4705. *Parent loans:* $5,675,009 (100% non-need-based). *Programs:* FFEL (Subsidized and Unsubsidized Stafford, PLUS), Perkins.

WORK-STUDY *Federal work-study:* Total amount: $1,327,414; 894 jobs averaging $1470.

APPLYING FOR FINANCIAL AID *Required financial aid forms:* FAFSA, institution's own form. *Financial aid deadline (priority):* 3/1. *Notification date:* Continuous beginning 3/1. Students must reply by 5/1 or within 2 weeks of notification.

CONTACT Mrs. Kendra M. Feigert, Director of Financial Aid, Lebanon Valley College, 101 North College Avenue, Annville, PA 17003, 866-582-4236 or toll-free 866-LVC-4ADM. *Fax:* 717-867-6027. *E-mail:* feigert@lvc.edu.

LEES-McRAE COLLEGE
Banner Elk, NC

Tuition & fees: N/R	Average undergraduate aid package: $12,600

ABOUT THE INSTITUTION Independent religious, coed. 29 undergraduate majors. Both federal and institutional methodology are used as a basis for awarding need-based institutional aid.

FRESHMAN FINANCIAL AID (Fall 2009, est.) 136 applied for aid; of those 85% were deemed to have need. 100% of freshmen with need received aid; of those 5% had need fully met. *Average percent of need met:* 73% (excluding resources awarded to replace EFC). *Average financial aid package:* $12,145 (excluding resources awarded to replace EFC). 11% of all full-time freshmen had no need and received non-need-based gift aid.

UNDERGRADUATE FINANCIAL AID (Fall 2009, est.) 741 applied for aid; of those 87% were deemed to have need. 100% of undergraduates with need received aid; of those 4% had need fully met. *Average percent of need met:* 74% (excluding resources awarded to replace EFC). *Average financial aid package:* $12,600 (excluding resources awarded to replace EFC). 6% of all full-time undergraduates had no need and received non-need-based gift aid.

GIFT AID (NEED-BASED) *Total amount:* $12,879,846 (13% federal, 15% state, 71% institutional, 1% external sources). *Receiving aid:* Freshmen: 48% (78); all full-time undergraduates: 49% (440). *Average award:* Freshmen: $9500; Undergraduates: $9700. *Scholarships, grants, and awards:* Federal Pell, FSEOG, state, private, college/university gift aid from institutional funds.

GIFT AID (NON-NEED-BASED) *Receiving aid:* Freshmen: 65% (106). Undergraduates: 66% (595). *Average award:* Freshmen: $5200. Undergraduates: $5600. *Scholarships, grants, and awards by category: Academic interests/achievement:* biological sciences, education, general academic interests/achievements, mathematics. *Creative arts/performance:* dance, journalism/publications, performing arts, theater/drama. *Special achievements/activities:* cheerleading/drum major, general special achievements/activities. *Special characteristics:* children of educators, children of faculty/staff, children with a deceased or disabled parent, international students, local/state students, previous college experience, relatives of clergy, religious affiliation, veterans. *Tuition waivers:* Full or partial for employees or children of employees.

LOANS *Student loans:* $4,505,131 (100% need-based). *Average need-based loan:* Freshmen: $3500. Undergraduates: $5000. *Parent loans:* $863,919 (100% need-based). *Programs:* FFEL (Subsidized and Unsubsidized Stafford, PLUS), Perkins, state, college/university.

WORK-STUDY *Federal work-study:* Total amount: $315,235; jobs available. *State or other work-study/employment:* Total amount: $104,915 (100% need-based). Part-time jobs available.

ATHLETIC AWARDS Total amount: $1,467,787 (100% need-based).

APPLYING FOR FINANCIAL AID *Required financial aid forms:* FAFSA, state aid form. *Financial aid deadline:* Continuous. *Notification date:* Continuous beginning 3/1.

CONTACT Cathy Shell, Director of Financial Aid, Lees-McRae College, PO Box 128, Banner Elk, NC 28604-0128, 828-898-8740 or toll-free 800-280-4562. *Fax:* 828-898-8746. *E-mail:* shell@lmc.edu.

LEE UNIVERSITY
Cleveland, TN

Tuition & fees: $11,610	Average undergraduate aid package: $10,108

ABOUT THE INSTITUTION Independent religious, coed. 36 undergraduate majors. Federal methodology is used as a basis for awarding need-based institutional aid.

UNDERGRADUATE EXPENSES for 2009–10 *Comprehensive fee:* $17,260 includes full-time tuition ($11,100), mandatory fees ($510), and room and board ($5650). *College room only:* $2720. Full-time tuition and fees vary according to course load. Room and board charges vary according to board plan and housing facility. *Part-time tuition:* $463 per credit hour. Part-time tuition and fees vary according to course load. *Payment plan:* Deferred payment.

FRESHMAN FINANCIAL AID (Fall 2009, est.) 724 applied for aid; of those 75% were deemed to have need. 99% of freshmen with need received aid; of those 31% had need fully met. *Average percent of need met:* 69% (excluding resources awarded to replace EFC). *Average financial aid package:* $10,688 (excluding resources awarded to replace EFC). 22% of all full-time freshmen had no need and received non-need-based gift aid.

UNDERGRADUATE FINANCIAL AID (Fall 2009, est.) 2,759 applied for aid; of those 81% were deemed to have need. 99% of undergraduates with need received aid; of those 17% had need fully met. *Average percent of need met:* 58% (excluding resources awarded to replace EFC). *Average financial aid package:* $10,108 (excluding resources awarded to replace EFC). 17% of all full-time undergraduates had no need and received non-need-based gift aid.

GIFT AID (NEED-BASED) *Total amount:* $14,034,390 (43% federal, 22% state, 32% institutional, 3% external sources). *Receiving aid:* Freshmen: 59% (487);

---

all full-time undergraduates: 56% (1,925). *Average award:* Freshmen: $9509; Undergraduates: $7803. *Scholarships, grants, and awards:* Federal Pell, FSEOG, state, private, college/university gift aid from institutional funds.

GIFT AID (NON-NEED-BASED) *Total amount:* $5,857,920 (25% state, 69% institutional, 6% external sources). *Receiving aid:* Freshmen: 14% (113). Undergraduates: 7% (246). *Average award:* Freshmen: $8634. Undergraduates: $6235. *Scholarships, grants, and awards by category: Academic interests/achievement:* biological sciences, business, communication, education, general academic interests/achievements, religion/biblical studies. *Creative arts/performance:* music, theater/drama. *Special achievements/activities:* cheerleading/drum major, leadership, religious involvement. *Special characteristics:* children of faculty/staff, local/state students, siblings of current students, spouses of current students. *Tuition waivers:* Full or partial for employees or children of employees.

LOANS *Student loans:* $16,546,478 (76% need-based, 24% non-need-based). 64% of past graduating class borrowed through all loan programs. *Average indebtedness per student:* $27,549. *Average need-based loan:* Freshmen: $3307. Undergraduates: $4189. *Parent loans:* $2,059,356 (34% need-based, 66% non-need-based). *Programs:* FFEL (Subsidized and Unsubsidized Stafford, PLUS), Perkins, college/university.

WORK-STUDY *Federal work-study:* Total amount: $456,796; 202 jobs averaging $1765. *State or other work-study/employment:* Total amount: $1,003,407 (100% non-need-based). Part-time jobs available.

ATHLETIC AWARDS Total amount: $1,610,144 (34% need-based, 66% non-need-based).

APPLYING FOR FINANCIAL AID *Required financial aid form:* FAFSA. *Financial aid deadline (priority):* 3/15. *Notification date:* Continuous beginning 2/1. Students must reply within 3 weeks of notification.

CONTACT Mr. Michael Ellis, Director of Student Financial Aid, Lee University, 1120 North Ocoee Street, Cleveland, TN 37320-3450, 423-614-8300 or toll-free 800-533-9930. *Fax:* 423-614-8308. *E-mail:* finaid@leeuniversity.edu.

LEHIGH UNIVERSITY
Bethlehem, PA

Tuition & fees: $38,630	Average undergraduate aid package: $33,008

ABOUT THE INSTITUTION Independent, coed. 84 undergraduate majors. Institutional methodology is used as a basis for awarding need-based institutional aid.

UNDERGRADUATE EXPENSES for 2009–10 *Comprehensive fee:* $48,830 includes full-time tuition ($38,330), mandatory fees ($300), and room and board ($10,200). *College room only:* $5910. Room and board charges vary according to board plan. *Part-time tuition:* $1600 per credit hour. *Payment plans:* Tuition prepayment, installment.

FRESHMAN FINANCIAL AID (Fall 2009, est.) 777 applied for aid; of those 71% were deemed to have need. 100% of freshmen with need received aid; of those 56% had need fully met. *Average percent of need met:* 97% (excluding resources awarded to replace EFC). *Average financial aid package:* $32,081 (excluding resources awarded to replace EFC). 6% of all full-time freshmen had no need and received non-need-based gift aid.

UNDERGRADUATE FINANCIAL AID (Fall 2009, est.) 2,804 applied for aid; of those 77% were deemed to have need. 100% of undergraduates with need received aid; of those 69% had need fully met. *Average percent of need met:* 96% (excluding resources awarded to replace EFC). *Average financial aid package:* $33,008 (excluding resources awarded to replace EFC). 7% of all full-time undergraduates had no need and received non-need-based gift aid.

GIFT AID (NEED-BASED) *Total amount:* $55,036,987 (6% federal, 2% state, 92% institutional). *Receiving aid:* Freshmen: 45% (540); all full-time undergraduates: 44% (2,087). *Average award:* Freshmen: $27,887; Undergraduates: $27,718. *Scholarships, grants, and awards:* Federal Pell, FSEOG, state, private, college/university gift aid from institutional funds, United Negro College Fund.

GIFT AID (NON-NEED-BASED) *Total amount:* $6,008,598 (1% federal, 57% institutional, 42% external sources). *Receiving aid:* Freshmen: 5% (55). Undergraduates: 5% (234). *Average award:* Freshmen: $10,139. Undergraduates: $10,524. *Scholarships, grants, and awards by category: Academic interests/achievement:* 415 awards ($4,465,460 total): business, communication, engineering/technologies, general academic interests/achievements, military science. *Creative arts/performance:* 35 awards ($101,600 total): general creative arts/performance, music, performing arts, theater/drama. *Special achievements/activities:* 2 awards ($15,000 total): general special achievements/activities.

Special characteristics: 119 awards ($4,054,862 total): children of faculty/staff, members of minority groups. *Tuition waivers:* Full or partial for employees or children of employees.

LOANS *Student loans:* $25,184,282 (40% need-based, 60% non-need-based). 54% of past graduating class borrowed through all loan programs. *Average indebtedness per student:* $31,123. *Average need-based loan:* Freshmen: $3388. Undergraduates: $4581. *Parent loans:* $6,647,547 (100% non-need-based). *Programs:* FFEL (Subsidized and Unsubsidized Stafford, PLUS), Perkins, college/ university, private alternative loans.

WORK-STUDY *Federal work-study:* Total amount: $2,032,864; 1,141 jobs averaging $1778. *State or other work-study/employment:* Total amount: $1,015,362 (10% need-based, 90% non-need-based). 52 part-time jobs averaging $1912.

ATHLETIC AWARDS Total amount: $3,159,376 (36% need-based, 64% non-need-based).

APPLYING FOR FINANCIAL AID *Required financial aid forms:* FAFSA, CSS Financial Aid PROFILE, noncustodial (divorced/separated) parent's statement, business/farm supplement. *Financial aid deadline:* 2/1. *Notification date:* 3/30. Students must reply by 5/1 or within 3 weeks of notification.

CONTACT Linda F. Bell, Director of Financial Aid, Lehigh University, 218 West Packer Avenue, Bethlehem, PA 18015-3094, 610-758-3181. *Fax:* 610-758-6211. *E-mail:* lfn0@lehigh.edu.

LEHMAN COLLEGE OF THE CITY UNIVERSITY OF NEW YORK
Bronx, NY

Tuition & fees (NY res): $4770	Average undergraduate aid package: $4002

ABOUT THE INSTITUTION State and locally supported, coed. 52 undergraduate majors. Federal methodology is used as a basis for awarding need-based institutional aid.

UNDERGRADUATE EXPENSES for 2009–10 *Tuition, state resident:* full-time $4600; part-time $195 per credit. *Tuition, nonresident:* full-time $9960; part-time $415 per credit. *Required fees:* full-time $170. Full-time tuition and fees vary according to program. Part-time tuition and fees vary according to program. *College room and board:* $12,569; *Room only:* $9612. *Payment plan:* Deferred payment.

FRESHMAN FINANCIAL AID (Fall 2009, est.) 646 applied for aid; of those 100% were deemed to have need. 100% of freshmen with need received aid; of those 4% had need fully met. *Average percent of need met:* 16% (excluding resources awarded to replace EFC). *Average financial aid package:* $3889 (excluding resources awarded to replace EFC). 1% of all full-time freshmen had no need and received non-need-based gift aid.

UNDERGRADUATE FINANCIAL AID (Fall 2009, est.) 4,922 applied for aid; of those 99% were deemed to have need. 100% of undergraduates with need received aid; of those 5% had need fully met. *Average percent of need met:* 66% (excluding resources awarded to replace EFC). *Average financial aid package:* $4002 (excluding resources awarded to replace EFC). 1% of all full-time undergraduates had no need and received non-need-based gift aid.

GIFT AID (NEED-BASED) *Total amount:* $35,938,353 (64% federal, 35% state, 1% institutional). *Receiving aid:* Freshmen: 85% (642); all full-time undergraduates: 78% (4,692). *Average award:* Freshmen: $1229; Undergraduates: $1455. *Scholarships, grants, and awards:* Federal Pell, FSEOG, state, college/university gift aid from institutional funds.

GIFT AID (NON-NEED-BASED) *Total amount:* $1,571,410 (21% state, 30% institutional, 49% external sources). *Receiving aid:* Freshmen: 50% (375). Undergraduates: 18% (1,089). *Average award:* Freshmen: $2824. Undergraduates: $3243.

LOANS *Student loans:* $12,493,833 (62% need-based, 38% non-need-based). 32% of past graduating class borrowed through all loan programs. *Average indebtedness per student:* $11,100. *Average need-based loan:* Freshmen: $1860. Undergraduates: $2006. *Parent loans:* $11,185 (100% non-need-based). *Programs:* Federal Direct (Subsidized and Unsubsidized Stafford, PLUS), Perkins.

WORK-STUDY *Federal work-study:* Total amount: $1,688,975; 1,272 jobs averaging $789.

APPLYING FOR FINANCIAL AID *Required financial aid forms:* FAFSA, state aid form. *Financial aid deadline:* Continuous. *Notification date:* Continuous beginning 3/1.

CONTACT David Martinez, Director of Financial Aid, Lehman College of the City University of New York, 250 Bedford Park Boulevard West, Bronx, NY 10468-1589, 718-960-8545 or toll-free 877-Lehman1 (out-of-state). *Fax:* 718-960-8328. *E-mail:* idmlc@cunyvm.cuny.edu.

LE MOYNE COLLEGE
Syracuse, NY

Tuition & fees: $25,830	Average undergraduate aid package: $19,390

ABOUT THE INSTITUTION Independent Roman Catholic (Jesuit), coed. 53 undergraduate majors. Both federal and institutional methodology are used as a basis for awarding need-based institutional aid.

UNDERGRADUATE EXPENSES for 2009–10 *Comprehensive fee:* $35,820 includes full-time tuition ($25,110), mandatory fees ($720), and room and board ($9990). *College room only:* $6340. Room and board charges vary according to board plan and housing facility. *Part-time tuition:* $526 per credit hour. Part-time tuition and fees vary according to class time. *Payment plans:* Installment, deferred payment.

FRESHMAN FINANCIAL AID (Fall 2008) 511 applied for aid; of those 88% were deemed to have need. 100% of freshmen with need received aid; of those 29% had need fully met. *Average percent of need met:* 81% (excluding resources awarded to replace EFC). *Average financial aid package:* $20,230 (excluding resources awarded to replace EFC). 10% of all full-time freshmen had no need and received non-need-based gift aid.

UNDERGRADUATE FINANCIAL AID (Fall 2008) 2,082 applied for aid; of those 90% were deemed to have need. 100% of undergraduates with need received aid; of those 23% had need fully met. *Average percent of need met:* 76% (excluding resources awarded to replace EFC). *Average financial aid package:* $19,390 (excluding resources awarded to replace EFC). 10% of all full-time undergraduates had no need and received non-need-based gift aid.

GIFT AID (NEED-BASED) *Total amount:* $27,461,803 (12% federal, 12% state, 74% institutional, 2% external sources). *Receiving aid:* Freshmen: 76% (412); all full-time undergraduates: 76% (1,744). *Average award:* Freshmen: $11,013; Undergraduates: $10,155. *Scholarships, grants, and awards:* Federal Pell, FSEOG, state, private, college/university gift aid from institutional funds.

GIFT AID (NON-NEED-BASED) *Total amount:* $3,358,713 (2% state, 94% institutional, 4% external sources). *Receiving aid:* Freshmen: 24% (133). Undergraduates: 19% (424). *Average award:* Freshmen: $10,399. Undergraduates: $10,745. *Scholarships, grants, and awards by category:* Academic interests/achievement: 374 awards ($5,292,967 total): general academic interests/achievements. Creative arts/performance: 3 awards ($960 total): music. Special achievements/activities: 613 awards ($4,593,170 total): leadership. Special characteristics: 148 awards ($584,250 total): children and siblings of alumni, members of minority groups. *Tuition waivers:* Full or partial for employees or children of employees.

LOANS *Student loans:* $17,538,767 (94% need-based, 6% non-need-based). 84% of past graduating class borrowed through all loan programs. *Average indebtedness per student:* $27,483. *Average need-based loan:* Freshmen: $3588. Undergraduates: $4635. *Parent loans:* $3,798,838 (89% need-based, 11% non-need-based). *Programs:* FFEL (Subsidized and Unsubsidized Stafford, PLUS), Perkins.

WORK-STUDY *Federal work-study:* Total amount: $314,606; 354 jobs averaging $1267. *State or other work-study/employment:* 509 part-time jobs averaging $970.

ATHLETIC AWARDS Total amount: $1,389,229 (68% need-based, 32% non-need-based).

APPLYING FOR FINANCIAL AID *Required financial aid forms:* FAFSA, institution's own form, state aid form. *Financial aid deadline (priority):* 2/1. *Notification date:* 3/15. Students must reply by 5/1 or within 2 weeks of notification.

CONTACT Mr. William C. Cheetham, Director of Financial Aid, Le Moyne College, 1419 Salt Springs Road, Syracuse, NY 13214-1301, 315-445-4400 or toll-free 800-333-4733. *Fax:* 315-445-4182. *E-mail:* cheethwc@lemoyne.edu.

LeMOYNE-OWEN COLLEGE
Memphis, TN

Tuition & fees: $10,318	Average undergraduate aid package: $10,224

ABOUT THE INSTITUTION Independent religious, coed. *Awards:* bachelor's degrees and post-bachelor's certificates. 22 undergraduate majors. *Total enrollment:* 592. Undergraduates: 592. Freshmen: 85. Federal methodology is used as a basis for awarding need-based institutional aid.

UNDERGRADUATE EXPENSES for 2009–10 *Application fee:* $25. *Comprehensive fee:* $15,170 includes full-time tuition ($10,098), mandatory fees ($220), and room and board ($4852). *Part-time tuition:* $421 per credit hour. *Payment plan:* Installment.

FRESHMAN FINANCIAL AID (Fall 2008) 166 applied for aid; of those 100% were deemed to have need. 99% of freshmen with need received aid; of those 9% had need fully met. *Average percent of need met:* 67% (excluding resources awarded to replace EFC). *Average financial aid package:* $10,235 (excluding resources awarded to replace EFC). 2% of all full-time freshmen had no need and received non-need-based gift aid.

UNDERGRADUATE FINANCIAL AID (Fall 2008) 680 applied for aid; of those 97% were deemed to have need. 99% of undergraduates with need received aid; of those 8% had need fully met. *Average percent of need met:* 62% (excluding resources awarded to replace EFC). *Average financial aid package:* $10,224 (excluding resources awarded to replace EFC). 2% of all full-time undergraduates had no need and received non-need-based gift aid.

GIFT AID (NEED-BASED) *Total amount:* $4,370,289 (56% federal, 26% state, 10% institutional, 8% external sources). *Receiving aid:* Freshmen: 92% (157); all full-time undergraduates: 89% (612). *Average award:* Freshmen: $7792; Undergraduates: $7356. *Scholarships, grants, and awards:* Federal Pell, FSEOG, state, private, college/university gift aid from institutional funds, United Negro College Fund.

GIFT AID (NON-NEED-BASED) *Total amount:* $203,353 (15% state, 68% institutional, 17% external sources). *Receiving aid:* Freshmen: 4% (6). Undergraduates: 3% (22). *Average award:* Freshmen: $9528. Undergraduates: $7793. *Scholarships, grants, and awards by category: Academic interests/achievement:* 68 awards ($347,759 total): general academic interests/achievements. *Creative arts/performance:* 21 awards ($87,032 total): journalism/publications, music. *Special characteristics:* 13 awards ($50,700 total): children of faculty/staff. *Tuition waivers:* Full or partial for employees or children of employees. *ROTC:* Army cooperative, Air Force cooperative.

LOANS *Student loans:* $4,025,043 (94% need-based, 6% non-need-based). 88% of past graduating class borrowed through all loan programs. *Average indebtedness per student:* $22,733. *Average need-based loan:* Freshmen: $2892. Undergraduates: $3478. *Parent loans:* $112,595 (61% need-based, 39% non-need-based). *Programs:* FFEL (Subsidized and Unsubsidized Stafford, PLUS).

WORK-STUDY *Federal work-study:* Total amount: $242,194; 154 jobs averaging $1573.

ATHLETIC AWARDS Total amount: $223,100 (76% need-based, 24% non-need-based).

APPLYING FOR FINANCIAL AID *Required financial aid forms:* FAFSA, institution's own form. *Financial aid deadline (priority):* 4/1. *Notification date:* Continuous beginning 5/1. Students must reply within 2 weeks of notification.

CONTACT Phyllis Nettles Torry, Director of Student Financial Services, LeMoyne-Owen College, 807 Walker Avenue, Memphis, TN 38126-6595, 901-435-1550 Ext. 1555. *Fax:* 901-435-1574. *E-mail:* phyllis_torry@loc.edu.

LENOIR-RHYNE UNIVERSITY
Hickory, NC

Tuition & fees: N/R	Average undergraduate aid package: $20,936

ABOUT THE INSTITUTION Independent Lutheran, coed. *Awards:* bachelor's and master's degrees and post-bachelor's certificates. 72 undergraduate majors. *Total enrollment:* 1,562. Undergraduates: 1,381. Freshmen: 346. Federal methodology is used as a basis for awarding need-based institutional aid.

FRESHMAN FINANCIAL AID (Fall 2008) 328 applied for aid; of those 89% were deemed to have need. 100% of freshmen with need received aid; of those 42% had need fully met. *Average percent of need met:* 88% (excluding resources awarded to replace EFC). *Average financial aid package:* $21,206 (excluding resources awarded to replace EFC). 16% of all full-time freshmen had no need and received non-need-based gift aid.

UNDERGRADUATE FINANCIAL AID (Fall 2008) 1,164 applied for aid; of those 88% were deemed to have need. 100% of undergraduates with need received aid; of those 41% had need fully met. *Average percent of need met:* 86% (excluding resources awarded to replace EFC). *Average financial aid package:* $20,936 (excluding resources awarded to replace EFC). 17% of all full-time undergraduates had no need and received non-need-based gift aid.

GIFT AID (NEED-BASED) *Total amount:* $16,930,600 (9% federal, 19% state, 70% institutional, 2% external sources). *Receiving aid:* Freshmen: 84% (291); all full-time undergraduates: 74% (1,020). *Average award:* Freshmen: $18,984; Undergraduates: $17,693. *Scholarships, grants, and awards:* Federal Pell, FSEOG, state, private, college/university gift aid from institutional funds.

GIFT AID (NON-NEED-BASED) *Total amount:* $4,596,911 (16% state, 77% institutional, 7% external sources). *Receiving aid:* Freshmen: 21% (73). Undergraduates: 19% (268). *Average award:* Freshmen: $9656. Undergraduates: $10,925. *Scholarships, grants, and awards by category: Academic interests/achievement:* general academic interests/achievements. *Creative arts/performance:* music. *Special achievements/activities:* cheerleading/drum major, leadership. *Special characteristics:* children and siblings of alumni, children of faculty/staff, ethnic background, local/state students, members of minority groups, relatives of clergy, religious affiliation, siblings of current students. *Tuition waivers:* Full or partial for employees or children of employees. *ROTC:* Army cooperative.

LOANS *Student loans:* $7,061,645 (64% need-based, 36% non-need-based). *Average need-based loan:* Freshmen: $3463. Undergraduates: $4955. *Parent loans:* $2,644,952 (19% need-based, 81% non-need-based). *Programs:* Federal Direct (Subsidized and Unsubsidized Stafford, PLUS), Perkins, state.

WORK-STUDY *Federal work-study:* Total amount: $57,500; jobs available. *State or other work-study/employment:* Part-time jobs available.

ATHLETIC AWARDS Total amount: $2,196,746 (60% need-based, 40% non-need-based).

APPLYING FOR FINANCIAL AID *Required financial aid forms:* FAFSA, state aid form. *Financial aid deadline:* Continuous. *Notification date:* Continuous beginning 2/15. Students must reply by 8/31.

CONTACT Eric Brandon, Director of Enrollment Services, Lenoir-Rhyne University, PO Box 7227, Hickory, NC 28603, 828-328-7301 or toll-free 800-277-5721. *Fax:* 828-328-7039. *E-mail:* admission@lrc.edu.

LESLEY UNIVERSITY
Cambridge, MA

Tuition & fees: $29,400	Average undergraduate aid package: $15,335

ABOUT THE INSTITUTION Independent, coed. 22 undergraduate majors. Both federal and institutional methodology are used as a basis for awarding need-based institutional aid.

UNDERGRADUATE EXPENSES for 2010–11 *Comprehensive fee:* $42,200 includes full-time tuition ($29,150), mandatory fees ($250), and room and board ($12,800). *College room only:* $7950. Room and board charges vary according to housing facility. *Payment plan:* Installment.

FRESHMAN FINANCIAL AID (Fall 2009, est.) 326 applied for aid; of those 90% were deemed to have need. 100% of freshmen with need received aid; of those 13% had need fully met. *Average percent of need met:* 74% (excluding resources awarded to replace EFC). *Average financial aid package:* $19,753 (excluding resources awarded to replace EFC). 2% of all full-time freshmen had no need and received non-need-based gift aid.

UNDERGRADUATE FINANCIAL AID (Fall 2009, est.) 1,230 applied for aid; of those 78% were deemed to have need. 99% of undergraduates with need received aid; of those 12% had need fully met. *Average percent of need met:* 70% (excluding resources awarded to replace EFC). *Average financial aid package:* $15,335 (excluding resources awarded to replace EFC). 18% of all full-time undergraduates had no need and received non-need-based gift aid.

GIFT AID (NEED-BASED) *Total amount:* $11,269,236 (16% federal, 4% state, 71% institutional, 9% external sources). *Receiving aid:* Freshmen: 76% (286); all full-time undergraduates: 69% (922). *Average award:* Freshmen: $15,193; Undergraduates: $14,014. *Scholarships, grants, and awards:* Federal Pell, FSEOG, state, private, college/university gift aid from institutional funds.

GIFT AID (NON-NEED-BASED) *Total amount:* $4,948,047 (100% institutional). *Receiving aid:* Freshmen: 11% (41). Undergraduates: 18% (233). *Average award:* Freshmen: $11,272. Undergraduates: $8885. *Scholarships, grants, and awards by category: Academic interests/achievement:* general academic interests/achievements. *Creative arts/performance:* art/fine arts. *Special achievements/activities:* general special achievements/activities. *Special characteristics:* ethnic background, local/state students, members of minority groups. *Tuition waivers:* Full or partial for employees or children of employees.

LOANS *Student loans:* $11,198,271 (52% need-based, 48% non-need-based). 90% of past graduating class borrowed through all loan programs. *Average indebtedness per student:* $17,000. *Average need-based loan:* Freshmen: $3715. Undergraduates: $4028. *Parent loans:* $3,419,190 (100% non-need-based). *Programs:* Federal Direct (Subsidized and Unsubsidized Stafford, PLUS), Perkins, state.

WORK-STUDY *Federal work-study:* Total amount: $450,000; jobs available. *State or other work-study/employment:* Part-time jobs available.

APPLYING FOR FINANCIAL AID *Required financial aid forms:* FAFSA, institution's own form. *Financial aid deadline (priority):* 3/15. *Notification date:* Continuous beginning 3/15.

CONTACT Scott A. Jewell, Director of Financial Aid, Lesley University, 29 Everett Street, Cambridge, MA 02138-2790, 617-349-8714 or toll-free 800-999-1959 Ext. 8800. *Fax:* 617-349-8717. *E-mail:* sjewell@lesley.edu.

LeTOURNEAU UNIVERSITY
Longview, TX

Tuition & fees: $21,980	Average undergraduate aid package: $10,706

ABOUT THE INSTITUTION Independent nondenominational, coed. 42 undergraduate majors. Federal methodology is used as a basis for awarding need-based institutional aid.

UNDERGRADUATE EXPENSES for 2010–11 *Comprehensive fee:* $30,370 includes full-time tuition ($21,510), mandatory fees ($470), and room and board ($8390). Room and board charges vary according to board plan. *Part-time tuition:* $858 per credit hour. Part-time tuition and fees vary according to course load. *Payment plan:* Installment.

FRESHMAN FINANCIAL AID (Fall 2009, est.) 314 applied for aid; of those 85% were deemed to have need. 99% of freshmen with need received aid; of those 17% had need fully met. *Average percent of need met:* 71% (excluding resources awarded to replace EFC). *Average financial aid package:* $16,301 (excluding resources awarded to replace EFC). 18% of all full-time freshmen had no need and received non-need-based gift aid.

UNDERGRADUATE FINANCIAL AID (Fall 2009, est.) 2,507 applied for aid; of those 90% were deemed to have need. 98% of undergraduates with need received aid; of those 7% had need fully met. *Average percent of need met:* 43% (excluding resources awarded to replace EFC). *Average financial aid package:* $10,706 (excluding resources awarded to replace EFC). 6% of all full-time undergraduates had no need and received non-need-based gift aid.

GIFT AID (NEED-BASED) *Total amount:* $13,177,559 (40% federal, 10% state, 46% institutional, 4% external sources). *Receiving aid:* Freshmen: 75% (256); all full-time undergraduates: 56% (1,615). *Average award:* Freshmen: $13,122; Undergraduates: $8618. *Scholarships, grants, and awards:* Federal Pell, FSEOG, state, college/university gift aid from institutional funds.

GIFT AID (NON-NEED-BASED) *Total amount:* $1,856,703 (1% federal, 94% institutional, 5% external sources). *Receiving aid:* Freshmen: 56% (193). Undergraduates: 18% (528). *Average award:* Freshmen: $2477. Undergraduates: $5862. *Scholarships, grants, and awards by category: Academic interests/achievement:* general academic interests/achievements. *Special characteristics:* children and siblings of alumni. *Tuition waivers:* Full or partial for employees or children of employees.

LOANS *Student loans:* $26,959,145 (36% need-based, 64% non-need-based). *Average need-based loan:* Freshmen: $2950. Undergraduates: $5206. *Parent loans:* $1,598,952 (100% non-need-based). *Programs:* Federal Direct (Subsidized and Unsubsidized Stafford, PLUS), Perkins, state.

WORK-STUDY *Federal work-study:* Total amount: $226,680; jobs available. *State or other work-study/employment:* Total amount: $49,300 (100% need-based). Part-time jobs available.

APPLYING FOR FINANCIAL AID *Required financial aid form:* FAFSA. *Financial aid deadline (priority):* 2/15. *Notification date:* Continuous beginning 3/1. Students must reply within 2 weeks of notification.

CONTACT Ms. Lindy Hall, Senior Director of Enrollment Services, LeTourneau University, PO Box 7001, Longview, TX 75607, 903-233-4312 or toll-free 800-759-8811. *Fax:* 903-233-4301. *E-mail:* finaid@letu.edu.

LEWIS & CLARK COLLEGE
Portland, OR

Tuition & fees: $35,233	Average undergraduate aid package: $27,618

ABOUT THE INSTITUTION Independent, coed. 27 undergraduate majors. Both federal and institutional methodology are used as a basis for awarding need-based institutional aid.

UNDERGRADUATE EXPENSES for 2009–10 *Comprehensive fee:* $44,239 includes full-time tuition ($34,995), mandatory fees ($238), and room and board ($9006). *College room only:* $4886. Room and board charges vary according to board plan and housing facility. *Part-time tuition:* $1762 per credit hour. *Payment plan:* Installment.

FRESHMAN FINANCIAL AID (Fall 2009, est.) 372 applied for aid; of those 76% were deemed to have need. 100% of freshmen with need received aid; of those 17% had need fully met. *Average percent of need met:* 83% (excluding resources awarded to replace EFC). *Average financial aid package:* $27,150 (excluding resources awarded to replace EFC). 11% of all full-time freshmen had no need and received non-need-based gift aid.

UNDERGRADUATE FINANCIAL AID (Fall 2009, est.) 1,304 applied for aid; of those 80% were deemed to have need. 100% of undergraduates with need received aid; of those 24% had need fully met. *Average percent of need met:* 83% (excluding resources awarded to replace EFC). *Average financial aid package:* $27,618 (excluding resources awarded to replace EFC). 13% of all full-time undergraduates had no need and received non-need-based gift aid.

GIFT AID (NEED-BASED) *Total amount:* $21,558,121 (9% federal, 1% state, 86% institutional, 4% external sources). *Receiving aid:* Freshmen: 55% (273); all full-time undergraduates: 54% (1,020). *Average award:* Freshmen: $21,303; Undergraduates: $20,201. *Scholarships, grants, and awards:* Federal Pell, FSEOG, state, private, college/university gift aid from institutional funds.

GIFT AID (NON-NEED-BASED) *Total amount:* $4,233,096 (96% institutional, 4% external sources). *Receiving aid:* Freshmen: 2% (8). Undergraduates: 2% (29). *Average award:* Freshmen: $11,010. Undergraduates: $10,371. *Scholarships, grants, and awards by category: Creative arts/performance:* 32 awards ($183,992 total): debating, music. *Special achievements/activities:* 89 awards ($587,813 total): community service, leadership. *Special characteristics:* 37 awards ($1,151,423 total): children of faculty/staff. *Tuition waivers:* Full or partial for employees or children of employees.

LOANS *Student loans:* $6,208,144 (65% need-based, 35% non-need-based). 58% of past graduating class borrowed through all loan programs. *Average indebtedness per student:* $17,084. *Average need-based loan:* Freshmen: $3414. Undergraduates: $4408. *Parent loans:* $673,792 (10% need-based, 90% non-need-based). *Programs:* FFEL (Subsidized and Unsubsidized Stafford, PLUS), Perkins.

WORK-STUDY *Federal work-study:* Total amount: $1,249,405; 494 jobs averaging $2529. *State or other work-study/employment:* Total amount: $429,706 (100% non-need-based). Part-time jobs available.

APPLYING FOR FINANCIAL AID *Required financial aid forms:* FAFSA, CSS Financial Aid PROFILE. *Financial aid deadline (priority):* 2/15. *Notification date:* Continuous beginning 3/1. Students must reply by 5/1.

CONTACT Glendi Gaddis, Director of Student Financial Services, Lewis & Clark College, Templeton Student Center, MS 56, Portland, OR 97219-7899, 503-768-7096 or toll-free 800-444-4111. *Fax:* 503-768-7074. *E-mail:* sfs@lclark.edu.

LEWIS-CLARK STATE COLLEGE
Lewiston, ID

Tuition & fees: N/R	Average undergraduate aid package: $8048

ABOUT THE INSTITUTION State-supported, coed. 50 undergraduate majors. Federal methodology is used as a basis for awarding need-based institutional aid.

FRESHMAN FINANCIAL AID (Fall 2008) 473 applied for aid; of those 78% were deemed to have need. 96% of freshmen with need received aid; of those 8% had need fully met. *Average percent of need met:* 8% (excluding resources awarded to replace EFC). *Average financial aid package:* $6702 (excluding resources awarded to replace EFC). 19% of all full-time freshmen had no need and received non-need-based gift aid.

UNDERGRADUATE FINANCIAL AID (Fall 2008) 1,763 applied for aid; of those 86% were deemed to have need. 98% of undergraduates with need received

aid; of those 10% had need fully met. *Average percent of need met:* 10% (excluding resources awarded to replace EFC). *Average financial aid package:* $8048 (excluding resources awarded to replace EFC). 11% of all full-time undergraduates had no need and received non-need-based gift aid.

GIFT AID (NEED-BASED) *Total amount:* $4,880,193 (83% federal, 4% state, 5% institutional, 8% external sources). *Receiving aid:* Freshmen: 38% (224); all full-time undergraduates: 43% (973). *Average award:* Freshmen: $3434; Undergraduates: $3796. *Scholarships, grants, and awards:* Federal Pell, FSEOG, state, private, college/university gift aid from institutional funds.

GIFT AID (NON-NEED-BASED) *Total amount:* $716,530 (36% state, 47% institutional, 17% external sources). *Receiving aid:* Freshmen: 40% (237). Undergraduates: 18% (416). *Average award:* Freshmen: $1792. Undergraduates: $2758. *Scholarships, grants, and awards by category:* Academic interests/achievement: 80 awards ($157,619 total): biological sciences, business, education, English, general academic interests/achievements, health fields, humanities, mathematics, physical sciences, social sciences. Creative arts/performance: 13 awards ($26,095 total): art/fine arts, creative writing, debating, music, theater/drama. Special achievements/activities: 193 awards ($211,713 total): community service, general special achievements/activities, junior miss, leadership, rodeo. Special characteristics: 374 awards ($893,405 total): children and siblings of alumni, ethnic background, first-generation college students, general special characteristics, members of minority groups, out-of-state students, previous college experience. *Tuition waivers:* Full or partial for employees or children of employees, senior citizens.

LOANS *Student loans:* $10,426,732 (59% need-based, 41% non-need-based). 61% of past graduating class borrowed through all loan programs. *Average need-based loan:* Freshmen: $2870. Undergraduates: $3918. *Parent loans:* $348,715 (100% non-need-based). *Programs:* FFEL (Subsidized and Unsubsidized Stafford, PLUS), Perkins, Federal Nursing.

WORK-STUDY *Federal work-study:* Total amount: $119,225; 93 jobs averaging $1282. *State or other work-study/employment:* Total amount: $165,003 (65% need-based, 35% non-need-based). 143 part-time jobs averaging $1154.

ATHLETIC AWARDS Total amount: $1,577,331 (100% non-need-based).

APPLYING FOR FINANCIAL AID *Required financial aid form:* FAFSA. *Financial aid deadline (priority):* 3/1. *Notification date:* Continuous beginning 4/15. Students must reply within 2 weeks of notification.

CONTACT Ms. Laura Hughes, Director of Financial Aid, Lewis-Clark State College, 500 8th Avenue, Lewiston, ID 83501-2698, 208-792-2224 or toll-free 800-933-5272. *Fax:* 208-792-2063. *E-mail:* lhughes@lcsc.edu.

LEWIS UNIVERSITY
Romeoville, IL

Tuition & fees: $22,990	Average undergraduate aid package: $18,419

ABOUT THE INSTITUTION Independent religious, coed. 69 undergraduate majors. Federal methodology is used as a basis for awarding need-based institutional aid.

UNDERGRADUATE EXPENSES for 2009–10 *Comprehensive fee:* $31,340 includes full-time tuition ($22,990) and room and board ($8350). *College room only:* $5450. Full-time tuition and fees vary according to course level, course load, and program. Room and board charges vary according to board plan and housing facility. *Part-time tuition:* $720 per credit hour. Part-time tuition and fees vary according to course level, course load, and program. *Payment plan:* Installment.

FRESHMAN FINANCIAL AID (Fall 2009, est.) 602 applied for aid; of those 85% were deemed to have need. 100% of freshmen with need received aid; of those 47% had need fully met. *Average percent of need met:* 81% (excluding resources awarded to replace EFC). *Average financial aid package:* $16,414 (excluding resources awarded to replace EFC). 11% of all full-time freshmen had no need and received non-need-based gift aid.

UNDERGRADUATE FINANCIAL AID (Fall 2009, est.) 2,763 applied for aid; of those 86% were deemed to have need. 99% of undergraduates with need received aid; of those 69% had need fully met. *Average percent of need met:* 84% (excluding resources awarded to replace EFC). *Average financial aid package:* $18,419 (excluding resources awarded to replace EFC). 9% of all full-time undergraduates had no need and received non-need-based gift aid.

GIFT AID (NEED-BASED) *Total amount:* $11,519,176 (41% federal, 41% state, 18% institutional). *Receiving aid:* Freshmen: 56% (365); all full-time undergraduates: 36% (1,155). *Average award:* Freshmen: $8121; Undergraduates: $8954.

Scholarships, grants, and awards: Federal Pell, FSEOG, state, private, college/university gift aid from institutional funds, Federal Nursing.

GIFT AID (NON-NEED-BASED) *Total amount:* $19,851,489 (5% federal, 1% state, 91% institutional, 3% external sources). *Receiving aid:* Freshmen: 77% (499). Undergraduates: 56% (1,809). *Average award:* Freshmen: $9359. Undergraduates: $7538. *Scholarships, grants, and awards by category:* Academic interests/achievement: 2,140 awards ($15,943,062 total): general academic interests/achievements. Creative arts/performance: 14 awards ($23,500 total): art/fine arts, music, theater/drama. Special achievements/activities: 333 awards ($1,673,425 total): community service, general special achievements/activities, memberships. Special characteristics: 333 awards ($1,673,425 total): children and siblings of alumni, children of faculty/staff, religious affiliation. *Tuition waivers:* Full or partial for children of alumni, employees or children of employees, adult students.

LOANS *Student loans:* $36,340,638 (37% need-based, 63% non-need-based). 26% of past graduating class borrowed through all loan programs. *Average indebtedness per student:* $20,413. *Average need-based loan:* Freshmen: $3378. Undergraduates: $4322. *Parent loans:* $4,156,472 (100% non-need-based). *Programs:* FFEL (Subsidized and Unsubsidized Stafford, PLUS), Perkins.

WORK-STUDY *Federal work-study:* Total amount: $409,287; 385 jobs averaging $3600. *State or other work-study/employment:* Total amount: $1,214,000 (100% non-need-based). 190 part-time jobs averaging $3600.

ATHLETIC AWARDS Total amount: $2,420,000 (100% non-need-based).

APPLYING FOR FINANCIAL AID *Required financial aid form:* FAFSA. *Financial aid deadline (priority):* 5/1. *Notification date:* Continuous. Students must reply within 2 weeks of notification.

CONTACT Ms. Janeen Decharinte, Director of Financial Aid, Lewis University, One University Parkway, Romeoville, IL 60446, 815-836-5262 or toll-free 800-897-9000. *Fax:* 815-836-5135. *E-mail:* decharja@lewisu.edu.

LEXINGTON COLLEGE
Chicago, IL

Tuition & fees: $23,800	Average undergraduate aid package: N/A

ABOUT THE INSTITUTION Independent, women only. 1 undergraduate major. Federal methodology is used as a basis for awarding need-based institutional aid.

UNDERGRADUATE EXPENSES for 2009–10 *One-time required fee:* $50. *Tuition:* full-time $22,800; part-time $760 per credit hour. Full-time tuition and fees vary according to course load. Part-time tuition and fees vary according to course load. *Payment plan:* Installment.

GIFT AID (NEED-BASED) *Scholarships, grants, and awards:* Federal Pell, FSEOG, state, private, college/university gift aid from institutional funds, Academic Competitiveness Grants.

GIFT AID (NON-NEED-BASED) *Tuition waivers:* Full or partial for employees or children of employees.

LOANS *Programs:* FFEL (Subsidized and Unsubsidized Stafford, PLUS), Sallie Mae Signature Student Loans, alternative loans.

APPLYING FOR FINANCIAL AID *Required financial aid form:* FAFSA. *Financial aid deadline:* 10/1 (priority: 5/15). *Notification date:* Continuous.

CONTACT Maria Lebron, Director of Financial Aid, Lexington College, 310 South Peoria Street, Suite 512, Chicago, IL 60607, 312-226-6294 Ext. 227. *Fax:* 312-226-6405. *E-mail:* finaid@lexingtoncollege.edu.

LIBERTY UNIVERSITY
Lynchburg, VA

ABOUT THE INSTITUTION Independent nondenominational, coed. 60 undergraduate majors.

GIFT AID (NEED-BASED) *Scholarships, grants, and awards:* Federal Pell, FSEOG, state, private, college/university gift aid from institutional funds, Academic Competitiveness Grants, National SMART Grants, TEACH Grants.

GIFT AID (NON-NEED-BASED) *Scholarships, grants, and awards by category:* Academic interests/achievement: general academic interests/achievements. Creative arts/performance: debating, journalism/publications, music, performing arts. Special characteristics: children of faculty/staff, international students, local/state students, public servants, religious affiliation, veterans.

LOANS *Programs:* FFEL (Subsidized and Unsubsidized Stafford, PLUS).

WORK-STUDY Federal work-study jobs available. *State or other work-study/employment:* Part-time jobs available.

APPLYING FOR FINANCIAL AID *Required financial aid forms:* FAFSA, state aid form.

CONTACT Robert Ritz, Director, Financial Aid Office, Liberty University, 1971 University Boulevard, Lynchburg, VA 24502, 434-582-2270 or toll-free 800-543-5317. *Fax:* 434-582-2053. *E-mail:* financialaid@liberty.edu.

LIFE PACIFIC COLLEGE
San Dimas, CA

CONTACT Mrs. Becky Huyck, Director of Financial Aid, Life Pacific College, 1100 Covina Boulevard, San Dimas, CA 91773-3298, 909-599-5433 Ext. 319 or toll-free 877-886-5433 Ext. 314. *Fax:* 909-599-6690. *E-mail:* bhuyck@lifepacific.edu.

LIFE UNIVERSITY
Marietta, GA

Tuition & fees: $8352	Average undergraduate aid package: $9750

ABOUT THE INSTITUTION Independent, coed. 5 undergraduate majors. Federal methodology is used as a basis for awarding need-based institutional aid.

UNDERGRADUATE EXPENSES for 2009–10 *Comprehensive fee:* $20,832 includes full-time tuition ($7605), mandatory fees ($747), and room and board ($12,480). *College room only:* $6300. Full-time tuition and fees vary according to course load. *Part-time tuition:* $169 per credit hour. *Part-time fees:* $249 per term. Part-time tuition and fees vary according to course load. *Payment plan:* Installment.

FRESHMAN FINANCIAL AID (Fall 2009, est.) 112 applied for aid; of those 88% were deemed to have need. 95% of freshmen with need received aid. *Average financial aid package:* $9800 (excluding resources awarded to replace EFC).

UNDERGRADUATE FINANCIAL AID (Fall 2009, est.) 426 applied for aid; of those 93% were deemed to have need. 96% of undergraduates with need received aid; of those 1% had need fully met. *Average percent of need met:* 1% (excluding resources awarded to replace EFC). *Average financial aid package:* $9750 (excluding resources awarded to replace EFC). 1% of all full-time undergraduates had no need and received non-need-based gift aid.

GIFT AID (NEED-BASED) *Total amount:* $1,958,000 (99% federal, 1% institutional). *Receiving aid:* Freshmen: 52% (75); all full-time undergraduates: 50% (255). *Average award:* Freshmen: $4600; Undergraduates: $4825. *Scholarships, grants, and awards:* Federal Pell, FSEOG, state, private, college/university gift aid from institutional funds.

GIFT AID (NON-NEED-BASED) *Total amount:* $320,000 (79% state, 15% institutional, 6% external sources). *Receiving aid:* Freshmen: 49% (71). Undergraduates: 37% (189). *Average award:* Undergraduates: $1000. *Scholarships, grants, and awards by category: Academic interests/achievement:* 9 awards ($19,875 total): general academic interests/achievements. *Special achievements/activities:* 56 awards ($462,000 total): general special achievements/activities. *Special characteristics:* 10 awards ($40,854 total): general special characteristics, international students. *Tuition waivers:* Full or partial for employees or children of employees.

LOANS *Student loans:* $7,875,000 (37% need-based, 63% non-need-based). 60% of past graduating class borrowed through all loan programs. *Average indebtedness per student:* $17,600. *Average need-based loan:* Freshmen: $3900. Undergraduates: $5000. *Parent loans:* $213,000 (100% need-based). *Programs:* FFEL (Subsidized and Unsubsidized Stafford, PLUS), Perkins, college/university, alternative loans.

WORK-STUDY *Federal work-study:* Total amount: $358,000; 232 jobs averaging $1500.

ATHLETIC AWARDS Total amount: $462,000 (100% non-need-based).

APPLYING FOR FINANCIAL AID *Required financial aid forms:* FAFSA, institution's own form. *Financial aid deadline (priority):* 3/1. *Notification date:* Continuous beginning 5/1.

CONTACT Melissa Waters, Director of Financial Aid, Life University, 1269 Barclay Circle, Marietta, GA 30060, 770-426-2901 or toll-free 800-543-3202 (in-state). *Fax:* 770-426-2926. *E-mail:* finaid@life.edu.

LIM COLLEGE
New York, NY

CONTACT Mr. Christopher Barto, Dean of Student Financial Services, LIM College, 12 East 53rd Street, New York, NY 10022-5268, 212-752-1530 or toll-free 800-677-1323. *Fax:* 212-317-8602. *E-mail:* cbarto@limcollege.edu.

LIMESTONE COLLEGE
Gaffney, SC

Tuition & fees: $19,200	Average undergraduate aid package: $13,082

ABOUT THE INSTITUTION Independent, coed. 49 undergraduate majors. Federal methodology is used as a basis for awarding need-based institutional aid.

UNDERGRADUATE EXPENSES for 2010–11 *Comprehensive fee:* $26,200 includes full-time tuition ($19,200) and room and board ($7000). *College room only:* $3500. Full-time tuition and fees vary according to class time and location. Room and board charges vary according to housing facility. *Part-time tuition:* $800 per semester hour. Part-time tuition and fees vary according to class time and location. *Payment plan:* Installment.

FRESHMAN FINANCIAL AID (Fall 2009, est.) 257 applied for aid; of those 82% were deemed to have need. 100% of freshmen with need received aid; of those 16% had need fully met. *Average percent of need met:* 52% (excluding resources awarded to replace EFC). *Average financial aid package:* $12,863 (excluding resources awarded to replace EFC). 9% of all full-time freshmen had no need and received non-need-based gift aid.

UNDERGRADUATE FINANCIAL AID (Fall 2009, est.) 740 applied for aid; of those 87% were deemed to have need. 100% of undergraduates with need received aid; of those 32% had need fully met. *Average percent of need met:* 45% (excluding resources awarded to replace EFC). *Average financial aid package:* $13,082 (excluding resources awarded to replace EFC). 9% of all full-time undergraduates had no need and received non-need-based gift aid.

GIFT AID (NEED-BASED) *Total amount:* $5,354,545 (29% federal, 14% state, 55% institutional, 2% external sources). *Receiving aid:* Freshmen: 76% (212); all full-time undergraduates: 69% (550). *Average award:* Freshmen: $11,764; Undergraduates: $11,174. *Scholarships, grants, and awards:* Federal Pell, FSEOG, state, private, college/university gift aid from institutional funds.

GIFT AID (NON-NEED-BASED) *Total amount:* $885,098 (76% state, 17% institutional, 7% external sources). *Receiving aid:* Freshmen: 10% (27). Undergraduates: 17% (137). *Average award:* Freshmen: $4337. Undergraduates: $4807. *Scholarships, grants, and awards by category: Academic interests/achievement:* biological sciences, business, communication, computer science, education, English, general academic interests/achievements, humanities, mathematics, physical sciences, religion/biblical studies, social sciences. *Creative arts/performance:* art/fine arts, music, performing arts, theater/drama. *Special achievements/activities:* cheerleading/drum major, general special achievements/activities, leadership, religious involvement. *Special characteristics:* children and siblings of alumni, children of faculty/staff, first-generation college students, local/state students, out-of-state students, siblings of current students. *Tuition waivers:* Full or partial for employees or children of employees.

LOANS *Student loans:* $4,465,524 (59% need-based, 41% non-need-based). *Average need-based loan:* Freshmen: $3033. Undergraduates: $3755. *Parent loans:* $855,854 (41% need-based, 59% non-need-based). *Programs:* FFEL (Subsidized and Unsubsidized Stafford, PLUS), Perkins.

WORK-STUDY *Federal work-study:* Total amount: $253,660; jobs available. *State or other work-study/employment:* Total amount: $54,882 (19% need-based, 81% non-need-based). Part-time jobs available.

ATHLETIC AWARDS Total amount: $2,195,404 (55% need-based, 45% non-need-based).

APPLYING FOR FINANCIAL AID *Required financial aid form:* FAFSA. *Financial aid deadline (priority):* 2/1. *Notification date:* Continuous. Students must reply within 3 weeks of notification.

CONTACT Mr. Bobby Greer, Acting Director of Financial Aid, Limestone College, 1115 College Drive, Gaffney, SC 29340-3799, 864-488-4567 or toll-free 800-795-7151 Ext. 554. *Fax:* 864-487-8706. *E-mail:* bgreer@limestone.edu.

LINCOLN CHRISTIAN UNIVERSITY
Lincoln, IL

ABOUT THE INSTITUTION Independent religious, coed. 13 undergraduate majors.

GIFT AID (NEED-BASED) *Scholarships, grants, and awards:* Federal Pell, FSEOG, state, college/university gift aid from institutional funds.

GIFT AID (NON-NEED-BASED) *Scholarships, grants, and awards by category:* *Academic interests/achievement:* general academic interests/achievements. *Special achievements/activities:* community service, leadership. *Special characteristics:* children of faculty/staff.

LOANS *Programs:* FFEL (Subsidized and Unsubsidized Stafford, PLUS), Perkins, college/university.

APPLYING FOR FINANCIAL AID *Required financial aid form:* FAFSA.

CONTACT Nancy Siddens, Financial Aid Director, Lincoln Christian University, 100 Campus View Drive, Lincoln, IL 62656, 217-732-3168 Ext. 2250 or toll-free 888-522-5228. *Fax:* 217-732-5914. *E-mail:* finaid@lccs.edu.

LINCOLN COLLEGE–NORMAL
Normal, IL

CONTACT Deb Keist, Assistant Director of Financial Aid, Lincoln College–Normal, 715 West Raab Road, Normal, IL 61761, 309-452-0500 or toll-free 800-569-0558. *Fax:* 309-454-5652.

LINCOLN COLLEGE OF NEW ENGLAND
Southington, CT

CONTACT Deborah Flinn, Director of Financial Aid, Lincoln College of New England, 2279 Mt. Vernon Road, Southington, CT 06489, 860-628-4751 Ext. 18 or toll-free 800-952-2444 (in-state). *Fax:* 860-628-6444. *E-mail:* 74623.74@compuserv.com.

LINCOLN MEMORIAL UNIVERSITY
Harrogate, TN

Tuition & fees: $15,700   **Average undergraduate aid package:** $16,166

ABOUT THE INSTITUTION Independent, coed. 42 undergraduate majors. Federal methodology is used as a basis for awarding need-based institutional aid.

UNDERGRADUATE EXPENSES for 2009–10 *Comprehensive fee:* $21,380 includes full-time tuition ($15,120), mandatory fees ($580), and room and board ($5680). *College room only:* $2540. Room and board charges vary according to board plan and housing facility. *Part-time tuition:* $630 per credit. *Part-time fees:* $630 per credit hour; $290 per term. *Payment plan:* Installment.

GIFT AID (NEED-BASED) *Total amount:* $13,960,797 (26% federal, 18% state, 53% institutional, 3% external sources). *Receiving aid:* Freshmen: 90% (282); all full-time undergraduates: 83% (1,064). *Average award:* Freshmen: $14,047; Undergraduates: $11,463. *Scholarships, grants, and awards:* Federal Pell, FSEOG, state, private, college/university gift aid from institutional funds.

GIFT AID (NON-NEED-BASED) *Total amount:* $1,914,980 (20% state, 70% institutional, 10% external sources). *Receiving aid:* Freshmen: 3% (9). Undergraduates: 10% (125). *Average award:* Freshmen: $4077. Undergraduates: $1793. *Scholarships, grants, and awards by category:* *Academic interests/achievement:* general academic interests/achievements. *Creative arts/performance:* music. *Special achievements/activities:* cheerleading/drum major. *Special characteristics:* children of faculty/staff. *Tuition waivers:* Full or partial for employees or children of employees, senior citizens.

LOANS *Student loans:* $7,226,293 (83% need-based, 17% non-need-based). 60% of past graduating class borrowed through all loan programs. *Average indebtedness per student:* $10,623. *Average need-based loan:* Freshmen: $3487. Undergraduates: $2625. *Parent loans:* $292,984 (28% need-based, 72% non-need-based). *Programs:* FFEL (Subsidized and Unsubsidized Stafford, PLUS), Perkins.

ATHLETIC AWARDS Total amount: $945,972 (46% need-based, 54% non-need-based).

APPLYING FOR FINANCIAL AID *Required financial aid form:* FAFSA. *Financial aid deadline (priority):* 4/1. *Notification date:* Continuous. Students must reply within 3 weeks of notification.

CONTACT Bryan Erslan, Director of Financial Aid, Lincoln Memorial University, Cumberland Gap Parkway, Harrogate, TN 37752-1901, 423-869-6465 or toll-free 800-325-0900. *Fax:* 423-869-6347. *E-mail:* bryan.erslan@lmunet.edu.

LINCOLN UNIVERSITY
Oakland, CA

CONTACT Mrs. Connie Lam, Director of Admissions, Lincoln University, 401 15th Street, Oakland, CA 94612, 415-221-1212.

LINCOLN UNIVERSITY
Jefferson City, MO

Tuition & fees (MO res): $5685   **Average undergraduate aid package:** $9587

ABOUT THE INSTITUTION State-supported, coed. 41 undergraduate majors. Federal methodology is used as a basis for awarding need-based institutional aid.

UNDERGRADUATE EXPENSES for 2010–11 *Tuition, state resident:* full-time $5685; part-time $189.50 per credit hour. *Tuition, nonresident:* full-time $10,395; part-time $346.50 per credit hour. *Required fees:* $15 per credit hour or $20 per term. Full-time tuition and fees vary according to location and reciprocity agreements. Part-time tuition and fees vary according to location and reciprocity agreements. Room and board charges vary according to board plan and housing facility. *Payment plan:* Installment.

FRESHMAN FINANCIAL AID (Fall 2009, est.) 631 applied for aid; of those 96% were deemed to have need. 100% of freshmen with need received aid; of those 6% had need fully met. *Average percent of need met:* 84% (excluding resources awarded to replace EFC). *Average financial aid package:* $9258 (excluding resources awarded to replace EFC).

UNDERGRADUATE FINANCIAL AID (Fall 2009, est.) 1,723 applied for aid; of those 95% were deemed to have need. 100% of undergraduates with need received aid; of those 11% had need fully met. *Average percent of need met:* 80% (excluding resources awarded to replace EFC). *Average financial aid package:* $9587 (excluding resources awarded to replace EFC). 1% of all full-time undergraduates had no need and received non-need-based gift aid.

GIFT AID (NEED-BASED) *Total amount:* $10,168,657 (65% federal, 9% state, 14% institutional, 12% external sources). *Receiving aid:* Freshmen: 76% (540); all full-time undergraduates: 67% (1,408). *Average award:* Freshmen: $5656; Undergraduates: $5422. *Scholarships, grants, and awards:* Federal Pell, FSEOG, state, private, college/university gift aid from institutional funds.

GIFT AID (NON-NEED-BASED) *Total amount:* $256,524 (10% federal, 3% state, 87% institutional). *Receiving aid:* Freshmen: 2% (14). Undergraduates: 2% (42). *Average award:* Undergraduates: $5534. *Scholarships, grants, and awards by category:* *Academic interests/achievement:* 211 awards ($423,993 total): agriculture, education, general academic interests/achievements, military science. *Creative arts/performance:* 120 awards ($199,687 total): art/fine arts, journalism/publications, music, performing arts, theater/drama. *Special achievements/activities:* 5 awards ($2592 total): cheerleading/drum major. *Special characteristics:* 253 awards ($338,147 total): adult students, children of faculty/staff, out-of-state students. *Tuition waivers:* Full or partial for employees or children of employees.

LOANS *Student loans:* $14,660,914 (45% need-based, 55% non-need-based). 66% of past graduating class borrowed through all loan programs. *Average indebtedness per student:* $26,114. *Average need-based loan:* Freshmen: $3394. Undergraduates: $3894. *Parent loans:* $726,860 (100% non-need-based). *Programs:* FFEL (Subsidized and Unsubsidized Stafford, PLUS).

WORK-STUDY *Federal work-study:* Total amount: $189,970; 164 jobs averaging $1161. *State or other work-study/employment:* Total amount: $712,904 (100% non-need-based). 223 part-time jobs averaging $3209.

ATHLETIC AWARDS Total amount: $986,568 (100% need-based).

APPLYING FOR FINANCIAL AID *Required financial aid forms:* FAFSA, institution's own form. *Financial aid deadline (priority):* 3/1. *Notification date:* Continuous beginning 3/15. Students must reply within 2 weeks of notification.

CONTACT Mr. Alfred Robinson, Director of Financial Aid, Lincoln University, 820 Chestnut Street, Jefferson City, MO 65102-0029, 573-681-6156 or toll-free 800-521-5052. *Fax:* 573-681-5871. *E-mail:* robinsona@lincolnu.edu.

LINCOLN UNIVERSITY
Lincoln University, PA

Tuition & fees (PA res): $8222   **Average undergraduate aid package:** $9060

Lincoln University

ABOUT THE INSTITUTION State-related, coed. 46 undergraduate majors. Federal methodology is used as a basis for awarding need-based institutional aid.

UNDERGRADUATE EXPENSES for 2009–10 *Tuition, state resident:* full-time $5862; part-time $246 per credit hour. *Tuition, nonresident:* full-time $9976; part-time $417 per credit hour. *Required fees:* full-time $2360; $102 per credit hour. Part-time tuition and fees vary according to course load. *College room and board:* $7770; *Room only:* $4218. Room and board charges vary according to board plan and housing facility. *Payment plans:* Installment, deferred payment.

FRESHMAN FINANCIAL AID (Fall 2009, est.) 562 applied for aid; of those 94% were deemed to have need. 94% of freshmen with need received aid; of those .2% had need fully met. *Average percent of need met:* 27% (excluding resources awarded to replace EFC). *Average financial aid package:* $5302 (excluding resources awarded to replace EFC). 1% of all full-time freshmen had no need and received non-need-based gift aid.

UNDERGRADUATE FINANCIAL AID (Fall 2009, est.) 1,913 applied for aid; of those 94% were deemed to have need. 97% of undergraduates with need received aid; of those 3% had need fully met. *Average percent of need met:* 49% (excluding resources awarded to replace EFC). *Average financial aid package:* $9060 (excluding resources awarded to replace EFC). 2% of all full-time undergraduates had no need and received non-need-based gift aid.

GIFT AID (NEED-BASED) *Total amount:* $7,058,394 (74% federal, 21% state, 4% institutional, 1% external sources). *Receiving aid:* Freshmen: 66% (382); all full-time undergraduates: 67% (1,349). *Average award:* Freshmen: $3520; Undergraduates: $5122. *Scholarships, grants, and awards:* Federal Pell, FSEOG, state, private, college/university gift aid from institutional funds, United Negro College Fund.

GIFT AID (NON-NEED-BASED) *Total amount:* $2,064,926 (10% state, 80% institutional, 10% external sources). *Receiving aid:* Freshmen: 23% (134). Undergraduates: 32% (635). *Average award:* Freshmen: $1787. Undergraduates: $3740. *Scholarships, grants, and awards by category: Academic interests/ achievement:* biological sciences, business, communication, computer science, education, English, general academic interests/achievements, humanities, mathematics, physical sciences, social sciences. *Creative arts/performance:* music. *Special achievements/activities:* general special achievements/activities. *Special characteristics:* children and siblings of alumni, children of faculty/staff, international students. *Tuition waivers:* Full or partial for employees or children of employees.

LOANS *Student loans:* $14,119,924 (96% need-based, 4% non-need-based). 89% of past graduating class borrowed through all loan programs. *Average indebtedness per student:* $30,818. *Average need-based loan:* Freshmen: $1912. Undergraduates: $3740. *Parent loans:* $2,757,375 (100% non-need-based). *Programs:* FFEL (Subsidized and Unsubsidized Stafford, PLUS), Perkins.

WORK-STUDY *Federal work-study:* Total amount: $189,020; 146 jobs averaging $1294.

ATHLETIC AWARDS Total amount: $482,902 (100% non-need-based).

APPLYING FOR FINANCIAL AID *Required financial aid form:* FAFSA. *Financial aid deadline:* 5/1. *Notification date:* Continuous. Students must reply within 2 weeks of notification.

CONTACT Thelma Ross, Director of Financial Aid, Lincoln University, PO Box 179, Lincoln University, PA 19352, 484-365-7583 or toll-free 800-790-0191. *Fax:* 484-365-8198. *E-mail:* tross@lincoln.edu.

LINDENWOOD UNIVERSITY
St. Charles, MO

Tuition & fees: $13,600	Average undergraduate aid package: $5855

ABOUT THE INSTITUTION Independent Presbyterian, coed. 91 undergraduate majors. Federal methodology is used as a basis for awarding need-based institutional aid.

UNDERGRADUATE EXPENSES for 2010–11 *Comprehensive fee:* $20,810 includes full-time tuition ($13,260), mandatory fees ($340), and room and board ($7210). *College room only:* $3980. Full-time tuition and fees vary according to program. *Part-time tuition:* $380 per credit hour. Part-time tuition and fees vary according to course load. *Payment plans:* Installment, deferred payment.

FRESHMAN FINANCIAL AID (Fall 2009, est.) 744 applied for aid; of those 86% were deemed to have need. 100% of freshmen with need received aid; of those 35% had need fully met. *Average percent of need met:* 90% (excluding resources awarded to replace EFC). *Average financial aid package:* $7175

(excluding resources awarded to replace EFC). 28% of all full-time freshmen had no need and received non-need-based gift aid.

UNDERGRADUATE FINANCIAL AID (Fall 2009, est.) 4,336 applied for aid; of those 91% were deemed to have need. 100% of undergraduates with need received aid; of those 42% had need fully met. *Average percent of need met:* 91% (excluding resources awarded to replace EFC). *Average financial aid package:* $5855 (excluding resources awarded to replace EFC). 15% of all full-time undergraduates had no need and received non-need-based gift aid.

GIFT AID (NEED-BASED) *Total amount:* $28,640,000 (25% federal, 19% state, 56% institutional). *Receiving aid:* Freshmen: 38% (403); all full-time undergraduates: 41% (2,536). *Average award:* Freshmen: $3274; Undergraduates: $3662. *Scholarships, grants, and awards:* Federal Pell, FSEOG, state, private, college/ university gift aid from institutional funds.

GIFT AID (NON-NEED-BASED) *Total amount:* $9,969,500 (3% state, 95% institutional, 2% external sources). *Receiving aid:* Freshmen: 29% (304). Undergraduates: 24% (1,469). *Average award:* Freshmen: $4431. Undergraduates: $4685. *Scholarships, grants, and awards by category: Academic interests/ achievement:* biological sciences, business, communication, computer science, education, engineering/technologies, English, foreign languages, general academic interests/achievements, health fields, humanities, international studies, library science, mathematics, military science, physical sciences, premedicine, religion/ biblical studies, social sciences. *Creative arts/performance:* applied art and design, art/fine arts, cinema/film/broadcasting, dance, general creative arts/ performance, journalism/publications, music, performing arts, theater/drama. *Special achievements/activities:* cheerleading/drum major, community service, general special achievements/activities, junior miss, leadership, rodeo. *Tuition waivers:* Full or partial for employees or children of employees, senior citizens.

LOANS *Student loans:* $37,000,000 (51% need-based, 49% non-need-based). *Average need-based loan:* Freshmen: $2472. Undergraduates: $1984. *Parent loans:* $1,700,000 (100% non-need-based). *Programs:* Federal Direct (Subsidized and Unsubsidized Stafford, PLUS), FFEL (Subsidized Stafford).

WORK-STUDY *Federal work-study:* Total amount: $500,000; jobs available (averaging $2400). *State or other work-study/employment:* Total amount: $6,400,000 (66% need-based, 34% non-need-based). Part-time jobs available.

APPLYING FOR FINANCIAL AID *Required financial aid form:* FAFSA. *Financial aid deadline (priority):* 4/1. *Notification date:* Continuous. Students must reply within 2 weeks of notification.

CONTACT Lori Bode, Director of Financial Aid, Lindenwood University, 209 South Kingshighway, St. Charles, MO 63301-1695, 636-949-4925. *Fax:* 636-949-4924.. *E-mail:* lbode@lindenwood.edu.

LINDSEY WILSON COLLEGE
Columbia, KY

Tuition & fees: $18,950	Average undergraduate aid package: $15,082

ABOUT THE INSTITUTION Independent United Methodist, coed. 34 undergraduate majors. Federal methodology is used as a basis for awarding need-based institutional aid.

UNDERGRADUATE EXPENSES for 2010–11 *Comprehensive fee:* $26,595 includes full-time tuition ($18,720), mandatory fees ($230), and room and board ($7645). *Part-time tuition:* $780 per credit hour. *Payment plan:* Installment.

FRESHMAN FINANCIAL AID (Fall 2009, est.) 562 applied for aid; of those 95% were deemed to have need. 100% of freshmen with need received aid; of those 33% had need fully met. *Average financial aid package:* $15,063 (excluding resources awarded to replace EFC).

UNDERGRADUATE FINANCIAL AID (Fall 2009, est.) 2,012 applied for aid; of those 94% were deemed to have need. 97% of undergraduates with need received aid; of those 38% had need fully met. *Average financial aid package:* $15,082 (excluding resources awarded to replace EFC).

GIFT AID (NEED-BASED) *Total amount:* $13,083,553 (45% federal, 22% state, 32% institutional, 1% external sources). *Receiving aid:* Freshmen: 95% (533); all full-time undergraduates: 91% (1,833). *Average award:* Freshmen: $14,797; Undergraduates: $11,907. *Scholarships, grants, and awards:* Federal Pell, FSEOG, state, private, college/university gift aid from institutional funds.

GIFT AID (NON-NEED-BASED) *Scholarships, grants, and awards by category: Academic interests/achievement:* biological sciences, business, education, English, general academic interests/achievements, mathematics, premedicine, religion/ biblical studies. *Creative arts/performance:* applied art and design, music. *Special achievements/activities:* cheerleading/drum major, general special achievements/ activities, junior miss, leadership, religious involvement. *Special characteristics:*

children and siblings of alumni, children of faculty/staff, relatives of clergy, religious affiliation. *Tuition waivers:* Full or partial for employees or children of employees, senior citizens.

LOANS *Student loans:* $9,216,167 (100% need-based). 88% of past graduating class borrowed through all loan programs. *Average indebtedness per student:* $24,741. *Average need-based loan:* Freshmen: $2905. Undergraduates: $4233. *Parent loans:* $454,625 (100% need-based). *Programs:* FFEL (Subsidized and Unsubsidized Stafford, PLUS), Perkins, college/university.

WORK-STUDY *Federal work-study:* Total amount: $244,926; 195 jobs averaging $1240. *State or other work-study/employment:* Part-time jobs available.

ATHLETIC AWARDS Total amount: $507,159 (100% need-based).

APPLYING FOR FINANCIAL AID *Required financial aid form:* FAFSA. *Financial aid deadline (priority):* 4/1. *Notification date:* Continuous beginning 4/15. Students must reply within 2 weeks of notification.

CONTACT Ms. Marilyn D. Radford, Director of Student Financial Services, Lindsey Wilson College, 210 Lindsey Wilson Street, Columbia, KY 42728, 270-384-8022 or toll-free 800-264-0138. *Fax:* 270-384-8591. *E-mail:* radfordm@lindsey.edu.

LINFIELD COLLEGE
McMinnville, OR

Tuition & fees: $29,034	Average undergraduate aid package: $19,168

ABOUT THE INSTITUTION Independent American Baptist Churches in the USA, coed. 41 undergraduate majors. Federal methodology is used as a basis for awarding need-based institutional aid.

UNDERGRADUATE EXPENSES for 2009–10 *Comprehensive fee:* $37,314 includes full-time tuition ($28,760), mandatory fees ($274), and room and board ($8280). *College room only:* $4480. Full-time tuition and fees vary according to location. Room and board charges vary according to board plan, housing facility, and location. *Part-time tuition:* $895 per semester hour. Part-time tuition and fees vary according to course load and location. *Payment plan:* Installment.

FRESHMAN FINANCIAL AID (Fall 2009, est.) 299 applied for aid; of those 100% were deemed to have need. 100% of freshmen with need received aid; of those 35% had need fully met. *Average percent of need met:* 84% (excluding resources awarded to replace EFC). *Average financial aid package:* $19,474 (excluding resources awarded to replace EFC). 29% of all full-time freshmen had no need and received non-need-based gift aid.

UNDERGRADUATE FINANCIAL AID (Fall 2009, est.) 1,106 applied for aid; of those 100% were deemed to have need. 100% of undergraduates with need received aid; of those 26% had need fully met. *Average percent of need met:* 85% (excluding resources awarded to replace EFC). *Average financial aid package:* $19,168 (excluding resources awarded to replace EFC). 31% of all full-time undergraduates had no need and received non-need-based gift aid.

GIFT AID (NEED-BASED) *Total amount:* $18,153,735 (12% federal, 2% state, 81% institutional, 5% external sources). *Receiving aid:* Freshmen: 60% (254); all full-time undergraduates: 60% (956). *Average award:* Freshmen: $13,361; Undergraduates: $9252. *Scholarships, grants, and awards:* Federal Pell, FSEOG, state, private, college/university gift aid from institutional funds.

GIFT AID (NON-NEED-BASED) *Total amount:* $4,319,024 (98% institutional, 2% external sources). *Receiving aid:* Freshmen: 40% (169). Undergraduates: 41% (645). *Average award:* Freshmen: $13,155. Undergraduates: $11,388. *Scholarships, grants, and awards by category: Academic interests/achievement:* 1,018 awards ($9,186,089 total): general academic interests/achievements. *Creative arts/performance:* 52 awards ($89,250 total): debating, music, theater/drama. *Special achievements/activities:* 79 awards ($97,850 total): community service, leadership. *Special characteristics:* 80 awards ($1,120,817 total): children of faculty/staff, members of minority groups. *Tuition waivers:* Full or partial for employees or children of employees, senior citizens.

LOANS *Student loans:* $8,630,832 (91% need-based, 9% non-need-based). 72% of past graduating class borrowed through all loan programs. *Average indebtedness per student:* $27,750. *Average need-based loan:* Freshmen: $3320. Undergraduates: $4280. *Parent loans:* $2,695,254 (100% non-need-based). *Programs:* Federal Direct (Subsidized and Unsubsidized Stafford, PLUS), Perkins, private loans.

WORK-STUDY *Federal work-study:* Total amount: $1,741,093; 759 jobs averaging $2201. *State or other work-study/employment:* Total amount: $1,371,410 (38% need-based, 62% non-need-based). 588 part-time jobs averaging $2273.

APPLYING FOR FINANCIAL AID *Required financial aid form:* FAFSA. *Financial aid deadline (priority):* 2/1. *Notification date:* 4/1. Students must reply by 5/1 or within 2 weeks of notification.

CONTACT Ms. Crisanne Werner, Director of Financial Aid, Linfield College, 900 Southeast Baker Street, A484, McMinnville, OR 97128-6894, 503-883-2225 or toll-free 800-640-2287. *Fax:* 503-883-2486. *E-mail:* finaid@linfield.edu.

LIPSCOMB UNIVERSITY
Nashville, TN

Tuition & fees: $20,390	Average undergraduate aid package: $16,409

ABOUT THE INSTITUTION Independent religious, coed. 85 undergraduate majors. Both federal and institutional methodology are used as a basis for awarding need-based institutional aid.

UNDERGRADUATE EXPENSES for 2009–10 *Comprehensive fee:* $28,240 includes full-time tuition ($19,330), mandatory fees ($1060), and room and board ($7850). *College room only:* $4720. Full-time tuition and fees vary according to class time, course load, and degree level. Room and board charges vary according to board plan and housing facility. *Part-time tuition:* $775 per hour. *Part-time fees:* $45 per credit hour. Part-time tuition and fees vary according to class time, course load, and degree level. *Payment plans:* Installment, deferred payment.

FRESHMAN FINANCIAL AID (Fall 2009, est.) 591 applied for aid; of those 70% were deemed to have need. 100% of freshmen with need received aid; of those 21% had need fully met. *Average percent of need met:* 62% (excluding resources awarded to replace EFC). *Average financial aid package:* $15,500 (excluding resources awarded to replace EFC). 21% of all full-time freshmen had no need and received non-need-based gift aid.

UNDERGRADUATE FINANCIAL AID (Fall 2009, est.) 2,196 applied for aid; of those 68% were deemed to have need. 100% of undergraduates with need received aid; of those 30% had need fully met. *Average percent of need met:* 62% (excluding resources awarded to replace EFC). *Average financial aid package:* $16,409 (excluding resources awarded to replace EFC). 17% of all full-time undergraduates had no need and received non-need-based gift aid.

GIFT AID (NEED-BASED) *Total amount:* $15,234,199 (18% federal, 25% state, 50% institutional, 7% external sources). *Receiving aid:* Freshmen: 32% (190); all full-time undergraduates: 28% (665). *Average award:* Freshmen: $6128; Undergraduates: $6819. *Scholarships, grants, and awards:* Federal Pell, FSEOG, state, private, college/university gift aid from institutional funds.

GIFT AID (NON-NEED-BASED) *Total amount:* $2,324,976 (56% state, 39% institutional, 5% external sources). *Receiving aid:* Freshmen: 67% (399). Undergraduates: 49% (1,175). *Average award:* Freshmen: $5490. Undergraduates: $6645. *Scholarships, grants, and awards by category: Academic interests/achievement:* biological sciences, business, communication, education, engineering/technologies, English, general academic interests/achievements, home economics, mathematics, premedicine, religion/biblical studies. *Creative arts/performance:* art/fine arts, journalism/publications, music, theater/drama. *Special achievements/activities:* cheerleading/drum major, community service, general special achievements/activities, leadership, religious involvement. *Special characteristics:* adult students, children and siblings of alumni, children of educators, children of faculty/staff, children with a deceased or disabled parent, international students, members of minority groups, relatives of clergy. *Tuition waivers:* Full or partial for employees or children of employees.

LOANS *Student loans:* $9,942,981 (90% need-based, 10% non-need-based). 64% of past graduating class borrowed through all loan programs. *Average indebtedness per student:* $19,523. *Average need-based loan:* Freshmen: $3538. Undergraduates: $4975. *Parent loans:* $3,748,528 (86% need-based, 14% non-need-based). *Programs:* FFEL (Subsidized and Unsubsidized Stafford, PLUS), Perkins, Federal Nursing.

WORK-STUDY *Federal work-study:* Total amount: $175,139; jobs available.

ATHLETIC AWARDS Total amount: $2,623,001 (65% need-based, 35% non-need-based).

APPLYING FOR FINANCIAL AID *Required financial aid form:* FAFSA. *Financial aid deadline (priority):* 2/15. *Notification date:* Continuous beginning 2/15.

CONTACT Mrs. Karita McCaleb Waters, Director of Financial Aid, Lipscomb University, One University Park Drive, Nashville, TN 37204-3951, 615-966-1791 or toll-free 877-582-4766. *Fax:* 615-966-7640. *E-mail:* karita.waters@lipscomb.edu.

LIVINGSTONE COLLEGE
Salisbury, NC

CONTACT Mrs. Terry Jefferies, Financial Aid Director, Livingstone College, 701 West Monroe Street, Price Building, Salisbury, NC 28144-5298, 704-216-6069 or toll-free 800-835-3435. *Fax:* 704-216-6319. *E-mail:* tjefferies@livingstone.edu.

LOCK HAVEN UNIVERSITY OF PENNSYLVANIA
Lock Haven, PA

Tuition & fees (PA res): $7201	Average undergraduate aid package: $8394

ABOUT THE INSTITUTION State-supported, coed. 47 undergraduate majors. Federal methodology is used as a basis for awarding need-based institutional aid.

UNDERGRADUATE EXPENSES for 2009–10 *One-time required fee:* $25. *Tuition, state resident:* full-time $5554; part-time $231 per credit hour. *Tuition, nonresident:* full-time $11,886; part-time $495 per credit hour. *Required fees:* full-time $1647; $44.35 per credit hour or $119 per term. Full-time tuition and fees vary according to course load and location. Part-time tuition and fees vary according to course load and location. *College room and board:* $6736; *Room only:* $3648. Room and board charges vary according to board plan and housing facility. *Payment plans:* Installment, deferred payment.

FRESHMAN FINANCIAL AID (Fall 2009, est.) 1,149 applied for aid; of those 77% were deemed to have need. 100% of freshmen with need received aid; of those 45% had need fully met. *Average percent of need met:* 75% (excluding resources awarded to replace EFC). *Average financial aid package:* $8394 (excluding resources awarded to replace EFC). 2% of all full-time freshmen had no need and received non-need-based gift aid.

UNDERGRADUATE FINANCIAL AID (Fall 2009, est.) 4,340 applied for aid; of those 77% were deemed to have need. 100% of undergraduates with need received aid; of those 55% had need fully met. *Average percent of need met:* 75% (excluding resources awarded to replace EFC). *Average financial aid package:* $8394 (excluding resources awarded to replace EFC). 5% of all full-time undergraduates had no need and received non-need-based gift aid.

GIFT AID (NEED-BASED) *Total amount:* $14,141,812 (60% federal, 37% state, 1% institutional, 2% external sources). *Receiving aid:* Freshmen: 49% (584); all full-time undergraduates: 48% (2,205). *Average award:* Freshmen: $6304; Undergraduates: $6304. *Scholarships, grants, and awards:* Federal Pell, FSEOG, state, private, college/university gift aid from institutional funds, United Negro College Fund.

GIFT AID (NON-NEED-BASED) *Total amount:* $729,077 (1% state, 25% institutional, 74% external sources). *Receiving aid:* Freshmen: 4% (48). Undergraduates: 5% (215). *Average award:* Freshmen: $1835. Undergraduates: $1076. *Scholarships, grants, and awards by category:* Academic interests/achievement: 113 awards ($257,936 total): biological sciences, communication, education, English, foreign languages, general academic interests/achievements, health fields, international studies, library science, mathematics, physical sciences, premedicine, social sciences. *Creative arts/performance:* 41 awards ($33,190 total): art/fine arts, journalism/publications, music. *Special achievements/activities:* leadership, memberships. *Special characteristics:* 82 awards ($179,169 total): handicapped students, local/state students, members of minority groups, previous college experience. *Tuition waivers:* Full or partial for minority students, employees or children of employees, senior citizens.

LOANS *Student loans:* $33,443,341 (41% need-based, 59% non-need-based). 85% of past graduating class borrowed through all loan programs. *Average indebtedness per student:* $22,585. *Average need-based loan:* Freshmen: $3233. Undergraduates: $4172. *Parent loans:* $2,591,935 (100% non-need-based). *Programs:* FFEL (Subsidized and Unsubsidized Stafford, PLUS), Perkins, college/university.

WORK-STUDY *Federal work-study:* Total amount: $319,053; 295 jobs averaging $1252. *State or other work-study/employment:* Total amount: $1,250,521 (100% non-need-based). 951 part-time jobs averaging $711.

ATHLETIC AWARDS Total amount: $755,137 (100% non-need-based).

APPLYING FOR FINANCIAL AID *Required financial aid form:* FAFSA. *Financial aid deadline:* 3/15. *Notification date:* Continuous beginning 4/1. Students must reply by 5/1 or within 2 weeks of notification.

CONTACT James Theeuwes, Director, Financial Services, Lock Haven University of Pennsylvania, Russell Hall 118, Lock Haven, PA 17745-2390, 570-484-2344 or toll-free 800-332-8900 (in-state), 800-233-8978 (out-of-state). *Fax:* 570-484-2918. *E-mail:* jtheeuwe@lhup.edu.

LOGAN UNIVERSITY–COLLEGE OF CHIROPRACTIC
Chesterfield, MO

CONTACT Linda K. Haman, Director of Financial Aid, Logan University–College of Chiropractic, 1851 Schoettler Road, PO Box 1065, Chesterfield, MO 63006-1065, 636-227-2100 Ext. 141 or toll-free 800-533-9210.

LOMA LINDA UNIVERSITY
Loma Linda, CA

CONTACT Verdell Schaefer, Director of Financial Aid, Loma Linda University, 11139 Anderson Street, Loma Linda, CA 92350, 909-558-4509. *Fax:* 909-558-4879. *E-mail:* finaid@univ.llu.edu.

LONG ISLAND UNIVERSITY, BROOKLYN CAMPUS
Brooklyn, NY

Tuition & fees: N/R	Average undergraduate aid package: $15,300

ABOUT THE INSTITUTION Independent, coed. 64 undergraduate majors. Federal methodology is used as a basis for awarding need-based institutional aid.

FRESHMAN FINANCIAL AID (Fall 2009, est.) 1,003 applied for aid; of those 81% were deemed to have need. 98% of freshmen with need received aid; of those 49% had need fully met. *Average percent of need met:* 52% (excluding resources awarded to replace EFC). *Average financial aid package:* $14,700 (excluding resources awarded to replace EFC). 11% of all full-time freshmen had no need and received non-need-based gift aid.

UNDERGRADUATE FINANCIAL AID (Fall 2009, est.) 3,893 applied for aid; of those 94% were deemed to have need. 94% of undergraduates with need received aid; of those 46% had need fully met. *Average percent of need met:* 45% (excluding resources awarded to replace EFC). *Average financial aid package:* $15,300 (excluding resources awarded to replace EFC). 5% of all full-time undergraduates had no need and received non-need-based gift aid.

GIFT AID (NEED-BASED) *Total amount:* $26,499,501 (48% federal, 29% state, 19% institutional, 4% external sources). *Receiving aid:* Freshmen: 71% (743); all full-time undergraduates: 69% (2,901). *Average award:* Freshmen: $11,400; Undergraduates: $11,300. *Scholarships, grants, and awards:* Federal Pell, FSEOG, state, private, college/university gift aid from institutional funds, Scholarships for Disadvantaged Students (Nursing and Pharmacy).

GIFT AID (NON-NEED-BASED) *Total amount:* $11,911,749 (99% institutional, 1% external sources). *Receiving aid:* Freshmen: 2% (24). Undergraduates: 2% (87). *Average award:* Freshmen: $19,300. Undergraduates: $22,100. *Scholarships, grants, and awards by category:* Academic interests/achievement: communication, education, general academic interests/achievements, health fields. *Creative arts/performance:* art/fine arts, cinema/film/broadcasting, dance, music, theater/drama. *Special achievements/activities:* cheerleading/drum major, general special achievements/activities, leadership. *Special characteristics:* children and siblings of alumni, children of faculty/staff, ethnic background, first-generation college students, general special characteristics, international students. *Tuition waivers:* Full or partial for employees or children of employees.

LOANS *Student loans:* $37,893,671 (70% need-based, 30% non-need-based). 97% of past graduating class borrowed through all loan programs. *Average indebtedness per student:* $41,000. *Average need-based loan:* Freshmen: $3600. Undergraduates: $4700. *Parent loans:* $12,498,888 (100% non-need-based). *Programs:* Federal Direct (Subsidized and Unsubsidized Stafford, PLUS), Perkins, Federal Health Professions Student Loans, alternative loans.

WORK-STUDY *Federal work-study:* Total amount: $1,069,127; jobs available. *State or other work-study/employment:* Total amount: $232,940 (100% non-need-based). Part-time jobs available.

ATHLETIC AWARDS Total amount: $5,003,655 (100% non-need-based).

APPLYING FOR FINANCIAL AID *Required financial aid forms:* FAFSA, state aid form. *Financial aid deadline:* Continuous. *Notification date:* Continuous beginning 4/1. Students must reply within 4 weeks of notification.

CONTACT Ms. Rose Iannicelli, Dean of Financial Services, Long Island University, Brooklyn Campus, 1 University Plaza, Brooklyn, NY 11201-8423, 718-488-1037 or toll-free 800-LIU-PLAN. *Fax:* 718-488-3343.

LONG ISLAND UNIVERSITY, C.W. POST CAMPUS
Brookville, NY

Tuition & fees: N/R	Average undergraduate aid package: $14,500

ABOUT THE INSTITUTION Independent, coed. 86 undergraduate majors. Federal methodology is used as a basis for awarding need-based institutional aid.

FRESHMAN FINANCIAL AID (Fall 2009, est.) 751 applied for aid; of those 82% were deemed to have need. 96% of freshmen with need received aid; of those 18% had need fully met. *Average percent of need met:* 75% (excluding resources awarded to replace EFC). *Average financial aid package:* $13,250 (excluding resources awarded to replace EFC). 13% of all full-time freshmen had no need and received non-need-based gift aid.

UNDERGRADUATE FINANCIAL AID (Fall 2009, est.) 3,347 applied for aid; of those 82% were deemed to have need. 97% of undergraduates with need received aid; of those 15% had need fully met. *Average percent of need met:* 75% (excluding resources awarded to replace EFC). *Average financial aid package:* $14,500 (excluding resources awarded to replace EFC). 14% of all full-time undergraduates had no need and received non-need-based gift aid.

GIFT AID (NEED-BASED) *Total amount:* $18,456,521 (24% federal, 29% state, 47% institutional). *Receiving aid:* Freshmen: 51% (437); all full-time undergraduates: 47% (1,915). *Average award:* Freshmen: $6400; Undergraduates: $5800. *Scholarships, grants, and awards:* Federal Pell, FSEOG, state, private, college/university gift aid from institutional funds.

GIFT AID (NON-NEED-BASED) *Total amount:* $17,614,756 (98% institutional, 2% external sources). *Receiving aid:* Freshmen: 63% (540). Undergraduates: 53% (2,124). *Average award:* Freshmen: $4270. Undergraduates: $6950. *Scholarships, grants, and awards by category: Academic interests/achievement:* biological sciences, business, computer science, education, general academic interests/achievements, health fields, mathematics. *Creative arts/performance:* art/fine arts, cinema/film/broadcasting, dance, journalism/publications, music, theater/drama. *Special achievements/activities:* leadership. *Special characteristics:* adult students, children and siblings of alumni, children of faculty/staff, international students, siblings of current students. *Tuition waivers:* Full or partial for employees or children of employees.

LOANS *Student loans:* $29,002,821 (77% need-based, 23% non-need-based). 65% of past graduating class borrowed through all loan programs. *Average need-based loan:* Freshmen: $3260. Undergraduates: $5350. *Parent loans:* $13,878,433 (100% non-need-based). *Programs:* Federal Direct (Subsidized and Unsubsidized Stafford, PLUS), Perkins, college/university.

WORK-STUDY *Federal work-study:* Total amount: $1,845,335; jobs available. *State or other work-study/employment:* Total amount: $43,649 (100% need-based). Part-time jobs available.

ATHLETIC AWARDS Total amount: $4,132,040 (100% non-need-based).

APPLYING FOR FINANCIAL AID *Required financial aid forms:* FAFSA, state aid form. *Financial aid deadline:* 3/1. *Notification date:* Continuous beginning 3/1. Students must reply by 5/1 or within 2 weeks of notification.

CONTACT Ms. Karen Urdahl, Office of Financial Assistance, Long Island University, C.W. Post Campus, 720 Northern Boulevard, Brookville, NY 11548-1300, 516-299-2338 or toll-free 800-LIU-PLAN. *Fax:* 516-299-3833. *E-mail:* finaid@cwpost.liu.edu.

LONGWOOD UNIVERSITY
Farmville, VA

Tuition & fees (VA res): $8925	Average undergraduate aid package: $10,118

ABOUT THE INSTITUTION State-supported, coed. 75 undergraduate majors. Federal methodology is used as a basis for awarding need-based institutional aid.

UNDERGRADUATE EXPENSES for 2009–10 *Tuition, state resident:* full-time $4680; part-time $156 per credit hour. *Tuition, nonresident:* full-time $13,590; part-time $453 per credit hour. *Required fees:* full-time $4245. Full-time tuition and fees vary according to course load. Part-time tuition and fees vary according to course load. *College room and board:* $7596; *Room only:* $4910. Room and board charges vary according to board plan, housing facility, and location. *Payment plan:* Installment.

FRESHMAN FINANCIAL AID (Fall 2008) 755 applied for aid; of those 58% were deemed to have need. 99% of freshmen with need received aid; of those 53% had need fully met. *Average percent of need met:* 85% (excluding resources awarded to replace EFC). *Average financial aid package:* $9813 (excluding resources awarded to replace EFC). 4% of all full-time freshmen had no need and received non-need-based gift aid.

UNDERGRADUATE FINANCIAL AID (Fall 2008) 2,536 applied for aid; of those 66% were deemed to have need. 99% of undergraduates with need received aid; of those 55% had need fully met. *Average percent of need met:* 85% (excluding resources awarded to replace EFC). *Average financial aid package:* $10,118 (excluding resources awarded to replace EFC). 6% of all full-time undergraduates had no need and received non-need-based gift aid.

GIFT AID (NEED-BASED) *Total amount:* $8,680,949 (30% federal, 42% state, 22% institutional, 6% external sources). *Receiving aid:* Freshmen: 42% (428); all full-time undergraduates: 40% (1,559). *Average award:* Freshmen: $5607; Undergraduates: $5380. *Scholarships, grants, and awards:* Federal Pell, FSEOG, state, private, college/university gift aid from institutional funds.

GIFT AID (NON-NEED-BASED) *Total amount:* $1,654,673 (9% federal, 7% state, 59% institutional, 25% external sources). *Receiving aid:* Freshmen: 1% (14). Undergraduates: 1% (47). *Average award:* Freshmen: $3413. Undergraduates: $3941. *Scholarships, grants, and awards by category: Academic interests/achievement:* biological sciences, business, computer science, education, English, general academic interests/achievements, humanities, international studies, mathematics, military science, social sciences. *Creative arts/performance:* art/fine arts, music, theater/drama. *Special achievements/activities:* memberships. *Special characteristics:* children and siblings of alumni, general special characteristics, local/state students. *Tuition waivers:* Full or partial for senior citizens.

LOANS *Student loans:* $15,027,046 (48% need-based, 52% non-need-based). 62% of past graduating class borrowed through all loan programs. *Average indebtedness per student:* $20,855. *Average need-based loan:* Freshmen: $4678. Undergraduates: $5504. *Parent loans:* $5,779,825 (10% need-based, 90% non-need-based). *Programs:* Federal Direct (Subsidized and Unsubsidized Stafford, PLUS), Perkins, private alternative loans.

WORK-STUDY *Federal work-study:* Total amount: $355,582; jobs available. *State or other work-study/employment:* Part-time jobs available.

ATHLETIC AWARDS Total amount: $1,787,096 (28% need-based, 72% non-need-based).

APPLYING FOR FINANCIAL AID *Required financial aid form:* FAFSA. *Financial aid deadline (priority):* 3/1. *Notification date:* Continuous beginning 4/1. Students must reply within 4 weeks of notification.

CONTACT Caroline Gibbs, Financial Aid Counselor, Longwood University, 201 High Street, Farmville, VA 23909, 434-395-2949 or toll-free 800-281-4677. *Fax:* 434-395-2829. *E-mail:* gibbsca@longwood.edu.

LORAS COLLEGE
Dubuque, IA

Tuition & fees: $26,234	Average undergraduate aid package: $16,558

ABOUT THE INSTITUTION Independent Roman Catholic, coed. 52 undergraduate majors. Federal methodology is used as a basis for awarding need-based institutional aid.

UNDERGRADUATE EXPENSES for 2010–11 *Comprehensive fee:* $33,505 includes full-time tuition ($24,912), mandatory fees ($1322), and room and board ($7271). *College room only:* $3643. Full-time tuition and fees vary according to course load and degree level. Room and board charges vary according to board plan and housing facility. *Part-time tuition:* $470 per credit hour. *Part-time fees:* $25 per credit hour. *Payment plan:* Installment.

FRESHMAN FINANCIAL AID (Fall 2009, est.) 389 applied for aid; of those 89% were deemed to have need. 100% of freshmen with need received aid; of those 45% had need fully met. *Average percent of need met:* 86% (excluding resources awarded to replace EFC). *Average financial aid package:* $20,546 (excluding resources awarded to replace EFC). 16% of all full-time freshmen had no need and received non-need-based gift aid.

UNDERGRADUATE FINANCIAL AID (Fall 2009, est.) 1,239 applied for aid; of those 90% were deemed to have need. 99% of undergraduates with need received aid; of those 40% had need fully met. *Average percent of need met:* 89% (excluding resources awarded to replace EFC). *Average financial aid package:* $16,558 (excluding resources awarded to replace EFC). 24% of all full-time undergraduates had no need and received non-need-based gift aid.

GIFT AID (NEED-BASED) *Total amount:* $14,329,918 (11% federal, 10% state, 79% institutional). *Receiving aid:* Freshmen: 75% (311); all full-time undergraduates: 67% (982). *Average award:* Freshmen: $10,162; Undergraduates: $8276. *Scholarships, grants, and awards:* Federal Pell, FSEOG, state, college/university gift aid from institutional funds.

GIFT AID (NON-NEED-BASED) *Total amount:* $6,610,316 (1% federal, 2% state, 92% institutional, 5% external sources). *Receiving aid:* Freshmen: 64% (263). Undergraduates: 66% (960). *Average award:* Freshmen: $9526. Undergraduates: $9620. *Scholarships, grants, and awards by category: Academic interests/achievement:* engineering/technologies, general academic interests/achievements, physical sciences. *Creative arts/performance:* music. *Special characteristics:* children and siblings of alumni, siblings of current students. *Tuition waivers:* Full or partial for employees or children of employees, senior citizens.

LOANS *Student loans:* $9,405,536 (45% need-based, 55% non-need-based). 82% of past graduating class borrowed through all loan programs. *Average indebtedness per student:* $30,100. *Average need-based loan:* Freshmen: $3771. Undergraduates: $3071. *Parent loans:* $1,259,015 (100% non-need-based). *Programs:* FFEL (Subsidized and Unsubsidized Stafford, PLUS), Perkins, college/university.

WORK-STUDY *Federal work-study:* Total amount: $250,000; 275 jobs averaging $2000. *State or other work-study/employment:* Total amount: $418,473 (2% need-based, 98% non-need-based). 200 part-time jobs averaging $1500.

APPLYING FOR FINANCIAL AID *Required financial aid form:* FAFSA. *Financial aid deadline (priority):* 4/15. *Notification date:* Continuous beginning 3/1. Students must reply within 3 weeks of notification.

CONTACT Ms. Julie A. Dunn, Director of Financial Planning, Loras College, 1450 Alta Vista Street, Dubuque, IA 52004-0178, 563-588-7136 or toll-free 800-245-6727. *Fax:* 563-588-7119. *E-mail:* julie.dunn@loras.edu.

LOUISIANA COLLEGE
Pineville, LA

CONTACT Shelley Jinks, Financial Aid Director, Louisiana College, 1140 College Drive, Pineville, LA 71359-0001, 318-487-7386 or toll-free 800-487-1906. *Fax:* 318-487-7449. *E-mail:* jinks@lacollege.edu.

LOUISIANA STATE UNIVERSITY AND AGRICULTURAL AND MECHANICAL COLLEGE
Baton Rouge, LA

Tuition & fees (LA res): $5233	Average undergraduate aid package: $9986

ABOUT THE INSTITUTION State-supported, coed. 74 undergraduate majors. Federal methodology is used as a basis for awarding need-based institutional aid.

UNDERGRADUATE EXPENSES for 2009–10 *Tuition, state resident:* full-time $3469. *Tuition, nonresident:* full-time $12,619. *Required fees:* full-time $1764. Part-time tuition and fees vary according to course load. *College room and board:* $7738; *Room only:* $4610. Room and board charges vary according to board plan and housing facility. *Payment plan:* Deferred payment.

FRESHMAN FINANCIAL AID (Fall 2008) 3,117 applied for aid; of those 56% were deemed to have need. 100% of freshmen with need received aid; of those 25% had need fully met. *Average percent of need met:* 74% (excluding resources awarded to replace EFC). *Average financial aid package:* $10,976 (excluding resources awarded to replace EFC). 29% of all full-time freshmen had no need and received non-need-based gift aid.

UNDERGRADUATE FINANCIAL AID (Fall 2008) 10,426 applied for aid; of those 67% were deemed to have need. 100% of undergraduates with need received aid; of those 17% had need fully met. *Average percent of need met:* 65% (excluding resources awarded to replace EFC). *Average financial aid package:*

$9986 (excluding resources awarded to replace EFC). 16% of all full-time undergraduates had no need and received non-need-based gift aid.

GIFT AID (NEED-BASED) *Total amount:* $41,680,287 (36% federal, 35% state, 26% institutional, 3% external sources). *Receiving aid:* Freshmen: 33% (1,693); all full-time undergraduates: 28% (6,010). *Average award:* Freshmen: $8549; Undergraduates: $7189. *Scholarships, grants, and awards:* Federal Pell, FSEOG, state, private, college/university gift aid from institutional funds.

GIFT AID (NON-NEED-BASED) *Total amount:* $50,784,672 (3% federal, 63% state, 30% institutional, 4% external sources). *Receiving aid:* Freshmen: 2% (79). Undergraduates: 1% (176). *Average award:* Freshmen: $3830. Undergraduates: $4126. *Scholarships, grants, and awards by category: Academic interests/achievement:* 920 awards ($941,400 total): agriculture, architecture, biological sciences, business, communication, computer science, education, engineering/technologies, English, foreign languages, general academic interests/achievements, home economics, humanities, mathematics, military science, physical sciences, premedicine. *Creative arts/performance:* 200 awards ($955,300 total): applied art and design, art/fine arts, journalism/publications, music, performing arts, theater/drama. *Special achievements/activities:* leadership. *Special characteristics:* 421 awards ($2,667,686 total): children and siblings of alumni, children with a deceased or disabled parent, general special characteristics. *Tuition waivers:* Full or partial for children of alumni, employees or children of employees.

LOANS *Student loans:* $44,654,821 (67% need-based, 33% non-need-based). 41% of past graduating class borrowed through all loan programs. *Average indebtedness per student:* $18,118. *Average need-based loan:* Freshmen: $3157. Undergraduates: $4274. *Parent loans:* $6,460,418 (23% need-based, 77% non-need-based). *Programs:* FFEL (Subsidized and Unsubsidized Stafford, PLUS), Perkins, college/university.

WORK-STUDY *Federal work-study:* Total amount: $1,855,708; 846 jobs averaging $1500. *State or other work-study/employment:* Total amount: $13,051,700 (19% need-based, 81% non-need-based). 4,038 part-time jobs averaging $2000.

ATHLETIC AWARDS Total amount: $7,133,628 (34% need-based, 66% non-need-based).

APPLYING FOR FINANCIAL AID *Required financial aid form:* FAFSA. *Financial aid deadline (priority):* 7/1. *Notification date:* 4/1. Students must reply by 5/1 or within 3 weeks of notification.

CONTACT Ms. Mary G. Parker, Executive Director of Undergraduate Admissions and Student Aid, Louisiana State University and Agricultural and Mechanical College, LSU 1146 Pleasant Hall, Baton Rouge, LA 70803-3103, 225-578-3113. *Fax:* 225-578-6300. *E-mail:* financialaid@lsu.edu.

LOUISIANA STATE UNIVERSITY HEALTH SCIENCES CENTER
New Orleans, LA

CONTACT Mr. Patrick Gorman, Director of Financial Aid, Louisiana State University Health Sciences Center, 433 Bolivar Street, New Orleans, LA 70112, 504-568-4821. *Fax:* 504-599-1390.

LOUISIANA STATE UNIVERSITY IN SHREVEPORT
Shreveport, LA

CONTACT Office of Student Financial Aid, Louisiana State University in Shreveport, One University Place, Shreveport, LA 71115-2399, 318-797-5363 or toll-free 800-229-5957 (in-state). *Fax:* 318-797-5366.

LOUISIANA TECH UNIVERSITY
Ruston, LA

Tuition & fees (LA res): $5220	Average undergraduate aid package: $9446

ABOUT THE INSTITUTION State-supported, coed. 79 undergraduate majors. Institutional methodology is used as a basis for awarding need-based institutional aid.

UNDERGRADUATE EXPENSES for 2009–10 *Tuition, state resident:* full-time $5220; part-time $180.75 per semester hour. *Tuition, nonresident:* full-time $10,617; part-time $180.75 per semester hour. Full-time tuition and fees vary according to course load, location, and program. Part-time tuition and fees vary according to course load, location, and program. **College room and board:** $5055; **Room only:** $2580. Room and board charges vary according to board plan and housing facility. **Payment plans:** Installment, deferred payment.

FRESHMAN FINANCIAL AID (Fall 2009, est.) 1,186 applied for aid; of those 59% were deemed to have need. 99% of freshmen with need received aid; of those 27% had need fully met. **Average percent of need met:** 71% (excluding resources awarded to replace EFC). **Average financial aid package:** $9278 (excluding resources awarded to replace EFC). 21% of all full-time freshmen had no need and received non-need-based gift aid.

UNDERGRADUATE FINANCIAL AID (Fall 2009, est.) 4,909 applied for aid; of those 67% were deemed to have need. 95% of undergraduates with need received aid; of those 22% had need fully met. **Average percent of need met:** 65% (excluding resources awarded to replace EFC). **Average financial aid package:** $9446 (excluding resources awarded to replace EFC). 16% of all full-time undergraduates had no need and received non-need-based gift aid.

GIFT AID (NEED-BASED) Total amount: $17,878,164 (49% federal, 36% state, 12% institutional, 3% external sources). **Receiving aid:** Freshmen: 40% (659); all full-time undergraduates: 41% (2,763). **Average award:** Freshmen: $7497; Undergraduates: $7171. **Scholarships, grants, and awards:** Federal Pell, FSEOG, state, private, college/university gift aid from institutional funds.

GIFT AID (NON-NEED-BASED) Total amount: $9,313,681 (59% state, 34% institutional, 7% external sources). **Receiving aid:** Freshmen: 8% (130). Undergraduates: 5% (350). **Average award:** Freshmen: $2032. Undergraduates: $2370. **Scholarships, grants, and awards by category:** Academic interests/achievement: agriculture, architecture, biological sciences, business, computer science, education, engineering/technologies, English, foreign languages, general academic interests/achievements, health fields, home economics, international studies, mathematics, military science, physical sciences, social sciences. Creative arts/performance: applied art and design, art/fine arts, creative writing, debating, general creative arts/performance, journalism/publications, music, performing arts, theater/drama. Special achievements/activities: cheerleading/drum major, junior miss. Special characteristics: children and siblings of alumni, children of faculty/staff, children of public servants, handicapped students, international students, members of minority groups, out-of-state students, veterans, veterans' children. **Tuition waivers:** Full or partial for children of alumni, employees or children of employees, senior citizens.

LOANS Student loans: $29,280,846 (59% need-based, 41% non-need-based). 51% of past graduating class borrowed through all loan programs. Average indebtedness per student: $12,408. **Average need-based loan:** Freshmen: $2784. Undergraduates: $3745. **Parent loans:** $14,228,188 (16% need-based, 84% non-need-based). **Programs:** Federal Direct (Subsidized and Unsubsidized Stafford, PLUS), Perkins.

WORK-STUDY Federal work-study: Total amount: $486,699; 268 jobs averaging $1815. **State or other work-study/employment:** Total amount: $2,044,587 (100% non-need-based). 989 part-time jobs averaging $1969.

ATHLETIC AWARDS Total amount: $2,858,264 (45% need-based, 55% non-need-based).

APPLYING FOR FINANCIAL AID Required financial aid forms: FAFSA, institution's own form. **Financial aid deadline (priority):** 4/15. **Notification date:** Continuous beginning 4/15. Students must reply within 3 weeks of notification.

CONTACT Financial Aid Office, Louisiana Tech University, PO Box 7925, Ruston, LA 71272, 318-257-2641 or toll-free 800-528-3241. Fax: 318-257-2628. E-mail: techaid@latech.edu.

LOURDES COLLEGE
Sylvania, OH

Tuition & fees: $15,300   **Average undergraduate aid package: $9732**

ABOUT THE INSTITUTION Independent Roman Catholic, coed. 26 undergraduate majors. Both federal and institutional methodology are used as a basis for awarding need-based institutional aid.

UNDERGRADUATE EXPENSES for 2009–10 Tuition: full-time $13,440; part-time $448 per credit hour. **Required fees:** full-time $1860; $62 per credit hour. Full-time tuition and fees vary according to course load and location. Part-time tuition and fees vary according to course load and location. **Payment plans:** Installment, deferred payment.

FRESHMAN FINANCIAL AID (Fall 2009, est.) 109 applied for aid; of those 83% were deemed to have need. 100% of freshmen with need received aid. **Average financial aid package:** $12,086 (excluding resources awarded to replace EFC).

UNDERGRADUATE FINANCIAL AID (Fall 2009, est.) 954 applied for aid; of those 90% were deemed to have need. 100% of undergraduates with need received aid. **Average financial aid package:** $9732 (excluding resources awarded to replace EFC).

GIFT AID (NEED-BASED) Total amount: $6,784,057 (62% federal, 19% state, 16% institutional, 3% external sources). **Receiving aid:** Freshmen: 61% (70); all full-time undergraduates: 63% (635). **Average award:** Freshmen: $6197; Undergraduates: $6590. **Scholarships, grants, and awards:** Federal Pell, FSEOG, state, private, college/university gift aid from institutional funds.

GIFT AID (NON-NEED-BASED) Receiving aid: Freshmen: 55% (63). Undergraduates: 45% (457). **Scholarships, grants, and awards by category:** Academic interests/achievement: 441 awards ($800,320 total): general academic interests/achievements. Creative arts/performance: art/fine arts. Special achievements/activities: general special achievements/activities. Special characteristics: adult students, ethnic background, local/state students, members of minority groups, out-of-state students, previous college experience. **Tuition waivers:** Full or partial for employees or children of employees, senior citizens.

LOANS Student loans: $12,744,864 (100% need-based). **Average need-based loan:** Freshmen: $3413. Undergraduates: $4134. **Parent loans:** $574,966 (100% need-based). **Programs:** Federal Direct (Subsidized and Unsubsidized Stafford, PLUS), Perkins, state, college/university, alternative loans.

WORK-STUDY Federal work-study: Total amount: $215,639; 116 jobs averaging $1859. **State or other work-study/employment:** Total amount: $100,000 (100% need-based). 100 part-time jobs averaging $1000.

APPLYING FOR FINANCIAL AID Required financial aid form: FAFSA. **Financial aid deadline (priority):** 3/1. **Notification date:** Continuous beginning 3/1. Students must reply within 4 weeks of notification.

CONTACT Denise McClusky, Director of Financial Aid, Lourdes College, 6832 Convent Boulevard, Sylvania, OH 43560-2898, 419-824-3732 or toll-free 800-878-3210 Ext. 1299. Fax: 419-882-3987. E-mail: finaid@lourdes.edu.

LOYOLA MARYMOUNT UNIVERSITY
Los Angeles, CA

CONTACT Financial Aid Office, Loyola Marymount University, One LMU Drive, Los Angeles, CA 90045-8350, 310-338-2753 or toll-free 800-LMU-INFO. E-mail: finaid@lmu.edu.

LOYOLA UNIVERSITY CHICAGO
Chicago, IL

Tuition & fees: $32,114   **Average undergraduate aid package: $27,092**

ABOUT THE INSTITUTION Independent Roman Catholic (Jesuit), coed. 76 undergraduate majors. Federal methodology is used as a basis for awarding need-based institutional aid.

UNDERGRADUATE EXPENSES for 2010–11 Comprehensive fee: $43,334 includes full-time tuition ($31,040), mandatory fees ($1074), and room and board ($11,220). **College room only:** $7370. Full-time tuition and fees vary according to course load, location, program, and student level. Room and board charges vary according to board plan and housing facility. **Part-time tuition:** $630 per credit hour. Part-time tuition and fees vary according to course load. **Payment plans:** Installment, deferred payment.

FRESHMAN FINANCIAL AID (Fall 2009, est.) 1,833 applied for aid; of those 84% were deemed to have need. 99% of freshmen with need received aid; of those 10% had need fully met. **Average percent of need met:** 84% (excluding resources awarded to replace EFC). **Average financial aid package:** $27,357 (excluding resources awarded to replace EFC). 19% of all full-time freshmen had no need and received non-need-based gift aid.

UNDERGRADUATE FINANCIAL AID (Fall 2009, est.) 7,520 applied for aid; of those 89% were deemed to have need. 100% of undergraduates with need received aid; of those 8% had need fully met. **Average percent of need met:** 82% (excluding resources awarded to replace EFC). **Average financial aid package:** $27,092 (excluding resources awarded to replace EFC). 17% of all full-time undergraduates had no need and received non-need-based gift aid.

GIFT AID (NEED-BASED) Total amount: $105,120,644 (15% federal, 11% state, 72% institutional, 2% external sources). **Receiving aid:** Freshmen: 73% (1,519); all full-time undergraduates: 70% (6,438). **Average award:** Freshmen: $17,781; Undergraduates: $16,380. **Scholarships, grants, and awards:** Federal Pell, FSEOG, state, private, college/university gift aid from institutional funds.

GIFT AID (NON-NEED-BASED) *Total amount:* $14,269,518 (6% federal, 88% institutional, 6% external sources). *Receiving aid:* Freshmen: 6% (129). Undergraduates: 4% (399). *Average award:* Freshmen: $7796. Undergraduates: $7524. *Scholarships, grants, and awards by category: Academic interests/ achievement:* 4,256 awards ($32,549,299 total): general academic interests/ achievements. *Creative arts/performance:* 40 awards ($113,700 total): art/fine arts, debating, journalism/publications, music, theater/drama. *Special achievements/ activities:* 368 awards ($1,813,137 total): community service, general special achievements/activities, leadership, memberships. *Special characteristics:* 1,365 awards ($3,476,708 total): adult students, general special characteristics, religious affiliation. *Tuition waivers:* Full or partial for employees or children of employees, senior citizens.

LOANS *Student loans:* $73,413,255 (75% need-based, 25% non-need-based). 77% of past graduating class borrowed through all loan programs. *Average indebtedness per student:* $35,526. *Average need-based loan:* Freshmen: $3810. Undergraduates: $4891. *Parent loans:* $16,681,182 (36% need-based, 64% non-need-based). *Programs:* FFEL (Subsidized and Unsubsidized Stafford, PLUS), Perkins, Federal Nursing.

WORK-STUDY *Federal work-study:* Total amount: $11,642,116; 5,108 jobs averaging $2201.

ATHLETIC AWARDS Total amount: $4,068,455 (45% need-based, 55% non-need-based).

APPLYING FOR FINANCIAL AID *Required financial aid form:* FAFSA. *Financial aid deadline:* Continuous. *Notification date:* Continuous beginning 2/15. Students must reply within 3 weeks of notification.

CONTACT Mr. Eric Weems, Director of Financial Aid; Loyola University Chicago, 6525 North Sheridan Road, Chicago, IL 60626, 773-508-3155 or toll-free 800-262-2373. *Fax:* 773-508-3177. *E-mail:* lufinaid@luc.edu.

LOYOLA UNIVERSITY MARYLAND
Baltimore, MD

Tuition & fees: $37,610	Average undergraduate aid package: $27,300

ABOUT THE INSTITUTION Independent Roman Catholic (Jesuit), coed. 32 undergraduate majors. Institutional methodology is used as a basis for awarding need-based institutional aid.

UNDERGRADUATE EXPENSES for 2009–10 *One-time required fee:* $165. *Comprehensive fee:* $48,890 includes full-time tuition ($36,510), mandatory fees ($1100), and room and board ($11,280). *College room only:* $9260. Full-time tuition and fees vary according to course load. Room and board charges vary according to board plan, housing facility, and location. *Part-time tuition:* $590 per credit. Part-time tuition and fees vary according to course load. *Payment plan:* Installment.

FRESHMAN FINANCIAL AID (Fall 2009, est.) 705 applied for aid; of those 78% were deemed to have need. 100% of freshmen with need received aid; of those 100% had need fully met. *Average percent of need met:* 100% (excluding resources awarded to replace EFC). *Average financial aid package:* $26,345 (excluding resources awarded to replace EFC). 8% of all full-time freshmen had no need and received non-need-based gift aid.

UNDERGRADUATE FINANCIAL AID (Fall 2009, est.) 2,203 applied for aid; of those 83% were deemed to have need. 100% of undergraduates with need received aid; of those 98% had need fully met. *Average percent of need met:* 97% (excluding resources awarded to replace EFC). *Average financial aid package:* $27,300 (excluding resources awarded to replace EFC). 10% of all full-time undergraduates had no need and received non-need-based gift aid.

GIFT AID (NEED-BASED) *Total amount:* $39,159,583 (7% federal, 2% state, 89% institutional, 2% external sources). *Receiving aid:* Freshmen: 51% (495); all full-time undergraduates: 44% (1,668). *Average award:* Freshmen: $18,750; Undergraduates: $19,275. *Scholarships, grants, and awards:* Federal Pell, FSEOG, state, private, college/university gift aid from institutional funds.

GIFT AID (NON-NEED-BASED) *Total amount:* $7,441,097 (14% federal, 1% state, 79% institutional, 6% external sources). *Receiving aid:* Freshmen: 10% (95). Undergraduates: 11% (395). *Average award:* Freshmen: $12,530. Undergraduates: $14,190. *Scholarships, grants, and awards by category: Academic interests/achievement:* general academic interests/achievements. *Tuition waivers:* Full or partial for employees or children of employees.

LOANS *Student loans:* $17,323,728 (46% need-based, 54% non-need-based). 72% of past graduating class borrowed through all loan programs. *Average indebtedness per student:* $26,855. *Average need-based loan:* Freshmen: $5445.

Undergraduates: $5875. *Parent loans:* $13,466,239 (100% non-need-based). *Programs:* Federal Direct (Subsidized and Unsubsidized Stafford, PLUS), Perkins, college/university.

WORK-STUDY *Federal work-study:* Total amount: $766,100; jobs available. *State or other work-study/employment:* Total amount: $864,341 (57% need-based, 43% non-need-based). Part-time jobs available.

ATHLETIC AWARDS Total amount: $4,887,037 (27% need-based, 73% non-need-based).

APPLYING FOR FINANCIAL AID *Required financial aid forms:* FAFSA, CSS Financial Aid PROFILE, noncustodial (divorced/separated) parent's statement, business/farm supplement. *Financial aid deadline:* 2/15. *Notification date:* 4/1. Students must reply by 5/1.

CONTACT Mr. Mark L. Lindenmeyer, Director of Financial Aid, Loyola University Maryland, 4501 North Charles Street, Baltimore, MD 21210-2699, 410-617-2576 or toll-free 800-221-9107 Ext. 2252 (in-state). *Fax:* 410-617-5149. *E-mail:* lindenmeyer@loyola.edu.

LOYOLA UNIVERSITY NEW ORLEANS
New Orleans, LA

Tuition & fees: $31,504	Average undergraduate aid package: $24,349

ABOUT THE INSTITUTION Independent Roman Catholic (Jesuit), coed. 48 undergraduate majors. Federal methodology is used as a basis for awarding need-based institutional aid.

UNDERGRADUATE EXPENSES for 2010–11 *Comprehensive fee:* $41,892 includes full-time tuition ($30,468), mandatory fees ($1036), and room and board ($10,388). *College room only:* $6160. Room and board charges vary according to board plan and housing facility. *Part-time tuition:* $869 per credit hour. *Payment plan:* Installment.

FRESHMAN FINANCIAL AID (Fall 2009, est.) 627 applied for aid; of those 81% were deemed to have need. 100% of freshmen with need received aid; of those 25% had need fully met. *Average percent of need met:* 88% (excluding resources awarded to replace EFC). *Average financial aid package:* $26,836 (excluding resources awarded to replace EFC). 30% of all full-time freshmen had no need and received non-need-based gift aid.

UNDERGRADUATE FINANCIAL AID (Fall 2009, est.) 1,806 applied for aid; of those 83% were deemed to have need. 100% of undergraduates with need received aid; of those 24% had need fully met. *Average percent of need met:* 82% (excluding resources awarded to replace EFC). *Average financial aid package:* $24,349 (excluding resources awarded to replace EFC). 34% of all full-time undergraduates had no need and received non-need-based gift aid.

GIFT AID (NEED-BASED) *Total amount:* $26,123,944 (14% federal, 8% state, 73% institutional, 5% external sources). *Receiving aid:* Freshmen: 69% (510); all full-time undergraduates: 63% (1,484). *Average award:* Freshmen: $18,146; Undergraduates: $14,571. *Scholarships, grants, and awards:* Federal Pell, FSEOG, state, private, college/university gift aid from institutional funds.

GIFT AID (NON-NEED-BASED) *Total amount:* $15,119,725 (4% state, 94% institutional, 2% external sources). *Receiving aid:* Freshmen: 68% (505). Undergraduates: 49% (1,140). *Average award:* Freshmen: $18,069. Undergraduates: $15,906. *Scholarships, grants, and awards by category: Academic interests/achievement:* general academic interests/achievements. *Creative arts/ performance:* general creative arts/performance. *Special characteristics:* children of faculty/staff. *Tuition waivers:* Full or partial for employees or children of employees, senior citizens.

LOANS *Student loans:* $11,446,280 (43% need-based, 57% non-need-based). 64% of past graduating class borrowed through all loan programs. *Average indebtedness per student:* $22,320. *Average need-based loan:* Freshmen: $3562. Undergraduates: $4390. *Parent loans:* $3,060,340 (74% need-based, 26% non-need-based). *Programs:* FFEL (Subsidized and Unsubsidized Stafford, PLUS), Perkins.

WORK-STUDY *Federal work-study:* Total amount: $1,145,942; jobs available.

ATHLETIC AWARDS Total amount: $665,390 (47% need-based, 53% non-need-based).

APPLYING FOR FINANCIAL AID *Required financial aid form:* FAFSA. *Financial aid deadline:* 6/1 (priority: 2/15). *Notification date:* 3/1. Students must reply by 5/1 or within 2 weeks of notification.

CONTACT Ms. Catherine M. Simoneaux, Director of Scholarships and Financial Aid, Loyola University New Orleans, 6363 St. Charles Avenue, Box 206, New Orleans, LA 70118-6195, 504-865-3231 or toll-free 800-4-LOYOLA. *Fax:* 504-865-3233. *E-mail:* finaid@loyno.edu.

LUBBOCK CHRISTIAN UNIVERSITY
Lubbock, TX

Tuition & fees: $15,120	Average undergraduate aid package: $13,010

ABOUT THE INSTITUTION Independent religious, coed. 67 undergraduate majors. Federal methodology is used as a basis for awarding need-based institutional aid.

UNDERGRADUATE EXPENSES for 2009–10 *Comprehensive fee:* $21,302 includes full-time tuition ($14,100), mandatory fees ($1020), and room and board ($6182). Full-time tuition and fees vary according to degree level and program. Room and board charges vary according to board plan and housing facility. *Part-time tuition:* $455 per semester hour. *Part-time fees:* $445 per term. Part-time tuition and fees vary according to course load, degree level, and program. *Payment plan:* Installment.

FRESHMAN FINANCIAL AID (Fall 2009, est.) 187 applied for aid; of those 87% were deemed to have need. 100% of freshmen with need received aid; of those 10% had need fully met. *Average percent of need met:* 72% (excluding resources awarded to replace EFC). *Average financial aid package:* $13,169 (excluding resources awarded to replace EFC). 14% of all full-time freshmen had no need and received non-need-based gift aid.

UNDERGRADUATE FINANCIAL AID (Fall 2009, est.) 1,093 applied for aid; of those 85% were deemed to have need. 100% of undergraduates with need received aid; of those 7% had need fully met. *Average percent of need met:* 67% (excluding resources awarded to replace EFC). *Average financial aid package:* $13,010 (excluding resources awarded to replace EFC). 15% of all full-time undergraduates had no need and received non-need-based gift aid.

GIFT AID (NEED-BASED) *Total amount:* $6,929,921 (39% federal, 27% state, 28% institutional, 6% external sources). *Receiving aid:* Freshmen: 63% (158); all full-time undergraduates: 67% (858). *Average award:* Freshmen: $9622; Undergraduates: $9089. *Scholarships, grants, and awards:* Federal Pell, FSEOG, state, college/university gift aid from institutional funds.

GIFT AID (NON-NEED-BASED) *Total amount:* $1,038,511 (1% state, 75% institutional, 24% external sources). *Receiving aid:* Freshmen: 6% (15). Undergraduates: 4% (53). *Average award:* Freshmen: $3995. Undergraduates: $3839. *Scholarships, grants, and awards by category: Academic interests/achievement:* agriculture, business, communication, computer science, education, English, foreign languages, general academic interests/achievements, humanities, physical sciences, religion/biblical studies, social sciences. *Creative arts/performance:* art/fine arts, journalism/publications, music, performing arts, theater/drama. *Special achievements/activities:* 43 awards ($38,800 total): cheerleading/drum major, leadership. *Special characteristics:* 40 awards ($347,495 total): children of faculty/staff, general special characteristics. *Tuition waivers:* Full or partial for employees or children of employees.

LOANS *Student loans:* $11,036,562 (75% need-based, 25% non-need-based). 79% of past graduating class borrowed through all loan programs. *Average indebtedness per student:* $26,320. *Average need-based loan:* Freshmen: $3244. Undergraduates: $4124. *Parent loans:* $3,003,762 (33% need-based, 67% non-need-based). *Programs:* FFEL (Subsidized and Unsubsidized Stafford, PLUS), Perkins, state.

WORK-STUDY *Federal work-study:* Total amount: $817,132; 688 jobs averaging $1778. *State or other work-study/employment:* Total amount: $25,036 (46% need-based, 54% non-need-based). 100 part-time jobs averaging $250.

ATHLETIC AWARDS Total amount: $1,315,555 (48% need-based, 52% non-need-based).

APPLYING FOR FINANCIAL AID *Required financial aid forms:* FAFSA, institution's own form. *Financial aid deadline (priority):* 6/1. *Notification date:* Continuous beginning 3/1.

CONTACT Amy Hardesty, Financial Aid Director, Lubbock Christian University, 5601 19th Street, Lubbock, TX 79407, 806-720-7176 or toll-free 800-933-7601. *Fax:* 806-720-7185. *E-mail:* amy.hardesty@lcu.edu.

LUTHER COLLEGE
Decorah, IA

Tuition & fees: $33,480	Average undergraduate aid package: $24,932

ABOUT THE INSTITUTION Independent religious, coed. 38 undergraduate majors. Federal methodology is used as a basis for awarding need-based institutional aid.

UNDERGRADUATE EXPENSES for 2010–11 *Comprehensive fee:* $39,280 includes full-time tuition ($33,330), mandatory fees ($150), and room and board ($5800). *College room only:* $2880. Full-time tuition and fees vary according to course load. Room and board charges vary according to board plan and housing facility. *Part-time tuition:* $1190 per credit hour. Part-time tuition and fees vary according to course load. *Payment plan:* Installment.

FRESHMAN FINANCIAL AID (Fall 2009, est.) 569 applied for aid; of those 84% were deemed to have need. 100% of freshmen with need received aid; of those 37% had need fully met. *Average percent of need met:* 91% (excluding resources awarded to replace EFC). *Average financial aid package:* $26,727 (excluding resources awarded to replace EFC). 14% of all full-time freshmen had no need and received non-need-based gift aid.

UNDERGRADUATE FINANCIAL AID (Fall 2009, est.) 1,969 applied for aid; of those 85% were deemed to have need. 100% of undergraduates with need received aid; of those 31% had need fully met. *Average percent of need met:* 88% (excluding resources awarded to replace EFC). *Average financial aid package:* $24,932 (excluding resources awarded to replace EFC). 10% of all full-time undergraduates had no need and received non-need-based gift aid.

GIFT AID (NEED-BASED) *Total amount:* $31,299,912 (16% federal, 5% state, 76% institutional, 3% external sources). *Receiving aid:* Freshmen: 73% (478); all full-time undergraduates: 68% (1,659). *Average award:* Freshmen: $18,292; Undergraduates: $17,454. *Scholarships, grants, and awards:* Federal Pell, FSEOG, state, private, college/university gift aid from institutional funds.

GIFT AID (NON-NEED-BASED) *Total amount:* $1,451,787 (3% federal, 78% institutional, 19% external sources). *Receiving aid:* Freshmen: 13% (86). Undergraduates: 9% (227). *Average award:* Freshmen: $13,347. Undergraduates: $9617. *Scholarships, grants, and awards by category: Academic interests/achievement:* 1,819 awards ($17,557,228 total): general academic interests/achievements. *Creative arts/performance:* 902 awards ($2,640,775 total): music. *Special characteristics:* 662 awards ($1,030,639 total): children and siblings of alumni, members of minority groups, religious affiliation. *Tuition waivers:* Full or partial for employees or children of employees.

LOANS *Student loans:* $10,980,212 (82% need-based, 18% non-need-based). 82% of past graduating class borrowed through all loan programs. *Average indebtedness per student:* $34,101. *Average need-based loan:* Freshmen: $5956. Undergraduates: $6406. *Parent loans:* $6,863,385 (17% need-based, 83% non-need-based). *Programs:* Federal Direct (Subsidized and Unsubsidized Stafford, PLUS), Perkins, college/university.

WORK-STUDY *Federal work-study:* Total amount: $1,981,301; 944 jobs averaging $2099. *State or other work-study/employment:* Total amount: $1,536,418 (18% need-based, 82% non-need-based). 1,080 part-time jobs averaging $2404.

APPLYING FOR FINANCIAL AID *Required financial aid forms:* FAFSA, institution's own form. *Financial aid deadline (priority):* 3/1. *Notification date:* Continuous beginning 3/15. Students must reply by 5/1.

CONTACT Ms. Janice Cordell, Director of Financial Aid, Luther College, 700 College Drive, Decorah, IA 52101-1045, 563-387-1018 or toll-free 800-458-8437. *Fax:* 563-387-2241. *E-mail:* cordellj@luther.edu.

LUTHER RICE UNIVERSITY
Lithonia, GA

Tuition & fees: N/R	Average undergraduate aid package: $5819

ABOUT THE INSTITUTION Independent Baptist, coed. *Awards:* bachelor's and master's degrees. 3 undergraduate majors. *Total enrollment:* 1,047. Undergraduates: 375. Federal methodology is used as a basis for awarding need-based institutional aid.

FRESHMAN FINANCIAL AID (Fall 2008) 2 applied for aid; of those 100% were deemed to have need. 100% of freshmen with need received aid; of those 100% had need fully met. *Average percent of need met:* 100% (excluding resources awarded to replace EFC). *Average financial aid package:* $10,292 (excluding resources awarded to replace EFC).

Luther Rice University

UNDERGRADUATE FINANCIAL AID (Fall 2008) 74 applied for aid; of those 100% were deemed to have need. 100% of undergraduates with need received aid; of those 64% had need fully met. *Average percent of need met:* 100% (excluding resources awarded to replace EFC). *Average financial aid package:* $5819 (excluding resources awarded to replace EFC).

GIFT AID (NEED-BASED) *Total amount:* $405,741 (100% federal). *Receiving aid:* Freshmen: 100% (2); all full-time undergraduates: 46% (47). *Average award:* Freshmen: $3253; Undergraduates: $3780. *Scholarships, grants, and awards:* Federal Pell, FSEOG, college/university gift aid from institutional funds.

LOANS *Student loans:* $4,304,495 (43% need-based, 57% non-need-based). *Programs:* FFEL (Subsidized and Unsubsidized Stafford, PLUS).

WORK-STUDY *Federal work-study:* Total amount: $14,706; 4 jobs averaging $3676.

APPLYING FOR FINANCIAL AID *Required financial aid form:* FAFSA. *Financial aid deadline (priority):* 1/1. *Notification date:* Continuous. Students must reply within 2 weeks of notification.

CONTACT Gary W. Cook, Director of Financial Aid, Luther Rice University, 3038 Evans Mill Road, Lithonia, GA 30038-2418, 770-484-1204 Ext. 241 or toll-free 800-442-1577. *Fax:* 678-990-5388. *E-mail:* gcook@lru.edu.

LYCOMING COLLEGE
Williamsport, PA

Tuition & fees: $29,894	Average undergraduate aid package: $23,264

ABOUT THE INSTITUTION Independent United Methodist, coed. 39 undergraduate majors. Federal methodology is used as a basis for awarding need-based institutional aid.

UNDERGRADUATE EXPENSES for 2010–11 *Comprehensive fee:* $38,028 includes full-time tuition ($29,344), mandatory fees ($550), and room and board ($8134). *College room only:* $4150. Room and board charges vary according to board plan and housing facility. *Part-time tuition:* $917 per credit hour. Part-time tuition and fees vary according to course load. *Payment plan:* Installment.

FRESHMAN FINANCIAL AID (Fall 2009, est.) 368 applied for aid; of those 94% were deemed to have need. 100% of freshmen with need received aid; of those 15% had need fully met. *Average percent of need met:* 81% (excluding resources awarded to replace EFC). *Average financial aid package:* $24,693 (excluding resources awarded to replace EFC). 9% of all full-time freshmen had no need and received non-need-based gift aid.

UNDERGRADUATE FINANCIAL AID (Fall 2009, est.) 1,220 applied for aid; of those 93% were deemed to have need. 100% of undergraduates with need received aid; of those 15% had need fully met. *Average percent of need met:* 78% (excluding resources awarded to replace EFC). *Average financial aid package:* $23,264 (excluding resources awarded to replace EFC). 12% of all full-time undergraduates had no need and received non-need-based gift aid.

GIFT AID (NEED-BASED) *Total amount:* $20,775,311 (10% federal, 8% state, 80% institutional, 2% external sources). *Receiving aid:* Freshmen: 90% (347); all full-time undergraduates: 85% (1,137). *Average award:* Freshmen: $20,267; Undergraduates: $18,340. *Scholarships, grants, and awards:* Federal Pell, FSEOG, state, private, college/university gift aid from institutional funds.

GIFT AID (NON-NEED-BASED) *Total amount:* $1,834,660 (99% institutional, 1% external sources). *Receiving aid:* Freshmen: 8% (32). Undergraduates: 7% (90). *Average award:* Freshmen: $12,406. Undergraduates: $10,852. *Scholarships, grants, and awards by category: Academic interests/achievement:* 959 awards ($9,220,983 total): biological sciences, business, communication, computer science, education, English, foreign languages, general academic interests/achievements, health fields, humanities, international studies, mathematics, physical sciences, premedicine, religion/biblical studies, social sciences. *Creative arts/performance:* 133 awards ($270,350 total): art/fine arts, creative writing, music, theater/drama. *Special achievements/activities:* 45 awards ($275,117 total): general special achievements/activities, leadership. *Special characteristics:* 49 awards ($927,675 total): children of educators, children of faculty/staff, relatives of clergy. *Tuition waivers:* Full or partial for employees or children of employees.

LOANS *Student loans:* $10,022,045 (74% need-based, 26% non-need-based). 85% of past graduating class borrowed through all loan programs. *Average indebtedness per student:* $29,478. *Average need-based loan:* Freshmen: $4044. Undergraduates: $4760. *Parent loans:* $5,138,103 (35% need-based, 65% non-need-based). *Programs:* FFEL (Subsidized and Unsubsidized Stafford, PLUS), Perkins, college/university.

WORK-STUDY *Federal work-study:* Total amount: $316,610; 364 jobs averaging $1102.

APPLYING FOR FINANCIAL AID *Required financial aid forms:* FAFSA, institution's own form, state aid form. *Financial aid deadline (priority):* 3/1. *Notification date:* Continuous beginning 3/1. Students must reply by 5/1.

CONTACT Mr. James S. Lakis, Director of Financial Aid, Lycoming College, 700 College Place, Williamsport, PA 17701-5192, 570-321-4040 or toll-free 800-345-3920 Ext. 4026. *Fax:* 570-321-4993. *E-mail:* lakis@lycoming.edu.

LYME ACADEMY COLLEGE OF FINE ARTS
Old Lyme, CT

Tuition & fees: $24,860	Average undergraduate aid package: $12,136

ABOUT THE INSTITUTION Independent, coed. 4 undergraduate majors. Federal methodology is used as a basis for awarding need-based institutional aid.

UNDERGRADUATE EXPENSES for 2010–11 *Tuition:* full-time $23,384; part-time $974.33 per credit. *Required fees:* full-time $1476; $50 per term. Full-time tuition and fees vary according to course load. Part-time tuition and fees vary according to course load. Room and board charges vary according to housing facility. *Payment plan:* Installment.

FRESHMAN FINANCIAL AID (Fall 2009, est.) 8 applied for aid; of those 88% were deemed to have need. 100% of freshmen with need received aid. *Average financial aid package:* $14,405 (excluding resources awarded to replace EFC). 11% of all full-time freshmen had no need and received non-need-based gift aid.

UNDERGRADUATE FINANCIAL AID (Fall 2009, est.) 45 applied for aid; of those 100% were deemed to have need. 89% of undergraduates with need received aid. *Average financial aid package:* $12,136 (excluding resources awarded to replace EFC). 15% of all full-time undergraduates had no need and received non-need-based gift aid.

GIFT AID (NEED-BASED) *Total amount:* $597,774 (19% federal, 13% state, 61% institutional, 7% external sources). *Receiving aid:* Freshmen: 56% (5); all full-time undergraduates: 56% (38). *Average award:* Freshmen: $4475; Undergraduates: $2219. *Scholarships, grants, and awards:* Federal Pell, FSEOG, state, private, college/university gift aid from institutional funds.

GIFT AID (NON-NEED-BASED) *Receiving aid:* Freshmen: 78% (7). Undergraduates: 59% (40). *Average award:* Freshmen: $7500. Undergraduates: $4000. *Scholarships, grants, and awards by category: Creative arts/performance:* art/fine arts. *Tuition waivers:* Full or partial for employees or children of employees.

LOANS *Student loans:* $466,875 (100% need-based). 67% of past graduating class borrowed through all loan programs. *Average indebtedness per student:* $18,460. *Average need-based loan:* Freshmen: $2882. Undergraduates: $3518. *Parent loans:* $224,843 (100% need-based). *Programs:* Federal Direct (Subsidized and Unsubsidized Stafford, PLUS), CHESLA alternative loans.

WORK-STUDY *Federal work-study:* Total amount: $5666; 10 jobs averaging $566. *State or other work-study/employment:* Total amount: $3885 (100% need-based). 2 part-time jobs averaging $3885.

APPLYING FOR FINANCIAL AID *Required financial aid form:* FAFSA. *Financial aid deadline:* Continuous. *Notification date:* Continuous beginning 3/1. Students must reply by 5/1 or within 2 weeks of notification.

CONTACT Mr. James Falconer, Director of Financial Aid, Lyme Academy College of Fine Arts, 84 Lyme Street, Old Lyme, CT 06371, 860-434-3571 Ext. 114. *Fax:* 860-434-8725. *E-mail:* jfalconer@lymeacademy.edu.

LYNCHBURG COLLEGE
Lynchburg, VA

Tuition & fees: $28,925	Average undergraduate aid package: $20,193

ABOUT THE INSTITUTION Independent religious, coed. 35 undergraduate majors. Federal methodology is used as a basis for awarding need-based institutional aid.

UNDERGRADUATE EXPENSES for 2009–10 *Comprehensive fee:* $35,895 includes full-time tuition ($27,980), mandatory fees ($945), and room and board ($6970). *College room only:* $3930. Room and board charges vary according to board plan and housing facility. *Part-time tuition:* $390 per credit hour. *Part-time fees:* $5.10 per credit hour. Part-time tuition and fees vary according to course load. *Payment plans:* Tuition prepayment, installment.

FRESHMAN FINANCIAL AID (Fall 2009, est.) 512 applied for aid; of those 82% were deemed to have need. 100% of freshmen with need received aid; of those 20% had need fully met. *Average percent of need met:* 83% (excluding resources awarded to replace EFC). *Average financial aid package:* $22,027 (excluding resources awarded to replace EFC). 25% of all full-time freshmen had no need and received non-need-based gift aid.

UNDERGRADUATE FINANCIAL AID (Fall 2009, est.) 1,715 applied for aid; of those 85% were deemed to have need. 99% of undergraduates with need received aid; of those 22% had need fully met. *Average percent of need met:* 78% (excluding resources awarded to replace EFC). *Average financial aid package:* $20,193 (excluding resources awarded to replace EFC). 27% of all full-time undergraduates had no need and received non-need-based gift aid.

GIFT AID (NEED-BASED) *Total amount:* $23,689,625 (12% federal, 10% state, 76% institutional, 2% external sources). *Receiving aid:* Freshmen: 71% (420); all full-time undergraduates: 69% (1,448). *Average award:* Freshmen: $18,465; Undergraduates: $16,607. *Scholarships, grants, and awards:* Federal Pell, FSEOG, state, private, college/university gift aid from institutional funds.

GIFT AID (NON-NEED-BASED) *Total amount:* $7,878,982 (15% state, 81% institutional, 4% external sources). *Receiving aid:* Freshmen: 9% (56). Undergraduates: 10% (200). *Average award:* Freshmen: $9987. Undergraduates: $9958. *Scholarships, grants, and awards by category:* Academic interests/achievement: general academic interests/achievements. *Creative arts/performance:* art/fine arts, music, theater/drama. *Tuition waivers:* Full or partial for employees or children of employees, adult students, senior citizens.

LOANS *Student loans:* $14,158,425 (58% need-based, 42% non-need-based). 67% of past graduating class borrowed through all loan programs. *Average indebtedness per student:* $30,954. *Average need-based loan:* Freshmen: $3126. Undergraduates: $3526. *Parent loans:* $3,968,292 (46% need-based, 54% non-need-based). *Programs:* Federal Direct (Subsidized and Unsubsidized Stafford, PLUS), Perkins.

WORK-STUDY *Federal work-study:* Total amount: $368,521; jobs available. *State or other work-study/employment:* Total amount: $797,860 (41% need-based, 59% non-need-based). Part-time jobs available.

APPLYING FOR FINANCIAL AID *Required financial aid forms:* FAFSA, state aid form. *Financial aid deadline (priority):* 3/5. *Notification date:* Continuous beginning 3/5. Students must reply by 5/1 or within 2 weeks of notification.

CONTACT Mrs. Michelle Davis, Director of Financial Aid, Lynchburg College, 1501 Lakeside Drive, Lynchburg, VA 24501-3199, 434-544-8228 or toll-free 800-426-8101. *Fax:* 434-544-8653.

LYNDON STATE COLLEGE
Lyndonville, VT

CONTACT Student Services Consultant, Lyndon State College, 1001 College Road, Lyndonville, VT 05851, 802-626-6396 or toll-free 800-225-1998. *Fax:* 802-626-9770. *E-mail:* financialaid@lyndonstate.edu.

LYNN UNIVERSITY
Boca Raton, FL

Tuition & fees: $30,100	Average undergraduate aid package: $20,853

ABOUT THE INSTITUTION Independent, coed. 15 undergraduate majors. Federal methodology is used as a basis for awarding need-based institutional aid.

UNDERGRADUATE EXPENSES for 2009–10 *Comprehensive fee:* $41,000 includes full-time tuition ($28,600), mandatory fees ($1500), and room and board ($10,900). Room and board charges vary according to housing facility. *Part-time tuition:* $825 per credit hour. *Part-time fees:* $30 per term. Part-time tuition and fees vary according to class time and course load. *Payment plans:* Installment, deferred payment.

FRESHMAN FINANCIAL AID (Fall 2009, est.) 237 applied for aid; of those 68% were deemed to have need. 98% of freshmen with need received aid; of those 99% had need fully met. *Average percent of need met:* 64% (excluding resources awarded to replace EFC). *Average financial aid package:* $22,852 (excluding resources awarded to replace EFC). 19% of all full-time freshmen had no need and received non-need-based gift aid.

UNDERGRADUATE FINANCIAL AID (Fall 2009, est.) 1,076 applied for aid; of those 62% were deemed to have need. 98% of undergraduates with need received aid; of those 100% had need fully met. *Average percent of need met:* 60% (excluding resources awarded to replace EFC). *Average financial aid package:* $20,853 (excluding resources awarded to replace EFC). 22% of all full-time undergraduates had no need and received non-need-based gift aid.

GIFT AID (NEED-BASED) *Total amount:* $8,433,871 (20% federal, 11% state, 68% institutional, 1% external sources). *Receiving aid:* Freshmen: 40% (137); all full-time undergraduates: 36% (559). *Average award:* Freshmen: $15,484; Undergraduates: $13,761. *Scholarships, grants, and awards:* Federal Pell, FSEOG, state, private, college/university gift aid from institutional funds.

GIFT AID (NON-NEED-BASED) *Total amount:* $3,187,865 (8% state, 84% institutional, 8% external sources). *Receiving aid:* Freshmen: 43% (148). Undergraduates: 39% (613). *Average award:* Freshmen: $11,934. Undergraduates: $11,381. *Scholarships, grants, and awards by category:* Academic interests/achievement: business, communication, general academic interests/achievements. *Creative arts/performance:* music. *Special achievements/activities:* leadership. *Special characteristics:* children of faculty/staff, local/state students, siblings of current students. *Tuition waivers:* Full or partial for employees or children of employees.

LOANS *Student loans:* $5,783,245 (87% need-based, 13% non-need-based). 43% of past graduating class borrowed through all loan programs. *Average indebtedness per student:* $34,075. *Average need-based loan:* Freshmen: $4497. Undergraduates: $5643. *Parent loans:* $3,458,798 (82% need-based, 18% non-need-based). *Programs:* Federal Direct (Subsidized and Unsubsidized Stafford, PLUS), FFEL (Subsidized and Unsubsidized Stafford, PLUS), Perkins, state, college/university.

WORK-STUDY *Federal work-study:* Total amount: $304,698; jobs available. *State or other work-study/employment:* Total amount: $267,185 (62% need-based, 38% non-need-based). Part-time jobs available.

ATHLETIC AWARDS Total amount: $2,931,798 (50% need-based, 50% non-need-based).

APPLYING FOR FINANCIAL AID *Required financial aid forms:* FAFSA, institution's own form. *Financial aid deadline (priority):* 3/1. *Notification date:* Continuous beginning 2/1. Students must reply within 2 weeks of notification.

CONTACT Mrs. Chan Park, Director of Student Financial Assistance, Lynn University, 3601 North Military Trail, Boca Raton, FL 33431-5598, 561-237-7186 or toll-free 800-888-5966. *Fax:* 561-237-7189. *E-mail:* cpark@lynn.edu.

LYON COLLEGE
Batesville, AR

ABOUT THE INSTITUTION Independent Presbyterian, coed. 18 undergraduate majors.

GIFT AID (NEED-BASED) *Scholarships, grants, and awards:* Federal Pell, FSEOG, state, private, college/university gift aid from institutional funds.

GIFT AID (NON-NEED-BASED) *Scholarships, grants, and awards by category:* Academic interests/achievement: business, general academic interests/achievements. *Creative arts/performance:* art/fine arts, music, theater/drama. *Special achievements/activities:* cheerleading/drum major, general special achievements/activities. *Special characteristics:* children of faculty/staff, ethnic background, first-generation college students, local/state students, members of minority groups, religious affiliation.

LOANS *Programs:* FFEL (Subsidized and Unsubsidized Stafford, PLUS), Perkins.

WORK-STUDY *Federal work-study:* Total amount: $105,426; 133 jobs averaging $1266. *State or other work-study/employment:* Total amount: $8000 (38% need-based, 62% non-need-based). Part-time jobs available.

APPLYING FOR FINANCIAL AID *Required financial aid form:* FAFSA.

CONTACT Mr. Tommy Tucker, Director of Student Assistance, Lyon College, 2300 Highland Road, Batesville, AR 72501, 870-307-7257 or toll-free 800-423-2542. *Fax:* 870-307-7542. *E-mail:* financialaid@lyon.edu.

MACALESTER COLLEGE
St. Paul, MN

Tuition & fees: $40,046	Average undergraduate aid package: $32,258

ABOUT THE INSTITUTION Independent Presbyterian, coed. 35 undergraduate majors. Institutional methodology is used as a basis for awarding need-based institutional aid.

UNDERGRADUATE EXPENSES for 2010–11 *Comprehensive fee:* $49,124 includes full-time tuition ($39,846), mandatory fees ($200), and room and board ($9078). *College room only:* $4854. Full-time tuition and fees vary according to reciprocity agreements. Room and board charges vary according to board plan and housing facility. *Part-time tuition:* $18,987 per term. *Part-time fees:* $1187 per credit hour. *Payment plan:* Installment.

FRESHMAN FINANCIAL AID (Fall 2009, est.) 454 applied for aid; of those 88% were deemed to have need. 100% of freshmen with need received aid; of those 100% had need fully met. *Average percent of need met:* 100% (excluding resources awarded to replace EFC). *Average financial aid package:* $32,533 (excluding resources awarded to replace EFC). 5% of all full-time freshmen had no need and received non-need-based gift aid.

UNDERGRADUATE FINANCIAL AID (Fall 2009, est.) 1,468 applied for aid; of those 90% were deemed to have need. 100% of undergraduates with need received aid; of those 100% had need fully met. *Average percent of need met:* 100% (excluding resources awarded to replace EFC). *Average financial aid package:* $32,258 (excluding resources awarded to replace EFC). 4% of all full-time undergraduates had no need and received non-need-based gift aid.

GIFT AID (NEED-BASED) *Total amount:* $35,919,712 (5% federal, 1% state, 92% institutional, 2% external sources). *Receiving aid:* Freshmen: 70% (397); all full-time undergraduates: 67% (1,311). *Average award:* Freshmen: $28,280; Undergraduates: $27,111. *Scholarships, grants, and awards:* Federal Pell, FSEOG, state, private, college/university gift aid from institutional funds.

GIFT AID (NON-NEED-BASED) *Total amount:* $790,440 (1% federal, 67% institutional, 32% external sources). *Receiving aid:* Freshmen: 7% (37). Undergraduates: 3% (65). *Average award:* Freshmen: $10,000. Undergraduates: $6293. *Scholarships, grants, and awards by category:* Academic interests/achievement: general academic interests/achievements. *Special characteristics:* ethnic background. *Tuition waivers:* Full or partial for employees or children of employees.

LOANS *Student loans:* $6,615,867 (91% need-based, 9% non-need-based). 76% of past graduating class borrowed through all loan programs. *Average indebtedness per student:* $17,275. *Average need-based loan:* Freshmen: $2909. Undergraduates: $3644. *Parent loans:* $1,419,606 (100% non-need-based). *Programs:* Federal Direct (Subsidized and Unsubsidized Stafford, PLUS), Perkins, state.

WORK-STUDY *Federal work-study:* Total amount: $500,972; jobs available. *State or other work-study/employment:* Total amount: $2,309,377 (95% need-based, 5% non-need-based). Part-time jobs available.

APPLYING FOR FINANCIAL AID *Required financial aid forms:* FAFSA, CSS Financial Aid PROFILE, noncustodial (divorced/separated) parent's statement. *Financial aid deadline:* 3/1 (priority: 2/8). *Notification date:* 4/1. Students must reply by 5/1.

CONTACT Financial Aid Office, Macalester College, 1600 Grand Avenue, St. Paul, MN 55105, 651-696-6214 or toll-free 800-231-7974. *Fax:* 651-696-6866. *E-mail:* finaid@macalester.edu.

MACHZIKEI HADATH RABBINICAL COLLEGE
Brooklyn, NY

CONTACT Rabbi Baruch Rozmarin, Director of Financial Aid, Machzikei Hadath Rabbinical College, 5407 16th Avenue, Brooklyn, NY 11204-1805, 718-854-8777.

MacMURRAY COLLEGE
Jacksonville, IL

Tuition & fees: $18,165	Average undergraduate aid package: $24,166

ABOUT THE INSTITUTION Independent United Methodist, coed. *Awards:* associate and bachelor's degrees. 39 undergraduate majors. *Total enrollment:* 602. Undergraduates: 602. Freshmen: 90. Federal methodology is used as a basis for awarding need-based institutional aid.

UNDERGRADUATE EXPENSES for 2009–10 *Comprehensive fee:* $25,703 includes full-time tuition ($17,940), mandatory fees ($225), and room and board ($7538). *College room only:* $3430. Room and board charges vary according to board plan. *Part-time tuition:* $600 per credit hour. *Part-time fees:* $25 per credit hour. Part-time tuition and fees vary according to course load. *Payment plan:* Installment.

FRESHMAN FINANCIAL AID (Fall 2009, est.) 92 applied for aid; of those 97% were deemed to have need. 100% of freshmen with need received aid; of those 53% had need fully met. *Average percent of need met:* 92% (excluding

resources awarded to replace EFC). *Average financial aid package:* $23,423 (excluding resources awarded to replace EFC). 1% of all full-time freshmen had no need and received non-need-based gift aid.

UNDERGRADUATE FINANCIAL AID (Fall 2009, est.) 463 applied for aid; of those 97% were deemed to have need. 100% of undergraduates with need received aid; of those 47% had need fully met. *Average percent of need met:* 93% (excluding resources awarded to replace EFC). *Average financial aid package:* $24,166 (excluding resources awarded to replace EFC). 3% of all full-time undergraduates had no need and received non-need-based gift aid.

GIFT AID (NEED-BASED) *Total amount:* $6,241,579 (20% federal, 17% state, 63% institutional). *Receiving aid:* Freshmen: 91% (87); all full-time undergraduates: 93% (438). *Average award:* Freshmen: $15,193; Undergraduates: $14,107. *Scholarships, grants, and awards:* Federal Pell, FSEOG, state, private, college/university gift aid from institutional funds.

GIFT AID (NON-NEED-BASED) *Total amount:* $2,214,602 (2% federal, 3% state, 89% institutional, 6% external sources). *Receiving aid:* Freshmen: 32% (31). Undergraduates: 27% (129). *Average award:* Freshmen: $8000. Undergraduates: $9212. *Scholarships, grants, and awards by category:* Academic interests/achievement: 261 awards ($1,062,609 total): biological sciences, English, foreign languages, general academic interests/achievements, religion/biblical studies. *Creative arts/performance:* 1 award ($5000 total): *Special characteristics:* 26 awards ($116,026 total): children and siblings of alumni, children of faculty/staff, international students, religious affiliation, siblings of current students. *Tuition waivers:* Full or partial for minority students, children of alumni, employees or children of employees, senior citizens.

LOANS *Student loans:* $5,060,284 (80% need-based, 20% non-need-based). 94% of past graduating class borrowed through all loan programs. *Average indebtedness per student:* $27,524. *Average need-based loan:* Freshmen: $8230. Undergraduates: $10,059. *Parent loans:* $283,863 (100% non-need-based). *Programs:* Federal Direct (Subsidized and Unsubsidized Stafford, PLUS), Perkins.

WORK-STUDY *Federal work-study:* Total amount: $64,173; 114 jobs averaging $564.

APPLYING FOR FINANCIAL AID *Required financial aid form:* FAFSA. *Financial aid deadline (priority):* 5/1. *Notification date:* 5/1. Students must reply within 2 weeks of notification.

CONTACT Charles R. Carothers, Director of Financial Aid, MacMurray College, 447 East College Avenue, Jacksonville, IL 62650, 217-479-7042 or toll-free 800-252-7485 (in-state). *Fax:* 217-291-0702. *E-mail:* charles.carothers@mac.edu.

MACON STATE COLLEGE
Macon, GA

CONTACT Office of Financial Aid, Macon State College, 100 College Station Drive, Macon, GA 31206, 478-471-2717 or toll-free 800-272-7619 Ext. 2800. *Fax:* 478-471-2790. *E-mail:* fainfo@mail.maconstate.edu.

MADONNA UNIVERSITY
Livonia, MI

CONTACT Cathy Durham, Financial Aid Secretary, Madonna University, 36600 Schoolcraft Road, Livonia, MI 48150-1173, 734-432-5663 or toll-free 800-852-4951. *Fax:* 734-432-5344. *E-mail:* finaid@madonna.edu.

MAGDALEN COLLEGE
Warner, NH

ABOUT THE INSTITUTION Independent Roman Catholic, coed. 1 undergraduate major.

GIFT AID (NEED-BASED) *Scholarships, grants, and awards:* private, college/university gift aid from institutional funds.

LOANS *Programs:* alternative loans.

APPLYING FOR FINANCIAL AID *Required financial aid form:* institution's own form.

CONTACT Bobbie Anne Abson, Financial Aid Director, Magdalen College, 511 Kearsarge Mountain Road, Warner, NH 03278, 603-456-2656 or toll-free 877-498-1723 (out-of-state). *Fax:* 603-456-2660. *E-mail:* babson@magdalen.edu.

MAHARISHI UNIVERSITY OF MANAGEMENT
Fairfield, IA

CONTACT Mr. Bill Christensen, Director of Financial Aid, Maharishi University of Management, 1000 North 4th Street, DB 1127, Fairfield, IA 52557-1127, 641-472-1156 or toll-free 800-369-6480. *Fax:* 641-472-1133. *E-mail:* bchrist@mum.edu.

MAINE COLLEGE OF ART
Portland, ME

ABOUT THE INSTITUTION Independent, coed. 9 undergraduate majors.
GIFT AID (NEED-BASED) *Scholarships, grants, and awards:* Federal Pell, FSEOG, state, private, college/university gift aid from institutional funds.
GIFT AID (NON-NEED-BASED) *Scholarships, grants, and awards by category: Creative arts/performance:* art/fine arts. *Special characteristics:* children of faculty/staff.
LOANS *Programs:* FFEL (Subsidized and Unsubsidized Stafford, PLUS), Perkins, alternative loans.
WORK-STUDY *Federal work-study:* Total amount: $115,677; 54 jobs averaging $2151.
APPLYING FOR FINANCIAL AID *Required financial aid form:* FAFSA.
CONTACT Adrienne J. Amari, Director of Financial Aid, Maine College of Art, 522 Congress Street, Portland, ME 04101-3987, 207-775-3052 or toll-free 800-639-4808. *Fax:* 207-772-5069. *E-mail:* aamari@meca.edu.

MAINE MARITIME ACADEMY
Castine, ME

Tuition & fees (ME res): $10,105   **Average undergraduate aid package: $8890**

ABOUT THE INSTITUTION State-supported, coed, primarily men. *Awards:* associate, bachelor's, and master's degrees. 11 undergraduate majors. *Total enrollment:* 860. Undergraduates: 842. Freshmen: 250. Federal methodology is used as a basis for awarding need-based institutional aid.
UNDERGRADUATE EXPENSES for 2009–10 *Application fee:* $15. *Tuition, state resident:* full-time $7900; part-time $300 per credit hour. *Tuition, nonresident:* full-time $15,600; part-time $550 per credit hour. *Required fees:* full-time $2205. Full-time tuition and fees vary according to course load and program. Part-time tuition and fees vary according to course load and program. *College room and board:* $8450; *Room only:* $5250. Room and board charges vary according to board plan. *Payment plan:* Installment.
FRESHMAN FINANCIAL AID (Fall 2009, est.) 200 applied for aid; of those 75% were deemed to have need. 100% of freshmen with need received aid; of those 11% had need fully met. *Average percent of need met:* 21% (excluding resources awarded to replace EFC). *Average financial aid package:* $7299 (excluding resources awarded to replace EFC). 10% of all full-time freshmen had no need and received non-need-based gift aid.
UNDERGRADUATE FINANCIAL AID (Fall 2009, est.) 794 applied for aid; of those 78% were deemed to have need. 100% of undergraduates with need received aid; of those 13% had need fully met. *Average percent of need met:* 35% (excluding resources awarded to replace EFC). *Average financial aid package:* $8890 (excluding resources awarded to replace EFC). 6% of all full-time undergraduates had no need and received non-need-based gift aid.
GIFT AID (NEED-BASED) *Total amount:* $3,880,799 (55% federal, 8% state, 24% institutional, 13% external sources). *Receiving aid:* Freshmen: 31% (95); all full-time undergraduates: 46% (421). *Average award:* Freshmen: $5650; Undergraduates: $6351. *Scholarships, grants, and awards:* Federal Pell, FSEOG, state, private, college/university gift aid from institutional funds.
GIFT AID (NON-NEED-BASED) *Total amount:* $507,290 (32% federal, 2% state, 40% institutional, 26% external sources). *Receiving aid:* Freshmen: 3% (10). Undergraduates: 4% (33). *Average award:* Freshmen: $3799. Undergraduates: $3373. *Scholarships, grants, and awards by category: Academic interests/achievement:* 372 awards ($976,705 total): biological sciences, business, engineering/technologies, general academic interests/achievements. *Special characteristics:* 7 awards ($59,250 total): children of faculty/staff. *ROTC:* Army, Naval.

LOANS *Student loans:* $7,725,099 (69% need-based, 31% non-need-based). 73% of past graduating class borrowed through all loan programs. *Average indebtedness per student:* $39,237. *Average need-based loan:* Freshmen: $3424. Undergraduates: $4370. *Parent loans:* $2,027,831 (39% need-based, 61% non-need-based). *Programs:* FFEL (Subsidized and Unsubsidized Stafford, PLUS), Perkins, college/university, alternative education loans.
WORK-STUDY *Federal work-study:* Total amount: $93,555; 179 jobs averaging $522.
APPLYING FOR FINANCIAL AID *Required financial aid form:* FAFSA. *Financial aid deadline (priority):* 4/15. *Notification date:* Continuous beginning 4/1. Students must reply within 4 weeks of notification.
CONTACT Ms. Holly Bayle, Assistant Director of Financial Aid, Maine Maritime Academy, Pleasant Street, Castine, ME 04420, 207-326-2205 or toll-free 800-464-6565 (in-state), 800-227-8465 (out-of-state). *Fax:* 207-326-2515. *E-mail:* bbayle@mma.edu.

MALONE UNIVERSITY
Canton, OH

Tuition & fees: $22,444   **Average undergraduate aid package: $15,984**

ABOUT THE INSTITUTION Independent religious, coed. 41 undergraduate majors. Federal methodology is used as a basis for awarding need-based institutional aid.
UNDERGRADUATE EXPENSES for 2010–11 *Comprehensive fee:* $29,992 includes full-time tuition ($21,954), mandatory fees ($490), and room and board ($7548). *College room only:* $3848. Room and board charges vary according to board plan. *Part-time tuition:* $425 per credit hour. *Part-time fees:* $122.50 per term. Part-time tuition and fees vary according to course load. *Payment plan:* Installment.
FRESHMAN FINANCIAL AID (Fall 2009, est.) 445 applied for aid; of those 93% were deemed to have need. 100% of freshmen with need received aid; of those 18% had need fully met. *Average percent of need met:* 78% (excluding resources awarded to replace EFC). *Average financial aid package:* $19,314 (excluding resources awarded to replace EFC). 11% of all full-time freshmen had no need and received non-need-based gift aid.
UNDERGRADUATE FINANCIAL AID (Fall 2009, est.) 1,581 applied for aid; of those 92% were deemed to have need. 100% of undergraduates with need received aid; of those 17% had need fully met. *Average percent of need met:* 72% (excluding resources awarded to replace EFC). *Average financial aid package:* $15,984 (excluding resources awarded to replace EFC). 10% of all full-time undergraduates had no need and received non-need-based gift aid.
GIFT AID (NEED-BASED) *Total amount:* $15,415,577 (25% federal, 7% state, 61% institutional, 7% external sources). *Receiving aid:* Freshmen: 87% (414); all full-time undergraduates: 76% (1,398). *Average award:* Freshmen: $15,254; Undergraduates: $12,173. *Scholarships, grants, and awards:* Federal Pell, FSEOG, state, private, college/university gift aid from institutional funds, Academic Competitiveness Grants, National SMART Grants.
GIFT AID (NON-NEED-BASED) *Total amount:* $1,661,187 (1% state, 93% institutional, 6% external sources). *Receiving aid:* Freshmen: 84% (402). Undergraduates: 63% (1,162). *Average award:* Freshmen: $8561. Undergraduates: $6959. *Scholarships, grants, and awards by category: Academic interests/achievement:* 1,072 awards ($6,901,327 total): biological sciences, business, communication, computer science, education, English, foreign languages, general academic interests/achievements, health fields, humanities, international studies, mathematics, physical sciences, premedicine, religion/biblical studies, social sciences. *Creative arts/performance:* 66 awards ($80,000 total): debating, journalism/publications, music, theater/drama. *Special achievements/activities:* 152 awards ($263,960 total): community service, general special achievements/activities, leadership, religious involvement. *Special characteristics:* 203 awards ($1,247,095 total): children and siblings of alumni, children of faculty/staff, general special characteristics, international students, parents of current students, relatives of clergy, religious affiliation, siblings of current students, spouses of current students. *Tuition waivers:* Full or partial for employees or children of employees, senior citizens.
LOANS *Student loans:* $14,124,487 (93% need-based, 7% non-need-based). 81% of past graduating class borrowed through all loan programs. *Average indebtedness per student:* $25,655. *Average need-based loan:* Freshmen: $3701. Undergraduates: $4520. *Parent loans:* $2,527,009 (91% need-based, 9% non-need-based). *Programs:* FFEL (Subsidized and Unsubsidized Stafford, PLUS), Perkins, state, college/university, alternative loans.

WORK-STUDY *Federal work-study:* Total amount: $843,132; 375 jobs averaging $2126. *State or other work-study/employment:* Total amount: $204,160 (84% need-based, 16% non-need-based). 81 part-time jobs averaging $2370.

ATHLETIC AWARDS Total amount: $2,553,040 (80% need-based, 20% non-need-based).

APPLYING FOR FINANCIAL AID *Required financial aid form:* FAFSA. *Financial aid deadline:* 7/31 (priority: 3/1). *Notification date:* Continuous beginning 3/1. Students must reply within 2 weeks of notification.

CONTACT Mrs. Pamela Pustay, Director of Financial Aid, Malone University, 2600 Cleveland Avenue NW, Canton, OH 44709, 330-471-8161 or toll-free 800-521-1146. *Fax:* 330-471-8652. *E-mail:* ppustay@malone.edu.

MANCHESTER COLLEGE
North Manchester, IN

Tuition & fees: $23,790	Average undergraduate aid package: $21,729

ABOUT THE INSTITUTION Independent religious, coed. 59 undergraduate majors. Federal methodology is used as a basis for awarding need-based institutional aid.

UNDERGRADUATE EXPENSES for 2009–10 *One-time required fee:* $250. *Comprehensive fee:* $32,340 includes full-time tuition ($23,000), mandatory fees ($790), and room and board ($8550). *College room only:* $5250. Room and board charges vary according to board plan and housing facility. *Part-time fees:* $350 per year. Part-time tuition and fees vary according to course load. *Payment plan:* Installment.

FRESHMAN FINANCIAL AID (Fall 2009, est.) 404 applied for aid; of those 89% were deemed to have need. 100% of freshmen with need received aid; of those 10% had need fully met. *Average percent of need met:* 87% (excluding resources awarded to replace EFC). *Average financial aid package:* $20,391 (excluding resources awarded to replace EFC). 11% of all full-time freshmen had no need and received non-need-based gift aid.

UNDERGRADUATE FINANCIAL AID (Fall 2009, est.) 1,069 applied for aid; of those 89% were deemed to have need. 100% of undergraduates with need received aid; of those 32% had need fully met. *Average percent of need met:* 92% (excluding resources awarded to replace EFC). *Average financial aid package:* $21,729 (excluding resources awarded to replace EFC). 9% of all full-time undergraduates had no need and received non-need-based gift aid.

GIFT AID (NEED-BASED) *Total amount:* $16,213,793 (8% federal, 21% state, 71% institutional). *Receiving aid:* Freshmen: 76% (324); all full-time undergraduates: 78% (884). *Average award:* Freshmen: $18,110; Undergraduates: $16,881. *Scholarships, grants, and awards:* Federal Pell, FSEOG, state, private, college/university gift aid from institutional funds.

GIFT AID (NON-NEED-BASED) *Total amount:* $3,065,595 (66% institutional, 34% external sources). *Receiving aid:* Freshmen: 84% (359). Undergraduates: 75% (847). *Average award:* Freshmen: $10,746. Undergraduates: $10,470. *Scholarships, grants, and awards by category: Academic interests/achievement:* business, English, foreign languages, general academic interests/achievements, humanities. *Creative arts/performance:* music, theater/drama. *Special achievements/activities:* leadership. *Special characteristics:* children and siblings of alumni, ethnic background, international students, members of minority groups, previous college experience, religious affiliation. *Tuition waivers:* Full or partial for employees or children of employees.

LOANS *Student loans:* $5,021,381 (100% need-based). 80% of past graduating class borrowed through all loan programs. *Average indebtedness per student:* $16,235. *Average need-based loan:* Freshmen: $3775. Undergraduates: $6024. *Parent loans:* $2,259,325 (100% need-based). *Programs:* FFEL (Subsidized and Unsubsidized Stafford, PLUS), Perkins.

WORK-STUDY *Federal work-study:* Total amount: $928,302; jobs available. *State or other work-study/employment:* Total amount: $259,163 (100% need-based). Part-time jobs available.

APPLYING FOR FINANCIAL AID *Required financial aid form:* FAFSA. *Financial aid deadline (priority):* 3/1. *Notification date:* Continuous beginning 3/15. Students must reply by 5/1 or within 3 weeks of notification.

CONTACT Mrs. Sherri Shockey, Director of Student Financial Services, Manchester College, 604 East College Avenue, North Manchester, IN 46962-1225, 260-982-5066 or toll-free 800-852-3648. *Fax:* 260-982-5043. *E-mail:* slshockey@manchester.edu.

MANHATTAN CHRISTIAN COLLEGE
Manhattan, KS

Tuition & fees: N/R	Average undergraduate aid package: $12,278

ABOUT THE INSTITUTION Independent religious, coed. *Awards:* associate and bachelor's degrees. 9 undergraduate majors. *Total enrollment:* 388. Undergraduates: 388. Federal methodology is used as a basis for awarding need-based institutional aid.

FRESHMAN FINANCIAL AID (Fall 2009, est.) 51 applied for aid; of those 84% were deemed to have need. 100% of freshmen with need received aid; of those 51% had need fully met. *Average percent of need met:* 75% (excluding resources awarded to replace EFC). *Average financial aid package:* $16,727 (excluding resources awarded to replace EFC). 19% of all full-time freshmen had no need and received non-need-based gift aid.

UNDERGRADUATE FINANCIAL AID (Fall 2009, est.) 299 applied for aid; of those 90% were deemed to have need. 100% of undergraduates with need received aid; of those 68% had need fully met. *Average percent of need met:* 70% (excluding resources awarded to replace EFC). *Average financial aid package:* $12,278 (excluding resources awarded to replace EFC). 13% of all full-time undergraduates had no need and received non-need-based gift aid.

GIFT AID (NEED-BASED) *Total amount:* $793,661 (72% federal, 28% state). *Receiving aid:* Freshmen: 75% (40); all full-time undergraduates: 49% (183). *Average award:* Freshmen: $4521; Undergraduates: $4459. *Scholarships, grants, and awards:* Federal Pell, FSEOG, state, private, college/university gift aid from institutional funds.

GIFT AID (NON-NEED-BASED) *Total amount:* $1,092,344 (10% federal, 2% state, 62% institutional, 26% external sources). *Receiving aid:* Freshmen: 81% (43). Undergraduates: 51% (188). *Average award:* Freshmen: $4500. Undergraduates: $3201. *Scholarships, grants, and awards by category: Academic interests/achievement:* 273 awards ($655,744 total): general academic interests/achievements, religion/biblical studies. *Creative arts/performance:* music. *Special achievements/activities:* 12 awards ($78,972 total): leadership. *Special characteristics:* 10 awards ($57,769 total): children of faculty/staff. *ROTC:* Army cooperative, Air Force cooperative.

LOANS *Student loans:* $1,548,261 (56% need-based, 44% non-need-based). 86% of past graduating class borrowed through all loan programs. *Average indebtedness per student:* $16,572. *Average need-based loan:* Freshmen: $2763. Undergraduates: $3731. *Parent loans:* $127,204 (100% non-need-based). *Programs:* Federal Direct (Subsidized and Unsubsidized Stafford, PLUS), Perkins.

WORK-STUDY *Federal work-study:* Total amount: $72,411; 56 jobs averaging $1293.

APPLYING FOR FINANCIAL AID *Required financial aid forms:* FAFSA, state aid form. *Financial aid deadline (priority):* 4/1. *Notification date:* Continuous. Students must reply within 2 weeks of notification.

CONTACT Mrs. Margaret Carlisle, Director of Financial Aid, Manhattan Christian College, 1415 Anderson Avenue, Manhattan, KS 66502-4081, 785-539-3571 or toll-free 877-246-4622. *E-mail:* carlisle@mccks.edu.

MANHATTAN COLLEGE
Riverdale, NY

Tuition & fees: $27,455	Average undergraduate aid package: $16,839

ABOUT THE INSTITUTION Independent religious, coed. 41 undergraduate majors. Federal methodology is used as a basis for awarding need-based institutional aid.

UNDERGRADUATE EXPENSES for 2010–11 *Comprehensive fee:* $38,125 includes full-time tuition ($25,520), mandatory fees ($1935), and room and board ($10,670). Full-time tuition and fees vary according to course load and program. Room and board charges vary according to board plan. *Part-time tuition:* $689 per credit hour. Part-time tuition and fees vary according to course load and program. *Payment plans:* Installment, deferred payment.

FRESHMAN FINANCIAL AID (Fall 2009, est.) 597 applied for aid; of those 79% were deemed to have need. 99% of freshmen with need received aid; of those 13% had need fully met. *Average percent of need met:* 67% (excluding resources awarded to replace EFC). *Average financial aid package:* $17,122 (excluding resources awarded to replace EFC). 29% of all full-time freshmen had no need and received non-need-based gift aid.

UNDERGRADUATE FINANCIAL AID (Fall 2009, est.) 2,332 applied for aid; of those 82% were deemed to have need. 99% of undergraduates with need received aid; of those 16% had need fully met. *Average percent of need met:* 67% (excluding resources awarded to replace EFC). *Average financial aid package:* $16,839 (excluding resources awarded to replace EFC). 33% of all full-time undergraduates had no need and received non-need-based gift aid.

GIFT AID (NEED-BASED) *Total amount:* $20,785,743 (16% federal, 13% state, 69% institutional, 2% external sources). *Receiving aid:* Freshmen: 63% (434); all full-time undergraduates: 61% (1,798). *Average award:* Freshmen: $8171; Undergraduates: $7690. *Scholarships, grants, and awards:* Federal Pell, FSEOG, state, private, college/university gift aid from institutional funds.

GIFT AID (NON-NEED-BASED) *Total amount:* $3,544,819 (1% federal, 6% state, 90% institutional, 3% external sources). *Receiving aid:* Freshmen: 32% (218). Undergraduates: 26% (759). *Average award:* Freshmen: $8312. Undergraduates: $8126. *Scholarships, grants, and awards by category: Academic interests/achievement:* biological sciences, business, computer science, foreign languages, general academic interests/achievements, mathematics, military science. *Creative arts/performance:* music. *Special achievements/activities:* community service, leadership. *Special characteristics:* children of faculty/staff. *Tuition waivers:* Full or partial for employees or children of employees.

LOANS *Student loans:* $17,810,120 (83% need-based, 17% non-need-based). 72% of past graduating class borrowed through all loan programs. *Average indebtedness per student:* $31,076. *Average need-based loan:* Freshmen: $3365. Undergraduates: $4369. *Parent loans:* $53,501,444 (97% need-based, 3% non-need-based). *Programs:* Federal Direct (Subsidized and Unsubsidized Stafford, PLUS), FFEL (Subsidized and Unsubsidized Stafford, PLUS), Perkins.

WORK-STUDY *Federal work-study:* Total amount: $600,000; 527 jobs averaging $1200. *State or other work-study/employment:* Total amount: $300,000 (100% non-need-based). 184 part-time jobs averaging $900.

ATHLETIC AWARDS Total amount: $3,464,968 (46% need-based, 54% non-need-based).

APPLYING FOR FINANCIAL AID *Required financial aid forms:* FAFSA, institution's own form, state aid form. *Financial aid deadline (priority):* 3/1. *Notification date:* 4/1. Students must reply by 5/1.

CONTACT Mr. Edward Keough, Director of Student Financial Services, Manhattan College, 4513 Manhattan College Parkway, Riverdale, NY 10471, 718-862-7100 or toll-free 800-622-9235 (in-state). *Fax:* 718-862-8027. *E-mail:* finaid@manhattan.edu.

MANHATTAN SCHOOL OF MUSIC
New York, NY

ABOUT THE INSTITUTION Independent, coed. 6 undergraduate majors.

GIFT AID (NEED-BASED) *Scholarships, grants, and awards:* Federal Pell, FSEOG, state, private, college/university gift aid from institutional funds.

GIFT AID (NON-NEED-BASED) *Scholarships, grants, and awards by category: Creative arts/performance:* music.

LOANS *Programs:* FFEL (Subsidized and Unsubsidized Stafford, PLUS), Perkins.

APPLYING FOR FINANCIAL AID *Required financial aid forms:* FAFSA, institution's own form, CSS Financial Aid PROFILE, verification worksheet.

CONTACT Ms. Amy Anderson, Assistant Dean for Enrollment Management, Manhattan School of Music, 120 Claremont Avenue, New York, NY 10027-4698, 212-749-2802 Ext. 4501. *Fax:* 212-749-3025. *E-mail:* aanderson@msmnyc.edu.

MANHATTANVILLE COLLEGE
Purchase, NY

Tuition & fees: $34,350 | **Average undergraduate aid package:** $26,779

ABOUT THE INSTITUTION Independent, coed. 41 undergraduate majors. Federal methodology is used as a basis for awarding need-based institutional aid.

UNDERGRADUATE EXPENSES for 2010–11 *Comprehensive fee:* $48,270 includes full-time tuition ($33,030), mandatory fees ($1320), and room and board ($13,920). *College room only:* $8250. Room and board charges vary according to board plan. *Part-time tuition:* $765 per credit. *Part-time fees:* $60 per term. Part-time tuition and fees vary according to program. *Payment plans:* Installment, deferred payment.

FRESHMAN FINANCIAL AID (Fall 2008) 377 applied for aid; of those 92% were deemed to have need. 100% of freshmen with need received aid; of those 10%

had need fully met. *Average percent of need met:* 97% (excluding resources awarded to replace EFC). *Average financial aid package:* $29,687 (excluding resources awarded to replace EFC). 24% of all full-time freshmen had no need and received non-need-based gift aid.

UNDERGRADUATE FINANCIAL AID (Fall 2008) 1,234 applied for aid; of those 92% were deemed to have need. 100% of undergraduates with need received aid; of those 10% had need fully met. *Average percent of need met:* 96% (excluding resources awarded to replace EFC). *Average financial aid package:* $26,779 (excluding resources awarded to replace EFC). 28% of all full-time undergraduates had no need and received non-need-based gift aid.

GIFT AID (NEED-BASED) *Total amount:* $15,149,786 (11% federal, 9% state, 80% institutional). *Receiving aid:* Freshmen: 68% (331); all full-time undergraduates: 62% (1,064). *Average award:* Freshmen: $18,740; Undergraduates: $17,427. *Scholarships, grants, and awards:* Federal Pell, FSEOG, state, private, college/university gift aid from institutional funds.

GIFT AID (NON-NEED-BASED) *Total amount:* $16,138,918 (100% institutional). *Receiving aid:* Freshmen: 54% (263). Undergraduates: 50% (868). *Average award:* Freshmen: $20,812. Undergraduates: $18,753. *Scholarships, grants, and awards by category: Academic interests/achievement:* general academic interests/achievements, mathematics. *Creative arts/performance:* dance, performing arts. *Special achievements/activities:* community service, leadership. *Special characteristics:* previous college experience. *Tuition waivers:* Full or partial for employees or children of employees, senior citizens.

LOANS *Student loans:* $13,661,932 (57% need-based, 43% non-need-based). *Average need-based loan:* Freshmen: $3927. Undergraduates: $4523. *Parent loans:* $265,566 (100% non-need-based). *Programs:* FFEL (Subsidized and Unsubsidized Stafford, PLUS), Perkins.

WORK-STUDY *Federal work-study:* Total amount: $269,248; jobs available. *State or other work-study/employment:* Total amount: $1,033,568 (73% need-based, 27% non-need-based). Part-time jobs available.

APPLYING FOR FINANCIAL AID *Required financial aid forms:* FAFSA, state aid form. *Financial aid deadline (priority):* 3/1. *Notification date:* Continuous. Students must reply by 5/1 or within 2 weeks of notification.

CONTACT Ms. Maria A. Barlaam, Director of Financial Aid, Manhattanville College, 2900 Purchase Street, Purchase, NY 10577-2132, 914-323-5357 or toll-free 800-328-4553. *Fax:* 914-323-5382. *E-mail:* barlaamm@mville.edu.

MANNES COLLEGE THE NEW SCHOOL FOR MUSIC
New York, NY

Tuition & fees: $33,600 | **Average undergraduate aid package:** $27,054

ABOUT THE INSTITUTION Independent, coed. 7 undergraduate majors. Federal methodology is used as a basis for awarding need-based institutional aid.

UNDERGRADUATE EXPENSES for 2009–10 *Comprehensive fee:* $48,860 includes full-time tuition ($32,860), mandatory fees ($740), and room and board ($15,260). *College room only:* $12,260. Room and board charges vary according to board plan and housing facility. *Part-time tuition:* $1076 per credit. Part-time tuition and fees vary according to course load. *Payment plan:* Installment.

FRESHMAN FINANCIAL AID (Fall 2009, est.) 13 applied for aid; of those 85% were deemed to have need. 100% of freshmen with need received aid. *Average percent of need met:* 54% (excluding resources awarded to replace EFC). *Average financial aid package:* $21,033 (excluding resources awarded to replace EFC). 4% of all full-time freshmen had no need and received non-need-based gift aid.

UNDERGRADUATE FINANCIAL AID (Fall 2009, est.) 67 applied for aid; of those 85% were deemed to have need. 100% of undergraduates with need received aid; of those 16% had need fully met. *Average percent of need met:* 71% (excluding resources awarded to replace EFC). *Average financial aid package:* $27,054 (excluding resources awarded to replace EFC). 4% of all full-time undergraduates had no need and received non-need-based gift aid.

GIFT AID (NEED-BASED) *Total amount:* $661,969 (19% federal, 5% state, 71% institutional, 5% external sources). *Receiving aid:* Freshmen: 21% (10); all full-time undergraduates: 27% (51). *Average award:* Freshmen: $12,079; Undergraduates: $10,386. *Scholarships, grants, and awards:* Federal Pell, FSEOG, state, private, college/university gift aid from institutional funds.

GIFT AID (NON-NEED-BASED) *Total amount:* $984,895 (99% institutional, 1% external sources). *Receiving aid:* Freshmen: 2% (1). Undergraduates: 4% (7).

Average award: Freshmen: $22,585. Undergraduates: $5880. **Scholarships, grants, and awards by category:** *Creative arts/performance:* music, performing arts. **Special characteristics:** international students. **Tuition waivers:** Full or partial for employees or children of employees.

LOANS *Student loans:* $438,300 (95% need-based, 5% non-need-based). 43% of past graduating class borrowed through all loan programs. *Average indebtedness per student:* $30,942. **Average need-based loan:** Freshmen: $10,636. Undergraduates: $12,904. **Parent loans:** $320,266 (100% need-based). **Programs:** FFEL (Subsidized and Unsubsidized Stafford, PLUS), Perkins.

WORK-STUDY *Federal work-study:* Total amount: $8000; jobs available.

APPLYING FOR FINANCIAL AID *Required financial aid forms:* FAFSA, state aid form. **Financial aid deadline:** Continuous. **Notification date:** Continuous beginning 3/1. Students must reply within 4 weeks of notification.

CONTACT Financial Aid Counselor, Mannes College The New School for Music, 150 West 85th Street, New York, NY 10024-4402, 212-229-8930 or toll-free 800-292-3040. *Fax:* 212-229-5919.

MANSFIELD UNIVERSITY OF PENNSYLVANIA
Mansfield, PA

Tuition & fees: N/R	Average undergraduate aid package: $2694

ABOUT THE INSTITUTION State-supported, coed. 71 undergraduate majors. Federal methodology is used as a basis for awarding need-based institutional aid.

FRESHMAN FINANCIAL AID (Fall 2008) 100% of freshmen with need received aid; of those 31% had need fully met. *Average percent of need met:* 81% (excluding resources awarded to replace EFC). *Average financial aid package:* $2269 (excluding resources awarded to replace EFC).

UNDERGRADUATE FINANCIAL AID (Fall 2008) 100% of undergraduates with need received aid; of those 33% had need fully met. *Average percent of need met:* 81% (excluding resources awarded to replace EFC). *Average financial aid package:* $2694 (excluding resources awarded to replace EFC). 1% of all full-time undergraduates had no need and received non-need-based gift aid.

GIFT AID (NEED-BASED) *Total amount:* $8,692,712 (47% federal, 35% state, 14% institutional, 4% external sources). **Receiving aid:** Freshmen: 68% (602); all full-time undergraduates: 66% (1,706). *Average award:* Freshmen: $2200; Undergraduates: $2404. **Scholarships, grants, and awards:** Federal Pell, FSEOG, state, private, college/university gift aid from institutional funds, Federal Nursing.

GIFT AID (NON-NEED-BASED) *Total amount:* $512,248 (16% federal, 1% institutional, 83% external sources). *Receiving aid:* Freshmen: 13% (113). Undergraduates: 8% (218). *Average award:* Undergraduates: $594. **Scholarships, grants, and awards by category:** *Academic interests/achievement:* biological sciences, communication, education, general academic interests/achievements, health fields, mathematics, physical sciences. *Creative arts/performance:* art/fine arts, journalism/publications, music. *Special achievements/activities:* leadership. *Special characteristics:* local/state students. **Tuition waivers:** Full or partial for employees or children of employees, senior citizens.

LOANS *Student loans:* $21,497,706 (41% need-based, 59% non-need-based). 81% of past graduating class borrowed through all loan programs. *Average indebtedness per student:* $28,937. **Average need-based loan:** Freshmen: $2664. Undergraduates: $3309. **Parent loans:** $1,542,945 (100% non-need-based). **Programs:** Federal Direct (Subsidized and Unsubsidized Stafford, PLUS), Perkins, Federal Nursing.

WORK-STUDY *Federal work-study:* Total amount: $217,367; jobs available. *State or other work-study/employment:* Total amount: $340,042 (100% need-based). Part-time jobs available.

ATHLETIC AWARDS Total amount: $313,289 (15% need-based, 85% non-need-based).

APPLYING FOR FINANCIAL AID *Required financial aid forms:* FAFSA, institution's own form. **Financial aid deadline:** Continuous. **Notification date:** Continuous beginning 3/15. Students must reply within 2 weeks of notification.

CONTACT Ms. Barbara Schmitt, Director of Financial Aid, Mansfield University of Pennsylvania, 224 South Hall, Mansfield, PA 16933, 570-662-4854 or toll-free 800-577-6826. *Fax:* 570-662-4136.

MAPLE SPRINGS BAPTIST BIBLE COLLEGE AND SEMINARY
Capitol Heights, MD

CONTACT Ms. Fannie G. Thompson, Director of Business Affairs, Maple Springs Baptist Bible College and Seminary, 4130 Belt Road, Capitol Heights, MD 20743, 301-736-3631. *Fax:* 301-735-6507.

MARANATHA BAPTIST BIBLE COLLEGE
Watertown, WI

ABOUT THE INSTITUTION Independent Baptist, coed. 34 undergraduate majors.

GIFT AID (NEED-BASED) *Scholarships, grants, and awards:* Federal Pell, FSEOG, state, private, college/university gift aid from institutional funds.

GIFT AID (NON-NEED-BASED) *Scholarships, grants, and awards by category:* *Academic interests/achievement:* business, general academic interests/achievements, religion/biblical studies. *Creative arts/performance:* music. *Special characteristics:* children and siblings of alumni, children of educators, children of faculty/staff, relatives of clergy, spouses of current students.

LOANS *Programs:* FFEL (Subsidized and Unsubsidized Stafford, PLUS), state, alternative loans.

WORK-STUDY *State or other work-study/employment:* Part-time jobs available.

APPLYING FOR FINANCIAL AID *Required financial aid form:* FAFSA.

CONTACT Mr. Bruce Roth, Associate Director of Financial Aid, Maranatha Baptist Bible College, 745 West Main Street, Watertown, WI 53094, 920-206-2318 or toll-free 800-622-2947. *Fax:* 920-261-9109. *E-mail:* financialaid@mbbc.edu.

MARIA COLLEGE
Albany, NY

CONTACT Sr. Mary Theresine Glock, Financial Aid Officer, Maria College, 700 New Scotland Avenue, Albany, NY 12208, 518-438-3111 Ext. 26. *Fax:* 518-438-7170.

MARIAN UNIVERSITY
Indianapolis, IN

ABOUT THE INSTITUTION Independent Roman Catholic, coed. 42 undergraduate majors.

GIFT AID (NEED-BASED) *Scholarships, grants, and awards:* Federal Pell, FSEOG, state, private, college/university gift aid from institutional funds.

GIFT AID (NON-NEED-BASED) *Scholarships, grants, and awards by category:* *Academic interests/achievement:* area/ethnic studies, general academic interests/achievements, religion/biblical studies. *Creative arts/performance:* applied art and design, art/fine arts, music, performing arts, theater/drama. *Special achievements/activities:* community service, religious involvement. *Special characteristics:* adult students, children and siblings of alumni, children of faculty/staff, international students, members of minority groups, religious affiliation, siblings of current students, spouses of current students.

LOANS *Programs:* FFEL (Subsidized and Unsubsidized Stafford, PLUS), Perkins, college/university.

WORK-STUDY *Federal work-study:* Total amount: $257,925; 200 jobs averaging $1500. *State or other work-study/employment:* Total amount: $28,500 (100% non-need-based). Part-time jobs available.

APPLYING FOR FINANCIAL AID *Required financial aid forms:* FAFSA, institution's own form.

CONTACT Mr. John E. Shelton, Dean of Financial Aid, Marian University, 3200 Cold Spring Road, Indianapolis, IN 46222-1997, 317-955-6040 or toll-free 800-772-7264 (in-state). *Fax:* 317-955-6424. *E-mail:* jshelton@marian.edu.

MARIAN UNIVERSITY
Fond du Lac, WI

Tuition & fees: $20,900	Average undergraduate aid package: $19,560

ABOUT THE INSTITUTION Independent Roman Catholic, coed. 50 undergraduate majors. Federal methodology is used as a basis for awarding need-based institutional aid.

UNDERGRADUATE EXPENSES for 2009–10 *One-time required fee:* $100. *Comprehensive fee:* $26,540 includes full-time tuition ($20,550), mandatory fees ($350), and room and board ($5640). *College room only:* $3910. Full-time tuition and fees vary according to class time, course load, degree level, and program. Room and board charges vary according to board plan and housing facility. *Part-time tuition:* $315 per credit. *Part-time fees:* $80 per term. Part-time tuition and fees vary according to class time, course load, degree level, and program. *Payment plan:* Installment.

FRESHMAN FINANCIAL AID (Fall 2009, est.) 283 applied for aid; of those 92% were deemed to have need. 100% of freshmen with need received aid; of those 40% had need fully met. *Average percent of need met:* 89% (excluding resources awarded to replace EFC). *Average financial aid package:* $19,855 (excluding resources awarded to replace EFC). 8% of all full-time freshmen had no need and received non-need-based gift aid.

UNDERGRADUATE FINANCIAL AID (Fall 2009, est.) 1,329 applied for aid; of those 88% were deemed to have need. 100% of undergraduates with need received aid; of those 47% had need fully met. *Average percent of need met:* 91% (excluding resources awarded to replace EFC). *Average financial aid package:* $19,560 (excluding resources awarded to replace EFC). 11% of all full-time undergraduates had no need and received non-need-based gift aid.

GIFT AID (NEED-BASED) *Total amount:* $12,517,286 (17% federal, 17% state, 64% institutional, 2% external sources). *Receiving aid:* Freshmen: 91% (259); all full-time undergraduates: 82% (1,129). *Average award:* Freshmen: $11,291; Undergraduates: $10,669. *Scholarships, grants, and awards:* Federal Pell, FSEOG, state, private, college/university gift aid from institutional funds, endowed scholarships.

GIFT AID (NON-NEED-BASED) *Total amount:* $906,325 (1% state, 96% institutional, 3% external sources). *Receiving aid:* Freshmen: 83% (235). Undergraduates: 70% (969). *Average award:* Freshmen: $5964. Undergraduates: $4931. *Scholarships, grants, and awards by category:* Academic interests/achievement: 1,203 awards ($5,727,534 total): general academic interests/achievements. Creative arts/performance: 38 awards ($77,250 total): music. Special characteristics: 78 awards ($310,512 total): children of faculty/staff, children with a deceased or disabled parent, siblings of current students. *Tuition waivers:* Full or partial for employees or children of employees, senior citizens.

LOANS *Student loans:* $12,481,614 (72% need-based, 28% non-need-based). 82% of past graduating class borrowed through all loan programs. *Average indebtedness per student:* $23,625. *Average need-based loan:* Freshmen: $5264. Undergraduates: $6758. *Parent loans:* $1,009,004 (80% need-based, 20% non-need-based). *Programs:* Federal Direct (Subsidized and Unsubsidized Stafford, PLUS), FFEL (Subsidized and Unsubsidized Stafford, PLUS), Perkins, Federal Nursing.

WORK-STUDY *Federal work-study:* Total amount: $124,835; 171 jobs averaging $730. *State or other work-study/employment:* Total amount: $311,845 (100% non-need-based). 189 part-time jobs averaging $1650.

APPLYING FOR FINANCIAL AID *Required financial aid forms:* FAFSA, institution's own form. *Financial aid deadline (priority):* 3/1. *Notification date:* Continuous beginning 3/1. Students must reply within 4 weeks of notification.

CONTACT Ms. Pam Warren, Associate Director of Financial Aid, Marian University, 45 South National Avenue, Fond du Lac, WI 54935-4699, 920-923-7614 or toll-free 800-2-MARIAN Ext. 7652 (in-state). *Fax:* 920-923-8767. *E-mail:* dmckinney@marianuniversity.edu.

MARIETTA COLLEGE
Marietta, OH

Tuition & fees: $27,066	Average undergraduate aid package: $24,875

ABOUT THE INSTITUTION Independent, coed. 41 undergraduate majors. Federal methodology is used as a basis for awarding need-based institutional aid.

UNDERGRADUATE EXPENSES for 2010–11 *Comprehensive fee:* $35,112 includes full-time tuition ($26,386), mandatory fees ($680), and room and board ($8046). *College room only:* $4400. Full-time tuition and fees vary according to course load and degree level. Room and board charges vary according to housing facility. *Part-time tuition:* $875 per credit hour. Part-time tuition and fees vary according to course load and degree level. *Payment plan:* Installment.

FRESHMAN FINANCIAL AID (Fall 2009, est.) 371 applied for aid; of those 86% were deemed to have need. 100% of freshmen with need received aid; of those 52% had need fully met. *Average percent of need met:* 94% (excluding

resources awarded to replace EFC). *Average financial aid package:* $25,970 (excluding resources awarded to replace EFC). 13% of all full-time freshmen had no need and received non-need-based gift aid.

UNDERGRADUATE FINANCIAL AID (Fall 2009, est.) 1,344 applied for aid; of those 81% were deemed to have need. 100% of undergraduates with need received aid; of those 50% had need fully met. *Average percent of need met:* 93% (excluding resources awarded to replace EFC). *Average financial aid package:* $24,875 (excluding resources awarded to replace EFC). 18% of all full-time undergraduates had no need and received non-need-based gift aid.

GIFT AID (NEED-BASED) *Total amount:* $16,761,094 (13% federal, 3% state, 84% institutional). *Receiving aid:* Freshmen: 80% (310); all full-time undergraduates: 74% (1,057). *Average award:* Freshmen: $14,468; Undergraduates: $12,858. *Scholarships, grants, and awards:* Federal Pell, FSEOG, state, private, college/university gift aid from institutional funds.

GIFT AID (NON-NEED-BASED) *Total amount:* $3,427,605 (86% institutional, 14% external sources). *Receiving aid:* Freshmen: 53% (204). Undergraduates: 52% (746). *Average award:* Freshmen: $10,231. Undergraduates: $8636. *Scholarships, grants, and awards by category:* Academic interests/achievement: 511 awards ($5,291,788 total): general academic interests/achievements, physical sciences. Creative arts/performance: 72 awards ($152,250 total): art/fine arts, music, performing arts, theater/drama. Special achievements/activities: 18 awards ($54,000 total): general special achievements/activities. Special characteristics: 164 awards ($679,725 total): children and siblings of alumni, ethnic background, members of minority groups. *Tuition waivers:* Full or partial for employees or children of employees.

LOANS *Student loans:* $7,824,010 (53% need-based, 47% non-need-based). 74% of past graduating class borrowed through all loan programs. *Average indebtedness per student:* $27,455. *Average need-based loan:* Freshmen: $2705. Undergraduates: $3755. *Parent loans:* $2,906,742 (100% non-need-based). *Programs:* Federal Direct (Subsidized and Unsubsidized Stafford, PLUS), Perkins.

WORK-STUDY *Federal work-study:* Total amount: $1,646,104; 884 jobs averaging $1744.

APPLYING FOR FINANCIAL AID *Required financial aid form:* FAFSA. *Financial aid deadline (priority):* 3/1. *Notification date:* 3/15. Students must reply by 5/1 or within 2 weeks of notification.

CONTACT Mr. Kevin Lamb, Director of Financial Aid, Marietta College, 215 Fifth Street, Marietta, OH 45750-4000, 740-376-4712 or toll-free 800-331-7896. *Fax:* 740-376-4990. *E-mail:* finaid@marietta.edu.

MARIST COLLEGE
Poughkeepsie, NY

Tuition & fees: $26,604	Average undergraduate aid package: $15,387

ABOUT THE INSTITUTION Independent, coed. 50 undergraduate majors. Federal methodology is used as a basis for awarding need-based institutional aid.

UNDERGRADUATE EXPENSES for 2009–10 *Comprehensive fee:* $37,829 includes full-time tuition ($26,104), mandatory fees ($500), and room and board ($11,225). *College room only:* $7235. Room and board charges vary according to board plan and housing facility. *Part-time tuition:* $610 per credit. *Part-time fees:* $40 per term. *Payment plan:* Installment.

FRESHMAN FINANCIAL AID (Fall 2009, est.) 865 applied for aid; of those 73% were deemed to have need. 100% of freshmen with need received aid; of those 20% had need fully met. *Average percent of need met:* 67% (excluding resources awarded to replace EFC). *Average financial aid package:* $15,558 (excluding resources awarded to replace EFC). 30% of all full-time freshmen had no need and received non-need-based gift aid.

UNDERGRADUATE FINANCIAL AID (Fall 2009, est.) 3,451 applied for aid; of those 80% were deemed to have need. 99% of undergraduates with need received aid; of those 16% had need fully met. *Average percent of need met:* 62% (excluding resources awarded to replace EFC). *Average financial aid package:* $15,387 (excluding resources awarded to replace EFC). 25% of all full-time undergraduates had no need and received non-need-based gift aid.

GIFT AID (NEED-BASED) *Total amount:* $29,178,814 (11% federal, 9% state, 77% institutional, 3% external sources). *Receiving aid:* Freshmen: 60% (622); all full-time undergraduates: 57% (2,571). *Average award:* Freshmen: $12,758; Undergraduates: $11,209. *Scholarships, grants, and awards:* Federal Pell, FSEOG, state, private, college/university gift aid from institutional funds.

GIFT AID (NON-NEED-BASED) *Total amount:* $8,994,476 (2% state, 96% institutional, 2% external sources). *Receiving aid:* Freshmen: 39% (409). Undergraduates: 29% (1,316). *Average award:* Freshmen: $7116. Undergraduates: $7101. **Scholarships, grants, and awards by category:** *Academic interests/achievement:* general academic interests/achievements. *Creative arts/performance:* debating, music. *Special characteristics:* local/state students. **Tuition waivers:** Full or partial for employees or children of employees.

LOANS *Student loans:* $30,596,496 (36% need-based, 64% non-need-based). 76% of past graduating class borrowed through all loan programs. *Average indebtedness per student:* $35,993. *Average need-based loan:* Freshmen: $5049. Undergraduates: $5931. *Parent loans:* $9,359,225 (100% non-need-based). *Programs:* FFEL (Subsidized and Unsubsidized Stafford, PLUS), Perkins, alternative loans.

WORK-STUDY *Federal work-study:* Total amount: $3,362,437; jobs available. *State or other work-study/employment:* Total amount: $1,417,900 (100% non-need-based). Part-time jobs available.

ATHLETIC AWARDS Total amount: $3,107,534 (43% need-based, 57% non-need-based).

APPLYING FOR FINANCIAL AID *Required financial aid forms:* FAFSA, institution's own form. *Financial aid deadline:* 5/1 (priority: 2/15). *Notification date:* Continuous beginning 3/15. Students must reply by 5/1 or within 2 weeks of notification.

CONTACT Joseph R. Weglarz, Executive Director, Student Financial Services, Marist College, 3399 North Road, Poughkeepsie, NY 12601, 845-575-3230 or toll-free 800-436-5483. *Fax:* 845-575-3099. *E-mail:* joseph.weglarz@marist.edu.

MARLBORO COLLEGE
Marlboro, VT

Tuition & fees: $33,660	Average undergraduate aid package: $21,011

ABOUT THE INSTITUTION Independent, coed. 75 undergraduate majors. Federal methodology is used as a basis for awarding need-based institutional aid.

UNDERGRADUATE EXPENSES for 2009–10 *Comprehensive fee:* $42,880 includes full-time tuition ($32,550), mandatory fees ($1110), and room and board ($9220). *College room only:* $5080. Full-time tuition and fees vary according to degree level, location, and program. *Part-time tuition:* $1085 per credit. Part-time tuition and fees vary according to course load, degree level, location, and program. *Payment plan:* Installment.

FRESHMAN FINANCIAL AID (Fall 2009, est.) 48 applied for aid; of those 98% were deemed to have need. 100% of freshmen with need received aid. *Average percent of need met:* 87% (excluding resources awarded to replace EFC). *Average financial aid package:* $21,326 (excluding resources awarded to replace EFC). 23% of all full-time freshmen had no need and received non-need-based gift aid.

UNDERGRADUATE FINANCIAL AID (Fall 2009, est.) 262 applied for aid; of those 87% were deemed to have need. 100% of undergraduates with need received aid. *Average percent of need met:* 87% (excluding resources awarded to replace EFC). *Average financial aid package:* $21,011 (excluding resources awarded to replace EFC). 21% of all full-time undergraduates had no need and received non-need-based gift aid.

GIFT AID (NEED-BASED) *Total amount:* $2,779,790 (16% federal, 2% state, 82% institutional). *Receiving aid:* Freshmen: 62% (40); all full-time undergraduates: 64% (196). *Average award:* Freshmen: $15,003; Undergraduates: $14,182. *Scholarships, grants, and awards:* Federal Pell, FSEOG, state, private, college/university gift aid from institutional funds.

GIFT AID (NON-NEED-BASED) *Total amount:* $1,650,146 (96% institutional, 4% external sources). *Receiving aid:* Freshmen: 72% (46). Undergraduates: 58% (179). *Average award:* Freshmen: $8250. Undergraduates: $6481. *Scholarships, grants, and awards by category:* *Academic interests/achievement:* general academic interests/achievements. *Tuition waivers:* Full or partial for employees or children of employees, senior citizens.

LOANS *Student loans:* $1,728,506 (50% need-based, 50% non-need-based). 66% of past graduating class borrowed through all loan programs. *Average indebtedness per student:* $6713. *Average need-based loan:* Freshmen: $3282. Undergraduates: $4167. *Parent loans:* $828,895 (100% non-need-based). *Programs:* FFEL (Subsidized and Unsubsidized Stafford, PLUS).

WORK-STUDY *Federal work-study:* Total amount: $364,526; jobs available. *State or other work-study/employment:* Part-time jobs available.

APPLYING FOR FINANCIAL AID *Required financial aid form:* FAFSA. *Financial aid deadline:* 3/1. *Notification date:* Continuous beginning 3/1. Students must reply by 5/1 or within 2 weeks of notification.

CONTACT Cathy S. Fuller, Associate Director of Financial Aid, Marlboro College, PO Box A, 2582 South Road, Marlboro, VT 05344-0300, 802-258-9237 or toll-free 800-343-0049. *Fax:* 802-258-9300. *E-mail:* finaid@marlboro.edu.

MARQUETTE UNIVERSITY
Milwaukee, WI

Tuition & fees: $30,462	Average undergraduate aid package: $21,428

ABOUT THE INSTITUTION Independent Roman Catholic (Jesuit), coed. 67 undergraduate majors. Federal methodology is used as a basis for awarding need-based institutional aid.

UNDERGRADUATE EXPENSES for 2010–11 *Tuition:* full-time $30,040; part-time $875 per credit. Full-time tuition and fees vary according to course load and program. Part-time tuition and fees vary according to program. Room and board charges vary according to board plan and housing facility. *Payment plan:* Installment.

FRESHMAN FINANCIAL AID (Fall 2009, est.) 1,628 applied for aid; of those 76% were deemed to have need. 100% of freshmen with need received aid; of those 27% had need fully met. *Average percent of need met:* 78% (excluding resources awarded to replace EFC). *Average financial aid package:* $21,961 (excluding resources awarded to replace EFC). 34% of all full-time freshmen had no need and received non-need-based gift aid.

UNDERGRADUATE FINANCIAL AID (Fall 2009, est.) 5,611 applied for aid; of those 83% were deemed to have need. 99% of undergraduates with need received aid; of those 28% had need fully met. *Average percent of need met:* 78% (excluding resources awarded to replace EFC). *Average financial aid package:* $21,428 (excluding resources awarded to replace EFC). 24% of all full-time undergraduates had no need and received non-need-based gift aid.

GIFT AID (NEED-BASED) *Total amount:* $64,880,137 (10% federal, 5% state, 78% institutional, 7% external sources). *Receiving aid:* Freshmen: 63% (1,228); all full-time undergraduates: 58% (4,479). *Average award:* Freshmen: $16,431; Undergraduates: $14,614. *Scholarships, grants, and awards:* Federal Pell, FSEOG, state, private, college/university gift aid from institutional funds.

GIFT AID (NON-NEED-BASED) *Total amount:* $20,979,181 (78% institutional, 22% external sources). *Receiving aid:* Freshmen: 6% (119). Undergraduates: 5% (376). *Average award:* Freshmen: $7186. Undergraduates: $8138. *Scholarships, grants, and awards by category:* *Academic interests/achievement:* 4,269 awards ($28,917,301 total): biological sciences, business, communication, engineering/technologies, foreign languages, general academic interests/achievements, health fields, mathematics. *Creative arts/performance:* theater/drama. *Special characteristics:* 193 awards ($5,285,838 total): children of faculty/staff. *Tuition waivers:* Full or partial for employees or children of employees, adult students, senior citizens.

LOANS *Student loans:* $46,950,259 (76% need-based, 24% non-need-based). 65% of past graduating class borrowed through all loan programs. *Average indebtedness per student:* $31,469. *Average need-based loan:* Freshmen: $4406. Undergraduates: $5440. *Parent loans:* $19,254,981 (26% need-based, 74% non-need-based). *Programs:* Federal Direct (Subsidized and Unsubsidized Stafford, PLUS), Perkins, Federal Nursing, state, college/university.

WORK-STUDY *Federal work-study:* Total amount: $6,444,315; jobs available. *State or other work-study/employment:* Part-time jobs available.

ATHLETIC AWARDS Total amount: $3,499,825 (32% need-based, 68% non-need-based).

APPLYING FOR FINANCIAL AID *Required financial aid form:* FAFSA. *Financial aid deadline:* Continuous. *Notification date:* Continuous beginning 3/20. Students must reply by 5/1 or within 3 weeks of notification.

CONTACT Susan Teerink, Director of Financial Aid, Marquette University, PO Box 1881, Milwaukee, WI 53201-1881, 414-288-4000 or toll-free 800-222-6544. *Fax:* 414-288-1718. *E-mail:* financialaid@marquette.edu.

MARSHALL UNIVERSITY
Huntington, WV

Tuition & fees (WV res): $5236	Average undergraduate aid package: $9498

ABOUT THE INSTITUTION State-supported, coed. 52 undergraduate majors. Federal methodology is used as a basis for awarding need-based institutional aid.

UNDERGRADUATE EXPENSES for 2009–10 *Tuition, state resident:* full-time $4319; part-time $180.25 per credit hour. *Tuition, nonresident:* full-time $11,565; part-time $482.25 per credit hour. *Required fees:* full-time $917; $38.50 per credit hour. Full-time tuition and fees vary according to degree level, location, program, and reciprocity agreements. Part-time tuition and fees vary according to course load, degree level, location, program, and reciprocity agreements. *College room and board:* $7556; *Room only:* $4474. Room and board charges vary according to board plan and housing facility. *Payment plan:* Installment. FRESHMAN FINANCIAL AID (Fall 2009, est.) 1,207 applied for aid; of those 74% were deemed to have need. 99% of freshmen with need received aid; of those 30% had need fully met. *Average percent of need met:* 55% (excluding resources awarded to replace EFC). *Average financial aid package:* $9688 (excluding resources awarded to replace EFC). 21% of all full-time freshmen had no need and received non-need-based gift aid.

UNDERGRADUATE FINANCIAL AID (Fall 2009, est.) 5,850 applied for aid; of those 78% were deemed to have need. 98% of undergraduates with need received aid; of those 30% had need fully met. *Average percent of need met:* 58% (excluding resources awarded to replace EFC). *Average financial aid package:* $9498 (excluding resources awarded to replace EFC). 18% of all full-time undergraduates had no need and received non-need-based gift aid.

GIFT AID (NEED-BASED) *Total amount:* $23,761,777 (74% federal, 26% state). *Receiving aid:* Freshmen: 47% (606); all full-time undergraduates: 44% (3,153). *Average award:* Freshmen: $6635; Undergraduates: $6177. *Scholarships, grants, and awards:* Federal Pell, FSEOG, state, private, college/university gift aid from institutional funds, Academic Competitiveness Grants, National SMART Grants, TEACH Grants.

GIFT AID (NON-NEED-BASED) *Total amount:* $14,710,948 (54% state, 34% institutional, 12% external sources). *Receiving aid:* Freshmen: 40% (522). Undergraduates: 24% (1,702). *Average award:* Freshmen: $6193. Undergraduates: $6062. *Scholarships, grants, and awards by category:* Academic interests/ achievement: 2,258 awards ($4,778,578 total): general academic interests/ achievements. Special characteristics: 53 awards ($189,274 total): children of faculty/staff. *Tuition waivers:* Full or partial for employees or children of employees, senior citizens.

LOANS *Student loans:* $37,234,025 (95% need-based, 5% non-need-based). 62% of past graduating class borrowed through all loan programs. *Average indebtedness per student:* $18,146. *Average need-based loan:* Freshmen: $5571. Undergraduates: $6800. *Parent loans:* $3,143,247 (100% non-need-based). *Programs:* Federal Direct (Subsidized and Unsubsidized Stafford, PLUS), Perkins, state, college/university, alternative loans.

WORK-STUDY *Federal work-study:* Total amount: $465,762; 256 jobs averaging $1819. *State or other work-study/employment:* Part-time jobs available.

ATHLETIC AWARDS Total amount: $4,456,037 (100% non-need-based).

APPLYING FOR FINANCIAL AID *Required financial aid form:* FAFSA. *Financial aid deadline (priority):* 3/1. *Notification date:* 3/15. Students must reply within 2 weeks of notification.

CONTACT Ms. Kathy Bialk, Director of Student Financial Aid, Marshall University, One John Marshall Drive, Huntington, WV 25755, 304-696-2280 or toll-free 800-642-3499 (in-state). *Fax:* 304-696-3242. *E-mail:* bialkk@marshall.edu.

MARS HILL COLLEGE
Mars Hill, NC

ABOUT THE INSTITUTION Independent Baptist, coed. 59 undergraduate majors.

GIFT AID (NEED-BASED) *Scholarships, grants, and awards:* Federal Pell, FSEOG, state, private, college/university gift aid from institutional funds.

GIFT AID (NON-NEED-BASED) *Scholarships, grants, and awards by category:* Academic interests/achievement: general academic interests/achievements. Creative arts/performance: dance, music, theater/drama. Special achievements/ activities: cheerleading/drum major. Special characteristics: children of faculty/ staff.

LOANS *Programs:* FFEL (Subsidized and Unsubsidized Stafford, PLUS), Perkins.

WORK-STUDY *Federal work-study:* Total amount: $215,494; 200 jobs averaging $1077.

APPLYING FOR FINANCIAL AID *Required financial aid forms:* FAFSA, state aid form.

CONTACT Amanda Randolph Willis, Director of Financial Aid, Mars Hill College, PO Box 370, Mars Hill, NC 28754, 828-689-1123 or toll-free 866-MHC-4-YOU. *Fax:* 828-689-1300. *E-mail:* awillis@mhc.edu.

MARTIN LUTHER COLLEGE
New Ulm, MN

Tuition & fees: $10,990   **Average undergraduate aid package: $10,085**

ABOUT THE INSTITUTION Independent religious, coed. 6 undergraduate majors. Federal methodology is used as a basis for awarding need-based institutional aid.

UNDERGRADUATE EXPENSES for 2010–11 *Comprehensive fee:* $15,250 includes full-time tuition ($10,990) and room and board ($4260).

FRESHMAN FINANCIAL AID (Fall 2008) 165 applied for aid; of those 79% were deemed to have need. 100% of freshmen with need received aid; of those 31% had need fully met. *Average percent of need met:* 60% (excluding resources awarded to replace EFC). *Average financial aid package:* $9294 (excluding resources awarded to replace EFC). 14% of all full-time freshmen had no need and received non-need-based gift aid.

UNDERGRADUATE FINANCIAL AID (Fall 2008) 650 applied for aid; of those 82% were deemed to have need. 100% of undergraduates with need received aid; of those 40% had need fully met. *Average percent of need met:* 63% (excluding resources awarded to replace EFC). *Average financial aid package:* $10,085 (excluding resources awarded to replace EFC). 10% of all full-time undergraduates had no need and received non-need-based gift aid.

GIFT AID (NEED-BASED) *Total amount:* $865,873 (23% federal, 5% state, 56% institutional, 16% external sources). *Receiving aid:* Freshmen: 62% (108); all full-time undergraduates: 59% (425). *Average award:* Freshmen: $4150; Undergraduates: $4025. *Scholarships, grants, and awards:* Federal Pell, FSEOG, state, private, college/university gift aid from institutional funds.

GIFT AID (NON-NEED-BASED) *Receiving aid:* Freshmen: 47% (83). Undergraduates: 45% (325). *Average award:* Freshmen: $1570. Undergraduates: $1595. *Scholarships, grants, and awards by category:* Academic interests/achievement: general academic interests/achievements. Creative arts/performance: music.

LOANS *Student loans:* $411,563 (100% need-based). 47% of past graduating class borrowed through all loan programs. *Average indebtedness per student:* $15,600. *Average need-based loan:* Freshmen: $3847. Undergraduates: $3950. *Parent loans:* $35,600 (100% need-based). *Programs:* FFEL (Subsidized and Unsubsidized Stafford, PLUS), Perkins, state, college/university.

WORK-STUDY *Federal work-study:* Total amount: $10,518; jobs available.

APPLYING FOR FINANCIAL AID *Required financial aid forms:* FAFSA, institution's own form. *Financial aid deadline:* 4/15. *Notification date:* Continuous beginning 3/15.

CONTACT Mr. Gene Slettedahl, Director of Financial Aid, Martin Luther College, 1995 Luther Court, New Ulm, MN 56073, 507-354-8221. *Fax:* 507-354-8225. *E-mail:* slettega@mlc-wels.edu.

MARTIN METHODIST COLLEGE
Pulaski, TN

CONTACT Ms. Anita Beecham, Financial Aid Assistant, Martin Methodist College, 433 West Madison Street, Pulaski, TN 38478-2716, 931-363-9808 or toll-free 800-467-1273. *Fax:* 931-363-9818. *E-mail:* abeecham@martinmethodist. edu.

MARTIN UNIVERSITY
Indianapolis, IN

ABOUT THE INSTITUTION Independent, coed. *Awards:* bachelor's and master's degrees. 14 undergraduate majors. *Total enrollment:* 1,236. Undergraduates: 1,074. Freshmen: 234.

GIFT AID (NEED-BASED) *Scholarships, grants, and awards:* Federal Pell, FSEOG, state, private, college/university gift aid from institutional funds.

LOANS *Programs:* FFEL (Subsidized and Unsubsidized Stafford, PLUS), Charles E. Schell Foundation loans.

WORK-STUDY *Federal work-study:* Total amount: $40,661; 28 jobs averaging $1450.

APPLYING FOR FINANCIAL AID *Required financial aid form:* FAFSA.

CONTACT Berdia Marshall, Director of Financial Aid, Martin University, 2171 Avondale Place, Indianapolis, IN 46218-3867, 317-543-3670. *Fax:* 317-543-4790. *E-mail:* bmarshall@martin.edu.

MARY BALDWIN COLLEGE
Staunton, VA

Tuition & fees: $24,585	Average undergraduate aid package: $19,749

ABOUT THE INSTITUTION Independent, coed, primarily women. 30 undergraduate majors. Federal methodology is used as a basis for awarding need-based institutional aid.

UNDERGRADUATE EXPENSES for 2009–10 *One-time required fee:* $215. *Comprehensive fee:* $31,655 includes full-time tuition ($24,370), mandatory fees ($215), and room and board ($7070). *College room only:* $4505. Full-time tuition and fees vary according to degree level. Room and board charges vary according to housing facility. *Part-time tuition:* $420 per semester hour. Part-time tuition and fees vary according to degree level. *Payment plan:* Installment.

FRESHMAN FINANCIAL AID (Fall 2009, est.) 257 applied for aid; of those 92% were deemed to have need. 99% of freshmen with need received aid; of those 18% had need fully met. *Average percent of need met:* 79% (excluding resources awarded to replace EFC). *Average financial aid package:* $20,319 (excluding resources awarded to replace EFC). 6% of all full-time freshmen had no need and received non-need-based gift aid.

UNDERGRADUATE FINANCIAL AID (Fall 2009, est.) 874 applied for aid; of those 92% were deemed to have need. 98% of undergraduates with need received aid; of those 14% had need fully met. *Average percent of need met:* 77% (excluding resources awarded to replace EFC). *Average financial aid package:* $19,749 (excluding resources awarded to replace EFC). 6% of all full-time undergraduates had no need and received non-need-based gift aid.

GIFT AID (NEED-BASED) *Total amount:* $13,462,885 (25% federal, 14% state, 59% institutional, 2% external sources). *Receiving aid:* Freshmen: 84% (223); all full-time undergraduates: 78% (757). *Average award:* Freshmen: $16,236; Undergraduates: $15,304. *Scholarships, grants, and awards:* Federal Pell, FSEOG, state, private, college/university gift aid from institutional funds.

GIFT AID (NON-NEED-BASED) *Total amount:* $815,391 (3% federal, 20% state, 76% institutional, 1% external sources). *Receiving aid:* Freshmen: 81% (216). Undergraduates: 79% (775). *Average award:* Freshmen: $11,753. Undergraduates: $10,768. *Scholarships, grants, and awards by category: Academic interests/achievement:* 632 awards ($4,766,953 total): general academic interests/achievements. *Special achievements/activities:* 30 awards ($77,361 total): leadership. *Special characteristics:* 10 awards ($187,835 total): children of educators, children of faculty/staff. *Tuition waivers:* Full or partial for employees or children of employees.

LOANS *Student loans:* $9,876,098 (93% need-based, 7% non-need-based). 73% of past graduating class borrowed through all loan programs. *Average indebtedness per student:* $25,665. *Average need-based loan:* Freshmen: $4428. Undergraduates: $4885. *Parent loans:* $1,474,106 (86% need-based, 14% non-need-based). *Programs:* FFEL (Subsidized and Unsubsidized Stafford, PLUS), Perkins, alternative loans.

WORK-STUDY *Federal work-study:* Total amount: $671,938; 382 jobs averaging $1759. *State or other work-study/employment:* 90 part-time jobs averaging $1334.

APPLYING FOR FINANCIAL AID *Required financial aid forms:* FAFSA, state aid form (for VA residents only). *Financial aid deadline:* Continuous. *Notification date:* Continuous beginning 3/15. Students must reply within 3 weeks of notification.

CONTACT Mrs. Robin Dietrich, Director of Financial Aid, Mary Baldwin College, 201 East Frederick Street, Staunton, VA 24401-3610, 540-887-7025 or toll-free 800-468-2262. *Fax:* 540-887-7229. *E-mail:* rdietric@mbc.edu.

MARYGROVE COLLEGE
Detroit, MI

CONTACT Mr. Donald Hurt, Director of Financial Aid, Marygrove College, 8425 West McNichols Road, Detroit, MI 48221-2599, 313-862-8000 Ext. 436 or toll-free 866-313-1297.

MARYLAND INSTITUTE COLLEGE OF ART
Baltimore, MD

CONTACT Ms. Diane Prengaman, Associate Vice President for Financial Aid, Maryland Institute College of Art, 1300 Mount Royal Avenue, Baltimore, MD 21217, 410-225-2285. *Fax:* 410-225-2337. *E-mail:* dprengam@mica.edu.

MARYLHURST UNIVERSITY
Marylhurst, OR

Tuition & fees: $16,920	Average undergraduate aid package: $10,510

ABOUT THE INSTITUTION Independent Roman Catholic, coed, primarily women. 22 undergraduate majors. Federal methodology is used as a basis for awarding need-based institutional aid.

UNDERGRADUATE EXPENSES for 2009–10 *Tuition:* full-time $16,920; part-time $376 per credit. Full-time tuition and fees vary according to course load, degree level, and program. Part-time tuition and fees vary according to course load, degree level, and program. *Payment plan:* Installment.

FRESHMAN FINANCIAL AID (Fall 2009, est.) 9 applied for aid; of those 100% were deemed to have need. 100% of freshmen with need received aid. *Average percent of need met:* 37% (excluding resources awarded to replace EFC). *Average financial aid package:* $8699 (excluding resources awarded to replace EFC).

UNDERGRADUATE FINANCIAL AID (Fall 2009, est.) 372 applied for aid; of those 92% were deemed to have need. 100% of undergraduates with need received aid; of those 4% had need fully met. *Average percent of need met:* 50% (excluding resources awarded to replace EFC). *Average financial aid package:* $10,510 (excluding resources awarded to replace EFC). 9% of all full-time undergraduates had no need and received non-need-based gift aid.

GIFT AID (NEED-BASED) *Total amount:* $3,006,497 (55% federal, 10% state, 28% institutional, 7% external sources). *Receiving aid:* Freshmen: 64% (7); all full-time undergraduates: 66% (268). *Average award:* Freshmen: $7160; Undergraduates: $7472. *Scholarships, grants, and awards:* Federal Pell, FSEOG, state, private, college/university gift aid from institutional funds, United Negro College Fund.

GIFT AID (NON-NEED-BASED) *Total amount:* $158,563 (72% institutional, 28% external sources). *Receiving aid:* Undergraduates: 1% (3). *Average award:* Undergraduates: $1882. *Tuition waivers:* Full or partial for employees or children of employees.

LOANS *Student loans:* $8,312,098 (83% need-based, 17% non-need-based). 71% of past graduating class borrowed through all loan programs. *Average indebtedness per student:* $27,846. *Average need-based loan:* Freshmen: $2771. Undergraduates: $4522. *Parent loans:* $235,303 (54% need-based, 46% non-need-based). *Programs:* FFEL (Subsidized and Unsubsidized Stafford, PLUS), Perkins.

WORK-STUDY *Federal work-study:* Total amount: $189,943; 51 jobs averaging $4583.

APPLYING FOR FINANCIAL AID *Required financial aid forms:* FAFSA, institution's own form. *Financial aid deadline:* Continuous. *Notification date:* Continuous beginning 5/15. Students must reply within 8 weeks of notification.

CONTACT Tracy Reisinger, Office of Financial Aid, Marylhurst University, 17600 Pacific Highway, PO Box 261, Marylhurst, OR 97036, 503-699-6253 or toll-free 800-634-9982. *Fax:* 503-635-6585. *E-mail:* treisinger@marylhurst.edu.

MARYMOUNT COLLEGE, PALOS VERDES, CALIFORNIA
Rancho Palos Verdes, CA

CONTACT Leslie A. Butler, Director of Financial Aid, Marymount College, Palos Verdes, California, 30800 Palos Verdes Drive East, Rancho Palos Verdes, CA 90275-6299, 310-377-5001 Ext. 216. *Fax:* 310-377-6223. *E-mail:* lbutler@marymountpv.edu.

MARYMOUNT MANHATTAN COLLEGE
New York, NY

Tuition & fees: $22,656	Average undergraduate aid package: $13,251

ABOUT THE INSTITUTION Independent, coed. 22 undergraduate majors. Federal methodology is used as a basis for awarding need-based institutional aid.

UNDERGRADUATE EXPENSES for 2009–10 *Comprehensive fee:* $35,530 includes full-time tuition ($21,578), mandatory fees ($1078), and room and board ($12,874). *College room only:* $10,874. *Part-time tuition:* $689 per credit hour. *Part-time fees:* $367 per term. *Payment plan:* Installment.

FRESHMAN FINANCIAL AID (Fall 2009, est.) 411 applied for aid; of those 83% were deemed to have need. 100% of freshmen with need received aid; of those 7% had need fully met. *Average percent of need met:* 50% (excluding resources awarded to replace EFC). *Average financial aid package:* $14,025 (excluding resources awarded to replace EFC). 15% of all full-time freshmen had no need and received non-need-based gift aid.

UNDERGRADUATE FINANCIAL AID (Fall 2009, est.) 1,303 applied for aid; of those 82% were deemed to have need. 100% of undergraduates with need received aid; of those 3% had need fully met. *Average percent of need met:* 47% (excluding resources awarded to replace EFC). *Average financial aid package:* $13,251 (excluding resources awarded to replace EFC). 17% of all full-time undergraduates had no need and received non-need-based gift aid.

GIFT AID (NEED-BASED) *Total amount:* $10,082,628 (22% federal, 10% state, 66% institutional, 2% external sources). *Receiving aid:* Freshmen: 70% (339); all full-time undergraduates: 62% (1,069). *Average award:* Freshmen: $11,158; Undergraduates: $9454. *Scholarships, grants, and awards:* Federal Pell, FSEOG, state, private, college/university gift aid from institutional funds.

GIFT AID (NON-NEED-BASED) *Total amount:* $1,668,311 (97% institutional, 3% external sources). *Receiving aid:* Freshmen: 4% (18). Undergraduates: 2% (32). *Average award:* Freshmen: $5674. Undergraduates: $5119. *Scholarships, grants, and awards by category: Academic interests/achievement:* general academic interests/achievements. *Creative arts/performance:* art/fine arts, dance, performing arts. *Special achievements/activities:* leadership. *Special characteristics:* local/state students.

LOANS *Student loans:* $10,365,311 (75% need-based, 25% non-need-based). 84% of past graduating class borrowed through all loan programs. *Average indebtedness per student:* $15,988. *Average need-based loan:* Freshmen: $3388. Undergraduates: $4236. *Parent loans:* $14,958,692 (75% need-based, 25% non-need-based). *Programs:* FFEL (Subsidized and Unsubsidized Stafford, PLUS).

WORK-STUDY *Federal work-study:* Total amount: $83,799; jobs available. *State or other work-study/employment:* Part-time jobs available.

APPLYING FOR FINANCIAL AID *Required financial aid form:* FAFSA. *Financial aid deadline (priority):* 3/15. *Notification date:* Continuous beginning 3/15. Students must reply by 5/1 or within 2 weeks of notification.

CONTACT Director of Financial Aid, Marymount Manhattan College, 221 East 71st Street, New York, NY 10021, 212-517-0500 or toll-free 800-MARYMOUNT (out-of-state). *Fax:* 212-517-0491.

MARYMOUNT UNIVERSITY
Arlington, VA

Tuition & fees: $22,620	Average undergraduate aid package: $15,574

ABOUT THE INSTITUTION Independent religious, coed. 26 undergraduate majors. Both federal and institutional methodology are used as a basis for awarding need-based institutional aid.

UNDERGRADUATE EXPENSES for 2009–10 *Comprehensive fee:* $32,365 includes full-time tuition ($22,370), mandatory fees ($250), and room and board ($9745). *Part-time tuition:* $725 per credit hour. *Part-time fees:* $7.50 per credit hour. *Payment plan:* Installment.

FRESHMAN FINANCIAL AID (Fall 2009, est.) 322 applied for aid; of those 81% were deemed to have need. 99% of freshmen with need received aid; of those 21% had need fully met. *Average percent of need met:* 73% (excluding resources awarded to replace EFC). *Average financial aid package:* $17,362 (excluding resources awarded to replace EFC). 27% of all full-time freshmen had no need and received non-need-based gift aid.

UNDERGRADUATE FINANCIAL AID (Fall 2009, est.) 1,361 applied for aid; of those 84% were deemed to have need. 99% of undergraduates with need received aid; of those 14% had need fully met. *Average percent of need met:* 67% (excluding resources awarded to replace EFC). *Average financial aid package:* $15,574 (excluding resources awarded to replace EFC). 20% of all full-time undergraduates had no need and received non-need-based gift aid.

GIFT AID (NEED-BASED) *Total amount:* $4,957,001 (46% federal, 1% state, 53% institutional). *Receiving aid:* Freshmen: 44% (168); all full-time undergraduates: 39% (741). *Average award:* Freshmen: $5295; Undergraduates: $6427. *Scholarships, grants, and awards:* Federal Pell, FSEOG, state, private, college/university gift aid from institutional funds.

GIFT AID (NON-NEED-BASED) *Total amount:* $11,693,679 (21% state, 78% institutional, 1% external sources). *Receiving aid:* Freshmen: 67% (258). Undergraduates: 48% (907). *Average award:* Freshmen: $8558. Undergraduates: $9553. *Scholarships, grants, and awards by category: Academic interests/*

achievement: 609 awards ($5,407,675 total): biological sciences, business, general academic interests/achievements, health fields, mathematics, social sciences. *Special achievements/activities:* 152 awards ($640,490 total): community service, general special achievements/activities, leadership. *Special characteristics:* 306 awards ($1,151,693 total): children of current students, children of faculty/staff, general special characteristics, international students, religious affiliation, veterans. *Tuition waivers:* Full or partial for children of alumni, employees or children of employees, senior citizens.

LOANS *Student loans:* $12,745,724 (35% need-based, 65% non-need-based). 76% of past graduating class borrowed through all loan programs. *Average indebtedness per student:* $22,946. *Average need-based loan:* Freshmen: $3525. Undergraduates: $4337. *Parent loans:* $4,400,684 (100% non-need-based). *Programs:* Federal Direct (Subsidized and Unsubsidized Stafford, PLUS), Perkins.

WORK-STUDY *Federal work-study:* Total amount: $1,233,182; 692 jobs averaging $1722.

APPLYING FOR FINANCIAL AID *Required financial aid form:* FAFSA. *Financial aid deadline (priority):* 3/1. *Notification date:* Continuous beginning 3/15. Students must reply within 2 weeks of notification.

CONTACT Ms. Debbie A. Raines, Director of Financial Aid, Marymount University, 2807 North Glebe Road, Arlington, VA 22207-4299, 703-284-1530 or toll-free 800-548-7638. *Fax:* 703-516-4771. *E-mail:* debbie.raines@marymount.edu.

MARYVILLE COLLEGE
Maryville, TN

Tuition & fees: $29,473	Average undergraduate aid package: $26,285

ABOUT THE INSTITUTION Independent Presbyterian, coed. 52 undergraduate majors. Federal methodology is used as a basis for awarding need-based institutional aid.

UNDERGRADUATE EXPENSES for 2010–11 *Comprehensive fee:* $38,505 includes full-time tuition ($28,798), mandatory fees ($675), and room and board ($9032). *College room only:* $4516. Full-time tuition and fees vary according to course load. Room and board charges vary according to board plan and housing facility. *Part-time tuition:* $1199 per credit hour. *Part-time fees:* $15 per credit hour. Part-time tuition and fees vary according to course load. *Payment plan:* Installment.

FRESHMAN FINANCIAL AID (Fall 2009, est.) 303 applied for aid; of those 89% were deemed to have need. 100% of freshmen with need received aid; of those 33% had need fully met. *Average percent of need met:* 92% (excluding resources awarded to replace EFC). *Average financial aid package:* $27,839 (excluding resources awarded to replace EFC). 11% of all full-time freshmen had no need and received non-need-based gift aid.

UNDERGRADUATE FINANCIAL AID (Fall 2009, est.) 1,103 applied for aid; of those 83% were deemed to have need. 100% of undergraduates with need received aid; of those 32% had need fully met. *Average percent of need met:* 87% (excluding resources awarded to replace EFC). *Average financial aid package:* $26,285 (excluding resources awarded to replace EFC). 12% of all full-time undergraduates had no need and received non-need-based gift aid.

GIFT AID (NEED-BASED) *Total amount:* $18,236,689 (11% federal, 15% state, 74% institutional). *Receiving aid:* Freshmen: 89% (269); all full-time undergraduates: 82% (909). *Average award:* Freshmen: $24,346; Undergraduates: $21,732. *Scholarships, grants, and awards:* Federal Pell, FSEOG, state, private, college/university gift aid from institutional funds.

GIFT AID (NON-NEED-BASED) *Total amount:* $3,804,211 (21% state, 78% institutional, 1% external sources). *Receiving aid:* Freshmen: 41% (125). Undergraduates: 37% (404). *Average award:* Freshmen: $16,824. Undergraduates: $15,380. *Scholarships, grants, and awards by category: Academic interests/achievement:* general academic interests/achievements. *Creative arts/performance:* art/fine arts, music, theater/drama. *Special achievements/activities:* community service, leadership. *Special characteristics:* children and siblings of alumni, children of faculty/staff, members of minority groups, religious affiliation. *Tuition waivers:* Full or partial for employees or children of employees.

LOANS *Student loans:* $6,214,052 (77% need-based, 23% non-need-based). 66% of past graduating class borrowed through all loan programs. *Average indebtedness per student:* $22,268. *Average need-based loan:* Freshmen: $2713. Undergraduates: $3459. *Parent loans:* $1,026,575 (24% need-based, 76% non-need-based). *Programs:* Federal Direct (Subsidized and Unsubsidized Stafford, PLUS), Perkins.

WORK-STUDY *Federal work-study:* Total amount: $791,833; 513 jobs averaging $1544. *State or other work-study/employment:* Total amount: $218,172 (61% need-based, 39% non-need-based). 4 part-time jobs averaging $1699.

APPLYING FOR FINANCIAL AID *Required financial aid form:* FAFSA. *Financial aid deadline (priority):* 3/1. *Notification date:* Continuous beginning 3/15. Students must reply within 4 weeks of notification.

CONTACT Mr. Richard Brand, Director of Financial Aid, Maryville College, 502 East Lamar Alexander Parkway, Maryville, TN 37804-5907, 865-981-8100 or toll-free 800-597-2687. *E-mail:* richard.brand@maryvillecollege.edu.

MARYVILLE UNIVERSITY OF SAINT LOUIS
St. Louis, MO

Tuition & fees: $20,994	Average undergraduate aid package: $17,959

ABOUT THE INSTITUTION Independent, coed. 55 undergraduate majors. Both federal and institutional methodology are used as a basis for awarding need-based institutional aid.

UNDERGRADUATE EXPENSES for 2009–10 *Comprehensive fee:* $29,204 includes full-time tuition ($20,384), mandatory fees ($610), and room and board ($8210). Full-time tuition and fees vary according to course load. Room and board charges vary according to housing facility. *Part-time tuition:* $612 per credit hour. *Part-time fees:* $152.50 per term. Part-time tuition and fees vary according to class time. *Payment plans:* Installment, deferred payment.

FRESHMAN FINANCIAL AID (Fall 2009, est.) 292 applied for aid; of those 87% were deemed to have need. 100% of freshmen with need received aid; of those 20% had need fully met. *Average percent of need met:* 79% (excluding resources awarded to replace EFC). *Average financial aid package:* $18,408 (excluding resources awarded to replace EFC). 20% of all full-time freshmen had no need and received non-need-based gift aid.

UNDERGRADUATE FINANCIAL AID (Fall 2009, est.) 1,465 applied for aid; of those 89% were deemed to have need. 100% of undergraduates with need received aid; of those 12% had need fully met. *Average percent of need met:* 70% (excluding resources awarded to replace EFC). *Average financial aid package:* $17,959 (excluding resources awarded to replace EFC). 19% of all full-time undergraduates had no need and received non-need-based gift aid.

GIFT AID (NEED-BASED) *Total amount:* $13,826,186 (22% federal, 13% state, 63% institutional, 2% external sources). *Receiving aid:* Freshmen: 74% (252); all full-time undergraduates: 75% (1,246). *Average award:* Freshmen: $13,040; Undergraduates: $10,244. *Scholarships, grants, and awards:* Federal Pell, FSEOG, state, private, college/university gift aid from institutional funds, Academic Competitiveness Grants, National SMART Grants, TEACH Grants.

GIFT AID (NON-NEED-BASED) *Total amount:* $2,660,780 (1% federal, 3% state, 94% institutional, 2% external sources). *Receiving aid:* Freshmen: 11% (39). Undergraduates: 6% (92). *Average award:* Freshmen: $10,718. Undergraduates: $6609. *Scholarships, grants, and awards by category: Academic interests/achievement:* 1,223 awards ($8,338,012 total): biological sciences, business, education, general academic interests/achievements, health fields. *Creative arts/performance:* 48 awards ($103,425 total): art/fine arts. *Special achievements/activities:* 205 awards ($346,265 total): community service, general special achievements/activities, leadership. *Special characteristics:* 169 awards ($235,933 total): children and siblings of alumni, children of current students, children of faculty/staff, ethnic background, general special characteristics, members of minority groups, parents of current students, siblings of current students, spouses of current students, twins, veterans. *Tuition waivers:* Full or partial for employees or children of employees, senior citizens.

LOANS *Student loans:* $18,058,537 (73% need-based, 27% non-need-based). 73% of past graduating class borrowed through all loan programs. *Average indebtedness per student:* $18,341. *Average need-based loan:* Freshmen: $3010. Undergraduates: $4021. *Parent loans:* $3,311,808 (41% need-based, 59% non-need-based). *Programs:* Federal Direct (Subsidized and Unsubsidized Stafford, PLUS), Perkins, Sallie Mae Signature Loans, KeyBank Loans, TERI Loans, CitiAssist Loans, Campus Door Loans.

WORK-STUDY *Federal work-study:* Total amount: $268,025; 238 jobs averaging $1959. *State or other work-study/employment:* Total amount: $512,846 (43% need-based, 57% non-need-based). 177 part-time jobs averaging $2364.

ATHLETIC AWARDS Total amount: $535,129 (57% need-based, 43% non-need-based).

APPLYING FOR FINANCIAL AID *Required financial aid form:* FAFSA. *Financial aid deadline (priority):* 3/1. *Notification date:* Continuous beginning 3/15. Students must reply by 5/1 or within 2 weeks of notification.

CONTACT Ms. Martha Harbaugh, Director of Financial Aid, Maryville University of Saint Louis, 650 Maryville University Drive, St. Louis, MO 63141-7299, 800-627-9855 Ext. 9360 or toll-free 800-627-9855. *Fax:* 314-529-9199. *E-mail:* fin_aid@maryville.edu.

MARYWOOD UNIVERSITY
Scranton, PA

Tuition & fees: $26,270	Average undergraduate aid package: $22,222

ABOUT THE INSTITUTION Independent Roman Catholic, coed. 63 undergraduate majors. Federal methodology is used as a basis for awarding need-based institutional aid.

UNDERGRADUATE EXPENSES for 2009–10 *One-time required fee:* $1120. *Comprehensive fee:* $37,768 includes full-time tuition ($25,150), mandatory fees ($1120), and room and board ($11,498). *College room only:* $6566. Full-time tuition and fees vary according to course load. Room and board charges vary according to board plan and housing facility. *Part-time tuition:* $575 per credit. *Part-time fees:* $200 per term. Part-time tuition and fees vary according to course load. *Payment plans:* Installment, deferred payment.

FRESHMAN FINANCIAL AID (Fall 2009, est.) 395 applied for aid; of those 93% were deemed to have need. 100% of freshmen with need received aid; of those 19% had need fully met. *Average percent of need met:* 82% (excluding resources awarded to replace EFC). *Average financial aid package:* $23,580 (excluding resources awarded to replace EFC). 11% of all full-time freshmen had no need and received non-need-based gift aid.

UNDERGRADUATE FINANCIAL AID (Fall 2009, est.) 1,884 applied for aid; of those 92% were deemed to have need. 100% of undergraduates with need received aid; of those 26% had need fully met. *Average percent of need met:* 81% (excluding resources awarded to replace EFC). *Average financial aid package:* $22,222 (excluding resources awarded to replace EFC). 14% of all full-time undergraduates had no need and received non-need-based gift aid.

GIFT AID (NEED-BASED) *Total amount:* $28,727,690 (13% federal, 11% state, 74% institutional, 2% external sources). *Receiving aid:* Freshmen: 75% (311); all full-time undergraduates: 72% (1,479). *Average award:* Freshmen: $7477; Undergraduates: $7524. *Scholarships, grants, and awards:* Federal Pell, FSEOG, state, private, college/university gift aid from institutional funds, Federal Nursing, Academic Competitiveness Grants, National SMART Grants, Disadvantaged Student Scholarships.

GIFT AID (NON-NEED-BASED) *Total amount:* $3,308,082 (4% federal, 90% institutional, 6% external sources). *Receiving aid:* Freshmen: 84% (349). Undergraduates: 82% (1,683). *Average award:* Freshmen: $13,606. Undergraduates: $10,678. *Scholarships, grants, and awards by category: Academic interests/achievement:* business, communication, education, foreign languages, general academic interests/achievements, health fields, mathematics, religion/biblical studies. *Creative arts/performance:* art/fine arts, cinema/film/broadcasting, journalism/publications, music, performing arts, theater/drama. *Special achievements/activities:* community service, general special achievements/activities, leadership. *Special characteristics:* adult students, children and siblings of alumni, children of current students, children of faculty/staff, children of workers in trades, ethnic background, general special characteristics, international students, local/state students, religious affiliation, siblings of current students, spouses of current students. *Tuition waivers:* Full or partial for employees or children of employees, senior citizens.

LOANS *Student loans:* $19,338,121 (94% need-based, 6% non-need-based). 94% of past graduating class borrowed through all loan programs. *Average indebtedness per student:* $31,471. *Average need-based loan:* Freshmen: $3694. Undergraduates: $5211. *Parent loans:* $2,959,606 (90% need-based, 10% non-need-based). *Programs:* Federal Direct (Subsidized and Unsubsidized Stafford, PLUS), Perkins, private alternative loans.

WORK-STUDY *Federal work-study:* Total amount: $1,456,324; 734 jobs averaging $2000.

APPLYING FOR FINANCIAL AID *Required financial aid forms:* FAFSA, institution's own form. *Financial aid deadline (priority):* 2/15. *Notification date:* Continuous beginning 2/15. Students must reply by 5/1 or within 3 weeks of notification.

CONTACT Mr. Stanley F. Skrutski, Director of Financial Aid, Marywood University, 2300 Adams Avenue, Scranton, PA 18509-1598, 570-348-6225 or toll-free 866-279-9663. *Fax:* 570-961-4739. *E-mail:* skrutski@ac.marywood.edu.

MASSACHUSETTS COLLEGE OF ART AND DESIGN
Boston, MA

ABOUT THE INSTITUTION State-supported, coed. 17 undergraduate majors.

GIFT AID (NEED-BASED) *Scholarships, grants, and awards:* Federal Pell, FSEOG, state, private, college/university gift aid from institutional funds.

GIFT AID (NON-NEED-BASED) *Scholarships, grants, and awards by category:* *Special characteristics:* children of faculty/staff, children of union members/company employees, veterans.

LOANS *Programs:* Federal Direct (Subsidized and Unsubsidized Stafford, PLUS), FFEL (Subsidized and Unsubsidized Stafford), Perkins, state, alternative loans.

WORK-STUDY *Federal work-study:* Total amount: $160,000; 187 jobs averaging $860.

APPLYING FOR FINANCIAL AID *Required financial aid form:* FAFSA.

CONTACT Auelio Ramirez, Director of Student Financial Assistance, Massachusetts College of Art and Design, 621 Huntington Avenue, Boston, MA 02115-5882, 617-879-7850. *Fax:* 617-879-7880. *E-mail:* aurelio.ramirez@massart.edu.

MASSACHUSETTS COLLEGE OF LIBERAL ARTS
North Adams, MA

Tuition & fees (MA res): $6875 | **Average undergraduate aid package: $9979**

ABOUT THE INSTITUTION State-supported, coed. 23 undergraduate majors. Federal methodology is used as a basis for awarding need-based institutional aid.

UNDERGRADUATE EXPENSES for 2009–10 *One-time required fee:* $140. *Tuition, state resident:* full-time $1030; part-time $42.92 per credit. *Tuition, nonresident:* full-time $9975; part-time $415.63 per credit. *Required fees:* full-time $5845; $198.01 per credit. Full-time tuition and fees vary according to program. Part-time tuition and fees vary according to course load and program. *College room and board:* $7868; *Room only:* $3418. Room and board charges vary according to board plan and housing facility. *Payment plan:* Installment.

FRESHMAN FINANCIAL AID (Fall 2009, est.) 332 applied for aid; of those 78% were deemed to have need. 100% of freshmen with need received aid. *Average percent of need met:* 87% (excluding resources awarded to replace EFC). *Average financial aid package:* $10,392 (excluding resources awarded to replace EFC). 5% of all full-time freshmen had no need and received non-need-based gift aid.

UNDERGRADUATE FINANCIAL AID (Fall 2009, est.) 1,259 applied for aid; of those 78% were deemed to have need. 99% of undergraduates with need received aid. *Average percent of need met:* 86% (excluding resources awarded to replace EFC). *Average financial aid package:* $9979 (excluding resources awarded to replace EFC). 5% of all full-time undergraduates had no need and received non-need-based gift aid.

GIFT AID (NEED-BASED) *Total amount:* $5,048,209 (51% federal, 16% state, 26% institutional, 7% external sources). *Receiving aid:* Freshmen: 60% (209); all full-time undergraduates: 54% (784). *Average award:* Freshmen: $5728; Undergraduates: $5367. *Scholarships, grants, and awards:* Federal Pell, FSEOG, state, private, college/university gift aid from institutional funds.

GIFT AID (NON-NEED-BASED) *Total amount:* $181,245 (9% state, 64% institutional, 27% external sources). *Receiving aid:* Freshmen: 37% (128). Undergraduates: 27% (390). *Average award:* Freshmen: $1914. Undergraduates: $2384. *Scholarships, grants, and awards by category:* Academic interests/achievement: biological sciences, business, communication, computer science, education, English, general academic interests/achievements, health fields, humanities, mathematics, physical sciences, social sciences. *Creative arts/performance:* applied art and design, art/fine arts, cinema/film/broadcasting, journalism/publications, music, performing arts, theater/drama. *Special achievements/activities:* general special achievements/activities, leadership, memberships. *Special characteristics:* first-generation college students, general special characteristics, handicapped students, local/state students, members of minority groups, out-of-state students. *Tuition waivers:* Full or partial for employees or children of employees, senior citizens.

LOANS *Student loans:* $8,289,844 (82% need-based, 18% non-need-based). 51% of past graduating class borrowed through all loan programs. *Average*

indebtedness per student: $17,297. *Average need-based loan:* Freshmen: $3270. Undergraduates: $3905. *Parent loans:* $558,325 (68% need-based, 32% non-need-based). *Programs:* FFEL (Subsidized and Unsubsidized Stafford, PLUS), Perkins, state.

WORK-STUDY *Federal work-study:* Total amount: $395,944; 204 jobs averaging $2017. *State or other work-study/employment:* Total amount: $600,546 (100% non-need-based). Part-time jobs available.

APPLYING FOR FINANCIAL AID *Required financial aid forms:* FAFSA, institution's own form. *Financial aid deadline (priority):* 3/1. *Notification date:* Continuous beginning 3/1. Students must reply by 5/1 or within 2 weeks of notification.

CONTACT Mrs. Elizabeth M. Petri, Director of Financial Aid, Massachusetts College of Liberal Arts, 375 Church Street, North Adams, MA 01247, 413-662-5219 or toll-free 800-292-6632 (in-state). *Fax:* 413-662-5105. *E-mail:* e.petri@mcla.edu.

MASSACHUSETTS COLLEGE OF PHARMACY AND HEALTH SCIENCES
Boston, MA

Tuition & fees: $24,550 | **Average undergraduate aid package: $12,035**

ABOUT THE INSTITUTION Independent, coed. 12 undergraduate majors. Federal methodology is used as a basis for awarding need-based institutional aid.

UNDERGRADUATE EXPENSES for 2009–10 *Comprehensive fee:* $36,450 includes full-time tuition ($23,800), mandatory fees ($750), and room and board ($11,900). Full-time tuition and fees vary according to course load, degree level, location, program, and student level. Room and board charges vary according to board plan, housing facility, and location. *Part-time tuition:* $875 per credit. *Part-time fees:* $190 per term. *Payment plan:* Installment.

FRESHMAN FINANCIAL AID (Fall 2009, est.) 618 applied for aid; of those 88% were deemed to have need. 100% of freshmen with need received aid; of those 52% had need fully met. *Average percent of need met:* 48% (excluding resources awarded to replace EFC). *Average financial aid package:* $14,986 (excluding resources awarded to replace EFC). 16% of all full-time freshmen had no need and received non-need-based gift aid.

UNDERGRADUATE FINANCIAL AID (Fall 2009, est.) 2,146 applied for aid; of those 91% were deemed to have need. 100% of undergraduates with need received aid; of those 49% had need fully met. *Average percent of need met:* 41% (excluding resources awarded to replace EFC). *Average financial aid package:* $12,035 (excluding resources awarded to replace EFC). 16% of all full-time undergraduates had no need and received non-need-based gift aid.

GIFT AID (NEED-BASED) *Total amount:* $15,371,637 (23% federal, 1% state, 74% institutional, 2% external sources). *Receiving aid:* Freshmen: 72% (465); all full-time undergraduates: 66% (1,533). *Average award:* Freshmen: $10,934; Undergraduates: $8612. *Scholarships, grants, and awards:* Federal Pell, FSEOG, state, private, college/university gift aid from institutional funds.

GIFT AID (NON-NEED-BASED) *Average award:* Freshmen: $10,331. Undergraduates: $11,269. *Scholarships, grants, and awards by category:* Academic interests/achievement: general academic interests/achievements. *Special characteristics:* children of faculty/staff. *Tuition waivers:* Full or partial for employees or children of employees.

LOANS *Student loans:* $31,000,921 (32% need-based, 68% non-need-based). *Average need-based loan:* Freshmen: $5165. Undergraduates: $5305. *Parent loans:* $1,800,771 (100% non-need-based). *Programs:* Federal Direct (Subsidized and Unsubsidized Stafford, PLUS), FFEL (Subsidized and Unsubsidized Stafford, PLUS), Perkins, Health Professions Loans.

WORK-STUDY *Federal work-study:* Total amount: $548,850; jobs available.

APPLYING FOR FINANCIAL AID *Required financial aid form:* FAFSA. *Financial aid deadline (priority):* 3/15. *Notification date:* Continuous. Students must reply by 5/1 or within 2 weeks of notification.

CONTACT Ms. Carrie Glass, Executive Director of Enrollment Services, Massachusetts College of Pharmacy and Health Sciences, 179 Longwood Avenue, Boston, MA 02115-5896, 617-732-2199 or toll-free 800-225-5506 (out-of-state). *Fax:* 617-732-2082. *E-mail:* carrie.glass@mcphs.edu.

MASSACHUSETTS INSTITUTE OF TECHNOLOGY
Cambridge, MA

Tuition & fees: $37,782	Average undergraduate aid package: $35,202

ABOUT THE INSTITUTION Independent, coed. 34 undergraduate majors. Both federal and institutional methodology are used as a basis for awarding need-based institutional aid.

UNDERGRADUATE EXPENSES for 2009–10 *Comprehensive fee:* $49,142 includes full-time tuition ($37,510), mandatory fees ($272), and room and board ($11,360). *College room only:* $6850. Room and board charges vary according to board plan and housing facility. *Part-time tuition:* $585 per unit. Part-time tuition and fees vary according to course load. *Payment plan:* Installment.

FRESHMAN FINANCIAL AID (Fall 2008) 834 applied for aid; of those 81% were deemed to have need. 100% of freshmen with need received aid; of those 100% had need fully met. *Average percent of need met:* 100% (excluding resources awarded to replace EFC). *Average financial aid package:* $35,919 (excluding resources awarded to replace EFC).

UNDERGRADUATE FINANCIAL AID (Fall 2008) 3,040 applied for aid; of those 83% were deemed to have need. 100% of undergraduates with need received aid; of those 100% had need fully met. *Average percent of need met:* 100% (excluding resources awarded to replace EFC). *Average financial aid package:* $35,202 (excluding resources awarded to replace EFC).

GIFT AID (NEED-BASED) *Total amount:* $82,952,912 (6% federal, 89% institutional, 5% external sources). *Receiving aid:* Freshmen: 63% (663); all full-time undergraduates: 60% (2,470). *Average award:* Freshmen: $34,136; Undergraduates: $33,112. *Scholarships, grants, and awards:* Federal Pell, FSEOG, state, private, college/university gift aid from institutional funds.

GIFT AID (NON-NEED-BASED) *Total amount:* $4,642,011 (26% federal, 74% external sources). *Receiving aid:* Freshmen: 3% (30). Undergraduates: 2% (74). *Tuition waivers:* Full or partial for employees or children of employees.

LOANS *Student loans:* $10,969,000 (34% need-based, 66% non-need-based). 45% of past graduating class borrowed through all loan programs. *Average indebtedness per student:* $15,043. *Average need-based loan:* Freshmen: $2127. Undergraduates: $3010. *Parent loans:* $4,420,507 (1% need-based, 99% non-need-based). *Programs:* Federal Direct (Subsidized and Unsubsidized Stafford, PLUS), Perkins, college/university.

WORK-STUDY *Federal work-study:* Total amount: $1,293,229; 733 jobs averaging $2415. *State or other work-study/employment:* Total amount: $2,332,909 (73% need-based, 27% non-need-based). 1,159 part-time jobs averaging $2013.

APPLYING FOR FINANCIAL AID *Required financial aid forms:* FAFSA, CSS Financial Aid PROFILE, noncustodial (divorced/separated) parent's statement, business/farm supplement, parents' complete federal income returns from prior year, W-2 forms. *Financial aid deadline:* 2/15. *Notification date:* 4/1. Students must reply by 5/1.

CONTACT Elizabeth Hicks, Executive Director of Student Financial Services, Massachusetts Institute of Technology, 77 Massachusetts Avenue, Room 11-320, Cambridge, MA 02139-4307, 617-253-4971. *Fax:* 617-253-9859. *E-mail:* finaid@mit.edu.

MASSACHUSETTS MARITIME ACADEMY
Buzzards Bay, MA

Tuition & fees (MA res): $6509	Average undergraduate aid package: N/A

ABOUT THE INSTITUTION State-supported, coed, primarily men. 13 undergraduate majors. Federal methodology is used as a basis for awarding need-based institutional aid.

UNDERGRADUATE EXPENSES for 2010–11 *One-time required fee:* $2285. *Tuition, state resident:* full-time $1242; part-time $255 per credit hour. *Tuition, nonresident:* full-time $13,881; part-time $782 per credit hour. *Required fees:* full-time $5267. Full-time tuition and fees vary according to course load, program, reciprocity agreements, and student level. Part-time tuition and fees vary according to class time, course load, program, reciprocity agreements, and student level. *College room and board:* $8917; *Room only:* $4978. Room and board charges vary according to location. *Payment plans:* Guaranteed tuition, installment, deferred payment.

GIFT AID (NEED-BASED) *Total amount:* $1,243,102 (69% federal, 30% state, 1% institutional). *Scholarships, grants, and awards:* Federal Pell, FSEOG, state, private, college/university gift aid from institutional funds.

GIFT AID (NON-NEED-BASED) *Total amount:* $951,488 (13% state, 82% institutional, 5% external sources). *Scholarships, grants, and awards by category: Academic interests/achievement:* general academic interests/achievements. *Creative arts/performance:* theater/drama. *Special achievements/activities:* leadership. *Special characteristics:* children and siblings of alumni, children of faculty/staff, international students, veterans. *Tuition waivers:* Full or partial for minority students, employees or children of employees, senior citizens.

LOANS *Student loans:* $7,276,377 (26% need-based, 74% non-need-based). 77% of past graduating class borrowed through all loan programs. *Average indebtedness per student:* $26,037. *Parent loans:* $1,429,113 (100% non-need-based). *Programs:* Federal Direct (Subsidized and Unsubsidized Stafford, PLUS).

WORK-STUDY *Federal work-study:* Total amount: $100,000; 118 jobs averaging $1000.

APPLYING FOR FINANCIAL AID *Required financial aid forms:* FAFSA, institution's own form. *Financial aid deadline (priority):* 5/1. *Notification date:* Continuous beginning 3/20.

CONTACT Ms. Catherine Kedski, Director of Financial Aid, Massachusetts Maritime Academy, 101 Academy Drive, Buzzards Bay, MA 02532, 508-830-5042 or toll-free 800-544-3411. *Fax:* 508-830-5077. *E-mail:* ckedski@maritime.edu.

THE MASTER'S COLLEGE AND SEMINARY
Santa Clarita, CA

Tuition & fees: $24,650	Average undergraduate aid package: $18,051

ABOUT THE INSTITUTION Independent nondenominational, coed. 47 undergraduate majors. Federal methodology is used as a basis for awarding need-based institutional aid.

UNDERGRADUATE EXPENSES for 2009–10 *Comprehensive fee:* $32,650 includes full-time tuition ($24,280), mandatory fees ($370), and room and board ($8000). *College room only:* $4480. Full-time tuition and fees vary according to course load, degree level, and program. Room and board charges vary according to board plan. *Part-time tuition:* $1015 per credit hour. *Part-time fees:* $1015 per credit hour. Part-time tuition and fees vary according to course load, degree level, and program. *Payment plan:* Installment.

FRESHMAN FINANCIAL AID (Fall 2009, est.) 125 applied for aid; of those 81% were deemed to have need. 99% of freshmen with need received aid; of those 25% had need fully met. *Average percent of need met:* 74% (excluding resources awarded to replace EFC). *Average financial aid package:* $18,617 (excluding resources awarded to replace EFC). 13% of all full-time freshmen had no need and received non-need-based gift aid.

UNDERGRADUATE FINANCIAL AID (Fall 2009, est.) 787 applied for aid; of those 89% were deemed to have need. 99% of undergraduates with need received aid; of those 18% had need fully met. *Average percent of need met:* 70% (excluding resources awarded to replace EFC). *Average financial aid package:* $18,051 (excluding resources awarded to replace EFC). 7% of all full-time undergraduates had no need and received non-need-based gift aid.

GIFT AID (NEED-BASED) *Total amount:* $7,928,058 (18% federal, 19% state, 50% institutional, 13% external sources). *Receiving aid:* Freshmen: 80% (100); all full-time undergraduates: 81% (641). *Average award:* Freshmen: $14,720; Undergraduates: $13,640. *Scholarships, grants, and awards:* Federal Pell, FSEOG, state, private, college/university gift aid from institutional funds.

GIFT AID (NON-NEED-BASED) *Total amount:* $866,910 (1% state, 55% institutional, 44% external sources). *Receiving aid:* Freshmen: 17% (21). Undergraduates: 10% (77). *Average award:* Freshmen: $6560. Undergraduates: $6274. *Scholarships, grants, and awards by category: Academic interests/achievement:* 482 awards ($3,027,062 total): biological sciences, business, education, general academic interests/achievements, mathematics, physical sciences, religion/biblical studies, social sciences. *Creative arts/performance:* 79 awards ($261,050 total): music. *Special achievements/activities:* 69 awards ($472,761 total): leadership. *Special characteristics:* 241 awards ($1,218,480 total): children and siblings of alumni, children of faculty/staff, general special characteristics, international students, relatives of clergy. *Tuition waivers:* Full or partial for employees or children of employees.

LOANS *Student loans:* $6,314,973 (77% need-based, 23% non-need-based). 68% of past graduating class borrowed through all loan programs. *Average indebtedness per student:* $30,003. *Average need-based loan:* Freshmen: $3912.

Undergraduates: $5246. *Parent loans:* $1,334,028 (45% need-based, 55% non-need-based). *Programs:* FFEL (Subsidized and Unsubsidized Stafford, PLUS), Perkins, alternative loans.

WORK-STUDY *Federal work-study:* Total amount: $173,911; 65 jobs averaging $2676. *State or other work-study/employment:* Total amount: $641,459 (87% need-based, 13% non-need-based). Part-time jobs available.

ATHLETIC AWARDS Total amount: $1,250,746 (76% need-based, 24% non-need-based).

APPLYING FOR FINANCIAL AID *Required financial aid forms:* FAFSA, institution's own form, state aid form. *Financial aid deadline (priority):* 3/2. *Notification date:* Continuous beginning 2/1. Students must reply by 5/1 or within 2 weeks of notification.

CONTACT Gary Edwards, Director of Financial Aid, The Master's College and Seminary, 21726 Placerita Canyon Road, Santa Clarita, CA 91321-1200, 661-362-2291 or toll-free 800-568-6248. *Fax:* 661-362-2693. *E-mail:* gedwards@masters.edu.

MATER ECCLESIAE COLLEGE
Greenville, RI

CONTACT Financial Aid Office, Mater Ecclesiae College, 60 Austin Avenue, Greenville, RI 02828, 401-949-2820.

MAYVILLE STATE UNIVERSITY
Mayville, ND

ABOUT THE INSTITUTION State-supported, coed. 34 undergraduate majors.

GIFT AID (NEED-BASED) *Scholarships, grants, and awards:* Federal Pell, FSEOG, state, private, college/university gift aid from institutional funds.

GIFT AID (NON-NEED-BASED) *Scholarships, grants, and awards by category: Academic interests/achievement:* biological sciences, business, computer science, education, English, general academic interests/achievements, health fields, library science, mathematics, physical sciences, premedicine, social sciences. *Creative arts/performance:* music, theater/drama. *Special characteristics:* international students, local/state students, members of minority groups, out-of-state students.

LOANS *Programs:* FFEL (Subsidized and Unsubsidized Stafford, PLUS), Perkins, college/university.

WORK-STUDY *Federal work-study:* Total amount: $54,616; 50 jobs averaging $1200.

APPLYING FOR FINANCIAL AID *Required financial aid form:* FAFSA.

CONTACT Ms. Shirley Hanson, Director of Financial Aid, Mayville State University, 330 3rd Street NE, Mayville, ND 58257-1299, 701-788-4767 or toll-free 800-437-4104. *Fax:* 701-788-4818. *E-mail:* shirley.hanson@mayvillestate.edu.

McDANIEL COLLEGE
Westminster, MD

Tuition & fees: $32,000	Average undergraduate aid package: $24,842

ABOUT THE INSTITUTION Independent, coed. 28 undergraduate majors. Both federal and institutional methodology are used as a basis for awarding need-based institutional aid.

UNDERGRADUATE EXPENSES for 2009–10 *Comprehensive fee:* $38,820 includes full-time tuition ($32,000) and room and board ($6820). *College room only:* $3500. Room and board charges vary according to board plan and housing facility. *Part-time tuition:* $1000 per credit. Part-time tuition and fees vary according to reciprocity agreements. *Payment plans:* Tuition prepayment, installment.

FRESHMAN FINANCIAL AID (Fall 2009, est.) 354 applied for aid; of those 85% were deemed to have need. 100% of freshmen with need received aid; of those 30% had need fully met. *Average percent of need met:* 95% (excluding resources awarded to replace EFC). *Average financial aid package:* $25,979 (excluding resources awarded to replace EFC). 20% of all full-time freshmen had no need and received non-need-based gift aid.

UNDERGRADUATE FINANCIAL AID (Fall 2009, est.) 1,299 applied for aid; of those 88% were deemed to have need. 100% of undergraduates with need received aid; of those 30% had need fully met. *Average percent of need met:* 97% (excluding resources awarded to replace EFC). *Average financial aid*

package: $24,842 (excluding resources awarded to replace EFC). 22% of all full-time undergraduates had no need and received non-need-based gift aid.

GIFT AID (NEED-BASED) *Total amount:* $20,962,208 (9% federal, 7% state, 84% institutional). *Receiving aid:* Freshmen: 70% (297); all full-time undergraduates: 67% (1,110). *Average award:* Freshmen: $21,937; Undergraduates: $20,147. *Scholarships, grants, and awards:* Federal Pell, FSEOG, state, private, college/university gift aid from institutional funds.

GIFT AID (NON-NEED-BASED) *Total amount:* $6,595,153 (3% state, 92% institutional, 5% external sources). *Average award:* Freshmen: $13,692. Undergraduates: $12,939. *Scholarships, grants, and awards by category: Academic interests/achievement:* 1,051 awards ($13,006,150 total): general academic interests/achievements. *Special achievements/activities:* 4 awards ($7000 total): junior miss, leadership. *Special characteristics:* 267 awards ($549,000 total): general special characteristics, local/state students, previous college experience, siblings of current students. *Tuition waivers:* Full or partial for employees or children of employees.

LOANS *Student loans:* $8,519,550 (47% need-based, 53% non-need-based). 63% of past graduating class borrowed through all loan programs. *Average indebtedness per student:* $25,325. *Average need-based loan:* Freshmen: $4393. Undergraduates: $4879. *Parent loans:* $2,578,074 (100% non-need-based). *Programs:* Federal Direct (Subsidized and Unsubsidized Stafford, PLUS), FFEL (Subsidized and Unsubsidized Stafford, PLUS), Perkins, college/university.

WORK-STUDY *Federal work-study:* Total amount: $256,949; 217 jobs averaging $926. *State or other work-study/employment:* Total amount: $240,805 (100% non-need-based). 274 part-time jobs averaging $954.

APPLYING FOR FINANCIAL AID *Required financial aid forms:* FAFSA, institution's own form, federal income tax form(s). *Financial aid deadline (priority):* 3/1. *Notification date:* Continuous beginning 3/1. Students must reply by 5/1 or within 2 weeks of notification.

CONTACT Ms. Patricia Williams, Financial Aid Office, McDaniel College, 2 College Hill, Westminster, MD 21157-4390, 410-857-2233 or toll-free 800-638-5005. *Fax:* 410-857-2729. *E-mail:* finaid@mcdaniel.edu.

McKENDREE UNIVERSITY
Lebanon, IL

Tuition & fees: $22,070	Average undergraduate aid package: $17,718

ABOUT THE INSTITUTION Independent religious, coed: 50 undergraduate majors. Federal methodology is used as a basis for awarding need-based institutional aid.

UNDERGRADUATE EXPENSES for 2010–11 *Comprehensive fee:* $29,920 includes full-time tuition ($21,370), mandatory fees ($700), and room and board ($7850). *College room only:* $4180. Full-time tuition and fees vary according to course load, degree level, and location. Room and board charges vary according to board plan and housing facility. *Part-time tuition:* $690 per hour. Part-time tuition and fees vary according to course load, degree level, and location. *Payment plan:* Installment.

FRESHMAN FINANCIAL AID (Fall 2009, est.) 289 applied for aid; of those 91% were deemed to have need. 100% of freshmen with need received aid; of those 19% had need fully met. *Average percent of need met:* 84% (excluding resources awarded to replace EFC). *Average financial aid package:* $20,472 (excluding resources awarded to replace EFC). 13% of all full-time freshmen had no need and received non-need-based gift aid.

UNDERGRADUATE FINANCIAL AID (Fall 2009, est.) 1,200 applied for aid; of those 87% were deemed to have need. 99% of undergraduates with need received aid; of those 28% had need fully met. *Average percent of need met:* 79% (excluding resources awarded to replace EFC). *Average financial aid package:* $17,718 (excluding resources awarded to replace EFC). 17% of all full-time undergraduates had no need and received non-need-based gift aid.

GIFT AID (NEED-BASED) *Total amount:* $16,911,516 (18% federal, 19% state, 59% institutional, 4% external sources). *Receiving aid:* Freshmen: 86% (262); all full-time undergraduates: 74% (993). *Average award:* Freshmen: $17,039; Undergraduates: $14,101. *Scholarships, grants, and awards:* Federal Pell, FSEOG, state, private, college/university gift aid from institutional funds.

GIFT AID (NON-NEED-BASED) *Total amount:* $2,692,065 (1% state, 88% institutional, 11% external sources). *Receiving aid:* Freshmen: 10% (31). Undergraduates: 11% (151). *Average award:* Freshmen: $9327. Undergraduates: $8591. *Scholarships, grants, and awards by category: Academic interests/achievement:* 772 awards ($4,369,722 total): biological sciences, business, general academic interests/achievements, religion/biblical studies. *Creative arts/*

performance: 122 awards ($451,345 total): music. *Special achievements/ activities:* 71 awards ($110,500 total): cheerleading/drum major, community service, leadership. *Special characteristics:* 56 awards ($445,669 total): children of faculty/staff, general special characteristics, out-of-state students, religious affiliation. *Tuition waivers:* Full or partial for employees or children of employees.
LOANS *Student loans:* $10,339,107 (69% need-based, 31% non-need-based). 73% of past graduating class borrowed through all loan programs. *Average indebtedness per student:* $19,445. *Average need-based loan:* Freshmen: $3196. Undergraduates: $3996. *Parent loans:* $3,232,363 (26% need-based, 74% non-need-based). *Programs:* Federal Direct (Subsidized and Unsubsidized Stafford, PLUS), Perkins.
WORK-STUDY *Federal work-study:* Total amount: $928,792; 780 jobs averaging $1690. *State or other work-study/employment:* Total amount: $156,830 (3% need-based, 97% non-need-based). 114 part-time jobs averaging $1424.
ATHLETIC AWARDS Total amount: $2,487,387 (48% need-based, 52% non-need-based).
APPLYING FOR FINANCIAL AID *Required financial aid form:* FAFSA. *Financial aid deadline (priority):* 5/31. *Notification date:* Continuous beginning 3/1.
CONTACT James A. Myers, Director of Financial Aid, McKendree University, 701 College Road, Lebanon, IL 62254-1299, 618-537-6529 or toll-free 800-232-7228 Ext. 6831. *Fax:* 618-537-6530. *E-mail:* jamyers@mckendree.edu.

McMURRY UNIVERSITY
Abilene, TX

Tuition & fees: $19,205	Average undergraduate aid package: $17,424

ABOUT THE INSTITUTION Independent United Methodist, coed. 44 undergraduate majors. Federal methodology is used as a basis for awarding need-based institutional aid.
UNDERGRADUATE EXPENSES for 2009–10 *One-time required fee:* $150. *Comprehensive fee:* $25,962 includes full-time tuition ($18,345), mandatory fees ($860), and room and board ($6757). *College room only:* $3264. Full-time tuition and fees vary according to course load. Room and board charges vary according to board plan and housing facility. *Part-time tuition:* $570 per semester hour. Part-time tuition and fees vary according to course load. *Payment plan:* Installment.
FRESHMAN FINANCIAL AID (Fall 2009, est.) 304 applied for aid; of those 89% were deemed to have need. 99% of freshmen with need received aid; of those 17% had need fully met. *Average percent of need met:* 86% (excluding resources awarded to replace EFC). *Average financial aid package:* $19,120 (excluding resources awarded to replace EFC). 7% of all full-time freshmen had no need and received non-need-based gift aid.
UNDERGRADUATE FINANCIAL AID (Fall 2009, est.) 1,111 applied for aid; of those 92% were deemed to have need. 100% of undergraduates with need received aid; of those 14% had need fully met. *Average percent of need met:* 84% (excluding resources awarded to replace EFC). *Average financial aid package:* $17,424 (excluding resources awarded to replace EFC). 6% of all full-time undergraduates had no need and received non-need-based gift aid.
GIFT AID (NEED-BASED) *Total amount:* $10,224,474 (31% federal, 25% state, 41% institutional, 3% external sources). *Receiving aid:* Freshmen: 82% (263); all full-time undergraduates: 78% (952). *Average award:* Freshmen: $11,759; Undergraduates: $9646. *Scholarships, grants, and awards:* Federal Pell, FSEOG, state, private, college/university gift aid from institutional funds, Academic Competitiveness Grants, National SMART Grants.
GIFT AID (NON-NEED-BASED) *Total amount:* $3,998,810 (1% federal, 4% state, 95% institutional). *Receiving aid:* Freshmen: 51% (164). Undergraduates: 53% (647). *Average award:* Freshmen: $5889. Undergraduates: $5458. *Scholarships, grants, and awards by category:* Academic interests/achievement: 236 awards ($502,419 total): biological sciences, business, communication, computer science, education, English, general academic interests/achievements, mathematics, physical sciences, premedicine, religion/biblical studies, social sciences. *Creative arts/performance:* 11 awards ($18,480 total): art/fine arts, music, theater/drama. *Special achievements/activities:* 63 awards ($95,300 total): general special achievements/activities, junior miss. *Special characteristics:* 403 awards ($2,589,039 total): children of faculty/staff, ethnic background, international students, local/state students, out-of-state students, previous college experience, relatives of clergy, religious affiliation. *Tuition waivers:* Full or partial for employees or children of employees.
LOANS *Student loans:* $9,479,453 (40% need-based, 60% non-need-based). 77% of past graduating class borrowed through all loan programs. *Average*

indebtedness per student: $27,935. *Average need-based loan:* Freshmen: $3390. Undergraduates: $4252. *Parent loans:* $425,297 (100% non-need-based). *Programs:* FFEL (Subsidized and Unsubsidized Stafford, PLUS), Perkins, state, alternative loans, United Methodist Student Loans, Bonner Price Loans.
WORK-STUDY *Federal work-study:* Total amount: $629,150; 302 jobs averaging $2055. *State or other work-study/employment:* Total amount: $115,601 (31% need-based, 69% non-need-based). 58 part-time jobs averaging $1897.
APPLYING FOR FINANCIAL AID *Required financial aid form:* FAFSA. *Financial aid deadline (priority):* 3/15. *Notification date:* Continuous beginning 2/1. Students must reply within 3 weeks of notification.
CONTACT Rachel Atkins, Director of Financial Aid, McMurry University, Box 908, Abilene, TX 79697, 325-793-4709 or toll-free 800-477-0077. *Fax:* 325-793-4718. *E-mail:* atkinsr@mcmurryadm.mcm.edu.

McNALLY SMITH COLLEGE OF MUSIC
Saint Paul, MN

Tuition & fees: $23,770	Average undergraduate aid package: N/A

ABOUT THE INSTITUTION Proprietary, coed. 5 undergraduate majors. Federal methodology is used as a basis for awarding need-based institutional aid.
UNDERGRADUATE EXPENSES for 2010–11 *Tuition:* full-time $21,970; part-time $845 per credit. *Required fees:* full-time $1800; $400 per term. Full-time tuition and fees vary according to course load. Part-time tuition and fees vary according to course load. *Payment plan:* Installment.
GIFT AID (NEED-BASED) *Total amount:* $2,106,180 (49% federal, 19% state, 28% institutional, 4% external sources). *Scholarships, grants, and awards:* Federal Pell, FSEOG, state, college/university gift aid from institutional funds.
GIFT AID (NON-NEED-BASED) *Total amount:* $123,088 (100% federal). *Scholarships, grants, and awards by category: Creative arts/performance:* music. *Tuition waivers:* Full or partial for employees or children of employees.
LOANS *Student loans:* $7,448,406 (100% need-based). *Parent loans:* $2,283,404 (100% need-based). *Programs:* Federal Direct (Subsidized and Unsubsidized Stafford, PLUS), state, college/university.
WORK-STUDY *Federal work-study:* Total amount: $60,000; jobs available. *State or other work-study/employment:* Total amount: $21,356 (100% need-based). Part-time jobs available.
APPLYING FOR FINANCIAL AID *Required financial aid forms:* FAFSA, institution's own form. *Financial aid deadline:* Continuous. *Notification date:* Continuous beginning 3/15.
CONTACT Mr. Paul Haugen, Financial Aid Administrator, McNally Smith College of Music, 19 Exchange Street East, Saint Paul, MN 55101-2220, 651-361-3321 or toll-free 800-594-9500. *Fax:* 651-291-0366. *E-mail:* paul.haugen@mcnallysmith.edu.

McNEESE STATE UNIVERSITY
Lake Charles, LA

ABOUT THE INSTITUTION State-supported, coed. 54 undergraduate majors.
GIFT AID (NEED-BASED) *Scholarships, grants, and awards:* Federal Pell, FSEOG, state, private, college/university gift aid from institutional funds, Federal Nursing, Academic Competitiveness Grants, National SMART Grants.
GIFT AID (NON-NEED-BASED) *Scholarships, grants, and awards by category: Academic interests/achievement:* agriculture, biological sciences, business, communication, computer science, education, engineering/technologies, English, foreign languages, general academic interests/achievements, health fields, home economics, humanities, library science, mathematics, physical sciences, premedicine, social sciences. *Creative arts/performance:* art/fine arts, cinema/film/broadcasting, creative writing, dance, debating, general creative arts/performance, journalism/publications, music, performing arts, theater/drama. *Special achievements/activities:* cheerleading/drum major, community service, general special achievements/activities, hobbies/interests, leadership, memberships, rodeo. *Special characteristics:* adult students, children and siblings of alumni, children of faculty/staff, children of workers in trades, children with a deceased or disabled parent, ethnic background, first-generation college students, general special characteristics, international students, local/state students, members of minority groups, out-of-state students, religious affiliation, spouses of deceased or disabled public servants, veterans, veterans' children.
LOANS *Programs:* FFEL (Subsidized and Unsubsidized Stafford, PLUS), Perkins.

APPLYING FOR FINANCIAL AID *Required financial aid forms:* FAFSA, institution's own form.

CONTACT Ms. Taina J. Savoit, Director of Financial Aid, McNeese State University, PO Box 93260, Lake Charles, LA 70609-3260, 337-475-5065 or toll-free 800-622-3352. *Fax:* 337-475-5068. *E-mail:* financialaid@mcneese.edu.

McPHERSON COLLEGE
McPherson, KS

Tuition & fees: $18,400	Average undergraduate aid package: $20,097

ABOUT THE INSTITUTION Independent religious, coed. 28 undergraduate majors. Federal methodology is used as a basis for awarding need-based institutional aid.

UNDERGRADUATE EXPENSES for 2009–10 *Comprehensive fee:* $25,310 includes full-time tuition ($17,900), mandatory fees ($500), and room and board ($6910). *College room only:* $2735. Full-time tuition and fees vary according to course load and program. *Part-time tuition:* $250 per credit hour. *Part-time fees:* $30 per credit hour. *Payment plan:* Installment.

FRESHMAN FINANCIAL AID (Fall 2009, est.) 128 applied for aid; of those 90% were deemed to have need. 100% of freshmen with need received aid; of those 36% had need fully met. *Average percent of need met:* 89% (excluding resources awarded to replace EFC). *Average financial aid package:* $19,181 (excluding resources awarded to replace EFC). 14% of all full-time freshmen had no need and received non-need-based gift aid.

UNDERGRADUATE FINANCIAL AID (Fall 2009, est.) 504 applied for aid; of those 92% were deemed to have need. 100% of undergraduates with need received aid; of those 34% had need fully met. *Average percent of need met:* 88% (excluding resources awarded to replace EFC). *Average financial aid package:* $20,097 (excluding resources awarded to replace EFC). 14% of all full-time undergraduates had no need and received non-need-based gift aid.

GIFT AID (NEED-BASED) *Total amount:* $2,638,906 (44% federal, 13% state, 43% institutional). *Receiving aid:* Freshmen: 74% (99); all full-time undergraduates: 73% (400). *Average award:* Freshmen: $6436; Undergraduates: $6464. *Scholarships, grants, and awards:* Federal Pell, FSEOG, state, private, college/university gift aid from institutional funds.

GIFT AID (NON-NEED-BASED) *Total amount:* $3,728,997 (96% institutional, 4% external sources). *Receiving aid:* Freshmen: 81% (109). Undergraduates: 81% (445). *Average award:* Freshmen: $9566. Undergraduates: $9344. *Scholarships, grants, and awards by category: Academic interests/achievement:* 444 awards ($1,961,297 total): general academic interests/achievements. *Creative arts/performance:* 34 awards ($75,050 total): art/fine arts, journalism/publications, music, theater/drama. *Special achievements/activities:* 38 awards ($72,133 total): cheerleading/drum major, community service, religious involvement. *Special characteristics:* 26 awards ($49,163 total): adult students, religious affiliation. *Tuition waivers:* Full or partial for employees or children of employees.

LOANS *Student loans:* $3,892,150 (55% need-based, 45% non-need-based). 85% of past graduating class borrowed through all loan programs. *Average indebtedness per student:* $25,787. *Average need-based loan:* Freshmen: $3990. Undergraduates: $5194. *Parent loans:* $682,838 (100% non-need-based). *Programs:* Federal Direct (Subsidized and Unsubsidized Stafford, PLUS), Perkins.

WORK-STUDY *Federal work-study:* Total amount: $287,318; 325 jobs averaging $910.

ATHLETIC AWARDS Total amount: $649,031 (100% non-need-based).

APPLYING FOR FINANCIAL AID *Required financial aid forms:* FAFSA, state aid form. *Financial aid deadline (priority):* 3/1. *Notification date:* Continuous beginning 3/1. Students must reply within 3 weeks of notification.

CONTACT Mr. Steven Frick, Director of Admissions and Financial Aid, McPherson College, 1600 East Euclid, McPherson, KS 67460-1402, 620-242-0400 Ext. 2415 or toll-free 800-365-7402. *Fax:* 620-241-8443. *E-mail:* fricks@mcpherson.edu.

MEDAILLE COLLEGE
Buffalo, NY

Tuition & fees: $19,590	Average undergraduate aid package: $24,000

ABOUT THE INSTITUTION Independent, coed. 20 undergraduate majors. Federal methodology is used as a basis for awarding need-based institutional aid.

UNDERGRADUATE EXPENSES for 2009–10 *Comprehensive fee:* $28,878 includes full-time tuition ($19,590) and room and board ($9288). Full-time tuition and fees vary according to location. Room and board charges vary according to housing facility. *Part-time tuition:* $677 per credit hour. Part-time tuition and fees vary according to course load. *Payment plan:* Installment.

FRESHMAN FINANCIAL AID (Fall 2009, est.) 387 applied for aid; of those 92% were deemed to have need. 100% of freshmen with need received aid; of those 8% had need fully met. *Average percent of need met:* 55% (excluding resources awarded to replace EFC). *Average financial aid package:* $24,000 (excluding resources awarded to replace EFC). 1% of all full-time freshmen had no need and received non-need-based gift aid.

UNDERGRADUATE FINANCIAL AID (Fall 2009, est.) 1,711 applied for aid; of those 96% were deemed to have need. 100% of undergraduates with need received aid; of those 2% had need fully met. *Average percent of need met:* 55% (excluding resources awarded to replace EFC). *Average financial aid package:* $24,000 (excluding resources awarded to replace EFC). 1% of all full-time undergraduates had no need and received non-need-based gift aid.

GIFT AID (NEED-BASED) *Total amount:* $15,148,518 (19% federal, 16% state, 64% institutional, 1% external sources). *Receiving aid:* Freshmen: 86% (355); all full-time undergraduates: 96% (1,650). *Average award:* Freshmen: $9859; Undergraduates: $8030. *Scholarships, grants, and awards:* Federal Pell, FSEOG, state, college/university gift aid from institutional funds.

GIFT AID (NON-NEED-BASED) *Total amount:* $394,000 (89% institutional, 11% external sources). *Receiving aid:* Freshmen: 86% (355). Undergraduates: 86% (1,477). *Average award:* Freshmen: $10,000. Undergraduates: $9000. *Scholarships, grants, and awards by category: Academic interests/achievement:* 15 awards ($11,250 total): general academic interests/achievements. *Special achievements/activities:* 61 awards ($136,750 total). *Special characteristics:* 10 awards ($28,000 total): adult students. *Tuition waivers:* Full or partial for employees or children of employees, adult students, senior citizens.

LOANS *Student loans:* $12,240,158 (87% need-based, 13% non-need-based). 95% of past graduating class borrowed through all loan programs. *Average indebtedness per student:* $21,000. *Average need-based loan:* Freshmen: $5000. Undergraduates: $7000. *Parent loans:* $1,135,587 (100% non-need-based). *Programs:* FFEL (Subsidized and Unsubsidized Stafford, PLUS).

WORK-STUDY *Federal work-study:* Total amount: $300,000; 150 jobs averaging $1500.

APPLYING FOR FINANCIAL AID *Required financial aid forms:* FAFSA, institution's own form, state aid form. *Financial aid deadline (priority):* 4/1. *Notification date:* Continuous. Students must reply within 2 weeks of notification.

CONTACT Ms. Catherine Buzanski, Director of Financial Aid, Medaille College, 18 Agassiz Circle, Buffalo, NY 14214-2695, 716-880-2179 or toll-free 800-292-1582 (in-state). *Fax:* 716-884-0291. *E-mail:* cbuzanski@medaille.edu.

MEDCENTER ONE COLLEGE OF NURSING
Bismarck, ND

Tuition & fees: $10,012	Average undergraduate aid package: $12,362

ABOUT THE INSTITUTION Independent, coed, primarily women. 1 undergraduate major. Both federal and institutional methodology are used as a basis for awarding need-based institutional aid.

UNDERGRADUATE EXPENSES for 2010–11 *Tuition:* full-time $10,012. Part-time tuition and fees vary according to course load.

UNDERGRADUATE FINANCIAL AID (Fall 2009, est.) 82 applied for aid; of those 83% were deemed to have need. 100% of undergraduates with need received aid; of those 29% had need fully met. *Average percent of need met:* 74% (excluding resources awarded to replace EFC). *Average financial aid package:* $12,362 (excluding resources awarded to replace EFC). 2% of all full-time undergraduates had no need and received non-need-based gift aid.

GIFT AID (NEED-BASED) *Total amount:* $230,907 (59% federal, 34% state, 2% institutional, 5% external sources). *Receiving aid:* All full-time undergraduates: 58% (52). *Average award:* Undergraduates: $3944. *Scholarships, grants, and awards:* Federal Pell, FSEOG, state, private, college/university gift aid from institutional funds.

GIFT AID (NON-NEED-BASED) *Total amount:* $21,857 (18% institutional, 82% external sources). *Receiving aid:* Undergraduates: 20% (18). *Average award:* Undergraduates: $250. *Scholarships, grants, and awards by category: Academic interests/achievement:* 19 awards ($5700 total): general academic interests/

achievements, health fields. *Special achievements/activities:* memberships. *Special characteristics:* 26 awards ($12,500 total): children and siblings of alumni, general special characteristics, local/state students.
LOANS *Student loans:* $1,112,939 (23% need-based, 77% non-need-based). *Average need-based loan:* Undergraduates: $4188. *Programs:* Federal Direct (Subsidized and Unsubsidized Stafford, PLUS), Perkins, Federal Nursing, college/university.
WORK-STUDY *Federal work-study:* Total amount: $6450; 5 jobs averaging $1200.
APPLYING FOR FINANCIAL AID *Financial aid deadline (priority):* 3/15. *Notification date:* Continuous beginning 5/1. Students must reply within 2 weeks of notification.
CONTACT Ms. Janell Thomas, Financial Aid Director, Medcenter One College of Nursing, 512 North 7th Street, Bismarck, ND 58501-4494, 701-323-6270. *Fax:* 701-323-6289. *E-mail:* jthomas@mohs.org.

MEDGAR EVERS COLLEGE OF THE CITY UNIVERSITY OF NEW YORK
Brooklyn, NY

Tuition & fees (NY res): $4902	Average undergraduate aid package: $3721

ABOUT THE INSTITUTION State and locally supported, coed. 15 undergraduate majors. Federal methodology is used as a basis for awarding need-based institutional aid.
UNDERGRADUATE EXPENSES for 2010–11 *Tuition, state resident:* full-time $4600; part-time $195 per credit hour. *Tuition, nonresident:* full-time $9960; part-time $415 per credit hour. *Required fees:* full-time $302; $150.85 per term. Full-time tuition and fees vary according to course load. Part-time tuition and fees vary according to course load. *Payment plans:* Installment, deferred payment.
FRESHMAN FINANCIAL AID (Fall 2009, est.) *Average financial aid package:* $3865 (excluding resources awarded to replace EFC).
UNDERGRADUATE FINANCIAL AID (Fall 2009, est.) *Average financial aid package:* $3721 (excluding resources awarded to replace EFC).
GIFT AID (NEED-BASED) *Total amount:* $18,723,391 (65% federal, 35% state). *Receiving aid:* Freshmen: 85% (1,094); all full-time undergraduates: 82% (3,805). *Average award:* Freshmen: $3724; Undergraduates: $3542. *Scholarships, grants, and awards:* Federal Pell, FSEOG, state, private, college/university gift aid from institutional funds, Thurgood Marshall Scholarship Fund.
GIFT AID (NON-NEED-BASED) *Scholarships, grants, and awards by category:* Academic interests/achievement: general academic interests/achievements.
LOANS *Student loans:* $1,754,599 (100% need-based). *Average need-based loan:* Freshmen: $1528. Undergraduates: $1621. *Programs:* Federal Direct (Subsidized and Unsubsidized Stafford, PLUS), FFEL (Subsidized and Unsubsidized Stafford, PLUS), Perkins.
WORK-STUDY *Federal work-study:* Total amount: $299,736; jobs available.
APPLYING FOR FINANCIAL AID *Required financial aid forms:* FAFSA, state aid form, University Financial Aid Information Supplemental Request (FASIR). *Financial aid deadline (priority):* 4/1. *Notification date:* Continuous beginning 9/1.
CONTACT Conley James, Acting Director of Financial Aid, Medgar Evers College of the City University of New York, 1650 Bedford Avenue, Brooklyn, NY 11225, 718-270-6038. *Fax:* 718-270-6194. *E-mail:* conley@mec.cuny.edu.

MEDICAL COLLEGE OF GEORGIA
Augusta, GA

Tuition & fees (GA res): $6782	Average undergraduate aid package: $8105

ABOUT THE INSTITUTION State-supported, coed. 8 undergraduate majors. Federal methodology is used as a basis for awarding need-based institutional aid.
UNDERGRADUATE EXPENSES for 2009–10 *Tuition, state resident:* full-time $6070; part-time $203 per credit hour. *Tuition, nonresident:* full-time $24,280; part-time $810 per credit hour. *Required fees:* full-time $712. Full-time tuition

and fees vary according to location. Part-time tuition and fees vary according to course load and location. Room and board charges vary according to housing facility.
UNDERGRADUATE FINANCIAL AID (Fall 2009, est.) 448 applied for aid; of those 100% were deemed to have need. 100% of undergraduates with need received aid. *Average financial aid package:* $8105 (excluding resources awarded to replace EFC).
GIFT AID (NEED-BASED) *Total amount:* $755,195 (82% federal, 4% institutional, 14% external sources). *Receiving aid:* All full-time undergraduates: 47% (253). *Average award:* Undergraduates: $2854. *Scholarships, grants, and awards:* Federal Pell, FSEOG, state, private, college/university gift aid from institutional funds, Federal Nursing.
GIFT AID (NON-NEED-BASED) *Total amount:* $1,487,074 (99% state, 1% external sources). *Receiving aid:* Undergraduates: 52% (276). *Scholarships, grants, and awards by category:* Academic interests/achievement: 634 awards ($2,667,320 total): health fields. Special characteristics: 42 awards ($89,226 total): religious affiliation. *Tuition waivers:* Full or partial for employees or children of employees.
LOANS *Student loans:* $2,850,946 (54% need-based, 46% non-need-based). *Average need-based loan:* Undergraduates: $6183. *Parent loans:* $19,000 (100% need-based). *Programs:* Federal Direct (Subsidized and Unsubsidized Stafford, PLUS), FFEL (Subsidized and Unsubsidized Stafford, PLUS), Perkins, Federal Nursing, state, college/university.
WORK-STUDY *Federal work-study:* Total amount: $46,254; 30 jobs averaging $1542.
APPLYING FOR FINANCIAL AID *Required financial aid forms:* FAFSA, institution's own form, state aid form. *Financial aid deadline:* Continuous. *Notification date:* Continuous beginning 6/10. Students must reply within 2 weeks of notification.
CONTACT Dr. Beverly Boggs, Executive Director of Academic Admissions and Student Financial Aid, Medical College of Georgia, 2013 Administration Building, Augusta, GA 30912-7320, 706-721-4901 or toll-free 800-519-3388 (in-state). *Fax:* 706-721-9407. *E-mail:* osfa@mail.mcg.edu.

MEDICAL UNIVERSITY OF SOUTH CAROLINA
Charleston, SC

ABOUT THE INSTITUTION State-supported, coed. 2 undergraduate majors.
GIFT AID (NEED-BASED) *Scholarships, grants, and awards:* Federal Pell, FSEOG, state, private, college/university gift aid from institutional funds, Federal Nursing, Scholarships for Disadvantaged Students (SDS).
GIFT AID (NON-NEED-BASED) *Scholarships, grants, and awards by category:* Academic interests/achievement: general academic interests/achievements, health fields. Special characteristics: ethnic background, general special characteristics, local/state students, members of minority groups.
LOANS *Programs:* FFEL (Subsidized and Unsubsidized Stafford, PLUS), Perkins, Federal Nursing, state, Health Professions Loans, Loans for Disadvantaged Students program, Primary Care Loans, alternative loans.
WORK-STUDY *Federal work-study:* Total amount: $20,257; jobs available.
CONTACT Cecile Kamath, PhD, Director for Financial Aid, Medical University of South Carolina, 45 Courtenay Drive, Charleston, SC 29425, 843-792-2536. *Fax:* 843-792-6356. *E-mail:* finaid@musc.edu.

MEMPHIS COLLEGE OF ART
Memphis, TN

Tuition & fees: $23,950	Average undergraduate aid package: $10,862

ABOUT THE INSTITUTION Independent, coed. 5 undergraduate majors. Both federal and institutional methodology are used as a basis for awarding need-based institutional aid.
UNDERGRADUATE EXPENSES for 2010–11 *Comprehensive fee:* $31,950 includes full-time tuition ($23,300), mandatory fees ($650), and room and board ($8000). *College room only:* $6000. Room and board charges vary according to housing facility. *Part-time tuition:* $1012 per credit hour. *Payment plan:* Installment.
FRESHMAN FINANCIAL AID (Fall 2009, est.) 92 applied for aid; of those 93% were deemed to have need. 100% of freshmen with need received aid; of those

23% had need fully met. *Average percent of need met:* 80% (excluding resources awarded to replace EFC). *Average financial aid package:* $10,424 (excluding resources awarded to replace EFC). 15% of all full-time freshmen had no need and received non-need-based gift aid.

UNDERGRADUATE FINANCIAL AID (Fall 2009, est.) 302 applied for aid; of those 92% were deemed to have need. 100% of undergraduates with need received aid; of those 23% had need fully met. *Average percent of need met:* 80% (excluding resources awarded to replace EFC). *Average financial aid package:* $10,862 (excluding resources awarded to replace EFC). 12% of all full-time undergraduates had no need and received non-need-based gift aid.

GIFT AID (NEED-BASED) *Total amount:* $1,189,982 (76% federal, 12% state, 12% institutional). *Receiving aid:* Freshmen: 50% (50); all full-time undergraduates: 52% (176). *Average award:* Freshmen: $6252; Undergraduates: $6252. *Scholarships, grants, and awards:* Federal Pell, FSEOG, state, private, college/university gift aid from institutional funds.

GIFT AID (NON-NEED-BASED) *Total amount:* $3,602,974 (9% state, 89% institutional, 2% external sources). *Receiving aid:* Freshmen: 83% (83). Undergraduates: 80% (269). *Average award:* Freshmen: $12,900. Undergraduates: $9000. *Scholarships, grants, and awards by category:* Academic interests/achievement: general academic interests/achievements. Creative arts/performance: applied art and design, art/fine arts. Special characteristics: 1 award ($11,000 total): children of faculty/staff, previous college experience. *Tuition waivers:* Full or partial for employees or children of employees.

LOANS *Student loans:* $2,752,904 (48% need-based, 52% non-need-based). 95% of past graduating class borrowed through all loan programs. *Average indebtedness per student:* $34,360. *Average need-based loan:* Freshmen: $3500. Undergraduates: $5500. *Parent loans:* $905,982 (100% non-need-based). *Programs:* Federal Direct (Subsidized and Unsubsidized Stafford, PLUS), FFEL (Subsidized and Unsubsidized Stafford, PLUS), college/university.

WORK-STUDY *Federal work-study:* Total amount: $110,400; 340 jobs averaging $500. *State or other work-study/employment:* Total amount: $41,250 (100% non-need-based). Part-time jobs available.

APPLYING FOR FINANCIAL AID *Required financial aid form:* FAFSA. *Financial aid deadline (priority):* 3/1. *Notification date:* Continuous beginning 4/1.

CONTACT Lynn Holladay, Director of Financial Aid, Memphis College of Art, 1930 Poplar Avenue, Overton Park, Memphis, TN 38104, 901-272-5136 or toll-free 800-727-1088. *Fax:* 901-272-5134. *E-mail:* lholladay@mca.edu.

MENLO COLLEGE
Atherton, CA

Tuition & fees: $33,550	Average undergraduate aid package: $26,274

ABOUT THE INSTITUTION Independent, coed. 10 undergraduate majors. Federal methodology is used as a basis for awarding need-based institutional aid.

UNDERGRADUATE EXPENSES for 2010–11 *Comprehensive fee:* $44,880 includes full-time tuition ($33,150), mandatory fees ($400), and room and board ($11,330). Full-time tuition and fees vary according to program. Room and board charges vary according to housing facility. *Part-time tuition:* $1381 per credit hour. Part-time tuition and fees vary according to program. *Payment plan:* Installment.

FRESHMAN FINANCIAL AID (Fall 2009, est.) 101 applied for aid; of those 85% were deemed to have need. 100% of freshmen with need received aid; of those 12% had need fully met. *Average percent of need met:* 73% (excluding resources awarded to replace EFC). *Average financial aid package:* $26,596 (excluding resources awarded to replace EFC). 29% of all full-time freshmen had no need and received non-need-based gift aid.

UNDERGRADUATE FINANCIAL AID (Fall 2009, est.) 373 applied for aid; of those 92% were deemed to have need. 100% of undergraduates with need received aid; of those 8% had need fully met. *Average percent of need met:* 70% (excluding resources awarded to replace EFC). *Average financial aid package:* $26,274 (excluding resources awarded to replace EFC). 33% of all full-time undergraduates had no need and received non-need-based gift aid.

GIFT AID (NEED-BASED) *Total amount:* $7,510,883 (10% federal, 7% state, 80% institutional, 3% external sources). *Receiving aid:* Freshmen: 59% (80); all full-time undergraduates: 58% (336). *Average award:* Freshmen: $25,343; Undergraduates: $22,421. *Scholarships, grants, and awards:* Federal Pell, FSEOG, state, college/university gift aid from institutional funds, Academic Competitiveness Grants.

GIFT AID (NON-NEED-BASED) *Total amount:* $1,993,640 (99% institutional, 1% external sources). *Receiving aid:* Freshmen: 7% (9). Undergraduates: 3%

(18). *Average award:* Freshmen: $11,525. Undergraduates: $9818. *Scholarships, grants, and awards by category:* Academic interests/achievement: 504 awards ($4,569,333 total): general academic interests/achievements. *Tuition waivers:* Full or partial for employees or children of employees.

LOANS *Student loans:* $2,855,542 (77% need-based, 23% non-need-based). 76% of past graduating class borrowed through all loan programs. *Average indebtedness per student:* $25,696. *Average need-based loan:* Freshmen: $2671. Undergraduates: $3780. *Parent loans:* $1,571,274 (43% need-based, 57% non-need-based). *Programs:* Federal Direct (Subsidized and Unsubsidized Stafford, PLUS).

WORK-STUDY *Federal work-study:* Total amount: $261,888; 261 jobs averaging $1000.

APPLYING FOR FINANCIAL AID *Required financial aid forms:* FAFSA, state aid form. *Financial aid deadline (priority):* 3/2. *Notification date:* Continuous beginning 3/15.

CONTACT Anne Heaton-Dunlap, Director of Financial Aid, Menlo College, 1000 El Camino Real, Atherton, CA 94027-4301, 650-543-3880 or toll-free 800-556-3656. *Fax:* 650-543-4103. *E-mail:* financialaid@menlo.edu.

MERCER UNIVERSITY
Macon, GA

Tuition & fees: $29,540	Average undergraduate aid package: $30,024

ABOUT THE INSTITUTION Independent Baptist, coed. 49 undergraduate majors. Federal methodology is used as a basis for awarding need-based institutional aid.

UNDERGRADUATE EXPENSES for 2009–10 *Comprehensive fee:* $38,328 includes full-time tuition ($29,340), mandatory fees ($200), and room and board ($8788). Full-time tuition and fees vary according to class time and location. Room and board charges vary according to board plan, housing facility, and location. *Part-time tuition:* $978 per credit hour. *Part-time fees:* $8.50 per credit hour. Part-time tuition and fees vary according to class time, course load, and location. *Payment plan:* Installment.

FRESHMAN FINANCIAL AID (Fall 2009, est.) 542 applied for aid; of those 88% were deemed to have need. 100% of freshmen with need received aid; of those 52% had need fully met. *Average percent of need met:* 88% (excluding resources awarded to replace EFC). *Average financial aid package:* $31,648 (excluding resources awarded to replace EFC). 23% of all full-time freshmen had no need and received non-need-based gift aid.

UNDERGRADUATE FINANCIAL AID (Fall 2009, est.) 1,817 applied for aid; of those 88% were deemed to have need. 100% of undergraduates with need received aid; of those 47% had need fully met. *Average percent of need met:* 88% (excluding resources awarded to replace EFC). *Average financial aid package:* $30,024 (excluding resources awarded to replace EFC). 28% of all full-time undergraduates had no need and received non-need-based gift aid.

GIFT AID (NEED-BASED) *Total amount:* $29,187,869 (11% federal, 10% state, 77% institutional, 2% external sources). *Receiving aid:* Freshmen: 77% (474); all full-time undergraduates: 71% (1,595). *Average award:* Freshmen: $21,619; Undergraduates: $19,558. *Scholarships, grants, and awards:* Federal Pell, FSEOG, state, college/university gift aid from institutional funds, Federal Nursing.

GIFT AID (NON-NEED-BASED) *Total amount:* $14,273,484 (16% state, 81% institutional, 3% external sources). *Receiving aid:* Freshmen: 25% (155). Undergraduates: 19% (422). *Average award:* Freshmen: $21,673. Undergraduates: $19,395. *Scholarships, grants, and awards by category:* Academic interests/achievement: $14,252,537 total: biological sciences, business, education, engineering/technologies, English, foreign languages, general academic interests/achievements, international studies, military science, religion/biblical studies. Creative arts/performance: $929,603 total: art/fine arts, debating, music, theater/drama. Special achievements/activities: $399,842 total: community service, general special achievements/activities, memberships. Special characteristics: $20,416,799 total: adult students, children of faculty/staff, children of public servants, children of union members/company employees, general special characteristics, international students, local/state students, members of minority groups, relatives of clergy, religious affiliation, siblings of current students. *Tuition waivers:* Full or partial for employees or children of employees.

LOANS *Student loans:* $12,665,561 (68% need-based, 32% non-need-based). 58% of past graduating class borrowed through all loan programs. *Average indebtedness per student:* $29,065. *Average need-based loan:* Freshmen: $6956. Undergraduates: $8304. *Parent loans:* $2,476,219 (38% need-based, 62%

non-need-based). *Programs:* Federal Direct (Subsidized and Unsubsidized Stafford, PLUS), Perkins, Federal Nursing, college/university.

WORK-STUDY *Federal work-study:* Total amount: $921,359; jobs available.

ATHLETIC AWARDS Total amount: $3,536,277 (37% need-based, 63% non-need-based).

APPLYING FOR FINANCIAL AID *Required financial aid forms:* FAFSA, institution's own form, state aid form (for GA residents only). *Financial aid deadline (priority):* 4/1. *Notification date:* Continuous. Students must reply within 2 weeks of notification.

CONTACT Ms. Carol Williams, Associate Vice President, Financial Planning, Mercer University, 1400 Coleman Avenue, Macon, GA 31207-0003, 478-301-2670 or toll-free 800-840-8577. *Fax:* 478-301-2671. *E-mail:* williams_ck@mercer.edu.

MERCY COLLEGE
Dobbs Ferry, NY

CONTACT Director of Financial Aid, Mercy College, 28 Wells Avenue, 5th Floor, Yonkers, NY 00701, 888-464-6737 or toll-free 800-MERCY-NY. *Fax:* 914-375-8582.

MERCY COLLEGE OF HEALTH SCIENCES
Des Moines, IA

CONTACT Lisa Croat, Financial Aid Assistant Coordinator, Mercy College of Health Sciences, 928 Sixth Avenue, Des Moines, IA 50309, 515-643-6720 or toll-free 800-637-2994. *Fax:* 515-643-6702. *E-mail:* lcroat@mercydesmoines.org.

MERCY COLLEGE OF NORTHWEST OHIO
Toledo, OH

Tuition & fees: $10,090	Average undergraduate aid package: $7464

ABOUT THE INSTITUTION Independent religious, coed, primarily women. 5 undergraduate majors. Federal methodology is used as a basis for awarding need-based institutional aid.

UNDERGRADUATE EXPENSES for 2009–10 *One-time required fee:* $15. *Tuition:* full-time $9440; part-time $326 per credit hour. *Required fees:* full-time $650; $5 per credit hour. Full-time tuition and fees vary according to course load. Part-time tuition and fees vary according to course load. Room and board charges vary according to housing facility. *Payment plans:* Installment, deferred payment.

FRESHMAN FINANCIAL AID (Fall 2008) 54 applied for aid; of those 87% were deemed to have need. 100% of freshmen with need received aid; of those 4% had need fully met. *Average percent of need met:* 53% (excluding resources awarded to replace EFC). *Average financial aid package:* $6470 (excluding resources awarded to replace EFC). 4% of all full-time freshmen had no need and received non-need-based gift aid.

UNDERGRADUATE FINANCIAL AID (Fall 2008) 373 applied for aid; of those 88% were deemed to have need. 100% of undergraduates with need received aid; of those 4% had need fully met. *Average percent of need met:* 61% (excluding resources awarded to replace EFC). *Average financial aid package:* $7464 (excluding resources awarded to replace EFC). 1% of all full-time undergraduates had no need and received non-need-based gift aid.

GIFT AID (NEED-BASED) *Total amount:* $1,658,726 (70% federal, 26% state, 1% institutional, 3% external sources). *Receiving aid:* Freshmen: 41% (23); all full-time undergraduates: 37% (167). *Average award:* Freshmen: $5739; Undergraduates: $3847. *Scholarships, grants, and awards:* Federal Pell, FSEOG, state, private, college/university gift aid from institutional funds, Federal Nursing.

GIFT AID (NON-NEED-BASED) *Total amount:* $423,516 (28% state, 30% institutional, 42% external sources). *Receiving aid:* Freshmen: 66% (37). Undergraduates: 44% (200). *Average award:* Freshmen: $3698. Undergraduates: $5565. *Scholarships, grants, and awards by category: Academic interests/achievement:* 75 awards ($140,000 total): health fields. *Tuition waivers:* Full or partial for employees or children of employees.

LOANS *Student loans:* $7,086,971 (37% need-based, 63% non-need-based). 77% of past graduating class borrowed through all loan programs. *Average indebtedness per student:* $19,620. *Average need-based loan:* Freshmen: $3310. Undergraduates: $3617. *Parent loans:* $100,798 (100% need-based). *Programs:*

Federal Direct (Subsidized and Unsubsidized Stafford, PLUS), FFEL (Subsidized and Unsubsidized Stafford, PLUS), state, college/university.

WORK-STUDY *Federal work-study:* Total amount: $42,943; 29 jobs averaging $1400. *State or other work-study/employment:* Total amount: $27,750 (86% need-based, 14% non-need-based). Part-time jobs available.

APPLYING FOR FINANCIAL AID *Required financial aid form:* FAFSA. *Financial aid deadline:* Continuous. *Notification date:* Continuous beginning 3/1. Students must reply by 8/15.

CONTACT Julie Leslie, Financial Aid Director, Mercy College of Northwest Ohio, 2221 Madison Avenue, Toledo, OH 43604, 419-251-1598 or toll-free 888-80-Mercy. *Fax:* 419-251-1462. *E-mail:* julie.leslie@mercycollege.edu.

MERCYHURST COLLEGE
Erie, PA

Tuition & fees: $26,346	Average undergraduate aid package: $19,803

ABOUT THE INSTITUTION Independent Roman Catholic, coed. 67 undergraduate majors. Federal methodology is used as a basis for awarding need-based institutional aid.

UNDERGRADUATE EXPENSES for 2010–11 *Comprehensive fee:* $35,541 includes full-time tuition ($24,648), mandatory fees ($1698), and room and board ($9195). *College room only:* $4542. Full-time tuition and fees vary according to program. Room and board charges vary according to board plan and housing facility. *Part-time tuition:* $822 per credit hour. Part-time tuition and fees vary according to class time, course load, degree level, and location. *Payment plan:* Installment.

FRESHMAN FINANCIAL AID (Fall 2009, est.) 596 applied for aid; of those 87% were deemed to have need. 100% of freshmen with need received aid; of those 50% had need fully met. *Average percent of need met:* 80% (excluding resources awarded to replace EFC). *Average financial aid package:* $23,226 (excluding resources awarded to replace EFC). 15% of all full-time freshmen had no need and received non-need-based gift aid.

UNDERGRADUATE FINANCIAL AID (Fall 2009, est.) 2,230 applied for aid; of those 84% were deemed to have need. 100% of undergraduates with need received aid; of those 31% had need fully met. *Average percent of need met:* 62% (excluding resources awarded to replace EFC). *Average financial aid package:* $19,803 (excluding resources awarded to replace EFC). 22% of all full-time undergraduates had no need and received non-need-based gift aid.

GIFT AID (NEED-BASED) *Total amount:* $29,744,903 (14% federal, 8% state, 77% institutional, 1% external sources). *Receiving aid:* Freshmen: 62% (414); all full-time undergraduates: 69% (1,828). *Average award:* Freshmen: $12,769; Undergraduates: $10,956. *Scholarships, grants, and awards:* Federal Pell, FSEOG, state, private, college/university gift aid from institutional funds.

GIFT AID (NON-NEED-BASED) *Total amount:* $6,321,212 (4% federal, 95% institutional, 1% external sources). *Receiving aid:* Freshmen: 77% (511). Undergraduates: 40% (1,067). *Average award:* Freshmen: $11,533. Undergraduates: $10,475. *Scholarships, grants, and awards by category: Academic interests/achievement:* 1,291 awards ($12,040,000 total): general academic interests/achievements. *Creative arts/performance:* 139 awards ($661,085 total): applied art and design, art/fine arts, dance, music. *Special achievements/activities:* 1,869 awards ($15,642,900 total): community service, general special achievements/activities, leadership, religious involvement. *Special characteristics:* 51 awards ($845,970 total): children and siblings of alumni, children of faculty/staff. *Tuition waivers:* Full or partial for employees or children of employees, adult students.

LOANS *Student loans:* $19,405,525 (92% need-based, 8% non-need-based). 76% of past graduating class borrowed through all loan programs. *Average indebtedness per student:* $22,630. *Average need-based loan:* Freshmen: $3352. Undergraduates: $5913. *Parent loans:* $3,398,665 (88% need-based, 12% non-need-based). *Programs:* Federal Direct (Subsidized and Unsubsidized Stafford, PLUS), Perkins, college/university.

WORK-STUDY *Federal work-study:* Total amount: $414,655; 345 jobs averaging $1208. *State or other work-study/employment:* Total amount: $844,305 (100% need-based). 853 part-time jobs averaging $1239.

ATHLETIC AWARDS Total amount: $5,589,341 (43% need-based, 57% non-need-based).

APPLYING FOR FINANCIAL AID *Required financial aid forms:* FAFSA, institution's own form. *Financial aid deadline:* 5/1 (priority: 3/1). *Notification date:* Continuous beginning 2/21. Students must reply within 2 weeks of notification.

CONTACT Carrie Newman, Director, Student Financial Services, Mercyhurst College, 501 East 38th Street, Erie, PA 16546, 814-824-2288 or toll-free 800-825-1926 Ext. 2202. *Fax:* 814-824-2300. *E-mail:* sfs@mercyhurst.edu.

MEREDITH COLLEGE
Raleigh, NC

Tuition & fees: N/R	Average undergraduate aid package: $18,638

ABOUT THE INSTITUTION Independent, undergraduate: women only; graduate: coed. 45 undergraduate majors. Federal methodology is used as a basis for awarding need-based institutional aid.

FRESHMAN FINANCIAL AID (Fall 2009, est.) 413 applied for aid; of those 86% were deemed to have need. 100% of freshmen with need received aid; of those 20% had need fully met. *Average percent of need met:* 83% (excluding resources awarded to replace EFC). *Average financial aid package:* $19,751 (excluding resources awarded to replace EFC). 12% of all full-time freshmen had no need and received non-need-based gift aid.

UNDERGRADUATE FINANCIAL AID (Fall 2009, est.) 1,434 applied for aid; of those 87% were deemed to have need. 100% of undergraduates with need received aid; of those 17% had need fully met. *Average percent of need met:* 78% (excluding resources awarded to replace EFC). *Average financial aid package:* $18,638 (excluding resources awarded to replace EFC). 8% of all full-time undergraduates had no need and received non-need-based gift aid.

GIFT AID (NEED-BASED) *Total amount:* $18,614,153 (14% federal, 27% state, 51% institutional, 8% external sources). *Receiving aid:* Freshmen: 75% (357); all full-time undergraduates: 70% (1,237). *Average award:* Freshmen: $16,829; Undergraduates: $14,917. *Scholarships, grants, and awards:* Federal Pell, FSEOG, state, private, college/university gift aid from institutional funds.

GIFT AID (NON-NEED-BASED) *Total amount:* $3,307,855 (21% state, 65% institutional, 14% external sources). *Average award:* Freshmen: $7334. Undergraduates: $6790. *Scholarships, grants, and awards by category: Academic interests/achievement:* biological sciences, business, computer science, education, English, foreign languages, general academic interests/achievements, mathematics, physical sciences, religion/biblical studies. *Creative arts/performance:* applied art and design, art/fine arts, creative writing, music. *Special achievements/activities:* community service, leadership. *Special characteristics:* adult students, children of faculty/staff, ethnic background, first-generation college students, international students, members of minority groups, out-of-state students, previous college experience, religious affiliation. *Tuition waivers:* Full or partial for employees or children of employees.

LOANS *Student loans:* $9,424,050 (87% need-based, 13% non-need-based). 76% of past graduating class borrowed through all loan programs. *Average indebtedness per student:* $32,350. *Average need-based loan:* Freshmen: $3148. Undergraduates: $4250. *Parent loans:* $2,287,512 (14% need-based, 86% non-need-based). *Programs:* FFEL (Subsidized and Unsubsidized Stafford, PLUS), Perkins, college/university.

WORK-STUDY *Federal work-study:* Total amount: $263,434; jobs available. *State or other work-study/employment:* Total amount: $77,122 (100% need-based). Part-time jobs available.

APPLYING FOR FINANCIAL AID *Required financial aid form:* FAFSA. *Financial aid deadline (priority):* 2/15. *Notification date:* Continuous beginning 3/15. Students must reply by 5/1 or within 2 weeks of notification.

CONTACT Mr. Kevin Michaelsen, Director of Financial Assistance, Meredith College, 3800 Hillsborough Street, Raleigh, NC 27607-5298, 919-760-8565 or toll-free 800-MEREDITH. *Fax:* 919-760-2375. *E-mail:* michaelsen@meredith.edu.

MERRIMACK COLLEGE
North Andover, MA

Tuition & fees: $29,810	Average undergraduate aid package: $15,668

ABOUT THE INSTITUTION Independent Roman Catholic, coed. 35 undergraduate majors. Federal methodology is used as a basis for awarding need-based institutional aid.

UNDERGRADUATE EXPENSES for 2009–10 *Comprehensive fee:* $40,000 includes full-time tuition ($29,310), mandatory fees ($500), and room and board ($10,190). *College room only:* $6040. Full-time tuition and fees vary according to program and student level. Room and board charges vary according to board plan and housing facility. *Part-time tuition:* $1045 per credit. *Part-time fees:* $62.50 per term. Part-time tuition and fees vary according to class time, course level, course load, and degree level. *Payment plans:* Guaranteed tuition, installment.

FRESHMAN FINANCIAL AID (Fall 2009, est.) 423 applied for aid; of those 82% were deemed to have need. 100% of freshmen with need received aid; of those 90% had need fully met. *Average percent of need met:* 72% (excluding resources awarded to replace EFC). *Average financial aid package:* $16,727 (excluding resources awarded to replace EFC). 20% of all full-time freshmen had no need and received non-need-based gift aid.

UNDERGRADUATE FINANCIAL AID (Fall 2009, est.) 1,451 applied for aid; of those 78% were deemed to have need. 100% of undergraduates with need received aid; of those 97% had need fully met. *Average percent of need met:* 70% (excluding resources awarded to replace EFC). *Average financial aid package:* $15,668 (excluding resources awarded to replace EFC). 16% of all full-time undergraduates had no need and received non-need-based gift aid.

GIFT AID (NEED-BASED) *Total amount:* $18,395,250 (10% federal, 4% state, 86% institutional). *Receiving aid:* Freshmen: 49% (259); all full-time undergraduates: 41% (766). *Average award:* Freshmen: $11,727; Undergraduates: $9868. *Scholarships, grants, and awards:* Federal Pell, FSEOG, state, private, college/university gift aid from institutional funds.

GIFT AID (NON-NEED-BASED) *Total amount:* $1,247,085 (76% institutional, 24% external sources). *Receiving aid:* Freshmen: 58% (306). Undergraduates: 56% (1,040). *Average award:* Freshmen: $9800. Undergraduates: $10,500. *Scholarships, grants, and awards by category: Academic interests/achievement:* 1,621 awards ($18,745,824 total): general academic interests/achievements. *Special characteristics:* 129 awards ($1,151,931 total): children and siblings of alumni, children of faculty/staff, international students, relatives of clergy, siblings of current students. *Tuition waivers:* Full or partial for employees or children of employees, senior citizens.

LOANS *Student loans:* $9,771,743 (55% need-based, 45% non-need-based). 66% of past graduating class borrowed through all loan programs. *Average indebtedness per student:* $24,000. *Average need-based loan:* Freshmen: $3944. Undergraduates: $4775. *Parent loans:* $4,852,446 (100% non-need-based). *Programs:* FFEL (Subsidized and Unsubsidized Stafford, PLUS), Perkins, state, college/university, MEFA Loans, alternative loans.

WORK-STUDY *Federal work-study:* Total amount: $200,000; 162 jobs averaging $1142. *State or other work-study/employment:* Total amount: $700,000 (100% non-need-based). 354 part-time jobs averaging $1600.

ATHLETIC AWARDS Total amount: $3,454,715 (100% non-need-based).

APPLYING FOR FINANCIAL AID *Required financial aid forms:* FAFSA, business/farm supplement. *Financial aid deadline:* 2/1. *Notification date:* Continuous beginning 3/1. Students must reply by 5/1.

CONTACT Christine A. Mordach, Director of Student Financial Aid and Scholarships, Merrimack College, 315 Turnpike Street, North Andover, MA 01845, 978-837-5186. *Fax:* 978-837-5067. *E-mail:* christine.mordach@merrimack.edu.

MESA STATE COLLEGE
Grand Junction, CO

Tuition & fees: N/R	Average undergraduate aid package: $6913

ABOUT THE INSTITUTION State-supported, coed. *Awards:* associate, bachelor's, and master's degrees. 42 undergraduate majors. *Total enrollment:* 6,261. Undergraduates: 6,165. Freshmen: 1,203. Federal methodology is used as a basis for awarding need-based institutional aid.

FRESHMAN FINANCIAL AID (Fall 2009, est.) 867 applied for aid; of those 73% were deemed to have need. 93% of freshmen with need received aid; of those 7% had need fully met. *Average percent of need met:* 59% (excluding resources awarded to replace EFC). *Average financial aid package:* $6078 (excluding resources awarded to replace EFC). 9% of all full-time freshmen had no need and received non-need-based gift aid.

UNDERGRADUATE FINANCIAL AID (Fall 2009, est.) 3,207 applied for aid; of those 79% were deemed to have need. 96% of undergraduates with need received aid; of those 6% had need fully met. *Average percent of need met:* 59% (excluding resources awarded to replace EFC). *Average financial aid package:* $6913 (excluding resources awarded to replace EFC). 8% of all full-time undergraduates had no need and received non-need-based gift aid.

GIFT AID (NEED-BASED) *Total amount:* $9,489,685 (62% federal, 35% state, 3% institutional). *Receiving aid:* Freshmen: 42% (462); all full-time undergraduates: 44% (1,870). *Average award:* Freshmen: $4460; Undergraduates: $4749. *Scholarships, grants, and awards:* Federal Pell, FSEOG, state, private, college/university gift aid from institutional funds.

GIFT AID (NON-NEED-BASED) *Total amount:* $3,496,737 (4% federal, 1% state, 64% institutional, 31% external sources). *Receiving aid:* Freshmen: 2% (22). Undergraduates: 2% (79). *Average award:* Freshmen: $2099. Undergraduates: $1938. *Scholarships, grants, and awards by category: Academic interests/achievement:* 764 awards ($1,343,994 total): biological sciences, business, communication, computer science, education, engineering/technologies, English, foreign languages, general academic interests/achievements, health fields, humanities, mathematics, physical sciences, social sciences. *Creative arts/performance:* 58 awards ($39,100 total): art/fine arts, creative writing, dance, journalism/publications, music, performing arts, theater/drama. *Special achievements/activities:* 5 awards ($1110 total): cheerleading/drum major, general special achievements/activities, hobbies/interests, leadership. *Special characteristics:* 55 awards ($49,332 total): adult students, first-generation college students, international students, local/state students, members of minority groups, out-of-state students. *Tuition waivers:* Full or partial for employees or children of employees.

LOANS *Student loans:* $19,817,554 (46% need-based, 54% non-need-based). 53% of past graduating class borrowed through all loan programs. *Average indebtedness per student:* $18,834. *Average need-based loan:* Freshmen: $3109. Undergraduates: $3721. *Parent loans:* $2,828,281 (100% non-need-based). *Programs:* Federal Direct (Subsidized and Unsubsidized Stafford, PLUS), Perkins.

WORK-STUDY *Federal work-study:* Total amount: $205,276; 116 jobs averaging $1770. *State or other work-study/employment:* Total amount: $1,945,589 (28% need-based, 72% non-need-based). 415 part-time jobs averaging $1727.

ATHLETIC AWARDS Total amount: $988,945 (100% non-need-based).

APPLYING FOR FINANCIAL AID *Required financial aid form:* FAFSA. *Financial aid deadline:* Continuous. *Notification date:* Continuous beginning 4/1. Students must reply within 4 weeks of notification.

CONTACT Mr. Curt Martin, Director of Financial Aid, Mesa State College, 1100 North Avenue, Grand Junction, CO 81501-3122, 970-248-1065 or toll-free 800-982-MESA. *Fax:* 970-248-1191. *E-mail:* cumartin@mesastate.edu.

MESIVTA OF EASTERN PARKWAY–YESHIVA ZICHRON MEILECH
Brooklyn, NY

CONTACT Rabbi Joseph Halberstadt, Dean, Mesivta of Eastern Parkway–Yeshiva Zichron Meilech, 510 Dahill Road, Brooklyn, NY 11218-5559, 718-438-1002.

MESIVTA TIFERETH JERUSALEM OF AMERICA
New York, NY

CONTACT Rabbi Dickstein, Director of Financial Aid, Mesivta Tifereth Jerusalem of America, 141 East Broadway, New York, NY 10002-6301, 212-964-2830.

MESIVTA TORAH VODAATH RABBINICAL SEMINARY
Brooklyn, NY

CONTACT Mrs. Kayla Goldring, Director of Financial Aid, Mesivta Torah Vodaath Rabbinical Seminary, 425 East Ninth Street, Brooklyn, NY 11218-5209, 718-941-8000.

MESSENGER COLLEGE
Joplin, MO

CONTACT Susan Aleckson, Financial Aid Director, Messenger College, 300 East 50th Street, Joplin, MO 64804, 417-624-7070 Ext. 308 or toll-free 800-385-8940 (in-state). *Fax:* 417-624-5070. *E-mail:* saleckson@messengercollege.edu.

MESSIAH COLLEGE
Grantham, PA

Tuition & fees: $27,480	Average undergraduate aid package: $18,236

ABOUT THE INSTITUTION Independent interdenominational, coed. 69 undergraduate majors. Federal methodology is used as a basis for awarding need-based institutional aid.

UNDERGRADUATE EXPENSES for 2010–11 *Comprehensive fee:* $35,640 includes full-time tuition ($26,680), mandatory fees ($800), and room and board ($8160). *College room only:* $4320. Room and board charges vary according to board plan, housing facility, and location. *Part-time tuition:* $1112 per credit. *Payment plan:* Installment.

FRESHMAN FINANCIAL AID (Fall 2009, est.) 609 applied for aid; of those 87% were deemed to have need. 100% of freshmen with need received aid; of those 21% had need fully met. *Average percent of need met:* 72% (excluding resources awarded to replace EFC). *Average financial aid package:* $18,939 (excluding resources awarded to replace EFC). 24% of all full-time freshmen had no need and received non-need-based gift aid.

UNDERGRADUATE FINANCIAL AID (Fall 2009, est.) 2,177 applied for aid; of those 89% were deemed to have need. 100% of undergraduates with need received aid; of those 18% had need fully met. *Average percent of need met:* 69% (excluding resources awarded to replace EFC). *Average financial aid package:* $18,236 (excluding resources awarded to replace EFC). 26% of all full-time undergraduates had no need and received non-need-based gift aid.

GIFT AID (NEED-BASED) *Total amount:* $24,220,322 (10% federal, 9% state, 77% institutional, 4% external sources). *Receiving aid:* Freshmen: 75% (524); all full-time undergraduates: 71% (1,913). *Average award:* Freshmen: $13,875; Undergraduates: $12,640. *Scholarships, grants, and awards:* Federal Pell, FSEOG, state, private, college/university gift aid from institutional funds.

GIFT AID (NON-NEED-BASED) *Total amount:* $7,707,433 (93% institutional, 7% external sources). *Receiving aid:* Freshmen: 10% (70). Undergraduates: 7% (177). *Average award:* Freshmen: $10,237. Undergraduates: $9283. *Scholarships, grants, and awards by category: Academic interests/achievement:* 2,004 awards ($13,690,524 total): general academic interests/achievements. *Creative arts/performance:* 37 awards ($436,003 total): art/fine arts, music, theater/drama. *Special achievements/activities:* 421 awards ($4,594,201 total): leadership. *Special characteristics:* 218 awards ($1,788,776 total): adult students, children of faculty/staff, local/state students, religious affiliation. *Tuition waivers:* Full or partial for minority students, children of alumni, employees or children of employees, adult students, senior citizens.

LOANS *Student loans:* $18,367,927 (71% need-based, 29% non-need-based). 76% of past graduating class borrowed through all loan programs. *Average indebtedness per student:* $33,867. *Average need-based loan:* Freshmen: $3719. Undergraduates: $4803. *Parent loans:* $4,528,178 (39% need-based, 61% non-need-based). *Programs:* Federal Direct (Subsidized and Unsubsidized Stafford, PLUS), Perkins, Federal Nursing.

WORK-STUDY *Federal work-study:* Total amount: $1,691,259; 844 jobs averaging $2097. *State or other work-study/employment:* Total amount: $2,066,851 (23% need-based, 77% non-need-based). 890 part-time jobs averaging $2487.

APPLYING FOR FINANCIAL AID *Required financial aid form:* FAFSA. *Financial aid deadline (priority):* 4/1. *Notification date:* Continuous beginning 3/15. Students must reply by 5/1 or within 4 weeks of notification.

CONTACT Mr. Michael Strite, Assistant Director of Financial Aid, Messiah College, PO Box 3006, Grantham, PA 17027, 717-691-6007 or toll-free 800-233-4220. *Fax:* 717-796-4791. *E-mail:* mstrite@messiah.edu.

METHODIST UNIVERSITY
Fayetteville, NC

Tuition & fees: $24,220	Average undergraduate aid package: $15,164

ABOUT THE INSTITUTION Independent United Methodist, coed. 57 undergraduate majors. Federal methodology is used as a basis for awarding need-based institutional aid.

UNDERGRADUATE EXPENSES for 2010–11 *Comprehensive fee:* $32,620 includes full-time tuition ($23,780), mandatory fees ($440), and room and board ($8400). Full-time tuition and fees vary according to class time. Room and board charges vary according to housing facility. Part-time tuition and fees vary according to class time and course load. *Payment plan:* Installment.

FRESHMAN FINANCIAL AID (Fall 2008) 439 applied for aid; of those 92% were deemed to have need. 98% of freshmen with need received aid; of those 19% had need fully met. *Average percent of need met:* 67% (excluding resources awarded to replace EFC). *Average financial aid package:* $17,546 (excluding resources awarded to replace EFC). 5% of all full-time freshmen had no need and received non-need-based gift aid.

UNDERGRADUATE FINANCIAL AID (Fall 2008) 1,683 applied for aid; of those 93% were deemed to have need. 94% of undergraduates with need received aid; of those 16% had need fully met. *Average percent of need met:* 67% (excluding resources awarded to replace EFC). *Average financial aid package:* $15,164 (excluding resources awarded to replace EFC). 4% of all full-time undergraduates had no need and received non-need-based gift aid.

GIFT AID (NEED-BASED) *Total amount:* $9,872,628 (22% federal, 17% state, 61% institutional). *Receiving aid:* Freshmen: 80% (350); all full-time undergraduates: 68% (1,151). *Average award:* Freshmen: $9686; Undergraduates: $7810. *Scholarships, grants, and awards:* Federal Pell, FSEOG, state, private, college/university gift aid from institutional funds.

GIFT AID (NON-NEED-BASED) *Total amount:* $7,045,480 (10% federal, 25% state, 50% institutional, 15% external sources). *Receiving aid:* Freshmen: 65% (287). Undergraduates: 70% (1,173). *Average award:* Freshmen: $2386. Undergraduates: $3274. *Scholarships, grants, and awards by category:* Academic interests/achievement: 438 awards ($3,226,513 total): English, general academic interests/achievements. Creative arts/performance: 41 awards ($68,695 total): debating, music, theater/drama. Special achievements/activities: 31 awards ($19,125 total): cheerleading/drum major, leadership. Special characteristics: 346 awards ($877,434 total): children and siblings of alumni, children of faculty/staff, relatives of clergy, religious affiliation. *Tuition waivers:* Full or partial for senior citizens.

LOANS *Student loans:* $10,754,495 (38% need-based, 62% non-need-based). 81% of past graduating class borrowed through all loan programs. *Average indebtedness per student:* $38,820. *Average need-based loan:* Freshmen: $3127. Undergraduates: $4001. *Parent loans:* $2,973,094 (100% non-need-based). *Programs:* FFEL (Subsidized and Unsubsidized Stafford, PLUS), Perkins.

WORK-STUDY *Federal work-study:* Total amount: $220,273; 495 jobs averaging $445. *State or other work-study/employment:* Total amount: $104,785 (100% non-need-based). 66 part-time jobs averaging $1588.

APPLYING FOR FINANCIAL AID *Required financial aid forms:* FAFSA, state aid form. *Financial aid deadline (priority):* 8/1. *Notification date:* Continuous beginning 3/6. Students must reply within 2 weeks of notification. **CONTACT** Bonnie Adamson, Financial Aid Office, Methodist University, 5400 Ramsey Street, Fayetteville, NC 28311-1420, 910-630-7307 or toll-free 800-488-7110 Ext. 7027. *Fax:* 910-630-7285. *E-mail:* adamson@methodist.edu.

METROPOLITAN COLLEGE OF NEW YORK
New York, NY

CONTACT Rosibel Gomez, Financial Aid Director, Metropolitan College of New York, 75 Varick Street, New York, NY 10013-1919, 212-343-1234 Ext. 5004 or toll-free 800-33-THINK Ext. 5001 (in-state). *Fax:* 212-343-7399.

METROPOLITAN STATE COLLEGE OF DENVER
Denver, CO

Tuition & fees (CO res): $3639	Average undergraduate aid package: $7052

ABOUT THE INSTITUTION State-supported, coed. 48 undergraduate majors. Federal methodology is used as a basis for awarding need-based institutional aid.

UNDERGRADUATE EXPENSES for 2009–10 *Tuition, state resident:* full-time $2850; part-time $118.75 per credit hour. *Tuition, nonresident:* full-time $12,343; part-time $514.30 per credit hour. *Required fees:* full-time $789; $320.10 per term. Full-time tuition and fees vary according to course load and location. Part-time tuition and fees vary according to course load and location. *Payment plans:* Installment, deferred payment.

FRESHMAN FINANCIAL AID (Fall 2008) 1,466 applied for aid; of those 67% were deemed to have need. 91% of freshmen with need received aid; of those 4% had need fully met. *Average percent of need met:* 56% (excluding resources

awarded to replace EFC). *Average financial aid package:* $6018 (excluding resources awarded to replace EFC). 16% of all full-time freshmen had no need and received non-need-based gift aid.

UNDERGRADUATE FINANCIAL AID (Fall 2008) 8,242 applied for aid; of those 78% were deemed to have need. 94% of undergraduates with need received aid; of those 3% had need fully met. *Average percent of need met:* 55% (excluding resources awarded to replace EFC). *Average financial aid package:* $7052 (excluding resources awarded to replace EFC). 17% of all full-time undergraduates had no need and received non-need-based gift aid.

GIFT AID (NEED-BASED) *Total amount:* $28,848,910 (65% federal, 26% state, 6% institutional, 3% external sources). *Receiving aid:* Freshmen: 41% (850); all full-time undergraduates: 44% (5,563). *Average award:* Freshmen: $4256; Undergraduates: $3890. *Scholarships, grants, and awards:* Federal Pell, FSEOG, state, private, college/university gift aid from institutional funds.

GIFT AID (NON-NEED-BASED) *Total amount:* $2,475,008 (31% federal, 5% state, 46% institutional, 18% external sources). *Average award:* Freshmen: $2172. Undergraduates: $1710. *Scholarships, grants, and awards by category:* Academic interests/achievement: 357 awards ($705,630 total): general academic interests/achievements. Creative arts/performance: 48 awards ($32,000 total): music. Special achievements/activities: 25 awards ($16,500 total): leadership. Special characteristics: 33 awards ($39,000 total): first-generation college students, veterans. *Tuition waivers:* Full or partial for senior citizens.

LOANS *Student loans:* $71,034,421 (84% need-based, 16% non-need-based). 57% of past graduating class borrowed through all loan programs. *Average indebtedness per student:* $20,620. *Average need-based loan:* Freshmen: $3079. Undergraduates: $4148. *Parent loans:* $2,198,736 (51% need-based, 49% non-need-based). *Programs:* FFEL (Subsidized and Unsubsidized Stafford, PLUS), Perkins.

WORK-STUDY *Federal work-study:* Total amount: $739,599; 210 jobs averaging $3522. *State or other work-study/employment:* Total amount: $1,298,651 (100% need-based). 545 part-time jobs averaging $3353.

ATHLETIC AWARDS Total amount: $1,096,126 (48% need-based, 52% non-need-based).

APPLYING FOR FINANCIAL AID *Required financial aid form:* FAFSA. *Financial aid deadline:* Continuous. *Notification date:* Continuous beginning 3/15.

CONTACT Office of Financial Aid, Metropolitan State College of Denver, PO Box 173362, Denver, CO 80217-3362, 303-556-8593. *Fax:* 303-556-4927.

METROPOLITAN STATE UNIVERSITY
St. Paul, MN

Tuition & fees (MN res): $5627	Average undergraduate aid package: N/A

ABOUT THE INSTITUTION State-supported, coed. *Awards:* bachelor's and master's degrees (offers primarily part-time evening degree programs). 53 undergraduate majors. *Total enrollment:* 8,237. Undergraduates: 8,237. Federal methodology is used as a basis for awarding need-based institutional aid.

UNDERGRADUATE EXPENSES for 2009–10 *Application fee:* $20. *Tuition, state resident:* full-time $5314; part-time $177.15 per credit hour. *Tuition, nonresident:* full-time $10,860; part-time $362 per credit hour. *Required fees:* full-time $313; $10.43 per credit hour. Full-time tuition and fees vary according to program and reciprocity agreements. Part-time tuition and fees vary according to course load, program, and reciprocity agreements. *Payment plan:* Installment.

GIFT AID (NEED-BASED) *Scholarships, grants, and awards:* Federal Pell, FSEOG, state, private, college/university gift aid from institutional funds.

GIFT AID (NON-NEED-BASED) *Scholarships, grants, and awards by category:* Academic interests/achievement: education, general academic interests/achievements. *Tuition waivers:* Full or partial for employees or children of employees, senior citizens.

LOANS *Programs:* FFEL (Subsidized and Unsubsidized Stafford, PLUS), state.

APPLYING FOR FINANCIAL AID *Required financial aid forms:* FAFSA, federal income tax form(s). *Financial aid deadline (priority):* 6/1. *Notification date:* Continuous beginning 6/15. Students must reply within 2 weeks of notification.

CONTACT Dr. Lois Larson, Interim Director of Financial Aid, Metropolitan State University, Founder's Hall, Room 147A, 700 East 7th Street, St. Paul, MN 55106-5000, 651-793-1411. *E-mail:* finaid@metrostate.edu.

MIAMI INTERNATIONAL UNIVERSITY OF ART & DESIGN
Miami, FL

UNDERGRADUATE EXPENSES Tuition cost varies by program. Prospective students should contact the school for current tuition costs. Other charges include a starting kit for all first-quarter students. Kits vary in price, depending on the program of study.

CONTACT Financial Aid Office, Miami International University of Art & Design, 1737 Bayshore Drive, Miami, FL 33132, 800-225-9023 Ext. 125 or toll-free 800-225-9023. *Fax:* 305-374-7946.

MIAMI UNIVERSITY
Oxford, OH

Tuition & fees (OH res): $11,910   Average undergraduate aid package: $11,374

ABOUT THE INSTITUTION State-related, coed. 111 undergraduate majors. Federal methodology is used as a basis for awarding need-based institutional aid.

UNDERGRADUATE EXPENSES for 2009–10 *Tuition, state resident:* full-time $11,442. *Tuition, nonresident:* full-time $26,202. *Required fees:* full-time $468. Full-time tuition and fees vary according to location and program. Part-time tuition and fees vary according to location and program. *College room and board:* $9458; *Room only:* $4786. Room and board charges vary according to board plan and housing facility. *Payment plan:* Installment.

FRESHMAN FINANCIAL AID (Fall 2009, est.) 2,304 applied for aid; of those 65% were deemed to have need. 99% of freshmen with need received aid; of those 30% had need fully met. *Average percent of need met:* 73% (excluding resources awarded to replace EFC). *Average financial aid package:* $14,052 (excluding resources awarded to replace EFC). 12% of all full-time freshmen had no need and received non-need-based gift aid.

UNDERGRADUATE FINANCIAL AID (Fall 2009, est.) 8,383 applied for aid; of those 73% were deemed to have need. 98% of undergraduates with need received aid; of those 14% had need fully met. *Average percent of need met:* 59% (excluding resources awarded to replace EFC). *Average financial aid package:* $11,374 (excluding resources awarded to replace EFC). 16% of all full-time undergraduates had no need and received non-need-based gift aid.

GIFT AID (NEED-BASED) *Total amount:* $25,684,346 (49% federal, 5% state, 46% institutional). *Receiving aid:* Freshmen: 41% (1,298); all full-time undergraduates: 25% (3,549). *Average award:* Freshmen: $7001; Undergraduates: $6359. *Scholarships, grants, and awards:* Federal Pell, FSEOG, state, private, college/university gift aid from institutional funds.

GIFT AID (NON-NEED-BASED) *Total amount:* $23,828,978 (1% state, 83% institutional, 16% external sources). *Receiving aid:* Freshmen: 27% (856). Undergraduates: 23% (3,171). *Average award:* Freshmen: $4909. Undergraduates: $4559. *Scholarships, grants, and awards by category:* Academic interests/achievement: architecture, education, engineering/technologies, general academic interests/achievements. Creative arts/performance: art/fine arts, music, theater/drama. Special achievements/activities: general special achievements/activities, leadership. Special characteristics: children of faculty/staff, local/state students, members of minority groups, out-of-state students. *Tuition waivers:* Full or partial for employees or children of employees.

LOANS *Student loans:* $56,005,491 (37% need-based, 63% non-need-based). 53% of past graduating class borrowed through all loan programs. *Average indebtedness per student:* $26,582. *Average need-based loan:* Freshmen: $3999. Undergraduates: $4699. *Parent loans:* $31,280,222 (100% non-need-based). *Programs:* Federal Direct (Subsidized and Unsubsidized Stafford, PLUS), Perkins, Federal Nursing, college/university, bank education loans.

WORK-STUDY *Federal work-study:* Total amount: $2,160,256; 932 jobs averaging $2244.

ATHLETIC AWARDS Total amount: $7,617,713 (100% non-need-based).

APPLYING FOR FINANCIAL AID *Required financial aid form:* FAFSA. *Financial aid deadline (priority):* 2/15. *Notification date:* Continuous beginning 3/20. Students must reply by 5/1 or within 3 weeks of notification.

CONTACT Mr. Chuck Knepfle, Office of Student Financial Aid, Miami University, Campus Avenue Building, Oxford, OH 45056-3427, 513-529-8734. *Fax:* 513-529-8713. *E-mail:* financialaid@muohio.edu.

MIAMI UNIVERSITY HAMILTON
Hamilton, OH

CONTACT Ken Rower, Coordinator of Financial Aid, Miami University Hamilton, 1601 Peck Boulevard, Hamilton, OH 45011, 513-785-3123. *Fax:* 513-785-3148.

MICHIGAN JEWISH INSTITUTE
Oak Park, MI

CONTACT Financial Aid Office, Michigan Jewish Institute, 25401 Coolidge Highway, Oak Park, MI 48237, 248-414-6900.

MICHIGAN STATE UNIVERSITY
East Lansing, MI

Tuition & fees (MI res): $10,880   Average undergraduate aid package: $10,620

ABOUT THE INSTITUTION State-supported, coed. 170 undergraduate majors. Federal methodology is used as a basis for awarding need-based institutional aid.

UNDERGRADUATE EXPENSES for 2009–10 *Tuition, state resident:* full-time $10,410; part-time $347 per credit hour. *Tuition, nonresident:* full-time $26,873; part-time $895.75 per credit hour. *Required fees:* full-time $470; $235 per term. Full-time tuition and fees vary according to course load, degree level, program, and student level. Part-time tuition and fees vary according to course load, degree level, program, and student level. *College room and board:* $7394; *Room only:* $3052. Room and board charges vary according to board plan and housing facility. *Payment plan:* Deferred payment.

FRESHMAN FINANCIAL AID (Fall 2009, est.) 5,427 applied for aid; of those 68% were deemed to have need. 99% of freshmen with need received aid; of those 24% had need fully met. *Average percent of need met:* 70% (excluding resources awarded to replace EFC). *Average financial aid package:* $11,357 (excluding resources awarded to replace EFC). 5% of all full-time freshmen had no need and received non-need-based gift aid.

UNDERGRADUATE FINANCIAL AID (Fall 2009, est.) 21,711 applied for aid; of those 75% were deemed to have need. 99% of undergraduates with need received aid; of those 19% had need fully met. *Average percent of need met:* 66% (excluding resources awarded to replace EFC). *Average financial aid package:* $10,620 (excluding resources awarded to replace EFC). 4% of all full-time undergraduates had no need and received non-need-based gift aid.

GIFT AID (NEED-BASED) *Total amount:* $83,203,924 (49% federal, 51% institutional). *Receiving aid:* Freshmen: 29% (2,106); all full-time undergraduates: 28% (9,263). *Average award:* Freshmen: $9119; Undergraduates: $8420. *Scholarships, grants, and awards:* Federal Pell, FSEOG, state, private, college/university gift aid from institutional funds, United Negro College Fund.

GIFT AID (NON-NEED-BASED) *Total amount:* $72,353,747 (2% federal, 45% state, 25% institutional, 28% external sources). *Receiving aid:* Freshmen: 33% (2,412). Undergraduates: 20% (6,842). *Average award:* Freshmen: $7044. Undergraduates: $7278. *Scholarships, grants, and awards by category:* Academic interests/achievement: agriculture, biological sciences, business, communication, computer science, education, engineering/technologies, English, foreign languages, general academic interests/achievements, health fields, international studies, mathematics, military science, physical sciences, social sciences. Creative arts/performance: creative writing, debating, journalism/publications, music, performing arts, theater/drama. Special achievements/activities: community service, hobbies/interests, junior miss, leadership, memberships, rodeo. Special characteristics: children and siblings of alumni, children of faculty/staff, children of union members/company employees, first-generation college students, handicapped students, international students, local/state students, out-of-state students, spouses of deceased or disabled public servants, veterans, veterans' children. *Tuition waivers:* Full or partial for employees or children of employees.

LOANS *Student loans:* $161,360,581 (40% need-based, 60% non-need-based). 44% of past graduating class borrowed through all loan programs. *Average indebtedness per student:* $19,696. *Average need-based loan:* Freshmen: $3464. Undergraduates: $4222. *Parent loans:* $65,263,351 (100% non-need-based). *Programs:* Federal Direct (Subsidized and Unsubsidized Stafford, PLUS), Perkins, college/university.

WORK-STUDY *Federal work-study:* Total amount: $2,495,831; 1,255 jobs averaging $1650. *State or other work-study/employment:* Part-time jobs available.

ATHLETIC AWARDS Total amount: $9,168,264 (44% need-based, 56% non-need-based).

APPLYING FOR FINANCIAL AID *Required financial aid form:* FAFSA. *Financial aid deadline:* Continuous. *Notification date:* Continuous beginning 3/15. Students must reply within 4 weeks of notification.

CONTACT Mr. Keith Williams, Associate Director, Michigan State University, 252 Student Services Building, East Lansing, MI 48824-1113, 517-353-5940. *Fax:* 517-432-1155. *E-mail:* willi398@msu.edu.

MICHIGAN TECHNOLOGICAL UNIVERSITY
Houghton, MI

Tuition & fees (MI res): $11,348   Average undergraduate aid package: $10,793

ABOUT THE INSTITUTION State-supported, coed. 88 undergraduate majors. Federal methodology is used as a basis for awarding need-based institutional aid.

UNDERGRADUATE EXPENSES for 2009–10 *Tuition, state resident:* full-time $10,500; part-time $350 per credit hour. *Tuition, nonresident:* full-time $22,770; part-time $759 per credit hour. *Required fees:* full-time $848; $423.75 per term. Full-time tuition and fees vary according to course load and program. Part-time tuition and fees vary according to course load and program. *College room and board:* $8121; *Room only:* $4401. Room and board charges vary according to board plan and housing facility. *Payment plans:* Installment, deferred payment.

FRESHMAN FINANCIAL AID (Fall 2009, est.) 1,038 applied for aid; of those 76% were deemed to have need. 100% of freshmen with need received aid; of those 13% had need fully met. *Average percent of need met:* 74% (excluding resources awarded to replace EFC). *Average financial aid package:* $11,961 (excluding resources awarded to replace EFC). 27% of all full-time freshmen had no need and received non-need-based gift aid.

UNDERGRADUATE FINANCIAL AID (Fall 2009, est.) 4,308 applied for aid; of those 82% were deemed to have need. 100% of undergraduates with need received aid; of those 14% had need fully met. *Average percent of need met:* 70% (excluding resources awarded to replace EFC). *Average financial aid package:* $10,793 (excluding resources awarded to replace EFC). 23% of all full-time undergraduates had no need and received non-need-based gift aid.

GIFT AID (NEED-BASED) *Total amount:* $25,937,505 (35% federal, 8% state, 52% institutional, 5% external sources). *Receiving aid:* Freshmen: 56% (649); all full-time undergraduates: 49% (2,721). *Average award:* Freshmen: $6037; Undergraduates: $5167. *Scholarships, grants, and awards:* Federal Pell, FSEOG, state, private, college/university gift aid from institutional funds.

GIFT AID (NON-NEED-BASED) *Total amount:* $5,332,894 (1% state, 93% institutional, 6% external sources). *Receiving aid:* Freshmen: 59% (681). Undergraduates: 46% (2,549). *Average award:* Freshmen: $4524. Undergraduates: $4162. *Scholarships, grants, and awards by category:* Academic interests/achievement: general academic interests/achievements. Special achievements/activities: leadership. Special characteristics: children and siblings of alumni, local/state students. *Tuition waivers:* Full or partial for children of alumni, employees or children of employees, senior citizens.

LOANS *Student loans:* $40,117,504 (83% need-based, 17% non-need-based). 68% of past graduating class borrowed through all loan programs. *Average indebtedness per student:* $26,764. *Average need-based loan:* Freshmen: $3366. Undergraduates: $4386. *Parent loans:* $5,822,600 (79% need-based, 21% non-need-based). *Programs:* Federal Direct (Subsidized and Unsubsidized Stafford, PLUS), Perkins, state, college/university.

WORK-STUDY *Federal work-study:* Total amount: $201,185; jobs available. *State or other work-study/employment:* Total amount: $3,058,587 (100% non-need-based). Part-time jobs available.

ATHLETIC AWARDS Total amount: $2,194,818 (41% need-based, 59% non-need-based).

APPLYING FOR FINANCIAL AID *Required financial aid form:* FAFSA. *Financial aid deadline (priority):* 3/1. *Notification date:* Continuous beginning 3/15.

CONTACT Mr. Bill Roberts, Director of Financial Aid, Michigan Technological University, 1400 Townsend Drive, Houghton, MI 49931-1295, 906-487-1742 or toll-free 888-MTU-1885. *Fax:* 906-487-3042. *E-mail:* wrrobert@mtu.edu.

MID-AMERICA CHRISTIAN UNIVERSITY
Oklahoma City, OK

CONTACT Mr. Todd Martin, Director of Financial Aid, Mid-America Christian University, 3500 Southwest 119th Street, Oklahoma City, OK 73170-4504, 405-691-3800. *Fax:* 405-692-3165. *E-mail:* tmartin@mabc.edu.

MIDAMERICA NAZARENE UNIVERSITY
Olathe, KS

ABOUT THE INSTITUTION Independent religious, coed. 45 undergraduate majors.

GIFT AID (NEED-BASED) *Scholarships, grants, and awards:* Federal Pell, FSEOG, state, private, college/university gift aid from institutional funds.

LOANS *Programs:* Federal Direct (Subsidized and Unsubsidized Stafford, PLUS), Perkins, college/university.

WORK-STUDY *Federal work-study:* Total amount: $12,000; jobs available.

APPLYING FOR FINANCIAL AID *Required financial aid form:* FAFSA.

CONTACT Rhonda L. Cole, Director of Student Financial Services, MidAmerica Nazarene University, 2030 East College Way, Olathe, KS 66062-1899, 913-791-3298 or toll-free 800-800-8887. *Fax:* 913-791-3482. *E-mail:* rcole@mnu.edu.

MID-ATLANTIC CHRISTIAN UNIVERSITY
Elizabeth City, NC

Tuition & fees: $10,320   Average undergraduate aid package: $14,067

ABOUT THE INSTITUTION Independent Christian, coed. 7 undergraduate majors. Federal methodology is used as a basis for awarding need-based institutional aid.

UNDERGRADUATE EXPENSES for 2009–10 *Comprehensive fee:* $17,110 includes full-time tuition ($9920), mandatory fees ($400), and room and board ($6790). *College room only:* $3590. Room and board charges vary according to housing facility. *Part-time tuition:* $310 per credit hour. *Part-time fees:* $21 per credit hour. *Payment plan:* Deferred payment.

FRESHMAN FINANCIAL AID (Fall 2008) 37 applied for aid; of those 100% were deemed to have need. 100% of freshmen with need received aid; of those 30% had need fully met. *Average percent of need met:* 78% (excluding resources awarded to replace EFC). *Average financial aid package:* $11,010 (excluding resources awarded to replace EFC).

UNDERGRADUATE FINANCIAL AID (Fall 2008) 141 applied for aid; of those 93% were deemed to have need. 100% of undergraduates with need received aid; of those 34% had need fully met. *Average percent of need met:* 81% (excluding resources awarded to replace EFC). *Average financial aid package:* $14,067 (excluding resources awarded to replace EFC). 6% of all full-time undergraduates had no need and received non-need-based gift aid.

GIFT AID (NEED-BASED) *Total amount:* $621,937 (45% federal, 2% state, 53% institutional). *Receiving aid:* Freshmen: 92% (34); all full-time undergraduates: 83% (118). *Average award:* Freshmen: $2366; Undergraduates: $3395. *Scholarships, grants, and awards:* Federal Pell, FSEOG, state, private, college/university gift aid from institutional funds.

GIFT AID (NON-NEED-BASED) *Total amount:* $47,671 (79% institutional, 21% external sources). *Receiving aid:* Freshmen: 14% (5). Undergraduates: 8% (11). *Average award:* Undergraduates: $2320. *Scholarships, grants, and awards by category:* Academic interests/achievement: 20 awards ($68,626 total): general academic interests/achievements, religion/biblical studies. Special achievements/activities: 11 awards ($12,121 total): general special achievements/activities, religious involvement. Special characteristics: 83 awards ($113,699 total): children and siblings of alumni, children of faculty/staff, general special characteristics, handicapped students, international students, married students, spouses of current students. *Tuition waivers:* Full or partial for children of alumni, employees or children of employees, senior citizens.

LOANS *Student loans:* $1,303,248 (77% need-based, 23% non-need-based). 81% of past graduating class borrowed through all loan programs. *Average indebtedness per student:* $26,953. *Average need-based loan:* Freshmen: $2623. Undergraduates: $3645. *Parent loans:* $45,830 (14% need-based, 86% non-need-based). *Programs:* Federal Direct (Subsidized and Unsubsidized Stafford, PLUS), alternative private loans.

WORK-STUDY *Federal work-study:* Total amount: $11,659; 12 jobs averaging $972.

Mid-Atlantic Christian University

APPLYING FOR FINANCIAL AID *Required financial aid forms:* FAFSA, institution's own form. *Financial aid deadline (priority):* 2/1. *Notification date:* Continuous beginning 4/1. Students must reply by 5/1 or within 2 weeks of notification.

CONTACT Lisa W. Pipkin, Financial Aid Administrator, Mid-Atlantic Christian University, 715 North Poindexter Street, Elizabeth City, NC 27909; 252-334-2020 or toll-free 800-RBC-8980. *Fax:* 252-334-2064. *E-mail:* lisa.pipkin@macuniversity.edu.

MID-CONTINENT UNIVERSITY
Mayfield, KY

Tuition & fees: $13,700	Average undergraduate aid package: $8244

ABOUT THE INSTITUTION Independent Southern Baptist, coed. 14 undergraduate majors. Federal methodology is used as a basis for awarding need-based institutional aid.

UNDERGRADUATE EXPENSES for 2009–10 *Comprehensive fee:* $20,200 includes full-time tuition ($12,450), mandatory fees ($1250), and room and board ($6500). Full-time tuition and fees vary according to course load and program. Room and board charges vary according to board plan and housing facility. *Part-time tuition:* $415 per credit hour. Part-time tuition and fees vary according to course load and program. *Payment plans:* Installment, deferred payment.

FRESHMAN FINANCIAL AID (Fall 2009, est.) 258 applied for aid; of those 98% were deemed to have need. 99% of freshmen with need received aid; of those 3% had need fully met. *Average percent of need met:* 35% (excluding resources awarded to replace EFC). *Average financial aid package:* $7718 (excluding resources awarded to replace EFC). 4% of all full-time freshmen had no need and received non-need-based gift aid.

UNDERGRADUATE FINANCIAL AID (Fall 2009, est.) 1,862 applied for aid; of those 98% were deemed to have need. 100% of undergraduates with need received aid; of those 3% had need fully met. *Average percent of need met:* 35% (excluding resources awarded to replace EFC). *Average financial aid package:* $8244 (excluding resources awarded to replace EFC). 2% of all full-time undergraduates had no need and received non-need-based gift aid.

GIFT AID (NEED-BASED) *Total amount:* $5,894,561 (40% federal, 44% state, 12% institutional, 4% external sources). *Receiving aid:* Freshmen: 89% (238); all full-time undergraduates: 84% (1,617). *Average award:* Freshmen: $6119; Undergraduates: $6021. *Scholarships, grants, and awards:* Federal Pell, FSEOG, state, private, college/university gift aid from institutional funds.

GIFT AID (NON-NEED-BASED) *Total amount:* $144,828 (100% state). *Receiving aid:* Freshmen: 3% (7). Undergraduates: 2% (34). *Average award:* Freshmen: $10,058. Undergraduates: $8359. *Scholarships, grants, and awards by category: Academic interests/achievement:* 28 awards ($33,672 total): education, English, general academic interests/achievements, humanities, religion/biblical studies, social sciences. *Special achievements/activities:* 8 awards ($16,682 total): cheerleading/drum major. *Special characteristics:* 8 awards ($3500 total): children and siblings of alumni, children of faculty/staff, children of union members/company employees, married students, relatives of clergy. *Tuition waivers:* Full or partial for employees or children of employees.

LOANS *Student loans:* $7,602,929 (77% need-based, 23% non-need-based). 78% of past graduating class borrowed through all loan programs. *Average indebtedness per student:* $10,782. *Average need-based loan:* Freshmen: $2537. Undergraduates: $3587. *Parent loans:* $104,936 (35% need-based, 65% non-need-based). *Programs:* Federal Direct (Subsidized and Unsubsidized Stafford, PLUS), FFEL (Subsidized and Unsubsidized Stafford, PLUS).

WORK-STUDY *Federal work-study:* Total amount: $173,303; 72 jobs averaging $2126. *State or other work-study/employment:* Total amount: $29,023 (100% need-based). Part-time jobs available.

ATHLETIC AWARDS Total amount: $792,916 (97% need-based, 3% non-need-based).

APPLYING FOR FINANCIAL AID *Required financial aid form:* FAFSA. *Financial aid deadline (priority):* 3/15. *Notification date:* Continuous beginning 8/18. Students must reply within 2 weeks of notification.

CONTACT Kent Youngblood, Director of Financial Aid, Mid-Continent University, 99 Powell Road East, Mayfield, KY 42066, 270-251-9400 Ext. 260. *Fax:* 270-251-9475. *E-mail:* kyoungblood@midcontinent.edu.

MIDDLEBURY COLLEGE
Middlebury, VT

Comprehensive fee: $50,780	Average undergraduate aid package: $33,345

ABOUT THE INSTITUTION Independent, coed. 44 undergraduate majors. Institutional methodology is used as a basis for awarding need-based institutional aid.

UNDERGRADUATE EXPENSES for 2009–10 *Comprehensive fee:* $50,780.

FRESHMAN FINANCIAL AID (Fall 2009, est.) 336 applied for aid; of those 74% were deemed to have need. 100% of freshmen with need received aid; of those 100% had need fully met. *Average percent of need met:* 100% (excluding resources awarded to replace EFC). *Average financial aid package:* $35,197 (excluding resources awarded to replace EFC).

UNDERGRADUATE FINANCIAL AID (Fall 2009, est.) 1,304 applied for aid; of those 92% were deemed to have need. 100% of undergraduates with need received aid; of those 100% had need fully met. *Average percent of need met:* 100% (excluding resources awarded to replace EFC). *Average financial aid package:* $33,345 (excluding resources awarded to replace EFC).

GIFT AID (NEED-BASED) *Total amount:* $35,949,671 (4% federal, 1% state, 93% institutional, 2% external sources). *Receiving aid:* Freshmen: 43% (249); all full-time undergraduates: 49% (1,194). *Average award:* Freshmen: $34,362; Undergraduates: $29,918. *Scholarships, grants, and awards:* Federal Pell, FSEOG, state, private, college/university gift aid from institutional funds.

LOANS *Student loans:* $5,248,404 (65% need-based, 35% non-need-based). 44% of past graduating class borrowed through all loan programs. *Average indebtedness per student:* $21,458. *Average need-based loan:* Freshmen: $2782. Undergraduates: $3659. *Parent loans:* $3,202,652 (100% non-need-based). *Programs:* FFEL (Subsidized and Unsubsidized Stafford, PLUS), Perkins, college/university.

WORK-STUDY *Federal work-study:* Total amount: $839,074; jobs available. *State or other work-study/employment:* Total amount: $510,930 (100% need-based). Part-time jobs available.

APPLYING FOR FINANCIAL AID *Required financial aid forms:* FAFSA, CSS Financial Aid PROFILE, noncustodial (divorced/separated) parent's statement, federal income tax return. *Financial aid deadline:* 2/1 (priority: 11/15). *Notification date:* 4/1. Students must reply by 5/1.

CONTACT Marguerite Corbin, Financial Aid Assistant, Middlebury College, Meeker House, 2nd Floor, 46 Porter Field Road, Middlebury, VT 05753, 802-443-5158. *E-mail:* financialaid@middlebury.edu.

MIDDLE TENNESSEE STATE UNIVERSITY
Murfreesboro, TN

CONTACT David Hutton, Financial Aid Director, Middle Tennessee State University, 218 Cope Administration Building, Murfreesboro, TN 37132, 615-898-2830. *Fax:* 615-898-5167.

MIDLAND COLLEGE
Midland, TX

ABOUT THE INSTITUTION State and locally supported, coed. 57 undergraduate majors.

GIFT AID (NEED-BASED) *Scholarships, grants, and awards:* Federal Pell, FSEOG, state, private, college/university gift aid from institutional funds.

LOANS *Programs:* FFEL (Subsidized Stafford, PLUS).

WORK-STUDY *Federal work-study:* Total amount: $128,000; 75 jobs averaging $2700. *State or other work-study/employment:* Total amount: $45,000 (100% need-based). 5 part-time jobs averaging $2700.

APPLYING FOR FINANCIAL AID *Required financial aid form:* FAFSA.

CONTACT Latisha Williams, Director, Midland College, 3600 North Garfield, Midland, TX 79705, 432-685-4507. *Fax:* 432-685-6857. *E-mail:* lwilliams@midland.edu.

MIDLAND LUTHERAN COLLEGE
Fremont, NE

ABOUT THE INSTITUTION Independent Lutheran, coed. *Awards:* associate and bachelor's degrees. 57 undergraduate majors. *Total enrollment:* 827. Undergraduates: 827. Freshmen: 215.

GIFT AID (NEED-BASED) *Scholarships, grants, and awards:* Federal Pell, FSEOG, state, private, college/university gift aid from institutional funds.

GIFT AID (NON-NEED-BASED) *Scholarships, grants, and awards by category: Academic interests/achievement:* biological sciences, business, communication, education, English, general academic interests/achievements, health fields, humanities, physical sciences, religion/biblical studies, social sciences. *Creative arts/performance:* art/fine arts, debating, journalism/publications, music, theater/drama. *Special achievements/activities:* community service, general special achievements/activities, leadership, religious involvement. *Special characteristics:* children and siblings of alumni, children of current students, children of faculty/staff, handicapped students, international students, members of minority groups, parents of current students, previous college experience, religious affiliation, siblings of current students, spouses of current students.

LOANS *Programs:* FFEL (Subsidized and Unsubsidized Stafford, PLUS), Perkins.

WORK-STUDY *Federal work-study:* Total amount: $100,000; 169 jobs averaging $1350. *State or other work-study/employment:* Total amount: $100,000 (50% need-based, 50% non-need-based). 121 part-time jobs averaging $1425.

APPLYING FOR FINANCIAL AID *Required financial aid form:* FAFSA.

CONTACT Penny James, Director of Financial Aid, Midland Lutheran College, 900 North Clarkson Street, Fremont, NE 68025-4200, 402-721-5480 Ext. 6520 or toll-free 800-642-8382 Ext. 6501. *Fax:* 402-721-0250. *E-mail:* finaid@mlc.edu.

MIDSTATE COLLEGE
Peoria, IL

CONTACT Janet Ozuna, Director of Financial Aid/Business Manager, Midstate College, 411 West Northmoor Road, Peoria, IL 61614, 309-692-4092. *Fax:* 309-692-3893.

MIDWAY COLLEGE
Midway, KY

ABOUT THE INSTITUTION Independent religious, coed, primarily women. 26 undergraduate majors.

GIFT AID (NEED-BASED) *Scholarships, grants, and awards:* Federal Pell, FSEOG, state, private, college/university gift aid from institutional funds.

GIFT AID (NON-NEED-BASED) *Scholarships, grants, and awards by category: Academic interests/achievement:* agriculture, business, general academic interests/achievements, health fields, premedicine. *Special achievements/activities:* general special achievements/activities, junior miss, leadership, religious involvement. *Special characteristics:* adult students, children and siblings of alumni, children of faculty/staff, members of minority groups, previous college experience, relatives of clergy, religious affiliation, veterans.

LOANS *Programs:* Federal Direct (Subsidized and Unsubsidized Stafford, PLUS), FFEL (Subsidized and Unsubsidized Stafford, PLUS), Perkins.

APPLYING FOR FINANCIAL AID *Required financial aid forms:* FAFSA, institution's own form.

CONTACT Katie Conrad, Director of Financial Aid, Midway College, 512 East Stephens Street, Midway, KY 40347-1120, 859-846-5410 or toll-free 800-755-0031. *Fax:* 859-846-5751. *E-mail:* kconrad@midway.edu.

MIDWESTERN STATE UNIVERSITY
Wichita Falls, TX

Tuition & fees (TX res): $6226	Average undergraduate aid package: $845

ABOUT THE INSTITUTION State-supported, coed. 79 undergraduate majors. Federal methodology is used as a basis for awarding need-based institutional aid.

UNDERGRADUATE EXPENSES for 2009–10 *Tuition, state resident:* full-time $1500; part-time $50 per credit hour. *Tuition, nonresident:* full-time $2400; part-time $80 per credit hour. *Required fees:* full-time $4726; $145.60 per credit hour or $179 per term. Full-time tuition and fees vary according to course load, location, and program. Part-time tuition and fees vary according to course load, location, and program. *College room and board:* $5560; *Room only:* $2990. Room and board charges vary according to board plan and housing facility. *Payment plan:* Installment.

FRESHMAN FINANCIAL AID (Fall 2009, est.) 563 applied for aid; of those 67% were deemed to have need. 99% of freshmen with need received aid; of those 29% had need fully met. *Average percent of need met:* 79% (excluding resources awarded to replace EFC). *Average financial aid package:* $9140 (excluding resources awarded to replace EFC). 17% of all full-time freshmen had no need and received non-need-based gift aid.

UNDERGRADUATE FINANCIAL AID (Fall 2009, est.) 2,433 applied for aid; of those 88% were deemed to have need. 99% of undergraduates with need received aid; of those 18% had need fully met. *Average percent of need met:* 70% (excluding resources awarded to replace EFC). *Average financial aid package:* $845 (excluding resources awarded to replace EFC). 18% of all full-time undergraduates had no need and received non-need-based gift aid.

GIFT AID (NEED-BASED) *Total amount:* $11,715,409 (63% federal, 25% state, 10% institutional, 2% external sources). *Receiving aid:* Freshmen: 49% (342); all full-time undergraduates: 42% (1,758). *Average award:* Freshmen: $7534; Undergraduates: $5886. *Scholarships, grants, and awards:* Federal Pell, FSEOG, state, private, college/university gift aid from institutional funds, state nursing scholarships.

GIFT AID (NON-NEED-BASED) *Total amount:* $1,361,279 (1% federal, 1% state, 79% institutional, 19% external sources). *Receiving aid:* Freshmen: 17% (122). Undergraduates: 15% (610). *Average award:* Freshmen: $2339. Undergraduates: $2096. *Scholarships, grants, and awards by category: Academic interests/achievement:* 895 awards ($1,155,073 total): biological sciences, business, communication, computer science, education, engineering/technologies, English, foreign languages, general academic interests/achievements, health fields, humanities, international studies, mathematics, physical sciences, premedicine, social sciences. *Creative arts/performance:* 189 awards ($109,850 total): art/fine arts, creative writing, general creative arts/performance, journalism/publications, music, theater/drama. *Special achievements/activities:* 165 awards ($192,750 total): cheerleading/drum major, general special achievements/activities, leadership. *Special characteristics:* 130 awards ($12,888 total): children and siblings of alumni, children of faculty/staff, children of union members/company employees, children of workers in trades, children with a deceased or disabled parent, first-generation college students, handicapped students, international students, members of minority groups, veterans, veterans' children. *Tuition waivers:* Full or partial for employees or children of employees, senior citizens.

LOANS *Student loans:* $21,673,164 (73% need-based, 27% non-need-based). 52% of past graduating class borrowed through all loan programs. *Average indebtedness per student:* $19,049. *Average need-based loan:* Freshmen: $4978. Undergraduates: $7136. *Parent loans:* $2,509,181 (34% need-based, 66% non-need-based). *Programs:* Federal Direct (Subsidized and Unsubsidized Stafford, PLUS), Perkins, state, college/university, alternative private loans.

WORK-STUDY *Federal work-study:* Total amount: $167,751; 54 jobs averaging $4059. *State or other work-study/employment:* Total amount: $34,331 (100% need-based). Part-time jobs available.

ATHLETIC AWARDS Total amount: $999,303 (36% need-based, 64% non-need-based).

APPLYING FOR FINANCIAL AID *Required financial aid forms:* FAFSA, institution's own form. *Financial aid deadline (priority):* 3/1. *Notification date:* Continuous beginning 4/15. Students must reply within 4 weeks of notification.

CONTACT Ms. Kathy Pennartz, Director of Financial Aid, Midwestern State University, 3410 Taft Boulevard, Wichita Falls, TX 76308-2099, 940-397-4214 or toll-free 800-842-1922. *Fax:* 940-397-4852. *E-mail:* financial-aid@mwsu.edu.

MIDWEST UNIVERSITY
Wentzville, MO

CONTACT Financial Aid Office, Midwest University, PO Box 365, 851 Parr Road, Wentzville, MO 63385, 636-327-4645.

MIDWIVES COLLEGE OF UTAH
Salt Lake City, UT

CONTACT Financial Aid Office, Midwives College of Utah, 1174 East 2700 South, Suite 2, Salt Lake City, UT 84106, 801-764-9068 or toll-free 866-764-9068.

MILES COLLEGE
Fairfield, AL

CONTACT P. N. Lanier, Financial Aid Administrator, Miles College, PO Box 3800, Birmingham, AL 35208, 205-929-1663 or toll-free 800-445-0708. *Fax:* 205-929-1668. *E-mail:* pnlani@netscape.net.

MILLERSVILLE UNIVERSITY OF PENNSYLVANIA
Millersville, PA

Tuition & fees (PA res): $7147   **Average undergraduate aid package: $8124**

ABOUT THE INSTITUTION State-supported, coed. 53 undergraduate majors. Federal methodology is used as a basis for awarding need-based institutional aid.

UNDERGRADUATE EXPENSES for 2009–10 *Tuition, state resident:* full-time $5554; part-time $231 per credit. *Tuition, nonresident:* full-time $13,886; part-time $579 per credit. *Required fees:* full-time $1593; $57.75 per credit or $60 per credit. Full-time tuition and fees vary according to degree level. Part-time tuition and fees vary according to course load and degree level. *College room and board:* $7766; *Room only:* $4608. Room and board charges vary according to board plan and housing facility. *Payment plan:* Installment.

FRESHMAN FINANCIAL AID (Fall 2009, est.) 1,188 applied for aid; of those 66% were deemed to have need. 97% of freshmen with need received aid; of those 15% had need fully met. *Average percent of need met:* 79% (excluding resources awarded to replace EFC). *Average financial aid package:* $8390 (excluding resources awarded to replace EFC). 3% of all full-time freshmen had no need and received non-need-based gift aid.

UNDERGRADUATE FINANCIAL AID (Fall 2009, est.) 5,298 applied for aid; of those 74% were deemed to have need. 97% of undergraduates with need received aid; of those 12% had need fully met. *Average percent of need met:* 77% (excluding resources awarded to replace EFC). *Average financial aid package:* $8124 (excluding resources awarded to replace EFC). 2% of all full-time undergraduates had no need and received non-need-based gift aid.

GIFT AID (NEED-BASED) *Total amount:* $15,019,175 (53% federal, 39% state, 5% institutional, 3% external sources). *Receiving aid:* Freshmen: 44% (581); all full-time undergraduates: 40% (2,659). *Average award:* Freshmen: $6004; Undergraduates: $5447. *Scholarships, grants, and awards:* Federal Pell, FSEOG, state, private, college/university gift aid from institutional funds, Schock Scholarships.

GIFT AID (NON-NEED-BASED) *Total amount:* $2,269,092 (3% federal, 9% state, 41% institutional, 47% external sources). *Receiving aid:* Freshmen: 12% (154). Undergraduates: 7% (452). *Average award:* Freshmen: $3341. Undergraduates: $3002. *Scholarships, grants, and awards by category:* Academic interests/achievement: 418 awards ($1,205,805 total): biological sciences, business, communication, computer science, education, English, foreign languages, general academic interests/achievements, health fields, humanities, mathematics, physical sciences, social sciences. Creative arts/performance: 19 awards ($18,659 total): art/fine arts, music. Special achievements/activities: 7 awards ($1100 total): community service. Special characteristics: 153 awards ($624,375 total): children of union members/company employees, international students. *Tuition waivers:* Full or partial for employees or children of employees, senior citizens.

LOANS *Student loans:* $33,466,042 (44% need-based, 56% non-need-based). 72% of past graduating class borrowed through all loan programs. *Average indebtedness per student:* $22,479. *Average need-based loan:* Freshmen: $3240. Undergraduates: $4099. *Parent loans:* $4,493,151 (100% non-need-based). *Programs:* FFEL (Subsidized and Unsubsidized Stafford, PLUS), Perkins.

WORK-STUDY *Federal work-study:* Total amount: $552,819; 270 jobs averaging $1602. *State or other work-study/employment:* Total amount: $1,651,647 (100% non-need-based). 1,559 part-time jobs averaging $1175.

ATHLETIC AWARDS Total amount: $382,896 (34% need-based, 66% non-need-based).

APPLYING FOR FINANCIAL AID *Required financial aid form:* FAFSA. *Financial aid deadline (priority):* 3/15. *Notification date:* Continuous beginning 3/15. Students must reply within 2 weeks of notification.

CONTACT Mr. Dwight G. Horsey, Director of Financial Aid, Millersville University of Pennsylvania, PO Box 1002, Millersville, PA 17551-0302, 717-872-3026 or toll-free 800-MU-ADMIT (out-of-state). *Fax:* 717-871-2248. *E-mail:* dwight.horsey@millersville.edu.

MILLIGAN COLLEGE
Milligan College, TN

Tuition & fees: $23,460   **Average undergraduate aid package: $16,483**

ABOUT THE INSTITUTION Independent Christian, coed. 27 undergraduate majors. Federal methodology is used as a basis for awarding need-based institutional aid.

UNDERGRADUATE EXPENSES for 2010–11 *One-time required fee:* $75. *Comprehensive fee:* $29,110 includes full-time tuition ($22,600), mandatory fees ($860), and room and board ($5650). *College room only:* $2650. Full-time tuition and fees vary according to course load. Room and board charges vary according to housing facility. *Part-time tuition:* $360 per credit hour. Part-time tuition and fees vary according to course load. *Payment plan:* Installment.

FRESHMAN FINANCIAL AID (Fall 2009, est.) 192 applied for aid; of those 86% were deemed to have need. 100% of freshmen with need received aid; of those 29% had need fully met. *Average percent of need met:* 82% (excluding resources awarded to replace EFC). *Average financial aid package:* $18,213 (excluding resources awarded to replace EFC). 18% of all full-time freshmen had no need and received non-need-based gift aid.

UNDERGRADUATE FINANCIAL AID (Fall 2009, est.) 741 applied for aid; of those 86% were deemed to have need. 100% of undergraduates with need received aid; of those 29% had need fully met. *Average percent of need met:* 79% (excluding resources awarded to replace EFC). *Average financial aid package:* $16,483 (excluding resources awarded to replace EFC). 15% of all full-time undergraduates had no need and received non-need-based gift aid.

GIFT AID (NEED-BASED) *Total amount:* $6,756,785 (19% federal, 14% state, 53% institutional, 14% external sources). *Receiving aid:* Freshmen: 78% (165); all full-time undergraduates: 77% (619). *Average award:* Freshmen: $15,830; Undergraduates: $13,293. *Scholarships, grants, and awards:* Federal Pell, FSEOG, state, private, college/university gift aid from institutional funds.

GIFT AID (NON-NEED-BASED) *Total amount:* $2,052,035 (21% state, 59% institutional, 20% external sources). *Receiving aid:* Freshmen: 18% (37). Undergraduates: 17% (133). *Average award:* Freshmen: $7759. Undergraduates: $7283. *Scholarships, grants, and awards by category:* Academic interests/achievement: 578 awards ($3,991,183 total): general academic interests/achievements, religion/biblical studies. Creative arts/performance: 42 awards ($68,118 total): art/fine arts, music, theater/drama. Special achievements/activities: 80 awards ($214,200 total): cheerleading/drum major, community service. Special characteristics: 24 awards ($400,755 total): children of faculty/staff. *Tuition waivers:* Full or partial for employees or children of employees.

LOANS *Student loans:* $4,372,619 (69% need-based, 31% non-need-based). 90% of past graduating class borrowed through all loan programs. *Average indebtedness per student:* $19,803. *Average need-based loan:* Freshmen: $3333. Undergraduates: $4458. *Parent loans:* $635,155 (35% need-based, 65% non-need-based). *Programs:* Federal Direct (Subsidized and Unsubsidized Stafford, PLUS), FFEL (Subsidized and Unsubsidized Stafford, PLUS), Perkins, alternative loans.

WORK-STUDY *Federal work-study:* Total amount: $132,938; 161 jobs averaging $1595. *State or other work-study/employment:* Total amount: $241,103 (17% need-based, 83% non-need-based). 145 part-time jobs averaging $1651.

ATHLETIC AWARDS Total amount: $2,343,793 (57% need-based, 43% non-need-based).

APPLYING FOR FINANCIAL AID *Required financial aid form:* FAFSA. *Financial aid deadline (priority):* 3/1. *Notification date:* Continuous beginning 3/1. Students must reply within 2 weeks of notification.

CONTACT Diane Keasling, Coordinator of Financial Aid, Milligan College, PO Box 250, Milligan College, TN 37682, 423-461-8968 or toll-free 800-262-8337 (in-state). *Fax:* 423-929-2368. *E-mail:* dlkeasling@milligan.edu.

MILLIKIN UNIVERSITY
Decatur, IL

Tuition & fees: $26,345	Average undergraduate aid package: $19,958

ABOUT THE INSTITUTION Independent religious, coed. 50 undergraduate majors. Institutional methodology is used as a basis for awarding need-based institutional aid.

UNDERGRADUATE EXPENSES for 2009–10 *Comprehensive fee:* $34,211 includes full-time tuition ($25,750), mandatory fees ($595), and room and board ($7866). *College room only:* $4306. Room and board charges vary according to board plan and housing facility. *Part-time tuition:* $860 per credit hour. *Part-time fees:* $75 per term. *Payment plan:* Installment.

FRESHMAN FINANCIAL AID (Fall 2009, est.) 519 applied for aid; of those 88% were deemed to have need. 100% of freshmen with need received aid; of those 43% had need fully met. *Average percent of need met:* 92% (excluding resources awarded to replace EFC). *Average financial aid package:* $22,656 (excluding resources awarded to replace EFC). 11% of all full-time freshmen had no need and received non-need-based gift aid.

UNDERGRADUATE FINANCIAL AID (Fall 2009, est.) 1,933 applied for aid; of those 87% were deemed to have need. 100% of undergraduates with need received aid; of those 54% had need fully met. *Average percent of need met:* 92% (excluding resources awarded to replace EFC). *Average financial aid package:* $19,958 (excluding resources awarded to replace EFC). 10% of all full-time undergraduates had no need and received non-need-based gift aid.

GIFT AID (NEED-BASED) *Total amount:* $14,413,400 (24% federal, 28% state, 48% institutional). *Receiving aid:* Freshmen: 82% (446); all full-time undergraduates: 74% (1,576). *Average award:* Freshmen: $10,228; Undergraduates: $8811. *Scholarships, grants, and awards:* Federal Pell, FSEOG, state, private, college/university gift aid from institutional funds.

GIFT AID (NON-NEED-BASED) *Total amount:* $17,318,255 (97% institutional, 3% external sources). *Receiving aid:* Freshmen: 85% (458). Undergraduates: 72% (1,537). *Average award:* Freshmen: $10,273. Undergraduates: $9108. *Scholarships, grants, and awards by category: Academic interests/achievement:* 2,044 awards ($15,504,190 total): biological sciences, business, communication, education, English, foreign languages, general academic interests/achievements, health fields, humanities, international studies, mathematics, physical sciences, premedicine. *Creative arts/performance:* 594 awards ($1,131,274 total): art/fine arts, dance, music, theater/drama. *Special achievements/activities:* 8 awards ($16,000 total): community service. *Special characteristics:* 211 awards ($1,011,174 total): children and siblings of alumni, children of union members/company employees, children with a deceased or disabled parent, international students, parents of current students, relatives of clergy, twins. *Tuition waivers:* Full or partial for employees or children of employees.

LOANS *Student loans:* $14,479,455 (41% need-based, 59% non-need-based). 82% of past graduating class borrowed through all loan programs. *Average indebtedness per student:* $28,449. *Average need-based loan:* Freshmen: $3426. Undergraduates: $4204. *Parent loans:* $2,457,761 (100% non-need-based). *Programs:* FFEL (Subsidized and Unsubsidized Stafford, PLUS), Perkins, state.

WORK-STUDY *Federal work-study:* Total amount: $458,955; 509 jobs averaging $902. *State or other work-study/employment:* Total amount: $140,717 (100% non-need-based). 206 part-time jobs averaging $683.

APPLYING FOR FINANCIAL AID *Required financial aid form:* FAFSA. *Financial aid deadline (priority):* 3/15. *Notification date:* Continuous beginning 3/15. Students must reply by 5/1 or within 4 weeks of notification.

CONTACT Cheryl Howerton, Director of Financial Aid, Millikin University, 1184 West Main Street, Decatur, IL 62522-2084, 217-424-6317 or toll-free 800-373-7733. *Fax:* 217-424-5070. *E-mail:* studentservicecenter@millikin.edu.

MILLSAPS COLLEGE
Jackson, MS

Tuition & fees: $26,240	Average undergraduate aid package: $24,659

ABOUT THE INSTITUTION Independent United Methodist, coed. 33 undergraduate majors. Federal methodology is used as a basis for awarding need-based institutional aid.

UNDERGRADUATE EXPENSES for 2009–10 *Comprehensive fee:* $35,492 includes full-time tuition ($24,608), mandatory fees ($1632), and room and board ($9252). *College room only:* $5216. Full-time tuition and fees vary according to reciprocity agreements. Room and board charges vary according to housing facility. *Part-time tuition:* $764 per credit hour. *Part-time fees:* $32 per credit hour. Part-time tuition and fees vary according to course load. *Payment plans:* Installment, deferred payment.

FRESHMAN FINANCIAL AID (Fall 2009, est.) 245 applied for aid; of those 76% were deemed to have need. 100% of freshmen with need received aid; of those 48% had need fully met. *Average percent of need met:* 92% (excluding resources awarded to replace EFC). *Average financial aid package:* $27,574 (excluding resources awarded to replace EFC). 33% of all full-time freshmen had no need and received non-need-based gift aid.

UNDERGRADUATE FINANCIAL AID (Fall 2009, est.) 707 applied for aid; of those 82% were deemed to have need. 100% of undergraduates with need received aid; of those 39% had need fully met. *Average percent of need met:* 84% (excluding resources awarded to replace EFC). *Average financial aid package:* $24,659 (excluding resources awarded to replace EFC). 39% of all full-time undergraduates had no need and received non-need-based gift aid.

GIFT AID (NEED-BASED) *Total amount:* $10,812,403 (10% federal, 2% state, 86% institutional, 2% external sources). *Receiving aid:* Freshmen: 66% (185); all full-time undergraduates: 57% (570). *Average award:* Freshmen: $22,158; Undergraduates: $18,969. *Scholarships, grants, and awards:* Federal Pell, FSEOG, state, private, college/university gift aid from institutional funds.

GIFT AID (NON-NEED-BASED) *Total amount:* $7,393,567 (3% state, 94% institutional, 3% external sources). *Receiving aid:* Freshmen: 19% (53). Undergraduates: 14% (144). *Average award:* Freshmen: $17,910. Undergraduates: $15,127. *Scholarships, grants, and awards by category: Academic interests/achievement:* business, general academic interests/achievements. *Creative arts/performance:* art/fine arts, music, theater/drama. *Special achievements/activities:* community service, general special achievements/activities, hobbies/interests, leadership, religious involvement. *Special characteristics:* adult students, children of faculty/staff, ethnic background, first-generation college students, local/state students, relatives of clergy, religious affiliation. *Tuition waivers:* Full or partial for employees or children of employees.

LOANS *Student loans:* $4,143,721 (58% need-based, 42% non-need-based). 59% of past graduating class borrowed through all loan programs. *Average indebtedness per student:* $31,304. *Average need-based loan:* Freshmen: $3071. Undergraduates: $4359. *Parent loans:* $739,188 (10% need-based, 90% non-need-based). *Programs:* FFEL (Subsidized and Unsubsidized Stafford, PLUS), Perkins, college/university.

WORK-STUDY *Federal work-study:* Total amount: $495,591; jobs available.

APPLYING FOR FINANCIAL AID *Required financial aid form:* FAFSA. *Financial aid deadline (priority):* 3/1. *Notification date:* Continuous beginning 3/15. Students must reply by 5/1 or within 2 weeks of notification.

CONTACT Patrick James, Director of Financial Aid, Millsaps College, 1701 North State Street, Jackson, MS 39210-0001, 601-974-1220 or toll-free 800-352-1050. *Fax:* 601-974-1224. *E-mail:* patrick.james@millsaps.edu.

MILLS COLLEGE
Oakland, CA

Tuition & fees: $37,605	Average undergraduate aid package: $30,193

ABOUT THE INSTITUTION Independent, undergraduate: women only; graduate: coed. 37 undergraduate majors. Federal methodology is used as a basis for awarding need-based institutional aid.

UNDERGRADUATE EXPENSES for 2010–11 *Comprehensive fee:* $49,249 includes full-time tuition ($36,428), mandatory fees ($1177), and room and board ($11,644). Full-time tuition and fees vary according to course load. Room and board charges vary according to board plan and housing facility. *Part-time tuition:* $6072 per course. *Part-time fees:* $1177 per year. Part-time tuition and fees vary according to course load. *Payment plan:* Installment.

FRESHMAN FINANCIAL AID (Fall 2008) 183 applied for aid; of those 93% were deemed to have need. 100% of freshmen with need received aid; of those 42% had need fully met. *Average percent of need met:* 87% (excluding resources awarded to replace EFC). *Average financial aid package:* $34,128 (excluding resources awarded to replace EFC). 12% of all full-time freshmen had no need and received non-need-based gift aid.

UNDERGRADUATE FINANCIAL AID (Fall 2008) 831 applied for aid; of those 96% were deemed to have need. 100% of undergraduates with need received aid; of those 47% had need fully met. *Average percent of need met:* 85% (excluding resources awarded to replace EFC). *Average financial aid package:*

$30,193 (excluding resources awarded to replace EFC). 8% of all full-time undergraduates had no need and received non-need-based gift aid.

GIFT AID (NEED-BASED) *Total amount:* $17,990,127 (9% federal, 14% state, 74% institutional, 3% external sources). *Receiving aid:* Freshmen: 91% (171); all full-time undergraduates: 84% (800). *Average award:* Freshmen: $27,283; Undergraduates: $23,193. *Scholarships, grants, and awards:* Federal Pell, FSEOG, state, private, college/university gift aid from institutional funds.

GIFT AID (NON-NEED-BASED) *Total amount:* $954,382 (89% institutional, 11% external sources). *Receiving aid:* Freshmen: 76% (143). Undergraduates: 71% (680). *Average award:* Freshmen: $17,345. Undergraduates: $14,955. *Scholarships, grants, and awards by category: Academic interests/achievement:* biological sciences, computer science, general academic interests/achievements, mathematics, physical sciences, premedicine. *Creative arts/performance:* art/fine arts, music. *Special characteristics:* children of faculty/staff. *Tuition waivers:* Full or partial for employees or children of employees.

LOANS *Student loans:* $6,501,793 (98% need-based, 2% non-need-based). 96% of past graduating class borrowed through all loan programs. *Average indebtedness per student:* $24,255. *Average need-based loan:* Freshmen: $5125. Undergraduates: $6515. *Parent loans:* $1,192,501 (86% need-based, 14% non-need-based). *Programs:* FFEL (Subsidized and Unsubsidized Stafford, PLUS), Perkins, college/university.

WORK-STUDY *Federal work-study:* Total amount: $200,007; jobs available. *State or other work-study/employment:* Total amount: $548,103 (88% need-based, 12% non-need-based). Part-time jobs available.

APPLYING FOR FINANCIAL AID *Required financial aid forms:* FAFSA, institution's own form, Non-custodial Parent Statement. *Financial aid deadline (priority):* 2/15. *Notification date:* Continuous beginning 3/1. Students must reply by 5/1 or within 2 weeks of notification.

CONTACT Mr. David Gin, The M Center/Financial Aid, Mills College, 5000 MacArthur Boulevard, Oakland, CA 94613, 510-430-2000 or toll-free 800-87-MILLS. *Fax:* 510-430-2003. *E-mail:* mcenter-finaid@mills.edu.

MILWAUKEE INSTITUTE OF ART AND DESIGN
Milwaukee, WI

Tuition & fees: N/R	Average undergraduate aid package: $19,455

ABOUT THE INSTITUTION Independent, coed. 10 undergraduate majors. Federal methodology is used as a basis for awarding need-based institutional aid.

FRESHMAN FINANCIAL AID (Fall 2008) 156 applied for aid; of those 91% were deemed to have need. 100% of freshmen with need received aid; of those 11% had need fully met. *Average percent of need met:* 67% (excluding resources awarded to replace EFC). *Average financial aid package:* $18,355 (excluding resources awarded to replace EFC). 28% of all full-time freshmen had no need and received non-need-based gift aid.

UNDERGRADUATE FINANCIAL AID (Fall 2008) 566 applied for aid; of those 94% were deemed to have need. 100% of undergraduates with need received aid; of those 11% had need fully met. *Average percent of need met:* 68% (excluding resources awarded to replace EFC). *Average financial aid package:* $19,455 (excluding resources awarded to replace EFC). 13% of all full-time undergraduates had no need and received non-need-based gift aid.

GIFT AID (NEED-BASED) *Total amount:* $6,925,277 (11% federal, 9% state, 78% institutional, 2% external sources). *Receiving aid:* Freshmen: 70% (142); all full-time undergraduates: 86% (527). *Average award:* Freshmen: $13,502; Undergraduates: $12,888. *Scholarships, grants, and awards:* Federal Pell, FSEOG, state, private, college/university gift aid from institutional funds.

GIFT AID (NON-NEED-BASED) *Receiving aid:* Freshmen: 5% (10). Undergraduates: 4% (27). *Average award:* Freshmen: $9486. Undergraduates: $9611. *Scholarships, grants, and awards by category: Creative arts/performance:* art/fine arts. *Special characteristics:* children of faculty/staff, ethnic background, local/state students, members of minority groups. *Tuition waivers:* Full or partial for employees or children of employees.

LOANS *Student loans:* $5,556,760 (100% need-based). 76% of past graduating class borrowed through all loan programs. *Average indebtedness per student:* $24,162. *Average need-based loan:* Freshmen: $4310. Undergraduates: $6236. *Parent loans:* $855,557 (100% need-based). *Programs:* Federal Direct (Subsidized and Unsubsidized Stafford, PLUS), alternative loans.

WORK-STUDY *Federal work-study:* Total amount: $102,940; jobs available.

APPLYING FOR FINANCIAL AID *Required financial aid form:* FAFSA. *Financial aid deadline:* 2/15. *Notification date:* 4/1. Students must reply by 5/1 or within 4 weeks of notification.

CONTACT Mr. Lloyd Mueller, Director of Financial Aid, Milwaukee Institute of Art and Design, 273 East Erie Street, Milwaukee, WI 53202-6003, 414-291-3272 or toll-free 888-749-MIAD. *Fax:* 414-291-8077. *E-mail:* llmuelle@miad.edu.

MILWAUKEE SCHOOL OF ENGINEERING
Milwaukee, WI

Tuition & fees: $29,520	Average undergraduate aid package: $17,687

ABOUT THE INSTITUTION Independent, coed, primarily men. 18 undergraduate majors. Federal methodology is used as a basis for awarding need-based institutional aid.

UNDERGRADUATE EXPENSES for 2010–11 *Comprehensive fee:* $36,951 includes full-time tuition ($29,520) and room and board ($7431). *College room only:* $4737. Room and board charges vary according to board plan and housing facility. *Part-time tuition:* $513 per quarter hour. Part-time tuition and fees vary according to course load. *Payment plan:* Installment.

FRESHMAN FINANCIAL AID (Fall 2008) 581 applied for aid; of those 88% were deemed to have need. 99% of freshmen with need received aid; of those 14% had need fully met. *Average percent of need met:* 70% (excluding resources awarded to replace EFC). *Average financial aid package:* $17,868 (excluding resources awarded to replace EFC). 17% of all full-time freshmen had no need and received non-need-based gift aid.

UNDERGRADUATE FINANCIAL AID (Fall 2008) 1,998 applied for aid; of those 90% were deemed to have need. 100% of undergraduates with need received aid; of those 15% had need fully met. *Average percent of need met:* 67% (excluding resources awarded to replace EFC). *Average financial aid package:* $17,687 (excluding resources awarded to replace EFC). 17% of all full-time undergraduates had no need and received non-need-based gift aid.

GIFT AID (NEED-BASED) *Total amount:* $25,932,247 (8% federal, 7% state, 81% institutional, 4% external sources). *Receiving aid:* Freshmen: 81% (506); all full-time undergraduates: 82% (1,774). *Average award:* Freshmen: $15,572; Undergraduates: $14,730. *Scholarships, grants, and awards:* Federal Pell, FSEOG, state, private, college/university gift aid from institutional funds.

GIFT AID (NON-NEED-BASED) *Total amount:* $4,918,407 (90% institutional, 10% external sources). *Receiving aid:* Freshmen: 8% (51). Undergraduates: 8% (171). *Average award:* Freshmen: $9824. Undergraduates: $9724. *Scholarships, grants, and awards by category: Academic interests/achievement:* 1,998 awards ($19,318,383 total): business, communication, computer science, engineering/technologies, health fields. *Special characteristics:* 34 awards ($692,992 total): children of faculty/staff. *Tuition waivers:* Full or partial for employees or children of employees.

LOANS *Student loans:* $20,606,408 (64% need-based, 36% non-need-based). 94% of past graduating class borrowed through all loan programs. *Average indebtedness per student:* $35,722. *Average need-based loan:* Freshmen: $2473. Undergraduates: $3246. *Parent loans:* $4,386,138 (60% need-based, 40% non-need-based). *Programs:* FFEL (Subsidized and Unsubsidized Stafford, PLUS), Perkins, state, college/university.

WORK-STUDY *Federal work-study:* Total amount: $327,689; 341 jobs averaging $961.

APPLYING FOR FINANCIAL AID *Required financial aid form:* FAFSA. *Financial aid deadline (priority):* 3/15. *Notification date:* Continuous beginning 3/1. Students must reply within 2 weeks of notification.

CONTACT Steve Midthun, Director of Financial Aid, Milwaukee School of Engineering, 1025 North Broadway, Milwaukee, WI 53202-3109, 414-277-7223 or toll-free 800-332-6763. *Fax:* 414-277-6952. *E-mail:* finaid@msoe.edu.

MINNEAPOLIS COLLEGE OF ART AND DESIGN
Minneapolis, MN

Tuition & fees: $29,700	Average undergraduate aid package: $16,229

ABOUT THE INSTITUTION Independent, coed. 11 undergraduate majors. Federal methodology is used as a basis for awarding need-based institutional aid.

UNDERGRADUATE EXPENSES for 2010–11 *Tuition:* full-time $29,500; part-time $985 per credit hour. *Required fees:* full-time $200; $100 per term.

Part-time tuition and fees vary according to course load. Room and board charges vary according to housing facility. *Payment plan:* Installment.

FRESHMAN FINANCIAL AID (Fall 2009, est.) 116 applied for aid; of those 84% were deemed to have need. 100% of freshmen with need received aid; of those 10% had need fully met. *Average percent of need met:* 60% (excluding resources awarded to replace EFC). *Average financial aid package:* $15,131 (excluding resources awarded to replace EFC). 11% of all full-time freshmen had no need and received non-need-based gift aid.

UNDERGRADUATE FINANCIAL AID (Fall 2009, est.) 622 applied for aid; of those 89% were deemed to have need. 100% of undergraduates with need received aid; of those 8% had need fully met. *Average percent of need met:* 60% (excluding resources awarded to replace EFC). *Average financial aid package:* $16,229 (excluding resources awarded to replace EFC). 8% of all full-time undergraduates had no need and received non-need-based gift aid.

GIFT AID (NEED-BASED) *Total amount:* $6,177,895 (16% federal, 10% state, 64% institutional, 10% external sources). *Receiving aid:* Freshmen: 75% (92); all full-time undergraduates: 76% (525). *Average award:* Freshmen: $11,651; Undergraduates: $11,679. *Scholarships, grants, and awards:* Federal Pell, FSEOG, state, private, college/university gift aid from institutional funds.

GIFT AID (NON-NEED-BASED) *Total amount:* $720,202 (70% institutional, 30% external sources). *Receiving aid:* Freshmen: 5% (6). Undergraduates: 3% (21). *Average award:* Freshmen: $9407. Undergraduates: $7879. *Scholarships, grants, and awards by category:* Creative arts/performance: 46 awards ($125,000 total): applied art and design, art/fine arts, cinema/film/broadcasting, general creative arts/performance. *Tuition waivers:* Full or partial for children of alumni, employees or children of employees.

LOANS *Student loans:* $6,933,657 (77% need-based, 23% non-need-based). 83% of past graduating class borrowed through all loan programs. *Average indebtedness per student:* $42,346. *Average need-based loan:* Freshmen: $3341. Undergraduates: $4616. *Parent loans:* $2,077,068 (49% need-based, 51% non-need-based). *Programs:* Federal Direct (Subsidized and Unsubsidized Stafford, PLUS), Perkins, state.

WORK-STUDY *Federal work-study:* Total amount: $78,972; 75 jobs averaging $2005. *State or other work-study/employment:* Total amount: $255,407 (56% need-based, 44% non-need-based). 20 part-time jobs averaging $2007.

APPLYING FOR FINANCIAL AID *Required financial aid form:* FAFSA. *Financial aid deadline:* 4/1 (priority: 3/15). *Notification date:* Continuous beginning 4/1. Students must reply by 5/1 or within 2 weeks of notification.

CONTACT Ms. Laura Link, Director of Financial Aid, Minneapolis College of Art and Design, 2501 Stevens Avenue South, Minneapolis, MN 55404-4347, 612-874-3733 or toll-free 800-874-6223. *Fax:* 612-874-3701. *E-mail:* laura_link@mead.edu.

MINNESOTA SCHOOL OF BUSINESS–BLAINE
Blaine, MN

CONTACT Financial Aid Office, Minnesota School of Business–Blaine, 3680 Pheasant Ridge Drive NE, Blaine, MN 55449, 763-225-8000.

MINNESOTA SCHOOL OF BUSINESS–ROCHESTER
Rochester, MN

CONTACT Financial Aid Office, Minnesota School of Business–Rochester, 2521 Pennington Drive, NW, Rochester, MN 55901, 507-536-9500 or toll-free 888-662-8772.

MINNESOTA STATE UNIVERSITY MANKATO
Mankato, MN

Tuition & fees (MN res): $6429   Average undergraduate aid package: $8130

ABOUT THE INSTITUTION State-supported, coed. 115 undergraduate majors. Federal methodology is used as a basis for awarding need-based institutional aid.

UNDERGRADUATE EXPENSES for 2009–10 *Tuition, state resident:* full-time $5631; part-time $225.15 per credit hour. *Tuition, nonresident:* full-time $12,063; part-time $481.05 per credit hour. *Required fees:* full-time $798; $33.14 per credit hour. Full-time tuition and fees vary according to course load, location, and reciprocity agreements. Part-time tuition and fees vary according to course load, location, and reciprocity agreements. *College room and board:* $6019. Room and board charges vary according to board plan and housing facility. *Payment plan:* Installment.

FRESHMAN FINANCIAL AID (Fall 2009, est.) 1,943 applied for aid; of those 64% were deemed to have need. 99% of freshmen with need received aid; of those 38% had need fully met. *Average percent of need met:* 86% (excluding resources awarded to replace EFC). *Average financial aid package:* $7969 (excluding resources awarded to replace EFC). 7% of all full-time freshmen had no need and received non-need-based gift aid.

UNDERGRADUATE FINANCIAL AID (Fall 2009, est.) 9,005 applied for aid; of those 67% were deemed to have need. 98% of undergraduates with need received aid; of those 38% had need fully met. *Average percent of need met:* 86% (excluding resources awarded to replace EFC). *Average financial aid package:* $8130 (excluding resources awarded to replace EFC). 4% of all full-time undergraduates had no need and received non-need-based gift aid.

GIFT AID (NEED-BASED) *Total amount:* $22,482,189 (63% federal, 28% state, 2% institutional, 7% external sources). *Receiving aid:* Freshmen: 43% (980); all full-time undergraduates: 40% (4,580). *Average award:* Freshmen: $5588; Undergraduates: $5236. *Scholarships, grants, and awards:* Federal Pell, FSEOG, state, private, college/university gift aid from institutional funds, Academic Competitiveness Grants, National SMART Grants.

GIFT AID (NON-NEED-BASED) *Total amount:* $3,005,144 (21% federal, 16% state, 18% institutional, 45% external sources). *Receiving aid:* Freshmen: 18% (411). Undergraduates: 11% (1,240). *Average award:* Freshmen: $1997. Undergraduates: $2273. *Tuition waivers:* Full or partial for employees or children of employees, senior citizens.

LOANS *Student loans:* $65,779,241 (63% need-based, 37% non-need-based). 82% of past graduating class borrowed through all loan programs. *Average indebtedness per student:* $25,667. *Average need-based loan:* Freshmen: $3106. Undergraduates: $3806. *Parent loans:* $2,735,463 (100% non-need-based). *Programs:* FFEL (Subsidized and Unsubsidized Stafford, PLUS), Perkins, state, alternative loans.

WORK-STUDY *Federal work-study:* Total amount: $1,535,422; 435 jobs averaging $3349. *State or other work-study/employment:* Total amount: $1,747,068 (100% need-based). 518 part-time jobs averaging $3366.

ATHLETIC AWARDS Total amount: $2,039,042 (33% need-based, 67% non-need-based).

APPLYING FOR FINANCIAL AID *Required financial aid forms:* FAFSA, SELF, alternative, or PLUS loan applications. *Financial aid deadline (priority):* 3/15. *Notification date:* Continuous beginning 3/30. Students must reply within 2 weeks of notification.

CONTACT Sandra Loerts, Director of Financial Aid, Minnesota State University Mankato, 228 Wiecking Center, Mankato, MN 56001, 507-389-1866 or toll-free 800-722-0544. *Fax:* 507-389-2227. *E-mail:* campushub@mnsu.edu.

MINNESOTA STATE UNIVERSITY MOORHEAD
Moorhead, MN

Tuition & fees (MN res): $6918   Average undergraduate aid package: $8172

ABOUT THE INSTITUTION State-supported, coed. 93 undergraduate majors. Federal methodology is used as a basis for awarding need-based institutional aid.

UNDERGRADUATE EXPENSES for 2010–11 *Tuition, state resident:* full-time $6140. *Tuition, nonresident:* full-time $6140. *Required fees:* full-time $778. Full-time tuition and fees vary according to program and reciprocity agreements. Part-time tuition and fees vary according to program and reciprocity agreements. *College room and board:* $6468. Room and board charges vary according to board plan and housing facility. *Payment plan:* Installment.

FRESHMAN FINANCIAL AID (Fall 2009, est.) 882 applied for aid; of those 80% were deemed to have need. 100% of freshmen with need received aid; of those 100% had need fully met. *Average financial aid package:* $7754 (excluding resources awarded to replace EFC).

UNDERGRADUATE FINANCIAL AID (Fall 2009, est.) 5,139 applied for aid; of those 75% were deemed to have need. 100% of undergraduates with need received aid; of those 100% had need fully met. *Average financial aid package:* $8172 (excluding resources awarded to replace EFC).

GIFT AID (NEED-BASED) *Total amount:* $12,984,454 (70% federal, 28% state, 2% institutional). *Receiving aid:* Freshmen: 45% (461); all full-time undergraduates: 37% (2,567). *Average award:* Freshmen: $4427; Undergraduates: $4001. *Scholarships, grants, and awards:* Federal Pell, FSEOG, state, private, college/university gift aid from institutional funds.

GIFT AID (NON-NEED-BASED) *Total amount:* $3,726,854 (5% federal, 72% institutional, 23% external sources). *Receiving aid:* Freshmen: 66% (676). Undergraduates: 26% (1,777). *Scholarships, grants, and awards by category: Academic interests/achievement:* biological sciences, business, communication, computer science, education, engineering/technologies, English, general academic interests/achievements, health fields, international studies, mathematics, physical sciences, premedicine, social sciences. *Creative arts/performance:* art/fine arts, cinema/film/broadcasting, creative writing, music, theater/drama. *Special achievements/activities:* community service, general special achievements/activities. *Special characteristics:* children of faculty/staff, first-generation college students, members of minority groups. *Tuition waivers:* Full or partial for employees or children of employees, senior citizens.

LOANS *Student loans:* $39,431,646 (37% need-based, 63% non-need-based). 70% of past graduating class borrowed through all loan programs. *Average indebtedness per student:* $27,918. *Average need-based loan:* Freshmen: $3377. Undergraduates: $4307. *Parent loans:* $561,282 (100% non-need-based). *Programs:* Federal Direct (Subsidized and Unsubsidized Stafford, PLUS), Perkins, state, alternative loans.

WORK-STUDY *Federal work-study:* Total amount: $614,439; 282 jobs averaging $2307. *State or other work-study/employment:* Total amount: $3,259,570 (15% need-based, 85% non-need-based). 212 part-time jobs averaging $2446.

ATHLETIC AWARDS Total amount: $343,204 (100% non-need-based).

APPLYING FOR FINANCIAL AID *Required financial aid form:* FAFSA. *Financial aid deadline (priority):* 2/15. *Notification date:* Continuous beginning 6/1. Students must reply within 2 weeks of notification.

CONTACT Ms. Carolyn Zehren, Director of Financial Aid, Minnesota State University Moorhead, 1104 7th Avenue South, Moorhead, MN 56563, 218-477-2085 or toll-free 800-593-7246. *Fax:* 218-477-2058. *E-mail:* zehren@mnstate.edu.

MINOT STATE UNIVERSITY
Minot, ND

ABOUT THE INSTITUTION State-supported, coed. 59 undergraduate majors.

GIFT AID (NEED-BASED) *Scholarships, grants, and awards:* Federal Pell, FSEOG, state, private, college/university gift aid from institutional funds, Federal Nursing.

GIFT AID (NON-NEED-BASED) *Scholarships, grants, and awards by category: Academic interests/achievement:* business, communication, computer science, education, English, general academic interests/achievements, health fields, humanities, mathematics, social sciences. *Special characteristics:* ethnic background, international students, local/state students, members of minority groups, out-of-state students, veterans, veterans' children.

LOANS *Programs:* FFEL (Subsidized and Unsubsidized Stafford, PLUS), Perkins, Federal Nursing, college/university.

WORK-STUDY *Federal work-study:* Total amount: $161,891; 140 jobs averaging $1053.

APPLYING FOR FINANCIAL AID *Required financial aid form:* FAFSA.

CONTACT Mr. Dale Gehring, Director of Financial Aid, Minot State University, 500 University Avenue, West, Minot, ND 58707-0002, 701-858-3862 or toll-free 800-777-0750 Ext. 3350. *Fax:* 701-858-4310. *E-mail:* dale.gehring@minotstateu.edu.

MIRRER YESHIVA
Brooklyn, NY

CONTACT Financial Aid Office, Mirrer Yeshiva, 1795 Ocean Parkway, Brooklyn, NY 11223-2010, 718-645-0536.

MISERICORDIA UNIVERSITY
Dallas, PA

Tuition & fees: $24,050	Average undergraduate aid package: $16,738

ABOUT THE INSTITUTION Independent Roman Catholic, coed, primarily women. 32 undergraduate majors. Federal methodology is used as a basis for awarding need-based institutional aid.

UNDERGRADUATE EXPENSES for 2009–10 *Comprehensive fee:* $34,100 includes full-time tuition ($22,850), mandatory fees ($1200), and room and board ($10,050). *College room only:* $5830. Room and board charges vary according to board plan and housing facility. *Part-time tuition:* $450 per credit. Part-time tuition and fees vary according to class time and location. *Payment plans:* Installment, deferred payment.

FRESHMAN FINANCIAL AID (Fall 2009, est.) 357 applied for aid; of those 86% were deemed to have need. 100% of freshmen with need received aid; of those 15% had need fully met. *Average percent of need met:* 73% (excluding resources awarded to replace EFC). *Average financial aid package:* $16,852 (excluding resources awarded to replace EFC). 13% of all full-time freshmen had no need and received non-need-based gift aid.

UNDERGRADUATE FINANCIAL AID (Fall 2009, est.) 1,546 applied for aid; of those 90% were deemed to have need. 100% of undergraduates with need received aid; of those 13% had need fully met. *Average percent of need met:* 71% (excluding resources awarded to replace EFC). *Average financial aid package:* $16,738 (excluding resources awarded to replace EFC). 9% of all full-time undergraduates had no need and received non-need-based gift aid.

GIFT AID (NEED-BASED) *Total amount:* $16,779,144 (14% federal, 13% state, 71% institutional, 2% external sources). *Receiving aid:* Freshmen: 83% (308); all full-time undergraduates: 82% (1,370). *Average award:* Freshmen: $13,218; Undergraduates: $12,018. *Scholarships, grants, and awards:* Federal Pell, FSEOG, state, private, college/university gift aid from institutional funds, Federal Nursing.

GIFT AID (NON-NEED-BASED) *Total amount:* $2,240,065 (94% institutional, 6% external sources). *Receiving aid:* Freshmen: 9% (33). Undergraduates: 7% (121). *Average award:* Freshmen: $7646. Undergraduates: $6835. *Scholarships, grants, and awards by category: Academic interests/achievement:* $6,746,295 total: business, computer science, education, general academic interests/achievements, health fields, physical sciences, social sciences. *Special achievements/activities:* $2,407,970 total: community service, general special achievements/activities, leadership. *Special characteristics:* $1,753,811 total: children and siblings of alumni, children of current students, children of faculty/staff, general special characteristics, members of minority groups, out-of-state students, previous college experience, relatives of clergy, religious affiliation, siblings of current students. *Tuition waivers:* Full or partial for employees or children of employees.

LOANS *Student loans:* $14,686,735 (75% need-based, 25% non-need-based). 78% of past graduating class borrowed through all loan programs. *Average indebtedness per student:* $33,641. *Average need-based loan:* Freshmen: $6800. Undergraduates: $8612. *Parent loans:* $3,267,900 (37% need-based, 63% non-need-based). *Programs:* FFEL (Subsidized and Unsubsidized Stafford, PLUS), Perkins, Federal Nursing, state.

WORK-STUDY *Federal work-study:* Total amount: $263,087; jobs available.

APPLYING FOR FINANCIAL AID *Required financial aid forms:* FAFSA, institution's own form. *Financial aid deadline (priority):* 3/1. *Notification date:* 3/15. Students must reply within 2 weeks of notification.

CONTACT Jane Dessoye, Executive Director of Enrollment Management, Misericordia University, 301 Lake Street, Dallas, PA 18612-1098, 570-674-6280 or toll-free 866-262-6363. *Fax:* 570-675-2441. *E-mail:* finaid@misericordia.edu.

MISSISSIPPI COLLEGE
Clinton, MS

Tuition & fees: $13,550	Average undergraduate aid package: $16,013

ABOUT THE INSTITUTION Independent Southern Baptist, coed. 68 undergraduate majors. Federal methodology is used as a basis for awarding need-based institutional aid.

UNDERGRADUATE EXPENSES for 2010–11 *Comprehensive fee:* $19,700 includes full-time tuition ($12,900), mandatory fees ($650), and room and board ($6150). Full-time tuition and fees vary according to course load, location, and program. Room and board charges vary according to housing facility. *Part-time tuition:* $405 per credit hour. *Part-time fees:* $170 per term. Part-time tuition and fees vary according to course load, location, and program. *Payment plans:* Installment, deferred payment.

FRESHMAN FINANCIAL AID (Fall 2009, est.) 452 applied for aid; of those 63% were deemed to have need. 100% of freshmen with need received aid; of those

37% had need fully met. *Average percent of need met:* 80% (excluding resources awarded to replace EFC). *Average financial aid package:* $15,070 (excluding resources awarded to replace EFC). 37% of all full-time freshmen had no need and received non-need-based gift aid.

UNDERGRADUATE FINANCIAL AID (Fall 2009, est.) 2,495 applied for aid; of those 63% were deemed to have need. 100% of undergraduates with need received aid; of those 33% had need fully met. *Average percent of need met:* 78% (excluding resources awarded to replace EFC). *Average financial aid package:* $16,013 (excluding resources awarded to replace EFC). 35% of all full-time undergraduates had no need and received non-need-based gift aid.

GIFT AID (NEED-BASED) *Total amount:* $14,062,962 (37% federal, 4% state, 56% institutional, 3% external sources). *Receiving aid:* Freshmen: 46% (206); all full-time undergraduates: 48% (1,218). *Average award:* Freshmen: $10,549; Undergraduates: $9484. *Scholarships, grants, and awards:* Federal Pell, FSEOG, state, private, college/university gift aid from institutional funds, Federal Nursing.

GIFT AID (NON-NEED-BASED) *Total amount:* $11,462,146 (9% state, 86% institutional, 5% external sources). *Receiving aid:* Freshmen: 17% (77). Undergraduates: 12% (301). *Average award:* Freshmen: $11,181. Undergraduates: $10,104. *Scholarships, grants, and awards by category: Academic interests/achievement:* $9,390,526 total: general academic interests/achievements. *Creative arts/performance:* $124,580 total: applied art and design, art/fine arts, music. *Special achievements/activities:* $3,636,650 total: general special achievements/activities, leadership, religious involvement. *Special characteristics:* $1,881,834 total: children and siblings of alumni, children of faculty/staff, general special characteristics, relatives of clergy. *Tuition waivers:* Full or partial for employees or children of employees.

LOANS *Student loans:* $16,724,353 (82% need-based, 18% non-need-based). 72% of past graduating class borrowed through all loan programs. *Average indebtedness per student:* $26,323. *Average need-based loan:* Freshmen: $5685. Undergraduates: $7582. *Parent loans:* $764,061 (100% need-based). *Programs:* FFEL (Subsidized and Unsubsidized Stafford, PLUS), Perkins, Federal Nursing, college/university.

WORK-STUDY *Federal work-study:* Total amount: $215,091; 229 jobs averaging $1088.

APPLYING FOR FINANCIAL AID *Required financial aid forms:* FAFSA, state aid form. *Financial aid deadline (priority):* 3/1. *Notification date:* Continuous beginning 3/1. Students must reply by 5/1.

CONTACT Karon McMillan, Director of Financial Aid, Mississippi College, PO Box 4035, Clinton, MS 39058, 601-925-3249 or toll-free 800-738-1236. *Fax:* 601-925-3950. *E-mail:* kmcmilla@mc.edu.

MISSISSIPPI STATE UNIVERSITY
Mississippi State, MS

Tuition & fees (MS res): $5151   **Average undergraduate aid package:** $10,155

ABOUT THE INSTITUTION State-supported, coed. 70 undergraduate majors. Federal methodology is used as a basis for awarding need-based institutional aid.

UNDERGRADUATE EXPENSES for 2009–10 *Tuition, state resident:* full-time $5151; part-time $214.75 per credit hour. *Tuition, nonresident:* full-time $13,021; part-time $542.75 per credit hour. Part-time tuition and fees vary according to course load. *College room and board:* $7520; *Room only:* $4285. Room and board charges vary according to board plan, housing facility, and student level. *Payment plan:* Installment.

FRESHMAN FINANCIAL AID (Fall 2008) 1,714 applied for aid; of those 82% were deemed to have need. 99% of freshmen with need received aid; of those 28% had need fully met. *Average percent of need met:* 68% (excluding resources awarded to replace EFC). *Average financial aid package:* $9743 (excluding resources awarded to replace EFC). 29% of all full-time freshmen had no need and received non-need-based gift aid.

UNDERGRADUATE FINANCIAL AID (Fall 2008) 8,102 applied for aid; of those 84% were deemed to have need. 98% of undergraduates with need received aid; of those 30% had need fully met. *Average percent of need met:* 66% (excluding resources awarded to replace EFC). *Average financial aid package:* $10,155 (excluding resources awarded to replace EFC). 20% of all full-time undergraduates had no need and received non-need-based gift aid.

GIFT AID (NEED-BASED) *Total amount:* $35,994,809 (46% federal, 10% state, 17% institutional, 27% external sources). *Receiving aid:* Freshmen: 53% (1,325); all full-time undergraduates: 49% (6,115). *Average award:* Freshmen: $5170;

Undergraduates: $5069. *Scholarships, grants, and awards:* Federal Pell, FSEOG, state, private, college/university gift aid from institutional funds, United Negro College Fund.

GIFT AID (NON-NEED-BASED) *Total amount:* $16,681,632 (21% state, 50% institutional, 29% external sources). *Receiving aid:* Freshmen: 10% (244). Undergraduates: 5% (655). *Average award:* Freshmen: $2950. Undergraduates: $2882. *Scholarships, grants, and awards by category: Academic interests/achievement:* agriculture, architecture, area/ethnic studies, biological sciences, business, communication, computer science, education, engineering/technologies, English, foreign languages, general academic interests/achievements, health fields, home economics, humanities, international studies, library science, mathematics, military science, physical sciences, premedicine, religion/biblical studies, social sciences. *Creative arts/performance:* applied art and design, art/fine arts, cinema/film/broadcasting, creative writing, dance, debating, general creative arts/performance, journalism/publications, music, performing arts, theater/drama. *Special achievements/activities:* cheerleading/drum major, general special achievements/activities, junior miss, leadership, memberships. *Special characteristics:* adult students, children and siblings of alumni, children of educators, children of faculty/staff, children of public servants, first-generation college students, handicapped students, local/state students, out-of-state students, previous college experience, spouses of deceased or disabled public servants. *Tuition waivers:* Full or partial for children of alumni, employees or children of employees, senior citizens.

LOANS *Student loans:* $76,222,313 (79% need-based, 21% non-need-based). 51% of past graduating class borrowed through all loan programs. *Average indebtedness per student:* $23,413. *Average need-based loan:* Freshmen: $3246. Undergraduates: $3935. *Parent loans:* $3,421,832 (28% need-based, 72% non-need-based). *Programs:* FFEL (Subsidized and Unsubsidized Stafford, PLUS), Perkins, college/university.

WORK-STUDY *Federal work-study:* Total amount: $2,816,152; 987 jobs averaging $2853.

ATHLETIC AWARDS Total amount: $5,830,997 (100% non-need-based).

APPLYING FOR FINANCIAL AID *Required financial aid forms:* FAFSA, state grant/scholarship application. *Financial aid deadline (priority):* 4/1. *Notification date:* Continuous beginning 12/1. Students must reply by 5/1.

CONTACT Mr. Bruce Crain, Director of Financial Aid, Mississippi State University, PO Box 6035, Mississippi State, MS 39762, 662-325-2450. *Fax:* 662-325-0702. *E-mail:* financialaid@saffairs.msstate.edu.

MISSISSIPPI UNIVERSITY FOR WOMEN
Columbus, MS

Tuition & fees (MS res): $4423   **Average undergraduate aid package:** $8408

ABOUT THE INSTITUTION State-supported, coed, primarily women. 26 undergraduate majors. Federal methodology is used as a basis for awarding need-based institutional aid.

UNDERGRADUATE EXPENSES for 2010–11 *Tuition, state resident:* full-time $4423; part-time $184.25 per credit hour. *Tuition, nonresident:* full-time $12,051; part-time $502.05 per credit hour. Part-time tuition and fees vary according to course load. *College room and board:* $5164; *Room only:* $3014. Room and board charges vary according to housing facility. *Payment plan:* Installment.

FRESHMAN FINANCIAL AID (Fall 2009, est.) 192 applied for aid; of those 88% were deemed to have need. 99% of freshmen with need received aid; of those 50% had need fully met. *Average percent of need met:* 50% (excluding resources awarded to replace EFC). *Average financial aid package:* $9132 (excluding resources awarded to replace EFC). 19% of all full-time freshmen had no need and received non-need-based gift aid.

UNDERGRADUATE FINANCIAL AID (Fall 2009, est.) 1,491 applied for aid; of those 88% were deemed to have need. 99% of undergraduates with need received aid; of those 67% had need fully met. *Average percent of need met:* 63% (excluding resources awarded to replace EFC). *Average financial aid package:* $8408 (excluding resources awarded to replace EFC). 16% of all full-time undergraduates had no need and received non-need-based gift aid.

GIFT AID (NEED-BASED) *Total amount:* $5,260,826 (100% federal). *Receiving aid:* Freshmen: 62% (130); all full-time undergraduates: 57% (1,005). *Average award:* Freshmen: $4983; Undergraduates: $5201. *Scholarships, grants, and awards:* Federal Pell, FSEOG, state, private, college/university gift aid from institutional funds.

GIFT AID (NON-NEED-BASED) *Total amount:* $4,456,506 (15% state, 77% institutional, 8% external sources). *Receiving aid:* Freshmen: 53% (112).

Mississippi University for Women

Undergraduates: 38% (658). *Average award:* Freshmen: $5868. Undergraduates: $4732. *Scholarships, grants, and awards by category: Academic interests/achievement:* 768 awards ($1,920,363 total): biological sciences, business, communication, computer science, education, English, general academic interests/achievements, health fields, home economics, humanities, mathematics, physical sciences. *Creative arts/performance:* 50 awards ($28,200 total): art/fine arts, journalism/publications, music, performing arts, theater/drama. *Special achievements/activities:* 11 awards ($16,541 total): junior miss, leadership. *Special characteristics:* 213 awards ($1,079,355 total): adult students, children and siblings of alumni, children of faculty/staff, ethnic background, international students, members of minority groups, out-of-state students, parents of current students. *Tuition waivers:* Full or partial for employees or children of employees.

LOANS *Student loans:* $9,825,273 (47% need-based, 53% non-need-based). 64% of past graduating class borrowed through all loan programs. *Average indebtedness per student:* $18,363. *Average need-based loan:* Freshmen: $3198. Undergraduates: $4494. *Parent loans:* $242,792 (100% non-need-based). *Programs:* FFEL (Subsidized and Unsubsidized Stafford, PLUS), Perkins.

WORK-STUDY *Federal work-study:* Total amount: $140,286; 93 jobs averaging $1693. *State or other work-study/employment:* Total amount: $267,480 (100% non-need-based). 194 part-time jobs averaging $1535.

APPLYING FOR FINANCIAL AID *Required financial aid forms:* FAFSA, institution's own form, state aid form. *Financial aid deadline (priority):* 3/1. *Notification date:* Continuous beginning 4/1. Students must reply within 2 weeks of notification.

CONTACT Mr. Dan Miller, Director of Financial Aid, Mississippi University for Women, 1100 College Street, MUW 1614, Columbus, MS 39701-4044, 662-329-7114 or toll-free 877-GO 2 THE W. *Fax:* 662-329-7325. *E-mail:* dmiller@finaid.muw.edu.

MISSISSIPPI VALLEY STATE UNIVERSITY
Itta Bena, MS

Tuition & fees: N/R	Average undergraduate aid package: N/A

ABOUT THE INSTITUTION State-supported, coed. 30 undergraduate majors. Federal methodology is used as a basis for awarding need-based institutional aid.

UNDERGRADUATE EXPENSES for 2010–11 *One-time required fee:* $50. *Tuition, state resident:* part-time $190.62 per credit hour. *Tuition, nonresident:* part-time $284.81 per credit hour. *Payment plan:* Installment.

GIFT AID (NEED-BASED) *Scholarships, grants, and awards:* Federal Pell, FSEOG, state, private, college/university gift aid from institutional funds.

GIFT AID (NON-NEED-BASED) *Scholarships, grants, and awards by category: Academic interests/achievement:* general academic interests/achievements. *Creative arts/performance:* art/fine arts, journalism/publications, music. *Special characteristics:* members of minority groups. *Tuition waivers:* Full or partial for children of alumni, employees or children of employees.

LOANS *Programs:* Federal Direct (Unsubsidized Stafford, PLUS), FFEL (Subsidized and Unsubsidized Stafford, PLUS).

WORK-STUDY Federal work-study jobs available. *State or other work-study/employment:* Part-time jobs available.

APPLYING FOR FINANCIAL AID *Required financial aid form:* FAFSA. *Financial aid deadline (priority):* 4/1. *Notification date:* 7/15.

CONTACT Mr. Lloyd E. Dixon, Director of Student Financial Aid, Mississippi Valley State University, 14000 Highway 82W #7268, Itta Bena, MS 38941-1400, 662-254-3335 or toll-free 800-844-6885 (in-state). *Fax:* 662-254-7900. *E-mail:* ldixon@mvsu.edu.

MISSOURI BAPTIST UNIVERSITY
St. Louis, MO

ABOUT THE INSTITUTION Independent Southern Baptist, coed. 37 undergraduate majors.

GIFT AID (NEED-BASED) *Scholarships, grants, and awards:* Federal Pell, FSEOG, state, private, college/university gift aid from institutional funds.

GIFT AID (NON-NEED-BASED) *Scholarships, grants, and awards by category: Academic interests/achievement:* general academic interests/achievements, religion/biblical studies. *Creative arts/performance:* music, theater/drama. *Special achievements/activities:* cheerleading/drum major, religious involvement. *Special characteristics:* children and siblings of alumni, children of current students, children of faculty/staff, parents of current students, public servants, relatives of clergy, religious affiliation, siblings of current students.

LOANS *Programs:* FFEL (Subsidized and Unsubsidized Stafford, PLUS).

WORK-STUDY *Federal work-study:* Total amount: $95,800; 63 jobs averaging $1521. *State or other work-study/employment:* Total amount: $24,923 (100% need-based). 5 part-time jobs averaging $4985.

APPLYING FOR FINANCIAL AID *Required financial aid forms:* FAFSA, institution's own form.

CONTACT Laurie Wallace, Director of Financial Services, Missouri Baptist University, One College Park Drive, St. Louis, MO 63141, 314-392-2366 or toll-free 877-434-1115 Ext. 2290. *Fax:* 314-434-7596. *E-mail:* wallace@mobap.edu.

MISSOURI SOUTHERN STATE UNIVERSITY
Joplin, MO

Tuition & fees (MO res): $4290	Average undergraduate aid package: $14,602

ABOUT THE INSTITUTION State-supported, coed. 38 undergraduate majors. Federal methodology is used as a basis for awarding need-based institutional aid.

UNDERGRADUATE EXPENSES for 2009–10 *Tuition, state resident:* full-time $4290; part-time $143 per credit hour. *Tuition, nonresident:* full-time $8580; part-time $286 per credit hour. Full-time tuition and fees vary according to course load. *College room and board:* $5500. Room and board charges vary according to board plan and housing facility.

FRESHMAN FINANCIAL AID (Fall 2009, est.) 739 applied for aid; of those 71% were deemed to have need. 94% of freshmen with need received aid; of those 16% had need fully met. *Average percent of need met:* 67% (excluding resources awarded to replace EFC). *Average financial aid package:* $7066 (excluding resources awarded to replace EFC). 18% of all full-time freshmen had no need and received non-need-based gift aid.

UNDERGRADUATE FINANCIAL AID (Fall 2009, est.) 3,418 applied for aid; of those 77% were deemed to have need. 97% of undergraduates with need received aid; of those 6% had need fully met. *Average percent of need met:* 55% (excluding resources awarded to replace EFC). *Average financial aid package:* $14,602 (excluding resources awarded to replace EFC). 9% of all full-time undergraduates had no need and received non-need-based gift aid.

GIFT AID (NEED-BASED) *Total amount:* $11,778,583 (83% federal, 17% state). *Receiving aid:* Freshmen: 54% (399); all full-time undergraduates: 58% (2,003). *Average award:* Freshmen: $4266; Undergraduates: $5953. *Scholarships, grants, and awards:* Federal Pell, FSEOG, state, private.

GIFT AID (NON-NEED-BASED) *Total amount:* $5,935,720 (2% state, 80% institutional, 18% external sources). *Receiving aid:* Freshmen: 52% (387). Undergraduates: 59% (2,052). *Average award:* Freshmen: $2509. Undergraduates: $4122. *Scholarships, grants, and awards by category: Academic interests/achievement:* 893 awards ($2,252,598 total): general academic interests/achievements. *Creative arts/performance:* 117 awards ($247,228 total): art/fine arts, debating, journalism/publications, music, theater/drama. *Special achievements/activities:* 29 awards ($23,278 total): general special achievements/activities. *Special characteristics:* 284 awards ($363,567 total): children and siblings of alumni, children of faculty/staff, ethnic background, local/state students, religious affiliation. *Tuition waivers:* Full or partial for employees or children of employees, senior citizens.

LOANS *Student loans:* $19,621,654 (49% need-based, 51% non-need-based). 51% of past graduating class borrowed through all loan programs. *Average indebtedness per student:* $10,006. *Average need-based loan:* Freshmen: $2880. Undergraduates: $4283. *Parent loans:* $220,115 (100% non-need-based). *Programs:* Federal Direct (Subsidized and Unsubsidized Stafford, PLUS), Perkins.

WORK-STUDY *Federal work-study:* Total amount: $250,000; 94 jobs averaging $2787. *State or other work-study/employment:* Total amount: $1,049,003 (100% non-need-based). 424 part-time jobs averaging $2474.

ATHLETIC AWARDS Total amount: $1,190,272 (100% non-need-based).

APPLYING FOR FINANCIAL AID *Required financial aid form:* FAFSA. *Financial aid deadline (priority):* 4/1. *Notification date:* Continuous beginning 3/1. Students must reply by 5/1 or within 3 weeks of notification.

CONTACT Ms. Kathy Feith, Director of Financial Aid, Missouri Southern State University, 3950 East Newman Road, Joplin, MO 64801-1595, 417-625-9325 or toll-free 866-818-MSSU. *Fax:* 417-659-4474. *E-mail:* feith-k@mssu.edu.

MISSOURI STATE UNIVERSITY
Springfield, MO

Tuition & fees (MO res): $6972   **Average undergraduate aid package: $7307**

ABOUT THE INSTITUTION State-supported, coed. 99 undergraduate majors. Federal methodology is used as a basis for awarding need-based institutional aid.

UNDERGRADUATE EXPENSES for 2009–10 *Tuition, state resident:* full-time $6276; part-time $186 per credit hour. *Tuition, nonresident:* full-time $11,556; part-time $362 per credit hour. *Required fees:* full-time $696. Full-time tuition and fees vary according to course level, location, and program. Part-time tuition and fees vary according to course level, course load, location, and program. *College room and board:* $5925. Room and board charges vary according to board plan and housing facility. *Payment plans:* Tuition prepayment, installment, deferred payment.

FRESHMAN FINANCIAL AID (Fall 2008) 1,945 applied for aid; of those 67% were deemed to have need. 98% of freshmen with need received aid; of those 28% had need fully met. *Average percent of need met:* 71% (excluding resources awarded to replace EFC). *Average financial aid package:* $7664 (excluding resources awarded to replace EFC). 19% of all full-time freshmen had no need and received non-need-based gift aid.

UNDERGRADUATE FINANCIAL AID (Fall 2008) 10,381 applied for aid; of those 74% were deemed to have need. 97% of undergraduates with need received aid; of those 21% had need fully met. *Average percent of need met:* 63% (excluding resources awarded to replace EFC). *Average financial aid package:* $7307 (excluding resources awarded to replace EFC). 16% of all full-time undergraduates had no need and received non-need-based gift aid.

GIFT AID (NEED-BASED) *Total amount:* $30,493,001 (46% federal, 23% state, 25% institutional, 6% external sources). *Receiving aid:* Freshmen: 52% (1,191); all full-time undergraduates: 49% (6,128). *Average award:* Freshmen: $5897; Undergraduates: $4971. *Scholarships, grants, and awards:* Federal Pell, FSEOG, state, private, college/university gift aid from institutional funds.

GIFT AID (NON-NEED-BASED) *Total amount:* $14,183,152 (10% state, 73% institutional, 17% external sources). *Receiving aid:* Freshmen: 9% (211). Undergraduates: 5% (629). *Average award:* Freshmen: $4159. Undergraduates: $4632. *Scholarships, grants, and awards by category: Academic interests/achievement:* general academic interests/achievements. *Creative arts/performance:* general creative arts/performance. *Special achievements/activities:* leadership. *Special characteristics:* children and siblings of alumni, local/state students, members of minority groups. *Tuition waivers:* Full or partial for children of alumni, employees or children of employees, senior citizens.

LOANS *Student loans:* $62,894,239 (63% need-based, 37% non-need-based). 85% of past graduating class borrowed through all loan programs. *Average indebtedness per student:* $19,813. *Average need-based loan:* Freshmen: $3122. Undergraduates: $3926. *Parent loans:* $7,353,119 (16% need-based, 84% non-need-based). *Programs:* FFEL (Subsidized and Unsubsidized Stafford, PLUS), Perkins, college/university.

WORK-STUDY *Federal work-study:* Total amount: $505,058; jobs available.

ATHLETIC AWARDS Total amount: $3,646,235 (25% need-based, 75% non-need-based).

APPLYING FOR FINANCIAL AID *Required financial aid form:* FAFSA. *Financial aid deadline (priority):* 3/31. *Notification date:* 4/30. Students must reply within 4 weeks of notification.

CONTACT Vicki Mattocks, Director of Financial Aid, Missouri State University, 901 South National Avenue, Springfield, MO 65804, 417-836-5262 or toll-free 800-492-7900. *E-mail:* financialaid@missouristate.edu.

MISSOURI TECH
St. Louis, MO

Tuition & fees: N/R   **Average undergraduate aid package: N/A**

ABOUT THE INSTITUTION Proprietary, coed, primarily men. *Awards:* associate and bachelor's degrees. 7 undergraduate majors. *Total enrollment:* 114. Undergraduates: 114. Both federal and institutional methodology are used as a basis for awarding need-based institutional aid.

GIFT AID (NEED-BASED) *Scholarships, grants, and awards:* Federal Pell, private, college/university gift aid from institutional funds.

GIFT AID (NON-NEED-BASED) *Scholarships, grants, and awards by category: Academic interests/achievement:* general academic interests/achievements.

LOANS *Programs:* FFEL (Subsidized and Unsubsidized Stafford, PLUS), college/university.

APPLYING FOR FINANCIAL AID *Required financial aid forms:* FAFSA, institution's own form. *Financial aid deadline:* Continuous. *Notification date:* Continuous.

CONTACT Director of Financial Aid, Missouri Tech, 1690 Country Club Plaza Drive, St. Charles, MO 63303, 636-573-9300. *Fax:* 636-573-9398. *E-mail:* contact@motech.edu.

MISSOURI UNIVERSITY OF SCIENCE AND TECHNOLOGY
Rolla, MO

Tuition & fees (MO res): $8488   **Average undergraduate aid package: $13,362**

ABOUT THE INSTITUTION State-supported, coed, primarily men. 35 undergraduate majors. Federal methodology is used as a basis for awarding need-based institutional aid.

UNDERGRADUATE EXPENSES for 2009–10 *Tuition, state resident:* full-time $7368; part-time $246 per credit hour. *Tuition, nonresident:* full-time $18,459; part-time $615 per credit hour. *Required fees:* full-time $1120; $120.52 per credit hour. Full-time tuition and fees vary according to course load, degree level, and program. Part-time tuition and fees vary according to course load, degree level, and program. *College room and board:* $7595; *Room only:* $4670. Room and board charges vary according to board plan, housing facility, and location. *Payment plan:* Installment.

FRESHMAN FINANCIAL AID (Fall 2009, est.) 1,074 applied for aid; of those 72% were deemed to have need. 100% of freshmen with need received aid; of those 60% had need fully met. *Average percent of need met:* 44% (excluding resources awarded to replace EFC). *Average financial aid package:* $14,282 (excluding resources awarded to replace EFC). 23% of all full-time freshmen had no need and received non-need-based gift aid.

UNDERGRADUATE FINANCIAL AID (Fall 2009, est.) 4,496 applied for aid; of those 82% were deemed to have need. 100% of undergraduates with need received aid; of those 60% had need fully met. *Average percent of need met:* 44% (excluding resources awarded to replace EFC). *Average financial aid package:* $13,362 (excluding resources awarded to replace EFC). 12% of all full-time undergraduates had no need and received non-need-based gift aid.

GIFT AID (NEED-BASED) *Total amount:* $17,234,757 (38% federal, 10% state, 50% institutional, 2% external sources). *Receiving aid:* Freshmen: 42% (459); all full-time undergraduates: 42% (2,040). *Average award:* Freshmen: $4107; Undergraduates: $4370. *Scholarships, grants, and awards:* Federal Pell, FSEOG, state, private, college/university gift aid from institutional funds, ROTC (Army and Air Force) scholarships.

GIFT AID (NON-NEED-BASED) *Total amount:* $9,375,610 (19% state, 76% institutional, 5% external sources). *Receiving aid:* Freshmen: 60% (664). Undergraduates: 57% (2,774). *Average award:* Freshmen: $5307. Undergraduates: $4889. *Scholarships, grants, and awards by category: Academic interests/achievement:* 3,324 awards ($13,410,316 total): biological sciences, business, computer science, education, engineering/technologies, English, general academic interests/achievements, humanities, mathematics, military science, physical sciences, premedicine, social sciences. *Creative arts/performance:* 9 awards ($2035 total): music, theater/drama. *Special characteristics:* 862 awards ($2,776,138 total): children and siblings of alumni, children of faculty/staff, members of minority groups, out-of-state students. *Tuition waivers:* Full or partial for employees or children of employees.

LOANS *Student loans:* $20,205,261 (61% need-based, 39% non-need-based). 83% of past graduating class borrowed through all loan programs. *Average indebtedness per student:* $24,235. *Average need-based loan:* Freshmen: $6471. Undergraduates: $5640. *Parent loans:* $3,851,932 (5% need-based, 95% non-need-based). *Programs:* Federal Direct (Subsidized and Unsubsidized Stafford), FFEL (Subsidized and Unsubsidized Stafford, PLUS), Perkins, state, college/university, alternative loans.

WORK-STUDY *Federal work-study:* Total amount: $335,556; 146 jobs averaging $2297. *State or other work-study/employment:* Total amount: $1,840,555 (57% need-based, 43% non-need-based). 1,191 part-time jobs averaging $1594.

ATHLETIC AWARDS Total amount: $2,092,997 (100% non-need-based).

APPLYING FOR FINANCIAL AID *Required financial aid form:* FAFSA. *Financial aid deadline (priority):* 3/1. *Notification date:* Continuous beginning 4/1. Students must reply within 3 weeks of notification.

CONTACT Lynn K. Stichnote, Director of Student Financial Assistance, Missouri University of Science and Technology, G1 Parker Hall, Rolla, MO 65409, 573-341-4282 or toll-free 800-522-0938. *Fax:* 573-341-4274. *E-mail:* lks@mst.edu.

MISSOURI VALLEY COLLEGE
Marshall, MO

Tuition & fees: N/R	Average undergraduate aid package: $14,600

ABOUT THE INSTITUTION Independent religious, coed. *Awards:* associate and bachelor's degrees. 38 undergraduate majors. *Total enrollment:* 1,639. Undergraduates: 1,639. Freshmen: 444. Federal methodology is used as a basis for awarding need-based institutional aid.

FRESHMAN FINANCIAL AID (Fall 2009, est.) 378 applied for aid; of those 85% were deemed to have need. 100% of freshmen with need received aid; of those 44% had need fully met. *Average percent of need met:* 86% (excluding resources awarded to replace EFC). *Average financial aid package:* $14,450 (excluding resources awarded to replace EFC). 24% of all full-time freshmen had no need and received non-need-based gift aid.

UNDERGRADUATE FINANCIAL AID (Fall 2009, est.) 1,237 applied for aid; of those 82% were deemed to have need. 100% of undergraduates with need received aid; of those 46% had need fully met. *Average percent of need met:* 83% (excluding resources awarded to replace EFC). *Average financial aid package:* $14,600 (excluding resources awarded to replace EFC). 27% of all full-time undergraduates had no need and received non-need-based gift aid.

GIFT AID (NEED-BASED) *Total amount:* $10,378,779 (37% federal, 15% state, 48% institutional). *Receiving aid:* Freshmen: 75% (322); all full-time undergraduates: 72% (1,019). *Average award:* Freshmen: $11,940; Undergraduates: $11,670. *Scholarships, grants, and awards:* Federal Pell, FSEOG, state, private, college/university gift aid from institutional funds.

GIFT AID (NON-NEED-BASED) *Total amount:* $323,344 (100% external sources). *Receiving aid:* Freshmen: 75% (322). Undergraduates: 72% (1,019). *Average award:* Freshmen: $11,200. Undergraduates: $10,900. *Scholarships, grants, and awards by category: Academic interests/achievement:* 247 awards ($280,365 total): biological sciences, business, communication, computer science, education, English, general academic interests/achievements, health fields, humanities, mathematics, military science, physical sciences, premedicine, social sciences. *Creative arts/performance:* 33 awards ($103,550 total): applied art and design, art/fine arts, cinema/film/broadcasting, dance, journalism/publications, music, performing arts, theater/drama. *Special achievements/activities:* 32 awards ($180,150 total): cheerleading/drum major, community service, general special achievements/activities, hobbies/interests, junior miss, leadership, rodeo. *Special characteristics:* 28 awards ($168,500 total): children and siblings of alumni, children of faculty/staff. *ROTC:* Army.

LOANS *Student loans:* $7,286,993 (49% need-based, 51% non-need-based). 82% of past graduating class borrowed through all loan programs. *Average indebtedness per student:* $23,200. *Average need-based loan:* Freshmen: $3050. Undergraduates: $3250. *Parent loans:* $459,830 (100% non-need-based). *Programs:* Federal Direct (Subsidized and Unsubsidized Stafford, PLUS), Perkins.

WORK-STUDY *Federal work-study:* Total amount: $244,405; 192 jobs averaging $1860. *State or other work-study/employment:* Total amount: $433,514 (100% non-need-based). 400 part-time jobs averaging $1860.

ATHLETIC AWARDS Total amount: $8,631,471 (100% need-based).

APPLYING FOR FINANCIAL AID *Required financial aid form:* FAFSA. *Financial aid deadline (priority):* 3/15. *Notification date:* Continuous beginning 10/1. Students must reply within 4 weeks of notification.

CONTACT Mr. Charles Richard Mayfield Jr., Director of Financial Aid, Missouri Valley College, 500 East College, Marshall, MO 65340-3197, 660-831-4176. *Fax:* 660-831-4003. *E-mail:* mayfieldb@moval.edu.

MISSOURI WESTERN STATE UNIVERSITY
St. Joseph, MO

ABOUT THE INSTITUTION State-supported, coed. 46 undergraduate majors.
GIFT AID (NEED-BASED) *Scholarships, grants, and awards:* Federal Pell, FSEOG, state, private, college/university gift aid from institutional funds.

GIFT AID (NON-NEED-BASED) *Scholarships, grants, and awards by category: Academic interests/achievement:* biological sciences, business, communication, computer science, education, engineering/technologies, English, general academic interests/achievements, health fields, humanities, mathematics, military science, physical sciences, social sciences. *Creative arts/performance:* art/fine arts, dance, music. *Special achievements/activities:* cheerleading/drum major, community service, general special achievements/activities, leadership. *Special characteristics:* children of faculty/staff, members of minority groups, out-of-state students.

LOANS *Programs:* FFEL (Subsidized and Unsubsidized Stafford, PLUS), Perkins.
WORK-STUDY *Federal work-study:* Total amount: $450,000; 277 jobs averaging $1447. *State or other work-study/employment:* 695 part-time jobs averaging $1688.

APPLYING FOR FINANCIAL AID *Required financial aid forms:* FAFSA, institution's own form.

CONTACT Angela Beam, Acting Director of Financial Aid, Missouri Western State University, 4525 Downs Drive, St. Joseph, MO 64507-2294, 816-271-5986 or toll-free 800-662-7041 Ext. 60. *Fax:* 816-271-5879. *E-mail:* lepley@missouriwestern.edu.

MITCHELL COLLEGE
New London, CT

CONTACT Jacklyn Stoltz, Director of Financial Aid, Mitchell College, 437 Pequot Avenue, New London, CT 06320-4498, 800-443-2811. *Fax:* 860-444-1209. *E-mail:* stoltz_j@mitchell.edu.

MOLLOY COLLEGE
Rockville Centre, NY

Tuition & fees: $20,960	Average undergraduate aid package: $12,545

ABOUT THE INSTITUTION Independent, coed. 44 undergraduate majors. Federal methodology is used as a basis for awarding need-based institutional aid.

UNDERGRADUATE EXPENSES for 2009–10 *One-time required fee:* $150. *Tuition:* full-time $19,970; part-time $660 per credit. *Payment plan:* Installment.

FRESHMAN FINANCIAL AID (Fall 2009, est.) 422 applied for aid; of those 83% were deemed to have need. 99% of freshmen with need received aid; of those 15% had need fully met. *Average percent of need met:* 61% (excluding resources awarded to replace EFC). *Average financial aid package:* $14,447 (excluding resources awarded to replace EFC). 10% of all full-time freshmen had no need and received non-need-based gift aid.

UNDERGRADUATE FINANCIAL AID (Fall 2009, est.) 2,314 applied for aid; of those 86% were deemed to have need. 100% of undergraduates with need received aid; of those 11% had need fully met. *Average percent of need met:* 53% (excluding resources awarded to replace EFC). *Average financial aid package:* $12,545 (excluding resources awarded to replace EFC). 7% of all full-time undergraduates had no need and received non-need-based gift aid.

GIFT AID (NEED-BASED) *Total amount:* $14,249,176 (31% federal, 20% state, 47% institutional, 2% external sources). *Receiving aid:* Freshmen: 79% (335); all full-time undergraduates: 77% (1,773). *Average award:* Freshmen: $11,887; Undergraduates: $8590. *Scholarships, grants, and awards:* Federal Pell, FSEOG, state, private, college/university gift aid from institutional funds, Federal Nursing, Academic Competitiveness Grants, National SMART Grants, TRiO Scholarships, TEACH Grants.

GIFT AID (NON-NEED-BASED) *Total amount:* $1,653,852 (6% state, 93% institutional, 1% external sources). *Receiving aid:* Freshmen: 10% (41). Undergraduates: 6% (133). *Average award:* Freshmen: $8103. Undergraduates: $6352. *Scholarships, grants, and awards by category: Academic interests/achievement:* 133 awards ($171,575 total): biological sciences, business, communication, education, English, general academic interests/achievements, health fields, mathematics. *Creative arts/performance:* 58 awards ($130,925 total): art/fine arts, music, performing arts, theater/drama. *Special achievements/activities:* 197 awards ($333,250 total): community service, leadership, memberships, religious involvement. *Special characteristics:* 153 awards ($146,000 total): children and siblings of alumni, children of faculty/staff, ethnic background, previous college experience, religious affiliation, siblings of current students. *Tuition waivers:* Full or partial for employees or children of employees.

LOANS *Student loans:* $22,932,542 (82% need-based, 18% non-need-based). 77% of past graduating class borrowed through all loan programs. *Average*

indebtedness per student: $29,823. **Average need-based loan:** Freshmen: $3664. Undergraduates: $5598. **Parent loans:** $3,718,975 (46% need-based, 54% non-need-based). **Programs:** Federal Direct (Subsidized and Unsubsidized Stafford, PLUS), FFEL (Subsidized and Unsubsidized Stafford, PLUS), Perkins, Federal Nursing, state, alternative loans.

WORK-STUDY **Federal work-study:** Total amount: $440,211; 418 jobs averaging $1231.

ATHLETIC AWARDS Total amount: $1,563,244 (71% need-based, 29% non-need-based).

APPLYING FOR FINANCIAL AID **Required financial aid forms:** FAFSA, state aid form. **Financial aid deadline:** 5/1. **Notification date:** 2/1. Students must reply within 5 weeks of notification.

CONTACT Ana C. Lockward, Director of Financial Aid, Molloy College, 1000 Hempstead Avenue, Rockville Centre, NY 11571, 516-678-5000 Ext. 6221 or toll-free 888-4MOLLOY. *Fax:* 516-256-2292. *E-mail:* alockward@molloy.edu.

MONMOUTH COLLEGE
Monmouth, IL

Tuition & fees: $24,950	Average undergraduate aid package: $20,775

ABOUT THE INSTITUTION Independent religious, coed. 37 undergraduate majors. Federal methodology is used as a basis for awarding need-based institutional aid.

UNDERGRADUATE EXPENSES for 2009–10 **Comprehensive fee:** $32,250 includes full-time tuition ($24,950) and room and board ($7300). **College room only:** $4250. Full-time tuition and fees vary according to course load. Room and board charges vary according to board plan and housing facility. **Part-time tuition:** $830 per credit hour. **Payment plan:** Installment.

FRESHMAN FINANCIAL AID (Fall 2009, est.) 373 applied for aid; of those 90% were deemed to have need. 100% of freshmen with need received aid; of those 22% had need fully met. **Average percent of need met:** 87% (excluding resources awarded to replace EFC). **Average financial aid package:** $22,388 (excluding resources awarded to replace EFC). 11% of all full-time freshmen had no need and received non-need-based gift aid.

UNDERGRADUATE FINANCIAL AID (Fall 2009, est.) 1,270 applied for aid; of those 90% were deemed to have need. 100% of undergraduates with need received aid; of those 20% had need fully met. **Average percent of need met:** 84% (excluding resources awarded to replace EFC). **Average financial aid package:** $20,775 (excluding resources awarded to replace EFC). 16% of all full-time undergraduates had no need and received non-need-based gift aid.

GIFT AID (NEED-BASED) **Total amount:** $19,556,574 (13% federal, 14% state, 73% institutional). **Receiving aid:** Freshmen: 89% (337); all full-time undergraduates: 84% (1,138). **Average award:** Freshmen: $18,189; Undergraduates: $16,052. **Scholarships, grants, and awards:** Federal Pell, FSEOG, state, private, college/university gift aid from institutional funds.

GIFT AID (NON-NEED-BASED) **Total amount:** $2,951,867 (85% institutional, 15% external sources). **Receiving aid:** Freshmen: 13% (51). Undergraduates: 11% (150). **Average award:** Freshmen: $12,081. Undergraduates: $10,425. **Scholarships, grants, and awards by category:** Academic interests/achievement: foreign languages, general academic interests/achievements. Creative arts/performance: art/fine arts, music, theater/drama. Special achievements/activities: general special achievements/activities. Special characteristics: international students, out-of-state students, siblings of current students, veterans. **Tuition waivers:** Full or partial for employees or children of employees.

LOANS **Student loans:** $8,527,611 (47% need-based, 53% non-need-based). 81% of past graduating class borrowed through all loan programs. Average indebtedness per student: $24,476. **Average need-based loan:** Freshmen: $3226. Undergraduates: $4085. **Parent loans:** $2,815,546 (100% non-need-based). **Programs:** Federal Direct (Subsidized and Unsubsidized Stafford, PLUS), Perkins.

WORK-STUDY **Federal work-study:** Total amount: $856,291; jobs available. **State or other work-study/employment:** Part-time jobs available.

APPLYING FOR FINANCIAL AID **Required financial aid forms:** FAFSA, verification documents/tax returns (if needed and requested). **Financial aid deadline (priority):** 3/1. **Notification date:** Continuous beginning 3/1. Students must reply by 8/1.

CONTACT Mrs. Jayne Schreck, Director of Financial Aid, Monmouth College, 700 East Broadway, Monmouth, IL 61462-1998, 309-457-2129 or toll-free 800-747-2687. *Fax:* 309-457-2373. *E-mail:* jayne@monm.edu.

MONMOUTH UNIVERSITY
West Long Branch, NJ

Tuition & fees: $25,013	Average undergraduate aid package: $17,601

ABOUT THE INSTITUTION Independent, coed. 33 undergraduate majors. Federal methodology is used as a basis for awarding need-based institutional aid.

UNDERGRADUATE EXPENSES for 2009–10 **One-time required fee:** $200. **Comprehensive fee:** $34,567 includes full-time tuition ($24,385), mandatory fees ($628), and room and board ($9554). **College room only:** $5436. Room and board charges vary according to board plan and housing facility. **Part-time tuition:** $706 per credit hour. **Part-time fees:** $157 per term. **Payment plan:** Installment.

FRESHMAN FINANCIAL AID (Fall 2009, est.) 878 applied for aid; of those 80% were deemed to have need. 100% of freshmen with need received aid; of those 5% had need fully met. **Average percent of need met:** 74% (excluding resources awarded to replace EFC). **Average financial aid package:** $18,930 (excluding resources awarded to replace EFC). 27% of all full-time freshmen had no need and received non-need-based gift aid.

UNDERGRADUATE FINANCIAL AID (Fall 2009, est.) 2,807 applied for aid; of those 100% were deemed to have need. 100% of undergraduates with need received aid; of those 7% had need fully met. **Average percent of need met:** 68% (excluding resources awarded to replace EFC). **Average financial aid package:** $17,601 (excluding resources awarded to replace EFC). 30% of all full-time undergraduates had no need and received non-need-based gift aid.

GIFT AID (NEED-BASED) **Total amount:** $13,889,603 (39% federal, 57% state, 4% institutional). **Receiving aid:** Freshmen: 30% (297); all full-time undergraduates: 26% (1,106). **Average award:** Freshmen: $12,972; Undergraduates: $12,348. **Scholarships, grants, and awards:** Federal Pell, FSEOG, state, private, college/university gift aid from institutional funds, Federal Nursing.

GIFT AID (NON-NEED-BASED) **Total amount:** $27,464,418 (1% federal, 96% institutional, 3% external sources). **Receiving aid:** Freshmen: 70% (694). Undergraduates: 61% (2,656). **Average award:** Freshmen: $8269. Undergraduates: $6689. **Scholarships, grants, and awards by category:** Academic interests/achievement: 3,916 awards ($29,551,639 total): business, communication, computer science, education, general academic interests/achievements, health fields, humanities, international studies, mathematics, social sciences. Special achievements/activities: 3 awards ($3000 total): leadership. Special characteristics: 278 awards ($771,745 total): adult students, children and siblings of alumni, children of faculty/staff, children of public servants, first-generation college students, general special characteristics, international students, local/state students, members of minority groups, out-of-state students, previous college experience, veterans. **Tuition waivers:** Full or partial for employees or children of employees, senior citizens.

LOANS **Student loans:** $34,287,699 (30% need-based, 70% non-need-based). 73% of past graduating class borrowed through all loan programs. Average indebtedness per student: $25,000. **Average need-based loan:** Freshmen: $3444. Undergraduates: $4828. **Parent loans:** $6,545,133 (100% non-need-based). **Programs:** Federal Direct (Subsidized and Unsubsidized Stafford, PLUS), Perkins, state, college/university, alternative private loans.

WORK-STUDY **Federal work-study:** Total amount: $630,000; 602 jobs averaging $1653.

ATHLETIC AWARDS Total amount: $4,021,963 (100% non-need-based).

APPLYING FOR FINANCIAL AID **Required financial aid form:** FAFSA. **Financial aid deadline:** Continuous. **Notification date:** Continuous beginning 2/1. Students must reply within 2 weeks of notification.

CONTACT Ms. Claire Alasio, Associate Vice President for Enrollment Management, Monmouth University, 400 Cedar Avenue, West Long Branch, NJ 07764-1898, 732-571-3463 or toll-free 800-543-9671. *Fax:* 732-923-4791. *E-mail:* finaid@monmouth.edu.

MONROE COLLEGE
Bronx, NY

ABOUT THE INSTITUTION Proprietary, coed. 15 undergraduate majors.

GIFT AID (NEED-BASED) **Scholarships, grants, and awards:** Federal Pell, FSEOG, state, private, college/university gift aid from institutional funds.

LOANS **Programs:** Federal Direct (Subsidized and Unsubsidized Stafford, PLUS), FFEL (Subsidized and Unsubsidized Stafford, PLUS), state, college/university.

APPLYING FOR FINANCIAL AID *Required financial aid forms:* FAFSA, state aid form.

CONTACT Howard Leslie, Dean of Student Financial Services, Monroe College, 434 Main Street, New Rochelle, NY 10468, 718-817-8203 or toll-free 800-55MONROE. *Fax:* 718-365-2363. *E-mail:* hleslie@monroecollege.edu.

MONROE COLLEGE
New Rochelle, NY

Tuition & fees: $11,744	Average undergraduate aid package: $11,343

ABOUT THE INSTITUTION Proprietary, coed. 6 undergraduate majors. Federal methodology is used as a basis for awarding need-based institutional aid.

UNDERGRADUATE EXPENSES for 2009–10 *Comprehensive fee:* $19,684 includes full-time tuition ($10,944), mandatory fees ($800), and room and board ($7940). Full-time tuition and fees vary according to degree level and program. Room and board charges vary according to board plan. *Part-time tuition:* $456 per credit. *Part-time fees:* $200 per term. Part-time tuition and fees vary according to degree level and program. *Payment plan:* Installment.

FRESHMAN FINANCIAL AID (Fall 2008) 442 applied for aid; of those 99% were deemed to have need. 100% of freshmen with need received aid; of those 60% had need fully met. *Average percent of need met:* 86% (excluding resources awarded to replace EFC). *Average financial aid package:* $11,256 (excluding resources awarded to replace EFC).

UNDERGRADUATE FINANCIAL AID (Fall 2008) 1,838 applied for aid; of those 99% were deemed to have need. 100% of undergraduates with need received aid; of those 61% had need fully met. *Average percent of need met:* 89% (excluding resources awarded to replace EFC). *Average financial aid package:* $11,343 (excluding resources awarded to replace EFC).

GIFT AID (NEED-BASED) *Total amount:* $9,063,017 (64% federal, 32% state, 4% institutional). *Receiving aid:* Freshmen: 82% (426); all full-time undergraduates: 90% (1,783). *Average award:* Freshmen: $6200; Undergraduates: $6315. *Scholarships, grants, and awards:* Federal Pell, FSEOG, state, private, college/university gift aid from institutional funds, county scholarships.

GIFT AID (NON-NEED-BASED) *Total amount:* $431,226 (100% external sources). *Receiving aid:* Freshmen: 23% (117). Undergraduates: 38% (751). *Tuition waivers:* Full or partial for employees or children of employees.

LOANS *Student loans:* $2,886,825 (100% need-based). 82% of past graduating class borrowed through all loan programs. *Average indebtedness per student:* $25,913. *Average need-based loan:* Freshmen: $2850. Undergraduates: $4725. *Parent loans:* $2,024,229 (100% need-based). *Programs:* Federal Direct (Subsidized and Unsubsidized Stafford, PLUS), FFEL (Subsidized and Unsubsidized Stafford, PLUS), state, college/university.

WORK-STUDY *Federal work-study:* Total amount: $194,355; 47 jobs averaging $2206.

ATHLETIC AWARDS Total amount: $233,295 (100% non-need-based).

APPLYING FOR FINANCIAL AID *Required financial aid forms:* FAFSA, state aid form. *Financial aid deadline:* Continuous. *Notification date:* Continuous beginning 3/1.

CONTACT James Gathard, Vice President, Student Financial Services, Monroe College, 2501 Jerome Avenue, Bronx, NY 10468, 718-933-6700 Ext. 8236 or toll-free 800-55MONROE. *Fax:* 718-365-2365. *E-mail:* hleslie@monroecollege.edu.

MONTANA STATE UNIVERSITY
Bozeman, MT

Tuition & fees (MT res): $5988	Average undergraduate aid package: $10,268

ABOUT THE INSTITUTION State-supported, coed. 58 undergraduate majors. Federal methodology is used as a basis for awarding need-based institutional aid.

UNDERGRADUATE EXPENSES for 2009–10 *Tuition, state resident:* full-time $5988. *Tuition, nonresident:* full-time $17,651. Full-time tuition and fees vary according to course load and degree level. Part-time tuition and fees vary according to course load and degree level. Room and board charges vary according to board plan and housing facility. *Payment plans:* Installment, deferred payment.

FRESHMAN FINANCIAL AID (Fall 2008) 1,207 applied for aid; of those 72% were deemed to have need. 97% of freshmen with need received aid; of those

8% had need fully met. *Average percent of need met:* 74% (excluding resources awarded to replace EFC). *Average financial aid package:* $10,635 (excluding resources awarded to replace EFC). 5% of all full-time freshmen had no need and received non-need-based gift aid.

UNDERGRADUATE FINANCIAL AID (Fall 2008) 5,593 applied for aid; of those 79% were deemed to have need. 97% of undergraduates with need received aid; of those 4% had need fully met. *Average percent of need met:* 72% (excluding resources awarded to replace EFC). *Average financial aid package:* $10,268 (excluding resources awarded to replace EFC). 4% of all full-time undergraduates had no need and received non-need-based gift aid.

GIFT AID (NEED-BASED) *Total amount:* $15,214,712 (60% federal, 7% state, 10% institutional, 23% external sources). *Receiving aid:* Freshmen: 36% (635); all full-time undergraduates: 33% (2,932). *Average award:* Freshmen: $4836; Undergraduates: $4530. *Scholarships, grants, and awards:* Federal Pell, FSEOG, state, private, college/university gift aid from institutional funds, Federal Nursing.

GIFT AID (NON-NEED-BASED) *Total amount:* $4,239,016 (4% state, 27% institutional, 69% external sources). *Receiving aid:* Freshmen: 3% (54). Undergraduates: 1% (119). *Average award:* Freshmen: $1949. Undergraduates: $2039. *Scholarships, grants, and awards by category:* Academic interests/achievement: agriculture, architecture, area/ethnic studies, biological sciences, business, communication, computer science, education, engineering/technologies, English, foreign languages, general academic interests/achievements, health fields, home economics, humanities, mathematics, military science, physical sciences, social sciences. Creative arts/performance: art/fine arts, cinema/film/broadcasting, dance, music, theater/drama. Special achievements/activities: general special achievements/activities, leadership. Special characteristics: children and siblings of alumni, general special characteristics, local/state students, members of minority groups. *Tuition waivers:* Full or partial for minority students, employees or children of employees, senior citizens.

LOANS *Student loans:* $37,105,018 (74% need-based, 26% non-need-based). 64% of past graduating class borrowed through all loan programs. *Average indebtedness per student:* $21,571. *Average need-based loan:* Freshmen: $3854. Undergraduates: $4422. *Parent loans:* $8,283,638 (30% need-based, 70% non-need-based). *Programs:* FFEL (Subsidized and Unsubsidized Stafford, PLUS), Perkins, Federal Nursing, college/university.

WORK-STUDY *Federal work-study:* Total amount: $463,486; jobs available. *State or other work-study/employment:* Total amount: $263,263 (100% need-based). Part-time jobs available.

ATHLETIC AWARDS Total amount: $1,335,461 (30% need-based, 70% non-need-based).

APPLYING FOR FINANCIAL AID *Required financial aid form:* FAFSA. *Financial aid deadline (priority):* 3/1. *Notification date:* Continuous beginning 4/1.

CONTACT Brandi Payne, Director of Financial Aid, Montana State University, Bozeman, MT 59717, 406-994-2845 or toll-free 888-MSU-CATS. *Fax:* 406-994-1893. *E-mail:* bpayne@montana.edu.

MONTANA STATE UNIVERSITY BILLINGS
Billings, MT

Tuition & fees (MT res): $5207	Average undergraduate aid package: $8806

ABOUT THE INSTITUTION State-supported, coed. 71 undergraduate majors. Federal methodology is used as a basis for awarding need-based institutional aid.

UNDERGRADUATE EXPENSES for 2009–10 *Tuition, state resident:* full-time $3988; part-time $144 per credit hour. *Tuition, nonresident:* full-time $14,648; part-time $407 per credit hour. *Required fees:* full-time $1219. Full-time tuition and fees vary according to course load, degree level, and location. Part-time tuition and fees vary according to course load, degree level, and location. *College room and board:* $5460. Room and board charges vary according to board plan and housing facility. *Payment plan:* Installment.

FRESHMAN FINANCIAL AID (Fall 2009, est.) 533 applied for aid; of those 79% were deemed to have need. 96% of freshmen with need received aid; of those 4% had need fully met. *Average percent of need met:* 67% (excluding resources awarded to replace EFC). *Average financial aid package:* $8055 (excluding resources awarded to replace EFC). 3% of all full-time freshmen had no need and received non-need-based gift aid.

UNDERGRADUATE FINANCIAL AID (Fall 2009, est.) 2,276 applied for aid; of those 82% were deemed to have need. 95% of undergraduates with need received aid; of those 3% had need fully met. *Average percent of need met:* 68% (excluding resources awarded to replace EFC). *Average financial aid*

package: $8806 (excluding resources awarded to replace EFC). 3% of all full-time undergraduates had no need and received non-need-based gift aid.

GIFT AID (NEED-BASED) *Total amount:* $7,115,567 (66% federal, 7% state, 18% institutional, 9% external sources). *Receiving aid:* Freshmen: 47% (320); all full-time undergraduates: 45% (1,359). *Average award:* Freshmen: $4044; Undergraduates: $4392. *Scholarships, grants, and awards:* Federal Pell, FSEOG, state, private, college/university gift aid from institutional funds.

GIFT AID (NON-NEED-BASED) *Total amount:* $425,915 (12% state, 48% institutional, 40% external sources). *Receiving aid:* Freshmen: 2% (12). Undergraduates: 1% (39). *Average award:* Freshmen: $2069. Undergraduates: $2071. *Scholarships, grants, and awards by category: Academic interests/ achievement:* biological sciences, business, communication, computer science, education, engineering/technologies, English, general academic interests/ achievements, health fields, humanities, mathematics, physical sciences, premedicine, social sciences. *Creative arts/performance:* art/fine arts, music, theater/drama. *Special achievements/activities:* cheerleading/drum major, general special achievements/activities. *Special characteristics:* adult students, children and siblings of alumni, children of faculty/staff, children of union members/ company employees, ethnic background, first-generation college students, local/ state students, members of minority groups, out-of-state students, veterans. *Tuition waivers:* Full or partial for employees or children of employees, senior citizens.

LOANS *Student loans:* $18,141,337 (55% need-based, 45% non-need-based). 73% of past graduating class borrowed through all loan programs. *Average indebtedness per student:* $23,189. *Average need-based loan:* Freshmen: $2850. Undergraduates: $3500. *Parent loans:* $760,460 (26% need-based, 74% non-need-based). *Programs:* FFEL (Subsidized and Unsubsidized Stafford, PLUS), Perkins, college/university.

WORK-STUDY *Federal work-study:* Total amount: $254,603; 206 jobs averaging $1236. *State or other work-study/employment:* Total amount: $105,172 (96% need-based, 4% non-need-based). 67 part-time jobs averaging $1570.

ATHLETIC AWARDS Total amount: $1,099,279 (61% need-based, 39% non-need-based).

APPLYING FOR FINANCIAL AID *Required financial aid form:* FAFSA. *Financial aid deadline (priority):* 3/1. *Notification date:* Continuous beginning 4/1. Students must reply within 3 weeks of notification.

CONTACT Ms. Judy Chapman, Director of Financial Aid, Montana State University Billings, 1500 University Drive, Billings, MT 59101, 406-657-2188 or toll-free 800-565-6782. *Fax:* 406-657-1789. *E-mail:* jchapman@msubillings.edu.

MONTANA STATE UNIVERSITY–NORTHERN
Havre, MT

Tuition & fees: N/R	Average undergraduate aid package: $9395

ABOUT THE INSTITUTION State-supported, coed. *Awards:* associate, bachelor's, and master's degrees. 27 undergraduate majors. *Total enrollment:* 1,215. Undergraduates: 1,143. Federal methodology is used as a basis for awarding need-based institutional aid.

FRESHMAN FINANCIAL AID (Fall 2008) 182 applied for aid; of those 85% were deemed to have need. 99% of freshmen with need received aid; of those 4% had need fully met. *Average percent of need met:* 61% (excluding resources awarded to replace EFC). *Average financial aid package:* $7700 (excluding resources awarded to replace EFC).

UNDERGRADUATE FINANCIAL AID (Fall 2008) 750 applied for aid; of those 90% were deemed to have need. 99% of undergraduates with need received aid; of those 3% had need fully met. *Average percent of need met:* 61% (excluding resources awarded to replace EFC). *Average financial aid package:* $9395 (excluding resources awarded to replace EFC).

GIFT AID (NEED-BASED) *Total amount:* $2,761,572 (68% federal, 11% state, 1% institutional, 20% external sources). *Receiving aid:* Freshmen: 68% (136); all full-time undergraduates: 65% (580). *Average award:* Freshmen: $3854; Undergraduates: $4186. *Scholarships, grants, and awards:* Federal Pell, FSEOG, state, private, college/university gift aid from institutional funds.

GIFT AID (NON-NEED-BASED) *Total amount:* $189,918 (2% state, 98% external sources). *Receiving aid:* Freshmen: 2% (4). Undergraduates: 1% (9). *Scholarships, grants, and awards by category: Academic interests/achievement:* agriculture, architecture, biological sciences, business, computer science, education, engineering/technologies, English, foreign languages, general academic interests/achievements, health fields, humanities, social sciences. *Creative arts/ performance:* art/fine arts. *Special achievements/activities:* community service,

general special achievements/activities, hobbies/interests, memberships, rodeo. *Special characteristics:* adult students, children and siblings of alumni, general special characteristics, international students, members of minority groups, out-of-state students, veterans.

LOANS *Student loans:* $3,585,295 (85% need-based, 15% non-need-based). 79% of past graduating class borrowed through all loan programs. *Average indebtedness per student:* $24,671. *Average need-based loan:* Freshmen: $2868. Undergraduates: $3811. *Parent loans:* $139,051 (38% need-based, 62% non-need-based). *Programs:* FFEL (Subsidized and Unsubsidized Stafford, PLUS), Perkins, Federal Nursing, college/university, alternative loans.

WORK-STUDY *Federal work-study:* Total amount: $87,593; jobs available. *State or other work-study/employment:* Total amount: $121,916 (100% need-based). Part-time jobs available.

ATHLETIC AWARDS Total amount: $194,483 (57% need-based, 43% non-need-based).

APPLYING FOR FINANCIAL AID *Required financial aid form:* FAFSA. *Financial aid deadline (priority):* 4/15. *Notification date:* Continuous beginning 4/1. Students must reply within 3 weeks of notification.

CONTACT Cindy Small, Director of Financial Aid, Montana State University– Northern, PO Box 7751, Havre, MT 59501, 406-265-3787 or toll-free 800-662-6132 (in-state).

MONTANA TECH OF THE UNIVERSITY OF MONTANA
Butte, MT

Tuition & fees (MT res): $6007	Average undergraduate aid package: $9086

ABOUT THE INSTITUTION State-supported, coed. 36 undergraduate majors. Federal methodology is used as a basis for awarding need-based institutional aid.

UNDERGRADUATE EXPENSES for 2009–10 *Tuition, state resident:* full-time $4696; part-time $195.65 per credit. *Tuition, nonresident:* full-time $15,510; part-time $646.25 per credit. *Required fees:* full-time $1311. Full-time tuition and fees vary according to course load, degree level, location, and program. Part-time tuition and fees vary according to course load, degree level, location, and program. *College room and board:* $6602; *Room only:* $2788. Room and board charges vary according to board plan. *Payment plans:* Installment, deferred payment.

FRESHMAN FINANCIAL AID (Fall 2009, est.) 382 applied for aid; of those 73% were deemed to have need. 100% of freshmen with need received aid; of those 28% had need fully met. *Average percent of need met:* 74% (excluding resources awarded to replace EFC). *Average financial aid package:* $8100 (excluding resources awarded to replace EFC). 18% of all full-time freshmen had no need and received non-need-based gift aid.

UNDERGRADUATE FINANCIAL AID (Fall 2009, est.) 1,333 applied for aid; of those 77% were deemed to have need. 100% of undergraduates with need received aid; of those 28% had need fully met. *Average percent of need met:* 76% (excluding resources awarded to replace EFC). *Average financial aid package:* $9086 (excluding resources awarded to replace EFC). 14% of all full-time undergraduates had no need and received non-need-based gift aid.

GIFT AID (NEED-BASED) *Total amount:* $4,207,924 (61% federal, 8% state, 21% institutional, 10% external sources). *Receiving aid:* Freshmen: 53% (256); all full-time undergraduates: 48% (908). *Average award:* Freshmen: $4690; Undergraduates: $4425. *Scholarships, grants, and awards:* Federal Pell, FSEOG, state, private, college/university gift aid from institutional funds.

GIFT AID (NON-NEED-BASED) *Total amount:* $1,231,666 (1% federal, 6% state, 72% institutional, 21% external sources). *Receiving aid:* Freshmen: 5% (23). Undergraduates: 3% (65). *Average award:* Freshmen: $2687. Undergraduates: $2862. *Scholarships, grants, and awards by category: Academic interests/ achievement:* business, computer science, engineering/technologies, general academic interests/achievements, health fields, mathematics, physical sciences. *Special achievements/activities:* community service, general special achievements/ activities. *Special characteristics:* children and siblings of alumni, children of faculty/staff, general special characteristics, local/state students, married students, out-of-state students, veterans. *Tuition waivers:* Full or partial for employees or children of employees.

LOANS *Student loans:* $6,803,468 (76% need-based, 24% non-need-based). 85% of past graduating class borrowed through all loan programs. *Average indebtedness per student:* $23,000. *Average need-based loan:* Freshmen: $3024.

Montana Tech of The University of Montana

Undergraduates: $3699. *Parent loans:* $486,338 (22% need-based, 78% non-need-based). *Programs:* FFEL (Subsidized and Unsubsidized Stafford, PLUS), Perkins, college/university.

WORK-STUDY *Federal work-study:* Total amount: $82,906; 52 jobs averaging $2500. *State or other work-study/employment:* Total amount: $3437 (100% need-based). 2 part-time jobs averaging $2500.

ATHLETIC AWARDS Total amount: $705,351 (26% need-based, 74% non-need-based).

APPLYING FOR FINANCIAL AID *Required financial aid forms:* FAFSA, institution's own form. *Financial aid deadline (priority):* 3/1. *Notification date:* Continuous beginning 4/1. Students must reply within 2 weeks of notification.

CONTACT Mike Richardson, Director of Financial Aid, Montana Tech of The University of Montana, West Park Street, Butte, MT 59701-8997, 406-496-4256 or toll-free 800-445-TECH Ext. 1. *Fax:* 406-496-4710. *E-mail:* mrichardson@mtech.edu.

MONTCLAIR STATE UNIVERSITY
Montclair, NJ

Tuition & fees (NJ res): $7042	Average undergraduate aid package: $9153

ABOUT THE INSTITUTION State-supported, coed. 53 undergraduate majors. Federal methodology is used as a basis for awarding need-based institutional aid.

UNDERGRADUATE EXPENSES for 2010–11 *Tuition, state resident:* full-time $7042; part-time $234.73 per credit. Room and board charges vary according to board plan and housing facility. *Payment plan:* Installment.

FRESHMAN FINANCIAL AID (Fall 2009, est.) 1,801 applied for aid; of those 82% were deemed to have need. 96% of freshmen with need received aid; of those 24% had need fully met. *Average percent of need met:* 58% (excluding resources awarded to replace EFC). *Average financial aid package:* $8988 (excluding resources awarded to replace EFC). 3% of all full-time freshmen had no need and received non-need-based gift aid.

UNDERGRADUATE FINANCIAL AID (Fall 2009, est.) 8,878 applied for aid; of those 86% were deemed to have need. 97% of undergraduates with need received aid; of those 25% had need fully met. *Average percent of need met:* 60% (excluding resources awarded to replace EFC). *Average financial aid package:* $9153 (excluding resources awarded to replace EFC). 2% of all full-time undergraduates had no need and received non-need-based gift aid.

GIFT AID (NEED-BASED) *Total amount:* $35,581,908 (53% federal, 47% state). *Receiving aid:* Freshmen: 37% (767); all full-time undergraduates: 35% (4,105). *Average award:* Freshmen: $3046; Undergraduates: $3573. *Scholarships, grants, and awards:* Federal Pell, FSEOG, state, college/university gift aid from institutional funds.

GIFT AID (NON-NEED-BASED) *Total amount:* $6,559,773 (13% state, 74% institutional, 13% external sources). *Receiving aid:* Freshmen: 14% (291). Undergraduates: 8% (953). *Average award:* Freshmen: $6863. Undergraduates: $6473. *Scholarships, grants, and awards by category: Academic interests/achievement:* 799 awards ($3,678,206 total): biological sciences, business, communication, education, English, foreign languages, general academic interests/achievements, home economics, humanities, international studies, mathematics, physical sciences, religion/biblical studies, social sciences. *Creative arts/performance:* 128 awards ($212,474 total): art/fine arts, cinema/film/broadcasting, dance, music, performing arts, theater/drama. *Special achievements/activities:* 30 awards ($23,406 total): community service, general special achievements/activities, leadership. *Special characteristics:* 18 awards ($61,372 total): children and siblings of alumni, international students. *Tuition waivers:* Full or partial for employees or children of employees, senior citizens.

LOANS *Student loans:* $76,554,040 (39% need-based, 61% non-need-based). 77% of past graduating class borrowed through all loan programs. *Average indebtedness per student:* $24,226. *Average need-based loan:* Freshmen: $3219. Undergraduates: $4154. *Parent loans:* $7,759,259 (100% non-need-based). *Programs:* FFEL (Subsidized and Unsubsidized Stafford, PLUS), Perkins, state, private loans.

WORK-STUDY *Federal work-study:* Total amount: $698,546; 555 jobs averaging $1383. *State or other work-study/employment:* Total amount: $2,880,297 (100% non-need-based). 1,485 part-time jobs averaging $1940.

APPLYING FOR FINANCIAL AID *Required financial aid form:* FAFSA. *Financial aid deadline (priority):* 3/1. *Notification date:* Continuous beginning 4/1. Students must reply within 2 weeks of notification.

CONTACT James T. Anderson, Director of Financial Aid, Montclair State University, College Hall, Room 222, Montclair, NJ 07043, 973-655-7022 or toll-free 800-331-9205. *Fax:* 973-655-7712. *E-mail:* cuozzof@mail.montclair.edu.

MONTREAT COLLEGE
Montreat, NC

Tuition & fees: N/R	Average undergraduate aid package: $12,337

ABOUT THE INSTITUTION Independent religious, coed. 14 undergraduate majors. Federal methodology is used as a basis for awarding need-based institutional aid.

FRESHMAN FINANCIAL AID (Fall 2009, est.) 116 applied for aid; of those 90% were deemed to have need. 100% of freshmen with need received aid; of those 12% had need fully met. *Average percent of need met:* 69% (excluding resources awarded to replace EFC). *Average financial aid package:* $16,157 (excluding resources awarded to replace EFC). 13% of all full-time freshmen had no need and received non-need-based gift aid.

UNDERGRADUATE FINANCIAL AID (Fall 2009, est.) 880 applied for aid; of those 90% were deemed to have need. 100% of undergraduates with need received aid; of those 19% had need fully met. *Average percent of need met:* 66% (excluding resources awarded to replace EFC). *Average financial aid package:* $12,337 (excluding resources awarded to replace EFC). 7% of all full-time undergraduates had no need and received non-need-based gift aid.

GIFT AID (NEED-BASED) *Total amount:* $5,539,526 (28% federal, 27% state, 36% institutional, 9% external sources). *Receiving aid:* Freshmen: 84% (101); all full-time undergraduates: 84% (763). *Average award:* Freshmen: $12,955; Undergraduates: $8571. *Scholarships, grants, and awards:* Federal Pell, FSEOG, state, private, college/university gift aid from institutional funds.

GIFT AID (NON-NEED-BASED) *Total amount:* $787,737 (16% state, 69% institutional, 15% external sources). *Receiving aid:* Freshmen: 4% (5). Undergraduates: 8% (74). *Average award:* Freshmen: $6173. Undergraduates: $8132. *Scholarships, grants, and awards by category: Academic interests/achievement:* 430 awards ($2,532,516 total): general academic interests/achievements. *Creative arts/performance:* 10 awards ($15,000 total): music. *Special achievements/activities:* 75 awards ($75,000 total): leadership. *Special characteristics:* 300 awards ($1,061,894 total): children of faculty/staff, first-generation college students, international students, local/state students, relatives of clergy, religious affiliation, veterans, veterans' children. *Tuition waivers:* Full or partial for employees or children of employees.

LOANS *Student loans:* $6,787,643 (72% need-based, 28% non-need-based). 82% of past graduating class borrowed through all loan programs. *Average indebtedness per student:* $19,295. *Average need-based loan:* Freshmen: $3152. Undergraduates: $4183. *Parent loans:* $340,362 (55% need-based, 45% non-need-based). *Programs:* Federal Direct (Subsidized and Unsubsidized Stafford, PLUS), Perkins.

WORK-STUDY *Federal work-study:* Total amount: $117,000; 85 jobs averaging $1800. *State or other work-study/employment:* Total amount: $79,335 (11% need-based, 89% non-need-based). 50 part-time jobs averaging $1800.

ATHLETIC AWARDS Total amount: $648,551 (74% need-based, 26% non-need-based).

APPLYING FOR FINANCIAL AID *Required financial aid forms:* FAFSA, state aid form. *Financial aid deadline (priority):* 4/1. *Notification date:* Continuous beginning 4/1. Students must reply within 2 weeks of notification.

CONTACT Beth Pocock, Financial Aid Office, Montreat College, PO Box 1267, Montreat, NC 28757, 828-669-8012 Ext. 3790 or toll-free 800-622-6968 (in-state). *Fax:* 828-669-0120. *E-mail:* financialaid@montreat.edu.

MONTSERRAT COLLEGE OF ART
Beverly, MA

CONTACT Creda Carney, Director of Financial Aid, Montserrat College of Art, 23 Essex Street, PO Box 26, Beverly, MA 01915, 978-922-8222 Ext. 1155 or toll-free 800-836-0487. *Fax:* 978-922-4268. *E-mail:* finaid@montserrat.edu.

MOODY BIBLE INSTITUTE
Chicago, IL

Tuition & fees: $1275	Average undergraduate aid package: N/A

ABOUT THE INSTITUTION Independent nondenominational, coed. 8 undergraduate majors. Institutional methodology is used as a basis for awarding need-based institutional aid.

UNDERGRADUATE EXPENSES for 2010–11 includes mandatory fees ($1275) and room and board ($8240). *College room only:* $4810. Full-time tuition and fees vary according to course load and degree level. Room and board charges vary according to board plan, housing facility, and location. Part-time tuition and fees vary according to course load and degree level. the college meets all of the tuition cost for each student. *Payment plan:* Installment.

GIFT AID (NEED-BASED) *Scholarships, grants, and awards:* private, college/university gift aid from institutional funds.

GIFT AID (NON-NEED-BASED) *Tuition waivers:* Full or partial for employees or children of employees.

LOANS *Programs:* alternative loans.

APPLYING FOR FINANCIAL AID *Required financial aid form:* institution's own form. *Financial aid deadline:* Continuous.

CONTACT Esther Kim, Director of Financial Aid, Moody Bible Institute, 820 North LaSalle Boulevard, Chicago, IL 60610-3284, 312-329-4178 or toll-free 800-967-4MBI. *Fax:* 312-329-4197. *E-mail:* esther.kim@moody.edu.

MOORE COLLEGE OF ART & DESIGN
Philadelphia, PA

CONTACT Kristina Fripps, Director of Financial Aid, Moore College of Art & Design, 20th and the Parkway, Philadelphia, PA 19103-1179, 215-965-4042 or toll-free 800-523-2025. *Fax:* 215-568-1773. *E-mail:* kfripps@moore.edu.

MORAVIAN COLLEGE
Bethlehem, PA

Tuition & fees: $32,177	Average undergraduate aid package: $23,421

ABOUT THE INSTITUTION Independent religious, coed. 61 undergraduate majors. Both federal and institutional methodology are used as a basis for awarding need-based institutional aid.

UNDERGRADUATE EXPENSES for 2010–11 *Comprehensive fee:* $41,341 includes full-time tuition ($31,662), mandatory fees ($515), and room and board ($9164). *College room only:* $5149. Room and board charges vary according to board plan and housing facility. *Part-time tuition:* $853.75 per credit hour. Part-time tuition and fees vary according to class time. *Payment plan:* Installment.

FRESHMAN FINANCIAL AID (Fall 2009, est.) 355 applied for aid; of those 90% were deemed to have need. 100% of freshmen with need received aid; of those 12% had need fully met. *Average percent of need met:* 80% (excluding resources awarded to replace EFC). *Average financial aid package:* $25,954 (excluding resources awarded to replace EFC). 14% of all full-time freshmen had no need and received non-need-based gift aid.

UNDERGRADUATE FINANCIAL AID (Fall 2009, est.) 1,336 applied for aid; of those 91% were deemed to have need. 100% of undergraduates with need received aid; of those 13% had need fully met. *Average percent of need met:* 79% (excluding resources awarded to replace EFC). *Average financial aid package:* $23,421 (excluding resources awarded to replace EFC). 14% of all full-time undergraduates had no need and received non-need-based gift aid.

GIFT AID (NEED-BASED) *Total amount:* $20,655,353 (10% federal, 9% state, 79% institutional, 2% external sources). *Receiving aid:* Freshmen: 84% (319); all full-time undergraduates: 78% (1,195). *Average award:* Freshmen: $20,141; Undergraduates: $17,584. *Scholarships, grants, and awards:* Federal Pell, FSEOG, state, private, college/university gift aid from institutional funds.

GIFT AID (NON-NEED-BASED) *Total amount:* $2,727,395 (3% federal, 1% state, 89% institutional, 7% external sources). *Receiving aid:* Freshmen: 6% (24). Undergraduates: 6% (87). *Average award:* Freshmen: $10,194. Undergraduates: $9240. *Scholarships, grants, and awards by category:* Academic interests/achievement: 733 awards ($8,996,000 total): biological sciences, business, computer science, foreign languages, general academic interests/achievements, health fields, mathematics, physical sciences. *Creative arts/performance:* 13 awards ($21,200 total): music. *Special achievements/activities:* 74 awards ($119,700 total): leadership, religious involvement. *Special characteristics:* 392 awards ($2,234,051 total): adult students, children and siblings of alumni,

---

children of educators, children of faculty/staff, ethnic background, international students, relatives of clergy, religious affiliation. *Tuition waivers:* Full or partial for employees or children of employees.

LOANS *Student loans:* $13,673,330 (69% need-based, 31% non-need-based). *Average need-based loan:* Freshmen: $4148. Undergraduates: $4706. *Parent loans:* $3,657,351 (38% need-based, 62% non-need-based). *Programs:* FFEL (Subsidized and Unsubsidized Stafford, PLUS), Perkins.

WORK-STUDY *Federal work-study:* Total amount: $1,961,950; 1,035 jobs averaging $1888. *State or other work-study/employment:* Total amount: $301,800 (12% need-based, 88% non-need-based). 252 part-time jobs averaging $1223.

APPLYING FOR FINANCIAL AID *Required financial aid forms:* FAFSA, institution's own form, state aid form, business/farm supplement. *Financial aid deadline (priority):* 2/14. *Notification date:* 3/31. Students must reply by 5/1 or within 2 weeks of notification.

CONTACT Mr. Stephen C. Cassel, Director of Financial Aid, Moravian College, 1200 Main Street, Bethlehem, PA 18018-6650, 610-861-1330 or toll-free 800-441-3191. *Fax:* 610-861-1346. *E-mail:* cassels@moravian.edu.

MOREHEAD STATE UNIVERSITY
Morehead, KY

Tuition & fees (KY res): $6036	Average undergraduate aid package: $9447

ABOUT THE INSTITUTION State-supported, coed. 48 undergraduate majors. Federal methodology is used as a basis for awarding need-based institutional aid.

UNDERGRADUATE EXPENSES for 2009–10 *Tuition, state resident:* full-time $6036; part-time $234 per credit hour. *Tuition, nonresident:* full-time $15,096; part-time $585 per credit hour. Full-time tuition and fees vary according to course load and reciprocity agreements. *College room and board:* $6192. Room and board charges vary according to board plan and housing facility. *Payment plans:* Installment, deferred payment.

FRESHMAN FINANCIAL AID (Fall 2009, est.) 1,139 applied for aid; of those 81% were deemed to have need. 99% of freshmen with need received aid; of those 33% had need fully met. *Average percent of need met:* 76% (excluding resources awarded to replace EFC). *Average financial aid package:* $9432 (excluding resources awarded to replace EFC). 12% of all full-time freshmen had no need and received non-need-based gift aid.

UNDERGRADUATE FINANCIAL AID (Fall 2009, est.) 4,674 applied for aid; of those 85% were deemed to have need. 98% of undergraduates with need received aid; of those 38% had need fully met. *Average percent of need met:* 74% (excluding resources awarded to replace EFC). *Average financial aid package:* $9447 (excluding resources awarded to replace EFC). 13% of all full-time undergraduates had no need and received non-need-based gift aid.

GIFT AID (NEED-BASED) *Total amount:* $15,832,917 (85% federal, 14% state, 1% institutional). *Receiving aid:* Freshmen: 48% (599); all full-time undergraduates: 48% (2,671). *Average award:* Freshmen: $5602; Undergraduates: $5224. *Scholarships, grants, and awards:* Federal Pell, FSEOG, state, private, college/university gift aid from institutional funds.

GIFT AID (NON-NEED-BASED) *Total amount:* $16,971,689 (26% state, 66% institutional, 8% external sources). *Receiving aid:* Freshmen: 66% (814). Undergraduates: 41% (2,294). *Average award:* Freshmen: $5782. Undergraduates: $6526. *Scholarships, grants, and awards by category:* Academic interests/achievement: 1,109 awards ($6,684,753 total): agriculture, biological sciences, business, communication, education, engineering/technologies, general academic interests/achievements, health fields, international studies, military science, physical sciences, social sciences. *Creative arts/performance:* 131 awards ($183,409 total): debating, journalism/publications, music, theater/drama. *Special achievements/activities:* 88 awards ($103,450 total): cheerleading/drum major, general special achievements/activities, junior miss, leadership. *Special characteristics:* 957 awards ($4,357,593 total): children and siblings of alumni, international students, local/state students, members of minority groups, out-of-state students. *Tuition waivers:* Full or partial for children of alumni, employees or children of employees, senior citizens.

LOANS *Student loans:* $25,497,982 (45% need-based, 55% non-need-based). 69% of past graduating class borrowed through all loan programs. *Average indebtedness per student:* $24,045. *Average need-based loan:* Freshmen: $2813. Undergraduates: $3657. *Parent loans:* $1,635,618 (100% non-need-based). *Programs:* Federal Direct (Subsidized and Unsubsidized Stafford, PLUS), FFEL (Subsidized and Unsubsidized Stafford, PLUS), Perkins, college/university.

WORK-STUDY *Federal work-study:* Total amount: $1,252,358; 623 jobs averaging $1888. *State or other work-study/employment:* Total amount: $1,444,882 (100% non-need-based). 688 part-time jobs averaging $2079.

ATHLETIC AWARDS Total amount: $1,680,196 (100% non-need-based).

APPLYING FOR FINANCIAL AID *Required financial aid forms:* FAFSA, institution's own form. *Financial aid deadline (priority):* 3/15. *Notification date:* Continuous.

CONTACT Donna King, Director of Financial Aid, Morehead State University, 100 Admissions Center, Morehead, KY 40351, 606-783-2000 or toll-free 800-585-6781. *Fax:* 606-783-2293. *E-mail:* d.king@moreheadstate.edu.

MOREHOUSE COLLEGE
Atlanta, GA

Tuition & fees: $21,376	Average undergraduate aid package: $12,425

ABOUT THE INSTITUTION Independent, men only. 26 undergraduate majors. Both federal and institutional methodology are used as a basis for awarding need-based institutional aid.

UNDERGRADUATE EXPENSES for 2009–10 *Comprehensive fee:* $32,322 includes full-time tuition ($19,424), mandatory fees ($1952), and room and board ($10,946). *College room only:* $6238. Full-time tuition and fees vary according to course load and student level. Room and board charges vary according to board plan. *Part-time tuition:* $809 per credit hour. *Part-time fees:* $976 per term. Part-time tuition and fees vary according to course load.

FRESHMAN FINANCIAL AID (Fall 2009, est.) 624 applied for aid; of those 100% were deemed to have need. 100% of freshmen with need received aid; of those 9% had need fully met. *Average percent of need met:* 29% (excluding resources awarded to replace EFC). *Average financial aid package:* $10,925 (excluding resources awarded to replace EFC).

UNDERGRADUATE FINANCIAL AID (Fall 2009, est.) 2,442 applied for aid; of those 100% were deemed to have need. 100% of undergraduates with need received aid; of those 8% had need fully met. *Average percent of need met:* 64% (excluding resources awarded to replace EFC). *Average financial aid package:* $12,425 (excluding resources awarded to replace EFC).

GIFT AID (NEED-BASED) *Total amount:* $6,019,641 (98% federal, 2% state). *Receiving aid:* Freshmen: 49% (313); all full-time undergraduates: 45% (1,120). *Average award:* Freshmen: $7600; Undergraduates: $10,850. *Scholarships, grants, and awards:* Federal Pell, FSEOG, state, private, college/university gift aid from institutional funds, United Negro College Fund.

GIFT AID (NON-NEED-BASED) *Total amount:* $13,675,389 (8% state, 81% institutional, 11% external sources). *Receiving aid:* Freshmen: 26% (164). Undergraduates: 22% (562). *Scholarships, grants, and awards by category:* Academic interests/achievement: business, general academic interests/achievements, military science. Creative arts/performance: art/fine arts, music. Special achievements/activities: community service, leadership, religious involvement. Special characteristics: children and siblings of alumni, children of faculty/staff, local/state students. *Tuition waivers:* Full or partial for employees or children of employees.

LOANS *Student loans:* $21,003,601 (75% need-based, 25% non-need-based). 90% of past graduating class borrowed through all loan programs. *Average indebtedness per student:* $32,125. *Average need-based loan:* Freshmen: $3500. Undergraduates: $5500. *Parent loans:* $19,153,579 (100% non-need-based). *Programs:* Federal Direct (Subsidized and Unsubsidized Stafford, PLUS), FFEL (Subsidized and Unsubsidized Stafford, PLUS), Perkins, state, college/university.

WORK-STUDY *Federal work-study:* Total amount: $530,151; jobs available. *State or other work-study/employment:* Total amount: $118,637 (100% non-need-based). Part-time jobs available.

ATHLETIC AWARDS Total amount: $1,495,289 (100% non-need-based).

APPLYING FOR FINANCIAL AID *Required financial aid forms:* FAFSA, institution's own form, CSS Financial Aid PROFILE, state aid form. *Financial aid deadline:* 4/1 (priority: 2/15). *Notification date:* Continuous beginning 3/18. Students must reply by 5/1 or within 4 weeks of notification.

CONTACT James A. Stotts, Director of Financial Aid, Morehouse College, 830 Westview Drive, SW, Atlanta, GA 30314, 404-681-2800 Ext. 2638 or toll-free 800-851-1254. *Fax:* 404-215-2711. *E-mail:* jstotts@morehouse.edu.

MORGAN STATE UNIVERSITY
Baltimore, MD

CONTACT Director of Financial Aid, Morgan State University, 1700 East Cold Spring Lane, Baltimore, MD 21251, 443-885-3170 or toll-free 800-332-6674.

MORNINGSIDE COLLEGE
Sioux City, IA

Tuition & fees: $22,980	Average undergraduate aid package: $18,517

ABOUT THE INSTITUTION Independent religious, coed. 45 undergraduate majors. Federal methodology is used as a basis for awarding need-based institutional aid.

UNDERGRADUATE EXPENSES for 2010–11 *Comprehensive fee:* $30,020 includes full-time tuition ($21,810), mandatory fees ($1170), and room and board ($7040). *College room only:* $3610. Full-time tuition and fees vary according to degree level, program, and student level. Room and board charges vary according to housing facility. Part-time tuition and fees vary according to course load and degree level. *Payment plan:* Installment.

FRESHMAN FINANCIAL AID (Fall 2009, est.) 313 applied for aid; of those 90% were deemed to have need. 100% of freshmen with need received aid; of those 30% had need fully met. *Average percent of need met:* 85% (excluding resources awarded to replace EFC). *Average financial aid package:* $19,430 (excluding resources awarded to replace EFC). 13% of all full-time freshmen had no need and received non-need-based gift aid.

UNDERGRADUATE FINANCIAL AID (Fall 2009, est.) 1,126 applied for aid; of those 92% were deemed to have need. 100% of undergraduates with need received aid; of those 28% had need fully met. *Average percent of need met:* 81% (excluding resources awarded to replace EFC). *Average financial aid package:* $18,517 (excluding resources awarded to replace EFC). 14% of all full-time undergraduates had no need and received non-need-based gift aid.

GIFT AID (NEED-BASED) *Total amount:* $5,310,996 (44% federal, 34% state, 22% institutional). *Receiving aid:* Freshmen: 72% (233); all full-time undergraduates: 65% (784). *Average award:* Freshmen: $6673; Undergraduates: $6774. *Scholarships, grants, and awards:* Federal Pell, FSEOG, state, private, college/university gift aid from institutional funds.

GIFT AID (NON-NEED-BASED) *Total amount:* $9,035,667 (1% federal, 2% state, 91% institutional, 6% external sources). *Receiving aid:* Freshmen: 87% (283). Undergraduates: 84% (1,006). *Average award:* Freshmen: $12,395. Undergraduates: $10,903. *Scholarships, grants, and awards by category:* Academic interests/achievement: $3,878,288 total: computer science, general academic interests/achievements. Creative arts/performance: $1,349,025 total: art/fine arts, cinema/film/broadcasting, creative writing, dance, journalism/publications, music, theater/drama. Special achievements/activities: $825,583 total: cheerleading/drum major, community service, leadership. Special characteristics: $1,798,818 total: children and siblings of alumni, children of faculty/staff, international students, out-of-state students, religious affiliation. *Tuition waivers:* Full or partial for children of alumni, employees or children of employees, senior citizens.

LOANS *Student loans:* $9,536,853 (42% need-based, 58% non-need-based). 89% of past graduating class borrowed through all loan programs. *Average indebtedness per student:* $37,479. *Average need-based loan:* Freshmen: $3930. Undergraduates: $4665. *Parent loans:* $1,064,891 (100% non-need-based). *Programs:* FFEL (Subsidized and Unsubsidized Stafford, PLUS), Perkins, state, college/university, private loans.

WORK-STUDY *Federal work-study:* Total amount: $820,308; 601 jobs averaging $1365. *State or other work-study/employment:* Total amount: $515,123 (100% non-need-based). 339 part-time jobs averaging $1520.

ATHLETIC AWARDS Total amount: $1,773,210 (100% non-need-based).

APPLYING FOR FINANCIAL AID *Required financial aid form:* FAFSA. *Financial aid deadline (priority):* 3/1. *Notification date:* 3/31.

CONTACT Karen Gagnon, Director of Student Financial Planning, Morningside College, 1501 Morningside Avenue, Sioux City, IA 51106, 712-274-5272 or toll-free 800-831-0806 Ext. 5111. *Fax:* 712-274-5605. *E-mail:* gagnon@morningside.edu.

MORRIS COLLEGE
Sumter, SC

CONTACT Ms. Sandra S. Gibson, Director of Financial Aid, Morris College, 100 West College Street, Sumter, SC 29150-3599, 803-934-3238 or toll-free 866-853-1345. *Fax:* 803-773-3687.

MORRISON UNIVERSITY
Reno, NV

CONTACT Kim Droniak, Financial Aid Administrator, Morrison University, 140 Washington Street, Reno, NV 89503-5600, 775-850-0700 or toll-free 800-369-6144. *Fax:* 775-850-0711.

MOUNTAIN STATE UNIVERSITY
Beckley, WV

Tuition & fees: $8700	Average undergraduate aid package: $7033

ABOUT THE INSTITUTION Independent, coed. 39 undergraduate majors. Federal methodology is used as a basis for awarding need-based institutional aid.

UNDERGRADUATE EXPENSES for 2010–11 *Comprehensive fee:* $14,816 includes full-time tuition ($6450), mandatory fees ($2250), and room and board ($6116). *College room only:* $3000. Full-time tuition and fees vary according to course load, degree level, location, and program. Room and board charges vary according to board plan. *Part-time tuition:* $215 per credit hour. *Part-time fees:* $75 per credit hour. Part-time tuition and fees vary according to course load, degree level, location, and program. *Payment plan:* Installment.

FRESHMAN FINANCIAL AID (Fall 2009, est.) 210 applied for aid; of those 93% were deemed to have need. 100% of freshmen with need received aid; of those 100% had need fully met. *Average percent of need met:* 39% (excluding resources awarded to replace EFC). *Average financial aid package:* $5651 (excluding resources awarded to replace EFC).

UNDERGRADUATE FINANCIAL AID (Fall 2009, est.) 2,052 applied for aid; of those 91% were deemed to have need. 100% of undergraduates with need received aid; of those 100% had need fully met. *Average percent of need met:* 48% (excluding resources awarded to replace EFC). *Average financial aid package:* $7033 (excluding resources awarded to replace EFC). 1% of all full-time undergraduates had no need and received non-need-based gift aid.

GIFT AID (NEED-BASED) *Total amount:* $7,242,282 (79% federal, 18% state, 1% institutional, 2% external sources). *Receiving aid:* Freshmen: 26% (149); all full-time undergraduates: 35% (1,294). *Average award:* Freshmen: $3915; Undergraduates: $4211. *Scholarships, grants, and awards:* Federal Pell, FSEOG, state, private, college/university gift aid from institutional funds, Federal Nursing.

GIFT AID (NON-NEED-BASED) *Total amount:* $334,920 (57% state, 43% institutional). *Receiving aid:* Freshmen: 1% (5). Undergraduates: 18. *Average award:* Undergraduates: $4214. *Scholarships, grants, and awards by category:* Academic interests/achievement: 32 awards ($149,100 total): general academic interests/achievements. *Special achievements/activities:* 10 awards ($8990 total): cheerleading/drum major. *Tuition waivers:* Full or partial for employees or children of employees, senior citizens.

LOANS *Student loans:* $26,760,491 (40% need-based, 60% non-need-based). 81% of past graduating class borrowed through all loan programs. *Average indebtedness per student:* $33,218. *Average need-based loan:* Freshmen: $2982. Undergraduates: $4592. *Parent loans:* $278,324 (100% non-need-based). *Programs:* FFEL (Subsidized and Unsubsidized Stafford, PLUS), private educational loans.

WORK-STUDY *Federal work-study:* Total amount: $199,197; 100 jobs averaging $1819.

ATHLETIC AWARDS Total amount: $413,723 (100% non-need-based).

APPLYING FOR FINANCIAL AID *Required financial aid form:* FAFSA. *Financial aid deadline:* Continuous. *Notification date:* Continuous beginning 4/1. Students must reply within 2 weeks of notification.

CONTACT Lynn Whitteker, Director of Financial Aid, Mountain State University, PO Box 9003, Beckley, WV 25802-9003, 304-929-1595 or toll-free 800-766-6067 Ext. 1433. *Fax:* 304-929-1390. *E-mail:* lwhitteker@mountainstate.edu.

MOUNT ALOYSIUS COLLEGE
Cresson, PA

Tuition & fees: $17,280	Average undergraduate aid package: $11,300

ABOUT THE INSTITUTION Independent Roman Catholic, coed. 25 undergraduate majors. Federal methodology is used as a basis for awarding need-based institutional aid.

UNDERGRADUATE EXPENSES for 2009–10 *Comprehensive fee:* $24,580 includes full-time tuition ($16,580), mandatory fees ($700), and room and board ($7300). *College room only:* $3750. *Part-time tuition:* $480 per credit. *Part-time fees:* $185 per term.

FRESHMAN FINANCIAL AID (Fall 2009, est.) 349 applied for aid; of those 94% were deemed to have need. 100% of freshmen with need received aid. *Average percent of need met:* 30% (excluding resources awarded to replace EFC). *Average financial aid package:* $14,980 (excluding resources awarded to replace EFC). 6% of all full-time freshmen had no need and received non-need-based gift aid.

UNDERGRADUATE FINANCIAL AID (Fall 2009, est.) 1,113 applied for aid; of those 97% were deemed to have need. 100% of undergraduates with need received aid. *Average percent of need met:* 35% (excluding resources awarded to replace EFC). *Average financial aid package:* $11,300 (excluding resources awarded to replace EFC). 3% of all full-time undergraduates had no need and received non-need-based gift aid.

GIFT AID (NEED-BASED) *Total amount:* $10,349,217 (30% federal, 24% state, 45% institutional, 1% external sources). *Receiving aid:* Freshmen: 94% (328); all full-time undergraduates: 97% (1,080). *Average award:* Freshmen: $2890; Undergraduates: $2000. *Scholarships, grants, and awards:* Federal Pell, FSEOG, state, private, college/university gift aid from institutional funds.

GIFT AID (NON-NEED-BASED) *Receiving aid:* Freshmen: 6% (21). Undergraduates: 3% (33). *Average award:* Freshmen: $3860. Undergraduates: $3500. *Scholarships, grants, and awards by category:* Academic interests/achievement: 1,145 awards ($2,932,093 total): general academic interests/achievements. Creative arts/performance: 20 awards ($17,500 total): music, performing arts. Special achievements/activities: 58 awards ($536,000 total): leadership. Special characteristics: 92 awards ($67,000 total): children of current students, parents of current students, religious affiliation, siblings of current students, spouses of current students, twins.

LOANS *Student loans:* $9,672,919 (100% need-based). 80% of past graduating class borrowed through all loan programs. *Average indebtedness per student:* $29,802. *Average need-based loan:* Freshmen: $3470. Undergraduates: $3400. *Parent loans:* $2,287,291 (100% need-based). *Programs:* Federal Direct (Subsidized and Unsubsidized Stafford, PLUS), FFEL (Subsidized and Unsubsidized Stafford, PLUS), Perkins, Federal Nursing, alternative loans.

WORK-STUDY *Federal work-study:* Total amount: $190,234; 223 jobs averaging $1030.

APPLYING FOR FINANCIAL AID *Required financial aid form:* FAFSA. *Financial aid deadline (priority):* 2/15. *Notification date:* Continuous beginning 3/15. Students must reply within 2 weeks of notification.

CONTACT Mrs. Stacy L. Schenk, Director of Financial Aid, Mount Aloysius College, 7373 Admiral Peary Highway, Cresson, PA 16630-1900, 814-886-6357 or toll-free 888-823-2220. *Fax:* 814-886-6463. *E-mail:* sschenk@mtaloy.edu.

MOUNT ANGEL SEMINARY
Saint Benedict, OR

CONTACT Dorene Preis, Director of Student Financial Aid/Registrar, Mount Angel Seminary, 1 Abbey Drive, Saint Benedict, OR 97373, 503-845-3951. *Fax:* 503-845-3126. *E-mail:* dpreis@mtangel.edu.

MOUNT CARMEL COLLEGE OF NURSING
Columbus, OH

CONTACT Carol Graham, Director of Financial Aid, Mount Carmel College of Nursing, 127 South Davis Avenue, Columbus, OH 43222, 614-234-5800 Ext. 5177. *E-mail:* cgraham@mchs.com.

MOUNT HOLYOKE COLLEGE
South Hadley, MA

Tuition & fees: $39,126	Average undergraduate aid package: $33,399

ABOUT THE INSTITUTION Independent, women only. 50 undergraduate majors. Institutional methodology is used as a basis for awarding need-based institutional aid.

UNDERGRADUATE EXPENSES for 2009–10 *Comprehensive fee:* $50,576 includes full-time tuition ($38,940), mandatory fees ($186), and room and board ($11,450). *College room only:* $5610. Full-time tuition and fees vary according to reciprocity agreements. *Part-time tuition:* $1220 per credit hour. Part-time tuition and fees vary according to reciprocity agreements. *Payment plans:* Tuition prepayment, installment.

FRESHMAN FINANCIAL AID (Fall 2009, est.) 469 applied for aid; of those 86% were deemed to have need. 100% of freshmen with need received aid; of those 100% had need fully met. *Average percent of need met:* 100% (excluding resources awarded to replace EFC). *Average financial aid package:* $35,797 (excluding resources awarded to replace EFC). 12% of all full-time freshmen had no need and received non-need-based gift aid.

UNDERGRADUATE FINANCIAL AID (Fall 2009, est.) 1,777 applied for aid; of those 91% were deemed to have need. 100% of undergraduates with need received aid; of those 100% had need fully met. *Average percent of need met:* 100% (excluding resources awarded to replace EFC). *Average financial aid package:* $33,399 (excluding resources awarded to replace EFC). 7% of all full-time undergraduates had no need and received non-need-based gift aid.

GIFT AID (NEED-BASED) *Total amount:* $43,713,686 (6% federal, 1% state, 91% institutional, 2% external sources). *Receiving aid:* Freshmen: 71% (397); all full-time undergraduates: 65% (1,542). *Average award:* Freshmen: $31,435; Undergraduates: $28,578. *Scholarships, grants, and awards:* Federal Pell, FSEOG, state, private, college/university gift aid from institutional funds.

GIFT AID (NON-NEED-BASED) *Total amount:* $3,782,959 (86% institutional, 14% external sources). *Average award:* Freshmen: $16,858. Undergraduates: $16,023. *Scholarships, grants, and awards by category:* Academic interests/ achievement: 201 awards ($3,171,360 total): general academic interests/ achievements. *Tuition waivers:* Full or partial for employees or children of employees.

LOANS *Student loans:* $9,615,353 (87% need-based, 13% non-need-based). 61% of past graduating class borrowed through all loan programs. *Average indebtedness per student:* $23,008. *Average need-based loan:* Freshmen: $3250. Undergraduates: $4675. *Parent loans:* $6,171,154 (100% non-need-based). *Programs:* Federal Direct (Subsidized and Unsubsidized Stafford, PLUS), Perkins, college/university.

WORK-STUDY *Federal work-study:* Total amount: $1,779,404; 886 jobs averaging $1863. *State or other work-study/employment:* Total amount: $787,302 (100% need-based). 402 part-time jobs averaging $1945.

APPLYING FOR FINANCIAL AID *Required financial aid forms:* FAFSA, CSS Financial Aid PROFILE, noncustodial (divorced/separated) parent's statement, federal tax returns and W-2 forms. *Financial aid deadline:* 3/1 (priority: 2/15). *Notification date:* 4/1. Students must reply by 5/1.

CONTACT Ms. Kathryn Blaisdell, Director of Student Financial Services, Mount Holyoke College, 50 College Street, South Hadley, MA 01075-1492, 413-538-2291. *Fax:* 413-538-2512. *E-mail:* kblaisde@mtholyoke.edu.

MOUNT IDA COLLEGE
Newton, MA

Tuition & fees: $24,500	Average undergraduate aid package: $15,105

ABOUT THE INSTITUTION Independent, coed. 22 undergraduate majors. Federal methodology is used as a basis for awarding need-based institutional aid.

UNDERGRADUATE EXPENSES for 2010–11 *Comprehensive fee:* $36,500 includes full-time tuition ($24,250), mandatory fees ($250), and room and board ($12,000). Part-time tuition and fees vary according to course load. *Payment plan:* Installment.

FRESHMAN FINANCIAL AID (Fall 2009, est.) 422 applied for aid; of those 92% were deemed to have need. 100% of freshmen with need received aid; of those 7% had need fully met. *Average percent of need met:* 63% (excluding resources awarded to replace EFC). *Average financial aid package:* $16,446 (excluding resources awarded to replace EFC). 21% of all full-time freshmen had no need and received non-need-based gift aid.

UNDERGRADUATE FINANCIAL AID (Fall 2009, est.) 1,231 applied for aid; of those 90% were deemed to have need. 100% of undergraduates with need received aid; of those 7% had need fully met. *Average percent of need met:* 58% (excluding resources awarded to replace EFC). *Average financial aid package:* $15,105 (excluding resources awarded to replace EFC). 17% of all full-time undergraduates had no need and received non-need-based gift aid.

GIFT AID (NEED-BASED) *Total amount:* $12,299,101 (19% federal, 5% state, 73% institutional, 3% external sources). *Receiving aid:* Freshmen: 74% (381); all full-time undergraduates: 78% (1,075). *Average award:* Freshmen: $13,379; Undergraduates: $11,328. *Scholarships, grants, and awards:* Federal Pell, FSEOG, state, private, college/university gift aid from institutional funds.

GIFT AID (NON-NEED-BASED) *Total amount:* $1,284,126 (4% state, 91% institutional, 5% external sources). *Receiving aid:* Freshmen: 4% (21). Undergraduates: 4% (52). *Average award:* Freshmen: $5017. *Scholarships, grants, and awards by category:* Creative arts/performance: 51 awards ($60,500 total): applied art and design, art/fine arts, general creative arts/performance. *Special achievements/activities:* 947 awards ($4,199,482 total): community service, general special achievements/activities, leadership. *Tuition waivers:* Full or partial for employees or children of employees.

LOANS *Student loans:* $12,504,001 (75% need-based, 25% non-need-based). 89% of past graduating class borrowed through all loan programs. *Average indebtedness per student:* $43,911. *Average need-based loan:* Freshmen: $3213. Undergraduates: $4063. *Parent loans:* $4,477,271 (46% need-based, 54% non-need-based). *Programs:* FFEL (Subsidized and Unsubsidized Stafford, PLUS), state, alternative loans.

WORK-STUDY *Federal work-study:* Total amount: $286,162; jobs available. *State or other work-study/employment:* Total amount: $61,354 (9% need-based, 91% non-need-based). Part-time jobs available.

ATHLETIC AWARDS Total amount: $512 (100% non-need-based).

APPLYING FOR FINANCIAL AID *Required financial aid form:* FAFSA. *Financial aid deadline (priority):* 5/1. *Notification date:* Continuous.

CONTACT David L. Goldman, Director of Financial Aid, Mount Ida College, 777 Dedham Street, Newton, MA 02459-3310, 617-928-4785. *Fax:* 617-332-7869. *E-mail:* finaid@mountida.edu.

MOUNT MARTY COLLEGE
Yankton, SD

Tuition & fees: $18,908	Average undergraduate aid package: $8937

ABOUT THE INSTITUTION Independent Roman Catholic, coed. 32 undergraduate majors. Federal methodology is used as a basis for awarding need-based institutional aid.

UNDERGRADUATE EXPENSES for 2009–10 *Comprehensive fee:* $24,274 includes full-time tuition ($17,078), mandatory fees ($1830), and room and board ($5366). Full-time tuition and fees vary according to location. Room and board charges vary according to board plan. *Part-time tuition:* $199 per credit hour. *Part-time fees:* $25 per credit hour. Part-time tuition and fees vary according to course load and location. *Payment plan:* Installment.

FRESHMAN FINANCIAL AID (Fall 2009, est.) 102 applied for aid; of those 90% were deemed to have need. 100% of freshmen with need received aid; of those 47% had need fully met. *Average percent of need met:* 84% (excluding resources awarded to replace EFC). *Average financial aid package:* $21,223 (excluding resources awarded to replace EFC). 11% of all full-time freshmen had no need and received non-need-based gift aid.

UNDERGRADUATE FINANCIAL AID (Fall 2009, est.) 554 applied for aid; of those 94% were deemed to have need. 100% of undergraduates with need received aid; of those 52% had need fully met. *Average percent of need met:* 89% (excluding resources awarded to replace EFC). *Average financial aid package:* $8937 (excluding resources awarded to replace EFC). 8% of all full-time undergraduates had no need and received non-need-based gift aid.

GIFT AID (NEED-BASED) *Total amount:* $4,745,508 (37% federal, 1% state, 58% institutional, 4% external sources). *Receiving aid:* Freshmen: 88% (92); all full-time undergraduates: 90% (522). *Average award:* Freshmen: $9781; Undergraduates: $7508. *Scholarships, grants, and awards:* Federal Pell, FSEOG, state, private, college/university gift aid from institutional funds.

GIFT AID (NON-NEED-BASED) *Total amount:* $187,150 (2% state, 95% institutional, 3% external sources). *Receiving aid:* Freshmen: 10% (11). Undergraduates: 6% (32). *Average award:* Freshmen: $17,137. Undergraduates: $14,147. *Scholarships, grants, and awards by category:* Academic interests/achievement: 477 awards ($2,862,295 total): general academic interests/achievements. Creative arts/performance: 62 awards ($64,745 total): music, theater/drama. Special characteristics: children of current students, children of faculty/staff, international students, parents of current students, religious affiliation, siblings of current students, spouses of current students. *Tuition waivers:* Full or partial for employees or children of employees.

LOANS *Student loans:* $3,049,373 (98% need-based, 2% non-need-based). 79% of past graduating class borrowed through all loan programs. *Average indebtedness per student:* $22,699. *Average need-based loan:* Freshmen: $4288. Undergraduates: $5168. *Parent loans:* $568,159 (90% need-based, 10% non-need-based). *Programs:* Federal Direct (Subsidized and Unsubsidized Stafford, PLUS), FFEL (Subsidized and Unsubsidized Stafford, PLUS), Perkins, Federal Nursing.

WORK-STUDY *Federal work-study:* Total amount: $303,084; 217 jobs averaging $1397. *State or other work-study/employment:* Total amount: $79,575 (75% need-based, 25% non-need-based). 57 part-time jobs averaging $1396.

ATHLETIC AWARDS Total amount: $635,111 (86% need-based, 14% non-need-based).

APPLYING FOR FINANCIAL AID *Required financial aid forms:* FAFSA, institution's own form. *Financial aid deadline (priority):* 3/1. *Notification date:* Continuous beginning 3/15. Students must reply within 2 weeks of notification.

CONTACT Mr. Ken Kocer, Director of Financial Assistance, Mount Marty College, 1105 West 8th Street, Yankton, SD 57078-3724, 605-668-1589 or toll-free 800-658-4552. *Fax:* 605-668-1585. *E-mail:* kkocer@mtmc.edu.

MOUNT MARY COLLEGE
Milwaukee, WI

Tuition & fees: $22,118	Average undergraduate aid package: $16,152

ABOUT THE INSTITUTION Independent Roman Catholic, undergraduate: women only; graduate: coed. 49 undergraduate majors. Federal methodology is used as a basis for awarding need-based institutional aid.

UNDERGRADUATE EXPENSES for 2010–11 *Comprehensive fee:* $29,616 includes full-time tuition ($21,668), mandatory fees ($450), and room and board ($7498). Full-time tuition and fees vary according to degree level and program. Room and board charges vary according to board plan. *Part-time tuition:* $648 per credit hour. *Part-time fees:* $120 per term. Part-time tuition and fees vary according to course load, degree level, and program. *Payment plan:* Installment.

FRESHMAN FINANCIAL AID (Fall 2009, est.) 149 applied for aid; of those 97% were deemed to have need. 100% of freshmen with need received aid; of those 6% had need fully met. *Average percent of need met:* 76% (excluding resources awarded to replace EFC). *Average financial aid package:* $19,419 (excluding resources awarded to replace EFC). 15% of all full-time freshmen had no need and received non-need-based gift aid.

UNDERGRADUATE FINANCIAL AID (Fall 2009, est.) 861 applied for aid; of those 91% were deemed to have need. 100% of undergraduates with need received aid; of those 8% had need fully met. *Average percent of need met:* 68% (excluding resources awarded to replace EFC). *Average financial aid package:* $16,152 (excluding resources awarded to replace EFC). 13% of all full-time undergraduates had no need and received non-need-based gift aid.

GIFT AID (NEED-BASED) *Total amount:* $10,001,543 (28% federal, 15% state, 56% institutional, 1% external sources). *Receiving aid:* Freshmen: 91% (144); all full-time undergraduates: 85% (779). *Average award:* Freshmen: $15,491; Undergraduates: $11,566. *Scholarships, grants, and awards:* Federal Pell, FSEOG, state, private, college/university gift aid from institutional funds, Metropolitan Milwaukee Association of Commerce Awards.

GIFT AID (NON-NEED-BASED) *Total amount:* $840,355 (99% institutional, 1% external sources). *Receiving aid:* Freshmen: 4% (6). Undergraduates: 4% (41). *Average award:* Freshmen: $8445. Undergraduates: $5355. *Scholarships, grants, and awards by category:* Academic interests/achievement: 356 awards ($1,338,418 total): business, communication, education, English, general academic interests/achievements, health fields, home economics, humanities, mathematics, physical sciences, social sciences. Creative arts/performance: 18 awards ($15,750 total): applied art and design, art/fine arts, music. Special achievements/activities: 7 awards ($49,657 total): general special achievements/

activities, leadership. Special characteristics: 13 awards ($170,766 total): children of faculty/staff, international students, parents of current students, siblings of current students. *Tuition waivers:* Full or partial for employees or children of employees, senior citizens.

LOANS *Student loans:* $10,705,070 (82% need-based, 18% non-need-based). 86% of past graduating class borrowed through all loan programs. *Average indebtedness per student:* $21,414. *Average need-based loan:* Freshmen: $3304. Undergraduates: $4495. *Parent loans:* $513,449 (25% need-based, 75% non-need-based). *Programs:* FFEL (Subsidized and Unsubsidized Stafford, PLUS), Perkins, state.

WORK-STUDY *Federal work-study:* Total amount: $158,948; 150 jobs averaging $1235. *State or other work-study/employment:* Total amount: $155,000 (100% non-need-based). 40 part-time jobs averaging $1254.

APPLYING FOR FINANCIAL AID *Required financial aid form:* FAFSA. *Financial aid deadline (priority):* 3/1. *Notification date:* Continuous. Students must reply within 2 weeks of notification.

CONTACT Debra Duff, Director of Financial Aid, Mount Mary College, 2900 North Menomonee River Parkway, Milwaukee, WI 53222-4597, 414-256-1258. *Fax:* 414-443-3602. *E-mail:* finaid@mtmary.edu.

MOUNT MERCY COLLEGE
Cedar Rapids, IA

Tuition & fees: $22,100	Average undergraduate aid package: $16,094

ABOUT THE INSTITUTION Independent Roman Catholic, coed. 49 undergraduate majors. Federal methodology is used as a basis for awarding need-based institutional aid.

UNDERGRADUATE EXPENSES for 2009–10 *Comprehensive fee:* $29,084 includes full-time tuition ($22,100) and room and board ($6984). Full-time tuition and fees vary according to course load. Room and board charges vary according to board plan and housing facility. *Part-time tuition:* $610 per credit hour. Part-time tuition and fees vary according to course load. *Payment plan:* Installment.

FRESHMAN FINANCIAL AID (Fall 2009, est.) 139 applied for aid; of those 89% were deemed to have need. 100% of freshmen with need received aid; of those 22% had need fully met. *Average percent of need met:* 80% (excluding resources awarded to replace EFC). *Average financial aid package:* $18,647 (excluding resources awarded to replace EFC). 18% of all full-time freshmen had no need and received non-need-based gift aid.

UNDERGRADUATE FINANCIAL AID (Fall 2009, est.) 994 applied for aid; of those 91% were deemed to have need. 99% of undergraduates with need received aid; of those 19% had need fully met. *Average percent of need met:* 72% (excluding resources awarded to replace EFC). *Average financial aid package:* $16,094 (excluding resources awarded to replace EFC). 14% of all full-time undergraduates had no need and received non-need-based gift aid.

GIFT AID (NEED-BASED) *Total amount:* $10,537,964 (18% federal, 21% state, 59% institutional, 2% external sources). *Receiving aid:* Freshmen: 82% (124); all full-time undergraduates: 81% (867). *Average award:* Freshmen: $13,992; Undergraduates: $11,589. *Scholarships, grants, and awards:* Federal Pell, FSEOG, state, private, college/university gift aid from institutional funds.

GIFT AID (NON-NEED-BASED) *Total amount:* $1,724,083 (1% state, 94% institutional, 5% external sources). *Receiving aid:* Freshmen: 14% (21). Undergraduates: 10% (110). *Average award:* Freshmen: $10,380. Undergraduates: $8107. *Scholarships, grants, and awards by category:* Academic interests/achievement: 1,094 awards ($6,230,829 total): general academic interests/achievements. Creative arts/performance: 32 awards ($37,635 total): art/fine arts, music, theater/drama. Special achievements/activities: 172 awards ($161,817 total): leadership. Special characteristics: 19 awards ($12,375 total): previous college experience. *Tuition waivers:* Full or partial for employees or children of employees.

LOANS *Student loans:* $10,376,016 (73% need-based, 27% non-need-based). 94% of past graduating class borrowed through all loan programs. *Average indebtedness per student:* $30,233. *Average need-based loan:* Freshmen: $4211. Undergraduates: $4952. *Parent loans:* $1,460,836 (45% need-based, 55% non-need-based). *Programs:* Federal Direct (Subsidized and Unsubsidized Stafford, PLUS), Perkins, state, college/university.

WORK-STUDY *Federal work-study:* Total amount: $414,296; 272 jobs averaging $1850. *State or other work-study/employment:* Total amount: $344,149 (20% need-based, 80% non-need-based). 125 part-time jobs averaging $1974.

ATHLETIC AWARDS Total amount: $676,689 (63% need-based, 37% non-need-based).

APPLYING FOR FINANCIAL AID *Required financial aid form:* FAFSA. *Financial aid deadline (priority):* 3/1. *Notification date:* Continuous beginning 3/15. Students must reply by 5/1 or within 3 weeks of notification.

CONTACT Bethany Rinderknecht, Director of Financial Aid, Mount Mercy College, 1330 Elmhurst Drive NE, Cedar Rapids, IA 52402-4797, 319-368-6467 Ext. 1545 or toll-free 800-248-4504. *Fax:* 319-364-3546. *E-mail:* brinderknecht@mtmercy.edu.

MOUNT OLIVE COLLEGE
Mount Olive, NC

Tuition & fees: $13,776	Average undergraduate aid package: $8887

ABOUT THE INSTITUTION Independent Free Will Baptist, coed. 22 undergraduate majors. Federal methodology is used as a basis for awarding need-based institutional aid.

UNDERGRADUATE EXPENSES for 2009–10 *Comprehensive fee:* $19,316 includes full-time tuition ($13,776) and room and board ($5540). *College room only:* $2300. *Part-time tuition:* $310 per credit hour.

FRESHMAN FINANCIAL AID (Fall 2008) 331 applied for aid; of those 85% were deemed to have need. 97% of freshmen with need received aid; of those 15% had need fully met. *Average percent of need met:* 72% (excluding resources awarded to replace EFC). *Average financial aid package:* $11,324 (excluding resources awarded to replace EFC). 1% of all full-time freshmen had no need and received non-need-based gift aid.

UNDERGRADUATE FINANCIAL AID (Fall 2008) 2,947 applied for aid; of those 85% were deemed to have need. 97% of undergraduates with need received aid; of those 15% had need fully met. *Average percent of need met:* 65% (excluding resources awarded to replace EFC). *Average financial aid package:* $8887 (excluding resources awarded to replace EFC). 1% of all full-time undergraduates had no need and received non-need-based gift aid.

GIFT AID (NEED-BASED) *Total amount:* $12,138,142 (36% federal, 58% state, 1% institutional, 5% external sources). *Receiving aid:* Freshmen: 82% (273); all full-time undergraduates: 79% (2,329). *Average award:* Freshmen: $8806; Undergraduates: $5815. *Scholarships, grants, and awards:* Federal Pell, FSEOG, state, private, college/university gift aid from institutional funds.

GIFT AID (NON-NEED-BASED) *Total amount:* $889,333 (2% federal, 64% state, 3% institutional, 31% external sources). *Receiving aid:* Freshmen: 4% (13). Undergraduates: 4% (108). *Average award:* Freshmen: $2187. Undergraduates: $2099. *Scholarships, grants, and awards by category: Academic interests/achievement:* general academic interests/achievements. *Creative arts/performance:* general creative arts/performance. *Special achievements/activities:* cheerleading/drum major, leadership, religious involvement. *Special characteristics:* children of faculty/staff, religious affiliation, veterans, veterans' children.

LOANS *Student loans:* $20,214,974 (70% need-based, 30% non-need-based). 93% of past graduating class borrowed through all loan programs. *Average indebtedness per student:* $16,117. *Average need-based loan:* Freshmen: $2846. Undergraduates: $3710. *Parent loans:* $301,165 (26% need-based, 74% non-need-based). *Programs:* Federal Direct (Subsidized and Unsubsidized Stafford, PLUS), FFEL (Subsidized and Unsubsidized Stafford, PLUS), Perkins, Federal Nursing, state.

WORK-STUDY *Federal work-study:* Total amount: $139,684; 160 jobs averaging $1169.

ATHLETIC AWARDS Total amount: $707,992 (68% need-based, 32% non-need-based).

APPLYING FOR FINANCIAL AID *Required financial aid forms:* FAFSA, state aid form. *Financial aid deadline:* Continuous. *Notification date:* Continuous beginning 2/14. Students must reply within 2 weeks of notification.

CONTACT Ms. Katrina K. Lee, Director of Financial Aid, Mount Olive College, 634 Henderson Street, Mount Olive, NC 28365, 919-658-7891 or toll-free 800-653-0854 (in-state). *Fax:* 919-658-9816. *E-mail:* klee@moc.edu.

MOUNT SAINT MARY COLLEGE
Newburgh, NY

Tuition & fees: $23,300	Average undergraduate aid package: $13,804

ABOUT THE INSTITUTION Independent, coed. 26 undergraduate majors. Federal methodology is used as a basis for awarding need-based institutional aid.

UNDERGRADUATE EXPENSES for 2010–11 *Comprehensive fee:* $35,200 includes full-time tuition ($22,350), mandatory fees ($950), and room and board ($11,900). *College room only:* $6900. Full-time tuition and fees vary according to class time, degree level, and location. Room and board charges vary according to board plan and housing facility. *Part-time tuition:* $745 per credit hour. *Part-time fees:* $70 per semester hour. Part-time tuition and fees vary according to class time, degree level, and location. *Payment plan:* Installment.

FRESHMAN FINANCIAL AID (Fall 2009, est.) 443 applied for aid; of those 82% were deemed to have need. 100% of freshmen with need received aid; of those 23% had need fully met. *Average percent of need met:* 66% (excluding resources awarded to replace EFC). *Average financial aid package:* $15,196 (excluding resources awarded to replace EFC). 17% of all full-time freshmen had no need and received non-need-based gift aid.

UNDERGRADUATE FINANCIAL AID (Fall 2009, est.) 1,676 applied for aid; of those 86% were deemed to have need. 99% of undergraduates with need received aid; of those 15% had need fully met. *Average percent of need met:* 58% (excluding resources awarded to replace EFC). *Average financial aid package:* $13,804 (excluding resources awarded to replace EFC). 12% of all full-time undergraduates had no need and received non-need-based gift aid.

GIFT AID (NEED-BASED) *Total amount:* $13,955,222 (25% federal, 16% state, 58% institutional, 1% external sources). *Receiving aid:* Freshmen: 76% (361); all full-time undergraduates: 73% (1,364). *Average award:* Freshmen: $11,818; Undergraduates: $10,089. *Scholarships, grants, and awards:* Federal Pell, FSEOG, state, private, college/university gift aid from institutional funds, Federal Nursing, Academic Competitiveness Grants, National SMART Grants.

GIFT AID (NON-NEED-BASED) *Total amount:* $2,432,696 (10% state, 85% institutional, 5% external sources). *Receiving aid:* Freshmen: 12% (55). Undergraduates: 7% (121). *Average award:* Freshmen: $7774. Undergraduates: $7667. *Scholarships, grants, and awards by category: Academic interests/achievement:* 817 awards ($5,689,700 total): general academic interests/achievements. *Special characteristics:* 38 awards ($619,324 total): children of faculty/staff. *Tuition waivers:* Full or partial for employees or children of employees.

LOANS *Student loans:* $19,261,452 (69% need-based, 31% non-need-based). 94% of past graduating class borrowed through all loan programs. *Average indebtedness per student:* $32,729. *Average need-based loan:* Freshmen: $3144. Undergraduates: $4171. *Parent loans:* $8,431,354 (31% need-based, 69% non-need-based). *Programs:* FFEL (Subsidized and Unsubsidized Stafford, PLUS), Federal Nursing.

WORK-STUDY *Federal work-study:* Total amount: $627,360; 386 jobs averaging $1255. *State or other work-study/employment:* Total amount: $4140 (100% need-based). Part-time jobs available.

APPLYING FOR FINANCIAL AID *Required financial aid form:* FAFSA. *Financial aid deadline:* 3/1 (priority: 2/15). *Notification date:* Continuous beginning 3/15. Students must reply by 5/1.

CONTACT Michelle Taylor, Director of Financial Aid, Mount Saint Mary College, 330 Powell Avenue, Newburgh, NY 12550-3494, 845-561-0800 or toll-free 888-937-6762. *Fax:* 845-569-3302. *E-mail:* taylor@msmc.edu.

MOUNT ST. MARY'S COLLEGE
Los Angeles, CA

Tuition & fees: $30,132	Average undergraduate aid package: $30,185

ABOUT THE INSTITUTION Independent Roman Catholic, coed. 29 undergraduate majors. Federal methodology is used as a basis for awarding need-based institutional aid.

UNDERGRADUATE EXPENSES for 2010–11 *Comprehensive fee:* $39,962 includes full-time tuition ($29,232), mandatory fees ($900), and room and board ($9830). Full-time tuition and fees vary according to degree level and program. Room and board charges vary according to board plan and housing facility. *Part-time tuition:* $1218 per unit. Part-time tuition and fees vary according to degree level and program. *Payment plan:* Installment.

FRESHMAN FINANCIAL AID (Fall 2009, est.) 398 applied for aid; of those 92% were deemed to have need. 100% of freshmen with need received aid; of those 7% had need fully met. *Average percent of need met:* 92% (excluding resources

awarded to replace EFC). *Average financial aid package:* $28,975 (excluding resources awarded to replace EFC). 2% of all full-time freshmen had no need and received non-need-based gift aid.

UNDERGRADUATE FINANCIAL AID (Fall 2009, est.) 1,387 applied for aid; of those 89% were deemed to have need. 100% of undergraduates with need received aid; of those 10% had need fully met. *Average percent of need met:* 93% (excluding resources awarded to replace EFC). *Average financial aid package:* $30,185 (excluding resources awarded to replace EFC). 2% of all full-time undergraduates had no need and received non-need-based gift aid.

GIFT AID (NEED-BASED) *Total amount:* $21,751,493 (19% federal, 23% state, 57% institutional, 1% external sources). *Receiving aid:* Freshmen: 85% (337); all full-time undergraduates: 60% (1,182). *Average award:* Freshmen: $1421; Undergraduates: $1701. *Scholarships, grants, and awards:* Federal Pell, FSEOG, state, private, college/university gift aid from institutional funds.

GIFT AID (NON-NEED-BASED) *Total amount:* $1,226,028 (100% institutional). *Receiving aid:* Freshmen: 92% (367). Undergraduates: 63% (1,238). *Average award:* Freshmen: $11,973. Undergraduates: $9821. *Scholarships, grants, and awards by category:* Academic interests/achievement: biological sciences, education, general academic interests/achievements. *Creative arts/performance:* music. *Special achievements/activities:* community service, leadership. *Special characteristics:* children and siblings of alumni. *Tuition waivers:* Full or partial for employees or children of employees.

LOANS *Student loans:* $23,275,381 (60% need-based, 40% non-need-based). 90% of past graduating class borrowed through all loan programs. *Average indebtedness per student:* $33,030. *Average need-based loan:* Freshmen: $3946. Undergraduates: $4451. *Parent loans:* $2,589,950 (100% non-need-based). *Programs:* FFEL (Subsidized and Unsubsidized Stafford, PLUS), Federal Nursing, college/university.

WORK-STUDY *Federal work-study:* Total amount: $445,414; jobs available. *State or other work-study/employment:* Total amount: $799,467 (100% need-based). Part-time jobs available.

APPLYING FOR FINANCIAL AID *Required financial aid forms:* FAFSA, institution's own form, state aid form. *Financial aid deadline (priority):* 2/15. *Notification date:* Continuous beginning 3/15. Students must reply by 5/1.

CONTACT La Royce Dodd, Financial Aid Director, Mount St. Mary's College, 12001 Chalon Road, Los Angeles, CA 90049, 310-954-4192 or toll-free 800-999-9893.

MOUNT ST. MARY'S UNIVERSITY
Emmitsburg, MD

Tuition & fees: $30,350	Average undergraduate aid package: $18,996

ABOUT THE INSTITUTION Independent Roman Catholic, coed. 28 undergraduate majors. Federal methodology is used as a basis for awarding need-based institutional aid.

UNDERGRADUATE EXPENSES for 2010–11 *Comprehensive fee:* $40,658 includes full-time tuition ($29,650), mandatory fees ($700), and room and board ($10,308). *College room only:* $5044. *Part-time tuition:* $990 per credit hour.

FRESHMAN FINANCIAL AID (Fall 2009, est.) 400 applied for aid; of those 86% were deemed to have need. 100% of freshmen with need received aid; of those 26% had need fully met. *Average percent of need met:* 76% (excluding resources awarded to replace EFC). *Average financial aid package:* $20,278 (excluding resources awarded to replace EFC). 24% of all full-time freshmen had no need and received non-need-based gift aid.

UNDERGRADUATE FINANCIAL AID (Fall 2009, est.) 1,173 applied for aid; of those 84% were deemed to have need. 100% of undergraduates with need received aid; of those 24% had need fully met. *Average percent of need met:* 72% (excluding resources awarded to replace EFC). *Average financial aid package:* $18,996 (excluding resources awarded to replace EFC). 32% of all full-time undergraduates had no need and received non-need-based gift aid.

GIFT AID (NEED-BASED) *Total amount:* $13,256,402 (11% federal, 8% state, 78% institutional, 3% external sources). *Receiving aid:* Freshmen: 74% (343); all full-time undergraduates: 65% (978). *Average award:* Freshmen: $16,102; Undergraduates: $14,784. *Scholarships, grants, and awards:* Federal Pell, FSEOG, state, private, college/university gift aid from institutional funds.

GIFT AID (NON-NEED-BASED) *Total amount:* $6,120,832 (9% federal, 1% state, 86% institutional, 4% external sources). *Receiving aid:* Freshmen: 15% (70). Undergraduates: 12% (184). *Average award:* Freshmen: $11,744. Undergraduates: $9586. *Scholarships, grants, and awards by category:*

Academic interests/achievement: 1,280 awards ($12,407,260 total): general academic interests/achievements. *Creative arts/performance:* 26 awards ($44,000 total): art/fine arts. *Special characteristics:* 283 awards ($1,089,900 total): children of educators, children of faculty/staff, members of minority groups, siblings of current students.

LOANS *Student loans:* $10,054,772 (60% need-based, 40% non-need-based). 67% of past graduating class borrowed through all loan programs. *Average indebtedness per student:* $26,160. *Average need-based loan:* Freshmen: $4150. Undergraduates: $4434. *Parent loans:* $3,856,835 (28% need-based, 72% non-need-based). *Programs:* FFEL (Subsidized and Unsubsidized Stafford, PLUS), Perkins.

WORK-STUDY *Federal work-study:* Total amount: $369,782; 216 jobs averaging $1700. *State or other work-study/employment:* Total amount: $370,145 (77% need-based, 23% non-need-based). 348 part-time jobs averaging $1000.

ATHLETIC AWARDS Total amount: $2,165,606 (44% need-based, 56% non-need-based).

APPLYING FOR FINANCIAL AID *Required financial aid forms:* FAFSA, institution's own form. *Financial aid deadline:* 3/1. *Notification date:* Continuous beginning 2/15. Students must reply by 5/1.

CONTACT Mr. David C. Reeder, Director of Financial Aid, Mount St. Mary's University, 16300 Old Emmitsburg Road, Emmitsburg, MD 21727-7799, 301-447-5207 or toll-free 800-448-4347. *Fax:* 301-447-5915. *E-mail:* reeder@msmary.edu.

MT. SIERRA COLLEGE
Monrovia, CA

CONTACT Financial Aid Office, Mt. Sierra College, 101 East Huntington Drive, Monrovia, CA 91016, 888-828-8800 or toll-free 888-828-8800.

MOUNT VERNON NAZARENE UNIVERSITY
Mount Vernon, OH

Tuition & fees: $21,330	Average undergraduate aid package: $15,619

ABOUT THE INSTITUTION Independent Nazarene, coed. 83 undergraduate majors. Federal methodology is used as a basis for awarding need-based institutional aid.

UNDERGRADUATE EXPENSES for 2010–11 *Comprehensive fee:* $27,510 includes full-time tuition ($20,700), mandatory fees ($630), and room and board ($6180). *College room only:* $3450. Full-time tuition and fees vary according to course load, program, and reciprocity agreements. *Part-time tuition:* $739 per credit hour. *Part-time fees:* $21 per credit hour. Part-time tuition and fees vary according to course load, program, and reciprocity agreements. *Payment plan:* Installment.

FRESHMAN FINANCIAL AID (Fall 2009, est.) 302 applied for aid; of those 92% were deemed to have need. 100% of freshmen with need received aid; of those 12% had need fully met. *Average percent of need met:* 70% (excluding resources awarded to replace EFC). *Average financial aid package:* $17,380 (excluding resources awarded to replace EFC). 7% of all full-time freshmen had no need and received non-need-based gift aid.

UNDERGRADUATE FINANCIAL AID (Fall 2009, est.) 1,356 applied for aid; of those 89% were deemed to have need. 100% of undergraduates with need received aid; of those 13% had need fully met. *Average percent of need met:* 70% (excluding resources awarded to replace EFC). *Average financial aid package:* $15,619 (excluding resources awarded to replace EFC). 6% of all full-time undergraduates had no need and received non-need-based gift aid.

GIFT AID (NEED-BASED) *Total amount:* $12,558,501 (24% federal, 8% state, 57% institutional, 11% external sources). *Receiving aid:* Freshmen: 89% (268); all full-time undergraduates: 66% (1,151). *Average award:* Freshmen: $11,360; Undergraduates: $9344. *Scholarships, grants, and awards:* Federal Pell, FSEOG, state, private, college/university gift aid from institutional funds.

GIFT AID (NON-NEED-BASED) *Total amount:* $1,250,388 (1% federal, 21% state, 71% institutional, 7% external sources). *Receiving aid:* Freshmen: 15% (44). Undergraduates: 10% (177). *Average award:* Freshmen: $5565. Undergraduates: $4102. *Scholarships, grants, and awards by category:* Academic interests/achievement: general academic interests/achievements. *Creative arts/performance:* music. *Special achievements/activities:* general special achievements/activities, junior miss, religious involvement. *Special characteristics:* children of faculty/staff, international students, members of minority groups, relatives of clergy,

religious affiliation, siblings of current students, spouses of current students. *Tuition waivers:* Full or partial for employees or children of employees, senior citizens.
LOANS *Student loans:* $13,060,113 (94% need-based, 6% non-need-based). 85% of past graduating class borrowed through all loan programs. *Average indebtedness per student:* $29,761. *Average need-based loan:* Freshmen: $3703. Undergraduates: $3984. *Parent loans:* $3,457,154 (47% need-based, 53% non-need-based). *Programs:* Federal Direct (Subsidized and Unsubsidized Stafford, PLUS), Perkins.
WORK-STUDY *Federal work-study:* Total amount: $280,000; 200 jobs averaging $1500. *State or other work-study/employment:* Total amount: $685,197 (45% need-based, 55% non-need-based). 415 part-time jobs averaging $1600.
ATHLETIC AWARDS Total amount: $685,522 (69% need-based, 31% non-need-based).
APPLYING FOR FINANCIAL AID *Required financial aid forms:* FAFSA, institution's own form. *Financial aid deadline (priority):* 3/15. *Notification date:* Continuous beginning 3/1. Students must reply within 2 weeks of notification.
CONTACT Financial Aid Office, Mount Vernon Nazarene University, 800 Martinsburg Road, Mount Vernon, OH 43050-9500, 740-397-9000 Ext. 4520 or toll-free 866-462-6868. *Fax:* 740-393-0511. *E-mail:* finaid@mvnu.edu.

MUHLENBERG COLLEGE
Allentown, PA

ABOUT THE INSTITUTION Independent religious, coed. 33 undergraduate majors.
GIFT AID (NEED-BASED) *Scholarships, grants, and awards:* Federal Pell, FSEOG, state, private, college/university gift aid from institutional funds.
LOANS *Programs:* FFEL (Subsidized and Unsubsidized Stafford, PLUS), Perkins.
WORK-STUDY *Federal work-study:* Total amount: $300,000; jobs available. *State or other work-study/employment:* Total amount: $167,624 (11% need-based, 89% non-need-based). Part-time jobs available.
APPLYING FOR FINANCIAL AID *Required financial aid forms:* institution's own form, CSS Financial Aid PROFILE, state aid form.
CONTACT Mr. Greg Mitton, Director of Financial Aid, Muhlenberg College, 2400 Chew Street, Allentown, PA 18104-5586, 484-664-3175. *Fax:* 484-664-3234. *E-mail:* mitton@muhlenberg.edu.

MULTNOMAH UNIVERSITY
Portland, OR

Tuition & fees: N/R	Average undergraduate aid package: $9211

ABOUT THE INSTITUTION Independent interdenominational, coed. 16 undergraduate majors. Federal methodology is used as a basis for awarding need-based institutional aid.
UNDERGRADUATE EXPENSES for 2010–11 *Tuition:* part-time $510 per credit hour. Full-time tuition and fees vary according to course load, location, and program. Part-time tuition and fees vary according to course load, location, and program. Room and board charges vary according to board plan and housing facility. *Payment plan:* Installment.
FRESHMAN FINANCIAL AID (Fall 2009, est.) 63 applied for aid; of those 84% were deemed to have need. 100% of freshmen with need received aid. *Average percent of need met:* 51% (excluding resources awarded to replace EFC). *Average financial aid package:* $9693 (excluding resources awarded to replace EFC). 9% of all full-time freshmen had no need and received non-need-based gift aid.
UNDERGRADUATE FINANCIAL AID (Fall 2009, est.) 503 applied for aid; of those 88% were deemed to have need. 100% of undergraduates with need received aid; of those 2% had need fully met. *Average percent of need met:* 50% (excluding resources awarded to replace EFC). *Average financial aid package:* $9211 (excluding resources awarded to replace EFC). 7% of all full-time undergraduates had no need and received non-need-based gift aid.
GIFT AID (NEED-BASED) *Total amount:* $2,351,979 (52% federal, 41% institutional, 7% external sources). *Receiving aid:* Freshmen: 73% (48); all full-time undergraduates: 74% (388). *Average award:* Freshmen: $6878; Undergraduates: $5846. *Scholarships, grants, and awards:* Federal Pell, FSEOG, private, college/university gift aid from institutional funds.
GIFT AID (NON-NEED-BASED) *Total amount:* $393,392 (77% institutional, 23% external sources). *Receiving aid:* Undergraduates: 1% (6). *Average award:* Freshmen: $2695. Undergraduates: $1848. *Scholarships, grants, and awards*

by category: *Academic interests/achievement:* 33 awards ($169,640 total): education, general academic interests/achievements, religion/biblical studies. *Special characteristics:* 62 awards ($105,171 total): children of current students, international students, religious affiliation, siblings of current students. *Tuition waivers:* Full or partial for employees or children of employees.
LOANS *Student loans:* $5,081,222 (56% need-based, 44% non-need-based). 98% of past graduating class borrowed through all loan programs. *Average indebtedness per student:* $21,020. *Average need-based loan:* Freshmen: $3052. Undergraduates: $4094. *Parent loans:* $626,434 (100% non-need-based). *Programs:* Federal Direct (Subsidized and Unsubsidized Stafford, PLUS).
WORK-STUDY *Federal work-study:* Total amount: $111,838; 75 jobs averaging $1500.
APPLYING FOR FINANCIAL AID *Required financial aid forms:* FAFSA, institution's own form. *Financial aid deadline (priority):* 4/1. *Notification date:* Continuous beginning 4/1. Students must reply within 3 weeks of notification.
CONTACT Mrs. Mary J. McGlothlan, Director of Financial Aid, Multnomah University, 8435 NE Glisan Street, Portland, OR 97220-5898, 503-251-5337 or toll-free 800-275-4672. *Fax:* 503-445-5199. *E-mail:* mmcglothlan@multnomah.edu.

MURRAY STATE UNIVERSITY
Murray, KY

Tuition & fees (KY res): $5976	Average undergraduate aid package: $5825

ABOUT THE INSTITUTION State-supported, coed. 104 undergraduate majors. Federal methodology is used as a basis for awarding need-based institutional aid.
UNDERGRADUATE EXPENSES for 2009–10 *Tuition, state resident:* full-time $5130; part-time $214 per credit hour. *Tuition, nonresident:* full-time $8006; part-time $301 per credit hour. *Required fees:* full-time $846; $35 per credit hour. Full-time tuition and fees vary according to reciprocity agreements. Part-time tuition and fees vary according to reciprocity agreements. *College room and board:* $6562; *Room only:* $3590. Room and board charges vary according to board plan and housing facility. *Payment plan:* Installment.
FRESHMAN FINANCIAL AID (Fall 2009, est.) 1,499 applied for aid; of those 77% were deemed to have need. 95% of freshmen with need received aid; of those 91% had need fully met. *Average financial aid package:* $5110 (excluding resources awarded to replace EFC). 36% of all full-time freshmen had no need and received non-need-based gift aid.
UNDERGRADUATE FINANCIAL AID (Fall 2009, est.) 4,518 applied for aid; of those 80% were deemed to have need. 88% of undergraduates with need received aid; of those 98% had need fully met. *Average financial aid package:* $5825 (excluding resources awarded to replace EFC). 35% of all full-time undergraduates had no need and received non-need-based gift aid.
GIFT AID (NEED-BASED) *Total amount:* $16,872,468 (73% federal, 12% state, 13% institutional, 2% external sources). *Receiving aid:* Freshmen: 57% (995); all full-time undergraduates: 38% (2,150). *Average award:* Freshmen: $2912; Undergraduates: $2738. *Scholarships, grants, and awards:* Federal Pell, FSEOG, state, private, college/university gift aid from institutional funds.
GIFT AID (NON-NEED-BASED) *Total amount:* $11,576,182 (39% state, 52% institutional, 9% external sources). *Receiving aid:* Freshmen: 33% (568). Undergraduates: 28% (1,604). *Average award:* Freshmen: $2275. Undergraduates: $2306. *Scholarships, grants, and awards by category:* *Academic interests/achievement:* $5,620,203 total: agriculture, biological sciences, business, communication, computer science, education, engineering/technologies, English, foreign languages, general academic interests/achievements, health fields, humanities, international studies, library science, mathematics. *Creative arts/performance:* $79,464 total: applied art and design, art/fine arts, creative writing, dance, debating, general creative arts/performance, journalism/publications, music, theater/drama. *Special achievements/activities:* $1,263,679 total: cheerleading/drum major, general special achievements/activities, junior miss, leadership, rodeo. *Special characteristics:* $8,173,724 total: adult students, children and siblings of alumni, children of faculty/staff, general special characteristics, handicapped students, international students, local/state students, members of minority groups, out-of-state students. *Tuition waivers:* Full or partial for children of alumni, employees or children of employees, senior citizens.
LOANS *Student loans:* $19,794,441 (56% need-based, 44% non-need-based). *Average indebtedness per student:* $18,000. *Average need-based loan:* Fresh-

men: $2044. Undergraduates: $2446. *Parent loans:* $2,077,091 (100% non-need-based). *Programs:* FFEL (Subsidized and Unsubsidized Stafford, PLUS), Perkins, Federal Nursing, state, college/university.

WORK-STUDY *Federal work-study:* Total amount: $816,347; 1,741 jobs averaging $2710. *State or other work-study/employment:* Total amount: $3,984,428 (100% non-need-based). 1,357 part-time jobs averaging $5420.

ATHLETIC AWARDS Total amount: $2,965,296 (30% need-based, 70% non-need-based).

APPLYING FOR FINANCIAL AID *Required financial aid forms:* FAFSA, institution's own form. *Financial aid deadline (priority):* 4/1. *Notification date:* Continuous beginning 4/15.

CONTACT Lori Mitchum, Director of Student Financial Aid, Murray State University, 500 Sparks Hall, Murray, KY 42071-0009, 270-809-2546 or toll-free 800-272-4678. *Fax:* 270-809-3116. *E-mail:* lori.mitchum@murraystate.edu.

MUSICIANS INSTITUTE
Hollywood, CA

CONTACT Director of Financial Aid, Musicians Institute, 1655 North McCadden Place, Hollywood, CA 90028, 323-462-1384 or toll-free 800-255-PLAY.

MUSKINGUM UNIVERSITY
New Concord, OH

Tuition & fees: N/R	Average undergraduate aid package: $17,950

ABOUT THE INSTITUTION Independent religious, coed. *Awards:* bachelor's and master's degrees. 57 undergraduate majors. *Total enrollment:* 2,099. Undergraduates: 1,709. Federal methodology is used as a basis for awarding need-based institutional aid.

FRESHMAN FINANCIAL AID (Fall 2009, est.) 434 applied for aid; of those 95% were deemed to have need. 100% of freshmen with need received aid; of those 20% had need fully met. *Average percent of need met:* 80% (excluding resources awarded to replace EFC). *Average financial aid package:* $19,361 (excluding resources awarded to replace EFC). 12% of all full-time freshmen had no need and received non-need-based gift aid.

UNDERGRADUATE FINANCIAL AID (Fall 2009, est.) 1,378 applied for aid; of those 92% were deemed to have need. 100% of undergraduates with need received aid; of those 22% had need fully met. *Average percent of need met:* 80% (excluding resources awarded to replace EFC). *Average financial aid package:* $17,950 (excluding resources awarded to replace EFC). 15% of all full-time undergraduates had no need and received non-need-based gift aid.

GIFT AID (NEED-BASED) *Total amount:* $18,030,244 (19% federal, 7% state, 71% institutional, 3% external sources). *Receiving aid:* Freshmen: 87% (413); all full-time undergraduates: 82% (1,274). *Average award:* Freshmen: $15,721; Undergraduates: $14,040. *Scholarships, grants, and awards:* Federal Pell, FSEOG, state, private, college/university gift aid from institutional funds.

GIFT AID (NON-NEED-BASED) *Total amount:* $1,903,597 (2% state, 97% institutional, 1% external sources). *Receiving aid:* Freshmen: 79% (375). Undergraduates: 73% (1,131). *Average award:* Freshmen: $8673. Undergraduates: $5114. *Scholarships, grants, and awards by category:* Academic interests/achievement: 662 awards ($6,084,592 total): biological sciences, computer science, engineering/technologies, general academic interests/achievements, mathematics, physical sciences, premedicine. Creative arts/performance: 164 awards ($227,385 total): art/fine arts, debating, journalism/publications, music, theater/drama. Special achievements/activities: 175 awards ($136,250 total): community service, leadership. Special characteristics: 951 awards ($1,117,582 total): children and siblings of alumni, ethnic background, local/state students, members of minority groups, relatives of clergy, religious affiliation, siblings of current students.

LOANS *Student loans:* $11,431,821 (71% need-based, 29% non-need-based). 79% of past graduating class borrowed through all loan programs. *Average indebtedness per student:* $28,343. *Average need-based loan:* Freshmen: $3584. Undergraduates: $4055. *Parent loans:* $1,522,137 (19% need-based, 81% non-need-based). *Programs:* Federal Direct (Subsidized and Unsubsidized Stafford, PLUS), Perkins, college/university.

WORK-STUDY *Federal work-study:* Total amount: $149,639; 450 jobs averaging $1000. *State or other work-study/employment:* Total amount: $450,000 (67% need-based, 33% non-need-based). 5 part-time jobs averaging $1000.

APPLYING FOR FINANCIAL AID *Required financial aid form:* FAFSA. *Financial aid deadline (priority):* 3/1. *Notification date:* Continuous beginning 3/1. Students must reply by 5/1 or within 2 weeks of notification.

CONTACT Mr. Jeff Zellers, Vice President of Enrollment, Muskingum University, 163 Stormont Street, New Concord, OH 43762, 740-826-8139 or toll-free 800-752-6082. *Fax:* 740-826-8100. *E-mail:* jzellers@muskingum.edu.

NAROPA UNIVERSITY
Boulder, CO

Tuition & fees: $23,520	Average undergraduate aid package: $25,123

ABOUT THE INSTITUTION Independent, coed. 12 undergraduate majors. Federal methodology is used as a basis for awarding need-based institutional aid.

UNDERGRADUATE EXPENSES for 2009–10 *Comprehensive fee:* $31,998 includes full-time tuition ($23,420), mandatory fees ($100), and room and board ($8478). *College room only:* $6174. Full-time tuition and fees vary according to course load. Room and board charges vary according to board plan. *Part-time tuition:* $760 per credit hour. *Part-time fees:* $300 per term. Part-time tuition and fees vary according to course load. *Payment plan:* Installment.

FRESHMAN FINANCIAL AID (Fall 2009, est.) 32 applied for aid; of those 91% were deemed to have need. 100% of freshmen with need received aid; of those 10% had need fully met. *Average percent of need met:* 86% (excluding resources awarded to replace EFC). *Average financial aid package:* $24,300 (excluding resources awarded to replace EFC).

UNDERGRADUATE FINANCIAL AID (Fall 2009, est.) 310 applied for aid; of those 91% were deemed to have need. 100% of undergraduates with need received aid; of those 2% had need fully met. *Average percent of need met:* 88% (excluding resources awarded to replace EFC). *Average financial aid package:* $25,123 (excluding resources awarded to replace EFC).

GIFT AID (NEED-BASED) *Total amount:* $4,469,718 (23% federal, 77% institutional). *Receiving aid:* Freshmen: 65% (28); all full-time undergraduates: 66% (283). *Average award:* Freshmen: $16,225; Undergraduates: $15,279. *Scholarships, grants, and awards:* Federal Pell, FSEOG, private, college/university gift aid from institutional funds.

GIFT AID (NON-NEED-BASED) *Tuition waivers:* Full or partial for employees or children of employees.

LOANS *Student loans:* $2,744,257 (94% need-based, 6% non-need-based). 71% of past graduating class borrowed through all loan programs. *Average indebtedness per student:* $23,717. *Average need-based loan:* Freshmen: $7547. Undergraduates: $9226. *Parent loans:* $909,394 (68% need-based, 32% non-need-based). *Programs:* Federal Direct (Subsidized and Unsubsidized Stafford, PLUS), Perkins.

WORK-STUDY *Federal work-study:* Total amount: $876,200; jobs available. *State or other work-study/employment:* Part-time jobs available.

APPLYING FOR FINANCIAL AID *Required financial aid form:* FAFSA. *Financial aid deadline (priority):* 3/1. *Notification date:* Continuous beginning 3/1. Students must reply within 3 weeks of notification.

CONTACT Nancy Morrell, Financial Aid Office, Naropa University, 2130 Arapahoe Avenue, Boulder, CO 80302-6697, 303-546-3534 or toll-free 800-772-0410 (out-of-state). *Fax:* 303-546-3536. *E-mail:* finaid@naropa.edu.

NATIONAL AMERICAN UNIVERSITY
Colorado Springs, CO

CONTACT Financial Aid Coordinator, National American University, 2577 North Chelton Road, Colorado Springs, CO 80909, 719-471-4205.

NATIONAL AMERICAN UNIVERSITY
Denver, CO

CONTACT Cheryl Schunneman, Director of Financial Aid, National American University, 321 Kansas City Street, Rapid City, SD 57701, 605-394-4800.

NATIONAL AMERICAN UNIVERSITY
Roseville, MN

CONTACT Financial Aid Office, National American University, 1500 West Highway 36, Roseville, MN 55113, 651-644-1265.

NATIONAL AMERICAN UNIVERSITY
Kansas City, MO

CONTACT Mary Anderson, Coordinator of Financial Aid, National American University, 4200 Blue Ridge, Kansas City, MO 64133, 816-353-4554. *Fax:* 816-353-1176.

NATIONAL AMERICAN UNIVERSITY
Albuquerque, NM

CONTACT Director of Financial Aid, National American University, 321 Kansas City Street, Rapid City, SD 57701, 605-394-4800 or toll-free 800-843-8892.

NATIONAL AMERICAN UNIVERSITY
Rapid City, SD

CONTACT Financial Aid Director, National American University, PO Box 1780, Rapid City, SD 57709-1780, 605-721-5213 or toll-free 800-843-8892.

NATIONAL AMERICAN UNIVERSITY—SIOUX FALLS BRANCH
Sioux Falls, SD

CONTACT Ms. Rhonda Kohnen, Financial Aid Coordinator, National American University–Sioux Falls Branch, 2801 South Kiwanis Avenue, Suite 100, Sioux Falls, SD 57105-4293, 605-334-5430 or toll-free 800-388-5430 (out-of-state). *Fax:* 605-334-1575. *E-mail:* rkohnen@national.edu.

NATIONAL COLLEGE
Bayamón, PR

CONTACT Mr. Desi Lopez, Vice President of Development and Financial Aid, National College, PO Box 2036, Bayamon, PR 00960, 787-780-5134 Ext. 230 or toll-free 800-780-5134. *Fax:* 787-740-7360. *E-mail:* 110106.1133@compuserve.com.

THE NATIONAL HISPANIC UNIVERSITY
San Jose, CA

CONTACT Takeo Kubo, Director of Financial Aid and Scholarship, The National Hispanic University, 14271 Story Road, San Jose, CA 95127-3823, 408-273-2708. *Fax:* 408-254-1369. *E-mail:* tkubo@nhu.edu.

NATIONAL LABOR COLLEGE
Silver Spring, MD

CONTACT Financial Aid Office, National Labor College, 10000 New Hampshire Avenue, Silver Spring, MD 20903, 301-431-6400 or toll-free 800-GMC-4CDP.

NATIONAL-LOUIS UNIVERSITY
Chicago, IL

CONTACT Janet Jazwiec, Assistant Director of Student Finance, National-Louis University, 1000 Capitol Drive, Wheeling, IL 60090, 847-947-5433 or toll-free 888-NLU-TODAY (in-state), 800-443-5522 (out-of-state). *Fax:* 847-947-5433. *E-mail:* jjazwiec@nl.edu.

NATIONAL PARALEGAL COLLEGE
Phoenix, AZ

CONTACT Financial Aid Office, National Paralegal College, 6516 N 7th Street, Suite 103, Phoenix, AZ 85014, 845-371-9101 or toll-free 800-371-6105 (out-of-state).

NATIONAL UNIVERSITY
La Jolla, CA

Tuition & fees: $10,788   **Average undergraduate aid package: $10,475**

ABOUT THE INSTITUTION Independent, coed. 45 undergraduate majors. Federal methodology is used as a basis for awarding need-based institutional aid.

UNDERGRADUATE EXPENSES for 2009–10 *Tuition:* full-time $10,728; part-time $298 per unit. Full-time tuition and fees vary according to course load and location. Part-time tuition and fees vary according to course load and location.

FRESHMAN FINANCIAL AID (Fall 2008) 472 applied for aid; of those 96% were deemed to have need. 57% of freshmen with need received aid; of those 1% had need fully met. *Average percent of need met:* 86% (excluding resources awarded to replace EFC). *Average financial aid package:* $8332 (excluding resources awarded to replace EFC). 1% of all full-time freshmen had no need and received non-need-based gift aid.

UNDERGRADUATE FINANCIAL AID (Fall 2008) 2,296 applied for aid; of those 96% were deemed to have need. 69% of undergraduates with need received aid; of those 2% had need fully met. *Average percent of need met:* 84% (excluding resources awarded to replace EFC). *Average financial aid package:* $10,475 (excluding resources awarded to replace EFC). 1% of all full-time undergraduates had no need and received non-need-based gift aid.

GIFT AID (NEED-BASED) *Total amount:* $6,673,637 (60% federal, 27% state, 13% institutional). *Receiving aid:* Freshmen: 15% (145); all full-time undergraduates: 17% (730). *Average award:* Freshmen: $9625; Undergraduates: $12,553. *Scholarships, grants, and awards:* Federal Pell, FSEOG, state, college/university gift aid from institutional funds.

GIFT AID (NON-NEED-BASED) *Total amount:* $301,840 (100% institutional). *Receiving aid:* Freshmen: 27% (257). Undergraduates: 35% (1,518). *Average award:* Freshmen: $7076. Undergraduates: $13,124. *Scholarships, grants, and awards by category: Academic interests/achievement:* general academic interests/ achievements. *Special achievements/activities:* leadership. *Tuition waivers:* Full or partial for employees or children of employees.

LOANS *Student loans:* $335,975,259 (47% need-based, 53% non-need-based). 46% of past graduating class borrowed through all loan programs. *Average indebtedness per student:* $18,468. *Average need-based loan:* Freshmen: $11,893. Undergraduates: $17,318. *Parent loans:* $210,997 (100% need-based). *Programs:* Federal Direct (Subsidized and Unsubsidized Stafford, PLUS), FFEL (Subsidized and Unsubsidized Stafford, PLUS), Perkins, college/university.

APPLYING FOR FINANCIAL AID *Required financial aid forms:* FAFSA, institution's own form. *Financial aid deadline:* Continuous. *Notification date:* Continuous beginning 6/30.

CONTACT Valerie Ryan, Financial Aid Office, National University, 11255 North Torrey Pines Road, La Jolla, CA 92037-1011, 858-642-8500 or toll-free 800-NAT-UNIV. *Fax:* 858-642-8720. *E-mail:* vryan@nu.edu.

NAZARENE BIBLE COLLEGE
Colorado Springs, CO

Tuition & fees: $8640   **Average undergraduate aid package: $6760**

ABOUT THE INSTITUTION Independent religious, coed. 6 undergraduate majors. Federal methodology is used as a basis for awarding need-based institutional aid.

UNDERGRADUATE EXPENSES for 2009–10 *Tuition:* full-time $8100; part-time $300 per credit hour. *Required fees:* full-time $540; $20 per credit hour. *Payment plan:* Installment.

FRESHMAN FINANCIAL AID (Fall 2008) 4 applied for aid; of those 100% were deemed to have need. 75% of freshmen with need received aid. *Average percent of need met:* 70% (excluding resources awarded to replace EFC). *Average financial aid package:* $4506 (excluding resources awarded to replace EFC).

UNDERGRADUATE FINANCIAL AID (Fall 2008) 190 applied for aid; of those 100% were deemed to have need. 90% of undergraduates with need received aid. *Average percent of need met:* 60% (excluding resources awarded to replace EFC). *Average financial aid package:* $6760 (excluding resources awarded to replace EFC).

GIFT AID (NEED-BASED) *Total amount:* $941,818 (82% federal, 14% institutional, 4% external sources). *Receiving aid:* Freshmen: 50% (2); all full-time undergraduates: 81% (171). *Average award:* Freshmen: $1880; Undergraduates: $3725. *Scholarships, grants, and awards:* Federal Pell, FSEOG, college/university gift aid from institutional funds.

GIFT AID (NON-NEED-BASED) *Scholarships, grants, and awards by category: Academic interests/achievement:* religion/biblical studies. *Tuition waivers:* Full or partial for employees or children of employees.

LOANS *Student loans:* $3,011,976 (55% need-based, 45% non-need-based). 70% of past graduating class borrowed through all loan programs. *Average indebtedness per student:* $28,448. *Parent loans:* $2910 (100% non-need-based). *Programs:* FFEL (Subsidized and Unsubsidized Stafford, PLUS), Perkins, college/university.

WORK-STUDY *Federal work-study:* Total amount: $19,632; 6 jobs averaging $3272.

APPLYING FOR FINANCIAL AID *Required financial aid form:* FAFSA. *Financial aid deadline:* Continuous. *Notification date:* Continuous beginning 2/1.

CONTACT Mr. Malcolm Britton, Director of Financial Aid, Nazarene Bible College, 1111 Academy Park Loop, Colorado Springs, CO 80910-3717, 719-884-5051 or toll-free 800-873-3873. *Fax:* 719-884-5199.

NAZARETH COLLEGE OF ROCHESTER
Rochester, NY

Tuition & fees: $26,140	Average undergraduate aid package: $18,541

ABOUT THE INSTITUTION Independent, coed. 65 undergraduate majors. Federal methodology is used as a basis for awarding need-based institutional aid.

UNDERGRADUATE EXPENSES for 2010–11 *Comprehensive fee:* $36,856 includes full-time tuition ($25,044), mandatory fees ($1096), and room and board ($10,716). Room and board charges vary according to board plan and housing facility. *Payment plans:* Installment, deferred payment.

FRESHMAN FINANCIAL AID (Fall 2009, est.) 455 applied for aid; of those 86% were deemed to have need. 100% of freshmen with need received aid; of those 23% had need fully met. *Average percent of need met:* 77% (excluding resources awarded to replace EFC). *Average financial aid package:* $19,324 (excluding resources awarded to replace EFC). 20% of all full-time freshmen had no need and received non-need-based gift aid.

UNDERGRADUATE FINANCIAL AID (Fall 2009, est.) 1,856 applied for aid; of those 90% were deemed to have need. 100% of undergraduates with need received aid; of those 20% had need fully met. *Average percent of need met:* 73% (excluding resources awarded to replace EFC). *Average financial aid package:* $18,541 (excluding resources awarded to replace EFC). 17% of all full-time undergraduates had no need and received non-need-based gift aid.

GIFT AID (NEED-BASED) *Total amount:* $22,698,311 (14% federal, 12% state, 67% institutional, 7% external sources). *Receiving aid:* Freshmen: 80% (393); all full-time undergraduates: 82% (1,677). *Average award:* Freshmen: $15,061; Undergraduates: $13,353. *Scholarships, grants, and awards:* Federal Pell, FSEOG, state, private, college/university gift aid from institutional funds, Federal Nursing.

GIFT AID (NON-NEED-BASED) *Total amount:* $4,776,279 (1% state, 84% institutional, 15% external sources). *Receiving aid:* Freshmen: 32% (158). Undergraduates: 31% (640). *Average award:* Freshmen: $15,769. Undergraduates: $14,749. *Scholarships, grants, and awards by category: Academic interests/achievement:* 1,930 awards ($14,499,771 total): general academic interests/achievements. *Creative arts/performance:* 210 awards ($731,275 total): art/fine arts, music, theater/drama. *Special characteristics:* 283 awards ($1,989,364 total): children and siblings of alumni, children of faculty/staff, siblings of current students. *Tuition waivers:* Full or partial for minority students, children of alumni, employees or children of employees.

LOANS *Student loans:* $17,754,291 (76% need-based, 24% non-need-based). 90% of past graduating class borrowed through all loan programs. *Average indebtedness per student:* $35,010. *Average need-based loan:* Freshmen: $3456. Undergraduates: $4916. *Parent loans:* $3,314,387 (47% need-based, 53% non-need-based). *Programs:* Federal Direct (Subsidized and Unsubsidized Stafford, PLUS), Perkins, Federal Nursing.

WORK-STUDY *Federal work-study:* Total amount: $1,917,719; 977 jobs averaging $2020.

APPLYING FOR FINANCIAL AID *Required financial aid forms:* FAFSA, state aid form. *Financial aid deadline (priority):* 2/15. *Notification date:* Continuous beginning 2/1. Students must reply by 5/1 or within 2 weeks of notification.

CONTACT Samantha Veeder, Director of Financial Aid, Nazareth College of Rochester, 4245 East Avenue, Rochester, NY 14618-3790, 585-389-2310 or toll-free 800-462-3944 (in-state). *Fax:* 585-389-2317. *E-mail:* sveeder0@naz.edu.

NEBRASKA CHRISTIAN COLLEGE
Papillion, NE

ABOUT THE INSTITUTION Independent religious, coed. *Awards:* associate and bachelor's degrees. 10 undergraduate majors. *Total enrollment:* 146. Undergraduates: 146. Freshmen: 48.

GIFT AID (NEED-BASED) *Scholarships, grants, and awards:* Federal Pell, FSEOG, state, private, college/university gift aid from institutional funds.

GIFT AID (NON-NEED-BASED) *Scholarships, grants, and awards by category: Academic interests/achievement:* general academic interests/achievements. *Special characteristics:* children of faculty/staff, international students, relatives of clergy.

LOANS *Programs:* FFEL (Subsidized and Unsubsidized Stafford, PLUS).

WORK-STUDY *Federal work-study:* Total amount: $11,751; 13 jobs averaging $1183.

APPLYING FOR FINANCIAL AID *Required financial aid forms:* FAFSA, institution's own form.

CONTACT Ms. Tina Larsen, Director of Financial Aid, Nebraska Christian College, 12550 South 114th Street, Papillion, NE 68046, 402-935-9400. *Fax:* 402-935-9500. *E-mail:* tlarsen@nechristian.edu.

NEBRASKA METHODIST COLLEGE
Omaha, NE

Tuition & fees: $12,740	Average undergraduate aid package: $9325

ABOUT THE INSTITUTION Independent religious, coed, primarily women. 8 undergraduate majors. Federal methodology is used as a basis for awarding need-based institutional aid.

UNDERGRADUATE EXPENSES for 2010–11 *One-time required fee:* $60. *Tuition:* full-time $12,090; part-time $485 per credit hour. *Required fees:* full-time $650; $20 per credit hour. Room and board charges vary according to housing facility. *Payment plan:* Installment.

FRESHMAN FINANCIAL AID (Fall 2009, est.) 28 applied for aid; of those 96% were deemed to have need. 100% of freshmen with need received aid; of those 26% had need fully met. *Average percent of need met:* 67% (excluding resources awarded to replace EFC). *Average financial aid package:* $10,367 (excluding resources awarded to replace EFC). 7% of all full-time freshmen had no need and received non-need-based gift aid.

UNDERGRADUATE FINANCIAL AID (Fall 2009, est.) 370 applied for aid; of those 89% were deemed to have need. 74% of undergraduates with need received aid; of those 11% had need fully met. *Average percent of need met:* 47% (excluding resources awarded to replace EFC). *Average financial aid package:* $9325 (excluding resources awarded to replace EFC). 6% of all full-time undergraduates had no need and received non-need-based gift aid.

GIFT AID (NEED-BASED) *Total amount:* $1,801,334 (46% federal, 5% state, 40% institutional, 9% external sources). *Receiving aid:* Freshmen: 90% (27); all full-time undergraduates: 62% (244). *Average award:* Freshmen: $7306; Undergraduates: $6377. *Scholarships, grants, and awards:* Federal Pell, FSEOG, state, private, college/university gift aid from institutional funds.

GIFT AID (NON-NEED-BASED) *Total amount:* $179,523 (78% institutional, 22% external sources). *Receiving aid:* Freshmen: 20% (6). Undergraduates: 4% (17). *Average award:* Freshmen: $6500. Undergraduates: $3165. *Scholarships, grants, and awards by category: Academic interests/achievement:* general academic interests/achievements. *Tuition waivers:* Full or partial for employees or children of employees.

LOANS *Student loans:* $4,571,339 (73% need-based, 27% non-need-based). 98% of past graduating class borrowed through all loan programs. *Average indebtedness per student:* $34,264. *Average need-based loan:* Freshmen: $4458. Undergraduates: $4418. *Parent loans:* $487,607 (30% need-based, 70% non-need-based). *Programs:* FFEL (Subsidized and Unsubsidized Stafford, PLUS), Perkins, Federal Nursing, college/university, alternative loans.

WORK-STUDY *Federal work-study:* Total amount: $28,100; jobs available.

APPLYING FOR FINANCIAL AID *Required financial aid forms:* FAFSA, institution's own form. *Financial aid deadline (priority):* 4/1. *Notification date:* Continuous. Students must reply within 3 weeks of notification.

CONTACT Ms. Penny James, Director of Financial Aid, Nebraska Methodist College, The Josie Harper Campus, 720 North 87th Street, Omaha, NE 68114-3426, 402-354-7225 or toll-free 800-335-5510. *Fax:* 402-354-7020. *E-mail:* penny.james@methodistcollege.edu.

NEBRASKA WESLEYAN UNIVERSITY
Lincoln, NE

Tuition & fees: $22,432	Average undergraduate aid package: $16,199

ABOUT THE INSTITUTION Independent United Methodist, coed. 49 undergraduate majors. Federal methodology is used as a basis for awarding need-based institutional aid.

UNDERGRADUATE EXPENSES for 2009–10 *One-time required fee:* $120. *Comprehensive fee:* $28,662 includes full-time tuition ($21,980), mandatory fees ($452), and room and board ($6230). Room and board charges vary according to board plan. *Part-time tuition:* $828 per credit hour. *Payment plans:* Installment, deferred payment.

FRESHMAN FINANCIAL AID (Fall 2009, est.) 345 applied for aid; of those 86% were deemed to have need. 100% of freshmen with need received aid; of those 17% had need fully met. *Average percent of need met:* 74% (excluding resources awarded to replace EFC). *Average financial aid package:* $16,854 (excluding resources awarded to replace EFC). 24% of all full-time freshmen had no need and received non-need-based gift aid.

UNDERGRADUATE FINANCIAL AID (Fall 2009, est.) 1,253 applied for aid; of those 87% were deemed to have need. 100% of undergraduates with need received aid; of those 20% had need fully met. *Average percent of need met:* 71% (excluding resources awarded to replace EFC). *Average financial aid package:* $16,199 (excluding resources awarded to replace EFC). 28% of all full-time undergraduates had no need and received non-need-based gift aid.

GIFT AID (NEED-BASED) *Total amount:* $12,571,157 (15% federal, 2% state, 79% institutional, 4% external sources). *Receiving aid:* Freshmen: 75% (294); all full-time undergraduates: 71% (1,073). *Average award:* Freshmen: $12,819; Undergraduates: $11,649. *Scholarships, grants, and awards:* Federal Pell, FSEOG, state, private, college/university gift aid from institutional funds.

GIFT AID (NON-NEED-BASED) *Total amount:* $3,546,919 (1% federal, 93% institutional, 6% external sources). *Receiving aid:* Freshmen: 9% (35). Undergraduates: 8% (119). *Average award:* Freshmen: $7669. Undergraduates: $6880. *Scholarships, grants, and awards by category: Academic interests/achievement:* general academic interests/achievements. *Creative arts/performance:* art/fine arts, music, theater/drama. *Special characteristics:* children and siblings of alumni, children of educators, children of faculty/staff, international students, relatives of clergy, siblings of current students. *Tuition waivers:* Full or partial for employees or children of employees, adult students, senior citizens.

LOANS *Student loans:* $8,441,478 (72% need-based, 28% non-need-based). 78% of past graduating class borrowed through all loan programs. *Average indebtedness per student:* $21,931. *Average need-based loan:* Freshmen: $4335. Undergraduates: $4636. *Parent loans:* $2,720,587 (36% need-based, 64% non-need-based). *Programs:* FFEL (Subsidized and Unsubsidized Stafford, PLUS), Perkins.

WORK-STUDY *Federal work-study:* Total amount: $130,000; jobs available. *State or other work-study/employment:* Total amount: $653,458 (31% need-based, 69% non-need-based). Part-time jobs available.

APPLYING FOR FINANCIAL AID *Required financial aid form:* FAFSA. *Financial aid deadline:* Continuous. *Notification date:* Continuous beginning 3/1. Students must reply within 4 weeks of notification.

CONTACT Mr. Thomas J. Ochsner, Director of Scholarships and Financial Aid, Nebraska Wesleyan University, 5000 Saint Paul Avenue, Lincoln, NE 68504, 402-465-2212 or toll-free 800-541-3818. *Fax:* 402-465-2194. *E-mail:* tjo@nebrwesleyan.edu.

NER ISRAEL RABBINICAL COLLEGE
Baltimore, MD

CONTACT Mr. Moshe Pelberg, Financial Aid Administrator, Ner Israel Rabbinical College, 400 Mount Wilson Lane, Baltimore, MD 21208, 410-484-7200.

NEUMANN UNIVERSITY
Aston, PA

Tuition & fees: $21,360	Average undergraduate aid package: $19,000

ABOUT THE INSTITUTION Independent Roman Catholic, coed. 19 undergraduate majors. Federal methodology is used as a basis for awarding need-based institutional aid.

UNDERGRADUATE EXPENSES for 2009–10 *Comprehensive fee:* $31,078 includes full-time tuition ($20,580), mandatory fees ($780), and room and board ($9718). *College room only:* $5732. Room and board charges vary according to board plan. *Part-time tuition:* $470 per credit hour. *Payment plan:* Installment.

FRESHMAN FINANCIAL AID (Fall 2009, est.) 470 applied for aid; of those 100% were deemed to have need. 100% of freshmen with need received aid; of those 66% had need fully met. *Average percent of need met:* 65% (excluding resources awarded to replace EFC). *Average financial aid package:* $19,000 (excluding resources awarded to replace EFC).

UNDERGRADUATE FINANCIAL AID (Fall 2009, est.) 1,820 applied for aid; of those 100% were deemed to have need. 100% of undergraduates with need received aid; of those 60% had need fully met. *Average percent of need met:* 65% (excluding resources awarded to replace EFC). *Average financial aid package:* $19,000 (excluding resources awarded to replace EFC).

GIFT AID (NEED-BASED) *Total amount:* $19,713,190 (16% federal, 11% state, 72% institutional, 1% external sources). *Receiving aid:* Freshmen: 90% (470); all full-time undergraduates: 81% (1,640). *Average award:* Freshmen: $11,000; Undergraduates: $11,000. *Scholarships, grants, and awards:* Federal Pell, FSEOG, state, private, college/university gift aid from institutional funds.

GIFT AID (NON-NEED-BASED) *Receiving aid:* Freshmen: 38% (200). Undergraduates: 30% (600). *Scholarships, grants, and awards by category: Creative arts/performance:* music. *Tuition waivers:* Full or partial for employees or children of employees.

LOANS *Student loans:* $20,308,011 (100% need-based). 80% of past graduating class borrowed through all loan programs. *Average indebtedness per student:* $30,000. *Average need-based loan:* Freshmen: $4000. Undergraduates: $5000. *Parent loans:* $4,466,892 (100% need-based). *Programs:* Federal Direct (Subsidized and Unsubsidized Stafford, PLUS), FFEL (Subsidized and Unsubsidized Stafford, PLUS), Perkins, Federal Nursing.

WORK-STUDY *Federal work-study:* Total amount: $250,000; 180 jobs averaging $1400. *State or other work-study/employment:* Part-time jobs available.

APPLYING FOR FINANCIAL AID *Required financial aid form:* FAFSA. *Financial aid deadline:* Continuous.

CONTACT Mrs. Katherine Markert, Director of Financial Aid, Neumann University, One Neumann Drive, Aston, PA 19014-1298, 610-558-5519 or toll-free 800-963-8626. *E-mail:* kmarkert@neumann.edu.

NEUMONT UNIVERSITY
South Jordan, UT

CONTACT Financial Aid Office, Neumont University, 10701 South River Front Parkway, Suite 300, South Jordan, UT 84095, 801-438-1100 or toll-free 866-622-3448.

NEVADA STATE COLLEGE AT HENDERSON
Henderson, NV

CONTACT Financial Aid Office, Nevada State College at Henderson, 1125 Nevada State Drive, Henderson, NV 89015, 702-992-2000.

NEWBERRY COLLEGE
Newberry, SC

Tuition & fees: $22,470	Average undergraduate aid package: $20,440

ABOUT THE INSTITUTION Independent Evangelical Lutheran, coed. 35 undergraduate majors. Federal methodology is used as a basis for awarding need-based institutional aid.

UNDERGRADUATE EXPENSES for 2009–10 *Comprehensive fee:* $30,220 includes full-time tuition ($20,500), mandatory fees ($1970), and room and board ($7750). *College room only:* $3800. Full-time tuition and fees vary according to class time, course load, and student level. Room and board charges vary according to housing facility. *Part-time tuition:* $500 per credit hour. *Part-time fees:* $100 per term. Part-time tuition and fees vary according to class time, course load, and student level. *Payment plan:* Installment.

FRESHMAN FINANCIAL AID (Fall 2009, est.) 318 applied for aid; of those 94% were deemed to have need. 100% of freshmen with need received aid; of those 20% had need fully met. *Average percent of need met:* 75% (excluding resources awarded to replace EFC). *Average financial aid package:* $21,205 (excluding resources awarded to replace EFC). 10% of all full-time freshmen had no need and received non-need-based gift aid.

UNDERGRADUATE FINANCIAL AID (Fall 2009, est.) 977 applied for aid; of those 92% were deemed to have need. 100% of undergraduates with need received aid; of those 24% had need fully met. *Average percent of need met:* 76% (excluding resources awarded to replace EFC). *Average financial aid package:* $20,440 (excluding resources awarded to replace EFC).

GIFT AID (NEED-BASED) *Total amount:* $13,960,811 (17% federal, 25% state, 56% institutional, 2% external sources). *Receiving aid:* Freshmen: 87% (300); all full-time undergraduates: 895. *Average award:* Freshmen: $18,600; Undergraduates: $16,969. *Scholarships, grants, and awards:* Federal Pell, FSEOG, state, private, college/university gift aid from institutional funds.

GIFT AID (NON-NEED-BASED) *Total amount:* $3,245,524 (28% state, 66% institutional, 6% external sources). *Receiving aid:* Freshmen: 17% (58). Undergraduates: 182. *Average award:* Freshmen: $10,958. Undergraduates: $11,552. *Scholarships, grants, and awards by category: Academic interests/ achievement:* biological sciences, business, communication, education, foreign languages, general academic interests/achievements, humanities, mathematics, physical sciences, religion/biblical studies, social sciences. *Creative arts/ performance:* music, theater/drama. *Special achievements/activities:* cheerleading/ drum major, religious involvement. *Special characteristics:* children and siblings of alumni, children of faculty/staff, international students, local/state students, relatives of clergy, religious affiliation, siblings of current students. *Tuition waivers:* Full or partial for employees or children of employees.

LOANS *Student loans:* $7,233,720 (76% need-based, 24% non-need-based). 86% of past graduating class borrowed through all loan programs. *Average indebtedness per student:* $30,693. *Average need-based loan:* Freshmen: $3468. Undergraduates: $4474. *Parent loans:* $1,035,172 (44% need-based, 56% non-need-based). *Programs:* Federal Direct (Subsidized and Unsubsidized Stafford, PLUS), Perkins, state.

WORK-STUDY *Federal work-study:* Total amount: $86,440; jobs available. *State or other work-study/employment:* Part-time jobs available.

ATHLETIC AWARDS Total amount: $1,697,170 (68% need-based, 32% non-need-based).

APPLYING FOR FINANCIAL AID *Required financial aid form:* FAFSA. *Financial aid deadline (priority):* 3/15. *Notification date:* Continuous beginning 3/15. Students must reply within 4 weeks of notification.

CONTACT Ms. Melissa A. Lutz, Director of Financial Aid, Newberry College, 2100 College Street, Newberry, SC 29108, 803-321-5127 or toll-free 800-845-4955 Ext. 5127. *Fax:* 803-321-5627. *E-mail:* missy.lutz@newberry.edu.

NEWBURY COLLEGE
Brookline, MA

CONTACT Office of Financial Assistance, Newbury College, 129 Fisher Avenue, Brookline, MA 02445-5796, 617-730-7100 or toll-free 800-NEWBURY. *Fax:* 617-730-7108.

NEW COLLEGE OF FLORIDA
Sarasota, FL

Tuition & fees (FL res): $4784	Average undergraduate aid package: $13,282

ABOUT THE INSTITUTION State-supported, coed. 42 undergraduate majors. Federal methodology is used as a basis for awarding need-based institutional aid.

UNDERGRADUATE EXPENSES for 2009–10 *Tuition, state resident:* full-time $4784. *Tuition, nonresident:* full-time $26,386. *College room and board:* $7783; *Room only:* $5252. Room and board charges vary according to board plan and housing facility. *Payment plans:* Installment, deferred payment.

FRESHMAN FINANCIAL AID (Fall 2009, est.) 172 applied for aid; of those 63% were deemed to have need. 100% of freshmen with need received aid; of those 67% had need fully met. *Average percent of need met:* 96% (excluding resources awarded to replace EFC). *Average financial aid package:* $13,471 (excluding resources awarded to replace EFC). 50% of all full-time freshmen had no need and received non-need-based gift aid.

UNDERGRADUATE FINANCIAL AID (Fall 2009, est.) 517 applied for aid; of those 72% were deemed to have need. 100% of undergraduates with need received aid; of those 57% had need fully met. *Average percent of need met:* 92% (excluding resources awarded to replace EFC). *Average financial aid package:* $13,282 (excluding resources awarded to replace EFC). 49% of all full-time undergraduates had no need and received non-need-based gift aid.

GIFT AID (NEED-BASED) *Total amount:* $3,063,852 (29% federal, 34% state, 33% institutional, 4% external sources). *Receiving aid:* Freshmen: 50% (108); all full-time undergraduates: 44% (364). *Average award:* Freshmen: $11,297; Undergraduates: $9844. *Scholarships, grants, and awards:* Federal Pell, FSEOG, state, private, college/university gift aid from institutional funds, Academic Competitiveness Grants.

GIFT AID (NON-NEED-BASED) *Total amount:* $164,123 (1% federal, 68% state, 18% institutional, 13% external sources). *Receiving aid:* Freshmen: 12% (27). Undergraduates: 7% (60). *Average award:* Freshmen: $2964. Undergraduates: $2778. *Scholarships, grants, and awards by category: Academic interests/ achievement:* $2,159,188 total: general academic interests/achievements. *Special achievements/activities:* $437,200 total: general special achievements/activities. *Special characteristics:* $1,156,374 total: out-of-state students.

LOANS *Student loans:* $1,727,183 (71% need-based, 29% non-need-based). 41% of past graduating class borrowed through all loan programs. *Average indebtedness per student:* $14,794. *Average need-based loan:* Freshmen: $2942. Undergraduates: $3857. *Parent loans:* $134,855 (20% need-based, 80% non-need-based). *Programs:* FFEL (Subsidized and Unsubsidized Stafford, PLUS), alternative loans.

WORK-STUDY *Federal work-study:* Total amount: $39,645; 14 jobs averaging $3417. *State or other work-study/employment:* Total amount: $156,006 (100% need-based). 60 part-time jobs averaging $2685.

APPLYING FOR FINANCIAL AID *Required financial aid form:* FAFSA. *Financial aid deadline (priority):* 2/15. *Notification date:* Continuous beginning 3/15. Students must reply by 5/1 or within 4 weeks of notification.

CONTACT Monica Baldwin, Director of Financial Aid, New College of Florida, 5800 Bay Shore Road, Sarasota, FL 34243-2109, 941-487-5000. *Fax:* 941-487-5010. *E-mail:* ncfinaid@ncf.edu.

NEW ENGLAND COLLEGE
Henniker, NH

Tuition & fees: $27,450	Average undergraduate aid package: $23,584

ABOUT THE INSTITUTION Independent, coed. 39 undergraduate majors. Both federal and institutional methodology are used as a basis for awarding need-based institutional aid.

UNDERGRADUATE EXPENSES for 2009–10 *Comprehensive fee:* $37,076 includes full-time tuition ($27,200), mandatory fees ($250), and room and board ($9626). *College room only:* $5000. Full-time tuition and fees vary according to class time, course load, degree level, location, program, and reciprocity agreements. Room and board charges vary according to board plan and housing facility. *Part-time tuition:* $1300 per credit. Part-time tuition and fees vary according to class time, course load, degree level, location, and program. *Payment plan:* Installment.

FRESHMAN FINANCIAL AID (Fall 2009, est.) 223 applied for aid; of those 94% were deemed to have need. 100% of freshmen with need received aid; of those 14% had need fully met. *Average percent of need met:* 81% (excluding resources awarded to replace EFC). *Average financial aid package:* $25,105 (excluding resources awarded to replace EFC). 18% of all full-time freshmen had no need and received non-need-based gift aid.

UNDERGRADUATE FINANCIAL AID (Fall 2009, est.) 738 applied for aid; of those 91% were deemed to have need. 99% of undergraduates with need received aid; of those 18% had need fully met. *Average percent of need met:* 78% (excluding resources awarded to replace EFC). *Average financial aid package:* $23,584 (excluding resources awarded to replace EFC). 23% of all full-time undergraduates had no need and received non-need-based gift aid.

GIFT AID (NEED-BASED) *Total amount:* $9,910,137 (16% federal, 84% institutional). *Receiving aid:* Freshmen: 80% (204); all full-time undergraduates: 69% (650). *Average award:* Freshmen: $16,469; Undergraduates: $15,259. *Scholarships, grants, and awards:* Federal Pell, FSEOG, state, private, college/university gift aid from institutional funds.

GIFT AID (NON-NEED-BASED) *Total amount:* $2,351,299 (100% institutional). *Receiving aid:* Freshmen: 5% (14). Undergraduates: 6% (56). *Average award:* Freshmen: $10,387. Undergraduates: $10,846. *Scholarships, grants, and awards by category: Academic interests/achievement:* 796 awards ($9,002,636 total): biological sciences, business, communication, computer science, education, engineering/technologies, English, general academic interests/achievements, health fields, humanities, international studies, mathematics, social sciences. *Creative arts/performance:* 9 awards ($97,000 total): applied art and design, art/fine arts, creative writing, theater/drama. *Special achievements/activities:* 161 awards ($838,227 total): community service, leadership. *Special characteristics:* 37 awards ($443,736 total): children and siblings of alumni, children of educators, children of faculty/staff, ethnic background, international students, local/state students, parents of current students, siblings of current students. *Tuition waivers:* Full or partial for children of alumni, employees or children of employees, adult students, senior citizens.

LOANS *Student loans:* $6,093,111 (95% need-based, 5% non-need-based). 77% of past graduating class borrowed through all loan programs. *Average indebtedness per student:* $33,466. *Average need-based loan:* Freshmen: $8098. Undergraduates: $8253. *Parent loans:* $1,995,674 (87% need-based, 13% non-need-based). *Programs:* Federal Direct (Subsidized and Unsubsidized Stafford, PLUS), FFEL (Subsidized and Unsubsidized Stafford, PLUS), Perkins, state.

WORK-STUDY *Federal work-study:* Total amount: $694,602; 384 jobs averaging $1705. *State or other work-study/employment:* Total amount: $40,460 (56% need-based, 44% non-need-based). 43 part-time jobs averaging $1163.

APPLYING FOR FINANCIAL AID *Required financial aid forms:* FAFSA, institution's own form. *Financial aid deadline (priority):* 4/1. *Notification date:* Continuous beginning 2/1. Students must reply by 9/7 or within 2 weeks of notification.

CONTACT Kristen Blase, Student Financial Services Director, New England College, 15 Main Street, Henniker, NH 03242-3293, 603-428-2226 or toll-free 800-521-7642. *Fax:* 603-428-2404. *E-mail:* rstein@nec.edu.

NEW ENGLAND COLLEGE OF BUSINESS
Boston, MA

CONTACT Financial Aid Office, New England College of Business, 10 High Street, Suite 204, Boston, MA 02111-2645, 617-951-2350 or toll-free 888-696-NECF.

NEW ENGLAND CONSERVATORY OF MUSIC
Boston, MA

Tuition & fees: $34,950	Average undergraduate aid package: $20,765

ABOUT THE INSTITUTION Independent, coed. 8 undergraduate majors. Federal methodology is used as a basis for awarding need-based institutional aid.

UNDERGRADUATE EXPENSES for 2010–11 *Comprehensive fee:* $47,050 includes full-time tuition ($34,500), mandatory fees ($450), and room and board ($12,100). Room and board charges vary according to board plan. *Part-time tuition:* $1100 per credit.

FRESHMAN FINANCIAL AID (Fall 2009, est.) 65 applied for aid; of those 89% were deemed to have need. 100% of freshmen with need received aid; of those 22% had need fully met. *Average percent of need met:* 58% (excluding resources awarded to replace EFC). *Average financial aid package:* $20,626 (excluding resources awarded to replace EFC). 27% of all full-time freshmen had no need and received non-need-based gift aid.

UNDERGRADUATE FINANCIAL AID (Fall 2009, est.) 232 applied for aid; of those 89% were deemed to have need. 100% of undergraduates with need received aid; of those 16% had need fully met. *Average percent of need met:* 60% (excluding resources awarded to replace EFC). *Average financial aid package:* $20,765 (excluding resources awarded to replace EFC). 36% of all full-time undergraduates had no need and received non-need-based gift aid.

GIFT AID (NEED-BASED) *Total amount:* $3,323,772 (13% federal, 1% state, 78% institutional, 8% external sources). *Receiving aid:* Freshmen: 52% (58); all full-time undergraduates: 55% (206). *Average award:* Freshmen: $16,771;

Undergraduates: $15,947. *Scholarships, grants, and awards:* Federal Pell, FSEOG, state, private, college/university gift aid from institutional funds.

GIFT AID (NON-NEED-BASED) *Total amount:* $2,313,988 (94% institutional, 6% external sources). *Receiving aid:* Freshmen: 7% (8). Undergraduates: 6% (22). *Average award:* Freshmen: $14,646. Undergraduates: $14,879. *Scholarships, grants, and awards by category: Creative arts/performance:* 297 awards ($2,687,419 total): music, theater/drama. *Tuition waivers:* Full or partial for employees or children of employees.

LOANS *Student loans:* $2,227,741 (69% need-based, 31% non-need-based). 74% of past graduating class borrowed through all loan programs. *Average indebtedness per student:* $38,509. *Average need-based loan:* Freshmen: $2913. Undergraduates: $3847. *Parent loans:* $871,748 (51% need-based, 49% non-need-based). *Programs:* FFEL (Subsidized and Unsubsidized Stafford, PLUS), Perkins, state.

WORK-STUDY *Federal work-study:* Total amount: $290,819; 142 jobs averaging $2062. *State or other work-study/employment:* Part-time jobs available.

APPLYING FOR FINANCIAL AID *Required financial aid forms:* FAFSA, institution's own form. *Financial aid deadline (priority):* 2/1. *Notification date:* Continuous beginning 4/1. Students must reply by 5/1.

CONTACT Lauren G. Urbanek, Director of Financial Aid, New England Conservatory of Music, 290 Huntington Avenue, Boston, MA 02115, 617-585-1113. *Fax:* 617-585-1115. *E-mail:* lauren.urbanek@necmusic.edu.

THE NEW ENGLAND INSTITUTE OF ART
Brookline, MA

UNDERGRADUATE EXPENSES Tuition cost varies by program. Prospective students should contact the school for current tuition costs. Other charges include a starting kit for all first-quarter students. Kits vary in price, depending on the program of study.

CONTACT Financial Aid Office, The New England Institute of Art, 142 Berkeley Street, Boston, MA 02116-5100, 617-267-7910 or toll-free 800-903-4425.

NEW ENGLAND SCHOOL OF COMMUNICATIONS
Bangor, ME

Tuition & fees: $11,500	Average undergraduate aid package: N/A

ABOUT THE INSTITUTION Independent, coed, primarily men. 20 undergraduate majors. Federal methodology is used as a basis for awarding need-based institutional aid.

UNDERGRADUATE EXPENSES for 2010–11 *Comprehensive fee:* $18,494 includes full-time tuition ($10,700), mandatory fees ($800), and room and board ($6994). *Part-time tuition:* $360 per credit. Part-time tuition and fees vary according to course load. *Payment plan:* Installment.

FRESHMAN FINANCIAL AID (Fall 2008) 195 applied for aid; of those 89% were deemed to have need. 100% of freshmen with need received aid; of those 71% had need fully met. 4% of all full-time freshmen had no need and received non-need-based gift aid.

UNDERGRADUATE FINANCIAL AID (Fall 2008) 416 applied for aid; of those 89% were deemed to have need. 100% of undergraduates with need received aid; of those 52% had need fully met. 2% of all full-time undergraduates had no need and received non-need-based gift aid.

GIFT AID (NEED-BASED) *Total amount:* $1,119,361 (60% federal, 21% state, 3% institutional, 16% external sources). *Receiving aid:* Freshmen: 66% (132); all full-time undergraduates: 64% (272). *Average award:* Freshmen: $2510; Undergraduates: $2590. *Scholarships, grants, and awards:* Federal Pell, FSEOG, state, private, college/university gift aid from institutional funds.

GIFT AID (NON-NEED-BASED) *Average award:* Freshmen: $403. Undergraduates: $403. *Scholarships, grants, and awards by category: Academic interests/achievement:* communication. *Special achievements/activities:* general special achievements/activities. *Tuition waivers:* Full or partial for employees or children of employees.

LOANS *Student loans:* $2,661,567 (49% need-based, 51% non-need-based). 85% of past graduating class borrowed through all loan programs. *Average indebtedness per student:* $33,000. *Average need-based loan:* Freshmen: $1812. Undergraduates: $2146. *Parent loans:* $775,066 (100% need-based). *Programs:* Federal Direct (Subsidized and Unsubsidized Stafford, PLUS), alternative loans.

WORK-STUDY *Federal work-study:* Total amount: $21,850; 39 jobs averaging $796. *State or other work-study/employment:* 10 part-time jobs averaging $1000.

APPLYING FOR FINANCIAL AID *Required financial aid form:* FAFSA. *Financial aid deadline (priority):* 5/1. *Notification date:* Continuous beginning 5/1. Students must reply within 4 weeks of notification.

CONTACT Mrs. Nicole Vachon, Director of Financial Aid, New England School of Communications, One College Circle, Bangor, ME 04401, 888-877-1876. *Fax:* 207-947-3987. *E-mail:* nicole@nescom.edu.

NEW HAMPSHIRE INSTITUTE OF ART
Manchester, NH

CONTACT Linda Lavallee, Director of Financial Aid, New Hampshire Institute of Art, 148 Concord Street, Manchester, NH 03104-4858, 603-623-0313 Ext. 577 or toll-free 866-241-4918 (in-state). *Fax:* 603-647-0658. *E-mail:* llavallee@nhia.edu.

NEW JERSEY CITY UNIVERSITY
Jersey City, NJ

Tuition & fees (NJ res): $8988	Average undergraduate aid package: $8440

ABOUT THE INSTITUTION State-supported, coed. 27 undergraduate majors. Institutional methodology is used as a basis for awarding need-based institutional aid.

UNDERGRADUATE EXPENSES for 2009–10 *Tuition, state resident:* full-time $6542; part-time $218 per credit hour. *Tuition, nonresident:* full-time $13,820; part-time $461 per credit hour. *Required fees:* full-time $2446; $79.40 per credit hour. Part-time tuition and fees vary according to course load. *College room and board:* $9043; *Room only:* $5788. *Payment plan:* Deferred payment.

FRESHMAN FINANCIAL AID (Fall 2008) 572 applied for aid; of those 90% were deemed to have need. 93% of freshmen with need received aid; of those 4% had need fully met. *Average percent of need met:* 58% (excluding resources awarded to replace EFC). *Average financial aid package:* $9098 (excluding resources awarded to replace EFC). 3% of all full-time freshmen had no need and received non-need-based gift aid.

UNDERGRADUATE FINANCIAL AID (Fall 2008) 3,611 applied for aid; of those 94% were deemed to have need. 95% of undergraduates with need received aid; of those 8% had need fully met. *Average percent of need met:* 59% (excluding resources awarded to replace EFC). *Average financial aid package:* $8440 (excluding resources awarded to replace EFC). 1% of all full-time undergraduates had no need and received non-need-based gift aid.

GIFT AID (NEED-BASED) *Total amount:* $16,164,928 (50% federal, 50% state). *Receiving aid:* Freshmen: 63% (410); all full-time undergraduates: 54% (2,395). *Average award:* Freshmen: $7661; Undergraduates: $6727. *Scholarships, grants, and awards:* Federal Pell, FSEOG, state, private, college/university gift aid from institutional funds, United Negro College Fund.

GIFT AID (NON-NEED-BASED) *Total amount:* $70,591 (100% state). *Receiving aid:* Freshmen: 10% (67). Undergraduates: 6% (283). *Average award:* Freshmen: $6052. Undergraduates: $4982. *Tuition waivers:* Full or partial for employees or children of employees, senior citizens.

LOANS *Student loans:* $13,177,120 (58% need-based, 42% non-need-based). 53% of past graduating class borrowed through all loan programs. *Average indebtedness per student:* $11,337. *Average need-based loan:* Freshmen: $3417. Undergraduates: $4280. *Parent loans:* $393,936 (100% non-need-based). *Programs:* FFEL (Subsidized and Unsubsidized Stafford, PLUS), Perkins, state.

WORK-STUDY *Federal work-study:* Total amount: $704,869; jobs available.

APPLYING FOR FINANCIAL AID *Required financial aid form:* FAFSA. *Financial aid deadline (priority):* 4/15. *Notification date:* 5/15.

CONTACT Ms. Carmen Panlilio, Assistant Vice President for Admissions and Enrollment Management, New Jersey City University, 2039 Kennedy Boulevard, Jersey City, NJ 07305-1597, 201-200-3173 or toll-free 888-441-NJCU.

NEW JERSEY INSTITUTE OF TECHNOLOGY
Newark, NJ

Tuition & fees (NJ res): $12,856	Average undergraduate aid package: $13,000

ABOUT THE INSTITUTION State-supported, coed. 41 undergraduate majors. Federal methodology is used as a basis for awarding need-based institutional aid.

UNDERGRADUATE EXPENSES for 2009–10 *Tuition, state resident:* full-time $10,816; part-time $412 per credit. *Tuition, nonresident:* full-time $20,560; part-time $879 per credit. *Required fees:* full-time $2040; $100 per credit or $102 per term. Full-time tuition and fees vary according to course load and degree level. Part-time tuition and fees vary according to course load and degree level. *College room and board:* $9806; *Room only:* $6890. Room and board charges vary according to board plan and housing facility. *Payment plans:* Installment, deferred payment.

FRESHMAN FINANCIAL AID (Fall 2009, est.) 809 applied for aid; of those 85% were deemed to have need. 100% of freshmen with need received aid; of those 17% had need fully met. *Average percent of need met:* 63% (excluding resources awarded to replace EFC). *Average financial aid package:* $13,500 (excluding resources awarded to replace EFC). 17% of all full-time freshmen had no need and received non-need-based gift aid.

UNDERGRADUATE FINANCIAL AID (Fall 2009, est.) 2,800 applied for aid; of those 86% were deemed to have need. 100% of undergraduates with need received aid; of those 8% had need fully met. *Average percent of need met:* 65% (excluding resources awarded to replace EFC). *Average financial aid package:* $13,000 (excluding resources awarded to replace EFC). 13% of all full-time undergraduates had no need and received non-need-based gift aid.

GIFT AID (NEED-BASED) *Total amount:* $22,387,664 (40% federal, 56% state, 4% external sources). *Receiving aid:* Freshmen: 59% (542); all full-time undergraduates: 38% (1,800). *Average award:* Freshmen: $15,000; Undergraduates: $8900. *Scholarships, grants, and awards:* Federal Pell, FSEOG, state, private, college/university gift aid from institutional funds.

GIFT AID (NON-NEED-BASED) *Total amount:* $9,250,000 (3% state, 86% institutional, 11% external sources). *Receiving aid:* Freshmen: 48% (440). Undergraduates: 31% (1,500). *Average award:* Freshmen: $14,200. Undergraduates: $7000. *Scholarships, grants, and awards by category:* Academic interests/achievement: architecture, biological sciences, business, communication, computer science, engineering/technologies, general academic interests/achievements, humanities, mathematics, physical sciences. *Special characteristics:* out-of-state students. *Tuition waivers:* Full or partial for employees or children of employees.

LOANS *Student loans:* $19,000,000 (32% need-based, 68% non-need-based). 40% of past graduating class borrowed through all loan programs. *Average indebtedness per student:* $20,000. *Average need-based loan:* Freshmen: $3100. Undergraduates: $5000. *Parent loans:* $1,843,256 (62% need-based, 38% non-need-based). *Programs:* Federal Direct (Subsidized and Unsubsidized Stafford, PLUS), Perkins, state, college/university.

WORK-STUDY *Federal work-study:* Total amount: $400,000; jobs available. *State or other work-study/employment:* Part-time jobs available.

ATHLETIC AWARDS Total amount: $800,000 (8% need-based, 92% non-need-based).

APPLYING FOR FINANCIAL AID *Required financial aid form:* FAFSA. *Financial aid deadline:* 5/5 (priority: 3/15). *Notification date:* Continuous beginning 3/10. Students must reply within 2 weeks of notification.

CONTACT Ivon Nunez, Director, Financial Aid Services, New Jersey Institute of Technology, Student Mall, University Heights, Newark, NJ 07102, 973-596-3476 or toll-free 800-925-NJIT. *Fax:* 973-596-6471. *E-mail:* ivon.nunez@njit.edu.

NEW LIFE THEOLOGICAL SEMINARY
Charlotte, NC

CONTACT Financial Aid Office, New Life Theological Seminary, PO Box 790106, Charlotte, NC 28206-7901, 704-334-6882.

NEWMAN UNIVERSITY
Wichita, KS

Tuition & fees: $20,712	Average undergraduate aid package: $14,370

ABOUT THE INSTITUTION Independent Roman Catholic, coed. 41 undergraduate majors. Federal methodology is used as a basis for awarding need-based institutional aid.

UNDERGRADUATE EXPENSES for 2010–11 *Comprehensive fee:* $27,650 includes full-time tuition ($19,872), mandatory fees ($840), and room and

board ($6938). *College room only:* $3520. Full-time tuition and fees vary according to class time, course load, location, and program. Room and board charges vary according to board plan and housing facility. *Part-time tuition:* $662 per credit hour. *Part-time fees:* $15 per credit hour; $40 per year. Part-time tuition and fees vary according to class time, course load, location, and program. *Payment plan:* Installment.

FRESHMAN FINANCIAL AID (Fall 2009, est.) 168 applied for aid; of those 89% were deemed to have need. 100% of freshmen with need received aid; of those 29% had need fully met. *Average percent of need met:* 74% (excluding resources awarded to replace EFC). *Average financial aid package:* $16,017 (excluding resources awarded to replace EFC). 5% of all full-time freshmen had no need and received non-need-based gift aid.

UNDERGRADUATE FINANCIAL AID (Fall 2009, est.) 1,074 applied for aid; of those 86% were deemed to have need. 100% of undergraduates with need received aid; of those 16% had need fully met. *Average percent of need met:* 62% (excluding resources awarded to replace EFC). *Average financial aid package:* $14,370 (excluding resources awarded to replace EFC). 4% of all full-time undergraduates had no need and received non-need-based gift aid.

GIFT AID (NEED-BASED) *Total amount:* $2,777,836 (74% federal, 26% state). *Receiving aid:* Freshmen: 71% (120); all full-time undergraduates: 67% (730). *Average award:* Freshmen: $4518; Undergraduates: $4869. *Scholarships, grants, and awards:* Federal Pell, FSEOG, state, private, college/university gift aid from institutional funds.

GIFT AID (NON-NEED-BASED) *Total amount:* $6,720,550 (95% institutional, 5% external sources). *Receiving aid:* Freshmen: 88% (148). Undergraduates: 73% (788). *Average award:* Freshmen: $7778. Undergraduates: $5673. *Scholarships, grants, and awards by category: Academic interests/achievement:* 596 awards ($3,743,860 total): general academic interests/achievements. *Creative arts/performance:* 37 awards ($78,000 total): art/fine arts, journalism/publications, music, theater/drama. *Special achievements/activities:* 97 awards ($461,500 total): community service, leadership, memberships, religious involvement. *Special characteristics:* 159 awards ($656,735 total): children and siblings of alumni, children of current students, children of faculty/staff, international students, married students, siblings of current students, spouses of current students. *Tuition waivers:* Full or partial for employees or children of employees.

LOANS *Student loans:* $12,628,916 (38% need-based, 62% non-need-based). 77% of past graduating class borrowed through all loan programs. *Average indebtedness per student:* $23,996. *Average need-based loan:* Freshmen: $2988. Undergraduates: $4065. *Parent loans:* $532,884 (100% non-need-based). *Programs:* Federal Direct (Subsidized and Unsubsidized Stafford, PLUS), Perkins.

WORK-STUDY *Federal work-study:* Total amount: $68,473; 66 jobs averaging $1037. *State or other work-study/employment:* Total amount: $79,551 (100% non-need-based). 80 part-time jobs averaging $994.

ATHLETIC AWARDS Total amount: $1,281,243 (100% non-need-based).

APPLYING FOR FINANCIAL AID *Required financial aid form:* FAFSA. *Financial aid deadline (priority):* 3/1. *Notification date:* Continuous.

CONTACT Kara Schwinn, Financial Aid Counselor, Newman University, 3100 McCormick Avenue, Wichita, KS 67213, 316-942-4291 Ext. 2302 or toll-free 877-NEWMANU Ext. 2144. *Fax:* 316-942-4483.

NEW MEXICO HIGHLANDS UNIVERSITY
Las Vegas, NM

CONTACT Eileen Sedillo, Director, Financial Aid and Scholarship, New Mexico Highlands University, Box 9000, Las Vegas, NM 87701, 505-454-3430 or toll-free 800-338-6648. *Fax:* 505-454-3398. *E-mail:* sedillo_e@nmhu.edu.

NEW MEXICO INSTITUTE OF MINING AND TECHNOLOGY
Socorro, NM

Tuition & fees (NM res): $4607   Average undergraduate aid package: $10,397

ABOUT THE INSTITUTION State-supported, coed. 23 undergraduate majors. Federal methodology is used as a basis for awarding need-based institutional aid.

UNDERGRADUATE EXPENSES for 2010–11 *Tuition, state resident:* full-time $3980; part-time $166 per credit hour. *Tuition, nonresident:* full-time $12,941; part-time $539 per credit hour. *Required fees:* full-time $627. Part-time tuition

and fees vary according to course load. *College room and board:* $5702. Room and board charges vary according to board plan and housing facility.

FRESHMAN FINANCIAL AID (Fall 2009, est.) 253 applied for aid; of those 46% were deemed to have need. 99% of freshmen with need received aid; of those 36% had need fully met. *Average percent of need met:* 91% (excluding resources awarded to replace EFC). *Average financial aid package:* $9886 (excluding resources awarded to replace EFC). 40% of all full-time freshmen had no need and received non-need-based gift aid.

UNDERGRADUATE FINANCIAL AID (Fall 2009, est.) 958 applied for aid; of those 49% were deemed to have need. 98% of undergraduates with need received aid; of those 43% had need fully met. *Average percent of need met:* 89% (excluding resources awarded to replace EFC). *Average financial aid package:* $10,397 (excluding resources awarded to replace EFC). 38% of all full-time undergraduates had no need and received non-need-based gift aid.

GIFT AID (NEED-BASED) *Total amount:* $1,916,897 (85% federal, 15% state). *Receiving aid:* Freshmen: 20% (60); all full-time undergraduates: 26% (275). *Average award:* Freshmen: $6020; Undergraduates: $6463. *Scholarships, grants, and awards:* Federal Pell, FSEOG, state, private, college/university gift aid from institutional funds.

GIFT AID (NON-NEED-BASED) *Total amount:* $3,275,457 (47% state, 53% institutional). *Receiving aid:* Freshmen: 30% (88). Undergraduates: 27% (286). *Average award:* Freshmen: $4164. Undergraduates: $5226. *Tuition waivers:* Full or partial for employees or children of employees.

LOANS *Student loans:* $1,937,007 (100% need-based). 90% of past graduating class borrowed through all loan programs. *Average indebtedness per student:* $7894. *Average need-based loan:* Freshmen: $4606. Undergraduates: $5089. *Parent loans:* $122,392 (100% need-based). *Programs:* FFEL (Subsidized and Unsubsidized Stafford, PLUS), Perkins.

WORK-STUDY *Federal work-study:* Total amount: $541,865; jobs available. *State or other work-study/employment:* Total amount: $131,853 (37% need-based, 63% non-need-based). Part-time jobs available.

APPLYING FOR FINANCIAL AID *Required financial aid form:* FAFSA. *Financial aid deadline (priority):* 6/1. *Notification date:* Continuous. Students must reply within 2 weeks of notification.

CONTACT Ms. Annette Kaus, Director of Financial Aid, New Mexico Institute of Mining and Technology, 801 Leroy Place, Socorro, NM 87801, 575-835-5333 or toll-free 800-428-TECH. *Fax:* 575-835-5959. *E-mail:* akaus@admin.nmt.edu.

NEW MEXICO STATE UNIVERSITY
Las Cruces, NM

Tuition & fees (NM res): $4998   Average undergraduate aid package: $7539

ABOUT THE INSTITUTION State-supported, coed. 82 undergraduate majors. Federal methodology is used as a basis for awarding need-based institutional aid.

UNDERGRADUATE EXPENSES for 2009–10 *Tuition, state resident:* full-time $3720; part-time $208.25 per credit hour. *Tuition, nonresident:* full-time $13,872; part-time $631.25 per credit hour. *Required fees:* full-time $1278. *College room and board:* $6338; *Room only:* $3628. Room and board charges vary according to board plan and housing facility. *Payment plans:* Installment, deferred payment.

FRESHMAN FINANCIAL AID (Fall 2009, est.) 1,470 applied for aid; of those 78% were deemed to have need. 81% of freshmen with need received aid; of those 8% had need fully met. *Average percent of need met:* 51% (excluding resources awarded to replace EFC). *Average financial aid package:* $6783 (excluding resources awarded to replace EFC). 1% of all full-time freshmen had no need and received non-need-based gift aid.

UNDERGRADUATE FINANCIAL AID (Fall 2009, est.) 7,907 applied for aid; of those 88% were deemed to have need. 88% of undergraduates with need received aid; of those 5% had need fully met. *Average percent of need met:* 48% (excluding resources awarded to replace EFC). *Average financial aid package:* $7539 (excluding resources awarded to replace EFC). 1% of all full-time undergraduates had no need and received non-need-based gift aid.

GIFT AID (NEED-BASED) *Total amount:* $27,815,692 (64% federal, 34% state, 2% external sources). *Receiving aid:* Freshmen: 48% (861); all full-time undergraduates: 48% (5,211). *Average award:* Freshmen: $5455; Undergraduates: $5125. *Scholarships, grants, and awards:* Federal Pell, FSEOG, state, private, college/university gift aid from institutional funds.

GIFT AID (NON-NEED-BASED) *Total amount:* $6,612,037 (2% federal, 95% state, 3% external sources). *Average award:* Freshmen: $424. Undergraduates: $315. *Scholarships, grants, and awards by category: Academic interests/achievement:* 1,147 awards ($7,026,722 total): agriculture, biological sciences, business, communication, computer science, education, engineering/technologies, English, foreign languages, general academic interests/achievements, health fields, home economics, humanities, mathematics, military science, physical sciences, social sciences. *Creative arts/performance:* 105 awards ($693,782 total): applied art and design, art/fine arts, general creative arts/performance, journalism/publications, music, performing arts, theater/drama. *Special achievements/activities:* leadership, rodeo. *Special characteristics:* adult students, children and siblings of alumni, children of faculty/staff, children of public servants, children of union members/company employees, children of workers in trades, children with a deceased or disabled parent, ethnic background, handicapped students, international students, local/state students, married students, members of minority groups, out-of-state students, previous college experience, spouses of current students, veterans, veterans' children. *Tuition waivers:* Full or partial for employees or children of employees, senior citizens.
LOANS *Student loans:* $35,605,163 (88% need-based, 12% non-need-based). 51% of past graduating class borrowed through all loan programs. *Average indebtedness per student:* $23,262. *Average need-based loan:* Freshmen: $3261. Undergraduates: $4130. *Parent loans:* $600,782 (50% need-based, 50% non-need-based). *Programs:* FFEL (Subsidized and Unsubsidized Stafford, PLUS), Perkins, state.
WORK-STUDY *Federal work-study:* Total amount: $591,709; 391 jobs averaging $1913. *State or other work-study/employment:* Total amount: $937,530 (84% need-based, 16% non-need-based). 458 part-time jobs averaging $2127.
ATHLETIC AWARDS Total amount: $2,074,030 (50% need-based, 50% non-need-based).
APPLYING FOR FINANCIAL AID *Required financial aid forms:* FAFSA, institution's own form. *Financial aid deadline (priority):* 3/1.
CONTACT Mr. Michael Zimmerman, Interim Director of Financial Aid, New Mexico State University, Box 30001, Department 5100, Las Cruces, NM 88003-8001, 575-646-4105 or toll-free 800-662-6678. *Fax:* 575-646-7381.

NEW ORLEANS BAPTIST THEOLOGICAL SEMINARY
New Orleans, LA

Tuition & fees: N/R	Average undergraduate aid package: $600

ABOUT THE INSTITUTION Independent Southern Baptist, coed, primarily men. *Awards:* associate, bachelor's, and master's degrees. 4 undergraduate majors. *Total enrollment:* 2,036. Undergraduates: 974. Institutional methodology is used as a basis for awarding need-based institutional aid.
FRESHMAN FINANCIAL AID (Fall 2009, est.) 56 applied for aid; of those 100% were deemed to have need. 91% of freshmen with need received aid. *Average percent of need met:* 20% (excluding resources awarded to replace EFC). *Average financial aid package:* $400 (excluding resources awarded to replace EFC).
UNDERGRADUATE FINANCIAL AID (Fall 2009, est.) 230 applied for aid; of those 100% were deemed to have need. 69% of undergraduates with need received aid. *Average percent of need met:* 30% (excluding resources awarded to replace EFC). *Average financial aid package:* $600 (excluding resources awarded to replace EFC).
GIFT AID (NEED-BASED) *Total amount:* $145,482 (23% state, 77% institutional). *Receiving aid:* Freshmen: 39% (51); all full-time undergraduates: 33% (159). *Average award:* Freshmen: $400; Undergraduates: $600. *Scholarships, grants, and awards:* state, private, college/university gift aid from institutional funds.
LOANS *Student loans:* $80,360 (100% need-based). 20% of past graduating class borrowed through all loan programs. *Average indebtedness per student:* $10,000. *Programs:* Signature Loans.
APPLYING FOR FINANCIAL AID *Required financial aid form:* institution's own form. *Financial aid deadline:* 6/15 (priority: 3/30). *Notification date:* 7/31. Students must reply within 4 weeks of notification.
CONTACT Owen Nease, Financial Aid Office, New Orleans Baptist Theological Seminary, 3939 Gentilly Boulevard, New Orleans, LA 70126-4858, 504-282-4455 Ext. 3348 or toll-free 800-662-8701. *Fax:* 504-816-8437. *E-mail:* financialaid@nobts.edu.

NEW SAINT ANDREWS COLLEGE
Moscow, ID

CONTACT Financial Aid Office, New Saint Andrews College, PO Box 9025, Moscow, ID 83843, 208-882-1566.

THE NEW SCHOOL FOR GENERAL STUDIES
New York, NY

Tuition & fees: $24,288	Average undergraduate aid package: $16,881

ABOUT THE INSTITUTION Independent, coed. 2 undergraduate majors. Federal methodology is used as a basis for awarding need-based institutional aid.
UNDERGRADUATE EXPENSES for 2009–10 *Comprehensive fee:* $39,548 includes full-time tuition ($24,288) and room and board ($15,260). *College room only:* $12,260. Room and board charges vary according to board plan and housing facility. *Part-time tuition:* $1012 per credit. Part-time tuition and fees vary according to course load. *Payment plan:* Installment.
UNDERGRADUATE FINANCIAL AID (Fall 2009, est.) 158 applied for aid; of those 92% were deemed to have need. 100% of undergraduates with need received aid; of those 4% had need fully met. *Average percent of need met:* 59% (excluding resources awarded to replace EFC). *Average financial aid package:* $16,881 (excluding resources awarded to replace EFC). 1% of all full-time undergraduates had no need and received non-need-based gift aid.
GIFT AID (NEED-BASED) *Total amount:* $3,199,598 (26% federal, 5% state, 66% institutional, 3% external sources). *Receiving aid:* All full-time undergraduates: 42% (142). *Average award:* Undergraduates: $7321. *Scholarships, grants, and awards:* Federal Pell, FSEOG, state, private, college/university gift aid from institutional funds.
GIFT AID (NON-NEED-BASED) *Total amount:* $91,836 (100% institutional). *Receiving aid:* Undergraduates: 1% (3). *Average award:* Undergraduates: $1825. *Scholarships, grants, and awards by category: Academic interests/achievement:* general academic interests/achievements. *Tuition waivers:* Full or partial for employees or children of employees.
LOANS *Student loans:* $3,999,696 (97% need-based, 3% non-need-based). *Average need-based loan:* Undergraduates: $9419. *Parent loans:* $193,043 (80% need-based, 20% non-need-based). *Programs:* FFEL (Subsidized and Unsubsidized Stafford, PLUS), Perkins.
WORK-STUDY *Federal work-study:* Total amount: $48,500; jobs available.
APPLYING FOR FINANCIAL AID *Required financial aid forms:* FAFSA, state aid form. *Financial aid deadline (priority):* 3/1. *Notification date:* Continuous beginning 3/1. Students must reply within 4 weeks of notification.
CONTACT Financial Aid Counselor, The New School for General Studies, 65 Fifth Avenue, New York, NY 10003, 212-229-8930 or toll-free 800-862-5039 (out-of-state). *Fax:* 212-229-5919.

THE NEW SCHOOL FOR JAZZ AND CONTEMPORARY MUSIC
New York, NY

Tuition & fees: $33,600	Average undergraduate aid package: $23,948

ABOUT THE INSTITUTION Independent, coed. 7 undergraduate majors. Federal methodology is used as a basis for awarding need-based institutional aid.
UNDERGRADUATE EXPENSES for 2009–10 *Comprehensive fee:* $48,860 includes full-time tuition ($32,860), mandatory fees ($740), and room and board ($15,260). *College room only:* $12,260. Room and board charges vary according to board plan and housing facility. *Part-time tuition:* $1076 per credit. Part-time tuition and fees vary according to course load and program. *Payment plan:* Installment.
FRESHMAN FINANCIAL AID (Fall 2009, est.) 29 applied for aid; of those 79% were deemed to have need. 100% of freshmen with need received aid. *Average percent of need met:* 65% (excluding resources awarded to replace EFC). *Average financial aid package:* $24,582 (excluding resources awarded to replace EFC). 23% of all full-time freshmen had no need and received non-need-based gift aid.
UNDERGRADUATE FINANCIAL AID (Fall 2009, est.) 114 applied for aid; of those 90% were deemed to have need. 100% of undergraduates with need received aid; of those 2% had need fully met. *Average percent of need met:*

54% (excluding resources awarded to replace EFC). *Average financial aid package:* $23,948 (excluding resources awarded to replace EFC). 3% of all full-time undergraduates had no need and received non-need-based gift aid.
GIFT AID (NEED-BASED) *Total amount:* $1,383,011 (12% federal, 3% state, 81% institutional, 4% external sources). *Receiving aid:* Freshmen: 42% (20); all full-time undergraduates: 38% (90). *Average award:* Freshmen: $19,905; Undergraduates: $14,475. *Scholarships, grants, and awards:* Federal Pell, FSEOG, state, private, college/university gift aid from institutional funds.
GIFT AID (NON-NEED-BASED) *Total amount:* $1,231,650 (99% institutional, 1% external sources). *Receiving aid:* Undergraduates: 5% (11). *Average award:* Freshmen: $12,258. Undergraduates: $9315. *Scholarships, grants, and awards by category:* Academic interests/achievement: general academic interests/achievements. Creative arts/performance: music. *Tuition waivers:* Full or partial for employees or children of employees.
LOANS *Student loans:* $974,137 (95% need-based, 5% non-need-based). 65% of past graduating class borrowed through all loan programs. *Average indebtedness per student:* $27,582. *Average need-based loan:* Freshmen: $8875. Undergraduates: $11,002. *Parent loans:* $392,133 (52% need-based, 48% non-need-based). *Programs:* FFEL (Subsidized and Unsubsidized Stafford, PLUS), Perkins.
WORK-STUDY *Federal work-study:* Total amount: $26,000; jobs available.
APPLYING FOR FINANCIAL AID *Required financial aid forms:* FAFSA, state aid form. *Financial aid deadline:* Continuous. *Notification date:* Continuous beginning 3/1. Students must reply within 4 weeks of notification.
CONTACT Eileen F. Doyle, Assistant Vice President for Student Financial Services, The New School for Jazz and Contemporary Music, 72 Fifth Avenue, New York, NY 10011, 212-229-8930. *E-mail:* sfs@newschool.edu.

NEWSCHOOL OF ARCHITECTURE & DESIGN
San Diego, CA

CONTACT Matt Wakeman, Director of Financial Aid, Newschool of Architecture & Design, 1249 F Street, San Diego, CA 92101-6634, 619-235-4100 Ext. 103. *Fax:* 619-235-4651.

NEW WORLD SCHOOL OF THE ARTS
Miami, FL

CONTACT Financial Aid Office, New World School of the Arts, 300 NE 2nd Avenue, Miami, FL 33132, 305-237-3135.

NEW YORK CITY COLLEGE OF TECHNOLOGY OF THE CITY UNIVERSITY OF NEW YORK
Brooklyn, NY

Tuition & fees (NY res): $4939	Average undergraduate aid package: $7863

ABOUT THE INSTITUTION State and locally supported, coed. 35 undergraduate majors. Both federal and institutional methodology are used as a basis for awarding need-based institutional aid.
UNDERGRADUATE EXPENSES for 2010–11 *Tuition, state resident:* full-time $4600; part-time $195 per credit. *Tuition, nonresident:* full-time $12,450; part-time $415 per credit. *Required fees:* full-time $339; $85.20 per term. *College room and board:* $1500. *Payment plan:* Deferred payment.
FRESHMAN FINANCIAL AID (Fall 2009, est.) 2,678 applied for aid; of those 90% were deemed to have need. 98% of freshmen with need received aid; of those 8% had need fully met. *Average percent of need met:* 64% (excluding resources awarded to replace EFC). *Average financial aid package:* $7839 (excluding resources awarded to replace EFC). 2% of all full-time freshmen had no need and received non-need-based gift aid.
UNDERGRADUATE FINANCIAL AID (Fall 2009, est.) 7,689 applied for aid; of those 93% were deemed to have need. 98% of undergraduates with need received aid; of those 5% had need fully met. *Average percent of need met:* 60% (excluding resources awarded to replace EFC). *Average financial aid package:* $7863 (excluding resources awarded to replace EFC). 1% of all full-time undergraduates had no need and received non-need-based gift aid.

GIFT AID (NEED-BASED) *Total amount:* $61,461,502 (60% federal, 39% state, 1% external sources). *Receiving aid:* Freshmen: 80% (2,361); all full-time undergraduates: 76% (6,915). *Average award:* Freshmen: $7679; Undergraduates: $7501. *Scholarships, grants, and awards:* Federal Pell, FSEOG, state, private, college/university gift aid from institutional funds, Federal Nursing.
GIFT AID (NON-NEED-BASED) *Total amount:* $118,859 (24% federal, 44% state, 32% external sources). *Receiving aid:* Freshmen: 22% (643). Undergraduates: 12% (1,107). *Average award:* Freshmen: $487. Undergraduates: $491. *Scholarships, grants, and awards by category:* Academic interests/achievement: general academic interests/achievements. Creative arts/performance: art/fine arts, music. *Special characteristics:* local/state students, members of minority groups. *Tuition waivers:* Full or partial for employees or children of employees.
LOANS *Student loans:* $4,968,604 (100% need-based). *Average need-based loan:* Freshmen: $2693. Undergraduates: $3859. *Programs:* Federal Direct (Subsidized and Unsubsidized Stafford, PLUS), Perkins, Federal Nursing.
WORK-STUDY *Federal work-study:* Total amount: $1,875,199; jobs available.
APPLYING FOR FINANCIAL AID *Required financial aid form:* FAFSA. *Financial aid deadline:* 4/30 (priority: 1/1). *Notification date:* 3/1.
CONTACT Sandra Higgins, Director of Financial Aid, New York City College of Technology of the City University of New York, 300 Jay Street, Namm Hall, Room G-13, Brooklyn, NY 11201, 718-260-5700. *Fax:* 718-254-8525. *E-mail:* shiggins@citytech.cuny.edu.

NEW YORK INSTITUTE OF TECHNOLOGY
Old Westbury, NY

Tuition & fees: $24,140	Average undergraduate aid package: $18,882

ABOUT THE INSTITUTION Independent, coed. 62 undergraduate majors. Federal methodology is used as a basis for awarding need-based institutional aid.
UNDERGRADUATE EXPENSES for 2009–10 *Comprehensive fee:* $34,660 includes full-time tuition ($23,380), mandatory fees ($760), and room and board ($10,520). Full-time tuition and fees vary according to course load and program. Room and board charges vary according to board plan, housing facility, and location. *Part-time tuition:* $790 per credit hour. *Part-time fees:* $330 per term. Part-time tuition and fees vary according to course load. *Payment plan:* Installment.
FRESHMAN FINANCIAL AID (Fall 2009, est.) 1,103 applied for aid; of those 87% were deemed to have need. 99% of freshmen with need received aid. *Average financial aid package:* $14,352 (excluding resources awarded to replace EFC). 13% of all full-time freshmen had no need and received non-need-based gift aid.
UNDERGRADUATE FINANCIAL AID (Fall 2009, est.) 3,207 applied for aid; of those 88% were deemed to have need. 98% of undergraduates with need received aid. *Average financial aid package:* $18,882 (excluding resources awarded to replace EFC). 11% of all full-time undergraduates had no need and received non-need-based gift aid.
GIFT AID (NEED-BASED) *Total amount:* $14,789,394 (38% federal, 35% state, 27% institutional). *Receiving aid:* Freshmen: 39% (633); all full-time undergraduates: 38% (2,020). *Average award:* Freshmen: $4227; Undergraduates: $5560. *Scholarships, grants, and awards:* Federal Pell, FSEOG, state, private, college/university gift aid from institutional funds.
GIFT AID (NON-NEED-BASED) *Total amount:* $17,249,420 (1% state, 99% institutional). *Receiving aid:* Freshmen: 57% (916). Undergraduates: 45% (2,406). *Average award:* Freshmen: $9212. Undergraduates: $12,385. *Scholarships, grants, and awards by category:* Academic interests/achievement: general academic interests/achievements. *Special characteristics:* children and siblings of alumni, children of educators, children of faculty/staff, children of public servants, local/state students, previous college experience, public servants, spouses of deceased or disabled public servants, veterans. *Tuition waivers:* Full or partial for employees or children of employees, senior citizens.
LOANS *Student loans:* $25,025,091 (41% need-based, 59% non-need-based). *Average need-based loan:* Freshmen: $3859. Undergraduates: $5779. *Parent loans:* $8,662,057 (100% non-need-based). *Programs:* Federal Direct (Subsidized and Unsubsidized Stafford, PLUS), Perkins, alternative loans.
WORK-STUDY *Federal work-study:* Total amount: $573,882; jobs available. *State or other work-study/employment:* Total amount: $593,123 (100% non-need-based). Part-time jobs available.
ATHLETIC AWARDS Total amount: $2,277,397 (100% non-need-based).

APPLYING FOR FINANCIAL AID *Required financial aid form:* FAFSA. *Financial aid deadline (priority):* 3/1. *Notification date:* Continuous beginning 3/1. Students must reply within 4 weeks of notification.

CONTACT Doreen Meyer, Director of Financial Aid, New York Institute of Technology, PO Box 8000, Old Westbury, NY 11568-8000, 516-686-1083 or toll-free 800-345-NYIT. *Fax:* 516-686-7997. *E-mail:* dmeyer@nyit.edu.

NEW YORK SCHOOL OF INTERIOR DESIGN
New York, NY

Tuition & fees: $22,895	Average undergraduate aid package: $7779

ABOUT THE INSTITUTION Independent, coed, primarily women. 1 undergraduate major. Federal methodology is used as a basis for awarding need-based institutional aid.

UNDERGRADUATE EXPENSES for 2010–11 *Tuition:* full-time $22,605; part-time $765 per credit. *Required fees:* full-time $290; $195 per term. Full-time tuition and fees vary according to course load. Part-time tuition and fees vary according to course load. *Payment plan:* Installment.

FRESHMAN FINANCIAL AID (Fall 2009, est.) 135 applied for aid; of those 95% were deemed to have need. 14% of freshmen with need received aid; of those 11% had need fully met. *Average percent of need met:* 1% (excluding resources awarded to replace EFC). *Average financial aid package:* $8441 (excluding resources awarded to replace EFC).

UNDERGRADUATE FINANCIAL AID (Fall 2009, est.) 402 applied for aid; of those 93% were deemed to have need. 29% of undergraduates with need received aid; of those 5% had need fully met. *Average percent of need met:* 1% (excluding resources awarded to replace EFC). *Average financial aid package:* $7779 (excluding resources awarded to replace EFC). 1% of all full-time undergraduates had no need and received non-need-based gift aid.

GIFT AID (NEED-BASED) *Total amount:* $615,927 (53% federal, 13% state, 29% institutional, 5% external sources). *Receiving aid:* Freshmen: 10% (13); all full-time undergraduates: 19% (77). *Average award:* Freshmen: $7823; Undergraduates: $5830. *Scholarships, grants, and awards:* Federal Pell, FSEOG, state, college/university gift aid from institutional funds.

GIFT AID (NON-NEED-BASED) *Total amount:* $11,628 (48% state, 52% institutional). *Receiving aid:* Undergraduates: 1. *Average award:* Undergraduates: $6000. *Tuition waivers:* Full or partial for employees or children of employees.

LOANS *Student loans:* $1,867,477 (81% need-based, 19% non-need-based). 71% of past graduating class borrowed through all loan programs. *Average indebtedness per student:* $21,000. *Average need-based loan:* Freshmen: $2922. Undergraduates: $3738. *Parent loans:* $462,733 (72% need-based, 28% non-need-based). *Programs:* Federal Direct (Subsidized and Unsubsidized Stafford, PLUS), state.

WORK-STUDY *Federal work-study:* Total amount: $33,091; 17 jobs averaging $1947.

APPLYING FOR FINANCIAL AID *Required financial aid forms:* FAFSA, state aid form. *Financial aid deadline (priority):* 5/1. *Notification date:* Continuous beginning 5/1. Students must reply within 2 weeks of notification.

CONTACT Mrs. Rashmi H. Wadhvani, Director of Financial Aid, New York School of Interior Design, 170 East 70th Street, New York, NY 10021-5110, 212-472-1500 Ext. 212 or toll-free 800-336-9743 Ext. 204. *Fax:* 212-472-1867. *E-mail:* nina@nysid.edu.

NEW YORK UNIVERSITY
New York, NY

Tuition & fees: $38,765	Average undergraduate aid package: $23,900

ABOUT THE INSTITUTION Independent, coed. 89 undergraduate majors. Federal methodology is used as a basis for awarding need-based institutional aid.

UNDERGRADUATE EXPENSES for 2009–10 *Comprehensive fee:* $51,993 includes full-time tuition ($36,586), mandatory fees ($2179), and room and board ($13,228). Full-time tuition and fees vary according to course load and program. Room and board charges vary according to board plan and housing facility. *Part-time tuition:* $1078 per credit. *Part-time fees:* $59 per credit; $403 per term. Part-time tuition and fees vary according to program. *Payment plans:* Guaranteed tuition, tuition prepayment, installment, deferred payment.

FRESHMAN FINANCIAL AID (Fall 2008) 3,004 applied for aid; of those 80% were deemed to have need. 98% of freshmen with need received aid. *Average percent of need met:* 71% (excluding resources awarded to replace EFC). *Average financial aid package:* $26,287 (excluding resources awarded to replace EFC). 5% of all full-time freshmen had no need and received non-need-based gift aid.

UNDERGRADUATE FINANCIAL AID (Fall 2008) 11,769 applied for aid; of those 86% were deemed to have need. 98% of undergraduates with need received aid. *Average percent of need met:* 64% (excluding resources awarded to replace EFC). *Average financial aid package:* $23,900 (excluding resources awarded to replace EFC). 8% of all full-time undergraduates had no need and received non-need-based gift aid.

GIFT AID (NEED-BASED) *Total amount:* $162,486,433 (11% federal, 6% state, 79% institutional, 4% external sources). *Receiving aid:* Freshmen: 51% (2,298); all full-time undergraduates: 49% (9,535). *Average award:* Freshmen: $19,120; Undergraduates: $16,870. *Scholarships, grants, and awards:* Federal Pell, FSEOG, state, private, college/university gift aid from institutional funds, Federal Nursing.

GIFT AID (NON-NEED-BASED) *Total amount:* $16,065,124 (3% state, 73% institutional, 24% external sources). *Average award:* Freshmen: $6683. Undergraduates: $7426. *Scholarships, grants, and awards by category:* Academic interests/achievement: 1,597 awards ($11,694,564 total): general academic interests/achievements. *Tuition waivers:* Full or partial for employees or children of employees.

LOANS *Student loans:* $136,033,795 (86% need-based, 14% non-need-based). 59% of past graduating class borrowed through all loan programs. *Average indebtedness per student:* $33,487. *Average need-based loan:* Freshmen: $4947. Undergraduates: $5583. *Parent loans:* $81,401,841 (79% need-based, 21% non-need-based). *Programs:* Federal Direct (Subsidized and Unsubsidized Stafford, PLUS), Perkins, Federal Nursing.

WORK-STUDY *Federal work-study:* Total amount: $5,588,642; 2,689 jobs averaging $2078.

APPLYING FOR FINANCIAL AID *Required financial aid forms:* FAFSA, state aid form. *Financial aid deadline (priority):* 2/15. *Notification date:* 4/1. Students must reply by 5/1.

CONTACT Financial Aid Office, New York University, 25 West Fourth Street, New York, NY 10012-1199, 212-998-4444. *Fax:* 212-995-4661. *E-mail:* financial.aid@nyu.edu.

NIAGARA UNIVERSITY
Niagara Falls, NY

Tuition & fees: $24,700	Average undergraduate aid package: $19,418

ABOUT THE INSTITUTION Independent religious, coed. 59 undergraduate majors. Federal methodology is used as a basis for awarding need-based institutional aid.

UNDERGRADUATE EXPENSES for 2009–10 *Comprehensive fee:* $34,950 includes full-time tuition ($23,700), mandatory fees ($1000), and room and board ($10,250). *Part-time tuition:* $790 per credit. *Payment plans:* Installment, deferred payment.

FRESHMAN FINANCIAL AID (Fall 2009, est.) 644 applied for aid; of those 89% were deemed to have need. 100% of freshmen with need received aid; of those 55% had need fully met. *Average percent of need met:* 85% (excluding resources awarded to replace EFC). *Average financial aid package:* $20,592 (excluding resources awarded to replace EFC). 14% of all full-time freshmen had no need and received non-need-based gift aid.

UNDERGRADUATE FINANCIAL AID (Fall 2009, est.) 2,339 applied for aid; of those 90% were deemed to have need. 100% of undergraduates with need received aid; of those 53% had need fully met. *Average percent of need met:* 82% (excluding resources awarded to replace EFC). *Average financial aid package:* $19,418 (excluding resources awarded to replace EFC). 17% of all full-time undergraduates had no need and received non-need-based gift aid.

GIFT AID (NEED-BASED) *Total amount:* $33,265,944 (16% federal, 10% state, 73% institutional, 1% external sources). *Receiving aid:* Freshmen: 84% (568); all full-time undergraduates: 70% (2,070). *Average award:* Freshmen: $16,843; Undergraduates: $15,144. *Scholarships, grants, and awards:* Federal Pell, FSEOG, state, private, college/university gift aid from institutional funds.

GIFT AID (NON-NEED-BASED) *Total amount:* $5,269,418 (6% federal, 1% state, 92% institutional, 1% external sources). *Receiving aid:* Freshmen: 63% (428). Undergraduates: 33% (966). *Average award:* Freshmen: $9495.

Undergraduates: $9291. *Scholarships, grants, and awards by category: Academic interests/achievement:* 2,559 awards ($21,805,262 total): general academic interests/achievements. *Creative arts/performance:* 52 awards ($224,838 total): theater/drama. *Special achievements/activities:* 7 awards ($13,000 total): community service. *Special characteristics:* 101 awards ($1,848,758 total): children of faculty/staff, relatives of clergy. *Tuition waivers:* Full or partial for employees or children of employees, senior citizens.

LOANS *Student loans:* $18,202,052 (92% need-based, 8% non-need-based). 78% of past graduating class borrowed through all loan programs. *Average indebtedness per student:* $27,215. *Average need-based loan:* Freshmen: $4116. Undergraduates: $4675. *Parent loans:* $4,082,876 (87% need-based, 13% non-need-based). *Programs:* Federal Direct (Subsidized and Unsubsidized Stafford, PLUS), Perkins, Federal Nursing, college/university.

WORK-STUDY *Federal work-study:* Total amount: $1,289,373; 413 jobs averaging $2957. *State or other work-study/employment:* Total amount: $272,819 (100% non-need-based). 49 part-time jobs averaging $4041.

ATHLETIC AWARDS Total amount: $3,682,034 (34% need-based, 66% non-need-based).

APPLYING FOR FINANCIAL AID *Required financial aid forms:* FAFSA, state aid form. *Financial aid deadline (priority):* 2/15. *Notification date:* Continuous beginning 3/15. Students must reply within 3 weeks of notification.

CONTACT Mrs. Maureen E. Salfi, Director of Financial Aid, Niagara University, Niagara University, NY 14109, 716-286-8686 or toll-free 800-462-2111. *Fax:* 716-286-8678. *E-mail:* finaid@niagara.edu.

NICHOLLS STATE UNIVERSITY
Thibodaux, LA

Tuition & fees (LA res): $3965	Average undergraduate aid package: $7415

ABOUT THE INSTITUTION State-supported, coed. 37 undergraduate majors. Federal methodology is used as a basis for awarding need-based institutional aid.

UNDERGRADUATE EXPENSES for 2009–10 *Tuition, state resident:* full-time $3965. *Tuition, nonresident:* full-time $10,433. Part-time tuition and fees vary according to course load. *College room and board:* $7310; *Room only:* $4850. Room and board charges vary according to board plan and housing facility. *Payment plans:* Installment, deferred payment.

FRESHMAN FINANCIAL AID (Fall 2008) 1,108 applied for aid; of those 52% were deemed to have need. 100% of freshmen with need received aid; of those 82% had need fully met. *Average percent of need met:* 95% (excluding resources awarded to replace EFC). *Average financial aid package:* $8124 (excluding resources awarded to replace EFC). 14% of all full-time freshmen had no need and received non-need-based gift aid.

UNDERGRADUATE FINANCIAL AID (Fall 2008) 4,084 applied for aid; of those 58% were deemed to have need. 99% of undergraduates with need received aid; of those 71% had need fully met. *Average percent of need met:* 90% (excluding resources awarded to replace EFC). *Average financial aid package:* $7415 (excluding resources awarded to replace EFC). 6% of all full-time undergraduates had no need and received non-need-based gift aid.

GIFT AID (NEED-BASED) *Total amount:* $9,470,293 (70% federal, 22% state, 4% institutional, 4% external sources). *Receiving aid:* Freshmen: 45% (545); all full-time undergraduates: 40% (2,042). *Average award:* Freshmen: $5070; Undergraduates: $4482. *Scholarships, grants, and awards:* Federal Pell, FSEOG, state, private, college/university gift aid from institutional funds.

GIFT AID (NON-NEED-BASED) *Total amount:* $7,387,211 (70% state, 14% institutional, 16% external sources). *Receiving aid:* Freshmen: 26% (312). Undergraduates: 14% (723). *Average award:* Freshmen: $3020. Undergraduates: $2811. *Scholarships, grants, and awards by category: Academic interests/achievement:* general academic interests/achievements. *Creative arts/performance:* dance, music. *Special achievements/activities:* cheerleading/drum major, leadership. *Special characteristics:* children of faculty/staff, general special characteristics, local/state students, members of minority groups, out-of-state students, previous college experience, public servants, veterans. *Tuition waivers:* Full or partial for employees or children of employees.

LOANS *Student loans:* $13,469,951 (31% need-based, 69% non-need-based). 56% of past graduating class borrowed through all loan programs. *Average indebtedness per student:* $18,822. *Average need-based loan:* Freshmen: $2743. Undergraduates: $3532. *Parent loans:* $371,785 (1% need-based, 99% non-need-based). *Programs:* FFEL (Subsidized and Unsubsidized Stafford, PLUS), Perkins, private loans.

WORK-STUDY *Federal work-study:* Total amount: $225,495; jobs available. *State or other work-study/employment:* Total amount: $1,394,336 (3% need-based, 97% non-need-based). Part-time jobs available.

ATHLETIC AWARDS Total amount: $1,557,119 (23% need-based, 77% non-need-based).

APPLYING FOR FINANCIAL AID *Required financial aid forms:* FAFSA, institution's own form, state aid form, noncustodial (divorced/separated) parent's statement. *Financial aid deadline:* 6/30 (priority: 4/15). *Notification date:* Continuous. Students must reply within 2 weeks of notification.

CONTACT Casie Triche, Director for the Office of Financial Aid, Nicholls State University, PO Box 2005, Thibodaux, LA 70310, 985-448-4077 or toll-free 877-NICHOLLS. *Fax:* 985-448-4124. *E-mail:* casie.triche@nicholls.edu.

NICHOLS COLLEGE
Dudley, MA

Tuition & fees: $28,870	Average undergraduate aid package: $26,532

ABOUT THE INSTITUTION Independent, coed. 20 undergraduate majors. Federal methodology is used as a basis for awarding need-based institutional aid.

UNDERGRADUATE EXPENSES for 2010–11 *Comprehensive fee:* $38,200 includes full-time tuition ($28,570), mandatory fees ($300), and room and board ($9330). *College room only:* $4900. *Part-time tuition:* $275 per credit hour. Part-time tuition and fees vary according to class time and course load. *Payment plan:* Installment.

FRESHMAN FINANCIAL AID (Fall 2009, est.) 347 applied for aid; of those 92% were deemed to have need. 100% of freshmen with need received aid; of those 9% had need fully met. *Average percent of need met:* 77% (excluding resources awarded to replace EFC). *Average financial aid package:* $22,773 (excluding resources awarded to replace EFC). 8% of all full-time freshmen had no need and received non-need-based gift aid.

UNDERGRADUATE FINANCIAL AID (Fall 2009, est.) 1,142 applied for aid; of those 92% were deemed to have need. 100% of undergraduates with need received aid; of those 6% had need fully met. *Average percent of need met:* 78% (excluding resources awarded to replace EFC). *Average financial aid package:* $26,532 (excluding resources awarded to replace EFC). 13% of all full-time undergraduates had no need and received non-need-based gift aid.

GIFT AID (NEED-BASED) *Total amount:* $14,927,785 (11% federal, 3% state, 85% institutional, 1% external sources). *Receiving aid:* Freshmen: 87% (303); all full-time undergraduates: 85% (989). *Average award:* Freshmen: $18,579; Undergraduates: $17,143. *Scholarships, grants, and awards:* Federal Pell, FSEOG, state, private, college/university gift aid from institutional funds.

GIFT AID (NON-NEED-BASED) *Total amount:* $425,225 (100% institutional). *Receiving aid:* Freshmen: 8% (28). Undergraduates: 5% (59). *Average award:* Freshmen: $9632. Undergraduates: $9871. *Scholarships, grants, and awards by category: Academic interests/achievement:* 689 awards ($5,539,600 total): general academic interests/achievements. *Special achievements/activities:* 7 awards ($16,200 total): community service, general special achievements/activities, leadership. *Special characteristics:* 62 awards ($421,300 total): children and siblings of alumni, children of faculty/staff, siblings of current students. *Tuition waivers:* Full or partial for employees or children of employees, senior citizens.

LOANS *Student loans:* $9,382,173 (97% need-based, 3% non-need-based). 86% of past graduating class borrowed through all loan programs. *Average indebtedness per student:* $27,112. *Average need-based loan:* Freshmen: $3028. Undergraduates: $3603. *Parent loans:* $4,616,825 (100% need-based). *Programs:* Federal Direct (Subsidized and Unsubsidized Stafford, PLUS).

WORK-STUDY *Federal work-study:* Total amount: $660,570; 303 jobs averaging $1432.

APPLYING FOR FINANCIAL AID *Required financial aid form:* FAFSA. *Financial aid deadline (priority):* 3/1. *Notification date:* Continuous. Students must reply within 2 weeks of notification.

CONTACT Ms. Denise Brindle, Director of Financial Aid, Nichols College, PO Box 5000, Dudley, MA 01571, 508-213-2372 or toll-free 800-470-3379. *Fax:* 508-213-2118. *E-mail:* denise.brindle@nichols.edu.

NORFOLK STATE UNIVERSITY
Norfolk, VA

Tuition & fees (VA res): $5138	Average undergraduate aid package: $13,168

ABOUT THE INSTITUTION State-supported, coed. 32 undergraduate majors. Federal methodology is used as a basis for awarding need-based institutional aid.

UNDERGRADUATE EXPENSES for 2010–11 *Tuition, state resident:* full-time $2652; part-time $260.69 per credit hour. *Tuition, nonresident:* full-time $14,411; part-time $622.26 per credit hour. *Required fees:* full-time $2486. Full-time tuition and fees vary according to course load. Part-time tuition and fees vary according to course load. Room and board charges vary according to board plan and housing facility. *Payment plan:* Installment.

FRESHMAN FINANCIAL AID (Fall 2008) 1,152 applied for aid; of those 90% were deemed to have need. 100% of freshmen with need received aid; of those 36% had need fully met. *Average percent of need met:* 78% (excluding resources awarded to replace EFC). *Average financial aid package:* $14,617 (excluding resources awarded to replace EFC).

UNDERGRADUATE FINANCIAL AID (Fall 2008) 5,073 applied for aid; of those 87% were deemed to have need. 100% of undergraduates with need received aid; of those 40% had need fully met. *Average percent of need met:* 82% (excluding resources awarded to replace EFC). *Average financial aid package:* $13,168 (excluding resources awarded to replace EFC).

GIFT AID (NEED-BASED) *Total amount:* $22,978,671 (69% federal, 27% state, 4% institutional). *Receiving aid:* Freshmen: 76% (884); all full-time undergraduates: 71% (3,693). *Average award:* Freshmen: $7144; Undergraduates: $6743. *Scholarships, grants, and awards:* Federal Pell, FSEOG, state, private, college/university gift aid from institutional funds.

GIFT AID (NON-NEED-BASED) *Receiving aid:* Freshmen: 30% (353). Undergraduates: 23% (1,173). *Scholarships, grants, and awards by category:* Creative arts/performance: music, performing arts. Special achievements/activities: general special achievements/activities.

LOANS *Student loans:* $38,312,575 (42% need-based, 58% non-need-based). 80% of past graduating class borrowed through all loan programs. *Average indebtedness per student:* $19,371. *Average need-based loan:* Freshmen: $3479. Undergraduates: $4140. *Parent loans:* $4,183,764 (100% non-need-based). *Programs:* Federal Direct (Subsidized and Unsubsidized Stafford), FFEL (PLUS), Perkins, state, alternative loans.

WORK-STUDY *Federal work-study:* Total amount: $857,047; jobs available. *State or other work-study/employment:* Part-time jobs available.

ATHLETIC AWARDS Total amount: $3,577,931 (100% non-need-based).

APPLYING FOR FINANCIAL AID *Required financial aid form:* FAFSA. *Financial aid deadline:* 5/31. *Notification date:* 6/15. Students must reply within 2 weeks of notification.

CONTACT Mr. Kevin Burns, Director of Financial Aid, Norfolk State University, 700 Park Avenue, Norfolk, VA 23504-3907, 757-823-8381. *Fax:* 757-823-9059. *E-mail:* kburns@nsu.edu.

NORTH CAROLINA AGRICULTURAL AND TECHNICAL STATE UNIVERSITY
Greensboro, NC

Tuition & fees (NC res): $3899	Average undergraduate aid package: $11,899

ABOUT THE INSTITUTION State-supported, coed. 50 undergraduate majors. Both federal and institutional methodology are used as a basis for awarding need-based institutional aid.

UNDERGRADUATE EXPENSES for 2010–11 *One-time required fee:* $140. *Tuition, state resident:* full-time $2104. *Tuition, nonresident:* full-time $11,546. *Required fees:* full-time $1795. Full-time tuition and fees vary according to course load. Part-time tuition and fees vary according to course load. *College room and board:* $5839; *Room only:* $3359. Room and board charges vary according to board plan.

FRESHMAN FINANCIAL AID (Fall 2008) 1,298 applied for aid; of those 100% were deemed to have need. 99% of freshmen with need received aid; of those 13% had need fully met. *Average percent of need met:* 88% (excluding

resources awarded to replace EFC). *Average financial aid package:* $12,389 (excluding resources awarded to replace EFC). 6% of all full-time freshmen had no need and received non-need-based gift aid.

UNDERGRADUATE FINANCIAL AID (Fall 2008) 5,996 applied for aid; of those 100% were deemed to have need. 98% of undergraduates with need received aid; of those 8% had need fully met. *Average percent of need met:* 84% (excluding resources awarded to replace EFC). *Average financial aid package:* $11,899 (excluding resources awarded to replace EFC). 5% of all full-time undergraduates had no need and received non-need-based gift aid.

GIFT AID (NEED-BASED) *Total amount:* $37,379,444 (42% federal, 37% state, 15% institutional, 6% external sources). *Receiving aid:* Freshmen: 57% (900); all full-time undergraduates: 49% (3,898). *Average award:* Freshmen: $5359; Undergraduates: $4764. *Scholarships, grants, and awards:* Federal Pell, FSEOG, state, private, college/university gift aid from institutional funds, United Negro College Fund.

GIFT AID (NON-NEED-BASED) *Total amount:* $3,424,031 (13% state, 56% institutional, 31% external sources). *Receiving aid:* Freshmen: 75% (1,189). Undergraduates: 57% (4,506). *Average award:* Freshmen: $6686. Undergraduates: $4815. *Tuition waivers:* Full or partial for senior citizens.

LOANS *Student loans:* $48,732,087 (79% need-based, 21% non-need-based). *Average indebtedness per student:* $16,289. *Average need-based loan:* Freshmen: $2728. Undergraduates: $3842. *Parent loans:* $3,931,221 (79% need-based, 21% non-need-based). *Programs:* Federal Direct (Subsidized and Unsubsidized Stafford, PLUS), FFEL (Subsidized and Unsubsidized Stafford, PLUS), Perkins, state.

WORK-STUDY *Federal work-study:* Total amount: $415,297; jobs available. *State or other work-study/employment:* Total amount: $3,818,355 (79% need-based, 21% non-need-based). Part-time jobs available.

ATHLETIC AWARDS Total amount: $1,545,961 (70% need-based, 30% non-need-based).

APPLYING FOR FINANCIAL AID *Required financial aid form:* FAFSA. *Financial aid deadline (priority):* 3/15. *Notification date:* 4/15.

CONTACT Mrs. Sherri Avent, Director of Student Financial Aid, North Carolina Agricultural and Technical State University, 1601 East Market Street, Dowdy Administration Building, Greensboro, NC 27411, 336-334-7973 or toll-free 800-443-8964 (in-state). *Fax:* 336-334-7954.

NORTH CAROLINA CENTRAL UNIVERSITY
Durham, NC

CONTACT Sharon J. Oliver, Director of Scholarships and Student Aid, North Carolina Central University, 106 Student Services Building, Durham, NC 27707-3129, 919-530-7412 or toll-free 877-667-7533.

NORTH CAROLINA STATE UNIVERSITY
Raleigh, NC

Tuition & fees (NC res): $5474	Average undergraduate aid package: $10,594

ABOUT THE INSTITUTION State-supported, coed. 109 undergraduate majors. Federal methodology is used as a basis for awarding need-based institutional aid.

UNDERGRADUATE EXPENSES for 2009–10 *Tuition, state resident:* full-time $3953. *Tuition, nonresident:* full-time $16,438. *Required fees:* full-time $1521. Full-time tuition and fees vary according to degree level and program. Part-time tuition and fees vary according to course load, degree level, and program. *College room and board:* $7966; *Room only:* $4798. Room and board charges vary according to board plan and housing facility. *Payment plan:* Installment.

FRESHMAN FINANCIAL AID (Fall 2009, est.) 3,529 applied for aid; of those 62% were deemed to have need. 99% of freshmen with need received aid; of those 57% had need fully met. *Average percent of need met:* 89% (excluding resources awarded to replace EFC). *Average financial aid package:* $10,943 (excluding resources awarded to replace EFC). 3% of all full-time freshmen had no need and received non-need-based gift aid.

UNDERGRADUATE FINANCIAL AID (Fall 2009, est.) 14,000 applied for aid; of those 71% were deemed to have need. 98% of undergraduates with need received aid; of those 52% had need fully met. *Average percent of need met:* 84% (excluding resources awarded to replace EFC). *Average financial aid package:* $10,594 (excluding resources awarded to replace EFC). 4% of all full-time undergraduates had no need and received non-need-based gift aid.

GIFT AID (NEED-BASED) *Total amount:* $79,925,088 (30% federal, 29% state, 36% institutional, 5% external sources). *Receiving aid:* Freshmen: 45% (2,130); all full-time undergraduates: 42% (9,297). *Average award:* Freshmen: $9356; Undergraduates: $8678. *Scholarships, grants, and awards:* Federal Pell, FSEOG, state, private, college/university gift aid from institutional funds.

GIFT AID (NON-NEED-BASED) *Total amount:* $11,649,479 (14% state, 49% institutional, 37% external sources). *Receiving aid:* Freshmen: 6% (272). Undergraduates: 4% (877). *Average award:* Freshmen: $6402. Undergraduates: $5293. *Scholarships, grants, and awards by category: Academic interests/achievement:* agriculture, biological sciences, business, education, engineering/technologies, general academic interests/achievements, humanities, mathematics, physical sciences, social sciences. *Creative arts/performance:* music. *Special achievements/activities:* leadership. *Tuition waivers:* Full or partial for employees or children of employees, senior citizens.

LOANS *Student loans:* $68,266,918 (41% need-based, 59% non-need-based). 48% of past graduating class borrowed through all loan programs. *Average indebtedness per student:* $19,011. *Average need-based loan:* Freshmen: $2174. Undergraduates: $2806. *Parent loans:* $9,470,326 (14% need-based, 86% non-need-based). *Programs:* Federal Direct (Subsidized and Unsubsidized Stafford, PLUS), FFEL (Subsidized and Unsubsidized Stafford, PLUS), Perkins, state, college/university.

WORK-STUDY *Federal work-study:* Total amount: $838,345; 731 jobs averaging $1162. *State or other work-study/employment:* Total amount: $1,729,068 (40% need-based, 60% non-need-based). 272 part-time jobs averaging $6910.

ATHLETIC AWARDS Total amount: $4,268,369 (36% need-based, 64% non-need-based).

APPLYING FOR FINANCIAL AID *Required financial aid forms:* FAFSA, institution's own form. *Financial aid deadline (priority):* 3/1. *Notification date:* Continuous beginning 4/1.

CONTACT Ms. Julia Rice Mallette, Director of Scholarships and Financial Aid, North Carolina State University, 2016 Harris Hall, Box 7302, Raleigh, NC 27695-7302, 919-515-2334. *Fax:* 919-515-8422. *E-mail:* julie_mallette@ncsu.edu.

NORTH CAROLINA WESLEYAN COLLEGE
Rocky Mount, NC

ABOUT THE INSTITUTION Independent religious, coed. *Awards:* bachelor's degrees (also offers adult part-time degree program with significant enrollment not reflected in profile). 26 undergraduate majors. *Total enrollment:* 1,510. Undergraduates: 1,510. Freshmen: 221.

GIFT AID (NEED-BASED) *Scholarships, grants, and awards:* Federal Pell, FSEOG, state, private, college/university gift aid from institutional funds.

LOANS *Programs:* FFEL (Subsidized and Unsubsidized Stafford, PLUS), Perkins, alternative loans.

WORK-STUDY *Federal work-study:* Total amount: $464,359; 323 jobs averaging $1438. *State or other work-study/employment:* Total amount: $145,337 (100% need-based). 67 part-time jobs averaging $565.

APPLYING FOR FINANCIAL AID *Required financial aid form:* FAFSA.

CONTACT Deana M. Summerlin, Director of Financial Aid, North Carolina Wesleyan College, 3400 North Wesleyan Boulevard, Rocky Mount, NC 27804, 252-985-5200 or toll-free 800-488-6292. *Fax:* 252-985-5295. *E-mail:* finaid@ncwc.edu.

NORTH CENTRAL COLLEGE
Naperville, IL

Tuition & fees: $26,916	Average undergraduate aid package: $19,870

ABOUT THE INSTITUTION Independent United Methodist, coed. 61 undergraduate majors. Federal methodology is used as a basis for awarding need-based institutional aid.

UNDERGRADUATE EXPENSES for 2009–10 *Comprehensive fee:* $35,481 includes full-time tuition ($26,676), mandatory fees ($240), and room and board ($8565). Room and board charges vary according to housing facility. *Part-time tuition:* $645 per credit hour. *Part-time fees:* $20 per term. Part-time tuition and fees vary according to course load. *Payment plan:* Installment.

FRESHMAN FINANCIAL AID (Fall 2009, est.) 502 applied for aid; of those 88% were deemed to have need. 100% of freshmen with need received aid; of those 32% had need fully met. *Average percent of need met:* 82% (excluding resources awarded to replace EFC). *Average financial aid package:* $21,663 (excluding resources awarded to replace EFC). 18% of all full-time freshmen had no need and received non-need-based gift aid.

UNDERGRADUATE FINANCIAL AID (Fall 2009, est.) 1,973 applied for aid; of those 89% were deemed to have need. 99% of undergraduates with need received aid; of those 25% had need fully met. *Average percent of need met:* 76% (excluding resources awarded to replace EFC). *Average financial aid package:* $19,870 (excluding resources awarded to replace EFC). 20% of all full-time undergraduates had no need and received non-need-based gift aid.

GIFT AID (NEED-BASED) *Total amount:* $26,242,716 (9% federal, 13% state, 77% institutional, 1% external sources). *Receiving aid:* Freshmen: 81% (439); all full-time undergraduates: 75% (1,725). *Average award:* Freshmen: $17,228; Undergraduates: $15,023. *Scholarships, grants, and awards:* Federal Pell, FSEOG, state, private, college/university gift aid from institutional funds.

GIFT AID (NON-NEED-BASED) *Total amount:* $6,349,910 (98% institutional, 2% external sources). *Receiving aid:* Freshmen: 16% (89). Undergraduates: 10% (236). *Average award:* Freshmen: $12,081. Undergraduates: $10,390. *Scholarships, grants, and awards by category: Academic interests/achievement:* biological sciences, business, communication, computer science, education, English, foreign languages, general academic interests/achievements, humanities, international studies, mathematics, physical sciences, premedicine, religion/biblical studies, social sciences. *Creative arts/performance:* art/fine arts, cinema/film/broadcasting, debating, journalism/publications, music, theater/drama. *Special achievements/activities:* community service, religious involvement. *Special characteristics:* adult students, children of faculty/staff, general special characteristics, international students, relatives of clergy. *Tuition waivers:* Full or partial for employees or children of employees, senior citizens.

LOANS *Student loans:* $16,625,290 (68% need-based, 32% non-need-based). 72% of past graduating class borrowed through all loan programs. *Average indebtedness per student:* $27,285. *Average need-based loan:* Freshmen: $3530. Undergraduates: $4531. *Parent loans:* $2,680,872 (17% need-based, 83% non-need-based). *Programs:* FFEL (Subsidized and Unsubsidized Stafford, PLUS), Perkins, state, college/university.

WORK-STUDY *Federal work-study:* Total amount: $209,996; 974 jobs averaging $215. *State or other work-study/employment:* Total amount: $327,738 (33% need-based, 67% non-need-based). Part-time jobs available.

APPLYING FOR FINANCIAL AID *Required financial aid forms:* FAFSA, institution's own form, federal income tax form(s). *Financial aid deadline:* Continuous. *Notification date:* Continuous beginning 3/1. Students must reply within 4 weeks of notification.

CONTACT Marty Rossman, Director of Financial Aid, North Central College, 30 North Brainard Street, Naperville, IL 60540, 630-637-5600 or toll-free 800-411-1861. *Fax:* 630-637-5608. *E-mail:* mprossman@noctrl.edu.

NORTH CENTRAL UNIVERSITY
Minneapolis, MN

CONTACT Mrs. Donna Jager, Director of Financial Aid, North Central University, 910 Elliot Avenue, Minneapolis, MN 55404-1322, 612-343-4485 or toll-free 800-289-6222. *Fax:* 612-343-8067. *E-mail:* finaid@northcentral.edu.

NORTH DAKOTA STATE UNIVERSITY
Fargo, ND

ABOUT THE INSTITUTION State-supported, coed. 100 undergraduate majors.

GIFT AID (NEED-BASED) *Scholarships, grants, and awards:* Federal Pell, FSEOG, state, private, college/university gift aid from institutional funds.

GIFT AID (NON-NEED-BASED) *Scholarships, grants, and awards by category: Academic interests/achievement:* agriculture, architecture, biological sciences, business, communication, computer science, education, engineering/technologies, English, general academic interests/achievements, health fields, home economics, humanities, mathematics, military science, physical sciences, premedicine, social sciences. *Creative arts/performance:* art/fine arts, debating, journalism/publications, music, theater/drama. *Special achievements/activities:* memberships, religious involvement. *Special characteristics:* children of faculty/staff, ethnic background.

LOANS *Programs:* FFEL (Subsidized and Unsubsidized Stafford, PLUS), Perkins, Federal Nursing, private loans.

APPLYING FOR FINANCIAL AID *Required financial aid form:* FAFSA.

CONTACT Jeanne Enebo, Director of Financial Aid, North Dakota State University, PO Box 5315, Fargo, ND 58105, 701-231-7537 or toll-free 800-488-NDSU. *Fax:* 701-231-6126. *E-mail:* j.enebo@ndsu.edu.

NORTHEASTERN ILLINOIS UNIVERSITY
Chicago, IL

Tuition & fees (IL res): $8508	Average undergraduate aid package: $8362

ABOUT THE INSTITUTION State-supported, coed. 42 undergraduate majors. Federal methodology is used as a basis for awarding need-based institutional aid.

UNDERGRADUATE EXPENSES for 2009–10 *Tuition, state resident:* full-time $7350; part-time $245 per credit hour. *Tuition, nonresident:* full-time $14,700; part-time $490 per credit hour. *Required fees:* full-time $1158; $49.85 per credit hour or $3 per term. Full-time tuition and fees vary according to location and student level. Part-time tuition and fees vary according to course load and location. *Payment plans:* Guaranteed tuition, deferred payment.

FRESHMAN FINANCIAL AID (Fall 2009, est.) 852 applied for aid; of those 83% were deemed to have need. 90% of freshmen with need received aid; of those 3% had need fully met. *Average percent of need met:* 50% (excluding resources awarded to replace EFC). *Average financial aid package:* $8042 (excluding resources awarded to replace EFC). 2% of all full-time freshmen had no need and received non-need-based gift aid.

UNDERGRADUATE FINANCIAL AID (Fall 2009, est.) 3,911 applied for aid; of those 86% were deemed to have need. 93% of undergraduates with need received aid; of those 4% had need fully met. *Average percent of need met:* 48% (excluding resources awarded to replace EFC). *Average financial aid package:* $8362 (excluding resources awarded to replace EFC). 3% of all full-time undergraduates had no need and received non-need-based gift aid.

GIFT AID (NEED-BASED) *Total amount:* $24,335,459 (64% federal, 36% state). *Receiving aid:* Freshmen: 58% (582); all full-time undergraduates: 51% (2,721). *Average award:* Freshmen: $7718; Undergraduates: $7038. *Scholarships, grants, and awards:* Federal Pell, FSEOG, state, private, college/university gift aid from institutional funds.

GIFT AID (NON-NEED-BASED) *Total amount:* $1,520,411 (66% state, 22% institutional, 12% external sources). *Receiving aid:* Freshmen: 4% (40). Undergraduates: 5% (245). *Average award:* Freshmen: $1348. Undergraduates: $3063. *Scholarships, grants, and awards by category: Academic interests/achievement:* biological sciences, business, communication, computer science, education, English, foreign languages, general academic interests/achievements, mathematics, physical sciences, social sciences. *Creative arts/performance:* art/fine arts, creative writing, dance, journalism/publications, music, performing arts, theater/drama. *Special achievements/activities:* general special achievements/activities, leadership. *Special characteristics:* adult students, children of faculty/staff, general special characteristics. *Tuition waivers:* Full or partial for employees or children of employees, senior citizens.

LOANS *Student loans:* $15,657,855 (56% need-based, 44% non-need-based). 16% of past graduating class borrowed through all loan programs. *Average indebtedness per student:* $10,903. *Average need-based loan:* Freshmen: $3188. Undergraduates: $4477. *Parent loans:* $257,426 (100% non-need-based). *Programs:* FFEL (Subsidized and Unsubsidized Stafford, PLUS), Perkins.

WORK-STUDY *Federal work-study:* Total amount: $218,290; jobs available. *State or other work-study/employment:* Total amount: $1,275,721 (100% non-need-based). Part-time jobs available.

APPLYING FOR FINANCIAL AID *Required financial aid form:* FAFSA. *Financial aid deadline (priority):* 2/15. *Notification date:* Continuous beginning 4/1. Students must reply within 2 weeks of notification.

CONTACT Financial Aid Office, Northeastern Illinois University, 5500 North St. Louis Avenue, Chicago, IL 60625, 773-442-5000. *Fax:* 773-442-5040. *E-mail:* financial-aid@neiu.edu.

NORTHEASTERN STATE UNIVERSITY
Tahlequah, OK

Tuition & fees (OK res): $4155	Average undergraduate aid package: $8680

ABOUT THE INSTITUTION State-supported, coed. 72 undergraduate majors. Federal methodology is used as a basis for awarding need-based institutional aid.

UNDERGRADUATE EXPENSES for 2009–10 *Tuition, state resident:* full-time $3210; part-time $107 per credit hour. *Tuition, nonresident:* full-time $9300; part-time $310 per credit hour. *Required fees:* full-time $945; $31.50 per credit hour. Full-time tuition and fees vary according to course load and program. Part-time tuition and fees vary according to course load and program. *College room and board:* $4826. Room and board charges vary according to board plan and housing facility.

FRESHMAN FINANCIAL AID (Fall 2009, est.) 917 applied for aid; of those 81% were deemed to have need. 86% of freshmen with need received aid; of those 68% had need fully met. *Average percent of need met:* 72% (excluding resources awarded to replace EFC). *Average financial aid package:* $8752 (excluding resources awarded to replace EFC). 5% of all full-time freshmen had no need and received non-need-based gift aid.

UNDERGRADUATE FINANCIAL AID (Fall 2009, est.) 4,621 applied for aid; of those 85% were deemed to have need. 84% of undergraduates with need received aid; of those 72% had need fully met. *Average percent of need met:* 71% (excluding resources awarded to replace EFC). *Average financial aid package:* $8680 (excluding resources awarded to replace EFC). 3% of all full-time undergraduates had no need and received non-need-based gift aid.

GIFT AID (NEED-BASED) *Total amount:* $18,684,102 (70% federal, 16% state, 3% institutional, 11% external sources). *Receiving aid:* Freshmen: 43% (459); all full-time undergraduates: 41% (2,365). *Average award:* Freshmen: $5207; Undergraduates: $5245. *Scholarships, grants, and awards:* Federal Pell, FSEOG, state, private, college/university gift aid from institutional funds.

GIFT AID (NON-NEED-BASED) *Total amount:* $3,741,615 (55% state, 9% institutional, 36% external sources). *Receiving aid:* Freshmen: 57% (607). Undergraduates: 52% (3,025). *Average award:* Freshmen: $2603. Undergraduates: $3374. *Scholarships, grants, and awards by category: Academic interests/achievement:* 1,339 awards ($2,544,730 total): biological sciences, business, communication, computer science, education, English, foreign languages, general academic interests/achievements, health fields, home economics, humanities, library science, mathematics, physical sciences, premedicine, social sciences. *Creative arts/performance:* 142 awards ($163,268 total): applied art and design, art/fine arts, dance, debating, journalism/publications, music, performing arts, theater/drama. *Special achievements/activities:* 102 awards ($214,180 total): cheerleading/drum major, community service, junior miss, leadership. *Special characteristics:* 89 awards ($142,523 total): children and siblings of alumni, children of faculty/staff, children with a deceased or disabled parent, out-of-state students, spouses of deceased or disabled public servants. *Tuition waivers:* Full or partial for employees or children of employees, senior citizens.

LOANS *Student loans:* $15,066,552 (13% need-based, 87% non-need-based). 68% of past graduating class borrowed through all loan programs. *Average indebtedness per student:* $2143. *Average need-based loan:* Freshmen: $2391. Undergraduates: $3825. *Parent loans:* $246,268 (60% need-based, 40% non-need-based). *Programs:* Federal Direct (Subsidized and Unsubsidized Stafford, PLUS), Perkins.

WORK-STUDY *Federal work-study:* Total amount: $546,966; 281 jobs averaging $1976. *State or other work-study/employment:* Total amount: $1,947,156 (100% non-need-based). 619 part-time jobs averaging $2463.

ATHLETIC AWARDS Total amount: $1,329,892 (100% non-need-based).

APPLYING FOR FINANCIAL AID *Required financial aid forms:* FAFSA, institution's own form. *Financial aid deadline (priority):* 4/1. *Notification date:* Continuous beginning 4/1. Students must reply within 2 weeks of notification.

CONTACT Dr. Teri Cochran, Director of Student Financial Services, Northeastern State University, 715 North Grand Avenue, Tahlequah, OK 74464-2399, 918-456-5511 Ext. 3410 or toll-free 800-722-9614 (in-state). *Fax:* 918-458-2510. *E-mail:* cochrant@nsuok.edu.

NORTHEASTERN UNIVERSITY
Boston, MA

Tuition & fees: $35,362	Average undergraduate aid package: $19,325

ABOUT THE INSTITUTION Independent, coed. 88 undergraduate majors. Both federal and institutional methodology are used as a basis for awarding need-based institutional aid.

UNDERGRADUATE EXPENSES for 2009–10 *Comprehensive fee:* $47,712 includes full-time tuition ($34,950), mandatory fees ($412), and room and board ($12,350). *College room only:* $6530. Room and board charges vary according to board plan and housing facility. *Payment plan:* Installment.

FRESHMAN FINANCIAL AID (Fall 2009, est.) 2,098 applied for aid; of those 79% were deemed to have need. 99% of freshmen with need received aid; of those 18% had need fully met. *Average percent of need met:* 69% (excluding resources awarded to replace EFC). *Average financial aid package:* $23,155 (excluding resources awarded to replace EFC). 23% of all full-time freshmen had no need and received non-need-based gift aid.

UNDERGRADUATE FINANCIAL AID (Fall 2009, est.) 10,208 applied for aid; of those 84% were deemed to have need. 99% of undergraduates with need received aid; of those 15% had need fully met. *Average percent of need met:* 59% (excluding resources awarded to replace EFC). *Average financial aid package:* $19,325 (excluding resources awarded to replace EFC). 23% of all full-time undergraduates had no need and received non-need-based gift aid.

GIFT AID (NEED-BASED) *Total amount:* $114,151,445 (11% federal, 2% state, 82% institutional, 5% external sources). *Receiving aid:* Freshmen: 56% (1,589); all full-time undergraduates: 51% (8,036). *Average award:* Freshmen: $18,814; Undergraduates: $14,627. *Scholarships, grants, and awards:* Federal Pell, FSEOG, state, private, college/university gift aid from institutional funds.

GIFT AID (NON-NEED-BASED) *Total amount:* $39,963,116 (92% institutional, 8% external sources). *Receiving aid:* Freshmen: 8% (234). Undergraduates: 5% (863). *Average award:* Freshmen: $12,010. Undergraduates: $9139. *Tuition waivers:* Full or partial for employees or children of employees.

LOANS *Student loans:* $110,349,096 (66% need-based, 34% non-need-based). *Average need-based loan:* Freshmen: $4472. Undergraduates: $4910. *Parent loans:* $26,455,461 (47% need-based, 53% non-need-based). *Programs:* Federal Direct (Subsidized and Unsubsidized Stafford, PLUS), Perkins, Federal Nursing, state.

WORK-STUDY *Federal work-study:* Total amount: $9,441,968; jobs available. *State or other work-study/employment:* Part-time jobs available.

ATHLETIC AWARDS Total amount: $9,962,735 (35% need-based, 65% non-need-based).

APPLYING FOR FINANCIAL AID *Required financial aid forms:* FAFSA, CSS Financial Aid PROFILE. *Financial aid deadline (priority):* 2/15. *Notification date:* Continuous beginning 3/15. Students must reply by 5/1.

CONTACT Mr. Anthony Erwin, Director of Student Financial Services, Northeastern University, 360 Huntington Avenue, Boston, MA 02115, 617-373-3190. *Fax:* 617-373-8735. *E-mail:* sfs@neu.edu.

NORTHERN ARIZONA UNIVERSITY
Flagstaff, AZ

Tuition & fees (AZ res): $6632	Average undergraduate aid package: $8729

ABOUT THE INSTITUTION State-supported, coed. 109 undergraduate majors. Federal methodology is used as a basis for awarding need-based institutional aid.

UNDERGRADUATE EXPENSES for 2010–11 *Tuition, state resident:* full-time $6092. *Tuition, nonresident:* full-time $17,318. *Required fees:* full-time $540. Full-time tuition and fees vary according to location and program. Part-time tuition and fees vary according to course load, location, and program. *College room and board:* $7872; *Room only:* $3344. Room and board charges vary according to board plan, housing facility, and location. *Payment plans:* Guaranteed tuition, installment.

FRESHMAN FINANCIAL AID (Fall 2008) 2,611 applied for aid; of those 62% were deemed to have need. 95% of freshmen with need received aid; of those 20% had need fully met. *Average percent of need met:* 69% (excluding resources awarded to replace EFC). *Average financial aid package:* $8623 (excluding resources awarded to replace EFC). 22% of all full-time freshmen had no need and received non-need-based gift aid.

UNDERGRADUATE FINANCIAL AID (Fall 2008) 9,621 applied for aid; of those 74% were deemed to have need. 97% of undergraduates with need received aid; of those 15% had need fully met. *Average percent of need met:* 65% (excluding resources awarded to replace EFC). *Average financial aid package:* $8729 (excluding resources awarded to replace EFC). 16% of all full-time undergraduates had no need and received non-need-based gift aid.

GIFT AID (NEED-BASED) *Total amount:* $43,357,659 (43% federal, 7% state, 41% institutional, 9% external sources). *Receiving aid:* Freshmen: 29% (947); all full-time undergraduates: 33% (4,577). *Average award:* Freshmen: $6074; Undergraduates: $5592. *Scholarships, grants, and awards:* Federal Pell, FSEOG, state, private, college/university gift aid from institutional funds, Federal Nursing, TEACH Grants.

GIFT AID (NON-NEED-BASED) *Total amount:* $13,446,237 (2% federal, 79% institutional, 19% external sources). *Receiving aid:* Freshmen: 25% (825). Undergraduates: 20% (2,785). *Average award:* Freshmen: $3530. Undergraduates: $3443. *Scholarships, grants, and awards by category: Academic interests/ achievement:* area/ethnic studies, biological sciences, business, communication, computer science, education, engineering/technologies, English, foreign languages, general academic interests/achievements, health fields, home economics, humanities, international studies, library science, mathematics, military science, physical sciences, premedicine, religion/biblical studies, social sciences. *Creative arts/performance:* applied art and design, art/fine arts, cinema/film/broadcasting, creative writing, debating, general creative arts/performance, journalism/publications, music, performing arts, theater/drama. *Special achievements/activities:* leadership. *Special characteristics:* adult students, children and siblings of alumni, children of educators, children of faculty/staff, children of public servants, first-generation college students, general special characteristics, handicapped students, international students, local/state students, members of minority groups, out-of-state students, public servants, spouses of deceased or disabled public servants, veterans, veterans' children. *Tuition waivers:* Full or partial for employees or children of employees.

LOANS *Student loans:* $63,856,920 (79% need-based, 21% non-need-based). 50% of past graduating class borrowed through all loan programs. *Average indebtedness per student:* $16,703. *Average need-based loan:* Freshmen: $3295. Undergraduates: $3947. *Parent loans:* $17,475,613 (60% need-based, 40% non-need-based). *Programs:* Federal Direct (Subsidized and Unsubsidized Stafford, PLUS), Perkins, Federal Nursing, state, college/university.

WORK-STUDY *Federal work-study:* Total amount: $1,061,017; jobs available. *State or other work-study/employment:* Total amount: $7,822,214 (51% need-based, 49% non-need-based). Part-time jobs available.

ATHLETIC AWARDS Total amount: $3,286,926 (39% need-based, 61% non-need-based).

APPLYING FOR FINANCIAL AID *Required financial aid form:* FAFSA. *Financial aid deadline (priority):* 2/14. *Notification date:* Continuous beginning 3/15.

CONTACT Michelle Castillo, Director, Financial Aid, Northern Arizona University, PO Box 4108, Flagstaff, AZ 86011-4108, 928-523-4951 or toll-free 888-MORE-NAU. *Fax:* 928-523-1551.

NORTHERN ILLINOIS UNIVERSITY
De Kalb, IL

Tuition & fees (IL res): $9079	Average undergraduate aid package: $11,087

ABOUT THE INSTITUTION State-supported, coed. *Awards:* bachelor's and master's degrees. 61 undergraduate majors. *Total enrollment:* 25,254. Undergraduates: 18,917. Freshmen: 3,013. Federal methodology is used as a basis for awarding need-based institutional aid.

UNDERGRADUATE EXPENSES for 2009–10 *Tuition, state resident:* full-time $7260; part-time $269 per credit hour. *Tuition, nonresident:* full-time $14,520; part-time $538 per credit hour. *Required fees:* full-time $1819; $75.77 per credit hour. Full-time tuition and fees vary according to course load, location, and student level. Part-time tuition and fees vary according to course load, location, and student level. *College room and board:* $9588. Room and board charges vary according to board plan and housing facility. *Payment plans:* Guaranteed tuition, installment.

FRESHMAN FINANCIAL AID (Fall 2009, est.) 2,670 applied for aid; of those 81% were deemed to have need. 99% of freshmen with need received aid; of those 9% had need fully met. *Average percent of need met:* 66% (excluding resources awarded to replace EFC). *Average financial aid package:* $11,877 (excluding resources awarded to replace EFC).

UNDERGRADUATE FINANCIAL AID (Fall 2009, est.) 12,791 applied for aid; of those 83% were deemed to have need. 99% of undergraduates with need received aid; of those 11% had need fully met. *Average percent of need met:* 65% (excluding resources awarded to replace EFC). *Average financial aid package:* $11,087 (excluding resources awarded to replace EFC). 1% of all full-time undergraduates had no need and received non-need-based gift aid.

GIFT AID (NEED-BASED) *Total amount:* $57,168,065 (46% federal, 45% state, 5% institutional, 4% external sources). *Receiving aid:* Freshmen: 50% (1,502); all full-time undergraduates: 42% (6,837). *Average award:* Freshmen: $8820; Undergraduates: $7582. *Scholarships, grants, and awards:* Federal Pell, FSEOG, state, private, college/university gift aid from institutional funds, United Negro College Fund, Federal Nursing, Academic Competitiveness Grants, National SMART Grants, TEACH Grants.

GIFT AID (NON-NEED-BASED) *Total amount:* $791,027 (4% institutional, 96% external sources). *Receiving aid:* Freshmen: 9. Undergraduates: 78. *Average award:* Undergraduates: $912. *Scholarships, grants, and awards by category: Academic interests/achievement:* biological sciences, business, communication, computer science, education, engineering/technologies, English, foreign languages, general academic interests/achievements, health fields, humanities, international studies, mathematics, physical sciences, social sciences. *Creative arts/performance:* applied art and design, art/fine arts, creative writing, dance, debating, journalism/publications, music, performing arts, theater/drama. *Special achievements/activities:* leadership. *Special characteristics:* adult students, children of faculty/staff, ethnic background, international students, members of minority groups, veterans. *Tuition waivers:* Full or partial for minority students, employees or children of employees, senior citizens. *ROTC:* Army, Air Force cooperative.
LOANS *Student loans:* $103,770,088 (43% need-based, 57% non-need-based). 63% of past graduating class borrowed through all loan programs. *Average indebtedness per student:* $24,154. *Average need-based loan:* Freshmen: $3425. Undergraduates: $4278. *Parent loans:* $15,515,864 (100% non-need-based). *Programs:* Federal Direct (Subsidized and Unsubsidized Stafford, PLUS), Perkins.
WORK-STUDY *Federal work-study:* Total amount: $19,375,470; 6,206 jobs averaging $3122.
ATHLETIC AWARDS Total amount: $5,329,336 (100% need-based).
APPLYING FOR FINANCIAL AID *Required financial aid form:* FAFSA. *Financial aid deadline (priority):* 3/1. *Notification date:* Continuous beginning 3/24. Students must reply within 2 weeks of notification.
CONTACT Ms. Kathleen D. Brunson, Director of Student Financial Aid, Northern Illinois University, De Kalb, IL 60115-2854, 815-753-1395 or toll-free 800-892-3050 (in-state). *Fax:* 815-753-9475.

NORTHERN KENTUCKY UNIVERSITY
Highland Heights, KY

Tuition & fees (KY res): $6792	Average undergraduate aid package: $7509

ABOUT THE INSTITUTION State-supported, coed. 62 undergraduate majors. Federal methodology is used as a basis for awarding need-based institutional aid.
UNDERGRADUATE EXPENSES for 2009–10 *Tuition, state resident:* full-time $6792; part-time $283 per credit hour. *Tuition, nonresident:* full-time $12,792; part-time $533 per credit hour. Full-time tuition and fees vary according to course load and reciprocity agreements. Part-time tuition and fees vary according to course load and reciprocity agreements. Room and board charges vary according to board plan, housing facility, and location. *Payment plan:* Installment.
FRESHMAN FINANCIAL AID (Fall 2008) 1,609 applied for aid; of those 73% were deemed to have need. 99% of freshmen with need received aid; of those 18% had need fully met. *Average percent of need met:* 58% (excluding resources awarded to replace EFC). *Average financial aid package:* $6886 (excluding resources awarded to replace EFC). 10% of all full-time freshmen had no need and received non-need-based gift aid.
UNDERGRADUATE FINANCIAL AID (Fall 2008) 6,722 applied for aid; of those 77% were deemed to have need. 97% of undergraduates with need received aid; of those 17% had need fully met. *Average percent of need met:* 54% (excluding resources awarded to replace EFC). *Average financial aid package:* $7509 (excluding resources awarded to replace EFC). 9% of all full-time undergraduates had no need and received non-need-based gift aid.
GIFT AID (NEED-BASED) *Total amount:* $13,389,248 (82% federal, 18% state). *Receiving aid:* Freshmen: 27% (533); all full-time undergraduates: 26% (2,460). *Average award:* Freshmen: $5379; Undergraduates: $4973. *Scholarships, grants, and awards:* Federal Pell, FSEOG, state, college/university gift aid from institutional funds.
GIFT AID (NON-NEED-BASED) *Total amount:* $14,035,693 (37% state, 55% institutional, 8% external sources). *Receiving aid:* Freshmen: 39% (775). Undergraduates: 22% (2,125). *Average award:* Freshmen: $3531. Undergraduates: $4087. *Scholarships, grants, and awards by category: Academic interests/achievement:* biological sciences, business, communication, computer science, education, engineering/technologies, English, general academic interests/achievements, health fields, mathematics, physical sciences, premedicine, social sciences. *Creative arts/performance:* art/fine arts, music, theater/drama. *Special achievements/activities:* community service, general special achievements/activities, leadership. *Special characteristics:* adult students, children and siblings of alumni, children of faculty/staff, children of public servants, children with a deceased or disabled parent, general special characteristics, handicapped students,

local/state students, members of minority groups, spouses of deceased or disabled public servants, veterans, veterans' children. *Tuition waivers:* Full or partial for employees or children of employees, senior citizens.
LOANS *Student loans:* $64,446,985 (43% need-based, 57% non-need-based). 40% of past graduating class borrowed through all loan programs. *Average indebtedness per student:* $23,129. *Average need-based loan:* Freshmen: $2971. Undergraduates: $3873. *Parent loans:* $6,773,257 (100% non-need-based). *Programs:* FFEL (Subsidized and Unsubsidized Stafford, PLUS), Perkins, private alternative loans.
WORK-STUDY *Federal work-study:* Total amount: $550,110; jobs available. *State or other work-study/employment:* Total amount: $3,002,638 (100% non-need-based). Part-time jobs available.
ATHLETIC AWARDS Total amount: $1,210,249 (100% non-need-based).
APPLYING FOR FINANCIAL AID *Required financial aid form:* FAFSA. *Financial aid deadline (priority):* 3/1. *Notification date:* Continuous beginning 4/1.
CONTACT Leah Stewart, Director of Student Financial Assistance, Northern Kentucky University, 416 Administrative Center, Highland Heights, KY 41099, 859-572-5144 or toll-free 800-637-9948. *Fax:* 859-572-6997. *E-mail:* ofa@nku.edu.

NORTHERN MICHIGAN UNIVERSITY
Marquette, MI

Tuition & fees (MI res): $7454	Average undergraduate aid package: $7979

ABOUT THE INSTITUTION State-supported, coed. 142 undergraduate majors. Federal methodology is used as a basis for awarding need-based institutional aid.
UNDERGRADUATE EXPENSES for 2010–11 *One-time required fee:* $225. *Tuition, state resident:* full-time $6840; part-time $285 per credit hour. *Tuition, nonresident:* full-time $11,214; part-time $467.25 per credit hour. *Required fees:* full-time $614; $31.13 per term. *College room and board:* $7846; *Room only:* $3948. Room and board charges vary according to board plan and housing facility. *Payment plans:* Installment, deferred payment.
FRESHMAN FINANCIAL AID (Fall 2008) 1,681 applied for aid; of those 68% were deemed to have need. 97% of freshmen with need received aid; of those 22% had need fully met. *Average percent of need met:* 60% (excluding resources awarded to replace EFC). *Average financial aid package:* $7596 (excluding resources awarded to replace EFC). 8% of all full-time freshmen had no need and received non-need-based gift aid.
UNDERGRADUATE FINANCIAL AID (Fall 2008) 6,650 applied for aid; of those 67% were deemed to have need. 97% of undergraduates with need received aid; of those 18% had need fully met. *Average percent of need met:* 64% (excluding resources awarded to replace EFC). *Average financial aid package:* $7979 (excluding resources awarded to replace EFC). 5% of all full-time undergraduates had no need and received non-need-based gift aid.
GIFT AID (NEED-BASED) *Total amount:* $13,422,564 (73% federal, 8% state, 18% institutional, 1% external sources). *Receiving aid:* Freshmen: 33% (585); all full-time undergraduates: 31% (2,348). *Average award:* Freshmen: $4544; Undergraduates: $4624. *Scholarships, grants, and awards:* Federal Pell, FSEOG, state, private, college/university gift aid from institutional funds, Federal Nursing.
GIFT AID (NON-NEED-BASED) *Total amount:* $12,540,467 (28% state, 51% institutional, 21% external sources). *Receiving aid:* Freshmen: 29% (514). Undergraduates: 22% (1,680). *Average award:* Freshmen: $2937. Undergraduates: $2755. *Scholarships, grants, and awards by category: Academic interests/achievement:* 277 awards ($411,754 total): biological sciences, business, communication, computer science, education, engineering/technologies, English, foreign languages, general academic interests/achievements, international studies, mathematics, military science, physical sciences, premedicine, social sciences. *Creative arts/performance:* 55 awards ($44,247 total): applied art and design, music, theater/drama. *Special achievements/activities:* 116 awards ($96,786 total): cheerleading/drum major, leadership, memberships. *Special characteristics:* 943 awards ($3,867,111 total): children of faculty/staff, children of union members/company employees, international students, members of minority groups, out-of-state students. *Tuition waivers:* Full or partial for employees or children of employees, senior citizens.
LOANS *Student loans:* $42,378,828 (43% need-based, 57% non-need-based). 67% of past graduating class borrowed through all loan programs. *Average indebtedness per student:* $24,074. *Average need-based loan:* Freshmen: $2921.

Undergraduates: $3801. *Parent loans:* $2,667,638 (100% non-need-based). *Programs:* Federal Direct (Subsidized and Unsubsidized Stafford, PLUS), Perkins, state, alternative loans.

WORK-STUDY *Federal work-study:* Total amount: $961,419; 454 jobs averaging $1840. *State or other work-study/employment:* Total amount: $201,163 (100% need-based). 107 part-time jobs averaging $1776.

ATHLETIC AWARDS Total amount: $2,142,951 (100% non-need-based).

APPLYING FOR FINANCIAL AID *Required financial aid form:* FAFSA. *Financial aid deadline (priority):* 3/1. *Notification date:* Continuous beginning 4/1. Students must reply within 2 weeks of notification.

CONTACT Michael Rotundo, Director of Financial Aid, Northern Michigan University, 1401 Presque Isle Avenue, Marquette, MI 49855, 906-227-1575 or toll-free 800-682-9797. *Fax:* 906-227-2321. *E-mail:* mrotundo@nmu.edu.

NORTHERN STATE UNIVERSITY
Aberdeen, SD

Tuition & fees (SD res): $6063	Average undergraduate aid package: $7047

ABOUT THE INSTITUTION State-supported, coed. 50 undergraduate majors. Federal methodology is used as a basis for awarding need-based institutional aid.

UNDERGRADUATE EXPENSES for 2009–10 *Tuition, state resident:* full-time $2751; part-time $91.70 per credit hour. *Tuition, nonresident:* full-time $8827; part-time $294.25 per credit hour. *Required fees:* full-time $3312; $110.40 per credit hour. Full-time tuition and fees vary according to course level, course load, and reciprocity agreements. Part-time tuition and fees vary according to course level, course load, and reciprocity agreements. *College room and board:* $4874; *Room only:* $2575. Room and board charges vary according to board plan. *Payment plan:* Installment.

FRESHMAN FINANCIAL AID (Fall 2009, est.) 262 applied for aid; of those 76% were deemed to have need. 100% of freshmen with need received aid; of those 19% had need fully met. *Average percent of need met:* 69% (excluding resources awarded to replace EFC). *Average financial aid package:* $6003 (excluding resources awarded to replace EFC). 12% of all full-time freshmen had no need and received non-need-based gift aid.

UNDERGRADUATE FINANCIAL AID (Fall 2009, est.) 1,140 applied for aid; of those 79% were deemed to have need. 100% of undergraduates with need received aid; of those 19% had need fully met. *Average percent of need met:* 69% (excluding resources awarded to replace EFC). *Average financial aid package:* $7047 (excluding resources awarded to replace EFC). 8% of all full-time undergraduates had no need and received non-need-based gift aid.

GIFT AID (NEED-BASED) *Total amount:* $3,060,015 (95% federal, 3% institutional, 2% external sources). *Receiving aid:* Freshmen: 59% (188); all full-time undergraduates: 55% (768). *Average award:* Freshmen: $3678; Undergraduates: $3574. *Scholarships, grants, and awards:* Federal Pell, FSEOG, state, private, college/university gift aid from institutional funds, Academic Competitiveness Grants, National SMART Grants, TEACH Grants, LEAP Grants.

GIFT AID (NON-NEED-BASED) *Total amount:* $1,580,197 (12% federal, 12% state, 52% institutional, 24% external sources). *Receiving aid:* Freshmen: 55% (175). Undergraduates: 51% (710). *Average award:* Freshmen: $2593. Undergraduates: $2138. *Scholarships, grants, and awards by category: Academic interests/achievement:* 538 awards ($657,514 total): biological sciences, business, communication, computer science, education, English, foreign languages, general academic interests/achievements, humanities, international studies, mathematics, physical sciences, social sciences. *Creative arts/performance:* 104 awards ($74,770 total): art/fine arts, music, theater/drama. *Special achievements/activities:* 11 awards ($6412 total): leadership. *Special characteristics:* 25 awards ($13,462 total): adult students, ethnic background, handicapped students, international students, local/state students, members of minority groups.

LOANS *Student loans:* $9,662,967 (47% need-based, 53% non-need-based). *Average need-based loan:* Freshmen: $2948. Undergraduates: $3543. *Parent loans:* $262,054 (100% non-need-based). *Programs:* Federal Direct (Subsidized and Unsubsidized Stafford, PLUS), FFEL (Subsidized and Unsubsidized Stafford, PLUS), Perkins, college/university, alternative loans.

WORK-STUDY *Federal work-study:* Total amount: $525,000; 271 jobs averaging $1858. *State or other work-study/employment:* Total amount: $550,000 (100% non-need-based). 378 part-time jobs averaging $1465.

ATHLETIC AWARDS Total amount: $706,201 (100% non-need-based).

APPLYING FOR FINANCIAL AID *Required financial aid form:* FAFSA. *Financial aid deadline (priority):* 3/1. *Notification date:* 4/15. Students must reply within 2 weeks of notification.

CONTACT Ms. Sharon Kienow, Director of Financial Aid, Northern State University, 1200 South Jay Street, Aberdeen, SD 57401-7198, 605-626-2640 or toll-free 800-678-5330. *Fax:* 605-626-2587. *E-mail:* kienows@northern.edu.

NORTH GEORGIA COLLEGE & STATE UNIVERSITY
Dahlonega, GA

Tuition & fees (GA res): $5036	Average undergraduate aid package: $8400

ABOUT THE INSTITUTION State-supported, coed. 48 undergraduate majors. Federal methodology is used as a basis for awarding need-based institutional aid.

UNDERGRADUATE EXPENSES for 2009–10 *Tuition, state resident:* full-time $3874; part-time $130 per credit hour. *Tuition, nonresident:* full-time $15,488; part-time $517 per credit hour. *Required fees:* full-time $1162. Part-time tuition and fees vary according to course load. *College room and board:* $5248; *Room only:* $2758. Room and board charges vary according to board plan and housing facility.

UNDERGRADUATE FINANCIAL AID (Fall 2008) 3,806 applied for aid; of those 42% were deemed to have need. 97% of undergraduates with need received aid; of those 68% had need fully met. *Average percent of need met:* 79% (excluding resources awarded to replace EFC). *Average financial aid package:* $8400 (excluding resources awarded to replace EFC). 4% of all full-time undergraduates had no need and received non-need-based gift aid.

GIFT AID (NEED-BASED) *Total amount:* $3,581,505 (98% federal, 2% institutional). *Receiving aid:* All full-time undergraduates: 34% (1,421). *Average award:* Undergraduates: $2000. *Scholarships, grants, and awards:* Federal Pell, FSEOG, state, private, college/university gift aid from institutional funds.

GIFT AID (NON-NEED-BASED) *Total amount:* $11,972,645 (1% federal, 90% state, 5% institutional, 4% external sources). *Receiving aid:* Undergraduates: 36% (1,497). *Average award:* Undergraduates: $1500. *Scholarships, grants, and awards by category: Academic interests/achievement:* biological sciences, business, education, English, general academic interests/achievements, health fields, humanities, mathematics, military science, physical sciences, premedicine. *Creative arts/performance:* applied art and design, general creative arts/performance, music. *Special achievements/activities:* cheerleading/drum major, community service, general special achievements/activities, leadership. *Special characteristics:* general special characteristics. *Tuition waivers:* Full or partial for employees or children of employees, senior citizens.

LOANS *Student loans:* $10,021,413 (45% need-based, 55% non-need-based). 65% of past graduating class borrowed through all loan programs. *Average indebtedness per student:* $9885. *Average need-based loan:* Undergraduates: $5500. *Parent loans:* $340,757 (100% non-need-based). *Programs:* Federal Direct (Subsidized and Unsubsidized Stafford, PLUS), FFEL (Subsidized and Unsubsidized Stafford, PLUS), Perkins, state, college/university.

WORK-STUDY *Federal work-study:* Total amount: $132,266; jobs available. *State or other work-study/employment:* Total amount: $310,000 (100% need-based). Part-time jobs available.

ATHLETIC AWARDS Total amount: $527,625 (100% non-need-based).

APPLYING FOR FINANCIAL AID *Required financial aid form:* FAFSA. *Financial aid deadline (priority):* 3/17. *Notification date:* Continuous beginning 3/1. Students must reply within 3 weeks of notification.

CONTACT Jill Rayner, Director, Financial Aid, North Georgia College & State University, 82 College Circle, Dahlonega, GA 30597-1001, 706-864-1688 or toll-free 800-498-9581. *Fax:* 706-864-1411. *E-mail:* jprayner@northgeorgia.edu.

NORTH GREENVILLE UNIVERSITY
Tigerville, SC

Tuition & fees: $12,264	Average undergraduate aid package: N/A

ABOUT THE INSTITUTION Independent Southern Baptist, coed. 37 undergraduate majors. Federal methodology is used as a basis for awarding need-based institutional aid.

UNDERGRADUATE EXPENSES for 2009–10 *Comprehensive fee:* $19,320 includes full-time tuition ($12,264) and room and board ($7056). *College room* *only:* $3192. Full-time tuition and fees vary according to course load. Room and board charges vary according to housing facility. *Part-time tuition:* $210 per credit hour. *Payment plan:* Installment.

FRESHMAN FINANCIAL AID (Fall 2009, est.) 472 applied for aid; of those 99% were deemed to have need. 100% of freshmen with need received aid; of those 90% had need fully met. *Average percent of need met:* 98% (excluding resources awarded to replace EFC).

UNDERGRADUATE FINANCIAL AID (Fall 2009, est.) 1,800 applied for aid; of those 99% were deemed to have need. 100% of undergraduates with need received aid; of those 90% had need fully met. *Average percent of need met:* 96% (excluding resources awarded to replace EFC).

GIFT AID (NEED-BASED) *Total amount:* $7,524,569 (33% federal, 37% state, 17% institutional, 13% external sources). *Receiving aid:* Freshmen: 57% (285); all full-time undergraduates: 57% (1,087). *Scholarships, grants, and awards:* Federal Pell, FSEOG, state, private, college/university gift aid from institutional funds.

GIFT AID (NON-NEED-BASED) *Total amount:* $11,742,750 (36% state, 64% institutional). *Scholarships, grants, and awards by category: Academic interests/achievement:* biological sciences, communication, education, general academic interests/achievements, military science, religion/biblical studies. *Creative arts/ performance:* journalism/publications, music, theater/drama. *Special characteristics:* children of faculty/staff. *Tuition waivers:* Full or partial for employees or children of employees.

LOANS *Student loans:* $7,004,622 (52% need-based, 48% non-need-based). 61% of past graduating class borrowed through all loan programs. *Average indebtedness per student:* $18,200. *Parent loans:* $819,931 (100% non-need-based). *Programs:* FFEL (Subsidized and Unsubsidized Stafford, PLUS), Perkins, state.

WORK-STUDY *Federal work-study:* Total amount: $148,000; jobs available. *State or other work-study/employment:* Total amount: $168,000 (100% non-need-based). Part-time jobs available.

ATHLETIC AWARDS Total amount: $961,930 (100% non-need-based).

APPLYING FOR FINANCIAL AID *Required financial aid form:* FAFSA. *Financial aid deadline:* Continuous.

CONTACT Mike Jordan, Director of Financial Aid, North Greenville University, PO Box 1892, Tigerville, SC 29688, 864-977-7058 or toll-free 800-468-6642 Ext. 7001. *Fax:* 864-977-7177. *E-mail:* mjordan@ngu.edu.

NORTHLAND COLLEGE
Ashland, WI

ABOUT THE INSTITUTION Independent religious, coed. 20 undergraduate majors.

GIFT AID (NEED-BASED) *Scholarships, grants, and awards:* Federal Pell, FSEOG, state, private, college/university gift aid from institutional funds, Bureau of Indian Affairs Grants, Academic Competitiveness Grants, National SMART Grants.

GIFT AID (NON-NEED-BASED) *Scholarships, grants, and awards by category: Academic interests/achievement:* general academic interests/achievements. *Creative arts/performance:* art/fine arts, music. *Special achievements/activities:* leadership. *Special characteristics:* ethnic background.

LOANS *Programs:* FFEL (Subsidized and Unsubsidized Stafford, PLUS), Perkins.

WORK-STUDY *Federal work-study:* Total amount: $491,053; 308 jobs averaging $1594. *State or other work-study/employment:* Total amount: $409,394 (60% need-based, 40% non-need-based). 150 part-time jobs averaging $1636.

APPLYING FOR FINANCIAL AID *Required financial aid form:* FAFSA.

CONTACT Debora L. Milanowski, Interim Director of Financial Aid, Northland College, 1411 Ellis Avenue, Ashland, WI 54806, 715-682-1255 or toll-free 800-753-1840 (in-state), 800-753-1040 (out-of-state). *Fax:* 715-682-1258. *E-mail:* dmilanow@northland.edu.

NORTH PARK UNIVERSITY
Chicago, IL

ABOUT THE INSTITUTION Independent religious, coed. *Awards:* bachelor's and master's degrees. 56 undergraduate majors. *Total enrollment:* 2,181. Undergraduates: 1,573. Freshmen: 320.

GIFT AID (NEED-BASED) *Scholarships, grants, and awards:* Federal Pell, FSEOG, state, private, college/university gift aid from institutional funds.

GIFT AID (NON-NEED-BASED) *Scholarships, grants, and awards by category: Academic interests/achievement:* general academic interests/achievements.

Creative arts/performance: art/fine arts, journalism/publications, music, theater/ drama. *Special achievements/activities:* religious involvement. *Special characteristics:* relatives of clergy.

LOANS *Programs:* Federal Direct (Subsidized and Unsubsidized Stafford, PLUS), Perkins, Federal Nursing.

WORK-STUDY *Federal work-study:* Total amount: $225,205; 158 jobs averaging $1500.

APPLYING FOR FINANCIAL AID *Required financial aid form:* FAFSA.

CONTACT Dr. Lucy Shaker, Director of Financial Aid, North Park University, 3225 West Foster Avenue, Chicago, IL 60625-4895, 773-244-5526 or toll-free 800-888-NPC8. *Fax:* 773-244-4953.

NORTHWEST CHRISTIAN UNIVERSITY
Eugene, OR

Tuition & fees: $22,900	Average undergraduate aid package: $19,146

ABOUT THE INSTITUTION Independent Christian, coed. 16 undergraduate majors. Federal methodology is used as a basis for awarding need-based institutional aid.

UNDERGRADUATE EXPENSES for 2009–10 *Comprehensive fee:* $29,700 includes full-time tuition ($22,900) and room and board ($6800). Full-time tuition and fees vary according to course load. Room and board charges vary according to board plan and housing facility. *Part-time tuition:* $770 per credit. Part-time tuition and fees vary according to course load. *Payment plans:* Installment, deferred payment.

FRESHMAN FINANCIAL AID (Fall 2009, est.) 73 applied for aid; of those 89% were deemed to have need. 100% of freshmen with need received aid; of those 22% had need fully met. *Average percent of need met:* 78% (excluding resources awarded to replace EFC). *Average financial aid package:* $18,806 (excluding resources awarded to replace EFC). 15% of all full-time freshmen had no need and received non-need-based gift aid.

UNDERGRADUATE FINANCIAL AID (Fall 2009, est.) 294 applied for aid; of those 92% were deemed to have need. 100% of undergraduates with need received aid; of those 19% had need fully met. *Average percent of need met:* 79% (excluding resources awarded to replace EFC). *Average financial aid package:* $19,146 (excluding resources awarded to replace EFC). 10% of all full-time undergraduates had no need and received non-need-based gift aid.

GIFT AID (NEED-BASED) *Total amount:* $3,610,633 (19% federal, 4% state, 68% institutional, 9% external sources). *Receiving aid:* Freshmen: 83% (65); all full-time undergraduates: 74% (270). *Average award:* Freshmen: $15,519; Undergraduates: $14,903. *Scholarships, grants, and awards:* Federal Pell, FSEOG, state, private, college/university gift aid from institutional funds.

GIFT AID (NON-NEED-BASED) *Total amount:* $311,650 (82% institutional, 18% external sources). *Receiving aid:* Freshmen: 9% (7). Undergraduates: 7% (27). *Average award:* Freshmen: $4880. Undergraduates: $6099. *Scholarships, grants, and awards by category: Academic interests/achievement:* general academic interests/achievements. *Creative arts/performance:* music. *Special achievements/ activities:* leadership. *Special characteristics:* children of faculty/staff, relatives of clergy, religious affiliation, siblings of current students. *Tuition waivers:* Full or partial for employees or children of employees.

LOANS *Student loans:* $2,027,784 (70% need-based, 30% non-need-based). 85% of past graduating class borrowed through all loan programs. *Average indebtedness per student:* $21,633. *Average need-based loan:* Freshmen: $3428. Undergraduates: $4290. *Parent loans:* $325,106 (58% need-based, 42% non-need-based). *Programs:* Federal Direct (Subsidized and Unsubsidized Stafford, PLUS), Perkins.

WORK-STUDY *Federal work-study:* Total amount: $191,630; jobs available. *State or other work-study/employment:* Total amount: $16,850 (85% need-based, 15% non-need-based). Part-time jobs available.

ATHLETIC AWARDS Total amount: $452,800 (74% need-based, 26% non-need-based).

APPLYING FOR FINANCIAL AID *Required financial aid forms:* FAFSA, merit worksheet. *Financial aid deadline (priority):* 3/1. *Notification date:* Continuous beginning 3/1. Students must reply within 2 weeks of notification.

CONTACT David Haggard, Director of Financial Aid, Northwest Christian University, 828 East 11th Avenue, Eugene, OR 97401-3727, 541-684-7218 or toll-free 877-463-6622. *Fax:* 541-684-7323. *E-mail:* dhaggard@northwestchristian.edu.

NORTHWEST COLLEGE OF ART
Poulsbo, WA

CONTACT Ms. Kim Y. Perigard, Director of Financial Aid, Northwest College of Art, 16464 State Highway 305, Poulsbo, WA 98370, 360-779-9993 or toll-free 800-769-ARTS.

NORTHWESTERN COLLEGE
Orange City, IA

CONTACT Mr. Gerry Korver, Director of Financial Aid, Northwestern College, 101 Seventh Street, SW, Orange City, IA 51041-1996, 712-707-7131 or toll-free 800-747-4757. *Fax:* 712-707-7164.

NORTHWESTERN COLLEGE
St. Paul, MN

Tuition & fees: $24,570	Average undergraduate aid package: $16,842

ABOUT THE INSTITUTION Independent nondenominational, coed. 48 undergraduate majors. Federal methodology is used as a basis for awarding need-based institutional aid.

UNDERGRADUATE EXPENSES for 2010–11 *Comprehensive fee:* $32,290 includes full-time tuition ($24,370), mandatory fees ($200), and room and board ($7720). *College room only:* $4480. Full-time tuition and fees vary according to course load. Room and board charges vary according to board plan. *Part-time tuition:* $1040 per semester hour. *Part-time fees:* $55 per term. Part-time tuition and fees vary according to course load. *Payment plan:* Installment.

FRESHMAN FINANCIAL AID (Fall 2009, est.) 414 applied for aid; of those 90% were deemed to have need. 100% of freshmen with need received aid; of those 11% had need fully met. *Average percent of need met:* 70% (excluding resources awarded to replace EFC). *Average financial aid package:* $17,247 (excluding resources awarded to replace EFC). 12% of all full-time freshmen had no need and received non-need-based gift aid.

UNDERGRADUATE FINANCIAL AID (Fall 2009, est.) 1,637 applied for aid; of those 90% were deemed to have need. 100% of undergraduates with need received aid; of those 11% had need fully met. *Average percent of need met:* 70% (excluding resources awarded to replace EFC). *Average financial aid package:* $16,842 (excluding resources awarded to replace EFC). 14% of all full-time undergraduates had no need and received non-need-based gift aid.

GIFT AID (NEED-BASED) *Total amount:* $17,621,023 (16% federal, 15% state, 65% institutional, 4% external sources). *Receiving aid:* Freshmen: 84% (369); all full-time undergraduates: 80% (1,448). *Average award:* Freshmen: $13,673; Undergraduates: $12,088. *Scholarships, grants, and awards:* Federal Pell, FSEOG, state, private, college/university gift aid from institutional funds.

GIFT AID (NON-NEED-BASED) *Total amount:* $1,837,575 (94% institutional, 6% external sources). *Receiving aid:* Freshmen: 6% (25). Undergraduates: 4% (64). *Average award:* Freshmen: $5133. Undergraduates: $5383. *Scholarships, grants, and awards by category: Academic interests/achievement:* 1,269 awards ($5,857,220 total): general academic interests/achievements. *Creative arts/performance:* 154 awards ($225,075 total): music, theater/drama. *Special achievements/activities:* 376 awards ($921,765 total): general special achievements/ activities, leadership. *Special characteristics:* 661 awards ($3,722,458 total): children of faculty/staff, ethnic background, international students, relatives of clergy, siblings of current students. *Tuition waivers:* Full or partial for children of alumni, employees or children of employees.

LOANS *Student loans:* $10,852,254 (89% need-based, 11% non-need-based). 84% of past graduating class borrowed through all loan programs. *Average indebtedness per student:* $26,259. *Average need-based loan:* Freshmen: $3562. Undergraduates: $4365. *Parent loans:* $4,965,955 (81% need-based, 19% non-need-based). *Programs:* Federal Direct (Subsidized and Unsubsidized Stafford, PLUS), Perkins, state.

WORK-STUDY *Federal work-study:* Total amount: $361,475; 169 jobs averaging $2139. *State or other work-study/employment:* Total amount: $760,807 (87% need-based, 13% non-need-based). 235 part-time jobs averaging $2080.

APPLYING FOR FINANCIAL AID *Required financial aid forms:* FAFSA, institution's own form. *Financial aid deadline (priority):* 3/1. *Notification date:* Continuous beginning 3/1. Students must reply within 2 weeks of notification.

CONTACT Mr. Richard L. Blatchley, Director of Financial Aid, Northwestern College, 3003 Snelling Avenue North, St. Paul, MN 55113-1598, 651-631-5321 or toll-free 800-827-6827. *Fax:* 651-628-3332. *E-mail:* rlb@nwc.edu.

NORTHWESTERN OKLAHOMA STATE UNIVERSITY
Alva, OK

Tuition & fees: N/R	Average undergraduate aid package: N/A

ABOUT THE INSTITUTION State-supported, coed. 45 undergraduate majors. Both federal and institutional methodology are used as a basis for awarding need-based institutional aid.

GIFT AID (NEED-BASED) *Total amount:* $4,090,604 (65% federal, 28% state, 7% institutional). *Scholarships, grants, and awards:* Federal Pell, FSEOG, state, private, college/university gift aid from institutional funds.

GIFT AID (NON-NEED-BASED) *Total amount:* $885,950 (8% state, 47% institutional, 45% external sources). *Scholarships, grants, and awards by category: Academic interests/achievement:* agriculture, biological sciences, business, communication, computer science, education, English, foreign languages, general academic interests/achievements, health fields, library science, mathematics, physical sciences, premedicine, social sciences. *Creative arts/performance:* art/fine arts, cinema/film/broadcasting, debating, general creative arts/ performance, journalism/publications, music, theater/drama. *Special achievements/ activities:* cheerleading/drum major, general special achievements/activities, leadership, memberships, rodeo. *Special characteristics:* children of faculty/staff. *Tuition waivers:* Full or partial for employees or children of employees, senior citizens.

LOANS *Student loans:* $4,069,441 (54% need-based, 46% non-need-based). 49% of past graduating class borrowed through all loan programs. *Average indebtedness per student:* $9381. *Parent loans:* $72,249 (100% non-need-based). *Programs:* FFEL (Subsidized and Unsubsidized Stafford, PLUS), Perkins.

WORK-STUDY *Federal work-study:* Total amount: $178,802; jobs available. *State or other work-study/employment:* Total amount: $246,006 (100% non-need-based). Part-time jobs available.

ATHLETIC AWARDS Total amount: $294,193 (76% need-based, 24% non-need-based).

APPLYING FOR FINANCIAL AID *Required financial aid forms:* FAFSA, institution's own form. *Financial aid deadline:* Continuous. *Notification date:* Continuous beginning 3/1. Students must reply by 8/15.

CONTACT Calleb N. Mosburg, Director of Financial Aid, Northwestern Oklahoma State University, 709 Oklahoma Boulevard, Alva, OK 73717-2799, 580-327-8542. *Fax:* 580-327-8177. *E-mail:* cnmosburg@nwosu.edu.

NORTHWESTERN STATE UNIVERSITY OF LOUISIANA
Natchitoches, LA

Tuition & fees (LA res): $3786	Average undergraduate aid package: $6741

ABOUT THE INSTITUTION State-supported, coed. 48 undergraduate majors. Both federal and institutional methodology are used as a basis for awarding need-based institutional aid.

UNDERGRADUATE EXPENSES for 2009–10 *Tuition, state resident:* full-time $2594; part-time $399 per credit hour. *Tuition, nonresident:* full-time $9280; part-time $678 per credit hour. *Required fees:* full-time $1192. Full-time tuition and fees vary according to course load and location. Part-time tuition and fees vary according to course load and location. *College room and board:* $6682; *Room only:* $4288. Room and board charges vary according to board plan, housing facility, and location. *Payment plan:* Installment.

FRESHMAN FINANCIAL AID (Fall 2009, est.) 1,047 applied for aid; of those 77% were deemed to have need. 98% of freshmen with need received aid; of those 52% had need fully met. *Average percent of need met:* 72% (excluding resources awarded to replace EFC). *Average financial aid package:* $6459 (excluding resources awarded to replace EFC). 29% of all full-time freshmen had no need and received non-need-based gift aid.

UNDERGRADUATE FINANCIAL AID (Fall 2009, est.) 4,124 applied for aid; of those 82% were deemed to have need. 96% of undergraduates with need received aid; of those 39% had need fully met. *Average percent of need met:*

54% (excluding resources awarded to replace EFC). *Average financial aid package:* $6741 (excluding resources awarded to replace EFC). 27% of all full-time undergraduates had no need and received non-need-based gift aid.
GIFT AID (NEED-BASED) *Total amount:* $12,660,720 (99% federal, 1% state). *Receiving aid:* Freshmen: 45% (561); all full-time undergraduates: 43% (2,316). *Average award:* Freshmen: $5078; Undergraduates: $4672. *Scholarships, grants, and awards:* Federal Pell, FSEOG, state, private, college/university gift aid from institutional funds, United Negro College Fund, Federal Nursing, third party scholarships.
GIFT AID (NON-NEED-BASED) *Total amount:* $10,561,781 (57% state, 23% institutional, 20% external sources). *Receiving aid:* Freshmen: 46% (571). Undergraduates: 29% (1,554). *Average award:* Freshmen: $4991. Undergraduates: $4874. *Scholarships, grants, and awards by category:* Academic interests/achievement: 2,354 awards ($1,971,332 total): biological sciences, education, engineering/technologies, general academic interests/achievements, health fields, humanities, mathematics, physical sciences. Creative arts/performance: 506 awards ($710,787 total): art/fine arts, cinema/film/broadcasting, creative writing, dance, general creative arts/performance, journalism/publications, music, performing arts, theater/drama. Special achievements/activities: 127 awards ($133,504 total): cheerleading/drum major, general special achievements/activities, leadership, memberships. Special characteristics: 654 awards ($2,733,466 total): adult students, children of faculty/staff, children of public servants, general special characteristics, international students, out-of-state students, public servants, veterans, veterans' children. *Tuition waivers:* Full or partial for employees or children of employees, senior citizens.
LOANS *Student loans:* $24,926,460 (44% need-based, 56% non-need-based). 68% of past graduating class borrowed through all loan programs. *Average indebtedness per student:* $21,773. *Average need-based loan:* Freshmen: $5204. Undergraduates: $6517. *Parent loans:* $163,214 (100% non-need-based). *Programs:* FFEL (Subsidized and Unsubsidized Stafford, PLUS), Perkins, alternative loans.
WORK-STUDY *Federal work-study:* Total amount: $340,172; 183 jobs averaging $1827. *State or other work-study/employment:* Total amount: $934,045 (100% non-need-based). 130 part-time jobs available.
ATHLETIC AWARDS Total amount: $2,445,893 (100% non-need-based).
APPLYING FOR FINANCIAL AID *Required financial aid forms:* FAFSA, institution's own form. *Financial aid deadline (priority):* 5/1. *Notification date:* Continuous beginning 5/1. Students must reply within 4 weeks of notification.
CONTACT Ms. Misti Adams, Director of Financial Aid, Northwestern State University of Louisiana, 103 Roy Hall, Natchitoches, LA 71497, 318-357-5961 or toll-free 800-327-1903. *Fax:* 318-357-5488. *E-mail:* nsufinaid@nsula.edu.

NORTHWESTERN UNIVERSITY
Evanston, IL

| Tuition & fees: $38,461 | Average undergraduate aid package: $30,080 |

ABOUT THE INSTITUTION Independent, coed. *Awards:* bachelor's and master's degrees and post-master's certificates. 111 undergraduate majors. *Total enrollment:* 18,431. Undergraduates: 8,476. Freshmen: 2,078. Both federal and institutional methodology are used as a basis for awarding need-based institutional aid.
UNDERGRADUATE EXPENSES for 2009–10 *Application fee:* $65. *Comprehensive fee:* $50,164 includes full-time tuition ($38,088), mandatory fees ($373), and room and board ($11,703). *College room only:* $6657.
FRESHMAN FINANCIAL AID (Fall 2009, est.) 1,312 applied for aid; of those 80% were deemed to have need. 100% of freshmen with need received aid; of those 100% had need fully met. *Average percent of need met:* 100% (excluding resources awarded to replace EFC). *Average financial aid package:* $30,424 (excluding resources awarded to replace EFC). 5% of all full-time freshmen had no need and received non-need-based gift aid.
UNDERGRADUATE FINANCIAL AID (Fall 2009, est.) 4,278 applied for aid; of those 86% were deemed to have need. 100% of undergraduates with need received aid; of those 100% had need fully met. *Average percent of need met:* 100% (excluding resources awarded to replace EFC). *Average financial aid package:* $30,080 (excluding resources awarded to replace EFC). 5% of all full-time undergraduates had no need and received non-need-based gift aid.
GIFT AID (NEED-BASED) *Total amount:* $94,971,642 (7% federal, 2% state, 87% institutional, 4% external sources). *Receiving aid:* Freshmen: 46% (983); all full-time undergraduates: 41% (3,478). *Average award:* Freshmen: $27,968;

Undergraduates: $26,817. *Scholarships, grants, and awards:* Federal Pell, FSEOG, state, college/university gift aid from institutional funds.
GIFT AID (NON-NEED-BASED) *Total amount:* $2,245,365 (45% institutional, 55% external sources). *Average award:* Freshmen: $2785. Undergraduates: $2521. *Scholarships, grants, and awards by category:* Creative arts/performance: 127 awards ($425,096 total): music. Special characteristics: 38 awards ($1,345,583 total): international students. *ROTC:* Army cooperative, Naval, Air Force cooperative.
LOANS *Student loans:* $22,880,826 (83% need-based, 17% non-need-based). 48% of past graduating class borrowed through all loan programs. *Average indebtedness per student:* $20,802. *Average need-based loan:* Freshmen: $3996. Undergraduates: $4625. *Parent loans:* $22,653,345 (100% non-need-based). *Programs:* Federal Direct (Subsidized and Unsubsidized Stafford, PLUS), FFEL (Subsidized and Unsubsidized Stafford, PLUS), Perkins, college/university.
WORK-STUDY *Federal work-study:* Total amount: $3,700,000; 2,301 jobs averaging $2050. *State or other work-study/employment:* Total amount: $1,419,868 (100% need-based). Part-time jobs available.
ATHLETIC AWARDS Total amount: $12,410,195 (100% non-need-based).
APPLYING FOR FINANCIAL AID *Required financial aid forms:* FAFSA, CSS Financial Aid PROFILE, noncustodial (divorced/separated) parent's statement, business/farm supplement, parent and student tax forms. *Financial aid deadline:* 2/15. *Notification date:* 4/15. Students must reply by 5/1 or within 2 weeks of notification.
CONTACT Office of Financial Aid, Northwestern University, 1801 Hinman Avenue, Evanston, IL 60204-1270, 847-491-7400. *E-mail:* ug-finaid@u.northwestern.edu.

NORTHWEST MISSOURI STATE UNIVERSITY
Maryville, MO

ABOUT THE INSTITUTION State-supported, coed. 83 undergraduate majors.
GIFT AID (NEED-BASED) *Scholarships, grants, and awards:* Federal Pell, FSEOG, state, private, college/university gift aid from institutional funds.
GIFT AID (NON-NEED-BASED) *Scholarships, grants, and awards by category:* Academic interests/achievement: agriculture, biological sciences, business, communication, computer science, education, English, foreign languages, general academic interests/achievements, health fields, home economics, humanities, mathematics, physical sciences, social sciences. Creative arts/performance: art/fine arts, cinema/film/broadcasting, debating, journalism/publications, music, theater/drama. Special achievements/activities: cheerleading/drum major, general special achievements/activities, leadership, memberships. Special characteristics: children and siblings of alumni, general special characteristics, members of minority groups, out-of-state students, previous college experience.
LOANS *Programs:* Federal Direct (Subsidized and Unsubsidized Stafford, PLUS), Perkins.
APPLYING FOR FINANCIAL AID *Required financial aid form:* FAFSA.
CONTACT Mr. Del Morley, Director of Financial Assistance, Northwest Missouri State University, 800 University Drive, Maryville, MO 64468-6001, 660-562-1138 or toll-free 800-633-1175.

NORTHWEST NAZARENE UNIVERSITY
Nampa, ID

| Tuition & fees: $23,090 | Average undergraduate aid package: $16,099 |

ABOUT THE INSTITUTION Independent religious, coed. 76 undergraduate majors. Federal methodology is used as a basis for awarding need-based institutional aid.
UNDERGRADUATE EXPENSES for 2010–11 *Comprehensive fee:* $29,110 includes full-time tuition ($22,810), mandatory fees ($280), and room and board ($6020). Full-time tuition and fees vary according to course load, degree level, program, and reciprocity agreements. Room and board charges vary according to board plan. *Payment plans:* Tuition prepayment, installment.
FRESHMAN FINANCIAL AID (Fall 2008) 271 applied for aid; of those 86% were deemed to have need. 100% of freshmen with need received aid; of those 25% had need fully met. *Average percent of need met:* 84% (excluding resources awarded to replace EFC). *Average financial aid package:* $16,586 (excluding resources awarded to replace EFC). 25% of all full-time freshmen had no need and received non-need-based gift aid.

UNDERGRADUATE FINANCIAL AID (Fall 2008) 874 applied for aid; of those 88% were deemed to have need. 100% of undergraduates with need received aid; of those 22% had need fully met. *Average percent of need met:* 83% (excluding resources awarded to replace EFC). *Average financial aid package:* $16,099 (excluding resources awarded to replace EFC). 27% of all full-time undergraduates had no need and received non-need-based gift aid.

GIFT AID (NEED-BASED) *Total amount:* $8,067,323 (17% federal, 1% state, 73% institutional, 9% external sources). *Receiving aid:* Freshmen: 61% (189); all full-time undergraduates: 61% (644). *Average award:* Freshmen: $8800; Undergraduates: $7888. *Scholarships, grants, and awards:* Federal Pell, FSEOG, state, private, college/university gift aid from institutional funds.

GIFT AID (NON-NEED-BASED) *Total amount:* $1,842,639 (2% state, 88% institutional, 10% external sources). *Receiving aid:* Freshmen: 75% (234). Undergraduates: 70% (743). *Average award:* Freshmen: $6843. Undergraduates: $5251. *Scholarships, grants, and awards by category: Academic interests/achievement:* 892 awards ($1,819,404 total): biological sciences, business, computer science, education, English, general academic interests/achievements, health fields, mathematics, military science, physical sciences, premedicine, religion/biblical studies, social sciences. *Creative arts/performance:* 62 awards ($35,074 total): art/fine arts, debating, general creative arts/performance, journalism/publications, music, performing arts, theater/drama. *Special achievements/activities:* 6 awards ($1263 total): cheerleading/drum major, general special achievements/activities, leadership, religious involvement. *Special characteristics:* 605 awards ($1,475,695 total): children and siblings of alumni, children of educators, children of faculty/staff, ethnic background, international students, members of minority groups, out-of-state students, relatives of clergy, religious affiliation, siblings of current students, veterans. *Tuition waivers:* Full or partial for minority students, children of alumni, employees or children of employees.

LOANS *Student loans:* $7,619,579 (69% need-based, 31% non-need-based). 83% of past graduating class borrowed through all loan programs. *Average indebtedness per student:* $25,758. *Average need-based loan:* Freshmen: $2501. Undergraduates: $3591. *Parent loans:* $1,448,903 (74% need-based, 26% non-need-based). *Programs:* FFEL (Subsidized and Unsubsidized Stafford, PLUS), Perkins, college/university.

WORK-STUDY *Federal work-study:* Total amount: $125,217; 144 jobs averaging $868. *State or other work-study/employment:* Total amount: $5347 (100% need-based). Part-time jobs available.

ATHLETIC AWARDS Total amount: $1,412,525 (67% need-based, 33% non-need-based).

APPLYING FOR FINANCIAL AID *Required financial aid forms:* FAFSA, institution's own form. *Financial aid deadline (priority):* 3/1. *Notification date:* Continuous beginning 4/1. Students must reply within 3 weeks of notification.

CONTACT Mr. Wes Maggard, Director of Financial Aid, Northwest Nazarene University, 623 Holly Street, Nampa, ID 83686, 208-467-8774 or toll-free 877-668-4968. *Fax:* 208-467-8375. *E-mail:* mwmaggard@nnu.edu.

NORTHWEST UNIVERSITY
Kirkland, WA

Tuition & fees: $22,650	Average undergraduate aid package: $15,580

ABOUT THE INSTITUTION Independent religious, coed. 43 undergraduate majors. Federal methodology is used as a basis for awarding need-based institutional aid.

UNDERGRADUATE EXPENSES for 2010–11 *Comprehensive fee:* $29,374 includes full-time tuition ($22,360), mandatory fees ($290), and room and board ($6724). Full-time tuition and fees vary according to class time and program. Room and board charges vary according to board plan and housing facility. *Part-time tuition:* $930 per credit hour. Part-time tuition and fees vary according to course load. *Payment plan:* Installment.

FRESHMAN FINANCIAL AID (Fall 2009, est.) 187 applied for aid; of those 88% were deemed to have need. 99% of freshmen with need received aid; of those 18% had need fully met. *Average percent of need met:* 72% (excluding resources awarded to replace EFC). *Average financial aid package:* $15,462 (excluding resources awarded to replace EFC). 14% of all full-time freshmen had no need and received non-need-based gift aid.

UNDERGRADUATE FINANCIAL AID (Fall 2009, est.) 902 applied for aid; of those 89% were deemed to have need. 99% of undergraduates with need received aid; of those 14% had need fully met. *Average percent of need met:* 71% (excluding resources awarded to replace EFC). *Average financial aid*

package: $15,580 (excluding resources awarded to replace EFC). 15% of all full-time undergraduates had no need and received non-need-based gift aid.

GIFT AID (NEED-BASED) *Total amount:* $8,222,774 (21% federal, 12% state, 64% institutional, 3% external sources). *Receiving aid:* Freshmen: 74% (161); all full-time undergraduates: 76% (792). *Average award:* Freshmen: $12,219; Undergraduates: $11,427. *Scholarships, grants, and awards:* Federal Pell, FSEOG, state, private, college/university gift aid from institutional funds.

GIFT AID (NON-NEED-BASED) *Total amount:* $1,408,430 (90% institutional, 10% external sources). *Receiving aid:* Freshmen: 8% (18). Undergraduates: 6% (63). *Average award:* Freshmen: $8143. Undergraduates: $6632. *Scholarships, grants, and awards by category: Academic interests/achievement:* 240 awards ($1,230,628 total): general academic interests/achievements. *Creative arts/performance:* 103 awards ($291,350 total): debating, music, performing arts, theater/drama. *Special achievements/activities:* 21 awards ($369,070 total): leadership. *Special characteristics:* 227 awards ($1,351,609 total): children of current students, children of faculty/staff, general special characteristics, international students, married students, parents of current students, relatives of clergy, religious affiliation, siblings of current students, spouses of current students. *Tuition waivers:* Full or partial for employees or children of employees.

LOANS *Student loans:* $7,275,957 (74% need-based, 26% non-need-based). 76% of past graduating class borrowed through all loan programs. *Average indebtedness per student:* $23,965. *Average need-based loan:* Freshmen: $2679. Undergraduates: $3791. *Parent loans:* $994,851 (48% need-based, 52% non-need-based). *Programs:* Federal Direct (Subsidized and Unsubsidized Stafford, PLUS), Perkins, state, alternative loans.

WORK-STUDY *Federal work-study:* Total amount: $191,187; 99 jobs averaging $3500. *State or other work-study/employment:* Total amount: $105,787 (81% need-based, 19% non-need-based). 33 part-time jobs averaging $3500.

ATHLETIC AWARDS Total amount: $739,680 (73% need-based, 27% non-need-based).

APPLYING FOR FINANCIAL AID *Required financial aid forms:* FAFSA, institution's own form. *Financial aid deadline:* 8/1 (priority: 2/15). *Notification date:* Continuous beginning 3/1. Students must reply within 4 weeks of notification.

CONTACT Ms. Lana J. Walter, Director of Financial Aid, Northwest University, PO Box 579, Kirkland, WA 98083-0579, 425-889-5336 or toll-free 800-669-3781. *Fax:* 425-889-5224. *E-mail:* lana.walter@northwestu.edu.

NORTHWOOD UNIVERSITY
Midland, MI

Tuition & fees: $18,408	Average undergraduate aid package: $15,831

ABOUT THE INSTITUTION Independent, coed. *Awards:* associate, bachelor's, and master's degrees. 5 undergraduate majors. *Total enrollment:* 2,269. Undergraduates: 1,950. Freshmen: 442. Federal methodology is used as a basis for awarding need-based institutional aid.

UNDERGRADUATE EXPENSES for 2009–10 *Application fee:* $25. *Tuition:* full-time $17,430; part-time $363 per quarter hour. Full-time tuition and fees vary according to class time. Part-time tuition and fees vary according to class time. Room and board charges vary according to board plan. *Payment plan:* Installment.

FRESHMAN FINANCIAL AID (Fall 2009, est.) 283 applied for aid; of those 90% were deemed to have need. 100% of freshmen with need received aid; of those 21% had need fully met. *Average percent of need met:* 59% (excluding resources awarded to replace EFC). *Average financial aid package:* $16,516 (excluding resources awarded to replace EFC). 14% of all full-time freshmen had no need and received non-need-based gift aid.

UNDERGRADUATE FINANCIAL AID (Fall 2009, est.) 1,377 applied for aid; of those 90% were deemed to have need. 100% of undergraduates with need received aid; of those 23% had need fully met. *Average percent of need met:* 54% (excluding resources awarded to replace EFC). *Average financial aid package:* $15,831 (excluding resources awarded to replace EFC). 14% of all full-time undergraduates had no need and received non-need-based gift aid.

GIFT AID (NEED-BASED) *Total amount:* $12,104,198 (23% federal, 21% state, 55% institutional, 1% external sources). *Receiving aid:* Freshmen: 66% (226); all full-time undergraduates: 61% (1,079). *Average award:* Freshmen: $5766; Undergraduates: $5585. *Scholarships, grants, and awards:* Federal Pell, FSEOG, state, private, college/university gift aid from institutional funds.

GIFT AID (NON-NEED-BASED) *Total amount:* $2,819,864 (10% state, 87% institutional, 3% external sources). *Receiving aid:* Freshmen: 29% (100). Undergraduates: 26% (458). *Average award:* Freshmen: $7594. Undergraduates: $6197. **Scholarships, grants, and awards by category:** Academic interests/achievement: business, general academic interests/achievements. **Special achievements/activities:** cheerleading/drum major, leadership, memberships. **Special characteristics:** children and siblings of alumni, children of faculty/staff, siblings of current students. **Tuition waivers:** Full or partial for employees or children of employees.

LOANS Student loans: $12,091,932 (71% need-based, 29% non-need-based). 72% of past graduating class borrowed through all loan programs. Average indebtedness per student: $28,634. **Average need-based loan:** Freshmen: $3307. Undergraduates: $4356. **Parent loans:** $1,830,219 (41% need-based, 59% non-need-based). **Programs:** FFEL (Subsidized and Unsubsidized Stafford, PLUS), state.

WORK-STUDY Federal work-study: Total amount: $275,044; jobs available. **State or other work-study/employment:** Part-time jobs available.

ATHLETIC AWARDS Total amount: $2,433,207 (53% need-based, 47% non-need-based).

APPLYING FOR FINANCIAL AID Required financial aid form: FAFSA. **Financial aid deadline:** Continuous. **Notification date:** Continuous beginning 3/1.

CONTACT Terri Mieler, Director of Financial Aid, Northwood University, 4000 Whiting Drive, Midland, MI 48640-2398, 989-837-4301 or toll-free 800-457-7878. Fax: 989-837-4130. E-mail: mieler@northwood.edu.

NORTHWOOD UNIVERSITY, FLORIDA CAMPUS
West Palm Beach, FL

Tuition & fees: $18,408	Average undergraduate aid package: $16,240

ABOUT THE INSTITUTION Independent, coed. **Awards:** associate and bachelor's degrees. 11 undergraduate majors. **Total enrollment:** 620. Undergraduates: 620. Freshmen: 109. Federal methodology is used as a basis for awarding need-based institutional aid.

UNDERGRADUATE EXPENSES for 2009–10 Application fee: $25. **Comprehensive fee:** $26,970 includes full-time tuition ($17,430), mandatory fees ($978), and room and board ($8562). Full-time tuition and fees vary according to class time. Room and board charges vary according to board plan. **Part-time tuition:** $363 per credit hour. Part-time tuition and fees vary according to class time. **Payment plan:** Installment.

FRESHMAN FINANCIAL AID (Fall 2009, est.) 69 applied for aid; of those 84% were deemed to have need. 100% of freshmen with need received aid; of those 12% had need fully met. **Average percent of need met:** 60% (excluding resources awarded to replace EFC). **Average financial aid package:** $17,741 (excluding resources awarded to replace EFC). 11% of all full-time freshmen had no need and received non-need-based gift aid.

UNDERGRADUATE FINANCIAL AID (Fall 2009, est.) 287 applied for aid; of those 87% were deemed to have need. 100% of undergraduates with need received aid; of those 18% had need fully met. **Average percent of need met:** 57% (excluding resources awarded to replace EFC). **Average financial aid package:** $16,240 (excluding resources awarded to replace EFC). 20% of all full-time undergraduates had no need and received non-need-based gift aid.

GIFT AID (NEED-BASED) Total amount: $2,501,882 (27% federal, 11% state, 61% institutional, 1% external sources). **Receiving aid:** Freshmen: 53% (51); all full-time undergraduates: 36% (197). **Average award:** Freshmen: $6941; Undergraduates: $6659. **Scholarships, grants, and awards:** Federal Pell, FSEOG, state, private, college/university gift aid from institutional funds.

GIFT AID (NON-NEED-BASED) Total amount: $1,203,598 (9% state, 90% institutional, 1% external sources). **Receiving aid:** Freshmen: 12% (12). Undergraduates: 14% (78). **Average award:** Freshmen: $9392. Undergraduates: $5298. **Scholarships, grants, and awards by category:** Academic interests/achievement: business, general academic interests/achievements. **Special achievements/activities:** memberships. **Special characteristics:** children and siblings of alumni, children of faculty/staff, siblings of current students. **Tuition waivers:** Full or partial for children of alumni, employees or children of employees.

LOANS Student loans: $2,512,910 (65% need-based, 35% non-need-based). 55% of past graduating class borrowed through all loan programs. Average indebtedness per student: $29,264. **Average need-based loan:** Freshmen: $3181. Undergraduates: $4119. **Parent loans:** $649,989 (33% need-based, 67% non-need-based). **Programs:** FFEL (Subsidized and Unsubsidized Stafford, PLUS).

WORK-STUDY Federal work-study: Total amount: $185,500; jobs available.

ATHLETIC AWARDS Total amount: $1,204,357 (28% need-based, 72% non-need-based).

APPLYING FOR FINANCIAL AID Required financial aid forms: FAFSA, state aid form. **Financial aid deadline:** Continuous. **Notification date:** Continuous beginning 3/1.

CONTACT Ms. Teresa A. Palmer, Director of Financial Aid, Northwood University, Florida Campus, 2600 North Military Trail, West Palm Beach, FL 33409-2911, 561-478-5590 or toll-free 800-458-8325. Fax: 561-681-7990. E-mail: palmer@northwood.edu.

NORTHWOOD UNIVERSITY, TEXAS CAMPUS
Cedar Hill, TX

Tuition & fees: $18,408	Average undergraduate aid package: $16,481

ABOUT THE INSTITUTION Independent, coed. **Awards:** bachelor's degrees. 3 undergraduate majors. **Total enrollment:** 461. Undergraduates: 461. Freshmen: 89. Federal methodology is used as a basis for awarding need-based institutional aid.

UNDERGRADUATE EXPENSES for 2009–10 Application fee: $25. **One-time required fee:** $125. **Comprehensive fee:** $25,998 includes full-time tuition ($17,430), mandatory fees ($978), and room and board ($7590). Full-time tuition and fees vary according to class time. Room and board charges vary according to board plan and housing facility. **Part-time tuition:** $363 per quarter hour. Part-time tuition and fees vary according to class time. **Payment plan:** Installment.

FRESHMAN FINANCIAL AID (Fall 2009, est.) 118 applied for aid; of those 92% were deemed to have need. 100% of freshmen with need received aid; of those 14% had need fully met. **Average percent of need met:** 64% (excluding resources awarded to replace EFC). **Average financial aid package:** $18,128 (excluding resources awarded to replace EFC). 12% of all full-time freshmen had no need and received non-need-based gift aid.

UNDERGRADUATE FINANCIAL AID (Fall 2009, est.) 384 applied for aid; of those 92% were deemed to have need. 100% of undergraduates with need received aid; of those 13% had need fully met. **Average percent of need met:** 62% (excluding resources awarded to replace EFC). **Average financial aid package:** $16,481 (excluding resources awarded to replace EFC). 12% of all full-time undergraduates had no need and received non-need-based gift aid.

GIFT AID (NEED-BASED) Total amount: $3,674,849 (28% federal, 71% institutional, 1% external sources). **Receiving aid:** Freshmen: 68% (94); all full-time undergraduates: 60% (302). **Average award:** Freshmen: $5088; Undergraduates: $5013. **Scholarships, grants, and awards:** Federal Pell, FSEOG, state, private, college/university gift aid from institutional funds.

GIFT AID (NON-NEED-BASED) Total amount: $811,005 (98% institutional, 2% external sources). **Receiving aid:** Freshmen: 17% (23). Undergraduates: 17% (86). **Average award:** Undergraduates: $6627. **Scholarships, grants, and awards by category:** Academic interests/achievement: business, general academic interests/achievements. **Special achievements/activities:** general special achievements/activities, memberships. **Special characteristics:** children and siblings of alumni, children of faculty/staff, siblings of current students. **Tuition waivers:** Full or partial for employees or children of employees.

LOANS Student loans: $3,076,418 (78% need-based, 22% non-need-based). 86% of past graduating class borrowed through all loan programs. Average indebtedness per student: $23,182. **Average need-based loan:** Freshmen: $3401. Undergraduates: $4223. **Parent loans:** $316,631 (31% need-based, 69% non-need-based). **Programs:** FFEL (Subsidized and Unsubsidized Stafford, PLUS).

WORK-STUDY Federal work-study: Total amount: $225,542; jobs available.

ATHLETIC AWARDS Total amount: $772,703 (57% need-based, 43% non-need-based).

APPLYING FOR FINANCIAL AID Required financial aid form: FAFSA. **Financial aid deadline:** Continuous. **Notification date:** Continuous beginning 3/1.

CONTACT Shana Thompson, Director of Financial Aid, Northwood University, Texas Campus, 1114 West FM 1382, Cedar Hill, TX 75104, 972-293-5479 or toll-free 800-927-9663. Fax: 972-293-7196. E-mail: sealsl@northwood.edu.

NORWICH UNIVERSITY
Northfield, VT

CONTACT Director of Student Financial Planning, Norwich University, 158 Harmon Drive, Northfield, VT 05663, 802-485-2015 or toll-free 800-468-6679.

NOTRE DAME COLLEGE
South Euclid, OH

Tuition & fees: $22,742	Average undergraduate aid package: N/A

ABOUT THE INSTITUTION Independent Roman Catholic, coed. 33 undergraduate majors. Federal methodology is used as a basis for awarding need-based institutional aid.

UNDERGRADUATE EXPENSES for 2009–10 *Comprehensive fee:* $30,334 includes full-time tuition ($22,192), mandatory fees ($550), and room and board ($7592). Full-time tuition and fees vary according to course load and degree level. Room and board charges vary according to board plan and housing facility. *Part-time tuition:* $460 per credit. Part-time tuition and fees vary according to course load and degree level. *Payment plan:* Installment.

GIFT AID (NEED-BASED) *Scholarships, grants, and awards:* Federal Pell, FSEOG, state, private, college/university gift aid from institutional funds, Academic Competitiveness Grants, National SMART Grants.

GIFT AID (NON-NEED-BASED) *Scholarships, grants, and awards by category: Academic interests/achievement:* general academic interests/achievements. *Creative arts/performance:* dance, general creative arts/performance, music, theater/drama. *Special achievements/activities:* community service, general special achievements/activities, leadership, memberships, religious involvement. *Special characteristics:* international students. *Tuition waivers:* Full or partial for employees or children of employees.

LOANS *Programs:* FFEL (Subsidized and Unsubsidized Stafford, PLUS), Perkins.

APPLYING FOR FINANCIAL AID *Required financial aid form:* FAFSA. *Financial aid deadline (priority):* 2/15. *Notification date:* Continuous beginning 3/1. Students must reply by 5/1.

CONTACT Ms. Dianna Roberts, Assistant Director of Financial Aid, Notre Dame College, 4545 College Road, South Euclid, OH 44118, 216-373-5213 or toll-free 800-632-1680. *Fax:* 216-373-5243. *E-mail:* droberts@ndc.edu.

NOTRE DAME DE NAMUR UNIVERSITY
Belmont, CA

Tuition & fees: $28,500	Average undergraduate aid package: $24,693

ABOUT THE INSTITUTION Independent Roman Catholic, coed. 30 undergraduate majors. Both federal and institutional methodology are used as a basis for awarding need-based institutional aid.

UNDERGRADUATE EXPENSES for 2010–11 *Comprehensive fee:* $40,100 includes full-time tuition ($28,200), mandatory fees ($300), and room and board ($11,600). *College room only:* $7610. Full-time tuition and fees vary according to degree level. Room and board charges vary according to board plan and housing facility. *Part-time tuition:* $700 per unit. *Part-time fees:* $3 per unit; $35 per term. Part-time tuition and fees vary according to degree level and program. *Payment plan:* Installment.

FRESHMAN FINANCIAL AID (Fall 2009, est.) 95 applied for aid; of those 96% were deemed to have need. 100% of freshmen with need received aid; of those 5% had need fully met. *Average percent of need met:* 69% (excluding resources awarded to replace EFC). *Average financial aid package:* $25,188 (excluding resources awarded to replace EFC).

UNDERGRADUATE FINANCIAL AID (Fall 2009, est.) 412 applied for aid; of those 95% were deemed to have need. 100% of undergraduates with need received aid; of those 10% had need fully met. *Average percent of need met:* 70% (excluding resources awarded to replace EFC). *Average financial aid package:* $24,693 (excluding resources awarded to replace EFC).

GIFT AID (NEED-BASED) *Total amount:* $7,243,230 (19% federal, 11% state, 67% institutional, 3% external sources). *Receiving aid:* Freshmen: 78% (91); all full-time undergraduates: 74% (386). *Average award:* Freshmen: $20,424; Undergraduates: $19,236. *Scholarships, grants, and awards:* Federal Pell, FSEOG, state, private, college/university gift aid from institutional funds.

GIFT AID (NON-NEED-BASED) *Total amount:* $113,365 (100% institutional). *Receiving aid:* Freshmen: 3% (4). Undergraduates: 4% (19). *Scholarships,*

grants, and awards by category: Academic interests/achievement: general academic interests/achievements. *Creative arts/performance:* applied art and design, art/fine arts, creative writing, music, performing arts, theater/drama. *Special achievements/activities:* general special achievements/activities. *Special characteristics:* children and siblings of alumni, children of faculty/staff, general special characteristics. *Tuition waivers:* Full or partial for employees or children of employees, senior citizens.

LOANS *Student loans:* $6,909,045 (89% need-based, 11% non-need-based). 82% of past graduating class borrowed through all loan programs. *Average indebtedness per student:* $21,758. *Average need-based loan:* Freshmen: $3733. Undergraduates: $4980. *Parent loans:* $4,164,113 (43% need-based, 57% non-need-based). *Programs:* Federal Direct (Subsidized and Unsubsidized Stafford, PLUS), Perkins.

WORK-STUDY *Federal work-study:* Total amount: $139,235; 87 jobs averaging $1600. *State or other work-study/employment:* Total amount: $155,260 (100% need-based). Part-time jobs available.

ATHLETIC AWARDS Total amount: $438,360 (94% need-based, 6% non-need-based).

APPLYING FOR FINANCIAL AID *Required financial aid form:* FAFSA. *Financial aid deadline (priority):* 3/2. *Notification date:* Continuous. Students must reply within 2 weeks of notification.

CONTACT Susan Pace, Director of Financial Aid, Notre Dame de Namur University, 1500 Ralston Avenue, Belmont, CA 94002, 650-508-3580 or toll-free 800-263-0545. *Fax:* 650-508-3635. *E-mail:* space@ndnu.edu.

NOVA SOUTHEASTERN UNIVERSITY
Fort Lauderdale, FL

Tuition & fees: $21,100	Average undergraduate aid package: $16,863

ABOUT THE INSTITUTION Independent, coed. 36 undergraduate majors. Federal methodology is used as a basis for awarding need-based institutional aid.

UNDERGRADUATE EXPENSES for 2009–10 *Comprehensive fee:* $29,460 includes full-time tuition ($20,550), mandatory fees ($550), and room and board ($8360). Full-time tuition and fees vary according to class time and program. Room and board charges vary according to board plan and housing facility. *Part-time tuition:* $680 per credit hour. Part-time tuition and fees vary according to class time, course load, and program. *Payment plans:* Installment, deferred payment.

FRESHMAN FINANCIAL AID (Fall 2009, est.) 1,494 applied for aid; of those 84% were deemed to have need. 99% of freshmen with need received aid; of those 12% had need fully met. *Average percent of need met:* 61% (excluding resources awarded to replace EFC). *Average financial aid package:* $18,542 (excluding resources awarded to replace EFC). 11% of all full-time freshmen had no need and received non-need-based gift aid.

UNDERGRADUATE FINANCIAL AID (Fall 2009, est.) 3,301 applied for aid; of those 89% were deemed to have need. 99% of undergraduates with need received aid; of those 7% had need fully met. *Average percent of need met:* 67% (excluding resources awarded to replace EFC). *Average financial aid package:* $16,863 (excluding resources awarded to replace EFC). 6% of all full-time undergraduates had no need and received non-need-based gift aid.

GIFT AID (NEED-BASED) *Total amount:* $24,192,842 (46% federal, 44% state, 4% institutional, 6% external sources). *Receiving aid:* Freshmen: 41% (717); all full-time undergraduates: 46% (1,769). *Average award:* Freshmen: $7066; Undergraduates: $6287. *Scholarships, grants, and awards:* Federal Pell, FSEOG, state, private, college/university gift aid from institutional funds.

GIFT AID (NON-NEED-BASED) *Total amount:* $1,594,620 (26% state, 55% institutional, 19% external sources). *Receiving aid:* Freshmen: 71% (1,236). Undergraduates: 75% (2,903). *Average award:* Freshmen: $5900. Undergraduates: $5631. *Scholarships, grants, and awards by category: Academic interests/achievement:* 3,220 awards ($6,250,010 total): general academic interests/achievements. *Tuition waivers:* Full or partial for employees or children of employees.

LOANS *Student loans:* $44,429,023 (37% need-based, 63% non-need-based). 71% of past graduating class borrowed through all loan programs. *Average indebtedness per student:* $36,908. *Average need-based loan:* Freshmen: $4822. Undergraduates: $5568. *Parent loans:* $16,709,108 (98% need-based, 2% non-need-based). *Programs:* Federal Direct (Subsidized and Unsubsidized Stafford, PLUS), FFEL (Subsidized and Unsubsidized Stafford, PLUS), Perkins, college/university.

WORK-STUDY *Federal work-study:* Total amount: $792,220; 278 jobs averaging $2850. *State or other work-study/employment:* Total amount: $5,525,925 (100% non-need-based). 1,511 part-time jobs averaging $3614.
ATHLETIC AWARDS Total amount: $2,886,419 (100% non-need-based).
APPLYING FOR FINANCIAL AID *Required financial aid forms:* FAFSA, institution's own form, state aid form. *Financial aid deadline (priority):* 4/15. *Notification date:* Continuous. Students must reply within 4 weeks of notification.
CONTACT Stephanie G. Brown, EdD, Associate Vice President for Enrollment and Student Services, Nova Southeastern University, 3301 College Avenue, Fort Lauderdale, FL 33314, 954-262-7456 or toll-free 800-541-NOVA. *Fax:* 954-262-3967. *E-mail:* browstep@nova.edu.

NYACK COLLEGE
Nyack, NY

Tuition & fees: $20,500	Average undergraduate aid package: $16,125

ABOUT THE INSTITUTION Independent religious, coed. 29 undergraduate majors. Federal methodology is used as a basis for awarding need-based institutional aid.
UNDERGRADUATE EXPENSES for 2010–11 *Comprehensive fee:* $28,700 includes full-time tuition ($19,500), mandatory fees ($1000), and room and board ($8200). Full-time tuition and fees vary according to course load, location, and program. Room and board charges vary according to board plan. *Part-time tuition:* $812 per credit hour. Part-time tuition and fees vary according to course load, location, and program. *Payment plan:* Installment.
FRESHMAN FINANCIAL AID (Fall 2009, est.) 299 applied for aid; of those 92% were deemed to have need. 100% of freshmen with need received aid; of those 13% had need fully met. *Average percent of need met:* 69% (excluding resources awarded to replace EFC). *Average financial aid package:* $16,493 (excluding resources awarded to replace EFC). 19% of all full-time freshmen had no need and received non-need-based gift aid.
UNDERGRADUATE FINANCIAL AID (Fall 2009, est.) 1,400 applied for aid; of those 94% were deemed to have need. 100% of undergraduates with need received aid; of those 13% had need fully met. *Average percent of need met:* 66% (excluding resources awarded to replace EFC). *Average financial aid package:* $16,125 (excluding resources awarded to replace EFC). 13% of all full-time undergraduates had no need and received non-need-based gift aid.
GIFT AID (NEED-BASED) *Total amount:* $12,618,604 (25% federal, 16% state, 58% institutional, 1% external sources). *Receiving aid:* Freshmen: 80% (275); all full-time undergraduates: 84% (1,292). *Average award:* Freshmen: $11,646; Undergraduates: $10,135. *Scholarships, grants, and awards:* Federal Pell, FSEOG, state, private, college/university gift aid from institutional funds.
GIFT AID (NON-NEED-BASED) *Total amount:* $1,523,123 (1% federal, 2% state, 93% institutional, 4% external sources). *Receiving aid:* Freshmen: 8% (29). Undergraduates: 6% (100). *Average award:* Freshmen: $6162. Undergraduates: $5585. *Scholarships, grants, and awards by category: Academic interests/achievement:* $1,477,695 total: general academic interests/achievements. *Creative arts/performance:* $352,000 total: journalism/publications, music, performing arts, theater/drama. *Special achievements/activities:* $1,474,615 total: cheerleading/drum major, community service, general special achievements/activities, leadership, religious involvement. *Special characteristics:* $2,471,089 total: children and siblings of alumni, children of faculty/staff, general special characteristics, international students, local/state students, out-of-state students, relatives of clergy, religious affiliation, spouses of current students. *Tuition waivers:* Full or partial for employees or children of employees.
LOANS *Student loans:* $14,655,573 (82% need-based, 18% non-need-based). 85% of past graduating class borrowed through all loan programs. *Average indebtedness per student:* $29,081. *Average need-based loan:* Freshmen: $4058. Undergraduates: $5250. *Parent loans:* $1,310,747 (49% need-based, 51% non-need-based). *Programs:* FFEL (Subsidized and Unsubsidized Stafford, PLUS), Perkins.
WORK-STUDY *Federal work-study:* Total amount: $309,762; 204 jobs averaging $1518. *State or other work-study/employment:* Total amount: $89,679 (88% need-based, 12% non-need-based). 58 part-time jobs averaging $1546.
ATHLETIC AWARDS Total amount: $1,133,920 (62% need-based, 38% non-need-based).
APPLYING FOR FINANCIAL AID *Required financial aid forms:* FAFSA, state aid form. *Financial aid deadline (priority):* 3/1. *Notification date:* Continuous beginning 3/1. Students must reply by 5/1 or within 4 weeks of notification.

CONTACT Steve Phillips, Director of Student Financial Services, Nyack College, 1 South Boulevard, Nyack, NY 10960-3698, 845-675-4747 or toll-free 800-33-NYACK. *Fax:* 845-358-7016. *E-mail:* sfs@nyack.edu.

OAK HILLS CHRISTIAN COLLEGE
Bemidji, MN

CONTACT Daniel Hovestol, Financial Aid Director, Oak Hills Christian College, 1600 Oak Hills Road, SW, Bemidji, MN 56601-8832, 218-751-8671 Ext. 1220 or toll-free 888-751-8670 Ext. 285. *Fax:* 218-444-1311. *E-mail:* ohfinaid@oakhills.edu.

OAKLAND CITY UNIVERSITY
Oakland City, IN

CONTACT Mrs. Caren K. Richeson, Director of Financial Aid, Oakland City University, 138 North Lucretia Street, Oakland City, IN 47660-1099, 812-749-1225 or toll-free 800-737-5125. *Fax:* 812-749-1438. *E-mail:* cricheson@oak.edu.

OAKLAND UNIVERSITY
Rochester, MI

Tuition & fees (MI res): $8783	Average undergraduate aid package: $10,874

ABOUT THE INSTITUTION State-supported, coed. 78 undergraduate majors. Federal methodology is used as a basis for awarding need-based institutional aid.
UNDERGRADUATE EXPENSES for 2009–10 *Tuition, state resident:* full-time $8783; part-time $292.75 per credit. *Tuition, nonresident:* full-time $20,498; part-time $683.25 per credit hour. Full-time tuition and fees vary according to program and student level. Part-time tuition and fees vary according to program and student level. *College room and board:* $7350. Room and board charges vary according to housing facility. *Payment plans:* Installment, deferred payment.
FRESHMAN FINANCIAL AID (Fall 2009, est.) 1,662 applied for aid; of those 71% were deemed to have need. 96% of freshmen with need received aid; of those 19% had need fully met. *Average percent of need met:* 74% (excluding resources awarded to replace EFC). *Average financial aid package:* $10,510 (excluding resources awarded to replace EFC). 17% of all full-time freshmen had no need and received non-need-based gift aid.
UNDERGRADUATE FINANCIAL AID (Fall 2009, est.) 6,691 applied for aid; of those 77% were deemed to have need. 97% of undergraduates with need received aid; of those 12% had need fully met. *Average percent of need met:* 73% (excluding resources awarded to replace EFC). *Average financial aid package:* $10,874 (excluding resources awarded to replace EFC). 10% of all full-time undergraduates had no need and received non-need-based gift aid.
GIFT AID (NEED-BASED) *Total amount:* $13,801,947 (64% federal, 6% state, 30% institutional). *Receiving aid:* Freshmen: 37% (830); all full-time undergraduates: 30% (3,064). *Average award:* Freshmen: $4960; Undergraduates: $4219. *Scholarships, grants, and awards:* Federal Pell, FSEOG, state, private, college/university gift aid from institutional funds.
GIFT AID (NON-NEED-BASED) *Total amount:* $13,723,905 (19% state, 41% institutional, 40% external sources). *Receiving aid:* Freshmen: 20% (459). Undergraduates: 13% (1,399). *Average award:* Freshmen: $1995. Undergraduates: $2510. *Scholarships, grants, and awards by category: Academic interests/achievement:* area/ethnic studies, biological sciences, business, education, engineering/technologies, English, foreign languages, general academic interests/achievements, health fields, humanities. *Creative arts/performance:* dance, music, performing arts. *Special characteristics:* adult students, ethnic background, out-of-state students. *Tuition waivers:* Full or partial for employees or children of employees.
LOANS *Student loans:* $44,899,260 (40% need-based, 60% non-need-based). 51% of past graduating class borrowed through all loan programs. *Average indebtedness per student:* $19,967. *Average need-based loan:* Freshmen: $6672. Undergraduates: $8358. *Parent loans:* $2,900,907 (100% need-based). *Programs:* Federal Direct (Subsidized and Unsubsidized Stafford, PLUS), Perkins, private loans.
WORK-STUDY *Federal work-study:* Total amount: $417,408; jobs available. *State or other work-study/employment:* Total amount: $116,928 (100% need-based). Part-time jobs available.

ATHLETIC AWARDS Total amount: $2,581,731 (100% non-need-based).
APPLYING FOR FINANCIAL AID *Required financial aid form:* FAFSA. *Financial aid deadline (priority):* 2/15. *Notification date:* Continuous beginning 3/15.
CONTACT Ms. Cindy Hermsen, Director of Financial Aid, Oakland University, 120 North Foundation Hall, Rochester, MI 48309-4401, 248-370-2550 or toll-free 800-OAK-UNIV. *E-mail:* finaid@oakland.edu.

OAKWOOD UNIVERSITY
Huntsville, AL

CONTACT Financial Aid Director, Oakwood University, 7000 Adventist Boulevard, Huntsville, AL 35896, 256-726-7210 or toll-free 800-358-3978 (in-state).

OBERLIN COLLEGE
Oberlin, OH

Tuition & fees: $40,004	Average undergraduate aid package: $32,508

ABOUT THE INSTITUTION Independent, coed. 54 undergraduate majors. Both federal and institutional methodology are used as a basis for awarding need-based institutional aid.
UNDERGRADUATE EXPENSES for 2009–10 *Comprehensive fee:* $50,484 includes full-time tuition ($39,686), mandatory fees ($318), and room and board ($10,480). *College room only:* $5450. Room and board charges vary according to board plan and housing facility. *Part-time tuition:* $1654 per credit hour. *Payment plan:* Installment.
FRESHMAN FINANCIAL AID (Fall 2009, est.) 544 applied for aid; of those 87% were deemed to have need. 100% of freshmen with need received aid; of those 100% had need fully met. *Average percent of need met:* 100% (excluding resources awarded to replace EFC). *Average financial aid package:* $30,403 (excluding resources awarded to replace EFC). 30% of all full-time freshmen had no need and received non-need-based gift aid.
UNDERGRADUATE FINANCIAL AID (Fall 2009, est.) 1,797 applied for aid; of those 87% were deemed to have need. 100% of undergraduates with need received aid; of those 100% had need fully met. *Average percent of need met:* 100% (excluding resources awarded to replace EFC). *Average financial aid package:* $32,508 (excluding resources awarded to replace EFC). 26% of all full-time undergraduates had no need and received non-need-based gift aid.
GIFT AID (NEED-BASED) *Total amount:* $41,747,984 (6% federal, 94% institutional). *Receiving aid:* Freshmen: 57% (461); all full-time undergraduates: 46% (1,306). *Average award:* Freshmen: $27,888; Undergraduates: $26,734. *Scholarships, grants, and awards:* Federal Pell, FSEOG, state, private, college/university gift aid from institutional funds.
GIFT AID (NON-NEED-BASED) *Total amount:* $8,135,144 (100% institutional). *Receiving aid:* Freshmen: 32% (255). Undergraduates: 38% (1,085). *Average award:* Freshmen: $11,275. Undergraduates: $11,812. *Scholarships, grants, and awards by category: Academic interests/achievement:* general academic interests/achievements, physical sciences. *Creative arts/performance:* music. *Tuition waivers:* Full or partial for employees or children of employees.
LOANS *Student loans:* $9,302,312 (90% need-based, 10% non-need-based). 54% of past graduating class borrowed through all loan programs. *Average indebtedness per student:* $18,604. *Average need-based loan:* Freshmen: $4448. Undergraduates: $4776. *Parent loans:* $2,988,952 (72% need-based, 28% non-need-based). *Programs:* FFEL (Subsidized and Unsubsidized Stafford, PLUS), Perkins, college/university.
WORK-STUDY *Federal work-study:* Total amount: $2,511,855; jobs available. *State or other work-study/employment:* Part-time jobs available.
APPLYING FOR FINANCIAL AID *Required financial aid forms:* FAFSA, institution's own form, CSS Financial Aid PROFILE, state aid form, noncustodial (divorced/separated) parent's statement, business/farm supplement. *Financial aid deadline:* 2/1 (priority: 1/15). *Notification date:* Continuous. Students must reply by 5/1.
CONTACT Robert Reddy Jr., Director of Financial Aid, Oberlin College, Carnegie Building #123, 52 West Lorain Street, Oberlin, OH 44074, 800-693-3173 or toll-free 800-622-OBIE. *Fax:* 440-775-8249. *E-mail:* financial.aid@oberlin.edu.

OCCIDENTAL COLLEGE
Los Angeles, CA

Tuition & fees: $40,903	Average undergraduate aid package: $36,048

ABOUT THE INSTITUTION Independent, coed. 32 undergraduate majors. Institutional methodology is used as a basis for awarding need-based institutional aid.
UNDERGRADUATE EXPENSES for 2010–11 *Comprehensive fee:* $52,263 includes full-time tuition ($39,870), mandatory fees ($1033), and room and board ($11,360). *College room only:* $6460. Room and board charges vary according to board plan. *Part-time tuition:* $1585 per credit. *Payment plans:* Tuition prepayment, installment.
FRESHMAN FINANCIAL AID (Fall 2009, est.) 427 applied for aid; of those 80% were deemed to have need. 100% of freshmen with need received aid; of those 100% had need fully met. *Average percent of need met:* 100% (excluding resources awarded to replace EFC). *Average financial aid package:* $33,612 (excluding resources awarded to replace EFC). 17% of all full-time freshmen had no need and received non-need-based gift aid.
UNDERGRADUATE FINANCIAL AID (Fall 2009, est.) 1,245 applied for aid; of those 87% were deemed to have need. 99% of undergraduates with need received aid; of those 100% had need fully met. *Average percent of need met:* 100% (excluding resources awarded to replace EFC). *Average financial aid package:* $36,048 (excluding resources awarded to replace EFC). 20% of all full-time undergraduates had no need and received non-need-based gift aid.
GIFT AID (NEED-BASED) *Total amount:* $30,630,249 (8% federal, 9% state, 79% institutional, 4% external sources). *Receiving aid:* Freshmen: 59% (338); all full-time undergraduates: 54% (1,054). *Average award:* Freshmen: $28,046; Undergraduates: $28,994. *Scholarships, grants, and awards:* Federal Pell, FSEOG, state, private, college/university gift aid from institutional funds.
GIFT AID (NON-NEED-BASED) *Total amount:* $4,938,863 (83% institutional, 17% external sources). *Receiving aid:* Freshmen: 9% (49). Undergraduates: 5% (95). *Average award:* Freshmen: $9580. Undergraduates: $9316. *Scholarships, grants, and awards by category: Academic interests/achievement:* 408 awards ($3,327,961 total): general academic interests/achievements. *Creative arts/performance:* 53 awards ($32,004 total): music. *Special achievements/activities:* 15 awards ($213,750 total): leadership. *Special characteristics:* 23 awards ($822,830 total): children of educators, children of faculty/staff. *Tuition waivers:* Full or partial for employees or children of employees.
LOANS *Student loans:* $9,085,868 (72% need-based, 28% non-need-based). 67% of past graduating class borrowed through all loan programs. *Average indebtedness per student:* $17,561. *Average need-based loan:* Freshmen: $4817. Undergraduates: $6346. *Parent loans:* $2,421,381 (21% need-based, 79% non-need-based). *Programs:* Federal Direct (Subsidized and Unsubsidized Stafford, PLUS), Perkins, college/university.
WORK-STUDY *Federal work-study:* Total amount: $1,630,110; 784 jobs averaging $2750. *State or other work-study/employment:* Total amount: $586,202 (59% need-based, 41% non-need-based). 170 part-time jobs averaging $1028.
APPLYING FOR FINANCIAL AID *Required financial aid forms:* FAFSA, CSS Financial Aid PROFILE, state aid form, noncustodial (divorced/separated) parent's statement. *Financial aid deadline:* 2/1. *Notification date:* 4/1. Students must reply by 5/1.
CONTACT Maureen McRae, Director of Financial Aid, Occidental College, 1600 Campus Road, Los Angeles, CA 90041, 323-259-2548 or toll-free 800-825-5262. *Fax:* 323-341-4961. *E-mail:* finaid@oxy.edu.

OGLALA LAKOTA COLLEGE
Kyle, SD

CONTACT Financial Aid Director, Oglala Lakota College, 490 Piya Wiconi Road, Kyle, SD 57752-0490, 605-455-6000.

OGLETHORPE UNIVERSITY
Atlanta, GA

Tuition & fees: $26,700	Average undergraduate aid package: $26,500

ABOUT THE INSTITUTION Independent, coed. 31 undergraduate majors. Both federal and institutional methodology are used as a basis for awarding need-based institutional aid.
UNDERGRADUATE EXPENSES for 2009–10 *Comprehensive fee:* $36,690 includes full-time tuition ($26,450), mandatory fees ($250), and room and board ($9990). Full-time tuition and fees vary according to degree level and program. Room and board charges vary according to housing facility and

location. *Part-time tuition:* $1217 per credit hour. Part-time tuition and fees vary according to course load, degree level, and program. *Payment plans:* Tuition prepayment, installment.

FRESHMAN FINANCIAL AID (Fall 2008) 206 applied for aid; of those 87% were deemed to have need. 100% of freshmen with need received aid; of those 38% had need fully met. *Average percent of need met:* 89% (excluding resources awarded to replace EFC). *Average financial aid package:* $26,585 (excluding resources awarded to replace EFC). 26% of all full-time freshmen had no need and received non-need-based gift aid.

UNDERGRADUATE FINANCIAL AID (Fall 2008) 569 applied for aid; of those 88% were deemed to have need. 100% of undergraduates with need received aid; of those 52% had need fully met. *Average percent of need met:* 86% (excluding resources awarded to replace EFC). *Average financial aid package:* $26,500 (excluding resources awarded to replace EFC). 28% of all full-time undergraduates had no need and received non-need-based gift aid.

GIFT AID (NEED-BASED) *Total amount:* $9,900,667 (9% federal, 11% state, 79% institutional, 1% external sources). *Receiving aid:* Freshmen: 73% (179); all full-time undergraduates: 58% (496). *Average award:* Freshmen: $20,797; Undergraduates: $19,876. *Scholarships, grants, and awards:* Federal Pell, FSEOG, state, private, college/university gift aid from institutional funds.

GIFT AID (NON-NEED-BASED) *Total amount:* $3,953,471 (11% state, 88% institutional, 1% external sources). *Receiving aid:* Freshmen: 50% (122). Undergraduates: 34% (289). *Average award:* Freshmen: $10,647. Undergraduates: $12,291. *Scholarships, grants, and awards by category:* Academic interests/achievement: general academic interests/achievements. Creative arts/performance: journalism/publications, music, performing arts, theater/drama. Special achievements/activities: community service, religious involvement. Special characteristics: children of faculty/staff, siblings of current students. *Tuition waivers:* Full or partial for employees or children of employees.

LOANS *Student loans:* $3,272,273 (100% need-based). 42% of past graduating class borrowed through all loan programs. *Average indebtedness per student:* $18,650. *Average need-based loan:* Freshmen: $5547. Undergraduates: $6326. *Parent loans:* $744,698 (100% non-need-based). *Programs:* Federal Direct (Subsidized and Unsubsidized Stafford, PLUS), Perkins.

WORK-STUDY *Federal work-study:* Total amount: $213,948; 116 jobs averaging $1844.

APPLYING FOR FINANCIAL AID *Required financial aid forms:* FAFSA, institution's own form. *Notification date:* Continuous beginning 3/1. Students must reply by 5/1 or within 3 weeks of notification.

CONTACT Ms. Meg McGinnis, Director of Financial Aid, Oglethorpe University, 4484 Peachtree Road NE, Atlanta, GA 30319, 404-364-8366 or toll-free 800-428-4484. *E-mail:* mmcginnis@oglethorpe.edu.

OHIO CHRISTIAN UNIVERSITY
Circleville, OH

ABOUT THE INSTITUTION Independent religious, coed. *Awards:* associate and bachelor's degrees. 11 undergraduate majors. *Total enrollment:* 636. Undergraduates: 636.

GIFT AID (NEED-BASED) *Scholarships, grants, and awards:* Federal Pell, FSEOG, state, private, college/university gift aid from institutional funds.

GIFT AID (NON-NEED-BASED) *Scholarships, grants, and awards by category:* Academic interests/achievement: business, education, general academic interests/achievements, health fields, religion/biblical studies. Creative arts/performance: music. Special achievements/activities: leadership. Special characteristics: adult students, children of faculty/staff, international students, out-of-state students, relatives of clergy, religious affiliation, siblings of current students, veterans, veterans' children.

LOANS *Programs:* FFEL (Subsidized and Unsubsidized Stafford, PLUS), college/university, state nursing loans.

APPLYING FOR FINANCIAL AID *Required financial aid form:* FAFSA.

CONTACT Michael Fracassa, Assistant Vice President of Finance, Ohio Christian University, 1476 Lancaster Pike, PO Box 458, Circleville, OH 43113-9487, 740-477-7758 or toll-free 800-701-0222. *Fax:* 740-477-5921. *E-mail:* mfracassa@ohiochristian.edu.

OHIO DOMINICAN UNIVERSITY
Columbus, OH

CONTACT Ms. Cynthia A. Hahn, Director of Financial Aid, Ohio Dominican University, 1216 Sunbury Road, Columbus, OH 43219, 614-251-4778 or toll-free 800-854-2670. *Fax:* 614-251-4456. *E-mail:* fin-aid@ohiodominican.edu.

OHIO NORTHERN UNIVERSITY
Ada, OH

Tuition & fees: $31,866	Average undergraduate aid package: $25,576

ABOUT THE INSTITUTION Independent religious, coed. 116 undergraduate majors. Federal methodology is used as a basis for awarding need-based institutional aid.

UNDERGRADUATE EXPENSES for 2009–10 *Comprehensive fee:* $40,146 includes full-time tuition ($31,626), mandatory fees ($240), and room and board ($8280). *College room only:* $4140. Full-time tuition and fees vary according to course load, degree level, program, and student level. Room and board charges vary according to board plan and housing facility. *Part-time tuition:* $880 per quarter hour. *Part-time fees:* $30 per term. Part-time tuition and fees vary according to course load, degree level, program, and student level. *Payment plan:* Installment.

FRESHMAN FINANCIAL AID (Fall 2009, est.) 626 applied for aid; of those 86% were deemed to have need. 100% of freshmen with need received aid; of those 18% had need fully met. *Average percent of need met:* 83% (excluding resources awarded to replace EFC). *Average financial aid package:* $27,073 (excluding resources awarded to replace EFC). 73% of all full-time freshmen had no need and received non-need-based gift aid.

UNDERGRADUATE FINANCIAL AID (Fall 2009, est.) 2,098 applied for aid; of those 90% were deemed to have need. 100% of undergraduates with need received aid; of those 16% had need fully met. *Average percent of need met:* 79% (excluding resources awarded to replace EFC). *Average financial aid package:* $25,576 (excluding resources awarded to replace EFC). 56% of all full-time undergraduates had no need and received non-need-based gift aid.

GIFT AID (NEED-BASED) *Total amount:* $34,961,591 (9% federal, 3% state, 86% institutional, 2% external sources). *Receiving aid:* Freshmen: 79% (508); all full-time undergraduates: 55% (1,336). *Average award:* Freshmen: $21,432; Undergraduates: $19,373. *Scholarships, grants, and awards:* Federal Pell, FSEOG, state, private, college/university gift aid from institutional funds.

GIFT AID (NON-NEED-BASED) *Total amount:* $8,552,642 (1% federal, 1% state, 94% institutional, 4% external sources). *Receiving aid:* Freshmen: 34% (218). Undergraduates: 23% (565). *Average award:* Freshmen: $16,254. Undergraduates: $17,458. *Scholarships, grants, and awards by category:* Academic interests/achievement: 2,011 awards ($26,863,310 total): biological sciences, business, communication, computer science, education, engineering/technologies, English, foreign languages, general academic interests/achievements, health fields, humanities, international studies, mathematics, physical sciences, premedicine, religion/biblical studies, social sciences. Creative arts/performance: 149 awards ($897,459 total): applied art and design, art/fine arts, creative writing, dance, journalism/publications, music, performing arts, theater/drama. Special achievements/activities: 284 awards ($2,917,986 total): community service, general special achievements/activities, junior miss, leadership. Special characteristics: 140 awards ($1,927,662 total): children of faculty/staff, international students, relatives of clergy, religious affiliation, siblings of current students. *Tuition waivers:* Full or partial for children of alumni, employees or children of employees.

LOANS *Student loans:* $13,227,953 (43% need-based, 57% non-need-based). 82% of past graduating class borrowed through all loan programs. *Average indebtedness per student:* $45,902. *Average need-based loan:* Freshmen: $8841. Undergraduates: $8021. *Parent loans:* $5,285,222 (100% need-based). *Programs:* FFEL (Subsidized and Unsubsidized Stafford, PLUS), Perkins, Federal Nursing, college/university.

WORK-STUDY *Federal work-study:* Total amount: $2,141,415; 1,331 jobs averaging $1563. *State or other work-study/employment:* Total amount: $434,071 (31% need-based, 69% non-need-based). 176 part-time jobs averaging $2420.

APPLYING FOR FINANCIAL AID *Required financial aid form:* FAFSA. *Financial aid deadline (priority):* 4/15. *Notification date:* Continuous beginning 3/1. Students must reply within 2 weeks of notification.

CONTACT Melanie Weaver, Director of Financial Aid, Ohio Northern University, 525 South Main Street, Ada, OH 45810, 419-772-2272 or toll-free 888-408-4ONU. *Fax:* 419-772-2313. *E-mail:* m-weaver.2@onu.edu.

THE OHIO STATE UNIVERSITY
Columbus, OH

Tuition & fees (OH res): $8706	Average undergraduate aid package: $10,725

ABOUT THE INSTITUTION State-supported, coed. 143 undergraduate majors. Federal methodology is used as a basis for awarding need-based institutional aid.

UNDERGRADUATE EXPENSES for 2010–11 *Tuition, state resident:* full-time $8406. *Tuition, nonresident:* full-time $21,978. *Required fees:* full-time $300. Full-time tuition and fees vary according to course load, program, and reciprocity agreements. Part-time tuition and fees vary according to course load, program, and reciprocity agreements. *College room and board:* $8409. Room and board charges vary according to board plan and housing facility. *Payment plan:* Installment.

FRESHMAN FINANCIAL AID (Fall 2009, est.) 5,464 applied for aid; of those 66% were deemed to have need. 100% of freshmen with need received aid; of those 26% had need fully met. *Average percent of need met:* 58% (excluding resources awarded to replace EFC). *Average financial aid package:* $10,575 (excluding resources awarded to replace EFC). 30% of all full-time freshmen had no need and received non-need-based gift aid.

UNDERGRADUATE FINANCIAL AID (Fall 2009, est.) 26,307 applied for aid; of those 79% were deemed to have need. 99% of undergraduates with need received aid; of those 18% had need fully met. *Average percent of need met:* 57% (excluding resources awarded to replace EFC). *Average financial aid package:* $10,725 (excluding resources awarded to replace EFC). 20% of all full-time undergraduates had no need and received non-need-based gift aid.

GIFT AID (NEED-BASED) *Total amount:* $109,085,258 (37% federal, 7% state, 52% institutional, 4% external sources). *Receiving aid:* Freshmen: 36% (2,348); all full-time undergraduates: 33% (12,505). *Average award:* Freshmen: $8430; Undergraduates: $8073. *Scholarships, grants, and awards:* Federal Pell, FSEOG, state, private, college/university gift aid from institutional funds.

GIFT AID (NON-NEED-BASED) *Total amount:* $51,855,182 (1% federal, 2% state, 87% institutional, 10% external sources). *Receiving aid:* Freshmen: 11% (729). Undergraduates: 6% (2,258). *Average award:* Freshmen: $4491. Undergraduates: $4645. *Scholarships, grants, and awards by category:* Academic interests/achievement: agriculture, architecture, area/ethnic studies, biological sciences, business, communication, computer science, education, engineering/technologies, English, foreign languages, general academic interests/achievements, health fields, home economics, humanities, international studies, mathematics, military science, physical sciences, premedicine, social sciences. *Creative arts/performance:* creative writing, dance, journalism/publications, music, performing arts, theater/drama. *Special achievements/activities:* cheerleading/drum major, hobbies/interests, leadership, memberships. *Special characteristics:* adult students, children and siblings of alumni, children of faculty/staff, children of public servants, children of union members/company employees, children of workers in trades, ethnic background, handicapped students, members of minority groups, out-of-state students, previous college experience. *Tuition waivers:* Full or partial for employees or children of employees, senior citizens.

LOANS *Student loans:* $207,068,321 (73% need-based, 27% non-need-based). 54% of past graduating class borrowed through all loan programs. *Average indebtedness per student:* $18,426. *Average need-based loan:* Freshmen: $3445. Undergraduates: $4671. *Parent loans:* $57,037,347 (100% non-need-based). *Programs:* Federal Direct (Subsidized and Unsubsidized Stafford, PLUS), Perkins, Federal Nursing, college/university.

WORK-STUDY *Federal work-study:* Total amount: $10,535,815; 3,544 jobs averaging $2973. *State or other work-study/employment:* Total amount: $492,760 (75% need-based, 25% non-need-based). 205 part-time jobs averaging $2404.

ATHLETIC AWARDS Total amount: $13,393,074 (100% non-need-based).

APPLYING FOR FINANCIAL AID *Required financial aid form:* FAFSA. *Financial aid deadline (priority):* 2/15. *Notification date:* 4/5. Students must reply by 5/1 or within 4 weeks of notification.

CONTACT Ms. Diane Stemper, Director of Student Financial Aid, The Ohio State University, 281 West Lane Avenue, 4th Floor, Columbus, OH 43210, 614-292-3600. *Fax:* 614-292-9264. *E-mail:* scsc@osu.edu.

OHIO UNIVERSITY
Athens, OH

Tuition & fees (OH res): $8973	Average undergraduate aid package: $8484

ABOUT THE INSTITUTION State-supported, coed. 126 undergraduate majors. Federal methodology is used as a basis for awarding need-based institutional aid.

UNDERGRADUATE EXPENSES for 2009–10 *Tuition, state resident:* full-time $8973; part-time $305 per quarter hour. *Tuition, nonresident:* full-time $17,937; part-time $600 per quarter hour. Full-time tuition and fees vary according to course load, degree level, location, and program. Part-time tuition and fees vary according to course load, degree level, location, and program. *College room and board:* $9408; *Room only:* $5196. Room and board charges vary according to board plan. *Payment plan:* Installment.

FRESHMAN FINANCIAL AID (Fall 2009, est.) 3,685 applied for aid; of those 67% were deemed to have need. 98% of freshmen with need received aid; of those 15% had need fully met. *Average percent of need met:* 58% (excluding resources awarded to replace EFC). *Average financial aid package:* $8272 (excluding resources awarded to replace EFC). 15% of all full-time freshmen had no need and received non-need-based gift aid.

UNDERGRADUATE FINANCIAL AID (Fall 2009, est.) 12,651 applied for aid; of those 72% were deemed to have need. 99% of undergraduates with need received aid; of those 15% had need fully met. *Average percent of need met:* 58% (excluding resources awarded to replace EFC). *Average financial aid package:* $8484 (excluding resources awarded to replace EFC). 13% of all full-time undergraduates had no need and received non-need-based gift aid.

GIFT AID (NEED-BASED) *Total amount:* $22,077,023 (81% federal, 19% institutional). *Receiving aid:* Freshmen: 57% (2,312); all full-time undergraduates: 51% (8,472). *Average award:* Freshmen: $6589; Undergraduates: $7145. *Scholarships, grants, and awards:* Federal Pell, FSEOG, state, college/university gift aid from institutional funds.

GIFT AID (NON-NEED-BASED) *Total amount:* $24,699,827 (4% state, 81% institutional, 15% external sources). *Receiving aid:* Freshmen: 32% (1,279). Undergraduates: 21% (3,525). *Average award:* Freshmen: $3944. Undergraduates: $3656. *Scholarships, grants, and awards by category:* Academic interests/achievement: area/ethnic studies, biological sciences, business, communication, computer science, education, engineering/technologies, English, foreign languages, general academic interests/achievements, health fields, home economics, humanities, international studies, mathematics, military science, physical sciences, premedicine, social sciences. *Creative arts/performance:* applied art and design, art/fine arts, cinema/film/broadcasting, dance, debating, journalism/publications, music, performing arts, theater/drama. *Special characteristics:* children of faculty/staff, members of minority groups. *Tuition waivers:* Full or partial for employees or children of employees.

LOANS *Student loans:* $86,684,123 (40% need-based, 60% non-need-based). 66% of past graduating class borrowed through all loan programs. *Average indebtedness per student:* $22,095. *Average need-based loan:* Freshmen: $3457. Undergraduates: $4287. *Parent loans:* $23,762,960 (100% non-need-based). *Programs:* Federal Direct (Subsidized and Unsubsidized Stafford, PLUS), Perkins, state, college/university.

WORK-STUDY *Federal work-study:* Total amount: $1,228,078; jobs available. *State or other work-study/employment:* Total amount: $13,634,072 (100% non-need-based). Part-time jobs available.

ATHLETIC AWARDS Total amount: $5,604,935 (100% non-need-based).

APPLYING FOR FINANCIAL AID *Required financial aid form:* FAFSA. *Financial aid deadline (priority):* 3/15. *Notification date:* 3/15.

CONTACT Ms. Sondra Williams, Director of Financial Aid, Ohio University, 020 Chubb Hall, Athens, OH 45701-2979, 740-593-4141. *Fax:* 740-593-4140. *E-mail:* willias1@ohio.edu.

OHIO UNIVERSITY–CHILLICOTHE
Chillicothe, OH

Tuition & fees: N/R	Average undergraduate aid package: $7751

ABOUT THE INSTITUTION State-supported, coed. *Awards:* associate, bachelor's, and master's degrees (offers first 2 years of most bachelor's degree programs available at the main campus in Athens; also offers several bachelor's degree programs that can be completed at this campus and several programs exclusive to this campus; also offers some graduate programs). 15 undergraduate majors. *Total enrollment:* 1,836. Undergraduates: 1,836. Federal methodology is used as a basis for awarding need-based institutional aid.

FRESHMAN FINANCIAL AID (Fall 2009, est.) 384 applied for aid; of those 86% were deemed to have need. 99% of freshmen with need received aid; of those 7% had need fully met. *Average percent of need met:* 59% (excluding resources awarded to replace EFC). *Average financial aid package:* $7417 (excluding resources awarded to replace EFC). 4% of all full-time freshmen had no need and received non-need-based gift aid.

UNDERGRADUATE FINANCIAL AID (Fall 2009, est.) 1,450 applied for aid; of those 90% were deemed to have need. 99% of undergraduates with need received aid; of those 6% had need fully met. *Average percent of need met:* 55% (excluding resources awarded to replace EFC). *Average financial aid package:* $7751 (excluding resources awarded to replace EFC). 2% of all full-time undergraduates had no need and received non-need-based gift aid.

GIFT AID (NEED-BASED) *Total amount:* $5,493,292 (96% federal, 4% institutional). *Receiving aid:* Freshmen: 83% (320); all full-time undergraduates: 82% (1,267). *Average award:* Freshmen: $7432; Undergraduates: $7730. *Scholarships, grants, and awards:* Federal Pell, FSEOG, state, college/university gift aid from institutional funds.

GIFT AID (NON-NEED-BASED) *Total amount:* $442,551 (6% state, 62% institutional, 32% external sources). *Receiving aid:* Freshmen: 10% (38). Undergraduates: 6% (97). *Average award:* Freshmen: $3623. Undergraduates: $4362. *Scholarships, grants, and awards by category: Academic interests/achievement:* area/ethnic studies, biological sciences, business, communication, computer science, education, engineering/technologies, English, foreign languages, general academic interests/achievements, health fields, home economics, humanities, international studies, mathematics, military science, physical sciences, premedicine, social sciences. *Creative arts/performance:* applied art and design, art/fine arts, cinema/film/broadcasting, dance, debating, journalism/publications, music, performing arts, theater/drama. *Special characteristics:* children of faculty/staff, members of minority groups. *ROTC:* Army cooperative, Air Force cooperative.

LOANS *Student loans:* $11,790,005 (43% need-based, 57% non-need-based). 66% of past graduating class borrowed through all loan programs. *Average indebtedness per student:* $22,095. *Average need-based loan:* Freshmen: $3439. Undergraduates: $3794. *Parent loans:* $9500 (100% non-need-based). *Programs:* Federal Direct (Subsidized and Unsubsidized Stafford, PLUS), Perkins, state, college/university.

WORK-STUDY *Federal work-study:* Total amount: $43,134; jobs available. *State or other work-study/employment:* Part-time jobs available.

APPLYING FOR FINANCIAL AID *Required financial aid form:* FAFSA. *Financial aid deadline (priority):* 3/15. *Notification date:* 3/15.

CONTACT Ms. Sondra Williams, Director of Financial Aid, Ohio University–Chillicothe, 020 Chubb Hall, Athens, OH 45701-2979, 740-593-4141 or toll-free 877-462-6824 (in-state). *Fax:* 740-593-4140. *E-mail:* willias1@ohio.edu.

OHIO UNIVERSITY–EASTERN
St. Clairsville, OH

Tuition & fees: N/R	Average undergraduate aid package: $6919

ABOUT THE INSTITUTION State-supported, coed. *Awards:* associate, bachelor's, and master's degrees (also offers some graduate courses). 11 undergraduate majors. *Total enrollment:* 751. Undergraduates: 751. Federal methodology is used as a basis for awarding need-based institutional aid.

FRESHMAN FINANCIAL AID (Fall 2009, est.) 146 applied for aid; of those 82% were deemed to have need. 98% of freshmen with need received aid; of those 10% had need fully met. *Average percent of need met:* 66% (excluding resources awarded to replace EFC). *Average financial aid package:* $6837 (excluding resources awarded to replace EFC). 7% of all full-time freshmen had no need and received non-need-based gift aid.

UNDERGRADUATE FINANCIAL AID (Fall 2009, est.) 490 applied for aid; of those 84% were deemed to have need. 98% of undergraduates with need received aid; of those 12% had need fully met. *Average percent of need met:* 63% (excluding resources awarded to replace EFC). *Average financial aid package:* $6919 (excluding resources awarded to replace EFC). 4% of all full-time undergraduates had no need and received non-need-based gift aid.

GIFT AID (NEED-BASED) *Total amount:* $1,390,581 (94% federal, 6% institutional). *Receiving aid:* Freshmen: 70% (115); all full-time undergraduates: 75% (389). *Average award:* Freshmen: $6718; Undergraduates: $7022. *Scholarships, grants, and awards:* Federal Pell, FSEOG, state, college/university gift aid from institutional funds.

GIFT AID (NON-NEED-BASED) *Total amount:* $163,000 (7% state, 93% institutional). *Receiving aid:* Freshmen: 18% (30). Undergraduates: 16% (82). *Average award:* Freshmen: $2675. Undergraduates: $2669. *Scholarships, grants, and awards by category: Academic interests/achievement:* area/ethnic studies, biological sciences, business, communication, computer science, education, engineering/technologies, English, foreign languages, general academic interests/achievements, health fields, home economics, humanities, international studies, mathematics, military science, physical sciences, premedicine, social sciences. *Creative arts/performance:* applied art and design, art/fine arts, cinema/film/broadcasting, dance, debating, journalism/publications, music, performing arts, theater/drama. *Special characteristics:* children of faculty/staff, members of minority groups. *Tuition waivers:* Full or partial for employees or children of employees, senior citizens.

LOANS *Student loans:* $2,911,550 (48% need-based, 52% non-need-based). 66% of past graduating class borrowed through all loan programs. *Average indebtedness per student:* $22,095. *Average need-based loan:* Freshmen: $3429. Undergraduates: $3944. *Parent loans:* $13,000 (100% non-need-based). *Programs:* Federal Direct (Subsidized and Unsubsidized Stafford, PLUS), Perkins, state, college/university.

WORK-STUDY *Federal work-study:* Total amount: $68,521; jobs available. *State or other work-study/employment:* Part-time jobs available.

APPLYING FOR FINANCIAL AID *Required financial aid form:* FAFSA. *Financial aid deadline (priority):* 3/15. *Notification date:* 3/15.

CONTACT Ms. Sondra Williams, Director of Financial Aid, Ohio University–Eastern, 020 Chubb Hall, Athens, OH 45701-2979, 740-593-4141 or toll-free 800-648-3331 (in-state). *Fax:* 740-593-4140. *E-mail:* willias1@ohio.edu.

OHIO UNIVERSITY–LANCASTER
Lancaster, OH

Tuition & fees: N/R	Average undergraduate aid package: $7386

ABOUT THE INSTITUTION State-supported, coed. *Awards:* associate, bachelor's, and master's degrees. 14 undergraduate majors. *Total enrollment:* 1,728. Undergraduates: 1,728. Federal methodology is used as a basis for awarding need-based institutional aid.

FRESHMAN FINANCIAL AID (Fall 2009, est.) 440 applied for aid; of those 77% were deemed to have need. 100% of freshmen with need received aid; of those 13% had need fully met. *Average percent of need met:* 64% (excluding resources awarded to replace EFC). *Average financial aid package:* $7043 (excluding resources awarded to replace EFC). 6% of all full-time freshmen had no need and received non-need-based gift aid.

UNDERGRADUATE FINANCIAL AID (Fall 2009, est.) 1,254 applied for aid; of those 83% were deemed to have need. 99% of undergraduates with need received aid; of those 10% had need fully met. *Average percent of need met:* 57% (excluding resources awarded to replace EFC). *Average financial aid package:* $7386 (excluding resources awarded to replace EFC). 4% of all full-time undergraduates had no need and received non-need-based gift aid.

GIFT AID (NEED-BASED) *Total amount:* $4,107,031 (96% federal, 4% institutional). *Receiving aid:* Freshmen: 70% (323); all full-time undergraduates: 80% (1,007). *Average award:* Freshmen: $6836; Undergraduates: $7264. *Scholarships, grants, and awards:* Federal Pell, FSEOG, state, college/university gift aid from institutional funds.

GIFT AID (NON-NEED-BASED) *Total amount:* $621,841 (10% state, 63% institutional, 27% external sources). *Receiving aid:* Freshmen: 12% (54). Undergraduates: 10% (120). *Average award:* Freshmen: $3441. Undergraduates: $2891. *Scholarships, grants, and awards by category: Academic interests/achievement:* area/ethnic studies, biological sciences, business, communication, computer science, education, engineering/technologies, English, foreign languages, general academic interests/achievements, health fields, home economics, humanities, international studies, mathematics, military science, physical sciences, premedicine, social sciences. *Creative arts/performance:* applied art and design, art/fine arts, cinema/film/broadcasting, dance, debating, journalism/publications, music, performing arts, theater/drama. *Special characteristics:* children of faculty/staff, members of minority groups. *ROTC:* Army cooperative, Air Force cooperative.

LOANS *Student loans:* $9,115,235 (42% need-based, 58% non-need-based). 66% of past graduating class borrowed through all loan programs. *Average*

indebtedness per student: $22,095. ***Average need-based loan:*** Freshmen: $3342. Undergraduates: $3798. ***Parent loans:*** $37,290 (100% non-need-based). ***Programs:*** Federal Direct (Subsidized and Unsubsidized Stafford, PLUS), Perkins, state, college/university.

WORK-STUDY *Federal work-study:* Total amount: $30,328; jobs available. ***State or other work-study/employment:*** Part-time jobs available.

APPLYING FOR FINANCIAL AID *Required financial aid form:* FAFSA. ***Financial aid deadline (priority):*** 3/15. ***Notification date:*** 3/15.

CONTACT Ms. Sondra Williams, Director of Financial Aid, Ohio University–Lancaster, 020 Chubb Hall, Athens, OH 45701-2979, 740-593-4141 or toll-free 888-446-4468 Ext. 215. *Fax:* 740-593-4140. *E-mail:* willias1@ohio.edu.

OHIO UNIVERSITY–SOUTHERN CAMPUS
Ironton, OH

Tuition & fees: N/R	Average undergraduate aid package: $7887

ABOUT THE INSTITUTION State-supported, coed. *Awards:* associate, bachelor's, and master's degrees. 17 undergraduate majors. *Total enrollment:* 1,836. Undergraduates: 1,699. Federal methodology is used as a basis for awarding need-based institutional aid.

FRESHMAN FINANCIAL AID (Fall 2009, est.) 320 applied for aid; of those 92% were deemed to have need. 99% of freshmen with need received aid; of those 6% had need fully met. *Average percent of need met:* 57% (excluding resources awarded to replace EFC). *Average financial aid package:* $7269 (excluding resources awarded to replace EFC). 3% of all full-time freshmen had no need and received non-need-based gift aid.

UNDERGRADUATE FINANCIAL AID (Fall 2009, est.) 1,319 applied for aid; of those 94% were deemed to have need. 99% of undergraduates with need received aid; of those 4% had need fully met. *Average percent of need met:* 54% (excluding resources awarded to replace EFC). *Average financial aid package:* $7887 (excluding resources awarded to replace EFC). 1% of all full-time undergraduates had no need and received non-need-based gift aid.

GIFT AID (NEED-BASED) *Total amount:* $5,316,764 (97% federal, 3% institutional). *Receiving aid:* Freshmen: 89% (284); all full-time undergraduates: 90% (1,206). *Average award:* Freshmen: $7169; Undergraduates: $7780. *Scholarships, grants, and awards:* Federal Pell, FSEOG, state, college/university gift aid from institutional funds.

GIFT AID (NON-NEED-BASED) *Total amount:* $363,937 (6% state, 79% institutional, 15% external sources). *Receiving aid:* Freshmen: 15% (47). Undergraduates: 13% (168). *Average award:* Freshmen: $2398. Undergraduates: $2194. *Scholarships, grants, and awards by category: Academic interests/ achievement:* area/ethnic studies, biological sciences, business, communication, computer science, education, engineering/technologies, English, foreign languages, general academic interests/achievements, health fields, home economics, humanities, international studies, mathematics, military science, physical sciences, premedicine, social sciences. *Creative arts/performance:* applied art and design, art/fine arts, cinema/film/broadcasting, dance, debating, journalism/ publications, music, performing arts, theater/drama. *Special characteristics:* children of faculty/staff, members of minority groups.

LOANS *Student loans:* $11,443,871 (43% need-based, 57% non-need-based). 66% of past graduating class borrowed through all loan programs. *Average indebtedness per student:* $22,095. *Average need-based loan:* Freshmen: $3439. Undergraduates: $3847. *Parent loans:* $41,173 (100% non-need-based). *Programs:* Federal Direct (Subsidized and Unsubsidized Stafford, PLUS), Perkins, state, college/university.

WORK-STUDY *Federal work-study:* Total amount: $53,723; jobs available. ***State or other work-study/employment:*** Part-time jobs available.

APPLYING FOR FINANCIAL AID *Required financial aid form:* FAFSA. ***Financial aid deadline (priority):*** 3/15. ***Notification date:*** 3/15.

CONTACT Ms. Sondra Williams, Director of Financial Aid, Ohio University–Southern Campus, 020 Chubb Hall, Athens, OH 45701-2979, 740-593-4141 or toll-free 800-626-0513. *Fax:* 740-593-4140. *E-mail:* willias1@ohio.edu.

OHIO UNIVERSITY–ZANESVILLE
Zanesville, OH

Tuition & fees (OH res): $4662	Average undergraduate aid package: $7147

ABOUT THE INSTITUTION State-supported, coed. 7 undergraduate majors. Federal methodology is used as a basis for awarding need-based institutional aid.

UNDERGRADUATE EXPENSES for 2009–10 *Tuition, state resident:* full-time $4662; part-time $137 per credit hour. *Tuition, nonresident:* full-time $8985; part-time $268 per credit hour. *Required fees:* $5 per term. Full-time tuition and fees vary according to student level. Part-time tuition and fees vary according to student level. *Payment plan:* Installment.

FRESHMAN FINANCIAL AID (Fall 2009, est.) 331 applied for aid; of those 81% were deemed to have need. 96% of freshmen with need received aid; of those 16% had need fully met. *Average percent of need met:* 65% (excluding resources awarded to replace EFC). *Average financial aid package:* $6315 (excluding resources awarded to replace EFC). 8% of all full-time freshmen had no need and received non-need-based gift aid.

UNDERGRADUATE FINANCIAL AID (Fall 2009, est.) 1,124 applied for aid; of those 85% were deemed to have need. 98% of undergraduates with need received aid; of those 10% had need fully met. *Average percent of need met:* 59% (excluding resources awarded to replace EFC). *Average financial aid package:* $7147 (excluding resources awarded to replace EFC). 5% of all full-time undergraduates had no need and received non-need-based gift aid.

GIFT AID (NEED-BASED) *Total amount:* $3,599,243 (93% federal, 7% institutional). *Receiving aid:* Freshmen: 71% (235); all full-time undergraduates: 79% (896). *Average award:* Freshmen: $6030; Undergraduates: $7009. *Scholarships, grants, and awards:* Federal Pell, FSEOG, state, college/university gift aid from institutional funds.

GIFT AID (NON-NEED-BASED) *Total amount:* $745,121 (6% state, 77% institutional, 17% external sources). *Receiving aid:* Freshmen: 28% (92). Undergraduates: 19% (216). *Average award:* Freshmen: $2736. Undergraduates: $2268. *Scholarships, grants, and awards by category: Academic interests/ achievement:* area/ethnic studies, biological sciences, business, communication, computer science, education, engineering/technologies, English, foreign languages, general academic interests/achievements, health fields, home economics, humanities, international studies, mathematics, military science, physical sciences, premedicine, social sciences. *Creative arts/performance:* applied art and design, art/fine arts, cinema/film/broadcasting, dance, debating, journalism/ publications, music, performing arts, theater/drama. *Special characteristics:* children of faculty/staff, members of minority groups. *Tuition waivers:* Full or partial for employees or children of employees, senior citizens.

LOANS *Student loans:* $7,708,751 (44% need-based, 56% non-need-based). 66% of past graduating class borrowed through all loan programs. *Average indebtedness per student:* $22,095. *Average need-based loan:* Freshmen: $3251. Undergraduates: $3867. *Parent loans:* $16,700 (100% non-need-based). *Programs:* Federal Direct (Subsidized and Unsubsidized Stafford, PLUS), Perkins, state, college/university.

WORK-STUDY *Federal work-study:* Total amount: $57,292; jobs available. ***State or other work-study/employment:*** Part-time jobs available.

APPLYING FOR FINANCIAL AID *Required financial aid form:* FAFSA. ***Financial aid deadline (priority):*** 3/15. ***Notification date:*** 3/15.

CONTACT Ms. Sondra Williams, Director of Financial Aid, Ohio University–Zanesville, 020 Chubb Hall, Athens, OH 45701-2979, 740-593-4141. *Fax:* 740-593-4140. *E-mail:* willias1@ohio.edu.

OHIO VALLEY UNIVERSITY
Vienna, WV

Tuition & fees: $17,200	Average undergraduate aid package: $12,283

ABOUT THE INSTITUTION Independent religious, coed. 16 undergraduate majors. Federal methodology is used as a basis for awarding need-based institutional aid.

UNDERGRADUATE EXPENSES for 2010–11 *One-time required fee:* $60. *Comprehensive fee:* $23,876 includes full-time tuition ($15,688), mandatory fees ($1512), and room and board ($6676). Full-time tuition and fees vary according to course load. Room and board charges vary according to board plan and housing facility. *Part-time tuition:* $525 per credit hour. Part-time tuition and fees vary according to course load. *Payment plan:* Installment.

FRESHMAN FINANCIAL AID (Fall 2009, est.) 76 applied for aid; of those 86% were deemed to have need. 100% of freshmen with need received aid; of those 18% had need fully met. *Average percent of need met:* 68% (excluding

resources awarded to replace EFC). *Average financial aid package:* $12,980 (excluding resources awarded to replace EFC). 12% of all full-time freshmen had no need and received non-need-based gift aid.

UNDERGRADUATE FINANCIAL AID (Fall 2009, est.) 400 applied for aid; of those 87% were deemed to have need. 98% of undergraduates with need received aid; of those 18% had need fully met. *Average percent of need met:* 67% (excluding resources awarded to replace EFC). *Average financial aid package:* $12,283 (excluding resources awarded to replace EFC). 10% of all full-time undergraduates had no need and received non-need-based gift aid.

GIFT AID (NEED-BASED) *Total amount:* $2,224,193 (40% federal, 9% state, 47% institutional, 4% external sources). *Receiving aid:* Freshmen: 75% (62); all full-time undergraduates: 69% (308). *Average award:* Freshmen: $10,404; Undergraduates: $9253. *Scholarships, grants, and awards:* Federal Pell, FSEOG, state, private, college/university gift aid from institutional funds.

GIFT AID (NON-NEED-BASED) *Total amount:* $472,050 (8% state, 87% institutional, 5% external sources). *Receiving aid:* Freshmen: 12% (10). Undergraduates: 11% (49). *Average award:* Freshmen: $4450. Undergraduates: $6372. *Scholarships, grants, and awards by category:* Academic interests/achievement: 215 awards ($824,103 total): education, English, general academic interests/achievements, religion/biblical studies. Creative arts/performance: 39 awards ($93,589 total): general creative arts/performance, journalism/publications, music, performing arts, theater/drama. Special achievements/activities: 45 awards ($28,125 total): community service, general special achievements/activities, leadership, religious involvement. Special characteristics: 87 awards ($413,389 total): adult students, children of faculty/staff, ethnic background, general special characteristics, international students, local/state students, relatives of clergy, religious affiliation. *Tuition waivers:* Full or partial for employees or children of employees.

LOANS *Student loans:* $2,602,270 (79% need-based, 21% non-need-based). 92% of past graduating class borrowed through all loan programs. *Average indebtedness per student:* $14,976. *Average need-based loan:* Freshmen: $2878. Undergraduates: $4183. *Parent loans:* $768,893 (51% need-based, 49% non-need-based). *Programs:* FFEL (Subsidized and Unsubsidized Stafford, PLUS), Perkins.

WORK-STUDY *Federal work-study:* Total amount: $125,051; 134 jobs averaging $1000. *State or other work-study/employment:* Total amount: $12,603 (100% non-need-based). 9 part-time jobs averaging $1400.

ATHLETIC AWARDS Total amount: $1,109,929 (59% need-based, 41% non-need-based).

APPLYING FOR FINANCIAL AID *Required financial aid form:* FAFSA. *Financial aid deadline (priority):* 3/1. *Notification date:* Continuous beginning 6/30. Students must reply within 4 weeks of notification.

CONTACT Summer Cook Boggess, Assistant Director of Financial Aid, Ohio Valley University, 1 Campus View Drive, Vienna, WV 26105-8000, 304-865-6207 or toll-free 877-446-8668 Ext. 6200 (out-of-state). *Fax:* 304-865-6001. *E-mail:* summer.cook@ovc.edu.

OHIO WESLEYAN UNIVERSITY
Delaware, OH

Tuition & fees: $35,030	Average undergraduate aid package: $28,014

ABOUT THE INSTITUTION Independent United Methodist, coed. 88 undergraduate majors. Federal methodology is used as a basis for awarding need-based institutional aid.

UNDERGRADUATE EXPENSES for 2009–10 *Comprehensive fee:* $44,254 includes full-time tuition ($34,570), mandatory fees ($460), and room and board ($9224). *College room only:* $4490. Room and board charges vary according to board plan. *Part-time tuition:* $3770 per course. *Payment plan:* Installment.

FRESHMAN FINANCIAL AID (Fall 2009, est.) 372 applied for aid; of those 83% were deemed to have need. 100% of freshmen with need received aid; of those 32% had need fully met. *Average percent of need met:* 92% (excluding resources awarded to replace EFC). *Average financial aid package:* $30,406 (excluding resources awarded to replace EFC). 37% of all full-time freshmen had no need and received non-need-based gift aid.

UNDERGRADUATE FINANCIAL AID (Fall 2009, est.) 1,250 applied for aid; of those 87% were deemed to have need. 100% of undergraduates with need received aid; of those 26% had need fully met. *Average percent of need met:* 85% (excluding resources awarded to replace EFC). *Average financial aid*

package: $28,014 (excluding resources awarded to replace EFC). 39% of all full-time undergraduates had no need and received non-need-based gift aid.

GIFT AID (NEED-BASED) *Total amount:* $24,210,191 (9% federal, 2% state, 87% institutional, 2% external sources). *Receiving aid:* Freshmen: 61% (304); all full-time undergraduates: 57% (1,057). *Average award:* Freshmen: $25,767; Undergraduates: $22,841. *Scholarships, grants, and awards:* Federal Pell, FSEOG, state, private, college/university gift aid from institutional funds.

GIFT AID (NON-NEED-BASED) *Total amount:* $12,609,743 (1% federal, 99% institutional). *Receiving aid:* Freshmen: 12% (62). Undergraduates: 8% (153). *Average award:* Freshmen: $18,976. Undergraduates: $16,509. *Scholarships, grants, and awards by category:* Academic interests/achievement: general academic interests/achievements. Creative arts/performance: general creative arts/performance. Special characteristics: children and siblings of alumni, local/state students, members of minority groups, religious affiliation. *Tuition waivers:* Full or partial for children of alumni, employees or children of employees.

LOANS *Student loans:* $6,136,712 (79% need-based, 21% non-need-based). 74% of past graduating class borrowed through all loan programs. *Average indebtedness per student:* $30,954. *Average need-based loan:* Freshmen: $4909. Undergraduates: $5378. *Parent loans:* $3,189,528 (100% non-need-based). *Programs:* Federal Direct (Subsidized and Unsubsidized Stafford, PLUS), Perkins, college/university.

WORK-STUDY *Federal work-study:* Total amount: $1,073,375; jobs available. *State or other work-study/employment:* Total amount: $398,560 (100% non-need-based). Part-time jobs available.

APPLYING FOR FINANCIAL AID *Required financial aid forms:* FAFSA, CSS Financial Aid PROFILE. *Financial aid deadline:* 5/1 (priority: 3/1). *Notification date:* Continuous beginning 2/15. Students must reply by 5/1 or within 2 weeks of notification.

CONTACT Mr. John L. Harrell Jr., Assistant Vice President for Admission and Financial Aid, Ohio Wesleyan University, 61 South Sandusky Street, Delaware, OH 43015, 740-368-3052 or toll-free 800-922-8953. *Fax:* 740-368-3066. *E-mail:* owfinaid@owu.edu.

OHR HAMEIR THEOLOGICAL SEMINARY
Cortlandt Manor, NY

CONTACT Financial Aid Office, Ohr Hameir Theological Seminary, Furnace Woods Road, Peekskill, NY 10566, 914-736-1500.

OHR SOMAYACH/JOSEPH TANENBAUM EDUCATIONAL CENTER
Monsey, NY

CONTACT Financial Aid Office, Ohr Somayach/Joseph Tanenbaum Educational Center, PO Box 334244, Route 306, Monsey, NY 10952-0334, 914-425-1370.

OKLAHOMA BAPTIST UNIVERSITY
Shawnee, OK

Tuition & fees: $18,670	Average undergraduate aid package: $13,131

ABOUT THE INSTITUTION Independent Southern Baptist, coed. 67 undergraduate majors. Federal methodology is used as a basis for awarding need-based institutional aid.

UNDERGRADUATE EXPENSES for 2010–11 *One-time required fee:* $50. *Comprehensive fee:* $24,300 includes full-time tuition ($17,220), mandatory fees ($1450), and room and board ($5630). Full-time tuition and fees vary according to course load. Room and board charges vary according to housing facility. *Part-time tuition:* $560 per credit hour. Part-time tuition and fees vary according to course load. *Payment plan:* Installment.

FRESHMAN FINANCIAL AID (Fall 2009, est.) 318 applied for aid; of those 87% were deemed to have need. 100% of freshmen with need received aid; of those 17% had need fully met. *Average percent of need met:* 71% (excluding resources awarded to replace EFC). *Average financial aid package:* $14,897 (excluding resources awarded to replace EFC). 22% of all full-time freshmen had no need and received non-need-based gift aid.

UNDERGRADUATE FINANCIAL AID (Fall 2009, est.) 1,130 applied for aid; of those 88% were deemed to have need. 100% of undergraduates with need received aid; of those 15% had need fully met. *Average percent of need met:*

70% (excluding resources awarded to replace EFC). *Average financial aid package:* $13,131 (excluding resources awarded to replace EFC). 17% of all full-time undergraduates had no need and received non-need-based gift aid.

GIFT AID (NEED-BASED) *Total amount:* $12,884,239 (17% federal, 10% state, 70% institutional, 3% external sources). *Receiving aid:* Freshmen: 58% (208); all full-time undergraduates: 44% (655). *Average award:* Freshmen: $5374; Undergraduates: $5477. *Scholarships, grants, and awards:* Federal Pell, FSEOG, state, private, college/university gift aid from institutional funds, Academic Competitiveness Grants, National SMART Grants, TEACH Grants.

GIFT AID (NON-NEED-BASED) *Total amount:* $1,213,500 (23% federal, 4% state, 69% institutional, 4% external sources). *Receiving aid:* Freshmen: 57% (203). Undergraduates: 43% (639). *Average award:* Freshmen: $2820. Undergraduates: $2704. *Scholarships, grants, and awards by category: Academic interests/achievement:* business, general academic interests/achievements, religion/biblical studies. *Creative arts/performance:* applied art and design, art/fine arts, music, performing arts, theater/drama. *Special achievements/activities:* leadership, religious involvement. *Special characteristics:* children and siblings of alumni, children of faculty/staff, general special characteristics, local/state students, out-of-state students, relatives of clergy, religious affiliation, veterans. *Tuition waivers:* Full or partial for employees or children of employees, senior citizens.

LOANS *Student loans:* $6,375,859 (97% need-based, 3% non-need-based). 68% of past graduating class borrowed through all loan programs. *Average indebtedness per student:* $21,554. *Average need-based loan:* Freshmen: $3510. Undergraduates: $4882. *Parent loans:* $862,184 (50% need-based, 50% non-need-based). *Programs:* Federal Direct (Subsidized and Unsubsidized Stafford, PLUS), Perkins, college/university.

WORK-STUDY *Federal work-study:* Total amount: $163,244; 144 jobs averaging $1212.

ATHLETIC AWARDS Total amount: $2,642,421 (78% need-based, 22% non-need-based).

APPLYING FOR FINANCIAL AID *Required financial aid form:* FAFSA. *Financial aid deadline:* Continuous. *Notification date:* Continuous beginning 2/1.

CONTACT Jonna Raney, Student Financial Services, Oklahoma Baptist University, 500 West University, Shawnee, OK 74804, 405-878-2016 or toll-free 800-654-3285. *Fax:* 405-878-2167. *E-mail:* jonna.raney@okbu.edu.

OKLAHOMA CHRISTIAN UNIVERSITY
Oklahoma City, OK

Tuition & fees: $17,456	Average undergraduate aid package: $15,488

ABOUT THE INSTITUTION Independent religious, coed. 58 undergraduate majors. Federal methodology is used as a basis for awarding need-based institutional aid.

UNDERGRADUATE EXPENSES for 2010–11 *Comprehensive fee:* $23,306 includes full-time tuition ($15,600), mandatory fees ($1856), and room and board ($5850). *College room only:* $2700. Full-time tuition and fees vary according to course load. Room and board charges vary according to board plan and housing facility. *Part-time tuition:* $650 per credit hour. *Part-time fees:* $915 per term. Part-time tuition and fees vary according to course load. *Payment plan:* Installment.

FRESHMAN FINANCIAL AID (Fall 2009, est.) 462 applied for aid; of those 75% were deemed to have need. 100% of freshmen with need received aid; of those 20% had need fully met. *Average percent of need met:* 49% (excluding resources awarded to replace EFC). *Average financial aid package:* $15,612 (excluding resources awarded to replace EFC). 19% of all full-time freshmen had no need and received non-need-based gift aid.

UNDERGRADUATE FINANCIAL AID (Fall 2009, est.) 1,913 applied for aid; of those 67% were deemed to have need. 100% of undergraduates with need received aid; of those 21% had need fully met. *Average percent of need met:* 55% (excluding resources awarded to replace EFC). *Average financial aid package:* $15,488 (excluding resources awarded to replace EFC). 22% of all full-time undergraduates had no need and received non-need-based gift aid.

GIFT AID (NEED-BASED) *Total amount:* $12,079,306 (21% federal, 6% state, 67% institutional, 6% external sources). *Receiving aid:* Freshmen: 42% (193); all full-time undergraduates: 36% (698). *Average award:* Freshmen: $2545; Undergraduates: $2445. *Scholarships, grants, and awards:* Federal Pell, FSEOG, state, private, college/university gift aid from institutional funds.

GIFT AID (NON-NEED-BASED) *Total amount:* $6,177,390 (95% institutional, 5% external sources). *Receiving aid:* Freshmen: 56% (257). Undergraduates:

50% (971). *Average award:* Freshmen: $3722. Undergraduates: $3935. *Scholarships, grants, and awards by category: Academic interests/achievement:* engineering/technologies, general academic interests/achievements, religion/biblical studies. *Creative arts/performance:* applied art and design, journalism/publications, music, theater/drama. *Special achievements/activities:* cheerleading/drum major, leadership. *Special characteristics:* children of faculty/staff, international students. *Tuition waivers:* Full or partial for employees or children of employees.

LOANS *Student loans:* $8,381,041 (67% need-based, 33% non-need-based). 76% of past graduating class borrowed through all loan programs. *Average indebtedness per student:* $26,612. *Average need-based loan:* Freshmen: $2824. Undergraduates: $3889. *Parent loans:* $3,719,530 (26% need-based, 74% non-need-based). *Programs:* Federal Direct (Subsidized and Unsubsidized Stafford, PLUS), FFEL (Subsidized and Unsubsidized Stafford, PLUS), Perkins, alternative loans.

WORK-STUDY *Federal work-study:* Total amount: $926,373; jobs available.

ATHLETIC AWARDS Total amount: $2,196,128 (34% need-based, 66% non-need-based).

APPLYING FOR FINANCIAL AID *Required financial aid form:* FAFSA. *Financial aid deadline:* 8/31 (priority: 3/15). *Notification date:* Continuous. Students must reply within 4 weeks of notification.

CONTACT Clint LaRue, Director of Financial Services, Oklahoma Christian University, Box 11000, Oklahoma City, OK 73136-1100, 405-425-5190 or toll-free 800-877-5010 (in-state). *Fax:* 405-425-5197. *E-mail:* clint.larue@oc.edu.

OKLAHOMA CITY UNIVERSITY
Oklahoma City, OK

Tuition & fees: $22,250	Average undergraduate aid package: $21,685

ABOUT THE INSTITUTION Independent United Methodist, coed. 74 undergraduate majors. Federal methodology is used as a basis for awarding need-based institutional aid.

UNDERGRADUATE EXPENSES for 2009–10 *Comprehensive fee:* $30,600 includes full-time tuition ($22,250) and room and board ($8350). *College room only:* $4650. Full-time tuition and fees vary according to program. Room and board charges vary according to board plan and housing facility. *Part-time tuition:* $760 per credit hour. *Part-time fees:* $60 per credit hour. Part-time tuition and fees vary according to program. *Payment plans:* Installment, deferred payment.

FRESHMAN FINANCIAL AID (Fall 2009, est.) 379 applied for aid; of those 98% were deemed to have need. 87% of freshmen with need received aid; of those 59% had need fully met. *Average percent of need met:* 83% (excluding resources awarded to replace EFC). *Average financial aid package:* $21,998 (excluding resources awarded to replace EFC). 12% of all full-time freshmen had no need and received non-need-based gift aid.

UNDERGRADUATE FINANCIAL AID (Fall 2009, est.) 975 applied for aid; of those 86% were deemed to have need. 94% of undergraduates with need received aid; of those 76% had need fully met. *Average percent of need met:* 81% (excluding resources awarded to replace EFC). *Average financial aid package:* $21,685 (excluding resources awarded to replace EFC). 12% of all full-time undergraduates had no need and received non-need-based gift aid.

GIFT AID (NEED-BASED) *Total amount:* $17,246,997 (7% federal, 7% state, 81% institutional, 5% external sources). *Receiving aid:* Freshmen: 72% (318); all full-time undergraduates: 50% (697). *Average award:* Freshmen: $15,115; Undergraduates: $14,224. *Scholarships, grants, and awards:* Federal Pell, FSEOG, state, private, college/university gift aid from institutional funds, United Negro College Fund, Federal Nursing, Native American Grants.

GIFT AID (NON-NEED-BASED) *Total amount:* $4,703,500 (2% state, 77% institutional, 21% external sources). *Receiving aid:* Freshmen: 46% (205). Undergraduates: 43% (597). *Average award:* Freshmen: $12,240. Undergraduates: $11,250. *Scholarships, grants, and awards by category: Academic interests/achievement:* $3,100,000 total: business, communication, education, general academic interests/achievements, health fields, religion/biblical studies. *Creative arts/performance:* $1,500,000 total: applied art and design, art/fine arts, dance, music, performing arts, theater/drama. *Special achievements/activities:* $250,000 total: cheerleading/drum major, general special achievements/activities, junior miss, leadership, religious involvement. *Special characteristics:* $1,450,000 total: children of faculty/staff, relatives of clergy. *Tuition waivers:* Full or partial for employees or children of employees.

LOANS *Student loans:* $9,760,407 (36% need-based, 64% non-need-based). 47% of past graduating class borrowed through all loan programs. *Average indebtedness per student:* $26,844. *Average need-based loan:* Freshmen: $4500. Undergraduates: $3600. *Parent loans:* $4,003,166 (100% non-need-based). *Programs:* Federal Direct (Subsidized and Unsubsidized Stafford, PLUS), FFEL (Subsidized and Unsubsidized Stafford, PLUS), Perkins, Federal Nursing.

WORK-STUDY *Federal work-study:* Total amount: $423,463; 248 jobs averaging $1707. *State or other work-study/employment:* Total amount: $350,000 (100% non-need-based). 50 part-time jobs averaging $2500.

ATHLETIC AWARDS Total amount: $3,926,833 (100% non-need-based).

APPLYING FOR FINANCIAL AID *Required financial aid forms:* FAFSA, institution's own form. *Financial aid deadline (priority):* 3/1. *Notification date:* Continuous beginning 3/25. Students must reply within 4 weeks of notification.

CONTACT Denise Flis, Senior Director Student Financial Services, Oklahoma City University, 2501 North Blackwelder, Oklahoma City, OK 73106-1493, 405-208-5848 or toll-free 800-633-7242. *Fax:* 405-208-5466. *E-mail:* dflis@okcu.edu.

OKLAHOMA PANHANDLE STATE UNIVERSITY
Goodwell, OK

Tuition & fees (OK res): $4242	Average undergraduate aid package: $7890

ABOUT THE INSTITUTION State-supported, coed. 25 undergraduate majors. Federal methodology is used as a basis for awarding need-based institutional aid.

UNDERGRADUATE EXPENSES for 2009–10 *Tuition, state resident:* full-time $2738; part-time $91.25 per credit hour. *Tuition, nonresident:* full-time $8077; part-time $269.25 per credit hour. *Required fees:* full-time $1504. Full-time tuition and fees vary according to course level, program, and student level. Part-time tuition and fees vary according to course level and student level. *College room and board:* $3320; *Room only:* $900. Room and board charges vary according to board plan and housing facility. *Payment plans:* Guaranteed tuition, installment.

FRESHMAN FINANCIAL AID (Fall 2008) *Average financial aid package:* $7418 (excluding resources awarded to replace EFC).

UNDERGRADUATE FINANCIAL AID (Fall 2008) *Average financial aid package:* $7890 (excluding resources awarded to replace EFC).

GIFT AID (NEED-BASED) *Total amount:* $2,230,128 (65% federal, 13% state, 8% institutional, 14% external sources). *Receiving aid:* Freshmen: 77% (220); all full-time undergraduates: 68% (650). *Average award:* Freshmen: $3328; Undergraduates: $3337. *Scholarships, grants, and awards:* Federal Pell, FSEOG, state, private, college/university gift aid from institutional funds.

GIFT AID (NON-NEED-BASED) *Scholarships, grants, and awards by category: Academic interests/achievement:* agriculture, biological sciences, business, computer science, education, English, general academic interests/achievements, health fields, mathematics, physical sciences. *Creative arts/performance:* art/fine arts, debating, music, performing arts, theater/drama. *Special achievements/activities:* cheerleading/drum major, general special achievements/activities, rodeo. *Special characteristics:* children of faculty/staff, general special characteristics, local/state students, out-of-state students, veterans, veterans' children. *Tuition waivers:* Full or partial for employees or children of employees, senior citizens.

LOANS *Student loans:* $3,085,938 (100% need-based). *Programs:* FFEL (Subsidized and Unsubsidized Stafford, PLUS), Perkins.

WORK-STUDY *Federal work-study:* Total amount: $34,936; 20 jobs averaging $1747. *State or other work-study/employment:* Total amount: $207,150 (100% need-based). 158 part-time jobs averaging $1311.

ATHLETIC AWARDS Total amount: $328,074 (100% need-based).

APPLYING FOR FINANCIAL AID *Required financial aid form:* FAFSA. *Financial aid deadline (priority):* 3/15. *Notification date:* 5/1. Students must reply by 8/1.

CONTACT Ms. Mary Ellen Riley, Director of Financial Aid, Oklahoma Panhandle State University, PO Box 430, Goodwell, OK 73939-0430, 580-349-2611 Ext. 324 or toll-free 800-664-6778. *E-mail:* mriley@opsu.edu.

OKLAHOMA STATE UNIVERSITY
Stillwater, OK

Tuition & fees (OK res): $6202	Average undergraduate aid package: $10,788

ABOUT THE INSTITUTION State-supported, coed. 82 undergraduate majors. Federal methodology is used as a basis for awarding need-based institutional aid.

UNDERGRADUATE EXPENSES for 2009–10 *One-time required fee:* $95. *Tuition, state resident:* full-time $3941; part-time $131.35 per credit hour. *Tuition, nonresident:* full-time $14,295; part-time $476.50 per credit hour. *Required fees:* full-time $2261; $75.35 per credit hour. Full-time tuition and fees vary according to program and student level. Part-time tuition and fees vary according to program and student level. *College room and board:* $6402; *Room only:* $3402. Room and board charges vary according to board plan and housing facility. *Payment plan:* Installment.

FRESHMAN FINANCIAL AID (Fall 2009, est.) 2,162 applied for aid; of those 70% were deemed to have need. 100% of freshmen with need received aid; of those 18% had need fully met. *Average percent of need met:* 76% (excluding resources awarded to replace EFC). *Average financial aid package:* $11,477 (excluding resources awarded to replace EFC). 28% of all full-time freshmen had no need and received non-need-based gift aid.

UNDERGRADUATE FINANCIAL AID (Fall 2009, est.) 9,848 applied for aid; of those 78% were deemed to have need. 99% of undergraduates with need received aid; of those 15% had need fully met. *Average percent of need met:* 72% (excluding resources awarded to replace EFC). *Average financial aid package:* $10,788 (excluding resources awarded to replace EFC). 23% of all full-time undergraduates had no need and received non-need-based gift aid.

GIFT AID (NEED-BASED) *Total amount:* $42,222,888 (50% federal, 28% state, 12% institutional, 10% external sources). *Receiving aid:* Freshmen: 39% (1,169); all full-time undergraduates: 36% (5,438). *Average award:* Freshmen: $6344; Undergraduates: $6022. *Scholarships, grants, and awards:* Federal Pell, FSEOG, state, private, college/university gift aid from institutional funds, Academic Competitiveness Grants, National SMART Grants, TEACH Grants.

GIFT AID (NON-NEED-BASED) *Total amount:* $10,672,532 (7% federal, 10% state, 41% institutional, 42% external sources). *Receiving aid:* Freshmen: 34% (1,008). Undergraduates: 23% (3,552). *Average award:* Freshmen: $4999. Undergraduates: $4305. *Scholarships, grants, and awards by category: Academic interests/achievement:* agriculture, architecture, area/ethnic studies, biological sciences, business, communication, computer science, education, engineering/technologies, English, foreign languages, general academic interests/achievements, home economics, humanities, international studies, mathematics, military science, physical sciences, premedicine, social sciences. *Creative arts/performance:* art/fine arts, creative writing, general creative arts/performance, journalism/publications, music, theater/drama. *Special achievements/activities:* cheerleading/drum major, community service, general special achievements/activities, leadership, memberships, rodeo. *Special characteristics:* adult students, children and siblings of alumni, ethnic background, first-generation college students, general special characteristics, handicapped students, out-of-state students, previous college experience. *Tuition waivers:* Full or partial for children of alumni.

LOANS *Student loans:* $51,585,436 (52% need-based, 48% non-need-based). 56% of past graduating class borrowed through all loan programs. *Average indebtedness per student:* $19,468. *Average need-based loan:* Freshmen: $3175. Undergraduates: $4161. *Parent loans:* $23,614,161 (17% need-based, 83% non-need-based). *Programs:* Federal Direct (Subsidized and Unsubsidized Stafford, PLUS), Perkins, college/university.

WORK-STUDY *Federal work-study:* Total amount: $949,333; 482 jobs averaging $1970. *State or other work-study/employment:* Total amount: $8,533,138 (100% non-need-based). 3,252 part-time jobs averaging $2624.

ATHLETIC AWARDS Total amount: $3,772,007 (46% need-based, 54% non-need-based).

APPLYING FOR FINANCIAL AID *Required financial aid forms:* FAFSA, institution's own form. *Financial aid deadline (priority):* 2/1. *Notification date:* Continuous beginning 3/1. Students must reply by 5/1 or within 2 weeks of notification.

CONTACT Office of Scholarships and Financial Aid, Oklahoma State University, 119 Student Union, Stillwater, OK 74078-5061, 405-744-6604 or toll-free 800-233-5019 Ext. 1 (in-state), 800-852-1255 (out-of-state). *Fax:* 405-744-6438. *E-mail:* finaid@okstate.edu.

OKLAHOMA WESLEYAN UNIVERSITY
Bartlesville, OK

Tuition & fees: $17,970	Average undergraduate aid package: $11,271

ABOUT THE INSTITUTION Independent religious, coed. 36 undergraduate majors. Both federal and institutional methodology are used as a basis for awarding need-based institutional aid.

UNDERGRADUATE EXPENSES for 2010–11 *Comprehensive fee:* $24,258 includes full-time tuition ($16,870), mandatory fees ($1100), and room and board ($6288). *College room only:* $3288. Full-time tuition and fees vary according to course load. Room and board charges vary according to board plan and housing facility. *Part-time tuition:* $700 per credit hour. *Part-time fees:* $55 per credit hour. *Payment plans:* Installment, deferred payment.

FRESHMAN FINANCIAL AID (Fall 2009, est.) 127 applied for aid; of those 89% were deemed to have need. 99% of freshmen with need received aid; of those 22% had need fully met. *Average percent of need met:* 68% (excluding resources awarded to replace EFC). *Average financial aid package:* $12,947 (excluding resources awarded to replace EFC). 9% of all full-time freshmen had no need and received non-need-based gift aid.

UNDERGRADUATE FINANCIAL AID (Fall 2009, est.) 674 applied for aid; of those 85% were deemed to have need. 99% of undergraduates with need received aid; of those 14% had need fully met. *Average percent of need met:* 63% (excluding resources awarded to replace EFC). *Average financial aid package:* $11,271 (excluding resources awarded to replace EFC). 8% of all full-time undergraduates had no need and received non-need-based gift aid.

GIFT AID (NEED-BASED) *Total amount:* $3,706,605 (41% federal, 10% state, 42% institutional, 7% external sources). *Receiving aid:* Freshmen: 69% (107); all full-time undergraduates: 67% (493). *Average award:* Freshmen: $9543; Undergraduates: $8203. *Scholarships, grants, and awards:* Federal Pell, FSEOG, state, private, college/university gift aid from institutional funds.

GIFT AID (NON-NEED-BASED) *Total amount:* $518,705 (2% federal, 2% state, 80% institutional, 16% external sources). *Receiving aid:* Freshmen: 13% (20). Undergraduates: 8% (55). *Average award:* Freshmen: $5608. Undergraduates: $5404. *Scholarships, grants, and awards by category: Academic interests/achievement:* 333 awards ($955,052 total): biological sciences, business, computer science, education, general academic interests/achievements, health fields, religion/biblical studies. *Creative arts/performance:* 24 awards ($21,825 total): music. *Special achievements/activities:* 297 awards ($174,822 total): religious involvement. *Special characteristics:* 343 awards ($638,202 total): children and siblings of alumni, children of educators, children of faculty/staff, international students, relatives of clergy, religious affiliation, siblings of current students. *Tuition waivers:* Full or partial for employees or children of employees, senior citizens.

LOANS *Student loans:* $7,672,637 (73% need-based, 27% non-need-based). 98% of past graduating class borrowed through all loan programs. *Average indebtedness per student:* $20,852. *Average need-based loan:* Freshmen: $3388. Undergraduates: $4079. *Parent loans:* $657,262 (37% need-based, 63% non-need-based). *Programs:* FFEL (Subsidized and Unsubsidized Stafford, PLUS), Perkins, college/university.

WORK-STUDY *Federal work-study:* Total amount: $223,492; 207 jobs averaging $1085. *State or other work-study/employment:* Total amount: $25,375 (8% need-based, 92% non-need-based). 16 part-time jobs averaging $1585.

ATHLETIC AWARDS Total amount: $780,144 (72% need-based, 28% non-need-based).

APPLYING FOR FINANCIAL AID *Required financial aid forms:* FAFSA, institution's own form. *Financial aid deadline (priority):* 3/31. *Notification date:* Continuous beginning 5/1. Students must reply within 1 week of notification.

CONTACT Lee Kanakis, Director of Student Financial Services, Oklahoma Wesleyan University, 2201 Silver Lake Road, Bartlesville, OK 74006, 918-335-6282 or toll-free 866-222-8226 (in-state). *Fax:* 918-335-6811. *E-mail:* financialaid@okwu.edu.

OLD DOMINION UNIVERSITY
Norfolk, VA

Tuition & fees (VA res): $7318	Average undergraduate aid package: $7701

ABOUT THE INSTITUTION State-supported, coed. 94 undergraduate majors. Federal methodology is used as a basis for awarding need-based institutional aid.

UNDERGRADUATE EXPENSES for 2010–11 *Tuition, state resident:* full-time $7080; part-time $236 per credit hour. *Tuition, nonresident:* full-time $19,530; part-time $651 per credit hour. *Required fees:* full-time $238; $59 per term. Full-time tuition and fees vary according to course level, course load, location, and student level. Part-time tuition and fees vary according to course level, course load, location, and student level. *College room and board:* $7868; *Room only:* $4552. Room and board charges vary according to board plan and housing facility. *Payment plans:* Installment, deferred payment.

FRESHMAN FINANCIAL AID (Fall 2009, est.) 2,186 applied for aid; of those 83% were deemed to have need. 91% of freshmen with need received aid; of those 58% had need fully met. *Average percent of need met:* 78% (excluding resources awarded to replace EFC). *Average financial aid package:* $7742 (excluding resources awarded to replace EFC). 3% of all full-time freshmen had no need and received non-need-based gift aid.

UNDERGRADUATE FINANCIAL AID (Fall 2009, est.) 10,413 applied for aid; of those 76% were deemed to have need. 94% of undergraduates with need received aid; of those 49% had need fully met. *Average percent of need met:* 74% (excluding resources awarded to replace EFC). *Average financial aid package:* $7701 (excluding resources awarded to replace EFC). 2% of all full-time undergraduates had no need and received non-need-based gift aid.

GIFT AID (NEED-BASED) *Total amount:* $36,625,615 (59% federal, 38% state, 2% institutional, 1% external sources). *Receiving aid:* Freshmen: 30% (824); all full-time undergraduates: 27% (3,630). *Average award:* Freshmen: $5103; Undergraduates: $4483. *Scholarships, grants, and awards:* Federal Pell, FSEOG, state, private, college/university gift aid from institutional funds, United Negro College Fund, Federal Nursing.

GIFT AID (NON-NEED-BASED) *Total amount:* $10,822,531 (5% state, 78% institutional, 17% external sources). *Receiving aid:* Freshmen: 28% (759). Undergraduates: 15% (2,025). *Average award:* Freshmen: $3233. Undergraduates: $3441. *Scholarships, grants, and awards by category: Academic interests/achievement:* 1,405 awards ($3,952,481 total): biological sciences, business, engineering/technologies, English, general academic interests/achievements, health fields, humanities, military science, physical sciences. *Creative arts/performance:* 86 awards ($98,453 total): art/fine arts, dance, music, performing arts, theater/drama. *Special achievements/activities:* 25 awards ($31,785 total): cheerleading/drum major, community service, leadership, memberships. *Special characteristics:* 38 awards ($15,687 total): children of faculty/staff, handicapped students, international students, local/state students, members of minority groups, previous college experience, veterans' children. *Tuition waivers:* Full or partial for employees or children of employees, senior citizens.

LOANS *Student loans:* $73,806,549 (43% need-based, 57% non-need-based). 81% of past graduating class borrowed through all loan programs. *Average indebtedness per student:* $17,250. *Average need-based loan:* Freshmen: $3220. Undergraduates: $4063. *Parent loans:* $8,851,753 (100% non-need-based). *Programs:* Federal Direct (Subsidized and Unsubsidized Stafford, PLUS), Perkins, Federal Nursing, college/university.

WORK-STUDY *Federal work-study:* Total amount: $1,170,472; 189 jobs averaging $1242.

ATHLETIC AWARDS Total amount: $4,011,385 (100% non-need-based).

APPLYING FOR FINANCIAL AID *Required financial aid form:* FAFSA. *Financial aid deadline:* 3/15 (priority: 2/15). *Notification date:* Continuous beginning 2/1. Students must reply within 2 weeks of notification.

CONTACT Veronica Finch, Director of Financial Aid, Old Dominion University, 121 Rollins Hall, Norfolk, VA 23529, 757-683-3683 or toll-free 800-348-7926. *E-mail:* vfinch@odu.edu.

OLIVET COLLEGE
Olivet, MI

Tuition & fees: $19,928	Average undergraduate aid package: $16,540

ABOUT THE INSTITUTION Independent religious, coed. *Awards:* bachelor's and master's degrees. 35 undergraduate majors. *Total enrollment:* 1,049. Undergraduates: 1,004. Federal methodology is used as a basis for awarding need-based institutional aid.

UNDERGRADUATE EXPENSES for 2009–10 *Application fee:* $25. *Comprehensive fee:* $26,800 includes full-time tuition ($19,138), mandatory fees ($790), and room and board ($6872). *College room only:* $3472. Full-time tuition and fees vary according to reciprocity agreements. Room and board charges vary according to board plan and housing facility. *Part-time tuition:* $637 per semester hour. *Part-time fees:* $395 per term. Part-time tuition and fees vary according to course load and reciprocity agreements. *Payment plan:* Installment.

FRESHMAN FINANCIAL AID (Fall 2009, est.) 226 applied for aid; of those 96% were deemed to have need. 100% of freshmen with need received aid; of those 30% had need fully met. *Average percent of need met:* 78% (excluding resources awarded to replace EFC). *Average financial aid package:* $15,440 (excluding resources awarded to replace EFC). 18% of all full-time freshmen had no need and received non-need-based gift aid.

UNDERGRADUATE FINANCIAL AID (Fall 2009, est.) 917 applied for aid; of those 92% were deemed to have need. 100% of undergraduates with need received aid; of those 16% had need fully met. *Average percent of need met:* 83% (excluding resources awarded to replace EFC). *Average financial aid package:* $16,540 (excluding resources awarded to replace EFC). 12% of all full-time undergraduates had no need and received non-need-based gift aid.

GIFT AID (NEED-BASED) *Total amount:* $12,672,769 (23% federal, 10% state, 65% institutional, 2% external sources). *Receiving aid:* Freshmen: 77% (217); all full-time undergraduates: 81% (834). *Average award:* Freshmen: $13,440; Undergraduates: $12,278. *Scholarships, grants, and awards:* Federal Pell, FSEOG, state, private, college/university gift aid from institutional funds.

GIFT AID (NON-NEED-BASED) *Total amount:* $1,468,149 (96% institutional, 4% external sources). *Receiving aid:* Freshmen: 13% (38). Undergraduates: 8% (79). *Average award:* Freshmen: $9588. Undergraduates: $11,090. *Scholarships, grants, and awards by category: Academic interests/achievement:* 501 awards ($2,285,063 total): business, communication, education, English, foreign languages, general academic interests/achievements. *Creative arts/performance:* 18 awards ($34,000 total): art/fine arts, journalism/publications, music. *Special achievements/activities:* 289 awards ($547,414 total): community service, leadership, memberships. *Special characteristics:* 231 awards ($922,236 total): children and siblings of alumni, children of faculty/staff, international students, religious affiliation, siblings of current students. *Tuition waivers:* Full or partial for employees or children of employees.

LOANS *Student loans:* $8,289,224 (72% need-based, 28% non-need-based). 91% of past graduating class borrowed through all loan programs. *Average indebtedness per student:* $21,820. *Average need-based loan:* Freshmen: $2765. Undergraduates: $4946. *Parent loans:* $750,694 (39% need-based, 61% non-need-based). *Programs:* FFEL (Subsidized and Unsubsidized Stafford, PLUS), Perkins, state, Key Alternative Loans, CitiAssist Loans, Smart Option Student Loans.

WORK-STUDY *Federal work-study:* Total amount: $172,021; 204 jobs averaging $843. *State or other work-study/employment:* Part-time jobs available.

APPLYING FOR FINANCIAL AID *Required financial aid form:* FAFSA. *Financial aid deadline:* Continuous. *Notification date:* Continuous beginning 3/1.

CONTACT Ms. Libby M. Jean, Director of Student Services, Olivet College, 320 South Main Street, Olivet, MI 49076-9701, 269-749-7655 Ext. 7655 or toll-free 800-456-7189. *Fax:* 269-749-3821. *E-mail:* ljean@olivetcollege.edu.

OLIVET NAZARENE UNIVERSITY
Bourbonnais, IL

Tuition & fees: N/R	Average undergraduate aid package: $17,812

ABOUT THE INSTITUTION Independent religious, coed. *Awards:* associate, bachelor's, and master's degrees. 66 undergraduate majors. *Total enrollment:* 4,636. Undergraduates: 3,190. Federal methodology is used as a basis for awarding need-based institutional aid.

FRESHMAN FINANCIAL AID (Fall 2009, est.) 722 applied for aid; of those 88% were deemed to have need. 100% of freshmen with need received aid; of those 36% had need fully met. *Average percent of need met:* 83% (excluding resources awarded to replace EFC). *Average financial aid package:* $19,075 (excluding resources awarded to replace EFC). 17% of all full-time freshmen had no need and received non-need-based gift aid.

UNDERGRADUATE FINANCIAL AID (Fall 2009, est.) 2,242 applied for aid; of those 90% were deemed to have need. 100% of undergraduates with need received aid; of those 32% had need fully met. *Average percent of need met:* 82% (excluding resources awarded to replace EFC). *Average financial aid package:* $17,812 (excluding resources awarded to replace EFC). 24% of all full-time undergraduates had no need and received non-need-based gift aid.

GIFT AID (NEED-BASED) *Total amount:* $20,778,634 (17% federal, 12% state, 60% institutional, 11% external sources). *Receiving aid:* Freshmen: 83% (637);

---

all full-time undergraduates: 76% (2,004). *Average award:* Freshmen: $14,561; Undergraduates: $13,112. *Scholarships, grants, and awards:* Federal Pell, FSEOG, state, private, college/university gift aid from institutional funds.

GIFT AID (NON-NEED-BASED) *Total amount:* $14,745,623 (8% federal, 2% state, 70% institutional, 20% external sources). *Receiving aid:* Freshmen: 17% (131). Undergraduates: 12% (308). *Average award:* Freshmen: $14,132. Undergraduates: $10,134. *Scholarships, grants, and awards by category: Academic interests/achievement:* $16,622,288 total: general academic interests/achievements, military science. *Creative arts/performance:* $638,147 total: art/fine arts, music, performing arts, theater/drama. *Special achievements/activities:* $814,558 total: cheerleading/drum major, religious involvement. *Special characteristics:* $7,699,477 total: children of faculty/staff, general special characteristics, relatives of clergy, religious affiliation. *Tuition waivers:* Full or partial for employees or children of employees. *ROTC:* Army.

LOANS *Student loans:* $16,969,355 (40% need-based, 60% non-need-based). 77% of past graduating class borrowed through all loan programs. *Average indebtedness per student:* $28,473. *Average need-based loan:* Freshmen: $3755. Undergraduates: $4419. *Parent loans:* $4,694,063 (72% need-based, 28% non-need-based). *Programs:* Federal Direct (Subsidized and Unsubsidized Stafford, PLUS), Perkins, private loans.

WORK-STUDY *Federal work-study:* Total amount: $319,434; 433 jobs averaging $738. *State or other work-study/employment:* Total amount: $943,240 (100% non-need-based). 846 part-time jobs averaging $1115.

ATHLETIC AWARDS Total amount: $2,451,479 (48% need-based, 52% non-need-based).

APPLYING FOR FINANCIAL AID *Financial aid deadline (priority):* 3/1. *Notification date:* Continuous beginning 2/1. Students must reply by 5/1.

CONTACT Mr. Greg Bruner, Financial Aid Director, Olivet Nazarene University, One University Avenue, Bourbonnais, IL 60914, 815-939-5249 or toll-free 800-648-1463. *Fax:* 815-939-5074. *E-mail:* gbruner@olivet.edu.

O'MORE COLLEGE OF DESIGN
Franklin, TN

CONTACT Office of Financial Aid, O'More College of Design, 423 South Margin Street, Franklin, TN 37064-2816, 615-794-4254 Ext. 30.

ORAL ROBERTS UNIVERSITY
Tulsa, OK

Tuition & fees: $18,916	Average undergraduate aid package: $18,229

ABOUT THE INSTITUTION Independent interdenominational, coed. 70 undergraduate majors. Federal methodology is used as a basis for awarding need-based institutional aid.

UNDERGRADUATE EXPENSES for 2009–10 *Comprehensive fee:* $26,832 includes full-time tuition ($18,476), mandatory fees ($440), and room and board ($7916). *College room only:* $3860. Full-time tuition and fees vary according to degree level. Room and board charges vary according to board plan and housing facility. *Part-time tuition:* $772 per credit hour. Part-time tuition and fees vary according to degree level. *Payment plan:* Installment.

FRESHMAN FINANCIAL AID (Fall 2008) 491 applied for aid; of those 85% were deemed to have need. 100% of freshmen with need received aid; of those 37% had need fully met. *Average percent of need met:* 86% (excluding resources awarded to replace EFC). *Average financial aid package:* $15,320 (excluding resources awarded to replace EFC). 25% of all full-time freshmen had no need and received non-need-based gift aid.

UNDERGRADUATE FINANCIAL AID (Fall 2008) 1,978 applied for aid; of those 88% were deemed to have need. 100% of undergraduates with need received aid; of those 37% had need fully met. *Average percent of need met:* 86% (excluding resources awarded to replace EFC). *Average financial aid package:* $18,229 (excluding resources awarded to replace EFC). 20% of all full-time undergraduates had no need and received non-need-based gift aid.

GIFT AID (NEED-BASED) *Total amount:* $4,670,402 (72% federal, 14% state, 14% institutional). *Receiving aid:* Freshmen: 69% (412); all full-time undergraduates: 67% (1,679). *Average award:* Freshmen: $9759; Undergraduates: $9304. *Scholarships, grants, and awards:* Federal Pell, FSEOG, state, private, college/university gift aid from institutional funds.

GIFT AID (NON-NEED-BASED) *Receiving aid:* Freshmen: 29% (173). Undergraduates: 25% (629). *Average award:* Freshmen: $6871. Undergraduates: $7151.

Scholarships, grants, and awards by category: Academic interests/achievement: biological sciences, business, communication, education, engineering/technologies, general academic interests/achievements, health fields, religion/biblical studies. *Creative arts/performance:* applied art and design, art/fine arts, cinema/film/broadcasting, journalism/publications, music. *Special achievements/activities:* cheerleading/drum major, community service, general special achievements/activities, leadership, memberships, religious involvement. *Special characteristics:* children and siblings of alumni, children of faculty/staff, general special characteristics, international students, relatives of clergy, siblings of current students. *Tuition waivers:* Full or partial for children of alumni, employees or children of employees.

LOANS *Student loans:* $20,668,979 (100% need-based). 67% of past graduating class borrowed through all loan programs. *Average indebtedness per student:* $34,555. *Average need-based loan:* Freshmen: $6534. Undergraduates: $10,159. *Parent loans:* $5,718,217 (100% need-based). *Programs:* FFEL (Subsidized and Unsubsidized Stafford, PLUS), Perkins.

WORK-STUDY *Federal work-study:* Total amount: $490,900; jobs available. *State or other work-study/employment:* Total amount: $323,702 (100% non-need-based). Part-time jobs available.

ATHLETIC AWARDS Total amount: $3,610,814 (100% non-need-based).

APPLYING FOR FINANCIAL AID *Required financial aid form:* FAFSA. *Financial aid deadline (priority):* 3/15. *Notification date:* Students must reply by 7/15.

CONTACT Director of Financial Aid, Oral Roberts University, 7777 South Lewis Avenue, Tulsa, OK 74171, 918-495-6510 or toll-free 800-678-8876. *Fax:* 918-495-6803. *E-mail:* finaid@oru.edu.

OREGON COLLEGE OF ART & CRAFT
Portland, OR

ABOUT THE INSTITUTION Independent, coed. 2 undergraduate majors.

GIFT AID (NEED-BASED) *Scholarships, grants, and awards:* Federal Pell, FSEOG, state, private, college/university gift aid from institutional funds.

GIFT AID (NON-NEED-BASED) *Scholarships, grants, and awards by category: Creative arts/performance:* art/fine arts.

LOANS *Programs:* FFEL (Subsidized and Unsubsidized Stafford, PLUS), state, alternative loans.

WORK-STUDY *Federal work-study:* Total amount: $17,653; 40 jobs averaging $459. *State or other work-study/employment:* Total amount: $27,250 (92% need-based, 8% non-need-based). 49 part-time jobs averaging $622.

APPLYING FOR FINANCIAL AID *Required financial aid form:* FAFSA.

CONTACT Lisa Newman, Director of Financial Aid, Oregon College of Art & Craft, 8245 Southwest Barnes Road, Portland, OR 97225, 503-297-5544 Ext. 124 or toll-free 800-390-0632 Ext. 129. *Fax:* 503-297-9651. *E-mail:* lnewman@ocac.edu.

OREGON HEALTH & SCIENCE UNIVERSITY
Portland, OR

Tuition & fees (OR res): $16,051   Average undergraduate aid package: $11,113

ABOUT THE INSTITUTION State-related, coed. 2 undergraduate majors. Federal methodology is used as a basis for awarding need-based institutional aid.

UNDERGRADUATE EXPENSES for 2009–10 *Tuition, state resident:* full-time $10,692; part-time $297 per credit. *Tuition, nonresident:* full-time $19,692; part-time $547 per credit. *Required fees:* full-time $5359. Full-time tuition and fees vary according to course level, degree level, location, program, reciprocity agreements, and student level. Part-time tuition and fees vary according to course level, course load, degree level, location, program, reciprocity agreements, and student level. *Payment plan:* Installment.

UNDERGRADUATE FINANCIAL AID (Fall 2009, est.) 407 applied for aid; of those 94% were deemed to have need. 99% of undergraduates with need received aid; of those 12% had need fully met. *Average percent of need met:* 40% (excluding resources awarded to replace EFC). *Average financial aid package:* $11,113 (excluding resources awarded to replace EFC). 1% of all full-time undergraduates had no need and received non-need-based gift aid.

GIFT AID (NEED-BASED) *Total amount:* $2,412,484 (46% federal, 14% state, 5% institutional, 35% external sources). *Receiving aid:* All full-time undergraduates: 54% (238). *Average award:* Undergraduates: $7820. *Scholarships, grants, and awards:* Federal Pell, FSEOG, state, private, college/university gift aid from institutional funds, Health Profession Scholarships.

GIFT AID (NON-NEED-BASED) *Total amount:* $30,569 (13% institutional, 87% external sources). *Receiving aid:* Undergraduates: 1% (3). *Average award:* Undergraduates: $2875. *Scholarships, grants, and awards by category: Academic interests/achievement:* 196 awards ($2,036,448 total): health fields. *Tuition waivers:* Full or partial for employees or children of employees.

LOANS *Student loans:* $12,999,203 (81% need-based, 19% non-need-based). *Average need-based loan:* Undergraduates: $3763. *Parent loans:* $861,584 (37% need-based, 63% non-need-based). *Programs:* Federal Direct (Subsidized and Unsubsidized Stafford, PLUS), Perkins, Federal Nursing, state, college/university, alternative loans.

WORK-STUDY *Federal work-study:* Total amount: $22,950; 18 jobs averaging $1275.

CONTACT Debbie Cox, Administrative Coordinator, Oregon Health & Science University, 3181 SW Sam Jackson Park Road, L-109, Portland, OR 97239-3089, 503-494-7800. *Fax:* 503-494-4629. *E-mail:* finaid@ohsu.edu.

OREGON INSTITUTE OF TECHNOLOGY
Klamath Falls, OR

Tuition & fees (OR res): $6765   Average undergraduate aid package: $5554

ABOUT THE INSTITUTION State-supported, coed. 19 undergraduate majors. Federal methodology is used as a basis for awarding need-based institutional aid.

UNDERGRADUATE EXPENSES for 2009–10 *Tuition, state resident:* full-time $5199; part-time $108 per credit. *Tuition, nonresident:* full-time $16,629; part-time $108 per credit. *Required fees:* full-time $1566. Full-time tuition and fees vary according to course level, course load, degree level, location, program, and reciprocity agreements. Part-time tuition and fees vary according to course level, course load, degree level, location, program, and reciprocity agreements. *College room and board:* $8615; *Room only:* $5330. Room and board charges vary according to board plan and housing facility.

FRESHMAN FINANCIAL AID (Fall 2008) 269 applied for aid; of those 88% were deemed to have need. 98% of freshmen with need received aid; of those 27% had need fully met. *Average percent of need met:* 20% (excluding resources awarded to replace EFC). *Average financial aid package:* $3725 (excluding resources awarded to replace EFC).

UNDERGRADUATE FINANCIAL AID (Fall 2008) 1,796 applied for aid; of those 93% were deemed to have need. 98% of undergraduates with need received aid; of those 24% had need fully met. *Average percent of need met:* 19% (excluding resources awarded to replace EFC). *Average financial aid package:* $5554 (excluding resources awarded to replace EFC). 1% of all full-time undergraduates had no need and received non-need-based gift aid.

GIFT AID (NEED-BASED) *Total amount:* $7,220,190 (41% federal, 21% state, 22% institutional, 16% external sources). *Receiving aid:* Freshmen: 34% (91); all full-time undergraduates: 41% (806). *Average award:* Freshmen: $5049; Undergraduates: $5361. *Scholarships, grants, and awards:* Federal Pell, FSEOG, state, private, college/university gift aid from institutional funds.

GIFT AID (NON-NEED-BASED) *Total amount:* $91,653 (37% institutional, 63% external sources). *Receiving aid:* Freshmen: 5% (14). Undergraduates: 3% (55). *Average award:* Undergraduates: $6617. *Scholarships, grants, and awards by category: Academic interests/achievement:* general academic interests/achievements. *Special achievements/activities:* general special achievements/activities, leadership.

LOANS *Student loans:* $12,512,929 (99% need-based, 1% non-need-based). 64% of past graduating class borrowed through all loan programs. *Average indebtedness per student:* $27,266. *Average need-based loan:* Freshmen: $2746. Undergraduates: $3988. *Parent loans:* $2,554,253 (72% need-based, 28% non-need-based). *Programs:* FFEL (Subsidized and Unsubsidized Stafford, PLUS), Perkins, college/university.

WORK-STUDY *Federal work-study:* Total amount: $234,427; jobs available.

ATHLETIC AWARDS Total amount: $364,358 (96% need-based, 4% non-need-based).

APPLYING FOR FINANCIAL AID *Required financial aid form:* FAFSA. *Financial aid deadline (priority):* 2/1. *Notification date:* Continuous beginning 4/1. Students must reply within 3 weeks of notification.

CONTACT Tracey Lehman, Financial Aid Director, Oregon Institute of Technology, 3201 Campus Drive, Klamath Falls, OR 97601, 541-885-1280 or toll-free 800-422-2017 (in-state), 800-343-6653 (out-of-state). *Fax:* 541-885-1024. *E-mail:* tracey.lehman@oit.edu.

OREGON STATE UNIVERSITY
Corvallis, OR

Tuition & fees (OR res): $6727	Average undergraduate aid package: $9856

ABOUT THE INSTITUTION State-supported, coed. 77 undergraduate majors. Federal methodology is used as a basis for awarding need-based institutional aid.

UNDERGRADUATE EXPENSES for 2009–10 *Tuition, state resident:* full-time $5436; part-time $151 per credit hour. *Tuition, nonresident:* full-time $18,360; part-time $510 per credit hour. *Required fees:* full-time $1291. Full-time tuition and fees vary according to course load. Part-time tuition and fees vary according to course load. *College room and board:* $8352. Room and board charges vary according to board plan and housing facility. *Payment plan:* Deferred payment.

FRESHMAN FINANCIAL AID (Fall 2009, est.) 2,565 applied for aid; of those 68% were deemed to have need. 98% of freshmen with need received aid; of those 19% had need fully met. *Average percent of need met:* 65% (excluding resources awarded to replace EFC). *Average financial aid package:* $9646 (excluding resources awarded to replace EFC). 1% of all full-time freshmen had no need and received non-need-based gift aid.

UNDERGRADUATE FINANCIAL AID (Fall 2009, est.) 10,599 applied for aid; of those 77% were deemed to have need. 97% of undergraduates with need received aid; of those 16% had need fully met. *Average percent of need met:* 62% (excluding resources awarded to replace EFC). *Average financial aid package:* $9856 (excluding resources awarded to replace EFC). 1% of all full-time undergraduates had no need and received non-need-based gift aid.

GIFT AID (NEED-BASED) *Total amount:* $41,864,984 (60% federal, 15% state, 17% institutional, 8% external sources). *Receiving aid:* Freshmen: 41% (1,323); all full-time undergraduates: 41% (6,129). *Average award:* Freshmen: $2669; Undergraduates: $2957. *Scholarships, grants, and awards:* Federal Pell, FSEOG, state, private, college/university gift aid from institutional funds.

GIFT AID (NON-NEED-BASED) *Total amount:* $8,011,740 (1% federal, 72% institutional, 27% external sources). *Receiving aid:* Freshmen: 2% (57). Undergraduates: 1% (192). *Average award:* Freshmen: $4068. Undergraduates: $3994. *Tuition waivers:* Full or partial for employees or children of employees.

LOANS *Student loans:* $72,107,934 (79% need-based, 21% non-need-based). *Average need-based loan:* Freshmen: $3207. Undergraduates: $3936. *Parent loans:* $36,858,772 (52% need-based, 48% non-need-based). *Programs:* Federal Direct (Subsidized and Unsubsidized Stafford, PLUS), Perkins, college/university.

WORK-STUDY *Federal work-study:* Total amount: $2,893,600; 2,055 jobs averaging $1471.

ATHLETIC AWARDS Total amount: $7,939,328 (26% need-based, 74% non-need-based).

APPLYING FOR FINANCIAL AID *Required financial aid form:* FAFSA. *Financial aid deadline (priority):* 2/28. *Notification date:* Continuous beginning 4/1. Students must reply within 4 weeks of notification.

CONTACT Doug Severs, Director, Financial Aid, Oregon State University, 218 Kerr Administration Building, Corvallis, OR 97331-2120, 541-737-2241 or toll-free 800-291-4192 (in-state). *E-mail:* doug.severs@oregonstate.edu.

OREGON STATE UNIVERSITY–CASCADES
Bend, OR

CONTACT Financial Aid Office, Oregon State University–Cascades, 2600 Northwest College Way, Bend, OR 97701, 541-322-3100.

OTIS COLLEGE OF ART AND DESIGN
Los Angeles, CA

Tuition & fees: $31,360	Average undergraduate aid package: $21,146

ABOUT THE INSTITUTION Independent, coed. 10 undergraduate majors. Federal methodology is used as a basis for awarding need-based institutional aid.

UNDERGRADUATE EXPENSES for 2009–10 *Tuition:* full-time $30,660; part-time $1022 per unit. *Payment plan:* Installment.

FRESHMAN FINANCIAL AID (Fall 2009, est.) 149 applied for aid; of those 81% were deemed to have need. 100% of freshmen with need received aid; of those

4% had need fully met. *Average percent of need met:* 49% (excluding resources awarded to replace EFC). *Average financial aid package:* $19,616 (excluding resources awarded to replace EFC). 17% of all full-time freshmen had no need and received non-need-based gift aid.

UNDERGRADUATE FINANCIAL AID (Fall 2009, est.) 923 applied for aid; of those 83% were deemed to have need. 100% of undergraduates with need received aid; of those 4% had need fully met. *Average percent of need met:* 52% (excluding resources awarded to replace EFC). *Average financial aid package:* $21,146 (excluding resources awarded to replace EFC). 14% of all full-time undergraduates had no need and received non-need-based gift aid.

GIFT AID (NEED-BASED) *Total amount:* $12,065,501 (22% federal, 20% state, 57% institutional, 1% external sources). *Receiving aid:* Freshmen: 67% (116); all full-time undergraduates: 66% (754). *Average award:* Freshmen: $15,662; Undergraduates: $15,903. *Scholarships, grants, and awards:* Federal Pell, FSEOG, state, private, college/university gift aid from institutional funds.

GIFT AID (NON-NEED-BASED) *Total amount:* $1,067,508 (96% institutional, 4% external sources). *Receiving aid:* Freshmen: 18% (31). Undergraduates: 15% (166). *Average award:* Freshmen: $7078. Undergraduates: $6432. *Scholarships, grants, and awards by category:* Academic interests/achievement: 147 awards ($915,700 total): general academic interests/achievements. *Creative arts/performance:* applied art and design, art/fine arts. *Tuition waivers:* Full or partial for employees or children of employees.

LOANS *Student loans:* $7,485,791 (93% need-based, 7% non-need-based). 65% of past graduating class borrowed through all loan programs. *Average indebtedness per student:* $27,903. *Average need-based loan:* Freshmen: $3531. Undergraduates: $4715. *Parent loans:* $2,669,751 (83% need-based, 17% non-need-based). *Programs:* Federal Direct (Subsidized and Unsubsidized Stafford, PLUS), FFEL (Subsidized and Unsubsidized Stafford, PLUS), Perkins, college/university.

WORK-STUDY *Federal work-study:* Total amount: $242,906; 185 jobs averaging $969. *State or other work-study/employment:* Total amount: $9000 (100% non-need-based). 12 part-time jobs averaging $608.

APPLYING FOR FINANCIAL AID *Required financial aid form:* FAFSA. *Financial aid deadline (priority):* 2/15. *Notification date:* 3/1.

CONTACT Jessika Huerta, Assistant Director of Financial Aid, Otis College of Art and Design, 9045 Lincoln Boulevard, Los Angeles, CA 90045-9785, 310-665-6898 or toll-free 800-527-OTIS. *Fax:* 310-665-6884. *E-mail:* jhuerta@otis.edu.

OTTAWA UNIVERSITY
Ottawa, KS

CONTACT Financial Aid Coordinator, Ottawa University, 1001 South Cedar, Ottawa, KS 66067-3399, 785-242-5200 or toll-free 800-755-5200 Ext. 5559. *E-mail:* finaid@ottawa.edu.

OTTERBEIN UNIVERSITY
Westerville, OH

ABOUT THE INSTITUTION Independent United Methodist, coed. *Awards:* bachelor's and master's degrees. 60 undergraduate majors. *Total enrollment:* 3,131. Undergraduates: 2,326. Freshmen: 654.

GIFT AID (NEED-BASED) *Scholarships, grants, and awards:* Federal Pell, FSEOG, state, private, college/university gift aid from institutional funds, Federal Nursing.

GIFT AID (NON-NEED-BASED) *Scholarships, grants, and awards by category:* Academic interests/achievement: general academic interests/achievements. Creative arts/performance: art/fine arts, music, theater/drama. Special achievements/ activities: community service, leadership. Special characteristics: children and siblings of alumni, children of faculty/staff, general special characteristics, international students, members of minority groups, previous college experience, relatives of clergy, siblings of current students, veterans.

LOANS *Programs:* FFEL (Subsidized and Unsubsidized Stafford, PLUS), Perkins, Federal Nursing, state, college/university.

WORK-STUDY *Federal work-study:* Total amount: $528,818; 500 jobs averaging $1000. *State or other work-study/employment:* Total amount: $240,982 (100% non-need-based). 250 part-time jobs averaging $1000.

APPLYING FOR FINANCIAL AID *Required financial aid form:* FAFSA.

CONTACT Mr. Thomas V. Yarnell, Director of Financial Aid, Otterbein University, One Otterbein College, Westerville, OH 43081-2006, 614-823-1502 or toll-free 800-488-8144. *Fax:* 614-823-1200. *E-mail:* tyarnell@otterbein.edu.

OUACHITA BAPTIST UNIVERSITY
Arkadelphia, AR

Tuition & fees: $19,820	Average undergraduate aid package: $15,237

ABOUT THE INSTITUTION Independent Baptist, coed. 59 undergraduate majors. Both federal and institutional methodology are used as a basis for awarding need-based institutional aid.

UNDERGRADUATE EXPENSES for 2010–11 *Comprehensive fee:* $25,660 includes full-time tuition ($19,360), mandatory fees ($460), and room and board ($5840). Room and board charges vary according to housing facility. *Part-time tuition:* $560 per semester hour. *Payment plans:* Installment, deferred payment.

FRESHMAN FINANCIAL AID (Fall 2009, est.) 307 applied for aid; of those 80% were deemed to have need. 100% of freshmen with need received aid; of those 43% had need fully met. *Average percent of need met:* 84% (excluding resources awarded to replace EFC). *Average financial aid package:* $16,975 (excluding resources awarded to replace EFC). 35% of all full-time freshmen had no need and received non-need-based gift aid.

UNDERGRADUATE FINANCIAL AID (Fall 2009, est.) 976 applied for aid; of those 82% were deemed to have need. 100% of undergraduates with need received aid; of those 30% had need fully met. *Average percent of need met:* 73% (excluding resources awarded to replace EFC). *Average financial aid package:* $15,237 (excluding resources awarded to replace EFC). 39% of all full-time undergraduates had no need and received non-need-based gift aid.

GIFT AID (NEED-BASED) *Total amount:* $8,326,035 (19% federal, 5% state, 76% institutional). *Receiving aid:* Freshmen: 62% (240); all full-time undergraduates: 56% (790). *Average award:* Freshmen: $12,254; Undergraduates: $11,957. *Scholarships, grants, and awards:* Federal Pell, FSEOG, state, private, college/university gift aid from institutional funds.

GIFT AID (NON-NEED-BASED) *Total amount:* $7,222,015 (7% state, 77% institutional, 16% external sources). *Receiving aid:* Freshmen: 37% (146). Undergraduates: 27% (376). *Average award:* Freshmen: $8224. Undergraduates: $8000. *Scholarships, grants, and awards by category: Academic interests/achievement:* area/ethnic studies, biological sciences, business, communication, computer science, education, engineering/technologies, English, foreign languages, general academic interests/achievements, health fields, home economics, humanities, international studies, mathematics, physical sciences, premedicine, religion/biblical studies, social sciences. *Creative arts/performance:* art/fine arts, journalism/publications, music, performing arts, theater/drama. *Special achievements/activities:* cheerleading/drum major, general special achievements/activities. *Special characteristics:* children and siblings of alumni, children of faculty/staff, ethnic background, first-generation college students, general special characteristics, handicapped students, international students, local/state students, married students, members of minority groups, out-of-state students, previous college experience, relatives of clergy, religious affiliation, twins. *Tuition waivers:* Full or partial for employees or children of employees.

LOANS *Student loans:* $3,899,697 (48% need-based, 52% non-need-based). 58% of past graduating class borrowed through all loan programs. *Average indebtedness per student:* $14,156. *Average need-based loan:* Freshmen: $1783. Undergraduates: $2289. *Parent loans:* $1,253,831 (15% need-based, 85% non-need-based). *Programs:* Federal Direct (Subsidized and Unsubsidized Stafford, PLUS), FFEL (Subsidized and Unsubsidized Stafford, PLUS), Perkins, state, college/university, alternative private loans.

WORK-STUDY *Federal work-study:* Total amount: $524,475; 305 jobs averaging $1800. *State or other work-study/employment:* Total amount: $309,006 (51% need-based, 49% non-need-based). Part-time jobs available.

ATHLETIC AWARDS Total amount: $2,041,883 (49% need-based, 51% non-need-based).

APPLYING FOR FINANCIAL AID *Required financial aid form:* FAFSA. *Financial aid deadline:* 6/1 (priority: 1/15). *Notification date:* Continuous beginning 11/1. Students must reply by 5/1.

CONTACT Ms. Susan Hurst, Director of Financial Aid, Ouachita Baptist University, Box 3774, Arkadelphia, AR 71998-0001, 870-245-5570 or toll-free 800-342-5628 (in-state). *Fax:* 870-245-5318. *E-mail:* hursts@obu.edu.

OUR LADY OF HOLY CROSS COLLEGE
New Orleans, LA

ABOUT THE INSTITUTION Independent Roman Catholic, coed. *Awards:* associate, bachelor's, and master's degrees and post-bachelor's certificates. 17 undergraduate majors. *Total enrollment:* 1,298. Undergraduates: 1,128.

GIFT AID (NEED-BASED) *Scholarships, grants, and awards:* Federal Pell, FSEOG, state, private, college/university gift aid from institutional funds.

GIFT AID (NON-NEED-BASED) *Scholarships, grants, and awards by category: Academic interests/achievement:* general academic interests/achievements. *Special characteristics:* children of faculty/staff, general special characteristics, relatives of clergy, religious affiliation.

LOANS *Programs:* FFEL (Subsidized and Unsubsidized Stafford, PLUS).

WORK-STUDY *Federal work-study:* Total amount: $129,845; 28 jobs averaging $5000.

APPLYING FOR FINANCIAL AID *Required financial aid form:* FAFSA.

CONTACT Mrs. Kristine Hatfield, Vice President of Enrollment Management and Student Development, Our Lady of Holy Cross College, 4123 Woodland Drive, New Orleans, LA 70131-7399, 504-398-2185 or toll-free 800-259-7744 Ext. 175. *Fax:* 504-394-1182. *E-mail:* khatfield@olhcc.edu.

OUR LADY OF THE LAKE COLLEGE
Baton Rouge, LA

Tuition & fees: N/R	Average undergraduate aid package: $5175

ABOUT THE INSTITUTION Independent Roman Catholic, coed, primarily women. 14 undergraduate majors. Federal methodology is used as a basis for awarding need-based institutional aid.

FRESHMAN FINANCIAL AID (Fall 2008) 90 applied for aid; of those 77% were deemed to have need. 99% of freshmen with need received aid; of those 3% had need fully met. *Average financial aid package:* $6513 (excluding resources awarded to replace EFC).

UNDERGRADUATE FINANCIAL AID (Fall 2008) 684 applied for aid; of those 80% were deemed to have need. 96% of undergraduates with need received aid; of those 2% had need fully met. *Average financial aid package:* $5175 (excluding resources awarded to replace EFC).

GIFT AID (NEED-BASED) *Total amount:* $3,065,610 (59% federal, 30% state, 7% institutional, 4% external sources). *Receiving aid:* Freshmen: 60% (57); all full-time undergraduates: 56% (445). *Average award:* Freshmen: $4910; Undergraduates: $2486. *Scholarships, grants, and awards:* Federal Pell, FSEOG, state, private, college/university gift aid from institutional funds.

GIFT AID (NON-NEED-BASED) *Receiving aid:* Freshmen: 42% (40). Undergraduates: 17% (137).

LOANS *Student loans:* $10,657,287 (100% need-based). 78% of past graduating class borrowed through all loan programs. *Average indebtedness per student:* $12,019. *Average need-based loan:* Freshmen: $9918. Undergraduates: $3664. *Parent loans:* $163,603 (100% need-based). *Programs:* FFEL (Subsidized and Unsubsidized Stafford, PLUS).

WORK-STUDY *Federal work-study:* Total amount: $90,540; jobs available.

APPLYING FOR FINANCIAL AID *Required financial aid form:* FAFSA. *Financial aid deadline (priority):* 3/1. *Notification date:* Continuous beginning 5/15.

CONTACT Tiffany D. Magee, Director of Financial Aid, Our Lady of the Lake College, 7434 Perkins Road, Baton Rouge, LA 70808, 225-768-1701 or toll-free 877-242-3509. *Fax:* 225-490-1632. *E-mail:* tiffany.magee@ololcollege.edu.

OUR LADY OF THE LAKE UNIVERSITY OF SAN ANTONIO
San Antonio, TX

Tuition & fees: $21,900	Average undergraduate aid package: N/A

ABOUT THE INSTITUTION Independent Roman Catholic, coed. 31 undergraduate majors. Both federal and institutional methodology are used as a basis for awarding need-based institutional aid.

UNDERGRADUATE EXPENSES for 2010–11 *Comprehensive fee:* $28,738 includes full-time tuition ($21,400), mandatory fees ($500), and room and board ($6838). *College room only:* $3988. Full-time tuition and fees vary according to degree level and location. Room and board charges vary according to board plan. *Part-time tuition:* $690 per credit hour. *Part-time fees:* $12 per credit hour; $58 per credit hour. Part-time tuition and fees vary according to degree level and location. *Payment plans:* Installment, deferred payment.

GIFT AID (NEED-BASED) *Total amount:* $11,808,203 (36% federal, 26% state, 36% institutional, 2% external sources). *Scholarships, grants, and awards:* Federal Pell, FSEOG, state, private, college/university gift aid from institutional funds.

GIFT AID (NON-NEED-BASED) *Scholarships, grants, and awards by category:* *Academic interests/achievement:* general academic interests/achievements. *Special characteristics:* children of faculty/staff, religious affiliation. *Tuition waivers:* Full or partial for employees or children of employees.

LOANS *Student loans:* $10,392,868 (100% need-based). *Parent loans:* $728,787 (100% need-based). *Programs:* FFEL (Subsidized and Unsubsidized Stafford, PLUS), Perkins, state.

WORK-STUDY *Federal work-study:* Total amount: $450,000; jobs available. *State or other work-study/employment:* Total amount: $550,000 (100% need-based). Part-time jobs available.

ATHLETIC AWARDS Total amount: $909,068 (100% need-based).

APPLYING FOR FINANCIAL AID *Required financial aid forms:* FAFSA, institution's own form. *Financial aid deadline (priority):* 5/1.

CONTACT Michael Fuller, Director of Financial Aid, Our Lady of the Lake University of San Antonio, 411 Southwest 24th Street, San Antonio, TX 78207-4689, 210-434-6711 Ext. 2541 or toll-free 800-436-6558. *Fax:* 210-431-3958. *E-mail:* mfuller@lake.ollusa.edu.

OZARK CHRISTIAN COLLEGE
Joplin, MO

CONTACT Jill Kaminsky, Application Processor, Ozark Christian College, 1111 North Main Street, Joplin, MO 64801-4804, 417-624-2518 Ext. 2017 or toll-free 800-299-4622. *Fax:* 417-624-0090. *E-mail:* finaid@occ.edu.

PACE UNIVERSITY
New York, NY

Tuition & fees: $33,542	Average undergraduate aid package: $28,055

ABOUT THE INSTITUTION Independent, coed. 71 undergraduate majors. Federal methodology is used as a basis for awarding need-based institutional aid.

UNDERGRADUATE EXPENSES for 2010–11 *Comprehensive fee:* $45,782 includes full-time tuition ($32,476), mandatory fees ($1066), and room and board ($12,240). Room and board charges vary according to board plan and housing facility. *Part-time tuition:* $937 per credit hour. Part-time tuition and fees vary according to course load. *Payment plan:* Installment.

FRESHMAN FINANCIAL AID (Fall 2009, est.) 1,446 applied for aid; of those 91% were deemed to have need. 100% of freshmen with need received aid; of those 12% had need fully met. *Average percent of need met:* 76% (excluding resources awarded to replace EFC). *Average financial aid package:* $27,786 (excluding resources awarded to replace EFC). 19% of all full-time freshmen had no need and received non-need-based gift aid.

UNDERGRADUATE FINANCIAL AID (Fall 2009, est.) 5,233 applied for aid; of those 92% were deemed to have need. 100% of undergraduates with need received aid; of those 13% had need fully met. *Average percent of need met:* 78% (excluding resources awarded to replace EFC), *Average financial aid package:* $28,055 (excluding resources awarded to replace EFC). 19% of all full-time undergraduates had no need and received non-need-based gift aid.

GIFT AID (NEED-BASED) *Total amount:* $109,701,468 (11% federal, 6% state, 81% institutional, 2% external sources). *Receiving aid:* Freshmen: 80% (1,309); all full-time undergraduates: 73% (4,736). *Average award:* Freshmen: $22,683; Undergraduates: $23,607. *Scholarships, grants, and awards:* Federal Pell, FSEOG, state, private, college/university gift aid from institutional funds, Federal Nursing, endowed and restricted scholarships and grants.

GIFT AID (NON-NEED-BASED) *Total amount:* $15,439,897 (1% state, 87% institutional, 12% external sources). *Receiving aid:* Freshmen: 6% (100). Undergraduates: 5% (310). *Average award:* Freshmen: $12,252. Undergraduates: $9602. *Scholarships, grants, and awards by category:* *Academic interests/achievement:* 5,198 awards ($47,744,921 total): biological sciences, business, communication, computer science, education, English, foreign languages, general academic interests/achievements, health fields, humanities, mathematics, physical sciences, social sciences. *Creative arts/performance:* 5 awards ($15,000

total): creative writing, debating, performing arts, theater/drama. *Special achievements/activities:* 429 awards ($4,788,657 total): community service, general special achievements/activities, leadership. *Special characteristics:* 76 awards ($1,020,958 total): adult students, children of faculty/staff, children with a deceased or disabled parent, general special characteristics, international students, parents of current students, previous college experience, spouses of deceased or disabled public servants, veterans. *Tuition waivers:* Full or partial for employees or children of employees, senior citizens.

LOANS *Student loans:* $41,580,554 (76% need-based, 24% non-need-based). 58% of past graduating class borrowed through all loan programs. *Average indebtedness per student:* $34,115. *Average need-based loan:* Freshmen: $3923. Undergraduates: $4517. *Parent loans:* $28,023,724 (35% need-based, 65% non-need-based). *Programs:* Federal Direct (Subsidized and Unsubsidized Stafford, PLUS), Perkins, Federal Nursing.

WORK-STUDY *Federal work-study:* Total amount: $1,452,318; 1,032 jobs averaging $3633.

ATHLETIC AWARDS Total amount: $2,213,995 (67% need-based, 33% non-need-based).

APPLYING FOR FINANCIAL AID *Required financial aid forms:* FAFSA, state aid form. *Financial aid deadline (priority):* 2/15. *Notification date:* Continuous beginning 2/25. Students must reply by 5/1 or within 2 weeks of notification.

CONTACT Mark Stephens, Pace University, 861 Bedford Road, Pleasantville, NY 10570, 914-773-3501 or toll-free 800-874-7223. *E-mail:* mstephens@pace.edu.

PACIFIC ISLANDS UNIVERSITY
Mangilao, GU

CONTACT Financial Aid Office, Pacific Islands University, PO Box 22619, Guam Main Facility, GU 96921-2619, 671-734-1812.

PACIFIC LUTHERAN UNIVERSITY
Tacoma, WA

Tuition & fees: $28,100	Average undergraduate aid package: $27,906

ABOUT THE INSTITUTION Independent religious, coed. 41 undergraduate majors. Federal methodology is used as a basis for awarding need-based institutional aid.

UNDERGRADUATE EXPENSES for 2009–10 *Comprehensive fee:* $36,700 includes full-time tuition ($28,100) and room and board ($8600). *College room only:* $4140. Room and board charges vary according to board plan and housing facility. *Part-time tuition:* $880 per credit hour.

FRESHMAN FINANCIAL AID (Fall 2009, est.) 628 applied for aid; of those 84% were deemed to have need. 100% of freshmen with need received aid; of those 35% had need fully met. *Average percent of need met:* 91% (excluding resources awarded to replace EFC). *Average financial aid package:* $28,330 (excluding resources awarded to replace EFC). 22% of all full-time freshmen had no need and received non-need-based gift aid.

UNDERGRADUATE FINANCIAL AID (Fall 2009, est.) 2,539 applied for aid; of those 88% were deemed to have need. 99% of undergraduates with need received aid; of those 30% had need fully met. *Average percent of need met:* 86% (excluding resources awarded to replace EFC). *Average financial aid package:* $27,906 (excluding resources awarded to replace EFC). 24% of all full-time undergraduates had no need and received non-need-based gift aid.

GIFT AID (NEED-BASED) *Total amount:* $34,610,882 (12% federal, 11% state, 74% institutional, 3% external sources). *Receiving aid:* Freshmen: 74% (525); all full-time undergraduates: 70% (2,178). *Average award:* Freshmen: $18,186; Undergraduates: $15,898. *Scholarships, grants, and awards:* Federal Pell, FSEOG, state, private, college/university gift aid from institutional funds, Federal Nursing.

GIFT AID (NON-NEED-BASED) *Total amount:* $12,568,695 (1% state, 81% institutional, 18% external sources). *Receiving aid:* Freshmen: 60% (427). Undergraduates: 54% (1,689). *Average award:* Freshmen: $12,954. Undergraduates: $11,635. *Scholarships, grants, and awards by category:* *Academic interests/achievement:* 2,276 awards ($25,317,971 total): general academic interests/achievements. *Creative arts/performance:* 225 awards ($661,954 total): art/fine arts, dance, debating, music, theater/drama. *Special achievements/activities:* 24 awards ($55,700 total): leadership. *Special characteristics:* 946 awards ($1,909,124 total): children and siblings of alumni, first-generation college students, international students, out-of-state students, relatives of clergy, religious affiliation. *Tuition waivers:* Full or partial for children of alumni, employees or children of employees.

LOANS *Student loans:* $18,737,277 (74% need-based, 26% non-need-based). 72% of past graduating class borrowed through all loan programs. *Average indebtedness per student:* $24,639. *Average need-based loan:* Freshmen: $6930. Undergraduates: $9067. *Parent loans:* $4,970,674 (31% need-based, 69% non-need-based). *Programs:* FFEL (Subsidized and Unsubsidized Stafford, PLUS), Perkins, Federal Nursing, state.

WORK-STUDY *Federal work-study:* Total amount: $1,298,244; 649 jobs averaging $2065. *State or other work-study/employment:* Total amount: $2,756,081 (42% need-based, 58% non-need-based). 292 part-time jobs averaging $3756.

APPLYING FOR FINANCIAL AID *Required financial aid form:* FAFSA. *Financial aid deadline (priority):* 1/31. *Notification date:* Continuous beginning 3/1. Students must reply by 5/1 or within 3 weeks of notification.

CONTACT Mrs. Katherine Walker Loffer, Associate Director, Financial Aid, Pacific Lutheran University, Hauge Administration Building, Room 130, Tacoma, WA 98447, 253-535-7167 or toll-free 800-274-6758. *Fax:* 253-535-8406. *E-mail:* walkerkl@plu.edu.

PACIFIC NORTHWEST COLLEGE OF ART
Portland, OR

CONTACT Peggy Burgus, Director of Financial Aid, Pacific Northwest College of Art, 1241 Northwest Johnson Street, Portland, OR 97209, 503-821-8976. *Fax:* 503-821-8978.

PACIFIC OAKS COLLEGE
Pasadena, CA

CONTACT Rosie Tristan, Financial Aid Specialist, Pacific Oaks College, 5 Westmoreland Place, Pasadena, CA 91103, 626-397-1350 or toll-free 800-684-0900. *Fax:* 626-577-6144. *E-mail:* financial@pacificoaks.edu.

PACIFIC UNION COLLEGE
Angwin, CA

Tuition & fees: $23,979	Average undergraduate aid package: $17,290

ABOUT THE INSTITUTION Independent Seventh-day Adventist, coed. 56 undergraduate majors. Federal methodology is used as a basis for awarding need-based institutional aid.

UNDERGRADUATE EXPENSES for 2009–10 *Comprehensive fee:* $30,729 includes full-time tuition ($23,844), mandatory fees ($135), and room and board ($6750). *College room only:* $3975. Full-time tuition and fees vary according to course load. *Part-time tuition:* $695 per quarter hour. Part-time tuition and fees vary according to course load. *Payment plans:* Guaranteed tuition, installment.

FRESHMAN FINANCIAL AID (Fall 2009, est.) 268 applied for aid; of those 100% were deemed to have need. 100% of freshmen with need received aid; of those 17% had need fully met. *Average percent of need met:* 52% (excluding resources awarded to replace EFC). *Average financial aid package:* $18,530 (excluding resources awarded to replace EFC). 26% of all full-time freshmen had no need and received non-need-based gift aid.

UNDERGRADUATE FINANCIAL AID (Fall 2009, est.) 1,054 applied for aid; of those 100% were deemed to have need. 100% of undergraduates with need received aid; of those 22% had need fully met. *Average percent of need met:* 44% (excluding resources awarded to replace EFC). *Average financial aid package:* $17,290 (excluding resources awarded to replace EFC). 32% of all full-time undergraduates had no need and received non-need-based gift aid.

GIFT AID (NEED-BASED) *Total amount:* $16,202,332 (14% federal, 15% state, 59% institutional, 12% external sources). *Receiving aid:* Freshmen: 99% (268); all full-time undergraduates: 97% (1,054). *Average award:* Freshmen: $15,600; Undergraduates: $14,400. *Scholarships, grants, and awards:* Federal Pell, FSEOG, state, private, college/university gift aid from institutional funds.

GIFT AID (NON-NEED-BASED) *Total amount:* $3,008,692 (56% institutional, 44% external sources). *Receiving aid:* Freshmen: 94% (254). Undergraduates: 86% (944). *Average award:* Freshmen: $1830. Undergraduates: $3444. *Scholarships, grants, and awards by category:* Academic interests/achievement: 13 awards ($62,500 total): education, religion/biblical studies. *Creative arts/*

performance: 15 awards ($15,000 total): art/fine arts, music, theater/drama. *Special achievements/activities:* 328 awards ($794,901 total): community service, general special achievements/activities, leadership, religious involvement. *Special characteristics:* $1,003,049 total: members of minority groups, religious affiliation, siblings of current students, spouses of current students. *Tuition waivers:* Full or partial for employees or children of employees, senior citizens.

LOANS *Student loans:* $12,881,866 (37% need-based, 63% non-need-based). 70% of past graduating class borrowed through all loan programs. *Average indebtedness per student:* $19,000. *Average need-based loan:* Freshmen: $2485. Undergraduates: $3488. *Parent loans:* $938,981 (100% need-based). *Programs:* FFEL (Subsidized and Unsubsidized Stafford, PLUS), Perkins, college/university.

WORK-STUDY *Federal work-study:* Total amount: $295,000; 125 jobs averaging $2284.

APPLYING FOR FINANCIAL AID *Required financial aid forms:* FAFSA, institution's own form. *Financial aid deadline (priority):* 3/2. *Notification date:* Continuous beginning 4/1. Students must reply within 3 weeks of notification.

CONTACT Laurie Wheeler, Director of Student Financial Services, Pacific Union College, One Angwin Avenue, Angwin, CA 94508, 707-965-7321 or toll-free 800-862-7080. *Fax:* 707-965-6595. *E-mail:* llwheeler@puc.edu.

PACIFIC UNIVERSITY
Forest Grove, OR

Tuition & fees: $29,966	Average undergraduate aid package: $26,485

ABOUT THE INSTITUTION Independent, coed. *Awards:* bachelor's and master's degrees. 50 undergraduate majors. *Total enrollment:* 3,167. Undergraduates: 1,481. Freshmen: 345. Federal methodology is used as a basis for awarding need-based institutional aid.

UNDERGRADUATE EXPENSES for 2009–10 *Application fee:* $40. *Comprehensive fee:* $38,084 includes full-time tuition ($29,290), mandatory fees ($676), and room and board ($8118). *College room only:* $4094. Room and board charges vary according to board plan and housing facility. *Part-time tuition:* $1219 per credit hour. Part-time tuition and fees vary according to course load. *Payment plans:* Installment, deferred payment.

FRESHMAN FINANCIAL AID (Fall 2009, est.) 316 applied for aid; of those 86% were deemed to have need. 100% of freshmen with need received aid; of those 32% had need fully met. *Average percent of need met:* 88% (excluding resources awarded to replace EFC). *Average financial aid package:* $26,379 (excluding resources awarded to replace EFC). 18% of all full-time freshmen had no need and received non-need-based gift aid.

UNDERGRADUATE FINANCIAL AID (Fall 2009, est.) 1,243 applied for aid; of those 90% were deemed to have need. 100% of undergraduates with need received aid; of those 24% had need fully met. *Average percent of need met:* 83% (excluding resources awarded to replace EFC). *Average financial aid package:* $26,485 (excluding resources awarded to replace EFC). 19% of all full-time undergraduates had no need and received non-need-based gift aid.

GIFT AID (NEED-BASED) *Total amount:* $16,478,810 (14% federal, 4% state, 78% institutional, 4% external sources). *Receiving aid:* Freshmen: 80% (267); all full-time undergraduates: 74% (1,021). *Average award:* Freshmen: $16,292; Undergraduates: $14,309. *Scholarships, grants, and awards:* Federal Pell, FSEOG, state, private, college/university gift aid from institutional funds.

GIFT AID (NON-NEED-BASED) *Total amount:* $5,483,746 (1% state, 96% institutional, 3% external sources). *Receiving aid:* Freshmen: 12% (40). Undergraduates: 7% (100). *Average award:* Freshmen: $12,170. Undergraduates: $10,908. *Scholarships, grants, and awards by category:* Academic interests/achievement: 1,161 awards ($10,127,750 total): biological sciences, business, communication, education, English, foreign languages, general academic interests/achievements, health fields, humanities, mathematics, physical sciences, premedicine, social sciences. *Creative arts/performance:* 78 awards ($190,275 total): art/fine arts, debating, journalism/publications, music, theater/drama. *Special achievements/activities:* 5 awards ($14,632 total): community service, memberships, religious involvement. *Special characteristics:* 741 awards ($3,174,201 total): children and siblings of alumni, children of faculty/staff, ethnic background, first-generation college students, general special characteristics, international students, local/state students, relatives of clergy, veterans. *Tuition waivers:* Full or partial for employees or children of employees. *ROTC:* Army cooperative, Air Force cooperative.

LOANS *Student loans:* $11,739,196 (73% need-based, 27% non-need-based). 85% of past graduating class borrowed through all loan programs. *Average indebtedness per student:* $27,770. *Average need-based loan:* Freshmen: $3344.

Undergraduates: $4448. *Parent loans:* $1,957,544 (44% need-based, 56% non-need-based). *Programs:* FFEL (Subsidized and Unsubsidized Stafford, PLUS), Perkins, private alternative loans.
WORK-STUDY *Federal work-study:* Total amount: $1,472,815; 753 jobs averaging $1951. *State or other work-study/employment:* Total amount: $147,930 (7% need-based, 93% non-need-based). 140 part-time jobs averaging $993.
APPLYING FOR FINANCIAL AID *Required financial aid form:* FAFSA. *Financial aid deadline (priority):* 3/1. *Notification date:* Continuous beginning 3/1.
CONTACT Financial Aid Front Desk, Pacific University, 2043 College Way, Forest Grove, OR 97116-1797, 503-352-2222 or toll-free 877-722-8648. *E-mail:* financialaid@pacificu.edu.

PAIER COLLEGE OF ART, INC.
Hamden, CT

CONTACT Mr. John DeRose, Director of Financial Aid, Paier College of Art, Inc., 20 Gorham Avenue, Hamden, CT 06514-3902, 203-287-3034. *Fax:* 203-287-3021. *E-mail:* paier.art@snet.net.

PAINE COLLEGE
Augusta, GA

CONTACT Ms. Gerri Bogan, Director of Financial Aid, Paine College, 1235 15th Street, Augusta, GA 30901, 706-821-8262 or toll-free 800-476-7703. *Fax:* 706-821-8691. *E-mail:* bogang@mail.paine.edu.

PALM BEACH ATLANTIC UNIVERSITY
West Palm Beach, FL

Tuition & fees: $22,700	Average undergraduate aid package: $20,405

ABOUT THE INSTITUTION Independent nondenominational, coed. Federal methodology is used as a basis for awarding need-based institutional aid.
UNDERGRADUATE EXPENSES for 2009–10 *Comprehensive fee:* $30,920 includes full-time tuition ($22,400), mandatory fees ($300), and room and board ($8220). *College room only:* $4570. Full-time tuition and fees vary according to course load, degree level, location, program, and reciprocity agreements. Room and board charges vary according to board plan and housing facility. *Part-time tuition:* $540 per credit hour. *Part-time fees:* $99 per term. Part-time tuition and fees vary according to course load, degree level, location, program, and reciprocity agreements. *Payment plan:* Installment.
FRESHMAN FINANCIAL AID (Fall 2009, est.) 391 applied for aid; of those 85% were deemed to have need. 100% of freshmen with need received aid; of those 33% had need fully met. *Average percent of need met:* 37% (excluding resources awarded to replace EFC). *Average financial aid package:* $19,644 (excluding resources awarded to replace EFC). 14% of all full-time freshmen had no need and received non-need-based gift aid.
UNDERGRADUATE FINANCIAL AID (Fall 2009, est.) 1,897 applied for aid; of those 88% were deemed to have need. 100% of undergraduates with need received aid; of those 30% had need fully met. *Average percent of need met:* 63% (excluding resources awarded to replace EFC). *Average financial aid package:* $20,405 (excluding resources awarded to replace EFC). 9% of all full-time undergraduates had no need and received non-need-based gift aid.
GIFT AID (NEED-BASED) *Total amount:* $5,655,545 (61% federal, 8% state, 31% institutional). *Receiving aid:* Freshmen: 69% (291); all full-time undergraduates: 50% (1,112). *Average award:* Freshmen: $7036; Undergraduates: $5521. *Scholarships, grants, and awards:* Federal Pell, FSEOG, state, private, college/university gift aid from institutional funds.
GIFT AID (NON-NEED-BASED) *Total amount:* $15,971,855 (27% state, 59% institutional, 14% external sources). *Receiving aid:* Freshmen: 79% (334). Undergraduates: 74% (1,622). *Average award:* Freshmen: $7944. Undergraduates: $5946. *Scholarships, grants, and awards by category:* Academic interests/achievement: 1,671 awards ($8,847,777 total): general academic interests/achievements. Creative arts/performance: 150 awards ($534,892 total): dance, music, theater/drama. Special achievements/activities: 5 awards ($8500 total): religious involvement. Special characteristics: 61 awards ($986,126 total): children and siblings of alumni, children of current students, children of educators, children of faculty/staff, previous college experience, siblings of current students, spouses of current students. *Tuition waivers:* Full or partial for employees or children of employees.

LOANS *Student loans:* $9,501,378 (38% need-based, 62% non-need-based). 68% of past graduating class borrowed through all loan programs. *Average indebtedness per student:* $22,443. *Average need-based loan:* Freshmen: $3357. Undergraduates: $4242. *Parent loans:* $1,399,896 (100% non-need-based). *Programs:* FFEL (Subsidized and Unsubsidized Stafford, PLUS), Perkins.
WORK-STUDY *Federal work-study:* Total amount: $591,182; 302 jobs averaging $1852. *State or other work-study/employment:* Total amount: $18,500 (100% need-based). 9 part-time jobs averaging $2056.
ATHLETIC AWARDS Total amount: $1,147,627 (100% non-need-based).
APPLYING FOR FINANCIAL AID *Required financial aid form:* FAFSA. *Financial aid deadline:* 8/1 (priority: 2/1). *Notification date:* Continuous beginning 2/15. Students must reply within 4 weeks of notification.
CONTACT Financial Aid Office, Palm Beach Atlantic University, PO Box 24708, West Palm Beach, FL 33416-4708, 561-803-2000 or toll-free 800-238-3998. *Fax:* 561-803-2130. *E-mail:* finaid@pba.edu.

PALMER COLLEGE OF CHIROPRACTIC
Davenport, IA

CONTACT Sue McCabe, Financial Planning Office, Palmer College of Chiropractic, 1000 Brady Street, Davenport, IA 52803, 563-884-5888 or toll-free 800-722-3648. *Fax:* 563-884-5299. *E-mail:* sue.mccabe@palmer.edu.

PARK UNIVERSITY
Parkville, MO

CONTACT Carla Boren, Director of Financial Aid, Park University, 8700 NW River Park Drive, Parkville, MO 64152, 816-584-6317 or toll-free 800-745-7275. *Fax:* 816-741-9668. *E-mail:* finaid@park.edu.

PARSONS THE NEW SCHOOL FOR DESIGN
New York, NY

Tuition & fees: $36,010	Average undergraduate aid package: $28,478

ABOUT THE INSTITUTION Independent, coed. 13 undergraduate majors. Federal methodology is used as a basis for awarding need-based institutional aid.
UNDERGRADUATE EXPENSES for 2009–10 *Comprehensive fee:* $51,270 includes full-time tuition ($35,220), mandatory fees ($790), and room and board ($15,260). *College room only:* $12,260. Room and board charges vary according to board plan and housing facility. *Part-time tuition:* $1202 per credit. Part-time tuition and fees vary according to course load. *Payment plan:* Installment.
FRESHMAN FINANCIAL AID (Fall 2009, est.) 513 applied for aid; of those 92% were deemed to have need. 96% of freshmen with need received aid; of those 5% had need fully met. *Average percent of need met:* 71% (excluding resources awarded to replace EFC). *Average financial aid package:* $30,776 (excluding resources awarded to replace EFC). 5% of all full-time freshmen had no need and received non-need-based gift aid.
UNDERGRADUATE FINANCIAL AID (Fall 2009, est.) 1,817 applied for aid; of those 93% were deemed to have need. 100% of undergraduates with need received aid; of those 8% had need fully met. *Average percent of need met:* 67% (excluding resources awarded to replace EFC). *Average financial aid package:* $28,478 (excluding resources awarded to replace EFC). 3% of all full-time undergraduates had no need and received non-need-based gift aid.
GIFT AID (NEED-BASED) *Total amount:* $28,059,725 (13% federal, 4% state, 81% institutional, 2% external sources). *Receiving aid:* Freshmen: 59% (444); all full-time undergraduates: 44% (1,615). *Average award:* Freshmen: $16,029; Undergraduates: $15,990. *Scholarships, grants, and awards:* Federal Pell, FSEOG, state, private, college/university gift aid from institutional funds.
GIFT AID (NON-NEED-BASED) *Total amount:* $6,865,108 (99% institutional, 1% external sources). *Receiving aid:* Freshmen: 2% (12). Undergraduates: 1% (42). *Average award:* Freshmen: $4800. Undergraduates: $4233. *Scholarships, grants, and awards by category:* Academic interests/achievement: general academic interests/achievements. Creative arts/performance: general creative arts/performance. *Tuition waivers:* Full or partial for employees or children of employees.
LOANS *Student loans:* $19,295,391 (95% need-based, 5% non-need-based). 51% of past graduating class borrowed through all loan programs. *Average indebtedness per student:* $33,576. *Average need-based loan:* Freshmen:

$11,300. Undergraduates: $12,703. *Parent loans:* $6,066,972 (90% need-based, 10% non-need-based). *Programs:* FFEL (Subsidized and Unsubsidized Stafford, PLUS), Perkins.

WORK-STUDY *Federal work-study:* Total amount: $254,597; jobs available. *State or other work-study/employment:* Part-time jobs available.

APPLYING FOR FINANCIAL AID *Required financial aid forms:* FAFSA, state aid form. *Financial aid deadline:* Continuous. *Notification date:* Continuous beginning 3/1. Students must reply within 4 weeks of notification.

CONTACT Financial Aid Counselor, Parsons The New School for Design, 66 Fifth Avenue, New York, NY 10011, 212-229-8930 or toll-free 877-528-3321.

PATRICIA STEVENS COLLEGE
St. Louis, MO

CONTACT Mr. Greg Elsenrath, Financial Aid Director, Patricia Stevens College, 1415 Olive Street, St. Louis, MO 63103, 314-421-0949 or toll-free 800-871-0949. *Fax:* 314-421-0304. *E-mail:* info@patriciastevens.com.

PATRICK HENRY COLLEGE
Purcellville, VA

Tuition & fees: $21,770	Average undergraduate aid package: N/A

ABOUT THE INSTITUTION Independent nondenominational, coed. 5 undergraduate majors. Institutional methodology is used as a basis for awarding need-based institutional aid.

UNDERGRADUATE EXPENSES for 2010–11 *Comprehensive fee:* $30,300 includes full-time tuition ($21,270), mandatory fees ($500), and room and board ($8530). Full-time tuition and fees vary according to course load. Room and board charges vary according to board plan. *Part-time tuition:* $645 per credit hour. Part-time tuition and fees vary according to course load. *Payment plan:* Installment.

GIFT AID (NEED-BASED) *Total amount:* $978,000 (100% institutional). *Scholarships, grants, and awards:* private, college/university gift aid from institutional funds.

GIFT AID (NON-NEED-BASED) *Total amount:* $1,700,000 (91% institutional, 9% external sources). *Scholarships, grants, and awards by category: Academic interests/achievement:* general academic interests/achievements. *Creative arts/performance:* debating, journalism/publications, music. *Special achievements/activities:* community service, leadership, memberships, religious involvement. *Special characteristics:* children of faculty/staff, children of public servants, public servants, relatives of clergy, veterans. *Tuition waivers:* Full or partial for employees or children of employees.

LOANS *Student loans:* $808,000 (100% non-need-based). *Programs:* private alternative loans.

APPLYING FOR FINANCIAL AID *Required financial aid form:* CSS Financial Aid PROFILE. *Financial aid deadline:* 6/15 (priority: 2/1). *Notification date:* Continuous beginning 3/1. Students must reply within 5 weeks of notification.

CONTACT Mr. William K. Kellaris Jr., Director of Financial Aid, Patrick Henry College, 10 Patrick Henry Circle, Purcellville, VA 20132, 540-441-8142. *Fax:* 540-441-8149. *E-mail:* wkkellaris@phc.edu.

PATTEN UNIVERSITY
Oakland, CA

CONTACT Mr. Robert A. Olivera, Dean of Enrollment Services, Patten University, 2433 Coolidge Avenue, Oakland, CA 94601-2699, 510-261-8500 Ext. 783. *Fax:* 510-534-8969. *E-mail:* oliverob@patten.edu.

PAUL QUINN COLLEGE
Dallas, TX

CONTACT Khaleelah Ali, Assistant Director of Financial Aid, Paul Quinn College, 3837 Simpson Stuart Road, Dallas, TX 75241, 214-302-3530 or toll-free 800-237-2648. *Fax:* 214-302-3535. *E-mail:* kali@pqc.edu.

PAUL SMITH'S COLLEGE
Paul Smiths, NY

ABOUT THE INSTITUTION Independent, coed, primarily men. *Awards:* associate and bachelor's degrees. 12 undergraduate majors. *Total enrollment:* 910. Undergraduates: 910.

GIFT AID (NEED-BASED) *Scholarships, grants, and awards:* Federal Pell, FSEOG, state, private, college/university gift aid from institutional funds.

GIFT AID (NON-NEED-BASED) *Scholarships, grants, and awards by category: Academic interests/achievement:* general academic interests/achievements.

LOANS *Programs:* FFEL (Subsidized and Unsubsidized Stafford, PLUS), Perkins.

WORK-STUDY *Federal work-study:* Total amount: $1,028,310; jobs available (averaging $2000). *State or other work-study/employment:* Total amount: $204,052 (2% need-based, 98% non-need-based). Part-time jobs available.

APPLYING FOR FINANCIAL AID *Required financial aid forms:* FAFSA, state aid form.

CONTACT Mary Ellen Chamberlain, Director of Financial Aid, Paul Smith's College, Routes 86 and 30, Paul Smiths, NY 12970, 518-327-6220 or toll-free 800-421-2605. *Fax:* 518-327-6055. *E-mail:* mchamberlain@paulsmiths.edu.

PEABODY CONSERVATORY OF THE JOHNS HOPKINS UNIVERSITY
Baltimore, MD

Tuition & fees: $34,675	Average undergraduate aid package: $15,451

ABOUT THE INSTITUTION Independent, coed. 8 undergraduate majors. Federal methodology is used as a basis for awarding need-based institutional aid.

UNDERGRADUATE EXPENSES for 2009–10 *One-time required fee:* $700. *Comprehensive fee:* $45,775 includes full-time tuition ($34,250), mandatory fees ($425), and room and board ($11,100). Full-time tuition and fees vary according to program. Room and board charges vary according to board plan. *Part-time tuition:* $975 per semester hour. Part-time tuition and fees vary according to course load. *Payment plan:* Installment.

FRESHMAN FINANCIAL AID (Fall 2009, est.) 75 applied for aid; of those 80% were deemed to have need. 97% of freshmen with need received aid; of those 29% had need fully met. *Average percent of need met:* 82% (excluding resources awarded to replace EFC). *Average financial aid package:* $19,838 (excluding resources awarded to replace EFC). 25% of all full-time freshmen had no need and received non-need-based gift aid.

UNDERGRADUATE FINANCIAL AID (Fall 2009, est.) 239 applied for aid; of those 87% were deemed to have need. 99% of undergraduates with need received aid; of those 24% had need fully met. *Average percent of need met:* 74% (excluding resources awarded to replace EFC). *Average financial aid package:* $15,451 (excluding resources awarded to replace EFC). 27% of all full-time undergraduates had no need and received non-need-based gift aid.

GIFT AID (NEED-BASED) *Total amount:* $3,918,071 (12% federal, 2% state, 81% institutional, 5% external sources). *Receiving aid:* Freshmen: 65% (55); all full-time undergraduates: 58% (190). *Average award:* Freshmen: $16,563; Undergraduates: $11,873. *Scholarships, grants, and awards:* Federal Pell, FSEOG, state, private, college/university gift aid from institutional funds.

GIFT AID (NON-NEED-BASED) *Total amount:* $1,335,964 (89% institutional, 11% external sources). *Receiving aid:* Freshmen: 25% (21). Undergraduates: 28% (94). *Average award:* Freshmen: $10,857. Undergraduates: $13,012. *Scholarships, grants, and awards by category: Creative arts/performance:* 356 awards ($4,361,833 total): music.

LOANS *Student loans:* $3,149,263 (88% need-based, 12% non-need-based). 51% of past graduating class borrowed through all loan programs. *Average indebtedness per student:* $39,482. *Average need-based loan:* Freshmen: $3097. Undergraduates: $5015. *Parent loans:* $1,201,047 (100% need-based). *Programs:* Federal Direct (Subsidized and Unsubsidized Stafford, PLUS), Perkins, college/university.

WORK-STUDY *Federal work-study:* Total amount: $227,697; 109 jobs averaging $2089.

APPLYING FOR FINANCIAL AID *Required financial aid forms:* FAFSA, Peabody International Student Financial Aid and Scholarship Application. *Financial aid deadline (priority):* 2/1. *Notification date:* 4/1. Students must reply by 5/1.

CONTACT Tom McDermott, Director of Financial Aid, Peabody Conservatory of The Johns Hopkins University, 1 East Mount Vernon Place, Baltimore, MD 21202-2397, 410-234-4900 or toll-free 800-368-2521 (out-of-state). *Fax:* 410-659-8102. *E-mail:* finaid@peabody.jhu.edu.

PEACE COLLEGE
Raleigh, NC

Tuition & fees: $24,308	Average undergraduate aid package: $19,858

ABOUT THE INSTITUTION Independent religious, women only. 17 undergraduate majors. Federal methodology is used as a basis for awarding need-based institutional aid.
UNDERGRADUATE EXPENSES for 2009–10 *Comprehensive fee:* $32,558 includes full-time tuition ($23,958), mandatory fees ($350), and room and board ($8250). Full-time tuition and fees vary according to course load. Room and board charges vary according to board plan and housing facility. *Part-time tuition:* $360 per semester hour. Part-time tuition and fees vary according to course load. *Payment plan:* Installment.
FRESHMAN FINANCIAL AID (Fall 2009, est.) 141 applied for aid; of those 92% were deemed to have need. 100% of freshmen with need received aid; of those 7% had need fully met. *Average percent of need met:* 78% (excluding resources awarded to replace EFC). *Average financial aid package:* $22,522 (excluding resources awarded to replace EFC). 15% of all full-time freshmen had no need and received non-need-based gift aid.
UNDERGRADUATE FINANCIAL AID (Fall 2009, est.) 601 applied for aid; of those 89% were deemed to have need. 100% of undergraduates with need received aid; of those 11% had need fully met. *Average percent of need met:* 72% (excluding resources awarded to replace EFC). *Average financial aid package:* $19,858 (excluding resources awarded to replace EFC). 18% of all full-time undergraduates had no need and received non-need-based gift aid.
GIFT AID (NEED-BASED) *Total amount:* $8,392,891 (18% federal, 23% state, 56% institutional, 3% external sources). *Receiving aid:* Freshmen: 86% (130); all full-time undergraduates: 81% (531). *Average award:* Freshmen: $18,915; Undergraduates: $15,690. *Scholarships, grants, and awards:* Federal Pell, FSEOG, state, private, college/university gift aid from institutional funds.
GIFT AID (NON-NEED-BASED) *Total amount:* $1,338,964 (19% state, 72% institutional, 9% external sources). *Receiving aid:* Freshmen: 5% (7). Undergraduates: 5% (36). *Average award:* Freshmen: $8423. Undergraduates: $7830. *Scholarships, grants, and awards by category: Academic interests/achievement:* 626 awards ($4,236,416 total): general academic interests/achievements. *Creative arts/performance:* 47 awards ($41,550 total): art/fine arts, music, theater/drama. *Special characteristics:* 13 awards ($79,826 total): children of faculty/staff, relatives of clergy, siblings of current students. *Tuition waivers:* Full or partial for employees or children of employees, senior citizens.
LOANS *Student loans:* $5,034,319 (77% need-based, 23% non-need-based). 78% of past graduating class borrowed through all loan programs. *Average indebtedness per student:* $22,428. *Average need-based loan:* Freshmen: $3120. Undergraduates: $3978. *Parent loans:* $986,251 (32% need-based, 68% non-need-based). *Programs:* Federal Direct (Subsidized and Unsubsidized Stafford, PLUS), alternative loans.
WORK-STUDY *Federal work-study:* Total amount: $303,500; 222 jobs averaging $1840. *State or other work-study/employment:* Total amount: $45,195 (55% need-based, 45% non-need-based). 17 part-time jobs averaging $1307.
APPLYING FOR FINANCIAL AID *Required financial aid form:* FAFSA. *Financial aid deadline (priority):* 3/15. *Notification date:* Continuous beginning 3/1. Students must reply within 4 weeks of notification.
CONTACT Ms. Angela J. Kirkley, Director of Financial Aid, Peace College, 15 East Peace Street, Raleigh, NC 27604, 919-508-2249 or toll-free 800-PEACE-47. *Fax:* 919-508-2325. *E-mail:* akirkley@peace.edu.

PEIRCE COLLEGE
Philadelphia, PA

Tuition & fees: $14,850	Average undergraduate aid package: $9971

ABOUT THE INSTITUTION Independent, coed. 13 undergraduate majors. Federal methodology is used as a basis for awarding need-based institutional aid.

UNDERGRADUATE EXPENSES for 2009–10 *Tuition:* full-time $13,800; part-time $460 per credit. *Required fees:* full-time $1050; $105 per course. Full-time tuition and fees vary according to course load. Part-time tuition and fees vary according to course load. *Payment plan:* Installment.
FRESHMAN FINANCIAL AID (Fall 2008) 15 applied for aid; of those 93% were deemed to have need. 100% of freshmen with need received aid. *Average percent of need met:* 47% (excluding resources awarded to replace EFC). *Average financial aid package:* $8470 (excluding resources awarded to replace EFC).
UNDERGRADUATE FINANCIAL AID (Fall 2008) 546 applied for aid; of those 86% were deemed to have need. 99% of undergraduates with need received aid; of those 2% had need fully met. *Average percent of need met:* 52% (excluding resources awarded to replace EFC). *Average financial aid package:* $9971 (excluding resources awarded to replace EFC). 4% of all full-time undergraduates had no need and received non-need-based gift aid.
GIFT AID (NEED-BASED) *Total amount:* $5,238,257 (57% federal, 28% state, 14% institutional, 1% external sources). *Receiving aid:* Freshmen: 65% (13); all full-time undergraduates: 52% (413). *Average award:* Freshmen: $4699; Undergraduates: $5587. *Scholarships, grants, and awards:* Federal Pell, FSEOG, state, college/university gift aid from institutional funds.
GIFT AID (NON-NEED-BASED) *Total amount:* $71,735 (100% institutional). *Receiving aid:* Undergraduates: 1% (5). *Average award:* Undergraduates: $2211. *Scholarships, grants, and awards by category: Academic interests/achievement:* 64 awards ($172,947 total): business, computer science. *Special achievements/activities:* 11 awards ($20,750 total): leadership, memberships. *Special characteristics:* 141 awards ($216,508 total): children and siblings of alumni, children of public servants, international students. *Tuition waivers:* Full or partial for children of alumni, employees or children of employees.
LOANS *Student loans:* $16,122,790 (43% need-based, 57% non-need-based). 87% of past graduating class borrowed through all loan programs. *Average indebtedness per student:* $19,748. *Average need-based loan:* Freshmen: $4107. Undergraduates: $5140. *Parent loans:* $86,350 (100% need-based). *Programs:* Federal Direct (Subsidized and Unsubsidized Stafford, PLUS), FFEL (Subsidized and Unsubsidized Stafford, PLUS).
WORK-STUDY *Federal work-study:* Total amount: $152,721; 25 jobs averaging $4000.
APPLYING FOR FINANCIAL AID *Required financial aid form:* FAFSA. *Financial aid deadline:* Continuous. *Notification date:* Continuous beginning 5/1.
CONTACT Lisa A. Gargiulo, Manager, Student Financial Services, Peirce College, 1420 Pine Street, Philadelphia, PA 19102, 215-670-9370 or toll-free 888-467-3472. *Fax:* 215-545-3671. *E-mail:* lagargiulo@peirce.edu.

PENN FOSTER COLLEGE
Scottsdale, AZ

CONTACT Financial Aid Office, Penn Foster College, 14300 North Northsight Boulevard, Suite 111, Scottsdale, AZ 85260, 480-947-6644 or toll-free 480-947-2680 (in-state).

PENN STATE ABINGTON
Abington, PA

Tuition & fees (PA res): $12,250	Average undergraduate aid package: $8915

ABOUT THE INSTITUTION State-related, coed. 118 undergraduate majors. Federal methodology is used as a basis for awarding need-based institutional aid.
UNDERGRADUATE EXPENSES for 2009–10 *Tuition, state resident:* full-time $11,442; part-time $463 per credit hour. *Tuition, nonresident:* full-time $17,460; part-time $728 per credit hour. *Required fees:* full-time $808.
FRESHMAN FINANCIAL AID (Fall 2008) 705 applied for aid; of those 76% were deemed to have need. 96% of freshmen with need received aid; of those 4% had need fully met. *Average percent of need met:* 66% (excluding resources awarded to replace EFC). *Average financial aid package:* $9306 (excluding resources awarded to replace EFC). 6% of all full-time freshmen had no need and received non-need-based gift aid.
UNDERGRADUATE FINANCIAL AID (Fall 2008) 2,094 applied for aid; of those 80% were deemed to have need. 97% of undergraduates with need received aid; of those 5% had need fully met. *Average percent of need met:* 64% (excluding resources awarded to replace EFC). *Average financial aid package:*

$8915 (excluding resources awarded to replace EFC). 3% of all full-time undergraduates had no need and received non-need-based gift aid.

GIFT AID (NEED-BASED) *Total amount:* **$9,572,753** (48% federal, 30% state, 13% institutional, 9% external sources). *Receiving aid:* Freshmen: 50% (402); all full-time undergraduates: 49% (1,246). *Average award:* Freshmen: $6764; Undergraduates: $6249. *Scholarships, grants, and awards:* Federal Pell, FSEOG, state, private, college/university gift aid from institutional funds.

GIFT AID (NON-NEED-BASED) *Total amount:* **$490,334** (34% federal, 1% state, 27% institutional, 38% external sources). *Receiving aid:* Freshmen: 34% (277). Undergraduates: 17% (426). *Average award:* Freshmen: $1612. Undergraduates: $1568. *Scholarships, grants, and awards by category: Academic interests/ achievement:* general academic interests/achievements. *Special characteristics:* children and siblings of alumni, general special characteristics.

LOANS *Student loans:* **$13,997,175** (80% need-based, 20% non-need-based). 68% of past graduating class borrowed through all loan programs. *Average indebtedness per student:* $28,680. *Average need-based loan:* Freshmen: $3287. Undergraduates: $3937. *Parent loans:* $1,458,662 (58% need-based, 42% non-need-based). *Programs:* Federal Direct (Subsidized and Unsubsidized Stafford, PLUS), Perkins, college/university, private loans.

WORK-STUDY *Federal work-study:* Total amount: $129,135; 75 jobs averaging $1701.

APPLYING FOR FINANCIAL AID *Required financial aid form:* FAFSA. *Financial aid deadline (priority):* 2/15. *Notification date:* Continuous.

CONTACT Debbie Meditz, Assistant Student Aid Coordinator, Penn State Abington, 106 Sutherland Building, 1600 Woodland Road, Abington, PA 19001, 215-881-7348. *Fax:* 215-881-7655. *E-mail:* dlm175@psu.edu.

PENN STATE ALTOONA
Altoona, PA

Tuition & fees (PA res): $12,750   Average undergraduate aid package: $8735

ABOUT THE INSTITUTION State-related, coed. 125 undergraduate majors. Federal methodology is used as a basis for awarding need-based institutional aid.

UNDERGRADUATE EXPENSES for 2009–10 *Tuition, state resident:* full-time $11,942; part-time $498 per credit hour. *Tuition, nonresident:* full-time $18,270; part-time $761 per credit hour. *Required fees:* full-time $808. Full-time tuition and fees vary according to course level, location, program, and student level. Part-time tuition and fees vary according to course level, course load, location, program, and student level. *College room and board:* $8170; *Room only:* $4430. Room and board charges vary according to board plan, housing facility, and location.

FRESHMAN FINANCIAL AID (Fall 2008) 1,238 applied for aid; of those 78% were deemed to have need. 95% of freshmen with need received aid; of those 6% had need fully met. *Average percent of need met:* 61% (excluding resources awarded to replace EFC). *Average financial aid package:* $8103 (excluding resources awarded to replace EFC). 2% of all full-time freshmen had no need and received non-need-based gift aid.

UNDERGRADUATE FINANCIAL AID (Fall 2008) 3,041 applied for aid; of those 81% were deemed to have need. 97% of undergraduates with need received aid; of those 6% had need fully met. *Average percent of need met:* 62% (excluding resources awarded to replace EFC). *Average financial aid package:* $8735 (excluding resources awarded to replace EFC). 2% of all full-time undergraduates had no need and received non-need-based gift aid.

GIFT AID (NEED-BASED) *Total amount:* **$11,282,546** (44% federal, 35% state, 14% institutional, 7% external sources). *Receiving aid:* Freshmen: 39% (577); all full-time undergraduates: 43% (1,574). *Average award:* Freshmen: $5588; Undergraduates: $5510. *Scholarships, grants, and awards:* Federal Pell, FSEOG, state, private, college/university gift aid from institutional funds.

GIFT AID (NON-NEED-BASED) *Total amount:* **$717,148** (50% federal, 2% state, 18% institutional, 30% external sources). *Receiving aid:* Freshmen: 22% (328). Undergraduates: 20% (736). *Average award:* Freshmen: $1100. Undergraduates: $1396. *Scholarships, grants, and awards by category: Academic interests/ achievement:* general academic interests/achievements. *Special characteristics:* children and siblings of alumni, general special characteristics.

LOANS *Student loans:* **$23,938,920** (84% need-based, 16% non-need-based). 68% of past graduating class borrowed through all loan programs. *Average indebtedness per student:* $28,680. *Average need-based loan:* Freshmen: $3387. Undergraduates: $3960. *Parent loans:* $6,824,902 (77% need-based, 23% non-need-based). *Programs:* Federal Direct (Subsidized and Unsubsidized Stafford, PLUS), Perkins, college/university, private loans.

WORK-STUDY *Federal work-study:* Total amount: $303,887; 152 jobs averaging $1987.

APPLYING FOR FINANCIAL AID *Required financial aid form:* FAFSA. *Financial aid deadline (priority):* 2/15. *Notification date:* Continuous beginning 3/1.

CONTACT Mr. David Pearlman, Assistant Director of Student Affairs, Penn State Altoona, W111 Smith Building, Altoona, PA 16601-3760, 814-949-5055 or toll-free 800-848-9843. *Fax:* 814-949-5536. *E-mail:* dpp1@psu.edu.

PENN STATE BERKS
Reading, PA

Tuition & fees (PA res): $12,750   Average undergraduate aid package: $7980

ABOUT THE INSTITUTION State-related, coed. 129 undergraduate majors. Federal methodology is used as a basis for awarding need-based institutional aid.

UNDERGRADUATE EXPENSES for 2009–10 *Tuition, state resident:* full-time $11,942; part-time $498 per credit hour. *Tuition, nonresident:* full-time $18,270; part-time $761 per credit hour. *Required fees:* full-time $808. Full-time tuition and fees vary according to course level, location, program, and student level. Part-time tuition and fees vary according to course level, course load, location, program, and student level. *College room and board:* $8940; *Room only:* $5200. Room and board charges vary according to board plan, housing facility, and location.

FRESHMAN FINANCIAL AID (Fall 2008) 840 applied for aid; of those 74% were deemed to have need. 96% of freshmen with need received aid; of those 4% had need fully met. *Average percent of need met:* 58% (excluding resources awarded to replace EFC). *Average financial aid package:* $7675 (excluding resources awarded to replace EFC). 2% of all full-time freshmen had no need and received non-need-based gift aid.

UNDERGRADUATE FINANCIAL AID (Fall 2008) 1,938 applied for aid; of those 75% were deemed to have need. 97% of undergraduates with need received aid; of those 5% had need fully met. *Average percent of need met:* 60% (excluding resources awarded to replace EFC). *Average financial aid package:* $7980 (excluding resources awarded to replace EFC). 2% of all full-time undergraduates had no need and received non-need-based gift aid.

GIFT AID (NEED-BASED) *Total amount:* **$6,038,292** (41% federal, 35% state, 16% institutional, 8% external sources). *Receiving aid:* Freshmen: 38% (371); all full-time undergraduates: 38% (906). *Average award:* Freshmen: $5799; Undergraduates: $5469. *Scholarships, grants, and awards:* Federal Pell, FSEOG, state, private, college/university gift aid from institutional funds.

GIFT AID (NON-NEED-BASED) *Total amount:* **$428,346** (32% federal, 3% state, 29% institutional, 36% external sources). *Receiving aid:* Freshmen: 16% (156). Undergraduates: 13% (319). *Average award:* Freshmen: $1811. Undergraduates: $2197. *Scholarships, grants, and awards by category: Academic interests/ achievement:* general academic interests/achievements. *Special characteristics:* children and siblings of alumni.

LOANS *Student loans:* **$14,454,788** (79% need-based, 21% non-need-based). 68% of past graduating class borrowed through all loan programs. *Average indebtedness per student:* $28,680. *Average need-based loan:* Freshmen: $3389. Undergraduates: $3908. *Parent loans:* $4,758,749 (72% need-based, 28% non-need-based). *Programs:* Federal Direct (Subsidized and Unsubsidized Stafford, PLUS), Perkins, college/university, private loans.

WORK-STUDY *Federal work-study:* Total amount: $119,041; 59 jobs averaging $2018.

APPLYING FOR FINANCIAL AID *Required financial aid form:* FAFSA. *Financial aid deadline (priority):* 2/15. *Notification date:* Continuous beginning 3/1.

CONTACT Maryann Hubick, Financial Aid Coordinator, Penn State Berks, Perkins Student Center, Room 6, Reading, PA 19610-6009, 610-396-6071. *Fax:* 610-396-6077. *E-mail:* mxh61@psu.edu.

PENN STATE ERIE, THE BEHREND COLLEGE
Erie, PA

Tuition & fees (PA res): $12,750   Average undergraduate aid package: $8847

ABOUT THE INSTITUTION State-related, coed. 129 undergraduate majors. Federal methodology is used as a basis for awarding need-based institutional aid.

UNDERGRADUATE EXPENSES for 2009–10 *Tuition, state resident:* full-time $11,942; part-time $498 per credit hour. *Tuition, nonresident:* full-time $18,270;

part-time $761 per credit hour. *Required fees:* full-time $808. Full-time tuition and fees vary according to course level, location, program, and student level. Part-time tuition and fees vary according to course level, course load, location, program, and student level. *College room and board:* $8170; *Room only:* $4430. Room and board charges vary according to board plan, housing facility, and location.

FRESHMAN FINANCIAL AID (Fall 2008) 975 applied for aid; of those 81% were deemed to have need. 97% of freshmen with need received aid; of those 5% had need fully met. *Average percent of need met:* 63% (excluding resources awarded to replace EFC). *Average financial aid package:* $8318 (excluding resources awarded to replace EFC). 2% of all full-time freshmen had no need and received non-need-based gift aid.

UNDERGRADUATE FINANCIAL AID (Fall 2008) 3,296 applied for aid; of those 85% were deemed to have need. 98% of undergraduates with need received aid; of those 6% had need fully met. *Average percent of need met:* 64% (excluding resources awarded to replace EFC). *Average financial aid package:* $8847 (excluding resources awarded to replace EFC). 2% of all full-time undergraduates had no need and received non-need-based gift aid.

GIFT AID (NEED-BASED) *Total amount:* $13,143,861 (36% federal, 36% state, 19% institutional, 9% external sources). *Receiving aid:* Freshmen: 48% (516); all full-time undergraduates: 46% (1,792). *Average award:* Freshmen: $5483; Undergraduates: $5396. *Scholarships, grants, and awards:* Federal Pell, FSEOG, state, private, college/university gift aid from institutional funds.

GIFT AID (NON-NEED-BASED) *Total amount:* $740,064 (13% federal, 6% state, 44% institutional, 37% external sources). *Receiving aid:* Freshmen: 24% (260). Undergraduates: 22% (845). *Average award:* Freshmen: $2079. Undergraduates: $3693. *Scholarships, grants, and awards by category:* Academic interests/achievement: general academic interests/achievements. *Special characteristics:* children and siblings of alumni.

LOANS *Student loans:* $26,448,743 (88% need-based, 12% non-need-based). 68% of past graduating class borrowed through all loan programs. *Average indebtedness per student:* $28,680. *Average need-based loan:* Freshmen: $3493. Undergraduates: $4239. *Parent loans:* $9,088,803 (86% need-based, 14% non-need-based). *Programs:* Federal Direct (Subsidized and Unsubsidized Stafford, PLUS), Perkins, college/university, private loans.

WORK-STUDY *Federal work-study:* Total amount: $317,229; 163 jobs averaging $1927.

APPLYING FOR FINANCIAL AID *Required financial aid form:* FAFSA. *Financial aid deadline (priority):* 2/15. *Notification date:* Continuous beginning 3/1.

CONTACT Ms. Jane Brady, Assistant Director of Admissions and Financial Aid, Penn State Erie, The Behrend College, 5091 Station Road, Erie, PA 16802, 814-898-6162 or toll-free 866-374-3378. *Fax:* 814-898-7595. *E-mail:* jub9@psu.edu.

PENN STATE HARRISBURG
Middletown, PA

Tuition & fees (PA res): $12,750   Average undergraduate aid package: $8990

ABOUT THE INSTITUTION State-related, coed. 29 undergraduate majors. Federal methodology is used as a basis for awarding need-based institutional aid.

UNDERGRADUATE EXPENSES for 2009–10 *Tuition, state resident:* full-time $11,942; part-time $498 per credit hour. *Tuition, nonresident:* full-time $18,270; part-time $761 per credit hour. *Required fees:* full-time $808. Full-time tuition and fees vary according to course level, location, program, and student level. Part-time tuition and fees vary according to course level, course load, location, program, and student level. *College room and board:* $9350; *Room only:* $5610. Room and board charges vary according to board plan, housing facility, and location.

FRESHMAN FINANCIAL AID (Fall 2008) 353 applied for aid; of those 77% were deemed to have need. 96% of freshmen with need received aid; of those 8% had need fully met. *Average percent of need met:* 60% (excluding resources awarded to replace EFC). *Average financial aid package:* $8208 (excluding resources awarded to replace EFC). 1% of all full-time freshmen had no need and received non-need-based gift aid.

UNDERGRADUATE FINANCIAL AID (Fall 2008) 1,602 applied for aid; of those 81% were deemed to have need. 97% of undergraduates with need received aid; of those 9% had need fully met. *Average percent of need met:* 61% (excluding resources awarded to replace EFC). *Average financial aid package:* $8990 (excluding resources awarded to replace EFC). 1% of all full-time undergraduates had no need and received non-need-based gift aid.

GIFT AID (NEED-BASED) *Total amount:* $6,047,809 (49% federal, 32% state, 13% institutional, 6% external sources). *Receiving aid:* Freshmen: 37% (163); all full-time undergraduates: 41% (828). *Average award:* Freshmen: $5420; Undergraduates: $5351. *Scholarships, grants, and awards:* Federal Pell, FSEOG, state, private, college/university gift aid from institutional funds.

GIFT AID (NON-NEED-BASED) *Total amount:* $563,509 (38% federal, 3% state, 8% institutional, 51% external sources). *Receiving aid:* Freshmen: 20% (89). Undergraduates: 16% (318). *Average award:* Freshmen: $2392. Undergraduates: $2946. *Scholarships, grants, and awards by category:* Academic interests/achievement: general academic interests/achievements. *Special characteristics:* children and siblings of alumni, general special characteristics.

LOANS *Student loans:* $15,231,264 (82% need-based, 18% non-need-based). 68% of past graduating class borrowed through all loan programs. *Average indebtedness per student:* $28,680. *Average need-based loan:* Freshmen: $3409. Undergraduates: $4344. *Parent loans:* $2,823,420 (77% need-based, 23% non-need-based). *Programs:* Federal Direct (Subsidized and Unsubsidized Stafford, PLUS), Perkins, college/university, private loans.

WORK-STUDY *Federal work-study:* Total amount: $92,725; 52 jobs averaging $1783.

APPLYING FOR FINANCIAL AID *Required financial aid form:* FAFSA. *Financial aid deadline (priority):* 2/15. *Notification date:* Continuous beginning 3/1.

CONTACT Ms. Carolyn Julian, Student Aid Adviser, Penn State Harrisburg, W112 Olmstead, 777 West Harrisburg Pike, Middletown, PA 17057-4898, 717-948-6307 or toll-free 800-222-2056. *Fax:* 717-948-6008. *E-mail:* czb3@psu.edu.

PENN STATE UNIVERSITY PARK
State College, PA

Tuition & fees (PA res): $14,416   Average undergraduate aid package: $9455

ABOUT THE INSTITUTION State-related, coed. 127 undergraduate majors. Federal methodology is used as a basis for awarding need-based institutional aid.

UNDERGRADUATE EXPENSES for 2009–10 *Tuition, state resident:* full-time $13,604; part-time $567 per credit hour. *Tuition, nonresident:* full-time $25,134; part-time $1047 per credit hour. *Required fees:* full-time $812. Full-time tuition and fees vary according to course level, degree level, location, program, and student level. Part-time tuition and fees vary according to course level, course load, degree level, location, program, and student level. *College room and board:* $8170; *Room only:* $4430. Room and board charges vary according to board plan, housing facility, and location. *Payment plans:* Installment, deferred payment.

FRESHMAN FINANCIAL AID (Fall 2008) 5,327 applied for aid; of those 64% were deemed to have need. 94% of freshmen with need received aid; of those 8% had need fully met. *Average percent of need met:* 63% (excluding resources awarded to replace EFC). *Average financial aid package:* $8531 (excluding resources awarded to replace EFC). 7% of all full-time freshmen had no need and received non-need-based gift aid.

UNDERGRADUATE FINANCIAL AID (Fall 2008) 24,223 applied for aid; of those 76% were deemed to have need. 97% of undergraduates with need received aid; of those 9% had need fully met. *Average percent of need met:* 64% (excluding resources awarded to replace EFC). *Average financial aid package:* $9455 (excluding resources awarded to replace EFC). 7% of all full-time undergraduates had no need and received non-need-based gift aid.

GIFT AID (NEED-BASED) *Total amount:* $84,427,731 (34% federal, 26% state, 31% institutional, 9% external sources). *Receiving aid:* Freshmen: 21% (1,503); all full-time undergraduates: 27% (9,738). *Average award:* Freshmen: $6122; Undergraduates: $5972. *Scholarships, grants, and awards:* Federal Pell, FSEOG, state, private, college/university gift aid from institutional funds.

GIFT AID (NON-NEED-BASED) *Total amount:* $24,498,246 (16% federal, 1% state, 35% institutional, 48% external sources). *Receiving aid:* Freshmen: 20% (1,457). Undergraduates: 16% (5,974). *Average award:* Freshmen: $3571. Undergraduates: $3384. *Scholarships, grants, and awards by category:* Academic interests/achievement: general academic interests/achievements. *Special characteristics:* children and siblings of alumni. *Tuition waivers:* Full or partial for employees or children of employees.

LOANS *Student loans:* $209,423,403 (80% need-based, 20% non-need-based). 68% of past graduating class borrowed through all loan programs. *Average indebtedness per student:* $28,680. *Average need-based loan:* Freshmen: $3414.

Undergraduates: $4513. *Parent loans:* $77,726,042 (77% need-based, 23% non-need-based). *Programs:* Federal Direct (Subsidized and Unsubsidized Stafford, PLUS), Perkins, college/university, private loans.

WORK-STUDY *Federal work-study:* Total amount: $1,642,634; 827 jobs averaging $1973. *State or other work-study/employment:* Total amount: $1240 (100% need-based). 1 part-time job averaging $1240.

ATHLETIC AWARDS Total amount: $11,199,582 (40% need-based, 60% non-need-based).

APPLYING FOR FINANCIAL AID *Required financial aid form:* FAFSA. *Financial aid deadline (priority):* 2/15. *Notification date:* Continuous.

CONTACT Ms. Anna Griswold, Assistant Vice Provost for Student Aid, Penn State University Park, 311 Shields Building, University Park, PA 16802, 814-863-0507. *Fax:* 814-863-0322. *E-mail:* amg5@psu.edu.

PENNSYLVANIA COLLEGE OF ART & DESIGN
Lancaster, PA

CONTACT J. David Hershey, Registrar/Director of Financial Aid, Pennsylvania College of Art & Design, 204 North Prince Street, PO Box 59, Lancaster, PA 17608-0059, 717-396-7833 Ext. 13. *Fax:* 717-396-1339. *E-mail:* finaid@pcad.edu.

PENNSYLVANIA COLLEGE OF TECHNOLOGY
Williamsport, PA

Tuition & fees (PA res): $12,480   Average undergraduate aid package: $13,348

ABOUT THE INSTITUTION State-related, coed. 114 undergraduate majors. Federal methodology is used as a basis for awarding need-based institutional aid.

UNDERGRADUATE EXPENSES for 2009–10 *Tuition, state resident:* full-time $10,500; part-time $416 per credit hour. *Tuition, nonresident:* full-time $13,650; part-time $521 per credit hour. *Required fees:* full-time $1980. Full-time tuition and fees vary according to course load and program. Part-time tuition and fees vary according to course load and program. *College room and board:* $8350. *Room only:* $5350. Room and board charges vary according to board plan, housing facility, and location. *Payment plan:* Deferred payment.

FRESHMAN FINANCIAL AID (Fall 2008) 1,419 applied for aid; of those 78% were deemed to have need. 100% of freshmen with need received aid.

UNDERGRADUATE FINANCIAL AID (Fall 2008) 6,510 applied for aid; of those 92% were deemed to have need. 100% of undergraduates with need received aid. *Average percent of need met:* 78% (excluding resources awarded to replace EFC). *Average financial aid package:* $13,348 (excluding resources awarded to replace EFC).

GIFT AID (NEED-BASED) *Receiving aid:* Freshmen: 78% (1,101); all full-time undergraduates: 92% (5,960). *Average award:* Undergraduates: $2666. *Scholarships, grants, and awards:* Federal Pell, FSEOG, state, private, college/university gift aid from institutional funds.

GIFT AID (NON-NEED-BASED) *Total amount:* $24,362,230 (29% federal, 32% state, 2% institutional, 37% external sources). *Tuition waivers:* Full or partial for employees or children of employees.

LOANS *Student loans:* $48,410,469 (100% non-need-based). *Parent loans:* $9,061,704 (100% non-need-based). *Programs:* FFEL (Subsidized and Unsubsidized Stafford, PLUS).

WORK-STUDY *Federal work-study:* Total amount: $304,224; 223 jobs averaging $1364. *State or other work-study/employment:* Total amount: $650,203 (100% non-need-based). 392 part-time jobs averaging $1659.

APPLYING FOR FINANCIAL AID *Required financial aid forms:* FAFSA, institution's own form. *Financial aid deadline (priority):* 4/1. *Notification date:* Continuous beginning 6/1. Students must reply within 2 weeks of notification.

CONTACT Candace Baran, Director of Financial Aid, Pennsylvania College of Technology, One College Avenue, Williamsport, PA 17701, 570-326-4766 or toll-free 800-367-9222 (in-state). *Fax:* 570-321-5552. *E-mail:* cbaran@pct.edu.

PEPPERDINE UNIVERSITY
Malibu, CA

Tuition & fees: $37,850   Average undergraduate aid package: $34,721

ABOUT THE INSTITUTION Independent religious, coed. 47 undergraduate majors. Federal methodology is used as a basis for awarding need-based institutional aid.

UNDERGRADUATE EXPENSES for 2009–10 *Comprehensive fee:* $48,750 includes full-time tuition ($37,730), mandatory fees ($120), and room and board ($10,900). *College room only:* $8380. Room and board charges vary according to board plan and housing facility. *Part-time tuition:* $1170 per credit hour. *Payment plan:* Installment.

FRESHMAN FINANCIAL AID (Fall 2009, est.) 559 applied for aid; of those 83% were deemed to have need. 100% of freshmen with need received aid; of those 32% had need fully met. *Average percent of need met:* 87% (excluding resources awarded to replace EFC). *Average financial aid package:* $34,936 (excluding resources awarded to replace EFC). 11% of all full-time freshmen had no need and received non-need-based gift aid.

UNDERGRADUATE FINANCIAL AID (Fall 2009, est.) 1,888 applied for aid; of those 85% were deemed to have need. 100% of undergraduates with need received aid; of those 33% had need fully met. *Average percent of need met:* 85% (excluding resources awarded to replace EFC). *Average financial aid package:* $34,721 (excluding resources awarded to replace EFC). 18% of all full-time undergraduates had no need and received non-need-based gift aid.

GIFT AID (NEED-BASED) *Total amount:* $36,302,954 (10% federal, 8% state, 80% institutional, 2% external sources). *Receiving aid:* Freshmen: 52% (397); all full-time undergraduates: 48% (1,458). *Average award:* Freshmen: $28,952; Undergraduates: $27,829. *Scholarships, grants, and awards:* Federal Pell, FSEOG, state, private, college/university gift aid from institutional funds, United Negro College Fund, Academic Competitiveness Grants, National SMART Grants.

GIFT AID (NON-NEED-BASED) *Total amount:* $18,444,674 (97% institutional, 3% external sources). *Receiving aid:* Freshmen: 25% (188). Undergraduates: 18% (549). *Average award:* Freshmen: $21,015. Undergraduates: $16,964. *Tuition waivers:* Full or partial for employees or children of employees.

LOANS *Student loans:* $15,355,222 (69% need-based, 31% non-need-based), 58% of past graduating class borrowed through all loan programs. *Average indebtedness per student:* $28,299. *Average need-based loan:* Freshmen: $3572. Undergraduates: $4823. *Parent loans:* $16,805,802 (61% need-based, 39% non-need-based). *Programs:* FFEL (Subsidized and Unsubsidized Stafford, PLUS), Perkins, college/university.

WORK-STUDY *Federal work-study:* Total amount: $875,000; jobs available. *State or other work-study/employment:* Total amount: $720,457 (17% need-based, 83% non-need-based). Part-time jobs available.

ATHLETIC AWARDS Total amount: $4,431,656 (17% need-based, 83% non-need-based).

APPLYING FOR FINANCIAL AID *Required financial aid form:* FAFSA. *Financial aid deadline:* 2/15. *Notification date:* 4/15.

CONTACT Janet Lockhart, Director of Financial Assistance, Pepperdine University, 24255 Pacific Coast Highway, Malibu, CA 90263-4301, 310-506-4301. *Fax:* 310-506-4746. *E-mail:* finaid2@pepperdine.edu.

PERELANDRA COLLEGE
La Mesa, CA

CONTACT Financial Aid Office, Perelandra College, 8697-C La Mesa Boulevard, PMB 21, La Mesa, CA 91941, 619-677-3308.

PERU STATE COLLEGE
Peru, NE

CONTACT Diana Lind, Director of Financial Aid, Peru State College, PO Box 10, Peru, NE 68421, 402-872-2228 or toll-free 800-742-4412 (in-state). *Fax:* 402-872-2419. *E-mail:* finaid@oakmail.peru.edu.

PFEIFFER UNIVERSITY
Misenheimer, NC

Tuition & fees: $19,040   Average undergraduate aid package: $16,246

ABOUT THE INSTITUTION Independent United Methodist, coed. *Awards:* bachelor's and master's degrees. 45 undergraduate majors. *Total enrollment:* 2,019. Undergraduates: 1,089. Institutional methodology is used as a basis for awarding need-based institutional aid.

UNDERGRADUATE EXPENSES for 2009–10 *Application fee:* $25. *Comprehensive fee:* $26,838 includes full-time tuition ($19,040) and room and board ($7798). *College room only:* $4658. Full-time tuition and fees vary according to course load. Room and board charges vary according to housing facility. *Part-time tuition:* $435 per credit hour. Part-time tuition and fees vary according to course load. *Payment plan:* Installment.

FRESHMAN FINANCIAL AID (Fall 2009, est.) 185 applied for aid; of those 83% were deemed to have need. 100% of freshmen with need received aid; of those 16% had need fully met. *Average percent of need met:* 76% (excluding resources awarded to replace EFC). *Average financial aid package:* $17,163 (excluding resources awarded to replace EFC).

UNDERGRADUATE FINANCIAL AID (Fall 2009, est.) 841 applied for aid; of those 85% were deemed to have need. 100% of undergraduates with need received aid; of those 15% had need fully met. *Average percent of need met:* 78% (excluding resources awarded to replace EFC). *Average financial aid package:* $16,246 (excluding resources awarded to replace EFC).

GIFT AID (NEED-BASED) *Total amount:* $8,000,022 (23% federal, 26% state, 45% institutional, 6% external sources). *Receiving aid:* Freshmen: 154; all full-time undergraduates: 713. *Average award:* Freshmen: $14,005; Undergraduates: $12,513. *Scholarships, grants, and awards:* Federal Pell, FSEOG, state, private, college/university gift aid from institutional funds, United Negro College Fund.

GIFT AID (NON-NEED-BASED) *Total amount:* $1,006,009 (25% state, 60% institutional, 15% external sources). *Receiving aid:* Freshmen: 21. Undergraduates: 67. *Average award:* Freshmen: $8743. Undergraduates: $6808. *Scholarships, grants, and awards by category:* Academic interests/achievement: general academic interests/achievements. Creative arts/performance: music. Special achievements/activities: leadership, religious involvement. Special characteristics: children and siblings of alumni, children of educators, children of faculty/staff. *Tuition waivers:* Full or partial for employees or children of employees. *ROTC:* Army cooperative.

LOANS *Student loans:* $5,958,175 (65% need-based, 35% non-need-based). 73% of past graduating class borrowed through all loan programs. *Average indebtedness per student:* $23,000. *Average need-based loan:* Freshmen: $3158. Undergraduates: $3953. *Parent loans:* $707,314 (29% need-based, 71% non-need-based). *Programs:* FFEL (Subsidized and Unsubsidized Stafford, PLUS), Perkins, state, college/university.

WORK-STUDY *Federal work-study:* Total amount: $256,396; jobs available.

ATHLETIC AWARDS Total amount: $1,416,173 (51% need-based, 49% non-need-based).

APPLYING FOR FINANCIAL AID *Required financial aid forms:* FAFSA, state aid form, noncustodial (divorced/separated) parent's statement. *Financial aid deadline (priority):* 4/15. *Notification date:* Continuous beginning 3/1.

CONTACT Amy Brown, Director of Financial Aid, Pfeiffer University, PO Box 960, Misenheimer, NC 28109, 704-463-1360 Ext. 3046 or toll-free 800-338-2060. *Fax:* 704-463-1363. *E-mail:* amy.brown@pfeiffer.edu.

PHILADELPHIA BIBLICAL UNIVERSITY
Langhorne, PA

Tuition & fees: $19,997	Average undergraduate aid package: $14,138

ABOUT THE INSTITUTION Independent nondenominational, coed. 11 undergraduate majors. Federal methodology is used as a basis for awarding need-based institutional aid.

UNDERGRADUATE EXPENSES for 2010–11 *Comprehensive fee:* $28,047 includes full-time tuition ($19,797), mandatory fees ($200), and room and board ($8050). *College room only:* $4300. Full-time tuition and fees vary according to course load, location, and program. Room and board charges vary according to board plan, housing facility, and location. *Part-time tuition:* $587 per credit hour. Part-time tuition and fees vary according to course load, location, and program. *Payment plan:* Installment.

FRESHMAN FINANCIAL AID (Fall 2009, est.) 175 applied for aid; of those 93% were deemed to have need. 99% of freshmen with need received aid; of those 16% had need fully met. *Average percent of need met:* 68% (excluding resources awarded to replace EFC). *Average financial aid package:* $13,544 (excluding resources awarded to replace EFC).

UNDERGRADUATE FINANCIAL AID (Fall 2009, est.) 884 applied for aid; of those 93% were deemed to have need. 99% of undergraduates with need received aid; of those 9% had need fully met. *Average percent of need met:*

66% (excluding resources awarded to replace EFC). *Average financial aid package:* $14,138 (excluding resources awarded to replace EFC).

GIFT AID (NEED-BASED) *Total amount:* $7,797,496 (22% federal, 11% state, 65% institutional, 2% external sources). *Receiving aid:* Freshmen: 83% (159); all full-time undergraduates: 79% (775). *Average award:* Freshmen: $10,419; Undergraduates: $10,131. *Scholarships, grants, and awards:* Federal Pell, FSEOG, state, private, college/university gift aid from institutional funds.

GIFT AID (NON-NEED-BASED) *Total amount:* $375,844 (2% federal, 96% institutional, 2% external sources). *Receiving aid:* Freshmen: 7% (14). Undergraduates: 4% (35). *Scholarships, grants, and awards by category:* Academic interests/achievement: 642 awards ($3,777,639 total): general academic interests/achievements. Creative arts/performance: 46 awards ($75,400 total): music. Special achievements/activities: 27 awards ($40,150 total): general special achievements/activities. Special characteristics: 145 awards ($52,583 total): children of faculty/staff, relatives of clergy. *Tuition waivers:* Full or partial for employees or children of employees.

LOANS *Student loans:* $6,452,316 (84% need-based, 16% non-need-based). 97% of past graduating class borrowed through all loan programs. *Average indebtedness per student:* $28,214. *Average need-based loan:* Freshmen: $3862. Undergraduates: $4955. *Parent loans:* $1,256,787 (38% need-based, 62% non-need-based). *Programs:* Federal Direct (Subsidized and Unsubsidized Stafford, PLUS), FFEL (Subsidized and Unsubsidized Stafford, PLUS), state.

WORK-STUDY *Federal work-study:* Total amount: $116,530; 133 jobs averaging $876.

APPLYING FOR FINANCIAL AID *Required financial aid form:* FAFSA. *Financial aid deadline:* Continuous. *Notification date:* Continuous. Students must reply by 2/15 or within 2 weeks of notification.

CONTACT Ms. Raye Thompson, Director of Financial Aid, Philadelphia Biblical University, 200 Manor Avenue, Langhorne, PA 19047-2990, 215-702-4243 or toll-free 800-366-0049. *Fax:* 215-702-4248. *E-mail:* rthompson@pbu.edu.

PHILADELPHIA UNIVERSITY
Philadelphia, PA

Tuition & fees: $27,498	Average undergraduate aid package: $21,048

ABOUT THE INSTITUTION Independent, coed. 32 undergraduate majors. Federal methodology is used as a basis for awarding need-based institutional aid.

UNDERGRADUATE EXPENSES for 2009–10 *Comprehensive fee:* $36,680 includes full-time tuition ($27,428), mandatory fees ($70), and room and board ($9182). *College room only:* $4540. Full-time tuition and fees vary according to degree level and program. Room and board charges vary according to board plan and housing facility. *Part-time tuition:* $486 per credit hour. Part-time tuition and fees vary according to class time, course load, degree level, and program. *Payment plans:* Installment, deferred payment.

FRESHMAN FINANCIAL AID (Fall 2009, est.) 653 applied for aid; of those 86% were deemed to have need. 100% of freshmen with need received aid; of those 12% had need fully met. *Average percent of need met:* 76% (excluding resources awarded to replace EFC). *Average financial aid package:* $22,240 (excluding resources awarded to replace EFC). 22% of all full-time freshmen had no need and received non-need-based gift aid.

UNDERGRADUATE FINANCIAL AID (Fall 2009, est.) 2,216 applied for aid; of those 88% were deemed to have need. 100% of undergraduates with need received aid; of those 9% had need fully met. *Average percent of need met:* 72% (excluding resources awarded to replace EFC). *Average financial aid package:* $21,048 (excluding resources awarded to replace EFC). 27% of all full-time undergraduates had no need and received non-need-based gift aid.

GIFT AID (NEED-BASED) *Total amount:* $25,518,278 (13% federal, 6% state, 80% institutional, 1% external sources). *Receiving aid:* Freshmen: 78% (557); all full-time undergraduates: 71% (1,909). *Average award:* Freshmen: $16,233; Undergraduates: $13,751. *Scholarships, grants, and awards:* Federal Pell, FSEOG, state, private, college/university gift aid from institutional funds, gift scholarships from outside sources (non-endowed) for which university chooses recipients.

GIFT AID (NON-NEED-BASED) *Total amount:* $4,179,364 (98% institutional, 2% external sources). *Receiving aid:* Freshmen: 7% (51). Undergraduates: 4% (118). *Average award:* Freshmen: $6542. Undergraduates: $5137. *Scholarships, grants, and awards by category:* Academic interests/achievement: engineering/technologies, general academic interests/achievements. *Tuition waivers:* Full or partial for employees or children of employees.

Philadelphia University

LOANS *Student loans:* $21,349,256 (72% need-based, 28% non-need-based). 81% of past graduating class borrowed through all loan programs. *Average indebtedness per student:* $32,037. *Average need-based loan:* Freshmen: $4011. Undergraduates: $5277. *Parent loans:* $7,661,965 (36% need-based, 64% non-need-based). *Programs:* Federal Direct (Subsidized and Unsubsidized Stafford, PLUS), Perkins, private loans.

WORK-STUDY *Federal work-study:* Total amount: $1,956,800; jobs available. *State or other work-study/employment:* Total amount: $502,810 (88% need-based, 12% non-need-based). Part-time jobs available.

ATHLETIC AWARDS Total amount: $2,216,124 (42% need-based, 58% non-need-based).

APPLYING FOR FINANCIAL AID *Required financial aid form:* FAFSA. *Financial aid deadline:* 4/15. *Notification date:* Continuous beginning 2/10. Students must reply by 5/1.

CONTACT Ms. Lisa J. Cooper, Director of Financial Aid, Philadelphia University, School House Lane and Henry Avenue, Philadelphia, PA 19144-5497, 215-951-2940. *Fax:* 215-951-2907. *E-mail:* cooperl@philau.edu.

PHILANDER SMITH COLLEGE
Little Rock, AR

Tuition & fees: N/R	Average undergraduate aid package: $10,770

ABOUT THE INSTITUTION Independent United Methodist, coed. 19 undergraduate majors. Federal methodology is used as a basis for awarding need-based institutional aid.

FRESHMAN FINANCIAL AID (Fall 2009, est.) 126 applied for aid; of those 97% were deemed to have need. 100% of freshmen with need received aid; of those 12% had need fully met. *Average percent of need met:* 66% (excluding resources awarded to replace EFC). *Average financial aid package:* $11,791 (excluding resources awarded to replace EFC). 8% of all full-time freshmen had no need and received non-need-based gift aid.

UNDERGRADUATE FINANCIAL AID (Fall 2009, est.) 563 applied for aid; of those 97% were deemed to have need. 100% of undergraduates with need received aid; of those 10% had need fully met. *Average percent of need met:* 56% (excluding resources awarded to replace EFC). *Average financial aid package:* $10,770 (excluding resources awarded to replace EFC). 4% of all full-time undergraduates had no need and received non-need-based gift aid.

GIFT AID (NEED-BASED) *Total amount:* $4,491,189 (54% federal, 3% state, 33% institutional, 10% external sources). *Receiving aid:* Freshmen: 84% (117); all full-time undergraduates: 88% (520). *Average award:* Freshmen: $9414; Undergraduates: $7537. *Scholarships, grants, and awards:* Federal Pell, FSEOG, state, private, college/university gift aid from institutional funds, United Negro College Fund.

GIFT AID (NON-NEED-BASED) *Receiving aid:* Freshmen: 8% (11). Undergraduates: 6% (38). *Average award:* Freshmen: $10,451. Undergraduates: $9194. *Scholarships, grants, and awards by category:* Academic interests/achievement: general academic interests/achievements. Creative arts/performance: 23 awards ($40,000 total): music. Special achievements/activities: general special achievements/activities.

LOANS *Student loans:* $4,816,690 (93% need-based, 7% non-need-based). 95% of past graduating class borrowed through all loan programs. *Average indebtedness per student:* $36,784. *Average need-based loan:* Freshmen: $3101. Undergraduates: $3723. *Parent loans:* $339,018 (100% non-need-based). *Programs:* Federal Direct (Subsidized and Unsubsidized Stafford, PLUS), state.

WORK-STUDY *Federal work-study:* Total amount: $152,692; 96 jobs averaging $2300.

ATHLETIC AWARDS Total amount: $92,688 (100% need-based).

APPLYING FOR FINANCIAL AID *Required financial aid forms:* FAFSA, institution's own form. *Financial aid deadline (priority):* 3/1. *Notification date:* Continuous. Students must reply within 2 weeks of notification.

CONTACT David D. Page, Director of Financial Aid, Philander Smith College, 900 Daisy Bates Drive, Little Rock, AR 72202-3799, 501-370-5270 or toll-free 800-446-6772.

PIEDMONT BAPTIST COLLEGE AND GRADUATE SCHOOL
Winston-Salem, NC

Tuition & fees: $11,170	Average undergraduate aid package: N/A

ABOUT THE INSTITUTION Independent Baptist, coed. 15 undergraduate majors. Federal methodology is used as a basis for awarding need-based institutional aid.

UNDERGRADUATE EXPENSES for 2009-10 *Comprehensive fee:* $16,930 includes full-time tuition ($10,380), mandatory fees ($790), and room and board ($5760). Full-time tuition and fees vary according to course load, degree level, location, and program. *Part-time tuition:* $450 per credit hour. *Part-time fees:* $220 per term. Part-time tuition and fees vary according to course load, degree level, location, and program. *Payment plan:* Installment.

GIFT AID (NEED-BASED) *Scholarships, grants, and awards:* Federal Pell, FSEOG.

GIFT AID (NON-NEED-BASED) *Scholarships, grants, and awards by category:* Academic interests/achievement: general academic interests/achievements. *Special characteristics:* children of faculty/staff, relatives of clergy, spouses of current students, veterans. *Tuition waivers:* Full or partial for employees or children of employees.

LOANS *Programs:* FFEL (Subsidized and Unsubsidized Stafford, PLUS), Signature Loans.

APPLYING FOR FINANCIAL AID *Required financial aid forms:* FAFSA, institution's own form. *Financial aid deadline:* 8/31 (priority: 6/1).

CONTACT Mrs. Sherry Melton, Director of Financial Aid, Piedmont Baptist College and Graduate School, 420 South Broad Street, Winston-Salem, NC 27101-5197, 336-714-7933 or toll-free 800-937-5097. *Fax:* 336-725-5522. *E-mail:* meltons@pbc.edu.

PIEDMONT COLLEGE
Demorest, GA

Tuition & fees: $18,000	Average undergraduate aid package: $18,780

ABOUT THE INSTITUTION Independent religious, coed. 32 undergraduate majors. Both federal and institutional methodology are used as a basis for awarding need-based institutional aid.

UNDERGRADUATE EXPENSES for 2010-11 *Tuition:* full-time $18,000; part-time $750 per semester hour. Full-time tuition and fees vary according to course load, degree level, location, and program. Part-time tuition and fees vary according to course load, degree level, location, and program. *Payment plan:* Installment.

FRESHMAN FINANCIAL AID (Fall 2009, est.) 167 applied for aid; of those 78% were deemed to have need. 98% of freshmen with need received aid; of those 34% had need fully met. *Average percent of need met:* 52% (excluding resources awarded to replace EFC). *Average financial aid package:* $18,230 (excluding resources awarded to replace EFC). 10% of all full-time freshmen had no need and received non-need-based gift aid.

UNDERGRADUATE FINANCIAL AID (Fall 2009, est.) 870 applied for aid; of those 77% were deemed to have need. 98% of undergraduates with need received aid; of those 30% had need fully met. *Average percent of need met:* 55% (excluding resources awarded to replace EFC). *Average financial aid package:* $18,780 (excluding resources awarded to replace EFC). 8% of all full-time undergraduates had no need and received non-need-based gift aid.

GIFT AID (NEED-BASED) *Total amount:* $3,891,333 (79% federal, 20% institutional, 1% external sources). *Receiving aid:* Freshmen: 17% (37); all full-time undergraduates: 19% (209). *Average award:* Freshmen: $1090; Undergraduates: $2460. *Scholarships, grants, and awards:* Federal Pell, FSEOG, state, private, college/university gift aid from institutional funds.

GIFT AID (NON-NEED-BASED) *Total amount:* $6,909,970 (13% federal, 35% state, 50% institutional, 2% external sources). *Receiving aid:* Freshmen: 57% (122). Undergraduates: 56% (622). *Average award:* Freshmen: $9480. Undergraduates: $8730. *Scholarships, grants, and awards by category:* Academic interests/achievement: 659 awards ($2,978,334 total): biological sciences, business, education, English, foreign languages, general academic interests/achievements, health fields, humanities, mathematics, premedicine, religion/biblical studies, social sciences. Creative arts/performance: 63 awards

---

($72,346 total): art/fine arts, music, theater/drama. *Special achievements/activities:* 240 awards ($896,438 total): leadership. *Special characteristics:* 254 awards ($1,956,884 total): adult students, children of faculty/staff, international students, out-of-state students. *Tuition waivers:* Full or partial for employees or children of employees.

LOANS *Student loans:* $7,396,593 (49% need-based, 51% non-need-based). 77% of past graduating class borrowed through all loan programs. *Average indebtedness per student:* $16,910. *Average need-based loan:* Freshmen: $3240. Undergraduates: $4370. *Parent loans:* $894,718 (100% non-need-based). *Programs:* Federal Direct (Subsidized and Unsubsidized Stafford, PLUS).

WORK-STUDY *Federal work-study:* Total amount: $171,490; 64 jobs averaging $3187. *State or other work-study/employment:* Total amount: $761,000 (21% need-based, 79% non-need-based). 230 part-time jobs averaging $2552.

APPLYING FOR FINANCIAL AID *Required financial aid forms:* FAFSA, state aid form. *Financial aid deadline (priority):* 3/1. *Notification date:* Continuous. Students must reply within 2 weeks of notification.

CONTACT Mrs. Kim Lovell, Director of Financial Aid, Piedmont College, PO Box 10, Demorest, GA 30535-0010, 706-778-3000 Ext. 1191 or toll-free 800-277-7020. *Fax:* 706-778-0708. *E-mail:* klovell@piedmont.edu.

PIKEVILLE COLLEGE
Pikeville, KY

Tuition & fees: $14,535	Average undergraduate aid package: $14,677

ABOUT THE INSTITUTION Independent religious, coed. 18 undergraduate majors. Federal methodology is used as a basis for awarding need-based institutional aid.

UNDERGRADUATE EXPENSES for 2009–10 *Comprehensive fee:* $20,535 includes full-time tuition ($14,535) and room and board ($6000). Full-time tuition and fees vary according to course load. *Part-time tuition:* $606 per credit hour. *Payment plan:* Installment.

FRESHMAN FINANCIAL AID (Fall 2009, est.) 185 applied for aid; of those 99% were deemed to have need. 100% of freshmen with need received aid; of those 74% had need fully met. *Average percent of need met:* 93% (excluding resources awarded to replace EFC). *Average financial aid package:* $15,558 (excluding resources awarded to replace EFC).

UNDERGRADUATE FINANCIAL AID (Fall 2009, est.) 597 applied for aid; of those 97% were deemed to have need. 100% of undergraduates with need received aid; of those 85% had need fully met. *Average percent of need met:* 92% (excluding resources awarded to replace EFC). *Average financial aid package:* $14,677 (excluding resources awarded to replace EFC).

GIFT AID (NEED-BASED) *Total amount:* $5,663,673 (33% federal, 31% state, 34% institutional, 2% external sources). *Receiving aid:* Freshmen: 97% (179); all full-time undergraduates: 92% (573). *Average award:* Freshmen: $12,894; Undergraduates: $11,834. *Scholarships, grants, and awards:* Federal Pell, FSEOG, state, private, college/university gift aid from institutional funds.

GIFT AID (NON-NEED-BASED) *Tuition waivers:* Full or partial for employees or children of employees, senior citizens.

LOANS *Student loans:* $3,004,979 (100% need-based). 76% of past graduating class borrowed through all loan programs. *Average indebtedness per student:* $18,103. *Average need-based loan:* Freshmen: $3457. Undergraduates: $4202. *Parent loans:* $127,761 (100% need-based). *Programs:* FFEL (Subsidized and Unsubsidized Stafford, PLUS), Perkins, college/university.

WORK-STUDY *Federal work-study:* Total amount: $366,200; 193 jobs averaging $1895.

ATHLETIC AWARDS Total amount: $1,311,806 (100% need-based).

APPLYING FOR FINANCIAL AID *Required financial aid forms:* FAFSA, institution's own form. *Financial aid deadline (priority):* 3/15. *Notification date:* Continuous. Students must reply by 5/1.

CONTACT Judy Vance Bradley, Assistant Dean of Student Financial Services, Pikeville College, 147 Sycamore Street, Pikeville, KY 41501, 606-218-5253 or toll-free 866-232-7700. *Fax:* 606-218-5255. *E-mail:* jbradley@pc.edu.

PINE MANOR COLLEGE
Chestnut Hill, MA

CONTACT Adrienne Hynek, Director of Financial Aid, Pine Manor College, 400 Heath Street, Chestnut Hill, MA 02467, 617-731-7053 or toll-free 800-762-1357. *Fax:* 617-731-7102. *E-mail:* hynekadrienne@pmc.edu.

PIONEER PACIFIC COLLEGE
Clackamas, OR

CONTACT Financial Aid Office, Pioneer Pacific College, 8800 SE Sunnyside Road, Clackamas, OR 97015, toll-free 866-772-4636 (out-of-state).

PIONEER PACIFIC COLLEGE
Wilsonville, OR

CONTACT Stacey Maurer, Financial Aid Director, Pioneer Pacific College, 25195 Southwest Parkway Avenue, Wilsonville, OR 97070, 503-682-3903 or toll-free 866-PPC-INFO (in-state). *Fax:* 503-682-1514. *E-mail:* smaurer@pioneerpacificcollege.com.

PIONEER PACIFIC COLLEGE–EUGENE/SPRINGFIELD BRANCH
Springfield, OR

CONTACT Financial Aid Office, Pioneer Pacific College–Eugene/Springfield Branch, 3800 Sports Way, Springfield, OR 97477, toll-free 866-772-4636 (out-of-state).

PITTSBURG STATE UNIVERSITY
Pittsburg, KS

Tuition & fees (KS res): $4592	Average undergraduate aid package: $9900

ABOUT THE INSTITUTION State-supported, coed. 106 undergraduate majors. Federal methodology is used as a basis for awarding need-based institutional aid.

UNDERGRADUATE EXPENSES for 2009–10 *Tuition, state resident:* full-time $3652; part-time $122 per credit hour. *Tuition, nonresident:* full-time $12,176; part-time $406 per credit hour. *Required fees:* full-time $940; $43 per credit hour. Part-time tuition and fees vary according to course load. *College room and board:* $5744. Room and board charges vary according to board plan and housing facility. *Payment plan:* Installment.

GIFT AID (NEED-BASED) *Total amount:* $13,236,009 (73% federal, 6% state, 11% institutional, 10% external sources). *Receiving aid:* Freshmen: 41% (405); all full-time undergraduates: 40% (2,208). *Average award:* Freshmen: $4595; Undergraduates: $4525. *Scholarships, grants, and awards:* Federal Pell, FSEOG, state, private, college/university gift aid from institutional funds.

GIFT AID (NON-NEED-BASED) *Total amount:* $2,348,459 (2% federal, 3% state, 55% institutional, 40% external sources). *Receiving aid:* Freshmen: 34% (336). Undergraduates: 22% (1,237). *Average award:* Freshmen: $2548. Undergraduates: $2450. *Scholarships, grants, and awards by category:* *Academic interests/achievement:* biological sciences, business, communication, computer science, education, engineering/technologies, English, foreign languages, general academic interests/achievements, health fields, home economics, mathematics, military science, physical sciences, social sciences. *Creative arts/performance:* music. *Special characteristics:* children and siblings of alumni, general special characteristics. *Tuition waivers:* Full or partial for employees or children of employees.

LOANS *Student loans:* $22,559,586 (58% need-based, 42% non-need-based). 67% of past graduating class borrowed through all loan programs. *Average indebtedness per student:* $18,516. *Average need-based loan:* Freshmen: $8230. Undergraduates: $3889. *Parent loans:* $947,734 (2% need-based, 98% non-need-based). *Programs:* Federal Direct (Subsidized and Unsubsidized Stafford, PLUS), Perkins, Federal Nursing, college/university.

ATHLETIC AWARDS Total amount: $1,254,982 (56% need-based, 44% non-need-based).

APPLYING FOR FINANCIAL AID *Required financial aid form:* FAFSA. *Financial aid deadline (priority):* 3/1. *Notification date:* Continuous beginning 3/1. Students must reply within 2 weeks of notification.

CONTACT Tammy Higgins, Director of Student Financial Assistance, Pittsburg State University, 1701 South Broadway, Pittsburg, KS 66762-5880, 620-235-4238 or toll-free 800-854-7488 Ext. 1. *Fax:* 620-235-4078. *E-mail:* thiggins@pittstate.edu.

PITZER COLLEGE
Claremont, CA

Tuition & fees: $39,330	Average undergraduate aid package: $36,498

ABOUT THE INSTITUTION Independent, coed. 52 undergraduate majors. Both federal and institutional methodology are used as a basis for awarding need-based institutional aid.

UNDERGRADUATE EXPENSES for 2009–10 *Comprehensive fee:* $50,770 includes full-time tuition ($35,840), mandatory fees ($3490), and room and board ($11,440). *College room only:* $7240. Full-time tuition and fees vary according to course load. Room and board charges vary according to board plan. *Part-time tuition:* $4480 per course. Part-time tuition and fees vary according to course load. *Payment plans:* Installment, deferred payment.

FRESHMAN FINANCIAL AID (Fall 2009, est.) 130 applied for aid; of those 80% were deemed to have need. 100% of freshmen with need received aid; of those 100% had need fully met. *Average percent of need met:* 100% (excluding resources awarded to replace EFC). *Average financial aid package:* $37,361 (excluding resources awarded to replace EFC). 4% of all full-time freshmen had no need and received non-need-based gift aid.

UNDERGRADUATE FINANCIAL AID (Fall 2009, est.) 430 applied for aid; of those 93% were deemed to have need. 100% of undergraduates with need received aid; of those 100% had need fully met. *Average percent of need met:* 100% (excluding resources awarded to replace EFC). *Average financial aid package:* $36,498 (excluding resources awarded to replace EFC). 5% of all full-time undergraduates had no need and received non-need-based gift aid.

GIFT AID (NEED-BASED) *Total amount:* $12,875,715 (7% federal, 8% state, 82% institutional, 3% external sources). *Receiving aid:* Freshmen: 42% (104); all full-time undergraduates: 37% (364). *Average award:* Freshmen: $32,831; Undergraduates: $33,872. *Scholarships, grants, and awards:* Federal Pell, FSEOG, state, private, college/university gift aid from institutional funds.

GIFT AID (NON-NEED-BASED) *Total amount:* $348,902 (70% institutional, 30% external sources). *Average award:* Freshmen: $5000. Undergraduates: $5000. *Scholarships, grants, and awards by category:* Academic interests/achievement: general academic interests/achievements. *Special achievements/activities:* community service, leadership. *Tuition waivers:* Full or partial for employees or children of employees.

LOANS *Student loans:* $2,510,138 (56% need-based, 44% non-need-based). 45% of past graduating class borrowed through all loan programs. *Average indebtedness per student:* $20,448. *Average need-based loan:* Freshmen: $2614. Undergraduates: $3647. *Parent loans:* $768,836 (100% non-need-based). *Programs:* Federal Direct (Subsidized and Unsubsidized Stafford, PLUS), Perkins, college/university.

WORK-STUDY *Federal work-study:* Total amount: $908,840; 355 jobs averaging $2542.

APPLYING FOR FINANCIAL AID *Required financial aid forms:* FAFSA, CSS Financial Aid PROFILE, state aid form, business/farm supplement. *Financial aid deadline:* 2/1. *Notification date:* 4/1. Students must reply by 5/1.

CONTACT Margaret Carothers, Director of Financial Aid, Pitzer College, 1050 North Mills Avenue, Claremont, CA 91711-6101, 909-621-8208 or toll-free 800-748-9371. *Fax:* 909-607-1205. *E-mail:* margaret_carothers@pitzer.edu.

PLATT COLLEGE SAN DIEGO
San Diego, CA

CONTACT Ms. Alice Diamond, Director of Financial Aid, Platt College San Diego, 6250 El Cajon Boulevard, San Diego, CA 92115-3919, 619-265-0107 or toll-free 866-752-8826.

PLYMOUTH STATE UNIVERSITY
Plymouth, NH

Tuition & fees (NH res): $8944	Average undergraduate aid package: $9403

ABOUT THE INSTITUTION State-supported, coed. 46 undergraduate majors. Federal methodology is used as a basis for awarding need-based institutional aid.

UNDERGRADUATE EXPENSES for 2009–10 *Tuition, state resident:* full-time $7000; part-time $292 per credit hour. *Tuition, nonresident:* full-time $15,170; part-time $632 per credit hour. *Required fees:* full-time $1944; $84 per credit hour. Full-time tuition and fees vary according to reciprocity agreements. Part-time tuition and fees vary according to course load and reciprocity agreements. *College room and board:* $8594; *Room only:* $5996. Room and board charges vary according to board plan and housing facility. *Payment plan:* Installment.

FRESHMAN FINANCIAL AID (Fall 2009, est.) 863 applied for aid; of those 69% were deemed to have need. 99% of freshmen with need received aid; of those 23% had need fully met. *Average percent of need met:* 62% (excluding resources awarded to replace EFC). *Average financial aid package:* $9285 (excluding resources awarded to replace EFC). 10% of all full-time freshmen had no need and received non-need-based gift aid.

UNDERGRADUATE FINANCIAL AID (Fall 2009, est.) 3,335 applied for aid; of those 73% were deemed to have need. 100% of undergraduates with need received aid; of those 18% had need fully met. *Average percent of need met:* 62% (excluding resources awarded to replace EFC). *Average financial aid package:* $9403 (excluding resources awarded to replace EFC). 8% of all full-time undergraduates had no need and received non-need-based gift aid.

GIFT AID (NEED-BASED) *Total amount:* $9,574,940 (47% federal, 9% state, 44% institutional). *Receiving aid:* Freshmen: 50% (479); all full-time undergraduates: 45% (1,829). *Average award:* Freshmen: $5609; Undergraduates: $5042. *Scholarships, grants, and awards:* Federal Pell, FSEOG, state, private, college/university gift aid from institutional funds.

GIFT AID (NON-NEED-BASED) *Total amount:* $3,193,868 (77% institutional, 23% external sources). *Receiving aid:* Freshmen: 28% (268). Undergraduates: 19% (767). *Average award:* Freshmen: $3077. Undergraduates: $2567. *Scholarships, grants, and awards by category:* Academic interests/achievement: 664 awards ($1,916,528 total): business, communication, education, English, general academic interests/achievements, health fields, mathematics, physical sciences, social sciences. *Creative arts/performance:* 29 awards ($33,500 total): creative writing, dance, music, theater/drama. *Special characteristics:* 85 awards ($251,815 total): children of faculty/staff, international students. *Tuition waivers:* Full or partial for employees or children of employees, senior citizens.

LOANS *Student loans:* $26,277,486 (40% need-based, 60% non-need-based). 82% of past graduating class borrowed through all loan programs. *Average indebtedness per student:* $29,709. *Average need-based loan:* Freshmen: $3295. Undergraduates: $4225. *Parent loans:* $11,718,576 (100% non-need-based). *Programs:* Federal Direct (Subsidized and Unsubsidized Stafford, PLUS), Perkins.

WORK-STUDY *Federal work-study:* Total amount: $3,536,800; 1,737 jobs averaging $2044.

APPLYING FOR FINANCIAL AID *Required financial aid form:* FAFSA. *Financial aid deadline (priority):* 3/1. *Notification date:* Continuous beginning 3/1. Students must reply by 5/1.

CONTACT June Louise Schlabach, Director of Financial Aid, Plymouth State University, 17 High Street, Plymouth, NH 03264-1595, 603-535-2338 or toll-free 800-842-6900. *Fax:* 603-535-2627. *E-mail:* jlschlabach@plymouth.edu.

POINT LOMA NAZARENE UNIVERSITY
San Diego, CA

Tuition & fees: $25,840	Average undergraduate aid package: $18,695

ABOUT THE INSTITUTION Independent Nazarene, coed. *Awards:* bachelor's and master's degrees and post-master's certificates. 59 undergraduate majors. *Total enrollment:* 3,490. Undergraduates: 2,394. Freshmen: 538. Federal methodology is used as a basis for awarding need-based institutional aid.

UNDERGRADUATE EXPENSES for 2009–10 *Application fee:* $50. *Comprehensive fee:* $33,940 includes full-time tuition ($25,300), mandatory fees ($540), and room and board ($8100). *College room only:* $4640. Full-time tuition and fees vary according to course load. Room and board charges vary according to board plan. *Part-time tuition:* $1055 per credit hour. Part-time tuition and fees vary according to course load. *Payment plan:* Installment.

FRESHMAN FINANCIAL AID (Fall 2009, est.) 447 applied for aid; of those 77% were deemed to have need. 99% of freshmen with need received aid; of those 9% had need fully met. *Average percent of need met:* 65% (excluding resources awarded to replace EFC). *Average financial aid package:* $17,046 (excluding resources awarded to replace EFC). 13% of all full-time freshmen had no need and received non-need-based gift aid.

UNDERGRADUATE FINANCIAL AID (Fall 2009, est.) 1,478 applied for aid; of those 96% were deemed to have need. 100% of undergraduates with need received aid; of those 19% had need fully met. *Average percent of need met:* 68% (excluding resources awarded to replace EFC). *Average financial aid*

package: $18,695 (excluding resources awarded to replace EFC). 19% of all full-time undergraduates had no need and received non-need-based gift aid. **GIFT AID (NEED-BASED)** *Total amount:* $15,568,053 (16% federal, 26% state, 51% institutional, 7% external sources). *Receiving aid:* Freshmen: 55% (292); all full-time undergraduates: 56% (1,254). *Average award:* Freshmen: $13,188; Undergraduates: $13,258. *Scholarships, grants, and awards:* Federal Pell, FSEOG, state, private, college/university gift aid from institutional funds, Federal Nursing.
GIFT AID (NON-NEED-BASED) *Total amount:* $3,943,653 (74% institutional, 26% external sources). *Receiving aid:* Freshmen: 6% (30). Undergraduates: 5% (116). *Average award:* Freshmen: $6472. Undergraduates: $6256. *Scholarships, grants, and awards by category: Academic interests/achievement:* biological sciences, business, communication, education, engineering/technologies, general academic interests/achievements, health fields, home economics, humanities, mathematics, religion/biblical studies, social sciences. *Creative arts/performance:* art/fine arts, debating, music, theater/drama. *Tuition waivers:* Full or partial for employees or children of employees, senior citizens. *ROTC:* Army cooperative, Naval cooperative, Air Force cooperative.
LOANS *Student loans:* $14,908,168 (69% need-based, 31% non-need-based). 87% of past graduating class borrowed through all loan programs. *Average indebtedness per student:* $29,491. *Average need-based loan:* Freshmen: $4226. Undergraduates: $5785. *Parent loans:* $5,717,121 (38% need-based, 62% non-need-based). *Programs:* FFEL (Subsidized and Unsubsidized Stafford, PLUS), Perkins, Federal Nursing, college/university.
WORK-STUDY *Federal work-study:* Total amount: $2,542,371; jobs available.
ATHLETIC AWARDS Total amount: $1,744,927 (37% need-based, 63% non-need-based).
APPLYING FOR FINANCIAL AID *Required financial aid forms:* FAFSA, institution's own form. *Financial aid deadline (priority):* 3/2. *Notification date:* Continuous beginning 3/1.
CONTACT Student Financial Services, Point Loma Nazarene University, 3900 Lomaland Drive, San Diego, CA 92106, 619-849-2538 or toll-free 800-733-7770. *Fax:* 619-849-7078. *E-mail:* sfs@pointloma.edu.

POINT PARK UNIVERSITY
Pittsburgh, PA

Tuition & fees: $21,334	Average undergraduate aid package: $15,767

ABOUT THE INSTITUTION Independent, coed. 57 undergraduate majors. Federal methodology is used as a basis for awarding need-based institutional aid.
UNDERGRADUATE EXPENSES for 2009–10 *Comprehensive fee:* $30,354 includes full-time tuition ($20,720), mandatory fees ($614), and room and board ($9020). *College room only:* $4300. Full-time tuition and fees vary according to program. Room and board charges vary according to board plan and housing facility. *Part-time tuition:* $574 per credit. *Part-time fees:* $22 per credit. Part-time tuition and fees vary according to program. *Payment plans:* Installment, deferred payment.
FRESHMAN FINANCIAL AID (Fall 2009, est.) 489 applied for aid; of those 89% were deemed to have need. 100% of freshmen with need received aid; of those 16% had need fully met. *Average percent of need met:* 74% (excluding resources awarded to replace EFC). *Average financial aid package:* $18,939 (excluding resources awarded to replace EFC). 32% of all full-time freshmen had no need and received non-need-based gift aid.
UNDERGRADUATE FINANCIAL AID (Fall 2009, est.) 2,563 applied for aid; of those 90% were deemed to have need. 100% of undergraduates with need received aid; of those 12% had need fully met. *Average percent of need met:* 65% (excluding resources awarded to replace EFC). *Average financial aid package:* $15,767 (excluding resources awarded to replace EFC). 15% of all full-time undergraduates had no need and received non-need-based gift aid.
GIFT AID (NEED-BASED) *Total amount:* $23,723,208 (25% federal, 14% state, 53% institutional, 8% external sources). *Receiving aid:* Freshmen: 61% (433); all full-time undergraduates: 79% (2,249). *Average award:* Freshmen: $13,547; Undergraduates: $10,080. *Scholarships, grants, and awards:* Federal Pell, FSEOG, state, private, college/university gift aid from institutional funds.
GIFT AID (NON-NEED-BASED) *Total amount:* $4,619,803 (1% federal, 1% state, 73% institutional, 25% external sources). *Receiving aid:* Freshmen: 8% (55). Undergraduates: 6% (172). *Average award:* Freshmen: $6310. Undergraduates: $6170. *Scholarships, grants, and awards by category: Academic interests/achievement:* 1,131 awards ($4,510,500 total): general academic interests/achievements. *Creative arts/performance:* 906 awards ($3,263,392 total): cinema/

film/broadcasting, dance, journalism/publications, performing arts, theater/drama. *Special achievements/activities:* 1,430 awards ($1,046,250 total): community service, junior miss. *Special characteristics:* 374 awards ($1,450,435 total): children and siblings of alumni, children of faculty/staff, international students, members of minority groups, previous college experience, siblings of current students. *Tuition waivers:* Full or partial for children of alumni, employees or children of employees.
LOANS *Student loans:* $28,249,084 (80% need-based, 20% non-need-based). 83% of past graduating class borrowed through all loan programs. *Average indebtedness per student:* $31,656. *Average need-based loan:* Freshmen: $4605. Undergraduates: $5159. *Parent loans:* $4,492,152 (45% need-based, 55% non-need-based). *Programs:* Federal Direct (Subsidized and Unsubsidized Stafford, PLUS), Perkins.
WORK-STUDY *Federal work-study:* Total amount: $367,093; 242 jobs averaging $2320. *State or other work-study/employment:* Total amount: $3,712,167 (68% need-based, 32% non-need-based). 325 part-time jobs averaging $2813.
ATHLETIC AWARDS Total amount: $1,192,341 (63% need-based, 37% non-need-based).
APPLYING FOR FINANCIAL AID *Required financial aid form:* FAFSA. *Financial aid deadline:* 4/1. *Notification date:* Continuous beginning 2/15. Students must reply by 8/30.
CONTACT Sandra M. Cronin, Director of Financial Aid, Point Park University, 201 Wood Street, Pittsburgh, PA 15222-1984, 412-392-3930 or toll-free 800-321-0129. *E-mail:* scronin@pointpark.edu.

POLYTECHNIC INSTITUTE OF NYU
Brooklyn, NY

Tuition & fees: $34,420	Average undergraduate aid package: $26,211

ABOUT THE INSTITUTION Independent, coed. 14 undergraduate majors. Federal methodology is used as a basis for awarding need-based institutional aid.
UNDERGRADUATE EXPENSES for 2009–10 *Comprehensive fee:* $43,420 includes full-time tuition ($33,274), mandatory fees ($1146), and room and board ($9000). *College room only:* $6961. Full-time tuition and fees vary according to course load. Room and board charges vary according to housing facility. *Part-time tuition:* $1058 per credit hour. *Part-time fees:* $418 per year. Part-time tuition and fees vary according to course load. *Payment plans:* Guaranteed tuition, tuition prepayment, installment, deferred payment.
FRESHMAN FINANCIAL AID (Fall 2009, est.) 363 applied for aid; of those 74% were deemed to have need. 99% of freshmen with need received aid; of those 77% had need fully met. *Average percent of need met:* 96% (excluding resources awarded to replace EFC). *Average financial aid package:* $30,099 (excluding resources awarded to replace EFC). 26% of all full-time freshmen had no need and received non-need-based gift aid.
UNDERGRADUATE FINANCIAL AID (Fall 2009, est.) 1,575 applied for aid; of those 76% were deemed to have need. 99% of undergraduates with need received aid; of those 55% had need fully met. *Average percent of need met:* 89% (excluding resources awarded to replace EFC). *Average financial aid package:* $26,211 (excluding resources awarded to replace EFC). 21% of all full-time undergraduates had no need and received non-need-based gift aid.
GIFT AID (NEED-BASED) *Total amount:* $13,496,889 (33% federal, 20% state, 47% institutional). *Receiving aid:* Freshmen: 66% (243); all full-time undergraduates: 65% (1,086). *Average award:* Freshmen: $12,578; Undergraduates: $12,353. *Scholarships, grants, and awards:* Federal Pell, FSEOG, state, private, college/university gift aid from institutional funds, United Negro College Fund.
GIFT AID (NON-NEED-BASED) *Total amount:* $19,565,032 (1% state, 99% institutional). *Receiving aid:* Freshmen: 65% (238). Undergraduates: 50% (840). *Average award:* Freshmen: $20,991. Undergraduates: $18,428. *Scholarships, grants, and awards by category: Academic interests/achievement:* computer science, engineering/technologies, general academic interests/achievements. *Special characteristics:* members of minority groups. *Tuition waivers:* Full or partial for employees or children of employees.
LOANS *Student loans:* $9,346,611 (48% need-based, 52% non-need-based). 74% of past graduating class borrowed through all loan programs. *Average indebtedness per student:* $31,035. *Average need-based loan:* Freshmen: $3855. Undergraduates: $4683. *Parent loans:* $1,626,596 (100% non-need-based). *Programs:* FFEL (Subsidized and Unsubsidized Stafford, PLUS), Perkins, college/university, alternative loans.
WORK-STUDY *Federal work-study:* Total amount: $200,000; 221 jobs averaging $3030.

APPLYING FOR FINANCIAL AID *Required financial aid forms:* FAFSA, state aid form. *Financial aid deadline:* Continuous. *Notification date:* Continuous beginning 2/15. Students must reply by 5/1 or within 2 weeks of notification.
CONTACT Ms. Christine Falzerano, Director of Financial Aid, Polytechnic Institute of NYU, 6 Metrotech Center, Brooklyn, NY 11201-2990, 718-260-3333 or toll-free 800-POLYTECH. *Fax:* 718-260-3052. *E-mail:* cfalzera@poly.edu.

POLYTECHNIC UNIVERSITY OF PUERTO RICO
Hato Rey, PR

Tuition & fees: $6837	Average undergraduate aid package: $5350

ABOUT THE INSTITUTION Independent, coed, primarily men. 13 undergraduate majors. Federal methodology is used as a basis for awarding need-based institutional aid.
UNDERGRADUATE EXPENSES for 2010–11 *Comprehensive fee:* $18,541 includes full-time tuition ($6192), mandatory fees ($645), and room and board ($11,704). Full-time tuition and fees vary according to course load, degree level, and program. *Part-time tuition:* $173 per credit hour. Part-time tuition and fees vary according to course load, degree level, and program. *Payment plan:* Deferred payment.
FRESHMAN FINANCIAL AID (Fall 2008) 684 applied for aid; of those 97% were deemed to have need. 83% of freshmen with need received aid; of those 1% had need fully met. *Average percent of need met:* 38% (excluding resources awarded to replace EFC). *Average financial aid package:* $4503 (excluding resources awarded to replace EFC).
UNDERGRADUATE FINANCIAL AID (Fall 2008) 2,749 applied for aid; of those 97% were deemed to have need. 82% of undergraduates with need received aid; of those 1% had need fully met. *Average percent of need met:* 63% (excluding resources awarded to replace EFC). *Average financial aid package:* $5350 (excluding resources awarded to replace EFC).
GIFT AID (NEED-BASED) *Total amount:* $23,081,537 (44% federal, 3% state, 1% institutional, 52% external sources). *Receiving aid:* Freshmen: 73% (552); all full-time undergraduates: 68% (2,199). *Average award:* Freshmen: $4565; Undergraduates: $4454. *Scholarships, grants, and awards:* Federal Pell, FSEOG, state, college/university gift aid from institutional funds.
GIFT AID (NON-NEED-BASED) *Receiving aid:* Freshmen: 9% (72). Undergraduates: 12% (381). *Scholarships, grants, and awards by category:* Academic interests/achievement: 485 awards ($557,326 total): architecture, business, engineering/technologies. *Tuition waivers:* Full or partial for employees or children of employees.
LOANS *Student loans:* $7,103,491 (100% need-based). *Average need-based loan:* Freshmen: $2848. Undergraduates: $4550. *Parent loans:* $684,596 (100% need-based). *Programs:* FFEL (Subsidized and Unsubsidized Stafford, PLUS).
WORK-STUDY *Federal work-study:* Total amount: $209,721; 121 jobs averaging $1733.
ATHLETIC AWARDS Total amount: $266,126 (100% need-based).
APPLYING FOR FINANCIAL AID *Required financial aid form:* FAFSA. *Financial aid deadline:* 5/15. *Notification date:* 7/15. Students must reply within 2 weeks of notification.
CONTACT Sergio E. Villoldo, Financial Aid Director, Polytechnic University of Puerto Rico, 377 Ponce de Leon Avenue, Hato Rey, PR 00919, 787-754-8000 Ext. 253. *Fax:* 787-766-1163.

POLYTECHNIC UNIVERSITY OF THE AMERICAS–MIAMI CAMPUS
Miami, FL

Tuition & fees: N/R	Average undergraduate aid package: N/A

ABOUT THE INSTITUTION Independent, coed. 2 undergraduate majors.
UNDERGRADUATE EXPENSES for 2009–10 *Tuition:* part-time $315 per credit hour. *Required fees:* $150 per term.
GIFT AID (NEED-BASED) *Scholarships, grants, and awards:* Federal Pell, college/university gift aid from institutional funds.
LOANS *Programs:* FFEL (Subsidized and Unsubsidized Stafford, PLUS), alternative loans.
WORK-STUDY Federal work-study jobs available.

CONTACT Maria Victoria Shehadeh, Administrative Affairs Coordinator/Financial Aid Officer, Polytechnic University of the Americas–Miami Campus, 8180 Northwest 36th Street, Suite 401, Miami, FL 33166, 305-418-8000 Ext. 204 or toll-free 888-729-7659 (out-of-state). *E-mail:* mshehadeh@pupr.edu.

POLYTECHNIC UNIVERSITY OF THE AMERICAS–ORLANDO CAMPUS
Winter Park, FL

Tuition & fees: N/R	Average undergraduate aid package: $7030

ABOUT THE INSTITUTION Independent, coed. 4 undergraduate majors. Federal methodology is used as a basis for awarding need-based institutional aid.
UNDERGRADUATE EXPENSES for 2009–10 *Tuition:* part-time $315 per credit hour. *Required fees:* $50 per term. tuition is $315 per credit hour for business and general courses, $345 per credit hour for engineering courses.
FRESHMAN FINANCIAL AID (Fall 2009, est.) 19 applied for aid; of those 100% were deemed to have need. 100% of freshmen with need received aid. *Average percent of need met:* 27% (excluding resources awarded to replace EFC). *Average financial aid package:* $6679 (excluding resources awarded to replace EFC).
UNDERGRADUATE FINANCIAL AID (Fall 2009, est.) 68 applied for aid; of those 100% were deemed to have need. 100% of undergraduates with need received aid. *Average percent of need met:* 27% (excluding resources awarded to replace EFC). *Average financial aid package:* $7030 (excluding resources awarded to replace EFC).
GIFT AID (NEED-BASED) *Total amount:* $547,386 (100% federal). *Receiving aid:* Freshmen: 85% (17); all full-time undergraduates: 63% (48). *Average award:* Freshmen: $4585; Undergraduates: $4411. *Scholarships, grants, and awards:* Federal Pell, FSEOG, state, private.
LOANS *Student loans:* $1,384,766 (100% need-based). 100% of past graduating class borrowed through all loan programs. *Average indebtedness per student:* $27,200. *Average need-based loan:* Freshmen: $3060. Undergraduates: $4321. *Parent loans:* $34,000 (100% need-based). *Programs:* FFEL (Subsidized and Unsubsidized Stafford, PLUS).
WORK-STUDY *Federal work-study:* Total amount: $1196; 1 job averaging $1196.
APPLYING FOR FINANCIAL AID *Required financial aid form:* FAFSA. *Financial aid deadline (priority):* 5/14. *Notification date:* Continuous beginning 3/1. Students must reply within 2 weeks of notification.
CONTACT Mrs. Ileana Diaz, Financial Aid Officer, Polytechnic University of the Americas–Orlando Campus, 4800 Howell Branch Road, Winter Park, FL 32792, 407-677-7000 Ext. 306 or toll-free 888-729-7659 (out-of-state). *Fax:* 407-677-5082. *E-mail:* idiaz@pupr.edu.

POMONA COLLEGE
Claremont, CA

Tuition & fees: $38,394	Average undergraduate aid package: $36,189

ABOUT THE INSTITUTION Independent, coed. 54 undergraduate majors. Both federal and institutional methodology are used as a basis for awarding need-based institutional aid.
UNDERGRADUATE EXPENSES for 2010–11 *Comprehensive fee:* $51,330 includes full-time tuition ($38,087), mandatory fees ($307), and room and board ($12,936). Room and board charges vary according to board plan. *Payment plan:* Installment.
FRESHMAN FINANCIAL AID (Fall 2009, est.) 271 applied for aid; of those 76% were deemed to have need. 100% of freshmen with need received aid; of those 100% had need fully met. *Average percent of need met:* 100% (excluding resources awarded to replace EFC). *Average financial aid package:* $37,045 (excluding resources awarded to replace EFC).
UNDERGRADUATE FINANCIAL AID (Fall 2009, est.) 928 applied for aid; of those 89% were deemed to have need. 100% of undergraduates with need received aid; of those 100% had need fully met. *Average percent of need met:* 100% (excluding resources awarded to replace EFC). *Average financial aid package:* $36,189 (excluding resources awarded to replace EFC).
GIFT AID (NEED-BASED) *Total amount:* $28,618,382 (6% federal, 3% state, 88% institutional, 3% external sources). *Receiving aid:* Freshmen: 54% (205);

all full-time undergraduates: 54% (823). *Average award:* Freshmen: $35,845; Undergraduates: $34,461. *Scholarships, grants, and awards:* Federal Pell, FSEOG, state, private, college/university gift aid from institutional funds.

GIFT AID (NON-NEED-BASED) *Total amount:* $685,503 (14% federal, 86% external sources). *Tuition waivers:* Full or partial for employees or children of employees.

LOANS *Student loans:* $1,206,195 (100% non-need-based). 51% of past graduating class borrowed through all loan programs. *Average indebtedness per student:* $11,700. *Parent loans:* $2,236,848 (100% non-need-based). *Programs:* Federal Direct (Subsidized and Unsubsidized Stafford, PLUS), Perkins, college/university.

WORK-STUDY *Federal work-study:* Total amount: $250,185; 240 jobs averaging $1042. *State or other work-study/employment:* Total amount: $1,042,692 (51% need-based, 49% non-need-based). 490 part-time jobs averaging $2123.

APPLYING FOR FINANCIAL AID *Required financial aid forms:* FAFSA, CSS Financial Aid PROFILE, state aid form, noncustodial (divorced/separated) parent's statement, business/farm supplement. *Financial aid deadline:* 2/1. *Notification date:* 4/10. Students must reply by 5/1.

CONTACT Mary Booker, Director of Financial Aid, Pomona College, 550 North College Avenue, Claremont, CA 91711, 909-621-8205. *Fax:* 909-607-7941. *E-mail:* financial_aid@pomadm.pomona.edu.

PONTIFICAL CATHOLIC UNIVERSITY OF PUERTO RICO
Ponce, PR

CONTACT Mrs. Margaret Alustiza, Director of Financial Aid, Pontifical Catholic University of Puerto Rico, 2250 Las Americas Avenue, Suite 549, Ponce, PR 00717-0777, 787-841-2000 Ext. 1065 or toll-free 800-981-5040. *Fax:* 787-651-2041. *E-mail:* malustiza@pucpr.edu.

PONTIFICAL COLLEGE JOSEPHINUM
Columbus, OH

CONTACT Marky Leichtnam, Financial Aid Director, Pontifical College Josephinum, 7625 North High Street, Columbus, OH 43235-1498, 614-985-2212 or toll-free 888-252-5812. *Fax:* 614-885-2307. *E-mail:* mleichtnam@pcj.edu.

PORTLAND STATE UNIVERSITY
Portland, OR

Tuition & fees (OR res): $6764	Average undergraduate aid package: $9343

ABOUT THE INSTITUTION State-supported, coed. 63 undergraduate majors. Federal methodology is used as a basis for awarding need-based institutional aid.

UNDERGRADUATE EXPENSES for 2009–10 *One-time required fee:* $265. *Tuition, state resident:* full-time $5321; part-time $118.25 per credit hour. *Tuition, nonresident:* full-time $19,755; part-time $439 per credit hour. *Required fees:* full-time $1443; $17 per credit hour or $95 per term. Full-time tuition and fees vary according to program and reciprocity agreements. Part-time tuition and fees vary according to course level. *College room and board:* $9774; *Room only:* $6891. Room and board charges vary according to board plan and housing facility. *Payment plan:* Installment.

FRESHMAN FINANCIAL AID (Fall 2009, est.) 1,167 applied for aid; of those 76% were deemed to have need. 99% of freshmen with need received aid; of those 9% had need fully met. *Average percent of need met:* 62% (excluding resources awarded to replace EFC). *Average financial aid package:* $8640 (excluding resources awarded to replace EFC). 1% of all full-time freshmen had no need and received non-need-based gift aid.

UNDERGRADUATE FINANCIAL AID (Fall 2009, est.) 9,712 applied for aid; of those 87% were deemed to have need. 100% of undergraduates with need received aid; of those 8% had need fully met. *Average percent of need met:* 61% (excluding resources awarded to replace EFC). *Average financial aid package:* $9343 (excluding resources awarded to replace EFC). 1% of all full-time undergraduates had no need and received non-need-based gift aid.

GIFT AID (NEED-BASED) *Total amount:* $46,307,500 (73% federal, 21% state, 2% institutional, 4% external sources). *Receiving aid:* Freshmen: 40% (613); all full-time undergraduates: 44% (6,000). *Average award:* Freshmen: $6361;

Undergraduates: $6302. *Scholarships, grants, and awards:* Federal Pell, FSEOG, state, private, college/university gift aid from institutional funds, United Negro College Fund.

GIFT AID (NON-NEED-BASED) *Total amount:* $670,757 (4% federal, 28% institutional, 68% external sources). *Receiving aid:* Freshmen: 1% (12). Undergraduates: 32. *Average award:* Freshmen: $1558. Undergraduates: $1988. *Scholarships, grants, and awards by category: Academic interests/achievement:* architecture, area/ethnic studies, business, computer science, education, engineering/technologies, foreign languages, general academic interests/achievements, humanities, international studies, physical sciences, social sciences. *Creative arts/performance:* art/fine arts, general creative arts/performance, music, theater/drama. *Special achievements/activities:* community service, general special achievements/activities, leadership, memberships. *Special characteristics:* adult students, ethnic background, handicapped students, international students, members of minority groups, out-of-state students. *Tuition waivers:* Full or partial for minority students, employees or children of employees, senior citizens.

LOANS *Student loans:* $106,725,092 (86% need-based, 14% non-need-based). 58% of past graduating class borrowed through all loan programs. *Average indebtedness per student:* $22,440. *Average need-based loan:* Freshmen: $3366. Undergraduates: $4536. *Parent loans:* $5,174,144 (52% need-based, 48% non-need-based). *Programs:* Federal Direct (Subsidized and Unsubsidized Stafford, PLUS), FFEL (Subsidized and Unsubsidized Stafford, PLUS), Perkins, state.

WORK-STUDY *Federal work-study:* Total amount: $3,306,055; 1,534 jobs averaging $2155.

ATHLETIC AWARDS Total amount: $2,329,142 (24% need-based, 76% non-need-based).

APPLYING FOR FINANCIAL AID *Required financial aid form:* FAFSA. *Financial aid deadline (priority):* 5/28. *Notification date:* Continuous. Students must reply within 4 weeks of notification.

CONTACT Phillip Rodgers, Director of Financial Aid, Portland State University, PO Box 751, Portland, OR 97207-0751, 800-547-8887. *Fax:* 503-725-5965. *E-mail:* askfa@pdx.edu.

POST UNIVERSITY
Waterbury, CT

ABOUT THE INSTITUTION Independent, coed. 23 undergraduate majors.

GIFT AID (NEED-BASED) *Scholarships, grants, and awards:* Federal Pell, FSEOG, state, private, college/university gift aid from institutional funds.

GIFT AID (NON-NEED-BASED) *Scholarships, grants, and awards by category: Academic interests/achievement:* agriculture, biological sciences, business, communication, computer science, education, English, general academic interests/achievements, humanities, international studies, social sciences. *Special characteristics:* children and siblings of alumni, local/state students, siblings of current students.

LOANS *Programs:* FFEL (Subsidized and Unsubsidized Stafford, PLUS), Perkins, college/university.

WORK-STUDY *Federal work-study:* Total amount: $242,000; 132 jobs averaging $1833. *State or other work-study/employment:* Total amount: $19,000 (100% need-based). 11 part-time jobs averaging $1727.

APPLYING FOR FINANCIAL AID *Required financial aid form:* FAFSA.

CONTACT Regina Faulds, Director of Financial Aid, Post University, 800 Country Club Road, Waterbury, CT 06723-2540, 203-596-4528 or toll-free 800-345-2562. *Fax:* 203-596-4599. *E-mail:* rfaulds@post.edu.

POTOMAC COLLEGE
Washington, DC

CONTACT Phyllis Crews, Financial Aid Counselor, Potomac College, 4000 Chesapeake Street NW, Washington, DC 20016, 202-686-0876 or toll-free 888-686-0876. *Fax:* 202-686-0818. *E-mail:* pcrews@potomac.edu.

POTOMAC COLLEGE
Herndon, VA

Tuition & fees: $16,020	Average undergraduate aid package: N/A

ABOUT THE INSTITUTION Proprietary, coed. 7 undergraduate majors. Federal methodology is used as a basis for awarding need-based institutional aid.

UNDERGRADUATE EXPENSES for 2009–10 *Tuition:* full-time $16,020; part-time $495 per credit.

GIFT AID (NEED-BASED) *Total amount:* $1,609,268 (99% federal, 1% institutional). *Scholarships, grants, and awards:* Federal Pell, FSEOG, private, college/university gift aid from institutional funds, Academic Competitiveness Grants, National SMART Grants.

LOANS *Student loans:* $5,810,710 (100% need-based). *Parent loans:* $4784 (100% need-based). *Programs:* FFEL (Subsidized and Unsubsidized Stafford, PLUS).

CONTACT Ms. Melva Carty, Director of Financial Aid, Potomac College, 4000 Chesapeake Street NW, Washington, DC 20016, 202-274-1783. *Fax:* 202-686-0818. *E-mail:* melva.carty@potomac.edu.

PRAIRIE VIEW A&M UNIVERSITY
Prairie View, TX

CONTACT Mr. A. D. James Jr., Executive Director, Student Financial Services and Scholarships, Prairie View A&M University, PO Box 2967, Prairie View, TX 77446-2967, 936-857-2423. *Fax:* 936-857-2425. *E-mail:* ad_james@pvamu.edu.

PRATT INSTITUTE
Brooklyn, NY

Tuition & fees: $36,790	Average undergraduate aid package: $13,039

ABOUT THE INSTITUTION Independent, coed. 26 undergraduate majors. Federal methodology is used as a basis for awarding need-based institutional aid.

UNDERGRADUATE EXPENSES for 2010–11 *Comprehensive fee:* $46,810 includes full-time tuition ($35,410), mandatory fees ($1380), and room and board ($10,020). *College room only:* $6340. *Part-time tuition:* $1142 per credit.

FRESHMAN FINANCIAL AID (Fall 2009, est.) 507 applied for aid; of those 86% were deemed to have need. 100% of freshmen with need received aid. *Average percent of need met:* 71% (excluding resources awarded to replace EFC). *Average financial aid package:* $12,926 (excluding resources awarded to replace EFC). 30% of all full-time freshmen had no need and received non-need-based gift aid.

UNDERGRADUATE FINANCIAL AID (Fall 2009, est.) 2,185 applied for aid; of those 89% were deemed to have need. 100% of undergraduates with need received aid. *Average percent of need met:* 64% (excluding resources awarded to replace EFC). *Average financial aid package:* $13,039 (excluding resources awarded to replace EFC). 12% of all full-time undergraduates had no need and received non-need-based gift aid.

GIFT AID (NEED-BASED) *Total amount:* $14,958,565 (21% federal, 10% state, 66% institutional, 3% external sources). *Receiving aid:* Freshmen: 61% (382); all full-time undergraduates: 63% (1,764). *Average award:* Freshmen: $9674; Undergraduates: $10,896. *Scholarships, grants, and awards:* Federal Pell, FSEOG, state, private, college/university gift aid from institutional funds.

GIFT AID (NON-NEED-BASED) *Total amount:* $18,049,813 (100% institutional). *Receiving aid:* Freshmen: 50% (318). Undergraduates: 48% (1,349). *Average award:* Freshmen: $8674. Undergraduates: $7432. *Scholarships, grants, and awards by category: Academic interests/achievement:* general academic interests/achievements.

LOANS *Student loans:* $20,082,219 (66% need-based, 34% non-need-based). *Average need-based loan:* Freshmen: $5140. Undergraduates: $6956. *Parent loans:* $14,059,688 (100% need-based). *Programs:* FFEL (Subsidized and Unsubsidized Stafford, PLUS), Perkins, college/university.

WORK-STUDY *Federal work-study:* Total amount: $805,779; jobs available. *State or other work-study/employment:* Total amount: $1,814,199 (100% non-need-based). Part-time jobs available.

APPLYING FOR FINANCIAL AID *Required financial aid form:* FAFSA. *Financial aid deadline:* 2/1. *Notification date:* Continuous beginning 3/10. Students must reply within 2 weeks of notification.

CONTACT Fiona Approo, Acting Director of Financial Aid, Pratt Institute, 200 Willoughby Avenue, Brooklyn, NY 11205-3899, 718-636-3715 or toll-free 800-331-0834. *Fax:* 718-636-3739. *E-mail:* faproo@pratt.edu.

PRESBYTERIAN COLLEGE
Clinton, SC

Tuition & fees: $28,880	Average undergraduate aid package: $29,765

ABOUT THE INSTITUTION Independent religious, coed. 35 undergraduate majors. Federal methodology is used as a basis for awarding need-based institutional aid.

UNDERGRADUATE EXPENSES for 2009–10 *One-time required fee:* $406. *Comprehensive fee:* $37,225 includes full-time tuition ($26,436), mandatory fees ($2444), and room and board ($8345). Full-time tuition and fees vary according to course level, program, and reciprocity agreements. Room and board charges vary according to board plan and housing facility. *Part-time tuition:* $1102 per credit hour. *Part-time fees:* $17 per credit hour; $22 per term. Part-time tuition and fees vary according to course level, course load, and program. *Payment plan:* Installment.

FRESHMAN FINANCIAL AID (Fall 2009, est.) 314 applied for aid; of those 84% were deemed to have need. 100% of freshmen with need received aid; of those 53% had need fully met. *Average percent of need met:* 91% (excluding resources awarded to replace EFC). *Average financial aid package:* $31,409 (excluding resources awarded to replace EFC). 23% of all full-time freshmen had no need and received non-need-based gift aid.

UNDERGRADUATE FINANCIAL AID (Fall 2009, est.) 935 applied for aid; of those 86% were deemed to have need. 100% of undergraduates with need received aid; of those 50% had need fully met. *Average percent of need met:* 88% (excluding resources awarded to replace EFC). *Average financial aid package:* $29,765 (excluding resources awarded to replace EFC). 28% of all full-time undergraduates had no need and received non-need-based gift aid.

GIFT AID (NEED-BASED) *Total amount:* $15,502,647 (8% federal, 27% state, 63% institutional, 2% external sources). *Receiving aid:* Freshmen: 73% (264); all full-time undergraduates: 68% (806). *Average award:* Freshmen: $29,691; Undergraduates: $27,536. *Scholarships, grants, and awards:* Federal Pell, FSEOG, state, private, college/university gift aid from institutional funds.

GIFT AID (NON-NEED-BASED) *Total amount:* $8,806,925 (10% state, 81% institutional, 9% external sources). *Receiving aid:* Freshmen: 53% (193). Undergraduates: 53% (630). *Average award:* Freshmen: $14,937. Undergraduates: $13,050. *Scholarships, grants, and awards by category: Academic interests/achievement:* general academic interests/achievements. *Creative arts/performance:* music. *Special achievements/activities:* leadership, religious involvement. *Special characteristics:* children of faculty/staff, relatives of clergy, religious affiliation. *Tuition waivers:* Full or partial for employees or children of employees, senior citizens.

LOANS *Student loans:* $3,643,505 (55% need-based, 45% non-need-based). 56% of past graduating class borrowed through all loan programs. *Average indebtedness per student:* $23,391. *Average need-based loan:* Freshmen: $3384. Undergraduates: $4111. *Parent loans:* $1,448,922 (24% need-based, 76% non-need-based). *Programs:* FFEL (Subsidized and Unsubsidized Stafford, PLUS), state, college/university, private loans.

WORK-STUDY Federal work-study jobs available. *State or other work-study/employment:* Total amount: $2,442,292 (100% need-based). Part-time jobs available.

ATHLETIC AWARDS Total amount: $5,261,308 (48% need-based, 52% non-need-based).

APPLYING FOR FINANCIAL AID *Required financial aid form:* FAFSA. *Financial aid deadline:* 6/30 (priority: 3/15).

CONTACT Mr. Jeff Holliday, Director of Financial Aid, Presbyterian College, 503 South Broad Street, Clinton, SC 29325, 864-833-8287 or toll-free 800-476-7272. *Fax:* 864-833-8481. *E-mail:* jsholli@presby.edu.

PRESCOTT COLLEGE
Prescott, AZ

Tuition & fees: $23,643	Average undergraduate aid package: $13,099

ABOUT THE INSTITUTION Independent, coed. 128 undergraduate majors. Federal methodology is used as a basis for awarding need-based institutional aid.

UNDERGRADUATE EXPENSES for 2009–10 *Tuition:* full-time $23,232; part-time $968 per term. *Required fees:* full-time $411; $205.50 per term. Full-time tuition and fees vary according to course load and degree level. Part-time tuition and fees vary according to course load and degree level. Room and board charges vary according to housing facility. *Payment plans:* Installment, deferred payment.

FRESHMAN FINANCIAL AID (Fall 2009, est.) 53 applied for aid; of those 83% were deemed to have need. 100% of freshmen with need received aid; of those 14% had need fully met. *Average percent of need met:* 58% (excluding resources awarded to replace EFC). *Average financial aid package:* $15,439 (excluding resources awarded to replace EFC). 26% of all full-time freshmen had no need and received non-need-based gift aid.

UNDERGRADUATE FINANCIAL AID (Fall 2009, est.) 422 applied for aid; of those 90% were deemed to have need. 99% of undergraduates with need received aid; of those 6% had need fully met. *Average percent of need met:* 47% (excluding resources awarded to replace EFC). *Average financial aid package:* $13,099 (excluding resources awarded to replace EFC). 22% of all full-time undergraduates had no need and received non-need-based gift aid.

GIFT AID (NEED-BASED) *Total amount:* $3,112,365 (36% federal, 1% state, 59% institutional, 4% external sources). *Receiving aid:* Freshmen: 63% (43); all full-time undergraduates: 57% (344). *Average award:* Freshmen: $12,131; Undergraduates: $9075. *Scholarships, grants, and awards:* Federal Pell, FSEOG, state, private, college/university gift aid from institutional funds, Academic Competitiveness Grants, National SMART Grants.

GIFT AID (NON-NEED-BASED) *Total amount:* $922,719 (1% state, 85% institutional, 14% external sources). *Receiving aid:* Freshmen: 3% (2). Undergraduates: 2% (10). *Average award:* Freshmen: $6611, Undergraduates: $5467. *Tuition waivers:* Full or partial for employees or children of employees.

LOANS *Student loans:* $4,084,065 (89% need-based, 11% non-need-based). 67% of past graduating class borrowed through all loan programs. *Average indebtedness per student:* $14,947. *Average need-based loan:* Freshmen: $3349. Undergraduates: $4589. *Parent loans:* $3,284,655 (35% need-based, 65% non-need-based). *Programs:* FFEL (Subsidized and Unsubsidized Stafford, PLUS).

WORK-STUDY *Federal work-study:* Total amount: $147,566; jobs available. *State or other work-study/employment:* Part-time jobs available.

APPLYING FOR FINANCIAL AID *Required financial aid form:* FAFSA. *Financial aid deadline (priority):* 3/1. *Notification date:* Continuous beginning 3/15. Students must reply within 12 weeks of notification.

CONTACT Financial Aid Office, Prescott College, 220 Grove Avenue, Prescott, AZ 86301-2990, 928-350-1111 or toll-free 800-628-6364. *Fax:* 928-776-5225. *E-mail:* finaid@prescott.edu.

PRESENTATION COLLEGE
Aberdeen, SD

ABOUT THE INSTITUTION Independent Roman Catholic, coed, primarily women. 19 undergraduate majors.

GIFT AID (NEED-BASED) *Scholarships, grants, and awards:* Federal Pell, FSEOG, state, private, college/university gift aid from institutional funds.

GIFT AID (NON-NEED-BASED) *Scholarships, grants, and awards by category:* *Special achievements/activities:* community service, general special achievements/activities, leadership, religious involvement. *Special characteristics:* children of faculty/staff.

LOANS *Programs:* FFEL (Subsidized and Unsubsidized Stafford, PLUS), Perkins, state, college/university.

APPLYING FOR FINANCIAL AID *Required financial aid forms:* FAFSA, state aid form.

CONTACT Ms. Janel Wagner, Director of Financial Aid, Presentation College, 1500 North Main Street, Aberdeen, SD 57401-1299, 605-229-8427 or toll-free 800-437-6060. *Fax:* 605-229-8537. *E-mail:* janel.wagner@presentation.edu.

PRINCETON UNIVERSITY
Princeton, NJ

Tuition & fees: $36,640	Average undergraduate aid package: $35,026

ABOUT THE INSTITUTION Independent, coed. 35 undergraduate majors. Both federal and institutional methodology are used as a basis for awarding need-based institutional aid.

UNDERGRADUATE EXPENSES for 2010–11 *Comprehensive fee:* $48,580 includes full-time tuition ($36,640) and room and board ($11,940). Room and board charges vary according to board plan. *Payment plans:* Installment, deferred payment.

FRESHMAN FINANCIAL AID (Fall 2008) 816 applied for aid; of those 85% were deemed to have need. 100% of freshmen with need received aid; of those 100% had need fully met. *Average percent of need met:* 100% (excluding resources awarded to replace EFC). *Average financial aid package:* $34,804 (excluding resources awarded to replace EFC).

UNDERGRADUATE FINANCIAL AID (Fall 2008) 3,151 applied for aid; of those 88% were deemed to have need. 100% of undergraduates with need received aid; of those 100% had need fully met. *Average percent of need met:* 100% (excluding resources awarded to replace EFC). *Average financial aid package:* $35,026 (excluding resources awarded to replace EFC).

GIFT AID (NEED-BASED) *Total amount:* $92,228,085 (4% federal, 93% institutional, 3% external sources). *Receiving aid:* Freshmen: 56% (697); all full-time undergraduates: 56% (2,759). *Average award:* Freshmen: $33,671; Undergraduates: $33,428. *Scholarships, grants, and awards:* Federal Pell, FSEOG, state, private, college/university gift aid from institutional funds.

GIFT AID (NON-NEED-BASED) *Tuition waivers:* Full or partial for employees or children of employees.

LOANS *Student loans:* 21% of past graduating class borrowed through all loan programs. *Average indebtedness per student:* $4957. *Parent loans:* $1,177,744 (100% non-need-based). *Programs:* FFEL (Subsidized and Unsubsidized Stafford, PLUS), Perkins, college/university.

WORK-STUDY *Federal work-study:* Total amount: $834,575; 628 jobs averaging $2314. *State or other work-study/employment:* Total amount: $1,571,242 (100% need-based). 1,253 part-time jobs averaging $2358.

APPLYING FOR FINANCIAL AID *Required financial aid forms:* FAFSA, institution's own form. *Financial aid deadline (priority):* 2/1. *Notification date:* 4/1. Students must reply by 5/1.

CONTACT Robin Moscato, Director of Financial Aid, Princeton University, Box 591, Princeton, NJ 08542, 609-258-3330. *Fax:* 609-258-0336. *E-mail:* moscato@princeton.edu.

PRINCIPIA COLLEGE
Elsah, IL

Tuition & fees: $23,625	Average undergraduate aid package: $24,175

ABOUT THE INSTITUTION Independent Christian Science, coed. 28 undergraduate majors. Institutional methodology is used as a basis for awarding need-based institutional aid.

UNDERGRADUATE EXPENSES for 2010–11 *One-time required fee:* $300. *Comprehensive fee:* $32,625 includes full-time tuition ($23,625) and room and board ($9000). *College room only:* $4380. Full-time tuition and fees vary according to course load. *Payment plan:* Installment.

FRESHMAN FINANCIAL AID (Fall 2009, est.) 84 applied for aid; of those 95% were deemed to have need. 100% of freshmen with need received aid; of those 88% had need fully met. *Average percent of need met:* 88% (excluding resources awarded to replace EFC). *Average financial aid package:* $23,837 (excluding resources awarded to replace EFC). 20% of all full-time freshmen had no need and received non-need-based gift aid.

UNDERGRADUATE FINANCIAL AID (Fall 2009, est.) 361 applied for aid; of those 97% were deemed to have need. 100% of undergraduates with need received aid; of those 85% had need fully met. *Average percent of need met:* 85% (excluding resources awarded to replace EFC). *Average financial aid package:* $24,175 (excluding resources awarded to replace EFC). 17% of all full-time undergraduates had no need and received non-need-based gift aid.

GIFT AID (NEED-BASED) *Total amount:* $4,779,100 (100% institutional). *Receiving aid:* Freshmen: 62% (62); all full-time undergraduates: 53% (265). *Average award:* Freshmen: $19,648; Undergraduates: $20,119. *Scholarships, grants, and awards:* private, college/university gift aid from institutional funds.

GIFT AID (NON-NEED-BASED) *Total amount:* $1,538,186 (100% institutional). *Receiving aid:* Freshmen: 32% (32). Undergraduates: 25% (126). *Average award:* Freshmen: $14,407. Undergraduates: $16,727. *Scholarships, grants, and awards by category:* *Academic interests/achievement:* 107 awards ($1,727,067 total): general academic interests/achievements. *Special achievements/activities:* 103 awards ($1,143,533 total): community service, general special achievements/activities, leadership, religious involvement. *Special characteristics:* 23 awards ($82,500 total): children and siblings of alumni, children of faculty/staff. *Tuition waivers:* Full or partial for employees or children of employees.

LOANS *Student loans:* $1,412,418 (100% need-based). 64% of past graduating class borrowed through all loan programs. *Average indebtedness per student:* $14,963. *Average need-based loan:* Freshmen: $5405. Undergraduates: $5342. *Programs:* college/university.

WORK-STUDY *State or other work-study/employment:* Total amount: $177,850 (100% need-based). 142 part-time jobs averaging $1252.

APPLYING FOR FINANCIAL AID *Required financial aid forms:* institution's own form, CSS Financial Aid PROFILE, income tax form(s). *Financial aid deadline (priority):* 3/1. *Notification date:* Continuous beginning 3/1. Students must reply by 5/1 or within 4 weeks of notification.

CONTACT Tami Gavaletz, Director of Financial Aid, Principia College, 1 Maybeck Place, Elsah, IL 62028-9799, 618-374-5187 or toll-free 800-277-4648 Ext. 2802. *Fax:* 618-374-5906. *E-mail:* tami.gavaletz@principia.edu.

PROVIDENCE COLLEGE
Providence, RI

Tuition & fees: $39,435	Average undergraduate aid package: $20,770

ABOUT THE INSTITUTION Independent Roman Catholic, coed. 46 undergraduate majors. Both federal and institutional methodology are used as a basis for awarding need-based institutional aid.

UNDERGRADUATE EXPENSES for 2010–11 *Comprehensive fee:* $51,125 includes full-time tuition ($38,610), mandatory fees ($825), and room and board ($11,690). *College room only:* $6790. Full-time tuition and fees vary according to degree level and student level. Room and board charges vary according to board plan and housing facility. *Part-time tuition:* $1120 per credit hour. Part-time tuition and fees vary according to degree level. *Payment plan:* Installment.

FRESHMAN FINANCIAL AID (Fall 2009, est.) 754 applied for aid; of those 77% were deemed to have need. 100% of freshmen with need received aid; of those 55% had need fully met. *Average percent of need met:* 77% (excluding resources awarded to replace EFC). *Average financial aid package:* $22,050 (excluding resources awarded to replace EFC). 8% of all full-time freshmen had no need and received non-need-based gift aid.

UNDERGRADUATE FINANCIAL AID (Fall 2009, est.) 2,615 applied for aid; of those 81% were deemed to have need. 100% of undergraduates with need received aid; of those 32% had need fully met. *Average percent of need met:* 78% (excluding resources awarded to replace EFC). *Average financial aid package:* $20,770 (excluding resources awarded to replace EFC). 6% of all full-time undergraduates had no need and received non-need-based gift aid.

GIFT AID (NEED-BASED) *Total amount:* $34,170,112 (9% federal, 1% state, 85% institutional, 5% external sources). *Receiving aid:* Freshmen: 52% (495); all full-time undergraduates: 49% (1,883). *Average award:* Freshmen: $17,180; Undergraduates: $17,013. *Scholarships, grants, and awards:* Federal Pell, FSEOG, state, private, college/university gift aid from institutional funds, Academic Competitiveness Grants, National SMART Grants.

GIFT AID (NON-NEED-BASED) *Total amount:* $8,269,064 (89% institutional, 11% external sources). *Receiving aid:* Freshmen: 6% (56). Undergraduates: 5% (211). *Average award:* Freshmen: $21,598. Undergraduates: $26,886. *Scholarships, grants, and awards by category: Academic interests/achievement:* 400 awards ($3,750,000 total): business, general academic interests/achievements, military science, premedicine. *Creative arts/performance:* 5 awards ($15,000 total): theater/drama. *Special achievements/activities:* 20 awards ($100,000 total): community service. *Special characteristics:* 74 awards ($72,500 total): siblings of current students. *Tuition waivers:* Full or partial for employees or children of employees, senior citizens.

LOANS *Student loans:* $23,512,601 (60% need-based, 40% non-need-based). 63% of past graduating class borrowed through all loan programs. *Average indebtedness per student:* $34,927. *Average need-based loan:* Freshmen: $4413. Undergraduates: $4745. *Parent loans:* $11,128,433 (65% need-based, 35% non-need-based). *Programs:* Federal Direct (Subsidized and Unsubsidized Stafford, PLUS), FFEL (Subsidized and Unsubsidized Stafford, PLUS), Perkins.

WORK-STUDY *Federal work-study:* Total amount: $1,873,771; 700 jobs averaging $1800. *State or other work-study/employment:* Total amount: $800,000 (100% non-need-based). 700 part-time jobs averaging $1800.

ATHLETIC AWARDS Total amount: $5,667,500 (23% need-based, 77% non-need-based).

APPLYING FOR FINANCIAL AID *Required financial aid forms:* FAFSA, CSS Financial Aid PROFILE, business/farm supplement. *Financial aid deadline:* 2/1. *Notification date:* 4/1. Students must reply by 5/1.

CONTACT Ms. Sandra J. Oliveira, Executive Director of Financial Aid, Providence College, 1 Cunningham Square, Providence, RI 02918, 401-865-2286 or toll-free 800-721-6444. *Fax:* 401-865-1186. *E-mail:* solivei6@providence.edu.

PURCHASE COLLEGE, STATE UNIVERSITY OF NEW YORK
Purchase, NY

Tuition & fees (NY res): $6431	Average undergraduate aid package: $9728

ABOUT THE INSTITUTION State-supported, coed. 43 undergraduate majors. Federal methodology is used as a basis for awarding need-based institutional aid.

UNDERGRADUATE EXPENSES for 2010–11 *One-time required fee:* $200. *Tuition, state resident:* full-time $4970; part-time $207 per credit hour. *Tuition, nonresident:* full-time $12,870; part-time $536 per credit hour. *Required fees:* full-time $1461; $.85 per credit hour. Full-time tuition and fees vary according to program. Part-time tuition and fees vary according to course load and program. *College room and board:* $9908; *Room only:* $6240. Room and board charges vary according to board plan and housing facility. *Payment plan:* Installment.

FRESHMAN FINANCIAL AID (Fall 2009, est.) 567 applied for aid; of those 67% were deemed to have need. 100% of freshmen with need received aid; of those 7% had need fully met. *Average percent of need met:* 53% (excluding resources awarded to replace EFC). *Average financial aid package:* $8175 (excluding resources awarded to replace EFC). 4% of all full-time freshmen had no need and received non-need-based gift aid.

UNDERGRADUATE FINANCIAL AID (Fall 2009, est.) 2,686 applied for aid; of those 75% were deemed to have need. 100% of undergraduates with need received aid; of those 7% had need fully met. *Average percent of need met:* 60% (excluding resources awarded to replace EFC). *Average financial aid package:* $9728 (excluding resources awarded to replace EFC). 3% of all full-time undergraduates had no need and received non-need-based gift aid.

GIFT AID (NEED-BASED) *Total amount:* $8,557,836 (49% federal, 37% state, 10% institutional, 4% external sources). *Receiving aid:* Freshmen: 42% (291); all full-time undergraduates: 46% (1,659). *Average award:* Freshmen: $6067; Undergraduates: $6001. *Scholarships, grants, and awards:* Federal Pell, FSEOG, state, private, college/university gift aid from institutional funds.

GIFT AID (NON-NEED-BASED) *Total amount:* $504,349 (31% state, 45% institutional, 24% external sources). *Receiving aid:* Freshmen: 1% (9). Undergraduates: 1% (38). *Average award:* Freshmen: $2175. Undergraduates: $1989. *Scholarships, grants, and awards by category: Academic interests/achievement:* area/ethnic studies, biological sciences, computer science, English, general academic interests/achievements, humanities, mathematics, social sciences. *Creative arts/performance:* art/fine arts, cinema/film/broadcasting, creative writing, dance, general creative arts/performance, music, performing arts, theater/drama. *Tuition waivers:* Full or partial for employees or children of employees.

LOANS *Student loans:* $18,095,181 (68% need-based, 32% non-need-based). 58% of past graduating class borrowed through all loan programs. *Average indebtedness per student:* $26,275. *Average need-based loan:* Freshmen: $3586. Undergraduates: $4787. *Parent loans:* $8,244,979 (73% need-based, 27% non-need-based). *Programs:* Federal Direct (Subsidized and Unsubsidized Stafford, PLUS), Perkins.

WORK-STUDY *Federal work-study:* Total amount: $68,920; jobs available. *State or other work-study/employment:* Total amount: $636,797 (42% need-based, 58% non-need-based). Part-time jobs available.

APPLYING FOR FINANCIAL AID *Required financial aid forms:* FAFSA, state aid form. *Financial aid deadline (priority):* 2/1. *Notification date:* Continuous beginning 3/1. Students must reply within 2 weeks of notification.

CONTACT Ms. Corey York, Director of Student Financial Services, Purchase College, State University of New York, 735 Anderson Hill Road, Purchase, NY 10577-1400, 914-251-6085. *Fax:* 914-251-6099. *E-mail:* corey.york@purchase.edu.

PURDUE UNIVERSITY
West Lafayette, IN

Tuition & fees (IN res): $8638	Average undergraduate aid package: $10,555

ABOUT THE INSTITUTION State-supported, coed. 85 undergraduate majors. Federal methodology is used as a basis for awarding need-based institutional aid.

UNDERGRADUATE EXPENSES for 2009–10 *Tuition, state resident:* full-time $8183; part-time $309 per credit hour. *Tuition, nonresident:* full-time $24,663; part-time $835 per credit hour. *Required fees:* full-time $455. Full-time tuition and fees vary according to course load and program. Part-time tuition and fees vary according to course load. *College room and board:* $8710; *Room only:* $3994. Room and board charges vary according to board plan and housing facility. *Payment plan:* Installment.

FRESHMAN FINANCIAL AID (Fall 2009, est.) 4,620 applied for aid; of those 68% were deemed to have need. 100% of freshmen with need received aid; of those 57% had need fully met. *Average percent of need met:* 96% (excluding resources awarded to replace EFC). *Average financial aid package:* $10,950 (excluding resources awarded to replace EFC). 7% of all full-time freshmen had no need and received non-need-based gift aid.

UNDERGRADUATE FINANCIAL AID (Fall 2009, est.) 19,158 applied for aid; of those 73% were deemed to have need. 100% of undergraduates with need received aid; of those 32% had need fully met. *Average percent of need met:* 95% (excluding resources awarded to replace EFC). *Average financial aid package:* $10,555 (excluding resources awarded to replace EFC). 7% of all full-time undergraduates had no need and received non-need-based gift aid.

GIFT AID (NEED-BASED) *Total amount:* $73,979,695 (39% federal, 24% state, 31% institutional, 6% external sources). *Receiving aid:* Freshmen: 37% (2,254). *Average award:* Freshmen: $10,052; Undergraduates: $8738. *Scholarships, grants, and awards:* Federal Pell, FSEOG, state, private, college/university gift aid from institutional funds, Academic Competitiveness Grants, National SMART Grants.

GIFT AID (NON-NEED-BASED) *Total amount:* $30,017,016 (20% federal, 7% state, 53% institutional, 20% external sources). *Receiving aid:* Freshmen: 29% (1,771). Undergraduates: 13% (4,069). *Average award:* Freshmen: $5945. Undergraduates: $5637. *Scholarships, grants, and awards by category:* Academic interests/achievement: agriculture, computer science, education, engineering/technologies, general academic interests/achievements, health fields, humanities, mathematics, military science, physical sciences. Creative arts/performance: music. Special achievements/activities: leadership. Special characteristics: children of faculty/staff. Tuition waivers: Full or partial for employees or children of employees, senior citizens.

LOANS *Student loans:* $151,210,968 (60% need-based, 40% non-need-based). 54% of past graduating class borrowed through all loan programs. *Average indebtedness per student:* $23,924. *Average need-based loan:* Freshmen: $3606. Undergraduates: $4562. *Parent loans:* $181,175,289 (22% need-based, 78% non-need-based). *Programs:* Federal Direct (Subsidized and Unsubsidized Stafford, PLUS), Perkins, college/university.

WORK-STUDY *Federal work-study:* Total amount: $788,577; 958 jobs averaging $1181.

ATHLETIC AWARDS Total amount: $7,419,661 (25% need-based, 75% non-need-based).

APPLYING FOR FINANCIAL AID *Required financial aid form:* FAFSA. *Financial aid deadline (priority):* 3/1. *Notification date:* 4/15.

CONTACT Joyce Hall, Division of Financial Aid, Purdue University, Schleman Hall of Student Services, Room 305, West Lafayette, IN 47907-2050, 765-494-5056. *Fax:* 765-494-6707.

PURDUE UNIVERSITY CALUMET
Hammond, IN

Tuition & fees (IN res): $6337 **Average undergraduate aid package: $6632**

ABOUT THE INSTITUTION State-supported, coed. 44 undergraduate majors. Federal methodology is used as a basis for awarding need-based institutional aid.

UNDERGRADUATE EXPENSES for 2009–10 *Tuition, state resident:* full-time $6337; part-time $210.25 per credit hour. *Tuition, nonresident:* full-time $13,624; part-time $470.50 per credit hour. *Required fees:* $20.65 per credit hour. Full-time tuition and fees vary according to course load and program. Part-time tuition and fees vary according to course load and program. *College room and board:* $6653; *Room only:* $4680. Room and board charges vary according to housing facility. *Payment plan:* Deferred payment.

FRESHMAN FINANCIAL AID (Fall 2008) 967 applied for aid; of those 77% were deemed to have need. 91% of freshmen with need received aid; of those 43%

had need fully met. *Average percent of need met:* 12% (excluding resources awarded to replace EFC). *Average financial aid package:* $3960 (excluding resources awarded to replace EFC). 5% of all full-time freshmen had no need and received non-need-based gift aid.

UNDERGRADUATE FINANCIAL AID (Fall 2008) 4,756 applied for aid; of those 82% were deemed to have need. 93% of undergraduates with need received aid; of those 11% had need fully met. *Average percent of need met:* 12% (excluding resources awarded to replace EFC). *Average financial aid package:* $6632 (excluding resources awarded to replace EFC). 5% of all full-time undergraduates had no need and received non-need-based gift aid.

GIFT AID (NEED-BASED) *Total amount:* $15,043,625 (63% federal, 35% state, 2% institutional). *Receiving aid:* Freshmen: 36% (455); all full-time undergraduates: 39% (2,544). *Average award:* Freshmen: $2947; Undergraduates: $4989. *Scholarships, grants, and awards:* Federal Pell, FSEOG, state, private, college/university gift aid from institutional funds.

GIFT AID (NON-NEED-BASED) *Total amount:* $3,046,650 (4% state, 69% institutional, 27% external sources). *Receiving aid:* Freshmen: 15% (186). Undergraduates: 9% (573). *Average award:* Freshmen: $2114. Undergraduates: $2370. *Scholarships, grants, and awards by category:* Academic interests/achievement: 706 awards ($2,055,988 total): general academic interests/achievements. *Tuition waivers:* Full or partial for employees or children of employees, senior citizens.

LOANS *Student loans:* $28,954,458 (97% need-based, 3% non-need-based). 62% of past graduating class borrowed through all loan programs. *Average indebtedness per student:* $19,706. *Average need-based loan:* Freshmen: $1908. Undergraduates: $3355. *Parent loans:* $2,169,010 (100% non-need-based). *Programs:* Federal Direct (Subsidized and Unsubsidized Stafford, PLUS), Perkins.

WORK-STUDY *Federal work-study:* Total amount: $239,609; 88 jobs averaging $1859. *State or other work-study/employment:* Part-time jobs available.

ATHLETIC AWARDS Total amount: $59,332 (100% non-need-based).

APPLYING FOR FINANCIAL AID *Required financial aid form:* FAFSA. *Financial aid deadline (priority):* 3/10. *Notification date:* Continuous beginning 4/15. Students must reply within 2 weeks of notification.

CONTACT Ms. Tanika House, Assistant Director of Financial Aid, Purdue University Calumet, 2200 169th Street, Hammond, IN 46323-2094, 219-989-2301 or toll-free 800-447-8738 (in-state). *Fax:* 219-989-2141. *E-mail:* finaid@calumet.purdue.edu.

PURDUE UNIVERSITY NORTH CENTRAL
Westville, IN

Tuition & fees (IN res): $6704 **Average undergraduate aid package: $6947**

ABOUT THE INSTITUTION State-supported, coed. 26 undergraduate majors. Federal methodology is used as a basis for awarding need-based institutional aid.

UNDERGRADUATE EXPENSES for 2010–11 *Tuition, state resident:* full-time $6128; part-time $204.25 per credit hour. *Tuition, nonresident:* full-time $15,384; part-time $512.80 per credit hour. *Required fees:* full-time $576; $19.20 per credit hour. Full-time tuition and fees vary according to course load, location, program, and reciprocity agreements. Part-time tuition and fees vary according to course load, location, program, and reciprocity agreements. *Payment plans:* Installment, deferred payment.

FRESHMAN FINANCIAL AID (Fall 2008) 565 applied for aid; of those 79% were deemed to have need. 91% of freshmen with need received aid; of those 12% had need fully met. *Average percent of need met:* 35% (excluding resources awarded to replace EFC). *Average financial aid package:* $5783 (excluding resources awarded to replace EFC). 2% of all full-time freshmen had no need and received non-need-based gift aid.

UNDERGRADUATE FINANCIAL AID (Fall 2008) 1,882 applied for aid; of those 82% were deemed to have need. 95% of undergraduates with need received aid; of those 4% had need fully met. *Average percent of need met:* 40% (excluding resources awarded to replace EFC). *Average financial aid package:* $6947 (excluding resources awarded to replace EFC). 1% of all full-time undergraduates had no need and received non-need-based gift aid.

GIFT AID (NEED-BASED) *Total amount:* $4,267,909 (89% federal, 10% state, 1% institutional). *Receiving aid:* Freshmen: 28% (212); all full-time undergraduates: 31% (795). *Average award:* Freshmen: $3730; Undergraduates: $4063. *Scholarships, grants, and awards:* Federal Pell, FSEOG, state, private, college/university gift aid from institutional funds.

Purdue University North Central

GIFT AID (NON-NEED-BASED) *Total amount:* $3,170,533 (82% state, 13% institutional, 5% external sources). *Receiving aid:* Freshmen: 31% (230). Undergraduates: 31% (791). *Average award:* Freshmen: $1523. Undergraduates: $1362. *Scholarships, grants, and awards by category: Academic interests/ achievement:* business, education, English, general academic interests/ achievements, health fields. *Special achievements/activities:* general special achievements/activities, leadership. *Special characteristics:* adult students, children of faculty/staff, veterans' children. *Tuition waivers:* Full or partial for employees or children of employees, senior citizens.

LOANS *Student loans:* $13,404,886 (44% need-based, 56% non-need-based). 75% of past graduating class borrowed through all loan programs. *Average indebtedness per student:* $20,859. *Average need-based loan:* Freshmen: $3014. Undergraduates: $3872. *Parent loans:* $499,912 (100% non-need-based). *Programs:* FFEL (Subsidized and Unsubsidized Stafford, PLUS), Perkins, alternative loans.

WORK-STUDY *Federal work-study:* Total amount: $132,000; jobs available. *State or other work-study/employment:* Part-time jobs available.

ATHLETIC AWARDS Total amount: $33,550 (100% non-need-based).

APPLYING FOR FINANCIAL AID *Required financial aid form:* FAFSA. *Financial aid deadline:* 6/30 (priority: 3/10). *Notification date:* Continuous beginning 4/15. Students must reply by 8/10.

CONTACT Anthony Cardenas, Assistant Dean of Enrollment and Outreach Recruitment, Purdue University North Central, 1401 South US Highway 421, Westville, IN 46391-9528, 219-785-5283 or toll-free 800-872-1231 (in-state). *Fax:* 219-785-5538. *E-mail:* acardenas@pnc.edu.

QUEENS COLLEGE OF THE CITY UNIVERSITY OF NEW YORK
Flushing, NY

Tuition & fees (NY res): $5047	Average undergraduate aid package: $7500

ABOUT THE INSTITUTION State and locally supported, coed. 63 undergraduate majors. Federal methodology is used as a basis for awarding need-based institutional aid.

UNDERGRADUATE EXPENSES for 2010–11 *Tuition, state resident:* full-time $4600; part-time $195 per credit. *Tuition, nonresident:* full-time $9960; part-time $415 per credit. *Required fees:* full-time $447; $140.75 per term. *College room and board:* $11,125. Room and board charges vary according to housing facility. *Payment plan:* Installment.

FRESHMAN FINANCIAL AID (Fall 2009, est.) 1,540 applied for aid; of those 91% were deemed to have need. 100% of freshmen with need received aid. *Average percent of need met:* 95% (excluding resources awarded to replace EFC). *Average financial aid package:* $7500 (excluding resources awarded to replace EFC). 2% of all full-time freshmen had no need and received non-need-based gift aid.

UNDERGRADUATE FINANCIAL AID (Fall 2009, est.) 10,450 applied for aid; of those 88% were deemed to have need. 100% of undergraduates with need received aid. *Average percent of need met:* 95% (excluding resources awarded to replace EFC). *Average financial aid package:* $7500 (excluding resources awarded to replace EFC). 1% of all full-time undergraduates had no need and received non-need-based gift aid.

GIFT AID (NEED-BASED) *Total amount:* $47,434,321 (55% federal, 41% state, 4% institutional). *Receiving aid:* Freshmen: 66% (1,108); all full-time undergraduates: 64% (7,483). *Average award:* Freshmen: $4800; Undergraduates: $4800. *Scholarships, grants, and awards:* Federal Pell, FSEOG, state, college/university gift aid from institutional funds, Peter Vallone Scholarships.

GIFT AID (NON-NEED-BASED) *Total amount:* $106,000 (100% institutional). *Receiving aid:* Freshmen: 31% (524). Undergraduates: 13% (1,480). *Average award:* Freshmen: $8300. Undergraduates: $8300. *Scholarships, grants, and awards by category: Academic interests/achievement:* general academic interests/ achievements. *Creative arts/performance:* music. *Special achievements/activities:* community service, leadership. *Tuition waivers:* Full or partial for senior citizens.

LOANS *Student loans:* $20,667,276 (56% need-based, 44% non-need-based). 41% of past graduating class borrowed through all loan programs. *Average indebtedness per student:* $14,000. *Average need-based loan:* Freshmen: $2800. Undergraduates: $4900. *Parent loans:* $300,668 (100% need-based). *Programs:* Federal Direct (Subsidized and Unsubsidized Stafford, PLUS), Perkins.

WORK-STUDY *Federal work-study:* Total amount: $396,363; jobs available. *State or other work-study/employment:* Total amount: $140,000 (100% need-based). Part-time jobs available.

ATHLETIC AWARDS Total amount: $215,925 (100% non-need-based).

APPLYING FOR FINANCIAL AID *Required financial aid forms:* FAFSA, institution's own form, state aid form. *Financial aid deadline (priority):* 2/15. *Notification date:* Continuous beginning 5/1. Students must reply within 3 weeks of notification.

CONTACT Rena Smith-Kiawu, Director of Financial Aid, Queens College of the City University of New York, 65-30 Kissena Boulevard, Flushing, NY 11367-1597, 718-997-5100.

QUEENS UNIVERSITY OF CHARLOTTE
Charlotte, NC

CONTACT Lauren H. Mack, Director of Financial Aid, Queens University of Charlotte, 1900 Selwyn Avenue, Charlotte, NC 28274-0002, 704-337-2230 or toll-free 800-849-0202. *Fax:* 704-337-2416. *E-mail:* mackl@queens.edu.

QUINCY UNIVERSITY
Quincy, IL

Tuition & fees: $22,030	Average undergraduate aid package: $20,172

ABOUT THE INSTITUTION Independent Roman Catholic, coed. 33 undergraduate majors. Federal methodology is used as a basis for awarding need-based institutional aid.

UNDERGRADUATE EXPENSES for 2009–10 *Comprehensive fee:* $30,410 includes full-time tuition ($21,300), mandatory fees ($730), and room and board ($8380). *College room only:* $4520. Room and board charges vary according to board plan and housing facility. *Part-time tuition:* $480 per credit hour. *Part-time fees:* $15 per credit hour. *Payment plan:* Installment.

FRESHMAN FINANCIAL AID (Fall 2009, est.) 237 applied for aid; of those 93% were deemed to have need. 100% of freshmen with need received aid; of those 24% had need fully met. *Average percent of need met:* 85% (excluding resources awarded to replace EFC). *Average financial aid package:* $22,199 (excluding resources awarded to replace EFC). 3% of all full-time freshmen had no need and received non-need-based gift aid.

UNDERGRADUATE FINANCIAL AID (Fall 2009, est.) 996 applied for aid; of those 91% were deemed to have need. 97% of undergraduates with need received aid; of those 22% had need fully met. *Average percent of need met:* 79% (excluding resources awarded to replace EFC). *Average financial aid package:* $20,172 (excluding resources awarded to replace EFC). 3% of all full-time undergraduates had no need and received non-need-based gift aid.

GIFT AID (NEED-BASED) *Total amount:* $12,358,319 (20% federal, 17% state, 62% institutional, 1% external sources). *Receiving aid:* Freshmen: 89% (221); all full-time undergraduates: 79% (864). *Average award:* Freshmen: $17,950; Undergraduates: $15,730. *Scholarships, grants, and awards:* Federal Pell, FSEOG, state, private, college/university gift aid from institutional funds.

GIFT AID (NON-NEED-BASED) *Total amount:* $1,086,933 (4% federal, 3% state, 86% institutional, 7% external sources). *Receiving aid:* Freshmen: 16% (40). Undergraduates: 11% (116). *Average award:* Freshmen: $11,875. Undergraduates: $9884. *Scholarships, grants, and awards by category: Academic interests/achievement:* 983 awards ($6,725,263 total): biological sciences, business, communication, computer science, education, English, general academic interests/achievements, health fields, international studies, mathematics, premedicine, religion/biblical studies, social sciences. *Creative arts/performance:* 51 awards ($109,837 total): art/fine arts, cinema/film/broadcasting, music. *Special achievements/activities:* 4 awards ($3400 total): community service, leadership. *Special characteristics:* 27 awards ($224,853 total): children of faculty/staff. *Tuition waivers:* Full or partial for employees or children of employees, senior citizens.

LOANS *Student loans:* $7,073,059 (71% need-based, 29% non-need-based). 77% of past graduating class borrowed through all loan programs. *Average indebtedness per student:* $21,785. *Average need-based loan:* Freshmen: $3907. Undergraduates: $4704. *Parent loans:* $765,629 (26% need-based, 74% non-need-based). *Programs:* FFEL (Subsidized and Unsubsidized Stafford, PLUS), Perkins.

WORK-STUDY *Federal work-study:* Total amount: $216,293; 515 jobs averaging $2000. *State or other work-study/employment:* Part-time jobs available.

ATHLETIC AWARDS Total amount: $2,938,790 (72% need-based, 28% non-need-based).

APPLYING FOR FINANCIAL AID *Required financial aid form:* FAFSA. *Financial aid deadline (priority):* 3/1. *Notification date:* Continuous beginning 2/15. Students must reply by 5/1 or within 2 weeks of notification.

CONTACT Lisa Flack, Director of Financial Aid, Quincy University, 1800 College Avenue, Quincy, IL 62301-2699, 217-228-5260 or toll-free 800-688-4295. *Fax:* 217-228-5635. *E-mail:* financialaid@quincy.edu.

QUINNIPIAC UNIVERSITY
Hamden, CT

Tuition & fees: $34,250	Average undergraduate aid package: $19,785

ABOUT THE INSTITUTION Independent, coed. 59 undergraduate majors. Federal methodology is used as a basis for awarding need-based institutional aid.

UNDERGRADUATE EXPENSES for 2010–11 *Comprehensive fee:* $46,980 includes full-time tuition ($32,850), mandatory fees ($1400), and room and board ($12,730). Room and board charges vary according to housing facility. *Part-time tuition:* $790 per credit hour. *Part-time fees:* $35 per credit hour. Part-time tuition and fees vary according to class time and course load. *Payment plans:* Installment, deferred payment.

FRESHMAN FINANCIAL AID (Fall 2009, est.) 1,263 applied for aid; of those 77% were deemed to have need. 100% of freshmen with need received aid; of those 13% had need fully met. *Average percent of need met:* 68% (excluding resources awarded to replace EFC). *Average financial aid package:* $20,351 (excluding resources awarded to replace EFC). 16% of all full-time freshmen had no need and received non-need-based gift aid.

UNDERGRADUATE FINANCIAL AID (Fall 2009, est.) 4,111 applied for aid; of those 81% were deemed to have need. 100% of undergraduates with need received aid; of those 13% had need fully met. *Average percent of need met:* 65% (excluding resources awarded to replace EFC). *Average financial aid package:* $19,785 (excluding resources awarded to replace EFC). 14% of all full-time undergraduates had no need and received non-need-based gift aid.

GIFT AID (NEED-BASED) *Total amount:* $34,303,917 (11% federal, 9% state, 76% institutional, 4% external sources). *Receiving aid:* Freshmen: 60% (955); all full-time undergraduates: 57% (3,263). *Average award:* Freshmen: $15,499; Undergraduates: $14,200. *Scholarships, grants, and awards:* Federal Pell, FSEOG, state, private, college/university gift aid from institutional funds.

GIFT AID (NON-NEED-BASED) *Total amount:* $20,041,011 (99% institutional, 1% external sources). *Receiving aid:* Freshmen: 27% (426). Undergraduates: 24% (1,377). *Average award:* Freshmen: $10,748. Undergraduates: $9748. *Scholarships, grants, and awards by category:* Academic interests/achievement: 1,963 awards ($19,801,664 total): general academic interests/achievements. Special characteristics: 327 awards ($2,755,269 total): children of faculty/staff, international students, siblings of current students. *Tuition waivers:* Full or partial for employees or children of employees.

LOANS *Student loans:* $43,725,129 (67% need-based, 33% non-need-based). 69% of past graduating class borrowed through all loan programs. *Average indebtedness per student:* $34,621. *Average need-based loan:* Freshmen: $3515. Undergraduates: $4476. *Parent loans:* $14,347,674 (100% non-need-based). *Programs:* Federal Direct (Subsidized and Unsubsidized Stafford, PLUS), Perkins, Federal Nursing.

WORK-STUDY *Federal work-study:* Total amount: $3,530,350; 1,744 jobs averaging $2032. *State or other work-study/employment:* Total amount: $87,774 (100% need-based). 48 part-time jobs averaging $1841.

ATHLETIC AWARDS Total amount: $7,247,236 (100% non-need-based).

APPLYING FOR FINANCIAL AID *Required financial aid forms:* FAFSA, CSS Financial Aid PROFILE. *Financial aid deadline (priority):* 3/1. *Notification date:* Continuous beginning 3/1. Students must reply by 5/1 or within 2 weeks of notification.

CONTACT Mr. Dominic Yoia, Senior Director of Financial Aid, Quinnipiac University, 275 Mount Carmel Avenue, Hamden, CT 06518, 203-582-5224 or toll-free 800-462-1944 (out-of-state). *Fax:* 203-582-5238. *E-mail:* finaid@quinnipiac.edu.

RABBI JACOB JOSEPH SCHOOL
Edison, NJ

CONTACT Financial Aid Office, Rabbi Jacob Joseph School, One Plainfield Ave, Edison, NJ 08817, 908-985-6533.

RABBINICAL ACADEMY MESIVTA RABBI CHAIM BERLIN
Brooklyn, NY

CONTACT Office of Financial Aid, Rabbinical Academy Mesivta Rabbi Chaim Berlin, 1605 Coney Island Avenue, Brooklyn, NY 11230-4715, 718-377-0777.

RABBINICAL COLLEGE BETH SHRAGA
Monsey, NY

CONTACT Financial Aid Office, Rabbinical College Beth Shraga, 28 Saddle River Road, Monsey, NY 10952-3035, 914-356-1980.

RABBINICAL COLLEGE BOBOVER YESHIVA B'NEI ZION
Brooklyn, NY

CONTACT Financial Aid Office, Rabbinical College Bobover Yeshiva B'nei Zion, 1577 48th Street, Brooklyn, NY 11219, 718-438-2018.

RABBINICAL COLLEGE CH'SAN SOFER
Brooklyn, NY

CONTACT Financial Aid Office, Rabbinical College Ch'san Sofer, 1876 50th Street, Brooklyn, NY 11204, 718-236-1171.

RABBINICAL COLLEGE OF AMERICA
Morristown, NJ

CONTACT Financial Aid Office, Rabbinical College of America, 226 Sussex Avenue, Morristown, NJ 07960, 973-267-9404. *Fax:* 973-267-5208.

RABBINICAL COLLEGE OF LONG ISLAND
Long Beach, NY

CONTACT Rabbi Cone, Financial Aid Administrator, Rabbinical College of Long Island, 201 Magnolia Boulevard, Long Beach, NY 11561-3305, 516-431-7414.

RABBINICAL COLLEGE OF OHR SHIMON YISROEL
Brooklyn, NY

CONTACT Financial Aid Office, Rabbinical College of Ohr Shimon Yisroel, 215-217 Hewes Street, Brooklyn, NY 11211, 718-855-4092.

RABBINICAL COLLEGE OF TELSHE
Wickliffe, OH

CONTACT Financial Aid Office, Rabbinical College of Telshe, 28400 Euclid Avenue, Wickliffe, OH 44092-2523, 216-943-5300.

RABBINICAL SEMINARY ADAS YEREIM
Brooklyn, NY

CONTACT Mr. Israel Weingarten, Financial Aid Administrator, Rabbinical Seminary Adas Yereim, 185 Wilson Street, Brooklyn, NY 11211-7206, 718-388-1751.

RABBINICAL SEMINARY M'KOR CHAIM
Brooklyn, NY

CONTACT Financial Aid Office, Rabbinical Seminary M'kor Chaim, 1571 55th Street, Brooklyn, NY 11219, 718-851-0183.

RABBINICAL SEMINARY OF AMERICA
Flushing, NY

CONTACT Ms. Leah Eisenstein, Director of Financial Aid, Rabbinical Seminary of America, 92-15 69th Avenue, Forest Hills, NY 11375, 718-268-4700. *Fax:* 718-268-4684.

RADFORD UNIVERSITY
Radford, VA

Tuition & fees (VA res): $6904   **Average undergraduate aid package:** $9394

ABOUT THE INSTITUTION State-supported, coed. 38 undergraduate majors. Federal methodology is used as a basis for awarding need-based institutional aid.

UNDERGRADUATE EXPENSES for 2009–10 *Tuition, state resident:* full-time $4396; part-time $183 per credit hour. *Tuition, nonresident:* full-time $14,060; part-time $586 per credit hour. *Required fees:* full-time $2508; $105 per credit hour. *College room and board:* $6970; *Room only:* $3698. Room and board charges vary according to board plan and housing facility. *Payment plan:* Installment.

FRESHMAN FINANCIAL AID (Fall 2009, est.) 1,040 applied for aid; of those 63% were deemed to have need. 93% of freshmen with need received aid; of those 21% had need fully met. *Average percent of need met:* 81% (excluding resources awarded to replace EFC). *Average financial aid package:* $8887 (excluding resources awarded to replace EFC). 2% of all full-time freshmen had no need and received non-need-based gift aid.

UNDERGRADUATE FINANCIAL AID (Fall 2009, est.) 4,839 applied for aid; of those 70% were deemed to have need. 96% of undergraduates with need received aid; of those 29% had need fully met. *Average percent of need met:* 83% (excluding resources awarded to replace EFC). *Average financial aid package:* $9394 (excluding resources awarded to replace EFC). 2% of all full-time undergraduates had no need and received non-need-based gift aid.

GIFT AID (NEED-BASED) *Total amount:* $18,950,905 (40% federal, 37% state, 19% institutional, 4% external sources). *Receiving aid:* Freshmen: 26% (383); all full-time undergraduates: 29% (2,121). *Average award:* Freshmen: $7927; Undergraduates: $7661. *Scholarships, grants, and awards:* Federal Pell, FSEOG, state, private, college/university gift aid from institutional funds.

GIFT AID (NON-NEED-BASED) *Total amount:* $1,594,894 (16% federal, 8% state, 45% institutional, 31% external sources). *Receiving aid:* Freshmen: 15% (220). Undergraduates: 9% (692). *Average award:* Freshmen: $5616. Undergraduates: $3895. *Tuition waivers:* Full or partial for employees or children of employees, senior citizens.

LOANS *Student loans:* $29,990,702 (71% need-based, 29% non-need-based). 59% of past graduating class borrowed through all loan programs. *Average indebtedness per student:* $18,817. *Average need-based loan:* Freshmen: $2888. Undergraduates: $3694. *Parent loans:* $4,260,113 (51% need-based, 49% non-need-based). *Programs:* Federal Direct (Subsidized and Unsubsidized Stafford, PLUS), Perkins, Federal Nursing, state, college/university.

WORK-STUDY *Federal work-study:* Total amount: $906,460; 352 jobs averaging $2610. *State or other work-study/employment:* Total amount: $900,144 (44% need-based, 56% non-need-based). 331 part-time jobs averaging $2610.

ATHLETIC AWARDS Total amount: $2,062,610 (92% need-based, 8% non-need-based).

APPLYING FOR FINANCIAL AID *Required financial aid form:* FAFSA. *Financial aid deadline (priority):* 2/15. *Notification date:* 4/15. Students must reply within 4 weeks of notification.

CONTACT Mrs. Barbara Porter, Director of Financial Aid, Radford University, PO Box 6905, Radford, VA 24142, 540-831-5408 or toll-free 800-890-4265. *Fax:* 540-831-5138. *E-mail:* bporter@radford.edu.

RAMAPO COLLEGE OF NEW JERSEY
Mahwah, NJ

Tuition & fees (NJ res): $11,416   **Average undergraduate aid package:** $8002

ABOUT THE INSTITUTION State-supported, coed. 36 undergraduate majors. Federal methodology is used as a basis for awarding need-based institutional aid.

UNDERGRADUATE EXPENSES for 2009–10 *Tuition, state resident:* full-time $7683; part-time $240.10 per credit. *Tuition, nonresident:* full-time $15,366; part-time $480.20 per credit. *Required fees:* full-time $3733; $116.65 per credit. Full-time tuition and fees vary according to degree level and reciprocity agreements. Part-time tuition and fees vary according to degree level and reciprocity agreements. *College room and board:* $11,290; *Room only:* $8200. Room and board charges vary according to board plan and housing facility. *Payment plan:* Installment.

FRESHMAN FINANCIAL AID (Fall 2009, est.) 784 applied for aid; of those 66% were deemed to have need. 95% of freshmen with need received aid; of those 19% had need fully met. *Average percent of need met:* 70% (excluding resources awarded to replace EFC). *Average financial aid package:* $11,783 (excluding resources awarded to replace EFC). 8% of all full-time freshmen had no need and received non-need-based gift aid.

UNDERGRADUATE FINANCIAL AID (Fall 2009, est.) 3,293 applied for aid; of those 74% were deemed to have need. 97% of undergraduates with need received aid; of those 5% had need fully met. *Average percent of need met:* 69% (excluding resources awarded to replace EFC). *Average financial aid package:* $8002 (excluding resources awarded to replace EFC). 5% of all full-time undergraduates had no need and received non-need-based gift aid.

GIFT AID (NEED-BASED) *Total amount:* $12,552,717 (46% federal, 48% state, 6% institutional). *Receiving aid:* Freshmen: 23% (216); all full-time undergraduates: 21% (1,081). *Average award:* Freshmen: $13,592; Undergraduates: $10,678. *Scholarships, grants, and awards:* Federal Pell, FSEOG, state, private, college/university gift aid from institutional funds, Federal Nursing.

GIFT AID (NON-NEED-BASED) *Total amount:* $7,222,773 (8% state, 82% institutional, 10% external sources). *Receiving aid:* Freshmen: 21% (199). Undergraduates: 14% (756). *Average award:* Freshmen: $10,021. Undergraduates: $12,174. *Scholarships, grants, and awards by category:* Academic interests/achievement: 579 awards ($5,814,533 total): general academic interests/achievements. Special characteristics: 94 awards ($1,265,001 total): children of faculty/staff, international students, out-of-state students. *Tuition waivers:* Full or partial for employees or children of employees, senior citizens.

LOANS *Student loans:* $31,666,425 (33% need-based, 67% non-need-based). 55% of past graduating class borrowed through all loan programs. *Average indebtedness per student:* $19,789. *Average need-based loan:* Freshmen: $3196. Undergraduates: $4563. *Parent loans:* $6,972,741 (100% non-need-based). *Programs:* Federal Direct (Subsidized and Unsubsidized Stafford, PLUS), Perkins, state.

WORK-STUDY *Federal work-study:* Total amount: $295,826; 134 jobs averaging $2207. *State or other work-study/employment:* Total amount: $1,716,263 (100% non-need-based). 761 part-time jobs averaging $2255.

APPLYING FOR FINANCIAL AID *Required financial aid form:* FAFSA. *Financial aid deadline (priority):* 3/1. *Notification date:* Continuous beginning 4/1. Students must reply by 5/1 or within 2 weeks of notification.

CONTACT Bernice Mulch, Assistant Director of Financial Aid, Ramapo College of New Jersey, 505 Ramapo Valley Road, Mahwah, NJ 07430-1680, 201-684-7252 or toll-free 800-9RAMAPO (in-state). *Fax:* 201-684-7085. *E-mail:* finaid@ramapo.edu.

RANDOLPH COLLEGE
Lynchburg, VA

Tuition & fees: $29,254   **Average undergraduate aid package:** $23,736

ABOUT THE INSTITUTION Independent Methodist, coed. 35 undergraduate majors. Federal methodology is used as a basis for awarding need-based institutional aid.

UNDERGRADUATE EXPENSES for 2010–11 *Comprehensive fee:* $39,249 includes full-time tuition ($28,744), mandatory fees ($510), and room and board ($9995). Part-time tuition and fees vary according to course load. *Payment plan:* Installment.

FRESHMAN FINANCIAL AID (Fall 2009, est.) 118 applied for aid; of those 86% were deemed to have need. 100% of freshmen with need received aid; of those 25% had need fully met. *Average percent of need met:* 78% (excluding resources awarded to replace EFC). *Average financial aid package:* $22,341 (excluding resources awarded to replace EFC). 24% of all full-time freshmen had no need and received non-need-based gift aid.

UNDERGRADUATE FINANCIAL AID (Fall 2009, est.) 377 applied for aid; of those 89% were deemed to have need. 99% of undergraduates with need received aid; of those 19% had need fully met. *Average percent of need met:* 77% (excluding resources awarded to replace EFC). *Average financial aid package:* $23,736 (excluding resources awarded to replace EFC). 30% of all full-time undergraduates had no need and received non-need-based gift aid.

GIFT AID (NEED-BASED) *Total amount:* $5,896,917 (12% federal, 8% state, 79% institutional, 1% external sources). *Receiving aid:* Freshmen: 76% (102); all full-time undergraduates: 70% (331). *Average award:* Freshmen: $17,863; Undergraduates: $18,184. *Scholarships, grants, and awards:* Federal Pell, FSEOG, state, private, college/university gift aid from institutional funds.

GIFT AID (NON-NEED-BASED) *Total amount:* $2,484,827 (8% state, 91% institutional, 1% external sources). *Receiving aid:* Freshmen: 16% (21). Undergraduates: 10% (48). *Average award:* Freshmen: $15,094. Undergraduates: $14,949. *Scholarships, grants, and awards by category:* Academic interests/achievement: 400 awards ($6,920,015 total): biological sciences, education, English, general academic interests/achievements, mathematics, physical sciences, premedicine, social sciences. *Creative arts/performance:* art/fine arts, creative writing, music, theater/drama. *Special achievements/activities:* community service, general special achievements/activities, leadership. *Special characteristics:* adult students, children of faculty/staff, international students, local/state students, relatives of clergy, religious affiliation, twins. *Tuition waivers:* Full or partial for employees or children of employees, adult students.

LOANS *Student loans:* $3,349,290 (70% need-based, 30% non-need-based). 78% of past graduating class borrowed through all loan programs. *Average indebtedness per student:* $26,395. *Average need-based loan:* Freshmen: $4461. Undergraduates: $5659. *Parent loans:* $1,252,135 (40% need-based, 60% non-need-based). *Programs:* Federal Direct (Subsidized and Unsubsidized Stafford, PLUS), FFEL (Subsidized and Unsubsidized Stafford, PLUS), Perkins.

WORK-STUDY *Federal work-study:* Total amount: $292,999; 80 jobs averaging $1860. *State or other work-study/employment:* Total amount: $183,876 (6% need-based, 94% non-need-based). 290 part-time jobs averaging $1200.

APPLYING FOR FINANCIAL AID *Required financial aid forms:* FAFSA, state aid form. *Financial aid deadline (priority):* 3/1. *Notification date:* Continuous beginning 3/1. Students must reply by 5/1 or within 2 weeks of notification.

CONTACT Kay G. Mattox, Director of Student Financial Services, Randolph College, 2500 Rivermont Avenue, Lynchburg, VA 24503-1526, 434-947-8128 or toll-free 800-745-7692. *Fax:* 434-947-8996. *E-mail:* kmattox@randolphcollege.edu.

RANDOLPH-MACON COLLEGE
Ashland, VA

Tuition & fees: $29,182	Average undergraduate aid package: $21,777

ABOUT THE INSTITUTION Independent United Methodist, coed. 29 undergraduate majors. Federal methodology is used as a basis for awarding need-based institutional aid.

UNDERGRADUATE EXPENSES for 2009–10 *Comprehensive fee:* $38,073 includes full-time tuition ($28,397), mandatory fees ($785), and room and board ($8891). Full-time tuition and fees vary according to reciprocity agreements. Room and board charges vary according to housing facility. *Part-time tuition:* $3155 per course. *Part-time fees:* $785 per year. *Payment plan:* Installment.

FRESHMAN FINANCIAL AID (Fall 2009, est.) 301 applied for aid; of those 82% were deemed to have need. 100% of freshmen with need received aid; of those 22% had need fully met. *Average percent of need met:* 80% (excluding resources awarded to replace EFC). *Average financial aid package:* $22,871 (excluding resources awarded to replace EFC). 32% of all full-time freshmen had no need and received non-need-based gift aid.

UNDERGRADUATE FINANCIAL AID (Fall 2009, est.) 935 applied for aid; of those 85% were deemed to have need. 100% of undergraduates with need received aid; of those 26% had need fully met. *Average percent of need met:* 79% (excluding resources awarded to replace EFC). *Average financial aid package:* $21,777 (excluding resources awarded to replace EFC). 33% of all full-time undergraduates had no need and received non-need-based gift aid.

GIFT AID (NEED-BASED) *Total amount:* $13,792,227 (9% federal, 11% state, 75% institutional, 5% external sources). *Receiving aid:* Freshmen: 68% (246); all full-time undergraduates: 65% (788). *Average award:* Freshmen: $18,530; Undergraduates: $17,689. *Scholarships, grants, and awards:* Federal Pell, FSEOG, state, private, college/university gift aid from institutional funds.

GIFT AID (NON-NEED-BASED) *Total amount:* $6,408,122 (16% state, 79% institutional, 5% external sources). *Receiving aid:* Freshmen: 13% (46). Undergraduates: 12% (147). *Average award:* Freshmen: $11,533. Undergraduates: $10,726. *Scholarships, grants, and awards by category:* Academic interests/achievement: 587 awards ($6,994,003 total): general academic interests/achievements. *Special achievements/activities:* 556 awards ($3,558,749 total): general special achievements/activities. *Special characteristics:* 559 awards ($1,413,930 total): children and siblings of alumni, children of faculty/staff, ethnic background, out-of-state students, relatives of clergy, siblings of current students. *Tuition waivers:* Full or partial for employees or children of employees.

LOANS *Student loans:* $8,112,654 (59% need-based, 41% non-need-based). 72% of past graduating class borrowed through all loan programs. *Average indebtedness per student:* $26,763. *Average need-based loan:* Freshmen: $4573. Undergraduates: $4627. *Parent loans:* $3,600,233 (26% need-based, 74% non-need-based). *Programs:* FFEL (Subsidized and Unsubsidized Stafford, PLUS), Perkins, college/university.

WORK-STUDY *Federal work-study:* Total amount: $383,293; 230 jobs averaging $2000.

APPLYING FOR FINANCIAL AID *Required financial aid forms:* FAFSA, state aid form. *Financial aid deadline (priority):* 2/15. *Notification date:* 3/1. Students must reply by 5/1 or within 2 weeks of notification.

CONTACT Ms. Mary Neal, Director of Financial Aid, Randolph-Macon College, PO Box 5005, Ashland, VA 23005-5505, 804-752-7259 or toll-free 800-888-1762. *Fax:* 804-752-3719. *E-mail:* mneal@rmc.edu.

REED COLLEGE
Portland, OR

Tuition & fees: $39,700	Average undergraduate aid package: $33,090

ABOUT THE INSTITUTION Independent, coed. 29 undergraduate majors. Institutional methodology is used as a basis for awarding need-based institutional aid.

UNDERGRADUATE EXPENSES for 2009–10 *Comprehensive fee:* $49,950 includes full-time tuition ($39,440), mandatory fees ($260), and room and board ($10,250). *College room only:* $5350. Room and board charges vary according to board plan and housing facility. *Part-time tuition:* $1675 per semester hour. Part-time tuition and fees vary according to course load. *Payment plan:* Installment.

FRESHMAN FINANCIAL AID (Fall 2009, est.) 241 applied for aid; of those 76% were deemed to have need. 100% of freshmen with need received aid; of those 97% had need fully met. *Average percent of need met:* 100% (excluding resources awarded to replace EFC). *Average financial aid package:* $33,161 (excluding resources awarded to replace EFC).

UNDERGRADUATE FINANCIAL AID (Fall 2009, est.) 841 applied for aid; of those 87% were deemed to have need. 100% of undergraduates with need received aid; of those 98% had need fully met. *Average percent of need met:* 100% (excluding resources awarded to replace EFC). *Average financial aid package:* $33,090 (excluding resources awarded to replace EFC).

GIFT AID (NEED-BASED) *Total amount:* $20,845,291 (8% federal, 91% institutional, 1% external sources). *Receiving aid:* Freshmen: 43% (156); all full-time undergraduates: 48% (671). *Average award:* Freshmen: $33,181; Undergraduates: $30,710. *Scholarships, grants, and awards:* Federal Pell, FSEOG, state, private, college/university gift aid from institutional funds.

GIFT AID (NON-NEED-BASED) *Total amount:* $46,990 (100% external sources). *Tuition waivers:* Full or partial for employees or children of employees.

LOANS *Student loans:* $3,312,641 (78% need-based, 22% non-need-based). 53% of past graduating class borrowed through all loan programs. *Average indebtedness per student:* $20,750. *Average need-based loan:* Freshmen: $3004. Undergraduates: $4234. *Parent loans:* $1,808,336 (5% need-based, 95% non-need-based). *Programs:* Federal Direct (Subsidized and Unsubsidized Stafford, PLUS), Perkins.

WORK-STUDY *Federal work-study:* Total amount: $381,871; 275 jobs averaging $1388. *State or other work-study/employment:* Total amount: $394,891 (100% need-based). 303 part-time jobs averaging $1304.

APPLYING FOR FINANCIAL AID *Required financial aid forms:* FAFSA, CSS Financial Aid PROFILE, noncustodial (divorced/separated) parent's statement, business/farm supplement. *Financial aid deadline:* 2/1. *Notification date:* 4/1. Students must reply by 5/1 or within 2 weeks of notification.

CONTACT Leslie Limper, Financial Aid Director, Reed College, 3203 Southeast Woodstock Boulevard, Portland, OR 97202-8199, 503-777-7223 or toll-free 800-547-4750 (out-of-state). *Fax:* 503-788-6682. *E-mail:* financial.aid@reed.edu.

REGENT UNIVERSITY
Virginia Beach, VA

Tuition & fees: $14,200	Average undergraduate aid package: N/A

ABOUT THE INSTITUTION Independent, coed. 24 undergraduate majors. Federal methodology is used as a basis for awarding need-based institutional aid.

UNDERGRADUATE EXPENSES for 2009–10 *Tuition:* full-time $13,950; part-time $465 per credit hour. Full-time tuition and fees vary according to course level, course load, program, and student level. Part-time tuition and fees vary according to course level, course load, program, and student level. Room and board charges vary according to housing facility. *Payment plan:* Installment.

GIFT AID (NEED-BASED) *Total amount:* $4,111,632 (74% federal, 26% institutional). *Scholarships, grants, and awards:* Federal Pell, state, college/university gift aid from institutional funds.

GIFT AID (NON-NEED-BASED) *Total amount:* $3,082,748 (3% federal, 92% institutional, 5% external sources). *Scholarships, grants, and awards by category: Academic interests/achievement:* business, communication, education, English, foreign languages, humanities, religion/biblical studies, social sciences. *Creative arts/performance:* cinema/film/broadcasting, journalism/publications. *Special achievements/activities:* leadership. *Special characteristics:* children and siblings of alumni, children of faculty/staff, public servants, siblings of current students. *Tuition waivers:* Full or partial for employees or children of employees.

LOANS *Student loans:* $11,518,804 (42% need-based, 58% non-need-based). *Parent loans:* $858,043 (100% non-need-based). *Programs:* Federal Direct (Subsidized and Unsubsidized Stafford, PLUS).

APPLYING FOR FINANCIAL AID *Required financial aid forms:* FAFSA, institution's own form, state aid form. *Financial aid deadline:* Continuous. *Notification date:* Continuous beginning 3/1. Students must reply within 2 weeks of notification.

CONTACT Central Financial Aid Office, Regent University, 1000 Regent University Drive, Student Center 251, Virginia Beach, VA 23707, 757-352-4125 or toll-free 800-373-5504. *Fax:* 757-352-4118. *E-mail:* finaid@regent.edu.

REGIS COLLEGE
Weston, MA

ABOUT THE INSTITUTION Independent Roman Catholic, coed. 21 undergraduate majors.

GIFT AID (NEED-BASED) *Scholarships, grants, and awards:* Federal Pell, FSEOG, state, private, college/university gift aid from institutional funds.

GIFT AID (NON-NEED-BASED) *Scholarships, grants, and awards by category: Academic interests/achievement:* general academic interests/achievements. *Special achievements/activities:* community service, leadership. *Special characteristics:* adult students, children of faculty/staff, international students, relatives of clergy, religious affiliation, siblings of current students.

LOANS *Programs:* Federal Direct (Subsidized and Unsubsidized Stafford, PLUS), Perkins, state.

WORK-STUDY *Federal work-study:* Total amount: $907,268; 436 jobs averaging $2000. *State or other work-study/employment:* Total amount: $47,050 (100% non-need-based). 40 part-time jobs averaging $1500.

APPLYING FOR FINANCIAL AID *Required financial aid forms:* FAFSA, institution's own form.

CONTACT Dee J. Ludwick, Director of Financial Aid, Regis College, Box 81, Weston, MA 02493, 781-768-7180 or toll-free 866-438-7344. *Fax:* 781-768-7225. *E-mail:* finaid@regiscollege.edu.

REGIS UNIVERSITY
Denver, CO

Tuition & fees: N/R	Average undergraduate aid package: $15,333

ABOUT THE INSTITUTION Independent Roman Catholic (Jesuit), coed. *Awards:* bachelor's and master's degrees. 33 undergraduate majors. *Total enrollment:* 11,038. Undergraduates: 5,705. Freshmen: 480. Federal methodology is used as a basis for awarding need-based institutional aid.

FRESHMAN FINANCIAL AID (Fall 2008) 383 applied for aid; of those 63% were deemed to have need. 100% of freshmen with need received aid; of those 64% had need fully met. *Average percent of need met:* 61% (excluding resources awarded to replace EFC). *Average financial aid package:* $17,534 (excluding resources awarded to replace EFC). 32% of all full-time freshmen had no need and received non-need-based gift aid.

UNDERGRADUATE FINANCIAL AID (Fall 2008) 1,210 applied for aid; of those 63% were deemed to have need. 99% of undergraduates with need received aid; of those 57% had need fully met. *Average percent of need met:* 54% (excluding resources awarded to replace EFC). *Average financial aid package:* $15,333 (excluding resources awarded to replace EFC). 24% of all full-time undergraduates had no need and received non-need-based gift aid.

GIFT AID (NEED-BASED) *Total amount:* $14,553,045 (11% federal, 12% state, 68% institutional, 9% external sources). *Receiving aid:* Freshmen: 46% (177); all full-time undergraduates: 40% (507). *Average award:* Freshmen: $12,788; Undergraduates: $10,756. *Scholarships, grants, and awards:* Federal Pell, FSEOG, state, private, college/university gift aid from institutional funds, Academic Competitiveness Grants, National SMART Grants.

GIFT AID (NON-NEED-BASED) *Total amount:* $6,714,280 (96% institutional, 4% external sources). *Receiving aid:* Freshmen: 36% (140). Undergraduates: 27% (346). *Average award:* Freshmen: $11,012. Undergraduates: $10,411. *Scholarships, grants, and awards by category: Academic interests/achievement:* 315 awards ($3,539,568 total): biological sciences, general academic interests/achievements, physical sciences. *Creative arts/performance:* 25 awards ($125,000 total): debating, music. *Special achievements/activities:* 49 awards ($31,616 total): leadership. *Special characteristics:* 23 awards ($359,456 total): children of faculty/staff, local/state students. *Tuition waivers:* Full or partial for employees or children of employees. *ROTC:* Army cooperative, Air Force cooperative.

LOANS *Student loans:* $5,560,549 (82% need-based, 18% non-need-based). 66% of past graduating class borrowed through all loan programs. *Average indebtedness per student:* $25,558. *Average need-based loan:* Freshmen: $1812. Undergraduates: $2226. *Parent loans:* $3,237,876 (59% need-based, 41% non-need-based). *Programs:* FFEL (Subsidized and Unsubsidized Stafford, PLUS), Perkins, Federal Nursing.

WORK-STUDY *Federal work-study:* Total amount: $422,389; 231 jobs averaging $1829. *State or other work-study/employment:* Total amount: $1,159,609 (64% need-based, 36% non-need-based). 443 part-time jobs averaging $1752.

ATHLETIC AWARDS Total amount: $2,196,154 (37% need-based, 63% non-need-based).

APPLYING FOR FINANCIAL AID *Required financial aid form:* FAFSA. *Financial aid deadline (priority):* 3/1. *Notification date:* Continuous beginning 3/15.

CONTACT Ellie Miller, Director of Financial Aid, Regis University, 3333 Regis Boulevard, Denver, CO 80221-1099, 303-964-5758 or toll-free 800-388-2366 Ext. 4900. *Fax:* 303-964-5449. *E-mail:* emiller@regis.edu.

REINHARDT UNIVERSITY
Waleska, GA

Tuition & fees: $16,670	Average undergraduate aid package: $9500

ABOUT THE INSTITUTION Independent religious, coed. 31 undergraduate majors. Federal methodology is used as a basis for awarding need-based institutional aid.

UNDERGRADUATE EXPENSES for 2009–10 *Comprehensive fee:* $22,942 includes full-time tuition ($16,500), mandatory fees ($170), and room and board ($6272). Full-time tuition and fees vary according to degree level, location, and program. Room and board charges vary according to board plan and housing facility. *Part-time tuition:* $550 per credit hour. *Part-time fees:* $85 per term. Part-time tuition and fees vary according to degree level, location, and program. *Payment plan:* Installment.

FRESHMAN FINANCIAL AID (Fall 2009, est.) 190 applied for aid; of those 85% were deemed to have need. 100% of freshmen with need received aid; of those 10% had need fully met. *Average percent of need met:* 18% (excluding resources awarded to replace EFC). *Average financial aid package:* $8071 (excluding resources awarded to replace EFC). 41% of all full-time freshmen had no need and received non-need-based gift aid.

UNDERGRADUATE FINANCIAL AID (Fall 2009, est.) 759 applied for aid; of those 89% were deemed to have need. 100% of undergraduates with need received aid; of those 8% had need fully met. *Average percent of need met:* 27% (excluding resources awarded to replace EFC). *Average financial aid package:* $9500 (excluding resources awarded to replace EFC). 25% of all full-time undergraduates had no need and received non-need-based gift aid.

GIFT AID (NEED-BASED) *Total amount:* $5,346,140 (27% federal, 28% state, 42% institutional, 3% external sources). *Receiving aid:* Freshmen: 53% (160); all full-time undergraduates: 64% (633). *Average award:* Freshmen: $6767; Undergraduates: $7403. *Scholarships, grants, and awards:* Federal Pell, FSEOG, state, private, college/university gift aid from institutional funds.

GIFT AID (NON-NEED-BASED) *Total amount:* $1,537,638 (34% state, 63% institutional, 3% external sources). *Receiving aid:* Freshmen: 41% (124). Undergraduates: 25% (246). *Average award:* Freshmen: $5304. Undergraduates: $5384. *Scholarships, grants, and awards by category: Academic interests/achievement:* 797 awards ($4,439,317 total): general academic interests/achievements. *Creative arts/performance:* 112 awards ($344,225 total): art/fine arts, music. *Special achievements/activities:* 14 awards ($18,975 total): leadership. *Special characteristics:* 87 awards ($464,655 total): religious affiliation. *Tuition waivers:* Full or partial for employees or children of employees, senior citizens.

LOANS *Student loans:* $5,684,045 (93% need-based, 7% non-need-based). 67% of past graduating class borrowed through all loan programs. *Average indebtedness per student:* $21,095. *Average need-based loan:* Freshmen: $3030. Undergraduates: $3631. *Parent loans:* $927,775 (87% need-based, 13% non-need-based). *Programs:* FFEL (Subsidized and Unsubsidized Stafford, PLUS).

WORK-STUDY *Federal work-study:* Total amount: $52,255; 97 jobs averaging $574. *State or other work-study/employment:* Total amount: $56,781 (100% non-need-based). 98 part-time jobs averaging $579.

ATHLETIC AWARDS Total amount: $991,085 (65% need-based, 35% non-need-based).

APPLYING FOR FINANCIAL AID *Required financial aid forms:* FAFSA, state aid form. *Financial aid deadline (priority):* 5/1. *Notification date:* Continuous. Students must reply by 6/1.

CONTACT Angela D. Harlow, Director of Financial Aid, Reinhardt University, 7300 Reinhardt College Circle, Waleska, GA 30183-2981, 770-720-5603. *Fax:* 770-720-9126.

RENSSELAER POLYTECHNIC INSTITUTE
Troy, NY

Tuition & fees: $39,165	Average undergraduate aid package: $32,065

ABOUT THE INSTITUTION Independent, coed. 39 undergraduate majors. Both federal and institutional methodology are used as a basis for awarding need-based institutional aid.

UNDERGRADUATE EXPENSES for 2009–10 *Comprehensive fee:* $50,310 includes full-time tuition ($38,100), mandatory fees ($1065), and room and board ($11,145). *College room only:* $6300. Room and board charges vary according to board plan and location. *Part-time tuition:* $1155 per credit hour. *Payment plan:* Installment.

FRESHMAN FINANCIAL AID (Fall 2009, est.) 1,097 applied for aid; of those 80% were deemed to have need. 100% of freshmen with need received aid; of those 44% had need fully met. *Average percent of need met:* 88% (excluding resources awarded to replace EFC). *Average financial aid package:* $33,062 (excluding resources awarded to replace EFC). 34% of all full-time freshmen had no need and received non-need-based gift aid.

UNDERGRADUATE FINANCIAL AID (Fall 2009, est.) 4,097 applied for aid; of those 88% were deemed to have need. 100% of undergraduates with need received aid; of those 36% had need fully met. *Average percent of need met:* 84% (excluding resources awarded to replace EFC). *Average financial aid package:* $32,065 (excluding resources awarded to replace EFC). 32% of all full-time undergraduates had no need and received non-need-based gift aid.

GIFT AID (NEED-BASED) *Total amount:* $77,642,786 (10% federal, 3% state, 85% institutional, 2% external sources). *Receiving aid:* Freshmen: 66% (877); all full-time undergraduates: 65% (3,586). *Average award:* Freshmen: $22,418;

Undergraduates: $22,268. *Scholarships, grants, and awards:* Federal Pell, FSEOG, state, private, college/university gift aid from institutional funds, Gates Millennium Scholarships, Academic Competitiveness Grants, National SMART Grants.

GIFT AID (NON-NEED-BASED) *Total amount:* $24,823,143 (8% federal, 1% state, 89% institutional, 2% external sources). *Receiving aid:* Freshmen: 17% (227). Undergraduates: 11% (631). *Average award:* Freshmen: $13,043. Undergraduates: $14,086. *Scholarships, grants, and awards by category: Academic interests/achievement:* general academic interests/achievements, humanities, mathematics, military science. *Creative arts/performance:* general creative arts/performance. *Special achievements/activities:* general special achievements/activities. *Special characteristics:* children and siblings of alumni, children of faculty/staff, ethnic background, general special characteristics, members of minority groups. *Tuition waivers:* Full or partial for employees or children of employees.

LOANS *Student loans:* $39,696,346 (60% need-based, 40% non-need-based). 71% of past graduating class borrowed through all loan programs. *Average indebtedness per student:* $30,838. *Average need-based loan:* Freshmen: $5741. Undergraduates: $6068. *Parent loans:* $6,968,530 (80% need-based, 20% non-need-based). *Programs:* Federal Direct (Subsidized and Unsubsidized Stafford, PLUS), Perkins, college/university, state loans from some states (not NY).

WORK-STUDY *Federal work-study:* Total amount: $1,118,944; 1,327 jobs averaging $2001.

ATHLETIC AWARDS Total amount: $1,769,274 (100% non-need-based).

APPLYING FOR FINANCIAL AID *Required financial aid forms:* FAFSA, CSS Financial Aid PROFILE. *Financial aid deadline (priority):* 2/15. *Notification date:* 3/25.

CONTACT Ms. Lynnette E. Koch, Acting Director of Financial Aid, Rensselaer Polytechnic Institute, Academy Hall, Troy, NY 12180-3590, 518-276-6813 or toll-free 800-448-6562. *Fax:* 518-276-4797. *E-mail:* financial_aid@rpi.edu.

RESEARCH COLLEGE OF NURSING
Kansas City, MO

CONTACT Ms. Stacie Withers, Financial Aid Director, Research College of Nursing, 2300 East Meyer Boulevard, Kansas City, MO 64132, 816-276-4728 or toll-free 800-842-6776. *Fax:* 816-276-3526. *E-mail:* stacie.withers@hcamidwest.com.

RHODE ISLAND COLLEGE
Providence, RI

Tuition & fees (RI res): $6976	Average undergraduate aid package: $8365

ABOUT THE INSTITUTION State-supported, coed. 72 undergraduate majors. Institutional methodology is used as a basis for awarding need-based institutional aid.

UNDERGRADUATE EXPENSES for 2010–11 *Tuition, state resident:* full-time $5988; part-time $250 per credit. *Tuition, nonresident:* full-time $15,880; part-time $604 per credit. *Required fees:* full-time $988; $28 per credit or $72 per term. Part-time tuition and fees vary according to course load. *College room and board:* $9270; *Room only:* $5266. Room and board charges vary according to board plan and housing facility. *Payment plan:* Installment.

FRESHMAN FINANCIAL AID (Fall 2009, est.) 1,085 applied for aid; of those 74% were deemed to have need. 97% of freshmen with need received aid; of those 25% had need fully met. *Average percent of need met:* 77% (excluding resources awarded to replace EFC). *Average financial aid package:* $8837 (excluding resources awarded to replace EFC). 4% of all full-time freshmen had no need and received non-need-based gift aid.

UNDERGRADUATE FINANCIAL AID (Fall 2009, est.) 4,417 applied for aid; of those 76% were deemed to have need. 95% of undergraduates with need received aid; of those 32% had need fully met. *Average percent of need met:* 75% (excluding resources awarded to replace EFC). *Average financial aid package:* $8365 (excluding resources awarded to replace EFC). 2% of all full-time undergraduates had no need and received non-need-based gift aid.

GIFT AID (NEED-BASED) *Total amount:* $16,617,372 (61% federal, 13% state, 22% institutional, 4% external sources). *Receiving aid:* Freshmen: 55% (671); all full-time undergraduates: 47% (2,693). *Average award:* Freshmen: $6160;

Undergraduates: $5360. *Scholarships, grants, and awards:* Federal Pell, FSEOG, state, private, college/university gift aid from institutional funds.
GIFT AID (NON-NEED-BASED) *Total amount:* $450,541 (62% institutional, 38% external sources). *Receiving aid:* Freshmen: 2% (24). Undergraduates: 1% (53). *Average award:* Freshmen: $1592. Undergraduates: $1819. *Scholarships, grants, and awards by category: Academic interests/achievement:* general academic interests/achievements. *Creative arts/performance:* art/fine arts, cinema/film/broadcasting, dance, journalism/publications, music, theater/drama. *Special characteristics:* children and siblings of alumni. *Tuition waivers:* Full or partial for employees or children of employees.
LOANS *Student loans:* $32,329,651 (61% need-based, 39% non-need-based). 71% of past graduating class borrowed through all loan programs. *Average indebtedness per student:* $18,352. *Average need-based loan:* Freshmen: $3265. Undergraduates: $3759. *Parent loans:* $1,885,066 (25% need-based, 75% non-need-based). *Programs:* FFEL (Subsidized and Unsubsidized Stafford, PLUS), Perkins, state, private loans.
WORK-STUDY *Federal work-study:* Total amount: $2,165,873; jobs available.
APPLYING FOR FINANCIAL AID *Required financial aid forms:* FAFSA, institution's own form. *Financial aid deadline (priority):* 3/1. *Notification date:* Continuous beginning 3/15. Students must reply by 5/1 or within 3 weeks of notification.
CONTACT James T. Hanbury, Director of Financial Aid, Rhode Island College, 600 Mount Pleasant Avenue, Providence, RI 02908, 401-456-8033 or toll-free 800-669-5760. *Fax:* 401-456-8686. *E-mail:* jhanbury@ric.edu.

RHODE ISLAND SCHOOL OF DESIGN
Providence, RI

CONTACT Director of Financial Aid, Rhode Island School of Design, 2 College Street, Providence, RI 02903-2784, 401-454-6661 or toll-free 800-364-7473. *Fax:* 401-454-6412.

RHODES COLLEGE
Memphis, TN

Tuition & fees: $33,710	Average undergraduate aid package: $31,373

ABOUT THE INSTITUTION Independent Presbyterian, coed. 33 undergraduate majors. Institutional methodology is used as a basis for awarding need-based institutional aid.
UNDERGRADUATE EXPENSES for 2009–10 *Comprehensive fee:* $42,024 includes full-time tuition ($33,400), mandatory fees ($310), and room and board ($8314). Room and board charges vary according to board plan and housing facility. *Part-time tuition:* $1350 per credit hour. *Payment plan:* Installment.
FRESHMAN FINANCIAL AID (Fall 2009, est.) 100% of freshmen with need received aid; of those 48% had need fully met. *Average percent of need met:* 87% (excluding resources awarded to replace EFC). *Average financial aid package:* $31,290 (excluding resources awarded to replace EFC). 42% of all full-time freshmen had no need and received non-need-based gift aid.
UNDERGRADUATE FINANCIAL AID (Fall 2009, est.) 100% of undergraduates with need received aid; of those 40% had need fully met. *Average percent of need met:* 80% (excluding resources awarded to replace EFC). *Average financial aid package:* $31,373 (excluding resources awarded to replace EFC). 36% of all full-time undergraduates had no need and received non-need-based gift aid.
GIFT AID (NEED-BASED) *Total amount:* $15,483,353 (8% federal, 6% state, 84% institutional, 2% external sources). *Receiving aid:* Freshmen: 47% (201); all full-time undergraduates: 45% (747). *Average award:* Freshmen: $21,487; Undergraduates: $20,727. *Scholarships, grants, and awards:* Federal Pell, FSEOG, state, private, college/university gift aid from institutional funds.
GIFT AID (NON-NEED-BASED) *Total amount:* $9,711,153 (1% federal, 5% state, 89% institutional, 5% external sources). *Receiving aid:* Freshmen: 16% (68). Undergraduates: 10% (157). *Average award:* Freshmen: $13,477. Undergraduates: $13,433. *Scholarships, grants, and awards by category: Academic interests/achievement:* general academic interests/achievements. *Creative arts/performance:* general creative arts/performance. *Special characteristics:* members of minority groups, religious affiliation. *Tuition waivers:* Full or partial for employees or children of employees.
LOANS *Student loans:* $4,555,197 (62% need-based, 38% non-need-based). 47% of past graduating class borrowed through all loan programs. *Average indebtedness per student:* $26,071. *Average need-based loan:* Freshmen: $4510.

Undergraduates: $6822. *Parent loans:* $1,700,629 (28% need-based, 72% non-need-based). *Programs:* Federal Direct (Subsidized and Unsubsidized Stafford, PLUS), FFEL (Subsidized and Unsubsidized Stafford, PLUS), Perkins.
WORK-STUDY *Federal work-study:* Total amount: $576,529; jobs available. *State or other work-study/employment:* Total amount: $851,044 (19% need-based, 81% non-need-based). Part-time jobs available.
APPLYING FOR FINANCIAL AID *Required financial aid forms:* FAFSA, CSS Financial Aid PROFILE, noncustodial (divorced/separated) parent's statement. *Financial aid deadline:* 3/1. *Notification date:* Continuous. Students must reply by 5/1.
CONTACT Art Weeden, Director of Financial Aid, Rhodes College, 2000 North Parkway, Memphis, TN 38112-1690, 901-843-3810 or toll-free 800-844-5969 (out-of-state). *Fax:* 901-843-3435. *E-mail:* weedena@rhodes.edu.

RICE UNIVERSITY
Houston, TX

ABOUT THE INSTITUTION Independent, coed. 58 undergraduate majors.
GIFT AID (NEED-BASED) *Scholarships, grants, and awards:* Federal Pell, FSEOG, state, private, college/university gift aid from institutional funds.
GIFT AID (NON-NEED-BASED) *Scholarships, grants, and awards by category: Academic interests/achievement:* engineering/technologies, general academic interests/achievements. *Creative arts/performance:* music. *Special achievements/activities:* general special achievements/activities, leadership.
LOANS *Programs:* FFEL (Subsidized and Unsubsidized Stafford, PLUS), Perkins.
WORK-STUDY *Federal work-study:* Total amount: $1,096,057; jobs available. *State or other work-study/employment:* Total amount: $10,000 (100% need-based). Part-time jobs available.
APPLYING FOR FINANCIAL AID *Required financial aid forms:* FAFSA, CSS Financial Aid PROFILE, business/farm supplement, tax returns and W-2 forms.
CONTACT Ms. Anne Walker, Director of Student Financial Services, Rice University, 116 Allen Center, MS 12, Houston, TX 77005, 713-348-4958 or toll-free 800-527-OWLS. *Fax:* 713-348-2139. *E-mail:* fina@rice.edu.

THE RICHARD STOCKTON COLLEGE OF NEW JERSEY
Pomona, NJ

Tuition & fees (NJ res): $11,041	Average undergraduate aid package: $15,435

ABOUT THE INSTITUTION State-supported, coed. 34 undergraduate majors. Federal methodology is used as a basis for awarding need-based institutional aid.
UNDERGRADUATE EXPENSES for 2009–10 *Tuition, state resident:* full-time $7067; part-time $235.55 per credit hour. *Tuition, nonresident:* full-time $12,750; part-time $425.01 per credit hour. *Required fees:* full-time $3974; $129.12 per credit hour or $50 per term. Full-time tuition and fees vary according to degree level. Part-time tuition and fees vary according to course load and degree level. *College room and board:* $10,189. Room and board charges vary according to board plan and housing facility. *Payment plans:* Installment, deferred payment.
FRESHMAN FINANCIAL AID (Fall 2009, est.) 779 applied for aid; of those 81% were deemed to have need. 98% of freshmen with need received aid; of those 30% had need fully met. *Average percent of need met:* 73% (excluding resources awarded to replace EFC). *Average financial aid package:* $16,224 (excluding resources awarded to replace EFC). 41% of all full-time freshmen had no need and received non-need-based gift aid.
UNDERGRADUATE FINANCIAL AID (Fall 2009, est.) 4,820 applied for aid; of those 85% were deemed to have need. 98% of undergraduates with need received aid; of those 27% had need fully met. *Average percent of need met:* 70% (excluding resources awarded to replace EFC). *Average financial aid package:* $15,435 (excluding resources awarded to replace EFC). 20% of all full-time undergraduates had no need and received non-need-based gift aid.
GIFT AID (NEED-BASED) *Total amount:* $23,283,317 (40% federal, 38% state, 21% institutional, 1% external sources). *Receiving aid:* Freshmen: 35% (302); all full-time undergraduates: 33% (1,987). *Average award:* Freshmen: $9531; Undergraduates: $8353. *Scholarships, grants, and awards:* Federal Pell, FSEOG, state, college/university gift aid from institutional funds.
GIFT AID (NON-NEED-BASED) *Total amount:* $2,004,375 (18% state, 77% institutional, 5% external sources). *Receiving aid:* Freshmen: 30% (263).

Undergraduates: 16% (971). *Average award:* Freshmen: $7518. Undergraduates: $6019. *Scholarships, grants, and awards by category: Academic interests/ achievement:* 129 awards ($186,675 total): area/ethnic studies, biological sciences, business, computer science, education, general academic interests/ achievements, health fields, humanities, mathematics, physical sciences, social sciences. *Creative arts/performance:* 14 awards ($15,637 total): applied art and design, art/fine arts, creative writing, dance, journalism/publications, music, performing arts, theater/drama. *Special achievements/activities:* 10 awards ($13,250 total): community service, general special achievements/activities, leadership. *Special characteristics:* 29 awards ($52,820 total): adult students, children of faculty/staff, children of union members/company employees, ethnic background, first-generation college students, general special characteristics, international students, local/state students, members of minority groups, previous college experience. *Tuition waivers:* Full or partial for employees or children of employees, senior citizens.

LOANS *Student loans:* $37,279,723 (83% need-based, 17% non-need-based). 69% of past graduating class borrowed through all loan programs. *Average indebtedness per student:* $27,847. *Average need-based loan:* Freshmen: $3417. Undergraduates: $4569. *Parent loans:* $4,035,211 (69% need-based, 31% non-need-based). *Programs:* Federal Direct (Subsidized and Unsubsidized Stafford, PLUS), Perkins, state.

WORK-STUDY *Federal work-study:* Total amount: $378,685; 221 jobs averaging $1999. *State or other work-study/employment:* Total amount: $994,314 (100% non-need-based). 605 part-time jobs averaging $1643.

APPLYING FOR FINANCIAL AID *Required financial aid form:* FAFSA. *Financial aid deadline (priority):* 3/1. *Notification date:* Continuous beginning 4/1. Students must reply within 2 weeks of notification.

CONTACT Ms. Jeanne S. Lewis, Director of Financial Aid, The Richard Stockton College of New Jersey, Jimmie Leeds Road, Pomona, NJ 08240-9988, 609-652-4203. *Fax:* 609-626-5517. *E-mail:* jeanne.lewis@stockton.edu.

RIDER UNIVERSITY
Lawrenceville, NJ

Tuition & fees: $29,060	Average undergraduate aid package: $21,152

ABOUT THE INSTITUTION Independent, coed. 55 undergraduate majors. Federal methodology is used as a basis for awarding need-based institutional aid.

UNDERGRADUATE EXPENSES for 2009–10 *Comprehensive fee:* $39,780 includes full-time tuition ($28,470), mandatory fees ($590), and room and board ($10,720). *College room only:* $6420. Full-time tuition and fees vary according to course load and program. Room and board charges vary according to board plan, housing facility, and location. *Part-time tuition:* $508 per credit. *Part-time fees:* $35 per course. Part-time tuition and fees vary according to course load and program. *Payment plan:* Installment.

FRESHMAN FINANCIAL AID (Fall 2009, est.) 938 applied for aid; of those 84% were deemed to have need. 100% of freshmen with need received aid; of those 22% had need fully met. *Average percent of need met:* 75% (excluding resources awarded to replace EFC). *Average financial aid package:* $22,721 (excluding resources awarded to replace EFC). 18% of all full-time freshmen had no need and received non-need-based gift aid.

UNDERGRADUATE FINANCIAL AID (Fall 2009, est.) 3,279 applied for aid; of those 87% were deemed to have need. 100% of undergraduates with need received aid; of those 19% had need fully met. *Average percent of need met:* 72% (excluding resources awarded to replace EFC). *Average financial aid package:* $21,152 (excluding resources awarded to replace EFC). 20% of all full-time undergraduates had no need and received non-need-based gift aid.

GIFT AID (NEED-BASED) *Total amount:* $39,629,166 (14% federal, 19% state, 66% institutional, 1% external sources). *Receiving aid:* Freshmen: 76% (783); all full-time undergraduates: 68% (2,785). *Average award:* Freshmen: $17,170; Undergraduates: $15,320. *Scholarships, grants, and awards:* state, college/ university gift aid from institutional funds.

GIFT AID (NON-NEED-BASED) *Total amount:* $10,546,830 (97% institutional, 3% external sources). *Receiving aid:* Freshmen: 14% (142). Undergraduates: 11% (444). *Average award:* Freshmen: $10,965. Undergraduates: $10,703. *Scholarships, grants, and awards by category: Academic interests/achievement:* general academic interests/achievements. *Creative arts/performance:* theater/ drama. *Special characteristics:* members of minority groups. *Tuition waivers:* Full or partial for employees or children of employees.

LOANS *Student loans:* $42,599,518 (61% need-based, 39% non-need-based). 72% of past graduating class borrowed through all loan programs. *Average*

---

indebtedness per student: $35,042. *Average need-based loan:* Freshmen: $3590. Undergraduates: $4178. *Parent loans:* $6,863,694 (35% need-based, 65% non-need-based). *Programs:* FFEL (Subsidized and Unsubsidized Stafford, PLUS), Perkins, state, alternative loans.

WORK-STUDY *Federal work-study:* Total amount: $4,342,379; 1,844 jobs averaging $2135. *State or other work-study/employment:* 541 part-time jobs averaging $1990.

ATHLETIC AWARDS Total amount: $3,123,675 (51% need-based, 49% non-need-based).

APPLYING FOR FINANCIAL AID *Required financial aid form:* FAFSA. *Financial aid deadline (priority):* 3/1. *Notification date:* Continuous beginning 2/20.

CONTACT Dr. Dennis Levy, Director of Financial Aid, Rider University, 2083 Lawrenceville Road, Lawrenceville, NJ 08648-3001, 609-896-5360 or toll-free 800-257-9026. *Fax:* 609-219-4487. *E-mail:* finaid@rider.edu.

RINGLING COLLEGE OF ART AND DESIGN
Sarasota, FL

Tuition & fees: $28,470	Average undergraduate aid package: $17,057

ABOUT THE INSTITUTION Independent, coed. 12 undergraduate majors. Federal methodology is used as a basis for awarding need-based institutional aid.

UNDERGRADUATE EXPENSES for 2009–10 *Comprehensive fee:* $38,940 includes full-time tuition ($27,620), mandatory fees ($850), and room and board ($10,470). *College room only:* $5520. Full-time tuition and fees vary according to course load, program, and student level. Room and board charges vary according to board plan and housing facility. *Part-time tuition:* $1304 per semester hour. Part-time tuition and fees vary according to course load, program, and student level. *Payment plan:* Installment.

FRESHMAN FINANCIAL AID (Fall 2009, est.) 263 applied for aid; of those 84% were deemed to have need. 98% of freshmen with need received aid; of those 4% had need fully met. *Average percent of need met:* 41% (excluding resources awarded to replace EFC). *Average financial aid package:* $15,103 (excluding resources awarded to replace EFC). 9% of all full-time freshmen had no need and received non-need-based gift aid.

UNDERGRADUATE FINANCIAL AID (Fall 2009, est.) 1,030 applied for aid; of those 89% were deemed to have need. 99% of undergraduates with need received aid; of those 4% had need fully met. *Average percent of need met:* 46% (excluding resources awarded to replace EFC). *Average financial aid package:* $17,057 (excluding resources awarded to replace EFC). 5% of all full-time undergraduates had no need and received non-need-based gift aid.

GIFT AID (NEED-BASED) *Total amount:* $6,966,093 (30% federal, 28% state, 35% institutional, 7% external sources). *Receiving aid:* Freshmen: 77% (203); all full-time undergraduates: 76% (785). *Average award:* Freshmen: $9061; Undergraduates: $8646. *Scholarships, grants, and awards:* Federal Pell, FSEOG, state, private, college/university gift aid from institutional funds.

GIFT AID (NON-NEED-BASED) *Total amount:* $449,131 (46% state, 46% institutional, 8% external sources). *Receiving aid:* Freshmen: 1% (3). Undergraduates: 1% (8). *Average award:* Freshmen: $3666. Undergraduates: $3310. *Scholarships, grants, and awards by category: Academic interests/ achievement:* 596 awards ($2,815,800 total): general academic interests/ achievements. *Creative arts/performance:* applied art and design, art/fine arts. *Tuition waivers:* Full or partial for employees or children of employees.

LOANS *Student loans:* $13,053,523 (86% need-based, 14% non-need-based). 78% of past graduating class borrowed through all loan programs. *Average indebtedness per student:* $52,173. *Average need-based loan:* Freshmen: $7224. Undergraduates: $9929. *Parent loans:* $7,511,224 (70% need-based, 30% non-need-based). *Programs:* Federal Direct (Subsidized and Unsubsidized Stafford, PLUS), FFEL (Subsidized and Unsubsidized Stafford, PLUS), alternative loans.

WORK-STUDY *Federal work-study:* Total amount: $287,407; jobs available. *State or other work-study/employment:* Part-time jobs available.

APPLYING FOR FINANCIAL AID *Required financial aid form:* FAFSA. *Financial aid deadline (priority):* 3/1. *Notification date:* Continuous beginning 3/15. Students must reply within 4 weeks of notification.

CONTACT Micah Jordan, Financial Aid Assistant Director, Ringling College of Art and Design, 2700 North Tamiami Trail, Sarasota, FL 34243, 941-359-7533 or toll-free 800-255-7695. *Fax:* 941-359-6107. *E-mail:* finaid@ringling.edu.

RIO GRANDE BIBLE INSTITUTE
Edinburg, TX

CONTACT Financial Aid Office, Rio Grande Bible Institute, 4300 S US Hwy 281, Edinburg, TX 78539, 956-380-8100.

RIPON COLLEGE
Ripon, WI

Tuition & fees: $25,445	Average undergraduate aid package: $22,365

ABOUT THE INSTITUTION Independent, coed. 38 undergraduate majors. Federal methodology is used as a basis for awarding need-based institutional aid.

UNDERGRADUATE EXPENSES for 2009–10 *Comprehensive fee:* $32,715 includes full-time tuition ($25,170), mandatory fees ($275), and room and board ($7270). *College room only:* $3790. *Part-time tuition:* $900 per credit. *Payment plan:* Installment.

FRESHMAN FINANCIAL AID (Fall 2009, est.) 228 applied for aid; of those 89% were deemed to have need. 100% of freshmen with need received aid; of those 21% had need fully met. *Average percent of need met:* 92% (excluding resources awarded to replace EFC). *Average financial aid package:* $23,714 (excluding resources awarded to replace EFC). 16% of all full-time freshmen had no need and received non-need-based gift aid.

UNDERGRADUATE FINANCIAL AID (Fall 2009, est.) 943 applied for aid; of those 91% were deemed to have need. 100% of undergraduates with need received aid; of those 31% had need fully met. *Average percent of need met:* 89% (excluding resources awarded to replace EFC). *Average financial aid package:* $22,365 (excluding resources awarded to replace EFC). 17% of all full-time undergraduates had no need and received non-need-based gift aid.

GIFT AID (NEED-BASED) *Total amount:* $15,903,622 (12% federal, 7% state, 65% institutional, 16% external sources). *Receiving aid:* Freshmen: 81% (202); all full-time undergraduates: 84% (847). *Average award:* Freshmen: $19,198; Undergraduates: $17,850. *Scholarships, grants, and awards:* Federal Pell, FSEOG, state, private, college/university gift aid from institutional funds.

GIFT AID (NON-NEED-BASED) *Total amount:* $3,258,751 (62% institutional, 38% external sources). *Receiving aid:* Freshmen: 10% (26). Undergraduates: 72% (723). *Average award:* Freshmen: $10,996. Undergraduates: $10,587. *Scholarships, grants, and awards by category: Academic interests/achievement:* 541 awards ($4,878,106 total): biological sciences, business, computer science, education, English, foreign languages, general academic interests/achievements, humanities, mathematics, military science, physical sciences, premedicine, religion/biblical studies, social sciences. *Creative arts/performance:* 107 awards ($287,500 total): art/fine arts, debating, music, theater/drama. *Special achievements/activities:* 176 awards ($716,948 total): general special achievements/activities, leadership, memberships. *Special characteristics:* 353 awards ($1,079,099 total): children and siblings of alumni, children of faculty/staff, ethnic background, first-generation college students, general special characteristics, international students, local/state students, members of minority groups, out-of-state students, previous college experience, religious affiliation, siblings of current students. *Tuition waivers:* Full or partial for employees or children of employees.

LOANS *Student loans:* $7,471,062 (63% need-based, 37% non-need-based). 76% of past graduating class borrowed through all loan programs. *Average indebtedness per student:* $26,073. *Average need-based loan:* Freshmen: $4002. Undergraduates: $4378. *Parent loans:* $823,481 (13% need-based, 87% non-need-based). *Programs:* Federal Direct (Subsidized and Unsubsidized Stafford, PLUS), Perkins, alternative loans.

WORK-STUDY *Federal work-study:* Total amount: $810,330; 454 jobs averaging $1531. *State or other work-study/employment:* Total amount: $881,330 (10% need-based, 90% non-need-based). 569 part-time jobs averaging $1449.

APPLYING FOR FINANCIAL AID *Required financial aid form:* FAFSA. *Financial aid deadline (priority):* 3/1. *Notification date:* Continuous. Students must reply within 2 weeks of notification.

CONTACT Steven M. Schuetz, Dean of Admission and Financial Aid, Ripon College, 300 Seward Street, Ripon, WI 54971, 920-748-8185 or toll-free 800-947-4766. *Fax:* 920-748-8335. *E-mail:* financialaid@ripon.edu.

RIVIER COLLEGE
Nashua, NH

Tuition & fees: $25,050	Average undergraduate aid package: $14,344

ABOUT THE INSTITUTION Independent Roman Catholic, coed. 41 undergraduate majors. Federal methodology is used as a basis for awarding need-based institutional aid.

UNDERGRADUATE EXPENSES for 2010–11 *One-time required fee:* $175. *Comprehensive fee:* $34,478 includes full-time tuition ($24,450), mandatory fees ($600), and room and board ($9428). Full-time tuition and fees vary according to degree level and program. Room and board charges vary according to board plan and housing facility. *Part-time tuition:* $815 per credit. *Part-time fees:* $25 per year. Part-time tuition and fees vary according to class time, course level, course load, degree level, and program. *Payment plans:* Installment, deferred payment.

FRESHMAN FINANCIAL AID (Fall 2009, est.) 229 applied for aid; of those 89% were deemed to have need. 100% of freshmen with need received aid; of those 6% had need fully met. *Average percent of need met:* 64% (excluding resources awarded to replace EFC). *Average financial aid package:* $16,773 (excluding resources awarded to replace EFC). 15% of all full-time freshmen had no need and received non-need-based gift aid.

UNDERGRADUATE FINANCIAL AID (Fall 2009, est.) 897 applied for aid; of those 89% were deemed to have need. 100% of undergraduates with need received aid; of those 9% had need fully met. *Average percent of need met:* 60% (excluding resources awarded to replace EFC). *Average financial aid package:* $14,344 (excluding resources awarded to replace EFC). 14% of all full-time undergraduates had no need and received non-need-based gift aid.

GIFT AID (NEED-BASED) *Total amount:* $7,638,277 (22% federal, 2% state, 71% institutional, 5% external sources). *Receiving aid:* Freshmen: 84% (199); all full-time undergraduates: 79% (761). *Average award:* Freshmen: $13,076; Undergraduates: $10,255. *Scholarships, grants, and awards:* Federal Pell, FSEOG, state, private, college/university gift aid from institutional funds.

GIFT AID (NON-NEED-BASED) *Total amount:* $784,440 (1% federal, 2% state, 87% institutional, 10% external sources). *Receiving aid:* Freshmen: 3% (7). Undergraduates: 3% (32). *Average award:* Freshmen: $5527. Undergraduates: $4849. *Scholarships, grants, and awards by category: Academic interests/achievement:* biological sciences, business, communication, computer science, education, English, foreign languages, general academic interests/achievements, humanities, mathematics, premedicine, social sciences. *Creative arts/performance:* applied art and design, art/fine arts, journalism/publications. *Special achievements/activities:* general special achievements/activities. *Special characteristics:* children and siblings of alumni, children of current students, international students, siblings of current students. *Tuition waivers:* Full or partial for employees or children of employees, senior citizens.

LOANS *Student loans:* $12,302,965 (69% need-based, 31% non-need-based). 94% of past graduating class borrowed through all loan programs. *Average indebtedness per student:* $36,389. *Average need-based loan:* Freshmen: $3457. Undergraduates: $4362. *Parent loans:* $2,216,473 (43% need-based, 57% non-need-based). *Programs:* Federal Direct (Subsidized and Unsubsidized Stafford, PLUS), Perkins, college/university.

WORK-STUDY *Federal work-study:* Total amount: $257,845; jobs available. *State or other work-study/employment:* Total amount: $130,674 (3% need-based, 97% non-need-based). Part-time jobs available.

APPLYING FOR FINANCIAL AID *Required financial aid form:* FAFSA. *Financial aid deadline (priority):* 3/1. *Notification date:* Continuous beginning 3/1. Students must reply within 3 weeks of notification.

CONTACT Valerie Patnaude, Director of Financial Aid, Rivier College, 420 Main Street, Nashua, NH 03060-5086, 603-897-8533 or toll-free 800-44RIVIER. *Fax:* 603-897-8810. *E-mail:* vpatnaude@rivier.edu.

ROANOKE COLLEGE
Salem, VA

Tuition & fees: $31,214	Average undergraduate aid package: $24,772

ABOUT THE INSTITUTION Independent religious, coed. 32 undergraduate majors. Federal methodology is used as a basis for awarding need-based institutional aid.

UNDERGRADUATE EXPENSES for 2010–11 *Comprehensive fee:* $41,522 includes full-time tuition ($30,314), mandatory fees ($900), and room and board ($10,308). *College room only:* $4788. Room and board charges vary according to board plan and housing facility. *Part-time tuition:* $1450 per course. Part-time tuition and fees vary according to course load. *Payment plan:* Installment.

FRESHMAN FINANCIAL AID (Fall 2009, est.) 482 applied for aid; of those 85% were deemed to have need. 100% of freshmen with need received aid; of those 35% had need fully met. *Average percent of need met:* 86% (excluding resources awarded to replace EFC). *Average financial aid package:* $24,994 (excluding resources awarded to replace EFC). 25% of all full-time freshmen had no need and received non-need-based gift aid.

UNDERGRADUATE FINANCIAL AID (Fall 2009, est.) 1,575 applied for aid; of those 81% were deemed to have need. 100% of undergraduates with need received aid; of those 32% had need fully met. *Average percent of need met:* 87% (excluding resources awarded to replace EFC). *Average financial aid package:* $24,772 (excluding resources awarded to replace EFC). 31% of all full-time undergraduates had no need and received non-need-based gift aid.

GIFT AID (NEED-BASED) *Total amount:* $24,821,899 (8% federal, 9% state, 80% institutional, 3% external sources). *Receiving aid:* Freshmen: 72% (401); all full-time undergraduates: 66% (1,270). *Average award:* Freshmen: $20,634; Undergraduates: $19,058. *Scholarships, grants, and awards:* Federal Pell, FSEOG, state, private, college/university gift aid from institutional funds.

GIFT AID (NON-NEED-BASED) *Total amount:* $6,718,388 (10% state, 87% institutional, 3% external sources). *Receiving aid:* Freshmen: 71% (400). Undergraduates: 67% (1,280). *Average award:* Freshmen: $10,357. Undergraduates: $10,405. *Tuition waivers:* Full or partial for employees or children of employees, senior citizens.

LOANS *Student loans:* $11,733,395 (88% need-based, 12% non-need-based). 66% of past graduating class borrowed through all loan programs. *Average indebtedness per student:* $25,932. *Average need-based loan:* Freshmen: $3941. Undergraduates: $4558. *Parent loans:* $2,495,314 (82% need-based, 18% non-need-based). *Programs:* FFEL (Subsidized and Unsubsidized Stafford, PLUS), Perkins, college/university, alternative loans.

WORK-STUDY *Federal work-study:* Total amount: $1,202,526; jobs available.

APPLYING FOR FINANCIAL AID *Required financial aid forms:* FAFSA, state aid form. *Financial aid deadline (priority):* 3/1. *Notification date:* Continuous. Students must reply within 2 weeks of notification.

CONTACT Mr. Thomas S. Blair Jr., Director of Financial Aid, Roanoke College, 221 College Lane, Salem, VA 24153-3794, 540-375-2235 or toll-free 800-388-2276. *E-mail:* finaid@roanoke.edu.

ROBERT MORRIS UNIVERSITY
Moon Township, PA

Tuition & fees: $20,560	Average undergraduate aid package: $16,548

ABOUT THE INSTITUTION Independent, coed. 30 undergraduate majors. Federal methodology is used as a basis for awarding need-based institutional aid.

UNDERGRADUATE EXPENSES for 2009–10 *Comprehensive fee:* $30,930 includes full-time tuition ($19,950), mandatory fees ($610), and room and board ($10,370). *College room only:* $5010. Full-time tuition and fees vary according to degree level and program. Room and board charges vary according to board plan and housing facility. *Part-time tuition:* $665 per credit hour. *Part-time fees:* $30 per credit hour. Part-time tuition and fees vary according to course load, degree level, and program. *Payment plans:* Installment, deferred payment.

FRESHMAN FINANCIAL AID (Fall 2009, est.) 647 applied for aid; of those 89% were deemed to have need. 100% of freshmen with need received aid; of those 13% had need fully met. *Average percent of need met:* 75% (excluding resources awarded to replace EFC). *Average financial aid package:* $18,482 (excluding resources awarded to replace EFC). 18% of all full-time freshmen had no need and received non-need-based gift aid.

UNDERGRADUATE FINANCIAL AID (Fall 2009, est.) 2,674 applied for aid; of those 90% were deemed to have need. 100% of undergraduates with need received aid; of those 15% had need fully met. *Average percent of need met:* 71% (excluding resources awarded to replace EFC). *Average financial aid package:* $16,548 (excluding resources awarded to replace EFC). 15% of all full-time undergraduates had no need and received non-need-based gift aid.

GIFT AID (NEED-BASED) *Total amount:* $21,897,537 (24% federal, 20% state, 53% institutional, 3% external sources). *Receiving aid:* Freshmen: 79% (569);

all full-time undergraduates: 73% (2,252). *Average award:* Freshmen: $13,211; Undergraduates: $10,397. *Scholarships, grants, and awards:* Federal Pell, FSEOG, state, private, college/university gift aid from institutional funds.

GIFT AID (NON-NEED-BASED) *Total amount:* $4,615,984 (2% federal, 1% state, 95% institutional, 2% external sources). *Receiving aid:* Freshmen: 9% (62). Undergraduates: 6% (178). *Average award:* Freshmen: $8728. Undergraduates: $7763. *Scholarships, grants, and awards by category:* Academic interests/achievement: general academic interests/achievements. *Tuition waivers:* Full or partial for employees or children of employees.

LOANS *Student loans:* $28,493,584 (72% need-based, 28% non-need-based). 84% of past graduating class borrowed through all loan programs. *Average indebtedness per student:* $35,055. *Average need-based loan:* Freshmen: $3960. Undergraduates: $5774. *Parent loans:* $5,471,583 (42% need-based, 58% non-need-based). *Programs:* FFEL (Subsidized and Unsubsidized Stafford, PLUS), Perkins, alternative private loans.

WORK-STUDY *Federal work-study:* Total amount: $3,763,002; jobs available. *State or other work-study/employment:* Part-time jobs available.

ATHLETIC AWARDS Total amount: $2,963,677 (52% need-based, 48% non-need-based).

APPLYING FOR FINANCIAL AID *Required financial aid form:* FAFSA. *Financial aid deadline:* Continuous. *Notification date:* Continuous beginning 3/15. Students must reply within 2 weeks of notification.

CONTACT Ms. Stephanie Hendershot, Director, Financial Aid, Robert Morris University, 6001 University Boulevard, Moon Township, PA 15108-1189, 412-397-2450 or toll-free 800-762-0097. *Fax:* 412-397-2200. *E-mail:* finaid@rmu.edu.

ROBERT MORRIS UNIVERSITY ILLINOIS
Chicago, IL

Tuition & fees: $20,100	Average undergraduate aid package: $12,121

ABOUT THE INSTITUTION Independent, coed. 16 undergraduate majors. Federal methodology is used as a basis for awarding need-based institutional aid.

UNDERGRADUATE EXPENSES for 2010–11 *Comprehensive fee:* $30,045 includes full-time tuition ($20,100) and room and board ($9945). *College room only:* $7800. Full-time tuition and fees vary according to location. Room and board charges vary according to housing facility and location. *Part-time tuition:* $558 per credit hour. Part-time tuition and fees vary according to course load and location. *Payment plan:* Installment.

FRESHMAN FINANCIAL AID (Fall 2009, est.) 1,357 applied for aid; of those 98% were deemed to have need. 98% of freshmen with need received aid; of those 4% had need fully met. *Average percent of need met:* 48% (excluding resources awarded to replace EFC). *Average financial aid package:* $11,980 (excluding resources awarded to replace EFC). 1% of all full-time freshmen had no need and received non-need-based gift aid.

UNDERGRADUATE FINANCIAL AID (Fall 2009, est.) 5,298 applied for aid; of those 95% were deemed to have need. 99% of undergraduates with need received aid; of those 3% had need fully met. *Average percent of need met:* 45% (excluding resources awarded to replace EFC). *Average financial aid package:* $12,121 (excluding resources awarded to replace EFC). 3% of all full-time undergraduates had no need and received non-need-based gift aid.

GIFT AID (NEED-BASED) *Total amount:* $27,623,646 (56% federal, 37% state, 7% institutional). *Receiving aid:* Freshmen: 78% (1,068); all full-time undergraduates: 65% (3,548). *Average award:* Freshmen: $8628; Undergraduates: $8739. *Scholarships, grants, and awards:* Federal Pell, FSEOG, state, private, college/university gift aid from institutional funds.

GIFT AID (NON-NEED-BASED) *Total amount:* $8,383,706 (100% institutional). *Receiving aid:* Freshmen: 43% (590). Undergraduates: 56% (3,061). *Average award:* Freshmen: $6804. Undergraduates: $6819. *Scholarships, grants, and awards by category:* Academic interests/achievement: architecture, business, computer science, general academic interests/achievements, health fields. *Creative arts/performance:* applied art and design, journalism/publications. *Special achievements/activities:* community service, general special achievements/activities. *Special characteristics:* children of faculty/staff, general special characteristics, out-of-state students, veterans. *Tuition waivers:* Full or partial for employees or children of employees.

LOANS *Student loans:* $37,621,184 (94% need-based, 6% non-need-based). 94% of past graduating class borrowed through all loan programs. *Average indebtedness per student:* $26,752. *Average need-based loan:* Freshmen: $4092. Undergraduates: $4482. *Parent loans:* $4,705,330 (80% need-based, 20%

Robert Morris University Illinois

non-need-based). **Programs:** Federal Direct (Subsidized and Unsubsidized Stafford, PLUS), FFEL (Subsidized and Unsubsidized Stafford, PLUS), Perkins.

WORK-STUDY *Federal work-study:* Total amount: $703,971; 419 jobs averaging $1680.

ATHLETIC AWARDS Total amount: $4,629,244 (85% need-based, 15% non-need-based).

APPLYING FOR FINANCIAL AID *Required financial aid form:* FAFSA. *Financial aid deadline:* Continuous. *Notification date:* Continuous.

CONTACT Leigh Taylor, Vice President of Financial Services, Robert Morris University Illinois, 401 South State Street, Suite 122, Chicago, IL 60605, 312-935-4408 or toll-free 800-RMC-5960. *Fax:* 312-935-4415. *E-mail:* ltaylor@robertmorris.edu.

ROBERTS WESLEYAN COLLEGE
Rochester, NY

Tuition & fees: $23,780	Average undergraduate aid package: $17,513

ABOUT THE INSTITUTION Independent religious, coed. 59 undergraduate majors. Federal methodology is used as a basis for awarding need-based institutional aid.

UNDERGRADUATE EXPENSES for 2009–10 *Comprehensive fee:* $32,300 includes full-time tuition ($22,580), mandatory fees ($1200), and room and board ($8520). *College room only:* $5816. Room and board charges vary according to board plan and housing facility. *Part-time tuition:* $493 per credit. Part-time tuition and fees vary according to course load. *Payment plan:* Installment.

FRESHMAN FINANCIAL AID (Fall 2009, est.) 244 applied for aid; of those 94% were deemed to have need. 100% of freshmen with need received aid; of those 10% had need fully met. *Average percent of need met:* 77% (excluding resources awarded to replace EFC). *Average financial aid package:* $21,741 (excluding resources awarded to replace EFC). 9% of all full-time freshmen had no need and received non-need-based gift aid.

UNDERGRADUATE FINANCIAL AID (Fall 2009, est.) 1,339 applied for aid; of those 95% were deemed to have need. 100% of undergraduates with need received aid; of those 9% had need fully met. *Average percent of need met:* 69% (excluding resources awarded to replace EFC). *Average financial aid package:* $17,513 (excluding resources awarded to replace EFC). 9% of all full-time undergraduates had no need and received non-need-based gift aid.

GIFT AID (NEED-BASED) *Total amount:* $14,399,434 (21% federal, 12% state, 53% institutional, 14% external sources). *Receiving aid:* Freshmen: 89% (229); all full-time undergraduates: 86% (1,240). *Average award:* Freshmen: $16,378; Undergraduates: $11,890. *Scholarships, grants, and awards:* Federal Pell, FSEOG, state, private, college/university gift aid from institutional funds, Academic Competitiveness Grants, National SMART Grants, TEACH Grants.

GIFT AID (NON-NEED-BASED) *Total amount:* $1,254,039 (1% federal, 2% state, 58% institutional, 39% external sources). *Receiving aid:* Freshmen: 7% (19). Undergraduates: 5% (73). *Average award:* Freshmen: $7809. Undergraduates: $4707. *Scholarships, grants, and awards by category:* Academic interests/achievement: 308 awards ($1,892,430 total): general academic interests/achievements. Creative arts/performance: 171 awards ($350,900 total): art/fine arts, music. Special achievements/activities: 416 awards ($717,775 total): general special achievements/activities, junior miss. Special characteristics: 576 awards ($1,697,692 total): children and siblings of alumni, children of faculty/staff, international students, out-of-state students, relatives of clergy, religious affiliation, siblings of current students. *Tuition waivers:* Full or partial for employees or children of employees, senior citizens.

LOANS *Student loans:* $11,739,786 (86% need-based, 14% non-need-based). 99% of past graduating class borrowed through all loan programs. *Average indebtedness per student:* $30,329. *Average need-based loan:* Freshmen: $4671. Undergraduates: $5450. *Parent loans:* $1,976,494 (55% need-based, 45% non-need-based). *Programs:* Federal Direct (Subsidized and Unsubsidized Stafford, PLUS), Perkins.

WORK-STUDY *Federal work-study:* Total amount: $508,000; 843 jobs averaging $1750. *State or other work-study/employment:* Total amount: $26,500 (100% non-need-based). 15 part-time jobs averaging $1767.

ATHLETIC AWARDS Total amount: $702,064 (71% need-based, 29% non-need-based).

APPLYING FOR FINANCIAL AID *Required financial aid forms:* FAFSA, state aid form. *Financial aid deadline (priority):* 3/15. *Notification date:* Continuous beginning 3/15. Students must reply by 5/1 or within 2 weeks of notification.

CONTACT Financial Aid Office, Roberts Wesleyan College, 2301 Westside Drive, Rochester, NY 14624-1997, 585-594-6150 or toll-free 800-777-4RWC. *Fax:* 585-594-6036. *E-mail:* finaid@roberts.edu.

ROCHESTER COLLEGE
Rochester Hills, MI

ABOUT THE INSTITUTION Independent religious, coed. 30 undergraduate majors.

GIFT AID (NEED-BASED) *Scholarships, grants, and awards:* Federal Pell, FSEOG, state, private, college/university gift aid from institutional funds.

GIFT AID (NON-NEED-BASED) *Scholarships, grants, and awards by category:* Academic interests/achievement: business, computer science, education, general academic interests/achievements, mathematics, religion/biblical studies. Creative arts/performance: journalism/publications, music, theater/drama. Special achievements/activities: general special achievements/activities, leadership. Special characteristics: adult students, children and siblings of alumni, children of faculty/staff, first-generation college students, general special characteristics, out-of-state students, previous college experience, relatives of clergy, siblings of current students.

LOANS *Programs:* Federal Direct (Subsidized and Unsubsidized Stafford, PLUS), Perkins.

APPLYING FOR FINANCIAL AID *Required financial aid forms:* FAFSA, institution's own form.

CONTACT Kara Miller, Director of Financial Aid, Rochester College, 800 West Avon Road, Rochester Hills, MI 48307, 248-218-2038 or toll-free 800-521-6010. *Fax:* 248-218-2065. *E-mail:* kmiller@rc.edu.

ROCHESTER INSTITUTE OF TECHNOLOGY
Rochester, NY

Tuition & fees: $29,283	Average undergraduate aid package: $22,500

ABOUT THE INSTITUTION Independent, coed. 114 undergraduate majors. Both federal and institutional methodology are used as a basis for awarding need-based institutional aid.

UNDERGRADUATE EXPENSES for 2009–10 *Comprehensive fee:* $38,925 includes full-time tuition ($28,866), mandatory fees ($417), and room and board ($9642). *College room only:* $5583. Full-time tuition and fees vary according to course load. Room and board charges vary according to board plan and housing facility. *Part-time tuition:* $641 per quarter hour. *Part-time fees:* $35 per term. Part-time tuition and fees vary according to class time and course load. *Payment plans:* Tuition prepayment, installment, deferred payment.

FRESHMAN FINANCIAL AID (Fall 2009, est.) 2,326 applied for aid; of those 87% were deemed to have need. 100% of freshmen with need received aid; of those 82% had need fully met. *Average percent of need met:* 88% (excluding resources awarded to replace EFC). *Average financial aid package:* $22,600 (excluding resources awarded to replace EFC). 11% of all full-time freshmen had no need and received non-need-based gift aid.

UNDERGRADUATE FINANCIAL AID (Fall 2009, est.) 9,068 applied for aid; of those 90% were deemed to have need. 100% of undergraduates with need received aid; of those 87% had need fully met. *Average percent of need met:* 88% (excluding resources awarded to replace EFC). *Average financial aid package:* $22,500 (excluding resources awarded to replace EFC). 11% of all full-time undergraduates had no need and received non-need-based gift aid.

GIFT AID (NEED-BASED) *Total amount:* $112,610,000 (17% federal, 7% state, 74% institutional, 2% external sources). *Receiving aid:* Freshmen: 73% (1,891); all full-time undergraduates: 66% (7,522). *Average award:* Freshmen: $16,500; Undergraduates: $16,000. *Scholarships, grants, and awards:* Federal Pell, FSEOG, state, private, college/university gift aid from institutional funds, NACME Scholarships, NSF Grants.

GIFT AID (NON-NEED-BASED) *Total amount:* $25,950,000 (9% federal, 24% state, 57% institutional, 10% external sources). *Receiving aid:* Freshmen: 21% (537). Undergraduates: 21% (2,378). *Average award:* Freshmen: $9000. Undergraduates: $8000. *Scholarships, grants, and awards by category:* Academic interests/achievement: 3,200 awards ($26,240,000 total): biological sciences, business, communication, computer science, engineering/technologies, general academic interests/achievements, health fields, international studies, mathematics, military science, physical sciences, premedicine, social sciences. *Creative arts/performance:* 320 awards ($1,804,000 total): applied art and design, art/fine arts, cinema/film/broadcasting. *Special achievements/activities:* community service, leadership. *Special characteristics:* children of faculty/staff, veterans. *Tuition waivers:* Full or partial for employees or children of employees.

LOANS *Student loans:* $81,000,000 (56% need-based, 44% non-need-based). *Average need-based loan:* Freshmen: $5100. Undergraduates: $5500. *Parent loans:* $20,400,000 (41% need-based, 59% non-need-based). *Programs:* Federal Direct (Subsidized and Unsubsidized Stafford, PLUS), Perkins, alternative loans.

WORK-STUDY *Federal work-study:* Total amount: $3,300,000; 2,000 jobs averaging $2400. *State or other work-study/employment:* Total amount: $7,500,000 (100% non-need-based). 5,000 part-time jobs averaging $2400.

APPLYING FOR FINANCIAL AID *Required financial aid forms:* FAFSA, state aid form. *Financial aid deadline (priority):* 3/1. *Notification date:* Continuous beginning 3/15. Students must reply by 5/1.

CONTACT Mrs. Verna Hazen, Assistant Vice President, Financial Aid and Scholarships, Rochester Institute of Technology, 56 Lomb Memorial Drive, Rochester, NY 14623-5604, 585-475-2186. *Fax:* 585-475-7270. *E-mail:* verna.hazen@rit.edu.

ROCKFORD COLLEGE
Rockford, IL

Tuition & fees: $24,750	Average undergraduate aid package: $17,247

ABOUT THE INSTITUTION Independent, coed. 46 undergraduate majors. Federal methodology is used as a basis for awarding need-based institutional aid.

UNDERGRADUATE EXPENSES for 2010–11 *Comprehensive fee:* $31,700 includes full-time tuition ($24,750) and room and board ($6950). *College room only:* $3950. Room and board charges vary according to board plan and housing facility. *Part-time tuition:* $650 per credit hour. *Part-time fees:* $40 per term. *Payment plan:* Installment.

FRESHMAN FINANCIAL AID (Fall 2009, est.) 96 applied for aid; of those 91% were deemed to have need. 100% of freshmen with need received aid; of those 14% had need fully met. *Average percent of need met:* 69% (excluding resources awarded to replace EFC). *Average financial aid package:* $17,362 (excluding resources awarded to replace EFC). 10% of all full-time freshmen had no need and received non-need-based gift aid.

UNDERGRADUATE FINANCIAL AID (Fall 2009, est.) 752 applied for aid; of those 94% were deemed to have need. 99% of undergraduates with need received aid; of those 13% had need fully met. *Average percent of need met:* 68% (excluding resources awarded to replace EFC). *Average financial aid package:* $17,247 (excluding resources awarded to replace EFC). 9% of all full-time undergraduates had no need and received non-need-based gift aid.

GIFT AID (NEED-BASED) *Total amount:* $8,738,733 (18% federal, 19% state, 61% institutional, 2% external sources). *Receiving aid:* Freshmen: 89% (86); all full-time undergraduates: 87% (682). *Average award:* Freshmen: $13,808; Undergraduates: $12,354. *Scholarships, grants, and awards:* Federal Pell, FSEOG, state, private, college/university gift aid from institutional funds.

GIFT AID (NON-NEED-BASED) *Total amount:* $1,071,128 (90% institutional, 10% external sources). *Receiving aid:* Freshmen: 11% (11). Undergraduates: 11% (84). *Average award:* Freshmen: $8245. Undergraduates: $8620. *Scholarships, grants, and awards by category: Academic interests/achievement:* 549 awards ($5,654,860 total): biological sciences, business, computer science, education, English, foreign languages, general academic interests/achievements, mathematics, physical sciences, premedicine, social sciences. *Creative arts/performance:* 33 awards ($64,050 total): dance, music, performing arts, theater/drama. *Special achievements/activities:* 10 awards ($15,400 total): community service, leadership. *Special characteristics:* 92 awards ($119,125 total): children and siblings of alumni, children of current students, children of educators, children of faculty/staff, general special characteristics, international students, out-of-state students, parents of current students, siblings of current students. *Tuition waivers:* Full or partial for employees or children of employees.

LOANS *Student loans:* $7,265,698 (85% need-based, 15% non-need-based). 100% of past graduating class borrowed through all loan programs. *Average indebtedness per student:* $25,845. *Average need-based loan:* Freshmen: $2953. Undergraduates: $4706. *Parent loans:* $583,454 (36% need-based, 64% non-need-based). *Programs:* Federal Direct (Subsidized and Unsubsidized Stafford, PLUS), Perkins, college/university, alternative loans.

WORK-STUDY *Federal work-study:* Total amount: $150,412; jobs available. *State or other work-study/employment:* Total amount: $128,546 (100% non-need-based). Part-time jobs available.

APPLYING FOR FINANCIAL AID *Required financial aid form:* FAFSA. *Financial aid deadline (priority):* 3/1. *Notification date:* Continuous beginning 3/15. Students must reply within 4 weeks of notification.

CONTACT Todd M. Free, Assistant Vice President for Student Administrative Services, Rockford College, 5050 East State Street, Rockford, IL 61108, 815-226-3385 or toll-free 800-892-2984. *Fax:* 815-394-5174. *E-mail:* tfree@rockford.edu.

ROCKHURST UNIVERSITY
Kansas City, MO

Tuition & fees: $25,890	Average undergraduate aid package: $25,772

ABOUT THE INSTITUTION Independent Roman Catholic (Jesuit), coed. 28 undergraduate majors. Federal methodology is used as a basis for awarding need-based institutional aid.

UNDERGRADUATE EXPENSES for 2009–10 *Comprehensive fee:* $32,970 includes full-time tuition ($24,950), mandatory fees ($940), and room and board ($7080). *College room only:* $4180. Full-time tuition and fees vary according to class time and course load. Room and board charges vary according to board plan and housing facility. *Part-time tuition:* $832 per credit hour. Part-time tuition and fees vary according to class time and course load. *Payment plans:* Installment, deferred payment.

FRESHMAN FINANCIAL AID (Fall 2009, est.) 417 applied for aid; of those 91% were deemed to have need. 100% of freshmen with need received aid; of those 21% had need fully met. *Average percent of need met:* 100% (excluding resources awarded to replace EFC). *Average financial aid package:* $26,952 (excluding resources awarded to replace EFC). 7% of all full-time freshmen had no need and received non-need-based gift aid.

UNDERGRADUATE FINANCIAL AID (Fall 2009, est.) 1,473 applied for aid; of those 84% were deemed to have need. 95% of undergraduates with need received aid; of those 15% had need fully met. *Average percent of need met:* 100% (excluding resources awarded to replace EFC). *Average financial aid package:* $25,772 (excluding resources awarded to replace EFC). 10% of all full-time undergraduates had no need and received non-need-based gift aid.

GIFT AID (NEED-BASED) *Total amount:* $12,749,779 (13% federal, 8% state, 77% institutional, 2% external sources). *Receiving aid:* Freshmen: 74% (308); all full-time undergraduates: 64% (984). *Average award:* Freshmen: $7413; Undergraduates: $8021. *Scholarships, grants, and awards:* Federal Pell, FSEOG, state, private, college/university gift aid from institutional funds.

GIFT AID (NON-NEED-BASED) *Total amount:* $8,637,164 (1% state, 96% institutional, 3% external sources). *Receiving aid:* Freshmen: 90% (375). Undergraduates: 76% (1,168). *Average award:* Freshmen: $13,266. Undergraduates: $12,904. *Scholarships, grants, and awards by category: Academic interests/achievement:* biological sciences, business, communication, English, foreign languages, general academic interests/achievements, health fields, humanities, mathematics, physical sciences, premedicine, religion/biblical studies, social sciences. *Creative arts/performance:* creative writing, music, performing arts, theater/drama. *Special achievements/activities:* community service, leadership. *Special characteristics:* children and siblings of alumni, children of faculty/staff, siblings of current students. *Tuition waivers:* Full or partial for children of alumni, employees or children of employees, senior citizens.

LOANS *Student loans:* $7,755,132 (51% need-based, 49% non-need-based). 79% of past graduating class borrowed through all loan programs. *Average indebtedness per student:* $21,950. *Average need-based loan:* Freshmen: $2988. Undergraduates: $3739. *Parent loans:* $1,309,002 (56% need-based, 44% non-need-based). *Programs:* FFEL (Subsidized and Unsubsidized Stafford, PLUS), Perkins.

WORK-STUDY *Federal work-study:* Total amount: $250,000; jobs available.

ATHLETIC AWARDS Total amount: $2,160,212 (15% need-based, 85% non-need-based).

APPLYING FOR FINANCIAL AID *Required financial aid form:* FAFSA. *Financial aid deadline (priority):* 3/1. *Notification date:* Continuous beginning 3/1. Students must reply by 6/1 or within 4 weeks of notification.

CONTACT Angela Karlin, Director of Financial Aid, Rockhurst University, 1100 Rockhurst Road, Kansas City, MO 64110-2561, 816-501-4238 or toll-free 800-842-6776. *Fax:* 816-501-3139. *E-mail:* angela.karlin@rockhurst.edu.

ROCKY MOUNTAIN COLLEGE
Billings, MT

Tuition & fees: $21,100	Average undergraduate aid package: $17,118

ABOUT THE INSTITUTION Independent interdenominational, coed. 53 undergraduate majors. Federal methodology is used as a basis for awarding need-based institutional aid.

UNDERGRADUATE EXPENSES for 2010–11 *Comprehensive fee:* $27,680 includes full-time tuition ($20,650), mandatory fees ($450), and room and board ($6580). Full-time tuition and fees vary according to course load, degree level, and program. Room and board charges vary according to board plan and housing facility. *Part-time tuition:* $860 per credit. Part-time tuition and fees vary according to course load, degree level, and program. *Payment plan:* Installment.

FRESHMAN FINANCIAL AID (Fall 2009, est.) 201 applied for aid; of those 86% were deemed to have need. 100% of freshmen with need received aid; of those 18% had need fully met. *Average percent of need met:* 67% (excluding resources awarded to replace EFC). *Average financial aid package:* $23,280 (excluding resources awarded to replace EFC). 22% of all full-time freshmen had no need and received non-need-based gift aid.

UNDERGRADUATE FINANCIAL AID (Fall 2009, est.) 641 applied for aid; of those 89% were deemed to have need. 100% of undergraduates with need received aid; of those 22% had need fully met. *Average percent of need met:* 69% (excluding resources awarded to replace EFC). *Average financial aid package:* $17,118 (excluding resources awarded to replace EFC). 20% of all full-time undergraduates had no need and received non-need-based gift aid.

GIFT AID (NEED-BASED) *Total amount:* $5,648,610 (21% federal, 2% state, 73% institutional, 4% external sources). *Receiving aid:* Freshmen: 73% (169); all full-time undergraduates: 46% (355). *Average award:* Freshmen: $12,701; Undergraduates: $11,959. *Scholarships, grants, and awards:* Federal Pell, FSEOG, state, private, college/university gift aid from institutional funds.

GIFT AID (NON-NEED-BASED) *Total amount:* $1,309,938 (82% institutional, 18% external sources). *Receiving aid:* Freshmen: 1. Undergraduates: 2% (14). *Average award:* Freshmen: $7189. Undergraduates: $6891. *Scholarships, grants, and awards by category: Academic interests/achievement:* $7,680,214 total: biological sciences, business, communication, computer science, education, English, general academic interests/achievements, health fields, humanities, mathematics, physical sciences, premedicine, religion/biblical studies, social sciences. *Creative arts/performance:* $49,735 total: art/fine arts, creative writing, debating, music, theater/drama. *Special achievements/activities:* $111,108 total: cheerleading/drum major, general special achievements/activities, leadership, religious involvement. *Special characteristics:* $851,707 total: children and siblings of alumni, children of faculty/staff, international students, members of minority groups, religious affiliation, siblings of current students, spouses of current students. *Tuition waivers:* Full or partial for employees or children of employees.

LOANS *Student loans:* $4,800,302 (39% need-based, 61% non-need-based). 68% of past graduating class borrowed through all loan programs. *Average indebtedness per student:* $24,361. *Average need-based loan:* Freshmen: $3470. Undergraduates: $3905. *Parent loans:* $692,777 (100% non-need-based). *Programs:* FFEL (Subsidized and Unsubsidized Stafford, PLUS), Perkins.

WORK-STUDY *Federal work-study:* Total amount: $694,122; 373 jobs averaging $1861. *State or other work-study/employment:* Total amount: $411,535 (33% need-based, 67% non-need-based). 224 part-time jobs averaging $1837.

ATHLETIC AWARDS Total amount: $2,032,448 (52% need-based, 48% non-need-based).

APPLYING FOR FINANCIAL AID *Required financial aid form:* FAFSA. *Financial aid deadline:* Continuous. *Notification date:* Continuous beginning 3/1. Students must reply by 4/3.

CONTACT Jessica Francischetti, Financial Aid Director, Rocky Mountain College, 1511 Poly Drive, Billings, MT 59102-1796, 406-657-1031 or toll-free 800-877-6259. *Fax:* 406-657-1169. *E-mail:* francisj@rocky.edu.

ROCKY MOUNTAIN COLLEGE OF ART + DESIGN
Lakewood, CO

Tuition & fees: $26,832	Average undergraduate aid package: $15,353

ABOUT THE INSTITUTION Proprietary, coed. 9 undergraduate majors. Federal methodology is used as a basis for awarding need-based institutional aid.

UNDERGRADUATE EXPENSES for 2010–11 *Tuition:* full-time $26,832; part-time $1118 per credit hour. Room and board charges vary according to board plan and housing facility. *Payment plan:* Installment.

FRESHMAN FINANCIAL AID (Fall 2009, est.) 102 applied for aid; of those 92% were deemed to have need. 100% of freshmen with need received aid; of those 3% had need fully met. *Average percent of need met:* 62% (excluding resources awarded to replace EFC). *Average financial aid package:* $14,687 (excluding resources awarded to replace EFC). 11% of all full-time freshmen had no need and received non-need-based gift aid.

UNDERGRADUATE FINANCIAL AID (Fall 2009, est.) 375 applied for aid; of those 92% were deemed to have need. 100% of undergraduates with need received aid; of those 5% had need fully met. *Average percent of need met:* 68% (excluding resources awarded to replace EFC). *Average financial aid package:* $15,353 (excluding resources awarded to replace EFC). 17% of all full-time undergraduates had no need and received non-need-based gift aid.

GIFT AID (NEED-BASED) *Total amount:* $2,504,090 (25% federal, 2% state, 70% institutional, 3% external sources). *Receiving aid:* Freshmen: 30% (39); all full-time undergraduates: 25% (131). *Average award:* Freshmen: $4424; Undergraduates: $4559. *Scholarships, grants, and awards:* Federal Pell, FSEOG, state, college/university gift aid from institutional funds.

GIFT AID (NON-NEED-BASED) *Total amount:* $514,536 (96% institutional, 4% external sources). *Receiving aid:* Freshmen: 72% (94). Undergraduates: 62% (323). *Average award:* Freshmen: $5927. Undergraduates: $5460. *Scholarships, grants, and awards by category: Academic interests/achievement:* 399 awards ($1,888,510 total): general academic interests/achievements. *Creative arts/performance:* 274 awards ($309,501 total): applied art and design, art/fine arts. *Special characteristics:* 4 awards ($83,386 total): children of faculty/staff. *Tuition waivers:* Full or partial for employees or children of employees.

LOANS *Student loans:* $3,998,322 (93% need-based, 7% non-need-based). 78% of past graduating class borrowed through all loan programs. *Average indebtedness per student:* $28,872. *Average need-based loan:* Freshmen: $3383. Undergraduates: $4397. *Parent loans:* $1,968,908 (93% need-based, 7% non-need-based). *Programs:* Federal Direct (Subsidized and Unsubsidized Stafford, PLUS), alternative loans.

WORK-STUDY *Federal work-study:* Total amount: $68,308; 33 jobs averaging $2070. *State or other work-study/employment:* Total amount: $105,665 (97% need-based, 3% non-need-based). 45 part-time jobs averaging $2349.

APPLYING FOR FINANCIAL AID *Required financial aid form:* FAFSA. *Financial aid deadline (priority):* 3/15. *Notification date:* Continuous beginning 4/1. Students must reply within 2 weeks of notification.

CONTACT Tammy Dybdahl, Director of Financial Aid, Rocky Mountain College of Art + Design, 1600 Pierce Street, Lakewood, CO 80214, 303-225-8551 or toll-free 800-888-ARTS. *Fax:* 303-567-7200. *E-mail:* tdybdahl@rmcad.edu.

ROGERS STATE UNIVERSITY
Claremore, OK

Tuition & fees (OK res): $4277	Average undergraduate aid package: $8004

ABOUT THE INSTITUTION State-supported, coed. 24 undergraduate majors. Federal methodology is used as a basis for awarding need-based institutional aid.

UNDERGRADUATE EXPENSES for 2010–11 *Tuition, state resident:* full-time $2729; part-time $90.95 per credit hour. *Tuition, nonresident:* full-time $8186; part-time $272.85 per credit hour. *Required fees:* full-time $1548; $51 per credit hour or $15 per term. Full-time tuition and fees vary according to course load, location, and program. Part-time tuition and fees vary according to course load, location, and program. *College room and board: Room only:* $4505. Room and board charges vary according to board plan and housing facility. *Payment plan:* Installment.

FRESHMAN FINANCIAL AID (Fall 2009, est.) 476 applied for aid; of those 82% were deemed to have need. 97% of freshmen with need received aid; of those 8% had need fully met. *Average percent of need met:* 63% (excluding resources awarded to replace EFC). *Average financial aid package:* $7529 (excluding resources awarded to replace EFC). 4% of all full-time freshmen had no need and received non-need-based gift aid.

UNDERGRADUATE FINANCIAL AID (Fall 2009, est.) 1,652 applied for aid; of those 84% were deemed to have need. 98% of undergraduates with need received aid; of those 10% had need fully met. *Average percent of need met:*

54% (excluding resources awarded to replace EFC). *Average financial aid package:* $8004 (excluding resources awarded to replace EFC). 3% of all full-time undergraduates had no need and received non-need-based gift aid.

GIFT AID (NEED-BASED) *Total amount:* $10,345,618 (64% federal, 26% state, 2% institutional, 8% external sources). *Receiving aid:* Freshmen: 51% (286); all full-time undergraduates: 51% (1,058). *Average award:* Freshmen: $5465; Undergraduates: $5267. *Scholarships, grants, and awards:* Federal Pell, FSEOG, state, private, college/university gift aid from institutional funds.

GIFT AID (NON-NEED-BASED) *Total amount:* $1,679,158 (64% state, 14% institutional, 22% external sources). *Receiving aid:* Freshmen: 28% (155). Undergraduates: 20% (422). *Average award:* Freshmen: $3419. Undergraduates: $2836. *Scholarships, grants, and awards by category: Academic interests/ achievement:* 487 awards: general academic interests/achievements. *Creative arts/performance:* 20 awards: music. *Special achievements/activities:* 60 awards: cheerleading/drum major, leadership, rodeo. *Special characteristics:* 207 awards: adult students, out-of-state students. *Tuition waivers:* Full or partial for employees or children of employees, senior citizens.

LOANS *Student loans:* $11,038,082 (88% need-based, 12% non-need-based). 55% of past graduating class borrowed through all loan programs. *Average indebtedness per student:* $11,880. *Average need-based loan:* Freshmen: $3115. Undergraduates: $3748. *Parent loans:* $36,810 (84% need-based, 16% non-need-based). *Programs:* FFEL (Subsidized and Unsubsidized Stafford, PLUS), alternative loans.

WORK-STUDY *Federal work-study:* Total amount: $146,375; 85 jobs averaging $1722. *State or other work-study/employment:* Total amount: $539,528 (62% need-based, 38% non-need-based). 244 part-time jobs averaging $2211.

ATHLETIC AWARDS Total amount: $683,571 (50% need-based, 50% non-need-based).

APPLYING FOR FINANCIAL AID *Required financial aid form:* FAFSA. *Financial aid deadline:* Continuous. *Notification date:* Continuous beginning 2/15. Students must reply within 2 weeks of notification.

CONTACT Mr. David Barron, Financial Aid Office, Rogers State University, 1701 West Will Rogers Boulevard, Claremore, OK 74017-3252, 918-343-7553 or toll-free 800-256-7511. *Fax:* 918-343-7598. *E-mail:* finaid@rsu.edu.

ROGER WILLIAMS UNIVERSITY
Bristol, RI

ABOUT THE INSTITUTION Independent, coed. *Awards:* associate, bachelor's, and master's degrees and post-bachelor's certificates. 47 undergraduate majors. *Total enrollment:* 5,159. Undergraduates: 4,345. Freshmen: 954.

GIFT AID (NEED-BASED) *Scholarships, grants, and awards:* Federal Pell, FSEOG, state, private, college/university gift aid from institutional funds.

GIFT AID (NON-NEED-BASED) *Scholarships, grants, and awards by category: Academic interests/achievement:* general academic interests/achievements.

LOANS *Programs:* FFEL (Subsidized and Unsubsidized Stafford, PLUS), Perkins, state.

WORK-STUDY *Federal work-study:* Total amount: $682,292; 403 jobs averaging $1626. *State or other work-study/employment:* 867 part-time jobs averaging $1034.

APPLYING FOR FINANCIAL AID *Required financial aid forms:* FAFSA, CSS Financial Aid PROFILE.

CONTACT Mr. Greg Rogers, Director of Institutional Research, Roger Williams University, 1 Old Ferry Road, Bristol, RI 02809, 401-254-3116 or toll-free 800-458-7144 (out-of-state). *Fax:* 401-254-3677. *E-mail:* grogers@rwu.edu.

ROLLINS COLLEGE
Winter Park, FL

Tuition & fees: $36,220	Average undergraduate aid package: $33,763

ABOUT THE INSTITUTION Independent, coed. 29 undergraduate majors. Federal methodology is used as a basis for awarding need-based institutional aid.

UNDERGRADUATE EXPENSES for 2009–10 *Comprehensive fee:* $47,540 includes full-time tuition ($36,220) and room and board ($11,320). *College room only:* $6660. *Payment plan:* Installment.

FRESHMAN FINANCIAL AID (Fall 2009, est.) 295 applied for aid; of those 83% were deemed to have need. 100% of freshmen with need received aid; of those 26% had need fully met. *Average percent of need met:* 86% (excluding

resources awarded to replace EFC). *Average financial aid package:* $33,073 (excluding resources awarded to replace EFC). 17% of all full-time freshmen had no need and received non-need-based gift aid.

UNDERGRADUATE FINANCIAL AID (Fall 2009, est.) 944 applied for aid; of those 88% were deemed to have need. 99% of undergraduates with need received aid; of those 21% had need fully met. *Average percent of need met:* 86% (excluding resources awarded to replace EFC). *Average financial aid package:* $33,763 (excluding resources awarded to replace EFC). 16% of all full-time undergraduates had no need and received non-need-based gift aid.

GIFT AID (NEED-BASED) *Total amount:* $21,141,785 (9% federal, 17% state, 73% institutional, 1% external sources). *Receiving aid:* Freshmen: 53% (244); all full-time undergraduates: 46% (824). *Average award:* Freshmen: $28,220; Undergraduates: $28,226. *Scholarships, grants, and awards:* Federal Pell, FSEOG, state, private, college/university gift aid from institutional funds.

GIFT AID (NON-NEED-BASED) *Total amount:* $7,519,208 (23% state, 75% institutional, 2% external sources). *Receiving aid:* Freshmen: 7% (31). Undergraduates: 5% (80). *Average award:* Freshmen: $15,827. Undergraduates: $15,291. *Scholarships, grants, and awards by category: Academic interests/achievement:* 614 awards ($8,987,943 total): computer science, engineering/technologies, general academic interests/achievements, mathematics, physical sciences. *Creative arts/performance:* 65 awards ($250,850 total): art/fine arts, music, theater/drama. *Tuition waivers:* Full or partial for employees or children of employees.

LOANS *Student loans:* $4,822,389 (54% need-based, 46% non-need-based). 51% of past graduating class borrowed through all loan programs. *Average indebtedness per student:* $22,255. *Average need-based loan:* Freshmen: $3806. Undergraduates: $4380. *Parent loans:* $3,146,872 (15% need-based, 85% non-need-based). *Programs:* Federal Direct (Subsidized and Unsubsidized Stafford, PLUS), Perkins, college/university.

WORK-STUDY *Federal work-study:* Total amount: $878,116; 375 jobs averaging $2342.

ATHLETIC AWARDS Total amount: $3,124,754 (28% need-based, 72% non-need-based).

APPLYING FOR FINANCIAL AID *Required financial aid forms:* FAFSA, institution's own form. *Financial aid deadline:* 3/1. *Notification date:* Continuous beginning 2/1.

CONTACT Mr. Steve Booker, Director of Student Financial Aid, Rollins College, 1000 Holt Avenue, #2721, Winter Park, FL 32789-4499, 407-646-2395. *Fax:* 407-646-2173. *E-mail:* sbooker@rollins.edu.

ROOSEVELT UNIVERSITY
Chicago, IL

CONTACT Mr. Walter J. H. O'Neill, Director of Financial Aid, Roosevelt University, 430 South Michigan Avenue, Chicago, IL 60605-1394, 312-341-2090 or toll-free 877-APPLYRU. *Fax:* 312-341-3545. *E-mail:* woneill@roosevelt.edu.

ROSE-HULMAN INSTITUTE OF TECHNOLOGY
Terre Haute, IN

Tuition & fees: $34,560	Average undergraduate aid package: $23,743

ABOUT THE INSTITUTION Independent, coed, primarily men. 16 undergraduate majors. Federal methodology is used as a basis for awarding need-based institutional aid.

UNDERGRADUATE EXPENSES for 2009–10 *One-time required fee:* $2800. *Comprehensive fee:* $44,001 includes full-time tuition ($33,900), mandatory fees ($660), and room and board ($9441). *College room only:* $5529. Full-time tuition and fees vary according to course load. Room and board charges vary according to board plan. *Part-time tuition:* $987 per credit hour. Part-time tuition and fees vary according to course load. *Payment plans:* Tuition prepayment, installment.

FRESHMAN FINANCIAL AID (Fall 2009, est.) 392 applied for aid; of those 86% were deemed to have need. 100% of freshmen with need received aid; of those 19% had need fully met. *Average percent of need met:* 88% (excluding resources awarded to replace EFC). *Average financial aid package:* $26,184 (excluding resources awarded to replace EFC). 26% of all full-time freshmen had no need and received non-need-based gift aid.

Rose-Hulman Institute of Technology

UNDERGRADUATE FINANCIAL AID (Fall 2009, est.) 1,482 applied for aid; of those 87% were deemed to have need. 100% of undergraduates with need received aid; of those 19% had need fully met. *Average percent of need met:* 82% (excluding resources awarded to replace EFC). *Average financial aid package:* $23,743 (excluding resources awarded to replace EFC). 27% of all full-time undergraduates had no need and received non-need-based gift aid.

GIFT AID (NEED-BASED) *Total amount:* $23,967,456 (8% federal, 4% state, 74% institutional, 14% external sources). *Receiving aid:* Freshmen: 72% (337); all full-time undergraduates: 70% (1,289). *Average award:* Freshmen: $21,563; Undergraduates: $18,278. *Scholarships, grants, and awards:* Federal Pell, FSEOG, state, college/university gift aid from institutional funds.

GIFT AID (NON-NEED-BASED) *Total amount:* $6,481,092 (79% institutional, 21% external sources). *Receiving aid:* Freshmen: 26% (121). Undergraduates: 24% (447). *Average award:* Freshmen: $11,092. Undergraduates: $9661. *Tuition waivers:* Full or partial for employees or children of employees.

LOANS *Student loans:* $35,817,456 (63% need-based, 37% non-need-based). 73% of past graduating class borrowed through all loan programs. *Average indebtedness per student:* $35,261. *Average need-based loan:* Freshmen: $4497. Undergraduates: $5014. *Parent loans:* $7,531,381 (85% need-based, 15% non-need-based). *Programs:* Federal Direct (Subsidized and Unsubsidized Stafford, PLUS), FFEL (Subsidized Stafford).

WORK-STUDY *Federal work-study:* Total amount: $983,973; 584 jobs averaging $1655. *State or other work-study/employment:* Total amount: $961,562 (93% need-based, 7% non-need-based). 581 part-time jobs averaging $1641.

APPLYING FOR FINANCIAL AID *Required financial aid form:* FAFSA. *Financial aid deadline (priority):* 3/1. *Notification date:* 3/10.

CONTACT Melinda L. Middleton, Director of Financial Aid, Rose-Hulman Institute of Technology, 5500 Wabash Avenue, Box #5, Terre Haute, IN 47803, 812-877-8259 or toll-free 800-248-7448. *Fax:* 812-877-8746. *E-mail:* melinda.middleton@rose-hulman.edu.

ROSEMONT COLLEGE
Rosemont, PA

Tuition & fees: $26,250 | **Average undergraduate aid package: $22,951**

ABOUT THE INSTITUTION Independent Roman Catholic, coed. 27 undergraduate majors. Federal methodology is used as a basis for awarding need-based institutional aid.

UNDERGRADUATE EXPENSES for 2009–10 *Comprehensive fee:* $36,830 includes full-time tuition ($25,000), mandatory fees ($1250), and room and board ($10,580). Room and board charges vary according to housing facility. *Part-time tuition:* $950 per credit hour. *Part-time fees:* $330 per term. *Payment plan:* Installment.

FRESHMAN FINANCIAL AID (Fall 2009, est.) 178 applied for aid; of those 98% were deemed to have need. 100% of freshmen with need received aid; of those 9% had need fully met. *Average percent of need met:* 74% (excluding resources awarded to replace EFC). *Average financial aid package:* $24,399 (excluding resources awarded to replace EFC). 5% of all full-time freshmen had no need and received non-need-based gift aid.

UNDERGRADUATE FINANCIAL AID (Fall 2009, est.) 409 applied for aid; of those 96% were deemed to have need. 100% of undergraduates with need received aid; of those 10% had need fully met. *Average percent of need met:* 71% (excluding resources awarded to replace EFC). *Average financial aid package:* $22,951 (excluding resources awarded to replace EFC). 6% of all full-time undergraduates had no need and received non-need-based gift aid.

GIFT AID (NEED-BASED) *Total amount:* $7,710,049 (17% federal, 11% state, 70% institutional, 2% external sources). *Receiving aid:* Freshmen: 94% (174); all full-time undergraduates: 93% (394). *Average award:* Freshmen: $21,560; Undergraduates: $19,749. *Scholarships, grants, and awards:* Federal Pell, FSEOG, state, private, college/university gift aid from institutional funds, Academic Competitiveness Grants, National SMART Grants.

GIFT AID (NON-NEED-BASED) *Total amount:* $435,076 (1% federal, 6% state, 88% institutional, 5% external sources). *Receiving aid:* Freshmen: 8% (15). Undergraduates: 8% (32). *Average award:* Freshmen: $13,950. Undergraduates: $10,490. *Scholarships, grants, and awards by category:* Academic interests/achievement: 240 awards ($1,820,000 total): general academic interests/achievements. Creative arts/performance: 7 awards ($15,500 total): art/fine arts. Special achievements/activities: 47 awards ($326,740 total): community service, general special achievements/activities, leadership, religious involvement. Special characteristics: children and siblings of alumni, children of educators,

children of faculty/staff, relatives of clergy, siblings of current students. *Tuition waivers:* Full or partial for employees or children of employees, senior citizens.

LOANS *Student loans:* $2,988,312 (84% need-based, 16% non-need-based). 87% of past graduating class borrowed through all loan programs. *Average indebtedness per student:* $21,338. *Average need-based loan:* Freshmen: $2987. Undergraduates: $3342. *Parent loans:* $1,055,106 (54% need-based, 46% non-need-based). *Programs:* Federal Direct (Subsidized and Unsubsidized Stafford, PLUS), Perkins.

WORK-STUDY *Federal work-study:* Total amount: $115,277; 114 jobs averaging $747.

ATHLETIC AWARDS Total amount: $187,147 (49% need-based, 51% non-need-based).

APPLYING FOR FINANCIAL AID *Required financial aid form:* FAFSA. *Financial aid deadline (priority):* 2/15. *Notification date:* Continuous beginning 3/15. Students must reply by 5/1 or within 4 weeks of notification.

CONTACT Chuck Walz, Director of Financial Aid, Rosemont College, 1400 Montgomery Avenue, Rosemont, PA 19010, 610-527-0200 Ext. 2220 or toll-free 800-331-0708. *Fax:* 610-527-0341. *E-mail:* cwalz@rosemont.edu.

ROWAN UNIVERSITY
Glassboro, NJ

Tuition & fees (NJ res): $11,234 | **Average undergraduate aid package: $8793**

ABOUT THE INSTITUTION State-supported, coed. 47 undergraduate majors. Both federal and institutional methodology are used as a basis for awarding need-based institutional aid.

UNDERGRADUATE EXPENSES for 2009–10 *Tuition, state resident:* full-time $8074; part-time $311 per credit hour. *Tuition, nonresident:* full-time $15,148; part-time $584 per credit hour. *Required fees:* full-time $3160; $135 per credit hour. Full-time tuition and fees vary according to course load, degree level, and program. Part-time tuition and fees vary according to degree level and program. *College room and board:* $9958; *Room only:* $6248. Room and board charges vary according to board plan and housing facility. *Payment plan:* Deferred payment.

FRESHMAN FINANCIAL AID (Fall 2008) 979 applied for aid; of those 63% were deemed to have need. 92% of freshmen with need received aid; of those 13% had need fully met. *Average percent of need met:* 81% (excluding resources awarded to replace EFC). *Average financial aid package:* $6977 (excluding resources awarded to replace EFC). 9% of all full-time freshmen had no need and received non-need-based gift aid.

UNDERGRADUATE FINANCIAL AID (Fall 2008) 6,111 applied for aid; of those 75% were deemed to have need. 96% of undergraduates with need received aid; of those 9% had need fully met. *Average percent of need met:* 81% (excluding resources awarded to replace EFC). *Average financial aid package:* $8793 (excluding resources awarded to replace EFC). 6% of all full-time undergraduates had no need and received non-need-based gift aid.

GIFT AID (NEED-BASED) *Total amount:* $23,641,514 (32% federal, 46% state, 19% institutional, 3% external sources). *Receiving aid:* Freshmen: 19% (219); all full-time undergraduates: 28% (2,222). *Average award:* Freshmen: $7589; Undergraduates: $8507. *Scholarships, grants, and awards:* Federal Pell, FSEOG, state, private, college/university gift aid from institutional funds.

GIFT AID (NON-NEED-BASED) *Total amount:* $2,782,108 (4% state, 81% institutional, 15% external sources). *Receiving aid:* Freshmen: 11% (127). Undergraduates: 8% (626). *Average award:* Freshmen: $5835. Undergraduates: $4972. *Scholarships, grants, and awards by category:* Academic interests/achievement: general academic interests/achievements. Creative arts/performance: general creative arts/performance, music. Special characteristics: members of minority groups. *Tuition waivers:* Full or partial for employees or children of employees.

LOANS *Student loans:* $51,256,736 (97% need-based, 3% non-need-based). 73% of past graduating class borrowed through all loan programs. *Average indebtedness per student:* $26,379. *Average need-based loan:* Freshmen: $3128. Undergraduates: $4303. *Parent loans:* $10,232,496 (70% need-based, 30% non-need-based). *Programs:* Federal Direct (Subsidized and Unsubsidized Stafford, PLUS), state.

WORK-STUDY *Federal work-study:* Total amount: $638,045; 413 jobs averaging $4176. *State or other work-study/employment:* Total amount: $989,013 (64% need-based, 36% non-need-based). 619 part-time jobs averaging $4416.

APPLYING FOR FINANCIAL AID *Required financial aid form:* FAFSA. *Financial aid deadline (priority):* 3/15. *Notification date:* Continuous beginning 3/15. Students must reply by 5/1.

CONTACT Luis Tavarez, Director of Financial Aid, Rowan University, 201 Mullica Hill Road, Glassboro, NJ 08028-1701, 856-256-4276 or toll-free 800-447-1165 (in-state). *Fax:* 856-256-4413. *E-mail:* tavarez@rowan.edu.

RUSH UNIVERSITY
Chicago, IL

CONTACT David Nelson, Acting Director, Student Financial Aid, Rush University, 600 South Paulina Street, Suite 440, Chicago, IL 60612-3832, 312-942-6256. *Fax:* 312-942-2732. *E-mail:* david_j_nelson@rush.edu.

RUSSELL SAGE COLLEGE
Troy, NY

Tuition & fees: $27,790   **Average undergraduate aid package: $31,024**

ABOUT THE INSTITUTION Independent, women only. 22 undergraduate majors. Both federal and institutional methodology are used as a basis for awarding need-based institutional aid.

UNDERGRADUATE EXPENSES for 2009–10 *Comprehensive fee:* $37,460, includes full-time tuition ($27,000), mandatory fees ($790), and room and board ($9670). *College room only:* $4940. Room and board charges vary according to board plan. *Part-time tuition:* $900 per credit hour. *Payment plans:* Installment, deferred payment.

FRESHMAN FINANCIAL AID (Fall 2009, est.) 128 applied for aid; of those 96% were deemed to have need. 100% of freshmen with need received aid; of those 67% had need fully met. *Average financial aid package:* $32,416 (excluding resources awarded to replace EFC). 4% of all full-time freshmen had no need and received non-need-based gift aid.

UNDERGRADUATE FINANCIAL AID (Fall 2009, est.) 687 applied for aid; of those 90% were deemed to have need. 100% of undergraduates with need received aid; of those 14% had need fully met. *Average financial aid package:* $31,024 (excluding resources awarded to replace EFC). 6% of all full-time undergraduates had no need and received non-need-based gift aid.

GIFT AID (NEED-BASED) *Total amount:* $6,445,423 (22% federal, 20% state, 55% institutional, 3% external sources). *Receiving aid:* Freshmen: 96% (123); all full-time undergraduates: 89% (616). *Average award:* Freshmen: $9190; Undergraduates: $7388. *Scholarships, grants, and awards:* Federal Pell, FSEOG, state, private, college/university gift aid from institutional funds, Federal Nursing.

GIFT AID (NON-NEED-BASED) *Total amount:* $4,999,047 (100% institutional). *Receiving aid:* Freshmen: 84% (107). Undergraduates: 82% (569). *Average award:* Freshmen: $10,200. Undergraduates: $12,800. *Scholarships, grants, and awards by category: Academic interests/achievement:* 458 awards ($5,367,750 total): general academic interests/achievements. *Creative arts/performance:* 6 awards ($131,250 total): theater/drama. *Special achievements/activities:* 24 awards ($49,000 total): community service, general special achievements/activities, leadership. *Special characteristics:* 331 awards ($858,800 total): adult students, children and siblings of alumni, children of educators, children of faculty/staff, first-generation college students, general special characteristics, siblings of current students, spouses of current students. *Tuition waivers:* Full or partial for employees or children of employees.

LOANS *Student loans:* $7,201,115 (53% need-based, 47% non-need-based). 96% of past graduating class borrowed through all loan programs. *Average indebtedness per student:* $29,000. *Average need-based loan:* Freshmen: $4595. Undergraduates: $5026. *Parent loans:* $819,000 (24% need-based, 76% non-need-based). *Programs:* FFEL (Subsidized and Unsubsidized Stafford, PLUS), Perkins.

WORK-STUDY *Federal work-study:* Total amount: $410,000; 401 jobs averaging $2000. *State or other work-study/employment:* Total amount: $132,000 (100% non-need-based). 88 part-time jobs averaging $1500.

APPLYING FOR FINANCIAL AID *Required financial aid forms:* FAFSA, state aid form. *Financial aid deadline (priority):* 3/1. *Notification date:* Continuous beginning 3/1. Students must reply within 2 weeks of notification.

CONTACT James K. Dease, Associate Vice President for Student Services, Russell Sage College, 45 Ferry Street, Troy, NY 12180, 518-244-2062 or toll-free 888-VERY-SAGE (in-state), 888-VERY SAGE (out-of-state). *Fax:* 518-244-2460. *E-mail:* deasej@sage.edu.

RUST COLLEGE
Holly Springs, MS

CONTACT Mrs. Helen L. Street, Director of Financial Aid, Rust College, 150 Rust Avenue, Holly Springs, MS 38635, 662-252-8000 Ext. 4061 or toll-free 888-886-8492 Ext. 4065. *Fax:* 662-252-8895.

RUTGERS, THE STATE UNIVERSITY OF NEW JERSEY, CAMDEN
Camden, NJ

Tuition & fees (NJ res): $11,698   **Average undergraduate aid package: $12,413**

ABOUT THE INSTITUTION State-supported, coed. 33 undergraduate majors. Federal methodology is used as a basis for awarding need-based institutional aid.

UNDERGRADUATE EXPENSES for 2009–10 *Tuition, state resident:* full-time $9546; part-time $307 per credit hour. *Tuition, nonresident:* full-time $20,178; part-time $654 per credit hour. *Required fees:* full-time $2152. Part-time tuition and fees vary according to course level. *College room and board:* $9788; *Room only:* $7048. Room and board charges vary according to board plan and housing facility. *Payment plan:* Installment.

FRESHMAN FINANCIAL AID (Fall 2009, est.) 392 applied for aid; of those 77% were deemed to have need. 95% of freshmen with need received aid; of those 51% had need fully met. *Average percent of need met:* 69% (excluding resources awarded to replace EFC). *Average financial aid package:* $11,915 (excluding resources awarded to replace EFC). 6% of all full-time freshmen had no need and received non-need-based gift aid.

UNDERGRADUATE FINANCIAL AID (Fall 2009, est.) 2,932 applied for aid; of those 84% were deemed to have need. 98% of undergraduates with need received aid; of those 44% had need fully met. *Average percent of need met:* 64% (excluding resources awarded to replace EFC). *Average financial aid package:* $12,413 (excluding resources awarded to replace EFC). 4% of all full-time undergraduates had no need and received non-need-based gift aid.

GIFT AID (NEED-BASED) *Total amount:* $18,292,457 (33% federal, 50% state, 15% institutional, 2% external sources). *Receiving aid:* Freshmen: 45% (194); all full-time undergraduates: 50% (1,684). *Average award:* Freshmen: $10,765; Undergraduates: $10,049. *Scholarships, grants, and awards:* Federal Pell, FSEOG, state, private, college/university gift aid from institutional funds, Federal Nursing.

GIFT AID (NON-NEED-BASED) *Total amount:* $338,278 (22% state, 68% institutional, 10% external sources). *Receiving aid:* Freshmen: 31% (134). Undergraduates: 15% (515). *Average award:* Freshmen: $3712. Undergraduates: $5544. *Tuition waivers:* Full or partial for employees or children of employees.

LOANS *Student loans:* $26,212,967 (58% need-based, 42% non-need-based). 70% of past graduating class borrowed through all loan programs. *Average indebtedness per student:* $22,552. *Average need-based loan:* Freshmen: $3234. Undergraduates: $4316. *Parent loans:* $1,562,420 (100% need-based). *Programs:* Federal Direct (Subsidized and Unsubsidized Stafford, PLUS), Perkins, state, college/university, alternative loans.

WORK-STUDY *Federal work-study:* Total amount: $662,187; jobs available. *State or other work-study/employment:* Total amount: $700,000 (100% non-need-based). Part-time jobs available.

APPLYING FOR FINANCIAL AID *Required financial aid form:* FAFSA. *Financial aid deadline:* Continuous. *Notification date:* Continuous beginning 2/15. Students must reply within 2 weeks of notification.

CONTACT Mr. Willie L. Williams, Manager, University Financial Aid Funds Control, Rutgers, The State University of New Jersey, Camden, 620 George Street, New Brunswick, NJ 08901, 732-932-7057 Ext. 603. *Fax:* 732-932-0516. *E-mail:* billw@rci.rutgers.edu.

RUTGERS, THE STATE UNIVERSITY OF NEW JERSEY, NEWARK
Newark, NJ

Tuition & fees (NJ res): $11,414   **Average undergraduate aid package: $13,090**

ABOUT THE INSTITUTION State-supported, coed. 50 undergraduate majors. Federal methodology is used as a basis for awarding need-based institutional aid.

UNDERGRADUATE EXPENSES for 2009–10 *Tuition, state resident:* full-time $9546; part-time $307 per credit hour. *Tuition, nonresident:* full-time $20,178; part-time $654 per credit hour. *Required fees:* full-time $1868. *College room and board:* $11,155; *Room only:* $6965. Room and board charges vary according to board plan and housing facility. *Payment plan:* Installment.

FRESHMAN FINANCIAL AID (Fall 2009, est.) 777 applied for aid; of those 83% were deemed to have need. 93% of freshmen with need received aid; of those 35% had need fully met. *Average percent of need met:* 78% (excluding resources awarded to replace EFC). *Average financial aid package:* $12,579 (excluding resources awarded to replace EFC). 2% of all full-time freshmen had no need and received non-need-based gift aid.

UNDERGRADUATE FINANCIAL AID (Fall 2009, est.) 4,523 applied for aid; of those 89% were deemed to have need. 97% of undergraduates with need received aid; of those 28% had need fully met. *Average percent of need met:* 77% (excluding resources awarded to replace EFC). *Average financial aid package:* $13,090 (excluding resources awarded to replace EFC). 2% of all full-time undergraduates had no need and received non-need-based gift aid.

GIFT AID (NEED-BASED) *Total amount:* $34,984,815 (33% federal, 50% state, 15% institutional, 2% external sources). *Receiving aid:* Freshmen: 50% (454); all full-time undergraduates: 53% (3,026). *Average award:* Freshmen: $11,369; Undergraduates: $10,680. *Scholarships, grants, and awards:* Federal Pell, FSEOG, state, private, college/university gift aid from institutional funds.

GIFT AID (NON-NEED-BASED) *Total amount:* $980,349 (25% state, 73% institutional, 2% external sources). *Receiving aid:* Freshmen: 30% (272). Undergraduates: 16% (918). *Average award:* Freshmen: $9800. Undergraduates: $6000. *Tuition waivers:* Full or partial for employees or children of employees.

LOANS *Student loans:* $31,075,091 (64% need-based, 36% non-need-based). 55% of past graduating class borrowed through all loan programs. *Average indebtedness per student:* $19,500. *Average need-based loan:* Freshmen: $3401. Undergraduates: $4474. *Parent loans:* $1,184,226 (87% need-based, 13% non-need-based). *Programs:* Federal Direct (Subsidized and Unsubsidized Stafford, PLUS), Perkins, state, college/university, alternative loans.

WORK-STUDY *Federal work-study:* Total amount: $1,200,000; jobs available. *State or other work-study/employment:* Total amount: $1,425,000 (100% non-need-based). Part-time jobs available.

ATHLETIC AWARDS Total amount: $89,750 (100% non-need-based).

APPLYING FOR FINANCIAL AID *Required financial aid form:* FAFSA. *Financial aid deadline (priority):* 3/15. *Notification date:* Continuous. Students must reply within 2 weeks of notification.

CONTACT Mr. Willie L. Williams, Manager, University Financial Aid Funds Control, Rutgers, The State University of New Jersey, Newark, 620 George Street, New Brunswick, NJ 08901, 732-932-7057 Ext. 603. *Fax:* 732-932-0516. *E-mail:* billw@rci.rutgers.edu.

RUTGERS, THE STATE UNIVERSITY OF NEW JERSEY, NEW BRUNSWICK
Piscataway, NJ

Tuition & fees (NJ res): $11,886	Average undergraduate aid package: $14,415

ABOUT THE INSTITUTION State-supported, coed. 120 undergraduate majors. Federal methodology is used as a basis for awarding need-based institutional aid.

UNDERGRADUATE EXPENSES for 2009–10 *Tuition, state resident:* full-time $9546; part-time $307 per credit hour. *Tuition, nonresident:* full-time $20,178; part-time $654 per credit hour. *Required fees:* full-time $2340. Part-time tuition and fees vary according to course level. *College room and board:* $10,676; *Room only:* $6526. Room and board charges vary according to board plan and housing facility. *Payment plan:* Installment.

FRESHMAN FINANCIAL AID (Fall 2009, est.) 4,843 applied for aid; of those 73% were deemed to have need. 94% of freshmen with need received aid; of those 48% had need fully met. *Average percent of need met:* 63% (excluding resources awarded to replace EFC). *Average financial aid package:* $14,625 (excluding resources awarded to replace EFC). 6% of all full-time freshmen had no need and received non-need-based gift aid.

UNDERGRADUATE FINANCIAL AID (Fall 2009, est.) 19,762 applied for aid; of those 81% were deemed to have need. 96% of undergraduates with need received aid; of those 41% had need fully met. *Average percent of need met:* 65% (excluding resources awarded to replace EFC). *Average financial aid package:* $14,415 (excluding resources awarded to replace EFC). 3% of all full-time undergraduates had no need and received non-need-based gift aid.

GIFT AID (NEED-BASED) *Total amount:* $125,415,145 (28% federal, 43% state, 25% institutional, 4% external sources). *Receiving aid:* Freshmen: 33% (1,906); all full-time undergraduates: 34% (9,487). *Average award:* Freshmen: $12,284; Undergraduates: $11,354. *Scholarships, grants, and awards:* Federal Pell, FSEOG, state, private, college/university gift aid from institutional funds.

GIFT AID (NON-NEED-BASED) *Total amount:* $14,587,705 (17% state, 80% institutional, 3% external sources). *Receiving aid:* Freshmen: 31% (1,807). Undergraduates: 24% (6,711). *Average award:* Freshmen: $8658. Undergraduates: $6098. *Tuition waivers:* Full or partial for employees or children of employees.

LOANS *Student loans:* $161,996,326 (70% need-based, 30% non-need-based). 52% of past graduating class borrowed through all loan programs. *Average indebtedness per student:* $19,760. *Average need-based loan:* Freshmen: $3427. Undergraduates: $4440. *Parent loans:* $14,247,209 (100% need-based). *Programs:* Federal Direct (Subsidized and Unsubsidized Stafford, PLUS), Perkins, state, college/university, alternative loans.

WORK-STUDY *Federal work-study:* Total amount: $5,174,450; jobs available. *State or other work-study/employment:* Total amount: $11,400,000 (100% non-need-based). Part-time jobs available.

ATHLETIC AWARDS Total amount: $7,955,451 (92% need-based, 8% non-need-based).

APPLYING FOR FINANCIAL AID *Required financial aid form:* FAFSA. *Financial aid deadline (priority):* 3/15. *Notification date:* Continuous. Students must reply within 2 weeks of notification.

CONTACT Mr. William Williams, Manager, University Financial Aid Funds Control, Rutgers, The State University of New Jersey, New Brunswick, 620 George Street, New Brunswick, NJ 08901, 732-932-7057 Ext. 603. *Fax:* 732-932-0516. *E-mail:* billw@rci.rutgers.edu.

SACRED HEART MAJOR SEMINARY
Detroit, MI

Tuition & fees: $14,390	Average undergraduate aid package: $3200

ABOUT THE INSTITUTION Independent Roman Catholic, coed. 3 undergraduate majors. Both federal and institutional methodology are used as a basis for awarding need-based institutional aid.

UNDERGRADUATE EXPENSES for 2009–10 *Comprehensive fee:* $22,190 includes full-time tuition ($14,310), mandatory fees ($80), and room and board ($7800). *Part-time tuition:* $335 per credit hour. *Part-time fees:* $40 per term. *Payment plans:* Installment, deferred payment.

UNDERGRADUATE FINANCIAL AID (Fall 2009, est.) 217 applied for aid; of those 88% were deemed to have need. 100% of undergraduates with need received aid. *Average percent of need met:* 70% (excluding resources awarded to replace EFC). *Average financial aid package:* $3200 (excluding resources awarded to replace EFC).

GIFT AID (NEED-BASED) *Total amount:* $437,862 (17% federal, 6% state, 77% institutional). *Scholarships, grants, and awards:* Federal Pell, FSEOG, state, private, college/university gift aid from institutional funds.

GIFT AID (NON-NEED-BASED) *Total amount:* $388,436 (100% institutional). *Scholarships, grants, and awards by category:* Academic interests/achievement: religion/biblical studies. *Special achievements/activities:* religious involvement. *Special characteristics:* local/state students, religious affiliation. *Tuition waivers:* Full or partial for employees or children of employees.

LOANS *Student loans:* $183,246 (100% need-based). 5% of past graduating class borrowed through all loan programs. *Programs:* Federal Direct (Subsidized and Unsubsidized Stafford), FFEL (Subsidized and Unsubsidized Stafford).

APPLYING FOR FINANCIAL AID *Required financial aid forms:* FAFSA, institution's own form. *Financial aid deadline (priority):* 2/20. *Notification date:* Continuous beginning 6/1. Students must reply within 2 weeks of notification.

CONTACT Financial Aid Office, Sacred Heart Major Seminary, 2701 Chicago Boulevard, Detroit, MI 48206-1799, 313-883-8500. *Fax:* 313-868-7028. *E-mail:* financialaid@shms.edu.

SACRED HEART UNIVERSITY
Fairfield, CT

Tuition & fees: $30,298	Average undergraduate aid package: $18,782

ABOUT THE INSTITUTION Independent Roman Catholic, coed. 55 undergraduate majors. Both federal and institutional methodology are used as a basis for awarding need-based institutional aid.

UNDERGRADUATE EXPENSES for 2009–10 *Comprehensive fee:* $41,982 includes full-time tuition ($30,090), mandatory fees ($208), and room and board ($11,684). *College room only:* $8840. Full-time tuition and fees vary according to program and student level. Room and board charges vary according to board plan and housing facility. *Part-time tuition:* $460 per credit hour. *Part-time fees:* $80 per term. Part-time tuition and fees vary according to program. *Payment plan:* Installment.

FRESHMAN FINANCIAL AID (Fall 2009, est.) 808 applied for aid; of those 79% were deemed to have need. 99% of freshmen with need received aid; of those 13% had need fully met. *Average percent of need met:* 65% (excluding resources awarded to replace EFC). *Average financial aid package:* $19,074 (excluding resources awarded to replace EFC). 19% of all full-time freshmen had no need and received non-need-based gift aid.

UNDERGRADUATE FINANCIAL AID (Fall 2009, est.) 2,979 applied for aid; of those 82% were deemed to have need. 99% of undergraduates with need received aid; of those 14% had need fully met. *Average percent of need met:* 65% (excluding resources awarded to replace EFC). *Average financial aid package:* $18,782 (excluding resources awarded to replace EFC). 16% of all full-time undergraduates had no need and received non-need-based gift aid.

GIFT AID (NEED-BASED) *Total amount:* $31,509,324 (11% federal, 8% state, 75% institutional, 6% external sources). *Receiving aid:* Freshmen: 70% (633); all full-time undergraduates: 68% (2,408). *Average award:* Freshmen: $15,411; Undergraduates: $14,508. *Scholarships, grants, and awards:* Federal Pell, FSEOG, state, private, college/university gift aid from institutional funds.

GIFT AID (NON-NEED-BASED) *Total amount:* $4,391,070 (83% institutional, 17% external sources). *Receiving aid:* Freshmen: 7% (60). Undergraduates: 5% (192). *Average award:* Freshmen: $6470. Undergraduates: $5541. *Scholarships, grants, and awards by category: Academic interests/achievement:* biological sciences, business, computer science, education, English, general academic interests/achievements, health fields, humanities, mathematics, physical sciences, premedicine. *Creative arts/performance:* applied art and design, art/fine arts, creative writing, music. *Special achievements/activities:* community service, general special achievements/activities, leadership, religious involvement. *Special characteristics:* children of current students, children of faculty/staff, ethnic background, handicapped students, members of minority groups, religious affiliation, siblings of current students, twins. *Tuition waivers:* Full or partial for employees or children of employees.

LOANS *Student loans:* $30,109,643 (60% need-based, 40% non-need-based). 96% of past graduating class borrowed through all loan programs. *Average indebtedness per student:* $27,000. *Average need-based loan:* Freshmen: $3498. Undergraduates: $4527. *Parent loans:* $7,474,273 (39% need-based, 61% non-need-based). *Programs:* Federal Direct (Subsidized and Unsubsidized Stafford, PLUS), FFEL (Subsidized and Unsubsidized Stafford, PLUS), Perkins, state.

WORK-STUDY *Federal work-study:* Total amount: $1,222,686; jobs available. *State or other work-study/employment:* Total amount: $1,011,665 (12% need-based, 88% non-need-based). Part-time jobs available.

ATHLETIC AWARDS Total amount: $7,795,705 (47% need-based, 53% non-need-based).

APPLYING FOR FINANCIAL AID *Required financial aid forms:* FAFSA, CSS Financial Aid PROFILE, noncustodial (divorced/separated) parent's statement. *Financial aid deadline (priority):* 2/15. *Notification date:* Continuous beginning 3/1. Students must reply within 2 weeks of notification.

CONTACT Ms. Julie B. Savino, Dean of University Financial Assistance, Sacred Heart University, 5151 Park Avenue, Fairfield, CT 06825, 203-371-7980. *Fax:* 203-365-7608. *E-mail:* savinoj@sacredheart.edu.

SAGE COLLEGE OF ALBANY
Albany, NY

Tuition & fees: $27,790	Average undergraduate aid package: $29,554

ABOUT THE INSTITUTION Independent, coed. 18 undergraduate majors. Both federal and institutional methodology are used as a basis for awarding need-based institutional aid.

UNDERGRADUATE EXPENSES for 2009–10 *Comprehensive fee:* $37,620 includes full-time tuition ($27,000), mandatory fees ($790), and room and board ($9830). *College room only:* $5100. Room and board charges vary according to board plan. *Part-time tuition:* $900 per credit hour. *Payment plans:* Installment, deferred payment.

FRESHMAN FINANCIAL AID (Fall 2009, est.) 104 applied for aid; of those 100% were deemed to have need. 100% of freshmen with need received aid; of those 73% had need fully met. *Average financial aid package:* $32,500 (excluding resources awarded to replace EFC). 5% of all full-time freshmen had no need and received non-need-based gift aid.

UNDERGRADUATE FINANCIAL AID (Fall 2009, est.) 483 applied for aid; of those 95% were deemed to have need. 100% of undergraduates with need received aid; of those 18% had need fully met. *Average financial aid package:* $29,554 (excluding resources awarded to replace EFC). 5% of all full-time undergraduates had no need and received non-need-based gift aid.

GIFT AID (NEED-BASED) *Total amount:* $5,330,050 (25% federal, 17% state, 56% institutional, 2% external sources). *Receiving aid:* Freshmen: 81% (85); all full-time undergraduates: 89% (436). *Average award:* Freshmen: $9615; Undergraduates: $7250. *Scholarships, grants, and awards:* Federal Pell, FSEOG, state, private, college/university gift aid from institutional funds.

GIFT AID (NON-NEED-BASED) *Total amount:* $4,117,888 (99% institutional, 1% external sources). *Receiving aid:* Freshmen: 66% (69). Undergraduates: 61% (301). *Average award:* Freshmen: $10,000. Undergraduates: $7450. *Scholarships, grants, and awards by category: Academic interests/achievement:* 326 awards ($2,006,494 total): general academic interests/achievements. *Creative arts/performance:* 17 awards ($52,500 total): art/fine arts. *Special achievements/activities:* 12 awards ($12,000 total): community service, general special achievements/activities. *Special characteristics:* 110 awards ($334,200 total): children and siblings of alumni, children of educators, children of faculty/staff, first-generation college students, general special characteristics, siblings of current students. *Tuition waivers:* Full or partial for employees or children of employees.

LOANS *Student loans:* $4,085,667 (57% need-based, 43% non-need-based). 96% of past graduating class borrowed through all loan programs. *Average indebtedness per student:* $24,000. *Average need-based loan:* Freshmen: $6780. Undergraduates: $5236. *Parent loans:* $775,000 (70% need-based, 30% non-need-based). *Programs:* FFEL (Subsidized and Unsubsidized Stafford, PLUS), Perkins, state, alternative loans.

WORK-STUDY *Federal work-study:* Total amount: $168,500; 196 jobs averaging $2000. *State or other work-study/employment:* Total amount: $46,000 (100% non-need-based). 32 part-time jobs averaging $1200.

APPLYING FOR FINANCIAL AID *Required financial aid forms:* FAFSA, state aid form. *Financial aid deadline (priority):* 3/1. *Notification date:* Continuous beginning 3/1. Students must reply within 2 weeks of notification.

CONTACT James K. Dease, Associate Vice President for Student Service, Sage College of Albany, 45 Ferry Street, Troy, NY 12180, 518-244-4525 or toll-free 888-VERY-SAGE. *Fax:* 518-244-2460. *E-mail:* deasej@sage.edu.

SAGINAW VALLEY STATE UNIVERSITY
University Center, MI

Tuition & fees (MI res): $6890	Average undergraduate aid package: $7086

ABOUT THE INSTITUTION State-supported, coed. 61 undergraduate majors. Federal methodology is used as a basis for awarding need-based institutional aid.

UNDERGRADUATE EXPENSES for 2009–10 *Tuition, state resident:* full-time $6452; part-time $215.40 per credit hour. *Tuition, nonresident:* full-time $15,762; part-time $525.40 per credit hour. *Required fees:* full-time $438; $14.60 per credit hour. Full-time tuition and fees vary according to course level, course load, location, and program. Part-time tuition and fees vary according to course level, course load, location, and program. *College room and board:* $7270; *Room only:* $4110. Room and board charges vary according to board plan, housing facility, and student level. *Payment plan:* Installment.

FRESHMAN FINANCIAL AID (Fall 2008) 1,596 applied for aid; of those 71% were deemed to have need. 98% of freshmen with need received aid; of those 22% had need fully met. *Average percent of need met:* 65% (excluding

Saginaw Valley State University

resources awarded to replace EFC). *Average financial aid package:* $7136 (excluding resources awarded to replace EFC). 13% of all full-time freshmen had no need and received non-need-based gift aid.

UNDERGRADUATE FINANCIAL AID (Fall 2008) 6,168 applied for aid; of those 70% were deemed to have need. 98% of undergraduates with need received aid; of those 17% had need fully met. *Average percent of need met:* 62% (excluding resources awarded to replace EFC). *Average financial aid package:* $7086 (excluding resources awarded to replace EFC). 11% of all full-time undergraduates had no need and received non-need-based gift aid.

GIFT AID (NEED-BASED) *Total amount:* $9,463,762 (83% federal, 10% state, 7% institutional). *Receiving aid:* Freshmen: 42% (693); all full-time undergraduates: 38% (2,541). *Average award:* Freshmen: $3542; Undergraduates: $3432. *Scholarships, grants, and awards:* Federal Pell, FSEOG, state, private, college/university gift aid from institutional funds.

GIFT AID (NON-NEED-BASED) *Total amount:* $12,441,132 (3% federal, 20% state, 54% institutional, 23% external sources). *Receiving aid:* Freshmen: 49% (801). Undergraduates: 30% (2,008). *Average award:* Freshmen: $3276. Undergraduates: $3745. *Scholarships, grants, and awards by category:* Academic interests/achievement: biological sciences, business, computer science, education, engineering/technologies, general academic interests/achievements, health fields, mathematics, physical sciences. Creative arts/performance: art/fine arts, music, theater/drama. Special achievements/activities: community service, leadership. Special characteristics: local/state students, members of minority groups. *Tuition waivers:* Full or partial for employees or children of employees.

LOANS *Student loans:* $38,427,179 (39% need-based, 61% non-need-based). 57% of past graduating class borrowed through all loan programs. *Average indebtedness per student:* $23,555. *Average need-based loan:* Freshmen: $2986. Undergraduates: $3816. *Parent loans:* $2,106,519 (100% non-need-based). *Programs:* Federal Direct (Subsidized and Unsubsidized Stafford, PLUS), state, CitiAssist Loans, Signature Student Loans.

WORK-STUDY *Federal work-study:* Total amount: $336,352; 174 jobs averaging $1938. *State or other work-study/employment:* Total amount: $147,786 (100% need-based). 78 part-time jobs averaging $1895.

ATHLETIC AWARDS Total amount: $1,313,355 (100% non-need-based).

APPLYING FOR FINANCIAL AID *Required financial aid form:* FAFSA. *Financial aid deadline (priority):* 2/14. *Notification date:* Continuous beginning 3/20. Students must reply within 10 weeks of notification.

CONTACT Robert Lemuel, Director of Scholarships and Financial Aid, Saginaw Valley State University, 7400 Bay Road, University Center, MI 48710, 989-964-4103 or toll-free 800-968-9500. *Fax:* 989-790-0180. *E-mail:* lemuel@svsy.edu.

ST. AMBROSE UNIVERSITY
Davenport, IA

Tuition & fees: $23,910	Average undergraduate aid package: $16,770

ABOUT THE INSTITUTION Independent Roman Catholic, coed. 71 undergraduate majors. Federal methodology is used as a basis for awarding need-based institutional aid.

UNDERGRADUATE EXPENSES for 2010–11 *Comprehensive fee:* $32,495 includes full-time tuition ($23,670), mandatory fees ($240), and room and board ($8585). *College room only:* $4375. Full-time tuition and fees vary according to course load, location, program, and reciprocity agreements. Room and board charges vary according to board plan and housing facility. *Part-time tuition:* $735 per credit hour. *Part-time fees:* $60 per term. Part-time tuition and fees vary according to course load and location. *Payment plan:* Installment.

FRESHMAN FINANCIAL AID (Fall 2009, est.) 576 applied for aid; of those 75% were deemed to have need. 99% of freshmen with need received aid; of those 49% had need fully met. *Average percent of need met:* 24% (excluding resources awarded to replace EFC). *Average financial aid package:* $17,785 (excluding resources awarded to replace EFC). 24% of all full-time freshmen had no need and received non-need-based gift aid.

UNDERGRADUATE FINANCIAL AID (Fall 2009, est.) 2,386 applied for aid; of those 76% were deemed to have need. 99% of undergraduates with need received aid; of those 26% had need fully met. *Average percent of need met:* 26% (excluding resources awarded to replace EFC). *Average financial aid package:* $16,770 (excluding resources awarded to replace EFC). 23% of all full-time undergraduates had no need and received non-need-based gift aid.

GIFT AID (NEED-BASED) *Total amount:* $18,482,503 (16% federal, 11% state, 71% institutional, 2% external sources). *Receiving aid:* Freshmen: 74% (429);

all full-time undergraduates: 73% (1,758). *Average award:* Freshmen: $11,544; Undergraduates: $10,732. *Scholarships, grants, and awards:* Federal Pell, FSEOG, state, private, college/university gift aid from institutional funds.

GIFT AID (NON-NEED-BASED) *Total amount:* $4,034,924 (99% institutional, 1% external sources). *Receiving aid:* Freshmen: 44% (256). Undergraduates: 31% (737). *Average award:* Freshmen: $7644. Undergraduates: $7158. *Scholarships, grants, and awards by category:* Academic interests/achievement: 2,182 awards ($14,270,530 total): general academic interests/achievements, international studies, religion/biblical studies. Creative arts/performance: 118 awards ($269,645 total): art/fine arts, dance, music, theater/drama. Special achievements/activities: 24 awards ($20,500 total): cheerleading/drum major. Special characteristics: 236 awards ($1,379,249 total): children and siblings of alumni, children of faculty/staff, international students, members of minority groups, out-of-state students, religious affiliation, veterans. *Tuition waivers:* Full or partial for minority students, children of alumni, employees or children of employees, adult students, senior citizens.

LOANS *Student loans:* $17,583,607 (91% need-based, 9% non-need-based). 77% of past graduating class borrowed through all loan programs. *Average indebtedness per student:* $33,216. *Average need-based loan:* Freshmen: $3896. Undergraduates: $4713. *Parent loans:* $3,536,850 (86% need-based, 14% non-need-based). *Programs:* Federal Direct (Subsidized and Unsubsidized Stafford, PLUS), Perkins, private loans.

WORK-STUDY *Federal work-study:* Total amount: $813,155; 477 jobs averaging $1822. *State or other work-study/employment:* Total amount: $294,439 (77% need-based, 23% non-need-based). 209 part-time jobs averaging $2260.

ATHLETIC AWARDS Total amount: $2,873,994 (74% need-based, 26% non-need-based).

APPLYING FOR FINANCIAL AID *Required financial aid form:* FAFSA. *Financial aid deadline (priority):* 3/15. *Notification date:* Continuous beginning 2/15. Students must reply within 2 weeks of notification.

CONTACT Ms. Julie Haack, Director of Financial Aid, St. Ambrose University, 518 West Locust Street, Davenport, IA 52803, 563-333-6314 or toll-free 800-383-2627. *Fax:* 563-333-6243. *E-mail:* haackjuliea@sau.edu.

ST. ANDREWS PRESBYTERIAN COLLEGE
Laurinburg, NC

Tuition & fees: $21,190	Average undergraduate aid package: $15,948

ABOUT THE INSTITUTION Independent Presbyterian, coed. 15 undergraduate majors. Federal methodology is used as a basis for awarding need-based institutional aid.

UNDERGRADUATE EXPENSES for 2009–10 *One-time required fee:* $150. *Comprehensive fee:* $29,862 includes full-time tuition ($21,190) and room and board ($8672). Full-time tuition and fees vary according to course load and location. Room and board charges vary according to housing facility. Part-time tuition and fees vary according to location. *Payment plan:* Installment.

FRESHMAN FINANCIAL AID (Fall 2009, est.) 132 applied for aid; of those 86% were deemed to have need. 100% of freshmen with need received aid; of those 20% had need fully met. *Average percent of need met:* 71% (excluding resources awarded to replace EFC). *Average financial aid package:* $16,117 (excluding resources awarded to replace EFC). 24% of all full-time freshmen had no need and received non-need-based gift aid.

UNDERGRADUATE FINANCIAL AID (Fall 2009, est.) 493 applied for aid; of those 87% were deemed to have need. 100% of undergraduates with need received aid; of those 23% had need fully met. *Average percent of need met:* 74% (excluding resources awarded to replace EFC). *Average financial aid package:* $15,948 (excluding resources awarded to replace EFC). 21% of all full-time undergraduates had no need and received non-need-based gift aid.

GIFT AID (NEED-BASED) *Total amount:* $4,301,327 (19% federal, 16% state, 53% institutional, 12% external sources). *Receiving aid:* Freshmen: 75% (113); all full-time undergraduates: 75% (428). *Average award:* Freshmen: $12,406; Undergraduates: $11,765. *Scholarships, grants, and awards:* Federal Pell, FSEOG, state, private, college/university gift aid from institutional funds.

GIFT AID (NON-NEED-BASED) *Total amount:* $1,006,024 (10% state, 75% institutional, 15% external sources). *Receiving aid:* Freshmen: 12% (18). Undergraduates: 12% (68). *Average award:* Freshmen: $5067. Undergraduates: $5228. *Scholarships, grants, and awards by category:* Academic interests/achievement: 419 awards ($1,736,664 total): general academic interests/achievements. Creative arts/performance: 20 awards ($19,050 total): general creative arts/performance, performing arts, theater/drama. Special achievements/

activities: 140 awards ($145,068 total): community service, general special achievements/activities, leadership. *Tuition waivers:* Full or partial for employees or children of employees, adult students, senior citizens.

LOANS *Student loans:* $3,346,885 (70% need-based, 30% non-need-based). 63% of past graduating class borrowed through all loan programs. *Average indebtedness per student:* $19,366. *Average need-based loan:* Freshmen: $3536. Undergraduates: $4327. *Parent loans:* $1,672,800 (36% need-based, 64% non-need-based). *Programs:* FFEL (Subsidized and Unsubsidized Stafford, PLUS), state.

WORK-STUDY *Federal work-study:* Total amount: $280,928; 274 jobs averaging $1800. *State or other work-study/employment:* Total amount: $27,904 (3% need-based, 97% non-need-based). 45 part-time jobs averaging $1800.

ATHLETIC AWARDS Total amount: $993,975 (70% need-based, 30% non-need-based).

APPLYING FOR FINANCIAL AID *Required financial aid forms:* FAFSA, state aid form. *Financial aid deadline:* Continuous. *Notification date:* Continuous beginning 2/1. Students must reply within 2 weeks of notification.

CONTACT Kimberly Driggers, Director of Student Financial Planning, St. Andrews Presbyterian College, 1700 Dogwood Mile, Laurinburg, NC 28352, 910-277-5562 or toll-free 800-763-0198. *Fax:* 910-277-5206.

SAINT ANSELM COLLEGE
Manchester, NH

Tuition & fees: $30,515	Average undergraduate aid package: $23,195

ABOUT THE INSTITUTION Independent Roman Catholic, coed. 37 undergraduate majors. Both federal and institutional methodology are used as a basis for awarding need-based institutional aid.

UNDERGRADUATE EXPENSES for 2009–10 *Comprehensive fee:* $42,065 includes full-time tuition ($29,720), mandatory fees ($795), and room and board ($11,550).

FRESHMAN FINANCIAL AID (Fall 2009, est.) 475 applied for aid; of those 82% were deemed to have need. 100% of freshmen with need received aid; of those 17% had need fully met. *Average percent of need met:* 84% (excluding resources awarded to replace EFC). *Average financial aid package:* $24,243 (excluding resources awarded to replace EFC). 21% of all full-time freshmen had no need and received non-need-based gift aid.

UNDERGRADUATE FINANCIAL AID (Fall 2009, est.) 1,588 applied for aid; of those 86% were deemed to have need. 100% of undergraduates with need received aid; of those 17% had need fully met. *Average percent of need met:* 82% (excluding resources awarded to replace EFC). *Average financial aid package:* $23,195 (excluding resources awarded to replace EFC). 17% of all full-time undergraduates had no need and received non-need-based gift aid.

GIFT AID (NEED-BASED) *Total amount:* $22,139,800 (8% federal, 90% institutional, 2% external sources). *Receiving aid:* Freshmen: 74% (389); all full-time undergraduates: 72% (1,355). *Average award:* Freshmen: $19,133; Undergraduates: $16,967. *Scholarships, grants, and awards:* Federal Pell, FSEOG, state, private, college/university gift aid from institutional funds.

GIFT AID (NON-NEED-BASED) *Total amount:* $3,058,543 (96% institutional, 4% external sources). *Receiving aid:* Freshmen: 7% (35). Undergraduates: 6% (108). *Average award:* Freshmen: $8384. Undergraduates: $8216. *Scholarships, grants, and awards by category:* Academic interests/achievement: 883 awards ($6,423,185 total): general academic interests/achievements. *Special characteristics:* 145 awards ($2,199,890 total): children of educators, children of faculty/staff, siblings of current students.

LOANS *Student loans:* $14,832,010 (60% need-based, 40% non-need-based). 75% of past graduating class borrowed through all loan programs. *Average indebtedness per student:* $36,823. *Average need-based loan:* Freshmen: $4584. Undergraduates: $5788. *Parent loans:* $6,194,205 (23% need-based, 77% non-need-based). *Programs:* Federal Direct (Subsidized and Unsubsidized Stafford, PLUS), Perkins.

WORK-STUDY *Federal work-study:* Total amount: $1,570,441; 1,060 jobs averaging $1482. *State or other work-study/employment:* Total amount: $11,000 (100% non-need-based). 7 part-time jobs averaging $1571.

ATHLETIC AWARDS Total amount: $936,000 (27% need-based, 73% non-need-based).

APPLYING FOR FINANCIAL AID *Required financial aid forms:* FAFSA, CSS Financial Aid PROFILE, noncustodial (divorced/separated) parent's statement.

Financial aid deadline: 3/15. *Notification date:* Continuous beginning 3/1. Students must reply by 5/1 or within 2 weeks of notification.
CONTACT Elizabeth Keuffel, Director of Financial Aid, Saint Anselm College, 100 Saint Anselm Drive, Manchester, NH 03102-1310, 603-641-7110 or toll-free 888-4ANSELM. *Fax:* 603-656-6015. *E-mail:* financial_aid@anselm.edu.

SAINT ANTHONY COLLEGE OF NURSING
Rockford, IL

Tuition & fees: $19,250	Average undergraduate aid package: $15,818

ABOUT THE INSTITUTION Independent Roman Catholic, coed, primarily women. 1 undergraduate major. Federal methodology is used as a basis for awarding need-based institutional aid.

UNDERGRADUATE EXPENSES for 2009–10 *Tuition:* full-time $18,846; part-time $590 per semester hour. *Required fees:* full-time $404; $30 per term. Full-time tuition and fees vary according to course load and degree level. Part-time tuition and fees vary according to course load and degree level. *Payment plans:* Installment, deferred payment.

UNDERGRADUATE FINANCIAL AID (Fall 2008) 152 applied for aid; of those 100% were deemed to have need. 100% of undergraduates with need received aid. *Average financial aid package:* $15,818 (excluding resources awarded to replace EFC).

GIFT AID (NEED-BASED) *Total amount:* $558,884 (45% federal, 50% state, 4% institutional, 1% external sources). *Receiving aid:* All full-time undergraduates: 51% (83). *Average award:* Undergraduates: $6636. *Scholarships, grants, and awards:* Federal Pell, state, private, college/university gift aid from institutional funds.

GIFT AID (NON-NEED-BASED) *Total amount:* $35,871 (85% state, 15% external sources). *Receiving aid:* Undergraduates: 6% (10).

LOANS *Student loans:* $1,506,703 (47% need-based, 53% non-need-based). 96% of past graduating class borrowed through all loan programs. *Average indebtedness per student:* $26,000. *Average need-based loan:* Undergraduates: $4861. *Parent loans:* $164,696 (100% non-need-based). *Programs:* FFEL (Subsidized and Unsubsidized Stafford, PLUS), alternative loans.

APPLYING FOR FINANCIAL AID *Financial aid deadline (priority):* 5/1.

CONTACT Serrita Woods, Financial Aid Officer, Saint Anthony College of Nursing, 5658 East State Street, Rockford, IL 61108-2468, 815-395-5089. *Fax:* 815-395-2730. *E-mail:* serritawoods@sacn.edu.

ST. AUGUSTINE COLLEGE
Chicago, IL

CONTACT Mrs. Maria Zambonino, Director of Financial Aid, St. Augustine College, 1345 W Angyle, Chicago, IL 60640, 773-878-3813. *Fax:* 773-878-9032. *E-mail:* mzambonino@hotmail.com.

SAINT AUGUSTINE'S COLLEGE
Raleigh, NC

CONTACT Ms. Wanda C. White, Director of Financial Aid, Saint Augustine's College, 1315 Oakwood Avenue, Raleigh, NC 27610-2298, 919-516-4131 or toll-free 800-948-1126. *Fax:* 919-516-4338. *E-mail:* wwhite@es.st-aug.edu.

ST. BONAVENTURE UNIVERSITY
St. Bonaventure, NY

Tuition & fees: $26,895	Average undergraduate aid package: $22,000

ABOUT THE INSTITUTION Independent religious, coed. 40 undergraduate majors. Federal methodology is used as a basis for awarding need-based institutional aid.

UNDERGRADUATE EXPENSES for 2010–11 *Comprehensive fee:* $35,966 includes full-time tuition ($25,930), mandatory fees ($965), and room and board ($9071). *College room only:* $4441. Room and board charges vary according to board plan and housing facility. *Part-time tuition:* $775 per credit hour.

FRESHMAN FINANCIAL AID (Fall 2009, est.) 422 applied for aid; of those 89% were deemed to have need. 100% of freshmen with need received aid; of those

24% had need fully met. *Average percent of need met:* 86% (excluding resources awarded to replace EFC). *Average financial aid package:* $24,153 (excluding resources awarded to replace EFC). 18% of all full-time freshmen had no need and received non-need-based gift aid.

UNDERGRADUATE FINANCIAL AID (Fall 2009, est.) 1,598 applied for aid; of those 88% were deemed to have need. 100% of undergraduates with need received aid; of those 29% had need fully met. *Average percent of need met:* 79% (excluding resources awarded to replace EFC). *Average financial aid package:* $22,000 (excluding resources awarded to replace EFC). 22% of all full-time undergraduates had no need and received non-need-based gift aid.

GIFT AID (NEED-BASED) *Total amount:* $27,589,770 (15% federal, 8% state, 76% institutional, 1% external sources). *Receiving aid:* Freshmen: 81% (375); all full-time undergraduates: 76% (1,409). *Average award:* Freshmen: $18,136; Undergraduates: $15,935. *Scholarships, grants, and awards:* Federal Pell, FSEOG, state, private, college/university gift aid from institutional funds.

GIFT AID (NON-NEED-BASED) *Total amount:* $3,226,331 (13% federal, 1% state, 85% institutional, 1% external sources). *Receiving aid:* Freshmen: 18% (84). Undergraduates: 12% (220). *Average award:* Freshmen: $11,435. Undergraduates: $10,307. *Scholarships, grants, and awards by category: Academic interests/achievement:* 1,000 awards ($5,500,000 total): business, general academic interests/achievements. *Creative arts/performance:* 40 awards ($40,000 total): journalism/publications, music, performing arts. *Special characteristics:* children of faculty/staff, local/state students, members of minority groups, relatives of clergy, religious affiliation, siblings of current students. *Tuition waivers:* Full or partial for employees or children of employees, senior citizens.

LOANS *Student loans:* $24,326,764 (61% need-based, 39% non-need-based). 83% of past graduating class borrowed through all loan programs. *Average indebtedness per student:* $36,832. *Average need-based loan:* Freshmen: $4077. Undergraduates: $4600. *Parent loans:* $3,786,376 (100% non-need-based). *Programs:* Federal Direct (Subsidized and Unsubsidized Stafford, PLUS), Perkins, college/university.

WORK-STUDY *Federal work-study:* Total amount: $1,035,967; 654 jobs averaging $1470. *State or other work-study/employment:* 100 part-time jobs averaging $1000.

ATHLETIC AWARDS Total amount: $2,691,234 (50% need-based, 50% non-need-based).

APPLYING FOR FINANCIAL AID *Required financial aid forms:* FAFSA, state aid form. *Financial aid deadline:* Continuous. *Notification date:* Continuous beginning 2/15. Students must reply by 5/1 or within 2 weeks of notification.

CONTACT Ms. Elisabeth T. Rankin, Director of Financial Aid, St. Bonaventure University, Route 417, St. Bonaventure, NY 14778-2284, 716-375-2528 or toll-free 800-462-5050. *Fax:* 716-375-2087. *E-mail:* erankin@sbu.edu.

ST. CATHERINE UNIVERSITY
St. Paul, MN

Tuition & fees: $28,758	Average undergraduate aid package: $26,870

ABOUT THE INSTITUTION Independent Roman Catholic, undergraduate: women only; graduate: coed. 78 undergraduate majors. Federal methodology is used as a basis for awarding need-based institutional aid.

UNDERGRADUATE EXPENSES for 2009–10 *One-time required fee:* $100. *Comprehensive fee:* $36,088 includes full-time tuition ($28,480), mandatory fees ($278), and room and board ($7330). *College room only:* $4110. Full-time tuition and fees vary according to class time and degree level. Room and board charges vary according to board plan and housing facility. *Part-time tuition:* $890 per credit hour. *Part-time fees:* $890 per credit hour; $139 per term. Part-time tuition and fees vary according to class time and degree level.

FRESHMAN FINANCIAL AID (Fall 2008) 393 applied for aid; of those 93% were deemed to have need. 100% of freshmen with need received aid; of those 10% had need fully met. *Average percent of need met:* 85% (excluding resources awarded to replace EFC). *Average financial aid package:* $28,870 (excluding resources awarded to replace EFC). 7% of all full-time freshmen had no need and received non-need-based gift aid.

UNDERGRADUATE FINANCIAL AID (Fall 2008) 1,662 applied for aid; of those 92% were deemed to have need. 100% of undergraduates with need received aid; of those 11% had need fully met. *Average percent of need met:* 83% (excluding resources awarded to replace EFC). *Average financial aid package:* $26,870 (excluding resources awarded to replace EFC). 6% of all full-time undergraduates had no need and received non-need-based gift aid.

GIFT AID (NEED-BASED) *Total amount:* $18,865,190 (30% federal, 20% state, 45% institutional, 5% external sources). *Receiving aid:* Freshmen: 83% (340); all full-time undergraduates: 76% (1,361). *Average award:* Freshmen: $13,680; Undergraduates: $10,925. *Scholarships, grants, and awards:* Federal Pell, FSEOG, state, private, college/university gift aid from institutional funds.

GIFT AID (NON-NEED-BASED) *Total amount:* $11,429,060 (1% state, 99% institutional). *Receiving aid:* Freshmen: 76% (312). Undergraduates: 62% (1,107). *Average award:* Freshmen: $9590. Undergraduates: $7170. *Scholarships, grants, and awards by category: Academic interests/achievement:* business, education, English, foreign languages, general academic interests/achievements, health fields, home economics, humanities, mathematics, physical sciences, premedicine, social sciences. *Creative arts/performance:* art/fine arts, music. *Special achievements/activities:* community service, general special achievements/activities, leadership, memberships. *Special characteristics:* adult students, children and siblings of alumni, children of current students, children of educators, children of faculty/staff, ethnic background, general special characteristics, international students, local/state students, out-of-state students, religious affiliation, siblings of current students, spouses of current students. *Tuition waivers:* Full or partial for employees or children of employees, senior citizens.

LOANS *Student loans:* $26,960,500 (39% need-based, 61% non-need-based). 96% of past graduating class borrowed through all loan programs. *Average indebtedness per student:* $24,400. *Average need-based loan:* Freshmen: $3530. Undergraduates: $4610. *Parent loans:* $3,800,080 (100% non-need-based). *Programs:* Federal Direct (Subsidized and Unsubsidized Stafford, PLUS), Perkins, Federal Nursing, state, alternative loans.

WORK-STUDY *Federal work-study:* Total amount: $288,340; jobs available. *State or other work-study/employment:* Total amount: $173,730 (100% need-based). Part-time jobs available.

APPLYING FOR FINANCIAL AID *Required financial aid forms:* FAFSA, institution's own form. *Financial aid deadline (priority):* 4/15. *Notification date:* Continuous. Students must reply within 2 weeks of notification.

CONTACT Beth Stevens, Director of Financial Aid, St. Catherine University, Mail #F-11, 2004 Randolph Avenue, St. Paul, MN 55105-1789, 651-690-6540 or toll-free 800-656-5283 (in-state). *Fax:* 651-690-6765. *E-mail:* finaid@stkate.edu.

ST. CHARLES BORROMEO SEMINARY, OVERBROOK
Wynnewood, PA

Tuition & fees: $15,190	Average undergraduate aid package: $15,080

ABOUT THE INSTITUTION Independent Roman Catholic, undergraduate: men only; graduate: coed. 1 undergraduate major. Federal methodology is used as a basis for awarding need-based institutional aid.

UNDERGRADUATE EXPENSES for 2009–10 *Comprehensive fee:* $24,750 includes full-time tuition ($14,240), mandatory fees ($950), and room and board ($9560). Room and board charges vary according to board plan. *Part-time tuition:* $777 per course. *Payment plan:* Installment.

FRESHMAN FINANCIAL AID (Fall 2009, est.) 6 applied for aid; of those 83% were deemed to have need. 100% of freshmen with need received aid; of those 80% had need fully met. *Average percent of need met:* 80% (excluding resources awarded to replace EFC). *Average financial aid package:* $15,795 (excluding resources awarded to replace EFC). 100% of all full-time freshmen had no need and received non-need-based gift aid.

UNDERGRADUATE FINANCIAL AID (Fall 2009, est.) 24 applied for aid; of those 100% were deemed to have need. 100% of undergraduates with need received aid; of those 58% had need fully met. *Average percent of need met:* 80% (excluding resources awarded to replace EFC). *Average financial aid package:* $15,080 (excluding resources awarded to replace EFC). 10% of all full-time undergraduates had no need and received non-need-based gift aid.

GIFT AID (NEED-BASED) *Total amount:* $570,962 (8% federal, 8% state, 81% institutional, 3% external sources). *Receiving aid:* Freshmen: 15% (2); all full-time undergraduates: 7% (6). *Average award:* Freshmen: $5000; Undergraduates: $5000. *Scholarships, grants, and awards:* Federal Pell, FSEOG, state, college/university gift aid from institutional funds.

GIFT AID (NON-NEED-BASED) *Receiving aid:* Freshmen: 38% (5). Undergraduates: 23% (20). *Average award:* Freshmen: $17,750. Undergraduates: $17,750.

Scholarships, grants, and awards by category: Academic interests/achievement: general academic interests/achievements.

LOANS *Student loans:* $294,847 (100% need-based). 45% of past graduating class borrowed through all loan programs. *Average indebtedness per student:* $19,000. *Average need-based loan:* Freshmen: $3500. Undergraduates: $5000. *Parent loans:* $24,625 (100% need-based). *Programs:* Federal Direct (Subsidized and Unsubsidized Stafford, PLUS).

APPLYING FOR FINANCIAL AID *Required financial aid forms:* FAFSA, institution's own form. *Financial aid deadline (priority):* 4/15. *Notification date:* 6/1. Students must reply by 6/15.

CONTACT Ms. Nora M. Downey, Coordinator of Financial Aid, St. Charles Borromeo Seminary, Overbrook, 100 East Wynnewood Road, Wynnewood, PA 19096-3099, 610-785-6582. *Fax:* 610-667-3971. *E-mail:* ndowney@adphila. org.

ST. CLOUD STATE UNIVERSITY
St. Cloud, MN

ABOUT THE INSTITUTION State-supported, coed. 146 undergraduate majors.
GIFT AID (NEED-BASED) *Scholarships, grants, and awards:* Federal Pell, FSEOG, state, private, college/university gift aid from institutional funds.
GIFT AID (NON-NEED-BASED) *Scholarships, grants, and awards by category: Academic interests/achievement:* biological sciences, business, communication, computer science, education, engineering/technologies, English, general academic interests/achievements, health fields, international studies, mathematics, physical sciences, social sciences. *Creative arts/performance:* applied art and design, art/fine arts, cinema/film/broadcasting, creative writing, journalism/publications, music, performing arts, theater/drama. *Special achievements/activities:* community service, general special achievements/activities. *Special characteristics:* children of faculty/staff, children of union members/company employees, local/state students, members of minority groups, out-of-state students.
LOANS *Programs:* FFEL (Subsidized and Unsubsidized Stafford, PLUS), Perkins, state.
WORK-STUDY *Federal work-study:* Total amount: $1,059,889; jobs available. *State or other work-study/employment:* Total amount: $946,324 (100% need-based). Part-time jobs available.
APPLYING FOR FINANCIAL AID *Required financial aid forms:* FAFSA, institution's own form.
CONTACT Frank P. Morrissey, Associate Director of Scholarships and Financial Aid, St. Cloud State University, 720 4th Avenue South, AS106, St. Cloud, MN 56301-4498, 320-308-2047 or toll-free 877-654-7278. *Fax:* 320-308-5424. *E-mail:* fpmorrissey@stcloudstate.edu.

ST. EDWARD'S UNIVERSITY
Austin, TX

Tuition & fees: $26,484	Average undergraduate aid package: $20,039

ABOUT THE INSTITUTION Independent Roman Catholic, coed. 52 undergraduate majors. Federal methodology is used as a basis for awarding need-based institutional aid.
UNDERGRADUATE EXPENSES for 2010–11 *Comprehensive fee:* $35,520 includes full-time tuition ($26,084), mandatory fees ($400), and room and board ($9036). *College room only:* $5036. Full-time tuition and fees vary according to course load and degree level. Room and board charges vary according to board plan and housing facility. *Part-time tuition:* $870 per credit hour. *Part-time fees:* $50 per term. Part-time tuition and fees vary according to course load and degree level. *Payment plans:* Installment, deferred payment.
FRESHMAN FINANCIAL AID (Fall 2009, est.) 643 applied for aid; of those 85% were deemed to have need. 100% of freshmen with need received aid; of those 12% had need fully met. *Average percent of need met:* 74% (excluding resources awarded to replace EFC). *Average financial aid package:* $22,340 (excluding resources awarded to replace EFC). 9% of all full-time freshmen had no need and received non-need-based gift aid.
UNDERGRADUATE FINANCIAL AID (Fall 2009, est.) 2,572 applied for aid; of those 86% were deemed to have need. 100% of undergraduates with need received aid; of those 13% had need fully met. *Average percent of need met:* 67% (excluding resources awarded to replace EFC). *Average financial aid package:* $20,039 (excluding resources awarded to replace EFC). 7% of all full-time undergraduates had no need and received non-need-based gift aid.

GIFT AID (NEED-BASED) *Total amount:* $25,464,604 (24% federal, 19% state, 57% institutional). *Receiving aid:* Freshmen: 67% (505); all full-time undergraduates: 58% (2,019). *Average award:* Freshmen: $13,705; Undergraduates: $11,815. *Scholarships, grants, and awards:* Federal Pell, FSEOG, state, private, college/university gift aid from institutional funds, endowed scholarships.
GIFT AID (NON-NEED-BASED) *Total amount:* $14,907,927 (94% institutional, 6% external sources). *Receiving aid:* Freshmen: 56% (423). Undergraduates: 45% (1,567). *Average award:* Freshmen: $8405. Undergraduates: $8167. *Scholarships, grants, and awards by category: Academic interests/achievement:* 2,003 awards ($12,425,639 total): biological sciences, business, communication, computer science, education, English, foreign languages, general academic interests/achievements, humanities, international studies, mathematics, military science, physical sciences, premedicine, religion/biblical studies, social sciences. *Creative arts/performance:* 40 awards ($109,183 total): art/fine arts, theater/drama. *Special achievements/activities:* 70 awards ($153,812 total): cheerleading/drum major, community service, general special achievements/activities, leadership. *Special characteristics:* 52 awards ($840,703 total): adult students, children of faculty/staff, religious affiliation. *Tuition waivers:* Full or partial for employees or children of employees.
LOANS *Student loans:* $27,419,317 (33% need-based, 67% non-need-based). 79% of past graduating class borrowed through all loan programs. *Average indebtedness per student:* $29,810. *Average need-based loan:* Freshmen: $3323. Undergraduates: $4360. *Parent loans:* $1,731,113 (100% non-need-based). *Programs:* Federal Direct (PLUS), FFEL (Subsidized and Unsubsidized Stafford, PLUS), Perkins, state, alternative educational loans.
WORK-STUDY *Federal work-study:* Total amount: $463,340; 239 jobs averaging $1939. *State or other work-study/employment:* Total amount: $17,630 (100% need-based). 10 part-time jobs averaging $1763.
ATHLETIC AWARDS Total amount: $2,146,516 (100% non-need-based).
APPLYING FOR FINANCIAL AID *Required financial aid form:* FAFSA. *Financial aid deadline:* 4/15 (priority: 3/1). *Notification date:* Continuous beginning 1/15. Students must reply by 5/1 or within 2 weeks of notification.
CONTACT Office of Student Financial Services, St. Edward's University, 3001 South Congress Avenue, Austin, TX 78704, 512-448-8523 or toll-free 800-555-0164. *Fax:* 512-416-5837. *E-mail:* seu.finaid@stedwards.edu.

ST. FRANCIS COLLEGE
Brooklyn Heights, NY

CONTACT Joseph Cummings, Director of Student Financial Services, St. Francis College, 180 Remsen Street, Brooklyn Heights, NY 11201-4398, 718-489-5390. *Fax:* 718-522-1274. *E-mail:* jcummings@stfranciscollege.edu.

SAINT FRANCIS MEDICAL CENTER COLLEGE OF NURSING
Peoria, IL

Tuition & fees: $15,436	Average undergraduate aid package: $11,693

ABOUT THE INSTITUTION Independent Roman Catholic, coed, primarily women. 1 undergraduate major. Federal methodology is used as a basis for awarding need-based institutional aid.
UNDERGRADUATE EXPENSES for 2010–11 *Tuition:* full-time $14,880; part-time $480 per semester hour. *Required fees:* full-time $556; $130 per term. Full-time tuition and fees vary according to course load. Part-time tuition and fees vary according to course load. *Payment plan:* Installment.
UNDERGRADUATE FINANCIAL AID (Fall 2009, est.) 244 applied for aid; of those 87% were deemed to have need. 100% of undergraduates with need received aid; of those 10% had need fully met. *Average percent of need met:* 58% (excluding resources awarded to replace EFC). *Average financial aid package:* $11,693 (excluding resources awarded to replace EFC). 9% of all full-time undergraduates had no need and received non-need-based gift aid.
GIFT AID (NEED-BASED) *Total amount:* $1,324,353 (33% federal, 56% state, 6% institutional, 5% external sources). *Receiving aid:* All full-time undergraduates: 63% (177). *Average award:* Undergraduates: $7321. *Scholarships, grants, and awards:* Federal Pell, state, private, college/university gift aid from institutional funds.
GIFT AID (NON-NEED-BASED) *Total amount:* $88,626 (32% state, 35% institutional, 33% external sources). *Receiving aid:* Undergraduates: 1% (2). *Average award:* Undergraduates: $1952. *Scholarships, grants, and awards by*

category: Academic interests/achievement: 81 awards ($52,815 total): general academic interests/achievements, health fields. *Tuition waivers:* Full or partial for employees or children of employees.

LOANS *Student loans:* $2,648,572 (80% need-based, 20% non-need-based). *Average need-based loan:* Undergraduates: $4047. *Parent loans:* $152,595 (13% need-based, 87% non-need-based). *Programs:* FFEL (Subsidized and Unsubsidized Stafford, PLUS), college/university.

APPLYING FOR FINANCIAL AID *Required financial aid forms:* FAFSA, institution's own form. *Financial aid deadline (priority):* 3/1. *Notification date:* Continuous beginning 5/1.

CONTACT Ms. Nancy Perryman, Coordinator Student Finance, Financial Assistance, Saint Francis Medical Center College of Nursing, 511 Northeast Greenleaf Street, Peoria, IL 61603-3783, 309-655-4119. *Fax:* 309-655-3962. *E-mail:* nancy.s.perryman@osfhealthcare.org.

SAINT FRANCIS UNIVERSITY
Loretto, PA

Tuition & fees: $25,554	Average undergraduate aid package: $17,896

ABOUT THE INSTITUTION Independent Roman Catholic, coed. 68 undergraduate majors. Federal methodology is used as a basis for awarding need-based institutional aid.

UNDERGRADUATE EXPENSES for 2009–10 *Comprehensive fee:* $34,270 includes full-time tuition ($24,504), mandatory fees ($1050), and room and board ($8716). *College room only:* $4380. Full-time tuition and fees vary according to course load and program. Room and board charges vary according to board plan and housing facility. *Part-time tuition:* $765 per credit hour. *Part-time fees:* $362 per credit hour. Part-time tuition and fees vary according to class time. *Payment plan:* Installment.

FRESHMAN FINANCIAL AID (Fall 2009, est.) 377 applied for aid; of those 91% were deemed to have need. 85% of freshmen with need received aid; of those 31% had need fully met. *Average percent of need met:* 78% (excluding resources awarded to replace EFC). *Average financial aid package:* $19,174 (excluding resources awarded to replace EFC). 17% of all full-time freshmen had no need and received non-need-based gift aid.

UNDERGRADUATE FINANCIAL AID (Fall 2009, est.) 1,457 applied for aid; of those 88% were deemed to have need. 97% of undergraduates with need received aid; of those 18% had need fully met. *Average percent of need met:* 69% (excluding resources awarded to replace EFC). *Average financial aid package:* $17,896 (excluding resources awarded to replace EFC). 15% of all full-time undergraduates had no need and received non-need-based gift aid.

GIFT AID (NEED-BASED) *Total amount:* $15,735,633 (11% federal, 13% state, 75% institutional, 1% external sources). *Receiving aid:* Freshmen: 69% (291); all full-time undergraduates: 82% (1,206). *Average award:* Freshmen: $16,460; Undergraduates: $15,543. *Scholarships, grants, and awards:* Federal Pell, FSEOG, state, private, college/university gift aid from institutional funds.

GIFT AID (NON-NEED-BASED) *Total amount:* $2,196,318 (1% federal, 2% state, 96% institutional, 1% external sources). *Receiving aid:* Freshmen: 17% (72). Undergraduates: 79% (1,163). *Average award:* Freshmen: $10,625. Undergraduates: $14,125. *Scholarships, grants, and awards by category: Academic interests/achievement:* 743 awards ($2,684,171 total): biological sciences, business, computer science, education, engineering/technologies, English, general academic interests/achievements, health fields, humanities, mathematics, religion/biblical studies, social sciences. *Creative arts/performance:* 37 awards ($34,000 total): art/fine arts, music. *Special achievements/activities:* 35 awards ($92,580 total): cheerleading/drum major, religious involvement. *Special characteristics:* 840 awards ($3,583,225 total): adult students, children and siblings of alumni, children of current students, children of educators, children of faculty/staff, international students, out-of-state students, previous college experience, religious affiliation, siblings of current students, spouses of current students. *Tuition waivers:* Full or partial for employees or children of employees.

LOANS *Student loans:* $9,788,752 (43% need-based, 57% non-need-based). 82% of past graduating class borrowed through all loan programs. *Average indebtedness per student:* $10,632. *Average need-based loan:* Freshmen: $3361. Undergraduates: $4317. *Parent loans:* $2,681,929 (90% need-based, 10% non-need-based). *Programs:* Federal Direct (Subsidized and Unsubsidized Stafford, PLUS), Perkins, private alternative loans.

WORK-STUDY *Federal work-study:* Total amount: $257,819; 257 jobs averaging $1000. *State or other work-study/employment:* Total amount: $49,644 (22% need-based, 78% non-need-based). 474 part-time jobs averaging $1000.

ATHLETIC AWARDS Total amount: $3,963,372 (54% need-based, 46% non-need-based).

APPLYING FOR FINANCIAL AID *Required financial aid form:* FAFSA. *Financial aid deadline (priority):* 5/1. *Notification date:* Continuous beginning 3/1. Students must reply by 5/1.

CONTACT Mr. Shane Himes, Financial Aid Counselor, Saint Francis University, PO Box 600, Loretto, PA 15931, 814-472-3010 or toll-free 800-342-5732. *Fax:* 814-472-3999. *E-mail:* shimes@francis.edu.

ST. GREGORY'S UNIVERSITY
Shawnee, OK

CONTACT Matt McCoin, Director of Financial Aid, St. Gregory's University, 1900 West MacArthur Drive, Shawnee, OK 74804, 405-878-5412 or toll-free 888-STGREGS. *Fax:* 405-878-5403. *E-mail:* mdmccoin@stgregorys.edu.

ST. GREGORY THE GREAT SEMINARY
Seward, NE

CONTACT Financial Aid Office, St. Gregory the Great Seminary, 800 Fletcher Road, Seward, NE 67434, 402-643-4052.

ST. JOHN FISHER COLLEGE
Rochester, NY

Tuition & fees: $24,320	Average undergraduate aid package: $17,795

ABOUT THE INSTITUTION Independent religious, coed. 39 undergraduate majors. Federal methodology is used as a basis for awarding need-based institutional aid.

UNDERGRADUATE EXPENSES for 2009–10 *Comprehensive fee:* $34,410 includes full-time tuition ($23,850), mandatory fees ($470), and room and board ($10,090). *College room only:* $6550. Room and board charges vary according to board plan. *Part-time tuition:* $650 per credit. *Part-time fees:* $25 per term. Part-time tuition and fees vary according to course load. *Payment plans:* Installment, deferred payment.

FRESHMAN FINANCIAL AID (Fall 2009, est.) 558 applied for aid; of those 84% were deemed to have need. 100% of freshmen with need received aid; of those 40% had need fully met. *Average percent of need met:* 85% (excluding resources awarded to replace EFC). *Average financial aid package:* $19,670 (excluding resources awarded to replace EFC). 16% of all full-time freshmen had no need and received non-need-based gift aid.

UNDERGRADUATE FINANCIAL AID (Fall 2009, est.) 2,411 applied for aid; of those 89% were deemed to have need. 100% of undergraduates with need received aid; of those 37% had need fully met. *Average percent of need met:* 81% (excluding resources awarded to replace EFC). *Average financial aid package:* $17,795 (excluding resources awarded to replace EFC). 16% of all full-time undergraduates had no need and received non-need-based gift aid.

GIFT AID (NEED-BASED) *Total amount:* $27,659,342 (15% federal, 12% state, 70% institutional, 3% external sources). *Receiving aid:* Freshmen: 84% (470); all full-time undergraduates: 81% (2,141). *Average award:* Freshmen: $16,121; Undergraduates: $13,219. *Scholarships, grants, and awards:* Federal Pell, FSEOG, state, private, college/university gift aid from institutional funds, Federal Nursing.

GIFT AID (NON-NEED-BASED) *Total amount:* $3,234,957 (1% federal, 1% state, 90% institutional, 8% external sources). *Receiving aid:* Freshmen: 64% (359). Undergraduates: 39% (1,021). *Average award:* Freshmen: $8359. Undergraduates: $7634. *Scholarships, grants, and awards by category: Academic interests/achievement:* 1,621 awards ($13,960,137 total): biological sciences, business, English, foreign languages, general academic interests/achievements, humanities, mathematics, physical sciences. *Special achievements/activities:* 101 awards ($1,027,028 total): community service. *Special characteristics:* 97 awards ($1,134,609 total): children and siblings of alumni, ethnic background, first-generation college students, local/state students, members of minority groups. *Tuition waivers:* Full or partial for employees or children of employees.

LOANS *Student loans:* $21,092,501 (92% need-based, 8% non-need-based). 84% of past graduating class borrowed through all loan programs. *Average indebtedness per student:* $30,281. *Average need-based loan:* Freshmen: $3308.

Undergraduates: $4594. *Parent loans:* $9,174,299 (85% need-based, 15% non-need-based). *Programs:* Federal Direct (Subsidized and Unsubsidized Stafford, PLUS), Perkins.

WORK-STUDY *Federal work-study:* Total amount: $1,465,533; 1,229 jobs averaging $1192.

APPLYING FOR FINANCIAL AID *Required financial aid forms:* FAFSA, state aid form. *Financial aid deadline (priority):* 2/15. *Notification date:* Continuous beginning 3/22. Students must reply by 5/1 or within 3 weeks of notification.

CONTACT Mrs. Angela Monnat, Director of Financial Aid, St. John Fisher College, 3690 East Avenue, Rochester, NY 14618-3597, 585-385-8042 or toll-free 800-444-4640. *Fax:* 585-385-8044. *E-mail:* amonnat@sjfc.edu.

ST. JOHN'S COLLEGE
Springfield, IL

Tuition & fees: N/R	Average undergraduate aid package: $16,202

ABOUT THE INSTITUTION Independent Roman Catholic, coed, primarily women. 1 undergraduate major. Federal methodology is used as a basis for awarding need-based institutional aid.

UNDERGRADUATE FINANCIAL AID (Fall 2009, est.) 67 applied for aid; of those 82% were deemed to have need. 100% of undergraduates with need received aid; of those 78% had need fully met. *Average percent of need met:* 78% (excluding resources awarded to replace EFC). *Average financial aid package:* $16,202 (excluding resources awarded to replace EFC).

GIFT AID (NEED-BASED) *Total amount:* $666,112 (14% federal, 35% state, 9% institutional, 42% external sources). *Receiving aid:* All full-time undergraduates: 57% (43). *Average award:* Undergraduates: $6211. *Scholarships, grants, and awards:* Federal Pell, FSEOG, state, private, college/university gift aid from institutional funds, Federal Nursing.

GIFT AID (NON-NEED-BASED) *Receiving aid:* Undergraduates: 67% (51).

LOANS *Student loans:* $429,580 (48% need-based, 52% non-need-based). *Average need-based loan:* Undergraduates: $4953. *Parent loans:* $46,168 (62% need-based, 38% non-need-based). *Programs:* Federal Direct (Subsidized and Unsubsidized Stafford), Federal Nursing.

WORK-STUDY *Federal work-study:* Total amount: $8589; 5 jobs averaging $1717.

CONTACT Mary M. Deatherage, Financial Aid Officer, St. John's College, 421 North Ninth Street, Springfield, IL 62702, 217-544-6464 Ext. 44705. *Fax:* 217-757-6870. *E-mail:* mdeather@st-johns.org.

ST. JOHN'S COLLEGE
Annapolis, MD

Tuition & fees: $42,192	Average undergraduate aid package: $27,256

ABOUT THE INSTITUTION Independent, coed. 3 undergraduate majors. Both federal and institutional methodology are used as a basis for awarding need-based institutional aid.

UNDERGRADUATE EXPENSES for 2010–11 *Comprehensive fee:* $52,176 includes full-time tuition ($41,792), mandatory fees ($400), and room and board ($9984). Room and board charges vary according to board plan. Part-time tuition and fees vary according to course load. *Payment plan:* Installment.

FRESHMAN FINANCIAL AID (Fall 2008) 126 applied for aid; of those 90% were deemed to have need. 100% of freshmen with need received aid; of those 75% had need fully met. *Average percent of need met:* 98% (excluding resources awarded to replace EFC). *Average financial aid package:* $28,282 (excluding resources awarded to replace EFC).

UNDERGRADUATE FINANCIAL AID (Fall 2008) 322 applied for aid; of those 87% were deemed to have need. 100% of undergraduates with need received aid; of those 98% had need fully met. *Average percent of need met:* 98% (excluding resources awarded to replace EFC). *Average financial aid package:* $27,256 (excluding resources awarded to replace EFC).

GIFT AID (NEED-BASED) *Total amount:* $7,193,429 (7% federal, 1% state, 92% institutional). *Receiving aid:* Freshmen: 58% (89); all full-time undergraduates: 57% (277). *Average award:* Freshmen: $24,280; Undergraduates: $24,391. *Scholarships, grants, and awards:* Federal Pell, FSEOG, state, private, college/university gift aid from institutional funds.

GIFT AID (NON-NEED-BASED) *Total amount:* $100,381 (14% state, 86% external sources). *Tuition waivers:* Full or partial for employees or children of employees.

LOANS *Student loans:* $2,382,680 (78% need-based, 22% non-need-based). 71% of past graduating class borrowed through all loan programs. *Average indebtedness per student:* $24,216. *Average need-based loan:* Freshmen: $4213. Undergraduates: $4973. *Parent loans:* $2,130,723 (100% non-need-based). *Programs:* Federal Direct (Subsidized and Unsubsidized Stafford, PLUS), Perkins, college/university.

WORK-STUDY *Federal work-study:* Total amount: $239,709; 130 jobs averaging $2600. *State or other work-study/employment:* Total amount: $161,282 (100% non-need-based). 156 part-time jobs averaging $1033.

APPLYING FOR FINANCIAL AID *Required financial aid forms:* FAFSA, CSS Financial Aid PROFILE, noncustodial (divorced/separated) parent's statement, business/farm supplement. *Financial aid deadline (priority):* 3/1. *Notification date:* Continuous beginning 1/1. Students must reply by 5/1.

CONTACT Ms. Dana Kennedy, Director of Financial Aid, St. John's College, PO Box 2800, Annapolis, MD 21404, 410-626-2502 or toll-free 800-727-9238. *Fax:* 410-626-2885. *E-mail:* dana.kennedy@sjca.edu.

ST. JOHN'S COLLEGE
Santa Fe, NM

Tuition & fees: $40,392	Average undergraduate aid package: $27,902

ABOUT THE INSTITUTION Independent, coed. *Awards:* bachelor's and master's degrees. 21 undergraduate majors. *Total enrollment:* 511. Undergraduates: 431. Freshmen: 110. Both federal and institutional methodology are used as a basis for awarding need-based institutional aid.

UNDERGRADUATE EXPENSES for 2009–10 *Comprehensive fee:* $49,954 includes full-time tuition ($39,992), mandatory fees ($400), and room and board ($9562). *College room only:* $4781.

FRESHMAN FINANCIAL AID (Fall 2008) 91 applied for aid; of those 97% were deemed to have need. 100% of freshmen with need received aid; of those 94% had need fully met. *Average percent of need met:* 97% (excluding resources awarded to replace EFC). *Average financial aid package:* $28,791 (excluding resources awarded to replace EFC).

UNDERGRADUATE FINANCIAL AID (Fall 2008) 330 applied for aid; of those 92% were deemed to have need. 100% of undergraduates with need received aid; of those 97% had need fully met. *Average percent of need met:* 94% (excluding resources awarded to replace EFC). *Average financial aid package:* $27,902 (excluding resources awarded to replace EFC).

GIFT AID (NEED-BASED) *Total amount:* $6,575,459 (8% federal, 2% state, 89% institutional, 1% external sources). *Receiving aid:* Freshmen: 71% (84); all full-time undergraduates: 61% (289). *Average award:* Freshmen: $24,521; Undergraduates: $19,210. *Scholarships, grants, and awards:* Federal Pell, FSEOG, state, private, college/university gift aid from institutional funds, Academic Competitiveness Grants, National SMART Grants.

GIFT AID (NON-NEED-BASED) *Scholarships, grants, and awards by category: Special characteristics:* children of faculty/staff.

LOANS *Student loans:* $2,135,504 (69% need-based, 31% non-need-based). 65% of past graduating class borrowed through all loan programs. *Average indebtedness per student:* $27,235. *Average need-based loan:* Freshmen: $3875. Undergraduates: $5047. *Parent loans:* $1,344,774 (100% non-need-based). *Programs:* FFEL (Subsidized and Unsubsidized Stafford, PLUS), Perkins, college/university.

WORK-STUDY *Federal work-study:* Total amount: $322,960; jobs available. *State or other work-study/employment:* Total amount: $20,750 (100% need-based). Part-time jobs available.

APPLYING FOR FINANCIAL AID *Required financial aid forms:* FAFSA, CSS Financial Aid PROFILE, noncustodial (divorced/separated) parent's statement, business/farm supplement. *Financial aid deadline:* 2/15. *Notification date:* Continuous beginning 12/10. Students must reply by 5/1.

CONTACT Michael Rodriguez, Director of Financial Aid, St. John's College, 1160 Camino Cruz Blanca, Santa Fe, NM 87505, 505-984-6058 or toll-free 800-331-5232. *Fax:* 505-984-6003. *E-mail:* mike.rodriguez@sjcsf.edu.

SAINT JOHN'S UNIVERSITY
Collegeville, MN

Tuition & fees: $29,936	Average undergraduate aid package: $22,414

Saint John's University

ABOUT THE INSTITUTION Independent Roman Catholic, coed, primarily men. 51 undergraduate majors. Federal methodology is used as a basis for awarding need-based institutional aid.

UNDERGRADUATE EXPENSES for 2009–10 *Comprehensive fee:* $37,650 includes full-time tuition ($29,388), mandatory fees ($548), and room and board ($7714). *College room only:* $3884. Room and board charges vary according to board plan and housing facility. *Part-time tuition:* $1225 per credit hour. Part-time tuition and fees vary according to course load. *Payment plan:* Installment.

FRESHMAN FINANCIAL AID (Fall 2009, est.) 364 applied for aid; of those 76% were deemed to have need. 100% of freshmen with need received aid; of those 60% had need fully met. *Average percent of need met:* 96% (excluding resources awarded to replace EFC). *Average financial aid package:* $25,930 (excluding resources awarded to replace EFC). 31% of all full-time freshmen had no need and received non-need-based gift aid.

UNDERGRADUATE FINANCIAL AID (Fall 2009, est.) 1,312 applied for aid; of those 84% were deemed to have need. 100% of undergraduates with need received aid; of those 46% had need fully met. *Average percent of need met:* 90% (excluding resources awarded to replace EFC). *Average financial aid package:* $22,414 (excluding resources awarded to replace EFC). 34% of all full-time undergraduates had no need and received non-need-based gift aid.

GIFT AID (NEED-BASED) *Total amount:* $19,743,106 (9% federal, 10% state, 77% institutional, 4% external sources). *Receiving aid:* Freshmen: 59% (270); all full-time undergraduates: 57% (1,070). *Average award:* Freshmen: $20,744; Undergraduates: $17,654. *Scholarships, grants, and awards:* Federal Pell, FSEOG, state, private, college/university gift aid from institutional funds.

GIFT AID (NON-NEED-BASED) *Total amount:* $10,096,354 (87% institutional, 13% external sources). *Receiving aid:* Freshmen: 58% (266). Undergraduates: 54% (1,010). *Average award:* Freshmen: $12,148. Undergraduates: $10,628. *Scholarships, grants, and awards by category:* Academic interests/achievement: 1,654 awards ($16,457,756 total): general academic interests/achievements. Creative arts/performance: 125 awards ($264,000 total): art/fine arts, music, theater/drama. Special characteristics: 136 awards ($2,696,921 total): international students.

LOANS *Student loans:* $11,745,303 (84% need-based, 16% non-need-based). *Average need-based loan:* Freshmen: $4234. Undergraduates: $4692. *Parent loans:* $1,069,690 (76% need-based, 24% non-need-based). *Programs:* Federal Direct (Subsidized and Unsubsidized Stafford, PLUS), Perkins, state, alternative loans.

WORK-STUDY *Federal work-study:* Total amount: $847,432; 302 jobs averaging $2596. *State or other work-study/employment:* Total amount: $1,989,467 (64% need-based, 36% non-need-based). 863 part-time jobs averaging $2550.

APPLYING FOR FINANCIAL AID *Required financial aid forms:* FAFSA, institution's own form, federal income tax form(s). *Financial aid deadline (priority):* 3/15. *Notification date:* Continuous beginning 3/15. Students must reply by 5/1 or within 3 weeks of notification.

CONTACT Ms. Mary Dehler, Associate Director of Financial Aid, Saint John's University, PO Box 5000, Collegeville, MN 56321-5000, 320-363-3664 or toll-free 800-544-1489. *Fax:* 320-363-3102. *E-mail:* mdehler@csbsju.edu.

awarded to replace EFC). *Average financial aid package:* $24,228 (excluding resources awarded to replace EFC). 6% of all full-time freshmen had no need and received non-need-based gift aid.

UNDERGRADUATE FINANCIAL AID (Fall 2008) 10,335 applied for aid; of those 93% were deemed to have need. 99% of undergraduates with need received aid; of those 10% had need fully met. *Average percent of need met:* 62% (excluding resources awarded to replace EFC). *Average financial aid package:* $20,524 (excluding resources awarded to replace EFC). 5% of all full-time undergraduates had no need and received non-need-based gift aid.

GIFT AID (NEED-BASED) *Total amount:* $86,603,529 (22% federal, 19% state, 59% institutional). *Receiving aid:* Freshmen: 72% (2,360); all full-time undergraduates: 69% (8,194). *Average award:* Freshmen: $13,428; Undergraduates: $10,506. *Scholarships, grants, and awards:* Federal Pell, FSEOG, state, private, college/university gift aid from institutional funds.

GIFT AID (NON-NEED-BASED) *Total amount:* $77,110,220 (1% state, 92% institutional, 7% external sources). *Receiving aid:* Freshmen: 65% (2,122). Undergraduates: 57% (6,767). *Average award:* Freshmen: $12,274. Undergraduates: $10,463. *Scholarships, grants, and awards by category:* Academic interests/achievement: 6,454 awards ($68,553,925 total): biological sciences, business, communication, computer science, education, English, foreign languages, general academic interests/achievements, health fields, humanities, mathematics, military science, physical sciences, premedicine, social sciences. Creative arts/performance: 124 awards ($308,941 total): art/fine arts, cinema/film/broadcasting, dance, debating, journalism/publications, music. Special achievements/activities: 333 awards ($893,964 total): cheerleading/drum major, community service, general special achievements/activities, hobbies/interests, leadership, religious involvement. Special characteristics: 2,353 awards ($12,268,319 total): children of faculty/staff, general special characteristics, local/state students, relatives of clergy, religious affiliation. *Tuition waivers:* Full or partial for employees or children of employees, senior citizens.

LOANS *Student loans:* $88,465,303 (65% need-based, 35% non-need-based). 70% of past graduating class borrowed through all loan programs. *Average indebtedness per student:* $30,692. *Average need-based loan:* Freshmen: $4190. Undergraduates: $6601. *Parent loans:* $22,293,013 (100% non-need-based). *Programs:* Federal Direct (Subsidized and Unsubsidized Stafford, PLUS), Perkins.

WORK-STUDY *Federal work-study:* Total amount: $2,564,464; 990 jobs averaging $2768.

ATHLETIC AWARDS Total amount: $5,258,200 (100% non-need-based).

APPLYING FOR FINANCIAL AID *Required financial aid form:* FAFSA. *Financial aid deadline (priority):* 2/1. *Notification date:* Continuous beginning 3/15. Students must reply within 2 weeks of notification.

CONTACT Mr. Jorge Rodriguez, Associate Vice President for Student Financial Services, St. John's University, 8000 Utopia Parkway, Queens, NY 11439, 718-990-2000 or toll-free 888-9STJOHNS. *Fax:* 718-990-5945. *E-mail:* financialaid@stjohns.edu.

ST. JOHN'S UNIVERSITY
Queens, NY

Tuition & fees: $30,040	Average undergraduate aid package: $20,524

ABOUT THE INSTITUTION Independent religious, coed. 66 undergraduate majors. Federal methodology is used as a basis for awarding need-based institutional aid.

UNDERGRADUATE EXPENSES for 2009–10 *Comprehensive fee:* $43,180 includes full-time tuition ($29,350), mandatory fees ($690), and room and board ($13,140). *College room only:* $8250. Full-time tuition and fees vary according to class time, course load, program, and student level. Room and board charges vary according to board plan, housing facility, and location. *Part-time tuition:* $978 per credit. *Part-time fees:* $247.50 per term. Part-time tuition and fees vary according to class time, course load, program, and student level. *Payment plans:* Installment, deferred payment.

FRESHMAN FINANCIAL AID (Fall 2008) 2,866 applied for aid; of those 92% were deemed to have need. 100% of freshmen with need received aid; of those 9% had need fully met. *Average percent of need met:* 71% (excluding resources

---

ST. JOHN VIANNEY COLLEGE SEMINARY
Miami, FL

CONTACT Ms. Bonnie DeAngulo, Director of Financial Aid, St. John Vianney College Seminary, 2900 Southwest 87th Avenue, Miami, FL 33165-3244, 305-223-4561 Ext. 10.

SAINT JOSEPH COLLEGE
West Hartford, CT

Tuition & fees: $27,202	Average undergraduate aid package: $20,293

ABOUT THE INSTITUTION Independent Roman Catholic, undergraduate: women only; graduate: coed. 23 undergraduate majors. Federal methodology is used as a basis for awarding need-based institutional aid.

UNDERGRADUATE EXPENSES for 2009–10 *Comprehensive fee:* $39,639 includes full-time tuition ($26,502), mandatory fees ($700), and room and board ($12,437). *College room only:* $5671. Full-time tuition and fees vary according to course load, degree level, program, and student level. Room and board charges vary according to board plan and housing facility. *Part-time tuition:* $595 per credit. *Part-time fees:* $30 per credit. Part-time tuition and fees vary according to course load, degree level, program, and student level. *Payment plan:* Installment.

FRESHMAN FINANCIAL AID (Fall 2009, est.) 178 applied for aid; of those 92% were deemed to have need. 100% of freshmen with need received aid; of those 10% had need fully met. *Average percent of need met:* 79% (excluding resources awarded to replace EFC). *Average financial aid package:* $23,828 (excluding resources awarded to replace EFC). 10% of all full-time freshmen had no need and received non-need-based gift aid.

UNDERGRADUATE FINANCIAL AID (Fall 2009, est.) 706 applied for aid; of those 92% were deemed to have need. 100% of undergraduates with need received aid; of those 8% had need fully met. *Average percent of need met:* 71% (excluding resources awarded to replace EFC). *Average financial aid package:* $20,293 (excluding resources awarded to replace EFC). 11% of all full-time undergraduates had no need and received non-need-based gift aid.

GIFT AID (NEED-BASED) *Total amount:* $10,504,689 (15% federal, 12% state, 70% institutional, 3% external sources). *Receiving aid:* Freshmen: 89% (164); all full-time undergraduates: 82% (631). *Average award:* Freshmen: $18,987; Undergraduates: $15,867. *Scholarships, grants, and awards:* Federal Pell, FSEOG, state, private, college/university gift aid from institutional funds.

GIFT AID (NON-NEED-BASED) *Total amount:* $457,485 (100% institutional). *Receiving aid:* Freshmen: 4% (8). Undergraduates: 4% (30). *Average award:* Freshmen: $10,158. Undergraduates: $8651. *Tuition waivers:* Full or partial for employees or children of employees.

LOANS *Student loans:* $7,544,916 (41% need-based, 59% non-need-based). 82% of past graduating class borrowed through all loan programs. *Average indebtedness per student:* $39,743. *Average need-based loan:* Freshmen: $3332. Undergraduates: $4536. *Parent loans:* $1,123,894 (100% non-need-based). *Programs:* Federal Direct (Subsidized and Unsubsidized Stafford, PLUS), Perkins, state, private bank loans.

WORK-STUDY *Federal work-study:* Total amount: $137,370; jobs available. *State or other work-study/employment:* Total amount: $398,702 (92% need-based, 8% non-need-based). Part-time jobs available.

APPLYING FOR FINANCIAL AID *Required financial aid form:* FAFSA. *Financial aid deadline (priority):* 2/15. *Notification date:* Continuous beginning 3/1. Students must reply within 2 weeks of notification.

CONTACT Beth Baker, Director of Financial Aid, Saint Joseph College, 1678 Asylum Avenue, West Hartford, CT 06117, 860-231-5319 or toll-free 866-442-8752. *E-mail:* ebaker@sjc.edu.

SAINT JOSEPH'S COLLEGE
Rensselaer, IN

ABOUT THE INSTITUTION Independent Roman Catholic, coed. *Awards:* associate, bachelor's, and master's degrees. 34 undergraduate majors. *Total enrollment:* 1,076. Undergraduates: 1,076. Freshmen: 298.

GIFT AID (NEED-BASED) *Scholarships, grants, and awards:* Federal Pell, FSEOG, state, private, college/university gift aid from institutional funds.

GIFT AID (NON-NEED-BASED) *Scholarships, grants, and awards by category:* Academic interests/achievement: general academic interests/achievements. Creative arts/performance: cinema/film/broadcasting, music, theater/drama. Special achievements/activities: cheerleading/drum major. Special characteristics: children and siblings of alumni, children of faculty/staff, siblings of current students.

LOANS *Programs:* FFEL (Subsidized and Unsubsidized Stafford, PLUS), Perkins.

WORK-STUDY *Federal work-study:* Total amount: $77,910; 71 jobs averaging $888.

APPLYING FOR FINANCIAL AID *Required financial aid forms:* FAFSA, combined institutional admission/financial aid form.

CONTACT Debra Sizemore, Director of Student Financial Services, Saint Joseph's College, US Highway 231, Rensselaer, IN 47978, 219-866-6163 or toll-free 800-447-8781 (out-of-state). *Fax:* 219-866-6144. *E-mail:* debbie@saintjoe.edu.

ST. JOSEPH'S COLLEGE, LONG ISLAND CAMPUS
Patchogue, NY

Tuition & fees: $16,765	Average undergraduate aid package: $10,009

ABOUT THE INSTITUTION Independent, coed. 22 undergraduate majors. Federal methodology is used as a basis for awarding need-based institutional aid.

UNDERGRADUATE EXPENSES for 2010–11 *Tuition:* full-time $16,200; part-time $530 per credit hour.

FRESHMAN FINANCIAL AID (Fall 2009, est.) 477 applied for aid; of those 69% were deemed to have need. 98% of freshmen with need received aid; of those 33% had need fully met. *Average percent of need met:* 83% (excluding resources awarded to replace EFC). *Average financial aid package:* $10,769 (excluding resources awarded to replace EFC). 24% of all full-time freshmen had no need and received non-need-based gift aid.

UNDERGRADUATE FINANCIAL AID (Fall 2009, est.) 2,728 applied for aid; of those 74% were deemed to have need. 97% of undergraduates with need received aid; of those 27% had need fully met. *Average percent of need met:* 71% (excluding resources awarded to replace EFC). *Average financial aid package:* $10,009 (excluding resources awarded to replace EFC). 14% of all full-time undergraduates had no need and received non-need-based gift aid.

GIFT AID (NEED-BASED) *Total amount:* $12,194,542 (30% federal, 22% state, 48% institutional). *Receiving aid:* Freshmen: 66% (324); all full-time undergraduates: 52% (1,618). *Average award:* Freshmen: $9477; Undergraduates: $7299. *Scholarships, grants, and awards:* Federal Pell, FSEOG, state, private, college/university gift aid from institutional funds.

GIFT AID (NON-NEED-BASED) *Total amount:* $3,419,403 (4% state, 93% institutional, 3% external sources). *Receiving aid:* Freshmen: 13% (62). Undergraduates: 6% (195). *Average award:* Freshmen: $7906. Undergraduates: $6848. *Scholarships, grants, and awards by category:* Academic interests/achievement: 1,512 awards ($9,724,044 total): general academic interests/achievements. Special characteristics: 145 awards ($373,944 total): children and siblings of alumni, children of faculty/staff, parents of current students, public servants, siblings of current students, spouses of current students, twins. *Tuition waivers:* Full or partial for employees or children of employees.

LOANS *Student loans:* $20,159,252 (43% need-based, 57% non-need-based). 64% of past graduating class borrowed through all loan programs. *Average indebtedness per student:* $21,023. *Average need-based loan:* Freshmen: $3109. Undergraduates: $4258. *Parent loans:* $4,730,647 (100% non-need-based). *Programs:* FFEL (Subsidized and Unsubsidized Stafford, PLUS), Perkins.

WORK-STUDY *Federal work-study:* Total amount: $285,917; 90 jobs averaging $3135. *State or other work-study/employment:* Total amount: $328,870 (100% non-need-based). 84 part-time jobs averaging $3915.

APPLYING FOR FINANCIAL AID *Required financial aid forms:* FAFSA, state aid form. *Financial aid deadline (priority):* 2/25. *Notification date:* Continuous beginning 3/15. Students must reply by 5/1 or within 2 weeks of notification.

CONTACT Amy Thompson, Director of Financial Aid, St. Joseph's College, Long Island Campus, 155 West Roe Boulevard, Patchogue, NY 11772-2399, 631-687-2611 or toll-free 866-AT ST JOE (in-state). *Fax:* 631-447-8883. *E-mail:* althompson@sjcny.edu.

ST. JOSEPH'S COLLEGE, NEW YORK
Brooklyn, NY

Tuition & fees: $16,765	Average undergraduate aid package: $11,786

ABOUT THE INSTITUTION Independent, coed. 22 undergraduate majors. Federal methodology is used as a basis for awarding need-based institutional aid.

UNDERGRADUATE EXPENSES for 2010–11 *Tuition:* full-time $16,200; part-time $530 per credit hour.

FRESHMAN FINANCIAL AID (Fall 2009, est.) 198 applied for aid; of those 82% were deemed to have need. 100% of freshmen with need received aid; of those 27% had need fully met. *Average percent of need met:* 76% (excluding resources awarded to replace EFC). *Average financial aid package:* $12,314 (excluding resources awarded to replace EFC). 15% of all full-time freshmen had no need and received non-need-based gift aid.

UNDERGRADUATE FINANCIAL AID (Fall 2009, est.) 769 applied for aid; of those 85% were deemed to have need. 98% of undergraduates with need received aid; of those 17% had need fully met. *Average percent of need met:* 66% (excluding resources awarded to replace EFC). *Average financial aid package:* $11,786 (excluding resources awarded to replace EFC). 11% of all full-time undergraduates had no need and received non-need-based gift aid.

GIFT AID (NEED-BASED) *Total amount:* $5,158,865 (41% federal, 19% state, 40% institutional). *Receiving aid:* Freshmen: 77% (163); all full-time undergraduates: 66% (551). *Average award:* Freshmen: $11,009; Undergraduates: $7847. *Scholarships, grants, and awards:* Federal Pell, FSEOG, state, private, college/university gift aid from institutional funds.

GIFT AID (NON-NEED-BASED) *Total amount:* $1,060,149 (3% state, 89% institutional, 8% external sources). *Receiving aid:* Freshmen: 15% (31). Undergraduates: 7% (59). *Average award:* Freshmen: $8545. Undergraduates: $6891. *Scholarships, grants, and awards by category: Academic interests/achievement:* 390 awards ($2,513,270 total): general academic interests/achievements. *Special characteristics:* 52 awards ($132,847 total): children and siblings of alumni, children of faculty/staff, parents of current students, public servants, siblings of current students, spouses of current students, twins. *Tuition waivers:* Full or partial for employees or children of employees.
LOANS *Student loans:* $4,987,474 (46% need-based, 54% non-need-based). 55% of past graduating class borrowed through all loan programs. *Average indebtedness per student:* $20,616. *Average need-based loan:* Freshmen: $3147. Undergraduates: $4284. *Parent loans:* $463,441 (100% non-need-based). *Programs:* FFEL (Subsidized and Unsubsidized Stafford, PLUS), Perkins.
WORK-STUDY *Federal work-study:* Total amount: $270,632; 118 jobs averaging $2379. *State or other work-study/employment:* Total amount: $21,479 (100% non-need-based). 20 part-time jobs averaging $1332.
APPLYING FOR FINANCIAL AID *Required financial aid forms:* FAFSA, state aid form. *Financial aid deadline (priority):* 2/25. *Notification date:* Continuous beginning 3/15. Students must reply by 5/1 or within 2 weeks of notification.
CONTACT Ms. Amy Thompson, Director of Financial Aid, St. Joseph's College, New York, 245 Clinton Avenue, Brooklyn, NY 11205-3688, 718-940-5713. *Fax:* 718-636-6827. *E-mail:* althompson@sjcny.edu.

SAINT JOSEPH'S COLLEGE OF MAINE
Standish, ME

Tuition & fees: $26,050	Average undergraduate aid package: $20,192

ABOUT THE INSTITUTION Independent religious, coed. 47 undergraduate majors. Both federal and institutional methodology are used as a basis for awarding need-based institutional aid.
UNDERGRADUATE EXPENSES for 2009–10 *Comprehensive fee:* $36,400 includes full-time tuition ($25,150), mandatory fees ($900), and room and board ($10,350). *Part-time tuition:* $450 per credit hour. Part-time tuition and fees vary according to course load. *Payment plan:* Installment.
FRESHMAN FINANCIAL AID (Fall 2009, est.) 265 applied for aid; of those 92% were deemed to have need. 100% of freshmen with need received aid; of those 9% had need fully met. *Average percent of need met:* 80% (excluding resources awarded to replace EFC). *Average financial aid package:* $21,499 (excluding resources awarded to replace EFC). 12% of all full-time freshmen had no need and received non-need-based gift aid.
UNDERGRADUATE FINANCIAL AID (Fall 2009, est.) 946 applied for aid; of those 91% were deemed to have need. 100% of undergraduates with need received aid; of those 11% had need fully met. *Average percent of need met:* 78% (excluding resources awarded to replace EFC). *Average financial aid package:* $20,192 (excluding resources awarded to replace EFC). 16% of all full-time undergraduates had no need and received non-need-based gift aid.
GIFT AID (NEED-BASED) *Total amount:* $11,586,992 (13% federal, 2% state, 78% institutional, 7% external sources). *Receiving aid:* Freshmen: 86% (242); all full-time undergraduates: 82% (861). *Average award:* Freshmen: $15,297; Undergraduates: $13,447. *Scholarships, grants, and awards:* Federal Pell, FSEOG, state, private, college/university gift aid from institutional funds, Federal Nursing.
GIFT AID (NON-NEED-BASED) *Total amount:* $1,931,739 (87% institutional, 13% external sources). *Receiving aid:* Freshmen: 7% (21). Undergraduates: 8% (81). *Average award:* Freshmen: $8220. Undergraduates: $8155. *Scholarships, grants, and awards by category: Academic interests/achievement:* 138 awards ($1,134,527 total): general academic interests/achievements. *Special characteristics:* 40 awards ($496,045 total): children of faculty/staff, siblings of current students, spouses of current students. *Tuition waivers:* Full or partial for employees or children of employees.
LOANS *Student loans:* $10,797,562 (66% need-based, 34% non-need-based). 87% of past graduating class borrowed through all loan programs. *Average indebtedness per student:* $36,071. *Average need-based loan:* Freshmen: $5832. Undergraduates: $6858. *Parent loans:* $2,241,251 (39% need-based, 61% non-need-based). *Programs:* Federal Direct (Subsidized and Unsubsidized Stafford, PLUS), Perkins, Federal Nursing, state.
WORK-STUDY *Federal work-study:* Total amount: $565,951; 408 jobs averaging $1382.

APPLYING FOR FINANCIAL AID *Required financial aid forms:* FAFSA, institution's own form. *Financial aid deadline (priority):* 3/1. *Notification date:* Continuous beginning 3/15. Students must reply by 5/1 or within 3 weeks of notification.
CONTACT Office of Financial Aid, Saint Joseph's College of Maine, 278 Whites Bridge Road, Standish, ME 04084-5263, 800-752-1266 or toll-free 800-338-7057. *Fax:* 207-893-6699. *E-mail:* finaid@sjcme.edu.

SAINT JOSEPH SEMINARY COLLEGE
Saint Benedict, LA

Tuition & fees: $12,882	Average undergraduate aid package: $4105

ABOUT THE INSTITUTION Independent Roman Catholic, men only. 1 undergraduate major. Federal methodology is used as a basis for awarding need-based institutional aid.
UNDERGRADUATE EXPENSES for 2010–11 *One-time required fee:* $150. *Comprehensive fee:* $24,050 includes full-time tuition ($11,582), mandatory fees ($1300), and room and board ($11,168). *College room only:* $5896. *Part-time tuition:* $185 per credit hour.
FRESHMAN FINANCIAL AID (Fall 2009, est.) 1 applied for aid; of those 100% were deemed to have need. 100% of freshmen with need received aid; of those 100% had need fully met. *Average percent of need met:* 100% (excluding resources awarded to replace EFC). *Average financial aid package:* $5350 (excluding resources awarded to replace EFC).
UNDERGRADUATE FINANCIAL AID (Fall 2009, est.) 33 applied for aid; of those 100% were deemed to have need. 100% of undergraduates with need received aid; of those 100% had need fully met. *Average percent of need met:* 100% (excluding resources awarded to replace EFC). *Average financial aid package:* $4105 (excluding resources awarded to replace EFC).
GIFT AID (NEED-BASED) *Total amount:* $78,950 (61% federal, 39% state). *Receiving aid:* Freshmen: 17% (1); all full-time undergraduates: 43% (33). *Average award:* Freshmen: $8120; Undergraduates: $4105. *Scholarships, grants, and awards:* Federal Pell, state, private, college/university gift aid from institutional funds.
LOANS *Student loans:* $11,000 (100% need-based). *Average indebtedness per student:* $5000. *Programs:* FFEL (Subsidized and Unsubsidized Stafford, PLUS).
WORK-STUDY Federal work-study jobs available. *State or other work-study/employment:* Part-time jobs available.
APPLYING FOR FINANCIAL AID *Required financial aid form:* FAFSA. *Financial aid deadline (priority):* 8/15. *Notification date:* Continuous beginning 7/1. Students must reply within 4 weeks of notification.
CONTACT George J. Binder Jr., Financial Aid Officer, Saint Joseph Seminary College, 75376 River Road, Saint Benedict, LA 70457, 985-867-2248. *Fax:* 985-867-2270. *E-mail:* gbinder@sjasc.edu.

SAINT JOSEPH'S UNIVERSITY
Philadelphia, PA

Tuition & fees: $34,090	Average undergraduate aid package: $19,271

ABOUT THE INSTITUTION Independent Roman Catholic (Jesuit), coed. 53 undergraduate majors. Federal methodology is used as a basis for awarding need-based institutional aid.
UNDERGRADUATE EXPENSES for 2009–10 *One-time required fee:* $225. *Comprehensive fee:* $45,665 includes full-time tuition ($33,940), mandatory fees ($150), and room and board ($11,575). *College room only:* $7320. Full-time tuition and fees vary according to course load. Room and board charges vary according to board plan and housing facility. *Part-time tuition:* $456 per credit. evening college, continuing education student tuition: $456 per credit. *Payment plans:* Installment, deferred payment.
FRESHMAN FINANCIAL AID (Fall 2009, est.) 888 applied for aid; of those 73% were deemed to have need. 100% of freshmen with need received aid; of those 25% had need fully met. *Average percent of need met:* 83% (excluding resources awarded to replace EFC). *Average financial aid package:* $19,574 (excluding resources awarded to replace EFC). 38% of all full-time freshmen had no need and received non-need-based gift aid.
UNDERGRADUATE FINANCIAL AID (Fall 2009, est.) 2,807 applied for aid; of those 80% were deemed to have need. 100% of undergraduates with need received aid; of those 23% had need fully met. *Average percent of need met:* 76% (excluding resources awarded to replace EFC). *Average financial aid*

package: $19,271 (excluding resources awarded to replace EFC). 40% of all full-time undergraduates had no need and received non-need-based gift aid.

GIFT AID (NEED-BASED) *Total amount:* $31,467,243 (7% federal, 4% state, 87% institutional, 2% external sources). *Receiving aid:* Freshmen: 54% (640); all full-time undergraduates: 48% (2,158). *Average award:* Freshmen: $16,206; Undergraduates: $14,947. *Scholarships, grants, and awards:* Federal Pell, FSEOG, state, private, college/university gift aid from institutional funds.

GIFT AID (NON-NEED-BASED) *Total amount:* $18,694,322 (98% institutional, 2% external sources). *Receiving aid:* Freshmen: 51% (601). Undergraduates: 46% (2,049). *Average award:* Freshmen: $10,125. Undergraduates: $10,206. *Scholarships, grants, and awards by category: Academic interests/achievement:* general academic interests/achievements. *Creative arts/performance:* art/fine arts, general creative arts/performance, music, theater/drama. *Special achievements/ activities:* general special achievements/activities. *Special characteristics:* children and siblings of alumni, members of minority groups. *Tuition waivers:* Full or partial for employees or children of employees.

LOANS *Student loans:* $26,171,978 (83% need-based, 17% non-need-based). *Average need-based loan:* Freshmen: $4063. Undergraduates: $5179. *Parent loans:* $17,435,120 (73% need-based, 27% non-need-based). *Programs:* Federal Direct (Subsidized and Unsubsidized Stafford, PLUS), FFEL (Subsidized and Unsubsidized Stafford, PLUS), Perkins.

WORK-STUDY *Federal work-study:* Total amount: $600,000; jobs available.

ATHLETIC AWARDS Total amount: $4,023,591 (48% need-based, 52% non-need-based).

APPLYING FOR FINANCIAL AID *Required financial aid form:* FAFSA. *Financial aid deadline (priority):* 2/15. *Notification date:* Continuous beginning 3/1. Students must reply by 5/1.

CONTACT Eileen M. Tucker, Director of Financial Assistance, Saint Joseph's University, 5600 City Avenue, Philadelphia, PA 19131-1395, 610-660-1556 or toll-free 888-BEAHAWK (in-state). *Fax:* 610-660-1342. *E-mail:* finaid@sju.edu.

ST. LAWRENCE UNIVERSITY
Canton, NY

Tuition & fees: $39,765	Average undergraduate aid package: $35,989

ABOUT THE INSTITUTION Independent, coed. 41 undergraduate majors. Both federal and institutional methodology are used as a basis for awarding need-based institutional aid.

UNDERGRADUATE EXPENSES for 2009–10 *Comprehensive fee:* $49,925 includes full-time tuition ($39,520), mandatory fees ($245), and room and board ($10,160). *College room only:* $5460. Room and board charges vary according to board plan. *Payment plan:* Installment.

FRESHMAN FINANCIAL AID (Fall 2009, est.) 446 applied for aid; of those 86% were deemed to have need. 100% of freshmen with need received aid; of those 41% had need fully met. *Average percent of need met:* 92% (excluding resources awarded to replace EFC). *Average financial aid package:* $30,029 (excluding resources awarded to replace EFC). 15% of all full-time freshmen had no need and received non-need-based gift aid.

UNDERGRADUATE FINANCIAL AID (Fall 2009, est.) 1,608 applied for aid; of those 89% were deemed to have need. 99% of undergraduates with need received aid; of those 42% had need fully met. *Average percent of need met:* 90% (excluding resources awarded to replace EFC). *Average financial aid package:* $35,989 (excluding resources awarded to replace EFC). 16% of all full-time undergraduates had no need and received non-need-based gift aid.

GIFT AID (NEED-BASED) *Total amount:* $38,217,933 (7% federal, 3% state, 86% institutional, 4% external sources). *Receiving aid:* Freshmen: 66% (383); all full-time undergraduates: 62% (1,401). *Average award:* Freshmen: $27,822; Undergraduates: $26,987. *Scholarships, grants, and awards:* Federal Pell, FSEOG, state, private, college/university gift aid from institutional funds.

GIFT AID (NON-NEED-BASED) *Total amount:* $5,099,481 (98% institutional, 2% external sources). *Receiving aid:* Freshmen: 11% (65). Undergraduates: 9% (196). *Average award:* Freshmen: $11,344. Undergraduates: $11,335. *Scholarships, grants, and awards by category: Academic interests/achievement:* general academic interests/achievements. *Special achievements/activities:* community service. *Special characteristics:* children and siblings of alumni, siblings of current students, veterans' children. *Tuition waivers:* Full or partial for employees or children of employees.

LOANS *Student loans:* $9,834,024 (48% need-based, 52% non-need-based). 74% of past graduating class borrowed through all loan programs. *Average*

---

indebtedness per student: $31,653. *Average need-based loan:* Freshmen: $3223. Undergraduates: $4282. *Parent loans:* $6,171,259 (100% non-need-based). *Programs:* Federal Direct (Subsidized and Unsubsidized Stafford, PLUS), Perkins, college/university.

WORK-STUDY *Federal work-study:* Total amount: $1,243,500; jobs available. *State or other work-study/employment:* Total amount: $718,368 (100% non-need-based). Part-time jobs available.

ATHLETIC AWARDS Total amount: $1,690,425 (100% non-need-based).

APPLYING FOR FINANCIAL AID *Required financial aid forms:* FAFSA, noncustodial (divorced/separated) parent's statement, business/farm supplement, income tax returns, W-2 forms. *Financial aid deadline:* 2/1. *Notification date:* 3/30. Students must reply by 5/1 or within 2 weeks of notification.

CONTACT Mrs. Patricia J. B. Farmer, Director of Financial Aid, St. Lawrence University, Payson Hall, 23 Romoda Drive, Canton, NY 13617-1455, 315-229-5265 or toll-free 800-285-1856. *Fax:* 315-229-5502. *E-mail:* pfarmer@stlawu.edu.

SAINT LEO UNIVERSITY
Saint Leo, FL

Tuition & fees: $17,646	Average undergraduate aid package: $16,532

ABOUT THE INSTITUTION Independent Roman Catholic, coed. 31 undergraduate majors. Federal methodology is used as a basis for awarding need-based institutional aid.

UNDERGRADUATE EXPENSES for 2009–10 *Comprehensive fee:* $26,370 includes full-time tuition ($16,996), mandatory fees ($650), and room and board ($8724). *College room only:* $4584. Room and board charges vary according to board plan and housing facility. *Payment plan:* Installment.

FRESHMAN FINANCIAL AID (Fall 2009, est.) 455 applied for aid; of those 83% were deemed to have need. 100% of freshmen with need received aid; of those 26% had need fully met. *Average percent of need met:* 80% (excluding resources awarded to replace EFC). *Average financial aid package:* $18,200 (excluding resources awarded to replace EFC).

UNDERGRADUATE FINANCIAL AID (Fall 2009, est.) 1,431 applied for aid; of those 83% were deemed to have need. 100% of undergraduates with need received aid; of those 28% had need fully met. *Average percent of need met:* 76% (excluding resources awarded to replace EFC). *Average financial aid package:* $16,532 (excluding resources awarded to replace EFC). 2% of all full-time undergraduates had no need and received non-need-based gift aid.

GIFT AID (NEED-BASED) *Total amount:* $14,793,552 (20% federal, 19% state, 58% institutional, 3% external sources). *Receiving aid:* Freshmen: 78% (379); all full-time undergraduates: 72% (1,179). *Average award:* Freshmen: $12,865; Undergraduates: $11,571. *Scholarships, grants, and awards:* Federal Pell, FSEOG, state, private, college/university gift aid from institutional funds, United Negro College Fund.

GIFT AID (NON-NEED-BASED) *Total amount:* $1,336,836 (64% state, 16% institutional, 20% external sources). *Receiving aid:* Freshmen: 8% (37). Undergraduates: 7% (109). *Average award:* Undergraduates: $7217. *Tuition waivers:* Full or partial for employees or children of employees.

LOANS *Student loans:* $10,939,413 (69% need-based, 31% non-need-based). 63% of past graduating class borrowed through all loan programs. *Average indebtedness per student:* $23,787. *Average need-based loan:* Freshmen: $3327. Undergraduates: $4111. *Parent loans:* $3,189,695 (56% need-based, 44% non-need-based). *Programs:* Federal Direct (Subsidized and Unsubsidized Stafford, PLUS), Perkins.

WORK-STUDY *Federal work-study:* Total amount: $1,207,320; 386 jobs averaging $3128.

ATHLETIC AWARDS Total amount: $1,662,578 (60% need-based, 40% non-need-based).

APPLYING FOR FINANCIAL AID *Required financial aid form:* FAFSA. *Financial aid deadline (priority):* 3/1. *Notification date:* Continuous beginning 1/31.

CONTACT Office of Student Financial Services, Saint Leo University, PO Box 6665, MC 2228, Saint Leo, FL 33574-6665, 800-240-7658 or toll-free 800-334-5532. *Fax:* 352-588-8403. *E-mail:* finaid@saintleo.edu.

ST. LOUIS CHRISTIAN COLLEGE
Florissant, MO

Tuition & fees: $11,000	Average undergraduate aid package: $14,102

ABOUT THE INSTITUTION Independent Christian, coed. 5 undergraduate majors. Federal methodology is used as a basis for awarding need-based institutional aid.

UNDERGRADUATE EXPENSES for 2009–10 *Comprehensive fee:* $14,600 includes full-time tuition ($10,350), mandatory fees ($650), and room and board ($3600). Room and board charges vary according to housing facility. *Part-time tuition:* $345 per credit hour.

FRESHMAN FINANCIAL AID (Fall 2009, est.) 54 applied for aid; of those 83% were deemed to have need. 100% of freshmen with need received aid; of those 22% had need fully met. *Average percent of need met:* 82% (excluding resources awarded to replace EFC). *Average financial aid package:* $15,520 (excluding resources awarded to replace EFC). 13% of all full-time freshmen had no need and received non-need-based gift aid.

UNDERGRADUATE FINANCIAL AID (Fall 2009, est.) 241 applied for aid; of those 93% were deemed to have need. 100% of undergraduates with need received aid; of those 19% had need fully met. *Average percent of need met:* 76% (excluding resources awarded to replace EFC). *Average financial aid package:* $14,102 (excluding resources awarded to replace EFC). 21% of all full-time undergraduates had no need and received non-need-based gift aid.

GIFT AID (NEED-BASED) *Total amount:* $4,892,150 (15% federal, 33% state, 2% institutional, 50% external sources). *Receiving aid:* Freshmen: 80% (45); all full-time undergraduates: 77% (225). *Average award:* Freshmen: $12,955; Undergraduates: $10,747. *Scholarships, grants, and awards:* Federal Pell, FSEOG, state, private, college/university gift aid from institutional funds.

GIFT AID (NON-NEED-BASED) *Average award:* Freshmen: $10,235. Undergraduates: $8274. *Tuition waivers:* Full or partial for employees or children of employees.

LOANS *Student loans:* $1,675,847 (95% need-based, 5% non-need-based). 80% of past graduating class borrowed through all loan programs. *Average indebtedness per student:* $11,654. *Average need-based loan:* Freshmen: $2524. Undergraduates: $3201. *Parent loans:* $43,380 (68% need-based, 32% non-need-based). *Programs:* Federal Direct (Subsidized and Unsubsidized Stafford, PLUS), private loans.

WORK-STUDY *Federal work-study:* Total amount: $26,800; 17 jobs averaging $1450. *State or other work-study/employment:* Total amount: $187,766 (100% non-need-based). 25 part-time jobs averaging $4200.

APPLYING FOR FINANCIAL AID *Required financial aid form:* FAFSA. *Financial aid deadline:* Continuous. *Notification date:* Continuous.

CONTACT Mrs. Catherine Wilhoit, Director of Financial Aid, St. Louis Christian College, 1360 Grandview Drive, Florissant, MO 63033-6499, 314-837-6777 Ext. 1101 or toll-free 800-887-SLCC. *Fax:* 314-837-8291.

ST. LOUIS COLLEGE OF PHARMACY
St. Louis, MO

Tuition & fees: $23,010	Average undergraduate aid package: $13,007

ABOUT THE INSTITUTION Independent, coed. 1 undergraduate major. Federal methodology is used as a basis for awarding need-based institutional aid.

UNDERGRADUATE EXPENSES for 2010–11 *Comprehensive fee:* $31,570 includes full-time tuition ($22,600), mandatory fees ($410), and room and board ($8560). *College room only:* $4829. Full-time tuition and fees vary according to student level. Room and board charges vary according to housing facility. *Part-time tuition:* $800 per credit hour. *Payment plan:* Installment.

FRESHMAN FINANCIAL AID (Fall 2009, est.) 241 applied for aid; of those 80% were deemed to have need. 92% of freshmen with need received aid; of those 9% had need fully met. *Average percent of need met:* 53% (excluding resources awarded to replace EFC). *Average financial aid package:* $14,172 (excluding resources awarded to replace EFC). 26% of all full-time freshmen had no need and received non-need-based gift aid.

UNDERGRADUATE FINANCIAL AID (Fall 2009, est.) 652 applied for aid; of those 87% were deemed to have need. 90% of undergraduates with need received aid; of those 8% had need fully met. *Average percent of need met:* 45% (excluding resources awarded to replace EFC). *Average financial aid package:* $13,007 (excluding resources awarded to replace EFC). 20% of all full-time undergraduates had no need and received non-need-based gift aid.

GIFT AID (NEED-BASED) *Total amount:* $4,112,540 (18% federal, 11% state, 60% institutional, 11% external sources). *Receiving aid:* Freshmen: 73% (178); all full-time undergraduates: 66% (441). *Average award:* Freshmen: $9842; Undergraduates: $9323. *Scholarships, grants, and awards:* Federal Pell, FSEOG, state, private, college/university gift aid from institutional funds.

GIFT AID (NON-NEED-BASED) *Total amount:* $974,470 (3% state, 83% institutional, 14% external sources). *Receiving aid:* Freshmen: 5% (12). Undergraduates: 4% (26). *Average award:* Freshmen: $5170. Undergraduates: $5640. *Scholarships, grants, and awards by category: Academic interests/ achievement:* 540 awards ($3,285,031 total): general academic interests/ achievements. *Special achievements/activities:* community service, leadership. *Special characteristics:* children of faculty/staff, local/state students. *Tuition waivers:* Full or partial for employees or children of employees.

LOANS *Student loans:* $6,156,983 (77% need-based, 23% non-need-based). 89% of past graduating class borrowed through all loan programs. *Average indebtedness per student:* $107,649. *Average need-based loan:* Freshmen: $4369. Undergraduates: $4982. *Parent loans:* $1,413,298 (52% need-based, 48% non-need-based). *Programs:* FFEL (Subsidized and Unsubsidized Stafford, PLUS), Perkins, Federal Health Professions Student Loans.

WORK-STUDY *Federal work-study:* Total amount: $279,967; 299 jobs averaging $933.

APPLYING FOR FINANCIAL AID *Required financial aid forms:* FAFSA, institution's own form. *Financial aid deadline (priority):* 3/15. *Notification date:* Continuous. Students must reply within 2 weeks of notification.

CONTACT Mr. David Rice, Director of Financial Aid, St. Louis College of Pharmacy, 4588 Parkview Place, St. Louis, MO 63110, 314-446-8320 or toll-free 800-278-5267 (in-state). *Fax:* 314-446-8310. *E-mail:* drice@stlcop.edu.

SAINT LOUIS UNIVERSITY
St. Louis, MO

Tuition & fees: $31,342	Average undergraduate aid package: $22,162

ABOUT THE INSTITUTION Independent Roman Catholic (Jesuit), coed. 73 undergraduate majors. Federal methodology is used as a basis for awarding need-based institutional aid.

UNDERGRADUATE EXPENSES for 2009–10 *Comprehensive fee:* $40,242 includes full-time tuition ($30,940), mandatory fees ($402), and room and board ($8900). *College room only:* $5000. Full-time tuition and fees vary according to location and program. Room and board charges vary according to board plan, housing facility, and location. *Part-time tuition:* $1080 per credit hour. *Part-time fees:* $120 per semester hour. Part-time tuition and fees vary according to location and program. *Payment plan:* Installment.

FRESHMAN FINANCIAL AID (Fall 2008) 1,260 applied for aid; of those 83% were deemed to have need. 100% of freshmen with need received aid; of those 20% had need fully met. *Average percent of need met:* 73% (excluding resources awarded to replace EFC). *Average financial aid package:* $24,100 (excluding resources awarded to replace EFC). 29% of all full-time freshmen had no need and received non-need-based gift aid.

UNDERGRADUATE FINANCIAL AID (Fall 2008) 4,569 applied for aid; of those 87% were deemed to have need. 100% of undergraduates with need received aid; of those 16% had need fully met. *Average percent of need met:* 67% (excluding resources awarded to replace EFC). *Average financial aid package:* $22,162 (excluding resources awarded to replace EFC). 28% of all full-time undergraduates had no need and received non-need-based gift aid.

GIFT AID (NEED-BASED) *Total amount:* $66,168,817 (13% federal, 5% state, 79% institutional, 3% external sources). *Receiving aid:* Freshmen: 63% (1,010); all full-time undergraduates: 51% (3,741). *Average award:* Freshmen: $19,795; Undergraduates: $17,184. *Scholarships, grants, and awards:* Federal Pell, FSEOG, state, private, college/university gift aid from institutional funds, Federal Nursing.

GIFT AID (NON-NEED-BASED) *Total amount:* $20,460,950 (1% state, 88% institutional, 11% external sources). *Receiving aid:* Freshmen: 8% (125). Undergraduates: 5% (366). *Average award:* Freshmen: $12,372. Undergraduates: $10,423. *Scholarships, grants, and awards by category: Academic interests/achievement:* 4,971 awards ($47,030,159 total): area/ethnic studies, biological sciences, business, communication, computer science, education, engineering/technologies, English, foreign languages, general academic interests/ achievements, health fields, humanities, international studies, mathematics, military science, physical sciences, premedicine, religion/biblical studies, social sciences. *Creative arts/performance:* 115 awards ($122,335 total): art/fine arts, music, performing arts, theater/drama. *Special achievements/activities:* 337 awards ($3,992,798 total): cheerleading/drum major, community service, general special achievements/activities, leadership, memberships, religious involvement. *Special characteristics:* 1,296 awards ($16,467,841 total): children of faculty/staff, first-generation college students, general special characteristics, international students, members of minority groups, previous college experience, religious affiliation, siblings of current students. *Tuition waivers:* Full or partial for children of alumni, employees or children of employees.

LOANS *Student loans:* $44,863,853 (39% need-based, 61% non-need-based). 64% of past graduating class borrowed through all loan programs. *Average indebtedness per student:* $33,747. *Average need-based loan:* Freshmen: $3973. Undergraduates: $5386. *Parent loans:* $9,614,122 (100% non-need-based). *Programs:* FFEL (Subsidized and Unsubsidized Stafford, PLUS), Perkins, Federal Nursing, college/university.

WORK-STUDY *Federal work-study:* Total amount: $612,139; 630 jobs averaging $972. *State or other work-study/employment:* Total amount: $16,522 (34% need-based, 66% non-need-based). 5 part-time jobs averaging $3304.

ATHLETIC AWARDS Total amount: $3,629,024 (40% need-based, 60% non-need-based).

APPLYING FOR FINANCIAL AID *Required financial aid form:* FAFSA. *Financial aid deadline (priority):* 3/1. *Notification date:* Continuous beginning 3/1. Students must reply by 5/1 or within 4 weeks of notification.

CONTACT Cari S. Wickliffe, Assistant Vice Provost, Student Financial Services, Saint Louis University, 221 North Grand Boulevard, DuBourg Hall, Room 121, St. Louis, MO 63103-2097, 314-977-3442 or toll-free 800-758-3678 (out-of-state). *Fax:* 314-977-3437. *E-mail:* wicklics@slu.edu.

SAINT LUKE'S COLLEGE
Kansas City, MO

Tuition & fees: $9520	Average undergraduate aid package: $10,000

ABOUT THE INSTITUTION Independent Episcopal, coed. *Awards:* bachelor's degrees. 1 undergraduate major. *Total enrollment:* 113. Undergraduates: 113. Both federal and institutional methodology are used as a basis for awarding need-based institutional aid.

UNDERGRADUATE EXPENSES for 2009–10 *Application fee:* $35. *Tuition:* full-time $8850.

UNDERGRADUATE FINANCIAL AID (Fall 2009, est.) 103 applied for aid; of those 86% were deemed to have need. 100% of undergraduates with need received aid; of those 3% had need fully met. *Average percent of need met:* 66% (excluding resources awarded to replace EFC). *Average financial aid package:* $10,000 (excluding resources awarded to replace EFC). 5% of all full-time undergraduates had no need and received non-need-based gift aid.

GIFT AID (NEED-BASED) *Total amount:* $402,918 (33% federal, 11% state, 50% institutional, 6% external sources). *Receiving aid:* All full-time undergraduates: 72% (89). *Average award:* Undergraduates: $2000. *Scholarships, grants, and awards:* Federal Pell, FSEOG, state, private, college/university gift aid from institutional funds.

GIFT AID (NON-NEED-BASED) *Total amount:* $24,500 (100% institutional). *Receiving aid:* Undergraduates: 2% (2). *Average award:* Undergraduates: $2000.

LOANS *Student loans:* $864,817 (66% need-based, 34% non-need-based). *Average need-based loan:* Undergraduates: $5500. *Parent loans:* $97,000 (100% need-based). *Programs:* FFEL (Subsidized and Unsubsidized Stafford, PLUS), Perkins, Federal Nursing, college/university.

WORK-STUDY Federal work-study jobs available.

CONTACT Marcia Shaw, Executive Director, Business Operations and Student Services, Saint Luke's College, 8320 Ward Parkway, Suite 300, Kansas City, MO 64114, 816-932-2194. *Fax:* 816-932-9064. *E-mail:* meshaw@saint-lukes.org.

SAINT MARTIN'S UNIVERSITY
Lacey, WA

Tuition & fees: $26,402	Average undergraduate aid package: $18,279

ABOUT THE INSTITUTION Independent Roman Catholic, coed. 31 undergraduate majors. Federal methodology is used as a basis for awarding need-based institutional aid.

UNDERGRADUATE EXPENSES for 2010–11 *Comprehensive fee:* $35,062 includes full-time tuition ($26,100), mandatory fees ($302), and room and board ($8660). *College room only:* $4290. Full-time tuition and fees vary according to location. Room and board charges vary according to board plan. *Part-time tuition:* $870 per credit hour. Part-time tuition and fees vary according to course load and location. *Payment plan:* Installment.

FRESHMAN FINANCIAL AID (Fall 2008) 164 applied for aid; of those 90% were deemed to have need. 100% of freshmen with need received aid; of those 29% had need fully met. *Average percent of need met:* 81% (excluding resources awarded to replace EFC). *Average financial aid package:* $20,109 (excluding resources awarded to replace EFC). 17% of all full-time freshmen had no need and received non-need-based gift aid.

UNDERGRADUATE FINANCIAL AID (Fall 2008) 798 applied for aid; of those 89% were deemed to have need. 100% of undergraduates with need received aid; of those 25% had need fully met. *Average percent of need met:* 77% (excluding resources awarded to replace EFC). *Average financial aid package:* $18,279 (excluding resources awarded to replace EFC). 17% of all full-time undergraduates had no need and received non-need-based gift aid.

GIFT AID (NEED-BASED) *Total amount:* $10,204,512 (15% federal, 18% state, 50% institutional, 17% external sources). *Receiving aid:* Freshmen: 81% (148); all full-time undergraduates: 79% (698). *Average award:* Freshmen: $16,664; Undergraduates: $13,848. *Scholarships, grants, and awards:* Federal Pell, FSEOG, state, private, college/university gift aid from institutional funds, Academic Competitiveness Grants, National SMART Grants, TEACH Grants.

GIFT AID (NON-NEED-BASED) *Total amount:* $1,815,946 (1% state, 73% institutional, 26% external sources). *Receiving aid:* Freshmen: 16% (30). Undergraduates: 10% (92). *Average award:* Freshmen: $9483. Undergraduates: $6990. *Scholarships, grants, and awards by category:* Academic interests/achievement: business, education, engineering/technologies, general academic interests/achievements, humanities, international studies, premedicine. *Creative arts/performance:* music, theater/drama. *Special achievements/activities:* community service, general special achievements/activities, leadership, religious involvement. *Special characteristics:* children and siblings of alumni, children of faculty/staff, general special characteristics, members of minority groups, siblings of current students, veterans' children. *Tuition waivers:* Full or partial for children of alumni, employees or children of employees.

LOANS *Student loans:* $7,950,905 (68% need-based, 32% non-need-based). 79% of past graduating class borrowed through all loan programs. *Average indebtedness per student:* $27,807. *Average need-based loan:* Freshmen: $2746. Undergraduates: $3883. *Parent loans:* $963,030 (30% need-based, 70% non-need-based). *Programs:* Federal Direct (Subsidized and Unsubsidized Stafford, PLUS), Perkins, state, college/university, private alternative loans.

WORK-STUDY *Federal work-study:* Total amount: $507,844; 275 jobs averaging $1861. *State or other work-study/employment:* Total amount: $764,287 (100% need-based). 174 part-time jobs averaging $3897.

ATHLETIC AWARDS Total amount: $1,229,868 (52% need-based, 48% non-need-based).

APPLYING FOR FINANCIAL AID *Required financial aid form:* FAFSA. *Financial aid deadline (priority):* 4/15. *Notification date:* Continuous beginning 2/15.

CONTACT Ms. Rachelle Shahan-Riehl, Director of Financial Aid, Saint Martin's University, 5300 Pacific Avenue SE, Lacey, WA 98503-7500, 360-438-4463 or toll-free 800-368-8803. *Fax:* 360-412-6190. *E-mail:* rshahanreihl@stmartin.edu.

SAINT MARY-OF-THE-WOODS COLLEGE
Saint Mary-of-the-Woods, IN

CONTACT Ms. Jan Benton, Director of Financial Aid, Saint Mary-of-the-Woods College, 106 Guerin Hall, Saint Mary-of-the-Woods, IN 47876, 812-535-5106 or toll-free 800-926-SMWC. *Fax:* 812-535-4900. *E-mail:* jbenton@smwc.edu.

SAINT MARY'S COLLEGE
Notre Dame, IN

Tuition & fees: $29,616	Average undergraduate aid package: $22,125

ABOUT THE INSTITUTION Independent Roman Catholic, women only. 36 undergraduate majors. Both federal and institutional methodology are used as a basis for awarding need-based institutional aid.

UNDERGRADUATE EXPENSES for 2009–10 *Comprehensive fee:* $38,822 includes full-time tuition ($28,980), mandatory fees ($636), and room and

board ($9206). *College room only:* $5672. Room and board charges vary according to board plan and housing facility. *Part-time tuition:* $1146 per credit hour. *Part-time fees:* $318 per term. *Payment plan:* Installment.

FRESHMAN FINANCIAL AID (Fall 2009, est.) 356 applied for aid; of those 88% were deemed to have need. 100% of freshmen with need received aid; of those 23% had need fully met. *Average percent of need met:* 82% (excluding resources awarded to replace EFC). *Average financial aid package:* $25,163 (excluding resources awarded to replace EFC). 24% of all full-time freshmen had no need and received non-need-based gift aid.

UNDERGRADUATE FINANCIAL AID (Fall 2009, est.) 1,332 applied for aid; of those 86% were deemed to have need. 99% of undergraduates with need received aid; of those 16% had need fully met. *Average percent of need met:* 71% (excluding resources awarded to replace EFC). *Average financial aid package:* $22,125 (excluding resources awarded to replace EFC). 23% of all full-time undergraduates had no need and received non-need-based gift aid.

GIFT AID (NEED-BASED) *Total amount:* $18,258,997 (9% federal, 4% state, 83% institutional, 4% external sources). *Receiving aid:* Freshmen: 68% (297); all full-time undergraduates: 64% (1,054). *Average award:* Freshmen: $20,093; Undergraduates: $15,340. *Scholarships, grants, and awards:* Federal Pell, FSEOG, state, private, college/university gift aid from institutional funds.

GIFT AID (NON-NEED-BASED) *Total amount:* $3,906,607 (97% institutional, 3% external sources). *Receiving aid:* Freshmen: 53% (230). Undergraduates: 50% (824). *Average award:* Freshmen: $11,165. Undergraduates: $10,227. *Tuition waivers:* Full or partial for employees or children of employees.

LOANS *Student loans:* $8,831,457 (95% need-based, 5% non-need-based). 72% of past graduating class borrowed through all loan programs. *Average indebtedness per student:* $25,531. *Average need-based loan:* Freshmen: $3493. Undergraduates: $4491. *Parent loans:* $3,889,162 (93% need-based, 7% non-need-based). *Programs:* Federal Direct (Subsidized and Unsubsidized Stafford, PLUS), FFEL (Subsidized and Unsubsidized Stafford, PLUS), Perkins, college/university.

WORK-STUDY *Federal work-study:* Total amount: $953,186; jobs available. *State or other work-study/employment:* Part-time jobs available.

APPLYING FOR FINANCIAL AID *Required financial aid forms:* FAFSA, CSS Financial Aid PROFILE, noncustodial (divorced/separated) parent's statement. *Financial aid deadline:* 3/1. *Notification date:* Continuous beginning 3/15. Students must reply within 3 weeks of notification.

CONTACT Kathleen M. Brown, Director of Financial Aid, Saint Mary's College, 141 Le Mans Hall, Notre Dame, IN 46556, 574-284-4557 or toll-free 800-551-7621. *Fax:* 574-284-4818. *E-mail:* kbrown@saintmarys.edu.

SAINT MARY'S COLLEGE OF CALIFORNIA
Moraga, CA

Tuition & fees: $33,910	Average undergraduate aid package: $25,104

ABOUT THE INSTITUTION Independent Roman Catholic, coed. 70 undergraduate majors. Federal methodology is used as a basis for awarding need-based institutional aid.

UNDERGRADUATE EXPENSES for 2009–10 *Comprehensive fee:* $45,850 includes full-time tuition ($33,760), mandatory fees ($150), and room and board ($11,940). *College room only:* $6570. Room and board charges vary according to board plan and housing facility. *Part-time tuition:* $4220 per course. *Payment plan:* Installment.

FRESHMAN FINANCIAL AID (Fall 2009, est.) 513 applied for aid; of those 94% were deemed to have need. 100% of freshmen with need received aid; of those 2% had need fully met. *Average percent of need met:* 85% (excluding resources awarded to replace EFC). *Average financial aid package:* $29,442 (excluding resources awarded to replace EFC). 4% of all full-time freshmen had no need and received non-need-based gift aid.

UNDERGRADUATE FINANCIAL AID (Fall 2009, est.) 1,921 applied for aid; of those 96% were deemed to have need. 98% of undergraduates with need received aid; of those 6% had need fully met. *Average percent of need met:* 75% (excluding resources awarded to replace EFC). *Average financial aid package:* $25,104 (excluding resources awarded to replace EFC). 4% of all full-time undergraduates had no need and received non-need-based gift aid.

GIFT AID (NEED-BASED) *Total amount:* $34,228,979 (10% federal, 15% state, 73% institutional, 2% external sources). *Receiving aid:* Freshmen: 71% (406); all full-time undergraduates: 59% (1,392). *Average award:* Freshmen: $24,254; Undergraduates: $21,692. *Scholarships, grants, and awards:* Federal Pell, FSEOG, state, private, college/university gift aid from institutional funds.

GIFT AID (NON-NEED-BASED) *Total amount:* $1,328,073 (98% institutional, 2% external sources). *Receiving aid:* Freshmen: 29% (165). Undergraduates: 25% (600). *Average award:* Freshmen: $14,333. Undergraduates: $12,574. *Scholarships, grants, and awards by category: Academic interests/achievement:* 298 awards ($3,570,655 total): general academic interests/achievements. *Creative arts/performance:* 12 awards ($150,000 total): dance, music, performing arts, theater/drama. *Special achievements/activities:* 104 awards ($890,734 total): leadership, memberships. *Special characteristics:* 48 awards ($1,497,837 total): children and siblings of alumni, children of educators, children of faculty/staff, general special characteristics, relatives of clergy. *Tuition waivers:* Full or partial for employees or children of employees.

LOANS *Student loans:* $14,710,207 (91% need-based, 9% non-need-based). 80% of past graduating class borrowed through all loan programs. *Average indebtedness per student:* $31,330. *Average need-based loan:* Freshmen: $3864. Undergraduates: $4789. *Parent loans:* $6,274,154 (79% need-based, 21% non-need-based). *Programs:* FFEL (Subsidized and Unsubsidized Stafford, PLUS), Perkins.

WORK-STUDY *Federal work-study:* Total amount: $1,334,796; 483 jobs averaging $2771.

ATHLETIC AWARDS Total amount: $4,826,475 (39% need-based, 61% non-need-based).

APPLYING FOR FINANCIAL AID *Required financial aid forms:* FAFSA, state aid form. *Financial aid deadline (priority):* 2/15. *Notification date:* Continuous beginning 3/30. Students must reply by 5/1 or within 2 weeks of notification.

CONTACT Priscilla Muha, Director of Financial Aid, Saint Mary's College of California, PO Box 4530, Moraga, CA 94575, 925-631-4370 or toll-free 800-800-4SMC. *Fax:* 925-376-2965. *E-mail:* finaid@stmarys-ca.edu.

ST. MARY'S COLLEGE OF MARYLAND
St. Mary's City, MD

Tuition & fees (MD res): $13,630	Average undergraduate aid package: $6500

ABOUT THE INSTITUTION State-supported, coed. 24 undergraduate majors. Federal methodology is used as a basis for awarding need-based institutional aid.

UNDERGRADUATE EXPENSES for 2010–11 *Tuition, state resident:* full-time $11,325; part-time $185 per credit hour. *Tuition, nonresident:* full-time $22,718; part-time $185 per credit hour. *Required fees:* full-time $2305. Full-time tuition and fees vary according to course load. Part-time tuition and fees vary according to course load. *College room and board:* $10,245; *Room only:* $5745. Room and board charges vary according to board plan and housing facility. *Payment plan:* Installment.

FRESHMAN FINANCIAL AID (Fall 2008) 320 applied for aid; of those 64% were deemed to have need. 100% of freshmen with need received aid. *Average percent of need met:* 59% (excluding resources awarded to replace EFC). *Average financial aid package:* $7500 (excluding resources awarded to replace EFC). 32% of all full-time freshmen had no need and received non-need-based gift aid.

UNDERGRADUATE FINANCIAL AID (Fall 2008) 1,222 applied for aid; of those 73% were deemed to have need. 100% of undergraduates with need received aid. *Average percent of need met:* 62% (excluding resources awarded to replace EFC). *Average financial aid package:* $6500 (excluding resources awarded to replace EFC). 24% of all full-time undergraduates had no need and received non-need-based gift aid.

GIFT AID (NEED-BASED) *Total amount:* $4,577,492 (18% federal, 26% state, 46% institutional, 10% external sources). *Receiving aid:* Freshmen: 17% (78); all full-time undergraduates: 19% (369). *Average award:* Freshmen: $3000; Undergraduates: $4000. *Scholarships, grants, and awards:* Federal Pell, FSEOG, state, private, college/university gift aid from institutional funds.

GIFT AID (NON-NEED-BASED) *Total amount:* $4,013,722 (13% state, 78% institutional, 9% external sources). *Receiving aid:* Freshmen: 17% (78). Undergraduates: 19% (369). *Average award:* Freshmen: $3000. Undergraduates: $4000. *Scholarships, grants, and awards by category: Academic interests/achievement:* 976 awards ($3,080,179 total): general academic interests/achievements. *Special characteristics:* 200 awards ($901,766 total): children and siblings of alumni, children of faculty/staff. *Tuition waivers:* Full or partial for employees or children of employees, senior citizens.

LOANS *Student loans:* $2,799,533 (100% need-based). 70% of past graduating class borrowed through all loan programs. *Average indebtedness per student:*

$17,125. *Average need-based loan:* Freshmen: $3500. Undergraduates: $6500. *Parent loans:* $5,049,908 (100% non-need-based). *Programs:* FFEL (Subsidized and Unsubsidized Stafford, PLUS), Perkins.

WORK-STUDY *Federal work-study:* Total amount: $61,214; 92 jobs averaging $562. *State or other work-study/employment:* Part-time jobs available.

APPLYING FOR FINANCIAL AID *Required financial aid form:* FAFSA. *Financial aid deadline:* 3/1. *Notification date:* 4/1. Students must reply by 5/1.

CONTACT Tim Wolfe, Director of Financial Aid, St. Mary's College of Maryland, 18952 East Fisher Road, St. Mary's City, MD 20686-3001, 240-895-3000 or toll-free 800-492-7181. *Fax:* 240-895-4959. *E-mail:* tawolfe@smcm.edu.

ST. MARY'S UNIVERSITY
San Antonio, TX

Tuition & fees: $22,556	Average undergraduate aid package: $20,138

ABOUT THE INSTITUTION Independent Roman Catholic, coed. 39 undergraduate majors. Federal methodology is used as a basis for awarding need-based institutional aid.

UNDERGRADUATE EXPENSES for 2010–11 *Comprehensive fee:* $30,106 includes full-time tuition ($21,980), mandatory fees ($576), and room and board ($7550). *College room only:* $4750. Room and board charges vary according to board plan and housing facility. *Part-time tuition:* $660 per credit hour. *Part-time fees:* $163 per term. *Payment plans:* Tuition prepayment, installment.

FRESHMAN FINANCIAL AID (Fall 2009, est.) 469 applied for aid; of those 93% were deemed to have need. 100% of freshmen with need received aid; of those 31% had need fully met. *Average percent of need met:* 83% (excluding resources awarded to replace EFC). *Average financial aid package:* $22,432 (excluding resources awarded to replace EFC). 18% of all full-time freshmen had no need and received non-need-based gift aid.

UNDERGRADUATE FINANCIAL AID (Fall 2009, est.) 1,747 applied for aid; of those 93% were deemed to have need. 100% of undergraduates with need received aid; of those 25% had need fully met. *Average percent of need met:* 76% (excluding resources awarded to replace EFC). *Average financial aid package:* $20,138 (excluding resources awarded to replace EFC). 25% of all full-time undergraduates had no need and received non-need-based gift aid.

GIFT AID (NEED-BASED) *Total amount:* $22,847,289 (22% federal, 27% state, 50% institutional, 1% external sources). *Receiving aid:* Freshmen: 81% (431); all full-time undergraduates: 77% (1,581). *Average award:* Freshmen: $16,094; Undergraduates: $14,206. *Scholarships, grants, and awards:* Federal Pell, FSEOG, state, private, college/university gift aid from institutional funds.

GIFT AID (NON-NEED-BASED) *Total amount:* $4,281,285 (99% institutional, 1% external sources). *Average award:* Freshmen: $8263. Undergraduates: $7292. *Scholarships, grants, and awards by category:* Academic interests/achievement: general academic interests/achievements, military science. *Creative arts/performance:* music. *Special achievements/activities:* cheerleading/drum major. *Tuition waivers:* Full or partial for employees or children of employees.

LOANS *Student loans:* $17,419,259 (76% need-based, 24% non-need-based). 79% of past graduating class borrowed through all loan programs. *Average indebtedness per student:* $22,592. *Average need-based loan:* Freshmen: $6549. Undergraduates: $6124. *Parent loans:* $1,214,138 (56% need-based, 44% non-need-based). *Programs:* FFEL (Subsidized and Unsubsidized Stafford, PLUS), Perkins, state, alternative loans.

WORK-STUDY *Federal work-study:* Total amount: $1,888,839; jobs available. *State or other work-study/employment:* Total amount: $452,301 (61% need-based, 39% non-need-based). Part-time jobs available.

ATHLETIC AWARDS Total amount: $2,069,139 (44% need-based, 56% non-need-based).

APPLYING FOR FINANCIAL AID *Required financial aid form:* FAFSA. *Financial aid deadline:* Continuous. *Notification date:* 3/15. Students must reply within 2 weeks of notification.

CONTACT Mr. David R. Krause, Director of Financial Assistance, St. Mary's University, One Camino Santa Maria, San Antonio, TX 78228-8541, 210-436-3141 or toll-free 800-FOR-STMU. *Fax:* 210-431-2221. *E-mail:* dkrause@alvin.stmarytx.edu.

SAINT MARY'S UNIVERSITY OF MINNESOTA
Winona, MN

Tuition & fees: $26,090	Average undergraduate aid package: $19,846

ABOUT THE INSTITUTION Independent Roman Catholic, coed. 60 undergraduate majors. Federal methodology is used as a basis for awarding need-based institutional aid.

UNDERGRADUATE EXPENSES for 2010–11 *Comprehensive fee:* $33,030 includes full-time tuition ($25,600), mandatory fees ($490), and room and board ($6940). *College room only:* $3880. Full-time tuition and fees vary according to course load, degree level, location, and program. Room and board charges vary according to housing facility. *Part-time tuition:* $850 per credit. *Part-time fees:* $490 per year. Part-time tuition and fees vary according to course load, degree level, location, and program. *Payment plan:* Installment.

FRESHMAN FINANCIAL AID (Fall 2009, est.) 300 applied for aid; of those 90% were deemed to have need. 100% of freshmen with need received aid; of those 19% had need fully met. *Average percent of need met:* 82% (excluding resources awarded to replace EFC). *Average financial aid package:* $20,617 (excluding resources awarded to replace EFC). 18% of all full-time freshmen had no need and received non-need-based gift aid.

UNDERGRADUATE FINANCIAL AID (Fall 2009, est.) 1,139 applied for aid; of those 90% were deemed to have need. 100% of undergraduates with need received aid; of those 21% had need fully met. *Average percent of need met:* 76% (excluding resources awarded to replace EFC). *Average financial aid package:* $19,846 (excluding resources awarded to replace EFC). 25% of all full-time undergraduates had no need and received non-need-based gift aid.

GIFT AID (NEED-BASED) *Total amount:* $16,537,478 (11% federal, 8% state, 79% institutional, 2% external sources). *Receiving aid:* Freshmen: 82% (269); all full-time undergraduates: 73% (1,021). *Average award:* Freshmen: $16,374; Undergraduates: $15,012. *Scholarships, grants, and awards:* Federal Pell, FSEOG, state, college/university gift aid from institutional funds.

GIFT AID (NON-NEED-BASED) *Average award:* Freshmen: $8672. Undergraduates: $9361. *Scholarships, grants, and awards by category:* Academic interests/achievement: 607 awards ($3,571,250 total): general academic interests/achievements. *Creative arts/performance:* 95 awards ($126,000 total): art/fine arts, music, theater/drama. *Special achievements/activities:* 152 awards ($813,500 total): leadership. *Special characteristics:* 302 awards ($2,325,079 total): children and siblings of alumni, children of faculty/staff, international students, members of minority groups. *Tuition waivers:* Full or partial for employees or children of employees.

LOANS *Student loans:* $8,888,010 (100% need-based). 77% of past graduating class borrowed through all loan programs. *Average indebtedness per student:* $32,166. *Average need-based loan:* Freshmen: $4091. Undergraduates: $4884. *Parent loans:* $968,620 (100% need-based). *Programs:* FFEL (Subsidized and Unsubsidized Stafford, PLUS), Perkins, state.

WORK-STUDY *Federal work-study:* Total amount: $318,550; 183 jobs averaging $1629. *State or other work-study/employment:* Total amount: $848,883 (100% need-based). 385 part-time jobs averaging $1635.

APPLYING FOR FINANCIAL AID *Required financial aid form:* FAFSA. *Financial aid deadline (priority):* 3/15. *Notification date:* Continuous. Students must reply within 3 weeks of notification.

CONTACT Ms. Jayne P. Wobig, Director of Financial Aid, Saint Mary's University of Minnesota, 700 Terrace Heights, #5, Winona, MN 55987-1399, 507-457-1437 or toll-free 800-635-5987. *Fax:* 507-457-6698. *E-mail:* jwobig@smumn.edu.

SAINT MICHAEL'S COLLEGE
Colchester, VT

Tuition & fees: $34,845	Average undergraduate aid package: $21,928

ABOUT THE INSTITUTION Independent Roman Catholic, coed. 37 undergraduate majors. Federal methodology is used as a basis for awarding need-based institutional aid.

UNDERGRADUATE EXPENSES for 2010–11 *Comprehensive fee:* $43,530 includes full-time tuition ($34,555), mandatory fees ($290), and room and board ($8685). Room and board charges vary according to housing facility. *Part-time tuition:* $1155 per credit. *Payment plan:* Installment.

FRESHMAN FINANCIAL AID (Fall 2009, est.) 388 applied for aid; of those 82% were deemed to have need. 100% of freshmen with need received aid; of those 27% had need fully met. *Average percent of need met:* 81% (excluding resources awarded to replace EFC). *Average financial aid package:* $28,393 (excluding resources awarded to replace EFC). 29% of all full-time freshmen had no need and received non-need-based gift aid.

UNDERGRADUATE FINANCIAL AID (Fall 2009, est.) 1,400 applied for aid; of those 84% were deemed to have need. 100% of undergraduates with need received aid; of those 23% had need fully met. *Average percent of need met:* 77% (excluding resources awarded to replace EFC). *Average financial aid package:* $21,928 (excluding resources awarded to replace EFC). 28% of all full-time undergraduates had no need and received non-need-based gift aid.

GIFT AID (NEED-BASED) *Total amount:* $18,551,814 (9% federal, 3% state, 86% institutional, 2% external sources). *Receiving aid:* Freshmen: 66% (312); all full-time undergraduates: 60% (1,131). *Average award:* Freshmen: $17,779; Undergraduates: $16,539. *Scholarships, grants, and awards:* Federal Pell, FSEOG, state, private, college/university gift aid from institutional funds.

GIFT AID (NON-NEED-BASED) *Total amount:* $5,533,308 (93% institutional, 7% external sources). *Receiving aid:* Freshmen: 12% (55). Undergraduates: 8% (150). *Average award:* Freshmen: $9195. Undergraduates: $8180. *Scholarships, grants, and awards by category:* Academic interests/achievement: general academic interests/achievements. Creative arts/performance: art/fine arts. Special characteristics: local/state students, members of minority groups, out-of-state students, religious affiliation, siblings of current students. *Tuition waivers:* Full or partial for employees or children of employees.

LOANS *Student loans:* $11,892,372 (72% need-based, 28% non-need-based). 76% of past graduating class borrowed through all loan programs. *Average indebtedness per student:* $30,742. *Average need-based loan:* Freshmen: $4846. Undergraduates: $5270. *Parent loans:* $5,567,868 (70% need-based, 30% non-need-based). *Programs:* Federal Direct (Subsidized and Unsubsidized Stafford, PLUS), FFEL (Subsidized and Unsubsidized Stafford, PLUS), Perkins.

WORK-STUDY *Federal work-study:* Total amount: $649,505; 359 jobs averaging $1430. *State or other work-study/employment:* Total amount: $357,245 (92% need-based, 8% non-need-based). 187 part-time jobs averaging $1375.

ATHLETIC AWARDS Total amount: $829,985 (8% need-based, 92% non-need-based).

APPLYING FOR FINANCIAL AID *Required financial aid forms:* FAFSA, federal income tax forms (student and parent). *Financial aid deadline (priority):* 2/15. *Notification date:* 4/1. Students must reply by 5/1 or within 2 weeks of notification.

CONTACT Mrs. Nelberta B. Lunde, Director of New Student Aid and Scholarship, Saint Michael's College, Winooski Park, Colchester, VT 05439, 802-654-3243 or toll-free 800-762-8000. *Fax:* 802-654-2591. *E-mail:* finaid@smcvt.edu.

ST. NORBERT COLLEGE
De Pere, WI

Tuition & fees: $26,972	Average undergraduate aid package: $24,799

ABOUT THE INSTITUTION Independent Roman Catholic, coed. 31 undergraduate majors. Federal methodology is used as a basis for awarding need-based institutional aid.

UNDERGRADUATE EXPENSES for 2009–10 *Comprehensive fee:* $34,024 includes full-time tuition ($26,522), mandatory fees ($450), and room and board ($7052). *College room only:* $3694. Full-time tuition and fees vary according to course load. Room and board charges vary according to board plan, housing facility, and student level. *Part-time tuition:* $829 per credit. Part-time tuition and fees vary according to course load. *Payment plans:* Installment, deferred payment.

FRESHMAN FINANCIAL AID (Fall 2009, est.) 469 applied for aid; of those 82% were deemed to have need. 100% of freshmen with need received aid; of those 42% had need fully met. *Average percent of need met:* 91% (excluding resources awarded to replace EFC). *Average financial aid package:* $24,838 (excluding resources awarded to replace EFC). 27% of all full-time freshmen had no need and received non-need-based gift aid.

UNDERGRADUATE FINANCIAL AID (Fall 2009, est.) 1,615 applied for aid; of those 85% were deemed to have need. 100% of undergraduates with need received aid; of those 40% had need fully met. *Average percent of need met:* 94% (excluding resources awarded to replace EFC). *Average financial aid package:* $24,799 (excluding resources awarded to replace EFC). 29% of all full-time undergraduates had no need and received non-need-based gift aid.

GIFT AID (NEED-BASED) *Total amount:* $20,703,626 (10% federal, 8% state, 78% institutional, 4% external sources). *Receiving aid:* Freshmen: 69% (374); all full-time undergraduates: 66% (1,337). *Average award:* Freshmen: $20,969; Undergraduates: $19,152. *Scholarships, grants, and awards:* Federal Pell, FSEOG, state, private, college/university gift aid from institutional funds.

GIFT AID (NON-NEED-BASED) *Total amount:* $5,735,503 (1% state, 90% institutional, 9% external sources). *Receiving aid:* Freshmen: 3% (15). Undergraduates: 2% (46). *Average award:* Freshmen: $10,567. Undergraduates: $8957. *Scholarships, grants, and awards by category:* Academic interests/achievement: 1,631 awards ($12,175,798 total): general academic interests/achievements. Creative arts/performance: 79 awards ($93,550 total): art/fine arts, music, theater/drama. Special characteristics: 234 awards ($2,781,070 total): children of faculty/staff, international students. *Tuition waivers:* Full or partial for employees or children of employees.

LOANS *Student loans:* $14,097,174 (91% need-based, 9% non-need-based). 72% of past graduating class borrowed through all loan programs. *Average indebtedness per student:* $30,001. *Average need-based loan:* Freshmen: $3428. Undergraduates: $4566. *Parent loans:* $3,303,817 (78% need-based, 22% non-need-based). *Programs:* Federal Direct (Subsidized and Unsubsidized Stafford, PLUS), Perkins, state, college/university.

WORK-STUDY *Federal work-study:* Total amount: $794,226; 347 jobs averaging $2218. *State or other work-study/employment:* Total amount: $1,970,093 (57% need-based, 43% non-need-based). 670 part-time jobs averaging $2480.

APPLYING FOR FINANCIAL AID *Required financial aid form:* FAFSA. *Financial aid deadline (priority):* 3/1. *Notification date:* Continuous beginning 3/15. Students must reply within 2 weeks of notification.

CONTACT Mr. Jeffrey A. Zahn, Director of Financial Aid, St. Norbert College, 100 Grant Street, De Pere, WI 54115-2099, 920-403-3071 or toll-free 800-236-4878. *Fax:* 920-403-3062. *E-mail:* jeff.zahn@snc.edu.

ST. OLAF COLLEGE
Northfield, MN

Tuition & fees: $35,500	Average undergraduate aid package: $26,401

ABOUT THE INSTITUTION Independent Lutheran, coed. 44 undergraduate majors. Both federal and institutional methodology are used as a basis for awarding need-based institutional aid.

UNDERGRADUATE EXPENSES for 2009–10 *Comprehensive fee:* $43,700 includes full-time tuition ($35,500) and room and board ($8200). *College room only:* $3800. Full-time tuition and fees vary according to course load. Room and board charges vary according to board plan and housing facility. *Part-time tuition:* $1110 per credit hour. Part-time tuition and fees vary according to course load. *Payment plan:* Installment.

FRESHMAN FINANCIAL AID (Fall 2009, est.) 634 applied for aid; of those 81% were deemed to have need. 100% of freshmen with need received aid; of those 100% had need fully met. *Average percent of need met:* 100% (excluding resources awarded to replace EFC). *Average financial aid package:* $28,081 (excluding resources awarded to replace EFC). 16% of all full-time freshmen had no need and received non-need-based gift aid.

UNDERGRADUATE FINANCIAL AID (Fall 2009, est.) 2,698 applied for aid; of those 75% were deemed to have need. 100% of undergraduates with need received aid; of those 100% had need fully met. *Average percent of need met:* 100% (excluding resources awarded to replace EFC). *Average financial aid package:* $26,401 (excluding resources awarded to replace EFC). 23% of all full-time undergraduates had no need and received non-need-based gift aid.

GIFT AID (NEED-BASED) *Total amount:* $42,966,921 (6% federal, 5% state, 85% institutional, 4% external sources). *Receiving aid:* Freshmen: 66% (512); all full-time undergraduates: 66% (2,011). *Average award:* Freshmen: $23,959; Undergraduates: $21,228. *Scholarships, grants, and awards:* Federal Pell, FSEOG, state, private, college/university gift aid from institutional funds.

GIFT AID (NON-NEED-BASED) *Total amount:* $5,056,726 (91% institutional, 9% external sources). *Receiving aid:* Freshmen: 34% (262). Undergraduates: 32% (955). *Average award:* Freshmen: $12,626. Undergraduates: $8048. *Scholarships, grants, and awards by category:* Academic interests/achievement: general academic interests/achievements. Creative arts/performance: music. Special achievements/activities: community service, religious involvement. Special characteristics: international students. *Tuition waivers:* Full or partial for employees or children of employees, senior citizens.

LOANS *Student loans:* $12,839,568 (100% need-based). 66% of past graduating class borrowed through all loan programs. *Average indebtedness per student:*

$25,853. *Average need-based loan:* Freshmen: $5064. Undergraduates: $6575. *Parent loans:* $6,913,733 (100% non-need-based). *Programs:* FFEL (Subsidized and Unsubsidized Stafford, PLUS), Perkins, Federal Nursing, state, college/university.

WORK-STUDY *Federal work-study:* Total amount: $2,061,402; jobs available. *State or other work-study/employment:* Total amount: $2,123,597 (80% need-based, 20% non-need-based). Part-time jobs available.

APPLYING FOR FINANCIAL AID *Required financial aid forms:* FAFSA, CSS Financial Aid PROFILE, noncustodial (divorced/separated) parent's statement, business/farm supplement. *Financial aid deadline:* 4/15 (priority: 1/15). *Notification date:* Continuous beginning 3/1. Students must reply by 5/1.

CONTACT Ms. Katharine Ruby, Assistant Vice President of Enrollment and Dean of Student Financial Aid, St. Olaf College, 1520 Saint Olaf Avenue, Northfield, MN 55057-1098, 507-786-3019 or toll-free 800-800-3025. *Fax:* 507-786-6688. *E-mail:* ruby@stolaf.edu.

SAINT PAUL'S COLLEGE
Lawrenceville, VA

Tuition & fees: $13,210	Average undergraduate aid package: $8147

ABOUT THE INSTITUTION Independent Episcopal, coed. 13 undergraduate majors. Federal methodology is used as a basis for awarding need-based institutional aid.

UNDERGRADUATE EXPENSES for 2009–10 *Comprehensive fee:* $19,850 includes full-time tuition ($11,880), mandatory fees ($1330), and room and board ($6640). *College room only:* $3140. *Part-time tuition:* $495 per credit hour. *Part-time fees:* $29 per credit hour. *Payment plans:* Installment, deferred payment.

FRESHMAN FINANCIAL AID (Fall 2009, est.) 201 applied for aid; of those 98% were deemed to have need. 95% of freshmen with need received aid; of those 3% had need fully met. *Average percent of need met:* 55% (excluding resources awarded to replace EFC). *Average financial aid package:* $8233 (excluding resources awarded to replace EFC).

UNDERGRADUATE FINANCIAL AID (Fall 2009, est.) 613 applied for aid; of those 98% were deemed to have need. 100% of undergraduates with need received aid; of those 11% had need fully met. *Average percent of need met:* 57% (excluding resources awarded to replace EFC). *Average financial aid package:* $8147 (excluding resources awarded to replace EFC).

GIFT AID (NEED-BASED) *Total amount:* $1,956,909 (95% federal, 5% state). *Receiving aid:* Freshmen: 70% (141); all full-time undergraduates: 70% (437). *Average award:* Freshmen: $4009; Undergraduates: $4508. *Scholarships, grants, and awards:* Federal Pell, FSEOG, state, private, college/university gift aid from institutional funds, United Negro College Fund.

GIFT AID (NON-NEED-BASED) *Total amount:* $2,103,577 (62% state, 26% institutional, 12% external sources). *Receiving aid:* Freshmen: 13% (27). Undergraduates: 19% (117). *Scholarships, grants, and awards by category:* Academic interests/achievement: general academic interests/achievements. Special achievements/activities: general special achievements/activities. Special characteristics: children and siblings of alumni, children of faculty/staff, children of union members/company employees. *Tuition waivers:* Full or partial for employees or children of employees.

LOANS *Student loans:* $3,232,885 (99% need-based, 1% non-need-based). 19% of past graduating class borrowed through all loan programs. *Average indebtedness per student:* $21,917. *Average need-based loan:* Freshmen: $997. Undergraduates: $1337. *Parent loans:* $830,448 (100% non-need-based). *Programs:* Federal Direct (Subsidized and Unsubsidized Stafford, PLUS), Perkins.

WORK-STUDY *Federal work-study:* Total amount: $273,276; jobs available.

ATHLETIC AWARDS Total amount: $1,213,256 (100% non-need-based).

APPLYING FOR FINANCIAL AID *Required financial aid form:* FAFSA. *Financial aid deadline (priority):* 5/29. *Notification date:* Continuous. Students must reply by 7/1 or within 4 weeks of notification.

CONTACT Ms. Joan Mayo, Financial Aid Assistant, Saint Paul's College, 115 College Drive, Lawrenceville, VA 23868-1202, 434-848-6496 or toll-free 800-678-7071. *Fax:* 434-848-6498. *E-mail:* aid@saintpauls.edu.

ST. PETERSBURG COLLEGE
St. Petersburg, FL

CONTACT Ray Pranske, Director, Scholarships and Student Financial Assistance, St. Petersburg College, PO Box 13489, St. Petersburg, FL 33733, 813-791-2442. *Fax:* 813-791-2436. *E-mail:* pransker@email.spjc.cc.fl.us.

SAINT PETER'S COLLEGE
Jersey City, NJ

ABOUT THE INSTITUTION Independent Roman Catholic (Jesuit), coed. *Awards:* associate, bachelor's, and master's degrees. 47 undergraduate majors. *Total enrollment:* 3,081. Undergraduates: 2,366. Freshmen: 567.

GIFT AID (NEED-BASED) *Scholarships, grants, and awards:* Federal Pell, FSEOG, state, private, college/university gift aid from institutional funds.

GIFT AID (NON-NEED-BASED) *Scholarships, grants, and awards by category:* Academic interests/achievement: general academic interests/achievements. Special achievements/activities: leadership. Special characteristics: children of faculty/staff, general special characteristics, relatives of clergy, religious affiliation.

LOANS *Programs:* FFEL (Subsidized and Unsubsidized Stafford, PLUS), state.

WORK-STUDY *Federal work-study:* Total amount: $484,025; 244 jobs averaging $1976.

APPLYING FOR FINANCIAL AID *Required financial aid form:* FAFSA.

CONTACT Jennifer Ragsdale, Acting Director of Financial Aid, Saint Peter's College, 2641 Kennedy Boulevard, Jersey City, NJ 07306, 201-761-6071 or toll-free 888-SPC-9933. *Fax:* 201-761-6073. *E-mail:* jragsdale@spc.edu.

ST. THOMAS AQUINAS COLLEGE
Sparkill, NY

CONTACT Margaret McGrail, Director of Financial Aid, St. Thomas Aquinas College, 125 Route 340, Sparkill, NY 10976, 914-398-4097 or toll-free 800-999-STAC.

ST. THOMAS UNIVERSITY
Miami Gardens, FL

Tuition & fees: $21,690	Average undergraduate aid package: N/A

ABOUT THE INSTITUTION Independent Roman Catholic, coed. 28 undergraduate majors. Federal methodology is used as a basis for awarding need-based institutional aid.

UNDERGRADUATE EXPENSES for 2009–10 *Comprehensive fee:* $28,206 includes full-time tuition ($21,690) and room and board ($6516). Full-time tuition and fees vary according to program. Room and board charges vary according to board plan and housing facility. *Part-time tuition:* $434 per credit hour. *Payment plan:* Installment.

FRESHMAN FINANCIAL AID (Fall 2009, est.) 215 applied for aid; of those 92% were deemed to have need. 100% of freshmen with need received aid; of those 19% had need fully met. 16% of all full-time freshmen had no need and received non-need-based gift aid.

UNDERGRADUATE FINANCIAL AID (Fall 2009, est.) 973 applied for aid; of those 83% were deemed to have need. 100% of undergraduates with need received aid; of those 24% had need fully met. 16% of all full-time undergraduates had no need and received non-need-based gift aid.

GIFT AID (NEED-BASED) *Total amount:* $13,341,164 (20% federal, 18% state, 61% institutional, 1% external sources). *Receiving aid:* Freshmen: 61% (146); all full-time undergraduates: 53% (587). *Average award:* Freshmen: $2411; Undergraduates: $2587. *Scholarships, grants, and awards:* Federal Pell, FSEOG, state, private, college/university gift aid from institutional funds.

GIFT AID (NON-NEED-BASED) *Receiving aid:* Freshmen: 83% (198). Undergraduates: 70% (775). *Average award:* Freshmen: $8737. Undergraduates: $6942. *Scholarships, grants, and awards by category:* Academic interests/achievement: general academic interests/achievements. Special achievements/activities: leadership. *Tuition waivers:* Full or partial for minority students, children of alumni, employees or children of employees.

LOANS *Student loans:* $5,287,784 (49% need-based, 51% non-need-based). *Average need-based loan:* Freshmen: $3528. Undergraduates: $4085. *Parent loans:* $125,160 (100% need-based). *Programs:* FFEL (Subsidized and Unsubsidized Stafford, PLUS), Perkins.

WORK-STUDY *Federal work-study:* Total amount: $533,852; jobs available.

ATHLETIC AWARDS Total amount: $1,031,399 (100% need-based).

APPLYING FOR FINANCIAL AID *Required financial aid forms:* FAFSA, state aid form. *Financial aid deadline (priority):* 4/1. *Notification date:* Continuous beginning 3/1.

CONTACT Ms. Anh Do, Director of Financial Aid, St. Thomas University, 16401 Northwest 37th Avenue, Miami, FL 33054, 305-474-6900 or toll-free 800-367-9010. *Fax:* 305-474-6930. *E-mail:* ado@stu.edu.

SAINT VINCENT COLLEGE
Latrobe, PA

Tuition & fees: $27,190	Average undergraduate aid package: $21,705

ABOUT THE INSTITUTION Independent Roman Catholic, coed. 49 undergraduate majors. Federal methodology is used as a basis for awarding need-based institutional aid.

UNDERGRADUATE EXPENSES for 2010–11 *Comprehensive fee:* $36,238 includes full-time tuition ($26,350), mandatory fees ($840), and room and board ($9048). *College room only:* $4896. Room and board charges vary according to board plan and housing facility. *Part-time tuition:* $824 per credit.

FRESHMAN FINANCIAL AID (Fall 2009, est.) 414 applied for aid; of those 79% were deemed to have need. 100% of freshmen with need received aid; of those 26% had need fully met. *Average percent of need met:* 88% (excluding resources awarded to replace EFC). *Average financial aid package:* $23,489 (excluding resources awarded to replace EFC). 26% of all full-time freshmen had no need and received non-need-based gift aid.

UNDERGRADUATE FINANCIAL AID (Fall 2009, est.) 1,492 applied for aid; of those 86% were deemed to have need. 100% of undergraduates with need received aid; of those 25% had need fully met. *Average percent of need met:* 81% (excluding resources awarded to replace EFC). *Average financial aid package:* $21,705 (excluding resources awarded to replace EFC). 23% of all full-time undergraduates had no need and received non-need-based gift aid.

GIFT AID (NEED-BASED) *Total amount:* $19,595,911 (11% federal, 11% state, 76% institutional, 2% external sources). *Receiving aid:* Freshmen: 74% (325); all full-time undergraduates: 77% (1,278). *Average award:* Freshmen: $18,036; Undergraduates: $16,506. *Scholarships, grants, and awards:* Federal Pell, FSEOG, state, private, college/university gift aid from institutional funds.

GIFT AID (NON-NEED-BASED) *Total amount:* $5,822,160 (100% institutional). *Receiving aid:* Freshmen: 10% (42). Undergraduates: 8% (130). *Average award:* Freshmen: $14,510. Undergraduates: $12,349. *Scholarships, grants, and awards by category: Academic interests/achievement:* general academic interests/achievements. *Special achievements/activities:* leadership. *Special characteristics:* children and siblings of alumni, general special characteristics, members of minority groups, religious affiliation.

LOANS *Student loans:* $15,422,087 (41% need-based, 59% non-need-based). 81% of past graduating class borrowed through all loan programs. *Average need-based loan:* Freshmen: $3676. Undergraduates: $4662. *Parent loans:* $4,542,553 (56% need-based, 44% non-need-based). *Programs:* FFEL (Subsidized and Unsubsidized Stafford, PLUS), Perkins.

WORK-STUDY *Federal work-study:* Total amount: $967,292; jobs available. *State or other work-study/employment:* Total amount: $1,156,898 (1% need-based, 99% non-need-based). Part-time jobs available.

APPLYING FOR FINANCIAL AID *Required financial aid forms:* FAFSA, state aid form. *Financial aid deadline:* 5/1 (priority: 3/1). *Notification date:* Continuous beginning 3/5. Students must reply within 4 weeks of notification.

CONTACT Kimberly Woodley, Director of Financial Aid, Saint Vincent College, 300 Fraser Purchase Road, Latrobe, PA 15650, 724-805-2500 or toll-free 800-782-5549. *E-mail:* kimberly.woodley@email.stvincent.edu.

SAINT XAVIER UNIVERSITY
Chicago, IL

Tuition & fees: $24,340	Average undergraduate aid package: $19,878

ABOUT THE INSTITUTION Independent Roman Catholic, coed. 39 undergraduate majors. Federal methodology is used as a basis for awarding need-based institutional aid.

UNDERGRADUATE EXPENSES for 2009–10 *Comprehensive fee:* $32,748 includes full-time tuition ($23,610), mandatory fees ($730), and room and board ($8408). *College room only:* $4897. Room and board charges vary according to board plan and housing facility. *Part-time tuition:* $790 per credit hour. *Part-time fees:* $490 per year. *Payment plan:* Installment.

FRESHMAN FINANCIAL AID (Fall 2009, est.) 433 applied for aid; of those 90% were deemed to have need. 100% of freshmen with need received aid; of those 19% had need fully met. *Average percent of need met:* 84% (excluding resources awarded to replace EFC). *Average financial aid package:* $22,370 (excluding resources awarded to replace EFC). 10% of all full-time freshmen had no need and received non-need-based gift aid.

UNDERGRADUATE FINANCIAL AID (Fall 2009, est.) 2,466 applied for aid; of those 85% were deemed to have need. 100% of undergraduates with need received aid; of those 19% had need fully met. *Average percent of need met:* 80% (excluding resources awarded to replace EFC). *Average financial aid package:* $19,878 (excluding resources awarded to replace EFC). 15% of all full-time undergraduates had no need and received non-need-based gift aid.

GIFT AID (NEED-BASED) *Total amount:* $28,534,625 (22% federal, 22% state, 55% institutional, 1% external sources). *Receiving aid:* Freshmen: 90% (390); all full-time undergraduates: 83% (2,079). *Average award:* Freshmen: $17,704; Undergraduates: $14,015. *Scholarships, grants, and awards:* Federal Pell, FSEOG, state, private, college/university gift aid from institutional funds, United Negro College Fund, Federal Nursing.

GIFT AID (NON-NEED-BASED) *Total amount:* $3,637,503 (2% federal, 96% institutional, 2% external sources). *Receiving aid:* Freshmen: 10% (43). Undergraduates: 8% (196). *Average award:* Freshmen: $11,339. Undergraduates: $9765. *Scholarships, grants, and awards by category: Academic interests/ achievement:* 2,352 awards ($14,467,740 total): general academic interests/ achievements. *Creative arts/performance:* 53 awards ($144,035 total): music. *Special achievements/activities:* leadership. *Special characteristics:* 74 awards ($1,154,790 total): children of faculty/staff. *Tuition waivers:* Full or partial for employees or children of employees, senior citizens.

LOANS *Student loans:* $24,308,792 (71% need-based, 29% non-need-based). 78% of past graduating class borrowed through all loan programs. *Average indebtedness per student:* $26,939. *Average need-based loan:* Freshmen: $3288. Undergraduates: $4626. *Parent loans:* $2,665,210 (25% need-based, 75% non-need-based). *Programs:* FFEL (Subsidized and Unsubsidized Stafford, PLUS), Perkins.

WORK-STUDY *Federal work-study:* Total amount: $4,290,286; 1,478 jobs averaging $2902. *State or other work-study/employment:* Total amount: $382,681 (38% need-based, 62% non-need-based). 49 part-time jobs averaging $7810.

ATHLETIC AWARDS Total amount: $1,981,690 (58% need-based, 42% non-need-based).

APPLYING FOR FINANCIAL AID *Required financial aid form:* FAFSA. *Financial aid deadline (priority):* 3/1. *Notification date:* Continuous beginning 2/16. Students must reply by 5/1 or within 2 weeks of notification.

CONTACT Ms. Susan Swisher, Assistant Vice President for Student Financial Services, Saint Xavier University, 3700 West 103rd Street, Chicago, IL 60655-3105, 773-298-3070 or toll-free 800-462-9288. *Fax:* 773-779-3084. *E-mail:* swisher@sxu.edu.

SALEM COLLEGE
Winston-Salem, NC

Tuition & fees: $21,965	Average undergraduate aid package: $18,755

ABOUT THE INSTITUTION Independent religious, undergraduate: women only; graduate: coed. 32 undergraduate majors. Federal methodology is used as a basis for awarding need-based institutional aid.

UNDERGRADUATE EXPENSES for 2010–11 *Comprehensive fee:* $33,485 includes full-time tuition ($21,610), mandatory fees ($355), and room and board ($11,520). *Part-time tuition:* $1074 per course. Part-time tuition and fees vary according to course load. *Payment plan:* Installment.

FRESHMAN FINANCIAL AID (Fall 2008) 79 applied for aid; of those 71% were deemed to have need. 100% of freshmen with need received aid; of those 100% had need fully met. *Average percent of need met:* 100% (excluding resources

awarded to replace EFC). *Average financial aid package:* $24,045 (excluding resources awarded to replace EFC). 6% of all full-time freshmen had no need and received non-need-based gift aid.

UNDERGRADUATE FINANCIAL AID (Fall 2008) 476 applied for aid; of those 92% were deemed to have need. 100% of undergraduates with need received aid; of those 100% had need fully met. *Average percent of need met:* 100% (excluding resources awarded to replace EFC). *Average financial aid package:* $18,755 (excluding resources awarded to replace EFC). 6% of all full-time undergraduates had no need and received non-need-based gift aid.

GIFT AID (NEED-BASED) *Total amount:* $4,498,786 (29% federal, 15% state, 56% institutional). *Receiving aid:* Freshmen: 45% (53); all full-time undergraduates: 50% (311). *Average award:* Freshmen: $12,023; Undergraduates: $8440. *Scholarships, grants, and awards:* Federal Pell, FSEOG, state, private, college/university gift aid from institutional funds.

GIFT AID (NON-NEED-BASED) *Total amount:* $4,085,420 (19% state, 76% institutional, 5% external sources). *Receiving aid:* Freshmen: 45% (53). Undergraduates: 67% (419). *Average award:* Freshmen: $12,263. Undergraduates: $13,316. *Scholarships, grants, and awards by category: Academic interests/achievement:* 294 awards ($2,582,305 total): general academic interests/achievements. *Creative arts/performance:* 13 awards ($57,340 total): music. *Special achievements/activities:* 17 awards ($324,220 total): leadership. *Special characteristics:* 64 awards ($142,724 total): children of educators, children of faculty/staff, relatives of clergy. *Tuition waivers:* Full or partial for employees or children of employees.

LOANS *Student loans:* $3,493,645 (50% need-based, 50% non-need-based). 70% of past graduating class borrowed through all loan programs. *Average indebtedness per student:* $19,000. *Average need-based loan:* Freshmen: $2924. Undergraduates: $4406. *Parent loans:* $334,643 (100% non-need-based). *Programs:* FFEL (Subsidized and Unsubsidized Stafford, PLUS), Perkins.

WORK-STUDY *Federal work-study:* Total amount: $98,853; 98 jobs averaging $1009. *State or other work-study/employment:* Total amount: $323,688 (100% need-based). Part-time jobs available.

APPLYING FOR FINANCIAL AID *Required financial aid forms:* FAFSA, institution's own form. *Financial aid deadline (priority):* 3/1. *Notification date:* Continuous beginning 3/1. Students must reply by 5/1 or within 2 weeks of notification.

CONTACT Lori A. Lewis, Director of Financial Aid, Salem College, 601 South Church Street, Winston-Salem, NC 27108, 336-721-2808 or toll-free 800-327-2536. *Fax:* 336-917-5584. *E-mail:* lori.lewis@salem.edu.

SALEM INTERNATIONAL UNIVERSITY
Salem, WV

CONTACT Pat Zinsmeister, Vice President for Financial Aid and Compliance, Salem International University, 223 West Main Street, Salem, WV 26426-0500, 304-326-1299 or toll-free 800-283-4562. *Fax:* 304-326-1509. *E-mail:* pzinsmeister@salemu.edu.

SALEM STATE COLLEGE
Salem, MA

Tuition & fees (MA res): $6790   **Average undergraduate aid package: N/A**

ABOUT THE INSTITUTION State-supported, coed. 74 undergraduate majors. Federal methodology is used as a basis for awarding need-based institutional aid.

UNDERGRADUATE EXPENSES for 2009–10 *Tuition, state resident:* full-time $910; part-time $37.92 per credit. *Tuition, nonresident:* full-time $7050; part-time $293.75 per credit. *Required fees:* full-time $5880; $245 per credit. Full-time tuition and fees vary according to class time and course load. Part-time tuition and fees vary according to class time and course load. *College room and board: Room only:* $6625. Room and board charges vary according to board plan and housing facility. *Payment plan:* Installment.

GIFT AID (NEED-BASED) *Total amount:* $14,936,617 (67% federal, 27% state, 6% institutional). *Scholarships, grants, and awards:* Federal Pell, FSEOG, state, private, college/university gift aid from institutional funds, Scholarships for Disadvantaged Students Nursing Grants, MSCBA Housing Grants.

GIFT AID (NON-NEED-BASED) *Total amount:* $1,739,223 (56% state, 21% institutional, 23% external sources). *Scholarships, grants, and awards by category: Academic interests/achievement:* general academic interests/achievements. *Creative arts/performance:* applied art and design, art/fine arts,

creative writing, dance, music, performing arts, theater/drama. *Special achievements/activities:* general special achievements/activities, memberships. *Special characteristics:* adult students, children and siblings of alumni, children of faculty/staff, children of public servants, children of union members/company employees, first-generation college students, general special characteristics, members of minority groups, public servants, veterans, veterans' children. *Tuition waivers:* Full or partial for employees or children of employees, senior citizens.

LOANS *Student loans:* $34,537,043 (47% need-based, 53% non-need-based). *Parent loans:* $2,078,928 (54% need-based, 46% non-need-based). *Programs:* FFEL (Subsidized and Unsubsidized Stafford, PLUS), Perkins, Federal Nursing, state, MEFA Loans, CitiAssist Loans, Sallie Mae SMART Loans.

WORK-STUDY *Federal work-study:* Total amount: $420,493; 286 jobs averaging $3000.

APPLYING FOR FINANCIAL AID *Required financial aid form:* FAFSA. *Financial aid deadline (priority):* 3/1. *Notification date:* Continuous beginning 3/12. Students must reply within 2 weeks of notification.

CONTACT Mary Benda, Director of Financial Aid, Salem State College, 352 Lafayette Street, Salem, MA 01970-5353, 978-542-6139. *Fax:* 978-542-6876.

SALISBURY UNIVERSITY
Salisbury, MD

Tuition & fees (MD res): $6618   **Average undergraduate aid package: $7027**

ABOUT THE INSTITUTION State-supported, coed. 39 undergraduate majors. Federal methodology is used as a basis for awarding need-based institutional aid.

UNDERGRADUATE EXPENSES for 2009–10 *Tuition, state resident:* full-time $4814; part-time $200 per credit hour. *Tuition, nonresident:* full-time $13,310; part-time $553 per credit hour. *Required fees:* full-time $1804; $61 per credit hour. *College room and board:* $8070; *Room only:* $4150. Room and board charges vary according to board plan and housing facility. *Payment plan:* Installment.

FRESHMAN FINANCIAL AID (Fall 2008) 961 applied for aid; of those 51% were deemed to have need. 98% of freshmen with need received aid; of those 23% had need fully met. *Average percent of need met:* 63% (excluding resources awarded to replace EFC). *Average financial aid package:* $6850 (excluding resources awarded to replace EFC). 23% of all full-time freshmen had no need and received non-need-based gift aid.

UNDERGRADUATE FINANCIAL AID (Fall 2008) 4,365 applied for aid; of those 64% were deemed to have need. 96% of undergraduates with need received aid; of those 21% had need fully met. *Average percent of need met:* 60% (excluding resources awarded to replace EFC). *Average financial aid package:* $7027 (excluding resources awarded to replace EFC). 8% of all full-time undergraduates had no need and received non-need-based gift aid.

GIFT AID (NEED-BASED) *Total amount:* $11,180,134 (40% federal, 34% state, 19% institutional, 7% external sources). *Receiving aid:* Freshmen: 35% (423); all full-time undergraduates: 31% (2,053). *Average award:* Freshmen: $5398; Undergraduates: $5256. *Scholarships, grants, and awards:* Federal Pell, FSEOG, state, private, college/university gift aid from institutional funds.

GIFT AID (NON-NEED-BASED) *Total amount:* $2,486,070 (6% federal, 21% state, 51% institutional, 22% external sources). *Average award:* Freshmen: $1730. Undergraduates: $2225. *Scholarships, grants, and awards by category: Academic interests/achievement:* 853 awards ($1,833,335 total): biological sciences, business, communication, computer science, education, English, foreign languages, general academic interests/achievements, health fields, humanities, mathematics, physical sciences, premedicine, social sciences. *Creative arts/performance:* 2 awards ($1500 total): applied art and design, music. *Special characteristics:* 24 awards ($45,000 total): children and siblings of alumni, first-generation college students. *Tuition waivers:* Full or partial for employees or children of employees, senior citizens.

LOANS *Student loans:* $23,496,186 (65% need-based, 35% non-need-based). 56% of past graduating class borrowed through all loan programs. *Average indebtedness per student:* $17,521. *Average need-based loan:* Freshmen: $3002. Undergraduates: $3764. *Parent loans:* $11,994,188 (53% need-based, 47% non-need-based). *Programs:* Federal Direct (Subsidized and Unsubsidized Stafford), Perkins.

WORK-STUDY *Federal work-study:* Total amount: $128,526; 70 jobs averaging $1840. *State or other work-study/employment:* Part-time jobs available.

APPLYING FOR FINANCIAL AID *Required financial aid form:* FAFSA. *Financial aid deadline (priority):* 3/1. *Notification date:* Continuous beginning 3/15. Students must reply by 5/1 or within 2 weeks of notification.

CONTACT Ms. Elizabeth B. Zimmerman, Director of Financial Aid, Salisbury University, 1101 Camden Avenue, Salisbury, MD 21801-6837, 410-543-6165 or toll-free 888-543-0148. *Fax:* 410-543-6138. *E-mail:* ebzimmerman@salisbury.edu.

SALVE REGINA UNIVERSITY
Newport, RI

Tuition & fees: $30,000	Average undergraduate aid package: $20,343

ABOUT THE INSTITUTION Independent Roman Catholic, coed. 45 undergraduate majors. Both federal and institutional methodology are used as a basis for awarding need-based institutional aid.

UNDERGRADUATE EXPENSES for 2009–10 *One-time required fee:* $2350. *Comprehensive fee:* $40,950 includes full-time tuition ($29,800), mandatory fees ($200), and room and board ($10,950). Room and board charges vary according to board plan and housing facility. *Part-time tuition:* $993 per credit hour. *Part-time fees:* $40 per term. Part-time tuition and fees vary according to course load. *Payment plan:* Installment.

FRESHMAN FINANCIAL AID (Fall 2009, est.) 447 applied for aid; of those 89% were deemed to have need. 100% of freshmen with need received aid; of those 7% had need fully met. *Average percent of need met:* 72% (excluding resources awarded to replace EFC). *Average financial aid package:* $22,822 (excluding resources awarded to replace EFC). 13% of all full-time freshmen had no need and received non-need-based gift aid.

UNDERGRADUATE FINANCIAL AID (Fall 2009, est.) 1,609 applied for aid; of those 88% were deemed to have need. 96% of undergraduates with need received aid; of those 6% had need fully met. *Average percent of need met:* 64% (excluding resources awarded to replace EFC). *Average financial aid package:* $20,343 (excluding resources awarded to replace EFC). 10% of all full-time undergraduates had no need and received non-need-based gift aid.

GIFT AID (NEED-BASED) *Total amount:* $21,135,827 (10% federal, 1% state, 86% institutional, 3% external sources). *Receiving aid:* Freshmen: 76% (381); all full-time undergraduates: 67% (1,289). *Average award:* Freshmen: $20,043; Undergraduates: $16,574. *Scholarships, grants, and awards:* Federal Pell, FSEOG, state, private, college/university gift aid from institutional funds.

GIFT AID (NON-NEED-BASED) *Total amount:* $1,764,277 (79% institutional, 21% external sources). *Receiving aid:* Freshmen: 4% (19). Undergraduates: 2% (43). *Average award:* Freshmen: $5815. Undergraduates: $6474. *Scholarships, grants, and awards by category: Academic interests/achievement:* 693 awards ($3,621,600 total): general academic interests/achievements. *Tuition waivers:* Full or partial for employees or children of employees.

LOANS *Student loans:* $14,548,803 (71% need-based, 29% non-need-based). 84% of past graduating class borrowed through all loan programs. *Average indebtedness per student:* $35,553. *Average need-based loan:* Freshmen: $3574. Undergraduates: $4656. *Parent loans:* $6,681,773 (37% need-based, 63% non-need-based). *Programs:* FFEL (Subsidized and Unsubsidized Stafford, PLUS), Perkins, Federal Nursing, college/university, alternative loans.

WORK-STUDY *Federal work-study:* Total amount: $538,547; 405 jobs averaging $1329. *State or other work-study/employment:* Total amount: $240,000 (100% non-need-based). 150 part-time jobs averaging $1400.

APPLYING FOR FINANCIAL AID *Required financial aid forms:* FAFSA, CSS Financial Aid PROFILE, business/farm supplement, Non-custodial Parent Statement. *Financial aid deadline (priority):* 3/1. *Notification date:* Continuous beginning 2/15. Students must reply by 5/1 or within 2 weeks of notification.

CONTACT Aida Mirante, Director of Financial Aid, Salve Regina University, 100 Ochre Point Avenue, Newport, RI 02840-4192, 401-341-2901 or toll-free 888-GO SALVE. *Fax:* 401-341-2928. *E-mail:* financial_aid@salve.edu.

SAMFORD UNIVERSITY
Birmingham, AL

Tuition & fees: $20,420	Average undergraduate aid package: $15,037

ABOUT THE INSTITUTION Independent Baptist, coed. 65 undergraduate majors. Federal methodology is used as a basis for awarding need-based institutional aid.

UNDERGRADUATE EXPENSES for 2009–10 *Comprehensive fee:* $27,044 includes full-time tuition ($20,200), mandatory fees ($220), and room and board ($6624). *College room only:* $3240. Full-time tuition and fees vary according to course load, degree level, and program. Room and board charges vary according to board plan and housing facility. *Part-time tuition:* $675 per credit. *Part-time fees:* $220 per year. Part-time tuition and fees vary according to course load, degree level, and program.

FRESHMAN FINANCIAL AID (Fall 2008) 511 applied for aid; of those 64% were deemed to have need. 100% of freshmen with need received aid; of those 16% had need fully met. *Average percent of need met:* 80% (excluding resources awarded to replace EFC). *Average financial aid package:* $17,144 (excluding resources awarded to replace EFC). 25% of all full-time freshmen had no need and received non-need-based gift aid.

UNDERGRADUATE FINANCIAL AID (Fall 2008) 1,524 applied for aid; of those 72% were deemed to have need. 100% of undergraduates with need received aid; of those 19% had need fully met. *Average percent of need met:* 72% (excluding resources awarded to replace EFC). *Average financial aid package:* $15,037 (excluding resources awarded to replace EFC). 21% of all full-time undergraduates had no need and received non-need-based gift aid.

GIFT AID (NEED-BASED) *Total amount:* $9,497,200 (15% federal, 3% state, 79% institutional, 3% external sources). *Receiving aid:* Freshmen: 44% (313); all full-time undergraduates: 38% (992). *Average award:* Freshmen: $11,672; Undergraduates: $9449. *Scholarships, grants, and awards:* Federal Pell, FSEOG, state, private, college/university gift aid from institutional funds, Federal Nursing.

GIFT AID (NON-NEED-BASED) *Total amount:* $5,224,521 (2% state, 75% institutional, 23% external sources). *Receiving aid:* Freshmen: 24% (170). Undergraduates: 27% (722). *Average award:* Freshmen: $4795. Undergraduates: $6155. *Scholarships, grants, and awards by category: Academic interests/achievement:* 468 awards ($2,861,101 total): biological sciences, business, communication, computer science, education, English, foreign languages, general academic interests/achievements, health fields, humanities, international studies, mathematics, physical sciences, premedicine, religion/biblical studies, social sciences. *Creative arts/performance:* 57 awards ($180,655 total): debating, journalism/publications, music, performing arts, theater/drama. *Special achievements/activities:* 8 awards ($26,500 total): leadership. *Special characteristics:* 72 awards ($854,519 total): children of faculty/staff, relatives of clergy. *Tuition waivers:* Full or partial for employees or children of employees.

LOANS *Student loans:* $14,203,589 (78% need-based, 22% non-need-based). 38% of past graduating class borrowed through all loan programs. *Average indebtedness per student:* $15,702. *Average need-based loan:* Freshmen: $4402. Undergraduates: $4750. *Parent loans:* $14,264,188 (52% need-based, 48% non-need-based). *Programs:* FFEL (Subsidized and Unsubsidized Stafford, PLUS), Perkins, Federal Nursing, college/university.

WORK-STUDY *Federal work-study:* Total amount: $512,880; 314 jobs averaging $1738. *State or other work-study/employment:* Total amount: $908,793 (66% need-based, 34% non-need-based). 598 part-time jobs averaging $1520.

ATHLETIC AWARDS Total amount: $5,313,439 (31% need-based, 69% non-need-based).

APPLYING FOR FINANCIAL AID *Required financial aid forms:* FAFSA, state aid form. *Financial aid deadline (priority):* 3/1. *Notification date:* 4/1. Students must reply by 5/1.

CONTACT Lane Smith, Director of Financial Aid, Samford University, 800 Lakeshore Drive, Birmingham, AL 35229, 205-726-2905 or toll-free 800-888-7218. *Fax:* 205-726-2738. *E-mail:* lsmith1@samford.edu.

SAM HOUSTON STATE UNIVERSITY
Huntsville, TX

Tuition & fees (TX res): $7000	Average undergraduate aid package: $4340

ABOUT THE INSTITUTION State-supported, coed. 43 undergraduate majors. Federal methodology is used as a basis for awarding need-based institutional aid.

UNDERGRADUATE EXPENSES for 2010–11 *Tuition, state resident:* full-time $4890; part-time $163 per credit hour. *Tuition, nonresident:* full-time $14,190; part-time $473 per credit hour. *Required fees:* full-time $2110. Full-time tuition and fees vary according to course level, course load, degree level, location, program, and student level. Part-time tuition and fees vary according to course level, course load, degree level, location, program, and student level. *College room and board:* $7022; *Room only:* $3914. Room and board charges vary according to board plan and housing facility. *Payment plan:* Installment.

FRESHMAN FINANCIAL AID (Fall 2008) 1,529 applied for aid; of those 71% were deemed to have need. 89% of freshmen with need received aid; of those .3% had need fully met. *Average percent of need met:* 36% (excluding resources awarded to replace EFC). *Average financial aid package:* $5832 (excluding resources awarded to replace EFC). 5% of all full-time freshmen had no need and received non-need-based gift aid.

UNDERGRADUATE FINANCIAL AID (Fall 2008) 8,023 applied for aid; of those 46% were deemed to have need. 86% of undergraduates with need received aid; of those .1% had need fully met. *Average percent of need met:* 31% (excluding resources awarded to replace EFC). *Average financial aid package:* $4340 (excluding resources awarded to replace EFC). 6% of all full-time undergraduates had no need and received non-need-based gift aid.

GIFT AID (NEED-BASED) *Total amount:* $22,373,767 (56% federal, 44% state). *Receiving aid:* Freshmen: 27% (556); all full-time undergraduates: 14% (1,652). *Average award:* Freshmen: $1204; Undergraduates: $906. **Scholarships, grants, and awards:** Federal Pell, FSEOG, state, private, college/university gift aid from institutional funds.

GIFT AID (NON-NEED-BASED) *Total amount:* $8,086,251 (1% federal, 13% state, 59% institutional, 27% external sources). *Receiving aid:* Freshmen: 23% (483). Undergraduates: 9% (1,069). *Average award:* Freshmen: $508. Undergraduates: $322. *Scholarships, grants, and awards by category: Academic interests/achievement:* agriculture, biological sciences, business, communication, computer science, education, engineering/technologies, English, foreign languages, general academic interests/achievements, home economics, humanities, library science, mathematics, military science, physical sciences, social sciences. *Creative arts/performance:* art/fine arts, dance, music. *Special achievements/activities:* cheerleading/drum major, general special achievements/activities, leadership, rodeo. *Special characteristics:* general special characteristics, handicapped students. *Tuition waivers:* Full or partial for employees or children of employees.

LOANS *Student loans:* $280,023,529 (93% need-based, 7% non-need-based). 55% of past graduating class borrowed through all loan programs. *Average indebtedness per student:* $6196. *Average need-based loan:* Freshmen: $215. Undergraduates: $189. *Parent loans:* $3,956,008 (100% need-based). *Programs:* Federal Direct (Subsidized and Unsubsidized Stafford, PLUS), FFEL (Subsidized and Unsubsidized Stafford, PLUS), Perkins, state, college/university.

WORK-STUDY *Federal work-study:* Total amount: $37,360; 291 jobs averaging $1563. *State or other work-study/employment:* Total amount: $6081 (100% need-based). 90 part-time jobs averaging $1206.

ATHLETIC AWARDS Total amount: $2,619,777 (100% non-need-based).

APPLYING FOR FINANCIAL AID *Required financial aid forms:* FAFSA, institution's own form. *Financial aid deadline (priority):* 5/31. *Notification date:* Continuous beginning 3/1. Students must reply within 4 weeks of notification.

CONTACT Lisa Tatom, Director of Financial Aid, Sam Houston State University, Box 2328, Huntsville, TX 77341-2328, 936-294-1774 or toll-free 866-232-7528 Ext. 1828. *Fax:* 936-294-3668. *E-mail:* fao.tatom@shsu.edu.

SAMUEL MERRITT UNIVERSITY
Oakland, CA

| Tuition & fees: $34,148 | Average undergraduate aid package: $32,000 |

ABOUT THE INSTITUTION Independent, coed, primarily women. 1 undergraduate major. Federal methodology is used as a basis for awarding need-based institutional aid.

UNDERGRADUATE EXPENSES for 2009–10 *One-time required fee:* $1323. *Tuition:* full-time $34,148; part-time $1439 per unit. Full-time tuition and fees vary according to degree level and program. Part-time tuition and fees vary according to degree level and program. *Payment plan:* Installment.

UNDERGRADUATE FINANCIAL AID (Fall 2009, est.) 495 applied for aid; of those 91% were deemed to have need. 100% of undergraduates with need received aid; of those 4% had need fully met. *Average percent of need met:* 69% (excluding resources awarded to replace EFC). *Average financial aid package:* $32,000 (excluding resources awarded to replace EFC).

GIFT AID (NEED-BASED) *Total amount:* $3,555,228 (23% federal, 18% state, 52% institutional, 7% external sources). *Receiving aid:* All full-time undergraduates: 54% (283). *Average award:* Undergraduates: $20,000. *Scholarships, grants, and awards:* Federal Pell, FSEOG, state, private, college/university gift aid from institutional funds, Federal Nursing.

GIFT AID (NON-NEED-BASED) *Total amount:* $508,333 (100% external sources). *Receiving aid:* Undergraduates: 9% (46).

LOANS *Student loans:* $19,653,052 (21% need-based, 79% non-need-based). *Average need-based loan:* Undergraduates: $10,457. *Parent loans:* $850,994 (70% need-based, 30% non-need-based). *Programs:* FFEL (Subsidized and Unsubsidized Stafford, PLUS), Perkins, Federal Nursing, college/university.

WORK-STUDY *Federal work-study:* Total amount: $190,000; 120 jobs averaging $1583. *State or other work-study/employment:* Part-time jobs available.

APPLYING FOR FINANCIAL AID *Required financial aid form:* FAFSA. *Financial aid deadline (priority):* 3/2. *Notification date:* Continuous beginning 4/15. Students must reply within 2 weeks of notification.

CONTACT Adel Mareghni, Financial Aid Counselor, Samuel Merritt University, 450 30th Street, Oakland, CA 94609, 510-869-6193 or toll-free 800-607-MERRITT. *Fax:* 510-869-1529. *E-mail:* amareghni@samuelmerritt.edu.

SAN DIEGO CHRISTIAN COLLEGE
El Cajon, CA

| Tuition & fees: $22,692 | Average undergraduate aid package: $17,231 |

ABOUT THE INSTITUTION Independent nondenominational, coed. 29 undergraduate majors. Federal methodology is used as a basis for awarding need-based institutional aid.

UNDERGRADUATE EXPENSES for 2010–11 *One-time required fee:* $100. *Comprehensive fee:* $30,952 includes full-time tuition ($21,610), mandatory fees ($1082), and room and board ($8260). Full-time tuition and fees vary according to class time, course load, and program. *Part-time tuition:* $874 per unit. *Part-time fees:* $204 per term. Part-time tuition and fees vary according to class time, course load, and program. *Payment plan:* Installment.

FRESHMAN FINANCIAL AID (Fall 2009, est.) 54 applied for aid; of those 89% were deemed to have need. 100% of freshmen with need received aid; of those 31% had need fully met. *Average percent of need met:* 52% (excluding resources awarded to replace EFC). *Average financial aid package:* $13,222 (excluding resources awarded to replace EFC). 8% of all full-time freshmen had no need and received non-need-based gift aid.

UNDERGRADUATE FINANCIAL AID (Fall 2009, est.) 334 applied for aid; of those 98% were deemed to have need. 92% of undergraduates with need received aid; of those 100% had need fully met. *Average percent of need met:* 80% (excluding resources awarded to replace EFC). *Average financial aid package:* $17,231 (excluding resources awarded to replace EFC). 9% of all full-time undergraduates had no need and received non-need-based gift aid.

GIFT AID (NEED-BASED) *Total amount:* $1,771,721 (42% federal, 42% state, 16% institutional). *Receiving aid:* Freshmen: 48% (30); all full-time undergraduates: 78% (300). *Average award:* Freshmen: $8957; Undergraduates: $15,650. *Scholarships, grants, and awards:* Federal Pell, FSEOG, state, private, college/university gift aid from institutional funds.

GIFT AID (NON-NEED-BASED) *Total amount:* $1,097,949 (94% institutional, 6% external sources). *Receiving aid:* Freshmen: 61% (38). Undergraduates: 72% (277). *Average award:* Freshmen: $4400. Undergraduates: $4792. *Scholarships, grants, and awards by category: Academic interests/achievement:* 196 awards ($514,897 total): general academic interests/achievements. *Creative arts/performance:* 33 awards ($72,350 total): music, performing arts, theater/drama. *Special achievements/activities:* 110 awards ($252,768 total): leadership, religious involvement. *Special characteristics:* 89 awards ($394,141 total): children of faculty/staff, international students, out-of-state students, relatives of clergy, religious affiliation, siblings of current students. *Tuition waivers:* Full or partial for employees or children of employees.

LOANS *Student loans:* $2,409,777 (54% need-based, 46% non-need-based). 72% of past graduating class borrowed through all loan programs. *Average indebtedness per student:* $24,722. *Average need-based loan:* Freshmen: $2493. Undergraduates: $4673. *Parent loans:* $634,482 (100% non-need-based). *Programs:* Federal Direct (Subsidized and Unsubsidized Stafford, PLUS), Perkins.

WORK-STUDY *Federal work-study:* Total amount: $25,900; 12 jobs averaging $2367. *State or other work-study/employment:* Total amount: $22,338 (100% need-based). 15 part-time jobs averaging $1339.

ATHLETIC AWARDS Total amount: $1,056,838 (100% non-need-based).

APPLYING FOR FINANCIAL AID *Required financial aid forms:* FAFSA, institution's own form, state aid form. *Financial aid deadline (priority):* 3/2. *Notification date:* Continuous beginning 2/1. Students must reply by 9/1 or within 4 weeks of notification.

CONTACT Susie Parks, Director of Enrollment Services, San Diego Christian College, 2100 Greenfield Drive, El Cajon, CA 92019, 619-201-8730 or toll-free 800-676-2242. *Fax:* 619-590-2184. *E-mail:* sparks@sdcc.edu.

SAN DIEGO STATE UNIVERSITY
San Diego, CA

Tuition & fees (CA res): $4902	Average undergraduate aid package: $8500

ABOUT THE INSTITUTION State-supported, coed. 103 undergraduate majors. Federal methodology is used as a basis for awarding need-based institutional aid.

UNDERGRADUATE EXPENSES for 2009–10 *Tuition, state resident:* full-time $0. *Tuition, nonresident:* full-time $11,160; part-time $372 per unit. *Required fees:* full-time $4902; $1605 per term. Full-time tuition and fees vary according to degree level. Part-time tuition and fees vary according to course load and degree level. *College room and board:* $11,485. Room and board charges vary according to board plan and housing facility. *Payment plan:* Installment.

FRESHMAN FINANCIAL AID (Fall 2009, est.) 3,200 applied for aid; of those 62% were deemed to have need. 100% of freshmen with need received aid; of those 20% had need fully met. *Average percent of need met:* 71% (excluding resources awarded to replace EFC). *Average financial aid package:* $7700 (excluding resources awarded to replace EFC). 5% of all full-time freshmen had no need and received non-need-based gift aid.

UNDERGRADUATE FINANCIAL AID (Fall 2009, est.) 17,200 applied for aid; of those 72% were deemed to have need. 97% of undergraduates with need received aid; of those 20% had need fully met. *Average percent of need met:* 73% (excluding resources awarded to replace EFC). *Average financial aid package:* $8500 (excluding resources awarded to replace EFC). 5% of all full-time undergraduates had no need and received non-need-based gift aid.

GIFT AID (NEED-BASED) *Total amount:* $66,086,000 (46% federal, 26% state, 28% institutional). *Receiving aid:* Freshmen: 43% (1,400); all full-time undergraduates: 39% (9,000). *Average award:* Freshmen: $7900; Undergraduates: $7100. *Scholarships, grants, and awards:* Federal Pell, FSEOG, state, private, college/university gift aid from institutional funds, Federal Nursing.

GIFT AID (NON-NEED-BASED) *Total amount:* $7,664,000 (37% federal, 26% institutional, 37% external sources). *Receiving aid:* Freshmen: 21% (700). Undergraduates: 11% (2,600). *Average award:* Freshmen: $2400. Undergraduates: $1800. *Scholarships, grants, and awards by category: Academic interests/achievement:* area/ethnic studies, biological sciences, business, communication, computer science, education, engineering/technologies, English, foreign languages, general academic interests/achievements, health fields, international studies, mathematics, military science, physical sciences, religion/biblical studies, social sciences. *Creative arts/performance:* applied art and design, art/fine arts, cinema/film/broadcasting, creative writing, dance, journalism/publications, music, performing arts, theater/drama. *Special achievements/activities:* leadership. *Special characteristics:* adult students, children and siblings of alumni, children of faculty/staff, children of workers in trades, first-generation college students, handicapped students, local/state students, veterans. *Tuition waivers:* Full or partial for employees or children of employees.

LOANS *Student loans:* $102,807,000 (58% need-based, 42% non-need-based). 44% of past graduating class borrowed through all loan programs. *Average indebtedness per student:* $14,700. *Average need-based loan:* Freshmen: $3000. Undergraduates: $4100. *Parent loans:* $61,584,000 (13% need-based, 87% non-need-based). *Programs:* Federal Direct (Subsidized and Unsubsidized Stafford, PLUS), Perkins, college/university.

WORK-STUDY *Federal work-study:* Total amount: $1,416,000; 5,167 jobs averaging $4000.

ATHLETIC AWARDS Total amount: $4,996,000 (100% non-need-based).

APPLYING FOR FINANCIAL AID *Required financial aid forms:* FAFSA, state aid form. *Financial aid deadline:* 3/2. *Notification date:* Continuous.

CONTACT Ms. Chrys Dutton, Director of Financial Aid and Scholarships, San Diego State University, 5500 Campanile Drive, SSW-3605, San Diego, CA 92182-7436, 619-594-6323.

SAN FRANCISCO ART INSTITUTE
San Francisco, CA

CONTACT Erin Zagaski, Interim Director of Financial Aid, San Francisco Art Institute, 800 Chestnut Street, San Francisco, CA 94133-2299, 415-749-4513 or toll-free 800-345-SFAI. *Fax:* 415-351-3503.

SAN FRANCISCO CONSERVATORY OF MUSIC
San Francisco, CA

Tuition & fees: $35,180	Average undergraduate aid package: $22,952

ABOUT THE INSTITUTION Independent, coed. 7 undergraduate majors. Federal methodology is used as a basis for awarding need-based institutional aid.

UNDERGRADUATE EXPENSES for 2010–11 *Tuition:* full-time $34,900; part-time $1540 per credit hour. *Required fees:* full-time $280; $280 per year. Part-time tuition and fees vary according to course load. *Payment plan:* Installment.

FRESHMAN FINANCIAL AID (Fall 2009, est.) 42 applied for aid; of those 83% were deemed to have need. 100% of freshmen with need received aid; of those 17% had need fully met. *Average percent of need met:* 67% (excluding resources awarded to replace EFC). *Average financial aid package:* $23,064 (excluding resources awarded to replace EFC). 33% of all full-time freshmen had no need and received non-need-based gift aid.

UNDERGRADUATE FINANCIAL AID (Fall 2009, est.) 127 applied for aid; of those 88% were deemed to have need. 100% of undergraduates with need received aid; of those 14% had need fully met. *Average percent of need met:* 66% (excluding resources awarded to replace EFC). *Average financial aid package:* $22,952 (excluding resources awarded to replace EFC). 37% of all full-time undergraduates had no need and received non-need-based gift aid.

GIFT AID (NEED-BASED) *Total amount:* $1,936,617 (14% federal, 9% state, 76% institutional, 1% external sources). *Receiving aid:* Freshmen: 64% (35); all full-time undergraduates: 60% (112). *Average award:* Freshmen: $19,257; Undergraduates: $17,133. *Scholarships, grants, and awards:* Federal Pell, FSEOG, state, private, college/university gift aid from institutional funds.

GIFT AID (NON-NEED-BASED) *Total amount:* $937,745 (98% institutional, 2% external sources). *Receiving aid:* Freshmen: 4% (2). Undergraduates: 5% (9). *Average award:* Freshmen: $12,777. Undergraduates: $12,389. *Scholarships, grants, and awards by category: Creative arts/performance:* music. *Tuition waivers:* Full or partial for employees or children of employees.

LOANS *Student loans:* $1,125,248 (79% need-based, 21% non-need-based). 69% of past graduating class borrowed through all loan programs. *Average indebtedness per student:* $15,454. *Average need-based loan:* Freshmen: $4038. Undergraduates: $6127. *Parent loans:* $1,902,699 (37% need-based, 63% non-need-based). *Programs:* FFEL (Subsidized and Unsubsidized Stafford, PLUS), Perkins.

WORK-STUDY *Federal work-study:* Total amount: $22,400; jobs available. *State or other work-study/employment:* Total amount: $5300 (100% non-need-based). Part-time jobs available.

APPLYING FOR FINANCIAL AID *Required financial aid forms:* FAFSA, institution's own form. *Financial aid deadline (priority):* 2/17. *Notification date:* Continuous beginning 4/1. Students must reply by 5/1 or within 2 weeks of notification.

CONTACT Doris Howard, Director of Financial Aid, San Francisco Conservatory of Music, 50 Oak Street, San Francisco, CA 94102-6011, 415-503-6214. *Fax:* 415-503-6299. *E-mail:* dbh@sfcm.edu.

SAN FRANCISCO STATE UNIVERSITY
San Francisco, CA

Tuition & fees (CA res): $4740	Average undergraduate aid package: $10,668

ABOUT THE INSTITUTION State-supported, coed. 91 undergraduate majors. Federal methodology is used as a basis for awarding need-based institutional aid.

UNDERGRADUATE EXPENSES for 2009–10 *Tuition, state resident:* full-time $0. *Tuition, nonresident:* full-time $11,160; part-time $372 per unit. *Required fees:* full-time $4740; $1524 per term. *College room and board:* $10,904; *Room only:* $7116. Room and board charges vary according to board plan and housing facility. *Payment plan:* Installment.

FRESHMAN FINANCIAL AID (Fall 2009, est.) 2,895 applied for aid; of those 75% were deemed to have need. 95% of freshmen with need received aid; of those 8% had need fully met. *Average percent of need met:* 65% (excluding resources awarded to replace EFC). *Average financial aid package:* $10,042 (excluding resources awarded to replace EFC). 1% of all full-time freshmen had no need and received non-need-based gift aid.

UNDERGRADUATE FINANCIAL AID (Fall 2009, est.) 12,475 applied for aid; of those 86% were deemed to have need. 97% of undergraduates with need received aid; of those 7% had need fully met. *Average percent of need met:* 64% (excluding resources awarded to replace EFC). *Average financial aid package:* $10,668 (excluding resources awarded to replace EFC). 1% of all full-time undergraduates had no need and received non-need-based gift aid.

GIFT AID (NEED-BASED) *Total amount:* $79,736,511 (47% federal, 50% state, 1% institutional, 2% external sources). *Receiving aid:* Freshmen: 37% (1,373); all full-time undergraduates: 41% (7,737). *Average award:* Freshmen: $9357; Undergraduates: $8635. *Scholarships, grants, and awards:* Federal Pell, FSEOG, state, private, college/university gift aid from institutional funds.

GIFT AID (NON-NEED-BASED) *Total amount:* $924,781 (35% institutional, 65% external sources). *Receiving aid:* Freshmen: 8% (290). Undergraduates: 4% (843). *Average award:* Freshmen: $3026. Undergraduates: $2799. *Tuition waivers:* Full or partial for employees or children of employees, senior citizens.

LOANS *Student loans:* $66,130,527 (89% need-based, 11% non-need-based). 39% of past graduating class borrowed through all loan programs. *Average indebtedness per student:* $15,684. *Average need-based loan:* Freshmen: $2567. Undergraduates: $3245. *Parent loans:* $21,630,957 (63% need-based, 37% non-need-based). *Programs:* Federal Direct (Subsidized and Unsubsidized Stafford, PLUS), FFEL (PLUS), Perkins.

WORK-STUDY *Federal work-study:* Total amount: $658,341; jobs available.

ATHLETIC AWARDS Total amount: $342,655 (55% need-based, 45% non-need-based).

APPLYING FOR FINANCIAL AID *Required financial aid form:* FAFSA. *Financial aid deadline (priority):* 3/2. *Notification date:* Continuous beginning 2/1. Students must reply within 2 weeks of notification.

CONTACT Barbara Hubler, Director of Financial Aid, San Francisco State University, 1600 Holloway Avenue, San Francisco, CA 94132-1722, 415-338-7000. *Fax:* 415-338-0949. *E-mail:* finaid@sfsu.edu.

SAN JOSE STATE UNIVERSITY
San Jose, CA

Tuition & fees (CA res): $3992	Average undergraduate aid package: $12,239

ABOUT THE INSTITUTION State-supported, coed. 89 undergraduate majors. Federal methodology is used as a basis for awarding need-based institutional aid.

UNDERGRADUATE EXPENSES for 2009–10 *Tuition, state resident:* full-time $0. *Tuition, nonresident:* full-time $10,170; part-time $339 per unit. *Required fees:* full-time $3992; $1399 per term. *College room and board:* $8663; *Room only:* $4968.

FRESHMAN FINANCIAL AID (Fall 2008) 2,488 applied for aid; of those 74% were deemed to have need. 96% of freshmen with need received aid; of those 46% had need fully met. *Average percent of need met:* 90% (excluding resources awarded to replace EFC). *Average financial aid package:* $12,124 (excluding resources awarded to replace EFC). 1% of all full-time freshmen had no need and received non-need-based gift aid.

UNDERGRADUATE FINANCIAL AID (Fall 2008) 12,503 applied for aid; of those 86% were deemed to have need. 96% of undergraduates with need received aid; of those 36% had need fully met. *Average percent of need met:* 85% (excluding resources awarded to replace EFC). *Average financial aid package:* $12,239 (excluding resources awarded to replace EFC). 1% of all full-time undergraduates had no need and received non-need-based gift aid.

GIFT AID (NEED-BASED) *Total amount:* $57,622,432 (49% federal, 47% state, 2% institutional, 2% external sources). *Receiving aid:* Freshmen: 43% (1,630); all full-time undergraduates: 39% (7,709). *Average award:* Freshmen: $6318; Undergraduates: $6033. *Scholarships, grants, and awards:* Federal Pell, FSEOG, state, private, college/university gift aid from institutional funds, Academic Competitiveness Grants, National SMART Grants, TEACH Grants.

GIFT AID (NON-NEED-BASED) *Total amount:* $1,225,008 (65% institutional, 35% external sources). *Receiving aid:* Freshmen: 1% (56). Undergraduates: 60. *Average award:* Freshmen: $2635. Undergraduates: $3405. *Scholarships, grants, and awards by category:* Academic interests/achievement: general academic interests/achievements.

LOANS *Student loans:* $39,955,654 (86% need-based, 14% non-need-based). 48% of past graduating class borrowed through all loan programs. *Average indebtedness per student:* $12,313. *Average need-based loan:* Freshmen: $4290.

Undergraduates: $5279. *Parent loans:* $3,270,311 (33% need-based, 67% non-need-based). *Programs:* FFEL (Subsidized and Unsubsidized Stafford, PLUS), Perkins, college/university.

WORK-STUDY *Federal work-study:* Total amount: $30,599,687; 6,663 jobs averaging $4592.

ATHLETIC AWARDS Total amount: $18,068,177 (8% need-based, 92% non-need-based).

APPLYING FOR FINANCIAL AID *Required financial aid form:* FAFSA. *Financial aid deadline (priority):* 3/2. *Notification date:* Continuous beginning 4/1.

CONTACT Coleetta McElroy, Interim Director of Financial Aid, San Jose State University, One Washington Square, San Jose, CA 95192-0036, 408-924-6086. *E-mail:* coleetta.mcelroy@sjsu.edu.

SANTA CLARA UNIVERSITY
Santa Clara, CA

Tuition & fees: $36,000	Average undergraduate aid package: $23,774

ABOUT THE INSTITUTION Independent Roman Catholic (Jesuit), coed. 50 undergraduate majors. Both federal and institutional methodology are used as a basis for awarding need-based institutional aid.

UNDERGRADUATE EXPENSES for 2009–10 *Comprehensive fee:* $47,400 includes full-time tuition ($36,000) and room and board ($11,400). Room and board charges vary according to housing facility and student level. *Part-time tuition:* $1200 per unit. Part-time tuition and fees vary according to course load. *Payment plan:* Installment.

FRESHMAN FINANCIAL AID (Fall 2009, est.) 714 applied for aid; of those 71% were deemed to have need. 97% of freshmen with need received aid; of those 42% had need fully met. *Average percent of need met:* 74% (excluding resources awarded to replace EFC). *Average financial aid package:* $26,456 (excluding resources awarded to replace EFC). 25% of all full-time freshmen had no need and received non-need-based gift aid.

UNDERGRADUATE FINANCIAL AID (Fall 2009, est.) 3,049 applied for aid; of those 76% were deemed to have need. 85% of undergraduates with need received aid; of those 39% had need fully met. *Average percent of need met:* 67% (excluding resources awarded to replace EFC). *Average financial aid package:* $23,774 (excluding resources awarded to replace EFC). 26% of all full-time undergraduates had no need and received non-need-based gift aid.

GIFT AID (NEED-BASED) *Total amount:* $33,976,741 (10% federal, 14% state, 76% institutional). *Receiving aid:* Freshmen: 35% (382); all full-time undergraduates: 30% (1,539). *Average award:* Freshmen: $22,031; Undergraduates: $18,666. *Scholarships, grants, and awards:* Federal Pell, FSEOG, state, private, college/university gift aid from institutional funds.

GIFT AID (NON-NEED-BASED) *Total amount:* $22,314,991 (89% institutional, 11% external sources). *Receiving aid:* Freshmen: 19% (204). Undergraduates: 14% (741). *Average award:* Freshmen: $10,373. Undergraduates: $11,557. *Scholarships, grants, and awards by category:* Academic interests/achievement: 2,352 awards ($25,324,717 total): business, engineering/technologies, general academic interests/achievements, military science. *Creative arts/performance:* 36 awards ($181,164 total): dance, debating, music, theater/drama. *Special characteristics:* 100 awards ($3,048,621 total): children and siblings of alumni, children of faculty/staff, children with a deceased or disabled parent, handicapped students. *Tuition waivers:* Full or partial for employees or children of employees.

LOANS *Student loans:* $16,560,447 (33% need-based, 67% non-need-based). 43% of past graduating class borrowed through all loan programs. *Average indebtedness per student:* $23,909. *Average need-based loan:* Freshmen: $3289. Undergraduates: $4461. *Parent loans:* $12,537,095 (100% non-need-based). *Programs:* Federal Direct (Subsidized and Unsubsidized Stafford, PLUS), FFEL (PLUS), Perkins, alternative private loans.

WORK-STUDY *Federal work-study:* Total amount: $1,755,512; 473 jobs averaging $3581.

ATHLETIC AWARDS Total amount: $4,626,647 (100% non-need-based).

APPLYING FOR FINANCIAL AID *Required financial aid forms:* FAFSA, CSS Financial Aid PROFILE. *Financial aid deadline (priority):* 2/1. *Notification date:* 4/1. Students must reply by 5/1 or within 2 weeks of notification.

CONTACT Marta I. Murchison, Associate Director, Systems and Data, Santa Clara University, 500 El Camino Real, Santa Clara, CA 95053, 408-551-6088. *Fax:* 408-551-6085. *E-mail:* mmurchison@scu.edu.

SANTA FE COLLEGE
Gainesville, FL

CONTACT Steven H. Fisher, Director of Financial Aid, Santa Fe College, 3000 NW 83rd Street, Gainesville, FL 32606-6200, 352-395-5480. *Fax:* 352-375-5642. *E-mail:* steve.fisher@santafe.cc.fl.us.

SARAH LAWRENCE COLLEGE
Bronxville, NY

Tuition & fees: N/R	Average undergraduate aid package: $30,802

ABOUT THE INSTITUTION Independent, coed. 110 undergraduate majors. Both federal and institutional methodology are used as a basis for awarding need-based institutional aid.

FRESHMAN FINANCIAL AID (Fall 2009, est.) 261 applied for aid; of those 90% were deemed to have need. 100% of freshmen with need received aid; of those 64% had need fully met. *Average percent of need met:* 87% (excluding resources awarded to replace EFC). *Average financial aid package:* $32,719 (excluding resources awarded to replace EFC).

UNDERGRADUATE FINANCIAL AID (Fall 2009, est.) 866 applied for aid; of those 93% were deemed to have need. 99% of undergraduates with need received aid; of those 64% had need fully met. *Average percent of need met:* 84% (excluding resources awarded to replace EFC). *Average financial aid package:* $30,802 (excluding resources awarded to replace EFC). 1% of all full-time undergraduates had no need and received non-need-based gift aid.

GIFT AID (NEED-BASED) *Total amount:* $21,518,212 (7% federal, 1% state, 91% institutional, 1% external sources). *Receiving aid:* Freshmen: 62% (224); all full-time undergraduates: 56% (736). *Average award:* Freshmen: $31,897; Undergraduates: $28,653. *Scholarships, grants, and awards:* Federal Pell, FSEOG, state, private, college/university gift aid from institutional funds.

GIFT AID (NON-NEED-BASED) *Total amount:* $13,900 (86% institutional, 14% external sources). *Receiving aid:* Freshmen: 1. Undergraduates: 4. *Average award:* Undergraduates: $12,000. *Tuition waivers:* Full or partial for employees or children of employees.

LOANS *Student loans:* $4,588,985 (96% need-based, 4% non-need-based). 52% of past graduating class borrowed through all loan programs. *Average indebtedness per student:* $17,246. *Average need-based loan:* Freshmen: $2435. Undergraduates: $3236. *Parent loans:* $3,899,698 (87% need-based, 13% non-need-based). *Programs:* Federal Direct (Subsidized and Unsubsidized Stafford, PLUS), FFEL (Subsidized and Unsubsidized Stafford, PLUS), Perkins, college/university, Signature Loans, CitiAssist Loans.

WORK-STUDY *Federal work-study:* Total amount: $1,162,660; 696 jobs averaging $1662. *State or other work-study/employment:* Total amount: $52,901 (82% need-based, 18% non-need-based). 33 part-time jobs averaging $1603.

APPLYING FOR FINANCIAL AID *Required financial aid forms:* FAFSA, CSS Financial Aid PROFILE, state aid form, noncustodial (divorced/separated) parent's statement. *Financial aid deadline:* 2/1. *Notification date:* 4/1. Students must reply by 5/1.

CONTACT Ms. Heather McDonnell, Director of Financial Aid, Sarah Lawrence College, One Mead Way, Bronxville, NY 10708, 914-395-2570 or toll-free 800-888-2858. *Fax:* 914-395-2676. *E-mail:* hmcdonn@sarahlawrence.edu.

SAVANNAH COLLEGE OF ART AND DESIGN
Savannah, GA

Tuition & fees: $29,570	Average undergraduate aid package: $14,040

ABOUT THE INSTITUTION Independent, coed. 31 undergraduate majors. Federal methodology is used as a basis for awarding need-based institutional aid.

UNDERGRADUATE EXPENSES for 2010–11 *Comprehensive fee:* $41,320 includes full-time tuition ($29,070), mandatory fees ($500), and room and board ($11,750). Full-time tuition and fees vary according to course load and degree level. Room and board charges vary according to board plan, housing facility, and location. *Part-time tuition:* $646 per quarter hour. Part-time tuition and fees vary according to course load and degree level. *Payment plan:* Installment.

FRESHMAN FINANCIAL AID (Fall 2008) 1,203 applied for aid; of those 84% were deemed to have need. 100% of freshmen with need received aid; of those 8% had need fully met. *Average percent of need met:* 20% (excluding resources awarded to replace EFC). *Average financial aid package:* $13,771 (excluding resources awarded to replace EFC). 28% of all full-time freshmen had no need and received non-need-based gift aid.

UNDERGRADUATE FINANCIAL AID (Fall 2008) 4,631 applied for aid; of those 87% were deemed to have need. 100% of undergraduates with need received aid; of those 7% had need fully met. *Average percent of need met:* 20% (excluding resources awarded to replace EFC). *Average financial aid package:* $14,040 (excluding resources awarded to replace EFC). 29% of all full-time undergraduates had no need and received non-need-based gift aid.

GIFT AID (NEED-BASED) *Total amount:* $11,992,860 (69% federal, 31% institutional). *Receiving aid:* Freshmen: 38% (616); all full-time undergraduates: 28% (2,014). *Average award:* Freshmen: $5149; Undergraduates: $5145. *Scholarships, grants, and awards:* Federal Pell, FSEOG, state, private, college/university gift aid from institutional funds.

GIFT AID (NON-NEED-BASED) *Total amount:* $51,471,445 (7% state, 93% institutional). *Receiving aid:* Freshmen: 55% (888). Undergraduates: 45% (3,225). *Average award:* Freshmen: $7830. Undergraduates: $9576. *Scholarships, grants, and awards by category: Academic interests/achievement:* architecture, education, general academic interests/achievements, humanities. *Creative arts/performance:* art/fine arts, general creative arts/performance. *Special achievements/activities:* general special achievements/activities. *Special characteristics:* general special characteristics. *Tuition waivers:* Full or partial for employees or children of employees.

LOANS *Student loans:* $56,964,906 (82% need-based, 18% non-need-based). *Average need-based loan:* Freshmen: $4413. Undergraduates: $4786. *Parent loans:* $54,345,305 (55% need-based, 45% non-need-based). *Programs:* Federal Direct (Subsidized and Unsubsidized Stafford, PLUS), state.

WORK-STUDY Federal work-study jobs available. *State or other work-study/employment:* Part-time jobs available.

ATHLETIC AWARDS Total amount: $3,909,809 (33% need-based, 67% non-need-based).

APPLYING FOR FINANCIAL AID *Required financial aid forms:* FAFSA, institution's own form, state aid form. *Financial aid deadline (priority):* 2/15. *Notification date:* Continuous beginning 6/1. Students must reply within 4 weeks of notification.

CONTACT Brenda Clark, Director of Financial Aid, Savannah College of Art and Design, PO Box 3146, Savannah, GA 31402-3146, 912-525-6119 or toll-free 800-869-7223. *E-mail:* bclark@scad.edu.

SAVANNAH STATE UNIVERSITY
Savannah, GA

Tuition & fees: N/R	Average undergraduate aid package: N/A

ABOUT THE INSTITUTION State-supported, coed. 30 undergraduate majors. Federal methodology is used as a basis for awarding need-based institutional aid.

GIFT AID (NEED-BASED) *Total amount:* $13,228,387 (100% federal). *Scholarships, grants, and awards:* Federal Pell, FSEOG, state, private, college/university gift aid from institutional funds.

GIFT AID (NON-NEED-BASED) *Total amount:* $4,014,081 (11% federal, 67% state, 3% institutional, 19% external sources). *Scholarships, grants, and awards by category: Academic interests/achievement:* biological sciences, business, computer science, engineering/technologies, English, general academic interests/achievements, humanities, mathematics, military science, physical sciences, social sciences. *Creative arts/performance:* music.

LOANS *Student loans:* $21,228,328 (100% non-need-based). *Parent loans:* $3,368,593 (100% non-need-based). *Programs:* Federal Direct (Subsidized and Unsubsidized Stafford, PLUS), Perkins, state, college/university.

WORK-STUDY *Federal work-study:* Total amount: $383,912; 272 jobs averaging $1411.

ATHLETIC AWARDS Total amount: $732,049 (100% non-need-based).

APPLYING FOR FINANCIAL AID *Required financial aid form:* FAFSA. *Financial aid deadline:* Continuous. *Notification date:* Continuous beginning 4/1. Students must reply within 2 weeks of notification.

CONTACT Adrienne Brown, Director of Financial Aid, Savannah State University, PO Box 20523, Savannah, GA 31404, 912-358-4162 or toll-free 800-788-0478. *Fax:* 912-353-3150. *E-mail:* finaid@savannahstate.edu.

SCHILLER INTERNATIONAL UNIVERSITY
Largo, FL

CONTACT Financial Aid Office, Schiller International University, 300 East Bay Drive, Largo, FL 33770, 727-736-5082 or toll-free 800-336-4133.

SCHOOL OF THE ART INSTITUTE OF CHICAGO
Chicago, IL

ABOUT THE INSTITUTION Independent, coed. 33 undergraduate majors.
GIFT AID (NEED-BASED) *Scholarships, grants, and awards:* Federal Pell, FSEOG, state, private, college/university gift aid from institutional funds.
GIFT AID (NON-NEED-BASED) *Scholarships, grants, and awards by category: Academic interests/achievement:* general academic interests/achievements. *Creative arts/performance:* art/fine arts.
LOANS *Programs:* FFEL (Subsidized and Unsubsidized Stafford, PLUS), Perkins.
WORK-STUDY *Federal work-study:* Total amount: $4,266,972; jobs available. *State or other work-study/employment:* Total amount: $209,652 (17% need-based, 83% non-need-based). Part-time jobs available.
APPLYING FOR FINANCIAL AID *Required financial aid form:* FAFSA.
CONTACT Student Financial Services, School of the Art Institute of Chicago, 36 South Wabash, Suite 1218, Chicago, IL 60603-3103, 312-629-6600 or toll-free 800-232-SAIC. *Fax:* 312-629-6601. *E-mail:* finaid@saic.edu.

SCHOOL OF THE MUSEUM OF FINE ARTS, BOSTON
Boston, MA

Tuition & fees: $30,660	Average undergraduate aid package: $18,204

ABOUT THE INSTITUTION Independent, coed. 20 undergraduate majors. Federal methodology is used as a basis for awarding need-based institutional aid.
UNDERGRADUATE EXPENSES for 2009–10 *One-time required fee:* $125. *Tuition:* full-time $29,540; part-time $1240 per credit hour. Full-time tuition and fees vary according to course load, degree level, and program. Part-time tuition and fees vary according to class time, course load, and program. Room and board charges vary according to housing facility. *Payment plan:* Installment.
FRESHMAN FINANCIAL AID (Fall 2009, est.) 81 applied for aid; of those 100% were deemed to have need. 100% of freshmen with need received aid; of those 16% had need fully met. *Average percent of need met:* 58% (excluding resources awarded to replace EFC). *Average financial aid package:* $19,081 (excluding resources awarded to replace EFC). 10% of all full-time freshmen had no need and received non-need-based gift aid.
UNDERGRADUATE FINANCIAL AID (Fall 2009, est.) 426 applied for aid; of those 100% were deemed to have need. 100% of undergraduates with need received aid; of those 13% had need fully met. *Average percent of need met:* 42% (excluding resources awarded to replace EFC). *Average financial aid package:* $18,204 (excluding resources awarded to replace EFC). 7% of all full-time undergraduates had no need and received non-need-based gift aid.
GIFT AID (NEED-BASED) *Total amount:* $5,924,216 (11% federal, 1% state, 87% institutional, 1% external sources). *Receiving aid:* Freshmen: 69% (70); all full-time undergraduates: 75% (404). *Average award:* Freshmen: $14,944; Undergraduates: $14,091. *Scholarships, grants, and awards:* Federal Pell, FSEOG, state, private, college/university gift aid from institutional funds.
GIFT AID (NON-NEED-BASED) *Total amount:* $473,513 (100% institutional). *Receiving aid:* Freshmen: 27% (28). Undergraduates: 4% (22). *Average award:* Freshmen: $5708. Undergraduates: $20,410. *Scholarships, grants, and awards by category: Creative arts/performance:* art/fine arts. *Special characteristics:* general special characteristics. *Tuition waivers:* Full or partial for employees or children of employees.
LOANS *Student loans:* $3,320,948 (100% need-based). *Average indebtedness per student:* $8179. *Average need-based loan:* Freshmen: $3441. Undergraduates: $4233. *Parent loans:* $2,158,695 (100% need-based). *Programs:* FFEL (Subsidized and Unsubsidized Stafford, PLUS), state.
WORK-STUDY *Federal work-study:* Total amount: $171,440; jobs available.

APPLYING FOR FINANCIAL AID *Required financial aid forms:* FAFSA, institution's own form. *Financial aid deadline (priority):* 3/15. *Notification date:* Continuous beginning 4/15. Students must reply by 5/1.
CONTACT Ms. Elizabeth Goreham, Director of Financial Aid, School of the Museum of Fine Arts, Boston, 230 The Fenway, Boston, MA 02115, 617-369-3684 or toll-free 800-643-6078 (in-state). *Fax:* 617-369-3041.

SCHOOL OF VISUAL ARTS
New York, NY

Tuition & fees: N/R	Average undergraduate aid package: $13,026

ABOUT THE INSTITUTION Proprietary, coed. 15 undergraduate majors. Federal methodology is used as a basis for awarding need-based institutional aid.
FRESHMAN FINANCIAL AID (Fall 2009, est.) 452 applied for aid; of those 88% were deemed to have need. 97% of freshmen with need received aid; of those 1% had need fully met. *Average percent of need met:* 41% (excluding resources awarded to replace EFC). *Average financial aid package:* $12,790 (excluding resources awarded to replace EFC). 5% of all full-time freshmen had no need and received non-need-based gift aid.
UNDERGRADUATE FINANCIAL AID (Fall 2009, est.) 2,010 applied for aid; of those 99% were deemed to have need. 90% of undergraduates with need received aid; of those 1% had need fully met. *Average percent of need met:* 37% (excluding resources awarded to replace EFC). *Average financial aid package:* $13,026 (excluding resources awarded to replace EFC). 7% of all full-time undergraduates had no need and received non-need-based gift aid.
GIFT AID (NEED-BASED) *Total amount:* $12,726,312 (38% federal, 14% state, 45% institutional, 3% external sources). *Receiving aid:* Freshmen: 42% (272); all full-time undergraduates: 38% (1,233). *Average award:* Freshmen: $9473; Undergraduates: $9128. *Scholarships, grants, and awards:* Federal Pell, FSEOG, state, private, college/university gift aid from institutional funds.
GIFT AID (NON-NEED-BASED) *Total amount:* $1,835,020 (3% state, 88% institutional, 9% external sources). *Receiving aid:* Freshmen: 12% (76). Undergraduates: 11% (358). *Average award:* Freshmen: $8600. Undergraduates: $7928. *Scholarships, grants, and awards by category: Creative arts/performance:* art/fine arts. *Tuition waivers:* Full or partial for employees or children of employees.
LOANS *Student loans:* $24,357,404 (90% need-based, 10% non-need-based). 75% of past graduating class borrowed through all loan programs. *Average indebtedness per student:* $37,699. *Average need-based loan:* Freshmen: $3581. Undergraduates: $4656. *Parent loans:* $13,125,424 (85% need-based, 15% non-need-based). *Programs:* Federal Direct (Subsidized and Unsubsidized Stafford, PLUS), FFEL (Subsidized and Unsubsidized Stafford, PLUS), Perkins, alternative loans.
WORK-STUDY *Federal work-study:* Total amount: $576,859; jobs available. *State or other work-study/employment:* Total amount: $336,233 (76% need-based, 24% non-need-based). Part-time jobs available.
APPLYING FOR FINANCIAL AID *Required financial aid forms:* FAFSA, state aid form. *Financial aid deadline:* 3/1 (priority: 2/1). *Notification date:* Continuous beginning 2/15. Students must reply within 4 weeks of notification.
CONTACT Director of Financial Aid, School of Visual Arts, 209 East 23rd Street, New York, NY 10010, 212-592-2030 or toll-free 800-436-4204. *Fax:* 212-592-2029. *E-mail:* fa@sva.edu.

SCHREINER UNIVERSITY
Kerrville, TX

Tuition & fees: $18,731	Average undergraduate aid package: $14,453

ABOUT THE INSTITUTION Independent Presbyterian, coed. 37 undergraduate majors. Federal methodology is used as a basis for awarding need-based institutional aid.
UNDERGRADUATE EXPENSES for 2009–10 *Comprehensive fee:* $27,457 includes full-time tuition ($18,131), mandatory fees ($600), and room and board ($8726). *College room only:* $5050. Room and board charges vary according to board plan and housing facility. *Part-time tuition:* $774 per credit hour. *Part-time fees:* $75 per term. *Payment plan:* Installment.
FRESHMAN FINANCIAL AID (Fall 2009, est.) 242 applied for aid; of those 79% were deemed to have need. 100% of freshmen with need received aid; of those 19% had need fully met. *Average percent of need met:* 75% (excluding

resources awarded to replace EFC). *Average financial aid package:* $14,469 (excluding resources awarded to replace EFC). 26% of all full-time freshmen had no need and received non-need-based gift aid.

UNDERGRADUATE FINANCIAL AID (Fall 2009, est.) 708 applied for aid; of those 86% were deemed to have need. 100% of undergraduates with need received aid; of those 17% had need fully met. *Average percent of need met:* 72% (excluding resources awarded to replace EFC). *Average financial aid package:* $14,453 (excluding resources awarded to replace EFC). 23% of all full-time undergraduates had no need and received non-need-based gift aid.

GIFT AID (NEED-BASED) *Total amount:* $7,210,080 (17% federal, 23% state, 44% institutional, 16% external sources). *Receiving aid:* Freshmen: 70% (191); all full-time undergraduates: 76% (607). *Average award:* Freshmen: $11,815; Undergraduates: $11,211. *Scholarships, grants, and awards:* Federal Pell, FSEOG, state, private, college/university gift aid from institutional funds.

GIFT AID (NON-NEED-BASED) *Total amount:* $1,881,194 (4% state, 78% institutional, 18% external sources). *Receiving aid:* Freshmen: 11% (29). Undergraduates: 9% (75). *Average award:* Freshmen: $6654. Undergraduates: $6612. *Scholarships, grants, and awards by category: Academic interests/achievement:* biological sciences, business, education, English, general academic interests/achievements, mathematics, physical sciences, premedicine, religion/biblical studies, social sciences. *Creative arts/performance:* art/fine arts, journalism/publications, music, theater/drama. *Special achievements/activities:* community service, leadership, memberships, religious involvement. *Special characteristics:* children of faculty/staff, general special characteristics, international students, local/state students, relatives of clergy, religious affiliation, siblings of current students. *Tuition waivers:* Full or partial for employees or children of employees.

LOANS *Student loans:* $5,638,751 (68% need-based, 32% non-need-based). 97% of past graduating class borrowed through all loan programs. *Average indebtedness per student:* $27,986. *Average need-based loan:* Freshmen: $2978. Undergraduates: $3608. *Parent loans:* $1,157,542 (23% need-based, 77% non-need-based). *Programs:* state, alternative loans.

WORK-STUDY *Federal work-study:* Total amount: $50,359; jobs available. *State or other work-study/employment:* Total amount: $413,533 (20% need-based, 80% non-need-based). Part-time jobs available.

APPLYING FOR FINANCIAL AID *Required financial aid forms:* FAFSA, Texas Application for State Financial Aid (TASFA). *Financial aid deadline:* 8/1 (priority: 4/1). *Notification date:* Continuous beginning 2/15. Students must reply within 2 weeks of notification.

CONTACT Toni Bryant, Director of Financial Aid, Schreiner University, 2100 Memorial Boulevard, Kerrville, TX 78028, 830-792-7217 or toll-free 800-343-4919. *Fax:* 830-792-7226. *E-mail:* finaid@schreiner.edu.

SCRIPPS COLLEGE
Claremont, CA

| Tuition & fees: $39,060 | Average undergraduate aid package: $34,330 |

ABOUT THE INSTITUTION Independent, women only. 60 undergraduate majors. Both federal and institutional methodology are used as a basis for awarding need-based institutional aid.

UNDERGRADUATE EXPENSES for 2009–10 *Comprehensive fee:* $50,910 includes full-time tuition ($38,846), mandatory fees ($214), and room and board ($11,850). Full-time tuition and fees vary according to program. Room and board charges vary according to board plan. *Part-time tuition:* $4811 per course. Part-time tuition and fees vary according to program. *Payment plans:* Tuition prepayment, installment.

FRESHMAN FINANCIAL AID (Fall 2009, est.) 96 applied for aid; of those 70% were deemed to have need. 100% of freshmen with need received aid; of those 100% had need fully met. *Average percent of need met:* 100% (excluding resources awarded to replace EFC). *Average financial aid package:* $36,163 (excluding resources awarded to replace EFC). 6% of all full-time freshmen had no need and received non-need-based gift aid.

UNDERGRADUATE FINANCIAL AID (Fall 2009, est.) 475 applied for aid; of those 78% were deemed to have need. 99% of undergraduates with need received aid; of those 100% had need fully met. *Average percent of need met:* 100% (excluding resources awarded to replace EFC). *Average financial aid package:* $34,330 (excluding resources awarded to replace EFC). 8% of all full-time undergraduates had no need and received non-need-based gift aid.

GIFT AID (NEED-BASED) *Total amount:* $11,104,154 (6% federal, 5% state, 87% institutional, 2% external sources). *Receiving aid:* Freshmen: 32% (65);

all full-time undergraduates: 39% (353). *Average award:* Freshmen: $32,284; Undergraduates: $31,456. *Scholarships, grants, and awards:* Federal Pell, FSEOG, state, private, college/university gift aid from institutional funds.

GIFT AID (NON-NEED-BASED) *Total amount:* $1,178,748 (1% state, 95% institutional, 4% external sources). *Average award:* Freshmen: $25,971. Undergraduates: $18,671. *Scholarships, grants, and awards by category: Academic interests/achievement:* general academic interests/achievements. *Special achievements/activities:* leadership. *Tuition waivers:* Full or partial for employees or children of employees.

LOANS *Student loans:* $1,719,415 (83% need-based, 17% non-need-based). 38% of past graduating class borrowed through all loan programs. *Average indebtedness per student:* $11,270. *Average need-based loan:* Freshmen: $2750. Undergraduates: $2614. *Parent loans:* $1,474,088 (100% non-need-based). *Programs:* Federal Direct (Subsidized and Unsubsidized Stafford, PLUS), Perkins, college/university.

WORK-STUDY *Federal work-study:* Total amount: $447,263; 286 jobs averaging $1576. *State or other work-study/employment:* Total amount: $21,600 (100% need-based). 17 part-time jobs averaging $1479.

APPLYING FOR FINANCIAL AID *Required financial aid forms:* FAFSA, CSS Financial Aid PROFILE, noncustodial (divorced/separated) parent's statement, business/farm supplement, verification worksheet, federal income tax form(s). *Financial aid deadline:* 5/1 (priority: 2/1). *Notification date:* 4/1. Students must reply by 5/1.

CONTACT David Levy, Director of Financial Aid, Scripps College, 1030 Columbia Avenue, PMB 1293, Claremont, CA 91711-3948, 909-621-8275 or toll-free 800-770-1333. *Fax:* 909-607-7742. *E-mail:* dlevy@scrippscollege.edu.

SEATTLE PACIFIC UNIVERSITY
Seattle, WA

| Tuition & fees: $27,810 | Average undergraduate aid package: $25,349 |

ABOUT THE INSTITUTION Independent Free Methodist, coed. 46 undergraduate majors. Federal methodology is used as a basis for awarding need-based institutional aid.

UNDERGRADUATE EXPENSES for 2009–10 *Comprehensive fee:* $36,354 includes full-time tuition ($27,450), mandatory fees ($360), and room and board ($8544). *College room only:* $4659. Room and board charges vary according to board plan and housing facility. *Part-time tuition:* $764 per credit. Part-time tuition and fees vary according to course load. *Payment plans:* Installment, deferred payment.

FRESHMAN FINANCIAL AID (Fall 2009, est.) 569 applied for aid; of those 85% were deemed to have need. 100% of freshmen with need received aid; of those 9% had need fully met. *Average percent of need met:* 84% (excluding resources awarded to replace EFC). *Average financial aid package:* $26,110 (excluding resources awarded to replace EFC). 21% of all full-time freshmen had no need and received non-need-based gift aid.

UNDERGRADUATE FINANCIAL AID (Fall 2009, est.) 2,063 applied for aid; of those 87% were deemed to have need. 100% of undergraduates with need received aid; of those 7% had need fully met. *Average percent of need met:* 83% (excluding resources awarded to replace EFC). *Average financial aid package:* $25,349 (excluding resources awarded to replace EFC). 24% of all full-time undergraduates had no need and received non-need-based gift aid.

GIFT AID (NEED-BASED) *Total amount:* $34,313,384 (13% federal, 7% state, 74% institutional, 6% external sources). *Receiving aid:* Freshmen: 73% (479); all full-time undergraduates: 66% (1,754). *Average award:* Freshmen: $24,156; Undergraduates: $21,173. *Scholarships, grants, and awards:* Federal Pell, FSEOG, state, private, college/university gift aid from institutional funds.

GIFT AID (NON-NEED-BASED) *Total amount:* $8,387,493 (88% institutional, 12% external sources). *Average award:* Freshmen: $12,641. Undergraduates: $13,114. *Scholarships, grants, and awards by category: Academic interests/achievement:* 559 awards ($4,189,756 total): engineering/technologies, general academic interests/achievements. *Creative arts/performance:* 36 awards ($58,766 total): art/fine arts, performing arts. *Special characteristics:* 242 awards ($1,268,320 total): children and siblings of alumni, children of faculty/staff, general special characteristics, international students, relatives of clergy, religious affiliation, veterans. *Tuition waivers:* Full or partial for employees or children of employees, senior citizens.

LOANS *Student loans:* $16,861,556 (89% need-based, 11% non-need-based). 70% of past graduating class borrowed through all loan programs. *Average indebtedness per student:* $25,800. *Average need-based loan:* Freshmen: $4975.

Undergraduates: $5136. *Parent loans:* $3,278,939 (79% need-based, 21% non-need-based). *Programs:* Federal Direct (Subsidized and Unsubsidized Stafford, PLUS), Perkins, Federal Nursing, college/university.

WORK-STUDY *Federal work-study:* Total amount: $540,824; 356 jobs averaging $1519. *State or other work-study/employment:* Total amount: $869,983 (100% need-based). 241 part-time jobs averaging $3610.

ATHLETIC AWARDS Total amount: $1,617,321 (56% need-based, 44% non-need-based).

APPLYING FOR FINANCIAL AID *Required financial aid form:* FAFSA. *Financial aid deadline (priority):* 2/1. *Notification date:* Continuous beginning 3/15. Students must reply by 5/1 or within 4 weeks of notification.

CONTACT Mr. Jordan Grant, Director of Student Financial Services, Seattle Pacific University, 3307 Third Avenue West, Seattle, WA 98119-1997, 206-281-2469 or toll-free 800-366-3344. *E-mail:* grantj@spu.edu.

SEATTLE UNIVERSITY
Seattle, WA

Tuition & fees: $29,340	Average undergraduate aid package: $28,428

ABOUT THE INSTITUTION Independent Roman Catholic, coed. 56 undergraduate majors. Federal methodology is used as a basis for awarding need-based institutional aid.

UNDERGRADUATE EXPENSES for 2009–10 *Comprehensive fee:* $38,145 includes full-time tuition ($29,340) and room and board ($8805). *College room only:* $5473. Full-time tuition and fees vary according to course load. Room and board charges vary according to board plan. *Part-time tuition:* $652 per credit hour. Part-time tuition and fees vary according to course load.

FRESHMAN FINANCIAL AID (Fall 2009, est.) 662 applied for aid; of those 76% were deemed to have need. 100% of freshmen with need received aid; of those 18% had need fully met. *Average percent of need met:* 77% (excluding resources awarded to replace EFC). *Average financial aid package:* $26,748 (excluding resources awarded to replace EFC). 1% of all full-time freshmen had no need and received non-need-based gift aid.

UNDERGRADUATE FINANCIAL AID (Fall 2009, est.) 3,316 applied for aid; of those 78% were deemed to have need. 98% of undergraduates with need received aid; of those 23% had need fully met. *Average percent of need met:* 77% (excluding resources awarded to replace EFC). *Average financial aid package:* $28,428 (excluding resources awarded to replace EFC). 1% of all full-time undergraduates had no need and received non-need-based gift aid.

GIFT AID (NEED-BASED) *Total amount:* $49,816,466 (11% federal, 8% state, 75% institutional, 6% external sources). *Receiving aid:* Freshmen: 67% (487); all full-time undergraduates: 60% (2,411). *Average award:* Freshmen: $16,022; Undergraduates: $16,432. *Scholarships, grants, and awards:* Federal Pell, FSEOG, state, private, college/university gift aid from institutional funds, Federal Nursing.

GIFT AID (NON-NEED-BASED) *Total amount:* $1,915,731 (77% federal, 19% institutional, 4% external sources). *Receiving aid:* Freshmen: 9% (63). Undergraduates: 8% (310). *Average award:* Freshmen: $4935. Undergraduates: $5402. *Scholarships, grants, and awards by category: Academic interests/achievement:* general academic interests/achievements. *Creative arts/performance:* art/fine arts, music, theater/drama. *Special achievements/activities:* leadership. *Special characteristics:* children and siblings of alumni, children of educators, children of faculty/staff, members of minority groups, religious affiliation. *Tuition waivers:* Full or partial for employees or children of employees.

LOANS *Student loans:* $23,689,204 (67% need-based, 33% non-need-based). 79% of past graduating class borrowed through all loan programs. *Average indebtedness per student:* $26,665. *Average need-based loan:* Freshmen: $4363. Undergraduates: $4766. *Parent loans:* $5,564,292 (6% need-based, 94% non-need-based). *Programs:* Federal Direct (Subsidized and Unsubsidized Stafford, PLUS), Perkins, Federal Nursing.

WORK-STUDY *Federal work-study:* Total amount: $3,449,281; jobs available. *State or other work-study/employment:* Total amount: $4,813,510 (100% need-based). Part-time jobs available.

ATHLETIC AWARDS Total amount: $3,178,779 (20% need-based, 80% non-need-based).

APPLYING FOR FINANCIAL AID *Required financial aid form:* FAFSA. *Financial aid deadline (priority):* 2/1. *Notification date:* 3/1. Students must reply by 5/1 or within 2 weeks of notification.

CONTACT Ms. Janet Cantelon, Director of Student Financial Services, Seattle University, 901 12th Avenue, PO Box 222000, Seattle, WA 98122-1090, 206-296-2000 or toll-free 800-542-0833 (in-state), 800-426-7123 (out-of-state). *Fax:* 206-296-5755. *E-mail:* financial-aid@seattleu.edu.

SETON HALL UNIVERSITY
South Orange, NJ

CONTACT Office of Enrollment Services, Seton Hall University, 400 South Orange Avenue, South Orange, NJ 07079, 973-761-9350 or toll-free 800-THE HALL (out-of-state). *Fax:* 973-275-2040. *E-mail:* thehall@shu.edu.

SETON HILL UNIVERSITY
Greensburg, PA

Tuition & fees: $26,622	Average undergraduate aid package: $21,411

ABOUT THE INSTITUTION Independent Roman Catholic, coed. 85 undergraduate majors. Federal methodology is used as a basis for awarding need-based institutional aid.

UNDERGRADUATE EXPENSES for 2009–10 *Comprehensive fee:* $35,432 includes full-time tuition ($26,322), mandatory fees ($300), and room and board ($8810). Room and board charges vary according to board plan and housing facility. *Part-time tuition:* $705 per credit. *Part-time fees:* $150 per term. Part-time tuition and fees vary according to course load. *Payment plans:* Installment, deferred payment.

FRESHMAN FINANCIAL AID (Fall 2009, est.) 260 applied for aid; of those 92% were deemed to have need. 100% of freshmen with need received aid; of those 19% had need fully met. *Average percent of need met:* 80% (excluding resources awarded to replace EFC). *Average financial aid package:* $23,712 (excluding resources awarded to replace EFC). 12% of all full-time freshmen had no need and received non-need-based gift aid.

UNDERGRADUATE FINANCIAL AID (Fall 2009, est.) 1,201 applied for aid; of those 93% were deemed to have need. 97% of undergraduates with need received aid; of those 16% had need fully met. *Average percent of need met:* 75% (excluding resources awarded to replace EFC). *Average financial aid package:* $21,411 (excluding resources awarded to replace EFC). 10% of all full-time undergraduates had no need and received non-need-based gift aid.

GIFT AID (NEED-BASED) *Total amount:* $17,214,606 (15% federal, 12% state, 71% institutional, 2% external sources). *Receiving aid:* Freshmen: 81% (237); all full-time undergraduates: 83% (1,078). *Average award:* Freshmen: $19,367; Undergraduates: $16,733. *Scholarships, grants, and awards:* Federal Pell, FSEOG, state, private, college/university gift aid from institutional funds.

GIFT AID (NON-NEED-BASED) *Total amount:* $2,095,570 (2% state, 94% institutional, 4% external sources). *Receiving aid:* Freshmen: 12% (36). Undergraduates: 11% (138). *Average award:* Freshmen: $10,662. Undergraduates: $11,798. *Scholarships, grants, and awards by category: Academic interests/achievement:* 532 awards ($5,013,256 total): biological sciences, business, communication, computer science, education, English, foreign languages, general academic interests/achievements, home economics, humanities, mathematics, physical sciences, premedicine, religion/biblical studies, social sciences. *Creative arts/performance:* 54 awards ($105,580 total): applied art and design, art/fine arts, creative writing, journalism/publications, music, performing arts, theater/drama. *Special achievements/activities:* 399 awards ($760,645 total): community service, general special achievements/activities, leadership, religious involvement. *Special characteristics:* 115 awards ($631,064 total): adult students, children and siblings of alumni, children of faculty/staff, children with a deceased or disabled parent, international students, parents of current students, siblings of current students. *Tuition waivers:* Full or partial for employees or children of employees.

LOANS *Student loans:* $9,724,866 (77% need-based, 23% non-need-based). 91% of past graduating class borrowed through all loan programs. *Average indebtedness per student:* $25,807. *Average need-based loan:* Freshmen: $4672. Undergraduates: $5108. *Parent loans:* $2,088,429 (41% need-based, 59% non-need-based). *Programs:* Federal Direct (Subsidized and Unsubsidized Stafford, PLUS), Perkins, college/university, alternative loans.

WORK-STUDY *Federal work-study:* Total amount: $655,236; 406 jobs averaging $1500. *State or other work-study/employment:* Total amount: $267,959 (12% need-based, 88% non-need-based). 162 part-time jobs averaging $1450.

ATHLETIC AWARDS Total amount: $3,219,045 (65% need-based, 35% non-need-based).

APPLYING FOR FINANCIAL AID *Required financial aid forms:* FAFSA, institution's own form, state aid form. *Financial aid deadline (priority):* 5/1. *Notification date:* Continuous beginning 11/15. Students must reply within 2 weeks of notification.

CONTACT Maryann Dudas, Director of Financial Aid, Seton Hill University, Seton Hill Drive, Greensburg, PA 15601, 724-838-4293 or toll-free 800-826-6234. *Fax:* 724-830-1194. *E-mail:* dudas@setonhill.edu.

SEWANEE: THE UNIVERSITY OF THE SOUTH
Sewanee, TN

ABOUT THE INSTITUTION Independent Episcopal, coed. 40 undergraduate majors.

GIFT AID (NEED-BASED) *Scholarships, grants, and awards:* Federal Pell, FSEOG, state, private, college/university gift aid from institutional funds.

GIFT AID (NON-NEED-BASED) *Scholarships, grants, and awards by category: Academic interests/achievement:* general academic interests/achievements. *Special characteristics:* children of faculty/staff, ethnic background, members of minority groups, relatives of clergy.

LOANS *Programs:* FFEL (Subsidized and Unsubsidized Stafford, PLUS), Perkins, state, college/university, private alternative loans.

APPLYING FOR FINANCIAL AID *Required financial aid forms:* FAFSA, institution's own form, student and/or parent U.S. income tax returns (if applicable).

CONTACT Beth A. Cragar, Associate Dean of Admission for Financial Aid, Sewanee: The University of the South, 735 University Avenue, Sewanee, TN 37383-1000, 931-598-1312 or toll-free 800-522-2234. *Fax:* 931-598-3273.

SHASTA BIBLE COLLEGE
Redding, CA

ABOUT THE INSTITUTION Independent nondenominational, coed. 3 undergraduate majors.

GIFT AID (NEED-BASED) *Scholarships, grants, and awards:* Federal Pell, FSEOG, state, private, college/university gift aid from institutional funds.

GIFT AID (NON-NEED-BASED) *Scholarships, grants, and awards by category: Academic interests/achievement:* education. *Creative arts/performance:* music. *Special achievements/activities:* general special achievements/activities. *Special characteristics:* relatives of clergy, veterans.

APPLYING FOR FINANCIAL AID *Required financial aid forms:* FAFSA, institution's own form, state aid form.

CONTACT Connie Barton, Financial Aid Administrator, Shasta Bible College, 2951 Goodwater Avenue, Redding, CA 96002, 530-221-4275 or toll-free 800-800-45BC (in-state), 800-800-6929 (out-of-state). *Fax:* 530-221-6929. *E-mail:* finaid@shasta.edu.

SHAWNEE STATE UNIVERSITY
Portsmouth, OH

CONTACT Barbara Bradbury, Director of Financial Aid, Shawnee State University, 940 Second Street, Portsmouth, OH 45662-4344, 740-351-3245 or toll-free 800-959-2SSU. *E-mail:* bbradbury@shawnee.edu.

SHAW UNIVERSITY
Raleigh, NC

CONTACT Rochelle King, Director of Financial Aid, Shaw University, 118 East South Street, Raleigh, NC 27601-2399, 919-546-8565 or toll-free 800-214-6683. *Fax:* 919-546-8356. *E-mail:* rking@shawu.edu.

SHENANDOAH UNIVERSITY
Winchester, VA

Tuition & fees: $25,080	Average undergraduate aid package: $16,575

ABOUT THE INSTITUTION Independent United Methodist, coed. 37 undergraduate majors. Federal methodology is used as a basis for awarding need-based institutional aid.

UNDERGRADUATE EXPENSES for 2010–11 *Comprehensive fee:* $33,950 includes full-time tuition ($24,780), mandatory fees ($300), and room and board ($8870). Full-time tuition and fees vary according to course load and program. Room and board charges vary according to board plan and housing facility. *Part-time tuition:* $723 per credit hour. Part-time tuition and fees vary according to course load and program. *Payment plan:* Installment.

FRESHMAN FINANCIAL AID (Fall 2009, est.) 345 applied for aid; of those 100% were deemed to have need. 100% of freshmen with need received aid; of those 26% had need fully met. *Average percent of need met:* 85% (excluding resources awarded to replace EFC). *Average financial aid package:* $16,250 (excluding resources awarded to replace EFC). 13% of all full-time freshmen had no need and received non-need-based gift aid.

UNDERGRADUATE FINANCIAL AID (Fall 2009, est.) 1,205 applied for aid; of those 92% were deemed to have need. 100% of undergraduates with need received aid; of those 26% had need fully met. *Average percent of need met:* 90% (excluding resources awarded to replace EFC). *Average financial aid package:* $16,575 (excluding resources awarded to replace EFC). 9% of all full-time undergraduates had no need and received non-need-based gift aid.

GIFT AID (NEED-BASED) *Total amount:* $4,081,786 (48% federal, 52% institutional). *Receiving aid:* Freshmen: 73% (297); all full-time undergraduates: 55% (891). *Average award:* Freshmen: $6000; Undergraduates: $6000. *Scholarships, grants, and awards:* Federal Pell, FSEOG, state, private, college/university gift aid from institutional funds, Federal Nursing.

GIFT AID (NON-NEED-BASED) *Total amount:* $10,255,233 (26% state, 70% institutional, 4% external sources). *Receiving aid:* Freshmen: 38% (156). Undergraduates: 29% (472). *Average award:* Freshmen: $6000. Undergraduates: $6000. *Scholarships, grants, and awards by category: Academic interests/achievement:* 598 awards ($1,801,223 total): business, general academic interests/achievements. *Creative arts/performance:* 422 awards ($967,862 total): dance, music, performing arts, theater/drama. *Special characteristics:* 173 awards ($763,728 total): children of faculty/staff, local/state students, relatives of clergy, religious affiliation. *Tuition waivers:* Full or partial for employees or children of employees.

LOANS *Student loans:* $13,564,696 (33% need-based, 67% non-need-based). 85% of past graduating class borrowed through all loan programs. *Average indebtedness per student:* $20,000. *Average need-based loan:* Freshmen: $3500. Undergraduates: $5000. *Parent loans:* $9,838,918 (41% need-based, 59% non-need-based). *Programs:* Federal Direct (Subsidized and Unsubsidized Stafford, PLUS), Perkins, Federal Nursing, college/university.

WORK-STUDY *Federal work-study:* Total amount: $901,050; 903 jobs averaging $1500. *State or other work-study/employment:* Total amount: $321,000 (100% non-need-based). 363 part-time jobs averaging $1500.

APPLYING FOR FINANCIAL AID *Required financial aid forms:* FAFSA, state aid form. *Financial aid deadline (priority):* 2/15. *Notification date:* Continuous beginning 3/15. Students must reply within 4 weeks of notification.

CONTACT Nancy Bragg, Director of Financial Aid, Shenandoah University, 1460 University Drive, Winchester, VA 22601-5195, 540-665-4538 or toll-free 800-432-2266. *Fax:* 540-665-4939. *E-mail:* nbragg@su.edu.

SHEPHERD UNIVERSITY
Shepherdstown, WV

Tuition & fees (WV res): $5234	Average undergraduate aid package: $10,791

ABOUT THE INSTITUTION State-supported, coed. 25 undergraduate majors. Federal methodology is used as a basis for awarding need-based institutional aid.

UNDERGRADUATE EXPENSES for 2009–10 *Tuition, state resident:* full-time $5234; part-time $214 per credit hour. *Tuition, nonresident:* full-time $13,574; part-time $561 per credit hour. Full-time tuition and fees vary according to program and reciprocity agreements. Part-time tuition and fees vary according to program. *College room and board:* $7228. Room and board charges vary according to board plan and housing facility. *Payment plan:* Installment.

FRESHMAN FINANCIAL AID (Fall 2008) 632 applied for aid; of those 58% were deemed to have need. 96% of freshmen with need received aid; of those 25% had need fully met. *Average percent of need met:* 89% (excluding resources awarded to replace EFC). *Average financial aid package:* $9881 (excluding resources awarded to replace EFC). 26% of all full-time freshmen had no need and received non-need-based gift aid.

UNDERGRADUATE FINANCIAL AID (Fall 2008) 2,740 applied for aid; of those 59% were deemed to have need. 98% of undergraduates with need received

aid; of those 24% had need fully met. *Average percent of need met:* 84% (excluding resources awarded to replace EFC). *Average financial aid package:* $10,791 (excluding resources awarded to replace EFC). 23% of all full-time undergraduates had no need and received non-need-based gift aid.

GIFT AID (NEED-BASED) *Total amount:* $4,656,749 (68% federal, 28% state, 4% institutional). *Receiving aid:* Freshmen: 34% (238); all full-time undergraduates: 33% (1,057). *Average award:* Freshmen: $4308; Undergraduates: $4145. *Scholarships, grants, and awards:* Federal Pell, FSEOG, state, private, college/university gift aid from institutional funds.

GIFT AID (NON-NEED-BASED) *Total amount:* $4,377,295 (36% state, 53% institutional, 11% external sources). *Receiving aid:* Freshmen: 21% (147). Undergraduates: 14% (447). *Average award:* Freshmen: $7851. Undergraduates: $8775. *Scholarships, grants, and awards by category: Academic interests/achievement:* 370 awards ($1,664,128 total): biological sciences, business, communication, computer science, education, engineering/technologies, English, general academic interests/achievements, health fields, home economics, humanities, mathematics, physical sciences, premedicine, social sciences. *Creative arts/performance:* 39 awards ($199,216 total): applied art and design, art/fine arts, music, performing arts, theater/drama. *Special achievements/activities:* 62 awards ($134,726 total): leadership. *Special characteristics:* 111 awards ($341,276 total): ethnic background, handicapped students, local/state students, members of minority groups, out-of-state students, previous college experience. *Tuition waivers:* Full or partial for minority students, senior citizens.

LOANS *Student loans:* $11,608,783 (46% need-based, 54% non-need-based). 65% of past graduating class borrowed through all loan programs. *Average indebtedness per student:* $20,053. *Average need-based loan:* Freshmen: $3053. Undergraduates: $3888. *Parent loans:* $2,255,590 (100% need-based). *Programs:* Federal Direct (Subsidized and Unsubsidized Stafford, PLUS), Perkins.

WORK-STUDY *Federal work-study:* Total amount: $203,086; 109 jobs averaging $1632. *State or other work-study/employment:* Total amount: $933,665 (100% non-need-based). 435 part-time jobs averaging $2233.

ATHLETIC AWARDS Total amount: $977,482 (100% non-need-based).

APPLYING FOR FINANCIAL AID *Required financial aid forms:* FAFSA, state aid form. *Financial aid deadline (priority):* 3/1. *Notification date:* Continuous beginning 3/30. Students must reply within 2 weeks of notification.

CONTACT Sandra Oerly-Bennett, Financial Aid Office, Shepherd University, PO Box 5000, Shepherdstown, WV 25443-5000, 304-876-5470 or toll-free 800-344-5231. *Fax:* 304-876-5238. *E-mail:* faoweb@shepherd.edu.

SHIMER COLLEGE
Chicago, IL

ABOUT THE INSTITUTION Independent, coed. 7 undergraduate majors.

GIFT AID (NEED-BASED) *Scholarships, grants, and awards:* Federal Pell, FSEOG, state, private, college/university gift aid from institutional funds.

GIFT AID (NON-NEED-BASED) *Scholarships, grants, and awards by category: Academic interests/achievement:* general academic interests/achievements. *Special characteristics:* children and siblings of alumni.

LOANS *Programs:* FFEL (Subsidized and Unsubsidized Stafford, PLUS), Perkins.

WORK-STUDY *Federal work-study:* Total amount: $85,900; 25 jobs averaging $1750. *State or other work-study/employment:* 5 part-time jobs averaging $1750.

APPLYING FOR FINANCIAL AID *Required financial aid forms:* FAFSA, institution's own form.

CONTACT Janet Henthorn, Director of Financial Aid, Shimer College, 3424 South State Street, Chicago, IL 60616, 312-235-3507 or toll-free 800-215-7173. *Fax:* 312-235-3502. *E-mail:* j.henthorn@shimer.edu.

SHIPPENSBURG UNIVERSITY OF PENNSYLVANIA
Shippensburg, PA

Tuition & fees (PA res): $7444	Average undergraduate aid package: $7738

ABOUT THE INSTITUTION State-supported, coed. 35 undergraduate majors. Federal methodology is used as a basis for awarding need-based institutional aid.

UNDERGRADUATE EXPENSES for 2009–10 *Tuition, state resident:* full-time $5554; part-time $231 per credit hour. *Tuition, nonresident:* full-time $13,886;

part-time $579 per credit hour. *Required fees:* full-time $1890; $186 per course or $60 per term. *College room and board:* $7086; *Room only:* $3750. Room and board charges vary according to board plan and housing facility. *Payment plan:* Installment.

FRESHMAN FINANCIAL AID (Fall 2009, est.) 1,508 applied for aid; of those 71% were deemed to have need. 96% of freshmen with need received aid; of those 16% had need fully met. *Average percent of need met:* 67% (excluding resources awarded to replace EFC). *Average financial aid package:* $7701 (excluding resources awarded to replace EFC). 9% of all full-time freshmen had no need and received non-need-based gift aid.

UNDERGRADUATE FINANCIAL AID (Fall 2009, est.) 5,286 applied for aid; of those 72% were deemed to have need. 96% of undergraduates with need received aid; of those 18% had need fully met. *Average percent of need met:* 69% (excluding resources awarded to replace EFC). *Average financial aid package:* $7738 (excluding resources awarded to replace EFC). 8% of all full-time undergraduates had no need and received non-need-based gift aid.

GIFT AID (NEED-BASED) *Total amount:* $14,353,326 (50% federal, 38% state, 5% institutional, 7% external sources). *Receiving aid:* Freshmen: 45% (757); all full-time undergraduates: 39% (2,599). *Average award:* Freshmen: $6298; Undergraduates: $5705. *Scholarships, grants, and awards:* Federal Pell, FSEOG, state, private, college/university gift aid from institutional funds, Academic Competitiveness Grants, National SMART Grants.

GIFT AID (NON-NEED-BASED) *Total amount:* $1,316,640 (1% federal, 2% state, 25% institutional, 72% external sources). *Receiving aid:* Freshmen: 4% (65). Undergraduates: 3% (223). *Average award:* Freshmen: $3978. Undergraduates: $3969. *Scholarships, grants, and awards by category: Academic interests/achievement:* 388 awards ($554,882 total): biological sciences, business, communication, computer science, education, English, foreign languages, general academic interests/achievements, humanities, mathematics, physical sciences, social sciences. *Creative arts/performance:* 5 awards ($3600 total): art/fine arts, music, theater/drama. *Special achievements/activities:* 312 awards ($580,369 total): community service, general special achievements/activities, leadership. *Special characteristics:* 58 awards ($60,354 total): children and siblings of alumni, general special characteristics, handicapped students, local/state students. *Tuition waivers:* Full or partial for employees or children of employees, senior citizens.

LOANS *Student loans:* $35,112,725 (57% need-based, 43% non-need-based). 74% of past graduating class borrowed through all loan programs. *Average indebtedness per student:* $21,163. *Average need-based loan:* Freshmen: $3217. Undergraduates: $3844. *Parent loans:* $4,322,874 (14% need-based, 86% non-need-based). *Programs:* FFEL (Subsidized and Unsubsidized Stafford, PLUS), Perkins, alternative loans.

WORK-STUDY *Federal work-study:* Total amount: $132,842; 114 jobs averaging $1165. *State or other work-study/employment:* Total amount: $220,080 (23% need-based, 77% non-need-based). 204 part-time jobs averaging $1079.

ATHLETIC AWARDS Total amount: $597,480 (48% need-based, 52% non-need-based).

APPLYING FOR FINANCIAL AID *Required financial aid form:* FAFSA. *Financial aid deadline (priority):* 3/15. *Notification date:* Continuous. Students must reply within 2 weeks of notification.

CONTACT Mrs. Trina Snyder, Interim Director of Financial Aid and Scholarships, Shippensburg University of Pennsylvania, 1871 Old Main Drive, Shippensburg, PA 17257-2299, 717-477-1131 or toll-free 800-822-8028 (in-state). *Fax:* 717-477-4028. *E-mail:* finaid@ship.edu.

SHORTER UNIVERSITY
Rome, GA

Tuition & fees: N/R	Average undergraduate aid package: $15,152

ABOUT THE INSTITUTION Independent Baptist, coed. 39 undergraduate majors. Federal methodology is used as a basis for awarding need-based institutional aid.

UNDERGRADUATE EXPENSES for 2010–11 *Tuition:* part-time $440 per credit hour. Full-time tuition and fees vary according to course load. Room and board charges vary according to board plan and housing facility. *Payment plan:* Installment.

FRESHMAN FINANCIAL AID (Fall 2009, est.) 304 applied for aid; of those 86% were deemed to have need. 100% of freshmen with need received aid; of those 26% had need fully met. *Average percent of need met:* 75% (excluding

resources awarded to replace EFC). *Average financial aid package:* $15,043 (excluding resources awarded to replace EFC). 16% of all full-time freshmen had no need and received non-need-based gift aid.

UNDERGRADUATE FINANCIAL AID (Fall 2009, est.) 1,004 applied for aid; of those 85% were deemed to have need. 100% of undergraduates with need received aid; of those 28% had need fully met. *Average percent of need met:* 71% (excluding resources awarded to replace EFC). *Average financial aid package:* $15,152 (excluding resources awarded to replace EFC). 16% of all full-time undergraduates had no need and received non-need-based gift aid.

GIFT AID (NEED-BASED) *Total amount:* $7,700,413 (30% federal, 25% state, 42% institutional, 3% external sources). *Receiving aid:* Freshmen: 78% (260); all full-time undergraduates: 73% (857). *Average award:* Freshmen: $12,687; Undergraduates: $12,411. *Scholarships, grants, and awards:* Federal Pell, FSEOG, state, private, college/university gift aid from institutional funds.

GIFT AID (NON-NEED-BASED) *Total amount:* $2,416,851 (1% federal, 48% state, 46% institutional, 5% external sources). *Receiving aid:* Freshmen: 15% (51). Undergraduates: 15% (176). *Average award:* Freshmen: $5800. Undergraduates: $4845. *Scholarships, grants, and awards by category: Academic interests/achievement:* English, foreign languages, general academic interests/achievements, religion/biblical studies. *Creative arts/performance:* art/fine arts, music, theater/drama. *Special achievements/activities:* cheerleading/drum major, religious involvement. *Special characteristics:* children of faculty/staff, children of union members/company employees, local/state students, out-of-state students, relatives of clergy, religious affiliation, siblings of current students. *Tuition waivers:* Full or partial for employees or children of employees, senior citizens.

LOANS *Student loans:* $5,405,944 (70% need-based, 30% non-need-based). 75% of past graduating class borrowed through all loan programs. *Average indebtedness per student:* $22,967. *Average need-based loan:* Freshmen: $3219. Undergraduates: $3939. *Parent loans:* $2,243,692 (32% need-based, 68% non-need-based). *Programs:* Federal Direct (Subsidized and Unsubsidized Stafford, PLUS), Perkins.

WORK-STUDY *Federal work-study:* Total amount: $233,384; jobs available. *State or other work-study/employment:* Total amount: $216,186 (4% need-based, 96% non-need-based). Part-time jobs available.

ATHLETIC AWARDS Total amount: $3,865,087 (51% need-based, 49% non-need-based).

APPLYING FOR FINANCIAL AID *Required financial aid forms:* FAFSA, institution's own form, state aid form. *Financial aid deadline (priority):* 4/1. *Notification date:* Continuous beginning 4/1. Students must reply within 2 weeks of notification.

CONTACT Tara Jones, Director of Financial Aid, Shorter University, 315 Shorter Avenue, Rome, GA 30165, 706-233-7227 or toll-free 800-868-6980. *Fax:* 706-233-7314. *E-mail:* tjones@shorter.edu.

SH'OR YOSHUV RABBINICAL COLLEGE
Lawrence, NY

CONTACT Office of Financial Aid, Sh'or Yoshuv Rabbinical College, 1526 Central Avenue, Far Rockaway, NY 11691-4002, 718-327-2048.

SIENA COLLEGE
Loudonville, NY

Tuition & fees: $25,285	Average undergraduate aid package: $16,796

ABOUT THE INSTITUTION Independent Roman Catholic, coed. 28 undergraduate majors. Federal methodology is used as a basis for awarding need-based institutional aid.

UNDERGRADUATE EXPENSES for 2009–10 *One-time required fee:* $280. *Comprehensive fee:* $35,215 includes full-time tuition ($25,060), mandatory fees ($225), and room and board ($9930). Full-time tuition and fees vary according to program. Room and board charges vary according to board plan and housing facility. *Part-time tuition:* $450 per credit hour. *Part-time fees:* $160 per term. Part-time tuition and fees vary according to program. *Payment plan:* Installment.

FRESHMAN FINANCIAL AID (Fall 2008) 737 applied for aid; of those 79% were deemed to have need. 100% of freshmen with need received aid; of those 13% had need fully met. *Average percent of need met:* 77% (excluding resources

awarded to replace EFC). *Average financial aid package:* $17,117 (excluding resources awarded to replace EFC). 17% of all full-time freshmen had no need and received non-need-based gift aid.

UNDERGRADUATE FINANCIAL AID (Fall 2008) 2,523 applied for aid; of those 82% were deemed to have need. 99% of undergraduates with need received aid; of those 15% had need fully met. *Average percent of need met:* 74% (excluding resources awarded to replace EFC). *Average financial aid package:* $16,796 (excluding resources awarded to replace EFC). 13% of all full-time undergraduates had no need and received non-need-based gift aid.

GIFT AID (NEED-BASED) *Total amount:* $26,533,706 (9% federal, 12% state, 79% institutional). *Receiving aid:* Freshmen: 68% (560); all full-time undergraduates: 65% (2,010). *Average award:* Freshmen: $14,505; Undergraduates: $12,865. *Scholarships, grants, and awards:* Federal Pell, FSEOG, state, private, college/university gift aid from institutional funds, Siena Grants, Franciscan Community Grants.

GIFT AID (NON-NEED-BASED) *Total amount:* $3,634,472 (3% state, 85% institutional, 12% external sources). *Receiving aid:* Freshmen: 48% (393). Undergraduates: 44% (1,359). *Average award:* Freshmen: $8059. Undergraduates: $8685. *Scholarships, grants, and awards by category: Academic interests/achievement:* biological sciences, business, communication, computer science, education, English, foreign languages, general academic interests/achievements, health fields, home economics, humanities, international studies, mathematics, military science, physical sciences, premedicine, religion/biblical studies, social sciences. *Creative arts/performance:* creative writing, general creative arts/performance, journalism/publications, music, performing arts, theater/drama. *Special achievements/activities:* community service, general special achievements/activities, hobbies/interests, leadership, memberships, religious involvement. *Special characteristics:* adult students, children and siblings of alumni, children of faculty/staff, children of public servants, children of union members/company employees, children of workers in trades, children with a deceased or disabled parent, ethnic background, general special characteristics, local/state students, out-of-state students, previous college experience, relatives of clergy, religious affiliation, veterans' children. *Tuition waivers:* Full or partial for employees or children of employees, senior citizens.

LOANS *Student loans:* $14,980,446 (50% need-based, 50% non-need-based). 77% of past graduating class borrowed through all loan programs. *Average indebtedness per student:* $28,200. *Average need-based loan:* Freshmen: $3307. Undergraduates: $4411. *Parent loans:* $5,357,783 (53% need-based, 47% non-need-based). *Programs:* FFEL (Subsidized and Unsubsidized Stafford, PLUS), Perkins.

WORK-STUDY *Federal work-study:* Total amount: $321,931; 500 jobs averaging $644.

ATHLETIC AWARDS Total amount: $3,262,540 (62% need-based, 38% non-need-based).

APPLYING FOR FINANCIAL AID *Required financial aid forms:* FAFSA, state aid form. *Financial aid deadline (priority):* 2/15. *Notification date:* 4/1. Students must reply by 5/1.

CONTACT Ms. Mary K. Lawyer, Assistant Vice President for Financial Aid, Siena College, 515 Loudon Road, Loudonville, NY 12211-1462, 518-783-2427 or toll-free 888-AT-SIENA. *Fax:* 518-783-2410. *E-mail:* aid@siena.edu.

SIENA HEIGHTS UNIVERSITY
Adrian, MI

CONTACT Office of Financial Aid, Siena Heights University, 1247 East Siena Heights Drive, Adrian, MI 49221, 517-264-7130 or toll-free 800-521-0009.

SIERRA NEVADA COLLEGE
Incline Village, NV

CONTACT Dorothy Caruso, Director of Financial Aid, Sierra Nevada College, 999 Tahoe Boulevard, Incline Village, NV 89451, 775-831-1314 Ext. 4066. *Fax:* 775-831-1347. *E-mail:* dcaruso@sierranevada.edu.

SILICON VALLEY UNIVERSITY
San Jose, CA

CONTACT Financial Aid Office, Silicon Valley University, 2160 Lundy Avenue, Suite 110, San Jose, CA 95131, 408-435-8989.

SILVER LAKE COLLEGE
Manitowoc, WI

Tuition & fees: $21,180	Average undergraduate aid package: $16,479

ABOUT THE INSTITUTION Independent Roman Catholic, coed. 25 undergraduate majors. Federal methodology is used as a basis for awarding need-based institutional aid.

UNDERGRADUATE EXPENSES for 2010–11 *Comprehensive fee:* $27,880 includes full-time tuition ($20,950), mandatory fees ($230), and room and board ($6700). *College room only:* $4800. Full-time tuition and fees vary according to location, program, and reciprocity agreements. Room and board charges vary according to board plan and housing facility. *Part-time tuition:* $625 per credit. *Part-time fees:* $60 per term. Part-time tuition and fees vary according to course load, location, and program. *Payment plans:* Installment, deferred payment.

FRESHMAN FINANCIAL AID (Fall 2009, est.) 30 applied for aid; of those 97% were deemed to have need. 100% of freshmen with need received aid; of those 28% had need fully met. *Average percent of need met:* 77% (excluding resources awarded to replace EFC). *Average financial aid package:* $18,013 (excluding resources awarded to replace EFC). 3% of all full-time freshmen had no need and received non-need-based gift aid.

UNDERGRADUATE FINANCIAL AID (Fall 2009, est.) 154 applied for aid; of those 97% were deemed to have need. 100% of undergraduates with need received aid; of those 15% had need fully met. *Average percent of need met:* 66% (excluding resources awarded to replace EFC). *Average financial aid package:* $16,479 (excluding resources awarded to replace EFC). 5% of all full-time undergraduates had no need and received non-need-based gift aid.

GIFT AID (NEED-BASED) *Total amount:* $1,868,527 (38% federal, 12% state, 48% institutional, 2% external sources). *Receiving aid:* Freshmen: 97% (29); all full-time undergraduates: 81% (144). *Average award:* Freshmen: $8835; Undergraduates: $9146. *Scholarships, grants, and awards:* Federal Pell, FSEOG, state, private, college/university gift aid from institutional funds.

GIFT AID (NON-NEED-BASED) *Total amount:* $116,336 (36% federal, 61% institutional, 3% external sources). *Receiving aid:* Freshmen: 87% (26). Undergraduates: 55% (97). *Average award:* Freshmen: $1000. Undergraduates: $6602. *Scholarships, grants, and awards by category: Academic interests/achievement:* 71 awards ($268,519 total): English, general academic interests/achievements. *Creative arts/performance:* 32 awards ($31,120 total): applied art and design, art/fine arts, music. *Special achievements/activities:* 31 awards ($30,832 total): community service, religious involvement. *Special characteristics:* 22 awards ($43,260 total): children and siblings of alumni, international students, local/state students. *Tuition waivers:* Full or partial for employees or children of employees, senior citizens.

LOANS *Student loans:* $1,765,323 (97% need-based, 3% non-need-based). 88% of past graduating class borrowed through all loan programs. *Average indebtedness per student:* $18,706. *Average need-based loan:* Freshmen: $3478. Undergraduates: $4388. *Parent loans:* $80,502 (100% need-based). *Programs:* Federal Direct (Subsidized and Unsubsidized Stafford, PLUS), state.

WORK-STUDY *Federal work-study:* Total amount: $170,848; 81 jobs averaging $1987. *State or other work-study/employment:* Total amount: $6950 (100% need-based). Part-time jobs available.

ATHLETIC AWARDS Total amount: $95,500 (94% need-based, 6% non-need-based).

APPLYING FOR FINANCIAL AID *Required financial aid form:* FAFSA. *Financial aid deadline (priority):* 3/15. *Notification date:* Continuous beginning 3/15.

CONTACT Ms. Michelle Leider, Associate Director of Financial Aid, Silver Lake College, 2406 South Alverno Road, Manitowoc, WI 54220-9319, 920-686-6122 or toll-free 800-236-4752 Ext. 175 (in-state). *Fax:* 920-684-7082. *E-mail:* financialaid@silver.sl.edu.

SIMMONS COLLEGE
Boston, MA

Tuition & fees: $31,450	Average undergraduate aid package: $21,304

ABOUT THE INSTITUTION Independent, undergraduate: women only; graduate: coed. 41 undergraduate majors. Federal methodology is used as a basis for awarding need-based institutional aid.

UNDERGRADUATE EXPENSES for 2009–10 *Comprehensive fee:* $43,500 includes full-time tuition ($30,520), mandatory fees ($930), and room and board ($12,050). Full-time tuition and fees vary according to course load and program. Room and board charges vary according to board plan. *Part-time tuition:* $954 per credit. Part-time tuition and fees vary according to course load and program. *Payment plan:* Installment.

FRESHMAN FINANCIAL AID (Fall 2009, est.) 313 applied for aid; of those 88% were deemed to have need. 100% of freshmen with need received aid; of those 7% had need fully met. *Average percent of need met:* 65% (excluding resources awarded to replace EFC). *Average financial aid package:* $21,704 (excluding resources awarded to replace EFC). 16% of all full-time freshmen had no need and received non-need-based gift aid.

UNDERGRADUATE FINANCIAL AID (Fall 2009, est.) 1,366 applied for aid; of those 90% were deemed to have need. 100% of undergraduates with need received aid; of those 7% had need fully met. *Average percent of need met:* 64% (excluding resources awarded to replace EFC). *Average financial aid package:* $21,304 (excluding resources awarded to replace EFC). 19% of all full-time undergraduates had no need and received non-need-based gift aid.

GIFT AID (NEED-BASED) *Total amount:* $17,689,440 (13% federal, 3% state, 80% institutional, 4% external sources). *Receiving aid:* Freshmen: 78% (276); all full-time undergraduates: 70% (1,215). *Average award:* Freshmen: $16,199; Undergraduates: $14,879. *Scholarships, grants, and awards:* Federal Pell, FSEOG, state, private, college/university gift aid from institutional funds.

GIFT AID (NON-NEED-BASED) *Total amount:* $3,093,845 (1% federal, 94% institutional, 5% external sources). *Receiving aid:* Freshmen: 4% (14). Undergraduates: 3% (47). *Average award:* Freshmen: $7737. Undergraduates: $8520. *Scholarships, grants, and awards by category: Academic interests/achievement:* general academic interests/achievements. *Special achievements/activities:* community service, general special achievements/activities. *Special characteristics:* children and siblings of alumni, general special characteristics. *Tuition waivers:* Full or partial for employees or children of employees.

LOANS *Student loans:* $18,255,589 (33% need-based, 67% non-need-based). 78% of past graduating class borrowed through all loan programs. *Average indebtedness per student:* $45,237. *Average need-based loan:* Freshmen: $4096. Undergraduates: $5140. *Parent loans:* $4,628,649 (100% non-need-based). *Programs:* Federal Direct (Subsidized and Unsubsidized Stafford, PLUS), Perkins, state, college/university.

WORK-STUDY *Federal work-study:* Total amount: $2,636,642; 1,165 jobs averaging $2296.

APPLYING FOR FINANCIAL AID *Required financial aid forms:* FAFSA, institution's own form. *Financial aid deadline (priority):* 2/15. *Notification date:* Continuous beginning 3/15. Students must reply by 5/1 or within 4 weeks of notification.

CONTACT Diane M. Hallisey, Director of Student Financial Services, Simmons College, 300 The Fenway, Boston, MA 02115, 617-521-2001 or toll-free 800-345-8468 (out-of-state). *Fax:* 617-521-3195. *E-mail:* hallisey@simmons.edu.

SIMPSON COLLEGE
Indianola, IA

Tuition & fees: $25,733	Average undergraduate aid package: $25,103

ABOUT THE INSTITUTION Independent United Methodist, coed. 45 undergraduate majors. Federal methodology is used as a basis for awarding need-based institutional aid.

UNDERGRADUATE EXPENSES for 2009–10 *One-time required fee:* $200. *Comprehensive fee:* $32,994 includes full-time tuition ($25,366), mandatory fees ($367), and room and board ($7261). *College room only:* $3485. Full-time tuition and fees vary according to course load, degree level, and program. Room and board charges vary according to board plan and housing facility. *Part-time tuition:* $290 per credit hour. Part-time tuition and fees vary according to course load and degree level. *Payment plan:* Installment.

FRESHMAN FINANCIAL AID (Fall 2009, est.) 390 applied for aid; of those 87% were deemed to have need. 100% of freshmen with need received aid; of those 25% had need fully met. *Average percent of need met:* 92% (excluding resources awarded to replace EFC). *Average financial aid package:* $25,779 (excluding resources awarded to replace EFC). 13% of all full-time freshmen had no need and received non-need-based gift aid.

UNDERGRADUATE FINANCIAL AID (Fall 2009, est.) 1,478 applied for aid; of those 86% were deemed to have need. 100% of undergraduates with need received aid; of those 25% had need fully met. *Average percent of need met:* 89% (excluding resources awarded to replace EFC). *Average financial aid*

package: $25,103 (excluding resources awarded to replace EFC). 14% of all full-time undergraduates had no need and received non-need-based gift aid.

GIFT AID (NEED-BASED) *Total amount:* $22,025,477 (12% federal, 13% state, 72% institutional, 3% external sources). *Receiving aid:* Freshmen: 87% (338); all full-time undergraduates: 86% (1,272). *Average award:* Freshmen: $19,122; Undergraduates: $16,915. *Scholarships, grants, and awards:* Federal Pell, FSEOG, state, private, college/university gift aid from institutional funds.

GIFT AID (NON-NEED-BASED) *Total amount:* $3,617,661 (3% federal, 91% institutional, 6% external sources). *Receiving aid:* Freshmen: 16% (62). Undergraduates: 13% (191). *Average award:* Freshmen: $14,480. Undergraduates: $12,819. *Scholarships, grants, and awards by category:* Academic interests/achievement: $9,018,872 total: general academic interests/achievements. Creative arts/performance: $568,098 total: art/fine arts, music, theater/drama. Special achievements/activities: $313,444 total: community service, leadership, religious involvement. Special characteristics: $2,470,382 total: adult students, children and siblings of alumni, children of educators, children of faculty/staff, ethnic background, international students, members of minority groups, relatives of clergy, religious affiliation, siblings of current students, twins. *Tuition waivers:* Full or partial for employees or children of employees.

LOANS *Student loans:* $12,877,313 (64% need-based, 36% non-need-based). 92% of past graduating class borrowed through all loan programs. *Average indebtedness per student:* $34,354. *Average need-based loan:* Freshmen: $2597. Undergraduates: $3506. *Parent loans:* $1,996,093 (25% need-based, 75% non-need-based). *Programs:* Federal Direct (Subsidized and Unsubsidized Stafford, PLUS), FFEL (Subsidized and Unsubsidized Stafford, PLUS), Perkins, state, college/university, alternative loans.

WORK-STUDY *Federal work-study:* Total amount: $322,932; 393 jobs averaging $982. *State or other work-study/employment:* Total amount: $523,742 (39% need-based, 61% non-need-based). 409 part-time jobs averaging $1307.

APPLYING FOR FINANCIAL AID *Required financial aid form:* FAFSA. *Financial aid deadline:* Continuous. *Notification date:* Continuous beginning 3/15. Students must reply by 5/1 or within 3 weeks of notification.

CONTACT Tracie Lynn Pavon, Assistant Vice President of Financial Aid, Simpson College, 701 North C Street, Indianola, IA 50125-1297, 515-961-1630 Ext. 1596 or toll-free 800-362-2454 (in-state), 800-362-2454 Ext. 1624 (out-of-state). *Fax:* 515-961-1300. *E-mail:* tracie.pavon@simpson.edu.

SIMPSON UNIVERSITY
Redding, CA

ABOUT THE INSTITUTION Independent religious, coed. 29 undergraduate majors.

GIFT AID (NEED-BASED) *Scholarships, grants, and awards:* Federal Pell, FSEOG, state, private, college/university gift aid from institutional funds.

GIFT AID (NON-NEED-BASED) *Scholarships, grants, and awards by category:* Academic interests/achievement: general academic interests/achievements. Creative arts/performance: music. Special achievements/activities: leadership, religious involvement. Special characteristics: children of faculty/staff, general special characteristics, members of minority groups, out-of-state students, relatives of clergy, religious affiliation, siblings of current students, spouses of current students.

LOANS *Programs:* FFEL (Subsidized and Unsubsidized Stafford, PLUS), Perkins, alternative loans.

WORK-STUDY *Federal work-study:* Total amount: $109,800; jobs available.

APPLYING FOR FINANCIAL AID *Required financial aid forms:* FAFSA, institution's own form.

CONTACT Melissa Hudson, Assistant Director of Student Financial Services, Simpson University, 2211 College View Drive, Redding, CA 96003-8606, 530-224-5600 or toll-free 800-598-2493. *Fax:* 530-226-4870. *E-mail:* financialaid@simpsonuniversity.edu.

SINTE GLESKA UNIVERSITY
Mission, SD

CONTACT Office of Financial Aid, Sinte Gleska University, PO Box 490, Rosebud, SD 57570-0490, 605-747-4258. *Fax:* 605-747-2098.

SKIDMORE COLLEGE
Saratoga Springs, NY

Tuition & fees: $40,420   **Average undergraduate aid package:** $34,104

ABOUT THE INSTITUTION Independent, coed. 43 undergraduate majors. Both federal and institutional methodology are used as a basis for awarding need-based institutional aid.

UNDERGRADUATE EXPENSES for 2009–10 *Comprehensive fee:* $51,196 includes full-time tuition ($39,600), mandatory fees ($820), and room and board ($10,776). *College room only:* $6376. Full-time tuition and fees vary according to course load. Room and board charges vary according to board plan and housing facility. *Part-time tuition:* $1320 per credit hour. *Part-time fees:* $25 per term. Part-time tuition and fees vary according to course load. *Payment plans:* Tuition prepayment, installment.

FRESHMAN FINANCIAL AID (Fall 2009, est.) 341 applied for aid; of those 80% were deemed to have need. 100% of freshmen with need received aid; of those 100% had need fully met. *Average percent of need met:* 100% (excluding resources awarded to replace EFC). *Average financial aid package:* $33,054 (excluding resources awarded to replace EFC). 1% of all full-time freshmen had no need and received non-need-based gift aid.

UNDERGRADUATE FINANCIAL AID (Fall 2009, est.) 1,264 applied for aid; of those 90% were deemed to have need. 100% of undergraduates with need received aid; of those 100% had need fully met. *Average percent of need met:* 87% (excluding resources awarded to replace EFC). *Average financial aid package:* $34,104 (excluding resources awarded to replace EFC). 1% of all full-time undergraduates had no need and received non-need-based gift aid.

GIFT AID (NEED-BASED) *Total amount:* $32,169,675 (8% federal, 3% state, 89% institutional). *Receiving aid:* Freshmen: 41% (272); all full-time undergraduates: 44% (1,135). *Average award:* Freshmen: $28,257; Undergraduates: $28,524. *Scholarships, grants, and awards:* Federal Pell, FSEOG, state, college/university gift aid from institutional funds.

GIFT AID (NON-NEED-BASED) *Total amount:* $934,635 (10% state, 36% institutional, 54% external sources). *Receiving aid:* Freshmen: 12% (83). Undergraduates: 10% (263). *Average award:* Freshmen: $10,000. Undergraduates: $10,000. *Scholarships, grants, and awards by category:* Academic interests/achievement: 20 awards ($200,000 total): biological sciences, computer science, mathematics, physical sciences. Creative arts/performance: 14 awards ($140,000 total): music. Special characteristics: 44 awards ($1,276,000 total): children of faculty/staff. *Tuition waivers:* Full or partial for employees or children of employees, senior citizens.

LOANS *Student loans:* $6,362,042 (57% need-based, 43% non-need-based). 51% of past graduating class borrowed through all loan programs. *Average indebtedness per student:* $18,303. *Average need-based loan:* Freshmen: $2708. Undergraduates: $3878. *Parent loans:* $4,439,706 (100% non-need-based). *Programs:* Federal Direct (Subsidized and Unsubsidized Stafford, PLUS), Perkins.

WORK-STUDY *Federal work-study:* Total amount: $1,281,767; 732 jobs averaging $2000. *State or other work-study/employment:* Total amount: $552,133 (100% non-need-based). 305 part-time jobs averaging $2000.

APPLYING FOR FINANCIAL AID *Required financial aid forms:* FAFSA, CSS Financial Aid PROFILE, noncustodial (divorced/separated) parent's statement. *Financial aid deadline:* 2/1. *Notification date:* 4/1. Students must reply by 5/1.

CONTACT Ms. Beth A. Post-Lundquist, Director of Financial Aid, Skidmore College, 815 North Broadway, Saratoga Springs, NY 12866-1632, 518-580-5750 or toll-free 800-867-6007. *Fax:* 518-580-5752. *E-mail:* bpostlun@skidmore.edu.

SLIPPERY ROCK UNIVERSITY OF PENNSYLVANIA
Slippery Rock, PA

Tuition & fees (PA res): $7235   **Average undergraduate aid package:** $8260

ABOUT THE INSTITUTION State-supported, coed. 78 undergraduate majors. Federal methodology is used as a basis for awarding need-based institutional aid.

UNDERGRADUATE EXPENSES for 2010–11 *Tuition, state resident:* full-time $5554; part-time $231 per credit hour. *Tuition, nonresident:* full-time $8331; part-time $463 per credit hour. *Required fees:* full-time $1681; $82 per credit hour or $60 per term. Full-time tuition and fees vary according to course load and degree level. Part-time tuition and fees vary according to course load and degree level. *College room and board:* $8454; *Room only:* $5846. Room and board charges vary according to board plan and housing facility. *Payment plan:* Installment.

FRESHMAN FINANCIAL AID (Fall 2009, est.) 1,474 applied for aid; of those 75% were deemed to have need. 99% of freshmen with need received aid; of those 42% had need fully met. *Average percent of need met:* 65% (excluding resources awarded to replace EFC). *Average financial aid package:* $8254 (excluding resources awarded to replace EFC). 22% of all full-time freshmen had no need and received non-need-based gift aid.

UNDERGRADUATE FINANCIAL AID (Fall 2009, est.) 6,577 applied for aid; of those 76% were deemed to have need. 98% of undergraduates with need received aid; of those 39% had need fully met. *Average percent of need met:* 67% (excluding resources awarded to replace EFC). *Average financial aid package:* $8260 (excluding resources awarded to replace EFC). 18% of all full-time undergraduates had no need and received non-need-based gift aid.

GIFT AID (NEED-BASED) *Total amount:* $17,705,182 (57% federal, 41% state, 2% external sources). *Receiving aid:* Freshmen: 49% (759); all full-time undergraduates: 45% (3,282). *Average award:* Freshmen: $3865; Undergraduates: $3563. *Scholarships, grants, and awards:* Federal Pell, FSEOG, state, private, college/university gift aid from institutional funds.

GIFT AID (NON-NEED-BASED) *Total amount:* $3,016,293 (46% institutional, 54% external sources). *Receiving aid:* Freshmen: 29% (453). Undergraduates: 18% (1,306). *Average award:* Freshmen: $6712. Undergraduates: $7241. *Scholarships, grants, and awards by category: Academic interests/achievement:* biological sciences, business, communication, computer science, education, English, general academic interests/achievements, health fields, physical sciences, social sciences. *Creative arts/performance:* applied art and design, art/fine arts, dance, music, performing arts, theater/drama. *Special achievements/activities:* community service, general special achievements/activities, leadership. *Special characteristics:* children and siblings of alumni, children of faculty/staff, children of union members/company employees, ethnic background, general special characteristics, local/state students, members of minority groups, out-of-state students, previous college experience. *Tuition waivers:* Full or partial for minority students, employees or children of employees, senior citizens.

LOANS *Student loans:* $45,423,359 (43% need-based, 57% non-need-based). 81% of past graduating class borrowed through all loan programs. *Average indebtedness per student:* $23,879. *Average need-based loan:* Freshmen: $3247. Undergraduates: $3863. *Parent loans:* $5,359,099 (100% non-need-based). *Programs:* Federal Direct (Subsidized and Unsubsidized Stafford, PLUS), FFEL (Subsidized and Unsubsidized Stafford, PLUS), Perkins.

WORK-STUDY *Federal work-study:* Total amount: $1,089,250; jobs available. *State or other work-study/employment:* Part-time jobs available.

ATHLETIC AWARDS Total amount: $911,340 (100% non-need-based).

APPLYING FOR FINANCIAL AID *Required financial aid form:* FAFSA. *Financial aid deadline (priority):* 3/15. *Notification date:* Continuous beginning 6/1.

CONTACT Ms. Patty A. Hladio, Director of Financial Aid, Slippery Rock University of Pennsylvania, 1 Morrow Way, Slippery Rock, PA 16057, 724-738-2044 or toll-free 800-SRU-9111. *Fax:* 724-738-2922. *E-mail:* financial.aid@sru.edu.

SMITH COLLEGE
Northampton, MA

Tuition & fees: $37,758	Average undergraduate aid package: $34,526

ABOUT THE INSTITUTION Independent, women only. 51 undergraduate majors. Both federal and institutional methodology are used as a basis for awarding need-based institutional aid.

UNDERGRADUATE EXPENSES for 2009–10 *Comprehensive fee:* $50,380 includes full-time tuition ($37,510), mandatory fees ($248), and room and board ($12,622). *College room only:* $6230. *Part-time tuition:* $1170 per credit hour. *Payment plans:* Tuition prepayment, installment.

FRESHMAN FINANCIAL AID (Fall 2009, est.) 526 applied for aid; of those 77% were deemed to have need. 100% of freshmen with need received aid; of those 100% had need fully met. *Average percent of need met:* 100% (excluding resources awarded to replace EFC). *Average financial aid package:* $33,269 (excluding resources awarded to replace EFC). 5% of all full-time freshmen had no need and received non-need-based gift aid.

UNDERGRADUATE FINANCIAL AID (Fall 2009, est.) 1,913 applied for aid; of those 86% were deemed to have need. 100% of undergraduates with need received aid; of those 100% had need fully met. *Average percent of need met:*

100% (excluding resources awarded to replace EFC). *Average financial aid package:* $34,526 (excluding resources awarded to replace EFC). 5% of all full-time undergraduates had no need and received non-need-based gift aid.

GIFT AID (NEED-BASED) *Total amount:* $49,315,117 (7% federal, 2% state, 89% institutional, 2% external sources). *Receiving aid:* Freshmen: 57% (378); all full-time undergraduates: 60% (1,545). *Average award:* Freshmen: $31,980; Undergraduates: $30,971. *Scholarships, grants, and awards:* Federal Pell, FSEOG, state, college/university gift aid from institutional funds.

GIFT AID (NON-NEED-BASED) *Total amount:* $1,779,429 (81% institutional, 19% external sources). *Receiving aid:* Freshmen: 1% (4). Undergraduates: 1% (19). *Average award:* Freshmen: $17,985. Undergraduates: $9805. *Tuition waivers:* Full or partial for employees or children of employees.

LOANS *Student loans:* $10,120,793 (66% need-based, 34% non-need-based). 62% of past graduating class borrowed through all loan programs. *Average indebtedness per student:* $21,573. *Average need-based loan:* Freshmen: $3198. Undergraduates: $4567. *Parent loans:* $5,375,726 (100% non-need-based). *Programs:* Federal Direct (Subsidized and Unsubsidized Stafford, PLUS), Perkins, state, college/university.

WORK-STUDY *Federal work-study:* Total amount: $2,633,023; jobs available. *State or other work-study/employment:* Total amount: $1,018,640 (83% need-based, 17% non-need-based). Part-time jobs available.

APPLYING FOR FINANCIAL AID *Required financial aid forms:* FAFSA, institution's own form, CSS Financial Aid PROFILE, noncustodial (divorced/separated) parent's statement, business/farm supplement. *Financial aid deadline:* 2/15. *Notification date:* 4/1. Students must reply by 5/1 or within 2 weeks of notification.

CONTACT David Belanger, Director of Student Financial Services, Smith College, College Hall, Northampton, MA 01063, 413-585-2530 or toll-free 800-383-3232. *Fax:* 413-585-2566. *E-mail:* sfs@smith.edu.

SOJOURNER-DOUGLASS COLLEGE
Baltimore, MD

Tuition & fees: N/R	Average undergraduate aid package: $4080

ABOUT THE INSTITUTION Independent, coed, primarily women. *Awards:* bachelor's and master's degrees (offers only evening and weekend programs). 21 undergraduate majors. *Total enrollment:* 1,151. Undergraduates: 1,078. Federal methodology is used as a basis for awarding need-based institutional aid.

FRESHMAN FINANCIAL AID (Fall 2008) 285 applied for aid; of those 100% were deemed to have need. 100% of freshmen with need received aid. *Average percent of need met:* 68% (excluding resources awarded to replace EFC). *Average financial aid package:* $7764 (excluding resources awarded to replace EFC).

UNDERGRADUATE FINANCIAL AID (Fall 2008) 1,412 applied for aid; of those 100% were deemed to have need. 100% of undergraduates with need received aid. *Average percent of need met:* 35% (excluding resources awarded to replace EFC). *Average financial aid package:* $4080 (excluding resources awarded to replace EFC).

GIFT AID (NEED-BASED) *Total amount:* $5,462,519 (74% federal, 23% state, 3% institutional). *Receiving aid:* Freshmen: 95% (270); all full-time undergraduates: 80% (1,128). *Average award:* Freshmen: $4411; Undergraduates: $4800. *Scholarships, grants, and awards:* Federal Pell, FSEOG, state, private, college/university gift aid from institutional funds.

GIFT AID (NON-NEED-BASED) *Total amount:* $728,119 (100% institutional). *Receiving aid:* Freshmen: 65% (184). Undergraduates: 34% (484).

LOANS *Student loans:* $9,383,179 (100% need-based). 91% of past graduating class borrowed through all loan programs. *Average indebtedness per student:* $34,750. *Average need-based loan:* Freshmen: $4760. Undergraduates: $6722. *Parent loans:* $36,000 (100% need-based). *Programs:* FFEL (Subsidized and Unsubsidized Stafford, PLUS).

WORK-STUDY *Federal work-study:* Total amount: $119,391; 16 jobs averaging $7462.

APPLYING FOR FINANCIAL AID *Required financial aid forms:* FAFSA, institution's own form. *Financial aid deadline:* Continuous.

CONTACT Ms. Rebecca Chalk, Financial Aid Director, Sojourner-Douglass College, 200 North Central Avenue, Baltimore, MD 21202, 410-276-0306 Ext. 258. *Fax:* 410-276-0148. *E-mail:* rchalk@host.sdc.edu.

SOKA UNIVERSITY OF AMERICA
Aliso Viejo, CA

CONTACT Financial Aid Office, Soka University of America, 1 University Drive, Aliso Viejo, CA 92656, 949-480-4000 or toll-free 888-600-SOKA (out-of-state).

SOMERSET CHRISTIAN COLLEGE
Zarephath, NJ

CONTACT Financial Aid Office, Somerset Christian College, 10 College Way, PO Box 9035, Zarephath, NJ 08890-9035, 732-356-1595 or toll-free 800-234-9305.

SONOMA STATE UNIVERSITY
Rohnert Park, CA

Tuition & fees (CA res): $5290	Average undergraduate aid package: $9782

ABOUT THE INSTITUTION State-supported, coed. 63 undergraduate majors. Federal methodology is used as a basis for awarding need-based institutional aid.

UNDERGRADUATE EXPENSES for 2009–10 *Tuition, state resident:* full-time $0. *Tuition, nonresident:* full-time $10,347; part-time $372 per unit. *Required fees:* full-time $5290; $1799 per term. Full-time tuition and fees vary according to course load and degree level. Part-time tuition and fees vary according to course load and degree level. *College room and board:* $10,086. Room and board charges vary according to housing facility.

FRESHMAN FINANCIAL AID (Fall 2009, est.) 701 applied for aid; of those 61% were deemed to have need. 92% of freshmen with need received aid; of those 14% had need fully met. *Average percent of need met:* 67% (excluding resources awarded to replace EFC). *Average financial aid package:* $8841 (excluding resources awarded to replace EFC). 1% of all full-time freshmen had no need and received non-need-based gift aid.

UNDERGRADUATE FINANCIAL AID (Fall 2009, est.) 3,755 applied for aid; of those 75% were deemed to have need. 96% of undergraduates with need received aid; of those 13% had need fully met. *Average percent of need met:* 70% (excluding resources awarded to replace EFC). *Average financial aid package:* $9782 (excluding resources awarded to replace EFC). 2% of all full-time undergraduates had no need and received non-need-based gift aid.

GIFT AID (NEED-BASED) *Total amount:* $15,998,891 (47% federal, 53% state). *Receiving aid:* Freshmen: 10% (211); all full-time undergraduates: 24% (1,616). *Average award:* Freshmen: $9863; Undergraduates: $8889. *Scholarships, grants, and awards:* Federal Pell, FSEOG, state, private, college/university gift aid from institutional funds, Academic Competitiveness Grants, National SMART Grants.

GIFT AID (NON-NEED-BASED) *Total amount:* $1,331,764 (21% state, 44% institutional, 35% external sources). *Receiving aid:* Freshmen: 3% (67). Undergraduates: 6% (384). *Average award:* Freshmen: $1525. Undergraduates: $1610. *Scholarships, grants, and awards by category: Academic interests/ achievement:* 129 awards ($263,815 total): area/ethnic studies, biological sciences, business, communication, computer science, education, engineering/ technologies, English, foreign languages, general academic interests/ achievements, health fields, humanities, mathematics, physical sciences, premedicine, social sciences. *Creative arts/performance:* 53 awards ($103,070 total): applied art and design, art/fine arts, cinema/film/broadcasting, creative writing, dance, journalism/publications, music, performing arts, theater/drama. *Special achievements/activities:* 3 awards ($2500 total): community service, leadership, memberships. *Special characteristics:* 92 awards ($110,500 total): adult students, children and siblings of alumni, children of educators, children of faculty/staff, children of public servants, children of union members/ company employees, children of workers in trades, ethnic background, first-generation college students, general special characteristics, handicapped students, international students, local/state students, married students, members of minority groups, out-of-state students, previous college experience, veterans. *Tuition waivers:* Full or partial for employees or children of employees.

LOANS *Student loans:* $25,615,664 (44% need-based, 56% non-need-based). 44% of past graduating class borrowed through all loan programs. *Average indebtedness per student:* $15,954. *Average need-based loan:* Freshmen: $3086. Undergraduates: $4251. *Parent loans:* $8,277,042 (100% non-need-based). *Programs:* Federal Direct (Subsidized and Unsubsidized Stafford, PLUS), Perkins.

WORK-STUDY *Federal work-study:* Total amount: $607,505; 218 jobs averaging $2894. *State or other work-study/employment:* Total amount: $1,600,000 (100% non-need-based). 620 part-time jobs averaging $2570.

ATHLETIC AWARDS Total amount: $416,852 (100% non-need-based).

APPLYING FOR FINANCIAL AID *Required financial aid form:* FAFSA. *Financial aid deadline (priority):* 1/31. *Notification date:* Continuous beginning 3/15. Students must reply within 2 weeks of notification.

CONTACT Susan Gutierrez, Director of Financial Aid, Sonoma State University, 1801 East Cotati Avenue, Rohnert Park, CA 94928-3609, 707-664-2287. *Fax:* 707-664-4242. *E-mail:* susan.gutierrez@sonoma.edu.

SOUTH CAROLINA STATE UNIVERSITY
Orangeburg, SC

ABOUT THE INSTITUTION State-supported, coed. 44 undergraduate majors.

GIFT AID (NEED-BASED) *Scholarships, grants, and awards:* Federal Pell, FSEOG, state, private, college/university gift aid from institutional funds.

GIFT AID (NON-NEED-BASED) *Scholarships, grants, and awards by category: Academic interests/achievement:* general academic interests/achievements. *Creative arts/performance:* music.

LOANS *Programs:* FFEL (Subsidized and Unsubsidized Stafford, PLUS), Perkins, college/university.

APPLYING FOR FINANCIAL AID *Required financial aid form:* FAFSA.

CONTACT Sandra S. Davis, Director of Financial Aid, South Carolina State University, 300 College Street Northeast, Orangeburg, SC 29117, 803-536-7067 or toll-free 800-260-5956. *Fax:* 803-536-8420. *E-mail:* sdavis@scsu.edu.

SOUTH COLLEGE
Knoxville, TN

CONTACT Larry Broadwater, Financial Aid Director, South College, 720 North Fifth Avenue, Knoxville, TN 37917, 423-524-3043. *Fax:* 423-637-0127.

SOUTH DAKOTA SCHOOL OF MINES AND TECHNOLOGY
Rapid City, SD

Tuition & fees (SD res): $6830	Average undergraduate aid package: $8764

ABOUT THE INSTITUTION State-supported, coed. 18 undergraduate majors. Both federal and institutional methodology are used as a basis for awarding need-based institutional aid.

UNDERGRADUATE EXPENSES for 2009–10 *Tuition, state resident:* full-time $2750; part-time $91.70 per credit hour. *Tuition, nonresident:* full-time $4130; part-time $137.45 per credit hour. *Required fees:* full-time $4080; $141.95 per credit hour. Full-time tuition and fees vary according to course load, location, program, and reciprocity agreements. Part-time tuition and fees vary according to course load, location, program, and reciprocity agreements. *College room and board:* $5080; *Room only:* $2640. Room and board charges vary according to board plan and housing facility. *Payment plans:* Installment, deferred payment.

FRESHMAN FINANCIAL AID (Fall 2009, est.) 349 applied for aid; of those 59% were deemed to have need. 100% of freshmen with need received aid; of those 21% had need fully met. *Average percent of need met:* 71% (excluding resources awarded to replace EFC). *Average financial aid package:* $9006 (excluding resources awarded to replace EFC). 30% of all full-time freshmen had no need and received non-need-based gift aid.

UNDERGRADUATE FINANCIAL AID (Fall 2009, est.) 1,346 applied for aid; of those 60% were deemed to have need. 100% of undergraduates with need received aid; of those 21% had need fully met. *Average percent of need met:* 66% (excluding resources awarded to replace EFC). *Average financial aid package:* $8764 (excluding resources awarded to replace EFC). 23% of all full-time undergraduates had no need and received non-need-based gift aid.

GIFT AID (NEED-BASED) *Total amount:* $3,003,434 (57% federal, 22% institutional, 21% external sources). *Receiving aid:* Freshmen: 44% (160); all full-time undergraduates: 35% (519). *Average award:* Freshmen: $4256; Undergraduates: $4176. *Scholarships, grants, and awards:* Federal Pell, FSEOG, state, college/university gift aid from institutional funds, Leveraging Educational Assistance Program (LEAP).

GIFT AID (NON-NEED-BASED) *Total amount;* $1,160,759 (57% institutional, 43% external sources). *Receiving aid:* Freshmen: 37% (132). Undergraduates: 20% (292). *Average award:* Freshmen: $2746. Undergraduates: $2947. *Scholarships, grants, and awards by category: Academic interests/achievement:* computer science, engineering/technologies, mathematics, physical sciences. *Special characteristics:* ethnic background, members of minority groups. *Tuition waivers:* Full or partial for employees or children of employees, senior citizens.
LOANS *Student loans:* $5,250,593 (100% need-based). 68% of past graduating class borrowed through all loan programs. *Average indebtedness per student:* $20,165. *Average need-based loan:* Freshmen: $3033. Undergraduates: $3796. *Parent loans:* $856,383 (65% need-based, 35% non-need-based). *Programs:* FFEL (Subsidized and Unsubsidized Stafford, PLUS), Perkins.
WORK-STUDY *Federal work-study:* Total amount: $269,018; 147 jobs averaging $1838.
ATHLETIC AWARDS Total amount: $469,250 (44% need-based, 56% non-need-based).
APPLYING FOR FINANCIAL AID *Required financial aid forms:* FAFSA, institution's own form, state aid form. *Financial aid deadline (priority):* 3/15. *Notification date:* Continuous beginning 5/15. Students must reply within 3 weeks of notification.
CONTACT David W. Martin, Financial Aid Director, South Dakota School of Mines and Technology, 501 East Saint Joseph Street, Rapid City, SD 57701-3995, 605-394-2274 or toll-free 800-544-8162 Ext. 2414. *Fax:* 605-394-1979. *E-mail:* david.martin@sdsmt.edu.

SOUTH DAKOTA STATE UNIVERSITY
Brookings, SD

Tuition & fees (SD res): $6155	Average undergraduate aid package: $9214

ABOUT THE INSTITUTION State-supported, coed. 75 undergraduate majors. Federal methodology is used as a basis for awarding need-based institutional aid.
UNDERGRADUATE EXPENSES for 2009–10 *Tuition, state resident:* full-time $2751; part-time $91.70 per credit hour. *Tuition, nonresident:* full-time $4124; part-time $137.45 per credit hour. *Required fees:* full-time $3404; $113.45 per credit hour. Full-time tuition and fees vary according to course level, course load, location, program, and reciprocity agreements. Part-time tuition and fees vary according to course level, course load, location, program, and reciprocity agreements. *College room and board:* $5668; *Room only:* $2540. Room and board charges vary according to board plan and housing facility. *Payment plans:* Installment, deferred payment.
FRESHMAN FINANCIAL AID (Fall 2009, est.) 1,739 applied for aid; of those 84% were deemed to have need. 100% of freshmen with need received aid; of those 81% had need fully met. *Average percent of need met:* 90% (excluding resources awarded to replace EFC). *Average financial aid package:* $8114 (excluding resources awarded to replace EFC). 24% of all full-time freshmen had no need and received non-need-based gift aid.
UNDERGRADUATE FINANCIAL AID (Fall 2009, est.) 7,354 applied for aid; of those 88% were deemed to have need. 100% of undergraduates with need received aid; of those 76% had need fully met. *Average percent of need met:* 86% (excluding resources awarded to replace EFC). *Average financial aid package:* $9214 (excluding resources awarded to replace EFC). 21% of all full-time undergraduates had no need and received non-need-based gift aid.
GIFT AID (NEED-BASED) *Total amount:* $20,193,473 (67% federal, 7% state, 17% institutional, 9% external sources). *Receiving aid:* Freshmen: 42% (853); all full-time undergraduates: 45% (3,814). *Average award:* Freshmen: $4270; Undergraduates: $4340. *Scholarships, grants, and awards:* Federal Pell, FSEOG, state, private, college/university gift aid from institutional funds, United Negro College Fund, Federal Nursing, Academic Competitiveness Grants, National SMART Grants, TEACH Grants, TRiO Scholarships.
GIFT AID (NON-NEED-BASED) *Total amount:* $3,873,878 (1% federal, 20% state, 54% institutional, 25% external sources). *Receiving aid:* Freshmen: 49% (1,012). Undergraduates: 63% (5,367). *Average award:* Freshmen: $1586. Undergraduates: $1422. *Scholarships, grants, and awards by category: Academic interests/achievement:* 3,144 awards ($3,358,522 total): agriculture, area/ethnic studies, biological sciences, business, communication, computer science, education, engineering/technologies, English, foreign languages, general academic interests/achievements, health fields, home economics, humanities, international studies, mathematics, military science, physical sciences, premedicine, social sciences. *Creative arts/performance:* 341 awards ($402,580 total): art/

fine arts, debating, general creative arts/performance, journalism/publications, music, performing arts, theater/drama. *Special achievements/activities:* 162 awards ($162,558 total): community service, general special achievements/activities, hobbies/interests, junior miss, leadership, memberships, rodeo. *Special characteristics:* 208 awards ($314,680 total): adult students, children of faculty/staff, children of workers in trades, ethnic background, first-generation college students, general special characteristics, handicapped students, international students, members of minority groups, veterans, veterans' children. *Tuition waivers:* Full or partial for children of alumni, employees or children of employees, senior citizens.
LOANS *Student loans:* $55,931,196 (68% need-based, 32% non-need-based). 74% of past graduating class borrowed through all loan programs. *Average indebtedness per student:* $22,914. *Average need-based loan:* Freshmen: $4524. Undergraduates: $5010. *Parent loans:* $2,132,713 (54% need-based, 46% non-need-based). *Programs:* Federal Direct (Subsidized and Unsubsidized Stafford, PLUS), FFEL (Subsidized and Unsubsidized Stafford, PLUS), Perkins, Federal Nursing, college/university, Health Professions Loans, private alternative loans.
WORK-STUDY *Federal work-study:* Total amount: $815,142; 694 jobs averaging $1240. *State or other work-study/employment:* Total amount: $3,637,775 (14% need-based, 86% non-need-based). 2,214 part-time jobs averaging $1566.
ATHLETIC AWARDS Total amount: $2,795,955 (65% need-based, 35% non-need-based).
APPLYING FOR FINANCIAL AID *Required financial aid form:* FAFSA. *Financial aid deadline (priority):* 3/11. *Notification date:* Continuous beginning 4/1. Students must reply within 3 weeks of notification.
CONTACT Mr. Jay Larsen, Director of Financial Aid, South Dakota State University, Box 2201, Administration 106, Brookings, SD 57007, 605-688-4703 or toll-free 800-952-3541. *Fax:* 605-688-5882. *E-mail:* jay.larsen@sdstate.edu.

SOUTHEASTERN BAPTIST COLLEGE
Laurel, MS

CONTACT Financial Aid Officer, Southeastern Baptist College, 4229 Highway 15 North, Laurel, MS 39440-1096, 601-426-6346.

SOUTHEASTERN BAPTIST THEOLOGICAL SEMINARY
Wake Forest, NC

CONTACT H. Allan Moseley, Vice President of Student Services/Dean of Students, Southeastern Baptist Theological Seminary, PO Box 1889, Wake Forest, NC 27588, 919-556-3101 Ext. 306 or toll-free 800-284-6317. *Fax:* 919-556-0998. *E-mail:* deanofstudents@sebts.edu.

SOUTHEASTERN BIBLE COLLEGE
Birmingham, AL

Tuition & fees: $11,150	Average undergraduate aid package: N/A

ABOUT THE INSTITUTION Independent nondenominational, coed. 1 undergraduate major. Federal methodology is used as a basis for awarding need-based institutional aid.
UNDERGRADUATE EXPENSES for 2009–10 *Tuition:* full-time $10,800; part-time $360 per semester hour. *Required fees:* full-time $350; $175 per term. Full-time tuition and fees vary according to course load and program. Part-time tuition and fees vary according to course load and program. *Payment plan:* Installment.
GIFT AID (NEED-BASED) *Scholarships, grants, and awards:* Federal Pell, FSEOG, college/university gift aid from institutional funds.
GIFT AID (NON-NEED-BASED) *Scholarships, grants, and awards by category: Academic interests/achievement:* general academic interests/achievements. *Creative arts/performance:* music. *Special characteristics:* children of faculty/staff, local/state students, veterans.
LOANS *Programs:* Federal Direct (Subsidized and Unsubsidized Stafford, PLUS).
WORK-STUDY Federal work-study jobs available. *State or other work-study/employment:* Part-time jobs available.

APPLYING FOR FINANCIAL AID *Required financial aid forms:* FAFSA, institution's own form. *Financial aid deadline (priority):* 4/1. *Notification date:* 5/1. Students must reply within 2 weeks of notification.

CONTACT Mr. Jay Powell, Financial Aid Administrator, Southeastern Bible College, 2545 Valleydale Road, Birmingham, AL 35244-2083, 205-970-9216 or toll-free 800-749-8878 (in-state). *Fax:* 205-970-9207. *E-mail:* finaid@sebc.edu.

SOUTHEASTERN LOUISIANA UNIVERSITY
Hammond, LA

Tuition & fees (LA res): $3932	Average undergraduate aid package: $5719

ABOUT THE INSTITUTION State-supported, coed. 52 undergraduate majors. Federal methodology is used as a basis for awarding need-based institutional aid.

UNDERGRADUATE EXPENSES for 2009–10 *Tuition, state resident:* full-time $2546; part-time $106 per credit hour. *Tuition, nonresident:* full-time $9802; part-time $106 per credit hour. *Required fees:* full-time $1386; $105 per credit hour. Full-time tuition and fees vary according to course load. Part-time tuition and fees vary according to course load. *College room and board:* $6450; *Room only:* $4020. Room and board charges vary according to board plan and housing facility. *Payment plans:* Installment, deferred payment.

FRESHMAN FINANCIAL AID (Fall 2009, est.) 2,276 applied for aid; of those 62% were deemed to have need. 95% of freshmen with need received aid; of those 36% had need fully met. *Average financial aid package:* $6118 (excluding resources awarded to replace EFC). 9% of all full-time freshmen had no need and received non-need-based gift aid.

UNDERGRADUATE FINANCIAL AID (Fall 2009, est.) 8,544 applied for aid; of those 70% were deemed to have need. 93% of undergraduates with need received aid; of those 28% had need fully met. *Average financial aid package:* $5719 (excluding resources awarded to replace EFC). 7% of all full-time undergraduates had no need and received non-need-based gift aid.

GIFT AID (NEED-BASED) *Total amount:* $16,198,828 (89% federal, 11% state). *Receiving aid:* Freshmen: 29% (769); all full-time undergraduates: 31% (3,433). *Average award:* Freshmen: $5876; Undergraduates: $4588. *Scholarships, grants, and awards:* Federal Pell, FSEOG, state, private, college/university gift aid from institutional funds, Federal Nursing.

GIFT AID (NON-NEED-BASED) *Total amount:* $10,401,305 (67% state, 30% institutional, 3% external sources). *Receiving aid:* Freshmen: 28% (742). Undergraduates: 22% (2,394). *Average award:* Freshmen: $1797. Undergraduates: $1071. *Scholarships, grants, and awards by category: Academic interests/achievement:* 3,517 awards ($3,441,289 total): agriculture, architecture, biological sciences, business, communication, computer science, education, engineering/technologies, English, foreign languages, general academic interests/achievements, health fields, home economics, humanities, international studies, mathematics, physical sciences, social sciences. *Creative arts/performance:* 217 awards ($248,861 total): applied art and design, art/fine arts, cinema/film/broadcasting, dance, general creative arts/performance, music, performing arts, theater/drama. *Special achievements/activities:* 180 awards ($196,220 total): cheerleading/drum major, community service, general special achievements/activities, leadership, memberships, rodeo. *Special characteristics:* 1,056 awards ($2,836,604 total): adult students, children and siblings of alumni, children of faculty/staff, children of public servants, first-generation college students, general special characteristics, handicapped students, international students, local/state students, members of minority groups, out-of-state students, veterans, veterans' children. *Tuition waivers:* Full or partial for employees or children of employees, senior citizens.

LOANS *Student loans:* $35,121,817 (50% need-based, 50% non-need-based). 60% of past graduating class borrowed through all loan programs. *Average indebtedness per student:* $18,947. *Average need-based loan:* Freshmen: $2844. Undergraduates: $2300. *Parent loans:* $615,519 (100% non-need-based). *Programs:* FFEL (Subsidized and Unsubsidized Stafford, PLUS), Perkins, college/university.

WORK-STUDY *Federal work-study:* Total amount: $478,370; 278 jobs averaging $1661. *State or other work-study/employment:* Total amount: $2,792,355 (100% non-need-based). 1,370 part-time jobs averaging $2038.

ATHLETIC AWARDS Total amount: $1,692,781 (100% non-need-based).

APPLYING FOR FINANCIAL AID *Required financial aid forms:* FAFSA, institution's own form. *Financial aid deadline (priority):* 5/1. *Notification date:* Continuous beginning 3/1. Students must reply within 2 weeks of notification.

CONTACT Sarah Schillage, Director of Financial Aid, Southeastern Louisiana University, SLU 10768, Hammond, LA 70402, 985-549-2244 or toll-free 800-222-7358. *Fax:* 985-549-5077. *E-mail:* finaid@selu.edu.

SOUTHEASTERN OKLAHOMA STATE UNIVERSITY
Durant, OK

Tuition & fees (OK res): $4316	Average undergraduate aid package: $1434

ABOUT THE INSTITUTION State-supported, coed. 50 undergraduate majors. Federal methodology is used as a basis for awarding need-based institutional aid.

UNDERGRADUATE EXPENSES for 2009–10 *Tuition, state resident:* full-time $3639; part-time $121.30 per credit hour. *Tuition, nonresident:* full-time $10,009; part-time $333.65 per credit hour. *Required fees:* full-time $677; $22.55 per credit hour. Full-time tuition and fees vary according to course level. Part-time tuition and fees vary according to course level and course load. *College room and board:* $4290; *Room only:* $1850. Room and board charges vary according to board plan and housing facility.

FRESHMAN FINANCIAL AID (Fall 2008) 449 applied for aid; of those 86% were deemed to have need. 98% of freshmen with need received aid; of those 12% had need fully met. *Average percent of need met:* 11% (excluding resources awarded to replace EFC). *Average financial aid package:* $1266 (excluding resources awarded to replace EFC). 1% of all full-time freshmen had no need and received non-need-based gift aid.

UNDERGRADUATE FINANCIAL AID (Fall 2008) 1,868 applied for aid; of those 87% were deemed to have need. 98% of undergraduates with need received aid; of those 11% had need fully met. *Average percent of need met:* 16% (excluding resources awarded to replace EFC). *Average financial aid package:* $1434 (excluding resources awarded to replace EFC). 1% of all full-time undergraduates had no need and received non-need-based gift aid.

GIFT AID (NEED-BASED) *Total amount:* $7,928,984 (64% federal, 36% state). *Receiving aid:* Freshmen: 52% (280); all full-time undergraduates: 48% (1,175). *Average award:* Freshmen: $1225; Undergraduates: $1382. *Scholarships, grants, and awards:* Federal Pell, FSEOG, state, private, college/university gift aid from institutional funds.

GIFT AID (NON-NEED-BASED) *Total amount:* $2,388,060 (4% state, 12% institutional, 84% external sources). *Receiving aid:* Freshmen: 32% (169). Undergraduates: 22% (545). *Average award:* Freshmen: $667. Undergraduates: $969. *Scholarships, grants, and awards by category: Academic interests/achievement:* 770 awards ($679,731 total): biological sciences, business, computer science, education, engineering/technologies, general academic interests/achievements, mathematics, physical sciences, social sciences. *Creative arts/performance:* 57 awards ($35,647 total): art/fine arts, dance, debating, music, performing arts, theater/drama. *Special achievements/activities:* 206 awards ($163,876 total): cheerleading/drum major, leadership, rodeo. *Special characteristics:* 2,173 awards ($4,726,615 total): children and siblings of alumni, out-of-state students. *Tuition waivers:* Full or partial for minority students, children of alumni, employees or children of employees, senior citizens.

LOANS *Student loans:* $9,066,597 (56% need-based, 44% non-need-based). 36% of past graduating class borrowed through all loan programs. *Average indebtedness per student:* $4967. *Average need-based loan:* Freshmen: $1321. Undergraduates: $1910. *Parent loans:* $294,181 (100% non-need-based). *Programs:* FFEL (Subsidized and Unsubsidized Stafford, PLUS), college/university.

WORK-STUDY *Federal work-study:* Total amount: $193,515; 464 jobs averaging $1699. *State or other work-study/employment:* Total amount: $737,971 (100% non-need-based). 707 part-time jobs averaging $2236.

ATHLETIC AWARDS Total amount: $967,581 (100% non-need-based).

APPLYING FOR FINANCIAL AID *Required financial aid forms:* FAFSA, institution's own form. *Financial aid deadline (priority):* 3/1. *Notification date:* Continuous beginning 4/15. Students must reply within 2 weeks of notification.

CONTACT Sherry Hudson, Director of Student Financial Aid, Southeastern Oklahoma State University, 1405 North 4th Avenue, Durant, OK 74701-0609, 580-745-2186 or toll-free 800-435-1327. *Fax:* 580-745-7469. *E-mail:* shudson@se.edu.

SOUTHEASTERN UNIVERSITY
Lakeland, FL

Tuition & fees: $15,000 — **Average undergraduate aid package: $9044**

ABOUT THE INSTITUTION Independent religious, coed. 38 undergraduate majors. Federal methodology is used as a basis for awarding need-based institutional aid.

UNDERGRADUATE EXPENSES for 2009–10 *Comprehensive fee:* $22,566 includes full-time tuition ($14,450), mandatory fees ($550), and room and board ($7566). Full-time tuition and fees vary according to class time, degree level, program, and reciprocity agreements. Room and board charges vary according to board plan and housing facility. *Part-time tuition:* $605 per credit. *Part-time fees:* $140 per term. Part-time tuition and fees vary according to class time, course load, degree level, program, and reciprocity agreements. *Payment plan:* Installment.

FRESHMAN FINANCIAL AID (Fall 2008) 486 applied for aid; of those 79% were deemed to have need. 100% of freshmen with need received aid; of those 15% had need fully met. *Average percent of need met:* 61% (excluding resources awarded to replace EFC). *Average financial aid package:* $10,088 (excluding resources awarded to replace EFC). 20% of all full-time freshmen had no need and received non-need-based gift aid.

UNDERGRADUATE FINANCIAL AID (Fall 2008) 2,174 applied for aid; of those 82% were deemed to have need. 99% of undergraduates with need received aid; of those 15% had need fully met. *Average percent of need met:* 56% (excluding resources awarded to replace EFC). *Average financial aid package:* $9044 (excluding resources awarded to replace EFC). 16% of all full-time undergraduates had no need and received non-need-based gift aid.

GIFT AID (NEED-BASED) *Total amount:* $9,774,546 (29% federal, 40% state, 22% institutional, 9% external sources). *Receiving aid:* Freshmen: 72% (378); all full-time undergraduates: 69% (1,647). *Average award:* Freshmen: $7629; Undergraduates: $6431. *Scholarships, grants, and awards:* Federal Pell, FSEOG, state, private, college/university gift aid from institutional funds.

GIFT AID (NON-NEED-BASED) *Total amount:* $3,116,923 (53% state, 31% institutional, 16% external sources). *Receiving aid:* Freshmen: 8% (42). Undergraduates: 8% (184). *Average award:* Freshmen: $2711. Undergraduates: $2230. *Scholarships, grants, and awards by category:* Academic interests/achievement: 758 awards ($1,973,649 total): communication, general academic interests/achievements, religion/biblical studies. *Creative arts/performance:* 133 awards ($261,889 total): journalism/publications, music, theater/drama. *Tuition waivers:* Full or partial for employees or children of employees.

LOANS *Student loans:* $15,490,525 (67% need-based, 33% non-need-based). 95% of past graduating class borrowed through all loan programs. *Average indebtedness per student:* $23,613. *Average need-based loan:* Freshmen: $3069. Undergraduates: $3598. *Parent loans:* $5,711,629 (30% need-based, 70% non-need-based). *Programs:* Federal Direct (Subsidized and Unsubsidized Stafford, PLUS), Perkins.

WORK-STUDY *Federal work-study:* Total amount: $143,028; jobs available.

APPLYING FOR FINANCIAL AID *Required financial aid forms:* FAFSA, institution's own form, state aid form, state aid form (for FL residents only). *Financial aid deadline (priority):* 4/15. *Notification date:* Continuous beginning 2/1. Students must reply by 5/1 or within 4 weeks of notification.

CONTACT Ms. Carol B. Bradley, Director, Student Financial Services, Southeastern University, 1000 Longfellow Boulevard, Lakeland, FL 33801-6099, 863-667-5000 or toll-free 800-500-8760. *Fax:* 863-667-5200. *E-mail:* cbradley@seuniversity.edu.

SOUTHEAST MISSOURI STATE UNIVERSITY
Cape Girardeau, MO

Tuition & fees (MO res): $6255 — **Average undergraduate aid package: $8317**

ABOUT THE INSTITUTION State-supported, coed. 70 undergraduate majors. Federal methodology is used as a basis for awarding need-based institutional aid.

UNDERGRADUATE EXPENSES for 2009–10 *Tuition, state resident:* full-time $5544; part-time $184.80 per credit hour. *Tuition, nonresident:* full-time $10,179; part-time $339.30 per credit hour. *Required fees:* full-time $711; $23.70 per credit hour. Full-time tuition and fees vary according to course load and location. Part-time tuition and fees vary according to course load and location.

College room and board: $6358; *Room only:* $3960. Room and board charges vary according to board plan and housing facility. *Payment plans:* Installment, deferred payment.

FRESHMAN FINANCIAL AID (Fall 2008) 1,318 applied for aid; of those 68% were deemed to have need. 100% of freshmen with need received aid; of those 25% had need fully met. *Average percent of need met:* 77% (excluding resources awarded to replace EFC). *Average financial aid package:* $8660 (excluding resources awarded to replace EFC). 31% of all full-time freshmen had no need and received non-need-based gift aid.

UNDERGRADUATE FINANCIAL AID (Fall 2008) 5,179 applied for aid; of those 74% were deemed to have need. 100% of undergraduates with need received aid; of those 24% had need fully met. *Average percent of need met:* 73% (excluding resources awarded to replace EFC). *Average financial aid package:* $8317 (excluding resources awarded to replace EFC). 17% of all full-time undergraduates had no need and received non-need-based gift aid.

GIFT AID (NEED-BASED) *Total amount:* $17,160,692 (50% federal, 23% state, 24% institutional, 3% external sources). *Receiving aid:* Freshmen: 52% (851); all full-time undergraduates: 47% (3,282). *Average award:* Freshmen: $5718; Undergraduates: $4832. *Scholarships, grants, and awards:* Federal Pell, FSEOG, state, private, college/university gift aid from institutional funds.

GIFT AID (NON-NEED-BASED) *Total amount:* $6,708,970 (1% federal, 5% state, 83% institutional, 11% external sources). *Receiving aid:* Freshmen: 8% (134). Undergraduates: 4% (287). *Average award:* Freshmen: $3593. Undergraduates: $4251. *Scholarships, grants, and awards by category:* Academic interests/achievement: 2,498 awards ($6,292,498 total): agriculture, biological sciences, business, communication, computer science, education, engineering/technologies, English, foreign languages, general academic interests/achievements, health fields, home economics, humanities, international studies, mathematics, military science, physical sciences, premedicine, religion/biblical studies, social sciences. *Creative arts/performance:* 256 awards ($205,450 total): music, performing arts, theater/drama. *Special achievements/activities:* 951 awards ($2,859,431 total): cheerleading/drum major, general special achievements/activities, leadership, memberships. *Special characteristics:* 593 awards ($2,103,002 total): children of faculty/staff, first-generation college students, general special characteristics, international students, members of minority groups, out-of-state students, previous college experience, veterans. *Tuition waivers:* Full or partial for employees or children of employees, senior citizens.

LOANS *Student loans:* $37,160,461 (60% need-based, 40% non-need-based). 63% of past graduating class borrowed through all loan programs. *Average indebtedness per student:* $19,613. *Average need-based loan:* Freshmen: $3054. Undergraduates: $3826. *Parent loans:* $16,674,761 (13% need-based, 87% non-need-based). *Programs:* FFEL (Subsidized and Unsubsidized Stafford, PLUS), Perkins.

WORK-STUDY *Federal work-study:* Total amount: $1,097,324; 150 jobs averaging $1674. *State or other work-study/employment:* 1,671 part-time jobs averaging $1782.

ATHLETIC AWARDS Total amount: $2,453,296 (44% need-based, 56% non-need-based).

APPLYING FOR FINANCIAL AID *Required financial aid form:* FAFSA. *Financial aid deadline (priority):* 3/1. *Notification date:* Continuous beginning 4/1. Students must reply within 3 weeks of notification.

CONTACT Kerri Saylor, Lead Customer Service Representative, Southeast Missouri State University, One University Plaza, Cape Girardeau, MO 63701, 573-651-2253. *Fax:* 573-651-5006. *E-mail:* sfs@semo.edu.

SOUTHERN ADVENTIST UNIVERSITY
Collegedale, TN

Tuition & fees: $17,712 — **Average undergraduate aid package: $20,165**

ABOUT THE INSTITUTION Independent Seventh-day Adventist, coed. 72 undergraduate majors. Both federal and institutional methodology are used as a basis for awarding need-based institutional aid.

UNDERGRADUATE EXPENSES for 2010–11 *Comprehensive fee:* $22,886 includes full-time tuition ($16,942), mandatory fees ($770), and room and board ($5174). *College room only:* $3174. Room and board charges vary according to housing facility. Part-time tuition and fees vary according to course load. *Payment plans:* Tuition prepayment, installment, deferred payment.

FRESHMAN FINANCIAL AID (Fall 2009, est.) 476 applied for aid; of those 59% were deemed to have need. 99% of freshmen with need received aid; of those 97% had need fully met. *Average percent of need met:* 82% (excluding

resources awarded to replace EFC). *Average financial aid package:* $20,130 (excluding resources awarded to replace EFC). 32% of all full-time freshmen had no need and received non-need-based gift aid.

UNDERGRADUATE FINANCIAL AID (Fall 2009, est.) 1,616 applied for aid; of those 63% were deemed to have need. 100% of undergraduates with need received aid; of those 95% had need fully met. *Average percent of need met:* 77% (excluding resources awarded to replace EFC). *Average financial aid package:* $20,165 (excluding resources awarded to replace EFC). 27% of all full-time undergraduates had no need and received non-need-based gift aid.

GIFT AID (NEED-BASED) *Total amount:* $12,208,409 (32% federal, 5% state, 45% institutional, 18% external sources). *Receiving aid:* Freshmen: 47% (280); all full-time undergraduates: 45% (992). *Average award:* Freshmen: $1272; Undergraduates: $11,272. *Scholarships, grants, and awards:* Federal Pell, FSEOG, state, private, college/university gift aid from institutional funds.

GIFT AID (NON-NEED-BASED) *Total amount:* $5,151,797 (11% state, 57% institutional, 32% external sources). *Receiving aid:* Freshmen: 39% (233). Undergraduates: 26% (565). *Average award:* Freshmen: $6990. Undergraduates: $5408. *Scholarships, grants, and awards by category:* Academic interests/achievement: business, communication, education, English, general academic interests/achievements, health fields, mathematics, religion/biblical studies. *Creative arts/performance:* art/fine arts, journalism/publications, music, theater/drama. *Special achievements/activities:* community service, general special achievements/activities, leadership, religious involvement. *Special characteristics:* children and siblings of alumni, general special characteristics, international students, local/state students, members of minority groups, out-of-state students, siblings of current students, spouses of current students. *Tuition waivers:* Full or partial for employees or children of employees, adult students, senior citizens.

LOANS *Student loans:* $12,311,509 (69% need-based, 31% non-need-based). 58% of past graduating class borrowed through all loan programs. *Average indebtedness per student:* $22,977. *Average need-based loan:* Freshmen: $3963. Undergraduates: $4793. *Parent loans:* $1,755,509 (31% need-based, 69% non-need-based). *Programs:* FFEL (Subsidized and Unsubsidized Stafford, PLUS), Perkins, Federal Nursing, college/university.

WORK-STUDY *Federal work-study:* Total amount: $1,959,637; jobs available. *State or other work-study/employment:* Part-time jobs available.

APPLYING FOR FINANCIAL AID *Required financial aid form:* FAFSA. *Financial aid deadline (priority):* 3/1. *Notification date:* Continuous. Students must reply within 2 weeks of notification.

CONTACT Mr. Marc Grundy, Director of Student Finance Office, Southern Adventist University, PO Box 370, Collegedale, TN 37315-0370, 423-236-2875 or toll-free 800-768-8437. *Fax:* 423-236-1835.

SOUTHERN ARKANSAS UNIVERSITY– MAGNOLIA
Magnolia, AR

Tuition & fees (AR res): $6066	Average undergraduate aid package: $7679

ABOUT THE INSTITUTION State-supported, coed. 58 undergraduate majors. Federal methodology is used as a basis for awarding need-based institutional aid.

UNDERGRADUATE EXPENSES for 2009–10 *Tuition, state resident:* full-time $5100; part-time $170 per hour. *Tuition, nonresident:* full-time $7740; part-time $258 per hour. *Required fees:* full-time $966; $31 per hour or $18 per term. Full-time tuition and fees vary according to course load. Part-time tuition and fees vary according to course load. *College room and board:* $4400; *Room only:* $2236. Room and board charges vary according to board plan and housing facility. *Payment plan:* Installment.

FRESHMAN FINANCIAL AID (Fall 2009, est.) 374 applied for aid; of those 90% were deemed to have need. 85% of freshmen with need received aid; of those 81% had need fully met. *Average percent of need met:* 100% (excluding resources awarded to replace EFC). *Average financial aid package:* $7486 (excluding resources awarded to replace EFC). 8% of all full-time freshmen had no need and received non-need-based gift aid.

UNDERGRADUATE FINANCIAL AID (Fall 2009, est.) 1,959 applied for aid; of those 90% were deemed to have need. 82% of undergraduates with need received aid; of those 82% had need fully met. *Average percent of need met:* 100% (excluding resources awarded to replace EFC). *Average financial aid*

package: $7679 (excluding resources awarded to replace EFC). 13% of all full-time undergraduates had no need and received non-need-based gift aid.

GIFT AID (NEED-BASED) *Total amount:* $7,811,339 (89% federal, 11% state). *Receiving aid:* Freshmen: 43% (267); all full-time undergraduates: 46% (1,043). *Average award:* Freshmen: $4241; Undergraduates: $4106. *Scholarships, grants, and awards:* Federal Pell, FSEOG, state, private, college/university gift aid from institutional funds.

GIFT AID (NON-NEED-BASED) *Total amount:* $6,017,402 (84% institutional, 16% external sources). *Receiving aid:* Freshmen: 32% (199). Undergraduates: 44% (987). *Average award:* Freshmen: $6036. Undergraduates: $5891. *Scholarships, grants, and awards by category:* Academic interests/achievement: 577 awards ($2,358,992 total): agriculture, business, computer science, education, English, foreign languages, general academic interests/achievements, health fields, mathematics, physical sciences, social sciences. *Creative arts/performance:* 21 awards ($76,632 total): art/fine arts, dance, music, theater/drama. *Special achievements/activities:* 67 awards ($181,093 total): cheerleading/drum major, leadership, rodeo. *Special characteristics:* 566 awards ($1,241,222 total): adult students, children and siblings of alumni, children of faculty/staff, members of minority groups, out-of-state students. *Tuition waivers:* Full or partial for children of alumni, employees or children of employees, senior citizens.

LOANS *Student loans:* $12,756,803 (54% need-based, 46% non-need-based). 72% of past graduating class borrowed through all loan programs. *Average indebtedness per student:* $15,672. *Average need-based loan:* Freshmen: $2880. Undergraduates: $3692. *Parent loans:* $104,630 (100% non-need-based). *Programs:* FFEL (Subsidized and Unsubsidized Stafford, PLUS), Perkins.

WORK-STUDY *Federal work-study:* Total amount: $3,791,480; 1,250 jobs averaging $3097. *State or other work-study/employment:* Total amount: $1,287,080 (100% non-need-based). 303 part-time jobs averaging $4268.

ATHLETIC AWARDS Total amount: $854,507 (100% non-need-based).

APPLYING FOR FINANCIAL AID *Required financial aid form:* FAFSA. *Financial aid deadline (priority):* 7/1. *Notification date:* Continuous beginning 4/1. Students must reply within 2 weeks of notification.

CONTACT Ms. Bronwyn C. Sneed, Director of Student Aid, Southern Arkansas University–Magnolia, PO Box 9344, Magnolia, AR 71754-9344, 870-235-4023 or toll-free 800-332-7286 (in-state). *Fax:* 870-235-4913. *E-mail:* bcsneed@ saumag.edu.

SOUTHERN BAPTIST THEOLOGICAL SEMINARY
Louisville, KY

Tuition & fees: N/R	Average undergraduate aid package: $1328

ABOUT THE INSTITUTION Independent Southern Baptist, coed. *Awards:* associate, bachelor's, and master's degrees. 6 undergraduate majors. *Total enrollment:* 3,190. Undergraduates: 668. Freshmen: 62. Institutional methodology is used as a basis for awarding need-based institutional aid.

FRESHMAN FINANCIAL AID (Fall 2009, est.) 19 applied for aid; of those 100% were deemed to have need. 100% of freshmen with need received aid. *Average financial aid package:* $840 (excluding resources awarded to replace EFC).

UNDERGRADUATE FINANCIAL AID (Fall 2009, est.) 71 applied for aid; of those 94% were deemed to have need. 100% of undergraduates with need received aid. *Average financial aid package:* $1328 (excluding resources awarded to replace EFC).

GIFT AID (NEED-BASED) *Total amount:* $267,656 (8% institutional, 92% external sources). *Receiving aid:* Freshmen: 40% (19); all full-time undergraduates: 18% (67). *Average award:* Freshmen: $703; Undergraduates: $1000. *Scholarships, grants, and awards:* private, college/university gift aid from institutional funds, local church and denominational scholarships, as well as scholarships from various ministries.

GIFT AID (NON-NEED-BASED) *Total amount:* $225,585 (100% institutional). *Receiving aid:* Freshmen: 4% (2). Undergraduates: 4% (15).

LOANS *Student loans:* $976,319 (100% need-based). 30% of past graduating class borrowed through all loan programs. *Average indebtedness per student:* $18,258. *Programs:* college/university, Non-Title IV loan programs (such as Sallie Mae Smart Option Loans).

APPLYING FOR FINANCIAL AID *Required financial aid form:* institution's own form. *Financial aid deadline:* 8/1. *Notification date:* Continuous.

CONTACT Mrs. Erin Joiner, Manager of Financial Aid, Southern Baptist Theological Seminary, 2825 Lexington Road, Louisville, KY 40280, 502-897-4206. *Fax:* 502-897-4031. *E-mail:* financialaid@sbts.edu.

SOUTHERN CALIFORNIA INSTITUTE OF ARCHITECTURE
Los Angeles, CA

CONTACT Lina Johnson, Financial Aid Director, Southern California Institute of Architecture, 960 East 3rd Street, Los Angeles, CA 90013, 213-613-2200 Ext. 345 or toll-free 800-774-7242. *Fax:* 213-613-2260. *E-mail:* financialaid@sciarc.edu.

SOUTHERN CALIFORNIA INSTITUTE OF TECHNOLOGY
Anaheim, CA

CONTACT Ziba Didehar, Financial Aid Officer, Southern California Institute of Technology, 1900 West Crescent Avenue, Building B, Anaheim, CA 92801, 714-520-5552. *Fax:* 714-520-4520. *E-mail:* scit@earthlink.net.

SOUTHERN CALIFORNIA SEMINARY
El Cajon, CA

CONTACT Financial Aid Office, Southern California Seminary, 2075 East Madison Avenue, El Cajon, CA 92019, 619-442-9841.

SOUTHERN CONNECTICUT STATE UNIVERSITY
New Haven, CT

Tuition & fees (CT res): $8050 | **Average undergraduate aid package: $8355**

ABOUT THE INSTITUTION State-supported, coed. 43 undergraduate majors. Federal methodology is used as a basis for awarding need-based institutional aid.

UNDERGRADUATE EXPENSES for 2010–11 *Tuition, state resident:* full-time $4023; part-time $403 per credit. *Tuition, nonresident:* full-time $13,020; part-time $416 per credit. *Required fees:* full-time $4027; $55 per term. Full-time tuition and fees vary according to course load. Part-time tuition and fees vary according to course load. *College room and board:* $9983; *Room only:* $5541. Room and board charges vary according to board plan and housing facility. *Payment plans:* Installment, deferred payment.

FRESHMAN FINANCIAL AID (Fall 2009, est.) 1,097 applied for aid; of those 67% were deemed to have need. 96% of freshmen with need received aid; of those 31% had need fully met. *Average percent of need met:* 79% (excluding resources awarded to replace EFC). *Average financial aid package:* $8291 (excluding resources awarded to replace EFC). 6% of all full-time freshmen had no need and received non-need-based gift aid.

UNDERGRADUATE FINANCIAL AID (Fall 2009, est.) 6,307 applied for aid; of those 67% were deemed to have need. 97% of undergraduates with need received aid; of those 33% had need fully met. *Average percent of need met:* 79% (excluding resources awarded to replace EFC). *Average financial aid package:* $8355 (excluding resources awarded to replace EFC). 4% of all full-time undergraduates had no need and received non-need-based gift aid.

GIFT AID (NEED-BASED) *Total amount:* $21,691,827 (44% federal, 26% state, 29% institutional, 1% external sources). *Receiving aid:* Freshmen: 46% (570); all full-time undergraduates: 45% (3,340). *Average award:* Freshmen: $6081; Undergraduates: $5784. *Scholarships, grants, and awards:* Federal Pell, FSEOG, state, private, college/university gift aid from institutional funds.

GIFT AID (NON-NEED-BASED) *Total amount:* $1,860,424 (2% federal, 57% institutional, 41% external sources). *Receiving aid:* Freshmen: 12% (143). Undergraduates: 8% (558). *Average award:* Freshmen: $3577. Undergraduates: $3677. *Scholarships, grants, and awards by category:* Special characteristics: children of faculty/staff, veterans. *Tuition waivers:* Full or partial for employees or children of employees, senior citizens.

LOANS *Student loans:* $54,808,614 (67% need-based, 33% non-need-based). 66% of past graduating class borrowed through all loan programs. *Average*

indebtedness per student: $17,374. *Average need-based loan:* Freshmen: $3408. Undergraduates: $3731. *Parent loans:* $10,479,075 (19% need-based, 81% non-need-based). *Programs:* Federal Direct (Subsidized and Unsubsidized Stafford, PLUS).

WORK-STUDY *Federal work-study:* Total amount: $442,825; 112 jobs averaging $3777.

ATHLETIC AWARDS Total amount: $1,480,195 (36% need-based, 64% non-need-based).

APPLYING FOR FINANCIAL AID *Required financial aid form:* FAFSA. *Financial aid deadline:* 3/9 (priority: 3/5). *Notification date:* Continuous beginning 4/11. Students must reply within 2 weeks of notification.

CONTACT Avon Dennis, Director of Financial Aid, Southern Connecticut State University, Wintergreen Building, New Haven, CT 06515-1355, 203-392-5448. *Fax:* 203-392-5229. *E-mail:* dennisa1@southernct.edu.

SOUTHERN ILLINOIS UNIVERSITY CARBONDALE
Carbondale, IL

Tuition & fees (IL res): $10,411 | **Average undergraduate aid package: $11,809**

ABOUT THE INSTITUTION State-supported, coed. 90 undergraduate majors. Federal methodology is used as a basis for awarding need-based institutional aid.

UNDERGRADUATE EXPENSES for 2009–10 *Tuition, state resident:* full-time $7290; part-time $243 per credit hour. *Tuition, nonresident:* full-time $18,225; part-time $607.50 per credit hour. *Required fees:* full-time $3121; $288 per credit hour. Full-time tuition and fees vary according to course load. Part-time tuition and fees vary according to course load. *College room and board:* $7673; *Room only:* $4405. Room and board charges vary according to board plan and housing facility. *Payment plans:* Guaranteed tuition, installment.

FRESHMAN FINANCIAL AID (Fall 2008) 2,233 applied for aid; of those 80% were deemed to have need. 97% of freshmen with need received aid; of those 88% had need fully met. *Average percent of need met:* 95% (excluding resources awarded to replace EFC). *Average financial aid package:* $11,811 (excluding resources awarded to replace EFC). 6% of all full-time freshmen had no need and received non-need-based gift aid.

UNDERGRADUATE FINANCIAL AID (Fall 2008) 10,510 applied for aid; of those 85% were deemed to have need. 97% of undergraduates with need received aid; of those 86% had need fully met. *Average percent of need met:* 95% (excluding resources awarded to replace EFC). *Average financial aid package:* $11,809 (excluding resources awarded to replace EFC). 9% of all full-time undergraduates had no need and received non-need-based gift aid.

GIFT AID (NEED-BASED) *Total amount:* $44,026,166 (41% federal, 49% state, 9% institutional, 1% external sources). *Receiving aid:* Freshmen: 49% (1,310); all full-time undergraduates: 45% (6,399). *Average award:* Freshmen: $7406; Undergraduates: $6934. *Scholarships, grants, and awards:* Federal Pell, FSEOG, state, private, college/university gift aid from institutional funds.

GIFT AID (NON-NEED-BASED) *Total amount:* $21,690,129 (31% federal, 32% state, 24% institutional, 13% external sources). *Receiving aid:* Freshmen: 35% (940). Undergraduates: 26% (3,732). *Average award:* Freshmen: $6718. Undergraduates: $6359. *Scholarships, grants, and awards by category:* Academic interests/achievement: agriculture, architecture, area/ethnic studies, biological sciences, business, communication, computer science, education, engineering/technologies, English, foreign languages, general academic interests/achievements, health fields, home economics, humanities, international studies, mathematics, military science, physical sciences, premedicine, religion/biblical studies, social sciences. Creative arts/performance: applied art and design, cinema/film/broadcasting, creative writing, dance, debating, general creative arts/performance, journalism/publications, performing arts. Special achievements/activities: cheerleading/drum major, community service, general special achievements/activities, leadership. Special characteristics: children and siblings of alumni, children of educators, children of faculty/staff, children of public servants, children with a deceased or disabled parent, general special characteristics, handicapped students, international students, members of minority groups, public servants, spouses of deceased or disabled public servants, veterans. *Tuition waivers:* Full or partial for employees or children of employees, senior citizens.

LOANS *Student loans:* $69,080,873 (59% need-based, 41% non-need-based). 50% of past graduating class borrowed through all loan programs. *Average*

indebtedness per student: $21,359. *Average need-based loan:* Freshmen: $3637. Undergraduates: $4121. *Parent loans:* $15,209,396 (17% need-based, 83% non-need-based). *Programs:* Federal Direct (Subsidized and Unsubsidized Stafford, PLUS), Perkins, college/university.

WORK-STUDY *Federal work-study:* Total amount: $7,777,587; jobs available. *State or other work-study/employment:* Total amount: $8,396,915 (19% need-based, 81% non-need-based). Part-time jobs available.

ATHLETIC AWARDS Total amount: $3,682,593 (34% need-based, 66% non-need-based).

APPLYING FOR FINANCIAL AID *Required financial aid form:* FAFSA. *Financial aid deadline (priority):* 4/1. *Notification date:* Continuous beginning 5/1. Students must reply within 4 weeks of notification.

CONTACT Linda Joy Clemons, Director of Financial Aid, Southern Illinois University Carbondale, Woody Hall, Third Floor, B-Wing, Carbondale, IL 62901-4702, 618-453-3102. *Fax:* 618-453-4606. *E-mail:* lclemons@siu.edu.

SOUTHERN ILLINOIS UNIVERSITY EDWARDSVILLE
Edwardsville, IL

Tuition & fees (IL res): $8336	Average undergraduate aid package: $15,749

ABOUT THE INSTITUTION State-supported, coed. 43 undergraduate majors. Federal methodology is used as a basis for awarding need-based institutional aid.

UNDERGRADUATE EXPENSES for 2009–10 *Tuition, state resident:* full-time $6201; part-time $206.70 per semester hour. *Tuition, nonresident:* full-time $15,503. *Required fees:* full-time $2135; $250.60 per semester hour. Full-time tuition and fees vary according to course load. Part-time tuition and fees vary according to course load. *College room and board:* $7461. Room and board charges vary according to board plan and housing facility. *Payment plans:* Guaranteed tuition, installment.

FRESHMAN FINANCIAL AID (Fall 2009, est.) 1,632 applied for aid; of those 87% were deemed to have need. 93% of freshmen with need received aid; of those 20% had need fully met. *Average percent of need met:* 45% (excluding resources awarded to replace EFC). *Average financial aid package:* $16,090 (excluding resources awarded to replace EFC). 2% of all full-time freshmen had no need and received non-need-based gift aid.

UNDERGRADUATE FINANCIAL AID (Fall 2009, est.) 7,027 applied for aid; of those 90% were deemed to have need. 94% of undergraduates with need received aid; of those 18% had need fully met. *Average percent of need met:* 46% (excluding resources awarded to replace EFC). *Average financial aid package:* $15,749 (excluding resources awarded to replace EFC). 4% of all full-time undergraduates had no need and received non-need-based gift aid.

GIFT AID (NEED-BASED) *Total amount:* $28,179,723 (56% federal, 36% state, 5% institutional, 3% external sources). *Receiving aid:* Freshmen: 36% (693); all full-time undergraduates: 34% (3,219). *Average award:* Freshmen: $9621; Undergraduates: $9606. *Scholarships, grants, and awards:* Federal Pell, FSEOG, state, private, college/university gift aid from institutional funds, Federal Nursing.

GIFT AID (NON-NEED-BASED) *Total amount:* $2,059,261 (19% federal, 31% state, 35% institutional, 15% external sources). *Receiving aid:* Freshmen: 2% (36). Undergraduates: 1% (140). *Average award:* Freshmen: $9091. Undergraduates: $7261. *Scholarships, grants, and awards by category:* Academic interests/achievement: business, education, general academic interests/achievements, health fields. Creative arts/performance: art/fine arts, dance, music, theater/drama. Special characteristics: children of faculty/staff. *Tuition waivers:* Full or partial for employees or children of employees, senior citizens.

LOANS *Student loans:* $42,174,151 (87% need-based, 13% non-need-based). 44% of past graduating class borrowed through all loan programs. *Average indebtedness per student:* $20,603. *Average need-based loan:* Freshmen: $9458. Undergraduates: $10,045. *Parent loans:* $11,960,113 (40% need-based, 60% non-need-based). *Programs:* Federal Direct (Subsidized and Unsubsidized Stafford, PLUS), FFEL (Subsidized and Unsubsidized Stafford, PLUS), Perkins, Federal Nursing, college/university, alternative loans.

WORK-STUDY *Federal work-study:* Total amount: $5,672,924; jobs available. *State or other work-study/employment:* Part-time jobs available.

ATHLETIC AWARDS Total amount: $598,563 (42% need-based, 58% non-need-based).

APPLYING FOR FINANCIAL AID *Required financial aid form:* FAFSA. *Financial aid deadline (priority):* 3/1. *Notification date:* Continuous beginning 3/15. Students must reply within 2 weeks of notification.

CONTACT Sharon Berry, Director of Financial Aid, Southern Illinois University Edwardsville, Campus Box 1060, Edwardsville, IL 62026-1060, 618-650-3834 or toll-free 800-447-SIUE. *Fax:* 618-650-3885. *E-mail:* shaberr@siue.edu.

SOUTHERN METHODIST COLLEGE
Orangeburg, SC

CONTACT Financial Aid Officer, Southern Methodist College, PO Box 1027, 541 Broughton Street, Orangeburg, SC 29116, 803-534-7826 Ext. 1326 or toll-free 800-360-1503. *Fax:* 803-534-7827.

SOUTHERN METHODIST UNIVERSITY
Dallas, TX

Tuition & fees: $35,160	Average undergraduate aid package: $30,985

ABOUT THE INSTITUTION Independent religious, coed. 66 undergraduate majors. Both federal and institutional methodology are used as a basis for awarding need-based institutional aid.

UNDERGRADUATE EXPENSES for 2009–10 *Comprehensive fee:* $47,605 includes full-time tuition ($31,200), mandatory fees ($3960), and room and board ($12,445). Full-time tuition and fees vary according to class time. Room and board charges vary according to board plan and housing facility. *Part-time tuition:* $1304 per credit hour. *Part-time fees:* $166 per credit hour. Part-time tuition and fees vary according to class time and course load. *Payment plans:* Tuition prepayment, installment.

FRESHMAN FINANCIAL AID (Fall 2009, est.) 726 applied for aid; of those 74% were deemed to have need. 100% of freshmen with need received aid; of those 44% had need fully met. *Average percent of need met:* 90% (excluding resources awarded to replace EFC). *Average financial aid package:* $33,921 (excluding resources awarded to replace EFC). 33% of all full-time freshmen had no need and received non-need-based gift aid.

UNDERGRADUATE FINANCIAL AID (Fall 2009, est.) 2,556 applied for aid; of those 83% were deemed to have need. 99% of undergraduates with need received aid; of those 35% had need fully met. *Average percent of need met:* 88% (excluding resources awarded to replace EFC). *Average financial aid package:* $30,985 (excluding resources awarded to replace EFC). 35% of all full-time undergraduates had no need and received non-need-based gift aid.

GIFT AID (NEED-BASED) *Total amount:* $46,658,097 (10% federal, 8% state, 81% institutional, 1% external sources). *Receiving aid:* Freshmen: 33% (440); all full-time undergraduates: 30% (1,750). *Average award:* Freshmen: $20,259; Undergraduates: $17,879. *Scholarships, grants, and awards:* Federal Pell, FSEOG, state, private, college/university gift aid from institutional funds.

GIFT AID (NON-NEED-BASED) *Total amount:* $23,789,144 (97% institutional, 3% external sources). *Receiving aid:* Freshmen: 29% (390). Undergraduates: 22% (1,295). *Average award:* Freshmen: $15,539. Undergraduates: $14,240. *Tuition waivers:* Full or partial for employees or children of employees.

LOANS *Student loans:* $16,384,820 (57% need-based, 43% non-need-based). 28% of past graduating class borrowed through all loan programs. *Average indebtedness per student:* $20,180. *Average need-based loan:* Freshmen: $2454. Undergraduates: $3433. *Parent loans:* $9,375,381 (30% need-based, 70% non-need-based). *Programs:* FFEL (Subsidized and Unsubsidized Stafford, PLUS), Perkins, state, college/university.

WORK-STUDY *Federal work-study:* Total amount: $4,277,497; 1,331 jobs averaging $3191. *State or other work-study/employment:* Total amount: $154,132 (26% need-based, 74% non-need-based). 16 part-time jobs averaging $2907.

ATHLETIC AWARDS Total amount: $11,363,514 (38% need-based, 62% non-need-based).

APPLYING FOR FINANCIAL AID *Required financial aid forms:* FAFSA, CSS Financial Aid PROFILE, noncustodial (divorced/separated) parent's statement, business/farm supplement. *Financial aid deadline (priority):* 3/1. *Notification date:* Continuous beginning 3/15.

CONTACT Marc Peterson, Director of Financial Aid, Southern Methodist University, PO Box 750181, Dallas, TX 75275, 214-768-3016 or toll-free 800-323-0672. *Fax:* 214-768-0202. *E-mail:* mpeterso@smu.edu.

SOUTHERN NAZARENE UNIVERSITY
Bethany, OK

Tuition & fees: $17,664   **Average undergraduate aid package:** N/A

ABOUT THE INSTITUTION Independent Nazarene, coed. **Awards:** associate, bachelor's, and master's degrees. 59 undergraduate majors. **Total enrollment:** 2,069. Undergraduates: 1,628. Freshmen: 270. Federal methodology is used as a basis for awarding need-based institutional aid.

UNDERGRADUATE EXPENSES for 2009–10 **Application fee:** $35. **Comprehensive fee:** $24,154 includes full-time tuition ($17,040), mandatory fees ($624), and room and board ($6490). **College room only:** $3200. **Part-time tuition:** $568 per credit hour. **Part-time fees:** $23 per credit hour.

FRESHMAN FINANCIAL AID (Fall 2009, est.) 257 applied for aid; of those 92% were deemed to have need. 96% of freshmen with need received aid.

UNDERGRADUATE FINANCIAL AID (Fall 2009, est.) 1,485 applied for aid; of those 92% were deemed to have need. 96% of undergraduates with need received aid.

GIFT AID (NEED-BASED) **Total amount:** $4,635,095 (63% federal, 26% state, 5% institutional, 6% external sources). **Scholarships, grants, and awards:** Federal Pell, FSEOG, state, private, college/university gift aid from institutional funds.

GIFT AID (NON-NEED-BASED) **Total amount:** $3,754,394 (93% institutional, 7% external sources). **Scholarships, grants, and awards by category:** Academic interests/achievement: biological sciences, business, communication, computer science, education, English, general academic interests/achievements, mathematics, physical sciences, religion/biblical studies, social sciences. Creative arts/performance: art/fine arts, music, performing arts. Special achievements/activities: cheerleading/drum major. Special characteristics: children and siblings of alumni, children of faculty/staff, first-generation college students, international students, local/state students, religious affiliation, siblings of current students, veterans, veterans' children. **ROTC:** Army cooperative, Air Force cooperative.

LOANS Student loans: $16,122,327 (45% need-based, 55% non-need-based). **Parent loans:** $2,187,167 (100% non-need-based). **Programs:** Federal Direct (Subsidized and Unsubsidized Stafford, PLUS), Perkins, alternative loans.

WORK-STUDY Federal work-study: Total amount: $221,000; 104 jobs averaging $2125. **State or other work-study/employment:** 115 part-time jobs averaging $3000.

ATHLETIC AWARDS Total amount: $2,531,568 (100% non-need-based).

APPLYING FOR FINANCIAL AID Required financial aid form: FAFSA. **Financial aid deadline (priority):** 3/1. **Notification date:** Continuous beginning 3/15. Students must reply within 2 weeks of notification.

CONTACT Diana Lee, Director of Financial Assistance, Southern Nazarene University, 6729 Northwest 39th Expressway, Bethany, OK 73008, 405-491-6310 or toll-free 800-648-9899. Fax: 405-717-6271. E-mail: dlee@snu.edu.

SOUTHERN NEW HAMPSHIRE UNIVERSITY
Manchester, NH

ABOUT THE INSTITUTION Independent, coed. 38 undergraduate majors.
GIFT AID (NEED-BASED) Scholarships, grants, and awards: Federal Pell, FSEOG, state, private, college/university gift aid from institutional funds.
LOANS Programs: FFEL (Subsidized and Unsubsidized Stafford, PLUS), Perkins.
APPLYING FOR FINANCIAL AID Required financial aid form: FAFSA.
CONTACT Financial Aid Office, Southern New Hampshire University, 2500 North River Road, Manchester, NH 03106, 603-645-9645 or toll-free 800-642-4968. Fax: 603-645-9639. E-mail: finaid@snhu.edu.

SOUTHERN OREGON UNIVERSITY
Ashland, OR

ABOUT THE INSTITUTION State-supported, coed. 40 undergraduate majors.
GIFT AID (NEED-BASED) Scholarships, grants, and awards: Federal Pell, FSEOG, state, private, college/university gift aid from institutional funds.
GIFT AID (NON-NEED-BASED) Scholarships, grants, and awards by category: Academic interests/achievement: biological sciences, business, education, English, foreign languages, general academic interests/achievements, health fields, mathematics, physical sciences, social sciences. Creative arts/performance: art/fine arts, creative writing, journalism/publications, music, theater/drama. Special achievements/activities: community service, general special achievements/activities, hobbies/interests, leadership, memberships. Special characteristics: adult students, international students, members of minority groups.

LOANS Programs: Federal Direct (Subsidized and Unsubsidized Stafford, PLUS), Perkins, state, college/university.

WORK-STUDY Federal work-study: Total amount: $696,004; jobs available.

APPLYING FOR FINANCIAL AID Required financial aid forms: FAFSA, institution's own form.

CONTACT Enrollment Services Center, Southern Oregon University, 1250 Siskiyou Boulevard, Ashland, OR 97520, 541-552-6600 or toll-free 800-482-7672 (in-state). Fax: 541-552-6614. E-mail: esc@sou.edu.

SOUTHERN POLYTECHNIC STATE UNIVERSITY
Marietta, GA

Tuition & fees (GA res): $4498   **Average undergraduate aid package:** $3678

ABOUT THE INSTITUTION State-supported, coed. 32 undergraduate majors. Federal methodology is used as a basis for awarding need-based institutional aid.

UNDERGRADUATE EXPENSES for 2009–10 Tuition, **state resident:** full-time $3502; part-time $146 per credit hour. **Tuition, nonresident:** full-time $13,998; part-time $584 per credit hour. **Required fees:** full-time $996; $498 per term. Full-time tuition and fees vary according to course load and degree level. Part-time tuition and fees vary according to course load and degree level. **College room and board:** $6350; **Room only:** $3550. Room and board charges vary according to board plan.

FRESHMAN FINANCIAL AID (Fall 2009, est.) 563 applied for aid; of those 100% were deemed to have need. 98% of freshmen with need received aid; of those 37% had need fully met. **Average percent of need met:** 91% (excluding resources awarded to replace EFC). **Average financial aid package:** $3101 (excluding resources awarded to replace EFC). 1% of all full-time freshmen had no need and received non-need-based gift aid.

UNDERGRADUATE FINANCIAL AID (Fall 2009, est.) 3,217 applied for aid; of those 80% were deemed to have need. 96% of undergraduates with need received aid; of those 15% had need fully met. **Average percent of need met:** 78% (excluding resources awarded to replace EFC). **Average financial aid package:** $3678 (excluding resources awarded to replace EFC). 1% of all full-time undergraduates had no need and received non-need-based gift aid.

GIFT AID (NEED-BASED) Total amount: $4,789,149 (97% federal, 3% external sources). **Receiving aid:** Freshmen: 44% (311); all full-time undergraduates: 46% (2,281). **Average award:** Freshmen: $3472; Undergraduates: $3739. **Scholarships, grants, and awards:** Federal Pell, FSEOG, state, private, college/university gift aid from institutional funds.

GIFT AID (NON-NEED-BASED) Total amount: $6,223,186 (2% federal, 92% state, 6% external sources). **Receiving aid:** Freshmen: 54% (379). Undergraduates: 17% (832). **Average award:** Freshmen: $10,626. Undergraduates: $8269. **Scholarships, grants, and awards by category:** Academic interests/achievement: general academic interests/achievements. Special characteristics: members of minority groups. **Tuition waivers:** Full or partial for employees or children of employees, senior citizens.

LOANS Student loans: $16,338,920 (46% need-based, 54% non-need-based). 50% of past graduating class borrowed through all loan programs. **Average indebtedness per student:** $16,280. **Average need-based loan:** Freshmen: $3714. Undergraduates: $4824. **Parent loans:** $613,809 (100% non-need-based). **Programs:** Federal Direct (Subsidized and Unsubsidized Stafford, PLUS).

WORK-STUDY Federal work-study: Total amount: $169,503; 105 jobs averaging $4000.

ATHLETIC AWARDS Total amount: $317,156 (100% non-need-based).

APPLYING FOR FINANCIAL AID Required financial aid form: FAFSA. **Financial aid deadline (priority):** 3/1. **Notification date:** Continuous beginning 4/1. Students must reply by 8/15.

CONTACT Mr. Gary Mann, Director of Financial Aid, Southern Polytechnic State University, 1100 South Marietta Parkway, Marietta, GA 30060-2896, 678-915-7290 or toll-free 800-635-3204. Fax: 678-915-4227. E-mail: gmann@spsu.edu.

SOUTHERN UNIVERSITY AND AGRICULTURAL AND MECHANICAL COLLEGE
Baton Rouge, LA

CONTACT Mr. Phillip Rodgers Sr., Director of Financial Aid, Southern University and Agricultural and Mechanical College, PO Box 9961, Baton Rouge, LA 70813, 225-771-2790 or toll-free 800-256-1531. *Fax:* 225-771-5898. *E-mail:* phillip_rodgers@cxs.subr.edu.

SOUTHERN UNIVERSITY AT NEW ORLEANS
New Orleans, LA

CONTACT Director of Financial Aid, Southern University at New Orleans, 6400 Press Drive, New Orleans, LA 70126, 504-286-5263. *Fax:* 504-286-5213.

SOUTHERN UTAH UNIVERSITY
Cedar City, UT

Tuition & fees (UT res): $4269 **Average undergraduate aid package: $6863**

ABOUT THE INSTITUTION State-supported, coed. 49 undergraduate majors. Federal methodology is used as a basis for awarding need-based institutional aid.

UNDERGRADUATE EXPENSES for 2009–10 *Tuition, state resident:* full-time $3730; part-time $182 per credit hour. *Tuition, nonresident:* full-time $12,308; part-time $600 per credit hour. *Required fees:* full-time $539; $539 per year. Part-time tuition and fees vary according to course load. *College room and board: Room only:* $1950. Room and board charges vary according to board plan and housing facility. *Payment plan:* Installment.

FRESHMAN FINANCIAL AID (Fall 2008) 795 applied for aid; of those 77% were deemed to have need. 100% of freshmen with need received aid; of those 14% had need fully met. *Average percent of need met:* 63% (excluding resources awarded to replace EFC). *Average financial aid package:* $5986 (excluding resources awarded to replace EFC). 51% of all full-time freshmen had no need and received non-need-based gift aid.

UNDERGRADUATE FINANCIAL AID (Fall 2008) 3,259 applied for aid; of those 86% were deemed to have need. 100% of undergraduates with need received aid; of those 11% had need fully met. *Average percent of need met:* 65% (excluding resources awarded to replace EFC). *Average financial aid package:* $6863 (excluding resources awarded to replace EFC). 42% of all full-time undergraduates had no need and received non-need-based gift aid.

GIFT AID (NEED-BASED) *Total amount:* $8,325,265 (94% federal, 2% state, 2% institutional, 2% external sources). *Receiving aid:* Freshmen: 51% (613); all full-time undergraduates: 59% (2,783). *Average award:* Freshmen: $4922; Undergraduates: $5100. *Scholarships, grants, and awards:* Federal Pell, FSEOG, state, private, college/university gift aid from institutional funds.

GIFT AID (NON-NEED-BASED) *Total amount:* $6,570,712 (85% institutional, 15% external sources). *Receiving aid:* Freshmen: 34% (405). Undergraduates: 19% (901). *Average award:* Freshmen: $5507. Undergraduates: $6654. *Scholarships, grants, and awards by category: Academic interests/achievement:* general academic interests/achievements. *Creative arts/performance:* general creative arts/performance, music, theater/drama. *Special achievements/activities:* general special achievements/activities, leadership. *Special characteristics:* children and siblings of alumni, local/state students, members of minority groups. *Tuition waivers:* Full or partial for employees or children of employees.

LOANS *Student loans:* $12,824,601 (74% need-based, 26% non-need-based). 51% of past graduating class borrowed through all loan programs. *Average indebtedness per student:* $10,485. *Average need-based loan:* Freshmen: $3015. Undergraduates: $3873. *Parent loans:* $386,584 (100% non-need-based). *Programs:* FFEL (Subsidized and Unsubsidized Stafford, PLUS), Perkins.

WORK-STUDY *Federal work-study:* Total amount: $284,371; jobs available. *State or other work-study/employment:* Total amount: $79,339 (100% need-based). Part-time jobs available.

ATHLETIC AWARDS Total amount: $1,980,185 (100% non-need-based).

APPLYING FOR FINANCIAL AID *Required financial aid form:* FAFSA. *Financial aid deadline (priority):* 12/1. *Notification date:* Continuous beginning 11/1. Students must reply by 5/1.

CONTACT Jan Carey-McDonald, Director of Financial Aid and Scholarships, Southern Utah University, 351 West University Boulevard, Cedar City, UT 84720-2498, 435-586-7735. *Fax:* 435-586-7736. *E-mail:* careymcdonald@suu.edu.

SOUTHERN VERMONT COLLEGE
Bennington, VT

CONTACT Office of Financial Aid, Southern Vermont College, 982 Mansion Drive, Bennington, VT 05201, 802-447-6306 or toll-free 800-378-2782. *Fax:* 802-447-4695. *E-mail:* financialaid@svc.edu.

SOUTHERN VIRGINIA UNIVERSITY
Buena Vista, VA

CONTACT Darin Hassell, Financial Aid Specialist, Southern Virginia University, One University Hill Drive, Buena Vista, VA 24416, 540-261-4351 or toll-free 800-229-8420. *Fax:* 540-261-8559. *E-mail:* finaid@svu.edu.

SOUTHERN WESLEYAN UNIVERSITY
Central, SC

CONTACT Mrs. Sherri Peters, Financial Aid Associate, Southern Wesleyan University, 907 Wesleyan Drive, Central, SC 29630-1020, 800-289-1292 Ext. 5517 or toll-free 800-289-1292 Ext. 5550. *Fax:* 864-644-5970. *E-mail:* finaid@swu.edu.

SOUTH UNIVERSITY
Montgomery, AL

UNDERGRADUATE EXPENSES Information about tuition and fees can be obtained by contacting the South University Admissions Office.

CONTACT Financial Aid Office, South University, 5355 Vaughn Road, Montgomery, AL 36116-1120, 334-395-8800 or toll-free 866-629-2962.

SOUTH UNIVERSITY
Royal Palm Beach, FL

UNDERGRADUATE EXPENSES Information about tuition and fees can be obtained by contacting the South University Admissions Office.

CONTACT Financial Aid Office, South University, 1760 North Congress Avenue, West Palm Beach, FL 33409, 561-697-9200 Ext. 230 or toll-free 866-629-2902. *Fax:* 561-697-9944. *E-mail:* lhartman@southcollege.edu.

SOUTH UNIVERSITY
Tampa, FL

UNDERGRADUATE EXPENSES Information about tuition and fees can be obtained by contacting the South University Admissions Office.

CONTACT Financial Aid Office, South University, 4401 North Himes Avenue, Suite 175, Tampa, FL 33614, 813-393-3800 or toll-free 800-846-1472.

SOUTH UNIVERSITY
Savannah, GA

UNDERGRADUATE EXPENSES Information about tuition and fees can be obtained by contacting the South University Admissions Office.

CONTACT Financial Aid Office, South University, 709 Mall Boulevard, Savannah, GA 31406, 912-201-8000 or toll-free 866-629-2901.

SOUTH UNIVERSITY
Columbia, SC

UNDERGRADUATE EXPENSES Information about tuition and fees can be obtained by contacting the South University Admissions Office.

CONTACT Sandra Gundlach, Financial Aid Coordinator, South University, 3810 Main Street, Columbia, SC 29203, 803-799-9082 or toll-free 866-629-3031. *Fax:* 803-799-9005.

SOUTH UNIVERSITY
Glen Allen, VA

CONTACT Financial Aid Office, South University, 2151 Old Brick Road, Glen Allen, VA 23060, 804-727-6800 or toll-free 888-422-5076.

SOUTH UNIVERSITY
Virginia Beach, VA

CONTACT Financial Aid Office, South University, 301 Bendix Road, Suite 100, Virginia Beach, VA 23452, 757-493-6900 or toll-free 877-206-1845.

SOUTHWEST BAPTIST UNIVERSITY
Bolivar, MO

Tuition & fees: $17,280 **Average undergraduate aid package: $14,821**

ABOUT THE INSTITUTION Independent Southern Baptist, coed. 54 undergraduate majors. Federal methodology is used as a basis for awarding need-based institutional aid.

UNDERGRADUATE EXPENSES for 2010–11 *Comprehensive fee:* $23,000 includes full-time tuition ($16,500), mandatory fees ($780), and room and board ($5720). *College room only:* $2860. Full-time tuition and fees vary according to course load. Room and board charges vary according to board plan and housing facility. Part-time tuition and fees vary according to course load and location. *Payment plan:* Installment.

FRESHMAN FINANCIAL AID (Fall 2009, est.) 405 applied for aid; of those 86% were deemed to have need. 100% of freshmen with need received aid; of those 28% had need fully met. *Average percent of need met:* 81% (excluding resources awarded to replace EFC). *Average financial aid package:* $15,610 (excluding resources awarded to replace EFC). 19% of all full-time freshmen had no need and received non-need-based gift aid.

UNDERGRADUATE FINANCIAL AID (Fall 2009, est.) 1,362 applied for aid; of those 88% were deemed to have need. 100% of undergraduates with need received aid; of those 26% had need fully met. *Average percent of need met:* 77% (excluding resources awarded to replace EFC). *Average financial aid package:* $14,821 (excluding resources awarded to replace EFC). 21% of all full-time undergraduates had no need and received non-need-based gift aid.

GIFT AID (NEED-BASED) *Total amount:* $6,922,050 (67% federal, 33% state). *Receiving aid:* Freshmen: 53% (227); all full-time undergraduates: 50% (773). *Average award:* Freshmen: $6010; Undergraduates: $5601. *Scholarships, grants, and awards:* Federal Pell, FSEOG, state, private, college/university gift aid from institutional funds.

GIFT AID (NON-NEED-BASED) *Total amount:* $10,288,915 (2% state, 88% institutional, 10% external sources). *Receiving aid:* Freshmen: 81% (349). Undergraduates: 77% (1,193). *Average award:* Freshmen: $8441. Undergraduates: $7361. *Scholarships, grants, and awards by category: Academic interests/achievement:* $7,210,712 total: general academic interests/achievements. *Creative arts/performance:* $214,325 total: art/fine arts, debating, general creative arts/performance, music, theater/drama. *Special achievements/activities:* $374,000 total: religious involvement. *Special characteristics:* $760,931 total: general special characteristics, local/state students, relatives of clergy. *Tuition waivers:* Full or partial for employees or children of employees.

LOANS *Student loans:* $12,778,362 (50% need-based, 50% non-need-based). 67% of past graduating class borrowed through all loan programs. *Average need-based loan:* Freshmen: $3598. Undergraduates: $4713. *Parent loans:* $857,480 (100% non-need-based). *Programs:* Federal Direct (Subsidized and Unsubsidized Stafford, PLUS), FFEL (Subsidized and Unsubsidized Stafford, PLUS), Perkins, Federal Nursing, state, alternative loans.

WORK-STUDY *Federal work-study:* Total amount: $637,489; 334 jobs averaging $1850.

ATHLETIC AWARDS Total amount: $2,314,767 (100% non-need-based).

APPLYING FOR FINANCIAL AID *Required financial aid forms:* FAFSA, institution's own form. *Financial aid deadline (priority):* 3/15. *Notification date:* Continuous. Students must reply within 2 weeks of notification.

CONTACT Mr. Brad Gamble, Director of Financial Aid, Southwest Baptist University, 1600 University Avenue, Bolivar, MO 65613-2597, 417-328-1823 or toll-free 800-526-5859. *Fax:* 417-328-1514. *E-mail:* bgamble@sbuniv.edu.

SOUTHWESTERN ADVENTIST UNIVERSITY
Keene, TX

CONTACT Student Financial Services, Southwestern Adventist University, PO Box 567, Keene, TX 76059, 817-645-3921 Ext. 262 or toll-free 800-433-2240. *Fax:* 817-556-4744.

SOUTHWESTERN ASSEMBLIES OF GOD UNIVERSITY
Waxahachie, TX

CONTACT Financial Aid Office, Southwestern Assemblies of God University, 1200 Sycamore Street, Waxahachie, TX 75165-2397, 972-825-4730 or toll-free 888-937-7248. *Fax:* 972-937-4001. *E-mail:* finaid@sagu.edu.

SOUTHWESTERN CHRISTIAN COLLEGE
Terrell, TX

CONTACT Financial Aid Office, Southwestern Christian College, PO Box 10, Terrell, TX 75160, 972-524-3341. *Fax:* 972-563-7133.

SOUTHWESTERN CHRISTIAN UNIVERSITY
Bethany, OK

ABOUT THE INSTITUTION Independent religious, coed. *Awards:* associate, bachelor's, and master's degrees. 11 undergraduate majors. *Total enrollment:* 264. Undergraduates: 180.

GIFT AID (NEED-BASED) *Scholarships, grants, and awards:* Federal Pell, FSEOG, state, private, college/university gift aid from institutional funds.

GIFT AID (NON-NEED-BASED) *Scholarships, grants, and awards by category: Academic interests/achievement:* business, education, general academic interests/achievements, religion/biblical studies. *Creative arts/performance:* music, theater/drama. *Special achievements/activities:* cheerleading/drum major, religious involvement. *Special characteristics:* children and siblings of alumni, children of faculty/staff, relatives of clergy, religious affiliation.

LOANS *Programs:* FFEL (Subsidized and Unsubsidized Stafford, PLUS).

WORK-STUDY *Federal work-study:* Total amount: $53,000; 60 jobs averaging $1500. *State or other work-study/employment:* Total amount: $15,000 (100% non-need-based). 10 part-time jobs averaging $1000.

APPLYING FOR FINANCIAL AID *Required financial aid form:* FAFSA.

CONTACT Mrs. Billie Stewart, Financial Aid Director, Southwestern Christian University, PO Box 340, Bethany, OK 73008, 405-789-7661 Ext. 3456. *Fax:* 405-495-0078. *E-mail:* billie.stewart@swcu.edu.

SOUTHWESTERN COLLEGE
Phoenix, AZ

CONTACT Mr. Pete Leonard, Director of Enrollment Management, Southwestern College, 2625 East Cactus Road, Phoenix, AZ 85032-7097, 602-992-6101 Ext. 114 or toll-free 800-247-2697. *Fax:* 602-404-2159.

SOUTHWESTERN COLLEGE
Winfield, KS

Tuition & fees: $19,630 **Average undergraduate aid package: $18,500**

ABOUT THE INSTITUTION Independent United Methodist, coed. 45 undergraduate majors. Federal methodology is used as a basis for awarding need-based institutional aid.

UNDERGRADUATE EXPENSES for 2009–10 *Comprehensive fee:* $25,380 includes full-time tuition ($19,530), mandatory fees ($100), and room and board ($5750). *College room only:* $2716. Full-time tuition and fees vary according to class time, course load, degree level, location, and program. Room and board charges vary according to board plan and housing facility. *Part-time tuition:* $814 per semester hour. Part-time tuition and fees vary according to class time, course load, degree level, location, and program. *Payment plan:* Installment.

FRESHMAN FINANCIAL AID (Fall 2009, est.) 108 applied for aid; of those 92% were deemed to have need. 100% of freshmen with need received aid; of those 20% had need fully met. *Average percent of need met:* 90% (excluding resources awarded to replace EFC). *Average financial aid package:* $20,328 (excluding resources awarded to replace EFC). 15% of all full-time freshmen had no need and received non-need-based gift aid.

UNDERGRADUATE FINANCIAL AID (Fall 2009, est.) 492 applied for aid; of those 92% were deemed to have need. 100% of undergraduates with need received aid; of those 24% had need fully met. *Average percent of need met:* 88% (excluding resources awarded to replace EFC). *Average financial aid package:* $18,500 (excluding resources awarded to replace EFC). 18% of all full-time undergraduates had no need and received non-need-based gift aid.

GIFT AID (NEED-BASED) *Total amount:* $5,555,607 (31% federal, 9% state, 56% institutional, 4% external sources). *Receiving aid:* Freshmen: 83% (99); all full-time undergraduates: 78% (444). *Average award:* Freshmen: $13,182; Undergraduates: $10,894. *Scholarships, grants, and awards:* Federal Pell, FSEOG, state, private, college/university gift aid from institutional funds.

GIFT AID (NON-NEED-BASED) *Total amount:* $1,002,948 (92% institutional, 8% external sources). *Receiving aid:* Freshmen: 8% (9). Undergraduates: 5% (30). *Average award:* Freshmen: $7978. Undergraduates: $7914. *Scholarships, grants, and awards by category: Academic interests/achievement:* $2,359,759 total: biological sciences, business, computer science, general academic interests/achievements, health fields, religion/biblical studies, social sciences. *Creative arts/performance:* $302,470 total: cinema/film/broadcasting, dance, journalism/publications, music, performing arts, theater/drama. *Special achievements/activities:* $1,109,452 total: cheerleading/drum major, community service, general special achievements/activities, leadership, memberships, religious involvement. *Special characteristics:* $752,810 total: children of educators, children of faculty/staff, ethnic background, international students, members of minority groups, religious affiliation. *Tuition waivers:* Full or partial for employees or children of employees, senior citizens.

LOANS *Student loans:* $7,770,504 (80% need-based, 20% non-need-based). 86% of past graduating class borrowed through all loan programs. *Average indebtedness per student:* $27,973. *Average need-based loan:* Freshmen: $4788. Undergraduates: $5630. *Parent loans:* $1,451,133 (33% need-based, 67% non-need-based). *Programs:* Federal Direct (Subsidized and Unsubsidized Stafford, PLUS), FFEL (Subsidized and Unsubsidized Stafford, PLUS), Perkins.

WORK-STUDY Federal work-study jobs available. *State or other work-study/employment:* Part-time jobs available.

ATHLETIC AWARDS Total amount: $782,200 (78% need-based, 22% non-need-based).

APPLYING FOR FINANCIAL AID *Required financial aid forms:* FAFSA, institution's own form. *Financial aid deadline:* 8/15 (priority: 4/1). *Notification date:* Continuous beginning 2/1. Students must reply within 2 weeks of notification.

CONTACT Mrs. Brenda D. Hicks, Director of Financial Aid, Southwestern College, 100 College Street, Winfield, KS 67156-2499, 620-229-6215 or toll-free 800-846-1543. *Fax:* 620-229-6363. *E-mail:* finaid@sckans.edu.

SOUTHWESTERN OKLAHOMA STATE UNIVERSITY
Weatherford, OK

Tuition & fees: N/R	Average undergraduate aid package: $4890

ABOUT THE INSTITUTION State-supported, coed. 53 undergraduate majors. Institutional methodology is used as a basis for awarding need-based institutional aid.

FRESHMAN FINANCIAL AID (Fall 2009, est.) 679 applied for aid; of those 76% were deemed to have need. 98% of freshmen with need received aid; of those 44% had need fully met. *Average percent of need met:* 87% (excluding resources awarded to replace EFC). *Average financial aid package:* $4934 (excluding resources awarded to replace EFC). 13% of all full-time freshmen had no need and received non-need-based gift aid.

UNDERGRADUATE FINANCIAL AID (Fall 2009, est.) 2,758 applied for aid; of those 81% were deemed to have need. 98% of undergraduates with need received aid; of those 42% had need fully met. *Average percent of need met:* 89% (excluding resources awarded to replace EFC). *Average financial aid package:* $4890 (excluding resources awarded to replace EFC). 33% of all full-time undergraduates had no need and received non-need-based gift aid.

GIFT AID (NEED-BASED) *Total amount:* $7,869,256 (89% federal, 11% state). *Receiving aid:* Freshmen: 56% (494); all full-time undergraduates: 55% (2,017). *Average award:* Freshmen: $1282; Undergraduates: $1463. *Scholarships, grants, and awards:* Federal Pell, FSEOG, state, private, college/university gift aid from institutional funds.

GIFT AID (NON-NEED-BASED) *Total amount:* $6,050,658 (9% federal, 61% state, 14% institutional, 16% external sources). *Receiving aid:* Freshmen: 42% (374). Undergraduates: 30% (1,095). *Average award:* Freshmen: $431. Undergraduates: $491. *Scholarships, grants, and awards by category: Academic interests/achievement:* biological sciences, business, communication, computer science, education, engineering/technologies, English, foreign languages, general academic interests/achievements, health fields, mathematics, physical sciences, social sciences. *Creative arts/performance:* applied art and design, art/fine arts, music, theater/drama. *Special achievements/activities:* cheerleading/drum major, leadership, rodeo. *Special characteristics:* children and siblings of alumni, local/state students, out-of-state students. *Tuition waivers:* Full or partial for employees or children of employees, senior citizens.

LOANS *Student loans:* $17,587,309 (40% need-based, 60% non-need-based). *Average need-based loan:* Freshmen: $1397. Undergraduates: $1677. *Parent loans:* $3,788,526 (100% non-need-based). *Programs:* Federal Direct (Subsidized and Unsubsidized Stafford, PLUS).

WORK-STUDY *Federal work-study:* Total amount: $1,806,482; jobs available.

ATHLETIC AWARDS Total amount: $1,058,195 (100% non-need-based).

APPLYING FOR FINANCIAL AID *Required financial aid forms:* FAFSA, institution's own form. *Financial aid deadline:* 3/1. *Notification date:* 3/15.

CONTACT Mr. Jerome Wichert, Director of Student Financial Services, Southwestern Oklahoma State University, 100 Campus Drive, Weatherford, OK 73096, 580-774-6003. *Fax:* 580-774-7066. *E-mail:* jerome.wichert@swosu.edu.

SOUTHWESTERN UNIVERSITY
Georgetown, TX

Tuition & fees: $30,220	Average undergraduate aid package: $26,810

ABOUT THE INSTITUTION Independent Methodist, coed. 46 undergraduate majors. Federal methodology is used as a basis for awarding need-based institutional aid.

UNDERGRADUATE EXPENSES for 2009–10 *Comprehensive fee:* $39,350 includes full-time tuition ($30,220) and room and board ($9130). *College room only:* $4860. Room and board charges vary according to board plan and housing facility. *Part-time tuition:* $1255 per semester hour. Part-time tuition and fees vary according to course load. *Payment plan:* Installment.

FRESHMAN FINANCIAL AID (Fall 2009, est.) 272 applied for aid; of those 81% were deemed to have need. 100% of freshmen with need received aid; of those 41% had need fully met. *Average percent of need met:* 97% (excluding resources awarded to replace EFC). *Average financial aid package:* $26,804 (excluding resources awarded to replace EFC). 37% of all full-time freshmen had no need and received non-need-based gift aid.

UNDERGRADUATE FINANCIAL AID (Fall 2009, est.) 858 applied for aid; of those 86% were deemed to have need. 100% of undergraduates with need received aid; of those 34% had need fully met. *Average percent of need met:* 90% (excluding resources awarded to replace EFC). *Average financial aid package:* $26,810 (excluding resources awarded to replace EFC). 32% of all full-time undergraduates had no need and received non-need-based gift aid.

GIFT AID (NEED-BASED) *Total amount:* $14,557,079 (11% federal, 12% state, 70% institutional, 7% external sources). *Receiving aid:* Freshmen: 59% (220); all full-time undergraduates: 57% (725). *Average award:* Freshmen: $22,025; Undergraduates: $20,735. *Scholarships, grants, and awards:* Federal Pell, FSEOG, state, private, college/university gift aid from institutional funds.

GIFT AID (NON-NEED-BASED) *Total amount:* $5,452,585 (94% institutional, 6% external sources). *Receiving aid:* Freshmen: 54% (201). Undergraduates: 41% (524). *Average award:* Freshmen: $15,630. Undergraduates: $12,688. *Scholarships, grants, and awards by category: Academic interests/achievement:* 1,202 awards ($10,387,684 total): business, general academic interests/achievements, humanities, international studies, mathematics, premedicine, social sciences. *Creative arts/performance:* 113 awards ($395,395 total): art/fine arts, music, theater/drama. *Special achievements/activities:* 5 awards ($4000 total): leadership. *Special characteristics:* 87 awards ($942,514 total): children of faculty/staff, general special characteristics, relatives of clergy, religious affiliation. *Tuition waivers:* Full or partial for employees or children of employees.

LOANS *Student loans:* $7,373,855 (87% need-based, 13% non-need-based). 61% of past graduating class borrowed through all loan programs. *Average indebtedness per student:* $24,036. *Average need-based loan:* Freshmen: $5114. Undergraduates: $5728. *Parent loans:* $4,768,501 (74% need-based, 26% non-need-based). *Programs:* Federal Direct (Subsidized and Unsubsidized Stafford, PLUS), Perkins, state, college/university.

WORK-STUDY *Federal work-study:* Total amount: $227,179; 138 jobs averaging $1874. *State or other work-study/employment:* Total amount: $1,418,174 (61% need-based, 39% non-need-based). 572 part-time jobs averaging $2629.

APPLYING FOR FINANCIAL AID *Required financial aid form:* FAFSA. *Financial aid deadline:* 3/1. *Notification date:* Continuous beginning 3/1. Students must reply by 5/1 or within 2 weeks of notification.

CONTACT Mr. James P. Gaeta, Director of Financial Aid, Southwestern University, PO Box 770, Georgetown, TX 78627-0770, 512-863-1259 or toll-free 800-252-3166. *Fax:* 512-863-1507. *E-mail:* gaetaj@southwestern.edu.

SOUTHWEST FLORIDA COLLEGE
Fort Myers, FL

CONTACT Mrs. Ingrid L. Sprandel, Director of Student Finance, Southwest Florida College, 1685 Medical Lane, Suite 200, Fort Myers, FL 33907, 941-939-4766 or toll-free 866-SWFC-NOW. *Fax:* 941-939-1332. *E-mail:* isprandel@swfc.edu.

SOUTHWEST MINNESOTA STATE UNIVERSITY
Marshall, MN

Tuition & fees (MN res): $7229	Average undergraduate aid package: $8541

ABOUT THE INSTITUTION State-supported, coed. 55 undergraduate majors. Federal methodology is used as a basis for awarding need-based institutional aid.

UNDERGRADUATE EXPENSES for 2010–11 *One-time required fee:* $20. *Tuition, state resident:* full-time $6250; part-time $201 per credit hour. *Tuition, nonresident:* full-time $6250; part-time $201 per credit hour. *Required fees:* full-time $979; $38 per credit hour or $38 per credit hour. Full-time tuition and fees vary according to course load, location, program, and reciprocity agreements. Part-time tuition and fees vary according to location, program, and reciprocity agreements. *College room and board:* $6846; *Room only:* $3927. Room and board charges vary according to board plan and housing facility. *Payment plan:* Installment.

FRESHMAN FINANCIAL AID (Fall 2009, est.) 396 applied for aid; of those 77% were deemed to have need. 99% of freshmen with need received aid; of those 15% had need fully met. *Average percent of need met:* 56% (excluding resources awarded to replace EFC). *Average financial aid package:* $8615 (excluding resources awarded to replace EFC). 24% of all full-time freshmen had no need and received non-need-based gift aid.

UNDERGRADUATE FINANCIAL AID (Fall 2009, est.) 1,830 applied for aid; of those 80% were deemed to have need. 99% of undergraduates with need received aid; of those 18% had need fully met. *Average percent of need met:* 57% (excluding resources awarded to replace EFC). *Average financial aid package:* $8541 (excluding resources awarded to replace EFC). 15% of all full-time undergraduates had no need and received non-need-based gift aid.

GIFT AID (NEED-BASED) *Total amount:* $6,045,071 (68% federal, 31% state, 1% institutional). *Receiving aid:* Freshmen: 48% (217); all full-time undergraduates: 48% (1,073). *Average award:* Freshmen: $5554; Undergraduates: $5128. *Scholarships, grants, and awards:* Federal Pell, FSEOG, state, private, college/university gift aid from institutional funds.

GIFT AID (NON-NEED-BASED) *Total amount:* $2,209,854 (12% federal, 1% state, 60% institutional, 27% external sources). *Receiving aid:* Freshmen: 39% (176). Undergraduates: 30% (669). *Average award:* Freshmen: $2714. Undergraduates: $2643. *Scholarships, grants, and awards by category:* Academic interests/achievement: 756 awards ($1,018,373 total): agriculture, biological sciences, business, communication, computer science, education, English, general academic interests/achievements, mathematics, physical sciences, premedicine, social sciences. *Creative arts/performance:* 72 awards ($38,566 total): art/fine arts, creative writing, debating, journalism/publications, music, performing arts, theater/drama. *Special achievements/activities:* 73 awards ($40,350 total): general special achievements/activities, hobbies/interests,

leadership. *Special characteristics:* 101 awards ($70,925 total): children and siblings of alumni, children of union members/company employees, ethnic background, first-generation college students, general special characteristics, handicapped students, international students, local/state students, members of minority groups, previous college experience, veterans, veterans' children. *Tuition waivers:* Full or partial for employees or children of employees, senior citizens.

LOANS *Student loans:* $15,848,157 (44% need-based, 56% non-need-based). 82% of past graduating class borrowed through all loan programs. *Average indebtedness per student:* $18,830. *Average need-based loan:* Freshmen: $3293. Undergraduates: $3946. *Parent loans:* $490,408 (100% non-need-based). *Programs:* Federal Direct (Subsidized and Unsubsidized Stafford, PLUS), Perkins, state.

WORK-STUDY *Federal work-study:* Total amount: $219,675; 101 jobs averaging $2173. *State or other work-study/employment:* Total amount: $432,104 (100% need-based). 205 part-time jobs averaging $2150.

ATHLETIC AWARDS Total amount: $716,552 (100% non-need-based).

APPLYING FOR FINANCIAL AID *Required financial aid forms:* FAFSA, institution's own form. *Financial aid deadline (priority):* 3/1. *Notification date:* Continuous beginning 5/1.

CONTACT Mr. David Vikander, Director of Financial Aid, Southwest Minnesota State University, 1501 State Street, Marshall, MN 56258, 507-537-6281 or toll-free 800-642-0684. *Fax:* 507-537-6275. *E-mail:* vikander@smsu.edu.

SOUTHWEST UNIVERSITY
Kenner, LA

CONTACT Financial Aid Office, Southwest University, 2200 Veterans Memorial Boulevard, Kenner, LA 70062, 504-468-2900 or toll-free 800-433-5923 (out-of-state).

SPALDING UNIVERSITY
Louisville, KY

CONTACT Director of Student Financial Services, Spalding University, 851 South Fourth Street, Louisville, KY 40203, 502-588-7185 or toll-free 800-896-8941 Ext. 2111. *Fax:* 502-585-7128. *E-mail:* onestop@spalding.edu.

SPELMAN COLLEGE
Atlanta, GA

ABOUT THE INSTITUTION Independent, women only. 25 undergraduate majors.

GIFT AID (NEED-BASED) *Scholarships, grants, and awards:* Federal Pell, FSEOG, state, private, college/university gift aid from institutional funds, United Negro College Fund.

LOANS *Programs:* FFEL (Subsidized and Unsubsidized Stafford, PLUS), Perkins.

APPLYING FOR FINANCIAL AID *Required financial aid form:* FAFSA.

CONTACT Lenora J. Jackson, Director, Student Financial Services, Spelman College, 350 Spelman Lane, SW, PO Box 771, Atlanta, GA 30314-4399, 404-270-5212 or toll-free 800-982-2411. *Fax:* 404-270-5220. *E-mail:* lenoraj@spelman.edu.

SPRING ARBOR UNIVERSITY
Spring Arbor, MI

Tuition & fees: $19,790	Average undergraduate aid package: $22,445

ABOUT THE INSTITUTION Independent Free Methodist, coed. 63 undergraduate majors. Federal methodology is used as a basis for awarding need-based institutional aid.

UNDERGRADUATE EXPENSES for 2009–10 *Comprehensive fee:* $26,740 includes full-time tuition ($19,250), mandatory fees ($540), and room and board ($6950). *College room only:* $3250. Full-time tuition and fees vary according to course load, degree level, and program. Room and board charges vary according to board plan and housing facility. *Part-time tuition:* $485 per credit hour. *Part-time fees:* $225 per term. Part-time tuition and fees vary according to course load, degree level, program, and reciprocity agreements. *Payment plan:* Installment.

FRESHMAN FINANCIAL AID (Fall 2009, est.) 371 applied for aid; of those 90% were deemed to have need. 100% of freshmen with need received aid; of those

Spring Arbor University

48% had need fully met. *Average percent of need met:* 92% (excluding resources awarded to replace EFC). *Average financial aid package:* $22,450 (excluding resources awarded to replace EFC).

UNDERGRADUATE FINANCIAL AID (Fall 2009, est.) 1,351 applied for aid; of those 91% were deemed to have need. 100% of undergraduates with need received aid; of those 50% had need fully met. *Average percent of need met:* 91% (excluding resources awarded to replace EFC). *Average financial aid package:* $22,445 (excluding resources awarded to replace EFC). 1% of all full-time undergraduates had no need and received non-need-based gift aid.

GIFT AID (NEED-BASED) *Total amount:* $19,349,924 (25% federal, 14% state, 61% institutional). *Receiving aid:* Freshmen: 88% (335); all full-time undergraduates: 85% (1,216). *Average award:* Freshmen: $12,681; Undergraduates: $12,196. *Scholarships, grants, and awards:* Federal Pell, FSEOG, state, private, college/university gift aid from institutional funds.

GIFT AID (NON-NEED-BASED) *Total amount:* $239,903 (1% federal, 43% state, 56% external sources). *Receiving aid:* Freshmen: 7% (25). Undergraduates: 5% (75). *Average award:* Undergraduates: $6155. *Scholarships, grants, and awards by category:* Academic interests/achievement: 976 awards ($3,533,481 total): general academic interests/achievements. *Creative arts/performance:* 148 awards ($87,725 total): art/fine arts, music. *Special achievements/activities:* junior miss. *Special characteristics:* 493 awards ($1,384,097 total): adult students, children of faculty/staff, general special characteristics, international students, members of minority groups, relatives of clergy, religious affiliation. *Tuition waivers:* Full or partial for employees or children of employees.

LOANS *Student loans:* $33,573,426 (39% need-based, 61% non-need-based). 86% of past graduating class borrowed through all loan programs. *Average indebtedness per student:* $26,052. *Average need-based loan:* Freshmen: $3681. Undergraduates: $4394. *Parent loans:* $1,511,658 (100% need-based). *Programs:* FFEL (Subsidized and Unsubsidized Stafford, PLUS), Perkins, alternative loans.

WORK-STUDY *Federal work-study:* Total amount: $376,765; 384 jobs averaging $794. *State or other work-study/employment:* 104 part-time jobs averaging $559.

ATHLETIC AWARDS Total amount: $1,368,221 (100% need-based).

APPLYING FOR FINANCIAL AID *Required financial aid form:* FAFSA. *Financial aid deadline (priority):* 3/1. *Notification date:* Continuous beginning 4/1. Students must reply within 2 weeks of notification.

CONTACT Geoff Marsh, Director of Financial Aid, Spring Arbor University, 106 East Main Street, Spring Arbor, MI 49283-9799, 517-750-6468 or toll-free 800-968-0011. *Fax:* 517-750-6620. *E-mail:* gmarsh@arbor.edu.

SPRINGFIELD COLLEGE
Springfield, MA

CONTACT Edward J. Ciosek, Director of Financial Aid, Springfield College, 263 Alden Street, Springfield, MA 01109-3797, 413-748-3108 or toll-free 800-343-1257 (out-of-state). *Fax:* 413-748-3462. *E-mail:* finaid@spfldcol.edu.

SPRING HILL COLLEGE
Mobile, AL

Tuition & fees: $25,450	Average undergraduate aid package: $23,948

ABOUT THE INSTITUTION Independent Roman Catholic (Jesuit), coed. 38 undergraduate majors. Federal methodology is used as a basis for awarding need-based institutional aid.

UNDERGRADUATE EXPENSES for 2009–10 *Comprehensive fee:* $35,180 includes full-time tuition ($23,910), mandatory fees ($1540), and room and board ($9730). *College room only:* $5100. Room and board charges vary according to board plan and housing facility. *Part-time tuition:* $890 per semester hour. *Part-time fees:* $50 per semester hour. *Payment plan:* Installment.

FRESHMAN FINANCIAL AID (Fall 2009, est.) 310 applied for aid; of those 81% were deemed to have need. 100% of freshmen with need received aid; of those 29% had need fully met. *Average percent of need met:* 85% (excluding resources awarded to replace EFC). *Average financial aid package:* $25,251 (excluding resources awarded to replace EFC). 27% of all full-time freshmen had no need and received non-need-based gift aid.

UNDERGRADUATE FINANCIAL AID (Fall 2009, est.) 956 applied for aid; of those 86% were deemed to have need. 100% of undergraduates with need received aid; of those 26% had need fully met. *Average percent of need met:*

82% (excluding resources awarded to replace EFC). *Average financial aid package:* $23,948 (excluding resources awarded to replace EFC). 28% of all full-time undergraduates had no need and received non-need-based gift aid.

GIFT AID (NEED-BASED) *Total amount:* $15,086,593 (14% federal, 2% state, 83% institutional, 1% external sources). *Receiving aid:* Freshmen: 69% (245); all full-time undergraduates: 66% (787). *Average award:* Freshmen: $17,633; Undergraduates: $17,473. *Scholarships, grants, and awards:* Federal Pell, FSEOG, state, private, college/university gift aid from institutional funds, Academic Competitiveness Grants, National SMART Grants, TEACH Grants.

GIFT AID (NON-NEED-BASED) *Total amount:* $5,516,203 (1% state, 98% institutional, 1% external sources). *Receiving aid:* Freshmen: 52% (182). Undergraduates: 51% (608). *Average award:* Freshmen: $14,332. Undergraduates: $13,699. *Scholarships, grants, and awards by category:* Academic interests/achievement: 1,130 awards ($14,072,927 total): general academic interests/achievements. *Special achievements/activities:* 448 awards ($896,000 total): community service. *Special characteristics:* 12 awards ($261,889 total): children of faculty/staff, siblings of current students. *Tuition waivers:* Full or partial for employees or children of employees.

LOANS *Student loans:* $7,783,360 (70% need-based, 30% non-need-based). 72% of past graduating class borrowed through all loan programs. *Average indebtedness per student:* $21,823. *Average need-based loan:* Freshmen: $4471. Undergraduates: $4732. *Parent loans:* $1,236,269 (27% need-based, 73% non-need-based). *Programs:* Federal Direct (Subsidized and Unsubsidized Stafford, PLUS), FFEL (Subsidized and Unsubsidized Stafford, PLUS), Perkins, alternative loans (CitiAssist, Signature).

WORK-STUDY *Federal work-study:* Total amount: $323,770; 231 jobs averaging $1126. *State or other work-study/employment:* Total amount: $217,140 (39% need-based, 61% non-need-based). 62 part-time jobs averaging $1068.

ATHLETIC AWARDS Total amount: $916,810 (46% need-based, 54% non-need-based).

APPLYING FOR FINANCIAL AID *Required financial aid forms:* FAFSA, state aid form. *Financial aid deadline (priority):* 3/1. *Notification date:* Continuous beginning 2/15. Students must reply by 5/1 or within 2 weeks of notification.

CONTACT Ms. Ellen Foster, Director of Financial Aid, Spring Hill College, 4000 Dauphin Street, Mobile, AL 36608, 251-380-3460 or toll-free 800-SHC-6704. *Fax:* 251-460-2176. *E-mail:* efoster@shc.edu.

STANFORD UNIVERSITY
Stanford, CA

Tuition & fees: $37,881	Average undergraduate aid package: $38,392

ABOUT THE INSTITUTION Independent, coed. 68 undergraduate majors. Both federal and institutional methodology are used as a basis for awarding need-based institutional aid.

UNDERGRADUATE EXPENSES for 2009–10 *Comprehensive fee:* $49,344 includes full-time tuition ($37,380), mandatory fees ($501), and room and board ($11,463). *College room only:* $6411. Room and board charges vary according to housing facility. *Payment plan:* Installment.

FRESHMAN FINANCIAL AID (Fall 2008) 1,051 applied for aid; of those 82% were deemed to have need. 100% of freshmen with need received aid; of those 96% had need fully met. *Average percent of need met:* 100% (excluding resources awarded to replace EFC). *Average financial aid package:* $40,204 (excluding resources awarded to replace EFC). 5% of all full-time freshmen had no need and received non-need-based gift aid.

UNDERGRADUATE FINANCIAL AID (Fall 2008) 3,761 applied for aid; of those 88% were deemed to have need. 99% of undergraduates with need received aid; of those 89% had need fully met. *Average percent of need met:* 100% (excluding resources awarded to replace EFC). *Average financial aid package:* $38,392 (excluding resources awarded to replace EFC). 12% of all full-time undergraduates had no need and received non-need-based gift aid.

GIFT AID (NEED-BASED) *Total amount:* $116,949,077 (5% federal, 3% state, 89% institutional, 3% external sources). *Receiving aid:* Freshmen: 50% (844); all full-time undergraduates: 47% (3,207). *Average award:* Freshmen: $38,037; Undergraduates: $36,419. *Scholarships, grants, and awards:* Federal Pell, FSEOG, state, private, college/university gift aid from institutional funds.

GIFT AID (NON-NEED-BASED) *Total amount:* $10,922,220 (2% federal, 44% institutional, 54% external sources). *Receiving aid:* Freshmen: 5% (81). Undergraduates: 8% (562). *Average award:* Freshmen: $3319. Undergraduates: $3601. *Tuition waivers:* Full or partial for employees or children of employees.

LOANS *Student loans:* $7,887,280 (22% need-based, 78% non-need-based). 36% of past graduating class borrowed through all loan programs. *Average indebtedness per student:* $16,219. *Average need-based loan:* Freshmen: $2614. Undergraduates: $3053. *Parent loans:* $6,222,623 (100% non-need-based). *Programs:* Federal Direct (Subsidized and Unsubsidized Stafford, PLUS), Perkins.

WORK-STUDY *Federal work-study:* Total amount: $2,343,591; 807 jobs averaging $2868. *State or other work-study/employment:* Total amount: $1,941,283 (100% need-based). 1,523 part-time jobs averaging $1934.

ATHLETIC AWARDS Total amount: $15,864,052 (14% need-based, 86% non-need-based).

APPLYING FOR FINANCIAL AID *Required financial aid forms:* FAFSA, CSS Financial Aid PROFILE, noncustodial (divorced/separated) parent's statement. *Financial aid deadline (priority):* 2/15. *Notification date:* Continuous beginning 4/3. Students must reply by 5/1.

CONTACT Financial Aid Office, Stanford University, Montag Hall, 355 Galvez Street, Stanford, CA 94305-3021, 650-723-3058. *Fax:* 650-725-0540. *E-mail:* financialaid@stanford.edu.

STATE UNIVERSITY OF NEW YORK AT BINGHAMTON
Binghamton, NY

Tuition & fees (NY res): $6761	Average undergraduate aid package: $11,940

ABOUT THE INSTITUTION State-supported, coed. 72 undergraduate majors. Federal methodology is used as a basis for awarding need-based institutional aid.

UNDERGRADUATE EXPENSES for 2009–10 *Tuition, state resident:* full-time $4970; part-time $207 per credit hour. *Tuition, nonresident:* full-time $12,870; part-time $536 per credit hour. *Required fees:* full-time $1791; $65.75 per credit hour or $105.50 per term. Part-time tuition and fees vary according to course load. *College room and board:* $10,614; *Room only:* $6546. Room and board charges vary according to board plan and housing facility.

FRESHMAN FINANCIAL AID (Fall 2009, est.) 1,626 applied for aid; of those 55% were deemed to have need. 100% of freshmen with need received aid; of those 18% had need fully met. *Average percent of need met:* 79% (excluding resources awarded to replace EFC). *Average financial aid package:* $11,083 (excluding resources awarded to replace EFC). 1% of all full-time freshmen had no need and received non-need-based gift aid.

UNDERGRADUATE FINANCIAL AID (Fall 2009, est.) 7,876 applied for aid; of those 66% were deemed to have need. 100% of undergraduates with need received aid; of those 22% had need fully met. *Average percent of need met:* 79% (excluding resources awarded to replace EFC). *Average financial aid package:* $11,940 (excluding resources awarded to replace EFC). 3% of all full-time undergraduates had no need and received non-need-based gift aid.

GIFT AID (NEED-BASED) *Total amount:* $30,251,478 (51% federal, 43% state, 4% institutional, 2% external sources). *Receiving aid:* Freshmen: 36% (725); all full-time undergraduates: 40% (4,471). *Average award:* Freshmen: $7395; Undergraduates: $6643. *Scholarships, grants, and awards:* Federal Pell, FSEOG, state, private, college/university gift aid from institutional funds.

GIFT AID (NON-NEED-BASED) *Total amount:* $1,748,385 (47% state, 26% institutional, 27% external sources). *Receiving aid:* Freshmen: 6% (121). Undergraduates: 5% (531). *Average award:* Freshmen: $2133. Undergraduates: $4311. *Scholarships, grants, and awards by category: Academic interests/achievement:* 238 awards ($403,828 total): area/ethnic studies, biological sciences, business, computer science, education, engineering/technologies, English, foreign languages, general academic interests/achievements, health fields, humanities, international studies, mathematics, physical sciences, premedicine, social sciences. *Creative arts/performance:* 11 awards ($14,850 total): art/fine arts, cinema/film/broadcasting, creative writing, dance, general creative arts/performance, journalism/publications, music, performing arts, theater/drama. *Special achievements/activities:* 206 awards ($343,715 total): community service, general special achievements/activities, leadership. *Special characteristics:* 74 awards ($175,750 total): adult students, children of faculty/staff, ethnic background, first-generation college students, handicapped students, local/state students, married students, members of minority groups, out-of-state students.

LOANS *Student loans:* $67,189,862 (73% need-based, 27% non-need-based). 49% of past graduating class borrowed through all loan programs. *Average indebtedness per student:* $14,560. *Average need-based loan:* Freshmen: $3791.

Undergraduates: $5358. *Parent loans:* $64,384,338 (56% need-based, 44% non-need-based). *Programs:* Federal Direct (Subsidized and Unsubsidized Stafford, PLUS), Perkins, Federal Nursing, college/university.

WORK-STUDY *Federal work-study:* Total amount: $730,000; 1,848 jobs averaging $1422.

ATHLETIC AWARDS Total amount: $2,818,604 (100% non-need-based).

APPLYING FOR FINANCIAL AID *Required financial aid forms:* FAFSA, state aid form. *Financial aid deadline (priority):* 2/1. *Notification date:* Continuous beginning 4/1. Students must reply within 2 weeks of notification.

CONTACT Mr. Dennis Chavez, Director of Student Financial Aid Services, State University of New York at Binghamton, PO Box 6000, Binghamton, NY 13902-6000, 607-777-2428.

STATE UNIVERSITY OF NEW YORK AT FREDONIA
Fredonia, NY

Tuition & fees (NY res): $6308	Average undergraduate aid package: $8119

ABOUT THE INSTITUTION State-supported, coed. 73 undergraduate majors. Federal methodology is used as a basis for awarding need-based institutional aid.

UNDERGRADUATE EXPENSES for 2010–11 *Tuition, state resident:* full-time $5020; part-time $207 per credit hour. *Tuition, nonresident:* full-time $12,920; part-time $536 per credit hour. *Required fees:* full-time $1288; $51.40 per credit hour. Full-time tuition and fees vary according to program. Part-time tuition and fees vary according to program. *College room and board:* $9330; *Room only:* $5650. Room and board charges vary according to board plan and housing facility. *Payment plan:* Installment.

FRESHMAN FINANCIAL AID (Fall 2009, est.) 991 applied for aid; of those 70% were deemed to have need. 99% of freshmen with need received aid; of those 22% had need fully met. *Average percent of need met:* 66% (excluding resources awarded to replace EFC). *Average financial aid package:* $7783 (excluding resources awarded to replace EFC). 11% of all full-time freshmen had no need and received non-need-based gift aid.

UNDERGRADUATE FINANCIAL AID (Fall 2009, est.) 4,405 applied for aid; of those 77% were deemed to have need. 99% of undergraduates with need received aid; of those 24% had need fully met. *Average percent of need met:* 65% (excluding resources awarded to replace EFC). *Average financial aid package:* $8119 (excluding resources awarded to replace EFC). 7% of all full-time undergraduates had no need and received non-need-based gift aid.

GIFT AID (NEED-BASED) *Total amount:* $15,495,528 (50% federal, 37% state, 9% institutional, 4% external sources). *Receiving aid:* Freshmen: 52% (563); all full-time undergraduates: 55% (2,816). *Average award:* Freshmen: $3939; Undergraduates: $4048. *Scholarships, grants, and awards:* Federal Pell, FSEOG, state, private, college/university gift aid from institutional funds, Academic Competitiveness Grants, National SMART Grants, TEACH Grants.

GIFT AID (NON-NEED-BASED) *Receiving aid:* Freshmen: 19% (210). Undergraduates: 12% (639). *Average award:* Freshmen: $1843. Undergraduates: $2051. *Scholarships, grants, and awards by category: Academic interests/achievement:* 425 awards ($442,276 total): biological sciences, business, communication, computer science, education, English, foreign languages, general academic interests/achievements, humanities, international studies, mathematics, physical sciences, social sciences. *Creative arts/performance:* 108 awards ($72,982 total): applied art and design, art/fine arts, dance, music, performing arts, theater/drama. *Special achievements/activities:* 18 awards ($47,875 total): general special achievements/activities, leadership. *Special characteristics:* 161 awards ($469,172 total): children and siblings of alumni, ethnic background, general special characteristics, international students, local/state students, members of minority groups, out-of-state students, parents of current students, previous college experience.

LOANS *Student loans:* $33,166,667 (43% need-based, 57% non-need-based). 86% of past graduating class borrowed through all loan programs. *Average indebtedness per student:* $34,935. *Average need-based loan:* Freshmen: $3632. Undergraduates: $4306. *Parent loans:* $3,440,518 (100% non-need-based). *Programs:* FFEL (Subsidized and Unsubsidized Stafford, PLUS), Perkins.

WORK-STUDY *Federal work-study:* Total amount: $244,523; 226 jobs averaging $1081.

State University of New York at Fredonia

APPLYING FOR FINANCIAL AID *Required financial aid forms:* FAFSA, state aid form. *Financial aid deadline:* Continuous. *Notification date:* Continuous beginning 3/1. Students must reply by 5/1.

CONTACT Jeremy Corrente, Assistant Director, State University of New York at Fredonia, 215 Maytum Hall, Fredonia, NY 14063, 716-673-3253 or toll-free 800-252-1212. *Fax:* 716-673-3785. *E-mail:* corrente@fredonia.edu.

STATE UNIVERSITY OF NEW YORK AT NEW PALTZ
New Paltz, NY

Tuition & fees (NY res): $6081   Average undergraduate aid package: $9023

ABOUT THE INSTITUTION State-supported, coed. 81 undergraduate majors. Federal methodology is used as a basis for awarding need-based institutional aid.

UNDERGRADUATE EXPENSES for 2009–10 *Tuition, state resident:* full-time $4970; part-time $207 per credit. *Tuition, nonresident:* full-time $12,870; part-time $536 per credit. *Required fees:* full-time $1111; $32.45 per credit or $165 per term. *College room and board:* $9202; *Room only:* $6020. Room and board charges vary according to board plan. *Payment plan:* Installment.

FRESHMAN FINANCIAL AID (Fall 2009, est.) 928 applied for aid; of those 60% were deemed to have need. 100% of freshmen with need received aid; of those 15% had need fully met. *Average percent of need met:* 57% (excluding resources awarded to replace EFC). *Average financial aid package:* $9748 (excluding resources awarded to replace EFC). 1% of all full-time freshmen had no need and received non-need-based gift aid.

UNDERGRADUATE FINANCIAL AID (Fall 2009, est.) 4,342 applied for aid; of those 69% were deemed to have need. 99% of undergraduates with need received aid; of those 16% had need fully met. *Average percent of need met:* 59% (excluding resources awarded to replace EFC). *Average financial aid package:* $9023 (excluding resources awarded to replace EFC). 1% of all full-time undergraduates had no need and received non-need-based gift aid.

GIFT AID (NEED-BASED) *Total amount:* $18,818,953 (40% federal, 59% state, 1% institutional). *Receiving aid:* Freshmen: 27% (289); all full-time undergraduates: 26% (1,520). *Average award:* Freshmen: $5214; Undergraduates: $4774. *Scholarships, grants, and awards:* Federal Pell, FSEOG, state, private, college/university gift aid from institutional funds.

GIFT AID (NON-NEED-BASED) *Total amount:* $1,254,354 (2% federal, 36% state, 12% institutional, 50% external sources). *Receiving aid:* Freshmen: 6% (60). Undergraduates: 3% (177). *Average award:* Freshmen: $1375. Undergraduates: $1591. *Scholarships, grants, and awards by category: Academic interests/achievement:* 37 awards ($114,200 total): business, communication, education, foreign languages, general academic interests/achievements, health fields. *Creative arts/performance:* 12 awards ($31,750 total): art/fine arts, music, performing arts, theater/drama. *Special characteristics:* 23 awards ($9500 total): children of faculty/staff, ethnic background, first-generation college students, handicapped students, members of minority groups.

LOANS *Student loans:* $36,332,430 (44% need-based, 56% non-need-based). 66% of past graduating class borrowed through all loan programs. *Average indebtedness per student:* $16,823. *Average need-based loan:* Freshmen: $3546. Undergraduates: $4287. *Parent loans:* $15,655,361 (100% non-need-based). *Programs:* FFEL (Subsidized and Unsubsidized Stafford, PLUS), Perkins, private alternative loans.

WORK-STUDY *Federal work-study:* Total amount: $1,064,749; 1,250 jobs averaging $900. *State or other work-study/employment:* Total amount: $800,640 (100% non-need-based). 500 part-time jobs averaging $1250.

APPLYING FOR FINANCIAL AID *Required financial aid forms:* FAFSA, state aid form. *Financial aid deadline (priority):* 3/15. *Notification date:* Continuous beginning 4/1. Students must reply within 4 weeks of notification.

CONTACT Mr. Daniel Sistarenik, Director of Financial Aid, State University of New York at New Paltz, 200 Hawk Drive, New Paltz, NY 12561-2437, 845-257-3250. *Fax:* 845-257-3568. *E-mail:* sistared@newpaltz.edu.

STATE UNIVERSITY OF NEW YORK AT OSWEGO
Oswego, NY

Tuition & fees (NY res): $6256   Average undergraduate aid package: $10,744

ABOUT THE INSTITUTION State-supported, coed. 66 undergraduate majors. Federal methodology is used as a basis for awarding need-based institutional aid.

UNDERGRADUATE EXPENSES for 2010–11 *Tuition, state resident:* full-time $4970; part-time $207 per credit hour. *Tuition, nonresident:* full-time $12,870; part-time $536 per credit hour. *Required fees:* full-time $1286; $49.21 per credit hour. Full-time tuition and fees vary according to degree level. Part-time tuition and fees vary according to course load and degree level. *College room and board:* $10,870; *Room only:* $6890. Room and board charges vary according to board plan and housing facility. *Payment plan:* Installment.

FRESHMAN FINANCIAL AID (Fall 2009, est.) 1,265 applied for aid; of those 72% were deemed to have need. 96% of freshmen with need received aid; of those 48% had need fully met. *Average percent of need met:* 84% (excluding resources awarded to replace EFC). *Average financial aid package:* $10,847 (excluding resources awarded to replace EFC). 17% of all full-time freshmen had no need and received non-need-based gift aid.

UNDERGRADUATE FINANCIAL AID (Fall 2009, est.) 5,896 applied for aid; of those 76% were deemed to have need. 97% of undergraduates with need received aid; of those 42% had need fully met. *Average percent of need met:* 84% (excluding resources awarded to replace EFC). *Average financial aid package:* $10,744 (excluding resources awarded to replace EFC). 17% of all full-time undergraduates had no need and received non-need-based gift aid.

GIFT AID (NEED-BASED) *Total amount:* $22,109,494 (51% federal, 38% state, 9% institutional, 2% external sources). *Receiving aid:* Freshmen: 56% (780); all full-time undergraduates: 56% (3,819). *Average award:* Freshmen: $6161; Undergraduates: $4642. *Scholarships, grants, and awards:* Federal Pell, FSEOG, state, private, college/university gift aid from institutional funds.

GIFT AID (NON-NEED-BASED) *Total amount:* $2,084,975 (1% federal, 2% state, 89% institutional, 8% external sources). *Receiving aid:* Freshmen: 10% (136). Undergraduates: 5% (328). *Average award:* Freshmen: $5804. Undergraduates: $7290. *Scholarships, grants, and awards by category: Academic interests/achievement:* area/ethnic studies, biological sciences, business, communication, computer science, education, English, foreign languages, general academic interests/achievements, humanities, international studies, mathematics, physical sciences, premedicine, social sciences.

LOANS *Student loans:* $37,083,628 (79% need-based, 21% non-need-based). 86% of past graduating class borrowed through all loan programs. *Average indebtedness per student:* $25,351. *Average need-based loan:* Freshmen: $4852. Undergraduates: $6146. *Parent loans:* $8,125,758 (67% need-based, 33% non-need-based). *Programs:* Federal Direct (Subsidized and Unsubsidized Stafford, PLUS), Perkins.

WORK-STUDY *Federal work-study:* Total amount: $778,288; 413 jobs averaging $950. *State or other work-study/employment:* Total amount: $1,098,971 (50% need-based, 50% non-need-based). 1,395 part-time jobs averaging $1541.

APPLYING FOR FINANCIAL AID *Required financial aid forms:* FAFSA, state aid form. *Financial aid deadline (priority):* 3/1. *Notification date:* Continuous beginning 3/1. Students must reply by 5/1 or within 3 weeks of notification.

CONTACT Mark C. Humbert, Director of Financial Aid, State University of New York at Oswego, 206 Culkin Hall, Oswego, NY 13126, 315-312-2248. *Fax:* 315-312-3696.

STATE UNIVERSITY OF NEW YORK AT PLATTSBURGH
Plattsburgh, NY

Tuition & fees (NY res): $6100   Average undergraduate aid package: $11,140

ABOUT THE INSTITUTION State-supported, coed. 63 undergraduate majors. Both federal and institutional methodology are used as a basis for awarding need-based institutional aid.

UNDERGRADUATE EXPENSES for 2009–10 *Tuition, state resident:* full-time $4970; part-time $207 per credit hour. *Tuition, nonresident:* full-time $12,870; part-time $536 per credit hour. *Required fees:* full-time $1130; $45.67 per credit hour. *College room and board:* $8600; *Room only:* $5500. Room and board charges vary according to board plan. *Payment plans:* Installment, deferred payment.

FRESHMAN FINANCIAL AID (Fall 2009, est.) 908 applied for aid; of those 69% were deemed to have need. 99% of freshmen with need received aid; of those 37% had need fully met. *Average percent of need met:* 94% (excluding resources awarded to replace EFC). *Average financial aid package:* $11,182 (excluding resources awarded to replace EFC). 33% of all full-time freshmen had no need and received non-need-based gift aid.

UNDERGRADUATE FINANCIAL AID (Fall 2009, est.) 4,442 applied for aid; of those 75% were deemed to have need. 99% of undergraduates with need received aid; of those 31% had need fully met. *Average percent of need met:* 90% (excluding resources awarded to replace EFC). *Average financial aid package:* $11,140 (excluding resources awarded to replace EFC). 28% of all full-time undergraduates had no need and received non-need-based gift aid.

GIFT AID (NEED-BASED) *Total amount:* $16,400,862 (49% federal, 36% state, 11% institutional, 4% external sources). *Receiving aid:* Freshmen: 53% (563); all full-time undergraduates: 52% (2,866). *Average award:* Freshmen: $6620; Undergraduates: $5723. *Scholarships, grants, and awards:* Federal Pell, FSEOG, state, private, college/university gift aid from institutional funds.

GIFT AID (NON-NEED-BASED) *Total amount:* $3,561,543 (4% federal, 9% state, 83% institutional, 4% external sources). *Receiving aid:* Freshmen: 26% (271). Undergraduates: 19% (1,044). *Average award:* Freshmen: $5543. Undergraduates: $6268. *Scholarships, grants, and awards by category:* Academic interests/achievement: 2,379 awards ($4,535,488 total): area/ethnic studies, biological sciences, business, communication, computer science, education, engineering/technologies, English, general academic interests/achievements, health fields, home economics, humanities, international studies, mathematics, physical sciences, premedicine, social sciences. *Creative arts/performance:* 164 awards ($281,985 total): art/fine arts, journalism/publications, music, theater/drama. *Special achievements/activities:* 11 awards ($17,000 total): community service, general special achievements/activities, leadership. *Special characteristics:* 1,158 awards ($2,547,596 total): international students, out-of-state students. *Tuition waivers:* Full or partial for employees or children of employees.

LOANS *Student loans:* $25,788,913 (76% need-based, 24% non-need-based). 72% of past graduating class borrowed through all loan programs. *Average indebtedness per student:* $21,010. *Average need-based loan:* Freshmen: $5518. Undergraduates: $6897. *Parent loans:* $4,181,734 (63% need-based, 37% non-need-based). *Programs:* Federal Direct (Subsidized and Unsubsidized Stafford, PLUS), Perkins, Federal Nursing, alternative loans.

WORK-STUDY *Federal work-study:* Total amount: $938,530; 635 jobs averaging $2096. *State or other work-study/employment:* 845 part-time jobs averaging $2200.

APPLYING FOR FINANCIAL AID *Required financial aid forms:* FAFSA, state aid form. *Financial aid deadline (priority):* 2/15. *Notification date:* Continuous beginning 3/1. Students must reply within 8 weeks of notification.

CONTACT Mr. Todd Moravec, Financial Aid Director, State University of New York at Plattsburgh, 101 Broad Street, Plattsburgh, NY 12901-2681, 518-564-2072 or toll-free 888-673-0012 (in-state). *Fax:* 518-564-4079. *E-mail:* todd.moravec@plattsburgh.edu.

STATE UNIVERSITY OF NEW YORK COLLEGE AT CORTLAND
Cortland, NY

Tuition & fees: N/R	Average undergraduate aid package: $11,858

ABOUT THE INSTITUTION State-supported, coed. 57 undergraduate majors. Federal methodology is used as a basis for awarding need-based institutional aid.

FRESHMAN FINANCIAL AID (Fall 2009, est.) 1,062 applied for aid; of those 62% were deemed to have need. 98% of freshmen with need received aid; of those 16% had need fully met. *Average percent of need met:* 71% (excluding resources awarded to replace EFC). *Average financial aid package:* $11,648 (excluding resources awarded to replace EFC). 22% of all full-time freshmen had no need and received non-need-based gift aid.

UNDERGRADUATE FINANCIAL AID (Fall 2009, est.) 5,072 applied for aid; of those 73% were deemed to have need. 98% of undergraduates with need received aid; of those 17% had need fully met. *Average percent of need met:* 71% (excluding resources awarded to replace EFC). *Average financial aid*

package: $11,858 (excluding resources awarded to replace EFC). 18% of all full-time undergraduates had no need and received non-need-based gift aid.

GIFT AID (NEED-BASED) *Total amount:* $11,894,574 (52% federal, 47% state, 1% institutional). *Receiving aid:* Freshmen: 43% (502); all full-time undergraduates: 49% (2,932). *Average award:* Freshmen: $4293; Undergraduates: $4673. *Scholarships, grants, and awards:* Federal Pell, FSEOG, state, private, college/university gift aid from institutional funds.

GIFT AID (NON-NEED-BASED) *Total amount:* $526,230 (27% institutional, 73% external sources). *Receiving aid:* Freshmen: 1% (15). Undergraduates: 3% (186). *Average award:* Freshmen: $7988. Undergraduates: $8868. *Scholarships, grants, and awards by category:* Academic interests/achievement: education, general academic interests/achievements, international studies, mathematics, physical sciences. *Creative arts/performance:* art/fine arts, music. *Special achievements/activities:* community service, general special achievements/activities, hobbies/interests, leadership. *Special characteristics:* adult students, local/state students, members of minority groups.

LOANS *Student loans:* $33,238,236 (40% need-based, 60% non-need-based). *Average need-based loan:* Freshmen: $3479. Undergraduates: $4183. *Parent loans:* $4,330,279 (100% non-need-based). *Programs:* FFEL (Subsidized and Unsubsidized Stafford, PLUS), Perkins.

WORK-STUDY *Federal work-study:* Total amount: $204,326; jobs available.

APPLYING FOR FINANCIAL AID *Required financial aid forms:* FAFSA, state aid form. *Financial aid deadline (priority):* 3/1. *Notification date:* Continuous beginning 3/15. Students must reply by 5/1 or within 4 weeks of notification.

CONTACT Karen Gallagher, Director of Financial Advisement, State University of New York College at Cortland, PO Box 2000, Cortland, NY 13045, 607-753-4717. *Fax:* 607-753-5990. *E-mail:* finaid@cortland.edu.

STATE UNIVERSITY OF NEW YORK COLLEGE AT GENESEO
Geneseo, NY

Tuition & fees (NY res): $6326	Average undergraduate aid package: $8041

ABOUT THE INSTITUTION State-supported, coed. 46 undergraduate majors. Federal methodology is used as a basis for awarding need-based institutional aid.

UNDERGRADUATE EXPENSES for 2009–10 *Tuition, state resident:* full-time $4970; part-time $207 per credit hour. *Tuition, nonresident:* full-time $12,870; part-time $536 per credit hour. *Required fees:* full-time $1356; $56.32 per credit hour. Part-time tuition and fees vary according to course load. *College room and board:* $9550. Room and board charges vary according to board plan and housing facility. *Payment plans:* Installment, deferred payment.

FRESHMAN FINANCIAL AID (Fall 2009, est.) 798 applied for aid; of those 49% were deemed to have need. 100% of freshmen with need received aid; of those 70% had need fully met. *Average percent of need met:* 70% (excluding resources awarded to replace EFC). *Average financial aid package:* $4213 (excluding resources awarded to replace EFC). 1% of all full-time freshmen had no need and received non-need-based gift aid.

UNDERGRADUATE FINANCIAL AID (Fall 2009, est.) 3,800 applied for aid; of those 62% were deemed to have need. 100% of undergraduates with need received aid; of those 72% had need fully met. *Average percent of need met:* 73% (excluding resources awarded to replace EFC). *Average financial aid package:* $8041 (excluding resources awarded to replace EFC). 10% of all full-time undergraduates had no need and received non-need-based gift aid.

GIFT AID (NEED-BASED) *Total amount:* $9,591,389 (52% federal, 48% state). *Receiving aid:* Freshmen: 20% (185); all full-time undergraduates: 44% (2,350). *Average award:* Freshmen: $3846; Undergraduates: $4018. *Scholarships, grants, and awards:* Federal Pell, FSEOG, state.

GIFT AID (NON-NEED-BASED) *Total amount:* $2,408,169 (1% federal, 26% state, 52% institutional, 21% external sources). *Receiving aid:* Freshmen: 20% (187). Undergraduates: 15% (830). *Average award:* Freshmen: $2297. Undergraduates: $2068. *Scholarships, grants, and awards by category:* Academic interests/achievement: 447 awards ($440,450 total): area/ethnic studies, biological sciences, business, communication, computer science, education, English, foreign languages, general academic interests/achievements, humanities, international studies, mathematics, physical sciences, premedicine, social sciences. *Creative arts/performance:* 28 awards ($22,400 total): applied art and design, art/fine arts, creative writing, dance, general creative arts/performance, journalism/publications, music, performing arts, theater/drama.

State University of New York College at Geneseo

Special achievements/activities: 10 awards ($6000 total): community service, leadership, memberships. *Special characteristics:* 33 awards ($22,700 total): adult students, ethnic background, local/state students, members of minority groups, religious affiliation.

LOANS *Student loans:* $21,125,812 (41% need-based, 59% non-need-based). 63% of past graduating class borrowed through all loan programs. *Average indebtedness per student:* $21,000. *Average need-based loan:* Freshmen: $3870. Undergraduates: $4466. *Parent loans:* $2,626,963 (100% non-need-based). *Programs:* FFEL (Subsidized and Unsubsidized Stafford, PLUS), Perkins.

WORK-STUDY *Federal work-study:* Total amount: $600,000; 395 jobs averaging $1395. *State or other work-study/employment:* Total amount: $678,000 (100% non-need-based). Part-time jobs available.

APPLYING FOR FINANCIAL AID *Required financial aid forms:* FAFSA, state aid form. *Financial aid deadline:* 2/15. *Notification date:* Continuous beginning 3/15. Students must reply by 5/1.

CONTACT Archie Cureton, Director of Financial Aid, State University of New York College at Geneseo, 1 College Circle, Erwin Hall 104, Geneseo, NY 14454, 585-245-5731 or toll-free 866-245-5211. *Fax:* 585-245-5717. *E-mail:* cureton@geneseo.edu.

STATE UNIVERSITY OF NEW YORK COLLEGE AT OLD WESTBURY
Old Westbury, NY

Tuition & fees (NY res): $5797   **Average undergraduate aid package:** $7115

ABOUT THE INSTITUTION State-supported, coed. 41 undergraduate majors. Both federal and institutional methodology are used as a basis for awarding need-based institutional aid.

UNDERGRADUATE EXPENSES for 2009–10 *Tuition, state resident:* full-time $4970; part-time $207 per credit hour. *Tuition, nonresident:* full-time $12,870; part-time $536 per credit hour. *Required fees:* full-time $827; $18.35 per credit hour or $105.50 per term. Part-time tuition and fees vary according to course load. *College room and board:* $9390; *Room only:* $6440. Room and board charges vary according to board plan and housing facility. *Payment plan:* Installment.

FRESHMAN FINANCIAL AID (Fall 2009, est.) 367 applied for aid; of those 82% were deemed to have need. 96% of freshmen with need received aid; of those 100% had need fully met. *Average percent of need met:* 46% (excluding resources awarded to replace EFC). *Average financial aid package:* $7402 (excluding resources awarded to replace EFC).

UNDERGRADUATE FINANCIAL AID (Fall 2009, est.) 2,510 applied for aid; of those 84% were deemed to have need. 92% of undergraduates with need received aid; of those 100% had need fully met. *Average percent of need met:* 44% (excluding resources awarded to replace EFC). *Average financial aid package:* $7115 (excluding resources awarded to replace EFC).

GIFT AID (NEED-BASED) *Total amount:* $12,120,235 (56% federal, 43% state, 1% institutional). *Receiving aid:* Freshmen: 69% (289); all full-time undergraduates: 61% (1,951). *Average award:* Freshmen: $7009; Undergraduates: $5785. *Scholarships, grants, and awards:* Federal Pell, FSEOG, state, private, college/university gift aid from institutional funds.

GIFT AID (NON-NEED-BASED) *Total amount:* $26,376 (100% external sources). *Receiving aid:* Freshmen: 8% (34). Undergraduates: 2% (76). *Scholarships, grants, and awards by category:* Academic interests/achievement: biological sciences, health fields, physical sciences. *Tuition waivers:* Full or partial for senior citizens.

LOANS *Student loans:* $5,548,799 (98% need-based, 2% non-need-based). 46% of past graduating class borrowed through all loan programs. *Average indebtedness per student:* $17,104. *Average need-based loan:* Freshmen: $1973. Undergraduates: $2561. *Parent loans:* $818,985 (97% need-based, 3% non-need-based). *Programs:* FFEL (Subsidized and Unsubsidized Stafford, PLUS), Perkins.

WORK-STUDY *Federal work-study:* Total amount: $172,132; 210 jobs averaging $819.

APPLYING FOR FINANCIAL AID *Required financial aid forms:* FAFSA, institution's own form, state aid form, income documentation. *Financial aid deadline (priority):* 4/12. *Notification date:* Continuous beginning 4/25. Students must reply within 2 weeks of notification.

CONTACT Ms. Dee Darrell, Financial Aid Assistant, State University of New York College at Old Westbury, PO Box 210, Old Westbury, NY 11568-0210, 516-876-3222. *Fax:* 516-876-3008. *E-mail:* finaid@oldwestbury.edu.

STATE UNIVERSITY OF NEW YORK COLLEGE AT ONEONTA
Oneonta, NY

Tuition & fees (NY res): $6185   **Average undergraduate aid package:** $11,712

ABOUT THE INSTITUTION State-supported, coed. 68 undergraduate majors. Federal methodology is used as a basis for awarding need-based institutional aid.

UNDERGRADUATE EXPENSES for 2010–11 *Tuition, state resident:* full-time $4970; part-time $207 per semester hour. *Tuition, nonresident:* full-time $12,870; part-time $536 per semester hour. *Required fees:* full-time $1215; $40.53 per semester hour. Part-time tuition and fees vary according to course load. *College room and board:* $8900; *Room only:* $5200. Room and board charges vary according to board plan and housing facility. *Payment plan:* Installment.

FRESHMAN FINANCIAL AID (Fall 2009, est.) 996 applied for aid; of those 63% were deemed to have need. 96% of freshmen with need received aid; of those 15% had need fully met. *Average percent of need met:* 60% (excluding resources awarded to replace EFC). *Average financial aid package:* $10,804 (excluding resources awarded to replace EFC). 23% of all full-time freshmen had no need and received non-need-based gift aid.

UNDERGRADUATE FINANCIAL AID (Fall 2009, est.) 4,444 applied for aid; of those 72% were deemed to have need. 98% of undergraduates with need received aid; of those 17% had need fully met. *Average percent of need met:* 63% (excluding resources awarded to replace EFC). *Average financial aid package:* $11,712 (excluding resources awarded to replace EFC). 19% of all full-time undergraduates had no need and received non-need-based gift aid.

GIFT AID (NEED-BASED) *Total amount:* $17,169,236 (44% federal, 37% state, 6% institutional, 13% external sources). *Receiving aid:* Freshmen: 45% (504); all full-time undergraduates: 46% (2,583). *Average award:* Freshmen: $5131; Undergraduates: $5001. *Scholarships, grants, and awards:* Federal Pell, FSEOG, state, private, college/university gift aid from institutional funds.

GIFT AID (NON-NEED-BASED) *Total amount:* $2,734,028 (7% federal, 3% state, 27% institutional, 63% external sources). *Average award:* Freshmen: $2200. Undergraduates: $2000. *Scholarships, grants, and awards by category:* Academic interests/achievement: 518 awards ($1,135,332 total): biological sciences, business, computer science, education, English, general academic interests/achievements, home economics, physical sciences, premedicine, social sciences. Creative arts/performance: 25 awards ($17,400 total): music, theater/drama. Special achievements/activities: 15 awards ($15,820 total): community service, general special achievements/activities, leadership. Special characteristics: 122 awards ($151,800 total): general special characteristics, international students, local/state students. *Tuition waivers:* Full or partial for employees or children of employees.

LOANS *Student loans:* $28,751,621 (43% need-based, 57% non-need-based). 75% of past graduating class borrowed through all loan programs. *Average indebtedness per student:* $16,490. *Average need-based loan:* Freshmen: $3685. Undergraduates: $4486. *Parent loans:* $7,336,532 (100% non-need-based). *Programs:* Federal Direct (Subsidized and Unsubsidized Stafford, PLUS), Perkins.

WORK-STUDY *Federal work-study:* Total amount: $450,747; 350 jobs averaging $1200.

APPLYING FOR FINANCIAL AID *Required financial aid forms:* FAFSA, state aid form. *Financial aid deadline (priority):* 3/15. *Notification date:* Continuous beginning 3/1. Students must reply by 5/1 or within 4 weeks of notification.

CONTACT Mr. Bill Goodhue, Director of Financial Aid, State University of New York College at Oneonta, Ravine Parkway, Oneonta, NY 13820, 607-436-2992 or toll-free 800-SUNY-123. *Fax:* 607-436-2659. *E-mail:* goodhucw@oneonta.edu.

STATE UNIVERSITY OF NEW YORK COLLEGE AT POTSDAM
Potsdam, NY

Tuition & fees (NY res): $6124   **Average undergraduate aid package:** $14,073

ABOUT THE INSTITUTION State-supported, coed. 49 undergraduate majors. Federal methodology is used as a basis for awarding need-based institutional aid.

UNDERGRADUATE EXPENSES for 2009–10 *Tuition, state resident:* full-time $4970; part-time $207 per credit hour. *Tuition, nonresident:* full-time $12,870; part-time $536 per credit hour. *Required fees:* full-time $1154; $52.20 per credit hour. *College room and board:* $9270; *Room only:* $5370. Room and board charges vary according to board plan and housing facility. *Payment plan:* Installment.

FRESHMAN FINANCIAL AID (Fall 2009, est.) 766 applied for aid; of those 76% were deemed to have need. 99% of freshmen with need received aid; of those 87% had need fully met. *Average percent of need met:* 87% (excluding resources awarded to replace EFC). *Average financial aid package:* $14,853 (excluding resources awarded to replace EFC). 10% of all full-time freshmen had no need and received non-need-based gift aid.

UNDERGRADUATE FINANCIAL AID (Fall 2009, est.) 3,100 applied for aid; of those 77% were deemed to have need. 99% of undergraduates with need received aid; of those 71% had need fully met. *Average percent of need met:* 71% (excluding resources awarded to replace EFC). *Average financial aid package:* $14,073 (excluding resources awarded to replace EFC). 6% of all full-time undergraduates had no need and received non-need-based gift aid.

GIFT AID (NEED-BASED) *Total amount:* $13,383,159 (48% federal, 38% state, 12% institutional, 2% external sources). *Receiving aid:* Freshmen: 65% (538); all full-time undergraduates: 60% (2,189). *Average award:* Freshmen: $6536; Undergraduates: $5956. *Scholarships, grants, and awards:* Federal Pell, FSEOG, state, private, college/university gift aid from institutional funds, VESID Awards, Veterans Administration Rehabilitation Awards, Bureau of Indian Affairs Grants.

GIFT AID (NON-NEED-BASED) *Total amount:* $3,153,364 (36% federal, 11% state, 50% institutional, 3% external sources). *Receiving aid:* Freshmen: 28% (230). Undergraduates: 22% (813). *Average award:* Freshmen: $7542. Undergraduates: $11,677. *Scholarships, grants, and awards by category:* Academic interests/achievement: 297 awards ($299,057 total): biological sciences, business, communication, computer science, education, engineering/technologies, English, foreign languages, general academic interests/achievements, humanities, mathematics, physical sciences, social sciences. Creative arts/performance: 141 awards ($172,551 total): art/fine arts, dance, music, performing arts, theater/drama. Special achievements/activities: 649 awards ($1,455,650 total): community service, general special achievements/activities, leadership. Special characteristics: 63 awards ($69,088 total): adult students, children and siblings of alumni, children of faculty/staff, ethnic background, handicapped students, local/state students, members of minority groups, previous college experience.

LOANS *Student loans:* $18,734,779 (48% need-based, 52% non-need-based). 80% of past graduating class borrowed through all loan programs. *Average indebtedness per student:* $19,220. *Average need-based loan:* Freshmen: $3843. Undergraduates: $4360. *Parent loans:* $6,908,651 (100% non-need-based). *Programs:* Federal Direct (Subsidized and Unsubsidized Stafford, PLUS), Perkins, college/university, alternative loans.

WORK-STUDY *Federal work-study:* Total amount: $290,006; 254 jobs averaging $1200.

APPLYING FOR FINANCIAL AID *Required financial aid forms:* FAFSA, state aid form. *Financial aid deadline (priority):* 3/1. *Notification date:* Continuous beginning 2/1. Students must reply by 5/1 or within 4 weeks of notification.

CONTACT Susan C. Aldrich, Director of Financial Aid, State University of New York College at Potsdam, 44 Pierrepont Avenue, Potsdam, NY 13676, 315-267-2162 or toll-free 877-POTSDAM. *Fax:* 315-267-3067. *E-mail:* finaid@potsdam.edu.

STATE UNIVERSITY OF NEW YORK COLLEGE OF AGRICULTURE AND TECHNOLOGY AT COBLESKILL
Cobleskill, NY

ABOUT THE INSTITUTION State-supported, coed. *Awards:* associate and bachelor's degrees. 34 undergraduate majors. *Total enrollment:* 2,619. Undergraduates: 2,619. Freshmen: 978.

GIFT AID (NEED-BASED) *Scholarships, grants, and awards:* Federal Pell, FSEOG, state, private, college/university gift aid from institutional funds.

LOANS *Programs:* FFEL (Subsidized and Unsubsidized Stafford, PLUS), Perkins.

APPLYING FOR FINANCIAL AID *Required financial aid forms:* FAFSA, state aid form.

CONTACT Brian Smith, Director of Financial Aid, State University of New York College of Agriculture and Technology at Cobleskill, Knapp Hall, Cobleskill, NY 12043, 518-255-5623 or toll-free 800-295-8988. *Fax:* 518-255-5844. *E-mail:* finaid@cobleskill.edu.

STATE UNIVERSITY OF NEW YORK COLLEGE OF AGRICULTURE AND TECHNOLOGY AT MORRISVILLE
Morrisville, NY

Tuition & fees: N/R   Average undergraduate aid package: $9249

ABOUT THE INSTITUTION State-supported, coed. *Awards:* associate and bachelor's degrees. 48 undergraduate majors. *Total enrollment:* 3,432. Undergraduates: 3,432. Freshmen: 1,277. Federal methodology is used as a basis for awarding need-based institutional aid.

FRESHMAN FINANCIAL AID (Fall 2009, est.) 1,079 applied for aid; of those 91% were deemed to have need. 99% of freshmen with need received aid; of those .3% had need fully met. *Average financial aid package:* $9021 (excluding resources awarded to replace EFC). 1% of all full-time freshmen had no need and received non-need-based gift aid.

UNDERGRADUATE FINANCIAL AID (Fall 2009, est.) 2,785 applied for aid; of those 90% were deemed to have need. 99% of undergraduates with need received aid; of those 1% had need fully met. *Average financial aid package:* $9249 (excluding resources awarded to replace EFC). 2% of all full-time undergraduates had no need and received non-need-based gift aid.

GIFT AID (NEED-BASED) *Total amount:* $14,602,896 (59% federal, 41% state). *Receiving aid:* Freshmen: 83% (932); all full-time undergraduates: 79% (2,355). *Average award:* Freshmen: $6040; Undergraduates: $5900. *Scholarships, grants, and awards:* Federal Pell, FSEOG, state, college/university gift aid from institutional funds.

GIFT AID (NON-NEED-BASED) *Total amount:* $1,012,276 (9% state, 65% institutional, 26% external sources). *Receiving aid:* Freshmen: 13% (151). Undergraduates: 16% (485). *Average award:* Freshmen: $1480. Undergraduates: $1597. *Scholarships, grants, and awards by category:* Academic interests/achievement: 428 awards ($432,270 total): general academic interests/achievements. Special achievements/activities: 33 awards ($13,750 total): memberships. Special characteristics: 95 awards ($102,850 total): children of faculty/staff, members of minority groups, out-of-state students. *Tuition waivers:* Full or partial for children of alumni, employees or children of employees. *ROTC:* Army cooperative.

LOANS *Student loans:* $19,640,473 (44% need-based, 56% non-need-based). 83% of past graduating class borrowed through all loan programs. *Average indebtedness per student:* $21,067. *Average need-based loan:* Freshmen: $3059. Undergraduates: $3659. *Parent loans:* $3,735,789 (100% non-need-based). *Programs:* Federal Direct (Subsidized and Unsubsidized Stafford, PLUS), Perkins, Federal Nursing.

WORK-STUDY *Federal work-study:* Total amount: $277,370; 160 jobs averaging $1740.

APPLYING FOR FINANCIAL AID *Required financial aid forms:* FAFSA, state aid form. *Financial aid deadline (priority):* 2/2. *Notification date:* Continuous beginning 3/1.

CONTACT Financial Aid Office, State University of New York College of Agriculture and Technology at Morrisville, PO Box 901, Morrisville, NY 13408-0901, 315-684-6289 or toll-free 800-258-0111 (in-state). *Fax:* 315-684-6628.

STATE UNIVERSITY OF NEW YORK COLLEGE OF ENVIRONMENTAL SCIENCE AND FORESTRY
Syracuse, NY

Tuition & fees (NY res): $5891   Average undergraduate aid package: $13,000

ABOUT THE INSTITUTION State-supported, coed. 48 undergraduate majors. Federal methodology is used as a basis for awarding need-based institutional aid.

State University of New York College of Environmental Science and Forestry

UNDERGRADUATE EXPENSES for 2010–11 *Tuition, state resident:* full-time $4970; part-time $207 per credit hour. *Tuition, nonresident:* full-time $12,870; part-time $536 per credit hour. *Required fees:* full-time $921. Full-time tuition and fees vary according to location. Part-time tuition and fees vary according to course load and location. *College room and board:* $12,460; *Room only:* $6250. Room and board charges vary according to board plan, housing facility, and location. *Payment plans:* Installment, deferred payment.

FRESHMAN FINANCIAL AID (Fall 2009, est.) 260 applied for aid; of those 64% were deemed to have need. 100% of freshmen with need received aid; of those 100% had need fully met. *Average percent of need met:* 100% (excluding resources awarded to replace EFC). *Average financial aid package:* $12,500 (excluding resources awarded to replace EFC). 18% of all full-time freshmen had no need and received non-need-based gift aid.

UNDERGRADUATE FINANCIAL AID (Fall 2009, est.) 1,267 applied for aid; of those 72% were deemed to have need. 100% of undergraduates with need received aid; of those 100% had need fully met. *Average percent of need met:* 100% (excluding resources awarded to replace EFC). *Average financial aid package:* $13,000 (excluding resources awarded to replace EFC). 6% of all full-time undergraduates had no need and received non-need-based gift aid.

GIFT AID (NEED-BASED) *Total amount:* $4,301,581 (43% federal, 35% state, 17% institutional, 5% external sources). *Receiving aid:* Freshmen: 59% (166); all full-time undergraduates: 60% (918). *Average award:* Freshmen: $4000; Undergraduates: $5000. *Scholarships, grants, and awards:* Federal Pell, FSEOG, state, private, college/university gift aid from institutional funds.

GIFT AID (NON-NEED-BASED) *Total amount:* $1,303,451 (21% federal, 6% state, 61% institutional, 12% external sources). *Receiving aid:* Freshmen: 44% (124). Undergraduates: 20% (312). *Average award:* Freshmen: $2500. Undergraduates: $2500. *Scholarships, grants, and awards by category:* Academic interests/achievement: 320 awards ($726,433 total): agriculture, architecture, biological sciences, engineering/technologies, physical sciences, premedicine. *Special achievements/activities:* leadership. *Special characteristics:* members of minority groups.

LOANS *Student loans:* $8,496,727 (49% need-based, 51% non-need-based). 80% of past graduating class borrowed through all loan programs. *Average indebtedness per student:* $27,000. *Average need-based loan:* Freshmen: $5500. Undergraduates: $6750. *Parent loans:* $2,067,720 (48% need-based, 52% non-need-based). *Programs:* Federal Direct (Subsidized and Unsubsidized Stafford, PLUS), Perkins, college/university.

WORK-STUDY *Federal work-study:* Total amount: $340,000; 300 jobs averaging $1500. *State or other work-study/employment:* Total amount: $278,544 (47% need-based, 53% non-need-based). 150 part-time jobs averaging $1200.

APPLYING FOR FINANCIAL AID *Required financial aid forms:* FAFSA, state aid form. *Financial aid deadline (priority):* 3/1. *Notification date:* 4/1. Students must reply within 2 weeks of notification.

CONTACT Mr. John E. View, Director of Financial Aid, State University of New York College of Environmental Science and Forestry, One Forestry Drive, Syracuse, NY 13210-2779, 315-470-6671 or toll-free 800-777-7373. *Fax:* 315-470-4734. *E-mail:* jeview@esf.edu.

STATE UNIVERSITY OF NEW YORK COLLEGE OF TECHNOLOGY AT CANTON
Canton, NY

Tuition & fees (NY res): $6279	Average undergraduate aid package: N/A

ABOUT THE INSTITUTION State-supported, coed. 33 undergraduate majors. Federal methodology is used as a basis for awarding need-based institutional aid.

UNDERGRADUATE EXPENSES for 2009–10 *One-time required fee:* $90. *Tuition, state resident:* full-time $4970; part-time $207 per credit hour. *Tuition, nonresident:* full-time $8750; part-time $536 per credit hour. *Required fees:* full-time $1309; $49 per credit hour or $5 per term. Full-time tuition and fees vary according to degree level, location, and program. Part-time tuition and fees vary according to degree level, location, and program. *College room and board:* $9320; *Room only:* $5400. Room and board charges vary according to housing facility. *Payment plans:* Installment, deferred payment.

GIFT AID (NEED-BASED) *Total amount:* $10,585,069 (45% federal, 48% state, 6% institutional, 1% external sources). *Scholarships, grants, and awards:* Federal Pell, FSEOG, state, private, college/university gift aid from institutional funds, Bureau of Indian Affairs Grants.

GIFT AID (NON-NEED-BASED) *Tuition waivers:* Full or partial for employees or children of employees.

LOANS *Student loans:* $12,307,917 (45% need-based, 55% non-need-based). *Parent loans:* $1,244,485 (100% need-based). *Programs:* Federal Direct (Subsidized and Unsubsidized Stafford, PLUS), Perkins, alternative loans.

WORK-STUDY *Federal work-study:* Total amount: $165,218; jobs available. *State or other work-study/employment:* Part-time jobs available.

ATHLETIC AWARDS Total amount: $3200 (100% need-based).

APPLYING FOR FINANCIAL AID *Required financial aid forms:* FAFSA, state aid form. *Financial aid deadline (priority):* 3/15. *Notification date:* Continuous beginning 2/15. Students must reply within 4 weeks of notification.

CONTACT Ms. Kerrie Cooper, Director of Financial Aid, State University of New York College of Technology at Canton, Student Service Center, Canton, NY 13617, 315-386-7616 or toll-free 800-388-7123. *Fax:* 315-386-7930. *E-mail:* cooper@canton.edu.

STATE UNIVERSITY OF NEW YORK COLLEGE OF TECHNOLOGY AT DELHI
Delhi, NY

Tuition & fees (NY res): $6360	Average undergraduate aid package: N/A

ABOUT THE INSTITUTION State-supported, coed. *Awards:* associate and bachelor's degrees. 33 undergraduate majors. *Total enrollment:* 2,971. Undergraduates: 2,971. Freshmen: 1,016. Federal methodology is used as a basis for awarding need-based institutional aid.

UNDERGRADUATE EXPENSES for 2009–10 *Application fee:* $40. *Tuition, state resident:* full-time $4970; part-time $207 per credit hour. *Tuition, nonresident:* full-time $12,870; part-time $536 per credit hour. *Required fees:* full-time $1390; $57.10 per credit hour or $695 per term. Full-time tuition and fees vary according to degree level. Part-time tuition and fees vary according to degree level. *College room and board:* $9300; *Room only:* $5400. Room and board charges vary according to board plan and location. *Payment plan:* Installment.

FRESHMAN FINANCIAL AID (Fall 2009, est.) 846 applied for aid.

UNDERGRADUATE FINANCIAL AID (Fall 2009, est.) 2,386 applied for aid.

GIFT AID (NEED-BASED) *Total amount:* $11,483,075 (52% federal, 41% state, 3% institutional, 4% external sources). *Receiving aid:* All full-time undergraduates: 74% (1,940). *Scholarships, grants, and awards:* Federal Pell, FSEOG, state, private, college/university gift aid from institutional funds.

GIFT AID (NON-NEED-BASED) *Scholarships, grants, and awards by category:* Academic interests/achievement: general academic interests/achievements. *Special achievements/activities:* community service.

LOANS *Student loans:* $13,743,851 (100% need-based). *Parent loans:* $3,515,371 (100% need-based). *Programs:* Federal Direct (Subsidized and Unsubsidized Stafford, PLUS), Perkins.

WORK-STUDY *Federal work-study:* Total amount: $145,850; 126 jobs averaging $1158. *State or other work-study/employment:* Total amount: $377,162 (100% need-based). Part-time jobs available.

ATHLETIC AWARDS Total amount: $955 (100% need-based).

APPLYING FOR FINANCIAL AID *Required financial aid forms:* FAFSA, state aid form. *Financial aid deadline (priority):* 2/15. *Notification date:* Continuous beginning 3/15.

CONTACT Director of Financial Aid, State University of New York College of Technology at Delhi, 109 Bush Hall, Delhi, NY 13753, 607-746-4570 or toll-free 800-96-DELHI. *Fax:* 607-746-4104.

STATE UNIVERSITY OF NEW YORK DOWNSTATE MEDICAL CENTER
Brooklyn, NY

CONTACT Financial Aid Office, State University of New York Downstate Medical Center, 450 Clarkson Avenue, Brooklyn, NY 11203-2098, 718-270-2488. *Fax:* 718-270-7592. *E-mail:* finaid1@downstate.edu.

STATE UNIVERSITY OF NEW YORK INSTITUTE OF TECHNOLOGY
Utica, NY

Tuition & fees: N/R   **Average undergraduate aid package: N/A**

ABOUT THE INSTITUTION State-supported, coed. *Awards:* bachelor's and master's degrees and post-master's certificates. 20 undergraduate majors. *Total enrollment:* 2,828. Undergraduates: 2,210. Freshmen: 204. Federal methodology is used as a basis for awarding need-based institutional aid.
FRESHMAN FINANCIAL AID (Fall 2009, est.) 179 applied for aid; of those 82% were deemed to have need. 99% of freshmen with need received aid. 7% of all full-time freshmen had no need and received non-need-based gift aid.
UNDERGRADUATE FINANCIAL AID (Fall 2009, est.) 1,289 applied for aid; of those 83% were deemed to have need. 99% of undergraduates with need received aid. 3% of all full-time undergraduates had no need and received non-need-based gift aid.
GIFT AID (NEED-BASED) *Total amount:* $5,421,071 (56% federal, 38% state, 4% institutional, 2% external sources). *Receiving aid:* Freshmen: 67% (137); all full-time undergraduates: 62% (952). *Average award:* Freshmen: $6232; Undergraduates: $5604. *Scholarships, grants, and awards:* Federal Pell, FSEOG, state, college/university gift aid from institutional funds.
GIFT AID (NON-NEED-BASED) *Total amount:* $276,910 (26% federal, 25% state, 35% institutional, 14% external sources). *Average award:* Freshmen: $1767. Undergraduates: $1747. *Scholarships, grants, and awards by category: Academic interests/achievement:* computer science, engineering/technologies, general academic interests/achievements. *Special characteristics:* local/state students, members of minority groups, previous college experience. *ROTC:* Army cooperative, Air Force cooperative.
LOANS *Student loans:* $6,853,332 (83% need-based, 17% non-need-based). *Average need-based loan:* Freshmen: $3187. Undergraduates: $4168. *Parent loans:* $1,501,749 (69% need-based, 31% non-need-based). *Programs:* Federal Direct (Subsidized and Unsubsidized Stafford, PLUS), Perkins, Federal Nursing.
WORK-STUDY *Federal work-study:* Total amount: $322,520; jobs available.
APPLYING FOR FINANCIAL AID *Required financial aid forms:* FAFSA, state aid form. *Financial aid deadline (priority):* 3/15. *Notification date:* Continuous beginning 3/15. Students must reply within 2 weeks of notification.
CONTACT Director of Financial Aid, State University of New York Institute of Technology, PO Box 3050, Utica, NY 13504-3050, 315-792-7210 or toll-free 800-SUNYTEC. *Fax:* 315-792-7220. *E-mail:* hoskeyl@sunyit.edu.

STATE UNIVERSITY OF NEW YORK MARITIME COLLEGE
Throggs Neck, NY

CONTACT Ms. Madeline Aponte, Director of Financial Aid, State University of New York Maritime College, 6 Pennyfield Avenue, Throgs Neck, NY 10465-4198, 718-409-7267 or toll-free 800-654-1874 (in-state), 800-642-1874 (out-of-state). *Fax:* 718-409-7275. *E-mail:* finaid@sunymaritime.edu.

STATE UNIVERSITY OF NEW YORK UPSTATE MEDICAL UNIVERSITY
Syracuse, NY

Tuition & fees (NY res): $5550   **Average undergraduate aid package: $11,847**

ABOUT THE INSTITUTION State-supported, coed. 6 undergraduate majors. Federal methodology is used as a basis for awarding need-based institutional aid.
UNDERGRADUATE EXPENSES for 2010–11 *Tuition, state resident:* full-time $4970; part-time $207 per credit. *Tuition, nonresident:* full-time $12,870; part-time $536 per credit. *Required fees:* full-time $580; $32 per credit. Full-time tuition and fees vary according to course load and program. Part-time tuition and fees vary according to course load and program. *College room and board:* $10,422; *Room only:* $6525. Room and board charges vary according to housing facility. *Payment plan:* Installment.
UNDERGRADUATE FINANCIAL AID (Fall 2009, est.) 227 applied for aid; of those 100% were deemed to have need. 100% of undergraduates with need

received aid. *Average percent of need met:* 86% (excluding resources awarded to replace EFC). *Average financial aid package:* $11,847 (excluding resources awarded to replace EFC).
GIFT AID (NEED-BASED) *Total amount:* $974,551 (52% federal, 23% state, 17% institutional, 8% external sources). *Receiving aid:* All full-time undergraduates: 44% (128). *Average award:* Undergraduates: $1608. *Scholarships, grants, and awards:* Federal Pell, FSEOG, state, college/university gift aid from institutional funds.
GIFT AID (NON-NEED-BASED) *Total amount:* $6385 (100% state). *Receiving aid:* Undergraduates: 1% (3). *Scholarships, grants, and awards by category: Academic interests/achievement:* 104 awards ($167,266 total): health fields.
LOANS *Student loans:* $1,483,055 (100% need-based). *Average need-based loan:* Undergraduates: $11,128. *Parent loans:* $33,164 (100% need-based). *Programs:* Federal Direct (Subsidized and Unsubsidized Stafford, PLUS), Perkins.
WORK-STUDY *Federal work-study:* Total amount: $50,826; jobs available.
APPLYING FOR FINANCIAL AID *Required financial aid form:* FAFSA. *Financial aid deadline (priority):* 3/1. *Notification date:* Continuous beginning 5/1. Students must reply within 3 weeks of notification.
CONTACT Michael Pede, Office of Financial Aid, State University of New York Upstate Medical University, 155 Elizabeth Blackwell Street, Syracuse, NY 13210-2375, 315-464-4329 or toll-free 800-736-2171. *E-mail:* finaid@upstate.edu.

STEPHEN F. AUSTIN STATE UNIVERSITY
Nacogdoches, TX

Tuition & fees (TX res): $6732   **Average undergraduate aid package: $8663**

ABOUT THE INSTITUTION State-supported, coed. 68 undergraduate majors. Federal methodology is used as a basis for awarding need-based institutional aid.
UNDERGRADUATE EXPENSES for 2009–10 *Tuition, state resident:* full-time $4830; part-time $161 per credit hour. *Tuition, nonresident:* full-time $13,140; part-time $438 per credit hour. *Required fees:* full-time $1902; $147 per credit hour. Full-time tuition and fees vary according to course load, degree level, and location. Part-time tuition and fees vary according to course load, degree level, and location. *College room and board:* $7377. Room and board charges vary according to board plan and housing facility. *Payment plan:* Installment.
FRESHMAN FINANCIAL AID (Fall 2008) 1,806 applied for aid; of those 78% were deemed to have need. 98% of freshmen with need received aid; of those 65% had need fully met. *Average percent of need met:* 84% (excluding resources awarded to replace EFC). *Average financial aid package:* $9059 (excluding resources awarded to replace EFC). 6% of all full-time freshmen had no need and received non-need-based gift aid.
UNDERGRADUATE FINANCIAL AID (Fall 2008) 6,828 applied for aid; of those 81% were deemed to have need. 98% of undergraduates with need received aid; of those 58% had need fully met. *Average percent of need met:* 86% (excluding resources awarded to replace EFC). *Average financial aid package:* $8663 (excluding resources awarded to replace EFC). 3% of all full-time undergraduates had no need and received non-need-based gift aid.
GIFT AID (NEED-BASED) *Total amount:* $23,409,263 (61% federal, 20% state, 19% institutional). *Receiving aid:* Freshmen: 47% (1,066); all full-time undergraduates: 45% (4,256). *Average award:* Freshmen: $3535; Undergraduates: $3723. *Scholarships, grants, and awards:* Federal Pell, FSEOG, state, college/university gift aid from institutional funds, Academic Competitiveness Grants, National SMART Grants, TEACH Grants.
GIFT AID (NON-NEED-BASED) *Total amount:* $10,297,250 (2% federal, 2% state, 72% institutional, 24% external sources). *Receiving aid:* Freshmen: 17% (396). Undergraduates: 16% (1,478). *Average award:* Freshmen: $2286. Undergraduates: $2472. *Scholarships, grants, and awards by category: Academic interests/achievement:* agriculture, biological sciences, business, communication, computer science, education, general academic interests/achievements, health fields, home economics, mathematics, military science, physical sciences, premedicine. *Creative arts/performance:* journalism/publications, music, theater/drama. *Special achievements/activities:* cheerleading/drum major, general special achievements/activities, hobbies/interests, leadership, rodeo. *Special characteristics:* adult students, children and siblings of alumni, children of faculty/staff, children of union members/company employees, first-generation college students, general special characteristics, local/state students, previous college experience. *Tuition waivers:* Full or partial for employees or children of employees, senior citizens.

Stephen F. Austin State University

LOANS *Student loans:* $63,891,527 (42% need-based, 58% non-need-based). 68% of past graduating class borrowed through all loan programs. *Average indebtedness per student:* $20,547. *Average need-based loan:* Freshmen: $3138. Undergraduates: $3981. *Parent loans:* $8,601,524 (100% non-need-based). *Programs:* FFEL (Subsidized and Unsubsidized Stafford, PLUS), Perkins, state, short-term emergency loans.

WORK-STUDY *Federal work-study:* Total amount: $687,373; jobs available. *State or other work-study/employment:* Total amount: $77,406 (100% need-based). Part-time jobs available.

ATHLETIC AWARDS Total amount: $3,084,896 (100% non-need-based).

APPLYING FOR FINANCIAL AID *Required financial aid form:* FAFSA. *Financial aid deadline:* Continuous. *Notification date:* Continuous beginning 4/1.

CONTACT Office of Financial Aid, Stephen F. Austin State University, PO Box 13052, Nacogdoches, TX 75962, 936-468-2403 or toll-free 800-731-2902. *Fax:* 936-468-1048. *E-mail:* finaid@sfasu.edu.

STEPHENS COLLEGE
Columbia, MO

Tuition & fees: $25,400	Average undergraduate aid package: $20,787

ABOUT THE INSTITUTION Independent, undergraduate: women only; graduate: coed. 33 undergraduate majors. Federal methodology is used as a basis for awarding need-based institutional aid.

UNDERGRADUATE EXPENSES for 2010–11 *Comprehensive fee:* $32,570 includes full-time tuition ($25,400) and room and board ($7170). *College room only:* $4770. Full-time tuition and fees vary according to degree level, program, and reciprocity agreements. Room and board charges vary according to board plan and housing facility. *Part-time tuition:* $700 per credit hour. Part-time tuition and fees vary according to degree level and program. *Payment plan:* Installment.

FRESHMAN FINANCIAL AID (Fall 2009, est.) 208 applied for aid; of those 89% were deemed to have need. 100% of freshmen with need received aid; of those 22% had need fully met. *Average percent of need met:* 77% (excluding resources awarded to replace EFC). *Average financial aid package:* $21,020 (excluding resources awarded to replace EFC). 46% of all full-time freshmen had no need and received non-need-based gift aid.

UNDERGRADUATE FINANCIAL AID (Fall 2009, est.) 651 applied for aid; of those 89% were deemed to have need. 100% of undergraduates with need received aid; of those 20% had need fully met. *Average percent of need met:* 78% (excluding resources awarded to replace EFC). *Average financial aid package:* $20,787 (excluding resources awarded to replace EFC). 23% of all full-time undergraduates had no need and received non-need-based gift aid.

GIFT AID (NEED-BASED) *Total amount:* $9,227,842 (14% federal, 6% state, 78% institutional, 2% external sources). *Receiving aid:* Freshmen: 78% (185); all full-time undergraduates: 77% (581). *Average award:* Freshmen: $17,653; Undergraduates: $16,735. *Scholarships, grants, and awards:* Federal Pell, FSEOG, state, private, college/university gift aid from institutional funds, Academic Competitiveness Grants, National SMART Grants.

GIFT AID (NON-NEED-BASED) *Total amount:* $1,945,014 (1% state, 94% institutional, 5% external sources). *Receiving aid:* Freshmen: 12% (28). Undergraduates: 11% (81). *Average award:* Freshmen: $8416. Undergraduates: $8629. *Scholarships, grants, and awards by category:* Academic interests/achievement: $4,222,347 total: English, general academic interests/achievements. *Creative arts/performance:* $120,250 total: dance, performing arts, theater/drama. *Special achievements/activities:* $1,012,029 total: leadership, memberships. *Special characteristics:* $174,427 total: children of faculty/staff, children of union members/company employees, parents of current students, siblings of current students, veterans, veterans' children. *Tuition waivers:* Full or partial for employees or children of employees.

LOANS *Student loans:* $4,067,967 (76% need-based, 24% non-need-based). 78% of past graduating class borrowed through all loan programs. *Average indebtedness per student:* $22,942. *Average need-based loan:* Freshmen: $3336. Undergraduates: $4334. *Parent loans:* $1,268,960 (34% need-based, 66% non-need-based). *Programs:* FFEL (Subsidized and Unsubsidized Stafford, PLUS), Perkins, alternative loans.

WORK-STUDY *Federal work-study:* Total amount: $159,180; 99 jobs averaging $1600. *State or other work-study/employment:* Total amount: $213,815 (80% need-based, 20% non-need-based). 140 part-time jobs averaging $1550.

ATHLETIC AWARDS Total amount: $334,000 (64% need-based, 36% non-need-based).

APPLYING FOR FINANCIAL AID *Required financial aid form:* FAFSA. *Financial aid deadline (priority):* 3/15. *Notification date:* Continuous beginning 3/1.

CONTACT Mrs. Rachel Touchatt, Financial Aid Director, Stephens College, 1200 East Broadway, Columbia, MO 65215-0002, 800-876-7207. *Fax:* 573-876-2320. *E-mail:* finaid@stephens.edu.

STERLING COLLEGE
Sterling, KS

CONTACT Ms. Jodi Lightner, Director of Financial Aid, Sterling College, PO Box 98, Sterling, KS 67579-0098, 620-278-4207 or toll-free 800-346-1017. *Fax:* 620-278-4416. *E-mail:* jlightner@sterling.edu.

STERLING COLLEGE
Craftsbury Common, VT

Tuition & fees: $23,621	Average undergraduate aid package: $20,010

ABOUT THE INSTITUTION Independent, coed. 23 undergraduate majors. Both federal and institutional methodology are used as a basis for awarding need-based institutional aid.

UNDERGRADUATE EXPENSES for 2009–10 *Comprehensive fee:* $31,175 includes full-time tuition ($23,196), mandatory fees ($425), and room and board ($7554). *College room only:* $3440. Full-time tuition and fees vary according to course load. Room and board charges vary according to board plan. *Part-time tuition:* $700 per credit hour. Part-time tuition and fees vary according to course load. *Payment plan:* Installment.

FRESHMAN FINANCIAL AID (Fall 2009, est.) 24 applied for aid; of those 92% were deemed to have need. 100% of freshmen with need received aid; of those 5% had need fully met. *Average percent of need met:* 65% (excluding resources awarded to replace EFC). *Average financial aid package:* $20,313 (excluding resources awarded to replace EFC). 4% of all full-time freshmen had no need and received non-need-based gift aid.

UNDERGRADUATE FINANCIAL AID (Fall 2009, est.) 90 applied for aid; of those 80% were deemed to have need. 100% of undergraduates with need received aid; of those 1% had need fully met. *Average percent of need met:* 64% (excluding resources awarded to replace EFC). *Average financial aid package:* $20,010 (excluding resources awarded to replace EFC). 12% of all full-time undergraduates had no need and received non-need-based gift aid.

GIFT AID (NEED-BASED) *Total amount:* $998,212 (20% federal, 6% state, 70% institutional, 4% external sources). *Receiving aid:* Freshmen: 88% (22); all full-time undergraduates: 76% (71). *Average award:* Freshmen: $15,694; Undergraduates: $14,747. *Scholarships, grants, and awards:* Federal Pell, FSEOG, state, private, college/university gift aid from institutional funds.

GIFT AID (NON-NEED-BASED) *Total amount:* $95,540 (95% institutional, 5% external sources). *Average award:* Freshmen: $4000. Undergraduates: $5442. *Scholarships, grants, and awards by category:* Academic interests/achievement: 7 awards ($23,500 total): general academic interests/achievements. *Special achievements/activities:* 14 awards ($50,000 total): general special achievements/activities. *Special characteristics:* 50 awards ($70,300 total): general special characteristics, local/state students, previous college experience. *Tuition waivers:* Full or partial for employees or children of employees, senior citizens.

LOANS *Student loans:* $421,959 (98% need-based, 2% non-need-based). 100% of past graduating class borrowed through all loan programs. *Average indebtedness per student:* $31,867. *Average need-based loan:* Freshmen: $3000. Undergraduates: $3714. *Parent loans:* $406,688 (86% need-based, 14% non-need-based). *Programs:* FFEL (Subsidized and Unsubsidized Stafford, PLUS).

WORK-STUDY *Federal work-study:* Total amount: $20,250; 45 jobs averaging $450. *State or other work-study/employment:* Total amount: $173,246 (81% need-based, 19% non-need-based). 88 part-time jobs averaging $1969.

APPLYING FOR FINANCIAL AID *Required financial aid forms:* FAFSA, institution's own form, state aid form. *Financial aid deadline:* Continuous. *Notification date:* Continuous beginning 1/31. Students must reply by 5/1 or within 2 weeks of notification.

CONTACT Barbara Stuart, Associate Director of Financial Aid, Sterling College, PO Box 72, Craftsbury Common, VT 05827, 800-648-3591 Ext. 2 or toll-free 800-648-3591 Ext. 100. *Fax:* 802-586-2596. *E-mail:* bstuart@sterlingcollege.edu.

STETSON UNIVERSITY
DeLand, FL

Tuition & fees: $33,424 · **Average undergraduate aid package: $27,435**

ABOUT THE INSTITUTION Independent, coed. 58 undergraduate majors. Federal methodology is used as a basis for awarding need-based institutional aid.
UNDERGRADUATE EXPENSES for 2010–11 *Comprehensive fee:* $43,229 includes full-time tuition ($31,374), mandatory fees ($2050), and room and board ($9805). *College room only:* $5620. Room and board charges vary according to board plan and housing facility. *Part-time tuition:* $960 per credit hour. *Payment plan:* Installment.
FRESHMAN FINANCIAL AID (Fall 2009, est.) 420 applied for aid; of those 85% were deemed to have need. 100% of freshmen with need received aid; of those 25% had need fully met. *Average percent of need met:* 85% (excluding resources awarded to replace EFC). *Average financial aid package:* $29,858 (excluding resources awarded to replace EFC). 24% of all full-time freshmen had no need and received non-need-based gift aid.
UNDERGRADUATE FINANCIAL AID (Fall 2009, est.) 1,484 applied for aid; of those 89% were deemed to have need. 100% of undergraduates with need received aid; of those 26% had need fully met. *Average percent of need met:* 81% (excluding resources awarded to replace EFC). *Average financial aid package:* $27,435 (excluding resources awarded to replace EFC). 28% of all full-time undergraduates had no need and received non-need-based gift aid.
GIFT AID (NEED-BASED) *Total amount:* $25,822,405 (14% federal, 20% state, 65% institutional, 1% external sources). *Receiving aid:* Freshmen: 71% (355); all full-time undergraduates: 63% (1,304). *Average award:* Freshmen: $23,402; Undergraduates: $20,704. *Scholarships, grants, and awards:* Federal Pell, FSEOG, state, private, college/university gift aid from institutional funds.
GIFT AID (NON-NEED-BASED) *Total amount:* $11,286,929 (24% state, 73% institutional, 3% external sources). *Receiving aid:* Freshmen: 11% (55). Undergraduates: 9% (193). *Average award:* Freshmen: $12,201. Undergraduates: $12,241. *Scholarships, grants, and awards by category: Academic interests/achievement:* area/ethnic studies, biological sciences, business, communication, computer science, education, English, foreign languages, general academic interests/achievements, humanities, mathematics, military science, physical sciences, premedicine, religion/biblical studies, social sciences. *Creative arts/performance:* applied art and design, art/fine arts, music, theater/drama. *Special achievements/activities:* cheerleading/drum major, community service, general special achievements/activities, leadership, religious involvement. *Special characteristics:* children and siblings of alumni, children of faculty/staff, ethnic background, general special characteristics, international students, local/state students, members of minority groups. *Tuition waivers:* Full or partial for employees or children of employees.
LOANS *Student loans:* $10,637,139 (72% need-based, 28% non-need-based). 83% of past graduating class borrowed through all loan programs. *Average indebtedness per student:* $30,914. *Average need-based loan:* Freshmen: $4159. Undergraduates: $4877. *Parent loans:* $2,119,426 (34% need-based, 66% non-need-based). *Programs:* Federal Direct (Subsidized and Unsubsidized Stafford, PLUS), Perkins, college/university.
WORK-STUDY *Federal work-study:* Total amount: $1,783,593; 739 jobs averaging $2414. *State or other work-study/employment:* Total amount: $835,276 (25% need-based, 75% non-need-based). 284 part-time jobs averaging $2941.
ATHLETIC AWARDS Total amount: $3,483,918 (40% need-based, 60% non-need-based).
APPLYING FOR FINANCIAL AID *Required financial aid forms:* FAFSA, institution's own form. *Financial aid deadline (priority):* 3/15. *Notification date:* Continuous. Students must reply within 2 weeks of notification.
CONTACT Robert D. Stewart, Director of Financial Aid, Stetson University, 421 North Woodland Boulevard, DeLand, FL 32723, 386-822-7120 or toll-free 800-688-0101. *Fax:* 386-822-7126. *E-mail:* finaid@stetson.edu.

STEVENS-HENAGER COLLEGE
Boise, ID

Tuition & fees: N/R · **Average undergraduate aid package: $8800**

ABOUT THE INSTITUTION Proprietary, coed. 9 undergraduate majors. Federal methodology is used as a basis for awarding need-based institutional aid.
FRESHMAN FINANCIAL AID (Fall 2008) 363 applied for aid; of those 75% were deemed to have need. 100% of freshmen with need received aid; of those 60% had need fully met. *Average percent of need met:* 60% (excluding resources awarded to replace EFC). *Average financial aid package:* $8800 (excluding resources awarded to replace EFC). 6% of all full-time freshmen had no need and received non-need-based gift aid.
UNDERGRADUATE FINANCIAL AID (Fall 2008) 903 applied for aid; of those 75% were deemed to have need. 100% of undergraduates with need received aid; of those 60% had need fully met. *Average percent of need met:* 60% (excluding resources awarded to replace EFC). *Average financial aid package:* $8800 (excluding resources awarded to replace EFC). 2% of all full-time undergraduates had no need and received non-need-based gift aid.
GIFT AID (NEED-BASED) *Total amount:* $3,623,788 (100% federal). *Receiving aid:* Freshmen: 75% (273); all full-time undergraduates: 75% (678). *Average award:* Freshmen: $5350; Undergraduates: $5350. *Scholarships, grants, and awards:* Federal Pell, FSEOG, state, private, college/university gift aid from institutional funds.
GIFT AID (NON-NEED-BASED) *Total amount:* $124,100 (98% institutional, 2% external sources). *Receiving aid:* Freshmen: 75% (273). Undergraduates: 75% (678). *Average award:* Freshmen: $7500. Undergraduates: $7500. *Scholarships, grants, and awards by category: Academic interests/achievement:* 60 awards ($450,000 total): business, computer science, health fields. *Creative arts/performance:* 10 awards ($70,000 total): applied art and design.
LOANS *Student loans:* $6,433,875 (37% need-based, 63% non-need-based). 95% of past graduating class borrowed through all loan programs. *Average indebtedness per student:* $11,000. *Average need-based loan:* Freshmen: $3500. Undergraduates: $3500. *Parent loans:* $42,000 (100% need-based). *Programs:* Federal Direct (Subsidized and Unsubsidized Stafford, PLUS), Perkins, college/university.
APPLYING FOR FINANCIAL AID *Required financial aid forms:* FAFSA, institution's own form, business/farm supplement. *Financial aid deadline:* Continuous. *Notification date:* Continuous beginning 5/1. Students must reply within 8 weeks of notification.
CONTACT Ms. Jaime L. Davis, Outreach and Admissions, Stevens-Henager College, 1444 South Entertainment Avenue, Boise, ID 83709, 208-283-5134. *Fax:* 208-345-6999. *E-mail:* jaime.davis@stevenshenager.edu.

STEVENS-HENAGER COLLEGE
West Haven, UT

CONTACT Michele A. Wilmoth, Director of Finance, Stevens-Henager College, 2168 Washington Boulevard, Ogden, UT 84401-1420, 801-394-7791 or toll-free 800-622-2640. *Fax:* 801-393-1748. *E-mail:* shcfad@stevenshenager.com.

STEVENS INSTITUTE OF TECHNOLOGY
Hoboken, NJ

CONTACT Ms. Adrienne Hynek, Associate Director of Financial Aid, Stevens Institute of Technology, Castle Point on Hudson, Hoboken, NJ 07030, 201-216-5555 or toll-free 800-458-5323. *Fax:* 201-216-8050. *E-mail:* ahynek@stevens.edu.

STEVENSON UNIVERSITY
Stevenson, MD

Tuition & fees: $20,644 · **Average undergraduate aid package: $14,124**

ABOUT THE INSTITUTION Independent, coed. 22 undergraduate majors. Institutional methodology is used as a basis for awarding need-based institutional aid.
UNDERGRADUATE EXPENSES for 2009–10 *Comprehensive fee:* $30,940 includes full-time tuition ($19,234), mandatory fees ($1410), and room and board ($10,296). *College room only:* $6750. Full-time tuition and fees vary according to degree level. Room and board charges vary according to board plan and housing facility. *Part-time tuition:* $487 per credit hour. *Part-time fees:* $75 per term. Part-time tuition and fees vary according to course load and degree level. *Payment plans:* Installment, deferred payment.
FRESHMAN FINANCIAL AID (Fall 2009, est.) 481 applied for aid; of those 85% were deemed to have need. 99% of freshmen with need received aid; of those 26% had need fully met. *Average percent of need met:* 64% (excluding

resources awarded to replace EFC). *Average financial aid package:* $15,294 (excluding resources awarded to replace EFC). 13% of all full-time freshmen had no need and received non-need-based gift aid.

UNDERGRADUATE FINANCIAL AID (Fall 2009, est.) 2,097 applied for aid; of those 86% were deemed to have need. 99% of undergraduates with need received aid; of those 30% had need fully met. *Average percent of need met:* 63% (excluding resources awarded to replace EFC). *Average financial aid package:* $14,124 (excluding resources awarded to replace EFC). 21% of all full-time undergraduates had no need and received non-need-based gift aid.

GIFT AID (NEED-BASED) *Total amount:* $18,700,166 (18% federal, 17% state, 62% institutional, 3% external sources). *Receiving aid:* Freshmen: 76% (397); all full-time undergraduates: 64% (1,687). *Average award:* Freshmen: $12,537; Undergraduates: $10,967. *Scholarships, grants, and awards:* Federal Pell, FSEOG, state, private, college/university gift aid from institutional funds.

GIFT AID (NON-NEED-BASED) *Total amount:* $5,145,023 (5% state, 86% institutional, 9% external sources). *Receiving aid:* Freshmen: 10% (53). Undergraduates: 7% (176). *Average award:* Freshmen: $8423. Undergraduates: $6920. *Scholarships, grants, and awards by category: Academic interests/ achievement:* general academic interests/achievements. *Creative arts/performance:* art/fine arts. *Tuition waivers:* Full or partial for employees or children of employees.

LOANS *Student loans:* $15,225,834 (69% need-based, 31% non-need-based). 65% of past graduating class borrowed through all loan programs. *Average indebtedness per student:* $20,779. *Average need-based loan:* Freshmen: $3170. Undergraduates: $4095. *Parent loans:* $9,105,133 (36% need-based, 64% non-need-based). *Programs:* Federal Direct (Subsidized and Unsubsidized Stafford, PLUS), Perkins.

WORK-STUDY *Federal work-study:* Total amount: $451,028; 225 jobs averaging $2000.

APPLYING FOR FINANCIAL AID *Required financial aid form:* FAFSA. *Financial aid deadline (priority):* 2/15. *Notification date:* Continuous beginning 3/15. Students must reply by 5/1 or within 2 weeks of notification.

CONTACT Ms. Barbara L. Miller, Director of Financial Aid, Stevenson University, 100 Campus Circle, Owings Mills, MD 21117, 443-352-4369 or toll-free 877-468-6852 (in-state), 877-468-3852 (out-of-state). *Fax:* 443-352-4370. *E-mail:* blmiller@stevenson.edu.

STILLMAN COLLEGE
Tuscaloosa, AL

Tuition & fees: $13,462	Average undergraduate aid package: $18,804

ABOUT THE INSTITUTION Independent religious, coed. 14 undergraduate majors. Federal methodology is used as a basis for awarding need-based institutional aid.

UNDERGRADUATE EXPENSES for 2009–10 *Comprehensive fee:* $19,798 includes full-time tuition ($12,160), mandatory fees ($1302), and room and board ($6336). Room and board charges vary according to housing facility. *Part-time tuition:* $503 per credit hour. *Part-time fees:* $91 per term. *Payment plan:* Deferred payment.

FRESHMAN FINANCIAL AID (Fall 2009, est.) 423 applied for aid; of those 95% were deemed to have need. 100% of freshmen with need received aid; of those 42% had need fully met. *Average financial aid package:* $19,798 (excluding resources awarded to replace EFC). 5% of all full-time freshmen had no need and received non-need-based gift aid.

UNDERGRADUATE FINANCIAL AID (Fall 2009, est.) 1,009 applied for aid; of those 95% were deemed to have need. 100% of undergraduates with need received aid; of those 56% had need fully met. *Average financial aid package:* $18,804 (excluding resources awarded to replace EFC). 6% of all full-time undergraduates had no need and received non-need-based gift aid.

GIFT AID (NEED-BASED) *Total amount:* $7,124,112 (52% federal, 3% state, 40% institutional, 5% external sources). *Receiving aid:* Freshmen: 85% (368); all full-time undergraduates: 50% (509). *Average award:* Freshmen: $3500; Undergraduates: $6000. *Scholarships, grants, and awards:* Federal Pell, FSEOG, state, private, college/university gift aid from institutional funds, United Negro College Fund.

GIFT AID (NON-NEED-BASED) *Total amount:* $4,540,384 (80% federal, 4% state, 2% institutional, 14% external sources). *Receiving aid:* Freshmen: 4% (17). Undergraduates: 6% (63). *Average award:* Freshmen: $3500. Undergraduates: $6489. *Scholarships, grants, and awards by category: Academic interests/ achievement:* 71 awards ($793,730 total): education, general academic interests/

achievements. *Creative arts/performance:* 135 awards ($645,385 total): music. *Special characteristics:* 18 awards ($69,872 total): children of faculty/staff. *Tuition waivers:* Full or partial for employees or children of employees.

LOANS *Student loans:* $11,471,639 (66% need-based, 34% non-need-based). 96% of past graduating class borrowed through all loan programs. *Average indebtedness per student:* $32,188. *Average need-based loan:* Freshmen: $3500. Undergraduates: $5500. *Parent loans:* $2,475,208 (50% need-based, 50% non-need-based). *Programs:* Federal Direct (Subsidized and Unsubsidized Stafford, PLUS), FFEL (Subsidized and Unsubsidized Stafford, PLUS), Perkins.

WORK-STUDY *Federal work-study:* Total amount: $213,000; 172 jobs averaging $1086.

ATHLETIC AWARDS Total amount: $1,500,000 (50% need-based, 50% non-need-based).

APPLYING FOR FINANCIAL AID *Required financial aid forms:* FAFSA, state aid form. *Financial aid deadline:* 6/1 (priority: 3/1). *Notification date:* 6/1. Students must reply within 2 weeks of notification.

CONTACT Jacqueline S. Morris, Director of Financial Aid, Stillman College, PO Box 1430, Tuscaloosa, AL 35403, 205-366-8950 or toll-free 800-841-5722. *Fax:* 205-247-8106. *E-mail:* jmorris@stillman.edu.

STONEHILL COLLEGE
Easton, MA

Tuition & fees: $31,210	Average undergraduate aid package: $20,975

ABOUT THE INSTITUTION Independent Roman Catholic, coed. 39 undergraduate majors. Both federal and institutional methodology are used as a basis for awarding need-based institutional aid.

UNDERGRADUATE EXPENSES for 2009–10 *Comprehensive fee:* $43,450 includes full-time tuition ($31,210) and room and board ($12,240). *College room only:* $7468. Room and board charges vary according to board plan. *Part-time tuition:* $1040 per course. *Part-time fees:* $25 per term. Part-time tuition and fees vary according to course load. *Payment plans:* Tuition prepayment, installment.

FRESHMAN FINANCIAL AID (Fall 2009, est.) 618 applied for aid; of those 78% were deemed to have need. 100% of freshmen with need received aid; of those 22% had need fully met. *Average percent of need met:* 77% (excluding resources awarded to replace EFC). *Average financial aid package:* $22,152 (excluding resources awarded to replace EFC). 26% of all full-time freshmen had no need and received non-need-based gift aid.

UNDERGRADUATE FINANCIAL AID (Fall 2009, est.) 1,965 applied for aid; of those 83% were deemed to have need. 100% of undergraduates with need received aid; of those 18% had need fully met. *Average percent of need met:* 60% (excluding resources awarded to replace EFC). *Average financial aid package:* $20,975 (excluding resources awarded to replace EFC). 19% of all full-time undergraduates had no need and received non-need-based gift aid.

GIFT AID (NEED-BASED) *Total amount:* $24,294,686 (8% federal, 3% state, 86% institutional, 3% external sources). *Receiving aid:* Freshmen: 75% (475); all full-time undergraduates: 66% (1,564). *Average award:* Freshmen: $18,831; Undergraduates: $16,538. *Scholarships, grants, and awards:* Federal Pell, FSEOG, state, private, college/university gift aid from institutional funds.

GIFT AID (NON-NEED-BASED) *Total amount:* $5,310,893 (5% federal, 88% institutional, 7% external sources). *Receiving aid:* Freshmen: 11% (70). Undergraduates: 8% (186). *Average award:* Freshmen: $9014. Undergraduates: $8689. *Scholarships, grants, and awards by category: Academic interests/ achievement:* general academic interests/achievements. *Special characteristics:* children of faculty/staff, children of union members/company employees, members of minority groups, relatives of clergy, siblings of current students, veterans, veterans' children. *Tuition waivers:* Full or partial for employees or children of employees.

LOANS *Student loans:* $15,273,871 (68% need-based, 32% non-need-based). 73% of past graduating class borrowed through all loan programs. *Average indebtedness per student:* $29,163. *Average need-based loan:* Freshmen: $3442. Undergraduates: $4750. *Parent loans:* $10,405,764 (35% need-based, 65% non-need-based). *Programs:* Federal Direct (Subsidized and Unsubsidized Stafford, PLUS), Perkins, state.

WORK-STUDY *Federal work-study:* Total amount: $1,130,658; 786 jobs averaging $2191. *State or other work-study/employment:* Total amount: $1,103,917 (23% need-based, 77% non-need-based). 392 part-time jobs averaging $1701.

ATHLETIC AWARDS Total amount: $1,939,180 (59% need-based, 41% non-need-based).
APPLYING FOR FINANCIAL AID *Required financial aid forms:* FAFSA, CSS Financial Aid PROFILE, noncustodial (divorced/separated) parent's statement, business/farm supplement. *Financial aid deadline (priority):* 2/1. *Notification date:* 4/1. Students must reply by 5/1.
CONTACT Rhonda Nickley, Office Manager, Stonehill College, 320 Washington Street, Easton, MA 02357, 508-565-1088. *Fax:* 508-565-1426. *E-mail:* finaid@stonehill.edu.

STONY BROOK UNIVERSITY, STATE UNIVERSITY OF NEW YORK
Stony Brook, NY

Tuition & fees (NY res): $6489	Average undergraduate aid package: $11,124

ABOUT THE INSTITUTION State-supported, coed. 62 undergraduate majors. Federal methodology is used as a basis for awarding need-based institutional aid.
UNDERGRADUATE EXPENSES for 2010–11 *Tuition, state resident:* full-time $4970; part-time $207 per credit. *Tuition, nonresident:* full-time $12,870; part-time $536 per credit. *Required fees:* full-time $1519; $74 per credit hour. *College room and board:* $9590; *Room only:* $6112. Room and board charges vary according to board plan and housing facility. *Payment plan:* Installment.
FRESHMAN FINANCIAL AID (Fall 2009, est.) 2,252 applied for aid; of those 70% were deemed to have need. 99% of freshmen with need received aid; of those 20% had need fully met. *Average percent of need met:* 75% (excluding resources awarded to replace EFC). *Average financial aid package:* $10,904 (excluding resources awarded to replace EFC). 14% of all full-time freshmen had no need and received non-need-based gift aid.
UNDERGRADUATE FINANCIAL AID (Fall 2009, est.) 10,611 applied for aid; of those 78% were deemed to have need. 98% of undergraduates with need received aid; of those 18% had need fully met. *Average percent of need met:* 71% (excluding resources awarded to replace EFC). *Average financial aid package:* $11,124 (excluding resources awarded to replace EFC). 7% of all full-time undergraduates had no need and received non-need-based gift aid.
GIFT AID (NEED-BASED) *Total amount:* $53,396,389 (54% federal, 40% state, 5% institutional, 1% external sources). *Receiving aid:* Freshmen: 52% (1,431); all full-time undergraduates: 49% (7,272). *Average award:* Freshmen: $7225; Undergraduates: $6953. *Scholarships, grants, and awards:* Federal Pell, FSEOG, state, private, college/university gift aid from institutional funds.
GIFT AID (NON-NEED-BASED) *Total amount:* $5,683,587 (3% federal, 9% state, 72% institutional, 16% external sources). *Receiving aid:* Freshmen: 4% (98). Undergraduates: 2% (288). *Average award:* Freshmen: $3786. Undergraduates: $3599. *Scholarships, grants, and awards by category: Academic interests/achievement:* 2,080 awards ($6,293,176 total): area/ethnic studies, biological sciences, business, computer science, engineering/technologies, English, foreign languages, general academic interests/achievements, health fields, international studies, mathematics, physical sciences, social sciences. *Creative arts/performance:* 25 awards ($125,398 total): cinema/film/broadcasting, journalism/publications, music. *Special achievements/activities:* 41 awards ($45,350 total): community service, leadership. *Special characteristics:* 22 awards ($152,370 total): ethnic background, general special characteristics.
LOANS *Student loans:* $80,530,583 (70% need-based, 30% non-need-based). 63% of past graduating class borrowed through all loan programs. *Average indebtedness per student:* $17,528. *Average need-based loan:* Freshmen: $3533. Undergraduates: $4545. *Parent loans:* $4,841,034 (29% need-based, 71% non-need-based). *Programs:* Federal Direct (Subsidized and Unsubsidized Stafford, PLUS), Perkins.
WORK-STUDY *Federal work-study:* Total amount: $920,041; 514 jobs averaging $1790. *State or other work-study/employment:* Total amount: $3,687,930 (34% need-based, 66% non-need-based). 1,835 part-time jobs averaging $2006.
ATHLETIC AWARDS Total amount: $5,062,712 (23% need-based, 77% non-need-based).
APPLYING FOR FINANCIAL AID *Required financial aid form:* FAFSA. *Financial aid deadline (priority):* 3/1. *Notification date:* Continuous beginning 3/15. Students must reply within 2 weeks of notification.
CONTACT Office of Student Financial Aid and Scholarship Services, Stony Brook University, State University of New York, Administration Building, Room 180, Stony Brook, NY 11794, 631-632-6840 or toll-free 800-872-7869 (out-of-state). *Fax:* 631-632-9525. *E-mail:* finaid@stonybrook.edu.

STRATFORD UNIVERSITY
Falls Church, VA

CONTACT Financial Aid Office, Stratford University, 7777 Leesburg Pike, Suite 100 South, Falls Church, VA 22043, 703-821-8570 or toll-free 800-444-0804.

STRATFORD UNIVERSITY
Woodbridge, VA

CONTACT Financial Aid Office, Stratford University, 14349 Gideon Drive, Woodbridge, VA 22192, toll-free 888-546-1250 (out-of-state).

STRAYER UNIVERSITY—AKRON CAMPUS
Akron, OH

CONTACT Financial Aid Office, Strayer University—Akron Campus, 51 Park West Boulevard, Akron, OH 44320, 330-734-6700.

STRAYER UNIVERSITY—ALEXANDRIA CAMPUS
Alexandria, VA

CONTACT Financial Aid Office, Strayer University—Alexandria Campus, 2730 Eisenhower Avenue, Alexandria, VA 22314, 703-317-2626.

STRAYER UNIVERSITY—ALLENTOWN CAMPUS
Center Valley, PA

CONTACT Financial Aid Office, Strayer University—Allentown Campus, 3800 Sierra Circle, Suite 300, Center Valley, PA 18034, 484-809-7770.

STRAYER UNIVERSITY—ANNE ARUNDEL CAMPUS
Millersville, MD

CONTACT Financial Aid Office, Strayer University—Anne Arundel Campus, 1520 Jabez Run, Millersville, MD 21108, 410-923-4500.

STRAYER UNIVERSITY—ARLINGTON CAMPUS
Arlington, VA

CONTACT Financial Aid Office, Strayer University—Arlington Campus, 2121 15th Street North, Arlington, VA 22201, 703-892-5100.

STRAYER UNIVERSITY—AUGUSTA CAMPUS
Augusta, GA

CONTACT Financial Aid Office, Strayer University—Augusta Campus, 1330 Augusta West Parkway, Augusta, GA 30909, 706-855-8233.

STRAYER UNIVERSITY—BAYMEADOWS CAMPUS
Jacksonville, FL

CONTACT Financial Aid Office, Strayer University—Baymeadows Campus, 8375 Dix Ellis Trail, Suite 200, Jacksonville, FL 32256, 904-538-1000.

STRAYER UNIVERSITY—BIRMINGHAM CAMPUS
Birmingham, AL
CONTACT Financial Aid Office, Strayer University—Birmingham Campus, 3570 Grandview Parkway, Suite 200, Birmingham, AL 35243, 205-453-6300.

STRAYER UNIVERSITY—BRICKELL CAMPUS
Miami, FL
CONTACT Financial Aid Office, Strayer University—Brickell Campus, 1201 Brickell Avenue, Suite 700, Miami, FL 33131, 305-507-5800.

STRAYER UNIVERSITY—CENTER CITY CAMPUS
Philadelphia, PA
CONTACT Financial Aid Office, Strayer University—Center City Campus, 1601 Cherry Street, Suite 100, Philadelphia, PA 19102, 267-256-0200.

STRAYER UNIVERSITY—CENTRAL AUSTIN CAMPUS
Austin, TX
CONTACT Financial Aid Office, Strayer University—Central Austin Campus, 8501 North Mopac Expressway, Suite 100, Austin, TX 78759, 512-568-3300.

STRAYER UNIVERSITY—CHAMBLEE CAMPUS
Atlanta, GA
CONTACT Financial Aid Office, Strayer University—Chamblee Campus, 3355 Northeast Expressway, Suite 100, Atlanta, GA 30341, 770-454-9270.

STRAYER UNIVERSITY—CHARLESTON CAMPUS
North Charleston, SC
CONTACT Financial Aid Office, Strayer University—Charleston Campus, 5010 Wetland Crossing, North Charleston, SC 29418, 843-746-5100.

STRAYER UNIVERSITY—CHERRY HILL CAMPUS
Cherry Hill, NJ
CONTACT Financial Aid Office, Strayer University—Cherry Hill Campus, 2201 Route 38, Suite 100, Cherry Hill, NJ 08002, 856-482-4200.

STRAYER UNIVERSITY—CHESAPEAKE CAMPUS
Chesapeake, VA
CONTACT Financial Aid Office, Strayer University—Chesapeake Campus, 700 Independent Parkway, Suite 400, Chesapeake, VA 23320, 757-382-9900.

STRAYER UNIVERSITY—CHESTERFIELD CAMPUS
Midlothian, VA
CONTACT Financial Aid Office, Strayer University—Chesterfield Campus, 2820 Waterford Lake Drive, Suite 100, Midlothian, VA 23112, 804-763-6300.

STRAYER UNIVERSITY—CHRISTIANA CAMPUS
Newark, DE
CONTACT Financial Aid Office, Strayer University—Christiana Campus, 240 Continental Drive, Suite 108, Newark, DE 19713, 302-292-6100.

STRAYER UNIVERSITY—COBB COUNTY CAMPUS
Atlanta, GA
CONTACT Financial Aid Office, Strayer University—Cobb County Campus, 3101 Towercreek Parkway, SE, Suite 700, Atlanta, GA 30339-3256, 770-612-2170.

STRAYER UNIVERSITY—COLUMBIA CAMPUS
Columbia, SC
CONTACT Financial Aid Office, Strayer University—Columbia Campus, 200 Center Point Circle, Suite 300, Columbia, SC 29210, 803-750-2500.

STRAYER UNIVERSITY—COLUMBUS CAMPUS
Columbus, OH
CONTACT Financial Aid Office, Strayer University—Columbus Campus, 8425 Pulsar Place, Suite 400, Columbus, OH 43240, 614-310-6700.

STRAYER UNIVERSITY—CORAL SPRINGS CAMPUS
Coral Springs, FL
CONTACT Financial Aid Office, Strayer University—Coral Springs Campus, 5830 Coral Ridge Drive, Suite 300, Coral Springs, FL 33076, 954-369-0700.

STRAYER UNIVERSITY—CRANBERRY WOODS CAMPUS
Cranberry Township, PA
CONTACT Financial Aid Office, Strayer University—Cranberry Woods Campus, Regional Learning Alliance, 850 Cranberry Woods Drive, Suite 2241, Cranberry Township, PA 16066, 724-741-1064.

STRAYER UNIVERSITY—DELAWARE COUNTY CAMPUS
Springfield, PA
CONTACT Financial Aid Office, Strayer University—Delaware County Campus, 760 West Sproul Road, Suite 200, Springfield, PA 19064-1215, 610-604-7700.

STRAYER UNIVERSITY—DORAL CAMPUS
Miami, FL
CONTACT Financial Aid Office, Strayer University—Doral Campus, 11430 Northwest 20th Street, Suite 150, Miami, FL 33172, 305-507-5700.

STRAYER UNIVERSITY—DOUGLASVILLE CAMPUS
Douglasville, GA
CONTACT Financial Aid Office, Strayer University—Douglasville Campus, 4655 Timber Ridge Drive, Douglasville, GA 30135, 678-715-2200.

STRAYER UNIVERSITY—FAIRVIEW PARK CAMPUS
Fairview Park, OH
CONTACT Financial Aid Office, Strayer University—Fairview Park Campus, 22730 Fairview Center Drive, Suite 150, Fairview Park, OH 44126-3616, 440-471-6400.

STRAYER UNIVERSITY—FLORENCE CAMPUS
Florence, KY
CONTACT Financial Aid Office, Strayer University—Florence Campus, 7300 Turfway Road, Suite 250, Florence, KY 41042, 859-692-2800.

STRAYER UNIVERSITY—FORT LAUDERDALE CAMPUS
Fort Lauderdale, FL
CONTACT Financial Aid Office, Strayer University—Fort Lauderdale Campus, 2307 West Broward Boulevard, Suite 100, Fort Lauderdale, FL 33312, 954-745-6960.

STRAYER UNIVERSITY—FREDERICKSBURG CAMPUS
Fredericksburg, VA
CONTACT Financial Aid Office, Strayer University—Fredericksburg Campus, 150 Riverside Parkway, Suite 100, Fredericksburg, VA 22406, 540-374-4300.

STRAYER UNIVERSITY—GARNER CAMPUS
Raleigh, NC
CONTACT Financial Aid Office, Strayer University—Garner Campus, 1812 Garner Station Boulevard, Raleigh, NC 27603, 919-890-7500.

STRAYER UNIVERSITY—GREENSBORO CAMPUS
Greensboro, NC
CONTACT Financial Aid Office, Strayer University—Greensboro Campus, 4900 Koger Boulevard, Suite 400, Greensboro, NC 27407, 336-315.7800.

STRAYER UNIVERSITY—GREENVILLE CAMPUS
Greenville, SC
CONTACT Financial Aid Office, Strayer University—Greenville Campus, 555 North Pleasantburg Drive, Suite 300, Greenville, SC 29607, 864-250-7000.

STRAYER UNIVERSITY—HENRICO CAMPUS
Glen Allen, VA
CONTACT Financial Aid Office, Strayer University—Henrico Campus, 11501 Nuckols Road, Glen Allen, VA 23059, 804-527-1000.

STRAYER UNIVERSITY—HUNTERSVILLE CAMPUS
Huntersville, NC
CONTACT Financial Aid Office, Strayer University—Huntersville Campus, 13620 Reese Boulevard, Suite 130, Huntersville, NC 28078, 704-379-6800.

STRAYER UNIVERSITY—HUNTSVILLE CAMPUS
Huntsville, AL
CONTACT Financial Aid Office, Strayer University—Huntsville Campus, 4955 Corporate Drive, NW, Suite 200, Huntsville, AL 35805, 256-665-9800.

STRAYER UNIVERSITY—KING OF PRUSSIA CAMPUS
King of Prussia, PA
CONTACT Financial Aid Office, Strayer University—King of Prussia Campus, 234 Mall Boulevard, Suite G-50, King of Prussia, PA 19406, 610-992-1700.

STRAYER UNIVERSITY—KNOXVILLE CAMPUS
Knoxville, TN
CONTACT Financial Aid Office, Strayer University—Knoxville Campus, 10118 Parkside Drive, Suite 200, Knoxville, TN 37922, 865-288-6000.

STRAYER UNIVERSITY—LAWRENCEVILLE CAMPUS
Lawrenceville, NJ
CONTACT Financial Aid Office, Strayer University—Lawrenceville Campus, 3150 Brunswick Pike, Suite 100, Lawrenceville, NJ 08648, 609-406-7600.

STRAYER UNIVERSITY—LEXINGTON CAMPUS
Lexington, KY
CONTACT Financial Aid Office, Strayer University—Lexington Campus, 220 Lexington Green Circle, Suite 550, Lexington, KY 40503, 859-971-4400.

STRAYER UNIVERSITY—LITHONIA CAMPUS
Lithonia, GA
CONTACT Financial Aid Office, Strayer University—Lithonia Campus, 3120 Stonecrest Boulevard, Suite 200, Lithonia, GA 30038, 678-323-7700.

STRAYER UNIVERSITY—LITTLE ROCK CAMPUS
Little Rock, AR
CONTACT Financial Aid Office, Strayer University—Little Rock Campus, 10825 Financial Centre Parkway, Suite 131, Little Rock, AR 72211.

STRAYER UNIVERSITY—LOUDOUN CAMPUS
Ashburn, VA
CONTACT Financial Aid Office, Strayer University—Loudoun Campus, 45150 Russell Branch Parkway, Suite 200, Ashburn, VA 20147, 703-729-8800.

STRAYER UNIVERSITY—LOUISVILLE CAMPUS
Louisville, KY
CONTACT Financial Aid Office, Strayer University—Louisville Campus, 2650 Eastpoint Parkway, Suite 100, Louisville, KY 40223, 502-253-5000.

STRAYER UNIVERSITY—LOWER BUCKS COUNTY CAMPUS
Trevose, PA
CONTACT Financial Aid Office, Strayer University—Lower Bucks County Campus, 3600 Horizon Boulevard, Suite 100, Trevose, PA 19053, 215-953-5999.

STRAYER UNIVERSITY—MAITLAND CAMPUS
Maitland, FL
CONTACT Financial Aid Office, Strayer University—Maitland Campus, 850 Trafalgar Court, Suite 360, Maitland, FL 32751, 407-618-5900.

STRAYER UNIVERSITY—MANASSAS CAMPUS
Manassas, VA
CONTACT Financial Aid Office, Strayer University—Manassas Campus, 9990 Battleview Parkway, Manassas, VA 20109, 703-330-8400.

STRAYER UNIVERSITY—MASON CAMPUS
Mason, OH
CONTACT Financial Aid Office, Strayer University—Mason Campus, 4605 Duke Drive, Suite 700, Mason, OH 45040, 513-234-6450.

STRAYER UNIVERSITY—METAIRIE CAMPUS
Metairie, LA
CONTACT Financial Aid Office, Strayer University—Metairie Campus, 111 Veterans Memorial Boulevard, Suite 420, Metairie, LA 70005, 504-799-1700.

STRAYER UNIVERSITY—MIRAMAR CAMPUS
Miramar, FL
CONTACT Financial Aid Office, Strayer University—Miramar Campus, 15620 Southwest 29th Street, Miramar, FL 33027, 954-378-2400.

STRAYER UNIVERSITY—MORROW CAMPUS
Morrow, GA
CONTACT Financial Aid Office, Strayer University—Morrow Campus, 3000 Corporate Center Drive, Suite 100, Morrow, GA 30260, 678-422-4100.

STRAYER UNIVERSITY—NASHVILLE CAMPUS
Nashville, TN
CONTACT Financial Aid Office, Strayer University—Nashville Campus, 1809 Dabbs Avenue, Nashville, TN 37210, 615-871-2260.

STRAYER UNIVERSITY—NEW BRUNSWICK CAMPUS
Piscataway, NJ
CONTACT Financial Aid Office, Strayer University—New Brunswick Campus, 242 Old New Brunswick Road, Suite 110, Piscataway, NJ 08854, 732-743-3800.

STRAYER UNIVERSITY—NEWPORT NEWS CAMPUS
Newport News, VA
CONTACT Financial Aid Office, Strayer University—Newport News Campus, 813 Diligence Drive, Suite 100, Newport News, VA 23606, 757-873-3100.

STRAYER UNIVERSITY—NORTH CHARLOTTE CAMPUS
Charlotte, NC
CONTACT Financial Aid Office, Strayer University—North Charlotte Campus, 8335 IBM Drive, Suite 150, Charlotte, NC 28262, 704-717-4000.

STRAYER UNIVERSITY—NORTH RALEIGH CAMPUS
Raleigh, NC
CONTACT Financial Aid Office, Strayer University—North Raleigh Campus, 3200 Spring Forest Road, Suite 214, Raleigh, NC 27616, 919-878-9900.

STRAYER UNIVERSITY—ORLANDO EAST CAMPUS
Orlando, FL
CONTACT Financial Aid Office, Strayer University—Orlando East Campus, 2200 North Alafaya Trail, Suite 500, Orlando, FL 32826, 407-926-2000.

STRAYER UNIVERSITY—OWINGS MILLS CAMPUS
Owings Mills, MD
CONTACT Financial Aid Office, Strayer University—Owings Mills Campus, 500 Redland Court, Suite 100, Owings Mills, MD 21117, 443-394-3339.

STRAYER UNIVERSITY—PALM BEACH GARDENS CAMPUS
Palm Beach Gardens, FL
CONTACT Financial Aid Office, Strayer University—Palm Beach Gardens Campus, 11025 RCA Center Drive, Suite 200, Palm Beach Gardens, FL 33410, 561-904-3000.

STRAYER UNIVERSITY—PENN CENTER WEST CAMPUS
Pittsburgh, PA
CONTACT Financial Aid Office, Strayer University—Penn Center West Campus, One Penn Center West, Suite 320, Pittsburgh, PA 15276, 412-747-7800.

STRAYER UNIVERSITY—PRINCE GEORGE'S CAMPUS
Suitland, MD
CONTACT Financial Aid Office, Strayer University—Prince George's Campus, 4710 Auth Place, First Floor, Suitland, MD 20746, 301-423-3600.

STRAYER UNIVERSITY—ROCKVILLE CAMPUS
Rockville, MD
CONTACT Financial Aid Office, Strayer University—Rockville Campus, 4 Research Place, Suite 100, Rockville, MD 20850, 301-548-5500.

STRAYER UNIVERSITY—ROSWELL CAMPUS
Roswell, GA

CONTACT Financial Aid Office, Strayer University—Roswell Campus, 100 Mansell Court East, Suite 100, Roswell, GA 30076, 770-650-3000.

STRAYER UNIVERSITY—RTP CAMPUS
Morrisville, NC

CONTACT Financial Aid Office, Strayer University—RTP Campus, 4 Copley Parkway, Morrisville, NC 27560, 919-466-4400.

STRAYER UNIVERSITY—SALT LAKE CAMPUS
Sandy, UT

CONTACT Financial Aid Office, Strayer University—Salt Lake Campus, 9815 South Monroe Street, Suite 200, Sandy, UT 84070, 801-432-5000.

STRAYER UNIVERSITY—SAND LAKE CAMPUS
Orlando, FL

CONTACT Financial Aid Office, Strayer University—Sand Lake Campus, 8541 South Park Circle, Building 900, Orlando, FL 32819, 407-264-9400.

STRAYER UNIVERSITY—SAVANNAH CAMPUS
Savannah, GA

CONTACT Financial Aid Office, Strayer University—Savannah Campus, 20 Martin Court, Savannah, GA 31419, 912-921-2900.

STRAYER UNIVERSITY—SHELBY OAKS CAMPUS
Memphis, TN

CONTACT Financial Aid Office, Strayer University—Shelby Oaks Campus, 6211 Shelby Oaks Drive, Suite 100, Memphis, TN 38134, 901-383-6750.

STRAYER UNIVERSITY—SOUTH CHARLOTTE CAMPUS
Charlotte, NC

CONTACT Financial Aid Office, Strayer University—South Charlotte Campus, 9101 Kings Parade Boulevard, Suite 200, Charlotte, NC 28273, 704-499-9200.

STRAYER UNIVERSITY—TAKOMA PARK CAMPUS
Washington, DC

CONTACT Financial Aid Office, Strayer University—Takoma Park Campus, 6830 Laurel Street, NW, Washington, DC 20012, 202-722-8100.

STRAYER UNIVERSITY—TAMPA EAST CAMPUS
Tampa, FL

CONTACT Financial Aid Office, Strayer University—Tampa East Campus, 6302 East Martin Luther King Boulevard, Suite 450, Tampa, FL 33619, 813-663-0100.

STRAYER UNIVERSITY—TAMPA WESTSHORE CAMPUS
Tampa, FL

CONTACT Financial Aid Office, Strayer University—Tampa Westshore Campus, 4902 Eisenhower Boulevard, Suite 100, Tampa, FL 33634, 813-882-0100.

STRAYER UNIVERSITY—TEAYS VALLEY CAMPUS
Scott Depot, WV

CONTACT Financial Aid Office, Strayer University—Teays Valley Campus, 100 Corporate Center Drive, Scott Depot, WV 25560, 304-760-1700.

STRAYER UNIVERSITY—THOUSAND OAKS CAMPUS
Memphis, TN

CONTACT Financial Aid Office, Strayer University—Thousand Oaks Campus, 2620 Thousand Oaks Boulevard, Suite 1100, Memphis, TN 38118, 901-369-0835.

STRAYER UNIVERSITY—VIRGINIA BEACH CAMPUS
Virginia Beach, VA

CONTACT Financial Aid Office, Strayer University—Virginia Beach Campus, 249 Central Park Avenue, Suite 350, Virginia Beach, VA 23462, 757-493-6000.

STRAYER UNIVERSITY—WASHINGTON CAMPUS
Washington, DC

CONTACT Financial Aid Office, Strayer University—Washington Campus, 1133 15th Street, NW, Washington, DC 200025, 202-408-2400.

STRAYER UNIVERSITY—WHITE MARSH CAMPUS
Baltimore, MD

CONTACT Financial Aid Office, Strayer University—White Marsh Campus, 9920 Franklin Square Drive, Suite 200, Baltimore, MD 21236, 410-238-9000.

STRAYER UNIVERSITY—WILLINGBORO CAMPUS
Willingboro, NJ

CONTACT Financial Aid Office, Strayer University—Willingboro Campus, 300 Willingboro Parkway, Willingboro Town Center, Suite 125, Willingboro, NJ 08046, 609-835-6000.

STRAYER UNIVERSITY—WOODBRIDGE CAMPUS
Woodbridge, VA

CONTACT Financial Aid Office, Strayer University—Woodbridge Campus, 13385 Minnieville Road, Woodbridge, VA 22192, 703-878-2800.

SUFFOLK UNIVERSITY
Boston, MA

| Tuition & fees: $27,208 | Average undergraduate aid package: $19,274 |

ABOUT THE INSTITUTION Independent, coed. 60 undergraduate majors. Both federal and institutional methodology are used as a basis for awarding need-based institutional aid.

UNDERGRADUATE EXPENSES for 2009–10 *Comprehensive fee:* $41,752 includes full-time tuition ($27,100), mandatory fees ($108), and room and board ($14,544). *College room only:* $12,204. Room and board charges vary according to board plan and housing facility. *Part-time tuition:* $665 per credit. *Part-time fees:* $10 per term. *Payment plans:* Installment, deferred payment.

FRESHMAN FINANCIAL AID (Fall 2009, est.) 1,016 applied for aid; of those 86% were deemed to have need. 99% of freshmen with need received aid; of those 11% had need fully met. *Average percent of need met:* 72% (excluding resources awarded to replace EFC). *Average financial aid package:* $20,415 (excluding resources awarded to replace EFC). 6% of all full-time freshmen had no need and received non-need-based gift aid.

UNDERGRADUATE FINANCIAL AID (Fall 2009, est.) 3,736 applied for aid; of those 86% were deemed to have need. 99% of undergraduates with need received aid; of those 12% had need fully met. *Average percent of need met:* 70% (excluding resources awarded to replace EFC). *Average financial aid package:* $19,274 (excluding resources awarded to replace EFC). 9% of all full-time undergraduates had no need and received non-need-based gift aid.

GIFT AID (NEED-BASED) *Total amount:* $35,338,867 (20% federal, 5% state, 73% institutional, 2% external sources). *Receiving aid:* Freshmen: 66% (821); all full-time undergraduates: 56% (2,971). *Average award:* Freshmen: $13,201; Undergraduates: $11,574. *Scholarships, grants, and awards:* Federal Pell, FSEOG, state, private, college/university gift aid from institutional funds.

GIFT AID (NON-NEED-BASED) *Total amount:* $11,882,529 (93% institutional, 7% external sources). *Receiving aid:* Freshmen: 19% (232). Undergraduates: 20% (1,053). *Average award:* Freshmen: $7047. Undergraduates: $8195. *Scholarships, grants, and awards by category: Academic interests/achievement:* 1,355 awards ($10,945,828 total): general academic interests/achievements. *Special achievements/activities:* 3 awards ($15,000 total): community service. *Special characteristics:* 213 awards ($607,200 total): children and siblings of alumni, children of faculty/staff, siblings of current students. *Tuition waivers:* Full or partial for employees or children of employees, senior citizens.

LOANS *Student loans:* $35,340,508 (40% need-based, 60% non-need-based). 73% of past graduating class borrowed through all loan programs. *Average need-based loan:* Freshmen: $3466. Undergraduates: $4603. *Parent loans:* $16,506,231 (100% non-need-based). *Programs:* Federal Direct (Subsidized and Unsubsidized Stafford, PLUS), Perkins, state, college/university.

WORK-STUDY *Federal work-study:* Total amount: $4,787,640; 2,049 jobs averaging $2335. *State or other work-study/employment:* Total amount: $1,350,308 (100% non-need-based). 421 part-time jobs averaging $3199.

APPLYING FOR FINANCIAL AID *Required financial aid forms:* FAFSA, institution's own form. *Financial aid deadline:* 3/1. *Notification date:* Continuous beginning 2/5. Students must reply by 5/1 or within 2 weeks of notification.

CONTACT Ms. Christine A. Perry, Director of Student Financial Services, Suffolk University, 8 Ashburton Place, Boston, MA 02108, 617-573-8470 or toll-free 800-6-SUFFOLK. *Fax:* 617-720-3579. *E-mail:* finaid@suffolk.edu.

SULLIVAN UNIVERSITY
Louisville, KY

CONTACT Charlene Geiser, Financial Planning Office, Sullivan University, 3101 Bardstown Road, Louisville, KY 40205, 502-456-6504 Ext. 311 or toll-free 800-844-1354. *Fax:* 502-456-0040. *E-mail:* cgeiser@sullivan.edu.

SUL ROSS STATE UNIVERSITY
Alpine, TX

Tuition & fees (TX res): $2928	Average undergraduate aid package: $11,857

ABOUT THE INSTITUTION State-supported, coed. 35 undergraduate majors. Federal methodology is used as a basis for awarding need-based institutional aid.

UNDERGRADUATE EXPENSES for 2010–11 *Tuition, state resident:* full-time $2928. *Tuition, nonresident:* full-time $9576. *College room and board:* $6370; *Room only:* $3820.

FRESHMAN FINANCIAL AID (Fall 2008) 243 applied for aid; of those 59% were deemed to have need. 100% of freshmen with need received aid. *Average percent of need met:* 22% (excluding resources awarded to replace EFC).

Average financial aid package: $11,428 (excluding resources awarded to replace EFC). 24% of all full-time freshmen had no need and received non-need-based gift aid.

UNDERGRADUATE FINANCIAL AID (Fall 2008) 999 applied for aid; of those 73% were deemed to have need. 100% of undergraduates with need received aid. *Average percent of need met:* 12% (excluding resources awarded to replace EFC). *Average financial aid package:* $11,857 (excluding resources awarded to replace EFC). 12% of all full-time undergraduates had no need and received non-need-based gift aid.

GIFT AID (NEED-BASED) *Total amount:* $5,463,651 (72% federal, 28% state). *Receiving aid:* Freshmen: 40% (125); all full-time undergraduates: 50% (643). *Average award:* Freshmen: $5960; Undergraduates: $5046. *Scholarships, grants, and awards:* Federal Pell, FSEOG, state, private, college/university gift aid from institutional funds.

GIFT AID (NON-NEED-BASED) *Total amount:* $842,292 (72% institutional, 28% external sources). *Receiving aid:* Freshmen: 23% (72). Undergraduates: 16% (208). *Average award:* Freshmen: $1090. Undergraduates: $1424. *Scholarships, grants, and awards by category: Academic interests/achievement:* agriculture, biological sciences, business, education, English, foreign languages, general academic interests/achievements, health fields. *Creative arts/performance:* art/fine arts, cinema/film/broadcasting, journalism/publications, music, theater/drama. *Special achievements/activities:* leadership. *Special characteristics:* local/state students.

LOANS *Student loans:* $8,737,982 (100% need-based). *Average need-based loan:* Freshmen: $4993. Undergraduates: $6482. *Programs:* FFEL (Subsidized and Unsubsidized Stafford, PLUS), Perkins, state, college/university.

WORK-STUDY *Federal work-study:* Total amount: $2,999,064; jobs available. *State or other work-study/employment:* Total amount: $82,708 (100% need-based). Part-time jobs available.

APPLYING FOR FINANCIAL AID *Required financial aid forms:* FAFSA, institution's own form. *Financial aid deadline:* 4/1 (priority: 3/1). *Notification date:* Continuous.

CONTACT Ms. Rena Gallego, Director of Financial Aid, Sul Ross State University, PO Box C-113, Alpine, TX 79832, 915-837-8059 or toll-free 888-722-7778.

SUSQUEHANNA UNIVERSITY
Selinsgrove, PA

Tuition & fees: $32,850	Average undergraduate aid package: $23,880

ABOUT THE INSTITUTION Independent religious, coed. 51 undergraduate majors. Both federal and institutional methodology are used as a basis for awarding need-based institutional aid.

UNDERGRADUATE EXPENSES for 2010–11 *Comprehensive fee:* $41,650 includes full-time tuition ($32,450), mandatory fees ($400), and room and board ($8800). *College room only:* $4600. Room and board charges vary according to board plan and housing facility. *Payment plans:* Tuition prepayment, installment.

FRESHMAN FINANCIAL AID (Fall 2009, est.) 511 applied for aid; of those 81% were deemed to have need. 100% of freshmen with need received aid; of those 20% had need fully met. *Average percent of need met:* 82% (excluding resources awarded to replace EFC). *Average financial aid package:* $23,903 (excluding resources awarded to replace EFC). 29% of all full-time freshmen had no need and received non-need-based gift aid.

UNDERGRADUATE FINANCIAL AID (Fall 2009, est.) 1,712 applied for aid; of those 87% were deemed to have need. 100% of undergraduates with need received aid; of those 17% had need fully met. *Average percent of need met:* 79% (excluding resources awarded to replace EFC). *Average financial aid package:* $23,880 (excluding resources awarded to replace EFC). 24% of all full-time undergraduates had no need and received non-need-based gift aid.

GIFT AID (NEED-BASED) *Total amount:* $26,943,191 (8% federal, 6% state, 83% institutional, 3% external sources). *Receiving aid:* Freshmen: 66% (410); all full-time undergraduates: 67% (1,476). *Average award:* Freshmen: $19,942; Undergraduates: $19,015. *Scholarships, grants, and awards:* Federal Pell, FSEOG, state, private, college/university gift aid from institutional funds.

GIFT AID (NON-NEED-BASED) *Total amount:* $6,751,414 (90% institutional, 10% external sources). *Receiving aid:* Freshmen: 11% (67). Undergraduates: 8% (172). *Average award:* Freshmen: $10,809. Undergraduates: $10,081. *Scholarships, grants, and awards by category: Academic interests/achievement:* business, general academic interests/achievements. *Creative arts/performance:* creative writing, music, theater/drama. *Special achievements/activities:* general special achievements/activities. *Special characteristics:* children and siblings of alumni, children of faculty/staff, members of minority groups, relatives of clergy, veterans. *Tuition waivers:* Full or partial for employees or children of employees.

LOANS *Student loans:* $12,778,890 (67% need-based, 33% non-need-based). 71% of past graduating class borrowed through all loan programs. *Average indebtedness per student:* $20,915. *Average need-based loan:* Freshmen: $3545. Undergraduates: $4390. *Parent loans:* $4,874,057 (37% need-based, 63% non-need-based). *Programs:* Federal Direct (Subsidized and Unsubsidized Stafford, PLUS), Perkins, college/university.

WORK-STUDY *Federal work-study:* Total amount: $1,661,554; 1,124 jobs averaging $2044. *State or other work-study/employment:* Total amount: $416,165 (44% need-based, 56% non-need-based). 84 part-time jobs averaging $4425.

APPLYING FOR FINANCIAL AID *Required financial aid forms:* FAFSA, CSS Financial Aid PROFILE, business/farm supplement, prior year federal income tax form(s). *Financial aid deadline (priority):* 3/1. *Notification date:* 3/15. Students must reply by 5/1.

CONTACT Ms. Helen S. Nunn, Director of Financial Aid, Susquehanna University, 514 University Avenue, Selinsgrove, PA 17870, 570-372-4450 or toll-free 800-326-9672. *Fax:* 570-372-2722. *E-mail:* nunn@susqu.edu.

SWARTHMORE COLLEGE
Swarthmore, PA

Tuition & fees: $37,860	Average undergraduate aid package: $35,342

ABOUT THE INSTITUTION Independent, coed. 45 undergraduate majors. Institutional methodology is used as a basis for awarding need-based institutional aid.

UNDERGRADUATE EXPENSES for 2009–10 *Comprehensive fee:* $49,600 includes full-time tuition ($37,510), mandatory fees ($350), and room and board ($11,740). *College room only:* $6018. Room and board charges vary according to board plan. *Payment plan:* Installment.

FRESHMAN FINANCIAL AID (Fall 2009, est.) 277 applied for aid; of those 78% were deemed to have need. 100% of freshmen with need received aid; of those 100% had need fully met. *Average percent of need met:* 100% (excluding resources awarded to replace EFC). *Average financial aid package:* $36,008 (excluding resources awarded to replace EFC). 1% of all full-time freshmen had no need and received non-need-based gift aid.

UNDERGRADUATE FINANCIAL AID (Fall 2009, est.) 813 applied for aid; of those 91% were deemed to have need. 100% of undergraduates with need received aid; of those 100% had need fully met. *Average percent of need met:* 100% (excluding resources awarded to replace EFC). *Average financial aid package:* $35,342 (excluding resources awarded to replace EFC). 1% of all full-time undergraduates had no need and received non-need-based gift aid.

GIFT AID (NEED-BASED) *Total amount:* $24,921,345 (5% federal, 93% institutional, 2% external sources). *Receiving aid:* Freshmen: 55% (216); all full-time undergraduates: 49% (742). *Average award:* Freshmen: $34,615; Undergraduates: $33,859. *Scholarships, grants, and awards:* Federal Pell, FSEOG, state, private, college/university gift aid from institutional funds.

GIFT AID (NON-NEED-BASED) *Total amount:* $741,710 (61% institutional, 39% external sources). *Average award:* Freshmen: $37,510. Undergraduates: $37,510. *Scholarships, grants, and awards by category: Academic interests/achievement:* 12 awards ($450,120 total): general academic interests/achievements. *Tuition waivers:* Full or partial for employees or children of employees.

LOANS *Student loans:* $2,026,699 (100% non-need-based). 45% of past graduating class borrowed through all loan programs. *Average indebtedness per student:* $15,737. *Parent loans:* $1,772,877 (100% non-need-based). *Programs:* FFEL (Subsidized and Unsubsidized Stafford, PLUS), Perkins, state, college/university.

WORK-STUDY *Federal work-study:* Total amount: $684,544; 668 jobs averaging $1643. *State or other work-study/employment:* Total amount: $592,400 (85% need-based, 15% non-need-based). Part-time jobs available.

APPLYING FOR FINANCIAL AID *Required financial aid forms:* FAFSA, institution's own form, CSS Financial Aid PROFILE, state aid form, noncustodial (divorced/separated) parent's statement, business/farm supplement, federal tax return, W-2 forms, year-end paycheck stub. *Financial aid deadline:* 2/15. *Notification date:* 4/1. Students must reply by 5/1.

CONTACT Laura Talbot, Director of Financial Aid, Swarthmore College, 500 College Avenue, Swarthmore, PA 19081-1397, 610-328-8358 or toll-free 800-667-3110. *Fax:* 610-690-5751. *E-mail:* finaid@swarthmore.edu.

SWEDISH INSTITUTE, COLLEGE OF HEALTH SCIENCES
New York, NY

CONTACT Financial Aid Office, Swedish Institute, College of Health Sciences, 226 West 26th Street, New York, NY 10001-6700, 212-924-5900.

SWEET BRIAR COLLEGE
Sweet Briar, VA

ABOUT THE INSTITUTION Independent, women only. 39 undergraduate majors.

GIFT AID (NEED-BASED) *Scholarships, grants, and awards:* Federal Pell, FSEOG, state, private, college/university gift aid from institutional funds.

GIFT AID (NON-NEED-BASED) *Scholarships, grants, and awards by category: Academic interests/achievement:* general academic interests/achievements, premedicine. *Creative arts/performance:* art/fine arts, general creative arts/performance, music. *Special achievements/activities:* community service. *Special characteristics:* adult students, general special characteristics, international students, local/state students.

LOANS *Programs:* Federal Direct (Subsidized and Unsubsidized Stafford, PLUS), Perkins, college/university.

WORK-STUDY *Federal work-study:* Total amount: $95,274; 99 jobs averaging $945. *State or other work-study/employment:* Total amount: $115,919 (100% need-based). 115 part-time jobs averaging $949.

APPLYING FOR FINANCIAL AID *Required financial aid forms:* FAFSA, noncustodial (divorced/separated) parent's statement.

CONTACT Bobbi Carpenter, Director of Financial Aid, Sweet Briar College, Box AS, Sweet Briar, VA 24595, 800-381-6156 or toll-free 800-381-6142. *Fax:* 434-381-6450. *E-mail:* bcarpenter@sbc.edu.

SYRACUSE UNIVERSITY
Syracuse, NY

Tuition & fees: $34,926	Average undergraduate aid package: $29,976

ABOUT THE INSTITUTION Independent, coed. 94 undergraduate majors. Institutional methodology is used as a basis for awarding need-based institutional aid.

UNDERGRADUATE EXPENSES for 2009–10 *Comprehensive fee:* $47,300 includes full-time tuition ($33,630), mandatory fees ($1296), and room and board ($12,374). *College room only:* $6560. Room and board charges vary according to board plan and housing facility. *Part-time tuition:* $1646 per credit hour. *Payment plan:* Installment.

FRESHMAN FINANCIAL AID (Fall 2009, est.) 2,524 applied for aid; of those 79% were deemed to have need. 100% of freshmen with need received aid; of those 84% had need fully met. *Average percent of need met:* 95% (excluding resources awarded to replace EFC). *Average financial aid package:* $32,500 (excluding resources awarded to replace EFC). 10% of all full-time freshmen had no need and received non-need-based gift aid.

UNDERGRADUATE FINANCIAL AID (Fall 2009, est.) 8,778 applied for aid; of those 86% were deemed to have need. 100% of undergraduates with need received aid; of those 65% had need fully met. *Average percent of need met:* 86% (excluding resources awarded to replace EFC). *Average financial aid package:* $29,976 (excluding resources awarded to replace EFC). 14% of all full-time undergraduates had no need and received non-need-based gift aid.

GIFT AID (NEED-BASED) *Total amount:* $174,019,776 (11% federal, 6% state, 81% institutional, 2% external sources). *Receiving aid:* Freshmen: 57% (1,839); all full-time undergraduates: 54% (6,850). *Average award:* Freshmen: $24,300; Undergraduates: $21,300. *Scholarships, grants, and awards:* Federal Pell, FSEOG, state, private, college/university gift aid from institutional funds.

GIFT AID (NON-NEED-BASED) *Total amount:* $18,040,334 (1% state, 91% institutional, 8% external sources). *Receiving aid:* Freshmen: 3% (101). Undergraduates: 3% (375). *Average award:* Freshmen: $8840. Undergraduates: $9130. *Scholarships, grants, and awards by category: Academic interests/achievement:* general academic interests/achievements. *Creative arts/performance:* art/fine arts, music. *Tuition waivers:* Full or partial for employees or children of employees.

LOANS *Student loans:* $74,963,449 (86% need-based, 14% non-need-based). 65% of past graduating class borrowed through all loan programs. *Average*

indebtedness per student: $28,358. **Average need-based loan:** Freshmen: $6280. Undergraduates: $7225. **Parent loans:** $26,473,769 (73% need-based, 27% non-need-based). **Programs:** Federal Direct (Subsidized and Unsubsidized Stafford, PLUS), Perkins.

WORK-STUDY **Federal work-study:** Total amount: $3,800,000; jobs available. **State or other work-study/employment:** Part-time jobs available.

ATHLETIC AWARDS Total amount: $12,860,727 (39% need-based, 61% non-need-based).

APPLYING FOR FINANCIAL AID **Required financial aid forms:** FAFSA, CSS Financial Aid PROFILE, noncustodial (divorced/separated) parent's statement. **Financial aid deadline:** 2/2. **Notification date:** 3/21. Students must reply by 5/1.

CONTACT Youlanda Copeland-Morgan, Director of Scholarship and Financial Aid, Syracuse University, 200 Archbold Gymnasium, Syracuse, NY 13244-1140, 315-443-1513. *E-mail:* finmail@syr.edu.

TABOR COLLEGE
Hillsboro, KS

Tuition & fees: $19,660	Average undergraduate aid package: $18,977

ABOUT THE INSTITUTION Independent Mennonite Brethren, coed. 85 undergraduate majors. Federal methodology is used as a basis for awarding need-based institutional aid.

UNDERGRADUATE EXPENSES for 2009–10 **One-time required fee:** $100. **Comprehensive fee:** $26,530 includes full-time tuition ($19,200), mandatory fees ($460), and room and board ($6870). **College room only:** $2700. Full-time tuition and fees vary according to course load. Room and board charges vary according to board plan, housing facility, and location. **Part-time tuition:** $800 per credit hour. **Part-time fees:** $10 per credit hour. Part-time tuition and fees vary according to course load. **Payment plan:** Installment.

FRESHMAN FINANCIAL AID (Fall 2009, est.) 140 applied for aid; of those 89% were deemed to have need. 100% of freshmen with need received aid; of those 15% had need fully met. **Average percent of need met:** 78% (excluding resources awarded to replace EFC). **Average financial aid package:** $19,133 (excluding resources awarded to replace EFC). 11% of all full-time freshmen had no need and received non-need-based gift aid.

UNDERGRADUATE FINANCIAL AID (Fall 2009, est.) 558 applied for aid; of those 86% were deemed to have need. 100% of undergraduates with need received aid; of those 23% had need fully met. **Average percent of need met:** 81% (excluding resources awarded to replace EFC). **Average financial aid package:** $18,977 (excluding resources awarded to replace EFC). 13% of all full-time undergraduates had no need and received non-need-based gift aid.

GIFT AID (NEED-BASED) **Total amount:** $1,550,951 (72% federal, 28% state). **Receiving aid:** Freshmen: 71% (100); all full-time undergraduates: 66% (378). **Average award:** Freshmen: $4156; Undergraduates: $4241. **Scholarships, grants, and awards:** Federal Pell, FSEOG, state, private, college/university gift aid from institutional funds.

GIFT AID (NON-NEED-BASED) **Total amount:** $3,582,138 (94% institutional, 6% external sources). **Receiving aid:** Freshmen: 89% (124). Undergraduates: 75% (425). **Average award:** Freshmen: $8774. Undergraduates: $7449. **Scholarships, grants, and awards by category:** Academic interests/achievement: $1,594,180 total: biological sciences, communication, general academic interests/achievements, humanities. Creative arts/performance: $171,990 total: journalism/publications, music, performing arts, theater/drama. Special achievements/activities: $1,030,640 total: cheerleading/drum major, general special achievements/activities, religious involvement. Special characteristics: $484,581 total: children and siblings of alumni, children of faculty/staff, general special characteristics, international students, local/state students, out-of-state students, religious affiliation. **Tuition waivers:** Full or partial for employees or children of employees.

LOANS **Student loans:** $4,181,223 (100% need-based). 81% of past graduating class borrowed through all loan programs. **Average indebtedness per student:** $20,500. **Average need-based loan:** Freshmen: $6143. Undergraduates: $8219. **Parent loans:** $481,984 (100% need-based). **Programs:** Federal Direct (Subsidized and Unsubsidized Stafford, PLUS), FFEL (Subsidized and Unsubsidized Stafford, PLUS), Perkins.

WORK-STUDY **Federal work-study:** Total amount: $106,340; 201 jobs averaging $550. **State or other work-study/employment:** Part-time jobs available.

ATHLETIC AWARDS Total amount: $1,082,545 (100% non-need-based).

APPLYING FOR FINANCIAL AID **Required financial aid forms:** FAFSA, state aid form. **Financial aid deadline:** 8/15 (priority: 3/1). **Notification date:** Continuous beginning 3/15. Students must reply within 4 weeks of notification.

CONTACT Mr. Scott Franz, Director of Student Financial Assistance, Tabor College, 400 South Jefferson, Hillsboro, KS 67063, 620-947-3121 Ext. 1726 or toll-free 800-822-6799. *Fax:* 620-947-6276. *E-mail:* scottf@tabor.edu.

TALLADEGA COLLEGE
Talladega, AL

CONTACT K. Michael Francois, Director of Financial Aid, Talladega College, 627 West Battle Street, Talladega, AL 35160, 256-761-6341 or toll-free 800-762-2468 (in-state), 800-633-2440 (out-of-state). *Fax:* 256-761-6462.

TALMUDICAL ACADEMY OF NEW JERSEY
Adelphia, NJ

CONTACT Office of Financial Aid, Talmudical Academy of New Jersey, Route 524, Adelphia, NJ 07710, 732-431-1600.

TALMUDICAL INSTITUTE OF UPSTATE NEW YORK
Rochester, NY

Tuition & fees: N/R	Average undergraduate aid package: N/A

ABOUT THE INSTITUTION Independent Jewish, men only. **Awards:** also offers some graduate courses. 1 undergraduate major. **Total enrollment:** 26. Undergraduates: 22. Institutional methodology is used as a basis for awarding need-based institutional aid.

GIFT AID (NEED-BASED) **Total amount:** $98,000 (36% federal, 64% institutional). **Scholarships, grants, and awards:** Federal Pell, FSEOG, college/university gift aid from institutional funds.

GIFT AID (NON-NEED-BASED) **Scholarships, grants, and awards by category:** Academic interests/achievement: religion/biblical studies.

WORK-STUDY **Federal work-study:** Total amount: $8000; jobs available.

APPLYING FOR FINANCIAL AID **Required financial aid form:** FAFSA. **Financial aid deadline:** Continuous. **Notification date:** Continuous.

CONTACT Mrs. Ella Berenstein, Financial Aid Administrator, Talmudical Institute of Upstate New York, 769 Park Avenue, Rochester, NY 14607-3046, 585-473-2810.

TALMUDICAL SEMINARY OHOLEI TORAH
Brooklyn, NY

CONTACT Financial Aid Administrator, Talmudical Seminary Oholei Torah, 667 Eastern Parkway, Brooklyn, NY 11213-3310, 718-774-5050.

TALMUDICAL YESHIVA OF PHILADELPHIA
Philadelphia, PA

CONTACT Director of Student Financial Aid/Registrar, Talmudical Yeshiva of Philadelphia, 6063 Drexel Road, Philadelphia, PA 19131-1296, 215-473-1212.

TALMUDIC COLLEGE OF FLORIDA
Miami Beach, FL

CONTACT Rabbi Ira Hill, Director of Financial Aid, Talmudic College of Florida, 1910 Alton Road, Miami Beach, FL 33139, 305-534-7050 or toll-free 888-825-6834. *Fax:* 305-534-8444.

TARLETON STATE UNIVERSITY
Stephenville, TX

Tuition & fees (TX res): $7150	Average undergraduate aid package: $9940

ABOUT THE INSTITUTION State-supported, coed. 77 undergraduate majors. Federal methodology is used as a basis for awarding need-based institutional aid.

UNDERGRADUATE EXPENSES for 2010–11 *Tuition, state resident:* full-time $5565; part-time $138.50 per credit hour. *Tuition, nonresident:* full-time $13,995; part-time $415.50 per credit hour. *Required fees:* full-time $1585. Full-time tuition and fees vary according to course load. Part-time tuition and fees vary according to course load. *College room and board:* $6591; *Room only:* $3291. Room and board charges vary according to board plan and housing facility. *Payment plan:* Installment.

FRESHMAN FINANCIAL AID (Fall 2008) 1,013 applied for aid; of those 62% were deemed to have need. *Average percent of need met:* 75% (excluding resources awarded to replace EFC). *Average financial aid package:* $10,022 (excluding resources awarded to replace EFC). 27% of all full-time freshmen had no need and received non-need-based gift aid.

UNDERGRADUATE FINANCIAL AID (Fall 2008) *Average percent of need met:* 71% (excluding resources awarded to replace EFC). *Average financial aid package:* $9940 (excluding resources awarded to replace EFC). 22% of all full-time undergraduates had no need and received non-need-based gift aid.

GIFT AID (NEED-BASED) *Total amount:* $16,886,927 (54% federal, 20% state, 9% institutional, 17% external sources). *Receiving aid:* Freshmen: 42% (524); all full-time undergraduates: 56% (3,273). *Average award:* Freshmen: $4278; Undergraduates: $3008. *Scholarships, grants, and awards:* Federal Pell, FSEOG, state, private, college/university gift aid from institutional funds.

GIFT AID (NON-NEED-BASED) *Total amount:* $3,957,827 (64% institutional, 36% external sources). *Receiving aid:* Freshmen: 24% (298). Undergraduates: 21% (1,250). *Average award:* Freshmen: $4762. Undergraduates: $1272.

LOANS *Student loans:* $32,098,102 (46% need-based, 54% non-need-based). 54% of past graduating class borrowed through all loan programs. *Average indebtedness per student:* $18,223. *Average need-based loan:* Freshmen: $2969. Undergraduates: $4032. *Parent loans:* $4,680,612 (100% non-need-based). *Programs:* Federal Direct (Subsidized and Unsubsidized Stafford, PLUS), FFEL (Subsidized and Unsubsidized Stafford, PLUS), state, college/university.

WORK-STUDY *Federal work-study:* Total amount: $141,394; jobs available. *State or other work-study/employment:* Total amount: $57,683 (100% need-based). Part-time jobs available.

ATHLETIC AWARDS Total amount: $1,188,340 (100% non-need-based).

APPLYING FOR FINANCIAL AID *Required financial aid form:* FAFSA. *Financial aid deadline:* 11/1 (priority: 4/1). *Notification date:* Continuous beginning 3/1. Students must reply within 2 weeks of notification.

CONTACT Ms. Betty Murray, Director of Student Financial Aid, Tarleton State University, Box T-0310, Stephenville, TX 76402, 254-968-9070 or toll-free 800-687-8236 (in-state). *Fax:* 254-968-9600. *E-mail:* finaid@tarleton.edu.

TAYLOR UNIVERSITY
Upland, IN

Tuition & fees: $25,396	Average undergraduate aid package: $18,002

ABOUT THE INSTITUTION Independent interdenominational, coed. 58 undergraduate majors. Federal methodology is used as a basis for awarding need-based institutional aid.

UNDERGRADUATE EXPENSES for 2009–10 *Comprehensive fee:* $32,104 includes full-time tuition ($25,164), mandatory fees ($232), and room and board ($6708). *College room only:* $3320. Full-time tuition and fees vary according to course load. Room and board charges vary according to board plan and housing facility. *Part-time tuition:* $901 per credit hour. *Part-time fees:* $36 per term. Part-time tuition and fees vary according to course load. *Payment plan:* Installment.

FRESHMAN FINANCIAL AID (Fall 2009, est.) 400 applied for aid; of those 78% were deemed to have need. 100% of freshmen with need received aid; of those 19% had need fully met. *Average percent of need met:* 75% (excluding resources awarded to replace EFC). *Average financial aid package:* $17,990 (excluding resources awarded to replace EFC). 25% of all full-time freshmen had no need and received non-need-based gift aid.

UNDERGRADUATE FINANCIAL AID (Fall 2009, est.) 1,378 applied for aid; of those 85% were deemed to have need. 100% of undergraduates with need received aid; of those 23% had need fully met. *Average percent of need met:* 76% (excluding resources awarded to replace EFC). *Average financial aid*

package: $18,002 (excluding resources awarded to replace EFC). 23% of all full-time undergraduates had no need and received non-need-based gift aid.

GIFT AID (NEED-BASED) *Total amount:* $14,052,473 (15% federal, 7% state, 72% institutional, 6% external sources). *Receiving aid:* Freshmen: 63% (307); all full-time undergraduates: 59% (1,112). *Average award:* Freshmen: $13,910; Undergraduates: $14,157. *Scholarships, grants, and awards:* Federal Pell, FSEOG, state, private, college/university gift aid from institutional funds, Academic Competitiveness Grants, National SMART Grants.

GIFT AID (NON-NEED-BASED) *Total amount:* $4,157,562 (83% institutional, 17% external sources). *Receiving aid:* Freshmen: 8% (39). Undergraduates: 7% (132). *Average award:* Freshmen: $6863. Undergraduates: $6520. *Scholarships, grants, and awards by category: Academic interests/achievement:* 906 awards ($4,929,561 total): general academic interests/achievements. *Creative arts/performance:* 88 awards ($237,128 total): music, theater/drama. *Special achievements/activities:* 99 awards ($511,244 total): leadership. *Special characteristics:* 850 awards ($3,002,546 total): children and siblings of alumni, children of faculty/staff, ethnic background, international students, religious affiliation. *Tuition waivers:* Full or partial for employees or children of employees, senior citizens.

LOANS *Student loans:* $10,029,146 (66% need-based, 34% non-need-based). 53% of past graduating class borrowed through all loan programs. *Average indebtedness per student:* $22,971. *Average need-based loan:* Freshmen: $4429. Undergraduates: $4542. *Parent loans:* $13,974,387 (28% need-based, 72% non-need-based). *Programs:* Federal Direct (Subsidized and Unsubsidized Stafford, PLUS), Perkins, college/university.

WORK-STUDY *Federal work-study:* Total amount: $645,305; 849 jobs averaging $2132.

ATHLETIC AWARDS Total amount: $1,640,271 (54% need-based, 46% non-need-based).

APPLYING FOR FINANCIAL AID *Required financial aid form:* FAFSA. *Financial aid deadline:* 3/10. *Notification date:* Continuous beginning 3/1. Students must reply by 5/1.

CONTACT Mr. Timothy A. Nace, Director of Financial Aid, Taylor University, 236 West Reade Avenue, Upland, IN 46989-1001, 765-998-5358 or toll-free 800-882-3456. *Fax:* 765-998-4910. *E-mail:* tmnace@taylor.edu.

TELSHE YESHIVA–CHICAGO
Chicago, IL

CONTACT Office of Financial Aid, Telshe Yeshiva–Chicago, 3535 West Foster Avenue, Chicago, IL 60625-5598, 773-463-7738.

TEMPLE BAPTIST COLLEGE
Cincinnati, OH

CONTACT Financial Aid Office, Temple Baptist College, 11965 Kenn Road, Cincinnati, OH 45240, 513-851-3800.

TEMPLE UNIVERSITY
Philadelphia, PA

Tuition & fees (PA res): $11,764	Average undergraduate aid package: $15,110

ABOUT THE INSTITUTION State-related, coed. 115 undergraduate majors. Federal methodology is used as a basis for awarding need-based institutional aid.

UNDERGRADUATE EXPENSES for 2009–10 *Tuition, state resident:* full-time $11,174; part-time $432 per credit. *Tuition, nonresident:* full-time $20,454; part-time $728 per credit. *Required fees:* full-time $590; $220 per year. Full-time tuition and fees vary according to course load, program, and reciprocity agreements. Part-time tuition and fees vary according to course load, program, and reciprocity agreements. *College room and board:* $9198; *Room only:* $6126. Room and board charges vary according to board plan and housing facility. *Payment plan:* Installment.

FRESHMAN FINANCIAL AID (Fall 2008) 3,746 applied for aid; of those 73% were deemed to have need. 98% of freshmen with need received aid; of those 36% had need fully met. *Average percent of need met:* 91% (excluding resources awarded to replace EFC). *Average financial aid package:* $15,722 (excluding resources awarded to replace EFC). 15% of all full-time freshmen had no need and received non-need-based gift aid.

UNDERGRADUATE FINANCIAL AID (Fall 2008) 20,481 applied for aid; of those 77% were deemed to have need. 94% of undergraduates with need received aid; of those 37% had need fully met. *Average percent of need met:* 89% (excluding resources awarded to replace EFC). *Average financial aid package:* $15,110 (excluding resources awarded to replace EFC). 13% of all full-time undergraduates had no need and received non-need-based gift aid.

GIFT AID (NEED-BASED) *Total amount:* $81,734,533 (38% federal, 24% state, 38% institutional). *Receiving aid:* Freshmen: 65% (2,684); all full-time undergraduates: 64% (14,639). *Average award:* Freshmen: $5804; Undergraduates: $5256. *Scholarships, grants, and awards:* Federal Pell, FSEOG, state, private, college/university gift aid from institutional funds, Federal Nursing.

GIFT AID (NON-NEED-BASED) *Total amount:* $64,841,274 (15% institutional, 85% external sources). *Receiving aid:* Freshmen: 38% (1,571). Undergraduates: 31% (7,108). *Average award:* Freshmen: $8437. Undergraduates: $9120. *Scholarships, grants, and awards by category: Academic interests/achievement:* general academic interests/achievements. *Creative arts/performance:* art/fine arts, general creative arts/performance, music, performing arts. *Special achievements/activities:* cheerleading/drum major. *Special characteristics:* children of faculty/staff, general special characteristics. *Tuition waivers:* Full or partial for employees or children of employees.

LOANS *Student loans:* $125,277,402 (54% need-based, 46% non-need-based). 75% of past graduating class borrowed through all loan programs. *Average indebtedness per student:* $29,886. *Average need-based loan:* Freshmen: $3427. Undergraduates: $4260. *Parent loans:* $638,600 (100% non-need-based). *Programs:* FFEL (Subsidized and Unsubsidized Stafford, PLUS), Perkins, Federal Nursing, state, college/university.

WORK-STUDY *Federal work-study:* Total amount: $1,694,992; jobs available.

ATHLETIC AWARDS Total amount: $7,228,609 (100% non-need-based).

APPLYING FOR FINANCIAL AID *Required financial aid form:* FAFSA. *Financial aid deadline (priority):* 3/1. *Notification date:* Continuous beginning 2/15. Students must reply by 5/1 or within 3 weeks of notification.

CONTACT Dr. John F. Morris, Director, Student Financial Services, Temple University, Conwell Hall, Ground Floor, Philadelphia, PA 19122-6096, 215-204-8760 or toll-free 888-340-2222. *Fax:* 215-204-2016. *E-mail:* john.morris@temple.edu.

TENNESSEE STATE UNIVERSITY
Nashville, TN

CONTACT Mary Chambliss, Director of Financial Aid, Tennessee State University, 3500 John Merritt Boulevard, Nashville, TN 37209-1561, 615-963-5772. *Fax:* 615-963-5108. *E-mail:* mchambliss@tnstate.edu.

TENNESSEE TECHNOLOGICAL UNIVERSITY
Cookeville, TN

Tuition & fees (TN res): $5498	Average undergraduate aid package: $7954

ABOUT THE INSTITUTION State-supported, coed. 68 undergraduate majors. Federal methodology is used as a basis for awarding need-based institutional aid.

UNDERGRADUATE EXPENSES for 2009–10 *Tuition, state resident:* full-time $5498; part-time $254 per hour. *Tuition, nonresident:* full-time $17,454; part-time $751 per hour. Full-time tuition and fees vary according to course load. Part-time tuition and fees vary according to course load. *College room and board:* $7124; *Room only:* $3560. Room and board charges vary according to board plan and housing facility. *Payment plan:* Installment.

FRESHMAN FINANCIAL AID (Fall 2009, est.) 1,506 applied for aid; of those 65% were deemed to have need. 99% of freshmen with need received aid; of those 31% had need fully met. *Average percent of need met:* 86% (excluding resources awarded to replace EFC). *Average financial aid package:* $8342 (excluding resources awarded to replace EFC). 29% of all full-time freshmen had no need and received non-need-based gift aid.

UNDERGRADUATE FINANCIAL AID (Fall 2009, est.) 7,739 applied for aid; of those 59% were deemed to have need. 98% of undergraduates with need received aid; of those 32% had need fully met. *Average percent of need met:* 82% (excluding resources awarded to replace EFC). *Average financial aid package:* $7954 (excluding resources awarded to replace EFC). 29% of all full-time undergraduates had no need and received non-need-based gift aid.

GIFT AID (NEED-BASED) *Total amount:* $32,569,151 (42% federal, 57% state, 1% institutional). *Receiving aid:* Freshmen: 32% (533); all full-time undergraduates: 30% (2,552). *Average award:* Freshmen: $4386; Undergraduates: $4182. *Scholarships, grants, and awards:* Federal Pell, FSEOG, state, private, college/university gift aid from institutional funds, United Negro College Fund.

GIFT AID (NON-NEED-BASED) *Total amount:* $8,210,148 (2% federal, 4% state, 58% institutional, 36% external sources). *Receiving aid:* Freshmen: 51% (844). Undergraduates: 48% (4,042). *Average award:* Freshmen: $5923. Undergraduates: $5647. *Scholarships, grants, and awards by category: Academic interests/achievement:* 6,566 awards ($17,369,701 total): agriculture, biological sciences, business, communication, computer science, education, engineering/technologies, English, foreign languages, general academic interests/achievements, health fields, home economics, humanities, international studies, mathematics, military science, physical sciences, premedicine, social sciences. *Creative arts/performance:* art/fine arts, debating, music. *Special achievements/activities:* 892 awards ($2,813,796 total): cheerleading/drum major, general special achievements/activities. *Special characteristics:* 1,615 awards ($1,774,190 total): children and siblings of alumni, children of educators, children of faculty/staff, children of public servants, ethnic background, first-generation college students, local/state students, members of minority groups, out-of-state students, public servants. *Tuition waivers:* Full or partial for employees or children of employees.

LOANS *Student loans:* $17,838,831 (56% need-based, 44% non-need-based). 44% of past graduating class borrowed through all loan programs. *Average indebtedness per student:* $14,691. *Average need-based loan:* Freshmen: $1892. Undergraduates: $1804. *Parent loans:* $1,096,056 (100% non-need-based). *Programs:* Federal Direct (Subsidized and Unsubsidized Stafford, PLUS), FFEL (PLUS), Perkins, college/university.

WORK-STUDY *Federal work-study:* Total amount: $309,519; 425 jobs averaging $868. *State or other work-study/employment:* Part-time jobs available.

ATHLETIC AWARDS Total amount: $2,813,796 (100% non-need-based).

APPLYING FOR FINANCIAL AID *Required financial aid form:* FAFSA. *Financial aid deadline (priority):* 3/15. *Notification date:* Continuous beginning 4/1. Students must reply within 2 weeks of notification.

CONTACT Lester McKenzie, Director of Financial Aid, Tennessee Technological University, Box 5076, 1000 North Dixie Avenue, Cookeville, TN 38501, 931-372-3073 or toll-free 800-255-8881. *Fax:* 931-372-6309. *E-mail:* lmckenzie@tntech.edu.

TENNESSEE TEMPLE UNIVERSITY
Chattanooga, TN

CONTACT Director of Financial Aid, Tennessee Temple University, 1815 Union Avenue, Chattanooga, TN 37404-3587, 423-493-4208 or toll-free 800-553-4050. *Fax:* 423-493-4497.

TENNESSEE WESLEYAN COLLEGE
Athens, TN

Tuition & fees: $18,600	Average undergraduate aid package: $14,087

ABOUT THE INSTITUTION Independent United Methodist, coed. 38 undergraduate majors. Federal methodology is used as a basis for awarding need-based institutional aid.

UNDERGRADUATE EXPENSES for 2009–10 *Comprehensive fee:* $24,700 includes full-time tuition ($18,000), mandatory fees ($600), and room and board ($6100). Full-time tuition and fees vary according to location. Room and board charges vary according to housing facility. *Part-time tuition:* $495 per credit hour. *Part-time fees:* $10 per credit hour. Part-time tuition and fees vary according to class time and location. *Payment plans:* Installment, deferred payment.

FRESHMAN FINANCIAL AID (Fall 2008) 250 applied for aid; of those 83% were deemed to have need. 99% of freshmen with need received aid; of those 30% had need fully met. *Average percent of need met:* 77% (excluding resources awarded to replace EFC). *Average financial aid package:* $14,731 (excluding resources awarded to replace EFC). 8% of all full-time freshmen had no need and received non-need-based gift aid.

UNDERGRADUATE FINANCIAL AID (Fall 2008) 871 applied for aid; of those 85% were deemed to have need. 97% of undergraduates with need received aid; of those 22% had need fully met. *Average percent of need met:* 70%

(excluding resources awarded to replace EFC). **Average financial aid package:** $14,087 (excluding resources awarded to replace EFC). 9% of all full-time undergraduates had no need and received non-need-based gift aid.

GIFT AID (NEED-BASED) **Total amount:** $6,486,671 (22% federal, 30% state, 43% institutional, 5% external sources). **Receiving aid:** Freshmen: 77% (204); all full-time undergraduates: 76% (702). **Average award:** Freshmen: $13,070; Undergraduates: $11,682. **Scholarships, grants, and awards:** Federal Pell, FSEOG, state, private, college/university gift aid from institutional funds.

GIFT AID (NON-NEED-BASED) **Total amount:** $1,323,456 (38% state, 53% institutional, 9% external sources). **Receiving aid:** Freshmen: 19% (49). Undergraduates: 13% (121). **Average award:** Freshmen: $7652. Undergraduates: $6221. **Scholarships, grants, and awards by category:** Academic interests/achievement: biological sciences, business, communication, computer science, education, English, foreign languages, general academic interests/achievements, health fields, humanities, international studies, mathematics, physical sciences, premedicine, religion/biblical studies, social sciences. Creative arts/performance: music. Special achievements/activities: cheerleading/drum major, general special achievements/activities, junior miss, memberships, religious involvement. Special characteristics: children and siblings of alumni, children of faculty/staff, general special characteristics, international students, members of minority groups, relatives of clergy, religious affiliation. **Tuition waivers:** Full or partial for employees or children of employees.

LOANS **Student loans:** $4,540,669 (75% need-based, 25% non-need-based). 45% of past graduating class borrowed through all loan programs. Average indebtedness per student: $16,304. **Average need-based loan:** Freshmen: $2731. Undergraduates: $3876. **Parent loans:** $527,984 (29% need-based, 71% non-need-based). **Programs:** FFEL (Subsidized and Unsubsidized Stafford, PLUS).

WORK-STUDY **Federal work-study:** Total amount: $57,809; jobs available. **State or other work-study/employment:** Total amount: $23,602 (2% need-based, 98% non-need-based). Part-time jobs available.

ATHLETIC AWARDS Total amount: $2,764,925 (65% need-based, 35% non-need-based).

APPLYING FOR FINANCIAL AID **Required financial aid forms:** FAFSA, institution's own form. **Financial aid deadline:** Continuous. **Notification date:** Continuous beginning 2/15.

CONTACT Mr. Bob Perry, Director of Financial Aid, Tennessee Wesleyan College, PO Box 40, Athens, TN 37371-0040, 423-746-5209 or toll-free 800-PICK-TWC. Fax: 423-744-9968. E-mail: rkperry@twcnet.edu.

TEXAS A&M INTERNATIONAL UNIVERSITY
Laredo, TX

CONTACT Laura Elizondo, Director of Financial Aid, Texas A&M International University, 5201 University Boulevard, Laredo, TX 78041, 956-326-2225 or toll-free 888-489-2648. Fax: 956-326-2224. E-mail: laura@tamiu.edu.

TEXAS A&M UNIVERSITY
College Station, TX

Tuition & fees (TX res): $8176	Average undergraduate aid package: $14,658

ABOUT THE INSTITUTION State-supported, coed. 110 undergraduate majors. Both federal and institutional methodology are used as a basis for awarding need-based institutional aid.

UNDERGRADUATE EXPENSES for 2009–10 Tuition, state resident: full-time $5152; part-time $171.74 per credit hour. Tuition, nonresident: full-time $19,582; part-time $652.74 per credit hour. Required fees: full-time $3024. College room and board: $8039. Room and board charges vary according to board plan, housing facility, and location. Payment plan: Installment.

FRESHMAN FINANCIAL AID (Fall 2009, est.) 5,358 applied for aid; of those 61% were deemed to have need. 99% of freshmen with need received aid; of those 61% had need fully met. Average percent of need met: 78% (excluding resources awarded to replace EFC). Average financial aid package: $16,119 (excluding resources awarded to replace EFC). 13% of all full-time freshmen had no need and received non-need-based gift aid.

UNDERGRADUATE FINANCIAL AID (Fall 2009, est.) 19,563 applied for aid; of those 69% were deemed to have need. 98% of undergraduates with need received aid; of those 48% had need fully met. Average percent of need met: 71% (excluding resources awarded to replace EFC). Average financial aid

package: $14,658 (excluding resources awarded to replace EFC). 5% of all full-time undergraduates had no need and received non-need-based gift aid.

GIFT AID (NEED-BASED) **Total amount:** $121,626,536 (28% federal, 28% state, 32% institutional, 12% external sources). **Receiving aid:** Freshmen: 42% (3,145); all full-time undergraduates: 33% (11,669). **Average award:** Freshmen: $10,653; Undergraduates: $8953. **Scholarships, grants, and awards:** Federal Pell, FSEOG, state, private, college/university gift aid from institutional funds.

GIFT AID (NON-NEED-BASED) **Total amount:** $15,013,486 (4% federal, 4% state, 54% institutional, 38% external sources). **Receiving aid:** Freshmen: 7% (540). Undergraduates: 3% (1,153). **Average award:** Freshmen: $4022. Undergraduates: $3441. **Scholarships, grants, and awards by category:** Academic interests/achievement: agriculture, architecture, biological sciences, business, computer science, education, engineering/technologies, general academic interests/achievements, health fields, physical sciences. Creative arts/performance: journalism/publications, performing arts, theater/drama. Special achievements/activities: general special achievements/activities, leadership, memberships, rodeo. Special characteristics: children of faculty/staff, first-generation college students, local/state students, veterans, veterans' children.

LOANS **Student loans:** $111,798,162 (52% need-based, 48% non-need-based). 54% of past graduating class borrowed through all loan programs. Average indebtedness per student: $21,276. **Average need-based loan:** Freshmen: $4926. Undergraduates: $6070. **Parent loans:** $24,115,703 (17% need-based, 83% non-need-based). **Programs:** Federal Direct (Subsidized and Unsubsidized Stafford, PLUS), Perkins, state, college/university.

WORK-STUDY **Federal work-study:** Total amount: $2,058,720; 847 jobs averaging $2431. **State or other work-study/employment:** Total amount: $816,091 (100% need-based). 380 part-time jobs averaging $2148.

ATHLETIC AWARDS Total amount: $5,164,819 (90% need-based, 10% non-need-based).

APPLYING FOR FINANCIAL AID **Required financial aid forms:** FAFSA, ApplyTexas scholarship questions/section. **Financial aid deadline (priority):** 3/31. **Notification date:** Continuous beginning 4/1. Students must reply within 4 weeks of notification.

CONTACT Scholarships and Financial Aid, Texas A&M University, The Pavilion 200, Spence Street, 1252 TAMU, College Station, TX 77842-3016, 979-845-3236. Fax: 979-847-9061. E-mail: financialaid@tamu.edu.

TEXAS A&M UNIVERSITY AT GALVESTON
Galveston, TX

CONTACT Dennis Carlton, Director for Financial Aid, Texas A&M University at Galveston, PO Box 1675, Galveston, TX 77553-1675, 409-740-4500. Fax: 409-740-4959. E-mail: carltond@tamug.tamu.edu.

TEXAS A&M UNIVERSITY–COMMERCE
Commerce, TX

Tuition & fees (TX res): $5500	Average undergraduate aid package: $9684

ABOUT THE INSTITUTION State-supported, coed. 76 undergraduate majors. Federal methodology is used as a basis for awarding need-based institutional aid.

UNDERGRADUATE EXPENSES for 2010–11 Tuition, state resident: full-time $5500. Tuition, nonresident: full-time $13,840. Full-time tuition and fees vary according to course load. Part-time tuition and fees vary according to course load. College room and board: $7090. Room and board charges vary according to board plan and housing facility. Payment plan: Installment.

FRESHMAN FINANCIAL AID (Fall 2009, est.) 639 applied for aid; of those 83% were deemed to have need. 99% of freshmen with need received aid; of those 44% had need fully met. Average percent of need met: 80% (excluding resources awarded to replace EFC). Average financial aid package: $11,581 (excluding resources awarded to replace EFC). 10% of all full-time freshmen had no need and received non-need-based gift aid.

UNDERGRADUATE FINANCIAL AID (Fall 2009, est.) 3,425 applied for aid; of those 85% were deemed to have need. 99% of undergraduates with need received aid; of those 31% had need fully met. Average percent of need met: 64% (excluding resources awarded to replace EFC). Average financial aid package: $9684 (excluding resources awarded to replace EFC). 7% of all full-time undergraduates had no need and received non-need-based gift aid.

GIFT AID (NEED-BASED) *Total amount:* $18,610,317 (67% federal, 18% state, 13% institutional, 2% external sources). *Receiving aid:* Freshmen: 71% (496); all full-time undergraduates: 61% (2,546). *Average award:* Freshmen: $9510; Undergraduates: $7161. *Scholarships, grants, and awards:* Federal Pell, FSEOG, state, private, college/university gift aid from institutional funds.

GIFT AID (NON-NEED-BASED) *Total amount:* $1,679,065 (1% federal, 87% institutional, 12% external sources). *Average award:* Freshmen: $2314. Undergraduates: $2581. *Scholarships, grants, and awards by category:* Academic interests/achievement: agriculture, general academic interests/ achievements. Creative arts/performance: art/fine arts, journalism/publications, music, theater/drama. Special achievements/activities: cheerleading/drum major, general special achievements/activities, leadership. *Tuition waivers:* Full or partial for senior citizens.

LOANS *Student loans:* $24,453,862 (90% need-based, 10% non-need-based). 74% of past graduating class borrowed through all loan programs. *Average indebtedness per student:* $21,918. *Average need-based loan:* Freshmen: $3556. Undergraduates: $4105. *Parent loans:* $1,017,899 (49% need-based, 51% non-need-based). *Programs:* Federal Direct (Subsidized and Unsubsidized Stafford, PLUS), FFEL (Subsidized and Unsubsidized Stafford, PLUS), Perkins, state.

WORK-STUDY *Federal work-study:* Total amount: $524,037; 151 jobs averaging $3187. *State or other work-study/employment:* Total amount: $83,331 (100% need-based). 35 part-time jobs averaging $2260.

ATHLETIC AWARDS Total amount: $921,337 (58% need-based, 42% non-need-based).

APPLYING FOR FINANCIAL AID *Required financial aid form:* FAFSA. *Financial aid deadline (priority):* 4/15. *Notification date:* Continuous beginning 5/15. Students must reply within 2 weeks of notification.

CONTACT Maria Ramos, Director of Financial Aid, Texas A&M University– Commerce, PO Box 3011, Commerce, TX 75429, 903-886-5091 or toll-free 800-331-3878. *Fax:* 903-886-5098. *E-mail:* maria_ramos@tamu-commerce. edu.

TEXAS A&M UNIVERSITY–CORPUS CHRISTI
Corpus Christi, TX

Tuition & fees (TX res): $6221	Average undergraduate aid package: $9277

ABOUT THE INSTITUTION State-supported, coed. 62 undergraduate majors. Federal methodology is used as a basis for awarding need-based institutional aid.

UNDERGRADUATE EXPENSES for 2010–11 *Tuition, state resident:* full-time $4456; part-time $155.50 per credit hour. *Tuition, nonresident:* full-time $13,016; part-time $440.81 per credit hour. *Required fees:* full-time $1765; $65.82 per credit hour. Full-time tuition and fees vary according to course load, degree level, and student level. Part-time tuition and fees vary according to course load, degree level, and student level. *College room and board:* $9528; *Room only:* $6677. Room and board charges vary according to housing facility and location. *Payment plan:* Installment.

FRESHMAN FINANCIAL AID (Fall 2009, est.) 983 applied for aid; of those 80% were deemed to have need. 98% of freshmen with need received aid; of those 13% had need fully met. *Average percent of need met:* 61% (excluding resources awarded to replace EFC). *Average financial aid package:* $10,137 (excluding resources awarded to replace EFC). 6% of all full-time freshmen had no need and received non-need-based gift aid.

UNDERGRADUATE FINANCIAL AID (Fall 2009, est.) 3,852 applied for aid; of those 83% were deemed to have need. 97% of undergraduates with need received aid; of those 12% had need fully met. *Average percent of need met:* 60% (excluding resources awarded to replace EFC). *Average financial aid package:* $9277 (excluding resources awarded to replace EFC). 3% of all full-time undergraduates had no need and received non-need-based gift aid.

GIFT AID (NEED-BASED) *Total amount:* $18,736,427 (74% federal, 22% state, 4% institutional). *Receiving aid:* Freshmen: 53% (673); all full-time undergraduates: 42% (2,473). *Average award:* Freshmen: $7136; Undergraduates: $5981. *Scholarships, grants, and awards:* Federal Pell, FSEOG, state, college/university gift aid from institutional funds.

GIFT AID (NON-NEED-BASED) *Total amount:* $2,643,795 (73% institutional, 27% external sources). *Receiving aid:* Freshmen: 20% (249). Undergraduates: 12% (707). *Average award:* Freshmen: $2233. Undergraduates: $2173. *Scholar-*

ships, grants, and awards by category: Academic interests/achievement: general academic interests/achievements. Creative arts/performance: art/fine arts, general creative arts/performance. Special characteristics: first-generation college students, international students. *Tuition waivers:* Full or partial for senior citizens.

LOANS *Student loans:* $30,083,722 (44% need-based, 56% non-need-based). 58% of past graduating class borrowed through all loan programs. *Average indebtedness per student:* $13,335. *Average need-based loan:* Freshmen: $3256. Undergraduates: $4280. *Parent loans:* $5,588,805 (100% non-need-based). *Programs:* FFEL (Subsidized and Unsubsidized Stafford, PLUS), Perkins, state, college/university.

WORK-STUDY *Federal work-study:* Total amount: $570,120; jobs available. *State or other work-study/employment:* Total amount: $449,707 (100% need-based). Part-time jobs available.

ATHLETIC AWARDS Total amount: $1,412,204 (100% non-need-based).

APPLYING FOR FINANCIAL AID *Required financial aid form:* FAFSA. *Financial aid deadline (priority):* 3/31. *Notification date:* Continuous beginning 4/1. Students must reply within 2 weeks of notification.

CONTACT Financial Assistance Advisor, Texas A&M University–Corpus Christi, 6300 Ocean Drive, Corpus Christi, TX 78412-5503, 361-825-2338 or toll-free 800-482-6822. *Fax:* 361-825-6095. *E-mail:* faoweb@tamucc.edu.

TEXAS A&M UNIVERSITY–KINGSVILLE
Kingsville, TX

CONTACT Ralph Perri, Director, Financial Aid, Texas A&M University–Kingsville, 700 University Boulevard, Kingsville, TX 78363, 361-593-2883 or toll-free 800-687-6000. *Fax:* 361-593-3036. *E-mail:* financial.aid@tamuk.edu.

TEXAS A&M UNIVERSITY–SAN ANTONIO
San Antonio, TX

CONTACT Financial Aid Office, Texas A&M University–San Antonio, 1450 Gillette Boulevard, San Antonio, TX 78224, 210-932-6299.

TEXAS A&M UNIVERSITY–TEXARKANA
Texarkana, TX

Tuition & fees: N/R	Average undergraduate aid package: N/A

ABOUT THE INSTITUTION State-supported, coed. 19 undergraduate majors. Federal methodology is used as a basis for awarding need-based institutional aid.

GIFT AID (NEED-BASED) *Total amount:* $2,472,802 (74% federal, 10% state, 14% institutional, 2% external sources). *Scholarships, grants, and awards:* Federal Pell, FSEOG, state, private, college/university gift aid from institutional funds.

GIFT AID (NON-NEED-BASED) *Scholarships, grants, and awards by category:* Academic interests/achievement: business, education, engineering/technologies, English, general academic interests/achievements, mathematics, social sciences. Special achievements/activities: community service, general special achievements/ activities, leadership, memberships.

LOANS *Student loans:* $1,877,900 (78% need-based, 22% non-need-based). *Programs:* FFEL (Subsidized and Unsubsidized Stafford, PLUS), college/ university.

WORK-STUDY *Federal work-study:* Total amount: $27,348; 12 jobs averaging $2279.

APPLYING FOR FINANCIAL AID *Required financial aid forms:* FAFSA, institution's own form, state aid form. *Financial aid deadline (priority):* 5/1. *Notification date:* Continuous beginning 6/1. Students must reply within 2 weeks of notification.

CONTACT Becky Ann Hejduk, Interim Director of Financial Aid and Veterans' Services, Texas A&M University–Texarkana, 2600 North Robison Road, Texarkana, TX 75505, 903-223-3059. *Fax:* 903-223-3118. *E-mail:* becky.hejduk@tamut. edu.

TEXAS CHRISTIAN UNIVERSITY
Fort Worth, TX

Tuition & fees: $30,048   **Average undergraduate aid package: $20,647**

ABOUT THE INSTITUTION Independent religious, coed. 99 undergraduate majors. Federal methodology is used as a basis for awarding need-based institutional aid.

UNDERGRADUATE EXPENSES for 2010–11 *Comprehensive fee:* $40,160 includes full-time tuition ($30,000), mandatory fees ($48), and room and board ($10,112). *College room only:* $6370. Room and board charges vary according to board plan and housing facility. Part-time tuition and fees vary according to course load. *Payment plans:* Tuition prepayment, installment.

FRESHMAN FINANCIAL AID (Fall 2009, est.) 1,000 applied for aid; of those 73% were deemed to have need. 99% of freshmen with need received aid; of those 30% had need fully met. *Average percent of need met:* 71% (excluding resources awarded to replace EFC). *Average financial aid package:* $19,821 (excluding resources awarded to replace EFC). 26% of all full-time freshmen had no need and received non-need-based gift aid.

UNDERGRADUATE FINANCIAL AID (Fall 2009, est.) 3,834 applied for aid; of those 81% were deemed to have need. 99% of undergraduates with need received aid; of those 29% had need fully met. *Average percent of need met:* 71% (excluding resources awarded to replace EFC). *Average financial aid package:* $20,647 (excluding resources awarded to replace EFC). 25% of all full-time undergraduates had no need and received non-need-based gift aid.

GIFT AID (NEED-BASED) *Total amount:* $46,055,245 (12% federal, 13% state, 72% institutional, 3% external sources). *Receiving aid:* Freshmen: 39% (712); all full-time undergraduates: 39% (2,835). *Average award:* Freshmen: $16,220; Undergraduates: $17,440. *Scholarships, grants, and awards:* Federal Pell, FSEOG, state, private, college/university gift aid from institutional funds.

GIFT AID (NON-NEED-BASED) *Total amount:* $22,503,145 (1% federal, 96% institutional, 3% external sources). *Receiving aid:* Freshmen: 27% (486). Undergraduates: 24% (1,757). *Average award:* Freshmen: $10,055. Undergraduates: $10,715. *Scholarships, grants, and awards by category: Academic interests/achievement:* 2,955 awards ($26,236,500 total): agriculture, biological sciences, business, communication, education, engineering/technologies, English, foreign languages, general academic interests/achievements, health fields, international studies, mathematics, military science, physical sciences, premedicine, religion/biblical studies, social sciences. *Creative arts/performance:* 363 awards ($2,526,000 total): applied art and design, art/fine arts, cinema/film/broadcasting, creative writing, dance, general creative arts/performance, journalism/publications, music, performing arts, theater/drama. *Special achievements/activities:* 493 awards ($4,195,000 total): general special achievements/activities, leadership, memberships, religious involvement. *Special characteristics:* 569 awards ($9,621,000 total): adult students, children of educators, children of faculty/staff, children of union members/company employees, children of workers in trades, ethnic background, general special characteristics, handicapped students, international students, local/state students, members of minority groups, previous college experience, relatives of clergy, religious affiliation, veterans, veterans' children. *Tuition waivers:* Full or partial for employees or children of employees.

LOANS *Student loans:* $36,437,589 (56% need-based, 44% non-need-based). 43% of past graduating class borrowed through all loan programs. *Average indebtedness per student:* $32,357. *Average need-based loan:* Freshmen: $3358. Undergraduates: $4368. *Parent loans:* $15,878,890 (19% need-based, 81% non-need-based). *Programs:* FFEL (Subsidized and Unsubsidized Stafford, PLUS), Perkins, Federal Nursing, state.

WORK-STUDY *Federal work-study:* Total amount: $3,112,790; 1,756 jobs averaging $2080. *State or other work-study/employment:* Total amount: $53,600 (100% need-based). 41 part-time jobs averaging $1763.

ATHLETIC AWARDS Total amount: $10,405,103 (47% need-based, 53% non-need-based).

APPLYING FOR FINANCIAL AID *Required financial aid form:* FAFSA. *Financial aid deadline:* 5/1. *Notification date:* Continuous beginning 3/15. Students must reply by 5/1.

CONTACT Michael Scott, Director, Scholarships and Student Financial Aid, Texas Christian University, PO Box 297012, Fort Worth, TX 76129-0002, 817-257-7858 or toll-free 800-828-3764. *Fax:* 817-257-7462. *E-mail:* m.scott@tcu.edu.

TEXAS COLLEGE
Tyler, TX

Tuition & fees: $9490   **Average undergraduate aid package: $9402**

ABOUT THE INSTITUTION Independent religious, coed. 18 undergraduate majors. Federal methodology is used as a basis for awarding need-based institutional aid.

UNDERGRADUATE EXPENSES for 2010–11 *One-time required fee:* $20. *Comprehensive fee:* $16,090 includes full-time tuition ($8000), mandatory fees ($1490), and room and board ($6600). *College room only:* $3600. *Part-time tuition:* $333 per credit hour. *Part-time fees:* $745 per term. *Payment plan:* Installment.

FRESHMAN FINANCIAL AID (Fall 2009, est.) 228 applied for aid; of those 98% were deemed to have need. 97% of freshmen with need received aid; of those 5% had need fully met. *Average percent of need met:* 61% (excluding resources awarded to replace EFC). *Average financial aid package:* $8905 (excluding resources awarded to replace EFC). 11% of all full-time freshmen had no need and received non-need-based gift aid.

UNDERGRADUATE FINANCIAL AID (Fall 2009, est.) 837 applied for aid; of those 97% were deemed to have need. 99% of undergraduates with need received aid; of those 4% had need fully met. *Average percent of need met:* 58% (excluding resources awarded to replace EFC). *Average financial aid package:* $9402 (excluding resources awarded to replace EFC). 3% of all full-time undergraduates had no need and received non-need-based gift aid.

GIFT AID (NEED-BASED) *Total amount:* $5,415,315 (65% federal, 21% state, 10% institutional, 4% external sources). *Receiving aid:* Freshmen: 93% (212); all full-time undergraduates: 80% (771). *Average award:* Freshmen: $6588; Undergraduates: $6375. *Scholarships, grants, and awards:* Federal Pell, FSEOG, state, private, college/university gift aid from institutional funds, United Negro College Fund.

GIFT AID (NON-NEED-BASED) *Total amount:* $277,982 (45% state, 39% institutional, 16% external sources). *Receiving aid:* Freshmen: 2% (4). Undergraduates: 1% (10). *Average award:* Freshmen: $3492. Undergraduates: $3099. *Scholarships, grants, and awards by category: Academic interests/achievement:* 54 awards ($89,490 total): general academic interests/achievements. *Special achievements/activities:* 2 awards ($15,762 total): leadership. *Tuition waivers:* Full or partial for employees or children of employees.

LOANS *Student loans:* $5,814,906 (47% need-based, 53% non-need-based). 92% of past graduating class borrowed through all loan programs. *Average indebtedness per student:* $18,735. *Average need-based loan:* Freshmen: $2566. Undergraduates: $3304. *Parent loans:* $323,939 (100% non-need-based). *Programs:* Federal Direct (Subsidized and Unsubsidized Stafford, PLUS), FFEL (Subsidized and Unsubsidized Stafford, PLUS), state.

WORK-STUDY *Federal work-study:* Total amount: $231,324; 130 jobs averaging $1589. *State or other work-study/employment:* Total amount: $40,403 (24% need-based, 76% non-need-based). 28 part-time jobs averaging $1438.

APPLYING FOR FINANCIAL AID *Required financial aid forms:* FAFSA, institution's own form. *Financial aid deadline (priority):* 6/1. *Notification date:* Continuous. Students must reply within 2 weeks of notification.

CONTACT Ms. Cecelia K. Jones, Director of Financial Aid, Texas College, 2404 North Grand Avenue, Tyler, TX 75702, 903-593-8311 Ext. 2241 or toll-free 800-306-6299 (out-of-state). *Fax:* 903-596-0001. *E-mail:* ckjones@texascollege.edu.

TEXAS LUTHERAN UNIVERSITY
Seguin, TX

Tuition & fees: $21,910   **Average undergraduate aid package: $18,482**

ABOUT THE INSTITUTION Independent religious, coed. 42 undergraduate majors. Federal methodology is used as a basis for awarding need-based institutional aid.

UNDERGRADUATE EXPENSES for 2009–10 *Comprehensive fee:* $28,310 includes full-time tuition ($21,780), mandatory fees ($130), and room and board ($6400). *College room only:* $3200. Full-time tuition and fees vary according to course load. Room and board charges vary according to board plan, housing facility, and location. *Part-time tuition:* $700 per semester hour. *Part-time fees:* $65 per term. Part-time tuition and fees vary according to course load. *Payment plan:* Installment.

Texas Lutheran University

FRESHMAN FINANCIAL AID (Fall 2009, est.) 316 applied for aid; of those 90% were deemed to have need. 100% of freshmen with need received aid; of those 42% had need fully met. **Average percent of need met:** 42% (excluding resources awarded to replace EFC). **Average financial aid package:** $20,591 (excluding resources awarded to replace EFC). 15% of all full-time freshmen had no need and received non-need-based gift aid.

UNDERGRADUATE FINANCIAL AID (Fall 2009, est.) 1,081 applied for aid; of those 88% were deemed to have need. 100% of undergraduates with need received aid; of those 37% had need fully met. **Average percent of need met:** 37% (excluding resources awarded to replace EFC). **Average financial aid package:** $18,482 (excluding resources awarded to replace EFC). 20% of all full-time undergraduates had no need and received non-need-based gift aid.

GIFT AID (NEED-BASED) Total amount: $12,701,506 (19% federal, 18% state, 61% institutional, 2% external sources). **Receiving aid:** Freshmen: 82% (284); all full-time undergraduates: 72% (944). **Average award:** Freshmen: $15,693; Undergraduates: $13,472. **Scholarships, grants, and awards:** Federal Pell, FSEOG, state, private, college/university gift aid from institutional funds, Academic Competitiveness Grants, National SMART Grants, TEACH Grants.

GIFT AID (NON-NEED-BASED) Total amount: $2,864,645 (94% institutional, 6% external sources). **Receiving aid:** Freshmen: 10% (33). Undergraduates: 7% (87). **Average award:** Freshmen: $10,909. Undergraduates: $8785. **Scholarships, grants, and awards by category:** Academic interests/achievement: 1,028 awards ($7,417,314 total): biological sciences, business, education, general academic interests/achievements, mathematics, physical sciences, premedicine. Creative arts/performance: 156 awards ($310,950 total): journalism/publications, music, theater/drama. Special achievements/activities: 112 awards ($129,780 total): general special achievements/activities, junior miss, leadership, memberships, religious involvement. Special characteristics: 528 awards ($1,032,575 total): children and siblings of alumni, children of faculty/staff, first-generation college students, religious affiliation. **Tuition waivers:** Full or partial for children of alumni, employees or children of employees.

LOANS Student loans: $8,751,041 (72% need-based, 28% non-need-based). 63% of past graduating class borrowed through all loan programs. Average indebtedness per student: $29,200. **Average need-based loan:** Freshmen: $4122. Undergraduates: $4844. **Parent loans:** $1,456,972 (30% need-based, 70% non-need-based). **Programs:** Federal Direct (Subsidized and Unsubsidized Stafford, PLUS), Perkins, state, alternative loans.

WORK-STUDY Federal work-study: Total amount: $1,041,621; 533 jobs averaging $1812. **State or other work-study/employment:** Total amount: $35,977 (100% need-based). 35 part-time jobs averaging $1662.

APPLYING FOR FINANCIAL AID Required financial aid form: FAFSA. **Financial aid deadline (priority):** 3/1. **Notification date:** Continuous beginning 3/1. Students must reply by 8/15.

CONTACT Cathleen Wright, Director of Financial Aid, Texas Lutheran University, 1000 West Court Street, Seguin, TX 78155-5999, 830-372-8075 or toll-free 800-771-8521. Fax: 830-372-8096. E-mail: cwright@tlu.edu.

TEXAS SOUTHERN UNIVERSITY
Houston, TX

CONTACT Financial Aid Office, Texas Southern University, 3100 Cleburne, Houston, TX 77004-4584, 713-313-7011. Fax: 713-313-1858.

TEXAS STATE UNIVERSITY–SAN MARCOS
San Marcos, TX

Tuition & fees (TX res): $7482	Average undergraduate aid package: $13,634

ABOUT THE INSTITUTION State-supported, coed. 93 undergraduate majors. Federal methodology is used as a basis for awarding need-based institutional aid.

UNDERGRADUATE EXPENSES for 2009–10 Tuition, state resident: full-time $5460; part-time $182 per credit hour. **Tuition, nonresident:** full-time $13,770; part-time $459 per credit hour. **Required fees:** full-time $2022; $46 per credit hour or $366 per term. Full-time tuition and fees vary according to course load. Part-time tuition and fees vary according to course load. **College room and board:** $6392; **Room only:** $4180. Room and board charges vary according to board plan and housing facility. **Payment plan:** Installment.

FRESHMAN FINANCIAL AID (Fall 2009, est.) 2,771 applied for aid; of those 69% were deemed to have need. 98% of freshmen with need received aid; of those 8% had need fully met. **Average percent of need met:** 69% (excluding resources awarded to replace EFC). **Average financial aid package:** $14,974 (excluding resources awarded to replace EFC). 5% of all full-time freshmen had no need and received non-need-based gift aid.

UNDERGRADUATE FINANCIAL AID (Fall 2009, est.) 14,672 applied for aid; of those 78% were deemed to have need. 96% of undergraduates with need received aid; of those 6% had need fully met. **Average percent of need met:** 65% (excluding resources awarded to replace EFC). **Average financial aid package:** $13,634 (excluding resources awarded to replace EFC). 2% of all full-time undergraduates had no need and received non-need-based gift aid.

GIFT AID (NEED-BASED) Total amount: $61,510,673 (58% federal, 42% state). **Receiving aid:** Freshmen: 38% (1,382); all full-time undergraduates: 39% (8,287). **Average award:** Freshmen: $7668; Undergraduates: $6374. **Scholarships, grants, and awards:** Federal Pell, FSEOG, state, private, college/university gift aid from institutional funds.

GIFT AID (NON-NEED-BASED) Total amount: $10,497,887 (42% institutional, 58% external sources). **Receiving aid:** Freshmen: 19% (691). Undergraduates: 8% (1,800). **Average award:** Freshmen: $2449. Undergraduates: $2611. **Scholarships, grants, and awards by category:** Academic interests/achievement: agriculture, business, education, English, general academic interests/achievements, home economics, international studies, military science. Creative arts/performance: applied art and design, journalism/publications, music, theater/drama. Special characteristics: children and siblings of alumni, first-generation college students, handicapped students. **Tuition waivers:** Full or partial for employees or children of employees.

LOANS Student loans: $125,200,073 (41% need-based, 59% non-need-based). 58% of past graduating class borrowed through all loan programs. Average indebtedness per student: $19,670. **Average need-based loan:** Freshmen: $4404. Undergraduates: $4438. **Parent loans:** $27,050,566 (100% non-need-based). **Programs:** Federal Direct (Subsidized and Unsubsidized Stafford, PLUS), FFEL (Subsidized and Unsubsidized Stafford, PLUS), Perkins, state, college/university, emergency tuition loans.

WORK-STUDY Federal work-study: Total amount: $1,436,904; 704 jobs averaging $2682. **State or other work-study/employment:** Total amount: $287,774 (100% need-based). 116 part-time jobs averaging $2825.

ATHLETIC AWARDS Total amount: $2,178,370 (100% non-need-based).

APPLYING FOR FINANCIAL AID Required financial aid form: FAFSA. **Financial aid deadline (priority):** 4/1. **Notification date:** Continuous beginning 5/1. Students must reply within 3 weeks of notification.

CONTACT Mr. Chris Murr, Director of Financial Aid, Texas State University–San Marcos, 601 University Drive, San Marcos, TX 78666-4602, 512-245-2315. Fax: 512-245-7920. E-mail: cm18@txstate.edu.

TEXAS TECH UNIVERSITY
Lubbock, TX

Tuition & fees (TX res): $7485	Average undergraduate aid package: $8738

ABOUT THE INSTITUTION State-supported, coed. 101 undergraduate majors. Federal methodology is used as a basis for awarding need-based institutional aid.

UNDERGRADUATE EXPENSES for 2009–10 Tuition, state resident: full-time $4875; part-time $162.50 per credit hour. **Tuition, nonresident:** full-time $13,185; part-time $439.50 per credit hour. **Required fees:** full-time $2610; $50 per credit hour or $555 per term. Full-time tuition and fees vary according to course load, program, and reciprocity agreements. Part-time tuition and fees vary according to course load, program, and reciprocity agreements. **College room and board:** $7527; **Room only:** $4100. Room and board charges vary according to board plan and housing facility. **Payment plan:** Installment.

FRESHMAN FINANCIAL AID (Fall 2008) 3,117 applied for aid; of those 58% were deemed to have need. 99% of freshmen with need received aid; of those 8% had need fully met. **Average percent of need met:** 49% (excluding resources awarded to replace EFC). **Average financial aid package:** $7362 (excluding resources awarded to replace EFC). 6% of all full-time freshmen had no need and received non-need-based gift aid.

UNDERGRADUATE FINANCIAL AID (Fall 2008) 13,547 applied for aid; of those 64% were deemed to have need. 99% of undergraduates with need received aid; of those 6% had need fully met. **Average percent of need met:** 61% (excluding resources awarded to replace EFC). **Average financial aid package:** $8738 (excluding resources awarded to replace EFC). 4% of all full-time undergraduates had no need and received non-need-based gift aid.

GIFT AID (NEED-BASED) *Total amount:* $40,448,892 (43% federal, 43% state, 14% institutional). *Receiving aid:* Freshmen: 24% (1,096); all full-time undergraduates: 28% (6,082). *Average award:* Freshmen: $6984; Undergraduates: $5580. *Scholarships, grants, and awards:* Federal Pell, FSEOG, state, private, college/university gift aid from institutional funds.

GIFT AID (NON-NEED-BASED) *Total amount:* $21,588,918 (74% institutional, 26% external sources). *Receiving aid:* Freshmen: 18% (792). Undergraduates: 10% (2,238). *Average award:* Freshmen: $3637. Undergraduates: $2715. *Scholarships, grants, and awards by category: Academic interests/achievement:* agriculture, architecture, biological sciences, business, communication, computer science, education, engineering/technologies, English, foreign languages, general academic interests/achievements, home economics, humanities, international studies, mathematics, military science, physical sciences, premedicine, social sciences. *Creative arts/performance:* applied art and design, art/fine arts, dance, journalism/publications, music, performing arts, theater/drama. *Special achievements/activities:* community service, memberships, rodeo. *Special characteristics:* children of faculty/staff, first-generation college students, handicapped students, out-of-state students, veterans, veterans' children. *Tuition waivers:* Full or partial for employees or children of employees, senior citizens.

LOANS *Student loans:* $128,216,050 (38% need-based, 62% non-need-based). 67% of past graduating class borrowed through all loan programs. *Average indebtedness per student:* $21,001. *Average need-based loan:* Freshmen: $3144. Undergraduates: $4069. *Parent loans:* $11,008,013 (100% non-need-based). *Programs:* FFEL (Subsidized and Unsubsidized Stafford, PLUS), Perkins, state, college/university.

WORK-STUDY *Federal work-study:* Total amount: $1,255,702; jobs available. *State or other work-study/employment:* Total amount: $776,308 (100% need-based). Part-time jobs available.

ATHLETIC AWARDS Total amount: $3,974,866 (100% non-need-based).

APPLYING FOR FINANCIAL AID *Required financial aid form:* FAFSA. *Financial aid deadline (priority):* 4/15. *Notification date:* Continuous. Students must reply within 2 weeks of notification.

CONTACT Becky Wilson, Managing Director, Student Financial Aid, Texas Tech University, PO Box 45011, Lubbock, TX 79409-5011, 806-742-0454. *Fax:* 806-742-0880.

TEXAS WESLEYAN UNIVERSITY
Fort Worth, TX

CONTACT Director of Financial Aid, Texas Wesleyan University, 1201 Wesleyan Street, Fort Worth, TX 76105-1536, 817-531-4420 or toll-free 800-580-8980 (in-state). *Fax:* 817-531-4231. *E-mail:* finaid@txwes.edu.

TEXAS WOMAN'S UNIVERSITY
Denton, TX

Tuition & fees (TX res): $6660 — **Average undergraduate aid package: $7813**

ABOUT THE INSTITUTION State-supported, coed, primarily women. 42 undergraduate majors. Both federal and institutional methodology are used as a basis for awarding need-based institutional aid.

UNDERGRADUATE EXPENSES for 2010–11 *Tuition, state resident:* full-time $4740; part-time $158 per credit hour. *Tuition, nonresident:* full-time $13,080; part-time $435 per credit hour. *Required fees:* full-time $1920. Full-time tuition and fees vary according to course load. Part-time tuition and fees vary according to course load. *College room and board:* $5967; *Room only:* $3058. Room and board charges vary according to board plan and housing facility. *Payment plan:* Installment.

FRESHMAN FINANCIAL AID (Fall 2009, est.) 655 applied for aid; of those 75% were deemed to have need. 98% of freshmen with need received aid; of those 64% had need fully met. *Average percent of need met:* 93% (excluding resources awarded to replace EFC). *Average financial aid package:* $9151 (excluding resources awarded to replace EFC). 37% of all full-time freshmen had no need and received non-need-based gift aid.

UNDERGRADUATE FINANCIAL AID (Fall 2009, est.) 4,198 applied for aid; of those 81% were deemed to have need. 97% of undergraduates with need received aid; of those 36% had need fully met. *Average percent of need met:* 88% (excluding resources awarded to replace EFC). *Average financial aid package:* $7813 (excluding resources awarded to replace EFC). 11% of all full-time undergraduates had no need and received non-need-based gift aid.

GIFT AID (NEED-BASED) *Total amount:* $26,128,521 (54% federal, 24% state, 17% institutional, 5% external sources). *Receiving aid:* Freshmen: 65% (477); all full-time undergraduates: 62% (3,287). *Average award:* Freshmen: $8900; Undergraduates: $7592. *Scholarships, grants, and awards:* Federal Pell, FSEOG, state, private, college/university gift aid from institutional funds.

GIFT AID (NON-NEED-BASED) *Total amount:* $2,315,171 (82% institutional, 18% external sources). *Receiving aid:* Freshmen: 39% (291). Undergraduates: 27% (1,415). *Average award:* Freshmen: $3000. Undergraduates: $3000. *Scholarships, grants, and awards by category: Academic interests/achievement:* biological sciences, business, communication, computer science, education, English, foreign languages, general academic interests/achievements, health fields, home economics, humanities, library science, mathematics, physical sciences, premedicine, social sciences. *Creative arts/performance:* applied art and design, art/fine arts, cinema/film/broadcasting, dance, journalism/publications, music, theater/drama. *Special characteristics:* 97 awards: international students. *Tuition waivers:* Full or partial for senior citizens.

LOANS *Student loans:* $43,592,220 (88% need-based, 12% non-need-based). 57% of past graduating class borrowed through all loan programs. *Average indebtedness per student:* $22,293. *Average need-based loan:* Freshmen: $2839. Undergraduates: $3703. *Parent loans:* $500,447 (54% need-based, 46% non-need-based). *Programs:* FFEL (Subsidized and Unsubsidized Stafford, PLUS), Perkins, Federal Nursing, state, college/university, alternative loans.

WORK-STUDY *Federal work-study:* Total amount: $377,125; 236 jobs averaging $2951. *State or other work-study/employment:* Total amount: $563,768 (16% need-based, 84% non-need-based). 52 part-time jobs averaging $1341.

ATHLETIC AWARDS Total amount: $451,000 (100% non-need-based).

APPLYING FOR FINANCIAL AID *Required financial aid form:* FAFSA. *Financial aid deadline (priority):* 4/1. *Notification date:* 5/1. Students must reply within 3 weeks of notification.

CONTACT Mr. Governor Jackson, Director of Financial Aid, Texas Woman's University, PO Box 425408, Denton, TX 76204-5408, 940-898-3051 or toll-free 866-809-6130. *Fax:* 940-898-3068. *E-mail:* gjackson@twu.edu.

THIEL COLLEGE
Greenville, PA

Tuition & fees: $20,998 — **Average undergraduate aid package: $19,313**

ABOUT THE INSTITUTION Independent religious, coed. 41 undergraduate majors. Federal methodology is used as a basis for awarding need-based institutional aid.

UNDERGRADUATE EXPENSES for 2009–10 *Comprehensive fee:* $29,788 includes full-time tuition ($20,998) and room and board ($8790). *College room only:* $4400. Room and board charges vary according to board plan and housing facility. *Part-time tuition:* $670 per credit hour. *Part-time fees:* $50 per credit hour. Part-time tuition and fees vary according to course load. *Payment plan:* Installment.

FRESHMAN FINANCIAL AID (Fall 2009, est.) 237 applied for aid; of those 97% were deemed to have need. 100% of freshmen with need received aid; of those 10% had need fully met. *Average percent of need met:* 71% (excluding resources awarded to replace EFC). *Average financial aid package:* $19,698 (excluding resources awarded to replace EFC). 5% of all full-time freshmen had no need and received non-need-based gift aid.

UNDERGRADUATE FINANCIAL AID (Fall 2009, est.) 780 applied for aid; of those 97% were deemed to have need. 100% of undergraduates with need received aid; of those 11% had need fully met. *Average percent of need met:* 71% (excluding resources awarded to replace EFC). *Average financial aid package:* $19,313 (excluding resources awarded to replace EFC). 11% of all full-time undergraduates had no need and received non-need-based gift aid.

GIFT AID (NEED-BASED) *Total amount:* $11,340,411 (18% federal, 11% state, 68% institutional, 3% external sources). *Receiving aid:* Freshmen: 85% (230); all full-time undergraduates: 80% (754). *Average award:* Freshmen: $15,767; Undergraduates: $15,071. *Scholarships, grants, and awards:* Federal Pell, FSEOG, state, private, college/university gift aid from institutional funds.

GIFT AID (NON-NEED-BASED) *Total amount:* $1,104,567 (2% state, 93% institutional, 5% external sources). *Receiving aid:* Freshmen: 8% (21). Undergraduates: 7% (66). *Average award:* Freshmen: $7521. Undergraduates: $7810. *Scholarships, grants, and awards by category: Academic interests/achievement:* biological sciences, business, computer science, education, English, general academic interests/achievements, mathematics, physical sciences, religion/biblical studies. *Creative arts/performance:* music. *Special achievements/*

activities: leadership. *Special characteristics:* children and siblings of alumni, children of faculty/staff, relatives of clergy, religious affiliation, siblings of current students. *Tuition waivers:* Full or partial for employees or children of employees, senior citizens.

LOANS *Student loans:* $6,934,006 (84% need-based, 16% non-need-based). 92% of past graduating class borrowed through all loan programs. *Average indebtedness per student:* $37,783. *Average need-based loan:* Freshmen: $4631. Undergraduates: $4548. *Parent loans:* $1,301,458 (53% need-based, 47% non-need-based). *Programs:* FFEL (Subsidized and Unsubsidized Stafford, PLUS), Perkins, college/university.

WORK-STUDY *Federal work-study:* Total amount: $146,579; jobs available. *State or other work-study/employment:* Total amount: $181,896 (50% need-based, 50% non-need-based). Part-time jobs available.

APPLYING FOR FINANCIAL AID *Required financial aid forms:* FAFSA, state aid form. *Financial aid deadline (priority):* 3/15. *Notification date:* Continuous. Students must reply within 2 weeks of notification.

CONTACT Ms. Cynthia H. Farrell, Director of Financial Aid, Thiel College, 75 College Avenue, Greenville, PA 16125-2181, 724-589-2178 or toll-free 800-248-4435. *Fax:* 724-589-2850. *E-mail:* cfarrell@thiel.edu.

THOMAS AQUINAS COLLEGE
Santa Paula, CA

Tuition & fees: $22,400	Average undergraduate aid package: $19,294

ABOUT THE INSTITUTION Independent Roman Catholic, coed. 1 undergraduate major. Institutional methodology is used as a basis for awarding need-based institutional aid.

UNDERGRADUATE EXPENSES for 2010–11 *Comprehensive fee:* $29,800 includes full-time tuition ($22,400) and room and board ($7400). *Part-time tuition:* $622 per credit hour. *Payment plan:* Installment.

FRESHMAN FINANCIAL AID (Fall 2009, est.) 91 applied for aid; of those 97% were deemed to have need. 100% of freshmen with need received aid; of those 100% had need fully met. *Average percent of need met:* 100% (excluding resources awarded to replace EFC). *Average financial aid package:* $19,716 (excluding resources awarded to replace EFC).

UNDERGRADUATE FINANCIAL AID (Fall 2009, est.) 267 applied for aid; of those 98% were deemed to have need. 100% of undergraduates with need received aid; of those 100% had need fully met. *Average percent of need met:* 100% (excluding resources awarded to replace EFC). *Average financial aid package:* $19,294 (excluding resources awarded to replace EFC).

GIFT AID (NEED-BASED) *Total amount:* $3,293,715 (17% federal, 9% state, 73% institutional, 1% external sources). *Receiving aid:* Freshmen: 78% (80); all full-time undergraduates: 68% (234). *Average award:* Freshmen: $14,893; Undergraduates: $14,076. *Scholarships, grants, and awards:* Federal Pell, state, private, college/university gift aid from institutional funds, Academic Competitiveness Grants.

GIFT AID (NON-NEED-BASED) *Total amount:* $13,600 (22% state, 78% external sources).

LOANS *Student loans:* $1,105,648 (78% need-based, 22% non-need-based). 76% of past graduating class borrowed through all loan programs. *Average indebtedness per student:* $14,303. *Average need-based loan:* Freshmen: $3002. Undergraduates: $3729. *Parent loans:* $333,919 (19% need-based, 81% non-need-based). *Programs:* FFEL (Subsidized and Unsubsidized Stafford, PLUS), college/university, Canada Student Loans.

WORK-STUDY *State or other work-study/employment:* Total amount: $900,078 (100% need-based). 235 part-time jobs averaging $3830.

APPLYING FOR FINANCIAL AID *Required financial aid forms:* FAFSA, institution's own form, state aid form, business/farm supplement, income tax return, Non-custodial Parent Statement. *Financial aid deadline:* 3/2. *Notification date:* Continuous beginning 1/1. Students must reply by 5/1 or within 2 weeks of notification.

CONTACT Mr. Gregory Becher, Director of Financial Aid, Thomas Aquinas College, 10000 North Ojai Road, Santa Paula, CA 93060-9980, 805-525-4419 Ext. 5936 or toll-free 800-634-9797. *Fax:* 805-525-9342. *E-mail:* gbecher@thomasaquinas.edu.

THOMAS COLLEGE
Waterville, ME

CONTACT Jeannine Bosse, Associate Director of Student Financial Aid, Thomas College, 180 West River Road, Waterville, ME 04901-5097, 800-339-7001. *Fax:* 207-859-1114. *E-mail:* sfsassistant@thomas.edu.

THOMAS EDISON STATE COLLEGE
Trenton, NJ

Tuition & fees (NJ res): $4695	Average undergraduate aid package: N/A

ABOUT THE INSTITUTION State-supported, coed. 93 undergraduate majors. Federal methodology is used as a basis for awarding need-based institutional aid.

UNDERGRADUATE EXPENSES for 2009–10 *Tuition, state resident:* full-time $4695; part-time $136 per credit hour. *Tuition, nonresident:* full-time $6720; part-time $180 per credit hour. *Required fees:* $103 per year. Part-time tuition and fees vary according to program and student level. students may choose either the Comprehensive Tuition Plan: $4,695 per year (state residents and military personnel), $6,720 (out-of-state), which covers up to 36 credits per year for all credit-earning options, or the Enrolled Options Plan: $1,390 per year (state residents and military personnel), $2,520 (out-of-state) and $3,440 (international) for annual enrollment tuition and a technology services fee ($103); tests, portfolios, courses and other fees at additional cost. Please visit www.tesc.edu for more details.

GIFT AID (NEED-BASED) *Total amount:* $2,595,000 (94% federal, 6% state). *Scholarships, grants, and awards:* Federal Pell, state, private.

GIFT AID (NON-NEED-BASED) *Tuition waivers:* Full or partial for employees or children of employees.

LOANS *Student loans:* $10,673,000 (100% need-based). *Programs:* FFEL (Subsidized and Unsubsidized Stafford, PLUS), state, private loans.

APPLYING FOR FINANCIAL AID *Required financial aid forms:* FAFSA, institution's own form. *Financial aid deadline:* Continuous. *Notification date:* Continuous. Students must reply within 4 weeks of notification.

CONTACT Financial Aid Office, Thomas Edison State College, 101 West State Street, Trenton, NJ 08608, 609-633-9658 or toll-free 888-442-8372. *Fax:* 609-633-6489. *E-mail:* finaid@tesc.edu.

THOMAS JEFFERSON UNIVERSITY
Philadelphia, PA

ABOUT THE INSTITUTION Independent, coed. 8 undergraduate majors.

GIFT AID (NEED-BASED) *Scholarships, grants, and awards:* Federal Pell, FSEOG, state, private, college/university gift aid from institutional funds, Scholarships for Disadvantaged Students (SDS).

GIFT AID (NON-NEED-BASED) *Scholarships, grants, and awards by category: Academic interests/achievement:* general academic interests/achievements, health fields. *Special characteristics:* members of minority groups, veterans.

LOANS *Programs:* FFEL (Subsidized and Unsubsidized Stafford, PLUS), Perkins, Federal Nursing, college/university.

APPLYING FOR FINANCIAL AID *Required financial aid forms:* FAFSA, institution's own form, parent and student income tax returns.

CONTACT Susan McFadden, University Director of Financial Aid, Thomas Jefferson University, 1025 Walnut Street, Philadelphia, PA 19107, 215-955-2867 or toll-free 877-533-3247. *Fax:* 215-955-5186. *E-mail:* financial.aid@jefferson.edu.

THOMAS MORE COLLEGE
Crestview Hills, KY

Tuition & fees: $24,720	Average undergraduate aid package: $14,988

ABOUT THE INSTITUTION Independent Roman Catholic, coed. 44 undergraduate majors. Federal methodology is used as a basis for awarding need-based institutional aid.

UNDERGRADUATE EXPENSES for 2010–11 *Comprehensive fee:* $31,250 includes full-time tuition ($24,000), mandatory fees ($720), and room and board ($6530). *College room only:* $3200. Full-time tuition and fees vary according to program and student level. Room and board charges vary according to board plan and housing facility. *Part-time tuition:* $545 per credit hour. *Part-time fees:* $30 per credit hour; $15 per term. Part-time tuition and fees vary according to course load and program. *Payment plans:* Installment, deferred payment.

FRESHMAN FINANCIAL AID (Fall 2009, est.) 279 applied for aid; of those 91% were deemed to have need. 100% of freshmen with need received aid; of those 28% had need fully met. *Average percent of need met:* 75% (excluding resources awarded to replace EFC). *Average financial aid package:* $18,249 (excluding resources awarded to replace EFC). 16% of all full-time freshmen had no need and received non-need-based gift aid.

UNDERGRADUATE FINANCIAL AID (Fall 2009, est.) 1,082 applied for aid; of those 86% were deemed to have need. 100% of undergraduates with need received aid; of those 23% had need fully met. *Average percent of need met:* 70% (excluding resources awarded to replace EFC). *Average financial aid package:* $14,988 (excluding resources awarded to replace EFC). 15% of all full-time undergraduates had no need and received non-need-based gift aid.

GIFT AID (NEED-BASED) *Total amount:* $9,777,479 (15% federal, 17% state, 65% institutional, 3% external sources). *Receiving aid:* Freshmen: 81% (248); all full-time undergraduates: 61% (807). *Average award:* Freshmen: $14,197; Undergraduates: $12,017. *Scholarships, grants, and awards:* Federal Pell, FSEOG, state, private, college/university gift aid from institutional funds, Federal Nursing.

GIFT AID (NON-NEED-BASED) *Total amount:* $3,454,357 (6% state, 90% institutional, 4% external sources). *Receiving aid:* Freshmen: 14% (44). Undergraduates: 10% (126). *Average award:* Freshmen: $13,047. Undergraduates: $12,022. *Scholarships, grants, and awards by category:* Academic interests/achievement: 88 awards ($280,209 total): biological sciences, business, communication, computer science, education, English, general academic interests/achievements, mathematics, physical sciences, premedicine, religion/biblical studies, social sciences. *Creative arts/performance:* 23 awards ($30,706 total): art/fine arts, theater/drama. *Special achievements/activities:* 95 awards ($205,551 total): community service, leadership, memberships, religious involvement. *Special characteristics:* 664 awards ($3,028,397 total): adult students, children and siblings of alumni, children of faculty/staff, children of union members/company employees, international students, members of minority groups, out-of-state students, religious affiliation, siblings of current students, veterans, veterans' children. *Tuition waivers:* Full or partial for employees or children of employees, senior citizens.

LOANS *Student loans:* $8,437,081 (36% need-based, 64% non-need-based). 73% of past graduating class borrowed through all loan programs. *Average indebtedness per student:* $26,862. *Average need-based loan:* Freshmen: $3429. Undergraduates: $4073. *Parent loans:* $1,061,751 (100% non-need-based). *Programs:* Federal Direct (Subsidized and Unsubsidized Stafford, PLUS), Perkins, Federal Nursing, college/university.

WORK-STUDY *Federal work-study:* Total amount: $194,756; 147 jobs averaging $1325. *State or other work-study/employment:* 187 part-time jobs averaging $988.

APPLYING FOR FINANCIAL AID *Required financial aid form:* FAFSA. *Financial aid deadline (priority):* 3/15. *Notification date:* Continuous beginning 3/1. Students must reply by 5/1.

CONTACT Ms. Mary Givhan, Director of Financial Aid, Thomas More College, 333 Thomas More Parkway, Crestview Hills, KY 41017-3495, 859-344-3531 or toll-free 800-825-4557. *Fax:* 859-344-3638. *E-mail:* mary.givhan@thomasmore.edu.

THOMAS MORE COLLEGE OF LIBERAL ARTS
Merrimack, NH

Tuition & fees: N/R	Average undergraduate aid package: $13,172

ABOUT THE INSTITUTION Independent religious, coed. 1 undergraduate major. Federal methodology is used as a basis for awarding need-based institutional aid.

FRESHMAN FINANCIAL AID (Fall 2009, est.) 19 applied for aid; of those 79% were deemed to have need. 100% of freshmen with need received aid; of those 13% had need fully met. *Average percent of need met:* 86% (excluding resources awarded to replace EFC). *Average financial aid package:* $14,215 (excluding resources awarded to replace EFC). 9% of all full-time freshmen had no need and received non-need-based gift aid.

UNDERGRADUATE FINANCIAL AID (Fall 2009, est.) 52 applied for aid; of those 87% were deemed to have need. 100% of undergraduates with need received aid; of those 11% had need fully met. *Average percent of need met:* 87% (excluding resources awarded to replace EFC). *Average financial aid package:* $13,172 (excluding resources awarded to replace EFC). 8% of all full-time undergraduates had no need and received non-need-based gift aid.

GIFT AID (NEED-BASED) *Total amount:* $421,341 (30% federal, 2% state, 68% institutional). *Receiving aid:* Freshmen: 68% (15); all full-time undergraduates: 66% (43). *Average award:* Freshmen: $11,415; Undergraduates: $9794. *Scholarships, grants, and awards:* Federal Pell, FSEOG, state, private, college/university gift aid from institutional funds.

GIFT AID (NON-NEED-BASED) *Total amount:* $77,750 (96% institutional, 4% external sources). *Receiving aid:* Freshmen: 45% (10). Undergraduates: 40% (26). *Average award:* Freshmen: $3000. Undergraduates: $3000. *Scholarships, grants, and awards by category:* Academic interests/achievement: 35 awards ($127,663 total): general academic interests/achievements. *Tuition waivers:* Full or partial for employees or children of employees.

LOANS *Student loans:* $278,550 (87% need-based, 13% non-need-based). 77% of past graduating class borrowed through all loan programs. *Average indebtedness per student:* $21,133. *Average need-based loan:* Freshmen: $3231. Undergraduates: $4290. *Parent loans:* $71,667 (89% need-based, 11% non-need-based). *Programs:* FFEL (Subsidized and Unsubsidized Stafford, PLUS).

WORK-STUDY *State or other work-study/employment:* Total amount: $60,911 (96% need-based, 4% non-need-based). 32 part-time jobs averaging $1293.

APPLYING FOR FINANCIAL AID *Required financial aid form:* FAFSA. *Financial aid deadline:* Continuous. *Notification date:* Continuous beginning 3/15. Students must reply within 2 weeks of notification.

CONTACT Clinton A. Hanson Jr., Director of Financial Aid, Thomas More College of Liberal Arts, 6 Manchester Street, Merrimack, NH 03054-4818, 603-880-8308 Ext. 23 or toll-free 800-880-8308. *Fax:* 603-880-9280. *E-mail:* chanson@thomasmorecollege.edu.

THOMAS UNIVERSITY
Thomasville, GA

CONTACT Ms. Angela Keys, Director of Financial Aid, Thomas University, 1501 Millpond Road, Thomasville, GA 31792-7499, 229-226-1621 Ext. 216 or toll-free 800-538-9784. *Fax:* 229-227-6919. *E-mail:* akeys@thomasu.edu.

TIFFIN UNIVERSITY
Tiffin, OH

Tuition & fees: $18,390	Average undergraduate aid package: $13,569

ABOUT THE INSTITUTION Independent, coed. 36 undergraduate majors. Federal methodology is used as a basis for awarding need-based institutional aid.

UNDERGRADUATE EXPENSES for 2010–11 *Comprehensive fee:* $26,730 includes full-time tuition ($18,390) and room and board ($8340). *College room only:* $4310. Full-time tuition and fees vary according to course load. Room and board charges vary according to board plan and housing facility. *Part-time tuition:* $613 per credit hour. *Payment plan:* Installment.

FRESHMAN FINANCIAL AID (Fall 2009, est.) 502 applied for aid; of those 99% were deemed to have need. 100% of freshmen with need received aid; of those 8% had need fully met. *Average percent of need met:* 8% (excluding resources awarded to replace EFC). *Average financial aid package:* $14,652 (excluding resources awarded to replace EFC). 3% of all full-time freshmen had no need and received non-need-based gift aid.

UNDERGRADUATE FINANCIAL AID (Fall 2009, est.) 1,800 applied for aid; of those 93% were deemed to have need. 100% of undergraduates with need received aid; of those 5% had need fully met. *Average percent of need met:* 5% (excluding resources awarded to replace EFC). *Average financial aid package:* $13,569 (excluding resources awarded to replace EFC). 4% of all full-time undergraduates had no need and received non-need-based gift aid.

GIFT AID (NEED-BASED) *Total amount:* $15,077,125 (39% federal, 10% state, 50% institutional, 1% external sources). *Receiving aid:* Freshmen: 70% (353); all full-time undergraduates: 63% (1,165). *Average award:* Freshmen: $5647; Undergraduates: $5747. *Scholarships, grants, and awards:* Federal Pell, FSEOG, state, private, college/university gift aid from institutional funds.

GIFT AID (NON-NEED-BASED) *Receiving aid:* Freshmen: 66% (333). Undergraduates: 53% (975). *Average award:* Freshmen: $7882. Undergraduates: $6870.

Scholarships, grants, and awards by category: Academic interests/achievement: 1,011 awards ($6,084,316 total): general academic interests/achievements. *Creative arts/performance:* 116 awards ($276,704 total): music, performing arts, theater/drama. *Special achievements/activities:* 29 awards ($29,100 total): cheerleading/drum major. *Special characteristics:* 16 awards ($181,055 total): children of faculty/staff. *Tuition waivers:* Full or partial for employees or children of employees, senior citizens.

LOANS *Student loans:* $17,464,592 (100% need-based). 82% of past graduating class borrowed through all loan programs. *Average indebtedness per student:* $26,345. *Average need-based loan:* Freshmen: $3209. Undergraduates: $3986. *Parent loans:* $1,588,176 (100% need-based). *Programs:* Federal Direct (Subsidized and Unsubsidized Stafford, PLUS), FFEL (Subsidized and Unsubsidized Stafford, PLUS), Perkins, college/university.

WORK-STUDY *Federal work-study:* Total amount: $128,081; 161 jobs averaging $2113.

ATHLETIC AWARDS Total amount: $2,678,445 (100% need-based).

APPLYING FOR FINANCIAL AID *Required financial aid form:* FAFSA. *Financial aid deadline (priority):* 1/1. *Notification date:* Continuous beginning 1/15. Students must reply within 2 weeks of notification.

CONTACT Ms. Cindy Little, Director of Financial Aid Operations, Tiffin University, 155 Miami Street, Tiffin, OH 44883, 419-448-3415 or toll-free 800-968-6446. *Fax:* 419-443-5006. *E-mail:* clittle@tiffin.edu.

TOCCOA FALLS COLLEGE
Toccoa Falls, GA

CONTACT Vince Welch, Director of Financial Aid, Toccoa Falls College, PO Box 800900, Toccoa Falls, GA 30598, 706-886-7299 Ext. 5234. *Fax:* 706-282-6041. *E-mail:* vwelch@tfc.edu.

TORAH TEMIMAH TALMUDICAL SEMINARY
Brooklyn, NY

CONTACT Financial Aid Office, Torah Temimah Talmudical Seminary, 507 Ocean Parkway, Brooklyn, NY 11218-5913, 718-853-8500.

TOUGALOO COLLEGE
Tougaloo, MS

CONTACT Director of Financial Aid, Tougaloo College, 500 West County Line Road, Tougaloo, MS 39174, 601-977-6134 or toll-free 888-42GALOO. *Fax:* 601-977-6164.

TOURO COLLEGE
New York, NY

CONTACT Office of Financial Aid, Touro College, 27 West 23rd Street, New York, NY 10010, 212-463-0400.

TOWSON UNIVERSITY
Towson, MD

Tuition & fees (MD res): $7418 | **Average undergraduate aid package:** $9182

ABOUT THE INSTITUTION State-supported, coed. 58 undergraduate majors. Federal methodology is used as a basis for awarding need-based institutional aid.

UNDERGRADUATE EXPENSES for 2009–10 *Tuition, state resident:* full-time $5180; part-time $225 per credit. *Tuition, nonresident:* full-time $15,994; part-time $611 per credit. *Required fees:* full-time $2238; $93 per credit. Full-time tuition and fees vary according to course load. *College room and board:* $8670; *Room only:* $5256. Room and board charges vary according to board plan and housing facility. *Payment plans:* Guaranteed tuition, tuition prepayment, installment.

FRESHMAN FINANCIAL AID (Fall 2009, est.) 1,941 applied for aid; of those 66% were deemed to have need. 94% of freshmen with need received aid; of those 18% had need fully met. *Average percent of need met:* 67% (excluding resources awarded to replace EFC). *Average financial aid package:* $8910 (excluding resources awarded to replace EFC). 10% of all full-time freshmen had no need and received non-need-based gift aid.

UNDERGRADUATE FINANCIAL AID (Fall 2009, est.) 9,814 applied for aid; of those 73% were deemed to have need. 95% of undergraduates with need received aid; of those 17% had need fully met. *Average percent of need met:* 67% (excluding resources awarded to replace EFC). *Average financial aid package:* $9182 (excluding resources awarded to replace EFC). 8% of all full-time undergraduates had no need and received non-need-based gift aid.

GIFT AID (NEED-BASED) *Total amount:* $35,539,661 (42% federal, 23% state, 34% institutional, 1% external sources). *Receiving aid:* Freshmen: 32% (757); all full-time undergraduates: 31% (4,600). *Average award:* Freshmen: $8753; Undergraduates: $7429. *Scholarships, grants, and awards:* Federal Pell, FSEOG, state, private, college/university gift aid from institutional funds.

GIFT AID (NON-NEED-BASED) *Total amount:* $13,986,884 (1% federal, 6% state, 61% institutional, 32% external sources). *Receiving aid:* Freshmen: 22% (532). Undergraduates: 13% (1,965). *Average award:* Freshmen: $4740. Undergraduates: $5229. *Scholarships, grants, and awards by category: Academic interests/achievement:* 1,514 awards ($6,520,174 total): biological sciences, business, communication, computer science, education, English, foreign languages, general academic interests/achievements, health fields, mathematics. *Creative arts/performance:* 195 awards ($602,574 total): art/fine arts, dance, debating, music, theater/drama. *Special achievements/activities:* 285 awards ($884,298 total): community service, memberships. *Special characteristics:* 654 awards ($3,163,656 total): adult students, children of faculty/staff, handicapped students, international students, veterans. *Tuition waivers:* Full or partial for employees or children of employees, senior citizens.

LOANS *Student loans:* $46,573,308 (53% need-based, 47% non-need-based). 23% of past graduating class borrowed through all loan programs. *Average indebtedness per student:* $13,245. *Average need-based loan:* Freshmen: $3237. Undergraduates: $4129. *Parent loans:* $34,650,068 (1% need-based, 99% non-need-based). *Programs:* Federal Direct (Subsidized and Unsubsidized Stafford, PLUS), Perkins.

WORK-STUDY *Federal work-study:* Total amount: $854,918; 485 jobs averaging $1701.

ATHLETIC AWARDS Total amount: $4,786,294 (1% need-based, 99% non-need-based).

APPLYING FOR FINANCIAL AID *Required financial aid form:* FAFSA. *Financial aid deadline:* 2/10 (priority: 1/31). *Notification date:* Continuous beginning 3/21. Students must reply within 2 weeks of notification.

CONTACT Vince Pecora, Director of Financial Aid, Towson University, 8000 York Road, Towson, MD 21252-0001, 410-704-4236 or toll-free 888-4TOWSON. *E-mail:* finaid@towson.edu.

TRANSYLVANIA UNIVERSITY
Lexington, KY

Tuition & fees: $25,280 | **Average undergraduate aid package:** $21,670

ABOUT THE INSTITUTION Independent religious, coed. 35 undergraduate majors. Federal methodology is used as a basis for awarding need-based institutional aid.

UNDERGRADUATE EXPENSES for 2009–10 *Comprehensive fee:* $33,050 includes full-time tuition ($24,250), mandatory fees ($1030), and room and board ($7770). Room and board charges vary according to board plan and location. *Part-time tuition:* $2805 per course. Part-time tuition and fees vary according to course load. *Payment plan:* Installment.

FRESHMAN FINANCIAL AID (Fall 2009, est.) 224 applied for aid; of those 82% were deemed to have need. 100% of freshmen with need received aid; of those 22% had need fully met. *Average percent of need met:* 85% (excluding resources awarded to replace EFC). *Average financial aid package:* $22,378 (excluding resources awarded to replace EFC). 33% of all full-time freshmen had no need and received non-need-based gift aid.

UNDERGRADUATE FINANCIAL AID (Fall 2009, est.) 808 applied for aid; of those 87% were deemed to have need. 100% of undergraduates with need received aid; of those 21% had need fully met. *Average percent of need met:* 83% (excluding resources awarded to replace EFC). *Average financial aid package:* $21,670 (excluding resources awarded to replace EFC). 33% of all full-time undergraduates had no need and received non-need-based gift aid.

GIFT AID (NEED-BASED) *Total amount:* $11,862,600 (11% federal, 23% state, 64% institutional, 2% external sources). *Receiving aid:* Freshmen: 65% (183);

all full-time undergraduates: 65% (704). *Average award:* Freshmen: $17,914; Undergraduates: $17,805. *Scholarships, grants, and awards:* Federal Pell, FSEOG, state, private, college/university gift aid from institutional funds.

GIFT AID (NON-NEED-BASED) *Total amount:* $4,816,048 (14% state, 84% institutional, 2% external sources). *Receiving aid:* Freshmen: 7% (21). Undergraduates: 6% (70). *Average award:* Freshmen: $9872. Undergraduates: $10,461. *Scholarships, grants, and awards by category: Academic interests/ achievement:* $8,638,405 total: computer science, general academic interests/ achievements. *Creative arts/performance:* $132,975 total: art/fine arts, music, theater/drama. *Special achievements/activities:* $1,137,114 total: general special achievements/activities, religious involvement. *Special characteristics:* $1,110,771 total: children of faculty/staff, members of minority groups, out-of-state students, relatives of clergy, religious affiliation. *Tuition waivers:* Full or partial for employees or children of employees.

LOANS *Student loans:* $5,303,749 (70% need-based, 30% non-need-based). 65% of past graduating class borrowed through all loan programs. *Average indebtedness per student:* $19,893. *Average need-based loan:* Freshmen: $4395. Undergraduates: $4457. *Parent loans:* $1,344,834 (32% need-based, 68% non-need-based). *Programs:* FFEL (Subsidized and Unsubsidized Stafford, PLUS), Perkins, college/university.

WORK-STUDY *Federal work-study:* Total amount: $503,659; 429 jobs averaging $1735. *State or other work-study/employment:* Total amount: $381,770 (37% need-based, 63% non-need-based). 63 part-time jobs averaging $6090.

APPLYING FOR FINANCIAL AID *Required financial aid form:* FAFSA. *Financial aid deadline (priority):* 3/1. *Notification date:* Continuous beginning 3/15. Students must reply within 2 weeks of notification.

CONTACT Mr. Dave Cecil, Director of Financial Aid, Transylvania University, 300 North Broadway, Lexington, KY 40508-1797, 859-233-8239 or toll-free 800-872-6798. *Fax:* 859-281-3650. *E-mail:* dcecil@transy.edu.

TREVECCA NAZARENE UNIVERSITY
Nashville, TN

Tuition & fees: $18,318	Average undergraduate aid package: N/A

ABOUT THE INSTITUTION Independent Nazarene, coed. 54 undergraduate majors. Federal methodology is used as a basis for awarding need-based institutional aid.

UNDERGRADUATE EXPENSES for 2010–11 *Comprehensive fee:* $26,052 includes full-time tuition ($18,318) and room and board ($7734). *College room only:* $3582. Full-time tuition and fees vary according to course load. Room and board charges vary according to board plan. Part-time tuition and fees vary according to course load. *Payment plans:* Tuition prepayment, installment.

GIFT AID (NEED-BASED) *Total amount:* $2,647,786 (43% federal, 49% state, 8% institutional). *Scholarships, grants, and awards:* Federal Pell, FSEOG, state, private, college/university gift aid from institutional funds.

GIFT AID (NON-NEED-BASED) *Total amount:* $5,651,442 (93% institutional, 7% external sources). *Scholarships, grants, and awards by category: Academic interests/achievement:* biological sciences, business, communication, education, English, general academic interests/achievements, physical sciences, religion/ biblical studies, social sciences. *Creative arts/performance:* cinema/film/ broadcasting, music. *Special achievements/activities:* general special achievements/ activities. *Special characteristics:* children of faculty/staff, general special characteristics, relatives of clergy, religious affiliation. *Tuition waivers:* Full or partial for employees or children of employees, senior citizens.

LOANS *Student loans:* $20,051,341 (44% need-based, 56% non-need-based). *Parent loans:* $1,670,022 (100% non-need-based). *Programs:* FFEL (Subsidized and Unsubsidized Stafford, PLUS), Perkins.

WORK-STUDY *Federal work-study:* Total amount: $90,268; jobs available.

ATHLETIC AWARDS Total amount: $1,240,134 (100% non-need-based).

APPLYING FOR FINANCIAL AID *Required financial aid form:* FAFSA. *Financial aid deadline:* 7/30 (priority: 2/25). *Notification date:* Continuous beginning 3/1.

CONTACT Eddie White, Assistant Director of Financial Aid, Trevecca Nazarene University, 333 Murfreesboro Road, Nashville, TN 37210-2834, 615-248-1242 or toll-free 888-210-4TNU. *Fax:* 615-248-7728. *E-mail:* ewhite@trevecca.edu.

TRINE UNIVERSITY
Angola, IN

Tuition & fees: $25,400	Average undergraduate aid package: $16,957

ABOUT THE INSTITUTION Independent, coed. 37 undergraduate majors. Federal methodology is used as a basis for awarding need-based institutional aid.

UNDERGRADUATE EXPENSES for 2010–11 *Comprehensive fee:* $33,900 includes full-time tuition ($25,300), mandatory fees ($100), and room and board ($8500). Full-time tuition and fees vary according to degree level and location. Room and board charges vary according to board plan and housing facility. *Part-time tuition:* $786 per credit hour. Part-time tuition and fees vary according to degree level and location. *Payment plan:* Installment.

FRESHMAN FINANCIAL AID (Fall 2009, est.) 439 applied for aid; of those 72% were deemed to have need. 100% of freshmen with need received aid; of those 100% had need fully met. *Average percent of need met:* 95% (excluding resources awarded to replace EFC). *Average financial aid package:* $19,118 (excluding resources awarded to replace EFC). 7% of all full-time freshmen had no need and received non-need-based gift aid.

UNDERGRADUATE FINANCIAL AID (Fall 2009, est.) 1,435 applied for aid; of those 74% were deemed to have need. 100% of undergraduates with need received aid; of those 43% had need fully met. *Average percent of need met:* 91% (excluding resources awarded to replace EFC). *Average financial aid package:* $16,957 (excluding resources awarded to replace EFC). 5% of all full-time undergraduates had no need and received non-need-based gift aid.

GIFT AID (NEED-BASED) *Total amount:* $7,508,767 (37% federal, 26% state, 37% institutional). *Receiving aid:* Freshmen: 40% (185); all full-time undergraduates: 31% (453). *Average award:* Freshmen: $4309; Undergraduates: $4373. *Scholarships, grants, and awards:* Federal Pell, FSEOG, state, private, college/ university gift aid from institutional funds.

GIFT AID (NON-NEED-BASED) *Total amount:* $12,168,433 (94% institutional, 6% external sources). *Receiving aid:* Freshmen: 69% (317). Undergraduates: 31% (453). *Average award:* Freshmen: $12,552. Undergraduates: $8604. *Scholarships, grants, and awards by category: Academic interests/achievement:* general academic interests/achievements. *Special characteristics:* children and siblings of alumni, children of faculty/staff, members of minority groups, siblings of current students. *Tuition waivers:* Full or partial for employees or children of employees.

LOANS *Student loans:* $8,078,331 (55% need-based, 45% non-need-based). 81% of past graduating class borrowed through all loan programs. *Average indebtedness per student:* $19,334. *Average need-based loan:* Freshmen: $3048. Undergraduates: $3573. *Parent loans:* $3,681,238 (100% non-need-based). *Programs:* FFEL (Subsidized and Unsubsidized Stafford, PLUS), alternative loans.

WORK-STUDY *Federal work-study:* Total amount: $1,774,432; jobs available.

APPLYING FOR FINANCIAL AID *Required financial aid form:* FAFSA. *Financial aid deadline (priority):* 3/10. *Notification date:* Continuous beginning 2/15. Students must reply by 5/1 or within 2 weeks of notification.

CONTACT Kim Bennett, Director of Financial Aid, Trine University, 1 University Avenue, Angola, IN 46703-1764, 260-665-4175 or toll-free 800-347-4TSU. *Fax:* 260-665-4511. *E-mail:* admit@trine.edu.

TRINITY BAPTIST COLLEGE
Jacksonville, FL

CONTACT Mr. Donald Schaffer, Financial Aid Administrator, Trinity Baptist College, 800 Hammond Boulevard, Jacksonville, FL 32221, 904-596-2445 or toll-free 800-786-2206 (out-of-state). *Fax:* 904-596-2531. *E-mail:* financialaid@tbc.edu.

TRINITY BIBLE COLLEGE
Ellendale, ND

Tuition & fees: N/R	Average undergraduate aid package: N/A

ABOUT THE INSTITUTION Independent Assemblies of God, coed. *Awards:* associate and bachelor's degrees. 12 undergraduate majors. *Total enrollment:* 292. Undergraduates: 292. Federal methodology is used as a basis for awarding need-based institutional aid.

GIFT AID (NEED-BASED) *Scholarships, grants, and awards:* Federal Pell, FSEOG, state, private, college/university gift aid from institutional funds.
GIFT AID (NON-NEED-BASED) *Scholarships, grants, and awards by category: Academic interests/achievement:* business, education, general academic interests/achievements, religion/biblical studies. *Creative arts/performance:* art/fine arts, creative writing, music, theater/drama. *Special achievements/activities:* community service, general special achievements/activities, leadership, religious involvement. *Special characteristics:* children and siblings of alumni, children of current students, children of faculty/staff, general special characteristics, international students, married students, parents of current students, relatives of clergy, siblings of current students, spouses of current students.
LOANS *Programs:* FFEL (Subsidized and Unsubsidized Stafford, PLUS), Perkins, alternative loans.
APPLYING FOR FINANCIAL AID *Required financial aid form:* FAFSA. *Financial aid deadline:* 9/1 (priority: 3/1). *Notification date:* Continuous. Students must reply within 3 weeks of notification.
CONTACT Susan Healy, Financial Aid Associate, Trinity Bible College, 50 South 6th Avenue, Ellendale, ND 58436-7150, 701-349-3621 Ext. 5787 or toll-free 888-TBC-2DAY. *Fax:* 701-349-5787. *E-mail:* shealy@trinitybiblecollege.edu.

TRINITY CHRISTIAN COLLEGE
Palos Heights, IL

Tuition & fees: $21,335	Average undergraduate aid package: $12,219

ABOUT THE INSTITUTION Independent Christian Reformed, coed. 60 undergraduate majors. Both federal and institutional methodology are used as a basis for awarding need-based institutional aid.
UNDERGRADUATE EXPENSES for 2010–11 *Comprehensive fee:* $29,460 includes full-time tuition ($21,225), mandatory fees ($110), and room and board ($8125). *College room only:* $4225. Room and board charges vary according to board plan. *Part-time tuition:* $710 per semester hour. Part-time tuition and fees vary according to course load. *Payment plan:* Installment.
FRESHMAN FINANCIAL AID (Fall 2009, est.) 192 applied for aid; of those 80% were deemed to have need. 100% of freshmen with need received aid; of those 7% had need fully met. *Average percent of need met:* 39% (excluding resources awarded to replace EFC). *Average financial aid package:* $15,134 (excluding resources awarded to replace EFC). 59% of all full-time freshmen had no need and received non-need-based gift aid.
UNDERGRADUATE FINANCIAL AID (Fall 2009, est.) 1,002 applied for aid; of those 90% were deemed to have need. 100% of undergraduates with need received aid; of those 5% had need fully met. *Average percent of need met:* 49% (excluding resources awarded to replace EFC). *Average financial aid package:* $12,219 (excluding resources awarded to replace EFC). 10% of all full-time undergraduates had no need and received non-need-based gift aid.
GIFT AID (NEED-BASED) *Total amount:* $4,147,878 (37% federal, 30% state, 33% institutional). *Receiving aid:* Freshmen: 74% (148); all full-time undergraduates: 65% (679). *Average award:* Freshmen: $4287; Undergraduates: $4120. *Scholarships, grants, and awards:* Federal Pell, FSEOG, state, private, college/university gift aid from institutional funds.
GIFT AID (NON-NEED-BASED) *Total amount:* $4,902,456 (1% federal, 93% institutional, 6% external sources). *Receiving aid:* Freshmen: 75% (151). Undergraduates: 7% (70). *Average award:* Freshmen: $7795. Undergraduates: $7024. *Scholarships, grants, and awards by category: Academic interests/achievement:* business, English, general academic interests/achievements, health fields, mathematics. *Creative arts/performance:* applied art and design, art/fine arts, journalism/publications, music, theater/drama. *Special achievements/activities:* general special achievements/activities, leadership, religious involvement. *Special characteristics:* adult students, children and siblings of alumni, children of faculty/staff, ethnic background, first-generation college students, local/state students, members of minority groups, out-of-state students, religious affiliation. *Tuition waivers:* Full or partial for employees or children of employees, senior citizens.
LOANS *Student loans:* $10,078,965 (42% need-based, 58% non-need-based). 77% of past graduating class borrowed through all loan programs. *Average indebtedness per student:* $33,133. *Average need-based loan:* Freshmen: $3710. Undergraduates: $4447. *Parent loans:* $1,036,618 (100% non-need-based). *Programs:* FFEL (Subsidized and Unsubsidized Stafford, PLUS), Perkins, Federal Nursing.

WORK-STUDY *Federal work-study:* Total amount: $159,625; 135 jobs averaging $1500. *State or other work-study/employment:* Total amount: $558,859 (100% non-need-based). Part-time jobs available.
ATHLETIC AWARDS Total amount: $938,675 (100% non-need-based).
APPLYING FOR FINANCIAL AID *Required financial aid forms:* FAFSA, institution's own form. *Financial aid deadline (priority):* 2/15. *Notification date:* Continuous beginning 3/1. Students must reply within 2 weeks of notification.
CONTACT L. Denise Coleman, Director of Financial Aid, Trinity Christian College, 6601 West College Drive, Palos Heights, IL 60463-0929, 708-239-4706 or toll-free 800-748-0085. *E-mail:* financialaid@trnty.edu.

TRINITY COLLEGE
Hartford, CT

Tuition & fees: $42,370	Average undergraduate aid package: $36,991

ABOUT THE INSTITUTION Independent, coed. 47 undergraduate majors. Both federal and institutional methodology are used as a basis for awarding need-based institutional aid.
UNDERGRADUATE EXPENSES for 2010–11 *One-time required fee:* $25. *Comprehensive fee:* $53,330 includes full-time tuition ($40,360), mandatory fees ($2010), and room and board ($10,960). *College room only:* $7120. Full-time tuition and fees vary according to course load and program. Room and board charges vary according to board plan. *Part-time tuition:* $4484 per course. Part-time tuition and fees vary according to course load and program. *Payment plan:* Installment.
FRESHMAN FINANCIAL AID (Fall 2009, est.) 279 applied for aid; of those 89% were deemed to have need. 100% of freshmen with need received aid; of those 100% had need fully met. *Average percent of need met:* 100% (excluding resources awarded to replace EFC). *Average financial aid package:* $36,504 (excluding resources awarded to replace EFC). 1% of all full-time freshmen had no need and received non-need-based gift aid.
UNDERGRADUATE FINANCIAL AID (Fall 2009, est.) 1,007 applied for aid; of those 91% were deemed to have need. 100% of undergraduates with need received aid; of those 100% had need fully met. *Average percent of need met:* 100% (excluding resources awarded to replace EFC). *Average financial aid package:* $36,991 (excluding resources awarded to replace EFC). 2% of all full-time undergraduates had no need and received non-need-based gift aid.
GIFT AID (NEED-BASED) *Total amount:* $31,171,049 (5% federal, 3% state, 90% institutional, 2% external sources). *Receiving aid:* Freshmen: 41% (234); all full-time undergraduates: 39% (850). *Average award:* Freshmen: $33,695; Undergraduates: $35,047. *Scholarships, grants, and awards:* Federal Pell, FSEOG, state, private, college/university gift aid from institutional funds, Academic Competitiveness Grants, National SMART Grants.
GIFT AID (NON-NEED-BASED) *Total amount:* $1,987,127 (96% institutional, 4% external sources). *Receiving aid:* Freshmen: 10% (60). Undergraduates: 8% (166). *Average award:* Freshmen: $38,900. Undergraduates: $29,375. *Scholarships, grants, and awards by category: Academic interests/achievement:* 3 awards ($3000 total): general academic interests/achievements. *Special achievements/activities:* 30 awards ($1,250,597 total): leadership. *Tuition waivers:* Full or partial for employees or children of employees, adult students.
LOANS *Student loans:* $5,802,048 (53% need-based, 47% non-need-based). 42% of past graduating class borrowed through all loan programs. *Average indebtedness per student:* $20,174. *Average need-based loan:* Freshmen: $3691. Undergraduates: $4341. *Parent loans:* $3,653,761 (100% non-need-based). *Programs:* Perkins, college/university, alternative loans.
WORK-STUDY *Federal work-study:* Total amount: $862,183; 691 jobs averaging $1747.
APPLYING FOR FINANCIAL AID *Required financial aid forms:* FAFSA, CSS Financial Aid PROFILE, noncustodial (divorced/separated) parent's statement, business/farm supplement, federal income tax form(s). *Financial aid deadline:* 3/1 (priority: 2/1). *Notification date:* 4/1. Students must reply by 5/1 or within 2 weeks of notification.
CONTACT Ms. Kelly O'Brien, Director of Financial Aid, Trinity College, 300 Summit Street, Hartford, CT 06106-3100, 860-297-2046. *Fax:* 860-987-6296.

TRINITY COLLEGE OF FLORIDA
New Port Richey, FL

ABOUT THE INSTITUTION Independent nondenominational, coed. 10 undergraduate majors.

GIFT AID (NEED-BASED) *Scholarships, grants, and awards:* Federal Pell, FSEOG, state, private, college/university gift aid from institutional funds.

GIFT AID (NON-NEED-BASED) *Scholarships, grants, and awards by category: Academic interests/achievement:* religion/biblical studies. *Special achievements/activities:* community service, leadership, religious involvement. *Special characteristics:* children of faculty/staff, relatives of clergy, spouses of current students.

LOANS *Programs:* FFEL (Subsidized and Unsubsidized Stafford, PLUS).

WORK-STUDY *Federal work-study:* Total amount: $37,750; 22 jobs averaging $1402. *State or other work-study/employment:* Part-time jobs available.

APPLYING FOR FINANCIAL AID *Required financial aid forms:* FAFSA, institution's own form.

CONTACT Sue Wayne, Financial Aid Director, Trinity College of Florida, 2430 Welbilt Boulevard, New Port Richey, FL 34655, 727-569-1413 or toll-free 800-388-0869. *Fax:* 727-376-0781. *E-mail:* swayne@trinitycollege.edu.

TRINITY COLLEGE OF NURSING AND HEALTH SCIENCES
Rock Island, IL

Tuition & fees: $5186   **Average undergraduate aid package:** N/A

ABOUT THE INSTITUTION Independent, coed. 5 undergraduate majors. Federal methodology is used as a basis for awarding need-based institutional aid.

UNDERGRADUATE EXPENSES for 2009–10 *Tuition:* full-time $4836; part-time $403 per credit hour. Full-time tuition and fees vary according to degree level. Part-time tuition and fees vary according to degree level. *Payment plans:* Installment, deferred payment.

FRESHMAN FINANCIAL AID (Fall 2009, est.) 33% of all full-time freshmen had no need and received non-need-based gift aid.

UNDERGRADUATE FINANCIAL AID (Fall 2009, est.) 172 applied for aid; of those 100% were deemed to have need. 100% of undergraduates with need received aid. 4% of all full-time undergraduates had no need and received non-need-based gift aid.

GIFT AID (NEED-BASED) *Total amount:* $443,723 (62% federal, 26% state, 4% institutional, 8% external sources). *Receiving aid:* All full-time undergraduates: 9% (19). *Scholarships, grants, and awards:* Federal Pell, FSEOG, state, private, college/university gift aid from institutional funds.

GIFT AID (NON-NEED-BASED) *Total amount:* $144,230 (100% institutional). *Average award:* Freshmen: $500. Undergraduates: $500.

LOANS *Student loans:* $1,157,012 (45% need-based, 55% non-need-based). 85% of past graduating class borrowed through all loan programs. *Parent loans:* $77,853 (100% need-based). *Programs:* Federal Direct (Subsidized and Unsubsidized Stafford, PLUS), Federal Nursing.

APPLYING FOR FINANCIAL AID *Required financial aid forms:* FAFSA, institution's own form. *Financial aid deadline:* Continuous. *Notification date:* Continuous beginning 6/1. Students must reply within 4 weeks of notification.

CONTACT Kris Hodgerson, Financial Aid Specialist, Trinity College of Nursing and Health Sciences, 2122 25th Avenue, Rock Island, IL 61201, 309-779-7700. *Fax:* 309-779-7748. *E-mail:* hodgersonk@ihs.org.

TRINITY INTERNATIONAL UNIVERSITY
Deerfield, IL

Tuition & fees: $21,980   **Average undergraduate aid package:** $20,273

ABOUT THE INSTITUTION Independent religious, coed. *Awards:* bachelor's and master's degrees and post-bachelor's certificates. 39 undergraduate majors. *Total enrollment:* 2,671. Undergraduates: 968. Freshmen: 134. Federal methodology is used as a basis for awarding need-based institutional aid.

UNDERGRADUATE EXPENSES for 2009–10 *Application fee:* $25. *Comprehensive fee:* $29,410 includes full-time tuition ($21,980) and room and board ($7430). *College room only:* $4050.

FRESHMAN FINANCIAL AID (Fall 2009, est.) 152 applied for aid; of those 86% were deemed to have need. 100% of freshmen with need received aid; of those 11% had need fully met. *Average percent of need met:* 89% (excluding resources awarded to replace EFC). *Average financial aid package:* $20,998 (excluding resources awarded to replace EFC). 8% of all full-time freshmen had no need and received non-need-based gift aid.

UNDERGRADUATE FINANCIAL AID (Fall 2009, est.) 590 applied for aid; of those 88% were deemed to have need. 100% of undergraduates with need received aid; of those 11% had need fully met. *Average percent of need met:* 96% (excluding resources awarded to replace EFC). *Average financial aid package:* $20,273 (excluding resources awarded to replace EFC). 7% of all full-time undergraduates had no need and received non-need-based gift aid.

GIFT AID (NEED-BASED) *Total amount:* $4,413,027 (33% federal, 17% state, 50% institutional). *Receiving aid:* Freshmen: 63% (98); all full-time undergraduates: 60% (406). *Average award:* Freshmen: $10,059; Undergraduates: $9420. *Scholarships, grants, and awards:* Federal Pell, FSEOG, state, private, college/university gift aid from institutional funds.

GIFT AID (NON-NEED-BASED) *Total amount:* $2,674,639 (94% institutional, 6% external sources). *Receiving aid:* Freshmen: 78% (121). Undergraduates: 70% (474). *Average award:* Freshmen: $5646. Undergraduates: $4591. *Scholarships, grants, and awards by category: Academic interests/achievement:* general academic interests/achievements. *Creative arts/performance:* music. *Special achievements/activities:* religious involvement. *Special characteristics:* children and siblings of alumni, members of minority groups, religious affiliation.

LOANS *Student loans:* $4,962,740 (46% need-based, 54% non-need-based). 88% of past graduating class borrowed through all loan programs. *Average indebtedness per student:* $23,864. *Average need-based loan:* Freshmen: $3795. Undergraduates: $4810. *Parent loans:* $847,363 (100% non-need-based). *Programs:* Federal Direct (Subsidized and Unsubsidized Stafford, PLUS), Perkins.

WORK-STUDY *Federal work-study:* Total amount: $72,636; jobs available.

ATHLETIC AWARDS Total amount: $2,448,193 (100% non-need-based).

APPLYING FOR FINANCIAL AID *Required financial aid form:* FAFSA. *Financial aid deadline (priority):* 4/1. *Notification date:* Continuous beginning 2/15. Students must reply within 4 weeks of notification.

CONTACT Pat Coles, Interim Director of Financial Aid, Trinity International University, 2065 Half Day Road, Deerfield, IL 60015-1284, 847-317-8060 or toll-free 800-822-3225 (out-of-state). *Fax:* 847-317-7081. *E-mail:* finaid@tiu.edu.

TRINITY LUTHERAN COLLEGE
Issaquah, WA

ABOUT THE INSTITUTION Independent Lutheran, coed. *Awards:* associate and bachelor's degrees and post-bachelor's certificates. 8 undergraduate majors. *Total enrollment:* 115. Undergraduates: 115.

GIFT AID (NEED-BASED) *Scholarships, grants, and awards:* Federal Pell, FSEOG, college/university gift aid from institutional funds.

GIFT AID (NON-NEED-BASED) *Scholarships, grants, and awards by category: Academic interests/achievement:* business, general academic interests/achievements, religion/biblical studies. *Creative arts/performance:* general creative arts/performance, music. *Special achievements/activities:* leadership, religious involvement. *Special characteristics:* children of faculty/staff, international students, religious affiliation.

LOANS *Programs:* FFEL (Subsidized and Unsubsidized Stafford, PLUS), college/university.

APPLYING FOR FINANCIAL AID *Required financial aid forms:* FAFSA, institution's own form.

CONTACT Ms. Susan Dalgleish, Director of Financial Aid, Trinity Lutheran College, 4221 228th Avenue SE, Issaquah, WA 98029-9299, 425-961-5514 or toll-free 800-843-5659. *Fax:* 425-392-0404. *E-mail:* susan.dalgleish@tlc.edu.

TRINITY UNIVERSITY
San Antonio, TX

Tuition & fees: $29,317   **Average undergraduate aid package:** $23,645

ABOUT THE INSTITUTION Independent religious, coed. 50 undergraduate majors. Federal methodology is used as a basis for awarding need-based institutional aid.

UNDERGRADUATE EXPENSES for 2009–10 *Comprehensive fee:* $38,212 includes full-time tuition ($28,272), mandatory fees ($1045), and room and board ($8895). *College room only:* $5825. Full-time tuition and fees vary according to course load. Room and board charges vary according to board plan. *Part-time tuition:* $1178 per credit hour. Part-time tuition and fees vary according to course load. *Payment plan:* Installment.
FRESHMAN FINANCIAL AID (Fall 2009, est.) 407 applied for aid; of those 70% were deemed to have need. 100% of freshmen with need received aid; of those 51% had need fully met. *Average percent of need met:* 94% (excluding resources awarded to replace EFC). *Average financial aid package:* $26,181 (excluding resources awarded to replace EFC). 44% of all full-time freshmen had no need and received non-need-based gift aid.
UNDERGRADUATE FINANCIAL AID (Fall 2009, est.) 1,245 applied for aid; of those 77% were deemed to have need. 100% of undergraduates with need received aid; of those 46% had need fully met. *Average percent of need met:* 90% (excluding resources awarded to replace EFC). *Average financial aid package:* $23,645 (excluding resources awarded to replace EFC). 44% of all full-time undergraduates had no need and received non-need-based gift aid.
GIFT AID (NEED-BASED) *Total amount:* $14,690,074 (11% federal, 9% state, 76% institutional, 4% external sources). *Receiving aid:* Freshmen: 44% (282); all full-time undergraduates: 38% (927). *Average award:* Freshmen: $19,259; Undergraduates: $16,619. *Scholarships, grants, and awards:* Federal Pell, FSEOG, state, private, college/university gift aid from institutional funds.
GIFT AID (NON-NEED-BASED) *Total amount:* $14,290,146 (95% institutional, 5% external sources). *Receiving aid:* Freshmen: 13% (82). Undergraduates: 8% (186). *Average award:* Freshmen: $14,865. Undergraduates: $12,112. *Scholarships, grants, and awards by category:* Academic interests/achievement: 1,438 awards ($14,852,571 total): general academic interests/achievements. Creative arts/performance: 88 awards ($553,250 total): art/fine arts, debating, music, theater/drama. Special characteristics: 3 awards ($30,029 total): first-generation college students. *Tuition waivers:* Full or partial for employees or children of employees.
LOANS *Student loans:* $7,324,569 (72% need-based, 28% non-need-based). *Average need-based loan:* Freshmen: $5491. Undergraduates: $6658. *Parent loans:* $8,875,441 (12% need-based, 88% non-need-based). *Programs:* FFEL (Subsidized and Unsubsidized Stafford, PLUS), Perkins, state, college/university.
WORK-STUDY *Federal work-study:* Total amount: $1,158,319; jobs available (averaging $2000). *State or other work-study/employment:* Part-time jobs available (averaging $2000).
APPLYING FOR FINANCIAL AID *Required financial aid form:* FAFSA. *Financial aid deadline:* 4/1 (priority: 2/15). *Notification date:* 4/1. Students must reply by 5/1 or within 3 weeks of notification.
CONTACT Sean Smith, Director of Financial Aid, Trinity University, 715 Stadium Drive, San Antonio, TX 78212-7200, 210-999-8315 or toll-free 800-TRINITY. *Fax:* 210-999-8316. *E-mail:* financialaid@trinity.edu.

TRINITY (WASHINGTON) UNIVERSITY
Washington, DC

CONTACT Catherine H. Geier, Director of Student Financial Services, Trinity (Washington) University, 125 Michigan Avenue, NE, Washington, DC 20017-1094, 202-884-9530 or toll-free 800-IWANTTC. *Fax:* 202-884-9524. *E-mail:* financialaid@trinitydc.edu.

TRI-STATE BIBLE COLLEGE
South Point, OH

CONTACT Financial Aid Office, Tri-State Bible College, 506 Margaret Street, PO Box 445, South Point, OH 45680-8402, 740-377-2520.

TROY UNIVERSITY
Troy, AL

Tuition & fees (AL res): $7016	Average undergraduate aid package: $4485

ABOUT THE INSTITUTION State-supported, coed. 42 undergraduate majors. Federal methodology is used as a basis for awarding need-based institutional aid.
UNDERGRADUATE EXPENSES for 2009–10 *Tuition, state resident:* full-time $6176; part-time $193 per credit hour. *Tuition, nonresident:* full-time $12,342;

part-time $386 per credit hour. *Required fees:* full-time $840; $8 per credit hour or $50 per term. Full-time tuition and fees vary according to program. *College room and board:* $6042. Room and board charges vary according to board plan and housing facility. *Payment plan:* Installment.
FRESHMAN FINANCIAL AID (Fall 2009, est.) 1,474 applied for aid; of those 100% were deemed to have need. 100% of freshmen with need received aid. *Average financial aid package:* $3854 (excluding resources awarded to replace EFC). 16% of all full-time freshmen had no need and received non-need-based gift aid.
UNDERGRADUATE FINANCIAL AID (Fall 2009, est.) 7,615 applied for aid; of those 100% were deemed to have need. 100% of undergraduates with need received aid. *Average financial aid package:* $4485 (excluding resources awarded to replace EFC). 12% of all full-time undergraduates had no need and received non-need-based gift aid.
GIFT AID (NEED-BASED) *Total amount:* $50,520,188 (99% federal, 1% state). *Receiving aid:* Freshmen: 52% (982); all full-time undergraduates: 50% (5,310). *Average award:* Freshmen: $4591; Undergraduates: $4485. *Scholarships, grants, and awards:* Federal Pell, FSEOG, state, private, college/university gift aid from institutional funds.
GIFT AID (NON-NEED-BASED) *Total amount:* $21,021,550 (48% institutional, 52% external sources). *Receiving aid:* Freshmen: 28% (536). Undergraduates: 16% (1,693). *Average award:* Freshmen: $3481. Undergraduates: $3927. *Scholarships, grants, and awards by category:* Academic interests/achievement: general academic interests/achievements. Creative arts/performance: music, theater/drama. Special achievements/activities: leadership. Special characteristics: general special characteristics. *Tuition waivers:* Full or partial for employees or children of employees.
LOANS *Student loans:* $235,190,387 (100% need-based). *Average need-based loan:* Freshmen: $3607. Undergraduates: $4531. *Parent loans:* $51,003,089 (100% need-based). *Programs:* FFEL (Subsidized and Unsubsidized Stafford, PLUS), Perkins.
WORK-STUDY *Federal work-study:* Total amount: $1,437,786; jobs available.
ATHLETIC AWARDS Total amount: $4,022,944 (100% non-need-based).
APPLYING FOR FINANCIAL AID *Required financial aid forms:* FAFSA, institution's own form. *Financial aid deadline (priority):* 3/1. *Notification date:* Continuous beginning 6/1. Students must reply within 2 weeks of notification.
CONTACT Ms. Carol Ballard, Associate Vice-Chancellor of Financial Aid, Troy University, 131 Adams Administration Building, Troy, AL 36082, 334-670-3186 or toll-free 800-551-9716. *Fax:* 334-670-3702. *E-mail:* csupri@troy.edu.

TRUETT-McCONNELL COLLEGE
Cleveland, GA

Tuition & fees: $14,000	Average undergraduate aid package: $12,784

ABOUT THE INSTITUTION Independent Baptist, coed. 11 undergraduate majors. Federal methodology is used as a basis for awarding need-based institutional aid.
UNDERGRADUATE EXPENSES for 2009–10 *Comprehensive fee:* $19,700 includes full-time tuition ($13,500), mandatory fees ($500), and room and board ($5700). Full-time tuition and fees vary according to course load. Room and board charges vary according to housing facility. *Part-time tuition:* $450 per semester hour. *Part-time fees:* $250 per term. Part-time tuition and fees vary according to course load.
FRESHMAN FINANCIAL AID (Fall 2009, est.) 124 applied for aid; of those 86% were deemed to have need. 100% of freshmen with need received aid; of those 16% had need fully met. *Average percent of need met:* 66% (excluding resources awarded to replace EFC). *Average financial aid package:* $11,888 (excluding resources awarded to replace EFC). 14% of all full-time freshmen had no need and received non-need-based gift aid.
UNDERGRADUATE FINANCIAL AID (Fall 2009, est.) 319 applied for aid; of those 89% were deemed to have need. 100% of undergraduates with need received aid; of those 15% had need fully met. *Average percent of need met:* 70% (excluding resources awarded to replace EFC). *Average financial aid package:* $12,784 (excluding resources awarded to replace EFC). 19% of all full-time undergraduates had no need and received non-need-based gift aid.
GIFT AID (NEED-BASED) *Total amount:* $3,239,989 (25% federal, 21% state, 44% institutional, 10% external sources). *Receiving aid:* Freshmen: 79% (106); all full-time undergraduates: 79% (281). *Average award:* Freshmen: $9545;

Undergraduates: $10,351. *Scholarships, grants, and awards:* Federal Pell, FSEOG, state, private, college/university gift aid from institutional funds.

GIFT AID (NON-NEED-BASED) *Receiving aid:* Freshmen: 12% (16). Undergraduates: 11% (40). *Average award:* Freshmen: $3968. Undergraduates: $5114. *Scholarships, grants, and awards by category: Academic interests/achievement:* 322 awards ($1,057,291 total): general academic interests/achievements. *Creative arts/performance:* 46 awards ($126,950 total): music. *Special achievements/ activities:* 25 awards ($50,000 total): leadership. *Special characteristics:* 65 awards ($132,256 total): international students, relatives of clergy, religious affiliation, siblings of current students, spouses of current students. *Tuition waivers:* Full or partial for employees or children of employees.

LOANS *Student loans:* $1,650,464 (45% need-based, 55% non-need-based). 65% of past graduating class borrowed through all loan programs. *Average indebtedness per student:* $16,742. *Average need-based loan:* Freshmen: $3197. Undergraduates: $3398. *Parent loans:* $268,831 (100% non-need-based). *Programs:* Federal Direct (Subsidized and Unsubsidized Stafford, PLUS).

WORK-STUDY *Federal work-study:* Total amount: $26,335; 18 jobs averaging $1535. *State or other work-study/employment:* Part-time jobs available.

ATHLETIC AWARDS Total amount: $423,687 (100% need-based).

APPLYING FOR FINANCIAL AID *Required financial aid forms:* FAFSA, institution's own form, state aid form. *Financial aid deadline:* Continuous. *Notification date:* Continuous beginning 3/15. Students must reply within 2 weeks of notification.

CONTACT Mrs. Becky Moore, Director of Financial Aid, Truett-McConnell College, 100 Alumni Drive, Cleveland, GA 30528, 706-865-2134 Ext. 144 or toll-free 800-226-8621 (in-state). *Fax:* 706-865-7615. *E-mail:* bmoore@truett. edu.

TRUMAN STATE UNIVERSITY
Kirksville, MO

Tuition & fees (MO res): $6692	Average undergraduate aid package: $8425

ABOUT THE INSTITUTION State-supported, coed. 64 undergraduate majors. Federal methodology is used as a basis for awarding need-based institutional aid.

UNDERGRADUATE EXPENSES for 2009–10 *One-time required fee:* $305. *Tuition, state resident:* full-time $6458; part-time $269 per credit. *Tuition, nonresident:* full-time $11,309; part-time $471 per credit. *Required fees:* full-time $234. Part-time tuition and fees vary according to course load. *College room and board:* $6854. Room and board charges vary according to housing facility. *Payment plan:* Installment.

FRESHMAN FINANCIAL AID (Fall 2008) 1,064 applied for aid; of those 60% were deemed to have need. 100% of freshmen with need received aid; of those 70% had need fully met. *Average percent of need met:* 85% (excluding resources awarded to replace EFC). *Average financial aid package:* $8875 (excluding resources awarded to replace EFC). 58% of all full-time freshmen had no need and received non-need-based gift aid.

UNDERGRADUATE FINANCIAL AID (Fall 2008) 3,476 applied for aid; of those 65% were deemed to have need. 100% of undergraduates with need received aid; of those 68% had need fully met. *Average percent of need met:* 82% (excluding resources awarded to replace EFC). *Average financial aid package:* $8425 (excluding resources awarded to replace EFC). 44% of all full-time undergraduates had no need and received non-need-based gift aid.

GIFT AID (NEED-BASED) *Total amount:* $5,947,026 (55% federal, 33% state, 12% institutional). *Receiving aid:* Freshmen: 35% (463); all full-time undergraduates: 30% (1,653). *Average award:* Freshmen: $3821; Undergraduates: $3607. *Scholarships, grants, and awards:* Federal Pell, FSEOG, state, private, college/ university gift aid from institutional funds, Academic Competitiveness Grants, National SMART Grants, TEACH Grants.

GIFT AID (NON-NEED-BASED) *Total amount:* $24,182,008 (1% federal, 10% state, 82% institutional, 7% external sources). *Receiving aid:* Freshmen: 44% (589). Undergraduates: 31% (1,684). *Average award:* Freshmen: $4926. Undergraduates: $4884. *Scholarships, grants, and awards by category: Academic interests/achievement:* 4,180 awards ($20,592,754 total): biological sciences, business, communication, education, English, foreign languages, general academic interests/achievements, mathematics, military science, physical sciences, premedicine, social sciences. *Creative arts/performance:* 100 awards ($96,294 total): art/fine arts, debating, music, theater/drama. *Special achievements/ activities:* 149 awards ($1,686,713 total): leadership. *Special characteristics:*

174 awards ($790,522 total): children and siblings of alumni, children of faculty/staff, international students. *Tuition waivers:* Full or partial for employees or children of employees, senior citizens.

LOANS *Student loans:* $14,788,060 (43% need-based, 57% non-need-based). 53% of past graduating class borrowed through all loan programs. *Average indebtedness per student:* $21,858. *Average need-based loan:* Freshmen: $3556. Undergraduates: $4312. *Parent loans:* $1,738,214 (100% non-need-based). *Programs:* FFEL (Subsidized and Unsubsidized Stafford, PLUS), Perkins, Federal Nursing, state, college/university, alternative loans.

WORK-STUDY *Federal work-study:* Total amount: $286,466; 239 jobs averaging $1213. *State or other work-study/employment:* Total amount: $1,868,325 (100% non-need-based). 837 part-time jobs averaging $1667.

ATHLETIC AWARDS Total amount: $1,313,540 (100% non-need-based).

APPLYING FOR FINANCIAL AID *Required financial aid forms:* FAFSA, institution's own form. *Financial aid deadline (priority):* 4/1. *Notification date:* Continuous beginning 4/1. Students must reply within 4 weeks of notification.

CONTACT Kathy Elsea, Director of Financial Aid, Truman State University, 103 McClain Hall, Kirksville, MO 63501-4221, 660-785-4130 or toll-free 800-892-7792 (in-state). *Fax:* 660-785-7389. *E-mail:* kelsea@truman.edu.

TUFTS UNIVERSITY
Medford, MA

Tuition & fees: $40,342	Average undergraduate aid package: $30,974

ABOUT THE INSTITUTION Independent, coed. 64 undergraduate majors. Both federal and institutional methodology are used as a basis for awarding need-based institutional aid.

UNDERGRADUATE EXPENSES for 2009–10 *Comprehensive fee:* $51,088 includes full-time tuition ($39,432), mandatory fees ($910), and room and board ($10,746). *College room only:* $5564. Room and board charges vary according to board plan. *Payment plans:* Tuition prepayment, installment.

FRESHMAN FINANCIAL AID (Fall 2009, est.) 680 applied for aid; of those 78% were deemed to have need. 100% of freshmen with need received aid; of those 100% had need fully met. *Average percent of need met:* 100% (excluding resources awarded to replace EFC). *Average financial aid package:* $29,559 (excluding resources awarded to replace EFC). 2% of all full-time freshmen had no need and received non-need-based gift aid.

UNDERGRADUATE FINANCIAL AID (Fall 2009, est.) 2,550 applied for aid; of those 87% were deemed to have need. 100% of undergraduates with need received aid; of those 97% had need fully met. *Average percent of need met:* 100% (excluding resources awarded to replace EFC). *Average financial aid package:* $30,974 (excluding resources awarded to replace EFC). 1% of all full-time undergraduates had no need and received non-need-based gift aid.

GIFT AID (NEED-BASED) *Total amount:* $58,522,492 (8% federal, 1% state, 88% institutional, 3% external sources). *Receiving aid:* Freshmen: 37% (484); all full-time undergraduates: 36% (1,983). *Average award:* Freshmen: $27,731; Undergraduates: $28,112. *Scholarships, grants, and awards:* Federal Pell, FSEOG, state, private, college/university gift aid from institutional funds.

GIFT AID (NON-NEED-BASED) *Total amount:* $586,273 (10% federal, 7% state, 6% institutional, 77% external sources). *Receiving aid:* Freshmen: 2% (23). Undergraduates: 1% (78). *Average award:* Freshmen: $500. Undergraduates: $500. *Scholarships, grants, and awards by category: Academic interests/ achievement:* general academic interests/achievements. *Tuition waivers:* Full or partial for employees or children of employees.

LOANS *Student loans:* $9,810,049 (80% need-based, 20% non-need-based). 41% of past graduating class borrowed through all loan programs. *Average indebtedness per student:* $23,731. *Average need-based loan:* Freshmen: $3280. Undergraduates: $3846. *Parent loans:* $12,536,071 (100% non-need-based). *Programs:* Federal Direct (Subsidized and Unsubsidized Stafford, PLUS), Perkins, college/university.

WORK-STUDY *Federal work-study:* Total amount: $3,087,181; 1,678 jobs averaging $1874. *State or other work-study/employment:* Total amount: $181,500 (100% need-based). 71 part-time jobs averaging $1983.

APPLYING FOR FINANCIAL AID *Required financial aid forms:* FAFSA, CSS Financial Aid PROFILE, noncustodial (divorced/separated) parent's statement, business/farm supplement, federal income tax form(s). *Financial aid deadline:* 2/15. *Notification date:* 4/5. Students must reply by 5/1.

CONTACT Patricia C. Reilly, Director of Financial Aid, Tufts University, Dowling Hall, Medford, MA 02155, 617-627-5912. *Fax:* 617-627-3987. *E-mail:* patricia. reilly@tufts.edu.

TUI UNIVERSITY
Cypress, CA

CONTACT Financial Aid Office, TUI University, 5665 Plaza Drive, 3rd Floor, Cypress, CA 90630, 714-816-0366.

TULANE UNIVERSITY
New Orleans, LA

Tuition & fees: $40,584	Average undergraduate aid package: $35,578

ABOUT THE INSTITUTION Independent, coed. 82 undergraduate majors. Both federal and institutional methodology are used as a basis for awarding need-based institutional aid.

UNDERGRADUATE EXPENSES for 2010–11 *Comprehensive fee:* $50,190 includes full-time tuition ($37,200), mandatory fees ($3384), and room and board ($9606). *College room only:* $5506. Room and board charges vary according to board plan and housing facility. *Payment plans:* Tuition prepayment, installment.

FRESHMAN FINANCIAL AID (Fall 2009, est.) 985 applied for aid; of those 64% were deemed to have need. 99% of freshmen with need received aid; of those 69% had need fully met. *Average percent of need met:* 91% (excluding resources awarded to replace EFC). *Average financial aid package:* $34,265 (excluding resources awarded to replace EFC). 42% of all full-time freshmen had no need and received non-need-based gift aid.

UNDERGRADUATE FINANCIAL AID (Fall 2009, est.) 2,936 applied for aid; of those 75% were deemed to have need. 100% of undergraduates with need received aid; of those 67% had need fully met. *Average percent of need met:* 92% (excluding resources awarded to replace EFC). *Average financial aid package:* $35,578 (excluding resources awarded to replace EFC). 39% of all full-time undergraduates had no need and received non-need-based gift aid.

GIFT AID (NEED-BASED) *Total amount:* $51,637;471 (11% federal, 2% state, 86% institutional, 1% external sources). *Receiving aid:* Freshmen: 41% (611); all full-time undergraduates: 39% (2,138). *Average award:* Freshmen: $23,528; Undergraduates: $25,177. *Scholarships, grants, and awards:* Federal Pell, FSEOG, state, private, college/university gift aid from institutional funds, Academic Competitiveness Grants, National SMART Grants.

GIFT AID (NON-NEED-BASED) *Total amount:* $50,347,850 (1% federal, 3% state, 93% institutional, 3% external sources). *Receiving aid:* Freshmen: 18% (265). Undergraduates: 12% (676). *Average award:* Freshmen: $21,718. Undergraduates: $21,230. *Scholarships, grants, and awards by category:* Academic interests/achievement: 3,043 awards ($65,182,585 total): general academic interests/achievements. Creative arts/performance: 36 awards ($149,458 total): music. Special achievements/activities: 46 awards ($542,650 total): community service. Special characteristics: 301 awards ($10,779,580 total): children of faculty/staff, local/state students. *Tuition waivers:* Full or partial for employees or children of employees.

LOANS *Student loans:* $25,758,102 (57% need-based, 43% non-need-based). 47% of past graduating class borrowed through all loan programs. *Average indebtedness per student:* $27,461. *Average need-based loan:* Freshmen: $6046. Undergraduates: $7108. *Parent loans:* $6,983,933 (10% need-based, 90% non-need-based). *Programs:* Federal Direct (Subsidized and Unsubsidized Stafford, PLUS), Perkins.

WORK-STUDY *Federal work-study:* Total amount: $1,429,511; 1,195 jobs averaging $2328. *State or other work-study/employment:* Total amount: $800,217 (23% need-based, 77% non-need-based). Part-time jobs available.

ATHLETIC AWARDS Total amount: $8,538,950 (29% need-based, 71% non-need-based).

APPLYING FOR FINANCIAL AID *Required financial aid forms:* FAFSA, CSS Financial Aid PROFILE, noncustodial (divorced/separated) parent's statement, business/farm supplement. *Financial aid deadline (priority):* 2/15. *Notification date:* Continuous beginning 3/1. Students must reply by 5/1 or within 2 weeks of notification.

CONTACT Mr. Michael T. Goodman, Director of Financial Aid, Tulane University, 6823 St. Charles Avenue, New Orleans, LA 70118-5669, 504-865-5723 or toll-free 800-873-9283. *Fax:* 504-862-8750. *E-mail:* finaid@tulane.edu.

TUSCULUM COLLEGE
Greeneville, TN

Tuition & fees: $19,530	Average undergraduate aid package: $17,651

ABOUT THE INSTITUTION Independent Presbyterian, coed. 37 undergraduate majors. Federal methodology is used as a basis for awarding need-based institutional aid.

UNDERGRADUATE EXPENSES for 2009–10 *Comprehensive fee:* $27,265 includes full-time tuition ($19,530) and room and board ($7735). Full-time tuition and fees vary according to degree level and reciprocity agreements. *Part-time tuition:* $825 per semester hour. Part-time tuition and fees vary according to degree level and reciprocity agreements. *Payment plan:* Installment.

FRESHMAN FINANCIAL AID (Fall 2008) 529 applied for aid; of those 74% were deemed to have need. 100% of freshmen with need received aid. *Average financial aid package:* $9845 (excluding resources awarded to replace EFC). 28% of all full-time freshmen had no need and received non-need-based gift aid.

UNDERGRADUATE FINANCIAL AID (Fall 2008) 2,069 applied for aid; of those 71% were deemed to have need. 100% of undergraduates with need received aid. *Average financial aid package:* $17,651 (excluding resources awarded to replace EFC). 30% of all full-time undergraduates had no need and received non-need-based gift aid.

GIFT AID (NEED-BASED) *Total amount:* $5,685,435 (48% federal, 52% state). *Receiving aid:* Freshmen: 74% (389); all full-time undergraduates: 71% (1,470). *Scholarships, grants, and awards:* Federal Pell, FSEOG, state, private, college/university gift aid from institutional funds.

GIFT AID (NON-NEED-BASED) *Total amount:* $15,836,661 (86% federal, 9% state, 4% institutional, 1% external sources). *Average award:* Freshmen: $2137. Undergraduates: $4088. *Scholarships, grants, and awards by category:* Academic interests/achievement: 482 awards ($2,522,535 total): general academic interests/achievements. Creative arts/performance: general creative arts/performance, music. Special achievements/activities: 36 awards ($52,166 total): cheerleading/drum major, community service, leadership. Special characteristics: 1,740 awards ($3,904,363 total): adult students, children of faculty/staff, local/state students. *Tuition waivers:* Full or partial for employees or children of employees.

LOANS *Student loans:* $6,974,574 (23% need-based, 77% non-need-based). 59% of past graduating class borrowed through all loan programs. *Average indebtedness per student:* $8632. *Parent loans:* $1,064,187 (100% non-need-based). *Programs:* FFEL (Subsidized and Unsubsidized Stafford, PLUS), Perkins.

WORK-STUDY *Federal work-study:* Total amount: $392,040; 264 jobs averaging $2285. *State or other work-study/employment:* Total amount: $16,000 (100% non-need-based). 16 part-time jobs averaging $2000.

ATHLETIC AWARDS Total amount: $1,732,282 (100% non-need-based).

APPLYING FOR FINANCIAL AID *Required financial aid form:* FAFSA. *Financial aid deadline (priority):* 2/15. *Notification date:* Continuous beginning 3/1. Students must reply within 3 weeks of notification.

CONTACT Melena Verity, Director of Financial Aid, Tusculum College, PO Box 5049, 60 Shiloh Road, Greeneville, TN 37743-9997, 423-636-7377 or toll-free 800-729-0256. *Fax:* 615-250-4968. *E-mail:* mverity@tusculum.edu.

TUSKEGEE UNIVERSITY
Tuskegee, AL

Tuition & fees: $16,750	Average undergraduate aid package: $13,824

ABOUT THE INSTITUTION Independent, coed. 43 undergraduate majors. Federal methodology is used as a basis for awarding need-based institutional aid.

UNDERGRADUATE EXPENSES for 2010–11 *Comprehensive fee:* $24,320 includes full-time tuition ($16,100), mandatory fees ($650), and room and board ($7570). Full-time tuition and fees vary according to course load and program. Room and board charges vary according to housing facility. *Part-time tuition:* $665 per credit hour. Part-time tuition and fees vary according to course load and program. *Payment plan:* Installment.

FRESHMAN FINANCIAL AID (Fall 2008) 635 applied for aid; of those 85% were deemed to have need. 94% of freshmen with need received aid; of those 68% had need fully met. *Average percent of need met:* 85% (excluding resources

awarded to replace EFC). *Average financial aid package:* $13,824 (excluding resources awarded to replace EFC). 28% of all full-time freshmen had no need and received non-need-based gift aid.

UNDERGRADUATE FINANCIAL AID (Fall 2008) 2,519 applied for aid; of those 85% were deemed to have need. 92% of undergraduates with need received aid; of those 70% had need fully met. *Average percent of need met:* 85% (excluding resources awarded to replace EFC). *Average financial aid package:* $13,824 (excluding resources awarded to replace EFC). 22% of all full-time undergraduates had no need and received non-need-based gift aid.

GIFT AID (NEED-BASED) *Total amount:* $6,122,249 (97% federal, 1% state, 2% institutional). *Receiving aid:* Freshmen: 58% (434); all full-time undergraduates: 61% (1,675). *Average award:* Freshmen: $8000; Undergraduates: $8000. *Scholarships, grants, and awards:* Federal Pell, FSEOG, state, private, college/university gift aid from institutional funds, United Negro College Fund.

GIFT AID (NON-NEED-BASED) *Total amount:* $3,524,421 (51% institutional, 49% external sources). *Receiving aid:* Freshmen: 38% (284). Undergraduates: 35% (951). *Average award:* Freshmen: $6000. Undergraduates: $6000. *Scholarships, grants, and awards by category:* Academic interests/achievement: 1,714 awards ($9,086,319 total): general academic interests/achievements. Creative arts/performance: 108 awards ($68,400 total): music. Special characteristics: 36 awards ($157,002 total): children of faculty/staff, local/state students. *Tuition waivers:* Full or partial for employees or children of employees.

LOANS *Student loans:* $19,099,842 (52% need-based, 48% non-need-based). 91% of past graduating class borrowed through all loan programs. *Average indebtedness per student:* $31,000. *Average need-based loan:* Freshmen: $5625. Undergraduates: $6006. *Parent loans:* $4,295,666 (100% non-need-based). *Programs:* Federal Direct (Subsidized and Unsubsidized Stafford, PLUS), Perkins.

WORK-STUDY *Federal work-study:* Total amount: $830,097; 525 jobs averaging $1879. *State or other work-study/employment:* Total amount: $1,425,900 (100% non-need-based). 424 part-time jobs averaging $4628.

ATHLETIC AWARDS Total amount: $1,408,216 (100% non-need-based).

APPLYING FOR FINANCIAL AID *Required financial aid forms:* FAFSA, institution's own form. *Financial aid deadline (priority):* 3/31. *Notification date:* Continuous. Students must reply within 2 weeks of notification.

CONTACT Mr. A. D. James Jr., Director of Student Financial Services, Tuskegee University, Tuskegee, AL 36088, 334-727-8201 or toll-free 800-622-6531. *Fax:* 334-724-4227. *E-mail:* jamesad@tuskegee.edu.

UNION COLLEGE
Barbourville, KY

Tuition & fees: $18,860	Average undergraduate aid package: $19,623

ABOUT THE INSTITUTION Independent United Methodist, coed. 21 undergraduate majors. Federal methodology is used as a basis for awarding need-based institutional aid.

UNDERGRADUATE EXPENSES for 2010–11 *Comprehensive fee:* $24,810 includes full-time tuition ($18,260), mandatory fees ($600), and room and board ($5950). *College room only:* $2550. Full-time tuition and fees vary according to course load. Room and board charges vary according to board plan and housing facility. *Part-time tuition:* $305 per credit hour. Part-time tuition and fees vary according to course load. *Payment plan:* Installment.

FRESHMAN FINANCIAL AID (Fall 2009, est.) 196 applied for aid; of those 93% were deemed to have need. 93% of freshmen with need received aid; of those 21% had need fully met. *Average percent of need met:* 75% (excluding resources awarded to replace EFC). *Average financial aid package:* $18,884 (excluding resources awarded to replace EFC). 9% of all full-time freshmen had no need and received non-need-based gift aid.

UNDERGRADUATE FINANCIAL AID (Fall 2009, est.) 797 applied for aid; of those 92% were deemed to have need. 97% of undergraduates with need received aid; of those 26% had need fully met. *Average percent of need met:* 80% (excluding resources awarded to replace EFC). *Average financial aid package:* $19,623 (excluding resources awarded to replace EFC). 8% of all full-time undergraduates had no need and received non-need-based gift aid.

GIFT AID (NEED-BASED) *Total amount:* $6,914,813 (45% federal, 23% state, 28% institutional, 4% external sources). *Receiving aid:* Freshmen: 84% (170); all full-time undergraduates: 85% (707). *Average award:* Freshmen: $12,644; Undergraduates: $12,442. *Scholarships, grants, and awards:* Federal Pell, FSEOG, state, college/university gift aid from institutional funds.

GIFT AID (NON-NEED-BASED) *Total amount:* $404,730 (100% state). *Receiving aid:* Freshmen: 9% (18). Undergraduates: 10% (87). *Average award:* Freshmen: $10,522. Undergraduates: $10,421. *Scholarships, grants, and awards by category:* Academic interests/achievement: 183 awards ($719,500 total): general academic interests/achievements. Creative arts/performance: 27 awards ($45,500 total): music. Special achievements/activities: 31 awards ($130,662 total): cheerleading/drum major. Special characteristics: 64 awards ($84,257 total): children and siblings of alumni, religious affiliation. *Tuition waivers:* Full or partial for employees or children of employees, senior citizens.

LOANS *Student loans:* $7,728,322 (55% need-based, 45% non-need-based). 73% of past graduating class borrowed through all loan programs. *Average indebtedness per student:* $22,388. *Average need-based loan:* Freshmen: $6280. Undergraduates: $7501. *Parent loans:* $600,456 (41% need-based, 59% non-need-based). *Programs:* Federal Direct (Subsidized and Unsubsidized Stafford, PLUS), FFEL (Subsidized and Unsubsidized Stafford, PLUS), Perkins, college/university.

WORK-STUDY *Federal work-study:* Total amount: $268,972; 166 jobs averaging $1324. *State or other work-study/employment:* 100 part-time jobs averaging $1324.

ATHLETIC AWARDS Total amount: $3,418,562 (100% need-based).

APPLYING FOR FINANCIAL AID *Required financial aid form:* FAFSA. *Financial aid deadline (priority):* 3/15. *Notification date:* Continuous beginning 4/1. Students must reply within 2 weeks of notification.

CONTACT Mrs. Jessica Cook, Associate Dean of Financial Services, Union College, 310 College Street, Barbourville, KY 40906-1499, 606-546-1607 or toll-free 800-489-8646. *Fax:* 606-546-1264. *E-mail:* jcook@unionky.edu.

UNION COLLEGE
Lincoln, NE

CONTACT Mr. John C. Burdick, IV, Director of Financial Aid, Union College, 3800 South 48th Street, Lincoln, NE 68506-4300, 800-228-4600. *Fax:* 402-486-2895. *E-mail:* financialaid@ucollege.edu.

UNION COLLEGE
Schenectady, NY

Comprehensive fee: $50,439	Average undergraduate aid package: $33,778

ABOUT THE INSTITUTION Independent, coed. 35 undergraduate majors. Both federal and institutional methodology are used as a basis for awarding need-based institutional aid.

UNDERGRADUATE EXPENSES for 2009–10 *Comprehensive fee:* $50,439. *Payment plan:* Installment.

FRESHMAN FINANCIAL AID (Fall 2009, est.) 342 applied for aid; of those 82% were deemed to have need. 99% of freshmen with need received aid; of those 99% had need fully met. *Average percent of need met:* 100% (excluding resources awarded to replace EFC). *Average financial aid package:* $35,815 (excluding resources awarded to replace EFC). 14% of all full-time freshmen had no need and received non-need-based gift aid.

UNDERGRADUATE FINANCIAL AID (Fall 2009, est.) 1,258 applied for aid; of those 81% were deemed to have need. 99% of undergraduates with need received aid; of those 98% had need fully met. *Average percent of need met:* 99% (excluding resources awarded to replace EFC). *Average financial aid package:* $33,778 (excluding resources awarded to replace EFC). 16% of all full-time undergraduates had no need and received non-need-based gift aid.

GIFT AID (NEED-BASED) *Total amount:* $30,975,329 (6% federal, 4% state, 88% institutional, 2% external sources). *Receiving aid:* Freshmen: 51% (265); all full-time undergraduates: 46% (973). *Average award:* Freshmen: $32,597; Undergraduates: $28,489. *Scholarships, grants, and awards:* Federal Pell, FSEOG, state, private, college/university gift aid from institutional funds.

GIFT AID (NON-NEED-BASED) *Total amount:* $3,993,365 (7% federal, 4% state, 88% institutional, 1% external sources). *Receiving aid:* Freshmen: 2% (9). Undergraduates: 2% (43). *Average award:* Freshmen: $10,016. Undergraduates: $10,002. *Scholarships, grants, and awards by category:* Academic interests/achievement: 355 awards ($3,538,925 total): general academic interests/achievements. Special characteristics: 30 awards: children of faculty/staff. *Tuition waivers:* Full or partial for employees or children of employees, senior citizens.

LOANS *Student loans:* $8,231,244 (47% need-based, 53% non-need-based). 61% of past graduating class borrowed through all loan programs. *Average*

indebtedness per student: $24,739. *Average need-based loan:* Freshmen: $2670. Undergraduates: $4007. *Parent loans:* $3,173,833 (100% non-need-based). *Programs:* Federal Direct (Subsidized and Unsubsidized Stafford, PLUS), Perkins, college/university.

WORK-STUDY *Federal work-study:* Total amount: $595,000; 552 jobs averaging $1555. *State or other work-study/employment:* Total amount: $105,000 (100% need-based). 146 part-time jobs averaging $1695.

APPLYING FOR FINANCIAL AID *Required financial aid forms:* FAFSA, CSS Financial Aid PROFILE, state aid form, noncustodial (divorced/separated) parent's statement, business/farm supplement. *Financial aid deadline:* 2/1. *Notification date:* 4/1. Students must reply by 5/1.

CONTACT Ms. Linda Parker, Director of Financial Aid and Family Financing, Union College, Grant Hall, Schenectady, NY 12308-2311, 518-388-6123 or toll-free 888-843-6688 (in-state). *Fax:* 518-388-8052. *E-mail:* finaid@union.edu.

UNION INSTITUTE & UNIVERSITY
Cincinnati, OH

CONTACT Ms. Rebecca Zackerman, Director of Financial Aid, Union Institute & University, 440 East McMillan Street, Cincinnati, OH 45206-1925, 513-861-6400 or toll-free 800-486-3116. *Fax:* 513-861-0779. *E-mail:* bzackerman@tui.edu.

UNION UNIVERSITY
Jackson, TN

Tuition & fees: $20,940	Average undergraduate aid package: $19,643

ABOUT THE INSTITUTION Independent Southern Baptist, coed. 66 undergraduate majors. Federal methodology is used as a basis for awarding need-based institutional aid.

UNDERGRADUATE EXPENSES for 2009–10 *Comprehensive fee:* $27,870 includes full-time tuition ($20,280), mandatory fees ($660), and room and board ($6930). Full-time tuition and fees vary according to course load. Room and board charges vary according to board plan and housing facility. *Part-time tuition:* $690 per credit hour. *Part-time fees:* $210 per term. *Payment plans:* Installment, deferred payment.

FRESHMAN FINANCIAL AID (Fall 2009, est.) 472 applied for aid; of those 82% were deemed to have need. 100% of freshmen with need received aid; of those 22% had need fully met. *Average percent of need met:* 74% (excluding resources awarded to replace EFC). *Average financial aid package:* $17,752 (excluding resources awarded to replace EFC). 13% of all full-time freshmen had no need and received non-need-based gift aid.

UNDERGRADUATE FINANCIAL AID (Fall 2009, est.) 1,521 applied for aid; of those 84% were deemed to have need. 100% of undergraduates with need received aid; of those 25% had need fully met. *Average percent of need met:* 69% (excluding resources awarded to replace EFC). *Average financial aid package:* $19,643 (excluding resources awarded to replace EFC). 11% of all full-time undergraduates had no need and received non-need-based gift aid.

GIFT AID (NEED-BASED) *Total amount:* $5,236,440 (46% federal, 18% state, 36% institutional). *Receiving aid:* Freshmen: 55% (294); all full-time undergraduates: 51% (910). *Average award:* Freshmen: $5613; Undergraduates: $5479. *Scholarships, grants, and awards:* Federal Pell, FSEOG, state, private, college/university gift aid from institutional funds.

GIFT AID (NON-NEED-BASED) *Total amount:* $14,745,312 (2% federal, 23% state, 69% institutional, 6% external sources). *Receiving aid:* Freshmen: 72% (383). Undergraduates: 68% (1,205). *Average award:* Freshmen: $7105. Undergraduates: $7432. *Scholarships, grants, and awards by category:* Academic interests/achievement: $7,215,557 total: business, communication, education, engineering/technologies, general academic interests/achievements, health fields, mathematics, military science, premedicine, religion/biblical studies. Creative arts/performance: $447,867 total: art/fine arts, cinema/film/broadcasting, journalism/publications, music, theater/drama. Special achievements/activities: $1,584,431 total: cheerleading/drum major, community service, general special achievements/activities, leadership, religious involvement. Special characteristics: $2,972,409 total: children and siblings of alumni, children of current students, children of educators, children of faculty/staff, ethnic background, general special characteristics, international students, members of minority groups, relatives of clergy, religious affiliation, siblings of current students, spouses of current students, twins, veterans, veterans' children. *Tuition waivers:* Full or partial for children of alumni, employees or children of employees.

LOANS *Student loans:* $8,099,968 (44% need-based, 56% non-need-based). 58% of past graduating class borrowed through all loan programs. *Average indebtedness per student:* $24,253. *Average need-based loan:* Freshmen: $3460. Undergraduates: $4453. *Parent loans:* $1,533,467 (100% non-need-based). *Programs:* Federal Direct (Subsidized and Unsubsidized Stafford, PLUS), Perkins, alternative loans.

WORK-STUDY *Federal work-study:* Total amount: $185,230; 141 jobs averaging $1235. *State or other work-study/employment:* Total amount: $350,185 (100% non-need-based). 373 part-time jobs averaging $1188.

ATHLETIC AWARDS Total amount: $1,123,498 (100% non-need-based).

APPLYING FOR FINANCIAL AID *Required financial aid forms:* FAFSA, institution's own form. *Financial aid deadline (priority):* 2/1. *Notification date:* Continuous beginning 3/1. Students must reply by 5/1 or within 2 weeks of notification.

CONTACT John Thomas Brandt, Director of Student Financial Planning, Union University, 1050 Union University Drive, Jackson, TN 38305-3697, 731-661-5015 or toll-free 800-33-UNION. *Fax:* 731-661-5570. *E-mail:* jbrandt@uu.edu.

UNITED STATES SPORTS ACADEMY
Daphne, AL

CONTACT Financial Aid Office, United States Sports Academy, One Academy Drive, Daphne, AL 36526-7055, 251-626-3303 or toll-free 800-223-2668 (out-of-state).

UNITED STATES UNIVERSITY
National City, CA

CONTACT Financial Aid Office, United States University, 140 West 16th Street, National City, CA 91950, 619-477-6310 or toll-free 888-422-3381 (out-of-state).

UNITED TALMUDICAL SEMINARY
Brooklyn, NY

CONTACT Financial Aid Office, United Talmudical Seminary, 82 Lee Avenue, Brooklyn, NY 11211-7900, 718-963-9770 Ext. 309.

UNITY COLLEGE
Unity, ME

Tuition & fees: N/R	Average undergraduate aid package: $17,369

ABOUT THE INSTITUTION Independent, coed. 14 undergraduate majors. Federal methodology is used as a basis for awarding need-based institutional aid.

FRESHMAN FINANCIAL AID (Fall 2009, est.) 165 applied for aid; of those 93% were deemed to have need. 100% of freshmen with need received aid; of those 3% had need fully met. *Average percent of need met:* 73% (excluding resources awarded to replace EFC). *Average financial aid package:* $17,693 (excluding resources awarded to replace EFC). 8% of all full-time freshmen had no need and received non-need-based gift aid.

UNDERGRADUATE FINANCIAL AID (Fall 2009, est.) 506 applied for aid; of those 91% were deemed to have need. 100% of undergraduates with need received aid; of those 7% had need fully met. *Average percent of need met:* 75% (excluding resources awarded to replace EFC). *Average financial aid package:* $17,369 (excluding resources awarded to replace EFC). 13% of all full-time undergraduates had no need and received non-need-based gift aid.

GIFT AID (NEED-BASED) *Total amount:* $5,107,890 (23% federal, 3% state, 70% institutional, 4% external sources). *Receiving aid:* Freshmen: 91% (153); all full-time undergraduates: 81% (457). *Average award:* Freshmen: $12,396; Undergraduates: $11,156. *Scholarships, grants, and awards:* Federal Pell, FSEOG, state, private, college/university gift aid from institutional funds.

GIFT AID (NON-NEED-BASED) *Total amount:* $290,758 (90% institutional, 10% external sources). *Receiving aid:* Freshmen: 1% (2). Undergraduates: 2% (12). *Average award:* Freshmen: $3623. Undergraduates: $3166. *Scholarships, grants, and awards by category:* Academic interests/achievement: 277 awards ($1,119,750 total): general academic interests/achievements. Special achievements/activities: 52 awards ($52,000 total): community service, leadership. Special characteristics: 93 awards ($217,170 total): children of educators, general special characteristics, local/state students, members of minority groups.

LOANS *Student loans:* $4,624,529 (78% need-based, 22% non-need-based). *Average need-based loan:* Freshmen: $4710. Undergraduates: $5677. *Parent loans:* $1,086,563 (35% need-based, 65% non-need-based). *Programs:* Federal Direct (Subsidized and Unsubsidized Stafford, PLUS), Perkins.

WORK-STUDY *Federal work-study:* Total amount: $589,907; 375 jobs averaging $1573. *State or other work-study/employment:* Total amount: $4800 (100% non-need-based). 4 part-time jobs averaging $1200.

APPLYING FOR FINANCIAL AID *Required financial aid form:* FAFSA. *Financial aid deadline:* Continuous. *Notification date:* Continuous beginning 3/10. Students must reply within 2 weeks of notification.

CONTACT Mr. Rand E. Newell, Director of Financial Aid, Unity College, 90 Quaker Hill Road, Unity, ME 04988, 207-948-3131 Ext. 201. *Fax:* 207-948-2018. *E-mail:* rnewell@unity.edu.

UNIVERSIDAD ADVENTISTA DE LAS ANTILLAS
Mayagüez, PR

Tuition & fees: $6170	Average undergraduate aid package: N/A

ABOUT THE INSTITUTION Independent Seventh-day Adventist, coed. 21 undergraduate majors. Both federal and institutional methodology are used as a basis for awarding need-based institutional aid.

UNDERGRADUATE EXPENSES for 2009–10 *Comprehensive fee:* $9070 includes full-time tuition ($6170) and room and board ($2900). *College room only:* $1100. Room and board charges vary according to board plan and housing facility. *Part-time tuition:* $155 per credit hour. *Payment plans:* Guaranteed tuition, tuition prepayment, installment.

FRESHMAN FINANCIAL AID (Fall 2009, est.) 174 applied for aid; of those 97% were deemed to have need. 100% of freshmen with need received aid. *Average percent of need met:* 70% (excluding resources awarded to replace EFC).

UNDERGRADUATE FINANCIAL AID (Fall 2009, est.) 955 applied for aid; of those 100% were deemed to have need. 100% of undergraduates with need received aid. *Average percent of need met:* 70% (excluding resources awarded to replace EFC).

GIFT AID (NEED-BASED) *Total amount:* $4,113,570 (92% federal, 5% state, 3% institutional). *Receiving aid:* Freshmen: 97% (168); all full-time undergraduates: 79% (752). *Average award:* Freshmen: $5972; Undergraduates: $6472. *Scholarships, grants, and awards:* Federal Pell, FSEOG, state, college/university gift aid from institutional funds.

GIFT AID (NON-NEED-BASED) *Scholarships, grants, and awards by category:* Special achievements/activities: community service. *Tuition waivers:* Full or partial for employees or children of employees.

LOANS *Student loans:* $2,056,850 (100% need-based). 10% of past graduating class borrowed through all loan programs. *Average indebtedness per student:* $4400. *Average need-based loan:* Freshmen: $1750. Undergraduates: $3250. *Parent loans:* $5300 (100% need-based). *Programs:* FFEL (Subsidized and Unsubsidized Stafford, PLUS).

WORK-STUDY *Federal work-study:* Total amount: $142,561; jobs available. *State or other work-study/employment:* Total amount: $131,570 (100% need-based). Part-time jobs available.

APPLYING FOR FINANCIAL AID *Required financial aid forms:* FAFSA, institution's own form. *Financial aid deadline:* Continuous.

CONTACT Mrs. Awilda Matos, Director of Financial Aid, Universidad Adventista de las Antillas, Box 118, Mayagüez, PR 00681-0118, 787-834-9595 Ext. 2263. *Fax:* 787-834-9597. *E-mail:* amatos@uaa.edu.

UNIVERSIDAD DEL ESTE
Carolina, PR

CONTACT Clotilde Santiago, Director of Financial Aid, Universidad del Este, Apartado 2010, Carolina, PR 00928, 787-257-7373 Ext. 3300.

UNIVERSIDAD DEL TURABO
Gurabo, PR

CONTACT Ms. Ivette Vázquez Ríos, Directora, Oficina de Asistencia Economica, Universidad del Turabo, Apartado 3030, Gurabo, PR 00778-3030, 787-743-7979 Ext. 4352. *Fax:* 787-743-7979.

UNIVERSIDAD FLET
Miami, FL

CONTACT Financial Aid Office, Universidad FLET, 14540 Southwest 136th Street, Suite 108, Miami, FL 33186, 305-232-5880 or toll-free 888-376-3538.

UNIVERSIDAD METROPOLITANA
San Juan, PR

CONTACT Economic Assistant Director, Universidad Metropolitana, Call Box 21150, Rio Piedras, PR 00928-1150, 787-766-1717 Ext. 6586 or toll-free 800-747-8362 (out-of-state).

UNIVERSIDAD TEOLÓGICA DEL CARIBE
St. Just, PR

CONTACT Mr. Eric Ayala, Director of Financial Aid, Universidad Teológica del Caribe, PO Box 901, St. Just, PR 00978-0901, 787-761-0640.

UNIVERSITY AT ALBANY, STATE UNIVERSITY OF NEW YORK
Albany, NY

Tuition & fees (NY res): $6748	Average undergraduate aid package: $9649

ABOUT THE INSTITUTION State-supported, coed. 63 undergraduate majors. Federal methodology is used as a basis for awarding need-based institutional aid.

UNDERGRADUATE EXPENSES for 2009–10 *Tuition, state resident:* full-time $4970; part-time $207 per credit. *Tuition, nonresident:* full-time $12,870; part-time $536 per credit. *Required fees:* full-time $1778. Part-time tuition and fees vary according to course load. *College room and board:* $10,238; *Room only:* $6324. Room and board charges vary according to board plan and housing facility. *Payment plan:* Installment.

FRESHMAN FINANCIAL AID (Fall 2009, est.) 1,990 applied for aid; of those 67% were deemed to have need. 97% of freshmen with need received aid; of those 13% had need fully met. *Average percent of need met:* 70% (excluding resources awarded to replace EFC). *Average financial aid package:* $10,008 (excluding resources awarded to replace EFC). 8% of all full-time freshmen had no need and received non-need-based gift aid.

UNDERGRADUATE FINANCIAL AID (Fall 2009, est.) 9,556 applied for aid; of those 76% were deemed to have need. 98% of undergraduates with need received aid; of those 11% had need fully met. *Average percent of need met:* 68% (excluding resources awarded to replace EFC). *Average financial aid package:* $9649 (excluding resources awarded to replace EFC). 5% of all full-time undergraduates had no need and received non-need-based gift aid.

GIFT AID (NEED-BASED) *Total amount:* $39,051,240 (53% federal, 41% state, 4% institutional, 2% external sources). *Receiving aid:* Freshmen: 50% (1,152); all full-time undergraduates: 51% (6,195). *Average award:* Freshmen: $7045; Undergraduates: $6398. *Scholarships, grants, and awards:* Federal Pell, FSEOG, state, private, college/university gift aid from institutional funds.

GIFT AID (NON-NEED-BASED) *Total amount:* $3,810,650 (1% federal, 32% state, 56% institutional, 11% external sources). *Receiving aid:* Freshmen: 2% (41). Undergraduates: 3% (326). *Average award:* Freshmen: $4069. Undergraduates: $3528. *Scholarships, grants, and awards by category:* Academic interests/achievement: 1,159 awards ($3,776,763 total): general academic interests/achievements.

LOANS *Student loans:* $59,449,251 (44% need-based, 56% non-need-based). 71% of past graduating class borrowed through all loan programs. *Average indebtedness per student:* $22,092. *Average need-based loan:* Freshmen: $3691. Undergraduates: $4408. *Parent loans:* $13,082,058 (100% non-need-based). *Programs:* Federal Direct (Subsidized and Unsubsidized Stafford, PLUS), Perkins.

WORK-STUDY *Federal work-study:* Total amount: $1,619,197; 1,034 jobs averaging $1566. *State or other work-study/employment:* Total amount: $1,352,716 (61% need-based, 39% non-need-based). 221 part-time jobs averaging $6115.

ATHLETIC AWARDS Total amount: $3,977,874 (31% need-based, 69% non-need-based).

APPLYING FOR FINANCIAL AID *Required financial aid form:* FAFSA. *Financial aid deadline (priority):* 3/15. *Notification date:* Continuous beginning 3/20. Students must reply by 5/1 or within 2 weeks of notification.

CONTACT Diane Corbett, Director of Financial Aid, University at Albany, State University of New York, Student Financial Center, Campus Center G-26, 1400 Washington Avenue, Albany, NY 12222-0001, 518-442-3202 or toll-free 800-293-7869 (in-state). *Fax:* 518-442-5295. *E-mail:* sscweb@uamail.albany.edu.

UNIVERSITY AT BUFFALO, THE STATE UNIVERSITY OF NEW YORK
Buffalo, NY

Tuition & fees (NY res): $7013 **Average undergraduate aid package: $2360**

ABOUT THE INSTITUTION State-supported, coed. 74 undergraduate majors. Federal methodology is used as a basis for awarding need-based institutional aid.

UNDERGRADUATE EXPENSES for 2009–10 *Tuition, state resident:* full-time $4970; part-time $207 per credit hour. *Tuition, nonresident:* full-time $12,870; part-time $536 per credit hour. *Required fees:* full-time $2043; $90 per credit hour. Part-time tuition and fees vary according to course load. *College room and board:* $9648; *Room only:* $5748. Room and board charges vary according to board plan and housing facility. *Payment plan:* Installment.

FRESHMAN FINANCIAL AID (Fall 2008) 2,588 applied for aid; of those 65% were deemed to have need. 100% of freshmen with need received aid; of those 25% had need fully met. *Average percent of need met:* 64% (excluding resources awarded to replace EFC). *Average financial aid package:* $2386 (excluding resources awarded to replace EFC). 5% of all full-time freshmen had no need and received non-need-based gift aid.

UNDERGRADUATE FINANCIAL AID (Fall 2008) 12,378 applied for aid; of those 75% were deemed to have need. 98% of undergraduates with need received aid; of those 67% had need fully met. *Average percent of need met:* 66% (excluding resources awarded to replace EFC). *Average financial aid package:* $2360 (excluding resources awarded to replace EFC). 2% of all full-time undergraduates had no need and received non-need-based gift aid.

GIFT AID (NEED-BASED) *Total amount:* $42,895,674 (46% federal, 48% state, 2% institutional, 4% external sources). *Receiving aid:* Freshmen: 26% (886); all full-time undergraduates: 13% (2,360). *Average award:* Freshmen: $1014; Undergraduates: $1567. *Scholarships, grants, and awards:* Federal Pell, FSEOG, state, private, college/university gift aid from institutional funds, Federal Nursing.

GIFT AID (NON-NEED-BASED) *Total amount:* $11,136,847 (4% state, 96% institutional). *Receiving aid:* Freshmen: 3% (98). Undergraduates: 4% (629). *Average award:* Freshmen: $4171. Undergraduates: $5171. *Tuition waivers:* Full or partial for minority students.

LOANS *Student loans:* $70,611,993 (100% need-based). 56% of past graduating class borrowed through all loan programs. *Average indebtedness per student:* $39,191. *Average need-based loan:* Freshmen: $2715. Undergraduates: $3394. *Parent loans:* $6,167,398 (100% non-need-based). *Programs:* Federal Direct (Subsidized and Unsubsidized Stafford, PLUS), Perkins, Federal Nursing, college/university.

WORK-STUDY *Federal work-study:* Total amount: $1,513,318; 1,101 jobs averaging $1375. *State or other work-study/employment:* Total amount: $8,003,839 (100% non-need-based). 2,279 part-time jobs averaging $3512.

ATHLETIC AWARDS Total amount: $4,086,914 (100% non-need-based).

APPLYING FOR FINANCIAL AID *Required financial aid form:* FAFSA. *Financial aid deadline (priority):* 3/1. *Notification date:* Continuous beginning 2/1. Students must reply by 5/1.

CONTACT Joseph V. Alongi, Assistant Coordinator, Student Financial Services (SARFS), University at Buffalo, the State University of New York, 232 Capen Hall, Buffalo, NY 14260, 716-645-2450 or toll-free 888-UB-ADMIT. *Fax:* 716-645-7760. *E-mail:* src@buffalo.edu.

UNIVERSITY OF ADVANCING TECHNOLOGY
Tempe, AZ

Tuition & fees: $18,900 **Average undergraduate aid package: N/A**

ABOUT THE INSTITUTION Proprietary, coed, primarily men. 7 undergraduate majors. Federal methodology is used as a basis for awarding need-based institutional aid.

UNDERGRADUATE EXPENSES for 2010–11 *Comprehensive fee:* $29,934 includes full-time tuition ($18,800), mandatory fees ($100), and room and board ($11,034). *College room only:* $7224. Room and board charges vary according to board plan. *Payment plan:* Installment.

GIFT AID (NEED-BASED) *Total amount:* $1,754,315 (100% federal). *Scholarships, grants, and awards:* Federal Pell, FSEOG, state, private, college/university gift aid from institutional funds.

GIFT AID (NON-NEED-BASED) *Total amount:* $970,586 (1% state, 82% institutional, 17% external sources). *Scholarships, grants, and awards by category:* Academic interests/achievement: computer science, general academic interests/achievements. *Special characteristics:* children of faculty/staff, local/state students, veterans, veterans' children. *Tuition waivers:* Full or partial for employees or children of employees.

LOANS *Student loans:* $12,772,195 (32% need-based, 68% non-need-based). *Parent loans:* $3,317,575 (100% non-need-based). *Programs:* Federal Direct (Subsidized and Unsubsidized Stafford, PLUS).

WORK-STUDY *Federal work-study:* Total amount: $125,297; jobs available (averaging $3000).

APPLYING FOR FINANCIAL AID *Required financial aid form:* FAFSA. *Financial aid deadline:* Continuous.

CONTACT Financial Aid Administrator, University of Advancing Technology, 2625 West Baseline Road, Tempe, AZ 85283-1042, 602-383-8228 or toll-free 800-658-5744 (out-of-state). *Fax:* 602-383-8222. *E-mail:* fa@uat.edu.

THE UNIVERSITY OF AKRON
Akron, OH

Tuition & fees (OH res): $8752 **Average undergraduate aid package: $7641**

ABOUT THE INSTITUTION State-supported, coed. 127 undergraduate majors. Federal methodology is used as a basis for awarding need-based institutional aid.

UNDERGRADUATE EXPENSES for 2009–10 *Tuition, state resident:* full-time $7345; part-time $306 per credit hour. *Tuition, nonresident:* full-time $16,593; part-time $614 per credit hour. *Required fees:* full-time $1407; $49 per credit hour. Full-time tuition and fees vary according to course load, degree level, and location. Part-time tuition and fees vary according to course load, degree level, and location. *College room and board:* $8697; *Room only:* $5499. Room and board charges vary according to board plan and housing facility. *Payment plan:* Installment.

FRESHMAN FINANCIAL AID (Fall 2009, est.) 3,748 applied for aid; of those 82% were deemed to have need. 100% of freshmen with need received aid; of those 7% had need fully met. *Average percent of need met:* 52% (excluding resources awarded to replace EFC). *Average financial aid package:* $7593 (excluding resources awarded to replace EFC). 10% of all full-time freshmen had no need and received non-need-based gift aid.

UNDERGRADUATE FINANCIAL AID (Fall 2009, est.) 14,077 applied for aid; of those 81% were deemed to have need. 100% of undergraduates with need received aid; of those 8% had need fully met. *Average percent of need met:* 52% (excluding resources awarded to replace EFC). *Average financial aid package:* $7641 (excluding resources awarded to replace EFC). 8% of all full-time undergraduates had no need and received non-need-based gift aid.

GIFT AID (NEED-BASED) *Total amount:* $41,033,659 (88% federal, 12% state). *Receiving aid:* Freshmen: 43% (1,786); all full-time undergraduates: 39% (6,391). *Average award:* Freshmen: $5301; Undergraduates: $5227. *Scholarships, grants, and awards:* Federal Pell, FSEOG, state, college/university gift aid from institutional funds.

GIFT AID (NON-NEED-BASED) *Total amount:* $24,857,208 (7% state, 77% institutional, 16% external sources). *Receiving aid:* Freshmen: 44% (1,850). Undergraduates: 33% (5,328). *Average award:* Freshmen: $4098. Undergraduates: $3802. *Scholarships, grants, and awards by category:* Academic interests/achievement: 3,382 awards ($8,244,379 total): biological sciences, business, communication, computer science, education, engineering/technologies, English, foreign languages, general academic interests/achievements, health fields, home economics, humanities, international studies, mathematics, military science, physical sciences, premedicine, social sciences. Creative arts/performance: 176 awards ($237,125 total): applied art and design, art/fine arts, creative writing, dance, debating, general creative arts/performance, journalism/publications, music, performing arts, theater/drama. Special achievements/activities: 110 awards ($332,701 total): community service, general special achievements/activities, leadership, memberships. Special characteristics: 2,075 awards

($7,389,943 total): adult students, general special characteristics, handicapped students, international students, local/state students, members of minority groups, out-of-state students. *Tuition waivers:* Full or partial for employees or children of employees, senior citizens.

LOANS *Student loans:* $118,215,781 (42% need-based, 58% non-need-based). 65% of past graduating class borrowed through all loan programs. *Average indebtedness per student:* $19,000. *Average need-based loan:* Freshmen: $3445. Undergraduates: $3973. *Parent loans:* $13,034,051 (100% non-need-based). *Programs:* FFEL (Subsidized and Unsubsidized Stafford, PLUS), Perkins, Federal Nursing, college/university.

WORK-STUDY *Federal work-study:* Total amount: $1,225,238; 718 jobs averaging $1706. *State or other work-study/employment:* Total amount: $5,411,067 (100% non-need-based). 2,674 part-time jobs averaging $2023.

ATHLETIC AWARDS Total amount: $5,598,494 (100% non-need-based).

APPLYING FOR FINANCIAL AID *Required financial aid forms:* FAFSA, institution's own form. *Financial aid deadline (priority):* 2/1. *Notification date:* Continuous beginning 4/1. Students must reply within 2 weeks of notification.

CONTACT Ms. Michelle Ellis, Interim Director of Student Financial Aid, The University of Akron, 302 Buchtel Common, Akron, OH 44325, 330-972-5860 or toll-free 800-655-4884. *Fax:* 330-972-7139. *E-mail:* mellis@uakron.edu.

THE UNIVERSITY OF ALABAMA
Tuscaloosa, AL

Tuition & fees (AL res): $7000   **Average undergraduate aid package:** $8888

ABOUT THE INSTITUTION State-supported, coed. 71 undergraduate majors. Federal methodology is used as a basis for awarding need-based institutional aid.

UNDERGRADUATE EXPENSES for 2009–10 *Tuition, state resident:* full-time $7000. *Tuition, nonresident:* full-time $19,200. Full-time tuition and fees vary according to course load. Part-time tuition and fees vary according to course load. *College room and board:* $7796; *Room only:* $4400. Room and board charges vary according to board plan and housing facility. *Payment plans:* Installment, deferred payment.

FRESHMAN FINANCIAL AID (Fall 2008) 2,309 applied for aid; of those 74% were deemed to have need. 100% of freshmen with need received aid; of those 14% had need fully met. *Average percent of need met:* 55% (excluding resources awarded to replace EFC). *Average financial aid package:* $9094 (excluding resources awarded to replace EFC). 24% of all full-time freshmen had no need and received non-need-based gift aid.

UNDERGRADUATE FINANCIAL AID (Fall 2008) 9,296 applied for aid; of those 84% were deemed to have need. 100% of undergraduates with need received aid; of those 9% had need fully met. *Average percent of need met:* 53% (excluding resources awarded to replace EFC). *Average financial aid package:* $8888 (excluding resources awarded to replace EFC). 19% of all full-time undergraduates had no need and received non-need-based gift aid.

GIFT AID (NEED-BASED) *Total amount:* $31,971,006 (48% federal, 2% state, 35% institutional, 15% external sources). *Receiving aid:* Freshmen: 25% (1,244); all full-time undergraduates: 26% (5,283). *Average award:* Freshmen: $7063; Undergraduates: $6155. *Scholarships, grants, and awards:* Federal Pell, FSEOG, state, private, college/university gift aid from institutional funds, Federal Nursing.

GIFT AID (NON-NEED-BASED) *Total amount:* $26,881,689 (89% institutional, 11% external sources). *Receiving aid:* Freshmen: 26% (1,320). Undergraduates: 21% (4,185). *Average award:* Freshmen: $6119. Undergraduates: $5819. *Scholarships, grants, and awards by category: Academic interests/achievement:* 6,421 awards ($26,949,083 total): area/ethnic studies, biological sciences, business, communication, computer science, education, engineering/technologies, English, foreign languages, general academic interests/achievements, home economics, library science, mathematics, military science, physical sciences, premedicine, social sciences. *Creative arts/performance:* 415 awards ($836,144 total): art/fine arts, cinema/film/broadcasting, creative writing, dance, debating, journalism/publications, music, theater/drama. *Special achievements/activities:* 507 awards ($865,333 total): cheerleading/drum major, community service, general special achievements/activities, hobbies/interests, junior miss. *Special characteristics:* children of union members/company employees, general special characteristics, international students, out-of-state students, spouses of deceased or disabled public servants. *Tuition waivers:* Full or partial for employees or children of employees.

LOANS *Student loans:* $80,065,901 (71% need-based, 29% non-need-based). 52% of past graduating class borrowed through all loan programs. *Average*

indebtedness per student: $23,964. *Average need-based loan:* Freshmen: $3621. Undergraduates: $4362. *Parent loans:* $19,915,681 (39% need-based, 61% non-need-based). *Programs:* Federal Direct (Subsidized and Unsubsidized Stafford, PLUS), Perkins, college/university, private loans.

WORK-STUDY *Federal work-study:* Total amount: $1,248,432; 509 jobs averaging $1938.

ATHLETIC AWARDS Total amount: $8,680,896 (27% need-based, 73% non-need-based).

APPLYING FOR FINANCIAL AID *Required financial aid form:* FAFSA. *Financial aid deadline (priority):* 3/1. *Notification date:* 4/1. Students must reply within 3 weeks of notification.

CONTACT Helen Leathers, Associate Director of Financial Aid, The University of Alabama, Box 870162, Tuscaloosa, AL 35487-0162, 205-348-6756 or toll-free 800-933-BAMA. *Fax:* 205-348-2989. *E-mail:* helen.leathers@ua.edu.

THE UNIVERSITY OF ALABAMA AT BIRMINGHAM
Birmingham, AL

Tuition & fees (AL res): $5096   **Average undergraduate aid package:** $9334

ABOUT THE INSTITUTION State-supported, coed. 48 undergraduate majors. Federal methodology is used as a basis for awarding need-based institutional aid.

UNDERGRADUATE EXPENSES for 2009–10 *Tuition, state resident:* full-time $4224; part-time $176 per credit hour. *Tuition, nonresident:* full-time $10,560; part-time $440 per credit hour. *Required fees:* full-time $872. *College room and board:* $8142; *Room only:* $4492.

FRESHMAN FINANCIAL AID (Fall 2009, est.) 1,094 applied for aid; of those 74% were deemed to have need. 98% of freshmen with need received aid; of those 21% had need fully met. *Average percent of need met:* 43% (excluding resources awarded to replace EFC). *Average financial aid package:* $9201 (excluding resources awarded to replace EFC). 26% of all full-time freshmen had no need and received non-need-based gift aid.

UNDERGRADUATE FINANCIAL AID (Fall 2009, est.) 5,217 applied for aid; of those 79% were deemed to have need. 98% of undergraduates with need received aid; of those 15% had need fully met. *Average percent of need met:* 50% (excluding resources awarded to replace EFC). *Average financial aid package:* $9334 (excluding resources awarded to replace EFC). 16% of all full-time undergraduates had no need and received non-need-based gift aid.

GIFT AID (NEED-BASED) *Total amount:* $15,241,740 (97% federal, 1% state, 1% institutional, 1% external sources). *Receiving aid:* Freshmen: 30% (447); all full-time undergraduates: 33% (2,560). *Average award:* Freshmen: $4844; Undergraduates: $5063. *Scholarships, grants, and awards:* Federal Pell, FSEOG, state, private, college/university gift aid from institutional funds, United Negro College Fund.

GIFT AID (NON-NEED-BASED) *Total amount:* $14,430,455 (1% state, 91% institutional, 8% external sources). *Receiving aid:* Freshmen: 32% (478). Undergraduates: 16% (1,273). *Average award:* Freshmen: $6400. Undergraduates: $6449. *Scholarships, grants, and awards by category: Academic interests/achievement:* business, communication, computer science, engineering/technologies, general academic interests/achievements, health fields, mathematics. *Creative arts/performance:* art/fine arts, music, performing arts, theater/drama. *Special achievements/activities:* cheerleading/drum major, junior miss, leadership, memberships, religious involvement. *Special characteristics:* adult students, children and siblings of alumni, children of current students, children of educators, children of faculty/staff, children of public servants, children of union members/company employees, children of workers in trades, children with a deceased or disabled parent, ethnic background, first-generation college students, general special characteristics, handicapped students, married students, members of minority groups, out-of-state students, parents of current students, previous college experience, public servants, relatives of clergy, siblings of current students, spouses of current students, spouses of deceased or disabled public servants, twins, veterans, veterans' children.

LOANS *Student loans:* $40,896,596 (45% need-based, 55% non-need-based). 53% of past graduating class borrowed through all loan programs. *Average indebtedness per student:* $21,670. *Average need-based loan:* Freshmen: $3162. Undergraduates: $4394. *Parent loans:* $3,213,976 (100% non-need-based). *Programs:* Federal Direct (Subsidized and Unsubsidized Stafford, PLUS), Perkins, state, college/university.

WORK-STUDY *Federal work-study:* Total amount: $1,586,306; jobs available.
ATHLETIC AWARDS Total amount: $4,898,522 (100% non-need-based).
APPLYING FOR FINANCIAL AID *Required financial aid form:* FAFSA. *Financial aid deadline (priority):* 3/1. *Notification date:* Continuous beginning 4/1. Students must reply within 4 weeks of notification.
CONTACT Ms. Janet B. May, Student Financial Aid Director, The University of Alabama at Birmingham, Hill University Center 317, 1530 3rd Avenue South, Birmingham, AL 35294-1150, 205-934-8132 or toll-free 800-421-8743.

THE UNIVERSITY OF ALABAMA IN HUNTSVILLE
Huntsville, AL

Tuition & fees (AL res): $6510   **Average undergraduate aid package: $8226**

ABOUT THE INSTITUTION State-supported, coed. 30 undergraduate majors. Federal methodology is used as a basis for awarding need-based institutional aid.
UNDERGRADUATE EXPENSES for 2009–10 *Tuition, state resident:* full-time $6510; part-time $227.95 per credit hour. *Tuition, nonresident:* full-time $15,628; part-time $551.47 per credit hour. *Required fees:* $31 per credit hour. Full-time tuition and fees vary according to course load. Part-time tuition and fees vary according to course load. *College room and board:* $7208; *Room only:* $5084. Room and board charges vary according to board plan and housing facility. *Payment plan:* Installment.
FRESHMAN FINANCIAL AID (Fall 2009, est.) 707 applied for aid; of those 51% were deemed to have need. 100% of freshmen with need received aid; of those 17% had need fully met. *Average percent of need met:* 62% (excluding resources awarded to replace EFC). *Average financial aid package:* $8925 (excluding resources awarded to replace EFC). 33% of all full-time freshmen had no need and received non-need-based gift aid.
UNDERGRADUATE FINANCIAL AID (Fall 2009, est.) 3,710 applied for aid; of those 61% were deemed to have need. 100% of undergraduates with need received aid; of those 9% had need fully met. *Average percent of need met:* 57% (excluding resources awarded to replace EFC). *Average financial aid package:* $8226 (excluding resources awarded to replace EFC). 18% of all full-time undergraduates had no need and received non-need-based gift aid.
GIFT AID (NEED-BASED) *Total amount:* $10,328,479 (76% federal, 1% state, 18% institutional, 5% external sources). *Receiving aid:* Freshmen: 42% (326); all full-time undergraduates: 37% (1,708). *Average award:* Freshmen: $6236; Undergraduates: $5372. *Scholarships, grants, and awards:* Federal Pell, FSEOG, state, private, college/university gift aid from institutional funds, Federal Nursing.
GIFT AID (NON-NEED-BASED) *Total amount:* $4,265,595 (90% institutional, 10% external sources). *Receiving aid:* Freshmen: 6% (47). Undergraduates: 2% (84). *Average award:* Freshmen: $4470. Undergraduates: $4332. *Scholarships, grants, and awards by category: Academic interests/achievement:* 1,818 awards ($5,557,297 total): biological sciences, business, communication, computer science, education, engineering/technologies, English, foreign languages, general academic interests/achievements, health fields, humanities, mathematics, physical sciences, social sciences. *Creative arts/performance:* 67 awards ($67,750 total): art/fine arts, music. *Special achievements/activities:* 486 awards ($1,842,550 total): cheerleading/drum major, community service, general special achievements/activities, junior miss, leadership. *Special characteristics:* 49 awards ($105,349 total): general special characteristics, local/state students, members of minority groups. *Tuition waivers:* Full or partial for employees or children of employees.
LOANS *Student loans:* $24,723,635 (79% need-based, 21% non-need-based). 26% of past graduating class borrowed through all loan programs. *Average indebtedness per student:* $24,938. *Average need-based loan:* Freshmen: $5340. Undergraduates: $7286. *Parent loans:* $1,207,191 (46% need-based, 54% non-need-based). *Programs:* Federal Direct (Subsidized and Unsubsidized Stafford, PLUS).
WORK-STUDY *Federal work-study:* Total amount: $434,661; 90 jobs averaging $4705.
ATHLETIC AWARDS Total amount: $1,749,172 (18% need-based, 82% non-need-based).
APPLYING FOR FINANCIAL AID *Required financial aid form:* FAFSA. *Financial aid deadline:* 7/31 (priority: 4/1). *Notification date:* Continuous beginning 4/1. Students must reply within 2 weeks of notification.

CONTACT Mr. Andrew Weaver, Director of Student Financial Services, The University of Alabama in Huntsville, 301 Sparkman Drive, UC Room 212, Huntsville, AL 35899, 256-824-6241 or toll-free 800-UAH-CALL. *Fax:* 256-824-6212. *E-mail:* finaid@uah.edu.

UNIVERSITY OF ALASKA ANCHORAGE
Anchorage, AK

Tuition & fees (AK res): $4580   **Average undergraduate aid package: $10,055**

ABOUT THE INSTITUTION State-supported, coed. 67 undergraduate majors. Federal methodology is used as a basis for awarding need-based institutional aid.
UNDERGRADUATE EXPENSES for 2009–10 *Tuition, state resident:* full-time $4020; part-time $134 per term. *Tuition, nonresident:* full-time $13,440; part-time $448 per term. *Required fees:* full-time $560. *College room and board:* $7962.
FRESHMAN FINANCIAL AID (Fall 2009, est.) 1,051 applied for aid; of those 65% were deemed to have need. 97% of freshmen with need received aid; of those 18% had need fully met. *Average percent of need met:* 87% (excluding resources awarded to replace EFC). *Average financial aid package:* $9427 (excluding resources awarded to replace EFC). 5% of all full-time freshmen had no need and received non-need-based gift aid.
UNDERGRADUATE FINANCIAL AID (Fall 2009, est.) 4,356 applied for aid; of those 73% were deemed to have need. 95% of undergraduates with need received aid; of those 17% had need fully met. *Average percent of need met:* 73% (excluding resources awarded to replace EFC). *Average financial aid package:* $10,055 (excluding resources awarded to replace EFC). 3% of all full-time undergraduates had no need and received non-need-based gift aid.
GIFT AID (NEED-BASED) *Total amount:* $16,459,362 (74% federal, 3% state, 11% institutional, 12% external sources). *Receiving aid:* Freshmen: 36% (503); all full-time undergraduates: 31% (2,144). *Average award:* Freshmen: $4578; Undergraduates: $4088. *Scholarships, grants, and awards:* Federal Pell, FSEOG, state, private, college/university gift aid from institutional funds.
GIFT AID (NON-NEED-BASED) *Total amount:* $5,035,920 (45% institutional, 55% external sources). *Receiving aid:* Freshmen: 16% (228). Undergraduates: 12% (795). *Average award:* Freshmen: $3022. Undergraduates: $2932. *Scholarships, grants, and awards by category: Academic interests/achievement:* biological sciences, business, communication, computer science, education, engineering/technologies, English, general academic interests/achievements, health fields, humanities, mathematics, social sciences. *Creative arts/performance:* debating. *Special achievements/activities:* general special achievements/activities.
LOANS *Student loans:* $35,354,581 (66% need-based, 34% non-need-based). 49% of past graduating class borrowed through all loan programs. *Average indebtedness per student:* $22,043. *Average need-based loan:* Freshmen: $3137. Undergraduates: $4042. *Parent loans:* $415,937 (70% need-based, 30% non-need-based). *Programs:* Federal Direct (Subsidized and Unsubsidized Stafford, PLUS), state.
WORK-STUDY *Federal work-study:* Total amount: $409,425; jobs available.
ATHLETIC AWARDS Total amount: $1,777,268 (14% need-based, 86% non-need-based).
APPLYING FOR FINANCIAL AID *Required financial aid form:* FAFSA. *Financial aid deadline (priority):* 4/1. *Notification date:* Continuous beginning 2/15. Students must reply within 4 weeks of notification.
CONTACT Theodore E. Malone, Director of Student Financial Assistance, University of Alaska Anchorage, PO Box 141608, Anchorage, AK 99514-1608, 907-786-1520. *Fax:* 907-786-6122.

UNIVERSITY OF ALASKA FAIRBANKS
Fairbanks, AK

Tuition & fees (AK res): $5668   **Average undergraduate aid package: $10,556**

ABOUT THE INSTITUTION State-supported, coed. 75 undergraduate majors. Federal methodology is used as a basis for awarding need-based institutional aid.
UNDERGRADUATE EXPENSES for 2010–11 *Tuition, state resident:* full-time $4755; part-time $147 per credit hour. *Tuition, nonresident:* full-time $15,345; part-time $500 per credit hour. *Required fees:* full-time $913; $16 per credit hour or $203 per term. Full-time tuition and fees vary according to course level,

course load, location, and reciprocity agreements. Part-time tuition and fees vary according to course level, course load, location, and reciprocity agreements. *College room and board:* $6800; *Room only:* $3610. Room and board charges vary according to board plan and housing facility. *Payment plan:* Installment. **FRESHMAN FINANCIAL AID (Fall 2009, est.)** 577 applied for aid; of those 61% were deemed to have need. 96% of freshmen with need received aid; of those 42% had need fully met. *Average percent of need met:* 56% (excluding resources awarded to replace EFC). *Average financial aid package:* $9655 (excluding resources awarded to replace EFC). 29% of all full-time freshmen had no need and received non-need-based gift aid.
UNDERGRADUATE FINANCIAL AID (Fall 2009, est.) 2,223 applied for aid; of those 65% were deemed to have need. 97% of undergraduates with need received aid; of those 41% had need fully met. *Average percent of need met:* 56% (excluding resources awarded to replace EFC). *Average financial aid package:* $10,556 (excluding resources awarded to replace EFC). 28% of all full-time undergraduates had no need and received non-need-based gift aid.
GIFT AID (NEED-BASED) *Total amount:* $5,563,373 (67% federal, 8% state, 20% institutional, 5% external sources). *Receiving aid:* Freshmen: 31% (238); all full-time undergraduates: 31% (1,004). *Average award:* Freshmen: $5574; Undergraduates: $5339. *Scholarships, grants, and awards:* Federal Pell, FSEOG, state, private, college/university gift aid from institutional funds.
GIFT AID (NON-NEED-BASED) *Total amount:* $2,042,770 (84% institutional, 16% external sources). *Receiving aid:* Freshmen: 4% (34). Undergraduates: 3% (109). *Average award:* Freshmen: $7834. Undergraduates: $7683. *Scholarships, grants, and awards by category: Academic interests/achievement:* biological sciences, general academic interests/achievements, military science, physical sciences. *Creative arts/performance:* art/fine arts, creative writing, music, theater/drama. *Special achievements/activities:* community service, general special achievements/activities, leadership. *Special characteristics:* local/state students, members of minority groups. *Tuition waivers:* Full or partial for children of alumni, employees or children of employees, senior citizens.
LOANS *Student loans:* $18,318,250 (74% need-based, 26% non-need-based). 54% of past graduating class borrowed through all loan programs. *Average indebtedness per student:* $29,485. *Average need-based loan:* Freshmen: $8377. Undergraduates: $9707. *Parent loans:* $281,311 (32% need-based, 68% non-need-based). *Programs:* FFEL (Subsidized and Unsubsidized Stafford, PLUS), state.
WORK-STUDY *Federal work-study:* Total amount: $126,214; 39 jobs averaging $3236.
ATHLETIC AWARDS Total amount: $943,834 (18% need-based, 82% non-need-based).
APPLYING FOR FINANCIAL AID *Required financial aid form:* FAFSA. *Financial aid deadline:* 7/1 (priority: 2/15). *Notification date:* Continuous beginning 3/1. Students must reply within 2 weeks of notification.
CONTACT Deanna Dierenger, Director of Financial Aid, University of Alaska Fairbanks, PO Box 756360, Fairbanks, AK 99775-6360, 907-474-7256 or toll-free 800-478-1823. *Fax:* 907-474-7065. *E-mail:* financialaid@uaf.edu.

UNIVERSITY OF ALASKA SOUTHEAST
Juneau, AK

Tuition & fees: N/R	Average undergraduate aid package: $5458

ABOUT THE INSTITUTION State-supported, coed. 17 undergraduate majors. Federal methodology is used as a basis for awarding need-based institutional aid.
FRESHMAN FINANCIAL AID (Fall 2008) 155 applied for aid; of those 46% were deemed to have need. 96% of freshmen with need received aid; of those 10% had need fully met. *Average percent of need met:* 46% (excluding resources awarded to replace EFC). *Average financial aid package:* $5741 (excluding resources awarded to replace EFC). 17% of all full-time freshmen had no need and received non-need-based gift aid.
UNDERGRADUATE FINANCIAL AID (Fall 2008) 506 applied for aid; of those 57% were deemed to have need. 96% of undergraduates with need received aid; of those 8% had need fully met. *Average percent of need met:* 45% (excluding resources awarded to replace EFC). *Average financial aid package:* $5458 (excluding resources awarded to replace EFC). 8% of all full-time undergraduates had no need and received non-need-based gift aid.
GIFT AID (NEED-BASED) *Total amount:* $990,250 (85% federal, 10% state, 5% institutional). *Receiving aid:* Freshmen: 33% (53); all full-time undergraduates:

31% (177). *Average award:* Freshmen: $1177; Undergraduates: $1290. *Scholarships, grants, and awards:* Federal Pell, FSEOG, state, private, college/university gift aid from institutional funds.
GIFT AID (NON-NEED-BASED) *Total amount:* $1,058,830 (23% federal, 32% institutional, 45% external sources). *Receiving aid:* Freshmen: 23% (37). Undergraduates: 21% (124). *Average award:* Freshmen: $1326. Undergraduates: $1196.
LOANS *Student loans:* $4,099,220 (32% need-based, 68% non-need-based). *Average need-based loan:* Freshmen: $1682. Undergraduates: $2026. *Parent loans:* $328,570 (100% non-need-based). *Programs:* Federal Direct (Subsidized and Unsubsidized Stafford, PLUS), FFEL (Subsidized and Unsubsidized Stafford, PLUS), state.
WORK-STUDY *Federal work-study:* Total amount: $68,740; 35 jobs available.
APPLYING FOR FINANCIAL AID *Required financial aid form:* FAFSA. *Financial aid deadline (priority):* 6/1. *Notification date:* Continuous beginning 2/15. Students must reply within 3 weeks of notification.
CONTACT Ms. Barbara Carlson Burnett, Financial Aid Director, University of Alaska Southeast, 11120 Glacier Highway, Juneau, AK 99801-8680, 907-796-6296 or toll-free 877-796-4827. *Fax:* 907-796-6250. *E-mail:* barbara.burnett@uas.alaska.edu.

THE UNIVERSITY OF ARIZONA
Tucson, AZ

Tuition & fees: N/R	Average undergraduate aid package: $10,021

ABOUT THE INSTITUTION State-supported, coed. 105 undergraduate majors. Federal methodology is used as a basis for awarding need-based institutional aid.
FRESHMAN FINANCIAL AID (Fall 2008) 4,048 applied for aid; of those 61% were deemed to have need. 97% of freshmen with need received aid; of those 13% had need fully met. *Average percent of need met:* 65% (excluding resources awarded to replace EFC). *Average financial aid package:* $9152 (excluding resources awarded to replace EFC). 35% of all full-time freshmen had no need and received non-need-based gift aid.
UNDERGRADUATE FINANCIAL AID (Fall 2008) 14,614 applied for aid; of those 73% were deemed to have need. 96% of undergraduates with need received aid; of those 11% had need fully met. *Average percent of need met:* 64% (excluding resources awarded to replace EFC). *Average financial aid package:* $10,021 (excluding resources awarded to replace EFC). 25% of all full-time undergraduates had no need and received non-need-based gift aid.
GIFT AID (NEED-BASED) *Total amount:* $81,247,741 (34% federal, 49% institutional, 17% external sources). *Receiving aid:* Freshmen: 36% (2,268); all full-time undergraduates: 36% (9,437). *Average award:* Freshmen: $7794; Undergraduates: $7849. *Scholarships, grants, and awards:* Federal Pell, FSEOG, state, private, college/university gift aid from institutional funds, Federal Nursing.
GIFT AID (NON-NEED-BASED) *Total amount:* $51,308,940 (74% institutional, 26% external sources). *Receiving aid:* Freshmen: 5% (293). Undergraduates: 3% (827). *Average award:* Freshmen: $4586. Undergraduates: $5064. *Scholarships, grants, and awards by category: Academic interests/achievement:* agriculture, architecture, biological sciences, business, education, engineering/technologies, general academic interests/achievements, humanities, military science, physical sciences, religion/biblical studies. *Creative arts/performance:* art/fine arts, dance, music, performing arts, theater/drama. *Special characteristics:* children of faculty/staff, ethnic background, international students. *Tuition waivers:* Full or partial for employees or children of employees.
LOANS *Student loans:* $76,613,000 (79% need-based, 21% non-need-based). 43% of past graduating class borrowed through all loan programs. *Average indebtedness per student:* $18,712. *Average need-based loan:* Freshmen: $3376. Undergraduates: $4325. *Parent loans:* $22,237,381 (58% need-based, 42% non-need-based). *Programs:* FFEL (Subsidized and Unsubsidized Stafford, PLUS), Perkins, Federal Nursing, college/university.
WORK-STUDY *Federal work-study:* Total amount: $2,076,445; jobs available. *State or other work-study/employment:* Total amount: $16,178,757 (46% need-based, 54% non-need-based). Part-time jobs available.
ATHLETIC AWARDS Total amount: $5,466,580 (31% need-based, 69% non-need-based).
APPLYING FOR FINANCIAL AID *Required financial aid form:* FAFSA. *Financial aid deadline:* Continuous. *Notification date:* Continuous.

CONTACT John Nametz, Director, Student Financial Aid, The University of Arizona, PO Box 210066, Tucson, AZ 85721-0066, 520-621-5200. *Fax:* 520-621-9473. *E-mail:* askaid@arizona.edu.

UNIVERSITY OF ARKANSAS
Fayetteville, AR

Tuition & fees (AR res): $6400	Average undergraduate aid package: $9030

ABOUT THE INSTITUTION State-supported, coed. 69 undergraduate majors. Federal methodology is used as a basis for awarding need-based institutional aid.

UNDERGRADUATE EXPENSES for 2009–10 *Tuition, state resident:* full-time $5010; part-time $167 per credit hour. *Tuition, nonresident:* full-time $13,888; part-time $463 per credit hour. *Required fees:* full-time $1390. Full-time tuition and fees vary according to course load and program. Part-time tuition and fees vary according to course load and program. *College room and board:* $7422; *Room only:* $4692. Room and board charges vary according to board plan and housing facility. *Payment plan:* Installment.

FRESHMAN FINANCIAL AID (Fall 2009, est.) 1,851 applied for aid; of those 65% were deemed to have need. 98% of freshmen with need received aid; of those 25% had need fully met. *Average percent of need met:* 68% (excluding resources awarded to replace EFC). *Average financial aid package:* $9074 (excluding resources awarded to replace EFC). 19% of all full-time freshmen had no need and received non-need-based gift aid.

UNDERGRADUATE FINANCIAL AID (Fall 2009, est.) 7,428 applied for aid; of those 74% were deemed to have need. 97% of undergraduates with need received aid; of those 19% had need fully met. *Average percent of need met:* 64% (excluding resources awarded to replace EFC). *Average financial aid package:* $9030 (excluding resources awarded to replace EFC). 17% of all full-time undergraduates had no need and received non-need-based gift aid.

GIFT AID (NEED-BASED) *Total amount:* $26,370,337 (57% federal, 17% state, 20% institutional, 6% external sources). *Receiving aid:* Freshmen: 33% (968); all full-time undergraduates: 30% (4,115). *Average award:* Freshmen: $6952; Undergraduates: $6343. *Scholarships, grants, and awards:* Federal Pell, FSEOG, state, private, college/university gift aid from institutional funds.

GIFT AID (NON-NEED-BASED) *Total amount:* $19,957,421 (23% state, 69% institutional, 8% external sources). *Receiving aid:* Freshmen: 6% (163). Undergraduates: 3% (424). *Average award:* Freshmen: $4642. Undergraduates: $5315. *Scholarships, grants, and awards by category: Academic interests/achievement:* general academic interests/achievements. *Creative arts/performance:* music, theater/drama. *Special achievements/activities:* community service, general special achievements/activities, leadership. *Special characteristics:* children and siblings of alumni, children of faculty/staff, ethnic background, international students, out-of-state students, previous college experience. *Tuition waivers:* Full or partial for employees or children of employees, senior citizens.

LOANS *Student loans:* $49,582,790 (67% need-based, 33% non-need-based). 43% of past graduating class borrowed through all loan programs. *Average indebtedness per student:* $20,171. *Average need-based loan:* Freshmen: $3284. Undergraduates: $4306. *Parent loans:* $6,311,219 (18% need-based, 82% non-need-based). *Programs:* FFEL (Subsidized and Unsubsidized Stafford, PLUS), Perkins, state, college/university, alternative loans.

WORK-STUDY *Federal work-study:* Total amount: $3,242,948; jobs available.

ATHLETIC AWARDS Total amount: $4,210,991 (32% need-based, 68% non-need-based).

APPLYING FOR FINANCIAL AID *Required financial aid form:* FAFSA. *Financial aid deadline (priority):* 3/15. *Notification date:* Continuous beginning 4/1. Students must reply within 4 weeks of notification.

CONTACT Kattie Wing, Director of Financial Aid, University of Arkansas, 114 Silas H. Hunt Hall, Fayetteville, AR 72701-1201, 479-575-3806 or toll-free 800-377-5346 (in-state), 800-377-8632 (out-of-state). *E-mail:* kattie@uark.edu.

UNIVERSITY OF ARKANSAS AT FORT SMITH
Fort Smith, AR

CONTACT Tammy Malone, Interim Financial Aid Director, University of Arkansas at Fort Smith, 5210 Grand Avenue, Fort Smith, AR 72913, 479-788-7099 or toll-free 888-512-5466. *Fax:* 479-788-7095. *E-mail:* tmalone@uafortsmith.edu.

UNIVERSITY OF ARKANSAS AT LITTLE ROCK
Little Rock, AR

CONTACT Financial Aid Office, University of Arkansas at Little Rock, 2801 South University Avenue, Little Rock, AR 72204-1099, 501-569-3127 or toll-free 800-482-8892 (in-state).

UNIVERSITY OF ARKANSAS AT MONTICELLO
Monticello, AR

CONTACT Susan Brewer, Director of Financial Aid, University of Arkansas at Monticello, PO Box 3470, Monticello, AR 71656, 870-460-1050 or toll-free 800-844-1826 (in-state). *Fax:* 870-460-1450. *E-mail:* brewers@uamont.edu.

UNIVERSITY OF ARKANSAS AT PINE BLUFF
Pine Bluff, AR

CONTACT Mrs. Carolyn Iverson, Director of Financial Aid, University of Arkansas at Pine Bluff, 1200 North University Drive, PO Box 4985, Pine Bluff, AR 71601, 870-575-8303 or toll-free 800-264-6585. *Fax:* 870-575-4622. *E-mail:* iverson_c@uapb.edu.

UNIVERSITY OF ARKANSAS FOR MEDICAL SCIENCES
Little Rock, AR

CONTACT Mr. Paul Carter, Director of Financial Aid, University of Arkansas for Medical Sciences, 4301 West Markham Street, MS 601, Little Rock, AR 72205, 501-686-5451. *Fax:* 501-686-5661. *E-mail:* pvcarter@uams.edu.

UNIVERSITY OF ATLANTA
Atlanta, GA

CONTACT Financial Aid Office, University of Atlanta, 6685 Peachtree Industrial Boulevard, Atlanta, GA 30360, 770-368-8877 or toll-free 800-533-3378.

UNIVERSITY OF BALTIMORE
Baltimore, MD

CONTACT Financial Aid Office, University of Baltimore, 1420 North Charles Street, CH 123, Baltimore, MD 21201-5779, 410-837-4763 or toll-free 877-APPLYUB. *Fax:* 410-837-5493. *E-mail:* financial-aid@ubalt.edu.

UNIVERSITY OF BRIDGEPORT
Bridgeport, CT

Tuition & fees: $25,465	Average undergraduate aid package: $22,618

ABOUT THE INSTITUTION Independent, coed. 33 undergraduate majors. Federal methodology is used as a basis for awarding need-based institutional aid.

UNDERGRADUATE EXPENSES for 2009–10 *Comprehensive fee:* $36,545 includes full-time tuition ($23,400), mandatory fees ($2065), and room and board ($11,080). Full-time tuition and fees vary according to course load and program. Room and board charges vary according to board plan and student level. *Part-time tuition:* $780 per credit hour. *Part-time fees:* $80 per term. Part-time tuition and fees vary according to course load and program. *Payment plans:* Installment, deferred payment.

FRESHMAN FINANCIAL AID (Fall 2009, est.) 405 applied for aid; of those 96% were deemed to have need. 100% of freshmen with need received aid; of those 11% had need fully met. *Average percent of need met:* 65% (excluding resources awarded to replace EFC). *Average financial aid package:* $25,307 (excluding resources awarded to replace EFC). 5% of all full-time freshmen had no need and received non-need-based gift aid.

UNDERGRADUATE FINANCIAL AID (Fall 2009, est.) 1,444 applied for aid; of those 82% were deemed to have need. 100% of undergraduates with need received aid; of those 12% had need fully met. *Average percent of need met:* 56% (excluding resources awarded to replace EFC). *Average financial aid package:* $22,618 (excluding resources awarded to replace EFC). 21% of all full-time undergraduates had no need and received non-need-based gift aid.

GIFT AID (NEED-BASED) *Total amount:* $21,060,515 (21% federal, 9% state, 69% institutional, 1% external sources). *Receiving aid:* Freshmen: 84% (367); all full-time undergraduates: 72% (1,077). *Average award:* Freshmen: $8261; Undergraduates: $8420. *Scholarships, grants, and awards:* Federal Pell, FSEOG, state, private, college/university gift aid from institutional funds.

GIFT AID (NON-NEED-BASED) *Receiving aid:* Freshmen: 87% (379). Undergraduates: 74% (1,113). *Average award:* Freshmen: $17,546. Undergraduates: $15,194. *Scholarships, grants, and awards by category: Academic interests/achievement:* 1,134 awards ($8,462,875 total): general academic interests/achievements. *Creative arts/performance:* 25 awards ($141,500 total): applied art and design, music. *Special characteristics:* children of faculty/staff, international students, local/state students, previous college experience. *Tuition waivers:* Full or partial for employees or children of employees, senior citizens.

LOANS *Student loans:* $13,525,272 (49% need-based, 51% non-need-based). *Average need-based loan:* Freshmen: $5294. Undergraduates: $5539. *Parent loans:* $3,299,712 (100% non-need-based). *Programs:* Federal Direct (Subsidized and Unsubsidized Stafford, PLUS), FFEL (Subsidized and Unsubsidized Stafford, PLUS), Perkins.

WORK-STUDY *Federal work-study:* Total amount: $399,985; 400 jobs averaging $2000. *State or other work-study/employment:* Total amount: $1,230,201 (100% need-based). Part-time jobs available.

ATHLETIC AWARDS Total amount: $2,632,603 (100% need-based).

APPLYING FOR FINANCIAL AID *Required financial aid form:* FAFSA. *Financial aid deadline (priority):* 3/1. *Notification date:* Continuous. Students must reply by 3/1 or within 4 weeks of notification.

CONTACT Kathleen E. Gailor, Director of Financial Aid, University of Bridgeport, 126 Park Avenue, Bridgeport, CT 06604, 203-576-4568 or toll-free 800-EXCEL-UB (in-state), 800-243-9496 (out-of-state). *Fax:* 203-576-4570. *E-mail:* finaid@bridgeport.edu.

UNIVERSITY OF CALIFORNIA, BERKELEY
Berkeley, CA

Tuition & fees (CA res): $9817	Average undergraduate aid package: $18,322

ABOUT THE INSTITUTION State-supported, coed. 93 undergraduate majors. Both federal and institutional methodology are used as a basis for awarding need-based institutional aid.

UNDERGRADUATE EXPENSES for 2009–10 *Tuition, state resident:* full-time $6888. *Tuition, nonresident:* full-time $29,557. *Required fees:* full-time $2929. Full-time tuition and fees vary according to course load and program. Part-time tuition and fees vary according to course load and program. *College room and board:* $15,308. Room and board charges vary according to board plan and housing facility. *Payment plan:* Installment.

FRESHMAN FINANCIAL AID (Fall 2009, est.) 3,424 applied for aid; of those 64% were deemed to have need. 97% of freshmen with need received aid; of those 51% had need fully met. *Average percent of need met:* 90% (excluding resources awarded to replace EFC). *Average financial aid package:* $20,400 (excluding resources awarded to replace EFC). 7% of all full-time freshmen had no need and received non-need-based gift aid.

UNDERGRADUATE FINANCIAL AID (Fall 2009, est.) 15,965 applied for aid; of those 81% were deemed to have need. 97% of undergraduates with need received aid; of those 49% had need fully met. *Average percent of need met:* 87% (excluding resources awarded to replace EFC). *Average financial aid package:* $18,322 (excluding resources awarded to replace EFC). 5% of all full-time undergraduates had no need and received non-need-based gift aid.

GIFT AID (NEED-BASED) *Total amount:* $169,756,049 (25% federal, 28% state, 43% institutional, 4% external sources). *Receiving aid:* Freshmen: 46% (1,978); all full-time undergraduates: 48% (12,000). *Average award:* Freshmen: $15,713; Undergraduates: $13,976. *Scholarships, grants, and awards:* Federal Pell, FSEOG, state, private, college/university gift aid from institutional funds.

GIFT AID (NON-NEED-BASED) *Total amount:* $13,923,920 (5% federal, 2% state, 59% institutional, 34% external sources). *Receiving aid:* Freshmen: 1%

(64). Undergraduates: 1% (169). *Average award:* Freshmen: $5210. Undergraduates: $5984. *Scholarships, grants, and awards by category: Academic interests/achievement:* general academic interests/achievements.

LOANS *Student loans:* $56,258,853 (71% need-based, 29% non-need-based). 41% of past graduating class borrowed through all loan programs. *Average indebtedness per student:* $14,493. *Average need-based loan:* Freshmen: $4204. Undergraduates: $5215. *Parent loans:* $26,561,115 (13% need-based, 87% non-need-based). *Programs:* Federal Direct (Subsidized and Unsubsidized Stafford, PLUS), Perkins.

WORK-STUDY *Federal work-study:* Total amount: $5,016,893; jobs available. *State or other work-study/employment:* Total amount: $14,992,902 (100% need-based). Part-time jobs available.

ATHLETIC AWARDS Total amount: $9,654,001 (30% need-based, 70% non-need-based).

APPLYING FOR FINANCIAL AID *Required financial aid forms:* FAFSA, state aid form, Cal Grant forms. *Financial aid deadline:* 3/2. *Notification date:* 4/15.

CONTACT Kathy Bradley, Administrative Specialist, University of California, Berkeley, 225 Sproul Hall, Berkeley, CA 94720-1960, 510-642-0649. *Fax:* 510-643-5526. *E-mail:* kbradley@berkeley.edu.

UNIVERSITY OF CALIFORNIA, DAVIS
Davis, CA

Tuition & fees (CA res): $9364	Average undergraduate aid package: $16,066

ABOUT THE INSTITUTION State-supported, coed. 83 undergraduate majors. Federal methodology is used as a basis for awarding need-based institutional aid.

UNDERGRADUATE EXPENSES for 2009–10 *Tuition, state resident:* full-time $0. *Tuition, nonresident:* full-time $22,021. *Required fees:* full-time $9364. *College room and board:* $12,361. Room and board charges vary according to board plan. *Payment plan:* Deferred payment.

FRESHMAN FINANCIAL AID (Fall 2009, est.) 3,712 applied for aid; of those 74% were deemed to have need. 97% of freshmen with need received aid; of those 15% had need fully met. *Average percent of need met:* 82% (excluding resources awarded to replace EFC). *Average financial aid package:* $17,676 (excluding resources awarded to replace EFC). 4% of all full-time freshmen had no need and received non-need-based gift aid.

UNDERGRADUATE FINANCIAL AID (Fall 2009, est.) 16,525 applied for aid; of those 84% were deemed to have need. 98% of undergraduates with need received aid; of those 22% had need fully met. *Average percent of need met:* 82% (excluding resources awarded to replace EFC). *Average financial aid package:* $16,066 (excluding resources awarded to replace EFC). 4% of all full-time undergraduates had no need and received non-need-based gift aid.

GIFT AID (NEED-BASED) *Total amount:* $168,421,432 (27% federal, 36% state, 35% institutional, 2% external sources). *Receiving aid:* Freshmen: 58% (2,535); all full-time undergraduates: 54% (12,889). *Average award:* Freshmen: $14,485; Undergraduates: $12,800. *Scholarships, grants, and awards:* Federal Pell, FSEOG, state, private, college/university gift aid from institutional funds, Academic Competitiveness Grants, National SMART Grants.

GIFT AID (NON-NEED-BASED) *Total amount:* $8,044,860 (2% federal, 68% institutional, 30% external sources). *Receiving aid:* Freshmen: 1% (30). Undergraduates: 102. *Average award:* Freshmen: $5496. Undergraduates: $5879. *Scholarships, grants, and awards by category: Academic interests/achievement:* agriculture, area/ethnic studies, biological sciences, business, communication, computer science, engineering/technologies, English, foreign languages, general academic interests/achievements, health fields, home economics, humanities, international studies, mathematics, premedicine, religion/biblical studies, social sciences.

LOANS *Student loans:* $60,200,189 (81% need-based, 19% non-need-based). 51% of past graduating class borrowed through all loan programs. *Average indebtedness per student:* $16,222. *Average need-based loan:* Freshmen: $5110. Undergraduates: $5140. *Parent loans:* $17,874,025 (9% need-based, 91% non-need-based). *Programs:* Federal Direct (Subsidized and Unsubsidized Stafford, PLUS), Perkins, college/university.

WORK-STUDY *Federal work-study:* Total amount: $3,374,824; jobs available.

ATHLETIC AWARDS Total amount: $3,913,326 (2% need-based, 98% non-need-based).

APPLYING FOR FINANCIAL AID *Required financial aid forms:* FAFSA, state aid form. *Financial aid deadline (priority):* 3/2. *Notification date:* Continuous beginning 3/23.

CONTACT Katy Maloney, Interim Director of Financial Aid, University of California, Davis, One Shields Avenue, 2128 Dutton Hall, Davis, CA 95616, 530-752-2396. *Fax:* 530-752-7339. *E-mail:* kamaloney@ucdavis.edu.

UNIVERSITY OF CALIFORNIA, IRVINE
Irvine, CA

Tuition & fees (CA res): $11,913   Average undergraduate aid package: $16,286

ABOUT THE INSTITUTION State-supported, coed. 75 undergraduate majors. Federal methodology is used as a basis for awarding need-based institutional aid.

UNDERGRADUATE EXPENSES for 2010–11 *Tuition, state resident:* full-time $0. *Tuition, nonresident:* full-time $22,879. *Required fees:* full-time $11,913. *College room and board:* $10,655. Room and board charges vary according to board plan and housing facility. *Payment plan:* Installment.

FRESHMAN FINANCIAL AID (Fall 2009, est.) 3,350 applied for aid; of those 69% were deemed to have need. 95% of freshmen with need received aid; of those 38% had need fully met. *Average percent of need met:* 84% (excluding resources awarded to replace EFC). *Average financial aid package:* $16,321 (excluding resources awarded to replace EFC). 2% of all full-time freshmen had no need and received non-need-based gift aid.

UNDERGRADUATE FINANCIAL AID (Fall 2009, est.) 14,850 applied for aid; of those 81% were deemed to have need. 97% of undergraduates with need received aid; of those 39% had need fully met. *Average percent of need met:* 84% (excluding resources awarded to replace EFC). *Average financial aid package:* $16,286 (excluding resources awarded to replace EFC). 3% of all full-time undergraduates had no need and received non-need-based gift aid.

GIFT AID (NEED-BASED) *Total amount:* $139,587,016 (26% federal, 36% state, 36% institutional, 2% external sources). *Receiving aid:* Freshmen: 50% (2,027); all full-time undergraduates: 49% (10,625). *Average award:* Freshmen: $12,406; Undergraduates: $13,035. *Scholarships, grants, and awards:* Federal Pell, FSEOG, state, private, college/university gift aid from institutional funds.

GIFT AID (NON-NEED-BASED) *Total amount:* $6,973,345 (2% federal, 83% institutional, 15% external sources). *Receiving aid:* Freshmen: 1% (23). Undergraduates: 105. *Average award:* Freshmen: $9275. Undergraduates: $8121. *Scholarships, grants, and awards by category: Academic interests/achievement:* 676 awards ($2,786,608 total): biological sciences, business, computer science, education, engineering/technologies, foreign languages, general academic interests/achievements, health fields, humanities, international studies, physical sciences, premedicine, social sciences. *Creative arts/performance:* 50 awards ($148,236 total): art/fine arts, cinema/film/broadcasting, dance, general creative arts/performance, music, theater/drama.

LOANS *Student loans:* $56,630,081 (71% need-based, 29% non-need-based). 48% of past graduating class borrowed through all loan programs. *Average indebtedness per student:* $15,529. *Average need-based loan:* Freshmen: $5941. Undergraduates: $6093. *Parent loans:* $33,691,847 (16% need-based, 84% non-need-based). *Programs:* Federal Direct (Subsidized and Unsubsidized Stafford, PLUS), FFEL (Subsidized and Unsubsidized Stafford, PLUS), Perkins, college/university, private loans.

WORK-STUDY *Federal work-study:* Total amount: $4,573,574; 3,488 jobs averaging $1843.

ATHLETIC AWARDS Total amount: $2,585,875 (28% need-based, 72% non-need-based).

APPLYING FOR FINANCIAL AID *Required financial aid forms:* FAFSA, state aid form. *Financial aid deadline:* 5/1 (priority: 3/2). *Notification date:* Continuous beginning 4/1.

CONTACT Ms. Penny Harrell, Associate Director of Student Services, University of California, Irvine, Office of Financial Aid and Scholarships, Irvine, CA 92697-2825, 949-824-8262. *Fax:* 949-824-4876. *E-mail:* finaid@uci.edu.

UNIVERSITY OF CALIFORNIA, LOS ANGELES
Los Angeles, CA

Tuition & fees (CA res): $9151   Average undergraduate aid package: $17,008

ABOUT THE INSTITUTION State-supported, coed. 100 undergraduate majors. Both federal and institutional methodology are used as a basis for awarding need-based institutional aid.

UNDERGRADUATE EXPENSES for 2009–10 *Tuition, state resident:* full-time $0. *Tuition, nonresident:* full-time $22,021. *Required fees:* full-time $9151. *College room and board:* $13,314. Room and board charges vary according to board plan and housing facility.

FRESHMAN FINANCIAL AID (Fall 2009, est.) 2,935 applied for aid; of those 82% were deemed to have need. 100% of freshmen with need received aid; of those 23% had need fully met. *Average percent of need met:* 81% (excluding resources awarded to replace EFC). *Average financial aid package:* $17,905 (excluding resources awarded to replace EFC). 4% of all full-time freshmen had no need and received non-need-based gift aid.

UNDERGRADUATE FINANCIAL AID (Fall 2009, est.) 15,224 applied for aid; of those 89% were deemed to have need. 100% of undergraduates with need received aid; of those 25% had need fully met. *Average percent of need met:* 81% (excluding resources awarded to replace EFC). *Average financial aid package:* $17,008 (excluding resources awarded to replace EFC). 4% of all full-time undergraduates had no need and received non-need-based gift aid.

GIFT AID (NEED-BASED) *Total amount:* $170,561,756 (25% federal, 32% state, 40% institutional, 3% external sources). *Receiving aid:* Freshmen: 52% (2,804); all full-time undergraduates: 50% (12,804). *Average award:* Freshmen: $14,232; Undergraduates: $13,302. *Scholarships, grants, and awards:* Federal Pell, FSEOG, state, private, college/university gift aid from institutional funds, United Negro College Fund, Federal Nursing.

GIFT AID (NON-NEED-BASED) *Total amount:* $7,312,180 (6% federal, 69% institutional, 25% external sources). *Receiving aid:* Freshmen: 1% (52). Undergraduates: 1% (135). *Average award:* Freshmen: $4601. Undergraduates: $4169. *Scholarships, grants, and awards by category: Academic interests/achievement:* general academic interests/achievements. *Special achievements/activities:* general special achievements/activities.

LOANS *Student loans:* $70,411,307 (77% need-based, 23% non-need-based). 46% of past graduating class borrowed through all loan programs. *Average indebtedness per student:* $16,824. *Average need-based loan:* Freshmen: $6200. Undergraduates: $6387. *Parent loans:* $24,866,029 (22% need-based, 78% non-need-based). *Programs:* FFEL (Subsidized and Unsubsidized Stafford, PLUS), Perkins, Federal Nursing, state, college/university.

WORK-STUDY *Federal work-study:* Total amount: $5,508,780; 2,830 jobs averaging $1460. *State or other work-study/employment:* Total amount: $400,000 (100% need-based). 774 part-time jobs averaging $1030.

ATHLETIC AWARDS Total amount: $8,636,321 (32% need-based, 68% non-need-based).

APPLYING FOR FINANCIAL AID *Required financial aid form:* FAFSA. *Financial aid deadline:* Continuous. *Notification date:* Continuous beginning 3/15.

CONTACT Ms. Yolanda Tan, Administrative Assistant, Financial Aid Office, University of California, Los Angeles, A-129 Murphy Hall, Los Angeles, CA 90095-1435, 310-206-0404. *E-mail:* finaid@saonet.ucla.edu.

UNIVERSITY OF CALIFORNIA, MERCED
Merced, CA

CONTACT Financial Aid Office, University of California, Merced, 5200 North Lake Road, Merced, CA 95343, 209-228-4400.

UNIVERSITY OF CALIFORNIA, RIVERSIDE
Riverside, CA

Tuition & fees (CA res): $8507   Average undergraduate aid package: $16,903

ABOUT THE INSTITUTION State-supported, coed. 60 undergraduate majors. Federal methodology is used as a basis for awarding need-based institutional aid.

UNDERGRADUATE EXPENSES for 2009–10 *Tuition, state resident:* full-time $0. *Tuition, nonresident:* full-time $22,671. *Required fees:* full-time $8507. *College room and board:* $10,900. Room and board charges vary according to board plan and housing facility. *Payment plan:* Deferred payment.

FRESHMAN FINANCIAL AID (Fall 2009, est.) 3,717 applied for aid; of those 81% were deemed to have need. 98% of freshmen with need received aid; of those 49% had need fully met. *Average percent of need met:* 91% (excluding

resources awarded to replace EFC). *Average financial aid package:* $18,067 (excluding resources awarded to replace EFC). 1% of all full-time freshmen had no need and received non-need-based gift aid.

UNDERGRADUATE FINANCIAL AID (Fall 2009, est.) 13,255 applied for aid; of those 87% were deemed to have need. 98% of undergraduates with need received aid; of those 35% had need fully met. *Average percent of need met:* 84% (excluding resources awarded to replace EFC). *Average financial aid package:* $16,903 (excluding resources awarded to replace EFC). 1% of all full-time undergraduates had no need and received non-need-based gift aid.

GIFT AID (NEED-BASED) *Total amount:* $137,887,894 (29% federal, 37% state, 33% institutional, 1% external sources). *Receiving aid:* Freshmen: 66% (2,801); all full-time undergraduates: 64% (10,576). *Average award:* Freshmen: $14,081; Undergraduates: $12,935. *Scholarships, grants, and awards:* Federal Pell, FSEOG, state, private, college/university gift aid from institutional funds.

GIFT AID (NON-NEED-BASED) *Total amount:* $5,936,429 (12% federal, 80% institutional, 8% external sources). *Receiving aid:* Freshmen: 1% (46). Undergraduates: 1% (185). *Average award:* Freshmen: $6221. Undergraduates: $7687. *Scholarships, grants, and awards by category:* Academic interests/ achievement: agriculture, area/ethnic studies, biological sciences, business, education, engineering/technologies, English, general academic interests/ achievements, humanities, mathematics, physical sciences, premedicine, social sciences. *Creative arts/performance:* art/fine arts, creative writing, dance, music, theater/drama.

LOANS *Student loans:* $57,620,750 (80% need-based, 20% non-need-based). 62% of past graduating class borrowed through all loan programs. *Average indebtedness per student:* $16,398. *Average need-based loan:* Freshmen: $4761. Undergraduates: $5991. *Parent loans:* $17,349,799 (21% need-based, 79% non-need-based). *Programs:* Federal Direct (Subsidized and Unsubsidized Stafford, PLUS), Perkins, college/university.

WORK-STUDY *Federal work-study:* Total amount: $5,152,083; 2,673 jobs averaging $1918. *State or other work-study/employment:* Part-time jobs available.

ATHLETIC AWARDS Total amount: $2,318,574 (38% need-based, 62% non-need-based).

APPLYING FOR FINANCIAL AID *Required financial aid forms:* FAFSA, state aid form. *Financial aid deadline:* 3/2. *Notification date:* Continuous. Students must reply by 5/1 or within 3 weeks of notification.

CONTACT Ms. Sheryl Hayes, Director of Financial Aid, University of California, Riverside, 2106 Student Services Building, Riverside, CA 92521-0209, 951-827-3878. *E-mail:* finaid@ucr.edu.

UNIVERSITY OF CALIFORNIA, SAN DIEGO
La Jolla, CA

Tuition & fees (CA res): $9698   **Average undergraduate aid package:** $18,560

ABOUT THE INSTITUTION State-supported, coed. 68 undergraduate majors. Both federal and institutional methodology are used as a basis for awarding need-based institutional aid.

UNDERGRADUATE EXPENSES for 2010–11 *Tuition, state resident:* full-time $0. *Tuition, nonresident:* full-time $22,669. *Required fees:* full-time $9698. *College room and board:* $11,057.

FRESHMAN FINANCIAL AID (Fall 2009, est.) 3,216 applied for aid; of those 76% were deemed to have need. 98% of freshmen with need received aid; of those 38% had need fully met. *Average percent of need met:* 89% (excluding resources awarded to replace EFC). *Average financial aid package:* $19,318 (excluding resources awarded to replace EFC). 3% of all full-time freshmen had no need and received non-need-based gift aid.

UNDERGRADUATE FINANCIAL AID (Fall 2009, est.) 15,627 applied for aid; of those 87% were deemed to have need. 98% of undergraduates with need received aid; of those 37% had need fully met. *Average percent of need met:* 86% (excluding resources awarded to replace EFC). *Average financial aid package:* $18,560 (excluding resources awarded to replace EFC). 3% of all full-time undergraduates had no need and received non-need-based gift aid.

GIFT AID (NEED-BASED) *Total amount:* $180,327,067 (29% federal, 35% state, 34% institutional, 2% external sources). *Receiving aid:* Freshmen: 62% (2,321); all full-time undergraduates: 57% (12,734). *Average award:* Freshmen: $14,304; Undergraduates: $13,983. *Scholarships, grants, and awards:* Federal Pell, FSEOG, state, private, college/university gift aid from institutional funds, Academic Competitiveness Grants, National SMART Grants.

GIFT AID (NON-NEED-BASED) *Total amount:* $9,171,822 (8% federal, 80% institutional, 12% external sources). *Receiving aid:* Freshmen: 1% (20). Undergraduates: 59. *Average award:* Freshmen: $10,265. Undergraduates: $9419. *Scholarships, grants, and awards by category:* Academic interests/achievement: biological sciences, business, communication, computer science, engineering/ technologies, general academic interests/achievements, mathematics, physical sciences, premedicine, social sciences. *Creative arts/performance:* applied art and design, cinema/film/broadcasting, dance, journalism/publications, performing arts. *Special achievements/activities:* community service, leadership. *Special characteristics:* ethnic background, first-generation college students, handicapped students, members of minority groups, veterans' children.

LOANS *Student loans:* $68,499,860 (83% need-based, 17% non-need-based). 51% of past graduating class borrowed through all loan programs. *Average indebtedness per student:* $17,679. *Average need-based loan:* Freshmen: $4891. Undergraduates: $5833. *Parent loans:* $10,558,656 (17% need-based, 83% non-need-based). *Programs:* Federal Direct (Subsidized and Unsubsidized Stafford, PLUS), FFEL (Subsidized and Unsubsidized Stafford, PLUS), Perkins, college/university, alternative loans.

WORK-STUDY *Federal work-study:* Total amount: $12,289,741; jobs available.

ATHLETIC AWARDS Total amount: $260,500 (39% need-based, 61% non-need-based).

APPLYING FOR FINANCIAL AID *Required financial aid forms:* FAFSA, state aid form. *Financial aid deadline (priority):* 3/2. *Notification date:* Continuous beginning 3/15.

CONTACT Ann Klein, Director of Financial Aid Office, University of California, San Diego, 9500 Gilman Drive, Mail Code 0013, La Jolla, CA 92093-0013, 858-534-3800. *Fax:* 858-534-5459. *E-mail:* aklein@ucsd.edu.

UNIVERSITY OF CALIFORNIA, SANTA BARBARA
Santa Barbara, CA

Tuition & fees (CA res): $9055   **Average undergraduate aid package:** $17,380

ABOUT THE INSTITUTION State-supported, coed. 75 undergraduate majors. Both federal and institutional methodology are used as a basis for awarding need-based institutional aid.

UNDERGRADUATE EXPENSES for 2009–10 *Tuition, state resident:* full-time $0. *Tuition, nonresident:* full-time $21,669. *Required fees:* full-time $9055. *College room and board:* $12,765. Room and board charges vary according to board plan and housing facility. *Payment plan:* Installment.

FRESHMAN FINANCIAL AID (Fall 2009, est.) 3,766 applied for aid; of those 72% were deemed to have need. 94% of freshmen with need received aid; of those 35% had need fully met. *Average percent of need met:* 84% (excluding resources awarded to replace EFC). *Average financial aid package:* $18,878 (excluding resources awarded to replace EFC). 2% of all full-time freshmen had no need and received non-need-based gift aid.

UNDERGRADUATE FINANCIAL AID (Fall 2009, est.) 12,791 applied for aid; of those 80% were deemed to have need. 94% of undergraduates with need received aid; of those 30% had need fully met. *Average percent of need met:* 82% (excluding resources awarded to replace EFC). *Average financial aid package:* $17,380 (excluding resources awarded to replace EFC). 2% of all full-time undergraduates had no need and received non-need-based gift aid.

GIFT AID (NEED-BASED) *Total amount:* $122,958,014 (26% federal, 36% state, 37% institutional, 1% external sources). *Receiving aid:* Freshmen: 51% (2,349); all full-time undergraduates: 45% (8,769). *Average award:* Freshmen: $15,409; Undergraduates: $13,876. *Scholarships, grants, and awards:* Federal Pell, FSEOG, state, private, college/university gift aid from institutional funds, endowed scholarships.

GIFT AID (NON-NEED-BASED) *Total amount:* $4,019,538 (16% federal, 1% state, 68% institutional, 15% external sources). *Receiving aid:* Freshmen: 1% (41). Undergraduates: 89. *Average award:* Freshmen: $6596. Undergraduates: $6021. *Scholarships, grants, and awards by category:* Academic interests/ achievement: general academic interests/achievements.

LOANS *Student loans:* $49,510,314 (79% need-based, 21% non-need-based). 47% of past graduating class borrowed through all loan programs. *Average indebtedness per student:* $17,768. *Average need-based loan:* Freshmen: $5948. Undergraduates: $6264. *Parent loans:* $28,770,006 (20% need-based, 80% non-need-based). *Programs:* Federal Direct (Subsidized and Unsubsidized Stafford, PLUS), Perkins.

University of California, Santa Barbara

WORK-STUDY *Federal work-study:* Total amount: $2,303,093; jobs available.
ATHLETIC AWARDS Total amount: $3,150,950 (18% need-based, 82% non-need-based).
APPLYING FOR FINANCIAL AID *Required financial aid form:* FAFSA. *Financial aid deadline (priority):* 3/2. *Notification date:* Continuous beginning 3/15. Students must reply within 2 weeks of notification.
CONTACT Office of Financial Aid, University of California, Santa Barbara, 2103 SAASB (Student Affairs/Administrative Services Building), Santa Barbara, CA 93106-3180, 805-893-2432. *Fax:* 805-893-8793.

UNIVERSITY OF CALIFORNIA, SANTA CRUZ
Santa Cruz, CA

Tuition & fees (CA res): $10,095	Average undergraduate aid package: $18,545

ABOUT THE INSTITUTION State-supported, coed. 56 undergraduate majors. Both federal and institutional methodology are used as a basis for awarding need-based institutional aid.
UNDERGRADUATE EXPENSES for 2009–10 *Tuition, state resident:* full-time $0. *Tuition, nonresident:* full-time $22,020. *Required fees:* full-time $10,095. Full-time tuition and fees vary according to course load. Part-time tuition and fees vary according to course load. *College room and board:* $13,641. Room and board charges vary according to board plan and housing facility. *Payment plans:* Installment, deferred payment.
FRESHMAN FINANCIAL AID (Fall 2009, est.) 2,722 applied for aid; of those 72% were deemed to have need. 95% of freshmen with need received aid; of those 51% had need fully met. *Average percent of need met:* 89% (excluding resources awarded to replace EFC). *Average financial aid package:* $19,228 (excluding resources awarded to replace EFC). 1% of all full-time freshmen had no need and received non-need-based gift aid.
UNDERGRADUATE FINANCIAL AID (Fall 2009, est.) 10,244 applied for aid; of those 80% were deemed to have need. 96% of undergraduates with need received aid; of those 49% had need fully met. *Average percent of need met:* 89% (excluding resources awarded to replace EFC). *Average financial aid package:* $18,545 (excluding resources awarded to replace EFC). 2% of all full-time undergraduates had no need and received non-need-based gift aid.
GIFT AID (NEED-BASED) *Total amount:* $100,995,238 (23% federal, 34% state, 42% institutional, 1% external sources). *Receiving aid:* Freshmen: 53% (1,702); all full-time undergraduates: 49% (7,237). *Average award:* Freshmen: $14,581; Undergraduates: $13,735. *Scholarships, grants, and awards:* Federal Pell, FSEOG, state, private, college/university gift aid from institutional funds.
GIFT AID (NON-NEED-BASED) *Total amount:* $3,280,555 (2% federal, 1% state, 84% institutional, 13% external sources). *Receiving aid:* Freshmen: 13. Undergraduates: 43. *Average award:* Freshmen: $9045. Undergraduates: $8010. *Scholarships, grants, and awards by category: Academic interests/achievement:* 195 awards ($763,559 total): general academic interests/achievements, humanities, physical sciences, social sciences. *Creative arts/performance:* 166 awards ($95,247 total): art/fine arts, cinema/film/broadcasting, music, theater/drama. *Special achievements/activities:* 14 awards ($8850 total): general special achievements/activities, leadership.
LOANS *Student loans:* $47,264,299 (71% need-based, 29% non-need-based). 53% of past graduating class borrowed through all loan programs. *Average indebtedness per student:* $16,024. *Average need-based loan:* Freshmen: $5277. Undergraduates: $5617. *Parent loans:* $23,196,236 (8% need-based, 92% non-need-based). *Programs:* Federal Direct (Subsidized and Unsubsidized Stafford, PLUS), Perkins.
WORK-STUDY *Federal work-study:* Total amount: $11,483,646; 5,793 jobs averaging $2103. *State or other work-study/employment:* Part-time jobs available.
APPLYING FOR FINANCIAL AID *Required financial aid forms:* FAFSA, state aid form. *Financial aid deadline:* 6/1 (priority: 3/17). *Notification date:* Continuous beginning 4/1. Students must reply within 4 weeks of notification.
CONTACT Ms. Ann Draper, Director of Financial Aid, University of California, Santa Cruz, 201 Hahn Student Services Building, Santa Cruz, CA 95064, 831-459-4358. *Fax:* 831-459-4631. *E-mail:* ann@ucsc.edu.

UNIVERSITY OF CENTRAL ARKANSAS
Conway, AR

Tuition & fees (AR res): $6699	Average undergraduate aid package: N/A

ABOUT THE INSTITUTION State-supported, coed. *Awards:* associate, bachelor's, and master's degrees and post-bachelor's and post-master's certificates. 60 undergraduate majors. *Total enrollment:* 12,974. Undergraduates: 11,048. Freshmen: 2,111. Federal methodology is used as a basis for awarding need-based institutional aid.
UNDERGRADUATE EXPENSES for 2009–10 *Tuition, state resident:* full-time $5206. *Tuition, nonresident:* full-time $10,412. *Required fees:* full-time $1493. Part-time tuition and fees vary according to course load. *College room and board:* $4880; *Room only:* $2780. Room and board charges vary according to board plan and housing facility. *Payment plan:* Installment.
GIFT AID (NEED-BASED) *Scholarships, grants, and awards:* Federal Pell, FSEOG, state, private, college/university gift aid from institutional funds, Federal Nursing.
GIFT AID (NON-NEED-BASED) *Scholarships, grants, and awards by category: Academic interests/achievement:* general academic interests/achievements. *Tuition waivers:* Full or partial for employees or children of employees, senior citizens. *ROTC:* Army.
LOANS *Programs:* FFEL (Subsidized and Unsubsidized Stafford, PLUS), Perkins, Federal Nursing, state, alternative loans.
WORK-STUDY Federal work-study jobs available. *State or other work-study/employment:* Part-time jobs available.
APPLYING FOR FINANCIAL AID *Required financial aid form:* FAFSA. *Financial aid deadline:* 7/1 (priority: 4/15). *Notification date:* Continuous.
CONTACT Cheryl Lyons, Director of Student Aid, University of Central Arkansas, 201 Donaghey Avenue, Conway, AR 72035, 501-450-3140 or toll-free 800-243-8245 (in-state). *Fax:* 501-450-5168. *E-mail:* clyons@uca.edu.

UNIVERSITY OF CENTRAL FLORIDA
Orlando, FL

Tuition & fees (FL res): $4526	Average undergraduate aid package: $7951

ABOUT THE INSTITUTION State-supported, coed. 81 undergraduate majors. Federal methodology is used as a basis for awarding need-based institutional aid.
UNDERGRADUATE EXPENSES for 2009–10 *Tuition, state resident:* full-time $4526; part-time $150.85 per credit. *Tuition, nonresident:* full-time $20,005; part-time $666.83 per credit. Full-time tuition and fees vary according to course load. Part-time tuition and fees vary according to course load. *College room and board:* $8540; *Room only:* $4940. Room and board charges vary according to board plan and housing facility. *Payment plans:* Tuition prepayment, deferred payment.
FRESHMAN FINANCIAL AID (Fall 2008) 4,441 applied for aid; of those 57% were deemed to have need. 99% of freshmen with need received aid; of those 19% had need fully met. *Average percent of need met:* 71% (excluding resources awarded to replace EFC). *Average financial aid package:* $7956 (excluding resources awarded to replace EFC). 11% of all full-time freshmen had no need and received non-need-based gift aid.
UNDERGRADUATE FINANCIAL AID (Fall 2008) 20,059 applied for aid; of those 71% were deemed to have need. 96% of undergraduates with need received aid; of those 17% had need fully met. *Average percent of need met:* 67% (excluding resources awarded to replace EFC). *Average financial aid package:* $7951 (excluding resources awarded to replace EFC). 6% of all full-time undergraduates had no need and received non-need-based gift aid.
GIFT AID (NEED-BASED) *Total amount:* $51,065,449 (66% federal, 15% state, 19% institutional). *Receiving aid:* Freshmen: 24% (1,445); all full-time undergraduates: 28% (8,895). *Average award:* Freshmen: $5018; Undergraduates: $4640. *Scholarships, grants, and awards:* Federal Pell, FSEOG, state, private, college/university gift aid from institutional funds.
GIFT AID (NON-NEED-BASED) *Total amount:* $75,446,439 (1% federal, 81% state, 11% institutional, 7% external sources). *Receiving aid:* Freshmen: 39% (2,385). Undergraduates: 27% (8,592). *Average award:* Freshmen: $2330. Undergraduates: $2327. *Scholarships, grants, and awards by category: Academic interests/achievement:* general academic interests/achievements. *Creative arts/performance:* cinema/film/broadcasting, music, theater/drama. *Special achievements/activities:* general special achievements/activities, leadership. *Special characteristics:* first-generation college students. *Tuition waivers:* Full or partial for employees or children of employees, senior citizens.
LOANS *Student loans:* $105,684,382 (47% need-based, 53% non-need-based). 41% of past graduating class borrowed through all loan programs. *Average*

indebtedness per student: $17,044. *Average need-based loan:* Freshmen: $3379. Undergraduates: $4681. *Parent loans:* $5,057,126 (100% non-need-based). *Programs:* Federal Direct (Subsidized and Unsubsidized Stafford, PLUS), Perkins. **WORK-STUDY** *Federal work-study:* Total amount: $1,566,142; jobs available. *State or other work-study/employment:* Part-time jobs available. **ATHLETIC AWARDS** Total amount: $2,301,033 (100% non-need-based). **APPLYING FOR FINANCIAL AID** *Required financial aid form:* FAFSA. *Financial aid deadline:* 6/30 (priority: 3/1). *Notification date:* Continuous beginning 3/15. Students must reply within 3 weeks of notification.

CONTACT Ms. Inez Ford, Assistant Director, Student Financial Assistance, University of Central Florida, 4000 Central Florida Boulevard, Orlando, FL 32816-0113, 407-823-2827. *Fax:* 407-823-5241. *E-mail:* iford@mail.ucf.edu.

UNIVERSITY OF CENTRAL MISSOURI
Warrensburg, MO

Tuition & fees (MO res): $7311   **Average undergraduate aid package:** $9426

ABOUT THE INSTITUTION State-supported, coed. 66 undergraduate majors. Federal methodology is used as a basis for awarding need-based institutional aid.

UNDERGRADUATE EXPENSES for 2010–11 *Tuition, state resident:* full-time $6585; part-time $219.50 per credit hour. *Tuition, nonresident:* full-time $12,444; part-time $414.80 per credit hour. *Required fees:* full-time $726; $24.20 per credit hour. Full-time tuition and fees vary according to course load and location. Part-time tuition and fees vary according to course load and location. *College room and board:* $6320; *Room only:* $4120. Room and board charges vary according to board plan and housing facility. *Payment plans:* Installment, deferred payment.

FRESHMAN FINANCIAL AID (Fall 2008) 1,193 applied for aid; of those 42% were deemed to have need. 100% of freshmen with need received aid; of those 21% had need fully met. *Average percent of need met:* 88% (excluding resources awarded to replace EFC). *Average financial aid package:* $9024 (excluding resources awarded to replace EFC). 17% of all full-time freshmen had no need and received non-need-based gift aid.

UNDERGRADUATE FINANCIAL AID (Fall 2008) 4,141 applied for aid; of those 46% were deemed to have need. 100% of undergraduates with need received aid; of those 16% had need fully met. *Average percent of need met:* 90% (excluding resources awarded to replace EFC). *Average financial aid package:* $9426 (excluding resources awarded to replace EFC). 14% of all full-time undergraduates had no need and received non-need-based gift aid.

GIFT AID (NEED-BASED) *Total amount:* $10,901,197 (100% federal). *Receiving aid:* Freshmen: 15% (217); all full-time undergraduates: 17% (983). *Average award:* Freshmen: $3406; Undergraduates: $3361. *Scholarships, grants, and awards:* Federal Pell, FSEOG, state, private, college/university gift aid from institutional funds.

GIFT AID (NON-NEED-BASED) *Total amount:* $14,812,445 (4% federal, 37% state, 35% institutional, 24% external sources). *Receiving aid:* Freshmen: 33% (477). Undergraduates: 32% (1,785). *Average award:* Freshmen: $8008. Undergraduates: $8345. *Scholarships, grants, and awards by category:* Academic interests/achievement: 2,310 awards ($4,725,000 total): agriculture, area/ethnic studies, biological sciences, business, communication, computer science, education, engineering/technologies, English, foreign languages, general academic interests/achievements, health fields, home economics, humanities, library science, mathematics, military science, physical sciences, premedicine, religion/biblical studies, social sciences. *Creative arts/performance:* 89 awards ($33,450 total): applied art and design, art/fine arts, cinema/film/broadcasting, creative writing, debating, journalism/publications, music, performing arts, theater/drama. *Special achievements/activities:* 71 awards ($46,800 total): cheerleading/drum major, leadership. *Special characteristics:* 675 awards ($975,000 total): adult students, children and siblings of alumni, children of faculty/staff, ethnic background, members of minority groups, out-of-state students, previous college experience. *Tuition waivers:* Full or partial for children of alumni, employees or children of employees, senior citizens.

LOANS *Student loans:* $32,335,226 (43% need-based, 57% non-need-based). 69% of past graduating class borrowed through all loan programs. *Average indebtedness per student:* $18,272. *Average need-based loan:* Freshmen: $4084. Undergraduates: $4543. *Parent loans:* $8,391,647 (100% non-need-based). *Programs:* Federal Direct (Subsidized and Unsubsidized Stafford, PLUS), Perkins, state.

WORK-STUDY *Federal work-study:* Total amount: $414,051; 221 jobs averaging $1324. *State or other work-study/employment:* Total amount: $2,040,714 (100% non-need-based). 1,150 part-time jobs averaging $1429. **ATHLETIC AWARDS** Total amount: $1,963,625 (100% non-need-based). **APPLYING FOR FINANCIAL AID** *Required financial aid forms:* FAFSA, institution's own form, CSS Financial Aid PROFILE, state aid form, noncustodial (divorced/separated) parent's statement, business/farm supplement. *Financial aid deadline (priority):* 4/1. *Notification date:* Continuous beginning 3/15. Students must reply within 3 weeks of notification.

CONTACT Mr. Phil Shreves, Director of Student Financial Assistance, University of Central Missouri, Ward Edwards Building 1100, Warrensburg, MO 64093, 660-543-4040 or toll-free 800-729-8266 (in-state). *Fax:* 660-543-8080. *E-mail:* sfs@ucmo.edu.

UNIVERSITY OF CENTRAL OKLAHOMA
Edmond, OK

Tuition & fees (OK res): $4223   **Average undergraduate aid package:** $7249

ABOUT THE INSTITUTION State-supported, coed. 87 undergraduate majors. Federal methodology is used as a basis for awarding need-based institutional aid.

UNDERGRADUATE EXPENSES for 2010–11 *Tuition, state resident:* full-time $3681; part-time $122.70 per credit hour. *Tuition, nonresident:* full-time $10,110; part-time $337 per credit hour. *Required fees:* full-time $542; $18.50 per credit hour. Full-time tuition and fees vary according to course load, degree level, and program. Part-time tuition and fees vary according to course load, degree level, and program. *College room and board:* $7776; *Room only:* $4716. Room and board charges vary according to board plan and housing facility. *Payment plans:* Guaranteed tuition, installment, deferred payment.

FRESHMAN FINANCIAL AID (Fall 2008) 1,083 applied for aid; of those 74% were deemed to have need. 90% of freshmen with need received aid; of those 9% had need fully met. *Average percent of need met:* 66% (excluding resources awarded to replace EFC). *Average financial aid package:* $6917 (excluding resources awarded to replace EFC). 8% of all full-time freshmen had no need and received non-need-based gift aid.

UNDERGRADUATE FINANCIAL AID (Fall 2008) 5,777 applied for aid; of those 83% were deemed to have need. 93% of undergraduates with need received aid; of those 9% had need fully met. *Average percent of need met:* 67% (excluding resources awarded to replace EFC). *Average financial aid package:* $7249 (excluding resources awarded to replace EFC). 54% of all full-time undergraduates had no need and received non-need-based gift aid.

GIFT AID (NEED-BASED) *Total amount:* $19,432,003 (62% federal, 27% state, 2% institutional, 9% external sources). *Receiving aid:* Freshmen: 46% (703); all full-time undergraduates: 48% (4,267). *Average award:* Freshmen: $6995; Undergraduates: $7378. *Scholarships, grants, and awards:* Federal Pell, FSEOG, state, private, college/university gift aid from institutional funds.

GIFT AID (NON-NEED-BASED) *Total amount:* $4,123,003 (44% state, 7% institutional, 49% external sources). *Receiving aid:* Freshmen: 2% (24). Undergraduates: 2% (162). *Average award:* Freshmen: $2628. Undergraduates: $5549. *Scholarships, grants, and awards by category:* Academic interests/achievement: biological sciences, business, computer science, education, foreign languages, general academic interests/achievements, health fields, home economics, mathematics, military science, physical sciences, social sciences. *Creative arts/performance:* applied art and design, art/fine arts, journalism/publications, music, theater/drama. *Special achievements/activities:* general special achievements/activities, leadership. *Special characteristics:* ethnic background, members of minority groups. *Tuition waivers:* Full or partial for employees or children of employees.

LOANS *Student loans:* $37,960,773 (87% need-based, 13% non-need-based). *Average need-based loan:* Freshmen: $3127. Undergraduates: $4339. *Parent loans:* $1,003,538 (67% need-based, 33% non-need-based). *Programs:* Federal Direct (Subsidized and Unsubsidized Stafford, PLUS), FFEL (Subsidized Stafford). **WORK-STUDY** Federal work-study jobs available. **ATHLETIC AWARDS** Total amount: $689,717 (53% need-based, 47% non-need-based).

APPLYING FOR FINANCIAL AID *Required financial aid forms:* FAFSA, institution's own form. *Financial aid deadline (priority):* 5/31. *Notification date:* Continuous beginning 5/1. Students must reply by 5/80 or within 4 weeks of notification.

CONTACT Ms. Becky Garrett, Assistant Director, Technical Services, University of Central Oklahoma, 100 North University Drive, Edmond, OK 73034-5209, 405-974-3334 or toll-free 800-254-4215. *Fax:* 405-340-7658. *E-mail:* bgarrett@uco.edu.

UNIVERSITY OF CHARLESTON
Charleston, WV

Tuition & fees: $24,000	Average undergraduate aid package: $21,500

ABOUT THE INSTITUTION Independent, coed. 29 undergraduate majors. Federal methodology is used as a basis for awarding need-based institutional aid.

UNDERGRADUATE EXPENSES for 2009–10 *Comprehensive fee:* $32,700 includes full-time tuition ($24,000) and room and board ($8700). *College room only:* $4750. Room and board charges vary according to board plan and housing facility. *Part-time tuition:* $400 per credit hour. *Part-time fees:* $75 per term. Part-time tuition and fees vary according to program. *Payment plan:* Installment.

FRESHMAN FINANCIAL AID (Fall 2008) 292 applied for aid; of those 88% were deemed to have need. 100% of freshmen with need received aid; of those 29% had need fully met. *Average percent of need met:* 84% (excluding resources awarded to replace EFC). *Average financial aid package:* $23,280 (excluding resources awarded to replace EFC).

UNDERGRADUATE FINANCIAL AID (Fall 2008) 995 applied for aid; of those 88% were deemed to have need. 100% of undergraduates with need received aid; of those 34% had need fully met. *Average percent of need met:* 87% (excluding resources awarded to replace EFC). *Average financial aid package:* $21,500 (excluding resources awarded to replace EFC).

GIFT AID (NEED-BASED) *Total amount:* $10,341,018 (14% federal, 6% state, 78% institutional, 2% external sources). *Receiving aid:* Freshmen: 80% (249); all full-time undergraduates: 59% (637). *Average award:* Freshmen: $5310; Undergraduates: $7150. *Scholarships, grants, and awards:* Federal Pell, FSEOG, state, private, college/university gift aid from institutional funds, Academic Competitiveness Grants, National SMART Grants, TEACH Grants.

GIFT AID (NON-NEED-BASED) *Total amount:* $4,006,985 (4% federal, 27% state, 64% institutional, 5% external sources). *Receiving aid:* Freshmen: 80% (248). Undergraduates: 73% (785). *Scholarships, grants, and awards by category:* Academic interests/achievement: general academic interests/achievements, military science. *Creative arts/performance:* music. *Special achievements/activities:* cheerleading/drum major, community service, general special achievements/activities, leadership. *Special characteristics:* children and siblings of alumni, children of educators, children of faculty/staff, international students. *Tuition waivers:* Full or partial for employees or children of employees, senior citizens.

LOANS *Student loans:* $8,340,294 (51% need-based, 49% non-need-based). 91% of past graduating class borrowed through all loan programs. *Average indebtedness per student:* $23,250. *Average need-based loan:* Freshmen: $7110. Undergraduates: $8100. *Parent loans:* $744,242 (100% non-need-based). *Programs:* FFEL (Subsidized and Unsubsidized Stafford, PLUS), Perkins, Federal Nursing.

WORK-STUDY *Federal work-study:* Total amount: $82,856; jobs available. *State or other work-study/employment:* Part-time jobs available.

ATHLETIC AWARDS Total amount: $2,520,462 (100% non-need-based).

APPLYING FOR FINANCIAL AID *Required financial aid form:* FAFSA. *Financial aid deadline:* Continuous. *Notification date:* Continuous beginning 3/1. Students must reply by 5/1.

CONTACT Ms. Janet M. Ruge, Director of Financial Aid, University of Charleston, 2300 MacCorkle Avenue SE, Charleston, WV 25304-1099, 304-357-4759 or toll-free 800-995-GOUC. *Fax:* 304-357-4769. *E-mail:* janetruge@ucwv.edu.

UNIVERSITY OF CHICAGO
Chicago, IL

Tuition & fees: $39,432	Average undergraduate aid package: $36,915

ABOUT THE INSTITUTION Independent, coed. 75 undergraduate majors. Both federal and institutional methodology are used as a basis for awarding need-based institutional aid.

UNDERGRADUATE EXPENSES for 2009–10 *Comprehensive fee:* $51,129 includes full-time tuition ($38,550), mandatory fees ($882), and room and board ($11,697). Room and board charges vary according to board plan and housing facility. Part-time tuition and fees vary according to course load. *Payment plans:* Tuition prepayment, installment.

FRESHMAN FINANCIAL AID (Fall 2009, est.) 923 applied for aid; of those 74% were deemed to have need. 100% of freshmen with need received aid; of those 100% had need fully met. *Average percent of need met:* 100% (excluding resources awarded to replace EFC). *Average financial aid package:* $39,153 (excluding resources awarded to replace EFC). 8% of all full-time freshmen had no need and received non-need-based gift aid.

UNDERGRADUATE FINANCIAL AID (Fall 2009, est.) 3,278 applied for aid; of those 74% were deemed to have need. 100% of undergraduates with need received aid; of those 80% had need fully met. *Average percent of need met:* 100% (excluding resources awarded to replace EFC). *Average financial aid package:* $36,915 (excluding resources awarded to replace EFC). 11% of all full-time undergraduates had no need and received non-need-based gift aid.

GIFT AID (NEED-BASED) *Total amount:* $79,193,162 (7% federal, 2% state, 87% institutional, 4% external sources). *Receiving aid:* Freshmen: 51% (676); all full-time undergraduates: 39% (1,954). *Average award:* Freshmen: $35,673; Undergraduates: $33,027. *Scholarships, grants, and awards:* Federal Pell, FSEOG, state, college/university gift aid from institutional funds.

GIFT AID (NON-NEED-BASED) *Total amount:* $10,881,745 (65% institutional, 35% external sources). *Average award:* Freshmen: $11,646. Undergraduates: $13,208. *Scholarships, grants, and awards by category:* Academic interests/achievement: general academic interests/achievements. *Tuition waivers:* Full or partial for employees or children of employees.

LOANS *Student loans:* $8,952,734 (72% need-based, 28% non-need-based). 48% of past graduating class borrowed through all loan programs. *Average indebtedness per student:* $24,238. *Average need-based loan:* Freshmen: $4367. Undergraduates: $5074. *Parent loans:* $7,354,296 (100% non-need-based). *Programs:* Federal Direct (Subsidized and Unsubsidized Stafford, PLUS), Perkins, alternative loans.

WORK-STUDY *Federal work-study:* Total amount: $2,385,802; jobs available. *State or other work-study/employment:* Total amount: $1,782,839 (100% need-based). Part-time jobs available.

APPLYING FOR FINANCIAL AID *Required financial aid forms:* FAFSA, institution's own form, CSS Financial Aid PROFILE, noncustodial (divorced/separated) parent's statement. *Financial aid deadline (priority):* 2/1. *Notification date:* 4/5. Students must reply by 5/1.

CONTACT Office of College Aid, University of Chicago, 1101 East 58th Street, Chicago, IL 60637, 773-702-8666. *Fax:* 773-702-5846.

UNIVERSITY OF CINCINNATI
Cincinnati, OH

Tuition & fees (OH res): $9399	Average undergraduate aid package: $7843

ABOUT THE INSTITUTION State-supported, coed. 140 undergraduate majors. Federal methodology is used as a basis for awarding need-based institutional aid.

UNDERGRADUATE EXPENSES for 2009–10 *Tuition, state resident:* full-time $7896; part-time $262 per credit hour. *Tuition, nonresident:* full-time $23,922; part-time $665 per credit hour. *Required fees:* full-time $1503; $42 per credit hour. Full-time tuition and fees vary according to course load, degree level, location, program, and reciprocity agreements. Part-time tuition and fees vary according to course load, degree level, location, program, and reciprocity agreements. *College room and board:* $9702; *Room only:* $5799. Room and board charges vary according to board plan and housing facility. *Payment plan:* Installment.

FRESHMAN FINANCIAL AID (Fall 2009, est.) 3,566 applied for aid; of those 75% were deemed to have need. 99% of freshmen with need received aid; of those 4% had need fully met. *Average percent of need met:* 64% (excluding resources awarded to replace EFC). *Average financial aid package:* $7650 (excluding resources awarded to replace EFC). 15% of all full-time freshmen had no need and received non-need-based gift aid.

UNDERGRADUATE FINANCIAL AID (Fall 2009, est.) 13,033 applied for aid; of those 80% were deemed to have need. 98% of undergraduates with need received aid; of those 5% had need fully met. *Average percent of need met:* 63% (excluding resources awarded to replace EFC). *Average financial aid package:* $7843 (excluding resources awarded to replace EFC). 17% of all full-time undergraduates had no need and received non-need-based gift aid.

GIFT AID (NEED-BASED) *Total amount:* $46,054,124 (55% federal, 8% state, 34% institutional, 3% external sources). *Receiving aid:* Freshmen: 29% (1,221); all full-time undergraduates: 26% (4,779). *Average award:* Freshmen: $6342; Undergraduates: $5883. *Scholarships, grants, and awards:* Federal Pell, FSEOG, state, private, college/university gift aid from institutional funds, United Negro College Fund, Federal Nursing, Academic Competitiveness Grants, National SMART Grants, TEACH Grants.

GIFT AID (NON-NEED-BASED) *Total amount:* $15,247,176 (95% institutional, 5% external sources). *Receiving aid:* Freshmen: 27% (1,151). Undergraduates: 19% (3,486). *Average award:* Freshmen: $4589. Undergraduates: $4755. *Tuition waivers:* Full or partial for employees or children of employees.

LOANS *Student loans:* $107,383,676 (58% need-based, 42% non-need-based). 69% of past graduating class borrowed through all loan programs. *Average indebtedness per student:* $25,878. *Average need-based loan:* Freshmen: $3365. Undergraduates: $4223. *Parent loans:* $82,123,573 (14% need-based, 86% non-need-based). *Programs:* FFEL (Subsidized and Unsubsidized Stafford, PLUS), Perkins, Federal Nursing, state, college/university.

WORK-STUDY *Federal work-study:* Total amount: $2,968,791; jobs available.

ATHLETIC AWARDS Total amount: $5,955,359 (38% need-based, 62% non-need-based).

APPLYING FOR FINANCIAL AID *Required financial aid form:* FAFSA. *Financial aid deadline:* Continuous. *Notification date:* Continuous beginning 3/10. Students must reply within 2 weeks of notification.

CONTACT Mrs. Dana Pawlowicz, Associate Director, University of Cincinnati, PO Box 210125, Cincinnati, OH 45221-0125, 513-556-2441. *Fax:* 513-556-9171. *E-mail:* dana.pawlowicz@uc.edu.

UNIVERSITY OF COLORADO AT BOULDER
Boulder, CO

Tuition & fees (CO res): $7932	Average undergraduate aid package: $14,790

ABOUT THE INSTITUTION State-supported, coed. 64 undergraduate majors. Federal methodology is used as a basis for awarding need-based institutional aid.

UNDERGRADUATE EXPENSES for 2009–10 *One-time required fee:* $182. *Tuition, state resident:* full-time $6446. *Tuition, nonresident:* full-time $26,700. *Required fees:* full-time $1486. Full-time tuition and fees vary according to program. Part-time tuition and fees vary according to course load and program. *College room and board:* $10,378. Room and board charges vary according to board plan, housing facility, and location. *Payment plan:* Deferred payment.

FRESHMAN FINANCIAL AID (Fall 2009, est.) 4,941 applied for aid; of those 44% were deemed to have need. 100% of freshmen with need received aid; of those 73% had need fully met. *Average percent of need met:* 92% (excluding resources awarded to replace EFC). *Average financial aid package:* $13,445 (excluding resources awarded to replace EFC). 45% of all full-time freshmen had no need and received non-need-based gift aid.

UNDERGRADUATE FINANCIAL AID (Fall 2009, est.) 16,949 applied for aid; of those 51% were deemed to have need. 99% of undergraduates with need received aid; of those 70% had need fully met. *Average percent of need met:* 92% (excluding resources awarded to replace EFC). *Average financial aid package:* $14,790 (excluding resources awarded to replace EFC). 26% of all full-time undergraduates had no need and received non-need-based gift aid.

GIFT AID (NEED-BASED) *Total amount:* $64,700,795 (32% federal, 11% state, 47% institutional, 10% external sources). *Receiving aid:* Freshmen: 35% (1,962); all full-time undergraduates: 29% (7,155). *Average award:* Freshmen: $7508; Undergraduates: $8125. *Scholarships, grants, and awards:* Federal Pell, FSEOG, state, private, college/university gift aid from institutional funds.

GIFT AID (NON-NEED-BASED) *Total amount:* $16,318,081 (17% federal, 62% institutional, 21% external sources). *Receiving aid:* Freshmen: 1% (72). Undergraduates: 1% (199). *Average award:* Freshmen: $4694. Undergraduates: $6707. *Scholarships, grants, and awards by category: Academic interests/achievement:* architecture, area/ethnic studies, biological sciences, business, communication, computer science, education, engineering/technologies, English, foreign languages, general academic interests/achievements, health fields, humanities, international studies, mathematics, military science, physical sciences, premedicine, social sciences. *Creative arts/performance:* art/fine arts, cinema/film/broadcasting, creative writing, dance, journalism/publications, music, performing arts, theater/drama. *Special achievements/activities:* community service, general special achievements/activities, leadership. *Special characteristics:*

first-generation college students, general special characteristics, local/state students. *Tuition waivers:* Full or partial for employees or children of employees, senior citizens.

LOANS *Student loans:* $95,936,980 (60% need-based, 40% non-need-based). 42% of past graduating class borrowed through all loan programs. *Average indebtedness per student:* $19,211. *Average need-based loan:* Freshmen: $5715. Undergraduates: $6796. *Parent loans:* $148,864,620 (24% need-based, 76% non-need-based). *Programs:* Federal Direct (Subsidized and Unsubsidized Stafford, PLUS), Perkins, college/university, private loans.

WORK-STUDY *Federal work-study:* Total amount: $1,538,963; 1,452 jobs averaging $1925. *State or other work-study/employment:* Total amount: $1,943,973 (96% need-based, 4% non-need-based). 822 part-time jobs averaging $2580.

ATHLETIC AWARDS Total amount: $5,459,304 (33% need-based, 67% non-need-based).

APPLYING FOR FINANCIAL AID *Required financial aid forms:* FAFSA, tax returns. *Financial aid deadline (priority):* 4/1. *Notification date:* Continuous beginning 3/1. Students must reply within 3 weeks of notification.

CONTACT Gwen E. Pomper, Director of Financial Aid, University of Colorado at Boulder, University Campus Box 77, Boulder, CO 80309, 303-492-8223. *Fax:* 303-492-0838. *E-mail:* finaid@colorado.edu.

UNIVERSITY OF COLORADO AT COLORADO SPRINGS
Colorado Springs, CO

Tuition & fees (CO res): $5693	Average undergraduate aid package: $8396

ABOUT THE INSTITUTION State-supported, coed. 39 undergraduate majors. Federal methodology is used as a basis for awarding need-based institutional aid.

UNDERGRADUATE EXPENSES for 2009–10 *Tuition, state resident:* full-time $4680. *Tuition, nonresident:* full-time $15,600. *Required fees:* full-time $1013. Full-time tuition and fees vary according to course load, degree level, program, reciprocity agreements, and student level. Part-time tuition and fees vary according to course load, degree level, program, reciprocity agreements, and student level. *College room and board:* $7490. Room and board charges vary according to board plan and housing facility. *Payment plan:* Installment.

FRESHMAN FINANCIAL AID (Fall 2009, est.) 682 applied for aid; of those 60% were deemed to have need. 91% of freshmen with need received aid; of those 10% had need fully met. *Average percent of need met:* 50% (excluding resources awarded to replace EFC). *Average financial aid package:* $7176 (excluding resources awarded to replace EFC). 10% of all full-time freshmen had no need and received non-need-based gift aid.

UNDERGRADUATE FINANCIAL AID (Fall 2009, est.) 4,623 applied for aid; of those 69% were deemed to have need. 94% of undergraduates with need received aid; of those 9% had need fully met. *Average percent of need met:* 53% (excluding resources awarded to replace EFC). *Average financial aid package:* $8396 (excluding resources awarded to replace EFC). 4% of all full-time undergraduates had no need and received non-need-based gift aid.

GIFT AID (NEED-BASED) *Total amount:* $17,662,933 (50% federal, 18% state, 26% institutional, 6% external sources). *Receiving aid:* Freshmen: 40% (308); all full-time undergraduates: 43% (2,356). *Average award:* Freshmen: $5916; Undergraduates: $6282. *Scholarships, grants, and awards:* Federal Pell, FSEOG, state, private, college/university gift aid from institutional funds.

GIFT AID (NON-NEED-BASED) *Average award:* Freshmen: $1136. Undergraduates: $1506. *Tuition waivers:* Full or partial for employees or children of employees.

LOANS *Student loans:* $22,236,880 (100% need-based). 61% of past graduating class borrowed through all loan programs. *Average indebtedness per student:* $20,923. *Average need-based loan:* Freshmen: $3071. Undergraduates: $4160. *Parent loans:* $3,300,595 (100% need-based). *Programs:* FFEL (Subsidized and Unsubsidized Stafford, PLUS), Perkins.

WORK-STUDY *Federal work-study:* Total amount: $360,238; 101 jobs averaging $3566. *State or other work-study/employment:* Total amount: $972,700 (86% need-based, 14% non-need-based). 290 part-time jobs averaging $3684.

ATHLETIC AWARDS Total amount: $568,235 (100% need-based).

APPLYING FOR FINANCIAL AID *Required financial aid form:* FAFSA. *Financial aid deadline (priority):* 3/1. *Notification date:* Continuous beginning 4/15.

University of Colorado at Colorado Springs

CONTACT Mr. Robert Bode, Director of Financial Aid, University of Colorado at Colorado Springs, 1420 Austin Bluffs Parkway, Colorado Springs, CO 80918, 719-255-3460 or toll-free 800-990-8227 Ext. 3383. *Fax:* 719-255-3650. *E-mail:* finaidse@uccs.edu.

UNIVERSITY OF COLORADO DENVER
Denver, CO

Tuition & fees (CO res): $6657	Average undergraduate aid package: $8804

ABOUT THE INSTITUTION State-supported, coed. 33 undergraduate majors. Federal methodology is used as a basis for awarding need-based institutional aid.

UNDERGRADUATE EXPENSES for 2010–11 *Tuition, state resident:* full-time $5712; part-time $238 per credit hour. *Tuition, nonresident:* full-time $18,744; part-time $781 per credit hour. *Required fees:* full-time $945. Full-time tuition and fees vary according to program and student level. Part-time tuition and fees vary according to program and student level. *College room and board:* $11,374; *Room only:* $6739. *Payment plans:* Installment, deferred payment.

FRESHMAN FINANCIAL AID (Fall 2008) 688 applied for aid; of those 81% were deemed to have need. 100% of freshmen with need received aid; of those 10% had need fully met. *Average percent of need met:* 59% (excluding resources awarded to replace EFC). *Average financial aid package:* $8129 (excluding resources awarded to replace EFC). 14% of all full-time freshmen had no need and received non-need-based gift aid.

UNDERGRADUATE FINANCIAL AID (Fall 2008) 4,154 applied for aid; of those 84% were deemed to have need. 100% of undergraduates with need received aid; of those 7% had need fully met. *Average percent of need met:* 55% (excluding resources awarded to replace EFC). *Average financial aid package:* $8804 (excluding resources awarded to replace EFC). 9% of all full-time undergraduates had no need and received non-need-based gift aid.

GIFT AID (NEED-BASED) *Total amount:* $18,701,122 (41% federal, 23% state, 28% institutional, 8% external sources). *Receiving aid:* Freshmen: 72% (533); all full-time undergraduates: 71% (3,178). *Average award:* Freshmen: $6292; Undergraduates: $5038. *Scholarships, grants, and awards:* Federal Pell, FSEOG, state, private, college/university gift aid from institutional funds, Federal Nursing.

GIFT AID (NON-NEED-BASED) *Total amount:* $2,140,857 (1% federal, 2% state, 56% institutional, 41% external sources). *Receiving aid:* Freshmen: 15% (112). Undergraduates: 10% (449). *Average award:* Freshmen: $3699. Undergraduates: $4268. *Tuition waivers:* Full or partial for employees or children of employees.

LOANS *Student loans:* $34,629,782 (78% need-based, 22% non-need-based). 66% of past graduating class borrowed through all loan programs. *Average indebtedness per student:* $21,264. *Average need-based loan:* Freshmen: $3074. Undergraduates: $4501. *Parent loans:* $5,513,428 (24% need-based, 76% non-need-based). *Programs:* FFEL (Subsidized and Unsubsidized Stafford, PLUS), Perkins, Federal Nursing, college/university.

WORK-STUDY *Federal work-study:* Total amount: $572,151; jobs available. *State or other work-study/employment:* Total amount: $934,016 (91% need-based, 9% non-need-based). Part-time jobs available.

APPLYING FOR FINANCIAL AID *Required financial aid forms:* FAFSA, institution's own form. *Financial aid deadline (priority):* 4/1. *Notification date:* Continuous beginning 5/1.

CONTACT Patrick McTee, Director of Financial Aid, University of Colorado Denver, PO Box 173364, Denver, CO 80217-3364, 303-556-2886. *Fax:* 303-556-2325. *E-mail:* patrick.mctee@ucdenver.edu.

UNIVERSITY OF CONNECTICUT
Storrs, CT

Tuition & fees (CT res): $10,416	Average undergraduate aid package: $12,238

ABOUT THE INSTITUTION State-supported, coed. 96 undergraduate majors. Federal methodology is used as a basis for awarding need-based institutional aid.

UNDERGRADUATE EXPENSES for 2010–11 *Tuition, state resident:* full-time $8064; part-time $336 per credit. *Tuition, nonresident:* full-time $24,528; part-time $1022 per credit. *Required fees:* full-time $2352. Part-time tuition and fees vary according to course load. *College room and board:* $10,782; *Room only:* $5774. Room and board charges vary according to board plan and housing facility. *Payment plans:* Installment, deferred payment.

FRESHMAN FINANCIAL AID (Fall 2009, est.) 2,694 applied for aid; of those 66% were deemed to have need. 98% of freshmen with need received aid; of those 19% had need fully met. *Average percent of need met:* 71% (excluding resources awarded to replace EFC). *Average financial aid package:* $12,930 (excluding resources awarded to replace EFC). 10% of all full-time freshmen had no need and received non-need-based gift aid.

UNDERGRADUATE FINANCIAL AID (Fall 2009, est.) 11,597 applied for aid; of those 75% were deemed to have need. 98% of undergraduates with need received aid; of those 18% had need fully met. *Average percent of need met:* 68% (excluding resources awarded to replace EFC). *Average financial aid package:* $12,238 (excluding resources awarded to replace EFC). 8% of all full-time undergraduates had no need and received non-need-based gift aid.

GIFT AID (NEED-BASED) *Total amount:* $62,818,280 (22% federal, 19% state, 55% institutional, 4% external sources). *Receiving aid:* Freshmen: 43% (1,392); all full-time undergraduates: 39% (6,392). *Average award:* Freshmen: $8071; Undergraduates: $7796. *Scholarships, grants, and awards:* Federal Pell, FSEOG, state, private, college/university gift aid from institutional funds.

GIFT AID (NON-NEED-BASED) *Total amount:* $11,164,311 (78% institutional, 22% external sources). *Receiving aid:* Freshmen: 39% (1,253). Undergraduates: 26% (4,197). *Average award:* Freshmen: $6866. Undergraduates: $6280. *Scholarships, grants, and awards by category: Academic interests/achievement:* 5,307 awards ($17,946,217 total): agriculture, biological sciences, business, computer science, education, engineering/technologies, English, foreign languages, general academic interests/achievements, health fields, humanities, international studies, mathematics, physical sciences, premedicine, religion/biblical studies, social sciences. *Creative arts/performance:* 116 awards ($199,900 total): art/fine arts, music, theater/drama. *Special achievements/activities:* 752 awards ($6,115,123 total): community service, leadership. *Special characteristics:* 4,708 awards ($14,637,142 total): adult students, children of faculty/staff, children of union members/company employees, local/state students, out-of-state students, spouses of deceased or disabled public servants, veterans. *Tuition waivers:* Full or partial for employees or children of employees, senior citizens.

LOANS *Student loans:* $70,341,589 (86% need-based, 14% non-need-based). 61% of past graduating class borrowed through all loan programs. *Average indebtedness per student:* $21,257. *Average need-based loan:* Freshmen: $3446. Undergraduates: $4204. *Parent loans:* $37,041,251 (31% need-based, 69% non-need-based). *Programs:* Federal Direct (Subsidized and Unsubsidized Stafford, PLUS), Perkins, Federal Nursing, state.

WORK-STUDY *Federal work-study:* Total amount: $2,828,624; 1,704 jobs averaging $1701. *State or other work-study/employment:* Total amount: $16,100,000 (30% need-based, 70% non-need-based). 5,503 part-time jobs averaging $2201.

ATHLETIC AWARDS Total amount: $8,552,052 (35% need-based, 65% non-need-based).

APPLYING FOR FINANCIAL AID *Required financial aid form:* FAFSA. *Financial aid deadline (priority):* 3/1. *Notification date:* Continuous beginning 3/1. Students must reply within 4 weeks of notification.

CONTACT Jean D. Main, Director, University of Connecticut, 233 Glenbrook Road, Unit 4116, Storrs, CT 06269-4116, 860-486-2819. *Fax:* 860-486-5098. *E-mail:* financialaid@uconn.edu.

UNIVERSITY OF DALLAS
Irving, TX

Tuition & fees: $27,815	Average undergraduate aid package: $20,532

ABOUT THE INSTITUTION Independent Roman Catholic, coed. 33 undergraduate majors. Federal methodology is used as a basis for awarding need-based institutional aid.

UNDERGRADUATE EXPENSES for 2010–11 *Comprehensive fee:* $36,465 includes full-time tuition ($26,100), mandatory fees ($1715), and room and board ($8650). *College room only:* $4820. Room and board charges vary according to board plan and housing facility. *Payment plan:* Installment.

FRESHMAN FINANCIAL AID (Fall 2009, est.) 256 applied for aid; of those 82% were deemed to have need. 100% of freshmen with need received aid; of those 28% had need fully met. *Average percent of need met:* 79% (excluding resources awarded to replace EFC). *Average financial aid package:* $21,054 (excluding resources awarded to replace EFC). 35% of all full-time freshmen had no need and received non-need-based gift aid.

UNDERGRADUATE FINANCIAL AID (Fall 2009, est.) 869 applied for aid; of those 88% were deemed to have need. 100% of undergraduates with need received aid; of those 23% had need fully met. *Average percent of need met:* 76% (excluding resources awarded to replace EFC). *Average financial aid package:* $20,532 (excluding resources awarded to replace EFC). 33% of all full-time undergraduates had no need and received non-need-based gift aid.
GIFT AID (NEED-BASED) *Total amount:* $15,317,304 (8% federal, 5% state, 85% institutional, 2% external sources). *Receiving aid:* Freshmen: 61% (208); all full-time undergraduates: 60% (759). *Average award:* Freshmen: $16,393; Undergraduates: $15,703. *Scholarships, grants, and awards:* Federal Pell, FSEOG, state, private, college/university gift aid from institutional funds.
GIFT AID (NON-NEED-BASED) *Total amount:* $2,009,065 (1% federal, 93% institutional, 6% external sources). *Receiving aid:* Freshmen: 7% (25). Undergraduates: 5% (68). *Average award:* Freshmen: $11,500. Undergraduates: $11,064. *Scholarships, grants, and awards by category: Academic interests/achievement:* 771 awards ($4,336,500 total): business, education, foreign languages, general academic interests/achievements, mathematics, physical sciences, premedicine, religion/biblical studies. *Creative arts/performance:* 40 awards ($86,000 total): art/fine arts, music, theater/drama. *Special achievements/activities:* 30 awards ($71,000 total): leadership. *Special characteristics:* 140 awards ($570,000 total): children of faculty/staff, religious affiliation, siblings of current students. *Tuition waivers:* Full or partial for employees or children of employees.
LOANS *Student loans:* $6,338,373 (47% need-based, 53% non-need-based). 57% of past graduating class borrowed through all loan programs. *Average indebtedness per student:* $24,650. *Average need-based loan:* Freshmen: $3865. Undergraduates: $4489. *Parent loans:* $952,202 (100% non-need-based). *Programs:* FFEL (Subsidized and Unsubsidized Stafford, PLUS), state.
WORK-STUDY *Federal work-study:* Total amount: $333,480; 292 jobs averaging $1655. *State or other work-study/employment:* Total amount: $87,573 (46% need-based, 54% non-need-based). 15 part-time jobs averaging $1250.
APPLYING FOR FINANCIAL AID *Required financial aid form:* FAFSA. *Financial aid deadline (priority):* 3/1. *Notification date:* Continuous. Students must reply by 5/1 or within 2 weeks of notification.
CONTACT Mrs. Laurie Rosenkrantz, Assistant Dean of Enrollment Management, University of Dallas, 1845 East Northgate Drive, Irving, TX 75062, 972-721-5266 or toll-free 800-628-6999. *Fax:* 972-721-5017. *E-mail:* ugadmis@udallas.edu.

UNIVERSITY OF DAYTON
Dayton, OH

Tuition & fees: $29,930	Average undergraduate aid package: $19,558

ABOUT THE INSTITUTION Independent Roman Catholic, coed. 73 undergraduate majors. Federal methodology is used as a basis for awarding need-based institutional aid.
UNDERGRADUATE EXPENSES for 2010–11 *Comprehensive fee:* $39,330 includes full-time tuition ($28,700), mandatory fees ($1230), and room and board ($9400). *College room only:* $5940. Full-time tuition and fees vary according to degree level and program. Room and board charges vary according to board plan, housing facility, and student level. *Part-time tuition:* $917 per credit hour. Part-time tuition and fees vary according to course load, degree level, and program. *Payment plan:* Deferred payment.
FRESHMAN FINANCIAL AID (Fall 2008) 1,540 applied for aid; of those 72% were deemed to have need. 100% of freshmen with need received aid; of those 47% had need fully met. *Average percent of need met:* 98% (excluding resources awarded to replace EFC). *Average financial aid package:* $19,992 (excluding resources awarded to replace EFC). 44% of all full-time freshmen had no need and received non-need-based gift aid.
UNDERGRADUATE FINANCIAL AID (Fall 2008) 5,092 applied for aid; of those 79% were deemed to have need. 96% of undergraduates with need received aid; of those 50% had need fully met. *Average percent of need met:* 94% (excluding resources awarded to replace EFC). *Average financial aid package:* $19,558 (excluding resources awarded to replace EFC). 42% of all full-time undergraduates had no need and received non-need-based gift aid.
GIFT AID (NEED-BASED) *Total amount:* $43,625,947 (9% federal, 6% state, 81% institutional, 4% external sources). *Receiving aid:* Freshmen: 39% (772); all full-time undergraduates: 48% (3,416). *Average award:* Freshmen: $13,467; Undergraduates: $12,883. *Scholarships, grants, and awards:* Federal Pell, FSEOG, state, private, college/university gift aid from institutional funds.

GIFT AID (NON-NEED-BASED) *Total amount:* $26,855,696 (5% federal, 4% state, 89% institutional, 2% external sources). *Receiving aid:* Freshmen: 53% (1,062). Undergraduates: 51% (3,629). *Average award:* Freshmen: $8913. Undergraduates: $7741. *Scholarships, grants, and awards by category: Academic interests/achievement:* 6,132 awards ($43,139,021 total): business, education, engineering/technologies, general academic interests/achievements, humanities. *Creative arts/performance:* 89 awards ($359,250 total): art/fine arts, music. *Special achievements/activities:* general special achievements/activities. *Special characteristics:* 421 awards ($9,247,741 total): children of faculty/staff, religious affiliation. *Tuition waivers:* Full or partial for employees or children of employees, senior citizens.
LOANS *Student loans:* $38,091,684 (81% need-based, 19% non-need-based). 58% of past graduating class borrowed through all loan programs. *Average indebtedness per student:* $35,865. *Average need-based loan:* Freshmen: $6962. Undergraduates: $7942. *Parent loans:* $7,700,189 (74% need-based, 26% non-need-based). *Programs:* Federal Direct (Subsidized and Unsubsidized Stafford, PLUS), Perkins, state, college/university.
WORK-STUDY *Federal work-study:* Total amount: $1,048,845; 780 jobs averaging $1401. *State or other work-study/employment:* Total amount: $6,436,846 (100% non-need-based). 2,483 part-time jobs averaging $1880.
ATHLETIC AWARDS Total amount: $3,131,549 (46% need-based, 54% non-need-based).
APPLYING FOR FINANCIAL AID *Required financial aid form:* FAFSA. *Financial aid deadline (priority):* 3/31. *Notification date:* Continuous beginning 3/5. Students must reply within 3 weeks of notification.
CONTACT Kathy Harmon, Director of Scholarships and Financial Aid, University of Dayton, 300 College Park Drive, Dayton, OH 45469-1305, 937-229-4311 or toll-free 800-837-7433. *Fax:* 937-229-4338. *E-mail:* kharmon@udayton.edu.

UNIVERSITY OF DELAWARE
Newark, DE

Tuition & fees (DE res): $9486	Average undergraduate aid package: $12,675

ABOUT THE INSTITUTION State-related, coed. 116 undergraduate majors. Federal methodology is used as a basis for awarding need-based institutional aid.
UNDERGRADUATE EXPENSES for 2009–10 *Tuition, state resident:* full-time $8540; part-time $356 per credit. *Tuition, nonresident:* full-time $22,240; part-time $927 per credit. *Required fees:* full-time $946. *College room and board:* $9066; *Room only:* $5466. Room and board charges vary according to board plan, housing facility, and student level. *Payment plan:* Installment.
FRESHMAN FINANCIAL AID (Fall 2009, est.) 3,319 applied for aid; of those 56% were deemed to have need. 96% of freshmen with need received aid; of those 56% had need fully met. *Average percent of need met:* 78% (excluding resources awarded to replace EFC). *Average financial aid package:* $12,610 (excluding resources awarded to replace EFC). 16% of all full-time freshmen had no need and received non-need-based gift aid.
UNDERGRADUATE FINANCIAL AID (Fall 2009, est.) 10,301 applied for aid; of those 64% were deemed to have need. 97% of undergraduates with need received aid; of those 51% had need fully met. *Average percent of need met:* 76% (excluding resources awarded to replace EFC). *Average financial aid package:* $12,675 (excluding resources awarded to replace EFC). 20% of all full-time undergraduates had no need and received non-need-based gift aid.
GIFT AID (NEED-BASED) *Total amount:* $28,667,994 (30% federal, 23% state, 39% institutional, 8% external sources). *Receiving aid:* Freshmen: 36% (1,336); all full-time undergraduates: 39% (4,394). *Average award:* Freshmen: $7156; Undergraduates: $6398. *Scholarships, grants, and awards:* Federal Pell, FSEOG, state, private, college/university gift aid from institutional funds.
GIFT AID (NON-NEED-BASED) *Total amount:* $16,875,370 (9% state, 78% institutional, 13% external sources). *Receiving aid:* Freshmen: 22% (823). Undergraduates: 16% (1,760). *Average award:* Freshmen: $5746. Undergraduates: $5965. *Scholarships, grants, and awards by category: Academic interests/achievement:* agriculture, biological sciences, business, communication, computer science, education, engineering/technologies, English, foreign languages, general academic interests/achievements, health fields, humanities, international studies, mathematics, military science, physical sciences, premedicine, religion/biblical studies, social sciences. *Creative arts/performance:* applied art and design, art/fine arts, music, theater/drama. *Special achievements/activities:* cheerleading/drum major, community service, general special achievements/activities, leadership. *Special characteristics:* children and siblings of alumni, children of faculty/staff, children of public servants, ethnic background, first-

generation college students, general special characteristics, local/state students, members of minority groups. *Tuition waivers:* Full or partial for employees or children of employees, senior citizens.

LOANS *Student loans:* $77,149,510 (54% need-based, 46% non-need-based). 44% of past graduating class borrowed through all loan programs. *Average indebtedness per student:* $17,200. *Average need-based loan:* Freshmen: $6075. Undergraduates: $7543. *Parent loans:* $26,956,079 (30% need-based, 70% non-need-based). *Programs:* Federal Direct (Subsidized and Unsubsidized Stafford, PLUS), Perkins, Federal Nursing.

WORK-STUDY *Federal work-study:* Total amount: $1,069,414; jobs available. *State or other work-study/employment:* Total amount: $290,229 (73% need-based, 27% non-need-based). Part-time jobs available.

ATHLETIC AWARDS Total amount: $7,936,190 (23% need-based, 77% non-need-based).

APPLYING FOR FINANCIAL AID *Required financial aid form:* FAFSA. *Financial aid deadline:* 3/15 (priority: 2/1). *Notification date:* Continuous beginning 3/15. Students must reply by 5/1 or within 3 weeks of notification.

CONTACT Mr. James Holloway, Associate Director of Financial Aid, University of Delaware, 140 University Visitors Center, Newark, DE 19716, 302-831-8081. *Fax:* 302-831-4334. *E-mail:* holloway@udel.edu.

UNIVERSITY OF DENVER
Denver, CO

Tuition & fees: $36,501	Average undergraduate aid package: $28,632

ABOUT THE INSTITUTION Independent, coed. 73 undergraduate majors. Both federal and institutional methodology are used as a basis for awarding need-based institutional aid.

UNDERGRADUATE EXPENSES for 2010–11 *Comprehensive fee:* $46,725 includes full-time tuition ($35,604), mandatory fees ($897), and room and board ($10,224). *College room only:* $6240. *Part-time tuition:* $989 per quarter hour.

FRESHMAN FINANCIAL AID (Fall 2009, est.) 771 applied for aid; of those 72% were deemed to have need. 100% of freshmen with need received aid; of those 30% had need fully met. *Average percent of need met:* 83% (excluding resources awarded to replace EFC). *Average financial aid package:* $29,211 (excluding resources awarded to replace EFC). 34% of all full-time freshmen had no need and received non-need-based gift aid.

UNDERGRADUATE FINANCIAL AID (Fall 2009, est.) 2,524 applied for aid; of those 80% were deemed to have need. 100% of undergraduates with need received aid; of those 27% had need fully met. *Average percent of need met:* 81% (excluding resources awarded to replace EFC). *Average financial aid package:* $28,632 (excluding resources awarded to replace EFC). 37% of all full-time undergraduates had no need and received non-need-based gift aid.

GIFT AID (NEED-BASED) *Total amount:* $45,114,959 (11% federal, 2% state, 79% institutional, 8% external sources). *Receiving aid:* Freshmen: 46% (552); all full-time undergraduates: 42% (1,976). *Average award:* Freshmen: $24,394; Undergraduates: $23,435. *Scholarships, grants, and awards:* Federal Pell, FSEOG, state, private, college/university gift aid from institutional funds.

GIFT AID (NON-NEED-BASED) *Total amount:* $22,162,814 (1% federal, 91% institutional, 8% external sources). *Receiving aid:* Freshmen: 9% (109). Undergraduates: 6% (304). *Average award:* Freshmen: $14,739. Undergraduates: $11,172. *Scholarships, grants, and awards by category: Academic interests/achievement:* biological sciences, business, communication, computer science, engineering/technologies, general academic interests/achievements, humanities, international studies, mathematics, physical sciences, social sciences. *Creative arts/performance:* art/fine arts, debating, music, theater/drama. *Special achievements/activities:* community service, leadership.

LOANS *Student loans:* $17,196,048 (62% need-based, 38% non-need-based). 45% of past graduating class borrowed through all loan programs. *Average indebtedness per student:* $26,986. *Average need-based loan:* Freshmen: $3339. Undergraduates: $4310. *Parent loans:* $6,578,822 (23% need-based, 77% non-need-based). *Programs:* Federal Direct (Subsidized and Unsubsidized Stafford, PLUS), Perkins, college/university.

WORK-STUDY *Federal work-study:* Total amount: $1,207,812; 552 jobs averaging $2280. *State or other work-study/employment:* Total amount: $536,896 (90% need-based, 10% non-need-based). 267 part-time jobs averaging $1820.

ATHLETIC AWARDS Total amount: $7,329,513 (15% need-based, 85% non-need-based).

APPLYING FOR FINANCIAL AID *Required financial aid forms:* FAFSA, CSS Financial Aid PROFILE, noncustodial (divorced/separated) parent's statement. *Financial aid deadline (priority):* 3/1. *Notification date:* 4/1. Students must reply by 5/1.

CONTACT Ms. Julia Benz, Assistant Vice Chancellor, Scholarships and Financial Aid, University of Denver, University Hall, Room 255A, 2197 South University Boulevard, Denver, CO 80208, 303-871-2880 or toll-free 800-525-9495 (out-of-state). *Fax:* 303-871-2341. *E-mail:* finaid@du.edu.

UNIVERSITY OF DETROIT MERCY
Detroit, MI

CONTACT Sandy Ross, Director of Financial Aid and Scholarships, University of Detroit Mercy, 4001 West McNichols Road, Detroit, MI 48221-3038, 313-993-3350 or toll-free 800-635-5020 (out-of-state). *Fax:* 313-993-3347.

UNIVERSITY OF DUBUQUE
Dubuque, IA

Tuition & fees: $21,590	Average undergraduate aid package: $18,863

ABOUT THE INSTITUTION Independent Presbyterian, coed. 32 undergraduate majors. Federal methodology is used as a basis for awarding need-based institutional aid.

UNDERGRADUATE EXPENSES for 2010–11 *One-time required fee:* $100. *Comprehensive fee:* $28,960 includes full-time tuition ($21,000), mandatory fees ($590), and room and board ($7370). *College room only:* $3640. Room and board charges vary according to board plan, housing facility, and location. *Part-time tuition:* $460 per credit hour. *Payment plan:* Installment.

FRESHMAN FINANCIAL AID (Fall 2009, est.) 348 applied for aid; of those 94% were deemed to have need. 100% of freshmen with need received aid; of those 29% had need fully met. *Average percent of need met:* 79% (excluding resources awarded to replace EFC). *Average financial aid package:* $19,471 (excluding resources awarded to replace EFC). 8% of all full-time freshmen had no need and received non-need-based gift aid.

UNDERGRADUATE FINANCIAL AID (Fall 2009, est.) 1,329 applied for aid; of those 93% were deemed to have need. 100% of undergraduates with need received aid; of those 26% had need fully met. *Average percent of need met:* 76% (excluding resources awarded to replace EFC). *Average financial aid package:* $18,863 (excluding resources awarded to replace EFC). 9% of all full-time undergraduates had no need and received non-need-based gift aid.

GIFT AID (NEED-BASED) *Total amount:* $15,520,083 (22% federal, 10% state, 50% institutional, 18% external sources). *Receiving aid:* Freshmen: 91% (326); all full-time undergraduates: 89% (1,226). *Average award:* Freshmen: $13,141; Undergraduates: $12,504. *Scholarships, grants, and awards:* Federal Pell, FSEOG, state, private, college/university gift aid from institutional funds.

GIFT AID (NON-NEED-BASED) *Total amount:* $2,449,112 (47% institutional, 53% external sources). *Receiving aid:* Freshmen: 14% (50). Undergraduates: 10% (141). *Average award:* Freshmen: $7158. Undergraduates: $6968. *Scholarships, grants, and awards by category: Academic interests/achievement:* general academic interests/achievements. *Special characteristics:* children and siblings of alumni, children of educators, children of faculty/staff, ethnic background, members of minority groups, out-of-state students, relatives of clergy, religious affiliation, siblings of current students. *Tuition waivers:* Full or partial for employees or children of employees.

LOANS *Student loans:* $13,857,719 (76% need-based, 24% non-need-based). 85% of past graduating class borrowed through all loan programs. *Average indebtedness per student:* $41,399. *Average need-based loan:* Freshmen: $7200. Undergraduates: $7135. *Parent loans:* $987,899 (49% need-based, 51% non-need-based). *Programs:* Federal Direct (Subsidized and Unsubsidized Stafford, PLUS), Perkins, state, college/university.

WORK-STUDY *Federal work-study:* Total amount: $212,683; 175 jobs averaging $1500. *State or other work-study/employment:* Total amount: $145,000 (100% need-based). Part-time jobs available.

APPLYING FOR FINANCIAL AID *Required financial aid form:* FAFSA. *Financial aid deadline:* Continuous. *Notification date:* Continuous beginning 3/1. Students must reply within 3 weeks of notification.

CONTACT Mr. Timothy Kremer, Dean of Student Financial Planning, University of Dubuque, 2000 University Avenue, Dubuque, IA 52001-5050, 563-589-3170 or toll-free 800-722-5583 (in-state). *Fax:* 563-589-3690.

UNIVERSITY OF EVANSVILLE
Evansville, IN

Tuition & fees: $26,756	Average undergraduate aid package: $22,537

ABOUT THE INSTITUTION Independent religious, coed. 82 undergraduate majors. Federal methodology is used as a basis for awarding need-based institutional aid.

UNDERGRADUATE EXPENSES for 2009–10 *Comprehensive fee:* $35,426 includes full-time tuition ($26,010), mandatory fees ($746), and room and board ($8670). *College room only:* $4470. Room and board charges vary according to board plan and housing facility. *Part-time tuition:* $725 per hour. *Part-time fees:* $45 per term. Part-time tuition and fees vary according to course load. *Payment plan:* Installment.

FRESHMAN FINANCIAL AID (Fall 2009, est.) 654 applied for aid; of those 85% were deemed to have need. 99% of freshmen with need received aid; of those 30% had need fully met. *Average percent of need met:* 92% (excluding resources awarded to replace EFC). *Average financial aid package:* $25,222 (excluding resources awarded to replace EFC). 18% of all full-time freshmen had no need and received non-need-based gift aid.

UNDERGRADUATE FINANCIAL AID (Fall 2009, est.) 2,123 applied for aid; of those 84% were deemed to have need. 100% of undergraduates with need received aid; of those 25% had need fully met. *Average percent of need met:* 83% (excluding resources awarded to replace EFC). *Average financial aid package:* $22,537 (excluding resources awarded to replace EFC). 21% of all full-time undergraduates had no need and received non-need-based gift aid.

GIFT AID (NEED-BASED) *Total amount:* $32,207,101 (11% federal, 11% state, 73% institutional, 5% external sources). *Receiving aid:* Freshmen: 78% (550); all full-time undergraduates: 71% (1,749). *Average award:* Freshmen: $22,648; Undergraduates: $19,392. *Scholarships, grants, and awards:* Federal Pell, FSEOG, state, college/university gift aid from institutional funds.

GIFT AID (NON-NEED-BASED) *Total amount:* $7,044,348 (94% institutional, 6% external sources). *Receiving aid:* Freshmen: 74% (522). Undergraduates: 62% (1,534). *Average award:* Freshmen: $15,676. Undergraduates: $12,866. *Scholarships, grants, and awards by category: Academic interests/achievement:* 1,369 awards ($14,710,808 total): biological sciences, business, communication, computer science, education, engineering/technologies, English, foreign languages, general academic interests/achievements, health fields, humanities, international studies, mathematics, physical sciences, premedicine, religion/biblical studies, social sciences. *Creative arts/performance:* 193 awards ($1,887,203 total): art/fine arts, music, theater/drama. *Special achievements/activities:* 83 awards ($45,835 total): leadership, memberships. *Special characteristics:* 478 awards ($4,758,466 total): children and siblings of alumni, children of faculty/staff, international students, members of minority groups, religious affiliation, siblings of current students. *Tuition waivers:* Full or partial for minority students, children of alumni, employees or children of employees, senior citizens.

LOANS *Student loans:* $10,011,638 (94% need-based, 6% non-need-based). 72% of past graduating class borrowed through all loan programs. *Average indebtedness per student:* $25,598. *Average need-based loan:* Freshmen: $3753. Undergraduates: $4615. *Parent loans:* $4,803,945 (91% need-based, 9% non-need-based). *Programs:* Federal Direct (Subsidized and Unsubsidized Stafford, PLUS), Perkins, Federal Nursing, college/university.

WORK-STUDY *Federal work-study:* Total amount: $618,600; 414 jobs averaging $1560. *State or other work-study/employment:* Total amount: $25,500 (33% need-based, 67% non-need-based). 15 part-time jobs averaging $1590.

ATHLETIC AWARDS Total amount: $3,925,630 (45% need-based, 55% non-need-based).

APPLYING FOR FINANCIAL AID *Required financial aid form:* FAFSA. *Financial aid deadline (priority):* 3/10. *Notification date:* Continuous beginning 3/25. Students must reply by 5/1.

CONTACT Ms. JoAnn E. Laugel, Director of Financial Aid, University of Evansville, 1800 Lincoln Avenue, Evansville, IN 47722, 812-488-2364 or toll-free 800-423-8633 Ext. 2468. *Fax:* 812-488-2028. *E-mail:* jl25@evansville.edu.

THE UNIVERSITY OF FINDLAY
Findlay, OH

Tuition & fees: $25,774	Average undergraduate aid package: $17,345

ABOUT THE INSTITUTION Independent religious, coed. 59 undergraduate majors. Federal methodology is used as a basis for awarding need-based institutional aid.

UNDERGRADUATE EXPENSES for 2009–10 *Comprehensive fee:* $34,328 includes full-time tuition ($25,016), mandatory fees ($758), and room and board ($8554). *College room only:* $4268. Full-time tuition and fees vary according to course load and program. *Part-time tuition:* $552 per semester hour. *Part-time fees:* $722 per term. Part-time tuition and fees vary according to course load and program. *Payment plan:* Installment.

FRESHMAN FINANCIAL AID (Fall 2009, est.) 585 applied for aid; of those 79% were deemed to have need. 100% of freshmen with need received aid; of those 10% had need fully met. *Average percent of need met:* 71% (excluding resources awarded to replace EFC). *Average financial aid package:* $19,022 (excluding resources awarded to replace EFC). 15% of all full-time freshmen had no need and received non-need-based gift aid.

UNDERGRADUATE FINANCIAL AID (Fall 2009, est.) 2,428 applied for aid; of those 79% were deemed to have need. 100% of undergraduates with need received aid; of those 10% had need fully met. *Average percent of need met:* 68% (excluding resources awarded to replace EFC). *Average financial aid package:* $17,345 (excluding resources awarded to replace EFC). 15% of all full-time undergraduates had no need and received non-need-based gift aid.

GIFT AID (NEED-BASED) *Total amount:* $27,820,700 (12% federal, 3% state, 82% institutional, 3% external sources). *Receiving aid:* Freshmen: 63% (409); all full-time undergraduates: 63% (1,695). *Average award:* Freshmen: $12,203; Undergraduates: $10,362. *Scholarships, grants, and awards:* Federal Pell, FSEOG, state, college/university gift aid from institutional funds.

GIFT AID (NON-NEED-BASED) *Total amount:* $3,821,300 (97% institutional, 3% external sources). *Receiving aid:* Freshmen: 72% (462). Undergraduates: 71% (1,915). *Average award:* Freshmen: $11,464. Undergraduates: $10,110. *Scholarships, grants, and awards by category: Academic interests/achievement:* general academic interests/achievements. *Creative arts/performance:* music, theater/drama. *Special characteristics:* children of faculty/staff. *Tuition waivers:* Full or partial for children of alumni, employees or children of employees, senior citizens.

LOANS *Student loans:* $25,525,000 (82% need-based, 18% non-need-based). 89% of past graduating class borrowed through all loan programs. *Average indebtedness per student:* $32,800. *Average need-based loan:* Freshmen: $2828. Undergraduates: $4950. *Parent loans:* $2,440,000 (80% need-based, 20% non-need-based). *Programs:* Federal Direct (Subsidized and Unsubsidized Stafford, PLUS), Perkins, college/university.

WORK-STUDY *Federal work-study:* Total amount: $550,000; 420 jobs averaging $830. *State or other work-study/employment:* 300 part-time jobs averaging $850.

ATHLETIC AWARDS Total amount: $2,827,000 (80% need-based, 20% non-need-based).

APPLYING FOR FINANCIAL AID *Required financial aid form:* FAFSA. *Financial aid deadline:* Continuous. *Notification date:* Continuous beginning 3/1. Students must reply within 2 weeks of notification.

CONTACT Mr. Arman Habegger, Director of Financial Aid, The University of Findlay, 1000 North Main Street, Findlay, OH 45840-3695, 419-434-4791 or toll-free 800-548-0932. *Fax:* 419-434-4344. *E-mail:* finaid@findlay.edu.

UNIVERSITY OF FLORIDA
Gainesville, FL

Tuition & fees (FL res): $4373	Average undergraduate aid package: $12,768

ABOUT THE INSTITUTION State-supported, coed. 100 undergraduate majors. Federal methodology is used as a basis for awarding need-based institutional aid.

UNDERGRADUATE EXPENSES for 2009–10 *Tuition, state resident:* full-time $4373; part-time $145.76 per credit hour. *Tuition, nonresident:* full-time $23,744; part-time $791.47 per credit hour. *College room and board:* $7500; *Room only:* $4860.

FRESHMAN FINANCIAL AID (Fall 2009, est.) 4,432 applied for aid; of those 60% were deemed to have need. 100% of freshmen with need received aid; of those 41% had need fully met. *Average percent of need met:* 86% (excluding resources awarded to replace EFC). *Average financial aid package:* $12,792 (excluding resources awarded to replace EFC). 56% of all full-time freshmen had no need and received non-need-based gift aid.

UNDERGRADUATE FINANCIAL AID (Fall 2009, est.) 18,087 applied for aid; of those 78% were deemed to have need. 99% of undergraduates with need received aid; of those 33% had need fully met. *Average percent of need met:* 82% (excluding resources awarded to replace EFC). *Average financial aid package:* $12,768 (excluding resources awarded to replace EFC). 51% of all full-time undergraduates had no need and received non-need-based gift aid. **GIFT AID (NEED-BASED)** *Total amount:* $48,310,873 (68% federal, 14% state, 18% institutional). *Receiving aid:* Freshmen: 25% (1,587); all full-time undergraduates: 26% (9,026). *Average award:* Freshmen: $6738; Undergraduates: $6415. *Scholarships, grants, and awards:* Federal Pell, FSEOG, state, private, college/university gift aid from institutional funds.

GIFT AID (NON-NEED-BASED) *Total amount:* $141,972,629 (1% federal, 59% state, 12% institutional, 28% external sources). *Receiving aid:* Freshmen: 40% (2,557). Undergraduates: 32% (11,016). *Average award:* Freshmen: $5881. Undergraduates: $4925. *Scholarships, grants, and awards by category:* Academic interests/achievement: agriculture, architecture, business, communication, computer science, education, engineering/technologies, general academic interests/achievements, health fields, military science. *Creative arts/performance:* art/fine arts, dance, general creative arts/performance, journalism/publications, music, performing arts, theater/drama. *Special achievements/activities:* community service, general special achievements/activities, leadership. *Special characteristics:* children of faculty/staff, members of minority groups, out-of-state students.

LOANS *Student loans:* $62,496,967 (45% need-based, 55% non-need-based). 41% of past graduating class borrowed through all loan programs. *Average indebtedness per student:* $15,932. *Average need-based loan:* Freshmen: $3098. Undergraduates: $4312. *Parent loans:* $5,081,978 (100% non-need-based). *Programs:* Federal Direct (Subsidized and Unsubsidized Stafford, PLUS), Perkins, college/university.

WORK-STUDY *Federal work-study:* Total amount: $1,675,601; 1,106 jobs averaging $1515. *State or other work-study/employment:* Total amount: $8,050,029 (100% non-need-based). 4,184 part-time jobs averaging $1924. **ATHLETIC AWARDS** Total amount: $7,257,984 (100% non-need-based). **APPLYING FOR FINANCIAL AID** *Required financial aid form:* FAFSA. *Financial aid deadline (priority):* 3/15. *Notification date:* Continuous beginning 3/20. **CONTACT** Ms. Karen L. Fooks, Director of Student Financial Affairs, University of Florida, S-107 Criser Hall, Gainesville, FL 32611-4025, 352-392-1271. *Fax:* 352-392-2861. *E-mail:* kfooks@ufl.edu.

UNIVERSITY OF GEORGIA
Athens, GA

Tuition & fees (GA res): $7530	Average undergraduate aid package: $9509

ABOUT THE INSTITUTION State-supported, coed. 126 undergraduate majors. Federal methodology is used as a basis for awarding need-based institutional aid.

UNDERGRADUATE EXPENSES for 2009–10 *Tuition, state resident:* full-time $6070; part-time $203 per credit. *Tuition, nonresident:* full-time $24,280; part-time $882 per credit. *Required fees:* full-time $1460; $730 per term. Full-time tuition and fees vary according to course load, location, and program. Part-time tuition and fees vary according to course load, location, and program. *College room and board:* $8046; *Room only:* $4524. Room and board charges vary according to board plan and housing facility. *Payment plan:* Guaranteed tuition.

FRESHMAN FINANCIAL AID (Fall 2009, est.) 3,359 applied for aid; of those 49% were deemed to have need. 99% of freshmen with need received aid; of those 29% had need fully met. *Average percent of need met:* 83% (excluding resources awarded to replace EFC). *Average financial aid package:* $11,122 (excluding resources awarded to replace EFC). 6% of all full-time freshmen had no need and received non-need-based gift aid.

UNDERGRADUATE FINANCIAL AID (Fall 2009, est.) 13,377 applied for aid; of those 60% were deemed to have need. 99% of undergraduates with need received aid; of those 18% had need fully met. *Average percent of need met:* 76% (excluding resources awarded to replace EFC). *Average financial aid package:* $9509 (excluding resources awarded to replace EFC). 5% of all full-time undergraduates had no need and received non-need-based gift aid.

GIFT AID (NEED-BASED) *Total amount:* $54,350,776 (41% federal, 53% state, 3% institutional, 3% external sources). *Receiving aid:* Freshmen: 34% (1,600); all full-time undergraduates: 29% (7,036). *Average award:* Freshmen: $9976;

Undergraduates: $7953. *Scholarships, grants, and awards:* Federal Pell, FSEOG, state, private, college/university gift aid from institutional funds. **GIFT AID (NON-NEED-BASED)** *Total amount:* $78,411,638 (1% federal, 92% state, 3% institutional, 4% external sources). *Receiving aid:* Freshmen: 10% (450). Undergraduates: 5% (1,297). *Average award:* Freshmen: $1507. Undergraduates: $1872. *Scholarships, grants, and awards by category:* Academic interests/achievement: 21,417 awards ($108,884,031 total): agriculture, business, education, general academic interests/achievements. *Creative arts/performance:* 93 awards ($103,100 total): music. *Special characteristics:* 248 awards ($413,250 total): local/state students. *Tuition waivers:* Full or partial for senior citizens.

LOANS *Student loans:* $61,155,344 (47% need-based, 53% non-need-based). 44% of past graduating class borrowed through all loan programs. *Average indebtedness per student:* $14,766. *Average need-based loan:* Freshmen: $2834. Undergraduates: $3809. *Parent loans:* $10,358,679 (22% need-based, 78% non-need-based). *Programs:* Federal Direct (Subsidized and Unsubsidized Stafford, PLUS), Perkins, state, college/university.

WORK-STUDY *Federal work-study:* Total amount: $1,110,082; 440 jobs averaging $2523. **ATHLETIC AWARDS** Total amount: $6,988,462 (25% need-based, 75% non-need-based).

APPLYING FOR FINANCIAL AID *Required financial aid form:* FAFSA. *Financial aid deadline (priority):* 3/1. *Notification date:* Continuous beginning 4/1. Students must reply within 2 weeks of notification. **CONTACT** Ms. Bonnie C. Joerschke, Financial Aid Director, University of Georgia, 220 Holmes/Hunter Academic Building, Athens, GA 30602-6114, 706-542-8208. *Fax:* 706-542-0977. *E-mail:* bonniej@uga.edu.

UNIVERSITY OF GREAT FALLS
Great Falls, MT

Tuition & fees: $18,856	Average undergraduate aid package: $15,294

ABOUT THE INSTITUTION Independent Roman Catholic, coed. 73 undergraduate majors. Both federal and institutional methodology are used as a basis for awarding need-based institutional aid.

UNDERGRADUATE EXPENSES for 2010–11 *Comprehensive fee:* $25,568 includes full-time tuition ($17,856), mandatory fees ($1000), and room and board ($6712). *College room only:* $3512. Full-time tuition and fees vary according to course load. Room and board charges vary according to housing facility. *Part-time tuition:* $566 per credit hour. Part-time tuition and fees vary according to course load, location, and program. *Payment plan:* Installment.

FRESHMAN FINANCIAL AID (Fall 2009, est.) 106 applied for aid; of those 100% were deemed to have need. 99% of freshmen with need received aid; of those 4% had need fully met. *Average percent of need met:* 64% (excluding resources awarded to replace EFC). *Average financial aid package:* $15,452 (excluding resources awarded to replace EFC). 6% of all full-time freshmen had no need and received non-need-based gift aid.

UNDERGRADUATE FINANCIAL AID (Fall 2009, est.) 428 applied for aid; of those 100% were deemed to have need. 100% of undergraduates with need received aid; of those 2% had need fully met. *Average percent of need met:* 60% (excluding resources awarded to replace EFC). *Average financial aid package:* $15,294 (excluding resources awarded to replace EFC). 4% of all full-time undergraduates had no need and received non-need-based gift aid.

GIFT AID (NEED-BASED) *Total amount:* $3,728,014 (53% federal, 47% institutional). *Receiving aid:* Freshmen: 39% (61); all full-time undergraduates: 49% (286). *Average award:* Freshmen: $4919; Undergraduates: $5238. *Scholarships, grants, and awards:* Federal Pell, private, college/university gift aid from institutional funds.

GIFT AID (NON-NEED-BASED) *Total amount:* $259,784 (100% institutional). *Receiving aid:* Freshmen: 64% (100). Undergraduates: 68% (401). *Average award:* Freshmen: $11,873. Undergraduates: $9542. *Scholarships, grants, and awards by category:* Academic interests/achievement: biological sciences, business, computer science, education, general academic interests/achievements, humanities, mathematics, physical sciences, premedicine, religion/biblical studies, social sciences. *Creative arts/performance:* art/fine arts, dance. *Special achievements/activities:* cheerleading/drum major, religious involvement. *Special characteristics:* children of current students, children of faculty/staff, ethnic background, first-generation college students, international students, parents of current students, religious affiliation, siblings of current students, spouses of current students.

LOANS *Student loans:* 67% of past graduating class borrowed through all loan programs. *Average need-based loan:* Freshmen: $3405. Undergraduates: $4364. *Programs:* Federal Direct (Subsidized and Unsubsidized Stafford, PLUS), FFEL (Subsidized and Unsubsidized Stafford, PLUS), Perkins, college/university.
WORK-STUDY Federal work-study jobs available. *State or other work-study/ employment:* Part-time jobs available.
ATHLETIC AWARDS Total amount: $1,590,326 (100% non-need-based).
APPLYING FOR FINANCIAL AID *Required financial aid form:* FAFSA. *Financial aid deadline (priority):* 5/1. *Notification date:* Continuous. Students must reply within 2 weeks of notification.
CONTACT Sandra Bauman, Director of Financial Aid, University of Great Falls, 1301 20th Street South, Great Falls, MT 59405, 406-791-5237 or toll-free 800-856-9544. *Fax:* 406-791-5242. *E-mail:* sbauman01@ugf.edu.

UNIVERSITY OF GUAM
Mangilao, GU

ABOUT THE INSTITUTION Territory-supported, coed. 37 undergraduate majors.
GIFT AID (NEED-BASED) *Scholarships, grants, and awards:* Federal Pell, FSEOG, state, private, college/university gift aid from institutional funds.
GIFT AID (NON-NEED-BASED) *Scholarships, grants, and awards by category:* Academic interests/achievement: agriculture, business, communication, computer science, education, general academic interests/achievements, health fields. Creative arts/performance: art/fine arts, general creative arts/performance, journalism/publications, music, performing arts. Special characteristics: children and siblings of alumni, children of faculty/staff, children of union members/ company employees, international students.
LOANS *Programs:* Federal Direct (Subsidized and Unsubsidized Stafford, PLUS), FFEL (Subsidized and Unsubsidized Stafford, PLUS), territory.
WORK-STUDY Federal work-study: Total amount: $361,380; jobs available.
APPLYING FOR FINANCIAL AID *Required financial aid form:* FAFSA.
CONTACT Office of Financial Aid, University of Guam, UOG Station, Mangilao, GU 96923, 671-735-2288. *Fax:* 671-734-2907.

UNIVERSITY OF HARTFORD
West Hartford, CT

Tuition & fees: $29,852	Average undergraduate aid package: $22,400

ABOUT THE INSTITUTION Independent, coed. 86 undergraduate majors. Federal methodology is used as a basis for awarding need-based institutional aid.
UNDERGRADUATE EXPENSES for 2010–11 *Comprehensive fee:* $41,424 includes full-time tuition ($28,582), mandatory fees ($1270), and room and board ($11,572). *College room only:* $7114. Full-time tuition and fees vary according to program. Room and board charges vary according to board plan and housing facility. *Part-time tuition:* $420 per credit hour. *Part-time fees:* $420 per credit hour. Part-time tuition and fees vary according to course load and program. *Payment plans:* Tuition prepayment, installment.
FRESHMAN FINANCIAL AID (Fall 2009, est.) 1,350 applied for aid; of those 87% were deemed to have need. 100% of freshmen with need received aid; of those 15% had need fully met. *Average percent of need met:* 78% (excluding resources awarded to replace EFC). *Average financial aid package:* $21,105 (excluding resources awarded to replace EFC).
UNDERGRADUATE FINANCIAL AID (Fall 2009, est.) 4,419 applied for aid; of those 83% were deemed to have need. 100% of undergraduates with need received aid; of those 26% had need fully met. *Average percent of need met:* 90% (excluding resources awarded to replace EFC). *Average financial aid package:* $22,400 (excluding resources awarded to replace EFC). 1% of all full-time undergraduates had no need and received non-need-based gift aid.
GIFT AID (NEED-BASED) *Total amount:* $56,172,626 (10% federal, 6% state, 82% institutional, 2% external sources). *Receiving aid:* Freshmen: 25% (348); all full-time undergraduates: 68% (3,198). *Average award:* Freshmen: $8970; Undergraduates: $8365. *Scholarships, grants, and awards:* Federal Pell, FSEOG, state, private, college/university gift aid from institutional funds.
GIFT AID (NON-NEED-BASED) *Total amount:* $5,979,509 (98% institutional, 2% external sources). *Receiving aid:* Freshmen: 10% (141). Undergraduates: 12% (565). *Average award:* Undergraduates: $6484. *Scholarships, grants, and awards by category:* Academic interests/achievement: engineering/ technologies, general academic interests/achievements, health fields, premedicine. Creative arts/performance: art/fine arts, dance, music, performing arts, theater/

drama. Special achievements/activities: community service. Special characteristics: adult students, children of current students, children of faculty/staff, children of union members/company employees, children with a deceased or disabled parent, ethnic background, first-generation college students, handicapped students, international students, local/state students, members of minority groups, parents of current students, previous college experience, religious affiliation, siblings of current students, twins. *Tuition waivers:* Full or partial for employees or children of employees, senior citizens.
LOANS *Student loans:* $33,171,536 (82% need-based, 18% non-need-based). 75% of past graduating class borrowed through all loan programs. *Average indebtedness per student:* $29,869. *Average need-based loan:* Freshmen: $3202. Undergraduates: $3979. *Parent loans:* $21,546,184 (94% need-based, 6% non-need-based). *Programs:* FFEL (Subsidized and Unsubsidized Stafford, PLUS), Perkins.
WORK-STUDY *Federal work-study:* Total amount: $889,886; 628 jobs averaging $1485. *State or other work-study/employment:* Total amount: $1,290,594 (88% need-based, 12% non-need-based). 112 part-time jobs averaging $4520.
ATHLETIC AWARDS Total amount: $4,558,361 (50% need-based, 50% non-need-based).
APPLYING FOR FINANCIAL AID *Required financial aid forms:* FAFSA, institution's own form. *Financial aid deadline (priority):* 2/1. *Notification date:* Continuous beginning 3/1. Students must reply by 5/1 or within 2 weeks of notification.
CONTACT Financial Aid Office, University of Hartford, 200 Bloomfield Avenue, West Hartford, CT 06117-1599, 860-768-4296 or toll-free 800-947-4303. *Fax:* 860-768-4961. *E-mail:* finaid@hartford.edu.

UNIVERSITY OF HAWAII AT HILO
Hilo, HI

Tuition & fees: N/R	Average undergraduate aid package: $8000

ABOUT THE INSTITUTION State-supported, coed. 29 undergraduate majors. Federal methodology is used as a basis for awarding need-based institutional aid.
FRESHMAN FINANCIAL AID (Fall 2009, est.) 339 applied for aid; of those 91% were deemed to have need. 100% of freshmen with need received aid; of those 14% had need fully met. *Average percent of need met:* 58% (excluding resources awarded to replace EFC). *Average financial aid package:* $7842 (excluding resources awarded to replace EFC).
UNDERGRADUATE FINANCIAL AID (Fall 2009, est.) 1,482 applied for aid; of those 100% were deemed to have need. 100% of undergraduates with need received aid; of those 12% had need fully met. *Average percent of need met:* 67% (excluding resources awarded to replace EFC). *Average financial aid package:* $8000 (excluding resources awarded to replace EFC).
GIFT AID (NEED-BASED) *Total amount:* $7,916,657 (86% federal, 9% state, 5% institutional). *Receiving aid:* Freshmen: 41% (221); all full-time undergraduates: 49% (1,043). *Average award:* Freshmen: $4057; Undergraduates: $4729. *Scholarships, grants, and awards:* Federal Pell, FSEOG, state, private, college/ university gift aid from institutional funds.
GIFT AID (NON-NEED-BASED) *Total amount:* $4,043,662 (9% institutional, 91% external sources). *Receiving aid:* Freshmen: 10% (55). Undergraduates: 8% (179). *Scholarships, grants, and awards by category:* Academic interests/ achievement: 52 awards ($72,000 total): business, computer science, English, general academic interests/achievements, health fields, social sciences. Creative arts/performance: 5 awards ($2500 total): art/fine arts, music, performing arts, theater/drama. Special achievements/activities: 18 awards ($20,500 total): community service, general special achievements/activities, leadership. Special characteristics: 23 awards ($78,186 total): general special characteristics, local/ state students.
LOANS *Student loans:* $10,936,484 (48% need-based, 52% non-need-based). 55% of past graduating class borrowed through all loan programs. *Average indebtedness per student:* $17,800. *Average need-based loan:* Freshmen: $1962. Undergraduates: $3063. *Parent loans:* $650,518 (100% non-need-based). *Programs:* Federal Direct (Subsidized and Unsubsidized Stafford, PLUS), Perkins, state.
WORK-STUDY *Federal work-study:* Total amount: $302,451; 200 jobs averaging $1738. *State or other work-study/employment:* Total amount: $780,102 (100% non-need-based). 500 part-time jobs averaging $2100.
ATHLETIC AWARDS Total amount: $366,500 (100% non-need-based).

APPLYING FOR FINANCIAL AID *Required financial aid form:* FAFSA. *Financial aid deadline (priority):* 3/1. *Notification date:* Continuous beginning 3/1. Students must reply within 3 weeks of notification.

CONTACT Financial Aid Director, University of Hawaii at Hilo, 200 West Kawili Street, Hilo, HI 96720-4091, 808-974-7324 or toll-free 800-897-4456 (out-of-state). *Fax:* 808-933-0861. *E-mail:* uhhfao@hawaii.edu.

UNIVERSITY OF HAWAII AT MANOA
Honolulu, HI

ABOUT THE INSTITUTION State-supported, coed. 82 undergraduate majors.

GIFT AID (NEED-BASED) *Scholarships, grants, and awards:* Federal Pell, FSEOG, state, private, college/university gift aid from institutional funds, Federal Nursing.

LOANS *Programs:* FFEL (Subsidized and Unsubsidized Stafford, PLUS), Perkins, Federal Nursing, state.

APPLYING FOR FINANCIAL AID *Required financial aid form:* FAFSA.

CONTACT Linda Clemons, Director of Financial Aid Services, University of Hawaii at Manoa, 2600 Campus Road, Suite 112, Honolulu, HI 96822, 808-956-3989 or toll-free 800-823-9771. *Fax:* 808-956-3985. *E-mail:* finaid@hawaii.edu.

UNIVERSITY OF HAWAII–WEST OAHU
Pearl City, HI

Tuition & fees (HI res): $4666	Average undergraduate aid package: $5051

ABOUT THE INSTITUTION State-supported, coed. 21 undergraduate majors. Federal methodology is used as a basis for awarding need-based institutional aid.

UNDERGRADUATE EXPENSES for 2010–11 *Tuition, state resident:* full-time $4656; part-time $194 per credit. *Tuition, nonresident:* full-time $14,352; part-time $598 per credit. *Required fees:* full-time $10.

FRESHMAN FINANCIAL AID (Fall 2008) *Average financial aid package:* $2470 (excluding resources awarded to replace EFC).

UNDERGRADUATE FINANCIAL AID (Fall 2008) *Average financial aid package:* $5051 (excluding resources awarded to replace EFC).

GIFT AID (NEED-BASED) *Total amount:* $1,420,847 (55% federal, 19% state, 10% institutional, 16% external sources). *Receiving aid:* Freshmen: 60% (15); all full-time undergraduates: 39% (154). *Average award:* Freshmen: $2470; Undergraduates: $4018. *Scholarships, grants, and awards:* Federal Pell, FSEOG, state, private, college/university gift aid from institutional funds.

GIFT AID (NON-NEED-BASED) *Tuition waivers:* Full or partial for employees or children of employees.

LOANS *Student loans:* $1,842,575 (100% need-based). *Average need-based loan:* Undergraduates: $4247. *Parent loans:* $22,074 (100% need-based). *Programs:* FFEL (Subsidized and Unsubsidized Stafford, PLUS).

WORK-STUDY *Federal work-study:* Total amount: $3000; jobs available. *State or other work-study/employment:* Total amount: $103,141 (100% need-based). Part-time jobs available.

APPLYING FOR FINANCIAL AID *Required financial aid form:* FAFSA. *Financial aid deadline (priority):* 4/1. *Notification date:* Continuous beginning 4/1. Students must reply within 2 weeks of notification.

CONTACT Financial Aid Office, University of Hawaii–West Oahu, 96-129 Ala Ike, Pearl City, HI 96782, 808-454-4700. *Fax:* 808-453-6075. *E-mail:* finaid@uhwo.hawaii.edu.

UNIVERSITY OF HOUSTON
Houston, TX

Tuition & fees (TX res): $8496	Average undergraduate aid package: $12,018

ABOUT THE INSTITUTION State-supported, coed. 87 undergraduate majors. Federal methodology is used as a basis for awarding need-based institutional aid.

UNDERGRADUATE EXPENSES for 2009–10 *Tuition, state resident:* full-time $5542; part-time $185 per credit hour. *Tuition, nonresident:* full-time $13,852; part-time $462 per credit hour. *Required fees:* full-time $2954. Full-time tuition and fees vary according to course level, course load, and program. Part-time tuition and fees vary according to course level, course load, and program.

College room and board: $7164; *Room only:* $4224. Room and board charges vary according to board plan and housing facility. *Payment plan:* Installment.

FRESHMAN FINANCIAL AID (Fall 2009, est.) 2,364 applied for aid; of those 81% were deemed to have need. 97% of freshmen with need received aid; of those 39% had need fully met. *Average percent of need met:* 83% (excluding resources awarded to replace EFC). *Average financial aid package:* $12,752 (excluding resources awarded to replace EFC). 6% of all full-time freshmen had no need and received non-need-based gift aid.

UNDERGRADUATE FINANCIAL AID (Fall 2009, est.) 13,792 applied for aid; of those 88% were deemed to have need. 96% of undergraduates with need received aid; of those 26% had need fully met. *Average percent of need met:* 76% (excluding resources awarded to replace EFC). *Average financial aid package:* $12,018 (excluding resources awarded to replace EFC). 2% of all full-time undergraduates had no need and received non-need-based gift aid.

GIFT AID (NEED-BASED) *Total amount:* $82,913,856 (50% federal, 21% state, 24% institutional, 5% external sources). *Receiving aid:* Freshmen: 55% (1,717); all full-time undergraduates: 50% (10,353). *Average award:* Freshmen: $9424; Undergraduates: $6649. *Scholarships, grants, and awards:* Federal Pell, FSEOG, state, private, college/university gift aid from institutional funds, United Negro College Fund.

GIFT AID (NON-NEED-BASED) *Total amount:* $2,914,561 (6% state, 75% institutional, 19% external sources). *Receiving aid:* Freshmen: 4% (131). Undergraduates: 1% (303). *Average award:* Freshmen: $5419. Undergraduates: $4544.

LOANS *Student loans:* $114,883,953 (78% need-based, 22% non-need-based). *Average indebtedness per student:* $22,573. *Average need-based loan:* Freshmen: $4870. Undergraduates: $6908. *Parent loans:* $2,923,107 (23% need-based, 77% non-need-based). *Programs:* FFEL (Subsidized and Unsubsidized Stafford, PLUS), Perkins, state.

WORK-STUDY *Federal work-study:* Total amount: $2,907,282; 700 jobs averaging $3610. *State or other work-study/employment:* Total amount: $183,223 (100% need-based). 43 part-time jobs averaging $3666.

ATHLETIC AWARDS Total amount: $4,164,450 (82% need-based, 18% non-need-based).

APPLYING FOR FINANCIAL AID *Required financial aid form:* FAFSA. *Financial aid deadline (priority):* 4/1. *Notification date:* Continuous beginning 5/1. Students must reply within 4 weeks of notification.

CONTACT Financial Aid Office, University of Houston, 4800 Calhoun Road, Houston, TX 77204-2160, 713-743-1010. *Fax:* 713-743-9098.

UNIVERSITY OF HOUSTON–CLEAR LAKE
Houston, TX

Tuition & fees (TX res): $5708	Average undergraduate aid package: $7469

ABOUT THE INSTITUTION State-supported, coed. 35 undergraduate majors. Federal methodology is used as a basis for awarding need-based institutional aid.

UNDERGRADUATE EXPENSES for 2009–10 *Tuition, state resident:* full-time $4560; part-time $152 per credit hour. *Tuition, nonresident:* full-time $13,770; part-time $459 per credit hour. *Required fees:* full-time $1148; $436 per term. Full-time tuition and fees vary according to course load, location, and program. Part-time tuition and fees vary according to course load, location, and program. *College room and board: Room only:* $7896. Room and board charges vary according to housing facility. *Payment plans:* Installment, deferred payment.

UNDERGRADUATE FINANCIAL AID (Fall 2009, est.) 1,383 applied for aid; of those 87% were deemed to have need. 97% of undergraduates with need received aid; of those 28% had need fully met. *Average percent of need met:* 43% (excluding resources awarded to replace EFC). *Average financial aid package:* $7469 (excluding resources awarded to replace EFC). 2% of all full-time undergraduates had no need and received non-need-based gift aid.

GIFT AID (NEED-BASED) *Total amount:* $9,357,933 (60% federal, 27% state, 8% institutional, 5% external sources). *Receiving aid:* All full-time undergraduates: 40% (722). *Average award:* Undergraduates: $2572. *Scholarships, grants, and awards:* Federal Pell, FSEOG, state, college/university gift aid from institutional funds.

GIFT AID (NON-NEED-BASED) *Total amount:* $1,639,272 (12% federal, 1% state, 67% institutional, 20% external sources). *Receiving aid:* Undergraduates: 33% (596). *Average award:* Undergraduates: $842. *Scholarships, grants, and awards by category:* Academic interests/achievement: biological sciences, business, computer science, education, humanities, mathematics, social sciences. *Special achievements/activities:* community service, general special achievements/ activities, leadership. *Special characteristics:* children and siblings of alumni. *Tuition waivers:* Full or partial for senior citizens.

LOANS *Student loans:* $18,105,947 (45% need-based, 55% non-need-based). *Average need-based loan:* Undergraduates: $4570. *Parent loans:* $41,956 (100% non-need-based). *Programs:* Federal Direct (Subsidized and Unsubsidized Stafford, PLUS), Perkins, state.

WORK-STUDY *Federal work-study:* Total amount: $120,690; 29 jobs averaging $2462. *State or other work-study/employment:* Total amount: $66,644 (100% need-based). 17 part-time jobs averaging $2703.

CONTACT Billy Satterfield, Executive Director of Student Financial Aid, University of Houston–Clear Lake, 2700 Bay Area Boulevard, Houston, TX 77058-1098, 281-283-2480. *Fax:* 281-283-2502. *E-mail:* satterfield@cl.uh.edu.

UNIVERSITY OF HOUSTON–DOWNTOWN
Houston, TX

Tuition & fees (TX res): $5232	Average undergraduate aid package: $8126

ABOUT THE INSTITUTION State-supported, coed. 38 undergraduate majors. Federal methodology is used as a basis for awarding need-based institutional aid.

UNDERGRADUATE EXPENSES for 2009–10 *One-time required fee:* $10. *Tuition, state resident:* full-time $4200; part-time $140 per credit hour. *Tuition, nonresident:* full-time $12,510; part-time $417 per credit hour. *Required fees:* full-time $1032. Full-time tuition and fees vary according to course load. Part-time tuition and fees vary according to course load. international students must also pay an international student service fee of $45 per semester. *Payment plan:* Installment.

FRESHMAN FINANCIAL AID (Fall 2009, est.) 839 applied for aid; of those 79% were deemed to have need. 98% of freshmen with need received aid; of those 5% had need fully met. *Average percent of need met:* 57% (excluding resources awarded to replace EFC). *Average financial aid package:* $9330 (excluding resources awarded to replace EFC). 10% of all full-time freshmen had no need and received non-need-based gift aid.

UNDERGRADUATE FINANCIAL AID (Fall 2009, est.) 4,890 applied for aid; of those 100% were deemed to have need. 96% of undergraduates with need received aid; of those 4% had need fully met. *Average percent of need met:* 49% (excluding resources awarded to replace EFC). *Average financial aid package:* $8126 (excluding resources awarded to replace EFC). 2% of all full-time undergraduates had no need and received non-need-based gift aid.

GIFT AID (NEED-BASED) *Total amount:* $31,519,903 (67% federal, 17% state, 14% institutional, 2% external sources). *Receiving aid:* Freshmen: 57% (613); all full-time undergraduates: 67% (4,062). *Average award:* Freshmen: $7371; Undergraduates: $5465. *Scholarships, grants, and awards:* Federal Pell, FSEOG, state, private, college/university gift aid from institutional funds.

GIFT AID (NON-NEED-BASED) *Total amount:* $662,388 (1% federal, 10% state, 70% institutional, 19% external sources). *Receiving aid:* Freshmen: 1% (6). Undergraduates: 24. *Average award:* Freshmen: $2395. Undergraduates: $2669. *Scholarships, grants, and awards by category:* Academic interests/achievement: 174 awards ($260,725 total): business, general academic interests/achievements. *Special achievements/activities:* community service, general special achievements/ activities, leadership. *Special characteristics:* general special characteristics. *Tuition waivers:* Full or partial for senior citizens.

LOANS *Student loans:* $46,005,128 (92% need-based, 8% non-need-based). 75% of past graduating class borrowed through all loan programs. *Average indebtedness per student:* $13,204. *Average need-based loan:* Freshmen: $3079. Undergraduates: $3819. *Parent loans:* $153,333 (80% need-based, 20% non-need-based). *Programs:* FFEL (Subsidized and Unsubsidized Stafford, PLUS), state.

WORK-STUDY *Federal work-study:* Total amount: $445,743; 169 jobs averaging $3265. *State or other work-study/employment:* Total amount: $63,957 (100% need-based). 26 part-time jobs averaging $2471.

APPLYING FOR FINANCIAL AID *Required financial aid form:* FAFSA. *Financial aid deadline (priority):* 4/1. *Notification date:* Continuous beginning 4/15. Students must reply within 4 weeks of notification.

CONTACT Office of Scholarships and Financial Aid, University of Houston– Downtown, One Main Street, Houston, TX 77002-1001, 713-221-8041. *Fax:* 713-221-8648. *E-mail:* uhd.finaid@uhd.edu.

UNIVERSITY OF HOUSTON–VICTORIA
Victoria, TX

ABOUT THE INSTITUTION State-supported, coed. 13 undergraduate majors.

GIFT AID (NEED-BASED) *Scholarships, grants, and awards:* Federal Pell, FSEOG, state, private, college/university gift aid from institutional funds.

GIFT AID (NON-NEED-BASED) *Scholarships, grants, and awards by category:* Academic interests/achievement: biological sciences, business, communication, computer science, education, general academic interests/achievements, humanities, mathematics, social sciences. *Special achievements/activities:* community service, leadership, memberships.

LOANS *Programs:* FFEL (Subsidized and Unsubsidized Stafford, PLUS), state, college/university.

APPLYING FOR FINANCIAL AID *Required financial aid form:* FAFSA.

CONTACT Carolyn Mallory, Financial Aid Director, University of Houston– Victoria, 3007 North Ben Wilson, Victoria, TX 77901-5731, 361-570-4131 or toll-free 877-970-4848 Ext. 110. *Fax:* 361-580-5555. *E-mail:* malloryc@uhv.edu.

UNIVERSITY OF IDAHO
Moscow, ID

Tuition & fees (ID res): $4932	Average undergraduate aid package: $11,751

ABOUT THE INSTITUTION State-supported, coed. 97 undergraduate majors. Federal methodology is used as a basis for awarding need-based institutional aid.

UNDERGRADUATE EXPENSES for 2009–10 *Tuition, state resident:* full-time $0. *Tuition, nonresident:* full-time $10,080; part-time $504 per credit. *Required fees:* full-time $4932; $251 per credit. Full-time tuition and fees vary according to course load, degree level, and program. Part-time tuition and fees vary according to course load, degree level, and program. *College room and board:* $7242. Room and board charges vary according to board plan and housing facility. *Payment plans:* Installment, deferred payment.

FRESHMAN FINANCIAL AID (Fall 2008) 1,354 applied for aid; of those 73% were deemed to have need. 98% of freshmen with need received aid; of those 30% had need fully met. *Average percent of need met:* 79% (excluding resources awarded to replace EFC). *Average financial aid package:* $11,284 (excluding resources awarded to replace EFC). 31% of all full-time freshmen had no need and received non-need-based gift aid.

UNDERGRADUATE FINANCIAL AID (Fall 2008) 6,193 applied for aid; of those 80% were deemed to have need. 98% of undergraduates with need received aid; of those 24% had need fully met. *Average percent of need met:* 74% (excluding resources awarded to replace EFC). *Average financial aid package:* $11,751 (excluding resources awarded to replace EFC). 23% of all full-time undergraduates had no need and received non-need-based gift aid.

GIFT AID (NEED-BASED) *Total amount:* $13,432,696 (85% federal, 15% institutional). *Receiving aid:* Freshmen: 34% (588); all full-time undergraduates: 37% (3,131). *Average award:* Freshmen: $3631; Undergraduates: $3825. *Scholarships, grants, and awards:* Federal Pell, FSEOG, state, private, college/ university gift aid from institutional funds.

GIFT AID (NON-NEED-BASED) *Total amount:* $9,837,427 (1% state, 72% institutional, 27% external sources). *Receiving aid:* Freshmen: 49% (852). Undergraduates: 47% (3,936). *Average award:* Freshmen: $4060. Undergraduates: $4652. *Scholarships, grants, and awards by category:* Academic interests/ achievement: agriculture, architecture, biological sciences, business, communication, computer science, education, engineering/technologies, English, foreign languages, general academic interests/achievements, home economics, humanities, library science, mathematics, military science, physical sciences, premedicine, social sciences. *Creative arts/performance:* applied art and design, art/fine arts, creative writing, dance, general creative arts/performance, journalism/publications, music, performing arts, theater/drama. *Special achievements/activities:* cheerleading/ drum major, general special achievements/activities, junior miss, leadership, rodeo. *Special characteristics:* children and siblings of alumni, children of faculty/staff, ethnic background, first-generation college students, general special characteristics, handicapped students, international students, local/state students, members of minority groups, out-of-state students, veterans. *Tuition waivers:* Full or partial for minority students, children of alumni, employees or children of employees, senior citizens.

LOANS *Student loans:* $37,602,500 (49% need-based, 51% non-need-based). 66% of past graduating class borrowed through all loan programs. *Average*

indebtedness per student: $21,702. *Average need-based loan:* Freshmen: $5173. Undergraduates: $7106. *Parent loans:* $5,796,312 (100% non-need-based). *Programs:* Federal Direct (Subsidized and Unsubsidized Stafford, PLUS), Perkins, college/university.

WORK-STUDY *Federal work-study:* Total amount: $623,170; 429 jobs averaging $2000. *State or other work-study/employment:* Total amount: $388,146 (100% need-based). 191 part-time jobs averaging $2000.

ATHLETIC AWARDS Total amount: $4,118,478 (100% non-need-based).

APPLYING FOR FINANCIAL AID *Required financial aid form:* FAFSA. *Financial aid deadline (priority):* 2/15. *Notification date:* Continuous beginning 3/30. Students must reply within 4 weeks of notification.

CONTACT Mr. Dan Davenport, Director of Student Financial Aid Services, University of Idaho, PO Box 444291, Moscow, ID 83844-4291, 208-885-6312 or toll-free 888-884-3246. *Fax:* 208-885-5592. *E-mail:* dand@uidaho.edu.

UNIVERSITY OF ILLINOIS AT CHICAGO
Chicago, IL

Tuition & fees (IL res): $12,034   Average undergraduate aid package: $12,497

ABOUT THE INSTITUTION State-supported, coed. 78 undergraduate majors. Federal methodology is used as a basis for awarding need-based institutional aid.

UNDERGRADUATE EXPENSES for 2009–10 *Tuition, state resident:* full-time $8342; part-time $1390 per term. *Tuition, nonresident:* full-time $20,732; part-time $3455 per term. *Required fees:* full-time $3692; $1147 per term. Full-time tuition and fees vary according to program. Part-time tuition and fees vary according to course load and program. *College room and board:* $9435; *Room only:* $6650. Room and board charges vary according to board plan and housing facility. *Payment plans:* Guaranteed tuition, installment.

FRESHMAN FINANCIAL AID (Fall 2008) 2,467 applied for aid; of those 81% were deemed to have need. 95% of freshmen with need received aid; of those 22% had need fully met. *Average percent of need met:* 73% (excluding resources awarded to replace EFC). *Average financial aid package:* $12,813 (excluding resources awarded to replace EFC). 6% of all full-time freshmen had no need and received non-need-based gift aid.

UNDERGRADUATE FINANCIAL AID (Fall 2008) 10,798 applied for aid; of those 85% were deemed to have need. 97% of undergraduates with need received aid; of those 21% had need fully met. *Average percent of need met:* 73% (excluding resources awarded to replace EFC). *Average financial aid package:* $12,497 (excluding resources awarded to replace EFC). 5% of all full-time undergraduates had no need and received non-need-based gift aid.

GIFT AID (NEED-BASED) *Total amount:* $71,633,775 (31% federal, 37% state, 30% institutional, 2% external sources). *Receiving aid:* Freshmen: 52% (1,528); all full-time undergraduates: 49% (7,099). *Average award:* Freshmen: $11,948; Undergraduates: $10,704. *Scholarships, grants, and awards:* Federal Pell, FSEOG, state, private, college/university gift aid from institutional funds.

GIFT AID (NON-NEED-BASED) *Total amount:* $2,674,866 (1% federal, 47% state, 28% institutional, 24% external sources). *Receiving aid:* Freshmen: 4% (110). Undergraduates: 2% (305). *Average award:* Freshmen: $2655. Undergraduates: $3703. *Scholarships, grants, and awards by category: Academic interests/achievement:* 1,238 awards ($1,961,671 total): architecture, business, general academic interests/achievements. *Creative arts/performance:* 172 awards ($522,946 total): applied art and design, art/fine arts, music, performing arts, theater/drama. *Tuition waivers:* Full or partial for employees or children of employees, senior citizens.

LOANS *Student loans:* $53,553,577 (82% need-based, 18% non-need-based). 57% of past graduating class borrowed through all loan programs. *Average indebtedness per student:* $17,276. *Average need-based loan:* Freshmen: $3277. Undergraduates: $4406. *Parent loans:* $16,854,507 (70% need-based, 30% non-need-based). *Programs:* Federal Direct (Subsidized and Unsubsidized Stafford, PLUS), Perkins, Federal Nursing, state, college/university, private alternative loans.

WORK-STUDY *Federal work-study:* Total amount: $1,598,696; 843 jobs averaging $1911. *State or other work-study/employment:* Total amount: $6,599,687 (66% need-based, 34% non-need-based). 2,646 part-time jobs averaging $2549.

ATHLETIC AWARDS Total amount: $3,297,630 (33% need-based, 67% non-need-based).

APPLYING FOR FINANCIAL AID *Required financial aid form:* FAFSA. *Financial aid deadline (priority):* 3/1. *Notification date:* Continuous beginning 3/15. Students must reply by 5/1.

CONTACT Deidre Rush, Associate Director of Financial Aid, University of Illinois at Chicago, 1200 West Harrison, M/C 334, Chicago, IL 60607-7128, 312-996-5563. *Fax:* 312-996-3385. *E-mail:* deidreb@uic.edu.

UNIVERSITY OF ILLINOIS AT SPRINGFIELD
Springfield, IL

Tuition & fees (IL res): $9532   Average undergraduate aid package: $10,264

ABOUT THE INSTITUTION State-supported, coed. 22 undergraduate majors. Federal methodology is used as a basis for awarding need-based institutional aid.

UNDERGRADUATE EXPENSES for 2009–10 *Tuition, state resident:* full-time $7402; part-time $246.75 per credit hour. *Tuition, nonresident:* full-time $16,552; part-time $551.75 per credit hour. *Required fees:* full-time $2130; $5 per credit hour or $726.50 per term. Full-time tuition and fees vary according to course load. Part-time tuition and fees vary according to course load. *College room and board:* $9200; *Room only:* $6250. Room and board charges vary according to board plan and housing facility. *Payment plans:* Guaranteed tuition, installment.

FRESHMAN FINANCIAL AID (Fall 2008) 289 applied for aid; of those 100% were deemed to have need. 75% of freshmen with need received aid; of those 14% had need fully met. *Average percent of need met:* 76% (excluding resources awarded to replace EFC). *Average financial aid package:* $11,499 (excluding resources awarded to replace EFC). 22% of all full-time freshmen had no need and received non-need-based gift aid.

UNDERGRADUATE FINANCIAL AID (Fall 2008) 1,396 applied for aid; of those 80% were deemed to have need. 98% of undergraduates with need received aid; of those 12% had need fully met. *Average percent of need met:* 72% (excluding resources awarded to replace EFC). *Average financial aid package:* $10,264 (excluding resources awarded to replace EFC). 14% of all full-time undergraduates had no need and received non-need-based gift aid.

GIFT AID (NEED-BASED) *Total amount:* $7,099,088 (37% federal, 47% state, 12% institutional, 4% external sources). *Receiving aid:* Freshmen: 68% (207); all full-time undergraduates: 50% (897). *Average award:* Freshmen: $8356; Undergraduates: $7585. *Scholarships, grants, and awards:* Federal Pell, FSEOG, state, private, college/university gift aid from institutional funds.

GIFT AID (NON-NEED-BASED) *Total amount:* $1,284,587 (50% state, 29% institutional, 21% external sources). *Receiving aid:* Freshmen: 18% (56). Undergraduates: 8% (151). *Average award:* Freshmen: $3316. Undergraduates: $3819. *Tuition waivers:* Full or partial for employees or children of employees, senior citizens.

LOANS *Student loans:* $9,613,378 (84% need-based, 16% non-need-based). 64% of past graduating class borrowed through all loan programs. *Average indebtedness per student:* $14,717. *Average need-based loan:* Freshmen: $3172. Undergraduates: $4138. *Parent loans:* $1,192,475 (61% need-based, 39% non-need-based). *Programs:* Federal Direct (Subsidized and Unsubsidized Stafford, PLUS), Perkins, college/university.

WORK-STUDY *Federal work-study:* Total amount: $181,226; jobs available. *State or other work-study/employment:* Total amount: $968,452 (62% need-based, 38% non-need-based). Part-time jobs available.

ATHLETIC AWARDS Total amount: $562,054 (56% need-based, 44% non-need-based).

APPLYING FOR FINANCIAL AID *Required financial aid form:* FAFSA. *Financial aid deadline:* 11/15 (priority: 4/1). *Notification date:* Continuous beginning 1/1. Students must reply within 3 weeks of notification.

CONTACT Mr. Gerard Joseph, Director of Financial Aid, University of Illinois at Springfield, One University Plaza, MS UHB 1015, Springfield, IL 62703-5407, 217-206-6724 or toll-free 888-977-4847. *Fax:* 217-206-7376. *E-mail:* finaid@uis.edu.

UNIVERSITY OF ILLINOIS AT URBANA–CHAMPAIGN
Champaign, IL

Tuition & fees (IL res): $12,660   Average undergraduate aid package: $12,076

ABOUT THE INSTITUTION State-supported, coed. 219 undergraduate majors. Federal methodology is used as a basis for awarding need-based institutional aid.

UNDERGRADUATE EXPENSES for 2009–10 *Tuition, state resident:* full-time $9484. *Tuition, nonresident:* full-time $23,626. *Required fees:* full-time $3176. Full-time tuition and fees vary according to course load, program, and student level. *College room and board:* $9284. Room and board charges vary according to board plan, housing facility, and location. *Payment plans:* Guaranteed tuition, installment.

FRESHMAN FINANCIAL AID (Fall 2008) 5,002 applied for aid; of those 68% were deemed to have need. 94% of freshmen with need received aid; of those 50% had need fully met. *Average percent of need met:* 71% (excluding resources awarded to replace EFC). *Average financial aid package:* $13,146 (excluding resources awarded to replace EFC). 14% of all full-time freshmen had no need and received non-need-based gift aid.

UNDERGRADUATE FINANCIAL AID (Fall 2008) 17,577 applied for aid; of those 75% were deemed to have need. 96% of undergraduates with need received aid; of those 46% had need fully met. *Average percent of need met:* 69% (excluding resources awarded to replace EFC). *Average financial aid package:* $12,076 (excluding resources awarded to replace EFC). 13% of all full-time undergraduates had no need and received non-need-based gift aid.

GIFT AID (NEED-BASED) *Total amount:* $81,201,146 (24% federal, 35% state, 35% institutional, 6% external sources). *Receiving aid:* Freshmen: 35% (2,575); all full-time undergraduates: 32% (9,804). *Average award:* Freshmen: $11,052; Undergraduates: $9868. *Scholarships, grants, and awards:* Federal Pell, FSEOG, state, private, college/university gift aid from institutional funds, United Negro College Fund.

GIFT AID (NON-NEED-BASED) *Total amount:* $11,451,073 (1% federal, 7% state, 64% institutional, 28% external sources). *Receiving aid:* Freshmen: 9% (667). Undergraduates: 5% (1,515). *Average award:* Freshmen: $3069. Undergraduates: $3046. *Scholarships, grants, and awards by category:* Academic interests/achievement: agriculture, architecture, area/ethnic studies, biological sciences, business, communication, computer science, education, engineering/technologies, English, foreign languages, general academic interests/ achievements, health fields, home economics, humanities, international studies, library science, mathematics, military science, physical sciences, premedicine, religion/biblical studies, social sciences. *Creative arts/performance:* applied art and design, art/fine arts, dance, general creative arts/performance, journalism/ publications, music, performing arts, theater/drama. *Special achievements/ activities:* general special achievements/activities, leadership. *Special characteristics:* children and siblings of alumni, children of faculty/staff, first-generation college students, general special characteristics, local/state students, veterans. *Tuition waivers:* Full or partial for employees or children of employees, senior citizens.

LOANS *Student loans:* $97,220,822 (79% need-based, 21% non-need-based). 51% of past graduating class borrowed through all loan programs. *Average indebtedness per student:* $19,378. *Average need-based loan:* Freshmen: $3851. Undergraduates: $4425. *Parent loans:* $50,630,625 (70% need-based, 30% non-need-based). *Programs:* Federal Direct (Subsidized and Unsubsidized Stafford, PLUS), Perkins, college/university.

WORK-STUDY *Federal work-study:* Total amount: $2,188,783; jobs available. *State or other work-study/employment:* Total amount: $17,592,797 (51% need-based, 49% non-need-based). Part-time jobs available.

ATHLETIC AWARDS Total amount: $6,394,671 (37% need-based, 63% non-need-based).

APPLYING FOR FINANCIAL AID *Required financial aid form:* FAFSA. *Financial aid deadline (priority):* 3/15. *Notification date:* 3/15.

CONTACT Daniel Mann, Director of Student Financial Aid, University of Illinois at Urbana–Champaign, Student Services Arcade Building, 620 East John Street, Champaign, IL 61820-5711, 217-333-0100.

UNIVERSITY OF INDIANAPOLIS
Indianapolis, IN

Tuition & fees: $21,170	Average undergraduate aid package: $15,526

ABOUT THE INSTITUTION Independent religious, coed. 62 undergraduate majors. Federal methodology is used as a basis for awarding need-based institutional aid.

UNDERGRADUATE EXPENSES for 2009–10 *Comprehensive fee:* $29,210 includes full-time tuition ($20,970), mandatory fees ($200), and room and board ($8040). *College room only:* $3820. Room and board charges vary

according to board plan and housing facility. *Part-time tuition:* $874 per credit hour. Part-time tuition and fees vary according to course load.

FRESHMAN FINANCIAL AID (Fall 2009, est.) 725 applied for aid; of those 87% were deemed to have need. 100% of freshmen with need received aid; of those 20% had need fully met. *Average percent of need met:* 79% (excluding resources awarded to replace EFC). *Average financial aid package:* $18,127 (excluding resources awarded to replace EFC). 73% of all full-time freshmen had no need and received non-need-based gift aid.

UNDERGRADUATE FINANCIAL AID (Fall 2009, est.) 3,258 applied for aid; of those 87% were deemed to have need. 99% of undergraduates with need received aid; of those 14% had need fully met. *Average percent of need met:* 70% (excluding resources awarded to replace EFC). *Average financial aid package:* $15,526 (excluding resources awarded to replace EFC). 45% of all full-time undergraduates had no need and received non-need-based gift aid.

GIFT AID (NEED-BASED) *Total amount:* $16,719,807 (36% federal, 36% state, 28% institutional). *Receiving aid:* Freshmen: 63% (471); all full-time undergraduates: 53% (2,044). *Average award:* Freshmen: $8796; Undergraduates: $8000. *Scholarships, grants, and awards:* Federal Pell, FSEOG, state, private, college/ university gift aid from institutional funds.

GIFT AID (NON-NEED-BASED) *Total amount:* $15,417,217 (3% state, 96% institutional, 1% external sources). *Receiving aid:* Freshmen: 81% (608). Undergraduates: 51% (1,957). *Average award:* Freshmen: $7654. Undergraduates: $7138. *Scholarships, grants, and awards by category:* Academic interests/ achievement: business, communication, general academic interests/achievements, health fields, physical sciences, religion/biblical studies. *Creative arts/performance:* art/fine arts, music, theater/drama. *Special achievements/activities:* community service, memberships. *Special characteristics:* children of faculty/staff, ethnic background, international students, out-of-state students, relatives of clergy, religious affiliation, veterans. *Tuition waivers:* Full or partial for employees or children of employees.

LOANS *Student loans:* $24,312,073 (40% need-based, 60% non-need-based). 79% of past graduating class borrowed through all loan programs. *Average indebtedness per student:* $27,070. *Average need-based loan:* Freshmen: $3439. Undergraduates: $4174. *Parent loans:* $3,279,268 (100% non-need-based). *Programs:* FFEL (Subsidized and Unsubsidized Stafford, PLUS), Perkins, Federal Nursing.

WORK-STUDY *Federal work-study:* Total amount: $1,928,231; jobs available.

ATHLETIC AWARDS Total amount: $3,623,842 (100% non-need-based).

APPLYING FOR FINANCIAL AID *Required financial aid forms:* FAFSA, institution's own form. *Financial aid deadline (priority):* 3/10. *Notification date:* Continuous beginning 3/1.

CONTACT Ms. Linda B. Handy, Director of Financial Aid, University of Indianapolis, 1400 East Hanna Avenue, Indianapolis, IN 46227-3697, 317-788-3217 or toll-free 800-232-8634 Ext. 3216. *Fax:* 317-788-6136. *E-mail:* handy@uindy.edu.

THE UNIVERSITY OF IOWA
Iowa City, IA

Tuition & fees (IA res): $7417	Average undergraduate aid package: $7781

ABOUT THE INSTITUTION State-supported, coed. 123 undergraduate majors. Federal methodology is used as a basis for awarding need-based institutional aid.

UNDERGRADUATE EXPENSES for 2010–11 *Tuition, state resident:* full-time $6128; part-time $255 per semester hour. *Tuition, nonresident:* full-time $22,424; part-time $934 per semester hour. *Required fees:* full-time $1289; $69 per semester hour. Full-time tuition and fees vary according to course load and program. Part-time tuition and fees vary according to course load and program. *College room and board:* $8331. Room and board charges vary according to board plan and housing facility. *Payment plan:* Installment.

FRESHMAN FINANCIAL AID (Fall 2009, est.) 3,002 applied for aid; of those 63% were deemed to have need. 96% of freshmen with need received aid; of those 54% had need fully met. *Average percent of need met:* 54% (excluding resources awarded to replace EFC). *Average financial aid package:* $7344 (excluding resources awarded to replace EFC). 23% of all full-time freshmen had no need and received non-need-based gift aid.

UNDERGRADUATE FINANCIAL AID (Fall 2009, est.) 12,582 applied for aid; of those 71% were deemed to have need. 95% of undergraduates with need received aid; of those 65% had need fully met. *Average percent of need met:* 65% (excluding resources awarded to replace EFC). *Average financial aid*

package: $7781 (excluding resources awarded to replace EFC). 15% of all full-time undergraduates had no need and received non-need-based gift aid.

GIFT AID (NEED-BASED) *Total amount:* $28,466,611 (41% federal, 5% state, 54% institutional). *Receiving aid:* Freshmen: 27% (1,094); all full-time undergraduates: 29% (5,350). *Average award:* Freshmen: $4862; Undergraduates: $5298. *Scholarships, grants, and awards:* Federal Pell, FSEOG, state, college/university gift aid from institutional funds.

GIFT AID (NON-NEED-BASED) *Total amount:* $31,639,256 (5% federal, 2% state, 76% institutional, 17% external sources). *Receiving aid:* Freshmen: 24% (963). Undergraduates: 16% (3,029). *Average award:* Freshmen: $3011. Undergraduates: $3279. *Scholarships, grants, and awards by category: Academic interests/achievement:* business, engineering/technologies, general academic interests/achievements, military science. *Creative arts/performance:* general creative arts/performance, music. *Special achievements/activities:* general special achievements/activities.

LOANS *Student loans:* $86,926,457 (33% need-based, 67% non-need-based). 61% of past graduating class borrowed through all loan programs. *Average indebtedness per student:* $22,684. *Average need-based loan:* Freshmen: $3186. Undergraduates: $4102. *Parent loans:* $28,360,154 (100% non-need-based). *Programs:* Federal Direct (Subsidized and Unsubsidized Stafford, PLUS), Perkins, Federal Nursing.

WORK-STUDY *Federal work-study:* Total amount: $1,937,876; jobs available. *State or other work-study/employment:* Part-time jobs available.

ATHLETIC AWARDS Total amount: $7,889,061 (100% non-need-based).

APPLYING FOR FINANCIAL AID *Required financial aid forms:* FAFSA, institution's own form. *Financial aid deadline:* Continuous. *Notification date:* Continuous beginning 3/1.

CONTACT Mark Warner, Director of Student Financial Aid, The University of Iowa, 208 Calvin Hall, Iowa City, IA 52242, 319-335-3127 or toll-free 800-553-4692.

THE UNIVERSITY OF KANSAS
Lawrence, KS

Tuition & fees (KS res): $8206   **Average undergraduate aid package:** $9630

ABOUT THE INSTITUTION State-supported, coed. 109 undergraduate majors. Federal methodology is used as a basis for awarding need-based institutional aid.

UNDERGRADUATE EXPENSES for 2009–10 *Tuition, state resident:* full-time $7359; part-time $245.30 per credit hour. *Tuition, nonresident:* full-time $19,327; part-time $644.25 per credit hour. *Required fees:* full-time $847; $70.56 per credit hour. Full-time tuition and fees vary according to program, reciprocity agreements, and student level. Part-time tuition and fees vary according to program, reciprocity agreements, and student level. *College room and board:* $6802; *Room only:* $3554. Room and board charges vary according to board plan and housing facility. *Payment plans:* Guaranteed tuition, installment.

FRESHMAN FINANCIAL AID (Fall 2008) 3,503 applied for aid; of those 49% were deemed to have need. 94% of freshmen with need received aid; of those 20% had need fully met. *Average percent of need met:* 44% (excluding resources awarded to replace EFC). *Average financial aid package:* $8437 (excluding resources awarded to replace EFC). 22% of all full-time freshmen had no need and received non-need-based gift aid.

UNDERGRADUATE FINANCIAL AID (Fall 2008) 14,447 applied for aid; of those 53% were deemed to have need. 96% of undergraduates with need received aid; of those 28% had need fully met. *Average percent of need met:* 53% (excluding resources awarded to replace EFC). *Average financial aid package:* $9630 (excluding resources awarded to replace EFC). 12% of all full-time undergraduates had no need and received non-need-based gift aid.

GIFT AID (NEED-BASED) *Total amount:* $22,617,995 (53% federal, 9% state, 38% institutional). *Receiving aid:* Freshmen: 25% (1,110); all full-time undergraduates: 25% (4,744). *Average award:* Freshmen: $4709; Undergraduates: $5052. *Scholarships, grants, and awards:* Federal Pell, FSEOG, state, private, college/university gift aid from institutional funds.

GIFT AID (NON-NEED-BASED) *Total amount:* $16,797,274 (78% institutional, 22% external sources). *Receiving aid:* Freshmen: 17% (742). Undergraduates: 12% (2,276). *Average award:* Freshmen: $3633, Undergraduates: $3379. *Scholarships, grants, and awards by category: Academic interests/achievement:* architecture, area/ethnic studies, biological sciences, business, communication, computer science, education, engineering/technologies, English, foreign languages, general academic interests/achievements, health fields, humanities,

international studies, mathematics, physical sciences, premedicine, religion/biblical studies, social sciences. *Creative arts/performance:* applied art and design, art/fine arts, cinema/film/broadcasting, creative writing, dance, debating, general creative arts/performance, journalism/publications, music, performing arts, theater/drama. *Special achievements/activities:* community service, general special achievements/activities, leadership. *Special characteristics:* adult students, children of faculty/staff, ethnic background, first-generation college students, general special characteristics, international students, local/state students, married students, members of minority groups, out-of-state students, previous college experience. *Tuition waivers:* Full or partial for employees or children of employees.

LOANS *Student loans:* $72,555,014 (40% need-based, 60% non-need-based). 45% of past graduating class borrowed through all loan programs. *Average indebtedness per student:* $22,478. *Average need-based loan:* Freshmen: $2873. Undergraduates: $3545. *Parent loans:* $30,995,175 (100% non-need-based). *Programs:* Federal Direct (Subsidized and Unsubsidized Stafford, PLUS), FFEL (Subsidized and Unsubsidized Stafford, PLUS), Perkins, college/university.

WORK-STUDY *Federal work-study:* Total amount: $1,899,566; 505 jobs averaging $3761. *State or other work-study/employment:* Total amount: $377,678 (100% non-need-based). 82 part-time jobs averaging $4606.

ATHLETIC AWARDS Total amount: $7,073,061 (100% non-need-based).

APPLYING FOR FINANCIAL AID *Required financial aid form:* FAFSA. *Financial aid deadline (priority):* 3/1. *Notification date:* Continuous beginning 4/1. Students must reply within 4 weeks of notification.

CONTACT Ms. Brenda Maigaard, Director of Student Financial Aid, The University of Kansas, 50 Strong Hall, Lawrence, KS 66045-7535, 785-864-4700 or toll-free 888-686-7323 (in-state). *Fax:* 785-864-5469. *E-mail:* financialaid@ku.edu.

UNIVERSITY OF KENTUCKY
Lexington, KY

Tuition & fees (KY res): $8123   **Average undergraduate aid package:** $13,029

ABOUT THE INSTITUTION State-supported, coed. 80 undergraduate majors. Federal methodology is used as a basis for awarding need-based institutional aid.

UNDERGRADUATE EXPENSES for 2009–10 *Tuition, state resident:* full-time $7214; part-time $301 per credit hour. *Tuition, nonresident:* full-time $15,769; part-time $658 per credit hour. *Required fees:* full-time $909; $21.50 per credit hour. Full-time tuition and fees vary according to degree level, program, reciprocity agreements, and student level. Part-time tuition and fees vary according to degree level, program, reciprocity agreements, and student level. *College room and board:* $9125; *Room only:* $3975. Room and board charges vary according to board plan and housing facility. *Payment plan:* Installment.

FRESHMAN FINANCIAL AID (Fall 2008) 2,815 applied for aid; of those 67% were deemed to have need. 98% of freshmen with need received aid; of those 20% had need fully met. *Average percent of need met:* 79% (excluding resources awarded to replace EFC). *Average financial aid package:* $13,180 (excluding resources awarded to replace EFC). 22% of all full-time freshmen had no need and received non-need-based gift aid.

UNDERGRADUATE FINANCIAL AID (Fall 2008) 9,732 applied for aid; of those 73% were deemed to have need. 94% of undergraduates with need received aid; of those 17% had need fully met. *Average percent of need met:* 78% (excluding resources awarded to replace EFC). *Average financial aid package:* $13,029 (excluding resources awarded to replace EFC). 19% of all full-time undergraduates had no need and received non-need-based gift aid.

GIFT AID (NEED-BASED) *Total amount:* $71,943,793 (18% federal, 28% state, 48% institutional, 6% external sources). *Receiving aid:* Freshmen: 18% (737); all full-time undergraduates: 17% (2,924). *Average award:* Freshmen: $5188; Undergraduates: $5074. *Scholarships, grants, and awards:* Federal Pell, FSEOG, state, private, college/university gift aid from institutional funds.

GIFT AID (NON-NEED-BASED) *Receiving aid:* Freshmen: 41% (1,688). Undergraduates: 29% (4,926). *Average award:* Freshmen: $4891. Undergraduates: $5579. *Scholarships, grants, and awards by category: Academic interests/achievement:* agriculture, architecture, area/ethnic studies, biological sciences, business, communication, computer science, education, engineering/technologies, English, foreign languages, general academic interests/achievements, health fields, home economics, international studies, mathematics, military science, physical sciences. *Creative arts/performance:* applied art and design, art/fine arts, cinema/film/broadcasting, creative writing, dance, debating, general creative arts/performance, journalism/publications, music, performing arts, theater/

drama. *Special achievements/activities:* cheerleading/drum major, general special achievements/activities, leadership. *Special characteristics:* adult students, children and siblings of alumni, children of educators, children of faculty/staff, children of public servants, children of union members/company employees, children of workers in trades, children with a deceased or disabled parent, ethnic background, first-generation college students, general special characteristics, handicapped students, international students, members of minority groups, public servants, spouses of deceased or disabled public servants, veterans, veterans' children. *Tuition waivers:* Full or partial for employees or children of employees, senior citizens.

LOANS *Student loans:* $59,362,150 (100% need-based). 33% of past graduating class borrowed through all loan programs. *Average indebtedness per student:* $22,943. *Average need-based loan:* Freshmen: $3287. Undergraduates: $3302. *Parent loans:* $11,985,429 (100% need-based). *Programs:* Federal Direct (Subsidized and Unsubsidized Stafford, PLUS), Perkins, college/university.

WORK-STUDY *Federal work-study:* Total amount: $613,248; jobs available. *State or other work-study/employment:* Total amount: $231,418 (100% need-based). Part-time jobs available.

ATHLETIC AWARDS Total amount: $8,028,369 (100% need-based).

APPLYING FOR FINANCIAL AID *Required financial aid form:* FAFSA. *Financial aid deadline (priority):* 2/15. *Notification date:* Continuous beginning 4/1. Students must reply within 3 weeks of notification.

CONTACT Ms. Lynda S. George, Director of Financial Aid, University of Kentucky, 128 Funkhouser Building, Lexington, KY 40506-0054, 859-257-3172 Ext. 241 or toll-free 800-432-0967 (in-state). *Fax:* 859-257-4398. *E-mail:* lgeorge@email.uky.edu.

UNIVERSITY OF LA VERNE
La Verne, CA

Tuition & fees: $29,800	Average undergraduate aid package: $24,932

ABOUT THE INSTITUTION Independent, coed. 46 undergraduate majors. Federal methodology is used as a basis for awarding need-based institutional aid.

UNDERGRADUATE EXPENSES for 2010–11 *Comprehensive fee:* $40,240 includes full-time tuition ($29,800) and room and board ($10,440). *College room only:* $5620. Full-time tuition and fees vary according to course load, degree level, location, program, and student level. Room and board charges vary according to board plan and housing facility. *Part-time tuition:* $845 per unit. Part-time tuition and fees vary according to course load, degree level, location, program, and student level. *Payment plans:* Installment, deferred payment.

FRESHMAN FINANCIAL AID (Fall 2009, est.) 296 applied for aid; of those 93% were deemed to have need. 100% of freshmen with need received aid; of those 9% had need fully met. *Average percent of need met:* 47% (excluding resources awarded to replace EFC). *Average financial aid package:* $26,195 (excluding resources awarded to replace EFC). 11% of all full-time freshmen had no need and received non-need-based gift aid.

UNDERGRADUATE FINANCIAL AID (Fall 2009, est.) 1,255 applied for aid; of those 95% were deemed to have need. 100% of undergraduates with need received aid; of those 13% had need fully met. *Average percent of need met:* 60% (excluding resources awarded to replace EFC). *Average financial aid package:* $24,932 (excluding resources awarded to replace EFC). 11% of all full-time undergraduates had no need and received non-need-based gift aid.

GIFT AID (NEED-BASED) *Total amount:* $23,213,749 (13% federal, 21% state, 65% institutional, 1% external sources). *Receiving aid:* Freshmen: 57% (186); all full-time undergraduates: 71% (1,017). *Average award:* Freshmen: $11,024; Undergraduates: $11,941. *Scholarships, grants, and awards:* Federal Pell, FSEOG, state, private, college/university gift aid from institutional funds.

GIFT AID (NON-NEED-BASED) *Total amount:* $1,695,416 (100% institutional). *Receiving aid:* Freshmen: 83% (272). Undergraduates: 72% (1,025). *Average award:* Freshmen: $17,758. Undergraduates: $15,146. *Scholarships, grants, and awards by category:* Academic interests/achievement: general academic interests/achievements. *Creative arts/performance:* art/fine arts, debating, journalism/publications, music, theater/drama. *Special achievements/activities:* community service, leadership. *Special characteristics:* children and siblings of alumni, children of faculty/staff, ethnic background, first-generation college students, general special characteristics, international students, religious affiliation. *Tuition waivers:* Full or partial for employees or children of employees.

LOANS *Student loans:* $11,335,012 (91% need-based, 9% non-need-based). 83% of past graduating class borrowed through all loan programs. *Average*

indebtedness per student: $25,491. *Average need-based loan:* Freshmen: $4111. Undergraduates: $4889. *Parent loans:* $2,086,386 (92% need-based, 8% non-need-based). *Programs:* FFEL (Subsidized and Unsubsidized Stafford, PLUS), Perkins, college/university, alternative loans.

WORK-STUDY *Federal work-study:* Total amount: $467,400; jobs available. *State or other work-study/employment:* Part-time jobs available.

APPLYING FOR FINANCIAL AID *Required financial aid forms:* FAFSA, state aid form. *Financial aid deadline (priority):* 3/2. *Notification date:* Continuous beginning 3/17. Students must reply within 2 weeks of notification.

CONTACT Leatha Webster, Director of Financial Aid, University of La Verne, 1950 3rd Street, La Verne, CA 91750-4443, 909-593-3511 Ext. 4180 or toll-free 800-876-4858. *Fax:* 909-392-2751. *E-mail:* lwebster@laverne.edu.

UNIVERSITY OF LOUISIANA AT LAFAYETTE
Lafayette, LA

ABOUT THE INSTITUTION State-supported, coed. *Awards:* bachelor's and master's degrees and post-master's certificates. 89 undergraduate majors. *Total enrollment:* 16,345. Undergraduates: 14,931. Freshmen: 2,763.

GIFT AID (NEED-BASED) *Scholarships, grants, and awards:* Federal Pell, FSEOG, state, college/university gift aid from institutional funds.

GIFT AID (NON-NEED-BASED) *Scholarships, grants, and awards by category:* Academic interests/achievement: general academic interests/achievements. *Creative arts/performance:* general creative arts/performance. *Special achievements/activities:* general special achievements/activities.

LOANS *Programs:* FFEL (Subsidized and Unsubsidized Stafford, PLUS), Perkins, Federal Nursing.

APPLYING FOR FINANCIAL AID *Required financial aid form:* FAFSA.

CONTACT Cindy S. Perez, Director of Financial Aid, University of Louisiana at Lafayette, PO Box 41206, Lafayette, LA 70504-1206, 337-482-6497 or toll-free 800-752-6553 (in-state). *Fax:* 337-482-6502. *E-mail:* cperez@louisiana.edu.

UNIVERSITY OF LOUISIANA AT MONROE
Monroe, LA

Tuition & fees: N/R	Average undergraduate aid package: N/A

ABOUT THE INSTITUTION State-supported, coed. 54 undergraduate majors. Federal methodology is used as a basis for awarding need-based institutional aid.

GIFT AID (NEED-BASED) *Scholarships, grants, and awards:* Federal Pell, FSEOG, state, private, college/university gift aid from institutional funds, Leveraging Educational Assistance Program (LEAP).

GIFT AID (NON-NEED-BASED) *Scholarships, grants, and awards by category:* Academic interests/achievement: agriculture, biological sciences, business, communication, computer science, education, English, foreign languages, general academic interests/achievements, health fields, home economics, library science, mathematics, military science, physical sciences, social sciences. *Creative arts/performance:* art/fine arts, creative writing, debating, journalism/publications, music, performing arts, theater/drama. *Special achievements/activities:* cheerleading/drum major, community service, leadership. *Special characteristics:* children of faculty/staff, children with a deceased or disabled parent, international students, out-of-state students. *Tuition waivers:* Full or partial for children of alumni, employees or children of employees.

LOANS *Programs:* FFEL (Subsidized and Unsubsidized Stafford, PLUS), Perkins, college/university, Federal Health Professions Student Loans.

WORK-STUDY Federal work-study jobs available. *State or other work-study/employment:* Part-time jobs available.

APPLYING FOR FINANCIAL AID *Required financial aid forms:* FAFSA, institution's own form. *Financial aid deadline (priority):* 4/1. *Notification date:* Continuous beginning 6/15. Students must reply within 2 weeks of notification.

CONTACT Ms. Teresa Smith, Director, Financial Aid, University of Louisiana at Monroe, 700 University Avenue, Monroe, LA 71209, 318-342-5320 or toll-free 800-372-5272 (in-state), 800-372-5127 (out-of-state). *Fax:* 318-342-3539. *E-mail:* tsmith@ulm.edu.

UNIVERSITY OF LOUISVILLE
Louisville, KY

Tuition & fees (KY res): $7944 | **Average undergraduate aid package: $10,170**

ABOUT THE INSTITUTION State-supported, coed. 53 undergraduate majors. Federal methodology is used as a basis for awarding need-based institutional aid.

UNDERGRADUATE EXPENSES for 2010–11 *Tuition, area resident:* part-time $331 per credit hour. *Tuition, state resident:* full-time $7944. *Tuition, nonresident:* full-time $19,272; part-time $803 per credit hour. Full-time tuition and fees vary according to reciprocity agreements. Part-time tuition and fees vary according to course load and reciprocity agreements. *College room and board:* $5437. Room and board charges vary according to board plan and housing facility. *Payment plan:* Installment.

FRESHMAN FINANCIAL AID (Fall 2009, est.) 2,002 applied for aid; of those 75% were deemed to have need. 99% of freshmen with need received aid; of those 26% had need fully met. *Average percent of need met:* 68% (excluding resources awarded to replace EFC). *Average financial aid package:* $10,465 (excluding resources awarded to replace EFC). 14% of all full-time freshmen had no need and received non-need-based gift aid.

UNDERGRADUATE FINANCIAL AID (Fall 2009, est.) 8,330 applied for aid; of those 81% were deemed to have need. 97% of undergraduates with need received aid; of those 22% had need fully met. *Average percent of need met:* 65% (excluding resources awarded to replace EFC). *Average financial aid package:* $10,170 (excluding resources awarded to replace EFC). 14% of all full-time undergraduates had no need and received non-need-based gift aid.

GIFT AID (NEED-BASED) *Total amount:* $43,836,072 (39% federal, 20% state, 30% institutional, 11% external sources). *Receiving aid:* Freshmen: 59% (1,451); all full-time undergraduates: 49% (5,839). *Average award:* Freshmen: $7989; Undergraduates: $7641. *Scholarships, grants, and awards:* Federal Pell, FSEOG, state, private, college/university gift aid from institutional funds.

GIFT AID (NON-NEED-BASED) *Total amount:* $24,669,193 (26% state, 57% institutional, 17% external sources). *Receiving aid:* Freshmen: 10% (240). Undergraduates: 6% (719). *Average award:* Freshmen: $6722. Undergraduates: $6948. *Scholarships, grants, and awards by category: Academic interests/achievement:* biological sciences, business, education, engineering/technologies, English, foreign languages, general academic interests/achievements, health fields, mathematics, military science, premedicine. *Creative arts/performance:* art/fine arts, creative writing, dance, debating, general creative arts/performance, music, theater/drama. *Special achievements/activities:* cheerleading/drum major, community service, general special achievements/activities, hobbies/interests, junior miss, leadership, memberships. *Special characteristics:* adult students, children and siblings of alumni, children of faculty/staff, children of union members/company employees, children with a deceased or disabled parent, ethnic background, general special characteristics, local/state students, members of minority groups, out-of-state students, previous college experience, veterans, veterans' children. *Tuition waivers:* Full or partial for employees or children of employees, senior citizens.

LOANS *Student loans:* $44,495,357 (71% need-based, 29% non-need-based). 47% of past graduating class borrowed through all loan programs. *Average indebtedness per student:* $17,651. *Average need-based loan:* Freshmen: $3031. Undergraduates: $4024. *Parent loans:* $3,387,647 (33% need-based, 67% non-need-based). *Programs:* Federal Direct (Subsidized and Unsubsidized Stafford, PLUS), Perkins, Federal Nursing.

WORK-STUDY *Federal work-study:* Total amount: $1,609,609; 1,020 jobs averaging $3449.

ATHLETIC AWARDS Total amount: $8,133,152 (36% need-based, 64% non-need-based).

APPLYING FOR FINANCIAL AID *Required financial aid form:* FAFSA. *Financial aid deadline (priority):* 3/15. *Notification date:* Continuous beginning 4/1. Students must reply by 5/1.

CONTACT Ms. Patricia O. Arauz, Director of Financial Aid, University of Louisville, 2301 South Third Street, Louisville, KY 40292-0001, 502-852-6145 or toll-free 800-334-8635 (out-of-state). *Fax:* 502-852-0182. *E-mail:* finaid@louisville.edu.

UNIVERSITY OF MAINE
Orono, ME

Tuition & fees (ME res): $9626 | **Average undergraduate aid package: $10,588**

ABOUT THE INSTITUTION State-supported, coed. 107 undergraduate majors. Federal methodology is used as a basis for awarding need-based institutional aid.

UNDERGRADUATE EXPENSES for 2009–10 *Tuition, state resident:* full-time $7590; part-time $253 per credit hour. *Tuition, nonresident:* full-time $21,840; part-time $728 per credit hour. *Required fees:* full-time $2036. Full-time tuition and fees vary according to course load and program. Part-time tuition and fees vary according to course load and program. *College room and board:* $8008. Room and board charges vary according to board plan and housing facility. *Payment plan:* Installment.

FRESHMAN FINANCIAL AID (Fall 2009, est.) 1,445 applied for aid; of those 82% were deemed to have need. 100% of freshmen with need received aid; of those 31% had need fully met. *Average percent of need met:* 74% (excluding resources awarded to replace EFC). *Average financial aid package:* $10,342 (excluding resources awarded to replace EFC).

UNDERGRADUATE FINANCIAL AID (Fall 2009, est.) 7,288 applied for aid; of those 85% were deemed to have need. 100% of undergraduates with need received aid; of those 32% had need fully met. *Average percent of need met:* 74% (excluding resources awarded to replace EFC). *Average financial aid package:* $10,588 (excluding resources awarded to replace EFC).

GIFT AID (NEED-BASED) *Total amount:* $35,010,329 (43% federal, 8% state, 41% institutional, 8% external sources). *Receiving aid:* Freshmen: 1,048; all full-time undergraduates: 4,831. *Average award:* Freshmen: $6766; Undergraduates: $6826. *Scholarships, grants, and awards:* Federal Pell, FSEOG, state, private, college/university gift aid from institutional funds, Academic Competitiveness Grants, National SMART Grants.

GIFT AID (NON-NEED-BASED) *Total amount:* $4,416,271 (3% federal, 3% state, 70% institutional, 24% external sources). *Receiving aid:* Freshmen: 56. Undergraduates: 185. *Average award:* Freshmen: $3490. Undergraduates: $4115. *Tuition waivers:* Full or partial for employees or children of employees, senior citizens.

LOANS *Student loans:* $64,897,554 (71% need-based, 29% non-need-based). 77% of past graduating class borrowed through all loan programs. *Average indebtedness per student:* $30,824. *Average need-based loan:* Freshmen: $5201. Undergraduates: $6392. *Parent loans:* $6,671,448 (33% need-based, 67% non-need-based). *Programs:* FFEL (Subsidized and Unsubsidized Stafford, PLUS), Perkins, state, college/university.

WORK-STUDY *Federal work-study:* Total amount: $2,882,732; 800 jobs averaging $2695.

ATHLETIC AWARDS Total amount: $5,447,311 (36% need-based, 64% non-need-based).

APPLYING FOR FINANCIAL AID *Required financial aid form:* FAFSA. *Financial aid deadline (priority):* 3/1. *Notification date:* Continuous beginning 3/15. Students must reply by 5/1 or within 2 weeks of notification.

CONTACT Ms. Peggy L. Crawford, Director of Student Aid, University of Maine, 5781 Wingate Hall, Orono, ME 04469, 207-581-1324 or toll-free 877-486-2364. *Fax:* 207-581-3261. *E-mail:* pcrawf@maine.edu.

UNIVERSITY OF MAINE AT AUGUSTA
Augusta, ME

ABOUT THE INSTITUTION State-supported, coed. 24 undergraduate majors.

GIFT AID (NEED-BASED) *Scholarships, grants, and awards:* Federal Pell, FSEOG, state, private, college/university gift aid from institutional funds.

GIFT AID (NON-NEED-BASED) *Scholarships, grants, and awards by category: Academic interests/achievement:* biological sciences, business, general academic interests/achievements, mathematics. *Creative arts/performance:* music. *Special achievements/activities:* general special achievements/activities, leadership. *Special characteristics:* children of faculty/staff, ethnic background, international students, local/state students, veterans' children.

LOANS *Programs:* Federal Direct (Subsidized and Unsubsidized Stafford, PLUS), FFEL (Subsidized and Unsubsidized Stafford, PLUS), Perkins, Federal Nursing.

WORK-STUDY *Federal work-study:* Total amount: $390,674; 220 jobs averaging $1500.

APPLYING FOR FINANCIAL AID *Required financial aid form:* FAFSA.

CONTACT Sherry McCollett, Director of Financial Aid, University of Maine at Augusta, 46 University Drive, Augusta, ME 04330-9410, 207-621-3455 or toll-free 877-862-1234 Ext. 3185 (in-state). *Fax:* 207-621-3116. *E-mail:* umafa@maine.edu.

UNIVERSITY OF MAINE AT FARMINGTON
Farmington, ME

CONTACT Mr. Ronald P. Milliken, Director of Financial Aid, University of Maine at Farmington, 224 Main Street, Farmington, ME 04938-1990, 207-778-7105. *Fax:* 207-778-8178. *E-mail:* milliken@maine.edu.

UNIVERSITY OF MAINE AT FORT KENT
Fort Kent, ME

Tuition & fees (ME res): $6803   **Average undergraduate aid package: $5422**

ABOUT THE INSTITUTION State-supported, coed. 25 undergraduate majors. Federal methodology is used as a basis for awarding need-based institutional aid.

UNDERGRADUATE EXPENSES for 2010–11 *Tuition, state resident:* full-time $6030. *Tuition, nonresident:* full-time $15,180. *Required fees:* full-time $773. *College room and board:* $7080; *Room only:* $4000.

FRESHMAN FINANCIAL AID (Fall 2009, est.) 98 applied for aid; of those 92% were deemed to have need. 100% of freshmen with need received aid; of those 47% had need fully met. *Average percent of need met:* 86% (excluding resources awarded to replace EFC). *Average financial aid package:* $6089 (excluding resources awarded to replace EFC). 7% of all full-time freshmen had no need and received non-need-based gift aid.

UNDERGRADUATE FINANCIAL AID (Fall 2009, est.) 363 applied for aid; of those 90% were deemed to have need. 100% of undergraduates with need received aid; of those 47% had need fully met. *Average percent of need met:* 82% (excluding resources awarded to replace EFC). *Average financial aid package:* $5422 (excluding resources awarded to replace EFC). 6% of all full-time undergraduates had no need and received non-need-based gift aid.

GIFT AID (NEED-BASED) *Total amount:* $1,341,372 (87% federal, 13% state). *Receiving aid:* Freshmen: 47% (55); all full-time undergraduates: 35% (200). *Average award:* Freshmen: $2627; Undergraduates: $2756. *Scholarships, grants, and awards:* Federal Pell, FSEOG, state, private, college/university gift aid from institutional funds.

GIFT AID (NON-NEED-BASED) *Total amount:* $623,750 (88% institutional, 12% external sources). *Receiving aid:* Freshmen: 76% (90). Undergraduates: 56% (322). *Average award:* Freshmen: $525. Undergraduates: $881. *Scholarships, grants, and awards by category: Academic interests/achievement:* biological sciences, business, communication, computer science, education, English, foreign languages, general academic interests/achievements, health fields, humanities, mathematics, social sciences. *Creative arts/performance:* general creative arts/performance, performing arts. *Special achievements/activities:* general special achievements/activities. *Special characteristics:* adult students, children of faculty/staff, general special characteristics, international students, members of minority groups.

LOANS *Student loans:* $3,053,310 (53% need-based, 47% non-need-based). *Average need-based loan:* Freshmen: $2561. Undergraduates: $2361. *Parent loans:* $108,163 (100% non-need-based). *Programs:* Federal Direct (Subsidized and Unsubsidized Stafford, PLUS), FFEL (Subsidized and Unsubsidized Stafford, PLUS), Perkins, state.

WORK-STUDY *Federal work-study:* Total amount: $550,662; jobs available. *State or other work-study/employment:* Part-time jobs available.

ATHLETIC AWARDS Total amount: $27,500 (100% need-based).

APPLYING FOR FINANCIAL AID *Required financial aid forms:* FAFSA, institution's own form, CSS Financial Aid PROFILE, state aid form. *Financial aid deadline (priority):* 3/1. *Notification date:* Continuous beginning 3/1.

CONTACT Ellen Cost, Director of Financial Aid, University of Maine at Fort Kent, 23 University Drive, Fort Kent, ME 04743-1292, 207-834-7606 or toll-free 888-TRY-UMFK. *Fax:* 207-834-7841. *E-mail:* ecost@maine.edu.

UNIVERSITY OF MAINE AT MACHIAS
Machias, ME

CONTACT Ms. Stephanie Larrabee, Director of Financial Aid, University of Maine at Machias, 9 O'Brien Avenue, Machias, ME 04654, 207-255-1203 or toll-free 888-GOTOUMM (in-state), 888-468-6866 (out-of-state). *Fax:* 207-255-4864.

UNIVERSITY OF MAINE AT PRESQUE ISLE
Presque Isle, ME

Tuition & fees (ME res): $6875   **Average undergraduate aid package: $9807**

ABOUT THE INSTITUTION State-supported, coed. 28 undergraduate majors. Federal methodology is used as a basis for awarding need-based institutional aid.

UNDERGRADUATE EXPENSES for 2009–10 *Tuition, state resident:* full-time $6030. *Tuition, nonresident:* full-time $15,180. *Required fees:* full-time $845. Full-time tuition and fees vary according to course load and reciprocity agreements. Part-time tuition and fees vary according to course load and reciprocity agreements. *College room and board:* $7300; *Room only:* $3752. Room and board charges vary according to board plan and housing facility. *Payment plans:* Installment, deferred payment.

FRESHMAN FINANCIAL AID (Fall 2008) 166 applied for aid; of those 89% were deemed to have need. 100% of freshmen with need received aid; of those 52% had need fully met. *Average percent of need met:* 83% (excluding resources awarded to replace EFC). *Average financial aid package:* $9268 (excluding resources awarded to replace EFC). 10% of all full-time freshmen had no need and received non-need-based gift aid.

UNDERGRADUATE FINANCIAL AID (Fall 2008) 673 applied for aid; of those 90% were deemed to have need. 100% of undergraduates with need received aid; of those 51% had need fully met. *Average percent of need met:* 82% (excluding resources awarded to replace EFC). *Average financial aid package:* $9807 (excluding resources awarded to replace EFC). 9% of all full-time undergraduates had no need and received non-need-based gift aid.

GIFT AID (NEED-BASED) *Total amount:* $3,809,169 (74% federal, 10% state, 12% institutional, 4% external sources). *Receiving aid:* Freshmen: 80% (147); all full-time undergraduates: 64% (592). *Average award:* Freshmen: $5866; Undergraduates: $5530. *Scholarships, grants, and awards:* Federal Pell, FSEOG, state, private, college/university gift aid from institutional funds.

GIFT AID (NON-NEED-BASED) *Total amount:* $372,222 (79% institutional, 21% external sources). *Receiving aid:* Freshmen: 6% (11). Undergraduates: 3% (32). *Average award:* Freshmen: $4729. Undergraduates: $4151. *Scholarships, grants, and awards by category: Academic interests/achievement:* general academic interests/achievements. *Creative arts/performance:* art/fine arts. *Special achievements/activities:* community service. *Special characteristics:* children of faculty/staff, ethnic background, international students, veterans' children. *Tuition waivers:* Full or partial for minority students, employees or children of employees, senior citizens.

LOANS *Student loans:* $3,563,328 (70% need-based, 30% non-need-based). *Average need-based loan:* Freshmen: $4039. Undergraduates: $4210. *Parent loans:* $107,635 (6% need-based, 94% non-need-based). *Programs:* Federal Direct (Subsidized and Unsubsidized Stafford, PLUS), Perkins, state, college/university.

WORK-STUDY *Federal work-study:* Total amount: $680,123; jobs available.

APPLYING FOR FINANCIAL AID *Required financial aid form:* FAFSA. *Financial aid deadline (priority):* 4/1. *Notification date:* Continuous. Students must reply within 2 weeks of notification.

CONTACT Christopher A. R. Bell, Director of Financial Aid, University of Maine at Presque Isle, 181 Main Street, Presque Isle, ME 04769-2888, 207-768-9511. *Fax:* 207-768-9608. *E-mail:* chris.bell@umpi.edu.

UNIVERSITY OF MANAGEMENT AND TECHNOLOGY
Arlington, VA

CONTACT Financial Aid Office, University of Management and Technology, 1901 North Fort Myer Drive, Arlington, VA 22209, 703-516-0035 or toll-free 800-924-4885 (in-state). *E-mail:* info@umtweb.edu.

UNIVERSITY OF MARY
Bismarck, ND

Tuition & fees: $13,126	Average undergraduate aid package: N/A

ABOUT THE INSTITUTION Independent Roman Catholic, coed. 46 undergraduate majors. Federal methodology is used as a basis for awarding need-based institutional aid.

UNDERGRADUATE EXPENSES for 2010–11 *Comprehensive fee:* $18,276 includes full-time tuition ($12,800), mandatory fees ($326), and room and board ($5150). *College room only:* $2350. Full-time tuition and fees vary according to course load, degree level, and program. Room and board charges vary according to board plan and housing facility. *Part-time tuition:* $400 per credit hour. Part-time tuition and fees vary according to course load, degree level, and program. *Payment plan:* Installment.

FRESHMAN FINANCIAL AID (Fall 2009, est.) 283 applied for aid; of those 77% were deemed to have need. 100% of freshmen with need received aid. *Average financial aid package:* $10,972 (excluding resources awarded to replace EFC). **GIFT AID (NEED-BASED)** *Total amount:* $9,151,107 (28% federal, 7% state, 60% institutional, 5% external sources). *Receiving aid:* Freshmen: 44% (138). *Average award:* Freshmen: $4030. *Scholarships, grants, and awards:* Federal Pell, FSEOG, state, private, college/university gift aid from institutional funds, Academic Competitiveness Grants, National SMART Grants, TEACH Grants. **GIFT AID (NON-NEED-BASED)** *Receiving aid:* Freshmen: 69% (214). *Scholarships, grants, and awards by category: Academic interests/achievement:* 1,265 awards ($4,320,116 total): general academic interests/achievements. *Creative arts/performance:* 52 awards ($143,950 total): debating, music, theater/drama. *Special achievements/activities:* 232 awards ($1,469,105 total): cheerleading/drum major, general special achievements/activities. *Special characteristics:* 349 awards ($960,282 total): children of faculty/staff, international students, local/state students, religious affiliation, siblings of current students, spouses of current students, veterans. *Tuition waivers:* Full or partial for employees or children of employees, senior citizens. **LOANS** *Student loans:* $12,972,888 (100% need-based). *Average need-based loan:* Freshmen: $3165. *Parent loans:* $386,737 (100% need-based). *Programs:* Federal Direct (Subsidized and Unsubsidized Stafford, PLUS), Perkins, Federal Nursing, alternative private loans. **WORK-STUDY** *Federal work-study:* Total amount: $173,530; 170 jobs averaging $1021. *State or other work-study/employment:* Total amount: $99,970 (100% need-based). 68 part-time jobs averaging $1470. **ATHLETIC AWARDS** Total amount: $1,452,455 (100% need-based).

APPLYING FOR FINANCIAL AID *Required financial aid form:* Federal FAFSA form is highly recommended. *Financial aid deadline (priority):* 3/15. *Notification date:* Continuous beginning 2/15. Students must reply within 2 weeks of notification.

CONTACT Brenda Zastoupil, Financial Assistance Director, University of Mary, 7500 University Drive, Bismarck, ND 58504-9652, 701-355-8244 or toll-free 800-288-6279. *Fax:* 701-255-7687. *E-mail:* brendaz@umary.edu.

UNIVERSITY OF MARY HARDIN-BAYLOR
Belton, TX

Tuition & fees: $20,650	Average undergraduate aid package: $15,535

ABOUT THE INSTITUTION Independent Southern Baptist, coed. 54 undergraduate majors. Federal methodology is used as a basis for awarding need-based institutional aid.

UNDERGRADUATE EXPENSES for 2009–10 *Comprehensive fee:* $26,000 includes full-time tuition ($18,300), mandatory fees ($2350), and room and board ($5350). Full-time tuition and fees vary according to course load. Room and board charges vary according to board plan and housing facility. *Part-time tuition:* $610 per credit hour. *Part-time fees:* $75 per credit hour; $50 per term. Part-time tuition and fees vary according to course load. *Payment plan:* Installment.

FRESHMAN FINANCIAL AID (Fall 2009, est.) 514 applied for aid; of those 85% were deemed to have need. 100% of freshmen with need received aid; of those 30% had need fully met. *Average percent of need met:* 65% (excluding resources awarded to replace EFC). *Average financial aid package:* $15,844 (excluding resources awarded to replace EFC). 16% of all full-time freshmen had no need and received non-need-based gift aid.

UNDERGRADUATE FINANCIAL AID (Fall 2009, est.) 2,049 applied for aid; of those 89% were deemed to have need. 100% of undergraduates with need received aid; of those 23% had need fully met. *Average percent of need met:* 62% (excluding resources awarded to replace EFC). *Average financial aid package:* $15,535 (excluding resources awarded to replace EFC). 9% of all full-time undergraduates had no need and received non-need-based gift aid. **GIFT AID (NEED-BASED)** *Total amount:* $15,493,854 (28% federal, 29% state, 43% institutional). *Receiving aid:* Freshmen: 69% (373); all full-time undergraduates: 77% (1,679). *Average award:* Freshmen: $8014; Undergraduates: $4657. *Scholarships, grants, and awards:* Federal Pell, FSEOG, state, private, college/university gift aid from institutional funds. **GIFT AID (NON-NEED-BASED)** *Total amount:* $6,208,665 (53% institutional, 47% external sources). *Receiving aid:* Freshmen: 49% (265). Undergraduates: 31% (686). *Average award:* Freshmen: $5468. Undergraduates: $4687. *Scholarships, grants, and awards by category: Academic interests/achievement:* 165 awards ($402,423 total): biological sciences, business, communication, computer science, education, English, foreign languages, general academic interests/achievements, health fields, humanities, international studies, mathematics, physical sciences, premedicine, religion/biblical studies, social sciences. *Creative arts/performance:* 110 awards ($217,235 total): art/fine arts, music. *Special achievements/activities:* 351 awards ($966,670 total): cheerleading/drum major, community service, leadership, religious involvement. *Special characteristics:* 173 awards ($1,210,259 total): children and siblings of alumni, children of faculty/staff, ethnic background, handicapped students, international students, local/state students, members of minority groups, out-of-state students, relatives of clergy, religious affiliation. *Tuition waivers:* Full or partial for employees or children of employees. **LOANS** *Student loans:* $17,634,772 (39% need-based, 61% non-need-based). 81% of past graduating class borrowed through all loan programs. *Average indebtedness per student:* $17,500. *Average need-based loan:* Freshmen: $2886. Undergraduates: $4203. *Parent loans:* $2,312,108 (100% non-need-based). *Programs:* Federal Direct (Subsidized and Unsubsidized Stafford, PLUS), Perkins, state. **WORK-STUDY** *Federal work-study:* Total amount: $490,800; 206 jobs averaging $2458. *State or other work-study/employment:* Total amount: $734,411 (25% need-based, 75% non-need-based). 347 part-time jobs averaging $2287. **APPLYING FOR FINANCIAL AID** *Required financial aid form:* FAFSA. *Financial aid deadline (priority):* 3/1. *Notification date:* Continuous beginning 2/1. Students must reply within 2 weeks of notification.

CONTACT Mr. David Orsag, Associate Director of Financial Aid, University of Mary Hardin-Baylor, Box 8080, Belton, TX 76513, 254-295-4517 or toll-free 800-727-8642. *Fax:* 254-295-5049. *E-mail:* dorsag@umhb.edu.

UNIVERSITY OF MARYLAND, BALTIMORE COUNTY
Baltimore, MD

Tuition & fees (MD res): $8872	Average undergraduate aid package: $11,409

ABOUT THE INSTITUTION State-supported, coed. 43 undergraduate majors. Federal methodology is used as a basis for awarding need-based institutional aid.

UNDERGRADUATE EXPENSES for 2009–10 *One-time required fee:* $125. *Tuition, state resident:* full-time $6484; part-time $270 per credit hour. *Tuition, nonresident:* full-time $15,825; part-time $658 per credit hour. *Required fees:* full-time $2388; $106 per credit hour. Full-time tuition and fees vary according to location and program. Part-time tuition and fees vary according to location and program. *College room and board:* $9303; *Room only:* $5670. Room and board charges vary according to board plan and housing facility. *Payment plan:* Installment.

FRESHMAN FINANCIAL AID (Fall 2008) 1,102 applied for aid; of those 61% were deemed to have need. 100% of freshmen with need received aid; of those 33% had need fully met. *Average percent of need met:* 88% (excluding resources awarded to replace EFC). *Average financial aid package:* $12,294 (excluding resources awarded to replace EFC). 34% of all full-time freshmen had no need and received non-need-based gift aid.

UNDERGRADUATE FINANCIAL AID (Fall 2008) 5,113 applied for aid; of those 75% were deemed to have need. 100% of undergraduates with need received aid; of those 41% had need fully met. *Average percent of need met:* 76% (excluding resources awarded to replace EFC). *Average financial aid package:*

$11,409 (excluding resources awarded to replace EFC). 12% of all full-time undergraduates had no need and received non-need-based gift aid.

GIFT AID (NEED-BASED) *Total amount:* $21,538,319 (35% federal, 32% state, 30% institutional, 3% external sources). *Receiving aid:* Freshmen: 38% (591); all full-time undergraduates: 39% (3,207). *Average award:* Freshmen: $9612; Undergraduates: $7920. *Scholarships, grants, and awards:* Federal Pell, FSEOG, state, private, college/university gift aid from institutional funds.

GIFT AID (NON-NEED-BASED) *Total amount:* $11,284,159 (2% federal, 5% state, 89% institutional, 4% external sources). *Receiving aid:* Freshmen: 7% (109). Undergraduates: 4% (348). *Average award:* Freshmen: $3811. Undergraduates: $3688. *Scholarships, grants, and awards by category:* Academic interests/achievement: 1,764 awards ($11,139,095 total): biological sciences, computer science, education, engineering/technologies, English, foreign languages, general academic interests/achievements, humanities, mathematics, physical sciences, social sciences. Creative arts/performance: 71 awards ($111,375 total): art/fine arts, cinema/film/broadcasting, creative writing, dance, music, performing arts, theater/drama. *Tuition waivers:* Full or partial for employees or children of employees, senior citizens.

LOANS *Student loans:* $29,995,064 (43% need-based, 57% non-need-based). 51% of past graduating class borrowed through all loan programs. *Average indebtedness per student:* $19,353. *Average need-based loan:* Freshmen: $3574. Undergraduates: $4496. *Parent loans:* $5,503,240 (100% non-need-based). *Programs:* Federal Direct (Subsidized and Unsubsidized Stafford, PLUS), Perkins.

WORK-STUDY *Federal work-study:* Total amount: $173,315; 71 jobs averaging $2441. *State or other work-study/employment:* Total amount: $905,379 (42% need-based, 58% non-need-based). Part-time jobs available.

ATHLETIC AWARDS Total amount: $2,054,992 (29% need-based, 71% non-need-based).

APPLYING FOR FINANCIAL AID *Required financial aid form:* FAFSA. *Financial aid deadline (priority):* 2/14. *Notification date:* Continuous beginning 3/15.

CONTACT Stephanie Johnson, Director, University of Maryland, Baltimore County, 1000 Hilltop Circle, Baltimore, MD 21250, 410-455-2387 or toll-free 800-UMBC-4U2 (in-state), 800-862-2402 (out-of-state). *Fax:* 410-455-1288. *E-mail:* finaid@umbc.edu.

UNIVERSITY OF MARYLAND, COLLEGE PARK
College Park, MD

Tuition & fees (MD res): $8053   Average undergraduate aid package: $9189

ABOUT THE INSTITUTION State-supported, coed. 96 undergraduate majors. Federal methodology is used as a basis for awarding need-based institutional aid.

UNDERGRADUATE EXPENSES for 2009–10 *Tuition, state resident:* full-time $6566; part-time $273 per credit hour. *Tuition, nonresident:* full-time $22,502; part-time $938 per credit hour. *Required fees:* full-time $1487; $338.94 per term. Part-time tuition and fees vary according to course load. *College room and board:* $9377; *Room only:* $5549. Room and board charges vary according to board plan. *Payment plans:* Installment, deferred payment.

FRESHMAN FINANCIAL AID (Fall 2008) 2,869 applied for aid; of those 56% were deemed to have need. 92% of freshmen with need received aid; of those 15% had need fully met. *Average percent of need met:* 62% (excluding resources awarded to replace EFC). *Average financial aid package:* $9920 (excluding resources awarded to replace EFC). 20% of all full-time freshmen had no need and received non-need-based gift aid.

UNDERGRADUATE FINANCIAL AID (Fall 2008) 13,509 applied for aid; of those 72% were deemed to have need. 92% of undergraduates with need received aid; of those 7% had need fully met. *Average percent of need met:* 56% (excluding resources awarded to replace EFC). *Average financial aid package:* $9189 (excluding resources awarded to replace EFC). 11% of all full-time undergraduates had no need and received non-need-based gift aid.

GIFT AID (NEED-BASED) *Total amount:* $37,546,810 (40% federal, 32% state, 28% institutional). *Receiving aid:* Freshmen: 22% (859); all full-time undergraduates: 24% (5,907). *Average award:* Freshmen: $7568; Undergraduates: $6232. *Scholarships, grants, and awards:* Federal Pell, FSEOG, state, private, college/university gift aid from institutional funds.

GIFT AID (NON-NEED-BASED) *Total amount:* $40,869,524 (11% state, 64% institutional, 25% external sources). *Receiving aid:* Freshmen: 23% (885). Undergraduates: 15% (3,723). *Average award:* Freshmen: $5167. Undergradu-

ates: $6211. *Scholarships, grants, and awards by category:* Academic interests/achievement: 4,758 awards ($21,101,816 total): agriculture, architecture, biological sciences, business, communication, computer science, education, engineering/technologies, English, foreign languages, general academic interests/achievements, health fields, humanities, international studies, library science, mathematics, military science, physical sciences, premedicine, social sciences. Creative arts/performance: 60 awards ($457,283 total): applied art and design, art/fine arts, dance, music, performing arts, theater/drama. Special achievements/activities: 64 awards ($359,830 total): cheerleading/drum major. Special characteristics: 1,734 awards ($6,988,500 total): adult students, out-of-state students. *Tuition waivers:* Full or partial for employees or children of employees.

LOANS *Student loans:* $76,954,533 (34% need-based, 66% non-need-based). 44% of past graduating class borrowed through all loan programs. *Average indebtedness per student:* $20,256. *Average need-based loan:* Freshmen: $3240. Undergraduates: $4152. *Parent loans:* $20,581,212 (40% need-based, 60% non-need-based). *Programs:* FFEL (Subsidized and Unsubsidized Stafford, PLUS), Perkins.

WORK-STUDY *Federal work-study:* Total amount: $582,496; 496 jobs averaging $1167.

ATHLETIC AWARDS Total amount: $11,058,391 (100% non-need-based).

APPLYING FOR FINANCIAL AID *Required financial aid form:* FAFSA. *Financial aid deadline (priority):* 2/15. *Notification date:* Continuous beginning 4/1.

CONTACT Sarah Bauder, Assistant Vice President for Enrollment Services and Financial Aid, University of Maryland, College Park, 0102 Lee Building, College Park, MD 20742, 301-314-8279 or toll-free 800-422-5867. *Fax:* 301-314-9587. *E-mail:* sbauder@umd.edu.

UNIVERSITY OF MARYLAND EASTERN SHORE
Princess Anne, MD

ABOUT THE INSTITUTION State-supported, coed. 52 undergraduate majors.

GIFT AID (NEED-BASED) *Scholarships, grants, and awards:* Federal Pell, FSEOG, state, college/university gift aid from institutional funds.

GIFT AID (NON-NEED-BASED) *Scholarships, grants, and awards by category:* Academic interests/achievement: agriculture, business, computer science, education, engineering/technologies, English, general academic interests/achievements, health fields, home economics, mathematics, physical sciences, social sciences. Creative arts/performance: art/fine arts, music, performing arts, theater/drama. Special characteristics: adult students, children of faculty/staff, first-generation college students, veterans.

LOANS *Programs:* Federal Direct (Subsidized and Unsubsidized Stafford, PLUS), Perkins.

WORK-STUDY *Federal work-study:* Total amount: $274,138; 156 jobs averaging $1757. *State or other work-study/employment:* Total amount: $1,500,000 (100% non-need-based). Part-time jobs available.

APPLYING FOR FINANCIAL AID *Required financial aid form:* FAFSA.

CONTACT Mr. James W. Kellam, Director of Financial Aid, University of Maryland Eastern Shore, Backbone Road, Princess Anne, MD 21853-1299, 410-651-6172. *Fax:* 410-651-7670. *E-mail:* jwkellam@umes.edu.

UNIVERSITY OF MARYLAND UNIVERSITY COLLEGE
Adelphi, MD

Tuition & fees (MD res): $5760   Average undergraduate aid package: $6795

ABOUT THE INSTITUTION State-supported, coed. 24 undergraduate majors. Federal methodology is used as a basis for awarding need-based institutional aid.

UNDERGRADUATE EXPENSES for 2010–11 *Tuition, state resident:* full-time $5520; part-time $230 per credit hour. *Tuition, nonresident:* full-time $11,976; part-time $499 per credit hour. *Required fees:* full-time $240; $10 per credit hour. *Payment plan:* Installment.

FRESHMAN FINANCIAL AID (Fall 2009, est.) 81 applied for aid; of those 91% were deemed to have need. 92% of freshmen with need received aid. *Average percent of need met:* 17% (excluding resources awarded to replace EFC). *Average financial aid package:* $5214 (excluding resources awarded to replace EFC).

University of Maryland University College

UNDERGRADUATE FINANCIAL AID (Fall 2009, est.) 1,920 applied for aid; of those 96% were deemed to have need. 92% of undergraduates with need received aid; of those .5% had need fully met. *Average percent of need met:* 23% (excluding resources awarded to replace EFC). *Average financial aid package:* $6795 (excluding resources awarded to replace EFC).
GIFT AID (NEED-BASED) *Total amount:* $12,401,090 (76% federal, 9% state, 14% institutional, 1% external sources). *Receiving aid:* Freshmen: 44% (48); all full-time undergraduates: 35% (993). *Average award:* Freshmen: $3447; Undergraduates: $3978. *Scholarships, grants, and awards:* Federal Pell, FSEOG, state, private, college/university gift aid from institutional funds.
GIFT AID (NON-NEED-BASED) *Total amount:* $2,062,360 (6% state, 67% institutional, 27% external sources). *Receiving aid:* Freshmen: 6% (6). Undergraduates: 10% (290). *Scholarships, grants, and awards by category:* Academic interests/achievement: general academic interests/achievements. *Special achievements/activities:* general special achievements/activities. *Tuition waivers:* Full or partial for employees or children of employees, senior citizens.
LOANS *Student loans:* $70,410,331 (42% need-based, 58% non-need-based). *Average need-based loan:* Freshmen: $2594. Undergraduates: $4200. *Parent loans:* $188,472 (100% non-need-based). *Programs:* Federal Direct (Subsidized and Unsubsidized Stafford, PLUS), FFEL (Subsidized and Unsubsidized Stafford, PLUS), Perkins.
WORK-STUDY *Federal work-study:* Total amount: $626,067; jobs available. *State or other work-study/employment:* Total amount: $260,974 (100% non-need-based). Part-time jobs available.
APPLYING FOR FINANCIAL AID *Required financial aid form:* FAFSA. *Financial aid deadline (priority):* 6/1. *Notification date:* Continuous. Students must reply within 2 weeks of notification.
CONTACT Cheryl Storie, Associate Vice President of Financial Aid, University of Maryland University College, 3501 University Boulevard East, Adelphi, MD 20783, 301-985-7847 or toll-free 800-888-8682 (in-state). *Fax:* 301-985-7462. *E-mail:* finaid@umuc.edu.

UNIVERSITY OF MARY WASHINGTON
Fredericksburg, VA

Tuition & fees (VA res): $3900   Average undergraduate aid package: $7960

ABOUT THE INSTITUTION State-supported, coed. 32 undergraduate majors. Federal methodology is used as a basis for awarding need-based institutional aid.
UNDERGRADUATE EXPENSES for 2010–11 *One-time required fee:* $75. *Tuition, state resident:* full-time $3900; part-time $172 per credit hour. *Tuition, nonresident:* full-time $16,810; part-time $700 per credit hour. Part-time tuition and fees vary according to course load and location. *College room and board:* $8200; *Room only:* $4850. Room and board charges vary according to board plan and housing facility. *Payment plan:* Installment.
FRESHMAN FINANCIAL AID (Fall 2009, est.) 665 applied for aid; of those 46% were deemed to have need. 90% of freshmen with need received aid; of those 12% had need fully met. *Average percent of need met:* 54% (excluding resources awarded to replace EFC). *Average financial aid package:* $8380 (excluding resources awarded to replace EFC). 12% of all full-time freshmen had no need and received non-need-based gift aid.
UNDERGRADUATE FINANCIAL AID (Fall 2009, est.) 2,080 applied for aid; of those 56% were deemed to have need. 93% of undergraduates with need received aid; of those 15% had need fully met. *Average percent of need met:* 53% (excluding resources awarded to replace EFC). *Average financial aid package:* $7960 (excluding resources awarded to replace EFC). 9% of all full-time undergraduates had no need and received non-need-based gift aid.
GIFT AID (NEED-BASED) *Total amount:* $3,973,800 (55% federal, 36% state, 9% institutional). *Receiving aid:* Freshmen: 18% (164); all full-time undergraduates: 15% (570). *Average award:* Freshmen: $7150; Undergraduates: $6440. *Scholarships, grants, and awards:* Federal Pell, FSEOG, state, private, college/university gift aid from institutional funds.
GIFT AID (NON-NEED-BASED) *Total amount:* $2,578,500 (7% federal, 60% institutional, 33% external sources). *Receiving aid:* Freshmen: 17% (159). Undergraduates: 9% (327). *Average award:* Freshmen: $2130. Undergraduates: $2540. *Scholarships, grants, and awards by category:* Academic interests/achievement: 750 awards ($1,250,000 total): biological sciences, business, computer science, education, English, foreign languages, general academic interests/achievements, humanities, international studies, mathematics, physical sciences, religion/biblical studies, social sciences. *Creative arts/performance:*

65 awards ($120,000 total): art/fine arts, dance, journalism/publications, music, theater/drama. *Special achievements/activities:* 3 awards ($18,200 total): leadership. *Special characteristics:* 12 awards ($36,000 total): adult students, children and siblings of alumni, children of faculty/staff, local/state students. *Tuition waivers:* Full or partial for senior citizens.
LOANS *Student loans:* $13,495,100 (37% need-based, 63% non-need-based). 57% of past graduating class borrowed through all loan programs. *Average indebtedness per student:* $16,000. *Average need-based loan:* Freshmen: $3500. Undergraduates: $4220. *Parent loans:* $3,510,000 (100% non-need-based). *Programs:* Federal Direct (Subsidized and Unsubsidized Stafford, PLUS), Perkins.
WORK-STUDY *Federal work-study:* Total amount: $55,600; 45 jobs averaging $1250. *State or other work-study/employment:* Total amount: $1,416,000 (100% non-need-based). 762 part-time jobs averaging $1850.
APPLYING FOR FINANCIAL AID *Required financial aid forms:* FAFSA, UMW Scholarship Information Form. *Financial aid deadline:* 5/15 (priority: 3/1). *Notification date:* 4/15. Students must reply by 5/1 or within 2 weeks of notification.
CONTACT Ms. Debra J. Harber, Director of Financial Aid, University of Mary Washington, 1301 College Avenue, Fredericksburg, VA 22401-5358, 540-654-2468 or toll-free 800-468-5614. *Fax:* 540-654-1858. *E-mail:* dharber@umw.edu.

UNIVERSITY OF MASSACHUSETTS AMHERST
Amherst, MA

Tuition & fees (MA res): $11,917   Average undergraduate aid package: $13,314

ABOUT THE INSTITUTION State-supported, coed. 84 undergraduate majors. Federal methodology is used as a basis for awarding need-based institutional aid.
UNDERGRADUATE EXPENSES for 2009–10 *One-time required fee:* $185. *Tuition, state resident:* full-time $1714; part-time $71.50 per credit. *Tuition, nonresident:* full-time $9937; part-time $414 per credit. *Required fees:* full-time $10,203. Full-time tuition and fees vary according to class time, course load, degree level, location, program, reciprocity agreements, and student level. Part-time tuition and fees vary according to class time, course load, degree level, location, program, reciprocity agreements, and student level. *College room and board:* $8276; *Room only:* $4612. Room and board charges vary according to board plan and housing facility. *Payment plan:* Installment.
FRESHMAN FINANCIAL AID (Fall 2008) 3,646 applied for aid; of those 60% were deemed to have need. 97% of freshmen with need received aid; of those 21% had need fully met. *Average percent of need met:* 84% (excluding resources awarded to replace EFC). *Average financial aid package:* $12,256 (excluding resources awarded to replace EFC). 6% of all full-time freshmen had no need and received non-need-based gift aid.
UNDERGRADUATE FINANCIAL AID (Fall 2008) 14,408 applied for aid; of those 69% were deemed to have need. 98% of undergraduates with need received aid; of those 25% had need fully met. *Average percent of need met:* 88% (excluding resources awarded to replace EFC). *Average financial aid package:* $13,314 (excluding resources awarded to replace EFC). 6% of all full-time undergraduates had no need and received non-need-based gift aid.
GIFT AID (NEED-BASED) *Total amount:* $59,663,436 (30% federal, 12% state, 51% institutional, 7% external sources). *Receiving aid:* Freshmen: 43% (1,796); all full-time undergraduates: 41% (7,744). *Average award:* Freshmen: $7952; Undergraduates: $8530. *Scholarships, grants, and awards:* Federal Pell, FSEOG, state, private, college/university gift aid from institutional funds.
GIFT AID (NON-NEED-BASED) *Total amount:* $8,227,214 (1% federal, 5% state, 51% institutional, 43% external sources). *Receiving aid:* Freshmen: 3% (135). Undergraduates: 3% (504). *Average award:* Freshmen: $3689. Undergraduates: $3134. *Scholarships, grants, and awards by category:* Academic interests/achievement: agriculture, architecture, biological sciences, business, communication, computer science, education, engineering/technologies, English, health fields, humanities, mathematics, military science, physical sciences, premedicine, social sciences. *Creative arts/performance:* art/fine arts, dance, journalism/publications, music, theater/drama. *Special achievements/activities:* cheerleading/drum major, general special achievements/activities, leadership. *Special characteristics:* children and siblings of alumni, children of faculty/staff, handicapped students, veterans. *Tuition waivers:* Full or partial for employees or children of employees, senior citizens.

LOANS *Student loans:* $99,414,517 (54% need-based, 46% non-need-based). 67% of past graduating class borrowed through all loan programs. *Average indebtedness per student:* $23,614. *Average need-based loan:* Freshmen: $3463. Undergraduates: $4374. *Parent loans:* $21,999,598 (20% need-based, 80% non-need-based). *Programs:* Federal Direct (Subsidized and Unsubsidized Stafford, PLUS), Perkins, state.

WORK-STUDY *Federal work-study:* Total amount: $8,339,790; 4,984 jobs averaging $1701.

ATHLETIC AWARDS Total amount: $5,658,585 (33% need-based, 67% non-need-based).

APPLYING FOR FINANCIAL AID *Required financial aid form:* FAFSA. *Financial aid deadline (priority):* 2/14. *Notification date:* Continuous beginning 3/1.

CONTACT Office of Financial Aid Services, University of Massachusetts Amherst, 255 Whitmore Administration Building, Amherst, MA 01003, 413-545-0801. *Fax:* 413-545-1700.

UNIVERSITY OF MASSACHUSETTS BOSTON
Boston, MA

Tuition & fees (MA res): $10,611   **Average undergraduate aid package:** $12,368

ABOUT THE INSTITUTION State-supported, coed. 39 undergraduate majors. Federal methodology is used as a basis for awarding need-based institutional aid.

UNDERGRADUATE EXPENSES for 2009–10 *Tuition, state resident:* full-time $1714; part-time $71.50 per credit hour. *Tuition, nonresident:* full-time $9758; part-time $406.50 per credit hour. *Required fees:* full-time $8897; $370 per credit hour. Full-time tuition and fees vary according to class time, course load, program, reciprocity agreements, and student level. Part-time tuition and fees vary according to class time, course load, program, reciprocity agreements, and student level. *Payment plan:* Installment.

FRESHMAN FINANCIAL AID (Fall 2008) 766 applied for aid; of those 78% were deemed to have need. 100% of freshmen with need received aid; of those 63% had need fully met. *Average percent of need met:* 93% (excluding resources awarded to replace EFC). *Average financial aid package:* $11,660 (excluding resources awarded to replace EFC). 10% of all full-time freshmen had no need and received non-need-based gift aid.

UNDERGRADUATE FINANCIAL AID (Fall 2008) 5,073 applied for aid; of those 85% were deemed to have need. 100% of undergraduates with need received aid; of those 73% had need fully met. *Average percent of need met:* 95% (excluding resources awarded to replace EFC). *Average financial aid package:* $12,368 (excluding resources awarded to replace EFC). 4% of all full-time undergraduates had no need and received non-need-based gift aid.

GIFT AID (NEED-BASED) *Total amount:* $24,481,615 (48% federal, 17% state, 32% institutional, 3% external sources). *Receiving aid:* Freshmen: 58% (558); all full-time undergraduates: 52% (3,695). *Average award:* Freshmen: $6945; Undergraduates: $6535. *Scholarships, grants, and awards:* Federal Pell, FSEOG, state, private, college/university gift aid from institutional funds, Academic Competitiveness Grants, National SMART Grants, TEACH Grants.

GIFT AID (NON-NEED-BASED) *Total amount:* $3,745,304 (4% federal, 2% state, 84% institutional, 10% external sources). *Receiving aid:* Freshmen: 3% (26). Undergraduates: 2% (108). *Average award:* Freshmen: $3856. Undergraduates: $3539. *Scholarships, grants, and awards by category:* Academic interests/achievement: general academic interests/achievements, health fields. *Special achievements/activities:* 1,247 awards ($1,944,883 total): general special achievements/activities, leadership. *Special characteristics:* 463 awards ($996,064 total): adult students, children of faculty/staff, children of union members/company employees, first-generation college students, veterans. *Tuition waivers:* Full or partial for employees or children of employees, senior citizens.

LOANS *Student loans:* $44,409,887 (60% need-based, 40% non-need-based). 67% of past graduating class borrowed through all loan programs. *Average indebtedness per student:* $19,327. *Average need-based loan:* Freshmen: $4329. Undergraduates: $5966. *Parent loans:* $1,874,141 (17% need-based, 83% non-need-based). *Programs:* Federal Direct (Subsidized and Unsubsidized Stafford, PLUS), Perkins.

WORK-STUDY *Federal work-study:* Total amount: $1,936,166; 523 jobs averaging $3061. *State or other work-study/employment:* Part-time jobs available.

APPLYING FOR FINANCIAL AID *Required financial aid form:* FAFSA. *Financial aid deadline (priority):* 3/1. *Notification date:* Continuous beginning 3/26.

CONTACT Judy L. Keyes, Director of Financial Aid Services, University of Massachusetts Boston, 100 Morrissey Boulevard, Boston, MA 02125-3393, 617-287-6300. *Fax:* 617-287-6323. *E-mail:* judy.keyes@umb.edu.

UNIVERSITY OF MASSACHUSETTS DARTMOUTH
North Dartmouth, MA

Tuition & fees (MA res): $10,358   **Average undergraduate aid package:** $13,949

ABOUT THE INSTITUTION State-supported, coed. 49 undergraduate majors. Federal methodology is used as a basis for awarding need-based institutional aid.

UNDERGRADUATE EXPENSES for 2009–10 *Tuition, state resident:* full-time $1417; part-time $59.04 per credit. *Tuition, nonresident:* full-time $8099; part-time $337.46 per credit. *Required fees:* full-time $8941; $372.54 per credit. Full-time tuition and fees vary according to program and reciprocity agreements. Part-time tuition and fees vary according to course load, program, and reciprocity agreements. *College room and board:* $8950; *Room only:* $6133. Room and board charges vary according to board plan and housing facility. *Payment plan:* Installment.

FRESHMAN FINANCIAL AID (Fall 2009, est.) 1,649 applied for aid; of those 76% were deemed to have need. 100% of freshmen with need received aid; of those 45% had need fully met. *Average percent of need met:* 90% (excluding resources awarded to replace EFC). *Average financial aid package:* $13,643 (excluding resources awarded to replace EFC). 21% of all full-time freshmen had no need and received non-need-based gift aid.

UNDERGRADUATE FINANCIAL AID (Fall 2009, est.) 5,788 applied for aid; of those 79% were deemed to have need. 100% of undergraduates with need received aid; of those 51% had need fully met. *Average percent of need met:* 90% (excluding resources awarded to replace EFC). *Average financial aid package:* $13,949 (excluding resources awarded to replace EFC). 17% of all full-time undergraduates had no need and received non-need-based gift aid.

GIFT AID (NEED-BASED) *Total amount:* $23,900,000 (44% federal, 13% state, 40% institutional, 3% external sources). *Receiving aid:* Freshmen: 69% (1,246); all full-time undergraduates: 64% (4,498). *Average award:* Freshmen: $6914; Undergraduates: $6461. *Scholarships, grants, and awards:* Federal Pell, FSEOG, state, private, college/university gift aid from institutional funds.

GIFT AID (NON-NEED-BASED) *Total amount:* $2,804,000 (1% federal, 1% state, 89% institutional, 9% external sources). *Receiving aid:* Freshmen: 3% (59). Undergraduates: 3% (192). *Average award:* Freshmen: $2440. Undergraduates: $2251. *Scholarships, grants, and awards by category:* Academic interests/achievement: general academic interests/achievements. *Special achievements/activities:* community service. *Special characteristics:* adult students, children of faculty/staff, children with a deceased or disabled parent, first-generation college students, members of minority groups, veterans. *Tuition waivers:* Full or partial for employees or children of employees, senior citizens.

LOANS *Student loans:* $49,000,000 (61% need-based, 39% non-need-based). 78% of past graduating class borrowed through all loan programs. *Average indebtedness per student:* $21,905. *Average need-based loan:* Freshmen: $6509. Undergraduates: $7223. *Parent loans:* $7,100,000 (31% need-based, 69% non-need-based). *Programs:* Federal Direct (Subsidized and Unsubsidized Stafford, PLUS), Perkins, Federal Nursing, state.

WORK-STUDY *Federal work-study:* Total amount: $2,211,995; jobs available. *State or other work-study/employment:* Total amount: $4,600,000 (75% need-based, 25% non-need-based). Part-time jobs available.

APPLYING FOR FINANCIAL AID *Required financial aid form:* FAFSA. *Financial aid deadline (priority):* 3/1. *Notification date:* Continuous beginning 3/25.

CONTACT Bruce Palmer, Director of Financial Aid, University of Massachusetts Dartmouth, 285 Old Westport Road, North Dartmouth, MA 02747-2300, 508-999-8643. *Fax:* 508-999-8935. *E-mail:* financialaid@umassd.edu.

UNIVERSITY OF MASSACHUSETTS LOWELL
Lowell, MA

Tuition & fees (MA res): $10,681   **Average undergraduate aid package:** $10,416

University of Massachusetts Lowell

ABOUT THE INSTITUTION State-supported, coed. 39 undergraduate majors. Federal methodology is used as a basis for awarding need-based institutional aid.

UNDERGRADUATE EXPENSES for 2010–11 *Tuition, state resident:* full-time $1454; part-time $60.58 per credit. *Tuition, nonresident:* full-time $13,474; part-time $357 per credit. *Required fees:* full-time $9227; $390.67 per credit. Part-time tuition and fees vary according to course load. *College room and board:* $8635; *Room only:* $5596. Room and board charges vary according to board plan and housing facility. *Payment plan:* Installment.

FRESHMAN FINANCIAL AID (Fall 2008) 1,274 applied for aid; of those 67% were deemed to have need. 100% of freshmen with need received aid; of those 71% had need fully met. *Average percent of need met:* 95% (excluding resources awarded to replace EFC). *Average financial aid package:* $10,614 (excluding resources awarded to replace EFC). 16% of all full-time freshmen had no need and received non-need-based gift aid.

UNDERGRADUATE FINANCIAL AID (Fall 2008) 5,015 applied for aid; of those 70% were deemed to have need. 100% of undergraduates with need received aid; of those 74% had need fully met. *Average percent of need met:* 96% (excluding resources awarded to replace EFC). *Average financial aid package:* $10,416 (excluding resources awarded to replace EFC). 9% of all full-time undergraduates had no need and received non-need-based gift aid.

GIFT AID (NEED-BASED) *Total amount:* $14,076,807 (49% federal, 19% state, 28% institutional, 4% external sources). *Receiving aid:* Freshmen: 51% (780); all full-time undergraduates: 44% (2,966). *Average award:* Freshmen: $6204; Undergraduates: $5385. *Scholarships, grants, and awards:* Federal Pell, FSEOG, state, private, college/university gift aid from institutional funds.

GIFT AID (NON-NEED-BASED) *Total amount:* $3,483,086 (1% federal, 1% state, 88% institutional, 10% external sources). *Receiving aid:* Freshmen: 3% (53). Undergraduates: 2% (155). *Average award:* Freshmen: $2874. Undergraduates: $2940. *Scholarships, grants, and awards by category: Academic interests/ achievement:* computer science, engineering/technologies, general academic interests/achievements, health fields, humanities. *Creative arts/performance:* music. *Special achievements/activities:* community service, general special achievements/activities. *Special characteristics:* general special characteristics. *Tuition waivers:* Full or partial for employees or children of employees, senior citizens.

LOANS *Student loans:* $37,784,767 (48% need-based, 52% non-need-based). 73% of past graduating class borrowed through all loan programs. *Average indebtedness per student:* $21,542. *Average need-based loan:* Freshmen: $4428. Undergraduates: $5608. *Parent loans:* $4,325,965 (11% need-based, 89% non-need-based). *Programs:* Federal Direct (Subsidized and Unsubsidized Stafford, PLUS), Perkins.

WORK-STUDY *Federal work-study:* Total amount: $265,356; 135 jobs averaging $2539. *State or other work-study/employment:* Total amount: $2,499,304 (100% need-based). 721 part-time jobs averaging $2718.

ATHLETIC AWARDS Total amount: $1,207,764 (29% need-based, 71% non-need-based).

APPLYING FOR FINANCIAL AID *Required financial aid form:* FAFSA. *Financial aid deadline (priority):* 3/1. *Notification date:* Continuous beginning 3/25.

CONTACT Joyce McLaughlin, Director of Financial Aid, University of Massachusetts Lowell, 883 Broadway Street, Room 102, Lowell, MA 01854, 978-934-4237 or toll-free 800-410-4607. *Fax:* 978-934-3009. *E-mail:* joyce_mclaughlin@uml.edu.

UNIVERSITY OF MEMPHIS
Memphis, TN

Tuition & fees (TN res): $7058	Average undergraduate aid package: $9005

ABOUT THE INSTITUTION State-supported, coed. 67 undergraduate majors. Federal methodology is used as a basis for awarding need-based institutional aid.

UNDERGRADUATE EXPENSES for 2009–10 *Tuition, state resident:* full-time $5304; part-time $221 per credit. *Tuition, nonresident:* full-time $18,024; part-time $751 per credit. *Required fees:* full-time $1754; $78 per credit. Full-time tuition and fees vary according to course load, degree level, program, and reciprocity agreements. Part-time tuition and fees vary according to course load, degree level, and program. *College room and board:* $5950; *Room only:* $3690. Room and board charges vary according to board plan and housing facility. *Payment plan:* Installment.

FRESHMAN FINANCIAL AID (Fall 2009, est.) 2,076 applied for aid; of those 76% were deemed to have need. 85% of freshmen with need received aid; of those 17% had need fully met. *Average percent of need met:* 82% (excluding resources awarded to replace EFC). *Average financial aid package:* $9539 (excluding resources awarded to replace EFC). 22% of all full-time freshmen had no need and received non-need-based gift aid.

UNDERGRADUATE FINANCIAL AID (Fall 2009, est.) 11,081 applied for aid; of those 80% were deemed to have need. 88% of undergraduates with need received aid; of those 9% had need fully met. *Average percent of need met:* 70% (excluding resources awarded to replace EFC). *Average financial aid package:* $9005 (excluding resources awarded to replace EFC). 16% of all full-time undergraduates had no need and received non-need-based gift aid.

GIFT AID (NEED-BASED) *Total amount:* $43,328,484 (83% federal, 15% state, 2% institutional). *Receiving aid:* Freshmen: 58% (1,291); all full-time undergraduates: 50% (6,210). *Average award:* Freshmen: $6987; Undergraduates: $5942. *Scholarships, grants, and awards:* Federal Pell, FSEOG, state, private, college/university gift aid from institutional funds.

GIFT AID (NON-NEED-BASED) *Total amount:* $26,820,207 (62% state, 35% institutional, 3% external sources). *Receiving aid:* Freshmen: 30% (668). Undergraduates: 38% (4,717). *Average award:* Freshmen: $7937. Undergraduates: $7945. *Scholarships, grants, and awards by category: Academic interests/ achievement:* biological sciences, business, communication, education, engineering/technologies, English, general academic interests/achievements, health fields, humanities, international studies, mathematics, military science, physical sciences, premedicine, social sciences. *Creative arts/performance:* art/fine arts, cinema/film/broadcasting, dance, journalism/publications, music. *Special achievements/activities:* cheerleading/drum major, general special achievements/ activities, leadership. *Special characteristics:* adult students, children of educators, children of faculty/staff, children of public servants, handicapped students, members of minority groups, public servants. *Tuition waivers:* Full or partial for employees or children of employees, senior citizens.

LOANS *Student loans:* $75,930,682 (42% need-based, 58% non-need-based). 29% of past graduating class borrowed through all loan programs. *Average indebtedness per student:* $23,342. *Average need-based loan:* Freshmen: $3382. Undergraduates: $4360. *Parent loans:* $2,562,095 (100% non-need-based). *Programs:* Federal Direct (Subsidized and Unsubsidized Stafford, PLUS), Perkins, college/university.

WORK-STUDY *Federal work-study:* Total amount: $543,891; 189 jobs averaging $2016. *State or other work-study/employment:* Total amount: $2,918,279 (100% non-need-based). Part-time jobs available.

ATHLETIC AWARDS Total amount: $3,753,887 (100% non-need-based).

APPLYING FOR FINANCIAL AID *Required financial aid form:* FAFSA. *Financial aid deadline (priority):* 3/1. *Notification date:* Continuous beginning 4/1. Students must reply by 8/1.

CONTACT Richard Ritzman, Director of Student Financial Aid, University of Memphis, Wilder Tower 103, Memphis, TN 38152, 901-678-2832 or toll-free 800-669-2678 (out-of-state). *Fax:* 901-678-3590. *E-mail:* rritzman@memphis.edu.

UNIVERSITY OF MIAMI
Coral Gables, FL

Tuition & fees: $37,836	Average undergraduate aid package: $30,640

ABOUT THE INSTITUTION Independent, coed. 112 undergraduate majors. Both federal and institutional methodology are used as a basis for awarding need-based institutional aid.

UNDERGRADUATE EXPENSES for 2010–11 *Comprehensive fee:* $48,898 includes full-time tuition ($36,962), mandatory fees ($874), and room and board ($11,062). *College room only:* $6448. Full-time tuition and fees vary according to course load, degree level, and program. Room and board charges vary according to board plan and housing facility. *Part-time tuition:* $1538 per credit hour. Part-time tuition and fees vary according to course load, degree level, and program. *Payment plans:* Tuition prepayment, installment, deferred payment.

FRESHMAN FINANCIAL AID (Fall 2009, est.) 1,223 applied for aid; of those 76% were deemed to have need. 100% of freshmen with need received aid; of those 35% had need fully met. *Average percent of need met:* 83% (excluding resources awarded to replace EFC). *Average financial aid package:* $31,230 (excluding resources awarded to replace EFC). 17% of all full-time freshmen had no need and received non-need-based gift aid.

UNDERGRADUATE FINANCIAL AID (Fall 2009, est.) 5,324 applied for aid; of those 84% were deemed to have need. 100% of undergraduates with need received aid; of those 35% had need fully met. *Average percent of need met:* 82% (excluding resources awarded to replace EFC). *Average financial aid package:* $30,640 (excluding resources awarded to replace EFC). 20% of all full-time undergraduates had no need and received non-need-based gift aid.

GIFT AID (NEED-BASED) *Total amount:* $91,277,819 (13% federal, 11% state, 74% institutional, 2% external sources). *Receiving aid:* Freshmen: 47% (895); all full-time undergraduates: 47% (4,323). *Average award:* Freshmen: $23,904; Undergraduates: $22,869. *Scholarships, grants, and awards:* Federal Pell, FSEOG, state, private, college/university gift aid from institutional funds, Federal Nursing, Academic Competitiveness Grants, National SMART Grants.

GIFT AID (NON-NEED-BASED) *Total amount:* $54,622,216 (21% state, 74% institutional, 5% external sources). *Receiving aid:* Freshmen: 16% (307). Undergraduates: 15% (1,379). *Average award:* Freshmen: $20,279. Undergraduates: $18,529. *Scholarships, grants, and awards by category: Academic interests/achievement:* 3,686 awards ($67,602,921 total): architecture, area/ethnic studies, biological sciences, business, communication, computer science, education, engineering/technologies, English, foreign languages, general academic interests/achievements, health fields, humanities, international studies, mathematics, physical sciences, premedicine, religion/biblical studies, social sciences. *Creative arts/performance:* 291 awards ($3,819,885 total): art/fine arts, cinema/film/broadcasting, debating, journalism/publications, music, performing arts, theater/drama. *Special characteristics:* 850 awards ($21,805,727 total): children of faculty/staff, international students. *Tuition waivers:* Full or partial for employees or children of employees.

LOANS *Student loans:* $51,642,833 (64% need-based, 36% non-need-based). 55% of past graduating class borrowed through all loan programs. *Average indebtedness per student:* $24,396. *Average need-based loan:* Freshmen: $3934. Undergraduates: $5078. *Parent loans:* $13,977,472 (26% need-based, 74% non-need-based). *Programs:* FFEL (Subsidized and Unsubsidized Stafford, PLUS), Perkins, Federal Nursing, college/university, private alternative loans.

WORK-STUDY *Federal work-study:* Total amount: $6,074,255; 2,102 jobs averaging $2892. *State or other work-study/employment:* Total amount: $1,489,374 (17% need-based, 83% non-need-based). 121 part-time jobs averaging $9675.

ATHLETIC AWARDS Total amount: $9,725,840 (41% need-based, 59% non-need-based).

APPLYING FOR FINANCIAL AID *Required financial aid form:* FAFSA. *Financial aid deadline (priority):* 2/1. *Notification date:* Continuous beginning 3/1.

CONTACT Mr. James M. Bauer, Assistant Vice President of Enrollment Management and Executive Director of Financial Assistance Services, University of Miami, Rhodes House, Building 37R, Coral Gables, FL 33124-5240, 305-284-2270. *Fax:* 305-284-8641. *E-mail:* jbauer@miami.edu.

UNIVERSITY OF MICHIGAN
Ann Arbor, MI

Tuition & fees (MI res): $12,589   Average undergraduate aid package: $11,511

ABOUT THE INSTITUTION State-supported, coed. 120 undergraduate majors. Federal methodology is used as a basis for awarding need-based institutional aid.

UNDERGRADUATE EXPENSES for 2009–10 *Tuition, state resident:* full-time $12,400; part-time $449 per credit hour. *Tuition, nonresident:* full-time $36,163; part-time $1419 per credit hour. *Required fees:* full-time $189; $95 per term. Full-time tuition and fees vary according to course load, program, and student level. Part-time tuition and fees vary according to course load, program, and student level. *College room and board:* $8924. Room and board charges vary according to board plan and housing facility. *Payment plan:* Installment.

FRESHMAN FINANCIAL AID (Fall 2009, est.) 3,788 applied for aid; of those 69% were deemed to have need. 100% of freshmen with need received aid; of those 90% had need fully met. *Average percent of need met:* 90% (excluding resources awarded to replace EFC). *Average financial aid package:* $8615 (excluding resources awarded to replace EFC). 45% of all full-time freshmen had no need and received non-need-based gift aid.

UNDERGRADUATE FINANCIAL AID (Fall 2009, est.) 15,151 applied for aid; of those 77% were deemed to have need. 100% of undergraduates with need received aid; of those 90% had need fully met. *Average percent of need met:* 90% (excluding resources awarded to replace EFC). *Average financial aid package:* $11,511 (excluding resources awarded to replace EFC). 34% of all full-time undergraduates had no need and received non-need-based gift aid.

GIFT AID (NEED-BASED) *Total amount:* $59,899,875 (25% federal, 75% institutional). *Receiving aid:* Freshmen: 24% (1,360); all full-time undergraduates: 25% (6,286). *Average award:* Freshmen: $8375; Undergraduates: $9529. *Scholarships, grants, and awards:* Federal Pell, FSEOG, state, private, college/university gift aid from institutional funds, Academic Competitiveness Grants, National SMART Grants.

GIFT AID (NON-NEED-BASED) *Total amount:* $87,849,335 (6% federal, 13% state, 64% institutional, 17% external sources). *Receiving aid:* Freshmen: 40% (2,282). Undergraduates: 30% (7,546). *Average award:* Freshmen: $5808. Undergraduates: $6479. *Scholarships, grants, and awards by category: Academic interests/achievement:* architecture, area/ethnic studies, biological sciences, business, communication, computer science, education, engineering/technologies, English, foreign languages, general academic interests/achievements, health fields, humanities, international studies, library science, mathematics, military science, physical sciences, premedicine, social sciences. *Creative arts/performance:* art/fine arts, cinema/film/broadcasting, creative writing, dance, journalism/publications, music, performing arts, theater/drama. *Special achievements/activities:* community service, general special achievements/activities, leadership. *Special characteristics:* children of faculty/staff, children of workers in trades, handicapped students, international students, local/state students, members of minority groups, out-of-state students.

LOANS *Student loans:* $106,196,467 (47% need-based, 53% non-need-based). 46% of past graduating class borrowed through all loan programs. *Average indebtedness per student:* $26,819. *Average need-based loan:* Freshmen: $4340. Undergraduates: $4305. *Parent loans:* $22,263,261 (100% non-need-based). *Programs:* Federal Direct (Subsidized and Unsubsidized Stafford, PLUS), Perkins, Federal Nursing, college/university, Health Professions Student Loans (HPSL).

WORK-STUDY *Federal work-study:* Total amount: $12,200,247; 2,296 jobs averaging $2506. *State or other work-study/employment:* Total amount: $461,664 (100% need-based). 148 part-time jobs averaging $1830.

ATHLETIC AWARDS Total amount: $14,667,331 (100% non-need-based).

APPLYING FOR FINANCIAL AID *Required financial aid forms:* FAFSA, CSS Financial Aid PROFILE, federal income tax form(s). *Financial aid deadline:* 5/31 (priority: 4/30). *Notification date:* Continuous beginning 3/15.

CONTACT Financial Aid Counseling and Advising Services, University of Michigan, 2500 Student Activities Building, 515 East Jefferson Street, Ann Arbor, MI 48109-1316, 734-763-6600. *Fax:* 734-647-3081. *E-mail:* financial.aid@umich.edu.

UNIVERSITY OF MICHIGAN–DEARBORN
Dearborn, MI

Tuition & fees (MI res): $9100   Average undergraduate aid package: $8515

ABOUT THE INSTITUTION State-supported, coed. 53 undergraduate majors. Federal methodology is used as a basis for awarding need-based institutional aid.

UNDERGRADUATE EXPENSES for 2009–10 *Tuition, state resident:* full-time $8573; part-time $339.25 per credit hour. *Tuition, nonresident:* full-time $19,356; part-time $770.35 per credit hour. *Required fees:* full-time $527; $163.25 per term. Full-time tuition and fees vary according to course level, course load, program, and student level. Part-time tuition and fees vary according to course level, course load, program, and student level. *Payment plan:* Installment.

FRESHMAN FINANCIAL AID (Fall 2009, est.) 801 applied for aid; of those 58% were deemed to have need. 98% of freshmen with need received aid; of those 10% had need fully met. *Average percent of need met:* 59% (excluding resources awarded to replace EFC). *Average financial aid package:* $5196 (excluding resources awarded to replace EFC). 60% of all full-time freshmen had no need and received non-need-based gift aid.

UNDERGRADUATE FINANCIAL AID (Fall 2009, est.) 4,092 applied for aid; of those 72% were deemed to have need. 93% of undergraduates with need received aid; of those 19% had need fully met. *Average percent of need met:* 33% (excluding resources awarded to replace EFC). *Average financial aid package:* $8515 (excluding resources awarded to replace EFC). 44% of all full-time undergraduates had no need and received non-need-based gift aid.

GIFT AID (NEED-BASED) *Total amount:* $14,834,083 (81% federal, 1% state, 18% institutional). *Receiving aid:* Freshmen: 30% (267); all full-time undergraduates: 41% (1,993). *Average award:* Freshmen: $4015; Undergraduates: $4035. *Scholarships, grants, and awards:* Federal Pell, FSEOG, state, private, college/university gift aid from institutional funds, United Negro College Fund.

GIFT AID (NON-NEED-BASED) *Total amount:* $5,656,413 (1% state, 91% institutional, 8% external sources). *Receiving aid:* Freshmen: 16% (139). Undergraduates: 7% (361). *Average award:* Freshmen: $3146. Undergraduates: $3256. *Scholarships, grants, and awards by category: Academic interests/achievement:* 815 awards ($2,934,708 total): biological sciences, business, communication, computer science, education, engineering/technologies, foreign languages, general academic interests/achievements, international studies, mathematics, physical sciences, social sciences. *Creative arts/performance:* 40 awards ($30,158 total): art/fine arts, cinema/film/broadcasting, creative writing, debating, general creative arts/performance, journalism/publications. *Special achievements/activities:* 153 awards ($719,449 total): community service, general special achievements/activities, leadership, memberships. *Special characteristics:* 361 awards ($3,831,592 total): adult students, children and siblings of alumni, children of current students, children of faculty/staff, children of workers in trades, ethnic background, general special characteristics, handicapped students, international students, members of minority groups, out-of-state students, previous college experience, public servants, siblings of current students, veterans, veterans' children. *Tuition waivers:* Full or partial for employees or children of employees, senior citizens.

LOANS *Student loans:* $26,834,021 (49% need-based, 51% non-need-based). 22% of past graduating class borrowed through all loan programs. *Average indebtedness per student:* $29,564. *Average need-based loan:* Freshmen: $2675. Undergraduates: $4330. *Parent loans:* $1,686,238 (100% non-need-based). *Programs:* Federal Direct (Subsidized and Unsubsidized Stafford, PLUS), Perkins, college/university, alternative loans.

WORK-STUDY *Federal work-study:* Total amount: $328,200; 189 jobs averaging $2160. *State or other work-study/employment:* Total amount: $17,630 (100% non-need-based). Part-time jobs available.

ATHLETIC AWARDS Total amount: $89,950 (100% non-need-based).

APPLYING FOR FINANCIAL AID *Required financial aid form:* FAFSA. *Financial aid deadline (priority):* 2/14. *Notification date:* Continuous beginning 3/10. Students must reply within 5 weeks of notification.

CONTACT Christopher W. Tremblay, Executive Director of Enrollment Managment, University of Michigan–Dearborn, 4901 Evergreen Road, 1183 UC, Dearborn, MI 48128-1491, 313-593-5300. *Fax:* 313-593-5313. *E-mail:* ask-ofa@umd.umich.edu.

UNIVERSITY OF MICHIGAN–FLINT
Flint, MI

Tuition & fees (MI res): $8279   **Average undergraduate aid package:** N/A

ABOUT THE INSTITUTION State-supported, coed. 82 undergraduate majors. Federal methodology is used as a basis for awarding need-based institutional aid.

UNDERGRADUATE EXPENSES for 2009–10 *One-time required fee:* $30. *Tuition, state resident:* full-time $7899; part-time $311.40 per credit hour. *Tuition, nonresident:* full-time $15,413; part-time $622.75 per credit hour. *Required fees:* full-time $380; $144.50 per term. Full-time tuition and fees vary according to course level, course load, degree level, program, and student level. Part-time tuition and fees vary according to course level, course load, degree level, program, and student level. *College room and board:* $6874; *Room only:* $4274. Room and board charges vary according to board plan. *Payment plan:* Installment.

GIFT AID (NEED-BASED) *Scholarships, grants, and awards:* Federal Pell, FSEOG, state, private, college/university gift aid from institutional funds, TEACH Grants.

GIFT AID (NON-NEED-BASED) *Scholarships, grants, and awards by category: Academic interests/achievement:* biological sciences, business, communication, computer science, education, engineering/technologies, English, foreign languages, general academic interests/achievements, health fields, humanities, international studies, mathematics, physical sciences, premedicine, social sciences. *Creative arts/performance:* art/fine arts, music, theater/drama. *Special achievements/activities:* community service, general special achievements/activities, hobbies/interests, leadership. *Special characteristics:* adult students, children and siblings of alumni, children of union members/company employees, first-generation college students, general special characteristics, handicapped students, international students, local/state students, members of minority groups. *Tuition waivers:* Full or partial for senior citizens.

LOANS *Programs:* Federal Direct (Subsidized and Unsubsidized Stafford, PLUS), Perkins.

WORK-STUDY Federal work-study jobs available. *State or other work-study/employment:* Part-time jobs available.

APPLYING FOR FINANCIAL AID *Required financial aid form:* FAFSA. *Financial aid deadline (priority):* 3/1. *Notification date:* Continuous beginning 3/15.

CONTACT Lori Vedder, Financial Aid Office, University of Michigan–Flint, Room 277 Pavilion, Flint, MI 48502-1950, 810-762-3444 or toll-free 800-942-5636 (in-state). *Fax:* 810-766-6757. *E-mail:* financial_aid@list.flint.umich.edu.

UNIVERSITY OF MINNESOTA, CROOKSTON
Crookston, MN

Tuition & fees (MN res): $10,647   **Average undergraduate aid package:** $11,016

ABOUT THE INSTITUTION State-supported, coed. 29 undergraduate majors. Federal methodology is used as a basis for awarding need-based institutional aid.

UNDERGRADUATE EXPENSES for 2010–11 *Tuition, state resident:* full-time $7956; part-time $306 per semester hour. *Tuition, nonresident:* full-time $7956; part-time $306 per semester hour. *Required fees:* full-time $2691; $306 per semester hour or $306 per semester hour. Full-time tuition and fees vary according to course load and reciprocity agreements. Part-time tuition and fees vary according to course load and reciprocity agreements. *College room and board:* $6563; *Room only:* $3087. Room and board charges vary according to board plan and housing facility. *Payment plans:* Guaranteed tuition, installment.

FRESHMAN FINANCIAL AID (Fall 2008) 241 applied for aid; of those 82% were deemed to have need. 99% of freshmen with need received aid; of those 35% had need fully met. *Average percent of need met:* 75% (excluding resources awarded to replace EFC). *Average financial aid package:* $11,188 (excluding resources awarded to replace EFC). 10% of all full-time freshmen had no need and received non-need-based gift aid.

UNDERGRADUATE FINANCIAL AID (Fall 2008) 878 applied for aid; of those 83% were deemed to have need. 100% of undergraduates with need received aid; of those 28% had need fully met. *Average percent of need met:* 74% (excluding resources awarded to replace EFC). *Average financial aid package:* $11,016 (excluding resources awarded to replace EFC). 8% of all full-time undergraduates had no need and received non-need-based gift aid.

GIFT AID (NEED-BASED) *Total amount:* $5,209,236 (34% federal, 37% state, 24% institutional, 5% external sources). *Receiving aid:* Freshmen: 69% (190); all full-time undergraduates: 65% (697). *Average award:* Freshmen: $8172; Undergraduates: $7088. *Scholarships, grants, and awards:* Federal Pell, FSEOG, state, private, college/university gift aid from institutional funds, Academic Competitiveness Grants, National SMART Grants.

GIFT AID (NON-NEED-BASED) *Total amount:* $304,215 (70% institutional, 30% external sources). *Receiving aid:* Freshmen: 15% (40). Undergraduates: 11% (113). *Average award:* Freshmen: $3329. Undergraduates: $2254. *Scholarships, grants, and awards by category: Academic interests/achievement:* agriculture, biological sciences, general academic interests/achievements. *Special characteristics:* children and siblings of alumni, children of faculty/staff, ethnic background, first-generation college students, general special characteristics, local/state students. *Tuition waivers:* Full or partial for senior citizens.

LOANS *Student loans:* $4,969,446 (98% need-based, 2% non-need-based). 86% of past graduating class borrowed through all loan programs. *Average indebtedness per student:* $26,199. *Average need-based loan:* Freshmen: $4056. Undergraduates: $4764. *Parent loans:* $712,557 (100% non-need-based). *Programs:* Federal Direct (Subsidized and Unsubsidized Stafford, PLUS), Perkins, state, private loans.

WORK-STUDY *Federal work-study:* Total amount: $185,721; 141 jobs averaging $1000. *State or other work-study/employment:* Total amount: $252,262 (100% need-based). 65 part-time jobs averaging $1000.

ATHLETIC AWARDS Total amount: $656,143 (100% non-need-based).

APPLYING FOR FINANCIAL AID *Required financial aid form:* FAFSA. *Financial aid deadline (priority):* 3/1. *Notification date:* 3/1. Students must reply within 8 weeks of notification.

CONTACT Melissa Dingmann, Director of Financial Aid, University of Minnesota, Crookston, 170 Owen Hall, Crookston, MN 56716-5001, 218-281-8576 or toll-free 800-862-6466. *Fax:* 218-281-8575. *E-mail:* dingmann@umn.edu.

UNIVERSITY OF MINNESOTA, DULUTH
Duluth, MN

Tuition & fees (MN res): $11,004   Average undergraduate aid package: $11,087

ABOUT THE INSTITUTION State-supported, coed. 71 undergraduate majors. Federal methodology is used as a basis for awarding need-based institutional aid.

UNDERGRADUATE EXPENSES for 2009–10 *Tuition, state resident:* full-time $8830; part-time $339.61 per credit. *Tuition, nonresident:* full-time $10,830; part-time $416.53 per credit. *Required fees:* full-time $2174; $60 per credit. Full-time tuition and fees vary according to class time, course load, degree level, program, and reciprocity agreements. Part-time tuition and fees vary according to class time, course load, degree level, program, and reciprocity agreements. *College room and board:* $6176. Room and board charges vary according to board plan and housing facility. *Payment plan:* Installment.

FRESHMAN FINANCIAL AID (Fall 2008) 1,797 applied for aid; of those 69% were deemed to have need. 100% of freshmen with need received aid; of those 33% had need fully met. *Average percent of need met:* 78% (excluding resources awarded to replace EFC). *Average financial aid package:* $10,805 (excluding resources awarded to replace EFC). 18% of all full-time freshmen had no need and received non-need-based gift aid.

UNDERGRADUATE FINANCIAL AID (Fall 2008) 7,092 applied for aid; of those 74% were deemed to have need. 100% of undergraduates with need received aid; of those 34% had need fully met. *Average percent of need met:* 76% (excluding resources awarded to replace EFC). *Average financial aid package:* $11,087 (excluding resources awarded to replace EFC). 10% of all full-time undergraduates had no need and received non-need-based gift aid.

GIFT AID (NEED-BASED) *Total amount:* $32,907,307 (28% federal, 44% state, 23% institutional, 5% external sources). *Receiving aid:* Freshmen: 58% (1,233); all full-time undergraduates: 57% (5,141). *Average award:* Freshmen: $7651; Undergraduates: $6432. *Scholarships, grants, and awards:* Federal Pell, FSEOG, state, private, college/university gift aid from institutional funds, Founders Opportunity Grants.

GIFT AID (NON-NEED-BASED) *Total amount:* $3,764,896 (38% state, 43% institutional, 19% external sources). *Receiving aid:* Freshmen: 14% (298). Undergraduates: 15% (1,387). *Average award:* Freshmen: $2245. Undergraduates: $2752. *Tuition waivers:* Full or partial for employees or children of employees.

LOANS *Student loans:* $51,664,916 (73% need-based, 27% non-need-based). 72% of past graduating class borrowed through all loan programs. *Average indebtedness per student:* $27,931. *Average need-based loan:* Freshmen: $4066. Undergraduates: $5705. *Parent loans:* $10,684,445 (59% need-based, 41% non-need-based). *Programs:* Federal Direct (Subsidized and Unsubsidized Stafford, PLUS), Perkins, state, college/university, Primary Care Loans.

WORK-STUDY *Federal work-study:* Total amount: $386,110; 235 jobs averaging $2020. *State or other work-study/employment:* Total amount: $638,537 (100% need-based). 295 part-time jobs averaging $2179.

ATHLETIC AWARDS Total amount: $1,169,405 (44% need-based, 56% non-need-based).

APPLYING FOR FINANCIAL AID *Required financial aid form:* FAFSA. *Financial aid deadline (priority):* 3/1. *Notification date:* Continuous beginning 3/1. Students must reply within 2 weeks of notification.

CONTACT Ms. Brenda Herzig, Director of Financial Aid, University of Minnesota, Duluth, 10 University Drive, 184 Darland Administration Building, Duluth, MN 55812-2496, 218-726-8000 or toll-free 800-232-1339. *Fax:* 218-726-8219.

UNIVERSITY OF MINNESOTA, MORRIS
Morris, MN

Tuition & fees (MN res): $10,716   Average undergraduate aid package: $14,261

ABOUT THE INSTITUTION State-supported, coed. *Awards:* bachelor's degrees. 42 undergraduate majors. *Total enrollment:* 1,607. Undergraduates: 1,607. Freshmen: 492. Federal methodology is used as a basis for awarding need-based institutional aid.

UNDERGRADUATE EXPENSES for 2009–10 *Application fee:* $35. *Tuition, state resident:* full-time $8830. *Tuition, nonresident:* full-time $8830. *Required fees:* full-time $1886. Full-time tuition and fees vary according to reciprocity agreements. Part-time tuition and fees vary according to course load and

reciprocity agreements. *College room and board:* $7050; *Room only:* $3290. Room and board charges vary according to board plan and housing facility. *Payment plan:* Installment.

FRESHMAN FINANCIAL AID (Fall 2009, est.) 375 applied for aid; of those 74% were deemed to have need. 100% of freshmen with need received aid; of those 52% had need fully met. *Average percent of need met:* 88% (excluding resources awarded to replace EFC). *Average financial aid package:* $14,707 (excluding resources awarded to replace EFC). 18% of all full-time freshmen had no need and received non-need-based gift aid.

UNDERGRADUATE FINANCIAL AID (Fall 2009, est.) 1,282 applied for aid; of those 80% were deemed to have need. 100% of undergraduates with need received aid; of those 44% had need fully met. *Average percent of need met:* 83% (excluding resources awarded to replace EFC). *Average financial aid package:* $14,261 (excluding resources awarded to replace EFC). 16% of all full-time undergraduates had no need and received non-need-based gift aid.

GIFT AID (NEED-BASED) *Total amount:* $9,712,911 (30% federal, 37% state, 26% institutional, 7% external sources). *Receiving aid:* Freshmen: 69% (278); all full-time undergraduates: 65% (1,004). *Average award:* Freshmen: $10,209; Undergraduates: $9147. *Scholarships, grants, and awards:* Federal Pell, FSEOG, state, private, college/university gift aid from institutional funds.

GIFT AID (NON-NEED-BASED) *Total amount:* $1,615,685 (75% institutional, 25% external sources). *Receiving aid:* Freshmen: 31% (126). Undergraduates: 26% (400). *Average award:* Freshmen: $3745. Undergraduates: $3589. *Scholarships, grants, and awards by category: Academic interests/achievement:* general academic interests/achievements. *Creative arts/performance:* music. *Special achievements/activities:* general special achievements/activities. *Special characteristics:* ethnic background, international students, members of minority groups, veterans, veterans' children. *Tuition waivers:* Full or partial for minority students, senior citizens.

LOANS *Student loans:* $6,414,087 (78% need-based, 22% non-need-based). 77% of past graduating class borrowed through all loan programs. *Average indebtedness per student:* $25,855. *Average need-based loan:* Freshmen: $6150. Undergraduates: $6633. *Parent loans:* $197,935 (100% non-need-based). *Programs:* Federal Direct (Subsidized and Unsubsidized Stafford, PLUS), Perkins, state.

WORK-STUDY *Federal work-study:* Total amount: $288,338; jobs available. *State or other work-study/employment:* Total amount: $224,675 (100% need-based). Part-time jobs available.

APPLYING FOR FINANCIAL AID *Required financial aid form:* FAFSA. *Financial aid deadline (priority):* 3/1. *Notification date:* Continuous. Students must reply within 3 weeks of notification.

CONTACT Ms. Jill Beauregard, Director of Financial Aid, University of Minnesota, Morris, 600 East 4th Street, Morris, MN 56267, 320-589-6035 or toll-free 800-992-8863. *Fax:* 320-589-1673. *E-mail:* morrisfa@morris.umn.edu.

UNIVERSITY OF MINNESOTA, TWIN CITIES CAMPUS
Minneapolis, MN

Tuition & fees (MN res): $11,017   Average undergraduate aid package: $13,189

ABOUT THE INSTITUTION State-supported, coed. 138 undergraduate majors. Federal methodology is used as a basis for awarding need-based institutional aid.

UNDERGRADUATE EXPENSES for 2009–10 *Tuition, state resident:* full-time $9120; part-time $350.76 per credit. *Tuition, nonresident:* full-time $13,120; part-time $504.61 per credit. *Required fees:* full-time $1897. Full-time tuition and fees vary according to program and reciprocity agreements. Part-time tuition and fees vary according to course load, program, and reciprocity agreements. *College room and board:* $7534; *Room only:* $4294. Room and board charges vary according to board plan, housing facility, and location. *Payment plan:* Installment.

FRESHMAN FINANCIAL AID (Fall 2009, est.) 4,292 applied for aid; of those 65% were deemed to have need. 100% of freshmen with need received aid; of those 52% had need fully met. *Average percent of need met:* 87% (excluding resources awarded to replace EFC). *Average financial aid package:* $12,948 (excluding resources awarded to replace EFC). 18% of all full-time freshmen had no need and received non-need-based gift aid.

UNDERGRADUATE FINANCIAL AID (Fall 2009, est.) 19,793 applied for aid; of those 74% were deemed to have need. 100% of undergraduates with need

University of Minnesota, Twin Cities Campus

received aid; of those 44% had need fully met. *Average percent of need met:* 83% (excluding resources awarded to replace EFC). *Average financial aid package:* $13,189 (excluding resources awarded to replace EFC). 13% of all full-time undergraduates had no need and received non-need-based gift aid.

GIFT AID (NEED-BASED) *Total amount:* $114,788,507 (30% federal, 39% state, 29% institutional, 2% external sources). *Receiving aid:* Freshmen: 51% (2,742); all full-time undergraduates: 50% (13,771). *Average award:* Freshmen: $8703; Undergraduates: $7832. *Scholarships, grants, and awards:* Federal Pell, state, private, college/university gift aid from institutional funds.

GIFT AID (NON-NEED-BASED) *Total amount:* $17,804,776 (91% institutional, 9% external sources). *Receiving aid:* Freshmen: 12% (637). Undergraduates: 11% (3,048). *Average award:* Freshmen: $4632. Undergraduates: $5020. *Scholarships, grants, and awards by category:* Academic interests/achievement: agriculture, architecture, area/ethnic studies, biological sciences, business, communication, computer science, education, engineering/technologies, English, foreign languages, general academic interests/achievements, health fields, home economics, humanities, international studies, library science, mathematics, military science, physical sciences, premedicine, religion/biblical studies, social sciences. *Creative arts/performance:* general creative arts/performance. *Special achievements/activities:* hobbies/interests, leadership. *Special characteristics:* general special characteristics, local/state students, members of minority groups. *Tuition waivers:* Full or partial for senior citizens.

LOANS *Student loans:* $139,870,092 (73% need-based, 27% non-need-based). 63% of past graduating class borrowed through all loan programs. *Average indebtedness per student:* $26,516. *Average need-based loan:* Freshmen: $4532. Undergraduates: $6073. *Parent loans:* $35,201,040 (100% non-need-based).

WORK-STUDY *Federal work-study:* Total amount: $6,132,465; jobs available. *State or other work-study/employment:* Total amount: $13,448,317 (100% need-based). Part-time jobs available.

APPLYING FOR FINANCIAL AID *Required financial aid forms:* FAFSA, institution's own form. *Financial aid deadline (priority):* 3/1. *Notification date:* Continuous beginning 2/15.

CONTACT Judy Swanson, Associate Director, Office of Student Finance, University of Minnesota, Twin Cities Campus, 200 Fraser Hall, 106 Pleasant Street SE, Minneapolis, MN 55455, 612-624-1111 or toll-free 800-752-1000. *Fax:* 612-624-9584. *E-mail:* helpingu@umn.edu.

UNIVERSITY OF MISSISSIPPI
Oxford, MS

Tuition & fees: N/R	Average undergraduate aid package: $7677

ABOUT THE INSTITUTION State-supported, coed. 61 undergraduate majors. Federal methodology is used as a basis for awarding need-based institutional aid.

FRESHMAN FINANCIAL AID (Fall 2008) 1,507 applied for aid; of those 65% were deemed to have need. 97% of freshmen with need received aid; of those 17% had need fully met. *Average percent of need met:* 77% (excluding resources awarded to replace EFC). *Average financial aid package:* $9280 (excluding resources awarded to replace EFC). 27% of all full-time freshmen had no need and received non-need-based gift aid.

UNDERGRADUATE FINANCIAL AID (Fall 2008) 6,876 applied for aid; of those 75% were deemed to have need. 97% of undergraduates with need received aid; of those 12% had need fully met. *Average percent of need met:* 76% (excluding resources awarded to replace EFC). *Average financial aid package:* $7677 (excluding resources awarded to replace EFC). 20% of all full-time undergraduates had no need and received non-need-based gift aid.

GIFT AID (NEED-BASED) *Total amount:* $25,632,375 (49% federal, 9% state, 34% institutional, 8% external sources). *Receiving aid:* Freshmen: 37% (857); all full-time undergraduates: 38% (4,387). *Average award:* Freshmen: $7169; Undergraduates: $6278. *Scholarships, grants, and awards:* Federal Pell, FSEOG, state, private, college/university gift aid from institutional funds.

GIFT AID (NON-NEED-BASED) *Total amount:* $14,040,179 (19% state, 66% institutional, 15% external sources). *Receiving aid:* Freshmen: 6% (144). Undergraduates: 4% (472). *Average award:* Freshmen: $4465. Undergraduates: $4106. *Scholarships, grants, and awards by category:* Academic interests/achievement: 6,292 awards ($14,396,832 total): biological sciences, business, communication, computer science, education, engineering/technologies, English, foreign languages, general academic interests/achievements, health fields, humanities, international studies, mathematics, military science, physical sciences, premedicine, religion/biblical studies, social sciences. Creative arts/performance:

724 awards ($1,022,334 total): art/fine arts, cinema/film/broadcasting, creative writing, debating, journalism/publications, music, performing arts, theater/drama. *Special achievements/activities:* 3,798 awards ($7,023,556 total): cheerleading/drum major, community service, general special achievements/activities, junior miss, leadership, memberships. *Special characteristics:* 4,882 awards ($8,783,945 total): adult students, children and siblings of alumni, children of faculty/staff, ethnic background, first-generation college students, general special characteristics, handicapped students, international students, local/state students, members of minority groups, out-of-state students, previous college experience, spouses of current students. *Tuition waivers:* Full or partial for children of alumni, employees or children of employees, senior citizens.

LOANS *Student loans:* $43,485,805 (72% need-based, 28% non-need-based). 39% of past graduating class borrowed through all loan programs. *Average indebtedness per student:* $22,866. *Average need-based loan:* Freshmen: $3513. Undergraduates: $4661. *Parent loans:* $9,422,190 (26% need-based, 74% non-need-based). *Programs:* FFEL (Subsidized and Unsubsidized Stafford, PLUS), Perkins, college/university.

WORK-STUDY *Federal work-study:* Total amount: $649,648; 456 jobs averaging $1396.

ATHLETIC AWARDS Total amount: $4,768,549 (45% need-based, 55% non-need-based).

APPLYING FOR FINANCIAL AID *Required financial aid form:* FAFSA. *Financial aid deadline (priority):* 3/15. *Notification date:* Continuous beginning 4/1. Students must reply within 3 weeks of notification.

CONTACT Ms. Laura Diven-Brown, Director of Financial Aid, University of Mississippi, 257 Martindale Center, University, MS 38677, 662-915-5788 or toll-free 800-653-6477 (in-state). *Fax:* 662-915-1164. *E-mail:* ldivenbr@olemiss.edu.

UNIVERSITY OF MISSISSIPPI MEDICAL CENTER
Jackson, MS

CONTACT Minetta Veazey, Administrative Secretary, University of Mississippi Medical Center, 2500 North State Street, Jackson, MS 39216, 601-984-1117. *Fax:* 601-984-6984. *E-mail:* mveazey@registrar.umsmed.edu.

UNIVERSITY OF MISSOURI
Columbia, MO

Tuition & fees (MO res): $8501	Average undergraduate aid package: $13,136

ABOUT THE INSTITUTION State-supported, coed. 115 undergraduate majors. Federal methodology is used as a basis for awarding need-based institutional aid.

UNDERGRADUATE EXPENSES for 2009–10 *Tuition, state resident:* full-time $7368; part-time $245.60 per credit hour. *Tuition, nonresident:* full-time $18,459; part-time $615.30 per credit hour. *Required fees:* full-time $1133. Full-time tuition and fees vary according to course load, program, and reciprocity agreements. Part-time tuition and fees vary according to course load, program, and reciprocity agreements. *College room and board:* $8100. Room and board charges vary according to board plan and housing facility. *Payment plan:* Installment.

FRESHMAN FINANCIAL AID (Fall 2009, est.) 4,239 applied for aid; of those 64% were deemed to have need. 98% of freshmen with need received aid; of those 19% had need fully met. *Average percent of need met:* 87% (excluding resources awarded to replace EFC). *Average financial aid package:* $14,346 (excluding resources awarded to replace EFC). 22% of all full-time freshmen had no need and received non-need-based gift aid.

UNDERGRADUATE FINANCIAL AID (Fall 2009, est.) 15,066 applied for aid; of those 71% were deemed to have need. 98% of undergraduates with need received aid; of those 19% had need fully met. *Average percent of need met:* 84% (excluding resources awarded to replace EFC). *Average financial aid package:* $13,136 (excluding resources awarded to replace EFC). 17% of all full-time undergraduates had no need and received non-need-based gift aid.

GIFT AID (NEED-BASED) *Total amount:* $56,258,004 (36% federal, 16% state, 42% institutional, 6% external sources). *Receiving aid:* Freshmen: 43% (2,378); all full-time undergraduates: 39% (8,753). *Average award:* Freshmen: $7857;

Undergraduates: $7152. *Scholarships, grants, and awards:* Federal Pell, FSEOG, state, private, college/university gift aid from institutional funds.

GIFT AID (NON-NEED-BASED) *Total amount:* $22,239,843 (5% federal, 13% state, 63% institutional, 19% external sources). *Receiving aid:* Freshmen: 3% (150). Undergraduates: 2% (400). *Average award:* Freshmen: $3454. Undergraduates: $3531. *Scholarships, grants, and awards by category:* Academic interests/achievement: agriculture, area/ethnic studies, biological sciences, business, communication, computer science, education, engineering/technologies, English, foreign languages, general academic interests/achievements, health fields, home economics, humanities, international studies, library science, mathematics, physical sciences, premedicine, religion/biblical studies, social sciences. *Creative arts/performance:* art/fine arts, cinema/film/broadcasting, creative writing, journalism/publications, music, theater/drama. *Special achievements/activities:* cheerleading/drum major, general special achievements/activities, memberships. *Special characteristics:* adult students, children and siblings of alumni, children of faculty/staff, ethnic background, first-generation college students, international students, local/state students, members of minority groups, out-of-state students. *Tuition waivers:* Full or partial for employees or children of employees, senior citizens.

LOANS *Student loans:* $87,392,355 (66% need-based, 34% non-need-based). 57% of past graduating class borrowed through all loan programs. *Average indebtedness per student:* $20,689. *Average need-based loan:* Freshmen: $3579. Undergraduates: $4441. *Parent loans:* $37,168,718 (42% need-based, 58% non-need-based). *Programs:* Federal Direct (Subsidized and Unsubsidized Stafford, PLUS), FFEL (PLUS), Perkins, Federal Nursing, state, college/university, alternative loans.

WORK-STUDY *Federal work-study:* Total amount: $2,151,674; jobs available.

ATHLETIC AWARDS Total amount: $5,873,020 (37% need-based, 63% non-need-based).

APPLYING FOR FINANCIAL AID *Required financial aid form:* FAFSA. *Financial aid deadline (priority):* 3/1. *Notification date:* Continuous beginning 4/1. Students must reply within 4 weeks of notification.

CONTACT James Brooks, Director, Student Financial Aid, University of Missouri, 11 Jesse Hall, Columbia, MO 65211, 573-882-7506 or toll-free 800-225-6075 (in-state). *Fax:* 573-884-5335. *E-mail:* finaidinfo@missouri.edu.

UNIVERSITY OF MISSOURI–KANSAS CITY
Kansas City, MO

Tuition & fees (MO res): $8273   **Average undergraduate aid package: $9704**

ABOUT THE INSTITUTION State-supported, coed. 63 undergraduate majors. Federal methodology is used as a basis for awarding need-based institutional aid.

UNDERGRADUATE EXPENSES for 2009–10 *Tuition, state resident:* full-time $7368; part-time $245.60 per credit hour. *Tuition, nonresident:* full-time $18,459; part-time $615.30 per credit hour. *Required fees:* full-time $905; $30.15 per credit hour or $30 per term. Full-time tuition and fees vary according to course load and program. Part-time tuition and fees vary according to course load and program. *College room and board:* $10,467. Room and board charges vary according to board plan and housing facility. *Payment plan:* Installment.

FRESHMAN FINANCIAL AID (Fall 2009, est.) 814 applied for aid; of those 81% were deemed to have need. 98% of freshmen with need received aid; of those 10% had need fully met. *Average percent of need met:* 57% (excluding resources awarded to replace EFC). *Average financial aid package:* $10,758 (excluding resources awarded to replace EFC). 21% of all full-time freshmen had no need and received non-need-based gift aid.

UNDERGRADUATE FINANCIAL AID (Fall 2009, est.) 4,798 applied for aid; of those 88% were deemed to have need. 96% of undergraduates with need received aid; of those 7% had need fully met. *Average percent of need met:* 51% (excluding resources awarded to replace EFC). *Average financial aid package:* $9704 (excluding resources awarded to replace EFC). 13% of all full-time undergraduates had no need and received non-need-based gift aid.

GIFT AID (NEED-BASED) *Total amount:* $22,975,699 (50% federal, 12% state, 34% institutional, 4% external sources). *Receiving aid:* Freshmen: 63% (613); all full-time undergraduates: 53% (3,321). *Average award:* Freshmen: $7882; Undergraduates: $6675. *Scholarships, grants, and awards:* Federal Pell, FSEOG, state, private, college/university gift aid from institutional funds, United Negro College Fund.

GIFT AID (NON-NEED-BASED) *Total amount:* $5,926,034 (5% state, 76% institutional, 19% external sources). *Receiving aid:* Freshmen: 3% (25).

Undergraduates: 1% (66). *Average award:* Freshmen: $4053. Undergraduates: $5101. *Scholarships, grants, and awards by category:* Academic interests/achievement: general academic interests/achievements. *Creative arts/performance:* debating, general creative arts/performance, music, performing arts. *Special achievements/activities:* general special achievements/activities. *Special characteristics:* ethnic background, members of minority groups, out-of-state students. *Tuition waivers:* Full or partial for employees or children of employees.

LOANS *Student loans:* $37,356,758 (88% need-based, 12% non-need-based). 65% of past graduating class borrowed through all loan programs. *Average indebtedness per student:* $20,512. *Average need-based loan:* Freshmen: $6358. Undergraduates: $8436. *Parent loans:* $10,121,802 (66% need-based, 34% non-need-based). *Programs:* Federal Direct (Subsidized and Unsubsidized Stafford, PLUS), Perkins, Federal Nursing, state, college/university.

WORK-STUDY *Federal work-study:* Total amount: $2,777,940; jobs available.

ATHLETIC AWARDS Total amount: $1,952,424 (39% need-based, 61% non-need-based).

APPLYING FOR FINANCIAL AID *Required financial aid form:* FAFSA. *Financial aid deadline (priority):* 3/1. *Notification date:* Continuous beginning 4/15. Students must reply within 2 weeks of notification.

CONTACT Jan Brandow, Director of Financial Aid and Scholarships, University of Missouri–Kansas City, 5100 Rockhill Road, Kansas City, MO 64110-2499, 816-235-1154 or toll-free 800-775-8652 (out-of-state). *Fax:* 816-235-5511. *E-mail:* brandowj@umkc.edu.

UNIVERSITY OF MISSOURI–ST. LOUIS
St. Louis, MO

Tuition & fees (MO res): $8595   **Average undergraduate aid package: $8707**

ABOUT THE INSTITUTION State-supported, coed. 69 undergraduate majors. Federal methodology is used as a basis for awarding need-based institutional aid.

UNDERGRADUATE EXPENSES for 2009–10 *Tuition, state resident:* full-time $7368; part-time $245.60 per credit hour. *Tuition, nonresident:* full-time $18,459; part-time $615.30 per credit hour. *Required fees:* full-time $1227; $47.09 per credit hour. Full-time tuition and fees vary according to course load, program, and reciprocity agreements. Part-time tuition and fees vary according to course load, program, and reciprocity agreements. *College room and board:* $8164; *Room only:* $4449. Room and board charges vary according to board plan and housing facility. *Payment plan:* Installment.

FRESHMAN FINANCIAL AID (Fall 2009, est.) 410 applied for aid; of those 87% were deemed to have need. 98% of freshmen with need received aid; of those 11% had need fully met. *Average percent of need met:* 54% (excluding resources awarded to replace EFC). *Average financial aid package:* $9205 (excluding resources awarded to replace EFC). 15% of all full-time freshmen had no need and received non-need-based gift aid.

UNDERGRADUATE FINANCIAL AID (Fall 2009, est.) 4,519 applied for aid; of those 90% were deemed to have need. 97% of undergraduates with need received aid; of those 6% had need fully met. *Average percent of need met:* 48% (excluding resources awarded to replace EFC). *Average financial aid package:* $8707 (excluding resources awarded to replace EFC). 9% of all full-time undergraduates had no need and received non-need-based gift aid.

GIFT AID (NEED-BASED) *Total amount:* $23,314,020 (65% federal, 12% state, 18% institutional, 5% external sources). *Receiving aid:* Freshmen: 67% (329); all full-time undergraduates: 54% (3,195). *Average award:* Freshmen: $6842; Undergraduates: $5815. *Scholarships, grants, and awards:* Federal Pell, FSEOG, state, private, college/university gift aid from institutional funds, Federal Nursing, Academic Competitiveness Grants, National Smart Grants, Federal TEACH Grants.

GIFT AID (NON-NEED-BASED) *Total amount:* $3,654,857 (5% state, 72% institutional, 23% external sources). *Receiving aid:* Freshmen: 5% (26). Undergraduates: 1% (88). *Average award:* Freshmen: $4028. Undergraduates: $4315. *Scholarships, grants, and awards by category:* Academic interests/achievement: biological sciences, business, communication, computer science, education, engineering/technologies, English, foreign languages, general academic interests/achievements, health fields, humanities, international studies, mathematics, physical sciences, premedicine, social sciences. *Creative arts/performance:* applied art and design, art/fine arts, dance, music, theater/drama. *Special achievements/activities:* memberships. *Special characteristics:* adult students, children and siblings of alumni, children of faculty/staff, ethnic background, general special characteristics, international students, local/state students, members of minority groups, out-of-state students, veterans. *Tuition waivers:* Full or partial for employees or children of employees, senior citizens.

LOANS *Student loans:* $48,515,634 (89% need-based, 11% non-need-based). 65% of past graduating class borrowed through all loan programs. *Average indebtedness per student:* $25,776. *Average need-based loan:* Freshmen: $3368. Undergraduates: $4543. *Parent loans:* $3,135,176 (42% need-based, 58% non-need-based). *Programs:* FFEL (Subsidized and Unsubsidized Stafford, PLUS), Perkins, Federal Nursing.

WORK-STUDY *Federal work-study:* Total amount: $320,136; 81 jobs averaging $3347.

ATHLETIC AWARDS Total amount: $1,411,679 (39% need-based, 61% non-need-based).

APPLYING FOR FINANCIAL AID *Required financial aid form:* FAFSA. *Financial aid deadline (priority):* 4/1. *Notification date:* Continuous beginning 4/1. Students must reply within 2 weeks of notification.

CONTACT Ms. Samantha M. Matchefts, Associate Director, Student Financial Aid, University of Missouri–St. Louis, One University Boulevard, 327 Millennium Student Center, St. Louis, MO 63121-4400, 314-516-6893 or toll-free 888-GO2-UMSL (in-state). *Fax:* 314-516-5408. *E-mail:* samantha.matchefts@umsl.edu.

UNIVERSITY OF MOBILE
Mobile, AL

Tuition & fees: $14,850	Average undergraduate aid package: $12,998

ABOUT THE INSTITUTION Independent Southern Baptist, coed. 30 undergraduate majors. Federal methodology is used as a basis for awarding need-based institutional aid.

UNDERGRADUATE EXPENSES for 2009–10 *Comprehensive fee:* $22,420 includes full-time tuition ($14,500), mandatory fees ($350), and room and board ($7570). *College room only:* $4470. Full-time tuition and fees vary according to course load and program. Room and board charges vary according to housing facility. *Part-time tuition:* $515 per credit hour. *Part-time fees:* $98 per degree program. Part-time tuition and fees vary according to course load. *Payment plan:* Installment.

FRESHMAN FINANCIAL AID (Fall 2009, est.) 221 applied for aid; of those 90% were deemed to have need. 95% of freshmen with need received aid. *Average percent of need met:* 62% (excluding resources awarded to replace EFC). *Average financial aid package:* $14,543 (excluding resources awarded to replace EFC). 14% of all full-time freshmen had no need and received non-need-based gift aid.

UNDERGRADUATE FINANCIAL AID (Fall 2009, est.) 840 applied for aid; of those 100% were deemed to have need. 94% of undergraduates with need received aid. *Average percent of need met:* 59% (excluding resources awarded to replace EFC). *Average financial aid package:* $12,998 (excluding resources awarded to replace EFC). 7% of all full-time undergraduates had no need and received non-need-based gift aid.

GIFT AID (NEED-BASED) *Total amount:* $9,340,974 (33% federal, 5% state, 57% institutional, 5% external sources). *Receiving aid:* Freshmen: 86% (189); all full-time undergraduates: 71% (781). *Average award:* Freshmen: $10,666; Undergraduates: $8765. *Scholarships, grants, and awards:* Federal Pell, FSEOG, state, private, college/university gift aid from institutional funds, Federal Nursing.

GIFT AID (NON-NEED-BASED) *Receiving aid:* Freshmen: 10% (22). Undergraduates: 11% (117). *Average award:* Freshmen: $6160. Undergraduates: $5830. *Tuition waivers:* Full or partial for employees or children of employees.

LOANS *Student loans:* $10,649,116 (42% need-based, 58% non-need-based). 25% of past graduating class borrowed through all loan programs. *Average indebtedness per student:* $18,840. *Average need-based loan:* Freshmen: $4097. Undergraduates: $5505. *Parent loans:* $641,219 (100% non-need-based). *Programs:* FFEL (Subsidized and Unsubsidized Stafford, PLUS), Perkins.

WORK-STUDY *Federal work-study:* Total amount: $154,075; 70 jobs averaging $2175.

ATHLETIC AWARDS Total amount: $2,184,513 (100% non-need-based).

APPLYING FOR FINANCIAL AID *Required financial aid forms:* FAFSA, institution's own form, state aid form. *Financial aid deadline (priority):* 2/15. *Notification date:* Continuous beginning 2/15. Students must reply within 2 weeks of notification.

CONTACT Marie Thomas Baston, Associate Vice President for Enrollment Services, University of Mobile, 5735 College Parkway, Mobile, AL 36613, 251-442-2370 or toll-free 800-946-7267. *Fax:* 251-442-2498. *E-mail:* mariet@umobile.edu.

THE UNIVERSITY OF MONTANA
Missoula, MT

ABOUT THE INSTITUTION State-supported, coed. *Awards:* associate, bachelor's, and master's degrees and post-master's certificates. 118 undergraduate majors. *Total enrollment:* 14,207. Undergraduates: 12,196. Freshmen: 2,430.

GIFT AID (NEED-BASED) *Scholarships, grants, and awards:* Federal Pell, FSEOG, state, private, college/university gift aid from institutional funds.

GIFT AID (NON-NEED-BASED) *Scholarships, grants, and awards by category: Academic interests/achievement:* biological sciences, business, computer science, education, English, foreign languages, general academic interests/achievements, health fields, humanities, international studies, mathematics, military science, physical sciences, premedicine, social sciences. *Creative arts/performance:* art/fine arts, creative writing, dance, journalism/publications, music, performing arts, theater/drama. *Special achievements/activities:* cheerleading/drum major, leadership, rodeo. *Special characteristics:* children and siblings of alumni, children with a deceased or disabled parent, general special characteristics, international students, members of minority groups, out-of-state students, veterans.

LOANS *Programs:* FFEL (Subsidized and Unsubsidized Stafford, PLUS), Perkins.

WORK-STUDY *Federal work-study:* Total amount: $3,170,350; jobs available. *State or other work-study/employment:* Total amount: $490,796 (100% need-based). Part-time jobs available.

APPLYING FOR FINANCIAL AID *Required financial aid forms:* FAFSA, UM Supplemental Information Sheet.

CONTACT Mick Hanson, Director of Financial Aid, The University of Montana, Enrollment Services, Missoula, MT 59812-0002, 406-243-5373 or toll-free 800-462-8636. *Fax:* 406-243-4930. *E-mail:* faid@mso.umt.edu.

THE UNIVERSITY OF MONTANA WESTERN
Dillon, MT

Tuition & fees (MT res): $4279	Average undergraduate aid package: $2858

ABOUT THE INSTITUTION State-supported, coed. 34 undergraduate majors. Federal methodology is used as a basis for awarding need-based institutional aid.

UNDERGRADUATE EXPENSES for 2010–11 *Tuition, state resident:* full-time $3355; part-time $139.77 per credit hour. *Tuition, nonresident:* full-time $12,035; part-time $501.45 per credit hour. *Required fees:* full-time $924. Full-time tuition and fees vary according to program and student level. Part-time tuition and fees vary according to program and student level. *College room and board:* $6420; *Room only:* $2180. Room and board charges vary according to housing facility. *Payment plan:* Deferred payment.

FRESHMAN FINANCIAL AID (Fall 2008) 293 applied for aid; of those 83% were deemed to have need. 100% of freshmen with need received aid; of those 6% had need fully met. *Average percent of need met:* 16% (excluding resources awarded to replace EFC). *Average financial aid package:* $2757 (excluding resources awarded to replace EFC). 1% of all full-time freshmen had no need and received non-need-based gift aid.

UNDERGRADUATE FINANCIAL AID (Fall 2008) 881 applied for aid; of those 84% were deemed to have need. 100% of undergraduates with need received aid; of those 3% had need fully met. *Average percent of need met:* 17% (excluding resources awarded to replace EFC). *Average financial aid package:* $2858 (excluding resources awarded to replace EFC). 1% of all full-time undergraduates had no need and received non-need-based gift aid.

GIFT AID (NEED-BASED) *Total amount:* $2,998,623 (56% federal, 8% state, 9% institutional, 27% external sources). *Receiving aid:* Freshmen: 58% (199); all full-time undergraduates: 65% (640). *Average award:* Freshmen: $2494; Undergraduates: $2525. *Scholarships, grants, and awards:* Federal Pell, FSEOG, state, private, college/university gift aid from institutional funds, Academic Competitiveness Grants, National Smart Grants, Federal TEACH Grants.

GIFT AID (NON-NEED-BASED) *Total amount:* $385,296 (2% state, 18% institutional, 80% external sources). *Receiving aid:* Freshmen: 20% (67). Undergraduates: 11% (104). *Average award:* Freshmen: $1000. Undergraduates: $1786. *Scholarships, grants, and awards by category: Academic interests/*

achievement: 24 awards ($37,975 total): biological sciences, business, education, English, general academic interests/achievements, humanities, mathematics, physical sciences, premedicine, social sciences. *Creative arts/performance:* 27 awards ($64,000 total): art/fine arts. *Special achievements/activities:* 48 awards ($141,427 total): general special achievements/activities, rodeo. *Special characteristics:* 58 awards ($170,617 total): children of faculty/staff, first-generation college students, international students, members of minority groups, out-of-state students, veterans. *Tuition waivers:* Full or partial for employees or children of employees, senior citizens.

LOANS *Student loans:* $4,562,723 (79% need-based, 21% non-need-based). 71% of past graduating class borrowed through all loan programs. *Average indebtedness per student:* $21,969. *Average need-based loan:* Freshmen: $3590. Undergraduates: $3774. *Parent loans:* $538,366 (68% need-based, 32% non-need-based). *Programs:* Federal Direct (Subsidized and Unsubsidized Stafford, PLUS), Perkins, college/university.

WORK-STUDY *Federal work-study:* Total amount: $285,643; 79 jobs averaging $2808. *State or other work-study/employment:* Total amount: $175,696 (74% need-based, 26% non-need-based). 126 part-time jobs averaging $2382.

ATHLETIC AWARDS Total amount: $780,052 (68% need-based, 32% non-need-based).

APPLYING FOR FINANCIAL AID *Required financial aid forms:* FAFSA, student data form, verification materials (if applicable). *Financial aid deadline (priority):* 3/1. *Notification date:* Continuous beginning 4/1. Students must reply within 4 weeks of notification.

CONTACT Erica L. Jones, Director of Financial Aid, The University of Montana Western, 710 South Atlantic Street, Dillon, MT 59725, 406-683-7511 or toll-free 866-869-6668 (in-state), 877-683-7493 (out-of-state). *Fax:* 406-683-7510. *E-mail:* e_jones@umwestern.edu.

UNIVERSITY OF MONTEVALLO
Montevallo, AL

Tuition & fees (AL res): $7750   **Average undergraduate aid package: $8531**

ABOUT THE INSTITUTION State-supported, coed. 25 undergraduate majors. Federal methodology is used as a basis for awarding need-based institutional aid.

UNDERGRADUATE EXPENSES for 2010–11 *Tuition, state resident:* full-time $7230; part-time $241 per credit hour. *Tuition, nonresident:* full-time $14,460; part-time $482 per credit hour. *Required fees:* full-time $520. Full-time tuition and fees vary according to course load. Part-time tuition and fees vary according to course load. *College room and board:* $4924. Room and board charges vary according to housing facility. *Payment plan:* Installment.

FRESHMAN FINANCIAL AID (Fall 2009, est.) 310 applied for aid; of those 72% were deemed to have need. 98% of freshmen with need received aid; of those 24% had need fully met. *Average percent of need met:* 70% (excluding resources awarded to replace EFC). *Average financial aid package:* $8777 (excluding resources awarded to replace EFC). 23% of all full-time freshmen had no need and received non-need-based gift aid.

UNDERGRADUATE FINANCIAL AID (Fall 2009, est.) 1,535 applied for aid; of those 77% were deemed to have need. 99% of undergraduates with need received aid; of those 29% had need fully met. *Average percent of need met:* 67% (excluding resources awarded to replace EFC). *Average financial aid package:* $8531 (excluding resources awarded to replace EFC). 17% of all full-time undergraduates had no need and received non-need-based gift aid.

GIFT AID (NEED-BASED) *Total amount:* $6,128,220 (63% federal, 1% state, 28% institutional, 8% external sources). *Receiving aid:* Freshmen: 49% (200); all full-time undergraduates: 43% (974). *Average award:* Freshmen: $6575; Undergraduates: $5979. *Scholarships, grants, and awards:* Federal Pell, FSEOG, state, private, college/university gift aid from institutional funds.

GIFT AID (NON-NEED-BASED) *Total amount:* $2,449,134 (85% institutional, 15% external sources). *Average award:* Freshmen: $6160. Undergraduates: $5370. *Scholarships, grants, and awards by category: Academic interests/achievement:* biological sciences, education, general academic interests/achievements, physical sciences. *Creative arts/performance:* art/fine arts, music. *Special achievements/activities:* junior miss. *Special characteristics:* international students, out-of-state students, veterans, veterans' children. *Tuition waivers:* Full or partial for employees or children of employees.

LOANS *Student loans:* $9,354,886 (80% need-based, 20% non-need-based). 54% of past graduating class borrowed through all loan programs. *Average indebtedness per student:* $16,581. *Average need-based loan:* Freshmen: $3201.

Undergraduates: $3880. *Parent loans:* $365,760 (46% need-based, 54% non-need-based). *Programs:* FFEL (Subsidized and Unsubsidized Stafford, PLUS), Perkins.

WORK-STUDY *Federal work-study:* Total amount: $193,365; 109 jobs averaging $1412. *State or other work-study/employment:* Part-time jobs available.

ATHLETIC AWARDS Total amount: $1,083,668 (26% need-based, 74% non-need-based).

APPLYING FOR FINANCIAL AID *Required financial aid form:* FAFSA. *Financial aid deadline (priority):* 4/1. *Notification date:* Continuous beginning 4/15. Students must reply within 2 weeks of notification.

CONTACT Ms. Maria Parker, Director of Student Financial Aid, University of Montevallo, Station 6050, Montevallo, AL 35115, 205-665-6050 or toll-free 800-292-4349. *Fax:* 205-665-6047. *E-mail:* finaid@montevallo.edu.

UNIVERSITY OF MOUNT UNION
Alliance, OH

Tuition & fees: $23,880   **Average undergraduate aid package: $19,081**

ABOUT THE INSTITUTION Independent United Methodist, coed. 48 undergraduate majors. Federal methodology is used as a basis for awarding need-based institutional aid.

UNDERGRADUATE EXPENSES for 2009–10 *Comprehensive fee:* $31,300 includes full-time tuition ($23,630), mandatory fees ($250), and room and board ($7420). Room and board charges vary according to board plan and housing facility. *Part-time tuition:* $995 per credit hour. *Payment plans:* Tuition prepayment, installment.

FRESHMAN FINANCIAL AID (Fall 2009, est.) 531 applied for aid; of those 91% were deemed to have need. 100% of freshmen with need received aid; of those 8% had need fully met. *Average percent of need met:* 75% (excluding resources awarded to replace EFC). *Average financial aid package:* $19,130 (excluding resources awarded to replace EFC). 15% of all full-time freshmen had no need and received non-need-based gift aid.

UNDERGRADUATE FINANCIAL AID (Fall 2009, est.) 1,916 applied for aid; of those 91% were deemed to have need. 100% of undergraduates with need received aid; of those 10% had need fully met. *Average percent of need met:* 77% (excluding resources awarded to replace EFC). *Average financial aid package:* $19,081 (excluding resources awarded to replace EFC). 17% of all full-time undergraduates had no need and received non-need-based gift aid.

GIFT AID (NEED-BASED) *Total amount:* $23,087,485 (15% federal, 5% state, 76% institutional, 4% external sources). *Receiving aid:* Freshmen: 82% (482); all full-time undergraduates: 81% (1,735). *Average award:* Freshmen: $14,420; Undergraduates: $13,650. *Scholarships, grants, and awards:* Federal Pell, FSEOG, state, private, college/university gift aid from institutional funds.

GIFT AID (NON-NEED-BASED) *Total amount:* $3,412,604 (1% federal, 88% institutional, 11% external sources). *Receiving aid:* Freshmen: 5% (28). Undergraduates: 5% (118). *Average award:* Freshmen: $8201. Undergraduates: $7307. *Scholarships, grants, and awards by category: Academic interests/achievement:* 1,209 awards ($8,682,788 total): general academic interests/achievements, physical sciences. *Creative arts/performance:* 111 awards ($420,710 total): art/fine arts, cinema/film/broadcasting, debating, journalism/publications, music, theater/drama. *Special characteristics:* 291 awards ($2,091,936 total): children and siblings of alumni, children of faculty/staff, ethnic background, international students, members of minority groups, relatives of clergy. *Tuition waivers:* Full or partial for children of alumni, employees or children of employees, senior citizens.

LOANS *Student loans:* $17,413,113 (71% need-based, 29% non-need-based). 70% of past graduating class borrowed through all loan programs. *Average indebtedness per student:* $25,804. *Average need-based loan:* Freshmen: $4268. Undergraduates: $5173. *Parent loans:* $3,505,146 (38% need-based, 62% non-need-based). *Programs:* FFEL (Subsidized and Unsubsidized Stafford, PLUS), Perkins, alternative loans.

WORK-STUDY *Federal work-study:* Total amount: $1,134,413; 1,385 jobs averaging $1239. *State or other work-study/employment:* Total amount: $468,127 (24% need-based, 76% non-need-based). 314 part-time jobs averaging $1505.

APPLYING FOR FINANCIAL AID *Required financial aid form:* FAFSA. *Financial aid deadline:* Continuous. *Notification date:* Continuous beginning 3/15. Students must reply within 4 weeks of notification.

UNIVERSITY OF NEBRASKA AT KEARNEY
Kearney, NE

Tuition & fees (NE res): $5634	Average undergraduate aid package: $9443

ABOUT THE INSTITUTION State-supported, coed. 41 undergraduate majors. Federal methodology is used as a basis for awarding need-based institutional aid.

UNDERGRADUATE EXPENSES for 2009–10 *Tuition, state resident:* full-time $4537; part-time $151.25 per hour. *Tuition, nonresident:* full-time $9300; part-time $310 per hour. *Required fees:* full-time $1097; $22.25 per hour or $75 per term. Full-time tuition and fees vary according to course level, course load, degree level, and location. Part-time tuition and fees vary according to course level, course load, degree level, and location. *College room and board:* $6830; *Room only:* $3450. Room and board charges vary according to board plan and housing facility. *Payment plan:* Installment.

FRESHMAN FINANCIAL AID (Fall 2009, est.) 820 applied for aid; of those 80% were deemed to have need. 99% of freshmen with need received aid; of those 33% had need fully met. *Average percent of need met:* 84% (excluding resources awarded to replace EFC). *Average financial aid package:* $10,019 (excluding resources awarded to replace EFC). 1% of all full-time freshmen had no need and received non-need-based gift aid.

UNDERGRADUATE FINANCIAL AID (Fall 2009, est.) 3,323 applied for aid; of those 83% were deemed to have need. 98% of undergraduates with need received aid; of those 30% had need fully met. *Average percent of need met:* 80% (excluding resources awarded to replace EFC). *Average financial aid package:* $9443 (excluding resources awarded to replace EFC). 12% of all full-time undergraduates had no need and received non-need-based gift aid.

GIFT AID (NEED-BASED) *Total amount:* $10,275,229 (69% federal, 10% state, 11% institutional, 10% external sources). *Receiving aid:* Freshmen: 49% (428); all full-time undergraduates: 39% (1,762). *Average award:* Freshmen: $6283; Undergraduates: $5582. *Scholarships, grants, and awards:* Federal Pell, FSEOG, state, private, college/university gift aid from institutional funds.

GIFT AID (NON-NEED-BASED) *Total amount:* $4,108,296 (2% federal, 63% institutional, 35% external sources). *Receiving aid:* Freshmen: 45% (391). Undergraduates: 24% (1,071). *Average award:* Freshmen: $3185. Undergraduates: $2200. *Scholarships, grants, and awards by category: Academic interests/achievement:* communication. *Creative arts/performance:* applied art and design, art/fine arts, debating, journalism/publications, music. *Special achievements/activities:* cheerleading/drum major. *Special characteristics:* children of faculty/staff, ethnic background, first-generation college students, international students, out-of-state students, veterans, veterans' children. *Tuition waivers:* Full or partial for employees or children of employees.

LOANS *Student loans:* $17,886,941 (53% need-based, 47% non-need-based). 73% of past graduating class borrowed through all loan programs. *Average indebtedness per student:* $19,160. *Average need-based loan:* Freshmen: $2573. Undergraduates: $3512. *Parent loans:* $1,836,110 (100% non-need-based). *Programs:* FFEL (Subsidized Stafford, PLUS), Perkins, college/university.

WORK-STUDY *Federal work-study:* Total amount: $1,181,979; jobs available.

ATHLETIC AWARDS Total amount: $747,835 (100% non-need-based).

APPLYING FOR FINANCIAL AID *Required financial aid forms:* FAFSA, institution's own form. *Financial aid deadline (priority):* 4/1. *Notification date:* Continuous beginning 3/15.

CONTACT Financial Aid Office, University of Nebraska at Kearney, Memorial Student Affairs Building, 905 West 25th Street, Kearney, NE 68849-0001, 308-865-8520 or toll-free 800-532-7639. *Fax:* 308-865-8096.

UNIVERSITY OF NEBRASKA AT OMAHA
Omaha, NE

Tuition & fees (NE res): $6229	Average undergraduate aid package: $2458

ABOUT THE INSTITUTION State-supported, coed. 66 undergraduate majors. Federal methodology is used as a basis for awarding need-based institutional aid.

UNDERGRADUATE EXPENSES for 2009–10 *Tuition, state resident:* full-time $5115; part-time $170.50 per credit hour. *Tuition, nonresident:* full-time $15,075; part-time $502.50 per credit hour. *Required fees:* full-time $1114. Full-time tuition and fees vary according to course load and reciprocity agreements. Part-time tuition and fees vary according to course load and reciprocity agreements. *College room and board:* $7230. Room and board charges vary according to board plan and housing facility. *Payment plans:* Installment, deferred payment.

FRESHMAN FINANCIAL AID (Fall 2009, est.) 1,304 applied for aid; of those 67% were deemed to have need. 97% of freshmen with need received aid. *Average financial aid package:* $2215 (excluding resources awarded to replace EFC). 10% of all full-time freshmen had no need and received non-need-based gift aid.

UNDERGRADUATE FINANCIAL AID (Fall 2009, est.) 5,733 applied for aid; of those 72% were deemed to have need. 97% of undergraduates with need received aid. *Average financial aid package:* $2458 (excluding resources awarded to replace EFC). 5% of all full-time undergraduates had no need and received non-need-based gift aid.

GIFT AID (NEED-BASED) *Total amount:* $19,025,752 (50% federal, 8% state, 27% institutional, 15% external sources). *Receiving aid:* Freshmen: 32% (559); all full-time undergraduates: 31% (2,684). *Average award:* Freshmen: $1888; Undergraduates: $2075. *Scholarships, grants, and awards:* Federal Pell, FSEOG, state, private, college/university gift aid from institutional funds.

GIFT AID (NON-NEED-BASED) *Receiving aid:* Freshmen: 34% (608). Undergraduates: 21% (1,866). *Average award:* Freshmen: $2236. Undergraduates: $2261. *Scholarships, grants, and awards by category: Academic interests/achievement:* biological sciences, business, communication, computer science, education, engineering/technologies, English, foreign languages, general academic interests/achievements, home economics, mathematics, physical sciences, premedicine, social sciences. *Creative arts/performance:* art/fine arts, creative writing, debating, journalism/publications, music, performing arts, theater/drama. *Special achievements/activities:* general special achievements/activities, leadership, memberships. *Special characteristics:* adult students, children and siblings of alumni, children of faculty/staff, ethnic background, first-generation college students, handicapped students, international students, members of minority groups, out-of-state students, veterans' children. *Tuition waivers:* Full or partial for children of alumni, employees or children of employees, senior citizens.

LOANS *Student loans:* $50,721,961 (41% need-based, 59% non-need-based). 49% of past graduating class borrowed through all loan programs. *Average indebtedness per student:* $19,500. *Average need-based loan:* Freshmen: $2643. Undergraduates: $3251. *Parent loans:* $1,543,716 (100% non-need-based). *Programs:* FFEL (Subsidized and Unsubsidized Stafford, PLUS), Perkins, college/university.

WORK-STUDY *Federal work-study:* Total amount: $630,431; 375 jobs averaging $1700.

ATHLETIC AWARDS Total amount: $932,621 (100% need-based).

APPLYING FOR FINANCIAL AID *Required financial aid form:* FAFSA. *Financial aid deadline (priority):* 3/1. *Notification date:* Continuous beginning 4/1. Students must reply within 2 weeks of notification.

CONTACT Office of Financial Aid, University of Nebraska at Omaha, 103 Eppley Administration Building, Omaha, NE 68182-0187, 402-554-2327 or toll-free 800-858-8648 (in-state). *Fax:* 402-554-3472. *E-mail:* finaid@unomaha.edu.

UNIVERSITY OF NEBRASKA–LINCOLN
Lincoln, NE

Tuition & fees (NE res): $6857	Average undergraduate aid package: $10,060

ABOUT THE INSTITUTION State-supported, coed. 129 undergraduate majors. Both federal and institutional methodology are used as a basis for awarding need-based institutional aid.

UNDERGRADUATE EXPENSES for 2009–10 *Tuition, state resident:* full-time $5610; part-time $187 per semester hour. *Tuition, nonresident:* full-time $16,650; part-time $555 per semester hour. *Required fees:* full-time $1247; $10.35 per semester hour or $272.70 per term. Full-time tuition and fees vary according to course load, program, and reciprocity agreements. Part-time tuition and fees vary according to course load, program, and reciprocity agreements. *College room and board:* $7260; *Room only:* $3828. Room and board charges vary according to board plan and housing facility. *Payment plan:* Installment.

FRESHMAN FINANCIAL AID (Fall 2008) 2,956 applied for aid; of those 65% were deemed to have need. 98% of freshmen with need received aid; of those

30% had need fully met. *Average percent of need met:* 89% (excluding resources awarded to replace EFC). *Average financial aid package:* $10,708 (excluding resources awarded to replace EFC). 16% of all full-time freshmen had no need and received non-need-based gift aid.

UNDERGRADUATE FINANCIAL AID (Fall 2008) 11,083 applied for aid; of those 70% were deemed to have need. 98% of undergraduates with need received aid; of those 26% had need fully met. *Average percent of need met:* 86% (excluding resources awarded to replace EFC). *Average financial aid package:* $10,060 (excluding resources awarded to replace EFC). 9% of all full-time undergraduates had no need and received non-need-based gift aid.

GIFT AID (NEED-BASED) *Total amount:* $36,998,581 (32% federal, 6% state, 47% institutional, 15% external sources). *Receiving aid:* Freshmen: 38% (1,616); all full-time undergraduates: 33% (5,744). *Average award:* Freshmen: $7585; Undergraduates: $6784. *Scholarships, grants, and awards:* Federal Pell, FSEOG, state, private, college/university gift aid from institutional funds.

GIFT AID (NON-NEED-BASED) *Total amount:* $24,535,012 (7% federal, 81% institutional, 12% external sources). *Receiving aid:* Freshmen: 6% (233). Undergraduates: 4% (657). *Average award:* Freshmen: $4778. Undergraduates: $5325. *Scholarships, grants, and awards by category: Academic interests/ achievement:* agriculture, architecture, biological sciences, business, computer science, education, engineering/technologies, English, foreign languages, general academic interests/achievements, health fields, home economics, humanities, international studies, mathematics, physical sciences, premedicine, social sciences. *Creative arts/performance:* art/fine arts, cinema/film/broadcasting, dance, journalism/publications, music, performing arts, theater/drama. *Special achievements/ activities:* cheerleading/drum major, community service, leadership. *Special characteristics:* children and siblings of alumni, ethnic background, handicapped students, international students, members of minority groups, out-of-state students, veterans' children. *Tuition waivers:* Full or partial for employees or children of employees.

LOANS *Student loans:* $59,506,969 (61% need-based, 39% non-need-based). 60% of past graduating class borrowed through all loan programs. *Average indebtedness per student:* $19,128. *Average need-based loan:* Freshmen: $3198. Undergraduates: $4016. *Parent loans:* $25,246,588 (43% need-based, 57% non-need-based). *Programs:* Federal Direct (Subsidized and Unsubsidized Stafford, PLUS), Perkins, college/university.

WORK-STUDY *Federal work-study:* Total amount: $2,840,019; 1,149 jobs averaging $2465.

ATHLETIC AWARDS Total amount: $6,578,711 (100% non-need-based).

APPLYING FOR FINANCIAL AID *Required financial aid form:* FAFSA. *Financial aid deadline (priority):* 4/1. *Notification date:* Continuous beginning 4/1.

CONTACT Ms. Jo Tederman, Assistant Director of Scholarships and Financial Aid, University of Nebraska–Lincoln, 17 Canfield Administration Building, Lincoln, NE 68588-0411, 402-472-2030 or toll-free 800-742-8800. *Fax:* 402-472-9826.

UNIVERSITY OF NEBRASKA MEDICAL CENTER
Omaha, NE

Tuition & fees: N/R	Average undergraduate aid package: $8239

ABOUT THE INSTITUTION State-supported, coed. 7 undergraduate majors. Federal methodology is used as a basis for awarding need-based institutional aid.

UNDERGRADUATE FINANCIAL AID (Fall 2008) 863 applied for aid; of those 84% were deemed to have need. 99% of undergraduates with need received aid; of those 14% had need fully met. *Average percent of need met:* 56% (excluding resources awarded to replace EFC). *Average financial aid package:* $8239 (excluding resources awarded to replace EFC). 18% of all full-time undergraduates had no need and received non-need-based gift aid.

GIFT AID (NEED-BASED) *Total amount:* $2,810,508 (27% federal, 13% state, 50% institutional, 10% external sources). *Receiving aid:* All full-time undergraduates: 56% (577). *Average award:* Undergraduates: $4760. *Scholarships, grants, and awards:* Federal Pell, FSEOG, state, private, college/university gift aid from institutional funds.

GIFT AID (NON-NEED-BASED) *Total amount:* $806,063 (9% state, 82% institutional, 9% external sources). *Receiving aid:* Undergraduates: 3% (28). *Average award:* Undergraduates: $8607.

LOANS *Student loans:* $7,347,410 (72% need-based, 28% non-need-based). 94% of past graduating class borrowed through all loan programs. *Average*

indebtedness per student: $29,188. *Average need-based loan:* Undergraduates: $4871. *Parent loans:* $855,046 (100% need-based). *Programs:* FFEL (Subsidized and Unsubsidized Stafford, PLUS), Perkins, Federal Nursing, state, college/university.

WORK-STUDY *Federal work-study:* Total amount: $35,158; 53 jobs averaging $663.

APPLYING FOR FINANCIAL AID *Required financial aid forms:* FAFSA, institution's own form. *Financial aid deadline (priority):* 3/15. *Notification date:* Continuous beginning 4/1. Students must reply within 2 weeks of notification.

CONTACT Judy D. Walker, Director of Financial Aid, University of Nebraska Medical Center, 984265 Nebraska Medical Center, Omaha, NE 68198-4265, 402-559-6409 or toll-free 800-626-8431 Ext. 6468. *Fax:* 402-559-6796. *E-mail:* jdwalker@unmc.edu.

UNIVERSITY OF NEVADA, LAS VEGAS
Las Vegas, NV

Tuition & fees (NV res): $5525	Average undergraduate aid package: $9706

ABOUT THE INSTITUTION State-supported, coed. 89 undergraduate majors. Federal methodology is used as a basis for awarding need-based institutional aid.

UNDERGRADUATE EXPENSES for 2010–11 *Tuition, state resident:* full-time $4913; part-time $156.75 per credit hour. *Tuition, nonresident:* full-time $18,203; part-time $313.75 per credit hour. *Required fees:* full-time $612. Full-time tuition and fees vary according to course level and reciprocity agreements. Part-time tuition and fees vary according to course level and reciprocity agreements. *College room and board:* $10,454; *Room only:* $6544. Room and board charges vary according to board plan. *Payment plan:* Deferred payment.

FRESHMAN FINANCIAL AID (Fall 2009, est.) 2,182 applied for aid; of those 76% were deemed to have need. 99% of freshmen with need received aid; of those 19% had need fully met. *Average percent of need met:* 51% (excluding resources awarded to replace EFC). *Average financial aid package:* $9291 (excluding resources awarded to replace EFC). 3% of all full-time freshmen had no need and received non-need-based gift aid.

UNDERGRADUATE FINANCIAL AID (Fall 2009, est.) 9,610 applied for aid; of those 83% were deemed to have need. 98% of undergraduates with need received aid; of those 17% had need fully met. *Average percent of need met:* 56% (excluding resources awarded to replace EFC). *Average financial aid package:* $9706 (excluding resources awarded to replace EFC). 2% of all full-time undergraduates had no need and received non-need-based gift aid.

GIFT AID (NEED-BASED) *Total amount:* $26,276,739 (68% federal, 17% state, 13% institutional, 2% external sources). *Receiving aid:* Freshmen: 36% (1,117); all full-time undergraduates: 32% (5,151). *Average award:* Freshmen: $5197; Undergraduates: $5123. *Scholarships, grants, and awards:* Federal Pell, FSEOG, state, private, college/university gift aid from institutional funds.

GIFT AID (NON-NEED-BASED) *Total amount:* $15,480,465 (28% federal, 56% state, 12% institutional, 4% external sources). *Receiving aid:* Freshmen: 41% (1,258). Undergraduates: 26% (4,256). *Average award:* Freshmen: $3633. Undergraduates: $3194. *Scholarships, grants, and awards by category: Academic interests/achievement:* architecture, biological sciences, business, communication, computer science, education, engineering/technologies, English, foreign languages, general academic interests/achievements, health fields, humanities, international studies, mathematics, physical sciences, premedicine, social sciences. *Creative arts/performance:* applied art and design, art/fine arts, cinema/ film/broadcasting, creative writing, dance, debating, general creative arts/ performance, journalism/publications, music, performing arts, theater/drama. *Special achievements/activities:* cheerleading/drum major, community service, general special achievements/activities, leadership, rodeo. *Special characteristics:* adult students, children and siblings of alumni, children of faculty/staff, children of public servants, children of union members/company employees, children with a deceased or disabled parent, ethnic background, first-generation college students, general special characteristics, handicapped students, international students, local/state students, members of minority groups, out-of-state students, previous college experience, veterans, veterans' children. *Tuition waivers:* Full or partial for children of alumni, employees or children of employees, senior citizens.

LOANS *Student loans:* $33,495,083 (71% need-based, 29% non-need-based). 37% of past graduating class borrowed through all loan programs. *Average indebtedness per student:* $17,256. *Average need-based loan:* Freshmen: $3077. Undergraduates: $4146. *Parent loans:* $15,128,216 (41% need-based, 59%

non-need-based). *Programs:* Federal Direct (Subsidized and Unsubsidized Stafford, PLUS), Perkins, Federal Nursing, state, college/university.

WORK-STUDY *Federal work-study:* Total amount: $1,322,830; 208 jobs averaging $4221. *State or other work-study/employment:* Total amount: $1,242,596 (96% need-based, 4% non-need-based). 473 part-time jobs averaging $3967.

ATHLETIC AWARDS Total amount: $4,373,157 (23% need-based, 77% non-need-based).

APPLYING FOR FINANCIAL AID *Required financial aid form:* FAFSA. *Financial aid deadline (priority):* 2/1. *Notification date:* Continuous beginning 3/20. Students must reply within 2 weeks of notification.

CONTACT Financial Aid and Scholarships, University of Nevada, Las Vegas, 4505 Maryland Parkway, Las Vegas, NV 89154-2016, 702-895-3424. *Fax:* 702-895-1353. *E-mail:* financialaid@unlv.edu.

UNIVERSITY OF NEVADA, RENO
Reno, NV

Tuition & fees (NV res): $5051	Average undergraduate aid package: $7375

ABOUT THE INSTITUTION State-supported, coed. 97 undergraduate majors. Federal methodology is used as a basis for awarding need-based institutional aid.

UNDERGRADUATE EXPENSES for 2009–10 *One-time required fee:* $106. *Tuition, state resident:* full-time $4635; part-time $154.50 per credit. *Tuition, nonresident:* full-time $16,975; part-time $304 per credit. *Required fees:* full-time $416. Full-time tuition and fees vary according to course load. Part-time tuition and fees vary according to course load. *College room and board:* $10,595; *Room only:* $6100. Room and board charges vary according to board plan and housing facility. *Payment plan:* Deferred payment.

FRESHMAN FINANCIAL AID (Fall 2008) 1,363 applied for aid; of those 63% were deemed to have need. 97% of freshmen with need received aid; of those 15% had need fully met. *Average percent of need met:* 55% (excluding resources awarded to replace EFC). *Average financial aid package:* $5860 (excluding resources awarded to replace EFC). 51% of all full-time freshmen had no need and received non-need-based gift aid.

UNDERGRADUATE FINANCIAL AID (Fall 2008) 5,025 applied for aid; of those 75% were deemed to have need. 96% of undergraduates with need received aid; of those 11% had need fully met. *Average percent of need met:* 57% (excluding resources awarded to replace EFC). *Average financial aid package:* $7375 (excluding resources awarded to replace EFC). 43% of all full-time undergraduates had no need and received non-need-based gift aid.

GIFT AID (NEED-BASED) *Total amount:* $17,649,986 (36% federal, 29% state, 29% institutional, 6% external sources). *Receiving aid:* Freshmen: 32% (714); all full-time undergraduates: 30% (3,109). *Average award:* Freshmen: $5605; Undergraduates: $5738. *Scholarships, grants, and awards:* Federal Pell, FSEOG, state, private, college/university gift aid from institutional funds, Federal Nursing.

GIFT AID (NON-NEED-BASED) *Total amount:* $13,723,503 (3% federal, 51% state, 35% institutional, 11% external sources). *Receiving aid:* Freshmen: 33% (738). Undergraduates: 25% (2,609). *Average award:* Freshmen: $2662. Undergraduates: $2702. *Scholarships, grants, and awards by category:* Academic interests/achievement: general academic interests/achievements. Creative arts/performance: general creative arts/performance, music, theater/drama. Special characteristics: adult students, children and siblings of alumni, ethnic background, first-generation college students, married students. *Tuition waivers:* Full or partial for children of alumni, employees or children of employees, senior citizens.

LOANS *Student loans:* $24,182,916 (77% need-based, 23% non-need-based). 36% of past graduating class borrowed through all loan programs. *Average indebtedness per student:* $15,854. *Average need-based loan:* Freshmen: $3182. Undergraduates: $4389. *Parent loans:* $2,462,381 (51% need-based, 49% non-need-based). *Programs:* FFEL (Subsidized and Unsubsidized Stafford, PLUS), Perkins, Federal Nursing, college/university.

WORK-STUDY *Federal work-study:* Total amount: $488,158; jobs available. *State or other work-study/employment:* Total amount: $33,000 (42% need-based, 58% non-need-based). Part-time jobs available.

ATHLETIC AWARDS Total amount: $5,088,236 (17% need-based, 83% non-need-based).

APPLYING FOR FINANCIAL AID *Required financial aid form:* FAFSA. *Financial aid deadline (priority):* 3/1. *Notification date:* Continuous beginning 4/1. Students must reply within 2 weeks of notification.

CONTACT Ms. Sandy Guidry, Interim Director of Student Financial Aid, University of Nevada, Reno, Mail Stop 076, Reno, NV 89557, 775-784-4666 or toll-free 866-263-8232. *Fax:* 775-784-1025. *E-mail:* sguidry@unr.nevada.edu.

UNIVERSITY OF NEW ENGLAND
Biddeford, ME

ABOUT THE INSTITUTION Independent, coed. 36 undergraduate majors.

GIFT AID (NEED-BASED) *Scholarships, grants, and awards:* Federal Pell, FSEOG, state, private, college/university gift aid from institutional funds.

GIFT AID (NON-NEED-BASED) *Scholarships, grants, and awards by category:* Academic interests/achievement: biological sciences, business, communication, education, English, general academic interests/achievements, health fields, humanities, international studies, mathematics, physical sciences, premedicine, social sciences. *Special achievements/activities:* community service, general special achievements/activities, leadership. *Special characteristics:* children and siblings of alumni, ethnic background, members of minority groups, siblings of current students.

LOANS *Programs:* FFEL (Subsidized and Unsubsidized Stafford, PLUS), Perkins, Federal Nursing, state, college/university.

WORK-STUDY *Federal work-study:* Total amount: $2,412,992; 850 jobs averaging $1946. *State or other work-study/employment:* Part-time jobs available.

APPLYING FOR FINANCIAL AID *Required financial aid form:* FAFSA.

CONTACT John R. Bowie, Director of Financial Aid, University of New England, 11 Hills Beach Road, Biddeford, ME 04005, 207-602-2342 or toll-free 800-477-4UNE. *Fax:* 207-602-5946. *E-mail:* finaid@une.edu.

UNIVERSITY OF NEW HAMPSHIRE
Durham, NH

Tuition & fees (NH res): $12,743	Average undergraduate aid package: $18,346

ABOUT THE INSTITUTION State-supported, coed. 85 undergraduate majors. Federal methodology is used as a basis for awarding need-based institutional aid.

UNDERGRADUATE EXPENSES for 2009–10 *Tuition, state resident:* full-time $10,080; part-time $420 per credit hour. *Tuition, nonresident:* full-time $24,050; part-time $1002 per credit hour. *Required fees:* full-time $2663; $665.75 per term. Full-time tuition and fees vary according to degree level. Part-time tuition and fees vary according to degree level. *College room and board:* $8874; *Room only:* $5420. Room and board charges vary according to board plan and housing facility. *Payment plan:* Installment.

FRESHMAN FINANCIAL AID (Fall 2008) 2,101 applied for aid; of those 73% were deemed to have need. 99% of freshmen with need received aid; of those 25% had need fully met. *Average percent of need met:* 84% (excluding resources awarded to replace EFC). *Average financial aid package:* $18,633 (excluding resources awarded to replace EFC). 21% of all full-time freshmen had no need and received non-need-based gift aid.

UNDERGRADUATE FINANCIAL AID (Fall 2008) 8,444 applied for aid; of those 79% were deemed to have need. 99% of undergraduates with need received aid; of those 22% had need fully met. *Average percent of need met:* 80% (excluding resources awarded to replace EFC). *Average financial aid package:* $18,346 (excluding resources awarded to replace EFC). 21% of all full-time undergraduates had no need and received non-need-based gift aid.

GIFT AID (NEED-BASED) *Total amount:* $39,314,579 (23% federal, 3% state, 57% institutional, 17% external sources). *Receiving aid:* Freshmen: 39% (978); all full-time undergraduates: 37% (4,140). *Average award:* Freshmen: $4283; Undergraduates: $3223. *Scholarships, grants, and awards:* Federal Pell, FSEOG, state, private, college/university gift aid from institutional funds, Veteran's Education Benefits.

GIFT AID (NON-NEED-BASED) *Total amount:* $14,127,475 (100% institutional). *Receiving aid:* Freshmen: 6% (139). Undergraduates: 4% (427). *Average award:* Freshmen: $7368. Undergraduates: $8640. *Scholarships, grants, and awards by category:* Academic interests/achievement: agriculture, business, education, engineering/technologies, English, general academic interests/achievements, health fields, humanities, mathematics, military science. *Creative arts/performance:* art/fine arts, dance, music, theater/drama. *Special achievements/activities:* community service. *Special characteristics:* children and siblings of alumni, children of faculty/staff, handicapped students, international students, local/state students. *Tuition waivers:* Full or partial for employees or children of employees.

LOANS *Student loans:* $92,868,308 (38% need-based, 62% non-need-based). 74% of past graduating class borrowed through all loan programs. *Average indebtedness per student:* $30,760. *Average need-based loan:* Freshmen: $2658. Undergraduates: $3456. *Parent loans:* $20,365,594 (100% non-need-based). *Programs:* FFEL (Subsidized and Unsubsidized Stafford, PLUS), Perkins, state, college/university.

WORK-STUDY *Federal work-study:* Total amount: $10,269,970; 3,942 jobs averaging $2402. *State or other work-study/employment:* Total amount: $5,902,418 (100% non-need-based). 2,620 part-time jobs averaging $1823.

ATHLETIC AWARDS Total amount: $7,215,246 (100% non-need-based).

APPLYING FOR FINANCIAL AID *Required financial aid form:* FAFSA. *Financial aid deadline (priority):* 3/1. *Notification date:* Continuous beginning 3/1.

CONTACT Susan K. Allen, Director of Financial Aid, University of New Hampshire, 11 Garrison Avenue, Durham, NH 03824, 603-862-3600. *Fax:* 603-862-1947. *E-mail:* financial.aid@unh.edu.

UNIVERSITY OF NEW HAMPSHIRE AT MANCHESTER
Manchester, NH

Tuition & fees (NH res): $11,126 **Average undergraduate aid package: $9982**

ABOUT THE INSTITUTION State-supported, coed. 13 undergraduate majors. Federal methodology is used as a basis for awarding need-based institutional aid.

UNDERGRADUATE EXPENSES for 2009–10 *Tuition, state resident:* full-time $9780; part-time $408 per credit hour. *Tuition, nonresident:* full-time $24,050; part-time $1002 per credit hour. *Required fees:* full-time $1346. Full-time tuition and fees vary according to course load and program. Part-time tuition and fees vary according to course load and program.

FRESHMAN FINANCIAL AID (Fall 2008) 90 applied for aid; of those 63% were deemed to have need. 100% of freshmen with need received aid; of those 12% had need fully met. *Average percent of need met:* 67% (excluding resources awarded to replace EFC). *Average financial aid package:* $8959 (excluding resources awarded to replace EFC).

UNDERGRADUATE FINANCIAL AID (Fall 2008) 523 applied for aid; of those 76% were deemed to have need. 98% of undergraduates with need received aid; of those 14% had need fully met. *Average percent of need met:* 64% (excluding resources awarded to replace EFC). *Average financial aid package:* $9982 (excluding resources awarded to replace EFC). 1% of all full-time undergraduates had no need and received non-need-based gift aid.

GIFT AID (NEED-BASED) *Total amount:* $811,617 (52% federal, 7% state, 26% institutional, 15% external sources). *Receiving aid:* Freshmen: 21% (23); all full-time undergraduates: 14% (107). *Average award:* Freshmen: $1621; Undergraduates: $1458. *Scholarships, grants, and awards:* Federal Pell, FSEOG, state, private, college/university gift aid from institutional funds.

GIFT AID (NON-NEED-BASED) *Total amount:* $45,530 (100% institutional). *Receiving aid:* Undergraduates: 3. *Average award:* Undergraduates: $983. *Scholarships, grants, and awards by category: Academic interests/achievement:* general academic interests/achievements. *Special characteristics:* children of faculty/staff. *Tuition waivers:* Full or partial for employees or children of employees, senior citizens.

LOANS *Student loans:* $4,200,736 (38% need-based, 62% non-need-based). 73% of past graduating class borrowed through all loan programs. *Average indebtedness per student:* $23,786. *Average need-based loan:* Freshmen: $2552. Undergraduates: $3636. *Parent loans:* $148,739 (100% non-need-based). *Programs:* FFEL (Subsidized and Unsubsidized Stafford, PLUS), Perkins, state, college/university.

WORK-STUDY *Federal work-study:* Total amount: $213,775; 100 jobs averaging $2263.

APPLYING FOR FINANCIAL AID *Required financial aid form:* FAFSA. *Financial aid deadline (priority):* 3/1. *Notification date:* Continuous beginning 4/1.

CONTACT Jodi Abad, Assistant Director of Financial Aid, University of New Hampshire at Manchester, French Hall, Manchester, NH 03101-1113, 603-641-4146. *Fax:* 603-641-4125.

UNIVERSITY OF NEW HAVEN
West Haven, CT

Tuition & fees: $29,470 **Average undergraduate aid package: $19,495**

ABOUT THE INSTITUTION Independent, coed. 48 undergraduate majors. Federal methodology is used as a basis for awarding need-based institutional aid.

UNDERGRADUATE EXPENSES for 2009–10 *One-time required fee:* $350. *Comprehensive fee:* $41,674 includes full-time tuition ($28,250), mandatory fees ($1220), and room and board ($12,204). *College room only:* $7600. Full-time tuition and fees vary according to course load. Room and board charges vary according to board plan and housing facility. *Part-time tuition:* $470 per credit hour. *Part-time fees:* $70 per term. Part-time tuition and fees vary according to course load. *Payment plan:* Installment.

FRESHMAN FINANCIAL AID (Fall 2009, est.) 1,145 applied for aid; of those 90% were deemed to have need. 100% of freshmen with need received aid; of those 15% had need fully met. *Average percent of need met:* 68% (excluding resources awarded to replace EFC). *Average financial aid package:* $20,193 (excluding resources awarded to replace EFC). 13% of all full-time freshmen had no need and received non-need-based gift aid.

UNDERGRADUATE FINANCIAL AID (Fall 2009, est.) 3,098 applied for aid; of those 91% were deemed to have need. 100% of undergraduates with need received aid; of those 16% had need fully met. *Average percent of need met:* 65% (excluding resources awarded to replace EFC). *Average financial aid package:* $19,495 (excluding resources awarded to replace EFC). 12% of all full-time undergraduates had no need and received non-need-based gift aid.

GIFT AID (NEED-BASED) *Total amount:* $42,099,094 (11% federal, 6% state, 79% institutional, 4% external sources). *Receiving aid:* Freshmen: 83% (1,035); all full-time undergraduates: 79% (2,800). *Average award:* Freshmen: $17,221; Undergraduates: $15,882. *Scholarships, grants, and awards:* Federal Pell, FSEOG, state, private, college/university gift aid from institutional funds.

GIFT AID (NON-NEED-BASED) *Total amount:* $5,332,283 (100% institutional). *Receiving aid:* Freshmen: 9% (116). Undergraduates: 8% (272). *Average award:* Freshmen: $10,430. Undergraduates: $9607. *Tuition waivers:* Full or partial for employees or children of employees.

LOANS *Student loans:* $34,865,960 (30% need-based, 70% non-need-based). 86% of past graduating class borrowed through all loan programs. *Average indebtedness per student:* $36,272. *Average need-based loan:* Freshmen: $3464. Undergraduates: $4129. *Parent loans:* $9,089,375 (100% non-need-based). *Programs:* FFEL (Subsidized and Unsubsidized Stafford, PLUS), Perkins.

WORK-STUDY *Federal work-study:* Total amount: $215,000; 157 jobs averaging $1290.

ATHLETIC AWARDS Total amount: $2,060,102 (78% need-based, 22% non-need-based).

APPLYING FOR FINANCIAL AID *Required financial aid forms:* FAFSA, federal tax returns. *Financial aid deadline:* 3/1. *Notification date:* Continuous beginning 3/15. Students must reply by 5/1 or within 2 weeks of notification.

CONTACT Mrs. Karen Flynn, Director of Financial Aid, University of New Haven, 300 Boston Post Road, West Haven, CT 06516-1916, 203-932-7315 or toll-free 800-DIAL-UNH. *Fax:* 203-931-6050. *E-mail:* financialaid@newhaven.edu.

UNIVERSITY OF NEW MEXICO
Albuquerque, NM

CONTACT Office of Student Financial Aid, University of New Mexico, Mesa Vista Hall North, Albuquerque, NM 87131, 505-277-2041 or toll-free 800-CALLUNM (in-state). *Fax:* 505-277-6326. *E-mail:* finaid@unm.edu.

UNIVERSITY OF NEW ORLEANS
New Orleans, LA

Tuition & fees (LA res): $4372 **Average undergraduate aid package: $8014**

ABOUT THE INSTITUTION State-supported, coed. 47 undergraduate majors. Federal methodology is used as a basis for awarding need-based institutional aid.

UNDERGRADUATE EXPENSES for 2009–10 *Tuition, state resident:* full-time $3704; part-time $123.47 per credit hour. *Tuition, nonresident:* full-time $11,860; part-time $395.33 per credit hour. *Required fees:* full-time $668. Full-time tuition and fees vary according to course load. Part-time tuition and fees vary according to course load. *College room and board:* $6700. Room and board charges vary according to board plan and housing facility. *Payment plans:* Installment, deferred payment.

FRESHMAN FINANCIAL AID (Fall 2009, est.) 1,110 applied for aid; of those 75% were deemed to have need. 96% of freshmen with need received aid; of those 21% had need fully met. *Average percent of need met:* 68% (excluding resources awarded to replace EFC). *Average financial aid package:* $8799 (excluding resources awarded to replace EFC). 8% of all full-time freshmen had no need and received non-need-based gift aid.

UNDERGRADUATE FINANCIAL AID (Fall 2009, est.) 5,356 applied for aid; of those 83% were deemed to have need. 93% of undergraduates with need received aid; of those 13% had need fully met. *Average percent of need met:* 59% (excluding resources awarded to replace EFC). *Average financial aid package:* $8014 (excluding resources awarded to replace EFC). 4% of all full-time undergraduates had no need and received non-need-based gift aid.

GIFT AID (NEED-BASED) *Total amount:* $18,201,825 (64% federal, 7% state, 29% institutional). *Receiving aid:* Freshmen: 43% (522); all full-time undergraduates: 42% (2,790). *Average award:* Freshmen: $6780; Undergraduates: $5799. *Scholarships, grants, and awards:* Federal Pell, FSEOG, state, private, college/university gift aid from institutional funds.

GIFT AID (NON-NEED-BASED) *Total amount:* $7,825,894 (78% state, 19% institutional, 3% external sources). *Receiving aid:* Freshmen: 40% (484). Undergraduates: 23% (1,508). *Average award:* Freshmen: $1666. Undergraduates: $1626. *Scholarships, grants, and awards by category: Academic interests/achievement:* 2,698 awards ($10,954,246 total): biological sciences, business, education, engineering/technologies, English, foreign languages, general academic interests/achievements, mathematics, physical sciences, social sciences. *Creative arts/performance:* 43 awards ($173,607 total): general creative arts/performance, music, theater/drama. *Special achievements/activities:* 103 awards ($816,169 total): general special achievements/activities, leadership. *Special characteristics:* 1,853 awards ($6,321,546 total): adult students, children and siblings of alumni, children of public servants, children with a deceased or disabled parent, general special characteristics, international students, local/state students, members of minority groups, out-of-state students, public servants. *Tuition waivers:* Full or partial for employees or children of employees, senior citizens.

LOANS *Student loans:* $22,394,204 (46% need-based, 54% non-need-based). 16% of past graduating class borrowed through all loan programs. *Average indebtedness per student:* $13,623. *Average need-based loan:* Freshmen: $3048. Undergraduates: $3925. *Parent loans:* $345,102 (100% non-need-based). *Programs:* Federal Direct (Subsidized and Unsubsidized Stafford, PLUS), FFEL (Subsidized and Unsubsidized Stafford, PLUS), Perkins, college/university.

WORK-STUDY *Federal work-study:* Total amount: $419,676; 151 jobs averaging $2779. *State or other work-study/employment:* Total amount: $709,217 (100% non-need-based). 419 part-time jobs averaging $1693.

ATHLETIC AWARDS Total amount: $1,423,907 (42% need-based, 58% non-need-based).

APPLYING FOR FINANCIAL AID *Required financial aid form:* FAFSA. *Financial aid deadline (priority):* 5/15. *Notification date:* Continuous beginning 4/10. Students must reply within 4 weeks of notification.

CONTACT Ms. Emily London-Jones, Director of Student Financial Aid, University of New Orleans, Administration Building, Room 1005, New Orleans, LA 70148, 504-280-6687 or toll-free 800-256-5866 (out-of-state). *Fax:* 504-280-3973. *E-mail:* elondon@uno.edu.

UNIVERSITY OF NORTH ALABAMA
Florence, AL

Tuition & fees (AL res): $6042	Average undergraduate aid package: $4993

ABOUT THE INSTITUTION State-supported, coed. 38 undergraduate majors. Federal methodology is used as a basis for awarding need-based institutional aid.

UNDERGRADUATE EXPENSES for 2010–11 *Tuition, state resident:* full-time $5010; part-time $167 per credit hour. *Tuition, nonresident:* full-time $10,020; part-time $334 per credit hour. *Required fees:* full-time $1032. Full-time tuition and fees vary according to course load and program. Part-time tuition and fees vary according to course load and program. *College room and board:* $4784. Room and board charges vary according to board plan and housing facility. *Payment plan:* Installment.

FRESHMAN FINANCIAL AID (Fall 2008) 689 applied for aid; of those 76% were deemed to have need. 97% of freshmen with need received aid; of those 48% had need fully met. *Average percent of need met:* 61% (excluding resources awarded to replace EFC). *Average financial aid package:* $4230 (excluding resources awarded to replace EFC). 32% of all full-time freshmen had no need and received non-need-based gift aid.

UNDERGRADUATE FINANCIAL AID (Fall 2008) 3,630 applied for aid; of those 61% were deemed to have need. 98% of undergraduates with need received aid; of those 44% had need fully met. *Average percent of need met:* 65% (excluding resources awarded to replace EFC). *Average financial aid package:* $4993 (excluding resources awarded to replace EFC). 25% of all full-time undergraduates had no need and received non-need-based gift aid.

GIFT AID (NEED-BASED) *Total amount:* $6,343,653 (96% federal, 4% state). *Receiving aid:* Freshmen: 32% (338); all full-time undergraduates: 29% (1,451). *Average award:* Freshmen: $4060; Undergraduates: $3819. *Scholarships, grants, and awards:* Federal Pell, FSEOG, state, private, college/university gift aid from institutional funds, Academic Competitiveness Grants, National SMART Grants.

GIFT AID (NON-NEED-BASED) *Total amount:* $4,471,818 (82% institutional, 18% external sources). *Receiving aid:* Freshmen: 37% (385). Undergraduates: 37% (1,874). *Average award:* Freshmen: $2726. Undergraduates: $2781. *Scholarships, grants, and awards by category: Academic interests/achievement:* general academic interests/achievements. *Creative arts/performance:* art/fine arts, journalism/publications, music. *Special achievements/activities:* cheerleading/drum major, general special achievements/activities, leadership. *Special characteristics:* children of faculty/staff, first-generation college students, general special characteristics, out-of-state students. *Tuition waivers:* Full or partial for employees or children of employees, senior citizens.

LOANS *Student loans:* $18,244,850 (73% need-based, 27% non-need-based). 64% of past graduating class borrowed through all loan programs. *Average indebtedness per student:* $24,500. *Average need-based loan:* Freshmen: $2115. Undergraduates: $2818. *Parent loans:* $507,058 (19% need-based, 81% non-need-based). *Programs:* FFEL (Subsidized and Unsubsidized Stafford, PLUS), Perkins.

WORK-STUDY *Federal work-study:* Total amount: $334,100; 215 jobs averaging $1200. *State or other work-study/employment:* Total amount: $649,827 (100% non-need-based). Part-time jobs available.

ATHLETIC AWARDS Total amount: $1,452,620 (100% non-need-based).

APPLYING FOR FINANCIAL AID *Required financial aid form:* FAFSA. *Financial aid deadline (priority):* 4/1. *Notification date:* 5/31. Students must reply within 2 weeks of notification.

CONTACT Mr. Ben Baker, Director of Student Financial Services, University of North Alabama, UNA Box 5014, Florence, AL 35632-0001, 256-765-4278 or toll-free 800-TALKUNA. *Fax:* 256-765-4920. *E-mail:* bjbaker@una.edu.

THE UNIVERSITY OF NORTH CAROLINA AT ASHEVILLE
Asheville, NC

Tuition & fees (NC res): $4411	Average undergraduate aid package: $10,553

ABOUT THE INSTITUTION State-supported, coed. 32 undergraduate majors. Federal methodology is used as a basis for awarding need-based institutional aid.

UNDERGRADUATE EXPENSES for 2010–11 *Tuition, state resident:* full-time $2389. *Tuition, nonresident:* full-time $14,106. *Required fees:* full-time $2022. Full-time tuition and fees vary according to course load. Part-time tuition and fees vary according to course load. *College room and board:* $6890; *Room only:* $3890. Room and board charges vary according to housing facility. *Payment plan:* Installment.

FRESHMAN FINANCIAL AID (Fall 2009, est.) 531 applied for aid; of those 55% were deemed to have need. 99% of freshmen with need received aid; of those 61% had need fully met. *Average percent of need met:* 88% (excluding resources awarded to replace EFC). *Average financial aid package:* $9967 (excluding resources awarded to replace EFC). 5% of all full-time freshmen had no need and received non-need-based gift aid.

UNDERGRADUATE FINANCIAL AID (Fall 2009, est.) 2,181 applied for aid; of those 66% were deemed to have need. 99% of undergraduates with need received aid; of those 54% had need fully met. *Average percent of need met:* 85% (excluding resources awarded to replace EFC). *Average financial aid*

package: $10,553 (excluding resources awarded to replace EFC). 5% of all full-time undergraduates had no need and received non-need-based gift aid.
GIFT AID (NEED-BASED) *Total amount:* $8,856,188 (46% federal, 39% state, 15% institutional). *Receiving aid:* Freshmen: 44% (278); all full-time undergraduates: 46% (1,375). *Average award:* Freshmen: $6403; Undergraduates: $6052. *Scholarships, grants, and awards:* Federal Pell, FSEOG, state, private, college/university gift aid from institutional funds.
GIFT AID (NON-NEED-BASED) *Total amount:* $1,070,949 (2% federal, 60% state, 38% institutional). *Receiving aid:* Freshmen: 7% (46). Undergraduates: 6% (183). *Average award:* Freshmen: $3616. Undergraduates: $3401. *Scholarships, grants, and awards by category: Academic interests/achievement:* biological sciences, business, communication, computer science, education, engineering/technologies, English, general academic interests/achievements, health fields, mathematics, physical sciences, premedicine, social sciences. *Creative arts/performance:* art/fine arts, general creative arts/performance, music, theater/drama. *Special achievements/activities:* community service, general special achievements/activities, junior miss, leadership. *Special characteristics:* adult students, children and siblings of alumni, children of faculty/staff, ethnic background, first-generation college students, general special characteristics, handicapped students, international students, local/state students, members of minority groups, veterans, veterans' children. *Tuition waivers:* Full or partial for employees or children of employees.
LOANS *Student loans:* $9,196,847 (53% need-based, 47% non-need-based). 50% of past graduating class borrowed through all loan programs. *Average indebtedness per student:* $14,596. *Average need-based loan:* Freshmen: $2890. Undergraduates: $3920. *Parent loans:* $581,941 (17% need-based, 83% non-need-based). *Programs:* Federal Direct (Subsidized and Unsubsidized Stafford, PLUS), Perkins, state, college/university.
WORK-STUDY *Federal work-study:* Total amount: $132,562; 52 jobs averaging $2549.
ATHLETIC AWARDS Total amount: $966,004 (25% need-based, 75% non-need-based).
APPLYING FOR FINANCIAL AID *Required financial aid form:* FAFSA. *Financial aid deadline (priority):* 3/1. *Notification date:* Continuous beginning 3/15. Students must reply within 2 weeks of notification.
CONTACT Ms. Elizabeth D. Bartlett, Associate Director of Financial Aid, The University of North Carolina at Asheville, 1 University Heights, Asheville, NC 28804-8510, 828-232-6535 or toll-free 800-531-9842. *Fax:* 828-251-2294. *E-mail:* bbartlett@unca.edu.

THE UNIVERSITY OF NORTH CAROLINA AT CHAPEL HILL
Chapel Hill, NC

Tuition & fees (NC res): $5626	Average undergraduate aid package: $12,380

ABOUT THE INSTITUTION State-supported, coed. 62 undergraduate majors. Both federal and institutional methodology are used as a basis for awarding need-based institutional aid.
UNDERGRADUATE EXPENSES for 2009–10 *Tuition, state resident:* full-time $3865. *Tuition, nonresident:* full-time $21,753. *Required fees:* full-time $1761. Full-time tuition and fees vary according to program. Part-time tuition and fees vary according to course load and program. *College room and board:* $8670; *Room only:* $5250. Room and board charges vary according to board plan, housing facility, and location. *Payment plans:* Installment, deferred payment.
FRESHMAN FINANCIAL AID (Fall 2008) 2,878 applied for aid; of those 42% were deemed to have need. 99% of freshmen with need received aid; of those 98% had need fully met. *Average percent of need met:* 100% (excluding resources awarded to replace EFC). *Average financial aid package:* $12,755 (excluding resources awarded to replace EFC). 21% of all full-time freshmen had no need and received non-need-based gift aid.
UNDERGRADUATE FINANCIAL AID (Fall 2008) 10,797 applied for aid; of those 51% were deemed to have need. 100% of undergraduates with need received aid; of those 98% had need fully met. *Average percent of need met:* 100% (excluding resources awarded to replace EFC). *Average financial aid package:* $12,380 (excluding resources awarded to replace EFC). 14% of all full-time undergraduates had no need and received non-need-based gift aid.
GIFT AID (NEED-BASED) *Total amount:* $55,239,213 (19% federal, 24% state, 49% institutional, 8% external sources). *Receiving aid:* Freshmen: 31% (1,197); all full-time undergraduates: 32% (5,414). *Average award:* Freshmen: $10,996;

Undergraduates: $9980. *Scholarships, grants, and awards:* Federal Pell, FSEOG, state, private, college/university gift aid from institutional funds.
GIFT AID (NON-NEED-BASED) *Total amount:* $15,807,969 (7% federal, 10% state, 34% institutional, 49% external sources). *Receiving aid:* Freshmen: 16% (611). Undergraduates: 10% (1,679). *Average award:* Freshmen: $4646. Undergraduates: $5219. *Scholarships, grants, and awards by category: Academic interests/achievement:* business, communication, education, English, general academic interests/achievements, health fields, mathematics. *Creative arts/performance:* applied art and design, art/fine arts, journalism/publications, music, theater/drama. *Special achievements/activities:* community service, general special achievements/activities, leadership. *Special characteristics:* children of faculty/staff, international students, out-of-state students, relatives of clergy, religious affiliation. *Tuition waivers:* Full or partial for employees or children of employees, senior citizens.
LOANS *Student loans:* $29,214,395 (62% need-based, 38% non-need-based). *Average need-based loan:* Freshmen: $3065. Undergraduates: $3849. *Parent loans:* $7,319,216 (32% need-based, 68% non-need-based). *Programs:* FFEL (Subsidized and Unsubsidized Stafford, PLUS), Perkins, state, college/university, alternative loans.
WORK-STUDY *Federal work-study:* Total amount: $2,000,941; 1,342 jobs averaging $1860.
ATHLETIC AWARDS Total amount: $6,367,585 (29% need-based, 71% non-need-based).
APPLYING FOR FINANCIAL AID *Required financial aid forms:* FAFSA, CSS Financial Aid PROFILE. *Financial aid deadline (priority):* 3/1. *Notification date:* Continuous beginning 3/15. Students must reply by 5/1.
CONTACT Ms. Shirley A. Ort, Associate Provost and Director, Office of Scholarships and Student Aid, The University of North Carolina at Chapel Hill, CB # 2300, Chapel Hill, NC 27514, 919-962-2315. *Fax:* 919-962-2716. *E-mail:* aidinfo@unc.edu.

THE UNIVERSITY OF NORTH CAROLINA AT CHARLOTTE
Charlotte, NC

Tuition & fees (NC res): $4427	Average undergraduate aid package: $8642

ABOUT THE INSTITUTION State-supported, coed. 70 undergraduate majors. Federal methodology is used as a basis for awarding need-based institutional aid.
UNDERGRADUATE EXPENSES for 2009–10 *Tuition, state resident:* full-time $2516. *Tuition, nonresident:* full-time $13,128. *Required fees:* full-time $1911. Full-time tuition and fees vary according to course load. Part-time tuition and fees vary according to course load. *College room and board:* $6796; *Room only:* $3466. Room and board charges vary according to board plan and housing facility. *Payment plan:* Installment.
FRESHMAN FINANCIAL AID (Fall 2009, est.) 2,469 applied for aid; of those 68% were deemed to have need. 98% of freshmen with need received aid; of those 28% had need fully met. *Average percent of need met:* 75% (excluding resources awarded to replace EFC). *Average financial aid package:* $8765 (excluding resources awarded to replace EFC). 1% of all full-time freshmen had no need and received non-need-based gift aid.
UNDERGRADUATE FINANCIAL AID (Fall 2009, est.) 11,270 applied for aid; of those 77% were deemed to have need. 98% of undergraduates with need received aid; of those 23% had need fully met. *Average percent of need met:* 74% (excluding resources awarded to replace EFC). *Average financial aid package:* $8642 (excluding resources awarded to replace EFC). 1% of all full-time undergraduates had no need and received non-need-based gift aid.
GIFT AID (NEED-BASED) *Total amount:* $53,645,526 (52% federal, 38% state, 10% institutional). *Receiving aid:* Freshmen: 51% (1,549); all full-time undergraduates: 48% (7,444). *Average award:* Freshmen: $6673; Undergraduates: $6096. *Scholarships, grants, and awards:* Federal Pell, FSEOG, state, private, college/university gift aid from institutional funds.
GIFT AID (NON-NEED-BASED) *Total amount:* $2,789,452 (15% state, 20% institutional, 65% external sources). *Receiving aid:* Freshmen: 2% (54). Undergraduates: 3% (540). *Average award:* Freshmen: $2124. Undergraduates: $2427. *Scholarships, grants, and awards by category: Academic interests/achievement:* architecture, business, computer science, education, engineering/technologies, general academic interests/achievements, health fields, humanities,

The University of North Carolina at Charlotte

mathematics, military science. *Creative arts/performance:* music, performing arts. *Special characteristics:* adult students. *Tuition waivers:* Full or partial for employees or children of employees.

LOANS *Student loans:* $80,035,562 (77% need-based, 23% non-need-based). 48% of past graduating class borrowed through all loan programs. *Average indebtedness per student:* $17,964. *Average need-based loan:* Freshmen: $2964. Undergraduates: $3724. *Parent loans:* $5,197,457 (52% need-based, 48% non-need-based). *Programs:* FFEL (Subsidized and Unsubsidized Stafford, PLUS), Perkins, state, college/university.

WORK-STUDY *Federal work-study:* Total amount: $891,649; 534 jobs averaging $1670. *State or other work-study/employment:* Total amount: $4,127,677 (60% need-based, 40% non-need-based). 1,993 part-time jobs averaging $2071.

ATHLETIC AWARDS Total amount: $2,089,255 (35% need-based, 65% non-need-based).

APPLYING FOR FINANCIAL AID *Required financial aid form:* FAFSA. *Financial aid deadline (priority):* 4/1. *Notification date:* 3/31. Students must reply within 3 weeks of notification.

CONTACT Anthony D. Carter, Director of Financial Aid, The University of North Carolina at Charlotte, 9201 University City Boulevard, Charlotte, NC 28223-0001, 704-687-2426. *Fax:* 704-687-3132. *E-mail:* acarte1@uncc.edu.

THE UNIVERSITY OF NORTH CAROLINA AT GREENSBORO
Greensboro, NC

Tuition & fees (NC res): $4234   **Average undergraduate aid package:** $9204

ABOUT THE INSTITUTION State-supported, coed. 71 undergraduate majors. Federal methodology is used as a basis for awarding need-based institutional aid.

UNDERGRADUATE EXPENSES for 2009–10 *Tuition, state resident:* full-time $2590; part-time $324 per course. *Tuition, nonresident:* full-time $14,351; part-time $1794 per course. *Required fees:* full-time $1644; $59.09 per credit hour. Part-time tuition and fees vary according to course load. *College room and board:* $6506; *Room only:* $3706. Room and board charges vary according to board plan and housing facility. *Payment plan:* Installment.

FRESHMAN FINANCIAL AID (Fall 2009, est.) 2,144 applied for aid; of those 90% were deemed to have need. 100% of freshmen with need received aid; of those 33% had need fully met. *Average percent of need met:* 62% (excluding resources awarded to replace EFC). *Average financial aid package:* $9173 (excluding resources awarded to replace EFC). 4% of all full-time freshmen had no need and received non-need-based gift aid.

UNDERGRADUATE FINANCIAL AID (Fall 2009, est.) 9,769 applied for aid; of those 97% were deemed to have need. 100% of undergraduates with need received aid; of those 29% had need fully met. *Average percent of need met:* 59% (excluding resources awarded to replace EFC). *Average financial aid package:* $9204 (excluding resources awarded to replace EFC). 4% of all full-time undergraduates had no need and received non-need-based gift aid.

GIFT AID (NEED-BASED) *Total amount:* $33,642,275 (76% federal, 9% state, 15% institutional). *Receiving aid:* Freshmen: 40% (995); all full-time undergraduates: 40% (5,071). *Average award:* Freshmen: $7805; Undergraduates: $6332. *Scholarships, grants, and awards:* Federal Pell, FSEOG, state, private, college/university gift aid from institutional funds.

GIFT AID (NON-NEED-BASED) *Total amount:* $18,811,869 (80% state, 19% institutional, 1% external sources). *Receiving aid:* Freshmen: 56% (1,407). Undergraduates: 52% (6,595). *Average award:* Freshmen: $1941. Undergraduates: $2348. *Scholarships, grants, and awards by category: Academic interests/achievement:* biological sciences, business, communication, education, English, foreign languages, general academic interests/achievements, health fields, home economics, humanities, library science, mathematics, physical sciences, premedicine, religion/biblical studies, social sciences. *Creative arts/performance:* art/fine arts, cinema/film/broadcasting, dance, music, performing arts, theater/drama. *Special achievements/activities:* community service, general special achievements/activities, junior miss, leadership, religious involvement. *Special characteristics:* adult students, children of faculty/staff, ethnic background, general special characteristics, handicapped students, international students, members of minority groups, out-of-state students, religious affiliation, veterans, veterans' children. *Tuition waivers:* Full or partial for employees or children of employees.

LOANS *Student loans:* $57,204,119 (41% need-based, 59% non-need-based). 67% of past graduating class borrowed through all loan programs. *Average indebtedness per student:* $18,604. *Average need-based loan:* Freshmen: $2625. Undergraduates: $4010. *Parent loans:* $9,052,642 (100% non-need-based). *Programs:* Federal Direct (Subsidized and Unsubsidized Stafford, PLUS), FFEL (Subsidized and Unsubsidized Stafford, PLUS), Perkins, college/university.

WORK-STUDY *Federal work-study:* Total amount: $770,646; 400 jobs averaging $1927.

ATHLETIC AWARDS Total amount: $1,726,029 (100% non-need-based).

APPLYING FOR FINANCIAL AID *Required financial aid form:* FAFSA. *Financial aid deadline (priority):* 3/1. *Notification date:* Continuous beginning 3/15. Students must reply within 3 weeks of notification.

CONTACT Mr. Bruce Cabiness, Associate Director of Financial Aid, The University of North Carolina at Greensboro, PO Box 26170, Greensboro, NC 27402-6170, 336-334-5702. *Fax:* 336-334-3010. *E-mail:* bruce_cabiness@uncg.edu.

THE UNIVERSITY OF NORTH CAROLINA AT PEMBROKE
Pembroke, NC

Tuition & fees (NC res): $3890   **Average undergraduate aid package:** $9268

ABOUT THE INSTITUTION State-supported, coed. 52 undergraduate majors. Federal methodology is used as a basis for awarding need-based institutional aid.

UNDERGRADUATE EXPENSES for 2010–11 *Tuition, state resident:* full-time $2173; part-time $145.86 per credit hour. *Tuition, nonresident:* full-time $11,380; part-time $146.91 per credit hour. *Required fees:* full-time $1717; $56.61 per unit or $56.61 per unit. *College room and board:* $5990; *Room only:* $5040. Room and board charges vary according to board plan and housing facility. *Payment plan:* Installment.

FRESHMAN FINANCIAL AID (Fall 2009, est.) 1,004 applied for aid; of those 82% were deemed to have need. 99% of freshmen with need received aid; of those 21% had need fully met. *Average percent of need met:* 82% (excluding resources awarded to replace EFC). *Average financial aid package:* $9666 (excluding resources awarded to replace EFC). 1% of all full-time freshmen had no need and received non-need-based gift aid.

UNDERGRADUATE FINANCIAL AID (Fall 2009, est.) 4,067 applied for aid; of those 86% were deemed to have need. 98% of undergraduates with need received aid; of those 19% had need fully met. *Average percent of need met:* 77% (excluding resources awarded to replace EFC). *Average financial aid package:* $9268 (excluding resources awarded to replace EFC). 1% of all full-time undergraduates had no need and received non-need-based gift aid.

GIFT AID (NEED-BASED) *Total amount:* $22,834,856 (57% federal, 39% state, 4% institutional). *Receiving aid:* Freshmen: 71% (783); all full-time undergraduates: 69% (3,240). *Average award:* Freshmen: $7719; Undergraduates: $6566. *Scholarships, grants, and awards:* Federal Pell, FSEOG, state, private, college/university gift aid from institutional funds.

GIFT AID (NON-NEED-BASED) *Total amount:* $311,287 (95% federal, 1% state, 3% institutional, 1% external sources). *Receiving aid:* Freshmen: 6% (70). Undergraduates: 4% (187). *Average award:* Freshmen: $2000. Undergraduates: $1050. *Scholarships, grants, and awards by category: Academic interests/achievement:* 12 awards ($9700 total): business, communication, education, English, general academic interests/achievements, health fields, physical sciences. *Creative arts/performance:* journalism/publications, music. *Special characteristics:* 1 award ($6250 total): children and siblings of alumni, general special characteristics. *Tuition waivers:* Full or partial for employees or children of employees.

LOANS *Student loans:* $20,225,113 (85% need-based, 15% non-need-based). *Average need-based loan:* Freshmen: $2802. Undergraduates: $3647. *Parent loans:* $1,139,897 (57% need-based, 43% non-need-based). *Programs:* FFEL (Subsidized and Unsubsidized Stafford, PLUS), Perkins, college/university.

WORK-STUDY *Federal work-study:* Total amount: $444,568; 310 jobs averaging $1434. *State or other work-study/employment:* Total amount: $2000 (100% non-need-based). 1 part-time job averaging $2000.

ATHLETIC AWARDS Total amount: $1,336,656 (100% need-based).

APPLYING FOR FINANCIAL AID *Required financial aid form:* FAFSA. *Financial aid deadline:* Continuous. *Notification date:* 4/15.

CONTACT Mildred Weber, Associate Director of Financial Aid, The University of North Carolina at Pembroke, PO Box 1510, Pembroke, NC 28372, 910-521-6612 or toll-free 800-949-UNCP. *Fax:* 910-775-4159. *E-mail:* mildred.weber@uncp.edu.

UNIVERSITY OF NORTH CAROLINA SCHOOL OF THE ARTS
Winston-Salem, NC

Tuition & fees (NC res): $5299   **Average undergraduate aid package: $15,304**

ABOUT THE INSTITUTION State-supported, coed. 8 undergraduate majors. Federal methodology is used as a basis for awarding need-based institutional aid.

UNDERGRADUATE EXPENSES for 2009–10 *Tuition, state resident:* full-time $3357; part-time $385 per credit hour. *Tuition, nonresident:* full-time $15,303. *Required fees:* full-time $1942. Full-time tuition and fees vary according to program. Part-time tuition and fees vary according to course load. *College room and board:* $7256; *Room only:* $3625. Room and board charges vary according to board plan and housing facility. *Payment plan:* Installment.

UNDERGRADUATE FINANCIAL AID (Fall 2008) 520 applied for aid; of those 77% were deemed to have need. 100% of undergraduates with need received aid; of those 14% had need fully met. *Average percent of need met:* 90% (excluding resources awarded to replace EFC). *Average financial aid package:* $15,304 (excluding resources awarded to replace EFC). 17% of all full-time undergraduates had no need and received non-need-based gift aid.

GIFT AID (NEED-BASED) *Total amount:* $2,810,846 (26% federal, 38% state, 31% institutional, 5% external sources). *Receiving aid:* All full-time undergraduates: 51% (389). *Average award:* Undergraduates: $7333. *Scholarships, grants, and awards:* Federal Pell, FSEOG, state, private, college/university gift aid from institutional funds.

GIFT AID (NON-NEED-BASED) *Total amount:* $473,644 (8% state, 75% institutional, 17% external sources). *Receiving aid:* Undergraduates: 3% (26). *Average award:* Undergraduates: $3527. *Scholarships, grants, and awards by category:* Creative arts/performance: applied art and design, cinema/film/broadcasting, dance, music, performing arts, theater/drama.

LOANS *Student loans:* $3,140,806 (63% need-based, 37% non-need-based). 69% of past graduating class borrowed through all loan programs. *Average indebtedness per student:* $26,616. *Average need-based loan:* Undergraduates: $4016. *Parent loans:* $1,785,911 (64% need-based, 36% non-need-based). *Programs:* Federal Direct (Subsidized and Unsubsidized Stafford, PLUS), FFEL (Subsidized and Unsubsidized Stafford, PLUS), Perkins.

WORK-STUDY *Federal work-study:* Total amount: $44,308; 92 jobs averaging $482.

APPLYING FOR FINANCIAL AID *Required financial aid form:* FAFSA. *Financial aid deadline (priority):* 3/1. *Notification date:* Continuous beginning 4/10. Students must reply within 2 weeks of notification.

CONTACT Jane C. Kamiab, Director of Financial Aid, University of North Carolina School of the Arts, 1533 South Main Street, Winston-Salem, NC 27127, 336-770-3297. *Fax:* 336-770-1489.

THE UNIVERSITY OF NORTH CAROLINA WILMINGTON
Wilmington, NC

Tuition & fees (NC res): $4873   **Average undergraduate aid package: $9078**

ABOUT THE INSTITUTION State-supported, coed. 59 undergraduate majors. Federal methodology is used as a basis for awarding need-based institutional aid.

UNDERGRADUATE EXPENSES for 2010–11 *Tuition, state resident:* full-time $2565. *Tuition, nonresident:* full-time $13,447. *Required fees:* full-time $2308. Full-time tuition and fees vary according to course load. Part-time tuition and fees vary according to course load. *College room and board:* $7798; *Room only:* $4648. Room and board charges vary according to board plan and housing facility. *Payment plan:* Installment.

FRESHMAN FINANCIAL AID (Fall 2008) 1,476 applied for aid; of those 57% were deemed to have need. 99% of freshmen with need received aid; of those 46% had need fully met. *Average percent of need met:* 85% (excluding

resources awarded to replace EFC). *Average financial aid package:* $9038 (excluding resources awarded to replace EFC). 2% of all full-time freshmen had no need and received non-need-based gift aid.

UNDERGRADUATE FINANCIAL AID (Fall 2008) 6,690 applied for aid; of those 69% were deemed to have need. 99% of undergraduates with need received aid; of those 41% had need fully met. *Average percent of need met:* 83% (excluding resources awarded to replace EFC). *Average financial aid package:* $9078 (excluding resources awarded to replace EFC). 3% of all full-time undergraduates had no need and received non-need-based gift aid.

GIFT AID (NEED-BASED) *Total amount:* $27,144,187 (42% federal, 38% state, 17% institutional, 3% external sources). *Receiving aid:* Freshmen: 38% (734); all full-time undergraduates: 39% (3,922). *Average award:* Freshmen: $6708; Undergraduates: $6030. *Scholarships, grants, and awards:* Federal Pell, FSEOG, state, private, college/university gift aid from institutional funds.

GIFT AID (NON-NEED-BASED) *Total amount:* $3,621,940 (20% state, 22% institutional, 58% external sources). *Receiving aid:* Freshmen: 19% (368). Undergraduates: 16% (1,663). *Average award:* Freshmen: $3168. Undergraduates: $2272. *Scholarships, grants, and awards by category:* Academic interests/achievement: 729 awards ($1,350,000 total): biological sciences, business, communication, computer science, education, engineering/technologies, English, foreign languages, general academic interests/achievements, health fields, humanities, international studies, mathematics, physical sciences, premedicine, social sciences. Creative arts/performance: 34 awards ($55,957 total): art/fine arts, cinema/film/broadcasting, creative writing, music, theater/drama. Special achievements/activities: 64 awards ($15,210 total): cheerleading/drum major, general special achievements/activities, leadership. Special characteristics: 4 awards ($7850 total): children of faculty/staff, children of union members/company employees, local/state students, married students, previous college experience. *Tuition waivers:* Full or partial for employees or children of employees.

LOANS *Student loans:* $55,530,982 (39% need-based, 61% non-need-based). 54% of past graduating class borrowed through all loan programs. *Average indebtedness per student:* $16,115. *Average need-based loan:* Freshmen: $2688. Undergraduates: $3547. *Parent loans:* $8,242,291 (100% non-need-based). *Programs:* Federal Direct (Subsidized and Unsubsidized Stafford, PLUS), FFEL (Subsidized and Unsubsidized Stafford, PLUS), Perkins, state, college/university.

WORK-STUDY *Federal work-study:* Total amount: $450,000; 243 jobs averaging $1481.

ATHLETIC AWARDS Total amount: $1,621,361 (24% need-based, 76% non-need-based).

APPLYING FOR FINANCIAL AID *Required financial aid form:* FAFSA. *Financial aid deadline (priority):* 4/1. *Notification date:* Continuous beginning 4/1. Students must reply within 3 weeks of notification.

CONTACT Emily Bliss, Director of Financial Aid and Veterans' Services Office, The University of North Carolina Wilmington, 601 South College Road, Wilmington, NC 28403-5951, 910-962-3177 or toll-free 800-228-5571 (out-of-state). *Fax:* 910-962-3851. *E-mail:* finaid@uncw.edu.

UNIVERSITY OF NORTH DAKOTA
Grand Forks, ND

Tuition & fees (ND res): $6727   **Average undergraduate aid package: $5723**

ABOUT THE INSTITUTION State-supported, coed. 85 undergraduate majors. Federal methodology is used as a basis for awarding need-based institutional aid.

UNDERGRADUATE EXPENSES for 2009–10 *Tuition, state resident:* full-time $5461; part-time $227 per credit hour. *Tuition, nonresident:* full-time $14,580; part-time $607 per credit hour. *Required fees:* full-time $1266. Full-time tuition and fees vary according to degree level, program, and reciprocity agreements. Part-time tuition and fees vary according to course load, degree level, program, and reciprocity agreements. *College room and board:* $5702; *Room only:* $2289. Room and board charges vary according to board plan and housing facility. *Payment plan:* Deferred payment.

FRESHMAN FINANCIAL AID (Fall 2009, est.) 1,721 applied for aid; of those 100% were deemed to have need. 98% of freshmen with need received aid; of those 43% had need fully met. *Average percent of need met:* 57% (excluding resources awarded to replace EFC). *Average financial aid package:* $4932 (excluding resources awarded to replace EFC). 42% of all full-time freshmen had no need and received non-need-based gift aid.

UNDERGRADUATE FINANCIAL AID (Fall 2009, est.) 6,900 applied for aid; of those 100% were deemed to have need. 93% of undergraduates with need

received aid; of those 30% had need fully met. *Average percent of need met:* 39% (excluding resources awarded to replace EFC). *Average financial aid package:* $5723 (excluding resources awarded to replace EFC). 29% of all full-time undergraduates had no need and received non-need-based gift aid.

GIFT AID (NEED-BASED) *Total amount:* $10,180,896 (64% federal, 7% state, 15% institutional, 14% external sources). *Receiving aid:* Freshmen: 48% (951); all full-time undergraduates: 38% (3,321). *Average award:* Freshmen: $2613; Undergraduates: $2892. *Scholarships, grants, and awards:* Federal Pell, FSEOG, state, private, college/university gift aid from institutional funds, Federal Nursing.

GIFT AID (NON-NEED-BASED) *Total amount:* $3,233,196 (2% federal, 9% state, 59% institutional, 30% external sources). *Receiving aid:* Freshmen: 8% (161). Undergraduates: 8% (681). *Average award:* Freshmen: $1392. Undergraduates: $1469. *Scholarships, grants, and awards by category: Academic interests/achievement:* biological sciences, business, communication, computer science, education, engineering/technologies, English, foreign languages, general academic interests/achievements, health fields, humanities, international studies, mathematics, military science, physical sciences, premedicine, social sciences. *Creative arts/performance:* art/fine arts, debating, music, theater/drama. *Special achievements/activities:* general special achievements/activities, leadership, memberships. *Special characteristics:* children of faculty/staff, ethnic background, general special characteristics, handicapped students, international students, members of minority groups, veterans' children. *Tuition waivers:* Full or partial for minority students, employees or children of employees, adult students, senior citizens.

LOANS *Student loans:* $56,974,584 (54% need-based, 46% non-need-based). 66% of past graduating class borrowed through all loan programs. *Average indebtedness per student:* $22,137. *Average need-based loan:* Freshmen: $3216. Undergraduates: $4130. *Parent loans:* $2,565,657 (23% need-based, 77% non-need-based). *Programs:* FFEL (Subsidized and Unsubsidized Stafford, PLUS), Perkins, Federal Nursing, alternative commercial loans.

WORK-STUDY *Federal work-study:* Total amount: $3,599,236; 1,972 jobs available.

ATHLETIC AWARDS Total amount: $2,462,654 (15% need-based, 85% non-need-based).

APPLYING FOR FINANCIAL AID *Required financial aid form:* FAFSA. *Financial aid deadline (priority):* 3/15. *Notification date:* Continuous beginning 5/15. Students must reply within 4 weeks of notification.

CONTACT Ms. Robin Holden, Director of Student Financial Aid Office, University of North Dakota, 264 Centennial Drive Stop 8371, Grand Forks, ND 58202, 701-777-3121 or toll-free 800-CALLUND. *Fax:* 701-777-2040. *E-mail:* robinholden@mail.und.nodak.edu.

UNIVERSITY OF NORTHERN COLORADO
Greeley, CO

Tuition & fees (CO res): $5116	Average undergraduate aid package: $14,315

ABOUT THE INSTITUTION State-supported, coed. 43 undergraduate majors. Federal methodology is used as a basis for awarding need-based institutional aid.

UNDERGRADUATE EXPENSES for 2009–10 *Tuition, state resident:* full-time $4296; part-time $179 per credit hour. *Tuition, nonresident:* full-time $14,544; part-time $606 per credit hour. *Required fees:* full-time $820; $41 per credit hour. Full-time tuition and fees vary according to program. Part-time tuition and fees vary according to program. *College room and board:* $8370; *Room only:* $3950. Room and board charges vary according to board plan, housing facility, and student level. *Payment plan:* Deferred payment.

FRESHMAN FINANCIAL AID (Fall 2008) 1,810 applied for aid; of those 53% were deemed to have need. 95% of freshmen with need received aid; of those 62% had need fully met. *Average percent of need met:* 100% (excluding resources awarded to replace EFC). *Average financial aid package:* $14,785 (excluding resources awarded to replace EFC). 27% of all full-time freshmen had no need and received non-need-based gift aid.

UNDERGRADUATE FINANCIAL AID (Fall 2008) 6,850 applied for aid; of those 59% were deemed to have need. 98% of undergraduates with need received aid; of those 58% had need fully met. *Average percent of need met:* 100% (excluding resources awarded to replace EFC). *Average financial aid package:* $14,315 (excluding resources awarded to replace EFC). 15% of all full-time undergraduates had no need and received non-need-based gift aid.

GIFT AID (NEED-BASED) *Total amount:* $16,678,480 (46% federal, 43% state, 8% institutional, 3% external sources). *Receiving aid:* Freshmen: 36% (739);

all full-time undergraduates: 36% (3,150). *Average award:* Freshmen: $5230; Undergraduates: $4745. *Scholarships, grants, and awards:* Federal Pell, FSEOG, state, private, college/university gift aid from institutional funds.

GIFT AID (NON-NEED-BASED) *Total amount:* $10,782,828 (5% federal, 3% state, 58% institutional, 34% external sources). *Receiving aid:* Freshmen: 28% (587). Undergraduates: 19% (1,648). *Average award:* Freshmen: $2520. Undergraduates: $3178. *Scholarships, grants, and awards by category: Academic interests/achievement:* biological sciences, business, communication, education, English, general academic interests/achievements, health fields, home economics, mathematics, military science, physical sciences, social sciences. *Creative arts/performance:* dance, music, performing arts, theater/drama. *Special characteristics:* adult students, children and siblings of alumni, children of faculty/staff, children of union members/company employees, ethnic background, general special characteristics, handicapped students, international students, local/state students, members of minority groups, out-of-state students, veterans.

LOANS *Student loans:* $37,413,568 (41% need-based, 59% non-need-based). *Average need-based loan:* Freshmen: $3547. Undergraduates: $4519. *Parent loans:* $16,821,367 (100% non-need-based). *Programs:* FFEL (Subsidized and Unsubsidized Stafford, PLUS), Perkins, college/university.

WORK-STUDY *Federal work-study:* Total amount: $530,520; jobs available. *State or other work-study/employment:* Total amount: $2,698,979 (50% need-based, 50% non-need-based). Part-time jobs available.

ATHLETIC AWARDS Total amount: $2,637,642 (100% non-need-based).

APPLYING FOR FINANCIAL AID *Required financial aid form:* FAFSA. *Financial aid deadline (priority):* 3/1. *Notification date:* Continuous beginning 4/15. Students must reply within 4 weeks of notification.

CONTACT Marty Somero, Director of Student Financial Aid, University of Northern Colorado, Carter Hall 1005, Campus Box 33, Greeley, CO 80639, 970-351-2502 or toll-free 888-700-4UNC (in-state). *Fax:* 970-351-3737. *E-mail:* ofa@unco.edu.

UNIVERSITY OF NORTHERN IOWA
Cedar Falls, IA

Tuition & fees (IA res): $7008	Average undergraduate aid package: $8243

ABOUT THE INSTITUTION State-supported, coed. 104 undergraduate majors. Federal methodology is used as a basis for awarding need-based institutional aid.

UNDERGRADUATE EXPENSES for 2010–11 *Tuition, state resident:* full-time $6102; part-time $254.25 per hour. *Tuition, nonresident:* full-time $14,442; part-time $395.55 per hour. *Required fees:* full-time $906. Full-time tuition and fees vary according to course load and program. Part-time tuition and fees vary according to course load and program. *College room and board:* $7189; *Room only:* $3435. Room and board charges vary according to board plan and housing facility. *Payment plan:* Installment.

FRESHMAN FINANCIAL AID (Fall 2009, est.) 1,686 applied for aid; of those 68% were deemed to have need. 96% of freshmen with need received aid; of those 27% had need fully met. *Average percent of need met:* 72% (excluding resources awarded to replace EFC). *Average financial aid package:* $7911 (excluding resources awarded to replace EFC). 24% of all full-time freshmen had no need and received non-need-based gift aid.

UNDERGRADUATE FINANCIAL AID (Fall 2009, est.) 8,297 applied for aid; of those 74% were deemed to have need. 95% of undergraduates with need received aid; of those 20% had need fully met. *Average percent of need met:* 65% (excluding resources awarded to replace EFC). *Average financial aid package:* $8243 (excluding resources awarded to replace EFC). 14% of all full-time undergraduates had no need and received non-need-based gift aid.

GIFT AID (NEED-BASED) *Total amount:* $17,166,172 (79% federal, 9% state, 12% institutional). *Receiving aid:* Freshmen: 29% (561); all full-time undergraduates: 32% (3,259). *Average award:* Freshmen: $4438; Undergraduates: $4691. *Scholarships, grants, and awards:* Federal Pell, FSEOG, state, private, college/university gift aid from institutional funds.

GIFT AID (NON-NEED-BASED) *Total amount:* $10,882,980 (4% state, 69% institutional, 27% external sources). *Receiving aid:* Freshmen: 40% (767). Undergraduates: 23% (2,318). *Average award:* Freshmen: $2587. Undergraduates: $2959. *Scholarships, grants, and awards by category: Academic interests/achievement:* biological sciences, business, education, general academic interests/achievements, mathematics, physical sciences, social sciences. *Creative arts/*

performance: applied art and design, art/fine arts, music, theater/drama. *Special achievements/activities:* leadership. *Special characteristics:* general special characteristics, members of minority groups.

LOANS *Student loans:* $48,150,189 (46% need-based, 54% non-need-based). 80% of past graduating class borrowed through all loan programs. *Average indebtedness per student:* $24,123. *Average need-based loan:* Freshmen: $3233. Undergraduates: $4261. *Parent loans:* $13,253,528 (100% non-need-based). *Programs:* Federal Direct (Subsidized and Unsubsidized Stafford, PLUS), Perkins, state, private alternative loans.

WORK-STUDY *Federal work-study:* Total amount: $1,109,147; 462 jobs averaging $1700. *State or other work-study/employment:* Total amount: $237,882 (80% need-based, 20% non-need-based). 107 part-time jobs averaging $1820.

ATHLETIC AWARDS Total amount: $3,189,748 (100% non-need-based).

APPLYING FOR FINANCIAL AID *Required financial aid form:* FAFSA. *Financial aid deadline:* Continuous. *Notification date:* Continuous beginning 3/1.

CONTACT Heather Soesbe, Associate Director, Office of Student Financial Aid, University of Northern Iowa, 105 Gilchrist Hall, Cedar Falls, IA 50614-0024, 319-273-2700 or toll-free 800-772-2037. *Fax:* 319-273-6950. *E-mail:* heather. soesbe@uni.edu.

UNIVERSITY OF NORTH FLORIDA
Jacksonville, FL

Tuition & fees (FL res): $4193	Average undergraduate aid package: $1822

ABOUT THE INSTITUTION State-supported, coed. 56 undergraduate majors. Federal methodology is used as a basis for awarding need-based institutional aid.

UNDERGRADUATE EXPENSES for 2009–10 *Tuition, state resident:* full-time $4193; part-time $139.78 per credit hour. *Tuition, nonresident:* full-time $17,582; part-time $586.06 per credit hour. *College room and board:* $9982; *Room only:* $6885. Room and board charges vary according to board plan and housing facility. *Payment plan:* Installment.

FRESHMAN FINANCIAL AID (Fall 2009, est.) 1,415 applied for aid; of those 65% were deemed to have need. 99% of freshmen with need received aid; of those 15% had need fully met. *Average percent of need met:* 91% (excluding resources awarded to replace EFC). *Average financial aid package:* $1635 (excluding resources awarded to replace EFC). 7% of all full-time freshmen had no need and received non-need-based gift aid.

UNDERGRADUATE FINANCIAL AID (Fall 2009, est.) 6,250 applied for aid; of those 77% were deemed to have need. 97% of undergraduates with need received aid; of those 9% had need fully met. *Average percent of need met:* 90% (excluding resources awarded to replace EFC). *Average financial aid package:* $1822 (excluding resources awarded to replace EFC). 13% of all full-time undergraduates had no need and received non-need-based gift aid.

GIFT AID (NEED-BASED) *Total amount:* $31,200,615 (55% federal, 31% state, 12% institutional, 2% external sources). *Receiving aid:* Freshmen: 33% (635); all full-time undergraduates: 29% (3,016). *Average award:* Freshmen: $1080; Undergraduates: $1500. *Scholarships, grants, and awards:* Federal Pell, FSEOG, state, private, college/university gift aid from institutional funds, 2+2 Scholarships (jointly sponsored with Florida Community College at Jacksonville).

GIFT AID (NON-NEED-BASED) *Total amount:* $12,201,584 (79% state, 19% institutional, 2% external sources). *Receiving aid:* Freshmen: 41% (785). Undergraduates: 24% (2,518). *Average award:* Freshmen: $1127. Undergraduates: $1210. *Scholarships, grants, and awards by category: Academic interests/ achievement:* 899 awards ($2,638,668 total): business, computer science, education, engineering/technologies, general academic interests/achievements, health fields, international studies. *Creative arts/performance:* 49 awards ($82,700 total): art/fine arts, music. *Special achievements/activities:* 99 awards ($101,299 total): community service, general special achievements/activities, leadership. *Special characteristics:* 21 awards ($48,029 total): first-generation college students, general special characteristics, international students, members of minority groups, out-of-state students. *Tuition waivers:* Full or partial for employees or children of employees, senior citizens.

LOANS *Student loans:* $35,739,351 (83% need-based, 17% non-need-based). 41% of past graduating class borrowed through all loan programs. *Average indebtedness per student:* $15,619. *Average need-based loan:* Freshmen: $1609. Undergraduates: $1793. *Parent loans:* $1,039,146 (57% need-based, 43% non-need-based). *Programs:* FFEL (Subsidized and Unsubsidized Stafford, PLUS).

WORK-STUDY *Federal work-study:* Total amount: $214,741; 87 jobs averaging $3119.

ATHLETIC AWARDS Total amount: $920,872 (23% need-based, 77% non-need-based).

APPLYING FOR FINANCIAL AID *Required financial aid forms:* FAFSA, financial aid transcript (for transfers). *Financial aid deadline (priority):* 4/1. *Notification date:* Continuous beginning 3/15. Students must reply within 2 weeks of notification.

CONTACT Ms. Anissa Agne, Director of Financial Aid, University of North Florida, 1 UNF Drive, Jacksonville, FL 32224-7699, 904-620-2604. *E-mail:* anissa.agne@unf.edu.

UNIVERSITY OF NORTH TEXAS
Denton, TX

Tuition & fees (TX res): $7301	Average undergraduate aid package: $10,811

ABOUT THE INSTITUTION State-supported, coed. 84 undergraduate majors. Federal methodology is used as a basis for awarding need-based institutional aid.

UNDERGRADUATE EXPENSES for 2010–11 *Tuition, state resident:* full-time $5360; part-time $178.67 per credit hour. *Tuition, nonresident:* full-time $13,670; part-time $455.67 per credit hour. *Required fees:* full-time $1941; $267.10 per credit hour. Full-time tuition and fees vary according to course load. Part-time tuition and fees vary according to course load. *College room and board:* $6534. Room and board charges vary according to board plan and housing facility. *Payment plan:* Installment.

FRESHMAN FINANCIAL AID (Fall 2009, est.) 2,558 applied for aid; of those 70% were deemed to have need. 99% of freshmen with need received aid; of those 45% had need fully met. *Average percent of need met:* 84% (excluding resources awarded to replace EFC). *Average financial aid package:* $12,122 (excluding resources awarded to replace EFC). 13% of all full-time freshmen had no need and received non-need-based gift aid.

UNDERGRADUATE FINANCIAL AID (Fall 2009, est.) 14,382 applied for aid; of those 77% were deemed to have need. 97% of undergraduates with need received aid; of those 30% had need fully met. *Average percent of need met:* 71% (excluding resources awarded to replace EFC). *Average financial aid package:* $10,811 (excluding resources awarded to replace EFC). 10% of all full-time undergraduates had no need and received non-need-based gift aid.

GIFT AID (NEED-BASED) *Total amount:* $83,965,490 (45% federal, 23% state, 23% institutional, 9% external sources). *Receiving aid:* Freshmen: 48% (1,533); all full-time undergraduates: 41% (8,813). *Average award:* Freshmen: $7367; Undergraduates: $6245. *Scholarships, grants, and awards:* Federal Pell, FSEOG, state, college/university gift aid from institutional funds.

GIFT AID (NON-NEED-BASED) *Total amount:* $7,207,835 (1% federal, 33% institutional, 66% external sources). *Receiving aid:* Freshmen: 23% (730). Undergraduates: 12% (2,505). *Average award:* Freshmen: $4787. Undergraduates: $4843. *Tuition waivers:* Full or partial for employees or children of employees, senior citizens.

LOANS *Student loans:* $118,160,909 (81% need-based, 19% non-need-based). *Average need-based loan:* Freshmen: $3473. Undergraduates: $4286. *Parent loans:* $50,276,450 (57% need-based, 43% non-need-based). *Programs:* Federal Direct (Subsidized and Unsubsidized Stafford, PLUS), Perkins, Federal Nursing, state, college/university.

WORK-STUDY *Federal work-study:* Total amount: $8,075,249; jobs available. *State or other work-study/employment:* Total amount: $1,081,623 (100% need-based). Part-time jobs available.

ATHLETIC AWARDS Total amount: $3,021,687 (43% need-based, 57% non-need-based).

APPLYING FOR FINANCIAL AID *Required financial aid form:* FAFSA. *Financial aid deadline (priority):* 3/31. *Notification date:* Continuous.

CONTACT Mrs. Carolyn Cunningham, Director of Financial Aid, University of North Texas, PO Box 311370, Denton, TX 76203-1370, 940-565-2302 or toll-free 800-868-8211 (in-state). *Fax:* 940-565-2738. *E-mail:* carolyn.cunningham@unt.edu.

UNIVERSITY OF NOTRE DAME
Notre Dame, IN

Tuition & fees: $38,477	Average undergraduate aid package: $34,101

University of Notre Dame

ABOUT THE INSTITUTION Independent Roman Catholic, coed. 55 undergraduate majors. Both federal and institutional methodology are used as a basis for awarding need-based institutional aid.

UNDERGRADUATE EXPENSES for 2009–10 *Comprehensive fee:* $48,845 includes full-time tuition ($37,970), mandatory fees ($507), and room and board ($10,368). *Part-time tuition:* $1582 per credit. *Payment plan:* Installment.

FRESHMAN FINANCIAL AID (Fall 2009, est.) 1,507 applied for aid; of those 72% were deemed to have need. 100% of freshmen with need received aid; of those 98% had need fully met. *Average percent of need met:* 99% (excluding resources awarded to replace EFC). *Average financial aid package:* $34,802 (excluding resources awarded to replace EFC). 2% of all full-time freshmen had no need and received non-need-based gift aid.

UNDERGRADUATE FINANCIAL AID (Fall 2009, est.) 5,181 applied for aid; of those 79% were deemed to have need. 100% of undergraduates with need received aid; of those 97% had need fully met. *Average percent of need met:* 99% (excluding resources awarded to replace EFC). *Average financial aid package:* $34,101 (excluding resources awarded to replace EFC). 3% of all full-time undergraduates had no need and received non-need-based gift aid.

GIFT AID (NEED-BASED) *Total amount:* $100,207,181 (9% federal, 87% institutional, 4% external sources). *Receiving aid:* Freshmen: 51% (1,054); all full-time undergraduates: 47% (3,907). *Average award:* Freshmen: $28,799; Undergraduates: $26,847. *Scholarships, grants, and awards:* Federal Pell, state, private, college/university gift aid from institutional funds, Academic Competitiveness Grants, National SMART Grants.

GIFT AID (NON-NEED-BASED) *Total amount:* $14,115,630 (32% federal, 1% state, 34% institutional, 33% external sources). *Receiving aid:* Freshmen: 34% (694). Undergraduates: 29% (2,396). *Average award:* Freshmen: $5806. Undergraduates: $6106. *Scholarships, grants, and awards by category:* Special characteristics: 253 awards ($8,873,302 total): children of faculty/staff. *Tuition waivers:* Full or partial for employees or children of employees.

LOANS *Student loans:* $38,778,577 (48% need-based, 52% non-need-based). 57% of past graduating class borrowed through all loan programs. *Average indebtedness per student:* $28,371. *Average need-based loan:* Freshmen: $3201. Undergraduates: $4782. *Parent loans:* $9,835,217 (2% need-based, 98% non-need-based). *Programs:* FFEL (Subsidized and Unsubsidized Stafford, PLUS), Perkins, Federal Nursing, Notre Dame Undergraduate Loans.

WORK-STUDY *Federal work-study:* Total amount: $4,251,990; 1,830 jobs averaging $2323. *State or other work-study/employment:* Total amount: $9,312,819 (11% need-based, 89% non-need-based). 3,204 part-time jobs averaging $2907.

ATHLETIC AWARDS Total amount: $14,586,940 (14% need-based, 86% non-need-based).

APPLYING FOR FINANCIAL AID *Required financial aid forms:* FAFSA, CSS Financial Aid PROFILE, business/farm supplement, income tax form(s), W-2 forms. *Financial aid deadline:* 2/15. *Notification date:* 4/1. Students must reply by 5/1.

CONTACT Mr. Joseph A. Russo, Director, Student Financial Strategies, University of Notre Dame, 115 Main Building, Notre Dame, IN 46556, 574-631-6436. *Fax:* 574-631-6899. *E-mail:* finaid.1@nd.edu.

UNIVERSITY OF OKLAHOMA
Norman, OK

Tuition & fees (OK res): $5245	Average undergraduate aid package: $11,884

ABOUT THE INSTITUTION State-supported, coed. 97 undergraduate majors. Federal methodology is used as a basis for awarding need-based institutional aid.

UNDERGRADUATE EXPENSES for 2009–10 *Tuition, state resident:* full-time $2830; part-time $117.90 per credit hour. *Tuition, nonresident:* full-time $10,814; part-time $450.60 per credit hour. *Required fees:* full-time $2415; $90.10 per credit hour or $126.50 per term. Full-time tuition and fees vary according to course load, location, program, and reciprocity agreements. Part-time tuition and fees vary according to course load, location, program, and reciprocity agreements. *College room and board:* $7598; *Room only:* $4160. Room and board charges vary according to board plan and housing facility. *Payment plans:* Guaranteed tuition, installment.

FRESHMAN FINANCIAL AID (Fall 2008) 2,406 applied for aid; of those 96% were deemed to have need. 100% of freshmen with need received aid; of those 53% had need fully met. *Average percent of need met:* 95% (excluding resources awarded to replace EFC). *Average financial aid package:* $11,348 (excluding resources awarded to replace EFC). 14% of all full-time freshmen had no need and received non-need-based gift aid.

UNDERGRADUATE FINANCIAL AID (Fall 2008) 9,082 applied for aid; of those 95% were deemed to have need. 100% of undergraduates with need received aid; of those 53% had need fully met. *Average percent of need met:* 95% (excluding resources awarded to replace EFC). *Average financial aid package:* $11,884 (excluding resources awarded to replace EFC). 12% of all full-time undergraduates had no need and received non-need-based gift aid.

GIFT AID (NEED-BASED) *Total amount:* $35,104,308 (44% federal, 29% state, 17% institutional, 10% external sources). *Receiving aid:* Freshmen: 5% (180); all full-time undergraduates: 12% (2,008). *Average award:* Freshmen: $5978; Undergraduates: $4801. *Scholarships, grants, and awards:* Federal Pell, FSEOG, state, private, college/university gift aid from institutional funds, United Negro College Fund.

GIFT AID (NON-NEED-BASED) *Total amount:* $9,440,724 (14% federal, 42% state, 27% institutional, 17% external sources). *Receiving aid:* Freshmen: 52% (1,947). Undergraduates: 32% (5,312). *Average award:* Freshmen: $1161. Undergraduates: $1234. *Scholarships, grants, and awards by category:* Academic interests/achievement: 9,371 awards ($22,159,806 total): architecture, area/ethnic studies, biological sciences, business, communication, computer science, education, engineering/technologies, foreign languages, general academic interests/achievements, humanities, international studies, mathematics, physical sciences, social sciences. Creative arts/performance: 106 awards ($1,905,540 total): art/fine arts, dance, journalism/publications, music, performing arts, theater/drama. Special achievements/activities: 40 awards ($96,325 total): leadership. Special characteristics: 417 awards ($1,135,905 total): children and siblings of alumni, members of minority groups, previous college experience. *Tuition waivers:* Full or partial for children of alumni, employees or children of employees, senior citizens.

LOANS *Student loans:* $53,692,564 (96% need-based, 4% non-need-based). 52% of past graduating class borrowed through all loan programs. *Average indebtedness per student:* $15,659. *Average need-based loan:* Freshmen: $3648. Undergraduates: $4522. *Parent loans:* $12,536,554 (98% need-based, 2% non-need-based). *Programs:* FFEL (Subsidized and Unsubsidized Stafford, PLUS), Perkins, college/university, alternative loans.

WORK-STUDY *Federal work-study:* Total amount: $1,480,151; 572 jobs averaging $2588.

ATHLETIC AWARDS Total amount: $6,053,157 (39% need-based, 61% non-need-based).

APPLYING FOR FINANCIAL AID *Required financial aid form:* FAFSA. *Financial aid deadline:* Continuous. *Notification date:* Continuous beginning 3/15. Students must reply within 6 weeks of notification.

CONTACT Financial Aid Assistant, University of Oklahoma, 1000 Asp Avenue, Room 216, Norman, OK 73019-4078, 405-325-4521 or toll-free 800-234-6868. *Fax:* 405-325-0819. *E-mail:* financialaid@ou.edu.

UNIVERSITY OF OREGON
Eugene, OR

Tuition & fees (OR res): $7428	Average undergraduate aid package: $9168

ABOUT THE INSTITUTION State-supported, coed. 81 undergraduate majors. Federal methodology is used as a basis for awarding need-based institutional aid.

UNDERGRADUATE EXPENSES for 2009–10 *One-time required fee:* $300. *Tuition, state resident:* full-time $6180; part-time $130 per credit hour. *Tuition, nonresident:* full-time $22,470; part-time $485 per credit hour. *Required fees:* full-time $1248. Full-time tuition and fees vary according to course load, degree level, and program. Part-time tuition and fees vary according to course load, degree level, and program. *College room and board:* $8620. Room and board charges vary according to board plan and housing facility. *Payment plan:* Installment.

FRESHMAN FINANCIAL AID (Fall 2009, est.) 2,559 applied for aid; of those 62% were deemed to have need. 94% of freshmen with need received aid; of those 15% had need fully met. *Average percent of need met:* 53% (excluding resources awarded to replace EFC). *Average financial aid package:* $9071 (excluding resources awarded to replace EFC). 12% of all full-time freshmen had no need and received non-need-based gift aid.

UNDERGRADUATE FINANCIAL AID (Fall 2009, est.) 10,022 applied for aid; of those 73% were deemed to have need. 95% of undergraduates with need

received aid; of those 14% had need fully met. *Average percent of need met:* 63% (excluding resources awarded to replace EFC). *Average financial aid package:* $9168 (excluding resources awarded to replace EFC). 6% of all full-time undergraduates had no need and received non-need-based gift aid.

GIFT AID (NEED-BASED) Total amount: $26,759,965 (75% federal, 21% state, 4% institutional). *Receiving aid:* Freshmen: 21% (786); all full-time undergraduates: 23% (3,944). *Average award:* Freshmen: $6794; Undergraduates: $6321. *Scholarships, grants, and awards:* Federal Pell, FSEOG, state, private, college/university gift aid from institutional funds.

GIFT AID (NON-NEED-BASED) Total amount: $14,249,717 (96% institutional, 4% external sources). *Receiving aid:* Freshmen: 22% (826). Undergraduates: 13% (2,237). *Average award:* Freshmen: $2812. Undergraduates: $2544. *Scholarships, grants, and awards by category: Academic interests/achievement:* 1,979 awards ($10,055,207 total): architecture, biological sciences, business, education, foreign languages, general academic interests/achievements, physical sciences, social sciences. *Creative arts/performance:* 451 awards ($1,398,183 total): art/fine arts, dance, journalism/publications, music, performing arts, theater/drama. *Special characteristics:* 377 awards ($3,276,892 total): children of faculty/staff, general special characteristics, international students, local/state students, veterans, veterans' children. *Tuition waivers:* Full or partial for employees or children of employees.

LOANS Student loans: $57,389,151 (45% need-based, 55% non-need-based). 55% of past graduating class borrowed through all loan programs. *Average indebtedness per student:* $19,336. *Average need-based loan:* Freshmen: $3529. Undergraduates: $4471. *Parent loans:* $37,053,836 (32% need-based, 68% non-need-based). *Programs:* Federal Direct (Subsidized and Unsubsidized Stafford, PLUS), Perkins, college/university.

WORK-STUDY Federal work-study: Total amount: $3,498,229; 2,163 jobs averaging $1416. *State or other work-study/employment:* Total amount: $141,600 (100% need-based). 54 part-time jobs averaging $2644.

ATHLETIC AWARDS Total amount: $7,554,543 (100% non-need-based).

APPLYING FOR FINANCIAL AID Required financial aid form: FAFSA. *Financial aid deadline (priority):* 3/1. *Notification date:* Continuous beginning 4/1. Students must reply within 4 weeks of notification.

CONTACT Elizabeth Bickford, Director of Financial Aid and Scholarships, University of Oregon, 1278 University of Oregon, Eugene, OR 97403-1278, 541-346-3221 or toll-free 800-232-3825 (in-state). *Fax:* 541-346-1175. *E-mail:* ebick@uoregon.edu.

UNIVERSITY OF PENNSYLVANIA
Philadelphia, PA

Tuition & fees: $40,514	Average undergraduate aid package: $33,060

ABOUT THE INSTITUTION Independent, coed. 97 undergraduate majors. Both federal and institutional methodology are used as a basis for awarding need-based institutional aid.

UNDERGRADUATE EXPENSES for 2010–11 Comprehensive fee: $51,944 includes full-time tuition ($36,208), mandatory fees ($4306), and room and board ($11,430). *College room only:* $7248. Room and board charges vary according to board plan. Part-time tuition and fees vary according to program. *Payment plans:* Tuition prepayment, installment.

FRESHMAN FINANCIAL AID (Fall 2008) 1,322 applied for aid; of those 78% were deemed to have need. 100% of freshmen with need received aid; of those 100% had need fully met. *Average percent of need met:* 100% (excluding resources awarded to replace EFC). *Average financial aid package:* $33,773 (excluding resources awarded to replace EFC).

UNDERGRADUATE FINANCIAL AID (Fall 2008) 4,658 applied for aid; of those 87% were deemed to have need. 100% of undergraduates with need received aid; of those 100% had need fully met. *Average percent of need met:* 100% (excluding resources awarded to replace EFC). *Average financial aid package:* $33,060 (excluding resources awarded to replace EFC).

GIFT AID (NEED-BASED) Total amount: $115,556,740 (6% federal, 1% state, 89% institutional, 4% external sources). *Receiving aid:* Freshmen: 41% (982); all full-time undergraduates: 40% (3,851). *Average award:* Freshmen: $31,452; Undergraduates: $30,043. *Scholarships, grants, and awards:* Federal Pell, FSEOG, state, private, college/university gift aid from institutional funds.

GIFT AID (NON-NEED-BASED) Total amount: $5,619,567 (1% federal, 99% external sources). *Tuition waivers:* Full or partial for employees or children of employees.

LOANS Student loans: $22,871,189 (26% need-based, 74% non-need-based). 41% of past graduating class borrowed through all loan programs. *Average indebtedness per student:* $17,787. *Average need-based loan:* Freshmen: $965. Undergraduates: $1491. *Parent loans:* $10,714,911 (100% non-need-based). *Programs:* FFEL (Subsidized and Unsubsidized Stafford, PLUS), Perkins, Federal Nursing, college/university, supplemental third-party loans (guaranteed by institution).

WORK-STUDY Federal work-study: Total amount: $10,622,872; 2,855 jobs averaging $2884. *State or other work-study/employment:* Total amount: $1,731,985 (100% need-based). 480 part-time jobs averaging $2905.

APPLYING FOR FINANCIAL AID Required financial aid forms: FAFSA, institution's own form, CSS Financial Aid PROFILE, noncustodial (divorced/separated) parent's statement, business/farm supplement, student's most recently completed income tax form. *Financial aid deadline (priority):* 2/15. *Notification date:* 4/1. Students must reply by 5/1.

CONTACT Mr. William Schilling, Director of Financial Aid, University of Pennsylvania, 212 Franklin Building, Philadelphia, PA 19104-6270, 215-898-6784. *Fax:* 215-573-2208. *E-mail:* schilling@sfs.upenn.edu.

UNIVERSITY OF PHOENIX
Phoenix, AZ

ABOUT THE INSTITUTION Proprietary, coed. *Awards:* associate, bachelor's, and master's degrees and post-bachelor's and post-master's certificates. 11 undergraduate majors. *Total enrollment:* 292,797. Undergraduates: 236,109. Freshmen: 31,010.

GIFT AID (NEED-BASED) Scholarships, grants, and awards: Federal Pell, FSEOG, state, private, college/university gift aid from institutional funds, Academic Competitiveness Grants, National SMART Grants.

GIFT AID (NON-NEED-BASED) Scholarships, grants, and awards by category: *Academic interests/achievement:* business, communication, computer science, social sciences.

LOANS Programs: FFEL (Subsidized and Unsubsidized Stafford, PLUS), Perkins.

APPLYING FOR FINANCIAL AID Required financial aid forms: FAFSA, institution's own form.

CONTACT ACS/AFS, University of Phoenix, 875 West Elliot Road, Tempe, AZ 85284, 480-735-3000 or toll-free 800-776-4867 (in-state), 800-228-7240 (out-of-state). *Fax:* 480-940-2060.

UNIVERSITY OF PHOENIX–ATLANTA CAMPUS
Sandy Springs, GA

ABOUT THE INSTITUTION Proprietary, coed. *Awards:* bachelor's and master's degrees. 23 undergraduate majors. *Total enrollment:* 1,573. Undergraduates: 1,196. Freshmen: 60.

GIFT AID (NEED-BASED) Scholarships, grants, and awards: Federal Pell, FSEOG, state, private, college/university gift aid from institutional funds, Academic Competitiveness Grants, National SMART Grants.

GIFT AID (NON-NEED-BASED) Scholarships, grants, and awards by category: *Academic interests/achievement:* business, communication, computer science, social sciences.

LOANS Programs: FFEL (Subsidized and Unsubsidized Stafford, PLUS), Perkins.

APPLYING FOR FINANCIAL AID Required financial aid forms: FAFSA, institution's own form.

CONTACT ACS/AFS, University of Phoenix–Atlanta Campus, 875 West Elliot Road, Tempe, AZ 85284, 480-735-3000 or toll-free 800-776-4867 (in-state), 800-228-7240 (out-of-state). *Fax:* 480-940-2060.

UNIVERSITY OF PHOENIX–BAY AREA CAMPUS
Pleasanton, CA

ABOUT THE INSTITUTION Proprietary, coed. *Awards:* bachelor's and master's degrees. 24 undergraduate majors. *Total enrollment:* 2,240. Undergraduates: 1,676. Freshmen: 91.

GIFT AID (NEED-BASED) Scholarships, grants, and awards: Federal Pell, FSEOG, state, private, college/university gift aid from institutional funds, Academic Competitiveness Grants, National SMART Grants.

GIFT AID (NON-NEED-BASED) *Scholarships, grants, and awards by category:* *Academic interests/achievement:* business, communication, computer science, social sciences.

LOANS *Programs:* FFEL (Subsidized and Unsubsidized Stafford, PLUS), Perkins.

APPLYING FOR FINANCIAL AID *Required financial aid forms:* FAFSA, institution's own form.

CONTACT ACS/AFS, University of Phoenix–Bay Area Campus, 875 West Elliot Road, Tempe, AZ 85284, 480-735-3000 or toll-free 877-4-STUDENT. *Fax:* 480-940-2060.

UNIVERSITY OF PHOENIX–BIRMINGHAM CAMPUS
Birmingham, AL

CONTACT Financial Aid Office, University of Phoenix–Birmingham Campus, One Corporate Center, Suite 400, Birmingham, AL 35244.

UNIVERSITY OF PHOENIX–BOSTON CAMPUS
Braintree, MA

ABOUT THE INSTITUTION Proprietary, coed. *Awards:* bachelor's and master's degrees. 3 undergraduate majors. *Total enrollment:* 361. Undergraduates: 265. Freshmen: 20.

GIFT AID (NEED-BASED) *Scholarships, grants, and awards:* Federal Pell, FSEOG, state, private, college/university gift aid from institutional funds, Academic Competitiveness Grants, National SMART Grants.

GIFT AID (NON-NEED-BASED) *Scholarships, grants, and awards by category:* *Academic interests/achievement:* business, communication, computer science, social sciences.

LOANS *Programs:* FFEL (Subsidized and Unsubsidized Stafford, PLUS), Perkins.

APPLYING FOR FINANCIAL AID *Required financial aid forms:* FAFSA, institution's own form.

CONTACT ACS/AFS, University of Phoenix–Boston Campus, 875 West Elliot Road, Tempe, AZ 85284, 480-735-3000 or toll-free 800-228-7240. *Fax:* 480-940-2060.

UNIVERSITY OF PHOENIX–CENTRAL FLORIDA CAMPUS
Maitland, FL

ABOUT THE INSTITUTION Proprietary, coed. *Awards:* bachelor's and master's degrees. 15 undergraduate majors. *Total enrollment:* 1,537. Undergraduates: 1,174. Freshmen: 53.

GIFT AID (NEED-BASED) *Scholarships, grants, and awards:* Federal Pell, FSEOG, state, private, college/university gift aid from institutional funds, Academic Competitiveness Grants, National SMART Grants.

GIFT AID (NON-NEED-BASED) *Scholarships, grants, and awards by category:* *Academic interests/achievement:* business, communication, computer science, social sciences.

LOANS *Programs:* FFEL (Subsidized and Unsubsidized Stafford, PLUS), Perkins.

APPLYING FOR FINANCIAL AID *Required financial aid forms:* FAFSA, institution's own form.

CONTACT ACS/AFS, University of Phoenix–Central Florida Campus, 875 West Elliot Road, Tempe, AZ 85284, 480-735-3000 or toll-free 800-776-4867 (in-state), 800-228-7240 (out-of-state). *Fax:* 480-940-2060.

UNIVERSITY OF PHOENIX–CENTRAL MASSACHUSETTS CAMPUS
Westborough, MA

ABOUT THE INSTITUTION Proprietary, coed. *Awards:* bachelor's and master's degrees. 4 undergraduate majors. *Total enrollment:* 148. Undergraduates: 117. Freshmen: 11.

GIFT AID (NEED-BASED) *Scholarships, grants, and awards:* Federal Pell, FSEOG, state, private, college/university gift aid from institutional funds, Academic Competitiveness Grants, National SMART Grants.

GIFT AID (NON-NEED-BASED) *Scholarships, grants, and awards by category:* *Academic interests/achievement:* business, communication, computer science, social sciences.

LOANS *Programs:* FFEL (Subsidized and Unsubsidized Stafford, PLUS), Perkins.

APPLYING FOR FINANCIAL AID *Required financial aid forms:* FAFSA, institution's own form.

CONTACT ACS/AFS, University of Phoenix–Central Massachusetts Campus, 875 West Elliot Road, Tempe, AZ 85284, 480-735-3000 or toll-free 800-776-4867 (in-state), 800-228-7240 (out-of-state). *Fax:* 480-940-2060.

UNIVERSITY OF PHOENIX–CENTRAL VALLEY CAMPUS
Fresno, CA

ABOUT THE INSTITUTION Proprietary, coed. *Awards:* bachelor's and master's degrees and post-bachelor's certificates. 8 undergraduate majors. *Total enrollment:* 2,235. Undergraduates: 1,928. Freshmen: 123.

GIFT AID (NEED-BASED) *Scholarships, grants, and awards:* Federal Pell, FSEOG, state, private, college/university gift aid from institutional funds, Academic Competitiveness Grants, National SMART Grants.

GIFT AID (NON-NEED-BASED) *Scholarships, grants, and awards by category:* *Academic interests/achievement:* business, communication, computer science, social sciences.

LOANS *Programs:* FFEL (Subsidized and Unsubsidized Stafford, PLUS), Perkins.

APPLYING FOR FINANCIAL AID *Required financial aid forms:* FAFSA, institution's own form.

CONTACT ACS/AFS, University of Phoenix–Central Valley Campus, 875 West Elliot Road, Tempe, AZ 85284, 480-735-3000 or toll-free 888-776-4867 (in-state), 888-228-7240 (out-of-state). *Fax:* 480-940-2060.

UNIVERSITY OF PHOENIX–CHARLOTTE CAMPUS
Charlotte, NC

ABOUT THE INSTITUTION Proprietary, coed. *Awards:* associate, bachelor's, and master's degrees. 5 undergraduate majors. *Total enrollment:* 1,149. Undergraduates: 866. Freshmen: 59.

GIFT AID (NEED-BASED) *Scholarships, grants, and awards:* Federal Pell, FSEOG, state, private, college/university gift aid from institutional funds, Academic Competitiveness Grants, National SMART Grants.

GIFT AID (NON-NEED-BASED) *Scholarships, grants, and awards by category:* *Academic interests/achievement:* business, communication, computer science, social sciences.

LOANS *Programs:* FFEL (Subsidized and Unsubsidized Stafford, PLUS), Perkins.

APPLYING FOR FINANCIAL AID *Required financial aid forms:* FAFSA, institution's own form.

CONTACT ACS/AFS, University of Phoenix–Charlotte Campus, 875 West Elliot Road, Tempe, AZ 85284, 480-735-3000 or toll-free 800-776-4867 (in-state), 800-228-7240 (out-of-state). *Fax:* 480-940-2060.

UNIVERSITY OF PHOENIX–CHICAGO CAMPUS
Schaumburg, IL

ABOUT THE INSTITUTION Proprietary, coed. *Awards:* bachelor's and master's degrees. 9 undergraduate majors. *Total enrollment:* 1,178. Undergraduates: 1,025. Freshmen: 164.

GIFT AID (NEED-BASED) *Scholarships, grants, and awards:* Federal Pell, FSEOG, state, private, college/university gift aid from institutional funds, Academic Competitiveness Grants, National SMART Grants.

GIFT AID (NON-NEED-BASED) *Scholarships, grants, and awards by category:* *Academic interests/achievement:* business, communication, computer science, social sciences.

LOANS *Programs:* FFEL (Subsidized and Unsubsidized Stafford, PLUS), Perkins.

APPLYING FOR FINANCIAL AID *Required financial aid forms:* FAFSA, institution's own form.

CONTACT ACS/AFS, University of Phoenix–Chicago Campus, 875 West Elliot Road, Tempe, AZ 85284, 480-735-3000 or toll-free 800-776-4867 (in-state), 800-228-7240 (out-of-state). *Fax:* 480-940-2060.

UNIVERSITY OF PHOENIX–CINCINNATI CAMPUS
West Chester, OH

ABOUT THE INSTITUTION Proprietary, coed. *Awards:* bachelor's and master's degrees. 1 undergraduate major. *Total enrollment:* 143. Undergraduates: 70.

GIFT AID (NEED-BASED) *Scholarships, grants, and awards:* Federal Pell, FSEOG, state, private, college/university gift aid from institutional funds, Academic Competitiveness Grants, National SMART Grants.

GIFT AID (NON-NEED-BASED) *Scholarships, grants, and awards by category: Academic interests/achievement:* business, communication, computer science, social sciences.

LOANS *Programs:* FFEL (Subsidized and Unsubsidized Stafford, PLUS), Perkins.

APPLYING FOR FINANCIAL AID *Required financial aid forms:* FAFSA, institution's own form.

CONTACT ACS/AFS, University of Phoenix–Cincinnati Campus, 875 West Elliot Road, Tempe, AZ 85284, 480-735-3000 or toll-free 800-776-4867 (in-state), 800-228-7240 (out-of-state). *Fax:* 480-940-2060.

UNIVERSITY OF PHOENIX–CLEVELAND CAMPUS
Independence, OH

ABOUT THE INSTITUTION Proprietary, coed. *Awards:* associate, bachelor's, and master's degrees. 27 undergraduate majors. *Total enrollment:* 664. Undergraduates: 394. Freshmen: 44.

GIFT AID (NEED-BASED) *Scholarships, grants, and awards:* Federal Pell, FSEOG, state, private, college/university gift aid from institutional funds, Academic Competitiveness Grants, National SMART Grants.

GIFT AID (NON-NEED-BASED) *Scholarships, grants, and awards by category: Academic interests/achievement:* business, communication, computer science, social sciences.

LOANS *Programs:* FFEL (Subsidized and Unsubsidized Stafford, PLUS), Perkins.

APPLYING FOR FINANCIAL AID *Required financial aid forms:* FAFSA, institution's own form.

CONTACT ACS/AFS, University of Phoenix–Cleveland Campus, 875 West Elliot Road, Tempe, AZ 85284, 480-735-3000 or toll-free 800-776-4867 (in-state), 800-228-7240 (out-of-state). *Fax:* 480-940-2060.

UNIVERSITY OF PHOENIX–COLUMBIA CAMPUS
Columbia, SC

CONTACT Financial Aid Office, University of Phoenix–Columbia Campus, 1001 Pinnacle Point Drive, Suite 200, Columbia, SC 29223, 803-699-5096.

UNIVERSITY OF PHOENIX–COLUMBUS GEORGIA CAMPUS
Columbus, GA

ABOUT THE INSTITUTION Proprietary, coed. *Awards:* associate, bachelor's, and master's degrees. 20 undergraduate majors. *Total enrollment:* 764. Undergraduates: 704. Freshmen: 121.

GIFT AID (NEED-BASED) *Scholarships, grants, and awards:* Federal Pell, FSEOG, state, private, college/university gift aid from institutional funds, Academic Competitiveness Grants, National SMART Grants.

GIFT AID (NON-NEED-BASED) *Scholarships, grants, and awards by category: Academic interests/achievement:* business, communication, computer science, social sciences.

LOANS *Programs:* FFEL (Subsidized and Unsubsidized Stafford, PLUS), Perkins.

APPLYING FOR FINANCIAL AID *Required financial aid forms:* FAFSA, institution's own form.

CONTACT ACS/AFS, University of Phoenix–Columbus Georgia Campus, 875 West Elliot Road, Tempe, AZ 85284, 480-735-3000 or toll-free 800-776-4867 (in-state), 800-228-7240 (out-of-state). *Fax:* 480-940-2060.

UNIVERSITY OF PHOENIX–COLUMBUS OHIO CAMPUS
Columbus, OH

ABOUT THE INSTITUTION Proprietary, coed. *Awards:* associate, bachelor's, and master's degrees. 1 undergraduate major. *Total enrollment:* 208. Undergraduates: 128. Freshmen: 17.

GIFT AID (NEED-BASED) *Scholarships, grants, and awards:* Federal Pell, FSEOG, state, private, college/university gift aid from institutional funds, Academic Competitiveness Grants, National SMART Grants.

GIFT AID (NON-NEED-BASED) *Scholarships, grants, and awards by category: Academic interests/achievement:* business, communication, computer science, social sciences.

LOANS *Programs:* FFEL (Subsidized and Unsubsidized Stafford, PLUS), Perkins.

APPLYING FOR FINANCIAL AID *Required financial aid forms:* FAFSA, institution's own form.

CONTACT ACS/AFS, University of Phoenix–Columbus Ohio Campus, 875 West Elliot Road, Tempe, AZ 85284, 480-735-3000 or toll-free 800-776-4867 (in-state), 800-228-7240 (out-of-state). *Fax:* 480-940-2060.

UNIVERSITY OF PHOENIX–DALLAS CAMPUS
Dallas, TX

ABOUT THE INSTITUTION Proprietary, coed. *Awards:* bachelor's and master's degrees. 22 undergraduate majors. *Total enrollment:* 1,371. Undergraduates: 1,075. Freshmen: 61.

GIFT AID (NEED-BASED) *Scholarships, grants, and awards:* Federal Pell, FSEOG, state, private, college/university gift aid from institutional funds, Academic Competitiveness Grants, National SMART Grants.

GIFT AID (NON-NEED-BASED) *Scholarships, grants, and awards by category: Academic interests/achievement:* business, communication, computer science, social sciences.

LOANS *Programs:* FFEL (Subsidized and Unsubsidized Stafford, PLUS), Perkins.

APPLYING FOR FINANCIAL AID *Required financial aid forms:* FAFSA, institution's own form.

CONTACT ACS/AFS, University of Phoenix–Dallas Campus, 875 West Elliot Road, Tempe, AZ 85284, 480-735-3000 or toll-free 800-776-4867 (in-state), 800-228-7240 (out-of-state). *Fax:* 480-940-2060.

UNIVERSITY OF PHOENIX–DENVER CAMPUS
Lone Tree, CO

ABOUT THE INSTITUTION Proprietary, coed. *Awards:* bachelor's and master's degrees and post-master's certificates. 23 undergraduate majors. *Total enrollment:* 2,264. Undergraduates: 1,289. Freshmen: 62.

GIFT AID (NEED-BASED) *Scholarships, grants, and awards:* Federal Pell, FSEOG, state, private, college/university gift aid from institutional funds, Academic Competitiveness Grants, National SMART Grants.

GIFT AID (NON-NEED-BASED) *Scholarships, grants, and awards by category: Academic interests/achievement:* business, communication, computer science, social sciences.

LOANS *Programs:* FFEL (Subsidized and Unsubsidized Stafford, PLUS), Perkins.

APPLYING FOR FINANCIAL AID *Required financial aid forms:* FAFSA, institution's own form.

CONTACT ACS/AFS, University of Phoenix–Denver Campus, 875 West Elliot Road, Tempe, AZ 85284, 480-735-3000 or toll-free 800-776-4867 (in-state), 800-228-7240 (out-of-state). *Fax:* 480-940-2060.

UNIVERSITY OF PHOENIX–DETROIT CAMPUS
Southfield, MI

ABOUT THE INSTITUTION Proprietary, coed. 16 undergraduate majors.

GIFT AID (NEED-BASED) *Scholarships, grants, and awards:* Federal Pell, FSEOG, state, private, college/university gift aid from institutional funds, Academic Competitiveness Grants, National SMART Grants.

GIFT AID (NON-NEED-BASED) *Scholarships, grants, and awards by category: Academic interests/achievement:* business, communication, computer science, social sciences.

LOANS *Programs:* FFEL (Subsidized and Unsubsidized Stafford, PLUS), Perkins.

APPLYING FOR FINANCIAL AID *Required financial aid forms:* FAFSA, institution's own form.

CONTACT ACS/AFS, University of Phoenix–Detroit Campus, 875 West Elliot Road, Tempe, AZ 85284, 480-735-3000. *Fax:* 480-940-2060.

UNIVERSITY OF PHOENIX–EASTERN WASHINGTON CAMPUS
Spokane Valley, WA

ABOUT THE INSTITUTION Proprietary, coed. *Awards:* bachelor's and master's degrees. 4 undergraduate majors. *Total enrollment:* 44. Undergraduates: 37.

GIFT AID (NEED-BASED) *Scholarships, grants, and awards:* Federal Pell, FSEOG, state, private, college/university gift aid from institutional funds, Academic Competitiveness Grants, National SMART Grants.

GIFT AID (NON-NEED-BASED) *Scholarships, grants, and awards by category: Academic interests/achievement:* business, communication, computer science, social sciences.

LOANS *Programs:* FFEL (Subsidized and Unsubsidized Stafford, PLUS), Perkins.

APPLYING FOR FINANCIAL AID *Required financial aid forms:* FAFSA, institution's own form.

CONTACT ACS/AFS, University of Phoenix–Eastern Washington Campus, 875 West Elliot Road, Tempe, AZ 85284, 480-735-3000 or toll-free 800-697-8223 (in-state), 800-228-7240 (out-of-state). *Fax:* 480-940-2060.

UNIVERSITY OF PHOENIX–HAWAII CAMPUS
Honolulu, HI

ABOUT THE INSTITUTION Proprietary, coed. *Awards:* bachelor's and master's degrees (courses conducted at 121 campuses and learning centers in 25 states). 29 undergraduate majors. *Total enrollment:* 955. Undergraduates: 743. Freshmen: 64.

GIFT AID (NEED-BASED) *Scholarships, grants, and awards:* Federal Pell, FSEOG, state, private, college/university gift aid from institutional funds, Academic Competitiveness Grants, National SMART Grants.

GIFT AID (NON-NEED-BASED) *Scholarships, grants, and awards by category: Academic interests/achievement:* business, communication, computer science, social sciences.

LOANS *Programs:* FFEL (Subsidized and Unsubsidized Stafford, PLUS), Perkins.

APPLYING FOR FINANCIAL AID *Required financial aid forms:* FAFSA, institution's own form.

CONTACT ACS/AFS, University of Phoenix–Hawaii Campus, 875 West Elliot Road, Tempe, AZ 85284, 480-735-3000 or toll-free 800-776-4867 (in-state), 800-228-7240 (out-of-state). *Fax:* 480-940-2060.

UNIVERSITY OF PHOENIX–HOUSTON CAMPUS
Houston, TX

ABOUT THE INSTITUTION Proprietary, coed. *Awards:* bachelor's and master's degrees. 27 undergraduate majors. *Total enrollment:* 2,748. Undergraduates: 2,286. Freshmen: 158.

GIFT AID (NEED-BASED) *Scholarships, grants, and awards:* Federal Pell, FSEOG, state, private, college/university gift aid from institutional funds, Academic Competitiveness Grants, National SMART Grants.

GIFT AID (NON-NEED-BASED) *Scholarships, grants, and awards by category: Academic interests/achievement:* business, communication, computer science, social sciences.

LOANS *Programs:* FFEL (Subsidized and Unsubsidized Stafford, PLUS), Perkins.

APPLYING FOR FINANCIAL AID *Required financial aid forms:* FAFSA, institution's own form.

CONTACT ACS/AFS, University of Phoenix–Houston Campus, 875 West Elliot Road, Tempe, AZ 85284, 480-735-3000 or toll-free 800-776-4867 (in-state), 800-228-7240 (out-of-state). *Fax:* 480-940-2060.

UNIVERSITY OF PHOENIX–IDAHO CAMPUS
Meridian, ID

ABOUT THE INSTITUTION Proprietary, coed. *Awards:* bachelor's and master's degrees. 23 undergraduate majors. *Total enrollment:* 545. Undergraduates: 456. Freshmen: 45.

GIFT AID (NEED-BASED) *Scholarships, grants, and awards:* Federal Pell, FSEOG, state, private, college/university gift aid from institutional funds, Academic Competitiveness Grants, National SMART Grants.

GIFT AID (NON-NEED-BASED) *Scholarships, grants, and awards by category: Academic interests/achievement:* business, communication, computer science, social sciences.

LOANS *Programs:* FFEL (Subsidized and Unsubsidized Stafford, PLUS), Perkins.

APPLYING FOR FINANCIAL AID *Required financial aid forms:* FAFSA, institution's own form.

CONTACT ACS/AFS, University of Phoenix–Idaho Campus, 875 West Elliot Road, Tempe, AZ 85284, 480-735-3000 or toll-free 800-776-4867 (in-state), 800-228-7240 (out-of-state). *Fax:* 480-940-2060.

UNIVERSITY OF PHOENIX–INDIANAPOLIS CAMPUS
Indianapolis, IN

ABOUT THE INSTITUTION Proprietary, coed. *Awards:* associate, bachelor's, and master's degrees. 30 undergraduate majors. *Total enrollment:* 339. Undergraduates: 271. Freshmen: 34.

GIFT AID (NEED-BASED) *Scholarships, grants, and awards:* Federal Pell, FSEOG, state, private, college/university gift aid from institutional funds, Academic Competitiveness Grants, National SMART Grants.

GIFT AID (NON-NEED-BASED) *Scholarships, grants, and awards by category: Academic interests/achievement:* business, communication, computer science, social sciences.

LOANS *Programs:* FFEL (Subsidized and Unsubsidized Stafford, PLUS), Perkins.

APPLYING FOR FINANCIAL AID *Required financial aid forms:* FAFSA, institution's own form.

CONTACT ACS/AFS, University of Phoenix–Indianapolis Campus, 875 West Elliot Road, Tempe, AZ 85284, 480-735-3000 or toll-free 800-776-4867 (in-state), 800-228-7240 (out-of-state). *Fax:* 480-940-2060.

UNIVERSITY OF PHOENIX–KANSAS CITY CAMPUS
Kansas City, MO

ABOUT THE INSTITUTION Proprietary, coed. *Awards:* bachelor's and master's degrees. 21 undergraduate majors. *Total enrollment:* 770. Undergraduates: 617. Freshmen: 57.

GIFT AID (NEED-BASED) *Scholarships, grants, and awards:* Federal Pell, FSEOG, state, private, college/university gift aid from institutional funds, Academic Competitiveness Grants, National SMART Grants.

GIFT AID (NON-NEED-BASED) *Scholarships, grants, and awards by category: Academic interests/achievement:* business, communication, computer science, social sciences.

LOANS *Programs:* FFEL (Subsidized and Unsubsidized Stafford, PLUS), Perkins.

APPLYING FOR FINANCIAL AID *Required financial aid forms:* FAFSA, institution's own form.

CONTACT ACS/AFS, University of Phoenix–Kansas City Campus, 875 West Elliot Road, Tempe, AZ 85284, 480-735-3000 or toll-free 800-776-4867 (in-state), 800-228-7240 (out-of-state). *Fax:* 480-940-2060.

UNIVERSITY OF PHOENIX–LAS VEGAS CAMPUS
Las Vegas, NV

ABOUT THE INSTITUTION Proprietary, coed. *Awards:* associate, bachelor's, and master's degrees and post-master's certificates. 27 undergraduate majors. *Total enrollment:* 3,162. Undergraduates: 2,301. Freshmen: 137.

GIFT AID (NEED-BASED) *Scholarships, grants, and awards:* Federal Pell, FSEOG, state, private, college/university gift aid from institutional funds, Academic Competitiveness Grants, National SMART Grants.

GIFT AID (NON-NEED-BASED) *Scholarships, grants, and awards by category:* *Academic interests/achievement:* business, communication, computer science, social sciences.

LOANS *Programs:* FFEL (Subsidized and Unsubsidized Stafford, PLUS), Perkins.

APPLYING FOR FINANCIAL AID *Required financial aid forms:* FAFSA, institution's own form.

CONTACT ACS/AFS, University of Phoenix–Las Vegas Campus, 875 West Elliot Road, Tempe, AZ 85284, 480-735-3000 or toll-free 800-776-4867 (in-state), 800-228-7240 (out-of-state). *Fax:* 480-940-2060.

UNIVERSITY OF PHOENIX–LITTLE ROCK CAMPUS
Little Rock, AR

ABOUT THE INSTITUTION Proprietary, coed. *Awards:* bachelor's and master's degrees. 5 undergraduate majors. *Total enrollment:* 773. Undergraduates: 622. Freshmen: 125.

GIFT AID (NEED-BASED) *Scholarships, grants, and awards:* Federal Pell, FSEOG, state, private, college/university gift aid from institutional funds, Academic Competitiveness Grants, National SMART Grants.

GIFT AID (NON-NEED-BASED) *Scholarships, grants, and awards by category:* *Academic interests/achievement:* business, communication, computer science, social sciences.

LOANS *Programs:* FFEL (Subsidized and Unsubsidized Stafford, PLUS), Perkins.

APPLYING FOR FINANCIAL AID *Required financial aid forms:* FAFSA, institution's own form.

CONTACT ACS/AFS, University of Phoenix–Little Rock Campus, 875 West Elliot Road, Tempe, AZ 85284, 480-735-3000 or toll-free 800-776-4867 (in-state), 800-228-7240 (out-of-state). *Fax:* 480-940-2060.

UNIVERSITY OF PHOENIX–LOUISIANA CAMPUS
Metairie, LA

ABOUT THE INSTITUTION Proprietary, coed. *Awards:* associate, bachelor's, and master's degrees. 31 undergraduate majors. *Total enrollment:* 1,919. Undergraduates: 1,530. Freshmen: 132.

GIFT AID (NEED-BASED) *Scholarships, grants, and awards:* Federal Pell, FSEOG, state, private, college/university gift aid from institutional funds, Academic Competitiveness Grants, National SMART Grants.

GIFT AID (NON-NEED-BASED) *Scholarships, grants, and awards by category:* *Academic interests/achievement:* business, communication, computer science, social sciences.

LOANS *Programs:* FFEL (Subsidized and Unsubsidized Stafford, PLUS), Perkins.

APPLYING FOR FINANCIAL AID *Required financial aid forms:* FAFSA, institution's own form.

CONTACT ACS/AFS, University of Phoenix–Louisiana Campus, 875 West Elliot Road, Tempe, AZ 85284, 480-735-3000 or toll-free 800-776-4867 (in-state), 800-228-7240 (out-of-state). *Fax:* 480-940-2060.

UNIVERSITY OF PHOENIX–MARYLAND CAMPUS
Columbia, MD

ABOUT THE INSTITUTION Proprietary, coed. *Awards:* bachelor's and master's degrees. 22 undergraduate majors. *Total enrollment:* 755. Undergraduates: 615. Freshmen: 24.

GIFT AID (NEED-BASED) *Scholarships, grants, and awards:* Federal Pell, FSEOG, state, private, college/university gift aid from institutional funds, Academic Competitiveness Grants, National SMART Grants.

GIFT AID (NON-NEED-BASED) *Scholarships, grants, and awards by category:* *Academic interests/achievement:* business, communication, computer science, social sciences.

LOANS *Programs:* FFEL (Subsidized and Unsubsidized Stafford, PLUS), Perkins.

APPLYING FOR FINANCIAL AID *Required financial aid forms:* FAFSA, institution's own form.

CONTACT ACS/AFS, University of Phoenix–Maryland Campus, 875 West Elliot Road, Tempe, AZ 85284, 480-735-3000 or toll-free 800-776-4867 (in-state), 800-228-7240 (out-of-state). *Fax:* 480-940-2060.

UNIVERSITY OF PHOENIX–METRO DETROIT CAMPUS
Troy, MI

CONTACT ACS/AFS, University of Phoenix–Metro Detroit Campus, 875 West Elliot Road, Suite 116, Tempe, AZ 85284, 480-735-3000 or toll-free 800-776-4867 (in-state), 800-228-7240 (out-of-state). *Fax:* 480-940-2060.

UNIVERSITY OF PHOENIX–NASHVILLE CAMPUS
Nashville, TN

ABOUT THE INSTITUTION Proprietary, coed. *Awards:* bachelor's and master's degrees. 11 undergraduate majors. *Total enrollment:* 917. Undergraduates: 751. Freshmen: 57.

GIFT AID (NEED-BASED) *Scholarships, grants, and awards:* Federal Pell, FSEOG, state, private, college/university gift aid from institutional funds, Academic Competitiveness Grants, National SMART Grants.

GIFT AID (NON-NEED-BASED) *Scholarships, grants, and awards by category:* *Academic interests/achievement:* business, communication, computer science, social sciences.

LOANS *Programs:* FFEL (Subsidized and Unsubsidized Stafford, PLUS), Perkins.

APPLYING FOR FINANCIAL AID *Required financial aid forms:* FAFSA, institution's own form.

CONTACT ACS/AFS, University of Phoenix–Nashville Campus, 875 West Elliot Road, Tempe, AZ 85284, 480-735-3000 or toll-free 800-776-4867 (in-state), 800-228-7240 (out-of-state). *Fax:* 480-940-2060.

UNIVERSITY OF PHOENIX–NEW MEXICO CAMPUS
Albuquerque, NM

ABOUT THE INSTITUTION Proprietary, coed. *Awards:* bachelor's and master's degrees. 12 undergraduate majors. *Total enrollment:* 4,170. Undergraduates: 3,452. Freshmen: 310.

GIFT AID (NEED-BASED) *Scholarships, grants, and awards:* Federal Pell, FSEOG, state, private, college/university gift aid from institutional funds, Academic Competitiveness Grants, National SMART Grants.

GIFT AID (NON-NEED-BASED) *Scholarships, grants, and awards by category:* *Academic interests/achievement:* business, communication, computer science, social sciences.

LOANS *Programs:* FFEL (Subsidized and Unsubsidized Stafford, PLUS), Perkins.

APPLYING FOR FINANCIAL AID *Required financial aid forms:* FAFSA, institution's own form.

CONTACT ACS/AFS, University of Phoenix–New Mexico Campus, 875 West Elliot Road, Tempe, AZ 85284, 480-735-3000 or toll-free 800-776-4867 (in-state), 800-228-7240 (out-of-state). *Fax:* 480-940-2060.

UNIVERSITY OF PHOENIX–NORTHERN NEVADA CAMPUS
Reno, NV

CONTACT Financial Aid Office, University of Phoenix–Northern Nevada Campus, 10345 Professional Circle, Suite 200, Reno, NV 89521-5862, 775-828-7999.

UNIVERSITY OF PHOENIX–NORTHERN VIRGINIA CAMPUS
Reston, VA

ABOUT THE INSTITUTION Proprietary, coed. *Awards:* bachelor's and master's degrees. 15 undergraduate majors. *Total enrollment:* 419. Undergraduates: 309. Freshmen: 23.

GIFT AID (NEED-BASED) *Scholarships, grants, and awards:* Federal Pell, FSEOG, state, private, college/university gift aid from institutional funds, Academic Competitiveness Grants, National SMART Grants.

GIFT AID (NON-NEED-BASED) *Scholarships, grants, and awards by category: Academic interests/achievement:* business, communication, computer science, social sciences.

LOANS *Programs:* FFEL (Subsidized and Unsubsidized Stafford, PLUS), Perkins.

APPLYING FOR FINANCIAL AID *Required financial aid forms:* FAFSA, institution's own form.

CONTACT ACS/AFS, University of Phoenix–Northern Virginia Campus, 875 West Elliott Road, Tempe, AZ 85284, 480-735-3000 or toll-free 800-776-4867 (in-state), 800-228-7240 (out-of-state). *Fax:* 480-940-2060.

UNIVERSITY OF PHOENIX–NORTH FLORIDA CAMPUS
Jacksonville, FL

ABOUT THE INSTITUTION Proprietary, coed. *Awards:* bachelor's and master's degrees. 16 undergraduate majors. *Total enrollment:* 1,276. Undergraduates: 1,019. Freshmen: 51.

GIFT AID (NEED-BASED) *Scholarships, grants, and awards:* Federal Pell, FSEOG, state, private, college/university gift aid from institutional funds, Academic Competitiveness Grants, National SMART Grants.

GIFT AID (NON-NEED-BASED) *Scholarships, grants, and awards by category: Academic interests/achievement:* business, communication, computer science, social sciences.

LOANS *Programs:* FFEL (Subsidized and Unsubsidized Stafford, PLUS), Perkins.

APPLYING FOR FINANCIAL AID *Required financial aid forms:* FAFSA, institution's own form.

CONTACT ACS/AFS, University of Phoenix–North Florida Campus, 875 West Elliot Road, Tempe, AZ 85284, 480-735-3000 or toll-free 800-776-4867 (in-state), 800-894-1758 (out-of-state). *Fax:* 480-940-2060.

UNIVERSITY OF PHOENIX–OKLAHOMA CITY CAMPUS
Oklahoma City, OK

ABOUT THE INSTITUTION Proprietary, coed. *Awards:* bachelor's and master's degrees. 16 undergraduate majors. *Total enrollment:* 801. Undergraduates: 732.

GIFT AID (NEED-BASED) *Scholarships, grants, and awards:* Federal Pell, FSEOG, state, private, college/university gift aid from institutional funds, Academic Competitiveness Grants, National SMART Grants.

GIFT AID (NON-NEED-BASED) *Scholarships, grants, and awards by category: Academic interests/achievement:* business, communication, computer science, social sciences.

LOANS *Programs:* FFEL (Subsidized and Unsubsidized Stafford, PLUS), Perkins.

APPLYING FOR FINANCIAL AID *Required financial aid forms:* FAFSA, institution's own form.

CONTACT ACS/AFS, University of Phoenix–Oklahoma City Campus, 875 West Elliot Road, Tempe, AZ 85284, 480-735-3000 or toll-free 800-776-4867 (in-state), 800-228-7240 (out-of-state). *Fax:* 480-940-2060.

UNIVERSITY OF PHOENIX–OREGON CAMPUS
Tigard, OR

ABOUT THE INSTITUTION Proprietary, coed. *Awards:* bachelor's and master's degrees. 18 undergraduate majors. *Total enrollment:* 1,265. Undergraduates: 1,042. Freshmen: 43.

GIFT AID (NEED-BASED) *Scholarships, grants, and awards:* Federal Pell, FSEOG, state, private, college/university gift aid from institutional funds, Academic Competitiveness Grants, National SMART Grants.

GIFT AID (NON-NEED-BASED) *Scholarships, grants, and awards by category: Academic interests/achievement:* business, communication, computer science, social sciences.

LOANS *Programs:* FFEL (Subsidized and Unsubsidized Stafford, PLUS), Perkins.

APPLYING FOR FINANCIAL AID *Required financial aid forms:* FAFSA, institution's own form.

CONTACT ACS/AFS, University of Phoenix–Oregon Campus, 875 West Elliot Road, Tempe, AZ 85284, 480-735-3000 or toll-free 800-776-4867 (in-state), 800-228-7240 (out-of-state). *Fax:* 480-940-2060.

UNIVERSITY OF PHOENIX–PHILADELPHIA CAMPUS
Wayne, PA

ABOUT THE INSTITUTION Proprietary, coed. *Awards:* bachelor's and master's degrees. 25 undergraduate majors. *Total enrollment:* 883. Undergraduates: 778. Freshmen: 72.

GIFT AID (NEED-BASED) *Scholarships, grants, and awards:* Federal Pell, FSEOG, state, private, college/university gift aid from institutional funds, Academic Competitiveness Grants, National SMART Grants.

GIFT AID (NON-NEED-BASED) *Scholarships, grants, and awards by category: Academic interests/achievement:* business, communication, computer science, social sciences.

LOANS *Programs:* FFEL (Subsidized and Unsubsidized Stafford, PLUS), Perkins.

APPLYING FOR FINANCIAL AID *Required financial aid forms:* FAFSA, institution's own form.

CONTACT ACS/AFS, University of Phoenix–Philadelphia Campus, 875 West Elliot Road, Tempe, AZ 85284, 480-735-3000 or toll-free 800-776-4867 (in-state), 800-228-7240 (out-of-state). *Fax:* 480-940-2060.

UNIVERSITY OF PHOENIX–PHOENIX CAMPUS
Phoenix, AZ

ABOUT THE INSTITUTION Proprietary, coed. *Awards:* bachelor's and master's degrees and post-bachelor's and post-master's certificates. 25 undergraduate majors. *Total enrollment:* 5,379. Undergraduates: 3,718. Freshmen: 193.

GIFT AID (NEED-BASED) *Scholarships, grants, and awards:* Federal Pell, FSEOG, state, private, college/university gift aid from institutional funds, Academic Competitiveness Grants, National SMART Grants.

GIFT AID (NON-NEED-BASED) *Scholarships, grants, and awards by category: Academic interests/achievement:* business, communication, computer science, social sciences.

LOANS *Programs:* FFEL (Subsidized and Unsubsidized Stafford, PLUS), Perkins.

APPLYING FOR FINANCIAL AID *Required financial aid forms:* FAFSA, institution's own form.

CONTACT ACS/AFS, University of Phoenix–Phoenix Campus, 875 West Elliot Road, Tempe, AZ 85284, 480-735-3000 or toll-free 800-776-4867 (in-state), 800-228-7240 (out-of-state). *Fax:* 480-940-2060.

UNIVERSITY OF PHOENIX–PITTSBURGH CAMPUS
Pittsburgh, PA

ABOUT THE INSTITUTION Proprietary, coed. *Awards:* bachelor's and master's degrees. 24 undergraduate majors. *Total enrollment:* 101. Undergraduates: 82.

GIFT AID (NEED-BASED) *Scholarships, grants, and awards:* Federal Pell, FSEOG, state, private, college/university gift aid from institutional funds, Academic Competitiveness Grants, National SMART Grants.

GIFT AID (NON-NEED-BASED) *Scholarships, grants, and awards by category: Academic interests/achievement:* business, communication, computer science, social sciences.

LOANS *Programs:* FFEL (Subsidized and Unsubsidized Stafford, PLUS), Perkins.

APPLYING FOR FINANCIAL AID *Required financial aid forms:* FAFSA, institution's own form.

CONTACT ACS/AFS, University of Phoenix–Pittsburgh Campus, 875 West Elliot Road, Tempe, AZ 85284, 480-735-3000 or toll-free 800-776-4867 (in-state), 800-228-7240 (out-of-state). *Fax:* 480-940-2060.

UNIVERSITY OF PHOENIX–PUERTO RICO CAMPUS
Guaynabo, PR

ABOUT THE INSTITUTION Proprietary, coed. *Awards:* bachelor's and master's degrees (courses conducted at 121 campuses and learning centers in 25 states). 2 undergraduate majors. *Total enrollment:* 2,815. Undergraduates: 1,117. Freshmen: 61.

GIFT AID (NEED-BASED) *Scholarships, grants, and awards:* Federal Pell, FSEOG, state, private, college/university gift aid from institutional funds, Academic Competitiveness Grants, National SMART Grants.

GIFT AID (NON-NEED-BASED) *Scholarships, grants, and awards by category:* *Academic interests/achievement:* business, communication, computer science, social sciences.

LOANS *Programs:* FFEL (Subsidized and Unsubsidized Stafford, PLUS), Perkins.

APPLYING FOR FINANCIAL AID *Required financial aid forms:* FAFSA, institution's own form.

CONTACT ACS/AFS, University of Phoenix–Puerto Rico Campus, 875 West Elliot Road, Tempe, AZ 85284, 480-735-3000 or toll-free 800-776-4867 (in-state), 800-228-7240 (out-of-state). *Fax:* 480-940-2060.

UNIVERSITY OF PHOENIX–RALEIGH CAMPUS
Raleigh, NC

ABOUT THE INSTITUTION Proprietary, coed. *Awards:* bachelor's and master's degrees. 7 undergraduate majors. *Total enrollment:* 500. Undergraduates: 372. Freshmen: 20.

GIFT AID (NEED-BASED) *Scholarships, grants, and awards:* Federal Pell, FSEOG, state, private, college/university gift aid from institutional funds, Academic Competitiveness Grants, National SMART Grants.

GIFT AID (NON-NEED-BASED) *Scholarships, grants, and awards by category:* *Academic interests/achievement:* business, communication, computer science, social sciences.

LOANS *Programs:* FFEL (Subsidized and Unsubsidized Stafford, PLUS), Perkins.

APPLYING FOR FINANCIAL AID *Required financial aid forms:* FAFSA, institution's own form.

CONTACT ACS/AFS, University of Phoenix–Raleigh Campus, 875 West Elliot Road, Tempe, AZ 85284, 480-735-3000 or toll-free 800-776-4867 (in-state), 800-228-7240 (out-of-state). *Fax:* 480-940-2060.

UNIVERSITY OF PHOENIX–RICHMOND CAMPUS
Richmond, VA

ABOUT THE INSTITUTION Proprietary, coed. *Awards:* bachelor's and master's degrees. 20 undergraduate majors. *Total enrollment:* 129. Undergraduates: 89.

GIFT AID (NEED-BASED) *Scholarships, grants, and awards:* Federal Pell, FSEOG, state, private, college/university gift aid from institutional funds, Academic Competitiveness Grants, National SMART Grants.

GIFT AID (NON-NEED-BASED) *Scholarships, grants, and awards by category:* *Academic interests/achievement:* business, communication, computer science, social sciences.

LOANS *Programs:* FFEL (Subsidized and Unsubsidized Stafford, PLUS), Perkins.

APPLYING FOR FINANCIAL AID *Required financial aid forms:* FAFSA, institution's own form.

CONTACT ACS/AFS, University of Phoenix–Richmond Campus, 875 West Elliot Road, Tempe, AZ 85284, 480-735-3000 or toll-free 800-776-4867 (in-state), 800-228-7240 (out-of-state). *Fax:* 480-940-2060.

UNIVERSITY OF PHOENIX–SACRAMENTO VALLEY CAMPUS
Sacramento, CA

ABOUT THE INSTITUTION Proprietary, coed. *Awards:* bachelor's and master's degrees. 27 undergraduate majors. *Total enrollment:* 3,842. Undergraduates: 3,162. Freshmen: 171.

GIFT AID (NEED-BASED) *Scholarships, grants, and awards:* Federal Pell, FSEOG, state, private, college/university gift aid from institutional funds, Academic Competitiveness Grants, National SMART Grants.

GIFT AID (NON-NEED-BASED) *Scholarships, grants, and awards by category:* *Academic interests/achievement:* business, communication, computer science, social sciences.

LOANS *Programs:* FFEL (Subsidized and Unsubsidized Stafford, PLUS), Perkins.

APPLYING FOR FINANCIAL AID *Required financial aid forms:* FAFSA, institution's own form.

CONTACT ACS/AFS, University of Phoenix–Sacramento Valley Campus, 875 West Elliot Road, Tempe, AZ 85284, 480-735-3000 or toll-free 800-776-4867 (in-state), 800-228-7240 (out-of-state). *Fax:* 480-940-2060.

UNIVERSITY OF PHOENIX–ST. LOUIS CAMPUS
St. Louis, MO

ABOUT THE INSTITUTION Proprietary, coed. *Awards:* associate, bachelor's, and master's degrees. 28 undergraduate majors. *Total enrollment:* 445. Undergraduates: 401. Freshmen: 60.

GIFT AID (NEED-BASED) *Scholarships, grants, and awards:* Federal Pell, FSEOG, state, private, college/university gift aid from institutional funds, Academic Competitiveness Grants, National SMART Grants.

GIFT AID (NON-NEED-BASED) *Scholarships, grants, and awards by category:* *Academic interests/achievement:* business, communication, computer science, social sciences.

LOANS *Programs:* FFEL (Subsidized and Unsubsidized Stafford, PLUS), Perkins.

APPLYING FOR FINANCIAL AID *Required financial aid forms:* FAFSA, institution's own form.

CONTACT ACS/AFS, University of Phoenix–St. Louis Campus, 875 West Elliot Road, Tempe, AZ 85284, 480-735-3000 or toll-free 800-776-4867 (in-state), 800-228-7240 (out-of-state). *Fax:* 480-940-2060.

UNIVERSITY OF PHOENIX–SAN DIEGO CAMPUS
San Diego, CA

ABOUT THE INSTITUTION Proprietary, coed. *Awards:* bachelor's and master's degrees. 12 undergraduate majors. *Total enrollment:* 3,212. Undergraduates: 2,500. Freshmen: 170.

GIFT AID (NEED-BASED) *Scholarships, grants, and awards:* Federal Pell, FSEOG, state, private, college/university gift aid from institutional funds, Academic Competitiveness Grants, National SMART Grants.

GIFT AID (NON-NEED-BASED) *Scholarships, grants, and awards by category:* *Academic interests/achievement:* business, communication, computer science, social sciences.

LOANS *Programs:* FFEL (Subsidized and Unsubsidized Stafford, PLUS), Perkins.

APPLYING FOR FINANCIAL AID *Required financial aid forms:* FAFSA, institution's own form.

CONTACT ACS/AFS, University of Phoenix–San Diego Campus, 875 West Elliot Road, Tempe, AZ 85284, 480-735-3000 or toll-free 888-776-4867 (in-state), 888-228-7240 (out-of-state). *Fax:* 480-940-2060.

UNIVERSITY OF PHOENIX–SOUTHERN ARIZONA CAMPUS
Tucson, AZ

ABOUT THE INSTITUTION Proprietary, coed. *Awards:* bachelor's and master's degrees and post-master's certificates. 12 undergraduate majors. *Total enrollment:* 2,229. Undergraduates: 1,631. Freshmen: 69.

GIFT AID (NEED-BASED) *Scholarships, grants, and awards:* Federal Pell, FSEOG, state, private, college/university gift aid from institutional funds, Academic Competitiveness Grants, National SMART Grants.

GIFT AID (NON-NEED-BASED) *Scholarships, grants, and awards by category: Academic interests/achievement:* business, communication, computer science, social sciences.

LOANS *Programs:* FFEL (Subsidized and Unsubsidized Stafford, PLUS), Perkins.

APPLYING FOR FINANCIAL AID *Required financial aid forms:* FAFSA, institution's own form.

CONTACT ACS/AFS, University of Phoenix–Southern Arizona Campus, 875 West Elliot Road, Tempe, AZ 85284, 480-735-3000 or toll-free 800-776-4867 (in-state), 800-228-7240 (out-of-state). *Fax:* 480-940-2060.

UNIVERSITY OF PHOENIX–SOUTHERN CALIFORNIA CAMPUS
Costa Mesa, CA

ABOUT THE INSTITUTION Proprietary, coed. *Awards:* bachelor's and master's degrees. 11 undergraduate majors. *Total enrollment:* 11,780. Undergraduates: 9,196. Freshmen: 458.

GIFT AID (NEED-BASED) *Scholarships, grants, and awards:* Federal Pell, FSEOG, state, private, college/university gift aid from institutional funds, Academic Competitiveness Grants, National SMART Grants.

GIFT AID (NON-NEED-BASED) *Scholarships, grants, and awards by category: Academic interests/achievement:* business, communication, computer science, social sciences.

LOANS *Programs:* FFEL (Subsidized and Unsubsidized Stafford, PLUS), Perkins.

APPLYING FOR FINANCIAL AID *Required financial aid forms:* FAFSA, institution's own form.

CONTACT ACS/AFS, University of Phoenix–Southern California Campus, 875 West Elliot Road, Tempe, AZ 85284, 480-735-3000 or toll-free 800-776-4867 (in-state), 800-228-7240 (out-of-state). *Fax:* 480-940-2060.

UNIVERSITY OF PHOENIX–SOUTHERN COLORADO CAMPUS
Colorado Springs, CO

ABOUT THE INSTITUTION Proprietary, coed. *Awards:* bachelor's and master's degrees. 18 undergraduate majors. *Total enrollment:* 560. Undergraduates: 311.

GIFT AID (NEED-BASED) *Scholarships, grants, and awards:* Federal Pell, FSEOG, state, private, college/university gift aid from institutional funds, Academic Competitiveness Grants, National SMART Grants.

GIFT AID (NON-NEED-BASED) *Scholarships, grants, and awards by category: Academic interests/achievement:* business, communication, computer science, social sciences.

LOANS *Programs:* FFEL (Subsidized and Unsubsidized Stafford, PLUS), Perkins.

APPLYING FOR FINANCIAL AID *Required financial aid forms:* FAFSA, institution's own form.

CONTACT ACS/AFS, University of Phoenix–Southern Colorado Campus, 875 West Elliot Road, Tempe, AZ 85284, 480-735-3000 or toll-free 800-776-4867 (in-state), 800-228-7240 (out-of-state). *Fax:* 480-940-2060.

UNIVERSITY OF PHOENIX–SOUTH FLORIDA CAMPUS
Fort Lauderdale, FL

ABOUT THE INSTITUTION Proprietary, coed. *Awards:* bachelor's and master's degrees. 14 undergraduate majors. *Total enrollment:* 2,439. Undergraduates: 1,961. Freshmen: 171.

GIFT AID (NEED-BASED) *Scholarships, grants, and awards:* Federal Pell, FSEOG, state, private, college/university gift aid from institutional funds, Academic Competitiveness Grants, National SMART Grants.

GIFT AID (NON-NEED-BASED) *Scholarships, grants, and awards by category: Academic interests/achievement:* business, communication, computer science, social sciences.

LOANS *Programs:* FFEL (Subsidized and Unsubsidized Stafford, PLUS), Perkins.

APPLYING FOR FINANCIAL AID *Required financial aid forms:* FAFSA, institution's own form.

CONTACT ACS/AFS, University of Phoenix–South Florida Campus, 875 West Elliot Road, Tempe, AZ 85284, 480-735-3000 or toll-free 800-228-7240. *Fax:* 480-940-2060.

UNIVERSITY OF PHOENIX–SPRINGFIELD CAMPUS
Springfield, MO

ABOUT THE INSTITUTION Proprietary, coed. *Awards:* associate, bachelor's, and master's degrees. 12 undergraduate majors. *Total enrollment:* 119. Undergraduates: 104. Freshmen: 23.

GIFT AID (NEED-BASED) *Scholarships, grants, and awards:* Federal Pell, FSEOG, state, private, college/university gift aid from institutional funds, Academic Competitiveness Grants, National SMART Grants.

GIFT AID (NON-NEED-BASED) *Scholarships, grants, and awards by category: Academic interests/achievement:* business, communication, computer science, social sciences.

LOANS *Programs:* FFEL (Subsidized and Unsubsidized Stafford, PLUS), Perkins.

APPLYING FOR FINANCIAL AID *Required financial aid forms:* FAFSA, institution's own form.

CONTACT ACS/AFS, University of Phoenix–Springfield Campus, 875 West Elliot Road, Tempe, AZ 85284, 480-735-3000 or toll-free 800-776-4867 (in-state), 800-228-7240 (out-of-state). *Fax:* 480-940-2060.

UNIVERSITY OF PHOENIX–TULSA CAMPUS
Tulsa, OK

ABOUT THE INSTITUTION Proprietary, coed. *Awards:* bachelor's and master's degrees. 16 undergraduate majors. *Total enrollment:* 785. Undergraduates: 703. Freshmen: 48.

GIFT AID (NEED-BASED) *Scholarships, grants, and awards:* Federal Pell, FSEOG, state, private, college/university gift aid from institutional funds, Academic Competitiveness Grants, National SMART Grants.

GIFT AID (NON-NEED-BASED) *Scholarships, grants, and awards by category: Academic interests/achievement:* business, communication, computer science, social sciences.

LOANS *Programs:* FFEL (Subsidized and Unsubsidized Stafford, PLUS), Perkins.

APPLYING FOR FINANCIAL AID *Required financial aid forms:* FAFSA, institution's own form.

CONTACT ACS/AFS, University of Phoenix–Tulsa Campus, 875 West Elliot Road, Tempe, AZ 85284, 480-735-3000 or toll-free 800-776-4867 (in-state), 800-228-7240 (out-of-state). *Fax:* 480-940-2060.

UNIVERSITY OF PHOENIX–UTAH CAMPUS
Salt Lake City, UT

ABOUT THE INSTITUTION Proprietary, coed. *Awards:* bachelor's and master's degrees. 17 undergraduate majors. *Total enrollment:* 3,169. Undergraduates: 1,936. Freshmen: 41.

GIFT AID (NEED-BASED) *Scholarships, grants, and awards:* Federal Pell, FSEOG, state, private, college/university gift aid from institutional funds, Academic Competitiveness Grants, National SMART Grants.

GIFT AID (NON-NEED-BASED) *Scholarships, grants, and awards by category: Academic interests/achievement:* business, communication, computer science, social sciences.

LOANS *Programs:* FFEL (Subsidized and Unsubsidized Stafford, PLUS), Perkins.

APPLYING FOR FINANCIAL AID *Required financial aid forms:* FAFSA, institution's own form.

CONTACT ACS/AFS, University of Phoenix–Utah Campus, 875 West Elliot Road, Tempe, AZ 85284, 480-735-3000 or toll-free 800-776-4867 (in-state), 800-228-7240 (out-of-state). *Fax:* 480-940-2060.

UNIVERSITY OF PHOENIX–WASHINGTON CAMPUS
Seattle, WA

ABOUT THE INSTITUTION Proprietary, coed. *Awards:* bachelor's and master's degrees. 24 undergraduate majors. *Total enrollment:* 749. Undergraduates: 572. Freshmen: 33.

GIFT AID (NEED-BASED) *Scholarships, grants, and awards:* Federal Pell, FSEOG, state, private, college/university gift aid from institutional funds, Academic Competitiveness Grants, National SMART Grants.

GIFT AID (NON-NEED-BASED) *Scholarships, grants, and awards by category:* *Academic interests/achievement:* business, communication, computer science, social sciences.

LOANS *Programs:* FFEL (Subsidized and Unsubsidized Stafford, PLUS), Perkins.

APPLYING FOR FINANCIAL AID *Required financial aid forms:* FAFSA, institution's own form.

CONTACT ACS/AFS, University of Phoenix–Washington Campus, 875 West Elliot Road, Tempe, AZ 85284, 480-735-3000 or toll-free 800-776-4867 (in-state), 800-228-7240 (out-of-state). *Fax:* 480-940-2060.

UNIVERSITY OF PHOENIX–WASHINGTON D.C. CAMPUS
Washington, DC

CONTACT Financial Aid Office, University of Phoenix–Washington D.C. Campus, 25 Massachusetts Avenue NW, Suite 150, Washington, DC 20001.

UNIVERSITY OF PHOENIX–WEST FLORIDA CAMPUS
Temple Terrace, FL

ABOUT THE INSTITUTION Proprietary, coed. *Awards:* bachelor's and master's degrees. 10 undergraduate majors. *Total enrollment:* 894. Undergraduates: 740. Freshmen: 29.

GIFT AID (NEED-BASED) *Scholarships, grants, and awards:* Federal Pell, FSEOG, state, private, college/university gift aid from institutional funds, Academic Competitiveness Grants, National SMART Grants.

GIFT AID (NON-NEED-BASED) *Scholarships, grants, and awards by category:* *Academic interests/achievement:* business, communication, computer science, social sciences.

LOANS *Programs:* FFEL (Subsidized and Unsubsidized Stafford, PLUS), Perkins.

APPLYING FOR FINANCIAL AID *Required financial aid forms:* FAFSA, institution's own form.

CONTACT ACS/AFS, University of Phoenix–West Florida Campus, 875 West Elliot Road, Tempe, AZ 85284, 480-735-3000 or toll-free 800-776-4867 (in-state), 800-228-7240 (out-of-state). *Fax:* 480-940-2060.

UNIVERSITY OF PHOENIX–WEST MICHIGAN CAMPUS
Walker, MI

ABOUT THE INSTITUTION Proprietary, coed. *Awards:* bachelor's and master's degrees. 14 undergraduate majors. *Total enrollment:* 524. Undergraduates: 456. Freshmen: 69.

GIFT AID (NEED-BASED) *Scholarships, grants, and awards:* Federal Pell, FSEOG, state, private, college/university gift aid from institutional funds, Academic Competitiveness Grants, National SMART Grants.

GIFT AID (NON-NEED-BASED) *Scholarships, grants, and awards by category:* *Academic interests/achievement:* business, communication, computer science, social sciences.

LOANS *Programs:* FFEL (Subsidized and Unsubsidized Stafford, PLUS), Perkins.

APPLYING FOR FINANCIAL AID *Required financial aid forms:* FAFSA, institution's own form.

CONTACT ACS/AFS, University of Phoenix–West Michigan Campus, 875 West Elliot Road, Tempe, AZ 85284, 480-735-3000 or toll-free 800-776-4867 (in-state), 800-228-7240 (out-of-state). *Fax:* 480-940-2060.

UNIVERSITY OF PHOENIX–WICHITA CAMPUS
Wichita, KS

ABOUT THE INSTITUTION Proprietary, coed. *Awards:* bachelor's and master's degrees. 4 undergraduate majors. *Total enrollment:* 135. Undergraduates: 125.

GIFT AID (NEED-BASED) *Scholarships, grants, and awards:* Federal Pell, FSEOG, state, private, college/university gift aid from institutional funds, Academic Competitiveness Grants, National SMART Grants.

GIFT AID (NON-NEED-BASED) *Scholarships, grants, and awards by category:* *Academic interests/achievement:* business, communication, computer science, social sciences.

LOANS *Programs:* FFEL (Subsidized and Unsubsidized Stafford, PLUS), Perkins.

APPLYING FOR FINANCIAL AID *Required financial aid forms:* FAFSA, institution's own form.

CONTACT ACS/AFS, University of Phoenix–Wichita Campus, 875 West Elliot Road, Tempe, AZ 85284, 480-735-3000 or toll-free 800-776-4867 (in-state), 800-228-7240 (out-of-state). *Fax:* 480-940-2060.

UNIVERSITY OF PHOENIX–WISCONSIN CAMPUS
Madison, WI

ABOUT THE INSTITUTION Proprietary, coed. *Awards:* bachelor's and master's degrees. 11 undergraduate majors. *Total enrollment:* 80. Undergraduates: 63.

GIFT AID (NEED-BASED) *Scholarships, grants, and awards:* Federal Pell, FSEOG, state, private, college/university gift aid from institutional funds, Academic Competitiveness Grants, National SMART Grants.

GIFT AID (NON-NEED-BASED) *Scholarships, grants, and awards by category:* *Academic interests/achievement:* business, communication, computer science, social sciences.

LOANS *Programs:* FFEL (Subsidized and Unsubsidized Stafford, PLUS), Perkins.

APPLYING FOR FINANCIAL AID *Required financial aid forms:* FAFSA, institution's own form.

CONTACT ACS/AFS, University of Phoenix–Wisconsin Campus, 875 West Elliot Road, Tempe, AZ 85284, 480-735-3000 or toll-free 800-776-4867 (in-state), 800-228-7240 (out-of-state). *Fax:* 480-940-2060.

UNIVERSITY OF PITTSBURGH
Pittsburgh, PA

Tuition & fees (PA res): $14,154　　**Average undergraduate aid package:** $10,132

ABOUT THE INSTITUTION State-related, coed. 91 undergraduate majors. Federal methodology is used as a basis for awarding need-based institutional aid.

UNDERGRADUATE EXPENSES for 2009–10 *Tuition, state resident:* full-time $13,344; part-time $556 per credit. *Tuition, nonresident:* full-time $23,042; part-time $960 per credit. *Required fees:* full-time $810; $189 per term. Full-time tuition and fees vary according to program. Part-time tuition and fees vary according to program. *College room and board:* $8900; *Room only:* $5300. Room and board charges vary according to board plan and housing facility. *Payment plans:* Installment, deferred payment.

FRESHMAN FINANCIAL AID (Fall 2009, est.) 3,007 applied for aid; of those 68% were deemed to have need. 98% of freshmen with need received aid; of those 39% had need fully met. *Average percent of need met:* 81% (excluding resources awarded to replace EFC). *Average financial aid package:* $10,530 (excluding resources awarded to replace EFC). 8% of all full-time freshmen had no need and received non-need-based gift aid.

UNDERGRADUATE FINANCIAL AID (Fall 2009, est.) 11,989 applied for aid; of those 78% were deemed to have need. 97% of undergraduates with need received aid; of those 36% had need fully met. *Average percent of need met:* 79% (excluding resources awarded to replace EFC). *Average financial aid package:* $10,132 (excluding resources awarded to replace EFC). 7% of all full-time undergraduates had no need and received non-need-based gift aid.

GIFT AID (NEED-BASED) *Total amount:* $52,691,664 (27% federal, 21% state, 38% institutional, 14% external sources). *Receiving aid:* Freshmen: 41% (1,503); all full-time undergraduates: 38% (6,432). *Average award:* Freshmen: $9623;

Undergraduates: $8321. *Scholarships, grants, and awards:* Federal Pell, FSEOG, state, private, college/university gift aid from institutional funds, Federal Nursing.

GIFT AID (NON-NEED-BASED) *Total amount:* $22,117,618 (1% state, 77% institutional, 22% external sources). *Receiving aid:* Freshmen: 22% (812). Undergraduates: 16% (2,695). *Average award:* Freshmen: $14,678. Undergraduates: $15,282. *Scholarships, grants, and awards by category: Academic interests/achievement:* 1,180 awards ($18,032,760 total): general academic interests/achievements. *Tuition waivers:* Full or partial for employees or children of employees.

LOANS *Student loans:* $100,529,476 (38% need-based, 62% non-need-based). *Average need-based loan:* Freshmen: $4318. Undergraduates: $4894. *Parent loans:* $19,952,514 (74% need-based, 26% non-need-based). *Programs:* FFEL (Subsidized and Unsubsidized Stafford, PLUS), Perkins, Federal Nursing, college/university.

WORK-STUDY *Federal work-study:* Total amount: $2,500,000; 1,500 jobs averaging $1934.

ATHLETIC AWARDS Total amount: $7,334,658 (45% need-based, 55% non-need-based).

APPLYING FOR FINANCIAL AID *Required financial aid form:* FAFSA. *Financial aid deadline (priority):* 3/1. *Notification date:* Continuous beginning 3/15.

CONTACT Dr. Betsy A. Porter, Director, Office of Admissions and Financial Aid, University of Pittsburgh, 4227 Fifth Avenue, First Floor, Pittsburgh, PA 15260, 412-624-7488. *Fax:* 412-648-8815. *E-mail:* oafa@pitt.edu.

UNIVERSITY OF PITTSBURGH AT BRADFORD
Bradford, PA

Tuition & fees (PA res): $11,722   Average undergraduate aid package: $12,600

ABOUT THE INSTITUTION State-related, coed. 33 undergraduate majors. Federal methodology is used as a basis for awarding need-based institutional aid.

UNDERGRADUATE EXPENSES for 2009–10 *Tuition, state resident:* full-time $11,012; part-time $458 per credit hour. *Tuition, nonresident:* full-time $20,572; part-time $857 per credit hour. *Required fees:* full-time $710; $105 per term. Full-time tuition and fees vary according to course load and program. Part-time tuition and fees vary according to course load and program. *College room and board:* $7480; *Room only:* $4540. Room and board charges vary according to board plan and housing facility. *Payment plan:* Installment.

FRESHMAN FINANCIAL AID (Fall 2009, est.) 412 applied for aid; of those 87% were deemed to have need. 100% of freshmen with need received aid; of those 98% had need fully met. *Average percent of need met:* 95% (excluding resources awarded to replace EFC). *Average financial aid package:* $13,628 (excluding resources awarded to replace EFC). 29% of all full-time freshmen had no need and received non-need-based gift aid.

UNDERGRADUATE FINANCIAL AID (Fall 2009, est.) 1,448 applied for aid; of those 91% were deemed to have need. 98% of undergraduates with need received aid; of those 60% had need fully met. *Average percent of need met:* 90% (excluding resources awarded to replace EFC). *Average financial aid package:* $12,600 (excluding resources awarded to replace EFC). 18% of all full-time undergraduates had no need and received non-need-based gift aid.

GIFT AID (NEED-BASED) *Total amount:* $8,784,314 (30% federal, 26% state, 40% institutional, 4% external sources). *Receiving aid:* Freshmen: 56% (233); all full-time undergraduates: 36% (530). *Average award:* Freshmen: $5482; Undergraduates: $5520. *Scholarships, grants, and awards:* Federal Pell, FSEOG, state, private, college/university gift aid from institutional funds, Academic Competitiveness Grants, National SMART Grants.

GIFT AID (NON-NEED-BASED) *Total amount:* $634,771 (1% state, 94% institutional, 5% external sources). *Receiving aid:* Freshmen: 61% (252). Undergraduates: 31% (449). *Average award:* Freshmen: $5942. Undergraduates: $5589. *Scholarships, grants, and awards by category: Academic interests/achievement:* 133 awards ($125,909 total): biological sciences, business, communication, computer science, education, engineering/technologies, English, general academic interests/achievements, health fields, humanities, mathematics, physical sciences, premedicine, social sciences. *Creative arts/performance:* 2 awards ($1379 total): cinema/film/broadcasting. *Special characteristics:* 1,130 awards ($4,429,088 total): adult students, children of faculty/staff, children of union members/company employees, local/state students, out-of-state students, veterans. *Tuition waivers:* Full or partial for employees or children of employees.

LOANS *Student loans:* $10,745,375 (93% need-based, 7% non-need-based). 82% of past graduating class borrowed through all loan programs. *Average indebtedness per student:* $21,683. *Average need-based loan:* Freshmen: $3408. Undergraduates: $4327. *Parent loans:* $1,386,647 (82% need-based, 18% non-need-based). *Programs:* FFEL (Subsidized and Unsubsidized Stafford, PLUS), Perkins.

WORK-STUDY *Federal work-study:* Total amount: $1,329,945; 193 jobs averaging $1740. *State or other work-study/employment:* Total amount: $10,624 (100% need-based). 1 part-time job averaging $1764.

APPLYING FOR FINANCIAL AID *Required financial aid form:* FAFSA. *Financial aid deadline (priority):* 3/1. *Notification date:* Continuous beginning 4/1. Students must reply within 2 weeks of notification.

CONTACT Melissa Ibanez, Director of Financial Aid, University of Pittsburgh at Bradford, 300 Campus Drive, Bradford, PA 16701-2812, 814-362-7550 or toll-free 800-872-1787. *Fax:* 814-362-7578. *E-mail:* ibanez@pitt.edu.

UNIVERSITY OF PITTSBURGH AT GREENSBURG
Greensburg, PA

Tuition & fees (PA res): $11,852   Average undergraduate aid package: $9367

ABOUT THE INSTITUTION State-related, coed. 23 undergraduate majors. Federal methodology is used as a basis for awarding need-based institutional aid.

UNDERGRADUATE EXPENSES for 2009–10 *Tuition, state resident:* full-time $11,012; part-time $458 per credit hour. *Tuition, nonresident:* full-time $20,572; part-time $857 per credit hour. *Required fees:* full-time $840. *College room and board:* $7840. Room and board charges vary according to board plan and housing facility. *Payment plan:* Installment.

FRESHMAN FINANCIAL AID (Fall 2009, est.) 383 applied for aid; of those 85% were deemed to have need. 99% of freshmen with need received aid; of those 21% had need fully met. *Average percent of need met:* 48% (excluding resources awarded to replace EFC). *Average financial aid package:* $9900 (excluding resources awarded to replace EFC). 1% of all full-time freshmen had no need and received non-need-based gift aid.

UNDERGRADUATE FINANCIAL AID (Fall 2009, est.) 1,443 applied for aid; of those 85% were deemed to have need. 97% of undergraduates with need received aid; of those 17% had need fully met. *Average percent of need met:* 49% (excluding resources awarded to replace EFC). *Average financial aid package:* $9367 (excluding resources awarded to replace EFC). 2% of all full-time undergraduates had no need and received non-need-based gift aid.

GIFT AID (NEED-BASED) *Total amount:* $5,442,809 (44% federal, 37% state, 12% institutional, 7% external sources). *Receiving aid:* Freshmen: 31% (129); all full-time undergraduates: 32% (529). *Average award:* Freshmen: $4601; Undergraduates: $4425. *Scholarships, grants, and awards:* Federal Pell, FSEOG, state, private, college/university gift aid from institutional funds, United Negro College Fund.

GIFT AID (NON-NEED-BASED) *Total amount:* $130,485 (3% state, 76% institutional, 21% external sources). *Receiving aid:* Freshmen: 19% (78). Undergraduates: 9% (148). *Average award:* Freshmen: $3750. Undergraduates: $3696. *Scholarships, grants, and awards by category: Special achievements/activities:* leadership. *Tuition waivers:* Full or partial for employees or children of employees, senior citizens.

LOANS *Student loans:* $7,595,335 (81% need-based, 19% non-need-based). 82% of past graduating class borrowed through all loan programs. *Average indebtedness per student:* $24,707. *Average need-based loan:* Freshmen: $3606. Undergraduates: $4339. *Parent loans:* $1,247,133 (79% need-based, 21% non-need-based). *Programs:* Federal Direct (Subsidized and Unsubsidized Stafford, PLUS), FFEL (Subsidized and Unsubsidized Stafford, PLUS), Perkins, college/university.

WORK-STUDY *Federal work-study:* Total amount: $502,617; jobs available.

APPLYING FOR FINANCIAL AID *Required financial aid forms:* FAFSA, state aid form. *Financial aid deadline (priority):* 2/15. *Notification date:* Continuous beginning 3/15. Students must reply within 3 weeks of notification.

CONTACT Ms. Brandi S. Darr, Director of Financial Aid, University of Pittsburgh at Greensburg, 150 Finoli Drive, Greensburg, PA 15601-5898, 724-836-7167. *E-mail:* upgfnaid@pitt.edu.

UNIVERSITY OF PITTSBURGH AT JOHNSTOWN
Johnstown, PA

Tuition & fees (PA res): $11,754   Average undergraduate aid package: $10,226

ABOUT THE INSTITUTION State-related, coed. 49 undergraduate majors. Federal methodology is used as a basis for awarding need-based institutional aid.

UNDERGRADUATE EXPENSES for 2009–10 *Tuition, state resident:* full-time $11,012; part-time $458 per credit. *Tuition, nonresident:* full-time $20,572; part-time $857 per credit hour. *Required fees:* full-time $742; $87 per term. Full-time tuition and fees vary according to program. Part-time tuition and fees vary according to program. *College room and board:* $7290; *Room only:* $4570. Room and board charges vary according to board plan and housing facility. *Payment plan:* Installment.

FRESHMAN FINANCIAL AID (Fall 2009, est.) 733 applied for aid; of those 80% were deemed to have need. 99% of freshmen with need received aid; of those 5% had need fully met. *Average percent of need met:* 57% (excluding resources awarded to replace EFC). *Average financial aid package:* $10,185 (excluding resources awarded to replace EFC). 2% of all full-time freshmen had no need and received non-need-based gift aid.

UNDERGRADUATE FINANCIAL AID (Fall 2009, est.) 2,586 applied for aid; of those 85% were deemed to have need. 98% of undergraduates with need received aid; of those 10% had need fully met. *Average percent of need met:* 57% (excluding resources awarded to replace EFC). *Average financial aid package:* $10,226 (excluding resources awarded to replace EFC). 1% of all full-time undergraduates had no need and received non-need-based gift aid.

GIFT AID (NEED-BASED) *Total amount:* $9,018,748 (44% federal, 44% state, 8% institutional, 4% external sources). *Receiving aid:* Freshmen: 56% (441); all full-time undergraduates: 52% (1,508). *Average award:* Freshmen: $5729; Undergraduates: $5373. *Scholarships, grants, and awards:* Federal Pell, FSEOG, state, private, college/university gift aid from institutional funds.

GIFT AID (NON-NEED-BASED) *Total amount:* $1,935,162 (11% state, 84% institutional, 5% external sources). *Receiving aid:* Freshmen: 23% (183). Undergraduates: 21% (617). *Average award:* Freshmen: $3717. Undergraduates: $2869. *Scholarships, grants, and awards by category: Academic interests/achievement:* 523 awards ($1,421,411 total): biological sciences, business, communication, computer science, education, engineering/technologies, English, general academic interests/achievements, humanities, mathematics, physical sciences, premedicine, social sciences. *Creative arts/performance:* 4 awards ($16,350 total): journalism/publications, theater/drama. *Special achievements/activities:* 137 awards ($182,500 total): leadership. *Special characteristics:* 199 awards ($1,945,522 total): children of faculty/staff. *Tuition waivers:* Full or partial for employees or children of employees.

LOANS *Student loans:* $19,690,661 (42% need-based, 58% non-need-based). 85% of past graduating class borrowed through all loan programs. *Average indebtedness per student:* $23,243. *Average need-based loan:* Freshmen: $3478. Undergraduates: $4297. *Parent loans:* $3,502,696 (100% non-need-based). *Programs:* Federal Direct (Subsidized and Unsubsidized Stafford, PLUS), Perkins.

WORK-STUDY *Federal work-study:* Total amount: $527,190; 160 jobs averaging $1807. *State or other work-study/employment:* Total amount: $516,736 (8% need-based, 92% non-need-based). 308 part-time jobs averaging $2640.

ATHLETIC AWARDS Total amount: $547,895 (100% non-need-based).

APPLYING FOR FINANCIAL AID *Required financial aid form:* FAFSA. *Financial aid deadline (priority):* 4/1. *Notification date:* Continuous beginning 4/1. Students must reply within 2 weeks of notification.

CONTACT Ms. Jeanine M. Lawn, Director of Student Financial Aid, University of Pittsburgh at Johnstown, 125 Biddle Hall, Johnstown, PA 15904-2990, 814-269-7045 or toll-free 800-765-4875. *Fax:* 814-269-7061. *E-mail:* lawn@pitt.edu.

UNIVERSITY OF PORTLAND
Portland, OR

Tuition & fees: $31,996   Average undergraduate aid package: $24,612

ABOUT THE INSTITUTION Independent Roman Catholic, coed. 42 undergraduate majors. Federal methodology is used as a basis for awarding need-based institutional aid.

UNDERGRADUATE EXPENSES for 2009–10 *Comprehensive fee:* $41,131 includes full-time tuition ($30,800), mandatory fees ($1196), and room and board ($9135). *College room only:* $4245. Full-time tuition and fees vary according to program. Room and board charges vary according to board plan and housing facility. *Part-time tuition:* $970 per credit hour. Part-time tuition and fees vary according to course load and program. *Payment plans:* Installment, deferred payment.

FRESHMAN FINANCIAL AID (Fall 2008) 676 applied for aid; of those 81% were deemed to have need. 100% of freshmen with need received aid; of those 10% had need fully met. *Average percent of need met:* 77% (excluding resources awarded to replace EFC). *Average financial aid package:* $23,598 (excluding resources awarded to replace EFC). 26% of all full-time freshmen had no need and received non-need-based gift aid.

UNDERGRADUATE FINANCIAL AID (Fall 2008) 2,264 applied for aid; of those 86% were deemed to have need. 100% of undergraduates with need received aid; of those 8% had need fully met. *Average percent of need met:* 75% (excluding resources awarded to replace EFC). *Average financial aid package:* $24,612 (excluding resources awarded to replace EFC). 26% of all full-time undergraduates had no need and received non-need-based gift aid.

GIFT AID (NEED-BASED) *Total amount:* $30,656,764 (12% federal, 2% state, 82% institutional, 4% external sources). *Receiving aid:* Freshmen: 50% (410); all full-time undergraduates: 48% (1,468). *Average award:* Freshmen: $8897; Undergraduates: $10,370. *Scholarships, grants, and awards:* Federal Pell, FSEOG, state, private, college/university gift aid from institutional funds.

GIFT AID (NON-NEED-BASED) *Total amount:* $12,994,478 (98% institutional, 2% external sources). *Receiving aid:* Freshmen: 67% (548). Undergraduates: 62% (1,896). *Average award:* Freshmen: $11,423. Undergraduates: $11,022. *Scholarships, grants, and awards by category: Academic interests/achievement:* 245 awards ($772,933 total): biological sciences, business, communication, computer science, education, engineering/technologies, English, foreign languages, general academic interests/achievements, health fields, humanities, mathematics, military science, physical sciences, premedicine, religion/biblical studies, social sciences. *Creative arts/performance:* 50 awards ($122,725 total): music, performing arts, theater/drama. *Special characteristics:* 29 awards ($850,885 total): children and siblings of alumni, children of faculty/staff, relatives of clergy, religious affiliation. *Tuition waivers:* Full or partial for employees or children of employees.

LOANS *Student loans:* $17,201,221 (84% need-based, 16% non-need-based). 10% of past graduating class borrowed through all loan programs. *Average indebtedness per student:* $9046. *Average need-based loan:* Freshmen: $3436. Undergraduates: $5084. *Parent loans:* $11,422,047 (73% need-based, 27% non-need-based). *Programs:* FFEL (Subsidized and Unsubsidized Stafford, PLUS), Perkins, Federal Nursing, college/university.

WORK-STUDY *Federal work-study:* Total amount: $3,050,316; 1,088 jobs averaging $2685.

ATHLETIC AWARDS Total amount: $3,794,054 (9% need-based, 91% non-need-based).

APPLYING FOR FINANCIAL AID *Required financial aid form:* FAFSA. *Financial aid deadline (priority):* 3/1. *Notification date:* Continuous beginning 3/15. Students must reply within 3 weeks of notification.

CONTACT Ms. Janet Turner, Director of Financial Aid, University of Portland, 5000 North Willamette Boulevard, Portland, OR 97203-5798, 503-943-7311 or toll-free 888-627-5601 (out-of-state). *Fax:* 503-943-7508. *E-mail:* finaid@up.edu.

UNIVERSITY OF PUERTO RICO, AGUADILLA UNIVERSITY COLLEGE
Aguadilla, PR

CONTACT Director of Financial Aid, University of Puerto Rico, Aguadilla University College, PO Box 250-160, Aguadilla, PR 00604-0160, 787-890-2681 Ext. 273.

UNIVERSITY OF PUERTO RICO AT ARECIBO
Arecibo, PR

CONTACT Mr. Luis Rodriguez, Director of Financial Aid, University of Puerto Rico at Arecibo, PO Box 4010, Arecibo, PR 00613, 787-878-2830 Ext. 2008.

UNIVERSITY OF PUERTO RICO AT BAYAMÓN
Bayamón, PR

Tuition & fees (PR res): $2076 | **Average undergraduate aid package: N/A**

ABOUT THE INSTITUTION Commonwealth-supported, coed. 18 undergraduate majors. Federal methodology is used as a basis for awarding need-based institutional aid.

UNDERGRADUATE EXPENSES for 2010–11 *Tuition, state resident:* full-time $1734; part-time $51 per credit. *Tuition, nonresident:* full-time $4039. *Required fees:* full-time $342; $144 per term. Full-time tuition and fees vary according to class time, course load, and program. Part-time tuition and fees vary according to class time, course load, and program. Room and board charges vary according to housing facility. *Payment plans:* Guaranteed tuition, deferred payment.

GIFT AID (NEED-BASED) *Scholarships, grants, and awards:* Federal Pell, FSEOG, state, college/university gift aid from institutional funds.

GIFT AID (NON-NEED-BASED) *Scholarships, grants, and awards by category: Academic interests/achievement:* general academic interests/achievements. *Creative arts/performance:* music, theater/drama. *Special achievements/activities:* cheerleading/drum major. *Special characteristics:* veterans, veterans' children. *Tuition waivers:* Full or partial for employees or children of employees.

LOANS *Programs:* Federal Direct (Unsubsidized Stafford, PLUS), Perkins.

WORK-STUDY Federal work-study jobs available.

APPLYING FOR FINANCIAL AID *Required financial aid forms:* FAFSA, institution's own form, state income tax form(s).

CONTACT Mr. Hector Cuadrado, Financial Aid Director, University of Puerto Rico at Bayamón, 170 Carretera 174 Parque Industrial Minillas, Bayamon, PR 00959-1911, 787-993-8953 Ext. 4033. *E-mail:* hector.cuadrado@upr.edu.

UNIVERSITY OF PUERTO RICO AT HUMACAO
Humacao, PR

CONTACT Larry Cruz, Director of Financial Aid, University of Puerto Rico at Humacao, HUC Station, Humacao, PR 00791-4300, 787-850-9342.

UNIVERSITY OF PUERTO RICO AT PONCE
Ponce, PR

CONTACT Carmelo Vega Montes, Director of Financial Aid, University of Puerto Rico at Ponce, Box 7186, Ponce, PR 00732-7186, 787-844-8181. *Fax:* 787-840-8108.

UNIVERSITY OF PUERTO RICO AT UTUADO
Utuado, PR

CONTACT Edgar Salvá, Director of Financial Assistance, University of Puerto Rico at Utuado, PO Box 2500, Utuado, PR 00641, 787-894-2828 Ext. 2603. *Fax:* 787-894-3810. *E-mail:* esalva@uprutuado.edu.

UNIVERSITY OF PUERTO RICO, CAYEY UNIVERSITY COLLEGE
Cayey, PR

CONTACT Mr. Hector Maldonado Otero, Director of Financial Aid, University of Puerto Rico, Cayey University College, Antonio Barcelo, Cayey, PR 00736, 787-738-2161. *Fax:* 787-263-0676.

UNIVERSITY OF PUERTO RICO, MAYAGÜEZ CAMPUS
Mayagüez, PR

ABOUT THE INSTITUTION Commonwealth-supported, coed. 54 undergraduate majors.

GIFT AID (NEED-BASED) *Scholarships, grants, and awards:* Federal Pell, FSEOG, state, private, college/university gift aid from institutional funds.

GIFT AID (NON-NEED-BASED) *Scholarships, grants, and awards by category: Academic interests/achievement:* military science. *Creative arts/performance:* dance, music. *Special achievements/activities:* cheerleading/drum major. *Special characteristics:* children of faculty/staff, veterans' children.

LOANS *Programs:* FFEL (Subsidized and Unsubsidized Stafford), college/university.

WORK-STUDY *Federal work-study:* Total amount: $730,280; 810 jobs averaging $982.

APPLYING FOR FINANCIAL AID *Required financial aid forms:* FAFSA, institution's own form, business/farm supplement.

CONTACT Ms. Ana I. Rodríguez, Director of Financial Aid, University of Puerto Rico, Mayagüez Campus, PO Box 9000, Mayagüez, PR 00681-9000, 787-265-3863. *Fax:* 787-265-1920. *E-mail:* a_rodriguez@rumad.uprm.edu.

UNIVERSITY OF PUERTO RICO, MEDICAL SCIENCES CAMPUS
San Juan, PR

ABOUT THE INSTITUTION Commonwealth-supported, coed, primarily women. 9 undergraduate majors.

GIFT AID (NEED-BASED) *Scholarships, grants, and awards:* Federal Pell, FSEOG, state, private, college/university gift aid from institutional funds, Department of Health and Human Services Scholarships.

GIFT AID (NON-NEED-BASED) *Scholarships, grants, and awards by category: Academic interests/achievement:* general academic interests/achievements. *Creative arts/performance:* performing arts. *Special achievements/activities:* general special achievements/activities. *Special characteristics:* children of faculty/staff, general special characteristics, veterans, veterans' children.

LOANS *Programs:* FFEL (Subsidized and Unsubsidized Stafford), alternative loans.

APPLYING FOR FINANCIAL AID *Required financial aid forms:* FAFSA, institution's own form.

CONTACT Mrs. Zoraida Figueroa, Financial Aid Director, University of Puerto Rico, Medical Sciences Campus, Terreno Centro Medico-Edificio Decanato Farmacia y Estudiantes, San Juan, PR 00936-5067, 787-763-2525. *Fax:* 787-282-7117. *E-mail:* zoraida.figueroa@upr.edu.

UNIVERSITY OF PUERTO RICO, RÍO PIEDRAS
San Juan, PR

Tuition & fees (PR res): $1320 | **Average undergraduate aid package: N/A**

ABOUT THE INSTITUTION Commonwealth-supported, coed. 57 undergraduate majors.

UNDERGRADUATE EXPENSES for 2009–10 *Tuition, state resident:* full-time $1176; part-time $49 per credit. *Tuition, nonresident:* full-time $3883; part-time $161.83 per credit. *Required fees:* full-time $144; $72 per term. Full-time tuition and fees vary according to degree level and reciprocity agreements. Part-time tuition and fees vary according to degree level and reciprocity agreements. *College room and board:* $8280. *Payment plan:* Deferred payment.

GIFT AID (NEED-BASED) *Scholarships, grants, and awards:* Federal Pell, FSEOG, state, private.

GIFT AID (NON-NEED-BASED) *Tuition waivers:* Full or partial for employees or children of employees.

LOANS *Programs:* Federal Direct (Subsidized and Unsubsidized Stafford, PLUS), Perkins, college/university, law access loans.

APPLYING FOR FINANCIAL AID *Required financial aid forms:* FAFSA, institution's own form. *Financial aid deadline:* 4/25 (priority: 2/25). *Notification date:* 7/26.

CONTACT Mr. Efraim Williams, EDP Manager, University of Puerto Rico, Río Piedras, PO Box 23300, San Juan, PR 00931-3300, 787-764-0000 Ext. 5573.

UNIVERSITY OF PUGET SOUND
Tacoma, WA

Tuition & fees: $37,225	Average undergraduate aid package: $27,595

ABOUT THE INSTITUTION Independent, coed. 36 undergraduate majors. Federal methodology is used as a basis for awarding need-based institutional aid.

UNDERGRADUATE EXPENSES for 2010–11 *Comprehensive fee:* $46,875 includes full-time tuition ($37,030), mandatory fees ($195), and room and board ($9650). *College room only:* $5390. Full-time tuition and fees vary according to course load. Room and board charges vary according to board plan and housing facility. *Part-time tuition:* $4670 per unit. Part-time tuition and fees vary according to course load. *Payment plans:* Installment, deferred payment.

FRESHMAN FINANCIAL AID (Fall 2009, est.) 551 applied for aid; of those 84% were deemed to have need. 100% of freshmen with need received aid; of those 29% had need fully met. *Average percent of need met:* 85% (excluding resources awarded to replace EFC). *Average financial aid package:* $28,277 (excluding resources awarded to replace EFC). 24% of all full-time freshmen had no need and received non-need-based gift aid.

UNDERGRADUATE FINANCIAL AID (Fall 2009, est.) 1,822 applied for aid; of those 90% were deemed to have need. 100% of undergraduates with need received aid; of those 23% had need fully met. *Average percent of need met:* 82% (excluding resources awarded to replace EFC). *Average financial aid package:* $27,595 (excluding resources awarded to replace EFC). 25% of all full-time undergraduates had no need and received non-need-based gift aid.

GIFT AID (NEED-BASED) *Total amount:* $34,963,573 (9% federal, 3% state, 84% institutional, 4% external sources). *Receiving aid:* Freshmen: 63% (455); all full-time undergraduates: 63% (1,617). *Average award:* Freshmen: $23,361; Undergraduates: $22,319. *Scholarships, grants, and awards:* Federal Pell, FSEOG, state, private, college/university gift aid from institutional funds.

GIFT AID (NON-NEED-BASED) *Total amount:* $5,852,722 (1% state, 93% institutional, 6% external sources). *Receiving aid:* Freshmen: 5% (33). Undergraduates: 4% (95). *Average award:* Freshmen: $10,172. Undergraduates: $8809. *Scholarships, grants, and awards by category: Academic interests/achievement:* 718 awards ($4,890,624 total): biological sciences, business, communication, computer science, English, foreign languages, general academic interests/achievements, humanities, international studies, mathematics, physical sciences, premedicine, social sciences. *Creative arts/performance:* 68 awards ($217,222 total): art/fine arts, debating, music, theater/drama. *Special achievements/activities:* 9 awards ($29,000 total): leadership, religious involvement. *Special characteristics:* 28 awards ($812,380 total): children of faculty/staff, international students. *Tuition waivers:* Full or partial for employees or children of employees.

LOANS *Student loans:* $12,337,635 (92% need-based, 8% non-need-based). 63% of past graduating class borrowed through all loan programs. *Average indebtedness per student:* $29,514. *Average need-based loan:* Freshmen: $4785. Undergraduates: $5357. *Parent loans:* $5,055,482 (78% need-based, 22% non-need-based). *Programs:* Federal Direct (Subsidized and Unsubsidized Stafford, PLUS), Perkins, Alaska Loans.

WORK-STUDY *Federal work-study:* Total amount: $1,406,000; 514 jobs averaging $2735. *State or other work-study/employment:* Total amount: $2,270,809 (100% need-based). 962 part-time jobs averaging $2360.

APPLYING FOR FINANCIAL AID *Required financial aid form:* FAFSA. *Financial aid deadline (priority):* 2/1. *Notification date:* Continuous beginning 3/15. Students must reply by 5/1.

CONTACT Maggie A. Mittuch, Associate Vice President for Student Financial Services, University of Puget Sound, 1500 North Warner Street #1039, Tacoma, WA 98416-1039, 253-879-3214 or toll-free 800-396-7191. *Fax:* 253-879-8508. *E-mail:* mmittuch@pugetsound.edu.

UNIVERSITY OF REDLANDS
Redlands, CA

Tuition & fees: $33,894	Average undergraduate aid package: $28,324

ABOUT THE INSTITUTION Independent, coed. 42 undergraduate majors. Federal methodology is used as a basis for awarding need-based institutional aid.

UNDERGRADUATE EXPENSES for 2009–10 *Comprehensive fee:* $44,366 includes full-time tuition ($33,594), mandatory fees ($300), and room and board ($10,472). *College room only:* $5814. Full-time tuition and fees vary according to program. Room and board charges vary according to board plan and housing facility. *Part-time tuition:* $1050 per credit. *Part-time fees:* $150 per term. Part-time tuition and fees vary according to course load and program. *Payment plan:* Installment.

FRESHMAN FINANCIAL AID (Fall 2009, est.) 491 applied for aid; of those 93% were deemed to have need. 99% of freshmen with need received aid; of those 19% had need fully met. *Average percent of need met:* 71% (excluding resources awarded to replace EFC). *Average financial aid package:* $29,994 (excluding resources awarded to replace EFC). 13% of all full-time freshmen had no need and received non-need-based gift aid.

UNDERGRADUATE FINANCIAL AID (Fall 2009, est.) 1,865 applied for aid; of those 96% were deemed to have need. 96% of undergraduates with need received aid; of those 17% had need fully met. *Average percent of need met:* 66% (excluding resources awarded to replace EFC). *Average financial aid package:* $28,324 (excluding resources awarded to replace EFC). 12% of all full-time undergraduates had no need and received non-need-based gift aid.

GIFT AID (NEED-BASED) *Total amount:* $40,034,529 (8% federal, 11% state, 81% institutional). *Receiving aid:* Freshmen: 79% (447); all full-time undergraduates: 75% (1,713). *Average award:* Freshmen: $25,240; Undergraduates: $23,039. *Scholarships, grants, and awards:* Federal Pell, FSEOG, state, private, college/university gift aid from institutional funds.

GIFT AID (NON-NEED-BASED) *Total amount:* $3,277,723 (75% institutional, 25% external sources). *Receiving aid:* Freshmen: 16% (92). Undergraduates: 9% (195). *Average award:* Freshmen: $14,297. *Scholarships, grants, and awards by category:* Academic interests/achievement: general academic interests/achievements. *Creative arts/performance:* art/fine arts, creative writing, debating, music. *Special achievements/activities:* general special achievements/activities. *Special characteristics:* international students. *Tuition waivers:* Full or partial for employees or children of employees.

LOANS *Student loans:* $13,586,554 (53% need-based, 47% non-need-based). 70% of past graduating class borrowed through all loan programs. *Average indebtedness per student:* $24,218. *Average need-based loan:* Freshmen: $4979. Undergraduates: $6122. *Parent loans:* $3,993,712 (100% non-need-based). *Programs:* FFEL (Subsidized and Unsubsidized Stafford, PLUS), Perkins, college/university.

WORK-STUDY *Federal work-study:* Total amount: $2,704,701; jobs available. *State or other work-study/employment:* Total amount: $897,450 (100% need-based). Part-time jobs available.

APPLYING FOR FINANCIAL AID *Required financial aid forms:* FAFSA, state aid form. *Financial aid deadline (priority):* 2/15. *Notification date:* Continuous beginning 2/28. Students must reply by 5/1.

CONTACT Bethann Corey, Director of Financial Aid, University of Redlands, PO Box 3080, Redlands, CA 92373-0999, 909-748-8261 or toll-free 800-455-5064. *Fax:* 909-335-4089. *E-mail:* financialaid@redlands.edu.

UNIVERSITY OF RHODE ISLAND
Kingston, RI

Tuition & fees (RI res): $9528	Average undergraduate aid package: $12,794

ABOUT THE INSTITUTION State-supported, coed. 80 undergraduate majors. Federal methodology is used as a basis for awarding need-based institutional aid.

UNDERGRADUATE EXPENSES for 2009–10 *Tuition, state resident:* full-time $8238; part-time $343 per credit hour. *Tuition, nonresident:* full-time $24,736; part-time $1031 per credit hour. *Required fees:* full-time $1290; $27 per credit hour or $49 per term. Full-time tuition and fees vary according to course load, location, and reciprocity agreements. Part-time tuition and fees vary according to course load, location, and reciprocity agreements. *College room and board:* $9892; *Room only:* $6182. Room and board charges vary according to board plan and housing facility. *Payment plan:* Installment.

FRESHMAN FINANCIAL AID (Fall 2009, est.) 2,577 applied for aid; of those 79% were deemed to have need. 86% of freshmen with need received aid; of those 97% had need fully met. *Average percent of need met:* 59% (excluding resources awarded to replace EFC). *Average financial aid package:* $12,463 (excluding resources awarded to replace EFC). 5% of all full-time freshmen had no need and received non-need-based gift aid.

UNDERGRADUATE FINANCIAL AID (Fall 2009, est.) 10,466 applied for aid; of those 84% were deemed to have need. 79% of undergraduates with need received aid; of those 87% had need fully met. *Average percent of need met:*

University of Rhode Island

57% (excluding resources awarded to replace EFC). *Average financial aid package:* $12,794 (excluding resources awarded to replace EFC). 3% of all full-time undergraduates had no need and received non-need-based gift aid.

GIFT AID (NEED-BASED) *Total amount:* $56,420,005 (25% federal, 5% state, 66% institutional, 4% external sources). *Receiving aid:* Freshmen: 60% (1,754); all full-time undergraduates: 60% (6,987). *Average award:* Freshmen: $7501; Undergraduates: $7540. *Scholarships, grants, and awards:* Federal Pell, FSEOG, state, private, college/university gift aid from institutional funds.

GIFT AID (NON-NEED-BASED) *Total amount:* $2,228,888 (88% institutional, 12% external sources). *Receiving aid:* Freshmen: 5% (147). Undergraduates: 4% (515). *Average award:* Freshmen: $3992. Undergraduates: $5057. *Tuition waivers:* Full or partial for minority students, employees or children of employees, senior citizens.

LOANS *Student loans:* $65,520,249 (79% need-based, 21% non-need-based). 72% of past graduating class borrowed through all loan programs. *Average indebtedness per student:* $23,000. *Average need-based loan:* Freshmen: $4191. Undergraduates: $5499. *Parent loans:* $38,923,978 (60% need-based, 40% non-need-based). *Programs:* Federal Direct (Subsidized and Unsubsidized Stafford, PLUS), Perkins, Federal Nursing, college/university.

WORK-STUDY *Federal work-study:* Total amount: $714,809; jobs available.

ATHLETIC AWARDS Total amount: $5,370,942 (98% need-based, 2% non-need-based).

APPLYING FOR FINANCIAL AID *Required financial aid form:* FAFSA. *Financial aid deadline (priority):* 3/1. *Notification date:* Continuous beginning 3/31. Students must reply by 5/1.

CONTACT Mr. Horace J. Amaral Jr., Director of Enrollment Services, University of Rhode Island, Green Hall, Kingston, RI 02881, 401-874-9500.

UNIVERSITY OF RICHMOND
Richmond, VA

Tuition & fees: $41,610	Average undergraduate aid package: $36,857

ABOUT THE INSTITUTION Independent, coed. 53 undergraduate majors. Federal methodology is used as a basis for awarding need-based institutional aid.

UNDERGRADUATE EXPENSES for 2010–11 *Comprehensive fee:* $50,420 includes full-time tuition ($41,610) and room and board ($8810). *College room only:* $3970. Full-time tuition and fees vary according to course load and student level. Room and board charges vary according to board plan and housing facility. *Payment plans:* Installment, deferred payment.

FRESHMAN FINANCIAL AID (Fall 2009, est.) 603 applied for aid; of those 81% were deemed to have need. 100% of freshmen with need received aid; of those 91% had need fully met. *Average percent of need met:* 100% (excluding resources awarded to replace EFC). *Average financial aid package:* $37,759 (excluding resources awarded to replace EFC). 5% of all full-time freshmen had no need and received non-need-based gift aid.

UNDERGRADUATE FINANCIAL AID (Fall 2009, est.) 1,712 applied for aid; of those 84% were deemed to have need. 100% of undergraduates with need received aid; of those 93% had need fully met. *Average percent of need met:* 100% (excluding resources awarded to replace EFC). *Average financial aid package:* $36,857 (excluding resources awarded to replace EFC). 14% of all full-time undergraduates had no need and received non-need-based gift aid.

GIFT AID (NEED-BASED) *Total amount:* $45,439,369 (5% federal, 2% state, 92% institutional, 1% external sources). *Receiving aid:* Freshmen: 52% (481); all full-time undergraduates: 46% (1,422). *Average award:* Freshmen: $33,712; Undergraduates: $33,404. *Scholarships, grants, and awards:* Federal Pell, FSEOG, state, private, college/university gift aid from institutional funds.

GIFT AID (NON-NEED-BASED) *Total amount:* $11,393,293 (7% federal, 6% state, 82% institutional, 5% external sources). *Receiving aid:* Freshmen: 5% (45). Undergraduates: 5% (153). *Average award:* Freshmen: $37,783. Undergraduates: $19,879. *Scholarships, grants, and awards by category: Academic interests/achievement:* 174 awards ($6,229,660 total): biological sciences, computer science, general academic interests/achievements, mathematics, physical sciences. *Creative arts/performance:* 30 awards ($850,200 total): art/fine arts, dance, music, performing arts, theater/drama. *Special achievements/ activities:* 96 awards ($240,000 total): community service. *Tuition waivers:* Full or partial for employees or children of employees.

LOANS *Student loans:* $10,452,091 (29% need-based, 71% non-need-based). 42% of past graduating class borrowed through all loan programs. *Average indebtedness per student:* $21,555. *Average need-based loan:* Freshmen: $2930.

Undergraduates: $3032. *Parent loans:* $4,831,960 (4% need-based, 96% non-need-based). *Programs:* Federal Direct (Subsidized and Unsubsidized Stafford, PLUS), Perkins.

WORK-STUDY *Federal work-study:* Total amount: $463,305; 432 jobs averaging $980.

ATHLETIC AWARDS Total amount: $8,052,913 (19% need-based, 81% non-need-based).

APPLYING FOR FINANCIAL AID *Required financial aid forms:* FAFSA, CSS Financial Aid PROFILE, prior year federal tax return. *Financial aid deadline:* 2/15. *Notification date:* 4/1. Students must reply within 4 weeks of notification.

CONTACT Financial Aid Office, University of Richmond, Sarah Brunet Hall, University of Richmond, VA 23173, 804-289-8438 or toll-free 800-700-1662. *Fax:* 804-484-1650. *E-mail:* finaid@richmond.edu.

UNIVERSITY OF RIO GRANDE
Rio Grande, OH

CONTACT Dr. John Hill, Director of Financial Aid, University of Rio Grande, 218 North College Avenue, Rio Grande, OH 45674, 740-245-7218 or toll-free 800-282-7201 (in-state). *Fax:* 740-245-7102.

UNIVERSITY OF ROCHESTER
Rochester, NY

Tuition & fees: $38,690	Average undergraduate aid package: $32,203

ABOUT THE INSTITUTION Independent, coed. 60 undergraduate majors. Institutional methodology is used as a basis for awarding need-based institutional aid.

UNDERGRADUATE EXPENSES for 2009–10 *Comprehensive fee:* $49,890 includes full-time tuition ($37,870), mandatory fees ($820), and room and board ($11,200). *College room only:* $6750. Room and board charges vary according to board plan. *Part-time tuition:* $1183 per credit hour. Part-time tuition and fees vary according to course load. *Payment plans:* Tuition prepayment, installment.

FRESHMAN FINANCIAL AID (Fall 2009, est.) 799 applied for aid; of those 83% were deemed to have need. 100% of freshmen with need received aid; of those 100% had need fully met. *Average percent of need met:* 100% (excluding resources awarded to replace EFC). *Average financial aid package:* $33,413 (excluding resources awarded to replace EFC). 27% of all full-time freshmen had no need and received non-need-based gift aid.

UNDERGRADUATE FINANCIAL AID (Fall 2009, est.) 2,968 applied for aid; of those 88% were deemed to have need. 100% of undergraduates with need received aid; of those 80% had need fully met. *Average percent of need met:* 96% (excluding resources awarded to replace EFC). *Average financial aid package:* $32,203 (excluding resources awarded to replace EFC). 31% of all full-time undergraduates had no need and received non-need-based gift aid.

GIFT AID (NEED-BASED) *Total amount:* $65,083,356 (10% federal, 6% state, 82% institutional, 2% external sources). *Receiving aid:* Freshmen: 61% (663); all full-time undergraduates: 57% (2,575). *Average award:* Freshmen: $29,089; Undergraduates: $26,741. *Scholarships, grants, and awards:* Federal Pell, FSEOG, state, college/university gift aid from institutional funds.

GIFT AID (NON-NEED-BASED) *Total amount:* $16,522,415 (7% federal, 1% state, 86% institutional, 6% external sources). *Receiving aid:* Freshmen: 7% (75). Undergraduates: 5% (215). *Average award:* Freshmen: $11,745. Undergraduates: $9508. *Scholarships, grants, and awards by category: Academic interests/achievement:* engineering/technologies, general academic interests/achievements, military science. *Creative arts/performance:* general creative arts/performance. *Special achievements/activities:* general special achievements/activities. *Special characteristics:* children and siblings of alumni, children of faculty/staff, general special characteristics, international students, veterans. *Tuition waivers:* Full or partial for employees or children of employees.

LOANS *Student loans:* $22,623,381 (74% need-based, 26% non-need-based). 55% of past graduating class borrowed through all loan programs. *Average indebtedness per student:* $27,121. *Average need-based loan:* Freshmen: $3914. Undergraduates: $4808. *Parent loans:* $7,875,783 (31% need-based, 69% non-need-based). *Programs:* Federal Direct (Subsidized and Unsubsidized Stafford, PLUS), Perkins, Federal Nursing.

WORK-STUDY *Federal work-study:* Total amount: $3,994,163; 1,620 jobs averaging $2466. *State or other work-study/employment:* Total amount: $1,335,819 (58% need-based, 42% non-need-based). Part-time jobs available.

APPLYING FOR FINANCIAL AID *Required financial aid forms:* FAFSA, CSS Financial Aid PROFILE, state aid form, noncustodial (divorced/separated) parent's statement. *Financial aid deadline (priority):* 2/1. *Notification date:* 4/1. Students must reply by 5/1.

CONTACT Charles W. Puls, Director of Financial Aid, University of Rochester, 124 Wallis Hall, Rochester, NY 14627-0261, 585-275-3226 or toll-free 888-822-2256. *Fax:* 585-756-7664.

UNIVERSITY OF ST. FRANCIS
Joliet, IL

Tuition & fees: $22,698	Average undergraduate aid package: $18,171

ABOUT THE INSTITUTION Independent Roman Catholic, coed. 48 undergraduate majors. Federal methodology is used as a basis for awarding need-based institutional aid.

UNDERGRADUATE EXPENSES for 2009–10 *Comprehensive fee:* $30,636 includes full-time tuition ($22,288), mandatory fees ($410), and room and board ($7938). Room and board charges vary according to board plan and housing facility. *Part-time tuition:* $743 per credit hour. *Payment plans:* Installment, deferred payment.

FRESHMAN FINANCIAL AID (Fall 2009, est.) 209 applied for aid; of those 85% were deemed to have need. 100% of freshmen with need received aid; of those 63% had need fully met. *Average percent of need met:* 78% (excluding resources awarded to replace EFC). *Average financial aid package:* $20,943 (excluding resources awarded to replace EFC). 20% of all full-time freshmen had no need and received non-need-based gift aid.

UNDERGRADUATE FINANCIAL AID (Fall 2009, est.) 1,199 applied for aid; of those 81% were deemed to have need. 100% of undergraduates with need received aid; of those 49% had need fully met. *Average percent of need met:* 72% (excluding resources awarded to replace EFC). *Average financial aid package:* $18,171 (excluding resources awarded to replace EFC). 17% of all full-time undergraduates had no need and received non-need-based gift aid.

GIFT AID (NEED-BASED) *Total amount:* $7,445,350 (24% federal, 29% state, 46% institutional, 1% external sources). *Receiving aid:* Freshmen: 48% (108); all full-time undergraduates: 56% (678). *Average award:* Freshmen: $7734; Undergraduates: $7816. *Scholarships, grants, and awards:* Federal Pell, FSEOG, state, private, college/university gift aid from institutional funds.

GIFT AID (NON-NEED-BASED) *Total amount:* $5,406,491 (2% federal, 1% state, 95% institutional, 2% external sources). *Receiving aid:* Freshmen: 47% (105). Undergraduates: 75% (903). *Average award:* Freshmen: $9040. Undergraduates: $6748. *Scholarships, grants, and awards by category: Academic interests/achievement:* $6,896,866 total: biological sciences, communication, education, general academic interests/achievements, health fields, international studies, social sciences. *Creative arts/performance:* $37,009 total: applied art and design, art/fine arts, music. *Special achievements/activities:* $3,703,913 total: cheerleading/drum major, community service, general special achievements/activities, leadership, religious involvement. *Special characteristics:* $435,971 total: children and siblings of alumni, children of educators, ethnic background, first-generation college students, religious affiliation, siblings of current students. *Tuition waivers:* Full or partial for children of alumni, employees or children of employees.

LOANS *Student loans:* $7,890,548 (41% need-based, 59% non-need-based). 96% of past graduating class borrowed through all loan programs. *Average indebtedness per student:* $21,594. *Average need-based loan:* Freshmen: $3676. Undergraduates: $4538. *Parent loans:* $2,101,472 (63% need-based, 37% non-need-based). *Programs:* Federal Direct (Subsidized and Unsubsidized Stafford, PLUS), Perkins, alternative loans.

WORK-STUDY *Federal work-study:* Total amount: $169,070; 122 jobs averaging $1386. *State or other work-study/employment:* Total amount: $362,849 (100% non-need-based). 232 part-time jobs averaging $1564.

ATHLETIC AWARDS Total amount: $3,105,105 (40% need-based, 60% non-need-based).

APPLYING FOR FINANCIAL AID *Required financial aid forms:* FAFSA, institution's own form. *Financial aid deadline (priority):* 4/1. *Notification date:* Continuous. Students must reply within 3 weeks of notification.

CONTACT Mrs. Mary V. Shaw, Director of Financial Aid Services, University of St. Francis, 500 North Wilcox Street, Joliet, IL 60435-6188, 815-740-3403 or toll-free 800-735-3500 (in-state), 800-735-7500 (out-of-state). *Fax:* 815-740-3822. *E-mail:* mshaw@stfrancis.edu.

UNIVERSITY OF SAINT FRANCIS
Fort Wayne, IN

Tuition & fees: $21,760	Average undergraduate aid package: $16,158

ABOUT THE INSTITUTION Independent Roman Catholic, coed. *Awards:* associate, bachelor's, and master's degrees and post-bachelor's certificates. 50 undergraduate majors. *Total enrollment:* 2,112. Undergraduates: 1,800. Freshmen: 322. Federal methodology is used as a basis for awarding need-based institutional aid.

UNDERGRADUATE EXPENSES for 2009–10 *Application fee:* $20. *Comprehensive fee:* $28,510 includes full-time tuition ($20,950), mandatory fees ($810), and room and board ($6750). Full-time tuition and fees vary according to course load. Room and board charges vary according to board plan and housing facility. *Part-time tuition:* $660 per semester hour. *Part-time fees:* $20 per semester hour; $135 per term. Part-time tuition and fees vary according to course load. *Payment plans:* Installment, deferred payment.

FRESHMAN FINANCIAL AID (Fall 2009, est.) 302 applied for aid; of those 89% were deemed to have need. 100% of freshmen with need received aid; of those 19% had need fully met. *Average percent of need met:* 80% (excluding resources awarded to replace EFC). *Average financial aid package:* $18,231 (excluding resources awarded to replace EFC). 11% of all full-time freshmen had no need and received non-need-based gift aid.

UNDERGRADUATE FINANCIAL AID (Fall 2009, est.) 1,477 applied for aid; of those 89% were deemed to have need. 100% of undergraduates with need received aid; of those 20% had need fully met. *Average percent of need met:* 72% (excluding resources awarded to replace EFC). *Average financial aid package:* $16,158 (excluding resources awarded to replace EFC). 10% of all full-time undergraduates had no need and received non-need-based gift aid.

GIFT AID (NEED-BASED) *Total amount:* $14,463,971 (22% federal, 21% state, 44% institutional, 13% external sources). *Receiving aid:* Freshmen: 86% (267); all full-time undergraduates: 86% (1,301). *Average award:* Freshmen: $14,867; Undergraduates: $12,247. *Scholarships, grants, and awards:* Federal Pell, FSEOG, state, private, college/university gift aid from institutional funds.

GIFT AID (NON-NEED-BASED) *Total amount:* $1,728,767 (3% state, 60% institutional, 37% external sources). *Receiving aid:* Freshmen: 10% (30). Undergraduates: 10% (154). *Average award:* Freshmen: $5807. Undergraduates: $5446. *Scholarships, grants, and awards by category: Academic interests/achievement:* 808 awards ($3,553,555 total): general academic interests/achievements, health fields. *Creative arts/performance:* 224 awards ($791,861 total): art/fine arts, dance, music. *Special achievements/activities:* 43 awards ($85,425 total): cheerleading/drum major, religious involvement. *Special characteristics:* 44 awards ($599,791 total): children of faculty/staff. *Tuition waivers:* Full or partial for children of alumni, employees or children of employees, senior citizens.

LOANS *Student loans:* $15,452,665 (72% need-based, 28% non-need-based). 98% of past graduating class borrowed through all loan programs. *Average indebtedness per student:* $28,428. *Average need-based loan:* Freshmen: $3276. Undergraduates: $4028. *Parent loans:* $1,368,982 (35% need-based, 65% non-need-based). *Programs:* FFEL (Subsidized and Unsubsidized Stafford, PLUS), Perkins.

WORK-STUDY *Federal work-study:* Total amount: $643,991; 629 jobs averaging $1411. *State or other work-study/employment:* Part-time jobs available.

ATHLETIC AWARDS Total amount: $3,324,528 (73% need-based, 27% non-need-based).

APPLYING FOR FINANCIAL AID *Required financial aid form:* FAFSA. *Financial aid deadline:* 6/30 (priority: 3/10). *Notification date:* Continuous beginning 3/1. Students must reply within 2 weeks of notification.

CONTACT Office of Financial Aid, University of Saint Francis, 2701 Spring Street, Fort Wayne, IN 46808, 260-399-8003 or toll-free 800-729-4732. *Fax:* 260-399-8162. *E-mail:* finaid@sf.edu.

UNIVERSITY OF SAINT MARY
Leavenworth, KS

CONTACT Mrs. Judy Wiedower, Financial Aid Director, University of Saint Mary, 4100 South Fourth Street, Leavenworth, KS 66048, 913-758-6314 or toll-free 800-752-7043 (out-of-state). *Fax:* 913-758-6146. *E-mail:* wiedower@hub.smcks.edu.

UNIVERSITY OF ST. THOMAS
St. Paul, MN

Tuition & fees: $29,467	Average undergraduate aid package: $23,858

ABOUT THE INSTITUTION Independent Roman Catholic, coed. 83 undergraduate majors. Federal methodology is used as a basis for awarding need-based institutional aid.
UNDERGRADUATE EXPENSES for 2009–10 *Comprehensive fee:* $37,509 includes full-time tuition ($28,944), mandatory fees ($523), and room and board ($8042). *College room only:* $5104. *Part-time tuition:* $904.50 per credit hour.
FRESHMAN FINANCIAL AID (Fall 2009, est.) 1,109 applied for aid; of those 76% were deemed to have need. 100% of freshmen with need received aid; of those 82% had need fully met. *Average percent of need met:* 94% (excluding resources awarded to replace EFC). *Average financial aid package:* $25,400 (excluding resources awarded to replace EFC). 18% of all full-time freshmen had no need and received non-need-based gift aid.
UNDERGRADUATE FINANCIAL AID (Fall 2009, est.) 4,139 applied for aid; of those 81% were deemed to have need. 100% of undergraduates with need received aid; of those 66% had need fully met. *Average percent of need met:* 92% (excluding resources awarded to replace EFC). *Average financial aid package:* $23,858 (excluding resources awarded to replace EFC). 11% of all full-time undergraduates had no need and received non-need-based gift aid.
GIFT AID (NEED-BASED) *Total amount:* $52,416,561 (11% federal, 10% state, 71% institutional, 8% external sources). *Receiving aid:* Freshmen: 62% (835); all full-time undergraduates: 57% (3,292). *Average award:* Freshmen: $19,162; Undergraduates: $15,779. *Scholarships, grants, and awards:* Federal Pell, FSEOG, state, private, college/university gift aid from institutional funds.
GIFT AID (NON-NEED-BASED) *Total amount:* $9,315,393 (96% institutional, 4% external sources). *Receiving aid:* Freshmen: 10% (130). Undergraduates: 6% (348). *Average award:* Freshmen: $13,206. Undergraduates: $11,065. *Scholarships, grants, and awards by category:* Academic interests/achievement: 2,874 awards ($22,304,038 total): biological sciences, business, education, English, general academic interests/achievements, humanities, international studies, mathematics, physical sciences, religion/biblical studies, social sciences. Creative arts/performance: 31 awards ($78,408 total): journalism/publications, music. Special characteristics: 199 awards ($2,912,975 total): children of educators, children of faculty/staff, general special characteristics.
LOANS *Student loans:* $33,506,957 (64% need-based, 36% non-need-based). 67% of past graduating class borrowed through all loan programs. *Average indebtedness per student:* $32,132. *Average need-based loan:* Freshmen: $5981. Undergraduates: $7447. *Parent loans:* $8,846,850 (29% need-based, 71% non-need-based). *Programs:* Federal Direct (Subsidized and Unsubsidized Stafford, PLUS), Perkins, state, alternative loans.
WORK-STUDY *Federal work-study:* Total amount: $3,290,676; 1,196 jobs averaging $2751. *State or other work-study/employment:* Total amount: $2,158,997 (67% need-based, 33% non-need-based). 806 part-time jobs averaging $2679.
APPLYING FOR FINANCIAL AID *Required financial aid form:* FAFSA. *Financial aid deadline:* Continuous. *Notification date:* Continuous beginning 3/1. Students must reply within 3 weeks of notification.
CONTACT Ms. Ginny Reese, Associate Director, Student Financial Services, University of St. Thomas, 2115 Summit Avenue, AQU 328, St. Paul, MN 55105-1096, 651-962-6557 or toll-free 800-328-6819 Ext. 26150. *Fax:* 651-962-6599. *E-mail:* ginny.reese@stthomas.edu.

UNIVERSITY OF ST. THOMAS
Houston, TX

Tuition & fees: $21,830	Average undergraduate aid package: $15,107

ABOUT THE INSTITUTION Independent Roman Catholic, coed. 39 undergraduate majors. Federal methodology is used as a basis for awarding need-based institutional aid.
UNDERGRADUATE EXPENSES for 2009–10 *Comprehensive fee:* $29,230 includes full-time tuition ($21,510), mandatory fees ($320), and room and board ($7400). *College room only:* $4400. Full-time tuition and fees vary according to course load. Room and board charges vary according to board plan and housing facility. *Part-time tuition:* $719 per credit hour. Part-time tuition and fees vary according to course load. *Payment plans:* Installment, deferred payment.
FRESHMAN FINANCIAL AID (Fall 2009, est.) 228 applied for aid; of those 81% were deemed to have need. 99% of freshmen with need received aid; of those 12% had need fully met. *Average percent of need met:* 71% (excluding resources awarded to replace EFC). *Average financial aid package:* $16,133 (excluding resources awarded to replace EFC). 29% of all full-time freshmen had no need and received non-need-based gift aid.
UNDERGRADUATE FINANCIAL AID (Fall 2009, est.) 886 applied for aid; of those 88% were deemed to have need. 99% of undergraduates with need received aid; of those 11% had need fully met. *Average percent of need met:* 65% (excluding resources awarded to replace EFC). *Average financial aid package:* $15,107 (excluding resources awarded to replace EFC). 24% of all full-time undergraduates had no need and received non-need-based gift aid.
GIFT AID (NEED-BASED) *Total amount:* $9,031,164 (26% federal, 21% state, 50% institutional, 3% external sources). *Receiving aid:* Freshmen: 64% (183); all full-time undergraduates: 57% (734). *Average award:* Freshmen: $13,259; Undergraduates: $11,859. *Scholarships, grants, and awards:* Federal Pell, FSEOG, state, private, college/university gift aid from institutional funds, Academic Competitiveness Grants, National SMART Grants.
GIFT AID (NON-NEED-BASED) *Total amount:* $2,634,201 (96% institutional, 4% external sources). *Receiving aid:* Freshmen: 7% (21). Undergraduates: 4% (57). *Average award:* Freshmen: $8587. Undergraduates: $7987. *Tuition waivers:* Full or partial for employees or children of employees, senior citizens.
LOANS *Student loans:* $6,071,914 (80% need-based, 20% non-need-based). 71% of past graduating class borrowed through all loan programs. *Average indebtedness per student:* $22,857. *Average need-based loan:* Freshmen: $3478. Undergraduates: $4684. *Parent loans:* $1,157,736 (27% need-based, 73% non-need-based). *Programs:* FFEL (Subsidized and Unsubsidized Stafford, PLUS), Perkins, state, private loans.
WORK-STUDY *Federal work-study:* Total amount: $127,113; 43 jobs averaging $3265. *State or other work-study/employment:* Total amount: $13,281 (100% need-based). Part-time jobs available.
ATHLETIC AWARDS Total amount: $173,450 (42% need-based, 58% non-need-based).
APPLYING FOR FINANCIAL AID *Required financial aid form:* FAFSA. *Financial aid deadline:* Continuous. *Notification date:* Continuous beginning 3/22. Students must reply within 2 weeks of notification.
CONTACT Lynda McKendree, Dean of Scholarships and Financial Aid, University of St. Thomas, 3800 Montrose Boulevard, Houston, TX 77006-4696, 713-525-2151 or toll-free 800-856-8565. *Fax:* 713-525-2142. *E-mail:* finaid@stthom.edu.

UNIVERSITY OF SAN DIEGO
San Diego, CA

Tuition & fees: $36,292	Average undergraduate aid package: $28,993

ABOUT THE INSTITUTION Independent Roman Catholic, coed. 39 undergraduate majors. Federal methodology is used as a basis for awarding need-based institutional aid.
UNDERGRADUATE EXPENSES for 2009–10 *Comprehensive fee:* $48,894 includes full-time tuition ($35,870), mandatory fees ($422), and room and board ($12,602). Room and board charges vary according to board plan and housing facility. *Part-time tuition:* $1240 per unit. *Part-time fees:* $151 per term. Part-time tuition and fees vary according to course load. *Payment plan:* Installment.
FRESHMAN FINANCIAL AID (Fall 2009, est.) 728 applied for aid; of those 84% were deemed to have need. 100% of freshmen with need received aid; of those 28% had need fully met. *Average percent of need met:* 82% (excluding resources awarded to replace EFC). *Average financial aid package:* $33,076 (excluding resources awarded to replace EFC). 19% of all full-time freshmen had no need and received non-need-based gift aid.

UNDERGRADUATE FINANCIAL AID (Fall 2009, est.) 2,668 applied for aid; of those 88% were deemed to have need. 100% of undergraduates with need received aid; of those 20% had need fully met. *Average percent of need met:* 74% (excluding resources awarded to replace EFC). *Average financial aid package:* $28,993 (excluding resources awarded to replace EFC). 16% of all full-time undergraduates had no need and received non-need-based gift aid.

GIFT AID (NEED-BASED) *Total amount:* $45,864,340 (11% federal, 10% state, 77% institutional, 2% external sources). *Receiving aid:* Freshmen: 55% (591); all full-time undergraduates: 45% (2,203). *Average award:* Freshmen: $26,425; Undergraduates: $21,139. *Scholarships, grants, and awards:* Federal Pell, FSEOG, state, private, college/university gift aid from institutional funds, Federal Nursing.

GIFT AID (NON-NEED-BASED) *Total amount:* $14,792,371 (19% federal, 78% institutional, 3% external sources). *Receiving aid:* Freshmen: 34% (368). Undergraduates: 21% (1,021). *Average award:* Freshmen: $14,609. Undergraduates: $13,385. *Scholarships, grants, and awards by category: Academic interests/achievement:* general academic interests/achievements. *Creative arts/performance:* music. *Special achievements/activities:* religious involvement. *Special characteristics:* children of faculty/staff. *Tuition waivers:* Full or partial for employees or children of employees.

LOANS *Student loans:* $22,595,722 (85% need-based, 15% non-need-based). 57% of past graduating class borrowed through all loan programs. *Average indebtedness per student:* $27,999. *Average need-based loan:* Freshmen: $5980. Undergraduates: $8037. *Parent loans:* $22,723,499 (38% need-based, 62% non-need-based). *Programs:* Federal Direct (Subsidized and Unsubsidized Stafford, PLUS), Perkins, college/university.

WORK-STUDY *Federal work-study:* Total amount: $2,412,833; 852 jobs averaging $2853. *State or other work-study/employment:* Total amount: $2,394,982 (15% need-based, 85% non-need-based). Part-time jobs available.

ATHLETIC AWARDS Total amount: $5,284,846 (19% need-based, 81% non-need-based).

APPLYING FOR FINANCIAL AID *Required financial aid form:* FAFSA. *Financial aid deadline (priority):* 3/2. *Notification date:* Continuous beginning 3/1. Students must reply by 5/1 or within 3 weeks of notification.

CONTACT Judith Lewis Logue, Director of Financial Aid Services, University of San Diego, 5998 Alcala Park, San Diego, CA 92110-2492, 619-260-4514 or toll-free 800-248-4873.

UNIVERSITY OF SAN FRANCISCO
San Francisco, CA

CONTACT Ms. Susan Murphy, Director of Financial Aid, University of San Francisco, 2130 Fulton Street, San Francisco, CA 94117-1080, 415-422-2620 or toll-free 800-CALLUSF (out-of-state). *Fax:* 415-422-6084. *E-mail:* murphy@usfca.edu.

UNIVERSITY OF SCIENCE AND ARTS OF OKLAHOMA
Chickasha, OK

Tuition & fees (OK res): $4440   **Average undergraduate aid package: $9044**

ABOUT THE INSTITUTION State-supported, coed. 25 undergraduate majors. Federal methodology is used as a basis for awarding need-based institutional aid.

UNDERGRADUATE EXPENSES for 2009–10 *Tuition, state resident:* full-time $3270; part-time $109 per credit hour. *Tuition, nonresident:* full-time $9390; part-time $313 per credit hour. *Required fees:* full-time $1170; $39 per credit hour. *College room and board:* $4850; *Room only:* $2530. Room and board charges vary according to board plan and housing facility. *Payment plans:* Guaranteed tuition, installment.

FRESHMAN FINANCIAL AID (Fall 2009, est.) 154 applied for aid; of those 87% were deemed to have need. 100% of freshmen with need received aid; of those 22% had need fully met. *Average percent of need met:* 77% (excluding resources awarded to replace EFC). *Average financial aid package:* $9208 (excluding resources awarded to replace EFC). 8% of all full-time freshmen had no need and received non-need-based gift aid.

UNDERGRADUATE FINANCIAL AID (Fall 2009, est.) 683 applied for aid; of those 85% were deemed to have need. 98% of undergraduates with need received aid; of those 20% had need fully met. *Average percent of need met:*

72% (excluding resources awarded to replace EFC). *Average financial aid package:* $9044 (excluding resources awarded to replace EFC). 13% of all full-time undergraduates had no need and received non-need-based gift aid.

GIFT AID (NEED-BASED) *Total amount:* $3,176,054 (61% federal, 23% state, 8% institutional, 8% external sources). *Receiving aid:* Freshmen: 71% (131); all full-time undergraduates: 58% (534). *Average award:* Freshmen: $7559; Undergraduates: $6991. *Scholarships, grants, and awards:* Federal Pell, FSEOG, state, private, college/university gift aid from institutional funds, USAO Foundation Grants.

GIFT AID (NON-NEED-BASED) *Total amount:* $602,611 (46% state, 40% institutional, 14% external sources). *Receiving aid:* Freshmen: 8% (15). Undergraduates: 5% (47). *Average award:* Freshmen: $2103. Undergraduates: $1872. *Scholarships, grants, and awards by category: Academic interests/achievement:* 199 awards ($400,834 total): general academic interests/achievements. *Creative arts/performance:* 17 awards ($28,200 total): art/fine arts, music, theater/drama. *Special achievements/activities:* 16 awards ($7667 total): cheerleading/drum major. *Special characteristics:* 105 awards ($313,540 total): children of faculty/staff, international students, out-of-state students, previous college experience. *Tuition waivers:* Full or partial for employees or children of employees, senior citizens.

LOANS *Student loans:* $2,396,286 (67% need-based, 33% non-need-based). 58% of past graduating class borrowed through all loan programs. *Average indebtedness per student:* $15,598. *Average need-based loan:* Freshmen: $2390. Undergraduates: $3085. *Parent loans:* $50,892 (6% need-based, 94% non-need-based). *Programs:* FFEL (Subsidized and Unsubsidized Stafford, PLUS), Perkins, college/university.

WORK-STUDY *Federal work-study:* Total amount: $248,709; 150 jobs averaging $1812.

ATHLETIC AWARDS Total amount: $951,403 (33% need-based, 67% non-need-based).

APPLYING FOR FINANCIAL AID *Required financial aid forms:* FAFSA, institution's own form. *Financial aid deadline (priority):* 3/15. *Notification date:* Continuous beginning 3/15. Students must reply within 4 weeks of notification.

CONTACT Nancy Moats, Director of Financial Aid, University of Science and Arts of Oklahoma, 1727 West Alabama, Chickasha, OK 73018-5322, 405-574-1251 or toll-free 800-933-8726 Ext. 1212. *Fax:* 405-574-1220. *E-mail:* nmoats@usao.edu.

THE UNIVERSITY OF SCRANTON
Scranton, PA

Tuition & fees: $34,536   **Average undergraduate aid package: $22,585**

ABOUT THE INSTITUTION Independent Roman Catholic (Jesuit), coed. 55 undergraduate majors. Federal methodology is used as a basis for awarding need-based institutional aid.

UNDERGRADUATE EXPENSES for 2010–11 *Comprehensive fee:* $46,398 includes full-time tuition ($34,236), mandatory fees ($300), and room and board ($11,862). *College room only:* $7002. Room and board charges vary according to board plan and housing facility. *Part-time tuition:* $882 per credit hour. *Payment plan:* Installment.

FRESHMAN FINANCIAL AID (Fall 2009, est.) 894 applied for aid; of those 83% were deemed to have need. 100% of freshmen with need received aid; of those 11% had need fully met. *Average percent of need met:* 72% (excluding resources awarded to replace EFC). *Average financial aid package:* $23,357 (excluding resources awarded to replace EFC). 17% of all full-time freshmen had no need and received non-need-based gift aid.

UNDERGRADUATE FINANCIAL AID (Fall 2009, est.) 3,161 applied for aid; of those 86% were deemed to have need. 99% of undergraduates with need received aid; of those 11% had need fully met. *Average percent of need met:* 74% (excluding resources awarded to replace EFC). *Average financial aid package:* $22,585 (excluding resources awarded to replace EFC). 16% of all full-time undergraduates had no need and received non-need-based gift aid.

GIFT AID (NEED-BASED) *Total amount:* $50,012,459 (8% federal, 5% state, 82% institutional, 5% external sources). *Receiving aid:* Freshmen: 70% (720); all full-time undergraduates: 66% (2,589). *Average award:* Freshmen: $18,194; Undergraduates: $16,794. *Scholarships, grants, and awards:* Federal Pell, FSEOG, state, private, college/university gift aid from institutional funds, TEACH Grants.

GIFT AID (NON-NEED-BASED) *Total amount:* $3,786,393 (91% institutional, 9% external sources). *Receiving aid:* Freshmen: 7% (69). Undergraduates: 5%

(184). *Average award:* Freshmen: $11,260. Undergraduates: $9932. *Scholarships, grants, and awards by category: Academic interests/achievement:* general academic interests/achievements, military science. *Special characteristics:* children of educators, children of faculty/staff, members of minority groups, siblings of current students. *Tuition waivers:* Full or partial for employees or children of employees, senior citizens.

LOANS *Student loans:* $26,864,782 (81% need-based, 19% non-need-based). 75% of past graduating class borrowed through all loan programs. *Average indebtedness per student:* $30,920. *Average need-based loan:* Freshmen: $3627. Undergraduates: $4590. *Parent loans:* $12,073,703 (55% need-based, 45% non-need-based). *Programs:* Federal Direct (Subsidized and Unsubsidized Stafford, PLUS), FFEL (Subsidized and Unsubsidized Stafford, PLUS), Perkins, Federal Nursing.

WORK-STUDY *Federal work-study:* Total amount: $2,296,046; 805 jobs averaging $1800. *State or other work-study/employment:* Total amount: $1,059,115 (34% need-based, 66% non-need-based). 620 part-time jobs averaging $1800.

APPLYING FOR FINANCIAL AID *Required financial aid form:* FAFSA. *Financial aid deadline (priority):* 2/15. *Notification date:* Continuous beginning 3/15. Students must reply by 5/1.

CONTACT Mr. William R. Burke, Director of Financial Aid, The University of Scranton, St. Thomas Hall 401, Scranton, PA 18510, 570-941-7887 or toll-free 888-SCRANTON. *Fax:* 570-941-4370. *E-mail:* finaid@scranton.edu.

UNIVERSITY OF SIOUX FALLS
Sioux Falls, SD

CONTACT Rachel Gunn, Financial Aid Counselor, University of Sioux Falls, 1101 West 22nd Street, Sioux Falls, SD 57105-1699, 605-331-6623 or toll-free 800-888-1047. *Fax:* 605-331-6615. *E-mail:* rachel.gunn@usiouxfalls.edu.

UNIVERSITY OF SOUTH ALABAMA
Mobile, AL

Tuition & fees (AL res): $5962   **Average undergraduate aid package: $3152**

ABOUT THE INSTITUTION State-supported, coed. 47 undergraduate majors. Federal methodology is used as a basis for awarding need-based institutional aid.

UNDERGRADUATE EXPENSES for 2010–11 *Tuition, state resident:* full-time $4860; part-time $162 per credit hour. *Tuition, nonresident:* full-time $10,200; part-time $340 per credit hour. *Required fees:* full-time $1102; $363 per term. Full-time tuition and fees vary according to class time, course level, course load, degree level, and program. Part-time tuition and fees vary according to class time, course level, course load, degree level, and program. *College room and board:* $5344; *Room only:* $2744. Room and board charges vary according to board plan, housing facility, and location. *Payment plan:* Installment.

FRESHMAN FINANCIAL AID (Fall 2008) 645 applied for aid; of those 100% were deemed to have need. 100% of freshmen with need received aid; of those 57% had need fully met. *Average percent of need met:* 23% (excluding resources awarded to replace EFC). *Average financial aid package:* $2722 (excluding resources awarded to replace EFC). 24% of all full-time freshmen had no need and received non-need-based gift aid.

UNDERGRADUATE FINANCIAL AID (Fall 2008) 3,257 applied for aid; of those 100% were deemed to have need. 100% of undergraduates with need received aid; of those 59% had need fully met. *Average percent of need met:* 25% (excluding resources awarded to replace EFC). *Average financial aid package:* $3152 (excluding resources awarded to replace EFC). 11% of all full-time undergraduates had no need and received non-need-based gift aid.

GIFT AID (NEED-BASED) *Total amount:* $11,664,215 (97% federal, 3% state). *Receiving aid:* Freshmen: 31% (462); all full-time undergraduates: 27% (2,143). *Average award:* Freshmen: $2135; Undergraduates: $2108. *Scholarships, grants, and awards:* Federal Pell, FSEOG, state, college/university gift aid from institutional funds.

GIFT AID (NON-NEED-BASED) *Total amount:* $7,939,321 (88% institutional, 12% external sources). *Receiving aid:* Freshmen: 38% (571). Undergraduates: 37% (2,946). *Average award:* Freshmen: $2182. Undergraduates: $2169. *Scholarships, grants, and awards by category: Academic interests/achievement:* business, computer science, general academic interests/achievements, humanities, international studies, military science. *Creative arts/performance:* art/fine arts, journalism/publications, music, theater/drama. *Special achievements/*

activities: general special achievements/activities, hobbies/interests, junior miss, leadership. *Special characteristics:* children and siblings of alumni, children of faculty/staff, members of minority groups. *Tuition waivers:* Full or partial for employees or children of employees.

LOANS *Student loans:* $67,722,861 (38% need-based, 62% non-need-based). *Average need-based loan:* Freshmen: $1560. Undergraduates: $2066. *Parent loans:* $1,860,715 (100% non-need-based). *Programs:* FFEL (Subsidized and Unsubsidized Stafford, PLUS), Perkins.

WORK-STUDY *Federal work-study:* Total amount: $233,914; jobs available. *State or other work-study/employment:* Part-time jobs available.

ATHLETIC AWARDS Total amount: $3,392,706 (100% non-need-based).

APPLYING FOR FINANCIAL AID *Required financial aid forms:* FAFSA, institution's own form. *Financial aid deadline:* Continuous. *Notification date:* Continuous beginning 5/1. Students must reply within 5 weeks of notification.

CONTACT Financial Aid Office, University of South Alabama, Meisler Hall, Suite 1200, Mobile, AL 36688-0002, 251-460-6231 or toll-free 800-872-5247. *Fax:* 251-460-6079. *E-mail:* finaid@usouthal.edu.

UNIVERSITY OF SOUTH CAROLINA
Columbia, SC

Tuition & fees (SC res): $9156   **Average undergraduate aid package: $12,016**

ABOUT THE INSTITUTION State-supported, coed. 68 undergraduate majors. Federal methodology is used as a basis for awarding need-based institutional aid.

UNDERGRADUATE EXPENSES for 2009–10 *Tuition, state resident:* full-time $8756; part-time $410 per credit hour. *Tuition, nonresident:* full-time $23,332; part-time $1065 per credit hour. *Required fees:* full-time $400; $17 per credit hour. Full-time tuition and fees vary according to course load, program, and reciprocity agreements. Part-time tuition and fees vary according to course load and program. *College room and board:* $7328; *Room only:* $4677. Room and board charges vary according to board plan, housing facility, and location. *Payment plans:* Installment, deferred payment.

FRESHMAN FINANCIAL AID (Fall 2008) 2,699 applied for aid; of those 58% were deemed to have need. 99% of freshmen with need received aid; of those 29% had need fully met. *Average percent of need met:* 75% (excluding resources awarded to replace EFC). *Average financial aid package:* $10,987 (excluding resources awarded to replace EFC). 50% of all full-time freshmen had no need and received non-need-based gift aid.

UNDERGRADUATE FINANCIAL AID (Fall 2008) 11,341 applied for aid; of those 72% were deemed to have need. 99% of undergraduates with need received aid; of those 26% had need fully met. *Average percent of need met:* 76% (excluding resources awarded to replace EFC). *Average financial aid package:* $12,016 (excluding resources awarded to replace EFC). 38% of all full-time undergraduates had no need and received non-need-based gift aid.

GIFT AID (NEED-BASED) *Total amount:* $46,520,934 (37% federal, 44% state, 11% institutional, 8% external sources). *Receiving aid:* Freshmen: 17% (628); all full-time undergraduates: 22% (3,953). *Average award:* Freshmen: $4650; Undergraduates: $4341. *Scholarships, grants, and awards:* Federal Pell, FSEOG, state, private, college/university gift aid from institutional funds, United Negro College Fund, Federal Nursing.

GIFT AID (NON-NEED-BASED) *Total amount:* $50,946,321 (49% state, 33% institutional, 18% external sources). *Receiving aid:* Freshmen: 37% (1,400). Undergraduates: 28% (5,027). *Average award:* Freshmen: $6160. Undergraduates: $6688. *Scholarships, grants, and awards by category: Academic interests/achievement:* 8,274 awards ($20,621,609 total): area/ethnic studies, biological sciences, business, communication, computer science, education, engineering/technologies, English, foreign languages, general academic interests/achievements, health fields, humanities, international studies, library science, mathematics, military science, physical sciences, premedicine, religion/biblical studies, social sciences. *Creative arts/performance:* 228 awards ($986,363 total): art/fine arts, dance, debating, journalism/publications, music, theater/drama. *Special achievements/activities:* 196 awards ($289,591 total): cheerleading/drum major, community service, general special achievements/activities, leadership, memberships, religious involvement. *Special characteristics:* 6,076 awards ($12,933,861 total): adult students, children and siblings of alumni, children of faculty/staff, children of union members/company employees, children of workers in trades, children with a deceased or disabled parent, ethnic background, first-generation college students, general special characteristics, handicapped students, international students, local/state students, members of minority groups, out-of-state students, relatives of clergy, religious affiliation, spouses of deceased or disabled public servants. *Tuition waivers:* Full or partial for employees or children of employees, senior citizens.

LOANS *Student loans:* $77,840,540 (47% need-based, 53% non-need-based). 46% of past graduating class borrowed through all loan programs. *Average indebtedness per student:* $21,755. *Average need-based loan:* Freshmen: $2703. Undergraduates: $3922. *Parent loans:* $11,809,294 (12% need-based, 88% non-need-based). *Programs:* Federal Direct (Subsidized and Unsubsidized Stafford, PLUS), Perkins, Federal Nursing.

WORK-STUDY *Federal work-study:* Total amount: $1,744,835; 626 jobs averaging $2814. *State or other work-study/employment:* Total amount: $9,507,015 (47% need-based, 53% non-need-based). 2,378 part-time jobs averaging $2203.

ATHLETIC AWARDS Total amount: $5,796,704 (37% need-based, 63% non-need-based).

APPLYING FOR FINANCIAL AID *Required financial aid form:* FAFSA. *Financial aid deadline (priority):* 4/1. *Notification date:* Continuous beginning 4/1.

CONTACT Dr. Ed Miller, Financial Aid Director, University of South Carolina, 1714 College Street, Columbia, SC 29208, 803-777-8134 or toll-free 800-868-5872 (in-state). *Fax:* 803-777-0941. *E-mail:* ewmiller@mailbox.sc.edu.

UNIVERSITY OF SOUTH CAROLINA AIKEN
Aiken, SC

Tuition & fees: N/R	Average undergraduate aid package: $9108

ABOUT THE INSTITUTION State-supported, coed. 20 undergraduate majors. Federal methodology is used as a basis for awarding need-based institutional aid.

FRESHMAN FINANCIAL AID (Fall 2008) 540 applied for aid; of those 65% were deemed to have need. 100% of freshmen with need received aid; of those 20% had need fully met. *Average percent of need met:* 74% (excluding resources awarded to replace EFC). *Average financial aid package:* $9766 (excluding resources awarded to replace EFC). 29% of all full-time freshmen had no need and received non-need-based gift aid.

UNDERGRADUATE FINANCIAL AID (Fall 2008) 2,172 applied for aid; of those 65% were deemed to have need. 99% of undergraduates with need received aid; of those 19% had need fully met. *Average percent of need met:* 69% (excluding resources awarded to replace EFC). *Average financial aid package:* $9108 (excluding resources awarded to replace EFC). 22% of all full-time undergraduates had no need and received non-need-based gift aid.

GIFT AID (NEED-BASED) *Total amount:* $8,102,772 (48% federal, 41% state, 7% institutional, 4% external sources). *Receiving aid:* Freshmen: 60% (335); all full-time undergraduates: 48% (1,139). *Average award:* Freshmen: $7871; Undergraduates: $6552. *Scholarships, grants, and awards:* Federal Pell, FSEOG, state, college/university gift aid from institutional funds.

GIFT AID (NON-NEED-BASED) *Total amount:* $3,518,049 (2% federal, 76% state, 17% institutional, 5% external sources). *Receiving aid:* Freshmen: 7% (38). Undergraduates: 7% (166). *Average award:* Freshmen: $5035. Undergraduates: $5686. *Scholarships, grants, and awards by category:* Academic interests/achievement: biological sciences, business, communication, computer science, education, engineering/technologies, English, general academic interests/achievements, humanities, mathematics, physical sciences, social sciences. Creative arts/performance: art/fine arts, creative writing, journalism/publications, music. Special achievements/activities: cheerleading/drum major. *Tuition waivers:* Full or partial for employees or children of employees, senior citizens.

LOANS *Student loans:* $13,833,547 (74% need-based, 26% non-need-based). *Average need-based loan:* Freshmen: $3170. Undergraduates: $4254. *Parent loans:* $594,392 (47% need-based, 53% non-need-based). *Programs:* Federal Direct (Subsidized and Unsubsidized Stafford, PLUS), FFEL (Subsidized and Unsubsidized Stafford, PLUS), Perkins.

WORK-STUDY *Federal work-study:* Total amount: $187,676; jobs available. *State or other work-study/employment:* Total amount: $580,834 (54% need-based, 46% non-need-based). Part-time jobs available.

ATHLETIC AWARDS Total amount: $700,629 (36% need-based, 64% non-need-based).

APPLYING FOR FINANCIAL AID *Required financial aid form:* FAFSA. *Financial aid deadline (priority):* 3/15. *Notification date:* Continuous beginning 5/1. Students must reply within 4 weeks of notification.

CONTACT Mr. Glenn Shumpert, Director of Financial Aid, University of South Carolina Aiken, 471 University Parkway, Aiken, SC 29801, 803-641-3476 or toll-free 888-WOW-USCA. *Fax:* 803-641-6840. *E-mail:* glens@usca.edu.

UNIVERSITY OF SOUTH CAROLINA BEAUFORT
Bluffton, SC

ABOUT THE INSTITUTION State-supported, coed. 10 undergraduate majors.

GIFT AID (NEED-BASED) *Scholarships, grants, and awards:* Federal Pell, FSEOG, state, private, college/university gift aid from institutional funds.

LOANS *Programs:* FFEL (Subsidized and Unsubsidized Stafford, PLUS).

WORK-STUDY *Federal work-study:* Total amount: $43,128; 30 jobs averaging $2800.

APPLYING FOR FINANCIAL AID *Required financial aid form:* FAFSA.

CONTACT Tina Wells, Financial Aid Administrative Assistant, University of South Carolina Beaufort, 801 Carteret Street, Beaufort, SC 29902, 843-521-3104. *Fax:* 843-521-3194. *E-mail:* uscbfina@uscb.edu.

UNIVERSITY OF SOUTH CAROLINA UPSTATE
Spartanburg, SC

ABOUT THE INSTITUTION State-supported, coed. 26 undergraduate majors.

GIFT AID (NEED-BASED) *Scholarships, grants, and awards:* Federal Pell, FSEOG, state, private, college/university gift aid from institutional funds.

GIFT AID (NON-NEED-BASED) *Scholarships, grants, and awards by category:* Academic interests/achievement: general academic interests/achievements. Special characteristics: first-generation college students.

LOANS *Programs:* FFEL (Subsidized and Unsubsidized Stafford, PLUS), Perkins, state, private loans.

WORK-STUDY *Federal work-study:* Total amount: $167,849; 97 jobs averaging $1730. *State or other work-study/employment:* Total amount: $546,246 (100% non-need-based). 439 part-time jobs averaging $1244.

APPLYING FOR FINANCIAL AID *Required financial aid form:* FAFSA.

CONTACT Kim Jenerette, Director of Financial Aid, University of South Carolina Upstate, 800 University Way, Spartanburg, SC 29303, 864-503-5340 or toll-free 800-277-8727. *Fax:* 864-503-5974. *E-mail:* kjenerette@uscupstate.edu.

THE UNIVERSITY OF SOUTH DAKOTA
Vermillion, SD

Tuition & fees (SD res): $6468	Average undergraduate aid package: $6067

ABOUT THE INSTITUTION State-supported, coed. 62 undergraduate majors. Federal methodology is used as a basis for awarding need-based institutional aid.

UNDERGRADUATE EXPENSES for 2010–11 *Tuition, state resident:* full-time $2751; part-time $92 per credit hour. *Tuition, nonresident:* full-time $4124; part-time $138 per credit hour. *Required fees:* full-time $3717; $124 per credit hour. Full-time tuition and fees vary according to course load and reciprocity agreements. Part-time tuition and fees vary according to course load and reciprocity agreements. *College room and board:* $5787; *Room only:* $2858. Room and board charges vary according to board plan and housing facility. *Payment plan:* Deferred payment.

FRESHMAN FINANCIAL AID (Fall 2009, est.) 901 applied for aid; of those 67% were deemed to have need. 99% of freshmen with need received aid; of those 23% had need fully met. *Average percent of need met:* 74% (excluding resources awarded to replace EFC). *Average financial aid package:* $5136 (excluding resources awarded to replace EFC). 23% of all full-time freshmen had no need and received non-need-based gift aid.

UNDERGRADUATE FINANCIAL AID (Fall 2009, est.) 3,940 applied for aid; of those 75% were deemed to have need. 98% of undergraduates with need received aid; of those 22% had need fully met. *Average percent of need met:* 72% (excluding resources awarded to replace EFC). *Average financial aid package:* $6067 (excluding resources awarded to replace EFC). 12% of all full-time undergraduates had no need and received non-need-based gift aid.

GIFT AID (NEED-BASED) *Total amount:* $6,569,817 (100% federal). *Receiving aid:* Freshmen: 26% (262); all full-time undergraduates: 26% (1,337). *Average award:* Freshmen: $3737; Undergraduates: $3859. *Scholarships, grants, and awards:* Federal Pell, FSEOG, private, college/university gift aid from institutional funds, Federal Nursing.

GIFT AID (NON-NEED-BASED) *Total amount:* $7,022,707 (18% federal, 11% state, 46% institutional, 25% external sources). *Receiving aid:* Freshmen: 42% (426). Undergraduates: 26% (1,340). *Average award:* Freshmen: $1997. Undergraduates: $1858. *Scholarships, grants, and awards by category: Academic interests/achievement:* biological sciences, business, communication, computer science, education, English, foreign languages, general academic interests/achievements, humanities, mathematics, military science, premedicine, social sciences. *Creative arts/performance:* art/fine arts, creative writing, debating, music, theater/drama. *Tuition waivers:* Full or partial for children of alumni, employees or children of employees, senior citizens.

LOANS *Student loans:* $19,649,715 (69% need-based, 31% non-need-based). 88% of past graduating class borrowed through all loan programs. *Average indebtedness per student:* $23,676. *Average need-based loan:* Freshmen: $3360. Undergraduates: $4076. *Parent loans:* $3,213,110 (100% non-need-based). *Programs:* FFEL (Subsidized and Unsubsidized Stafford, PLUS), Perkins, Federal Nursing, college/university, alternative loans.

WORK-STUDY *Federal work-study:* Total amount: $865,467; 545 jobs averaging $1792. *State or other work-study/employment:* 692 part-time jobs averaging $1135.

ATHLETIC AWARDS Total amount: $1,429,533 (100% non-need-based).

APPLYING FOR FINANCIAL AID *Required financial aid form:* FAFSA. *Financial aid deadline (priority):* 3/15. *Notification date:* Continuous.

CONTACT Julie Pier, Director of Student Financial Aid, The University of South Dakota, Belbas Center, Vermillion, SD 57069-2390, 605-677-5446 or toll-free 877-269-6837. *Fax:* 605-677-5238.

UNIVERSITY OF SOUTHERN CALIFORNIA
Los Angeles, CA

Tuition & fees: $39,184	Average undergraduate aid package: $34,960

ABOUT THE INSTITUTION Independent, coed. 97 undergraduate majors. Both federal and institutional methodology are used as a basis for awarding need-based institutional aid.

UNDERGRADUATE EXPENSES for 2009–10 *One-time required fee:* $150. *Comprehensive fee:* $50,642 includes full-time tuition ($38,570), mandatory fees ($614), and room and board ($11,458). *College room only:* $6416. Full-time tuition and fees vary according to program. Room and board charges vary according to board plan and housing facility. *Part-time tuition:* $1299 per unit. Part-time tuition and fees vary according to course load and program. *Payment plans:* Tuition prepayment, installment.

FRESHMAN FINANCIAL AID (Fall 2008) 1,761 applied for aid; of those 67% were deemed to have need. 100% of freshmen with need received aid; of those 97% had need fully met. *Average percent of need met:* 100% (excluding resources awarded to replace EFC). *Average financial aid package:* $35,653 (excluding resources awarded to replace EFC). 25% of all full-time freshmen had no need and received non-need-based gift aid.

UNDERGRADUATE FINANCIAL AID (Fall 2008) 8,276 applied for aid; of those 80% were deemed to have need. 100% of undergraduates with need received aid; of those 95% had need fully met. *Average percent of need met:* 100% (excluding resources awarded to replace EFC). *Average financial aid package:* $34,960 (excluding resources awarded to replace EFC). 20% of all full-time undergraduates had no need and received non-need-based gift aid.

GIFT AID (NEED-BASED) *Total amount:* $174,949,115 (8% federal, 9% state, 80% institutional, 3% external sources). *Receiving aid:* Freshmen: 37% (1,012); all full-time undergraduates: 37% (5,855). *Average award:* Freshmen: $25,657; Undergraduates: $24,658. *Scholarships, grants, and awards:* Federal Pell, FSEOG, state, private, college/university gift aid from institutional funds.

GIFT AID (NON-NEED-BASED) *Total amount:* $50,293,353 (80% institutional, 20% external sources). *Receiving aid:* Freshmen: 25% (700). Undergraduates: 18% (2,898). *Average award:* Freshmen: $15,726. Undergraduates: $15,695. *Scholarships, grants, and awards by category: Academic interests/achievement:* 5,310 awards ($79,912,098 total): general academic interests/achievements. *Creative arts/performance:* 14 awards ($371,140 total): debating. *Special achievements/activities:* 74 awards ($746,000 total): leadership. *Special characteristics:* 1,010 awards ($17,942,564 total): children and siblings of alumni, children of faculty/staff, international students, members of minority groups. *Tuition waivers:* Full or partial for employees or children of employees.

LOANS *Student loans:* $62,073,146 (54% need-based, 46% non-need-based). 45% of past graduating class borrowed through all loan programs. *Average indebtedness per student:* $30,097. *Average need-based loan:* Freshmen: $3757. Undergraduates: $6013. *Parent loans:* $64,071,909 (100% non-need-based). *Programs:* FFEL (Subsidized and Unsubsidized Stafford, PLUS), Perkins, 'Credit Ready' and credit-based loans.

WORK-STUDY *Federal work-study:* Total amount: $12,641,167; 4,835 jobs averaging $2601.

ATHLETIC AWARDS Total amount: $14,574,467 (30% need-based, 70% non-need-based).

APPLYING FOR FINANCIAL AID *Required financial aid forms:* FAFSA, CSS Financial Aid PROFILE, W-2 forms, USC non-filing forms. *Financial aid deadline (priority):* 2/2. *Notification date:* Continuous beginning 3/15. Students must reply by 5/1.

CONTACT Katharine Harrington, Dean of Admission and Financial Aid, University of Southern California, 700 Childs Way, Los Angeles, CA 90089-0914, 213-740-5445. *Fax:* 213-740-0680. *E-mail:* fao@usc.edu.

UNIVERSITY OF SOUTHERN INDIANA
Evansville, IN

Tuition & fees (IN res): $5474	Average undergraduate aid package: $8198

ABOUT THE INSTITUTION State-supported, coed. 55 undergraduate majors. Federal methodology is used as a basis for awarding need-based institutional aid.

UNDERGRADUATE EXPENSES for 2010–11 *Tuition, state resident:* full-time $5274; part-time $175.80 per credit hour. *Tuition, nonresident:* full-time $12,555; part-time $418.50 per credit hour. *Required fees:* full-time $200; $22.75 per term. Full-time tuition and fees vary according to course load and reciprocity agreements. Part-time tuition and fees vary according to course load and reciprocity agreements. *College room and board:* $6700; *Room only:* $3450. Room and board charges vary according to board plan and housing facility. *Payment plan:* Installment.

FRESHMAN FINANCIAL AID (Fall 2009, est.) 1,876 applied for aid; of those 71% were deemed to have need. 99% of freshmen with need received aid; of those 17% had need fully met. *Average percent of need met:* 80% (excluding resources awarded to replace EFC). *Average financial aid package:* $8172 (excluding resources awarded to replace EFC). 11% of all full-time freshmen had no need and received non-need-based gift aid.

UNDERGRADUATE FINANCIAL AID (Fall 2009, est.) 6,738 applied for aid; of those 73% were deemed to have need. 97% of undergraduates with need received aid; of those 16% had need fully met. *Average percent of need met:* 78% (excluding resources awarded to replace EFC). *Average financial aid package:* $8198 (excluding resources awarded to replace EFC). 10% of all full-time undergraduates had no need and received non-need-based gift aid.

GIFT AID (NEED-BASED) *Total amount:* $22,085,270 (54% federal, 32% state, 12% institutional, 2% external sources). *Receiving aid:* Freshmen: 48% (995); all full-time undergraduates: 43% (3,461). *Average award:* Freshmen: $4887; Undergraduates: $4433. *Scholarships, grants, and awards:* Federal Pell, FSEOG, state, private, college/university gift aid from institutional funds, Federal Nursing.

GIFT AID (NON-NEED-BASED) *Total amount:* $3,615,142 (67% institutional, 33% external sources). *Receiving aid:* Freshmen: 6% (133). Undergraduates: 4% (323). *Average award:* Freshmen: $2593. Undergraduates: $2730. *Scholarships, grants, and awards by category: Academic interests/achievement:* 1,761 awards ($1,224,645 total): biological sciences, business, education, engineering/technologies, general academic interests/achievements, health fields, humanities, mathematics, premedicine, social sciences. *Creative arts/performance:* 27 awards ($16,925 total): art/fine arts, creative writing, theater/drama. *Special achievements/activities:* leadership. *Special characteristics:* 205 awards ($516,205 total): children of faculty/staff, members of minority groups, out-of-state students, spouses of current students, veterans' children. *Tuition waivers:* Full or partial for employees or children of employees.

LOANS *Student loans:* $48,496,312 (70% need-based, 30% non-need-based). *Average need-based loan:* Freshmen: $2886. Undergraduates: $3494. *Parent loans:* $3,377,809 (23% need-based, 77% non-need-based). *Programs:* Federal Direct (Subsidized and Unsubsidized Stafford, PLUS).

WORK-STUDY *Federal work-study:* Total amount: $291,727; 94 jobs averaging $1577.

ATHLETIC AWARDS Total amount: $1,033,042 (34% need-based, 66% non-need-based).

APPLYING FOR FINANCIAL AID *Required financial aid forms:* FAFSA, institution's own form. *Financial aid deadline:* 3/1. *Notification date:* Continuous beginning 4/1.

CONTACT Financial Aid Counselor, University of Southern Indiana, 8600 University Boulevard, Evansville, IN 47712-3590, 812-464-1767 or toll-free 800-467-1965. *Fax:* 812-465-7154. *E-mail:* finaid@usi.edu.

UNIVERSITY OF SOUTHERN MAINE
Portland, ME

Tuition & fees: N/R	Average undergraduate aid package: $13,618

ABOUT THE INSTITUTION State-supported, coed. 46 undergraduate majors. Federal methodology is used as a basis for awarding need-based institutional aid.

FRESHMAN FINANCIAL AID (Fall 2009, est.) 795 applied for aid; of those 83% were deemed to have need. 100% of freshmen with need received aid; of those 58% had need fully met. *Average percent of need met:* 66% (excluding resources awarded to replace EFC). *Average financial aid package:* $13,094 (excluding resources awarded to replace EFC). 6% of all full-time freshmen had no need and received non-need-based gift aid.

UNDERGRADUATE FINANCIAL AID (Fall 2009, est.) 4,497 applied for aid; of those 88% were deemed to have need. 100% of undergraduates with need received aid; of those 60% had need fully met. *Average percent of need met:* 69% (excluding resources awarded to replace EFC). *Average financial aid package:* $13,618 (excluding resources awarded to replace EFC). 4% of all full-time undergraduates had no need and received non-need-based gift aid.

GIFT AID (NEED-BASED) *Total amount:* $19,122,514 (64% federal, 10% state, 15% institutional, 11% external sources). *Receiving aid:* Freshmen: 57% (550); all full-time undergraduates: 59% (2,874). *Average award:* Freshmen: $5593; Undergraduates: $5518. *Scholarships, grants, and awards:* Federal Pell, FSEOG, state, college/university gift aid from institutional funds.

GIFT AID (NON-NEED-BASED) *Total amount:* $1,187,090 (46% institutional, 54% external sources). *Receiving aid:* Freshmen: 1% (6). Undergraduates: 1% (70). *Average award:* Freshmen: $2445. Undergraduates: $3474. *Scholarships, grants, and awards by category: Academic interests/achievement:* general academic interests/achievements. *Creative arts/performance:* music, theater/drama. *Special achievements/activities:* community service. *Special characteristics:* children of faculty/staff, general special characteristics, local/state students, out-of-state students. *Tuition waivers:* Full or partial for minority students, employees or children of employees.

LOANS *Student loans:* $59,529,785 (77% need-based, 23% non-need-based). *Average indebtedness per student:* $25,892. *Average need-based loan:* Freshmen: $5453. Undergraduates: $7613. *Parent loans:* $5,034,569 (34% need-based, 66% non-need-based). *Programs:* Federal Direct (Subsidized and Unsubsidized Stafford, PLUS), Perkins, Federal Nursing, college/university.

WORK-STUDY *Federal work-study:* Total amount: $3,630,530; jobs available.

APPLYING FOR FINANCIAL AID *Required financial aid form:* FAFSA. *Financial aid deadline (priority):* 2/15. *Notification date:* Continuous beginning 3/15. Students must reply within 2 weeks of notification.

CONTACT Mr. Keith P. Dubois, Director of Student Financial Aid, University of Southern Maine, 96 Falmouth Street, PO Box 9300, Portland, ME 04104-9300, 207-780-5122 or toll-free 800-800-4USM Ext. 5670. *Fax:* 207-780-5143. *E-mail:* dubois@maine.edu.

UNIVERSITY OF SOUTHERN MISSISSIPPI
Hattiesburg, MS

Tuition & fees (MS res): $5096	Average undergraduate aid package: $9018

ABOUT THE INSTITUTION State-supported, coed. 68 undergraduate majors. Federal methodology is used as a basis for awarding need-based institutional aid.

UNDERGRADUATE EXPENSES for 2010–11 *Tuition, state resident:* full-time $5096; part-time $213 per credit hour. *Tuition, nonresident:* full-time $12,746; part-time $545 per credit hour. Part-time tuition and fees vary according to course load and degree level. *College room and board:* $6200; *Room only:* $3762. Room and board charges vary according to board plan and housing facility. *Payment plan:* Installment.

FRESHMAN FINANCIAL AID (Fall 2008) 1,433 applied for aid; of those 82% were deemed to have need. 98% of freshmen with need received aid; of those 27% had need fully met. *Average percent of need met:* 84% (excluding resources awarded to replace EFC). *Average financial aid package:* $9433 (excluding resources awarded to replace EFC). 12% of all full-time freshmen had no need and received non-need-based gift aid.

UNDERGRADUATE FINANCIAL AID (Fall 2008) 7,939 applied for aid; of those 86% were deemed to have need. 97% of undergraduates with need received aid; of those 27% had need fully met. *Average percent of need met:* 82% (excluding resources awarded to replace EFC). *Average financial aid package:* $9018 (excluding resources awarded to replace EFC). 8% of all full-time undergraduates had no need and received non-need-based gift aid.

GIFT AID (NEED-BASED) *Total amount:* $23,059,692 (78% federal, 7% state, 11% institutional, 4% external sources). *Receiving aid:* Freshmen: 43% (744); all full-time undergraduates: 42% (4,345). *Average award:* Freshmen: $4771; Undergraduates: $3978. *Scholarships, grants, and awards:* Federal Pell, FSEOG, state, private, college/university gift aid from institutional funds.

GIFT AID (NON-NEED-BASED) *Total amount:* $13,364,310 (6% federal, 20% state, 62% institutional, 12% external sources). *Receiving aid:* Freshmen: 39% (672). Undergraduates: 29% (3,028). *Average award:* Freshmen: $4310. Undergraduates: $3585. *Scholarships, grants, and awards by category: Academic interests/achievement:* 2,795 awards ($4,956,009 total): general academic interests/achievements. *Creative arts/performance:* 450 awards ($477,145 total): art/fine arts, dance, music, theater/drama. *Special achievements/activities:* 122 awards ($139,080 total): cheerleading/drum major, leadership. *Special characteristics:* 7,817 awards ($14,953,030 total): children and siblings of alumni, children of faculty/staff, ethnic background, local/state students, out-of-state students, veterans. *Tuition waivers:* Full or partial for children of alumni, employees or children of employees, senior citizens.

LOANS *Student loans:* $59,932,833 (49% need-based, 51% non-need-based). 63% of past graduating class borrowed through all loan programs. *Average indebtedness per student:* $19,915. *Average need-based loan:* Freshmen: $4057. Undergraduates: $4878. *Parent loans:* $4,071,934 (14% need-based, 86% non-need-based). *Programs:* Federal Direct (Subsidized and Unsubsidized Stafford, PLUS), FFEL (Subsidized Stafford).

WORK-STUDY *Federal work-study:* Total amount: $472,355; jobs available.

ATHLETIC AWARDS Total amount: $3,319,580 (38% need-based, 62% non-need-based).

APPLYING FOR FINANCIAL AID *Required financial aid forms:* FAFSA, institution's own form. *Financial aid deadline (priority):* 3/15. *Notification date:* Continuous. Students must reply within 2 weeks of notification.

CONTACT Mr. David Williamson, Interim Director of Financial Aid, University of Southern Mississippi, 118 College Drive #5101, Hattiesburg, MS 39406-0001, 601-266-4774. *E-mail:* david.williamson@usm.edu.

UNIVERSITY OF SOUTH FLORIDA
Tampa, FL

ABOUT THE INSTITUTION State-supported, coed. 87 undergraduate majors.

GIFT AID (NEED-BASED) *Scholarships, grants, and awards:* Federal Pell, FSEOG, state, private, college/university gift aid from institutional funds.

GIFT AID (NON-NEED-BASED) *Scholarships, grants, and awards by category: Academic interests/achievement:* architecture, biological sciences, business, communication, computer science, education, engineering/technologies, English, foreign languages, general academic interests/achievements, health fields, humanities, international studies, library science, mathematics, military science, physical sciences, premedicine, religion/biblical studies, social sciences. *Creative arts/performance:* applied art and design, art/fine arts, cinema/film/broadcasting, creative writing, dance, debating, journalism/publications, music, performing arts, theater/drama. *Special achievements/activities:* general special achievements/activities. *Special characteristics:* general special characteristics.

LOANS *Programs:* FFEL (Subsidized and Unsubsidized Stafford, PLUS), Perkins, college/university.

APPLYING FOR FINANCIAL AID *Required financial aid form:* FAFSA.

CONTACT Ms. Billie Jo Hamilton, Director of Student Financial Aid, University of South Florida, 4202 East Fowler Avenue, SVC 1102, Tampa, FL 33620-6960, 813-974-4700. *Fax:* 813-974-5144. *E-mail:* bjhamilton@admin.usf.edu.

THE UNIVERSITY OF TAMPA
Tampa, FL

Tuition & fees: $22,482	Average undergraduate aid package: $16,003

ABOUT THE INSTITUTION Independent, coed. 49 undergraduate majors. Federal methodology is used as a basis for awarding need-based institutional aid.

UNDERGRADUATE EXPENSES for 2009–10 *Comprehensive fee:* $30,778 includes full-time tuition ($21,420), mandatory fees ($1062), and room and board ($8296). *College room only:* $4430. Full-time tuition and fees vary according to class time. Room and board charges vary according to board plan and housing facility. *Part-time tuition:* $455 per credit hour. *Part-time fees:* $35 per term. Part-time tuition and fees vary according to class time. *Payment plan:* Installment.

FRESHMAN FINANCIAL AID (Fall 2009, est.) 1,080 applied for aid; of those 77% were deemed to have need. 100% of freshmen with need received aid; of those 22% had need fully met. *Average percent of need met:* 81% (excluding resources awarded to replace EFC). *Average financial aid package:* $15,900 (excluding resources awarded to replace EFC). 33% of all full-time freshmen had no need and received non-need-based gift aid.

UNDERGRADUATE FINANCIAL AID (Fall 2009, est.) 3,616 applied for aid; of those 82% were deemed to have need. 100% of undergraduates with need received aid; of those 19% had need fully met. *Average percent of need met:* 83% (excluding resources awarded to replace EFC). *Average financial aid package:* $16,003 (excluding resources awarded to replace EFC). 33% of all full-time undergraduates had no need and received non-need-based gift aid.

GIFT AID (NEED-BASED) *Total amount:* $25,659,359 (23% federal, 19% state, 55% institutional, 3% external sources). *Receiving aid:* Freshmen: 47% (653); all full-time undergraduates: 39% (2,113). *Average award:* Freshmen: $6222; Undergraduates: $5644. *Scholarships, grants, and awards:* Federal Pell, FSEOG, state, private, college/university gift aid from institutional funds.

GIFT AID (NON-NEED-BASED) *Total amount:* $5,792,553 (42% state, 54% institutional, 4% external sources). *Receiving aid:* Freshmen: 58% (799). Undergraduates: 51% (2,746). *Average award:* Freshmen: $5347. Undergraduates: $5443. *Scholarships, grants, and awards by category:* Academic interests/achievement: 4,807 awards ($22,063,032 total): biological sciences, general academic interests/achievements, international studies, military science, social sciences. Creative arts/performance: 153 awards ($261,000 total): art/fine arts, creative writing, journalism/publications, music, performing arts. Special achievements/activities: 162 awards ($141,000 total): general special achievements/activities, leadership, memberships. Special characteristics: 437 awards ($1,696,688 total): children and siblings of alumni, children of faculty/staff, international students. *Tuition waivers:* Full or partial for employees or children of employees.

LOANS *Student loans:* $12,410,906 (74% need-based, 26% non-need-based). 62% of past graduating class borrowed through all loan programs. *Average indebtedness per student:* $28,129. *Average need-based loan:* Freshmen: $3368. Undergraduates: $4315. *Parent loans:* $10,373,075 (77% need-based, 23% non-need-based). *Programs:* Federal Direct (Subsidized and Unsubsidized Stafford, PLUS), Perkins, state, college/university.

WORK-STUDY *Federal work-study:* Total amount: $538,648; 375 jobs averaging $2000. *State or other work-study/employment:* Total amount: $4041 (100% need-based). 2 part-time jobs averaging $2000.

ATHLETIC AWARDS Total amount: $1,276,168 (48% need-based, 52% non-need-based).

APPLYING FOR FINANCIAL AID *Required financial aid form:* FAFSA. *Financial aid deadline:* Continuous. *Notification date:* Continuous beginning 2/1. Students must reply within 3 weeks of notification.

CONTACT Financial Aid Counselor, The University of Tampa, 401 West Kennedy Boulevard, Tampa, FL 33606-1490, 813-253-6219 or toll-free 888-646-2438 (in-state), 888-MINARET (out-of-state). Fax: 813-258-7439. E-mail: finaid@ut.edu.

THE UNIVERSITY OF TENNESSEE
Knoxville, TN

Tuition & fees (TN res): $6850	Average undergraduate aid package: $10,679

ABOUT THE INSTITUTION State-supported, coed. 95 undergraduate majors. Federal methodology is used as a basis for awarding need-based institutional aid.

UNDERGRADUATE EXPENSES for 2009–10 *Tuition, state resident:* full-time $6850; part-time $248 per hour. *Tuition, nonresident:* full-time $20,946; part-time $823 per hour. *Required fees:* $36 per hour. Full-time tuition and fees vary according to location and program. Part-time tuition and fees vary according to location and program. *College room and board:* $7254. Room and board charges vary according to board plan and housing facility. *Payment plan:* Installment.

FRESHMAN FINANCIAL AID (Fall 2009, est.) 3,554 applied for aid; of those 55% were deemed to have need. 99% of freshmen with need received aid; of those 38% had need fully met. *Average percent of need met:* 81% (excluding resources awarded to replace EFC). *Average financial aid package:* $11,408 (excluding resources awarded to replace EFC). 17% of all full-time freshmen had no need and received non-need-based gift aid.

UNDERGRADUATE FINANCIAL AID (Fall 2009, est.) 17,029 applied for aid; of those 59% were deemed to have need. 97% of undergraduates with need received aid; of those 29% had need fully met. *Average percent of need met:* 73% (excluding resources awarded to replace EFC). *Average financial aid package:* $10,679 (excluding resources awarded to replace EFC). 12% of all full-time undergraduates had no need and received non-need-based gift aid.

GIFT AID (NEED-BASED) *Total amount:* $97,781,236 (25% federal, 53% state, 19% institutional, 3% external sources). *Receiving aid:* Freshmen: 51% (1,893); all full-time undergraduates: 44% (8,554). *Average award:* Freshmen: $2717; Undergraduates: $3104. *Scholarships, grants, and awards:* Federal Pell, FSEOG, state, private, college/university gift aid from institutional funds, Federal Nursing.

GIFT AID (NON-NEED-BASED) *Total amount:* $54,741,368 *Average award:* Freshmen: $1884. Undergraduates: $2461. *Scholarships, grants, and awards by category:* Academic interests/achievement: 2,980 awards ($6,750,172 total): agriculture, architecture, business, communication, computer science, education, engineering/technologies, general academic interests/achievements, health fields, humanities, international studies, library science, military science, social sciences. Creative arts/performance: art/fine arts. Special characteristics: children and siblings of alumni. *Tuition waivers:* Full or partial for employees or children of employees, senior citizens.

LOANS *Student loans:* $54,741,368 (100% need-based). 46% of past graduating class borrowed through all loan programs. *Average indebtedness per student:* $24,593. *Average need-based loan:* Freshmen: $3560. Undergraduates: $4304. *Parent loans:* $7,153,675 (100% need-based). *Programs:* FFEL (Subsidized and Unsubsidized Stafford, PLUS), Perkins, college/university.

WORK-STUDY *Federal work-study:* Total amount: $912,528; 421 jobs averaging $2168.

ATHLETIC AWARDS Total amount: $6,470,789 (100% need-based).

APPLYING FOR FINANCIAL AID *Required financial aid form:* FAFSA. *Financial aid deadline (priority):* 3/1. *Notification date:* Continuous beginning 3/15. Students must reply within 3 weeks of notification.

CONTACT Office of Financial Aid and Scholarships, The University of Tennessee, 115 Student Services Building, Knoxville, TN 37996-0210, 865-974-3131 or toll-free 800-221-8657 (in-state). Fax: 865-974-2175. E-mail: finaid@utk.edu.

THE UNIVERSITY OF TENNESSEE AT CHATTANOOGA
Chattanooga, TN

Tuition & fees (TN res): $5656	Average undergraduate aid package: $9853

ABOUT THE INSTITUTION State-supported, coed. 45 undergraduate majors. Both federal and institutional methodology are used as a basis for awarding need-based institutional aid.

UNDERGRADUATE EXPENSES for 2009–10 *Tuition, state resident:* full-time $4506; part-time $188 per credit hour. *Tuition, nonresident:* full-time $15,804; part-time $471 per credit hour. *Required fees:* full-time $1150; $33 per credit hour or $85 per term. *College room and board:* $8056; *Room only:* $5200. Room and board charges vary according to board plan and housing facility. *Payment plan:* Deferred payment.

FRESHMAN FINANCIAL AID (Fall 2009, est.) 2,103 applied for aid; of those 64% were deemed to have need. 100% of freshmen with need received aid; of those 65% had need fully met. *Average percent of need met:* 87% (excluding resources awarded to replace EFC). *Average financial aid package:* $9220 (excluding resources awarded to replace EFC). 18% of all full-time freshmen had no need and received non-need-based gift aid.

UNDERGRADUATE FINANCIAL AID (Fall 2009, est.) 6,923 applied for aid; of those 69% were deemed to have need. 98% of undergraduates with need received aid; of those 18% had need fully met. *Average percent of need met:* 83% (excluding resources awarded to replace EFC). *Average financial aid package:* $9853 (excluding resources awarded to replace EFC). 13% of all full-time undergraduates had no need and received non-need-based gift aid.

GIFT AID (NEED-BASED) *Total amount:* $22,358,641 (57% federal, 43% state). *Receiving aid:* Freshmen:· 57% (1,258); all full-time undergraduates: 52% (4,144). *Average award:* Freshmen: $4480; Undergraduates: $4320. *Scholarships, grants, and awards:* Federal Pell, FSEOG, state, private, college/university gift aid from institutional funds, United Negro College Fund, Federal Nursing.

GIFT AID (NON-NEED-BASED) *Total amount:* $11,244,150 (54% institutional, 46% external sources). *Receiving aid:* Freshmen: 45% (982). Undergraduates: 40% (3,176). *Average award:* Freshmen: $3015. Undergraduates: $2720. *Scholarships, grants, and awards by category: Academic interests/achievement:* biological sciences, business, education, general academic interests/achievements, military science. *Creative arts/performance:* music. *Special achievements/activities:* community service. *Special characteristics:* children and siblings of alumni, ethnic background. *Tuition waivers:* Full or partial for employees or children of employees, senior citizens.

LOANS *Student loans:* $32,976,041 (44% need-based, 56% non-need-based). 65% of past graduating class borrowed through all loan programs. *Average indebtedness per student:* $19,456. *Average need-based loan:* Freshmen: $3904. Undergraduates: $4310. *Parent loans:* $1,353,387 (100% non-need-based). *Programs:* FFEL (Subsidized and Unsubsidized Stafford, PLUS), Perkins, college/university.

WORK-STUDY *Federal work-study:* Total amount: $424,024; jobs available. *State or other work-study/employment:* Total amount: $170,100 (100% non-need-based). Part-time jobs available.

ATHLETIC AWARDS Total amount: $3,033,101 (100% non-need-based).

APPLYING FOR FINANCIAL AID *Required financial aid forms:* FAFSA, institution's own form. *Financial aid deadline (priority):* 4/1. *Notification date:* Continuous beginning 3/1. Students must reply within 6 weeks of notification.

CONTACT Dianne Cox, Financial Aid Director, The University of Tennessee at Chattanooga, 615 McCallie Avenue, Chattanooga, TN 37403-2598, 423-425-4677 or toll-free 800-UTC-MOCS (in-state). *Fax:* 423-425-2292. *E-mail:* dianne-cox@utc.edu.

THE UNIVERSITY OF TENNESSEE AT MARTIN
Martin, TN

Tuition & fees (TN res): $5769	Average undergraduate aid package: $11,491

ABOUT THE INSTITUTION State-supported, coed. 85 undergraduate majors. Federal methodology is used as a basis for awarding need-based institutional aid.

UNDERGRADUATE EXPENSES for 2009–10 *Tuition, state resident:* full-time $4708; part-time $197 per credit hour. *Tuition, nonresident:* full-time $16,094; part-time $672 per credit hour. *Required fees:* full-time $1061; $44 per credit hour. Part-time tuition and fees vary according to course load. *College room and board:* $4914; *Room only:* $2390. Room and board charges vary according to board plan and housing facility. *Payment plan:* Deferred payment.

FRESHMAN FINANCIAL AID (Fall 2009, est.) 1,346 applied for aid; of those 74% were deemed to have need. 99% of freshmen with need received aid; of those 42% had need fully met. *Average percent of need met:* 83% (excluding resources awarded to replace EFC). *Average financial aid package:* $11,877 (excluding resources awarded to replace EFC). 24% of all full-time freshmen had no need and received non-need-based gift aid.

UNDERGRADUATE FINANCIAL AID (Fall 2009, est.) 5,569 applied for aid; of those 74% were deemed to have need. 98% of undergraduates with need received aid; of those 32% had need fully met. *Average percent of need met:* 78% (excluding resources awarded to replace EFC). *Average financial aid package:* $11,491 (excluding resources awarded to replace EFC). 20% of all full-time undergraduates had no need and received non-need-based gift aid.

GIFT AID (NEED-BASED) *Total amount:* $17,107,046 (75% federal, 21% state, 4% institutional). *Receiving aid:* Freshmen: 48% (655); all full-time undergraduates: 47% (2,742). *Average award:* Freshmen: $6455; Undergraduates: $5687. *Scholarships, grants, and awards:* Federal Pell, FSEOG, state, private, college/university gift aid from institutional funds.

GIFT AID (NON-NEED-BASED) *Total amount:* $21,371,893 (79% state, 14% institutional, 7% external sources). *Receiving aid:* Freshmen: 64% (882). Undergraduates: 42% (2,460). *Average award:* Freshmen: $5379. Undergraduates: $5229. *Scholarships, grants, and awards by category: Academic interests/achievement:* 2,344 awards ($3,101,414 total): agriculture, biological sciences, business, communication, computer science, education, engineering/technologies, English, general academic interests/achievements, health fields, home economics, humanities, mathematics, military science, physical sciences, premedicine, social sciences. *Creative arts/performance:* 241 awards ($153,730 total): art/fine arts, journalism/publications, music, theater/drama. *Special achievements/activities:* 194 awards ($360,183 total): cheerleading/drum major, general special achievements/activities, leadership, rodeo. *Special characteristics:* 2,275 awards ($3,548,273 total): adult students, children of educators, children of faculty/staff, ethnic background, handicapped students, members of minority groups, out-of-state students. *Tuition waivers:* Full or partial for employees or children of employees, senior citizens.

LOANS *Student loans:* $22,067,825 (49% need-based, 51% non-need-based). 71% of past graduating class borrowed through all loan programs. *Average indebtedness per student:* $20,997. *Average need-based loan:* Freshmen: $2779. Undergraduates: $3886. *Parent loans:* $772,466 (100% non-need-based). *Programs:* FFEL (Subsidized and Unsubsidized Stafford, PLUS), Perkins.

WORK-STUDY *Federal work-study:* Total amount: $602,296; 263 jobs averaging $2500.

ATHLETIC AWARDS Total amount: $2,478,609 (100% non-need-based).

APPLYING FOR FINANCIAL AID *Required financial aid form:* FAFSA. *Financial aid deadline (priority):* 3/1. *Notification date:* Continuous beginning 4/1. Students must reply within 2 weeks of notification.

CONTACT Sheryl L. Frazier, Interim Director of Student Financial Assistance, The University of Tennessee at Martin, 205 Administration Building, Martin, TN 38238-1000, 731-881-7040 or toll-free 800-829-8861. *Fax:* 731-881-7036. *E-mail:* sneel@utm.edu.

THE UNIVERSITY OF TEXAS AT ARLINGTON
Arlington, TX

Tuition & fees (TX res): $8186	Average undergraduate aid package: $9939

ABOUT THE INSTITUTION State-supported, coed. 60 undergraduate majors. Federal methodology is used as a basis for awarding need-based institutional aid.

UNDERGRADUATE EXPENSES for 2009–10 *Tuition, state resident:* full-time $8186. *Tuition, nonresident:* full-time $16,496. Full-time tuition and fees vary according to course level, course load, and program. Part-time tuition and fees vary according to course level, course load, and program. *College room and board:* $6658; *Room only:* $3493. Room and board charges vary according to board plan and housing facility. *Payment plan:* Installment.

FRESHMAN FINANCIAL AID (Fall 2009, est.) 1,901 applied for aid; of those 83% were deemed to have need. 100% of freshmen with need received aid; of those 24% had need fully met. *Average percent of need met:* 74% (excluding resources awarded to replace EFC). *Average financial aid package:* $10,858 (excluding resources awarded to replace EFC). 8% of all full-time freshmen had no need and received non-need-based gift aid.

UNDERGRADUATE FINANCIAL AID (Fall 2009, est.) 10,428 applied for aid; of those 88% were deemed to have need. 100% of undergraduates with need received aid; of those 9% had need fully met. *Average percent of need met:* 73% (excluding resources awarded to replace EFC). *Average financial aid package:* $9939 (excluding resources awarded to replace EFC). 2% of all full-time undergraduates had no need and received non-need-based gift aid.

GIFT AID (NEED-BASED) *Total amount:* $72,359,601 (46% federal, 20% state, 29% institutional, 5% external sources). *Receiving aid:* Freshmen: 51% (1,226); all full-time undergraduates: 51% (7,238). *Average award:* Freshmen: $8103; Undergraduates: $6493. *Scholarships, grants, and awards:* Federal Pell, FSEOG, state, private, college/university gift aid from institutional funds, United Negro College Fund.

GIFT AID (NON-NEED-BASED) *Total amount:* $4,796,155 (8% state, 73% institutional, 19% external sources). *Receiving aid:* Freshmen: 35% (831).

Undergraduates: 19% (2,716). *Average award:* Freshmen: $5606. Undergraduates: $5050. *Scholarships, grants, and awards by category: Academic interests/ achievement:* architecture, biological sciences, business, communication, computer science, education, engineering/technologies, English, foreign languages, general academic interests/achievements, health fields, humanities, international studies, mathematics, military science, physical sciences, social sciences. *Creative arts/performance:* journalism/publications, music, theater/ drama. *Special achievements/activities:* cheerleading/drum major, community service, general special achievements/activities, leadership. *Special characteristics:* children with a deceased or disabled parent, first-generation college students, general special characteristics, handicapped students, public servants. *Tuition waivers:* Full or partial for employees or children of employees.

LOANS *Student loans:* $83,211,629 (79% need-based, 21% non-need-based). 53% of past graduating class borrowed through all loan programs. *Average indebtedness per student:* $18,749. *Average need-based loan:* Freshmen: $3134. Undergraduates: $4162. *Parent loans:* $2,288,035 (40% need-based, 60% non-need-based). *Programs:* Federal Direct (Subsidized and Unsubsidized Stafford, PLUS), Perkins, state.

WORK-STUDY *Federal work-study:* Total amount: $5,959,269; jobs available. *State or other work-study/employment:* Total amount: $193,324 (100% need-based). Part-time jobs available.

ATHLETIC AWARDS Total amount: $1,790,217 (89% need-based, 11% non-need-based).

APPLYING FOR FINANCIAL AID *Required financial aid form:* FAFSA. *Financial aid deadline (priority):* 5/15. *Notification date:* Continuous. Students must reply within 3 weeks of notification.

CONTACT Karen Krause, Director of Financial Aid, The University of Texas at Arlington, UTA Box 19199, Arlington, TX 76019, 817-272-3561. *Fax:* 817-272-3555. *E-mail:* kkrause@uta.edu.

THE UNIVERSITY OF TEXAS AT AUSTIN
Austin, TX

Tuition & fees (TX res): $8930   **Average undergraduate aid package: $12,388**

ABOUT THE INSTITUTION State-supported, coed. 81 undergraduate majors. Federal methodology is used as a basis for awarding need-based institutional aid.

UNDERGRADUATE EXPENSES for 2009–10 *Tuition, state resident:* full-time $8930. *Tuition, nonresident:* full-time $30,006. Full-time tuition and fees vary according to course load and program. Part-time tuition and fees vary according to course load and program. *College room and board:* $9602. Room and board charges vary according to housing facility. *Payment plan:* Installment.

FRESHMAN FINANCIAL AID (Fall 2009, est.) 5,477 applied for aid; of those 63% were deemed to have need. 100% of freshmen with need received aid; of those 34% had need fully met. *Average percent of need met:* 85% (excluding resources awarded to replace EFC). *Average financial aid package:* $13,378 (excluding resources awarded to replace EFC). 13% of all full-time freshmen had no need and received non-need-based gift aid.

UNDERGRADUATE FINANCIAL AID (Fall 2009, est.) 21,253 applied for aid; of those 72% were deemed to have need. 100% of undergraduates with need received aid; of those 24% had need fully met. *Average percent of need met:* 75% (excluding resources awarded to replace EFC). *Average financial aid package:* $12,388 (excluding resources awarded to replace EFC). 5% of all full-time undergraduates had no need and received non-need-based gift aid.

GIFT AID (NEED-BASED) *Total amount:* $131,481,679 (33% federal, 26% state, 34% institutional, 7% external sources). *Receiving aid:* Freshmen: 45% (3,247); all full-time undergraduates: 36% (12,484). *Average award:* Freshmen: $9453; Undergraduates: $8822. *Scholarships, grants, and awards:* Federal Pell, FSEOG, state, private, college/university gift aid from institutional funds.

GIFT AID (NON-NEED-BASED) *Total amount:* $7,509,625 (28% institutional, 72% external sources). *Receiving aid:* Freshmen: 24% (1,744). Undergraduates: 12% (4,259). *Scholarships, grants, and awards by category: Academic interests/achievement:* general academic interests/achievements. *Creative arts/ performance:* general creative arts/performance. *Special achievements/activities:* leadership. *Special characteristics:* local/state students. *Tuition waivers:* Full or partial for senior citizens.

LOANS *Student loans:* $121,160,298 (63% need-based, 37% non-need-based). 50% of past graduating class borrowed through all loan programs. *Average indebtedness per student:* $22,102. *Average need-based loan:* Freshmen: $3001.

Undergraduates: $4204. *Parent loans:* $81,037,959 (10% need-based, 90% non-need-based). *Programs:* FFEL (Subsidized and Unsubsidized Stafford, PLUS), Perkins, Federal Nursing, state, college/university.

WORK-STUDY *Federal work-study:* Total amount: $4,305,730; jobs available. *State or other work-study/employment:* Part-time jobs available.

APPLYING FOR FINANCIAL AID *Required financial aid form:* FAFSA. *Financial aid deadline:* Continuous. *Notification date:* Continuous beginning 3/15. Students must reply within 4 weeks of notification.

CONTACT Tom Melecki, PhD, Director of Student Financial Services, The University of Texas at Austin, PO Box 7758, UT Station, Austin, TX 78713-7758, 512-475-6203. *Fax:* 512-475-6349. *E-mail:* tom.melecki@austin.utexas.edu.

THE UNIVERSITY OF TEXAS AT BROWNSVILLE
Brownsville, TX

Tuition & fees (TX res): $4547   **Average undergraduate aid package: $8685**

ABOUT THE INSTITUTION State-supported, coed. 37 undergraduate majors. Federal methodology is used as a basis for awarding need-based institutional aid.

UNDERGRADUATE EXPENSES for 2009–10 *Tuition, state resident:* full-time $3180; part-time $132.50 per credit hour. *Tuition, nonresident:* full-time $9828; part-time $409.50 per credit hour. *Required fees:* full-time $1367; $36 per credit hour or $251.30 per term. Full-time tuition and fees vary according to class time, course level, course load, location, and program. Part-time tuition and fees vary according to class time, course level, course load, location, and program. *College room and board:* $5742; *Room only:* $2992. Room and board charges vary according to board plan. *Payment plan:* Installment.

FRESHMAN FINANCIAL AID (Fall 2009, est.) 1,404 applied for aid; of those 94% were deemed to have need. 100% of freshmen with need received aid. *Average percent of need met:* 70% (excluding resources awarded to replace EFC). *Average financial aid package:* $8431 (excluding resources awarded to replace EFC). 3% of all full-time freshmen had no need and received non-need-based gift aid.

UNDERGRADUATE FINANCIAL AID (Fall 2009, est.) 4,026 applied for aid; of those 95% were deemed to have need. 100% of undergraduates with need received aid. *Average percent of need met:* 59% (excluding resources awarded to replace EFC). *Average financial aid package:* $8685 (excluding resources awarded to replace EFC). 2% of all full-time undergraduates had no need and received non-need-based gift aid.

GIFT AID (NEED-BASED) *Total amount:* $36,491,045 (81% federal, 19% state). *Receiving aid:* Freshmen: 79% (1,227); all full-time undergraduates: 74% (3,481). *Average award:* Freshmen: $7639; Undergraduates: $7045. *Scholarships, grants, and awards:* Federal Pell, FSEOG, state, private, college/university gift aid from institutional funds.

GIFT AID (NON-NEED-BASED) *Total amount:* $5,482,237 (10% state, 78% institutional, 12% external sources). *Receiving aid:* Freshmen: 79% (1,231). Undergraduates: 72% (3,388). *Average award:* Freshmen: $3887. Undergraduates: $3577. *Scholarships, grants, and awards by category: Academic interests/ achievement:* biological sciences, business, communication, computer science, education, engineering/technologies, English, foreign languages, general academic interests/achievements, health fields, international studies, mathematics, physical sciences, social sciences. *Creative arts/performance:* art/fine arts, music, performing arts. *Special characteristics:* children of faculty/staff, first-generation college students, general special characteristics, international students. *Tuition waivers:* Full or partial for senior citizens.

LOANS *Student loans:* $24,915,519 (67% need-based, 33% non-need-based). *Average need-based loan:* Freshmen: $3030. Undergraduates: $3845. *Parent loans:* $36,464 (100% non-need-based). *Programs:* FFEL (Subsidized and Unsubsidized Stafford, PLUS), state, college/university.

WORK-STUDY *Federal work-study:* Total amount: $613,117; 192 jobs averaging $3193. *State or other work-study/employment:* Total amount: $108,979 (100% need-based). 31 part-time jobs averaging $3515.

ATHLETIC AWARDS Total amount: $360,364 (100% non-need-based).

APPLYING FOR FINANCIAL AID *Required financial aid form:* FAFSA. *Financial aid deadline (priority):* 3/1. *Notification date:* 5/1. Students must reply by 7/1 or within 12 weeks of notification.

CONTACT Ms. Georgiana M. Velarde, Assistant Director of Financial Aid, The University of Texas at Brownsville, 80 Fort Brown, Brownsville, TX 78520-4991, 956-882-8830 or toll-free 800-850-0160 (in-state). *Fax:* 956-882-8229. *E-mail:* georgiana.velarde@utb.edu.

THE UNIVERSITY OF TEXAS AT DALLAS
Richardson, TX

Tuition & fees (TX res): $10,340   **Average undergraduate aid package: $14,322**

ABOUT THE INSTITUTION State-supported, coed. 41 undergraduate majors. Both federal and institutional methodology are used as a basis for awarding need-based institutional aid.

UNDERGRADUATE EXPENSES for 2009–10 *Tuition, state resident:* full-time $10,340; part-time $344.67 per credit hour. *Tuition, nonresident:* full-time $23,730; part-time $791 per credit hour. Full-time tuition and fees vary according to course load and degree level. Part-time tuition and fees vary according to course load and degree level. *College room and board:* $7733. Room and board charges vary according to board plan and housing facility. *Payment plans:* Guaranteed tuition, installment.

FRESHMAN FINANCIAL AID (Fall 2008) 712 applied for aid; of those 70% were deemed to have need. 96% of freshmen with need received aid; of those 8% had need fully met. *Average percent of need met:* 68% (excluding resources awarded to replace EFC). *Average financial aid package:* $14,509 (excluding resources awarded to replace EFC). 29% of all full-time freshmen had no need and received non-need-based gift aid.

UNDERGRADUATE FINANCIAL AID (Fall 2008) 4,072 applied for aid; of those 81% were deemed to have need. 97% of undergraduates with need received aid; of those 5% had need fully met. *Average percent of need met:* 67% (excluding resources awarded to replace EFC). *Average financial aid package:* $14,322 (excluding resources awarded to replace EFC). 21% of all full-time undergraduates had no need and received non-need-based gift aid.

GIFT AID (NEED-BASED) *Total amount:* $18,490,815 (40% federal, 13% state, 42% institutional, 5% external sources). *Receiving aid:* Freshmen: 41% (451); all full-time undergraduates: 42% (2,899). *Average award:* Freshmen: $8016; Undergraduates: $5068. *Scholarships, grants, and awards:* Federal Pell, FSEOG, state, private, college/university gift aid from institutional funds.

GIFT AID (NON-NEED-BASED) *Total amount:* $13,324,609 (95% institutional, 5% external sources). *Receiving aid:* Freshmen: 8% (86). Undergraduates: 3% (188). *Average award:* Freshmen: $10,245. Undergraduates: $8218. *Scholarships, grants, and awards by category: Academic interests/achievement:* biological sciences, business, computer science, engineering/technologies, general academic interests/achievements, mathematics, physical sciences. *Special achievements/activities:* general special achievements/activities, leadership. *Special characteristics:* adult students, children of public servants, general special characteristics, handicapped students, international students, local/state students, members of minority groups, out-of-state students, public servants, veterans, veterans' children. *Tuition waivers:* Full or partial for senior citizens.

LOANS *Student loans:* $26,904,654 (72% need-based, 28% non-need-based). 42% of past graduating class borrowed through all loan programs. *Average indebtedness per student:* $17,483. *Average need-based loan:* Freshmen: $3208. Undergraduates: $4457. *Parent loans:* $2,855,778 (21% need-based, 79% non-need-based). *Programs:* FFEL (Subsidized and Unsubsidized Stafford, PLUS), Perkins, state, college/university.

WORK-STUDY *Federal work-study:* Total amount: $349,716; jobs available. *State or other work-study/employment:* Total amount: $73,054 (76% need-based, 24% non-need-based). Part-time jobs available.

APPLYING FOR FINANCIAL AID *Required financial aid form:* FAFSA. *Financial aid deadline (priority):* 3/31. *Notification date:* Continuous beginning 3/1. Students must reply within 2 weeks of notification.

CONTACT Dr. Karen M. Jarrell, University Registrar and Assistant Vice President of Student Financial Aid and Academic Records, The University of Texas at Dallas, 800 West Campbell Road, MC12, Richardson, TX 75080-3021, 972-883-2941 or toll-free 800-889-2443. *Fax:* 972-883-2947. *E-mail:* karenl@utdallas.edu.

THE UNIVERSITY OF TEXAS AT EL PASO
El Paso, TX

Tuition & fees: N/R   **Average undergraduate aid package: $12,159**

ABOUT THE INSTITUTION State-supported, coed. 61 undergraduate majors. Federal methodology is used as a basis for awarding need-based institutional aid.

FRESHMAN FINANCIAL AID (Fall 2008) 1,641 applied for aid; of those 82% were deemed to have need. 99% of freshmen with need received aid; of those 32% had need fully met. *Average percent of need met:* 82% (excluding resources awarded to replace EFC). *Average financial aid package:* $11,558 (excluding resources awarded to replace EFC).

UNDERGRADUATE FINANCIAL AID (Fall 2008) 8,115 applied for aid; of those 80% were deemed to have need. 98% of undergraduates with need received aid; of those 33% had need fully met. *Average percent of need met:* 80% (excluding resources awarded to replace EFC). *Average financial aid package:* $12,159 (excluding resources awarded to replace EFC).

GIFT AID (NEED-BASED) *Total amount:* $51,488,258 (64% federal, 22% state, 14% institutional). *Receiving aid:* Freshmen: 1,133; all full-time undergraduates: 5,421. *Average award:* Freshmen: $8218; Undergraduates: $6460. *Scholarships, grants, and awards:* Federal Pell, FSEOG, state, private, college/university gift aid from institutional funds, United Negro College Fund, Federal Nursing.

GIFT AID (NON-NEED-BASED) *Total amount:* $6,139,487 (7% federal, 8% state, 63% institutional, 22% external sources). *Receiving aid:* Freshmen: 141. Undergraduates: 648. *Average award:* Freshmen: $1086. Undergraduates: $2429. *Scholarships, grants, and awards by category: Academic interests/achievement:* biological sciences, business, communication, computer science, education, engineering/technologies, English, general academic interests/achievements, health fields, humanities, international studies, mathematics, military science, physical sciences. *Creative arts/performance:* applied art and design, art/fine arts, journalism/publications, music, performing arts, theater/drama. *Special achievements/activities:* cheerleading/drum major, leadership. *Special characteristics:* ethnic background, international students, local/state students, members of minority groups, out-of-state students. *Tuition waivers:* Full or partial for employees or children of employees.

LOANS *Student loans:* $69,943,386 (98% need-based, 2% non-need-based). 64% of past graduating class borrowed through all loan programs. *Average indebtedness per student:* $17,476. *Average need-based loan:* Freshmen: $4033. Undergraduates: $6526. *Parent loans:* $19,802,489 (100% non-need-based). *Programs:* FFEL (Subsidized and Unsubsidized Stafford, PLUS), Perkins, Federal Nursing, state, college/university.

WORK-STUDY *Federal work-study:* Total amount: $2,720,166; 381 jobs averaging $2686. *State or other work-study/employment:* Total amount: $201,886 (100% need-based). 42 part-time jobs averaging $3036.

ATHLETIC AWARDS Total amount: $3,820,640 (100% non-need-based).

APPLYING FOR FINANCIAL AID *Required financial aid forms:* FAFSA, institution's own form. *Financial aid deadline (priority):* 3/15. *Notification date:* Continuous beginning 6/30. Students must reply within 2 weeks of notification.

CONTACT Mr. Raul Lerma, Director of Financial Aid, The University of Texas at El Paso, 500 West University Avenue, El Paso, TX 79968-0001, 915-747-5204 or toll-free 877-746-4636. *Fax:* 915-747-5631. *E-mail:* rlerma@utep.edu.

THE UNIVERSITY OF TEXAS AT SAN ANTONIO
San Antonio, TX

Tuition & fees (TX res): $7527   **Average undergraduate aid package: $8057**

ABOUT THE INSTITUTION State-supported, coed. 56 undergraduate majors. Federal methodology is used as a basis for awarding need-based institutional aid.

UNDERGRADUATE EXPENSES for 2010–11 *Tuition, state resident:* full-time $5126; part-time $170.85 per hour. *Tuition, nonresident:* full-time $13,436; part-time $447.85 per hour. *Required fees:* full-time $2401. Full-time tuition and fees vary according to course level, course load, and degree level. Part-time tuition and fees vary according to course level, course load, and degree level.

College room and board: $8937; *Room only:* $6075. Room and board charges vary according to board plan and housing facility. *Payment plans:* Installment, deferred payment.

FRESHMAN FINANCIAL AID (Fall 2008) 3,381 applied for aid; of those 73% were deemed to have need. 95% of freshmen with need received aid; of those 26% had need fully met. *Average percent of need met:* 61% (excluding resources awarded to replace EFC). *Average financial aid package:* $9137 (excluding resources awarded to replace EFC). 7% of all full-time freshmen had no need and received non-need-based gift aid.

UNDERGRADUATE FINANCIAL AID (Fall 2008) 13,659 applied for aid; of those 83% were deemed to have need. 96% of undergraduates with need received aid; of those 17% had need fully met. *Average percent of need met:* 52% (excluding resources awarded to replace EFC). *Average financial aid package:* $8057 (excluding resources awarded to replace EFC). 4% of all full-time undergraduates had no need and received non-need-based gift aid.

GIFT AID (NEED-BASED) *Total amount:* $48,897,114 (62% federal, 21% state, 17% institutional). *Receiving aid:* Freshmen: 41% (1,972); all full-time undergraduates: 45% (8,759). *Average award:* Freshmen: $7089; Undergraduates: $5069. *Scholarships, grants, and awards:* Federal Pell, FSEOG, state, private, college/university gift aid from institutional funds.

GIFT AID (NON-NEED-BASED) *Total amount:* $7,373,971 (1% state, 43% institutional, 56% external sources). *Receiving aid:* Freshmen: 15% (729). Undergraduates: 10% (1,953). *Average award:* Freshmen: $1431. Undergraduates: $1877. *Scholarships, grants, and awards by category:* Academic interests/achievement: agriculture, architecture, area/ethnic studies, biological sciences, business, communication, computer science, education, engineering/technologies, English, foreign languages, general academic interests/achievements, humanities, international studies, mathematics, physical sciences, social sciences. *Creative arts/performance:* art/fine arts, creative writing, debating, music. *Special achievements/activities:* cheerleading/drum major, general special achievements/activities. *Special characteristics:* ethnic background, first-generation college students, general special characteristics, handicapped students, local/state students, members of minority groups, out-of-state students. *Tuition waivers:* Full or partial for employees or children of employees.

LOANS *Student loans:* $89,988,577 (48% need-based, 52% non-need-based). 64% of past graduating class borrowed through all loan programs. *Average indebtedness per student:* $23,152. *Average need-based loan:* Freshmen: $3191. Undergraduates: $4087. *Parent loans:* $8,177,939 (100% non-need-based). *Programs:* Federal Direct (Subsidized and Unsubsidized Stafford, PLUS), Perkins, state, college/university.

WORK-STUDY *Federal work-study:* Total amount: $1,238,320; 504 jobs averaging $2457. *State or other work-study/employment:* Total amount: $1,018,574 (100% need-based). 85 part-time jobs averaging $1969.

ATHLETIC AWARDS Total amount: $2,168,684 (100% non-need-based).

APPLYING FOR FINANCIAL AID *Required financial aid forms:* FAFSA, institution's own form. *Financial aid deadline (priority):* 3/15. *Notification date:* Continuous beginning 4/1. Students must reply within 4 weeks of notification.

CONTACT Kim Canady, Assistant Director of Student Financial Aid, The University of Texas at San Antonio, One UTSA Cirlce, San Antonio, TX 78249, 210-458-8000 or toll-free 800-669-0919. *Fax:* 210-458-4638. *E-mail:* financialaid@utsa.edu.

THE UNIVERSITY OF TEXAS AT TYLER
Tyler, TX

Tuition & fees (TX res): $6042	Average undergraduate aid package: $8496

ABOUT THE INSTITUTION State-supported, coed. 38 undergraduate majors. Federal methodology is used as a basis for awarding need-based institutional aid.

UNDERGRADUATE EXPENSES for 2009–10 *Tuition, state resident:* full-time $4650; part-time $50 per semester hour. *Tuition, nonresident:* full-time $13,080; part-time $331 per semester hour. *Required fees:* full-time $1392. Full-time tuition and fees vary according to course level, course load, and degree level. *College room and board:* $8016; *Room only:* $5102. Room and board charges vary according to board plan and housing facility. *Payment plan:* Installment.

FRESHMAN FINANCIAL AID (Fall 2008) 414 applied for aid; of those 69% were deemed to have need. 98% of freshmen with need received aid; of those 24% had need fully met. *Average percent of need met:* 58% (excluding resources

awarded to replace EFC). *Average financial aid package:* $8342 (excluding resources awarded to replace EFC). 19% of all full-time freshmen had no need and received non-need-based gift aid.

UNDERGRADUATE FINANCIAL AID (Fall 2008) 2,488 applied for aid; of those 81% were deemed to have need. 99% of undergraduates with need received aid; of those 12% had need fully met. *Average percent of need met:* 57% (excluding resources awarded to replace EFC). *Average financial aid package:* $8496 (excluding resources awarded to replace EFC). 9% of all full-time undergraduates had no need and received non-need-based gift aid.

GIFT AID (NEED-BASED) *Total amount:* $10,775,479 (55% federal, 19% state, 19% institutional, 7% external sources). *Receiving aid:* Freshmen: 42% (244); all full-time undergraduates: 42% (1,595). *Average award:* Freshmen: $7496; Undergraduates: $5899. *Scholarships, grants, and awards:* Federal Pell, FSEOG, state, private, college/university gift aid from institutional funds, Texas Grants, Institutional Grants (Education Affordability Program).

GIFT AID (NON-NEED-BASED) *Total amount:* $2,985,720 (2% state, 55% institutional, 43% external sources). *Receiving aid:* Freshmen: 6% (33). Undergraduates: 3% (109). *Average award:* Freshmen: $3228. Undergraduates: $2451. *Scholarships, grants, and awards by category:* Academic interests/achievement: 889 awards ($2,140,900 total): communication, engineering/technologies, general academic interests/achievements, health fields. *Creative arts/performance:* 53 awards ($39,375 total): art/fine arts, music. *Special characteristics:* 23 awards ($173,802 total): children of faculty/staff. *Tuition waivers:* Full or partial for employees or children of employees, senior citizens.

LOANS *Student loans:* $19,979,714 (72% need-based, 28% non-need-based). 51% of past graduating class borrowed through all loan programs. *Average indebtedness per student:* $18,041. *Average need-based loan:* Freshmen: $2256. Undergraduates: $4077. *Parent loans:* $5,284,072 (18% need-based, 82% non-need-based). *Programs:* FFEL (Subsidized and Unsubsidized Stafford, PLUS), Federal Nursing.

WORK-STUDY *Federal work-study:* Total amount: $385,983; 105 jobs averaging $3408. *State or other work-study/employment:* Total amount: $195,610 (35% need-based, 65% non-need-based). 14 part-time jobs averaging $4444.

APPLYING FOR FINANCIAL AID *Required financial aid forms:* FAFSA, institution's own form. *Financial aid deadline (priority):* 4/1. *Notification date:* Continuous beginning 4/15. Students must reply within 2 weeks of notification.

CONTACT Candice A. Lindsey, Executive Director of Enrollment Management and Marketing, The University of Texas at Tyler, 3900 University Boulevard, Tyler, TX 75799, 903-566-7221 or toll-free 800-UTTYLER (in-state). *Fax:* 903-566-7183. *E-mail:* clindsey@uttyler.edu.

THE UNIVERSITY OF TEXAS HEALTH SCIENCE CENTER AT HOUSTON
Houston, TX

Tuition & fees: N/R	Average undergraduate aid package: $9508

ABOUT THE INSTITUTION State-supported, coed. 2 undergraduate majors. Federal methodology is used as a basis for awarding need-based institutional aid.

UNDERGRADUATE EXPENSES for 2010–11 *Tuition, state resident:* part-time $149 per credit hour. *Tuition, nonresident:* part-time $623 per credit hour. *Required fees:* $157 per credit hour. *Payment plan:* Installment.

UNDERGRADUATE FINANCIAL AID (Fall 2008) 266 applied for aid; of those 91% were deemed to have need. 100% of undergraduates with need received aid; of those 12% had need fully met. *Average percent of need met:* 45% (excluding resources awarded to replace EFC). *Average financial aid package:* $9508 (excluding resources awarded to replace EFC). 7% of all full-time undergraduates had no need and received non-need-based gift aid.

GIFT AID (NEED-BASED) *Total amount:* $1,011,399 (32% federal, 5% state, 56% institutional, 7% external sources). *Receiving aid:* All full-time undergraduates: 34% (154). *Average award:* Undergraduates: $5195. *Scholarships, grants, and awards:* Federal Pell, FSEOG, state, private, college/university gift aid from institutional funds.

GIFT AID (NON-NEED-BASED) *Average award:* Undergraduates: $2176. *Scholarships, grants, and awards by category:* Academic interests/achievement: health fields.

LOANS *Student loans:* $3,407,756 (100% need-based). *Average need-based loan:* Undergraduates: $5158. *Parent loans:* $787,521 (100% need-based).

Programs: FFEL (Subsidized and Unsubsidized Stafford, PLUS), Perkins, Federal Nursing, state, college/university, alternative loans.
APPLYING FOR FINANCIAL AID *Required financial aid forms:* FAFSA, institution's own form. *Financial aid deadline:* Continuous. *Notification date:* Continuous.
CONTACT Ms. Wanda Williams, Director, The University of Texas Health Science Center at Houston, PO Box 20036, Houston, TX 77225, 713-500-3860. *Fax:* 713-500-3863. *E-mail:* wanda.k.williams@uth.tmc.edu.

THE UNIVERSITY OF TEXAS HEALTH SCIENCE CENTER AT SAN ANTONIO
San Antonio, TX

CONTACT Robert T. Lawson, Financial Aid Administrator, The University of Texas Health Science Center at San Antonio, 7703 Floyd Curl Drive, MSC 7708, San Antonio, TX 78284, 210-567-0025. *Fax:* 210-567-6643.

THE UNIVERSITY OF TEXAS MEDICAL BRANCH
Galveston, TX

Tuition & fees (TX res): $5502   Average undergraduate aid package: $14,903

ABOUT THE INSTITUTION State-supported, coed. 3 undergraduate majors. Federal methodology is used as a basis for awarding need-based institutional aid.
UNDERGRADUATE EXPENSES for 2009–10 *Tuition, state resident:* full-time $4695; part-time $156.50 per credit hour. *Tuition, nonresident:* full-time $13,125; part-time $437.50 per credit hour. *Required fees:* full-time $807; $10.99 per credit hour or $201.33 per term. Full-time tuition and fees vary according to course load, degree level, and program. Part-time tuition and fees vary according to course load, degree level, and program. *College room and board: Room only:* $4620. Room and board charges vary according to housing facility. *Payment plan:* Installment.
UNDERGRADUATE FINANCIAL AID (Fall 2009, est.) 237 applied for aid; of those 78% were deemed to have need. 100% of undergraduates with need received aid; of those 83% had need fully met. *Average percent of need met:* 90% (excluding resources awarded to replace EFC). *Average financial aid package:* $14,903 (excluding resources awarded to replace EFC). 4% of all full-time undergraduates had no need and received non-need-based gift aid.
GIFT AID (NEED-BASED) *Total amount:* $863,199 (74% federal, 8% state, 16% institutional, 2% external sources). *Receiving aid:* All full-time undergraduates: 29% (90). *Average award:* Undergraduates: $4788. *Scholarships, grants, and awards:* Federal Pell, FSEOG, state, private, college/university gift aid from institutional funds.
GIFT AID (NON-NEED-BASED) *Total amount:* $29,700 (87% institutional, 13% external sources). *Receiving aid:* Undergraduates: 22% (69). *Average award:* Undergraduates: $1558. *Scholarships, grants, and awards by category:* Academic interests/achievement: health fields.
LOANS *Student loans:* $3,572,125 (99% need-based, 1% non-need-based). *Average need-based loan:* Undergraduates: $4975. *Parent loans:* $42,500 (100% need-based). *Programs:* Federal Direct (Subsidized and Unsubsidized Stafford, PLUS), Perkins, Federal Nursing, state, college/university.
WORK-STUDY *Federal work-study:* Total amount: $51,023; 23 jobs averaging $2262.
CONTACT Mrs. Carol A. Cromie, University Financial Aid Officer, The University of Texas Medical Branch, 301 University Boulevard, Galveston, TX 77555-1305, 409-772-9795. *Fax:* 409-772-4466. *E-mail:* cacromie@umtb.edu.

THE UNIVERSITY OF TEXAS OF THE PERMIAN BASIN
Odessa, TX

Tuition & fees (TX res): $5378   Average undergraduate aid package: $7384

ABOUT THE INSTITUTION State-supported, coed. 36 undergraduate majors. Institutional methodology is used as a basis for awarding need-based institutional aid.

UNDERGRADUATE EXPENSES for 2009–10 *Tuition, state resident:* full-time $4380; part-time $146 per semester hour. *Tuition, nonresident:* full-time $12,690; part-time $423 per semester hour. *Required fees:* full-time $998. Full-time tuition and fees vary according to course load and location. Part-time tuition and fees vary according to course load and location. *College room and board:* $6445; *Room only:* $3744. Room and board charges vary according to board plan and housing facility. *Payment plan:* Installment.
FRESHMAN FINANCIAL AID (Fall 2009, est.) 244 applied for aid; of those 68% were deemed to have need. 100% of freshmen with need received aid; of those 26% had need fully met. *Average percent of need met:* 74% (excluding resources awarded to replace EFC). *Average financial aid package:* $8021 (excluding resources awarded to replace EFC). 17% of all full-time freshmen had no need and received non-need-based gift aid.
UNDERGRADUATE FINANCIAL AID (Fall 2009, est.) 1,364 applied for aid; of those 80% were deemed to have need. 100% of undergraduates with need received aid; of those 23% had need fully met. *Average percent of need met:* 81% (excluding resources awarded to replace EFC). *Average financial aid package:* $7384 (excluding resources awarded to replace EFC). 13% of all full-time undergraduates had no need and received non-need-based gift aid.
GIFT AID (NEED-BASED) *Total amount:* $4,941,067 (81% federal, 17% state, 2% institutional). *Receiving aid:* Freshmen: 34% (109); all full-time undergraduates: 40% (767). *Average award:* Freshmen: $6937; Undergraduates: $6842. *Scholarships, grants, and awards:* Federal Pell, FSEOG, state, private, college/university gift aid from institutional funds.
GIFT AID (NON-NEED-BASED) *Total amount:* $4,296,732 (1% federal, 5% state, 72% institutional, 22% external sources). *Receiving aid:* Freshmen: 47% (153). Undergraduates: 37% (722). *Average award:* Freshmen: $2484. Undergraduates: $2460. *Scholarships, grants, and awards by category:* Academic interests/achievement: 1,308 awards ($2,517,691 total): general academic interests/achievements. Creative arts/performance: 58 awards ($84,050 total): art/fine arts, dance, general creative arts/performance, music, theater/drama. Special achievements/activities: 8 awards ($9300 total): cheerleading/drum major. *Tuition waivers:* Full or partial for employees or children of employees, senior citizens.
LOANS *Student loans:* $7,860,028 (50% need-based, 50% non-need-based). 64% of past graduating class borrowed through all loan programs. *Average indebtedness per student:* $18,507. *Average need-based loan:* Freshmen: $2281. Undergraduates: $3540. *Parent loans:* $142,648 (100% non-need-based). *Programs:* Federal Direct (Subsidized and Unsubsidized Stafford, PLUS), state.
WORK-STUDY *Federal work-study:* Total amount: $49,478; 20 jobs averaging $2474. *State or other work-study/employment:* Total amount: $20,738 (100% need-based). 15 part-time jobs averaging $1382.
ATHLETIC AWARDS Total amount: $347,203 (100% non-need-based).
APPLYING FOR FINANCIAL AID *Required financial aid form:* FAFSA. *Financial aid deadline (priority):* 2/1. *Notification date:* Continuous beginning 3/1. Students must reply within 2 weeks of notification.
CONTACT Mr. Robert L. Vasquez, Director, Office of Student Financial Aid, The University of Texas of the Permian Basin, 4901 East University Bouelvard, Odessa, TX 79762, 432-552-2620 or toll-free 866-552-UTPB. *Fax:* 432-552-2621. *E-mail:* finaid@utpb.edu.

THE UNIVERSITY OF TEXAS–PAN AMERICAN
Edinburg, TX

Tuition & fees (TX res): $4304   Average undergraduate aid package: $9033

ABOUT THE INSTITUTION State-supported, coed. 50 undergraduate majors. Federal methodology is used as a basis for awarding need-based institutional aid.
UNDERGRADUATE EXPENSES for 2009–10 *Tuition, state resident:* full-time $3305; part-time $137.70 per credit hour. *Tuition, nonresident:* full-time $10,049; part-time $418.70 per credit hour. *Required fees:* full-time $999; $116.05 per credit hour or $137.20 per term. Full-time tuition and fees vary according to course load and location. Part-time tuition and fees vary according to course load and location. *College room and board:* $5294; *Room only:* $3200. Room and board charges vary according to board plan and housing facility. *Payment plan:* Installment.
FRESHMAN FINANCIAL AID (Fall 2008) 2,148 applied for aid; of those 96% were deemed to have need. 100% of freshmen with need received aid; of those

6% had need fully met. *Average percent of need met:* 76% (excluding resources awarded to replace EFC). *Average financial aid package:* $9560 (excluding resources awarded to replace EFC). 3% of all full-time freshmen had no need and received non-need-based gift aid.

UNDERGRADUATE FINANCIAL AID (Fall 2008) 9,047 applied for aid; of those 96% were deemed to have need. 100% of undergraduates with need received aid; of those 7% had need fully met. *Average percent of need met:* 71% (excluding resources awarded to replace EFC). *Average financial aid package:* $9033 (excluding resources awarded to replace EFC). 3% of all full-time undergraduates had no need and received non-need-based gift aid.

GIFT AID (NEED-BASED) *Total amount:* $66,944,547 (52% federal, 35% state, 12% institutional, 1% external sources). *Receiving aid:* Freshmen: 80% (2,007); all full-time undergraduates: 74% (8,349). *Average award:* Freshmen: $9769; Undergraduates: $9716. *Scholarships, grants, and awards:* Federal Pell, FSEOG, state, private, college/university gift aid from institutional funds.

GIFT AID (NON-NEED-BASED) *Total amount:* $1,878,875 (9% federal, 2% state, 77% institutional, 12% external sources). *Receiving aid:* Freshmen: 1% (16). Undergraduates: 1% (72). *Average award:* Freshmen: $4606. Undergraduates: $5018. *Scholarships, grants, and awards by category: Academic interests/ achievement:* 1,536 awards ($4,670,488 total): biological sciences, business, communication, computer science, education, engineering/technologies, English, general academic interests/achievements, health fields, mathematics, military science, premedicine, social sciences. *Creative arts/performance:* 126 awards ($107,858 total): art/fine arts, dance, journalism/publications, music, theater/ drama. *Special achievements/activities:* 86 awards ($53,051 total): cheerleading/ drum major, community service, general special achievements/activities, leadership, memberships. *Special characteristics:* 77 awards ($154,962 total): ethnic background, general special characteristics, international students, local/state students, out-of-state students, veterans. *Tuition waivers:* Full or partial for senior citizens.

LOANS *Student loans:* $29,584,497 (88% need-based, 12% non-need-based). 64% of past graduating class borrowed through all loan programs. *Average indebtedness per student:* $13,088. *Average need-based loan:* Freshmen: $2295. Undergraduates: $4568. *Parent loans:* $165,875 (12% need-based, 88% non-need-based). *Programs:* Federal Direct (Subsidized and Unsubsidized Stafford, PLUS), Perkins, state, college/university.

WORK-STUDY *Federal work-study:* Total amount: $1,888,193; 863 jobs averaging $2188. *State or other work-study/employment:* Total amount: $363,005 (100% need-based). 241 part-time jobs averaging $1506.

ATHLETIC AWARDS Total amount: $972,554 (37% need-based, 63% non-need-based).

APPLYING FOR FINANCIAL AID *Required financial aid form:* FAFSA. *Financial aid deadline (priority):* 4/1. *Notification date:* Continuous beginning 4/1. Students must reply within 2 weeks of notification.

CONTACT Mrs. Elaine Rivera, Executive Director of Student Financial Services, The University of Texas–Pan American, 1201 West University Drive, Edinburg, TX 78541, 956-381-5372. *Fax:* 956-381-2396. *E-mail:* eriverall@utpa.edu.

THE UNIVERSITY OF TEXAS SOUTHWESTERN MEDICAL CENTER AT DALLAS
Dallas, TX

ABOUT THE INSTITUTION State-supported, coed. 4 undergraduate majors.

GIFT AID (NEED-BASED) *Scholarships, grants, and awards:* Federal Pell, FSEOG, state, private, college/university gift aid from institutional funds.

GIFT AID (NON-NEED-BASED) *Scholarships, grants, and awards by category: Special achievements/activities:* community service.

LOANS *Programs:* FFEL (Subsidized and Unsubsidized Stafford, PLUS), Perkins, state, college/university, alternative loans.

WORK-STUDY *Federal work-study:* Total amount: $69,376; 10 jobs averaging $1933.

CONTACT Ms. Lisa J. McGaha, Associate Director of Student Financial Aid, The University of Texas Southwestern Medical Center at Dallas, 5323 Harry Hines Boulevard, Dallas, TX 75390-9064, 214-648-3611. *Fax:* 214-648-3289. *E-mail:* lisa.mcgaha@utsouthwestern.edu.

THE UNIVERSITY OF THE ARTS
Philadelphia, PA

CONTACT Office of Financial Aid, The University of the Arts, 320 South Broad Street, Philadelphia, PA 19102-4944, 800-616-ARTS Ext. 6170 or toll-free 800-616-ARTS. *E-mail:* finaid@uarts.edu.

UNIVERSITY OF THE CUMBERLANDS
Williamsburg, KY

ABOUT THE INSTITUTION Independent Kentucky Baptist, coed. 41 undergraduate majors.

GIFT AID (NEED-BASED) *Scholarships, grants, and awards:* Federal Pell, FSEOG, state, private, college/university gift aid from institutional funds.

GIFT AID (NON-NEED-BASED) *Scholarships, grants, and awards by category: Academic interests/achievement:* general academic interests/achievements. *Creative arts/performance:* art/fine arts, debating, journalism/publications, music, theater/drama. *Special achievements/activities:* cheerleading/drum major, community service, leadership, religious involvement. *Special characteristics:* children and siblings of alumni, children of faculty/staff, relatives of clergy, religious affiliation, siblings of current students.

LOANS *Programs:* FFEL (Subsidized and Unsubsidized Stafford, PLUS), Perkins, college/university.

WORK-STUDY *Federal work-study:* Total amount: $960,090; 491 jobs averaging $1947. *State or other work-study/employment:* Total amount: $396,033 (75% need-based, 25% non-need-based). 210 part-time jobs averaging $1567.

APPLYING FOR FINANCIAL AID *Required financial aid form:* FAFSA.

CONTACT Mr. Steve Allen, Vice President of Student Financial Planning, University of the Cumberlands, 6190 College Station Drive, Williamsburg, KY 40769-1372, 606-549-2200 or toll-free 800-343-1609. *Fax:* 606-539-4515. *E-mail:* finplan@ucumberlands.edu.

UNIVERSITY OF THE DISTRICT OF COLUMBIA
Washington, DC

Tuition & fees (DC res): $5370	Average undergraduate aid package: $5500

ABOUT THE INSTITUTION District-supported, coed. 83 undergraduate majors. Federal methodology is used as a basis for awarding need-based institutional aid.

UNDERGRADUATE EXPENSES for 2010–11 *Tuition, state resident:* full-time $4750; part-time $198 per credit hour. *Tuition, nonresident:* full-time $11,680; part-time $487 per credit hour. *Required fees:* full-time $620; $30 per credit hour or $30 per credit hour. Part-time tuition and fees vary according to course load. *Payment plans:* Installment, deferred payment.

FRESHMAN FINANCIAL AID (Fall 2009, est.) 278 applied for aid; of those 100% were deemed to have need. 100% of freshmen with need received aid; of those 32% had need fully met. *Average percent of need met:* 55% (excluding resources awarded to replace EFC). *Average financial aid package:* $5250 (excluding resources awarded to replace EFC). 45% of all full-time freshmen had no need and received non-need-based gift aid.

UNDERGRADUATE FINANCIAL AID (Fall 2009, est.) 2,028 applied for aid; of those 90% were deemed to have need. 79% of undergraduates with need received aid; of those 52% had need fully met. *Average percent of need met:* 93% (excluding resources awarded to replace EFC). *Average financial aid package:* $5500 (excluding resources awarded to replace EFC). 7% of all full-time undergraduates had no need and received non-need-based gift aid.

GIFT AID (NEED-BASED) *Total amount:* $7,416,619 (96% federal, 2% state, 1% institutional, 1% external sources). *Receiving aid:* Freshmen: 49% (246); all full-time undergraduates: 42% (926). *Average award:* Freshmen: $3275; Undergraduates: $3275. *Scholarships, grants, and awards:* Federal Pell, FSEOG, state, college/university gift aid from institutional funds.

GIFT AID (NON-NEED-BASED) *Total amount:* $208,400 (50% institutional, 50% external sources). *Receiving aid:* Freshmen: 16% (79). Undergraduates: 8% (176). *Average award:* Freshmen: $2750. Undergraduates: $2750. *Scholarships, grants, and awards by category: Academic interests/achievement:* general academic interests/achievements. *Creative arts/performance:* music. *Special characteristics:* children of faculty/staff. *Tuition waivers:* Full or partial for employees or children of employees, senior citizens.

LOANS *Student loans:* $460,520 (87% need-based, 13% non-need-based). 93% of past graduating class borrowed through all loan programs. *Average indebtedness per student:* $17,547. *Average need-based loan:* Freshmen: $2750. Undergraduates: $2750. *Parent loans:* $54,674 (100% need-based). *Programs:* FFEL (Subsidized and Unsubsidized Stafford, PLUS), Perkins, college/university.

WORK-STUDY *Federal work-study:* Total amount: $76,431; jobs available. *State or other work-study/employment:* Part-time jobs available.

ATHLETIC AWARDS Total amount: $255,247 (100% need-based).

APPLYING FOR FINANCIAL AID *Required financial aid forms:* FAFSA, institution's own form, district aid form. *Financial aid deadline (priority):* 3/31. *Notification date:* Continuous beginning 4/1. Students must reply within 2 weeks of notification.

CONTACT Willis Parker, Director, Officer of Financial Aid, University of the District of Columbia, 4200 Connecticut Avenue NW, Washington, DC 20008-1175, 202-274-6053. *E-mail:* wparker@udc.edu.

UNIVERSITY OF THE INCARNATE WORD
San Antonio, TX

Tuition & fees: $21,890	Average undergraduate aid package: $15,618

ABOUT THE INSTITUTION Independent Roman Catholic, coed. 58 undergraduate majors. Federal methodology is used as a basis for awarding need-based institutional aid.

UNDERGRADUATE EXPENSES for 2010–11 *Comprehensive fee:* $31,110 includes full-time tuition ($21,000), mandatory fees ($890), and room and board ($9220). *College room only:* $5540. Full-time tuition and fees vary according to course load, degree level, location, and reciprocity agreements. Room and board charges vary according to board plan and housing facility. *Part-time tuition:* $675 per semester hour. Part-time tuition and fees vary according to course load, degree level, location, and reciprocity agreements. *Payment plan:* Installment.

FRESHMAN FINANCIAL AID (Fall 2009, est.) 637 applied for aid; of those 90% were deemed to have need. 100% of freshmen with need received aid; of those 29% had need fully met. *Average percent of need met:* 66% (excluding resources awarded to replace EFC). *Average financial aid package:* $18,080 (excluding resources awarded to replace EFC). 9% of all full-time freshmen had no need and received non-need-based gift aid.

UNDERGRADUATE FINANCIAL AID (Fall 2009, est.) 3,171 applied for aid; of those 92% were deemed to have need. 100% of undergraduates with need received aid; of those 22% had need fully met. *Average percent of need met:* 64% (excluding resources awarded to replace EFC). *Average financial aid package:* $15,618 (excluding resources awarded to replace EFC). 5% of all full-time undergraduates had no need and received non-need-based gift aid.

GIFT AID (NEED-BASED) *Total amount:* $26,620,419 (34% federal, 17% state, 47% institutional, 2% external sources). *Receiving aid:* Freshmen: 79% (569); all full-time undergraduates: 80% (2,698). *Average award:* Freshmen: $13,345; Undergraduates: $10,754. *Scholarships, grants, and awards:* Federal Pell, FSEOG, state, private, college/university gift aid from institutional funds, United Negro College Fund, Federal Nursing.

GIFT AID (NON-NEED-BASED) *Total amount:* $3,426,913 (79% institutional, 21% external sources). *Receiving aid:* Freshmen: 77% (556). Undergraduates: 58% (1,949). *Average award:* Freshmen: $8416. Undergraduates: $6908. *Scholarships, grants, and awards by category:* Academic interests/achievement: general academic interests/achievements. *Creative arts/performance:* art/fine arts. *Special achievements/activities:* religious involvement. *Special characteristics:* children and siblings of alumni, children of faculty/staff, parents of current students. *Tuition waivers:* Full or partial for employees or children of employees, senior citizens.

LOANS *Student loans:* $22,748,381 (94% need-based, 6% non-need-based). *Average need-based loan:* Freshmen: $3372. Undergraduates: $4576. *Parent loans:* $4,548,871 (93% need-based, 7% non-need-based). *Programs:* Federal Direct (Subsidized and Unsubsidized Stafford, PLUS), FFEL (Subsidized and Unsubsidized Stafford, PLUS), Perkins, Federal Nursing, state, alternative loans.

WORK-STUDY *Federal work-study:* Total amount: $661,757; jobs available. *State or other work-study/employment:* Total amount: $38,217 (100% need-based). Part-time jobs available.

ATHLETIC AWARDS Total amount: $3,935,106 (83% need-based, 17% non-need-based).

APPLYING FOR FINANCIAL AID *Required financial aid form:* FAFSA. *Financial aid deadline (priority):* 4/1. *Notification date:* Continuous beginning 2/15. Students must reply within 2 weeks of notification.

CONTACT Amy Carcanagues, Director of Financial Assistance, University of the Incarnate Word, 4301 Broadway, San Antonio, TX 78209, 210-829-6008 or toll-free 800-749-WORD. *Fax:* 210-283-5053. *E-mail:* finaid@uiwtx.edu.

UNIVERSITY OF THE OZARKS
Clarksville, AR

Tuition & fees: $20,530	Average undergraduate aid package: $18,877

ABOUT THE INSTITUTION Independent Presbyterian, coed. 30 undergraduate majors. Federal methodology is used as a basis for awarding need-based institutional aid.

UNDERGRADUATE EXPENSES for 2010–11 *Comprehensive fee:* $26,830 includes full-time tuition ($19,930), mandatory fees ($600), and room and board ($6300). *College room only:* $2900. Room and board charges vary according to board plan and housing facility. *Payment plan:* Installment.

FRESHMAN FINANCIAL AID (Fall 2009, est.) 119 applied for aid; of those 88% were deemed to have need. 100% of freshmen with need received aid; of those 22% had need fully met. *Average percent of need met:* 82% (excluding resources awarded to replace EFC). *Average financial aid package:* $19,491 (excluding resources awarded to replace EFC). 25% of all full-time freshmen had no need and received non-need-based gift aid.

UNDERGRADUATE FINANCIAL AID (Fall 2009, est.) 389 applied for aid; of those 91% were deemed to have need. 100% of undergraduates with need received aid; of those 18% had need fully met. *Average percent of need met:* 77% (excluding resources awarded to replace EFC). *Average financial aid package:* $18,877 (excluding resources awarded to replace EFC). 32% of all full-time undergraduates had no need and received non-need-based gift aid.

GIFT AID (NEED-BASED) *Total amount:* $4,842,304 (21% federal, 8% state, 68% institutional, 3% external sources). *Receiving aid:* Freshmen: 67% (102); all full-time undergraduates: 58% (343). *Average award:* Freshmen: $15,308; Undergraduates: $13,990. *Scholarships, grants, and awards:* Federal Pell, FSEOG, state, private, college/university gift aid from institutional funds, United Negro College Fund, Federal Nursing.

GIFT AID (NON-NEED-BASED) *Total amount:* $3,347,037 (1% state, 98% institutional, 1% external sources). *Average award:* Freshmen: $14,691. Undergraduates: $16,569. *Scholarships, grants, and awards by category:* Academic interests/achievement: $2,328,001 total: biological sciences, business, communication, education, English, general academic interests/achievements, humanities, mathematics, premedicine, religion/biblical studies, social sciences. *Creative arts/performance:* $144,045 total: art/fine arts, music, theater/drama. *Special achievements/activities:* $1,612,721 total: leadership. *Special characteristics:* $633,827 total: children and siblings of alumni, children of faculty/staff, ethnic background, general special characteristics, international students, members of minority groups, relatives of clergy, religious affiliation, siblings of current students. *Tuition waivers:* Full or partial for children of alumni, employees or children of employees.

LOANS *Student loans:* $2,647,823 (96% need-based, 4% non-need-based). 56% of past graduating class borrowed through all loan programs. *Average indebtedness per student:* $18,425. *Average need-based loan:* Freshmen: $8703. Undergraduates: $10,173. *Parent loans:* $2,647,823 (96% need-based, 4% non-need-based). *Programs:* FFEL (Subsidized and Unsubsidized Stafford, PLUS), Perkins, college/university.

WORK-STUDY *Federal work-study:* Total amount: $150,316; 133 jobs averaging $1130. *State or other work-study/employment:* Total amount: $123,500 (51% need-based, 49% non-need-based). 23 part-time jobs averaging $5370.

ATHLETIC AWARDS Total amount: $123,500 (51% need-based, 49% non-need-based).

APPLYING FOR FINANCIAL AID *Required financial aid form:* FAFSA. *Financial aid deadline (priority):* 2/15. *Notification date:* Continuous beginning 3/1. Students must reply within 2 weeks of notification.

CONTACT Ms. Jana D. Hart, Director of Financial Aid, University of the Ozarks, 415 North College Avenue, Clarksville, AR 72830-2880, 479-979-1221 or toll-free 800-264-8636. *Fax:* 479-979-1417. *E-mail:* jhart@ozarks.edu.

UNIVERSITY OF THE PACIFIC
Stockton, CA

Tuition & fees: $32,230	Average undergraduate aid package: $29,320

ABOUT THE INSTITUTION Independent, coed. 54 undergraduate majors. Federal methodology is used as a basis for awarding need-based institutional aid.

UNDERGRADUATE EXPENSES for 2010–11 *Comprehensive fee:* $42,846 includes full-time tuition ($31,730), mandatory fees ($500), and room and board ($10,616). Room and board charges vary according to board plan and housing facility. Part-time tuition and fees vary according to course load. *Payment plan:* Deferred payment.

FRESHMAN FINANCIAL AID (Fall 2009, est.) 786 applied for aid; of those 85% were deemed to have need. 100% of freshmen with need received aid; of those 37% had need fully met. *Average financial aid package:* $29,490 (excluding resources awarded to replace EFC). 17% of all full-time freshmen had no need and received non-need-based gift aid.

UNDERGRADUATE FINANCIAL AID (Fall 2009, est.) 2,648 applied for aid; of those 89% were deemed to have need. 100% of undergraduates with need received aid; of those 28% had need fully met. *Average financial aid package:* $29,320 (excluding resources awarded to replace EFC). 14% of all full-time undergraduates had no need and received non-need-based gift aid.

GIFT AID (NEED-BASED) *Total amount:* $50,318,917 (14% federal, 20% state, 66% institutional). *Receiving aid:* Freshmen: 72% (640); all full-time undergraduates: 66% (2,240). *Average award:* Freshmen: $23,613; Undergraduates: $22,044. *Scholarships, grants, and awards:* Federal Pell, FSEOG, state, private, college/university gift aid from institutional funds.

GIFT AID (NON-NEED-BASED) *Total amount:* $4,490,527 (100% institutional). *Average award:* Freshmen: $8824. Undergraduates: $9534. *Scholarships, grants, and awards by category:* Academic interests/achievement: general academic interests/achievements. Creative arts/performance: debating, music. Special achievements/activities: religious involvement. *Tuition waivers:* Full or partial for employees or children of employees.

LOANS *Student loans:* $16,014,452 (91% need-based, 9% non-need-based). *Average need-based loan:* Freshmen: $3947. Undergraduates: $5013. *Parent loans:* $7,866,959 (85% need-based, 15% non-need-based). *Programs:* Federal Direct (Subsidized and Unsubsidized Stafford, PLUS), FFEL (Subsidized and Unsubsidized Stafford, PLUS), Perkins, state.

WORK-STUDY *Federal work-study:* Total amount: $4,543,674; jobs available.

ATHLETIC AWARDS Total amount: $5,045,389 (42% need-based, 58% non-need-based).

APPLYING FOR FINANCIAL AID *Required financial aid form:* FAFSA. *Financial aid deadline (priority):* 2/15. *Notification date:* Continuous beginning 3/15.

CONTACT Lynn Fox, Director of Financial Aid, University of the Pacific, 3601 Pacific Avenue, Stockton, CA 95211-0197, 209-946-2421 or toll-free 800-959-2867.

UNIVERSITY OF THE SACRED HEART
San Juan, PR

CONTACT Ms. Maria Torres, Director of Financial Aid, University of the Sacred Heart, PO Box 12383, San Juan, PR 00914-0383, 787-728-1515 Ext. 3605.

UNIVERSITY OF THE SCIENCES IN PHILADELPHIA
Philadelphia, PA

Tuition & fees: $29,630	Average undergraduate aid package: $8554

ABOUT THE INSTITUTION Independent, coed. 21 undergraduate majors. Federal methodology is used as a basis for awarding need-based institutional aid.

UNDERGRADUATE EXPENSES for 2009–10 *Comprehensive fee:* $41,212 includes full-time tuition ($28,190), mandatory fees ($1440), and room and board ($11,582). *College room only:* $7076. Full-time tuition and fees vary according to degree level and program. Room and board charges vary according to board plan. *Part-time tuition:* $1175 per credit hour. *Part-time fees:* $45 per credit hour. Part-time tuition and fees vary according to course load and degree level. *Payment plans:* Tuition prepayment, installment.

FRESHMAN FINANCIAL AID (Fall 2008) 475 applied for aid; of those 88% were deemed to have need. 100% of freshmen with need received aid; of those 52% had need fully met. *Average percent of need met:* 96% (excluding resources awarded to replace EFC). *Average financial aid package:* $8764 (excluding resources awarded to replace EFC). 11% of all full-time freshmen had no need and received non-need-based gift aid.

UNDERGRADUATE FINANCIAL AID (Fall 2008) 1,778 applied for aid; of those 95% were deemed to have need. 100% of undergraduates with need received aid; of those 38% had need fully met. *Average percent of need met:* 98% (excluding resources awarded to replace EFC). *Average financial aid package:* $8554 (excluding resources awarded to replace EFC). 5% of all full-time undergraduates had no need and received non-need-based gift aid.

GIFT AID (NEED-BASED) *Total amount:* $6,126,302 (10% federal, 7% state, 78% institutional, 5% external sources). *Receiving aid:* Freshmen: 76% (390); all full-time undergraduates: 41% (846). *Average award:* Freshmen: $9416; Undergraduates: $7361. *Scholarships, grants, and awards:* Federal Pell, FSEOG, state, college/university gift aid from institutional funds.

GIFT AID (NON-NEED-BASED) *Receiving aid:* Freshmen: 81% (419). Undergraduates: 78% (1,630). *Average award:* Freshmen: $8939. Undergraduates: $7984. *Scholarships, grants, and awards by category:* Academic interests/achievement: general academic interests/achievements. *Tuition waivers:* Full or partial for employees or children of employees.

LOANS *Student loans:* $2,254,996 (59% need-based, 41% non-need-based). 83% of past graduating class borrowed through all loan programs. *Average indebtedness per student:* $34,019. *Average need-based loan:* Freshmen: $3303. Undergraduates: $6047. *Parent loans:* $956,361 (100% need-based). *Programs:* Federal Direct (Subsidized and Unsubsidized Stafford, PLUS), Perkins, Health Professions Loans.

WORK-STUDY *Federal work-study:* Total amount: $122,830; jobs available. *State or other work-study/employment:* Part-time jobs available.

APPLYING FOR FINANCIAL AID *Required financial aid form:* FAFSA. *Financial aid deadline (priority):* 3/15. *Notification date:* Continuous beginning 2/15. Students must reply within 2 weeks of notification.

CONTACT Ms. Paula Lehrberger, Director of Financial Aid, University of the Sciences in Philadelphia, 600 South 43rd Street, Philadelphia, PA 19104-4495, 215-596-8894 or toll-free 888-996-8747 (in-state). *Fax:* 215-596-8554.

UNIVERSITY OF THE SOUTHWEST
Hobbs, NM

Tuition & fees: $12,964	Average undergraduate aid package: $2614

ABOUT THE INSTITUTION Independent, coed. 16 undergraduate majors. Both federal and institutional methodology are used as a basis for awarding need-based institutional aid.

UNDERGRADUATE EXPENSES for 2010–11 *Comprehensive fee:* $22,349 includes full-time tuition ($12,964) and room and board ($9385). *College room only:* $3370. Full-time tuition and fees vary according to course load. Room and board charges vary according to housing facility. *Part-time tuition:* $486 per semester hour. Part-time tuition and fees vary according to course load. *Payment plan:* Deferred payment.

FRESHMAN FINANCIAL AID (Fall 2009, est.) 59 applied for aid; of those 85% were deemed to have need. 100% of freshmen with need received aid; of those 10% had need fully met. *Average percent of need met:* 70% (excluding resources awarded to replace EFC). *Average financial aid package:* $1216 (excluding resources awarded to replace EFC). 10% of all full-time freshmen had no need and received non-need-based gift aid.

UNDERGRADUATE FINANCIAL AID (Fall 2009, est.) 280 applied for aid; of those 87% were deemed to have need. 100% of undergraduates with need received aid; of those 12% had need fully met. *Average percent of need met:* 70% (excluding resources awarded to replace EFC). *Average financial aid package:* $2614 (excluding resources awarded to replace EFC). 6% of all full-time undergraduates had no need and received non-need-based gift aid.

GIFT AID (NEED-BASED) *Total amount:* $1,111,244 (68% federal, 32% state). *Receiving aid:* Freshmen: 46% (27); all full-time undergraduates: 57% (162). *Average award:* Freshmen: $3051; Undergraduates: $2534. *Scholarships, grants, and awards:* Federal Pell, FSEOG, state, private, college/university gift aid from institutional funds.

GIFT AID (NON-NEED-BASED) *Total amount:* $489,475 (85% institutional, 15% external sources). *Receiving aid:* Freshmen: 32% (19). Undergraduates: 25% (71). *Average award:* Freshmen: $1333. Undergraduates: $1240. *Scholar-*

ships, grants, and awards by category: *Academic interests/achievement:* 160 awards ($298,828 total): biological sciences, business, education, English, general academic interests/achievements, humanities, mathematics, physical sciences, premedicine, religion/biblical studies, social sciences. *Creative arts/ performance:* 4 awards ($6000 total): debating, music. *Special achievements/ activities:* 8 awards ($8500 total): general special achievements/activities, leadership. *Special characteristics:* 1 award ($6019 total): children of faculty/ staff. *Tuition waivers:* Full or partial for employees or children of employees.
LOANS *Student loans:* $2,175,690 (43% need-based, 57% non-need-based). 86% of past graduating class borrowed through all loan programs. *Average indebtedness per student:* $32,200. *Average need-based loan:* Freshmen: $2481. Undergraduates: $1585. *Parent loans:* $148,257 (100% non-need-based). *Programs:* Federal Direct (Subsidized and Unsubsidized Stafford, PLUS), FFEL (Subsidized and Unsubsidized Stafford, PLUS).
WORK-STUDY *Federal work-study:* Total amount: $55,000; 27 jobs averaging $2037. *State or other work-study/employment:* Total amount: $37,030 (92% need-based, 8% non-need-based). 15 part-time jobs averaging $2268.
ATHLETIC AWARDS Total amount: $497,000 (100% non-need-based).
APPLYING FOR FINANCIAL AID *Required financial aid forms:* FAFSA, institution's own form. *Financial aid deadline:* Continuous. *Notification date:* Continuous beginning 4/15. Students must reply within 2 weeks of notification.
CONTACT Kerrie Mitchell, Director of Financial Aid, University of the Southwest, 6610 North Lovington Highway, Hobbs, NM 88240-9129, 575-492-2114 or toll-free 800-530-4400. *Fax:* 575-392-6006. *E-mail:* kmitchell@usw.edu.

UNIVERSITY OF THE VIRGIN ISLANDS
Saint Thomas, VI

ABOUT THE INSTITUTION Territory-supported, coed. 21 undergraduate majors.
GIFT AID (NEED-BASED) *Scholarships, grants, and awards:* Federal Pell, FSEOG, state, college/university gift aid from institutional funds, Federal Nursing.
GIFT AID (NON-NEED-BASED) *Scholarships, grants, and awards by category:* Special characteristics: children of faculty/staff, veterans.
LOANS *Programs:* Federal Direct (Subsidized and Unsubsidized Stafford, PLUS), Perkins, college/university.
APPLYING FOR FINANCIAL AID *Required financial aid form:* FAFSA.
CONTACT Mavis M. Gilchrist, Director of Financial Aid, University of the Virgin Islands, RR #2, Box 10,000, Kingshill, St. Thomas, VI 00850, 340-692-4186. *Fax:* 340-692-4145. *E-mail:* mgilchr@uvi.edu.

UNIVERSITY OF THE WEST
Rosemead, CA

CONTACT Dr. Teresa Ku, Director of Student Services, University of the West, 1409 Walnut Grove Avenue, Rosemead, CA 91770, 626-571-8811 Ext. 355. *Fax:* 626-571-1413. *E-mail:* naikuangk@hlu.edu.

THE UNIVERSITY OF TOLEDO
Toledo, OH

Tuition & fees (OH res): $8066	Average undergraduate aid package: $14,129

ABOUT THE INSTITUTION State-supported, coed. 173 undergraduate majors. Federal methodology is used as a basis for awarding need-based institutional aid.
UNDERGRADUATE EXPENSES for 2010–11 *Tuition, state resident:* full-time $6935; part-time $294 per semester hour. *Tuition, nonresident:* full-time $15,746; part-time $661 per semester hour. *Required fees:* full-time $1131; $47.92 per semester hour. Full-time tuition and fees vary according to course load, program, and reciprocity agreements. Part-time tuition and fees vary according to course load, program, and reciprocity agreements. *College room and board:* $9478; *Room only:* $6348. Room and board charges vary according to board plan and housing facility. *Payment plan:* Installment.
FRESHMAN FINANCIAL AID (Fall 2009, est.) 3,803 applied for aid; of those 82% were deemed to have need. 100% of freshmen with need received aid; of those 20% had need fully met. *Average percent of need met:* 86% (excluding resources awarded to replace EFC). *Average financial aid package:* $14,094 (excluding resources awarded to replace EFC). 23% of all full-time freshmen had no need and received non-need-based gift aid.

UNDERGRADUATE FINANCIAL AID (Fall 2009, est.) 12,133 applied for aid; of those 82% were deemed to have need. 100% of undergraduates with need received aid; of those 23% had need fully met. *Average percent of need met:* 86% (excluding resources awarded to replace EFC). *Average financial aid package:* $14,129 (excluding resources awarded to replace EFC). 22% of all full-time undergraduates had no need and received non-need-based gift aid.
GIFT AID (NEED-BASED) *Total amount:* $59,813,469 (48% federal, 8% state, 40% institutional, 4% external sources). *Receiving aid:* Freshmen: 75% (3,080); all full-time undergraduates: 59% (8,820). *Average award:* Freshmen: $6917; Undergraduates: $6514. *Scholarships, grants, and awards:* Federal Pell, FSEOG, state, private, college/university gift aid from institutional funds, Academic Competitiveness Grants, National SMART Grants, TEACH Grants.
GIFT AID (NON-NEED-BASED) *Total amount:* $18,202,903 (4% state, 77% institutional, 19% external sources). *Average award:* Freshmen: $3828. Undergraduates: $3921. *Scholarships, grants, and awards by category:* *Academic interests/achievement:* biological sciences, business, communication, education, engineering/technologies, English, foreign languages, general academic interests/achievements, health fields, humanities, international studies, library science, mathematics, physical sciences, premedicine, social sciences. *Creative arts/performance:* art/fine arts, general creative arts/performance, music, performing arts, theater/drama. *Special achievements/activities:* cheerleading/drum major, general special achievements/activities, hobbies/interests, leadership, memberships, religious involvement. *Special characteristics:* adult students, children and siblings of alumni, children of faculty/staff, children of public servants, children of union members/company employees, ethnic background, general special characteristics, handicapped students, international students, members of minority groups, previous college experience, public servants, religious affiliation, veterans, veterans' children. *Tuition waivers:* Full or partial for children of alumni, employees or children of employees.
LOANS *Student loans:* $87,314,583 (87% need-based, 13% non-need-based). 71% of past graduating class borrowed through all loan programs. *Average indebtedness per student:* $27,066. *Average need-based loan:* Freshmen: $6322. Undergraduates: $7599. *Parent loans:* $19,523,823 (80% need-based, 20% non-need-based). *Programs:* Federal Direct (Subsidized and Unsubsidized Stafford, PLUS), Perkins, alternative loans.
WORK-STUDY *Federal work-study:* Total amount: $993,707; 499 jobs averaging $1991.
ATHLETIC AWARDS Total amount: $3,807,099 (48% need-based, 52% non-need-based).
APPLYING FOR FINANCIAL AID *Required financial aid form:* FAFSA. *Financial aid deadline (priority):* 4/1. *Notification date:* Continuous beginning 4/1. Students must reply within 4 weeks of notification.
CONTACT Carolyn Baumgartner, Director, The University of Toledo, 2801 West Bancroft Street, MS-314, Toledo, OH 43606, 419-530-5812 or toll-free 800-5TOLEDO (in-state). *Fax:* 419-530-5835. *E-mail:* cbaumga@utnet.utoledo.edu.

UNIVERSITY OF TULSA
Tulsa, OK

Tuition & fees: $25,144	Average undergraduate aid package: $26,961

ABOUT THE INSTITUTION Independent religious, coed. 63 undergraduate majors. Federal methodology is used as a basis for awarding need-based institutional aid.
UNDERGRADUATE EXPENSES for 2009–10 *One-time required fee:* $425. *Comprehensive fee:* $33,688 includes full-time tuition ($25,054), mandatory fees ($90), and room and board ($8544). *College room only:* $4724. Room and board charges vary according to board plan and housing facility. *Part-time tuition:* $899 per credit. *Payment plans:* Tuition prepayment, installment.
FRESHMAN FINANCIAL AID (Fall 2008) 646 applied for aid; of those 53% were deemed to have need. 100% of freshmen with need received aid; of those 53% had need fully met. *Average percent of need met:* 87% (excluding resources awarded to replace EFC). *Average financial aid package:* $28,783 (excluding resources awarded to replace EFC). 38% of all full-time freshmen had no need and received non-need-based gift aid.
UNDERGRADUATE FINANCIAL AID (Fall 2008) 2,559 applied for aid; of those 48% were deemed to have need. 100% of undergraduates with need received aid; of those 48% had need fully met. *Average percent of need met:* 85% (excluding resources awarded to replace EFC). *Average financial aid package:* $26,961 (excluding resources awarded to replace EFC). 37% of all full-time undergraduates had no need and received non-need-based gift aid.

University of Tulsa

GIFT AID (NEED-BASED) *Total amount:* $3,411,783 (72% federal, 20% state, 8% institutional). *Receiving aid:* Freshmen: 19% (134); all full-time undergraduates: 19% (553). *Average award:* Freshmen $6594; Undergraduates: $5996. *Scholarships, grants, and awards:* Federal Pell, FSEOG, state, private, college/university gift aid from institutional funds.

GIFT AID (NON-NEED-BASED) *Total amount:* $26,872,652 (1% federal, 8% state, 87% institutional, 4% external sources). *Receiving aid:* Freshmen: 49% (340). Undergraduates: 40% (1,161). *Average award:* Freshmen: $13,115. Undergraduates: $13,567. *Scholarships, grants, and awards by category:* Academic interests/achievement: biological sciences, business, communication, computer science, education, engineering/technologies, English, foreign languages, general academic interests/achievements, health fields, international studies, mathematics, physical sciences, premedicine, religion/biblical studies, social sciences. *Creative arts/performance:* art/fine arts, music, performing arts, theater/drama. *Special achievements/activities:* cheerleading/drum major, community service, leadership. *Special characteristics:* children and siblings of alumni, children of faculty/staff, relatives of clergy, religious affiliation, siblings of current students. *Tuition waivers:* Full or partial for employees or children of employees.

LOANS *Student loans:* $9,245,317 (35% need-based, 65% non-need-based). 51% of past graduating class borrowed through all loan programs. *Average indebtedness per student:* $35,816. *Average need-based loan:* Freshmen: $3141. Undergraduates: $4211. *Parent loans:* $3,629,111 (100% non-need-based). *Programs:* Federal Direct (Subsidized and Unsubsidized Stafford, PLUS), Perkins.

WORK-STUDY *Federal work-study:* Total amount: $1,878,300; 604 jobs averaging $2964. *State or other work-study/employment:* Total amount: $407 (100% non-need-based). 3 part-time jobs averaging $1269.

ATHLETIC AWARDS Total amount: $8,385,560 (100% non-need-based).

APPLYING FOR FINANCIAL AID *Required financial aid forms:* FAFSA, institution's own form. *Financial aid deadline (priority):* 4/1. *Notification date:* Continuous. Students must reply by 5/1 or within 2 weeks of notification.

CONTACT Ms. Vicki Hendrickson, Director of Student Financial Services, University of Tulsa, 600 South College, Tulsa, OK 74104, 918-631-2526 or toll-free 800-331-3050. *Fax:* 918-631-5105. *E-mail:* vicki-hendrickson@utulsa.edu.

UNIVERSITY OF UTAH
Salt Lake City, UT

ABOUT THE INSTITUTION State-supported, coed. 94 undergraduate majors.

GIFT AID (NEED-BASED) *Scholarships, grants, and awards:* Federal Pell, FSEOG, state, private, college/university gift aid from institutional funds, Federal Nursing.

GIFT AID (NON-NEED-BASED) *Scholarships, grants, and awards by category:* Academic interests/achievement: architecture, area/ethnic studies, biological sciences, business, communication, computer science, education, engineering/technologies, English, foreign languages, general academic interests/achievements, health fields, humanities, international studies, mathematics, military science, physical sciences, social sciences. *Creative arts/performance:* art/fine arts, cinema/film/broadcasting, creative writing, dance, journalism/publications, music, performing arts, theater/drama. *Special achievements/activities:* cheerleading/drum major, general special achievements/activities, leadership. *Special characteristics:* children of faculty/staff, children of public servants, children with a deceased or disabled parent, ethnic background, first-generation college students, handicapped students, out-of-state students, spouses of deceased or disabled public servants.

LOANS *Programs:* FFEL (Subsidized and Unsubsidized Stafford, PLUS), Perkins, Federal Nursing, college/university.

WORK-STUDY *Federal work-study:* Total amount: $1,434,000; jobs available.

APPLYING FOR FINANCIAL AID *Required financial aid forms:* FAFSA, institution's own form.

CONTACT Amy Capps, Assistant Director, University of Utah, 201 South 1460 East, Room 105, Salt Lake City, UT 84112-9055, 801-581-6211 or toll-free 800-444-8638. *Fax:* 801-585-6350. *E-mail:* fawin1@saff.utah.edu.

UNIVERSITY OF VERMONT
Burlington, VT

Tuition & fees (VT res): **$13,524**   Average undergraduate aid package: **$18,364**

ABOUT THE INSTITUTION State-supported, coed. 100 undergraduate majors. Federal methodology is used as a basis for awarding need-based institutional aid.

UNDERGRADUATE EXPENSES for 2009–10 *Tuition, state resident:* full-time $11,712; part-time $488 per credit hour. *Tuition, nonresident:* full-time $29,568; part-time $1232 per credit hour. *Required fees:* full-time $1812. Part-time tuition and fees vary according to course load. *College room and board:* $9026; *Room only:* $5964. Room and board charges vary according to board plan and housing facility. *Payment plans:* Installment, deferred payment.

FRESHMAN FINANCIAL AID (Fall 2009, est.) 2,060 applied for aid; of those 80% were deemed to have need. 100% of freshmen with need received aid; of those 18% had need fully met. *Average percent of need met:* 76% (excluding resources awarded to replace EFC). *Average financial aid package:* $20,894 (excluding resources awarded to replace EFC). 20% of all full-time freshmen had no need and received non-need-based gift aid.

UNDERGRADUATE FINANCIAL AID (Fall 2009, est.) 7,084 applied for aid; of those 83% were deemed to have need. 99% of undergraduates with need received aid; of those 20% had need fully met. *Average percent of need met:* 71% (excluding resources awarded to replace EFC). *Average financial aid package:* $18,364 (excluding resources awarded to replace EFC). 18% of all full-time undergraduates had no need and received non-need-based gift aid.

GIFT AID (NEED-BASED) *Total amount:* $82,772,887 (15% federal, 7% state, 75% institutional, 3% external sources). *Receiving aid:* Freshmen: 61% (1,600); all full-time undergraduates: 50% (5,022). *Average award:* Freshmen: $17,767; Undergraduates: $14,576. *Scholarships, grants, and awards:* Federal Pell, FSEOG, state, private, college/university gift aid from institutional funds, Federal Nursing.

GIFT AID (NON-NEED-BASED) *Total amount:* $6,252,809 (79% institutional, 21% external sources). *Receiving aid:* Freshmen: 3% (72). Undergraduates: 2% (241). *Average award:* Freshmen: $2393. Undergraduates: $2426. *Scholarships, grants, and awards by category:* Academic interests/achievement: 5,300 awards ($12,678,087 total): agriculture, area/ethnic studies, business, computer science, education, engineering/technologies, English, foreign languages, general academic interests/achievements, health fields, home economics, humanities, international studies, mathematics, military science, physical sciences, premedicine, social sciences. *Creative arts/performance:* 15 awards ($11,277 total): debating, music, theater/drama. *Special achievements/activities:* 86 awards ($363,662 total): community service, leadership, memberships. *Special characteristics:* 159 awards ($578,035 total): adult students, ethnic background, first-generation college students. *Tuition waivers:* Full or partial for employees or children of employees, senior citizens.

LOANS *Student loans:* $45,295,354 (44% need-based, 56% non-need-based). 63% of past graduating class borrowed through all loan programs. *Average indebtedness per student:* $27,696. *Average need-based loan:* Freshmen: $5338. Undergraduates: $6413. *Parent loans:* $49,699,009 (100% non-need-based). *Programs:* FFEL (Subsidized and Unsubsidized Stafford, PLUS), Perkins, Federal Nursing, state, college/university.

WORK-STUDY *Federal work-study:* Total amount: $3,563,489; 2,437 jobs averaging $1462.

ATHLETIC AWARDS Total amount: $4,915,996 (25% need-based, 75% non-need-based).

APPLYING FOR FINANCIAL AID *Required financial aid form:* FAFSA. *Financial aid deadline (priority):* 2/10. *Notification date:* Continuous beginning 3/15. Students must reply within 4 weeks of notification.

CONTACT Student Financial Services, University of Vermont, 221 Waterman Building, Burlington, VT 05405-0160, 802-656-5700. *Fax:* 802-656-4076. *E-mail:* sfs@uvm.edu.

UNIVERSITY OF VIRGINIA
Charlottesville, VA

Tuition & fees (VA res): **$9672**   Average undergraduate aid package: **$20,138**

ABOUT THE INSTITUTION State-supported, coed. 47 undergraduate majors. Federal methodology is used as a basis for awarding need-based institutional aid.

UNDERGRADUATE EXPENSES for 2009–10 *Tuition, state resident:* full-time $7496; part-time $250 per credit hour. *Tuition, nonresident:* full-time $29,054; part-time $968 per credit hour. *Required fees:* full-time $2176; $2176 per year. *College room and board:* $8290; *Room only:* $4510. Room and board charges vary according to board plan and housing facility. *Payment plan:* Installment.

FRESHMAN FINANCIAL AID (Fall 2009, est.) 2,404 applied for aid; of those 44% were deemed to have need. 95% of freshmen with need received aid; of those 58% had need fully met. *Average percent of need met:* 89% (excluding resources awarded to replace EFC). *Average financial aid package:* $19,578 (excluding resources awarded to replace EFC). 12% of all full-time freshmen had no need and received non-need-based gift aid.

UNDERGRADUATE FINANCIAL AID (Fall 2009, est.) 8,051 applied for aid; of those 53% were deemed to have need. 94% of undergraduates with need received aid; of those 58% had need fully met. *Average percent of need met:* 89% (excluding resources awarded to replace EFC). *Average financial aid package:* $20,138 (excluding resources awarded to replace EFC). 11% of all full-time undergraduates had no need and received non-need-based gift aid.

GIFT AID (NEED-BASED) *Total amount:* $50,487,405 (14% federal, 13% state, 64% institutional, 9% external sources). *Receiving aid:* Freshmen: 28% (914); all full-time undergraduates: 25% (3,514). *Average award:* Freshmen: $14,382; Undergraduates: $14,955. *Scholarships, grants, and awards:* Federal Pell, FSEOG, state, private, college/university gift aid from institutional funds, Federal Nursing.

GIFT AID (NON-NEED-BASED) *Total amount:* $15,203,135 (3% state, 13% institutional, 84% external sources). *Receiving aid:* Freshmen: 4% (126). Undergraduates: 3% (419). *Average award:* Freshmen: $8773. Undergraduates: $9880. *Scholarships, grants, and awards by category: Academic interests/ achievement:* general academic interests/achievements. *Creative arts/performance:* music. *Tuition waivers:* Full or partial for employees or children of employees, senior citizens.

LOANS *Student loans:* $28,215,304 (51% need-based, 49% non-need-based). 34% of past graduating class borrowed through all loan programs. *Average indebtedness per student:* $19,939. *Average need-based loan:* Freshmen: $4989. Undergraduates: $5589. *Parent loans:* $8,106,233 (5% need-based, 95% non-need-based). *Programs:* FFEL (Subsidized and Unsubsidized Stafford, PLUS), Perkins, Federal Nursing, college/university, alternative private loans.

WORK-STUDY *Federal work-study:* Total amount: $1,692,284; jobs available.

ATHLETIC AWARDS Total amount: $10,388,137 (34% need-based, 66% non-need-based).

APPLYING FOR FINANCIAL AID *Required financial aid forms:* FAFSA, institution's own form. *Financial aid deadline (priority):* 3/1. *Notification date:* 4/5. Students must reply by 5/1.

CONTACT Ms. Yvonne B. Hubbard, Director, Student Financial Services, University of Virginia, PO Box 400207, Charlottesville, VA 22904-4207, 434-982-6000. *E-mail:* faid@virginia.edu.

THE UNIVERSITY OF VIRGINIA'S COLLEGE AT WISE
Wise, VA

Tuition & fees (VA res): $6748	Average undergraduate aid package: $9212

ABOUT THE INSTITUTION State-supported, coed. 25 undergraduate majors. Federal methodology is used as a basis for awarding need-based institutional aid.

UNDERGRADUATE EXPENSES for 2009–10 *Tuition, state resident:* full-time $3586; part-time $153 per semester hour. *Tuition, nonresident:* full-time $15,714; part-time $666 per semester hour. *Required fees:* full-time $3162; $81.31 per semester hour or $894.43 per term. Part-time tuition and fees vary according to course load. *College room and board:* $7323; *Room only:* $3994. Room and board charges vary according to board plan and housing facility. *Payment plans:* Installment, deferred payment.

FRESHMAN FINANCIAL AID (Fall 2009, est.) 347 applied for aid; of those 83% were deemed to have need. 100% of freshmen with need received aid; of those 79% had need fully met. *Average percent of need met:* 79% (excluding resources awarded to replace EFC). *Average financial aid package:* $13,128 (excluding resources awarded to replace EFC). 10% of all full-time freshmen had no need and received non-need-based gift aid.

UNDERGRADUATE FINANCIAL AID (Fall 2009, est.) 1,347 applied for aid; of those 84% were deemed to have need. 99% of undergraduates with need received aid; of those 74% had need fully met. *Average percent of need met:* 74% (excluding resources awarded to replace EFC). *Average financial aid package:* $9212 (excluding resources awarded to replace EFC). 8% of all full-time undergraduates had no need and received non-need-based gift aid.

GIFT AID (NEED-BASED) *Total amount:* $5,835,443 (56% federal, 35% state, 7% institutional, 2% external sources). *Receiving aid:* Freshmen: 63% (249); all full-time undergraduates: 65% (966). *Average award:* Freshmen: $6056; Undergraduates: $5474. *Scholarships, grants, and awards:* Federal Pell, FSEOG, state, private, college/university gift aid from institutional funds.

GIFT AID (NON-NEED-BASED) *Total amount:* $1,676,839 (78% institutional, 22% external sources). *Receiving aid:* Freshmen: 69% (275). Undergraduates: 49% (734). *Average award:* Freshmen: $3180. Undergraduates: $3456. *Scholarships, grants, and awards by category: Academic interests/achievement:* agriculture, biological sciences, business, computer science, education, English, general academic interests/achievements, health fields, humanities, mathematics, physical sciences, premedicine, social sciences. *Creative arts/performance:* creative writing, general creative arts/performance, journalism/publications, music, performing arts, theater/drama. *Special achievements/activities:* community service, religious involvement. *Special characteristics:* children with a deceased or disabled parent, ethnic background, local/state students, veterans, veterans' children. *Tuition waivers:* Full or partial for employees or children of employees, senior citizens.

LOANS *Student loans:* $4,872,259 (49% need-based, 51% non-need-based). 58% of past graduating class borrowed through all loan programs. *Average indebtedness per student:* $12,120. *Average need-based loan:* Freshmen: $2519. Undergraduates: $3168. *Parent loans:* $749,300 (100% non-need-based). *Programs:* FFEL (Subsidized and Unsubsidized Stafford, PLUS), Perkins, state, college/university.

WORK-STUDY *Federal work-study:* Total amount: $300,000; jobs available.

ATHLETIC AWARDS Total amount: $451,592 (100% non-need-based).

APPLYING FOR FINANCIAL AID *Required financial aid form:* FAFSA. *Financial aid deadline (priority):* 4/1. *Notification date:* Continuous. Students must reply within 4 weeks of notification.

CONTACT Bill Wendle, Director of Financial Aid, The University of Virginia's College at Wise, 1 College Avenue, Wise, VA 24293, 276-328-0103 or toll-free 888-282-9324. *Fax:* 276-328-0251. *E-mail:* wdw8m@uvawise.edu.

UNIVERSITY OF WASHINGTON
Seattle, WA

Tuition & fees (WA res): $7692	Average undergraduate aid package: $11,560

ABOUT THE INSTITUTION State-supported, coed. 154 undergraduate majors. Federal methodology is used as a basis for awarding need-based institutional aid.

UNDERGRADUATE EXPENSES for 2009–10 *Tuition, state resident:* full-time $7125. *Tuition, nonresident:* full-time $23,800. *Required fees:* full-time $567. Full-time tuition and fees vary according to course load. Part-time tuition and fees vary according to course load. *College room and board:* $7800. Room and board charges vary according to board plan and housing facility.

FRESHMAN FINANCIAL AID (Fall 2008) 3,741 applied for aid; of those 59% were deemed to have need. 92% of freshmen with need received aid; of those 39% had need fully met. *Average percent of need met:* 80% (excluding resources awarded to replace EFC). *Average financial aid package:* $10,580 (excluding resources awarded to replace EFC). 1% of all full-time freshmen had no need and received non-need-based gift aid.

UNDERGRADUATE FINANCIAL AID (Fall 2008) 13,572 applied for aid; of those 72% were deemed to have need. 94% of undergraduates with need received aid; of those 35% had need fully met. *Average percent of need met:* 79% (excluding resources awarded to replace EFC). *Average financial aid package:* $11,560 (excluding resources awarded to replace EFC). 3% of all full-time undergraduates had no need and received non-need-based gift aid.

GIFT AID (NEED-BASED) *Total amount:* $72,063,000 (32% federal, 45% state, 18% institutional, 5% external sources). *Receiving aid:* Freshmen: 29% (1,608); all full-time undergraduates: 29% (7,138). *Average award:* Freshmen: $7580; Undergraduates: $8720. *Scholarships, grants, and awards:* Federal Pell, FSEOG, state, private, college/university gift aid from institutional funds.

GIFT AID (NON-NEED-BASED) *Total amount:* $9,952,000 (2% federal, 5% state, 55% institutional, 38% external sources). *Receiving aid:* Freshmen: 7% (385). Undergraduates: 4% (973). *Average award:* Freshmen: $4790. Undergraduates: $4430. *Scholarships, grants, and awards by category: Academic interests/ achievement:* architecture, business, computer science, education, engineering/ technologies, general academic interests/achievements, health fields. *Creative arts/performance:* art/fine arts, general creative arts/performance, music, perform-

ing arts. *Special achievements/activities:* general special achievements/activities, leadership, memberships. *Tuition waivers:* Full or partial for senior citizens.
LOANS *Student loans:* $61,925,000 (75% need-based, 25% non-need-based). 50% of past graduating class borrowed through all loan programs. *Average indebtedness per student:* $16,800. *Average need-based loan:* Freshmen: $1960. Undergraduates: $2860. *Parent loans:* $23,946,000 (28% need-based, 72% non-need-based). *Programs:* Federal Direct (Subsidized and Unsubsidized Stafford, PLUS), Perkins, Federal Nursing, college/university.
WORK-STUDY *Federal work-study:* Total amount: $2,596,000; 478 jobs averaging $2800. *State or other work-study/employment:* Total amount: $525,000 (100% need-based). 327 part-time jobs averaging $3160.
ATHLETIC AWARDS Total amount: $3,954,000 (54% need-based, 46% non-need-based).
APPLYING FOR FINANCIAL AID *Required financial aid form:* FAFSA. *Financial aid deadline (priority):* 2/28. *Notification date:* 3/31.
CONTACT Office of Student Financial Aid, University of Washington, Box 355880, Seattle, WA 98195-5880, 206-543-6101. *E-mail:* osfa@u.washington.edu.

UNIVERSITY OF WASHINGTON, BOTHELL
Bothell, WA

CONTACT Financial Aid Office, University of Washington, Bothell, 18115 Campus Way NE, Bothell, WA 98011-8246, 425-352-5000.

UNIVERSITY OF WASHINGTON, TACOMA
Tacoma, WA

Tuition & fees (WA res): $7653   **Average undergraduate aid package: $13,800**

ABOUT THE INSTITUTION State-supported, coed. 24 undergraduate majors. Federal methodology is used as a basis for awarding need-based institutional aid.
UNDERGRADUATE EXPENSES for 2009–10 *Tuition, state resident:* full-time $7653; part-time $255 per credit. *Tuition, nonresident:* full-time $24,328; part-time $811 per credit. Full-time tuition and fees vary according to course load. Part-time tuition and fees vary according to course load. *College room and board: Room only:* $8949. Room and board charges vary according to housing facility. *Payment plan:* Installment.
FRESHMAN FINANCIAL AID (Fall 2009, est.) 170 applied for aid; of those 65% were deemed to have need. 86% of freshmen with need received aid; of those 23% had need fully met. *Average percent of need met:* 78% (excluding resources awarded to replace EFC). *Average financial aid package:* $11,200 (excluding resources awarded to replace EFC).
UNDERGRADUATE FINANCIAL AID (Fall 2009, est.) 1,486 applied for aid; of those 85% were deemed to have need. 96% of undergraduates with need received aid; of those 27% had need fully met. *Average percent of need met:* 77% (excluding resources awarded to replace EFC). *Average financial aid package:* $13,800 (excluding resources awarded to replace EFC).
GIFT AID (NEED-BASED) *Total amount:* $12,286,500 (40% federal, 43% state, 16% institutional, 1% external sources). *Receiving aid:* Freshmen: 73; all full-time undergraduates: 966. *Average award:* Freshmen: $9800; Undergraduates: $11,200. *Scholarships, grants, and awards:* Federal Pell, FSEOG, state, private, college/university gift aid from institutional funds.
GIFT AID (NON-NEED-BASED) *Total amount:* $379,000 (66% institutional, 34% external sources). *Receiving aid:* Freshmen: 21. Undergraduates: 37. *Average award:* Freshmen: $3000. Undergraduates: $6300. *Tuition waivers:* Full or partial for employees or children of employees, senior citizens.
LOANS *Student loans:* $10,640,000 (79% need-based, 21% non-need-based). 58% of past graduating class borrowed through all loan programs. *Average indebtedness per student:* $17,900. *Average need-based loan:* Freshmen: $4100. Undergraduates: $6900. *Parent loans:* $1,181,000 (19% need-based, 81% non-need-based). *Programs:* Federal Direct (Subsidized and Unsubsidized Stafford, PLUS), Perkins, Federal Nursing.
WORK-STUDY *Federal work-study:* Total amount: $179,000; jobs available. *State or other work-study/employment:* Total amount: $260,000 (100% need-based). Part-time jobs available.
APPLYING FOR FINANCIAL AID *Required financial aid form:* FAFSA. *Financial aid deadline (priority):* 2/28. *Notification date:* 4/1. Students must reply within 3 weeks of notification.

CONTACT Ms. Shari King, Associate Director of Financial Aid and Veterans Affairs, University of Washington, Tacoma, 1900 Commerce Street, Box 358400, Tacoma, WA 98402-3100, 253-692-4400 or toll-free 800-736-7750 (out-of-state). *Fax:* 253-692-4414. *E-mail:* osfatac@uw.edu.

THE UNIVERSITY OF WEST ALABAMA
Livingston, AL

Tuition & fees (AL res): $5420   **Average undergraduate aid package: N/A**

ABOUT THE INSTITUTION State-supported, coed. 19 undergraduate majors. Federal methodology is used as a basis for awarding need-based institutional aid.
UNDERGRADUATE EXPENSES for 2010–11 *Tuition, state resident:* full-time $5060; part-time $215 per semester hour. *Tuition, nonresident:* full-time $10,120; part-time $430 per semester hour. *Required fees:* full-time $360. Full-time tuition and fees vary according to course load, degree level, and program. Part-time tuition and fees vary according to course load, degree level, and program. *College room and board:* $3748; *Room only:* $2200. Room and board charges vary according to board plan and housing facility.
FRESHMAN FINANCIAL AID (Fall 2009, est.) 173 applied for aid; of those 99% were deemed to have need. 72% of freshmen with need received aid; of those 77% had need fully met. *Average percent of need met:* 77% (excluding resources awarded to replace EFC). 15% of all full-time freshmen had no need and received non-need-based gift aid.
UNDERGRADUATE FINANCIAL AID (Fall 2009, est.) 982 applied for aid; of those 89% were deemed to have need. 87% of undergraduates with need received aid; of those 68% had need fully met. *Average percent of need met:* 68% (excluding resources awarded to replace EFC). 9% of all full-time undergraduates had no need and received non-need-based gift aid.
GIFT AID (NEED-BASED) *Total amount:* $3,952,869 (98% federal, 2% state). *Receiving aid:* Freshmen: 47% (115); all full-time undergraduates: 48% (737). *Average award:* Freshmen: $3243; Undergraduates: $3729. *Scholarships, grants, and awards:* Federal Pell, FSEOG, state, private, college/university gift aid from institutional funds.
GIFT AID (NON-NEED-BASED) *Total amount:* $1,351,925 (6% federal, 89% institutional, 5% external sources). *Receiving aid:* Freshmen: 39% (95). Undergraduates: 37% (576). *Average award:* Freshmen: $1894. Undergraduates: $1739. *Scholarships, grants, and awards by category:* Academic interests/achievement: general academic interests/achievements. *Special achievements/activities:* cheerleading/drum major, general special achievements/activities, rodeo. *Special characteristics:* children of faculty/staff, first-generation college students. *Tuition waivers:* Full or partial for employees or children of employees.
LOANS *Student loans:* $8,431,841 (47% need-based, 53% non-need-based). 61% of past graduating class borrowed through all loan programs. *Average indebtedness per student:* $17,406. *Average need-based loan:* Freshmen: $2556. Undergraduates: $2961. *Parent loans:* $283,840 (100% non-need-based). *Programs:* FFEL (Subsidized and Unsubsidized Stafford, PLUS), Perkins, Stafford Federal Loan Teacher Loan Forgiveness.
WORK-STUDY *Federal work-study:* Total amount: $272,895; 112 jobs averaging $3336. *State or other work-study/employment:* Total amount: $35,000 (100% non-need-based). Part-time jobs available.
ATHLETIC AWARDS Total amount: $1,070,419 (100% non-need-based).
APPLYING FOR FINANCIAL AID *Required financial aid form:* FAFSA. *Financial aid deadline (priority):* 4/1. *Notification date:* Continuous beginning 6/1. Students must reply within 2 weeks of notification.
CONTACT Mr. Don Rainer, Director of Financial Aid, The University of West Alabama, Station 3, Livingston, AL 35470, 205-652-3576 or toll-free 800-621-7742 (in-state), 800-621-8044 (out-of-state). *Fax:* 205-652-3847. *E-mail:* drainer@uwa.edu.

UNIVERSITY OF WEST FLORIDA
Pensacola, FL

Tuition & fees (FL res): $4210   **Average undergraduate aid package: N/A**

ABOUT THE INSTITUTION State-supported, coed. 49 undergraduate majors. Federal methodology is used as a basis for awarding need-based institutional aid.

UNDERGRADUATE EXPENSES for 2009–10 *Tuition, state resident:* full-time $2658; part-time $140.34 per semester hour. *Tuition, nonresident:* full-time $14,926; part-time $569.73 per semester hour. *Required fees:* full-time $1552. Full-time tuition and fees vary according to location and reciprocity agreements. Part-time tuition and fees vary according to location and reciprocity agreements. *College room and board:* $6900. Room and board charges vary according to housing facility. *Payment plans:* Tuition prepayment, deferred payment.

GIFT AID (NEED-BASED) Total amount: $17,546,690 (81% federal, 11% state, 8% institutional). *Scholarships, grants, and awards:* Federal Pell, FSEOG, state, private, college/university gift aid from institutional funds.

GIFT AID (NON-NEED-BASED) Total amount: $10,166,466 (80% state, 14% institutional, 6% external sources). *Scholarships, grants, and awards by category: Academic interests/achievement:* biological sciences, business, general academic interests/achievements, military science. *Creative arts/performance:* applied art and design, art/fine arts, music, theater/drama. *Special characteristics:* children and siblings of alumni, first-generation college students, handicapped students, members of minority groups. *Tuition waivers:* Full or partial for employees or children of employees, senior citizens.

LOANS Student loans: $34,987,776 (46% need-based, 54% non-need-based). *Parent loans:* $1,206,100 (100% non-need-based). *Programs:* Federal Direct (Subsidized and Unsubsidized Stafford, PLUS), Perkins, college/university.

WORK-STUDY *Federal work-study:* Total amount: $414,515; jobs available. *State or other work-study/employment:* Part-time jobs available.

ATHLETIC AWARDS Total amount: $963,980 (100% non-need-based).

APPLYING FOR FINANCIAL AID *Required financial aid forms:* FAFSA, institution's own form. *Financial aid deadline:* Continuous. *Notification date:* Continuous beginning 2/1.

CONTACT Ms. Georganne E. Major, Coordinator, University of West Florida, 11000 University Parkway, Pensacola, FL 32514-5750, 850-474-2397 or toll-free 800-263-1074. *E-mail:* gmajor@uwf.edu.

UNIVERSITY OF WEST GEORGIA
Carrollton, GA

Tuition & fees (GA res): $4582	Average undergraduate aid package: $8224

ABOUT THE INSTITUTION State-supported, coed. 52 undergraduate majors. Federal methodology is used as a basis for awarding need-based institutional aid.

UNDERGRADUATE EXPENSES for 2009–10 *Tuition, state resident:* full-time $3196; part-time $134 per semester hour. *Tuition, nonresident:* full-time $12,778; part-time $533 per semester hour. *Required fees:* full-time $1386; $42.90 per semester hour or $307 per term. Full-time tuition and fees vary according to course load. Part-time tuition and fees vary according to course load. *College room and board:* $6254; *Room only:* $3300. Room and board charges vary according to board plan and housing facility.

FRESHMAN FINANCIAL AID (Fall 2009, est.) 1,686 applied for aid; of those 75% were deemed to have need. 98% of freshmen with need received aid; of those 22% had need fully met. *Average percent of need met:* 65% (excluding resources awarded to replace EFC). *Average financial aid package:* $8427 (excluding resources awarded to replace EFC). 2% of all full-time freshmen had no need and received non-need-based gift aid.

UNDERGRADUATE FINANCIAL AID (Fall 2009, est.) 6,520 applied for aid; of those 76% were deemed to have need. 99% of undergraduates with need received aid; of those 17% had need fully met. *Average percent of need met:* 60% (excluding resources awarded to replace EFC). *Average financial aid package:* $8224 (excluding resources awarded to replace EFC). 3% of all full-time undergraduates had no need and received non-need-based gift aid.

GIFT AID (NEED-BASED) Total amount: $26,175,766 (71% federal, 27% state, 1% institutional, 1% external sources). *Receiving aid:* Freshmen: 57% (1,103); all full-time undergraduates: 50% (4,042). *Average award:* Freshmen: $6614; Undergraduates: $5804. *Scholarships, grants, and awards:* Federal Pell, FSEOG, state, private, college/university gift aid from institutional funds, United Negro College Fund.

GIFT AID (NON-NEED-BASED) Total amount: $5,802,397 (93% state, 4% institutional, 3% external sources). *Receiving aid:* Freshmen: 17% (326). Undergraduates: 11% (893). *Average award:* Freshmen: $2125. Undergraduates: $1532. *Scholarships, grants, and awards by category: Academic interests/achievement:* biological sciences, business, communication, computer science, education, English, foreign languages, general academic interests/achievements, health fields, humanities, mathematics, physical sciences, premedicine, social

sciences. *Creative arts/performance:* applied art and design, art/fine arts, debating, general creative arts/performance, journalism/publications, music, performing arts, theater/drama. *Special achievements/activities:* community service, leadership, memberships, religious involvement. *Special characteristics:* adult students, children and siblings of alumni, general special characteristics, handicapped students, international students, local/state students, members of minority groups. *Tuition waivers:* Full or partial for senior citizens.

LOANS Student loans: $38,773,418 (58% need-based, 42% non-need-based). 76% of past graduating class borrowed through all loan programs. *Average indebtedness per student:* $14,347. *Average need-based loan:* Freshmen: $3232. Undergraduates: $3980. *Parent loans:* $2,623,351 (100% non-need-based). *Programs:* Federal Direct (Subsidized and Unsubsidized Stafford, PLUS), Perkins, state, college/university.

WORK-STUDY *Federal work-study:* Total amount: $380,000; jobs available. *State or other work-study/employment:* Part-time jobs available.

ATHLETIC AWARDS Total amount: $994,605 (45% need-based, 55% non-need-based).

APPLYING FOR FINANCIAL AID *Required financial aid form:* FAFSA. *Financial aid deadline:* 7/1 (priority: 4/1). *Notification date:* Continuous beginning 6/1.

CONTACT Kimberly Jordan, Director of Financial Aid, University of West Georgia, 1601 Maple Street, Aycock Hall, Carrollton, GA 30118, 678-839-6421. *Fax:* 678-839-6422. *E-mail:* kjordan@westga.edu.

UNIVERSITY OF WISCONSIN–EAU CLAIRE
Eau Claire, WI

Tuition & fees (WI res): $6633	Average undergraduate aid package: $8037

ABOUT THE INSTITUTION State-supported, coed. 49 undergraduate majors. Federal methodology is used as a basis for awarding need-based institutional aid.

UNDERGRADUATE EXPENSES for 2009–10 *Tuition, state resident:* full-time $5527; part-time $276 per credit. *Tuition, nonresident:* full-time $13,100; part-time $592 per credit. *Required fees:* full-time $1106; $46 per credit or $2 per credit. Full-time tuition and fees vary according to reciprocity agreements. Part-time tuition and fees vary according to reciprocity agreements. *College room and board:* $5730; *Room only:* $2830. Room and board charges vary according to board plan and housing facility. *Payment plan:* Installment.

FRESHMAN FINANCIAL AID (Fall 2008) 1,574 applied for aid; of those 53% were deemed to have need. 99% of freshmen with need received aid; of those 64% had need fully met. *Average percent of need met:* 92% (excluding resources awarded to replace EFC). *Average financial aid package:* $7731 (excluding resources awarded to replace EFC). 17% of all full-time freshmen had no need and received non-need-based gift aid.

UNDERGRADUATE FINANCIAL AID (Fall 2008) 6,708 applied for aid; of those 64% were deemed to have need. 99% of undergraduates with need received aid; of those 67% had need fully met. *Average percent of need met:* 92% (excluding resources awarded to replace EFC). *Average financial aid package:* $8037 (excluding resources awarded to replace EFC). 9% of all full-time undergraduates had no need and received non-need-based gift aid.

GIFT AID (NEED-BASED) Total amount: $14,068,232 (57% federal, 30% state, 4% institutional, 9% external sources). *Receiving aid:* Freshmen: 26% (541); all full-time undergraduates: 26% (2,479). *Average award:* Freshmen: $5603; Undergraduates: $5461. *Scholarships, grants, and awards:* Federal Pell, FSEOG, state, private, college/university gift aid from institutional funds, Federal Nursing, Academic Competitiveness Grants, National SMART Grants, Bureau of Indian Affairs Grants.

GIFT AID (NON-NEED-BASED) Total amount: $1,704,857 (6% federal, 5% state, 34% institutional, 55% external sources). *Average award:* Freshmen: $1894. Undergraduates: $1835. *Scholarships, grants, and awards by category: Academic interests/achievement:* biological sciences, business, communication, computer science, education, English, foreign languages, general academic interests/achievements, health fields, international studies, mathematics, physical sciences, premedicine, social sciences. *Creative arts/performance:* debating, music, theater/drama. *Special achievements/activities:* community service, general special achievements/activities, hobbies/interests, leadership, memberships. *Special characteristics:* adult students, ethnic background, first-generation college students, general special characteristics, international students, local/state students, members of minority groups, previous college experience. *Tuition waivers:* Full or partial for minority students.

LOANS *Student loans:* $35,913,718 (53% need-based, 47% non-need-based). 68% of past graduating class borrowed through all loan programs. *Average indebtedness per student:* $19,687. *Average need-based loan:* Freshmen: $3881. Undergraduates: $4427. *Parent loans:* $1,640,849 (100% non-need-based). *Programs:* Federal Direct (Subsidized and Unsubsidized Stafford, PLUS), Perkins, state, college/university, alternative loans.

WORK-STUDY *Federal work-study:* Total amount: $3,412,692; 2,079 jobs averaging $1642. *State or other work-study/employment:* Total amount: $2,379,514 (51% need-based, 49% non-need-based). 1,698 part-time jobs averaging $1401.

APPLYING FOR FINANCIAL AID *Required financial aid form:* FAFSA. *Financial aid deadline (priority):* 4/15. *Notification date:* Continuous beginning 4/15. Students must reply within 3 weeks of notification.

CONTACT Ms. Kathleen Sahlhoff, Director of Financial Aid, University of Wisconsin–Eau Claire, 115 Schofield Hall, Eau Claire, WI 54701, 715-836-3373. *Fax:* 715-836-3846. *E-mail:* sahlhoka@uwec.edu.

UNIVERSITY OF WISCONSIN–GREEN BAY
Green Bay, WI

Tuition & fees (WI res): $6909	Average undergraduate aid package: $10,169

ABOUT THE INSTITUTION State-supported, coed. 37 undergraduate majors. Federal methodology is used as a basis for awarding need-based institutional aid.

UNDERGRADUATE EXPENSES for 2010–11 *Tuition, state resident:* full-time $5659; part-time $236 per credit hour. *Tuition, nonresident:* full-time $13,649; part-time $569 per credit hour. *Required fees:* full-time $1250; $53 per credit hour. Full-time tuition and fees vary according to reciprocity agreements. Part-time tuition and fees vary according to reciprocity agreements. *College room and board:* $6500; *Room only:* $3600. Room and board charges vary according to board plan and housing facility. *Payment plan:* Installment.

FRESHMAN FINANCIAL AID (Fall 2009, est.) 917 applied for aid; of those 73% were deemed to have need. 96% of freshmen with need received aid; of those 43% had need fully met. *Average percent of need met:* 85% (excluding resources awarded to replace EFC). *Average financial aid package:* $10,053 (excluding resources awarded to replace EFC). 1% of all full-time freshmen had no need and received non-need-based gift aid.

UNDERGRADUATE FINANCIAL AID (Fall 2009, est.) 4,085 applied for aid; of those 78% were deemed to have need. 96% of undergraduates with need received aid; of those 46% had need fully met. *Average percent of need met:* 86% (excluding resources awarded to replace EFC). *Average financial aid package:* $10,169 (excluding resources awarded to replace EFC). 1% of all full-time undergraduates had no need and received non-need-based gift aid.

GIFT AID (NEED-BASED) *Total amount:* $11,460,502 (62% federal, 29% state, 1% institutional, 8% external sources). *Receiving aid:* Freshmen: 39% (399); all full-time undergraduates: 35% (1,743). *Average award:* Freshmen: $6046; Undergraduates: $6129. *Scholarships, grants, and awards:* Federal Pell, FSEOG, state, private, college/university gift aid from institutional funds.

GIFT AID (NON-NEED-BASED) *Total amount:* $445,861 (17% state, 32% institutional, 51% external sources). *Receiving aid:* Freshmen: 24% (245). Undergraduates: 23% (1,131). *Average award:* Freshmen: $2043. Undergraduates: $2255. *Scholarships, grants, and awards by category: Academic interests/achievement:* 50 awards ($300,000 total): area/ethnic studies, biological sciences, business, communication, education, engineering/technologies, general academic interests/achievements, health fields, humanities, physical sciences, premedicine, social sciences. *Creative arts/performance:* 20 awards ($25,000 total): art/fine arts, dance, journalism/publications, music, theater/drama. *Special achievements/activities:* 5 awards ($15,000 total): community service, general special achievements/activities, leadership. *Special characteristics:* 15 awards ($200,000 total): adult students, children and siblings of alumni, children of public servants, ethnic background, handicapped students, local/state students, members of minority groups, veterans. *Tuition waivers:* Full or partial for senior citizens.

LOANS *Student loans:* $24,622,660 (55% need-based, 45% non-need-based). 71% of past graduating class borrowed through all loan programs. *Average indebtedness per student:* $19,636. *Average need-based loan:* Freshmen: $4302. Undergraduates: $5117. *Parent loans:* $1,242,837 (100% non-need-based). *Programs:* FFEL (Subsidized and Unsubsidized Stafford, PLUS), Perkins.

WORK-STUDY *Federal work-study:* Total amount: $487,490; 225 jobs averaging $1812. *State or other work-study/employment:* Part-time jobs available.

ATHLETIC AWARDS Total amount: $2,128,586 (66% need-based, 34% non-need-based).

APPLYING FOR FINANCIAL AID *Required financial aid form:* FAFSA. *Financial aid deadline (priority):* 4/15. *Notification date:* Continuous. Students must reply within 3 weeks of notification.

CONTACT Mr. Ron Ronnenberg, Director of Financial Aid, University of Wisconsin–Green Bay, 2420 Nicolet Drive, Green Bay, WI 54311-7001, 920-465-2073 or toll-free 888-367-8942 (out-of-state). *E-mail:* ronnenbr@uwgb.edu.

UNIVERSITY OF WISCONSIN–LA CROSSE
La Crosse, WI

Tuition & fees (WI res): $7509	Average undergraduate aid package: $6397

ABOUT THE INSTITUTION State-supported, coed. 47 undergraduate majors. Federal methodology is used as a basis for awarding need-based institutional aid.

UNDERGRADUATE EXPENSES for 2009–10 *Tuition, state resident:* full-time $6425; part-time $268 per credit hour. *Tuition, nonresident:* full-time $13,998; part-time $583 per credit hour. *Required fees:* full-time $1084. Full-time tuition and fees vary according to degree level, program, and reciprocity agreements. Part-time tuition and fees vary according to course load, degree level, program, and reciprocity agreements. *College room and board:* $5630; *Room only:* $3240. Room and board charges vary according to board plan and housing facility. *Payment plan:* Installment.

FRESHMAN FINANCIAL AID (Fall 2008) 1,331 applied for aid; of those 55% were deemed to have need. 94% of freshmen with need received aid; of those 29% had need fully met. *Average percent of need met:* 76% (excluding resources awarded to replace EFC). *Average financial aid package:* $5931 (excluding resources awarded to replace EFC). 3% of all full-time freshmen had no need and received non-need-based gift aid.

UNDERGRADUATE FINANCIAL AID (Fall 2008) 5,311 applied for aid; of those 63% were deemed to have need. 96% of undergraduates with need received aid; of those 30% had need fully met. *Average percent of need met:* 81% (excluding resources awarded to replace EFC). *Average financial aid package:* $6397 (excluding resources awarded to replace EFC). 2% of all full-time undergraduates had no need and received non-need-based gift aid.

GIFT AID (NEED-BASED) *Total amount:* $9,090,859 (61% federal, 35% state, 2% institutional, 2% external sources). *Receiving aid:* Freshmen: 16% (276); all full-time undergraduates: 18% (1,409). *Average award:* Freshmen: $5784; Undergraduates: $5523. *Scholarships, grants, and awards:* Federal Pell, FSEOG, state, private, college/university gift aid from institutional funds.

GIFT AID (NON-NEED-BASED) *Total amount:* $3,695,075 (4% federal, 12% state, 27% institutional, 57% external sources). *Receiving aid:* Freshmen: 5% (86). Undergraduates: 4% (280). *Average award:* Freshmen: $1763. Undergraduates: $1524. *Scholarships, grants, and awards by category: Academic interests/achievement:* area/ethnic studies, biological sciences, business, communication, computer science, education, English, foreign languages, general academic interests/achievements, health fields, humanities, international studies, mathematics, military science, physical sciences, social sciences. *Creative arts/performance:* art/fine arts, music, theater/drama. *Special achievements/activities:* community service, leadership, memberships. *Special characteristics:* adult students, children and siblings of alumni, children of union members/company employees, ethnic background, first-generation college students, general special characteristics, international students, local/state students, members of minority groups, out-of-state students, veterans, veterans' children. *Tuition waivers:* Full or partial for minority students.

LOANS *Student loans:* $32,056,913 (39% need-based, 61% non-need-based). 65% of past graduating class borrowed through all loan programs. *Average indebtedness per student:* $21,998. *Average need-based loan:* Freshmen: $3048. Undergraduates: $3817. *Parent loans:* $2,263,347 (100% non-need-based). *Programs:* FFEL (Subsidized and Unsubsidized Stafford, PLUS), Perkins.

WORK-STUDY *Federal work-study:* Total amount: $473,919; jobs available. *State or other work-study/employment:* Total amount: $332,698 (100% non-need-based). Part-time jobs available.

APPLYING FOR FINANCIAL AID *Required financial aid form:* FAFSA. *Financial aid deadline (priority):* 3/15. *Notification date:* Continuous beginning 4/1.

CONTACT Louise Larson Janke, Director of Financial Aid, University of Wisconsin–La Crosse, 1725 State Street, La Crosse, WI 54601-3742, 608-785-8604. *Fax:* 608-785-8843. *E-mail:* finaid@uwlax.edu.

UNIVERSITY OF WISCONSIN–MADISON
Madison, WI

Tuition & fees (WI res): $8314   **Average undergraduate aid package: $11,141**

ABOUT THE INSTITUTION State-supported, coed. 115 undergraduate majors. Federal methodology is used as a basis for awarding need-based institutional aid.

UNDERGRADUATE EXPENSES for 2009–10 *Tuition, state resident:* full-time $7296; part-time $303.99 per credit hour. *Tuition, nonresident:* full-time $22,045; part-time $918.56 per credit hour. *Required fees:* full-time $1018; $44.25 per credit hour or $44.25 per credit hour. Full-time tuition and fees vary according to program and reciprocity agreements. Part-time tuition and fees vary according to course load, program, and reciprocity agreements. *College room and board:* $7157. Room and board charges vary according to board plan and housing facility.

FRESHMAN FINANCIAL AID (Fall 2009, est.) 3,745 applied for aid; of those 56% were deemed to have need. 97% of freshmen with need received aid; of those 22% had need fully met. *Average percent of need met:* 75% (excluding resources awarded to replace EFC). *Average financial aid package:* $11,050 (excluding resources awarded to replace EFC). 12% of all full-time freshmen had no need and received non-need-based gift aid.

UNDERGRADUATE FINANCIAL AID (Fall 2009, est.) 15,044 applied for aid; of those 67% were deemed to have need. 98% of undergraduates with need received aid; of those 20% had need fully met. *Average percent of need met:* 76% (excluding resources awarded to replace EFC). *Average financial aid package:* $11,141 (excluding resources awarded to replace EFC). 10% of all full-time undergraduates had no need and received non-need-based gift aid.

GIFT AID (NEED-BASED) *Total amount:* $38,746,577 (52% federal, 20% state, 28% institutional). *Receiving aid:* Freshmen: 22% (1,221); all full-time undergraduates: 23% (6,405). *Average award:* Freshmen: $6290; Undergraduates: $5850. *Scholarships, grants, and awards:* Federal Pell, FSEOG, state, private, college/university gift aid from institutional funds.

GIFT AID (NON-NEED-BASED) *Total amount:* $31,984,703 (2% federal, 17% state, 56% institutional, 25% external sources). *Receiving aid:* Freshmen: 29% (1,648). Undergraduates: 27% (7,396). *Average award:* Freshmen: $3335. Undergraduates: $3234. *Scholarships, grants, and awards by category:* Academic interests/achievement: general academic interests/achievements. Creative arts/performance: general creative arts/performance. Special achievements/activities: general special achievements/activities. Special characteristics: general special characteristics.

LOANS *Student loans:* $94,258,299 (42% need-based, 58% non-need-based). 50% of past graduating class borrowed through all loan programs. *Average indebtedness per student:* $21,552. *Average need-based loan:* Freshmen: $4102. Undergraduates: $4896. *Parent loans:* $14,591,510 (100% non-need-based). *Programs:* Federal Direct (Subsidized and Unsubsidized Stafford, PLUS), Perkins, Federal Nursing, state.

WORK-STUDY *Federal work-study:* Total amount: $9,063,905; jobs available.

ATHLETIC AWARDS Total amount: $8,752,146 (100% non-need-based).

APPLYING FOR FINANCIAL AID *Required financial aid form:* FAFSA. *Financial aid deadline:* Continuous. *Notification date:* Continuous beginning 4/1. Students must reply within 3 weeks of notification.

CONTACT Office of Student Financial Aid, University of Wisconsin–Madison, 333 East Campus Mall #9701, Madison, WI 53715-1382, 608-262-3060. *Fax:* 608-262-9068. *E-mail:* finaid@finaid.wisc.edu.

UNIVERSITY OF WISCONSIN–MILWAUKEE
Milwaukee, WI

ABOUT THE INSTITUTION State-supported, coed. 103 undergraduate majors.

GIFT AID (NEED-BASED) *Scholarships, grants, and awards:* Federal Pell, FSEOG, state, private, college/university gift aid from institutional funds, Federal Nursing.

GIFT AID (NON-NEED-BASED) *Scholarships, grants, and awards by category:* Academic interests/achievement: general academic interests/achievements. Creative arts/performance: general creative arts/performance. Special achievements/activities: general special achievements/activities. Special characteristics: general special characteristics.

LOANS *Programs:* FFEL (Subsidized and Unsubsidized Stafford, PLUS), Perkins, Federal Nursing, state, alternative loans.

WORK-STUDY *Federal work-study:* Total amount: $1,539,315; jobs available.

APPLYING FOR FINANCIAL AID *Required financial aid form:* FAFSA.

CONTACT Ms. Jane Hojan-Clark, Director of Financial Aid and Student Employment Services, University of Wisconsin–Milwaukee, Mellencamp Hall 162, Milwaukee, WI 53201, 414-229-6300. *E-mail:* jhojan@uwm.edu.

UNIVERSITY OF WISCONSIN–OSHKOSH
Oshkosh, WI

ABOUT THE INSTITUTION State-supported, coed. 56 undergraduate majors.

GIFT AID (NEED-BASED) *Scholarships, grants, and awards:* Federal Pell, FSEOG, state, private, college/university gift aid from institutional funds, Federal Nursing.

LOANS *Programs:* FFEL (Subsidized and Unsubsidized Stafford, PLUS), Perkins, Federal Nursing, state, college/university.

WORK-STUDY *Federal work-study:* Total amount: $664,391; jobs available. *State or other work-study/employment:* Total amount: $3,000,000 (100% non-need-based). Part-time jobs available.

APPLYING FOR FINANCIAL AID *Required financial aid form:* FAFSA.

CONTACT Ms. Sheila Denney, Financial Aid Counselor, University of Wisconsin–Oshkosh, 800 Algoma Boulevard, Oshkosh, WI 54901, 920-424-3377. *E-mail:* denney@uwosh.edu.

UNIVERSITY OF WISCONSIN–PARKSIDE
Kenosha, WI

Tuition & fees (WI res): $7196   **Average undergraduate aid package: $8487**

ABOUT THE INSTITUTION State-supported, coed. 37 undergraduate majors. Federal methodology is used as a basis for awarding need-based institutional aid.

UNDERGRADUATE EXPENSES for 2009–10 *Tuition, state resident:* full-time $6280; part-time $223.49 per credit hour. *Tuition, nonresident:* full-time $13,853; part-time $539.03 per credit hour. *Required fees:* full-time $916; $40 per credit hour. Full-time tuition and fees vary according to course load and reciprocity agreements. Part-time tuition and fees vary according to course load. *College room and board:* $6252; *Room only:* $3987. Room and board charges vary according to board plan and housing facility. *Payment plan:* Installment.

FRESHMAN FINANCIAL AID (Fall 2008) 663 applied for aid; of those 79% were deemed to have need. 96% of freshmen with need received aid; of those 31% had need fully met. *Average percent of need met:* 71% (excluding resources awarded to replace EFC). *Average financial aid package:* $8160 (excluding resources awarded to replace EFC).

UNDERGRADUATE FINANCIAL AID (Fall 2008) 2,843 applied for aid; of those 81% were deemed to have need. 97% of undergraduates with need received aid; of those 36% had need fully met. *Average percent of need met:* 68% (excluding resources awarded to replace EFC). *Average financial aid package:* $8487 (excluding resources awarded to replace EFC).

GIFT AID (NEED-BASED) *Total amount:* $9,914,137 (60% federal, 39% state, 1% external sources). *Receiving aid:* Freshmen: 35% (291); all full-time undergraduates: 34% (1,238). *Average award:* Freshmen: $6932; Undergraduates: $6315. *Scholarships, grants, and awards:* Federal Pell, FSEOG, state, private, college/university gift aid from institutional funds, Federal Nursing.

GIFT AID (NON-NEED-BASED) *Total amount:* $1,258,439 (49% federal, 8% state, 43% external sources). *Receiving aid:* Freshmen: 13% (106). Undergraduates: 11% (421). *Scholarships, grants, and awards by category:* Academic interests/achievement: biological sciences, business, communication, education, engineering/technologies, English, foreign languages, general academic interests/achievements, health fields, mathematics, physical sciences, premedicine. Creative arts/performance: applied art and design, art/fine arts, music, theater/drama. Special achievements/activities: community service, leadership. Special characteristics: adult students, children of union members/company employees, children of workers in trades, ethnic background, general special characteristics, international students, local/state students, members of minority groups. *Tuition waivers:* Full or partial for senior citizens.

LOANS *Student loans:* $18,527,011 (43% need-based, 57% non-need-based). 65% of past graduating class borrowed through all loan programs. *Average indebtedness per student:* $18,254. *Parent loans:* $1,000,517 (100% non-need-based). *Programs:* FFEL (Subsidized and Unsubsidized Stafford, PLUS), Perkins, Federal Nursing, state.

WORK-STUDY *Federal work-study:* Total amount: $116,736; jobs available. *State or other work-study/employment:* Part-time jobs available.

ATHLETIC AWARDS Total amount: $1,153,082 (100% non-need-based).

APPLYING FOR FINANCIAL AID *Required financial aid form:* FAFSA. *Financial aid deadline (priority):* 11/15. *Notification date:* Continuous beginning 4/1. Students must reply within 2 weeks of notification.

CONTACT Dr. Randall McCready, Director of Financial Aid and Scholarships, University of Wisconsin–Parkside, 900 Wood Road, Kenosha, WI 53141-2000, 262-595-2004. *Fax:* 262-595-2216. *E-mail:* randall.mccready@uwp.edu.

UNIVERSITY OF WISCONSIN–PLATTEVILLE
Platteville, WI

CONTACT Elizabeth Tucker, Director of Financial Aid, University of Wisconsin–Platteville, 1 University Plaza, Platteville, WI 53818-3099, 608-342-1836 or toll-free 800-362-5515. *Fax:* 608-342-1281. *E-mail:* tucker@uwplatt.edu.

UNIVERSITY OF WISCONSIN–RIVER FALLS
River Falls, WI

Tuition & fees (WI res): $6460   **Average undergraduate aid package:** $2810

ABOUT THE INSTITUTION State-supported, coed. 95 undergraduate majors. Federal methodology is used as a basis for awarding need-based institutional aid.

UNDERGRADUATE EXPENSES for 2009–10 *Tuition, state resident:* full-time $5364; part-time $446.98 per credit. *Tuition, nonresident:* full-time $13,009; part-time $1084.06 per credit. *Required fees:* full-time $1096; $257.88 per credit. Full-time tuition and fees vary according to course load, degree level, and reciprocity agreements. Part-time tuition and fees vary according to course load, degree level, and reciprocity agreements. *College room and board:* $5372; *Room only:* $3238. Room and board charges vary according to board plan and housing facility. *Payment plan:* Installment.

FRESHMAN FINANCIAL AID (Fall 2008) 1,204 applied for aid; of those 89% were deemed to have need. 86% of freshmen with need received aid. *Average percent of need met:* 87% (excluding resources awarded to replace EFC). *Average financial aid package:* $2326 (excluding resources awarded to replace EFC).

UNDERGRADUATE FINANCIAL AID (Fall 2008) 5,068 applied for aid; of those 95% were deemed to have need. 73% of undergraduates with need received aid. *Average percent of need met:* 84% (excluding resources awarded to replace EFC). *Average financial aid package:* $2810 (excluding resources awarded to replace EFC).

GIFT AID (NEED-BASED) *Total amount:* $7,871,747 (63% federal, 26% state, 11% institutional). *Receiving aid:* Freshmen: 34% (445); all full-time undergraduates: 25% (1,427). *Average award:* Freshmen: $1782; Undergraduates: $2062. *Scholarships, grants, and awards:* Federal Pell, FSEOG, state, private, college/university gift aid from institutional funds.

GIFT AID (NON-NEED-BASED) *Total amount:* $1,736,906 (3% state, 35% institutional, 62% external sources). *Receiving aid:* Freshmen: 52% (689). Undergraduates: 47% (2,691). *Scholarships, grants, and awards by category:* Academic interests/achievement: agriculture, area/ethnic studies, biological sciences, business, communication, computer science, education, English, foreign languages, general academic interests/achievements, health fields, humanities, international studies, mathematics, physical sciences, premedicine, social sciences. Creative arts/performance: art/fine arts, music, theater/drama. *Tuition waivers:* Full or partial for children of alumni.

LOANS *Student loans:* $28,163,265 (45% need-based, 55% non-need-based). 72% of past graduating class borrowed through all loan programs. *Average indebtedness per student:* $8000. *Parent loans:* $1,145,779 (100% non-need-based). *Programs:* FFEL (Subsidized and Unsubsidized Stafford, PLUS), Perkins, state.

WORK-STUDY *Federal work-study:* Total amount: $334,434; jobs available. *State or other work-study/employment:* Total amount: $183,556 (40% need-based, 60% non-need-based). Part-time jobs available.

APPLYING FOR FINANCIAL AID *Required financial aid forms:* FAFSA, institution's own form. *Financial aid deadline (priority):* 3/15. *Notification date:* 4/1. Students must reply within 3 weeks of notification.

CONTACT Ms. Barbara J. Stinson, Director of Financial Aid, University of Wisconsin–River Falls, 410 South Third Street, River Falls, WI 54022-5001, 715-425-4111. *Fax:* 715-425-0708.

UNIVERSITY OF WISCONSIN–STEVENS POINT
Stevens Point, WI

Tuition & fees (WI res): $6530   **Average undergraduate aid package:** $7723

ABOUT THE INSTITUTION State-supported, coed. 55 undergraduate majors. Federal methodology is used as a basis for awarding need-based institutional aid.

UNDERGRADUATE EXPENSES for 2010–11 *Tuition, state resident:* full-time $6530; part-time $272 per credit hour. *Tuition, nonresident:* full-time $14,104; part-time $587 per credit hour. *Required fees:* $272 per credit hour. Full-time tuition and fees vary according to course load and reciprocity agreements. Part-time tuition and fees vary according to course load and reciprocity agreements. *College room and board:* $5612; *Room only:* $3336. *Payment plan:* Installment.

FRESHMAN FINANCIAL AID (Fall 2008) 1,262 applied for aid; of those 62% were deemed to have need. 94% of freshmen with need received aid; of those 70% had need fully met. *Average percent of need met:* 76% (excluding resources awarded to replace EFC). *Average financial aid package:* $6446 (excluding resources awarded to replace EFC). 7% of all full-time freshmen had no need and received non-need-based gift aid.

UNDERGRADUATE FINANCIAL AID (Fall 2008) 6,165 applied for aid; of those 70% were deemed to have need. 97% of undergraduates with need received aid; of those 72% had need fully met. *Average percent of need met:* 72% (excluding resources awarded to replace EFC). *Average financial aid package:* $7723 (excluding resources awarded to replace EFC). 7% of all full-time undergraduates had no need and received non-need-based gift aid.

GIFT AID (NEED-BASED) *Total amount:* $13,249,289 (61% federal, 33% state, 3% institutional, 3% external sources). *Receiving aid:* Freshmen: 23% (372); all full-time undergraduates: 26% (2,208). *Average award:* Freshmen: $5359; Undergraduates: $5654. *Scholarships, grants, and awards:* Federal Pell, FSEOG, state, college/university gift aid from institutional funds.

GIFT AID (NON-NEED-BASED) *Total amount:* $2,571,283 (3% state, 33% institutional, 64% external sources). *Receiving aid:* Freshmen: 5% (84). Undergraduates: 6% (488). *Average award:* Freshmen: $2519. Undergraduates: $2763. *Scholarships, grants, and awards by category:* Academic interests/achievement: agriculture, architecture, biological sciences, business, communication, computer science, education, engineering/technologies, English, foreign languages, general academic interests/achievements, health fields, home economics, humanities, international studies, mathematics, military science, physical sciences, premedicine, social sciences. Creative arts/performance: applied art and design, creative writing, dance, music, performing arts, theater/drama. Special achievements/activities: general special achievements/activities, leadership. Special characteristics: adult students, ethnic background, general special characteristics, international students, members of minority groups, out-of-state students, veterans.

LOANS *Student loans:* $32,544,850 (58% need-based, 42% non-need-based). 73% of past graduating class borrowed through all loan programs. *Average indebtedness per student:* $19,738. *Average need-based loan:* Freshmen: $3774. Undergraduates: $4708. *Parent loans:* $2,921,386 (6% need-based, 94% non-need-based). *Programs:* FFEL (Subsidized and Unsubsidized Stafford, PLUS), Perkins.

WORK-STUDY *Federal work-study:* Total amount: $1,897,091; jobs available. *State or other work-study/employment:* Part-time jobs available.

APPLYING FOR FINANCIAL AID *Required financial aid form:* FAFSA. *Financial aid deadline (priority):* 5/15. *Notification date:* Continuous. Students must reply within 4 weeks of notification.

CONTACT Mr. Paul Watson, Director of Financial Aid, University of Wisconsin–Stevens Point, 105 Student Services Center, Stevens Point, WI 54481-3897, 715-346-4771. *Fax:* 715-346-3526. *E-mail:* pwatson@uwsp.edu.

UNIVERSITY OF WISCONSIN–STOUT
Menomonie, WI

Tuition & fees (WI res): $7821   **Average undergraduate aid package:** $9291

ABOUT THE INSTITUTION State-supported, coed. 40 undergraduate majors. Federal methodology is used as a basis for awarding need-based institutional aid.

UNDERGRADUATE EXPENSES for 2009–10 *Tuition, state resident:* full-time $5974; part-time $199 per credit hour. *Tuition, nonresident:* full-time $13,719; part-time $457 per credit hour. *Required fees:* full-time $1847; $62 per credit hour or $62 per credit hour. Full-time tuition and fees vary according to degree level and reciprocity agreements. Part-time tuition and fees vary according to degree level and reciprocity agreements. *College room and board:* $5336; *Room only:* $3200. Room and board charges vary according to board plan and housing facility. *Payment plan:* Installment.

FRESHMAN FINANCIAL AID (Fall 2009, est.) 1,262 applied for aid; of those 65% were deemed to have need. 99% of freshmen with need received aid; of those 54% had need fully met. *Average percent of need met:* 90% (excluding resources awarded to replace EFC). *Average financial aid package:* $8805 (excluding resources awarded to replace EFC). 3% of all full-time freshmen had no need and received non-need-based gift aid.

UNDERGRADUATE FINANCIAL AID (Fall 2009, est.) 5,383 applied for aid; of those 71% were deemed to have need. 99% of undergraduates with need received aid; of those 55% had need fully met. *Average percent of need met:* 90% (excluding resources awarded to replace EFC). *Average financial aid package:* $9291 (excluding resources awarded to replace EFC). 3% of all full-time undergraduates had no need and received non-need-based gift aid.

GIFT AID (NEED-BASED) *Total amount:* $12,112,201 (71% federal, 25% state, 1% institutional, 3% external sources). *Receiving aid:* Freshmen: 28% (426); all full-time undergraduates: 31% (2,112). *Average award:* Freshmen: $5689; Undergraduates: $5346. *Scholarships, grants, and awards:* Federal Pell, FSEOG, state, private, college/university gift aid from institutional funds, Bureau of Indian Affairs Grants, GEAR UP grants, Academic Competitiveness Grants.

GIFT AID (NON-NEED-BASED) *Total amount:* $1,344,600 (3% federal, 4% state, 39% institutional, 54% external sources). *Receiving aid:* Freshmen: 11% (172). Undergraduates: 7% (481). *Average award:* Freshmen: $1620. Undergraduates: $1707. *Scholarships, grants, and awards by category: Academic interests/achievement:* 232 awards ($282,325 total): business, computer science, education, engineering/technologies, general academic interests/achievements, home economics, international studies, mathematics, physical sciences. *Creative arts/performance:* 14 awards ($14,050 total): applied art and design, art/fine arts, music. *Special achievements/activities:* 33 awards ($36,900 total): community service, general special achievements/activities, leadership, memberships, religious involvement. *Special characteristics:* 51 awards ($70,175 total): adult students, first-generation college students, handicapped students, international students, local/state students, members of minority groups, out-of-state students, previous college experience, veterans, veterans' children.

LOANS *Student loans:* $40,816,046 (39% need-based, 61% non-need-based). 75% of past graduating class borrowed through all loan programs. *Average indebtedness per student:* $27,478. *Average need-based loan:* Freshmen: $3403. Undergraduates: $4207. *Parent loans:* $2,651,497 (100% non-need-based). *Programs:* Federal Direct (Subsidized and Unsubsidized Stafford, PLUS), Perkins, alternative loans.

WORK-STUDY *Federal work-study:* Total amount: $2,184,932; 1,170 jobs averaging $1796.

APPLYING FOR FINANCIAL AID *Required financial aid form:* FAFSA. *Financial aid deadline (priority):* 3/15. *Notification date:* Continuous beginning 4/1. Students must reply within 4 weeks of notification.

CONTACT Beth M. Boisen, Director of Financial Aid, University of Wisconsin–Stout, 210 Bowman Hall, Menomonie, WI 54751, 715-232-1363 or toll-free 800-HI-STOUT (in-state). *Fax:* 715-232-5246. *E-mail:* boisenb@uwstout.edu.

UNIVERSITY OF WISCONSIN–SUPERIOR
Superior, WI

Tuition & fees (WI res): $6736   **Average undergraduate aid package:** N/A

ABOUT THE INSTITUTION State-supported, coed. 65 undergraduate majors. Federal methodology is used as a basis for awarding need-based institutional aid.

UNDERGRADUATE EXPENSES for 2009–10 *Tuition, state resident:* full-time $5571; part-time $401 per semester hour. *Tuition, nonresident:* full-time $13,144; part-time $717 per semester hour. *Required fees:* full-time $1165. Full-time tuition and fees vary according to course load, program, and reciprocity agreements. Part-time tuition and fees vary according to program and reciprocity agreements. *College room and board:* $5485; *Room only:* $2960. Room and board charges vary according to board plan, housing facility, and student level. *Payment plan:* Installment.

FRESHMAN FINANCIAL AID (Fall 2009, est.) 259 applied for aid; of those 76% were deemed to have need. 99% of freshmen with need received aid; of those 26% had need fully met. 4% of all full-time freshmen had no need and received non-need-based gift aid.

UNDERGRADUATE FINANCIAL AID (Fall 2009, est.) 1,450 applied for aid; of those 83% were deemed to have need. 99% of undergraduates with need received aid; of those 24% had need fully met. 2% of all full-time undergraduates had no need and received non-need-based gift aid.

GIFT AID (NEED-BASED) *Total amount:* $4,714,588 (78% federal, 20% state, 2% external sources). *Receiving aid:* Freshmen: 33% (121); all full-time undergraduates: 37% (770). *Average award:* Freshmen: $6160; Undergraduates: $5452. *Scholarships, grants, and awards:* Federal Pell, FSEOG, state, private, college/university gift aid from institutional funds.

GIFT AID (NON-NEED-BASED) *Total amount:* $985,729 (6% state, 63% institutional, 31% external sources). *Receiving aid:* Freshmen: 23% (83). Undergraduates: 13% (278). *Average award:* Freshmen: $1488. Undergraduates: $1769. *Scholarships, grants, and awards by category: Academic interests/achievement:* biological sciences, business, communication, computer science, education, English, general academic interests/achievements, health fields, humanities, mathematics, physical sciences, social sciences. *Creative arts/performance:* general creative arts/performance. *Special characteristics:* general special characteristics, members of minority groups.

LOANS *Student loans:* $10,437,169 (45% need-based, 55% non-need-based). 75% of past graduating class borrowed through all loan programs. *Average indebtedness per student:* $22,516. *Average need-based loan:* Freshmen: $2870. Undergraduates: $3811. *Parent loans:* $407,686 (100% non-need-based). *Programs:* Federal Direct (Subsidized and Unsubsidized Stafford, PLUS), Perkins, college/university.

WORK-STUDY *Federal work-study:* Total amount: $300,000; jobs available. *State or other work-study/employment:* Part-time jobs available.

APPLYING FOR FINANCIAL AID *Required financial aid form:* FAFSA. *Financial aid deadline:* Continuous. *Notification date:* Continuous beginning 3/15.

CONTACT Tammi Reijo, Assistant Director, Financial Aid, University of Wisconsin–Superior, Belknap and Catlin, Old Main 110, PO Box 2000, Superior, WI 54880, 715-394-8200. *Fax:* 715-394-8027. *E-mail:* treijo@uwsuper.edu.

UNIVERSITY OF WISCONSIN–WHITEWATER
Whitewater, WI

Tuition & fees (WI res): $7439   **Average undergraduate aid package:** $7957

ABOUT THE INSTITUTION State-supported, coed. 56 undergraduate majors. Federal methodology is used as a basis for awarding need-based institutional aid.

UNDERGRADUATE EXPENSES for 2010–11 *Tuition, state resident:* full-time $5551; part-time $179 per credit hour. *Tuition, nonresident:* full-time $13,124; part-time $431 per credit hour. *Required fees:* full-time $1888. Full-time tuition and fees vary according to degree level and reciprocity agreements. *College room and board:* $5028; *Room only:* $3072. Room and board charges vary according to board plan. *Payment plan:* Installment.

FRESHMAN FINANCIAL AID (Fall 2009, est.) 1,900 applied for aid; of those 67% were deemed to have need. 96% of freshmen with need received aid; of those 57% had need fully met. *Average percent of need met:* 68% (excluding resources awarded to replace EFC). *Average financial aid package:* $7408 (excluding resources awarded to replace EFC). 7% of all full-time freshmen had no need and received non-need-based gift aid.

UNDERGRADUATE FINANCIAL AID (Fall 2009, est.) 7,074 applied for aid; of those 70% were deemed to have need. 97% of undergraduates with need received aid; of those 63% had need fully met. *Average percent of need met:* 73% (excluding resources awarded to replace EFC). *Average financial aid*

package: $7957 (excluding resources awarded to replace EFC). 4% of all full-time undergraduates had no need and received non-need-based gift aid.

GIFT AID (NEED-BASED) *Total amount:* $16,140,000 (66% federal, 34% state). *Receiving aid:* Freshmen: 37% (709); all full-time undergraduates: 32% (2,876). *Average award:* Freshmen: $5758; Undergraduates: $5220. *Scholarships, grants, and awards:* Federal Pell, FSEOG, state, private, college/university gift aid from institutional funds.

GIFT AID (NON-NEED-BASED) *Total amount:* $3,539,000 (1% federal, 3% state, 32% institutional, 64% external sources). *Receiving aid:* Freshmen: 17% (323). Undergraduates: 9% (815). *Average award:* Freshmen: $1233. Undergraduates: $1424. *Scholarships, grants, and awards by category: Academic interests/ achievement:* biological sciences, business, communication, computer science, education, English, foreign languages, general academic interests/achievements, humanities, mathematics, physical sciences, premedicine, social sciences. *Creative arts/performance:* art/fine arts, cinema/film/broadcasting, creative writing, journalism/publications, music, theater/drama. *Special achievements/activities:* leadership. *Special characteristics:* adult students, ethnic background, handicapped students, international students, local/state students, members of minority groups, out-of-state students. *Tuition waivers:* Full or partial for children of alumni, senior citizens.

LOANS *Student loans:* $50,680,000 (40% need-based, 60% non-need-based). 67% of past graduating class borrowed through all loan programs. *Average indebtedness per student:* $20,715. *Average need-based loan:* Freshmen: $3267. Undergraduates: $3984. *Parent loans:* $7,000,000 (100% non-need-based). *Programs:* Federal Direct (Subsidized and Unsubsidized Stafford, PLUS), Perkins.

WORK-STUDY *Federal work-study:* Total amount: $700,000; 505 jobs averaging $1261. *State or other work-study/employment:* Total amount: $3,500,000 (100% non-need-based). 1,723 part-time jobs averaging $2031.

APPLYING FOR FINANCIAL AID *Required financial aid form:* FAFSA. *Financial aid deadline (priority):* 3/15. *Notification date:* Continuous beginning 4/1. Students must reply within 3 weeks of notification.

CONTACT Ms. Carol Miller, Director of Financial Aid, University of Wisconsin–Whitewater, 800 West Main Street, Whitewater, WI 53190-1790, 262-472-1130. *Fax:* 262-472-5655.

UNIVERSITY OF WYOMING
Laramie, WY

Tuition & fees (WY res): $3927	Average undergraduate aid package: $9332

ABOUT THE INSTITUTION State-supported, coed. 80 undergraduate majors. Federal methodology is used as a basis for awarding need-based institutional aid.

UNDERGRADUATE EXPENSES for 2010–11 *One-time required fee:* $100. *Tuition, state resident:* full-time $2970; part-time $99 per credit hour. *Tuition, nonresident:* full-time $11,280; part-time $376 per credit hour. *Required fees:* full-time $957; $239 per term. Full-time tuition and fees vary according to course load, location, and reciprocity agreements. Part-time tuition and fees vary according to course load, location, and reciprocity agreements. *College room and board:* $8360; *Room only:* $3612. Room and board charges vary according to board plan and housing facility. *Payment plan:* Installment.

FRESHMAN FINANCIAL AID (Fall 2009, est.) 1,224 applied for aid; of those 59% were deemed to have need. 99% of freshmen with need received aid; of those 36% had need fully met. *Average percent of need met:* 34% (excluding resources awarded to replace EFC). *Average financial aid package:* $9535 (excluding resources awarded to replace EFC). 47% of all full-time freshmen had no need and received non-need-based gift aid.

UNDERGRADUATE FINANCIAL AID (Fall 2009, est.) 5,101 applied for aid; of those 70% were deemed to have need. 99% of undergraduates with need received aid; of those 23% had need fully met. *Average percent of need met:* 44% (excluding resources awarded to replace EFC). *Average financial aid package:* $9332 (excluding resources awarded to replace EFC). 40% of all full-time undergraduates had no need and received non-need-based gift aid.

GIFT AID (NEED-BASED) *Total amount:* $10,363,661 (81% federal, 9% state, 4% institutional, 6% external sources). *Receiving aid:* Freshmen: 24% (383); all full-time undergraduates: 27% (2,183). *Average award:* Freshmen: $4009; Undergraduates: $4660. *Scholarships, grants, and awards:* Federal Pell, FSEOG, state, private, college/university gift aid from institutional funds.

GIFT AID (NON-NEED-BASED) *Total amount:* $26,063,388 (68% state, 25% institutional, 7% external sources). *Receiving aid:* Freshmen: 40% (626). Undergraduates: 29% (2,371). *Average award:* Freshmen: $4993. Undergradu-ates: $4751. *Scholarships, grants, and awards by category: Academic interests/ achievement:* 5,287 awards ($14,328,752 total): agriculture, business, communication, computer science, education, engineering/technologies, English, foreign languages, general academic interests/achievements, health fields, home economics, international studies, mathematics, military science, physical sciences, social sciences. *Creative arts/performance:* 659 awards ($734,637 total): art/fine arts, dance, debating, music, theater/drama. *Special achievements/ activities:* 164 awards ($317,885 total): cheerleading/drum major, junior miss, leadership, rodeo. *Special characteristics:* 1,939 awards ($6,414,360 total): adult students, children and siblings of alumni, ethnic background, first-generation college students, handicapped students, international students, local/ state students, out-of-state students, veterans. *Tuition waivers:* Full or partial for children of alumni, employees or children of employees, senior citizens.

LOANS *Student loans:* $30,858,712 (91% need-based, 9% non-need-based). 50% of past graduating class borrowed through all loan programs. *Average indebtedness per student:* $17,084. *Average need-based loan:* Freshmen: $2320. Undergraduates: $3446. *Parent loans:* $2,068,302 (100% non-need-based). *Programs:* FFEL (Subsidized and Unsubsidized Stafford, PLUS), Perkins, alternative loans.

WORK-STUDY *Federal work-study:* Total amount: $587,264; 292 jobs averaging $2011.

ATHLETIC AWARDS Total amount: $3,567,910 (100% non-need-based).

APPLYING FOR FINANCIAL AID *Required financial aid form:* FAFSA. *Financial aid deadline (priority):* 2/1. *Notification date:* Continuous beginning 3/15. Students must reply within 3 weeks of notification.

CONTACT Mr. David Gruen, Director of Student Financial Aid, University of Wyoming, Department 3335, Laramie, WY 82071, 307-766-2116 or toll-free 800-342-5996. *Fax:* 307-766-3800. *E-mail:* finaid@uwyo.edu.

UPPER IOWA UNIVERSITY
Fayette, IA

CONTACT Jobyna Johnston, Director of Financial Aid, Upper Iowa University, Parker Fox Hall, Box 1859, Fayette, IA 52142-1859, 563-425-5393 or toll-free 800-553-4150 Ext. 2. *Fax:* 563-425-5277. *E-mail:* jobyna@uiu.edu.

URBANA UNIVERSITY
Urbana, OH

CONTACT Mrs. Amy M. Barnhart, Director of Financial Aid, Urbana University, 579 College Way, Urbana, OH 43078-2091, 937-484-1359 or toll-free 800-7-URBANA. *Fax:* 937-652-6870. *E-mail:* abarnhart@urbana.edu.

URSINUS COLLEGE
Collegeville, PA

Tuition & fees: $40,120	Average undergraduate aid package: $27,194

ABOUT THE INSTITUTION Independent, coed. 34 undergraduate majors. Both federal and institutional methodology are used as a basis for awarding need-based institutional aid.

UNDERGRADUATE EXPENSES for 2010–11 *Comprehensive fee:* $49,870 includes full-time tuition ($39,950), mandatory fees ($170), and room and board ($9750). *College room only:* $4875. *Part-time tuition:* $1249 per credit hour. *Part-time fees:* $170 per year. *Payment plan:* Installment.

FRESHMAN FINANCIAL AID (Fall 2009, est.) 457 applied for aid; of those 79% were deemed to have need. 100% of freshmen with need received aid; of those 24% had need fully met. *Average percent of need met:* 84% (excluding resources awarded to replace EFC). *Average financial aid package:* $29,053 (excluding resources awarded to replace EFC). 23% of all full-time freshmen had no need and received non-need-based gift aid.

UNDERGRADUATE FINANCIAL AID (Fall 2009, est.) 1,440 applied for aid; of those 84% were deemed to have need. 100% of undergraduates with need received aid; of those 22% had need fully met. *Average percent of need met:* 80% (excluding resources awarded to replace EFC). *Average financial aid package:* $27,194 (excluding resources awarded to replace EFC). 24% of all full-time undergraduates had no need and received non-need-based gift aid.

GIFT AID (NEED-BASED) *Total amount:* $27,112,135 (7% federal, 5% state, 86% institutional, 2% external sources). *Receiving aid:* Freshmen: 71% (362); all full-time undergraduates: 70% (1,205). *Average award:* Freshmen: $25,319;

Undergraduates: $22,868. **Scholarships, grants, and awards:** Federal Pell, FSEOG, state, private, college/university gift aid from institutional funds.

GIFT AID (NON-NEED-BASED) Total amount: $6,992,832 (96% institutional, 4% external sources). **Receiving aid:** Freshmen: 12% (60). Undergraduates: 11% (187). **Average award:** Freshmen: $14,688. Undergraduates: $13,512. **Scholarships, grants, and awards by category:** Academic interests/achievement: 914 awards ($13,084,942 total): general academic interests/achievements. Creative arts/performance: 8 awards ($110,000 total): creative writing. Special achievements/activities: 20 awards ($78,000 total): leadership. Special characteristics: 219 awards ($1,951,400 total): children and siblings of alumni, children of faculty/staff, international students, siblings of current students. **Tuition waivers:** Full or partial for employees or children of employees.

LOANS Student loans: $12,298,012 (61% need-based, 39% non-need-based). 80% of past graduating class borrowed through all loan programs. Average indebtedness per student: $25,875. **Average need-based loan:** Freshmen: $3596. Undergraduates: $4306. **Parent loans:** $3,836,260 (27% need-based, 73% non-need-based). **Programs:** FFEL (Subsidized and Unsubsidized Stafford, PLUS), Perkins.

WORK-STUDY Federal work-study: Total amount: $987,667; 743 jobs averaging $1822. **State or other work-study/employment:** Total amount: $23,620 (100% non-need-based). Part-time jobs available.

APPLYING FOR FINANCIAL AID Required financial aid forms: FAFSA, institution's own form, CSS Financial Aid PROFILE. **Financial aid deadline:** 2/15. **Notification date:** 4/1. Students must reply by 5/1.

CONTACT Ms. Suzanne B. Sparrow, Director of Student Financial Services, Ursinus College, PO Box 1000, Collegeville, PA 19426-1000, 610-409-3600 Ext. 2242. Fax: 610-409-3662. E-mail: ssparrow@ursinus.edu.

URSULINE COLLEGE
Pepper Pike, OH

Tuition & fees: $23,000	Average undergraduate aid package: $16,825

ABOUT THE INSTITUTION Independent Roman Catholic, coed, primarily women. 43 undergraduate majors. Federal methodology is used as a basis for awarding need-based institutional aid.

UNDERGRADUATE EXPENSES for 2009–10 Comprehensive fee: $30,664 includes full-time tuition ($22,770), mandatory fees ($230), and room and board ($7664). **College room only:** $3916. Full-time tuition and fees vary according to location. Room and board charges vary according to board plan and housing facility. **Part-time tuition:** $759 per credit hour. Part-time tuition and fees vary according to location. **Payment plan:** Installment.

FRESHMAN FINANCIAL AID (Fall 2008) 109 applied for aid; of those 95% were deemed to have need. 100% of freshmen with need received aid; of those 24% had need fully met. **Average percent of need met:** 86% (excluding resources awarded to replace EFC). **Average financial aid package:** $20,296 (excluding resources awarded to replace EFC). 5% of all full-time freshmen had no need and received non-need-based gift aid.

UNDERGRADUATE FINANCIAL AID (Fall 2008) 575 applied for aid; of those 91% were deemed to have need. 100% of undergraduates with need received aid; of those 20% had need fully met. **Average percent of need met:** 74% (excluding resources awarded to replace EFC). **Average financial aid package:** $16,825 (excluding resources awarded to replace EFC). 10% of all full-time undergraduates had no need and received non-need-based gift aid.

GIFT AID (NEED-BASED) Total amount: $6,742,198 (24% federal, 16% state, 56% institutional, 4% external sources). **Receiving aid:** Freshmen: 95% (104); all full-time undergraduates: 84% (512). **Average award:** Freshmen: $15,692; Undergraduates: $11,566. **Scholarships, grants, and awards:** Federal Pell, FSEOG, state, private, college/university gift aid from institutional funds, United Negro College Fund.

GIFT AID (NON-NEED-BASED) Total amount: $510,117 (14% state, 79% institutional, 7% external sources). **Receiving aid:** Freshmen: 6% (7). Undergraduates: 5% (30). **Average award:** Freshmen: $5822. Undergraduates: $4608. **Scholarships, grants, and awards by category:** Academic interests/achievement: general academic interests/achievements. Special achievements/activities: community service, leadership. Special characteristics: children and siblings of alumni, children of faculty/staff, relatives of clergy, religious affiliation, siblings of current students. **Tuition waivers:** Full or partial for employees or children of employees.

LOANS Student loans: $10,071,563 (78% need-based, 22% non-need-based). 94% of past graduating class borrowed through all loan programs. Average

indebtedness per student: $25,830. **Average need-based loan:** Freshmen: $4416. Undergraduates: $5487. **Parent loans:** $388,246 (39% need-based, 61% non-need-based). **Programs:** FFEL (Subsidized and Unsubsidized Stafford, PLUS), Perkins, college/university.

WORK-STUDY Federal work-study: Total amount: $219,078; jobs available.

ATHLETIC AWARDS Total amount: $432,969 (77% need-based, 23% non-need-based).

APPLYING FOR FINANCIAL AID Required financial aid form: FAFSA. **Financial aid deadline:** Continuous. **Notification date:** Continuous beginning 3/1. Students must reply within 4 weeks of notification.

CONTACT Ms. Mary Lynn Perri, Director of Financial Aid and Enrollment Services, Ursuline College, 2550 Lander Road, Pepper Pike, OH 44124-4398, 440-646-8330 or toll-free 888-URSULINE. Fax: 440-684-6114. E-mail: mperri@ursuline.edu.

UTAH STATE UNIVERSITY
Logan, UT

Tuition & fees (UT res): $4828	Average undergraduate aid package: $7300

ABOUT THE INSTITUTION State-supported, coed. 118 undergraduate majors. Federal methodology is used as a basis for awarding need-based institutional aid.

UNDERGRADUATE EXPENSES for 2009–10 Tuition, state resident: full-time $4043. **Tuition, nonresident:** full-time $13,017. **Required fees:** full-time $785. Full-time tuition and fees vary according to course load, program, reciprocity agreements, and student level. Part-time tuition and fees vary according to course load, program, reciprocity agreements, and student level. **College room and board:** $4900; **Room only:** $1650. Room and board charges vary according to board plan and housing facility. **Payment plan:** Deferred payment.

FRESHMAN FINANCIAL AID (Fall 2009, est.) 1,402 applied for aid; of those 76% were deemed to have need. 98% of freshmen with need received aid; of those 16% had need fully met. **Average percent of need met:** 67% (excluding resources awarded to replace EFC). **Average financial aid package:** $7974 (excluding resources awarded to replace EFC). 6% of all full-time freshmen had no need and received non-need-based gift aid.

UNDERGRADUATE FINANCIAL AID (Fall 2009, est.) 6,900 applied for aid; of those 87% were deemed to have need. 97% of undergraduates with need received aid; of those 10% had need fully met. **Average percent of need met:** 63% (excluding resources awarded to replace EFC). **Average financial aid package:** $7300 (excluding resources awarded to replace EFC). 3% of all full-time undergraduates had no need and received non-need-based gift aid.

GIFT AID (NEED-BASED) Total amount: $23,243,000 (99% federal, 1% state). **Receiving aid:** Freshmen: 22% (577); all full-time undergraduates: 37% (4,220). **Average award:** Freshmen: $3957; Undergraduates: $4959. **Scholarships, grants, and awards:** Federal Pell, FSEOG, state, private, college/university gift aid from institutional funds.

GIFT AID (NON-NEED-BASED) Total amount: $12,894,000 (67% institutional, 33% external sources). **Receiving aid:** Freshmen: 19% (493). Undergraduates: 16% (1,876). **Average award:** Freshmen: $2900. Undergraduates: $2500. **Scholarships, grants, and awards by category:** Academic interests/achievement: agriculture, architecture, biological sciences, business, communication, computer science, education, engineering/technologies, English, foreign languages, general academic interests/achievements, health fields, home economics, humanities, international studies, library science, mathematics, physical sciences, premedicine, social sciences. Creative arts/performance: applied art and design, art/fine arts, general creative arts/performance, journalism/publications, music, performing arts, theater/drama. Special characteristics: children and siblings of alumni, children of faculty/staff, international students. **Tuition waivers:** Full or partial for minority students, children of alumni, employees or children of employees, adult students, senior citizens.

LOANS Student loans: $24,680,000 (63% need-based, 37% non-need-based). **Average need-based loan:** Freshmen: $3300. Undergraduates: $4080. **Parent loans:** $505,259 (100% non-need-based). **Programs:** FFEL (Subsidized and Unsubsidized Stafford, PLUS), Perkins, college/university.

WORK-STUDY Federal work-study: Total amount: $860,000; jobs available. **State or other work-study/employment:** Total amount: $780,000 (100% need-based). Part-time jobs available.

ATHLETIC AWARDS Total amount: $2,570,200 (100% non-need-based).

APPLYING FOR FINANCIAL AID *Required financial aid forms:* FAFSA, federal income tax forms. *Financial aid deadline:* Continuous. *Notification date:* Continuous beginning 4/1. Students must reply within 4 weeks of notification.

CONTACT Tamara Allen, Associate Director of Financial Aid, Utah State University, Old Main Hill, Logan, UT 84322, 435-797-3369 or toll-free 800-488-8108. *Fax:* 435-797-0654. *E-mail:* tamara.allen@usu.edu.

UTAH VALLEY UNIVERSITY
Orem, UT

Tuition & fees (UT res): $4258   **Average undergraduate aid package: $7433**

ABOUT THE INSTITUTION State-supported, coed. 90 undergraduate majors. Both federal and institutional methodology are used as a basis for awarding need-based institutional aid.

UNDERGRADUATE EXPENSES for 2010–11 *Tuition, state resident:* full-time $3674; part-time $144.33 per credit hour. *Tuition, nonresident:* full-time $11,304; part-time $471 per credit hour. *Required fees:* full-time $584; $584 per term. Full-time tuition and fees vary according to course load. Part-time tuition and fees vary according to course load. *College room and board:* $8670; *Room only:* $6503. Room and board charges vary according to housing facility. *Payment plans:* Installment, deferred payment.

FRESHMAN FINANCIAL AID (Fall 2009, est.) 1,561 applied for aid; of those 89% were deemed to have need. 95% of freshmen with need received aid; of those 6% had need fully met. *Average percent of need met:* 46% (excluding resources awarded to replace EFC). *Average financial aid package:* $6243 (excluding resources awarded to replace EFC). 15% of all full-time freshmen had no need and received non-need-based gift aid.

UNDERGRADUATE FINANCIAL AID (Fall 2009, est.) 9,424 applied for aid; of those 94% were deemed to have need. 95% of undergraduates with need received aid; of those 4% had need fully met. *Average percent of need met:* 47% (excluding resources awarded to replace EFC). *Average financial aid package:* $7433 (excluding resources awarded to replace EFC). 7% of all full-time undergraduates had no need and received non-need-based gift aid.

GIFT AID (NEED-BASED) *Total amount:* $37,997,077 (98% federal, 2% external sources). *Receiving aid:* Freshmen: 38% (1,009); all full-time undergraduates: 46% (6,599). *Average award:* Freshmen: $4532; Undergraduates: $4710. *Scholarships, grants, and awards:* Federal Pell, FSEOG, state, private, college/university gift aid from institutional funds.

GIFT AID (NON-NEED-BASED) *Total amount:* $668,634 (5% federal, 26% state, 29% institutional, 40% external sources). *Average award:* Freshmen: $3233. Undergraduates: $3050. *Tuition waivers:* Full or partial for employees or children of employees.

LOANS *Student loans:* $70,198,814 (95% need-based, 5% non-need-based). 63% of past graduating class borrowed through all loan programs. *Average indebtedness per student:* $17,274. *Average need-based loan:* Freshmen: $3263. Undergraduates: $4178. *Parent loans:* $942,087 (81% need-based, 19% non-need-based). *Programs:* FFEL (Subsidized and Unsubsidized Stafford, PLUS), Perkins, state, college/university.

WORK-STUDY *Federal work-study:* Total amount: $2,999,944; jobs available. *State or other work-study/employment:* Total amount: $2,479,590 (98% need-based, 2% non-need-based). Part-time jobs available.

ATHLETIC AWARDS Total amount: $902,735 (33% need-based, 67% non-need-based).

APPLYING FOR FINANCIAL AID *Required financial aid forms:* FAFSA, institution's own form. *Financial aid deadline (priority):* 5/1. *Notification date:* Continuous beginning 5/15. Students must reply by 6/15.

CONTACT Joanna McCormick, Senior Director, Utah Valley University, 800 West University Parkway, Orem, UT 84058, 801-863-8442 Ext. 8440. *Fax:* 801-863-8448. *E-mail:* joanna.mccormick@uvu.edu.

U.T.A. MESIVTA OF KIRYAS JOEL
Monroe, NY

CONTACT Financial Aid Office, U.T.A. Mesivta of Kiryas Joel, 9 Nickelsburg Road, Unit 312, Monroe, NY 10950, 845-873-9901.

UTICA COLLEGE
Utica, NY

Tuition & fees: $27,284   **Average undergraduate aid package: $20,690**

ABOUT THE INSTITUTION Independent, coed. 46 undergraduate majors. Federal methodology is used as a basis for awarding need-based institutional aid.

UNDERGRADUATE EXPENSES for 2009–10 *Comprehensive fee:* $38,134 includes full-time tuition ($26,764), mandatory fees ($520), and room and board ($10,850). Full-time tuition and fees vary according to class time and course load. Room and board charges vary according to board plan and housing facility. *Part-time tuition:* $905 per credit hour. Part-time tuition and fees vary according to class time and course load. *Payment plans:* Installment, deferred payment.

FRESHMAN FINANCIAL AID (Fall 2009, est.) 535 applied for aid; of those 94% were deemed to have need. 100% of freshmen with need received aid; of those 8% had need fully met. *Average percent of need met:* 70% (excluding resources awarded to replace EFC). *Average financial aid package:* $22,824 (excluding resources awarded to replace EFC). 5% of all full-time freshmen had no need and received non-need-based gift aid.

UNDERGRADUATE FINANCIAL AID (Fall 2009, est.) 1,943 applied for aid; of those 94% were deemed to have need. 100% of undergraduates with need received aid; of those 11% had need fully met. *Average percent of need met:* 68% (excluding resources awarded to replace EFC). *Average financial aid package:* $20,690 (excluding resources awarded to replace EFC). 7% of all full-time undergraduates had no need and received non-need-based gift aid.

GIFT AID (NEED-BASED) *Total amount:* $28,572,926 (16% federal, 12% state, 70% institutional, 2% external sources). *Receiving aid:* Freshmen: 93% (504); all full-time undergraduates: 90% (1,806). *Average award:* Freshmen: $8635; Undergraduates: $7886. *Scholarships, grants, and awards:* Federal Pell, FSEOG, state, private, college/university gift aid from institutional funds, Federal Nursing.

GIFT AID (NON-NEED-BASED) *Total amount:* $2,254,176 (1% state, 95% institutional, 4% external sources). *Receiving aid:* Freshmen: 5% (27). Undergraduates: 6% (111). *Average award:* Freshmen: $13,203. Undergraduates: $9954. *Scholarships, grants, and awards by category:* Academic interests/achievement: general academic interests/achievements. *Tuition waivers:* Full or partial for employees or children of employees, senior citizens.

LOANS *Student loans:* $14,688,692 (89% need-based, 11% non-need-based). 86% of past graduating class borrowed through all loan programs. *Average indebtedness per student:* $35,534. *Average need-based loan:* Freshmen: $3444. Undergraduates: $4300. *Parent loans:* $5,649,770 (93% need-based, 7% non-need-based). *Programs:* Federal Direct (Subsidized and Unsubsidized Stafford, PLUS), Perkins.

WORK-STUDY *Federal work-study:* Total amount: $879,714; jobs available. *State or other work-study/employment:* Part-time jobs available.

APPLYING FOR FINANCIAL AID *Required financial aid form:* FAFSA. *Financial aid deadline (priority):* 2/15. *Notification date:* Continuous. Students must reply by 5/1 or within 4 weeks of notification.

CONTACT Laura Bedford, Director of Student Financial Services, Utica College, 1600 Burrstone Road, Utica, NY 13502-4892, 315-792-3179 or toll-free 800-782-8884. *Fax:* 315-792-3368. *E-mail:* lbedford@utica.edu.

VALDOSTA STATE UNIVERSITY
Valdosta, GA

Tuition & fees (GA res): $4488   **Average undergraduate aid package: $9152**

ABOUT THE INSTITUTION State-supported, coed. 60 undergraduate majors. Federal methodology is used as a basis for awarding need-based institutional aid.

UNDERGRADUATE EXPENSES for 2010–11 *Tuition, state resident:* full-time $2978; part-time $125 per credit hour. *Tuition, nonresident:* full-time $11,907; part-time $497 per credit hour. *Required fees:* full-time $1510. Part-time tuition and fees vary according to course load. *College room and board:* $6480; *Room only:* $3250. Room and board charges vary according to board plan and housing facility.

FRESHMAN FINANCIAL AID (Fall 2008) 1,781 applied for aid; of those 73% were deemed to have need. 99% of freshmen with need received aid; of those 53% had need fully met. *Average percent of need met:* 90% (excluding

resources awarded to replace EFC). *Average financial aid package:* $11,142 (excluding resources awarded to replace EFC). 2% of all full-time freshmen had no need and received non-need-based gift aid.

UNDERGRADUATE FINANCIAL AID (Fall 2008) 6,481 applied for aid; of those 100% were deemed to have need. 83% of undergraduates with need received aid; of those 48% had need fully met. *Average percent of need met:* 85% (excluding resources awarded to replace EFC). *Average financial aid package:* $9152 (excluding resources awarded to replace EFC). 2% of all full-time undergraduates had no need and received non-need-based gift aid.

GIFT AID (NEED-BASED) *Total amount:* $21,811,054 (55% federal, 41% state, 1% institutional, 3% external sources). *Receiving aid:* Freshmen: 49% (1,019); all full-time undergraduates: 47% (3,990). *Average award:* Freshmen: $5725; Undergraduates: $5345. *Scholarships, grants, and awards:* Federal Pell, FSEOG, state, private, college/university gift aid from institutional funds.

GIFT AID (NON-NEED-BASED) *Total amount:* $8,025,780 (93% state, 2% institutional, 5% external sources). *Receiving aid:* Freshmen: 4% (85). Undergraduates: 3% (245). *Average award:* Freshmen: $2366. Undergraduates: $1585. *Scholarships, grants, and awards by category: Academic interests/ achievement:* biological sciences, business, communication, computer science, education, engineering/technologies, English, foreign languages, general academic interests/achievements, health fields, humanities, library science, mathematics, military science, physical sciences, premedicine, social sciences. *Creative arts/ performance:* art/fine arts, music, theater/drama. *Special achievements/activities:* community service, general special achievements/activities, hobbies/interests. *Special characteristics:* children of public servants, general special characteristics, international students, members of minority groups. *Tuition waivers:* Full or partial for employees or children of employees, senior citizens.

LOANS *Student loans:* $50,124,534 (72% need-based, 28% non-need-based). 65% of past graduating class borrowed through all loan programs. *Average indebtedness per student:* $18,221. *Average need-based loan:* Freshmen: $4457. Undergraduates: $5224. *Parent loans:* $33,990,882 (32% need-based, 68% non-need-based). *Programs:* Federal Direct (Subsidized and Unsubsidized Stafford, PLUS), college/university.

WORK-STUDY *Federal work-study:* Total amount: $499,302; 254 jobs averaging $2755.

ATHLETIC AWARDS Total amount: $952,124 (51% need-based, 49% non-need-based).

APPLYING FOR FINANCIAL AID *Required financial aid form:* FAFSA. *Financial aid deadline (priority):* 5/1. *Notification date:* Continuous beginning 5/15.

CONTACT Mr. Douglas R. Tanner, Director of Financial Aid, Valdosta State University, 1500 North Patterson Street, Valdosta, GA 31698, 229-333-5935 or toll-free 800-618-1878 Ext. 1. *Fax:* 229-333-5430.

VALLEY CITY STATE UNIVERSITY
Valley City, ND

Tuition & fees (ND res): $6075	Average undergraduate aid package: $8480

ABOUT THE INSTITUTION State-supported, coed. 40 undergraduate majors. Federal methodology is used as a basis for awarding need-based institutional aid.

UNDERGRADUATE EXPENSES for 2010–11 *Tuition, state resident:* full-time $4433; part-time $147.76 per semester hour. *Tuition, nonresident:* full-time $11,835; part-time $394.50 per semester hour. *Required fees:* full-time $1642; $68.45 per semester hour. Full-time tuition and fees vary according to course load, location, program, and reciprocity agreements. Part-time tuition and fees vary according to course load, location, program, and reciprocity agreements. *College room and board:* $4528; *Room only:* $1812. Room and board charges vary according to board plan and housing facility.

FRESHMAN FINANCIAL AID (Fall 2009, est.) 126 applied for aid; of those 76% were deemed to have need. 100% of freshmen with need received aid; of those 99% had need fully met. *Average percent of need met:* 80% (excluding resources awarded to replace EFC). *Average financial aid package:* $8770 (excluding resources awarded to replace EFC). 78% of all full-time freshmen had no need and received non-need-based gift aid.

UNDERGRADUATE FINANCIAL AID (Fall 2009, est.) 519 applied for aid; of those 76% were deemed to have need. 100% of undergraduates with need received aid; of those 99% had need fully met. *Average percent of need met:* 76% (excluding resources awarded to replace EFC). *Average financial aid package:* $8480 (excluding resources awarded to replace EFC). 45% of all full-time undergraduates had no need and received non-need-based gift aid.

GIFT AID (NEED-BASED) *Total amount:* $1,711,091 (63% federal, 12% state, 17% institutional, 8% external sources). *Receiving aid:* Freshmen: 58% (90); all full-time undergraduates: 58% (350). *Average award:* Freshmen: $5158; Undergraduates: $4339. *Scholarships, grants, and awards:* Federal Pell, FSEOG, state, private, college/university gift aid from institutional funds.

GIFT AID (NON-NEED-BASED) *Total amount:* $14,115 (42% institutional, 58% external sources). *Receiving aid:* Freshmen: 3% (4). Undergraduates: 1% (5). *Average award:* Freshmen: $2063. Undergraduates: $1761. *Scholarships, grants, and awards by category: Academic interests/achievement:* biological sciences, business, communication, computer science, education, English, general academic interests/achievements, humanities, library science, mathematics, physical sciences, social sciences. *Creative arts/performance:* applied art and design, art/ fine arts, journalism/publications, music, theater/drama. *Special achievements/ activities:* general special achievements/activities. *Special characteristics:* children of faculty/staff, ethnic background, general special characteristics, international students, members of minority groups. *Tuition waivers:* Full or partial for children of alumni, employees or children of employees.

LOANS *Student loans:* $2,732,869 (74% need-based, 26% non-need-based). 88% of past graduating class borrowed through all loan programs. *Average indebtedness per student:* $25,929. *Average need-based loan:* Freshmen: $3201. Undergraduates: $3891. *Parent loans:* $10,800 (1% need-based, 99% non-need-based). *Programs:* FFEL (Subsidized and Unsubsidized Stafford, PLUS), Perkins, college/university.

WORK-STUDY *Federal work-study:* Total amount: $73,690; 50 jobs averaging $1517. *State or other work-study/employment:* Part-time jobs available.

ATHLETIC AWARDS Total amount: $94,034 (49% need-based, 51% non-need-based).

APPLYING FOR FINANCIAL AID *Required financial aid form:* FAFSA. *Financial aid deadline (priority):* 3/15. *Notification date:* Continuous beginning 2/15. Students must reply within 4 weeks of notification.

CONTACT Betty Kuss Schumacher, Director of Student Financial Aid, Valley City State University, 101 College Street SW, Valley City, ND 58072, 701-845-7412 or toll-free 800-532-8641 Ext. 37101. *Fax:* 701-845-7410. *E-mail:* betty.schumacher@vcsu.edu.

VALLEY FORGE CHRISTIAN COLLEGE
Phoenixville, PA

Tuition & fees: $16,250	Average undergraduate aid package: $8841

ABOUT THE INSTITUTION Independent Assemblies of God, coed. 18 undergraduate majors. Federal methodology is used as a basis for awarding need-based institutional aid.

UNDERGRADUATE EXPENSES for 2010–11 *One-time required fee:* $75. *Comprehensive fee:* $23,806 includes full-time tuition ($14,600), mandatory fees ($1650), and room and board ($7556). *College room only:* $3860. *Part-time tuition:* $564 per credit. *Part-time fees:* $250 per term.

FRESHMAN FINANCIAL AID (Fall 2009, est.) 161 applied for aid; of those 93% were deemed to have need. 100% of freshmen with need received aid; of those 5% had need fully met. *Average percent of need met:* 51% (excluding resources awarded to replace EFC). *Average financial aid package:* $10,205 (excluding resources awarded to replace EFC). 11% of all full-time freshmen had no need and received non-need-based gift aid.

UNDERGRADUATE FINANCIAL AID (Fall 2009, est.) 1,189 applied for aid; of those 91% were deemed to have need. 95% of undergraduates with need received aid; of those 8% had need fully met. *Average percent of need met:* 44% (excluding resources awarded to replace EFC). *Average financial aid package:* $8841 (excluding resources awarded to replace EFC). 20% of all full-time undergraduates had no need and received non-need-based gift aid.

GIFT AID (NEED-BASED) *Total amount:* $5,792,397 (46% federal, 14% state, 34% institutional, 6% external sources). *Receiving aid:* Freshmen: 74% (131); all full-time undergraduates: 66% (929). *Average award:* Freshmen: $7150; Undergraduates: $6048. *Scholarships, grants, and awards:* Federal Pell, FSEOG, state, private, college/university gift aid from institutional funds.

GIFT AID (NON-NEED-BASED) *Total amount:* $779,186 (92% institutional, 8% external sources). *Receiving aid:* Freshmen: 2% (3). Undergraduates: 3% (42). *Average award:* Freshmen: $3462. Undergraduates: $2283. *Scholarships, grants, and awards by category: Academic interests/achievement:* 190 awards ($529,549 total): general academic interests/achievements. *Creative arts/performance:* 353 awards ($787,230 total): art/fine arts, music. *Special achievements/activities:* 365 awards ($359,884 total): community service, general special achievements/

activities, leadership, religious involvement. *Special characteristics:* 552 awards ($558,634 total): children of current students, children of faculty/staff, general special characteristics, local/state students, married students, parents of current students, relatives of clergy, siblings of current students, spouses of current students.
LOANS *Student loans:* $8,446,578 (79% need-based, 21% non-need-based). 96% of past graduating class borrowed through all loan programs. *Average indebtedness per student:* $42,894. *Average need-based loan:* Freshmen: $3222. Undergraduates: $3980. *Parent loans:* $3,366,085 (60% need-based, 40% non-need-based). *Programs:* Federal Direct (Subsidized and Unsubsidized Stafford, PLUS), Perkins.
WORK-STUDY *Federal work-study:* Total amount: $70,845; 65 jobs averaging $1090.
APPLYING FOR FINANCIAL AID *Required financial aid form:* FAFSA. *Financial aid deadline (priority):* 5/1. *Notification date:* Continuous beginning 3/1. Students must reply within 3 weeks of notification.
CONTACT Mrs. Linda Stein, Director of Financial Aid, Valley Forge Christian College, 1401 Charlestown Road, Phoenixville, PA 19460-2399, 610-917-1416 or toll-free 800-432-8322. *Fax:* 610-917-2069. *E-mail:* listein@vfcc.edu.

VALLEY FORGE CHRISTIAN COLLEGE WOODBRIDGE CAMPUS
Woodbridge, VA

Tuition & fees: $7150	Average undergraduate aid package: N/A

ABOUT THE INSTITUTION Independent Assemblies of God, coed.
UNDERGRADUATE EXPENSES for 2010–11 *Tuition:* full-time $7150.
GIFT AID (NEED-BASED) *Scholarships, grants, and awards:* Federal Pell, FSEOG.
LOANS *Programs:* FFEL (Subsidized and Unsubsidized Stafford, PLUS), alternative loans.
APPLYING FOR FINANCIAL AID *Required financial aid form:* FAFSA. *Financial aid deadline (priority):* 5/1.
CONTACT Christiana Bruwaa-Frimpong, Student Accounts/Financial Aid Counselor, Valley Forge Christian College Woodbridge Campus, 13909 Smoketown Road, Woodbridge, VA 22192, 703-580-4810 Ext. 172 or toll-free 800-432-8322 (in-state). *Fax:* 703-580-4806.

VALPARAISO UNIVERSITY
Valparaiso, IN

Tuition & fees: $28,320	Average undergraduate aid package: $20,787

ABOUT THE INSTITUTION Independent religious, coed. 87 undergraduate majors. Federal methodology is used as a basis for awarding need-based institutional aid.
UNDERGRADUATE EXPENSES for 2009–10 *Comprehensive fee:* $36,280 includes full-time tuition ($27,360), mandatory fees ($960), and room and board ($7960). *College room only:* $4910. Full-time tuition and fees vary according to course load. Room and board charges vary according to housing facility and student level. *Part-time tuition:* $1240 per credit hour. *Part-time fees:* $25 per credit hour. Part-time tuition and fees vary according to course load. *Payment plans:* Installment, deferred payment.
FRESHMAN FINANCIAL AID (Fall 2008) 598 applied for aid; of those 83% were deemed to have need. 100% of freshmen with need received aid; of those 24% had need fully met. *Average percent of need met:* 82% (excluding resources awarded to replace EFC). *Average financial aid package:* $21,739 (excluding resources awarded to replace EFC). 22% of all full-time freshmen had no need and received non-need-based gift aid.
UNDERGRADUATE FINANCIAL AID (Fall 2008) 2,236 applied for aid; of those 88% were deemed to have need. 100% of undergraduates with need received aid; of those 24% had need fully met. *Average percent of need met:* 81% (excluding resources awarded to replace EFC). *Average financial aid package:* $20,787 (excluding resources awarded to replace EFC). 22% of all full-time undergraduates had no need and received non-need-based gift aid.
GIFT AID (NEED-BASED) *Total amount:* $28,351,684 (11% federal, 11% state, 74% institutional, 4% external sources). *Receiving aid:* Freshmen: 75% (491); all full-time undergraduates: 71% (1,923). *Average award:* Freshmen: $18,200;

Undergraduates: $15,320. *Scholarships, grants, and awards:* Federal Pell, FSEOG, state, private, college/university gift aid from institutional funds.
GIFT AID (NON-NEED-BASED) *Total amount:* $7,180,135 (2% federal, 91% institutional, 7% external sources). *Receiving aid:* Freshmen: 9% (60). Undergraduates: 9% (241). *Average award:* Freshmen: $9268. Undergraduates: $9002. *Scholarships, grants, and awards by category: Academic interests/ achievement:* 2,025 awards ($16,400,000 total): business, engineering/ technologies, foreign languages, general academic interests/achievements, health fields, physical sciences, religion/biblical studies. *Creative arts/performance:* 106 awards ($125,000 total): art/fine arts, music, performing arts, theater/ drama. *Special characteristics:* 407 awards ($2,335,000 total): children and siblings of alumni, children of faculty/staff, international students, relatives of clergy, religious affiliation. *Tuition waivers:* Full or partial for employees or children of employees.
LOANS *Student loans:* $16,243,357 (69% need-based, 31% non-need-based). 73% of past graduating class borrowed through all loan programs. *Average indebtedness per student:* $31,783. *Average need-based loan:* Freshmen: $3980. Undergraduates: $5036. *Parent loans:* $4,216,012 (28% need-based, 72% non-need-based). *Programs:* Federal Direct (Subsidized and Unsubsidized Stafford, PLUS), Perkins, college/university, private loans.
WORK-STUDY *Federal work-study:* Total amount: $1,120,785; 575 jobs averaging $2000. *State or other work-study/employment:* Total amount: $1,559,921 (11% need-based, 89% non-need-based). 511 part-time jobs averaging $2000.
ATHLETIC AWARDS Total amount: $2,842,927 (39% need-based, 61% non-need-based).
APPLYING FOR FINANCIAL AID *Required financial aid form:* FAFSA. *Financial aid deadline (priority):* 3/1. *Notification date:* Continuous beginning 3/1. Students must reply by 5/1.
CONTACT Mr. Robert Helgeson, Director of Financial Aid, Valparaiso University, 1700 Chapel Drive, Valparaiso, IN 46383-6493, 219-464-5015 or toll-free 888-GO-VALPO. *Fax:* 219-464-5012. *E-mail:* robert.helgeson@valpo.edu.

VANDERBILT UNIVERSITY
Nashville, TN

Tuition & fees: $38,578	Average undergraduate aid package: $40,507

ABOUT THE INSTITUTION Independent, coed. 72 undergraduate majors. Both federal and institutional methodology are used as a basis for awarding need-based institutional aid.
UNDERGRADUATE EXPENSES for 2009–10 *One-time required fee:* $620. *Comprehensive fee:* $51,228 includes full-time tuition ($37,632), mandatory fees ($946), and room and board ($12,650). *College room only:* $8200. Room and board charges vary according to board plan. *Part-time tuition:* $1568 per credit hour. *Payment plans:* Tuition prepayment, installment.
FRESHMAN FINANCIAL AID (Fall 2009, est.) 860 applied for aid; of those 86% were deemed to have need. 100% of freshmen with need received aid; of those 100% had need fully met. *Average percent of need met:* 99% (excluding resources awarded to replace EFC). *Average financial aid package:* $41,002 (excluding resources awarded to replace EFC). 8% of all full-time freshmen had no need and received non-need-based gift aid.
UNDERGRADUATE FINANCIAL AID (Fall 2009, est.) 3,198 applied for aid; of those 92% were deemed to have need. 100% of undergraduates with need received aid; of those 100% had need fully met. *Average percent of need met:* 99% (excluding resources awarded to replace EFC). *Average financial aid package:* $40,507 (excluding resources awarded to replace EFC). 9% of all full-time undergraduates had no need and received non-need-based gift aid.
GIFT AID (NEED-BASED) *Total amount:* $114,717,666 (4% federal, 3% state, 91% institutional, 2% external sources). *Receiving aid:* Freshmen: 42% (673); all full-time undergraduates: 41% (2,778). *Average award:* Freshmen: $34,489; Undergraduates: $33,928. *Scholarships, grants, and awards:* Federal Pell, FSEOG, state, private, college/university gift aid from institutional funds.
GIFT AID (NON-NEED-BASED) *Total amount:* $17,790,509 (11% federal, 5% state, 81% institutional, 3% external sources). *Receiving aid:* Freshmen: 26% (412). Undergraduates: 20% (1,342). *Average award:* Freshmen: $20,488. Undergraduates: $20,506. *Scholarships, grants, and awards by category: Academic interests/achievement:* general academic interests/achievements. *Creative arts/performance:* general creative arts/performance. *Special achievements/ activities:* general special achievements/activities, leadership. *Special characteristics:* general special characteristics, local/state students, members of minority groups. *Tuition waivers:* Full or partial for employees or children of employees.

LOANS *Student loans:* $7,636,668 (12% need-based, 88% non-need-based). 40% of past graduating class borrowed through all loan programs. *Average indebtedness per student:* $19,563. *Average need-based loan:* Freshmen: $238. Undergraduates: $526. *Parent loans:* $5,865,986 (100% non-need-based). *Programs:* FFEL (Subsidized and Unsubsidized Stafford, PLUS), Perkins, Federal Nursing, college/university.

WORK-STUDY *Federal work-study:* Total amount: $2,622,272; jobs available. *State or other work-study/employment:* Total amount: $793,978 (100% need-based). Part-time jobs available.

ATHLETIC AWARDS Total amount: $9,277,413 (29% need-based, 71% non-need-based).

APPLYING FOR FINANCIAL AID *Required financial aid forms:* FAFSA, CSS Financial Aid PROFILE. *Financial aid deadline (priority):* 2/1. *Notification date:* 4/1. Students must reply by 5/1.

CONTACT David Mohning, Executive Director of Student Financial Aid, Vanderbilt University, 2309 West End Avenue, Nashville, TN 37235, 615-322-3591 or toll-free 800-288-0432. *Fax:* 615-343-8512. *E-mail:* finaid@vanderbilt.edu.

VANDERCOOK COLLEGE OF MUSIC
Chicago, IL

CONTACT Ms. D. Denny, Director of Financial Aid, VanderCook College of Music, 3140 South Federal Street, Chicago, IL 60616-3731, 312-225-6288 Ext. 233 or toll-free 800-448-2655. *Fax:* 312-225-5211. *E-mail:* ddenny@vandercook.edu.

VANGUARD UNIVERSITY OF SOUTHERN CALIFORNIA
Costa Mesa, CA

Tuition & fees: $26,342	Average undergraduate aid package: $18,766

ABOUT THE INSTITUTION Independent religious, coed. 46 undergraduate majors. Federal methodology is used as a basis for awarding need-based institutional aid.

UNDERGRADUATE EXPENSES for 2010–11 *Comprehensive fee:* $34,616 includes full-time tuition ($26,342) and room and board ($8274). *College room only:* $4074. Full-time tuition and fees vary according to course load. Room and board charges vary according to board plan and housing facility. *Part-time tuition:* $1098 per unit. Part-time tuition and fees vary according to course load. *Payment plan:* Installment.

FRESHMAN FINANCIAL AID (Fall 2009, est.) 372 applied for aid; of those 90% were deemed to have need. 100% of freshmen with need received aid; of those 13% had need fully met. *Average percent of need met:* 72% (excluding resources awarded to replace EFC). *Average financial aid package:* $19,528 (excluding resources awarded to replace EFC). 13% of all full-time freshmen had no need and received non-need-based gift aid.

UNDERGRADUATE FINANCIAL AID (Fall 2009, est.) 1,085 applied for aid; of those 89% were deemed to have need. 100% of undergraduates with need received aid; of those 15% had need fully met. *Average percent of need met:* 68% (excluding resources awarded to replace EFC). *Average financial aid package:* $18,766 (excluding resources awarded to replace EFC). 16% of all full-time undergraduates had no need and received non-need-based gift aid.

GIFT AID (NEED-BASED) *Total amount:* $13,122,528 (14% federal, 16% state, 67% institutional, 3% external sources). *Receiving aid:* Freshmen: 63% (283); all full-time undergraduates: 64% (780). *Average award:* Freshmen: $8132; Undergraduates: $9347. *Scholarships, grants, and awards:* Federal Pell, FSEOG, state, private, college/university gift aid from institutional funds.

GIFT AID (NON-NEED-BASED) *Total amount:* $1,806,309 (94% institutional, 6% external sources). *Receiving aid:* Freshmen: 69% (313). Undergraduates: 65% (796). *Average award:* Freshmen: $8805. Undergraduates: $8187. *Scholarships, grants, and awards by category:* Academic interests/achievement: 868 awards ($5,899,176 total): general academic interests/achievements. *Creative arts/performance:* 246 awards ($642,465 total): debating, music, theater/drama. *Special characteristics:* 28 awards ($485,843 total): children of faculty/staff. *Tuition waivers:* Full or partial for employees or children of employees.

LOANS *Student loans:* $8,369,873 (76% need-based, 24% non-need-based). 77% of past graduating class borrowed through all loan programs. *Average indebtedness per student:* $26,435. *Average need-based loan:* Freshmen: $4105.

Undergraduates: $4681. *Parent loans:* $2,762,095 (41% need-based, 59% non-need-based). *Programs:* FFEL (Subsidized and Unsubsidized Stafford, PLUS), Perkins.

WORK-STUDY *Federal work-study:* Total amount: $421,017; 148 jobs averaging $2960.

ATHLETIC AWARDS Total amount: $1,846,095 (41% need-based, 59% non-need-based).

APPLYING FOR FINANCIAL AID *Required financial aid forms:* FAFSA, state aid form. *Financial aid deadline (priority):* 3/2. *Notification date:* Continuous beginning 3/15. Students must reply within 3 weeks of notification.

CONTACT Undergraduate Admissions Office, Vanguard University of Southern California, 55 Fair Drive, Costa Mesa, CA 92626-6597, 800-722-6279. *Fax:* 714-966-5471. *E-mail:* admissions@vanguard.edu.

VASSAR COLLEGE
Poughkeepsie, NY

Tuition & fees: $41,930	Average undergraduate aid package: $37,512

ABOUT THE INSTITUTION Independent, coed. 52 undergraduate majors. Institutional methodology is used as a basis for awarding need-based institutional aid.

UNDERGRADUATE EXPENSES for 2009–10 *Comprehensive fee:* $51,300 includes full-time tuition ($41,335), mandatory fees ($595), and room and board ($9370). *College room only:* $5090. Room and board charges vary according to board plan and housing facility. *Part-time tuition:* $4890 per course. Part-time tuition and fees vary according to course load. *Payment plan:* Installment.

FRESHMAN FINANCIAL AID (Fall 2009, est.) 478 applied for aid; of those 83% were deemed to have need. 100% of freshmen with need received aid; of those 100% had need fully met. *Average percent of need met:* 100% (excluding resources awarded to replace EFC). *Average financial aid package:* $39,069 (excluding resources awarded to replace EFC).

UNDERGRADUATE FINANCIAL AID (Fall 2009, est.) 1,643 applied for aid; of those 87% were deemed to have need. 100% of undergraduates with need received aid; of those 100% had need fully met. *Average percent of need met:* 100% (excluding resources awarded to replace EFC). *Average financial aid package:* $37,512 (excluding resources awarded to replace EFC).

GIFT AID (NEED-BASED) *Total amount:* $46,885,544 (5% federal, 1% state, 92% institutional, 2% external sources). *Receiving aid:* Freshmen: 60% (399); all full-time undergraduates: 56% (1,432). *Average award:* Freshmen: $35,696; Undergraduates: $33,155. *Scholarships, grants, and awards:* Federal Pell, FSEOG, state, private, college/university gift aid from institutional funds.

GIFT AID (NON-NEED-BASED) *Total amount:* $162,356 (7% federal, 19% state, 74% external sources). *Tuition waivers:* Full or partial for employees or children of employees.

LOANS *Student loans:* $3,351,051 (48% need-based, 52% non-need-based). 49% of past graduating class borrowed through all loan programs. *Average indebtedness per student:* $18,876. *Average need-based loan:* Freshmen: $1754. Undergraduates: $2614. *Parent loans:* $2,935,657 (100% non-need-based). *Programs:* Federal Direct (Subsidized and Unsubsidized Stafford, PLUS), Perkins.

WORK-STUDY *Federal work-study:* Total amount: $1,700,840; jobs available. *State or other work-study/employment:* Total amount: $638,767 (95% need-based, 5% non-need-based). Part-time jobs available.

APPLYING FOR FINANCIAL AID *Required financial aid forms:* FAFSA, CSS Financial Aid PROFILE, noncustodial (divorced/separated) parent's statement, business/farm supplement. *Financial aid deadline:* 2/1. *Notification date:* 3/29. Students must reply by 5/1.

CONTACT Mr. Michael Fraher, Director of Financial Aid, Vassar College, 124 Raymond Avenue, Poughkeepsie, NY 12604, 845-437-5320 or toll-free 800-827-7270. *Fax:* 845-437-5325. *E-mail:* mafraher@vassar.edu.

VAUGHN COLLEGE OF AERONAUTICS AND TECHNOLOGY
Flushing, NY

ABOUT THE INSTITUTION Independent, coed, primarily men. 11 undergraduate majors.

Vaughn College of Aeronautics and Technology

GIFT AID (NEED-BASED) *Scholarships, grants, and awards:* Federal Pell, FSEOG, state, private, college/university gift aid from institutional funds, Academic Competitiveness Grants, National SMART Grants, TEACH Grants.

GIFT AID (NON-NEED-BASED) *Scholarships, grants, and awards by category: Academic interests/achievement:* computer science, education, engineering/technologies. *Special characteristics:* veterans, veterans' children.

LOANS *Programs:* Federal Direct (Subsidized and Unsubsidized Stafford, PLUS), FFEL (Subsidized and Unsubsidized Stafford, PLUS), private loans.

WORK-STUDY *Federal work-study:* Total amount: $21,510; 25 jobs averaging $3000. *State or other work-study/employment:* Part-time jobs available.

APPLYING FOR FINANCIAL AID *Required financial aid forms:* FAFSA, state aid form.

CONTACT Dorothy Martin, Director of Financial Aid, Vaughn College of Aeronautics and Technology, 86-01 23rd Avenue, Flushing, NY 11369, 718-429-6600 Ext. 187 or toll-free 800-776-2376 Ext. 145 (in-state). *Fax:* 718-779-2231. *E-mail:* dorothy.martin@vaughn.edu.

VERMONT TECHNICAL COLLEGE
Randolph Center, VT

Tuition & fees (VT res): $10,892   **Average undergraduate aid package: $8152**

ABOUT THE INSTITUTION State-supported, coed. 23 undergraduate majors. Federal methodology is used as a basis for awarding need-based institutional aid.

UNDERGRADUATE EXPENSES for 2009–10 *Tuition, state resident:* full-time $9960; part-time $415 per credit. *Tuition, nonresident:* full-time $19,008; part-time $792 per credit. *Required fees:* full-time $932. Full-time tuition and fees vary according to course load and program. Part-time tuition and fees vary according to program. *College room and board:* $7808. Room and board charges vary according to board plan. *Payment plan:* Installment.

FRESHMAN FINANCIAL AID (Fall 2009, est.) 260 applied for aid; of those 85% were deemed to have need. 99% of freshmen with need received aid; of those 15% had need fully met. *Average percent of need met:* 68% (excluding resources awarded to replace EFC). *Average financial aid package:* $8194 (excluding resources awarded to replace EFC). 9% of all full-time freshmen had no need and received non-need-based gift aid.

UNDERGRADUATE FINANCIAL AID (Fall 2009, est.) 1,028 applied for aid; of those 86% were deemed to have need. 99% of undergraduates with need received aid; of those 13% had need fully met. *Average percent of need met:* 68% (excluding resources awarded to replace EFC). *Average financial aid package:* $8152 (excluding resources awarded to replace EFC). 2% of all full-time undergraduates had no need and received non-need-based gift aid.

GIFT AID (NEED-BASED) *Total amount:* $4,141,175 (39% federal, 25% state, 16% institutional, 20% external sources). *Receiving aid:* Freshmen: 64% (185); all full-time undergraduates: 55% (673). *Average award:* Freshmen: $5420; Undergraduates: $5272. *Scholarships, grants, and awards:* Federal Pell, FSEOG, state, private, college/university gift aid from institutional funds.

GIFT AID (NON-NEED-BASED) *Total amount:* $604,851 (25% institutional, 75% external sources). *Receiving aid:* Freshmen: 3% (9). Undergraduates: 3% (33). *Average award:* Freshmen: $4184. Undergraduates: $4632. *Scholarships, grants, and awards by category: Academic interests/achievement:* 40 awards ($286,860 total): agriculture, general academic interests/achievements. *Tuition waivers:* Full or partial for employees or children of employees.

LOANS *Student loans:* $9,481,446 (84% need-based, 16% non-need-based). 80% of past graduating class borrowed through all loan programs. *Average indebtedness per student:* $26,000. *Average need-based loan:* Freshmen: $3310. Undergraduates: $3484. *Parent loans:* $2,146,023 (63% need-based, 37% non-need-based). *Programs:* Federal Direct (Subsidized and Unsubsidized Stafford, PLUS), FFEL (Subsidized and Unsubsidized Stafford, PLUS), Perkins.

WORK-STUDY *Federal work-study:* Total amount: $144,245; 144 jobs averaging $1000.

APPLYING FOR FINANCIAL AID *Required financial aid forms:* FAFSA, state aid form. *Financial aid deadline (priority):* 3/1. *Notification date:* Continuous beginning 3/19.

CONTACT Catherine R. McCullough, Director of Financial Aid, Vermont Technical College, PO Box 500, Randolph Center, VT 05061-0500, 802-728-1248 or toll-free 800-442-VTC1. *Fax:* 802-728-1390.

VICTORY UNIVERSITY
Memphis, TN

Tuition & fees: $10,320   **Average undergraduate aid package: $4709**

ABOUT THE INSTITUTION Independent, coed. 13 undergraduate majors. Federal methodology is used as a basis for awarding need-based institutional aid.

UNDERGRADUATE EXPENSES for 2009–10 *Tuition:* full-time $9750; part-time $325 per credit hour. Full-time tuition and fees vary according to course load. Part-time tuition and fees vary according to course load. *Payment plan:* Installment.

FRESHMAN FINANCIAL AID (Fall 2009, est.) 8 applied for aid; of those 100% were deemed to have need. 100% of freshmen with need received aid. *Average percent of need met:* 51% (excluding resources awarded to replace EFC). *Average financial aid package:* $4212 (excluding resources awarded to replace EFC).

UNDERGRADUATE FINANCIAL AID (Fall 2009, est.) 465 applied for aid; of those 92% were deemed to have need. 100% of undergraduates with need received aid; of those 2% had need fully met. *Average percent of need met:* 47% (excluding resources awarded to replace EFC). *Average financial aid package:* $4709 (excluding resources awarded to replace EFC).

GIFT AID (NEED-BASED) *Total amount:* $2,780,520 (82% federal, 18% state). *Receiving aid:* Freshmen: 70% (7); all full-time undergraduates: 73% (355). *Average award:* Freshmen: $2903; Undergraduates: $3146. *Scholarships, grants, and awards:* Federal Pell, FSEOG, state, private.

GIFT AID (NON-NEED-BASED) *Total amount:* $139,262 (13% federal, 50% state, 37% external sources). *Receiving aid:* Freshmen: 30% (3). Undergraduates: 7% (35). *Tuition waivers:* Full or partial for employees or children of employees, senior citizens.

LOANS *Student loans:* $6,220,604 (31% need-based, 69% non-need-based). 58% of past graduating class borrowed through all loan programs. *Average indebtedness per student:* $21,505. *Average need-based loan:* Freshmen: $1750. Undergraduates: $2226. *Parent loans:* $45,650 (100% non-need-based). *Programs:* Federal Direct (Subsidized and Unsubsidized Stafford, PLUS).

WORK-STUDY *Federal work-study:* Total amount: $92,165; 45 jobs averaging $2048.

APPLYING FOR FINANCIAL AID *Required financial aid form:* FAFSA. *Financial aid deadline (priority):* 2/15. *Notification date:* Continuous beginning 4/1. Students must reply within 2 weeks of notification.

CONTACT Ms. LaTonya Branch, Financial Aid Director, Victory University, 255 North Highland, Memphis, TN 38111, 901-320-9787 Ext. 1032 or toll-free 800-960-9777. *Fax:* 901-320-9724. *E-mail:* lbranch@victory.edu.

VILLA MARIA COLLEGE OF BUFFALO
Buffalo, NY

Tuition & fees: $14,380   **Average undergraduate aid package: $7328**

ABOUT THE INSTITUTION Independent religious, coed. 16 undergraduate majors. Federal methodology is used as a basis for awarding need-based institutional aid.

UNDERGRADUATE EXPENSES for 2009–10 *Tuition:* full-time $14,380; part-time $485 per credit. *Required fees:* $125 per term. Full-time tuition and fees vary according to course level, course load, degree level, program, and student level. Part-time tuition and fees vary according to course level, course load, degree level, program, and student level. *Payment plan:* Installment.

FRESHMAN FINANCIAL AID (Fall 2009, est.) 143 applied for aid; of those 90% were deemed to have need. 100% of freshmen with need received aid. *Average percent of need met:* 50% (excluding resources awarded to replace EFC). *Average financial aid package:* $5335 (excluding resources awarded to replace EFC). 5% of all full-time freshmen had no need and received non-need-based gift aid.

UNDERGRADUATE FINANCIAL AID (Fall 2009, est.) 408 applied for aid; of those 75% were deemed to have need. 100% of undergraduates with need received aid; of those 4% had need fully met. *Average percent of need met:* 50% (excluding resources awarded to replace EFC). *Average financial aid package:* $7328 (excluding resources awarded to replace EFC). 4% of all full-time undergraduates had no need and received non-need-based gift aid.

GIFT AID (NEED-BASED) *Total amount:* $2,477,820 (49% federal, 35% state, 11% institutional, 5% external sources). *Receiving aid:* Freshmen: 72% (106);

all full-time undergraduates: 61% (253). *Average award:* Freshmen: $2856; Undergraduates: $4971. *Scholarships, grants, and awards:* Federal Pell, FSEOG, state, private, college/university gift aid from institutional funds.

GIFT AID (NON-NEED-BASED) *Receiving aid:* Freshmen: 16% (24). Undergraduates: 15% (63). *Average award:* Freshmen: $1500. Undergraduates: $1333. *Tuition waivers:* Full or partial for employees or children of employees.

LOANS *Student loans:* $3,075,218 (100% need-based). *Average need-based loan:* Freshmen: $2677. Undergraduates: $4195. *Parent loans:* $423,935 (100% need-based). *Programs:* Federal Direct (Subsidized and Unsubsidized Stafford, PLUS), private loans.

WORK-STUDY *Federal work-study:* Total amount: $27,936; 65 jobs averaging $430.

APPLYING FOR FINANCIAL AID *Required financial aid forms:* FAFSA, state aid form. *Financial aid deadline:* Continuous. *Notification date:* Continuous beginning 5/1. Students must reply within 3 weeks of notification.

CONTACT Christina Horner, Director of Financial Aid, Villa Maria College of Buffalo, 240 Pine Ridge Road, Buffalo, NY 14225, 716-961-1849. *Fax:* 716-896-0705. *E-mail:* chorner@villa.edu.

VILLANOVA UNIVERSITY
Villanova, PA

Tuition & fees: $38,305	Average undergraduate aid package: $26,967

ABOUT THE INSTITUTION Independent Roman Catholic, coed. 45 undergraduate majors. Both federal and institutional methodology are used as a basis for awarding need-based institutional aid.

UNDERGRADUATE EXPENSES for 2009–10 *Comprehensive fee:* $48,625 includes full-time tuition ($37,725), mandatory fees ($580), and room and board ($10,320). *College room only:* $5460. Full-time tuition and fees vary according to class time, course level, program, and student level. Room and board charges vary according to board plan and housing facility. *Part-time tuition:* $1545 per course. Part-time tuition and fees vary according to class time, course level, and program. *Payment plan:* Installment.

FRESHMAN FINANCIAL AID (Fall 2009, est.) 1,187 applied for aid; of those 73% were deemed to have need. 100% of freshmen with need received aid; of those 27% had need fully met. *Average percent of need met:* 87% (excluding resources awarded to replace EFC). *Average financial aid package:* $30,122 (excluding resources awarded to replace EFC). 8% of all full-time freshmen had no need and received non-need-based gift aid.

UNDERGRADUATE FINANCIAL AID (Fall 2009, est.) 3,691 applied for aid; of those 87% were deemed to have need. 99% of undergraduates with need received aid; of those 19% had need fully met. *Average percent of need met:* 80% (excluding resources awarded to replace EFC). *Average financial aid package:* $26,967 (excluding resources awarded to replace EFC). 7% of all full-time undergraduates had no need and received non-need-based gift aid.

GIFT AID (NEED-BASED) *Total amount:* $63,549,512 (10% federal, 2% state, 85% institutional, 3% external sources). *Receiving aid:* Freshmen: 49% (810); all full-time undergraduates: 42% (2,798). *Average award:* Freshmen: $25,493; Undergraduates: $22,101. *Scholarships, grants, and awards:* Federal Pell, FSEOG, state, private, college/university gift aid from institutional funds, endowed and restricted grants.

GIFT AID (NON-NEED-BASED) *Total amount:* $8,820,399 (31% federal, 56% institutional, 13% external sources). *Receiving aid:* Freshmen: 16% (260). Undergraduates: 13% (883). *Average award:* Freshmen: $8492. Undergraduates: $11,337. *Scholarships, grants, and awards by category:* Academic interests/achievement: 846 awards ($6,308,977 total): general academic interests/achievements, international studies, military science. *Special achievements/activities:* 22 awards ($21,500 total): general special achievements/activities. *Special characteristics:* 263 awards ($7,639,500 total): children of educators, children of faculty/staff, general special characteristics, members of minority groups, religious affiliation. *Tuition waivers:* Full or partial for employees or children of employees, senior citizens.

LOANS *Student loans:* $35,465,251 (81% need-based, 19% non-need-based). 55% of past graduating class borrowed through all loan programs. *Average indebtedness per student:* $31,048. *Average need-based loan:* Freshmen: $3462. Undergraduates: $4643. *Parent loans:* $14,053,134 (72% need-based, 28% non-need-based). *Programs:* FFEL (Subsidized and Unsubsidized Stafford, PLUS), Perkins, Federal Nursing, Villanova Loan.

WORK-STUDY *Federal work-study:* Total amount: $6,815,663; 2,618 jobs averaging $2542. *State or other work-study/employment:* 55 part-time jobs averaging $2881.

ATHLETIC AWARDS Total amount: $9,337,839 (28% need-based, 72% non-need-based).

APPLYING FOR FINANCIAL AID *Required financial aid forms:* FAFSA, institution's own form, CSS Financial Aid PROFILE, federal income tax forms, W-2 forms. *Financial aid deadline (priority):* 2/1. *Notification date:* 4/1. Students must reply by 5/1.

CONTACT Bonnie Lee Behm, Director of Financial Assistance, Villanova University, 800 Lancaster Avenue, Villanova, PA 19085-1699, 610-519-4010. *Fax:* 610-519-7599. *E-mail:* bonnie.behm@villanova.edu.

VIRGINIA COLLEGE AT BIRMINGHAM
Birmingham, AL

CONTACT Vice President, Campus Administration, Virginia College at Birmingham, 65 Bagby Drive, Birmingham, AL 35209, 205-802-1200. *Fax:* 205-271-8273.

VIRGINIA COLLEGE AT HUNTSVILLE
Huntsville, AL

CONTACT David W. Hall, Student Finance Director, Virginia College at Huntsville, 2800-A Bob Wallace Avenue, Huntsville, AL 35805, 205-533-7387 Ext. 106. *Fax:* 205-533-7785.

VIRGINIA COMMONWEALTH UNIVERSITY
Richmond, VA

Tuition & fees (VA res): $7117	Average undergraduate aid package: $8344

ABOUT THE INSTITUTION State-supported, coed. 60 undergraduate majors. Federal methodology is used as a basis for awarding need-based institutional aid.

UNDERGRADUATE EXPENSES for 2009–10 *Tuition, state resident:* full-time $5253; part-time $221 per credit hour. *Tuition, nonresident:* full-time $18,477; part-time $772 per credit hour. *Required fees:* full-time $1864; $73.20 per credit hour. *College room and board:* $8335; *Room only:* $5059. Room and board charges vary according to board plan. *Payment plan:* Installment.

FRESHMAN FINANCIAL AID (Fall 2008) 2,274 applied for aid; of those 76% were deemed to have need. 100% of freshmen with need received aid; of those 11% had need fully met. *Average percent of need met:* 58% (excluding resources awarded to replace EFC). *Average financial aid package:* $8381 (excluding resources awarded to replace EFC). 11% of all full-time freshmen had no need and received non-need-based gift aid.

UNDERGRADUATE FINANCIAL AID (Fall 2008) 10,469 applied for aid; of those 79% were deemed to have need. 100% of undergraduates with need received aid; of those 12% had need fully met. *Average percent of need met:* 59% (excluding resources awarded to replace EFC). *Average financial aid package:* $8344 (excluding resources awarded to replace EFC). 7% of all full-time undergraduates had no need and received non-need-based gift aid.

GIFT AID (NEED-BASED) *Total amount:* $39,341,464 (41% federal, 41% state, 8% institutional, 10% external sources). *Receiving aid:* Freshmen: 31% (1,183); all full-time undergraduates: 34% (6,088). *Average award:* Freshmen: $5344; Undergraduates: $4830. *Scholarships, grants, and awards:* Federal Pell, FSEOG, state, private, college/university gift aid from institutional funds, United Negro College Fund.

GIFT AID (NON-NEED-BASED) *Total amount:* $7,846,029 (4% federal, 2% state, 25% institutional, 69% external sources). *Receiving aid:* Freshmen: 23% (884). Undergraduates: 14% (2,463). *Average award:* Freshmen: $2854. Undergraduates: $5615. *Scholarships, grants, and awards by category:* Academic interests/achievement: 2,460 awards ($7,870,454 total): biological sciences, business, computer science, education, engineering/technologies, foreign languages, general academic interests/achievements, health fields, humanities, mathematics, military science, physical sciences. *Creative arts/performance:* 121 awards ($209,070 total): art/fine arts, dance, music, performing arts, theater/drama. *Special characteristics:* 57 awards ($399,055 total): veterans' children. *Tuition waivers:* Full or partial for employees or children of employees, senior citizens.

Virginia Commonwealth University

LOANS *Student loans:* $88,652,312 (77% need-based, 23% non-need-based). 61% of past graduating class borrowed through all loan programs. *Average indebtedness per student:* $22,864. *Average need-based loan:* Freshmen: $3427. Undergraduates: $4177. *Parent loans:* $10,104,562 (66% need-based, 34% non-need-based). *Programs:* Federal Direct (Subsidized and Unsubsidized Stafford, PLUS), Perkins, Federal Nursing, college/university.

WORK-STUDY *Federal work-study:* Total amount: $672,509; 398 jobs averaging $1773. *State or other work-study/employment:* Total amount: $1055 (100% non-need-based). Part-time jobs available.

ATHLETIC AWARDS Total amount: $2,631,966 (28% need-based, 72% non-need-based).

APPLYING FOR FINANCIAL AID *Required financial aid form:* FAFSA. *Financial aid deadline (priority):* 3/1. *Notification date:* Continuous beginning 4/1. Students must reply within 2 weeks of notification.

CONTACT Financial Aid Office, Virginia Commonwealth University, 901 West Franklin Street, Richmond, VA 23284-3026, 804-828-6669 or toll-free 800-841-3638. *Fax:* 804-827-0060. *E-mail:* faidmail@vcu.edu.

VIRGINIA INTERMONT COLLEGE
Bristol, VA

Tuition & fees: $23,373	Average undergraduate aid package: $15,499

ABOUT THE INSTITUTION Independent religious, coed. 36 undergraduate majors. Federal methodology is used as a basis for awarding need-based institutional aid.

UNDERGRADUATE EXPENSES for 2010–11 *Comprehensive fee:* $30,697 includes full-time tuition ($23,373) and room and board ($7324). *College room only:* $3581. Full-time tuition and fees vary according to class time, program, reciprocity agreements, and student level. Room and board charges vary according to housing facility. *Part-time tuition:* $240 per credit hour. Part-time tuition and fees vary according to class time, course level, course load, program, reciprocity agreements, and student level. *Payment plan:* Installment.

FRESHMAN FINANCIAL AID (Fall 2009, est.) 99 applied for aid; of those 89% were deemed to have need. 100% of freshmen with need received aid; of those 11% had need fully met. *Average percent of need met:* 74% (excluding resources awarded to replace EFC). *Average financial aid package:* $18,862 (excluding resources awarded to replace EFC). 18% of all full-time freshmen had no need and received non-need-based gift aid.

UNDERGRADUATE FINANCIAL AID (Fall 2009, est.) 479 applied for aid; of those 93% were deemed to have need. 100% of undergraduates with need received aid; of those 5% had need fully met. *Average percent of need met:* 60% (excluding resources awarded to replace EFC). *Average financial aid package:* $15,499 (excluding resources awarded to replace EFC). 11% of all full-time undergraduates had no need and received non-need-based gift aid.

GIFT AID (NEED-BASED) *Total amount:* $4,146,871 (24% federal, 17% state, 52% institutional, 7% external sources). *Receiving aid:* Freshmen: 44% (46); all full-time undergraduates: 44% (232). *Average award:* Freshmen: $4359; Undergraduates: $11,767. *Scholarships, grants, and awards:* Federal Pell, FSEOG, state, private, college/university gift aid from institutional funds.

GIFT AID (NON-NEED-BASED) *Total amount:* $660,898 (12% state, 87% institutional, 1% external sources). *Receiving aid:* Freshmen: 81% (85). Undergraduates: 61% (321). *Average award:* Freshmen: $9032. Undergraduates: $8961. *Scholarships, grants, and awards by category:* Academic interests/achievement: general academic interests/achievements. Creative arts/performance: applied art and design, art/fine arts, dance, general creative arts/performance, music, performing arts, theater/drama. Special achievements/activities: cheerleading/drum major, religious involvement. Special characteristics: children of faculty/staff, first-generation college students, members of minority groups, religious affiliation. *Tuition waivers:* Full or partial for employees or children of employees, senior citizens.

LOANS *Student loans:* $3,393,324 (89% need-based, 11% non-need-based). 76% of past graduating class borrowed through all loan programs. *Average indebtedness per student:* $16,337. *Average need-based loan:* Freshmen: $3437. Undergraduates: $3853. *Parent loans:* $907,392 (51% need-based, 49% non-need-based). *Programs:* Federal Direct (Subsidized and Unsubsidized Stafford, PLUS), Perkins, alternative loans.

WORK-STUDY *Federal work-study:* Total amount: $151,660; 98 jobs averaging $1000.

ATHLETIC AWARDS Total amount: $966,640 (87% need-based, 13% non-need-based).

APPLYING FOR FINANCIAL AID *Required financial aid forms:* FAFSA, state aid form. *Financial aid deadline (priority):* 2/15. *Notification date:* Continuous beginning 2/15. Students must reply within 2 weeks of notification.

CONTACT Ms. Denise Posey, Director of Financial Aid, Virginia Intermont College, 1013 Moore Street, Bristol, VA 24201-4298, 276-466-7872 or toll-free 800-451-1842. *Fax:* 276-466-7855.

VIRGINIA INTERNATIONAL UNIVERSITY
Fairfax, VA

CONTACT Financial Aid Office, Virginia International University, 11200 Waples Mill Road, Fairfax, VA 22030, 703-591-7042 or toll-free 800-514 6848.

VIRGINIA MILITARY INSTITUTE
Lexington, VA

Tuition & fees (VA res): $11,190	Average undergraduate aid package: $19,330

ABOUT THE INSTITUTION State-supported, coed, primarily men. 14 undergraduate majors. Federal methodology is used as a basis for awarding need-based institutional aid.

UNDERGRADUATE EXPENSES for 2009–10 *One-time required fee:* $2368. *Tuition, state resident:* full-time $5500. *Tuition, nonresident:* full-time $23,048. *Required fees:* full-time $5690. *College room and board:* $6792. *Payment plan:* Installment.

FRESHMAN FINANCIAL AID (Fall 2008) 291 applied for aid; of those 66% were deemed to have need. 98% of freshmen with need received aid; of those 65% had need fully met. *Average percent of need met:* 90% (excluding resources awarded to replace EFC). *Average financial aid package:* $17,634 (excluding resources awarded to replace EFC). 16% of all full-time freshmen had no need and received non-need-based gift aid.

UNDERGRADUATE FINANCIAL AID (Fall 2008) 861 applied for aid; of those 73% were deemed to have need. 99% of undergraduates with need received aid; of those 65% had need fully met. *Average percent of need met:* 90% (excluding resources awarded to replace EFC). *Average financial aid package:* $19,330 (excluding resources awarded to replace EFC). 21% of all full-time undergraduates had no need and received non-need-based gift aid.

GIFT AID (NEED-BASED) *Total amount:* $4,842,754 (18% federal, 15% state, 63% institutional, 4% external sources). *Receiving aid:* Freshmen: 44% (184); all full-time undergraduates: 42% (610). *Average award:* Freshmen: $16,228; Undergraduates: $15,802. *Scholarships, grants, and awards:* Federal Pell, FSEOG, state, private, college/university gift aid from institutional funds.

GIFT AID (NON-NEED-BASED) *Total amount:* $8,949,991 (83% federal, 15% institutional, 2% external sources). *Receiving aid:* Freshmen: 27% (114). Undergraduates: 25% (360). *Average award:* Freshmen: $14,728. Undergraduates: $14,966. *Scholarships, grants, and awards by category:* Academic interests/achievement: 75 awards ($800,000 total): biological sciences, business, computer science, engineering/technologies, English, general academic interests/achievements, international studies, mathematics, military science, premedicine. Creative arts/performance: 12 awards ($7500 total): music. Special achievements/activities: 20 awards ($75,000 total): general special achievements/activities, leadership. Special characteristics: 315 awards ($1,050,000 total): children and siblings of alumni, children of faculty/staff, general special characteristics, local/state students, out-of-state students. *Tuition waivers:* Full or partial for senior citizens.

LOANS *Student loans:* $3,338,173 (37% need-based, 63% non-need-based). 34% of past graduating class borrowed through all loan programs. *Average indebtedness per student:* $19,046. *Average need-based loan:* Freshmen: $4033. Undergraduates: $4053. *Parent loans:* $1,558,842 (100% non-need-based). *Programs:* Federal Direct (Subsidized and Unsubsidized Stafford, PLUS), Perkins.

WORK-STUDY *Federal work-study:* Total amount: $3598; 5 jobs averaging $719.

ATHLETIC AWARDS Total amount: $2,771,304 (31% need-based, 69% non-need-based).

APPLYING FOR FINANCIAL AID *Required financial aid forms:* FAFSA, institution's own form. *Financial aid deadline (priority):* 3/1. *Notification date:* Continuous beginning 3/15. Students must reply by 5/1.

CONTACT Col. Timothy P. Golden, Director of Financial Aid, Virginia Military Institute, 306 Carroll Hall, Lexington, VA 24450, 540-464-7208 or toll-free 800-767-4207. *Fax:* 540-464-7629. *E-mail:* goldentp@vmi.edu.

VIRGINIA POLYTECHNIC INSTITUTE AND STATE UNIVERSITY
Blacksburg, VA

Tuition & fees: N/R **Average undergraduate aid package:** $10,909

ABOUT THE INSTITUTION State-supported, coed. 66 undergraduate majors. Federal methodology is used as a basis for awarding need-based institutional aid.

FRESHMAN FINANCIAL AID (Fall 2008) 3,837 applied for aid; of those 59% were deemed to have need. 89% of freshmen with need received aid; of those 18% had need fully met. *Average percent of need met:* 63% (excluding resources awarded to replace EFC). *Average financial aid package:* $11,315 (excluding resources awarded to replace EFC). 12% of all full-time freshmen had no need and received non-need-based gift aid.

UNDERGRADUATE FINANCIAL AID (Fall 2008) 13,931 applied for aid; of those 61% were deemed to have need. 97% of undergraduates with need received aid; of those 26% had need fully met. *Average percent of need met:* 71% (excluding resources awarded to replace EFC). *Average financial aid package:* $10,909 (excluding resources awarded to replace EFC). 9% of all full-time undergraduates had no need and received non-need-based gift aid.

GIFT AID (NEED-BASED) *Total amount:* $33,899,872 (33% federal, 38% state, 7% institutional, 22% external sources). *Receiving aid:* Freshmen: 26% (1,407); all full-time undergraduates: 27% (6,218). *Average award:* Freshmen: $6653; Undergraduates: $5579. *Scholarships, grants, and awards:* Federal Pell, FSEOG, state, college/university gift aid from institutional funds.

GIFT AID (NON-NEED-BASED) *Total amount:* $32,441,860 (24% institutional, 76% external sources). *Receiving aid:* Freshmen: 8% (449). Undergraduates: 6% (1,458). *Average award:* Freshmen: $2853. Undergraduates: $2667. *Scholarships, grants, and awards by category: Academic interests/achievement:* library science. *Creative arts/performance:* applied-art and design, art/fine arts, cinema/film/broadcasting, creative writing, journalism/publications, music, performing arts, theater/drama. *Special achievements/activities:* cheerleading/drum major, community service, general special achievements/activities, leadership, memberships, religious involvement. *Special characteristics:* children of faculty/staff, first-generation college students, local/state students, members of minority groups, out-of-state students, twins, veterans' children. *Tuition waivers:* Full or partial for senior citizens.

LOANS *Student loans:* $81,180,017 (34% need-based, 66% non-need-based). 52% of past graduating class borrowed through all loan programs. *Average indebtedness per student:* $22,070. *Average need-based loan:* Freshmen: $3837. Undergraduates: $4104. *Parent loans:* $16,422,165 (100% non-need-based). **WORK-STUDY** *Federal work-study:* Total amount: $881,071; jobs available. *State or other work-study/employment:* Total amount: $7,454,039 (100% non-need-based). Part-time jobs available.

ATHLETIC AWARDS Total amount: $6,893,374 (35% need-based, 65% non-need-based).

APPLYING FOR FINANCIAL AID *Required financial aid forms:* FAFSA, general scholarship application. *Financial aid deadline (priority):* 3/1. *Notification date:* Continuous beginning 3/30. Students must reply by 5/1 or within 4 weeks of notification.

CONTACT Dr. Barry Simmons, Director, Virginia Polytechnic Institute and State University, 300 Student Service Building, Blacksburg, VA 24061, 540-231-5179. *Fax:* 540-231-9139. *E-mail:* simmonsb@vt.edu.

VIRGINIA STATE UNIVERSITY
Petersburg, VA

CONTACT Henry DeBose, Director, Virginia State University, PO Box 9031, Petersburg, VA 23806-2096, 804-524-5992 or toll-free 800-871-7611. *Fax:* 804-524-6818. *E-mail:* hedebose@vsu.edu.

VIRGINIA UNION UNIVERSITY
Richmond, VA

Tuition & fees: $14,630 **Average undergraduate aid package:** $10,921

ABOUT THE INSTITUTION Independent Baptist, coed. 22 undergraduate majors. Federal methodology is used as a basis for awarding need-based institutional aid.

UNDERGRADUATE EXPENSES for 2010–11 *Comprehensive fee:* $21,460 includes full-time tuition ($13,314), mandatory fees ($1316), and room and board ($6830). *College room only:* $3084. Full-time tuition and fees vary according to course level and course load. Room and board charges vary according to housing facility. *Part-time tuition:* $422 per credit hour. *Part-time fees:* $40 per credit hour. Part-time tuition and fees vary according to course level and course load. *Payment plans:* Installment, deferred payment.

FRESHMAN FINANCIAL AID (Fall 2009, est.) 511 applied for aid; of those 94% were deemed to have need. 97% of freshmen with need received aid. *Average financial aid package:* $9816 (excluding resources awarded to replace EFC).

UNDERGRADUATE FINANCIAL AID (Fall 2009, est.) 1,163 applied for aid; of those 95% were deemed to have need. 99% of undergraduates with need received aid. *Average financial aid package:* $10,921 (excluding resources awarded to replace EFC).

GIFT AID (NEED-BASED) *Receiving aid:* Freshmen: 73% (384); all full-time undergraduates: 65% (849). *Average award:* Freshmen: $5543; Undergraduates: $5371. *Scholarships, grants, and awards:* Federal Pell, FSEOG, state, private, college/university gift aid from institutional funds.

GIFT AID (NON-NEED-BASED) *Receiving aid:* Freshmen: 47% (247). Undergraduates: 52% (671). *Scholarships, grants, and awards by category: Academic interests/achievement:* general academic interests/achievements. *Tuition waivers:* Full or partial for employees or children of employees.

LOANS *Average need-based loan:* Freshmen: $3359. Undergraduates: $3894. *Programs:* Federal Direct (Subsidized and Unsubsidized Stafford), FFEL (PLUS), Perkins.

WORK-STUDY Federal work-study jobs available.

APPLYING FOR FINANCIAL AID *Required financial aid forms:* FAFSA, state aid form. *Financial aid deadline (priority):* 5/1. *Notification date:* Continuous. Students must reply within 2 weeks of notification.

CONTACT Mrs. Donna Mack-Tatum, Director of Financial Aid, Virginia Union University, 1500 North Lombardy Street, Richmond, VA 23220-1170, 804-257-5882 or toll-free 800-368-3227 (out-of-state). *E-mail:* dtatum@vuu.edu.

VIRGINIA UNIVERSITY OF LYNCHBURG
Lynchburg, VA

Tuition & fees: $5300 **Average undergraduate aid package:** N/A

ABOUT THE INSTITUTION Independent religious, coed. 4 undergraduate majors. Federal methodology is used as a basis for awarding need-based institutional aid.

UNDERGRADUATE EXPENSES for 2010–11 *Comprehensive fee:* $8900 includes full-time tuition ($5000), mandatory fees ($300), and room and board ($3600). Full-time tuition and fees vary according to location and program. *Part-time tuition:* $167 per credit hour. Part-time tuition and fees vary according to location and program. *Payment plan:* Installment.

FRESHMAN FINANCIAL AID (Fall 2009, est.) 24 applied for aid; of those 100% were deemed to have need. 100% of freshmen with need received aid; of those 100% had need fully met. *Average percent of need met:* 100% (excluding resources awarded to replace EFC). *Average financial aid package:* $4013 (excluding resources awarded to replace EFC).

GIFT AID (NEED-BASED) *Total amount:* $779,171 (98% federal, 2% external sources). *Receiving aid:* Freshmen: 100% (24). *Average award:* Freshmen: $1338. *Scholarships, grants, and awards:* Federal Pell, FSEOG.

GIFT AID (NON-NEED-BASED) *Tuition waivers:* Full or partial for employees or children of employees.

LOANS *Student loans:* $3,391,734 (100% need-based). 90% of past graduating class borrowed through all loan programs. *Average indebtedness per student:* $9500. *Average need-based loan:* Freshmen: $3500. *Parent loans:* $15,840 (100% need-based). *Programs:* FFEL (Subsidized and Unsubsidized Stafford).

WORK-STUDY *Federal work-study:* Total amount: $9194; 9 jobs available.

APPLYING FOR FINANCIAL AID *Required financial aid form:* FAFSA. *Financial aid deadline:* Continuous. *Notification date:* Continuous beginning 6/1. Students must reply by 8/31.

CONTACT Mrs. Charlene P. Scruggs, Financial Aid Director, Virginia University of Lynchburg, 2058 Garfield Avenue, Lynchburg, VA 24572, 434-528-5276. *Fax:* 434-455-5958. *E-mail:* cscruggs@vul.edu.

VIRGINIA WESLEYAN COLLEGE
Norfolk, VA

Tuition & fees: $27,476   **Average undergraduate aid package:** $23,356

ABOUT THE INSTITUTION Independent United Methodist, coed. 50 undergraduate majors. Federal methodology is used as a basis for awarding need-based institutional aid.

UNDERGRADUATE EXPENSES for 2009–10 *Comprehensive fee:* $34,860 includes full-time tuition ($26,976), mandatory fees ($500), and room and board ($7384). Room and board charges vary according to board plan and housing facility. *Part-time tuition:* $1124 per hour. *Payment plans:* Installment, deferred payment.

FRESHMAN FINANCIAL AID (Fall 2008) 308 applied for aid; of those 83% were deemed to have need. 98% of freshmen with need received aid; of those 13% had need fully met. *Average percent of need met:* 86% (excluding resources awarded to replace EFC). *Average financial aid package:* $22,996 (excluding resources awarded to replace EFC). 19% of all full-time freshmen had no need and received non-need-based gift aid.

UNDERGRADUATE FINANCIAL AID (Fall 2008) 1,038 applied for aid; of those 86% were deemed to have need. 99% of undergraduates with need received aid; of those 11% had need fully met. *Average percent of need met:* 85% (excluding resources awarded to replace EFC). *Average financial aid package:* $23,356 (excluding resources awarded to replace EFC). 18% of all full-time undergraduates had no need and received non-need-based gift aid.

GIFT AID (NEED-BASED) *Total amount:* $11,840,744 (11% federal, 15% state, 72% institutional, 2% external sources). *Receiving aid:* Freshmen: 76% (251); all full-time undergraduates: 73% (873). *Average award:* Freshmen: $15,330; Undergraduates: $13,507. *Scholarships, grants, and awards:* Federal Pell, FSEOG, state, private, college/university gift aid from institutional funds, United Negro College Fund.

GIFT AID (NON-NEED-BASED) *Total amount:* $2,663,269 (26% state, 69% institutional, 5% external sources). *Receiving aid:* Freshmen: 18% (60). Undergraduates: 15% (175). *Average award:* Freshmen: $7634. Undergraduates: $7171. *Scholarships, grants, and awards by category: Academic interests/achievement:* general academic interests/achievements. *Creative arts/performance:* art/fine arts, music, theater/drama. *Special achievements/activities:* community service, leadership, religious involvement. *Special characteristics:* children of faculty/staff, relatives of clergy, religious affiliation. *Tuition waivers:* Full or partial for employees or children of employees, senior citizens.

LOANS *Student loans:* $8,707,923 (78% need-based, 22% non-need-based). 80% of past graduating class borrowed through all loan programs. *Average indebtedness per student:* $27,658. *Average need-based loan:* Freshmen: $5828. Undergraduates: $7170. *Parent loans:* $3,237,328 (44% need-based, 56% non-need-based). *Programs:* FFEL (Subsidized and Unsubsidized Stafford, PLUS), Perkins, alternative loans.

WORK-STUDY *Federal work-study:* Total amount: $193,886; 189 jobs averaging $1026.

APPLYING FOR FINANCIAL AID *Required financial aid forms:* FAFSA, state aid form. *Financial aid deadline (priority):* 3/1. *Notification date:* Continuous. Students must reply by 5/1 or within 2 weeks of notification.

CONTACT Mrs. Angie T. Hawkins, Director of Financial Aid, Virginia Wesleyan College, 1584 Wesleyan Drive, Norfolk, VA 23502-5599, 757-455-3345 or toll-free 800-737-8684. *Fax:* 757-455-6779. *E-mail:* finaid@vwc.edu.

VITERBO UNIVERSITY
La Crosse, WI

CONTACT Ms. Terry Norman, Director of Financial Aid, Viterbo University, 900 Viterbo Drive, La Crosse, WI 54601-4797, 608-796-3900 or toll-free 800-VITERBO Ext. 3010. *Fax:* 608-796-3050. *E-mail:* twnorman@viterbo.edu.

VOORHEES COLLEGE
Denmark, SC

CONTACT Augusta L. Kitchen, Director of Financial Aid, Voorhees College, PO Box 678, Denmark, SC 29042, 803-703-7109 Ext. 7106 or toll-free 866-685-9904. *Fax:* 803-793-0831. *E-mail:* akitchen@voorhees.edu.

WABASH COLLEGE
Crawfordsville, IN

Tuition & fees: $29,750   **Average undergraduate aid package:** $27,083

ABOUT THE INSTITUTION Independent, men only. 24 undergraduate majors. Both federal and institutional methodology are used as a basis for awarding need-based institutional aid.

UNDERGRADUATE EXPENSES for 2009–10 *Comprehensive fee:* $37,350 includes full-time tuition ($29,100), mandatory fees ($650), and room and board ($7600). *College room only:* $3500. Full-time tuition and fees vary according to reciprocity agreements. Room and board charges vary according to board plan and housing facility. *Part-time tuition:* $4850 per course. *Part-time fees:* $450 per year. Part-time tuition and fees vary according to course load and reciprocity agreements. *Payment plans:* Tuition prepayment, installment.

FRESHMAN FINANCIAL AID (Fall 2009, est.) 233 applied for aid; of those 87% were deemed to have need. 100% of freshmen with need received aid; of those 94% had need fully met. *Average percent of need met:* 98% (excluding resources awarded to replace EFC). *Average financial aid package:* $28,136 (excluding resources awarded to replace EFC). 12% of all full-time freshmen had no need and received non-need-based gift aid.

UNDERGRADUATE FINANCIAL AID (Fall 2009, est.) 772 applied for aid; of those 90% were deemed to have need. 100% of undergraduates with need received aid; of those 88% had need fully met. *Average percent of need met:* 96% (excluding resources awarded to replace EFC). *Average financial aid package:* $27,083 (excluding resources awarded to replace EFC). 17% of all full-time undergraduates had no need and received non-need-based gift aid.

GIFT AID (NEED-BASED) *Total amount:* $13,750,962 (7% federal, 7% state, 83% institutional, 3% external sources). *Receiving aid:* Freshmen: 82% (201); all full-time undergraduates: 79% (692). *Average award:* Freshmen: $19,459; Undergraduates: $18,638. *Scholarships, grants, and awards:* Federal Pell, state, private, college/university gift aid from institutional funds.

GIFT AID (NON-NEED-BASED) *Total amount:* $3,296,863 (1% federal, 89% institutional, 10% external sources). *Receiving aid:* Freshmen: 24% (58). Undergraduates: 30% (259). *Average award:* Freshmen: $14,262. Undergraduates: $16,398. *Scholarships, grants, and awards by category: Academic interests/achievement:* 1,044 awards ($7,921,678 total): general academic interests/achievements. *Creative arts/performance:* 50 awards ($180,110 total): art/fine arts, creative writing, journalism/publications, music, theater/drama. *Special achievements/activities:* 38 awards ($615,749 total): community service, leadership. *Special characteristics:* 7 awards ($149,363 total): children of faculty/staff. *Tuition waivers:* Full or partial for employees or children of employees.

LOANS *Student loans:* $5,100,472 (58% need-based, 42% non-need-based). 70% of past graduating class borrowed through all loan programs. *Average indebtedness per student:* $28,383. *Average need-based loan:* Freshmen: $5674. Undergraduates: $5319. *Programs:* Federal Direct (Subsidized and Unsubsidized Stafford, PLUS), college/university.

WORK-STUDY *State or other work-study/employment:* Total amount: $2,153,698 (83% need-based, 17% non-need-based). 786 part-time jobs averaging $2635.

APPLYING FOR FINANCIAL AID *Required financial aid forms:* FAFSA, CSS Financial Aid PROFILE, noncustodial (divorced/separated) parent's statement, federal income tax form(s), W-2 forms. *Financial aid deadline:* 3/1 (priority: 2/15). *Notification date:* 3/31. Students must reply by 5/1 or within 2 weeks of notification.

CONTACT Mr. Clint Gasaway, Financial Aid Director, Wabash College, PO Box 352, Crawfordsville, IN 47933-0352, 800-718-9746 or toll-free 800-345-5385. *Fax:* 765-361-6166. *E-mail:* financialaid@wabash.edu.

WAGNER COLLEGE
Staten Island, NY

Tuition & fees: $32,580   **Average undergraduate aid package:** $20,457

ABOUT THE INSTITUTION Independent, coed. 38 undergraduate majors. Federal methodology is used as a basis for awarding need-based institutional aid.

UNDERGRADUATE EXPENSES for 2009–10 *Comprehensive fee:* $42,280 includes full-time tuition ($32,430), mandatory fees ($150), and room and board ($9700). Full-time tuition and fees vary according to course load. *Part-time tuition:* $4054 per unit. Part-time tuition and fees vary according to course load.

FRESHMAN FINANCIAL AID (Fall 2009, est.) 430 applied for aid; of those 83% were deemed to have need. 100% of freshmen with need received aid; of those 25% had need fully met. *Average percent of need met:* 74% (excluding resources awarded to replace EFC). *Average financial aid package:* $21,102 (excluding resources awarded to replace EFC). 24% of all full-time freshmen had no need and received non-need-based gift aid.

UNDERGRADUATE FINANCIAL AID (Fall 2009, est.) 1,290 applied for aid; of those 82% were deemed to have need. 100% of undergraduates with need received aid; of those 27% had need fully met. *Average percent of need met:* 73% (excluding resources awarded to replace EFC). *Average financial aid package:* $20,457 (excluding resources awarded to replace EFC). 31% of all full-time undergraduates had no need and received non-need-based gift aid.

GIFT AID (NEED-BASED) *Total amount:* $12,555,272 (9% federal, 5% state, 84% institutional, 2% external sources). *Receiving aid:* Freshmen: 68% (352); all full-time undergraduates: 57% (1,034). *Average award:* Freshmen: $12,489; Undergraduates: $16,157. *Scholarships, grants, and awards:* Federal Pell, FSEOG, state, private, college/university gift aid from institutional funds.

GIFT AID (NON-NEED-BASED) *Total amount:* $7,333,728 (1% state, 99% institutional). *Average award:* Freshmen: $11,473. Undergraduates: $12,072. *Scholarships, grants, and awards by category:* Academic interests/achievement: 1,221 awards ($12,546,705 total): general academic interests/achievements. Creative arts/performance: 235 awards ($2,846,751 total): music, theater/drama. Special characteristics: 127 awards ($1,542,395 total): children of faculty/staff, siblings of current students. *Tuition waivers:* Full or partial for employees or children of employees.

LOANS *Student loans:* $11,914,337 (75% need-based, 25% non-need-based). 61% of past graduating class borrowed through all loan programs. *Average indebtedness per student:* $36,988. *Average need-based loan:* Freshmen: $3808. Undergraduates: $4643. *Parent loans:* $3,818,242 (68% need-based, 32% non-need-based). *Programs:* Federal Direct (Subsidized and Unsubsidized Stafford, PLUS), Perkins, Federal Nursing.

WORK-STUDY *Federal work-study:* Total amount: $847,407; 596 jobs averaging $1500.

ATHLETIC AWARDS Total amount: $2,219,205 (86% need-based, 14% non-need-based).

APPLYING FOR FINANCIAL AID *Required financial aid forms:* FAFSA, institution's own form, state aid form. *Financial aid deadline (priority):* 2/15. *Notification date:* 3/1. Students must reply within 3 weeks of notification.

CONTACT Mr. Angelo Araimo, Vice President for Enrollment and Planning, Wagner College, One Campus Road, Staten Island, NY 10301, 718-390-3411 or toll-free 800-221-1010 (out-of-state). *Fax:* 718-390-3105.

WAKE FOREST UNIVERSITY
Winston-Salem, NC

Tuition & fees: $39,970	Average undergraduate aid package: $32,965

ABOUT THE INSTITUTION Independent, coed. 39 undergraduate majors. Institutional methodology is used as a basis for awarding need-based institutional aid.

UNDERGRADUATE EXPENSES for 2010–11 *Comprehensive fee:* $50,980 includes full-time tuition ($39,544), mandatory fees ($426), and room and board ($11,010). *College room only:* $7150. *Part-time tuition:* $1640 per semester hour.

FRESHMAN FINANCIAL AID (Fall 2009, est.) 432 applied for aid; of those 82% were deemed to have need. 99% of freshmen with need received aid; of those 93% had need fully met. *Average percent of need met:* 99% (excluding resources awarded to replace EFC). *Average financial aid package:* $33,285 (excluding resources awarded to replace EFC). 6% of all full-time freshmen had no need and received non-need-based gift aid.

UNDERGRADUATE FINANCIAL AID (Fall 2009, est.) 1,915 applied for aid; of those 91% were deemed to have need. 99% of undergraduates with need received aid; of those 64% had need fully met. *Average percent of need met:* 99% (excluding resources awarded to replace EFC). *Average financial aid package:* $32,965 (excluding resources awarded to replace EFC). 9% of all full-time undergraduates had no need and received non-need-based gift aid.

GIFT AID (NEED-BASED) *Total amount:* $36,407,786 (10% federal, 8% state, 78% institutional, 4% external sources). *Receiving aid:* Freshmen: 28% (336); all full-time undergraduates: 35% (1,617). *Average award:* Freshmen: $28,085; Undergraduates: $26,473. *Scholarships, grants, and awards:* Federal Pell, FSEOG, state, private, college/university gift aid from institutional funds.

GIFT AID (NON-NEED-BASED) *Total amount:* $8,164,901 (15% federal, 11% state, 57% institutional, 17% external sources). *Receiving aid:* Freshmen: 17% (202). Undergraduates: 25% (1,125). *Average award:* Freshmen: $16,327. Undergraduates: $13,864. *Scholarships, grants, and awards by category:* Academic interests/achievement: general academic interests/achievements. Creative arts/performance: general creative arts/performance. Special achievements/activities: leadership. Special characteristics: children and siblings of alumni, local/state students, religious affiliation.

LOANS *Student loans:* $20,299,206 (80% need-based, 20% non-need-based). 38% of past graduating class borrowed through all loan programs. *Average indebtedness per student:* $24,561. *Average need-based loan:* Freshmen: $8028. Undergraduates: $11,305. *Parent loans:* $7,871,614 (93% need-based, 7% non-need-based). *Programs:* FFEL (Subsidized and Unsubsidized Stafford, PLUS), Perkins, state, college/university.

WORK-STUDY *Federal work-study:* Total amount: $2,188,658; jobs available. *State or other work-study/employment:* Part-time jobs available.

ATHLETIC AWARDS Total amount: $9,849,703 (31% need-based, 69% non-need-based).

APPLYING FOR FINANCIAL AID *Required financial aid forms:* FAFSA, CSS Financial Aid PROFILE, state aid form, noncustodial (divorced/separated) parent's statement. *Financial aid deadline:* 3/1 (priority: 2/15). *Notification date:* Continuous beginning 4/1. Students must reply by 5/1 or within 4 weeks of notification.

CONTACT Adam Holyfield, Associate Director of Financial Aid, Wake Forest University, PO Box 7246, Winston-Salem, NC 27109-7246, 336-758-5154. *Fax:* 336-758-4924. *E-mail:* financial-aid@wfu.edu.

WALDEN UNIVERSITY
Minneapolis, MN

CONTACT Financial Aid Office, Walden University, 155 Fifth Avenue South, Minneapolis, MN 55401, 800-444-6795 or toll-free 866-492-5336 (out-of-state). *Fax:* 410-843-6211. *E-mail:* finaid@waldenu.edu.

WALDORF COLLEGE
Forest City, IA

Tuition & fees: $18,760	Average undergraduate aid package: $17,520

ABOUT THE INSTITUTION Independent Lutheran, coed. 28 undergraduate majors. Federal methodology is used as a basis for awarding need-based institutional aid.

UNDERGRADUATE EXPENSES for 2010–11 *Comprehensive fee:* $24,714 includes full-time tuition ($17,900), mandatory fees ($860), and room and board ($5954). Full-time tuition and fees vary according to class time, course load, and program. Room and board charges vary according to board plan and housing facility. *Payment plans:* Installment, deferred payment.

FRESHMAN FINANCIAL AID (Fall 2009, est.) 146 applied for aid; of those 82% were deemed to have need. 99% of freshmen with need received aid; of those 18% had need fully met. *Average percent of need met:* 80% (excluding resources awarded to replace EFC). *Average financial aid package:* $16,104 (excluding resources awarded to replace EFC). 15% of all full-time freshmen had no need and received non-need-based gift aid.

UNDERGRADUATE FINANCIAL AID (Fall 2009, est.) 502 applied for aid; of those 89% were deemed to have need. 100% of undergraduates with need received aid; of those 18% had need fully met. *Average percent of need met:* 80% (excluding resources awarded to replace EFC). *Average financial aid package:* $17,520 (excluding resources awarded to replace EFC). 15% of all full-time undergraduates had no need and received non-need-based gift aid.

GIFT AID (NEED-BASED) *Total amount:* $4,691,860 (26% federal, 11% state, 56% institutional, 7% external sources). *Receiving aid:* Freshmen: 76% (119); all full-time undergraduates: 80% (442). *Average award:* Freshmen: $12,556; Undergraduates: $12,934. *Scholarships, grants, and awards:* Federal Pell, FSEOG, state, private, college/university gift aid from institutional funds.

GIFT AID (NON-NEED-BASED) *Total amount:* $710,586 (1% federal, 89% institutional, 10% external sources). *Receiving aid:* Freshmen: 10% (15). Undergraduates: 8% (46). *Average award:* Freshmen: $5239. Undergraduates: $6221. *Scholarships, grants, and awards by category:* Academic interests/achievement: communication, general academic interests/achievements. Creative arts/performance: music, theater/drama. Special achievements/activities: cheerleading/

Waldorf College

drum major, junior miss, leadership. *Special characteristics:* children of faculty/staff, religious affiliation. *Tuition waivers:* Full or partial for employees or children of employees.

LOANS *Student loans:* $3,850,324 (77% need-based, 23% non-need-based). 97% of past graduating class borrowed through all loan programs. *Average indebtedness per student:* $30,348. *Average need-based loan:* Freshmen: $3601. Undergraduates: $4715. *Parent loans:* $2,190,279 (30% need-based, 70% non-need-based). *Programs:* Federal Direct (Subsidized and Unsubsidized Stafford, PLUS), Perkins, state, alternative loans.

WORK-STUDY *Federal work-study:* Total amount: $257,614; 365 jobs averaging $1419. *State or other work-study/employment:* 215 part-time jobs averaging $719.

ATHLETIC AWARDS Total amount: $1,444,128 (74% need-based, 26% non-need-based).

APPLYING FOR FINANCIAL AID *Required financial aid form:* FAFSA. *Financial aid deadline (priority):* 3/1. *Notification date:* Continuous beginning 3/1. Students must reply within 2 weeks of notification.

CONTACT Duane Polsdofer, Director of Financial Aid, Waldorf College, 106 South 6th Street, Forest City, IA 50436, 641-585-8120 or toll-free 800-292-1903. *Fax:* 641-585-8125.

WALLA WALLA UNIVERSITY
College Place, WA

ABOUT THE INSTITUTION Independent Seventh-day Adventist, coed. *Awards:* associate, bachelor's, and master's degrees. 84 undergraduate majors. *Total enrollment:* 1,800. Undergraduates: 1,563. Freshmen: 315.

GIFT AID (NEED-BASED) *Scholarships, grants, and awards:* Federal Pell, FSEOG, state, private, college/university gift aid from institutional funds, Federal Nursing.

GIFT AID (NON-NEED-BASED) *Scholarships, grants, and awards by category: Academic interests/achievement:* biological sciences, business, communication, education, engineering/technologies, English, foreign languages, general academic interests/achievements, humanities, mathematics, religion/biblical studies. *Creative arts/performance:* general creative arts/performance, music, theater/drama. *Special achievements/activities:* leadership. *Special characteristics:* children of faculty/staff, veterans.

LOANS *Programs:* FFEL (Subsidized and Unsubsidized Stafford, PLUS), Perkins, Federal Nursing, college/university.

APPLYING FOR FINANCIAL AID *Required financial aid forms:* FAFSA, institution's own form.

CONTACT Ms. Nancy Caldera, Associate Director of Financial Aid, Walla Walla University, 204 South College Avenue, College Place, WA 99324-1198, 509-527-2315 or toll-free 800-541-8900. *Fax:* 509-527-2556. *E-mail:* nancy.caldera@wallawalla.edu.

WALSH COLLEGE OF ACCOUNTANCY AND BUSINESS ADMINISTRATION
Troy, MI

CONTACT Howard Thomas, Director of Student Financial Resources, Walsh College of Accountancy and Business Administration, 3838 Livernois Road, PO Box 7006, Troy, MI 48007-7006, 248-823-1285 or toll-free 800-925-7401 (in-state). *Fax:* 248-524-2520. *E-mail:* hthomas@walshcollege.edu.

WALSH UNIVERSITY
North Canton, OH

CONTACT Holly Van Gilder, Director of Financial Aid, Walsh University, 2020 East Maple NW, North Canton, OH 44720-3396, 330-490-7147 or toll-free 800-362-9846 (in-state), 800-362-8846 (out-of-state). *Fax:* 330-490-7372. *E-mail:* hvangilder@walsh.edu.

WARNER PACIFIC COLLEGE
Portland, OR

Tuition & fees: $17,110	Average undergraduate aid package: $15,928

ABOUT THE INSTITUTION Independent religious, coed. 31 undergraduate majors. Federal methodology is used as a basis for awarding need-based institutional aid.

UNDERGRADUATE EXPENSES for 2010–11 *Comprehensive fee:* $23,756 includes full-time tuition ($16,480), mandatory fees ($630), and room and board ($6646). Full-time tuition and fees vary according to course load, degree level, location, reciprocity agreements, and student level. Room and board charges vary according to board plan and housing facility. *Part-time tuition:* $750 per credit. *Part-time fees:* $475 per credit. Part-time tuition and fees vary according to course load, degree level, location, and reciprocity agreements. *Payment plan:* Installment.

FRESHMAN FINANCIAL AID (Fall 2009, est.) 90 applied for aid; of those 88% were deemed to have need. 100% of freshmen with need received aid; of those 11% had need fully met. *Average percent of need met:* 71% (excluding resources awarded to replace EFC). *Average financial aid package:* $13,992 (excluding resources awarded to replace EFC). 13% of all full-time freshmen had no need and received non-need-based gift aid.

UNDERGRADUATE FINANCIAL AID (Fall 2009, est.) 409 applied for aid; of those 92% were deemed to have need. 100% of undergraduates with need received aid; of those 16% had need fully met. *Average percent of need met:* 72% (excluding resources awarded to replace EFC). *Average financial aid package:* $15,928 (excluding resources awarded to replace EFC). 9% of all full-time undergraduates had no need and received non-need-based gift aid.

GIFT AID (NEED-BASED) *Total amount:* $3,463,090 (33% federal, 9% state, 51% institutional, 7% external sources). *Receiving aid:* Freshmen: 77% (70); all full-time undergraduates: 79% (331). *Average award:* Freshmen: $5130; Undergraduates: $5436. *Scholarships, grants, and awards:* Federal Pell, FSEOG, state, private, college/university gift aid from institutional funds.

GIFT AID (NON-NEED-BASED) *Total amount:* $169,906 (93% institutional, 7% external sources). *Receiving aid:* Freshmen: 84% (76). Undergraduates: 85% (356). *Average award:* Freshmen: $2750. Undergraduates: $3346. *Scholarships, grants, and awards by category: Academic interests/achievement:* 320 awards ($901,234 total): area/ethnic studies, biological sciences, general academic interests/achievements, humanities, mathematics, physical sciences, religion/biblical studies, social sciences. *Creative arts/performance:* 42 awards ($87,979 total): music, theater/drama. *Special achievements/activities:* 33 awards ($44,000 total): leadership. *Special characteristics:* 213 awards ($216,721 total): children and siblings of alumni, members of minority groups, religious affiliation. *Tuition waivers:* Full or partial for children of alumni, employees or children of employees.

LOANS *Student loans:* $3,192,254 (80% need-based, 20% non-need-based). 93% of past graduating class borrowed through all loan programs. *Average indebtedness per student:* $22,433. *Average need-based loan:* Freshmen: $3462. Undergraduates: $4423. *Parent loans:* $681,288 (36% need-based, 64% non-need-based). *Programs:* Federal Direct (Subsidized and Unsubsidized Stafford, PLUS), FFEL (Subsidized and Unsubsidized Stafford, PLUS), Perkins.

WORK-STUDY *Federal work-study:* Total amount: $576,520; 297 jobs averaging $1941.

ATHLETIC AWARDS Total amount: $644,494 (83% need-based, 17% non-need-based).

APPLYING FOR FINANCIAL AID *Required financial aid form:* FAFSA. *Financial aid deadline:* Continuous. *Notification date:* Continuous beginning 3/1. Students must reply within 2 weeks of notification.

CONTACT Bryan Cook, Interim Director of Student Financial Services and Financial Aid, Warner Pacific College, 2219 Southeast 68th Avenue, Portland, OR 97215-4099, 503-517-1018 or toll-free 800-804-1510 (out-of-state). *Fax:* 503-517-1352. *E-mail:* bcook@warnerpacific.edu.

WARNER UNIVERSITY
Lake Wales, FL

CONTACT Student Financial Services, Warner University, 13895 Highway 27, Lake Wales, FL 33859, 863-638-7202 or toll-free 800-949-7248 (in-state). *Fax:* 863-638-7603. *E-mail:* financialaid@warner.edu.

WARREN WILSON COLLEGE
Swannanoa, NC

Tuition & fees: $24,196	Average undergraduate aid package: $21,323

ABOUT THE INSTITUTION Independent religious, coed. *Awards:* bachelor's and master's degrees. 27 undergraduate majors. *Total enrollment:* 1,002. Undergraduates: 927. Freshmen: 249. Both federal and institutional methodology are used as a basis for awarding need-based institutional aid.

UNDERGRADUATE EXPENSES for 2009–10 *Comprehensive fee:* $31,966 includes full-time tuition ($23,896), mandatory fees ($300), and room and board ($7770). *Part-time tuition:* $996 per credit.

FRESHMAN FINANCIAL AID (Fall 2009, est.) 201 applied for aid; of those 80% were deemed to have need. 100% of freshmen with need received aid; of those 18% had need fully met. *Average percent of need met:* 72% (excluding resources awarded to replace EFC). *Average financial aid package:* $21,716 (excluding resources awarded to replace EFC). 24% of all full-time freshmen had no need and received non-need-based gift aid.

UNDERGRADUATE FINANCIAL AID (Fall 2009, est.) 706 applied for aid; of those 85% were deemed to have need. 100% of undergraduates with need received aid; of those 15% had need fully met. *Average percent of need met:* 74% (excluding resources awarded to replace EFC). *Average financial aid package:* $21,323 (excluding resources awarded to replace EFC). 16% of all full-time undergraduates had no need and received non-need-based gift aid.

GIFT AID (NEED-BASED) *Total amount:* $7,123,889 (18% federal, 6% state, 72% institutional, 4% external sources). *Receiving aid:* Freshmen: 69% (154); all full-time undergraduates: 58% (549). *Average award:* Freshmen: $13,330; Undergraduates: $12,522. *Scholarships, grants, and awards:* Federal Pell, FSEOG, state, college/university gift aid from institutional funds, Academic Competitiveness Grants, National SMART Grants.

GIFT AID (NON-NEED-BASED) *Total amount:* $1,152,174 (5% state, 73% institutional, 22% external sources). *Receiving aid:* Freshmen: 21% (47). Undergraduates: 15% (141). *Average award:* Freshmen: $4583. Undergraduates: $5461. *Scholarships, grants, and awards by category: Academic interests/achievement:* 202 awards ($561,949 total): general academic interests/achievements. *Creative arts/performance:* 15 awards ($15,250 total): art/fine arts, creative writing. *Special achievements/activities:* 56 awards ($101,500 total): community service, leadership. *Special characteristics:* 144 awards ($384,461 total): children of faculty/staff, general special characteristics, local/state students, previous college experience, religious affiliation.

LOANS *Student loans:* $3,657,567 (87% need-based, 13% non-need-based). 34% of past graduating class borrowed through all loan programs. *Average indebtedness per student:* $20,441. *Average need-based loan:* Freshmen: $2445. Undergraduates: $3165. *Parent loans:* $1,594,630 (76% need-based, 24% non-need-based). *Programs:* Federal Direct (Subsidized and Unsubsidized Stafford, PLUS), Perkins, college/university.

WORK-STUDY *Federal work-study:* Total amount: $900,000; 530 jobs averaging $3480. *State or other work-study/employment:* Total amount: $950,000 (42% need-based, 58% non-need-based). 400 part-time jobs averaging $3480.

APPLYING FOR FINANCIAL AID *Required financial aid forms:* FAFSA, institution's own form, state aid form. *Financial aid deadline (priority):* 4/1. *Notification date:* Continuous. Students must reply by 5/1 or within 3 weeks of notification.

CONTACT Admissions Office, Warren Wilson College, PO Box 9000, Asheville, NC 28815-9000, 800-934-3536. *Fax:* 828-298-1440.

WARTBURG COLLEGE
Waverly, IA

Tuition & fees: $29,020	Average undergraduate aid package: $20,496

ABOUT THE INSTITUTION Independent Lutheran, coed. 56 undergraduate majors. Federal methodology is used as a basis for awarding need-based institutional aid.

UNDERGRADUATE EXPENSES for 2010–11 *Comprehensive fee:* $36,995 includes full-time tuition ($28,220), mandatory fees ($800), and room and board ($7975). *College room only:* $3810.

FRESHMAN FINANCIAL AID (Fall 2008) 474 applied for aid; of those 84% were deemed to have need. 100% of freshmen with need received aid; of those 21% had need fully met. *Average percent of need met:* 85% (excluding resources awarded to replace EFC). *Average financial aid package:* $21,441 (excluding resources awarded to replace EFC). 23% of all full-time freshmen had no need and received non-need-based gift aid.

UNDERGRADUATE FINANCIAL AID (Fall 2008) 1,537 applied for aid; of those 86% were deemed to have need. 100% of undergraduates with need received aid; of those 42% had need fully met. *Average percent of need met:* 83% (excluding resources awarded to replace EFC). *Average financial aid package:*

$20,496 (excluding resources awarded to replace EFC). 23% of all full-time undergraduates had no need and received non-need-based gift aid.

GIFT AID (NEED-BASED) *Total amount:* $21,252,337 (8% federal, 13% state, 69% institutional, 10% external sources). *Receiving aid:* Freshmen: 77% (397); all full-time undergraduates: 77% (1,325). *Average award:* Freshmen: $17,841; Undergraduates: $16,018. *Scholarships, grants, and awards:* Federal Pell, FSEOG, state, private, college/university gift aid from institutional funds.

GIFT AID (NON-NEED-BASED) *Total amount:* $6,746,289 (85% institutional, 15% external sources). *Receiving aid:* Freshmen: 15% (75). Undergraduates: 11% (196). *Average award:* Freshmen: $18,373. Undergraduates: $16,552. *Scholarships, grants, and awards by category: Academic interests/achievement:* biological sciences, business, communication, computer science, education, English, general academic interests/achievements, international studies, mathematics, physical sciences, religion/biblical studies. *Creative arts/performance:* art/fine arts, journalism/publications, music. *Special characteristics:* children and siblings of alumni, children of faculty/staff, ethnic background, international students, members of minority groups, out-of-state students, religious affiliation, siblings of current students.

LOANS *Student loans:* $12,075,703 (58% need-based, 42% non-need-based). 81% of past graduating class borrowed through all loan programs. *Average indebtedness per student:* $27,225. *Average need-based loan:* Freshmen: $3411. Undergraduates: $4604. *Parent loans:* $1,526,888 (52% need-based, 48% non-need-based). *Programs:* FFEL (Subsidized and Unsubsidized Stafford, PLUS), Perkins, alternative loans.

WORK-STUDY *Federal work-study:* Total amount: $812,839; jobs available. *State or other work-study/employment:* Part-time jobs available.

APPLYING FOR FINANCIAL AID *Required financial aid form:* FAFSA. *Financial aid deadline (priority):* 3/1. *Notification date:* Continuous beginning 3/21. Students must reply within 2 weeks of notification.

CONTACT Ms. Jennifer Sassman, Director of Financial Aid, Wartburg College, 100 Wartburg Boulevard, PO Box 1003, Waverly, IA 50677-0903, 319-352-8262 or toll-free 800-772-2085. *Fax:* 319-352-8514. *E-mail:* jennifer.sassman@wartburg.edu.

WASHBURN UNIVERSITY
Topeka, KS

Tuition & fees (KS res): $6116	Average undergraduate aid package: $8748

ABOUT THE INSTITUTION City-supported, coed. 79 undergraduate majors. Federal methodology is used as a basis for awarding need-based institutional aid.

UNDERGRADUATE EXPENSES for 2009–10 *Tuition, state resident:* full-time $6030; part-time $201 per credit hour. *Tuition, nonresident:* full-time $13,680; part-time $456 per credit hour. *Required fees:* full-time $86; $21 per term. Full-time tuition and fees vary according to program. Part-time tuition and fees vary according to program. *College room and board:* $5792; *Room only:* $3242. Room and board charges vary according to board plan and housing facility. *Payment plan:* Installment.

FRESHMAN FINANCIAL AID (Fall 2009, est.) 655 applied for aid; of those 69% were deemed to have need. 99% of freshmen with need received aid; of those 14% had need fully met. *Average percent of need met:* 35% (excluding resources awarded to replace EFC). *Average financial aid package:* $7670 (excluding resources awarded to replace EFC). 13% of all full-time freshmen had no need and received non-need-based gift aid.

UNDERGRADUATE FINANCIAL AID (Fall 2009, est.) 3,420 applied for aid; of those 70% were deemed to have need. 99% of undergraduates with need received aid; of those 13% had need fully met. *Average percent of need met:* 39% (excluding resources awarded to replace EFC). *Average financial aid package:* $8748 (excluding resources awarded to replace EFC). 15% of all full-time undergraduates had no need and received non-need-based gift aid.

GIFT AID (NEED-BASED) *Total amount:* $10,210,289 (82% federal, 3% state, 12% institutional, 3% external sources). *Receiving aid:* Freshmen: 39% (273); all full-time undergraduates: 35% (1,345). *Average award:* Freshmen: $4693; Undergraduates: $4778. *Scholarships, grants, and awards:* Federal Pell, FSEOG, state, private, college/university gift aid from institutional funds.

GIFT AID (NON-NEED-BASED) *Total amount:* $1,900,022 (1% federal, 5% state, 65% institutional, 29% external sources). *Receiving aid:* Freshmen: 27% (193). Undergraduates: 26% (1,000). *Average award:* Freshmen: $2055. Undergraduates: $1888. *Scholarships, grants, and awards by category: Academic interests/achievement:* 1,811 awards ($1,924,640 total): biological sciences, business, communication, computer science, education, engineering/technologies, English, foreign languages, general academic interests/achievements, health fields, humanities, international studies, mathematics, physical sciences, premedicine, religion/biblical studies, social sciences. *Creative arts/performance:* 218 awards ($195,349 total): art/fine arts, cinema/film/broadcasting, debating, journalism/publications, music, performing arts, theater/drama. *Special achievements/activities:* 617 awards ($1,498,771 total): cheerleading/drum major, community service, general special achievements/activities, leadership. *Special characteristics:* 142 awards ($214,505 total): adult students, children and siblings of alumni, children of faculty/staff, ethnic background, international students, local/state students. *Tuition waivers:* Full or partial for employees or children of employees, senior citizens.

LOANS *Student loans:* $30,058,301 (57% need-based, 43% non-need-based). 66% of past graduating class borrowed through all loan programs. *Average indebtedness per student:* $17,031. *Average need-based loan:* Freshmen: $3331. Undergraduates: $4295. *Parent loans:* $7,449,493 (57% need-based, 43% non-need-based). *Programs:* Federal Direct (Subsidized and Unsubsidized Stafford, PLUS), FFEL (Subsidized and Unsubsidized Stafford, PLUS), Perkins, college/university, alternative private loans.

WORK-STUDY *Federal work-study:* Total amount: $762,600; 37 jobs averaging $2662. *State or other work-study/employment:* Total amount: $21,482 (100% need-based). Part-time jobs available.

ATHLETIC AWARDS Total amount: $1,419,098 (51% need-based, 49% non-need-based).

APPLYING FOR FINANCIAL AID *Required financial aid forms:* FAFSA, institution's own form. *Financial aid deadline (priority):* 2/15. *Notification date:* Continuous beginning 3/15. Students must reply within 2 weeks of notification.

CONTACT Gail Palmer, Director of Financial Aid, Washburn University, 1700 SW College Avenue, Topeka, KS 66621, 785-670-1151 or toll-free 800-332-0291 (in-state). *Fax:* 785-670-1079. *E-mail:* gail.palmer@washburn.edu.

WASHINGTON ADVENTIST UNIVERSITY
Takoma Park, MD

CONTACT Elaine Oliver, Director, Financial Aid, Washington Adventist University, 7600 Flower Avenue, Takoma Park, MD 20912, 301-891-4005 or toll-free 800-835-4212.

WASHINGTON & JEFFERSON COLLEGE
Washington, PA

Tuition & fees: $32,895 | **Average undergraduate aid package: $24,008**

ABOUT THE INSTITUTION Independent, coed. 31 undergraduate majors. Both federal and institutional methodology are used as a basis for awarding need-based institutional aid.

UNDERGRADUATE EXPENSES for 2009–10 *Comprehensive fee:* $41,820 includes full-time tuition ($32,495), mandatory fees ($400), and room and board ($8925). *College room only:* $5256. Room and board charges vary according to board plan and housing facility. *Part-time tuition:* $815 per credit hour. Part-time tuition and fees vary according to course load. *Payment plans:* Installment, deferred payment.

FRESHMAN FINANCIAL AID (Fall 2009, est.) 359 applied for aid; of those 86% were deemed to have need. 100% of freshmen with need received aid; of those 20% had need fully met. *Average percent of need met:* 82% (excluding resources awarded to replace EFC). *Average financial aid package:* $24,661 (excluding resources awarded to replace EFC). 21% of all full-time freshmen had no need and received non-need-based gift aid.

UNDERGRADUATE FINANCIAL AID (Fall 2009, est.) 1,267 applied for aid; of those 90% were deemed to have need. 100% of undergraduates with need received aid; of those 18% had need fully met. *Average percent of need met:* 79% (excluding resources awarded to replace EFC). *Average financial aid package:* $24,008 (excluding resources awarded to replace EFC). 19% of all full-time undergraduates had no need and received non-need-based gift aid.

GIFT AID (NEED-BASED) *Total amount:* $20,040,332 (9% federal, 8% state, 81% institutional, 2% external sources). *Receiving aid:* Freshmen: 65% (255); all full-time undergraduates: 65% (955). *Average award:* Freshmen: $9524; Undergraduates: $9786. *Scholarships, grants, and awards:* Federal Pell, FSEOG, state, private, college/university gift aid from institutional funds, Academic Competitiveness Grants, National SMART Grants.

GIFT AID (NON-NEED-BASED) *Total amount:* $3,506,421 (98% institutional, 2% external sources). *Receiving aid:* Freshmen: 71% (280). Undergraduates: 65% (950). *Average award:* Freshmen: $11,851. Undergraduates: $10,736. *Scholarships, grants, and awards by category:* Academic interests/achievement: 1,230 awards ($12,930,789 total): business, general academic interests/achievements. *Special characteristics:* 28 awards ($816,542 total): children and siblings of alumni, children of faculty/staff. *Tuition waivers:* Full or partial for employees or children of employees.

LOANS *Student loans:* $12,497,210 (67% need-based, 33% non-need-based). 75% of past graduating class borrowed through all loan programs. *Average indebtedness per student:* $23,000. *Average need-based loan:* Freshmen: $3730. Undergraduates: $4809. *Parent loans:* $3,485,958 (60% need-based, 40% non-need-based). *Programs:* FFEL (Subsidized and Unsubsidized Stafford, PLUS), Perkins, college/university.

WORK-STUDY *Federal work-study:* Total amount: $1,192,488; 639 jobs averaging $1680. *State or other work-study/employment:* Total amount: $230,000 (100% non-need-based). 207 part-time jobs averaging $600.

APPLYING FOR FINANCIAL AID *Required financial aid form:* FAFSA. *Financial aid deadline (priority):* 2/15. *Notification date:* Continuous beginning 3/1. Students must reply by 5/1.

CONTACT Michelle Anderson, Director of Financial Aid, Washington & Jefferson College, 60 South Lincoln Street, Washington, PA 15301-4801, 724-503-1001 Ext. 6019 or toll-free 888-WANDJAY. *Fax:* 724-250-3340. *E-mail:* manderson@washjeff.edu.

WASHINGTON AND LEE UNIVERSITY
Lexington, VA

Tuition & fees: $38,877 | **Average undergraduate aid package: $37,052**

ABOUT THE INSTITUTION Independent, coed. 39 undergraduate majors. Both federal and institutional methodology are used as a basis for awarding need-based institutional aid.

UNDERGRADUATE EXPENSES for 2009–10 *Comprehensive fee:* $47,287 includes full-time tuition ($37,990), mandatory fees ($887), and room and board ($8410). *College room only:* $3285. Full-time tuition and fees vary according to degree level. Room and board charges vary according to board plan and housing facility. *Part-time tuition:* $1267 per credit hour. Part-time tuition and fees vary according to degree level.

FRESHMAN FINANCIAL AID (Fall 2009, est.) 282 applied for aid; of those 69% were deemed to have need. 100% of freshmen with need received aid; of those 100% had need fully met. *Average percent of need met:* 100% (excluding resources awarded to replace EFC). *Average financial aid package:* $38,620 (excluding resources awarded to replace EFC). 6% of all full-time freshmen had no need and received non-need-based gift aid.

UNDERGRADUATE FINANCIAL AID (Fall 2009, est.) 711 applied for aid; of those 86% were deemed to have need. 100% of undergraduates with need received aid; of those 100% had need fully met. *Average percent of need met:* 100% (excluding resources awarded to replace EFC). *Average financial aid package:* $37,052 (excluding resources awarded to replace EFC). 9% of all full-time undergraduates had no need and received non-need-based gift aid.

GIFT AID (NEED-BASED) *Total amount:* $19,224,952 (3% federal, 2% state, 92% institutional, 3% external sources). *Receiving aid:* Freshmen: 40% (187); all full-time undergraduates: 33% (585). *Average award:* Freshmen: $29,643; Undergraduates: $31,111. *Scholarships, grants, and awards:* Federal Pell, FSEOG, state, private, college/university gift aid from institutional funds.

GIFT AID (NON-NEED-BASED) *Total amount:* $10,187,831 (4% state, 91% institutional, 5% external sources). *Receiving aid:* Freshmen: 25% (116). Undergraduates: 21% (372). *Average award:* Freshmen: $30,405. Undergraduates: $27,499. *Scholarships, grants, and awards by category:* Academic interests/achievement: 392 awards ($8,565,869 total): general academic interests/achievements. *Tuition waivers:* Full or partial for employees or children of employees.

LOANS *Student loans:* $5,193,558 (31% need-based, 69% non-need-based). 31% of past graduating class borrowed through all loan programs. *Average indebtedness per student:* $23,615. *Average need-based loan:* Freshmen: $2557. Undergraduates: $3700. *Parent loans:* $3,933,214 (100% non-need-based). *Programs:* Federal Direct (Subsidized and Unsubsidized Stafford, PLUS), Perkins, college/university.

WORK-STUDY *Federal work-study:* Total amount: $264,080; 139 jobs averaging $1862. *State or other work-study/employment:* Total amount: $816,000 (100% non-need-based). 453 part-time jobs averaging $1857.

APPLYING FOR FINANCIAL AID *Required financial aid forms:* FAFSA, CSS Financial Aid PROFILE, noncustodial (divorced/separated) parent's statement, business/farm supplement, federal tax returns. *Financial aid deadline:* 3/1. *Notification date:* 4/1. Students must reply by 5/1.

CONTACT John DeCourcy, Director, Financial Aid, Washington and Lee University, Gilliam House, 204 West Washington Street, Lexington, VA 24450, 540-458-8717. *Fax:* 540-458-8614. *E-mail:* financialaid@wlu.edu.

WASHINGTON BIBLE COLLEGE
Lanham, MD

Tuition & fees: N/R	Average undergraduate aid package: $7250

ABOUT THE INSTITUTION Independent nondenominational, coed. *Awards:* associate, bachelor's, and master's degrees and post-bachelor's certificates (graduate degrees offered by Capital Bible Seminary). 7 undergraduate majors. *Total enrollment:* 616. Undergraduates: 254. Freshmen: 29. Both federal and institutional methodology are used as a basis for awarding need-based institutional aid.

FRESHMAN FINANCIAL AID (Fall 2009, est.) 17 applied for aid; of those 76% were deemed to have need. 100% of freshmen with need received aid. *Average percent of need met:* 59% (excluding resources awarded to replace EFC). *Average financial aid package:* $6500 (excluding resources awarded to replace EFC).

UNDERGRADUATE FINANCIAL AID (Fall 2009, est.) 139 applied for aid; of those 94% were deemed to have need. 94% of undergraduates with need received aid; of those 7% had need fully met. *Average percent of need met:* 63% (excluding resources awarded to replace EFC). *Average financial aid package:* $7250 (excluding resources awarded to replace EFC). 13% of all full-time undergraduates had no need and received non-need-based gift aid.

GIFT AID (NEED-BASED) *Total amount:* $722,167 (56% federal, 16% state, 10% institutional, 18% external sources). *Receiving aid:* Freshmen: 65% (13); all full-time undergraduates: 70% (107). *Average award:* Freshmen: $2175; Undergraduates: $2992. *Scholarships, grants, and awards:* Federal Pell, FSEOG, state, private, college/university gift aid from institutional funds.

GIFT AID (NON-NEED-BASED) *Total amount:* $234,304 (100% institutional). *Receiving aid:* Freshmen: 50% (10). Undergraduates: 73% (111). *Average award:* Undergraduates: $1518. *Scholarships, grants, and awards by category: Academic interests/achievement:* 131 awards ($104,501 total): general academic interests/achievements. *Creative arts/performance:* 19 awards ($32,500 total): music. *Special achievements/activities:* 41 awards ($85,263 total): general special achievements/activities, leadership, religious involvement. *Special characteristics:* 19 awards ($59,944 total): children of faculty/staff, international students, relatives of clergy, siblings of current students, spouses of current students. *Tuition waivers:* Full or partial for employees or children of employees.

LOANS *Student loans:* $1,750,081 (38% need-based, 62% non-need-based). 50% of past graduating class borrowed through all loan programs. *Average indebtedness per student:* $27,375. *Average need-based loan:* Freshmen: $3208. Undergraduates: $3602. *Parent loans:* $53,650 (100% non-need-based). *Programs:* FFEL (Subsidized and Unsubsidized Stafford, PLUS).

WORK-STUDY *Federal work-study:* Total amount: $45,362; 19 jobs averaging $2388.

APPLYING FOR FINANCIAL AID *Required financial aid forms:* FAFSA, institution's own form, CSS Financial Aid PROFILE. *Financial aid deadline (priority):* 7/1. *Notification date:* Continuous beginning 7/1. Students must reply within 2 weeks of notification.

CONTACT Nichole Sefiane, Financial Aid Director, Washington Bible College, 6511 Princess Garden Parkway, Lanham, MD 20706-3599, 301-552-1400 Ext. 1222 or toll-free 877-793-7227 Ext. 1212. *Fax:* 240-387-1351. *E-mail:* nsefiane@bible.edu.

WASHINGTON COLLEGE
Chestertown, MD

ABOUT THE INSTITUTION Independent, coed. 34 undergraduate majors.

GIFT AID (NEED-BASED) *Scholarships, grants, and awards:* Federal Pell, FSEOG, state, private, college/university gift aid from institutional funds.

GIFT AID (NON-NEED-BASED) *Scholarships, grants, and awards by category: Academic interests/achievement:* general academic interests/achievements. *Special characteristics:* children of faculty/staff.

LOANS *Programs:* FFEL (Subsidized and Unsubsidized Stafford, PLUS), Perkins.

WORK-STUDY *Federal work-study:* Total amount: $582,913; 290 jobs averaging $2000.

APPLYING FOR FINANCIAL AID *Required financial aid forms:* FAFSA, institution's own form.

CONTACT Ms. Jean M. Narcum, Director of Financial Aid, Washington College, 300 Washington Avenue, Chestertown, MD 21620-1197, 410-778-7214 or toll-free 800-422-1782. *Fax:* 410-778-7287. *E-mail:* jnarcum2@washcoll.edu.

WASHINGTON STATE UNIVERSITY
Pullman, WA

Tuition & fees (WA res): $8489	Average undergraduate aid package: $11,347

ABOUT THE INSTITUTION State-supported, coed. 129 undergraduate majors. Federal methodology is used as a basis for awarding need-based institutional aid.

UNDERGRADUATE EXPENSES for 2009–10 *Tuition, state resident:* full-time $7088; part-time $380 per credit hour. *Tuition, nonresident:* full-time $18,164; part-time $934 per credit hour. *Required fees:* full-time $1401. Full-time tuition and fees vary according to location and reciprocity agreements. Part-time tuition and fees vary according to course load, location, and reciprocity agreements. *College room and board:* $8886; *Room only:* $4852. Room and board charges vary according to board plan, housing facility, and location.

FRESHMAN FINANCIAL AID (Fall 2008) 2,642 applied for aid; of those 61% were deemed to have need. 100% of freshmen with need received aid; of those 32% had need fully met. *Average percent of need met:* 77% (excluding resources awarded to replace EFC). *Average financial aid package:* $10,887 (excluding resources awarded to replace EFC). 19% of all full-time freshmen had no need and received non-need-based gift aid.

UNDERGRADUATE FINANCIAL AID (Fall 2008) 11,924 applied for aid; of those 74% were deemed to have need. 99% of undergraduates with need received aid; of those 25% had need fully met. *Average percent of need met:* 77% (excluding resources awarded to replace EFC). *Average financial aid package:* $11,347 (excluding resources awarded to replace EFC). 6% of all full-time undergraduates had no need and received non-need-based gift aid.

GIFT AID (NEED-BASED) *Total amount:* $47,182,016 (39% federal, 51% state, 10% institutional). *Receiving aid:* Freshmen: 27% (997); all full-time undergraduates: 34% (6,188). *Average award:* Freshmen: $6890; Undergraduates: $7403. *Scholarships, grants, and awards:* Federal Pell, FSEOG, state, private, college/university gift aid from institutional funds, United Negro College Fund, Federal Nursing.

GIFT AID (NON-NEED-BASED) *Total amount:* $14,072,192 (5% state, 41% institutional, 54% external sources). *Receiving aid:* Freshmen: 32% (1,183). Undergraduates: 19% (3,331). *Average award:* Freshmen: $3751. Undergraduates: $2284. *Scholarships, grants, and awards by category: Academic interests/achievement:* agriculture, architecture, area/ethnic studies, biological sciences, business, communication, computer science, education, engineering/technologies, English, foreign languages, general academic interests/achievements, health fields, home economics, humanities, international studies, mathematics, military science, physical sciences, premedicine, social sciences. *Creative arts/performance:* applied art and design, art/fine arts, cinema/film/broadcasting, creative writing, general creative arts/performance, journalism/publications, music, performing arts, theater/drama. *Special achievements/activities:* community service, general special achievements/activities, junior miss, leadership, memberships, religious involvement, rodeo. *Special characteristics:* children and siblings of alumni, children of faculty/staff, children of public servants, children with a deceased or disabled parent, first-generation college students, handicapped students, international students, out-of-state students, public servants, religious affiliation, veterans, veterans' children. *Tuition waivers:* Full or partial for employees or children of employees, senior citizens.

LOANS *Student loans:* $65,525,102 (49% need-based, 51% non-need-based). *Average need-based loan:* Freshmen: $3268. Undergraduates: $4438. *Parent loans:* $19,387,962 (100% non-need-based). *Programs:* Federal Direct (Subsidized and Unsubsidized Stafford, PLUS), Perkins, Federal Nursing, college/university, alternative loans.

WORK-STUDY *Federal work-study:* Total amount: $565,109; 273 jobs averaging $2500. *State or other work-study/employment:* Total amount: $1,926,898 (100% need-based). 861 part-time jobs averaging $2500.

ATHLETIC AWARDS Total amount: $6,116,394 (100% non-need-based).

APPLYING FOR FINANCIAL AID *Required financial aid form:* FAFSA. *Financial aid deadline (priority):* 2/15. *Notification date:* Continuous beginning 4/1.

CONTACT Mike Whaley, Office of Financial Aid and Scholarships, Washington State University, PO Box 641068, Pullman, WA 99164-1068, 509-335-9721 or toll-free 888-468-6978. *Fax:* 509-335-3689. *E-mail:* whaley@wsu.edu.

WASHINGTON UNIVERSITY IN ST. LOUIS
St. Louis, MO

Tuition & fees: $40,374	Average undergraduate aid package: $32,350

ABOUT THE INSTITUTION Independent, coed. 165 undergraduate majors. Institutional methodology is used as a basis for awarding need-based institutional aid.

UNDERGRADUATE EXPENSES for 2010–11 *Comprehensive fee:* $53,315 includes full-time tuition ($39,400), mandatory fees ($974), and room and board ($12,941). *College room only:* $8405. Room and board charges vary according to board plan and housing facility. *Payment plans:* Tuition prepayment, installment.

FRESHMAN FINANCIAL AID (Fall 2009, est.) 996 applied for aid; of those 57% were deemed to have need. 98% of freshmen with need received aid; of those 100% had need fully met. *Average percent of need met:* 100% (excluding resources awarded to replace EFC). *Average financial aid package:* $31,489 (excluding resources awarded to replace EFC). 18% of all full-time freshmen had no need and received non-need-based gift aid.

UNDERGRADUATE FINANCIAL AID (Fall 2009, est.) 4,260 applied for aid; of those 61% were deemed to have need. 99% of undergraduates with need received aid; of those 100% had need fully met. *Average percent of need met:* 100% (excluding resources awarded to replace EFC). *Average financial aid package:* $32,350 (excluding resources awarded to replace EFC). 15% of all full-time undergraduates had no need and received non-need-based gift aid.

GIFT AID (NEED-BASED) *Total amount:* $71,564,594 (4% federal, 1% state, 90% institutional, 5% external sources). *Receiving aid:* Freshmen: 36% (542); all full-time undergraduates: 41% (2,498). *Average award:* Freshmen: $27,699; Undergraduates: $28,649. *Scholarships, grants, and awards:* Federal Pell, FSEOG, state, private, college/university gift aid from institutional funds, United Negro College Fund.

GIFT AID (NON-NEED-BASED) *Total amount:* $7,180,631 (2% federal, 5% state, 79% institutional, 14% external sources). *Receiving aid:* Freshmen: 4% (59). Undergraduates: 3% (176). *Average award:* Freshmen: $9195. Undergraduates: $7865. *Scholarships, grants, and awards by category:* Academic interests/achievement: architecture, biological sciences, business, communication, computer science, education, engineering/technologies, English, foreign languages, general academic interests/achievements, health fields, humanities, international studies, mathematics, military science, physical sciences, premedicine, religion/biblical studies, social sciences. Creative arts/performance: applied art and design, art/fine arts, cinema/film/broadcasting, creative writing, dance, music, performing arts, theater/drama. *Tuition waivers:* Full or partial for employees or children of employees.

LOANS *Student loans:* $12,175,145 (90% need-based, 10% non-need-based). 39% of past graduating class borrowed through all loan programs. *Average need-based loan:* Freshmen: $5275. Undergraduates: $6193. *Parent loans:* $1,098,763 (60% need-based, 40% non-need-based). *Programs:* Federal Direct (Subsidized and Unsubsidized Stafford, PLUS), Perkins, state, college/university.

WORK-STUDY *Federal work-study:* Total amount: $2,115,848; 1,107 jobs averaging $1911.

APPLYING FOR FINANCIAL AID *Required financial aid forms:* FAFSA, CSS Financial Aid PROFILE, noncustodial (divorced/separated) parent's statement, student and parent 1040 tax return (or signed waiver if there is no tax return). *Financial aid deadline:* 2/15. *Notification date:* 4/1. Students must reply by 5/1 or within 2 weeks of notification.

CONTACT Mr. William Witbrodt, Director of Financial Aid, Washington University in St. Louis, Campus Box 1041, St. Louis, MO 63130-4899, 314-935-5900 or toll-free 800-638-0700. *Fax:* 314-935-4037. *E-mail:* financial@wustl.edu.

WATKINS COLLEGE OF ART, DESIGN, & FILM
Nashville, TN

Tuition & fees: $18,600	Average undergraduate aid package: $11,150

ABOUT THE INSTITUTION Independent, coed. 6 undergraduate majors. Federal methodology is used as a basis for awarding need-based institutional aid.

UNDERGRADUATE EXPENSES for 2010–11 *Tuition:* full-time $17,250; part-time $575 per credit. *Required fees:* full-time $1350; $45 per credit. *Payment plan:* Installment.

FRESHMAN FINANCIAL AID (Fall 2008) 39 applied for aid; of those 100% were deemed to have need. 100% of freshmen with need received aid; of those 13% had need fully met. *Average percent of need met:* 30% (excluding resources awarded to replace EFC). *Average financial aid package:* $9327 (excluding resources awarded to replace EFC). 7% of all full-time freshmen had no need and received non-need-based gift aid.

UNDERGRADUATE FINANCIAL AID (Fall 2008) 174 applied for aid; of those 100% were deemed to have need. 100% of undergraduates with need received aid; of those 17% had need fully met. *Average percent of need met:* 45% (excluding resources awarded to replace EFC). *Average financial aid package:* $11,150 (excluding resources awarded to replace EFC). 14% of all full-time undergraduates had no need and received non-need-based gift aid.

GIFT AID (NEED-BASED) *Total amount:* $448,335 (74% federal, 11% state, 15% institutional). *Receiving aid:* Freshmen: 31% (13); all full-time undergraduates: 43% (95). *Average award:* Freshmen: $3526; Undergraduates: $4000. *Scholarships, grants, and awards:* Federal Pell, FSEOG, state, private, college/university gift aid from institutional funds, Academic Competitiveness Grants.

GIFT AID (NON-NEED-BASED) *Total amount:* $474,680 (60% state, 37% institutional, 3% external sources). *Receiving aid:* Freshmen: 5% (2). Undergraduates: 32% (70). *Average award:* Freshmen: $3000. Undergraduates: $4000. *Scholarships, grants, and awards by category:* Academic interests/achievement: general academic interests/achievements. Creative arts/performance: applied art and design, art/fine arts, cinema/film/broadcasting. Special achievements/activities: general special achievements/activities. *Tuition waivers:* Full or partial for employees or children of employees.

LOANS *Student loans:* $1,900,685 (47% need-based, 53% non-need-based). 47% of past graduating class borrowed through all loan programs. *Average indebtedness per student:* $15,000. *Average need-based loan:* Freshmen: $3500. Undergraduates: $4750. *Parent loans:* $486,468 (100% non-need-based). *Programs:* Federal Direct (Subsidized and Unsubsidized Stafford, PLUS), private alternative loans.

WORK-STUDY *Federal work-study:* Total amount: $20,293; 17 jobs averaging $1300. *State or other work-study/employment:* Total amount: $20,000 (100% non-need-based). 25 part-time jobs averaging $2000.

APPLYING FOR FINANCIAL AID *Required financial aid forms:* FAFSA, institution's own form. *Financial aid deadline (priority):* 4/1. *Notification date:* Continuous beginning 5/1. Students must reply within 2 weeks of notification.

CONTACT Lyle Jones, Financial Aid Coordinator, Watkins College of Art, Design, & Film, 2298 Rosa L. Parks Boulevard, Nashville, TN 37228, 615-383-4848 Ext. 7421. *Fax:* 615-383-4849. *E-mail:* financialaid@watkins.edu.

WAYLAND BAPTIST UNIVERSITY
Plainview, TX

Tuition & fees: $12,470	Average undergraduate aid package: $11,850

ABOUT THE INSTITUTION Independent Baptist, coed. 41 undergraduate majors. Federal methodology is used as a basis for awarding need-based institutional aid.

UNDERGRADUATE EXPENSES for 2009–10 *One-time required fee:* $270. *Comprehensive fee:* $16,334 includes full-time tuition ($11,850), mandatory fees ($620), and room and board ($3864). *College room only:* $1328. Full-time tuition and fees vary according to course load and location. Room and board charges vary according to board plan and housing facility. *Part-time tuition:* $395 per credit hour. *Part-time fees:* $60 per term. Part-time tuition and fees vary according to course load and location. *Payment plan:* Installment.

FRESHMAN FINANCIAL AID (Fall 2009, est.) 188 applied for aid; of those 82% were deemed to have need. 99% of freshmen with need received aid; of those

23% had need fully met. *Average percent of need met:* 74% (excluding resources awarded to replace EFC). *Average financial aid package:* $11,447 (excluding resources awarded to replace EFC). 21% of all full-time freshmen had no need and received non-need-based gift aid.

UNDERGRADUATE FINANCIAL AID (Fall 2009, est.) 651 applied for aid; of those 83% were deemed to have need. 99% of undergraduates with need received aid; of those 21% had need fully met. *Average percent of need met:* 73% (excluding resources awarded to replace EFC). *Average financial aid package:* $11,850 (excluding resources awarded to replace EFC). 20% of all full-time undergraduates had no need and received non-need-based gift aid.

GIFT AID (NEED-BASED) *Total amount:* $4,949,908 (35% federal, 23% state, 40% institutional, 2% external sources). *Receiving aid:* Freshmen: 71% (153); all full-time undergraduates: 70% (526). *Average award:* Freshmen: $9472; Undergraduates: $9044. *Scholarships, grants, and awards:* Federal Pell, FSEOG, state, private, college/university gift aid from institutional funds.

GIFT AID (NON-NEED-BASED) *Total amount:* $1,738,414 (1% federal, 1% state, 94% institutional, 4% external sources). *Receiving aid:* Freshmen: 13% (29). Undergraduates: 8% (58). *Average award:* Freshmen: $7576. Undergraduates: $7202. *Scholarships, grants, and awards by category: Academic interests/ achievement:* 318 awards ($1,018,112 total): biological sciences, business, communication, education, English, general academic interests/achievements, mathematics, physical sciences, religion/biblical studies, social sciences. *Creative arts/performance:* 137 awards ($167,006 total): art/fine arts, journalism/publications, music, theater/drama. *Special achievements/activities:* 159 awards ($80,075 total): cheerleading/drum major, leadership, memberships, religious involvement. *Special characteristics:* 343 awards ($705,945 total): children and siblings of alumni, children of faculty/staff, ethnic background, general special characteristics, international students, local/state students, members of minority groups, relatives of clergy, religious affiliation. *Tuition waivers:* Full or partial for employees or children of employees.

LOANS *Student loans:* $3,593,171 (73% need-based, 27% non-need-based). 78% of past graduating class borrowed through all loan programs. *Average indebtedness per student:* $25,387. *Average need-based loan:* Freshmen: $3038. Undergraduates: $3665. *Parent loans:* $148,724 (23% need-based, 77% non-need-based). *Programs:* FFEL (Subsidized and Unsubsidized Stafford, PLUS), Perkins, state.

WORK-STUDY *Federal work-study:* Total amount: $117,547; 132 jobs averaging $1840. *State or other work-study/employment:* Total amount: $95,397 (15% need-based, 85% non-need-based). 77 part-time jobs averaging $1718.

APPLYING FOR FINANCIAL AID *Required financial aid forms:* FAFSA, institution's own form. *Financial aid deadline (priority):* 5/1. *Notification date:* Continuous beginning 1/1. Students must reply within 3 weeks of notification.

CONTACT Karen LaQuey, Director of Financial Aid, Wayland Baptist University, 1900 West 7th Street, Plainview, TX 79072-6998, 806-291-3520 or toll-free 800-588-1928. *Fax:* 806-291-1956. *E-mail:* laquey@wbu.edu.

WAYNESBURG UNIVERSITY
Waynesburg, PA

Tuition & fees: $17,760 — **Average undergraduate aid package:** $12,878

ABOUT THE INSTITUTION Independent religious, coed. 50 undergraduate majors. Federal methodology is used as a basis for awarding need-based institutional aid.

UNDERGRADUATE EXPENSES for 2009–10 *Comprehensive fee:* $25,130 includes full-time tuition ($17,400), mandatory fees ($360), and room and board ($7370). *College room only:* $3750. Full-time tuition and fees vary according to class time. Room and board charges vary according to board plan. *Part-time tuition:* $730 per credit hour. Part-time tuition and fees vary according to class time, course load, and location. *Payment plan:* Installment.

FRESHMAN FINANCIAL AID (Fall 2009, est.) 391 applied for aid; of those 89% were deemed to have need. 100% of freshmen with need received aid; of those 18% had need fully met. *Average percent of need met:* 79% (excluding resources awarded to replace EFC). *Average financial aid package:* $14,316 (excluding resources awarded to replace EFC). 8% of all full-time freshmen had no need and received non-need-based gift aid.

UNDERGRADUATE FINANCIAL AID (Fall 2009, est.) 1,581 applied for aid; of those 87% were deemed to have need. 99% of undergraduates with need received aid; of those 20% had need fully met. *Average percent of need met:* 76% (excluding resources awarded to replace EFC). *Average financial aid*

package: $12,878 (excluding resources awarded to replace EFC). 7% of all full-time undergraduates had no need and received non-need-based gift aid.

GIFT AID (NEED-BASED) *Total amount:* $12,830,000 (21% federal, 19% state, 56% institutional, 4% external sources). *Receiving aid:* Freshmen: 50% (346); all full-time undergraduates: 65% (1,262). *Average award:* Freshmen: $11,393; Undergraduates: $10,058. *Scholarships, grants, and awards:* Federal Pell, FSEOG, state, private, college/university gift aid from institutional funds.

GIFT AID (NON-NEED-BASED) *Total amount:* $1,739,000 (1% federal, 1% state, 86% institutional, 12% external sources). *Receiving aid:* Freshmen: 5% (38). Undergraduates: 6% (113). *Average award:* Freshmen: $6058. Undergraduates: $7076. *Scholarships, grants, and awards by category: Academic interests/ achievement:* 60 awards ($150,000 total): biological sciences, business, communication, computer science, education, English, general academic interests/ achievements, international studies, mathematics, religion/biblical studies. *Creative arts/performance:* music. *Special achievements/activities:* community service. *Special characteristics:* children of faculty/staff. *Tuition waivers:* Full or partial for employees or children of employees.

LOANS *Student loans:* $12,050,000 (65% need-based, 35% non-need-based). 88% of past graduating class borrowed through all loan programs. *Average indebtedness per student:* $22,000. *Average need-based loan:* Freshmen: $3090. Undergraduates: $3876. *Parent loans:* $2,100,000 (19% need-based, 81% non-need-based). *Programs:* FFEL (Subsidized and Unsubsidized Stafford, PLUS), Perkins, Federal Nursing.

WORK-STUDY *Federal work-study:* Total amount: $176,000; jobs available.

APPLYING FOR FINANCIAL AID *Required financial aid form:* FAFSA. *Financial aid deadline:* Continuous. *Notification date:* Continuous beginning 2/15. Students must reply within 2 weeks of notification.

CONTACT Matthew C. Stokan, Director of Financial Aid, Waynesburg University, 51 West College Street, Waynesburg, PA 15370-1222, 724-852-3208 or toll-free 800-225-7393. *Fax:* 724-852-3269. *E-mail:* mstokan@waynesburg.edu.

WAYNE STATE COLLEGE
Wayne, NE

Tuition & fees (NE res): $4805 — **Average undergraduate aid package:** $6771

ABOUT THE INSTITUTION State-supported, coed. 53 undergraduate majors. Federal methodology is used as a basis for awarding need-based institutional aid.

UNDERGRADUATE EXPENSES for 2009–10 *Tuition, state resident:* full-time $3675; part-time $122.50 per credit hour. *Tuition, nonresident:* full-time $7350; part-time $245 per credit hour. *Required fees:* full-time $1130; $44.50 per credit hour. Full-time tuition and fees vary according to course level and course load. Part-time tuition and fees vary according to course level and course load. *College room and board:* $5280; *Room only:* $2510. Room and board charges vary according to board plan and housing facility. *Payment plan:* Installment.

FRESHMAN FINANCIAL AID (Fall 2009, est.) 596 applied for aid; of those 80% were deemed to have need. 97% of freshmen with need received aid; of those 49% had need fully met. *Average percent of need met:* 60% (excluding resources awarded to replace EFC). *Average financial aid package:* $6787 (excluding resources awarded to replace EFC). 5% of all full-time freshmen had no need and received non-need-based gift aid.

UNDERGRADUATE FINANCIAL AID (Fall 2009, est.) 2,261 applied for aid; of those 80% were deemed to have need. 100% of undergraduates with need received aid; of those 36% had need fully met. *Average percent of need met:* 73% (excluding resources awarded to replace EFC). *Average financial aid package:* $6771 (excluding resources awarded to replace EFC). 12% of all full-time undergraduates had no need and received non-need-based gift aid.

GIFT AID (NEED-BASED) *Total amount:* $5,368,262 (87% federal, 13% state). *Receiving aid:* Freshmen: 54% (357); all full-time undergraduates: 49% (1,325). *Average award:* Freshmen: $3916; Undergraduates: $3797. *Scholarships, grants, and awards:* Federal Pell, FSEOG, state, private, college/university gift aid from institutional funds.

GIFT AID (NON-NEED-BASED) *Total amount:* $2,465,846 (74% institutional, 26% external sources). *Receiving aid:* Freshmen: 27% (182). Undergraduates: 23% (623). *Average award:* Freshmen: $1486. Undergraduates: $2805. *Scholarships, grants, and awards by category: Academic interests/achievement:* biological sciences, business, communication, computer science, education, English, foreign languages, general academic interests/achievements, health fields, home economics, humanities, mathematics, physical sciences, premedicine, social sciences. *Creative arts/performance:* applied art and design, art/fine arts, creative writing, debating, general creative arts/performance, journalism/publications, music, performing arts, theater/drama. *Special achievements/activities:* general special achievements/activities, leadership. *Special characteristics:* children of faculty/staff, children with a deceased or disabled parent, ethnic background, general special characteristics, local/state students, members of minority groups, out-of-state students, veterans, veterans' children. *Tuition waivers:* Full or partial for employees or children of employees.

LOANS *Student loans:* $11,570,172 (47% need-based, 53% non-need-based). *Average need-based loan:* Freshmen: $3329. Undergraduates: $3747. *Parent loans:* $541,726 (100% non-need-based). *Programs:* FFEL (Subsidized and Unsubsidized Stafford, PLUS), Perkins.

WORK-STUDY *Federal work-study:* Total amount: $119,875; jobs available.

ATHLETIC AWARDS Total amount: $414,516 (100% non-need-based).

APPLYING FOR FINANCIAL AID *Required financial aid form:* FAFSA. *Financial aid deadline (priority):* 4/1. *Notification date:* Continuous beginning 3/1. Students must reply within 4 weeks of notification.

CONTACT Kyle M. Rose, Director of Financial Aid, Wayne State College, 1111 Main Street, Wayne, NE 68787, 402-375-7230 or toll-free 800-228-9972 (in-state). *Fax:* 402-375-7067. *E-mail:* kyrose1@wsc.edu.

WAYNE STATE UNIVERSITY
Detroit, MI

Tuition & fees (MI res): $8643	Average undergraduate aid package: $12,125

ABOUT THE INSTITUTION State-supported, coed. 86 undergraduate majors. Federal methodology is used as a basis for awarding need-based institutional aid.

UNDERGRADUATE EXPENSES for 2009–10 *Tuition, state resident:* full-time $7571; part-time $252.35 per credit hour. *Tuition, nonresident:* full-time $17,340; part-time $578 per credit hour. *Required fees:* full-time $1072; $23.70 per credit hour or $180.45 per term. Full-time tuition and fees vary according to course load, program, and student level. Part-time tuition and fees vary according to course load, program, and student level. *College room and board:* $7210. Room and board charges vary according to board plan and housing facility. *Payment plan:* Installment.

FRESHMAN FINANCIAL AID (Fall 2008) 2,241 applied for aid; of those 80% were deemed to have need. 98% of freshmen with need received aid; of those 22% had need fully met. *Average percent of need met:* 72% (excluding resources awarded to replace EFC). *Average financial aid package:* $11,934 (excluding resources awarded to replace EFC). 11% of all full-time freshmen had no need and received non-need-based gift aid.

UNDERGRADUATE FINANCIAL AID (Fall 2008) 8,831 applied for aid; of those 86% were deemed to have need. 98% of undergraduates with need received aid; of those 21% had need fully met. *Average percent of need met:* 67% (excluding resources awarded to replace EFC). *Average financial aid package:* $12,125 (excluding resources awarded to replace EFC). 10% of all full-time undergraduates had no need and received non-need-based gift aid.

GIFT AID (NEED-BASED) *Total amount:* $35,649,437 (78% federal, 4% state, 18% institutional). *Receiving aid:* Freshmen: 52% (1,376); all full-time undergraduates: 46% (5,582). *Average award:* Freshmen: $5546; Undergraduates: $4895. *Scholarships, grants, and awards:* Federal Pell, FSEOG, state, private, college/university gift aid from institutional funds, United Negro College Fund.

GIFT AID (NON-NEED-BASED) *Total amount:* $19,395,500 (14% state, 63% institutional, 23% external sources). *Receiving aid:* Freshmen: 35% (930). Undergraduates: 23% (2,823). *Average award:* Freshmen: $4720. Undergraduates: $5158. *Scholarships, grants, and awards by category:* Academic interests/achievement: 2,410 awards ($6,666,706 total): area/ethnic studies, biological sciences, business, communication, computer science, education, engineering/technologies, English, foreign languages, general academic interests/achievements, health fields, humanities, international studies, library science, mathematics, military science, physical sciences, premedicine, social sciences. Creative arts/performance: 352 awards ($870,060 total): art/fine arts, dance, debating, journalism/publications, music, theater/drama. Special achievements/activities: leadership. Special characteristics: 94 awards ($325,199 total): children of faculty/staff. *Tuition waivers:* Full or partial for employees or children of employees, senior citizens.

LOANS *Student loans:* $80,319,085 (93% need-based, 7% non-need-based). 56% of past graduating class borrowed through all loan programs. *Average indebtedness per student:* $19,781. *Average need-based loan:* Freshmen: $3549.

Undergraduates: $4328. *Parent loans:* $22,701,473 (100% non-need-based). *Programs:* Federal Direct (Subsidized and Unsubsidized Stafford, PLUS), Perkins, Federal Nursing, college/university.

WORK-STUDY *Federal work-study:* Total amount: $986,371; 268 jobs averaging $3536. *State or other work-study/employment:* Total amount: $280,410 (100% need-based). 83 part-time jobs averaging $3312.

ATHLETIC AWARDS Total amount: $2,593,930 (100% non-need-based).

APPLYING FOR FINANCIAL AID *Required financial aid forms:* FAFSA, income tax forms, W-2 forms. *Financial aid deadline:* 4/30 (priority: 2/15). *Notification date:* Continuous beginning 3/1. Students must reply within 2 weeks of notification.

CONTACT Albert Hermsen, Director of Scholarships and Financial Aid, Wayne State University, 3W HNJ Student Services Building, Detroit, MI 48202, 313-577-3378 or toll-free 877-WSU-INFO. *Fax:* 313-577-6648.

WEBBER INTERNATIONAL UNIVERSITY
Babson Park, FL

Tuition & fees: $17,850	Average undergraduate aid package: $17,601

ABOUT THE INSTITUTION Independent, coed. 11 undergraduate majors. Federal methodology is used as a basis for awarding need-based institutional aid.

UNDERGRADUATE EXPENSES for 2010–11 *Comprehensive fee:* $24,822 includes full-time tuition ($17,850) and room and board ($6972). *College room only:* $4500. Full-time tuition and fees vary according to class time and course load. Room and board charges vary according to board plan and gender. *Part-time tuition:* $247 per credit hour. Part-time tuition and fees vary according to course load. *Payment plan:* Installment.

FRESHMAN FINANCIAL AID (Fall 2009, est.) 137 applied for aid; of those 78% were deemed to have need. 100% of freshmen with need received aid; of those 18% had need fully met. *Average percent of need met:* 55% (excluding resources awarded to replace EFC). *Average financial aid package:* $17,870 (excluding resources awarded to replace EFC). 30% of all full-time freshmen had no need and received non-need-based gift aid.

UNDERGRADUATE FINANCIAL AID (Fall 2009, est.) 435 applied for aid; of those 81% were deemed to have need. 100% of undergraduates with need received aid; of those 11% had need fully met. *Average percent of need met:* 50% (excluding resources awarded to replace EFC). *Average financial aid package:* $17,601 (excluding resources awarded to replace EFC). 27% of all full-time undergraduates had no need and received non-need-based gift aid.

GIFT AID (NEED-BASED) *Total amount:* $3,136,050 (41% federal, 38% state, 19% institutional, 2% external sources). *Receiving aid:* Freshmen: 62% (107); all full-time undergraduates: 63% (351). *Average award:* Freshmen: $14,965; Undergraduates: $13,616. *Scholarships, grants, and awards:* Federal Pell, FSEOG, state, private, college/university gift aid from institutional funds.

GIFT AID (NON-NEED-BASED) *Total amount:* $1,536,235 (23% state, 74% institutional, 3% external sources). *Receiving aid:* Freshmen: 59% (102). Undergraduates: 55% (303). *Average award:* Freshmen: $7488. Undergraduates: $7491. *Scholarships, grants, and awards by category:* Academic interests/achievement: $749,170 total: business, general academic interests/achievements. Creative arts/performance: $44,750 total: general creative arts/performance, journalism/publications. Special achievements/activities: $2,561,209 total: cheerleading/drum major, community service, general special achievements/activities, leadership, memberships. Special characteristics: $1,003,041 total: children and siblings of alumni, children of faculty/staff, first-generation college students, general special characteristics, international students, local/state students, out-of-state students, siblings of current students. *Tuition waivers:* Full or partial for children of alumni, employees or children of employees, adult students, senior citizens.

LOANS *Student loans:* $2,862,824 (89% need-based, 11% non-need-based). 57% of past graduating class borrowed through all loan programs. *Average indebtedness per student:* $25,962. *Average need-based loan:* Freshmen: $4515. Undergraduates: $5001. *Parent loans:* $555,358 (74% need-based, 26% non-need-based). *Programs:* FFEL (Subsidized and Unsubsidized Stafford, PLUS), Perkins, alternative loans.

WORK-STUDY *Federal work-study:* Total amount: $41,371; 33 jobs averaging $1254. *State or other work-study/employment:* Total amount: $39,305 (18% need-based, 82% non-need-based). 28 part-time jobs averaging $1404.

ATHLETIC AWARDS Total amount: $2,540,170 (66% need-based, 34% non-need-based).

APPLYING FOR FINANCIAL AID *Required financial aid forms:* FAFSA, state aid form. *Financial aid deadline:* 8/1 (priority: 5/1). *Notification date:* Continuous beginning 3/1. Students must reply within 4 weeks of notification.

CONTACT Ms. Kathleen Wilson, Director of Financial Aid, Webber International University, PO Box 96, 1201 Scenic Highway, Babson Park, FL 33827-0096, 863-638-2930 or toll-free 800-741-1844. *Fax:* 863-638-1317. *E-mail:* wilsonka@webber.edu.

WEBB INSTITUTE
Glen Cove, NY

Tuition & fees: See below.	Average undergraduate aid package: $5200

ABOUT THE INSTITUTION Independent, coed. 1 undergraduate major. Federal methodology is used as a basis for awarding need-based institutional aid.

UNDERGRADUATE EXPENSES for 2009–10 includes room and board ($10,200). All students are awarded full-tuition scholarships.

FRESHMAN FINANCIAL AID (Fall 2009, est.) 3 applied for aid; of those 100% were deemed to have need. 100% of freshmen with need received aid. *Average financial aid package:* $3500 (excluding resources awarded to replace EFC).

UNDERGRADUATE FINANCIAL AID (Fall 2009, est.) 19 applied for aid; of those 100% were deemed to have need. 100% of undergraduates with need received aid; of those 100% had need fully met. *Average percent of need met:* 53% (excluding resources awarded to replace EFC). *Average financial aid package:* $5200 (excluding resources awarded to replace EFC).

GIFT AID (NEED-BASED) *Total amount:* $42,600 (30% federal, 6% state, 64% institutional). *Receiving aid:* All full-time undergraduates: 11% (10). *Average award:* Undergraduates: $2710. *Scholarships, grants, and awards:* Federal Pell, state, private, college/university gift aid from institutional funds.

GIFT AID (NON-NEED-BASED) *Total amount:* $23,250 (28% state, 72% external sources). *Receiving aid:* Undergraduates: 8% (7).

LOANS *Student loans:* $35,000 (100% need-based). 33% of past graduating class borrowed through all loan programs. *Average indebtedness per student:* $8545. *Average need-based loan:* Freshmen: $3500. Undergraduates: $5200. *Parent loans:* $20,500 (100% need-based). *Programs:* FFEL (Subsidized and Unsubsidized Stafford, PLUS).

APPLYING FOR FINANCIAL AID *Required financial aid form:* FAFSA. *Financial aid deadline (priority):* 7/1. *Notification date:* Continuous beginning 8/15.

CONTACT William G. Murray, Director of Enrollment Management, Webb Institute, Crescent Beach Road, Glen Cove, NY 11542-1398, 516-671-2213 Ext. 104. *Fax:* 516-674-9838. *E-mail:* bmurray@webb-institute.edu.

WEBER STATE UNIVERSITY
Ogden, UT

ABOUT THE INSTITUTION State-supported, coed. 85 undergraduate majors.

GIFT AID (NEED-BASED) *Scholarships, grants, and awards:* Federal Pell, FSEOG, state, private, college/university gift aid from institutional funds.

LOANS *Programs:* FFEL (Subsidized and Unsubsidized Stafford, PLUS), Perkins, college/university, short-term tuition loans.

APPLYING FOR FINANCIAL AID *Required financial aid forms:* FAFSA, institution's own form.

CONTACT Mr. Richard O. Effiong, Financial Aid Director, Weber State University, 120 Student Service Center, 1136 University Circle, Ogden, UT 84408-1136, 801-626-7569 or toll-free 800-634-6568 (in-state), 800-848-7770 (out-of-state). *E-mail:* finaid@weber.edu.

WEBSTER UNIVERSITY
St. Louis, MO

Tuition & fees: $21,056	Average undergraduate aid package: $22,542

ABOUT THE INSTITUTION Independent, coed. 52 undergraduate majors. Federal methodology is used as a basis for awarding need-based institutional aid.

UNDERGRADUATE EXPENSES for 2009–10 *Comprehensive fee:* $30,126 includes full-time tuition ($21,056) and room and board ($9070). *College room only:* $4830. Full-time tuition and fees vary according to program. Room and board charges vary according to board plan and housing facility. *Part-time tuition:* $550 per credit hour. Part-time tuition and fees vary according to location. *Payment plan:* Installment.

FRESHMAN FINANCIAL AID (Fall 2009, est.) 425 applied for aid; of those 87% were deemed to have need. 100% of freshmen with need received aid. *Average financial aid package:* $23,852 (excluding resources awarded to replace EFC). 22% of all full-time freshmen had no need and received non-need-based gift aid.

UNDERGRADUATE FINANCIAL AID (Fall 2009, est.) 2,131 applied for aid; of those 87% were deemed to have need. 100% of undergraduates with need received aid. *Average financial aid package:* $22,542 (excluding resources awarded to replace EFC). 17% of all full-time undergraduates had no need and received non-need-based gift aid.

GIFT AID (NEED-BASED) *Total amount:* $21,508,499 (19% federal, 13% state, 66% institutional, 2% external sources). *Receiving aid:* Freshmen: 59% (290); all full-time undergraduates: 55% (1,519). *Average award:* Freshmen: $8534; Undergraduates: $7033. *Scholarships, grants, and awards:* Federal Pell, FSEOG, state, private, college/university gift aid from institutional funds.

GIFT AID (NON-NEED-BASED) *Total amount:* $3,639,616 (3% state, 91% institutional, 6% external sources). *Receiving aid:* Freshmen: 58% (288). Undergraduates: 45% (1,236). *Average award:* Freshmen: $10,567. Undergraduates: $8343. *Scholarships, grants, and awards by category: Academic interests/achievement:* 1,746 awards ($12,042,500 total): biological sciences, business, communication, computer science, education, English, foreign languages, general academic interests/achievements, humanities, international studies. *Creative arts/performance:* 58 awards ($115,563 total): art/fine arts, creative writing, debating, music, theater/drama. *Special achievements/activities:* 12 awards ($24,000 total): leadership. *Special characteristics:* 132 awards ($1,127,340 total): children and siblings of alumni, children of faculty/staff, ethnic background, international students, members of minority groups, out-of-state students. *Tuition waivers:* Full or partial for employees or children of employees.

LOANS *Student loans:* $18,200,889 (90% need-based, 10% non-need-based). 57% of past graduating class borrowed through all loan programs. *Average indebtedness per student:* $26,184. *Average need-based loan:* Freshmen: $3292. Undergraduates: $4475. *Parent loans:* $2,763,281 (79% need-based, 21% non-need-based). *Programs:* FFEL (Subsidized and Unsubsidized Stafford, PLUS), Perkins.

WORK-STUDY *Federal work-study:* Total amount: $2,266,032; 1,086 jobs averaging $2166. *State or other work-study/employment:* Total amount: $1,049,478 (67% need-based, 33% non-need-based). 505 part-time jobs averaging $2145.

APPLYING FOR FINANCIAL AID *Required financial aid forms:* FAFSA, institution's own form. *Financial aid deadline (priority):* 4/1. *Notification date:* Continuous beginning 2/1.

CONTACT Marilynn Shelton, Financial Aid Counselor, Webster University, 470 East Lockwood Avenue, St. Louis, MO 63119, 314-968-6992 Ext. 7671 or toll-free 800-75-ENROL. *Fax:* 314-968-7125. *E-mail:* sheltoma@webster.edu.

WELLESLEY COLLEGE
Wellesley, MA

Tuition & fees: $38,062	Average undergraduate aid package: $35,951

ABOUT THE INSTITUTION Independent, women only. 59 undergraduate majors. Both federal and institutional methodology are used as a basis for awarding need-based institutional aid.

UNDERGRADUATE EXPENSES for 2009–10 *Comprehensive fee:* $49,794 includes full-time tuition ($37,826), mandatory fees ($236), and room and board ($11,732). *College room only:* $5980. *Part-time tuition:* $1182 per credit hour. *Part-time fees:* $30 per credit. Part-time tuition and fees vary according to course load. *Payment plans:* Tuition prepayment, installment.

FRESHMAN FINANCIAL AID (Fall 2009, est.) 413 applied for aid; of those 83% were deemed to have need. 100% of freshmen with need received aid; of those 100% had need fully met. *Average percent of need met:* 100% (excluding resources awarded to replace EFC). *Average financial aid package:* $36,064 (excluding resources awarded to replace EFC).

UNDERGRADUATE FINANCIAL AID (Fall 2009, est.) 1,551 applied for aid; of those 87% were deemed to have need. 100% of undergraduates with need received aid; of those 100% had need fully met. *Average percent of need met:* 100% (excluding resources awarded to replace EFC). *Average financial aid package:* $35,951 (excluding resources awarded to replace EFC).

GIFT AID (NEED-BASED) *Total amount:* $44,592,163 (5% federal, 1% state, 92% institutional, 2% external sources). *Receiving aid:* Freshmen: 57% (334); all full-time undergraduates: 60% (1,311). *Average award:* Freshmen: $34,246;

Undergraduates: $34,014. *Scholarships, grants, and awards:* Federal Pell, FSEOG, state, college/university gift aid from institutional funds.

GIFT AID (NON-NEED-BASED) *Total amount:* $592,805 (100% external sources). *Tuition waivers:* Full or partial for employees or children of employees.

LOANS *Student loans:* $4,225,225 (64% need-based, 36% non-need-based). 56% of past graduating class borrowed through all loan programs. *Average indebtedness per student:* $13,324. *Average need-based loan:* Freshmen: $2601. Undergraduates: $3104. *Parent loans:* $3,486,334 (100% non-need-based). *Programs:* Federal Direct (Subsidized and Unsubsidized Stafford, PLUS), Perkins, state, college/university.

WORK-STUDY *Federal work-study:* Total amount: $973,856; 796 jobs averaging $1223. *State or other work-study/employment:* Total amount: $480,105 (100% need-based). 366 part-time jobs averaging $1312.

APPLYING FOR FINANCIAL AID *Required financial aid forms:* FAFSA, CSS Financial Aid PROFILE, noncustodial (divorced/separated) parent's statement, business/farm supplement, parents' federal income tax and W-2 forms. *Financial aid deadline (priority):* 1/15. *Notification date:* 4/1. Students must reply by 5/1.

CONTACT Ms. Kathryn Osmond, Executive Director of Financial Aid, Wellesley College, 106 Central Street, Wellesley, MA 02481-8203, 781-283-2360. *Fax:* 781-283-3946. *E-mail:* finaid@wellesley.edu.

WELLS COLLEGE
Aurora, NY

Tuition & fees: $29,680	Average undergraduate aid package: $21,009

ABOUT THE INSTITUTION Independent, coed, primarily women. 40 undergraduate majors. Federal methodology is used as a basis for awarding need-based institutional aid.

UNDERGRADUATE EXPENSES for 2009–10 *Comprehensive fee:* $38,680 includes full-time tuition ($28,180), mandatory fees ($1500), and room and board ($9000). *Part-time tuition:* $790 per credit hour. *Payment plan:* Installment.

FRESHMAN FINANCIAL AID (Fall 2009, est.) 136 applied for aid; of those 92% were deemed to have need. 100% of freshmen with need received aid; of those 13% had need fully met. *Average percent of need met:* 79% (excluding resources awarded to replace EFC). *Average financial aid package:* $24,878 (excluding resources awarded to replace EFC). 11% of all full-time freshmen had no need and received non-need-based gift aid.

UNDERGRADUATE FINANCIAL AID (Fall 2009, est.) 494 applied for aid; of those 92% were deemed to have need. 100% of undergraduates with need received aid; of those 21% had need fully met. *Average percent of need met:* 82% (excluding resources awarded to replace EFC). *Average financial aid package:* $21,009 (excluding resources awarded to replace EFC). 12% of all full-time undergraduates had no need and received non-need-based gift aid.

GIFT AID (NEED-BASED) *Total amount:* $7,245,735 (16% federal, 9% state, 72% institutional, 3% external sources). *Receiving aid:* Freshmen: 86% (124); all full-time undergraduates: 83% (453). *Average award:* Freshmen: $21,320; Undergraduates: $16,271. *Scholarships, grants, and awards:* Federal Pell, FSEOG, state, private, college/university gift aid from institutional funds.

GIFT AID (NON-NEED-BASED) *Total amount:* $526,456 (3% state, 94% institutional, 3% external sources). *Receiving aid:* Freshmen: 57% (83). Undergraduates: 49% (267). *Average award:* Freshmen: $11,656. Undergraduates: $8069. *Scholarships, grants, and awards by category:* Academic interests/achievement: 109 awards ($789,000 total): general academic interests/achievements. Special achievements/activities: 185 awards ($1,448,750 total): leadership. Special characteristics: 32 awards ($140,250 total): children and siblings of alumni, international students. *Tuition waivers:* Full or partial for employees or children of employees, senior citizens.

LOANS *Student loans:* $4,395,667 (40% need-based, 60% non-need-based). 82% of past graduating class borrowed through all loan programs. *Average indebtedness per student:* $24,180. *Average need-based loan:* Freshmen: $3680. Undergraduates: $4562. *Parent loans:* $735,755 (100% non-need-based). *Programs:* Federal Direct (Subsidized and Unsubsidized Stafford, PLUS), Perkins, state.

WORK-STUDY *Federal work-study:* Total amount: $100,000; 90 jobs averaging $1100. *State or other work-study/employment:* Total amount: $391,460 (94% need-based, 6% non-need-based). 355 part-time jobs averaging $1100.

APPLYING FOR FINANCIAL AID *Required financial aid form:* FAFSA. *Financial aid deadline (priority):* 2/15. *Notification date:* 3/1. Students must reply by 5/1.

CONTACT Ms. Cathleen A. Patella, Director of Financial Aid, Wells College, Route 90, Aurora, NY 13026, 315-364-3289 or toll-free 800-952-9355. *Fax:* 315-364-3227. *E-mail:* cpatella@wells.edu.

WENTWORTH INSTITUTE OF TECHNOLOGY
Boston, MA

CONTACT Anne-marie Caruso, Director of Financial Aid, Wentworth Institute of Technology, 550 Huntington Avenue, Boston, MA 02115-5998, 617-989-4174 or toll-free 800-556-0610. *Fax:* 617-989-4201. *E-mail:* carusoa@wit.edu.

WESLEYAN COLLEGE
Macon, GA

Tuition & fees: $17,500	Average undergraduate aid package: $15,787

ABOUT THE INSTITUTION Independent United Methodist, undergraduate: women only; graduate: coed. 29 undergraduate majors. Federal methodology is used as a basis for awarding need-based institutional aid.

UNDERGRADUATE EXPENSES for 2009–10 *Comprehensive fee:* $25,500 includes full-time tuition ($17,500) and room and board ($8000). Full-time tuition and fees vary according to class time, course load, and program. Room and board charges vary according to board plan and housing facility. *Part-time tuition:* $415 per credit hour. Part-time tuition and fees vary according to class time, course load, and program.

FRESHMAN FINANCIAL AID (Fall 2008) 73 applied for aid; of those 82% were deemed to have need. 100% of freshmen with need received aid; of those 37% had need fully met. *Average percent of need met:* 84% (excluding resources awarded to replace EFC). *Average financial aid package:* $14,567 (excluding resources awarded to replace EFC). 27% of all full-time freshmen had no need and received non-need-based gift aid.

UNDERGRADUATE FINANCIAL AID (Fall 2008) 283 applied for aid; of those 83% were deemed to have need. 100% of undergraduates with need received aid; of those 29% had need fully met. *Average percent of need met:* 82% (excluding resources awarded to replace EFC). *Average financial aid package:* $15,787 (excluding resources awarded to replace EFC). 33% of all full-time undergraduates had no need and received non-need-based gift aid.

GIFT AID (NEED-BASED) *Total amount:* $3,036,640 (25% federal, 14% state, 59% institutional, 2% external sources). *Receiving aid:* Freshmen: 71% (60); all full-time undergraduates: 59% (231). *Average award:* Freshmen: $12,154; Undergraduates: $12,098. *Scholarships, grants, and awards:* Federal Pell, FSEOG, state, private, college/university gift aid from institutional funds.

GIFT AID (NON-NEED-BASED) *Total amount:* $2,513,461 (12% state, 86% institutional, 2% external sources). *Receiving aid:* Freshmen: 24% (20). Undergraduates: 15% (59). *Average award:* Freshmen: $13,937. Undergraduates: $15,310. *Scholarships, grants, and awards by category:* Academic interests/achievement: 207 awards ($2,112,489 total): biological sciences, business, communication, education, English, foreign languages, general academic interests/achievements, humanities, mathematics, premedicine, religion/biblical studies, social sciences. Creative arts/performance: 44 awards ($138,156 total): art/fine arts, music, theater/drama. Special achievements/activities: 105 awards ($293,337 total): community service, general special achievements/activities, leadership, memberships, religious involvement. Special characteristics: 94 awards ($278,200 total): adult students, children and siblings of alumni, children of current students, children of faculty/staff, ethnic background, first-generation college students, general special characteristics, handicapped students, international students, out-of-state students, parents of current students, relatives of clergy, religious affiliation, siblings of current students, spouses of current students, veterans. *Tuition waivers:* Full or partial for employees or children of employees, senior citizens.

LOANS *Student loans:* $2,546,152 (70% need-based, 30% non-need-based). 63% of past graduating class borrowed through all loan programs. *Average indebtedness per student:* $20,983. *Average need-based loan:* Freshmen: $3314. Undergraduates: $4851. *Parent loans:* $303,437 (26% need-based, 74% non-need-based). *Programs:* Federal Direct (Subsidized and Unsubsidized Stafford, PLUS), FFEL (Subsidized and Unsubsidized Stafford, PLUS), Perkins, college/university, alternative loans.

WORK-STUDY *Federal work-study:* Total amount: $42,971; 47 jobs averaging $946. *State or other work-study/employment:* Total amount: $140,031 (13% need-based, 87% non-need-based). 119 part-time jobs averaging $1113.

APPLYING FOR FINANCIAL AID *Required financial aid forms:* FAFSA, institution's own form, state aid form. *Financial aid deadline (priority):* 2/15. *Notification date:* Continuous beginning 3/1. Students must reply by 5/1 or within 3 weeks of notification.

CONTACT Kizzy K. Holmes, Director of Financial Aid, Wesleyan College, 4760 Forsyth Road, Macon, GA 31210-4462, 478-757-5205 or toll-free 800-447-6610. *Fax:* 478-757-3780. *E-mail:* financialaid@wesleyancollege.edu.

WESLEYAN UNIVERSITY
Middletown, CT

Tuition & fees: $40,092	Average undergraduate aid package: $34,488

ABOUT THE INSTITUTION Independent, coed. 47 undergraduate majors. Both federal and institutional methodology are used as a basis for awarding need-based institutional aid.

UNDERGRADUATE EXPENSES for 2009–10 *One-time required fee:* $300. *Comprehensive fee:* $51,132 includes full-time tuition ($39,822), mandatory fees ($270), and room and board ($11,040). Room and board charges vary according to board plan and housing facility. *Payment plan:* Installment.

FRESHMAN FINANCIAL AID (Fall 2008) 405 applied for aid; of those 83% were deemed to have need. 100% of freshmen with need received aid; of those 100% had need fully met. *Average percent of need met:* 100% (excluding resources awarded to replace EFC). *Average financial aid package:* $34,382 (excluding resources awarded to replace EFC). 2% of all full-time freshmen had no need and received non-need-based gift aid.

UNDERGRADUATE FINANCIAL AID (Fall 2008) 1,397 applied for aid; of those 92% were deemed to have need. 100% of undergraduates with need received aid; of those 100% had need fully met. *Average percent of need met:* 100% (excluding resources awarded to replace EFC). *Average financial aid package:* $34,488 (excluding resources awarded to replace EFC). 3% of all full-time undergraduates had no need and received non-need-based gift aid.

GIFT AID (NEED-BASED) *Total amount:* $34,937,792 (6% federal, 2% state, 90% institutional, 2% external sources). *Receiving aid:* Freshmen: 43% (305); all full-time undergraduates: 42% (1,164). *Average award:* Freshmen: $32,975; Undergraduates: $30,462. *Scholarships, grants, and awards:* Federal Pell, FSEOG, state, private, college/university gift aid from institutional funds.

GIFT AID (NON-NEED-BASED) *Total amount:* $3,373,400 (100% institutional). *Average award:* Freshmen: $36,634. Undergraduates: $48,191.

LOANS *Student loans:* $5,831,733 (100% need-based). 44% of past graduating class borrowed through all loan programs. *Average indebtedness per student:* $29,174. *Average need-based loan:* Freshmen: $2496. Undergraduates: $4944. *Parent loans:* $3,922,561 (100% need-based). *Programs:* Federal Direct (Subsidized and Unsubsidized Stafford, PLUS), Perkins, college/university.

WORK-STUDY *Federal work-study:* Total amount: $2,274,063; 1,012 jobs averaging $2213. *State or other work-study/employment:* Total amount: $292,410 (100% need-based). 84 part-time jobs averaging $2010.

APPLYING FOR FINANCIAL AID *Required financial aid forms:* FAFSA, CSS Financial Aid PROFILE, noncustodial (divorced/separated) parent's statement. *Financial aid deadline:* 2/15. *Notification date:* 4/1. Students must reply by 5/1.

CONTACT Jennifer Garratt Lawton, Director of Financial Aid, Wesleyan University, 237 High Street, Middletown, CT 06459-0260, 860-685-2800. *Fax:* 860-685-2801. *E-mail:* finaid@wesleyan.edu.

WESLEY COLLEGE
Dover, DE

CONTACT James Marks, Director of Student Financial Planning, Wesley College, 120 North State Street, Dover, DE 19901-3875, 302-736-2334 or toll-free 800-937-5398 Ext. 2400 (out-of-state). *Fax:* 302-736-2594. *E-mail:* marksja@wesley.edu.

WESLEY COLLEGE
Florence, MS

CONTACT William Devore Jr., Director of Financial Aid, Wesley College, PO Box 1070, Florence, MS 39073-1070, 601-845-4086 or toll-free 800-748-9972. *Fax:* 601-845-2266. *E-mail:* wdevore@wesleycollege.edu.

WEST CHESTER UNIVERSITY OF PENNSYLVANIA
West Chester, PA

Tuition & fees (PA res): $7211	Average undergraduate aid package: $7129

ABOUT THE INSTITUTION State-supported, coed. 52 undergraduate majors. Federal methodology is used as a basis for awarding need-based institutional aid.

UNDERGRADUATE EXPENSES for 2009–10 *Tuition, state resident:* full-time $5554; part-time $231 per credit. *Tuition, nonresident:* full-time $13,886; part-time $579 per credit. *Required fees:* full-time $1657; $60.18 per credit. Full-time tuition and fees vary according to course load. Part-time tuition and fees vary according to course load. *College room and board:* $7032; *Room only:* $4692. Room and board charges vary according to board plan and housing facility. *Payment plan:* Installment.

FRESHMAN FINANCIAL AID (Fall 2008) 1,661 applied for aid; of those 62% were deemed to have need. 95% of freshmen with need received aid; of those 46% had need fully met. *Average percent of need met:* 57% (excluding resources awarded to replace EFC). *Average financial aid package:* $6962 (excluding resources awarded to replace EFC). 3% of all full-time freshmen had no need and received non-need-based gift aid.

UNDERGRADUATE FINANCIAL AID (Fall 2008) 7,307 applied for aid; of those 68% were deemed to have need. 95% of undergraduates with need received aid; of those 46% had need fully met. *Average percent of need met:* 60% (excluding resources awarded to replace EFC). *Average financial aid package:* $7129 (excluding resources awarded to replace EFC). 3% of all full-time undergraduates had no need and received non-need-based gift aid.

GIFT AID (NEED-BASED) *Total amount:* $15,458,278 (44% federal, 39% state, 9% institutional, 8% external sources). *Receiving aid:* Freshmen: 33% (663); all full-time undergraduates: 29% (2,996). *Average award:* Freshmen: $4266; Undergraduates: $4617. *Scholarships, grants, and awards:* Federal Pell, FSEOG, state, college/university gift aid from institutional funds.

GIFT AID (NON-NEED-BASED) *Total amount:* $1,546,623 (1% state, 58% institutional, 41% external sources). *Receiving aid:* Freshmen: 1. Undergraduates: 3. *Average award:* Freshmen: $3118. Undergraduates: $3152. *Scholarships, grants, and awards by category:* Academic interests/achievement: business, general academic interests/achievements, mathematics, social sciences. Creative arts/performance: music, theater/drama. Special characteristics: children of faculty/staff. *Tuition waivers:* Full or partial for employees or children of employees, senior citizens.

LOANS *Student loans:* $54,852,044 (70% need-based, 30% non-need-based). 72% of past graduating class borrowed through all loan programs. *Average indebtedness per student:* $19,820. *Average need-based loan:* Freshmen: $3523. Undergraduates: $4313. *Parent loans:* $7,090,179 (100% non-need-based). *Programs:* FFEL (Subsidized and Unsubsidized Stafford, PLUS), Perkins, Federal Nursing.

WORK-STUDY *Federal work-study:* Total amount: $809,491; jobs available. *State or other work-study/employment:* Part-time jobs available.

ATHLETIC AWARDS Total amount: $659,942 (49% need-based, 51% non-need-based).

APPLYING FOR FINANCIAL AID *Required financial aid form:* FAFSA. *Financial aid deadline (priority):* 3/1. *Notification date:* Students must reply within 4 weeks of notification.

CONTACT Mr. Dana Parker, Financial Aid Office, West Chester University of Pennsylvania, 25 University Avenue, Suite #030, West Chester, PA 19383, 610-436-2627 or toll-free 877-315-2165 (in-state). *Fax:* 610-436-2574. *E-mail:* finaid@wcupa.edu.

WEST COAST UNIVERSITY
North Hollywood, CA

CONTACT Financial Aid Office, West Coast University, 12215 Victory Boulevard, North Hollywood, CA 91606, 323-315-5207 or toll-free 866-508-2684 (in-state).

WESTERN CAROLINA UNIVERSITY
Cullowhee, NC

Tuition & fees (NC res): $4330 | **Average undergraduate aid package: $8681**

ABOUT THE INSTITUTION State-supported, coed. 69 undergraduate majors. Federal methodology is used as a basis for awarding need-based institutional aid.

UNDERGRADUATE EXPENSES for 2009–10 *Tuition, state resident:* full-time $2106. *Tuition, nonresident:* full-time $11,703. *Required fees:* full-time $2224. Full-time tuition and fees vary according to degree level. Part-time tuition and fees vary according to course load and degree level. *College room and board:* $5912; *Room only:* $3062. Room and board charges vary according to board plan and housing facility. *Payment plan:* Installment.

FRESHMAN FINANCIAL AID (Fall 2009, est.) 1,341 applied for aid; of those 69% were deemed to have need. 99% of freshmen with need received aid; of those 33% had need fully met. *Average percent of need met:* 81% (excluding resources awarded to replace EFC). *Average financial aid package:* $8865 (excluding resources awarded to replace EFC). 4% of all full-time freshmen had no need and received non-need-based gift aid.

UNDERGRADUATE FINANCIAL AID (Fall 2009, est.) 4,736 applied for aid; of those 76% were deemed to have need. 97% of undergraduates with need received aid; of those 40% had need fully met. *Average percent of need met:* 81% (excluding resources awarded to replace EFC). *Average financial aid package:* $8681 (excluding resources awarded to replace EFC). 5% of all full-time undergraduates had no need and received non-need-based gift aid.

GIFT AID (NEED-BASED) *Total amount:* $21,858,248 (43% federal, 45% state, 8% institutional, 4% external sources). *Receiving aid:* Freshmen: 58% (898); all full-time undergraduates: 53% (3,266). *Average award:* Freshmen: $7351; Undergraduates: $6722. *Scholarships, grants, and awards:* Federal Pell, FSEOG, state, private, college/university gift aid from institutional funds.

GIFT AID (NON-NEED-BASED) *Total amount:* $2,617,878 (2% federal, 53% state, 25% institutional, 20% external sources). *Receiving aid:* Freshmen: 6% (97). Undergraduates: 6% (349). *Average award:* Freshmen: $2157. Undergraduates: $1799. *Scholarships, grants, and awards by category: Academic interests/ achievement:* 448 awards ($743,636 total): biological sciences, business, communication, education, English, general academic interests/achievements, mathematics. *Creative arts/performance:* 221 awards ($54,600 total): art/fine arts, music, theater/drama. *Special characteristics:* 45 awards ($49,981 total): ethnic background, handicapped students, local/state students, members of minority groups. *Tuition waivers:* Full or partial for employees or children of employees.

LOANS *Student loans:* $21,882,391 (64% need-based, 36% non-need-based). 51% of past graduating class borrowed through all loan programs. *Average indebtedness per student:* $11,609. *Average need-based loan:* Freshmen: $3963. Undergraduates: $4390. *Parent loans:* $4,788,144 (33% need-based, 67% non-need-based). *Programs:* Federal Direct (Subsidized and Unsubsidized Stafford, PLUS), FFEL (Subsidized and Unsubsidized Stafford, PLUS), Perkins.

WORK-STUDY *Federal work-study:* Total amount: $729,897; 405 jobs averaging $1581.

ATHLETIC AWARDS Total amount: $2,465,708 (49% need-based, 51% non-need-based).

APPLYING FOR FINANCIAL AID *Required financial aid forms:* FAFSA, institution's own form. *Financial aid deadline (priority):* 3/15. *Notification date:* Continuous beginning 4/1.

CONTACT Ms. Trina F. Orr, Director of Financial Aid, Western Carolina University, 123 Killian Annex, Cullowhee, NC 28723, 828-227-7292 or toll-free 877-WCU4YOU. *Fax:* 828-227-7042. *E-mail:* torr@email.wcu.edu.

WESTERN CONNECTICUT STATE UNIVERSITY
Danbury, CT

Tuition & fees (CT res): $7909 | **Average undergraduate aid package: $4719**

ABOUT THE INSTITUTION State-supported, coed. 37 undergraduate majors. Federal methodology is used as a basis for awarding need-based institutional aid.

UNDERGRADUATE EXPENSES for 2010–11 *Tuition, state resident:* full-time $4023; part-time $364 per credit hour. *Tuition, nonresident:* full-time $13,020; part-time $367 per credit hour. *Required fees:* full-time $3886. Full-time tuition and fees vary according to reciprocity agreements. *College room and board: Room only:* $5858. Room and board charges vary according to housing facility. *Payment plan:* Installment.

FRESHMAN FINANCIAL AID (Fall 2008) 758 applied for aid; of those 89% were deemed to have need. 85% of freshmen with need received aid; of those 41% had need fully met. *Average percent of need met:* 57% (excluding resources awarded to replace EFC). *Average financial aid package:* $4662 (excluding resources awarded to replace EFC). 3% of all full-time freshmen had no need and received non-need-based gift aid.

UNDERGRADUATE FINANCIAL AID (Fall 2008) 3,254 applied for aid; of those 90% were deemed to have need. 86% of undergraduates with need received aid; of those 43% had need fully met. *Average percent of need met:* 61% (excluding resources awarded to replace EFC). *Average financial aid package:* $4719 (excluding resources awarded to replace EFC). 2% of all full-time undergraduates had no need and received non-need-based gift aid.

GIFT AID (NEED-BASED) *Total amount:* $1,208,357 (16% federal, 47% state, 5% institutional, 32% external sources). *Receiving aid:* Freshmen: 19% (177); all full-time undergraduates: 12% (558). *Average award:* Freshmen: $2362; Undergraduates: $2694. *Scholarships, grants, and awards:* Federal Pell, FSEOG, state, private, college/university gift aid from institutional funds.

GIFT AID (NON-NEED-BASED) *Total amount:* $357,320 (3% state, 38% institutional, 59% external sources). *Receiving aid:* Freshmen: 11% (105). Undergraduates: 8% (355). *Average award:* Freshmen: $1281. Undergraduates: $1686. *Scholarships, grants, and awards by category: Academic interests/ achievement:* general academic interests/achievements. *Tuition waivers:* Full or partial for employees or children of employees, senior citizens.

LOANS *Student loans:* $3,396,388 (66% need-based, 34% non-need-based). 36% of past graduating class borrowed through all loan programs. *Average indebtedness per student:* $26,024. *Average need-based loan:* Freshmen: $9230. Undergraduates: $7042. *Parent loans:* $7,636,620 (57% need-based, 43% non-need-based). *Programs:* Federal Direct (Subsidized and Unsubsidized Stafford, PLUS), FFEL (Subsidized and Unsubsidized Stafford, PLUS), Perkins.

WORK-STUDY *Federal work-study:* Total amount: $88,900; jobs available. *State or other work-study/employment:* Total amount: $32,700 (100% need-based). Part-time jobs available.

APPLYING FOR FINANCIAL AID *Required financial aid forms:* FAFSA, institution's own form. *Financial aid deadline:* 4/15. *Notification date:* Continuous beginning 4/15. Students must reply by 5/1.

CONTACT Nancy Barton, Director of Student Financial Services, Western Connecticut State University, 181 White Street, Danbury, CT 06810-6860, 203-837-8588 or toll-free 877-837-WCSU. *Fax:* 203-837-8528. *E-mail:* bartonn@wcsu.edu.

WESTERN GOVERNORS UNIVERSITY
Salt Lake City, UT

Tuition & fees: N/R | **Average undergraduate aid package: $2856**

ABOUT THE INSTITUTION Independent, coed. *Awards:* bachelor's and master's degrees and post-bachelor's certificates. 7 undergraduate majors. *Total enrollment:* 9,022. Undergraduates: 6,491. Federal methodology is used as a basis for awarding need-based institutional aid.

FRESHMAN FINANCIAL AID (Fall 2008) 994 applied for aid; of those 100% were deemed to have need. 100% of freshmen with need received aid; of those 30% had need fully met. *Average percent of need met:* 30% (excluding resources awarded to replace EFC). *Average financial aid package:* $2038 (excluding resources awarded to replace EFC).

UNDERGRADUATE FINANCIAL AID (Fall 2008) 14,170 applied for aid; of those 42% were deemed to have need. 100% of undergraduates with need received aid; of those 30% had need fully met. *Average percent of need met:* 30% (excluding resources awarded to replace EFC). *Average financial aid package:* $2856 (excluding resources awarded to replace EFC). 1831% of all full-time undergraduates had no need and received non-need-based gift aid.

GIFT AID (NEED-BASED) *Total amount:* $15,692,525 (97% federal, 3% institutional). *Receiving aid:* Freshmen: 44% (611); all full-time undergraduates: 38% (5,324). *Average award:* Freshmen: $2651; Undergraduates: $2856. *Scholarships, grants, and awards:* Federal Pell, private, college/university gift aid from institutional funds.

GIFT AID (NON-NEED-BASED) *Total amount:* $259,500 (100% institutional). *Average award:* Undergraduates: $4290.

LOANS *Student loans:* $72,326,444 (38% need-based, 62% non-need-based). 72% of past graduating class borrowed through all loan programs. *Average indebtedness per student:* $9560. *Average need-based loan:* Freshmen: $2038. Undergraduates: $2943. *Parent loans:* $45,329 (100% non-need-based). *Programs:* Federal Direct (Subsidized and Unsubsidized Stafford, PLUS), FFEL (Subsidized and Unsubsidized Stafford, PLUS).

APPLYING FOR FINANCIAL AID *Required financial aid forms:* FAFSA, institution's own form. *Financial aid deadline:* Continuous. *Notification date:* Continuous.

CONTACT Jenny Allen Ryan, Director of Financial Aid, Western Governors University, 4001 South 700 East, Suite 700, Salt Lake City, UT 84107, 877-435-7948 Ext. 5731 or toll-free 877-435-7948. *Fax:* 801-907-7727. *E-mail:* jallenryan@wgu.edu.

WESTERN ILLINOIS UNIVERSITY
Macomb, IL

Tuition & fees (IL res): $8958	Average undergraduate aid package: $9261

ABOUT THE INSTITUTION State-supported, coed. 64 undergraduate majors. Federal methodology is used as a basis for awarding need-based institutional aid.

UNDERGRADUATE EXPENSES for 2009–10 *Tuition, state resident:* full-time $6779; part-time $226 per credit hour. *Tuition, nonresident:* full-time $10,168; part-time $339 per credit hour. *Required fees:* full-time $2179; $72.62 per credit hour. Full-time tuition and fees vary according to course load, location, and student level. Part-time tuition and fees vary according to course load, location, and student level. *College room and board:* $7642; *Room only:* $4612. Room and board charges vary according to board plan, housing facility, and student level. *Payment plan:* Guaranteed tuition.

FRESHMAN FINANCIAL AID (Fall 2009, est.) 1,378 applied for aid; of those 81% were deemed to have need. 97% of freshmen with need received aid; of those 37% had need fully met. *Average percent of need met:* 59% (excluding resources awarded to replace EFC). *Average financial aid package:* $9087 (excluding resources awarded to replace EFC). 4% of all full-time freshmen had no need and received non-need-based gift aid.

UNDERGRADUATE FINANCIAL AID (Fall 2009, est.) 7,842 applied for aid; of those 82% were deemed to have need. 97% of undergraduates with need received aid; of those 37% had need fully met. *Average percent of need met:* 61% (excluding resources awarded to replace EFC). *Average financial aid package:* $9261 (excluding resources awarded to replace EFC). 5% of all full-time undergraduates had no need and received non-need-based gift aid.

GIFT AID (NEED-BASED) *Total amount:* $32,214,675 (49% federal, 40% state, 8% institutional, 3% external sources). *Receiving aid:* Freshmen: 47% (777); all full-time undergraduates: 46% (4,439). *Average award:* Freshmen: $8480; Undergraduates: $7479. *Scholarships, grants, and awards:* Federal Pell, FSEOG, state, private, college/university gift aid from institutional funds.

GIFT AID (NON-NEED-BASED) *Total amount:* $3,338,966 (5% federal, 32% state, 45% institutional, 18% external sources). *Average award:* Freshmen: $3630. Undergraduates: $3081. *Scholarships, grants, and awards by category:* *Academic interests/achievement:* 3,642 awards ($3,436,508 total): agriculture, biological sciences, business, education, foreign languages, general academic interests/achievements, home economics, mathematics, physical sciences, social sciences. *Creative arts/performance:* 590 awards ($788,624 total): applied art and design, cinema/film/broadcasting, dance, debating, journalism/publications, music, performing arts, theater/drama. *Special achievements/activities:* 291 awards ($200,390 total): community service, leadership. *Special characteristics:* 1,301 awards ($2,335,990 total): children of faculty/staff, general special

characteristics, international students, members of minority groups, veterans' children. *Tuition waivers:* Full or partial for employees or children of employees, senior citizens.

LOANS *Student loans:* $56,270,130 (49% need-based, 51% non-need-based). 68% of past graduating class borrowed through all loan programs. *Average indebtedness per student:* $20,550. *Average need-based loan:* Freshmen: $3257. Undergraduates: $4159. *Parent loans:* $10,529,575 (71% need-based, 29% non-need-based). *Programs:* FFEL (Subsidized and Unsubsidized Stafford, PLUS), Perkins, college/university.

WORK-STUDY *Federal work-study:* Total amount: $453,774; 207 jobs averaging $2180. *State or other work-study/employment:* Total amount: $2,691,679 (68% need-based, 32% non-need-based). 1,762 part-time jobs averaging $1505.

ATHLETIC AWARDS Total amount: $2,678,438 (46% need-based, 54% non-need-based).

APPLYING FOR FINANCIAL AID *Required financial aid form:* FAFSA. *Financial aid deadline (priority):* 2/15. *Notification date:* Continuous beginning 1/15.

CONTACT Financial Aid Office, Western Illinois University, 1 University Circle, Macomb, IL 61455-1390, 309-298-2446 or toll-free 877-742-5948. *Fax:* 309-298-2353. *E-mail:* financial-aid@wiu.edu.

WESTERN INTERNATIONAL UNIVERSITY
Phoenix, AZ

Tuition & fees: $11,250	Average undergraduate aid package: $3321

ABOUT THE INSTITUTION Proprietary, coed. 9 undergraduate majors.

UNDERGRADUATE EXPENSES for 2010–11 *Tuition:* full-time $11,250; part-time $375 per credit hour. Full-time tuition and fees vary according to course level, degree level, and student level. Part-time tuition and fees vary according to course level, degree level, and student level. *Payment plan:* Deferred payment.

FRESHMAN FINANCIAL AID (Fall 2009, est.) *Average financial aid package:* $2617 (excluding resources awarded to replace EFC).

UNDERGRADUATE FINANCIAL AID (Fall 2009, est.) *Average financial aid package:* $3321 (excluding resources awarded to replace EFC).

LOANS *Student loans:* 80% of past graduating class borrowed through all loan programs. *Average indebtedness per student:* $5285.

CONTACT Ms. Ella Owen, Compliance Officer, Western International University, 9215 North Black Canyon Highway, Phoenix, AZ 85021, 602-429-1056. *Fax:* 602-383-9812. *E-mail:* ella.owen@west.edu.

WESTERN KENTUCKY UNIVERSITY
Bowling Green, KY

Tuition & fees (KY res): $7200	Average undergraduate aid package: $11,854

ABOUT THE INSTITUTION State-supported, coed. 86 undergraduate majors. Federal methodology is used as a basis for awarding need-based institutional aid.

UNDERGRADUATE EXPENSES for 2009–10 *Tuition, state resident:* full-time $7200; part-time $300 per hour. *Tuition, nonresident:* full-time $17,784; part-time $741 per hour. Full-time tuition and fees vary according to course level, course load, location, program, and reciprocity agreements. Part-time tuition and fees vary according to course level, course load, location, program, and reciprocity agreements. *College room and board:* $6351; *Room only:* $3645. Room and board charges vary according to board plan and housing facility. *Payment plan:* Installment.

FRESHMAN FINANCIAL AID (Fall 2008) 2,654 applied for aid; of those 73% were deemed to have need. 99% of freshmen with need received aid; of those 32% had need fully met. *Average percent of need met:* 32% (excluding resources awarded to replace EFC). *Average financial aid package:* $11,180 (excluding resources awarded to replace EFC). 10% of all full-time freshmen had no need and received non-need-based gift aid.

UNDERGRADUATE FINANCIAL AID (Fall 2008) 10,286 applied for aid; of those 76% were deemed to have need. 99% of undergraduates with need received aid; of those 33% had need fully met. *Average percent of need met:* 33% (excluding resources awarded to replace EFC). *Average financial aid package:* $11,854 (excluding resources awarded to replace EFC). 9% of all full-time undergraduates had no need and received non-need-based gift aid.

GIFT AID (NEED-BASED) *Total amount:* $29,587,303 (67% federal, 26% state, 7% institutional). *Receiving aid:* Freshmen: 41% (1,320); all full-time undergraduates: 38% (5,099). *Average award:* Freshmen: $5247; Undergraduates: $4981. *Scholarships, grants, and awards:* Federal Pell, FSEOG, state, private, college/university gift aid from institutional funds, United Negro College Fund.

GIFT AID (NON-NEED-BASED) *Total amount:* $26,350,572 (12% federal, 39% state, 42% institutional, 7% external sources). *Receiving aid:* Freshmen: 50% (1,618). Undergraduates: 32% (4,307). *Average award:* Freshmen: $5226. Undergraduates: $4836. *Scholarships, grants, and awards by category:* Academic interests/achievement: 2,321 awards ($8,521,281 total): agriculture, biological sciences, business, communication, education, engineering/technologies, English, foreign languages, general academic interests/achievements, health fields, home economics, mathematics, military science, physical sciences, premedicine, social sciences. *Creative arts/performance:* 366 awards ($1,129,090 total): art/fine arts, cinema/film/broadcasting, dance, debating, general creative arts/performance, journalism/publications, music, theater/drama. *Special achievements/activities:* 348 awards ($469,495 total): general special achievements/activities, leadership, memberships. *Special characteristics:* 1,383 awards ($2,326,350 total): adult students, children of union members/company employees, ethnic background, general special characteristics, handicapped students, international students, local/state students, members of minority groups, out-of-state students, religious affiliation, veterans. *Tuition waivers:* Full or partial for children of alumni, employees or children of employees, senior citizens.

LOANS *Student loans:* $63,903,083 (41% need-based, 59% non-need-based). 56% of past graduating class borrowed through all loan programs. *Average indebtedness per student:* $17,436. *Average need-based loan:* Freshmen: $3018. Undergraduates: $3814. *Parent loans:* $6,447,260 (100% non-need-based). *Programs:* FFEL (Subsidized and Unsubsidized Stafford, PLUS), Perkins, alternative loans.

WORK-STUDY *Federal work-study:* Total amount: $1,337,922; 670 jobs averaging $1997. *State or other work-study/employment:* Total amount: $4,372,362 (100% non-need-based). 1,829 part-time jobs averaging $2391.

ATHLETIC AWARDS Total amount: $4,589,544 (100% non-need-based).

APPLYING FOR FINANCIAL AID *Required financial aid form:* FAFSA. *Financial aid deadline (priority):* 3/15. *Notification date:* Continuous beginning 3/1.

CONTACT Cindy Burnette, Student Financial Assistance Director, Western Kentucky University, Potter Hall, Room 317, Bowling Green, KY 42101-1018, 270-745-2758 or toll-free 800-495-8463 (in-state). *Fax:* 270-745-6586. *E-mail:* cindy.burnette@wku.edu.

WESTERN MICHIGAN UNIVERSITY
Kalamazoo, MI

ABOUT THE INSTITUTION State-supported, coed. 117 undergraduate majors.

GIFT AID (NEED-BASED) *Scholarships, grants, and awards:* Federal Pell, FSEOG, state, private, college/university gift aid from institutional funds, Federal Nursing.

GIFT AID (NON-NEED-BASED) *Scholarships, grants, and awards by category:* Academic interests/achievement: general academic interests/achievements. *Creative arts/performance:* general creative arts/performance. *Special characteristics:* children of faculty/staff, veterans.

LOANS *Programs:* Federal Direct (Subsidized and Unsubsidized Stafford, PLUS), Perkins, alternative loans.

APPLYING FOR FINANCIAL AID *Required financial aid form:* FAFSA.

CONTACT Mr. David Ladd, Associate Director of Student Financial Aid, Western Michigan University, 1903 West Michigan Avenue, Faunce Student Services Building, Room 3306, Kalamazoo, MI 49008-5337, 269-387-6000. *E-mail:* david.ladd@wmich.edu.

WESTERN NEW ENGLAND COLLEGE
Springfield, MA

Tuition & fees: $28,816	Average undergraduate aid package: $18,654

ABOUT THE INSTITUTION Independent, coed. 38 undergraduate majors. Federal methodology is used as a basis for awarding need-based institutional aid.

UNDERGRADUATE EXPENSES for 2009–10 *Comprehensive fee:* $39,796 includes full-time tuition ($26,822), mandatory fees ($1994), and room and board ($10,980). Full-time tuition and fees vary according to program. Room and board charges vary according to board plan and housing facility. *Part-time*

tuition: $505 per credit hour. Part-time tuition and fees vary according to location and program. *Payment plans:* Tuition prepayment, installment.

FRESHMAN FINANCIAL AID (Fall 2009, est.) 612 applied for aid; of those 87% were deemed to have need. 100% of freshmen with need received aid; of those 13% had need fully met. *Average percent of need met:* 70% (excluding resources awarded to replace EFC). *Average financial aid package:* $20,409 (excluding resources awarded to replace EFC). 14% of all full-time freshmen had no need and received non-need-based gift aid.

UNDERGRADUATE FINANCIAL AID (Fall 2009, est.) 2,099 applied for aid; of those 88% were deemed to have need. 100% of undergraduates with need received aid; of those 12% had need fully met. *Average percent of need met:* 67% (excluding resources awarded to replace EFC). *Average financial aid package:* $18,654 (excluding resources awarded to replace EFC). 12% of all full-time undergraduates had no need and received non-need-based gift aid.

GIFT AID (NEED-BASED) *Total amount:* $23,316,679 (11% federal, 3% state, 84% institutional, 2% external sources). *Receiving aid:* Freshmen: 79% (535); all full-time undergraduates: 74% (1,826). *Average award:* Freshmen: $15,024; Undergraduates: $13,383. *Scholarships, grants, and awards:* Federal Pell, FSEOG, state, private, college/university gift aid from institutional funds, Academic Competitiveness Grants, National SMART Grants.

GIFT AID (NON-NEED-BASED) *Total amount:* $3,630,471 (21% federal, 77% institutional, 2% external sources). *Receiving aid:* Freshmen: 6% (44). Undergraduates: 4% (105). *Average award:* Freshmen: $9767. Undergraduates: $9625. *Scholarships, grants, and awards by category:* Academic interests/achievement: general academic interests/achievements. *Creative arts/performance:* 1 award ($500 total): music. *Special achievements/activities:* community service, leadership. *Special characteristics:* children of faculty/staff, children of union members/company employees, international students, local/state students, members of minority groups, out-of-state students, siblings of current students. *Tuition waivers:* Full or partial for employees or children of employees, senior citizens.

LOANS *Student loans:* $22,262,433 (37% need-based, 63% non-need-based). *Average need-based loan:* Freshmen: $4122. Undergraduates: $4775. *Parent loans:* $10,789,564 (100% non-need-based). *Programs:* Federal Direct (Subsidized and Unsubsidized Stafford, PLUS), FFEL (PLUS), Perkins, state.

WORK-STUDY *Federal work-study:* Total amount: $1,934,644; 969 jobs averaging $1700. *State or other work-study/employment:* Total amount: $700,000 (100% non-need-based). Part-time jobs available.

APPLYING FOR FINANCIAL AID *Required financial aid forms:* FAFSA, federal income tax form(s), W-2 forms. *Financial aid deadline (priority):* 4/15. *Notification date:* Continuous beginning 3/15. Students must reply by 5/1 or within 2 weeks of notification.

CONTACT Mrs. Kathy M. Chambers, Associate Director of Student Administrative Services, Western New England College, 1215 Wilbraham Road, Springfield, MA 01119-2684, 413-796-2080 or toll-free 800-325-1122 Ext. 1321. *Fax:* 413-796-2081. *E-mail:* finaid@wnec.edu.

WESTERN NEW MEXICO UNIVERSITY
Silver City, NM

Tuition & fees (NM res): $3589	Average undergraduate aid package: $8662

ABOUT THE INSTITUTION State-supported, coed. *Awards:* associate, bachelor's, and master's degrees. 58 undergraduate majors. *Total enrollment:* 2,697. Undergraduates: 2,219. Freshmen: 277. Federal methodology is used as a basis for awarding need-based institutional aid.

UNDERGRADUATE EXPENSES for 2009–10 *Tuition, state resident:* full-time $2616. *Tuition, nonresident:* full-time $11,832. *Required fees:* full-time $973. Full-time tuition and fees vary according to course load, location, and reciprocity agreements. Part-time tuition and fees vary according to course load and location. *College room and board:* $5200; *Room only:* $2000. Room and board charges vary according to board plan and housing facility. *Payment plan:* Installment.

FRESHMAN FINANCIAL AID (Fall 2008) 290 applied for aid; of those 81% were deemed to have need. 99% of freshmen with need received aid; of those 6% had need fully met. *Average percent of need met:* 72% (excluding resources awarded to replace EFC). *Average financial aid package:* $7297 (excluding resources awarded to replace EFC). 7% of all full-time freshmen had no need and received non-need-based gift aid.

UNDERGRADUATE FINANCIAL AID (Fall 2008) 1,166 applied for aid; of those 86% were deemed to have need. 99% of undergraduates with need received

aid; of those 11% had need fully met. *Average percent of need met:* 75% (excluding resources awarded to replace EFC). *Average financial aid package:* $8662 (excluding resources awarded to replace EFC). 5% of all full-time undergraduates had no need and received non-need-based gift aid.

GIFT AID (NEED-BASED) *Total amount:* $5,162,575 (77% federal, 7% state, 16% institutional). *Receiving aid:* Freshmen: 63% (199); all full-time undergraduates: 67% (871). *Average award:* Freshmen: $4671; Undergraduates: $4412. *Scholarships, grants, and awards:* Federal Pell, FSEOG, state, private, college/university gift aid from institutional funds.

GIFT AID (NON-NEED-BASED) *Total amount:* $1,023,133 (100% external sources). *Receiving aid:* Freshmen: 2% (6). Undergraduates: 4% (57). *Average award:* Freshmen: $2900. Undergraduates: $4019. *Scholarships, grants, and awards by category: Academic interests/achievement:* 380 awards ($775,155 total): general academic interests/achievements. *Creative arts/performance:* performing arts. *Special achievements/activities:* 27 awards ($40,415 total): general special achievements/activities. *Special characteristics:* 7 awards ($45,020 total): general special characteristics, veterans. *Tuition waivers:* Full or partial for employees or children of employees, senior citizens.

LOANS *Student loans:* $6,615,899 (100% need-based). 40% of past graduating class borrowed through all loan programs. *Average indebtedness per student:* $5500. *Average need-based loan:* Freshmen: $2953. Undergraduates: $3683. *Parent loans:* $34,830 (100% need-based). *Programs:* FFEL (Subsidized and Unsubsidized Stafford, PLUS), Perkins, state, college/university.

WORK-STUDY *Federal work-study:* Total amount: $187,810; 79 jobs averaging $2279. *State or other work-study/employment:* Total amount: $381,456 (49% need-based, 51% non-need-based). 219 part-time jobs averaging $1495.

ATHLETIC AWARDS Total amount: $599,171 (100% non-need-based).

APPLYING FOR FINANCIAL AID *Required financial aid forms:* FAFSA, institution's own form. *Financial aid deadline (priority):* 4/1. *Notification date:* Continuous beginning 4/1. Students must reply within 2 weeks of notification.

CONTACT Debra Reyes, Assistant Director, Western New Mexico University, PO Box 680, Silver City, NM 88062, 575-538-6173 or toll-free 800-872-WNMU (in-state). *Fax:* 575-538-6189. *E-mail:* reyesd@wnmu.edu.

WESTERN OREGON UNIVERSITY
Monmouth, OR

Tuition & fees (OR res): $7458	Average undergraduate aid package: $8626

ABOUT THE INSTITUTION State-supported, coed. 36 undergraduate majors. Federal methodology is used as a basis for awarding need-based institutional aid.

UNDERGRADUATE EXPENSES for 2010–11 *One-time required fee:* $171. *Tuition, state resident:* full-time $6285; part-time $130 per credit hour. *Tuition, nonresident:* full-time $17,376; part-time $371 per credit hour. *Required fees:* full-time $1173. Full-time tuition and fees vary according to course level, course load, degree level, and reciprocity agreements. Part-time tuition and fees vary according to course level, course load, degree level, and reciprocity agreements. *College room and board:* $8208. Room and board charges vary according to board plan and housing facility. *Payment plans:* Guaranteed tuition, deferred payment.

FRESHMAN FINANCIAL AID (Fall 2009, est.) 662 applied for aid; of those 78% were deemed to have need. 100% of freshmen with need received aid; of those 20% had need fully met. *Average percent of need met:* 71% (excluding resources awarded to replace EFC). *Average financial aid package:* $8944 (excluding resources awarded to replace EFC). 9% of all full-time freshmen had no need and received non-need-based gift aid.

UNDERGRADUATE FINANCIAL AID (Fall 2009, est.) 2,986 applied for aid; of those 81% were deemed to have need. 100% of undergraduates with need received aid; of those 17% had need fully met. *Average percent of need met:* 67% (excluding resources awarded to replace EFC). *Average financial aid package:* $8626 (excluding resources awarded to replace EFC). 7% of all full-time undergraduates had no need and received non-need-based gift aid.

GIFT AID (NEED-BASED) *Total amount:* $10,541,880 (61% federal, 18% state, 6% institutional, 15% external sources). *Receiving aid:* Freshmen: 62% (438); all full-time undergraduates: 58% (1,864). *Average award:* Freshmen: $7006; Undergraduates: $6271. *Scholarships, grants, and awards:* Federal Pell, FSEOG, state, private, college/university gift aid from institutional funds, Academic Competitiveness Grants, National SMART Grants, TEACH Grants.

GIFT AID (NON-NEED-BASED) *Total amount:* $1,034,687 (3% federal, 52% institutional, 45% external sources). *Receiving aid:* Freshmen: 6% (42).

Undergraduates: 3% (89). *Average award:* Freshmen: $1662. Undergraduates: $2159. *Scholarships, grants, and awards by category: Academic interests/achievement:* 961 awards ($1,757,477 total): biological sciences, business, computer science, education, English, foreign languages, general academic interests/achievements, humanities, mathematics, physical sciences, premedicine, social sciences. *Creative arts/performance:* 98 awards ($118,716 total): art/fine arts, dance, music, performing arts, theater/drama. *Special achievements/activities:* 335 awards ($838,763 total): community service, general special achievements/activities, leadership. *Special characteristics:* 27 awards ($132,364 total): adult students, ethnic background, handicapped students, international students, local/state students, veterans. *Tuition waivers:* Full or partial for employees or children of employees.

LOANS *Student loans:* $19,478,254 (70% need-based, 30% non-need-based). 61% of past graduating class borrowed through all loan programs. *Average indebtedness per student:* $25,063. *Average need-based loan:* Freshmen: $3229. Undergraduates: $3969. *Parent loans:* $5,041,899 (23% need-based, 77% non-need-based). *Programs:* Federal Direct (Subsidized and Unsubsidized Stafford, PLUS), Perkins, college/university.

WORK-STUDY *Federal work-study:* Total amount: $205,000; 260 jobs averaging $913.

ATHLETIC AWARDS Total amount: $437,735 (49% need-based, 51% non-need-based).

APPLYING FOR FINANCIAL AID *Required financial aid form:* FAFSA. *Financial aid deadline (priority):* 3/1. *Notification date:* Continuous beginning 3/10. Students must reply within 3 weeks of notification.

CONTACT Ms. Donna Fossum, Director of Financial Aid, Western Oregon University, 345 North Monmouth Avenue, Monmouth, OR 97361, 503-838-8475 or toll-free 877-877-1593. *Fax:* 503-838-8200. *E-mail:* finaid@wou.edu.

WESTERN STATE COLLEGE OF COLORADO
Gunnison, CO

Tuition & fees (CO res): $4064	Average undergraduate aid package: $4500

ABOUT THE INSTITUTION State-supported, coed. 70 undergraduate majors. Federal methodology is used as a basis for awarding need-based institutional aid.

UNDERGRADUATE EXPENSES for 2009–10 *Tuition, state resident:* full-time $3140; part-time $130.84 per credit hour. *Tuition, nonresident:* full-time $12,336; part-time $514 per credit hour. *Required fees:* full-time $924; $289 per term. Full-time tuition and fees vary according to course load. Part-time tuition and fees vary according to course load. *College room and board:* $8324; *Room only:* $4292. Room and board charges vary according to board plan and housing facility. *Payment plans:* Installment, deferred payment.

FRESHMAN FINANCIAL AID (Fall 2009, est.) 374 applied for aid; of those 67% were deemed to have need. 85% of freshmen with need received aid; of those 15% had need fully met. *Average percent of need met:* 50% (excluding resources awarded to replace EFC). *Average financial aid package:* $7500 (excluding resources awarded to replace EFC). 35% of all full-time freshmen had no need and received non-need-based gift aid.

UNDERGRADUATE FINANCIAL AID (Fall 2009, est.) 1,357 applied for aid; of those 67% were deemed to have need. 85% of undergraduates with need received aid; of those 10% had need fully met. *Average percent of need met:* 40% (excluding resources awarded to replace EFC). *Average financial aid package:* $4500 (excluding resources awarded to replace EFC). 22% of all full-time undergraduates had no need and received non-need-based gift aid.

GIFT AID (NEED-BASED) *Total amount:* $3,325,000 (59% federal, 23% state, 13% institutional, 5% external sources). *Receiving aid:* Freshmen: 21% (107); all full-time undergraduates: 19% (386). *Average award:* Freshmen: $2500; Undergraduates: $2500. *Scholarships, grants, and awards:* Federal Pell, FSEOG, state, private, college/university gift aid from institutional funds.

GIFT AID (NON-NEED-BASED) *Total amount:* $2,020,000 (79% institutional, 21% external sources). *Receiving aid:* Freshmen: 6% (28). Undergraduates: 8% (155). *Average award:* Freshmen: $1900. Undergraduates: $1700. *Scholarships, grants, and awards by category: Academic interests/achievement:* 455 awards ($755,000 total): general academic interests/achievements. *Creative arts/performance:* 75 awards ($35,000 total): art/fine arts, music. *Special achievements/activities:* 55 awards ($77,000 total): leadership. *Special characteristics:* 14 awards ($7300 total): children and siblings of alumni. *Tuition waivers:* Full or partial for senior citizens.

LOANS *Student loans:* $6,400,000 (47% need-based, 53% non-need-based). 75% of past graduating class borrowed through all loan programs. *Average indebtedness per student:* $17,750. *Average need-based loan:* Freshmen: $3500. Undergraduates: $5300. *Parent loans:* $1,600,000 (100% non-need-based). *Programs:* FFEL (Subsidized and Unsubsidized Stafford, PLUS), Perkins.

WORK-STUDY *Federal work-study:* Total amount: $220,000; 218 jobs averaging $1362. *State or other work-study/employment:* Total amount: $1,060,000 (20% need-based, 80% non-need-based). 229 part-time jobs averaging $1418.

ATHLETIC AWARDS Total amount: $920,000 (100% non-need-based).

APPLYING FOR FINANCIAL AID *Required financial aid form:* FAFSA. *Financial aid deadline (priority):* 4/1. *Notification date:* Continuous beginning 4/1. Students must reply within 3 weeks of notification.

CONTACT Eric Cronkright, Director, Financial Aid, Western State College of Colorado, Room 115, Ute Hall, Gunnison, CO 81231, 970-943-3026 or toll-free 800-876-5309. *Fax:* 970-943-3086. *E-mail:* ecronkright@western.edu.

WESTERN WASHINGTON UNIVERSITY
Bellingham, WA

Tuition & fees (WA res): $6159   **Average undergraduate aid package:** $11,001

ABOUT THE INSTITUTION State-supported, coed. 112 undergraduate majors. Federal methodology is used as a basis for awarding need-based institutional aid.

UNDERGRADUATE EXPENSES for 2009–10 *Tuition, state resident:* full-time $5397. *Tuition, nonresident:* full-time $16,428. *Required fees:* full-time $762. Full-time tuition and fees vary according to course load and location. Part-time tuition and fees vary according to course load and location. *College room and board:* $8393. Room and board charges vary according to board plan and housing facility. *Payment plan:* Installment.

FRESHMAN FINANCIAL AID (Fall 2009, est.) 2,032 applied for aid; of those 57% were deemed to have need. 96% of freshmen with need received aid; of those 25% had need fully met. *Average percent of need met:* 88% (excluding resources awarded to replace EFC). *Average financial aid package:* $11,233 (excluding resources awarded to replace EFC). 1% of all full-time freshmen had no need and received non-need-based gift aid.

UNDERGRADUATE FINANCIAL AID (Fall 2009, est.) 7,711 applied for aid; of those 68% were deemed to have need. 97% of undergraduates with need received aid; of those 24% had need fully met. *Average percent of need met:* 85% (excluding resources awarded to replace EFC). *Average financial aid package:* $11,001 (excluding resources awarded to replace EFC). 2% of all full-time undergraduates had no need and received non-need-based gift aid.

GIFT AID (NEED-BASED) *Total amount:* $27,576,313 (45% federal, 37% state, 12% institutional, 6% external sources). *Receiving aid:* Freshmen: 34% (909); all full-time undergraduates: 31% (3,848). *Average award:* Freshmen: $7779; Undergraduates: $7788. *Scholarships, grants, and awards:* Federal Pell, FSEOG, state, private, college/university gift aid from institutional funds.

GIFT AID (NON-NEED-BASED) *Total amount:* $1,624,208 (13% federal, 8% state, 22% institutional, 57% external sources). *Receiving aid:* Freshmen: 2% (52). Undergraduates: 1% (104). *Average award:* Freshmen: $1365. Undergraduates: $1510. *Scholarships, grants, and awards by category:* Academic interests/achievement: biological sciences, business, communication, computer science, education, engineering/technologies, English, foreign languages, general academic interests/achievements, health fields, humanities, library science, mathematics, physical sciences, premedicine, social sciences. *Creative arts/performance:* applied art and design, art/fine arts, cinema/film/broadcasting, creative writing, dance, general creative arts/performance, journalism/publications, music, performing arts, theater/drama. *Special achievements/activities:* community service, leadership, memberships. *Special characteristics:* children of public servants, children of union members/company employees, ethnic background, general special characteristics, international students, local/state students, members of minority groups, previous college experience, veterans. *Tuition waivers:* Full or partial for minority students, employees or children of employees.

LOANS *Student loans:* $38,902,597 (59% need-based, 41% non-need-based). 50% of past graduating class borrowed through all loan programs. *Average indebtedness per student:* $15,929. *Average need-based loan:* Freshmen: $3521. Undergraduates: $4326. *Parent loans:* $20,422,733 (11% need-based, 89% non-need-based). *Programs:* Federal Direct (Subsidized and Unsubsidized Stafford, PLUS), Perkins, college/university, alternative loans.

WORK-STUDY *Federal work-study:* Total amount: $652,748; 200 jobs averaging $3264. *State or other work-study/employment:* Total amount: $1,728,282 (100% need-based). 478 part-time jobs averaging $3616.

ATHLETIC AWARDS Total amount: $882,495 (30% need-based, 70% non-need-based).

APPLYING FOR FINANCIAL AID *Required financial aid form:* FAFSA. *Financial aid deadline (priority):* 2/15. *Notification date:* Continuous beginning 3/15. Students must reply within 3 weeks of notification.

CONTACT Ms. Fidele Dent, Office Support Supervisor II, Financial Aid, Western Washington University, Old Main 255, MS 9006, 516 High Street, Bellingham, WA 98225-9006, 360-650-3470. *E-mail:* financialaid@wwu.edu.

WESTFIELD STATE COLLEGE
Westfield, MA

Tuition & fees (MA res): $7016   **Average undergraduate aid package:** $7812

ABOUT THE INSTITUTION State-supported, coed. 28 undergraduate majors. Federal methodology is used as a basis for awarding need-based institutional aid.

UNDERGRADUATE EXPENSES for 2009–10 *Tuition, state resident:* full-time $970; part-time $85 per credit hour. *Tuition, nonresident:* full-time $7050; part-time $95 per credit hour. *Required fees:* full-time $6046; $110 per credit hour or $150 per term. Full-time tuition and fees vary according to reciprocity agreements. *College room and board:* $7728. Room and board charges vary according to board plan, housing facility, and location. *Payment plan:* Installment.

FRESHMAN FINANCIAL AID (Fall 2009, est.) 1,013 applied for aid; of those 64% were deemed to have need. 98% of freshmen with need received aid; of those 17% had need fully met. *Average percent of need met:* 71% (excluding resources awarded to replace EFC). *Average financial aid package:* $7853 (excluding resources awarded to replace EFC). 2% of all full-time freshmen had no need and received non-need-based gift aid.

UNDERGRADUATE FINANCIAL AID (Fall 2009, est.) 3,694 applied for aid; of those 67% were deemed to have need. 98% of undergraduates with need received aid; of those 20% had need fully met. *Average percent of need met:* 73% (excluding resources awarded to replace EFC). *Average financial aid package:* $7812 (excluding resources awarded to replace EFC). 1% of all full-time undergraduates had no need and received non-need-based gift aid.

GIFT AID (NEED-BASED) *Total amount:* $9,333,692 (54% federal, 25% state, 15% institutional, 6% external sources). *Receiving aid:* Freshmen: 39% (439); all full-time undergraduates: 34% (1,544). *Average award:* Freshmen: $5687; Undergraduates: $5058. *Scholarships, grants, and awards:* Federal Pell, FSEOG, state, private, college/university gift aid from institutional funds.

GIFT AID (NON-NEED-BASED) *Total amount:* $594,951 (36% state, 31% institutional, 33% external sources). *Receiving aid:* Freshmen: 16% (179). Undergraduates: 8% (365). *Average award:* Freshmen: $3955. Undergraduates: $4695. *Scholarships, grants, and awards by category:* Academic interests/achievement: general academic interests/achievements. *Tuition waivers:* Full or partial for employees or children of employees, senior citizens.

LOANS *Student loans:* $23,039,588 (55% need-based, 45% non-need-based). 73% of past graduating class borrowed through all loan programs. *Average indebtedness per student:* $18,648. *Average need-based loan:* Freshmen: $3115. Undergraduates: $3955. *Parent loans:* $3,226,022 (12% need-based, 88% non-need-based). *Programs:* FFEL (Subsidized and Unsubsidized Stafford, PLUS), Perkins.

WORK-STUDY *Federal work-study:* Total amount: $522,823; 327 jobs averaging $1558.

APPLYING FOR FINANCIAL AID *Required financial aid form:* FAFSA. *Financial aid deadline (priority):* 3/1. *Notification date:* 4/15.

CONTACT Catherine Ryan, Financial Aid Director, Westfield State College, 333 Western Avenue, Westfield, MA 01086, 413-572-5218 or toll-free 800-322-8401 (in-state).

WEST LIBERTY UNIVERSITY
West Liberty, WV

Tuition & fees (WV res): $4880   **Average undergraduate aid package:** $8023

ABOUT THE INSTITUTION State-supported, coed. 35 undergraduate majors. Federal methodology is used as a basis for awarding need-based institutional aid.

UNDERGRADUATE EXPENSES for 2009–10 *One-time required fee:* $100. *Tuition, state resident:* full-time $4880; part-time $203 per credit hour. *Tuition, nonresident:* full-time $11,950; part-time $498 per credit hour. *College room and board:* $6870. Room and board charges vary according to board plan and housing facility. *Payment plans:* Installment, deferred payment.

FRESHMAN FINANCIAL AID (Fall 2009, est.) 527 applied for aid; of those 78% were deemed to have need. 100% of freshmen with need received aid. *Average financial aid package:* $6357 (excluding resources awarded to replace EFC).

UNDERGRADUATE FINANCIAL AID (Fall 2009, est.) 2,005 applied for aid; of those 75% were deemed to have need. 100% of undergraduates with need received aid. *Average financial aid package:* $8023 (excluding resources awarded to replace EFC).

GIFT AID (NEED-BASED) *Total amount:* $5,844,603 (77% federal, 23% state). *Receiving aid:* Freshmen: 48% (275); all full-time undergraduates: 47% (1,074). *Average award:* Freshmen: $5034; Undergraduates: $5177. *Scholarships, grants, and awards:* Federal Pell, FSEOG, state, private, college/university gift aid from institutional funds.

GIFT AID (NON-NEED-BASED) *Total amount:* $2,521,998 (1% federal, 53% state, 35% institutional, 11% external sources). *Receiving aid:* Freshmen: 27% (155). Undergraduates: 25% (558). *Scholarships, grants, and awards by category:* Academic interests/achievement: business, communication, education, English, general academic interests/achievements, health fields, mathematics, physical sciences. *Creative arts/performance:* art/fine arts, music, theater/drama. *Special achievements/activities:* cheerleading/drum major. *Special characteristics:* children and siblings of alumni, children of faculty/staff. *Tuition waivers:* Full or partial for employees or children of employees, senior citizens.

LOANS *Student loans:* $11,329,862 (49% need-based, 51% non-need-based). *Average need-based loan:* Freshmen: $3598. Undergraduates: $4311. *Parent loans:* $1,816,992 (100% non-need-based). *Programs:* Federal Direct (Subsidized and Unsubsidized Stafford, PLUS), Perkins, Federal Nursing, alternative loans.

WORK-STUDY *Federal work-study:* Total amount: $133,000; jobs available. *State or other work-study/employment:* Total amount: $341,599 (100% non-need-based). Part-time jobs available.

ATHLETIC AWARDS Total amount: $954,073 (100% non-need-based).

APPLYING FOR FINANCIAL AID *Required financial aid form:* FAFSA. *Financial aid deadline (priority):* 3/1. *Notification date:* Continuous. Students must reply within 2 weeks of notification.

CONTACT Mr. Scott A. Cook, Dean of Students, Registrar, and Director of Financial Aid, West Liberty University, PO Box 295, West Liberty, WV 26074-0295, 304-336-8016 or toll-free 800-732-6204 Ext. 8076. *Fax:* 304-336-8088. *E-mail:* cookscot@westliberty.edu.

WESTMINSTER COLLEGE
Fulton, MO

Tuition & fees: $17,990	Average undergraduate aid package: $17,676

ABOUT THE INSTITUTION Independent religious, coed. 29 undergraduate majors. Federal methodology is used as a basis for awarding need-based institutional aid.

UNDERGRADUATE EXPENSES for 2009–10 *Comprehensive fee:* $25,110 includes full-time tuition ($17,990) and room and board ($7120). *College room only:* $3700. Room and board charges vary according to board plan and housing facility. *Part-time tuition:* $750 per credit hour. *Payment plan:* Installment.

FRESHMAN FINANCIAL AID (Fall 2009, est.) 249 applied for aid; of those 75% were deemed to have need. 100% of freshmen with need received aid; of those 59% had need fully met. *Average percent of need met:* 82% (excluding resources awarded to replace EFC). *Average financial aid package:* $18,906 (excluding resources awarded to replace EFC). 39% of all full-time freshmen had no need and received non-need-based gift aid.

UNDERGRADUATE FINANCIAL AID (Fall 2009, est.) 758 applied for aid; of those 80% were deemed to have need. 100% of undergraduates with need received aid; of those 56% had need fully met. *Average percent of need met:* 80% (excluding resources awarded to replace EFC). *Average financial aid package:* $17,676 (excluding resources awarded to replace EFC). 40% of all full-time undergraduates had no need and received non-need-based gift aid.

GIFT AID (NEED-BASED) *Total amount:* $13,641,863 (10% federal, 8% state, 67% institutional, 15% external sources). *Receiving aid:* Freshmen: 60% (186); all full-time undergraduates: 57% (603). *Average award:* Freshmen: $14,707; Undergraduates: $13,156. *Scholarships, grants, and awards:* Federal Pell, FSEOG, state, private, college/university gift aid from institutional funds.

GIFT AID (NON-NEED-BASED) *Average award:* Freshmen: $9098. Undergraduates: $9144. *Scholarships, grants, and awards by category:* Academic interests/achievement: 551 awards ($4,242,730 total): general academic interests/achievements. *Creative arts/performance:* 10 awards ($10,000 total): music. *Special achievements/activities:* 65 awards ($59,065 total): general special achievements/activities, leadership. *Special characteristics:* 293 awards ($1,976,653 total): children and siblings of alumni, children of faculty/staff, ethnic background, international students, local/state students, relatives of clergy, religious affiliation, siblings of current students, twins. *Tuition waivers:* Full or partial for children of alumni, employees or children of employees.

LOANS *Student loans:* $4,691,147 (41% need-based, 59% non-need-based). 58% of past graduating class borrowed through all loan programs. *Average indebtedness per student:* $20,018. *Average need-based loan:* Freshmen: $3403. Undergraduates: $3849. *Parent loans:* $939,666 (100% non-need-based). *Programs:* FFEL (Subsidized and Unsubsidized Stafford, PLUS), Perkins.

WORK-STUDY *Federal work-study:* Total amount: $325,000; 230 jobs averaging $1413. *State or other work-study/employment:* Total amount: $350,000 (100% non-need-based). 216 part-time jobs averaging $2124.

APPLYING FOR FINANCIAL AID *Required financial aid form:* FAFSA. *Financial aid deadline (priority):* 2/15. *Notification date:* Continuous beginning 3/15. Students must reply within 3 weeks of notification.

CONTACT Ms. Aimee Bristow, Director of Financial Aid, Westminster College, 501 Westminster Avenue, Fulton, MO 65251-1299, 800-475-3361. *Fax:* 573-592-5255. *E-mail:* aimee.bristow@westminster-mo.edu.

WESTMINSTER COLLEGE
New Wilmington, PA

Tuition & fees: $29,150	Average undergraduate aid package: $23,163

ABOUT THE INSTITUTION Independent religious, coed. 52 undergraduate majors. Federal methodology is used as a basis for awarding need-based institutional aid.

UNDERGRADUATE EXPENSES for 2010–11 *Comprehensive fee:* $37,990 includes full-time tuition ($28,020), mandatory fees ($1130), and room and board ($8840). *College room only:* $4770.

FRESHMAN FINANCIAL AID (Fall 2009, est.) 419 applied for aid; of those 92% were deemed to have need. 100% of freshmen with need received aid; of those 26% had need fully met. *Average percent of need met:* 81% (excluding resources awarded to replace EFC). *Average financial aid package:* $23,090 (excluding resources awarded to replace EFC). 14% of all full-time freshmen had no need and received non-need-based gift aid.

UNDERGRADUATE FINANCIAL AID (Fall 2009, est.) 1,313 applied for aid; of those 91% were deemed to have need. 100% of undergraduates with need received aid; of those 28% had need fully met. *Average percent of need met:* 83% (excluding resources awarded to replace EFC). *Average financial aid package:* $23,163 (excluding resources awarded to replace EFC). 16% of all full-time undergraduates had no need and received non-need-based gift aid.

GIFT AID (NEED-BASED) *Total amount:* $22,053,219 (9% federal, 9% state, 77% institutional, 5% external sources). *Receiving aid:* Freshmen: 84% (380); all full-time undergraduates: 83% (1,184). *Average award:* Freshmen: $19,537; Undergraduates: $18,663. *Scholarships, grants, and awards:* Federal Pell, FSEOG, state, private, college/university gift aid from institutional funds.

GIFT AID (NON-NEED-BASED) *Total amount:* $2,939,374 (98% institutional, 2% external sources). *Receiving aid:* Freshmen: 83% (373). Undergraduates: 80% (1,151). *Average award:* Freshmen: $14,522. Undergraduates: $12,701. *Scholarships, grants, and awards by category:* Academic interests/achievement: general academic interests/achievements. *Creative arts/performance:* cinema/film/broadcasting, general creative arts/performance, music, theater/drama. *Special characteristics:* children and siblings of alumni, general special characteristics, international students, religious affiliation.

LOANS *Student loans:* $10,032,147 (95% need-based, 5% non-need-based). 80% of past graduating class borrowed through all loan programs. *Average indebtedness per student:* $28,262. *Average need-based loan:* Freshmen: $3469.

Undergraduates: $4312. *Parent loans:* $2,597,211 (90% need-based, 10% non-need-based). *Programs:* FFEL (Subsidized and Unsubsidized Stafford, PLUS), Perkins, Resource Loans.

WORK-STUDY *Federal work-study:* Total amount: $775,394; jobs available. *State or other work-study/employment:* Total amount: $273,922 (77% need-based, 23% non-need-based). Part-time jobs available.

APPLYING FOR FINANCIAL AID *Required financial aid forms:* FAFSA, institution's own form, W-2 forms. *Financial aid deadline:* Continuous. *Notification date:* Continuous beginning 3/1. Students must reply by 5/1 or within 3 weeks of notification.

CONTACT Mrs. Cheryl A. Gerber, Director of Financial Aid, Westminster College, 319 South Market Street, New Wilmington, PA 16172-0001, 724-946-7102 or toll-free 800-942-8033 (in-state). *Fax:* 724-946-6171. *E-mail:* gerberca@westminster.edu.

WESTMINSTER COLLEGE
Salt Lake City, UT

Tuition & fees: $24,996	Average undergraduate aid package: $18,640

ABOUT THE INSTITUTION Independent, coed. 38 undergraduate majors. Federal methodology is used as a basis for awarding need-based institutional aid.

UNDERGRADUATE EXPENSES for 2009–10 *Comprehensive fee:* $32,002 includes full-time tuition ($24,576), mandatory fees ($420), and room and board ($7006). Full-time tuition and fees vary according to course load. Room and board charges vary according to board plan. *Part-time tuition:* $1024 per credit hour. *Part-time fees:* $122 per term. Part-time tuition and fees vary according to course load. *Payment plans:* Installment, deferred payment.

FRESHMAN FINANCIAL AID (Fall 2009, est.) 343 applied for aid; of those 81% were deemed to have need. 100% of freshmen with need received aid; of those 35% had need fully met. *Average percent of need met:* 89% (excluding resources awarded to replace EFC). *Average financial aid package:* $20,571 (excluding resources awarded to replace EFC). 36% of all full-time freshmen had no need and received non-need-based gift aid.

UNDERGRADUATE FINANCIAL AID (Fall 2009, est.) 1,410 applied for aid; of those 86% were deemed to have need. 100% of undergraduates with need received aid; of those 35% had need fully met. *Average percent of need met:* 78% (excluding resources awarded to replace EFC). *Average financial aid package:* $18,640 (excluding resources awarded to replace EFC). 33% of all full-time undergraduates had no need and received non-need-based gift aid.

GIFT AID (NEED-BASED) *Total amount:* $15,939,801 (17% federal, 75% institutional, 8% external sources). *Receiving aid:* Freshmen: 59% (277); all full-time undergraduates: 60% (1,205). *Average award:* Freshmen: $15,732; Undergraduates: $13,657. *Scholarships, grants, and awards:* Federal Pell, FSEOG, state, private, college/university gift aid from institutional funds.

GIFT AID (NON-NEED-BASED) *Total amount:* $7,279,667 (1% state, 78% institutional, 21% external sources). *Receiving aid:* Freshmen: 8% (38). Undergraduates: 6% (117). *Average award:* Freshmen: $12,341. Undergraduates: $10,995. *Scholarships, grants, and awards by category: Academic interests/achievement:* biological sciences, business, communication, computer science, education, English, general academic interests/achievements, health fields, humanities, international studies, mathematics, military science, physical sciences, premedicine, social sciences. *Creative arts/performance:* art/fine arts, journalism/publications, music, theater/drama. *Special achievements/activities:* leadership. *Special characteristics:* adult students, children and siblings of alumni, children of faculty/staff, children of public servants, ethnic background, first-generation college students, handicapped students, international students, local/state students, members of minority groups, public servants, relatives of clergy, religious affiliation, siblings of current students, spouses of current students, veterans, veterans' children. *Tuition waivers:* Full or partial for employees or children of employees.

LOANS *Student loans:* $11,036,381 (79% need-based, 21% non-need-based). 54% of past graduating class borrowed through all loan programs. *Average indebtedness per student:* $20,251. *Average need-based loan:* Freshmen: $4171. Undergraduates: $4980. *Parent loans:* $851,814 (76% need-based, 24% non-need-based). *Programs:* FFEL (Subsidized and Unsubsidized Stafford, PLUS), Perkins.

WORK-STUDY *Federal work-study:* Total amount: $660,590; jobs available. *State or other work-study/employment:* Total amount: $530,000 (100% non-need-based). Part-time jobs available.

ATHLETIC AWARDS Total amount: $334,836 (66% need-based, 34% non-need-based).

APPLYING FOR FINANCIAL AID *Required financial aid form:* FAFSA. *Financial aid deadline:* Continuous. *Notification date:* Continuous beginning 3/1. Students must reply within 3 weeks of notification.

CONTACT Elizabeth Key, Director of Financial Aid, Westminster College, 1840 South 1300 East, Salt Lake City, UT 84105, 801-832-2500 or toll-free 800-748-4753 (out-of-state). *Fax:* 801-832-2501. *E-mail:* ekey@westminstercollege.edu.

WESTMONT COLLEGE
Santa Barbara, CA

Tuition & fees: $34,460	Average undergraduate aid package: $24,129

ABOUT THE INSTITUTION Independent nondenominational, coed. 43 undergraduate majors. Federal methodology is used as a basis for awarding need-based institutional aid.

UNDERGRADUATE EXPENSES for 2010–11 *Comprehensive fee:* $45,420 includes full-time tuition ($33,400), mandatory fees ($1060), and room and board ($10,960). *College room only:* $6810.

FRESHMAN FINANCIAL AID (Fall 2009, est.) 252 applied for aid; of those 82% were deemed to have need. 100% of freshmen with need received aid; of those 10% had need fully met. *Average percent of need met:* 71% (excluding resources awarded to replace EFC). *Average financial aid package:* $24,160 (excluding resources awarded to replace EFC). 30% of all full-time freshmen had no need and received non-need-based gift aid.

UNDERGRADUATE FINANCIAL AID (Fall 2009, est.) 910 applied for aid; of those 88% were deemed to have need. 100% of undergraduates with need received aid; of those 10% had need fully met. *Average percent of need met:* 70% (excluding resources awarded to replace EFC). *Average financial aid package:* $24,129 (excluding resources awarded to replace EFC). 27% of all full-time undergraduates had no need and received non-need-based gift aid.

GIFT AID (NEED-BASED) *Total amount:* $14,334,022 (9% federal, 13% state, 76% institutional, 2% external sources). *Receiving aid:* Freshmen: 62% (206); all full-time undergraduates: 62% (801). *Average award:* Freshmen: $20,396; Undergraduates: $19,229. *Scholarships, grants, and awards:* Federal Pell, FSEOG, state, private, college/university gift aid from institutional funds.

GIFT AID (NON-NEED-BASED) *Total amount:* $3,846,301 (97% institutional, 3% external sources). *Receiving aid:* Freshmen: 5% (18). Undergraduates: 5% (65). *Average award:* Freshmen: $9769. Undergraduates: $10,128. *Scholarships, grants, and awards by category: Academic interests/achievement:* 862 awards ($7,644,385 total): general academic interests/achievements. *Creative arts/performance:* 95 awards ($179,930 total): art/fine arts, music, theater/drama. *Special achievements/activities:* 95 awards ($142,500 total): general special achievements/activities, leadership. *Special characteristics:* 287 awards ($1,259,937 total): children of faculty/staff, ethnic background, international students.

LOANS *Student loans:* $7,154,021 (76% need-based, 24% non-need-based). 61% of past graduating class borrowed through all loan programs. *Average indebtedness per student:* $25,565. *Average need-based loan:* Freshmen: $4070. Undergraduates: $5483. *Parent loans:* $2,512,485 (44% need-based, 56% non-need-based). *Programs:* FFEL (Subsidized and Unsubsidized Stafford, PLUS), Perkins, college/university, alternative loans.

WORK-STUDY *Federal work-study:* Total amount: $135,255; 143 jobs averaging $946.

ATHLETIC AWARDS Total amount: $1,235,724 (56% need-based, 44% non-need-based).

APPLYING FOR FINANCIAL AID *Required financial aid form:* FAFSA. *Financial aid deadline (priority):* 3/1. *Notification date:* 3/1. Students must reply by 5/1 or within 2 weeks of notification.

CONTACT Mrs. Diane L. Horvath, Director of Financial Aid, Westmont College, 955 La Paz Road, Santa Barbara, CA 93108, 805-565-6061 or toll-free 800-777-9011. *Fax:* 805-565-7157. *E-mail:* dhorvath@westmont.edu.

WEST SUBURBAN COLLEGE OF NURSING
Oak Park, IL

Tuition & fees: $21,536	Average undergraduate aid package: $8159

ABOUT THE INSTITUTION Independent, coed, primarily women. 2 undergraduate majors. Both federal and institutional methodology are used as a basis for awarding need-based institutional aid.

UNDERGRADUATE EXPENSES for 2009–10 *Tuition:* full-time $20,986; part-time $711 per credit hour. *Required fees:* full-time $550; $135 per term. Full-time tuition and fees vary according to program. Part-time tuition and fees vary according to course load and program. *Payment plan:* Installment.

UNDERGRADUATE FINANCIAL AID (Fall 2009, est.) 199 applied for aid; of those 95% were deemed to have need. 100% of undergraduates with need received aid; of those 94% had need fully met. *Average percent of need met:* 84% (excluding resources awarded to replace EFC). *Average financial aid package:* $8159 (excluding resources awarded to replace EFC). 3% of all full-time undergraduates had no need and received non-need-based gift aid.

GIFT AID (NEED-BASED) *Total amount:* $730,111 (41% federal, 35% state, 24% institutional). *Receiving aid:* All full-time undergraduates: 80% (189). *Average award:* Undergraduates: $3000. *Scholarships, grants, and awards:* Federal Pell, FSEOG, state, college/university gift aid from institutional funds.

GIFT AID (NON-NEED-BASED) *Total amount:* $330,414 (91% institutional, 9% external sources). *Receiving aid:* Undergraduates: 80% (189). *Average award:* Undergraduates: $5000. *Tuition waivers:* Full or partial for employees or children of employees.

LOANS *Student loans:* $2,205,855 (81% need-based, 19% non-need-based). *Average need-based loan:* Undergraduates: $5500. *Parent loans:* $152,176 (100% need-based). *Programs:* Federal Direct (Subsidized and Unsubsidized Stafford, PLUS).

WORK-STUDY *Federal work-study:* Total amount: $20,100; 4 jobs averaging $5000.

CONTACT Ms. Shirley Howell, Financial Aid Officer, West Suburban College of Nursing, 3 Erie Court, Oak Park, IL 60302, 708-763-1426. *Fax:* 708-763-1531. *E-mail:* shirley.howell@wscn.edu.

WEST TEXAS A&M UNIVERSITY
Canyon, TX

CONTACT Mr. Jim Reed, Director of Financial Aid, West Texas A&M University, WTAMU Box 60939, Canyon, TX 79016-0001, 806-651-2055 or toll-free 800-99-WTAMU. *Fax:* 806-651-2924. *E-mail:* jreed@mail.wtamu.edu.

WEST VIRGINIA STATE UNIVERSITY
Institute, WV

CONTACT Mrs. Mary Blizzard, Director, Office of Student Financial Assistance, West Virginia State University, PO Box 1000, Ferrell Hall 324, Institute, WV 25112-1000, 304-766-3131 or toll-free 800-987-2112.

WEST VIRGINIA UNIVERSITY
Morgantown, WV

Tuition & fees (WV res): $5304	Average undergraduate aid package: $6959

ABOUT THE INSTITUTION State-supported, coed. 79 undergraduate majors. Federal methodology is used as a basis for awarding need-based institutional aid.

UNDERGRADUATE EXPENSES for 2009–10 *Tuition, state resident:* full-time $5304; part-time $221 per credit hour. *Tuition, nonresident:* full-time $16,402; part-time $683 per credit hour. Full-time tuition and fees vary according to location, program, and reciprocity agreements. Part-time tuition and fees vary according to course load, location, program, and reciprocity agreements. *College room and board:* $7770. Room and board charges vary according to board plan, housing facility, and location. *Payment plan:* Installment.

FRESHMAN FINANCIAL AID (Fall 2009, est.) 3,765 applied for aid; of those 78% were deemed to have need. 70% of freshmen with need received aid; of those 30% had need fully met. *Average percent of need met:* 72% (excluding resources awarded to replace EFC). *Average financial aid package:* $4124 (excluding resources awarded to replace EFC). 29% of all full-time freshmen had no need and received non-need-based gift aid.

UNDERGRADUATE FINANCIAL AID (Fall 2009, est.) 16,189 applied for aid; of those 78% were deemed to have need. 79% of undergraduates with need received aid; of those 30% had need fully met. *Average percent of need met:* 75% (excluding resources awarded to replace EFC). *Average financial aid*

package: $6959 (excluding resources awarded to replace EFC). 16% of all full-time undergraduates had no need and received non-need-based gift aid.

GIFT AID (NEED-BASED) *Total amount:* $37,024,896 (72% federal, 22% state, 6% institutional). *Receiving aid:* Freshmen: 33% (1,490); all full-time undergraduates: 34% (6,864). *Average award:* Freshmen: $5384; Undergraduates: $6266. *Scholarships, grants, and awards:* Federal Pell, FSEOG, state, private, college/university gift aid from institutional funds.

GIFT AID (NON-NEED-BASED) *Total amount:* $31,624,546 (1% federal, 74% state, 19% institutional, 6% external sources). *Receiving aid:* Freshmen: 33% (1,518). Undergraduates: 36% (7,328). *Average award:* Freshmen: $1601. Undergraduates: $1912. *Scholarships, grants, and awards by category: Academic interests/achievement:* agriculture, architecture, area/ethnic studies, biological sciences, business, communication, computer science, education, engineering/technologies, English, foreign languages, general academic interests/achievements, health fields, home economics, humanities, international studies, library science, mathematics, military science, physical sciences, premedicine, religion/biblical studies, social sciences. *Creative arts/performance:* art/fine arts, debating, music, theater/drama. *Special achievements/activities:* general special achievements/activities, leadership. *Special characteristics:* children of faculty/staff, children of union members/company employees, children of workers in trades, ethnic background, general special characteristics, international students, local/state students, members of minority groups. *Tuition waivers:* Full or partial for employees or children of employees, senior citizens.

LOANS *Student loans:* $112,447,558 (32% need-based, 68% non-need-based). *Average need-based loan:* Freshmen: $3804. Undergraduates: $4433. *Parent loans:* $50,460,376 (100% non-need-based). *Programs:* Federal Direct (Subsidized and Unsubsidized Stafford, PLUS), Perkins, college/university.

WORK-STUDY *Federal work-study:* Total amount: $1,800,000; jobs available. *State or other work-study/employment:* Total amount: $1,831,267 (100% non-need-based). Part-time jobs available.

ATHLETIC AWARDS Total amount: $4,724,300 (100% non-need-based).

APPLYING FOR FINANCIAL AID *Required financial aid forms:* FAFSA, state aid form. *Financial aid deadline:* 3/1. *Notification date:* Continuous beginning 3/15. Students must reply within 4 weeks of notification.

CONTACT Kaye Widney, Director of Financial Aid, West Virginia University, PO Box 6004, Morgantown, WV 26506-6004, 304-293-5242 or toll-free 800-344-9881. *Fax:* 304-293-4890. *E-mail:* kaye.widney@mail.wvu.edu.

WEST VIRGINIA UNIVERSITY INSTITUTE OF TECHNOLOGY
Montgomery, WV

CONTACT Nina M. Morton, Director of Financial Aid, West Virginia University Institute of Technology, 405 Fayette Pike, Montgomery, WV 25136, 304-442-3032 or toll-free 888-554-8324.

WEST VIRGINIA WESLEYAN COLLEGE
Buckhannon, WV

Tuition & fees: $23,980	Average undergraduate aid package: $23,785

ABOUT THE INSTITUTION Independent religious, coed. 64 undergraduate majors. Federal methodology is used as a basis for awarding need-based institutional aid.

UNDERGRADUATE EXPENSES for 2010–11 *Comprehensive fee:* $31,120 includes full-time tuition ($23,130), mandatory fees ($850), and room and board ($7140). Full-time tuition and fees vary according to course load. Room and board charges vary according to board plan and housing facility. Part-time tuition and fees vary according to course load. *Payment plan:* Installment.

FRESHMAN FINANCIAL AID (Fall 2009, est.) 378 applied for aid; of those 87% were deemed to have need. 100% of freshmen with need received aid; of those 22% had need fully met. *Average percent of need met:* 86% (excluding resources awarded to replace EFC). *Average financial aid package:* $24,424 (excluding resources awarded to replace EFC). 12% of all full-time freshmen had no need and received non-need-based gift aid.

UNDERGRADUATE FINANCIAL AID (Fall 2009, est.) 1,302 applied for aid; of those 77% were deemed to have need. 100% of undergraduates with need received aid; of those 33% had need fully met. *Average percent of need met:* 78% (excluding resources awarded to replace EFC). *Average financial aid*

package: $23,785 (excluding resources awarded to replace EFC). 20% of all full-time undergraduates had no need and received non-need-based gift aid.

GIFT AID (NEED-BASED) *Total amount:* $18,040,256 (11% federal, 12% state, 73% institutional, 4% external sources). *Receiving aid:* Freshmen: 82% (329); all full-time undergraduates: 76% (1,008). *Average award:* Freshmen: $19,436; Undergraduates: $18,591. *Scholarships, grants, and awards:* Federal Pell, FSEOG, state, private, college/university gift aid from institutional funds, Federal Nursing.

GIFT AID (NON-NEED-BASED) *Total amount:* $3,618,206 (8% state, 89% institutional, 3% external sources). *Receiving aid:* Freshmen: 19% (74). Undergraduates: 16% (215). *Average award:* Freshmen: $13,020. Undergraduates: $12,053. *Scholarships, grants, and awards by category: Academic interests/achievement:* English, general academic interests/achievements, physical sciences. *Creative arts/performance:* art/fine arts, music, performing arts, theater/drama. *Special achievements/activities:* community service, leadership, religious involvement. *Special characteristics:* children and siblings of alumni, children of faculty/staff, general special characteristics, international students, relatives of clergy, religious affiliation. *Tuition waivers:* Full or partial for employees or children of employees.

LOANS *Student loans:* $6,469,072 (13% need-based, 87% non-need-based). 71% of past graduating class borrowed through all loan programs. *Average indebtedness per student:* $21,502. *Average need-based loan:* Freshmen: $3388. Undergraduates: $4189. *Parent loans:* $783,183 (100% non-need-based). *Programs:* Federal Direct (Subsidized and Unsubsidized Stafford, PLUS), Perkins, Federal Nursing, college/university.

WORK-STUDY *Federal work-study:* Total amount: $594,040; jobs available. *State or other work-study/employment:* Total amount: $235,816 (70% need-based, 30% non-need-based). Part-time jobs available.

ATHLETIC AWARDS Total amount: $3,564,361 (31% need-based, 69% non-need-based).

APPLYING FOR FINANCIAL AID *Required financial aid form:* FAFSA. *Financial aid deadline (priority):* 2/15. *Notification date:* Continuous beginning 3/15. Students must reply within 4 weeks of notification.

CONTACT Susan George, Director of Financial Aid, West Virginia Wesleyan College, 59 College Avenue, Buckhannon, WV 26201, 304-473-8080 or toll-free 800-722-9933 (out-of-state). *E-mail:* george_s@wvwc.edu.

WESTWOOD COLLEGE–ANAHEIM
Anaheim, CA

CONTACT Financial Aid Office, Westwood College–Anaheim, 1551 South Douglass Road, Anaheim, CA 92806, 714-226-9990 or toll-free 877-650-6050 (in-state).

WESTWOOD COLLEGE–ANNANDALE CAMPUS
Annandale, VA

CONTACT Financial Aid Office, Westwood College–Annandale Campus, 7611 Little River Turnpike, 5th Floor, Annandale, VA 22003, 706-642-3770 or toll-free 800-281-2978.

WESTWOOD COLLEGE–ARLINGTON BALLSTON CAMPUS
Arlington, VA

CONTACT Financial Aid Office, Westwood College–Arlington Ballston Campus, 4300 Wilson Boulevard, Suite 200, Arlington, VA 22203, 703-243-3900.

WESTWOOD COLLEGE–ATLANTA MIDTOWN
Atlanta, GA

CONTACT Financial Aid Office, Westwood College–Atlanta Midtown, 1100 Spring Street, Atlanta, GA 30309, 404-745-9096.

WESTWOOD COLLEGE–ATLANTA NORTHLAKE
Atlanta, GA

CONTACT Financial Aid Office, Westwood College–Atlanta Northlake, 2309 Parklake Drive, NE, Building 10, Atlanta, GA 30345, 404-962-2999.

WESTWOOD COLLEGE–CHICAGO DU PAGE
Woodridge, IL

CONTACT Patty Zavala, Senior Student Finance Specialist, Westwood College–Chicago Du Page, 7155 Janes Avenue, Woodridge, IL 60517, 630-434-8244 or toll-free 888-721-7646 (in-state).

WESTWOOD COLLEGE–CHICAGO LOOP CAMPUS
Chicago, IL

CONTACT Financial Aid Office, Westwood College–Chicago Loop Campus, 17 North State Street, Suite 300, Chicago, IL 60602, 312-739-0850.

WESTWOOD COLLEGE–CHICAGO O'HARE AIRPORT
Chicago, IL

CONTACT Financial Aid Office, Westwood College–Chicago O'Hare Airport, 8501 West Higgins Road, Suite 100, Chicago, IL 60631, 773-380-6801 or toll-free 877-877-8857 (in-state).

WESTWOOD COLLEGE–CHICAGO RIVER OAKS
Calumet City, IL

CONTACT Financial Aid Office, Westwood College–Chicago River Oaks, 80 River Oaks Drive, Suite D-49, Calumet City, IL 60409, 708-832-1988 or toll-free 888-549-6873 (in-state).

WESTWOOD COLLEGE–DALLAS
Dallas, TX

CONTACT Financial Aid Office, Westwood College–Dallas, 8390 LBJ Freeway, Executive Center 1, Suite 100, Dallas, TX 75243, 214-570-0100 or toll-free 800-281-2978.

WESTWOOD COLLEGE–DENVER NORTH
Denver, CO

CONTACT Admissions Office, Westwood College–Denver North, 7350 North Broadway, Denver, CO 80221, 800-875-6050 or toll-free 800-992-5050.

WESTWOOD COLLEGE–DENVER SOUTH
Denver, CO

CONTACT Financial Aid Office, Westwood College–Denver South, 3150 South Sheridan Boulevard, Denver, CO 80227, 303-934-2790 or toll-free 800-281-2978.

WESTWOOD COLLEGE–FORT WORTH
Fort Worth, TX

CONTACT Financial Aid Office, Westwood College–Fort Worth, 4232 North Freeway, Fort Worth, TX 76137, 817-605-8111 or toll-free 866-533-9997 (in-state).

WESTWOOD COLLEGE–INLAND EMPIRE
Upland, CA

CONTACT Financial Aid Office, Westwood College–Inland Empire, 20 West 7th Street, Upland, CA 91786, 909-931-7550 or toll-free 866-288-9488 (in-state).

WESTWOOD COLLEGE–LOS ANGELES
Los Angeles, CA

CONTACT Financial Aid Office, Westwood College–Los Angeles, 3250 Wilshire Boulevard, 4th Floor, Los Angeles, CA 90010, 213-739-9999 or toll-free 877-377-4600 (in-state).

WESTWOOD COLLEGE–SOUTH BAY CAMPUS
Torrance, CA

CONTACT Financial Aid Office, Westwood College–South Bay Campus, 19700 South Vermont Avenue, Suite 100, Torrance, CA 90502, 310-522-2088 or toll-free 800-281-2978.

WHEATON COLLEGE
Wheaton, IL

Tuition & fees: $27,580   **Average undergraduate aid package: $22,934**

ABOUT THE INSTITUTION Independent nondenominational, coed. 39 undergraduate majors. Both federal and institutional methodology are used as a basis for awarding need-based institutional aid.

UNDERGRADUATE EXPENSES for 2010–11 *Comprehensive fee:* $35,630 includes full-time tuition ($27,580) and room and board ($8050). *College room only:* $4750. *Part-time tuition:* $1149 per credit hour. Part-time tuition and fees vary according to course load.

FRESHMAN FINANCIAL AID (Fall 2009, est.) 486 applied for aid; of those 70% were deemed to have need. 99% of freshmen with need received aid; of those 25% had need fully met. *Average percent of need met:* 86% (excluding resources awarded to replace EFC). *Average financial aid package:* $24,042 (excluding resources awarded to replace EFC). 16% of all full-time freshmen had no need and received non-need-based gift aid.

UNDERGRADUATE FINANCIAL AID (Fall 2009, est.) 1,747 applied for aid; of those 72% were deemed to have need. 98% of undergraduates with need received aid; of those 29% had need fully met. *Average percent of need met:* 84% (excluding resources awarded to replace EFC). *Average financial aid package:* $22,934 (excluding resources awarded to replace EFC). 16% of all full-time undergraduates had no need and received non-need-based gift aid.

GIFT AID (NEED-BASED) *Total amount:* $21,468,016 (12% federal, 2% state, 82% institutional, 4% external sources). *Receiving aid:* Freshmen: 50% (311); all full-time undergraduates: 50% (1,159). *Average award:* Freshmen: $18,058; Undergraduates: $16,241. *Scholarships, grants, and awards:* Federal Pell, FSEOG, state, college/university gift aid from institutional funds.

GIFT AID (NON-NEED-BASED) *Total amount:* $1,422,686 (2% federal, 84% institutional, 14% external sources). *Receiving aid:* Freshmen: 18% (111). Undergraduates: 19% (441). *Average award:* Freshmen: $4002. Undergraduates: $5397. *Scholarships, grants, and awards by category:* Academic interests/achievement: 660 awards ($900,251 total): biological sciences, business, computer science, education, foreign languages, general academic interests/achievements, health fields, humanities, mathematics, military science, physical sciences, premedicine, religion/biblical studies, social sciences. *Creative arts/performance:* 92 awards ($239,157 total): art/fine arts, music. *Special achievements/activities:* 18 awards ($81,526 total): general special achievements/activities. *Special characteristics:* 138 awards ($1,436,417 total): ethnic background, general special characteristics, handicapped students.

LOANS *Student loans:* $9,108,650 (85% need-based, 15% non-need-based). 51% of past graduating class borrowed through all loan programs. *Average indebtedness per student:* $20,455. *Average need-based loan:* Freshmen: $4460. Undergraduates: $4803. *Parent loans:* $2,100,173 (71% need-based, 29% non-need-based). *Programs:* FFEL (Subsidized and Unsubsidized Stafford, PLUS), Perkins.

WORK-STUDY *Federal work-study:* Total amount: $447,816; 279 jobs averaging $1472.

APPLYING FOR FINANCIAL AID *Required financial aid forms:* FAFSA, institution's own form. *Financial aid deadline (priority):* 2/15. *Notification date:* Continuous beginning 3/1.

CONTACT Ms. Karen Belling, Director of Financial Aid, Wheaton College, 501 College Avenue, Wheaton, IL 60187-5593, 630-752-5021 or toll-free 800-222-2419 (out-of-state). *E-mail:* finaid@wheaton.edu.

WHEATON COLLEGE
Norton, MA

Tuition & fees: $41,084   **Average undergraduate aid package: $31,770**

ABOUT THE INSTITUTION Independent, coed. 42 undergraduate majors. Institutional methodology is used as a basis for awarding need-based institutional aid.

UNDERGRADUATE EXPENSES for 2010–11 *One-time required fee:* $50. *Comprehensive fee:* $51,264 includes full-time tuition ($40,790), mandatory fees ($294), and room and board ($10,180). *College room only:* $5350. *Payment plans:* Tuition prepayment, installment.

FRESHMAN FINANCIAL AID (Fall 2009, est.) 289 applied for aid; of those 89% were deemed to have need. 100% of freshmen with need received aid; of those 51% had need fully met. *Average percent of need met:* 96% (excluding resources awarded to replace EFC). *Average financial aid package:* $31,605 (excluding resources awarded to replace EFC). 16% of all full-time freshmen had no need and received non-need-based gift aid.

UNDERGRADUATE FINANCIAL AID (Fall 2009, est.) 1,011 applied for aid; of those 90% were deemed to have need. 100% of undergraduates with need received aid; of those 57% had need fully met. *Average percent of need met:* 97% (excluding resources awarded to replace EFC). *Average financial aid package:* $31,770 (excluding resources awarded to replace EFC). 13% of all full-time undergraduates had no need and received non-need-based gift aid.

GIFT AID (NEED-BASED) *Total amount:* $23,776,998 (7% federal, 2% state, 88% institutional, 3% external sources). *Receiving aid:* Freshmen: 59% (250); all full-time undergraduates: 53% (867). *Average award:* Freshmen: $25,818; Undergraduates: $25,214. *Scholarships, grants, and awards:* Federal Pell, FSEOG, state, private, college/university gift aid from institutional funds.

GIFT AID (NON-NEED-BASED) *Total amount:* $2,502,562 (89% institutional, 11% external sources). *Receiving aid:* Freshmen: 1% (6). Undergraduates: 1% (15). *Average award:* Freshmen: $11,250. Undergraduates: $10,725. *Scholarships, grants, and awards by category:* Academic interests/achievement: 470 awards ($4,841,875 total): general academic interests/achievements. *Tuition waivers:* Full or partial for employees or children of employees.

LOANS *Student loans:* $6,551,417 (61% need-based, 39% non-need-based). 53% of past graduating class borrowed through all loan programs. *Average indebtedness per student:* $25,540. *Average need-based loan:* Freshmen: $3897. Undergraduates: $4614. *Parent loans:* $4,886,491 (100% non-need-based). *Programs:* Federal Direct (Subsidized and Unsubsidized Stafford, PLUS), Perkins, MEFA Loans, private educational loans.

WORK-STUDY *Federal work-study:* Total amount: $1,509,864; 766 jobs averaging $1828. *State or other work-study/employment:* Total amount: $664,150 (47% need-based, 53% non-need-based). 314 part-time jobs averaging $1760.

APPLYING FOR FINANCIAL AID *Required financial aid forms:* FAFSA, CSS Financial Aid PROFILE, business/farm supplement, federal income tax form(s). *Financial aid deadline:* 2/1. *Notification date:* 4/1. Students must reply by 5/1.

CONTACT Ms. Susan Beard, Director of Financial Aid Programs, Wheaton College, 26 East Main Street, Norton, MA 02766, 508-286-8232 or toll-free 800-394-6003. *Fax:* 508-286-3787. *E-mail:* sfs@wheatonma.edu.

WHEELING JESUIT UNIVERSITY
Wheeling, WV

Tuition & fees: $24,390   **Average undergraduate aid package: $21,466**

ABOUT THE INSTITUTION Independent Roman Catholic (Jesuit), coed. 55 undergraduate majors. Federal methodology is used as a basis for awarding need-based institutional aid.

UNDERGRADUATE EXPENSES for 2009–10 *Tuition:* full-time $23,590; part-time $655 per hour.

FRESHMAN FINANCIAL AID (Fall 2009, est.) 256 applied for aid; of those 86% were deemed to have need. 100% of freshmen with need received aid; of those 35% had need fully met. *Average percent of need met:* 89% (excluding resources awarded to replace EFC). *Average financial aid package:* $23,733 (excluding resources awarded to replace EFC). 16% of all full-time freshmen had no need and received non-need-based gift aid.

UNDERGRADUATE FINANCIAL AID (Fall 2009, est.) 823 applied for aid; of those 87% were deemed to have need. 100% of undergraduates with need received aid; of those 35% had need fully met. *Average percent of need met:* 86% (excluding resources awarded to replace EFC). *Average financial aid package:* $21,466 (excluding resources awarded to replace EFC). 20% of all full-time undergraduates had no need and received non-need-based gift aid.

GIFT AID (NEED-BASED) *Total amount:* $3,196,599 (45% federal, 9% state, 46% institutional). *Receiving aid:* Freshmen: 59% (156); all full-time undergraduates: 53% (478). *Average award:* Freshmen: $7436; Undergraduates: $6559. *Scholarships, grants, and awards:* Federal Pell, FSEOG, state, private, college/university gift aid from institutional funds, Federal Nursing.

GIFT AID (NON-NEED-BASED) *Total amount:* $9,726,159 (1% federal, 6% state, 90% institutional, 3% external sources). *Receiving aid:* Freshmen: 84% (221). Undergraduates: 74% (667). *Average award:* Freshmen: $11,094. Undergraduates: $10,869. *Scholarships, grants, and awards by category: Academic interests/achievement:* 773 awards ($7,619,754 total): general academic interests/achievements, premedicine. *Creative arts/performance:* 27 awards ($49,500 total): music. *Special achievements/activities:* 91 awards ($266,960 total): community service, general special achievements/activities. *Special characteristics:* 355 awards ($1,466,850 total): children and siblings of alumni, children of faculty/staff, general special characteristics, religious affiliation.

LOANS *Student loans:* $8,186,935 (46% need-based, 54% non-need-based). 89% of past graduating class borrowed through all loan programs. *Average indebtedness per student:* $26,334. *Average need-based loan:* Freshmen: $4401. Undergraduates: $4767. *Parent loans:* $808,424 (100% non-need-based). *Programs:* Federal Direct (Subsidized and Unsubsidized Stafford, PLUS), Perkins, Federal Nursing, alternative loans.

WORK-STUDY *Federal work-study:* Total amount: $193,752; 162 jobs averaging $2200. *State or other work-study/employment:* Total amount: $355,300 (100% non-need-based). 176 part-time jobs averaging $2200.

ATHLETIC AWARDS Total amount: $829,293 (100% non-need-based).

APPLYING FOR FINANCIAL AID *Required financial aid forms:* FAFSA, institution's own form. *Financial aid deadline (priority):* 3/1. *Notification date:* Continuous beginning 3/15. Students must reply within 2 weeks of notification.

CONTACT Christie Tomczyk, Director of Financial Aid, Wheeling Jesuit University, 316 Washington Avenue, Wheeling, WV 26003-6295, 304-243-2304 or toll-free 800-624-6992 Ext. 2359. *Fax:* 304-243-4397. *E-mail:* finaid@wju.edu.

WHEELOCK COLLEGE
Boston, MA

Tuition & fees: $28,160	Average undergraduate aid package: $20,806

ABOUT THE INSTITUTION Independent, coed, primarily women. 16 undergraduate majors. Federal methodology is used as a basis for awarding need-based institutional aid.

UNDERGRADUATE EXPENSES for 2009–10 *One-time required fee:* $225. *Comprehensive fee:* $39,360 includes full-time tuition ($27,150), mandatory fees ($1010), and room and board ($11,200). Full-time tuition and fees vary according to program. *Part-time tuition:* $850 per credit. Part-time tuition and fees vary according to program. *Payment plan:* Installment.

FRESHMAN FINANCIAL AID (Fall 2009, est.) 177 applied for aid; of those 96% were deemed to have need. 100% of freshmen with need received aid; of those 18% had need fully met. *Average percent of need met:* 74% (excluding resources awarded to replace EFC). *Average financial aid package:* $22,857 (excluding resources awarded to replace EFC). 5% of all full-time freshmen had no need and received non-need-based gift aid.

UNDERGRADUATE FINANCIAL AID (Fall 2009, est.) 646 applied for aid; of those 92% were deemed to have need. 99% of undergraduates with need received aid; of those 15% had need fully met. *Average percent of need met:* 69% (excluding resources awarded to replace EFC). *Average financial aid package:* $20,806 (excluding resources awarded to replace EFC). 13% of all full-time undergraduates had no need and received non-need-based gift aid.

GIFT AID (NEED-BASED) *Total amount:* $9,276,930 (12% federal, 4% state, 81% institutional, 3% external sources). *Receiving aid:* Freshmen: 94% (170);

all full-time undergraduates: 83% (584). *Average award:* Freshmen: $18,775; Undergraduates: $15,922. *Scholarships, grants, and awards:* Federal Pell, FSEOG, state, private, college/university gift aid from institutional funds.

GIFT AID (NON-NEED-BASED) *Total amount:* $1,232,364 (93% institutional, 7% external sources). *Receiving aid:* Freshmen: 13% (23). Undergraduates: 8% (56). *Average award:* Freshmen: $10,095. Undergraduates: $10,010. *Scholarships, grants, and awards by category: Academic interests/achievement:* general academic interests/achievements. *Tuition waivers:* Full or partial for employees or children of employees.

LOANS *Student loans:* $7,179,759 (72% need-based, 28% non-need-based). 96% of past graduating class borrowed through all loan programs. *Average indebtedness per student:* $43,319. *Average need-based loan:* Freshmen: $3815. Undergraduates: $5097. *Parent loans:* $1,395,027 (40% need-based, 60% non-need-based). *Programs:* FFEL (Subsidized and Unsubsidized Stafford, PLUS), Perkins, state, college/university.

WORK-STUDY *Federal work-study:* Total amount: $308,172; 233 jobs averaging $1800.

APPLYING FOR FINANCIAL AID *Required financial aid form:* FAFSA. *Financial aid deadline (priority):* 2/15. *Notification date:* Continuous beginning 3/1. Students must reply by 5/1.

CONTACT Roxanne Dumas, Director of Financial Aid, Wheelock College, 200 The Riverway, Boston, MA 02215-4176, 617-879-2208 or toll-free 800-734-5212 (out-of-state). *Fax:* 617-879-2470. *E-mail:* rdumas@wheelock.edu.

WHITMAN COLLEGE
Walla Walla, WA

Tuition & fees: $38,770	Average undergraduate aid package: $29,197

ABOUT THE INSTITUTION Independent, coed. 41 undergraduate majors. Institutional methodology is used as a basis for awarding need-based institutional aid.

UNDERGRADUATE EXPENSES for 2010–11 *Comprehensive fee:* $48,490 includes full-time tuition ($38,450), mandatory fees ($320), and room and board ($9720). *College room only:* $4480. Room and board charges vary according to board plan and housing facility. *Part-time tuition:* $1602 per credit hour. *Payment plan:* Deferred payment.

FRESHMAN FINANCIAL AID (Fall 2009, est.) 282 applied for aid; of those 69% were deemed to have need. 100% of freshmen with need received aid; of those 84% had need fully met. *Average percent of need met:* 94% (excluding resources awarded to replace EFC). *Average financial aid package:* $28,133 (excluding resources awarded to replace EFC). 31% of all full-time freshmen had no need and received non-need-based gift aid.

UNDERGRADUATE FINANCIAL AID (Fall 2009, est.) 855 applied for aid; of those 81% were deemed to have need. 100% of undergraduates with need received aid; of those 91% had need fully met. *Average percent of need met:* 94% (excluding resources awarded to replace EFC). *Average financial aid package:* $29,197 (excluding resources awarded to replace EFC). 29% of all full-time undergraduates had no need and received non-need-based gift aid.

GIFT AID (NEED-BASED) *Total amount:* $15,649,982 (5% federal, 3% state, 92% institutional). *Receiving aid:* Freshmen: 48% (190); all full-time undergraduates: 44% (686). *Average award:* Freshmen: $24,003; Undergraduates: $24,366. *Scholarships, grants, and awards:* Federal Pell, FSEOG, state, private, college/university gift aid from institutional funds.

GIFT AID (NON-NEED-BASED) *Total amount:* $6,296,248 (3% state, 80% institutional, 17% external sources). *Receiving aid:* Freshmen: 22% (89). Undergraduates: 13% (211). *Average award:* Freshmen: $9775. Undergraduates: $10,686. *Scholarships, grants, and awards by category: Academic interests/achievement:* 594 awards ($5,346,805 total): general academic interests/achievements. *Creative arts/performance:* 115 awards ($205,500 total): art/fine arts, debating, music, theater/drama. *Special achievements/activities:* 3 awards ($7500 total): leadership. *Special characteristics:* 56 awards ($331,366 total): ethnic background, first-generation college students, international students. *Tuition waivers:* Full or partial for employees or children of employees.

LOANS *Student loans:* $3,111,549 (70% need-based, 30% non-need-based). 49% of past graduating class borrowed through all loan programs. *Average indebtedness per student:* $16,782. *Average need-based loan:* Freshmen: $4145. Undergraduates: $4361. *Parent loans:* $1,724,987 (100% non-need-based). *Programs:* Federal Direct (Subsidized and Unsubsidized Stafford, PLUS), FFEL (Subsidized and Unsubsidized Stafford, PLUS), Perkins, alternative loans.

WORK-STUDY *Federal work-study:* Total amount: $948,184; 499 jobs averaging $1944. *State or other work-study/employment:* Total amount: $271,046 (77% need-based, 23% non-need-based). 191 part-time jobs averaging $1256.

APPLYING FOR FINANCIAL AID *Required financial aid forms:* FAFSA, CSS Financial Aid PROFILE. *Financial aid deadline:* 2/1 (priority: 11/15). *Notification date:* Continuous beginning 12/18. Students must reply within 2 weeks of notification.

CONTACT Tyson Harlow, Financial Aid Assistant, Whitman College, 345 Boyer Avenue, Walla Walla, WA 99362-2046, 509-527-5178 or toll-free 877-462-9448. *Fax:* 509-527-4967.

WHITTIER COLLEGE
Whittier, CA

ABOUT THE INSTITUTION Independent, coed. 25 undergraduate majors.

GIFT AID (NEED-BASED) *Scholarships, grants, and awards:* Federal Pell, FSEOG, state, private, college/university gift aid from institutional funds.

GIFT AID (NON-NEED-BASED) *Scholarships, grants, and awards by category:* Academic interests/achievement: general academic interests/achievements. Creative arts/performance: art/fine arts, music, theater/drama. Special characteristics: children and siblings of alumni, children of faculty/staff, international students.

LOANS *Programs:* Federal Direct (PLUS), FFEL (Subsidized and Unsubsidized Stafford, PLUS), Perkins, alternative financing loans.

WORK-STUDY *Federal work-study:* Total amount: $1,818,989; jobs available. *State or other work-study/employment:* Total amount: $740,724 (100% non-need-based). Part-time jobs available.

APPLYING FOR FINANCIAL AID *Required financial aid forms:* FAFSA, CSS Financial Aid PROFILE.

CONTACT Mr. David Carnevale, Director of Student Financing, Whittier College, 13406 East Philadelphia Street, Whittier, CA 90608-0634, 562-907-4285. *Fax:* 562-464-4560. *E-mail:* dcarneva@whittier.edu.

WHITWORTH UNIVERSITY
Spokane, WA

Tuition & fees: N/R	Average undergraduate aid package: $23,442

ABOUT THE INSTITUTION Independent Presbyterian, coed. *Awards:* bachelor's and master's degrees. 43 undergraduate majors. *Total enrollment:* 2,607. Undergraduates: 2,331. Freshmen: 533. Federal methodology is used as a basis for awarding need-based institutional aid.

FRESHMAN FINANCIAL AID (Fall 2009, est.) 484 applied for aid; of those 88% were deemed to have need. 100% of freshmen with need received aid; of those 23% had need fully met. *Average percent of need met:* 86% (excluding resources awarded to replace EFC). *Average financial aid package:* $26,895 (excluding resources awarded to replace EFC). 19% of all full-time freshmen had no need and received non-need-based gift aid.

UNDERGRADUATE FINANCIAL AID (Fall 2009, est.) 1,809 applied for aid; of those 89% were deemed to have need. 100% of undergraduates with need received aid; of those 19% had need fully met. *Average percent of need met:* 81% (excluding resources awarded to replace EFC). *Average financial aid package:* $23,442 (excluding resources awarded to replace EFC). 22% of all full-time undergraduates had no need and received non-need-based gift aid.

GIFT AID (NEED-BASED) *Total amount:* $25,643,702 (12% federal, 9% state, 75% institutional, 4% external sources). *Receiving aid:* Freshmen: 75% (419); all full-time undergraduates: 68% (1,550). *Average award:* Freshmen: $19,575; Undergraduates: $16,353. *Scholarships, grants, and awards:* Federal Pell, FSEOG, state, private, college/university gift aid from institutional funds.

GIFT AID (NON-NEED-BASED) *Total amount:* $6,799,490 (5% federal, 1% state, 90% institutional, 4% external sources). *Receiving aid:* Freshmen: 11% (61). Undergraduates: 7% (163). *Average award:* Freshmen: $10,706. Undergraduates: $10,424. *Scholarships, grants, and awards by category:* Academic interests/achievement: 1,604 awards ($14,526,598 total): biological sciences, computer science, general academic interests/achievements, military science, physical sciences, premedicine. Creative arts/performance: 176 awards ($404,769 total): art/fine arts, journalism/publications, music, theater/drama. Special achievements/activities: 45 awards ($31,500 total): religious involvement. Special characteristics: 669 awards ($2,459,670 total): children and siblings of alumni, ethnic background, international students, members of minority groups,

relatives of clergy, siblings of current students. *Tuition waivers:* Full or partial for employees or children of employees. *ROTC:* Army cooperative.

LOANS *Student loans:* $12,028,199 (82% need-based, 18% non-need-based). 68% of past graduating class borrowed through all loan programs. *Average indebtedness per student:* $18,801. *Average need-based loan:* Freshmen: $4243. Undergraduates: $4818. *Parent loans:* $2,879,416 (33% need-based, 67% non-need-based). *Programs:* Federal Direct (Subsidized and Unsubsidized Stafford, PLUS), Perkins.

WORK-STUDY *Federal work-study:* Total amount: $1,780,077; 739 jobs averaging $2214. *State or other work-study/employment:* Total amount: $1,425,959 (98% need-based, 2% non-need-based). 374 part-time jobs averaging $3008.

APPLYING FOR FINANCIAL AID *Required financial aid form:* FAFSA. *Financial aid deadline (priority):* 3/1. *Notification date:* Continuous beginning 3/15.

CONTACT Ms. Wendy Z. Olson, Director of Financial Aid, Whitworth University, 300 West Hawthorne Road, Spokane, WA 99251-0001, 509-777-4306 or toll-free 800-533-4668 (out-of-state). *Fax:* 509-777-4601. *E-mail:* wolson@whitworth.edu.

WICHITA STATE UNIVERSITY
Wichita, KS

Tuition & fees (KS res): $5450	Average undergraduate aid package: $7278

ABOUT THE INSTITUTION State-supported, coed. 61 undergraduate majors. Federal methodology is used as a basis for awarding need-based institutional aid.

UNDERGRADUATE EXPENSES for 2009–10 *Tuition, state resident:* full-time $4497; part-time $149.90 per credit hour. *Tuition, nonresident:* full-time $12,531; part-time $417.70 per credit hour. *Required fees:* full-time $953; $31.20 per credit hour or $17 per term. Full-time tuition and fees vary according to course load and degree level. Part-time tuition and fees vary according to course load and degree level. *College room and board:* $6700. Room and board charges vary according to board plan and housing facility. *Payment plan:* Installment.

FRESHMAN FINANCIAL AID (Fall 2009, est.) 1,062 applied for aid; of those 37% were deemed to have need. 97% of freshmen with need received aid; of those 73% had need fully met. *Average percent of need met:* 49% (excluding resources awarded to replace EFC). *Average financial aid package:* $6676 (excluding resources awarded to replace EFC). 41% of all full-time freshmen had no need and received non-need-based gift aid.

UNDERGRADUATE FINANCIAL AID (Fall 2009, est.) 6,118 applied for aid; of those 47% were deemed to have need. 98% of undergraduates with need received aid; of those 68% had need fully met. *Average percent of need met:* 50% (excluding resources awarded to replace EFC). *Average financial aid package:* $7278 (excluding resources awarded to replace EFC). 21% of all full-time undergraduates had no need and received non-need-based gift aid.

GIFT AID (NEED-BASED) *Total amount:* $11,482,801 (84% federal, 15% state, 1% external sources). *Receiving aid:* Freshmen: 21% (247); all full-time undergraduates: 20% (1,458). *Average award:* Freshmen: $3582; Undergraduates: $3604. *Scholarships, grants, and awards:* Federal Pell, FSEOG, state, private, college/university gift aid from institutional funds, Academic Competitiveness Grants, National SMART Grants.

GIFT AID (NON-NEED-BASED) *Total amount:* $8,624,769 (87% institutional, 13% external sources). *Receiving aid:* Freshmen: 18% (213). Undergraduates: 12% (929). *Average award:* Freshmen: $2337. Undergraduates: $1704. *Scholarships, grants, and awards by category:* Academic interests/achievement: area/ethnic studies, biological sciences, business, communication, computer science, education, engineering/technologies, English, foreign languages, general academic interests/achievements, health fields, humanities, international studies, mathematics, physical sciences, premedicine, social sciences. Creative arts/performance: applied art and design, art/fine arts, creative writing, dance, debating, journalism/publications, music, performing arts, theater/drama. Special achievements/activities: cheerleading/drum major, general special achievements/activities, leadership, memberships. Special characteristics: adult students, first-generation college students, international students, members of minority groups. *Tuition waivers:* Full or partial for employees or children of employees, senior citizens.

LOANS *Student loans:* $38,153,298 (49% need-based, 51% non-need-based). 57% of past graduating class borrowed through all loan programs. *Average indebtedness per student:* $15,769. *Average need-based loan:* Freshmen: $3201. Undergraduates: $4729. *Parent loans:* $769,705 (100% non-need-based). *Programs:* FFEL (Subsidized and Unsubsidized Stafford, PLUS), Perkins.

WORK-STUDY *Federal work-study:* Total amount: $211,772; 72 jobs averaging $2941. *State or other work-study/employment:* Total amount: $94,678 (100% need-based). Part-time jobs available.

ATHLETIC AWARDS Total amount: $1,482,308 (100% non-need-based).

APPLYING FOR FINANCIAL AID *Required financial aid forms:* FAFSA, institution's own form. *Financial aid deadline (priority):* 3/1. *Notification date:* Continuous beginning 3/1. Students must reply within 2 weeks of notification.

CONTACT Deborah D. Byers, Director of Financial Aid, Wichita State University, 1845 Fairmount, Wichita, KS 67260-0024, 316-978-3430 or toll-free 800-362-2594. *Fax:* 316-978-3396. *E-mail:* deb.byers@wichita.edu.

WIDENER UNIVERSITY
Chester, PA

Tuition & fees: $31,840	Average undergraduate aid package: $23,048

ABOUT THE INSTITUTION Independent, coed. 73 undergraduate majors. Both federal and institutional methodology are used as a basis for awarding need-based institutional aid.

UNDERGRADUATE EXPENSES for 2009–10 *Comprehensive fee:* $43,110 includes full-time tuition ($31,340), mandatory fees ($500), and room and board ($11,270). *College room only:* $5820. Full-time tuition and fees vary according to class time, course. load, and program. Room and board charges vary according to board plan and housing facility. *Part-time tuition:* $1045 per credit hour. *Payment plan:* Installment.

FRESHMAN FINANCIAL AID (Fall 2009, est.) 667 applied for aid; of those 93% were deemed to have need. 100% of freshmen with need received aid; of those 14% had need fully met. *Average percent of need met:* 77% (excluding resources awarded to replace EFC). *Average financial aid package:* $25,475 (excluding resources awarded to replace EFC). 10% of all full-time freshmen had no need and received non-need-based gift aid.

UNDERGRADUATE FINANCIAL AID (Fall 2009, est.) 2,369 applied for aid; of those 92% were deemed to have need. 99% of undergraduates with need received aid; of those 15% had need fully met. *Average percent of need met:* 72% (excluding resources awarded to replace EFC). *Average financial aid package:* $23,048 (excluding resources awarded to replace EFC). 12% of all full-time undergraduates had no need and received non-need-based gift aid.

GIFT AID (NEED-BASED) *Total amount:* $36,782,297 (14% federal, 7% state, 76% institutional, 3% external sources). *Receiving aid:* Freshmen: 73% (521); all full-time undergraduates: 64% (1,745). *Average award:* Freshmen: $9460; Undergraduates: $8804. *Scholarships, grants, and awards:* Federal Pell, FSEOG, state, private, college/university gift aid from institutional funds, Federal Nursing.

GIFT AID (NON-NEED-BASED) *Total amount:* $4,135,609 (5% federal, 1% state, 90% institutional, 4% external sources). *Receiving aid:* Freshmen: 72% (514). Undergraduates: 63% (1,712). *Average award:* Freshmen: $14,600. Undergraduates: $11,490. *Scholarships, grants, and awards by category:* Academic interests/achievement: 2,180 awards ($21,236,971 total): biological sciences, business, communication, computer science, education, engineering/technologies, English, foreign languages, general academic interests/achievements, health fields, humanities, international studies, mathematics, military science, physical sciences, premedicine, social sciences. *Creative arts/performance:* 45 awards ($90,000 total): music. *Special achievements/activities:* 51 awards ($241,000 total): community service, general special achievements/activities, leadership. *Special characteristics:* 173 awards ($2,466,445 total): adult students, children of faculty/staff, ethnic background, international students. *Tuition waivers:* Full or partial for employees or children of employees, senior citizens.

LOANS *Student loans:* $28,150,156 (93% need-based, 7% non-need-based). 87% of past graduating class borrowed through all loan programs. *Average indebtedness per student:* $38,372. *Average need-based loan:* Freshmen: $4130. Undergraduates: $4794. *Parent loans:* $5,893,443 (90% need-based, 10% non-need-based). *Programs:* FFEL (Subsidized and Unsubsidized Stafford, PLUS), Perkins.

WORK-STUDY *Federal work-study:* Total amount: $2,517,076; 1,680 jobs averaging $1400. *State or other work-study/employment:* Total amount: $578,161 (71% need-based, 29% non-need-based). 500 part-time jobs averaging $1200.

APPLYING FOR FINANCIAL AID *Required financial aid form:* FAFSA. *Financial aid deadline (priority):* 2/15. *Notification date:* Continuous beginning 3/15. Students must reply within 4 weeks of notification.

CONTACT Thomas K. Malloy, Director of Student Financial Services, Widener University, One University Place, Chester, PA 19013-5792, 610-499-4161 or toll-free 888-WIDENER. *Fax:* 610-499-4687. *E-mail:* finaidmc@mail.widener.edu.

WILBERFORCE UNIVERSITY
Wilberforce, OH

CONTACT Director of Financial Aid, Wilberforce University, 1055 North Bickett Road, Wilberforce, OH 45384, 937-708-5727 or toll-free 800-367-8568. *Fax:* 937-376-4752.

WILEY COLLEGE
Marshall, TX

CONTACT Cecelia Jones, Interim Director of Financial Aid, Wiley College, 711 Wiley Avenue, Marshall, TX 75670-5199, 903-927-3210 or toll-free 800-658-6889. *Fax:* 903-927-3366.

WILKES UNIVERSITY
Wilkes-Barre, PA

Tuition & fees: $26,010	Average undergraduate aid package: $20,291

ABOUT THE INSTITUTION Independent, coed. 34 undergraduate majors. Federal methodology is used as a basis for awarding need-based institutional aid.

UNDERGRADUATE EXPENSES for 2009–10 *Comprehensive fee:* $37,110 includes full-time tuition ($24,690), mandatory fees ($1320), and room and board ($11,100). *College room only:* $6680. Room and board charges vary according to board plan and housing facility. *Part-time tuition:* $685 per credit hour. *Part-time fees:* $60 per credit hour. *Payment plans:* Installment, deferred payment.

FRESHMAN FINANCIAL AID (Fall 2009, est.) 500 applied for aid; of those 90% were deemed to have need. 100% of freshmen with need received aid; of those 15% had need fully met. *Average percent of need met:* 77% (excluding resources awarded to replace EFC). *Average financial aid package:* $21,111 (excluding resources awarded to replace EFC). 12% of all full-time freshmen had no need and received non-need-based gift aid.

UNDERGRADUATE FINANCIAL AID (Fall 2009, est.) 1,806 applied for aid; of those 92% were deemed to have need. 100% of undergraduates with need received aid; of those 14% had need fully met. *Average percent of need met:* 73% (excluding resources awarded to replace EFC). *Average financial aid package:* $20,291 (excluding resources awarded to replace EFC). 12% of all full-time undergraduates had no need and received non-need-based gift aid.

GIFT AID (NEED-BASED) *Total amount:* $23,212,022 (13% federal, 11% state, 73% institutional, 3% external sources). *Receiving aid:* Freshmen: 86% (451); all full-time undergraduates: 80% (1,616). *Average award:* Freshmen: $16,250; Undergraduates: $14,948. *Scholarships, grants, and awards:* Federal Pell, FSEOG, state, private, college/university gift aid from institutional funds.

GIFT AID (NON-NEED-BASED) *Total amount:* $2,604,246 (1% federal, 88% institutional, 11% external sources). *Receiving aid:* Freshmen: 77% (407). Undergraduates: 63% (1,274). *Average award:* Freshmen: $10,631. Undergraduates: $9743. *Scholarships, grants, and awards by category:* Academic interests/achievement: general academic interests/achievements. *Creative arts/performance:* performing arts, theater/drama. *Special achievements/activities:* general special achievements/activities, leadership. *Special characteristics:* children of faculty/staff. *Tuition waivers:* Full or partial for employees or children of employees.

LOANS *Student loans:* $17,387,520 (88% need-based, 12% non-need-based). 87% of past graduating class borrowed through all loan programs. *Average indebtedness per student:* $34,775. *Average need-based loan:* Freshmen: $3500. Undergraduates: $4433. *Parent loans:* $3,249,376 (73% need-based, 27% non-need-based). *Programs:* Federal Direct (Subsidized and Unsubsidized Stafford, PLUS), FFEL (Subsidized and Unsubsidized Stafford, PLUS), Perkins, Federal Nursing, state, college/university, Gulf Oil Loan Fund, Rulison Evans Loan Fund.

WORK-STUDY *Federal work-study:* Total amount: $2,267,570; jobs available. *State or other work-study/employment:* Part-time jobs available.

APPLYING FOR FINANCIAL AID *Required financial aid form:* FAFSA. *Financial aid deadline (priority):* 3/1. *Notification date:* Continuous.

CONTACT Melanie Mickelson, Vice President, Enrollment Services, Wilkes University, 84 West South Street, Wilkes-Barre, PA 18766, 570-408-4000 or toll-free 800-945-5378 Ext. 4400. *Fax:* 570-408-3000. *E-mail:* melanie.mickelson@wilkes.edu.

WILLAMETTE UNIVERSITY
Salem, OR

Tuition & fees: $35,610	Average undergraduate aid package: $29,387

ABOUT THE INSTITUTION Independent United Methodist, coed. 40 undergraduate majors. Federal methodology is used as a basis for awarding need-based institutional aid.

UNDERGRADUATE EXPENSES for 2009–10 *Comprehensive fee:* $43,960 includes full-time tuition ($35,400), mandatory fees ($210), and room and board ($8350). Full-time tuition and fees vary according to course load. Room and board charges vary according to board plan and housing facility. *Part-time tuition:* $4425 per course. Part-time tuition and fees vary according to course load. *Payment plans:* Tuition prepayment, installment.

FRESHMAN FINANCIAL AID (Fall 2009, est.) 459 applied for aid; of those 78% were deemed to have need. 100% of freshmen with need received aid; of those 15% had need fully met. *Average percent of need met:* 89% (excluding resources awarded to replace EFC). *Average financial aid package:* $29,353 (excluding resources awarded to replace EFC). 31% of all full-time freshmen had no need and received non-need-based gift aid.

UNDERGRADUATE FINANCIAL AID (Fall 2009, est.) 1,346 applied for aid; of those 86% were deemed to have need. 100% of undergraduates with need received aid; of those 17% had need fully met. *Average percent of need met:* 89% (excluding resources awarded to replace EFC). *Average financial aid package:* $29,387 (excluding resources awarded to replace EFC). 32% of all full-time undergraduates had no need and received non-need-based gift aid.

GIFT AID (NEED-BASED) *Total amount:* $27,830,605 (10% federal, 1% state, 84% institutional, 5% external sources). *Receiving aid:* Freshmen: 65% (354); all full-time undergraduates: 62% (1,142). *Average award:* Freshmen: $24,061; Undergraduates: $23,226. *Scholarships, grants, and awards:* Federal Pell, FSEOG, state, private, college/university gift aid from institutional funds.

GIFT AID (NON-NEED-BASED) *Total amount:* $6,985,794 (97% institutional, 3% external sources). *Receiving aid:* Freshmen: 25% (137). Undergraduates: 14% (265). *Average award:* Freshmen: $13,072. Undergraduates: $11,727. *Scholarships, grants, and awards by category: Academic interests/achievement:* general academic interests/achievements. *Creative arts/performance:* debating, music, theater/drama. *Special achievements/activities:* community service, leadership. *Special characteristics:* children and siblings of alumni, international students, members of minority groups, religious affiliation. *Tuition waivers:* Full or partial for employees or children of employees.

LOANS *Student loans:* $7,931,352 (91% need-based, 9% non-need-based). 63% of past graduating class borrowed through all loan programs. *Average indebtedness per student:* $23,643. *Average need-based loan:* Freshmen: $3426. Undergraduates: $4334. *Parent loans:* $2,905,897 (70% need-based, 30% non-need-based). *Programs:* FFEL (Subsidized and Unsubsidized Stafford, PLUS), Perkins.

WORK-STUDY *Federal work-study:* Total amount: $1,741,277; jobs available. *State or other work-study/employment:* Part-time jobs available.

APPLYING FOR FINANCIAL AID *Required financial aid form:* FAFSA. *Financial aid deadline (priority):* 2/1. *Notification date:* Continuous beginning 4/1. Students must reply by 5/1 or within 2 weeks of notification.

CONTACT Patty Hoban, Director of Financial Aid, Willamette University, 900 State Street, Salem, OR 97301-3931, 503-370-6273 or toll-free 877-542-2787. *Fax:* 503-370-6588. *E-mail:* phoban@willamette.edu.

WILLIAM CAREY UNIVERSITY
Hattiesburg, MS

Tuition & fees: $9750	Average undergraduate aid package: N/A

ABOUT THE INSTITUTION Independent Southern Baptist, coed. 32 undergraduate majors. Federal methodology is used as a basis for awarding need-based institutional aid.

UNDERGRADUATE EXPENSES for 2009–10 *Comprehensive fee:* $14,565 includes full-time tuition ($9300), mandatory fees ($450), and room and board

($4815). *College room only:* $2640. Full-time tuition and fees vary according to degree level and location. Room and board charges vary according to board plan, housing facility, and location. *Part-time tuition:* $310 per credit hour. *Part-time fees:* $310 per semester hour; $150 per term. Part-time tuition and fees vary according to degree level and location. *Payment plan:* Deferred payment.

FRESHMAN FINANCIAL AID (Fall 2009, est.) 1,740 applied for aid; of those 99% were deemed to have need. 100% of freshmen with need received aid; of those 94% had need fully met. *Average percent of need met:* 90% (excluding resources awarded to replace EFC). *Average financial aid package:* $15,000 (excluding resources awarded to replace EFC). 13% of all full-time freshmen had no need and received non-need-based gift aid.

GIFT AID (NEED-BASED) *Total amount:* $6,400,000 (62% federal, 30% state, 8% external sources). *Receiving aid:* Freshmen: 90% (1,720). *Average award:* Freshmen: $8000. *Scholarships, grants, and awards:* Federal Pell, FSEOG, state, private, college/university gift aid from institutional funds.

GIFT AID (NON-NEED-BASED) *Total amount:* $5,400,000 (100% institutional). *Receiving aid:* Freshmen: 43% (825). *Average award:* Freshmen: $7400. *Scholarships, grants, and awards by category: Academic interests/achievement:* 925 awards ($5,300,000 total): general academic interests/achievements. *Creative arts/performance:* 80 awards ($375,000 total): art/fine arts, debating, journalism/publications, music, theater/drama. *Special achievements/activities:* 215 awards ($230,000 total): cheerleading/drum major, junior miss, leadership, religious involvement. *Special characteristics:* 212 awards ($340,000 total): children and siblings of alumni, children of educators, children of faculty/staff, first-generation college students, international students, relatives of clergy, religious affiliation, veterans. *Tuition waivers:* Full or partial for employees or children of employees.

LOANS *Student loans:* $25,000,000 (100% need-based). 85% of past graduating class borrowed through all loan programs. *Average indebtedness per student:* $17,500. *Average need-based loan:* Freshmen: $7000. *Parent loans:* $210,000 (100% need-based). *Programs:* FFEL (Subsidized and Unsubsidized Stafford, PLUS), Perkins, Federal Nursing, college/university.

WORK-STUDY *Federal work-study:* Total amount: $300,000; 260 jobs averaging $2100. *State or other work-study/employment:* Total amount: $125,000 (100% non-need-based). 110 part-time jobs averaging $2100.

ATHLETIC AWARDS Total amount: $830,000 (100% non-need-based).

APPLYING FOR FINANCIAL AID *Required financial aid forms:* FAFSA, institution's own form, state aid form. *Financial aid deadline (priority):* 4/1. *Notification date:* Continuous beginning 5/1. Students must reply within 2 weeks of notification.

CONTACT Ms. Brenda Pittman, Associate Director of Financial Aid, William Carey University, 498 Tuscan Avenue, Hattiesburg, MS 39401-5499, 601-318-6153 or toll-free 800-962-5991 (in-state).

WILLIAM JESSUP UNIVERSITY
Rocklin, CA

ABOUT THE INSTITUTION Independent nondenominational, coed. 8 undergraduate majors.

GIFT AID (NEED-BASED) *Scholarships, grants, and awards:* Federal Pell, FSEOG, state, private, college/university gift aid from institutional funds.

GIFT AID (NON-NEED-BASED) *Scholarships, grants, and awards by category: Academic interests/achievement:* education, general academic interests/achievements, international studies, religion/biblical studies. *Creative arts/performance:* music. *Special achievements/activities:* leadership, religious involvement. *Special characteristics:* adult students, children of faculty/staff, international students, previous college experience, relatives of clergy, veterans, veterans' children.

LOANS *Programs:* FFEL (Subsidized and Unsubsidized Stafford, PLUS).

WORK-STUDY *Federal work-study:* Total amount: $50,000; 18 jobs averaging $1792. *State or other work-study/employment:* Total amount: $150,000 (33% need-based, 67% non-need-based). Part-time jobs available.

APPLYING FOR FINANCIAL AID *Required financial aid form:* FAFSA.

CONTACT Kristi Kindberg, Financial Aid Administrator, William Jessup University, 790 South 12th Street, San Jose, CA 95112-2381, 408-278-4328 or toll-free 800-355-7522. *Fax:* 408-293-9299. *E-mail:* finaid@sjchristian.edu.

WILLIAM JEWELL COLLEGE
Liberty, MO

Tuition & fees: $28,750   **Average undergraduate aid package:** $20,258

ABOUT THE INSTITUTION Independent Baptist, coed. 47 undergraduate majors. Federal methodology is used as a basis for awarding need-based institutional aid.

UNDERGRADUATE EXPENSES for 2010–11 *Comprehensive fee:* $35,950 includes full-time tuition ($28,450), mandatory fees ($300), and room and board ($7200). Full-time tuition and fees vary according to class time, course load, program, and student level. Room and board charges vary according to board plan and housing facility. *Part-time tuition:* $825 per credit hour. *Payment plan:* Installment.

FRESHMAN FINANCIAL AID (Fall 2009, est.) 258 applied for aid; of those 84% were deemed to have need. 100% of freshmen with need received aid; of those 28% had need fully met. *Average percent of need met:* 89% (excluding resources awarded to replace EFC). *Average financial aid package:* $23,595 (excluding resources awarded to replace EFC). 13% of all full-time freshmen had no need and received non-need-based gift aid.

UNDERGRADUATE FINANCIAL AID (Fall 2009, est.) 852 applied for aid; of those 86% were deemed to have need. 100% of undergraduates with need received aid; of those 22% had need fully met. *Average percent of need met:* 79% (excluding resources awarded to replace EFC). *Average financial aid package:* $20,258 (excluding resources awarded to replace EFC). 16% of all full-time undergraduates had no need and received non-need-based gift aid.

GIFT AID (NEED-BASED) *Total amount:* $9,480,896 (16% federal, 10% state, 70% institutional, 4% external sources). *Receiving aid:* Freshmen: 77% (217); all full-time undergraduates: 70% (719). *Average award:* Freshmen: $18,845; Undergraduates: $15,963. *Scholarships, grants, and awards:* Federal Pell, FSEOG, state, college/university gift aid from institutional funds.

GIFT AID (NON-NEED-BASED) *Total amount:* $2,412,662 (2% state, 94% institutional, 4% external sources). *Receiving aid:* Freshmen: 77% (217). Undergraduates: 68% (702). *Average award:* Freshmen: $12,522. Undergraduates: $9994. *Scholarships, grants, and awards by category:* Academic interests/achievement: general academic interests/achievements. Creative arts/performance: art/fine arts, debating, journalism/publications, music, theater/drama. Special achievements/activities: cheerleading/drum major, religious involvement. Special characteristics: children and siblings of alumni, children of faculty/staff, siblings of current students. *Tuition waivers:* Full or partial for children of alumni, employees or children of employees.

LOANS *Student loans:* $5,812,804 (48% need-based, 52% non-need-based). 75% of past graduating class borrowed through all loan programs. *Average indebtedness per student:* $24,102. *Average need-based loan:* Freshmen: $5205. Undergraduates: $5335. *Parent loans:* $1,206,387 (81% need-based, 19% non-need-based). *Programs:* FFEL (Subsidized and Unsubsidized Stafford, PLUS), Perkins, Federal Nursing, alternative loans.

WORK-STUDY *Federal work-study:* Total amount: $1,001,000; jobs available. *State or other work-study/employment:* Total amount: $125,625 (100% non-need-based). Part-time jobs available.

ATHLETIC AWARDS Total amount: $2,755,053 (68% need-based, 32% non-need-based).

APPLYING FOR FINANCIAL AID *Required financial aid form:* FAFSA. *Financial aid deadline (priority):* 3/1. *Notification date:* Continuous. Students must reply within 2 weeks of notification.

CONTACT Sue Karnes, Director of Financial Aid, William Jewell College, 500 College Hill, Liberty, MO 64068, 816-415-5973 or toll-free 888-2JEWELL. *Fax:* 816-415-5006. *E-mail:* karness@william.jewell.edu.

WILLIAM PATERSON UNIVERSITY OF NEW JERSEY
Wayne, NJ

Tuition & fees (NJ res): $10,838   **Average undergraduate aid package:** $14,598

ABOUT THE INSTITUTION State-supported, coed. 53 undergraduate majors. Federal methodology is used as a basis for awarding need-based institutional aid.

UNDERGRADUATE EXPENSES for 2009–10 *Tuition, state resident:* full-time $6567; part-time $210.47 per credit. *Tuition, nonresident:* full-time $13,321;

part-time $431.47 per credit. *Required fees:* full-time $4271; $137.53 per credit. Full-time tuition and fees vary according to program. Part-time tuition and fees vary according to course load and program. *College room and board:* $10,280; *Room only:* $6800. Room and board charges vary according to board plan and housing facility. *Payment plan:* Installment.

FRESHMAN FINANCIAL AID (Fall 2009, est.) 1,301 applied for aid; of those 76% were deemed to have need. 98% of freshmen with need received aid; of those 38% had need fully met. *Average financial aid package:* $14,180 (excluding resources awarded to replace EFC). 8% of all full-time freshmen had no need and received non-need-based gift aid.

UNDERGRADUATE FINANCIAL AID (Fall 2009, est.) 6,181 applied for aid; of those 82% were deemed to have need. 98% of undergraduates with need received aid; of those 32% had need fully met. *Average financial aid package:* $14,598 (excluding resources awarded to replace EFC). 5% of all full-time undergraduates had no need and received non-need-based gift aid.

GIFT AID (NEED-BASED) *Total amount:* $25,650,708 (53% federal, 43% state, 4% institutional). *Receiving aid:* Freshmen: 37% (532); all full-time undergraduates: 37% (2,884). *Average award:* Freshmen: $9680; Undergraduates: $8850. *Scholarships, grants, and awards:* Federal Pell, FSEOG, state, private, college/university gift aid from institutional funds.

GIFT AID (NON-NEED-BASED) *Total amount:* $7,072,142 (1% federal, 4% state, 90% institutional, 5% external sources). *Receiving aid:* Freshmen: 17% (251). Undergraduates: 10% (792). *Average award:* Freshmen: $4932. Undergraduates: $6271. *Tuition waivers:* Full or partial for employees or children of employees, senior citizens.

LOANS *Student loans:* $56,154,236 (41% need-based, 59% non-need-based). 64% of past graduating class borrowed through all loan programs. *Average indebtedness per student:* $25,893. *Average need-based loan:* Freshmen: $3427. Undergraduates: $4405. *Parent loans:* $5,157,414 (100% non-need-based). *Programs:* Federal Direct (Subsidized and Unsubsidized Stafford, PLUS), Perkins, Federal Nursing, state.

WORK-STUDY *Federal work-study:* Total amount: $364,000; jobs available. *State or other work-study/employment:* Total amount: $278,000 (100% non-need-based). Part-time jobs available.

APPLYING FOR FINANCIAL AID *Required financial aid form:* FAFSA. *Financial aid deadline (priority):* 4/1. *Notification date:* Continuous.

CONTACT Elizabeth Riquez, Director of Financial Aid, William Paterson University of New Jersey, 300 Pompton Road, Wayne, NJ 07470, 973-720-2928 or toll-free 877-WPU-EXCEL (in-state). *Fax:* 973-720-3133. *E-mail:* riqueze@wpunj.edu.

WILLIAM PENN UNIVERSITY
Oskaloosa, IA

CONTACT Cyndi Peiffer, Director of Financial Aid, William Penn University, 201 Trueblood Avenue, Oskaloosa, IA 52577-1799, 641-673-1060 or toll-free 800-779-7366. *Fax:* 641-673-1115. *E-mail:* peifferc@wmpenn.edu.

WILLIAMS BAPTIST COLLEGE
Walnut Ridge, AR

Tuition & fees: $11,400   **Average undergraduate aid package:** $12,992

ABOUT THE INSTITUTION Independent Southern Baptist, coed. 26 undergraduate majors. Federal methodology is used as a basis for awarding need-based institutional aid.

UNDERGRADUATE EXPENSES for 2009–10 *Comprehensive fee:* $16,600 includes full-time tuition ($10,600), mandatory fees ($800), and room and board ($5200). *Payment plan:* Installment.

FRESHMAN FINANCIAL AID (Fall 2008) 112 applied for aid; of those 57% were deemed to have need. 100% of freshmen with need received aid. *Average financial aid package:* $13,676 (excluding resources awarded to replace EFC).

UNDERGRADUATE FINANCIAL AID (Fall 2008) 409 applied for aid; of those 63% were deemed to have need. 100% of undergraduates with need received aid. *Average financial aid package:* $12,992 (excluding resources awarded to replace EFC).

GIFT AID (NEED-BASED) *Total amount:* $1,333,394 (75% federal, 25% state). *Receiving aid:* Freshmen: 44% (64); all full-time undergraduates: 52% (257).

Average award: Freshmen: $5343; Undergraduates: $4513. **Scholarships, grants, and awards:** Federal Pell, FSEOG, state, private, college/university gift aid from institutional funds.

GIFT AID (NON-NEED-BASED) Total amount: $1,867,431 (7% state, 76% institutional, 17% external sources). **Receiving aid:** Freshmen: 44% (64). Undergraduates: 49% (242). **Scholarships, grants, and awards by category:** Academic interests/achievement: 432 awards ($1,464,473 total): biological sciences, business, education, general academic interests/achievements, humanities, religion/biblical studies. Creative arts/performance: 38 awards ($39,300 total): art/fine arts, music. Special achievements/activities: 11 awards ($4700 total): cheerleading/drum major. Special characteristics: 147 awards ($192,201 total): children of faculty/staff, international students, members of minority groups, relatives of clergy, religious affiliation. **Tuition waivers:** Full or partial for employees or children of employees, senior citizens.

LOANS Student loans: $2,183,160 (51% need-based, 49% non-need-based). 80% of past graduating class borrowed through all loan programs. Average indebtedness per student: $16,826. **Average need-based loan:** Freshmen: $2523. Undergraduates: $3611. **Parent loans:** $110,150 (100% non-need-based). **Programs:** Federal Direct (Subsidized and Unsubsidized Stafford, PLUS).

WORK-STUDY Federal work-study: Total amount: $278,616; 199 jobs averaging $1372. **State or other work-study/employment:** Total amount: $38,355 (100% non-need-based). 34 part-time jobs averaging $1128.

ATHLETIC AWARDS Total amount: $631,223 (100% non-need-based).

APPLYING FOR FINANCIAL AID Required financial aid form: FAFSA. **Financial aid deadline:** Continuous. **Notification date:** Continuous beginning 4/1. Students must reply within 2 weeks of notification.

CONTACT Mrs. Barbara Turner, Director of Financial Aid, Williams Baptist College, 60 West Fulbright Avenue, Walnut Ridge, AR 72476, 870-759-4112 or toll-free 800-722-4434. Fax: 870-759-4209. E-mail: bturner@wbcoll.edu.

WILLIAMS COLLEGE
Williamstown, MA

Tuition & fees: $39,490	Average undergraduate aid package: $39,012

ABOUT THE INSTITUTION Independent, coed. 33 undergraduate majors. Institutional methodology is used as a basis for awarding need-based institutional aid.

UNDERGRADUATE EXPENSES for 2009–10 Comprehensive fee: $49,880 includes full-time tuition ($39,250), mandatory fees ($240), and room and board ($10,390). **College room only:** $5280. Room and board charges vary according to board plan. **Payment plan:** Installment.

FRESHMAN FINANCIAL AID (Fall 2009, est.) 344 applied for aid; of those 83% were deemed to have need. 100% of freshmen with need received aid; of those 100% had need fully met. **Average percent of need met:** 100% (excluding resources awarded to replace EFC). **Average financial aid package:** $38,531 (excluding resources awarded to replace EFC).

UNDERGRADUATE FINANCIAL AID (Fall 2009, est.) 1,284 applied for aid; of those 89% were deemed to have need. 100% of undergraduates with need received aid; of those 100% had need fully met. **Average percent of need met:** 100% (excluding resources awarded to replace EFC). **Average financial aid package:** $39,012 (excluding resources awarded to replace EFC).

GIFT AID (NEED-BASED) Total amount: $42,413,563 (6% federal, 92% institutional, 2% external sources). **Receiving aid:** Freshmen: 52% (285); all full-time undergraduates: 52% (1,135). **Average award:** Freshmen: $33,382; Undergraduates: $34,269. **Scholarships, grants, and awards:** Federal Pell, FSEOG, state, private, college/university gift aid from institutional funds.

GIFT AID (NON-NEED-BASED) Total amount: $1,100,497 (100% external sources).

LOANS Student loans: $2,066,483 (100% non-need-based). 46% of past graduating class borrowed through all loan programs. Average indebtedness per student: $7960. **Parent loans:** $3,066,807 (100% non-need-based). **Programs:** Federal Direct (Subsidized and Unsubsidized Stafford, PLUS), Perkins, college/university.

WORK-STUDY Federal work-study: Total amount: $914,780; 477 jobs averaging $1918. **State or other work-study/employment:** Total amount: $3,420,039 (32% need-based, 68% non-need-based). 421 part-time jobs averaging $1956.

APPLYING FOR FINANCIAL AID Required financial aid forms: FAFSA, CSS Financial Aid PROFILE, noncustodial (divorced/separated) parent's statement, parents' and student's most recent federal tax returns and W-2 forms. **Financial aid deadline:** 2/1. **Notification date:** 4/1. Students must reply by 5/1.

CONTACT Paul J. Boyer, Director of Financial Aid, Williams College, PO Box 37, Williamstown, MA 01267, 413-597-4181. Fax: 413-597-2999. E-mail: paul.j.boyer@williams.edu.

WILLIAMSON CHRISTIAN COLLEGE
Franklin, TN

CONTACT Jeanie Maguire, Director of Financial Aid, Williamson Christian College, 200 Seaboard Lane, Franklin, TN 37067, 615-771-7821. Fax: 615-771-7810. E-mail: info@williamsoncc.edu.

WILLIAM WOODS UNIVERSITY
Fulton, MO

CONTACT Deana Ready, Director of Student Financial Services, William Woods University, One University Avenue, Fulton, MO 65251, 573-592-4232 or toll-free 800-995-3159 Ext. 4221. Fax: 573-592-1180.

WILMINGTON COLLEGE
Wilmington, OH

ABOUT THE INSTITUTION Independent Friends, coed. 42 undergraduate majors.

GIFT AID (NEED-BASED) Scholarships, grants, and awards: Federal Pell, FSEOG, state, private, college/university gift aid from institutional funds.

GIFT AID (NON-NEED-BASED) Scholarships, grants, and awards by category: Academic interests/achievement: agriculture, biological sciences, business, communication, education, general academic interests/achievements, international studies, mathematics, physical sciences, premedicine, religion/biblical studies. Creative arts/performance: theater/drama. Special achievements/activities: leadership. Special characteristics: children and siblings of alumni, members of minority groups, religious affiliation, siblings of current students.

LOANS Programs: FFEL (Subsidized and Unsubsidized Stafford, PLUS), Perkins.

WORK-STUDY Federal work-study: Total amount: $851,580; jobs available.

APPLYING FOR FINANCIAL AID Required financial aid form: FAFSA.

CONTACT Donna Barton, Coordinator of Financial Aid, Wilmington College, Pyle Center Box 1184, Wilmington, OH 45177, 937-382-6661 Ext. 466 or toll-free 800-341-9318. Fax: 937-383-8564.

WILMINGTON UNIVERSITY
New Castle, DE

CONTACT J. Lynn Iocono, Director of Financial Aid, Wilmington University, 320 DuPont Highway, New Castle, DE 19720, 302-328-9437 or toll-free 877-967-5464. Fax: 302-328-5902.

WILSON COLLEGE
Chambersburg, PA

Tuition & fees: $28,220	Average undergraduate aid package: $22,148

ABOUT THE INSTITUTION Independent religious, coed, primarily women. 29 undergraduate majors. Federal methodology is used as a basis for awarding need-based institutional aid.

UNDERGRADUATE EXPENSES for 2010–11 Comprehensive fee: $37,650 includes full-time tuition ($27,640), mandatory fees ($580), and room and board ($9430). **College room only:** $4910. Room and board charges vary according to board plan. **Part-time tuition:** $2765 per course. **Part-time fees:** $45 per course; $50 per term. Part-time tuition and fees vary according to course load. **Payment plan:** Installment.

FRESHMAN FINANCIAL AID (Fall 2009, est.) 99 applied for aid; of those 93% were deemed to have need. 100% of freshmen with need received aid; of those 22% had need fully met. **Average percent of need met:** 82% (excluding resources awarded to replace EFC). **Average financial aid package:** $23,512 (excluding resources awarded to replace EFC). 11% of all full-time freshmen had no need and received non-need-based gift aid.

UNDERGRADUATE FINANCIAL AID (Fall 2009, est.) 317 applied for aid; of those 91% were deemed to have need. 100% of undergraduates with need received aid; of those 18% had need fully met. **Average percent of need met:** 78% (excluding resources awarded to replace EFC). **Average financial aid**

package: $22,148 (excluding resources awarded to replace EFC). 14% of all full-time undergraduates had no need and received non-need-based gift aid.

GIFT AID (NEED-BASED) *Total amount:* $6,072,592 (22% federal, 10% state, 65% institutional, 3% external sources). *Receiving aid:* Freshmen: 89% (92); all full-time undergraduates: 83% (287). *Average award:* Freshmen: $20,572; Undergraduates: $18,314. *Scholarships, grants, and awards:* Federal Pell, FSEOG, state, private, college/university gift aid from institutional funds.

GIFT AID (NON-NEED-BASED) *Total amount:* $979,599 (6% federal, 4% state, 80% institutional, 10% external sources). *Receiving aid:* Freshmen: 14% (14). Undergraduates: 9% (32). *Average award:* Freshmen: $12,489. Undergraduates: $12,357. *Scholarships, grants, and awards by category: Academic interests/achievement:* 243 awards ($1,967,669 total): biological sciences, business, communication, computer science, education, English, foreign languages, general academic interests/achievements, humanities, international studies, mathematics, physical sciences, premedicine, religion/biblical studies, social sciences. *Creative arts/performance:* 1 award ($1800 total): music. *Special achievements/activities:* 22 awards ($100,247 total): community service, general special achievements/activities, leadership. *Special characteristics:* 19 awards ($351,050 total): adult students, children and siblings of alumni, children of current students, children of faculty/staff, international students, local/state students, relatives of clergy, religious affiliation, veterans. *Tuition waivers:* Full or partial for employees or children of employees.

LOANS *Student loans:* $4,102,796 (71% need-based, 29% non-need-based). 87% of past graduating class borrowed through all loan programs. *Average indebtedness per student:* $33,673. *Average need-based loan:* Freshmen: $3262. Undergraduates: $4344. *Parent loans:* $1,326,541 (25% need-based, 75% non-need-based). *Programs:* Federal Direct (Subsidized and Unsubsidized Stafford, PLUS), Perkins.

WORK-STUDY *Federal work-study:* Total amount: $51,312; 42 jobs averaging $2000. *State or other work-study/employment:* Total amount: $196,071 (44% need-based, 56% non-need-based). 115 part-time jobs averaging $2000.

APPLYING FOR FINANCIAL AID *Required financial aid forms:* FAFSA, institution's own form. *Financial aid deadline (priority):* 4/30. *Notification date:* Continuous beginning 9/15.

CONTACT Ms. Linda Brittain, Dean of Financial Aid/Senior Enrollment Associate, Wilson College, 1015 Philadelphia Avenue, Chambersburg, PA 17201-1285, 717-262-2002 or toll-free 800-421-8402. *Fax:* 717-262-2530. *E-mail:* finaid@wilson.edu.

WINGATE UNIVERSITY
Wingate, NC

ABOUT THE INSTITUTION Independent Baptist, coed. 37 undergraduate majors.

GIFT AID (NEED-BASED) *Scholarships, grants, and awards:* state, college/university gift aid from institutional funds.

GIFT AID (NON-NEED-BASED) *Scholarships, grants, and awards by category: Academic interests/achievement:* general academic interests/achievements. *Creative arts/performance:* music. *Special achievements/activities:* religious involvement. *Special characteristics:* children and siblings of alumni, relatives of clergy, religious affiliation.

WORK-STUDY *Federal work-study:* Total amount: $104,477; jobs available. *State or other work-study/employment:* Total amount: $340,000 (100% non-need-based). Part-time jobs available.

APPLYING FOR FINANCIAL AID *Required financial aid form:* FAFSA.

CONTACT Teresa G. Williams, Director of Financial Planning, Wingate University, Campus Box 3001, Wingate, NC 28174, 704-233-8209 or toll-free 800-755-5550. *Fax:* 704-233-9396. *E-mail:* tgwilliam@wingate.edu.

WINONA STATE UNIVERSITY
Winona, MN

Tuition & fees (MN res): $7916   **Average undergraduate aid package:** $6728

ABOUT THE INSTITUTION State-supported, coed. 96 undergraduate majors. Federal methodology is used as a basis for awarding need-based institutional aid.

UNDERGRADUATE EXPENSES for 2010–11 *Tuition, state resident:* full-time $6056. *Tuition, nonresident:* full-time $10,890. *Required fees:* full-time $1860. Full-time tuition and fees vary according to location and reciprocity agreements. Part-time tuition and fees vary according to location and reciprocity agreements.

College room and board: $6556. Room and board charges vary according to board plan, housing facility, and location. *Payment plan:* Installment.

FRESHMAN FINANCIAL AID (Fall 2008) 1,512 applied for aid; of those 64% were deemed to have need. 98% of freshmen with need received aid; of those 5% had need fully met. *Average percent of need met:* 31% (excluding resources awarded to replace EFC). *Average financial aid package:* $6028 (excluding resources awarded to replace EFC). 20% of all full-time freshmen had no need and received non-need-based gift aid.

UNDERGRADUATE FINANCIAL AID (Fall 2008) 5,316 applied for aid; of those 71% were deemed to have need. 98% of undergraduates with need received aid; of those 12% had need fully met. *Average percent of need met:* 44% (excluding resources awarded to replace EFC). *Average financial aid package:* $6728 (excluding resources awarded to replace EFC). 12% of all full-time undergraduates had no need and received non-need-based gift aid.

GIFT AID (NEED-BASED) *Total amount:* $8,468,099 (59% federal, 39% state, 2% institutional). *Receiving aid:* Freshmen: 25% (465); all full-time undergraduates: 26% (1,897). *Average award:* Freshmen: $4254; Undergraduates: $4078. *Scholarships, grants, and awards:* Federal Pell, FSEOG, state, private, college/university gift aid from institutional funds.

GIFT AID (NON-NEED-BASED) *Total amount:* $6,480,300 (1% federal, 54% institutional, 45% external sources). *Receiving aid:* Freshmen: 28% (517). Undergraduates: 16% (1,182). *Average award:* Freshmen: $1531. Undergraduates: $2557. *Scholarships, grants, and awards by category: Academic interests/achievement:* 1,246 awards ($1,284,772 total): general academic interests/achievements. *Creative arts/performance:* 54 awards ($71,800 total): art/fine arts, debating, music, theater/drama. *Special characteristics:* 350 awards ($1,536,177 total): children and siblings of alumni, children of faculty/staff, local/state students, members of minority groups, out-of-state students. *Tuition waivers:* Full or partial for employees or children of employees.

LOANS *Student loans:* $45,392,388 (33% need-based, 67% non-need-based). 74% of past graduating class borrowed through all loan programs. *Average indebtedness per student:* $27,190. *Average need-based loan:* Freshmen: $3224. Undergraduates: $4045. *Parent loans:* $2,676,617 (100% non-need-based). *Programs:* FFEL (Subsidized and Unsubsidized Stafford, PLUS), Perkins, state, college/university.

WORK-STUDY *Federal work-study:* Total amount: $438,407; 213 jobs averaging $1987. *State or other work-study/employment:* Total amount: $3,772,016 (16% need-based, 84% non-need-based). 292 part-time jobs averaging $1979.

ATHLETIC AWARDS Total amount: $722,469 (100% non-need-based).

APPLYING FOR FINANCIAL AID *Required financial aid form:* FAFSA. *Financial aid deadline:* Continuous. *Notification date:* 5/1. Students must reply within 3 weeks of notification.

CONTACT Cindy Groth, Counselor, Winona State University, PO Box 5838, Winona, MN 55987-5838, 507-457-5090 Ext. 5561 or toll-free 800-DIAL WSU.

WINSTON-SALEM STATE UNIVERSITY
Winston-Salem, NC

CONTACT Raymond Solomon, Director of Financial Aid Office, Winston-Salem State University, 601 Martin Luther King Jr. Drive, PO Box 19524, Winston-Salem, NC 27110-0003, 336-750-3299 or toll-free 800-257-4052. *Fax:* 336-750-3297.

WINTHROP UNIVERSITY
Rock Hill, SC

Tuition & fees (SC res): $11,606   **Average undergraduate aid package:** $10,109

ABOUT THE INSTITUTION State-supported, coed. 33 undergraduate majors. Federal methodology is used as a basis for awarding need-based institutional aid.

UNDERGRADUATE EXPENSES for 2009–10 *Tuition, state resident:* full-time $11,606; part-time $484 per semester hour. *Tuition, nonresident:* full-time $21,596; part-time $900 per semester hour. Full-time tuition and fees vary according to degree level. Part-time tuition and fees vary according to degree level. *College room and board:* $6530; *Room only:* $4130. Room and board charges vary according to board plan and housing facility. *Payment plan:* Installment.

FRESHMAN FINANCIAL AID (Fall 2009, est.) 935 applied for aid; of those 81% were deemed to have need. 99% of freshmen with need received aid; of those

19% had need fully met. *Average percent of need met:* 68% (excluding resources awarded to replace EFC). *Average financial aid package:* $11,228 (excluding resources awarded to replace EFC). 10% of all full-time freshmen had no need and received non-need-based gift aid.

UNDERGRADUATE FINANCIAL AID (Fall 2009, est.) 3,597 applied for aid; of those 85% were deemed to have need. 99% of undergraduates with need received aid; of those 17% had need fully met. *Average percent of need met:* 59% (excluding resources awarded to replace EFC). *Average financial aid package:* $10,109 (excluding resources awarded to replace EFC). 8% of all full-time undergraduates had no need and received non-need-based gift aid.

GIFT AID (NEED-BASED) *Total amount:* $19,707,416 (42% federal, 38% state, 17% institutional, 3% external sources). *Receiving aid:* Freshmen: 69% (730); all full-time undergraduates: 57% (2,537). *Average award:* Freshmen: $8898; Undergraduates: $7768. *Scholarships, grants, and awards:* Federal Pell, FSEOG, state, private, college/university gift aid from institutional funds, TEACH Grants.

GIFT AID (NON-NEED-BASED) *Total amount:* $8,973,044 (3% federal, 45% state, 46% institutional, 6% external sources). *Receiving aid:* Freshmen: 9% (91). Undergraduates: 6% (260). *Average award:* Freshmen: $5780. Undergraduates: $4539. *Scholarships, grants, and awards by category: Academic interests/achievement:* 463 awards ($2,218,142 total): general academic interests/achievements. *Creative arts/performance:* 124 awards ($176,682 total): art/fine arts, dance, music, performing arts, theater/drama. *Special characteristics:* 8 awards ($4800 total): children of faculty/staff. *Tuition waivers:* Full or partial for employees or children of employees, senior citizens.

LOANS *Student loans:* $27,166,142 (38% need-based, 62% non-need-based). 68% of past graduating class borrowed through all loan programs. *Average indebtedness per student:* $24,463. *Average need-based loan:* Freshmen: $3258. Undergraduates: $4281. *Parent loans:* $4,464,198 (100% non-need-based). *Programs:* Federal Direct (Subsidized and Unsubsidized Stafford, PLUS), Perkins.

WORK-STUDY *Federal work-study:* Total amount: $250,000; 273 jobs averaging $916. *State or other work-study/employment:* Total amount: $1,899,434 (100% non-need-based). Part-time jobs available.

ATHLETIC AWARDS Total amount: $1,770,898 (17% need-based, 83% non-need-based).

APPLYING FOR FINANCIAL AID *Required financial aid form:* FAFSA. *Financial aid deadline (priority):* 3/1. *Notification date:* Continuous beginning 3/15. Students must reply within 4 weeks of notification.

CONTACT Ms. Leah Sturgis, Associate Director, Office of Financial Aid, Winthrop University, 119 Tillman Hall, Rock Hill, SC 29733, 803-323-2189 or toll-free 800-763-0230. *Fax:* 803-323-2557. *E-mail:* finaid@winthrop.edu.

WISCONSIN LUTHERAN COLLEGE
Milwaukee, WI

ABOUT THE INSTITUTION Independent religious, coed. *Awards:* bachelor's degrees. 29 undergraduate majors. *Total enrollment:* 753. Undergraduates: 753. Freshmen: 225.

GIFT AID (NEED-BASED) *Scholarships, grants, and awards:* Federal Pell, FSEOG, state, private, college/university gift aid from institutional funds.

GIFT AID (NON-NEED-BASED) *Scholarships, grants, and awards by category: Academic interests/achievement:* biological sciences, business, communication, education, general academic interests/achievements, health fields, international studies, mathematics, religion/biblical studies, social sciences. *Creative arts/performance:* art/fine arts, music, theater/drama. *Special achievements/activities:* general special achievements/activities, leadership. *Special characteristics:* children of faculty/staff, ethnic background, first-generation college students, international students, members of minority groups.

LOANS *Programs:* FFEL (Subsidized and Unsubsidized Stafford, PLUS), private loans.

WORK-STUDY *Federal work-study:* Total amount: $420,472; 242 jobs averaging $1721. *State or other work-study/employment:* Total amount: $202,395 (34% need-based, 66% non-need-based). 54 part-time jobs averaging $4027.

APPLYING FOR FINANCIAL AID *Required financial aid forms:* FAFSA, institution's own form.

CONTACT Mrs. Linda Loeffel, Director of Financial Aid, Wisconsin Lutheran College, 8800 West Bluemound Road, Milwaukee, WI 53226-4699, 414-443-8856 or toll-free 888-WIS LUTH. *Fax:* 414-443-8514. *E-mail:* linda.loeffel@wlc.edu.

WITTENBERG UNIVERSITY
Springfield, OH

Tuition & fees: $34,190	Average undergraduate aid package: $27,562

ABOUT THE INSTITUTION Independent religious, coed. 31 undergraduate majors. Federal methodology is used as a basis for awarding need-based institutional aid.

UNDERGRADUATE EXPENSES for 2009–10 *Comprehensive fee:* $42,962 includes full-time tuition ($33,890), mandatory fees ($300), and room and board ($8772). *College room only:* $4554. Room and board charges vary according to board plan and housing facility. *Part-time tuition:* $1130 per credit hour. Part-time tuition and fees vary according to course load. *Payment plan:* Installment.

FRESHMAN FINANCIAL AID (Fall 2009, est.) 426 applied for aid; of those 87% were deemed to have need. 100% of freshmen with need received aid; of those 32% had need fully met. *Average percent of need met:* 87% (excluding resources awarded to replace EFC). *Average financial aid package:* $30,966 (excluding resources awarded to replace EFC). 24% of all full-time freshmen had no need and received non-need-based gift aid.

UNDERGRADUATE FINANCIAL AID (Fall 2009, est.) 1,507 applied for aid; of those 88% were deemed to have need. 100% of undergraduates with need received aid; of those 32% had need fully met. *Average percent of need met:* 85% (excluding resources awarded to replace EFC). *Average financial aid package:* $27,562 (excluding resources awarded to replace EFC). 27% of all full-time undergraduates had no need and received non-need-based gift aid.

GIFT AID (NEED-BASED) *Total amount:* $28,358,315 (8% federal, 2% state, 87% institutional, 3% external sources). *Receiving aid:* Freshmen: 75% (368); all full-time undergraduates: 72% (1,304). *Average award:* Freshmen: $24,348; Undergraduates: $21,660. *Scholarships, grants, and awards:* Federal Pell, FSEOG, state, private, college/university gift aid from institutional funds.

GIFT AID (NON-NEED-BASED) *Total amount:* $6,807,402 (97% institutional, 3% external sources). *Average award:* Freshmen: $13,657. Undergraduates: $13,539. *Scholarships, grants, and awards by category: Academic interests/achievement:* general academic interests/achievements. *Creative arts/performance:* art/fine arts, dance, music, theater/drama. *Special achievements/activities:* community service, general special achievements/activities, leadership. *Special characteristics:* adult students, children and siblings of alumni, children of faculty/staff, ethnic background, international students, local/state students, members of minority groups, relatives of clergy, religious affiliation. *Tuition waivers:* Full or partial for minority students, children of alumni, employees or children of employees, adult students, senior citizens.

LOANS *Student loans:* $13,348,017 (91% need-based, 9% non-need-based). 68% of past graduating class borrowed through all loan programs. *Average indebtedness per student:* $28,729. *Average need-based loan:* Freshmen: $4239. Undergraduates: $4546. *Parent loans:* $4,765,368 (85% need-based, 15% non-need-based). *Programs:* Federal Direct (Subsidized and Unsubsidized Stafford, PLUS), Perkins, college/university, alternative loans.

WORK-STUDY *Federal work-study:* Total amount: $1,845,374; jobs available. *State or other work-study/employment:* Total amount: $2,075,316 (66% need-based, 34% non-need-based). Part-time jobs available.

APPLYING FOR FINANCIAL AID *Required financial aid form:* FAFSA. *Financial aid deadline (priority):* 3/1. *Notification date:* Continuous beginning 3/1. Students must reply within 2 weeks of notification.

CONTACT Mr. J. Randy Green, Director of Financial Aid, Wittenberg University, PO Box 720, Springfield, OH 45501-0720, 937-327-7321 or toll-free 800-677-7558 Ext. 6314. *Fax:* 937-327-6379. *E-mail:* jgreen@wittenberg.edu.

WOFFORD COLLEGE
Spartanburg, SC

Tuition & fees: $30,280	Average undergraduate aid package: $28,954

ABOUT THE INSTITUTION Independent religious, coed. 31 undergraduate majors. Federal methodology is used as a basis for awarding need-based institutional aid.

UNDERGRADUATE EXPENSES for 2009–10 *Comprehensive fee:* $38,760 includes full-time tuition ($30,280) and room and board ($8480). *Part-time tuition:* $1195 per credit hour. *Payment plan:* Installment.

FRESHMAN FINANCIAL AID (Fall 2009, est.) 300 applied for aid; of those 74% were deemed to have need. 100% of freshmen with need received aid; of those 49% had need fully met. *Average percent of need met:* 88% (excluding resources awarded to replace EFC). *Average financial aid package:* $29,406 (excluding resources awarded to replace EFC). 25% of all full-time freshmen had no need and received non-need-based gift aid.

UNDERGRADUATE FINANCIAL AID (Fall 2009, est.) 970 applied for aid; of those 83% were deemed to have need. 100% of undergraduates with need received aid; of those 51% had need fully met. *Average percent of need met:* 87% (excluding resources awarded to replace EFC). *Average financial aid package:* $28,954 (excluding resources awarded to replace EFC). 25% of all full-time undergraduates had no need and received non-need-based gift aid.

GIFT AID (NEED-BASED) *Total amount:* $15,954,437 (8% federal, 24% state, 65% institutional, 3% external sources). *Receiving aid:* Freshmen: 52% (204); all full-time undergraduates: 52% (735). *Average award:* Freshmen: $26,184; Undergraduates: $24,703. *Scholarships, grants, and awards:* Federal Pell, FSEOG, state, college/university gift aid from institutional funds.

GIFT AID (NON-NEED-BASED) *Total amount:* $9,107,851 (26% state, 66% institutional, 8% external sources). *Receiving aid:* Freshmen: 19% (75). Undergraduates: 20% (281). *Average award:* Freshmen: $14,219. Undergraduates: $13,278. *Scholarships, grants, and awards by category: Academic interests/achievement:* general academic interests/achievements. *Creative arts/performance:* music. *Special achievements/activities:* cheerleading/drum major, community service, general special achievements/activities, leadership, religious involvement. *Special characteristics:* children of faculty/staff, general special characteristics, relatives of clergy. *Tuition waivers:* Full or partial for employees or children of employees.

LOANS *Student loans:* $4,113,747 (65% need-based, 35% non-need-based). 45% of past graduating class borrowed through all loan programs. *Average indebtedness per student:* $22,199. *Average need-based loan:* Freshmen: $3016. Undergraduates: $4364. *Parent loans:* $1,278,817 (36% need-based, 64% non-need-based). *Programs:* FFEL (Subsidized and Unsubsidized Stafford, PLUS), Perkins.

WORK-STUDY *Federal work-study:* Total amount: $354,854; jobs available.

ATHLETIC AWARDS Total amount: $3,993,282 (43% need-based, 57% non-need-based).

APPLYING FOR FINANCIAL AID *Required financial aid form:* FAFSA. *Financial aid deadline (priority):* 3/15. *Notification date:* Continuous beginning 3/31. Students must reply by 5/1.

CONTACT Kay C. Walton, Director of Financial Aid, Wofford College, 429 North Church Street, Spartanburg, SC 29303-3663, 864-597-4160. *Fax:* 864-597-4149. *E-mail:* finaid@wofford.edu.

WOODBURY UNIVERSITY
Burbank, CA

Tuition & fees: $28,855	Average undergraduate aid package: $18,693

ABOUT THE INSTITUTION Independent, coed. 17 undergraduate majors. Federal methodology is used as a basis for awarding need-based institutional aid.

UNDERGRADUATE EXPENSES for 2010–11 *Comprehensive fee:* $38,148 includes full-time tuition ($28,465), mandatory fees ($390), and room and board ($9293). *College room only:* $5788. Full-time tuition and fees vary according to course load and degree level. *Part-time tuition:* $965 per credit hour. Part-time tuition and fees vary according to course load and degree level.

FRESHMAN FINANCIAL AID (Fall 2008) 113 applied for aid; of those 95% were deemed to have need. 100% of freshmen with need received aid; of those 5% had need fully met. *Average percent of need met:* 58% (excluding resources awarded to replace EFC). *Average financial aid package:* $18,655 (excluding resources awarded to replace EFC). 21% of all full-time freshmen had no need and received non-need-based gift aid.

UNDERGRADUATE FINANCIAL AID (Fall 2008) 895 applied for aid; of those 96% were deemed to have need. 100% of undergraduates with need received aid; of those 4% had need fully met. *Average percent of need met:* 53% (excluding resources awarded to replace EFC). *Average financial aid package:* $18,693 (excluding resources awarded to replace EFC). 13% of all full-time undergraduates had no need and received non-need-based gift aid.

GIFT AID (NEED-BASED) *Total amount:* $12,163,578 (19% federal, 27% state, 51% institutional, 3% external sources). *Receiving aid:* Freshmen: 78% (105); all full-time undergraduates: 83% (826). *Average award:* Freshmen: $15,303;

Undergraduates: $14,144. *Scholarships, grants, and awards:* Federal Pell, FSEOG, state, private, college/university gift aid from institutional funds.

GIFT AID (NON-NEED-BASED) *Total amount:* $991,857 (1% state, 95% institutional, 4% external sources). *Receiving aid:* Freshmen: 3% (4). Undergraduates: 2% (22). *Average award:* Freshmen: $6753. Undergraduates: $6602. *Scholarships, grants, and awards by category: Academic interests/achievement:* 680 awards ($3,908,521 total): architecture, general academic interests/achievements.

LOANS *Student loans:* $12,488,255 (88% need-based, 12% non-need-based). 91% of past graduating class borrowed through all loan programs. *Average indebtedness per student:* $47,059. *Average need-based loan:* Freshmen: $3792. Undergraduates: $5202. *Parent loans:* $3,831,139 (63% need-based, 37% non-need-based). *Programs:* FFEL (Subsidized and Unsubsidized Stafford, PLUS), Perkins, alternative loans.

WORK-STUDY *Federal work-study:* Total amount: $191,486; jobs available.

APPLYING FOR FINANCIAL AID *Required financial aid forms:* FAFSA, institution's own form. *Financial aid deadline:* Continuous. *Notification date:* Continuous beginning 3/15. Students must reply within 2 weeks of notification.

CONTACT Celeastia Williams, Director of Enrollment Services, Woodbury University, 7500 Glenoaks Boulevard, Burbank, CA 91510, 818-767-0888 Ext. 273 or toll-free 800-784-WOOD. *Fax:* 818-767-4816.

WORCESTER POLYTECHNIC INSTITUTE
Worcester, MA

Tuition & fees: $38,920	Average undergraduate aid package: $25,306

ABOUT THE INSTITUTION Independent, coed. 50 undergraduate majors. Both federal and institutional methodology are used as a basis for awarding need-based institutional aid.

UNDERGRADUATE EXPENSES for 2010–11 *One-time required fee:* $200. *Comprehensive fee:* $50,530 includes full-time tuition ($38,360), mandatory fees ($560), and room and board ($11,610). *College room only:* $6790. Room and board charges vary according to board plan and housing facility. *Part-time tuition:* $1025 per credit hour. Part-time tuition and fees vary according to course load. *Payment plans:* Installment, deferred payment.

FRESHMAN FINANCIAL AID (Fall 2009, est.) 842 applied for aid; of those 85% were deemed to have need. 100% of freshmen with need received aid; of those 47% had need fully met. *Average percent of need met:* 74% (excluding resources awarded to replace EFC). *Average financial aid package:* $26,408 (excluding resources awarded to replace EFC). 21% of all full-time freshmen had no need and received non-need-based gift aid.

UNDERGRADUATE FINANCIAL AID (Fall 2009, est.) 2,641 applied for aid; of those 88% were deemed to have need. 99% of undergraduates with need received aid; of those 34% had need fully met. *Average percent of need met:* 70% (excluding resources awarded to replace EFC). *Average financial aid package:* $25,306 (excluding resources awarded to replace EFC). 28% of all full-time undergraduates had no need and received non-need-based gift aid.

GIFT AID (NEED-BASED) *Total amount:* $42,110,377 (8% federal, 2% state, 84% institutional, 6% external sources). *Receiving aid:* Freshmen: 76% (702); all full-time undergraduates: 67% (2,181). *Average award:* Freshmen: $20,797; Undergraduates: $17,979. *Scholarships, grants, and awards:* Federal Pell, FSEOG, state, private, college/university gift aid from institutional funds.

GIFT AID (NON-NEED-BASED) *Total amount:* $16,111,635 (81% institutional, 19% external sources). *Receiving aid:* Freshmen: 26% (244). Undergraduates: 18% (598). *Average award:* Freshmen: $15,865. Undergraduates: $15,384. *Scholarships, grants, and awards by category: Academic interests/achievement:* 2,514 awards ($30,365,169 total): general academic interests/achievements, premedicine. *Special characteristics:* 44 awards ($143,615 total): children of workers in trades. *Tuition waivers:* Full or partial for employees or children of employees.

LOANS *Student loans:* $30,503,962 (41% need-based, 59% non-need-based). 74% of past graduating class borrowed through all loan programs. *Average indebtedness per student:* $44,340. *Average need-based loan:* Freshmen: $5813. Undergraduates: $6836. *Parent loans:* $8,196,375 (100% non-need-based). *Programs:* FFEL (Subsidized and Unsubsidized Stafford, PLUS), Perkins, state, college/university.

WORK-STUDY *Federal work-study:* Total amount: $810,571; 612 jobs averaging $1324.

APPLYING FOR FINANCIAL AID *Required financial aid forms:* FAFSA, CSS Financial Aid PROFILE. *Financial aid deadline:* 2/1. *Notification date:* 4/1. Students must reply by 5/1.

CONTACT Office of Financial Aid, Worcester Polytechnic Institute, 100 Institute Road, Worcester, MA 01609-2280, 508-831-5469. *Fax:* 508-831-5039. *E-mail:* finaid@wpi.edu.

WORCESTER STATE COLLEGE
Worcester, MA

Tuition & fees (MA res): $6605	Average undergraduate aid package: $9679

ABOUT THE INSTITUTION State-supported, coed. 28 undergraduate majors. Federal methodology is used as a basis for awarding need-based institutional aid.

UNDERGRADUATE EXPENSES for 2009–10 *Tuition, state resident:* full-time $970; part-time $40.42 per credit. *Tuition, nonresident:* full-time $7050; part-time $293.75 per credit. *Required fees:* full-time $5635; $224.37 per credit. Full-time tuition and fees vary according to class time, course load, degree level, and reciprocity agreements. Part-time tuition and fees vary according to class time, course load, degree level, and reciprocity agreements. *College room and board:* $9067; *Room only:* $6267. Room and board charges vary according to board plan and housing facility. *Payment plan:* Installment.

FRESHMAN FINANCIAL AID (Fall 2008) 598 applied for aid; of those 63% were deemed to have need. 98% of freshmen with need received aid; of those 44% had need fully met. *Average percent of need met:* 82% (excluding resources awarded to replace EFC). *Average financial aid package:* $9591 (excluding resources awarded to replace EFC).

UNDERGRADUATE FINANCIAL AID (Fall 2008) 2,558 applied for aid; of those 65% were deemed to have need. 98% of undergraduates with need received aid; of those 51% had need fully met. *Average percent of need met:* 85% (excluding resources awarded to replace EFC). *Average financial aid package:* $9679 (excluding resources awarded to replace EFC).

GIFT AID (NEED-BASED) *Total amount:* $6,667,875 (47% federal, 26% state, 21% institutional, 6% external sources). *Receiving aid:* Freshmen: 49% (323); all full-time undergraduates: 36% (1,205). *Average award:* Freshmen: $4643; Undergraduates: $4555. *Scholarships, grants, and awards:* Federal Pell, FSEOG, state, private, college/university gift aid from institutional funds.

GIFT AID (NON-NEED-BASED) *Total amount:* $301,088 (75% federal, 25% state). *Receiving aid:* Freshmen: 28% (180). Undergraduates: 16% (524). *Tuition waivers:* Full or partial for employees or children of employees, senior citizens.

LOANS *Student loans:* $13,087,615 (34% need-based, 66% non-need-based). 42% of past graduating class borrowed through all loan programs. *Average indebtedness per student:* $17,819. *Average need-based loan:* Freshmen: $1876. Undergraduates: $2615. *Parent loans:* $1,369,189 (100% non-need-based). *Programs:* FFEL (Subsidized and Unsubsidized Stafford, PLUS), Perkins, state.

WORK-STUDY *Federal work-study:* Total amount: $263,051; 244 jobs averaging $1500.

APPLYING FOR FINANCIAL AID *Required financial aid form:* FAFSA. *Financial aid deadline:* 5/1 (priority: 3/1). *Notification date:* Continuous beginning 3/1. Students must reply within 2 weeks of notification.

CONTACT Ms. Jayne McGinn, Director of Financial Aid, Worcester State College, 486 Chandler Street, Worcester, MA 01602, 508-929-8058 or toll-free 866-WSC-CALL. *Fax:* 508-929-8194. *E-mail:* jmcginn@worcester.edu.

WRIGHT STATE UNIVERSITY
Dayton, OH

Tuition & fees (OH res): $7797	Average undergraduate aid package: $9177

ABOUT THE INSTITUTION State-supported, coed. 163 undergraduate majors. Federal methodology is used as a basis for awarding need-based institutional aid.

UNDERGRADUATE EXPENSES for 2010–11 *Tuition, state resident:* full-time $7797; part-time $235 per credit hour. *Tuition, nonresident:* full-time $15,213; part-time $462 per credit hour.

FRESHMAN FINANCIAL AID (Fall 2009, est.) 2,248 applied for aid; of those 82% were deemed to have need. 99% of freshmen with need received aid; of those 11% had need fully met. *Average percent of need met:* 56% (excluding resources awarded to replace EFC). *Average financial aid package:* $8785 (excluding resources awarded to replace EFC). 10% of all full-time freshmen had no need and received non-need-based gift aid.

UNDERGRADUATE FINANCIAL AID (Fall 2009, est.) 8,944 applied for aid; of those 87% were deemed to have need. 99% of undergraduates with need received aid; of those 9% had need fully met. *Average percent of need met:* 54% (excluding resources awarded to replace EFC). *Average financial aid package:* $9177 (excluding resources awarded to replace EFC). 8% of all full-time undergraduates had no need and received non-need-based gift aid.

GIFT AID (NEED-BASED) *Total amount:* $38,137,438 (58% federal, 12% state, 28% institutional, 2% external sources). *Receiving aid:* Freshmen: 58% (1,463); all full-time undergraduates: 50% (5,646). *Average award:* Freshmen: $6099; Undergraduates: $6113. *Scholarships, grants, and awards:* Federal Pell, FSEOG, state, private, college/university gift aid from institutional funds, United Negro College Fund, Federal Nursing, Choose Ohio First Scholarships.

GIFT AID (NON-NEED-BASED) *Total amount:* $5,875,484 (21% state, 72% institutional, 7% external sources). *Receiving aid:* Freshmen: 5% (134). Undergraduates: 3% (284). *Average award:* Freshmen: $3249. Undergraduates: $4091. *Scholarships, grants, and awards by category: Academic interests/ achievement:* 2,195 awards ($6,118,130 total): area/ethnic studies, biological sciences, business, communication, computer science, education, engineering/ technologies, English, foreign languages, general academic interests/ achievements, health fields, humanities, international studies, mathematics, military science, physical sciences, premedicine, religion/biblical studies, social sciences. *Creative arts/performance:* 307 awards ($616,345 total): applied art and design, art/fine arts, cinema/film/broadcasting, creative writing, dance, general creative arts/performance, music, performing arts, theater/drama. *Special achievements/activities:* 470 awards ($3,272,445 total): cheerleading/drum major, community service, general special achievements/activities, leadership, memberships. *Special characteristics:* 757 awards ($2,625,675 total): adult students, children and siblings of alumni, children of educators, children of faculty/staff, ethnic background, first-generation college students, handicapped students, international students, out-of-state students.

LOANS *Student loans:* $87,115,394 (81% need-based, 19% non-need-based). 73% of past graduating class borrowed through all loan programs. *Average indebtedness per student:* $25,357. *Average need-based loan:* Freshmen: $3288. Undergraduates: $4106. *Parent loans:* $63,245,775 (33% need-based, 67% non-need-based). *Programs:* FFEL (Subsidized and Unsubsidized Stafford, PLUS), Perkins, Federal Nursing, state, college/university, private loans.

WORK-STUDY *Federal work-study:* Total amount: $3,448,951; 1,433 jobs averaging $2448.

ATHLETIC AWARDS Total amount: $2,477,538 (30% need-based, 70% non-need-based).

APPLYING FOR FINANCIAL AID *Required financial aid form:* FAFSA. *Financial aid deadline (priority):* 2/15. *Notification date:* Continuous beginning 3/15.

CONTACT Mrs. Jennifer L. Penick, Director of Financial Aid, Wright State University, 3640 Colonel Glenn Highway, Dayton, OH 45435, 937-775-5721 or toll-free 800-247-1770. *Fax:* 937-775-5795. *E-mail:* jennifer.penick@wright.edu.

XAVIER UNIVERSITY
Cincinnati, OH

Tuition & fees: $28,570	Average undergraduate aid package: $17,748

ABOUT THE INSTITUTION Independent Roman Catholic, coed. 55 undergraduate majors. Federal methodology is used as a basis for awarding need-based institutional aid.

UNDERGRADUATE EXPENSES for 2009–10 *One-time required fee:* $190. *Comprehensive fee:* $38,100 includes full-time tuition ($27,900), mandatory fees ($670), and room and board ($9530). *College room only:* $5250. Full-time tuition and fees vary according to course load and program. Room and board charges vary according to board plan and housing facility. *Part-time tuition:* $550 per credit hour. Part-time tuition and fees vary according to course load and location. *Payment plans:* Installment, deferred payment.

FRESHMAN FINANCIAL AID (Fall 2009, est.) 979 applied for aid; of those 79% were deemed to have need. 100% of freshmen with need received aid; of those 22% had need fully met. *Average percent of need met:* 78% (excluding resources awarded to replace EFC). *Average financial aid package:* $19,215 (excluding resources awarded to replace EFC). 32% of all full-time freshmen had no need and received non-need-based gift aid.

UNDERGRADUATE FINANCIAL AID (Fall 2009, est.) 2,669 applied for aid; of those 83% were deemed to have need. 99% of undergraduates with need received aid; of those 18% had need fully met. **Average percent of need met:** 70% (excluding resources awarded to replace EFC). **Average financial aid package:** $17,748 (excluding resources awarded to replace EFC). 30% of all full-time undergraduates had no need and received non-need-based gift aid.

GIFT AID (NEED-BASED) Total amount: $27,831,071 (13% federal, 2% state, 81% institutional, 4% external sources). **Receiving aid:** Freshmen: 63% (746); all full-time undergraduates: 56% (2,087). **Average award:** Freshmen: $14,248; Undergraduates: $12,753. **Scholarships, grants, and awards:** Federal Pell, FSEOG, state, private, college/university gift aid from institutional funds.

GIFT AID (NON-NEED-BASED) Total amount: $15,492,739 (89% institutional, 11% external sources). **Receiving aid:** Freshmen: 10% (123). Undergraduates: 7% (267). **Average award:** Freshmen: $11,803. Undergraduates: $10,906. **Scholarships, grants, and awards by category:** Academic interests/achievement: 1,415 awards ($15,122,602 total): foreign languages, general academic interests/achievements, mathematics, military science, physical sciences, social sciences. Creative arts/performance: 118 awards ($552,445 total): art/fine arts, music, performing arts, theater/drama. Special characteristics: 231 awards ($742,452 total): children and siblings of alumni, international students, members of minority groups, siblings of current students. **Tuition waivers:** Full or partial for employees or children of employees, senior citizens.

LOANS Student loans: $23,889,546 (69% need-based, 31% non-need-based). 67% of past graduating class borrowed through all loan programs. Average indebtedness per student: $27,098. **Average need-based loan:** Freshmen: $4003. Undergraduates: $4593. **Parent loans:** $6,255,173 (35% need-based, 65% non-need-based). **Programs:** Federal Direct (Subsidized and Unsubsidized Stafford, PLUS), Perkins.

WORK-STUDY Federal work-study: Total amount: $1,694,306; 756 jobs averaging $2247. **State or other work-study/employment:** 29 part-time jobs averaging $1952.

ATHLETIC AWARDS Total amount: $3,202,465 (40% need-based, 60% non-need-based).

APPLYING FOR FINANCIAL AID Required financial aid form: FAFSA. **Financial aid deadline (priority):** 2/15. **Notification date:** Continuous beginning 2/15. Students must reply by 5/1.

CONTACT Office of Financial Aid, Xavier University, 3800 Victory Parkway, Cincinnati, OH 45207-5411, 513-745-3142 or toll-free 800-344-4698. Fax: 513-745-2806.

XAVIER UNIVERSITY OF LOUISIANA
New Orleans, LA

Tuition & fees: $15,300	Average undergraduate aid package: $15,724

ABOUT THE INSTITUTION Independent Roman Catholic, coed. 54 undergraduate majors. Federal methodology is used as a basis for awarding need-based institutional aid.

UNDERGRADUATE EXPENSES for 2009–10 One-time required fee: $150. **Comprehensive fee:** $22,300 includes full-time tuition ($15,300) and room and board ($7000). Room and board charges vary according to housing facility. **Part-time tuition:** $700 per semester hour. Part-time tuition and fees vary according to course load. **Payment plan:** Installment.

FRESHMAN FINANCIAL AID (Fall 2008) 750 applied for aid; of those 88% were deemed to have need. 100% of freshmen with need received aid; of those 1% had need fully met. **Average percent of need met:** 11% (excluding resources awarded to replace EFC). **Average financial aid package:** $15,114 (excluding resources awarded to replace EFC). 6% of all full-time freshmen had no need and received non-need-based gift aid.

UNDERGRADUATE FINANCIAL AID (Fall 2008) 2,433 applied for aid; of those 89% were deemed to have need. 100% of undergraduates with need received aid; of those 1% had need fully met. **Average percent of need met:** 13% (excluding resources awarded to replace EFC). **Average financial aid package:** $15,724 (excluding resources awarded to replace EFC). 3% of all full-time undergraduates had no need and received non-need-based gift aid.

GIFT AID (NEED-BASED) Total amount: $4,713,780 (78% federal, 10% state, 12% institutional). **Receiving aid:** Freshmen: 62% (479); all full-time undergraduates: 53% (1,405). **Average award:** Freshmen: $5137; Undergraduates: $5374. **Scholarships, grants, and awards:** Federal Pell, FSEOG, state, private, college/university gift aid from institutional funds, United Negro College Fund.

GIFT AID (NON-NEED-BASED) Total amount: $3,776,412 (1% federal, 23% state, 76% institutional). **Receiving aid:** Freshmen: 74% (574). Undergraduates: 56% (1,489). **Average award:** Freshmen: $8341. Undergraduates: $9039. **Scholarships, grants, and awards by category:** Academic interests/achievement: 1,576 awards ($4,030,007 total): biological sciences, business, communication, computer science, education, engineering/technologies, English, foreign languages, general academic interests/achievements, humanities, mathematics, physical sciences, premedicine, religion/biblical studies, social sciences. **Tuition waivers:** Full or partial for employees or children of employees.

LOANS Student loans: $10,845,949 (82% need-based, 18% non-need-based). 78% of past graduating class borrowed through all loan programs. Average indebtedness per student: $32,872. **Average need-based loan:** Freshmen: $3373. Undergraduates: $4495. **Parent loans:** $2,257,676 (100% non-need-based). **Programs:** Federal Direct (Subsidized and Unsubsidized Stafford, PLUS), FFEL (Subsidized and Unsubsidized Stafford, PLUS), Perkins.

WORK-STUDY Federal work-study: Total amount: $278,410; 278 jobs averaging $1186.

ATHLETIC AWARDS Total amount: $567,745 (100% non-need-based).

APPLYING FOR FINANCIAL AID Required financial aid form: FAFSA. **Financial aid deadline (priority):** 1/1. **Notification date:** Continuous beginning 4/1. Students must reply within 2 weeks of notification.

CONTACT Mrs. Mildred Higgins, Financial Aid Director, Xavier University of Louisiana, One Drexel Drive, New Orleans, LA 70125-1098, 504-520-7517 or toll-free 877-XAVIERU.

YALE UNIVERSITY
New Haven, CT

Tuition & fees: $36,500	Average undergraduate aid package: $39,270

ABOUT THE INSTITUTION Independent, coed. 66 undergraduate majors. Both federal and institutional methodology are used as a basis for awarding need-based institutional aid.

UNDERGRADUATE EXPENSES for 2009–10 Comprehensive fee: $47,500 includes full-time tuition ($36,500) and room and board ($11,000). **College room only:** $6000. Room and board charges vary according to board plan. **Payment plan:** Installment.

FRESHMAN FINANCIAL AID (Fall 2009, est.) 813 applied for aid; of those 96% were deemed to have need. 100% of freshmen with need received aid; of those 100% had need fully met. **Average percent of need met:** 100% (excluding resources awarded to replace EFC). **Average financial aid package:** $39,282 (excluding resources awarded to replace EFC).

UNDERGRADUATE FINANCIAL AID (Fall 2009, est.) 2,958 applied for aid; of those 97% were deemed to have need. 100% of undergraduates with need received aid; of those 100% had need fully met. **Average percent of need met:** 100% (excluding resources awarded to replace EFC). **Average financial aid package:** $39,270 (excluding resources awarded to replace EFC).

GIFT AID (NEED-BASED) Total amount: $107,348,942 (5% federal, 91% institutional, 4% external sources). **Receiving aid:** Freshmen: 60% (780); all full-time undergraduates: 54% (2,852). **Average award:** Freshmen: $38,090; Undergraduates: $37,639. **Scholarships, grants, and awards:** Federal Pell, FSEOG, state, private, college/university gift aid from institutional funds, United Negro College Fund.

GIFT AID (NON-NEED-BASED) Total amount: $1,100,485 (100% external sources).

LOANS Student loans: $2,338,489 (26% need-based, 74% non-need-based). 31% of past graduating class borrowed through all loan programs. Average indebtedness per student: $10,717. **Average need-based loan:** Freshmen: $1772. Undergraduates: $2136. **Parent loans:** $2,887,635 (100% non-need-based). **Programs:** Federal Direct (Subsidized and Unsubsidized Stafford, PLUS), Perkins, state, college/university.

WORK-STUDY Federal work-study: Total amount: $1,136,224; 606 jobs averaging $1895. **State or other work-study/employment:** Total amount: $3,256,922 (100% need-based). 1,564 part-time jobs averaging $2070.

APPLYING FOR FINANCIAL AID Required financial aid forms: FAFSA, CSS Financial Aid PROFILE, noncustodial (divorced/separated) parent's statement, business/farm supplement, parent tax returns. **Financial aid deadline:** 3/1. **Notification date:** 4/1. Students must reply by 5/1 or within 1 week of notification.

CONTACT Mr. Caesar T. Storlazzi, Student Financial Services, Yale University, PO Box 208288, New Haven, CT 06520-8288, 203-432-0371. *Fax:* 203-777-6100. *E-mail:* sfs@yale.edu.

YESHIVA AND KOLEL BAIS MEDRASH ELYON
Monsey, NY
CONTACT Financial Aid Office, Yeshiva and Kolel Bais Medrash Elyon, 73 Main Street, Monsey, NY 10952, 845-356-7064.

YESHIVA AND KOLLEL HARBOTZAS TORAH
Brooklyn, NY
CONTACT Financial Aid Office, Yeshiva and Kollel Harbotzas Torah, 1049 East 15th Street, Brooklyn, NY 11230, 718-692-0208.

YESHIVA BETH MOSHE
Scranton, PA
CONTACT Financial Aid Office, Yeshiva Beth Moshe, 930 Hickory Street, Scranton, PA 18505-2124, 717-346-1747.

YESHIVA COLLEGE OF THE NATION'S CAPITAL
Silver Spring, MD
CONTACT Financial Aid Office, Yeshiva College of the Nation's Capital, 1216 Arcola Avenue, Silver Spring, MD 20902, 301-593-2534.

YESHIVA DERECH CHAIM
Brooklyn, NY
CONTACT Financial Aid Office, Yeshiva Derech Chaim, 1573 39th Street, Brooklyn, NY 11218, 718-438-5426.

YESHIVA D'MONSEY RABBINICAL COLLEGE
Monsey, NY
CONTACT Financial Aid Office, Yeshiva D'Monsey Rabbinical College, 2 Roman Boulevard, Monsey, NY 10952, 914-352-5852.

YESHIVA GEDOLAH IMREI YOSEF D'SPINKA
Brooklyn, NY
CONTACT Financial Aid Office, Yeshiva Gedolah Imrei Yosef D'Spinka, 1466 56th Street, Brooklyn, NY 11219, 718-851-8721.

YESHIVA GEDOLAH OF GREATER DETROIT
Oak Park, MI
CONTACT Rabbi P. Rushnawitz, Executive Administrator, Yeshiva Gedolah of Greater Detroit, 24600 Greenfield Road, Oak Park, MI 48237-1544, 810-968-3360. *Fax:* 810-968-8613.

YESHIVA GEDOLAH RABBINICAL COLLEGE
Miami Beach, FL
CONTACT Financial Aid Office, Yeshiva Gedolah Rabbinical College, 1140 Alton Road, Miami Beach, FL 33139, 305-673-5664.

YESHIVA KARLIN STOLIN RABBINICAL INSTITUTE
Brooklyn, NY
CONTACT Mr. Daniel Ross, Financial Aid Administrator, Yeshiva Karlin Stolin Rabbinical Institute, 1818 Fifty-fourth Street, Brooklyn, NY 11204, 718-232-7800 Ext. 116. *Fax:* 718-331-4833.

YESHIVA OF NITRA RABBINICAL COLLEGE
Mount Kisco, NY
CONTACT Mr. Yosef Rosen, Financial Aid Administrator, Yeshiva of Nitra Rabbinical College, 194 Division Avenue, Mount Kisco, NY 10549, 718-384-5460. *Fax:* 718-387-9400.

YESHIVA OF THE TELSHE ALUMNI
Riverdale, NY
CONTACT Financial Aid Office, Yeshiva of the Telshe Alumni, 4904 Independence Avenue, Riverdale, NY 10471, 718-601-3523.

YESHIVA OHR ELCHONON CHABAD/WEST COAST TALMUDICAL SEMINARY
Los Angeles, CA
CONTACT Ms. Hendy Tauber, Director of Financial Aid, Yeshiva Ohr Elchonon Chabad/West Coast Talmudical Seminary, 7215 Waring Avenue, Los Angeles, CA 90046-7660, 213-937-3763. *Fax:* 213-937-9456.

YESHIVA SHAAREI TORAH OF ROCKLAND
Suffern, NY
CONTACT Financial Aid Office, Yeshiva Shaarei Torah of Rockland, 91 West Carlton Road, Suffern, NY 10901, 845-352-3431.

YESHIVA SHAAR HATORAH TALMUDIC RESEARCH INSTITUTE
Kew Gardens, NY
CONTACT Mr. Yoel Yankelewitz, Executive Director, Financial Aid, Yeshiva Shaar Hatorah Talmudic Research Institute, 117-06 84th Avenue, Kew Gardens, NY 11418-1469, 718-846-1940.

YESHIVAS NOVOMINSK
Brooklyn, NY
CONTACT Financial Aid Office, Yeshivas Novominsk, 1569 47th Street, Brooklyn, NY 11219, 718-438-2727.

YESHIVATH VIZNITZ
Monsey, NY
CONTACT Financial Aid Office, Yeshivath Viznitz, Phyllis Terrace, PO Box 446, Monsey, NY 10952, 914-356-1010.

YESHIVATH ZICHRON MOSHE
South Fallsburg, NY
CONTACT Ms. Miryom R. Miller, Director of Financial Aid, Yeshivath Zichron Moshe, Laurel Park Road, South Fallsburg, NY 12779, 914-434-5240. *Fax:* 914-434-1009. *E-mail:* lehus@aol.com.

YESHIVAT MIKDASH MELECH
Brooklyn, NY

CONTACT Financial Aid Office, Yeshivat Mikdash Melech, 1326 Ocean Parkway, Brooklyn, NY 11230-5601, 718-339-1090.

YESHIVA TORAS CHAIM TALMUDICAL SEMINARY
Denver, CO

CONTACT Office of Financial Aid, Yeshiva Toras Chaim Talmudical Seminary, 1400 Quitman Street, Denver, CO 80204-1415, 303-629-8200.

YESHIVA UNIVERSITY
New York, NY

CONTACT Jean Belmont, Director of Student Finances, Yeshiva University, 500 West 185th Street, Room 121, New York, NY 10033-3201, 212-960-5269. *Fax:* 212-960-0037. *E-mail:* jbelmont@ymail.yu.edu.

YORK COLLEGE
York, NE

Tuition & fees: $14,998	Average undergraduate aid package: $13,765

ABOUT THE INSTITUTION Independent religious, coed. 38 undergraduate majors. Institutional methodology is used as a basis for awarding need-based institutional aid.

UNDERGRADUATE EXPENSES for 2010–11 *Comprehensive fee:* $20,678 includes full-time tuition ($13,158), mandatory fees ($1840), and room and board ($5680). Full-time tuition and fees vary according to course load. Room and board charges vary according to board plan and housing facility. *Part-time tuition:* $460 per credit hour. *Part-time fees:* $220 per credit hour. Part-time tuition and fees vary according to course load. *Payment plan:* Installment.

FRESHMAN FINANCIAL AID (Fall 2009, est.) 111 applied for aid; of those 94% were deemed to have need. 100% of freshmen with need received aid; of those 27% had need fully met. *Average percent of need met:* 85% (excluding resources awarded to replace EFC). *Average financial aid package:* $13,531 (excluding resources awarded to replace EFC). 8% of all full-time freshmen had no need and received non-need-based gift aid.

UNDERGRADUATE FINANCIAL AID (Fall 2009, est.) 414 applied for aid; of those 90% were deemed to have need. 100% of undergraduates with need received aid; of those 17% had need fully met. *Average percent of need met:* 77% (excluding resources awarded to replace EFC). *Average financial aid package:* $13,765 (excluding resources awarded to replace EFC). 7% of all full-time undergraduates had no need and received non-need-based gift aid.

GIFT AID (NEED-BASED) *Total amount:* $2,315,363 (38% federal, 2% state, 54% institutional, 6% external sources). *Receiving aid:* Freshmen: 90% (104); all full-time undergraduates: 83% (366). *Average award:* Freshmen: $9064; Undergraduates: $9266. *Scholarships, grants, and awards:* Federal Pell, FSEOG, state, private, college/university gift aid from institutional funds.

GIFT AID (NON-NEED-BASED) *Total amount:* $218,850 (90% institutional, 10% external sources). *Receiving aid:* Freshmen: 10% (12). Undergraduates: 9% (40). *Average award:* Freshmen: $3778. Undergraduates: $4207. *Scholarships, grants, and awards by category:* Academic interests/achievement: 209 awards ($562,875 total): biological sciences, business, communication, computer science, education, English, general academic interests/achievements, mathematics, premedicine, religion/biblical studies. *Creative arts/performance:* 64 awards ($154,755 total): music, theater/drama. *Special achievements/activities:* 133 awards ($95,648 total): leadership. *Special characteristics:* 72 awards ($265,543 total): children and siblings of alumni, children of faculty/staff, previous college experience, siblings of current students. *Tuition waivers:* Full or partial for employees or children of employees.

LOANS *Student loans:* $2,872,305 (76% need-based, 24% non-need-based). 78% of past graduating class borrowed through all loan programs. *Average indebtedness per student:* $22,020. *Average need-based loan:* Freshmen: $4576. Undergraduates: $4352. *Parent loans:* $349,971 (26% need-based, 74% non-need-based). *Programs:* FFEL (Subsidized and Unsubsidized Stafford, PLUS), Perkins, alternative loans.

WORK-STUDY *Federal work-study:* Total amount: $74,931; 64 jobs averaging $1160. *State or other work-study/employment:* Total amount: $153,985 (67% need-based, 33% non-need-based). 112 part-time jobs averaging $1287.

ATHLETIC AWARDS Total amount: $1,210,036 (68% need-based, 32% non-need-based).

APPLYING FOR FINANCIAL AID *Required financial aid form:* FAFSA. *Financial aid deadline (priority):* 6/15. *Notification date:* Continuous. Students must reply within 4 weeks of notification.

CONTACT Brien Alley, Director of Financial Aid, York College, 1125 East 8th Street, York, NE 68467, 402-363-5624 or toll-free 800-950-9675. *Fax:* 402-363-5623. *E-mail:* balley@york.edu.

YORK COLLEGE OF PENNSYLVANIA
York, PA

Tuition & fees: $15,140	Average undergraduate aid package: $10,915

ABOUT THE INSTITUTION Independent, coed. 52 undergraduate majors. Federal methodology is used as a basis for awarding need-based institutional aid.

UNDERGRADUATE EXPENSES for 2010–11 *Comprehensive fee:* $23,670 includes full-time tuition ($13,640), mandatory fees ($1500), and room and board ($8530). *College room only:* $4750. Room and board charges vary according to housing facility. *Part-time tuition:* $425 per credit hour. *Part-time fees:* $330 per term. *Payment plans:* Tuition prepayment, installment.

FRESHMAN FINANCIAL AID (Fall 2009, est.) 996 applied for aid; of those 71% were deemed to have need. 99% of freshmen with need received aid; of those 24% had need fully met. *Average percent of need met:* 73% (excluding resources awarded to replace EFC). *Average financial aid package:* $11,110 (excluding resources awarded to replace EFC). 16% of all full-time freshmen had no need and received non-need-based gift aid.

UNDERGRADUATE FINANCIAL AID (Fall 2009, est.) 3,746 applied for aid; of those 75% were deemed to have need. 99% of undergraduates with need received aid; of those 25% had need fully met. *Average percent of need met:* 70% (excluding resources awarded to replace EFC). *Average financial aid package:* $10,915 (excluding resources awarded to replace EFC). 11% of all full-time undergraduates had no need and received non-need-based gift aid.

GIFT AID (NEED-BASED) *Total amount:* $14,909,528 (31% federal, 19% state, 46% institutional, 4% external sources). *Receiving aid:* Freshmen: 50% (548); all full-time undergraduates: 44% (2,009). *Average award:* Freshmen: $5659; Undergraduates: $5383. *Scholarships, grants, and awards:* Federal Pell, FSEOG, state, private, college/university gift aid from institutional funds.

GIFT AID (NON-NEED-BASED) *Total amount:* $1,884,947 (1% state, 89% institutional, 10% external sources). *Receiving aid:* Freshmen: 37% (409). Undergraduates: 20% (935). *Average award:* Freshmen: $4133. Undergraduates: $3717. *Scholarships, grants, and awards by category:* Academic interests/achievement: 629 awards ($3,172,730 total): general academic interests/achievements. *Creative arts/performance:* 18 awards ($18,353 total): music. *Special characteristics:* 34 awards ($60,863 total): children and siblings of alumni, children of union members/company employees, international students, members of minority groups. *Tuition waivers:* Full or partial for employees or children of employees.

LOANS *Student loans:* $25,635,873 (44% need-based, 56% non-need-based). 74% of past graduating class borrowed through all loan programs. *Average indebtedness per student:* $27,583. *Average need-based loan:* Freshmen: $4822. Undergraduates: $5961. *Parent loans:* $4,775,908 (69% need-based, 31% non-need-based). *Programs:* Federal Direct (Subsidized and Unsubsidized Stafford, PLUS), FFEL (Subsidized and Unsubsidized Stafford, PLUS), Perkins, Federal Nursing, college/university.

WORK-STUDY *Federal work-study:* Total amount: $571,502; 305 jobs averaging $1937. *State or other work-study/employment:* Total amount: $36,100 (100% non-need-based). 17 part-time jobs averaging $2059.

APPLYING FOR FINANCIAL AID *Required financial aid form:* FAFSA. *Financial aid deadline (priority):* 3/1. *Notification date:* Continuous beginning 3/1. Students must reply within 4 weeks of notification.

CONTACT Calvin Williams, Director of Financial Aid, York College of Pennsylvania, Country Club Road, York, PA 17405-7199, 717-849-1682 or toll-free 800-455-8018. *Fax:* 717-849-1685. *E-mail:* financialaid@ycp.edu.

YORK COLLEGE OF THE CITY UNIVERSITY OF NEW YORK
Jamaica, NY

ABOUT THE INSTITUTION State and locally supported, coed. 45 undergraduate majors.

GIFT AID (NEED-BASED) *Scholarships, grants, and awards:* Federal Pell, FSEOG, state, college/university gift aid from institutional funds.

LOANS *Programs:* Federal Direct (Subsidized and Unsubsidized Stafford, PLUS), Perkins.

WORK-STUDY *Federal work-study:* Total amount: $1,555,344; 1,022 jobs averaging $1517.

APPLYING FOR FINANCIAL AID *Required financial aid form:* FAFSA.

CONTACT Ms. Cathy Tsiapanos, Director of Student Financial Services, York College of the City University of New York, 94-20 Guy R. Brewer Boulevard, Jamaica, NY 11451-0001, 718-262-2238. *E-mail:* ctsia@york.cuny.edu.

YORKTOWN UNIVERSITY
Denver, CO

CONTACT Financial Aid Office, Yorktown University, 4340 East Kentucky Avenue, Suite 457, Denver, CO 80246, 877-757-0059.

YOUNG HARRIS COLLEGE
Young Harris, GA

CONTACT Joanne W. Putnam, Financial Aid Director, Young Harris College, PO Box 247, 1 College Street, Young Harris, GA 30582, 706-379-3111 Ext. 5163 or toll-free 800-241-3754 (in-state). *Fax:* 706-379-4306. *E-mail:* jwputnam@yhc.edu.

YOUNGSTOWN STATE UNIVERSITY
Youngstown, OH

Tuition & fees (OH res): $6956 **Average undergraduate aid package: $8163**

ABOUT THE INSTITUTION State-supported, coed. 122 undergraduate majors. Federal methodology is used as a basis for awarding need-based institutional aid.

UNDERGRADUATE EXPENSES for 2009–10 *Tuition, state resident:* full-time $6727; part-time $290 per credit. *Tuition, nonresident:* full-time $12,400; part-time $526 per credit. *Required fees:* full-time $229; $10 per credit. Full-time tuition and fees vary according to course load. Part-time tuition and fees vary according to course load. *College room and board:* $7400. Room and board charges vary according to board plan and housing facility. *Payment plan:* Installment.

FRESHMAN FINANCIAL AID (Fall 2008) 1,936 applied for aid; of those 85% were deemed to have need. 86% of freshmen with need received aid; of those 12% had need fully met. *Average percent of need met:* 34% (excluding resources awarded to replace EFC). *Average financial aid package:* $7949 (excluding resources awarded to replace EFC). 10% of all full-time freshmen had no need and received non-need-based gift aid.

UNDERGRADUATE FINANCIAL AID (Fall 2008) 7,996 applied for aid; of those 87% were deemed to have need. 88% of undergraduates with need received aid; of those 8% had need fully met. *Average percent of need met:* 32% (excluding resources awarded to replace EFC). *Average financial aid package:* $8163 (excluding resources awarded to replace EFC). 10% of all full-time undergraduates had no need and received non-need-based gift aid.

GIFT AID (NEED-BASED) *Total amount:* $29,528,702 (68% federal, 20% state, 3% institutional, 9% external sources). *Receiving aid:* Freshmen: 47% (1,053); all full-time undergraduates: 45% (4,358). *Average award:* Freshmen: $5285; Undergraduates: $5142. *Scholarships, grants, and awards:* Federal Pell, FSEOG, state, private, college/university gift aid from institutional funds.

GIFT AID (NON-NEED-BASED) *Total amount:* $8,209,799 (2% federal, 22% state, 24% institutional, 52% external sources). *Receiving aid:* Freshmen: 29% (636). Undergraduates: 25% (2,419). *Average award:* Freshmen: $2414. Undergraduates: $2099. *Scholarships, grants, and awards by category: Academic interests/achievement:* biological sciences, business, communication, computer science, education, engineering/technologies, English, foreign languages, general academic interests/achievements, health fields, humanities, mathematics, military science, physical sciences, premedicine, religion/biblical studies, social sciences. *Creative arts/performance:* art/fine arts, creative writing, journalism/publications, music, performing arts, theater/drama. *Special achievements/activities:* cheerleading/drum major, community service, leadership, memberships, religious involvement. *Special characteristics:* adult students, children and siblings of alumni, children of faculty/staff, children of union members/company employees, children of workers in trades, children with a deceased or disabled parent, ethnic background, handicapped students, international students, local/state students, members of minority groups, out-of-state students, public servants, religious affiliation, spouses of deceased or disabled public servants, veterans, veterans' children. *Tuition waivers:* Full or partial for employees or children of employees, senior citizens.

LOANS *Student loans:* $63,540,730 (43% need-based, 57% non-need-based). *Average need-based loan:* Freshmen: $3154. Undergraduates: $3763. *Parent loans:* $37,227,811 (100% non-need-based). *Programs:* FFEL (Subsidized and Unsubsidized Stafford, PLUS), Perkins, state, Charles E. Schell Foundation loans, George W. Wright Student Aid Loans, Rogers Student Loans.

WORK-STUDY *Federal work-study:* Total amount: $898,113; 328 jobs averaging $2738. *State or other work-study/employment:* Total amount: $4,338,824 (100% non-need-based). Part-time jobs available.

ATHLETIC AWARDS Total amount: $3,545,860 (100% non-need-based).

APPLYING FOR FINANCIAL AID *Required financial aid forms:* FAFSA, institution's own form. *Financial aid deadline (priority):* 2/15. *Notification date:* 5/1. Students must reply within 4 weeks of notification.

CONTACT Ms. Beth Bartlett, Administrative Assistant, Youngstown State University, One University Plaza, Youngstown, OH 44555, 330-941-3504 or toll-free 877-468-6978. *Fax:* 330-941-1659. *E-mail:* babartlett@ysu.edu.

ZION BIBLE COLLEGE
Haverhill, MA

CONTACT Financial Aid Office, Zion Bible College, 320 South Main Street, Haverhill, MA 01835, 978-478-3400 or toll-free 800-356-4014.

Appendix

State Scholarship and Grant Programs

Each state government has established one or more state-administered financial aid programs for qualified students. In many instances, these state programs are restricted to legal residents of the state. However, they often are available to out-of-state students who will be or are attending colleges or universities within the state. In addition to residential status, other qualifications frequently exist.

Gift aid and forgivable loan programs open to undergraduate students for all states and the District of Columbia are described on the following pages. They are arranged in alphabetical order, first by state name, then by program name. The annotation for each program provides information about the program, eligibility, and the contact addresses for applications or further information. Unless otherwise stated, this information refers to awards for 2009–10. Information is provided by the state-sponsoring agency in response to *Peterson's Annual Survey of Non-institutional Aid*, which was conducted between January 2009 and April 2009. Information is accurate when Peterson's receives it. However, it is always advisable to check with the sponsor to ascertain that the information remains correct.

You should write to the address given for each program to request that award details for 2010–11 be sent to you as soon as they are available. Descriptive information, brochures, and application forms for state scholarship programs are usually available from the financial aid offices of public colleges or universities within the specific state. High school guidance offices often have information and relevant forms for awards for which high school seniors may be eligible. Increasingly, state government agencies are putting state scholarship information on state government agency Web sites. In searching state government Web sites, however, you should be aware that the higher education agency in many states is separate from the state's general education office, which is often responsible only for elementary and secondary education. Also, the page at public university Web sites that provides information about student financial aid frequently has a list of state-sponsored scholarships and financial aid programs. College and university Web sites can be easily accessed through www.petersons.com.

Names of scholarship programs are frequently used inconsistently or become abbreviated in popular usage. Many programs have variant names by which they are known. The program's sponsor has approved the title of the program that Peterson's uses in this guide, yet this name may differ from the program's official name or from its most commonly used name.

In addition to the grant aid and forgivable loan programs listed on the following pages, states may also offer internship or work-study programs, graduate fellowships and grants, or low-interest loans. If you are interested in learning more about these other kinds of programs, the state education office that supplies information or applications for the undergraduate scholarship programs listed here should be able to provide information about other kinds of higher education financial aid programs that are sponsored by the state.

ALABAMA

Air Force ROTC College Scholarship.

Scholarship program provides three- and four-year scholarships in three different types to high school seniors. All scholarship cadets receive a nontaxable monthly allowance (stipend) during the academic year. For more details refer to Web Site http://www.afrotc.com/scholarships/hsschol/types.php. *Award:* Scholarship for use in freshman, sophomore, junior, or senior year; renewable. *Award amount:* $9000–$15,000. *Number of awards:* 2000–4000. *Eligibility Requirements:* Applicant must be age 17-30 and enrolled or expecting to enroll full-time at a two-year or four-year institution or university. Applicant must have 3.0 GPA or higher. Available to U.S. citizens. Applicant or parent must meet one or more of the following requirements: Air Force experience; retired from active duty; disabled or killed as a result of military service; prisoner of war; or missing in action. *Application Requirements:* Application, interview, test scores, transcript. **Deadline:** December 1.

Contact Ty Christian, Chief Air Force ROTC Advertising Manager, Air Force Reserve Officer Training Corps, 551 East Maxwell Boulevard, Maxwell Air Force Base, AL 36112-6106. *E-mail:* ty.christian@maxwell.af.mil. *Phone:* 334-953-2278. *Fax:* 334-953-4384. *Web site:* http://www.afrotc.com.

Alabama G.I. Dependents Scholarship Program.

Full scholarship for dependents of Alabama disabled, prisoner of war, or missing-in-action veterans. Child or stepchild must initiate training before 26th birthday; age 30 deadline may apply in certain situations. No age deadline for spouses or widows. *Award:* Scholarship for use in freshman, sophomore, junior, or senior year; renewable. *Award amount:* varies. *Number of awards:* varies. *Eligibility Requirements:* Applicant must be age 30 or under; enrolled or expecting to enroll full- or part-time at a four-year institution or university; resident of Alabama and studying in Alabama. Available to U.S. and non-U.S. citizens. Applicant or parent must meet one or more of the following requirements: general military experience; retired from active duty; disabled or killed as a result of military service; prisoner of war; or missing in action. *Application Requirements:* Application. **Deadline:** varies.

Contact Willie E. Moore, Scholarship Administrator, Alabama Department of Veterans Affairs, PO Box 1509, Montgomery, AL 36102-1509. *E-mail:* wmoore@va.state.al.us. *Phone:* 334-242-5077. *Fax:* 334-242-5102. *Web site:* http://www.va.alabama.gov.

Alabama National Guard Educational Assistance Program.

Renewable award aids Alabama residents who are members of the Alabama National Guard and are enrolled in an accredited college in Alabama. Forms must be signed by a representative of the Alabama Military Department and financial aid officer. Recipient must be in a degree-seeking program. *Award:* Scholarship for use in freshman, sophomore, junior, senior, or graduate year; renewable. *Award amount:* $25–$1000. *Number of awards:* up to 575. *Eligibility Requirements:* Applicant must be age 17 and over; enrolled or expecting to enroll full- or part-time at a two-year, four-year, or technical institution or university; resident of Alabama and studying in Alabama. Available to U.S. citizens. Applicant must have served in the Air Force National Guard or Army National Guard. *Application Requirements:* Application. **Deadline:** continuous.

Contact Cheryl Newton, Grants Coordinator, Alabama Commission on Higher Education, 100 North Union Street, PO Box 302000, Montgomery, AL 36130-2000. *E-mail:* cheryl.newton@ache.alabama.gov. *Phone:* 334-242-2273. *Web site:* http://www.ache.alabama.gov.

Alabama Student Assistance Program.

Scholarship award of $300 to $5000 per academic year given to undergraduate students residing in the state of Alabama and attending a college or university in Alabama. *Award:* Grant for use in freshman, sophomore, junior, or senior year; not renewable. *Award amount:* $300–$5000. *Number of awards:* varies. *Eligibility Requirements:* Applicant must be enrolled or expecting to enroll full- or part-time at a two-year, four-year, or technical institution or university; resident of Alabama and studying in Alabama. Available to U.S. citizens. *Application Requirements:* Application. **Deadline:** continuous.

Contact Cheryl Newton, Grants Coordinator, Alabama Commission on Higher Education, 100 North Union Street, PO Box 302000, Montgomery, AL 36130-2000. *E-mail:* cheryl.newton@ache.alabama.gov. *Phone:* 334-242-2273. *Web site:* http://www.ache.alabama.gov.

Alabama Student Grant Program.

Nonrenewable awards available to Alabama residents for undergraduate study at certain independent colleges within the state. Both full and half-time students are eligible. Deadlines: September 15, January 15, and February 15. *Award:* Grant for use in freshman, sophomore, junior, or senior year; not renewable. *Award amount:* up to $1200. *Number of awards:* up to 1200. *Eligibility*

Requirements: Applicant must be enrolled or expecting to enroll full- or part-time at a four-year institution or university; resident of Alabama and studying in Alabama. Available to U.S. citizens. *Application Requirements:* Application.

Contact Cheryl Newton, Grants Coordinator, Alabama Commission on Higher Education, 100 North Union Street, PO Box 302000, Montgomery, AL 36130-2000. *E-mail:* cheryl.newton@ache.alabama.gov. *Phone:* 334-242-2273. *Web site:* http://www.ache.alabama.gov.

Police Officers and Firefighters Survivors Education Assistance Program-Alabama.

Provides tuition, fees, books, and supplies to dependents of full-time police officers and firefighters killed in the line of duty. Must attend any Alabama public college as an undergraduate. Must be Alabama resident. *Award:* Scholarship for use in freshman, sophomore, junior, or senior year; renewable. *Award amount:* $2000–$5000. *Number of awards:* 15–30. *Eligibility Requirements:* Applicant must be age 21 or under; enrolled or expecting to enroll full- or part-time at a two-year, four-year, or technical institution or university; single; resident of Alabama and studying in Alabama. Available to U.S. citizens. *Application Requirements:* Application, transcript, birth certificate, marriage license, death certificate, letter from medical doctor. **Deadline:** continuous.

Contact Cheryl Newton, Grants Coordinator, Alabama Commission on Higher Education, 100 North Union Street, PO Box 302000, Montgomery, AL 36130-2000. *E-mail:* cheryl.newton@ache.alabama.gov. *Phone:* 334-242-2273. *Web site:* http://www.ache.alabama.gov.

ALASKA

GEAR UP Alaska Scholarship.

Scholarship provides up to $7000 each year for up to four years of undergraduate study (up to $3500 each year for half-time study) for students who participated in the GEAR UP Programs in 6th, 7th, and 8th grade and have met the academic milestones established by their district. Must reapply each year and application must be signed by GEAR UP program director. Must be an Alaska high school senior or have an Alaska diploma or GED. Must submit FAFSA and have financial need. Must be under age 22. *Award:* Scholarship for use in freshman, sophomore, junior, or senior year; not renewable. *Award amount:* $3500–$7000. *Number of awards:* varies. *Eligibility Requirements:* Applicant must be age 22 or under; enrolled or expecting to enroll full- or part-time at a two-year or four-year institution or university and resident of Alaska. Available to U.S. citizens. *Application Requirements:* Application, financial need analysis, references, transcript, FAFSA, SAR. **Deadline:** May 31.

Contact Adam Weed, Special Projects Coordinator, Alaska State Department of Education, 801 West 10th Street, Suite 200, PO Box 110500, Juneau, AK 99811-0500. *E-mail:* adam.weed@alaska.gov. *Phone:* 907-465-6685. *Web site:* http://www.eed.state.ak.us.

ARIZONA

Arizona Private Postsecondary Education Student Financial Assistance Program. Provides grants to financially needy Arizona Community College graduates, to attend a private postsecondary baccalaureate degree-granting institution. *Award:* Forgivable loan for use in junior or senior year; renewable. *Award amount:* $1000–$2000. *Number of awards:* varies. *Eligibility Requirements:* Applicant must be enrolled or expecting to enroll full-time at a four-year institution or university; resident of Arizona and studying in Arizona. Applicant must have 2.5 GPA or higher. Available to U.S. citizens. *Application Requirements:* Application, financial need analysis, transcript, promissory note. **Deadline:** June 30.

Contact Mila Zaporteza, Business Manager, Arizona Commission for Postsecondary Education, 2020 North Central Avenue, Suite 650, Phoenix, AZ 85004-4503. *E-mail:* mila@azhighered.gov. *Phone:* 602-258-2435 Ext. 102. *Fax:* 602-258-2483. *Web site:* http://www.azhighered.gov.

Leveraging Educational Assistance Partnership. Grants to financially needy students, who enroll in and attend postsecondary education or training in Arizona schools. Program was formerly known as the State Student Incentive Grant or SSIG Program. *Award:* Grant for use in freshman, sophomore, junior, senior, or graduate year; not renewable. *Award amount:* $100–$2500. *Number of awards:* varies. *Eligibility Requirements:* Applicant must be enrolled or expecting to enroll full- or part-time at a two-year, four-year, or technical institution or university; resident of Arizona and studying in Arizona. Available to U.S. citizens. *Application Requirements:* Application, financial need analysis, transcript. **Deadline:** April 30.

Contact Mila A. Zaporteza, Business Manager and LEAP Financial Aid Manager, Arizona Commission for Postsecondary Education, 2020 North Central Avenue, Suite 650,

Phoenix, AZ 85004-4503. *E-mail:* mila@azhighered.gov. *Phone:* 602-258-2435 Ext. 102. *Fax:* 602-258-2483. *Web site:* http://www.azhighered.gov.

Postsecondary Education Grant Program. Awards of up to $2000 to Arizona residents studying in Arizona. May be renewed annually for a maximum of four calendar years. Minimum 2.5 GPA required. Deadline June 30. *Award:* Forgivable loan for use in freshman, sophomore, junior, or senior year; renewable. *Award amount:* $1000–$2000. *Number of awards:* varies. *Eligibility Requirements:* Applicant must be enrolled or expecting to enroll full- or part-time at a four-year institution or university; resident of Arizona and studying in Arizona. Applicant must have 2.5 GPA or higher. Available to U.S. citizens. *Application Requirements:* Application, driver's license, transcript, promissory note. **Deadline:** June 30.

Contact Dr. April L. Osborn, Executive Director, Arizona Commission for Postsecondary Education, 2020 North Central Avenue, Suite 650, Phoenix, AZ 85004-4503. *E-mail:* aosborn@azhighered.gov. *Phone:* 602-258-2435. *Fax:* 602-258-2483. *Web site:* http://www.azhighered.gov.

ARKANSAS

Arkansas Academic Challenge Scholarship Program. Awards for Arkansas residents who are graduating high school seniors, currently enrolled college students and nontraditional students to study at an approved Arkansas institution. Must have at least a 2.5 GPA or 19 ACT composite score (or the equivalent). Renewable up to three additional years. *Award:* Scholarship for use in freshman, sophomore, junior, or senior year; renewable. *Award amount:* $1250–$5000. *Number of awards:* 25,000–30,000. *Eligibility Requirements:* Applicant must be enrolled or expecting to enroll full-time at a two-year or four-year institution or university; resident of Arkansas and studying in Arkansas. Applicant must have 2.5 GPA or higher. Available to U.S. citizens. *Application Requirements:* Application, test scores, transcript. **Deadline:** June 1.

Contact Tara Smith, Director of Financial Aid, Arkansas Department of Higher Education, 114 East Capitol Avenue, Little Rock, AR 72201-3818. *E-mail:* finaid@adhe.arknet.edu. *Phone:* 501-371-2000. *Fax:* 501-371-2001. *Web site:* http://www.adhe.edu.

Arkansas Governor's Scholars Program. Awards for outstanding Arkansas high school seniors. Must be an Arkansas resident and have a high school GPA of at

least 3.5 or have scored at least 27 on the ACT. Award is $4000 per year for four years of full-time undergraduate study. Applicants who attain 32 or above on ACT, 1410 or above on SAT and have an academic 3.5 GPA, or are selected as National Merit or National Achievement finalists may receive an award equal to tuition, mandatory fees, room, and board up to $10,000 per year at any Arkansas institution. *Award:* Scholarship for use in freshman, sophomore, junior, or senior year; renewable. *Award amount:* $4000–$10,000. *Number of awards:* up to 375. *Eligibility Requirements:* Applicant must be enrolled or expecting to enroll full-time at a two-year or four-year institution or university; resident of Arkansas and studying in Arkansas. Applicant must have 3.5 GPA or higher. Available to U.S. citizens. *Application Requirements:* Application, test scores, transcript. **Deadline:** February 1.

Contact Tara Smith, Director of Financial Aid, Arkansas Department of Higher Education, 114 East Capitol Avenue, Little Rock, AR 72201-3818. *E-mail:* taras@adhe.edu. *Phone:* 501-371-2000. *Fax:* 501-371-2001. *Web site:* http://www.adhe.edu.

Arkansas Single Parent Scholarship. Scholarships are awarded to economically disadvantaged single parents who reside in Arkansas who have custodial care of at least one minor child and have not already received a baccalaureate degree. Award values, application deadlines, and other criteria vary by county. Visit http://www.aspsf.org for more information. *Award:* Scholarship for use in freshman, sophomore, junior, or senior year; not renewable. *Award amount:* $200–$1800. *Number of awards:* up to 1600. *Eligibility Requirements:* Applicant must be enrolled or expecting to enroll full- or part-time at a two-year, four-year, or technical institution or university; single; resident of Arkansas and must have an interest in designated field specified by sponsor. Available to U.S. citizens. *Application Requirements:* Application, financial need analysis, interview, references, transcript, statement of goals, FAFSA SAR. **Deadline:** varies.

Contact varies by county, Arkansas Single Parent Scholarship Fund. *Web site:* http://www.aspsf.org.

Law Enforcement Officers' Dependents Scholarship-Arkansas. Scholarship for dependents, under 23 years old, of Arkansas law-enforcement officers killed or permanently disabled in the line of duty. Renewable award is a waiver of tuition, fees, and room at two- or four-year Arkansas institution. Submit birth certificate, death certificate, and claims commission report of findings of fact. Proof of disability from State Claims Commission may also be submitted. *Award:* Scholarship for use in freshman, sophomore, junior, or senior year; renewable. *Number of awards:* 27–32. *Eligibility Requirements:* Applicant must be age 23 or under; enrolled or expecting to enroll full- or part-time at a two-year, four-year, or technical institution or university; resident of Arkansas and studying in Arkansas. Available to U.S. citizens. *Application Requirements:* Application. **Deadline:** continuous.

Contact Tara Smith, Director of Financial Aid, Arkansas Department of Higher Education, 114 East Capitol Avenue, Little Rock, AR 72201-3818. *E-mail:* taras@adhe.edu. *Phone:* 501-371-2000. *Fax:* 501-371-2001. *Web site:* http://www.adhe.edu.

Military Dependent's Scholarship Program. Renewable waiver of tuition, fees, room and board undergraduate students seeking a bachelor's degree or certificate of completion at any public college, university or technical school in Arkansas who qualify as a spouse or dependent child of an Arkansas resident who has been declared to be missing in action, killed in action, a POW, or killed on ordnance delivery, or a veteran who has been declared to be 100 percent totally and permanently disabled during, or as a result of, active military service. *Award:* Scholarship for use in freshman, sophomore, junior, or senior year; renewable. *Number of awards:* 1–60. *Eligibility Requirements:* Applicant must be enrolled or expecting to enroll full-time at a two-year, four-year, or technical institution or university; resident of Arkansas and studying in Arkansas. Available to U.S. citizens. Applicant or parent must meet one or more of the following requirements: general military experience; retired from active duty; disabled or killed as a result of military service; prisoner of war; or missing in action. *Application Requirements:* Application, references, report of casualty. **Deadline:** June 1.

Contact Tara Smith, Director of Financial Aid, Arkansas Department of Higher Education, 114 East Capitol Avenue, Little Rock, AR 72201-3818. *E-mail:* taras@adhe.edu. *Phone:* 501-371-2000. *Fax:* 501-371-2001. *Web site:* http://www.adhe.edu.

Robert C. Byrd Honors Scholarship-Arkansas. Applicant must be a graduate of a public or private school or receive a recognized equivalent of a high school diploma. Must be a resident of Arkansas. Must be admitted to an institution of higher education, demonstrate outstanding academic achievement and show promise of continued academic achievement. Award is $1500 for each academic year for a maximum of four years. *Award:* Scholarship for use in freshman year; renewable. *Award amount:* $1500. *Number of awards:* 62. *Eligibility Requirements:* Applicant must be high school student; planning to enroll or expecting to enroll full-time at a two-year, four-year, or technical institution or university and resident of Arkansas. Available to U.S. citizens. *Application Requirements:* Application, transcript. **Deadline:** February 16.

Contact Margaret Amps, Program Coordinator, Arkansas State Department of Education, Four Capitol Mall, Little Rock, AR 72201. *E-mail:* margaret.amps@arkansas.gov. *Phone:* 501-682-4396. *Web site:* http://www.arkansased.org.

Second Effort Scholarship. Awarded to those scholars who achieved one of the 10 highest scores on the Arkansas High School Diploma Test (GED). Must be at least age 18 and not have graduated from high school. Students do not apply for this award, they are contacted by the Arkansas Department of Higher Education. *Award:* Scholarship for use in freshman year; renewable. *Award amount:* up to $1000. *Number of awards:* 10. *Eligibility Requirements:* Applicant must be high school student; planning to enroll or expecting to enroll full- or part-time at a two-year or four-year institution or university; resident of Arkansas and studying in Arkansas. Available to U.S. citizens. *Application Requirements:* Application. **Deadline:** varies.

Contact Tara Smith, Director of Financial Aid, Arkansas Department of Higher Education, 114 East Capitol Avenue, Little Rock, AR 72201-3818. *E-mail:* taras@adhe.edu. *Phone:* 501-371-2000. *Fax:* 501-371-2001. *Web site:* http://www.adhe.edu.

CALIFORNIA

Cal Grant C. Award for California residents who are enrolled in a short-term vocational training program. Program must lead to a recognized degree or certificate. Course length must be a minimum of 4 months and no longer than 24 months. Students must be attending an approved California institution and show financial need. *Award:* Grant for use in freshman or sophomore year; renewable. *Award amount:* $576–$3168. *Number of awards:* up to 7761. *Eligibility Requirements:* Applicant must be enrolled or expecting to enroll full- or part-time at a two-year or technical institution; resident of California and studying in California. Available to U.S. citizens.

Application Requirements: Application, financial need analysis, GPA verification. **Deadline:** March 2.

Contact Catalina Mistler, Chief, Program Administration & Services Division, California Student Aid Commission, PO Box 419026, Rancho Cordova, CA 95741-9026. *E-mail:* studentsupport@csac.ca.gov. *Phone:* 916-526-7268. *Fax:* 916-526-8002. *Web site:* http://www.csac.ca.gov.

Child Development Teacher and Supervisor Grant Program. Award is for those students pursuing an approved course of study leading to a Child Development Permit issued by the California Commission on Teacher Credentialing. In exchange for each year funding is received, recipients agree to provide one year of service in a licensed childcare center. *Academic Fields/Career Goals:* Child and Family Studies; Education. *Award:* Grant for use in freshman, sophomore, junior, senior, or graduate year; renewable. *Award amount:* $1000–$2000. *Number of awards:* up to 300. *Eligibility Requirements:* Applicant must be enrolled or expecting to enroll full- or part-time at a two-year or four-year institution or university; resident of California and studying in California. Applicant or parent of applicant must have employment or volunteer experience in teaching/education. Available to U.S. citizens. *Application Requirements:* Application, financial need analysis, references, GPA verification. **Deadline:** April 16.

Contact Catalina Mistler, Chief, Program Administration & Services Division, California Student Aid Commission, PO Box 419026, Rancho Cordova, CA 95741-9026. *E-mail:* studentsupport@csac.ca.gov. *Phone:* 916-526-7268. *Fax:* 916-526-8002. *Web site:* http://www.csac.ca.gov.

Competitive Cal Grant A. Award for California residents who are not recent high school graduates attending an approved college or university within the state. Must show financial need and meet minimum 3.0 GPA requirement. *Award:* Grant for use in freshman, sophomore, junior, or senior year; renewable. *Award amount:* $2772–$6636. *Number of awards:* 22,500. *Eligibility Requirements:* Applicant must be enrolled or expecting to enroll full- or part-time at a two-year or four-year institution or university; resident of California and studying in California. Applicant must have 3.0 GPA or higher. Available to U.S. citizens. *Application Requirements:* Application, financial need analysis, GPA verification. **Deadline:** March 2.

Contact Catalina Mistler, Chief, Program Administration & Services Division, California

Student Aid Commission, PO Box 419026, Rancho Cordova, CA 95741-9026. *E-mail:* studentsupport@csac.ca.gov. *Phone:* 916-526-7268. *Fax:* 916-526-8002. *Web site:* http://www.csac.ca.gov.

Cooperative Agencies Resources for Education Program. Renewable award available to California resident enrolled as a full-time student at a two-year California community college. Must currently receive CalWORKs/TANF and have at least one child under fourteen years of age at time of acceptance into CARE program. Must be in EOPS, a single head of household, and age 18 or older. Contact local college EOPS-CARE office for application and more information. To locate nearest campus, see http://www.icanaffordcollege.com/applications/homepage2.cfm. *Award:* Grant for use in freshman or sophomore year; renewable. *Award amount:* varies. *Number of awards:* 10,000–11,000. *Eligibility Requirements:* Applicant must be age 18 and over; enrolled or expecting to enroll full-time at a two-year institution; single; resident of California and studying in California. Available to U.S. citizens. *Application Requirements:* Application, financial need analysis, test scores, transcript. **Deadline:** continuous.

Contact Contact local community college EOPS/CARE program, California Community Colleges. *Web site:* http://www.cccco.edu.

Entitlement Cal Grant B. Provide grant funds for access costs for low-income students in an amount not to exceed $1551. Must be California residents and enroll in an undergraduate academic program of not less than one academic year at a qualifying postsecondary institution. Must show financial need and meet the minimum 2.0 GPA requirement. *Award:* Grant for use in freshman, sophomore, junior, or senior year; renewable. *Award amount:* $700–$1551. *Number of awards:* varies. *Eligibility Requirements:* Applicant must be age 23 or under; enrolled or expecting to enroll full- or part-time at a two-year, four-year, or technical institution or university; resident of California and studying in California. Available to U.S. citizens. *Application Requirements:* Application, financial need analysis. **Deadline:** March 2.

Contact Catalina Mistler, Chief, Program Administration & Services Division, California Student Aid Commission, PO Box 419026, Rancho Cordova, CA 95741-9026. *E-mail:* studentsupport@csac.ca.gov. *Phone:* 916-526-7268. *Fax:* 916-526-8002. *Web site:* http://www.csac.ca.gov.

Law Enforcement Personnel Dependents Scholarship. Provides college grants to needy dependents of California law enforcement officers, officers and employees of the Department of Corrections and Department of Youth Authority, and firefighters killed or disabled in the line of duty. *Award:* Grant for use in freshman, sophomore, junior, or senior year; renewable. *Award amount:* $100–$11,259. *Number of awards:* varies. *Eligibility Requirements:* Applicant must be enrolled or expecting to enroll full- or part-time at a two-year or four-year institution or university; resident of California and studying in California. Applicant or parent of applicant must have employment or volunteer experience in police/firefighting. Available to U.S. citizens. *Application Requirements:* Application, financial need analysis, transcript, birth certificate, death certificate of parents or spouse, police report. **Deadline:** continuous.

Contact Catalina Mistler, Chief, Program Administration & Services Division, California Student Aid Commission, PO Box 419026, Rancho Cordova, CA 95741-9026. *E-mail:* studentsupport@csac.ca.gov. *Phone:* 916-526-7268. *Fax:* 916-526-8002. *Web site:* http://www.csac.ca.gov.

COLORADO

American Legion Auxiliary Department of Colorado Department President's Scholarship for Junior Member. Open to children, spouses, grandchildren, and great-grandchildren of veterans, and veterans who served in the Armed Forces during eligibility dates for membership in the American Legion. Applicants must be Colorado residents who have been accepted by an accredited school in Colorado. *Award:* Scholarship for use in freshman year; not renewable. *Award amount:* up to $500. *Number of awards:* 1–2. *Eligibility Requirements:* Applicant must be high school student; planning to enroll or expecting to enroll full- or part-time at a four-year institution or university; resident of Colorado and studying in Colorado. Available to U.S. citizens. Applicant or parent must meet one or more of the following requirements: general military experience; retired from active duty; disabled or killed as a result of military service; prisoner of war; or missing in action. *Application Requirements:* Application, essay, references, transcript. **Deadline:** April 15.

Contact Jean Lennie, Department Secretary and Treasurer, American Legion Auxiliary Department of Colorado, 7465 East First Avenue, Suite D, Denver, CO 80230. *E-mail:* ala@coloradolegion.org. *Phone:* 303-367-5388. *Fax:* 303-367-0688. *Web site:* http://www.coloradolegion.org.

American Legion Auxiliary Department of Colorado Past Presidents' Parley Nurses Scholarship. Open to children, spouses, grandchildren, and great-grandchildren of American Legion veterans, and veterans who served in the armed forces during eligibility dates for membership in the American Legion. Must be Colorado residents who have been accepted by an accredited school of nursing in Colorado. *Academic Fields/Career Goals:* Nursing. *Award:* Scholarship for use in freshman, sophomore, junior, senior, or graduate year; not renewable. *Award amount:* up to $500. *Number of awards:* 3–5. *Eligibility Requirements:* Applicant must be enrolled or expecting to enroll full- or part-time at a four-year institution or university; resident of Colorado and studying in Colorado. Applicant or parent of applicant must be member of American Legion or Auxiliary. Available to U.S. citizens. Applicant or parent must meet one or more of the following requirements: general military experience; retired from active duty; disabled or killed as a result of military service; prisoner of war; or missing in action. *Application Requirements:* Application, essay, financial need analysis, references. **Deadline:** April 1.

Contact American Legion Auxiliary Department of Colorado, 7465 East First Avenue, Suite D, Denver, CO 80230. *E-mail:* ala@coloradolegion.org. *Phone:* 303-367-5388. *Web site:* http://www.coloradolegion.org.

Colorado Leveraging Educational Assistance Partnership (CLEAP). Scholarship of up to $5000 awarded for an undergraduate student enrolled at least half time. Applicant must be a U.S citizen and Colorado resident. *Award:* Scholarship for use in freshman, sophomore, junior, or senior year; not renewable. *Award amount:* up to $5000. *Number of awards:* varies. *Eligibility Requirements:* Applicant must be enrolled or expecting to enroll full- or part-time at a two-year, four-year, or technical institution or university and resident of Colorado. Available to U.S. citizens. *Application Requirements:* Application.

Contact Celina Duran, Financial Aid Administrator, Colorado Commission on Higher Education, 1560 Broadway, Suite 1600, Denver, CO 80202. *E-mail:* celina.duran@dhe.state.co.us. *Phone:* 303-866-2723. *Fax:* 303-866-4266. *Web site:* http://www.highered.colorado.gov/dhedefault.html.

Colorado Student Grant. Grants for Colorado residents attending eligible public, private, or vocational institutions within the state. Students must complete a Free Application for Federal Student Aid (FAFSA) and qualify at 150% of Pell eligibility. Application deadlines vary by institution. Renewable award for undergraduates. Contact the financial aid office at the college/institution for application and more information. *Award:* Grant for use in freshman, sophomore, junior, or senior year; renewable. *Award amount:* $850–$5000. *Number of awards:* 50,202. *Eligibility Requirements:* Applicant must be enrolled or expecting to enroll full- or part-time at a two-year, four-year, or technical institution or university; resident of Colorado and studying in Colorado. Available to U.S. citizens. *Application Requirements:* Application, financial need analysis, student must have an active FAFSA on file at the institution.

Contact Celina Duran, Financial Aid Administrator, Colorado Commission on Higher Education, 1560 Broadway, Suite 1600, Denver, CO 80202. *E-mail:* celina.duran@dhe.state. co.us. *Phone:* 303-866-2723. *Fax:* 303-866-4266. *Web site:* http://www.highered.colorado. gov/dhedefault.html.

Colorado Undergraduate Merit Scholarships. Renewable awards for students who are Colorado residents attending Colorado state-supported institutions at the undergraduate level. Must demonstrate superior scholarship or talent. Contact college financial aid office for complete information and deadlines. *Award:* Scholarship for use in freshman, sophomore, junior, or senior year; renewable. *Award amount:* up to $5000. *Number of awards:* 1127. *Eligibility Requirements:* Applicant must be enrolled or expecting to enroll full- or part-time at a two-year, four-year, or technical institution or university; resident of Colorado and studying in Colorado. Available to U.S. citizens. *Application Requirements:* Application, test scores, transcript.

Contact Celina Duran, Financial Aid Administrator, Colorado Commission on Higher Education, 1560 Broadway, Suite 1600, Denver, CO 80202. *E-mail:* celina.duran@dhe.state. co.us. *Phone:* 303-866-2723. *Fax:* 303-866-4266. *Web site:* http://www.highered.colorado. gov/dhedefault.html.

Governor's Opportunity Scholarship. Scholarship available for the most needy first-time freshman whose parents' adjusted gross income is less than $26,000. Must be U.S. citizen or permanent legal resident. Work-study is part of the program. This program is in phase out and will sunset in 2012. *Award:* Scholarship for use in freshman, sophomore, junior, or senior year; renewable. *Award amount:* up to $10,700. *Number of awards:* 470. *Eligibility Requirements:* Applicant must be high school

student; planning to enroll or expecting to enroll full-time at a two-year, four-year, or technical institution or university; resident of Colorado and studying in Colorado. Available to U.S. citizens. *Application Requirements:* Application, financial need analysis, test scores, transcript. **Deadline:** continuous.

Contact Celina Duran, Financial Aid Administrator, Colorado Commission on Higher Education, 1560 Broadway, Suite 1600, Denver, CO 80202. *E-mail:* celina.duran@dhe.state. co.us. *Phone:* 303-866-2723. *Fax:* 303-866-4266. *Web site:* http://www.highered.colorado. gov/dhedefault.html.

Western Undergraduate Exchange (WUE). Students in designated states can enroll in two- and four-year undergraduate programs at 145 public institutions in participating states and pay 150 percent of resident tuition. Applicants apply directly to the admissions office at participating institution. Applicants must indicate that they want to be considered for the "WUE tuition discount". Participating institutions and the programs of study offered at the WUE rate are listed at http://wiche.edu/ wue. *Award:* Scholarship for use in freshman, sophomore, junior, or senior year; renewable. *Award amount:* varies. *Number of awards:* varies. *Eligibility Requirements:* Applicant must be enrolled or expecting to enroll full-time at a two-year or four-year institution; resident of Alaska, Arizona, California, Colorado, Hawaii, Idaho, Montana, Nevada, New Mexico, North Dakota, Oregon, South Dakota, Utah, Washington, or Wyoming and studying in Alaska, Arizona, California, Colorado, Hawaii, Idaho, Montana, Nevada, New Mexico, North Dakota, Oregon, or South Dakota. Available to U.S. citizens. *Application Requirements:* Application, test scores, transcript, varies by institution.

Contact Ms. Laura Ewing, Administrative Assistant, Student Exchange, Western Interstate Commission for Higher Education, 3035 Center Green Drive, Boulder, CO 80301. *E-mail:* info-sep@wiche.edu. *Phone:* 303-541-0270. *Web site:* http://www.wiche.edu/.

CONNECTICUT

AIFS-HACU Scholarships. Scholarships to outstanding Hispanic students to study abroad with AIFS. Available to students attending HACU member schools. Students will receive scholarships of up to 50 percent of the full program fee. Students must meet all standard AIFS eligibility requirements. Deadlines: April 15 for fall, October 1 for spring, and March 15 for summer. *Award:* Scholarship for use in

freshman, sophomore, junior, or senior year; not renewable. *Award amount:* $6000–$8000. *Number of awards:* varies. *Eligibility Requirements:* Applicant must be Hispanic; age 17 and over; enrolled or expecting to enroll full-time at a two-year or four-year institution or university and must have an interest in international exchange. Applicant must have 3.0 GPA or higher. Available to U.S. and non-U.S. citizens. *Application Requirements:* Application, essay, photo, references, transcript. *Fee:* $95. **Deadline:** varies.

Contact David Mauro, Admissions Counselor, American Institute for Foreign Study, River Plaza, 9 West Broad Street, Stamford, CT 06902-3788. *E-mail:* dmauro@ aifs.com. *Phone:* 800-727-2437 Ext. 5163. *Fax:* 203-399-5463. *Web site:* http://www. aifsabroad.com.

Capitol Scholarship Program. Award for Connecticut residents attending eligible institutions in Connecticut or in a state with reciprocity with Connecticut (Massachusetts, Maine, New Hampshire, Pennsylvania, Rhode Island, Vermont, or Washington, D.C). Must be U.S. citizen or permanent resident alien who is a high school senior or graduate. Must rank in top 20% of class or score at least 1800 on SAT or score at least 27 on the ACT. Students must also demonstrate financial need as a result of filing the FAFSA. *Award:* Scholarship for use in freshman, sophomore, junior, or senior year; renewable. *Award amount:* $500–$3000. *Number of awards:* 4500–5500. *Eligibility Requirements:* Applicant must be enrolled or expecting to enroll full- or part-time at a two-year, four-year, or technical institution or university; resident of Connecticut and studying in Connecticut, District of Columbia, Maine, Massachusetts, New Hampshire, Pennsylvania, Rhode Island, or Vermont. Available to U.S. citizens. *Application Requirements:* Application, financial need analysis, test scores, FAFSA. **Deadline:** February 15.

Contact Mrs. Linda Diamond, Senior Associate, Connecticut Department of Higher Education, 61 Woodland Street, Hartford, CT 06105. *E-mail:* csp@ctdhe.org. *Phone:* 860-947-1855. *Fax:* 860-947-1313. *Web site:* http://www.ctdhe.org.

Connecticut Aid to Public College Students Grant. Award for Connecticut residents attending public colleges or universities within the state. Renewable awards based on financial need. Application deadline varies by institution. Apply at college financial aid office. *Award:* Grant for use in freshman, sophomore, junior, or senior year; renewable. *Award amount:* varies. *Number of awards:* varies. *Eligibility Requirements:* Applicant must be enrolled or expecting to enroll full- or part-time at a two-year or four-year institution or university; resident of Connecticut and studying in Connecticut. Available to U.S. citizens. *Application Requirements:* Financial need analysis, FAFSA. **Deadline:** continuous.

Contact Ms. Lynne Little, Executive Assistant, Connecticut Department of Higher Education, 61 Woodland Street, Hartford, CT 06105. *E-mail:* caps@ctdhe.org. *Phone:* 860-947-1855. *Fax:* 860-947-1838. *Web site:* http://www.ctdhe.org.

Connecticut Army National Guard 100% Tuition Waiver. Program is for any active member of the Connecticut Army National Guard in good standing. Must be a resident of Connecticut attending any Connecticut state (public) university, community-technical college or regional vocational-technical school. The total number of available awards is unlimited. *Award:* Scholarship for use in freshman, sophomore, junior, or senior year; not renewable. *Award amount:* $16,000. *Number of awards:* varies. *Eligibility Requirements:* Applicant must be age 17-65; enrolled or expecting to enroll full- or part-time at a two-year, four-year, or technical institution or university; resident of Connecticut and studying in Connecticut. Available to U.S. and non-U.S. citizens. Applicant or parent must meet one or more of the following requirements: Army National Guard experience; retired from active duty; disabled or killed as a result of military service; prisoner of war; or missing in action. *Application Requirements:* Application. **Deadline:** July 1.

Contact Capt. Jeremy Lingenfelser, Education Services Officer, Connecticut Army National Guard, 360 Broad Street, Hartford, CT 06105-3795. *E-mail:* education@ct.ngb.army.mil. *Phone:* 860-524-4816. *Fax:* 860-524-4904. *Web site:* http://www.ct.ngb.army.mil.

Connecticut Independent College Student Grants. Award for Connecticut residents attending an independent college or university within the state on at least a half-time basis. Renewable awards based on financial need. Application deadline varies by institution. Apply at college financial aid office. *Award:* Grant for use in freshman, sophomore, junior, or senior year; renewable. *Award amount:* $250–$8500. *Number of awards:* varies. *Eligibility Requirements:* Applicant must be enrolled or expecting to enroll full- or part-time at a two-year or four-year institution or

university; resident of Connecticut and studying in Connecticut. Available to U.S. citizens. *Application Requirements:* Financial need analysis, FAFSA. **Deadline:** continuous.

Contact Ms. Lynne Little, Executive Assistant, Connecticut Department of Higher Education, 61 Woodland Street, Hartford, CT 06105. *E-mail:* cics@ctdhe.org. *Phone:* 860-947-1855. *Fax:* 860-947-1838. *Web site:* http://www.ctdhe.org.

Minority Teacher Incentive Grant Program. Program provides up to $5,000 a year for two years of full-time study in a teacher preparation program for the junior or senior year at a Connecticut college or university. Applicant must be African-American, Hispanic/Latino, Asian American or Native American heritage and be nominated by the Education Dean. Program graduates who teach in Connecticut public schools may be eligible for loan reimbursement stipends up to $2,500 per year for up to four years. *Academic Fields/Career Goals:* Education. *Award:* Grant for use in junior or senior year; renewable. *Award amount:* $2500–$5000. *Number of awards:* 1–75. *Eligibility Requirements:* Applicant must be American Indian/Alaska Native, Asian/Pacific Islander, Black (non-Hispanic), or Hispanic; enrolled or expecting to enroll full-time at a four-year institution or university and studying in Connecticut. Available to U.S. citizens. *Application Requirements:* Application. **Deadline:** October 1.

Contact Ms. Judy-Ann Staple, Associate, Connecticut Department of Higher Education, 61 Woodland Street, Hartford, CT 06105. *E-mail:* mtip@ctdhe.org. *Phone:* 860-947-1855. *Fax:* 860-947-1838. *Web site:* http://www.ctdhe.org.

DELAWARE

Christa McAuliffe Teacher Scholarship Loan-Delaware. Award for legal residents of Delaware who are U.S. citizens or eligible non-citizens. Must be full-time student enrolled at a Delaware college in an undergraduate program leading to teacher certification. High school seniors must rank in upper half of class and have a combined score of 1570 on the SAT. Undergraduates must have at least a 2.75 cumulative GPA. For details visit Web site http://www.doe.k12.de.us. *Academic Fields/Career Goals:* Education. *Award:* Forgivable loan for use in freshman, sophomore, junior, or senior year; renewable. *Award amount:* $1000–$5000. *Number of awards:* 1–60. *Eligibility Requirements:* Applicant must be enrolled or expecting to enroll full-time at a four-

year institution or university; resident of Delaware and studying in Delaware. Available to U.S. citizens. *Application Requirements:* Application, essay, test scores, transcript. **Deadline:** March 28.

Contact Carylin Brinkley, Program Administrator, Delaware Higher Education Commission, Carvel State Office Building, 820 North French Street, Fifth Floor, Wilmington, DE 19801-3509. *E-mail:* cbrinkley@doe.k12.de.us. *Phone:* 302-577-5240. *Fax:* 302-577-6765. *Web site:* http://www.doe.k12.de.us.

Delaware Nursing Incentive Scholarship Loan. Award for legal residents of Delaware who are U.S. citizens or eligible non-citizens. Must be full-time student enrolled in an accredited program leading to certification as an RN or LPN. High school seniors must rank in upper half of class with at least a 2.5 cumulative GPA. *Academic Fields/Career Goals:* Nursing. *Award:* Forgivable loan for use in freshman, sophomore, junior, or senior year; renewable. *Award amount:* $1000–$5000. *Number of awards:* 1–40. *Eligibility Requirements:* Applicant must be enrolled or expecting to enroll full- or part-time at a two-year or four-year institution and resident of Delaware. Applicant must have 2.5 GPA or higher. Available to U.S. citizens. *Application Requirements:* Application, essay, test scores, transcript. **Deadline:** March 28.

Contact Carylin Brinkley, Program Administrator, Delaware Higher Education Commission, Carvel State Office Building, 820 North French Street, Fifth Floor, Wilmington, DE 19801-3509. *E-mail:* cbrinkley@doe.k12.de.us. *Phone:* 302-577-5240. *Fax:* 302-577-6765. *Web site:* http://www.doe.k12.de.us.

Delaware Solid Waste Authority John P. "Pat" Healy Scholarship. Award for legal residents of Delaware who are U.S. citizens or eligible non-citizens. Must be high school seniors or full-time college students in their freshman or sophomore years. Must major in either environmental engineering or environmental sciences at a Delaware college. Selection based on financial need, academic performance, community and school involvement, and leadership ability. *Academic Fields/Career Goals:* Engineering-Related Technologies; Environmental Science. *Award:* Scholarship for use in freshman or sophomore year; renewable. *Award amount:* $2000. *Number of awards:* 1. *Eligibility Requirements:* Applicant must be enrolled or expecting to enroll full-time at a two-year or four-year institution or university; resident of Delaware; studying in Delaware and must have an interest in leadership. Applicant or parent of applicant must have employment or volunteer experience in community service. Applicant must have 3.0 GPA or higher. Available to U.S. citizens. *Application Requirements:* Application, financial need analysis, FAFSA, Student Aid Report (SAR). **Deadline:** March 14.

Contact Carylin Brinkley, Program Administrator, Delaware Higher Education Commission, Carvel State Office Building, 820 North French Street, Fifth Floor, Wilmington, DE 19801-3509. *E-mail:* cbrinkley@doe.k12.de.us. *Phone:* 302-577-5240. *Fax:* 302-577-6765. *Web site:* http://www.doe.k12.de.us.

Diamond State Scholarship. Award for legal residents of Delaware who are U.S. citizens or eligible non-citizens. Must be enrolled as a full-time student in a degree program at a nonprofit, regionally accredited institution. Minimum 3.0 GPA required. High school seniors should rank in upper quarter of class and have a combined score of at least 1800 on the SAT. *Award:* Scholarship for use in freshman year; renewable. *Award amount:* $1250. *Number of awards:* 50. *Eligibility Requirements:* Applicant must be high school student; planning to enroll or expecting to enroll full-time at a four-year institution or university and resident of Delaware. Applicant must have 3.0 GPA or higher. Available to U.S. citizens. *Application Requirements:* Application, essay, test scores, transcript. **Deadline:** March 28.

Contact Carylin Brinkley, Program Administrator, Delaware Higher Education Commission, Carvel State Office Building, 820 North French Street, Fifth Floor, Wilmington, DE 19801-3509. *E-mail:* cbrinkley@doe.k12.de.us. *Phone:* 302-577-5240. *Fax:* 302-577-6765. *Web site:* http://www.doe.k12.de.us.

Educational Benefits for Children of Deceased Veterans and Others Award. Award for children between the ages of 16 and 24 of deceased/MIA/POW veterans or state police officers. Must have been a resident of Delaware for 3 or more years prior to the date of application. If the applicant's parent is a member of the armed forces, the parent must have been a resident of Delaware at the time of death or declaration of missing in action or prisoner of war status. Award will not exceed tuition and fees at a Delaware public college. *Award:* Grant for use in freshman, sophomore, junior, or senior year; renewable. *Award amount:* varies. *Number of awards:* varies. *Eligibility Requirements:* Applicant must be age 16-24; enrolled or expecting to enroll full-time at a two-year or four-year institution or university and resident of Delaware. Applicant or parent of applicant must have employment or volunteer experience in police/firefighting. Available to U.S. citizens. Applicant or parent must meet one or more of the following requirements: general military experience; retired from active duty; disabled or killed as a result of military service; prisoner of war; or missing in action. *Application Requirements:* Application, verification of service-related death. **Deadline:** continuous.

Contact Delaware Higher Education Commission. *Phone:* 302-577-5240. *Fax:* 302-577-6765. *Web site:* http://www.doe.k12.de.us.

Governor's Workforce Development Grant. Grants for part-time undergraduate students attending Delaware College of Art and Design, Delaware State University, Delaware Technical and Community College, Goldey-Beacom College, University of Delaware, Wesley College, Widener University (Delaware Campus), or Wilmington College. Must be at least 18 years old, a resident of Delaware, and employed by a company in Delaware that contributes to the Blue Collar Training Fund Program. *Award:* Grant for use in freshman, sophomore, junior, or senior year; renewable. *Award amount:* $2000. *Number of awards:* 40. *Eligibility Requirements:* Applicant must be age 18 and over; enrolled or expecting to enroll full- or part-time at a two-year or four-year institution or university; resident of Delaware and studying in Delaware. Available to U.S. and non-U.S. citizens. *Application Requirements:* Application. **Deadline:** varies.

Contact Carylin Brinkley, Program Administrator, Delaware Higher Education Commission, Carvel State Office Building, 820 North French Street, Fifth Floor, Wilmington, DE 19801-3509. *E-mail:* cbrinkley@doe.k12.de.us. *Phone:* 302-577-5240. *Fax:* 302-577-6765. *Web site:* http://www.doe.k12.de.us.

Legislative Essay Scholarship. Award for legal residents of Delaware who are U.S. citizens or eligible non-citizens. Must be high school seniors in public or private schools or in home school programs who plans to enroll full-time at a nonprofit, regionally accredited college. Must submit an essay on topic: "Pluribus Unum: Is this motto adopted in 1782 relevant to our country today?". *Award:* Prize for use in freshman year; not renewable. *Award amount:* $1000–$10,000. *Number of awards:* up to 62. *Eligibility Requirements:* Applicant must be high school student; planning to enroll or expecting to enroll full- or part-time at a two-year, four-year, or technical institution or university and resident of Delaware. Available to U.S. citizens. *Application Requirements:* Application, applicant must enter a contest, essay. **Deadline:** November 30.

Contact Carylin Brinkley, Program Administrator, Delaware Higher Education Commission, Carvel State Office Building, 820 North French Street, Fifth Floor, Wilmington, DE 19801-3509. *E-mail:* cbrinkley@doe.k12.de.us. *Phone:* 302-577-5240. *Fax:* 302-577-6765. *Web site:* http://www.doe.k12.de.us.

Robert C. Byrd Honors Scholarship-Delaware. Award for legal residents of Delaware who are U.S. citizens or eligible non-citizens. For high school seniors who rank in upper quarter of class or GED recipients with a minimum score of 300 and a combined score of at least 1800 on the SAT. Minimum 3.5 GPA required. Must be enrolled at least half-time at a nonprofit, regionally accredited institution. *Award:* Scholarship for use in freshman year; renewable. *Award amount:* $1500. *Number of awards:* 20. *Eligibility Requirements:* Applicant must be high school student; planning to enroll or expecting to enroll full-time at a two-year or four-year institution or university and resident of Delaware. Applicant must have 3.5 GPA or higher. Available to U.S. citizens. *Application Requirements:* Application, essay, test scores, transcript. **Deadline:** March 28.

Contact Carylin Brinkley, Program Administrator, Delaware Higher Education Commission, Carvel State Office Building, 820 North French Street, Fifth Floor, Wilmington, DE 19801-3509. *E-mail:* cbrinkley@doe.k12.de.us. *Phone:* 302-577-5240. *Fax:* 302-577-6765. *Web site:* http://www.doe.k12.de.us.

Scholarship Incentive Program-Delaware. Award for legal residents of Delaware who are U.S. citizens or eligible non-citizens. Must demonstrate substantial financial need and enroll full-time in an undergraduate degree program at a nonprofit, regionally accredited institution in Delaware or Pennsylvania. Minimum 2.5 GPA required. *Award:* Grant for use in freshman, sophomore, junior, senior, or graduate year; not renewable. *Award amount:* $700–$2200. *Number of awards:* 1000–1300. *Eligibility Requirements:* Applicant must be enrolled or expecting to enroll full-time at a two-year or four-year institution or university; resident of Delaware and studying in Delaware or Pennsylvania. Applicant must have 2.5 GPA or higher.

Available to U.S. citizens. *Application Requirements:* Application, financial need analysis, transcript, FAFSA. **Deadline:** April 15.

Contact Carylin Brinkley, Program Administrator, Delaware Higher Education Commission, Carvel State Office Building, 820 North French Street, Fifth Floor, Wilmington, DE 19801-3509. *E-mail:* cbrinkley@doe.k12.de.us. *Phone:* 302-577-5240. *Fax:* 302-577-6765. *Web site:* http://www.doe.k12.de.us.

State Tuition Assistance. You must enlist in the Delaware National Guard to be eligible for this scholarship award. Award providing tuition assistance for any member of the Air or Army National Guard attending a Delaware two-year or four-year college. Awards are renewable. Applicant's minimum GPA must be 2.0. *Award:* Scholarship for use in freshman, sophomore, junior, or senior year; renewable. *Award amount:* up to $10,000. *Number of awards:* 1–300. *Eligibility Requirements:* Applicant must be enrolled or expecting to enroll full- or part-time at a two-year or four-year institution or university and studying in Delaware. Available to U.S. citizens. Applicant or parent must meet one or more of the following requirements: Air Force National Guard or Army National Guard experience; retired from active duty; disabled or killed as a result of military service; prisoner of war; or missing in action. *Application Requirements:* Application, transcript.

Contact Robert Csizmadia, State Tuition Assistance Manager, Delaware National Guard, 1st Regiment Road, Wilmington, DE 19808-2191. *E-mail:* robert.csizmadi@de.ngb.army.mil. *Phone:* 302-326-7012. *Fax:* 302-326-7029. *Web site:* http://www.delawarenationalguard.com.

DISTRICT OF COLUMBIA

American Council of the Blind Scholarships. Merit-based award available to undergraduate students who are legally blind in both eyes. Submit certificate of legal blindness and proof of acceptance at an accredited postsecondary institution. *Award:* Scholarship for use in freshman, sophomore, junior, or senior year; renewable. *Award amount:* $1000–$2500. *Number of awards:* 16–20. *Eligibility Requirements:* Applicant must be enrolled or expecting to enroll full- or part-time at a four-year institution or university. Applicant must be visually impaired. Applicant must have 3.5 GPA or higher. Available to U.S. citizens. *Application Requirements:* Application, autobiography, essay, references, transcript, evidence of legal blindness, proof of post-secondary school acceptance. **Deadline:** March 1.

Contact Tatricia Castillo, Scholarship Coordinator, American Council of the Blind, 1155 15th Street, NW, Suite 1004, Washington, DC 20005. *E-mail:* tcastillo@acp.org. *Phone:* 202-467-5081. *Fax:* 202-467-5085. *Web site:* http://www.acb.org.

Bureau of Indian Education Grant Program. Grants are provided to supplement financial assistance to eligible American Indian/Alaska Native students entering college seeking a baccalaureate degree. A student must be a member of, or at least one-quarter degree Indian blood descendent of a member of an American Indian tribe who are eligible for the special programs and services provided by the United States through the Bureau of Indian Affairs to Indians because of their status as Indians. *Award:* Grant for use in freshman year; not renewable. *Award amount:* varies. *Number of awards:* varies. *Eligibility Requirements:* Applicant must be American Indian/Alaska Native; high school student and planning to enroll or expecting to enroll full-time at a two-year or four-year institution or university. Available to U.S. citizens. *Application Requirements:* Application, references, test scores, transcript. **Deadline:** varies.

Contact Paulina Bell, Office Automation Assistant, Bureau of Indian Affairs Office of Indian Education Programs, 1849 C Street, NW, MS 3609-MIB, Washington, DC 20240-0001. *Phone:* 202-208-6123. *Fax:* 202-208-3312. *Web site:* http://www.oiep.bia.edu.

Central Intelligence Agency Undergraduate Scholarship Program. Need and merit-based award for students with minimum 3.0 GPA, who are interested in working for the Central Intelligence Agency upon graduation. Renewable for four years of undergraduate study. Must apply in senior year of high school or sophomore year in college. For further information refer to Web site http://www.cia.gov. *Academic Fields/Career Goals:* Accounting; Business/Consumer Services; Computer Science/Data Processing; Economics; Electrical Engineering/Electronics; Foreign Language; Geography; Graphics/Graphic Arts/Printing; International Studies; Political Science; Surveying; Surveying Technology, Cartography, or Geographic Information Science. *Award:* Scholarship for use in freshman, sophomore, junior, or senior year; renewable. *Award amount:* up to $18,000. *Number of awards:* varies. *Eligibility Requirements:* Applicant must be age 18 and over and enrolled or expecting to enroll full-time at a four-year institution or university. Applicant must have 3.0 GPA or higher. Available to U.S. citizens. *Application Requirements:* Application, financial need analysis, resume, references, test scores, transcript. **Deadline:** November 1.

Contact Van Patrick, Chief, College Relations, Central Intelligence Agency, Recruitment Center, L 100 LF7, Washington, DC 20505. *E-mail:* ivanilp0@ucia.gov. *Phone:* 703-613-8388. *Fax:* 703-613-7676. *Web site:* http://www.cia.gov.

Costas G. Lemonopoulos Scholarship. Scholarships to children of NALC members attending public, four-year colleges or universities supported by the state of Florida or St. Petersburg Junior College. Scholarships are renewable one time. *Award:* Scholarship for use in freshman, sophomore, junior, or senior year; renewable. *Award amount:* varies. *Number of awards:* 1–20. *Eligibility Requirements:* Applicant must be enrolled or expecting to enroll full-time at a two-year or four-year institution or university and studying in Florida. Applicant or parent of applicant must be member of National Association of Letter Carriers. Available to U.S. citizens. *Application Requirements:* Application, references, transcript. **Deadline:** June 1.

Contact Ann Porch, Membership Committee, National Association of Letter Carriers, 100 Indiana Avenue, NW, Washington, DC 20001-2144 USA. *E-mail:* nalcinf@nalc.org. *Phone:* 202-393-4695. *Fax:* 202-737-1540. *Web site:* http://www.nalc.org.

DC Leveraging Educational Assistance Partnership Program (LEAP). $250 to $1500 grants available to District of Columbia residents, who qualify for federal need-based aid and are enrolled in undergraduate programs, and pursuing a first baccalaureate degree. Must attend a Title IV eligible college or university at least half-time. *Award:* Grant for use in freshman, sophomore, junior, or senior year; renewable. *Award amount:* $250–$1500. *Number of awards:* up to 3200. *Eligibility Requirements:* Applicant must be enrolled or expecting to enroll full- or part-time at a two-year or four-year institution or university and resident of District of Columbia. Available to U.S. citizens. *Application Requirements:* Application, financial need analysis, transcript, Student Aid Report (SAR), FAFSA. **Deadline:** June 30.

Contact Ms. Rehva D. Jones, Director, Higher Education Financial Services and Preparatory Programs, District of Columbia Office of the State Superintendent, 810 First Street, NW, Washington, DC 20002. *E-mail:*

rehva.jones@dc.gov. *Phone:* 202-481-3948. *Fax:* 202-741-6491. *Web site:* http://www.osse.dc.gov.

Federal Cyber Service: Scholarship For Service (SFS) Program. This program provides scholarships that generally fund books, tuition, room and board, and a stipend while attending a participating institution in an Information Assurance program. Participants must apply directly to participating institutions. *Award:* Scholarship for use in junior, senior, graduate, or postgraduate years; not renewable. *Eligibility Requirements:* Applicant must be enrolled or expecting to enroll full-time at a four-year institution or university. Available to U.S. citizens. *Application Requirements:* Application, Will vary by participating institution.

Contact Kathy Roberson, Program Manager, National Science Foundation, Washington, DC 20415. *E-mail:* sfs@opm.gov. *Web site:* http://www.sfs.opm.gov.

Harry S. Truman Scholarship. Scholarships for U.S. citizens or U.S. nationals who are college or university students with junior-level academic standing and who wish to attend professional or graduate school to prepare for careers in government or the nonprofit and advocacy sectors. Candidates must be nominated by their institution. Public service and leadership record considered. Visit Web site http://www.truman.gov for further information and application. *Academic Fields/Career Goals:* Political Science; Public Policy and Administration. *Award:* Scholarship for use in junior year; renewable. *Award amount:* $30,000. *Number of awards:* 65. *Eligibility Requirements:* Applicant must be enrolled or expecting to enroll full-time at a four-year institution or university and must have an interest in leadership. Available to U.S. citizens. *Application Requirements:* Application, interview, references, policy proposal. **Deadline:** February 5.

Contact Tonji Wade, Program Officer, Harry S. Truman Scholarship Foundation, 712 Jackson Place, NW, Washington, DC 20006. *E-mail:* office@truman.gov. *Phone:* 202-395-4831. *Fax:* 202-395-6995. *Web site:* http://www.truman.gov.

Montgomery GI Bill (Active Duty) Chapter 30. Award provides up to thirty-six months of education benefits to eligible veterans for college, business school, technical courses, vocational courses, correspondence courses, apprenticeships/job training, or flight training. Must be an eligible veteran with an Honorable Discharge and have high school diploma or GED before applying for benefits. *Award:* Scholarship for use in freshman, sophomore, junior, senior, or graduate year; renewable. *Award amount:* $1101–$37,224. *Number of awards:* varies. *Eligibility Requirements:* Applicant must be enrolled or expecting to enroll full- or part-time at a two-year, four-year, or technical institution or university. Available to U.S. citizens. Applicant or parent must meet one or more of the following requirements: general military experience; retired from active duty; disabled or killed as a result of military service; prisoner of war; or missing in action. *Application Requirements:* Application, proof of active military service of at least 2 years. **Deadline:** continuous.

Contact Keith M. Wilson, Director, Education Service, Department of Veterans Affairs (VA), 810 Vermont Avenue, NW, Washington, DC 20420. *E-mail:* co225a@vba.va.gov. *Phone:* 202-273-7132. *Web site:* http://www.gibill.va.gov.

Montgomery GI Bill (Selected Reserve). Educational assistance program for members of the selected reserve of the Army, Navy, Air Force, Marine Corps and Coast Guard, as well as the Army and Air National Guard. Available to all reservists and National Guard personnel who commit to a six-year obligation, and remain in the Reserve or Guard during the six years. Award is renewable. Monthly benefit is $309 for up to thirty-six months for full-time. *Award:* Scholarship for use in freshman, sophomore, junior, senior, or postgraduate years; renewable. *Award amount:* up to $3708. *Number of awards:* varies. *Eligibility Requirements:* Applicant must be enrolled or expecting to enroll full- or part-time at a two-year, four-year, or technical institution or university. Available to U.S. citizens. Applicant or parent must meet one or more of the following requirements: general military experience; retired from active duty; disabled or killed as a result of military service; prisoner of war; or missing in action. *Application Requirements:* Application, proof of military service of six years in the reserve or guard. **Deadline:** continuous.

Contact Keith M. Wilson, Director, Education Service, Department of Veterans Affairs (VA), 810 Vermont Avenue, NW, Washington, DC 20420. *E-mail:* co225a@vba.va.gov. *Phone:* 202-273-7132. *Web site:* http://www.gibill.va.gov.

Reserve Education Assistance Program. The program provides educational assistance to members of National Guard and reserve components. Selected Reserve and Individual Ready Reserve (IRR) who are called or ordered to active duty service in response to a war or national emergency as declared by the president or Congress are eligible. For further information see Web site http://www.GIBILL.va.gov. *Award:* Scholarship for use in freshman, sophomore, junior, senior, graduate, or postgraduate years; renewable. *Award amount:* $215–$860. *Number of awards:* 1. *Eligibility Requirements:* Applicant must be enrolled or expecting to enroll full- or part-time at a two-year, four-year, or technical institution or university. Available to U.S. citizens. Applicant or parent must meet one or more of the following requirements: general military experience; retired from active duty; disabled or killed as a result of military service; prisoner of war; or missing in action. *Application Requirements:* Application. **Deadline:** continuous.

Contact Keith M. Wilson, Director, Education Service, Department of Veterans Affairs (VA), 810 Vermont Avenue, NW, Washington, DC 20420. *E-mail:* co225a@vba.va.gov. *Phone:* 202-273-7132. *Web site:* http://www.gibill.va.gov.

Survivors and Dependents Educational Assistance (Chapter 35)-VA. Monthly $860 benefits for up to 45 months. Must be spouses or children under age 26 of current veterans missing in action or of deceased or totally and permanently disabled (service-related) service persons. For more information visit the following Web site http://www.gibill.va.gov. *Award:* Scholarship for use in freshman, sophomore, junior, or senior year; renewable. *Award amount:* up to $10,320. *Number of awards:* 10,733. *Eligibility Requirements:* Applicant must be age 25 or under and enrolled or expecting to enroll full- or part-time at a two-year, four-year, or technical institution or university. Available to U.S. and non-U.S. citizens. Applicant or parent must meet one or more of the following requirements: general military experience; retired from active duty; disabled or killed as a result of military service; prisoner of war; or missing in action. *Application Requirements:* Application, proof of parent or spouse's qualifying service. **Deadline:** continuous.

Contact Keith M. Wilson, Director, Education Service, Department of Veterans Affairs (VA), 810 Vermont Avenue, NW, Washington, DC 20420. *E-mail:* co225a@vba.va.gov. *Phone:* 202-273-7132. *Web site:* http://www.gibill.va.gov.

FLORIDA

Access to Better Learning and Education Grant. Grant program provides tuition assistance to Florida undergraduate students enrolled in degree programs at eligible private Florida colleges or universities. Must be a U.S. citizen or eligible non-citizen and must meet Florida residency requirements. The participating institution determines application procedures, deadlines, and student eligibility. *Award:* Grant for use in freshman, sophomore, junior, or senior year; renewable. *Award amount:* up to $1182. *Number of awards:* varies. *Eligibility Requirements:* Applicant must be enrolled or expecting to enroll full-time at a four-year institution or university; resident of Florida and studying in Florida. Available to U.S. citizens. *Application Requirements:* Application.

Contact Customer Service, Florida State Department of Education, Talllahassee, FL 32399. *E-mail:* osfa@fldoe.org. *Phone:* 888-827-2007. *Web site:* http://www. floridastudentfinancialaid.org.

Critical Teacher Shortage Student Loan Forgiveness Program-Florida. Award program provides financial assistance to eligible Florida teachers who hold a valid Florida teachers certificate or Florida department of health license, by assisting them in the repayment of undergraduate and graduate educational loans that led to certification in a critical teacher shortage subject area. Must teach full-time at a publicly-funded school. *Academic Fields/Career Goals:* Education. *Award:* Forgivable loan for use in freshman, sophomore, junior, or senior year; renewable. *Award amount:* up to $10,000. *Number of awards:* varies. *Eligibility Requirements:* Applicant must be enrolled or expecting to enroll full- or part-time at a two-year or four-year institution or university and resident of Florida. Available to U.S. citizens. *Application Requirements:* Application, transcript. **Deadline:** July 15.

Contact Customer Service, Florida State Department of Education, Tallahassee, FL 32399. *E-mail:* osfa@fldoe.org. *Phone:* 888-827-2004. *Web site:* http://www. floridastudentfinancialaid.org.

First Generation Matching Grant Program. Need-based grants to Florida resident undergraduate students who are enrolled in state universities in Florida and whose parents have not earned baccalaureate degrees. Available state funds are contingent upon matching contributions from private sources on a dollar-for-dollar basis. *Award:* Grant for use in freshman, sophomore, junior, or senior year; renewable. *Award amount:* varies. *Number of awards:* varies. *Eligibility Requirements:* Applicant must be enrolled or expecting to enroll full- or part-time at a two-year institution

or university; resident of Florida and studying in Florida. Available to U.S. citizens. *Application Requirements:* Application, financial need analysis.

Contact Customer Service, Florida State Department of Education, Tallahassee, FL 32399. *E-mail:* osfa@fldoe.org. *Phone:* 888-828-2004. *Web site:* http://www. floridastudentfinancialaid.org.

Florida Bright Futures Scholarship Program. Three lottery-funded scholarships reward Florida high school graduates for high academic achievement. Program is comprised of the following three awards: Florida Academic Scholars Award, Florida Medallion Scholars Award and Florida Gold Seal Vocational Scholars Award. *Award:* Scholarship for use in freshman, sophomore, junior, or senior year; renewable. *Eligibility Requirements:* Applicant must be high school student; planning to enroll or expecting to enroll full- or part-time at a two-year, four-year, or technical institution or university; resident of Florida and studying in Florida. Applicant must have 3.0 GPA or higher. Available to U.S. citizens. *Application Requirements:* Application, test scores, transcript.

Contact Customer Service, Florida State Department of Education, Tallahassee, FL 32399. *E-mail:* osfa@fldoe.org. *Phone:* 888-827-2004. *Web site:* http://www. floridastudentfinancialaid.org.

Florida Postsecondary Student Assistance Grant. Scholarships to degree-seeking, resident, undergraduate students who demonstrate substantial financial need and are enrolled in eligible degree-granting private colleges and universities not eligible under the Florida Private Student Assistance Grant. FSAG is a decentralized program, and each participating institution determines application procedures, deadlines and student eligibility. Number of awards varies. *Award:* Grant for use in freshman, sophomore, junior, or senior year; renewable. *Award amount:* $200–$1916. *Number of awards:* varies. *Eligibility Requirements:* Applicant must be enrolled or expecting to enroll full-time at a two-year or four-year institution or university; resident of Florida and studying in Florida. Available to U.S. citizens. *Application Requirements:* Application, financial need analysis.

Contact Customer Service, Florida State Department of Education, Tallahassee, FL 32399. *E-mail:* osfa@fldoe.org. *Phone:* 888-827-2004. *Web site:* http://www. floridastudentfinancialaid.org.

Florida Private Student Assistance Grant. Grants for Florida residents who are U.S. citizens or eligible non-citizens

attending eligible private, nonprofit, four-year colleges and universities in Florida. Must be a full-time student and demonstrate substantial financial need. For renewal, must have earned a minimum cumulative GPA of 2.0 at the last institution attended. *Award:* Grant for use in freshman, sophomore, junior, or senior year; renewable. *Award amount:* $200–$2069. *Number of awards:* varies. *Eligibility Requirements:* Applicant must be enrolled or expecting to enroll full-time at a four-year institution or university; resident of Florida and studying in Florida. Available to U.S. citizens. *Application Requirements:* Application, financial need analysis.

Contact Customer Service, Florida State Department of Education, Tallahassee, FL 32399. *E-mail:* osfa@fldoe.org. *Phone:* 888-827-2004. *Web site:* http://www. floridastudentfinancialaid.org.

Florida Public Student Assistance Grant. Grants for Florida residents, U.S. citizens or eligible non-citizens who attend state universities and public community colleges. For renewal, must have earned a minimum cumulative GPA of 2.0 at the last institution attended. Students with documented disabilities are able to qualify for part-time status. *Award:* Grant for use in freshman, sophomore, junior, or senior year; renewable. *Award amount:* $200–$2069. *Number of awards:* varies. *Eligibility Requirements:* Applicant must be enrolled or expecting to enroll full- or part-time at a two-year or four-year institution or university; resident of Florida and studying in Florida. Available to U.S. citizens. *Application Requirements:* Application, financial need analysis.

Contact Customer Service, Florida State Department of Education, Tallahassee, FL 32399. *E-mail:* osfa@fldoe.org. *Phone:* 888-827-2004. *Web site:* http://www. floridastudentfinancialaid.org.

Florida Student Assistance Grant-Career Education. Need-based grant program available to Florida residents enrolled in certificate programs of 450 or more clock hours at participating community colleges or career centers operated by district school boards. FSAG-CE is a decentralized state of Florida program, which means that each participating institution determines application procedures, deadlines, student eligibility, and award amounts. *Award:* Grant for use in freshman, sophomore, junior, or senior year; renewable. *Award amount:* $200–$1916. *Eligibility Requirements:* Applicant must be enrolled or expecting to enroll full- or part-time at a two-year or technical institution; resident of Florida and studying in Florida. Available to U.S. citizens. *Application Requirements:* Application, financial need analysis.

Contact Customer Service, Florida State Department of Education, Tallahassee, FL 32399. *E-mail:* osfa@fldoe.org. *Phone:* 888-847-2004. *Web site:* http://www.floridastudentfinancialaid.org.

Florida Work Experience Program. Need-based program providing eligible Florida students work experiences that will complement and reinforce their educational and career goals. Must maintain GPA of 2.0. Postsecondary institution will determine applicant's eligibility, number of hours to be worked per week, and the award amount. *Award:* Grant for use in freshman, sophomore, junior, or senior year; renewable. *Award amount:* varies. *Number of awards:* varies. *Eligibility Requirements:* Applicant must be enrolled or expecting to enroll full- or part-time at a two-year or four-year institution or university; resident of Florida and studying in Florida. Available to U.S. citizens. *Application Requirements:* Application, financial need analysis.

Contact Customer Service, Florida State Department of Education, Tallahassee, FL 32399. *E-mail:* osfa@fldoe.com. *Phone:* 888-827-2004. *Web site:* http://www.floridastudentfinancialaid.org.

Jose Marti Scholarship Challenge Grant Fund. Award available to Hispanic-American students who were born in, or whose parent was born in a Hispanic country. Must have lived in Florida for one year, be enrolled full-time in Florida at an eligible school, and have a GPA of 3.0 or above. Must be U.S. citizen or eligible non-citizen. FAFSA must be processed by May 15. For more information, visit Web site http://www.floridastudentfinancialaid.org/ssfad/home/applyhere.htm. *Award:* Scholarship for use in freshman, sophomore, junior, or senior year; renewable. *Award amount:* $2000. *Number of awards:* varies. *Eligibility Requirements:* Applicant must be of Hispanic heritage; high school student; planning to enroll or expecting to enroll full-time at a two-year or four-year institution or university; resident of Florida and studying in Florida. Applicant must have 3.0 GPA or higher. Available to U.S. citizens. *Application Requirements:* Application, financial need analysis. **Deadline:** April 1.

Contact Customer Service, Florida State Department of Education, Tallahassee, FL 32303. *E-mail:* osfa@fldoe.org. *Phone:* 888-827-2004. *Web site:* http://www.floridastudentfinancialaid.org.

Mary McLeod Bethune Scholarship. Renewable award to Florida students with a GPA of 3.0 or above, who will attend Bethune-Cookman College, Edward Waters College, Florida A&M University, or Florida Memorial University. Must not have previously received a baccalaureate degree. Must demonstrate financial need as specified by the institution. *Award:* Scholarship for use in freshman, sophomore, junior, or senior year; renewable. *Award amount:* $3000. *Number of awards:* varies. *Eligibility Requirements:* Applicant must be enrolled or expecting to enroll full-time at a four-year institution or university; resident of Florida and studying in Florida. Applicant must have 3.0 GPA or higher. Available to U.S. citizens. *Application Requirements:* Application, financial need analysis.

Contact Customer Service, Florida State Department of Education, Tallahassee, FL 32399. *E-mail:* osfa@fldoe.org. *Phone:* 888-827-2004. *Web site:* http://www.floridastudentfinancialaid.org.

Robert C. Byrd Honors Scholarship-Florida. One applicant per Florida high school may be nominated by the high school principal or designee by May 15. Must be U.S. citizen or eligible non-citizen and Florida resident. Application must be submitted in the same year as graduation. Must meet selective service system registration requirements. May attend any postsecondary accredited institution. *Award:* Scholarship for use in freshman, sophomore, junior, or senior year; renewable. *Award amount:* $1500. *Eligibility Requirements:* Applicant must be high school student; planning to enroll or expecting to enroll full-time at a two-year, four-year, or technical institution or university and resident of Florida. Applicant must have 3.5 GPA or higher. Available to U.S. citizens. *Application Requirements:* Application, references, test scores, transcript. **Deadline:** April 15.

Contact Customer Service, Florida State Department of Education, Tallahassee, FL 32399. *E-mail:* osfa@fldoe.org. *Phone:* 888-827-2004. *Web site:* http://www.floridastudentfinancialaid.org.

Rosewood Family Scholarship Fund. Renewable award for eligible direct descendants of African-American Rosewood families affected by the incident of January 1923. Must not have previously received a baccalaureate degree. *Award:* Scholarship for use in freshman, sophomore, junior, or senior year; renewable. *Award amount:* up to $4000. *Number of awards:* up to 25. *Eligibility Requirements:* Applicant must be enrolled or expecting to enroll full-time

at a two-year, four-year, or technical institution or university and studying in Florida. Available to U.S. citizens. *Application Requirements:* Application, financial need analysis. **Deadline:** April 1.

Contact Customer Service, Florida State Department of Education, Tallahassee, FL 32399. *E-mail:* osfa@fldoe.org. *Phone:* 888-827-2004. *Web site:* http://www.floridastudentfinancialaid.org.

Scholarships for Children & Spouses of Deceased or Disabled Veterans or Servicemembers. Renewable scholarships for children and spouses of deceased or disabled veterans and service members. Children must be between the ages of 16 and 22, and attend an eligible Florida public, nonpublic postsecondary institution or enrolled part-time. Must ensure that the Florida Department of Veterans Affairs certifies the applicants eligibility. Must maintain GPA of 2.0. *Award:* Scholarship for use in freshman, sophomore, junior, or senior year; renewable. *Award amount:* varies. *Number of awards:* varies. *Eligibility Requirements:* Applicant must be age 16-22; enrolled or expecting to enroll full- or part-time at a two-year, four-year, or technical institution or university; resident of Florida and studying in Florida. Available to U.S. citizens. Applicant or parent must meet one or more of the following requirements: general military experience; retired from active duty; disabled or killed as a result of military service; prisoner of war; or missing in action. *Application Requirements:* Application. **Deadline:** April 1.

Contact Customer Service, Florida State Department of Education, Tallahassee, FL 32399. *Phone:* 888-827-2004. *Web site:* http://www.floridastudentfinancialaid.org.

William L. Boyd IV Florida Resident Access Grant. Renewable awards to Florida undergraduate students attending an eligible private, nonprofit Florida college or university. Postsecondary institution will determine applicant's eligibility. Renewal applicant must have earned a minimum institutional GPA of 2.0. *Award:* Grant for use in freshman, sophomore, junior, or senior year; renewable. *Award amount:* up to $2837. *Number of awards:* varies. *Eligibility Requirements:* Applicant must be enrolled or expecting to enroll full-time at a four-year institution or university; resident of Florida and studying in Florida. Available to U.S. citizens. *Application Requirements:* Application.

Contact Customer Service, Florida State Department of Education, Tallahassee, FL 32399. *E-mail:* osfa@fldoe.org. *Phone:* 888-

827-2004. *Web site:* http://www. floridastudentfinancialaid.org.

GEORGIA

American Indian Nurse Scholarship Awards. Renewable award of $500 to $1000. Currently able to fund between 10 and 15 students. Intended originally to benefit females only, the program has expanded to include males and the career goals now include not only nursing careers, but jobs in health care and health education, as well. *Academic Fields/Career Goals:* Health Administration; Nursing. *Award:* Scholarship for use in freshman, sophomore, junior, senior, graduate, or postgraduate years; renewable. *Award amount:* $500–$1000. *Number of awards:* 10–15. *Eligibility Requirements:* Applicant must be American Indian/Alaska Native and enrolled or expecting to enroll full-time at a two-year, four-year, or technical institution or university. Applicant must have 2.5 GPA or higher. Available to U.S. citizens. *Application Requirements:* Application, autobiography, financial need analysis, photo, references, transcript. **Deadline:** continuous.

Contact Mrs. Joe Calvin, Scholarship Awards Consultant, National Society of The Colonial Dames of America, Nine Cross Creek Drive, Birmingham, AL 35213. *E-mail:* info@ nscda.org. *Phone:* 205-871-4072. *Web site:* http://www.nscda.org.

Georgia HOPE Scholarship Program. Scholarship and Grant program for Georgia residents who are college undergraduates to attend an accredited two or four-year Georgia institution. Pays actual undergraduate tuition charged at public postsecondary institutions plus mandatory fees as capped in 2004 plus a $300 per year book allowance. At private postsecondary institutions in Georgia, students may receive up to $3500 per year for full-time study or $1750 per year for part-time. Minimum 3.0 GPA required. Renewable if student maintains grades. Write for deadlines. *Award:* Scholarship for use in freshman, sophomore, junior, or senior year; renewable. *Award amount:* up to $6000. *Number of awards:* 200,000–230,000. *Eligibility Requirements:* Applicant must be enrolled or expecting to enroll full- or part-time at a two-year or four-year institution or university; resident of Georgia and studying in Georgia. Applicant must have 3.0 GPA or higher. Available to U.S. citizens. *Application Requirements:* Application, high schools must report transcripts to GSFC. **Deadline:** continuous.

Contact Tracy Ireland, Vice President, Georgia Student Finance Commission, 2082 East Exchange Place, Suite 100, Tucker, GA 30084. *E-mail:* tracyi@gsfc.org. *Phone:* 800-505-4732. *Web site:* http://www.GAcollege411. org.

Georgia Leveraging Educational Assistance Partnership Grant Program. Awards based on financial need. Recipients must be eligible for the Federal Pell Grant. Renewable award for Georgia residents enrolled in a state postsecondary institution. Must be U.S. citizen. *Award:* Grant for use in freshman, sophomore, junior, or senior year; renewable. *Award amount:* $300–$2000. *Number of awards:* 2500–3000. *Eligibility Requirements:* Applicant must be enrolled or expecting to enroll full- or part-time at a two-year, four-year, or technical institution or university; resident of Georgia and studying in Georgia. Available to U.S. citizens. *Application Requirements:* Application, financial need analysis. **Deadline:** continuous.

Contact Mr. Tracy A. Ireland, Vice President, Financial Aid Operations, Georgia Student Finance Commission, 2082 East Exchange Place, Suite 100, Tucker, GA 30084. *E-mail:* tracyi@gsfc.org. *Phone:* 770-724-9066. *Web site:* http://www.GAcollege411.org.

Georgia National Guard Service Cancelable Loan Program. Forgivable loans will be awarded to residents of Georgia maintaining good military standing as an eligible member of the Georgia National Guard who are enrolled at least half-time in an undergraduate degree program at an eligible college, university or technical school within the state of Georgia. *Award:* Forgivable loan for use in freshman, sophomore, junior, or senior year; not renewable. *Award amount:* $150–$1821. *Number of awards:* 200–250. *Eligibility Requirements:* Applicant must be enrolled or expecting to enroll full- or part-time at a two-year, four-year, or technical institution or university; resident of Georgia and studying in Georgia. Available to U.S. citizens. Applicant or parent must meet one or more of the following requirements: Air Force National Guard or Army National Guard experience; retired from active duty; disabled or killed as a result of military service; prisoner of war; or missing in action. *Application Requirements:* Application, financial need analysis. **Deadline:** June 4.

Contact Ms. Caylee French, AVP, Financial Aid Operations, Georgia Student Finance Commission, 2082 East Exchange Place, Tucker, GA 30084. *E-mail:* cayleef@gsfc. org. *Phone:* 770-724-9244. *Fax:* 770-724-9205. *Web site:* http://www.GAcollege411. org.

Georgia Public Safety Memorial Grant. Award for children of Georgia law enforcement officers, prison guards, or fire fighters killed or permanently disabled in the line of duty. Must attend an accredited postsecondary Georgia school. Complete the Law Enforcement Personnel Dependents application. *Award:* Grant for use in freshman, sophomore, junior, or senior year; not renewable. *Award amount:* $2000. *Number of awards:* 20–40. *Eligibility Requirements:* Applicant must be enrolled or expecting to enroll full-time at a two-year, four-year, or technical institution or university; resident of Georgia and studying in Georgia. Available to U.S. citizens. *Application Requirements:* Application, selective service registration. **Deadline:** continuous.

Contact Tracy Ireland, Vice President, Georgia Student Finance Commission, 2082 East Exchange Place, Suite 100, Tucker, GA 30084. *E-mail:* tracyi@gsfc.org. *Phone:* 770-724-9066. *Web site:* http://www.GAcollege411. org.

Georgia Tuition Equalization Grant (GTEG). Award for Georgia residents pursuing undergraduate study at an accredited two- or four-year Georgia private postsecondary institution. Also available to residents of Georgia who live near the State borders to attend certain four-year public colleges out-of-state. *Award:* Grant for use in freshman, sophomore, junior, or senior year; renewable. *Award amount:* $750. *Number of awards:* 1–35,000. *Eligibility Requirements:* Applicant must be enrolled or expecting to enroll full-time at a two-year or four-year institution or university; resident of Georgia and studying in Alabama, Florida, Georgia, South Carolina, or Tennessee. Available to U.S. citizens. *Application Requirements:* Application, social security number. **Deadline:** continuous.

Contact Tracy Ireland, Vice President, Georgia Student Finance Commission, 2082 East Exchange Place, Suite 100, Tucker, GA 30084. *E-mail:* tracyi@gsfc.org. *Phone:* 800-505-4732. *Web site:* http://www.GAcollege411. org.

Service-Cancelable Loans–Georgia. Scholarship assists Georgia students enrolled in critical fields of study in allied health. For use at GSFA-approved schools. Awards $4500 forgivable loan for dentistry students only. Contact school financial aid officer for more details. *Academic Fields/Career Goals:* Dental Health/Services; Health and Medical Sciences; Nursing; Therapy/ Rehabilitation. *Award:* Forgivable loan for use in freshman, sophomore, junior, or senior year; not renewable. *Award amount:* $2000–$4500. *Number of awards:* 500–1200. *Eligibility Requirements:* Applicant must be enrolled or expecting to enroll full- or part-time at a two-year, four-year, or technical institution or university; resident of Georgia and studying in Georgia. Available to U.S. citizens. *Application Requirements:* Application, financial need analysis. **Deadline:** continuous.

Contact Ms. Caylee French, AVP, Financial Aid Operations, Georgia Student Finance Commission, 2082 East Exchange Place, Tucker, GA 30084. *E-mail:* cayleef@gsfc. org. *Phone:* 770-724-9244. *Fax:* 770-724-9205. *Web site:* http://www.GAcollege411. org.

HAWAII

Hawaii State Student Incentive Grant. Grants are given to residents of Hawaii who are enrolled in a participating Hawaiian state school. Funds are for undergraduate tuition only. Applicants must submit a financial need analysis. *Award:* Grant for use in freshman, sophomore, junior, or senior year; renewable. *Award amount:* $200–$2000. *Number of awards:* 470. *Eligibility Requirements:* Applicant must be enrolled or expecting to enroll full- or part-time at a two-year, four-year, or technical institution or university; resident of Hawaii and studying in Hawaii. Available to U.S. citizens. *Application Requirements:* Application, financial need analysis. **Deadline:** continuous.

Contact Janine Oyama, Financial Aid Specialist, Hawaii State Postsecondary Education Commission, University of Hawaii, Honolulu, HI 96822. *Phone:* 808-956-6066.

IDAHO

Freedom Scholarship. Full tuition, room and board scholarship and up to $500 for books per semester for children of Idaho citizens determined by the federal government to have been prisoners of war, missing in action, or killed in action or died of injuries or wounds sustained in action in southeast Asia, including Korea, or who shall become so hereafter, in any area of armed conflicts. Applicant must attend an Idaho public college or university and meet all requirements for regular admission. The award value and the number of awards granted varies. For additional information, see Web site http://www.boardofed.idaho. gov/scholarships/. *Award:* Scholarship for use in freshman, sophomore, junior, or senior year; not renewable. *Award amount:* varies. *Number of awards:* varies. *Eligibil-*

ity Requirements: Applicant must be enrolled or expecting to enroll full- or part-time at a two-year, four-year, or technical institution or university; resident of Idaho and studying in Idaho. Available to U.S. citizens. Applicant or parent must meet one or more of the following requirements: general military experience; retired from active duty; disabled or killed as a result of military service; prisoner of war; or missing in action. *Application Requirements:* Application. **Deadline:** January 15.

Contact Dana Kelly, Program Manager, Idaho State Board of Education, PO Box 83720, Boise, ID 83720-0037. *E-mail:* dana. kelly@osbe.idaho.gov. *Phone:* 208-332-1574. *Web site:* http://www.boardofed.idaho.gov.

Idaho Minority and "At Risk"; Student Scholarship. Renewable award for Idaho residents who are disabled or members of a minority group and have financial need. Must attend one of eight postsecondary institutions in the state for undergraduate study. Deadlines vary by institution. Must be a U.S. citizen and be a graduate of an Idaho high school. Contact college financial aid office. The awards range up to $3000 a year for a maximum of four years. For additional information, go to Web site http://www.boardofed.idaho.gov/ scholarships/. *Award:* Scholarship for use in freshman, sophomore, junior, or senior year; renewable. *Award amount:* up to $3000. *Number of awards:* 35–40. *Eligibility Requirements:* Applicant must be American Indian/Alaska Native, Black (non-Hispanic), or Hispanic; enrolled or expecting to enroll full-time at a two-year, four-year, or technical institution or university; resident of Idaho and studying in Idaho. Applicant must be hearing impaired, physically disabled, or visually impaired. Available to U.S. citizens. *Application Requirements:* Application, financial need analysis, transcript. **Deadline:** varies.

Contact Dana Kelly, Program Manager, Idaho State Board of Education, PO Box 83720, Boise, ID 83720-0037. *E-mail:* dana. kelly@osbe.idaho.gov. *Phone:* 208-332-1574. *Web site:* http://www.boardofed.idaho.gov.

Idaho Promise Category A Scholarship Program. Renewable award available to Idaho residents who are graduating high school seniors. Must attend an approved Idaho institution of higher education on full-time basis and be enrolled in an eligible program. Must have a minimum GPA of 3.5 and an ACT score of 28 or above if enrolling in an academic program, and a GPA of 2.8 and must take the COMPASS test if enrolling in a professional-technical program. For additional information, list

of eligible programs, and application, go to Web site http://www.boardofed.idaho. gov/scholarships/. *Award:* Scholarship for use in freshman year; renewable. *Award amount:* $3000. *Number of awards:* 25. *Eligibility Requirements:* Applicant must be high school student; planning to enroll or expecting to enroll full-time at a two-year, four-year, or technical institution or university; resident of Idaho and studying in Idaho. Available to U.S. citizens. *Application Requirements:* Application, applicant must enter a contest, test scores. **Deadline:** January 15.

Contact Dana Kelly, Program Manager, Student Affairs, Idaho State Board of Education, PO Box 83720, Boise, ID 83720-0037 USA. *E-mail:* dana.kelly@osbe.idaho.gov. *Phone:* 208-332-1574. *Fax:* 208-334-2632. *Web site:* http://www.boardofed.idaho.gov.

Idaho Promise Category B Scholarship Program. Available to Idaho residents entering college for the first time prior to the age of 22. Must have completed high school or its equivalent in Idaho and have a minimum GPA of 3.0 or an ACT score of 20 or higher. Scholarship limited to four semesters. Please go to Web site for complete information http://www.boardofed. idaho.gov/scholarships/. *Award:* Scholarship for use in freshman year; renewable. *Award amount:* up to $600. *Number of awards:* varies. *Eligibility Requirements:* Applicant must be high school student; age 22 or under; planning to enroll or expecting to enroll full-time at a two-year, four-year, or technical institution or university; resident of Idaho and studying in Idaho. Applicant must have 3.0 GPA or higher. Available to U.S. citizens. *Application Requirements:* Application, transcript. **Deadline:** continuous.

Contact Dana Kelly, Program Manager, Idaho State Board of Education, PO Box 83720, Boise, ID 83720-0037. *E-mail:* dana. kelly@osbe.idaho.gov. *Phone:* 208-332-1574. *Fax:* 208-334-2632. *Web site:* http://www. boardofed.idaho.gov.

Leveraging Educational Assistance State Partnership Program (LEAP). One-time award assists students from any state, attending participating Idaho trade schools, colleges, and universities, and majoring in any field except theology or divinity. Must be enrolled for at least six credits and show financial need. Must be U.S. citizen or permanent resident. Deadlines vary by institution. For a list of eligible institutions, go to Web site http://www.boardofed. idaho.gov/scholarships/. *Award:* Grant for use in freshman, sophomore, junior, or senior year; not renewable. *Award amount:*

$400–$5000. *Number of awards:* varies. *Eligibility Requirements:* Applicant must be enrolled or expecting to enroll full- or part-time at a two-year, four-year, or technical institution or university and studying in Idaho. Available to U.S. citizens. *Application Requirements:* Application, financial need analysis, self-addressed stamped envelope. **Deadline:** varies.

Contact Dana Kelly, Student Affairs, Idaho State Board of Education, PO Box 83720, Boise, ID 83720-0037. *Phone:* 208-332-1574. *Fax:* 208-334-2632. *Web site:* http://www.boardofed.idaho.gov.

Public Safety Officer Dependent Scholarship. Scholarship for dependents of full-time Idaho public safety officers who were killed or disabled in the line of duty. Recipients will attend an Idaho postsecondary institution with a full waiver of fees, including tuition, on-campus housing and campus meal plan, and up to $500 per semester for books and supplies. For complete information, see Web site http://www.boardofed.idaho.gov/scholarships/. *Award:* Scholarship for use in freshman year; renewable. *Number of awards:* varies. *Eligibility Requirements:* Applicant must be enrolled or expecting to enroll full- or part-time at a two-year or four-year institution or university; resident of Idaho and studying in Idaho. Applicant or parent of applicant must have employment or volunteer experience in police/firefighting. Available to U.S. citizens. *Application Requirements:* Application. **Deadline:** January 15.

Contact Dana Kelly, Program Manager, Idaho State Board of Education, PO Box 83720, Boise, ID 83720-0037. *E-mail:* dana.kelly@osbe.idaho.gov. *Phone:* 208-332-1574. *Web site:* http://www.boardofed.idaho.gov.

ILLINOIS

Brill Family Scholarship. One $1000 award available to an upper-level female undergraduate majoring in aerospace or biomedical engineering. *Award:* Scholarship for use in sophomore, junior, or senior year; not renewable. *Award amount:* $1000. *Number of awards:* 1. *Eligibility Requirements:* Applicant must be enrolled or expecting to enroll full-time at a four-year institution or university and female. Applicant must have 3.0 GPA or higher. *Application Requirements:* **Deadline:** February 15.

Contact Scholarship Committee, Society of Women Engineers, 120 South La Salle Street, Suite 1515, Chicago, IL 60603. *E-mail:* scholarshipapplication@swe.org. *Phone:* 312-596-5223. *Fax:* 312-596-5252. *Web site:* http://www.swe.org.

Golden Apple Scholars of Illinois. Applicants must be between the ages of 16 and 21 and maintain a GPA of 2.5. Eligible applicants must be residents of Illinois studying in Illinois. Recipients must agree to teach in high-need Illinois schools. *Academic Fields/Career Goals:* Education. *Award:* Scholarship for use in freshman, sophomore, junior, or senior year; renewable. *Award amount:* $23,000. *Number of awards:* 100–150. *Eligibility Requirements:* Applicant must be age 16-21; enrolled or expecting to enroll full-time at a four-year institution or university; resident of Illinois and studying in Illinois. Available to U.S. citizens. *Application Requirements:* Application, driver's license, essay, interview, photo, references, test scores, transcript, Social Security card. **Deadline:** November 15.

Contact Ms. Patricia Kilduff, Director of Recruitment and Placement, Golden Apple Foundation, 8 South Michigan Avenue, Suite 700, Chicago, IL 60603-3318. *E-mail:* kilduff@goldenapple.org. *Phone:* 312-407-0006 Ext. 105. *Fax:* 312-407-0344. *Web site:* http://www.goldenapple.org.

Grant Program for Dependents of Police, Fire, or Correctional Officers. Awards available to Illinois residents who are dependents of police, fire, and correctional officers killed or disabled in line of duty. Provides for tuition and fees at approved Illinois institutions. Number of grants and individual dollar amount awarded vary. *Award:* Grant for use in freshman, sophomore, junior, senior, graduate, or postgraduate years; renewable. *Award amount:* varies. *Number of awards:* varies. *Eligibility Requirements:* Applicant must be enrolled or expecting to enroll full- or part-time at a two-year, four-year, or technical institution or university; resident of Illinois and studying in Illinois. Available to U.S. citizens. *Application Requirements:* Application, proof of status. **Deadline:** varies.

Contact College Zone Counselor, Illinois Student Assistance Commission (ISAC), 1755 Lake Cook Road, Deerfield, IL 60015-5209. *E-mail:* collegezone@isac.org. *Phone:* 800-899-4722. *Fax:* 847-831-8549. *Web site:* http://www.collegezone.org.

Higher Education License Plate Program-HELP. Grants for students who attend Illinois colleges for which the special collegiate license plates are available. The Illinois Secretary of State issues the license plates, and part of the proceeds are used for grants for undergraduate students attending these colleges, to pay tuition and mandatory fees. *Award:* Grant for use in freshman, sophomore, junior, or senior year; not renewable. *Award amount:* varies. *Number of awards:* varies. *Eligibility Requirements:* Applicant must be enrolled or expecting to enroll full- or part-time at a two-year or four-year institution or university; resident of Illinois and studying in Illinois. Available to U.S. citizens. *Application Requirements:* Application, financial need analysis. **Deadline:** varies.

Contact College Zone Counselor, Illinois Student Assistance Commission (ISAC), 1755 Lake Cook Road, Deerfield, IL 60015-5209. *E-mail:* collegezone@isac.org. *Phone:* 800-899-4722. *Fax:* 847-831-8549. *Web site:* http://www.collegezone.org.

Illinois College Savings Bond Bonus Incentive Grant Program. Program offers Illinois college savings bond holders a grant for each year of bond maturity payable upon bond redemption if at least 70 percent of proceeds are used to attend college in Illinois. The amount of grant will depend on the amount of the bond, ranging from a $40 to $440 grant per $5000 of the bond. Applications are accepted between August 1 and May 30 of the academic year in which the bonds matured, or in the academic year immediately following maturity. *Award:* Grant for use in freshman, sophomore, junior, senior, graduate, or postgraduate years; not renewable. *Number of awards:* varies. *Eligibility Requirements:* Applicant must be enrolled or expecting to enroll full- or part-time at a two-year, four-year, or technical institution or university and studying in Illinois. Available to U.S. citizens. *Application Requirements:* Application. **Deadline:** varies.

Contact College Zone Counselor, Illinois Student Assistance Commission (ISAC), 1755 Lake Cook Road, Deerfield, IL 60015-5209. *E-mail:* collegezone@isac.org. *Phone:* 800-899-4722. *Fax:* 847-831-8549. *Web site:* http://www.collegezone.org.

Illinois Future Teachers Corps Program. Scholarships are available for students planning to become teachers in Illinois. Students must be Illinois residents, enrolled or accepted as a junior or above in a Teacher Education Program at an Illinois college or university. By receiving the award, students agree to teach for five years at either a public, private, or parochial Illinois preschool, or at a public elementary or secondary school. *Academic Fields/Career Goals:* Education. *Award:* Scholarship for use in junior, senior, or graduate year; renewable. *Award amount:* $5000–$10,000. *Eligibility Requirements:* Applicant must be enrolled or expecting to enroll full- or part-time at a four-year institution or university; resident of Illinois and studying in Illinois. Available to U.S. citizens. *Application Requirements:* Application, financial need analysis, FAFSA. **Deadline:** March 1.

Contact College Zone Counselor, Illinois Student Assistance Commission (ISAC), 1755 Lake Cook Road, Deerfield, IL 60015-5209. *E-mail:* collegezone@isac.org. *Phone:* 800-899-4722. *Fax:* 847-831-8549. *Web site:* http://www.collegezone.org.

Illinois General Assembly Scholarship. Scholarships available for Illinois students enrolled at an Illinois four-year state-supported college. Must contact the general assembly member for eligibility criteria. Deadline varies. *Award:* Scholarship for use in freshman, sophomore, junior, or senior year; not renewable. *Award amount:* varies. *Number of awards:* varies. *Eligibility Requirements:* Applicant must be enrolled or expecting to enroll full- or part-time at a four-year institution or university; resident of Illinois and studying in Illinois. Available to U.S. citizens. *Application Requirements:* Application. **Deadline:** varies.

Contact College Zone Counselor, Illinois Student Assistance Commission (ISAC), 1755 Lake Cook Road, Deerfield, IL 60015-5209. *E-mail:* collegezone@isac.org. *Phone:* 800-899-4722. *Fax:* 847-831-8549. *Web site:* http://www.collegezone.org.

Illinois Monetary Award Program. Awards to Illinois residents enrolled in a minimum of 3 hours per term in a degree program at an approved Illinois institution. See Web site for complete list of participating schools. Must demonstrate financial need, based on the information provided on the Free Application for Federal Student Aid. Number of grants and the individual dollar amount awarded vary. Deadline: As soon as possible after January 1 of the year in which the student will enter college. *Award:* Grant for use in freshman, sophomore, junior, or senior year; renewable. *Award amount:* $2637. *Eligibility Requirements:* Applicant must be enrolled or expecting to enroll full- or part-time at a two-year, four-year, or technical institution or university; resident of Illinois and studying in Illinois. Available to U.S. citizens. *Application Requirements:* Financial need analysis, FAFSA online. **Deadline:** varies.

Contact College Zone Counselor, Illinois Student Assistance Commission (ISAC), 1755 Lake Cook Road, Deerfield, IL 60015-5209. *E-mail:* collegezone@isac.org. *Phone:* 800-899-4722. *Fax:* 847-831-8549. *Web site:* http://www.collegezone.org.

Illinois National Guard Grant Program. Active duty members of the Illinois National Guard, or who are within 12 months of discharge, and who have completed one full year of service are eligible. May be used for study at Illinois two- or four-year public colleges for a maximum of the equivalent of four academic years of full-time enrollment. Deadlines: October 1 of the academic year for full year, March 1 for second/third term, or June 15 for the summer term. *Award:* Grant for use in freshman, sophomore, junior, senior, or graduate year; renewable. *Award amount:* varies. *Number of awards:* varies. *Eligibility Requirements:* Applicant must be enrolled or expecting to enroll full- or part-time at a two-year or four-year institution or university; resident of Illinois and studying in Illinois. Available to U.S. citizens. Applicant or parent must meet one or more of the following requirements: Air Force National Guard or Army National Guard experience; retired from active duty; disabled or killed as a result of military service; prisoner of war; or missing in action. *Application Requirements:* Application, documentation of service. **Deadline:** varies.

Contact College Zone Counselor, Illinois Student Assistance Commission (ISAC), 1755 Lake Cook Road, Deerfield, IL 60015-5209. *E-mail:* collegezone@isac.org. *Phone:* 800-899-4722. *Fax:* 847-831-8549. *Web site:* http://www.collegezone.org.

Illinois Special Education Teacher Tuition Waiver. Teachers or students who are pursuing a career in special education as public, private or parochial preschool, elementary or secondary school teachers in Illinois may be eligible for this program. This program will exempt such individuals from paying tuition and mandatory fees at an eligible institution, for up to four years. The individual dollar amount awarded are subject to sufficient annual appropriations by the Illinois General Assembly. *Academic Fields/Career Goals:* Special Education. *Award:* Scholarship for use in freshman, sophomore, junior, senior, or graduate year; renewable. *Award amount:* varies. *Eligibility Requirements:* Applicant must be enrolled or expecting to enroll full- or part-time at a four-year institution or university; resident of Illinois and studying in Illinois. Available to U.S. citizens. *Application Requirements:* Application. **Deadline:** March 1.

Contact College Zone Counselor, Illinois Student Assistance Commission (ISAC), 1755 Lake Cook Road, Deerfield, IL 60015-5209. *E-mail:* collegezone@isac.org. *Phone:* 800-

899-4722. *Fax:* 847-831-8549. *Web site:* http://www.collegezone.org.

Illinois Student-to-Student Program of Matching Grants. Matching grant is available to undergraduates at participating state-supported colleges. Number of grants and the individual dollar amount awarded vary. Contact financial aid office at institution. *Award:* Grant for use in freshman, sophomore, junior, or senior year; not renewable. *Award amount:* $300–$1000. *Number of awards:* varies. *Eligibility Requirements:* Applicant must be enrolled or expecting to enroll full- or part-time at a two-year or four-year institution or university; resident of Illinois and studying in Illinois. Available to U.S. citizens. *Application Requirements:* Application, financial need analysis. **Deadline:** varies.

Contact College Zone Counselor, Illinois Student Assistance Commission (ISAC), 1755 Lake Cook Road, Deerfield, IL 60015-5209. *E-mail:* collegezone@isac.org. *Phone:* 800-899-4722. *Fax:* 847-831-8549. *Web site:* http://www.collegezone.org.

Illinois Veteran Grant Program-IVG. Awards qualified veterans and pays eligible tuition and fees for study in Illinois public universities or community colleges. Program eligibility units are based on the enrolled hours for a particular term, not the dollar amount of the benefits paid. Applications are available at college financial aid office and can be submitted any time during the academic year for which assistance is being requested. *Award:* Grant for use in freshman, sophomore, junior, senior, or graduate year; renewable. *Eligibility Requirements:* Applicant must be enrolled or expecting to enroll full- or part-time at a two-year or four-year institution or university; resident of Illinois and studying in Illinois. Available to U.S. citizens. Applicant or parent must meet one or more of the following requirements: general military experience; retired from active duty; disabled or killed as a result of military service; prisoner of war; or missing in action. *Application Requirements:* Application. **Deadline:** continuous.

Contact College Zone Counselor, Illinois Student Assistance Commission (ISAC), 1755 Lake Cook Road, Deerfield, IL 60015-5209. *E-mail:* collegezone@isac.org. *Phone:* 800-899-4722. *Fax:* 847-831-8549. *Web site:* http://www.collegezone.org.

Merit Recognition Scholarship (MRS) Program. One-time awards available to Illinois residents for use at Illinois institutions. Must be ranked in the top 5 percent of high school class or have scored among the top 5 percent on the ACT, SAT, or Prairie State Achievement Exam. Number of scholarships granted varies. Program not currently funded. *Award:* Scholarship for use in freshman year; not renewable. *Award amount:* up to $1000. *Number of awards:* varies. *Eligibility Requirements:* Applicant must be high school student; planning to enroll or expecting to enroll full- or part-time at a two-year or four-year institution or university; resident of Illinois and studying in Illinois. Available to U.S. citizens. *Application Requirements:* Application, transcript. **Deadline:** June 15.

Contact College Zone Counselor, Illinois Student Assistance Commission (ISAC), 1755 Lake Cook Road, Deerfield, IL 60015-5209. *E-mail:* collegezone@isac.org. *Phone:* 800-899-4722. *Fax:* 847-831-8549. *Web site:* http://www.collegezone.org.

MIA/POW Scholarships. One-time award for spouse, child, or step-child of veterans who are missing in action or were a prisoner of war. Must be enrolled at a state-supported school in Illinois. Candidate must be U.S. citizen. Must apply and be accepted before beginning of school. Also for children and spouses of veterans who are determined to be 100 percent disabled as established by the Veterans Administration. Scholarship value and the number of awards granted varies. *Award:* Scholarship for use in freshman, sophomore, junior, or senior year; renewable. *Award amount:* varies. *Number of awards:* varies. *Eligibility Requirements:* Applicant must be enrolled or expecting to enroll full- or part-time at a two-year or four-year institution or university; resident of Illinois and studying in Illinois. Available to U.S. citizens. Applicant or parent must meet one or more of the following requirements: general military experience; retired from active duty; disabled or killed as a result of military service; prisoner of war; or missing in action. *Application Requirements:* Application. **Deadline:** continuous.

Contact Ms. Tracy Smith, Grants Section, Illinois Department of Veterans' Affairs, 833 South Spring Street, Springfield, IL 62794-9432. *Phone:* 217-782-3564. *Fax:* 217-782-4161. *Web site:* http://www.state.il.us/agency/dva.

Minority Teachers of Illinois Scholarship Program. Award for minority students intending to become school teachers; teaching commitment attached to receipt. Number of scholarships and the individual dollar amounts vary. *Academic Fields/Career Goals:* Education; Special Education. *Award:* Scholarship for use in freshman, sophomore, junior, senior, graduate, or postgraduate years; renewable. *Award*

amount: up to $5000. *Eligibility Requirements:* Applicant must be American Indian/Alaska Native, Asian/Pacific Islander, Black (non-Hispanic), or Hispanic; enrolled or expecting to enroll full- or part-time at a two-year or four-year institution or university; resident of Illinois and studying in Illinois. Available to U.S. citizens. *Application Requirements:* Application, transcript. **Deadline:** March 1.

Contact College Zone Counselor, Illinois Student Assistance Commission (ISAC), 1755 Lake Cook Road, Deerfield, IL 60015-5209. *E-mail:* collegezone@isac.org. *Phone:* 800-899-4722. *Fax:* 847-831-8549. *Web site:* http://www.collegezone.org.

Robert C. Byrd Honors Scholarship-Illinois. Scholarship for Illinois residents and graduating high school seniors accepted on a full-time basis as an undergraduate student at an Illinois college or university. The award is up to $1500 per year, for a maximum of four years. Minimum 3.5 GPA required. Students are automatically considered for this scholarship if they meet the eligibility requirements. High school counselors submit information to selection process. *Award:* Scholarship for use in freshman, sophomore, junior, or senior year; renewable. *Award amount:* up to $1500. *Number of awards:* varies. *Eligibility Requirements:* Applicant must be high school student; planning to enroll or expecting to enroll full-time at a two-year or four-year institution or university; resident of Illinois and studying in Illinois. Available to U.S. citizens. *Application Requirements:* Application, test scores, transcript. **Deadline:** July 15.

Contact College Zone Counselor, Illinois Student Assistance Commission (ISAC), 1755 Lake Cook Road, Deerfield, IL 60015-5209. *E-mail:* collegezone@isac.org. *Phone:* 800-899-4722. *Fax:* 847-931-8549. *Web site:* http://www.collegezone.org.

Silas Purnell Illinois Incentive for Access Program. Students whose information provided on the FAFSA results in a calculated zero expected family contribution when they are college freshmen may be eligible to receive a grant of up to $500. Must be a U.S. citizen and an Illinois resident studying at a participating Illinois institution. See Web site for complete list of schools and additional requirements. *Award:* Grant for use in freshman year; not renewable. *Award amount:* up to $500. *Number of awards:* varies. *Eligibility Requirements:* Applicant must be high school student; planning to enroll or expecting to enroll full- or part-time at a two-year, four-year, or technical institution or

university; resident of Illinois and studying in Illinois. Available to U.S. citizens. *Application Requirements:* Financial need analysis, FAFSA. **Deadline:** July 1.

Contact College Zone Counselor, Illinois Student Assistance Commission (ISAC), 1755 Lake Cook Road, Deerfield, IL 60015-5209. *E-mail:* collegezone@isac.org. *Phone:* 800-899-4722. *Fax:* 847-831-8549. *Web site:* http://www.collegezone.org.

Veterans' Children Educational Opportunities. $250 award for each child aged 10 to 18 of a veteran who died or became totally disabled as a result of service during World War I, World War II, Korean, or Vietnam War. Must be Illinois resident studying in Illinois. Death must be service-connected. Disability must be rated 100 percent for two or more years. *Award:* Grant for use in freshman year; not renewable. *Award amount:* $250. *Number of awards:* varies. *Eligibility Requirements:* Applicant must be age 10-18; enrolled or expecting to enroll full- or part-time at a two-year or four-year institution or university; resident of Illinois and studying in Illinois. Available to U.S. citizens. Applicant or parent must meet one or more of the following requirements: general military experience; retired from active duty; disabled or killed as a result of military service; prisoner of war; or missing in action. *Application Requirements:* Application. **Deadline:** June 30.

Contact Tracy Smith, Grants Section, Illinois Department of Veterans' Affairs, 833 South Spring Street, Springfield, IL 62794-9432. *Phone:* 217-782-3564. *Fax:* 217-782-4161. *Web site:* http://www.state.il.us/agency/dva.

INDIANA

Child of Disabled Veteran Grant or Purple Heart Recipient Grant. Free tuition at Indiana state-supported colleges or universities for children of disabled veterans or Purple Heart recipients. Must submit form DD214 or service record. Covers tuition and mandatory fees. *Award:* Grant for use in freshman, sophomore, junior, senior, graduate, or postgraduate years; renewable. *Award amount:* varies. *Number of awards:* varies. *Eligibility Requirements:* Applicant must be enrolled or expecting to enroll full- or part-time at a two-year or four-year institution or university; resident of Indiana and studying in Indiana. Available to U.S. citizens. Applicant or parent must meet one or more of the following requirements: general military experience; retired from active duty; disabled or killed as a result of military service; prisoner of war; or missing in action. *Application Requirements:* Application, FAFSA. **Deadline:** continuous.

Contact Jon Brinkley, State Service Officer, Indiana Department of Veterans Affairs, 302 West Washington Street, Room E-120, Indianapolis, IN 46204-2738. *E-mail:* jbrinkley@dva.in.gov. *Phone:* 317-232-3910. *Fax:* 317-232-7721. *Web site:* http://www.in.gov/dva.

Department of Veterans Affairs Free Tuition for Children of POW/MIA's in Vietnam. Renewable award for residents of Indiana who are the children of veterans declared missing in action or prisoner-of-war after January 1, 1960. Provides tuition at Indiana state-supported institutions for undergraduate study. *Award:* Grant for use in freshman, sophomore, junior, senior, graduate, or postgraduate years; renewable. *Award amount:* varies. *Number of awards:* varies. *Eligibility Requirements:* Applicant must be age 24 or under; enrolled or expecting to enroll full- or part-time at a two-year or four-year institution or university; resident of Indiana and studying in Indiana. Available to U.S. citizens. Applicant or parent must meet one or more of the following requirements: general military experience; retired from active duty; disabled or killed as a result of military service; prisoner of war; or missing in action. *Application Requirements:* Application. **Deadline:** continuous.

Contact Jon Brinkley, State Service Officer, Indiana Department of Veterans Affairs, 302 West Washington Street, Room E-120, Indianapolis, IN 46204-2738. *E-mail:* jbrinkley@dva.in.gov. *Phone:* 317-232-3910. *Fax:* 317-232-7721. *Web site:* http://www.in.gov/dva.

Frank O'Bannon Grant Program. A need-based, tuition-restricted program for students attending Indiana public, private, or proprietary institutions seeking a first undergraduate degree. Students (and parents of dependent students) who are U.S. citizens and Indiana residents must file the FAFSA yearly by the March 10 deadline. *Award:* Grant for use in freshman, sophomore, junior, or senior year; not renewable. *Award amount:* $200–$10,992. *Number of awards:* 48,408–70,239. *Eligibility Requirements:* Applicant must be enrolled or expecting to enroll full-time at a two-year, four-year, or technical institution or university; resident of Indiana and studying in Indiana. Available to U.S. citizens. *Application Requirements:* Application, financial need analysis, FAFSA. **Deadline:** March 10.

Contact Grants Counselor, State Student Assistance Commission of Indiana (SSACI), 150 West Market Street, Suite 500, Indianapolis, IN 46204-2805. *E-mail:* grants@ssaci.state.in.us. *Phone:* 317-232-2350. *Fax:* 317-232-3260. *Web site:* http://www.in.gov/ssaci.

Hoosier Scholar Award. A $500 nonrenewable award. Based on the size of the senior class, one to three scholars are selected by the guidance counselor's) of each accredited high school in Indiana. The award is based on academic merit and may be used for any educational expense at an eligible Indiana institution of higher education. *Award:* Scholarship for use in freshman year; not renewable. *Award amount:* $500. *Number of awards:* 666–840. *Eligibility Requirements:* Applicant must be high school student; planning to enroll or expecting to enroll full-time at a two-year or four-year institution or university; resident of Indiana and studying in Indiana. Applicant must have 3.5 GPA or higher. Available to U.S. citizens. *Application Requirements:* Application, references. **Deadline:** March 10.

Contact Ada Sparkman, Program Coordinator, State Student Assistance Commission of Indiana (SSACI), 150 West Market Street, Suite 500, Indianapolis, IN 46204-2805. *Phone:* 317-232-2350. *Fax:* 317-232-3260. *Web site:* http://www.in.gov/ssaci.

Indiana National Guard Supplemental Grant. The award is a supplement to the Indiana Higher Education Grant program. Applicants must be members of the Indiana National Guard. All Guard paperwork must be completed prior to the start of each semester. The FAFSA must be received by March 10. Award covers certain tuition and fees at select public colleges. *Award:* Grant for use in freshman, sophomore, junior, or senior year; not renewable. *Award amount:* $20–$7110. *Number of awards:* 503–925. *Eligibility Requirements:* Applicant must be enrolled or expecting to enroll full- or part-time at a two-year or four-year institution or university; resident of Indiana and studying in Indiana. Available to U.S. citizens. Applicant or parent must meet one or more of the following requirements: Air Force National Guard or Army National Guard experience; retired from active duty; disabled or killed as a result of military service; prisoner of war; or missing in action. *Application Requirements:* Application. **Deadline:** March 10.

Contact Kathryn Moore, Grants Counselor, State Student Assistance Commission of Indiana (SSACI), 150 West Market Street, Suite 500, Indianapolis, IN 46204-2805. *E-mail:* kmoore@ssaci.in.gov. *Phone:* 317-232-2350. *Fax:* 317-232-2360. *Web site:* http://www.in.gov/ssaci.

Indiana Nursing Scholarship Fund. Need-based tuition funding for nursing students enrolled full- or part-time at an eligible Indiana institution. Must be a U.S. citizen and an Indiana resident and have a minimum 2.0 GPA or meet the minimum requirements for the nursing program. Upon graduation, recipients must practice as a nurse in an Indiana health care setting for two years. *Academic Fields/Career Goals:* Nursing. *Award:* Scholarship for use in freshman, sophomore, junior, or senior year; not renewable. *Award amount:* $200–$5000. *Number of awards:* 490–690. *Eligibility Requirements:* Applicant must be enrolled or expecting to enroll full- or part-time at a two-year or four-year institution or university; resident of Indiana and studying in Indiana. Available to U.S. citizens. *Application Requirements:* Application, financial need analysis, FAFSA. **Deadline:** continuous.

Contact Yvonne Heflin, Director, Special Programs, State Student Assistance Commission of Indiana (SSACI), 150 West Market Street, Suite 500, Indianapolis, IN 46204-2805. *Phone:* 317-232-2350. *Fax:* 317-232-3260. *Web site:* http://www.in.gov/ssaci.

National Guard Scholarship Extension Program. A scholarship extension applicant is eligible for a tuition scholarship under Indiana Code 21-13-5-4 for a period not to exceed the period of scholarship extension the applicant served on active duty as a member of the National Guard (mobilized and deployed). Must apply not later than one (1) year after the applicant ceases to be a member of the Indiana National Guard. Applicant should apply through the education officer of their last unit of assignment. *Award:* Grant for use in freshman, sophomore, junior, or senior year; renewable. *Award amount:* varies. *Number of awards:* varies. *Eligibility Requirements:* Applicant must be enrolled or expecting to enroll full- or part-time at a two-year, four-year, or technical institution or university and studying in Indiana. Available to U.S. citizens. Applicant must have served in the Air Force National Guard or Army National Guard. *Application Requirements:* Application. **Deadline:** continuous.

Contact Pamela Moody, National Guard Education Officer, Indiana Department of Veterans Affairs, 302 West Washington Street, Suite E120, Indianapolis, IN 46204. *E-mail:* pamela.moody@in.ngb.army.mil. *Phone:* 317-964-7017. *Fax:* 317-232-7721. *Web site:* http://www.in.gov/dva.

National Guard Tuition Supplement Program. Applicant must be a member of the Indiana National Guard, in active drilling status, who has not been AWOL during the last 12 months, does not possess a bachelor's degree, possesses the requisite academic qualifications, meets the requirements of the state-supported college or university, and meets all National Guard requirements. *Award:* Grant for use in freshman, sophomore, junior, or senior year; renewable. *Award amount:* varies. *Number of awards:* varies. *Eligibility Requirements:* Applicant must be enrolled or expecting to enroll full- or part-time at a two-year, four-year, or technical institution or university and studying in Indiana. Available to U.S. citizens. Applicant must have served in the Air Force National Guard or Army National Guard. *Application Requirements:* Application, FAFSA. **Deadline:** continuous.

Contact Jon Brinkley, State Service Officer, Indiana Department of Veterans Affairs, 302 West Washington Street, Room E-120, Indianapolis, IN 46204-2738. *E-mail:* jbrinkley@dva.in.gov. *Phone:* 317-232-3910. *Fax:* 317-232-7721. *Web site:* http://www.in.gov/dva.

Part-Time Grant Program. Program is designed to encourage part-time undergraduates to start and complete their associate or baccalaureate degrees or certificates by subsidizing part-time tuition costs. It is a term-based award that is based on need. State residency requirements must be met and a FAFSA must be filed. Eligibility is determined at the institutional level subject to approval by SSACI. *Award:* Grant for use in freshman, sophomore, junior, or senior year; not renewable. *Award amount:* $20–$4000. *Number of awards:* 4680–6700. *Eligibility Requirements:* Applicant must be enrolled or expecting to enroll part-time at a two-year, four-year, or technical institution or university; resident of Indiana and studying in Indiana. Available to U.S. citizens. *Application Requirements:* Application, financial need analysis. **Deadline:** continuous.

Contact Grants Counselor, State Student Assistance Commission of Indiana (SSACI), 150 West Market Street, Suite 500, Indianapolis, IN 46204-2805. *E-mail:* grants@ssaci.state.in.us. *Phone:* 317-232-2350. *Fax:* 317-232-3260. *Web site:* http://www.in.gov/ssaci.

Resident Tuition for Active Duty Military Personnel. Applicant must be a nonresident of Indiana serving on active duty and stationed in Indiana and attending any state-supported college or university. Dependents remain eligible for the duration of their enrollment, even if the active duty person is no longer in Indiana. Entitlement is to the resident tuition rate. *Award:* Grant for use in freshman, sophomore, junior, senior, graduate, or postgraduate years; renewable. *Award amount:* varies. *Number of awards:* varies. *Eligibility Requirements:* Applicant must be enrolled or expecting to enroll full- or part-time at a two-year, four-year, or technical institution or university and studying in Indiana. Available to U.S. citizens. Applicant or parent must meet one or more of the following requirements: Air Force, Army, Marine Corps, or Navy experience; retired from active duty; disabled or killed as a result of military service; prisoner of war; or missing in action. *Application Requirements:* Application. **Deadline:** continuous.

Contact Jon Brinkley, State Service Officer, Indiana Department of Veterans Affairs, 302 West Washington Street, Room E-120, Indianapolis, IN 46204-2738. *E-mail:* jbrinkley@dva.in.gov. *Phone:* 317-232-3910. *Fax:* 317-232-7721. *Web site:* http://www.in.gov/dva.

Tuition and Fee Remission for Children and Spouses of National Guard Members. Award to an individual whose father, mother or spouse was a member of the Indiana National Guard and suffered a service-connected death while serving on state active duty (which includes mobilized and deployed for federal active duty). The student must be eligible to pay the resident tuition rate at the state-supported college or university and must possess the requisite academic qualifications. *Award:* Grant for use in freshman, sophomore, junior, or senior year; renewable. *Award amount:* varies. *Number of awards:* varies. *Eligibility Requirements:* Applicant must be enrolled or expecting to enroll full- or part-time at a two-year, four-year, or technical institution or university and studying in Indiana. Available to U.S. citizens. Applicant or parent must meet one or more of the following requirements: Air Force National Guard or Army National Guard experience; retired from active duty; disabled or killed as a result of military service; prisoner of war; or missing in action. *Application Requirements:* Application, FAFSA. **Deadline:** continuous.

Contact R. Martin Umbarger, Adjutant General, Indiana Department of Veterans Affairs, 2002 South Holt Road, Indianapolis, IN 46241. *E-mail:* r.martin.umbarger@in.ngb.army.mil. *Phone:* 317-247-3559. *Fax:* 317-247-3540. *Web site:* http://www.in.gov/dva.

Twenty-first Century Scholars Gear Up Summer Scholarship. Grant of up to $3000 that pays for summer school tuition and regularly assessed course fees (does not cover other costs such as textbooks or room and board). *Award:* Scholarship for use in freshman, sophomore, junior, or senior year; not renewable. *Award amount:* up to $3000. *Number of awards:* 1. *Eligibility Requirements:* Applicant must be enrolled or expecting to enroll full-time at a two-year or four-year institution or university; resident of Indiana and studying in Indiana. Available to U.S. citizens. *Application Requirements:* Application, must be in twenty-first century scholars program, high school diploma. **Deadline:** varies.

Contact Coordinator, Office of Twenty-First Century Scholars, State Student Assistance Commission of Indiana (SSACI), 150 West Market Street, Suite 500, Indianapolis, IN 46204. *E-mail:* 21stscholars@ssaci.in.gov. *Phone:* 317-234-1394. *Web site:* http://www.in.gov/ssaci.

IOWA

All Iowa Opportunity Scholarship. Students attending eligible Iowa colleges and universities may receive awards of up to $6420. Minimum 2.5 GPA. Priority will be given to students who participated in the Federal TRIO Programs, graduated from alternative high schools, and to homeless youth. Applicant must enroll within two academic years of graduating from high school. Maximum individual awards cannot exceed more than the resident tuition rate at Iowa Regent Universities. *Award:* Scholarship for use in freshman or sophomore year; not renewable. *Number of awards:* 200–800. *Eligibility Requirements:* Applicant must be enrolled or expecting to enroll full- or part-time at a two-year or four-year institution or university; resident of Iowa and studying in Iowa. Applicant must have 2.5 GPA or higher. Available to U.S. citizens. *Application Requirements:* Application, financial need analysis. **Deadline:** May 1.

Contact Todd Brown, Director, Scholarships, Grants, and Loan Forgiveness, Iowa College Student Aid Commission, 200 Tenth Street, Fourth Floor, Des Moines, IA 50309-3609. *E-mail:* todd.brown@iowa.gov. *Phone:* 515-725-3405. *Fax:* 515-725-3401. *Web site:* http://www.iowacollegeaid.gov.

Governor Terry E. Branstad Iowa State Fair Scholarship. Awards up to four scholarships ranging from $500 to $1000 to students graduating from an Iowa high school. Must actively participate at the Iowa State fair. For more details see Web site http://www.iowacollegeaid.org. *Award:* Scholarship for use in freshman year; not renewable. *Award amount:* $500–$1000. *Number of awards:* up to 4. *Eligibility Requirements:* Applicant must be high school student; planning to enroll or expecting to enroll full- or part-time at a four-year institution or university; resident of Iowa and studying in Iowa. Available to U.S. citizens. *Application Requirements:* Application, essay, financial need analysis, references, transcript. **Deadline:** May 1.

Contact Misty Burke, Program Planner, Iowa College Student Aid Commission, 200 Tenth Street, Fourth Floor, Des Moines, IA 50309-3609. *E-mail:* misty.burke@iowa.gov. *Phone:* 515-725-3424. *Fax:* 515-725-3401. *Web site:* http://www.iowacollegeaid.gov.

Iowa Grants. Statewide need-based program to assist high-need Iowa residents. Recipients must demonstrate a high level of financial need to receive awards ranging from $100 to $1000. Awards are prorated for students enrolled for less than full-time. Awards must be used at Iowa postsecondary institutions. *Award:* Grant for use in freshman, sophomore, junior, or senior year; not renewable. *Award amount:* $100–$1000. *Number of awards:* 2000–3000. *Eligibility Requirements:* Applicant must be enrolled or expecting to enroll full- or part-time at a two-year, four-year, or technical institution or university; resident of Iowa and studying in Iowa. Available to U.S. citizens. *Application Requirements:* Application, financial need analysis. **Deadline:** continuous.

Contact Todd Brown, Director, Scholarships, Grants, and Loan Forgiveness, Iowa College Student Aid Commission, 200 Tenth Street, Fourth Floor, Des Moines, IA 50309-3609. *E-mail:* todd.brown@iowa.gov. *Phone:* 515-725-3405. *Fax:* 515-725-3401. *Web site:* http://www.iowacollegeaid.gov.

Iowa National Guard Education Assistance Program. Program provides postsecondary tuition assistance to members of Iowa National Guard Units. Must study at a postsecondary institution in Iowa. Contact the office for additional information. *Award:* Grant for use in freshman, sophomore, junior, or senior year; not renewable. *Number of awards:* 700–1500. *Eligibility Requirements:* Applicant must be enrolled or expecting to enroll full- or part-time at a two-year, four-year, or technical institution or university; resident of Iowa and studying in Iowa. Available to U.S. citizens. Applicant or parent must meet one or more of the following requirements: Air Force National Guard or Army National Guard experience; retired from active duty; disabled or killed as a result of military service; prisoner of war; or missing in action. *Application Requirements:* Application. **Deadline:** continuous.

Contact Todd Brown, Director, Scholarships, Grants, and Loan Forgiveness, Iowa College Student Aid Commission, 200 Tenth Street, Fourth Floor, Des Moines, IA 50309-3609. *E-mail:* todd.brown@iowa.gov. *Phone:* 515-725-3405. *Fax:* 515-725-3401. *Web site:* http://www.iowacollegeaid.gov.

Iowa Tuition Grant Program. Program assists students who attend independent postsecondary institutions in Iowa. Iowa residents currently enrolled, or planning to enroll, for at least 3 semester hours at one of the eligible Iowa postsecondary institutions may apply. Awards currently range from $100 to $4000. Grants may not exceed the difference between independent college and university tuition fees and the average tuition fees at the three public Regent universities. *Award:* Grant for use in freshman, sophomore, junior, or senior year; renewable. *Award amount:* $100–$4000. *Number of awards:* 16,000–17,500. *Eligibility Requirements:* Applicant must be enrolled or expecting to enroll full- or part-time at a four-year institution or university; resident of Iowa and studying in Iowa. Available to U.S. citizens. *Application Requirements:* Application, financial need analysis. **Deadline:** July 1.

Contact Todd Brown, Director, Scholarships, Grants, and Loan Forgiveness, Iowa College Student Aid Commission, 200 Tenth Street, Fourth Floor, Des Moines, IA 50309-3609. *E-mail:* todd.brown@iowa.gov. *Phone:* 515-725-3420. *Fax:* 515-725-3401. *Web site:* http://www.iowacollegeaid.gov.

Iowa Vocational-Technical Tuition Grant Program. Program provides need-based financial assistance to Iowa residents enrolled in career education (vocational-technical), and career option programs at Iowa area community colleges. Grants range from $150 to $1200, depending on the length of the program, financial need, and available funds. *Award:* Grant for use in freshman or sophomore year; not renewable. *Award amount:* $150–$1200. *Number of awards:* 2500–3500. *Eligibility Requirements:* Applicant must be enrolled or expecting to enroll full- or part-time at a technical institution; resident of Iowa and studying in Iowa. Available to U.S. citizens. *Application Requirements:* Application, financial need analysis. **Deadline:** July 1.

Contact Todd Brown, Director, Program Administration, Iowa College Student Aid Commission, 200 Tenth Street, Fourth Floor, Des Moines, IA 50309-3609. *E-mail:* julie.leeper@iowa.gov. *Phone:* 515-725-3405. *Fax:* 515-725-3401. *Web site:* http://www.iowacollegeaid.gov.

KANSAS

Kansas Educational Benefits for Children of MIA, POW, and Deceased Veterans of the Vietnam War. Scholarship awarded to students who are children of veterans. Must show proof of parent's status as missing in action, prisoner of war, or killed in action in the Vietnam War. Kansas residence required of veteran at time of entry to service. Must attend a state-supported postsecondary school. *Award:* Scholarship for use in freshman, sophomore, junior, or senior year; not renewable. *Award amount:* varies. *Number of awards:* 1. *Eligibility Requirements:* Applicant must be enrolled or expecting to enroll full-time at a two-year, four-year, or technical institution or university and studying in Kansas. Available to U.S. citizens. Applicant or parent must meet one or more of the following requirements: general military experience; retired from active duty; disabled or killed as a result of military service; prisoner of war; or missing in action. *Application Requirements:* Application, birth certificate, school acceptance letter, military discharge of veteran. **Deadline:** varies.

Contact Wayne Bollig, Program Director, Kansas Commission on Veterans Affairs, 700 Jackson, SW, Suite 701, Topeka, KS 66603-3743. *E-mail:* wbollig@kcva.org. *Phone:* 785-296-3976. *Fax:* 785-296-1462. *Web site:* http://www.kcva.org.

Kansas Ethnic Minority Scholarship. Scholarship program designed to assist financially needy, academically competitive students who are identified as members of any of the following ethnic/racial groups: African-American, American Indian or Alaskan Native, Asian or Pacific Islander, or Hispanic. Priority is given to applicants who are freshmen. Students must be Kansas residents attending postsecondary institutions in Kansas. For more details refer to Web site http://www.kansasregents.org/financial_aid/minority.html. *Award:* Scholarship for use in freshman, sophomore, junior, or senior year; renewable. *Award amount:* up to $1850. *Number of awards:* varies. *Eligibility Requirements:* Applicant must be American Indian/Alaska Native, Asian/Pacific Islander, Black (non-Hispanic), or Hispanic; enrolled or expecting to enroll full-time at a two-year or four-year institution or university; resident of Kansas and studying in Kansas. Applicant must have 3.0 GPA or higher. Available to U.S. citizens. *Application Requirements:* Application, financial need analysis, test scores. *Fee:* $12. **Deadline:** May 1.

Contact Diane Lindeman, Director of Student Financial Assistance, Kansas Board of Regents, 1000 Jackson, SW, Suite 520, Topeka, KS 66612-1368. *E-mail:* dlindeman@ ksbor.org. *Phone:* 785-296-3517. *Web site:* http://www.kansasregents.org.

Kansas Nursing Service Scholarship Program. This is a service scholarship loan program available to students attending two-year or four-year public and private postsecondary institutions as well as vocational technical schools with nursing education programs. Students can be pursuing either LPN or RN licensure. This is a service obligation scholarship, therefore students must agree to work in the field of nursing one year for each year they have received the scholarship or must repay the amount of the scholarship award that they received plus interest. Students must be Kansas residents attending a postsecondary institution in Kansas. *Academic Fields/ Career Goals:* Nursing. *Award:* Scholarship for use in freshman, sophomore, junior, or senior year; renewable. *Award amount:* $2500–$3500. *Number of awards:* varies. *Eligibility Requirements:* Applicant must be enrolled or expecting to enroll full-time at a two-year, four-year, or technical institution or university. Available to U.S. citizens. *Application Requirements:* Application, financial need analysis, test scores, transcript. *Fee:* $12. **Deadline:** May 1.

Contact Diane Lindeman, Director of Student Financial Assistance, Kansas Board of Regents, 1000 Jackson, SW, Suite 520, Topeka, KS 66612-1368. *E-mail:* dlindeman@ ksbor.org. *Phone:* 785-296-3517. *Web site:* http://www.kansasregents.org.

Kansas Teacher Service Scholarship. Scholarship to encourage talented students to enter the teaching profession and teach in Kansas in specific curriculum areas or in underserved areas of Kansas. Students must be Kansas residents attending a postsecondary institution in Kansas. For more details, refer to Web site http://www. kansasregents.org *Academic Fields/Career Goals:* Education. *Award:* Scholarship for use in junior, senior, or graduate year; renewable. *Award amount:* $2150–$5374. *Number of awards:* varies. *Eligibility Requirements:* Applicant must be enrolled or expecting to enroll full- or part-time at a four-year institution or university. Applicant must have 3.0 GPA or higher. Available to U.S. citizens. *Application Requirements:* Application, essay, financial need analysis, resume, references, test scores, transcript. *Fee:* $12. **Deadline:** May 1.

Contact Diane Lindeman, Director of Student Financial Assistance, Kansas Board of Regents, 1000 Jackson, SW, Suite 520, Topeka, KS 66612-1368. *E-mail:* dlindeman@ ksbor.org. *Phone:* 785-296-3517. *Web site:* http://www.kansasregents.org.

Marsha's Angels Scholarship. Scholarship for students who have completed all prerequisites to enter their first year of an accredited nursing program. Applicants living in Sedgwick County, Kansas or one of the surrounding counties may attend an accredited nursing program anywhere in the U.S.; applicants from any other state in the U.S. may use the scholarship to attend a program in Sedgwick County, Kansas, one of the surrounding counties, or St. Luke's College in Missouri. *Academic Fields/Career Goals:* Nursing. *Award:* Scholarship for use in freshman year; not renewable. *Award amount:* $1600– $1800. *Number of awards:* varies. *Eligibility Requirements:* Applicant must be high school student and planning to enroll or expecting to enroll full- or part-time at a four-year institution or university. Available to U.S. citizens. *Application Requirements:* Application, transcript. **Deadline:** June 30.

Contact Scholarship Committee, Marsha's Angels Scholarship Fund, PO Box 401, Valley Center, KS 67147-0401. *E-mail:* marshasangels@gmail.com. *Web site:* http:// www.marshasangels.org.

Ted and Nora Anderson Scholarships. Scholarship of $250 for each semester (one year only) given to the children of American Legion members or Auxiliary members who are holding membership for the past three consecutive years. Children of a deceased member can also apply. Parent of the applicant must be a veteran. Must be high school seniors or college freshmen or sophomores in a Kansas institution. Scholarship for use at an approved college, university, or trade school in Kansas. Must maintain a C average in college. *Award:* Scholarship for use in freshman or sophomore year; not renewable. *Award amount:* $250–$500. *Number of awards:* 4. *Eligibility Requirements:* Applicant must be enrolled or expecting to enroll full-time at a two-year, four-year, or technical institution or university; resident of Kansas and studying in Kansas. Applicant or parent of applicant must be member of American Legion or Auxiliary. Available to U.S. citizens. Applicant or parent must meet one or more of the following requirements: general military experience; retired from active duty; disabled or killed as a result of military service; prisoner of war; or missing in action. *Application Requirements:* Application, essay, financial need analysis, photo, references, transcript. **Deadline:** February 15.

Contact Jim Gravenstein, Chairman, Scholarship Committee, American Legion Department of Kansas, 1314 Topeka Boulevard, SW, Topeka, KS 66612. *Phone:* 785-232-9315. *Fax:* 785-232-1399. *Web site:* http:// www.ksamlegion.org.

KENTUCKY

College Access Program (CAP) Grant. Award for U.S. citizens and Kentucky residents seeking their first undergraduate degree. Applicants enrolled in sectarian institutions are not eligible. Must submit Free Application for Federal Student Aid to demonstrate financial need. Funding is limited. Awards are made on a first-come, first-serve basis. *Award:* Grant for use in freshman, sophomore, junior, or senior year; not renewable. *Award amount:* up to $1900. *Number of awards:* 35,000–45,000. *Eligibility Requirements:* Applicant must be enrolled or expecting to enroll full- or part-time at a two-year, four-year, or technical institution or university; resident of Kentucky and studying in Kentucky. Available to U.S. citizens. *Application Requirements:* Application, financial need analysis, FAFSA. **Deadline:** March 15.

Contact Sheila Roe, Program Coordinator, Kentucky Higher Education Assistance Authority (KHEAA), PO Box 798, Frankfort, KY 40602-0798. *E-mail:* sroe@kheaa.com. *Phone:* 800-928-8926 Ext. 67393. *Fax:* 502-696-7373. *Web site:* http://www.kheaa.com.

Department of Veterans Affairs Tuition Waiver-KY KRS 164-507. Scholarship available to college students who are residents of Kentucky under the age of 26. *Award:* Scholarship for use in freshman, sophomore, junior, or senior year; not renewable. *Award amount:* varies. *Number of awards:* 400. *Eligibility Requirements:* Applicant must be age 26 or under; enrolled or expecting to enroll full- or part-time at a two-year or four-year institution or university and resident of Kentucky. Available to U.S. citizens. *Application Requirements:* Application. **Deadline:** varies.

Contact Barbara Sipek, Tuition Waiver Coordinator, Kentucky Department of Veterans Affairs, 321 West Main Street, Suite 390, Louisville, KY 40213-9095 USA. *E-mail:* barbaraa.sipek@ky.gov. *Phone:* 502-595-4447. *Fax:* 502-595-4448. *Web site:* http://www. veterans.ky.gov.

Early Childhood Development Scholarship. Awards scholarship with conditional service commitment for part-time students currently employed by participating ECD facility or providing training in ECD for an approved organization. For more information, visit

Web site http://www.kheaa.com. *Academic Fields/Career Goals:* Child and Family Studies; Education. *Award:* Scholarship for use in freshman, sophomore, junior, or senior year; not renewable. *Award amount:* up to $1800. *Number of awards:* 1000–1300. *Eligibility Requirements:* Applicant must be enrolled or expecting to enroll part-time at a two-year or four-year institution or university; resident of Kentucky and studying in Kentucky. Available to U.S. citizens. *Application Requirements:* Application, financial need analysis, FAFSA. **Deadline:** continuous.

Contact David Lawhorn, Program Coordinator, Kentucky Higher Education Assistance Authority (KHEAA), PO Box 798, Frankfort, KY 40602-0798. *E-mail:* dlawhorn@kheaa. com. *Phone:* 800-928-8926 Ext. 67383. *Fax:* 502-696-7373. *Web site:* http://www.kheaa. com.

Environmental Protection Scholarship. Renewable awards for college juniors, seniors, and graduate students for tuition, fees, and room and board and a book allowance at a Kentucky public university. Minimum 3.0 GPA required. Must agree to work full-time for the Kentucky Natural Resources and Environmental Protection Cabinet upon graduation. Interview is required. *Academic Fields/Career Goals:* Biology; Civil Engineering; Earth Science; Environmental Science; Hydrology; Mechanical Engineering; Natural Resources; Natural Sciences. *Award:* Scholarship for use in junior, senior, or graduate year; renewable. *Award amount:* $15,500–$31,000. *Number of awards:* 1–4. *Eligibility Requirements:* Applicant must be enrolled or expecting to enroll full-time at a four-year institution or university and studying in Kentucky. Applicant must have 3.0 GPA or higher. Available to U.S. and non-U.S. citizens. *Application Requirements:* Application, essay, interview, references, transcript, valid work permit for non-citizens. **Deadline:** February 15.

Contact James Kipp, Scholarship Program Coordinator, Kentucky Natural Resources and Environmental Protection Cabinet, 233 Mining/Mineral Resources Building, Lexington, KY 40506-0107. *E-mail:* kipp@uky.edu. *Phone:* 859-257-1299. *Fax:* 859-323-1049. *Web site:* http://www.dep.ky.gov.

Go Higher Grant. Need-based grant for adult students pursuing their first undergraduate degree. Completion of the FAFSA is required. *Award:* Grant for use in freshman, sophomore, junior, or senior year; not renewable. *Award amount:* up to $1000. *Number of awards:* 100–300. *Eligibility Requirements:* Applicant must be age 24

and over; enrolled or expecting to enroll full- or part-time at a two-year, four-year, or technical institution or university; resident of Kentucky and studying in Kentucky. Available to U.S. citizens. *Application Requirements:* Application, FAFSA. **Deadline:** continuous.

Contact Sheila Roe, Grant Program Coordinator, Kentucky Higher Education Assistance Authority (KHEAA), PO Box 798, Frankfort, KY 40206-0798. *E-mail:* sroe@kheaa.com. *Phone:* 800-928-8926 Ext. 67393. *Web site:* http://www.kheaa.com.

Kentucky Educational Excellence Scholarship (KEES). Annual award based on yearly high school GPA and highest ACT or SAT score received by high school graduation. Awards are renewable, if required cumulative GPA is maintained at a Kentucky postsecondary school. Must be a Kentucky resident, and a graduate of a Kentucky high school. *Award:* Scholarship for use in freshman, sophomore, junior, or senior year; renewable. *Award amount:* $125–$2500. *Number of awards:* 63,000–67,000. *Eligibility Requirements:* Applicant must be high school student; planning to enroll or expecting to enroll full- or part-time at a two-year, four-year, or technical institution or university; resident of Kentucky and studying in Kentucky. Applicant must have 2.5 GPA or higher. Available to U.S. citizens. *Application Requirements:* Test scores, Data submitted by KY high schools. **Deadline:** continuous.

Contact Megan Cummins, KEES Coordinator, Kentucky Higher Education Assistance Authority (KHEAA). *E-mail:* mcummins@kheaa.com. *Phone:* 800-928-8926 Ext. 67397. *Fax:* 502-696-7373. *Web site:* http://www.kheaa.com.

Kentucky Minority Educator Recruitment and Retention (KMERR) Scholarship. Scholarship for minority teacher candidates who rank in the upper half of their class or have a minimum 2.5 GPA. Must be a U.S. citizen and Kentucky resident enrolled in one of Kentucky's eight public institutions. Must teach one semester in Kentucky for each semester the scholarship is received. *Academic Fields/Career Goals:* Education. *Award:* Forgivable loan for use in freshman, sophomore, junior, or senior year; renewable. *Award amount:* $2500–$5000. *Number of awards:* 400. *Eligibility Requirements:* Applicant must be American Indian/Alaska Native, Asian/Pacific Islander, Black (non-Hispanic), or Hispanic; enrolled or expecting to enroll full-time at a two-year or four-year institution or university; resident of Kentucky and studying in Kentucky. Applicant must

have 2.5 GPA or higher. Available to U.S. citizens. *Application Requirements:* Application, references, test scores, transcript. **Deadline:** continuous.

Contact Natasha Murray, State Program Coordinator, Kentucky Department of Education, 500 Mero Street, 17th Floor, Frankfort, KY 40601. *E-mail:* michael.dailey@education.ky.gov. *Phone:* 502-564-1479. *Fax:* 502-564-6952. *Web site:* http://www.education.ky.gov.

Kentucky Office of Vocational Rehabilitation. Grant provides services necessary to secure employment. Eligible individual must possess physical or mental impairment that results in a substantial impediment to employment; benefit from vocational rehabilitation services in terms of an employment outcome; and require vocational rehabilitation services to prepare for, enter, or retain employment. *Award:* Grant for use in freshman, sophomore, junior, senior, graduate, or postgraduate years; renewable. *Award amount:* varies. *Number of awards:* varies. *Eligibility Requirements:* Applicant must be enrolled or expecting to enroll full- or part-time at a two-year, four-year, or technical institution or university. Available to U.S. citizens. *Application Requirements:* Application, financial need analysis, interview, transcript, Eligibility for OVR services and in proper priority category. **Deadline:** continuous.

Contact Charles Puckett, Program Administrator, Kentucky Office of Vocational Rehabilitation, 600 West Cedar Street, Suite 2E, Louisville, KY 40202. *E-mail:* marianu.spencer@mail.state.ky.us. *Phone:* 502-595-4173. *Fax:* 502-564-2358. *Web site:* http://www.ovr.ky.gov.

Kentucky Teacher Scholarship Program. Awards Kentucky residents attending Kentucky institutions and pursuing initial teacher certification programs. Must teach one semester for each semester of award received. In critical shortage areas, must teach one semester for every two semesters of award received. If teaching service is not rendered, the scholarship converts to a loan that must be repaid with interest. For more information, see Web http://www.kheaa.com. *Academic Fields/Career Goals:* Education. *Award:* Forgivable loan for use in freshman, sophomore, junior, or senior year; renewable. *Award amount:* $325–$5000. *Number of awards:* 300–600. *Eligibility Requirements:* Applicant must be enrolled or expecting to enroll full-time at a two-year or four-year institution or university; resident of Kentucky and studying in Kentucky. Available to U.S. citizens. *Application Requirements:* Application, financial need analysis. **Deadline:** May 1.

Contact Jennifer Toth, Scholarship Coordinator, Kentucky Higher Education Assistance Authority (KHEAA), PO Box 798, Frankfort, KY 40602. *E-mail:* jtoth@kheaa.com. *Phone:* 800-928-8926 Ext. 67392. *Fax:* 502-696-7473. *Web site:* http://www.kheaa.com.

Kentucky Transportation Cabinet Civil Engineering Scholarship Program. Scholarships awarded to qualified Kentucky residents who wish to study civil engineering at University of Kentucky, Western Kentucky University, University of Louisville or Kentucky State University. Applicant should be a graduate of an accredited Kentucky high school or a Kentucky resident. Scholarship recipients are given opportunities to work for the Cabinet during summers and job opportunities upon graduation within the state of KY. *Academic Fields/Career Goals:* Civil Engineering. *Award:* Scholarship for use in freshman, sophomore, junior, or senior year; renewable. *Award amount:* $10,400–$40,000. *Number of awards:* 15–25. *Eligibility Requirements:* Applicant must be enrolled or expecting to enroll full-time at a four-year institution or university; resident of Kentucky and studying in Kentucky. Applicant must have 3.0 GPA or higher. Available to U.S. and non-U.S. citizens. *Application Requirements:* Application, essay, interview, references, test scores, transcript. **Deadline:** March 1.

Contact Jamie Bewley Byrd, Scholarship Program Administrator, Kentucky Transportation Cabinet, 200 Mero Street, Frankfort, KY 40622. *E-mail:* jamie.bewleybyrd@ky.gov. *Web site:* http://www.transportation.ky.gov.

Kentucky Tuition Grant (KTG). Grants available to Kentucky residents who are full-time undergraduates at an independent college within the state. Based on financial need. Must submit FAFSA. *Award:* Grant for use in freshman, sophomore, junior, or senior year; not renewable. *Award amount:* $200–$3000. *Number of awards:* 12,000–13,000. *Eligibility Requirements:* Applicant must be enrolled or expecting to enroll full-time at a two-year or four-year institution or university; resident of Kentucky and studying in Kentucky. Available to U.S. citizens. *Application Requirements:* Application, financial need analysis, FAFSA. **Deadline:** March 15.

Contact Sheila Roe, Grant Program Coordinator, Kentucky Higher Education Assistance Authority (KHEAA), PO Box 798, Frankfort, KY 40602-0798. *E-mail:* sroe@kheaa.com. *Phone:* 800-928-8926 Ext. 67393. *Fax:* 502-696-7496. *Web site:* http://www.kheaa.com.

Minority Educator Recruitment and Retention Scholarship. Conversion loan or scholarship for Kentucky residents. Provides up to $5000 per academic year to minority students majoring in teacher education and pursuing initial teacher certification. Must be repaid with interest if scholarship requirements are not met. *Academic Fields/Career Goals:* Education; Special Education. *Award:* Forgivable loan for use in freshman, sophomore, junior, or senior year; not renewable. *Award amount:* up to $5000. *Number of awards:* 200–300. *Eligibility Requirements:* Applicant must be American Indian/Alaska Native, Asian/Pacific Islander, Black (non-Hispanic), or Hispanic; enrolled or expecting to enroll full-time at a two-year or four-year institution or university; resident of Kentucky and studying in Kentucky. Available to U.S. citizens. *Application Requirements:* Application. **Deadline:** continuous.

Contact Natasha Murray, Program Director, Kentucky Department of Education, Kentucky Higher Education Assistance Authority (KHEAA), 500 Metro Street, Frankfort, KY 40601. *E-mail:* natasha.murray@education.ky.gov. *Phone:* 502-564-1479. *Web site:* http://www.kheaa.com.

Touchstone Energy All "A" Classic Scholarship. Award of $1000 for senior student in good standing at a Kentucky high school which is a member of the All Classic. Applicant must be a U.S. citizen and must plan to attend a postsecondary institution in Kentucky in the upcoming year as a full-time student and be drug free. *Award:* Scholarship for use in freshman year; not renewable. *Award amount:* $1000. *Number of awards:* 12. *Eligibility Requirements:* Applicant must be high school student; planning to enroll or expecting to enroll full-time at a two-year, four-year, or technical institution or university; resident of Kentucky and studying in Kentucky. Available to U.S. citizens. *Application Requirements:* Application, essay, photo, references, transcript. **Deadline:** December 3.

Contact David Cowden, Chairperson, Scholarship Committee, Kentucky Touchstone Energy Cooperatives, 1320 Lincoln Road, Lewisport, KY 42351. *E-mail:* allaclassic@alltel.net. *Phone:* 859-744-4812. *Web site:* http://www.ekpc.coop.

WIRE Scholarships. Scholarship available to Kentucky students who are juniors or seniors in a Kentucky college or university and have 60 credit hours by fall semester. Immediate family of student must be served by one of the state's 24 rural electric distribution cooperatives. Awards based on academic achievement, extracurricular activities, career goals, recommendations. *Award:* Scholarship for use in junior or senior year; not renewable. *Award amount:* $1000. *Number of awards:* 3. *Eligibility Requirements:* Applicant must be enrolled or expecting to enroll full-time at a four-year, or technical institution or university; resident of Kentucky and studying in Kentucky. Available to U.S. citizens. *Application Requirements:* Application, transcript, a letter explaining how this scholarship would enhance your academic goals. **Deadline:** June 18.

Contact Ellie Hobgood, Scholarship Coordinator, Kentucky Association of Electric Cooperatives, Inc., PO Box 32170, Louisville, KY 40232. *E-mail:* ehobgood@kentuckyliving.com. *Phone:* 800-595-4846. *Web site:* http://www.kaec.com.

LOUISIANA

Hemophilia Federation of America Educational Scholarship. One-time scholarship for persons with hemophilia, attending either full-time or part-time in any accredited two- or four-year college, university, or vocation/technical school in the United States. *Award:* Scholarship for use in freshman, sophomore, junior, or senior year; not renewable. *Award amount:* $1500. *Number of awards:* 1–3. *Eligibility Requirements:* Applicant must be enrolled or expecting to enroll full- or part-time at a two-year, four-year, or technical institution or university. Applicant must be physically disabled. Available to U.S. citizens. *Application Requirements:* Application, essay, financial need analysis, references. **Deadline:** April 30.

Contact Scholarship Committee, Hemophilia Federation of America, 1405 West Pinhook Road, Suite 101, Lafayette, LA 70503. *E-mail:* info@hemophiliafed.org. *Phone:* 337-261-9787. *Web site:* http://www.hemophiliaed.org.

Leveraging Educational Assistance Program (LEAP)/Special Leveraging Educational Assistance Program (SLEAP). Apply by completing the FAFSA each year. Must be a resident of Louisiana and must be attending an institution in Louisiana. Institution the student plans to attend must recommend student for award. When you submit the FAFSA, you have automatically applied for all four levels of TOPS, for the LA LEAP/SLEAP Grant, for Louisiana Guaranteed Loans, and for Federal Pell Grants and Go Grants. Please do not send separate letters to application to the TOPS office. *Award:* Grant for use in freshman, sophomore, junior, or senior year; renewable. *Award amount:* $200–$2000. *Number of awards:* 4951. *Eligibility Requirements:* Applicant must be enrolled or expecting to enroll full-time at a two-year, four-year, or technical institution or university; resident of Louisiana and studying in Louisiana. Available to U.S. citizens. *Application Requirements:* Application, financial need analysis, FAFSA. **Deadline:** July 1.

Contact Bonnie Lavergne, Public Information, Louisiana Office of Student Financial Assistance, PO Box 91202, Baton Rouge, LA 70821-9202. *E-mail:* custserv@osfa.state.la.us. *Phone:* 800-259-5626 Ext. 1012. *Fax:* 225-922-0412. *Web site:* http://www.osfa.la.gov.

Louisiana Department of Veterans Affairs State Aid Program. Tuition exemption at any state-supported college, university, or technical institute in Louisiana for children (dependents between the ages of 18-25) of veterans that are rated 90 percent or above service connected disabled by the U.S. Department of Veterans Affairs. Tuition exemption also available for the surviving spouse and children (dependents between the ages of 18-25) of veterans who died on active duty, in line of duty, or where death was the result of a disability incurred in or aggravated by military service. For residents of Louisiana. *Award:* Scholarship for use in freshman, sophomore, junior, or senior year; not renewable. *Award amount:* varies. *Number of awards:* varies. *Eligibility Requirements:* Applicant must be age 18-25; enrolled or expecting to enroll full-time at a two-year, four-year, or technical institution or university; resident of Louisiana and studying in Louisiana. Available to U.S. citizens. Applicant or parent must meet one or more of the following requirements: general military experience; retired from active duty; disabled or killed as a result of military service; prisoner of war; or missing in action. *Application Requirements:* Application. **Deadline:** continuous.

Contact Mr. Richard Blackwell, Veterans Affairs Deputy Assistant Secretary, Louisiana Department of Veteran Affairs, PO Box 94095, Capitol Station, Baton Rouge, LA 70804-4095 USA. *E-mail:* richard.blackwell@vetaffairs.la.gov. *Phone:* 225-922-0500 Ext. 203. *Fax:* 225-922-0511. *Web site:* http://www.vetaffairs.com.

Louisiana National Guard State Tuition Exemption Program. Renewable award for college undergraduates to receive tuition exemption upon satisfactory performance in the Louisiana National Guard. Applicant must attend a state-funded institution in Louisiana, be a resident and registered voter in Louisiana, meet the academic and residency requirements of the university attended, and provide documentation of Louisiana National Guard enlistment. The exemption can be used for up to 15 semesters. Minimum 2.5 GPA required. *Award:* Scholarship for use in freshman, sophomore, junior, or senior year; renewable. *Award amount:* varies. *Number of awards:* varies. *Eligibility Requirements:* Applicant must be enrolled or expecting to enroll full- or part-time at a two-year, four-year, or technical institution or university; resident of Louisiana and studying in Louisiana. Applicant must have 2.5 GPA or higher. Available to U.S. citizens. Applicant or parent must meet one or more of the following requirements: Air Force National Guard or Army National Guard experience; retired from active duty; disabled or killed as a result of military service; prisoner of war; or missing in action. *Application Requirements:* Application, test scores, transcript. **Deadline:** continuous.

Contact Jona M. Hughes, Education Services Officer, Louisiana National Guard, Joint Task Force LA, Building 35, Jackson Barracks, JI-PD, New Orleans, LA 70146-0330. *E-mail:* hughesj@la-arng.ngb.army.mil. *Phone:* 504-278-8531 Ext. 8304. *Fax:* 504-278-8025. *Web site:* http://www.la.ngb.army.mil.

Robert C. Byrd Honors Scholarship-Louisiana. Applicant must have earned a high school diploma or equivalent (GED) in Louisiana in the same academic year in which the scholarship is to be awarded. Minimum 3.5 GPA required. Must be a U.S. citizen and legal resident of Louisiana. Total number of awards vary each year. *Award:* Scholarship for use in freshman, sophomore, junior, or senior year; renewable. *Award amount:* up to $6000. *Number of awards:* 110. *Eligibility Requirements:* Applicant must be enrolled or expecting to enroll full-time at a four-year institution or university and resident of Louisiana. Applicant must have 2.5 GPA or higher. Available to U.S. citizens. *Application Requirements:* Application, essay, test scores, transcript, selective service form. **Deadline:** March 10.

Contact Melissa Hollins, Scholarship Coordinator, Louisiana State Department of Education, PO Box 94064, Baton Rouge, LA 70804. *E-mail:* melissa.hollins@la.gov. *Phone:* 225-342-2098. *Fax:* 225-342-7316. *Web site:* http://www.doe.state.la.us.

Rockefeller State Wildlife Scholarship. For high school graduates, college undergraduates, and college graduate students majoring in forestry, wildlife, or marine science. High school graduates and college undergraduates with fewer than 24 hours, must have at least a 2.5 grade point average and have scored at least a 20 on the ACT or a 940 on the SAT. College graduate students must have a grade point average of at least 3.0 in order to apply. Renewable up to five years as an undergraduate and two years as a graduate student. *Academic Fields/Career Goals:* Biology; Marine Biology; Marine/Ocean Engineering; Natural Resources; Oceanography. *Award:* Scholarship for use in freshman, sophomore, junior, senior, graduate, or postgraduate years; renewable. *Award amount:* $1000. *Number of awards:* 60. *Eligibility Requirements:* Applicant must be enrolled or expecting to enroll full-time at a four-year institution or university; resident of Louisiana and studying in Louisiana. Applicant must have 2.5 GPA or higher. Available to U.S. citizens. *Application Requirements:* Application, test scores, transcript, FAFSA. **Deadline:** July 1.

Contact Bonnie Lavergne, Public Information, Louisiana Office of Student Financial Assistance, PO Box 91202, Baton Rouge, LA 70821-9202. *E-mail:* custserv@osfa.state.la.us. *Phone:* 800-259-5626 Ext. 1012. *Fax:* 225-922-0412. *Web site:* http://www.osfa.la.gov.

Taylor Opportunity Program for Students. Program awards 8 semesters or 12 quarters of tuition to any Louisiana State postsecondary institution. Program awards 8 semesters of an amount equal to the weighted average public tuition fee, to students attending a LAICU (Louisiana Association of Independent Colleges and Universities) institution. When you submit the FAFSA, you have automatically applied for all four levels of TOPS, for the LA LEAP/SLEAP Grant, for Louisiana Guaranteed Loans, and for Federal Pell Grants and Go Grants. Please do not send separate letters to application to the TOPS office. *Award:* Scholarship for use in freshman, sophomore, junior, or senior year; renewable. *Award amount:* $308–$3725. *Number of awards:* 24,372. *Eligibility Requirements:* Applicant must be enrolled or expecting to enroll full-time at a two-year, four-year, or technical institution or university; resident of Louisiana and studying in Louisiana. Available to U.S. citizens. *Application Requirements:* Application, test scores, transcript. **Deadline:** July 1.

Contact Public Information, Louisiana Office of Student Financial Assistance, PO Box 91202, Baton Rouge, LA 70821-9202. *E-mail:* custserv@osfa.state.la.us. *Phone:* 800-

259-5626 Ext. 1012. *Fax:* 225-922-0790. *Web site:* http://www.osfa.la.gov.

Taylor Opportunity Program for Students–Honors Level. Program awards 8 semesters or 12 quarters of tuition to any Louisiana State postsecondary institution. Program awards an amount equal to the weighted average public tuition fee, to students attending a LAICU (Louisiana Association of Independent Colleges and Universities) institution. In addition $400 per semester is provided. When you submit the FAFSA, you have automatically applied for all four levels of TOPS, for the LA LEAP/SLEAP Grant, for Louisiana Guaranteed Loans, and for Federal Pell Grants and Go Grants. Please do not send separate letters to application to the TOPS office. For more information, see Web http://www.fafsa.ed.gov. *Award:* Scholarship for use in freshman, sophomore, junior, or senior year; renewable. *Award amount:* $708–$4525. *Number of awards:* 6977. *Eligibility Requirements:* Applicant must be enrolled or expecting to enroll full-time at a two-year, four-year, or technical institution or university; resident of Louisiana and studying in Louisiana. Applicant must have 3.0 GPA or higher. Available to U.S. citizens. *Application Requirements:* Application, test scores, transcript. **Deadline:** July 1.

Contact Public Information, Louisiana Office of Student Financial Assistance, PO Box 91202, Baton Rouge, LA 70821-9202. *E-mail:* custserv@osfa.state.la.us. *Phone:* 800-259-5626 Ext. 1012. *Fax:* 225-922-0790. *Web site:* http://www.osfa.la.gov.

Taylor Opportunity Program for Students–Performance Level. Program awards 8 semesters or 12 quarters of tuition to any Louisiana State postsecondary institution. Program awards an amount equal to the weighted average public tuition fee, to students attending a LAICU (Louisiana Association of Independent Colleges and Universities) institution. When you submit the FAFSA, you have automatically applied for all four levels of TOPS, for the LA LEAP/SLEAP Grant, for Louisiana Guaranteed Loans, and for Federal Pell Grants and Go Grants. Please do not send separate letters to application to the TOPS office. *Award:* Scholarship for use in freshman, sophomore, junior, or senior year; renewable. *Award amount:* $508–$4125. *Number of awards:* 9225. *Eligibility Requirements:* Applicant must be enrolled or expecting to enroll full-time at a two-year, four-year, or technical institution or university; resident of Louisiana and studying in Louisiana. Applicant must have 3.0 GPA or higher. Available to U.S. citizens. *Application Requirements:* Application, test scores, transcript. **Deadline:** July 1.

Contact Public Information, Louisiana Office of Student Financial Assistance, PO Box 91202, Baton Rouge, LA 70821-9202. *E-mail:* custserv@osfa.state.la.us. *Phone:* 800-259-5626 Ext. 1012. *Fax:* 225-922-0790. *Web site:* http://www.osfa.la.gov.

Taylor Opportunity Program for Students–Tech Award. Program awards an amount equal to tuition for up to 4 semesters of technical training at a Louisiana postsecondary institution that offers a vocational or technical education certificate or diploma program, or a non-academic degree program. Must have completed the TOPS Opportunity core curriculum or the TOPS Tech core curriculum, must have achieved a 2.50 grade point average over the core curriculum only, and must have achieved an ACT score of 17. Program awards an amount equal to the weighted average public tuition fee for technical programs to students attending a LAICU private institution for technical training. When you submit the FAFSA, you have automatically applied for all four levels of TOPS, for the LA LEAP/SLEAP Grant, for Louisiana Guaranteed Loans, and for Federal Pell Grants and Go Grants. Please do not send separate letters to application to the TOPS office. *Award:* Scholarship for use in freshman or sophomore year; renewable. *Award amount:* $308–$1624. *Number of awards:* 737. *Eligibility Requirements:* Applicant must be enrolled or expecting to enroll full-time at a technical institution; resident of Louisiana and studying in Louisiana. Applicant must have 2.5 GPA or higher. Available to U.S. citizens. *Application Requirements:* Application, test scores, transcript, ACT of 17 OR SAT of 810. **Deadline:** July 1.

Contact Public Information, Louisiana Office of Student Financial Assistance, PO Box 91202, Baton Rouge, LA 70821-9202. *E-mail:* custserv@osfa.state.la.us. *Phone:* 800-259-5626 Ext. 1012. *Fax:* 225-922-0790. *Web site:* http://www.osfa.la.gov.

MAINE

American Legion Auxiliary Department of Maine Daniel E. Lambert Memorial Scholarship. Scholarships to assist young men and women in continuing their education beyond high school. Must demonstrate financial need, must be a resident of the State of Maine, U.S. citizen, and parent must be a veteran. *Award:* Scholarship for use in freshman year; not renewable. *Award amount:* $1000. *Number of awards:* up to

2. *Eligibility Requirements:* Applicant must be high school student; planning to enroll or expecting to enroll full-time at a four-year institution or university and resident of Maine. Available to U.S. citizens. Applicant or parent must meet one or more of the following requirements: general military experience; retired from active duty; disabled or killed as a result of military service; prisoner of war; or missing in action. *Application Requirements:* Application, financial need analysis. **Deadline:** May 1.

Contact Mary Wells, Education Chairman, American Legion Auxiliary Department of Maine, 21 Limerock Street, PO Box 434, Rockland, ME 04841 USA. *E-mail:* aladeptsecme@verizon.net. *Phone:* 207-532-6007. *Web site:* http://www.mainelegion.org.

American Legion Auxiliary Department of Maine National President's Scholarship. Scholarships to children of veterans who served in the Armed Forces during the eligibility dates for The American Legion. One $2500, one $2000, and one $1000 scholarship will be awarded. Applicant must complete 50 hours of community service during his/her high school years. *Award:* Scholarship for use in freshman year; not renewable. *Award amount:* $1000–$2500. *Number of awards:* 3. *Eligibility Requirements:* Applicant must be high school student; planning to enroll or expecting to enroll full-time at a four-year institution or university and resident of Maine. Applicant or parent of applicant must have employment or volunteer experience in community service. Available to U.S. citizens. Applicant or parent must meet one or more of the following requirements: general military experience; retired from active duty; disabled or killed as a result of military service; prisoner of war; or missing in action. *Application Requirements:* Application, essay, references, test scores, transcript. **Deadline:** March 1.

Contact Mary Wells, Education Chairman, American Legion Auxiliary Department of Maine, 21 Limerock Street, PO Box 434, Rockland, ME 04841 USA. *E-mail:* aladeptsecme@verizon.net. *Phone:* 207-532-6007. *Web site:* http://www.mainelegion.org.

American Legion Auxiliary Department of Maine Past Presidents' Parley Nurses Scholarship. One-time award for child, grandchild, sister, or brother of veteran. Must be resident of Maine and wishing to continue education at accredited school in medical field. Must submit photo, doctor's statement, and evidence of civic activity. Minimum 3.5 GPA required. *Academic Fields/Career Goals:* Health and Medical

Sciences; Nursing. *Award:* Scholarship for use in freshman, sophomore, junior, or senior year; not renewable. *Award amount:* $300. *Number of awards:* 1. *Eligibility Requirements:* Applicant must be age 18 and over; enrolled or expecting to enroll full-time at a two-year, four-year, or technical institution or university and resident of Maine. Applicant or parent of applicant must have employment or volunteer experience in community service. Applicant must have 2.5 GPA or higher. Available to U.S. citizens. Applicant or parent must meet one or more of the following requirements: general military experience; retired from active duty; disabled or killed as a result of military service; prisoner of war; or missing in action. *Application Requirements:* Application, photo, references, transcript, doctor's statement. **Deadline:** March 31.

Contact Mary Wells, Education Chairman, American Legion Auxiliary Department of Maine, 21 Limerock Street, PO Box 434, Rockland, ME 04841 USA. *E-mail:* aladeptsecme@verizon.net. *Phone:* 207-532-6007. *Web site:* http://www.mainelegion.org.

Early College For ME. Scholarship for high school students who have not made plans for college but are academically capable of success in college. Recipients are selected by their school principal or director. Students must be entering a Maine Community College. Refer to Web site http://www.mccs.me.edu/scholarships.html. *Award:* Scholarship for use in freshman year; renewable. *Award amount:* $2000. *Number of awards:* 200. *Eligibility Requirements:* Applicant must be high school student; planning to enroll or expecting to enroll full-time at a two-year or four-year institution or university; resident of Maine and studying in Maine. Available to U.S. citizens. *Application Requirements:* Application, financial need analysis, references, transcript. **Deadline:** varies.

Contact Charles P. Collins, State Director, Center for Career Development, Maine Community College System, 323 State Street, Augusta, ME 04330. *E-mail:* ccollins@mccs.me.edu. *Phone:* 207-767-5210 Ext. 4115. *Fax:* 207-629-4048. *Web site:* http://www.mccs.me.edu.

Educators for Maine Forgivable Loan Program. Forgivable loan for residents of Maine who are high school seniors, college students, or college graduates with a minimum 3.0 GPA, studying or preparing to study teacher education. Must teach in Maine upon graduation. Award based on merit. For application information see Web site http://www.famemaine.com. *Academic Fields/Career Goals:* Education. *Award:* Forgivable loan for use in freshman, sophomore, junior, or senior year; renewable. *Award amount:* $2000–$3000. *Number of awards:* up to 500. *Eligibility Requirements:* Applicant must be enrolled or expecting to enroll full-time at a two-year or four-year institution or university and resident of Maine. Applicant must have 3.0 GPA or higher. Available to U.S. citizens. *Application Requirements:* Application, essay, test scores, transcript. **Deadline:** May 15.

Contact Lisa Bongiovanni, Manager, Operations, Finance Authority of Maine, Five Community Drive, PO Box 949, Augusta, ME 04332-0949 USA. *E-mail:* education@famemaine.com. *Phone:* 207-623-3263. *Fax:* 207-623-0095. *Web site:* http://www.famemaine.com.

Maine Rural Rehabilitation Fund Scholarship Program. One-time scholarship open to Maine residents enrolled in or accepted by any school, college, or university. Must be full time and demonstrate financial need. Those opting for a Maine institution given preference. Major must lead to an agricultural career. Minimum 3.0 GPA required. *Academic Fields/Career Goals:* Agribusiness; Agriculture; Animal/Veterinary Sciences. *Award:* Scholarship for use in freshman, sophomore, junior, senior, graduate, or postgraduate years; not renewable. *Award amount:* $800–$2000. *Number of awards:* 10–20. *Eligibility Requirements:* Applicant must be enrolled or expecting to enroll full-time at a two-year, four-year, or technical institution or university and resident of Maine. Applicant must have 3.0 GPA or higher. Available to U.S. citizens. *Application Requirements:* Application, autobiography, financial need analysis, transcript. **Deadline:** June 15.

Contact Jane Aiudi, Director of Marketing, Maine Department of Agriculture, Food and Rural Resources, 28 State House Station, Augusta, ME 04333-0028. *E-mail:* jane.aiudi@maine.gov. *Phone:* 207-287-7628. *Fax:* 207-287-5576. *Web site:* http://www.maine.gov/agriculture.

Robert C. Byrd Honors Scholarship-Maine. Merit-based, renewable scholarship of up to $1500 annually for graduating high school seniors. Must have a minimum of 3.0 GPA. Must be a resident of Maine. Superior academic performance is the primary criterion. For application, see Web site http://www.famemaine.com. *Award:* Scholarship for use in freshman year; renewable. *Award amount:* up to $1500. *Number of awards:* up to 30. *Eligibility Requirements:* Applicant must be high school student; planning to enroll or expecting to enroll full-time at a two-year, four-year, or technical institution or university and resident of Maine. Applicant must have 3.0 GPA or higher. Available to U.S. citizens. *Application Requirements:* Application, essay, transcript, high school profile. **Deadline:** May 1.

Contact Lisa Bongiovanni, Manager, Operations, Finance Authority of Maine, Five Community Drive, PO Box 949, Augusta, ME 04332-0949 USA. *E-mail:* education@famemaine.com. *Phone:* 207-623-3263. *Fax:* 207-623-0095. *Web site:* http://www.famemaine.com.

State of Maine Grant Program. Scholarship for residents of Maine, attending an eligible school in Connecticut, Maine, Massachusetts, New Hampshire, Pennsylvania, Rhode Island, Washington, D.C., or Vermont. Award based on need. Must apply annually. Complete free application for Federal Student Aid to apply. One-time award for undergraduate study. For further information see Web site http://www.famemaine.com. *Award:* Grant for use in freshman, sophomore, junior, or senior year; not renewable. *Award amount:* $500–$1250. *Number of awards:* up to 13,000. *Eligibility Requirements:* Applicant must be enrolled or expecting to enroll full- or part-time at a two-year, four-year, or technical institution or university; resident of Maine and studying in Connecticut, District of Columbia, Maine, Massachusetts, New Hampshire, Pennsylvania, Rhode Island, or Vermont. Available to U.S. citizens. *Application Requirements:* Application, financial need analysis, FAFSA. **Deadline:** May 1.

Contact Lisa Bongiovanni, Manager, Operations, Finance Authority of Maine, Five Community Drive, PO Box 949, Augusta, ME 04332-0949 USA. *E-mail:* education@famemaine.com. *Phone:* 207-623-3263. *Fax:* 207-623-0095. *Web site:* http://www.famemaine.com.

Tuition Waiver Programs. Provides tuition waivers for children and spouses of EMS personnel, firefighters, and law enforcement officers who have been killed in the line of duty and for students who were foster children under the custody of the Department of Human Services when they graduated from high school. Waivers valid at the University of Maine System, the Maine Technical College System, and Maine Maritime Academy. Applicant must reside and study in Maine. *Award:* Grant for use in freshman, sophomore, junior, or senior year; renewable. *Award amount:* varies. *Number of awards:* up to 30.

Eligibility Requirements: Applicant must be enrolled or expecting to enroll full- or part-time at a four-year institution or university; resident of Maine and studying in Maine. Applicant or parent of applicant must have employment or volunteer experience in police/firefighting. Available to U.S. citizens. *Application Requirements:* Application, letter from the Department of Human Services documenting that applicant is in their custody and residing in foster care at the time of graduation from high school or its equivalent. **Deadline:** continuous.

Contact Lisa Bongiovanni, Manager, Operations, Finance Authority of Maine, Five Community Drive, PO Box 949, Augusta, ME 04332-0949 USA. *E-mail:* education@famemaine.com. *Phone:* 207-623-3263. *Fax:* 207-623-0095. *Web site:* http://www.famemaine.com.

U.S. Department of Education Fulbright-Hays Project Abroad Scholarship for Programs in China. Scholarships offered to students who are participating in a CIEE Chinese language programs in China or Taiwan. Must be a U.S. citizen enrolled in a CIEE program. Students must have completed the equivalent of two years study in Chinese language (documented). Deadlines: April 1 and November 1. There is also a return requirement for scholarship awardees to submit a program report and evaluation. *Academic Fields/Career Goals:* Asian Studies; Education. *Award:* Scholarship for use in junior or senior year; not renewable. *Award amount:* $1000–$12,000. *Number of awards:* 1–20. *Eligibility Requirements:* Applicant must be enrolled or expecting to enroll full-time at a four-year institution or university and must have an interest in foreign language. Applicant must have 3.0 GPA or higher. Available to U.S. citizens. *Application Requirements:* Application, essay, financial need analysis, references, transcript, copy of passport or birth certificate. **Deadline:** varies.

Contact CIEE Scholarship Committee, CIEE: Council on International Educational Exchange, 300 Fore Street, Portland, ME 04101 USA. *E-mail:* studyinfo@ciee.org. *Phone:* 800-407-8839. *Fax:* 207-553-4299. *Web site:* http://www.ciee.org.

Veterans Dependents Educational Benefits-Maine. Tuition waiver award for dependent children or spouses of veterans permanently and totally disabled resulting from service-connected disability; died from a service-connected disability ; at time of death was totally and permanently disabled due to service-connected disability, but whose death was not related to the service-connected disability; or member of the Armed Forces on active duty who has been listed for more than 90 days as missing in action, captured or forcibly detained or interned in the line of duty. Benefits apply only to the University of Maine System, Maine community colleges and Maine Maritime Academy. Must be high school graduate. Must submit with application proof of veteran's VA disability along with dependent verification paperwork such as birth, marriage, or adoption certificate and proof of enrollment in degree program. *Award:* Scholarship for use in freshman, sophomore, junior, or senior year; not renewable. *Award amount:* varies. *Number of awards:* varies. *Eligibility Requirements:* Applicant must be enrolled or expecting to enroll full- or part-time at a two-year or four-year institution or university; resident of Maine and studying in Maine. Available to U.S. citizens. Applicant must have general military experience. *Application Requirements:* Application, see Web site for complete application instructions.

Contact Mrs. Paula Gagnon, Office Associate II, Maine Division of Veterans Services, State House, Station 117, Augusta, ME 04333-0117. *E-mail:* mainebvs@maine.gov. *Phone:* 207-626-4464. *Fax:* 207-626-4471. *Web site:* http://www.maine.gov/dvem/bvs.

MARYLAND

Charles W. Riley Fire and Emergency Medical Services Tuition Reimbursement Program. Award intended to reimburse members of rescue organizations serving Maryland communities for tuition costs of course work towards a degree or certificate in fire service or medical technology. Must attend a two- or four-year school in Maryland. Minimum 2.0 GPA. The scholarship is worth up to $6500. *Academic Fields/Career Goals:* Fire Sciences; Health and Medical Sciences; Trade/Technical Specialties. *Award:* Scholarship for use in freshman, sophomore, junior, or senior year; not renewable. *Award amount:* up to $6500. *Number of awards:* up to 150. *Eligibility Requirements:* Applicant must be enrolled or expecting to enroll full- or part-time at a two-year or four-year institution or university; resident of Maryland and studying in Maryland. Applicant or parent of applicant must have employment or volunteer experience in police/firefighting. Available to U.S. citizens. *Application Requirements:* Application, transcript, tuition receipt, proof of enrollment. **Deadline:** July 1.

Contact Maura Sappington, Office of Student Financial Assistance, Maryland State Higher Education Commission, 839 Bestgate Road, Suite 400, Annapolis, MD 21401-3013. *E-mail:* msapping@mhec.state.md.us. *Phone:* 410-260-4569. *Fax:* 410-260-3203. *Web site:* http://www.mhec.state.md.us.

Delegate Scholarship Program-Maryland. Delegate scholarships help Maryland residents attending Maryland degree-granting institutions, certain career schools, or nursing diploma schools. May attend out-of-state institution if Maryland Higher Education Commission deems major to be unique and not offered at a Maryland institution. Free Application for Federal Student Aid may be required. Students interested in this program should apply by contacting their legislative district delegate. *Award:* Scholarship for use in freshman, sophomore, junior, or senior year; not renewable. *Award amount:* $200–$8650. *Number of awards:* up to 3500. *Eligibility Requirements:* Applicant must be enrolled or expecting to enroll full- or part-time at a two-year, four-year, or technical institution or university; resident of Maryland and studying in Maryland. Available to U.S. citizens. *Application Requirements:* Application, FAFSA. **Deadline:** continuous.

Contact Monica Wheatley, Office of Student Financial Assistance, Maryland State Higher Education Commission, 839 Bestgate Road, Suite 400, Annapolis, MD 21401-3013. *E-mail:* osfamail@mhec.state.md.us. *Phone:* 800-974-1024. *Fax:* 410-260-3200. *Web site:* http://www.mhec.state.md.us.

Distinguished Scholar Award-Maryland. Renewable award for Maryland students enrolled full-time at Maryland institutions. National Merit Scholar Finalists automatically offered award. Others may qualify for the award in satisfying criteria of a minimum 3.7 GPA or in combination with high test scores, or for Talent in Arts competition in categories of music, drama, dance, or visual arts. Must maintain annual 3.0 GPA in college for award to be renewed. *Award:* Scholarship for use in freshman, sophomore, junior, or senior year; renewable. *Award amount:* up to $3000. *Number of awards:* up to 1400. *Eligibility Requirements:* Applicant must be high school student; planning to enroll or expecting to enroll full-time at a two-year or four-year institution or university; resident of Maryland and studying in Maryland. Available to U.S. citizens. *Application Requirements:* Application, test scores, transcript.

Contact Tamika McKelvin, Program Administrator, Maryland State Higher Education Commission, 839 Bestgate Road, Suite 400, Annapolis, MD 21401-3013. *E-mail:* tmckelvi@mhec.state.md.us. *Phone:* 410-260-

4546. *Fax:* 410-260-3200. *Web site:* http://www.mhec.state.md.us.

Distinguished Scholar Community College Transfer Program. Scholarship available for Maryland residents who have completed 60 credit hours or an associate degree at a Maryland community college and are transferring to a Maryland four-year institution. *Award:* Scholarship for use in freshman or sophomore year; renewable. *Award amount:* $3000. *Number of awards:* 127. *Eligibility Requirements:* Applicant must be enrolled or expecting to enroll full-time at a two-year institution; resident of Maryland and studying in Maryland. Available to U.S. citizens. *Application Requirements:* Application, transcript. **Deadline:** March 1.

Contact Maura Sappington, Program Manager, Maryland State Higher Education Commission, 839 Bestgate Road, Suite 400, Annapolis, MD 21401-3013. *E-mail:* msapping@mhec.state.md.us. *Phone:* 410-260-4569. *Fax:* 410-260-3203. *Web site:* http://www.mhec.state.md.us.

Edward T. Conroy Memorial Scholarship Program. Scholarship for dependents of deceased or 100 percent disabled U.S. Armed Forces personnel; the son, daughter, or surviving spouse of a victim of the September 11, 2001 terrorist attacks who died as a result of the attacks on the World Trade Center in New York City, the attack on the Pentagon in Virginia, or the crash of United Airlines Flight 93 in Pennsylvania; a POW/MIA of the Vietnam Conflict or his/her son or daughter; the son, daughter or surviving spouse (who has not remarried) of a state or local public safety employee or volunteer who died in the line of duty; or a state or local public safety employee or volunteer who was 100 percent disabled in the line of duty. Must be Maryland resident at time of disability. Submit applicable VA certification. Must be at least 16 years of age and attend Maryland institution. *Award:* Scholarship for use in freshman, sophomore, junior, or senior year; renewable. *Award amount:* $7200–$9000. *Number of awards:* up to 121. *Eligibility Requirements:* Applicant must be age 16-24; enrolled or expecting to enroll full- or part-time at a two-year or four-year institution or university; resident of Maryland and studying in Maryland. Applicant or parent of applicant must have employment or volunteer experience in police/firefighting. Available to U.S. citizens. Applicant or parent must meet one or more of the following requirements: general military experience; retired from active duty; disabled or killed as a result of

military service; prisoner of war; or missing in action. *Application Requirements:* Application, birth and death certificate, disability papers. **Deadline:** July 15.

Contact Linda Asplin, Office of Student Financial Assistance, Maryland State Higher Education Commission, 839 Bestgate Road, Suite 400, Annapolis, MD 21401-3013. *E-mail:* lasplin@mhec.state.md.us. *Phone:* 410-260-4563. *Fax:* 410-260-3203. *Web site:* http://www.mhec.state.md.us.

Graduate and Professional Scholarship Program-Maryland. Graduate and professional scholarships provide need-based financial assistance to students attending a Maryland school of medicine, dentistry, law, pharmacy, social work, or nursing. Funds are provided to specific Maryland colleges and universities. Students must demonstrate financial need and be Maryland residents. Contact institution financial aid office for more information. *Academic Fields/Career Goals:* Dental Health/Services; Health and Medical Sciences; Law/Legal Services; Nursing; Social Services. *Award:* Scholarship for use in freshman, sophomore, junior, or senior year; renewable. *Award amount:* $1000–$5000. *Number of awards:* up to 584. *Eligibility Requirements:* Applicant must be enrolled or expecting to enroll full- or part-time at a four-year institution or university; resident of Maryland and studying in Maryland. Available to U.S. citizens. *Application Requirements:* Application, financial need analysis, contact institution financial aid office. **Deadline:** March 1.

Contact Monica Wheatley, Program Manager, Maryland State Higher Education Commission, 839 Bestgate Road, Suite 400, Annapolis, MD 21401. *E-mail:* mwheatle@mhec.state.md.us. *Phone:* 410-260-4560. *Fax:* 410-260-3202. *Web site:* http://www.mhec.state.md.us.

Howard P. Rawlings Educational Excellence Awards Educational Assistance Grant. Award for Maryland residents accepted or enrolled in a full-time undergraduate degree or certificate program at a Maryland institution or hospital nursing school. Must submit financial aid form by March 1. Must earn 2.0 GPA in college to maintain award. *Award:* Grant for use in freshman, sophomore, junior, or senior year; renewable. *Award amount:* $400–$2700. *Number of awards:* 15,000–30,000. *Eligibility Requirements:* Applicant must be enrolled or expecting to enroll full-time at a two-year or four-year institution or university; resident of Maryland and studying in Maryland. Available to U.S. citizens.

Application Requirements: Application, financial need analysis. **Deadline:** March 1.

Contact Office of Student Financial Assistance, Maryland State Higher Education Commission, 839 Bestgate Road, Suite 400, Annapolis, MD 21401-3013. *E-mail:* osfamail@mhec.state.md.us. *Phone:* 800-974-1024. *Fax:* 410-260-3200. *Web site:* http://www.mhec.state.md.us.

Howard P. Rawlings Educational Excellence Awards Guaranteed Access Grant. Award for Maryland resident enrolling full-time in an undergraduate program at a Maryland institution. Must be under 21 at time of first award and begin college within one year of completing high school in Maryland with a minimum 2.5 GPA. Must have an annual family income less than 130 percent of the federal poverty level guideline. *Award:* Grant for use in freshman, sophomore, junior, or senior year; renewable. *Award amount:* $400–$14,800. *Number of awards:* up to 1000. *Eligibility Requirements:* Applicant must be age 21 or under; enrolled or expecting to enroll full-time at a two-year or four-year institution or university; resident of Maryland and studying in Maryland. Applicant must have 3.5 GPA or higher. Available to U.S. citizens. *Application Requirements:* Application, financial need analysis, transcript. **Deadline:** March 1.

Contact Theresa Lowe, Office of Student Financial Assistance, Maryland State Higher Education Commission, 839 Bestgate Road, Suite 400, Annapolis, MD 21401-3013. *E-mail:* osfamail@mhec.state.md.us. *Phone:* 410-260-4555. *Fax:* 410-260-3200. *Web site:* http://www.mhec.state.md.us.

Janet L. Hoffmann Loan Assistance Repayment Program. Provides assistance for repayment of loan debt to Maryland residents working full-time in nonprofit organizations and state or local governments. Must submit Employment Verification Form and Lender Verification Form. *Academic Fields/Career Goals:* Education; Law/Legal Services; Nursing; Social Services; Therapy/Rehabilitation. *Award:* Grant for use in freshman, sophomore, junior, or senior year; not renewable. *Award amount:* $1500–$10,000. *Number of awards:* up to 700. *Eligibility Requirements:* Applicant must be enrolled or expecting to enroll full-time at a four-year institution or university; resident of Maryland and studying in Maryland. Applicant or parent of applicant must have employment or volunteer experience in government/politics. Available to U.S. citizens. *Application Requirements:* Application, transcript, IRS 1040 form. **Deadline:** September 30.

Contact Tamika McKelvin, Office of Student Financial Assistance, Maryland State Higher Education Commission, 839 Bestgate Road, Suite 400, Annapolis, MD 21401. *E-mail:* tmckelvil@mhec.state.md.us. *Phone:* 410-260-4546. *Fax:* 410-260-3203. *Web site:* http://www.mhec.state.md.us.

J.F. Tolbert Memorial Student Grant Program. Awards of $500 granted to Maryland residents attending a private career school in Maryland. The scholarship deadline continues. *Award:* Grant for use in freshman or sophomore year; not renewable. *Award amount:* $500. *Number of awards:* 522. *Eligibility Requirements:* Applicant must be enrolled or expecting to enroll full-time at a technical institution; resident of Maryland and studying in Maryland. Available to U.S. citizens. *Application Requirements:* Application, financial need analysis. **Deadline:** continuous.

Contact Glenda Hamlet, Office of Student Financial Assistance, Maryland State Higher Education Commission, 839 Bestgate Road, Suite 400, Annapolis, MD 21401-3013. *E-mail:* osfamail@mhec.state.md.us. *Phone:* 800-974-1024. *Fax:* 410-260-3200. *Web site:* http://www.mhec.state.md.us.

Part-Time Grant Program-Maryland. Funds provided to Maryland colleges and universities. Eligible students must be enrolled on a part-time basis (6 to 11 credits) in an undergraduate degree program. Must demonstrate financial need and also be Maryland resident. Contact financial aid office at institution for more information. *Award:* Grant for use in freshman, sophomore, junior, or senior year; renewable. *Award amount:* $200–$1500. *Number of awards:* 1800–9000. *Eligibility Requirements:* Applicant must be enrolled or expecting to enroll part-time at a two-year or four-year institution or university; resident of Maryland and studying in Maryland. Available to U.S. citizens. *Application Requirements:* Application, financial need analysis. **Deadline:** March 1.

Contact Monica Wheatley, Program Manager, Maryland State Higher Education Commission, 839 Bestgate Road, Suite 400, Annapolis, MD 21401. *E-mail:* mwheatle@mhec.state.md.us. *Phone:* 410-260-4560. *Fax:* 410-260-3202. *Web site:* http://www.mhec.state.md.us.

Senatorial Scholarships-Maryland. Renewable award for Maryland residents attending a Maryland degree-granting institution, nursing diploma school, or certain private career schools. May be used out-of-state only if Maryland Higher Education Commission deems major to be unique and not offered at Maryland institution. The scholarship value is $400 to $7000. *Award:* Scholarship for use in freshman, sophomore, junior, or senior year; renewable. *Award amount:* $400–$7000. *Number of awards:* up to 7000. *Eligibility Requirements:* Applicant must be enrolled or expecting to enroll full- or part-time at a two-year, four-year, or technical institution or university; resident of Maryland and studying in Maryland. Available to U.S. citizens. *Application Requirements:* Application, financial need analysis, test scores. **Deadline:** March 1.

Contact Monica Wheatley, Office of Student Financial Assistance, Maryland State Higher Education Commission, 839 Bestgate Road, Suite 400, Annapolis, MD 21401-3013. *E-mail:* osfamail@mhec.state.md.us. *Phone:* 800-974-1024. *Fax:* 410-260-3200. *Web site:* http://www.mhec.state.md.us.

Tuition Reduction for Non-Resident Nursing Students. Available to nonresidents of Maryland who attend a two-year or four-year public institution in Maryland. It is renewable provided student maintains academic requirements designated by institution attended. Recipient must agree to serve as a full-time nurse in a hospital or related institution for two to four years. *Academic Fields/Career Goals:* Nursing. *Award:* Scholarship for use in freshman, sophomore, junior, or senior year; renewable. *Award amount:* varies. *Number of awards:* varies. *Eligibility Requirements:* Applicant must be enrolled or expecting to enroll full- or part-time at a two-year or four-year institution and studying in Maryland. Available to U.S. citizens. *Application Requirements:* Application. **Deadline:** varies.

Contact Robert Parker, Director, Maryland State Higher Education Commission, 839 Bestgate Road, Suite 400, Annapolis, MD 21401-3013. *E-mail:* rparker@mhec.state.md.us. *Phone:* 410-260-4558. *Web site:* http://www.mhec.state.md.us.

Tuition Waiver for Foster Care Recipients. Applicant must be a high school graduate or GED recipient and under the age of 21. Must either have resided in a foster care home in Maryland at the time of high school graduation or GED reception, or until 14th birthday, and been adopted after 14th birthday. Applicant, if status approved, will be exempt from paying tuition and mandatory fees at a public college in Maryland. *Award:* Grant for use in freshman, sophomore, junior, senior, or graduate year; renewable. *Award amount:* varies. *Number of awards:* varies. *Eligibility Requirements:* Applicant must be age 21 or under; enrolled or expecting to enroll full- or part-time at a two-year or four-year institution or university; resident of Maryland and studying in Maryland. Available to U.S. citizens. *Application Requirements:* Application, financial need analysis, must inquire at financial aid office of schools. **Deadline:** March 1.

Contact Robert Parker, Director, Maryland State Higher Education Commission, 839 Bestgate Road, Suite 400, Annapolis, MD 21401-3013. *E-mail:* rparker@mhec.state.md.us. *Phone:* 410-260-4558. *Web site:* http://www.mhec.state.md.us.

Veterans of the Afghanistan and Iraq Conflicts Scholarship Program. Provides financial assistance to Maryland resident U.S. Armed Forces personnel who served in Afghanistan or Iraq Conflicts and their children or spouses who are attending Maryland institutions. *Award:* Scholarship for use in freshman, sophomore, junior, or senior year; renewable. *Award amount:* $8850. *Number of awards:* 123. *Eligibility Requirements:* Applicant must be enrolled or expecting to enroll full- or part-time at a two-year or four-year institution or university; resident of Maryland and studying in Maryland. Available to U.S. citizens. Applicant or parent must meet one or more of the following requirements: general military experience; retired from active duty; disabled or killed as a result of military service; prisoner of war; or missing in action. *Application Requirements:* Application, financial need analysis, birth certificate/marriage certificate, documentation of military order. **Deadline:** March 1.

Contact Linda Asplin, Program Administrator, Maryland State Higher Education Commission, 839 Bestgate Road, Suite 400, Annapolis, MD 21401-3013. *E-mail:* lasplin@mhec.state.md.us. *Phone:* 410-260-4563. *Fax:* 410-260-3203. *Web site:* http://www.mhec.state.md.us.

Workforce Shortage Student Assistance Grant Program. Scholarship of $4000 available to students who will be required to major in specific areas and will be obligated to serve in the state of Maryland after completion of degree. *Award:* Scholarship for use in freshman, sophomore, junior, or senior year; renewable. *Award amount:* $4000. *Number of awards:* 1300. *Eligibility Requirements:* Applicant must be enrolled or expecting to enroll full- or part-time at a two-year or four-year institution or university; resident of Maryland and studying in Maryland. Available to U.S. citizens. *Application Requirements:* Application, essay, financial need analysis, resume, references, transcript, certain majors require additional documentation. **Deadline:** July 1.

Contact Maura Sappington, Program Manager, Maryland State Higher Education Commission, 839 Bestgate Road, Suite 400, Annapolis, MD 21401-3013. *E-mail:* msapping@mhec.state.md.us. *Phone:* 410-260-4569. *Fax:* 410-260-3203. *Web site:* http://www.mhec.state.md.us.

MASSACHUSETTS

Agnes M. Lindsay Scholarship. Scholarships for students with demonstrated financial need who are from rural areas of Massachusetts and attend public institutions of higher education in Massachusetts. Deadline varies. *Award:* Scholarship for use in freshman, sophomore, junior, or senior year; not renewable. *Award amount:* varies. *Number of awards:* varies. *Eligibility Requirements:* Applicant must be enrolled or expecting to enroll full-time at a two-year or four-year institution or university; resident of Massachusetts and studying in Massachusetts. Available to U.S. citizens. *Application Requirements:* Application, financial need analysis. **Deadline:** varies.

Contact Robert Brun, Director of Scholarships and Grants, Massachusetts Office of Student Financial Assistance, 454 Broadway, Suite 200, Revere, MA 02151. *E-mail:* osfa@osfa.mass.edu. *Phone:* 617-727-9420. *Fax:* 617-727-0667. *Web site:* http://www.osfa.mass.edu.

Christian A. Herter Memorial Scholarship. Renewable award for Massachusetts residents who are in the tenth and eleventh grades, and whose socioeconomic backgrounds and environment may inhibit their ability to attain educational goals. Must exhibit severe personal or family-related difficulties, medical problems, or have overcome a personal obstacle. Provides up to 50 percent of the student's calculated need, as determined by federal methodology, at the college of their choice within the continental United States. *Award:* Scholarship for use in freshman year; renewable. *Award amount:* up to $15,000. *Number of awards:* 25. *Eligibility Requirements:* Applicant must be high school student; planning to enroll or expecting to enroll full-time at a two-year, four-year, or technical institution or university and resident of Massachusetts. Applicant must have 2.5 GPA or higher. Available to U.S. citizens. *Application Requirements:* Application, autobiography, financial need analysis, interview, references. **Deadline:** March 14.

Contact Robert Brun, Director of Scholarships and Grants, Massachusetts Office of Student Financial Assistance, 454 Broadway, Suite 200, Revere, MA 02151. *E-mail:* osfa@

osfa.mass.edu. *Phone:* 617-727-9420. *Fax:* 617-727-0667. *Web site:* http://www.osfa.mass.edu.

DSS Adopted Children Tuition Waiver. Need-based tuition waiver for Massachusetts residents who are full-time undergraduate students. Must attend a Massachusetts public institution of higher education and be under 24 years of age. File the FAFSA after January 1. Contact school financial aid office for more information. *Award:* Scholarship for use in freshman, sophomore, junior, or senior year; renewable. *Award amount:* varies. *Number of awards:* varies. *Eligibility Requirements:* Applicant must be age 24 or under; enrolled or expecting to enroll full-time at a two-year or four-year institution and resident of Massachusetts. Available to U.S. and non-Canadian citizens. *Application Requirements:* Application, financial need analysis, FAFSA. **Deadline:** varies.

Contact Robert Brun, Director of Scholarships and Grants, Massachusetts Office of Student Financial Assistance, 454 Broadway, Suite 200, Revere, MA 02151. *E-mail:* osfa@osfa.mass.edu. *Phone:* 617-727-9420. *Fax:* 617-727-0667. *Web site:* http://www.osfa.mass.edu.

Early Childhood Educators Scholarship Program. Scholarship to provide financial assistance for currently employed early childhood educators and providers who enroll in an associate or bachelor degree program in Early Childhood Education or related programs. Awards are not based on financial need. Individuals taking their first college-level ECE course are eligible for 100 percent tuition, while subsequent ECE courses are awarded at 50 percent tuition. Can be used for one class each semester. *Academic Fields/Career Goals:* Education. *Award:* Scholarship for use in freshman, sophomore, junior, or senior year; not renewable. *Award amount:* $150–$3600. *Number of awards:* varies. *Eligibility Requirements:* Applicant must be enrolled or expecting to enroll full- or part-time at a four-year institution or university. Available to U.S. citizens. *Application Requirements:* Application. **Deadline:** July 1.

Contact Robert Brun, Director of Scholarships and Grants, Massachusetts Office of Student Financial Assistance, 454 Broadway, Suite 200, Revere, MA 02151. *E-mail:* osfa@osfa.mass.edu. *Phone:* 617-727-9420. *Fax:* 617-727-0667. *Web site:* http://www.osfa.mass.edu.

John and Abigail Adams Scholarship. Scholarship to reward and inspire student achievement, attract more high-performing

students to Massachusetts public higher education, and provide families of college-bound students with financial assistance. Must be a U.S. citizen or an eligible non-citizen. There is no application process for the scholarship. Students who are eligible will be notified in the fall of their senior year in high school. *Award:* Scholarship for use in freshman year; not renewable. *Award amount:* varies. *Number of awards:* varies. *Eligibility Requirements:* Applicant must be high school student; planning to enroll or expecting to enroll full-time at a two-year or four-year institution or university; resident of Massachusetts and studying in Massachusetts. Applicant must have 3.0 GPA or higher. Available to U.S. citizens. *Application Requirements:* **Deadline:** varies.

Contact Robert Brun, Director of Scholarships and Grants, Massachusetts Office of Student Financial Assistance, 454 Broadway, Suite 200, Revere, MA 02151. *E-mail:* osfa@osfa.mass.edu. *Phone:* 617-727-9420. *Fax:* 617-727-0667. *Web site:* http://www.osfa.mass.edu.

Massachusetts Assistance for Student Success Program. Provides need-based financial assistance to Massachusetts residents to attend undergraduate postsecondary institutions in Connecticut, Maine, Massachusetts, New Hampshire, Pennsylvania, Rhode Island, Vermont, and District of Columbia. High school seniors may apply. Expected Family Contribution (EFC) should be $3850. Timely filing of FAFSA required. *Award:* Grant for use in freshman, sophomore, junior, or senior year; not renewable. *Award amount:* $300–$2400. *Number of awards:* 25,000–30,000. *Eligibility Requirements:* Applicant must be enrolled or expecting to enroll full-time at a two-year, four-year, or technical institution or university; resident of Massachusetts and studying in Connecticut, District of Columbia, Maine, Massachusetts, New Hampshire, Pennsylvania, Rhode Island, or Vermont. Available to U.S. citizens. *Application Requirements:* Financial need analysis, FAFSA. **Deadline:** May 1.

Contact Robert Brun, Director of Scholarships and Grants, Massachusetts Office of Student Financial Assistance, 454 Broadway, Suite 200, Revere, MA 02151. *E-mail:* osfa@osfa.mass.edu. *Phone:* 617-727-9420. *Fax:* 617-727-0667. *Web site:* http://www.osfa.mass.edu.

Massachusetts Cash Grant Program. A need-based grant to assist with mandatory fees and non-state supported tuition. This supplemental award is available to Massachusetts residents, who are undergraduates at public two-year, four-year colleges and universities in Massachusetts. Must file FAFSA before May 1. Contact college financial aid office for information. *Award:* Grant for use in freshman, sophomore, junior, or senior year; not renewable. *Award amount:* varies. *Number of awards:* varies. *Eligibility Requirements:* Applicant must be enrolled or expecting to enroll full-time at a two-year or four-year institution or university and resident of Massachusetts. Available to U.S. citizens. *Application Requirements:* Application, financial need analysis, FAFSA. **Deadline:** continuous.

Contact Robert Brun, Director of Scholarships and Grants, Massachusetts Office of Student Financial Assistance, 454 Broadway, Suite 200, Revere, MA 02151. *E-mail:* osfa@osfa.mass.edu. *Phone:* 617-727-9420. *Fax:* 617-727-0667. *Web site:* http://www.osfa.mass.edu.

Massachusetts Gilbert Matching Student Grant Program. Grants for permanent Massachusetts residents attending an independent, regionally accredited Massachusetts school or school of nursing full time. Must be U.S. citizen and permanent legal resident of Massachusetts. File the Free Application for Federal Student Aid after January 1. Contact college financial aid office for complete details and deadlines. *Award:* Grant for use in freshman, sophomore, junior, or senior year; not renewable. *Award amount:* $200–$2500. *Number of awards:* varies. *Eligibility Requirements:* Applicant must be enrolled or expecting to enroll full-time at a four-year institution or university; resident of Massachusetts and studying in Massachusetts. Available to U.S. citizens. *Application Requirements:* Financial need analysis, FAFSA. **Deadline:** varies.

Contact Robert Brun, Director of Scholarships and Grants, Massachusetts Office of Student Financial Assistance, 454 Broadway, Suite 200, Revere, MA 02151. *E-mail:* rbrun@osfa.mass.edu. *Phone:* 617-727-9420. *Fax:* 617-727-0667. *Web site:* http://www.osfa.mass.edu.

Massachusetts Part-Time Grant Program. Award for permanent Massachusetts residents who have enrolled part-time for at least one year in a state-approved postsecondary school. The recipient must not have a bachelor's degree. FAFSA must be filed before May 1. Contact college financial aid office for further information. *Award:* Grant for use in freshman, sophomore, junior, or senior year; not renewable. *Award amount:* $200–$1150. *Number of awards:* 200. *Eligibility Requirements:* Applicant must be enrolled or expecting to enroll part-time at a two-

year, four-year, or technical institution or university and resident of Massachusetts. Available to U.S. citizens. *Application Requirements:* Application, financial need analysis, FAFSA. **Deadline:** varies.

Contact Robert Brun, Director of Scholarships and Grants, Massachusetts Office of Student Financial Assistance, 454 Broadway, Suite 200, Revere, MA 02151. *E-mail:* osfa@osfa.mass.edu. *Phone:* 617-727-9420. *Fax:* 617-727-0667. *Web site:* http://www.osfa.mass.edu.

Massachusetts Public Service Grant Program. Scholarships for children and/or spouses of deceased members of fire, police, and corrections departments, who were killed in the line of duty. Awards Massachusetts residents attending Massachusetts institutions. Applicant should have not received a prior bachelor's degree or its equivalent. *Award:* Grant for use in freshman, sophomore, junior, or senior year; not renewable. *Award amount:* varies. *Number of awards:* varies. *Eligibility Requirements:* Applicant must be enrolled or expecting to enroll full-time at a four-year institution or university and resident of Massachusetts. Applicant or parent of applicant must have employment or volunteer experience in police/firefighting. Available to U.S. and non-U.S. citizens. Applicant or parent must meet one or more of the following requirements: general military experience; retired from active duty; disabled or killed as a result of military service; prisoner of war; or missing in action. *Application Requirements:* Application, financial need analysis, copy of birth certificate, copy of veteran's death certificate. **Deadline:** May 1.

Contact Alison Leary, Director of Scholarships and Grants, Massachusetts Office of Student Financial Assistance, 454 Broadway, Suite 200, Revere, MA 02151. *E-mail:* osfa@osfa.mass.edu. *Phone:* 617-727-9420. *Fax:* 617-727-0667. *Web site:* http://www.osfa.mass.edu.

New England Regional Student Program-Tuition Break. Tuition discount for residents of New England. Students pay reduced out-of-state tuition at public colleges or universities in other New England states when enrolling in certain majors not offered at public institutions in home state. Details are available at http://www.nebhe.org/tuitionbreak. *Award:* Scholarship for use in freshman, sophomore, junior, or senior year; renewable. *Award amount:* varies. *Eligibility Requirements:* Applicant must be enrolled or expecting to enroll full- or part-time at a two-year or four-year institution or university; resident of Connecticut,

Maine, Massachusetts, New Hampshire, Rhode Island, or Vermont and studying in Connecticut, Maine, Massachusetts, New Hampshire, Quebec, or Vermont. Available to U.S. citizens. *Application Requirements:* College application for admission. **Deadline:** continuous.

Contact Wendy Lindsay, Senior Director of Regional Student Program, New England Board of Higher Education, 45 Temple Place, Boston, MA 02111. *E-mail:* tuitionbreak@nebhe.org. *Phone:* 617-357-9620 Ext. 111. *Fax:* 617-338-1577. *Web site:* http://www.nebhe.org.

Paraprofessional Teacher Preparation Grant. Grant providing financial aid assistance to Massachusetts residents, who are currently employed as paraprofessionals in Massachusetts public schools and wish to obtain higher education and become certified as full-time teachers. *Academic Fields/Career Goals:* Education. *Award:* Grant for use in freshman, sophomore, junior, or senior year; not renewable. *Award amount:* $250–$7500. *Number of awards:* varies. *Eligibility Requirements:* Applicant must be enrolled or expecting to enroll full- or part-time at a two-year or four-year institution or university and resident of Massachusetts. Available to U.S. citizens. *Application Requirements:* Application, FAFSA. **Deadline:** August 1.

Contact Robert Brun, Director of Scholarships and Grants, Massachusetts Office of Student Financial Assistance, 454 Broadway, Suite 200, Revere, MA 02151. *E-mail:* osfa@osfa.mass.edu. *Phone:* 617-727-9420. *Fax:* 617-727-0667. *Web site:* http://www.osfa.mass.edu.

Robert C. Byrd Honors Scholarship-Massachusetts. Scholarship for high school senior who is a resident of Massachusetts for at least one year prior to the beginning of the academic year he/she will enter college. Must have applied or been accepted to an accredited institution of higher education and be a U.S. citizen, national or permanent resident. *Award:* Scholarship for use in freshman year; renewable. *Award amount:* $1500. *Number of awards:* varies. *Eligibility Requirements:* Applicant must be high school student; planning to enroll or expecting to enroll full-time at a four-year institution or university and resident of Massachusetts. Applicant must have 3.5 GPA or higher. Available to U.S. citizens. *Application Requirements:* Application, transcript. **Deadline:** June 1.

Contact Sally Teixeira, Scholarship Coordinator, Massachusetts Department of Education, 350 Main Street, Malden, MA

02148-5023. *E-mail:* steixeira@doe.mass.edu. *Phone:* 781-338-6304. *Web site:* http://www. doe.mass.edu.

MICHIGAN

American Legion Auxiliary Department of Michigan Medical Career Scholarship. Award for training in Michigan as registered nurse, licensed practical nurse, physical therapist, respiratory therapist, or in any medical career. Must be child, grandchild, great-grandchild, wife, or widow of honorably discharged or deceased veteran who has served during the eligibility dates for American Legion membership. Must be Michigan resident attending a Michigan school. *Academic Fields/Career Goals:* Health and Medical Sciences; Nursing; Therapy/Rehabilitation. *Award:* Scholarship for use in freshman year; not renewable. *Award amount:* $500–$500. *Number of awards:* 10–20. *Eligibility Requirements:* Applicant must be high school student; planning to enroll or expecting to enroll full-time at a two-year, four-year, or technical institution or university; resident of Michigan and studying in Michigan. Available to U.S. citizens. Applicant must have general military experience. *Application Requirements:* Application, financial need analysis, references, transcript, veterans discharge papers, copy of pages 1 and 2 of federal income tax return. **Deadline:** March 15.

Contact Ms. LeAnn Knott, Scholarship Coordinator, American Legion Auxiliary Department of Michigan, 212 North Verlinden Avenue, Suite B, Lansing, MI 48915. *E-mail:* lknott@michalaux.org. *Phone:* 517-267-8809 Ext. 22. *Fax:* 517-371-3698. *Web site:* http://www.michalaux.org.

American Legion Auxiliary Department of Michigan Memorial Scholarship. Scholarship for daughter, granddaughter, and great-granddaughter of any honorably discharged or deceased veteran of U.S. wars or conflicts. Must be Michigan resident for minimum of one year, female between 16 and 21 years, and attend college in Michigan. Must include copy of discharge and copy of parent or guardian's IRS 1040 form. *Award:* Scholarship for use in freshman or sophomore year; not renewable. *Award amount:* $500–$500. *Number of awards:* 10–35. *Eligibility Requirements:* Applicant must be age 16-21; enrolled or expecting to enroll full-time at a two-year, four-year, or technical institution or university; female; resident of Michigan and studying in Michigan. Available to U.S. citizens. Applicant must have general military experience. *Application Require-*

ments: Application, financial need analysis, references, transcript, discharge papers. **Deadline:** March 15.

Contact LeAnn Knott, Scholarship Coordinator, American Legion Auxiliary Department of Michigan, 212 North Verlinden Avenue, Suite B, Lansing, MI 48915. *E-mail:* lknott@michalaux.org. *Phone:* 517-267-8809 Ext. 22. *Fax:* 517-371-3698. *Web site:* http://www.michalaux.org.

American Legion Auxiliary Department of Michigan Scholarship for Non-Traditional Student. Applicant must be a dependent of a veteran. Must be one of the following: nontraditional student returning to classroom after some period of time in which their education was interrupted, student over the age of 22 attending college for the first time to pursue a degree, or student over the age of 22 attending a trade or vocational school. Applicants must be Michigan residents only and attend Michigan institution. Judging based on: need-25 points, character/leadership-25 points, scholastic standing-25 points, initiative/goal-25 points. *Award:* Scholarship for use in freshman, sophomore, junior, or senior year; renewable. *Award amount:* $500–$500. *Number of awards:* 1–1. *Eligibility Requirements:* Applicant must be age 23 and over; enrolled or expecting to enroll full-time at a two-year, four-year, or technical institution or university; resident of Michigan and studying in Michigan. Available to U.S. citizens. Applicant must have general military experience. *Application Requirements:* Application, financial need analysis, transcript, copy of veterans discharge papers. **Deadline:** March 15.

Contact LeAnn Knott, Scholarship Coordinator, American Legion Auxiliary Department of Michigan, 212 North Verlinden Avenue, Suite B, Lansing, MI 48915. *E-mail:* lknott@michalaux.org. *Phone:* 517-267-8809 Ext. 22. *Fax:* 517-371-3698. *Web site:* http://www.michalaux.org.

Michigan Competitive Scholarship. Renewable awards for Michigan resident to pursue undergraduate study at a Michigan institution. Awards limited to tuition. Must maintain at least a 2.0 grade point average and meet the college's academic progress requirements. Must file Free Application for Federal Student Aid. *Award:* Scholarship for use in freshman, sophomore, junior, or senior year; renewable. *Award amount:* $510–$1610. *Number of awards:* varies. *Eligibility Requirements:* Applicant must be enrolled or expecting to enroll full- or part-time at a two-year or four-year institution or university; resident of Michigan and studying in Michigan. Available to

U.S. citizens. *Application Requirements:* Application, financial need analysis, test scores. **Deadline:** March 1.

Contact Scholarship and Grant Director, Michigan Higher Education Assistance Authority, PO Box 30466, Lansing, MI 48909-7962. *E-mail:* osg@michigan.gov. *Phone:* 888-447-2687. *Web site:* http://www.michigan.gov/studentaid.

Michigan Indian Tuition Waiver. Renewable award provides free tuition for Native-American of 1/4 or more blood degree who attend a Michigan public college or university. Must be a Michigan resident for at least one year. The tuition waiver program covers full-time, part-time or summer school student attending a public, state, community, junior college, public college, or public university. Deadline: continuous. *Award:* Scholarship for use in freshman, sophomore, junior, senior, graduate, or postgraduate years; renewable. *Award amount:* varies. *Number of awards:* varies. *Eligibility Requirements:* Applicant must be American Indian/Alaska Native; enrolled or expecting to enroll full- or part-time at a two-year, four-year, or technical institution or university; resident of Michigan and studying in Michigan. Available to U.S. citizens. *Application Requirements:* Application, driver's license, transcript, tribal certification, proof of residency. **Deadline:** continuous.

Contact Christin McKerchie, Executive Assistant to Programs, Inter-Tribal Council of Michigan Inc., 2956 Ashmun Street, Suite A, Sault Ste. Marie, MI 49783. *Phone:* 906-632-6896 Ext. 136. *Fax:* 906-632-6878. *Web site:* http://www.itcmi.org.

Michigan Tuition Grant. Need-based program. Students must be Michigan residents and attend a Michigan private, nonprofit, degree-granting college. Must file the Free Application for Federal Student Aid and meet the college's academic progress requirements. *Award:* Grant for use in freshman, sophomore, junior, or senior year; renewable. *Award amount:* up to $1610. *Number of awards:* varies. *Eligibility Requirements:* Applicant must be enrolled or expecting to enroll full- or part-time at a four-year institution or university; resident of Michigan and studying in Michigan. Available to U.S. citizens. *Application Requirements:* Financial need analysis. **Deadline:** July 1.

Contact Scholarship and Grant Director, Michigan Higher Education Assistance Authority, PO Box 30462, Lansing, MI 48909-7962. *E-mail:* osg@michigan.gov. *Phone:* 888-447-2687. *Web site:* http://www.michigan.gov/studentaid.

Tuition Incentive Program. Award for Michigan residents who receive or have received Medicaid for required period of time through the Department of Human Services. Scholarship provides two years tuition towards an associate degree at a Michigan college or university and $2000 total assistance for third and fourth years. Must apply before graduating from high school or earning a general education development diploma. *Award:* Grant for use in freshman, sophomore, junior, or senior year; renewable. *Award amount:* varies. *Number of awards:* varies. *Eligibility Requirements:* Applicant must be high school student; planning to enroll or expecting to enroll full- or part-time at a two-year or four-year institution or university; resident of Michigan and studying in Michigan. Available to U.S. citizens. *Application Requirements:* Application, Medicaid eligibility for specified period of time. **Deadline:** continuous.

Contact Scholarship and Grant Director, Michigan Higher Education Assistance Authority, PO Box 30462, Lansing, MI 48909-7962. *E-mail:* osg@michigan.gov. *Phone:* 888-447-2687. *Web site:* http://www.michigan.gov/studentaid.

MINNESOTA

Leadership, Excellence and Dedicated Service Scholarship. Scholarship provides a maximum of thirty $1000 to selected high school seniors who become a member of the Minnesota National Guard and complete the application process. The award recognizes demonstrated leadership, community services and potential for success in the Minnesota National Guard. *Award:* Scholarship for use in freshman year; not renewable. *Award amount:* $1000. *Number of awards:* up to 30. *Eligibility Requirements:* Applicant must be high school student; planning to enroll or expecting to enroll full- or part-time at a two-year, four-year, or technical institution or university; resident of Minnesota and must have an interest in leadership. Applicant or parent of applicant must have employment or volunteer experience in community service. Available to U.S. citizens. Applicant or parent must meet one or more of the following requirements: Air Force National Guard or Army National Guard experience; retired from active duty; disabled or killed as a result of military service; prisoner of war; or missing in action. *Application Requirements:* Essay, resume, references, transcript. **Deadline:** March 15.

Contact Barbara O'Reilly, Education Services Officer, Minnesota Department of Military Affairs, 20 West 12th Street, Veterans Services Building, St. Paul, MN 55155-2098. *E-mail:* barbara.oreilly@mn.ngb.army.mil. *Phone:* 651-282-4508. *Web site:* http://www.minnesotanationalguard.org.

Minnesota Achieve Scholarship. Eligible Minnesota high school graduates who complete any one of four sets of courses defined as rigorous earn a one-time scholarship to help pay for college at a public or private university or college in Minnesota. Eligible students who graduated between January 1, 2008 and December 31, 2008 can receive a one-time scholarship of $1,200 available for use within the four years immediately following their high school graduation. Eligible students who graduate after January 1, 2009 and enroll full time (15 credits) in an eligible college or university in the academic year immediately following their high school graduation can receive a one-time scholarship for use in their first academic year ranging from $1,200 to approximately $4,000 depending on financial need and funds availability. *Award:* Scholarship for use in freshman year; not renewable. *Award amount:* up to $1200. *Number of awards:* varies. *Eligibility Requirements:* Applicant must be enrolled or expecting to enroll full-time at a two-year, four-year, or technical institution or university; resident of Minnesota and studying in Minnesota. Applicant must have 2.5 GPA or higher. Available to U.S. citizens. *Application Requirements:* Application, financial need analysis, test scores, transcript. **Deadline:** continuous.

Contact Scholarship Staff, Minnesota Office of Higher Education, 1450 Energy Park Drive, St. Paul, MN 55108. *Phone:* 651-642-0567. *Fax:* 651-642-0675. *Web site:* http://www.getreadyforcollege.org.

Minnesota GI Bill Program. Provides financial assistance to eligible Minnesota veterans and non-veterans who have served 5 or more years cumulatively as a member of the National Guard or Reserves, and served on or after September 11, 2001. Surviving spouses and children of service members who have died or have a total and permanent disability and who served on or after September 11, 2001, may also be eligible. Full-time students may receive up to $1000 per term, and part-time students up to $500 per term up to $3,000 per year. Maximum lifetime benefit is $10,000. *Award:* Scholarship for use in freshman, sophomore, junior, senior, graduate, or postgraduate years; not renewable. *Award amount:* up to $3000. *Number of awards:* varies. *Eligibility Requirements:*

Applicant must be enrolled or expecting to enroll full- or part-time at a two-year, four-year, or technical institution or university; resident of Minnesota and studying in Minnesota. Available to U.S. citizens. Applicant or parent must meet one or more of the following requirements: general military experience; retired from active duty; disabled or killed as a result of military service; prisoner of war; or missing in action. *Application Requirements:* Application, financial need analysis, military records. **Deadline:** continuous.

Contact Scholarship Staff, Minnesota Office of Higher Education, 1450 Energy Park Drive, St. Paul, MN 55108. *Phone:* 651-642-0567. *Fax:* 651-642-0675. *Web site:* http://www.getreadyforcollege.org.

Minnesota Indian Scholarship. Scholarship for Minnesota residents who are one-fourth or more American Indian ancestry and attending an eligible Minnesota postsecondary institution. Maximum award is $4000 for undergraduate students and $6000 for graduate students. Scholarships are limited to 3 years for certificate or AA/AS programs, 5 years for bachelor's degree programs, and 5 years for graduate programs. Applicants must maintain satisfactory academic progress, not be in default on student loans, and be eligible to receive Pell or State Grant and have remaining need. *Award:* Scholarship for use in freshman, sophomore, junior, senior, graduate, or postgraduate years; not renewable. *Award amount:* up to $6000. *Number of awards:* 500–600. *Eligibility Requirements:* Applicant must be American Indian/Alaska Native; enrolled or expecting to enroll full- or part-time at a two-year, four-year, or technical institution or university; resident of Minnesota and studying in Minnesota. Available to U.S. citizens. *Application Requirements:* Application, financial need analysis, American Indian ancestry documentation. **Deadline:** continuous.

Contact Scholarship Staff, Minnesota Office of Higher Education, 1450 Energy Park Drive, Suite 350, St. Paul, MN 55108. *E-mail:* sandy.bowes@state.mn.us. *Phone:* 651-642-0567 Ext. 1. *Fax:* 651-642-0675. *Web site:* http://www.getreadyforcollege.org.

Minnesota Reciprocal Agreement. Renewable tuition waiver for Minnesota residents. Waives all or part of non-resident tuition surcharge at public institutions in Iowa, Kansas, Michigan, Missouri, Nebraska, North Dakota, South Dakota, Wisconsin and Manitoba. Deadline: last day of academic term. *Award:* Scholarship for use in freshman, sophomore, junior, senior, graduate, or postgraduate years; renewable.

Award amount: varies. *Number of awards:* varies. *Eligibility Requirements:* Applicant must be enrolled or expecting to enroll full- or part-time at a two-year, four-year, or technical institution or university; resident of Minnesota and studying in Iowa, Kansas, Manitoba, Michigan, Missouri, Nebraska, North Dakota, South Dakota, or Wisconsin. Available to U.S. citizens. *Application Requirements:* Application. **Deadline:** continuous.

Contact Jodi Rouland, Program Assistant, Minnesota Office of Higher Education. *E-mail:* jodi.rouland@state.mn.us. *Phone:* 651-355-0614. *Fax:* 651-642-0675. *Web site:* http://www.getreadyforcollege.org.

Minnesota State Grant Program. Need-based grant program available for Minnesota residents attending Minnesota colleges. Student covers 46% of cost with remainder covered by Pell Grant, parent contribution and state grant. Students apply with FAFSA and college administers the program on campus. *Award:* Grant for use in freshman, sophomore, junior, or senior year; renewable. *Award amount:* $100–$8661. *Number of awards:* 71,000–85,000. *Eligibility Requirements:* Applicant must be age 17 and over; enrolled or expecting to enroll full- or part-time at a two-year, four-year, or technical institution or university; resident of Minnesota and studying in Minnesota. Available to U.S. citizens. *Application Requirements:* Application, financial need analysis. **Deadline:** continuous.

Contact Grant Staff, Minnesota Office of Higher Education, 1450 Energy Park Drive, Suite 350, St. Paul, MN 55108. *Phone:* 651-642-0567 Ext. 1. *Web site:* http://www.getreadyforcollege.org.

Minnesota State Veterans' Dependents Assistance Program. Tuition assistance to dependents of persons considered to be prisoner-of-war or missing in action after August 1, 1958. Must be Minnesota resident attending Minnesota two- or four-year school. *Award:* Scholarship for use in freshman, sophomore, junior, or senior year; renewable. *Award amount:* varies. *Number of awards:* varies. *Eligibility Requirements:* Applicant must be enrolled or expecting to enroll full- or part-time at a two-year or four-year institution; resident of Minnesota and studying in Minnesota. Available to U.S. citizens. Applicant or parent must meet one or more of the following requirements: general military experience; retired from active duty; disabled or killed as a result of military service; prisoner of war; or missing in action. *Application Requirements:* Application. **Deadline:** continuous.

Contact Ginny Dodds, Manager, Minnesota Office of Higher Education, 1450 Energy Park Drive, Suite 350, St. Paul, MN 55108-5227. *E-mail:* ginny.dodds@state.mn.us. *Phone:* 651-355-0610. *Web site:* http://www.getreadyforcollege.org.

Paul and Fern Yocum Scholarship. Scholarship to dependent children of full-time Yocum Oil employees. *Award:* Scholarship for use in freshman, sophomore, junior, senior, or graduate year; not renewable. *Award amount:* $1000. *Number of awards:* 3. *Eligibility Requirements:* Applicant must be enrolled or expecting to enroll full- or part-time at a four-year institution or university. Applicant or parent of applicant must be affiliated with Yocum Oil Company. Available to U.S. and non-Canadian citizens. *Application Requirements:* Application. **Deadline:** April 15.

Contact Donna Paulson, Administrative Assistant, Minnesota Community Foundation, 55 Fifth Street East, Suite 600, St. Paul, MN 55101-1797. *E-mail:* dkp@mncommunityfoundation.org. *Phone:* 651-325-4212. *Web site:* http://www.mncommunityfoundation.org.

Postsecondary Child Care Grant Program-Minnesota. Grant available for students not receiving MFIP. Based on financial need. Cannot exceed actual child care costs or maximum award chart (based on income). Must be Minnesota resident. For use at Minnesota two- or four-year school, including public technical colleges. *Award:* Grant for use in freshman, sophomore, junior, or senior year; renewable. *Award amount:* $100–$2600. *Number of awards:* varies. *Eligibility Requirements:* Applicant must be enrolled or expecting to enroll full- or part-time at a two-year, four-year, or technical institution or university; resident of Minnesota and studying in Minnesota. Available to U.S. citizens. *Application Requirements:* Application, financial need analysis. **Deadline:** continuous.

Contact Brenda Larter, Program Administrator, Minnesota Office of Higher Education, 1450 Energy Park Drive, Suite 350, St. Paul, MN 55108-5227. *E-mail:* brenda.larter@state.mn.us. *Phone:* 651-355-0612. *Fax:* 651-642-0675. *Web site:* http://www.getreadyforcollege.org.

Safety Officers' Survivor Grant Program. Grant for eligible survivors of Minnesota public safety officers killed in the line of duty. Safety officers who have been permanently or totally disabled in the line of duty are also eligible. Must be used at a Minnesota institution participating in State Grant Program. Write for details. Must submit proof of death or disability and Public Safety Officers Benefit Fund Certificate. Must apply for renewal each year for four years. *Award:* Grant for use in freshman, sophomore, junior, or senior year; not renewable. *Award amount:* up to $9438. *Number of awards:* 1. *Eligibility Requirements:* Applicant must be age 23 or under; enrolled or expecting to enroll full- or part-time at a two-year, four-year, or technical institution or university; resident of Minnesota and studying in Minnesota. Available to U.S. citizens. *Application Requirements:* Application, proof of death or disability. **Deadline:** continuous.

Contact Brenda Larter, Program Administrator, Minnesota Office of Higher Education. *E-mail:* brenda.larter@state.mn.us. *Phone:* 651-355-0612. *Fax:* 651-642-0675. *Web site:* http://www.getreadyforcollege.org.

MISSISSIPPI

Critical Needs Teacher Loan/Scholarship. Eligible applicants will agree to employment immediately upon degree completion as a full-time classroom teacher in a public school located in a critical teacher shortage area in the state of Mississippi. Must verify the intention to pursue a first bachelor's degree in teacher education. Award covers tuition and required fees, average cost of room and meals plus allowance for books. Must be enrolled at a Mississippi college or university. *Academic Fields/Career Goals:* Education; Psychology; Therapy/Rehabilitation. *Award:* Forgivable loan for use in junior or senior year; not renewable. *Award amount:* varies. *Number of awards:* varies. *Eligibility Requirements:* Applicant must be enrolled or expecting to enroll full- or part-time at a four-year institution or university; resident of Mississippi and studying in Mississippi. Available to U.S. and non-U.S. citizens. *Application Requirements:* Application, test scores, transcript. **Deadline:** March 31.

Contact Apryll Washington, Program Administrator, Mississippi Office of Student Financial Aid, 3825 Ridgewood Road, Jackson, MS 39211. *E-mail:* awashington@mississippi.edu. *Phone:* 601-432-6997. *Fax:* 601-432-6527. *Web site:* http://www.mississippi.edu/ihl.

Higher Education Legislative Plan (HELP). Eligible applicant must be resident of Mississippi and be freshman and/or sophomore student who graduated from high school within the immediate past two years. Must demonstrate need as determined by the results of the FAFSA: documenting an average family adjusted gross income of $36,500 or less over the prior two years.

Must be enrolled full-time at a Mississippi college or university, have a GPA of 2.5 and have scored 20 on the ACT. *Award:* Scholarship for use in freshman or sophomore year; renewable. *Award amount:* varies. *Number of awards:* varies. *Eligibility Requirements:* Applicant must be enrolled or expecting to enroll full-time at a four-year institution or university; resident of Mississippi and studying in Mississippi. Applicant must have 2.5 GPA or higher. Available to U.S. citizens. *Application Requirements:* Application, financial need analysis, test scores, transcript, FAFSA. **Deadline:** March 31.

Contact Babs McAlpin, Program Administrator, Mississippi Office of Student Financial Aid, 3825 Ridgewood Road, Jackson, MS 39211. *E-mail:* bmcalpin@mississippi. edu. *Phone:* 601-432-6997. *Fax:* 601-432-6527. *Web site:* http://www.mississippi.edu/ ihl.

Mississippi Eminent Scholars Grant. Award for an entering freshmen or as a renewal for sophomore, junior or senior. who are residents of Mississippi. Applicants must achieve a GPA of 3.5 and must have scored 29 on the ACT. Must enroll full-time at an eligible Mississippi college or university. *Award:* Grant for use in freshman, sophomore, junior, or senior year; renewable. *Award amount:* up to $2500. *Number of awards:* varies. *Eligibility Requirements:* Applicant must be enrolled or expecting to enroll full-time at a two-year or four-year institution or university; resident of Mississippi and studying in Mississippi. Applicant must have 3.5 GPA or higher. Available to U.S. citizens. *Application Requirements:* Application, test scores, transcript. **Deadline:** September 15.

Contact Mrs. Jennifer Rogers, Director of Student Financial Aid, Mississippi Office of Student Financial Aid, 3825 Ridgewood Road, Jackson, MS 39211-6453. *E-mail:* sfa@ mississippi.edu. *Phone:* 800-327-2980. *Fax:* 601-432-6527. *Web site:* http://www.mississippi. edu/ihl.

Mississippi Health Care Professions Loan/ Scholarship Program. Renewable award for junior and senior undergraduates studying psychology or speech pathology, and graduate students studying physical therapy or occupational therapy. Must be Mississippi residents attending four-year colleges or universities in Mississippi. Must fulfill work obligation in Mississippi on the basis of one year's service for one year's loan received, or pay back as loan. *Academic Fields/Career Goals:* Health and Medical Sciences; Psychology; Therapy/ Rehabilitation. *Award:* Forgivable loan for use in junior, senior, or graduate year; renewable. *Award amount:* $1500–$6000. *Number of awards:* varies. *Eligibility Requirements:* Applicant must be enrolled or expecting to enroll full-time at a four-year institution or university; resident of Mississippi and studying in Mississippi. Available to U.S. citizens. *Application Requirements:* Application, references, transcript. **Deadline:** March 31.

Contact Susan Eckels, Program Administrator, Mississippi Office of Student Financial Aid, 3825 Ridgewood Road, Jackson, MS 39211-6453. *E-mail:* seckels@mississippi. edu. *Phone:* 601-432-6997. *Web site:* http:// www.mississippi.edu/ihl.

Mississippi Leveraging Educational Assistance Partnership (LEAP). Award for Mississippi residents enrolled for full-time study at a Mississippi college or university. Based on financial need. Contact college financial aid office. Award value and deadline varies. *Award:* Grant for use in freshman, sophomore, junior, or senior year; renewable. *Award amount:* varies. *Number of awards:* varies. *Eligibility Requirements:* Applicant must be enrolled or expecting to enroll full-time at a two-year or four-year institution or university; resident of Mississippi and studying in Mississippi. Available to U.S. citizens. *Application Requirements:* Application, financial need analysis, FAFSA. **Deadline:** varies.

Contact Mrs. Jennifer Rogers, Director of Student Financial Aid, Mississippi Office of Student Financial Aid, 3825 Ridgewood Road, Jackson, MS 39211-6453. *E-mail:* sfa@ mississippi.edu. *Phone:* 800-327-2980. *Fax:* 601-432-6527. *Web site:* http://www.mississippi. edu/ihl.

Mississippi Resident Tuition Assistance Grant. Must be a resident of Mississippi enrolled full-time at an eligible Mississippi college or university. Must maintain a minimum 2.5 GPA each semester. MTAG awards may be up to $500 per academic year for freshman and sophomores and $1000 per academic year for juniors and seniors. *Award:* Grant for use in freshman, sophomore, junior, or senior year; renewable. *Award amount:* $500–$1000. *Number of awards:* varies. *Eligibility Requirements:* Applicant must be enrolled or expecting to enroll full-time at a two-year or four-year institution or university; resident of Mississippi and studying in Mississippi. Applicant must have 2.5 GPA or higher. Available to U.S. citizens. *Application Requirements:* Application, test scores, transcript. **Deadline:** September 15.

Contact Mrs. Jennifer Rogers, Director of Student Financial Aid, Mississippi Office of Student Financial Aid, 3825 Ridgewood Road, Jackson, MS 39211-6453. *E-mail:* sfa@ mississippi.edu. *Phone:* 800-327-2980. *Fax:* 601-432-6527. *Web site:* http://www.mississippi. edu/ihl.

Nursing Education Loan/Scholarship-BSN. Award available to junior and senior students pursuing a baccalaureate degree in nursing as well as to the licensed registered nurse who wishes to continue education to the baccalaureate degree. Include transcript and references with application. Minimum 2.5 GPA required. Must be a Mississippi resident and agree to employment in professional nursing (patient care) in Mississippi. *Academic Fields/Career Goals:* Nursing. *Award:* Forgivable loan for use in junior or senior year; renewable. *Award amount:* $4000–$8000. *Number of awards:* varies. *Eligibility Requirements:* Applicant must be enrolled or expecting to enroll full- or part-time at a four-year institution or university; resident of Mississippi and studying in Mississippi. Applicant must have 2.5 GPA or higher. Available to U.S. citizens. *Application Requirements:* Application, financial need analysis, references, transcript. **Deadline:** March 31.

Contact Mrs. Jennifer Rogers, Director of Student Financial Aid, Mississippi Office of Student Financial Aid, 3825 Ridgewood Road, Jackson, MS 39211-6453. *E-mail:* sfa@ mississippi.edu. *Phone:* 800-327-2980. *Fax:* 601-432-6527. *Web site:* http://www.mississippi. edu/ihl.

William Winter Teacher Scholar Loan. Scholarship available to a junior or senior student at a four-year Mississippi college or university. Applicants must enroll in a program of study leading to a Class "A" teacher educator license. *Academic Fields/ Career Goals:* Education. *Award:* Forgivable loan for use in junior or senior year; renewable. *Award amount:* up to $4000. *Number of awards:* varies. *Eligibility Requirements:* Applicant must be enrolled or expecting to enroll full-time at a four-year institution or university; resident of Mississippi and studying in Mississippi. Available to U.S. citizens. *Application Requirements:* Application, test scores. **Deadline:** March 31.

Contact Meg Harris, Program Administrator, Mississippi Office of Student Financial Aid, 3825 Ridgewood Road, Jackson, MS 39211. *E-mail:* mharris@mississippi.edu. *Phone:* 601-432-6997. *Fax:* 601-432-6527. *Web site:* http://www.mississippi.edu/ihl.

MISSOURI

Access Missouri Financial Assistance Program. Need-based program that provides awards to students who are enrolled full time and have an expected family contribution (EFC) of $12,000 or less based on their Free Application for Federal Student Aid (FAFSA). Awards vary depending on EFC and the type of postsecondary school. *Award:* Grant for use in freshman, sophomore, junior, or senior year; not renewable. *Eligibility Requirements:* Applicant must be enrolled or expecting to enroll full-time at a two-year, four-year, or technical institution or university; resident of Missouri and studying in Missouri. Applicant must have 2.5 GPA or higher. Available to U.S. citizens. *Application Requirements:* FAFSA on file by April 1.

Contact Information Center, Missouri Department of Higher Education, 3515 Amazonas Drive, Jefferson City, MO 65109-5717. *E-mail:* info@dhe.mo.gov. *Phone:* 800-473-6757 Ext. 4. *Fax:* 573-751-6635. *Web site:* http://www.dhe.mo.gov.

Environmental Education Scholarship Program (EESP). Scholarship to minority and other underrepresented students pursuing a bachelor's or master's degree in an environmental course of study. Must be a Missouri resident having a cumulative high school GPA of 3.0 or if enrolled in college, must have cumulative GPA of 2.5. *Academic Fields/Career Goals:* Environmental Science. *Award:* Scholarship for use in freshman, sophomore, junior, senior, or graduate year; renewable. *Award amount:* $2000. *Number of awards:* 16. *Eligibility Requirements:* Applicant must be American Indian/Alaska Native, Asian/Pacific Islander, Black (non-Hispanic), or Hispanic; enrolled or expecting to enroll full-time at a four-year institution or university and resident of Missouri. Applicant must have 3.0 GPA or higher. Available to U.S. citizens. *Application Requirements:* Application, essay, references, transcript. **Deadline:** June 1.

Contact Dana Muessig, Executive, Missouri Department of Natural Resources, PO Box 176, Jefferson City, MO 65102. *E-mail:* danamuessig@dnr.mo.gov. *Phone:* 800-361-4827. *Fax:* 573-526-3878. *Web site:* http://www.dnr.mo.gov.

Lillie Lois Ford Scholarship Fund. Two awards of $1000 each are given each year to one boy and one girl. Applicant must have attended a full session of Missouri Boys/Girls State or Missouri Cadet Patrol Academy. Must be a Missouri resident below age 21, attending an accredited college/university as a full-time student.

Must be an unmarried descendant of a veteran having served at least 90 days on active duty in the Army, Air Force, Navy, Marine Corps or Coast Guard of the United States. *Award:* Scholarship for use in freshman year; not renewable. *Award amount:* $1000. *Number of awards:* 2. *Eligibility Requirements:* Applicant must be high school student; age 21 or under; planning to enroll or expecting to enroll full-time at a two-year or four-year institution or university; single and resident of Missouri. Available to U.S. citizens. Applicant or parent must meet one or more of the following requirements: general military experience; retired from active duty; disabled or killed as a result of military service; prisoner of war; or missing in action. *Application Requirements:* Application, financial need analysis, test scores, copy of the veteran's discharge certificate. **Deadline:** April 20.

Contact John Doane, Chairman, Education and Scholarship Committee, American Legion Department of Missouri, PO Box 179, Jefferson City, MO 65102-0179. *Phone:* 417-924-8186. *Web site:* http://www.missourilegion.org.

Marguerite Ross Barnett Memorial Scholarship. Scholarship was established for students who are employed while attending school part-time. Must be enrolled at least half-time but less than full-time at a participating Missouri postsecondary school, be employed and compensated for at least 20 hours per week, be 18 years of age, be a Missouri resident and a U.S. citizen or a permanent resident. *Award:* Scholarship for use in freshman, sophomore, junior, or senior year; renewable. *Award amount:* varies. *Number of awards:* varies. *Eligibility Requirements:* Applicant must be age 18 and over; enrolled or expecting to enroll part-time at a two-year, four-year, or technical institution or university; resident of Missouri and studying in Missouri. Applicant must have 2.5 GPA or higher. Available to U.S. citizens. *Application Requirements:* FAFSA on file by August 1. **Deadline:** August 1.

Contact Information Center, Missouri Department of Higher Education, 3515 Amazonas Drive, Jefferson City, MO 65109-5717. *E-mail:* info@dhe.mo.gov. *Phone:* 800-473-6757 Ext. 4. *Fax:* 573-751-6635. *Web site:* http://www.dhe.mo.gov.

Missouri Higher Education Academic Scholarship (Bright Flight). Program encourages top-ranked high school seniors to attend approved Missouri postsecondary schools. Must be a Missouri resident and a U.S. citizen. Must have a composite score

on the ACT or SAT in the top 3 percent of all Missouri students taking those tests. Students with scores in the top 3 percent are eligible for an annual award of up to $3,000 (up to $1,500 each semester). For 2010 high school seniors, ACT or SAT scores in the top 5% will qualify. Students with scores in the top 5% are eligible for an annual award of up to $1,000 (up to $500 each semester). Award amounts, and the availability of the award for students in the top 5%, are subject to change based on the amount of funding allocated for the program in the legislative session. *Award:* Scholarship for use in freshman, sophomore, junior, or senior year; renewable. *Number of awards:* varies. *Eligibility Requirements:* Applicant must be enrolled or expecting to enroll full-time at a two-year, four-year, or technical institution or university; resident of Missouri and studying in Missouri. Applicant must have 2.5 GPA or higher. Available to U.S. citizens. *Application Requirements:* Test scores. **Deadline:** June 11.

Contact Information Center, Missouri Department of Higher Education, 3515 Amazonas Drive, Jefferson City, MO 65109-5717. *E-mail:* info@dhe.mo.gov. *Phone:* 800-473-6757 Ext. 4. *Fax:* 573-751-6635. *Web site:* http://www.dhe.mo.gov.

Primary Care Resource Initiative for Missouri Loan Program. Forgivable loans for Missouri residents attending Missouri institutions pursuing a degree as a primary care physician or dentist, dental hygienist, psychiatrist, psychologist, licensed professional counselor, licensed clinical social worker or dietitian/nutritionist . To be forgiven participant must work in a Missouri health professional shortage area. *Academic Fields/Career Goals:* Behavioral Science; Dental Health/Services; Health and Medical Sciences; Nursing. *Award:* Forgivable loan for use in freshman, sophomore, junior, senior, graduate, or postgraduate years; not renewable. *Award amount:* $5000–$20,000. *Number of awards:* 100. *Eligibility Requirements:* Applicant must be enrolled or expecting to enroll full-time at a four-year institution or university; resident of Missouri and studying in Missouri. Available to U.S. and non-U.S. citizens. *Application Requirements:* Application, proof of Missouri residency. **Deadline:** June 30.

Contact Cheryl Thomas, Health and Senior Services Manager, Missouri Department of Health and Senior Services, PO Box 570, Jefferson City, MO 65102-0570. *E-mail:* cheryl.thomas@dhss.mo.gov. *Phone:* 800-891-7415. *Fax:* 573-522-8146. *Web site:* http://www.dhss.mo.gov.

Robert C. Byrd Honors Scholarship-Missouri. Award for high school seniors who are residents of Missouri. Amount of the award each year depends on the amount the state is allotted by the U.S. Department of Education. Maximum amount awarded per student is $1500. Students must score above 10th percentile on ACT. *Award:* Scholarship for use in freshman year; renewable. *Award amount:* up to $1500. *Number of awards:* 100–150. *Eligibility Requirements:* Applicant must be American Indian/Alaska Native, Asian/Pacific Islander, Black (non-Hispanic), or Hispanic; high school student; planning to enroll or expecting to enroll full-time at a four-year institution or university and resident of Missouri. Available to U.S. citizens. *Application Requirements:* Application, test scores, transcript. **Deadline:** April 15.

Contact Laura Harrison, Administrative Assistant II, Missouri Department of Elementary and Secondary Education, PO Box 480, Jefferson City, MO 65102-0480. *E-mail:* laura.harrison@dese.mo.gov. *Phone:* 573-751-1668. *Fax:* 573-526-3580. *Web site:* http://www.dese.mo.gov.

MONTANA

Montana Higher Education Opportunity Grant. This grant is awarded based on need to undergraduate students attending either part-time or full-time who are residents of Montana and attending participating Montana schools. Awards are limited to the most needy students. A specific major or program of study is not required. This grant does not need to be repaid, and students may apply each year. Apply by filing FAFSA by March 1 and contacting the financial aid office at the admitting college. *Award:* Grant for use in freshman, sophomore, junior, or senior year; not renewable. *Award amount:* $400–$600. *Number of awards:* up to 800. *Eligibility Requirements:* Applicant must be enrolled or expecting to enroll full- or part-time at a two-year or four-year institution or university; resident of Montana and studying in Montana. Available to U.S. citizens. *Application Requirements:* Application, financial need analysis, resume, FAFSA. **Deadline:** March 1.

Contact Jamie Dushin, Budget Analyst, Montana Guaranteed Student Loan Program, Office of Commissioner of Higher Education, PO Box 203101, Helena, MT 59620-3101. *E-mail:* jdushin@mgslp.state.mt.us. *Phone:* 406-444-0638. *Fax:* 406-444-1869. *Web site:* http://www.mgslp.state.mt.us.

Montana Tuition Assistance Program-Baker Grant. Need-based grant for Montana residents attending participating Montana schools who have earned at least $2575 during the previous calendar year. Must be enrolled full time. Grant does not need to be repaid. Award covers the first undergraduate degree or certificate. Apply by filing FAFSA by March 1 and contacting the financial aid office at the admitting college. *Award:* Grant for use in freshman, sophomore, junior, or senior year; not renewable. *Award amount:* $100–$1000. *Number of awards:* 1000–3000. *Eligibility Requirements:* Applicant must be enrolled or expecting to enroll full-time at a two-year or four-year institution or university; resident of Montana and studying in Montana. Available to U.S. citizens. *Application Requirements:* Application, financial need analysis, resume, FAFSA. **Deadline:** March 1.

Contact Jamie Dushin, Budget Analyst, Montana Guaranteed Student Loan Program, Office of Commissioner of Higher Education, PO Box 203101, Helena, MT 59620-3101. *E-mail:* jdushin@mgslp.state.mt.us. *Phone:* 406-444-0638. *Fax:* 406-444-1869. *Web site:* http://www.mgslp.state.mt.us.

Montana University System Honor Scholarship. Scholarship will be awarded annually to high school seniors graduating from accredited Montana high schools. The MUS Honor Scholarship is a four year renewable scholarship that waives the tuition and registration fee at one of the Montana University System campuses or one of the three community colleges (Flathead Valley in Kalispell, Miles in Miles City or Dawson in Glendive). The scholarship must be used within 9 months after high school graduation. Applicant should have a GPA of 3.4. *Award:* Scholarship for use in freshman year; renewable. *Award amount:* up to $4020. *Number of awards:* up to 200. *Eligibility Requirements:* Applicant must be high school student; planning to enroll or expecting to enroll full-time at a two-year or four-year institution or university; resident of Montana and studying in Montana. Applicant must have 3.5 GPA or higher. Available to U.S. citizens. *Application Requirements:* Application, test scores, transcript, college acceptance letter. **Deadline:** February 15.

Contact Janice Kirkpatrick, Grant and Scholarship Coordinator, Montana Guaranteed Student Loan Program, Office of Commissioner of Higher Education, PO Box 203101, Helena, MT 59620-3101. *E-mail:* jkirkpatrick@mgslp.state.mt.us. *Phone:* 406-444-0638. *Fax:* 406-444-1869. *Web site:* http://www.mgslp.state.mt.us.

NEBRASKA

Nebraska State Grant. Available to undergraduates attending a participating postsecondary institution in Nebraska. Available to Pell Grant recipients only. Nebraska residency required. Awards determined by each participating institution. Student must complete the Free Application for Federal Student Aid (FAFSA) to apply. Contact financial aid office at institution for additional information. *Award:* Grant for use in freshman, sophomore, junior, or senior year; not renewable. *Award amount:* $100–$1600. *Number of awards:* varies. *Eligibility Requirements:* Applicant must be enrolled or expecting to enroll full- or part-time at a two-year, four-year, or technical institution or university; resident of Nebraska and studying in Nebraska. Available to U.S. citizens. *Application Requirements:* Application, financial need analysis. **Deadline:** continuous.

Contact Mr. J. Ritchie Morrow, Financial Aid Coordinator, Nebraska's Coordinating Commission for Postsecondary Education, 140 North Eighth Street, Suite 300, PO Box 95005, Lincoln, NE 68509-5005. *E-mail:* Ritchie.Morrow@nebraska.gov. *Phone:* 402-471-2847. *Fax:* 402-471-2886. *Web site:* http://www.ccpe.state.ne.us.

NEVADA

Governor Guinn Millennium Scholarship. Scholarship for high school graduates with a diploma from a Nevada public or private high school in the graduating class of the year 2000 or later. Must complete high school with at least 3.25 GPA. *Award:* Scholarship for use in freshman, sophomore, junior, or senior year; not renewable. *Award amount:* $10,000. *Number of awards:* 1. *Eligibility Requirements:* Applicant must be enrolled or expecting to enroll full-time at a two-year or four-year institution or university and resident of Nevada. Available to U.S. citizens. *Application Requirements:* Application. **Deadline:** varies.

Contact Reba Coombs, Executive Director, Nevada Office of the State Treasurer, 555 East Washington Avenue, Suite 4600, Las Vegas, NV 89101. *E-mail:* info@nevadatreasurer.gov. *Phone:* 702-486-3383. *Fax:* 702-486-3246. *Web site:* http://www.nevadatreasurer.gov.

National Space Grant College and Fellowship Program. The grant provides graduate fellowships and undergraduate scholarship to qualified students majoring in science, technology, engineering and mathematics. Must be a U.S. citizen (permanent residence status, green card or student visa is not accepted)and enrolled full-time in an accredited educational institution in the state of Nevada. Minimum 3.0 GPA required. Awardees cannot receive other federal funds during the time they are receiving a Nevada NASA Space Grant award. *Academic Fields/Career Goals:* Applied Sciences; Aviation/Aerospace; Chemical Engineering; Civil Engineering; Computer Science/Data Processing; Earth Science; Engineering/Technology; Mathematics; Mechanical Engineering; Natural Sciences; Physical Sciences. *Award:* Scholarship for use in freshman, sophomore, junior, senior, or graduate year; not renewable. *Award amount:* $1250–$13,333. *Number of awards:* 1–25. *Eligibility Requirements:* Applicant must be enrolled or expecting to enroll full-time at a two-year or four-year institution or university; resident of Nevada and studying in Nevada. Applicant must have 3.0 GPA or higher. Available to U.S. citizens. *Application Requirements:* Application, essay, resume, references, transcript. **Deadline:** April 15.

Contact Leone Thierman, Program Coordinator, Nevada NASA Space Grant Consortium, 2215 Raggio Parkway, Reno, NV 89512. *E-mail:* nvsg@dri.edu. *Phone:* 775-673-7674. *Fax:* 775-673-7485. *Web site:* http://www.nvspacegrant.org.

Nevada Student Incentive Grant. Grants awarded to undergraduate and graduate students who are Nevada residents pursuing their first degree. Recipients must be enrolled at least halftime and have financial need. Awards may range from $200 to $4000. High school students may not apply. *Award:* Grant for use in freshman, sophomore, junior, senior, or graduate year; not renewable. *Award amount:* $200–$4000. *Number of awards:* 400–800. *Eligibility Requirements:* Applicant must be enrolled or expecting to enroll full- or part-time at a two-year, four-year, or technical institution or university; resident of Nevada and studying in Nevada. Available to U.S. citizens. *Application Requirements:* Application, financial need analysis. **Deadline:** continuous.

Contact Ms. Vicki Graves, Scholarship Coordinator, Nevada Department of Education, 700 East Fifth Street, Carson City, NV 89701. *E-mail:* vgraves@doe.nv.gov. *Phone:* 775-687-9150. *Fax:* 775-687-9113. *Web site:* http://www.doe.nv.gov.

NEW HAMPSHIRE

Leveraged Incentive Grant Program. Grants to provide assistance on the basis of merit and need to full-time undergraduate New Hampshire students at New Hampshire accredited institutions. Must be a New Hampshire resident, and demonstrate financial need as determined by the federal formula and by merit as determined by the institution. Must be a sophomore, junior or senior undergraduate student. *Award:* Grant for use in sophomore, junior, or senior year; not renewable. *Award amount:* $250–$7500. *Number of awards:* varies. *Eligibility Requirements:* Applicant must be enrolled or expecting to enroll full-time at a two-year, four-year, or technical institution or university; resident of New Hampshire and studying in New Hampshire. Available to U.S. citizens. *Application Requirements:* FAFSA. **Deadline:** varies.

Contact Ms. Cynthia Capodestria, Coordinator of Student Financial Aid Programs, New Hampshire Postsecondary Education Commission, Three Barrell Court, Suite 300, Concord, NH 03301-8543. *E-mail:* cynthia.capodestria@pec.state.nh.us. *Phone:* 603-271-2555 Ext. 360. *Fax:* 603-271-2696. *Web site:* http://www.nh.gov/postsecondary.

New Hampshire Incentive Program (NHIP). Grants to provide financial assistance to New Hampshire students attending eligible institutions in New England. Must demonstrate financial need. May be a part- or full-time undergraduate student with no previous bachelor's degree. *Award:* Grant for use in freshman, sophomore, junior, or senior year; renewable. *Award amount:* $125–$1000. *Number of awards:* 4300–4500. *Eligibility Requirements:* Applicant must be enrolled or expecting to enroll full- or part-time at a two-year or four-year institution or university; resident of New Hampshire and studying in Connecticut, Maine, Massachusetts, New Hampshire, Rhode Island, or Vermont. Available to U.S. citizens. *Application Requirements:* FAFSA. **Deadline:** May 1.

Contact Ms. Cynthia Capodestria, Coordinator of Student Financial Aid Programs, New Hampshire Postsecondary Education Commission, Three Barrell Court, Suite 300, Concord, NH 03301-8543. *E-mail:* cynthia.capodestria@pec.state.nh.us. *Phone:* 603-271-2555 Ext. 360. *Fax:* 603-271-2696. *Web site:* http://www.nh.gov/postsecondary.

Scholarships for Orphans of Veterans–New Hampshire. Scholarship to provide financial assistance (room, board, books and supplies) to children of parents) who served in World War II, Korean Conflict, Vietnam (Southeast Asian Conflict) or the Gulf Wars, or any other operation for which the armed forces expeditionary medal or theater of operations service medal was awarded to the veteran. *Award:* Scholarship for use in freshman, sophomore, junior, or senior year; renewable. *Award amount:* up to $2500. *Number of awards:* 1–10. *Eligibility Requirements:* Applicant must be age 16-25; enrolled or expecting to enroll full-time at a two-year or four-year institution or university; resident of New Hampshire and studying in New Hampshire. Available to U.S. citizens. Applicant or parent must meet one or more of the following requirements: general military experience; retired from active duty; disabled or killed as a result of military service; prisoner of war; or missing in action. *Application Requirements:* Application. **Deadline:** varies.

Contact Ms. Cynthia Capodestria, Coordinator of Student Financial Aid Programs, New Hampshire Postsecondary Education Commission, Three Barrell Court, Suite 300, Concord, NH 03301-8543. *E-mail:* cynthia.capodestria@pec.state.nh.us. *Phone:* 603-271-2555 Ext. 360. *Fax:* 603-271-2696. *Web site:* http://www.nh.gov/postsecondary.

Workforce Incentive Program. The program provides incentive for students to pursue careers in critical workforce shortage areas at appropriate New Hampshire institutions and to encourage students to then seek employment in New Hampshire after completion of their career program. May be a part- or full-time student in an approved program, and should demonstrate financial need as determined by the institution. *Academic Fields/Career Goals:* Education; Foreign Language; Nursing; Special Education. *Award:* Forgivable loan for use in freshman, sophomore, junior, senior, graduate, or postgraduate years; not renewable. *Award amount:* varies. *Number of awards:* varies. *Eligibility Requirements:* Applicant must be enrolled or expecting to enroll full- or part-time at a four-year institution or university; resident of New Hampshire and studying in New Hampshire. Available to U.S. citizens. *Application Requirements:* Application. **Deadline:** varies.

Contact Ms. Cynthia Capodestria, Coordinator of Student Financial Aid Programs, New Hampshire Postsecondary Education Commission, Three Barrell Court, Suite 300, Concord, NH 03301-8543. *E-mail:* cynthia.capodestria@pec.state.nh.us. *Phone:* 603-271-2555 Ext. 360. *Fax:* 603-271-2696. *Web site:* http://www.nh.gov/postsecondary.

NEW JERSEY

American Legion Department of New Jersey High School Oratorical Contest. Award to promote and coordinate the Oratorical Contest Program at the Department, District, County and Post Levels. High School Oratorical Contest is to develop a deeper knowledge and understanding of the constitution of the United States. *Award:* Prize for use in freshman year; not renewable. *Award amount:* $1000–$4000. *Number of awards:* 5. *Eligibility Requirements:* Applicant must be high school student; planning to enroll or expecting to enroll full-time at a four-year institution or university and must have an interest in public speaking. Available to U.S. citizens. *Application Requirements:* Application, applicant must enter a contest. **Deadline:** March 8.

Contact Raymond L. Zawacki, Department Adjutant, American Legion Department of New Jersey, 135 West Hanover Street, Trenton, NJ 08618. *E-mail:* ray@njamericanlegion.org. *Phone:* 609-695-5418. *Fax:* 609-394-1532. *Web site:* http://www.njamericanlegion.org.

ANNA Alcavis International, Inc. Career Mobility Scholarship. Scholarship to students accepted or enrolled in a baccalaureate or higher degree program in nursing. Applicant must hold a current credential as a Certified Nephrology Nurse (CNN) or Certified Dialysis Nurse (CDN) administered by the Nephrology Nursing Certification Commission (NNCC). *Academic Fields/Career Goals:* Nursing. *Award:* Forgivable loan for use in freshman, sophomore, junior, senior, or graduate year; renewable. *Award amount:* $2000. *Number of awards:* 5. *Eligibility Requirements:* Applicant must be enrolled or expecting to enroll full-time at a four-year institution or university. Applicant or parent of applicant must be member of American Nephrology Nurses' Association. Applicant or parent of applicant must have employment or volunteer experience in nursing. Available to U.S. and non-Canadian citizens. *Application Requirements:* Application, essay, financial need analysis, transcript. **Deadline:** October 15.

Contact Sharon Longton, Awards, Scholarships, and Grants Chairperson, American Nephrology Nurses' Association, East Holly Avenue, PO Box 56, Pitman, NJ 08071-0056. *E-mail:* slongton@dmc.org. *Phone:* 313-966-2674. *Web site:* http://www.annanurse.org.

Dana Christmas Scholarship for Heroism. Honors young New Jersey residents for acts of heroism. Scholarship is a nonrenewable award of up to $10,000 for 5 students. This scholarship may be used for undergraduate or graduate study. Deadline varies. *Award:* Scholarship for use in freshman, sophomore, junior, senior, or graduate year; not renewable. *Award amount:* up to $10,000. *Number of awards:*

up to 5. *Eligibility Requirements:* Applicant must be age 21 or under; enrolled or expecting to enroll full- or part-time at a two-year, four-year, or technical institution or university and resident of New Jersey. Available to U.S. citizens. *Application Requirements:* Application. **Deadline:** varies.

Contact Gisele Joachim, Director, Financial Aid Services, New Jersey Higher Education Student Assistance Authority, 4 Quakerbridge Plaza, PO Box 540, Trenton, NJ 08625. *E-mail:* gjoachim@hesaa.org. *Phone:* 800-792-8670 Ext. 2349. *Fax:* 609-588-7389. *Web site:* http://www.hesaa.org.

Edward J. Bloustein Distinguished Scholars. Renewable scholarship for students who are placed in top 10 percent of their classes and have a minimum combined SAT score of 1260, or ranked first, second or third in their classes as of end of junior year. Must be New Jersey resident and must attend a New Jersey two-year college, four-year college or university, or approved programs at proprietary institutions. Secondary schools must forward to HESAA, the names and class standings for all nominees. Award value up to $1000 and deadline varies. *Award:* Scholarship for use in freshman, sophomore, junior, senior, or graduate year; renewable. *Award amount:* up to $1000. *Number of awards:* varies. *Eligibility Requirements:* Applicant must be enrolled or expecting to enroll full-time at a two-year or four-year institution or university; resident of New Jersey and studying in New Jersey. Available to U.S. citizens. *Application Requirements:* Application, test scores, nomination by high school. **Deadline:** varies.

Contact Carol Muka, Assistant Director of Grants and Scholarships, New Jersey Higher Education Student Assistance Authority, PO Box 540, Trenton, NJ 08625. *E-mail:* cmuka@hesaa.org. *Phone:* 800-792-8670 Ext. 3266. *Fax:* 609-588-2228. *Web site:* http://www.hesaa.org.

Law Enforcement Officer Memorial Scholarship. Scholarships for full-time undergraduate study at approved New Jersey institutions for the dependent children of New Jersey law enforcement officers killed in the line of duty. Value of scholarship will be established annually. Deadline varies. *Award:* Scholarship for use in freshman, sophomore, junior, or senior year; renewable. *Award amount:* varies. *Number of awards:* varies. *Eligibility Requirements:* Applicant must be enrolled or expecting to enroll full-time at a four-year institution or university; resident of New Jersey and studying in New Jersey. Applicant or par-

ent of applicant must have employment or volunteer experience in police/firefighting. Available to U.S. citizens. *Application Requirements:* Application. **Deadline:** varies.

Contact Carol Muka, Assistant Director of Grants and Scholarships, New Jersey Higher Education Student Assistance Authority, PO Box 540, Trenton, NJ 08625. *E-mail:* cmuka@hesaa.org. *Phone:* 800-792-8670 Ext. 3266. *Fax:* 609-588-2228. *Web site:* http://www.hesaa.org.

Luterman Scholarship. Applicant must be a natural or adopted descendant of a member of American Legion, Department of New Jersey. Applicant must be a member of the graduating class of high school including Vo-tech. *Award:* Scholarship for use in freshman year; not renewable. *Award amount:* $1000–$4000. *Number of awards:* 7. *Eligibility Requirements:* Applicant must be high school student and planning to enroll or expecting to enroll full-time at a two-year, four-year, or technical institution or university. Applicant or parent of applicant must be member of American Legion or Auxiliary. Available to U.S. citizens. Applicant or parent must meet one or more of the following requirements: Army experience; retired from active duty; disabled or killed as a result of military service; prisoner of war; or missing in action. *Application Requirements:* Application. **Deadline:** February 15.

Contact Raymond L. Zawacki, Department Adjutant, American Legion Department of New Jersey, 135 West Hanover Street, Trenton, NJ 08618. *E-mail:* ray@njamericanlegion.org. *Phone:* 609-695-5418. *Fax:* 609-394-1532. *Web site:* http://www.njamericanlegion.org.

New Jersey Student Tuition Assistance Reward Scholarship II. Scholarship for high school graduates who plan to pursue a baccalaureate degree at a New Jersey four-year public institution. Scholarship will cover the cost of tuition and approved fees for up to 18 credits per semester when combined with other state, federal and institutional aid. Deadline varies. *Award:* Scholarship for use in freshman year; renewable. *Award amount:* $2000. *Number of awards:* varies. *Eligibility Requirements:* Applicant must be enrolled or expecting to enroll full-time at a four-year institution or university; resident of New Jersey and studying in New Jersey. Applicant must have 3.0 GPA or higher. Available to U.S. citizens. *Application Requirements:* Application, FAFSA. **Deadline:** varies.

Contact Cathleen Lewis, Assistant Director, Client Services, New Jersey Higher Education Student Assistance Authority, 4

Quaker Bridge Plaza, PO Box 540, Trenton, NJ 08625-0540. *E-mail:* clewis@hesaa.org. *Phone:* 609-588-3280. *Fax:* 609-588-2228. *Web site:* http://www.hesaa.org.

New Jersey War Orphans Tuition Assistance. $500 scholarship to children of those service personnel who died while in the military or due to service-connected disabilities, or who are officially listed as missing in action by the U.S. Department of Defense. Must be a resident of New Jersey for at least one year immediately preceding the filing of the application and be between the ages of 16 and 21 at the time of application. *Award:* Scholarship for use in freshman, sophomore, junior, or senior year; renewable. *Award amount:* $500. *Number of awards:* varies. *Eligibility Requirements:* Applicant must be age 16-21; enrolled or expecting to enroll full-time at a four-year institution or university and resident of New Jersey. Available to U.S. citizens. Applicant or parent must meet one or more of the following requirements: general military experience; retired from active duty; disabled or killed as a result of military service; prisoner of war; or missing in action. *Application Requirements:* Application, transcript. **Deadline:** varies.

Contact Patricia Richter, Grants Manager, New Jersey Department of Military and Veterans Affairs, PO Box 340, Trenton, NJ 08625-0340. *E-mail:* patricia.richter@njdmava.state.nj.us. *Phone:* 609-530-6854. *Fax:* 609-530-6970. *Web site:* http://www.state.nj.us/military.

New Jersey World Trade Center Scholarship. Scholarship was established by the legislature to aid the dependent children and surviving spouses of New Jersey residents who were killed in the terrorist attacks, or who are missing and officially presumed dead as a direct result of the attacks; applies to instate and out-of-state institutions for students seeking undergraduate degrees. Deadlines: March 1 for fall, October 1 for spring. *Award:* Scholarship for use in freshman, sophomore, junior, or senior year; renewable. *Award amount:* up to $6500. *Number of awards:* varies. *Eligibility Requirements:* Applicant must be enrolled or expecting to enroll full-time at a four-year institution or university and resident of New Jersey. Available to U.S. citizens. *Application Requirements:* Application. **Deadline:** varies.

Contact Giselle Joachim, Director of Financial Aid Services, New Jersey Higher Education Student Assistance Authority, PO Box 540, Trenton, NJ 08625. *E-mail:* gjoachim@hesaa.org. *Phone:* 800-792-8670 Ext. 2349. *Fax:* 609-588-7389. *Web site:* http://www.hesaa.org.

NJ Student Tuition Assistance Reward Scholarship. Scholarship for students who graduate in the top 20 percent of their high school class. Recipients may be awarded up to five semesters of tuition (up to 15 credits per term) and approved fees at one of New Jersey's nineteen county colleges. *Award:* Scholarship for use in freshman, sophomore, junior, or senior year; renewable. *Award amount:* $2500–$7500. *Number of awards:* varies. *Eligibility Requirements:* Applicant must be enrolled or expecting to enroll full-time at a two-year or four-year institution or university; resident of New Jersey and studying in New Jersey. Applicant must have 3.0 GPA or higher. Available to U.S. citizens. *Application Requirements:* Application, transcript. **Deadline:** varies.

Contact Carol Muka, Assistant Director of Grants and Scholarships, New Jersey Higher Education Student Assistance Authority, PO Box 540, Trenton, NJ 08625. *E-mail:* cmuka@hessa.org. *Phone:* 800-792-8670 Ext. 3266. *Fax:* 609-588-2228. *Web site:* http://www.hesaa.org.

Outstanding Scholar Recruitment Program. Awards students who meet the eligibility criteria and who are enrolled as first-time freshmen at participating New Jersey institutions receive annual scholarship awards of up to $7500. *Award:* Scholarship for use in freshman, sophomore, junior, or senior year; renewable. *Award amount:* $2500–$7500. *Number of awards:* varies. *Eligibility Requirements:* Applicant must be enrolled or expecting to enroll full-time at a four-year institution or university; resident of New Jersey and studying in New Jersey. Available to U.S. citizens. *Application Requirements:* Application. **Deadline:** varies.

Contact Carol Muka, Assistant Director of Grants and Scholarships, New Jersey Higher Education Student Assistance Authority, PO Box 540, Trenton, NJ 08625. *E-mail:* cmuka@hesaa.org. *Phone:* 800-792-8670 Ext. 3266. *Fax:* 609-588-2228. *Web site:* http://www.hesaa.org.

Part-Time Tuition Aid Grant (TAG) for County Colleges. Provides financial aid to eligible part-time undergraduate students enrolled for 9 to 11 credits at participating New Jersey community colleges. Deadlines: March 1 for spring and October 1 for fall. *Award:* Grant for use in freshman, sophomore, junior, or senior year; not renewable. *Award amount:* $419–$628. *Number of awards:* varies. *Eligibility*

Requirements: Applicant must be enrolled or expecting to enroll part-time at a two-year or four-year institution or university; resident of New Jersey and studying in New Jersey. Available to U.S. citizens. *Application Requirements:* Application, financial need analysis. **Deadline:** varies.

Contact Sherri Fox, Acting Director of Grants and Scholarships, New Jersey Higher Education Student Assistance Authority, PO Box 540, Trenton, NJ 08625. *Phone:* 800-792-8670. *Fax:* 609-588-2228. *Web site:* http://www.hesaa.org.

POW-MIA Tuition Benefit Program. Free undergraduate college tuition provided to any child born or adopted before or during the period of time his or her parent was officially declared a prisoner of war or person missing in action after January 1, 1960. The POW-MIA must have been a New Jersey resident at the time he or she entered the service. Child of veteran must attend either a public or private institution in New Jersey. A copy of DD 1300 must be furnished with the application. Minimum 2.5 GPA required. *Award:* Scholarship for use in freshman, sophomore, junior, or senior year; renewable. *Award amount:* varies. *Number of awards:* varies. *Eligibility Requirements:* Applicant must be enrolled or expecting to enroll full-time at a two-year, four-year, or technical institution or university; resident of New Jersey and studying in New Jersey. Applicant must have 2.5 GPA or higher. Available to U.S. citizens. Applicant or parent must meet one or more of the following requirements: general military experience; retired from active duty; disabled or killed as a result of military service; prisoner of war; or missing in action. *Application Requirements:* Application, transcript, copy of DD 1300. **Deadline:** varies.

Contact Patricia Richter, Grants Manager, New Jersey Department of Military and Veterans Affairs, PO Box 340, Trenton, NJ 08625-0340. *E-mail:* patricia.richter@njdmava.state.nj.us. *Phone:* 609-530-6854. *Fax:* 609-530-6970. *Web site:* http://www.state.nj.us/military.

Stutz Scholarship. Award to natural or adopted son or daughter of a member of The American Legion, Department of New Jersey. Applicant must be a member of the graduating class of high school including Vo-tech. *Award:* Scholarship for use in freshman year; not renewable. *Award amount:* $4000. *Number of awards:* 1. *Eligibility Requirements:* Applicant must be high school student and planning to enroll or expecting to enroll full-time at a two-year, four-year, or technical institution or university. Applicant or parent of applicant must be member of American Legion or Auxiliary. Available to U.S. citizens. Applicant or parent must meet one or more of the following requirements: Army experience; retired from active duty; disabled or killed as a result of military service; prisoner of war; or missing in action. *Application Requirements:* Application. **Deadline:** February 15.

Contact Raymond L. Zawacki, Department Adjutant, American Legion Department of New Jersey, 135 West Hanover Street, Trenton, NJ 08618. *E-mail:* ray@njamericanlegion.org. *Phone:* 609-695-5418. *Fax:* 609-394-1532. *Web site:* http://www.njamericanlegion.org.

Survivor Tuition Benefits Program. The scholarship provides tuition fees for spouses and dependents of law enforcement officers, fire, or emergency services personnel killed in the line of duty. Eligible recipients may attend any independent institution in the state; however, the annual value of the grant cannot exceed the highest tuition charged at a New Jersey public institution. *Award:* Scholarship for use in freshman, sophomore, junior, or senior year; renewable. *Award amount:* varies. *Number of awards:* varies. *Eligibility Requirements:* Applicant must be enrolled or expecting to enroll full- or part-time at a two-year or four-year institution or university; resident of New Jersey and studying in New Jersey. Applicant or parent of applicant must have employment or volunteer experience in police/firefighting. Available to U.S. citizens. *Application Requirements:* Application. **Deadline:** varies.

Contact Carol Muka, Scholarship Coordinator, New Jersey Higher Education Student Assistance Authority, PO Box 540, Trenton, NJ 08625. *E-mail:* cmuka@hesaa.org. *Phone:* 800-792-8670 Ext. 3266. *Fax:* 609-588-2228. *Web site:* http://www.hesaa.org.

Tuition Aid Grant. The program provides tuition fees to eligible undergraduate students attending participating in-state institutions. Deadlines: March 1 for fall, October 1 for spring. *Award:* Grant for use in freshman, sophomore, junior, or senior year; not renewable. *Award amount:* $868–$7272. *Number of awards:* varies. *Eligibility Requirements:* Applicant must be enrolled or expecting to enroll full-time at a two-year or four-year institution or university; resident of New Jersey and studying in New Jersey. Available to U.S. citizens. *Application Requirements:* Application, financial need analysis. **Deadline:** varies.

Contact Sherri Fox, Acting Director of Grants and Scholarships, New Jersey Higher Education Student Assistance Authority, PO Box 540, Trenton, NJ 08625. *Phone:* 800-792-8670. *Fax:* 609-588-2228. *Web site:* http://www.hesaa.org.

Urban Scholars. Renewable scholarship to high achieving students attending public secondary schools in the urban and economically distressed areas of New Jersey. Students must rank in the top 10 percent of their class and have a GPA of at least 3.0 at the end of their junior year. Must be New Jersey resident and attend a New Jersey two-year college, four-year college or university, or approved programs at proprietary institutions. Students do not apply directly for scholarship consideration. Deadline varies. *Award:* Scholarship for use in freshman, sophomore, junior, or senior year; renewable. *Award amount:* up to $1000. *Number of awards:* varies. *Eligibility Requirements:* Applicant must be enrolled or expecting to enroll full-time at a two-year or four-year institution or university; resident of New Jersey and studying in New Jersey. Applicant must have 3.0 GPA or higher. Available to U.S. citizens. *Application Requirements:* Application, test scores, nomination by school. **Deadline:** varies.

Contact Carol Muka, Assistant Director of Grants and Scholarships, New Jersey Higher Education Student Assistance Authority, PO Box 540, Trenton, NJ 08625. *E-mail:* cmuka@hesaa.org. *Phone:* 800-792-8670 Ext. 3266. *Fax:* 609-588-2228. *Web site:* http://www.hesaa.org.

Veterans Tuition Credit Program-New Jersey. Award for New Jersey resident veterans who served in the armed forces between December 31, 1960, and May 7, 1975. Must have been a New Jersey resident at time of induction or discharge or for two years immediately prior to application. *Award:* Scholarship for use in freshman, sophomore, junior, or senior year; renewable. *Award amount:* $200–$400. *Number of awards:* varies. *Eligibility Requirements:* Applicant must be enrolled or expecting to enroll full- or part-time at a two-year, four-year, or technical institution or university and resident of New Jersey. Available to U.S. citizens. Applicant or parent must meet one or more of the following requirements: general military experience; retired from active duty; disabled or killed as a result of military service; prisoner of war; or missing in action. *Application Requirements:* Application. **Deadline:** varies.

Contact Patricia Richter, Grants Manager, New Jersey Department of Military and Veterans Affairs, PO Box 340, Trenton, NJ 08625-0340. *E-mail:* patricia.richter@njdmava.state.nj.us. *Phone:* 609-530-6854. *Fax:* 609-530-6970. *Web site:* http://www.state.nj.us/military.

NEW MEXICO

Allied Health Student Loan Program-New Mexico. Award to New Mexico residents studying in New Mexico to increase the number of physician assistants in areas of the state which have experienced shortages of health practitioners. Provides educational loans to students seeking certification/licensers in an eligible health field. As a condition of each loan, the student must declare intent to practice as a health professional in a designated shortage area. For every year of service, a portion of the loan will be forgiven. *Academic Fields/Career Goals:* Dental Health/Services; Health and Medical Sciences; Nursing; Therapy/Rehabilitation. *Award:* Forgivable loan for use in freshman, sophomore, junior, or senior year; renewable. *Award amount:* up to $12,000. *Number of awards:* 1–40. *Eligibility Requirements:* Applicant must be enrolled or expecting to enroll full- or part-time at a four-year institution or university; resident of New Mexico and studying in New Mexico. Available to U.S. citizens. *Application Requirements:* Application, financial need analysis, transcript, FAFSA. **Deadline:** July 1.

Contact Theresa Acker, Financial Aid Division, New Mexico Commission on Higher Education, 1068 Cerrillos Road, Santa Fe, NM 87505-1650. *E-mail:* theresa.acker@state.nm.us. *Phone:* 505-476-6506. *Fax:* 505-476-6511. *Web site:* http://www.hed.state.nm.us.

Children of Deceased Veterans Scholarship-New Mexico. Award for New Mexico residents who are children of veterans killed or disabled as a result of service, prisoner of war, or veterans missing in action. Must be between ages 16 and 26. For use at New Mexico schools for undergraduate study. Must submit parent's death certificate and DD form 214. *Award:* Scholarship for use in freshman, sophomore, junior, or senior year; renewable. *Award amount:* $300. *Number of awards:* varies. *Eligibility Requirements:* Applicant must be age 16-26; enrolled or expecting to enroll full- or part-time at a two-year or four-year institution or university; resident of New Mexico and studying in New Mexico. Available to U.S. citizens. Applicant or parent must meet one or more of the following requirements: general military experience; retired from active duty; disabled or killed as a result of military service;

prisoner of war; or missing in action. *Application Requirements:* Application, transcript, death certificate or notice of casualty, DD form 214. **Deadline:** continuous.

Contact Alan Martinez, Deputy Secretary, New Mexico Department of Veterans' Services, Bataan Memorial Building, PO BOX 2324, Santa Fe, NM 87504. *E-mail:* alan.martinez@state.nm.us. *Phone:* 505-827-6300. *Fax:* 505-827-6372. *Web site:* http://www.dvs.state.nm.us.

College Affordability Grant. Grant available to New Mexico students with financial need who do not qualify for other state grants and scholarships to attend and complete educational programs at a New Mexico public college or university. Student must have unmet need after all other financial aid has been awarded. Student may not be receiving any other state grants or scholarships. Renewable upon satisfactory academic progress. *Award:* Grant for use in freshman, sophomore, junior, or senior year; renewable. *Award amount:* up to $1000. *Number of awards:* 1. *Eligibility Requirements:* Applicant must be enrolled or expecting to enroll full- or part-time at a two-year or four-year institution or university; resident of New Mexico and studying in New Mexico. Available to U.S. citizens. *Application Requirements:* Application, financial need analysis, FAFSA. **Deadline:** continuous.

Contact Tashina Banks Acker, Director of Financial Aid, New Mexico Commission on Higher Education, 1068 Cerrillos Road, Santa Fe, NM 87505-1650. *E-mail:* tashina.banks-moore@state.nm.us. *Phone:* 505-476-6549. *Fax:* 505-476-6511. *Web site:* http://www.hed.state.nm.us.

Legislative Endowment Scholarships. Renewable scholarships to provide aid for undergraduate students with substantial financial need who are attending public postsecondary institutions in New Mexico. Four-year schools may award up to $2500 per academic year, two-year schools may award up to $1000 per academic year. Deadlines varies. *Award:* Scholarship for use in freshman, sophomore, junior, or senior year; renewable. *Award amount:* $1000–$2500. *Number of awards:* 1. *Eligibility Requirements:* Applicant must be enrolled or expecting to enroll full- or part-time at a two-year or four-year institution or university; resident of New Mexico and studying in New Mexico. Available to U.S. citizens. *Application Requirements:* Application, financial need analysis, FAFSA. **Deadline:** varies.

Contact Tashina Banks Moore, Director of Financial Aid, New Mexico Commission on Higher Education, 1068 Cerrillos Road, Santa Fe, NM 87505-1650. *E-mail:* tashina.banks-moore@state.nm.us. *Phone:* 505-475-6549. *Fax:* 505-476-6511. *Web site:* http://www.hed.state.nm.us.

Legislative Lottery Scholarship. Renewable Scholarship for New Mexico high school graduates or GED recipients who plan to attend an eligible New Mexico public college or university. Must be enrolled full-time and maintain 2.5 GPA. *Award:* Scholarship for use in freshman year; renewable. *Award amount:* varies. *Number of awards:* 1. *Eligibility Requirements:* Applicant must be high school student; planning to enroll or expecting to enroll full-time at a four-year institution or university; resident of New Mexico and studying in New Mexico. Applicant must have 3.5 GPA or higher. Available to U.S. citizens. *Application Requirements:* Application, FAFSA. **Deadline:** varies.

Contact Tashina Banks Moore, Director of Financial Aid, New Mexico Commission on Higher Education, 1068 Cerrillos Road, Santa Fe, NM 87505. *E-mail:* tashina.banks-moore@state.nm.us. *Phone:* 505-476-6549. *Fax:* 505-476-6511. *Web site:* http://www.hed.state.nm.us.

Minority Doctoral Assistance Loan-For-Service Program. Award program enacted to increase the number of ethnic minorities and women available to teach engineering, physical or life sciences, mathematics, and other academic disciplines in which ethnic minorities or women are demonstrably underrepresented in New Mexico colleges and universities. Award may be renewable for up to four years. *Academic Fields/Career Goals:* Chemical Engineering; Engineering/Technology; Mathematics; Mechanical Engineering; Natural Sciences; Physical Sciences. *Award:* Forgivable loan for use in freshman, sophomore, junior, senior, or graduate year; renewable. *Award amount:* $15,000. *Number of awards:* varies. *Eligibility Requirements:* Applicant must be American Indian/Alaska Native, Asian/Pacific Islander, Black (non-Hispanic), or Hispanic; enrolled or expecting to enroll full-time at a four-year institution or university; resident of New Mexico and studying in New Mexico. Available to U.S. citizens. *Application Requirements:* Application, essay, references, transcript. **Deadline:** March 15.

Contact Theresa Acker, Financial Aid Division, New Mexico Commission on Higher Education, 1068 Cerrillos Road, Santa Fe, NM 87505-1650. *E-mail:* tashina.banks-moore@state.nm.us. *Phone:* 505-476-6506. *Fax:* 505-476-6511. *Web site:* http://www.hed.state.nm.us.

New Mexico Competitive Scholarship. Scholarships for non-residents or non-citizens of the United States to encourage out-of-state students who have demonstrated high academic achievement in high school to enroll in public four-year universities in New Mexico. Renewable for up to four years. For details visit http://fin.hed.state.nm.us. *Award:* Scholarship for use in freshman year; renewable. *Award amount:* varies. *Number of awards:* varies. *Eligibility Requirements:* Applicant must be high school student; planning to enroll or expecting to enroll full-time at a four-year institution or university and studying in New Mexico. Available to Canadian and non-U.S. citizens. *Application Requirements:* Application, essay, references, test scores. **Deadline:** varies.

Contact Tashina Banks Moore, Director of Financial Aid, New Mexico Commission on Higher Education, 1068 Cerrillos Road, Santa Fe, NM 87505. *E-mail:* tashina.banks-moore@state.nm.us. *Phone:* 505-476-6549. *Fax:* 505-476-6511. *Web site:* http://www.hed.state.nm.us.

New Mexico Scholars' Program. Renewable award program created to encourage New Mexico high school students to attend public postsecondary institutions or the following private colleges in New Mexico: College of Santa Fe, St. John's College, College of the Southwest. For details visit http://fin.hed.state.nm.us. *Award:* Scholarship for use in freshman year; renewable. *Award amount:* varies. *Number of awards:* 1. *Eligibility Requirements:* Applicant must be high school student; age 21 or under; planning to enroll or expecting to enroll full-time at a two-year or four-year institution; resident of New Mexico and studying in New Mexico. Available to U.S. citizens. *Application Requirements:* Application, financial need analysis, test scores, FAFSA. **Deadline:** varies.

Contact Tashina Banks Moore, Director of Financial Aid, New Mexico Commission on Higher Education, 1068 Cerrillos Road, Santa Fe, NM 87505-1650. *E-mail:* tashina.banks-moore@state.nm.us. *Phone:* 505-476-6549. *Fax:* 505-476-6511. *Web site:* http://www.hed.state.nm.us.

New Mexico Student Incentive Grant. Grant created to provide aid for undergraduate students with substantial financial need who are attending public colleges or universities or the following eligible colleges in New Mexico: College of Santa Fe, St. John's College, College of the

Southwest, Institute of American Indian Art, Crownpoint Institute of Technology, Dine College and Southwestern Indian Polytechnic Institute. Part-time students are eligible for pro-rated awards. *Award:* Grant for use in freshman, sophomore, junior, or senior year; not renewable. *Award amount:* $200–$2500. *Number of awards:* 1. *Eligibility Requirements:* Applicant must be enrolled or expecting to enroll full- or part-time at a two-year, four-year, or technical institution or university; resident of New Mexico and studying in New Mexico. Available to U.S. citizens. *Application Requirements:* Application, financial need analysis, FAFSA. **Deadline:** varies.

Contact Tashina Banks Moore, Director of Financial Aid, New Mexico Commission on Higher Education, 1068 Cerrillos Road, Santa Fe, NM 87505-1650. *E-mail:* tashina.banks-moore@state.nm.us. *Phone:* 505-476-6549. *Fax:* 505-476-6511. *Web site:* http://www.hed.state.nm.us.

New Mexico Vietnam Veteran Scholarship. Award for Vietnam veterans who have been New Mexico residents for a minimum of ten years and are attending state-funded postsecondary schools. Must have been awarded the Vietnam Campaign medal. Must submit DD 214 and discharge papers. *Award:* Scholarship for use in freshman, sophomore, junior, or senior year; renewable. *Award amount:* $3500–$4000. *Number of awards:* 100. *Eligibility Requirements:* Applicant must be enrolled or expecting to enroll full- or part-time at a two-year, four-year, or technical institution or university; resident of New Mexico and studying in New Mexico. Available to U.S. citizens. Applicant or parent must meet one or more of the following requirements: general military experience; retired from active duty; disabled or killed as a result of military service; prisoner of war; or missing in action. *Application Requirements:* Application, copy of DD Form 214. **Deadline:** continuous.

Contact Alan Martinez, Deputy Secretary, New Mexico Department of Veterans' Services, Bataan Memorial Building, PO BOX 2324, Santa Fe, NM 87504. *E-mail:* alan.martinez@state.nm.us. *Phone:* 505-827-6300. *Fax:* 505-827-6372. *Web site:* http://www.dvs.state.nm.us.

Nurse Educator Loan-for-Service. Forgivable loan of up to $5000 for New Mexico nursing majors to obtain an undergraduate, graduate, or post graduate degree in the state of New Mexico. Each loan has a service agreement wherein the student declares his/her intent to serve in a nurse faculty position in a New Mexico public,

post-secondary institution. For every academic year of service, a portion of the loan is forgiven and if the entire service agreement is fulfilled, the entire loan is eligible for forgiveness. Must be a U.S. citizen. *Academic Fields/Career Goals:* Nursing. *Award:* Forgivable loan for use in senior year; renewable. *Award amount:* up to $5000. *Number of awards:* 1. *Eligibility Requirements:* Applicant must be enrolled or expecting to enroll full- or part-time at a four-year institution or university; resident of New Mexico and studying in New Mexico. Available to U.S. citizens. *Application Requirements:* Application, essay, transcript. **Deadline:** July 1.

Contact Theresa Acker, Financial Aid Division, New Mexico Commission on Higher Education, 1068 Cerrillos Road, Santa Fe, NM 85705-1650. *E-mail:* theresa.acker@state.nm.us. *Phone:* 505-476-6506. *Fax:* 505-476-6511. *Web site:* http://www.hed.state.nm.us.

Nursing Student Loan-For-Service Program. Award to increase the number of nurses in areas of New Mexico which have experienced shortages by making educational loans to students entering nursing programs. As a condition of each loan, the student shall declare his/her intent to practice as a health professional in a designated shortage area. For every year of service, a portion of the loan will be forgiven. *Academic Fields/Career Goals:* Nursing. *Award:* Forgivable loan for use in freshman, sophomore, junior, or senior year; renewable. *Award amount:* up to $12,000. *Number of awards:* 1. *Eligibility Requirements:* Applicant must be enrolled or expecting to enroll full- or part-time at a four-year institution or university; resident of New Mexico and studying in New Mexico. Available to U.S. citizens. *Application Requirements:* Application, financial need analysis, transcript, FAFSA. **Deadline:** July 1.

Contact Theresa Acker, Financial Aid Division, New Mexico Commission on Higher Education, 1068 Cerrillos Road, Santa Fe, NM 87505-1650. *E-mail:* theresa.acker@state.nm.us. *Phone:* 505-476-6506. *Fax:* 505-476-6511. *Web site:* http://www.hed.state.nm.us.

Public Service Law Loan Repayment Assistance Program. Program to provide legal educational loan repayment assistance to individuals providing public service in state or local government or the nonprofit sector in New Mexico to low income or underserved residents. *Academic Fields/Career Goals:* Law/Legal Services. *Award:* Forgivable loan for use in freshman, sophomore, junior, or senior year; renewable. *Award amount:* up to $7200. *Number of*

awards: 1–16. *Eligibility Requirements:* Applicant must be enrolled or expecting to enroll full-time at a four-year institution or university; resident of New Mexico and studying in New Mexico. Available to U.S. citizens. *Application Requirements:* Application. **Deadline:** February 28.

Contact Theresa Acker, Financial Aid Division, New Mexico Commission on Higher Education, 1068 Cerrillos Road, Santa Fe, NM 87505. *E-mail:* theresa.acker@state.nm.us. *Phone:* 505-476-6506. *Fax:* 505-475-6511. *Web site:* http://www.hed.state.nm.us.

Teacher Loan-For-Service. Purpose is to proactively address New Mexico's teacher shortage by providing students with the financial resources to complete or enhance their post-secondary teacher preparation education. *Academic Fields/Career Goals:* Education. *Award:* Forgivable loan for use in freshman, sophomore, junior, or senior year; renewable. *Award amount:* up to $4000. *Number of awards:* 1. *Eligibility Requirements:* Applicant must be enrolled or expecting to enroll full- or part-time at a four-year institution or university; resident of New Mexico and studying in New Mexico. Available to U.S. citizens. *Application Requirements:* Application, financial need analysis, FAFSA. **Deadline:** July 1.

Contact Theresa Acker, Financial Aid Division, New Mexico Commission on Higher Education, 1068 Cerrillos Road, Santa Fe, NM 87505-1650. *E-mail:* theresa.acker@state.nm.us. *Phone:* 505-476-6506. *Fax:* 505-476-6511. *Web site:* http://www.hed.state.nm.us.

Vietnam Veterans' Scholarship Program. Renewable scholarship program created to provide aid for Vietnam veterans who are undergraduate and graduate students attending public postsecondary institutions or select private colleges in New Mexico. Private colleges include: College of Santa Fe, St. John's College and College of the Southwest. *Award:* Scholarship for use in freshman, sophomore, junior, or senior year; renewable. *Award amount:* varies. *Number of awards:* 1. *Eligibility Requirements:* Applicant must be enrolled or expecting to enroll full-time at a two-year or four-year institution; resident of New Mexico and studying in New Mexico. Available to U.S. citizens. Applicant or parent must meet one or more of the following requirements: general military experience; retired from active duty; disabled or killed as a result of military service; prisoner of war; or missing in action. *Application Requirements:* Application, certification by the NM Veteran's commission. **Deadline:** varies.

Contact Tashina Banks Moore, Director of Financial Aid, New Mexico Commission on Higher Education, 1068 Cerrillos Road, Santa Fe, NM 87505-1650. *E-mail:* tashina. banks-moore@state.nm.us. *Phone:* 505-476-6549. *Fax:* 505-476-6511. *Web site:* http://www.hed.state.nm.us.

NEW YORK

DAAD University Summer Course Grant. Scholarships are awarded to students pursuing full-time study at Canadian or US colleges or universities. There are no restrictions as to field of study, but applicants must have attained at least Sophomore standing (second-year standing in Canada) at the time of application. Scholarships are available for courses lasting a minimum of three weeks. The scholarship is approximately 850 Euro, which covers tuition, room and board in whole or in part. Accommodations are arranged by the host institution. In addition, DAAD will provide an international travel subsidy of 300-450 Euro. Scholarship recipients are expected to devote their full attention to the course and may not concurrently undertake individual research. A written report is requested within four weeks of the end of the course. *Academic Fields/Career Goals:* Foreign Language. *Award:* Grant for use in sophomore, junior, senior, or graduate year; not renewable. *Award amount:* varies. *Number of awards:* varies. *Eligibility Requirements:* Applicant must be enrolled or expecting to enroll full-time at a four-year institution or university and must have an interest in German language/culture. Available to U.S. and non-U.S. citizens. *Application Requirements:* Application, applicant must enter a contest, essay, resume, references, transcript. **Deadline:** December 15.

Contact Jane Fu, Information Officer, German Academic Exchange Service (DAAD), 871 United Nations Plaza, New York, NY 10017. *E-mail:* daadny@daad.org. *Phone:* 212-758-3223 Ext. 201. *Fax:* 212-755-5780. *Web site:* http://www.daad.org.

Japan-U.S. Friendship Commission Prize for the Translation of Japanese Literature. Annual prize for the best translation into English of a modern work of literature or for the best classical literary translation, or the prize is divided between a classical and a modern work. To qualify, works must be book-length translations of Japanese literary works: novels, collections of short stories, literary essays, memoirs, drama or poetry. *Academic Fields/Career Goals:* Foreign Language. *Award:* Prize for use in freshman, sophomore, junior, or senior year; not renewable. *Award amount:* $3000. *Number of awards:* 2. *Eligibility Requirements:* Applicant must be enrolled or expecting to enroll full- or part-time at a two-year, four-year, or technical institution or university. Available to U.S. citizens. *Application Requirements:* Application, applicant must enter a contest, resume, unpublished manuscripts. **Deadline:** February 29.

Contact Kia Cheleen, Assistant Director, Donald Keene Center of Japanese Culture, 507 Kent Hall, MC 3920, 1140 Amsterdam Avenue, Columbia University, New York, NY 10027 USA. *E-mail:* donald-keene-center@columbia.edu. *Phone:* 212-854-5036. *Fax:* 212-854-4019. *Web site:* http://www.donaldkeenecenter.org.

New York Aid for Part-Time Study (APTS). Renewable scholarship provides tuition assistance to part-time undergraduate students who are New York residents, meet income eligibility requirements and are attending New York accredited institutions. Deadline varies. Must be U.S. citizen. *Award:* Grant for use in freshman, sophomore, junior, or senior year; renewable. *Award amount:* up to $2000. *Number of awards:* varies. *Eligibility Requirements:* Applicant must be enrolled or expecting to enroll part-time at a two-year or four-year institution or university; resident of New York and studying in New York. Available to U.S. citizens. *Application Requirements:* Application, financial need analysis. **Deadline:** varies.

Contact Student Information, New York State Higher Education Services Corporation, 99 Washington Avenue, Room 1320, Albany, NY 12255. *Phone:* 518-473-3887. *Fax:* 518-474-2839. *Web site:* http://www.hesc.com.

New York Lottery Leaders of Tomorrow (Lot) Scholarship. Scholarship to one eligible graduating senior from every participating public and private high school in New York State is awarded a $1250, four-year college scholarship. Scholarships can only be used toward the cost of tuition. *Award:* Scholarship for use in freshman year; renewable. *Award amount:* $1250. *Number of awards:* varies. *Eligibility Requirements:* Applicant must be high school student; planning to enroll or expecting to enroll full-time at a four-year institution; resident of New York and studying in New York. Applicant must have 3.0 GPA or higher. Available to U.S. citizens. *Application Requirements:* Application, essay, transcript. **Deadline:** March 26.

Contact Scholarship Coordinator, New York Lottery, One Broadway Center, PO Box 7540, Schenectady, NY 12301-7540. *E-mail:* lotscholar@lottery.state.ny.us. *Phone:* 518-525-2686. *Fax:* 518-525-2689. *Web site:* http://www.nylottery.org.

New York Memorial Scholarships for Families of Deceased Police Officers, Fire Fighters and Peace Officers. Renewable scholarship for children, spouses and financial dependents of deceased fire fighters, volunteer firefighters, police officers, peace officers and emergency medical service workers who died in the line of duty. Provides up to the cost of SUNY educational expenses. *Award:* Scholarship for use in freshman, sophomore, junior, or senior year; renewable. *Award amount:* varies. *Number of awards:* varies. *Eligibility Requirements:* Applicant must be enrolled or expecting to enroll full-time at a four-year institution or university; resident of New York and studying in New York. Available to U.S. citizens. *Application Requirements:* Application, financial need analysis, transcript. **Deadline:** May 1.

Contact Scholarships, New York State Higher Education Services Corporation. *Phone:* 888-697-4372. *Web site:* http://www.hesc.com.

New York State Aid to Native Americans. Award for enrolled members of a New York State tribe and their children who are attending or planning to attend a New York State college and who are New York State residents. Deadlines: July 15 for the fall semester, December 31 for the spring semester, and May 20 for summer session. *Award:* Scholarship for use in freshman, sophomore, junior, or senior year; renewable. *Award amount:* $85–$2000. *Number of awards:* varies. *Eligibility Requirements:* Applicant must be American Indian/Alaska Native; enrolled or expecting to enroll full- or part-time at a two-year, four-year, or technical institution or university; resident of New York and studying in New York. Available to U.S. citizens. *Application Requirements:* Application, financial need analysis, references, transcript. **Deadline:** varies.

Contact Native American Education Unit, New York State Higher Education Services Corporation, EBA Room 475, Albany, NY 12234. *Phone:* 518-474-0537. *Web site:* http://www.hesc.com.

New York State Tuition Assistance Program. Award for New York state residents attending a New York postsecondary institution. Must be full-time student in approved program with tuition over $200 per year. Must show financial need and not be in default in any other state program. Renewable award of $500 to $5000 dependent on family income and tuition charged. *Award:* Grant for use in freshman, sophomore, junior, or senior year; renewable. *Award amount:* up to $5000. *Number of awards:* 350,000–360,000. *Eligibility Requirements:* Applicant must be enrolled or expecting to enroll full-time at a two-year or four-year institution or university; resident of New York and studying in New York. Available to U.S. citizens. *Application Requirements:* Application, financial need analysis. **Deadline:** May 1.

Contact Student Information, New York State Higher Education Services Corporation, 99 Washington Avenue, Room 1400, Albany, NY 12255. *Phone:* 888-697-4372. *Web site:* http://www.hesc.com.

New York Vietnam/Persian Gulf/Afghanistan Veterans Tuition Awards. Scholarship for veterans who served in Vietnam, the Persian Gulf, or Afghanistan. Must be a New York resident attending a New York institution. Must establish eligibility by September 1. *Award:* Scholarship for use in freshman, sophomore, junior, or senior year; renewable. *Number of awards:* varies. *Eligibility Requirements:* Applicant must be enrolled or expecting to enroll full- or part-time at a two-year, four-year, or technical institution or university; resident of New York and studying in New York. Available to U.S. citizens. Applicant or parent must meet one or more of the following requirements: general military experience; retired from active duty; disabled or killed as a result of military service; prisoner of war; or missing in action. *Application Requirements:* Application, financial need analysis. **Deadline:** May 1.

Contact Associate HESC Information Representative, New York State Higher Education Services Corporation, 99 Washington Avenue, Grants & Scholarships Unit, Albany, NY 12255. *E-mail:* scholarship@hesc.com. *Phone:* 888-NYS-HESC (697. *Web site:* http://www.hesc.com.

Regents Award for Child of Veteran. Award for students whose parent, as a result of service in U.S. Armed Forces during war or national emergency, died; suffered a 40 percent or more disability; or is classified as missing in action or a prisoner of war. Veteran must be current New York State resident or have been so at time of death. Student must be a New York resident, attending, or planning to attend, college in New York State. Must establish eligibility before applying for payment. *Award:* Scholarship for use in freshman,

sophomore, junior, or senior year; not renewable. *Award amount:* up to $450. *Number of awards:* varies. *Eligibility Requirements:* Applicant must be enrolled or expecting to enroll full-time at a two-year or four-year institution or university; resident of New York and studying in New York. Available to U.S. citizens. Applicant or parent must meet one or more of the following requirements: general military experience; retired from active duty; disabled or killed as a result of military service; prisoner of war; or missing in action. *Application Requirements:* Application, proof of eligibility. **Deadline:** May 1.

Contact Rita McGivern, Student Information, New York State Higher Education Services Corporation, 99 Washington Avenue, Room 1320, Albany, NY 12255. *E-mail:* rmcgivern@hesc.com. *Web site:* http://www.hesc.com.

Regents Professional Opportunity Scholarship. Scholarship for New York residents beginning or already enrolled in an approved degree-granting program of study in New York that leads to licensure in a particular profession. See the Web site for the list of eligible professions. Must be U.S. citizen or permanent resident. Award recipients must agree to practice upon licensure in their profession in New York for 12 months for each annual payment received. Priority given to economically disadvantaged members of minority groups underrepresented in the professions. *Academic Fields/Career Goals:* Accounting; Architecture; Dental Health/Services; Engineering/Technology; Health and Medical Sciences; Interior Design; Landscape Architecture; Law/Legal Services; Nursing; Pharmacy; Psychology; Social Services. *Award:* Scholarship for use in freshman, sophomore, junior, senior, or graduate year; renewable. *Award amount:* up to $5000. *Number of awards:* 220. *Eligibility Requirements:* Applicant must be enrolled or expecting to enroll full-time at a two-year or four-year institution or university; resident of New York and studying in New York. Available to U.S. citizens. *Application Requirements:* Application. **Deadline:** May 31.

Contact Lewis J. Hall, Supervisor, New York State Education Department, 89 Washington Avenue, Room 1078 EBA, Albany, NY 12234. *E-mail:* scholar@mail.nysed.gov. *Phone:* 518-486-1319. *Fax:* 518-486-5346. *Web site:* http://www.highered.nysed.gov.

Regents Professional Opportunity Scholarships. Award for New York State residents pursuing career in certain licensed professions. Must attend New York State

college. Priority given to economically disadvantaged members of minority group underrepresented in chosen profession and graduates of SEEK, College Discovery, EOP, and HEOP. Must work in New York State in chosen profession one year for each annual payment. Scholarships are awarded to undergraduate or graduate students, depending on the program. *Award:* Scholarship for use in freshman, sophomore, junior, senior, graduate, or postgraduate years; not renewable. *Award amount:* $1000–$5000. *Eligibility Requirements:* Applicant must be enrolled or expecting to enroll full-time at a two-year or four-year institution or university; resident of New York and studying in New York. Available to U.S. citizens. *Application Requirements:* Application. **Deadline:** May 3.

Contact Scholarship Coordinator, New York State Higher Education Services Corporation, Education Building Addition Room 1071, Albany, NY 12234. *Phone:* 518-486-1319. *Web site:* http://www.hesc.com.

Robert C. Byrd Honors Scholarship-New York. Award for outstanding high school seniors accepted to U.S. college or university. Based on SAT score and high school average. Minimum 1875 combined SAT score from one sitting. Must be legal resident of New York and a U.S. citizen. Renewable for up to four years. *Award:* Scholarship for use in freshman year; renewable. *Award amount:* $1500. *Number of awards:* 400. *Eligibility Requirements:* Applicant must be high school student; planning to enroll or expecting to enroll full-time at a two-year or four-year institution or university and resident of New York. Available to U.S. citizens. *Application Requirements:* Application. **Deadline:** March 1.

Contact Lewis J. Hall, Supervisor, New York State Education Department, 89 Washington Avenue, Room 1078 EBA, Albany, NY 12234. *E-mail:* scholar@mail.nysed.gov. *Phone:* 518-486-1319. *Fax:* 518-486-5346. *Web site:* http://www.highered.nysed.gov.

Scholarship for Academic Excellence. Renewable award for New York residents. Scholarship winners must attend a college or university in New York. 2000 scholarships are for $1500 and 6000 are for $500. The selection criteria used are based on Regents test scores or rank in class or local exam. Must be U.S. citizen or permanent resident. *Award:* Scholarship for use in freshman year; renewable. *Award amount:* $500–$1500. *Number of awards:* up to 8000. *Eligibility Requirements:* Applicant must be high school student; planning to enroll or expecting to enroll full-time at a two-year or four-year institution or university; resident of New York and studying in New York. Available to U.S. citizens. *Application Requirements:* Application. **Deadline:** December 19.

Contact Lewis J. Hall, Supervisor, New York State Education Department, 89 Washington Avenue, Room 1078 EBA, Albany, NY 12234. *E-mail:* scholar@mail.nysed.gov. *Phone:* 518-486-1319. *Fax:* 518-486-5346. *Web site:* http://www.highered.nysed.gov.

Scholarships for Academic Excellence. Renewable awards of up to $1500 for academically outstanding New York State high school graduates planning to attend an approved postsecondary institution in New York State. For full-time study only. Contact high school guidance counselor to apply. *Award:* Scholarship for use in freshman, sophomore, junior, or senior year; renewable. *Award amount:* $500–$1500. *Number of awards:* up to 8000. *Eligibility Requirements:* Applicant must be high school student; planning to enroll or expecting to enroll full-time at a four-year institution or university; resident of New York and studying in New York. Available to U.S. citizens. *Application Requirements:* Application. **Deadline:** varies.

Contact Rita McGivern, Student Information, New York State Higher Education Services Corporation, 99 Washington Avenue, Room 1320, Albany, NY 12255. *E-mail:* scholarship@hesc.com. *Web site:* http://www.hesc.com.

World Trade Center Memorial Scholarship. Renewable awards of up to the cost of educational expenses at a State University of New York four-year college. Available to the children, spouses and financial dependents of victims who died or were severely disabled as a result of the September 11, 2001 terrorist attacks on the U.S. and the rescue and recovery efforts. *Award:* Scholarship for use in freshman, sophomore, junior, or senior year; renewable. *Award amount:* varies. *Number of awards:* varies. *Eligibility Requirements:* Applicant must be enrolled or expecting to enroll full-time at a four-year institution or university and studying in New York. Available to U.S. and non-U.S. citizens. *Application Requirements:* Application, financial need analysis, references, transcript. **Deadline:** May 1.

Contact Scholarship Unit, New York State Higher Education Services Corporation, 99 Washington Avenue, Room 1320, Albany, NY 12255. *Phone:* 888-697-4372. *Web site:* http://www.hesc.com.

NORTH CAROLINA

Federal Supplemental Educational Opportunity Grant Program. Applicant must have exceptional financial need to qualify for this award. Amount of financial need is determined by the educational institution the student attends. Available only to undergraduate students. Recipient must be a U.S. citizen or permanent resident. Priority is given to a students who receive Federal Pell Grants. *Award:* Grant for use in freshman, sophomore, junior, or senior year; not renewable. *Award amount:* $100–$4400. *Number of awards:* varies. *Eligibility Requirements:* Applicant must be enrolled or expecting to enroll full-time at a four-year institution or university and resident of North Carolina. Available to U.S. citizens. *Application Requirements:* Application, financial need analysis, transcript. **Deadline:** continuous.

Contact Federal Student Aid Information Center, College Foundation of North Carolina Inc., PO Box 84, Washington, DC 20044. *Phone:* 800-433-3243. *Web site:* http://www.cfnc.org.

North Carolina Community College Grant Program. Annual award for North Carolina residents enrolled at least part-time in a North Carolina community college curriculum program. Priority given to those enrolled in college transferable curriculum programs, persons seeking new job skills, women in non-traditional curricula, and those participating in an ABE, GED, or high school diploma program. Contact financial aid office of institution the student attends for information and deadline. Must complete Free Application for Federal Student Aid. *Award:* Grant for use in freshman or sophomore year; renewable. *Award amount:* $683. *Number of awards:* varies. *Eligibility Requirements:* Applicant must be enrolled or expecting to enroll full- or part-time at a two-year or technical institution; resident of North Carolina and studying in North Carolina. Available to U.S. citizens. *Application Requirements:* Application, financial need analysis, FAFSA. **Deadline:** varies.

Contact Bill Carswell, Manager, Scholarship and Grants Division, North Carolina State Education Assistance Authority, PO Box 14103, Research Triangle Park, NC 27709. *E-mail:* carswellb@ncseaa.edu. *Phone:* 919-549-8614. *Fax:* 919-248-4687. *Web site:* http://www.ncseaa.edu.

North Carolina Division of Services for the Blind Rehabilitation Services. Financial assistance is available for North Carolina residents who are blind or visually impaired and who require vocational rehabilitation to help find employment. Tuition and other assistance provided based on need. Open to U.S. citizens and legal residents of United States. Applicants goal must be to work after receiving vocational services. To apply, contact the local DSB office and apply for vocational rehabilitation services. *Award:* Scholarship for use in freshman, sophomore, junior, or senior year; renewable. *Award amount:* varies. *Number of awards:* varies. *Eligibility Requirements:* Applicant must be enrolled or expecting to enroll full-time at a two-year, four-year, or technical institution or university and resident of North Carolina. Applicant must be visually impaired. Available to U.S. citizens. *Application Requirements:* Application, financial need analysis, interview, proof of eligibility. **Deadline:** continuous.

Contact JoAnn Strader, Chief of Rehabilitation Field Services, North Carolina Division of Services for the Blind, 2601 Mail Service Center, Raleigh, NC 27699-2601. *E-mail:* joann.strader@ncmail.net. *Phone:* 919-733-9700. *Fax:* 919-715-8771. *Web site:* http://www.ncdhhs.gov.

North Carolina Legislative Tuition Grant Program (NCLTG). Renewable aid for North Carolina residents attending approved private colleges or universities within the state. Must be enrolled full or part-time in an undergraduate program not leading to a religious vocation. Contact college financial aid office for deadlines. *Award:* Grant for use in freshman, sophomore, junior, or senior year; renewable. *Award amount:* $1950. *Number of awards:* varies. *Eligibility Requirements:* Applicant must be enrolled or expecting to enroll full- or part-time at a two-year or four-year institution or university; resident of North Carolina and studying in North Carolina. Available to U.S. citizens. *Application Requirements:* Application. **Deadline:** varies.

Contact Bill Carswell, Manager of Scholarship and Grant Division, North Carolina State Education Assistance Authority, PO Box 13663, Research Triangle Park, NC 27709. *E-mail:* carswellb@ncseaa.edu. *Phone:* 919-549-8614. *Fax:* 919-248-4687. *Web site:* http://www.ncseaa.edu.

North Carolina National Guard Tuition Assistance Program. Scholarship for members of the North Carolina Air and Army National Guard who will remain in the service for two years following the period for which assistance is provided. Must reapply for each academic period. For use at approved North Carolina institutions. *Award:* Grant for use in freshman, sophomore, junior, senior, or graduate year; not renewable. *Award amount:* up to $2000. *Number of awards:* varies. *Eligibility Requirements:* Applicant must be enrolled or expecting to enroll full- or part-time at a two-year, four-year, or technical institution or university; resident of North Carolina and studying in North Carolina. Available to U.S. citizens. Applicant or parent must meet one or more of the following requirements: Air Force National Guard or Army National Guard experience; retired from active duty; disabled or killed as a result of military service; prisoner of war; or missing in action. *Application Requirements:* Application. **Deadline:** varies.

Contact Anne Gildhouse, Education Services Officer, North Carolina National Guard, Claude T. Bowers Military Center, 4105 Reedy Creek Road, Raleigh, NC 27607-6410. *E-mail:* anne.gildhouse@nc.ngb.army.mil. *Phone:* 919-664-6000. *Fax:* 919-664-6520. *Web site:* http://www.nc.ngb.army.mil.

North Carolina Sheriffs' Association Undergraduate Criminal Justice Scholarships. One-time award for full-time North Carolina resident undergraduate students majoring in criminal justice at a University of North Carolina school. Priority given to child of any North Carolina law enforcement officer. Letter of recommendation from county sheriff required. *Academic Fields/Career Goals:* Criminal Justice/Criminology; Law Enforcement/Police Administration. *Award:* Scholarship for use in freshman, sophomore, junior, or senior year; not renewable. *Award amount:* $1000–$2000. *Number of awards:* up to 10. *Eligibility Requirements:* Applicant must be enrolled or expecting to enroll full-time at a four-year institution or university; resident of North Carolina and studying in North Carolina. Applicant or parent of applicant must have employment or volunteer experience in police/firefighting. Available to U.S. citizens. *Application Requirements:* Application, financial need analysis, references, transcript, statement of career goals. **Deadline:** continuous.

Contact Nolita Goldston, Assistant, Scholarship and Grant Division, North Carolina State Education Assistance Authority, PO Box 13663, Research Triangle Park, NC 27709. *E-mail:* ngoldston@ncseaa.edu. *Phone:* 919-549-8614. *Fax:* 919-248-4687. *Web site:* http://www.ncseaa.edu.

North Carolina Student Loan Program for Health, Science, and Mathematics. Renewable award for North Carolina residents studying health-related fields, or science or math education. Based on merit, need, and promise of service as a health professional or educator in an under-served area of North Carolina. Need two co-signers. Submit surety statement. *Academic Fields/Career Goals:* Dental Health/Services; Health Administration; Health and Medical Sciences; Nursing; Physical Sciences; Therapy/Rehabilitation. *Award:* Forgivable loan for use in freshman, sophomore, junior, senior, or graduate year; renewable. *Award amount:* $3000–$8500. *Number of awards:* 1. *Eligibility Requirements:* Applicant must be enrolled or expecting to enroll full-time at a two-year or four-year institution or university and resident of North Carolina. Available to U.S. citizens. *Application Requirements:* Application, financial need analysis, transcript. **Deadline:** June 1.

Contact Edna Williams, Manager, Selection and Origination, North Carolina State Education Assistance Authority, PO Box 14223, Research Triangle Park, NC 27709. *E-mail:* eew@ncseaa.edu. *Phone:* 800-700-1775 Ext. 4658. *Web site:* http://www.ncseaa.edu.

North Carolina Teaching Fellows Scholarship Program. Award for North Carolina high school seniors planning to pursue teacher training studies. Must agree to teach in a North Carolina public or government school for four years or repay award. For more details visit Web site http://www.teachingfellows.org. *Academic Fields/Career Goals:* Education. *Award:* Forgivable loan for use in freshman year; renewable. *Award amount:* $6500. *Number of awards:* 500. *Eligibility Requirements:* Applicant must be high school student; planning to enroll or expecting to enroll full-time at a four-year institution or university; resident of North Carolina and studying in North Carolina. Applicant must have 3.5 GPA or higher. Available to U.S. citizens. *Application Requirements:* Application, essay, interview, references, test scores, transcript. **Deadline:** varies.

Contact Lynne Stewart, Program Officer, North Carolina Teaching Fellows Commission, 3739 National Drive, Suite 100, Raleigh, NC 27612. *E-mail:* tfellows@ncforum.org. *Phone:* 919-781-6833 Ext. 103. *Fax:* 919-781-6527. *Web site:* http://www.teachingfellows.org.

North Carolina Veterans Scholarships Class I-A. Scholarships for children of certain deceased, disabled or POW/MIA veterans. Award value is $4500 per nine-month academic year in private colleges and junior colleges. No limit on number awarded each year. *Award:* Scholarship for use in freshman, sophomore, junior, or senior year; renewable. *Award amount:* $4500. *Number of awards:* varies. *Eligibility Requirements:* Applicant must be enrolled or expecting to enroll full-time at a two-year, four-year, or technical institution or university; resident of North Carolina and studying in North Carolina. Available to U.S. citizens. Applicant or parent must meet one or more of the following requirements: general military experience; retired from active duty; disabled or killed as a result of military service; prisoner of war; or missing in action. *Application Requirements:* Application, financial need analysis, interview, transcript. **Deadline:** continuous.

Contact Charles Smith, Assistant Secretary, North Carolina Division of Veterans Affairs, 325 North Salisbury Street, Raleigh, NC 27603. *E-mail:* charlie.smith@ncmail.net. *Phone:* 919-733-3851. *Fax:* 919-733-2834. *Web site:* http://www.doa.state.nc.us/vets/va.htm.

North Carolina Veterans Scholarships Class I-B. Awards for children of veterans rated by USDVA as 100 percent disabled due to wartime service as defined in the law, and currently or at time of death drawing compensation for such disability. Parent must have been a North Carolina resident at time of entry into service. Duration of the scholarship is four academic years (8 semesters) if used within 8 years. No limit on number awarded each year. *Award:* Scholarship for use in freshman, sophomore, junior, or senior year; renewable. *Award amount:* $1500. *Number of awards:* varies. *Eligibility Requirements:* Applicant must be enrolled or expecting to enroll full- or part-time at a two-year, four-year, or technical institution or university; resident of North Carolina and studying in North Carolina. Available to U.S. citizens. Applicant or parent must meet one or more of the following requirements: general military experience; retired from active duty; disabled or killed as a result of military service; prisoner of war; or missing in action. *Application Requirements:* Application, financial need analysis, interview, transcript. **Deadline:** continuous.

Contact Charles Smith, Assistant Secretary, North Carolina Division of Veterans Affairs, 325 North Salisbury Street, Raleigh, NC 27603. *E-mail:* charlie.smith@ncmail.net. *Phone:* 919-733-3851. *Fax:* 919-733-2834. *Web site:* http://www.doa.state.nc.us/vets/va.htm.

North Carolina Veterans Scholarships Class II. Awards for children of veterans rated by USDVA as much as 20 percent but less than 100 percent disabled due to wartime service as defined in the law, or awarded Purple Heart Medal for wounds received. Parent must have been a North Carolina resident at time of entry into service. Duration of the scholarship is four academic years (8 semesters) if used within 8 years. Free tuition and exemption from certain mandatory fees as set forth in the law in Public, Community and Technical Colleges. *Award:* Scholarship for use in freshman, sophomore, junior, or senior year; renewable. *Award amount:* $4500. *Number of awards:* up to 100. *Eligibility Requirements:* Applicant must be enrolled or expecting to enroll full- or part-time at a two-year, four-year, or technical institution or university; resident of North Carolina and studying in North Carolina. Available to U.S. citizens. Applicant or parent must meet one or more of the following requirements: general military experience; retired from active duty; disabled or killed as a result of military service; prisoner of war; or missing in action. *Application Requirements:* Application, financial need analysis, interview, transcript. **Deadline:** March 1.

Contact Charles Smith, Assistant Secretary, North Carolina Division of Veterans Affairs, 325 North Salisbury Street, Raleigh, NC 27603. *E-mail:* charlie.smith@ncmail.net. *Phone:* 919-733-3851. *Fax:* 919-733-2834. *Web site:* http://www.doa.state.nc.us/vets/va. htm.

North Carolina Veterans Scholarships Class III. Awards for children of a deceased war veteran, who was honorably discharged and who does not qualify under any other provision within this synopsis or veteran who served in a combat zone or waters adjacent to a combat zone and received a campaign badge or medal and who does not qualify under any other provision within this synopsis. Duration of the scholarship is four academic years (8 semesters) if used within 8 years. *Award:* Scholarship for use in freshman, sophomore, junior, or senior year; renewable. *Award amount:* $4500. *Number of awards:* up to 100. *Eligibility Requirements:* Applicant must be enrolled or expecting to enroll full- or part-time at a two-year, four-year, or technical institution or university; resident of North Carolina and studying in North Carolina. Available to U.S. citizens. Applicant or parent must meet one or more of the following requirements: general military experience; retired from active duty; disabled or killed as a result of military service; prisoner of war; or missing in action. *Application Requirements:* Application, financial need analysis, interview, transcript. **Deadline:** March 1.

Contact Charles Smith, Assistant Secretary, North Carolina Division of Veterans Affairs, 325 North Salisbury Street, Raleigh, NC 27603. *E-mail:* charlie.smith@ncmail.net. *Phone:* 919-733-3851. *Fax:* 919-733-2834. *Web site:* http://www.doa.state.nc.us/vets/va. htm.

North Carolina Veterans Scholarships Class IV. Awards for children of veterans, who were prisoner of war or missing in action. Duration of the scholarship is four academic years (8 semesters) if used within 8 years. No limit on number awarded each year. Award value is $4500 per nine-month academic year in private colleges and junior colleges. *Award:* Scholarship for use in freshman, sophomore, junior, or senior year; renewable. *Award amount:* $4500. *Number of awards:* varies. *Eligibility Requirements:* Applicant must be enrolled or expecting to enroll full- or part-time at a two-year, four-year, or technical institution or university; resident of North Carolina and studying in North Carolina. Available to U.S. citizens. Applicant or parent must meet one or more of the following requirements: general military experience; retired from active duty; disabled or killed as a result of military service; prisoner of war; or missing in action. *Application Requirements:* Application, financial need analysis, interview, transcript. **Deadline:** continuous.

Contact Charles Smith, Assistant Secretary, North Carolina Division of Veterans Affairs, 325 North Salisbury Street, Raleigh, NC 27603. *E-mail:* charlie.smith@ncmail.net. *Phone:* 919-733-3851. *Fax:* 919-733-2834. *Web site:* http://www.doa.state.nc.us/vets/va. htm.

Nurse Education Scholarship Loan Program (NESLP). Must be U.S. citizen and North Carolina resident. Award available through financial aid offices of North Carolina colleges and universities that offer programs to prepare students for licensure in the state as LPN or RN. Recipients enter contract with the State of North Carolina to work full time as a licensed nurse. Loans not repaid through service must be repaid in cash. Award based upon financial need. Maximum award for students enrolled in Associate Degree Nursing and Practical Nurse Education programs is $5000. Maximum award for students enrolled in a baccalaureate program is $400. *Academic Fields/Career Goals:* Nursing. *Award:* Forgivable loan for use in freshman, sophomore, junior, or senior year; renewable. *Award amount:* $400–$5000. *Number of awards:* varies. *Eligibility Requirements:* Applicant must be enrolled or expecting to enroll full- or part-time at

a four-year institution or university; resident of North Carolina and studying in North Carolina. Available to U.S. citizens. *Application Requirements:* Application, financial need analysis. **Deadline:** continuous.

Contact Bill Carswell, Manager of Scholarship and Grant Division, North Carolina State Education Assistance Authority, PO Box 14103, Research Triangle Park, NC 27709. *E-mail:* carswellb@ncseaa.edu. *Phone:* 919-549-8614. *Fax:* 919-248-4687. *Web site:* http://www.ncseaa.edu.

State Contractual Scholarship Fund Program-North Carolina. Renewable award for North Carolina residents already attending an approved private college or university in the state and pursuing an undergraduate degree. Must have financial need. Contact college financial aid office for deadline and information. May not be enrolled in a program leading to a religious vocation. *Award:* Scholarship for use in freshman, sophomore, junior, or senior year; renewable. *Award amount:* up to $1350. *Number of awards:* varies. *Eligibility Requirements:* Applicant must be enrolled or expecting to enroll full- or part-time at a four-year institution or university; resident of North Carolina and studying in North Carolina. Available to U.S. citizens. *Application Requirements:* Application, financial need analysis. **Deadline:** varies.

Contact Bill Carswell, Manager of Scholarship and Grant Division, North Carolina State Education Assistance Authority, PO Box 13663, Research Triangle Park, NC 27709. *E-mail:* carswellb@ncseaa.edu. *Phone:* 919-549-8614. *Fax:* 919-248-4687. *Web site:* http://www.ncseaa.edu.

Teacher Assistant Scholarship Fund. Funding to attend a public or private four-year college or university in North Carolina with an approved teacher education program. Applicant must be employed full-time as a teacher assistant in an instructional area while pursuing licensure and maintain employment to remain eligible. Must have at least 3.0 cumulative GPA. Refer to Web site for further details http://www.ncseaa. edu/tas.htm. *Academic Fields/Career Goals:* Education. *Award:* Scholarship for use in freshman, sophomore, junior, or senior year; renewable. *Award amount:* $600–$3600. *Number of awards:* varies. *Eligibility Requirements:* Applicant must be enrolled or expecting to enroll full- or part-time at a four-year institution or university; resident of North Carolina and studying in North Carolina. Applicant or parent of applicant must have employment or volunteer experience in teaching/ education. Applicant must have 3.0 GPA or higher. Available to U.S. citizens. *Application Requirements:* Application, financial need analysis, transcript, FAFSA. **Deadline:** March 31.

Contact Rashonn Albritton, Processing Assistant, North Carolina State Education Assistance Authority, PO Box 13663, Research Triangle Park, NC 27709. *E-mail:* ralbritton@ncseaa.edu. *Phone:* 919-549-8614. *Fax:* 919-248-4687. *Web site:* http://www.ncseaa.edu.

Training Support for Youth with Disabilities. Public service program that helps persons with disabilities obtain competitive employment. To qualify: student must have a mental, physical or learning disability that is an impediment to employment. An individually designed program is developed for and with each eligible student. Assistance is based on financial need and type of program in which the student enrolls. *Award:* Grant for use in freshman, sophomore, junior, or senior year; renewable. *Award amount:* $2400. *Number of awards:* varies. *Eligibility Requirements:* Applicant must be enrolled or expecting to enroll full- or part-time at a two-year, four-year, or technical institution or university and resident of North Carolina. Applicant must be hearing impaired, learning disabled, physically disabled, or visually impaired. Available to U.S. citizens. *Application Requirements:* Application, financial need analysis, interview, test scores, transcript, medical and psychological records. **Deadline:** continuous.

Contact Alma Taylor, Program Specialist for Transition, North Carolina Division of Vocational Rehabilitation Services, 2801 Mail Service Center, Raleigh, NC 27699-2801. *E-mail:* alma.taylor@ncmail.net. *Phone:* 919-855-3572. *Fax:* 919-715-0616. *Web site:* http://www.dhhs.state.nc.us.

University of North Carolina Need-Based Grant. Applicants must be enrolled in at least 6 credit hours at one of sixteen UNC system universities. Eligibility based on need; award varies, consideration for grant automatic when FAFSA is filed. Late applications may be denied due to insufficient funds. *Award:* Grant for use in freshman, sophomore, junior, or senior year; renewable. *Award amount:* varies. *Number of awards:* varies. *Eligibility Requirements:* Applicant must be enrolled or expecting to enroll full- or part-time at an institution or university; resident of North Carolina and studying in North Carolina. Available to U.S. citizens. *Application Requirements:* Application, financial need analysis, FAFSA. **Deadline:** varies.

Contact Bill Carswell, Manager of Scholarship and Grant Division, North Carolina State Education Assistance Authority, PO Box 13663, Research Triangle Park, NC 27709. *E-mail:* carswellb@ncseaa.edu. *Phone:* 919-549-8614. *Fax:* 919-248-4687. *Web site:* http://www.ncseaa.edu.

University of North Carolina Need-Based Grant. Grants available for eligible students attending one of the 16 campuses of the University of North Carolina. Students must be enrolled in at least 6 credit hours at one of the 16 constituent institutions of The University of North Carolina. Award amounts vary based on legislative appropriations. *Award:* Grant for use in freshman, sophomore, junior, or senior year; not renewable. *Award amount:* varies. *Number of awards:* varies. *Eligibility Requirements:* Applicant must be enrolled or expecting to enroll full- or part-time at a four-year institution or university; resident of North Carolina and studying in North Carolina. Available to U.S. citizens. *Application Requirements:* Financial need analysis. **Deadline:** continuous.

Contact College Foundation of North Carolina, College Foundation of North Carolina Inc. *E-mail:* programinformation@cfnc.org. *Phone:* 866-866-CFNC. *Fax:* 919-248-4687. *Web site:* http://www.cfnc.org.

NORTH DAKOTA

North Dakota Indian Scholarship Program. Award of $500 to $2000 per year to assist American Indian students who are North Dakota residents in obtaining a college education. Must have been accepted for admission at an institution of higher learning or state vocational education program within North Dakota. Based upon scholastic ability and unmet financial need. Minimum 2.0 GPA required. *Award:* Scholarship for use in freshman, sophomore, junior, or senior year; renewable. *Award amount:* $800–$2000. *Number of awards:* 175–230. *Eligibility Requirements:* Applicant must be American Indian/Alaska Native; enrolled or expecting to enroll full- or part-time at a two-year, four-year, or technical institution or university; resident of North Dakota and studying in North Dakota. Available to U.S. citizens. *Application Requirements:* Application, financial need analysis, transcript, proof of tribal enrollment, budget. **Deadline:** July 15.

Contact Rhonda Schauer, Coordinator of American Indian Higher Education, North Dakota University System, BSC Horizon Building, Suite 202, 1815 Schafer Street, Bismarck, ND 58501-1217. *E-mail:* rhonda.

schauer@ndus.edu. *Phone:* 701-224-2497. *Web site:* http://www.ndus.edu.

North Dakota Scholars Program. Provides scholarships equal to cost of tuition at the public colleges in North Dakota for North Dakota residents. To be eligible for consideration for a ND Scholars scholarship, a high school junior must take the ACT Assessment between October and June of their junior year and score in the upper five percentile of all ND ACT test takers. The numeric sum of the English, Math, reading and science reasoning scores will be used as a second selection criteria. The numeric sum of a student's English and mathematics scores will be used as selection criteria if a tie-breaker is needed. *Award:* Scholarship for use in freshman, sophomore, junior, or senior year; renewable. *Award amount:* $4160–$5461. *Number of awards:* 45–50. *Eligibility Requirements:* Applicant must be high school student; planning to enroll or expecting to enroll full-time at a two-year or four-year institution or university; resident of North Dakota and studying in North Dakota. Available to U.S. citizens. *Application Requirements:* References, test scores.

Contact Peggy Wipf, Director of Financial Aid, North Dakota University System, 600 East Boulevard Avenue, Department 215, Bismarck, ND 58505-0230. *E-mail:* peggy.wipf@ndus.nodak.edu. *Phone:* 701-328-4114. *Web site:* http://www.ndus.edu.

North Dakota State Student Incentive Grant Program. Aids North Dakota residents attending an approved college or university in North Dakota. Must be enrolled in a program of at least nine months in length. Must be a U.S. citizen. Must complete the FAFSAA. Needs-based. *Award:* Grant for use in freshman, sophomore, junior, or senior year; not renewable. *Award amount:* $1200. *Number of awards:* 7500–8300. *Eligibility Requirements:* Applicant must be enrolled or expecting to enroll full-time at a two-year or four-year institution or university; resident of North Dakota and studying in North Dakota. Available to U.S. citizens. *Application Requirements:* Financial need analysis. **Deadline:** March 15.

Contact Peggy Wipf, Director of Financial Aid, North Dakota University System, 600 East Boulevard Avenue, Department 215, Bismarck, ND 58505-0230. *Phone:* 701-328-4114. *Web site:* http://www.ndus.edu.

OHIO

Ohio Environmental Science & Engineering Scholarships. Merit-based, non-renewable, tuition-only scholarships awarded to undergraduate students admitted to Ohio state or private colleges and universities. Must be able to demonstrate knowledge of, and commitment to, careers in environmental sciences or environmental engineering. *Academic Fields/Career Goals:* Environmental Science. *Award:* Scholarship for use in senior year; not renewable. *Award amount:* $1250–$2500. *Number of awards:* 18. *Eligibility Requirements:* Applicant must be enrolled or expecting to enroll full- or part-time at a two-year or four-year institution or university and studying in Ohio. Applicant must have 3.0 GPA or higher. Available to U.S. citizens. *Application Requirements:* Application, essay, resume, references, self-addressed stamped envelope, transcript. **Deadline:** June 1.

Contact Mr. Lynn E. Elfner, Chief Executive Officer, Ohio Academy of Science/Ohio Environmental Education Fund, 1500 West Third Avenue, Suite 228, Columbus, OH 43212-2817. *E-mail:* oas@iwaynet.net. *Phone:* 614-488-2228. *Fax:* 614-488-7629. *Web site:* http://www.ohiosci.org.

Ohio Missing in Action and Prisoners of War Orphans Scholarship. Renewable award aids children of Vietnam conflict servicemen who have been classified as missing in action or prisoner of war. Applicants must be under the age of 25 and be enrolled full-time at an Ohio college. A percentage of tuition is awarded. Dollar value of each award varies. *Award:* Scholarship for use in freshman, sophomore, junior, or senior year; renewable. *Award amount:* varies. *Number of awards:* 1–5. *Eligibility Requirements:* Applicant must be age 25 or under; enrolled or expecting to enroll full-time at a four-year institution or university; resident of Ohio and studying in Ohio. Available to U.S. citizens. Applicant or parent must meet one or more of the following requirements: general military experience; retired from active duty; disabled or killed as a result of military service; prisoner of war; or missing in action. *Application Requirements:* Application. **Deadline:** July 1.

Contact Jathiya Abdullah-Simmons, Program Administrator, Ohio Board of Regents, 30 East Broad Street, 36th Floor, Columbus, OH 43215-3414. *E-mail:* jabdullah-simmons@regents.state.oh.us. *Phone:* 614-752-9528. *Fax:* 614-752-5903. *Web site:* http://www.uso.edu.

Ohio National Guard Scholarship Program. Scholarships are for undergraduate studies at an approved Ohio post-secondary institution. Applicants must enlist for six or three years of Selective Service Reserve Duty in the Ohio National Guard. Scholarship pays 100% instructional and general fees for public institutions and an average of cost of public universities is available for private schools. May reapply up to four years of studies (12 quarters or 8 semesters) for six year enlistment and two years of studies (6 quarters or 4 semesters) for three year enlistment. Deadlines: July 1 (fall), November 1 (winter quarter/spring semester), February 1 (spring quarter), April 1 (summer). *Award:* Scholarship for use in freshman, sophomore, junior, or senior year; not renewable. *Award amount:* up to $4006. *Number of awards:* up to 3500. *Eligibility Requirements:* Applicant must be enrolled or expecting to enroll full- or part-time at a two-year, four-year, or technical institution or university; resident of Ohio and studying in Ohio. Available to U.S. citizens. Applicant must have served in the Air Force National Guard or Army National Guard. *Application Requirements:* Application. **Deadline:** varies.

Contact Mrs. Toni E. Davis, Grants Administrator, Ohio National Guard, 2825 West Dublin Granville Road, ONGSP, Columbus, OH 43235-2789. *E-mail:* toni.davis7@us.army.mil. *Phone:* 614-336-7143. *Fax:* 614-336-7318. *Web site:* http://www.ongsp.org.

Ohio Safety Officers College Memorial Fund. Renewable award covering up to full tuition is available to children and surviving spouses of peace officers, other safety officers and fire fighters killed in the line of duty in any state. Children must be under 26 years of age. Dollar value of each award varies. Must be an Ohio resident and enroll full-time or part-time at an Ohio college or university. Any spouse/child of a member of the armed services of the U.S., who has been killed in the line duty during Operation Enduring Freedom, Operation Iraqi Freedom or a combat zone designated by the President of the United States. Dollar value of each award varies. *Award:* Scholarship for use in freshman, sophomore, junior, or senior year; renewable. *Award amount:* varies. *Number of awards:* 50–65. *Eligibility Requirements:* Applicant must be age 26 or under; enrolled or expecting to enroll full- or part-time at a two-year or four-year institution or university; resident of Ohio and studying in Ohio. Available to U.S. citizens. *Application Requirements:* **Deadline:** continuous.

Contact Barbara Thoma, Program Administrator, Ohio Board of Regents, 30 East Broad Street, 36th Floor, Columbus, OH 43215-3414. *E-mail:* bthoma@regents.state.oh.us. *Phone:* 614-752-9535. *Fax:* 614-752-5903. *Web site:* http://www.uso.edu.

Ohio War Orphans Scholarship. Aids Ohio residents attending an eligible college in Ohio. Must be between the ages of 16 and 25, the child of a disabled or deceased veteran, and enrolled full-time. Renewable up to five years. Amount of award varies. Must include Form DD214. *Award:* Scholarship for use in freshman, sophomore, junior, or senior year; renewable. *Award amount:* varies. *Number of awards:* 300–450. *Eligibility Requirements:* Applicant must be age 16-25; enrolled or expecting to enroll full-time at a two-year or four-year institution or university; resident of Ohio and studying in Ohio. Available to U.S. citizens. Applicant or parent must meet one or more of the following requirements: general military experience; retired from active duty; disabled or killed as a result of military service; prisoner of war; or missing in action. *Application Requirements:* Application. **Deadline:** July 1.

Contact Jathiya Abdullah-Simmons, Program Administrator, Ohio Board of Regents, 30 East Broad Street, 36th Floor, Columbus, OH 43215-3414. *E-mail:* jabdullah-simmons@regents.state.oh.us. *Phone:* 614-752-9528. *Fax:* 614-752-5903. *Web site:* http://www.uso.edu.

OKLAHOMA

Academic Scholars Program. Awards for students of high academic ability to attend institutions in Oklahoma. Renewable up to four years. ACT or SAT scores must fall between 99.5 and 100th percentiles, or applicant must be designated as a National Merit scholar or finalist. Oklahoma public institutions can also select institutional nominees. *Award:* Scholarship for use in freshman year; renewable. *Award amount:* $1800–$5500. *Number of awards:* varies. *Eligibility Requirements:* Applicant must be high school student; planning to enroll or expecting to enroll full-time at a two-year or four-year institution or university and studying in Oklahoma. Available to U.S. citizens. *Application Requirements:* Application, test scores, transcript. **Deadline:** continuous.

Contact Scholarship Programs Coordinator, Oklahoma State Regents for Higher Education, PO Box 108850, Oklahoma City, OK 73101-8850. *E-mail:* studentinfo@osrhe.edu. *Phone:* 800-858-1840. *Fax:* 405-225-9230. *Web site:* http://www.okhighered.org.

Future Teacher Scholarship-Oklahoma. Open to outstanding Oklahoma high school graduates who agree to teach in shortage areas. Must rank in top 15 percent of graduating class or score above 85th percentile on ACT or similar test, or be accepted in an educational program. Students nominated by institution. Reapply to renew. Must attend college/university in Oklahoma. *Academic Fields/Career Goals:* Education. *Award:* Scholarship for use in freshman, sophomore, junior, senior, or graduate year; renewable. *Award amount:* $500–$1500. *Eligibility Requirements:* Applicant must be enrolled or expecting to enroll full- or part-time at a two-year or four-year institution or university; resident of Oklahoma and studying in Oklahoma. Available to U.S. citizens. *Application Requirements:* Application, essay, test scores, transcript. **Deadline:** varies.

Contact Scholarship Programs Coordinator, Oklahoma State Regents for Higher Education, PO Box 108850, Oklahoma City, OK 73101-8850. *E-mail:* studentinfo@osrhe. edu. *Phone:* 800-858-1840. *Fax:* 405-225-9230. *Web site:* http://www.okhighered.org.

Oklahoma Tuition Aid Grant. Award for Oklahoma residents enrolled at an Oklahoma institution at least part time each semester in a degree program. May be enrolled in two- or four-year or approved vocational-technical institution. Award for students attending public institutions or private colleges. Application is made through FAFSA. *Award:* Grant for use in freshman, sophomore, junior, or senior year; renewable. *Award amount:* $1000–$1300. *Number of awards:* varies. *Eligibility Requirements:* Applicant must be enrolled or expecting to enroll full- or part-time at a two-year, four-year, or technical institution or university; resident of Oklahoma and studying in Oklahoma. Available to U.S. citizens. *Application Requirements:* Application, financial need analysis, FAFSA. **Deadline:** varies.

Contact Oklahoma State Regents for Higher Education, PO Box 108850, Oklahoma City, OK 73101-8850. *E-mail:* studentinfo@osrhe. edu. *Phone:* 405-858-1840. *Fax:* 405-225-9230. *Web site:* http://www.okhighered.org.

Regional University Baccalaureate Scholarship. Renewable award for Oklahoma residents attending one of 11 participating Oklahoma public universities. Must have an ACT composite score of at least 30 or be a National Merit semifinalist or commended student. In addition to the award amount, each recipient will receive a resident tuition waiver from the institution. Must maintain a 3.25 GPA. Deadlines vary depending upon the institution attended. *Award:* Scholarship for use in freshman, sophomore, junior, or senior

year; renewable. *Award amount:* $3000. *Number of awards:* varies. *Eligibility Requirements:* Applicant must be enrolled or expecting to enroll full-time at an institution or university; resident of Oklahoma and studying in Oklahoma. Available to U.S. citizens. *Application Requirements:* Application. **Deadline:** varies.

Contact Scholarship Programs Coordinator, Oklahoma State Regents for Higher Education, PO Box 108850, Oklahoma City, OK 73101-8850. *E-mail:* studentinfo@osrhe. edu. *Phone:* 405-858-1840. *Fax:* 405-225-9230. *Web site:* http://www.okhighered.org.

Robert C. Byrd Honors Scholarship-Oklahoma. Scholarships available to high school seniors. Applicants must be U.S. citizens or national, or be permanent residents of the United States. Must be legal residents of Oklahoma. Must have a minimum ACT composite score of 32 and/or a minimum SAT combined score of 1420 and/or 2130 or a minimum GED score of 700. Application URL http://www. sde.state.ok.us/pro/Byrd/application.pdf. *Award:* Scholarship for use in freshman year; not renewable. *Award amount:* $1500. *Number of awards:* 10. *Eligibility Requirements:* Applicant must be high school student; planning to enroll or expecting to enroll full-time at a four-year institution or university and resident of Oklahoma. Available to U.S. citizens. *Application Requirements:* Application, essay, references, transcript. **Deadline:** April 11.

Contact Certification Specialist, Oklahoma State Department of Education, 2500 North Lincoln Boulevard, Suite 212, Oklahoma City, OK 73105-4599. *Phone:* 405-521-2808. *Web site:* http://www.sde.state.ok.us.

OREGON

American Legion Auxiliary Department of Oregon Department Grants. One-time award for educational use in the state of Oregon. Must be a resident of Oregon who is the child or widow of a veteran or the wife of a disabled veteran. *Award:* Grant for use in freshman, sophomore, junior, or senior year; not renewable. *Award amount:* $1000. *Number of awards:* 2. *Eligibility Requirements:* Applicant must be enrolled or expecting to enroll full- or part-time at a two-year, four-year, or technical institution or university and resident of Oregon. Available to U.S. citizens. Applicant or parent must meet one or more of the following requirements: general military experience; retired from active duty; disabled or killed as a result of military service; prisoner of war; or missing in action. *Application Requirements:* Application,

essay, financial need analysis, interview, references, test scores, transcript. **Deadline:** March 10.

Contact Virginia Biddle, Secretary/ Treasurer, American Legion Auxiliary Department of Oregon, PO Box 1730, Wilsonville, OR 97070. *E-mail:* alaor@pcez.com. *Phone:* 503-682-3162. *Fax:* 503-685-5008.

American Legion Auxiliary Department of Oregon National President's Scholarship. One-time award for children of veterans who served in the Armed Forces during eligibility dates for American Legion membership. Must be high school senior and Oregon resident. Must be entered by a local American Legion auxiliary unit. Three scholarships of varying amounts. *Award:* Scholarship for use in freshman year; not renewable. *Award amount:* $1000–$2500. *Number of awards:* 3. *Eligibility Requirements:* Applicant must be high school student; planning to enroll or expecting to enroll full- or part-time at a four-year institution or university and resident of Oregon. Available to U.S. citizens. Applicant or parent must meet one or more of the following requirements: general military experience; retired from active duty; disabled or killed as a result of military service; prisoner of war; or missing in action. *Application Requirements:* Application, essay, financial need analysis, interview, references, transcript. **Deadline:** March 1.

Contact Virginia Biddle, Secretary/ Treasurer, American Legion Auxiliary Department of Oregon, PO Box 1730, Wilsonville, OR 97070. *E-mail:* alaor@pcez.com. *Phone:* 503-682-3162. *Fax:* 503-685-5008.

American Legion Auxiliary Department of Oregon Nurses Scholarship. One-time award for Oregon residents who are in their senior year of High School, who are the children of veterans who served during eligibility dates for American Legion membership. Must enroll in a nursing program. Contact local units for application. *Academic Fields/Career Goals:* Nursing. *Award:* Scholarship for use in freshman year; not renewable. *Award amount:* $1500. *Number of awards:* 1. *Eligibility Requirements:* Applicant must be high school student; planning to enroll or expecting to enroll full- or part-time at a four-year institution or university and resident of Oregon. Available to U.S. citizens. Applicant or parent must meet one or more of the following requirements: general military experience; retired from active duty; disabled or killed as a result of military service; prisoner of war; or missing in action. *Application Requirements:* Application, essay, financial need analysis, interview, transcript. **Deadline:** May 15.

Contact Virginia Biddle, Secretary/Treasurer, American Legion Auxiliary Department of Oregon, PO Box 1730, Wilsonville, OR 97070. *E-mail:* alaor@pcez.com. *Phone:* 503-682-3162. *Fax:* 503-685-5008.

American Legion Auxiliary Department of Oregon Spirit of Youth Scholarship. One-time award available to Oregon high school seniors. Must be a current female junior member of the American Legion Auxiliary with a three-year membership history. Apply through local units. *Award:* Scholarship for use in freshman year; not renewable. *Award amount:* $1000. *Number of awards:* 1. *Eligibility Requirements:* Applicant must be high school student; planning to enroll or expecting to enroll full- or part-time at a four-year institution or university; female and resident of Oregon. Applicant or parent of applicant must be member of American Legion or Auxiliary. Available to U.S. citizens. Applicant or parent must meet one or more of the following requirements: general military experience; retired from active duty; disabled or killed as a result of military service; prisoner of war; or missing in action. *Application Requirements:* Application, essay, financial need analysis, interview, references, transcript. **Deadline:** March 1.

Contact Virginia Biddle, Secretary/Treasurer, American Legion Auxiliary Department of Oregon, PO Box 1730, Wilsonville, OR 97070. *E-mail:* alaor@pcez.com. *Phone:* 503-682-3162. *Fax:* 503-685-5008.

Dorothy Campbell Memorial Scholarship. Renewable award for female Oregon high school graduates with a minimum 2.75 GPA. Must submit essay describing strong, continuing interest in golf and the contribution that sport has made to applicant's development. Must have played on high school golf team, if available. For more information, see Web http://www.getcollegefunds.org. *Award:* Scholarship for use in freshman, sophomore, junior, or senior year; renewable. *Award amount:* varies. *Number of awards:* varies. *Eligibility Requirements:* Applicant must be enrolled or expecting to enroll full-time at a four-year institution; female; resident of Oregon; studying in Oregon and must have an interest in golf. Available to U.S. citizens. *Application Requirements:* Application, essay, financial need analysis, transcript. **Deadline:** March 1.

Contact Alan Baas, Scholarship Coordinator, Oregon Student Assistance Commission, 1500 Valley River Drive, Suite 100, Eugene,

OR 97401-7020. *Phone:* 800-452-8807. *Web site:* http://www.GetCollegeFunds.org.

Glenn Jackson Scholars Scholarships (OCF). Renewable award for Oregon graduating high school seniors who are dependents of employees or retirees of Oregon Department of Transportation or Parks and Recreation Department. Employees must have worked in their department at least three years as of the March 1 scholarship deadline. Must submit essays on topics announced on Web site http://www.osac.state.or.us. *Award:* Scholarship for use in freshman, sophomore, junior, or senior year; renewable. *Award amount:* varies. *Number of awards:* varies. *Eligibility Requirements:* Applicant must be high school student; planning to enroll or expecting to enroll full- or part-time at a two-year or four-year institution or university and resident of Oregon. Applicant or parent of applicant must be affiliated with Oregon Department of Transportation Parks and Recreation. Available to U.S. citizens. *Application Requirements:* Application, essay, financial need analysis, references, transcript, activity chart. **Deadline:** March 1.

Contact Director of Grant Programs, Oregon Student Assistance Commission, 1500 Valley River Drive, Suite 100, Eugene, OR 97401-7020. *Phone:* 800-452-8807 Ext. 7395. *Web site:* http://www.GetCollegeFunds.org.

Laurence R. Foster Memorial Scholarship. One-time award to students enrolled or planning to enroll in a public health degree program. First preference given to those working in the public health field and those pursuing a graduate degree in public health. Undergraduates entering junior or senior year health programs may apply if seeking a public health career, and not private practice. Prefer applicants from diverse cultures. Must provide three references. Additional essay required. Must be resident of Oregon. *Academic Fields/Career Goals:* Public Health. *Award:* Scholarship for use in freshman, sophomore, junior, or senior year; renewable. *Award amount:* varies. *Number of awards:* varies. *Eligibility Requirements:* Applicant must be enrolled or expecting to enroll full- or part-time at a four-year institution and resident of Oregon. Available to U.S. citizens. *Application Requirements:* Application, essay, financial need analysis, references, transcript, activity chart. **Deadline:** March 1.

Contact Rachel Cummings, Scholarship Coordinator, Oregon Student Assistance Commission, 1500 Valley River Drive, Suite 100,

Eugene, OR 97401-7020. *Phone:* 800-452-8807 Ext. 7395. *Web site:* http://www.GetCollegeFunds.org.

Oregon Opportunity Grant. Available to Oregon residents who are undergraduate students enrolled at least half-time in a participating Oregon institution. Must establish financial need, have completed the FAFSA and be eligible for a Federal Pell Grant. Award amounts vary but for full-time students can range from about $1400 per semester for community college students to $2100 to 5000 at a 4-year private college or university. For additional information, and to apply online visit Web site http://www.getcollegefunds.org. *Award:* Scholarship for use in freshman, sophomore, junior, or senior year; renewable. *Award amount:* varies. *Eligibility Requirements:* Applicant must be enrolled or expecting to enroll full- or part-time at a two-year or four-year institution or university; resident of Oregon and studying in Oregon. Available to U.S. citizens. *Application Requirements:* Application, financial need analysis, transcript, FAFSA. **Deadline:** March 1.

Contact Director of Grant Programs, Oregon Student Assistance Commission, 1500 Valley River Drive, Suite 100, Eugene, OR 97401-7020. *Phone:* 800-452-8807 Ext. 7395. *Web site:* http://www.GetCollegeFunds.org.

Oregon Scholarship Fund Community College Student Award. Scholarship open to Oregon residents enrolled or planning to enroll in Oregon community college programs. Recipients may reapply for one additional year. Must enroll at least half-time. Apply at http://www.getcollegefunds.org. *Award:* Scholarship for use in freshman or sophomore year; not renewable. *Award amount:* varies. *Number of awards:* varies. *Eligibility Requirements:* Applicant must be enrolled or expecting to enroll full-time at a two-year institution; resident of Oregon and studying in Oregon. Available to U.S. citizens. *Application Requirements:* Application, essay, financial need analysis, transcript, activity chart. **Deadline:** March 1.

Contact Director of Grant Programs, Oregon Student Assistance Commission, 1500 Valley River Drive, Suite 100, Eugene, OR 97401-7020. *Phone:* 800-452-8807 Ext. 7395. *Web site:* http://www.GetCollegeFunds.org.

Oregon Scholarship Fund Transfer Student Award. Award open to Oregon residents who are currently enrolled in their second year at an Oregon community college and are planning to transfer to a four-year college in Oregon. Prior recipients may apply for one additional year. Must enroll at least half-time. Apply at http://

www.getcollegefunds.org. *Award:* Scholarship for use in junior or senior year; not renewable. *Award amount:* varies. *Number of awards:* varies. *Eligibility Requirements:* Applicant must be enrolled or expecting to enroll full-time at a two-year or four-year institution; resident of Oregon and studying in Oregon. Available to U.S. citizens. *Application Requirements:* Application, essay, financial need analysis, transcript, activity chart. **Deadline:** March 1.

Contact Director of Grant Programs, Oregon Student Assistance Commission, 1500 Valley River Drive, Suite 100, Eugene, OR 97401-7020. *Phone:* 800-452-8807 Ext. 7395. *Web site:* http://www.GetCollegeFunds.org.

Oregon Trucking Association Safety Council Scholarship. One-time award available to a child of an Oregon Trucking Association member, or child of an employee. Applicants must be graduating high school seniors from an Oregon high school, Oregon residency not required . For additional information, see Web site http://www.osac.state.or.us. *Award:* Scholarship for use in freshman year; not renewable. *Award amount:* varies. *Eligibility Requirements:* Applicant must be high school student and planning to enroll or expecting to enroll full-time at a four-year institution. Applicant or parent of applicant must be affiliated with Oregon Trucking Association. Available to U.S. citizens. *Application Requirements:* Application, essay, financial need analysis, references, transcript, activity chart. **Deadline:** March 1.

Contact Director of Grant Programs, Oregon Student Assistance Commission, 1500 Valley River Drive, Suite 100, Eugene, OR 97401-7020. *Phone:* 800-452-8807 Ext. 7395. *Web site:* http://www.GetCollegeFunds.org.

Oregon Veterans' Education Aid. To be eligible, veteran must have actively served in U.S. armed forces 90 days and been discharged under honorable conditions. Must be U.S. citizen and Oregon resident. Korean War veteran or received campaign or expeditionary medal or ribbon awarded by U.S. armed forces for services after June 30, 1958. Full-time students receive up to $150 per month, and part-time students receive up to $100 per month for a maximum of 36 months. Length of benefits depend on length of service. *Award:* Grant for use in freshman, sophomore, junior, senior, graduate, or postgraduate years; not renewable. *Award amount:* $3600–$5400. *Number of awards:* 1–200. *Eligibility Requirements:* Applicant must be enrolled or expecting to enroll full- or part-time at a two-year, four-year, or technical institution or university; resident

of Oregon and studying in Oregon. Available to U.S. citizens. Applicant must have general military experience. *Application Requirements:* Application, certified copy of DD Form 214. **Deadline:** continuous.

Contact Loriann Sheridan, Educational Aid Coordinator, Oregon Department of Veterans' Affairs, 700 Summer Street, NE, Salem, OR 97301-1289. *E-mail:* sheridl@odva.state.or.us. *Phone:* 503-373-2264. *Fax:* 503-373-2392. *Web site:* http://www.oregon.gov/odva.

Peter Connacher Memorial Scholarship. Renewable award for American prisoners-of-war and their descendants. Written proof of prisoner-of-war status and discharge papers from the U.S. Armed Forces must accompany application. Statement of relationship between applicant and former prisoner-of-war is required. See Web site at http://www.osac.state.or.us for details. *Award:* Scholarship for use in freshman, sophomore, junior, or senior year; renewable. *Award amount:* varies. *Number of awards:* varies. *Eligibility Requirements:* Applicant must be enrolled or expecting to enroll full-time at a two-year or four-year institution and resident of Oregon. Available to U.S. citizens. Applicant or parent must meet one or more of the following requirements: general military experience; retired from active duty; disabled or killed as a result of military service; prisoner of war; or missing in action. *Application Requirements:* Application, essay, financial need analysis, transcript, military discharge papers, documentation of POW status. **Deadline:** March 1.

Contact Director of Grant Programs, Oregon Student Assistance Commission, 1500 Valley River Drive, Suite 100, Eugene, OR 97401-7020. *Phone:* 800-452-8807 Ext. 7395. *Web site:* http://www.GetCollegeFunds.org.

PENNSYLVANIA

Armed Forces Loan Forgiveness Program. Loan forgiveness for non-residents of Pennsylvania who served in Armed Forces in an active duty status after September 11, 2001. Must be a student who either left a PA approved institution of postsecondary education due to call to active duty, or was living in PA at time of enlistment, or enlisted in military immediately after attending a PA approved institution of postsecondary education. Number of loans forgiven varies. *Award:* Forgivable loan for use in freshman, sophomore, junior, or senior year; not renewable. *Award amount:* up to $2500. *Number of awards:* varies. *Eligibility Requirements:* Applicant must be enrolled or expecting to enroll full- or part-time at

a two-year, four-year, or technical institution or university. Available to U.S. citizens. Applicant or parent must meet one or more of the following requirements: general military experience; retired from active duty; disabled or killed as a result of military service; prisoner of war; or missing in action. *Application Requirements:* Application. **Deadline:** December 31.

Contact Keith R. New, Director of Public Relations, Pennsylvania Higher Education Assistance Agency, 1200 North Seventh Street, Harrisburg, PA 17102-1444. *E-mail:* knew@pheaa.org. *Phone:* 717-720-2509. *Fax:* 717-720-3903. *Web site:* http://www.pheaa.org.

New Economy Technology and SciTech Scholarships. Renewable award for Pennsylvania residents pursuing a degree in science or technology at a PHEAA-approved two- or four-year Pennsylvania college or university. Must maintain minimum GPA of 3.0. Must commence employment in Pennsylvania in a field related to degree within one year after graduation, and work one year for each year the scholarship was awarded. *Academic Fields/Career Goals:* Engineering/Technology; Engineering-Related Technologies; Natural Sciences; Physical Sciences. *Award:* Scholarship for use in freshman, sophomore, junior, or senior year; renewable. *Award amount:* $1000–$3000. *Number of awards:* varies. *Eligibility Requirements:* Applicant must be age 18 and over; enrolled or expecting to enroll full-time at a two-year, four-year, or technical institution or university; resident of Pennsylvania and studying in Pennsylvania. Applicant must have 3.0 GPA or higher. Available to U.S. citizens. *Application Requirements:* Application, FAFSA. **Deadline:** December 31.

Contact State Grant and Special Programs Division, Pennsylvania Higher Education Assistance Agency, 1200 North Seventh Street, Harrisburg, PA 17102-1444. *Phone:* 800-692-7392. *Web site:* http://www.pheaa.org.

Pennsylvania State Grant. Award for Pennsylvania residents attending an approved postsecondary institution as undergraduates in a program of at least two years duration. Renewable for up to eight semesters if applicants show continued need and academic progress. Must submit FAFSA. Number of awards granted varies annually. Scholarship value is $200 to $4120. Deadlines: May 1 and August 1. *Award:* Grant for use in freshman, sophomore, junior, or senior year; renewable. *Award amount:* $200–$4120. *Number of awards:*

varies. *Eligibility Requirements:* Applicant must be enrolled or expecting to enroll full- or part-time at a two-year, four-year, or technical institution or university and resident of Pennsylvania. Available to U.S. citizens. *Application Requirements:* Financial need analysis, FAFSA. **Deadline:** varies.

Contact Keith New, Director of Public Relations, Pennsylvania Higher Education Assistance Agency, 1200 North Seventh Street, Harrisburg, PA 17102-1444. *Phone:* 717-720-2509. *Fax:* 717-720-3903. *Web site:* http://www.pheaa.org.

Postsecondary Education Gratuity Program. The program offers waiver of tuition and fees for children of Pennsylvania police officers, firefighters, rescue or ambulance squad members, corrections facility employees, or National Guard members who died in line of duty after January 1, 1976. *Award:* Grant for use in freshman, sophomore, junior, or senior year; renewable. *Award amount:* varies. *Number of awards:* varies. *Eligibility Requirements:* Applicant must be age 25 or under; enrolled or expecting to enroll full-time at a two-year or four-year institution or university; resident of Pennsylvania and studying in Pennsylvania. Available to U.S. citizens. Applicant or parent must meet one or more of the following requirements: Air Force National Guard or Army National Guard experience; retired from active duty; disabled or killed as a result of military service; prisoner of war; or missing in action. *Application Requirements:* Application. **Deadline:** August 1.

Contact Keith R. New, Director of Public Relations, Pennsylvania Higher Education Assistance Agency, 1200 North Seventh Street, Harrisburg, PA 17102-1444. *E-mail:* knew@pheaa.org. *Phone:* 717-720-2509. *Fax:* 717-720-3903. *Web site:* http://www.pheaa.org.

Robert C. Byrd Honors Scholarship-Pennsylvania. Awards Pennsylvania residents who are graduating high school seniors. Must rank in the top 5 percent of graduating class, have at least a 3.5 GPA and score 1150 or above on the SAT, 25 or above on the ACT, or 355 or above on the GED. Renewable award and the amount granted varies. Applicants are expected to be a full-time freshman student enrolled at an eligible institution of higher education, following high school graduation. *Award:* Scholarship for use in freshman year; renewable. *Award amount:* $1500. *Number of awards:* varies. *Eligibility Requirements:* Applicant must be high school student; planning to enroll or expecting to enroll full-time at a four-year institution or

university and resident of Pennsylvania. Available to U.S. citizens. *Application Requirements:* Application, references, test scores, transcript, letter of acceptance. **Deadline:** April 1.

Contact Keith R. New, Director of Public Relations, Pennsylvania Higher Education Assistance Agency, 1200 North Seventh Street, Harrisburg, PA 17102. *Phone:* 717-720-2509. *Fax:* 717-720-3903. *Web site:* http://www.pheaa.org.

RHODE ISLAND

Rhode Island State Grant Program. Grants for residents of Rhode Island attending an approved school in United States. Based on need. Renewable for up to four years if in good academic standing and meet financial need requirements. *Award:* Grant for use in freshman, sophomore, junior, or senior year; renewable. *Award amount:* $250–$900. *Number of awards:* 10,000–12,900. *Eligibility Requirements:* Applicant must be enrolled or expecting to enroll full- or part-time at a two-year, four-year, or technical institution or university and resident of Rhode Island. Available to U.S. citizens. *Application Requirements:* Application, financial need analysis. **Deadline:** March 1.

Contact Mr. Michael Joyce, Director of Program Administration, Rhode Island Higher Education Assistance Authority, 560 Jefferson Boulevard, Suite 100, Warwick, RI 02886. *E-mail:* mjoyce@riheaa.org. *Phone:* 401-736-1172. *Fax:* 401-736-1178. *Web site:* http://www.riheaa.org.

SOUTH CAROLINA

Educational Assistance for Certain War Veterans Dependents Scholarship-South Carolina. Free tuition for South Carolina residents whose parent is a resident, wartime veteran, and meets one of these criteria; awarded Purple Heart or Congressional Medal of Honor; permanently and totally disabled or killed as a result of military service; prisoner of war; or missing in action. Must be age 18-26 and enrolled or expecting to enroll full or part-time at a two-year or four-year technical institution or university in South Carolina. Complete information and qualifications for this award are on Web site http://www.govoepp.state.sc.us. *Award:* Scholarship for use in freshman, sophomore, junior, or senior year; not renewable. *Award amount:* varies. *Number of awards:* varies. *Eligibility Requirements:* Applicant must be age 18-26; enrolled or expecting to enroll full- or part-time at a two-year, four-year, or technical institution or university; resident

of South Carolina and studying in South Carolina. Available to U.S. citizens. Applicant or parent must meet one or more of the following requirements: general military experience; retired from active duty; disabled or killed as a result of military service; prisoner of war; or missing in action. *Application Requirements:* Application, transcript, proof of qualification of veteran. **Deadline:** continuous.

Contact Dianne Coley, Free Tuition Program Assistant, South Carolina Division of Veterans Affairs, South Carolina Governor's Office, 1205 Pendleton Street, Suite 369, Columbia, SC 29201 USA. *E-mail:* va@oepp.sc.gov. *Phone:* 803-255-4317. *Fax:* 803-255-4257. *Web site:* http://www.govoepp.state.sc.us/vetaff.htm.

Palmetto Fellows Scholarship Program. Renewable award for qualified high school seniors in South Carolina to attend a four-year South Carolina institution. The scholarship must be applied directly towards the cost of attendance, less any other gift aid received. *Award:* Scholarship for use in freshman year; renewable. *Award amount:* $6700–$7500. *Number of awards:* 4846. *Eligibility Requirements:* Applicant must be high school student; planning to enroll or expecting to enroll full-time at a four-year institution or university; resident of South Carolina and studying in South Carolina. Applicant must have 3.5 GPA or higher. Available to U.S. citizens. *Application Requirements:* Application, test scores, transcript. **Deadline:** December 15.

Contact Dr. Karen Woodfaulk, Director of Student Services, South Carolina Commission on Higher Education, 1333 Main Street, Suite 200, Columbia, SC 29201. *E-mail:* kwoodfaulk@che.sc.gov. *Phone:* 803-737-2244. *Fax:* 803-737-3610. *Web site:* http://www.che.sc.gov.

Robert C. Byrd Honors Scholarship-South Carolina. Renewable award for a graduating high school senior from South Carolina, who will be attending a two- or four-year institution. Applicants should be superior students who demonstrate academic achievement and show promise of continued success at a postsecondary institution. Interested applicants should contact their high school counselors after the first week of December for an application. *Award:* Scholarship for use in freshman year; renewable. *Award amount:* varies. *Number of awards:* varies. *Eligibility Requirements:* Applicant must be high school student; planning to enroll or expecting to enroll full-time at a two-year or four-year institution or university and resident of South Carolina. Available to U.S. citizens. *Applica-*

tion Requirements: Application, test scores, ACT or SAT scores. **Deadline:** varies.

Contact Beth Cope, Program Coordinator, South Carolina Department of Education, 1424 Senate Street, Columbia, SC 29201. *E-mail:* bcope@sde.state.sc.us. *Phone:* 803-734-8116. *Fax:* 803-734-4387. *Web site:* http://www.ed.sc.gov.

South Carolina HOPE Scholarship. A merit-based scholarship for eligible first-time entering freshman attending a four-year South Carolina institution. Minimum GPA of 3.0 required. Must be a resident of South Carolina. *Award:* Scholarship for use in freshman year; not renewable. *Award amount:* $2800. *Number of awards:* 2605. *Eligibility Requirements:* Applicant must be high school student; planning to enroll or expecting to enroll full-time at a four-year institution or university; resident of South Carolina and studying in South Carolina. Applicant must have 3.0 GPA or higher. Available to U.S. citizens. *Application Requirements:* Transcript. **Deadline:** continuous.

Contact Gerrick Hampton, Scholarship Coordinator, South Carolina Commission on Higher Education, 1333 Main Street, Suite 200, Columbia, SC 29201. *E-mail:* ghampton@che.sc.gov. *Phone:* 803-737-4544. *Fax:* 803-737-3610. *Web site:* http://www.che.sc.gov.

South Carolina Need-Based Grants Program. Award based on FAFSA. A student may receive up to $2500 annually for full-time and up to $1250 annually for part-time study. The grant must be applied directly towards the cost of college attendance for a maximum of eight full-time equivalent terms. *Award:* Grant for use in freshman, sophomore, junior, senior, or graduate year; renewable. *Award amount:* $1250–$2500. *Number of awards:* 1–26,730. *Eligibility Requirements:* Applicant must be enrolled or expecting to enroll full- or part-time at a two-year, four-year, or technical institution or university; resident of South Carolina and studying in South Carolina. Available to U.S. citizens. *Application Requirements:* Application, financial need analysis. **Deadline:** continuous.

Contact Dr. Karen Woodfaulk, Director of Student Service, South Carolina Commission on Higher Education, 1333 Main Street, Suite 200, Columbia, SC 29201. *E-mail:* kwoodfaulk@che.sc.gov. *Phone:* 803-737-2244. *Fax:* 803-737-2297. *Web site:* http://www.che.sc.gov.

South Carolina Teacher Loan Program. One-time awards for South Carolina residents attending four-year postsecondary institutions in South Carolina. Recipients must teach in the South Carolina public school

system in a critical-need area after graduation. Twenty percent of loan forgiven for each year of service. Write for additional requirements. *Academic Fields/Career Goals:* Education; Special Education. *Award:* Forgivable loan for use in freshman, sophomore, junior, senior, or graduate year; not renewable. *Award amount:* $2500–$5000. *Number of awards:* up to 1121. *Eligibility Requirements:* Applicant must be enrolled or expecting to enroll full- or part-time at a four-year institution or university; resident of South Carolina and studying in South Carolina. Applicant must have 3.0 GPA or higher. Available to U.S. citizens. *Application Requirements:* Application, references, test scores, promissory note. **Deadline:** June 1.

Contact Jennifer Jones-Gaddy, Vice President, South Carolina Student Loan Corporation, PO Box 21487, Columbia, SC 29221. *E-mail:* jgaddy@slc.sc.edu. *Phone:* 803-798-0916. *Fax:* 803-772-9410. *Web site:* http://www.scstudentloan.org.

South Carolina Tuition Grants Program. Award assists South Carolina residents attending one of twenty-one approved South Carolina independent colleges. Freshmen must be in upper 3/4 of high school class or have SAT score of at least 900 or ACT of 19 or 2.0 final GAP on SC uniform grading scale. Upper-class students must complete 24 semester hours per year to be eligible. Must complete FAFSA annually to apply. *Award:* Grant for use in freshman, sophomore, junior, or senior year; renewable. *Award amount:* $100–$2600. *Eligibility Requirements:* Applicant must be enrolled or expecting to enroll full-time at a two-year or four-year institution or university; resident of South Carolina and studying in South Carolina. Available to U.S. citizens. *Application Requirements:* Application, FAFSA. **Deadline:** June 30.

Contact Katie Harrison, Deputy Director, South Carolina Tuition Grants Commission, 800 Dutch Square Boulevard, Suite 260A, Columbia, SC 29210. *E-mail:* katie@sctuitiongrants.org. *Phone:* 803-896-1120. *Fax:* 803-896-1126. *Web site:* http://www.sctuitiongrants.com.

SOUTH DAKOTA

Haines Memorial Scholarship. One-time scholarship for South Dakota public university students who are sophomores, juniors, or seniors having at least a 2.5 GPA and majoring in a teacher education program. Must include resume with application. Must be South Dakota resident. *Academic Fields/Career Goals:* Education. *Award:* Scholarship for use in sophomore,

junior, or senior year; not renewable. *Award amount:* $2150. *Number of awards:* 1. *Eligibility Requirements:* Applicant must be enrolled or expecting to enroll full-time at an institution or university; resident of South Dakota and studying in South Dakota. Applicant must have 3.5 GPA or higher. Available to U.S. citizens. *Application Requirements:* Application, driver's license, essay, resume, typed statement describing personal philosophy and philosophy of education. **Deadline:** February 8.

Contact Dr. Paul D. Turman, Director of Academic Assessment, South Dakota Board of Regents, 306 East Capitol Avenue, Suite 200, Pierre, SD 57501-2545. *E-mail:* pault@sdbor.edu. *Phone:* 605-773-3455. *Web site:* http://www.sdbor.edu.

South Dakota Opportunity Scholarship. Renewable scholarship may be worth up to $5000 over four years to students who take a rigorous college-prep curriculum while in high school and stay in the state for their postsecondary education. *Award:* Scholarship for use in freshman, sophomore, junior, or senior year; renewable. *Award amount:* $1000. *Number of awards:* 1000. *Eligibility Requirements:* Applicant must be high school student; planning to enroll or expecting to enroll full-time at a two-year, four-year, or technical institution or university; resident of South Dakota and studying in South Dakota. Applicant must have 3.0 GPA or higher. Available to U.S. citizens. *Application Requirements:* Application, test scores, transcript. **Deadline:** September 1.

Contact Janelle Toman, Scholarship Committee, South Dakota Board of Regents, 306 East Capitol, Suite 200, Pierre, SD 57501-2545. *E-mail:* info@sdbor.edu. *Phone:* 605-773-3455. *Fax:* 605-773-2422. *Web site:* http://www.sdbor.edu.

TENNESSEE

Christa McAuliffe Scholarship Program. Scholarship to assist and support Tennessee students who have demonstrated a commitment to a career in educating the youth of Tennessee. Offered to college seniors for a period of one academic year. Must have a minimum college GPA of 3.5. Must have attained scores on either the ACT or SAT which meet or exceed the national norms. Award is made on a periodic basis as funding becomes available. *Academic Fields/Career Goals:* Education. *Award:* Scholarship for use in senior year; not renewable. *Award amount:* up to $500. *Number of awards:* up to 1. *Eligibility Requirements:* Applicant must be enrolled or expecting to enroll full-time at a four-year institution or university; resident of Tennessee and studying in Tennessee. Applicant must have 3.5 GPA or higher. Available to U.S. citizens. *Application Requirements:* Application, essay. **Deadline:** April 1.

Contact Ms. Kathy Stripling, Scholarship Administrator, Tennessee Student Assistance Corporation, Parkway Towers, 404 James Robertson Parkway, Suite 1510, Nashville, TN 37243-0820. *E-mail:* kathy.stripling@tn.gov. *Phone:* 866-291-2675 Ext. 155. *Fax:* 615-741-6101. *Web site:* http://www.tn.gov/collegepays.

Dependent Children Scholarship Program. Scholarship for Tennessee residents who are dependent children of a Tennessee law enforcement officer, fireman, or an emergency medical service technician who has been killed or totally and permanently disabled while performing duties within the scope of such employment. The scholarship is awarded to full-time undergraduate students for a maximum of four academic years or the period required for the completion of the program of study. *Award:* Scholarship for use in freshman, sophomore, junior, or senior year; renewable. *Award amount:* varies. *Number of awards:* up to 31. *Eligibility Requirements:* Applicant must be enrolled or expecting to enroll full-time at a two-year or four-year institution or university; resident of Tennessee and studying in Tennessee. Available to U.S. citizens. *Application Requirements:* Application, FAFSA. **Deadline:** July 15.

Contact Ms. Naomi Derryberry, Director of Grants, Tennessee Student Assistance Corporation, Parkway Towers, 404 James Robertson Parkway, Suite 1510, Nashville, TN 37243-0820. *E-mail:* naomi.derryberry@tn.gov. *Phone:* 866-291-2675 Ext. 125. *Fax:* 615-741-6101. *Web site:* http://www.tn.gov/collegepays.

Helping Heroes Grant. Provides assistance to Tennessee veterans who meet eligibility requirements for the program. Award is up to $2000 per year. For more information, visit http://www.tn.gov/collegepays *Award:* Grant for use in freshman, sophomore, junior, or senior year; not renewable. *Award amount:* up to $2000. *Eligibility Requirements:* Applicant must be enrolled or expecting to enroll full- or part-time at a two-year or four-year institution or university. Available to U.S. citizens. *Application Requirements:* Application, 00-214. **Deadline:** September 1.

Contact Mr. Robert Biggers, Director of Lottery Programs, Tennessee Student Assistance Corporation, Parkway Towers, Suite 1510, 404 James Robertson Parkway, Nashville, TN

37243. *E-mail:* robert.biggers@tn.gov. *Phone:* 866-291-2675. *Fax:* 615-741-6101. *Web site:* http://www.tn.gov/collegepays.

HOPE with ASPIRE Award. HOPE Scholarship of $4,000 with $1500 supplement. Must meet Tennessee HOPE Scholarship requirements and Adjusted Gross Income (AGI) attributable to the student must be $36,000 or less. *Award:* Scholarship for use in freshman, sophomore, junior, or senior year; renewable. *Award amount:* up to $5500. *Number of awards:* varies. *Eligibility Requirements:* Applicant must be enrolled or expecting to enroll full- or part-time at a two-year or four-year institution or university; resident of Tennessee and studying in Tennessee. Applicant must have 3.0 GPA or higher. Available to U.S. citizens. *Application Requirements:* Application, financial need analysis. **Deadline:** September 1.

Contact Mr. Robert Biggers, Director of Lottery Scholarship Programs, Tennessee Student Assistance Corporation, Parkway Towers, 404 James Robertson Parkway, Suite 1510, Nashville, TN 37243-0820. *E-mail:* robert.biggers@tn.gov. *Phone:* 866-291-2675 Ext. 106. *Fax:* 615-741-6101. *Web site:* http://www.tn.gov/collegepays.

Minority Teaching Fellows Program/Tennessee. Forgivable loan for minority Tennessee residents pursuing teaching careers. Minimum 2.75 GPA required for high school applicant, minimum 2.5 GPA required for college applicant. Must be in the top quarter of the class or score an 18 on ACT. Must teach one year for each year the award is received, or repay loan. *Academic Fields/Career Goals:* Education; Special Education. *Award:* Forgivable loan for use in freshman, sophomore, junior, or senior year; renewable. *Award amount:* up to $5000. *Number of awards:* 19–116. *Eligibility Requirements:* Applicant must be American Indian/Alaska Native, Asian/Pacific Islander, Black (non-Hispanic), or Hispanic; enrolled or expecting to enroll full-time at a two-year or four-year institution or university; resident of Tennessee and studying in Tennessee. Available to U.S. citizens. *Application Requirements:* Application, essay, references, test scores, transcript, statement of intent. **Deadline:** April 15.

Contact Mike McCormack, Scholarship Administrator, Tennessee Student Assistance Corporation, Parkway Towers, 404 James Robertson Parkway, Suite 1510, Nashville, TN 37243-0820. *E-mail:* mike.mccormack@tn.gov. *Phone:* 866-291-2675 Ext. 140. *Fax:* 615-741-6101. *Web site:* http://www.tn.gov/collegepays.

Ned McWherter Scholars Program. Award for Tennessee high school seniors with high academic ability. Must have minimum high school GPA of 3.5 and a score of 29 on the ACT or SAT equivalent. Must attend a college or university in Tennessee and be a permanent U.S. citizen. For more information, visit Web site http://tn.gov/collegepays. *Award:* Scholarship for use in freshman, sophomore, junior, or senior year; renewable. *Award amount:* up to $3000. *Number of awards:* up to 180. *Eligibility Requirements:* Applicant must be enrolled or expecting to enroll full-time at a two-year, four-year, or technical institution or university; resident of Tennessee and studying in Tennessee. Applicant must have 3.5 GPA or higher. Available to U.S. citizens. *Application Requirements:* Application, test scores, transcript. **Deadline:** February 15.

Contact Kathy Stripling, Scholarship Administrator, Tennessee Student Assistance Corporation, 404 James Robertson Parkway, Suite 1510, Parkway Towers, Nashville, TN 37243-0820. *E-mail:* kathy.stripling@tn.gov. *Phone:* 866-291-2675 Ext. 155. *Fax:* 615-741-6101. *Web site:* http://www.tn.gov/collegepays.

Tennessee Education Lottery Scholarship Program-HOPE with General Assembly Merit Scholarship (GAMS). HOPE Scholarship of $4,000 with supplemental award of $1,000. Entering freshmen must have 3.75 GPA and 29 ACT (1280 SAT). Must be a U.S. citizen and a resident of Tennessee. *Award:* Scholarship for use in freshman, sophomore, junior, or senior year; renewable. *Award amount:* up to $5000. *Number of awards:* varies. *Eligibility Requirements:* Applicant must be enrolled or expecting to enroll full- or part-time at a two-year or four-year institution or university; resident of Tennessee and studying in Tennessee. Available to U.S. citizens. *Application Requirements:* Application. **Deadline:** September 1.

Contact Mr. Robert Biggers, Director of Lottery Scholarship Programs, Tennessee Student Assistance Corporation, Parkway Towers, 404 James Robertson Parkway, Suite 1510, Nashville, TN 37243-0820. *E-mail:* robert.biggers@tn.gov. *Phone:* 866-291-2675 Ext. 106. *Fax:* 615-741-6101. *Web site:* http://www.tn.gov/collegepays.

Tennessee Education Lottery Scholarship Program Tennessee HOPE Access Grant. Non-renewable award of $2,750 for students at four-year colleges or $1,750 for students at two-year colleges. Entering freshmen must have a minimum GPA of 2.75, ACT score of 18-20 (or SAT equivalent), and adjusted gross income attributable to the student must be $36,000 or less. Recipients will become eligible for Tennessee HOPE Scholarship by meeting HOPE Scholarship renewal criteria. *Award:* Scholarship for use in freshman, sophomore, junior, or senior year; not renewable. *Award amount:* $1750–$2750. *Number of awards:* varies. *Eligibility Requirements:* Applicant must be enrolled or expecting to enroll full- or part-time at a two-year or four-year institution or university; resident of Tennessee and studying in Tennessee. Available to U.S. citizens. *Application Requirements:* Application, financial need analysis. **Deadline:** September 1.

Contact Mr. Robert Biggers, Director of Lottery Scholarship Programs, Tennessee Student Assistance Corporation, Parkway Towers, 404 James Robertson Parkway, Suite 1510, Nashville, TN 37243-0820. *E-mail:* robert.biggers@tn.gov. *Phone:* 866-291-2675 Ext. 106. *Fax:* 615-741-6101. *Web site:* http://www.tn.gov/collegepays.

Tennessee Education Lottery Scholarship Program Tennessee HOPE Scholarship. Award amount is $4,000 for 4-year institutions and $2,000 for 2-year institutions. Must be a Tennessee resident attending an eligible postsecondary institution in Tennessee. For more information, visit http://www.TN.gov/CollegePays *Award:* Scholarship for use in freshman, sophomore, junior, or senior year; renewable. *Award amount:* $2000–$4000. *Number of awards:* varies. *Eligibility Requirements:* Applicant must be enrolled or expecting to enroll full- or part-time at a two-year or four-year institution or university; resident of Tennessee and studying in Tennessee. Applicant must have 3.0 GPA or higher. Available to U.S. citizens. *Application Requirements:* Application. **Deadline:** September 1.

Contact Mr. Robert Biggers, Director of Lottery Scholarship Programs, Tennessee Student Assistance Corporation, Parkway Towers, 404 James Robertson Parkway, Suite 1510, Nashville, TN 37243-0820. *E-mail:* robert.biggers@tn.gov. *Phone:* 866-291-2675 Ext. 106. *Fax:* 615-741-6101. *Web site:* http://www.tn.gov/collegepays.

Tennessee Education Lottery Scholarship Program Wilder-Naifeh Technical Skills Grant. Award up to $2,000 for students enrolled in a certificate or diploma program at a Tennessee Technology Center. Cannot be prior recipient of Tennessee HOPE Scholarship. For more information, visit http://www.TN.gov/CollegePays. *Award:* Grant for use in freshman or

sophomore year; renewable. *Award amount:* up to $2000. *Number of awards:* varies. *Eligibility Requirements:* Applicant must be enrolled or expecting to enroll full- or part-time at a technical institution; resident of Tennessee and studying in Tennessee. Available to U.S. citizens. *Application Requirements:* Application. **Deadline:** November 1.

Contact Mr. Robert Biggers, Director of Lottery Scholarship Programs, Tennessee Student Assistance Corporation, Parkway Towers, 404 James Robertson Parkway, Suite 1510, Nashville, TN 37243-0820. *E-mail:* robert.biggers@tn.gov. *Phone:* 866-291-2675 Ext. 106. *Fax:* 615-741-6101. *Web site:* http://www.tn.gov/collegepays.

Tennessee HOPE Foster Child Tuition Grant. Renewable tuition award available for recipients of the HOPE Scholarship or HOPE Access Grant. Student must have been in Tennessee state custody as a foster child for at least one year after reaching age 14. Award amount varies and shall not exceed the tuition and mandatory fees at an eligible Tennessee public postsecondary institution. For additional information, visit Web site http://www.tn.gov/collegepays. *Award:* Scholarship for use in freshman, sophomore, junior, or senior year; renewable. *Eligibility Requirements:* Applicant must be enrolled or expecting to enroll full- or part-time at a two-year or four-year institution or university; resident of Tennessee and studying in Tennessee. Applicant must have 3.0 GPA or higher. Available to U.S. citizens. *Application Requirements:* Application. **Deadline:** September 1.

Contact Mr. Robert Biggers, Director of Lottery Scholarship Programs, Tennessee Student Assistance Corporation, Parkway Towers, 404 James Robertson Parkway, Suite 1510, Nashville, TN 37243-0820. *E-mail:* robert.biggers@tn.gov. *Phone:* 866-291-2675 Ext. 106. *Fax:* 615-741-6101. *Web site:* http://www.tn.gov/collegepays.

Tennessee Student Assistance Award Program. Award to assist Tennessee residents attending an approved college or university within the state. Complete a Free Application for Federal Student Aid form. FAFSA must be processed by February 15 for priority consideration. For more information, see Web http://www.fafsa.ed.gov. *Award:* Grant for use in freshman, sophomore, junior, or senior year; renewable. *Award amount:* $100–$4000. *Number of awards:* 25,000–28,000. *Eligibility Requirements:* Applicant must be enrolled or expecting to enroll full- or part-time at a two-year, four-year, or technical institution or university; resident of Tennessee

and studying in Tennessee. Available to U.S. citizens. *Application Requirements:* Application, financial need analysis. **Deadline:** February 15.

Contact Naomi Derryberry, Director of Grants, Tennessee Student Assistance Corporation, Parkway Towers, 404 James Robertson Parkway, Suite 1510, Nashville, TN 37243-0820. *E-mail:* naomi.derryberry@tn.gov. *Phone:* 866-291-2675 Ext. 125. *Fax:* 615-741-6101. *Web site:* http://www.tn.gov/collegepays.

Tennessee Teaching Scholars Program. Forgivable loan for college juniors, seniors, and college graduates admitted to an education program in Tennessee with a minimum GPA of 2.75. Students must commit to teach in a Tennessee public school one year for each year of the award. Must be a U.S. citizen and resident of Tennessee. *Academic Fields/Career Goals:* Education. *Award:* Forgivable loan for use in junior, senior, or graduate year; renewable. *Award amount:* up to $4500. *Number of awards:* up to 180. *Eligibility Requirements:* Applicant must be enrolled or expecting to enroll full- or part-time at a four-year institution or university; resident of Tennessee and studying in Tennessee. Available to U.S. citizens. *Application Requirements:* Application, references, test scores, transcript. **Deadline:** April 15.

Contact Mike McCormack, Scholarship Administrator, Tennessee Student Assistance Corporation, 404 James Robertson Parkway, Suite 1510, Parkway Towers, Nashville, TN 37243-0820. *E-mail:* mike.mccormack@tn.gov. *Phone:* 615-741-1346. *Fax:* 615-741-6101. *Web site:* http://www.tn.gov/collegepays.

TEXAS

Conditional Grant Program. Renewable award to students who are considered economically disadvantaged based on federal guidelines. The maximum amount awarded per semester is $3,000 not to exceed $6000 per academic year. Students already enrolled in an undergraduate program should have minimum GPA 2.5 and students newly enrolling should have minimum GPA 3.0. *Academic Fields/Career Goals:* Civil Engineering; Computer Science/Data Processing; Occupational Safety and Health. *Award:* Grant for use in freshman, sophomore, junior, or senior year; renewable. *Award amount:* up to $6000. *Number of awards:* varies. *Eligibility Requirements:* Applicant must be enrolled or expecting to enroll full-time at a four-year institution or university; resident of Texas and studying in Texas. Available to U.S. citizens. *Application Requirements:* Application, essay, interview, references, test scores, transcript. **Deadline:** March 1.

Contact Minnie Brown, Program Coordinator, Texas Department of Transportation, 125 East 11th Street, Austin, TX 78701-2483. *E-mail:* mbrown2@dot.state.tx.us. *Phone:* 512-416-4979. *Fax:* 512-416-4980. *Web site:* http://www.txdot.gov.

Texas National Guard Tuition Assistance Program. Provides exemption from the payment of tuition to certain members of the Texas National Guard, Texas Air Guard or the State Guard. Must be Texas resident and attend school in Texas. Deadline varies. *Award:* Scholarship for use in freshman, sophomore, junior, or senior year; renewable. *Award amount:* varies. *Number of awards:* varies. *Eligibility Requirements:* Applicant must be enrolled or expecting to enroll full- or part-time at a four-year institution or university; resident of Texas and studying in Texas. Available to U.S. citizens. Applicant or parent must meet one or more of the following requirements: Air Force National Guard or Army National Guard experience; retired from active duty; disabled or killed as a result of military service; prisoner of war; or missing in action. *Application Requirements:* Application. **Deadline:** varies.

Contact State Adjutant General's Office, Texas Higher Education Coordinating Board, PO Box 5218, Austin, TX 78763-5218. *E-mail:* education.office@tx.ngb.army.mil. *Phone:* 512-465-5515. *Web site:* http://www.collegefortexans.com.

Toward EXcellence Access and Success (TEXAS Grant). Renewable aid for students enrolled in public colleges or universities in Texas. Must be a resident of Texas and have completed the Recommended High School Curriculum or Distinguished Achievement Curriculum in high school. For renewal awards, must maintain a minimum GPA of 2.5. Based on need. Amount of award is determined by the financial aid office of each school. Deadlines vary. Contact the college/university financial aid office for application information. *Award:* Grant for use in freshman, sophomore, junior, or senior year; renewable. *Award amount:* $2680–$6080. *Eligibility Requirements:* Applicant must be enrolled or expecting to enroll full- or part-time at a two-year, four-year, or technical institution or university; resident of Texas and studying in Texas. Available to U.S. citizens. *Application Requirements:* Financial need analysis, transcript.

Contact Financial Aid Office of relevant school, Texas Higher Education Coordinating Board. *Web site:* http://www.collegefortexans.com.

Tuition Equalization Grant (TEG) Program. Renewable award for Texas residents enrolled full-time at an independent college or university within the state. Based on financial need. Renewal awards require the student to maintain an overall college GPA of at least 2.5. Deadlines vary by institution. Must not be receiving athletic scholarship. Contact college/university financial aid office for application information. Nonresidents who are National Merit Finalists may also receive awards. *Award:* Grant for use in freshman, sophomore, junior, or senior year; renewable. *Award amount:* $3808–$5712. *Eligibility Requirements:* Applicant must be enrolled or expecting to enroll full-time at a two-year or four-year institution or university; resident of Texas and studying in Texas. Available to U.S. citizens. *Application Requirements:* Financial need analysis, FAFSA.

Contact Financial Aid Office of Relevant Institution, Texas Higher Education Coordinating Board. *Web site:* http://www.collegefortexans.com.

Vanessa Rudloff Scholarship Program. Scholarships of $1000 awarded to qualified TWLE members and their dependents who are entering or continuing students at an accredited college or university. For details refer to Web Site http://www.twle.net/. *Award:* Scholarship for use in freshman, sophomore, junior, senior, graduate, or postgraduate years; not renewable. *Award amount:* $1000. *Number of awards:* 4. *Eligibility Requirements:* Applicant must be enrolled or expecting to enroll full- or part-time at a two-year, four-year, or technical institution or university. Applicant or parent of applicant must be member of Texas Women in Law Enforcement. Applicant must have 3.0 GPA or higher. Available to U.S. and non-U.S. citizens. *Application Requirements:* Application, essay, references. **Deadline:** April 15.

Contact Glenda Baker, Scholarship Awards Chairperson, Texas Women in Law Enforcement, 12605 Rhea Court, Austin, TX 78727. *E-mail:* gbakerab@aol.com. *Web site:* http://www.twle.com.

UTAH

New Century Scholarship. The New Century Scholarship is for Utah high school students who complete the requirements for an Associate's Degree by September 1st of the year they graduate from high school. Recipients receive an award of up to 75% of Bachelor Degree tuition at eligible institutions in Utah for up to 60 credit hours. *Award:* Scholarship for use in junior or senior year; renewable. *Award amount:* $457–$2682. *Number of awards:* 1. *Eligibility Requirements:* Applicant must be enrolled or expecting to enroll full-time at a four-year institution or university; resident of Utah and studying in Utah. Applicant must have 3.0 GPA or higher. Available to U.S. citizens. *Application Requirements:* Application, transcript, GPA/copy of enrollment verification from an eligible Utah 4-year institution, verification from registrar of completion of requirements for associates degree. **Deadline:** January 8.

Contact David Hughes, Manager of Financial Aid, State of Utah, Board of Regents Building, The Gateway, 60 South 400 West, Salt Lake City, UT 84101-1284. *E-mail:* dhughes@utahsbr.edu. *Phone:* 801-321-7221. *Web site:* http://www.utahsbr.edu.

T.H. Bell Teaching Incentive Loan-Utah. Renewable awards for Utah residents who are high school seniors wishing to pursue teaching careers. The award value varies depending upon tuition and fees at a Utah institution. Must agree to teach in a Utah public school or pay back loan through monthly installments. *Academic Fields/Career Goals:* Education. *Award:* Forgivable loan for use in freshman, sophomore, junior, or senior year; renewable. *Award amount:* varies. *Number of awards:* 25–50. *Eligibility Requirements:* Applicant must be enrolled or expecting to enroll full-time at a four-year institution or university; resident of Utah and studying in Utah. Available to U.S. citizens. *Application Requirements:* Application, essay, test scores, transcript. **Deadline:** March 26.

Contact Linda Alder, Education Specialist, Utah State Office of Education, 250 East 500 South, PO Box 144200, Salt Lake City, UT 84114-4200. *E-mail:* linda.alder@schools.utah.gov. *Phone:* 801-538-7923. *Fax:* 801-538-7973. *Web site:* http://www.schools.utah.gov/cert.

Utah Centennial Opportunity Program for Education. Award available to students with substantial financial need for use at any of the participating Utah institutions. The student must be a Utah resident. Contact the financial aid office of the participating institution for requirements and deadlines. *Award:* Grant for use in freshman, sophomore, junior, or senior year; not renewable. *Award amount:* $300–$5000. *Number of awards:* up to 7375. *Eligibility Requirements:* Applicant must be enrolled or expecting to enroll full- or part-time at a two-year, four-year, or technical institution or university; resident of Utah and studying in Utah. Available to U.S. citizens. *Application Requirements:* Financial need analysis, FAFSA. **Deadline:** continuous.

Contact Ms. Lynda L. Reid, Student Aid Specialist III, Utah State Board of Regents, 60 South 400 West, The Board of Regents Building, The Gateway, Salt Lake City, UT 84101-1284 USA. *E-mail:* lreid@utahsbr. edu. *Phone:* 801-321-7207. *Fax:* 801-366-7168. *Web site:* http://www.uheaa.org.

Utah Leveraging Educational Assistance Partnership. Award available to Utah resident students with substantial financial need for use at any of the participating Utah institutions. Contact the financial aid office of the participating institution for requirements and deadlines. *Award:* Grant for use in freshman, sophomore, junior, or senior year; not renewable. *Award amount:* $300–$2500. *Number of awards:* up to 3985. *Eligibility Requirements:* Applicant must be enrolled or expecting to enroll full- or part-time at a two-year, four-year, or technical institution or university; resident of Utah and studying in Utah. Available to U.S. citizens. *Application Requirements:* Financial need analysis, FAFSA. **Deadline:** continuous.

Contact Ms. Lynda L. Reid, Student Aid Specialist III, Utah State Board of Regents, 60 South 400 West, The Board of Regents Building, The Gateway, Salt Lake City, UT 84101-1284 USA. *E-mail:* lreid@utahsbr. edu. *Phone:* 801-321-7207. *Fax:* 801-366-7168. *Web site:* http://www.uheaa.org.

VERMONT

Vermont Incentive Grants. Renewable grants for Vermont residents based on financial need. Must meet needs test. Must be college undergraduate or graduate student enrolled full-time at an approved post secondary institution. Only available to Vermont residents. *Award:* Grant for use in freshman, sophomore, junior, or senior year; renewable. *Award amount:* $500–$10,800. *Number of awards:* varies. *Eligibility Requirements:* Applicant must be enrolled or expecting to enroll full-time at a two-year, four-year, or technical institution or university and resident of Vermont. Available to U.S. citizens. *Application Requirements:* Application, financial need analysis, FAFSA. **Deadline:** continuous.

Contact Grant Program, Vermont Student Assistance Corporation, PO Box 2000,

Winooski, VT 05404-2000. *Phone:* 802-655-9602. *Fax:* 802-654-3765. *Web site:* http://www.vsac.org.

Vermont Non-Degree Student Grant Program. Need-based, renewable grants for Vermont residents enrolled in non-degree programs in a college, vocational school, or high school adult program, that will improve employability or encourage further study. Award amounts vary. *Award:* Grant for use in freshman, sophomore, junior, or senior year; renewable. *Award amount:* varies. *Number of awards:* varies. *Eligibility Requirements:* Applicant must be enrolled or expecting to enroll full- or part-time at a two-year, four-year, or technical institution or university and resident of Vermont. Available to U.S. citizens. *Application Requirements:* Application, financial need analysis. **Deadline:** continuous.

Contact Grant Program Department, Vermont Student Assistance Corporation, 10 East Allen Street, PO Box 2000, Winooski, VT 05404-2000. *Phone:* 802-655-9602. *Web site:* http://www.vsac.org.

Vermont Part-Time Student Grants. For undergraduates carrying less than twelve credits per semester who have not received a bachelor's degree. Must be Vermont resident. Based on financial need. Complete Vermont Financial Aid Packet to apply. May be used at any approved post-secondary institution. *Award:* Grant for use in freshman, sophomore, junior, or senior year; renewable. *Award amount:* $250–$8100. *Number of awards:* varies. *Eligibility Requirements:* Applicant must be enrolled or expecting to enroll part-time at a four-year institution or university and resident of Vermont. Available to U.S. citizens. *Application Requirements:* Application, financial need analysis. **Deadline:** continuous.

Contact Grant Program, Vermont Student Assistance Corporation, PO Box 2000, Winooski, VT 05404-2000. *Phone:* 802-655-9602. *Fax:* 802-654-3765. *Web site:* http://www.vsac.org.

VIRGINIA

College Scholarship Assistance Program. Need-based scholarship for undergraduate study by a Virginia resident at a participating Virginia two- or four-year college, or university. Contact financial aid office at the participating Virginia public or nonprofit private institution. The program does not have its own application; institutions use results from the federal FAFSA form. *Award:* Grant for use in freshman, sophomore, junior, or senior year; not renewable. *Award amount:* $400–$5000.

Number of awards: varies. *Eligibility Requirements:* Applicant must be enrolled or expecting to enroll full- or part-time at a two-year or four-year institution or university; resident of Virginia and studying in Virginia. Available to U.S. citizens. *Application Requirements:* Financial need analysis.

Contact Contact the financial aid office of participating Virginia college. For additional details, visit www.schev.edu, Virginia State Council of Higher Education. *Web site:* http://www.schev.edu.

Gheens Foundation Scholarship. Scholarship supports African American students from greater Louisville, KY. For use in one of the following universities: Clark Atlanta University, Morehouse College, Morris Brown College, Spelman College, Tuskegee University, Howard University, Florida A&M, Southern University, Tennessee State or Prairie View University. Apply online at http://www.uncf.org. *Award:* Scholarship for use in freshman, sophomore, junior, or senior year; not renewable. *Award amount:* up to $2000. *Number of awards:* varies. *Eligibility Requirements:* Applicant must be Black (non-Hispanic); enrolled or expecting to enroll full- or part-time at a four-year institution or university; resident of Kentucky and studying in Alabama, District of Columbia, Florida, Georgia, Louisiana, Tennessee, or Texas. Applicant must have 2.5 GPA or higher. Available to U.S. citizens. *Application Requirements:* Application, financial need analysis, transcript.

Contact Director, Program Services, United Negro College Fund, 8260 Willow Oaks Corporate Drive, PO Box 10444, Fairfax, VA 22031-8044. *E-mail:* rebecca.bennett@uncf. org. *Phone:* 800-331-2244. *Web site:* http://www.uncf.org.

Mary Marshall Practical Nursing Scholarships. Award for practical nursing students who are Virginia residents. Must attend a nursing program in Virginia. Recipient must agree to work in Virginia after graduation. Minimum 3.0 GPA required. Scholarship value and the number of scholarships granted varies annually. *Academic Fields/Career Goals:* Nursing. *Award:* Scholarship for use in freshman, sophomore, junior, or senior year; not renewable. *Award amount:* $150–$500. *Number of awards:* 50–150. *Eligibility Requirements:* Applicant must be age 18 and over; enrolled or expecting to enroll full- or part-time at a four-year institution or university; resident of Virginia and studying in Virginia. Applicant must have 3.0 GPA or higher. Available to U.S.

citizens. *Application Requirements:* Application, financial need analysis, references, transcript. **Deadline:** June 30.

Contact Mrs. Aileen Harris, Healthcare Workforce Manager, Virginia Department of Health, Office of Minority Health and Public Health Policy, PO Box 2448, 109 Governor Street, Suite 1016-E, Richmond, VA 23218-2448. *E-mail:* aileen.harris@vdh.virginia.gov. *Phone:* 804-864-7435. *Fax:* 804-864-7440. *Web site:* http://www.vdh.virginia.gov.

Mary Marshall Registered Nurse Scholarships. Award for registered nursing students who are Virginia residents. Must attend a nursing program in Virginia. Recipient must agree to work in Virginia after graduation. Minimum 3.0 GPA required. The amount of each scholarship award is dependent upon the amount of money appropriated by the Virginia General Assembly and the number of qualified applicants. *Academic Fields/Career Goals:* Nursing. *Award:* Scholarship for use in freshman, sophomore, junior, or senior year; not renewable. *Award amount:* $2000. *Eligibility Requirements:* Applicant must be enrolled or expecting to enroll full- or part-time at a four-year institution or university; resident of Virginia and studying in Virginia. Applicant must have 3.0 GPA or higher. Available to U.S. citizens. *Application Requirements:* Application, financial need analysis, references, transcript. **Deadline:** June 30.

Contact Mrs. Aileen Harris, Healthcare Workforce Manager, Virginia Department of Health, Office of Minority Health and Public Health Policy, PO Box 2448, 109 Governor Street, Suite 1016-E, Richmond, VA 23218-2448. *E-mail:* aileen.harris@vdh.virginia.gov. *Phone:* 804-864-7435. *Fax:* 804-864-7440. *Web site:* http://www.vdh.virginia.gov.

NRA Youth Educational Summit (YES) Scholarships. Awards for Youth Educational Summit participants based on the initial application, on-site debate, and degree of participation during the week-long event. Must be graduating high school seniors enrolled in undergraduate program. Must have a minimum GPA of 3.0. *Award:* Scholarship for use in freshman year; not renewable. *Award amount:* $1000–$10,000. *Number of awards:* 1–6. *Eligibility Requirements:* Applicant must be high school student and planning to enroll or expecting to enroll full- or part-time at a two-year, four-year, or technical institution or university. Applicant must have 3.0 GPA or higher. Available to U.S. citizens. *Application Requirements:* Application, applicant must enter a contest, essay, references, transcript. **Deadline:** March 1.

Contact Event Services Manager, National Rifle Association, 11250 Waples Mill Road, Fairfax, VA 22030. *E-mail:* fnra@nrahq.org. *Phone:* 703-267-1354. *Web site:* http://www.nrafoundation.org.

Nurse Practitioners/Nurse Midwife Program Scholarships. One-time award for nurse practitioner/nurse midwife students who have been residents of Virginia for at least one year. Must attend a nursing program in Virginia. Recipient must agree to work in an under-served community in Virginia following graduation. The amount of each scholarship award is dependent upon the amount of funds appropriated by the Virginia General Assembly. Minimum 3.0 GPA required. *Academic Fields/Career Goals:* Nursing. *Award:* Scholarship for use in freshman, sophomore, junior, or senior year; not renewable. *Award amount:* $5000. *Number of awards:* 5. *Eligibility Requirements:* Applicant must be enrolled or expecting to enroll full- or part-time at a four-year institution or university; resident of Virginia and studying in Virginia. Applicant must have 3.0 GPA or higher. Available to U.S. citizens. *Application Requirements:* Application, essay, references, transcript. **Deadline:** July 31.

Contact Mrs. Aileen Harris, Healthcare Workforce Manager, Virginia Department of Health, Office of Minority Health and Public Health Policy, PO Box 2448, 109 Governor Street, Suite 1016-E, Richmond, VA 23218-2448. *E-mail:* aileen.harris@vdh.virginia.gov. *Phone:* 804-864-7435. *Fax:* 804-864-7440. *Web site:* http://www.vdh.virginia.gov.

State Department Federal Credit Union Annual Scholarship Program. Scholarships available to members who are currently enrolled in a degree program and have completed 12 credit hours of coursework at an accredited college or university. Must have own account in good standing with SDFCU, have a minimum 2.5 GPA, submit official cumulative transcripts, and describe need for financial assistance to continue their education. Scholarship only open to members of State Department Federal Credit Union. *Award:* Scholarship for use in sophomore, junior, or senior year; not renewable. *Award amount:* varies. *Number of awards:* varies. *Eligibility Requirements:* Applicant must be enrolled or expecting to enroll full-time at a four-year institution or university. Applicant must have 2.5 GPA or higher. Available to U.S. and non-U.S. citizens. *Application Requirements:* Application, applicant must enter a contest, financial need analysis, transcript, personal statement. **Deadline:** April 10.

Contact Scholarship Coordinator, State Department Federal Credit Union Annual Scholarship Program, 1630 King Street, Alexandria, VA 22314. *E-mail:* sdfcu@sdfcu.org. *Phone:* 703-706-5187. *Web site:* http://www.sdfcu.org.

Virginia Commonwealth Award. Need-based award for undergraduate or graduate study at a Virginia public two- or four-year college, or university. Undergraduates must be Virginia residents. The application and awards process are administered by the financial aid office at the Virginia public institution where student is enrolled. Dollar value of each award varies. Contact financial aid office for application and deadlines. *Award:* Grant for use in freshman, sophomore, junior, or senior year; not renewable. *Award amount:* varies. *Number of awards:* varies. *Eligibility Requirements:* Applicant must be enrolled or expecting to enroll full- or part-time at a two-year or four-year institution or university; resident of Virginia and studying in Virginia. Available to U.S. citizens. *Application Requirements:* Financial need analysis.

Contact Contact the financial aid office of participating Virginia college. For additional details, visit www.schev.edu, Virginia State Council of Higher Education. *Web site:* http://www.schev.edu.

Virginia Guaranteed Assistance Program. Awards to undergraduate students proportional to their need, up to full tuition, fees and book allowance. Must be a graduate of a Virginia high school. High school GPA of 2.5 required. Must be enrolled full-time in a Virginia two- or four-year institution and demonstrate financial need. Must maintain minimum college GPA of 2.0 for renewal awards. *Award:* Grant for use in freshman, sophomore, junior, or senior year; not renewable. *Award amount:* varies. *Number of awards:* varies. *Eligibility Requirements:* Applicant must be enrolled or expecting to enroll full-time at a two-year or four-year institution or university; resident of Virginia and studying in Virginia. Applicant must have 2.5 GPA or higher. Available to U.S. citizens. *Application Requirements:* Financial need analysis, transcript.

Contact Contact the financial aid office of participating Virginia college. For additional details, visit www.schev.edu, Virginia State Council of Higher Education. *Web site:* http://www.schev.edu.

Virginia Military Survivors and Dependents Education Program. Scholarships for post-secondary students between ages 16 and 19 to attend Virginia state-supported institutions. Must be child or surviving child of veteran who has either been permanently or totally disabled due to war or other armed conflict; died as a result of war or other armed conflict; or been listed as a POW or MIA. Parent must also meet Virginia residency requirements. *Award:* Scholarship for use in freshman, sophomore, junior, senior, or graduate year; renewable. *Award amount:* varies. *Number of awards:* varies. *Eligibility Requirements:* Applicant must be age 16-19; enrolled or expecting to enroll full-time at a two-year, four-year, or technical institution or university; resident of Virginia and studying in Virginia. Available to U.S. citizens. Applicant or parent must meet one or more of the following requirements: general military experience; retired from active duty; disabled or killed as a result of military service; prisoner of war; or missing in action. *Application Requirements:* Application, references. **Deadline:** varies.

Contact Doris Sullivan, Coordinator, Virginia Department of Veterans Services, Poff Federal Building, 270 Franklin Road, SW, Room 503, Roanoke, VA 24011-2215. *Phone:* 540-857-7101 Ext. 213. *Fax:* 540-857-7573. *Web site:* http://www.dvs.virginia.gov.

Virginia Tuition Assistance Grant Program (Private Institutions). Awards for undergraduate students. Also available to graduate and first professional degree students pursuing a health-related degree program. Not to be used for religious study. Must be US citizen or eligible non-citizen, Virginia domiciled, and enrolled full-time at an approved private, nonprofit college within Virginia. Awards amounts for 2010-11 are not known as of the timing of this submission. Information and application available from participating Virginia colleges financial aid office. Visit http://www.schev.edu and click on "Financial Aid." *Award:* Grant for use in freshman, sophomore, junior, senior, or graduate year; renewable. *Award amount:* $1000–$3000. *Number of awards:* 22,000. *Eligibility Requirements:* Applicant must be enrolled or expecting to enroll full-time at a four-year institution or university; resident of Virginia and studying in Virginia. Available to U.S. citizens. *Application Requirements:* Application. **Deadline:** July 31.

Contact Contact the financial aid office of participating private, nonprofit Virginia college. For additional details, visit www.schev.edu, Virginia State Council of Higher Education. *Web site:* http://www.schev.edu.

Walter Reed Smith Scholarship. Award for full-time female undergraduate students who are descendant of a Confederate soldier, studying nutrition, home economics, nursing, business administration, or computer science in accredited college or university. Minimum 3.0 GPA required. Submit application and letter of endorsement from sponsoring chapter of the United Daughters of the Confederacy. *Academic Fields/Career Goals:* Business/Consumer Services; Computer Science/Data Processing; Food Science/Nutrition; Home Economics; Nursing. *Award:* Scholarship for use in freshman, sophomore, junior, or senior year; renewable. *Award amount:* $800–$1000. *Number of awards:* 1–2. *Eligibility Requirements:* Applicant must be enrolled or expecting to enroll full-time at a four-year institution or university and female. Applicant or parent of applicant must be member of United Daughters of the Confederacy. Applicant must have 3.0 GPA or higher. Available to U.S. citizens. *Application Requirements:* Application, essay, financial need analysis, photo, references, self-addressed stamped envelope, transcript, copy of applicant's birth certificate, copy of confederate ancestor's proof of service. **Deadline:** March 15.

Contact United Daughters of the Confederacy, 328 North Boulevard, Richmond, VA 23220-4009 USA. *E-mail:* hqudc@rcn.com. *Phone:* 804-355-1636. *Fax:* 804-353-1396. *Web site:* http://www.hqudc.org.

WASHINGTON

American Indian Endowed Scholarship. Awarded to financially needy undergraduate and graduate students with close social and cultural ties with a Native-American community. Must be Washington resident and enrolled full-time at Washington public or private school. Must be committed to use education to return service to the state's American Indian community. *Award:* Scholarship for use in freshman, sophomore, junior, senior, graduate, or postgraduate years; not renewable. *Award amount:* $500–$2000. *Number of awards:* 10–20. *Eligibility Requirements:* Applicant must be American Indian/Alaska Native; enrolled or expecting to enroll full-time at a two-year, four-year, or technical institution or university; resident of Washington and studying in Washington. Available to U.S. citizens. *Application Requirements:* Application, essay, references, transcript. **Deadline:** February 1.

Contact Ann Voyles, Program Manager, Washington Higher Education Coordinating Board (replaced the Council for Postsecondary Education), 917 Lakeridge Way, PO Box 43430, Olympia, WA 98504-3430. *E-mail:* annv@hecb.wa.gov. *Phone:* 360-753-7843. *Fax:* 360-704-6243. *Web site:* http://www.hecb.wa.gov.

Future Teachers Conditional Scholarship and Loan Repayment Program. Participants must agree to teach in Washington K-12 schools in return for conditional scholarships or loan repayments. Applicants must be Washington residents, attend an eligible institution in Washington, and pursue a teaching certificate or specific additional endorsements. Select priority may or may not be available when applying. *Academic Fields/Career Goals:* Education. *Award:* Forgivable loan for use in freshman, sophomore, junior, senior, or graduate year; renewable. *Award amount:* $2928–$7512. *Number of awards:* 80–120. *Eligibility Requirements:* Applicant must be enrolled or expecting to enroll full- or part-time at a two-year or four-year institution or university; resident of Washington and studying in Washington. Available to U.S. citizens. *Application Requirements:* Application, essay, references, transcript, bilingual verification (if applicable). **Deadline:** October 9.

Contact Mary Knutson, Program Manager, Washington Higher Education Coordinating Board (replaced the Council for Postsecondary Education), 917 Lakeridge Way, PO Box 43430, Olympia, WA 98504-3430. *E-mail:* FUT@hecb.wa.gov. *Phone:* 360-753-7845. *Fax:* 360-704-6245. *Web site:* http://www.hecb.wa.gov.

Health Professionals Scholarship Program. Program was created to attract and retain licensed primary care health professionals, to serve in critical shortage areas in Washington state. Must sign a promissory note agreeing to serve for a minimum of three years in a designated shortage area in Washington state or pay back funds at double penalty with the interest. *Academic Fields/Career Goals:* Health and Medical Sciences. *Award:* Scholarship for use in sophomore, junior, or senior year; renewable. *Award amount:* $5000–$75,000. *Number of awards:* 10–50. *Eligibility Requirements:* Applicant must be enrolled or expecting to enroll full- or part-time at a two-year, four-year, or technical institution or university. Available to U.S. citizens. *Application Requirements:* Application, essay, references, transcript. **Deadline:** April 30.

Contact Rochelle Wambach, Program Administrator, Washington Higher Education Coordinating Board (replaced the Council for Postsecondary Education), PO Box 43430, Olympia, WA 98504-3430. *E-mail:* rochellew@

hecb.wa.gov. *Phone:* 360-753-7847. *Web site:* http://www.hecb.wa.gov.

Passport to College Promise Scholarship. Scholarship to encourage Washington residents who are former foster care youth to prepare for and succeed in college. Recipients must have spent at least one year in foster care after their 16th birthday. *Award:* Scholarship for use in freshman, sophomore, junior, or senior year; renewable. *Award amount:* $1–$6700. *Number of awards:* 1–150. *Eligibility Requirements:* Applicant must be age 18-26; enrolled or expecting to enroll full- or part-time at a two-year, four-year, or technical institution or university; resident of Washington and studying in Washington. Available to U.S. citizens. *Application Requirements:* Application, financial need analysis, consent form. **Deadline:** continuous.

Contact Ms. Dawn Cypriano-McAferty, Program Manager, Washington Higher Education Coordinating Board (replaced the Council for Postsecondary Education), 917 Lakeridge Way SW, PO Box 43430, Olympia, WA 98504-3430. *E-mail:* passporttocollege@hecb. wa.gov. *Phone:* 888-535-0747 Ext. 5. *Fax:* 360-704-6246. *Web site:* http://www.hecb.wa. gov.

Washington Award for Vocational Excellence (WAVE). Award to honor vocational students from the legislative districts of Washington. Grants for up to two years of undergraduate resident tuition. Must be enrolled in Washington high school, skills center, or community or technical college at time of application. To be eligible to apply student must complete 360 hours in single vocational program in high school or one year at technical college. Contact principal, guidance counselor, or on-campus WAVE coordinator for more information. *Award:* Scholarship for use in freshman, sophomore, junior, or senior year; renewable. *Award amount:* $1–$6720. *Number of awards:* 147. *Eligibility Requirements:* Applicant must be enrolled or expecting to enroll full- or part-time at a two-year, four-year, or technical institution or university; resident of Washington and studying in Washington. Available to U.S. citizens. *Application Requirements:* Application. **Deadline:** February 12.

Contact Terri Colbert, Program Specialist, Washington Higher Education Coordinating Board (replaced the Council for Postsecondary Education), Workforce Training and Education Coordinating Board, PO Box 43105, Olympia, WA 98504-3105. *E-mail:* tcolbert@ wtb.wa.gov. *Phone:* 360-753-5680. *Fax:* 360-586-5862. *Web site:* http://www.hecb.wa.gov.

Washington Scholars Program. Awards high school students from the legislative districts of Washington. Must enroll in college or university in Washington. Scholarships up to four years of full-time resident undergraduate tuition and fees. Student must not pursue a degree in theology. Contact principal or guidance counselor for more information. Requires nomination by high school principal and be in the top 1 percent of his or her graduating senior class. *Award:* Scholarship for use in freshman, sophomore, junior, or senior year; renewable. *Award amount:* $1–$6720. *Number of awards:* 147. *Eligibility Requirements:* Applicant must be high school student; planning to enroll or expecting to enroll full- or part-time at a two-year or four-year institution or university; resident of Washington and studying in Washington. Available to U.S. citizens. *Application Requirements:* Application, test scores, transcript. **Deadline:** January 19.

Contact Ann Voyles, Program Manager, Washington Higher Education Coordinating Board (replaced the Council for Postsecondary Education), 917 Lakeridge Way, PO Box 43430, Olympia, WA 98504-3430. *E-mail:* annv@hecb.wa.gov. *Phone:* 360-753-7843. *Fax:* 360-704-6243. *Web site:* http://www. hecb.wa.gov.

Washington State Need Grant Program. The program helps Washington's lowest-income undergraduate students to pursue degrees, hone skills, or retrain for new careers. Students with family incomes equal to or less than 50 percent of the state median are eligible for up to 100 percent of the maximum grant. Students with incomes between 51-70% of the state median are prorated dependent on income. All grants are subject to funding. *Award:* Grant for use in freshman, sophomore, junior, or senior year; not renewable. *Award amount:* $106–$6876. *Number of awards:* 71,233. *Eligibility Requirements:* Applicant must be enrolled or expecting to enroll full- or part-time at a two-year, four-year, or technical institution or university; resident of Washington and studying in Washington. Available to U.S. citizens. *Application Requirements:* Application, financial need analysis, FAFSA. **Deadline:** continuous.

Contact Program Manager, Washington Higher Education Coordinating Board (replaced the Council for Postsecondary Education). *E-mail:* finaid@hecb.wa.gov. *Web site:* http:// www.hecb.wa.gov.

WEST VIRGINIA

Robert C. Byrd Honors Scholarship-West Virginia. Award for West Virginia residents who have demonstrated outstanding academic achievement. Must be a graduating high school senior. May apply for renewal consideration for a total of four years of assistance. For full-time study only. *Award:* Scholarship for use in freshman year; renewable. *Award amount:* $1500. *Number of awards:* 36. *Eligibility Requirements:* Applicant must be high school student; planning to enroll or expecting to enroll full-time at a two-year, four-year, or technical institution or university and resident of West Virginia. Applicant must have 3.0 GPA or higher. Available to U.S. citizens. *Application Requirements:* Application, test scores, transcript, letter of acceptance from a college/university. **Deadline:** March 1.

Contact Darlene Elmore, Scholarship Coordinator, West Virginia Higher Education Policy Commission-Student Services, 1018 Kanawha Boulevard East, Suite 700, Charleston, WV 25301. *E-mail:* elmore@hepc.wvnet.edu. *Phone:* 304-558-4618 Ext. 278. *Fax:* 304-558-4622. *Web site:* http://www.wvhepcnew. wvnet.edu/.

Underwood-Smith Teacher Scholarship Program. Award for West Virginia residents at West Virginia institutions pursuing teaching careers. Must have a 3.5 GPA after completion of two years of course work. Must teach two years in West Virginia public schools for each year the award is received. Recipients will be required to sign an agreement acknowledging an understanding of the program's requirements and their willingness to repay the award if appropriate teaching service is not rendered. *Academic Fields/Career Goals:* Education. *Award:* Scholarship for use in junior, senior, graduate, or postgraduate years; renewable. *Award amount:* $1620–$5000. *Number of awards:* 53–60. *Eligibility Requirements:* Applicant must be enrolled or expecting to enroll full-time at a four-year institution or university; resident of West Virginia and studying in West Virginia. Applicant must have 3.0 GPA or higher. Available to U.S. citizens. *Application Requirements:* Application, essay, references. **Deadline:** March 1.

Contact Darlene Elmore, Scholarship Coordinator, West Virginia Higher Education Policy Commission-Student Services, 1018 Kanawha Boulevard East, Suite 700, Charleston, WV 25301. *E-mail:* elmore@hepc.wvnet.edu. *Phone:* 304-558-4618 Ext. 278. *Fax:* 304-558-4622. *Web site:* http://www.wvhepcnew. wvnet.edu/.

West Virginia Engineering, Science and Technology Scholarship Program. Award for full-time students attending West Virginia institutions, pursuing a degree in engineering, science, or technology. Must be a resident of West Virginia. Must have a 3.0 GPA, and after graduation, must work in the fields of engineering, science, or technology in West Virginia one year for each year the award was received. *Academic Fields/Career Goals:* Electrical Engineering/Electronics; Engineering/ Technology; Engineering-Related Technologies; Science, Technology, and Society. *Award:* Scholarship for use in freshman, sophomore, junior, or senior year; renewable. *Award amount:* $1500–$3000. *Number of awards:* 200–300. *Eligibility Requirements:* Applicant must be enrolled or expecting to enroll full-time at a two-year, four-year, or technical institution or university; resident of West Virginia and studying in West Virginia. Applicant must have 3.0 GPA or higher. Available to U.S. citizens. *Application Requirements:* Application, essay, test scores, transcript. **Deadline:** March 1.

Contact Darlene Elmore, Scholarship Coordinator, West Virginia Higher Education Policy Commission-Student Services, 1018 Kanawha Boulevard East, Suite 700, Charleston, WV 25301. *E-mail:* elmore@hepc.wvnet.edu. *Phone:* 304-558-4618. *Web site:* http://www. wvhepcnew.wvnet.edu/.

West Virginia Higher Education Grant Program. Award available for West Virginia resident for one year immediately preceding the date of application, high school graduate or the equivalent, demonstrate financial need, and enroll as a full-time undergraduate at an approved university or college located in West Virginia or Pennsylvania. *Award:* Grant for use in freshman year; not renewable. *Award amount:* $375–$3542. *Number of awards:* 10,755–11,000. *Eligibility Requirements:* Applicant must be high school student; planning to enroll or expecting to enroll full-time at a four-year institution or university; resident of West Virginia and studying in Pennsylvania or West Virginia. Available to U.S. citizens. *Application Requirements:* Application, financial need analysis, references, test scores, transcript. **Deadline:** March 1.

Contact Judy Smith, Senior Project Coordinator, West Virginia Higher Education Policy Commission-Student Services, 1018 Kanawha Boulevard East, Suite 700, Charleston, WV 25301-2827. *E-mail:* kee@hepc.wvnet. edu. *Phone:* 304-558-4618. *Fax:* 304-558-4622. *Web site:* http://www.wvhepcnew.wvnet. edu/.

WISCONSIN

Handicapped Student Grant-Wisconsin. One-time award available to residents of Wisconsin who have severe or profound hearing or visual impairment. Must be enrolled at least half-time at a nonprofit institution. If the handicap prevents the student from attending a Wisconsin school, the award may be used out-of-state in a specialized college. Refer to Web site for further details http://www.heab.state.wi. us. *Award:* Grant for use in freshman, sophomore, junior, or senior year; not renewable. *Award amount:* $250–$1800. *Number of awards:* varies. *Eligibility Requirements:* Applicant must be enrolled or expecting to enroll full- or part-time at a four-year institution or university and resident of Wisconsin. Applicant must be hearing impaired or visually impaired. Available to U.S. citizens. *Application Requirements:* Application, financial need analysis. **Deadline:** continuous.

Contact Sandy Thomas, Program Coordinator, Wisconsin Higher Educational Aid Board, PO Box 7885, Madison, WI 53707-7885. *E-mail:* sandy.thomas@wi.gov. *Phone:* 608-266-0888. *Fax:* 608-267-2808. *Web site:* http://www.heab.wi.gov.

Menominee Indian Tribe Adult Vocational Training Program. Renewable award for enrolled Menominee tribal members to use at vocational or technical schools. Must be at least 1/4 Menominee and show proof of Indian blood. Must complete financial aid form. Deadlines: March 1 and November 1. *Award:* Grant for use in freshman or sophomore year; renewable. *Award amount:* $100–$2200. *Number of awards:* 50–70. *Eligibility Requirements:* Applicant must be American Indian/Alaska Native and enrolled or expecting to enroll full- or part-time at a technical institution. Available to U.S. citizens. *Application Requirements:* Application, financial need analysis, proof of Indian blood. **Deadline:** varies.

Contact Virginia Nuske, Education Director, Menominee Indian Tribe of Wisconsin, PO Box 910, Keshena, WI 54135. *E-mail:* vnuske@mitw.org. *Phone:* 715-799-5110. *Fax:* 715-799-5102. *Web site:* http://www. menominee-nsn.gov.

Minority Undergraduate Retention Grant-Wisconsin. The grant provides financial assistance to African-American, Native-American, Hispanic, and former citizens of Laos, Vietnam, and Cambodia, for study in Wisconsin. Must be Wisconsin resident, enrolled at least half-time in Wisconsin Technical College System schools, nonprofit independent colleges and universities, and tribal colleges. Refer to Web site

for further details http://www.heab.state. wi.us. *Award:* Grant for use in sophomore, junior, or senior year; not renewable. *Award amount:* $250–$2500. *Number of awards:* varies. *Eligibility Requirements:* Applicant must be American Indian/Alaska Native, Asian/Pacific Islander, Black (non-Hispanic), or Hispanic; enrolled or expecting to enroll full- or part-time at a two-year, four-year, or technical institution or university; resident of Wisconsin and studying in Wisconsin. Available to U.S. and non-U.S. citizens. *Application Requirements:* Application, financial need analysis. **Deadline:** continuous.

Contact Mary Lou Kuzdas, Program Coordinator, Wisconsin Higher Educational Aid Board, PO Box 7885, Madison, WI 53707-7885. *E-mail:* mary.kuzdas@wi.gov. *Phone:* 608-267-2212. *Fax:* 608-267-2808. *Web site:* http://www.heab.wi.gov.

Talent Incentive Program Grant. Grant assists residents of Wisconsin who are attending a nonprofit institution in Wisconsin, and who have substantial financial need. Must meet income criteria, be considered economically and educationally disadvantaged, and be enrolled at least half-time. Refer to Web site for further details http://www.heab.state.wi.us. *Award:* Grant for use in freshman, sophomore, junior, or senior year; renewable. *Award amount:* $250–$1800. *Number of awards:* varies. *Eligibility Requirements:* Applicant must be enrolled or expecting to enroll full- or part-time at a two-year, four-year, or technical institution or university; resident of Wisconsin and studying in Wisconsin. Available to U.S. citizens. *Application Requirements:* Application, financial need analysis, nomination by financial aid office. **Deadline:** continuous.

Contact Colette Brown, Program Coordinator, Wisconsin Higher Educational Aid Board, PO Box 7885, Madison, WI 53707-7885. *E-mail:* colette.brown@wi.gov. *Phone:* 608-266-1665. *Fax:* 608-267-2808. *Web site:* http://www.heab.wi.gov.

Veterans Education (VetEd) Reimbursement Grant. Open only to Wisconsin veterans enrolled at approved schools for undergraduate study. Benefit is based on length of time serving on active duty in the armed forces (active duty for training does not apply). Application due no later than 60 days after the course start date. Veterans may be reimbursed up to 100 percent of tuition and fees at UW–Madison rate for the same number of credits. Veteran must earn a 2.0 or better for the semester. *Award:* Grant for use in freshman, sophomore, junior, or senior year; renewable.

Award amount: up to $3594. *Number of awards:* varies. *Eligibility Requirements:* Applicant must be enrolled or expecting to enroll full- or part-time at a two-year, four-year, or technical institution or university; resident of Wisconsin and studying in Minnesota or Wisconsin. Available to U.S. citizens. Applicant must have served in the Air Force, Army, Coast Guard, Marine Corps, or Navy. *Application Requirements:* Application, Be certified as a Wisconsin veteran. **Deadline:** continuous.

Contact Ms. Leslie Busby-Amegashie, Analyst, Wisconsin Department of Veterans Affairs (WDVA), PO Box 7843, Madison, WI 53707-7843. *E-mail:* leslie.busby-amegashie@dva.state.wi.us. *Phone:* 800-947-8387. *Web site:* http://www.dva.state.wi.us.

Wisconsin Academic Excellence Scholarship. Renewable award for high school seniors with the highest GPA in graduating class. Must be a Wisconsin resident attending a nonprofit Wisconsin institution full-time. Scholarship value is $2250 toward tuition each year for up to four years. Must maintain 3.0 GPA for renewal. Refer to your high school counselor for more details. *Award:* Scholarship for use in freshman year; renewable. *Award amount:* up to $2250. *Number of awards:* varies. *Eligibility Requirements:* Applicant must be high school student; planning to enroll or expecting to enroll full-time at a two-year, four-year, or technical institution or university; resident of Wisconsin and studying in Wisconsin. Applicant must have 3.0 GPA or higher. Available to U.S. citizens. *Application Requirements:* Application, test scores, transcript. **Deadline:** continuous.

Contact Nancy Wilkison, Program Coordinator, Wisconsin Higher Educational Aid Board, PO Box 7885, Madison, WI 53707-7885. *E-mail:* nancy.wilkison@wi.gov. *Phone:* 608-267-2213. *Fax:* 608-267-2808. *Web site:* http://www.heab.wi.gov.

Wisconsin Higher Education Grants (WHEG). Grants for residents of Wisconsin enrolled at least half-time in degree or certificate programs at a University of Wisconsin Institution, Wisconsin Technical College or an approved Tribal College . Must show financial need. Refer to Web site for further details http://www.heab.wi. gov. *Award:* Grant for use in freshman, sophomore, junior, or senior year; not renewable. *Award amount:* $250–$3000. *Number of awards:* varies. *Eligibility Requirements:* Applicant must be enrolled or expecting to enroll full- or part-time at a two-year, four-year, or technical institution or university; resident of Wisconsin

and studying in Wisconsin. Available to U.S. citizens. *Application Requirements:* Application, financial need analysis. **Deadline:** continuous.

Contact Sandra Thomas, Program Coordinator, Wisconsin Higher Educational Aid Board, PO Box 7885, Madison, WI 53707-7885. *E-mail:* sandy.thomas@heab.state.wi.us. *Phone:* 608-266-0888. *Fax:* 608-267-2808. *Web site:* http://www.heab.wi.gov.

Wisconsin League for Nursing Inc., Scholarship. One-time award for Wisconsin residents who have completed half of an accredited Wisconsin school of nursing program. Financial need of student must be demonstrated. Scholarship applications are mailed by WLN office ONLY to Wisconsin nursing schools in January for distribution to students. Students interested in obtaining an application must contact their nursing school and submit completed applications to their school. Applications sent directly to WLN office will be returned to applicant. For further information visit Web site http://www.wisconsinwln.org/ Scholarships.htm. *Academic Fields/Career Goals:* Nursing. *Award:* Scholarship for use in junior or senior year; not renewable. *Award amount:* $500–$1000. *Number of awards:* 11–35. *Eligibility Requirements:* Applicant must be enrolled or expecting to enroll full-time at a two-year, four-year, or technical institution or university; resident of Wisconsin and studying in Wisconsin. Available to U.S. citizens. *Application Requirements:* Application, essay, financial need analysis. **Deadline:** March 1.

Contact Mary Ann Tanner, Administrative Secretary, Wisconsin League for Nursing, Inc., 2121 East Newport Avenue, Milwaukee, WI 53211-2952 USA. *E-mail:* wln@wisconsinwln. org. *Phone:* 888-755-3329. *Fax:* 888-755-3329. *Web site:* http://www.wisconsinwln. org.

Wisconsin Native American/Indian Student Assistance Grant. Grants for Wisconsin residents who are at least one-quarter American Indian. Must be attending a college or university within the state. Refer to Web site for further details http:// www.heab.state.wi.us. *Award:* Grant for use in freshman, sophomore, junior, or senior year; not renewable. *Award amount:* $250– $1100. *Number of awards:* varies. *Eligibility Requirements:* Applicant must be American Indian/Alaska Native; enrolled or expecting to enroll full- or part-time at a two-year, four-year, or technical institution or university; resident of Wisconsin and studying in Wisconsin. Available to U.S. citizens. *Application Requirements:*

Application, financial need analysis. **Deadline:** continuous.

Contact Sandra Thomas, Program Coordinator, Wisconsin Higher Educational Aid Board, PO Box 7885, Madison, WI 53707-7885. *E-mail:* sandy.thomas@wi.gov. *Phone:* 608-266-0888. *Fax:* 608-267-2808. *Web site:* http://www.heab.wi.gov.

WYOMING

Douvas Memorial Scholarship. Available to Wyoming residents who are first-generation Americans. Must be between 18 and 22 years old. Must be used at any Wyoming public institution of higher education for study in freshman year. *Award:* Scholarship for use in freshman year; not renewable. *Award amount:* $500. *Number of awards:* 1. *Eligibility Requirements:* Applicant must be age 18-22; enrolled or expecting to enroll full- or part-time at a two-year or four-year institution or university; resident of Wyoming and studying in Wyoming. Available to U.S. citizens. *Application Requirements:* Application. **Deadline:** March 24.

Contact Gerry Maas, Director, Health and Safety, Wyoming Department of Education, 2300 Capitol Avenue, Hathaway Building, 2nd Floor, Cheyenne, WY 82002-0050. *E-mail:* gmaas@educ.state.wy.us. *Phone:* 307-777-6282. *Fax:* 307-777-6234.

Hathaway Scholarship. Scholarship for Wyoming students to pursue postsecondary education within the state. Award ranges from $1000 to $1600. Deadline varies. *Award:* Scholarship for use in freshman, sophomore, junior, or senior year; not renewable. *Award amount:* $1000–$1600. *Number of awards:* 1. *Eligibility Requirements:* Applicant must be enrolled or expecting to enroll full-time at a two-year or four-year institution or university; resident of Wyoming and studying in Wyoming. Available to U.S. citizens. *Application Requirements:* Application. **Deadline:** varies.

Contact Kay Post, Director, Wyoming Department of Education, 2020 Grand Avenue, Suite 500, Laramie, WY 82070. *E-mail:* kpost@educ.state.wy.us. *Phone:* 307-777-5599.

Superior Student in Education Scholarship-Wyoming. Scholarship available each year to sixteen new Wyoming high school graduates who plan to teach in Wyoming. The award covers costs of undergraduate tuition at the University of Wyoming or any Wyoming community college. *Academic Fields/Career Goals:* Education. *Award:* Scholarship for use in freshman, sophomore, junior, or senior year; renewable. *Award amount:* $1000–

$1000. *Number of awards:* 16–16. *Eligibility Requirements:* Applicant must be high school student; planning to enroll or expecting to enroll full-time at a two-year or four-year institution or university; resident of Wyoming and studying in Wyoming. Applicant must have 3.0 GPA or higher. Available to U.S. citizens. *Application Requirements:* Application, references, test scores, transcript. **Deadline:** October 31.

Contact Tammy Mack, Assistant Director, Scholarships, State of Wyoming, Administered by University of Wyoming, Student Financial Aid Department 3335, 1000 East University Avenue, Laramie, WY 82071-3335. *E-mail:* westmack@uwyo.edu. *Phone:* 307-766-2412. *Fax:* 307-766-3800. *Web site:* http://www.uwyo.edu/scholarships.

Vietnam Veterans Award-Wyoming. Scholarship available to Wyoming residents who served in the armed forces between August 5, 1964 and May 7, 1975, and received a Vietnam service medal. *Award:* Scholarship for use in freshman, sophomore, junior, or senior year; renewable. *Award amount:* varies. *Number of awards:* varies. *Eligibility Requirements:* Applicant must be enrolled or expecting to enroll full- or part-time at a two-year or four-year institution or university and resident of Wyoming. Available to U.S. citizens. Applicant or parent must meet one or more of the following requirements: general military experience; retired from active duty; disabled or killed as a result of military service; prisoner of war; or missing in action. *Application Requirements:* Application. **Deadline:** continuous.

Contact Tammy Mack, Assistant Director, Scholarships, State of Wyoming, Administered by University of Wyoming, Student Financial Aid Department 3335, 1000 East University Avenue, Laramie, WY 82071-3335. *E-mail:* westmack@uwyo.edu. *Phone:* 307-766-2412. *Fax:* 307-766-3800. *Web site:* http://www.uwyo.edu/scholarships.

Indexes

Non-Need Scholarships for Undergraduates

Academic Interests/ Achievements

Agriculture

Abilene Christian University, TX
Angelo State University, TX
Arkansas State University—Jonesboro, AR
Arkansas Tech University, AR
Auburn University, AL
Austin Peay State University, TN
Berry College, GA
California Polytechnic State University, San Luis Obispo, CA
California State Polytechnic University, Pomona, CA
California State University, Chico, CA
California State University, Fresno, CA
California State University, Stanislaus, CA
Cameron University, OK
Clemson University, SC
Dickinson State University, ND
Dordt College, IA
Eastern Michigan University, MI
Eastern New Mexico University, NM
Ferris State University, MI
Florida Agricultural and Mechanical University, FL
Florida Southern College, FL
Fort Lewis College, CO
Fort Valley State University, GA
Illinois State University, IL
Iowa State University of Science and Technology, IA
Kentucky State University, KY
Langston University, OK
Lincoln University, MO
Louisiana State University and Agricultural and Mechanical College, LA
Louisiana Tech University, LA
Lubbock Christian University, TX
Michigan State University, MI
Mississippi State University, MS
Montana State University, MT
Montana State University–Northern, MT
Morehead State University, KY
Murray State University, KY
New Mexico State University, NM
North Carolina State University, NC
Northwestern Oklahoma State University, OK
The Ohio State University, OH
Oklahoma Panhandle State University, OK
Oklahoma State University, OK
Purdue University, IN
Sam Houston State University, TX
South Dakota State University, SD
Southeastern Louisiana University, LA
Southeast Missouri State University, MO

Southern Arkansas University–Magnolia, AR
Southern Illinois University Carbondale, IL
Southwest Minnesota State University, MN
State University of New York College of Environmental Science and Forestry, NY
Stephen F. Austin State University, TX
Sul Ross State University, TX
Tennessee Technological University, TN
Texas A&M University, TX
Texas A&M University–Commerce, TX
Texas Christian University, TX
Texas State University–San Marcos, TX
Texas Tech University, TX
The University of Arizona, AZ
University of California, Davis, CA
University of California, Riverside, CA
University of Central Missouri, MO
University of Connecticut, CT
University of Delaware, DE
University of Florida, FL
University of Georgia, GA
University of Idaho, ID
University of Illinois at Urbana–Champaign, IL
University of Kentucky, KY
University of Louisiana at Monroe, LA
University of Maryland, College Park, MD
University of Massachusetts Amherst, MA
University of Minnesota, Crookston, MN
University of Minnesota, Twin Cities Campus, MN
University of Missouri, MO
University of Nebraska–Lincoln, NE
University of New Hampshire, NH
The University of Tennessee, TN
The University of Tennessee at Martin, TN
The University of Texas at San Antonio, TX
University of Vermont, VT
The University of Virginia's College at Wise, VA
University of Wisconsin–River Falls, WI
University of Wisconsin–Stevens Point, WI
University of Wyoming, WY
Utah State University, UT
Vermont Technical College, VT
Washington State University, WA
Western Illinois University, IL
Western Kentucky University, KY
West Virginia University, WV

Architecture

Arizona State University, AZ
Auburn University, AL
Ball State University, IN
Boston Architectural College, MA
California College of the Arts, CA
California Polytechnic State University, San Luis Obispo, CA

California State Polytechnic University, Pomona, CA
City College of the City University of New York, NY
Clemson University, SC
Cooper Union for the Advancement of Science and Art, NY
Drury University, MO
Eastern Michigan University, MI
Ferris State University, MI
Georgia Institute of Technology, GA
Hampton University, VA
Illinois Institute of Technology, IL
Iowa State University of Science and Technology, IA
James Madison University, VA
Kent State University, OH
Lawrence Technological University, MI
Louisiana State University and Agricultural and Mechanical College, LA
Louisiana Tech University, LA
Miami University, OH
Mississippi State University, MS
Montana State University, MT
Montana State University–Northern, MT
New Jersey Institute of Technology, NJ
The Ohio State University, OH
Oklahoma State University, OK
Polytechnic University of Puerto Rico, PR
Portland State University, OR
Robert Morris University Illinois, IL
Savannah College of Art and Design, GA
Southeastern Louisiana University, LA
Southern Illinois University Carbondale, IL
State University of New York College of Environmental Science and Forestry, NY
Texas A&M University, TX
Texas Tech University, TX
The University of Arizona, AZ
University of Colorado at Boulder, CO
University of Florida, FL
University of Idaho, ID
University of Illinois at Chicago, IL
University of Illinois at Urbana–Champaign, IL
The University of Kansas, KS
University of Kentucky, KY
University of Maryland, College Park, MD
University of Massachusetts Amherst, MA
University of Miami, FL
University of Michigan, MI
University of Minnesota, Twin Cities Campus, MN
University of Nebraska–Lincoln, NE
University of Nevada, Las Vegas, NV
The University of North Carolina at Charlotte, NC

University of Oklahoma, OK
University of Oregon, OR
The University of Tennessee, TN
The University of Texas at Arlington, TX
The University of Texas at San Antonio, TX
University of Washington, WA
University of Wisconsin–Stevens Point, WI
Utah State University, UT
Washington State University, WA
Washington University in St. Louis, MO
West Virginia University, WV
Woodbury University, CA

Area/Ethnic Studies

Arizona State University, AZ
Arkansas State University—Jonesboro, AR
Birmingham-Southern College, AL
California State University, Chico, CA
California State University, Fresno, CA
California State University, Stanislaus, CA
City College of the City University of New
  York, NY
The College of New Rochelle, NY
Eastern Washington University, WA
Fort Lewis College, CO
Furman University, SC
Indiana University of Pennsylvania, PA
Iowa State University of Science and
  Technology, IA
Kean University, NJ
Kent State University, OH
Mississippi State University, MS
Montana State University, MT
Northern Arizona University, AZ
Oakland University, MI
The Ohio State University, OH
Ohio University, OH
Ohio University–Chillicothe, OH
Ohio University–Eastern, OH
Ohio University–Lancaster, OH
Ohio University–Southern Campus, OH
Ohio University–Zanesville, OH
Oklahoma State University, OK
Ouachita Baptist University, AR
Portland State University, OR
Purchase College, State University of New
  York, NY
The Richard Stockton College of New
  Jersey, NJ
Saint Louis University, MO
San Diego State University, CA
Sonoma State University, CA
South Dakota State University, SD
Southern Illinois University Carbondale, IL
State University of New York at
  Binghamton, NY
State University of New York at Oswego, NY
State University of New York at
  Plattsburgh, NY
State University of New York College at
  Geneseo, NY
Stetson University, FL
Stony Brook University, State University of
  New York, NY
The University of Alabama, AL
University of California, Davis, CA
University of California, Riverside, CA
University of Central Missouri, MO
University of Colorado at Boulder, CO
University of Illinois at Urbana–
  Champaign, IL
The University of Kansas, KS
University of Kentucky, KY

University of Miami, FL
University of Michigan, MI
University of Minnesota, Twin Cities
  Campus, MN
University of Missouri, MO
University of Oklahoma, OK
University of South Carolina, SC
The University of Texas at San Antonio, TX
University of Vermont, VT
University of Wisconsin–Green Bay, WI
University of Wisconsin–La Crosse, WI
University of Wisconsin–River Falls, WI
Warner Pacific College, OR
Washington State University, WA
Wayne State University, MI
West Virginia University, WV
Wichita State University, KS
Wright State University, OH

Biological Sciences

Abilene Christian University, TX
Alaska Pacific University, AK
Alderson-Broaddus College, WV
Alfred University, NY
Angelo State University, TX
Arizona State University, AZ
Arkansas State University—Jonesboro, AR
Arkansas Tech University, AR
Armstrong Atlantic State University, GA
Auburn University, AL
Augsburg College, MN
Augustana College, IL
Augustana College, SD
Austin College, TX
Austin Peay State University, TN
Averett University, VA
Bard College, NY
Barton College, NC
Belhaven University, MS
Bellarmine University, KY
Bethel College, IN
Bethel College, KS
Biola University, CA
Birmingham-Southern College, AL
Black Hills State University, SD
Bloomfield College, NJ
Bloomsburg University of Pennsylvania, PA
Blue Mountain College, MS
Boise State University, ID
Bowie State University, MD
Bowling Green State University, OH
Brenau University, GA
Brescia University, KY
Brevard College, NC
Briar Cliff University, IA
Bryan College, TN
Buena Vista University, IA
Butler University, IN
California Lutheran University, CA
California Polytechnic State University,
  San Luis Obispo, CA
California State Polytechnic University,
  Pomona, CA
California State University, Chico, CA
California State University, Fresno, CA
California State University,
  San Bernardino, CA
California State University, Stanislaus, CA
Calvin College, MI
Cameron University, OK
Campbellsville University, KY
Carroll University, WI
Carson-Newman College, TN

Carthage College, WI
Case Western Reserve University, OH
Centenary College of Louisiana, LA
Central College, IA
Central Michigan University, MI
Chapman University, CA
Chatham University, PA
Christopher Newport University, VA
The Citadel, The Military College of South
  Carolina, SC
City College of the City University of New
  York, NY
Clarkson University, NY
Clemson University, SC
Cleveland State University, OH
Coastal Carolina University, SC
Coe College, IA
The College at Brockport, State University of
  New York, NY
College of Charleston, SC
The College of New Rochelle, NY
College of Saint Mary, NE
College of Staten Island of the City University
  of New York, NY
The Colorado College, CO
Columbia College, MO
Columbus State University, GA
Concordia University Chicago, IL
Concordia University, Nebraska, NE
Concordia University Texas, TX
Dalton State College, GA
Davidson College, NC
Defiance College, OH
Delta State University, MS
DePauw University, IN
DeSales University, PA
Dickinson State University, ND
Dordt College, IA
Drury University, MO
D'Youville College, NY
East Carolina University, NC
Eastern Michigan University, MI
Eastern New Mexico University, NM
Eastern Washington University, WA
East Stroudsburg University of
  Pennsylvania, PA
East Texas Baptist University, TX
Edinboro University of Pennsylvania, PA
Elizabethtown College, PA
Elmhurst College, IL
Elon University, NC
Emmanuel College, MA
Emporia State University, KS
Erskine College, SC
Fairfield University, CT
Ferris State University, MI
Fitchburg State College, MA
Florida Gulf Coast University, FL
Florida International University, FL
Florida Southern College, FL
Fordham University, NY
Fort Lewis College, CO
Framingham State College, MA
Francis Marion University, SC
Frostburg State University, MD
Furman University, SC
Gannon University, PA
Gardner-Webb University, NC
George Fox University, OR
Georgia Institute of Technology, GA
Georgian Court University, NJ
Georgia Southern University, GA
Glenville State College, WV

Non-Need Scholarships for Undergraduates
Academic Interests/Achievements

Green Mountain College, VT
Greenville College, IL
Grove City College, PA
Guilford College, NC
Hamline University, MN
Hampden-Sydney College, VA
Hampton University, VA
Hardin-Simmons University, TX
Harrisburg University of Science and
  Technology, PA
Hawai'i Pacific University, HI
Henderson State University, AR
High Point University, NC
Howard Payne University, TX
Huntingdon College, AL
Huntington University, IN
Idaho State University, ID
Illinois State University, IL
Indiana University of Pennsylvania, PA
Iowa State University of Science and
  Technology, IA
Jacksonville State University, AL
James Madison University, VA
Jefferson College of Health Sciences, VA
John Carroll University, OH
Judson College, AL
Juniata College, PA
Kean University, NJ
Kennesaw State University, GA
Kent State University, OH
King's College, PA
Kutztown University of Pennsylvania, PA
LaGrange College, GA
Lake Erie College, OH
Lake Forest College, IL
Lebanon Valley College, PA
Lees-McRae College, NC
Lee University, TN
Lewis-Clark State College, ID
Limestone College, SC
Lincoln University, PA
Lindenwood University, MO
Lindsey Wilson College, KY
Lipscomb University, TN
Lock Haven University of Pennsylvania, PA
Long Island University, C.W. Post
  Campus, NY
Longwood University, VA
Louisiana State University and Agricultural
  and Mechanical College, LA
Louisiana Tech University, LA
Lycoming College, PA
MacMurray College, IL
Maine Maritime Academy, ME
Malone University, OH
Manhattan College, NY
Mansfield University of Pennsylvania, PA
Marquette University, WI
Marymount University, VA
Maryville University of Saint Louis, MO
Massachusetts College of Liberal Arts, MA
The Master's College and Seminary, CA
McKendree University, IL
McMurry University, TX
Mercer University, GA
Meredith College, NC
Mesa State College, CO
Michigan State University, MI
Midwestern State University, TX
Millersville University of Pennsylvania, PA
Millikin University, IL
Mills College, CA
Minnesota State University Moorhead, MN

Mississippi State University, MS
Mississippi University for Women, MS
Missouri University of Science and
  Technology, MO
Missouri Valley College, MO
Molloy College, NY
Montana State University, MT
Montana State University Billings, MT
Montana State University–Northern, MT
Montclair State University, NJ
Moravian College, PA
Morehead State University, KY
Mount St. Mary's College, CA
Murray State University, KY
Muskingum University, OH
Newberry College, SC
New England College, NH
New Jersey Institute of Technology, NJ
New Mexico State University, NM
North Carolina State University, NC
North Central College, IL
Northeastern Illinois University, IL
Northeastern State University, OK
Northern Arizona University, AZ
Northern Illinois University, IL
Northern Kentucky University, KY
Northern Michigan University, MI
Northern State University, SD
North Georgia College & State University, GA
North Greenville University, SC
Northwestern Oklahoma State University, OK
Northwestern State University of
  Louisiana, LA
Northwest Nazarene University, ID
Oakland University, MI
Ohio Northern University, OH
The Ohio State University, OH
Ohio University, OH
Ohio University–Chillicothe, OH
Ohio University–Eastern, OH
Ohio University–Lancaster, OH
Ohio University–Southern Campus, OH
Ohio University–Zanesville, OH
Oklahoma Panhandle State University, OK
Oklahoma State University, OK
Oklahoma Wesleyan University, OK
Old Dominion University, VA
Oral Roberts University, OK
Ouachita Baptist University, AR
Pace University, NY
Pacific University, OR
Piedmont College, GA
Pittsburg State University, KS
Point Loma Nazarene University, CA
Purchase College, State University of New
  York, NY
Quincy University, IL
Randolph College, VA
Regis University, CO
The Richard Stockton College of New
  Jersey, NJ
Ripon College, WI
Rivier College, NH
Rochester Institute of Technology, NY
Rockford College, IL
Rockhurst University, MO
Rocky Mountain College, MT
Sacred Heart University, CT
Saginaw Valley State University, MI
St. Edward's University, TX
Saint Francis University, PA
St. John Fisher College, NY
St. John's University, NY

Saint Louis University, MO
Salisbury University, MD
Samford University, AL
Sam Houston State University, TX
San Diego State University, CA
Savannah State University, GA
Schreiner University, TX
Seton Hill University, PA
Shepherd University, WV
Shippensburg University of Pennsylvania, PA
Siena College, NY
Skidmore College, NY
Slippery Rock University of Pennsylvania, PA
Sonoma State University, CA
South Dakota State University, SD
Southeastern Louisiana University, LA
Southeastern Oklahoma State University, OK
Southeast Missouri State University, MO
Southern Illinois University Carbondale, IL
Southern Nazarene University, OK
Southwestern College, KS
Southwestern Oklahoma State University, OK
Southwest Minnesota State University, MN
State University of New York at
  Binghamton, NY
State University of New York at Fredonia, NY
State University of New York at Oswego, NY
State University of New York at
  Plattsburgh, NY
State University of New York College at
  Geneseo, NY
State University of New York College at Old
  Westbury, NY
State University of New York College at
  Oneonta, NY
State University of New York College at
  Potsdam, NY
State University of New York College of
  Environmental Science and Forestry, NY
Stephen F. Austin State University, TX
Stetson University, FL
Stony Brook University, State University of
  New York, NY
Sul Ross State University, TX
Tabor College, KS
Tennessee Technological University, TN
Tennessee Wesleyan College, TN
Texas A&M University, TX
Texas Christian University, TX
Texas Lutheran University, TX
Texas Tech University, TX
Texas Woman's University, TX
Thiel College, PA
Thomas More College, KY
Towson University, MD
Trevecca Nazarene University, TN
Truman State University, MO
The University of Akron, OH
The University of Alabama, AL
The University of Alabama in Huntsville, AL
University of Alaska Anchorage, AK
University of Alaska Fairbanks, AK
The University of Arizona, AZ
University of California, Davis, CA
University of California, Irvine, CA
University of California, Riverside, CA
University of California, San Diego, CA
University of Central Missouri, MO
University of Central Oklahoma, OK
University of Colorado at Boulder, CO
University of Connecticut, CT
University of Delaware, DE
University of Denver, CO

University of Evansville, IN
University of Great Falls, MT
University of Houston–Clear Lake, TX
University of Idaho, ID
University of Illinois at Urbana–
  Champaign, IL
The University of Kansas, KS
University of Kentucky, KY
University of Louisiana at Monroe, LA
University of Louisville, KY
University of Maine at Fort Kent, ME
University of Mary Hardin-Baylor, TX
University of Maryland, Baltimore
  County, MD
University of Maryland, College Park, MD
University of Mary Washington, VA
University of Massachusetts Amherst, MA
University of Memphis, TN
University of Miami, FL
University of Michigan, MI
University of Michigan–Dearborn, MI
University of Michigan–Flint, MI
University of Minnesota, Crookston, MN
University of Minnesota, Twin Cities
  Campus, MN
University of Mississippi, MS
University of Missouri, MO
University of Missouri–St. Louis, MO
The University of Montana Western, MT
University of Montevallo, AL
University of Nebraska at Omaha, NE
University of Nebraska–Lincoln, NE
University of Nevada, Las Vegas, NV
University of New Orleans, LA
The University of North Carolina at
  Asheville, NC
The University of North Carolina at
  Greensboro, NC
The University of North Carolina
  Wilmington, NC
University of North Dakota, ND
University of Northern Colorado, CO
University of Northern Iowa, IA
University of Oklahoma, OK
University of Oregon, OR
University of Pittsburgh at Bradford, PA
University of Pittsburgh at Johnstown, PA
University of Portland, OR
University of Puget Sound, WA
University of Richmond, VA
University of St. Francis, IL
University of St. Thomas, MN
University of South Carolina, SC
University of South Carolina Aiken, SC
The University of South Dakota, SD
University of Southern Indiana, IN
The University of Tampa, FL
The University of Tennessee at
  Chattanooga, TN
The University of Tennessee at Martin, TN
The University of Texas at Arlington, TX
The University of Texas at Brownsville, TX
The University of Texas at Dallas, TX
The University of Texas at El Paso, TX
The University of Texas at San Antonio, TX
The University of Texas–Pan American, TX
University of the Ozarks, AR
University of the Southwest, NM
The University of Toledo, OH
University of Tulsa, OK
The University of Virginia's College at
  Wise, VA
University of West Florida, FL

University of West Georgia, GA
University of Wisconsin–Eau Claire, WI
University of Wisconsin–Green Bay, WI
University of Wisconsin–La Crosse, WI
University of Wisconsin–Parkside, WI
University of Wisconsin–River Falls, WI
University of Wisconsin–Stevens Point, WI
University of Wisconsin–Superior, WI
University of Wisconsin–Whitewater, WI
Utah State University, UT
Valdosta State University, GA
Valley City State University, ND
Virginia Commonwealth University, VA
Virginia Military Institute, VA
Warner Pacific College, OR
Wartburg College, IA
Washburn University, KS
Washington State University, WA
Washington University in St. Louis, MO
Wayland Baptist University, TX
Waynesburg University, PA
Wayne State College, NE
Wayne State University, MI
Webster University, MO
Wesleyan College, GA
Western Carolina University, NC
Western Illinois University, IL
Western Kentucky University, KY
Western Oregon University, OR
Western Washington University, WA
Westminster College, UT
West Virginia University, WV
Wheaton College, IL
Whitworth University, WA
Wichita State University, KS
Widener University, PA
Williams Baptist College, AR
Wilson College, PA
Wright State University, OH
Xavier University of Louisiana, LA
York College, NE
Youngstown State University, OH

Business

Abilene Christian University, TX
Adrian College, MI
Alaska Pacific University, AK
Albion College, MI
Alderson-Broaddus College, WV
Alfred University, NY
Alliant International University, CA
Angelo State University, TX
Aquinas College, TN
Arizona State University, AZ
Arkansas State University—Jonesboro, AR
Arkansas Tech University, AR
Atlantic Union College, MA
Auburn University, AL
Augsburg College, MN
Augustana College, IL
Augustana College, SD
Austin College, TX
Austin Peay State University, TN
Averett University, VA
Ball State University, IN
Barton College, NC
Baylor University, TX
Belhaven University, MS
Bellarmine University, KY
Bethel College, IN
Birmingham-Southern College, AL
Black Hills State University, SD
Bloomfield College, NJ

Bloomsburg University of Pennsylvania, PA
Blue Mountain College, MS
Boise State University, ID
Bowie State University, MD
Bowling Green State University, OH
Brenau University, GA
Brescia University, KY
Brevard College, NC
Briar Cliff University, IA
Bryan College, TN
Bucknell University, PA
Buena Vista University, IA
Butler University, IN
California Lutheran University, CA
California Polytechnic State University,
  San Luis Obispo, CA
California State Polytechnic University,
  Pomona, CA
California State University, Chico, CA
California State University, Fresno, CA
California State University, Fullerton, CA
California State University, Monterey Bay, CA
California State University, Northridge, CA
California State University,
  San Bernardino, CA
California State University, Stanislaus, CA
Calvin College, MI
Cameron University, OK
Campbellsville University, KY
Carroll University, WI
Carson-Newman College, TN
Carthage College, WI
Case Western Reserve University, OH
Cedar Crest College, PA
Centenary College of Louisiana, LA
Central College, IA
Central Michigan University, MI
Chatham University, PA
Christopher Newport University, VA
The Citadel, The Military College of South
  Carolina, SC
Clarkson University, NY
Clearwater Christian College, FL
Cleary University, MI
Clemson University, SC
Cleveland State University, OH
Coastal Carolina University, SC
Coe College, IA
The College at Brockport, State University of
  New York, NY
College of Charleston, SC
The College of New Rochelle, NY
The College of Saint Rose, NY
College of Staten Island of the City University
  of New York, NY
Colorado School of Mines, CO
Columbia College, MO
Columbia College Chicago, IL
Columbus State University, GA
Concordia University, MI
Concordia University Chicago, IL
Concordia University, Nebraska, NE
Concordia University Texas, TX
Concord University, WV
Cornerstone University, MI
Creighton University, NE
Dakota State University, SD
Dallas Baptist University, TX
Dalton State College, GA
Davidson College, NC
Defiance College, OH
Delta State University, MS
DePauw University, IN

Non-Need Scholarships for Undergraduates
Academic Interests/Achievements

DeSales University, PA
Dickinson State University, ND
Dordt College, IA
Dowling College, NY
Drury University, MO
D'Youville College, NY
East Carolina University, NC
Eastern Michigan University, MI
Eastern New Mexico University, NM
Eastern Washington University, WA
East Stroudsburg University of
  Pennsylvania, PA
East Texas Baptist University, TX
ECPI College of Technology, VA
ECPI Technical College, VA
Edinboro University of Pennsylvania, PA
Elizabethtown College, PA
Elmhurst College, IL
Elon University, NC
Emporia State University, KS
Endicott College, MA
Erskine College, SC
Evangel University, MO
Everest University, FL
Fairfield University, CT
Felician College, NJ
Ferris State University, MI
Fitchburg State College, MA
Five Towns College, NY
Flagler College, FL
Florida Agricultural and Mechanical
  University, FL
Florida Atlantic University, FL
Florida Gulf Coast University, FL
Florida International University, FL
Florida Southern College, FL
Fordham University, NY
Fort Lewis College, CO
Fort Valley State University, GA
Francis Marion University, SC
Fresno Pacific University, CA
Frostburg State University, MD
Furman University, SC
Gannon University, PA
Gardner-Webb University, NC
Georgia College & State University, GA
Georgian Court University, NJ
Georgia Southern University, GA
Glenville State College, WV
Goldey-Beacom College, DE
Gonzaga University, WA
Grace College, IN
Grace University, NE
Grand Valley State University, MI
Green Mountain College, VT
Greenville College, IL
Grove City College, PA
Hampton University, VA
Hardin-Simmons University, TX
Harrisburg University of Science and
  Technology, PA
Hawai'i Pacific University, HI
High Point University, NC
Hillsdale Free Will Baptist College, OK
Howard Payne University, TX
Humphreys College, CA
Huntington University, IN
Husson University, ME
Idaho State University, ID
Illinois Institute of Technology, IL
Illinois State University, IL
Indiana University of Pennsylvania, PA

Iowa State University of Science and
  Technology, IA
Jacksonville State University, AL
Jacksonville University, FL
James Madison University, VA
John Carroll University, OH
Johnson Bible College, TN
Juniata College, PA
Kean University, NJ
Kennesaw State University, GA
Kent State University, OH
Kettering University, MI
King's College, PA
Kutztown University of Pennsylvania, PA
Lake Erie College, OH
Lakeland College, WI
Langston University, OK
Lawrence Technological University, MI
Lee University, TN
Lehigh University, PA
Lewis-Clark State College, ID
Limestone College, SC
Lincoln University, PA
Lindenwood University, MO
Lindsey Wilson College, KY
Lipscomb University, TN
Long Island University, C.W. Post
  Campus, NY
Longwood University, VA
Louisiana State University and Agricultural
  and Mechanical College, LA
Louisiana Tech University, LA
Lubbock Christian University, TX
Lycoming College, PA
Lynn University, FL
Maine Maritime Academy, ME
Malone University, OH
Manchester College, IN
Manhattan College, NY
Marquette University, WI
Marymount University, VA
Maryville University of Saint Louis, MO
Marywood University, PA
Massachusetts College of Liberal Arts, MA
The Master's College and Seminary, CA
McKendree University, IL
McMurry University, TX
Mercer University, GA
Meredith College, NC
Mesa State College, CO
Michigan State University, MI
Midwestern State University, TX
Millersville University of Pennsylvania, PA
Millikin University, IL
Millsaps College, MS
Milwaukee School of Engineering, WI
Minnesota State University Moorhead, MN
Misericordia University, PA
Mississippi State University, MS
Mississippi University for Women, MS
Missouri University of Science and
  Technology, MO
Missouri Valley College, MO
Molloy College, NY
Monmouth University, NJ
Montana State University, MT
Montana State University Billings, MT
Montana State University–Northern, MT
Montana Tech of The University of
  Montana, MT
Montclair State University, NJ
Moravian College, PA
Morehead State University, KY

Morehouse College, GA
Mount Mary College, WI
Murray State University, KY
Newberry College, SC
New England College, NH
New Jersey Institute of Technology, NJ
New Mexico State University, NM
North Carolina State University, NC
North Central College, IL
Northeastern Illinois University, IL
Northeastern State University, OK
Northern Arizona University, AZ
Northern Illinois University, IL
Northern Kentucky University, KY
Northern Michigan University, MI
Northern State University, SD
North Georgia College & State University, GA
Northwestern Oklahoma State University, OK
Northwest Nazarene University, ID
Northwood University, MI
Northwood University, Florida Campus, FL
Northwood University, Texas Campus, TX
Oakland University, MI
Ohio Northern University, OH
The Ohio State University, OH
Ohio University, OH
Ohio University–Chillicothe, OH
Ohio University–Eastern, OH
Ohio University–Lancaster, OH
Ohio University–Southern Campus, OH
Ohio University–Zanesville, OH
Oklahoma Baptist University, OK
Oklahoma City University, OK
Oklahoma Panhandle State University, OK
Oklahoma State University, OK
Oklahoma Wesleyan University, OK
Old Dominion University, VA
Olivet College, MI
Oral Roberts University, OK
Ouachita Baptist University, AR
Pace University, NY
Pacific University, OR
Peirce College, PA
Piedmont College, GA
Pittsburg State University, KS
Plymouth State University, NH
Point Loma Nazarene University, CA
Polytechnic University of Puerto Rico, PR
Portland State University, OR
Providence College, RI
Purdue University North Central, IN
Quincy University, IL
Regent University, VA
The Richard Stockton College of New
  Jersey, NJ
Ripon College, WI
Rivier College, NH
Robert Morris University Illinois, IL
Rochester Institute of Technology, NY
Rockford College, IL
Rockhurst University, MO
Rocky Mountain College, MT
Sacred Heart University, CT
Saginaw Valley State University, MI
St. Bonaventure University, NY
St. Catherine University, MN
St. Edward's University, TX
Saint Francis University, PA
St. John Fisher College, NY
St. John's University, NY
Saint Louis University, MO
Saint Martin's University, WA
Salisbury University, MD

Samford University, AL
Sam Houston State University, TX
San Diego State University, CA
Santa Clara University, CA
Savannah State University, GA
Schreiner University, TX
Seton Hill University, PA
Shenandoah University, VA
Shepherd University, WV
Shippensburg University of Pennsylvania, PA
Siena College, NY
Slippery Rock University of Pennsylvania, PA
Sonoma State University, CA
South Dakota State University, SD
Southeastern Louisiana University, LA
Southeastern Oklahoma State University, OK
Southeast Missouri State University, MO
Southern Adventist University, TN
Southern Arkansas University–Magnolia, AR
Southern Illinois University Carbondale, IL
Southern Illinois University Edwardsville, IL
Southern Nazarene University, OK
Southwestern College, KS
Southwestern Oklahoma State University, OK
Southwestern University, TX
Southwest Minnesota State University, MN
State University of New York at
  Binghamton, NY
State University of New York at Fredonia, NY
State University of New York at New
  Paltz, NY
State University of New York at Oswego, NY
State University of New York at
  Plattsburgh, NY
State University of New York College at
  Geneseo, NY
State University of New York College at
  Oneonta, NY
State University of New York College at
  Potsdam, NY
Stephen F. Austin State University, TX
Stetson University, FL
Stevens-Henager College, ID
Stony Brook University, State University of
  New York, NY
Sul Ross State University, TX
Susquehanna University, PA
Tennessee Technological University, TN
Tennessee Wesleyan College, TN
Texas A&M University, TX
Texas A&M University–Texarkana, TX
Texas Christian University, TX
Texas Lutheran University, TX
Texas State University–San Marcos, TX
Texas Tech University, TX
Texas Woman's University, TX
Thiel College, PA
Thomas More College, KY
Towson University, MD
Trevecca Nazarene University, TN
Trinity Bible College, ND
Trinity Christian College, IL
Truman State University, MO
Union University, TN
The University of Akron, OH
The University of Alabama, AL
The University of Alabama at
  Birmingham, AL
The University of Alabama in Huntsville, AL
University of Alaska Anchorage, AK
The University of Arizona, AZ
University of California, Davis, CA
University of California, Irvine, CA

University of California, Riverside, CA
University of California, San Diego, CA
University of Central Missouri, MO
University of Central Oklahoma, OK
University of Colorado at Boulder, CO
University of Connecticut, CT
University of Dallas, TX
University of Dayton, OH
University of Delaware, DE
University of Denver, CO
University of Evansville, IN
University of Florida, FL
University of Georgia, GA
University of Great Falls, MT
University of Hawaii at Hilo, HI
University of Houston–Clear Lake, TX
University of Houston–Downtown, TX
University of Idaho, ID
University of Illinois at Chicago, IL
University of Illinois at Urbana–
  Champaign, IL
University of Indianapolis, IN
The University of Iowa, IA
The University of Kansas, KS
University of Kentucky, KY
University of Louisiana at Monroe, LA
University of Louisville, KY
University of Maine at Fort Kent, ME
University of Mary Hardin-Baylor, TX
University of Maryland, College Park, MD
University of Mary Washington, VA
University of Massachusetts Amherst, MA
University of Memphis, TN
University of Miami, FL
University of Michigan, MI
University of Michigan–Dearborn, MI
University of Michigan–Flint, MI
University of Minnesota, Twin Cities
  Campus, MN
University of Mississippi, MS
University of Missouri, MO
University of Missouri–St. Louis, MO
The University of Montana Western, MT
University of Nebraska at Omaha, NE
University of Nebraska–Lincoln, NE
University of Nevada, Las Vegas, NV
University of New Hampshire, NH
University of New Orleans, LA
The University of North Carolina at
  Asheville, NC
The University of North Carolina at Chapel
  Hill, NC
The University of North Carolina at
  Charlotte, NC
The University of North Carolina at
  Greensboro, NC
The University of North Carolina at
  Pembroke, NC
The University of North Carolina
  Wilmington, NC
University of North Dakota, ND
University of Northern Colorado, CO
University of Northern Iowa, IA
University of North Florida, FL
University of Oklahoma, OK
University of Oregon, OR
University of Pittsburgh at Bradford, PA
University of Pittsburgh at Johnstown, PA
University of Portland, OR
University of Puget Sound, WA
University of St. Thomas, MN
University of South Alabama, AL
University of South Carolina, SC

University of South Carolina Aiken, SC
The University of South Dakota, SD
University of Southern Indiana, IN
The University of Tennessee, TN
The University of Tennessee at
  Chattanooga, TN
The University of Tennessee at Martin, TN
The University of Texas at Arlington, TX
The University of Texas at Brownsville, TX
The University of Texas at Dallas, TX
The University of Texas at El Paso, TX
The University of Texas at San Antonio, TX
The University of Texas–Pan American, TX
University of the Ozarks, AR
University of the Southwest, NM
The University of Toledo, OH
University of Tulsa, OK
University of Vermont, VT
The University of Virginia's College at
  Wise, VA
University of Washington, WA
University of West Florida, FL
University of West Georgia, GA
University of Wisconsin–Eau Claire, WI
University of Wisconsin–Green Bay, WI
University of Wisconsin–La Crosse, WI
University of Wisconsin–Parkside, WI
University of Wisconsin–River Falls, WI
University of Wisconsin–Stevens Point, WI
University of Wisconsin–Stout, WI
University of Wisconsin–Superior, WI
University of Wisconsin–Whitewater, WI
University of Wyoming, WY
Utah State University, UT
Valdosta State University, GA
Valley City State University, ND
Valparaiso University, IN
Virginia Commonwealth University, VA
Virginia Military Institute, VA
Wartburg College, IA
Washburn University, KS
Washington & Jefferson College, PA
Washington State University, WA
Washington University in St. Louis, MO
Wayland Baptist University, TX
Waynesburg University, PA
Wayne State College, NE
Wayne State University, MI
Webber International University, FL
Webster University, MO
Wesleyan College, GA
West Chester University of Pennsylvania, PA
Western Carolina University, NC
Western Illinois University, IL
Western Kentucky University, KY
Western Oregon University, OR
Western Washington University, WA
West Liberty University, WV
Westminster College, UT
West Virginia University, WV
Wheaton College, IL
Wichita State University, KS
Widener University, PA
Williams Baptist College, AR
Wilson College, PA
Wright State University, OH
Xavier University of Louisiana, LA
York College, NE
Youngstown State University, OH

Communication

Abilene Christian University, TX
Adelphi University, NY

Non-Need Scholarships for Undergraduates
Academic Interests/Achievements

Albion College, MI
Alderson-Broaddus College, WV
Alfred University, NY
Alliant International University, CA
Angelo State University, TX
Arizona State University, AZ
Arkansas State University—Jonesboro, AR
Auburn University, AL
Augsburg College, MN
Augustana College, IL
Augustana College, SD
Austin College, TX
Austin Peay State University, TN
Ball State University, IN
Barton College, NC
Baylor University, TX
Belhaven University, MS
Bethel College, IN
Biola University, CA
Birmingham-Southern College, AL
Black Hills State University, SD
Bloomsburg University of Pennsylvania, PA
Boise State University, ID
Bowie State University, MD
Bowling Green State University, OH
Brenau University, GA
Briar Cliff University, IA
Bryan College, TN
Butler University, IN
California Lutheran University, CA
California Polytechnic State University,
  San Luis Obispo, CA
California State University, Chico, CA
California State University, Fresno, CA
California State University, Fullerton, CA
California State University, Northridge, CA
California State University, Stanislaus, CA
Calvin College, MI
Cameron University, OK
Campbellsville University, KY
Case Western Reserve University, OH
Cedar Crest College, PA
Centenary College of Louisiana, LA
Central College, IA
Central Michigan University, MI
Chatham University, PA
Christopher Newport University, VA
City College of the City University of New
  York, NY
Clarkson University, NY
Clemson University, SC
Cleveland State University, OH
The College at Brockport, State University of
  New York, NY
College of Charleston, SC
The College of New Rochelle, NY
Columbia College Chicago, IL
Columbus State University, GA
Concordia University Chicago, IL
Concordia University, Nebraska, NE
Concord University, WV
Dakota State University, SD
Dallas Baptist University, TX
Defiance College, OH
DePauw University, IN
DeSales University, PA
Dickinson State University, ND
Dordt College, IA
Drury University, MO
East Carolina University, NC
Eastern Michigan University, MI
Eastern New Mexico University, NM
Eastern Washington University, WA

East Stroudsburg University of
  Pennsylvania, PA
East Texas Baptist University, TX
Edinboro University of Pennsylvania, PA
Elizabethtown College, PA
Elmhurst College, IL
Elon University, NC
Emporia State University, KS
Evangel University, MO
Ferris State University, MI
Fitchburg State College, MA
Flagler College, FL
Florida International University, FL
Florida Southern College, FL
Fordham University, NY
Fort Lewis College, CO
Frostburg State University, MD
Furman University, SC
Gardner-Webb University, NC
Georgia Southern University, GA
Grand Valley State University, MI
Grove City College, PA
Hamline University, MN
Hampton University, VA
Harding University, AR
Hardin-Simmons University, TX
Hawai'i Pacific University, HI
Hofstra University, NY
Howard Payne University, TX
Huntington University, IN
Idaho State University, ID
Illinois State University, IL
Indiana University of Pennsylvania, PA
Iowa State University of Science and
  Technology, IA
Ithaca College, NY
Jacksonville State University, AL
John Carroll University, OH
Johnson Bible College, TN
Juniata College, PA
Kean University, NJ
Kennesaw State University, GA
Kent State University, OH
King's College, PA
Kutztown University of Pennsylvania, PA
Lee University, TN
Lehigh University, PA
Limestone College, SC
Lincoln University, PA
Lindenwood University, MO
Lipscomb University, TN
Lock Haven University of Pennsylvania, PA
Long Island University, Brooklyn
  Campus, NY
Louisiana State University and Agricultural
  and Mechanical College, LA
Lubbock Christian University, TX
Lycoming College, PA
Lynn University, FL
Malone University, OH
Mansfield University of Pennsylvania, PA
Marquette University, WI
Marywood University, PA
Massachusetts College of Liberal Arts, MA
McMurry University, TX
Mesa State College, CO
Michigan State University, MI
Midwestern State University, TX
Millersville University of Pennsylvania, PA
Millikin University, IL
Milwaukee School of Engineering, WI
Minnesota State University Moorhead, MN
Mississippi State University, MS

Mississippi University for Women, MS
Missouri Valley College, MO
Molloy College, NY
Monmouth University, NJ
Montana State University, MT
Montana State University Billings, MT
Montclair State University, NJ
Morehead State University, KY
Mount Mary College, WI
Murray State University, KY
Newberry College, SC
New England College, NH
New England School of Communications, ME
New Jersey Institute of Technology, NJ
New Mexico State University, NM
North Central College, IL
Northeastern Illinois University, IL
Northeastern State University, OK
Northern Arizona University, AZ
Northern Illinois University, IL
Northern Kentucky University, KY
Northern Michigan University, MI
Northern State University, SD
North Greenville University, SC
Northwestern Oklahoma State University, OK
Ohio Northern University, OH
The Ohio State University, OH
Ohio University, OH
Ohio University–Chillicothe, OH
Ohio University–Eastern, OH
Ohio University–Lancaster, OH
Ohio University–Southern Campus, OH
Ohio University–Zanesville, OH
Oklahoma City University, OK
Oklahoma State University, OK
Olivet College, MI
Oral Roberts University, OK
Ouachita Baptist University, AR
Pace University, NY
Pacific University, OR
Pittsburg State University, KS
Plymouth State University, NH
Point Loma Nazarene University, CA
Quincy University, IL
Regent University, VA
Rivier College, NH
Rochester Institute of Technology, NY
Rockhurst University, MO
Rocky Mountain College, MT
St. Edward's University, TX
St. John's University, NY
Saint Louis University, MO
Salisbury University, MD
Samford University, AL
Sam Houston State University, TX
San Diego State University, CA
Seton Hill University, PA
Shepherd University, WV
Shippensburg University of Pennsylvania, PA
Siena College, NY
Slippery Rock University of Pennsylvania, PA
Sonoma State University, CA
South Dakota State University, SD
Southeastern Louisiana University, LA
Southeastern University, FL
Southeast Missouri State University, MO
Southern Adventist University, TN
Southern Illinois University Carbondale, IL
Southern Nazarene University, OK
Southwestern Oklahoma State University, OK
Southwest Minnesota State University, MN
State University of New York at Fredonia, NY

State University of New York at New Paltz, NY
State University of New York at Oswego, NY
State University of New York at Plattsburgh, NY
State University of New York College at Geneseo, NY
State University of New York College at Potsdam, NY
Stephen F. Austin State University, TX
Stetson University, FL
Tabor College, KS
Tennessee Technological University, TN
Tennessee Wesleyan College, TN
Texas Christian University, TX
Texas Tech University, TX
Texas Woman's University, TX
Thomas More College, KY
Towson University, MD
Trevecca Nazarene University, TN
Truman State University, MO
Union University, TN
The University of Akron, OH
The University of Alabama, AL
The University of Alabama at Birmingham, AL
The University of Alabama in Huntsville, AL
University of Alaska Anchorage, AK
University of California, Davis, CA
University of California, San Diego, CA
University of Central Missouri, MO
University of Colorado at Boulder, CO
University of Delaware, DE
University of Denver, CO
University of Evansville, IN
University of Florida, FL
University of Idaho, ID
University of Illinois at Urbana–Champaign, IL
University of Indianapolis, IN
The University of Kansas, KS
University of Kentucky, KY
University of Louisiana at Monroe, LA
University of Maine at Fort Kent, ME
University of Mary Hardin-Baylor, TX
University of Maryland, College Park, MD
University of Massachusetts Amherst, MA
University of Memphis, TN
University of Miami, FL
University of Michigan, MI
University of Michigan–Dearborn, MI
University of Michigan–Flint, MI
University of Minnesota, Twin Cities Campus, MN
University of Mississippi, MS
University of Missouri, MO
University of Missouri–St. Louis, MO
University of Nebraska at Kearney, NE
University of Nebraska at Omaha, NE
University of Nevada, Las Vegas, NV
The University of North Carolina at Asheville, NC
The University of North Carolina at Chapel Hill, NC
The University of North Carolina at Greensboro, NC
The University of North Carolina at Pembroke, NC
The University of North Carolina Wilmington, NC
University of North Dakota, ND
University of Northern Colorado, CO
University of Oklahoma, OK

University of Pittsburgh at Bradford, PA
University of Pittsburgh at Johnstown, PA
University of Portland, OR
University of Puget Sound, WA
University of St. Francis, IL
University of South Carolina, SC
University of South Carolina Aiken, SC
The University of South Dakota, SD
The University of Tennessee, TN
The University of Tennessee at Martin, TN
The University of Texas at Arlington, TX
The University of Texas at Brownsville, TX
The University of Texas at El Paso, TX
The University of Texas at San Antonio, TX
The University of Texas at Tyler, TX
The University of Texas–Pan American, TX
University of the Ozarks, AR
The University of Toledo, OH
University of Tulsa, OK
University of West Georgia, GA
University of Wisconsin–Eau Claire, WI
University of Wisconsin–Green Bay, WI
University of Wisconsin–La Crosse, WI
University of Wisconsin–Parkside, WI
University of Wisconsin–River Falls, WI
University of Wisconsin–Stevens Point, WI
University of Wisconsin–Superior, WI
University of Wisconsin–Whitewater, WI
University of Wyoming, WY
Utah State University, UT
Valdosta State University, GA
Valley City State University, ND
Waldorf College, IA
Wartburg College, IA
Washburn University, KS
Washington State University, WA
Washington University in St. Louis, MO
Wayland Baptist University, TX
Waynesburg University, PA
Wayne State College, NE
Wayne State University, MI
Webster University, MO
Wesleyan College, GA
Western Carolina University, NC
Western Kentucky University, KY
Western Washington University, WA
West Liberty University, WV
Westminster College, UT
West Virginia University, WV
Wichita State University, KS
Widener University, PA
Wilson College, PA
Wright State University, OH
Xavier University of Louisiana, LA
York College, NE
Youngstown State University, OH

Computer Science
Alderson-Broaddus College, WV
Alliant International University, CA
Angelo State University, TX
Arizona State University, AZ
Arkansas State University—Jonesboro, AR
Arkansas Tech University, AR
Armstrong Atlantic State University, GA
Atlantic Union College, MA
Auburn University, AL
Augsburg College, MN
Augustana College, IL
Augustana College, SD
Austin Peay State University, TN
Bard College, NY
Barton College, NC

Baylor University, TX
Bethel College, IN
Birmingham-Southern College, AL
Black Hills State University, SD
Bloomfield College, NJ
Bloomsburg University of Pennsylvania, PA
Boise State University, ID
Bowie State University, MD
Bowling Green State University, OH
Briar Cliff University, IA
Bryan College, TN
Buena Vista University, IA
Butler University, IN
California Lutheran University, CA
California Polytechnic State University, San Luis Obispo, CA
California State Polytechnic University, Pomona, CA
California State University, Chico, CA
California State University, Northridge, CA
California State University, San Bernardino, CA
California State University, Stanislaus, CA
Calvin College, MI
Cameron University, OK
Campbellsville University, KY
Carroll University, WI
Carthage College, WI
Case Western Reserve University, OH
Central College, IA
Central Michigan University, MI
Christopher Newport University, VA
City College of the City University of New York, NY
Clarke College, IA
Clarkson University, NY
Cleary University, MI
Clemson University, SC
Cleveland State University, OH
The College at Brockport, State University of New York, NY
College of Charleston, SC
College of Staten Island of the City University of New York, NY
Colorado School of Mines, CO
Columbus State University, GA
Concordia University Chicago, IL
Concordia University, Nebraska, NE
Concordia University Texas, TX
Dakota State University, SD
Dallas Baptist University, TX
Dalton State College, GA
Defiance College, OH
Delta State University, MS
DePauw University, IN
DeSales University, PA
Dickinson State University, ND
Dordt College, IA
Drury University, MO
Eastern Michigan University, MI
Eastern New Mexico University, NM
Eastern Washington University, WA
East Stroudsburg University of Pennsylvania, PA
ECPI College of Technology, VA
ECPI Technical College, VA
Edinboro University of Pennsylvania, PA
Elizabethtown College, PA
Elmhurst College, IL
Elon University, NC
Emporia State University, KS
Evangel University, MO
Everest University, FL

Non-Need Scholarships for Undergraduates
Academic Interests/Achievements

Ferris State University, MI
Fitchburg State College, MA
Florida International University, FL
Fort Lewis College, CO
Francis Marion University, SC
Frostburg State University, MD
Furman University, SC
Gardner-Webb University, NC
George Fox University, OR
Georgia College & State University, GA
Georgia Institute of Technology, GA
Georgia Southern University, GA
Graceland University, IA
Grand Valley State University, MI
Hampton University, VA
Harding University, AR
Hardin-Simmons University, TX
Harrisburg University of Science and
    Technology, PA
Humphreys College, CA
Huntingdon College, AL
Huntington University, IN
Husson University, ME
Idaho State University, ID
Illinois State University, IL
Indiana University of Pennsylvania, PA
Iowa State University of Science and
    Technology, IA
Jacksonville State University, AL
James Madison University, VA
John Carroll University, OH
Johnson C. Smith University, NC
Juniata College, PA
Kean University, NJ
Kennesaw State University, GA
Kent State University, OH
Kettering University, MI
Keystone College, PA
King's College, PA
Kutztown University of Pennsylvania, PA
Lake Forest College, IL
Lawrence Technological University, MI
Limestone College, SC
Lincoln University, PA
Lindenwood University, MO
Long Island University, C.W. Post
    Campus, NY
Longwood University, VA
Louisiana State University and Agricultural
    and Mechanical College, LA
Louisiana Tech University, LA
Lubbock Christian University, TX
Lycoming College, PA
Malone University, OH
Manhattan College, NY
Massachusetts College of Liberal Arts, MA
McMurry University, TX
Meredith College, NC
Mesa State College, CO
Michigan State University, MI
Midwestern State University, TX
Millersville University of Pennsylvania, PA
Mills College, CA
Milwaukee School of Engineering, WI
Minnesota State University Moorhead, MN
Misericordia University, PA
Mississippi State University, MS
Mississippi University for Women, MS
Missouri University of Science and
    Technology, MO
Missouri Valley College, MO
Monmouth University, NJ
Montana State University, MT

Montana State University Billings, MT
Montana State University–Northern, MT
Montana Tech of The University of
    Montana, MT
Moravian College, PA
Morningside College, IA
Murray State University, KY
Muskingum University, OH
New England College, NH
New Jersey Institute of Technology, NJ
New Mexico State University, NM
North Central College, IL
Northeastern Illinois University, IL
Northeastern State University, OK
Northern Arizona University, AZ
Northern Illinois University, IL
Northern Kentucky University, KY
Northern Michigan University, MI
Northern State University, SD
Northwestern Oklahoma State University, OK
Northwest Nazarene University, ID
Ohio Northern University, OH
The Ohio State University, OH
Ohio University, OH
Ohio University–Chillicothe, OH
Ohio University–Eastern, OH
Ohio University–Lancaster, OH
Ohio University–Southern Campus, OH
Ohio University–Zanesville, OH
Oklahoma Panhandle State University, OK
Oklahoma State University, OK
Oklahoma Wesleyan University, OK
Ouachita Baptist University, AR
Pace University, NY
Peirce College, PA
Pittsburg State University, KS
Polytechnic Institute of NYU, NY
Portland State University, OR
Purchase College, State University of New
    York, NY
Purdue University, IN
Quincy University, IL
The Richard Stockton College of New
    Jersey, NJ
Ripon College, WI
Rivier College, NH
Robert Morris University Illinois, IL
Rochester Institute of Technology, NY
Rockford College, IL
Rocky Mountain College, MT
Rollins College, FL
Sacred Heart University, CT
Saginaw Valley State University, MI
St. Edward's University, TX
Saint Francis University, PA
St. John's University, NY
Saint Louis University, MO
Salisbury University, MD
Samford University, AL
Sam Houston State University, TX
San Diego State University, CA
Savannah State University, GA
Seton Hill University, PA
Shepherd University, WV
Shippensburg University of Pennsylvania, PA
Siena College, NY
Skidmore College, NY
Slippery Rock University of Pennsylvania, PA
Sonoma State University, CA
South Dakota School of Mines and
    Technology, SD
South Dakota State University, SD
Southeastern Louisiana University, LA

Southeastern Oklahoma State University, OK
Southeast Missouri State University, MO
Southern Arkansas University–Magnolia, AR
Southern Illinois University Carbondale, IL
Southern Nazarene University, OK
Southwestern College, KS
Southwestern Oklahoma State University, OK
Southwest Minnesota State University, MN
State University of New York at
    Binghamton, NY
State University of New York at Fredonia, NY
State University of New York at Oswego, NY
State University of New York at
    Plattsburgh, NY
State University of New York College at
    Geneseo, NY
State University of New York College at
    Oneonta, NY
State University of New York College at
    Potsdam, NY
State University of New York Institute of
    Technology, NY
Stephen F. Austin State University, TX
Stetson University, FL
Stevens-Henager College, ID
Stony Brook University, State University of
    New York, NY
Tennessee Technological University, TN
Tennessee Wesleyan College, TN
Texas A&M University, TX
Texas Tech University, TX
Texas Woman's University, TX
Thiel College, PA
Thomas More College, KY
Towson University, MD
Transylvania University, KY
University of Advancing Technology, AZ
The University of Akron, OH
The University of Alabama, AL
The University of Alabama at
    Birmingham, AL
The University of Alabama in Huntsville, AL
University of Alaska Anchorage, AK
University of California, Davis, CA
University of California, Irvine, CA
University of California, San Diego, CA
University of Central Missouri, MO
University of Central Oklahoma, OK
University of Colorado at Boulder, CO
University of Connecticut, CT
University of Delaware, DE
University of Denver, CO
University of Evansville, IN
University of Florida, FL
University of Great Falls, MT
University of Hawaii at Hilo, HI
University of Houston–Clear Lake, TX
University of Idaho, ID
University of Illinois at Urbana–
    Champaign, IL
The University of Kansas, KS
University of Kentucky, KY
University of Louisiana at Monroe, LA
University of Maine at Fort Kent, ME
University of Mary Hardin-Baylor, TX
University of Maryland, Baltimore
    County, MD
University of Maryland, College Park, MD
University of Mary Washington, VA
University of Massachusetts Amherst, MA
University of Massachusetts Lowell, MA
University of Miami, FL
University of Michigan, MI

f www.facebook.com/pay4undergrad

University of Michigan–Dearborn, MI
University of Michigan–Flint, MI
University of Minnesota, Twin Cities
  Campus, MN
University of Mississippi, MS
University of Missouri, MO
University of Missouri–St. Louis, MO
University of Nebraska at Omaha, NE
University of Nebraska–Lincoln, NE
University of Nevada, Las Vegas, NV
The University of North Carolina at
  Asheville, NC
The University of North Carolina at
  Charlotte, NC
The University of North Carolina
  Wilmington, NC
University of North Dakota, ND
University of North Florida, FL
University of Oklahoma, OK
University of Pittsburgh at Bradford, PA
University of Pittsburgh at Johnstown, PA
University of Portland, OR
University of Puget Sound, WA
University of Richmond, VA
University of South Alabama, AL
University of South Carolina, SC
University of South Carolina Aiken, SC
The University of South Dakota, SD
The University of Tennessee, TN
The University of Tennessee at Martin, TN
The University of Texas at Arlington, TX
The University of Texas at Brownsville, TX
The University of Texas at Dallas, TX
The University of Texas at El Paso, TX
The University of Texas at San Antonio, TX
The University of Texas–Pan American, TX
University of Tulsa, OK
University of Vermont, VT
The University of Virginia's College at
  Wise, VA
University of Washington, WA
University of West Georgia, GA
University of Wisconsin–Eau Claire, WI
University of Wisconsin–La Crosse, WI
University of Wisconsin–River Falls, WI
University of Wisconsin–Stevens Point, WI
University of Wisconsin–Stout, WI
University of Wisconsin–Superior, WI
University of Wisconsin–Whitewater, WI
University of Wyoming, WY
Utah State University, UT
Valdosta State University, GA
Valley City State University, ND
Virginia Commonwealth University, VA
Virginia Military Institute, VA
Wartburg College, IA
Washburn University, KS
Washington State University, WA
Washington University in St. Louis, MO
Waynesburg University, PA
Wayne State College, NE
Wayne State University, MI
Webster University, MO
Western Oregon University, OR
Western Washington University, WA
Westminster College, UT
West Virginia University, WV
Wheaton College, IL
Whitworth University, WA
Wichita State University, KS
Widener University, PA
Wilson College, PA
Wright State University, OH

Xavier University of Louisiana, LA
York College, NE
Youngstown State University, OH

Education

Abilene Christian University, TX
Alaska Pacific University, AK
Alderson-Broaddus College, WV
Alfred University, NY
Alliant International University, CA
Angelo State University, TX
Aquinas College, TN
Arizona State University, AZ
Arkansas State University—Jonesboro, AR
Arkansas Tech University, AR
Armstrong Atlantic State University, GA
Atlantic Union College, MA
Auburn University, AL
Augsburg College, MN
Augustana College, IL
Augustana College, SD
Aurora University, IL
Austin College, TX
Austin Peay State University, TN
Averett University, VA
Ball State University, IN
The Baptist College of Florida, FL
Barton College, NC
Baylor University, TX
Belhaven University, MS
Bellarmine University, KY
Berklee College of Music, MA
Berry College, GA
Bethel College, IN
Bethesda Christian University, CA
Birmingham-Southern College, AL
Black Hills State University, SD
Bloomfield College, NJ
Bloomsburg University of Pennsylvania, PA
Blue Mountain College, MS
Boise State University, ID
Boston University, MA
Bowling Green State University, OH
Brenau University, GA
Brescia University, KY
Brevard College, NC
Briar Cliff University, IA
Bryan College, TN
Buena Vista University, IA
Butler University, IN
California Lutheran University, CA
California Polytechnic State University,
  San Luis Obispo, CA
California State Polytechnic University,
  Pomona, CA
California State University, Chico, CA
California State University, Fresno, CA
California State University, Northridge, CA
California State University,
  San Bernardino, CA
California State University, Stanislaus, CA
Calvin College, MI
Cambridge College, MA
Cameron University, OK
Campbellsville University, KY
Carroll University, WI
Carson-Newman College, TN
Case Western Reserve University, OH
Catawba College, NC
Centenary College of Louisiana, LA
Central College, IA
Central Michigan University, MI
Chatham University, PA

Christopher Newport University, VA
City College of the City University of New
  York, NY
Clearwater Christian College, FL
Clemson University, SC
Cleveland State University, OH
Coastal Carolina University, SC
The College at Brockport, State University of
  New York, NY
College of Charleston, SC
The College of New Rochelle, NY
College of Saint Mary, NE
The College of Saint Rose, NY
College of Staten Island of the City University
  of New York, NY
Columbia College, MO
Columbia College Chicago, IL
Columbus State University, GA
Concordia University, MI
Concordia University Chicago, IL
Concordia University, Nebraska, NE
Concordia University Texas, TX
Concord University, WV
Cornerstone University, MI
Creighton University, NE
Dakota State University, SD
Dallas Baptist University, TX
Dalton State College, GA
Davidson College, NC
Defiance College, OH
Delta State University, MS
DeSales University, PA
Dickinson State University, ND
Dominican College, NY
Dordt College, IA
Dowling College, NY
Drury University, MO
D'Youville College, NY
East Carolina University, NC
Eastern Michigan University, MI
Eastern New Mexico University, NM
Eastern Washington University, WA
East Stroudsburg University of
  Pennsylvania, PA
East Texas Baptist University, TX
Edinboro University of Pennsylvania, PA
Elizabethtown College, PA
Elmhurst College, IL
Elon University, NC
Emmanuel College, MA
Emporia State University, KS
Endicott College, MA
Erskine College, SC
Evangel University, MO
Fairfield University, CT
Felician College, NJ
Ferris State University, MI
Fitchburg State College, MA
Five Towns College, NY
Flagler College, FL
Florida Gulf Coast University, FL
Florida International University, FL
Florida Southern College, FL
Fort Lewis College, CO
Framingham State College, MA
Francis Marion University, SC
Frostburg State University, MD
Furman University, SC
Gannon University, PA
Gardner-Webb University, NC
George Fox University, OR
Georgia College & State University, GA
Georgia Southern University, GA

Non-Need Scholarships for Undergraduates
Academic Interests/Achievements

Glenville State College, WV
Grace University, NE
Grand Valley State University, MI
Green Mountain College, VT
Greenville College, IL
Grove City College, PA
Hampden-Sydney College, VA
Hampton University, VA
Hardin-Simmons University, TX
Henderson State University, AR
High Point University, NC
Hillsdale Free Will Baptist College, OK
Howard Payne University, TX
Huntington University, IN
Husson University, ME
Idaho State University, ID
Illinois State University, IL
Indiana University of Pennsylvania, PA
Iowa State University of Science and
 Technology, IA
Jacksonville State University, AL
James Madison University, VA
Jarvis Christian College, TX
John Carroll University, OH
Johnson Bible College, TN
Juniata College, PA
Kean University, NJ
Kennesaw State University, GA
Kent State University, OH
Keystone College, PA
King's College, PA
Kutztown University of Pennsylvania, PA
LaGrange College, GA
Lake Erie College, OH
Langston University, OK
Lawrence Technological University, MI
Lees-McRae College, NC
Lee University, TN
Lewis-Clark State College, ID
Limestone College, SC
Lincoln University, MO
Lincoln University, PA
Lindenwood University, MO
Lindsey Wilson College, KY
Lipscomb University, TN
Lock Haven University of Pennsylvania, PA
Long Island University, Brooklyn
 Campus, NY
Long Island University, C.W. Post
 Campus, NY
Longwood University, VA
Louisiana State University and Agricultural
 and Mechanical College, LA
Louisiana Tech University, LA
Lubbock Christian University, TX
Lycoming College, PA
Malone University, OH
Mansfield University of Pennsylvania, PA
Maryville University of Saint Louis, MO
Marywood University, PA
Massachusetts College of Liberal Arts, MA
The Master's College and Seminary, CA
McMurry University, TX
Mercer University, GA
Meredith College, NC
Mesa State College, CO
Metropolitan State University, MN
Miami University, OH
Michigan State University, MI
Mid-Continent University, KY
Midwestern State University, TX
Millersville University of Pennsylvania, PA
Millikin University, IL

Minnesota State University Moorhead, MN
Misericordia University, PA
Mississippi State University, MS
Mississippi University for Women, MS
Missouri University of Science and
 Technology, MO
Missouri Valley College, MO
Molloy College, NY
Monmouth University, NJ
Montana State University, MT
Montana State University Billings, MT
Montana State University–Northern, MT
Montclair State University, NJ
Morehead State University, KY
Mount Mary College, WI
Mount St. Mary's College, CA
Multnomah University, OR
Murray State University, KY
Newberry College, SC
New England College, NH
New Mexico State University, NM
North Carolina State University, NC
North Central College, IL
Northeastern Illinois University, IL
Northeastern State University, OK
Northern Arizona University, AZ
Northern Illinois University, IL
Northern Kentucky University, KY
Northern Michigan University, MI
Northern State University, SD
North Georgia College & State University, GA
North Greenville University, SC
Northwestern Oklahoma State University, OK
Northwestern State University of
 Louisiana, LA
Northwest Nazarene University, ID
Oakland University, MI
Ohio Northern University, OH
The Ohio State University, OH
Ohio University, OH
Ohio University–Chillicothe, OH
Ohio University–Eastern, OH
Ohio University–Lancaster, OH
Ohio University–Southern Campus, OH
Ohio University–Zanesville, OH
Ohio Valley University, WV
Oklahoma City University, OK
Oklahoma Panhandle State University, OK
Oklahoma State University, OK
Oklahoma Wesleyan University, OK
Olivet College, MI
Oral Roberts University, OK
Ouachita Baptist University, AR
Pace University, NY
Pacific Union College, CA
Pacific University, OR
Piedmont College, GA
Pittsburg State University, KS
Plymouth State University, NH
Point Loma Nazarene University, CA
Portland State University, OR
Purdue University, IN
Purdue University North Central, IN
Quincy University, IL
Randolph College, VA
Regent University, VA
The Richard Stockton College of New
 Jersey, NJ
Ripon College, WI
Rivier College, NH
Rockford College, IL
Rocky Mountain College, MT
Sacred Heart University, CT

Saginaw Valley State University, MI
St. Catherine University, MN
St. Edward's University, TX
Saint Francis University, PA
St. John's University, NY
Saint Louis University, MO
Saint Martin's University, WA
Salisbury University, MD
Samford University, AL
Sam Houston State University, TX
San Diego State University, CA
Savannah College of Art and Design, GA
Schreiner University, TX
Seton Hill University, PA
Shepherd University, WV
Shippensburg University of Pennsylvania, PA
Siena College, NY
Slippery Rock University of Pennsylvania, PA
Sonoma State University, CA
South Dakota State University, SD
Southeastern Louisiana University, LA
Southeastern Oklahoma State University, OK
Southeast Missouri State University, MO
Southern Adventist University, TN
Southern Arkansas University–Magnolia, AR
Southern Illinois University Carbondale, IL
Southern Illinois University Edwardsville, IL
Southern Nazarene University, OK
Southwestern Oklahoma State University, OK
Southwest Minnesota State University, MN
State University of New York at
 Binghamton, NY
State University of New York at Fredonia, NY
State University of New York at New
 Paltz, NY
State University of New York at Oswego, NY
State University of New York at
 Plattsburgh, NY
State University of New York College at
 Cortland, NY
State University of New York College at
 Geneseo, NY
State University of New York College at
 Oneonta, NY
State University of New York College at
 Potsdam, NY
Stephen F. Austin State University, TX
Stetson University, FL
Stillman College, AL
Sul Ross State University, TX
Tennessee Technological University, TN
Tennessee Wesleyan College, TN
Texas A&M University, TX
Texas A&M University–Texarkana, TX
Texas Christian University, TX
Texas Lutheran University, TX
Texas State University–San Marcos, TX
Texas Tech University, TX
Texas Woman's University, TX
Thiel College, PA
Thomas More College, KY
Towson University, MD
Trevecca Nazarene University, TN
Trinity Bible College, ND
Truman State University, MO
Union University, TN
The University of Akron, OH
The University of Alabama, AL
The University of Alabama in Huntsville, AL
University of Alaska Anchorage, AK
The University of Arizona, AZ
University of California, Irvine, CA
University of California, Riverside, CA

University of Central Missouri, MO
University of Central Oklahoma, OK
University of Colorado at Boulder, CO
University of Connecticut, CT
University of Dallas, TX
University of Dayton, OH
University of Delaware, DE
University of Evansville, IN
University of Florida, FL
University of Georgia, GA
University of Great Falls, MT
University of Houston–Clear Lake, TX
University of Idaho, ID
University of Illinois at Urbana–
  Champaign, IL
The University of Kansas, KS
University of Kentucky, KY
University of Louisiana at Monroe, LA
University of Louisville, KY
University of Maine at Fort Kent, ME
University of Mary Hardin-Baylor, TX
University of Maryland, Baltimore
  County, MD
University of Maryland, College Park, MD
University of Mary Washington, VA
University of Massachusetts Amherst, MA
University of Memphis, TN
University of Miami, FL
University of Michigan, MI
University of Michigan–Dearborn, MI
University of Michigan–Flint, MI
University of Minnesota, Twin Cities
  Campus, MN
University of Mississippi, MS
University of Missouri, MO
University of Missouri–St. Louis, MO
The University of Montana Western, MT
University of Montevallo, AL
University of Nebraska at Omaha, NE
University of Nebraska–Lincoln, NE
University of Nevada, Las Vegas, NV
University of New Hampshire, NH
University of New Orleans, LA
The University of North Carolina at
  Asheville, NC
The University of North Carolina at Chapel
  Hill, NC
The University of North Carolina at
  Charlotte, NC
The University of North Carolina at
  Greensboro, NC
The University of North Carolina at
  Pembroke, NC
The University of North Carolina
  Wilmington, NC
University of North Dakota, ND
University of Northern Colorado, CO
University of Northern Iowa, IA
University of North Florida, FL
University of Oklahoma, OK
University of Oregon, OR
University of Pittsburgh at Bradford, PA
University of Pittsburgh at Johnstown, PA
University of Portland, OR
University of St. Francis, IL
University of St. Thomas, MN
University of South Carolina, SC
University of South Carolina Aiken, SC
The University of South Dakota, SD
University of Southern Indiana, IN
The University of Tennessee, TN
The University of Tennessee at
  Chattanooga, TN

The University of Tennessee at Martin, TN
The University of Texas at Arlington, TX
The University of Texas at Brownsville, TX
The University of Texas at El Paso, TX
The University of Texas at San Antonio, TX
The University of Texas–Pan American, TX
University of the Ozarks, AR
University of the Southwest, NM
The University of Toledo, OH
University of Tulsa, OK
University of Vermont, VT
The University of Virginia's College at
  Wise, VA
University of Washington, WA
University of West Georgia, GA
University of Wisconsin–Eau Claire, WI
University of Wisconsin–Green Bay, WI
University of Wisconsin–La Crosse, WI
University of Wisconsin–Parkside, WI
University of Wisconsin–River Falls, WI
University of Wisconsin–Stevens Point, WI
University of Wisconsin–Stout, WI
University of Wisconsin–Superior, WI
University of Wisconsin–Whitewater, WI
University of Wyoming, WY
Utah State University, UT
Valdosta State University, GA
Valley City State University, ND
Virginia Commonwealth University, VA
Wartburg College, IA
Washburn University, KS
Washington State University, WA
Washington University in St. Louis, MO
Wayland Baptist University, TX
Waynesburg University, PA
Wayne State College, NE
Wayne State University, MI
Webster University, MO
Wesleyan College, GA
Western Carolina University, NC
Western Illinois University, IL
Western Kentucky University, KY
Western Oregon University, OR
Western Washington University, WA
West Liberty University, WV
Westminster College, UT
West Virginia University, WV
Wheaton College, IL
Wichita State University, KS
Widener University, PA
Williams Baptist College, AR
Wilson College, PA
Wright State University, OH
Xavier University of Louisiana, LA
York College, NE
Youngstown State University, OH

Engineering/Technologies

Alfred University, NY
Arizona State University, AZ
Arkansas State University—Jonesboro, AR
Arkansas Tech University, AR
Armstrong Atlantic State University, GA
Auburn University, AL
Austin College, TX
Averett University, VA
Ball State University, IN
Baylor University, TX
Berklee College of Music, MA
Birmingham-Southern College, AL
Bluefield State College, WV
Boise State University, ID
Boston University, MA

Bowie State University, MD
Bowling Green State University, OH
Bryant University, RI
Bucknell University, PA
Butler University, IN
California Polytechnic State University,
  San Luis Obispo, CA
California State Polytechnic University,
  Pomona, CA
California State University, Chico, CA
California State University, Fresno, CA
California State University, Fullerton, CA
California State University, Northridge, CA
Calvin College, MI
Cameron University, OK
Carthage College, WI
Case Western Reserve University, OH
Centenary College of Louisiana, LA
Central Michigan University, MI
Christian Brothers University, TN
Christopher Newport University, VA
The Citadel, The Military College of South
  Carolina, SC
City College of the City University of New
  York, NY
Clarkson University, NY
Clemson University, SC
Cleveland State University, OH
College of Charleston, SC
The College of Saint Rose, NY
College of Staten Island of the City University
  of New York, NY
Colorado School of Mines, CO
Cooper Union for the Advancement of Science
  and Art, NY
Dalton State College, GA
Dordt College, IA
East Carolina University, NC
Eastern Michigan University, MI
Eastern New Mexico University, NM
Eastern Washington University, WA
ECPI College of Technology, VA
ECPI Technical College, VA
Edinboro University of Pennsylvania, PA
Elizabethtown College, PA
Elon University, NC
Emmanuel College, MA
Emporia State University, KS
Evangel University, MO
Fairfield University, CT
Ferris State University, MI
Florida Agricultural and Mechanical
  University, FL
Florida Atlantic University, FL
Florida Gulf Coast University, FL
Florida International University, FL
Frostburg State University, MD
Furman University, SC
Gannon University, PA
Geneva College, PA
George Fox University, OR
Georgia Institute of Technology, GA
Georgia Southern University, GA
Gonzaga University, WA
Graceland University, IA
Grand Valley State University, MI
Greenville College, IL
Grove City College, PA
Hampton University, VA
Harding University, AR
Idaho State University, ID
Illinois Institute of Technology, IL
Illinois State University, IL

Non-Need Scholarships for Undergraduates
Academic Interests/Achievements

Indiana University of Pennsylvania, PA
Iowa State University of Science and
  Technology, IA
James Madison University, VA
The Johns Hopkins University, MD
Kent State University, OH
Kettering University, MI
Lakeland College, WI
Langston University, OK
Lawrence Technological University, MI
Lehigh University, PA
Lindenwood University, MO
Lipscomb University, TN
Loras College, IA
Louisiana State University and Agricultural
  and Mechanical College, LA
Louisiana Tech University, LA
Maine Maritime Academy, ME
Marquette University, WI
Mercer University, GA
Mesa State College, CO
Miami University, OH
Michigan State University, MI
Midwestern State University, TX
Milwaukee School of Engineering, WI
Minnesota State University Moorhead, MN
Mississippi State University, MS
Missouri University of Science and
  Technology, MO
Montana State University, MT
Montana State University Billings, MT
Montana State University–Northern, MT
Montana Tech of The University of
  Montana, MT
Morehead State University, KY
Murray State University, KY
Muskingum University, OH
New England College, NH
New Jersey Institute of Technology, NJ
New Mexico State University, NM
North Carolina State University, NC
Northern Arizona University, AZ
Northern Illinois University, IL
Northern Kentucky University, KY
Northern Michigan University, MI
Northwestern State University of
  Louisiana, LA
Oakland University, MI
Ohio Northern University, OH
The Ohio State University, OH
Ohio University, OH
Ohio University–Chillicothe, OH
Ohio University–Eastern, OH
Ohio University–Lancaster, OH
Ohio University–Southern Campus, OH
Ohio University–Zanesville, OH
Oklahoma Christian University, OK
Oklahoma State University, OK
Old Dominion University, VA
Oral Roberts University, OK
Ouachita Baptist University, AR
Philadelphia University, PA
Pittsburg State University, KS
Point Loma Nazarene University, CA
Polytechnic Institute of NYU, NY
Polytechnic University of Puerto Rico, PR
Portland State University, OR
Purdue University, IN
Rochester Institute of Technology, NY
Rollins College, FL
Saginaw Valley State University, MI
Saint Francis University, PA
Saint Louis University, MO

Saint Martin's University, WA
Sam Houston State University, TX
San Diego State University, CA
Santa Clara University, CA
Savannah State University, GA
Seattle Pacific University, WA
Shepherd University, WV
Sonoma State University, CA
South Dakota School of Mines and
  Technology, SD
South Dakota State University, SD
Southeastern Louisiana University, LA
Southeastern Oklahoma State University, OK
Southeast Missouri State University, MO
Southern Illinois University Carbondale, IL
Southwestern Oklahoma State University, OK
State University of New York at
  Binghamton, NY
State University of New York at
  Plattsburgh, NY
State University of New York College at
  Potsdam, NY
State University of New York College of
  Environmental Science and Forestry, NY
State University of New York Institute of
  Technology, NY
Stony Brook University, State University of
  New York, NY
Tennessee Technological University, TN
Texas A&M University, TX
Texas A&M University–Texarkana, TX
Texas Christian University, TX
Texas Tech University, TX
Union University, TN
The University of Akron, OH
The University of Alabama, AL
The University of Alabama at
  Birmingham, AL
The University of Alabama in Huntsville, AL
University of Alaska Anchorage, AK
The University of Arizona, AZ
University of California, Davis, CA
University of California, Irvine, CA
University of California, Riverside, CA
University of California, San Diego, CA
University of Central Missouri, MO
University of Colorado at Boulder, CO
University of Connecticut, CT
University of Dayton, OH
University of Delaware, DE
University of Denver, CO
University of Evansville, IN
University of Florida, FL
University of Hartford, CT
University of Idaho, ID
University of Illinois at Urbana–
  Champaign, IL
The University of Iowa, IA
The University of Kansas, KS
University of Kentucky, KY
University of Louisville, KY
University of Maryland, Baltimore
  County, MD
University of Maryland, College Park, MD
University of Massachusetts Amherst, MA
University of Massachusetts Lowell, MA
University of Memphis, TN
University of Miami, FL
University of Michigan, MI
University of Michigan–Dearborn, MI
University of Michigan–Flint, MI
University of Minnesota, Twin Cities
  Campus, MN

University of Mississippi, MS
University of Missouri, MO
University of Missouri–St. Louis, MO
University of Nebraska at Omaha, NE
University of Nebraska–Lincoln, NE
University of Nevada, Las Vegas, NV
University of New Hampshire, NH
University of New Orleans, LA
The University of North Carolina at
  Asheville, NC
The University of North Carolina at
  Charlotte, NC
The University of North Carolina
  Wilmington, NC
University of North Dakota, ND
University of North Florida, FL
University of Oklahoma, OK
University of Pittsburgh at Bradford, PA
University of Pittsburgh at Johnstown, PA
University of Portland, OR
University of Rochester, NY
University of South Carolina, SC
University of South Carolina Aiken, SC
University of Southern Indiana, IN
The University of Tennessee, TN
The University of Tennessee at Martin, TN
The University of Texas at Arlington, TX
The University of Texas at Brownsville, TX
The University of Texas at Dallas, TX
The University of Texas at El Paso, TX
The University of Texas at San Antonio, TX
The University of Texas at Tyler, TX
The University of Texas–Pan American, TX
The University of Toledo, OH
University of Tulsa, OK
University of Vermont, VT
University of Washington, WA
University of Wisconsin–Green Bay, WI
University of Wisconsin–Parkside, WI
University of Wisconsin–Stevens Point, WI
University of Wisconsin–Stout, WI
University of Wyoming, WY
Utah State University, UT
Valdosta State University, GA
Valparaiso University, IN
Virginia Commonwealth University, VA
Virginia Military Institute, VA
Washburn University, KS
Washington State University, WA
Washington University in St. Louis, MO
Wayne State University, MI
Western Kentucky University, KY
Western Washington University, WA
West Virginia University, WV
Wichita State University, KS
Widener University, PA
Wright State University, OH
Xavier University of Louisiana, LA
Youngstown State University, OH

English

Abilene Christian University, TX
Alfred University, NY
Alliant International University, CA
Angelo State University, TX
Arizona State University, AZ
Arkansas State University—Jonesboro, AR
Arkansas Tech University, AR
Armstrong Atlantic State University, GA
Atlantic Union College, MA
Auburn University, AL
Augsburg College, MN
Augustana College, IL

Augustana College, SD
Austin College, TX
Austin Peay State University, TN
Averett University, VA
Ball State University, IN
Barton College, NC
Baylor University, TX
Belhaven University, MS
Berry College, GA
Bethel College, IN
Birmingham-Southern College, AL
Black Hills State University, SD
Bloomfield College, NJ
Bloomsburg University of Pennsylvania, PA
Blue Mountain College, MS
Boise State University, ID
Bowling Green State University, OH
Brescia University, KY
Brevard College, NC
Briar Cliff University, IA
Bryan College, TN
Butler University, IN
California Lutheran University, CA
California Polytechnic State University,
  San Luis Obispo, CA
California State University, Chico, CA
California State University, Fresno, CA
California State University, Northridge, CA
California State University, Stanislaus, CA
Calvin College, MI
Cameron University, OK
Campbellsville University, KY
Case Western Reserve University, OH
Cedar Crest College, PA
Centenary College of Louisiana, LA
Central Michigan University, MI
Chatham University, PA
Christopher Newport University, VA
City College of the City University of New
  York, NY
Clemson University, SC
Cleveland State University, OH
Coe College, IA
The College at Brockport, State University of
  New York, NY
College of Charleston, SC
The College of New Rochelle, NY
The College of Saint Rose, NY
Columbia College, MO
Columbus State University, GA
Concordia University Chicago, IL
Concordia University, Nebraska, NE
Concord University, WV
Dakota State University, SD
Dalton State College, GA
Defiance College, OH
Delta State University, MS
DePauw University, IN
DeSales University, PA
Dickinson State University, ND
Dordt College, IA
Drury University, MO
D'Youville College, NY
East Carolina University, NC
Eastern Michigan University, MI
Eastern New Mexico University, NM
Eastern Washington University, WA
East Stroudsburg University of
  Pennsylvania, PA
East Texas Baptist University, TX
Edinboro University of Pennsylvania, PA
Elizabethtown College, PA
Elmhurst College, IL

Emporia State University, KS
Erskine College, SC
Evangel University, MO
Felician College, NJ
Fitchburg State College, MA
Flagler College, FL
Florida International University, FL
Fort Lewis College, CO
Francis Marion University, SC
Frostburg State University, MD
Furman University, SC
Gannon University, PA
Gardner-Webb University, NC
Georgia College & State University, GA
Georgian Court University, NJ
Georgia Southern University, GA
Glenville State College, WV
Graceland University, IA
Grand Valley State University, MI
Green Mountain College, VT
Grove City College, PA
Hamline University, MN
Harding University, AR
Hardin-Simmons University, TX
High Point University, NC
Hillsdale Free Will Baptist College, OK
Howard Payne University, TX
Idaho State University, ID
Illinois State University, IL
Indiana University of Pennsylvania, PA
Iowa State University of Science and
  Technology, IA
Jacksonville State University, AL
James Madison University, VA
John Carroll University, OH
Juniata College, PA
Kean University, NJ
Kennesaw State University, GA
Kent State University, OH
King's College, PA
Kutztown University of Pennsylvania, PA
LaGrange College, GA
Lake Erie College, OH
Lakeland College, WI
Lewis-Clark State College, ID
Limestone College, SC
Lincoln University, PA
Lindenwood University, MO
Lindsey Wilson College, KY
Lipscomb University, TN
Lock Haven University of Pennsylvania, PA
Longwood University, VA
Louisiana State University and Agricultural
  and Mechanical College, LA
Louisiana Tech University, LA
Lubbock Christian University, TX
Lycoming College, PA
MacMurray College, IL
Malone University, OH
Manchester College, IN
Massachusetts College of Liberal Arts, MA
McMurry University, TX
Mercer University, GA
Meredith College, NC
Mesa State College, CO
Methodist University, NC
Michigan State University, MI
Mid-Continent University, KY
Midwestern State University, TX
Millersville University of Pennsylvania, PA
Millikin University, IL
Minnesota State University Moorhead, MN
Mississippi State University, MS

Mississippi University for Women, MS
Missouri University of Science and
  Technology, MO
Missouri Valley College, MO
Molloy College, NY
Montana State University, MT
Montana State University Billings, MT
Montana State University–Northern, MT
Montclair State University, NJ
Mount Mary College, WI
Murray State University, KY
New England College, NH
New Mexico State University, NM
North Central College, IL
Northeastern Illinois University, IL
Northeastern State University, OK
Northern Arizona University, AZ
Northern Illinois University, IL
Northern Kentucky University, KY
Northern Michigan University, MI
Northern State University, SD
North Georgia College & State University, GA
Northwestern Oklahoma State University, OK
Northwest Nazarene University, ID
Oakland University, MI
Ohio Northern University, OH
The Ohio State University, OH
Ohio University, OH
Ohio University–Chillicothe, OH
Ohio University–Eastern, OH
Ohio University–Lancaster, OH
Ohio University–Southern Campus, OH
Ohio University–Zanesville, OH
Ohio Valley University, WV
Oklahoma Panhandle State University, OK
Oklahoma State University, OK
Old Dominion University, VA
Olivet College, MI
Ouachita Baptist University, AR
Pace University, NY
Pacific University, OR
Piedmont College, GA
Pittsburg State University, KS
Plymouth State University, NH
Purchase College, State University of New
  York, NY
Purdue University North Central, IN
Quincy University, IL
Randolph College, VA
Regent University, VA
Ripon College, WI
Rivier College, NH
Rockford College, IL
Rockhurst University, MO
Rocky Mountain College, MT
Sacred Heart University, CT
St. Catherine University, MN
St. Edward's University, TX
Saint Francis University, PA
St. John Fisher College, NY
St. John's University, NY
Saint Louis University, MO
Salisbury University, MD
Samford University, AL
Sam Houston State University, TX
San Diego State University, CA
Savannah State University, GA
Schreiner University, TX
Seton Hill University, PA
Shepherd University, WV
Shippensburg University of Pennsylvania, PA
Shorter University, GA
Siena College, NY

Non-Need Scholarships for Undergraduates
Academic Interests/Achievements

Silver Lake College, WI
Slippery Rock University of Pennsylvania, PA
Sonoma State University, CA
South Dakota State University, SD
Southeastern Louisiana University, LA
Southeast Missouri State University, MO
Southern Adventist University, TN
Southern Arkansas University–Magnolia, AR
Southern Illinois University Carbondale, IL
Southern Nazarene University, OK
Southwestern Oklahoma State University, OK
Southwest Minnesota State University, MN
State University of New York at
 Binghamton, NY
State University of New York at Fredonia, NY
State University of New York at Oswego, NY
State University of New York at
 Plattsburgh, NY
State University of New York College at
 Geneseo, NY
State University of New York College at
 Oneonta, NY
State University of New York College at
 Potsdam, NY
Stephens College, MO
Stetson University, FL
Stony Brook University, State University of
 New York, NY
Sul Ross State University, TX
Tennessee Technological University, TN
Tennessee Wesleyan College, TN
Texas A&M University–Texarkana, TX
Texas Christian University, TX
Texas State University–San Marcos, TX
Texas Tech University, TX
Texas Woman's University, TX
Thiel College, PA
Thomas More College, KY
Towson University, MD
Trevecca Nazarene University, TN
Trinity Christian College, IL
Truman State University, MO
The University of Akron, OH
The University of Alabama, AL
The University of Alabama in Huntsville, AL
University of Alaska Anchorage, AK
University of California, Davis, CA
University of California, Riverside, CA
University of Central Missouri, MO
University of Colorado at Boulder, CO
University of Connecticut, CT
University of Delaware, DE
University of Evansville, IN
University of Hawaii at Hilo, HI
University of Idaho, ID
University of Illinois at Urbana–
 Champaign, IL
The University of Kansas, KS
University of Kentucky, KY
University of Louisiana at Monroe, LA
University of Louisville, KY
University of Maine at Fort Kent, ME
University of Mary Hardin-Baylor, TX
University of Maryland, Baltimore
 County, MD
University of Maryland, College Park, MD
University of Mary Washington, VA
University of Massachusetts Amherst, MA
University of Memphis, TN
University of Miami, FL
University of Michigan, MI
University of Michigan–Flint, MI

University of Minnesota, Twin Cities
 Campus, MN
University of Mississippi, MS
University of Missouri, MO
University of Missouri–St. Louis, MO
The University of Montana Western, MT
University of Nebraska at Omaha, NE
University of Nebraska–Lincoln, NE
University of Nevada, Las Vegas, NV
University of New Hampshire, NH
University of New Orleans, LA
The University of North Carolina at
 Asheville, NC
The University of North Carolina at Chapel
 Hill, NC
The University of North Carolina at
 Greensboro, NC
The University of North Carolina at
 Pembroke, NC
The University of North Carolina
 Wilmington, NC
University of North Dakota, ND
University of Northern Colorado, CO
University of Pittsburgh at Bradford, PA
University of Pittsburgh at Johnstown, PA
University of Portland, OR
University of Puget Sound, WA
University of St. Thomas, MN
University of South Carolina, SC
University of South Carolina Aiken, SC
The University of South Dakota, SD
The University of Tennessee at Martin, TN
The University of Texas at Arlington, TX
The University of Texas at Brownsville, TX
The University of Texas at El Paso, TX
The University of Texas at San Antonio, TX
The University of Texas–Pan American, TX
University of the Ozarks, AR
University of the Southwest, NM
The University of Toledo, OH
University of Tulsa, OK
University of Vermont, VT
The University of Virginia's College at
 Wise, VA
University of West Georgia, GA
University of Wisconsin–Eau Claire, WI
University of Wisconsin–La Crosse, WI
University of Wisconsin–Parkside, WI
University of Wisconsin–River Falls, WI
University of Wisconsin–Stevens Point, WI
University of Wisconsin–Superior, WI
University of Wisconsin–Whitewater, WI
University of Wyoming, WY
Utah State University, UT
Valdosta State University, GA
Valley City State University, ND
Virginia Military Institute, VA
Wartburg College, IA
Washburn University, KS
Washington State University, WA
Washington University in St. Louis, MO
Wayland Baptist University, TX
Waynesburg University, PA
Wayne State College, NE
Wayne State University, MI
Webster University, MO
Wesleyan College, GA
Western Carolina University, NC
Western Kentucky University, KY
Western Oregon University, OR
Western Washington University, WA
West Liberty University, WV
Westminster College, UT

West Virginia University, WV
West Virginia Wesleyan College, WV
Wichita State University, KS
Widener University, PA
Wilson College, PA
Wright State University, OH
Xavier University of Louisiana, LA
York College, NE
Youngstown State University, OH

Foreign Languages

Abilene Christian University, TX
Adelphi University, NY
Alfred University, NY
Alliant International University, CA
Angelo State University, TX
Arizona State University, AZ
Armstrong Atlantic State University, GA
Auburn University, AL
Augsburg College, MN
Augustana College, IL
Augustana College, SD
Austin College, TX
Austin Peay State University, TN
Averett University, VA
Ball State University, IN
Baylor University, TX
Belhaven University, MS
Birmingham-Southern College, AL
Black Hills State University, SD
Bloomsburg University of Pennsylvania, PA
Boise State University, ID
Boston University, MA
Bowling Green State University, OH
Briar Cliff University, IA
Bryan College, TN
Butler University, IN
California Lutheran University, CA
California Polytechnic State University,
 San Luis Obispo, CA
California State University, Chico, CA
California State University, Fresno, CA
California State University,
 San Bernardino, CA
California State University, Stanislaus, CA
Calvin College, MI
Cameron University, OK
Carthage College, WI
Case Western Reserve University, OH
Centenary College of Louisiana, LA
Central College, IA
Central Michigan University, MI
Christopher Newport University, VA
City College of the City University of New
 York, NY
Clarke College, IA
Clemson University, SC
Coe College, IA
The College at Brockport, State University of
 New York, NY
College of Charleston, SC
The College of New Rochelle, NY
The College of Saint Rose, NY
Concordia University Chicago, IL
Concordia University Texas, TX
Davidson College, NC
Delta State University, MS
DePauw University, IN
DeSales University, PA
Dickinson State University, ND
Dordt College, IA
Drury University, MO
East Carolina University, NC

Eastern Michigan University, MI
Eastern New Mexico University, NM
Eastern Washington University, WA
East Stroudsburg University of
  Pennsylvania, PA
Edgewood College, WI
Edinboro University of Pennsylvania, PA
Elizabethtown College, PA
Elmhurst College, IL
Emmanuel College, MA
Emporia State University, KS
Erskine College, SC
Evangel University, MO
Fairfield University, CT
Flagler College, FL
Florida International University, FL
Fordham University, NY
Frostburg State University, MD
Furman University, SC
Gannon University, PA
Gardner-Webb University, NC
Georgia College & State University, GA
Georgian Court University, NJ
Georgia Southern University, GA
Grand Valley State University, MI
Grove City College, PA
Hamline University, MN
Hardin-Simmons University, TX
High Point University, NC
Idaho State University, ID
Illinois Institute of Technology, IL
Illinois State University, IL
Indiana University of Pennsylvania, PA
Iowa State University of Science and
  Technology, IA
John Carroll University, OH
Juniata College, PA
Kean University, NJ
Kennesaw State University, GA
King's College, PA
Kutztown University of Pennsylvania, PA
Lake Erie College, OH
Lake Forest College, IL
Lindenwood University, MO
Lock Haven University of Pennsylvania, PA
Louisiana State University and Agricultural
  and Mechanical College, LA
Louisiana Tech University, LA
Lubbock Christian University, TX
Lycoming College, PA
MacMurray College, IL
Malone University, OH
Manchester College, IN
Manhattan College, NY
Marquette University, WI
Marywood University, PA
Mercer University, GA
Meredith College, NC
Mesa State College, CO
Michigan State University, MI
Midwestern State University, TX
Millersville University of Pennsylvania, PA
Millikin University, IL
Mississippi State University, MS
Monmouth College, IL
Montana State University, MT
Montana State University–Northern, MT
Montclair State University, NJ
Moravian College, PA
Murray State University, KY
Newberry College, SC
New Mexico State University, NM
North Central College, IL

Northeastern Illinois University, IL
Northeastern State University, OK
Northern Arizona University, AZ
Northern Illinois University, IL
Northern Michigan University, MI
Northern State University, SD
Northwestern Oklahoma State University, OK
Oakland University, MI
Ohio Northern University, OH
The Ohio State University, OH
Ohio University, OH
Ohio University–Chillicothe, OH
Ohio University–Eastern, OH
Ohio University–Lancaster, OH
Ohio University–Southern Campus, OH
Ohio University–Zanesville, OH
Oklahoma State University, OK
Olivet College, MI
Ouachita Baptist University, AR
Pace University, NY
Pacific University, OR
Piedmont College, GA
Pittsburg State University, KS
Portland State University, OR
Regent University, VA
Ripon College, WI
Rivier College, NH
Rockford College, IL
Rockhurst University, MO
St. Catherine University, MN
St. Edward's University, TX
St. John Fisher College, NY
St. John's University, NY
Saint Louis University, MO
Salisbury University, MD
Samford University, AL
Sam Houston State University, TX
San Diego State University, CA
Seton Hill University, PA
Shippensburg University of Pennsylvania, PA
Shorter University, GA
Siena College, NY
Sonoma State University, CA
South Dakota State University, SD
Southeastern Louisiana University, LA
Southeast Missouri State University, MO
Southern Arkansas University–Magnolia, AR
Southern Illinois University Carbondale, IL
Southwestern Oklahoma State University, OK
State University of New York at
  Binghamton, NY
State University of New York at Fredonia, NY
State University of New York at New
  Paltz, NY
State University of New York at Oswego, NY
State University of New York College at
  Geneseo, NY
State University of New York College at
  Potsdam, NY
Stetson University, FL
Stony Brook University, State University of
  New York, NY
Sul Ross State University, TX
Tennessee Technological University, TN
Tennessee Wesleyan College, TN
Texas Christian University, TX
Texas Tech University, TX
Texas Woman's University, TX
Towson University, MD
Truman State University, MO
The University of Akron, OH
The University of Alabama, AL
The University of Alabama in Huntsville, AL

University of California, Davis, CA
University of California, Irvine, CA
University of Central Missouri, MO
University of Central Oklahoma, OK
University of Colorado at Boulder, CO
University of Connecticut, CT
University of Dallas, TX
University of Delaware, DE
University of Evansville, IN
University of Idaho, ID
University of Illinois at Urbana–
  Champaign, IL
The University of Kansas, KS
University of Kentucky, KY
University of Louisiana at Monroe, LA
University of Louisville, KY
University of Maine at Fort Kent, ME
University of Mary Hardin-Baylor, TX
University of Maryland, Baltimore
  County, MD
University of Maryland, College Park, MD
University of Mary Washington, VA
University of Miami, FL
University of Michigan, MI
University of Michigan–Dearborn, MI
University of Michigan–Flint, MI
University of Minnesota, Twin Cities
  Campus, MN
University of Mississippi, MS
University of Missouri, MO
University of Missouri–St. Louis, MO
University of Nebraska at Omaha, NE
University of Nebraska–Lincoln, NE
University of Nevada, Las Vegas, NV
University of New Orleans, LA
The University of North Carolina at
  Greensboro, NC
The University of North Carolina
  Wilmington, NC
University of North Dakota, ND
University of Oklahoma, OK
University of Oregon, OR
University of Portland, OR
University of Puget Sound, WA
University of South Carolina, SC
The University of South Dakota, SD
The University of Texas at Arlington, TX
The University of Texas at Brownsville, TX
The University of Texas at San Antonio, TX
The University of Toledo, OH
University of Tulsa, OK
University of Vermont, VT
University of West Georgia, GA
University of Wisconsin–Eau Claire, WI
University of Wisconsin–La Crosse, WI
University of Wisconsin–Parkside, WI
University of Wisconsin–River Falls, WI
University of Wisconsin–Stevens Point, WI
University of Wisconsin–Whitewater, WI
University of Wyoming, WY
Utah State University, UT
Valdosta State University, GA
Valparaiso University, IN
Virginia Commonwealth University, VA
Washburn University, KS
Washington State University, WA
Washington University in St. Louis, MO
Wayne State College, NE
Wayne State University, MI
Webster University, MO
Wesleyan College, GA
Western Illinois University, IL
Western Kentucky University, KY

Western Oregon University, OR
Western Washington University, WA
West Virginia University, WV
Wheaton College, IL
Wichita State University, KS
Widener University, PA
Wilson College, PA
Wright State University, OH
Xavier University, OH
Xavier University of Louisiana, LA
Youngstown State University, OH

Health Fields

Alderson-Broaddus College, WV
Aquinas College, TN
Arizona State University, AZ
Arkansas State University—Jonesboro, AR
Arkansas Tech University, AR
Armstrong Atlantic State University, GA
Atlantic Union College, MA
Auburn University, AL
Augsburg College, MN
Augustana College, SD
Austin College, TX
Austin Peay State University, TN
Averett University, VA
Ball State University, IN
Barton College, NC
Bastyr University, WA
Baylor University, TX
Bellarmine University, KY
Bethel College, IN
Birmingham-Southern College, AL
Black Hills State University, SD
Bloomfield College, NJ
Bloomsburg University of Pennsylvania, PA
Blue Mountain College, MS
Boise State University, ID
Bowling Green State University, OH
Brenau University, GA
Brescia University, KY
Brevard College, NC
Briar Cliff University, IA
California Polytechnic State University,
  San Luis Obispo, CA
California State University, Chico, CA
California State University, Fresno, CA
California State University,
  San Bernardino, CA
California State University, Stanislaus, CA
Calvin College, MI
Carroll University, WI
Carthage College, WI
Case Western Reserve University, OH
Centenary College of Louisiana, LA
Central College, IA
Central Michigan University, MI
Chamberlain College of Nursing, MO
Clemson University, SC
Cleveland State University, OH
The College at Brockport, State University of
  New York, NY
College of Charleston, SC
The College of New Rochelle, NY
College of Staten Island of the City University
  of New York, NY
Columbus State University, GA
Concordia University, Nebraska, NE
Concordia University Texas, TX
Dalton State College, GA
Defiance College, OH
Delta State University, MS
DePauw University, IN

DeSales University, PA
Dickinson State University, ND
Dominican College, NY
Drury University, MO
D'Youville College, NY
East Carolina University, NC
Eastern Michigan University, MI
Eastern New Mexico University, NM
Eastern Washington University, WA
East Stroudsburg University of
  Pennsylvania, PA
East Texas Baptist University, TX
ECPI College of Technology, VA
ECPI Technical College, VA
Edinboro University of Pennsylvania, PA
Elizabethtown College, PA
Elmhurst College, IL
Emmanuel College, MA
Emporia State University, KS
Endicott College, MA
Everest University, FL
Felician College, NJ
Ferris State University, MI
Fitchburg State College, MA
Florida Agricultural and Mechanical
  University, FL
Florida Gulf Coast University, FL
Florida International University, FL
Florida Southern College, FL
Francis Marion University, SC
Frostburg State University, MD
Furman University, SC
Gardner-Webb University, NC
Georgia College & State University, GA
Georgia Southern University, GA
Grace University, NE
Grand Valley State University, MI
Hampden-Sydney College, VA
Hampton University, VA
Harding University, AR
Hardin-Simmons University, TX
Hawai'i Pacific University, HI
Houston Baptist University, TX
Husson University, ME
Idaho State University, ID
Illinois Institute of Technology, IL
Illinois State University, IL
Indiana University of Pennsylvania, PA
Iowa State University of Science and
  Technology, IA
Jacksonville State University, AL
James Madison University, VA
Jefferson College of Health Sciences, VA
John Carroll University, OH
Juniata College, PA
Kean University, NJ
Kennesaw State University, GA
Kent State University, OH
King's College, PA
Kutztown University of Pennsylvania, PA
LaGrange College, GA
Lakeview College of Nursing, IL
Langston University, OK
Lewis-Clark State College, ID
Lindenwood University, MO
Lock Haven University of Pennsylvania, PA
Long Island University, Brooklyn
  Campus, NY
Long Island University, C.W. Post
  Campus, NY
Louisiana Tech University, LA
Lycoming College, PA
Malone University, OH

Mansfield University of Pennsylvania, PA
Marquette University, WI
Marymount University, VA
Maryville University of Saint Louis, MO
Marywood University, PA
Massachusetts College of Liberal Arts, MA
Medcenter One College of Nursing, ND
Medical College of Georgia, GA
Mercy College of Northwest Ohio, OH
Mesa State College, CO
Michigan State University, MI
Midwestern State University, TX
Millersville University of Pennsylvania, PA
Millikin University, IL
Milwaukee School of Engineering, WI
Minnesota State University Moorhead, MN
Misericordia University, PA
Mississippi State University, MS
Mississippi University for Women, MS
Missouri Valley College, MO
Molloy College, NY
Monmouth University, NJ
Montana State University, MT
Montana State University Billings, MT
Montana State University–Northern, MT
Montana Tech of The University of
  Montana, MT
Moravian College, PA
Morehead State University, KY
Mount Mary College, WI
Murray State University, KY
New England College, NH
New Mexico State University, NM
Northeastern State University, OK
Northern Arizona University, AZ
Northern Illinois University, IL
Northern Kentucky University, KY
Northern Michigan University, MI
North Georgia College & State University, GA
Northwestern Oklahoma State University, OK
Northwestern State University of
  Louisiana, LA
Northwest Nazarene University, ID
Oakland University, MI
Ohio Northern University, OH
The Ohio State University, OH
Ohio University, OH
Ohio University–Chillicothe, OH
Ohio University–Eastern, OH
Ohio University–Lancaster, OH
Ohio University–Southern Campus, OH
Ohio University–Zanesville, OH
Oklahoma City University, OK
Oklahoma Panhandle State University, OK
Oklahoma Wesleyan University, OK
Old Dominion University, VA
Oral Roberts University, OK
Oregon Health & Science University, OR
Ouachita Baptist University, AR
Pace University, NY
Pacific University, OR
Piedmont College, GA
Pittsburg State University, KS
Plymouth State University, NH
Point Loma Nazarene University, CA
Purdue University, IN
Purdue University North Central, IN
Quincy University, IL
The Richard Stockton College of New
  Jersey, NJ
Robert Morris University Illinois, IL
Rochester Institute of Technology, NY
Rockhurst University, MO

Rocky Mountain College, MT
Sacred Heart University, CT
Saginaw Valley State University, MI
St. Catherine University, MN
Saint Francis Medical Center College of
  Nursing, IL
Saint Francis University, PA
St. John's University, NY
Saint Louis University, MO
Salisbury University, MD
Samford University, AL
San Diego State University, CA
Shepherd University, WV
Siena College, NY
Slippery Rock University of Pennsylvania, PA
Sonoma State University, CA
South Dakota State University, SD
Southeastern Louisiana University, LA
Southeast Missouri State University, MO
Southern Adventist University, TN
Southern Arkansas University–Magnolia, AR
Southern Illinois University Carbondale, IL
Southern Illinois University Edwardsville, IL
Southwestern College, KS
Southwestern Oklahoma State University, OK
State University of New York at
  Binghamton, NY
State University of New York at New
  Paltz, NY
State University of New York at
  Plattsburgh, NY
State University of New York College at Old
  Westbury, NY
State University of New York Upstate Medical
  University, NY
Stephen F. Austin State University, TX
Stevens-Henager College, ID
Stony Brook University, State University of
  New York, NY
Sul Ross State University, TX
Tennessee Technological University, TN
Tennessee Wesleyan College, TN
Texas A&M University, TX
Texas Christian University, TX
Texas Woman's University, TX
Towson University, MD
Trinity Christian College, IL
Union University, TN
The University of Akron, OH
The University of Alabama at
  Birmingham, AL
The University of Alabama in Huntsville, AL
University of Alaska Anchorage, AK
University of California, Davis, CA
University of California, Irvine, CA
University of Central Missouri, MO
University of Central Oklahoma, OK
University of Colorado at Boulder, CO
University of Connecticut, CT
University of Delaware, DE
University of Evansville, IN
University of Florida, FL
University of Hartford, CT
University of Hawaii at Hilo, HI
University of Illinois at Urbana–
  Champaign, IL
University of Indianapolis, IN
The University of Kansas, KS
University of Kentucky, KY
University of Louisiana at Monroe, LA
University of Louisville, KY
University of Maine at Fort Kent, ME
University of Mary Hardin-Baylor, TX

University of Maryland, College Park, MD
University of Massachusetts Amherst, MA
University of Massachusetts Boston, MA
University of Massachusetts Lowell, MA
University of Memphis, TN
University of Miami, FL
University of Michigan, MI
University of Michigan–Flint, MI
University of Minnesota, Twin Cities
  Campus, MN
University of Mississippi, MS
University of Missouri, MO
University of Missouri–St. Louis, MO
University of Nebraska–Lincoln, NE
University of Nevada, Las Vegas, NV
University of New Hampshire, NH
The University of North Carolina at
  Asheville, NC
The University of North Carolina at Chapel
  Hill, NC
The University of North Carolina at
  Charlotte, NC
The University of North Carolina at
  Greensboro, NC
The University of North Carolina at
  Pembroke, NC
The University of North Carolina
  Wilmington, NC
University of North Dakota, ND
University of Northern Colorado, CO
University of North Florida, FL
University of Pittsburgh at Bradford, PA
University of Portland, OR
University of St. Francis, IL
University of Saint Francis, IN
University of South Carolina, SC
University of Southern Indiana, IN
The University of Tennessee, TN
The University of Tennessee at Martin, TN
The University of Texas at Arlington, TX
The University of Texas at Brownsville, TX
The University of Texas at El Paso, TX
The University of Texas at Tyler, TX
The University of Texas Health Science
  Center at Houston, TX
The University of Texas Medical Branch, TX
The University of Texas–Pan American, TX
The University of Toledo, OH
University of Tulsa, OK
University of Vermont, VT
The University of Virginia's College at
  Wise, VA
University of Washington, WA
University of West Georgia, GA
University of Wisconsin–Eau Claire, WI
University of Wisconsin–Green Bay, WI
University of Wisconsin–La Crosse, WI
University of Wisconsin–Parkside, WI
University of Wisconsin–River Falls, WI
University of Wisconsin–Stevens Point, WI
University of Wisconsin–Superior, WI
University of Wyoming, WY
Utah State University, UT
Valdosta State University, GA
Valparaiso University, IN
Virginia Commonwealth University, VA
Washburn University, KS
Washington State University, WA
Washington University in St. Louis, MO
Wayne State College, NE
Wayne State University, MI
Western Kentucky University, KY
Western Washington University, WA

West Liberty University, WV
Westminster College, UT
West Virginia University, WV
Wheaton College, IL
Wichita State University, KS
Widener University, PA
Wright State University, OH
Youngstown State University, OH

Home Economics

Arizona State University, AZ
Auburn University, AL
Averett University, VA
Baylor University, TX
Bowling Green State University, OH
California Polytechnic State University,
  San Luis Obispo, CA
Carson-Newman College, TN
East Carolina University, NC
Eastern Michigan University, MI
Eastern New Mexico University, NM
Fort Valley State University, GA
Framingham State College, MA
Idaho State University, ID
Illinois State University, IL
Indiana University of Pennsylvania, PA
Iowa State University of Science and
  Technology, IA
Jacksonville State University, AL
Lipscomb University, TN
Louisiana State University and Agricultural
  and Mechanical College, LA
Louisiana Tech University, LA
Mississippi State University, MS
Mississippi University for Women, MS
Montana State University, MT
Montclair State University, NJ
Mount Mary College, WI
New Mexico State University, NM
Northeastern State University, OK
Northern Arizona University, AZ
The Ohio State University, OH
Ohio University, OH
Ohio University–Chillicothe, OH
Ohio University–Eastern, OH
Ohio University–Lancaster, OH
Ohio University–Southern Campus, OH
Ohio University–Zanesville, OH
Oklahoma State University, OK
Ouachita Baptist University, AR
Pittsburg State University, KS
Point Loma Nazarene University, CA
St. Catherine University, MN
Sam Houston State University, TX
Seton Hill University, PA
Shepherd University, WV
Siena College, NY
South Dakota State University, SD
Southeastern Louisiana University, LA
Southeast Missouri State University, MO
Southern Illinois University Carbondale, IL
State University of New York at
  Plattsburgh, NY
State University of New York College at
  Oneonta, NY
Stephen F. Austin State University, TX
Tennessee Technological University, TN
Texas State University–San Marcos, TX
Texas Tech University, TX
Texas Woman's University, TX
The University of Akron, OH
The University of Alabama, AL
University of California, Davis, CA

Non-Need Scholarships for Undergraduates
Academic Interests/Achievements

University of Central Missouri, MO
University of Central Oklahoma, OK
University of Idaho, ID
University of Illinois at Urbana–
 Champaign, IL
University of Kentucky, KY
University of Louisiana at Monroe, LA
University of Minnesota, Twin Cities
 Campus, MN
University of Missouri, MO
University of Nebraska at Omaha, NE
University of Nebraska–Lincoln, NE
The University of North Carolina at
 Greensboro, NC
University of Northern Colorado, CO
The University of Tennessee at Martin, TN
University of Vermont, VT
University of Wisconsin–Stevens Point, WI
University of Wisconsin–Stout, WI
University of Wyoming, WY
Utah State University, UT
Washington State University, WA
Wayne State College, NE
Western Illinois University, IL
Western Kentucky University, KY
West Virginia University, WV

Humanities

Alaska Pacific University, AK
Alderson-Broaddus College, WV
Alfred University, NY
Alliant International University, CA
Arizona State University, AZ
Arkansas State University—Jonesboro, AR
Armstrong Atlantic State University, GA
Auburn University, AL
Augustana College, IL
Augustana College, SD
Austin College, TX
Austin Peay State University, TN
Averett University, VA
Ball State University, IN
Barton College, NC
Baylor University, TX
Belhaven University, MS
Berry College, GA
Birmingham-Southern College, AL
Black Hills State University, SD
Bloomfield College, NJ
Bloomsburg University of Pennsylvania, PA
Blue Mountain College, MS
Boise State University, ID
Bowling Green State University, OH
Brenau University, GA
Briar Cliff University, IA
Bryan College, TN
Buena Vista University, IA
Butler University, IN
California Lutheran University, CA
California Polytechnic State University,
 San Luis Obispo, CA
California State Polytechnic University,
 Pomona, CA
California State University, Chico, CA
California State University, Fresno, CA
California State University, Fullerton, CA
California State University, Stanislaus, CA
Calvin College, MI
Campbellsville University, KY
Carroll University, WI
Case Western Reserve University, OH
Centenary College of Louisiana, LA
Central College, IA

Central Michigan University, MI
Christopher Newport University, VA
The Citadel, The Military College of South
 Carolina, SC
City College of the City University of New
 York, NY
Clarkson University, NY
Clemson University, SC
Cleveland State University, OH
Coastal Carolina University, SC
The College at Brockport, State University of
 New York, NY
College of Charleston, SC
The College of New Rochelle, NY
College of Staten Island of the City University
 of New York, NY
College of the Holy Cross, MA
Columbia College, MO
Columbus State University, GA
Concordia University, Nebraska, NE
Dallas Baptist University, TX
Dalton State College, GA
Defiance College, OH
Delta State University, MS
DeSales University, PA
Dickinson State University, ND
Dordt College, IA
Drury University, MO
D'Youville College, NY
East Carolina University, NC
Eastern Michigan University, MI
Eastern New Mexico University, NM
East Texas Baptist University, TX
Edinboro University of Pennsylvania, PA
Elizabethtown College, PA
Elmhurst College, IL
Emmanuel College, MA
Emporia State University, KS
Evangel University, MO
Flagler College, FL
Florida Gulf Coast University, FL
Florida International University, FL
Fort Lewis College, CO
Francis Marion University, SC
Fresno Pacific University, CA
Frostburg State University, MD
Furman University, SC
Gannon University, PA
Gardner-Webb University, NC
Georgia College & State University, GA
Georgia Southern University, GA
Grand Valley State University, MI
Hardin-Simmons University, TX
High Point University, NC
Idaho State University, ID
Illinois State University, IL
Indiana University of Pennsylvania, PA
Iowa State University of Science and
 Technology, IA
Jacksonville State University, AL
James Madison University, VA
Juniata College, PA
Kean University, NJ
Kennesaw State University, GA
King's College, PA
Kutztown University of Pennsylvania, PA
Lake Erie College, OH
Lawrence Technological University, MI
Lewis-Clark State College, ID
Limestone College, SC
Lincoln University, PA
Lindenwood University, MO
Longwood University, VA

Louisiana State University and Agricultural
 and Mechanical College, LA
Lubbock Christian University, TX
Lycoming College, PA
Malone University, OH
Manchester College, IN
Massachusetts College of Liberal Arts, MA
Mesa State College, CO
Mid-Continent University, KY
Midwestern State University, TX
Millersville University of Pennsylvania, PA
Millikin University, IL
Mississippi State University, MS
Mississippi University for Women, MS
Missouri University of Science and
 Technology, MO
Missouri Valley College, MO
Monmouth University, NJ
Montana State University, MT
Montana State University Billings, MT
Montana State University–Northern, MT
Montclair State University, NJ
Mount Mary College, WI
Murray State University, KY
Newberry College, SC
New England College, NH
New Jersey Institute of Technology, NJ
New Mexico State University, NM
North Carolina State University, NC
North Central College, IL
Northeastern State University, OK
Northern Arizona University, AZ
Northern Illinois University, IL
Northern State University, SD
North Georgia College & State University, GA
Northwestern State University of
 Louisiana, LA
Oakland University, MI
Ohio Northern University, OH
The Ohio State University, OH
Ohio University, OH
Ohio University–Chillicothe, OH
Ohio University–Eastern, OH
Ohio University–Lancaster, OH
Ohio University–Southern Campus, OH
Ohio University–Zanesville, OH
Oklahoma State University, OK
Old Dominion University, VA
Ouachita Baptist University, AR
Pace University, NY
Pacific University, OR
Piedmont College, GA
Point Loma Nazarene University, CA
Portland State University, OR
Purchase College, State University of New
 York, NY
Purdue University, IN
Regent University, VA
Rensselaer Polytechnic Institute, NY
The Richard Stockton College of New
 Jersey, NJ
Ripon College, WI
Rivier College, NH
Rockhurst University, MO
Rocky Mountain College, MT
Sacred Heart University, CT
St. Catherine University, MN
St. Edward's University, TX
Saint Francis University, PA
St. John Fisher College, NY
St. John's University, NY
Saint Louis University, MO
Saint Martin's University, WA

Salisbury University, MD
Samford University, AL
Sam Houston State University, TX
Savannah College of Art and Design, GA
Savannah State University, GA
Seton Hill University, PA
Shepherd University, WV
Shippensburg University of Pennsylvania, PA
Siena College, NY
Sonoma State University, CA
South Dakota State University, SD
Southeastern Louisiana University, LA
Southeast Missouri State University, MO
Southern Illinois University Carbondale, IL
Southwestern University, TX
State University of New York at
  Binghamton, NY
State University of New York at Fredonia, NY
State University of New York at Oswego, NY
State University of New York at
  Plattsburgh, NY
State University of New York College at
  Geneseo, NY
State University of New York College at
  Potsdam, NY
Stetson University, FL
Tabor College, KS
Tennessee Technological University, TN
Tennessee Wesleyan College, TN
Texas Tech University, TX
Texas Woman's University, TX
The University of Akron, OH
The University of Alabama in Huntsville, AL
University of Alaska Anchorage, AK
The University of Arizona, AZ
University of California, Davis, CA
University of California, Irvine, CA
University of California, Riverside, CA
University of California, Santa Cruz, CA
University of Central Missouri, MO
University of Colorado at Boulder, CO
University of Connecticut, CT
University of Dayton, OH
University of Delaware, DE
University of Denver, CO
University of Evansville, IN
University of Great Falls, MT
University of Houston–Clear Lake, TX
University of Idaho, ID
University of Illinois at Urbana–
  Champaign, IL
The University of Kansas, KS
University of Maine at Fort Kent, ME
University of Mary Hardin-Baylor, TX
University of Maryland, Baltimore
  County, MD
University of Maryland, College Park, MD
University of Mary Washington, VA
University of Massachusetts Amherst, MA
University of Massachusetts Lowell, MA
University of Memphis, TN
University of Miami, FL
University of Michigan, MI
University of Michigan–Flint, MI
University of Minnesota, Twin Cities
  Campus, MN
University of Mississippi, MS
University of Missouri, MO
University of Missouri–St. Louis, MO
The University of Montana Western, MT
University of Nebraska–Lincoln, NE
University of Nevada, Las Vegas, NV
University of New Hampshire, NH

The University of North Carolina at
  Charlotte, NC
The University of North Carolina at
  Greensboro, NC
The University of North Carolina
  Wilmington, NC
University of North Dakota, ND
University of Oklahoma, OK
University of Pittsburgh at Bradford, PA
University of Pittsburgh at Johnstown, PA
University of Portland, OR
University of Puget Sound, WA
University of St. Thomas, MN
University of South Alabama, AL
University of South Carolina, SC
University of South Carolina Aiken, SC
The University of South Dakota, SD
University of Southern Indiana, IN
The University of Tennessee, TN
The University of Tennessee at Martin, TN
The University of Texas at Arlington, TX
The University of Texas at El Paso, TX
The University of Texas at San Antonio, TX
University of the Ozarks, AR
University of the Southwest, NM
The University of Toledo, OH
University of Vermont, VT
The University of Virginia's College at
  Wise, VA
University of West Georgia, GA
University of Wisconsin–Green Bay, WI
University of Wisconsin–La Crosse, WI
University of Wisconsin–River Falls, WI
University of Wisconsin–Stevens Point, WI
University of Wisconsin–Superior, WI
University of Wisconsin–Whitewater, WI
Utah State University, UT
Valdosta State University, GA
Valley City State University, ND
Virginia Commonwealth University, VA
Warner Pacific College, OR
Washburn University, KS
Washington State University, WA
Washington University in St. Louis, MO
Wayne State College, NE
Wayne State University, MI
Webster University, MO
Wesleyan College, GA
Western Oregon University, OR
Western Washington University, WA
Westminster College, UT
West Virginia University, WV
Wheaton College, IL
Wichita State University, KS
Widener University, PA
Williams Baptist College, AR
Wilson College, PA
Wright State University, OH
Xavier University of Louisiana, LA
Youngstown State University, OH

International Studies

Alfred University, NY
Alliant International University, CA
Angelo State University, TX
Armstrong Atlantic State University, GA
Augsburg College, MN
Augustana College, SD
Austin College, TX
Austin Peay State University, TN
Ball State University, IN
Barton College, NC
Baylor University, TX

Belhaven University, MS
Birmingham-Southern College, AL
Bloomsburg University of Pennsylvania, PA
Boise State University, ID
Bowling Green State University, OH
Buena Vista University, IA
Butler University, IN
California Lutheran University, CA
California Polytechnic State University,
  San Luis Obispo, CA
California State University, Chico, CA
California State University, Stanislaus, CA
Calvin College, MI
Carroll University, WI
Case Western Reserve University, OH
Central College, IA
Central Michigan University, MI
Chatham University, PA
City College of the City University of New
  York, NY
Clemson University, SC
The College at Brockport, State University of
  New York, NY
College of Staten Island of the City University
  of New York, NY
Columbus State University, GA
Concordia University Texas, TX
Culver-Stockton College, MO
Defiance College, OH
DePauw University, IN
D'Youville College, NY
Elizabethtown College, PA
Elmhurst College, IL
Frostburg State University, MD
Furman University, SC
Gannon University, PA
Georgia College & State University, GA
Georgia Southern University, GA
Grace University, NE
Grand Valley State University, MI
Hampden-Sydney College, VA
Hampshire College, MA
Henderson State University, AR
High Point University, NC
Idaho State University, ID
Illinois State University, IL
Indiana University of Pennsylvania, PA
Iowa State University of Science and
  Technology, IA
James Madison University, VA
Juniata College, PA
Kean University, NJ
Kennesaw State University, GA
Kent State University, OH
Keuka College, NY
Kutztown University of Pennsylvania, PA
Lake Erie College, OH
Lawrence Technological University, MI
Lindenwood University, MO
Lock Haven University of Pennsylvania, PA
Longwood University, VA
Louisiana Tech University, LA
Lycoming College, PA
Malone University, OH
Mercer University, GA
Michigan State University, MI
Midwestern State University, TX
Millikin University, IL
Minnesota State University Moorhead, MN
Mississippi State University, MS
Monmouth University, NJ
Montclair State University, NJ
Morehead State University, KY

Murray State University, KY
New England College, NH
North Central College, IL
Northern Arizona University, AZ
Northern Illinois University, IL
Northern Michigan University, MI
Northern State University, SD
Ohio Northern University, OH
The Ohio State University, OH
Ohio University, OH
Ohio University–Chillicothe, OH
Ohio University–Eastern, OH
Ohio University–Lancaster, OH
Ohio University–Southern Campus, OH
Ohio University–Zanesville, OH
Oklahoma State University, OK
Ouachita Baptist University, AR
Portland State University, OR
Quincy University, IL
Rochester Institute of Technology, NY
St. Ambrose University, IA
St. Edward's University, TX
Saint Louis University, MO
Saint Martin's University, WA
Samford University, AL
San Diego State University, CA
Siena College, NY
South Dakota State University, SD
Southeastern Louisiana University, LA
Southeast Missouri State University, MO
Southern Illinois University Carbondale, IL
Southwestern University, TX
State University of New York at
  Binghamton, NY
State University of New York at Fredonia, NY
State University of New York at Oswego, NY
State University of New York at
  Plattsburgh, NY
State University of New York College at
  Cortland, NY
State University of New York College at
  Geneseo, NY
Stony Brook University, State University of
  New York, NY
Tennessee Technological University, TN
Tennessee Wesleyan College, TN
Texas Christian University, TX
Texas State University–San Marcos, TX
Texas Tech University, TX
The University of Akron, OH
University of California, Davis, CA
University of California, Irvine, CA
University of Colorado at Boulder, CO
University of Connecticut, CT
University of Delaware, DE
University of Denver, CO
University of Evansville, IN
University of Illinois at Urbana–
  Champaign, IL
The University of Kansas, KS
University of Kentucky, KY
University of Mary Hardin-Baylor, TX
University of Maryland, College Park, MD
University of Mary Washington, VA
University of Memphis, TN
University of Miami, FL
University of Michigan, MI
University of Michigan–Dearborn, MI
University of Michigan–Flint, MI
University of Minnesota, Twin Cities
  Campus, MN
University of Mississippi, MS
University of Missouri, MO

University of Missouri–St. Louis, MO
University of Nebraska–Lincoln, NE
University of Nevada, Las Vegas, NV
The University of North Carolina
  Wilmington, NC
University of North Dakota, ND
University of North Florida, FL
University of Oklahoma, OK
University of Puget Sound, WA
University of St. Francis, IL
University of St. Thomas, MN
University of South Alabama, AL
University of South Carolina, SC
The University of Tampa, FL
The University of Tennessee, TN
The University of Texas at Arlington, TX
The University of Texas at Brownsville, TX
The University of Texas at El Paso, TX
The University of Texas at San Antonio, TX
The University of Toledo, OH
University of Tulsa, OK
University of Vermont, VT
University of Wisconsin–Eau Claire, WI
University of Wisconsin–La Crosse, WI
University of Wisconsin–River Falls, WI
University of Wisconsin–Stevens Point, WI
University of Wisconsin–Stout, WI
University of Wyoming, WY
Utah State University, UT
Villanova University, PA
Virginia Military Institute, VA
Wartburg College, IA
Washburn University, KS
Washington State University, WA
Washington University in St. Louis, MO
Waynesburg University, PA
Wayne State University, MI
Webster University, MO
Westminster College, UT
West Virginia University, WV
Wichita State University, KS
Widener University, PA
Wilson College, PA
Wright State University, OH

Library Science

Arkansas State University—Jonesboro, AR
Blue Mountain College, MS
California Polytechnic State University,
  San Luis Obispo, CA
Emporia State University, KS
Illinois State University, IL
Iowa State University of Science and
  Technology, IA
Kent State University, OH
Kutztown University of Pennsylvania, PA
Lindenwood University, MO
Lock Haven University of Pennsylvania, PA
Mississippi State University, MS
Murray State University, KY
Northeastern State University, OK
Northern Arizona University, AZ
Northwestern Oklahoma State University, OK
Sam Houston State University, TX
Texas Woman's University, TX
The University of Alabama, AL
University of Central Missouri, MO
University of Idaho, ID
University of Illinois at Urbana–
  Champaign, IL
University of Louisiana at Monroe, LA
University of Maryland, College Park, MD
University of Michigan, MI

University of Minnesota, Twin Cities
  Campus, MN
University of Missouri, MO
The University of North Carolina at
  Greensboro, NC
University of South Carolina, SC
The University of Tennessee, TN
The University of Toledo, OH
Utah State University, UT
Valdosta State University, GA
Valley City State University, ND
Virginia Polytechnic Institute and State
  University, VA
Wayne State University, MI
Western Washington University, WA
West Virginia University, WV

Mathematics

Abilene Christian University, TX
Albion College, MI
Alderson-Broaddus College, WV
Alfred University, NY
Angelo State University, TX
Arizona State University, AZ
Arkansas State University—Jonesboro, AR
Arkansas Tech University, AR
Armstrong Atlantic State University, GA
Ashland University, OH
Atlantic Union College, MA
Auburn University, AL
Augsburg College, MN
Augustana College, IL
Augustana College, SD
Aurora University, IL
Austin Peay State University, TN
Averett University, VA
Ball State University, IN
Bard College, NY
Barton College, NC
Baylor University, TX
Belhaven University, MS
Bethel College, IN
Birmingham-Southern College, AL
Black Hills State University, SD
Bloomfield College, NJ
Bloomsburg University of Pennsylvania, PA
Blue Mountain College, MS
Boise State University, ID
Bowie State University, MD
Bowling Green State University, OH
Brevard College, NC
Briar Cliff University, IA
Bryan College, TN
Bucknell University, PA
Buena Vista University, IA
Butler University, IN
California Lutheran University, CA
California Polytechnic State University,
  San Luis Obispo, CA
California State Polytechnic University,
  Pomona, CA
California State University, Chico, CA
California State University, Fresno, CA
California State University, Fullerton, CA
California State University, Northridge, CA
California State University,
  San Bernardino, CA
California State University, Stanislaus, CA
Calvin College, MI
Cameron University, OK
Campbellsville University, KY
Carroll University, WI
Carson-Newman College, TN

Carthage College, WI
Case Western Reserve University, OH
Centenary College of Louisiana, LA
Central College, IA
Central Michigan University, MI
Chatham University, PA
Christopher Newport University, VA
City College of the City University of New York, NY
Clarkson University, NY
Clemson University, SC
Cleveland State University, OH
Coastal Carolina University, SC
Coe College, IA
The College at Brockport, State University of New York, NY
College of Charleston, SC
The College of New Rochelle, NY
College of Saint Mary, NE
The College of Saint Rose, NY
College of Staten Island of the City University of New York, NY
The Colorado College, CO
Colorado School of Mines, CO
Columbia College, MO
Columbus State University, GA
Concordia University Chicago, IL
Concordia University, Nebraska, NE
Concordia University, St. Paul, MN
Concordia University Texas, TX
Dakota State University, SD
Dallas Baptist University, TX
Davidson College, NC
Defiance College, OH
Delta State University, MS
DePauw University, IN
DeSales University, PA
Dickinson State University, ND
Dordt College, IA
Dowling College, NY
Drury University, MO
Duke University, NC
D'Youville College, NY
East Carolina University, NC
Eastern Michigan University, MI
Eastern New Mexico University, NM
Eastern Washington University, WA
East Stroudsburg University of Pennsylvania, PA
East Texas Baptist University, TX
Edinboro University of Pennsylvania, PA
Elizabethtown College, PA
Elmhurst College, IL
Elon University, NC
Emmanuel College, MA
Emporia State University, KS
Erskine College, SC
Evangel University, MO
Ferris State University, MI
Fitchburg State College, MA
Florida Gulf Coast University, FL
Florida International University, FL
Fort Lewis College, CO
Francis Marion University, SC
Frostburg State University, MD
Furman University, SC
Gannon University, PA
Gardner-Webb University, NC
George Fox University, OR
Georgia College & State University, GA
Georgian Court University, NJ
Georgia Southern University, GA
Glenville State College, WV

Grand Valley State University, MI
Greenville College, IL
Hardin-Simmons University, TX
Henderson State University, AR
High Point University, NC
Hillsdale Free Will Baptist College, OK
Howard Payne University, TX
Huntingdon College, AL
Huntington University, IN
Idaho State University, ID
Illinois State University, IL
Indiana University of Pennsylvania, PA
Iowa State University of Science and Technology, IA
Jacksonville State University, AL
James Madison University, VA
John Carroll University, OH
Johnson C. Smith University, NC
Juniata College, PA
Kean University, NJ
Kennesaw State University, GA
Kent State University, OH
Kettering University, MI
King's College, PA
Knox College, IL
Kutztown University of Pennsylvania, PA
Lake Erie College, OH
Lake Forest College, IL
Lawrence Technological University, MI
Lees-McRae College, NC
Lewis-Clark State College, ID
Limestone College, SC
Lincoln University, PA
Lindenwood University, MO
Lindsey Wilson College, KY
Lipscomb University, TN
Lock Haven University of Pennsylvania, PA
Long Island University, C.W. Post Campus, NY
Longwood University, VA
Louisiana State University and Agricultural and Mechanical College, LA
Louisiana Tech University, LA
Lycoming College, PA
Malone University, OH
Manhattan College, NY
Manhattanville College, NY
Mansfield University of Pennsylvania, PA
Marquette University, WI
Marymount University, VA
Marywood University, PA
Massachusetts College of Liberal Arts, MA
The Master's College and Seminary, CA
McMurry University, TX
Meredith College, NC
Mesa State College, CO
Michigan State University, MI
Midwestern State University, TX
Millersville University of Pennsylvania, PA
Millikin University, IL
Mills College, CA
Minnesota State University Moorhead, MN
Mississippi State University, MS
Mississippi University for Women, MS
Missouri University of Science and Technology, MO
Missouri Valley College, MO
Molloy College, NY
Monmouth University, NJ
Montana State University, MT
Montana State University Billings, MT
Montana Tech of The University of Montana, MT

Montclair State University, NJ
Moravian College, PA
Mount Mary College, WI
Murray State University, KY
Muskingum University, OH
Newberry College, SC
New England College, NH
New Jersey Institute of Technology, NJ
New Mexico State University, NM
North Carolina State University, NC
North Central College, IL
Northeastern Illinois University, IL
Northeastern State University, OK
Northern Arizona University, AZ
Northern Illinois University, IL
Northern Kentucky University, KY
Northern Michigan University, MI
Northern State University, SD
North Georgia College & State University, GA
Northwestern Oklahoma State University, OK
Northwestern State University of Louisiana, LA
Northwest Nazarene University, ID
Ohio Northern University, OH
The Ohio State University, OH
Ohio University, OH
Ohio University–Chillicothe, OH
Ohio University–Eastern, OH
Ohio University–Lancaster, OH
Ohio University–Southern Campus, OH
Ohio University–Zanesville, OH
Oklahoma Panhandle State University, OK
Oklahoma State University, OK
Ouachita Baptist University, AR
Pace University, NY
Pacific University, OR
Piedmont College, GA
Pittsburg State University, KS
Plymouth State University, NH
Point Loma Nazarene University, CA
Purchase College, State University of New York, NY
Purdue University, IN
Quincy University, IL
Randolph College, VA
Rensselaer Polytechnic Institute, NY
The Richard Stockton College of New Jersey, NJ
Ripon College, WI
Rivier College, NH
Rochester Institute of Technology, NY
Rockford College, IL
Rockhurst University, MO
Rocky Mountain College, MT
Rollins College, FL
Sacred Heart University, CT
Saginaw Valley State University, MI
St. Catherine University, MN
St. Edward's University, TX
Saint Francis University, PA
St. John Fisher College, NY
St. John's University, NY
Saint Louis University, MO
Salisbury University, MD
Samford University, AL
Sam Houston State University, TX
San Diego State University, CA
Savannah State University, GA
Schreiner University, TX
Seton Hill University, PA
Shepherd University, WV
Shippensburg University of Pennsylvania, PA
Siena College, NY

Non-Need Scholarships for Undergraduates
Academic Interests/Achievements

Skidmore College, NY
Sonoma State University, CA
South Dakota School of Mines and
  Technology, SD
South Dakota State University, SD
Southeastern Louisiana University, LA
Southeastern Oklahoma State University, OK
Southeast Missouri State University, MO
Southern Adventist University, TN
Southern Arkansas University–Magnolia, AR
Southern Illinois University Carbondale, IL
Southern Nazarene University, OK
Southwestern Oklahoma State University, OK
Southwestern University, TX
Southwest Minnesota State University, MN
State University of New York at
  Binghamton, NY
State University of New York at Fredonia, NY
State University of New York at Oswego, NY
State University of New York at
  Plattsburgh, NY
State University of New York College at
  Cortland, NY
State University of New York College at
  Geneseo, NY
State University of New York College at
  Potsdam, NY
Stephen F. Austin State University, TX
Stetson University, FL
Stony Brook University, State University of
  New York, NY
Tennessee Technological University, TN
Tennessee Wesleyan College, TN
Texas A&M University–Texarkana, TX
Texas Christian University, TX
Texas Lutheran University, TX
Texas Tech University, TX
Texas Woman's University, TX
Thiel College, PA
Thomas More College, KY
Towson University, MD
Trinity Christian College, IL
Truman State University, MO
Union University, TN
The University of Akron, OH
The University of Alabama, AL
The University of Alabama at
  Birmingham, AL
The University of Alabama in Huntsville, AL
University of Alaska Anchorage, AK
University of California, Davis, CA
University of California, Riverside, CA
University of California, San Diego, CA
University of Central Missouri, MO
University of Central Oklahoma, OK
University of Colorado at Boulder, CO
University of Connecticut, CT
University of Dallas, TX
University of Delaware, DE
University of Denver, CO
University of Evansville, IN
University of Great Falls, MT
University of Houston–Clear Lake, TX
University of Idaho, ID
University of Illinois at Urbana–
  Champaign, IL
The University of Kansas, KS
University of Kentucky, KY
University of Louisiana at Monroe, LA
University of Louisville, KY
University of Maine at Fort Kent, ME
University of Mary Hardin-Baylor, TX

University of Maryland, Baltimore
  County, MD
University of Maryland, College Park, MD
University of Mary Washington, VA
University of Massachusetts Amherst, MA
University of Memphis, TN
University of Miami, FL
University of Michigan, MI
University of Michigan–Dearborn, MI
University of Michigan–Flint, MI
University of Minnesota, Twin Cities
  Campus, MN
University of Mississippi, MS
University of Missouri, MO
University of Missouri–St. Louis, MO
The University of Montana Western, MT
University of Nebraska at Omaha, NE
University of Nebraska–Lincoln, NE
University of Nevada, Las Vegas, NV
University of New Hampshire, NH
University of New Orleans, LA
The University of North Carolina at
  Asheville, NC
The University of North Carolina at Chapel
  Hill, NC
The University of North Carolina at
  Charlotte, NC
The University of North Carolina at
  Greensboro, NC
The University of North Carolina
  Wilmington, NC
University of North Dakota, ND
University of Northern Colorado, CO
University of Northern Iowa, IA
University of Oklahoma, OK
University of Pittsburgh at Bradford, PA
University of Pittsburgh at Johnstown, PA
University of Portland, OR
University of Puget Sound, WA
University of Richmond, VA
University of St. Thomas, MN
University of South Carolina, SC
University of South Carolina Aiken, SC
The University of South Dakota, SD
University of Southern Indiana, IN
The University of Tennessee at Martin, TN
The University of Texas at Arlington, TX
The University of Texas at Brownsville, TX
The University of Texas at Dallas, TX
The University of Texas at El Paso, TX
The University of Texas at San Antonio, TX
The University of Texas–Pan American, TX
University of the Ozarks, AR
University of the Southwest, NM
The University of Toledo, OH
University of Tulsa, OK
University of Vermont, VT
The University of Virginia's College at
  Wise, VA
University of West Georgia, GA
University of Wisconsin–Eau Claire, WI
University of Wisconsin–La Crosse, WI
University of Wisconsin–Parkside, WI
University of Wisconsin–River Falls, WI
University of Wisconsin–Stevens Point, WI
University of Wisconsin–Stout, WI
University of Wisconsin–Superior, WI
University of Wisconsin–Whitewater, WI
University of Wyoming, WY
Utah State University, UT
Valdosta State University, GA
Valley City State University, ND
Virginia Commonwealth University, VA

Virginia Military Institute, VA
Warner Pacific College, OR
Wartburg College, IA
Washburn University, KS
Washington State University, WA
Washington University in St. Louis, MO
Wayland Baptist University, TX
Waynesburg University, PA
Wayne State College, NE
Wayne State University, MI
Wesleyan College, GA
West Chester University of Pennsylvania, PA
Western Carolina University, NC
Western Illinois University, IL
Western Kentucky University, KY
Western Oregon University, OR
Western Washington University, WA
West Liberty University, WV
Westminster College, UT
West Virginia University, WV
Wheaton College, IL
Wichita State University, KS
Widener University, PA
Wilson College, PA
Wright State University, OH
Xavier University, OH
Xavier University of Louisiana, LA
York College, NE
Youngstown State University, OH

Military Science

Alfred University, NY
Angelo State University, TX
Arizona State University, AZ
Arkansas State University—Jonesboro, AR
Arkansas Tech University, AR
Armstrong Atlantic State University, GA
Austin Peay State University, TN
Ball State University, IN
Baylor University, TX
Black Hills State University, SD
Boise State University, ID
Boston College, MA
Bowie State University, MD
Bowling Green State University, OH
California Polytechnic State University,
  San Luis Obispo, CA
California State University, Fullerton, CA
Cameron University, OK
Carson-Newman College, TN
Central Michigan University, MI
Christopher Newport University, VA
The Citadel, The Military College of South
  Carolina, SC
Clarkson University, NY
Clemson University, SC
The College at Brockport, State University of
  New York, NY
College of Saint Benedict, MN
College of the Holy Cross, MA
Colorado School of Mines, CO
Columbus State University, GA
Creighton University, NE
Dickinson College, PA
East Carolina University, NC
Eastern New Mexico University, NM
Eastern Washington University, WA
Edinboro University of Pennsylvania, PA
Elon University, NC
Florida Institute of Technology, FL
Fort Valley State University, GA
Furman University, SC
Georgia Southern University, GA

Gonzaga University, WA
Idaho State University, ID
Illinois State University, IL
Iowa State University of Science and
   Technology, IA
Jacksonville State University, AL
James Madison University, VA
John Carroll University, OH
Kent State University, OH
Lawrence Technological University, MI
Lehigh University, PA
Lincoln University, MO
Lindenwood University, MO
Longwood University, VA
Louisiana State University and Agricultural
   and Mechanical College, LA
Louisiana Tech University, LA
Manhattan College, NY
Mercer University, GA
Michigan State University, MI
Mississippi State University, MS
Missouri University of Science and
   Technology, MO
Missouri Valley College, MO
Montana State University, MT
Morehead State University, KY
Morehouse College, GA
New Mexico State University, NM
Northern Arizona University, AZ
Northern Michigan University, MI
North Georgia College & State University, GA
North Greenville University, SC
Northwest Nazarene University, ID
The Ohio State University, OH
Ohio University, OH
Ohio University–Chillicothe, OH
Ohio University–Eastern, OH
Ohio University–Lancaster, OH
Ohio University–Southern Campus, OH
Ohio University–Zanesville, OH
Oklahoma State University, OK
Old Dominion University, VA
Olivet Nazarene University, IL
Pittsburg State University, KS
Providence College, RI
Purdue University, IN
Rensselaer Polytechnic Institute, NY
Ripon College, WI
Rochester Institute of Technology, NY
St. Edward's University, TX
St. John's University, NY
Saint Louis University, MO
St. Mary's University, TX
Sam Houston State University, TX
San Diego State University, CA
Santa Clara University, CA
Savannah State University, GA
Siena College, NY
South Dakota State University, SD
Southeast Missouri State University, MO
Southern Illinois University Carbondale, IL
Stephen F. Austin State University, TX
Stetson University, FL
Tennessee Technological University, TN
Texas Christian University, TX
Texas State University–San Marcos, TX
Texas Tech University, TX
Truman State University, MO
Union University, TN
The University of Akron, OH
The University of Alabama, AL
University of Alaska Fairbanks, AK
The University of Arizona, AZ

University of Central Missouri, MO
University of Central Oklahoma, OK
University of Charleston, WV
University of Colorado at Boulder, CO
University of Delaware, DE
University of Florida, FL
University of Idaho, ID
University of Illinois at Urbana–
   Champaign, IL
The University of Iowa, IA
University of Kentucky, KY
University of Louisiana at Monroe, LA
University of Louisville, KY
University of Maryland, College Park, MD
University of Massachusetts Amherst, MA
University of Memphis, TN
University of Michigan, MI
University of Minnesota, Twin Cities
   Campus, MN
University of Mississippi, MS
University of New Hampshire, NH
The University of North Carolina at
   Charlotte, NC
University of North Dakota, ND
University of Northern Colorado, CO
University of Portland, OR
University of Rochester, NY
The University of Scranton, PA
University of South Alabama, AL
University of South Carolina, SC
The University of South Dakota, SD
The University of Tampa, FL
The University of Tennessee, TN
The University of Tennessee at
   Chattanooga, TN
The University of Tennessee at Martin, TN
The University of Texas at Arlington, TX
The University of Texas at El Paso, TX
The University of Texas–Pan American, TX
University of Vermont, VT
University of West Florida, FL
University of Wisconsin–La Crosse, WI
University of Wisconsin–Stevens Point, WI
University of Wyoming, WY
Valdosta State University, GA
Villanova University, PA
Virginia Commonwealth University, VA
Virginia Military Institute, VA
Washington State University, WA
Washington University in St. Louis, MO
Wayne State University, MI
Western Kentucky University, KY
Westminster College, UT
West Virginia University, WV
Wheaton College, IL
Whitworth University, WA
Widener University, PA
Wright State University, OH
Xavier University, OH
Youngstown State University, OH

Physical Sciences

Abilene Christian University, TX
Alaska Pacific University, AK
Alderson-Broaddus College, WV
Alfred University, NY
Angelo State University, TX
Arizona State University, AZ
Arkansas State University—Jonesboro, AR
Arkansas Tech University, AR
Armstrong Atlantic State University, GA
Ashland University, OH
Auburn University, AL

Augsburg College, MN
Augustana College, IL
Augustana College, SD
Austin College, TX
Austin Peay State University, TN
Averett University, VA
Ball State University, IN
Bard College, NY
Barton College, NC
Baylor University, TX
Bethel College, IN
Birmingham-Southern College, AL
Black Hills State University, SD
Bloomfield College, NJ
Bloomsburg University of Pennsylvania, PA
Blue Mountain College, MS
Boise State University, ID
Bowling Green State University, OH
Brescia University, KY
Brevard College, NC
Briar Cliff University, IA
Bryan College, TN
Bucknell University, PA
Butler University, IN
California Lutheran University, CA
California Polytechnic State University,
   San Luis Obispo, CA
California State Polytechnic University,
   Pomona, CA
California State University, Chico, CA
California State University, Fresno, CA
California State University,
   San Bernardino, CA
California State University, Stanislaus, CA
Calvin College, MI
Campbellsville University, KY
Carroll University, WI
Carthage College, WI
Case Western Reserve University, OH
Centenary College of Louisiana, LA
Central College, IA
Central Michigan University, MI
Chapman University, CA
Chatham University, PA
Clarkson University, NY
Clemson University, SC
Cleveland State University, OH
Coe College, IA
The College at Brockport, State University of
   New York, NY
College of Charleston, SC
The College of New Rochelle, NY
College of Staten Island of the City University
   of New York, NY
The Colorado College, CO
Colorado School of Mines, CO
Columbia College, MO
Columbus State University, GA
Concordia University, Nebraska, NE
Concordia University, St. Paul, MN
Concordia University Texas, TX
Davidson College, NC
Defiance College, OH
Delta State University, MS
DePauw University, IN
DeSales University, PA
Dickinson State University, ND
Dominican University, IL
Dordt College, IA
Drury University, MO
East Carolina University, NC
Eastern Michigan University, MI
Eastern New Mexico University, NM

Eastern Washington University, WA
East Stroudsburg University of
  Pennsylvania, PA
East Texas Baptist University, TX
Edinboro University of Pennsylvania, PA
Elizabethtown College, PA
Elmhurst College, IL
Elon University, NC
Emmanuel College, MA
Emporia State University, KS
Evangel University, MO
Fairfield University, CT
Florida Atlantic University, FL
Florida Gulf Coast University, FL
Florida International University, FL
Florida Southern College, FL
Fort Lewis College, CO
Framingham State College, MA
Frostburg State University, MD
Furman University, SC
Gardner-Webb University, NC
George Fox University, OR
Georgia College & State University, GA
Georgia Institute of Technology, GA
Georgian Court University, NJ
Graceland University, IA
Grand Valley State University, MI
Green Mountain College, VT
Greenville College, IL
Grove City College, PA
Hamline University, MN
Hampshire College, MA
Hampton University, VA
Hardin-Simmons University, TX
Harrisburg University of Science and
  Technology, PA
High Point University, NC
Howard Payne University, TX
Idaho State University, ID
Illinois State University, IL
Indiana University of Pennsylvania, PA
Iowa State University of Science and
  Technology, IA
Jacksonville State University, AL
James Madison University, VA
Jamestown College, ND
John Carroll University, OH
Juniata College, PA
Kean University, NJ
Kennesaw State University, GA
Kent State University, OH
Kettering University, MI
King's College, PA
Kutztown University of Pennsylvania, PA
Lake Erie College, OH
Lake Forest College, IL
Lawrence Technological University, MI
Lewis-Clark State College, ID
Limestone College, SC
Lincoln University, PA
Lindenwood University, MO
Lock Haven University of Pennsylvania, PA
Loras College, IA
Louisiana State University and Agricultural
  and Mechanical College, LA
Louisiana Tech University, LA
Lubbock Christian University, TX
Lycoming College, PA
Malone University, OH
Mansfield University of Pennsylvania, PA
Marietta College, OH
Massachusetts College of Liberal Arts, MA
The Master's College and Seminary, CA

McMurry University, TX
Meredith College, NC
Mesa State College, CO
Michigan State University, MI
Midwestern State University, TX
Millersville University of Pennsylvania, PA
Millikin University, IL
Mills College, CA
Minnesota State University Moorhead, MN
Misericordia University, PA
Mississippi State University, MS
Mississippi University for Women, MS
Missouri University of Science and
  Technology, MO
Missouri Valley College, MO
Montana State University, MT
Montana State University Billings, MT
Montana Tech of The University of
  Montana, MT
Montclair State University, NJ
Moravian College, PA
Morehead State University, KY
Mount Mary College, WI
Muskingum University, OH
Newberry College, SC
New Jersey Institute of Technology, NJ
New Mexico State University, NM
North Carolina State University, NC
North Central College, IL
Northeastern Illinois University, IL
Northeastern State University, OK
Northern Arizona University, AZ
Northern Illinois University, IL
Northern Kentucky University, KY
Northern Michigan University, MI
Northern State University, SD
North Georgia College & State University, GA
Northwestern Oklahoma State University, OK
Northwestern State University of
  Louisiana, LA
Northwest Nazarene University, ID
Oberlin College, OH
Ohio Northern University, OH
The Ohio State University, OH
Ohio University, OH
Ohio University–Chillicothe, OH
Ohio University–Eastern, OH
Ohio University–Lancaster, OH
Ohio University–Southern Campus, OH
Ohio University–Zanesville, OH
Oklahoma Panhandle State University, OK
Oklahoma State University, OK
Old Dominion University, VA
Ouachita Baptist University, AR
Pace University, NY
Pacific University, OR
Pittsburg State University, KS
Plymouth State University, NH
Portland State University, OR
Purdue University, IN
Randolph College, VA
Regis University, CO
The Richard Stockton College of New
  Jersey, NJ
Ripon College, WI
Rochester Institute of Technology, NY
Rockford College, IL
Rockhurst University, MO
Rocky Mountain College, MT
Rollins College, FL
Sacred Heart University, CT
Saginaw Valley State University, MI
St. Catherine University, MN

St. Edward's University, TX
St. John Fisher College, NY
St. John's University, NY
Saint Louis University, MO
Salisbury University, MD
Samford University, AL
Sam Houston State University, TX
San Diego State University, CA
Savannah State University, GA
Schreiner University, TX
Seton Hill University, PA
Shepherd University, WV
Shippensburg University of Pennsylvania, PA
Siena College, NY
Skidmore College, NY
Slippery Rock University of Pennsylvania, PA
Sonoma State University, CA
South Dakota School of Mines and
  Technology, SD
South Dakota State University, SD
Southeastern Louisiana University, LA
Southeastern Oklahoma State University, OK
Southeast Missouri State University, MO
Southern Arkansas University–Magnolia, AR
Southern Illinois University Carbondale, IL
Southern Nazarene University, OK
Southwestern Oklahoma State University, OK
Southwest Minnesota State University, MN
State University of New York at
  Binghamton, NY
State University of New York at Fredonia, NY
State University of New York at Oswego, NY
State University of New York at
  Plattsburgh, NY
State University of New York College at
  Cortland, NY
State University of New York College at
  Geneseo, NY
State University of New York College at Old
  Westbury, NY
State University of New York College at
  Oneonta, NY
State University of New York College at
  Potsdam, NY
State University of New York College of
  Environmental Science and Forestry, NY
Stephen F. Austin State University, TX
Stetson University, FL
Stony Brook University, State University of
  New York, NY
Tennessee Technological University, TN
Tennessee Wesleyan College, TN
Texas A&M University, TX
Texas Christian University, TX
Texas Lutheran University, TX
Texas Tech University, TX
Texas Woman's University, TX
Thiel College, PA
Thomas More College, KY
Trevecca Nazarene University, TN
Truman State University, MO
The University of Akron, OH
The University of Alabama, AL
The University of Alabama in Huntsville, AL
University of Alaska Fairbanks, AK
The University of Arizona, AZ
University of California, Irvine, CA
University of California, Riverside, CA
University of California, San Diego, CA
University of California, Santa Cruz, CA
University of Central Missouri, MO
University of Central Oklahoma, OK
University of Colorado at Boulder, CO

University of Connecticut, CT
University of Dallas, TX
University of Delaware, DE
University of Denver, CO
University of Evansville, IN
University of Great Falls, MT
University of Idaho, ID
University of Illinois at Urbana–Champaign, IL
University of Indianapolis, IN
The University of Kansas, KS
University of Kentucky, KY
University of Louisiana at Monroe, LA
University of Mary Hardin-Baylor, TX
University of Maryland, Baltimore County, MD
University of Maryland, College Park, MD
University of Mary Washington, VA
University of Massachusetts Amherst, MA
University of Memphis, TN
University of Miami, FL
University of Michigan, MI
University of Michigan–Dearborn, MI
University of Michigan–Flint, MI
University of Minnesota, Twin Cities Campus, MN
University of Mississippi, MS
University of Missouri, MO
University of Missouri–St. Louis, MO
The University of Montana Western, MT
University of Montevallo, AL
University of Mount Union, OH
University of Nebraska at Omaha, NE
University of Nebraska–Lincoln, NE
University of Nevada, Las Vegas, NV
University of New Orleans, LA
The University of North Carolina at Asheville, NC
The University of North Carolina at Greensboro, NC
The University of North Carolina at Pembroke, NC
The University of North Carolina Wilmington, NC
University of North Dakota, ND
University of Northern Colorado, CO
University of Northern Iowa, IA
University of Oklahoma, OK
University of Oregon, OR
University of Pittsburgh at Bradford, PA
University of Pittsburgh at Johnstown, PA
University of Portland, OR
University of Puget Sound, WA
University of Richmond, VA
University of St. Thomas, MN
University of South Carolina, SC
University of South Carolina Aiken, SC
The University of Tennessee at Martin, TN
The University of Texas at Arlington, TX
The University of Texas at Brownsville, TX
The University of Texas at Dallas, TX
The University of Texas at El Paso, TX
The University of Texas at San Antonio, TX
University of the Southwest, NM
The University of Toledo, OH
University of Tulsa, OK
University of Vermont, VT
The University of Virginia's College at Wise, VA
University of West Georgia, GA
University of Wisconsin–Eau Claire, WI
University of Wisconsin–Green Bay, WI
University of Wisconsin–La Crosse, WI

University of Wisconsin–Parkside, WI
University of Wisconsin–River Falls, WI
University of Wisconsin–Stevens Point, WI
University of Wisconsin–Stout, WI
University of Wisconsin–Superior, WI
University of Wisconsin–Whitewater, WI
University of Wyoming, WY
Utah State University, UT
Valdosta State University, GA
Valley City State University, ND
Valparaiso University, IN
Virginia Commonwealth University, VA
Warner Pacific College, OR
Wartburg College, IA
Washburn University, KS
Washington State University, WA
Washington University in St. Louis, MO
Wayland Baptist University, TX
Wayne State College, NE
Wayne State University, MI
Western Illinois University, IL
Western Kentucky University, KY
Western Oregon University, OR
Western Washington University, WA
West Liberty University, WV
Westminster College, UT
West Virginia University, WV
West Virginia Wesleyan College, WV
Wheaton College, IL
Whitworth University, WA
Wichita State University, KS
Widener University, PA
Wilson College, PA
Wright State University, OH
Xavier University, OH
Xavier University of Louisiana, LA
Youngstown State University, OH

Premedicine

Alderson-Broaddus College, WV
Alfred University, NY
American Jewish University, CA
Angelo State University, TX
Arizona State University, AZ
Arkansas State University—Jonesboro, AR
Atlantic Union College, MA
Auburn University, AL
Augustana College, SD
Austin College, TX
Averett University, VA
Baylor University, TX
Belhaven University, MS
Bethel College, IN
Birmingham-Southern College, AL
Blue Mountain College, MS
Boise State University, ID
Brescia University, KY
Brevard College, NC
Bryan College, TN
California State University, Stanislaus, CA
Calvin College, MI
Campbellsville University, KY
Carroll University, WI
Carthage College, WI
Case Western Reserve University, OH
Centenary College of Louisiana, LA
Central College, IA
Chatham University, PA
City College of the City University of New York, NY
Clearwater Christian College, FL
Clemson University, SC
Cleveland State University, OH

Coe College, IA
The College at Brockport, State University of New York, NY
College of Charleston, SC
The College of New Rochelle, NY
The College of Saint Rose, NY
College of Staten Island of the City University of New York, NY
Concordia University, Nebraska, NE
Dallas Baptist University, TX
Davidson College, NC
Defiance College, OH
Delta State University, MS
DeSales University, PA
Dickinson State University, ND
Dordt College, IA
Drury University, MO
D'Youville College, NY
Eastern New Mexico University, NM
Edinboro University of Pennsylvania, PA
Elizabethtown College, PA
Elmhurst College, IL
Elon University, NC
Emory & Henry College, VA
Emporia State University, KS
Erskine College, SC
Fort Valley State University, GA
Francis Marion University, SC
Frostburg State University, MD
Furman University, SC
Gannon University, PA
Gardner-Webb University, NC
Grand Valley State University, MI
Hamline University, MN
Hampden-Sydney College, VA
Hardin-Simmons University, TX
High Point University, NC
Howard Payne University, TX
Idaho State University, ID
Illinois State University, IL
Indiana State University, IN
Indiana University of Pennsylvania, PA
Iowa State University of Science and Technology, IA
James Madison University, VA
John Carroll University, OH
Judson College, AL
Juniata College, PA
Kennesaw State University, GA
King's College, PA
Lindenwood University, MO
Lindsey Wilson College, KY
Lipscomb University, TN
Lock Haven University of Pennsylvania, PA
Louisiana State University and Agricultural and Mechanical College, LA
Lycoming College, PA
Malone University, OH
McMurry University, TX
Midwestern State University, TX
Millikin University, IL
Mills College, CA
Minnesota State University Moorhead, MN
Mississippi State University, MS
Missouri University of Science and Technology, MO
Missouri Valley College, MO
Montana State University Billings, MT
Muskingum University, OH
North Central College, IL
Northeastern State University, OK
Northern Arizona University, AZ
Northern Kentucky University, KY

Northern Michigan University, MI
North Georgia College & State University, GA
Northwestern Oklahoma State University, OK
Northwest Nazarene University, ID
Ohio Northern University, OH
The Ohio State University, OH
Ohio University, OH
Ohio University–Chillicothe, OH
Ohio University–Eastern, OH
Ohio University–Lancaster, OH
Ohio University–Southern Campus, OH
Ohio University–Zanesville, OH
Oklahoma State University, OK
Ouachita Baptist University, AR
Pacific University, OR
Piedmont College, GA
Providence College, RI
Quincy University, IL
Randolph College, VA
Ripon College, WI
Rivier College, NH
Rochester Institute of Technology, NY
Rockford College, IL
Rockhurst University, MO
Rocky Mountain College, MT
Sacred Heart University, CT
St. Catherine University, MN
St. Edward's University, TX
St. John's University, NY
Saint Louis University, MO
Saint Martin's University, WA
Salisbury University, MD
Samford University, AL
Schreiner University, TX
Seton Hill University, PA
Shepherd University, WV
Siena College, NY
Sonoma State University, CA
South Dakota State University, SD
Southeast Missouri State University, MO
Southern Illinois University Carbondale, IL
Southwestern University, TX
Southwest Minnesota State University, MN
State University of New York at
  Binghamton, NY
State University of New York at Oswego, NY
State University of New York at
  Plattsburgh, NY
State University of New York College at
  Geneseo, NY
State University of New York College at
  Oneonta, NY
State University of New York College of
  Environmental Science and Forestry, NY
Stephen F. Austin State University, TX
Stetson University, FL
Tennessee Technological University, TN
Tennessee Wesleyan College, TN
Texas Christian University, TX
Texas Lutheran University, TX
Texas Tech University, TX
Texas Woman's University, TX
Thomas More College, KY
Truman State University, MO
Union University, TN
The University of Akron, OH
The University of Alabama, AL
University of California, Davis, CA
University of California, Irvine, CA
University of California, Riverside, CA
University of California, San Diego, CA
University of Central Missouri, MO
University of Colorado at Boulder, CO

University of Connecticut, CT
University of Dallas, TX
University of Delaware, DE
University of Evansville, IN
University of Great Falls, MT
University of Hartford, CT
University of Idaho, ID
University of Illinois at Urbana–
  Champaign, IL
The University of Kansas, KS
University of Louisville, KY
University of Mary Hardin-Baylor, TX
University of Maryland, College Park, MD
University of Massachusetts Amherst, MA
University of Memphis, TN
University of Miami, FL
University of Michigan, MI
University of Michigan–Flint, MI
University of Minnesota, Twin Cities
  Campus, MN
University of Mississippi, MS
University of Missouri, MO
University of Missouri–St. Louis, MO
The University of Montana Western, MT
University of Nebraska at Omaha, NE
University of Nebraska–Lincoln, NE
University of Nevada, Las Vegas, NV
The University of North Carolina at
  Asheville, NC
The University of North Carolina at
  Greensboro, NC
The University of North Carolina
  Wilmington, NC
University of North Dakota, ND
University of Pittsburgh at Bradford, PA
University of Pittsburgh at Johnstown, PA
University of Portland, OR
University of Puget Sound, WA
University of South Carolina, SC
The University of South Dakota, SD
University of Southern Indiana, IN
The University of Tennessee at Martin, TN
The University of Texas–Pan American, TX
University of the Ozarks, AR
University of the Southwest, NM
The University of Toledo, OH
University of Tulsa, OK
University of Vermont, VT
The University of Virginia's College at
  Wise, VA
University of West Georgia, GA
University of Wisconsin–Eau Claire, WI
University of Wisconsin–Green Bay, WI
University of Wisconsin–Parkside, WI
University of Wisconsin–River Falls, WI
University of Wisconsin–Stevens Point, WI
University of Wisconsin–Whitewater, WI
Utah State University, UT
Valdosta State University, GA
Virginia Military Institute, VA
Washburn University, KS
Washington State University, WA
Washington University in St. Louis, MO
Wayne State College, NE
Wayne State University, MI
Wesleyan College, GA
Western Kentucky University, KY
Western Oregon University, OR
Western Washington University, WA
Westminster College, UT
West Virginia University, WV
Wheaton College, IL
Wheeling Jesuit University, WV

Whitworth University, WA
Wichita State University, KS
Widener University, PA
Wilson College, PA
Worcester Polytechnic Institute, MA
Wright State University, OH
Xavier University of Louisiana, LA
York College, NE
Youngstown State University, OH

Religion/Biblical Studies

Abilene Christian University, TX
Alaska Bible College, AK
Alderson-Broaddus College, WV
American Baptist College of American Baptist
  Theological Seminary, TN
Appalachian Bible College, WV
Atlantic Union College, MA
Augsburg College, MN
Augustana College, IL
Augustana College, SD
Austin College, TX
Austin Graduate School of Theology, TX
Averett University, VA
The Baptist College of Florida, FL
Baptist University of the Americas, TX
Barton College, NC
Baylor University, TX
Belhaven University, MS
Belmont University, TN
Berry College, GA
Bethel College, IN
Bethesda Christian University, CA
Birmingham-Southern College, AL
Bloomfield College, NJ
Bloomsburg University of Pennsylvania, PA
Blue Mountain College, MS
Brescia University, KY
Brevard College, NC
Briar Cliff University, IA
Bryan College, TN
California Baptist University, CA
California Lutheran University, CA
Calvin College, MI
Campbellsville University, KY
Carson-Newman College, TN
Carthage College, WI
Case Western Reserve University, OH
Centenary College of Louisiana, LA
Central College, IA
Christopher Newport University, VA
Cincinnati Christian University, OH
The Citadel, The Military College of South
  Carolina, SC
Clearwater Christian College, FL
The College of New Rochelle, NY
Columbia College, MO
Concordia University, MI
Concordia University Chicago, IL
Concordia University, Nebraska, NE
Concordia University, St. Paul, MN
Concordia University Texas, TX
Concordia University Wisconsin, WI
Cornerstone University, MI
Crossroads College, MN
Dallas Baptist University, TX
Davidson College, NC
Defiance College, OH
DeSales University, PA
Dordt College, IA
Eastern Michigan University, MI
Eastern New Mexico University, NM
East Texas Baptist University, TX

Edinboro University of Pennsylvania, PA
Elizabethtown College, PA
Elmhurst College, IL
Elon University, NC
Emmanuel College, MA
Emory & Henry College, VA
Erskine College, SC
Evangel University, MO
Faulkner University, AL
Felician College, NJ
Flagler College, FL
Florida Gulf Coast University, FL
Florida Southern College, FL
Furman University, SC
Gannon University, PA
Gardner-Webb University, NC
Geneva College, PA
George Fox University, OR
Grace University, NE
Greenville College, IL
Grove City College, PA
Hampden-Sydney College, VA
Hannibal-LaGrange College, MO
Harding University, AR
Hardin-Simmons University, TX
High Point University, NC
Hillsdale Free Will Baptist College, OK
Houston Baptist University, TX
Howard Payne University, TX
Idaho State University, ID
James Madison University, VA
John Carroll University, OH
Johnson Bible College, TN
King's College, PA
LaGrange College, GA
Lakeland College, WI
Lebanon Valley College, PA
Lee University, TN
Limestone College, SC
Lindenwood University, MO
Lindsey Wilson College, KY
Lipscomb University, TN
Lubbock Christian University, TX
Lycoming College, PA
MacMurray College, IL
Malone University, OH
Manhattan Christian College, KS
Marywood University, PA
The Master's College and Seminary, CA
McKendree University, IL
McMurry University, TX
Mercer University, GA
Meredith College, NC
Mid-Atlantic Christian University, NC
Mid-Continent University, KY
Milligan College, TN
Mississippi State University, MS
Montclair State University, NJ
Multnomah University, OR
Nazarene Bible College, CO
Newberry College, SC
North Central College, IL
Northern Arizona University, AZ
North Greenville University, SC
Northwest Nazarene University, ID
Ohio Northern University, OH
Ohio Valley University, WV
Oklahoma Baptist University, OK
Oklahoma Christian University, OK
Oklahoma City University, OK
Oklahoma Wesleyan University, OK
Oral Roberts University, OK
Ouachita Baptist University, AR

Pacific Union College, CA
Piedmont College, GA
Point Loma Nazarene University, CA
Quincy University, IL
Regent University, VA
Ripon College, WI
Rockhurst University, MO
Rocky Mountain College, MT
Sacred Heart Major Seminary, MI
St. Ambrose University, IA
St. Edward's University, TX
Saint Francis University, PA
Saint Louis University, MO
Samford University, AL
San Diego State University, CA
Schreiner University, TX
Seton Hill University, PA
Shorter University, GA
Siena College, NY
Southeastern University, FL
Southeast Missouri State University, MO
Southern Adventist University, TN
Southern Illinois University Carbondale, IL
Southern Nazarene University, OK
Southwestern College, KS
Stetson University, FL
Talmudical Institute of Upstate New York, NY
Tennessee Wesleyan College, TN
Texas Christian University, TX
Thiel College, PA
Thomas More College, KY
Trevecca Nazarene University, TN
Trinity Bible College, ND
Union University, TN
The University of Arizona, AZ
University of California, Davis, CA
University of Central Missouri, MO
University of Connecticut, CT
University of Dallas, TX
University of Delaware, DE
University of Evansville, IN
University of Great Falls, MT
University of Illinois at Urbana–
  Champaign, IL
University of Indianapolis, IN
The University of Kansas, KS
University of Mary Hardin-Baylor, TX
University of Mary Washington, VA
University of Miami, FL
University of Minnesota, Twin Cities
  Campus, MN
University of Mississippi, MS
University of Missouri, MO
The University of North Carolina at
  Greensboro, NC
University of Portland, OR
University of St. Thomas, MN
University of South Carolina, SC
University of the Ozarks, AR
University of the Southwest, NM
University of Tulsa, OK
Valparaiso University, IN
Warner Pacific College, OR
Wartburg College, IA
Washburn University, KS
Washington University in St. Louis, MO
Wayland Baptist University, TX
Waynesburg University, PA
Wesleyan College, GA
West Virginia University, WV
Wheaton College, IL
Williams Baptist College, AR
Wilson College, PA

Wright State University, OH
Xavier University of Louisiana, LA
York College, NE
Youngstown State University, OH

Social Sciences

Abilene Christian University, TX
Alaska Pacific University, AK
Alderson-Broaddus College, WV
Alfred University, NY
Alliant International University, CA
Angelo State University, TX
Arizona State University, AZ
Arkansas State University—Jonesboro, AR
Arkansas Tech University, AR
Ashland University, OH
Auburn University, AL
Augsburg College, MN
Augustana College, IL
Augustana College, SD
Austin College, TX
Austin Peay State University, TN
Ball State University, IN
Barton College, NC
Baylor University, TX
Belhaven University, MS
Bethel College, IN
Birmingham-Southern College, AL
Black Hills State University, SD
Bloomfield College, NJ
Bloomsburg University of Pennsylvania, PA
Blue Mountain College, MS
Boise State University, ID
Bowling Green State University, OH
Brescia University, KY
Brevard College, NC
Briar Cliff University, IA
Bryan College, TN
Butler University, IN
California Lutheran University, CA
California Polytechnic State University,
  San Luis Obispo, CA
California State Polytechnic University,
  Pomona, CA
California State University, Chico, CA
California State University, Fresno, CA
California State University, Fullerton, CA
California State University, Northridge, CA
California State University,
  San Bernardino, CA
California State University, Stanislaus, CA
Calvin College, MI
Cameron University, OK
Campbellsville University, KY
Carlos Albizu University, PR
Carroll University, WI
Case Western Reserve University, OH
Centenary College of Louisiana, LA
Central College, IA
Central Michigan University, MI
Chatham University, PA
City College of the City University of New
  York, NY
Clarkson University, NY
Clemson University, SC
Cleveland State University, OH
The College at Brockport, State University of
  New York, NY
College of Charleston, SC
The College of New Rochelle, NY
The College of Saint Rose, NY
College of Staten Island of the City University
  of New York, NY

Non-Need Scholarships for Undergraduates
Academic Interests/Achievements

Columbia College, MO
Concordia University, Nebraska, NE
Concordia University Texas, TX
Concord University, WV
Dalton State College, GA
Davidson College, NC
Defiance College, OH
Delta State University, MS
DeSales University, PA
Dickinson State University, ND
Dordt College, IA
Dowling College, NY
Drury University, MO
D'Youville College, NY
Eastern Michigan University, MI
Eastern New Mexico University, NM
Eastern Washington University, WA
East Stroudsburg University of
  Pennsylvania, PA
East Texas Baptist University, TX
Edinboro University of Pennsylvania, PA
Elizabethtown College, PA
Elmhurst College, IL
Elon University, NC
Emmanuel College, MA
Emporia State University, KS
Erskine College, SC
Evangel University, MO
Fitchburg State College, MA
Flagler College, FL
Florida Atlantic University, FL
Florida Gulf Coast University, FL
Florida International University, FL
Florida Southern College, FL
Fort Lewis College, CO
Fort Valley State University, GA
Francis Marion University, SC
Fresno Pacific University, CA
Frostburg State University, MD
Furman University, SC
Gannon University, PA
Gardner-Webb University, NC
Georgia College & State University, GA
Georgia Southern University, GA
Glenville State College, WV
Grand Valley State University, MI
Green Mountain College, VT
Grove City College, PA
Hampshire College, MA
Hardin-Simmons University, TX
Hawai'i Pacific University, HI
Howard Payne University, TX
Idaho State University, ID
Illinois State University, IL
Indiana University of Pennsylvania, PA
Iowa State University of Science and
  Technology, IA
Jacksonville State University, AL
James Madison University, VA
John Carroll University, OH
Juniata College, PA
Kean University, NJ
Kennesaw State University, GA
Kent State University, OH
King's College, PA
LaGrange College, GA
Lake Erie College, OH
Lewis-Clark State College, ID
Limestone College, SC
Lincoln University, PA
Lindenwood University, MO
Lock Haven University of Pennsylvania, PA
Longwood University, VA

Louisiana Tech University, LA
Lubbock Christian University, TX
Lycoming College, PA
Malone University, OH
Marymount University, VA
Massachusetts College of Liberal Arts, MA
The Master's College and Seminary, CA
McMurry University, TX
Mesa State College, CO
Michigan State University, MI
Mid-Continent University, KY
Midwestern State University, TX
Millersville University of Pennsylvania, PA
Minnesota State University Moorhead, MN
Misericordia University, PA
Mississippi State University, MS
Missouri University of Science and
  Technology, MO
Missouri Valley College, MO
Monmouth University, NJ
Montana State University, MT
Montana State University Billings, MT
Montana State University–Northern, MT
Montclair State University, NJ
Morehead State University, KY
Mount Mary College, WI
Newberry College, SC
New England College, NH
New Mexico State University, NM
North Carolina State University, NC
North Central College, IL
Northeastern Illinois University, IL
Northeastern State University, OK
Northern Arizona University, AZ
Northern Illinois University, IL
Northern Kentucky University, KY
Northern Michigan University, MI
Northern State University, SD
Northwestern Oklahoma State University, OK
Northwest Nazarene University, ID
Ohio Northern University, OH
The Ohio State University, OH
Ohio University, OH
Ohio University–Chillicothe, OH
Ohio University–Eastern, OH
Ohio University–Lancaster, OH
Ohio University–Southern Campus, OH
Ohio University–Zanesville, OH
Oklahoma State University, OK
Ouachita Baptist University, AR
Pace University, NY
Pacific University, OR
Piedmont College, GA
Pittsburg State University, KS
Plymouth State University, NH
Point Loma Nazarene University, CA
Portland State University, OR
Purchase College, State University of New
  York, NY
Quincy University, IL
Randolph College, VA
Regent University, VA
The Richard Stockton College of New
  Jersey, NJ
Ripon College, WI
Rivier College, NH
Rochester Institute of Technology, NY
Rockford College, IL
Rockhurst University, MO
Rocky Mountain College, MT
St. Catherine University, MN
St. Edward's University, TX
Saint Francis University, PA

St. John's University, NY
Saint Louis University, MO
Salisbury University, MD
Samford University, AL
Sam Houston State University, TX
San Diego State University, CA
Savannah State University, GA
Schreiner University, TX
Seton Hill University, PA
Shepherd University, WV
Shippensburg University of Pennsylvania, PA
Siena College, NY
Slippery Rock University of Pennsylvania, PA
Sonoma State University, CA
South Dakota State University, SD
Southeastern Louisiana University, LA
Southeastern Oklahoma State University, OK
Southeast Missouri State University, MO
Southern Arkansas University–Magnolia, AR
Southern Illinois University Carbondale, IL
Southern Nazarene University, OK
Southwestern College, KS
Southwestern Oklahoma State University, OK
Southwestern University, TX
Southwest Minnesota State University, MN
State University of New York at
  Binghamton, NY
State University of New York at Fredonia, NY
State University of New York at Oswego, NY
State University of New York at
  Plattsburgh, NY
State University of New York College at
  Geneseo, NY
State University of New York College at
  Oneonta, NY
State University of New York College at
  Potsdam, NY
Stetson University, FL
Stony Brook University, State University of
  New York, NY
Tennessee Technological University, TN
Tennessee Wesleyan College, TN
Texas A&M University–Texarkana, TX
Texas Christian University, TX
Texas Tech University, TX
Texas Woman's University, TX
Thomas More College, KY
Trevecca Nazarene University, TN
Truman State University, MO
The University of Akron, OH
The University of Alabama, AL
The University of Alabama in Huntsville, AL
University of Alaska Anchorage, AK
University of California, Davis, CA
University of California, Irvine, CA
University of California, Riverside, CA
University of California, San Diego, CA
University of California, Santa Cruz, CA
University of Central Missouri, MO
University of Central Oklahoma, OK
University of Colorado at Boulder, CO
University of Connecticut, CT
University of Delaware, DE
University of Denver, CO
University of Evansville, IN
University of Great Falls, MT
University of Hawaii at Hilo, HI
University of Houston–Clear Lake, TX
University of Idaho, ID
University of Illinois at Urbana–
  Champaign, IL
The University of Kansas, KS
University of Louisiana at Monroe, LA

www.facebook.com/pay4undergrad

University of Maine at Fort Kent, ME
University of Mary Hardin-Baylor, TX
University of Maryland, Baltimore
County, MD
University of Maryland, College Park, MD
University of Mary Washington, VA
University of Massachusetts Amherst, MA
University of Memphis, TN
University of Miami, FL
University of Michigan, MI
University of Michigan–Dearborn, MI
University of Michigan–Flint, MI
University of Minnesota, Twin Cities
Campus, MN
University of Mississippi, MS
University of Missouri, MO
University of Missouri–St. Louis, MO
The University of Montana Western, MT
University of Nebraska at Omaha, NE
University of Nebraska–Lincoln, NE
University of Nevada, Las Vegas, NV
University of New Orleans, LA
The University of North Carolina at
Asheville, NC
The University of North Carolina at
Greensboro, NC
The University of North Carolina
Wilmington, NC
University of North Dakota, ND
University of Northern Colorado, CO
University of Northern Iowa, IA
University of Oklahoma, OK
University of Oregon, OR
University of Pittsburgh at Bradford, PA
University of Pittsburgh at Johnstown, PA
University of Portland, OR
University of Puget Sound, WA
University of St. Francis, IL
University of St. Thomas, MN
University of South Carolina, SC
University of South Carolina Aiken, SC
The University of South Dakota, SD
University of Southern Indiana, IN
The University of Tampa, FL
The University of Tennessee, TN
The University of Tennessee at Martin, TN
The University of Texas at Arlington, TX
The University of Texas at Brownsville, TX
The University of Texas at San Antonio, TX
The University of Texas–Pan American, TX
University of the Ozarks, AR
University of the Southwest, NM
The University of Toledo, OH
University of Tulsa, OK
University of Vermont, VT
The University of Virginia's College at
Wise, VA
University of West Georgia, GA
University of Wisconsin–Eau Claire, WI
University of Wisconsin–Green Bay, WI
University of Wisconsin–La Crosse, WI
University of Wisconsin–River Falls, WI
University of Wisconsin–Stevens Point, WI
University of Wisconsin–Superior, WI
University of Wisconsin–Whitewater, WI
University of Wyoming, WY
Utah State University, UT
Valdosta State University, GA
Valley City State University, ND
Warner Pacific College, OR
Washburn University, KS
Washington State University, WA
Washington University in St. Louis, MO

Wayland Baptist University, TX
Wayne State College, NE
Wayne State University, MI
Wesleyan College, GA
West Chester University of Pennsylvania, PA
Western Illinois University, IL
Western Kentucky University, KY
Western Oregon University, OR
Western Washington University, WA
Westminster College, UT
West Virginia University, WV
Wheaton College, IL
Wichita State University, KS
Widener University, PA
Wilson College, PA
Wright State University, OH
Xavier University, OH
Xavier University of Louisiana, LA
Youngstown State University, OH

Creative Arts/Performance

Applied Art and Design

Arcadia University, PA
Arizona State University, AZ
Auburn University, AL
Belhaven University, MS
Bethesda Christian University, CA
Bloomfield College, NJ
Bowie State University, MD
Brenau University, GA
California College of the Arts, CA
California Institute of the Arts, CA
California Polytechnic State University,
San Luis Obispo, CA
California State University, Chico, CA
Carthage College, WI
Central Michigan University, MI
City College of the City University of New
York, NY
Clemson University, SC
College for Creative Studies, MI
The College of New Rochelle, NY
Columbia College Chicago, IL
Concordia University, CA
Concordia University, Nebraska, NE
Converse College, SC
Corcoran College of Art and Design, DC
East Carolina University, NC
Eastern Michigan University, MI
Eastern New Mexico University, NM
East Stroudsburg University of
Pennsylvania, PA
The Evergreen State College, WA
Fashion Institute of Technology, NY
Ferris State University, MI
Flagler College, FL
Georgia College & State University, GA
Grace College, IN
Graceland University, IA
Grand Valley State University, MI
Greenville College, IL
Hardin-Simmons University, TX
Huntington University, IN
Illinois State University, IL
Indiana University of Pennsylvania, PA
Iowa State University of Science and
Technology, IA
Kean University, NJ
Keene State College, NH
Kutztown University of Pennsylvania, PA
Lindenwood University, MO
Lindsey Wilson College, KY

Louisiana State University and Agricultural
and Mechanical College, LA
Louisiana Tech University, LA
Massachusetts College of Liberal Arts, MA
Memphis College of Art, TN
Mercyhurst College, PA
Meredith College, NC
Minneapolis College of Art and Design, MN
Mississippi College, MS
Mississippi State University, MS
Missouri Valley College, MO
Mount Ida College, MA
Mount Mary College, WI
Murray State University, KY
New England College, NH
New Mexico State University, NM
Northeastern State University, OK
Northern Arizona University, AZ
Northern Illinois University, IL
Northern Michigan University, MI
North Georgia College & State University, GA
Notre Dame de Namur University, CA
Ohio Northern University, OH
Ohio University, OH
Ohio University–Chillicothe, OH
Ohio University–Eastern, OH
Ohio University–Lancaster, OH
Ohio University–Southern Campus, OH
Ohio University–Zanesville, OH
Oklahoma Baptist University, OK
Oklahoma Christian University, OK
Oklahoma City University, OK
Oral Roberts University, OK
Otis College of Art and Design, CA
The Richard Stockton College of New
Jersey, NJ
Ringling College of Art and Design, FL
Rivier College, NH
Robert Morris University Illinois, IL
Rochester Institute of Technology, NY
Rocky Mountain College of Art + Design, CO
Sacred Heart University, CT
Salem State College, MA
Salisbury University, MD
San Diego State University, CA
Seton Hill University, PA
Shepherd University, WV
Silver Lake College, WI
Slippery Rock University of Pennsylvania, PA
Sonoma State University, CA
Southeastern Louisiana University, LA
Southern Illinois University Carbondale, IL
Southwestern Oklahoma State University, OK
State University of New York at Fredonia, NY
State University of New York College at
Geneseo, NY
Stetson University, FL
Stevens-Henager College, ID
Texas Christian University, TX
Texas State University–San Marcos, TX
Texas Tech University, TX
Texas Woman's University, TX
Trinity Christian College, IL
The University of Akron, OH
University of Bridgeport, CT
University of California, San Diego, CA
University of Central Missouri, MO
University of Central Oklahoma, OK
University of Delaware, DE
University of Idaho, ID
University of Illinois at Chicago, IL
University of Illinois at Urbana–
Champaign, IL

The University of Kansas, KS
University of Kentucky, KY
University of Maryland, College Park, MD
University of Missouri–St. Louis, MO
University of Nebraska at Kearney, NE
University of Nevada, Las Vegas, NV
The University of North Carolina at Chapel
  Hill, NC
University of North Carolina School of the
  Arts, NC
University of Northern Iowa, IA
University of St. Francis, IL
The University of Texas at El Paso, TX
University of West Florida, FL
University of West Georgia, GA
University of Wisconsin–Parkside, WI
University of Wisconsin–Stevens Point, WI
University of Wisconsin–Stout, WI
Utah State University, UT
Valley City State University, ND
Virginia Intermont College, VA
Virginia Polytechnic Institute and State
  University, VA
Washington State University, WA
Washington University in St. Louis, MO
Watkins College of Art, Design, & Film, TN
Wayne State College, NE
Western Illinois University, IL
Western Washington University, WA
Wichita State University, KS
Wright State University, OH

Art/Fine Arts

Abilene Christian University, TX
Adelphi University, NY
Adrian College, MI
Alabama Agricultural and Mechanical
  University, AL
Alaska Pacific University, AK
Albion College, MI
Albright College, PA
Alderson-Broaddus College, WV
Alfred University, NY
Alma College, MI
Alverno College, WI
Anderson University, IN
Angelo State University, TX
Arcadia University, PA
Arizona State University, AZ
Arkansas State University—Jonesboro, AR
Arkansas Tech University, AR
Armstrong Atlantic State University, GA
Ashland University, OH
Auburn University, AL
Augsburg College, MN
Augustana College, IL
Augustana College, SD
Austin College, TX
Austin Peay State University, TN
Averett University, VA
Ball State University, IN
Barton College, NC
Baylor University, TX
Belhaven University, MS
Bellarmine University, KY
Berry College, GA
Bethany College, KS
Bethany Lutheran College, MN
Bethel College, IN
Bethel College, KS
Bethel University, MN
Biola University, CA
Birmingham-Southern College, AL

Black Hills State University, SD
Bloomfield College, NJ
Bluefield College, VA
Blue Mountain College, MS
Bluffton University, OH
Boise State University, ID
Boston University, MA
Bowie State University, MD
Bowling Green State University, OH
Bradley University, IL
Brenau University, GA
Brescia University, KY
Brevard College, NC
Briar Cliff University, IA
Bucknell University, PA
Buena Vista University, IA
Butler University, IN
Caldwell College, NJ
California Baptist University, CA
California College of the Arts, CA
California Institute of the Arts, CA
California Lutheran University, CA
California Polytechnic State University,
  San Luis Obispo, CA
California State University, Chico, CA
California State University, Fresno, CA
California State University, Fullerton, CA
California State University,
  San Bernardino, CA
California State University, Stanislaus, CA
Calvin College, MI
Cameron University, OK
Campbellsville University, KY
Campbell University, NC
Canisius College, NY
Carnegie Mellon University, PA
Carroll University, WI
Carson-Newman College, TN
Carthage College, WI
Case Western Reserve University, OH
Cedar Crest College, PA
Centenary College of Louisiana, LA
Central College, IA
Central Michigan University, MI
Chapman University, CA
Christopher Newport University, VA
City College of the City University of New
  York, NY
Clarke College, IA
Clemson University, SC
The Cleveland Institute of Art, OH
Cleveland State University, OH
Coastal Carolina University, SC
Coe College, IA
Coker College, SC
The College at Brockport, State University of
  New York, NY
College for Creative Studies, MI
College of Charleston, SC
College of Mount St. Joseph, OH
The College of New Rochelle, NY
College of Notre Dame of Maryland, MD
College of Saint Benedict, MN
College of Saint Mary, NE
The College of Saint Rose, NY
College of Staten Island of the City University
  of New York, NY
College of Visual Arts, MN
Colorado State University, CO
Columbia College, MO
Columbia College Chicago, IL
Columbus College of Art & Design, OH
Columbus State University, GA

Concordia College, MN
Concordia University, MI
Concordia University Chicago, IL
Concordia University, Nebraska, NE
Concordia University, St. Paul, MN
Concord University, WV
Cooper Union for the Advancement of Science
  and Art, NY
Cornell College, IA
Creighton University, NE
Culver-Stockton College, MO
Daemen College, NY
Davidson College, NC
Delta State University, MS
DePaul University, IL
DePauw University, IN
Dickinson State University, ND
Dillard University, LA
Doane College, NE
Drake University, IA
Drury University, MO
East Carolina University, NC
Eastern Michigan University, MI
Eastern New Mexico University, NM
Eastern Washington University, WA
Eckerd College, FL
Edgewood College, WI
Edinboro University of Pennsylvania, PA
Elizabethtown College, PA
Elmhurst College, IL
Elon University, NC
Emory & Henry College, VA
Emory University, GA
Emporia State University, KS
Endicott College, MA
Eureka College, IL
Evangel University, MO
The Evergreen State College, WA
Fairfield University, CT
Ferris State University, MI
Flagler College, FL
Florida Gulf Coast University, FL
Florida Southern College, FL
Fort Lewis College, CO
Francis Marion University, SC
Franklin College, IN
Frostburg State University, MD
Furman University, SC
Gardner-Webb University, NC
George Fox University, OR
Georgetown College, KY
Georgia College & State University, GA
Georgian Court University, NJ
Georgia Southern University, GA
Georgia Southwestern State University, GA
Gordon College, MA
Goucher College, MD
Grace College, IN
Grand Valley State University, MI
Grand View University, IA
Green Mountain College, VT
Greenville College, IL
Gustavus Adolphus College, MN
Hamline University, MN
Hannibal-LaGrange College, MO
Hanover College, IN
Harding University, AR
Hardin-Simmons University, TX
Henderson State University, AR
Hendrix College, AR
High Point University, NC
Hobart and William Smith Colleges, NY
Hofstra University, NY

Hollins University, VA
Hope College, MI
Houghton College, NY
Houston Baptist University, TX
Howard Payne University, TX
Huntington University, IN
Idaho State University, ID
Illinois State University, IL
Indiana State University, IN
Indiana University of Pennsylvania, PA
Indiana Wesleyan University, IN
Iowa State University of Science and
   Technology, IA
Iowa Wesleyan College, IA
Jacksonville State University, AL
James Madison University, VA
Jamestown College, ND
John Brown University, AR
Johnson Bible College, TN
Judson College, AL
Juniata College, PA
Kansas City Art Institute, MO
Kean University, NJ
Keene State College, NH
Kent State University, OH
Kent State University at Stark, OH
Kentucky State University, KY
Kentucky Wesleyan College, KY
Kenyon College, OH
Knox College, IL
Kutztown University of Pennsylvania, PA
Lake Erie College, OH
Lake Forest College, IL
Lakeland College, WI
Lesley University, MA
Lewis-Clark State College, ID
Lewis University, IL
Limestone College, SC
Lincoln University, MO
Lindenwood University, MO
Lipscomb University, TN
Lock Haven University of Pennsylvania, PA
Long Island University, Brooklyn
   Campus, NY
Long Island University, C.W. Post
   Campus, NY
Longwood University, VA
Louisiana State University and Agricultural
   and Mechanical College, LA
Louisiana Tech University, LA
Lourdes College, OH
Loyola University Chicago, IL
Lubbock Christian University, TX
Lycoming College, PA
Lyme Academy College of Fine Arts, CT
Lynchburg College, VA
Mansfield University of Pennsylvania, PA
Marietta College, OH
Marymount Manhattan College, NY
Maryville College, TN
Maryville University of Saint Louis, MO
Marywood University, PA
Massachusetts College of Liberal Arts, MA
McMurry University, TX
McPherson College, KS
Memphis College of Art, TN
Mercer University, GA
Mercyhurst College, PA
Meredith College, NC
Mesa State College, CO
Messiah College, PA
Miami University, OH
Midwestern State University, TX

Millersville University of Pennsylvania, PA
Milligan College, TN
Millikin University, IL
Millsaps College, MS
Mills College, CA
Milwaukee Institute of Art and Design, WI
Minneapolis College of Art and Design, MN
Minnesota State University Moorhead, MN
Mississippi College, MS
Mississippi State University, MS
Mississippi University for Women, MS
Mississippi Valley State University, MS
Missouri Southern State University, MO
Missouri Valley College, MO
Molloy College, NY
Monmouth College, IL
Montana State University, MT
Montana State University Billings, MT
Montana State University–Northern, MT
Montclair State University, NJ
Morehouse College, GA
Morningside College, IA
Mount Ida College, MA
Mount Mary College, WI
Mount Mercy College, IA
Mount St. Mary's University, MD
Murray State University, KY
Muskingum University, OH
Nazareth College of Rochester, NY
Nebraska Wesleyan University, NE
New England College, NH
Newman University, KS
New Mexico State University, NM
New York City College of Technology of the
   City University of New York, NY
North Central College, IL
Northeastern Illinois University, IL
Northeastern State University, OK
Northern Arizona University, AZ
Northern Illinois University, IL
Northern Kentucky University, KY
Northern State University, SD
Northwestern Oklahoma State University, OK
Northwestern State University of
   Louisiana, LA
Northwest Nazarene University, ID
Notre Dame de Namur University, CA
Ohio Northern University, OH
Ohio University, OH
Ohio University–Chillicothe, OH
Ohio University–Eastern, OH
Ohio University–Lancaster, OH
Ohio University–Southern Campus, OH
Ohio University–Zanesville, OH
Oklahoma Baptist University, OK
Oklahoma City University, OK
Oklahoma Panhandle State University, OK
Oklahoma State University, OK
Old Dominion University, VA
Olivet College, MI
Olivet Nazarene University, IL
Oral Roberts University, OK
Otis College of Art and Design, CA
Ouachita Baptist University, AR
Pacific Lutheran University, WA
Pacific Union College, CA
Pacific University, OR
Peace College, NC
Piedmont College, GA
Point Loma Nazarene University, CA
Portland State University, OR
Purchase College, State University of New
   York, NY

Quincy University, IL
Randolph College, VA
Reinhardt University, GA
Rhode Island College, RI
The Richard Stockton College of New
   Jersey, NJ
Ringling College of Art and Design, FL
Ripon College, WI
Rivier College, NH
Roberts Wesleyan College, NY
Rochester Institute of Technology, NY
Rocky Mountain College, MT
Rocky Mountain College of Art + Design, CO
Rollins College, FL
Rosemont College, PA
Sacred Heart University, CT
Sage College of Albany, NY
Saginaw Valley State University, MI
St. Ambrose University, IA
St. Catherine University, MN
St. Edward's University, TX
Saint Francis University, PA
Saint John's University, MN
St. John's University, NY
Saint Joseph's University, PA
Saint Louis University, MO
Saint Mary's University of Minnesota, MN
Saint Michael's College, VT
St. Norbert College, WI
Salem State College, MA
Sam Houston State University, TX
San Diego State University, CA
Savannah College of Art and Design, GA
School of the Museum of Fine Arts,
   Boston, MA
School of Visual Arts, NY
Schreiner University, TX
Seattle Pacific University, WA
Seattle University, WA
Seton Hill University, PA
Shepherd University, WV
Shippensburg University of Pennsylvania, PA
Shorter University, GA
Silver Lake College, WI
Simpson College, IA
Slippery Rock University of Pennsylvania, PA
Sonoma State University, CA
South Dakota State University, SD
Southeastern Louisiana University, LA
Southeastern Oklahoma State University, OK
Southern Adventist University, TN
Southern Arkansas University–Magnolia, AR
Southern Illinois University Edwardsville, IL
Southern Nazarene University, OK
Southwest Baptist University, MO
Southwestern Oklahoma State University, OK
Southwestern University, TX
Southwest Minnesota State University, MN
Spring Arbor University, MI
State University of New York at
   Binghamton, NY
State University of New York at Fredonia, NY
State University of New York at New
   Paltz, NY
State University of New York at
   Plattsburgh, NY
State University of New York College at
   Cortland, NY
State University of New York College at
   Geneseo, NY
State University of New York College at
   Potsdam, NY
Stetson University, FL

Stevenson University, MD
Sul Ross State University, TX
Syracuse University, NY
Temple University, PA
Tennessee Technological University, TN
Texas A&M University–Commerce, TX
Texas A&M University–Corpus Christi, TX
Texas Christian University, TX
Texas Tech University, TX
Texas Woman's University, TX
Thomas More College, KY
Towson University, MD
Transylvania University, KY
Trinity Bible College, ND
Trinity Christian College, IL
Trinity University, TX
Truman State University, MO
Union University, TN
The University of Akron, OH
The University of Alabama, AL
The University of Alabama at
  Birmingham, AL
The University of Alabama in Huntsville, AL
University of Alaska Fairbanks, AK
The University of Arizona, AZ
University of California, Irvine, CA
University of California, Riverside, CA
University of California, Santa Cruz, CA
University of Central Missouri, MO
University of Central Oklahoma, OK
University of Colorado at Boulder, CO
University of Connecticut, CT
University of Dallas, TX
University of Dayton, OH
University of Delaware, DE
University of Denver, CO
University of Evansville, IN
University of Florida, FL
University of Great Falls, MT
University of Hartford, CT
University of Hawaii at Hilo, HI
University of Idaho, ID
University of Illinois at Chicago, IL
University of Illinois at Urbana–
  Champaign, IL
University of Indianapolis, IN
The University of Kansas, KS
University of Kentucky, KY
University of La Verne, CA
University of Louisiana at Monroe, LA
University of Louisville, KY
University of Maine at Presque Isle, ME
University of Mary Hardin-Baylor, TX
University of Maryland, Baltimore
  County, MD
University of Maryland, College Park, MD
University of Mary Washington, VA
University of Massachusetts Amherst, MA
University of Memphis, TN
University of Miami, FL
University of Michigan, MI
University of Michigan–Dearborn, MI
University of Michigan–Flint, MI
University of Mississippi, MS
University of Missouri, MO
University of Missouri–St. Louis, MO
The University of Montana Western, MT
University of Montevallo, AL
University of Mount Union, OH
University of Nebraska at Kearney, NE
University of Nebraska at Omaha, NE
University of Nebraska–Lincoln, NE
University of Nevada, Las Vegas, NV

University of New Hampshire, NH
University of North Alabama, AL
The University of North Carolina at
  Asheville, NC
The University of North Carolina at Chapel
  Hill, NC
The University of North Carolina at
  Greensboro, NC
The University of North Carolina
  Wilmington, NC
University of North Dakota, ND
University of Northern Iowa, IA
University of North Florida, FL
University of Oklahoma, OK
University of Oregon, OR
University of Puget Sound, WA
University of Redlands, CA
University of Richmond, VA
University of St. Francis, IL
University of Saint Francis, IN
University of Science and Arts of
  Oklahoma, OK
University of South Alabama, AL
University of South Carolina, SC
University of South Carolina Aiken, SC
The University of South Dakota, SD
University of Southern Indiana, IN
University of Southern Mississippi, MS
The University of Tampa, FL
The University of Tennessee, TN
The University of Tennessee at Martin, TN
The University of Texas at Brownsville, TX
The University of Texas at El Paso, TX
The University of Texas at San Antonio, TX
The University of Texas at Tyler, TX
The University of Texas of the Permian
  Basin, TX
The University of Texas–Pan American, TX
University of the Incarnate Word, TX
University of the Ozarks, AR
The University of Toledo, OH
University of Tulsa, OK
University of Washington, WA
University of West Florida, FL
University of West Georgia, GA
University of Wisconsin–Green Bay, WI
University of Wisconsin–La Crosse, WI
University of Wisconsin–Parkside, WI
University of Wisconsin–River Falls, WI
University of Wisconsin–Stout, WI
University of Wisconsin–Whitewater, WI
University of Wyoming, WY
Utah State University, UT
Valdosta State University, GA
Valley City State University, ND
Valley Forge Christian College, PA
Valparaiso University, IN
Virginia Commonwealth University, VA
Virginia Intermont College, VA
Virginia Polytechnic Institute and State
  University, VA
Virginia Wesleyan College, VA
Wabash College, IN
Warren Wilson College, NC
Wartburg College, IA
Washburn University, KS
Washington State University, WA
Washington University in St. Louis, MO
Watkins College of Art, Design, & Film, TN
Wayland Baptist University, TX
Wayne State College, NE
Wayne State University, MI
Webster University, MO

Wesleyan College, GA
Western Carolina University, NC
Western Kentucky University, KY
Western Oregon University, OR
Western State College of Colorado, CO
Western Washington University, WA
West Liberty University, WV
Westminster College, UT
Westmont College, CA
West Virginia University, WV
West Virginia Wesleyan College, WV
Wheaton College, IL
Whitman College, WA
Whitworth University, WA
Wichita State University, KS
William Carey University, MS
William Jewell College, MO
Williams Baptist College, AR
Winona State University, MN
Winthrop University, SC
Wittenberg University, OH
Wright State University, OH
Xavier University, OH
Youngstown State University, OH

Cinema/Film/Broadcasting
Arizona State University, AZ
Arkansas State University—Jonesboro, AR
Arkansas Tech University, AR
Auburn University, AL
Ball State University, IN
Baylor University, TX
Biola University, CA
Bloomfield College, NJ
Bowling Green State University, OH
Brenau University, GA
Butler University, IN
California Institute of the Arts, CA
California Polytechnic State University,
  San Luis Obispo, CA
California State University, Chico, CA
Central Michigan University, MI
Chapman University, CA
City College of the City University of New
  York, NY
The College at Brockport, State University of
  New York, NY
The College of New Rochelle, NY
Columbia College Chicago, IL
DeSales University, PA
Eastern Michigan University, MI
Eastern New Mexico University, NM
Eastern Washington University, WA
Edinboro University of Pennsylvania, PA
Everest University, FL
Five Towns College, NY
Flagler College, FL
Florida State University, FL
Georgia Southern University, GA
Grace University, NE
Grand Valley State University, MI
Harding University, AR
Henderson State University, AR
Huntington University, IN
Illinois State University, IL
Ithaca College, NY
James Madison University, VA
Kean University, NJ
Keene State College, NH
Lindenwood University, MO
Long Island University, Brooklyn
  Campus, NY

Long Island University, C.W. Post
  Campus, NY
Marywood University, PA
Massachusetts College of Liberal Arts, MA
Minneapolis College of Art and Design, MN
Minnesota State University Moorhead, MN
Mississippi State University, MS
Missouri Valley College, MO
Montana State University, MT
Montclair State University, NJ
Morningside College, IA
North Central College, IL
Northern Arizona University, AZ
Northwestern Oklahoma State University, OK
Northwestern State University of
  Louisiana, LA
Ohio University, OH
Ohio University–Chillicothe, OH
Ohio University–Eastern, OH
Ohio University–Lancaster, OH
Ohio University–Southern Campus, OH
Ohio University–Zanesville, OH
Oral Roberts University, OK
Point Park University, PA
Purchase College, State University of New
  York, NY
Quincy University, IL
Regent University, VA
Rhode Island College, RI
Rochester Institute of Technology, NY
St. John's University, NY
San Diego State University, CA
Sonoma State University, CA
Southeastern Louisiana University, LA
Southern Illinois University Carbondale, IL
Southwestern College, KS
State University of New York at
  Binghamton, NY
Stony Brook University, State University of
  New York, NY
Sul Ross State University, TX
Texas Christian University, TX
Texas Woman's University, TX
Trevecca Nazarene University, TN
Union University, TN
The University of Alabama, AL
University of California, Irvine, CA
University of California, San Diego, CA
University of California, Santa Cruz, CA
University of Central Florida, FL
University of Central Missouri, MO
University of Colorado at Boulder, CO
The University of Kansas, KS
University of Kentucky, KY
University of Maryland, Baltimore
  County, MD
University of Memphis, TN
University of Miami, FL
University of Michigan, MI
University of Michigan–Dearborn, MI
University of Mississippi, MS
University of Missouri, MO
University of Mount Union, OH
University of Nebraska–Lincoln, NE
University of Nevada, Las Vegas, NV
The University of North Carolina at
  Greensboro, NC
University of North Carolina School of the
  Arts, NC
The University of North Carolina
  Wilmington, NC
University of Pittsburgh at Bradford, PA
University of Wisconsin–Whitewater, WI

Virginia Polytechnic Institute and State
  University, VA
Washburn University, KS
Washington State University, WA
Washington University in St. Louis, MO
Watkins College of Art, Design, & Film, TN
Western Illinois University, IL
Western Kentucky University, KY
Western Washington University, WA
Westminster College, PA
Wright State University, OH

Creative Writing
Alderson-Broaddus College, WV
Arizona State University, AZ
Arkansas Tech University, AR
Auburn University, AL
Augustana College, IL
Augustana College, SD
Austin Peay State University, TN
Belhaven University, MS
Bowling Green State University, OH
Brenau University, GA
Brescia University, KY
Bucknell University, PA
California College of the Arts, CA
California Institute of the Arts, CA
California Lutheran University, CA
California Polytechnic State University,
  San Luis Obispo, CA
California State University, Chico, CA
Cameron University, OK
Campbell University, NC
Case Western Reserve University, OH
Central College, IA
Central Michigan University, MI
Chapman University, CA
City College of the City University of New
  York, NY
Cleveland State University, OH
Coe College, IA
Coker College, SC
The College at Brockport, State University of
  New York, NY
The College of New Rochelle, NY
Colorado State University, CO
Columbia College, MO
Columbia College Chicago, IL
Creighton University, NE
Davidson College, NC
Delta State University, MS
Dickinson State University, ND
Drury University, MO
Duke University, NC
Eastern Michigan University, MI
Eastern New Mexico University, NM
Eastern Washington University, WA
Eckerd College, FL
Edgewood College, WI
Emporia State University, KS
The Evergreen State College, WA
Frostburg State University, MD
Furman University, SC
Georgia College & State University, GA
Georgian Court University, NJ
Graceland University, IA
Green Mountain College, VT
Grove City College, PA
Hamline University, MN
Hampshire College, MA
Hardin-Simmons University, TX
Hobart and William Smith Colleges, NY
Hollins University, VA

Hood College, MD
Hope College, MI
Huntington University, IN
Illinois State University, IL
Kentucky Wesleyan College, KY
Kenyon College, OH
Knox College, IL
Lake Forest College, IL
Lakeland College, WI
Lewis-Clark State College, ID
Louisiana Tech University, LA
Lycoming College, PA
Meredith College, NC
Mesa State College, CO
Michigan State University, MI
Midwestern State University, TX
Minnesota State University Moorhead, MN
Mississippi State University, MS
Morningside College, IA
Murray State University, KY
New England College, NH
Northeastern Illinois University, IL
Northern Arizona University, AZ
Northern Illinois University, IL
Northwestern State University of
  Louisiana, LA
Notre Dame de Namur University, CA
Ohio Northern University, OH
The Ohio State University, OH
Oklahoma State University, OK
Pace University, NY
Plymouth State University, NH
Purchase College, State University of New
  York, NY
Randolph College, VA
The Richard Stockton College of New
  Jersey, NJ
Rockhurst University, MO
Rocky Mountain College, MT
Sacred Heart University, CT
Salem State College, MA
San Diego State University, CA
Seton Hill University, PA
Siena College, NY
Sonoma State University, CA
Southern Illinois University Carbondale, IL
Southwest Minnesota State University, MN
State University of New York at
  Binghamton, NY
State University of New York College at
  Geneseo, NY
Susquehanna University, PA
Texas Christian University, TX
Trinity Bible College, ND
The University of Akron, OH
The University of Alabama, AL
University of Alaska Fairbanks, AK
University of California, Riverside, CA
University of Central Missouri, MO
University of Colorado at Boulder, CO
University of Idaho, ID
The University of Kansas, KS
University of Kentucky, KY
University of Louisiana at Monroe, LA
University of Louisville, KY
University of Maryland, Baltimore
  County, MD
University of Michigan, MI
University of Michigan–Dearborn, MI
University of Mississippi, MS
University of Missouri, MO
University of Nebraska at Omaha, NE
University of Nevada, Las Vegas, NV

The University of North Carolina Wilmington, NC
University of Redlands, CA
University of South Carolina Aiken, SC
The University of South Dakota, SD
University of Southern Indiana, IN
The University of Tampa, FL
The University of Texas at San Antonio, TX
The University of Virginia's College at Wise, VA
University of Wisconsin–Stevens Point, WI
University of Wisconsin–Whitewater, WI
Ursinus College, PA
Virginia Polytechnic Institute and State University, VA
Wabash College, IN
Warren Wilson College, NC
Washington State University, WA
Washington University in St. Louis, MO
Wayne State College, NE
Webster University, MO
Western Washington University, WA
Wichita State University, KS
Wright State University, OH
Youngstown State University, OH

Dance

Adelphi University, NY
Albion College, MI
Alma College, MI
Angelo State University, TX
Arizona State University, AZ
Ball State University, IN
Belhaven University, MS
Birmingham-Southern College, AL
Boise State University, ID
Bowling Green State University, OH
Brenau University, GA
Bucknell University, PA
Butler University, IN
California Institute of the Arts, CA
California Polytechnic State University, San Luis Obispo, CA
California State University, Chico, CA
California State University, Fullerton, CA
Case Western Reserve University, OH
Cedar Crest College, PA
Centenary College of Louisiana, LA
Central Michigan University, MI
Chapman University, CA
Cleveland State University, OH
Coker College, SC
The College at Brockport, State University of New York, NY
The College of New Rochelle, NY
The College of Wooster, OH
Colorado State University, CO
Columbia College Chicago, IL
Columbus State University, GA
Concordia University, Nebraska, NE
Creighton University, NE
DeSales University, PA
Duquesne University, PA
Eastern Michigan University, MI
Eastern New Mexico University, NM
Florida International University, FL
Florida State University, FL
Fordham University, NY
Goucher College, MD
Graceland University, IA
Grand Valley State University, MI
Gustavus Adolphus College, MN
Hawai'i Pacific University, HI

Henderson State University, AR
Hendrix College, AR
Hobart and William Smith Colleges, NY
Hofstra University, NY
Hollins University, VA
Hope College, MI
Idaho State University, ID
Indiana University of Pennsylvania, PA
Ithaca College, NY
James Madison University, VA
The Juilliard School, NY
Keene State College, NH
Kent State University, OH
Knox College, IL
Kutztown University of Pennsylvania, PA
Lake Erie College, OH
Lees-McRae College, NC
Lindenwood University, MO
Long Island University, Brooklyn Campus, NY
Long Island University, C.W. Post Campus, NY
Manhattanville College, NY
Marymount Manhattan College, NY
Mercyhurst College, PA
Mesa State College, CO
Millikin University, IL
Mississippi State University, MS
Missouri Valley College, MO
Montana State University, MT
Montclair State University, NJ
Morningside College, IA
Murray State University, KY
Nicholls State University, LA
Northeastern Illinois University, IL
Northeastern State University, OK
Northern Illinois University, IL
Northwestern State University of Louisiana, LA
Notre Dame College, OH
Oakland University, MI
Ohio Northern University, OH
The Ohio State University, OH
Ohio University, OH
Ohio University–Chillicothe, OH
Ohio University–Eastern, OH
Ohio University–Lancaster, OH
Ohio University–Southern Campus, OH
Ohio University–Zanesville, OH
Oklahoma City University, OK
Old Dominion University, VA
Pacific Lutheran University, WA
Palm Beach Atlantic University, FL
Plymouth State University, NH
Point Park University, PA
Purchase College, State University of New York, NY
Rhode Island College, RI
The Richard Stockton College of New Jersey, NJ
Rockford College, IL
St. Ambrose University, IA
St. John's University, NY
Saint Mary's College of California, CA
Salem State College, MA
Sam Houston State University, TX
San Diego State University, CA
Santa Clara University, CA
Shenandoah University, VA
Slippery Rock University of Pennsylvania, PA
Sonoma State University, CA
Southeastern Louisiana University, LA
Southeastern Oklahoma State University, OK

Southern Arkansas University–Magnolia, AR
Southern Illinois University Carbondale, IL
Southern Illinois University Edwardsville, IL
Southwestern College, KS
State University of New York at Binghamton, NY
State University of New York at Fredonia, NY
State University of New York College at Geneseo, NY
State University of New York College at Potsdam, NY
Stephens College, MO
Texas Christian University, TX
Texas Tech University, TX
Texas Woman's University, TX
Towson University, MD
The University of Akron, OH
The University of Alabama, AL
The University of Arizona, AZ
University of California, Irvine, CA
University of California, Riverside, CA
University of California, San Diego, CA
University of Colorado at Boulder, CO
University of Florida, FL
University of Great Falls, MT
University of Hartford, CT
University of Idaho, ID
University of Illinois at Urbana–Champaign, IL
The University of Kansas, KS
University of Kentucky, KY
University of Louisville, KY
University of Maryland, Baltimore County, MD
University of Maryland, College Park, MD
University of Mary Washington, VA
University of Massachusetts Amherst, MA
University of Memphis, TN
University of Michigan, MI
University of Missouri–St. Louis, MO
University of Nebraska–Lincoln, NE
University of Nevada, Las Vegas, NV
University of New Hampshire, NH
The University of North Carolina at Greensboro, NC
University of North Carolina School of the Arts, NC
University of Northern Colorado, CO
University of Oklahoma, OK
University of Oregon, OR
University of Richmond, VA
University of Saint Francis, IN
University of South Carolina, SC
University of Southern Mississippi, MS
The University of Texas of the Permian Basin, TX
The University of Texas–Pan American, TX
University of Wisconsin–Green Bay, WI
University of Wisconsin–Stevens Point, WI
University of Wyoming, WY
Virginia Commonwealth University, VA
Virginia Intermont College, VA
Washington University in St. Louis, MO
Wayne State University, MI
Western Illinois University, IL
Western Kentucky University, KY
Western Oregon University, OR
Western Washington University, WA
Wichita State University, KS
Winthrop University, SC
Wittenberg University, OH
Wright State University, OH

Debating

Abilene Christian University, TX
Alderson-Broaddus College, WV
Arizona State University, AZ
Arkansas State University—Jonesboro, AR
Augustana College, IL
Austin Peay State University, TN
Ball State University, IN
Baylor University, TX
Berry College, GA
Bethany Lutheran College, MN
Bethel College, KS
Bethel University, MN
Boise State University, ID
Bowling Green State University, OH
California Polytechnic State University,
  San Luis Obispo, CA
California State University, Chico, CA
Cameron University, OK
Carson-Newman College, TN
Cedarville University, OH
The College of New Rochelle, NY
Concordia College, MN
Concordia University, CA
Concordia University, Nebraska, NE
Creighton University, NE
Culver-Stockton College, MO
DePaul University, IL
Doane College, NE
Drury University, MO
Eastern Michigan University, MI
Eastern New Mexico University, NM
Emporia State University, KS
Ferris State University, MI
Florida College, FL
George Fox University, OR
Gonzaga University, WA
Gustavus Adolphus College, MN
Harding University, AR
Henderson State University, AR
Houston Baptist University, TX
Idaho State University, ID
Illinois State University, IL
Lewis & Clark College, OR
Lewis-Clark State College, ID
Linfield College, OR
Louisiana Tech University, LA
Loyola University Chicago, IL
Malone University, OH
Marist College, NY
Mercer University, GA
Methodist University, NC
Michigan State University, MI
Mississippi State University, MS
Missouri Southern State University, MO
Morehead State University, KY
Murray State University, KY
Muskingum University, OH
North Central College, IL
Northeastern State University, OK
Northern Arizona University, AZ
Northern Illinois University, IL
Northwestern Oklahoma State University, OK
Northwest Nazarene University, ID
Northwest University, WA
Ohio University, OH
Ohio University–Chillicothe, OH
Ohio University–Eastern, OH
Ohio University–Lancaster, OH
Ohio University–Southern Campus, OH
Ohio University–Zanesville, OH
Oklahoma Panhandle State University, OK
Pace University, NY

Pacific Lutheran University, WA
Pacific University, OR
Patrick Henry College, VA
Point Loma Nazarene University, CA
Regis University, CO
Ripon College, WI
Rocky Mountain College, MT
St. John's University, NY
Samford University, AL
Santa Clara University, CA
South Dakota State University, SD
Southeastern Oklahoma State University, OK
Southern Illinois University Carbondale, IL
Southwest Baptist University, MO
Southwest Minnesota State University, MN
Tennessee Technological University, TN
Towson University, MD
Trinity University, TX
Truman State University, MO
The University of Akron, OH
The University of Alabama, AL
University of Alaska Anchorage, AK
University of Central Missouri, MO
University of Denver, CO
The University of Kansas, KS
University of Kentucky, KY
University of La Verne, CA
University of Louisiana at Monroe, LA
University of Louisville, KY
University of Mary, ND
University of Miami, FL
University of Michigan–Dearborn, MI
University of Mississippi, MS
University of Missouri–Kansas City, MO
University of Mount Union, OH
University of Nebraska at Kearney, NE
University of Nebraska at Omaha, NE
University of Nevada, Las Vegas, NV
University of North Dakota, ND
University of Puget Sound, WA
University of Redlands, CA
University of South Carolina, SC
The University of South Dakota, SD
University of Southern California, CA
The University of Texas at San Antonio, TX
University of the Pacific, CA
University of the Southwest, NM
University of Vermont, VT
University of West Georgia, GA
University of Wisconsin–Eau Claire, WI
University of Wyoming, WY
Vanguard University of Southern
  California, CA
Washburn University, KS
Wayne State College, NE
Wayne State University, MI
Webster University, MO
Western Illinois University, IL
Western Kentucky University, KY
West Virginia University, WV
Whitman College, WA
Wichita State University, KS
Willamette University, OR
William Carey University, MS
William Jewell College, MO
Winona State University, MN

Journalism/Publications

Abilene Christian University, TX
Albright College, PA
Alderson-Broaddus College, WV
Angelo State University, TX
Arizona State University, AZ

Arkansas State University—Jonesboro, AR
Auburn University, AL
Austin Peay State University, TN
Averett University, VA
Ball State University, IN
Baylor University, TX
Belhaven University, MS
Berry College, GA
Bethany Lutheran College, MN
Bethel College, IN
Biola University, CA
Boise State University, ID
Bowling Green State University, OH
Brenau University, GA
Brevard College, NC
Bryan College, TN
California Lutheran University, CA
California Polytechnic State University,
  San Luis Obispo, CA
California State University, Chico, CA
California State University, Fresno, CA
California State University, Northridge, CA
California State University,
  San Bernardino, CA
Cameron University, OK
Campbellsville University, KY
Campbell University, NC
Carroll University, WI
Carson-Newman College, TN
Central Michigan University, MI
The Citadel, The Military College of South
  Carolina, SC
The College at Brockport, State University of
  New York, NY
The College of New Rochelle, NY
Columbia College Chicago, IL
Concord University, WV
Creighton University, NE
Delta State University, MS
DePauw University, IN
Dickinson State University, ND
Dordt College, IA
Eastern New Mexico University, NM
Eastern Washington University, WA
Edinboro University of Pennsylvania, PA
Elon University, NC
Emory & Henry College, VA
Faulkner University, AL
Ferris State University, MI
Florida College, FL
Florida International University, FL
Fort Valley State University, GA
Franklin College, IN
Frostburg State University, MD
Georgia College & State University, GA
Glenville State College, WV
Grand Valley State University, MI
Hannibal-LaGrange College, MO
Harding University, AR
Hardin-Simmons University, TX
Hawai'i Pacific University, HI
Henderson State University, AR
Huntington University, IN
Indiana University of Pennsylvania, PA
Iowa State University of Science and
  Technology, IA
Ithaca College, NY
Jacksonville State University, AL
James Madison University, VA
John Brown University, AR
Kent State University, OH
Kentucky State University, KY
Lakeland College, WI

Lees-McRae College, NC
LeMoyne-Owen College, TN
Lincoln University, MO
Lindenwood University, MO
Lipscomb University, TN
Lock Haven University of Pennsylvania, PA
Long Island University, C.W. Post Campus, NY
Louisiana State University and Agricultural and Mechanical College, LA
Louisiana Tech University, LA
Loyola University Chicago, IL
Lubbock Christian University, TX
Malone University, OH
Mansfield University of Pennsylvania, PA
Marywood University, PA
Massachusetts College of Liberal Arts, MA
McPherson College, KS
Mesa State College, CO
Michigan State University, MI
Midwestern State University, TX
Mississippi State University, MS
Mississippi University for Women, MS
Mississippi Valley State University, MS
Missouri Southern State University, MO
Missouri Valley College, MO
Morehead State University, KY
Morningside College, IA
Murray State University, KY
Muskingum University, OH
Newman University, KS
New Mexico State University, NM
North Central College, IL
Northeastern Illinois University, IL
Northeastern State University, OK
Northern Arizona University, AZ
Northern Illinois University, IL
North Greenville University, SC
Northwestern Oklahoma State University, OK
Northwestern State University of Louisiana, LA
Northwest Nazarene University, ID
Nyack College, NY
Oglethorpe University, GA
Ohio Northern University, OH
The Ohio State University, OH
Ohio University, OH
Ohio University–Chillicothe, OH
Ohio University–Eastern, OH
Ohio University–Lancaster, OH
Ohio University–Southern Campus, OH
Ohio University–Zanesville, OH
Ohio Valley University, WV
Oklahoma Christian University, OK
Oklahoma State University, OK
Olivet College, MI
Oral Roberts University, OK
Ouachita Baptist University, AR
Pacific University, OR
Patrick Henry College, VA
Point Park University, PA
Regent University, VA
Rhode Island College, RI
The Richard Stockton College of New Jersey, NJ
Rivier College, NH
Robert Morris University Illinois, IL
St. Bonaventure University, NY
St. John's University, NY
Samford University, AL
San Diego State University, CA
Schreiner University, TX
Seton Hill University, PA

Siena College, NY
Sonoma State University, CA
South Dakota State University, SD
Southeastern University, FL
Southern Adventist University, TN
Southern Illinois University Carbondale, IL
Southwestern College, KS
Southwest Minnesota State University, MN
State University of New York at Binghamton, NY
State University of New York at Plattsburgh, NY
State University of New York College at Geneseo, NY
Stephen F. Austin State University, TX
Stony Brook University, State University of New York, NY
Sul Ross State University, TX
Tabor College, KS
Texas A&M University, TX
Texas A&M University–Commerce, TX
Texas Christian University, TX
Texas Lutheran University, TX
Texas State University–San Marcos, TX
Texas Tech University, TX
Texas Woman's University, TX
Trinity Christian College, IL
Union University, TN
The University of Akron, OH
The University of Alabama, AL
University of California, San Diego, CA
University of Central Missouri, MO
University of Central Oklahoma, OK
University of Colorado at Boulder, CO
University of Florida, FL
University of Idaho, ID
University of Illinois at Urbana–Champaign, IL
The University of Kansas, KS
University of Kentucky, KY
University of La Verne, CA
University of Louisiana at Monroe, LA
University of Mary Washington, VA
University of Massachusetts Amherst, MA
University of Memphis, TN
University of Miami, FL
University of Michigan, MI
University of Michigan–Dearborn, MI
University of Mississippi, MS
University of Missouri, MO
University of Mount Union, OH
University of Nebraska at Kearney, NE
University of Nebraska at Omaha, NE
University of Nebraska–Lincoln, NE
University of Nevada, Las Vegas, NV
University of North Alabama, AL
The University of North Carolina at Chapel Hill, NC
The University of North Carolina at Pembroke, NC
University of Oklahoma, OK
University of Oregon, OR
University of Pittsburgh at Johnstown, PA
University of St. Thomas, MN
University of South Alabama, AL
University of South Carolina, SC
University of South Carolina Aiken, SC
The University of Tampa, FL
The University of Tennessee at Martin, TN
The University of Texas at Arlington, TX
The University of Texas at El Paso, TX
The University of Texas–Pan American, TX

The University of Virginia's College at Wise, VA
University of West Georgia, GA
University of Wisconsin–Green Bay, WI
University of Wisconsin–Whitewater, WI
Utah State University, UT
Valley City State University, ND
Virginia Polytechnic Institute and State University, VA
Wabash College, IN
Wartburg College, IA
Washburn University, KS
Washington State University, WA
Wayland Baptist University, TX
Wayne State College, NE
Wayne State University, MI
Webber International University, FL
Western Illinois University, IL
Western Kentucky University, KY
Western Washington University, WA
Westminster College, UT
Whitworth University, WA
Wichita State University, KS
William Carey University, MS
William Jewell College, MO
Youngstown State University, OH

Music

Abilene Christian University, TX
Adelphi University, NY
Adrian College, MI
Agnes Scott College, GA
Alabama Agricultural and Mechanical University, AL
Alabama State University, AL
Alaska Bible College, AK
Alaska Pacific University, AK
Albion College, MI
Albright College, PA
Alderson-Broaddus College, WV
Alma College, MI
Alverno College, WI
Anderson University, IN
Andrews University, MI
Angelo State University, TX
Arizona State University, AZ
Arkansas State University—Jonesboro, AR
Arkansas Tech University, AR
Armstrong Atlantic State University, GA
Asbury University, KY
Ashland University, OH
Atlantic Union College, MA
Auburn University, AL
Augsburg College, MN
Augustana College, IL
Augustana College, SD
Aurora University, IL
Austin College, TX
Austin Peay State University, TN
Averett University, VA
Baldwin-Wallace College, OH
Ball State University, IN
The Baptist College of Florida, FL
Barton College, NC
Baylor University, TX
Belhaven University, MS
Bellarmine University, KY
Belmont University, TN
Beloit College, WI
Benedict College, SC
Benedictine College, KS
Benedictine University, IL
Berklee College of Music, MA

Berry College, GA
Bethany College, KS
Bethany College, WV
Bethany Lutheran College, MN
Bethel College, IN
Bethel College, KS
Bethel University, MN
Bethesda Christian University, CA
Biola University, CA
Birmingham-Southern College, AL
Black Hills State University, SD
Bluefield College, VA
Blue Mountain College, MS
Bluffton University, OH
Boise State University, ID
Boston University, MA
Bowie State University, MD
Bowling Green State University, OH
Bradley University, IL
Brenau University, GA
Brescia University, KY
Brevard College, NC
Brewton-Parker College, GA
Briar Cliff University, IA
Bridgewater College, VA
Bryan College, TN
Bucknell University, PA
Buena Vista University, IA
Butler University, IN
Caldwell College, NJ
California Baptist University, CA
California Institute of the Arts, CA
California Lutheran University, CA
California Polytechnic State University,
  San Luis Obispo, CA
California State University, Chico, CA
California State University, East Bay, CA
California State University, Fresno, CA
California State University, Fullerton, CA
California State University, Northridge, CA
California State University,
  San Bernardino, CA
California State University, Stanislaus, CA
Calvin College, MI
Cameron University, OK
Campbellsville University, KY
Campbell University, NC
Canisius College, NY
Carleton College, MN
Carnegie Mellon University, PA
Carroll University, WI
Carson-Newman College, TN
Carthage College, WI
Case Western Reserve University, OH
Catawba College, NC
The Catholic University of America, DC
Cedarville University, OH
Centenary College of Louisiana, LA
Central College, IA
Central Michigan University, MI
Centre College, KY
Chapman University, CA
Chestnut Hill College, PA
Chowan University, NC
Christopher Newport University, VA
Cincinnati Christian University, OH
The Citadel, The Military College of South
  Carolina, SC
City College of the City University of New
  York, NY
Clarke College, IA
Clear Creek Baptist Bible College, KY
Clearwater Christian College, FL

Cleveland Institute of Music, OH
Cleveland State University, OH
Coastal Carolina University, SC
Coe College, IA
Coker College, SC
The College at Brockport, State University of
  New York, NY
College of Charleston, SC
College of Mount St. Joseph, OH
The College of New Jersey, NJ
The College of New Rochelle, NY
College of Saint Benedict, MN
College of Saint Mary, NE
The College of Saint Rose, NY
The College of St. Scholastica, MN
College of Staten Island of the City University
  of New York, NY
College of the Holy Cross, MA
The College of William and Mary, VA
The College of Wooster, OH
Colorado State University, CO
Columbia College, MO
Columbia College Chicago, IL
Columbus State University, GA
Concordia College, MN
Concordia University, CA
Concordia University, MI
Concordia University Chicago, IL
Concordia University, Nebraska, NE
Concordia University, St. Paul, MN
Concordia University Texas, TX
Concordia University Wisconsin, WI
Concord University, WV
Converse College, SC
Corban University, OR
Cornell College, IA
Cornerstone University, MI
Covenant College, GA
Creighton University, NE
Crossroads College, MN
Crown College, MN
Culver-Stockton College, MO
Dakota State University, SD
Dallas Baptist University, TX
Davidson College, NC
Delta State University, MS
DePaul University, IL
DePauw University, IN
Dickinson State University, ND
Dillard University, LA
Doane College, NE
Dominican University of California, CA
Dordt College, IA
Drake University, IA
Drury University, MO
Duquesne University, PA
East Carolina University, NC
Eastern Kentucky University, KY
Eastern Michigan University, MI
Eastern New Mexico University, NM
Eastern Washington University, WA
East Stroudsburg University of
  Pennsylvania, PA
East Texas Baptist University, TX
Eckerd College, FL
Edgewood College, WI
Edinboro University of Pennsylvania, PA
Elizabethtown College, PA
Elmhurst College, IL
Elon University, NC
Emory & Henry College, VA
Emory University, GA
Emporia State University, KS

Erskine College, SC
Eureka College, IL
Evangel University, MO
Fairfield University, CT
Faulkner University, AL
Fayetteville State University, NC
Ferris State University, MI
Five Towns College, NY
Florida Atlantic University, FL
Florida College, FL
Florida Gulf Coast University, FL
Florida International University, FL
Florida Southern College, FL
Florida State University, FL
Fordham University, NY
Fort Lewis College, CO
Fort Valley State University, GA
Francis Marion University, SC
Franklin & Marshall College, PA
Franklin College, IN
Fresno Pacific University, CA
Frostburg State University, MD
Furman University, SC
Gannon University, PA
Gardner-Webb University, NC
Geneva College, PA
George Fox University, OR
Georgetown College, KY
Georgia College & State University, GA
Georgian Court University, NJ
Georgia Southern University, GA
Georgia Southwestern State University, GA
Gettysburg College, PA
Glenville State College, WV
God's Bible School and College, OH
Gonzaga University, WA
Gordon College, MA
Goucher College, MD
Grace Bible College, MI
Grace College, IN
Graceland University, IA
Grace University, NE
Grand Valley State University, MI
Grand View University, IA
Green Mountain College, VT
Greenville College, IL
Grove City College, PA
Guilford College, NC
Gustavus Adolphus College, MN
Hamline University, MN
Hampden-Sydney College, VA
Hampton University, VA
Hannibal-LaGrange College, MO
Hanover College, IN
Harding University, AR
Hardin-Simmons University, TX
Hawai'i Pacific University, HI
Heidelberg University, OH
Henderson State University, AR
Hendrix College, AR
High Point University, NC
Hillsdale Free Will Baptist College, OK
Hobart and William Smith Colleges, NY
Hofstra University, NY
Hollins University, VA
Hope College, MI
Houghton College, NY
Houston Baptist University, TX
Howard Payne University, TX
Huntingdon College, AL
Huntington University, IN
Huston-Tillotson University, TX
Idaho State University, ID

Illinois College, IL
Illinois State University, IL
Illinois Wesleyan University, IL
Indiana University of Pennsylvania, PA
Indiana Wesleyan University, IN
Iona College, NY
Iowa State University of Science and
  Technology, IA
Iowa Wesleyan College, IA
Ithaca College, NY
Jacksonville State University, AL
James Madison University, VA
Jamestown College, ND
John Brown University, AR
Johnson Bible College, TN
Johnson C. Smith University, NC
Judson College, AL
The Juilliard School, NY
Juniata College, PA
Kean University, NJ
Keene State College, NH
Kennesaw State University, GA
Kent State University, OH
Kent State University at Stark, OH
Kentucky Mountain Bible College, KY
Kentucky State University, KY
Kentucky Wesleyan College, KY
Kenyon College, OH
King College, TN
Knox College, IL
Kutztown University of Pennsylvania, PA
LaGrange College, GA
Lake Erie College, OH
Lake Forest College, IL
Lakeland College, WI
Lancaster Bible College & Graduate
  School, PA
Langston University, OK
Lawrence University, WI
Lebanon Valley College, PA
Lee University, TN
Lehigh University, PA
Le Moyne College, NY
LeMoyne-Owen College, TN
Lenoir-Rhyne University, NC
Lewis & Clark College, OR
Lewis-Clark State College, ID
Lewis University, IL
Limestone College, SC
Lincoln Memorial University, TN
Lincoln University, MO
Lincoln University, PA
Lindenwood University, MO
Lindsey Wilson College, KY
Linfield College, OR
Lipscomb University, TN
Lock Haven University of Pennsylvania, PA
Long Island University, Brooklyn
  Campus, NY
Long Island University, C.W. Post
  Campus, NY
Longwood University, VA
Loras College, IA
Louisiana State University and Agricultural
  and Mechanical College, LA
Louisiana Tech University, LA
Loyola University Chicago, IL
Lubbock Christian University, TX
Luther College, IA
Lycoming College, PA
Lynchburg College, VA
Lynn University, FL
Malone University, OH

Manchester College, IN
Manhattan Christian College, KS
Manhattan College, NY
Mannes College The New School for
  Music, NY
Mansfield University of Pennsylvania, PA
Marian University, WI
Marietta College, OH
Marist College, NY
Martin Luther College, MN
Maryville College, TN
Marywood University, PA
Massachusetts College of Liberal Arts, MA
The Master's College and Seminary, CA
McKendree University, IL
McMurry University, TX
McNally Smith College of Music, MN
McPherson College, KS
Mercer University, GA
Mercyhurst College, PA
Meredith College, NC
Mesa State College, CO
Messiah College, PA
Methodist University, NC
Metropolitan State College of Denver, CO
Miami University, OH
Michigan State University, MI
Midwestern State University, TX
Millersville University of Pennsylvania, PA
Milligan College, TN
Millikin University, IL
Millsaps College, MS
Mills College, CA
Minnesota State University Moorhead, MN
Mississippi College, MS
Mississippi State University, MS
Mississippi University for Women, MS
Mississippi Valley State University, MS
Missouri Southern State University, MO
Missouri University of Science and
  Technology, MO
Missouri Valley College, MO
Molloy College, NY
Monmouth College, IL
Montana State University, MT
Montana State University Billings, MT
Montclair State University, NJ
Montreat College, NC
Moravian College, PA
Morehead State University, KY
Morehouse College, GA
Morningside College, IA
Mount Aloysius College, PA
Mount Marty College, SD
Mount Mary College, WI
Mount Mercy College, IA
Mount St. Mary's College, CA
Mount Vernon Nazarene University, OH
Murray State University, KY
Muskingum University, OH
Nazareth College of Rochester, NY
Nebraska Wesleyan University, NE
Neumann University, PA
Newberry College, SC
New England Conservatory of Music, MA
Newman University, KS
New Mexico State University, NM
The New School for Jazz and Contemporary
  Music, NY
New York City College of Technology of the
  City University of New York, NY
Nicholls State University, LA
Norfolk State University, VA

North Carolina State University, NC
North Central College, IL
Northeastern Illinois University, IL
Northeastern State University, OK
Northern Arizona University, AZ
Northern Illinois University, IL
Northern Kentucky University, KY
Northern Michigan University, MI
Northern State University, SD
North Georgia College & State University, GA
North Greenville University, SC
Northwest Christian University, OR
Northwestern College, MN
Northwestern Oklahoma State University, OK
Northwestern State University of
  Louisiana, LA
Northwestern University, IL
Northwest Nazarene University, ID
Northwest University, WA
Notre Dame College, OH
Notre Dame de Namur University, CA
Nyack College, NY
Oakland University, MI
Oberlin College, OH
Occidental College, CA
Oglethorpe University, GA
Ohio Northern University, OH
The Ohio State University, OH
Ohio University, OH
Ohio University–Chillicothe, OH
Ohio University–Eastern, OH
Ohio University–Lancaster, OH
Ohio University–Southern Campus, OH
Ohio University–Zanesville, OH
Ohio Valley University, WV
Oklahoma Baptist University, OK
Oklahoma Christian University, OK
Oklahoma City University, OK
Oklahoma Panhandle State University, OK
Oklahoma State University, OK
Oklahoma Wesleyan University, OK
Old Dominion University, VA
Olivet College, MI
Olivet Nazarene University, IL
Oral Roberts University, OK
Ouachita Baptist University, AR
Pacific Lutheran University, WA
Pacific Union College, CA
Pacific University, OR
Palm Beach Atlantic University, FL
Patrick Henry College, VA
Peabody Conservatory of The Johns Hopkins
  University, MD
Peace College, NC
Pfeiffer University, NC
Philadelphia Biblical University, PA
Philander Smith College, AR
Piedmont College, GA
Pittsburg State University, KS
Plymouth State University, NH
Point Loma Nazarene University, CA
Portland State University, OR
Presbyterian College, SC
Purchase College, State University of New
  York, NY
Purdue University, IN
Queens College of the City University of New
  York, NY
Quincy University, IL
Randolph College, VA
Regis University, CO
Reinhardt University, GA
Rhode Island College, RI

The Richard Stockton College of New Jersey, NJ
Ripon College, WI
Roberts Wesleyan College, NY
Rockford College, IL
Rockhurst University, MO
Rocky Mountain College, MT
Rogers State University, OK
Rollins College, FL
Rowan University, NJ
Sacred Heart University, CT
Saginaw Valley State University, MI
St. Ambrose University, IA
St. Bonaventure University, NY
St. Catherine University, MN
Saint Francis University, PA
Saint John's University, MN
St. John's University, NY
Saint Joseph's University, PA
Saint Louis University, MO
Saint Martin's University, WA
Saint Mary's College of California, CA
St. Mary's University, TX
Saint Mary's University of Minnesota, MN
St. Norbert College, WI
St. Olaf College, MN
Saint Xavier University, IL
Salem College, NC
Salem State College, MA
Salisbury University, MD
Samford University, AL
Sam Houston State University, TX
San Diego Christian College, CA
San Diego State University, CA
San Francisco Conservatory of Music, CA
Santa Clara University, CA
Savannah State University, GA
Schreiner University, TX
Seattle University, WA
Seton Hill University, PA
Shenandoah University, VA
Shepherd University, WV
Shippensburg University of Pennsylvania, PA
Shorter University, GA
Siena College, NY
Silver Lake College, WI
Simpson College, IA
Skidmore College, NY
Slippery Rock University of Pennsylvania, PA
Sonoma State University, CA
South Dakota State University, SD
Southeastern Bible College, AL
Southeastern Louisiana University, LA
Southeastern Oklahoma State University, OK
Southeastern University, FL
Southeast Missouri State University, MO
Southern Adventist University, TN
Southern Arkansas University–Magnolia, AR
Southern Illinois University Edwardsville, IL
Southern Nazarene University, OK
Southern Utah University, UT
Southwest Baptist University, MO
Southwestern College, KS
Southwestern Oklahoma State University, OK
Southwestern University, TX
Southwest Minnesota State University, MN
Spring Arbor University, MI
State University of New York at Binghamton, NY
State University of New York at Fredonia, NY
State University of New York at New Paltz, NY

State University of New York at Plattsburgh, NY
State University of New York College at Cortland, NY
State University of New York College at Geneseo, NY
State University of New York College at Oneonta, NY
State University of New York College at Potsdam, NY
Stephen F. Austin State University, TX
Stetson University, FL
Stillman College, AL
Stony Brook University, State University of New York, NY
Sul Ross State University, TX
Susquehanna University, PA
Syracuse University, NY
Tabor College, KS
Taylor University, IN
Temple University, PA
Tennessee Technological University, TN
Tennessee Wesleyan College, TN
Texas A&M University–Commerce, TX
Texas Christian University, TX
Texas Lutheran University, TX
Texas State University–San Marcos, TX
Texas Tech University, TX
Texas Woman's University, TX
Thiel College, PA
Tiffin University, OH
Towson University, MD
Transylvania University, KY
Trevecca Nazarene University, TN
Trinity Bible College, ND
Trinity Christian College, IL
Trinity International University, IL
Trinity University, TX
Troy University, AL
Truett-McConnell College, GA
Truman State University, MO
Tulane University, LA
Tusculum College, TN
Tuskegee University, AL
Union College, KY
Union University, TN
The University of Akron, OH
The University of Alabama, AL
The University of Alabama at Birmingham, AL
The University of Alabama in Huntsville, AL
University of Alaska Fairbanks, AK
The University of Arizona, AZ
University of Arkansas, AR
University of Bridgeport, CT
University of California, Irvine, CA
University of California, Riverside, CA
University of California, Santa Cruz, CA
University of Central Florida, FL
University of Central Missouri, MO
University of Central Oklahoma, OK
University of Charleston, WV
University of Colorado at Boulder, CO
University of Connecticut, CT
University of Dallas, TX
University of Dayton, OH
University of Delaware, DE
University of Denver, CO
University of Evansville, IN
The University of Findlay, OH
University of Florida, FL
University of Georgia, GA
University of Hartford, CT

University of Hawaii at Hilo, HI
University of Idaho, ID
University of Illinois at Chicago, IL
University of Illinois at Urbana–Champaign, IL
University of Indianapolis, IN
The University of Iowa, IA
The University of Kansas, KS
University of Kentucky, KY
University of La Verne, CA
University of Louisiana at Monroe, LA
University of Louisville, KY
University of Mary, ND
University of Mary Hardin-Baylor, TX
University of Maryland, Baltimore County, MD
University of Maryland, College Park, MD
University of Mary Washington, VA
University of Massachusetts Amherst, MA
University of Massachusetts Lowell, MA
University of Memphis, TN
University of Miami, FL
University of Michigan, MI
University of Michigan–Flint, MI
University of Minnesota, Morris, MN
University of Mississippi, MS
University of Missouri, MO
University of Missouri–Kansas City, MO
University of Missouri–St. Louis, MO
University of Montevallo, AL
University of Mount Union, OH
University of Nebraska at Kearney, NE
University of Nebraska at Omaha, NE
University of Nebraska–Lincoln, NE
University of Nevada, Las Vegas, NV
University of Nevada, Reno, NV
University of New Hampshire, NH
University of New Orleans, LA
University of North Alabama, AL
The University of North Carolina at Asheville, NC
The University of North Carolina at Chapel Hill, NC
The University of North Carolina at Charlotte, NC
The University of North Carolina at Greensboro, NC
The University of North Carolina at Pembroke, NC
University of North Carolina School of the Arts, NC
The University of North Carolina Wilmington, NC
University of North Dakota, ND
University of Northern Colorado, CO
University of Northern Iowa, IA
University of North Florida, FL
University of Oklahoma, OK
University of Oregon, OR
University of Portland, OR
University of Puerto Rico at Bayamón, PR
University of Puget Sound, WA
University of Redlands, CA
University of Richmond, VA
University of St. Francis, IL
University of Saint Francis, IN
University of St. Thomas, MN
University of San Diego, CA
University of Science and Arts of Oklahoma, OK
University of South Alabama, AL
University of South Carolina, SC
University of South Carolina Aiken, SC

The University of South Dakota, SD
University of Southern Maine, ME
University of Southern Mississippi, MS
The University of Tampa, FL
The University of Tennessee at Chattanooga, TN
The University of Tennessee at Martin, TN
The University of Texas at Arlington, TX
The University of Texas at Brownsville, TX
The University of Texas at El Paso, TX
The University of Texas at San Antonio, TX
The University of Texas at Tyler, TX
The University of Texas of the Permian Basin, TX
The University of Texas–Pan American, TX
University of the District of Columbia, DC
University of the Ozarks, AR
University of the Pacific, CA
University of the Southwest, NM
The University of Toledo, OH
University of Tulsa, OK
University of Vermont, VT
University of Virginia, VA
The University of Virginia's College at Wise, VA
University of Washington, WA
University of West Florida, FL
University of West Georgia, GA
University of Wisconsin–Eau Claire, WI
University of Wisconsin–Green Bay, WI
University of Wisconsin–La Crosse, WI
University of Wisconsin–Parkside, WI
University of Wisconsin–River Falls, WI
University of Wisconsin–Stevens Point, WI
University of Wisconsin–Stout, WI
University of Wisconsin–Whitewater, WI
University of Wyoming, WY
Utah State University, UT
Valdosta State University, GA
Valley City State University, ND
Valley Forge Christian College, PA
Valparaiso University, IN
Vanguard University of Southern California, CA
Virginia Commonwealth University, VA
Virginia Intermont College, VA
Virginia Military Institute, VA
Virginia Polytechnic Institute and State University, VA
Virginia Wesleyan College, VA
Wabash College, IN
Wagner College, NY
Waldorf College, IA
Warner Pacific College, OR
Wartburg College, IA
Washburn University, KS
Washington Bible College, MD
Washington State University, WA
Washington University in St. Louis, MO
Wayland Baptist University, TX
Waynesburg University, PA
Wayne State College, NE
Wayne State University, MI
Webster University, MO
Wesleyan College, GA
West Chester University of Pennsylvania, PA
Western Carolina University, NC
Western Illinois University, IL
Western Kentucky University, KY
Western New England College, MA
Western Oregon University, OR
Western State College of Colorado, CO
Western Washington University, WA

West Liberty University, WV
Westminster College, MO
Westminster College, PA
Westminster College, UT
Westmont College, CA
West Virginia University, WV
West Virginia Wesleyan College, WV
Wheaton College, IL
Wheeling Jesuit University, WV
Whitman College, WA
Whitworth University, WA
Wichita State University, KS
Widener University, PA
Willamette University, OR
William Carey University, MS
William Jewell College, MO
Williams Baptist College, AR
Wilson College, PA
Winona State University, MN
Winthrop University, SC
Wittenberg University, OH
Wofford College, SC
Wright State University, OH
Xavier University, OH
York College, NE
York College of Pennsylvania, PA
Youngstown State University, OH

Performing Arts

Adelphi University, NY
Albion College, MI
Alderson-Broaddus College, WV
Alfred University, NY
Alma College, MI
Angelo State University, TX
Arizona State University, AZ
Arkansas State University—Jonesboro, AR
Auburn University, AL
Augsburg College, MN
Augustana College, SD
Ball State University, IN
Belhaven University, MS
Birmingham-Southern College, AL
Bloomfield College, NJ
Bluefield College, VA
Boise State University, ID
Bowling Green State University, OH
Brenau University, GA
Bryan College, TN
Bucknell University, PA
California Institute of the Arts, CA
California Lutheran University, CA
California Polytechnic State University, San Luis Obispo, CA
California State University, Chico, CA
California State University, Fullerton, CA
Calvin College, MI
Carroll University, WI
Case Western Reserve University, OH
Cedar Crest College, PA
Centenary College of Louisiana, LA
Central Michigan University, MI
Chapman University, CA
City College of the City University of New York, NY
Clemson University, SC
Cleveland State University, OH
Coe College, IA
The College at Brockport, State University of New York, NY
College of Charleston, SC
The College of New Rochelle, NY
Columbia College Chicago, IL

Columbus State University, GA
Concordia University, MI
Corban University, OR
Cornell College, IA
Creighton University, NE
Davidson College, NC
Delta State University, MS
DePaul University, IL
DePauw University, IN
DeSales University, PA
Doane College, NE
Eastern Michigan University, MI
Eastern New Mexico University, NM
Edgewood College, WI
Elizabethtown College, PA
Elon University, NC
Emerson College, MA
Eureka College, IL
Fairfield University, CT
Flagler College, FL
Florida Atlantic University, FL
Florida International University, FL
Fort Lewis College, CO
Franklin College, IN
Fresno Pacific University, CA
Frostburg State University, MD
Gannon University, PA
Georgetown College, KY
Georgia College & State University, GA
Goucher College, MD
Green Mountain College, VT
Greenville College, IL
Hannibal-LaGrange College, MO
Hardin-Simmons University, TX
Heidelberg University, OH
Henderson State University, AR
Hillsdale Free Will Baptist College, OK
Hobart and William Smith Colleges, NY
Huntingdon College, AL
Idaho State University, ID
Illinois State University, IL
Indiana State University, IN
Indiana University of Pennsylvania, PA
Ithaca College, NY
The Juilliard School, NY
Juniata College, PA
Kean University, NJ
Kennesaw State University, GA
Kent State University, OH
Kentucky State University, KY
Kentucky Wesleyan College, KY
King College, TN
Lake Erie College, OH
Lakeland College, WI
Lees-McRae College, NC
Lehigh University, PA
Limestone College, SC
Lincoln University, MO
Lindenwood University, MO
Louisiana State University and Agricultural and Mechanical College, LA
Louisiana Tech University, LA
Lubbock Christian University, TX
Manhattanville College, NY
Mannes College The New School for Music, NY
Marietta College, OH
Marymount Manhattan College, NY
Marywood University, PA
Massachusetts College of Liberal Arts, MA
Mesa State College, CO
Michigan State University, MI
Mississippi State University, MS

Mississippi University for Women, MS
Missouri Valley College, MO
Molloy College, NY
Montclair State University, NJ
Mount Aloysius College, PA
New Mexico State University, NM
Norfolk State University, VA
Northeastern Illinois University, IL
Northeastern State University, OK
Northern Arizona University, AZ
Northern Illinois University, IL
Northwestern State University of
  Louisiana, LA
Northwest Nazarene University, ID
Northwest University, WA
Notre Dame de Namur University, CA
Nyack College, NY
Oakland University, MI
Oglethorpe University, GA
Ohio Northern University, OH
The Ohio State University, OH
Ohio University, OH
Ohio University–Chillicothe, OH
Ohio University–Eastern, OH
Ohio University–Lancaster, OH
Ohio University–Southern Campus, OH
Ohio University–Zanesville, OH
Ohio Valley University, WV
Oklahoma Baptist University, OK
Oklahoma City University, OK
Oklahoma Panhandle State University, OK
Old Dominion University, VA
Olivet Nazarene University, IL
Ouachita Baptist University, AR
Pace University, NY
Point Park University, PA
Purchase College, State University of New
  York, NY
The Richard Stockton College of New
  Jersey, NJ
Rockford College, IL
Rockhurst University, MO
St. Andrews Presbyterian College, NC
St. Bonaventure University, NY
Saint Louis University, MO
Saint Mary's College of California, CA
Salem State College, MA
Samford University, AL
San Diego Christian College, CA
San Diego State University, CA
Seattle Pacific University, WA
Seton Hill University, PA
Shenandoah University, VA
Shepherd University, WV
Siena College, NY
Slippery Rock University of Pennsylvania, PA
Sonoma State University, CA
South Dakota State University, SD
Southeastern Louisiana University, LA
Southeastern Oklahoma State University, OK
Southeast Missouri State University, MO
Southern Illinois University Carbondale, IL
Southern Nazarene University, OK
Southwestern College, KS
Southwest Minnesota State University, MN
State University of New York at
  Binghamton, NY
State University of New York at Fredonia, NY
State University of New York at New
  Paltz, NY
State University of New York College at
  Geneseo, NY

State University of New York College at
  Potsdam, NY
Stephens College, MO
Tabor College, KS
Temple University, PA
Texas A&M University, TX
Texas Christian University, TX
Texas Tech University, TX
Tiffin University, OH
The University of Akron, OH
The University of Alabama at
  Birmingham, AL
The University of Arizona, AZ
University of California, San Diego, CA
University of Central Missouri, MO
University of Colorado at Boulder, CO
University of Florida, FL
University of Hartford, CT
University of Hawaii at Hilo, HI
University of Idaho, ID
University of Illinois at Chicago, IL
University of Illinois at Urbana–
  Champaign, IL
The University of Kansas, KS
University of Kentucky, KY
University of Louisiana at Monroe, LA
University of Maine at Fort Kent, ME
University of Maryland, Baltimore
  County, MD
University of Maryland, College Park, MD
University of Miami, FL
University of Michigan, MI
University of Mississippi, MS
University of Missouri–Kansas City, MO
University of Nebraska at Omaha, NE
University of Nebraska–Lincoln, NE
University of Nevada, Las Vegas, NV
The University of North Carolina at
  Charlotte, NC
The University of North Carolina at
  Greensboro, NC
University of North Carolina School of the
  Arts, NC
University of Northern Colorado, CO
University of Oklahoma, OK
University of Oregon, OR
University of Portland, OR
University of Richmond, VA
The University of Tampa, FL
The University of Texas at Brownsville, TX
The University of Texas at El Paso, TX
The University of Toledo, OH
University of Tulsa, OK
The University of Virginia's College at
  Wise, VA
University of Washington, WA
University of West Georgia, GA
University of Wisconsin–Stevens Point, WI
Utah State University, UT
Valparaiso University, IN
Virginia Commonwealth University, VA
Virginia Intermont College, VA
Virginia Polytechnic Institute and State
  University, VA
Washburn University, KS
Washington State University, WA
Washington University in St. Louis, MO
Wayne State College, NE
Western Illinois University, IL
Western New Mexico University, NM
Western Oregon University, OR
Western Washington University, WA
West Virginia Wesleyan College, WV

Wichita State University, KS
Wilkes University, PA
Winthrop University, SC
Wright State University, OH
Xavier University, OH
Youngstown State University, OH

Theater/Drama

Abilene Christian University, TX
Adelphi University, NY
Adrian College, MI
Alabama State University, AL
Alaska Pacific University, AK
Albion College, MI
Albright College, PA
Alderson-Broaddus College, WV
Alma College, MI
Angelo State University, TX
Arcadia University, PA
Arizona State University, AZ
Arkansas State University—Jonesboro, AR
Ashland University, OH
Auburn University, AL
Augsburg College, MN
Augustana College, IL
Augustana College, SD
Aurora University, IL
Austin College, TX
Austin Peay State University, TN
Averett University, VA
Ball State University, IN
Barton College, NC
Baylor University, TX
Belhaven University, MS
Belmont Abbey College, NC
Benedictine College, KS
Berry College, GA
Bethany College, KS
Bethany Lutheran College, MN
Bethel College, IN
Bethel College, KS
Bethel University, MN
Biola University, CA
Birmingham-Southern College, AL
Black Hills State University, SD
Bloomfield College, NJ
Bluefield College, VA
Blue Mountain College, MS
Boise State University, ID
Boston University, MA
Bowling Green State University, OH
Bradley University, IL
Brenau University, GA
Brevard College, NC
Briar Cliff University, IA
Bryan College, TN
Bucknell University, PA
Buena Vista University, IA
Butler University, IN
California Baptist University, CA
California Institute of the Arts, CA
California Lutheran University, CA
California Polytechnic State University,
  San Luis Obispo, CA
California State University, Chico, CA
California State University, Fresno, CA
California State University, Fullerton, CA
California State University,
  San Bernardino, CA
Calvin College, MI
Cameron University, OK
Campbellsville University, KY
Campbell University, NC

Carroll University, WI
Carthage College, WI
Case Western Reserve University, OH
Catawba College, NC
The Catholic University of America, DC
Cedar Crest College, PA
Centenary College of Louisiana, LA
Central College, IA
Central Michigan University, MI
Centre College, KY
Chapman University, CA
Chatham University, PA
Chestnut Hill College, PA
Christopher Newport University, VA
Clarke College, IA
Clemson University, SC
Cleveland State University, OH
Coastal Carolina University, SC
Coe College, IA
Coker College, SC
The College at Brockport, State University of New York, NY
College of Charleston, SC
The College of New Rochelle, NY
College of Saint Benedict, MN
College of Staten Island of the City University of New York, NY
The College of William and Mary, VA
The College of Wooster, OH
Colorado State University, CO
Columbia College Chicago, IL
Columbus State University, GA
Concordia College, MN
Concordia University, CA
Concordia University, MI
Concordia University, Nebraska, NE
Concordia University, St. Paul, MN
Concord University, WV
Converse College, SC
Cornell College, IA
Creighton University, NE
Culver-Stockton College, MO
Davidson College, NC
DePaul University, IL
DeSales University, PA
Dickinson State University, ND
Dillard University, LA
Doane College, NE
Dordt College, IA
Drake University, IA
Drury University, MO
Eastern Michigan University, MI
Eastern New Mexico University, NM
Eastern Washington University, WA
East Stroudsburg University of Pennsylvania, PA
East Texas Baptist University, TX
Eckerd College, FL
Edgewood College, WI
Elizabethtown College, PA
Elmhurst College, IL
Elon University, NC
Emory & Henry College, VA
Emory University, GA
Emporia State University, KS
Erskine College, SC
Eureka College, IL
Evangel University, MO
Faulkner University, AL
Ferris State University, MI
Five Towns College, NY
Flagler College, FL
Florida College, FL

Florida International University, FL
Florida Southern College, FL
Florida State University, FL
Fort Lewis College, CO
Francis Marion University, SC
Franklin College, IN
Fresno Pacific University, CA
Frostburg State University, MD
Furman University, SC
Gannon University, PA
Gardner-Webb University, NC
George Fox University, OR
Georgetown College, KY
Georgia College & State University, GA
Georgia Southern University, GA
Gordon College, MA
Goucher College, MD
Grace College, IN
Graceland University, IA
Grand Valley State University, MI
Grand View University, IA
Green Mountain College, VT
Guilford College, NC
Gustavus Adolphus College, MN
Hamline University, MN
Hannibal-LaGrange College, MO
Hanover College, IN
Hardin-Simmons University, TX
Henderson State University, AR
Hendrix College, AR
Hofstra University, NY
Hope College, MI
Howard Payne University, TX
Huntington University, IN
Idaho State University, ID
Illinois College, IL
Illinois State University, IL
Illinois Wesleyan University, IL
Indiana University of Pennsylvania, PA
Indiana Wesleyan University, IN
Iowa State University of Science and Technology, IA
Ithaca College, NY
Jacksonville State University, AL
James Madison University, VA
Jamestown College, ND
John Brown University, AR
The Juilliard School, NY
Kean University, NJ
Keene State College, NH
Kennesaw State University, GA
Kent State University, OH
Kent State University at Stark, OH
Kentucky Mountain Bible College, KY
King College, TN
Knox College, IL
LaGrange College, GA
Lake Erie College, OH
Lake Forest College, IL
Lees-McRae College, NC
Lee University, TN
Lehigh University, PA
Lewis-Clark State College, ID
Lewis University, IL
Limestone College, SC
Lincoln University, MO
Lindenwood University, MO
Linfield College, OR
Lipscomb University, TN
Long Island University, Brooklyn Campus, NY
Long Island University, C.W. Post Campus, NY

Longwood University, VA
Louisiana State University and Agricultural and Mechanical College, LA
Louisiana Tech University, LA
Loyola University Chicago, IL
Lubbock Christian University, TX
Lycoming College, PA
Lynchburg College, VA
Malone University, OH
Manchester College, IN
Marietta College, OH
Marquette University, WI
Maryville College, TN
Marywood University, PA
Massachusetts College of Liberal Arts, MA
Massachusetts Maritime Academy, MA
McMurry University, TX
McPherson College, KS
Mercer University, GA
Mesa State College, CO
Messiah College, PA
Methodist University, NC
Miami University, OH
Michigan State University, MI
Midwestern State University, TX
Milligan College, TN
Millikin University, IL
Millsaps College, MS
Minnesota State University Moorhead, MN
Mississippi State University, MS
Mississippi University for Women, MS
Missouri Southern State University, MO
Missouri University of Science and Technology, MO
Missouri Valley College, MO
Molloy College, NY
Monmouth College, IL
Montana State University, MT
Montana State University Billings, MT
Montclair State University, NJ
Morehead State University, KY
Morningside College, IA
Mount Marty College, SD
Mount Mercy College, IA
Murray State University, KY
Muskingum University, OH
Nazareth College of Rochester, NY
Nebraska Wesleyan University, NE
Newberry College, SC
New England College, NH
New England Conservatory of Music, MA
Newman University, KS
New Mexico State University, NM
Niagara University, NY
North Central College, IL
Northeastern Illinois University, IL
Northeastern State University, OK
Northern Arizona University, AZ
Northern Illinois University, IL
Northern Kentucky University, KY
Northern Michigan University, MI
Northern State University, SD
North Greenville University, SC
Northwestern College, MN
Northwestern Oklahoma State University, OK
Northwestern State University of Louisiana, LA
Northwest Nazarene University, ID
Northwest University, WA
Notre Dame College, OH
Notre Dame de Namur University, CA
Nyack College, NY
Oglethorpe University, GA

Ohio Northern University, OH
The Ohio State University, OH
Ohio University, OH
Ohio University–Chillicothe, OH
Ohio University–Eastern, OH
Ohio University–Lancaster, OH
Ohio University–Southern Campus, OH
Ohio University–Zanesville, OH
Ohio Valley University, WV
Oklahoma Baptist University, OK
Oklahoma Christian University, OK
Oklahoma City University, OK
Oklahoma Panhandle State University, OK
Oklahoma State University, OK
Old Dominion University, VA
Olivet Nazarene University, IL
Ouachita Baptist University, AR
Pace University, NY
Pacific Lutheran University, WA
Pacific Union College, CA
Pacific University, OR
Palm Beach Atlantic University, FL
Peace College, NC
Piedmont College, GA
Plymouth State University, NH
Point Loma Nazarene University, CA
Point Park University, PA
Portland State University, OR
Providence College, RI
Purchase College, State University of New
 York, NY
Randolph College, VA
Rhode Island College, RI
The Richard Stockton College of New
 Jersey, NJ
Rider University, NJ
Ripon College, WI
Rockford College, IL
Rockhurst University, MO
Rocky Mountain College, MT
Rollins College, FL
Russell Sage College, NY
Saginaw Valley State University, MI
St. Ambrose University, IA
St. Andrews Presbyterian College, NC
St. Edward's University, TX
Saint John's University, MN
Saint Joseph's University, PA
Saint Louis University, MO
Saint Martin's University, WA
Saint Mary's College of California, CA
Saint Mary's University of Minnesota, MN
St. Norbert College, WI
Salem State College, MA
Samford University, AL
San Diego Christian College, CA
San Diego State University, CA
Santa Clara University, CA
Schreiner University, TX
Seattle University, WA
Seton Hill University, PA
Shenandoah University, VA
Shepherd University, WV
Shippensburg University of Pennsylvania, PA
Shorter University, GA
Siena College, NY
Simpson College, IA
Slippery Rock University of Pennsylvania, PA
Sonoma State University, CA
South Dakota State University, SD
Southeastern Louisiana University, LA
Southeastern Oklahoma State University, OK
Southeastern University, FL

Southeast Missouri State University, MO
Southern Adventist University, TN
Southern Arkansas University–Magnolia, AR
Southern Illinois University Edwardsville, IL
Southern Utah University, UT
Southwest Baptist University, MO
Southwestern College, KS
Southwestern Oklahoma State University, OK
Southwestern University, TX
Southwest Minnesota State University, MN
State University of New York at
 Binghamton, NY
State University of New York at Fredonia, NY
State University of New York at New
 Paltz, NY
State University of New York at
 Plattsburgh, NY
State University of New York College at
 Geneseo, NY
State University of New York College at
 Oneonta, NY
State University of New York College at
 Potsdam, NY
Stephen F. Austin State University, TX
Stephens College, MO
Stetson University, FL
Sul Ross State University, TX
Susquehanna University, PA
Tabor College, KS
Taylor University, IN
Texas A&M University, TX
Texas A&M University–Commerce, TX
Texas Christian University, TX
Texas Lutheran University, TX
Texas State University–San Marcos, TX
Texas Tech University, TX
Texas Woman's University, TX
Thomas More College, KY
Tiffin University, OH
Towson University, MD
Transylvania University, KY
Trinity Bible College, ND
Trinity Christian College, IL
Trinity University, TX
Troy University, AL
Truman State University, MO
Union University, TN
The University of Akron, OH
The University of Alabama, AL
The University of Alabama at
 Birmingham, AL
University of Alaska Fairbanks, AK
The University of Arizona, AZ
University of Arkansas, AR
University of California, Irvine, CA
University of California, Riverside, CA
University of California, Santa Cruz, CA
University of Central Florida, FL
University of Central Missouri, MO
University of Central Oklahoma, OK
University of Colorado at Boulder, CO
University of Connecticut, CT
University of Dallas, TX
University of Delaware, DE
University of Denver, CO
University of Evansville, IN
The University of Findlay, OH
University of Florida, FL
University of Hartford, CT
University of Hawaii at Hilo, HI
University of Idaho, ID
University of Illinois at Chicago, IL

University of Illinois at Urbana–
 Champaign, IL
University of Indianapolis, IN
The University of Kansas, KS
University of Kentucky, KY
University of La Verne, CA
University of Louisiana at Monroe, LA
University of Louisville, KY
University of Mary, ND
University of Maryland, Baltimore
 County, MD
University of Maryland, College Park, MD
University of Mary Washington, VA
University of Massachusetts Amherst, MA
University of Miami, FL
University of Michigan, MI
University of Michigan–Flint, MI
University of Mississippi, MS
University of Missouri, MO
University of Missouri–St. Louis, MO
University of Mount Union, OH
University of Nebraska at Omaha, NE
University of Nebraska–Lincoln, NE
University of Nevada, Las Vegas, NV
University of Nevada, Reno, NV
University of New Hampshire, NH
University of New Orleans, LA
The University of North Carolina at
 Asheville, NC
The University of North Carolina at Chapel
 Hill, NC
The University of North Carolina at
 Greensboro, NC
University of North Carolina School of the
 Arts, NC
The University of North Carolina
 Wilmington, NC
University of North Dakota, ND
University of Northern Colorado, CO
University of Northern Iowa, IA
University of Oklahoma, OK
University of Oregon, OR
University of Pittsburgh at Johnstown, PA
University of Portland, OR
University of Puerto Rico at Bayamón, PR
University of Puget Sound, WA
University of Richmond, VA
University of Science and Arts of
 Oklahoma, OK
University of South Alabama, AL
University of South Carolina, SC
The University of South Dakota, SD
University of Southern Indiana, IN
University of Southern Maine, ME
University of Southern Mississippi, MS
The University of Tennessee at Martin, TN
The University of Texas at Arlington, TX
The University of Texas at El Paso, TX
The University of Texas of the Permian
 Basin, TX
The University of Texas–Pan American, TX
University of the Ozarks, AR
The University of Toledo, OH
University of Tulsa, OK
University of Vermont, VT
The University of Virginia's College at
 Wise, VA
University of West Florida, FL
University of West Georgia, GA
University of Wisconsin–Eau Claire, WI
University of Wisconsin–Green Bay, WI
University of Wisconsin–La Crosse, WI
University of Wisconsin–Parkside, WI

University of Wisconsin–River Falls, WI
University of Wisconsin–Stevens Point, WI
University of Wisconsin–Whitewater, WI
University of Wyoming, WY
Utah State University, UT
Valdosta State University, GA
Valley City State University, ND
Valparaiso University, IN
Vanguard University of Southern
  California, CA
Virginia Commonwealth University, VA
Virginia Intermont College, VA
Virginia Polytechnic Institute and State
  University, VA
Virginia Wesleyan College, VA
Wabash College, IN
Wagner College, NY
Waldorf College, IA
Warner Pacific College, OR
Washburn University, KS
Washington State University, WA
Washington University in St. Louis, MO
Wayland Baptist University, TX
Wayne State College, NE
Wayne State University, MI
Webster University, MO
Wesleyan College, GA
West Chester University of Pennsylvania, PA
Western Carolina University, NC
Western Illinois University, IL
Western Kentucky University, KY
Western Oregon University, OR
Western Washington University, WA
West Liberty University, WV
Westminster College, PA
Westminster College, UT
Westmont College, CA
West Virginia University, WV
West Virginia Wesleyan College, WV
Whitman College, WA
Whitworth University, WA
Wichita State University, KS
Wilkes University, PA
Willamette University, OR
William Carey University, MS
William Jewell College, MO
Winona State University, MN
Winthrop University, SC
Wittenberg University, OH
Wright State University, OH
Xavier University, OH
York College, NE
Youngstown State University, OH

Special Achievements/ Activities

Cheerleading/Drum Major

Abilene Christian University, TX
Angelo State University, TX
Arkansas State University—Jonesboro, AR
Arkansas Tech University, AR
Ashland University, OH
Auburn University, AL
Belhaven University, MS
Bellarmine University, KY
Bethany College, KS
Bethel College, IN
Bluefield State College, WV
Boise State University, ID
Brevard College, NC
Brewton-Parker College, GA

California Baptist University, CA
Campbellsville University, KY
Campbell University, NC
Cleveland State University, OH
Coastal Carolina University, SC
Columbus State University, GA
Culver-Stockton College, MO
Delta State University, MS
Dickinson State University, ND
Drury University, MO
Eastern Kentucky University, KY
East Texas Baptist University, TX
Evangel University, MO
Faulkner University, AL
Florida Institute of Technology, FL
Francis Marion University, SC
Gardner-Webb University, NC
Georgia Institute of Technology, GA
Georgia Southern University, GA
Glenville State College, WV
Graceland University, IA
Harding University, AR
Hawai'i Pacific University, HI
Henderson State University, AR
Houston Baptist University, TX
Huntingdon College, AL
Huntington University, IN
Idaho State University, ID
Indiana Wesleyan University, IN
James Madison University, VA
John Brown University, AR
Kentucky State University, KY
Langston University, OK
Lees-McRae College, NC
Lee University, TN
Lenoir-Rhyne University, NC
Limestone College, SC
Lincoln Memorial University, TN
Lincoln University, MO
Lindenwood University, MO
Lindsey Wilson College, KY
Lipscomb University, TN
Long Island University, Brooklyn
  Campus, NY
Louisiana Tech University, LA
Lubbock Christian University, TX
McKendree University, IL
McPherson College, KS
Mesa State College, CO
Methodist University, NC
Mid-Continent University, KY
Midwestern State University, TX
Milligan College, TN
Mississippi State University, MS
Missouri Valley College, MO
Montana State University Billings, MT
Morehead State University, KY
Morningside College, IA
Mountain State University, WV
Mount Olive College, NC
Murray State University, KY
Newberry College, SC
Nicholls State University, LA
Northeastern State University, OK
Northern Michigan University, MI
North Georgia College & State University, GA
Northwestern Oklahoma State University, OK
Northwestern State University of
  Louisiana, LA
Northwest Nazarene University, ID
Northwood University, MI
Nyack College, NY
The Ohio State University, OH

Oklahoma Christian University, OK
Oklahoma City University, OK
Oklahoma Panhandle State University, OK
Oklahoma State University, OK
Old Dominion University, VA
Olivet Nazarene University, IL
Oral Roberts University, OK
Ouachita Baptist University, AR
Rocky Mountain College, MT
Rogers State University, OK
St. Ambrose University, IA
St. Edward's University, TX
Saint Francis University, PA
St. John's University, NY
Saint Louis University, MO
St. Mary's University, TX
Sam Houston State University, TX
Shorter University, GA
Southeastern Louisiana University, LA
Southeastern Oklahoma State University, OK
Southeast Missouri State University, MO
Southern Arkansas University–Magnolia, AR
Southern Illinois University Carbondale, IL
Southern Nazarene University, OK
Southwestern College, KS
Southwestern Oklahoma State University, OK
Stephen F. Austin State University, TX
Stetson University, FL
Tabor College, KS
Temple University, PA
Tennessee Technological University, TN
Tennessee Wesleyan College, TN
Texas A&M University–Commerce, TX
Tiffin University, OH
Tusculum College, TN
Union College, KY
Union University, TN
The University of Alabama, AL
The University of Alabama at
  Birmingham, AL
The University of Alabama in Huntsville, AL
University of Central Missouri, MO
University of Charleston, WV
University of Delaware, DE
University of Great Falls, MT
University of Idaho, ID
University of Kentucky, KY
University of Louisiana at Monroe, LA
University of Louisville, KY
University of Mary, ND
University of Mary Hardin-Baylor, TX
University of Maryland, College Park, MD
University of Massachusetts Amherst, MA
University of Memphis, TN
University of Mississippi, MS
University of Missouri, MO
University of Nebraska at Kearney, NE
University of Nebraska–Lincoln, NE
University of Nevada, Las Vegas, NV
University of North Alabama, AL
The University of North Carolina
  Wilmington, NC
University of Puerto Rico at Bayamón, PR
University of St. Francis, IL
University of Saint Francis, IN
University of Science and Arts of
  Oklahoma, OK
University of South Carolina, SC
University of South Carolina Aiken, SC
University of Southern Mississippi, MS
The University of Tennessee at Martin, TN
The University of Texas at Arlington, TX
The University of Texas at El Paso, TX

The University of Texas at San Antonio, TX
The University of Texas of the Permian
  Basin, TX
The University of Texas–Pan American, TX
The University of Toledo, OH
University of Tulsa, OK
The University of West Alabama, AL
University of Wyoming, WY
Virginia Intermont College, VA
Virginia Polytechnic Institute and State
  University, VA
Waldorf College, IA
Washburn University, KS
Wayland Baptist University, TX
Webber International University, FL
West Liberty University, WV
Wichita State University, KS
William Carey University, MS
William Jewell College, MO
Williams Baptist College, AR
Wofford College, SC
Wright State University, OH
Youngstown State University, OH

Community Service
Adelphi University, NY
Agnes Scott College, GA
Alaska Pacific University, AK
Alliant International University, CA
Alverno College, WI
Arcadia University, PA
Arkansas State University—Jonesboro, AR
Arkansas Tech University, AR
Armstrong Atlantic State University, GA
Augsburg College, MN
Austin College, TX
Ball State University, IN
Baylor University, TX
Bellarmine University, KY
Beloit College, WI
Benedictine University, IL
Bentley University, MA
Berry College, GA
Bethel University, MN
Biola University, CA
Bloomfield College, NJ
Boise State University, ID
Bradley University, IL
Brevard College, NC
Bryan College, TN
Burlington College, VT
California Lutheran University, CA
California Maritime Academy, CA
California Polytechnic State University,
  San Luis Obispo, CA
California State University, Chico, CA
California State University, Fresno, CA
California State University,
  San Bernardino, CA
California State University, Stanislaus, CA
Calvin College, MI
Cedar Crest College, PA
Centenary College of Louisiana, LA
Central College, IA
Centre College, KY
The Citadel, The Military College of South
  Carolina, SC
City College of the City University of New
  York, NY
Clark University, MA
Clemson University, SC
The College at Brockport, State University of
  New York, NY

College of Mount St. Joseph, OH
The College of New Rochelle, NY
College of Notre Dame of Maryland, MD
College of Saint Mary, NE
The College of Saint Rose, NY
College of Staten Island of the City University
  of New York, NY
The College of Wooster, OH
Columbus State University, GA
Concord University, WV
Cornell College, IA
Dallas Baptist University, TX
Dalton State College, GA
Davidson College, NC
Defiance College, OH
DePaul University, IL
DePauw University, IN
DigiPen Institute of Technology, WA
Dominican University of California, CA
Eastern New Mexico University, NM
Eckerd College, FL
ECPI College of Technology, VA
ECPI Technical College, VA
Edgewood College, WI
Elon University, NC
Emmanuel College, MA
Endicott College, MA
The Evergreen State College, WA
Florida Gulf Coast University, FL
Florida Southern College, FL
Frostburg State University, MD
Furman University, SC
Gannon University, PA
Georgia College & State University, GA
Georgia Southern University, GA
Green Mountain College, VT
Hampshire College, MA
Hendrix College, AR
Hillsdale Free Will Baptist College, OK
Hollins University, VA
Houston Baptist University, TX
Howard Payne University, TX
Humphreys College, CA
Huntingdon College, AL
Illinois Institute of Technology, IL
Illinois State University, IL
Indiana University of Pennsylvania, PA
Iowa State University of Science and
  Technology, IA
Jamestown College, ND
John Carroll University, OH
Johnson Bible College, TN
Johnson C. Smith University, NC
Juniata College, PA
Kean University, NJ
Kennesaw State University, GA
Kent State University, OH
Keuka College, NY
King's College, PA
Knox College, IL
Kutztown University of Pennsylvania, PA
Lake Erie College, OH
Lakeland College, WI
Lasell College, MA
Lewis & Clark College, OR
Lewis-Clark State College, ID
Lewis University, IL
Lindenwood University, MO
Linfield College, OR
Lipscomb University, TN
Loyola University Chicago, IL
Malone University, OH
Manhattan College, NY

Manhattanville College, NY
Marymount University, VA
Maryville College, TN
Maryville University of Saint Louis, MO
Marywood University, PA
McKendree University, IL
McPherson College, KS
Mercer University, GA
Mercyhurst College, PA
Meredith College, NC
Michigan State University, MI
Millersville University of Pennsylvania, PA
Milligan College, TN
Millikin University, IL
Millsaps College, MS
Minnesota State University Moorhead, MN
Misericordia University, PA
Missouri Valley College, MO
Molloy College, NY
Montana State University–Northern, MT
Montana Tech of The University of
  Montana, MT
Montclair State University, NJ
Morehouse College, GA
Morningside College, IA
Mount Ida College, MA
Mount St. Mary's College, CA
Muskingum University, OH
New England College, NH
Newman University, KS
Niagara University, NY
Nichols College, MA
North Central College, IL
Northeastern State University, OK
Northern Kentucky University, KY
North Georgia College & State University, GA
Notre Dame College, OH
Nyack College, NY
Oglethorpe University, GA
Ohio Northern University, OH
Ohio Valley University, WV
Oklahoma State University, OK
Old Dominion University, VA
Olivet College, MI
Oral Roberts University, OK
Pace University, NY
Pacific Union College, CA
Pacific University, OR
Patrick Henry College, VA
Pitzer College, CA
Point Park University, PA
Portland State University, OR
Principia College, IL
Providence College, RI
Queens College of the City University of New
  York, NY
Quincy University, IL
Randolph College, VA
The Richard Stockton College of New
  Jersey, NJ
Robert Morris University Illinois, IL
Rochester Institute of Technology, NY
Rockford College, IL
Rockhurst University, MO
Rosemont College, PA
Russell Sage College, NY
Sacred Heart University, CT
Sage College of Albany, NY
Saginaw Valley State University, MI
St. Andrews Presbyterian College, NC
St. Catherine University, MN
St. Edward's University, TX
St. John Fisher College, NY

Non-Need Scholarships for Undergraduates
Special Achievements/Activities

St. John's University, NY
St. Lawrence University, NY
St. Louis College of Pharmacy, MO
Saint Louis University, MO
Saint Martin's University, WA
St. Olaf College, MN
Schreiner University, TX
Seton Hill University, PA
Shippensburg University of Pennsylvania, PA
Siena College, NY
Silver Lake College, WI
Simmons College, MA
Simpson College, IA
Slippery Rock University of Pennsylvania, PA
Sonoma State University, CA
South Dakota State University, SD
Southeastern Louisiana University, LA
Southern Adventist University, TN
Southern Illinois University Carbondale, IL
Southwestern College, KS
Spring Hill College, AL
State University of New York at Binghamton, NY
State University of New York at Plattsburgh, NY
State University of New York College at Cortland, NY
State University of New York College at Geneseo, NY
State University of New York College at Oneonta, NY
State University of New York College at Potsdam, NY
State University of New York College of Technology at Delhi, NY
Stetson University, FL
Stony Brook University, State University of New York, NY
Suffolk University, MA
Texas A&M University–Texarkana, TX
Texas Tech University, TX
Thomas More College, KY
Towson University, MD
Trinity Bible College, ND
Tulane University, LA
Tusculum College, TN
Union University, TN
Unity College, ME
Universidad Adventista de las Antillas, PR
The University of Akron, OH
The University of Alabama, AL
The University of Alabama in Huntsville, AL
University of Alaska Fairbanks, AK
University of Arkansas, AR
University of California, San Diego, CA
University of Charleston, WV
University of Colorado at Boulder, CO
University of Connecticut, CT
University of Delaware, DE
University of Denver, CO
University of Florida, FL
University of Hartford, CT
University of Hawaii at Hilo, HI
University of Houston–Clear Lake, TX
University of Houston–Downtown, TX
University of Indianapolis, IN
The University of Kansas, KS
University of La Verne, CA
University of Louisiana at Monroe, LA
University of Louisville, KY
University of Maine at Presque Isle, ME
University of Mary Hardin-Baylor, TX
University of Massachusetts Dartmouth, MA

University of Massachusetts Lowell, MA
University of Michigan, MI
University of Michigan–Dearborn, MI
University of Michigan–Flint, MI
University of Mississippi, MS
University of Nebraska–Lincoln, NE
University of Nevada, Las Vegas, NV
University of New Hampshire, NH
The University of North Carolina at Asheville, NC
The University of North Carolina at Chapel Hill, NC
The University of North Carolina at Greensboro, NC
University of North Florida, FL
University of Richmond, VA
University of St. Francis, IL
University of South Carolina, SC
University of Southern Maine, ME
The University of Tennessee at Chattanooga, TN
The University of Texas at Arlington, TX
The University of Texas–Pan American, TX
University of Tulsa, OK
University of Vermont, VT
The University of Virginia's College at Wise, VA
University of West Georgia, GA
University of Wisconsin–Eau Claire, WI
University of Wisconsin–Green Bay, WI
University of Wisconsin–La Crosse, WI
University of Wisconsin–Parkside, WI
University of Wisconsin–Stout, WI
Ursuline College, OH
Valdosta State University, GA
Valley Forge Christian College, PA
Virginia Polytechnic Institute and State University, VA
Virginia Wesleyan College, VA
Wabash College, IN
Warren Wilson College, NC
Washburn University, KS
Washington State University, WA
Waynesburg University, PA
Webber International University, FL
Wesleyan College, GA
Western Illinois University, IL
Western New England College, MA
Western Oregon University, OR
Western Washington University, WA
West Virginia Wesleyan College, WV
Wheeling Jesuit University, WV
Widener University, PA
Willamette University, OR
Wilson College, PA
Wittenberg University, OH
Wofford College, SC
Wright State University, OH
Youngstown State University, OH

Hobbies/Interests

Angelo State University, TX
Arkansas Tech University, AR
Brevard College, NC
California State Polytechnic University, Pomona, CA
California State University, Chico, CA
California State University, San Bernardino, CA
Centenary College of Louisiana, LA
The College at Brockport, State University of New York, NY
The College of New Rochelle, NY

Corban University, OR
Dalton State College, GA
Eastern New Mexico University, NM
Florida Institute of Technology, FL
Hawai'i Pacific University, HI
Illinois Institute of Technology, IL
Indiana University of Pennsylvania, PA
Lake Erie College, OH
Mesa State College, CO
Michigan State University, MI
Millsaps College, MS
Missouri Valley College, MO
Montana State University–Northern, MT
The Ohio State University, OH
St. John's University, NY
Siena College, NY
South Dakota State University, SD
Southwest Minnesota State University, MN
State University of New York College at Cortland, NY
Stephen F. Austin State University, TX
The University of Alabama, AL
University of Louisville, KY
University of Michigan–Flint, MI
University of Minnesota, Twin Cities Campus, MN
University of South Alabama, AL
The University of Toledo, OH
University of Wisconsin–Eau Claire, WI
Valdosta State University, GA

Junior Miss

Augsburg College, MN
Belhaven University, MS
Bethel University, MN
Birmingham-Southern College, AL
Bluefield State College, WV
Campbellsville University, KY
Carroll University, WI
Cedar Crest College, PA
The College of New Rochelle, NY
College of Saint Benedict, MN
Concordia University Texas, TX
Georgetown College, KY
Georgia Southern University, GA
Grace College, IN
Grand View University, IA
Gustavus Adolphus College, MN
Hardin-Simmons University, TX
Huntingdon College, AL
Idaho State University, ID
Kentucky Wesleyan College, KY
Lewis-Clark State College, ID
Lindenwood University, MO
Lindsey Wilson College, KY
Louisiana Tech University, LA
McDaniel College, MD
McMurry University, TX
Michigan State University, MI
Mississippi State University, MS
Mississippi University for Women, MS
Missouri Valley College, MO
Morehead State University, KY
Mount Vernon Nazarene University, OH
Murray State University, KY
Northeastern State University, OK
Ohio Northern University, OH
Oklahoma City University, OK
Point Park University, PA
Roberts Wesleyan College, NY
South Dakota State University, SD
Spring Arbor University, MI
Tennessee Wesleyan College, TN

Texas Lutheran University, TX
The University of Alabama, AL
The University of Alabama at
  Birmingham, AL
The University of Alabama in Huntsville, AL
University of Idaho, ID
University of Louisville, KY
University of Mississippi, MS
University of Montevallo, AL
The University of North Carolina at
  Asheville, NC
The University of North Carolina at
  Greensboro, NC
University of South Alabama, AL
University of Wyoming, WY
Waldorf College, IA
Washington State University, WA
William Carey University, MS

Leadership

Abilene Christian University, TX
Agnes Scott College, GA
Alabama State University, AL
Alaska Pacific University, AK
Albright College, PA
Alderson-Broaddus College, WV
Alfred University, NY
Alliant International University, CA
American Jewish University, CA
American University, DC
Anderson University, IN
Andrews University, MI
Angelo State University, TX
Aquinas College, TN
Arcadia University, PA
Arkansas State University—Jonesboro, AR
Arkansas Tech University, AR
Asbury University, KY
Atlantic Union College, MA
Auburn University, AL
Augsburg College, MN
Augustana College, SD
Austin College, TX
Austin Peay State University, TN
Ave Maria University, FL
Averett University, VA
Azusa Pacific University, CA
Babson College, MA
Baldwin-Wallace College, OH
Ball State University, IN
Bard College, NY
Barton College, NC
Baylor University, TX
Becker College, MA
Belhaven University, MS
Bellarmine University, KY
Benedictine University, IL
Bethany College, WV
Bethel College, IN
Bethel University, MN
Biola University, CA
Bloomfield College, NJ
Bluefield State College, WV
Blue Mountain College, MS
Bluffton University, OH
Boise State University, ID
Boston University, MA
Bowdoin College, ME
Bowling Green State University, OH
Bradley University, IL
Brenau University, GA
Brescia University, KY
Brevard College, NC

Briar Cliff University, IA
Bridgewater State College, MA
Bryan College, TN
Bucknell University, PA
Buena Vista University, IA
Burlington College, VT
California Lutheran University, CA
California Maritime Academy, CA
California Polytechnic State University,
  San Luis Obispo, CA
California State Polytechnic University,
  Pomona, CA
California State University, Chico, CA
California State University, Fresno, CA
California State University, Fullerton, CA
California State University, Monterey Bay, CA
California State University, Northridge, CA
California State University, Stanislaus, CA
Cameron University, OK
Campbellsville University, KY
Carnegie Mellon University, PA
Carroll University, WI
Carson-Newman College, TN
Carthage College, WI
Case Western Reserve University, OH
Cedar Crest College, PA
Cedarville University, OH
Centenary College, NJ
Central Michigan University, MI
Chamberlain College of Nursing, MO
Chowan University, NC
Christian Brothers University, TN
Christopher Newport University, VA
Cincinnati Christian University, OH
The Citadel, The Military College of South
  Carolina, SC
City College of the City University of New
  York, NY
Claremont McKenna College, CA
Clarke College, IA
Clarkson University, NY
Clearwater Christian College, FL
Clemson University, SC
The College at Brockport, State University of
  New York, NY
College of Mount St. Joseph, OH
The College of New Rochelle, NY
College of Notre Dame of Maryland, MD
College of Saint Mary, NE
Columbia College, MO
Columbia College Chicago, IL
Columbus State University, GA
Concordia University Texas, TX
Concord University, WV
Converse College, SC
Corban University, OR
Cornell College, IA
Cornerstone University, MI
Covenant College, GA
Creighton University, NE
Crown College, MN
Culver-Stockton College, MO
Dallas Baptist University, TX
Dalton State College, GA
Davidson College, NC
Defiance College, OH
Delta State University, MS
DePaul University, IL
DePauw University, IN
Dickinson State University, ND
Dominican University, IL
Dominican University of California, CA
Dordt College, IA

Drury University, MO
Duke University, NC
Eastern Michigan University, MI
Eastern New Mexico University, NM
Eastern Oregon University, OR
East Stroudsburg University of
  Pennsylvania, PA
East Texas Baptist University, TX
Eckerd College, FL
Elmira College, NY
Elon University, NC
Embry-Riddle Aeronautical University, AZ
Embry-Riddle Aeronautical University, FL
Embry-Riddle Aeronautical University
  Worldwide, FL
Emmanuel College, MA
Emory University, GA
Endicott College, MA
Erskine College, SC
Eugene Lang College The New School for
  Liberal Arts, NY
Eureka College, IL
Evangel University, MO
Faulkner University, AL
Fitchburg State College, MA
Flagler College, FL
Florida Gulf Coast University, FL
Florida Southern College, FL
Fort Lewis College, CO
Frostburg State University, MD
Furman University, SC
Gallaudet University, DC
Gannon University, PA
George Fox University, OR
Georgetown College, KY
Georgia College & State University, GA
Georgia Institute of Technology, GA
Georgia Southern University, GA
Georgia Southwestern State University, GA
Gonzaga University, WA
Gordon College, MA
Graceland University, IA
Grace University, NE
Green Mountain College, VT
Greenville College, IL
Grove City College, PA
Hamline University, MN
Hampden-Sydney College, VA
Hampshire College, MA
Hampton University, VA
Harding University, AR
Hardin-Simmons University, TX
Hawai'i Pacific University, HI
Henderson State University, AR
Hendrix College, AR
Hobart and William Smith Colleges, NY
Hofstra University, NY
Hollins University, VA
Hope International University, CA
Houston Baptist University, TX
Howard Payne University, TX
Husson University, ME
Idaho State University, ID
Illinois Institute of Technology, IL
Illinois State University, IL
Indiana University of Pennsylvania, PA
Iowa State University of Science and
  Technology, IA
Ithaca College, NY
Jacksonville University, FL
James Madison University, VA
Jamestown College, ND
John Brown University, AR

Non-Need Scholarships for Undergraduates
Special Achievements/Activities

John Carroll University, OH
Johnson & Wales University, CO
Johnson & Wales University, FL
Johnson & Wales University, RI
Johnson & Wales University—Charlotte
  Campus, NC
Johnson Bible College, TN
Johnson C. Smith University, NC
Juniata College, PA
Kean University, NJ
Kennesaw State University, GA
Kent State University, OH
Kent State University at Stark, OH
Kentucky Wesleyan College, KY
Kettering University, MI
Keuka College, NY
King's College, PA
Kutztown University of Pennsylvania, PA
Kuyper College, MI
LaGrange College, GA
Lake Forest College, IL
Lakeland College, WI
Lancaster Bible College & Graduate
  School, PA
Langston University, OK
Lasell College, MA
Lee University, TN
Le Moyne College, NY
Lenoir-Rhyne University, NC
Lewis & Clark College, OR
Lewis-Clark State College, ID
Limestone College, SC
Lindenwood University, MO
Lindsey Wilson College, KY
Linfield College, OR
Lipscomb University, TN
Lock Haven University of Pennsylvania, PA
Long Island University, Brooklyn
  Campus, NY
Long Island University, C.W. Post
  Campus, NY
Louisiana State University and Agricultural
  and Mechanical College, LA
Loyola University Chicago, IL
Lubbock Christian University, TX
Lycoming College, PA
Lynn University, FL
Malone University, OH
Manchester College, IN
Manhattan Christian College, KS
Manhattan College, NY
Manhattanville College, NY
Mansfield University of Pennsylvania, PA
Mary Baldwin College, VA
Marymount Manhattan College, NY
Marymount University, VA
Maryville College, TN
Maryville University of Saint Louis, MO
Marywood University, PA
Massachusetts College of Liberal Arts, MA
Massachusetts Maritime Academy, MA
The Master's College and Seminary, CA
McDaniel College, MD
McKendree University, IL
Mercyhurst College, PA
Meredith College, NC
Mesa State College, CO
Messiah College, PA
Methodist University, NC
Metropolitan State College of Denver, CO
Miami University, OH
Michigan State University, MI
Michigan Technological University, MI

Midwestern State University, TX
Millsaps College, MS
Misericordia University, PA
Mississippi College, MS
Mississippi State University, MS
Mississippi University for Women, MS
Missouri State University, MO
Missouri Valley College, MO
Molloy College, NY
Monmouth University, NJ
Montana State University, MT
Montclair State University, NJ
Montreat College, NC
Moravian College, PA
Morehead State University, KY
Morehouse College, GA
Morningside College, IA
Mount Aloysius College, PA
Mount Ida College, MA
Mount Mary College, WI
Mount Mercy College, IA
Mount Olive College, NC
Mount St. Mary's College, CA
Murray State University, KY
Muskingum University, OH
National University, CA
New England College, NH
Newman University, KS
New Mexico State University, NM
Nicholls State University, LA
Nichols College, MA
North Carolina State University, NC
Northeastern Illinois University, IL
Northeastern State University, OK
Northern Arizona University, AZ
Northern Illinois University, IL
Northern Kentucky University, KY
Northern Michigan University, MI
Northern State University, SD
North Georgia College & State University, GA
Northwest Christian University, OR
Northwestern College, MN
Northwestern Oklahoma State University, OK
Northwestern State University of
  Louisiana, LA
Northwest Nazarene University, ID
Northwest University, WA
Northwood University, MI
Notre Dame College, OH
Nyack College, NY
Occidental College, CA
Ohio Northern University, OH
The Ohio State University, OH
Ohio Valley University, WV
Oklahoma Baptist University, OK
Oklahoma Christian University, OK
Oklahoma City University, OK
Oklahoma State University, OK
Old Dominion University, VA
Olivet College, MI
Oral Roberts University, OK
Oregon Institute of Technology, OR
Pace University, NY
Pacific Lutheran University, WA
Pacific Union College, CA
Patrick Henry College, VA
Peirce College, PA
Pfeiffer University, NC
Piedmont College, GA
Pitzer College, CA
Portland State University, OR
Presbyterian College, SC
Principia College, IL

Purdue University, IN
Purdue University North Central, IN
Queens College of the City University of New
  York, NY
Quincy University, IL
Randolph College, VA
Regent University, VA
Regis University, CO
Reinhardt University, GA
The Richard Stockton College of New
  Jersey, NJ
Ripon College, WI
Rochester Institute of Technology, NY
Rockford College, IL
Rockhurst University, MO
Rocky Mountain College, MT
Rogers State University, OK
Rosemont College, PA
Russell Sage College, NY
Sacred Heart University, CT
Saginaw Valley State University, MI
St. Andrews Presbyterian College, NC
St. Catherine University, MN
St. Edward's University, TX
St. John's University, NY
St. Louis College of Pharmacy, MO
Saint Louis University, MO
Saint Martin's University, WA
Saint Mary's College of California, CA
Saint Mary's University of Minnesota, MN
St. Thomas University, FL
Saint Vincent College, PA
Saint Xavier University, IL
Salem College, NC
Samford University, AL
Sam Houston State University, TX
San Diego Christian College, CA
San Diego State University, CA
Schreiner University, TX
Scripps College, CA
Seattle University, WA
Seton Hill University, PA
Shepherd University, WV
Shippensburg University of Pennsylvania, PA
Siena College, NY
Simpson College, IA
Slippery Rock University of Pennsylvania, PA
Sonoma State University, CA
South Dakota State University, SD
Southeastern Louisiana University, LA
Southeastern Oklahoma State University, OK
Southeast Missouri State University, MO
Southern Adventist University, TN
Southern Arkansas University–Magnolia, AR
Southern Illinois University Carbondale, IL
Southern Utah University, UT
Southwestern College, KS
Southwestern Oklahoma State University, OK
Southwestern University, TX
Southwest Minnesota State University, MN
State University of New York at
  Binghamton, NY
State University of New York at Fredonia, NY
State University of New York at
  Plattsburgh, NY
State University of New York College at
  Cortland, NY
State University of New York College at
  Geneseo, NY
State University of New York College at
  Oneonta, NY
State University of New York College at
  Potsdam, NY

State University of New York College of Environmental Science and Forestry, NY
Stephen F. Austin State University, TX
Stephens College, MO
Stetson University, FL
Stony Brook University, State University of New York, NY
Sul Ross State University, TX
Taylor University, IN
Texas A&M University, TX
Texas A&M University–Commerce, TX
Texas A&M University–Texarkana, TX
Texas Christian University, TX
Texas College, TX
Texas Lutheran University, TX
Thiel College, PA
Thomas More College, KY
Trinity Bible College, ND
Trinity Christian College, IL
Trinity College, CT
Troy University, AL
Truett-McConnell College, GA
Truman State University, MO
Tusculum College, TN
Union University, TN
Unity College, ME
The University of Akron, OH
The University of Alabama at Birmingham, AL
The University of Alabama in Huntsville, AL
University of Alaska Fairbanks, AK
University of Arkansas, AR
University of California, San Diego, CA
University of California, Santa Cruz, CA
University of Central Florida, FL
University of Central Missouri, MO
University of Central Oklahoma, OK
University of Charleston, WV
University of Colorado at Boulder, CO
University of Connecticut, CT
University of Dallas, TX
University of Delaware, DE
University of Denver, CO
University of Evansville, IN
University of Florida, FL
University of Hawaii at Hilo, HI
University of Houston–Clear Lake, TX
University of Houston–Downtown, TX
University of Idaho, ID
University of Illinois at Urbana–Champaign, IL
The University of Kansas, KS
University of Kentucky, KY
University of La Verne, CA
University of Louisiana at Monroe, LA
University of Louisville, KY
University of Mary Hardin-Baylor, TX
University of Mary Washington, VA
University of Massachusetts Amherst, MA
University of Massachusetts Boston, MA
University of Memphis, TN
University of Michigan, MI
University of Michigan–Dearborn, MI
University of Michigan–Flint, MI
University of Minnesota, Twin Cities Campus, MN
University of Mississippi, MS
University of Nebraska at Omaha, NE
University of Nebraska–Lincoln, NE
University of Nevada, Las Vegas, NV
University of New Orleans, LA
University of North Alabama, AL

The University of North Carolina at Asheville, NC
The University of North Carolina at Chapel Hill, NC
The University of North Carolina at Greensboro, NC
The University of North Carolina Wilmington, NC
University of North Dakota, ND
University of Northern Iowa, IA
University of North Florida, FL
University of Oklahoma, OK
University of Pittsburgh at Greensburg, PA
University of Pittsburgh at Johnstown, PA
University of Puget Sound, WA
University of St. Francis, IL
University of South Alabama, AL
University of South Carolina, SC
University of Southern California, CA
University of Southern Indiana, IN
University of Southern Mississippi, MS
The University of Tampa, FL
The University of Tennessee at Martin, TN
The University of Texas at Arlington, TX
The University of Texas at Austin, TX
The University of Texas at Dallas, TX
The University of Texas at El Paso, TX
The University of Texas–Pan American, TX
University of the Ozarks, AR
University of the Southwest, NM
The University of Toledo, OH
University of Tulsa, OK
University of Vermont, VT
University of Washington, WA
University of West Georgia, GA
University of Wisconsin–Eau Claire, WI
University of Wisconsin–Green Bay, WI
University of Wisconsin–La Crosse, WI
University of Wisconsin–Parkside, WI
University of Wisconsin–Stevens Point, WI
University of Wisconsin–Stout, WI
University of Wisconsin–Whitewater, WI
University of Wyoming, WY
Ursinus College, PA
Ursuline College, OH
Valley Forge Christian College, PA
Vanderbilt University, TN
Virginia Military Institute, VA
Virginia Polytechnic Institute and State University, VA
Virginia Wesleyan College, VA
Wabash College, IN
Wake Forest University, NC
Waldorf College, IA
Warner Pacific College, OR
Warren Wilson College, NC
Washburn University, KS
Washington Bible College, MD
Washington State University, WA
Wayland Baptist University, TX
Wayne State College, NE
Wayne State University, MI
Webber International University, FL
Webster University, MO
Wells College, NY
Wesleyan College, GA
Western Illinois University, IL
Western Kentucky University, KY
Western New England College, MA
Western Oregon University, OR
Western State College of Colorado, CO
Western Washington University, WA
Westminster College, MO

Westminster College, UT
Westmont College, CA
West Virginia University, WV
West Virginia Wesleyan College, WV
Whitman College, WA
Wichita State University, KS
Widener University, PA
Wilkes University, PA
Willamette University, OR
William Carey University, MS
Wilson College, PA
Wittenberg University, OH
Wofford College, SC
Wright State University, OH
York College, NE
Youngstown State University, OH

Memberships

Adelphi University, NY
Albright College, PA
American University, DC
Angelo State University, TX
Arcadia University, PA
Auburn University, AL
Averett University, VA
Birmingham-Southern College, AL
Blue Mountain College, MS
Boston University, MA
California State University, Chico, CA
California State University, San Bernardino, CA
California State University, Stanislaus, CA
Carroll University, WI
Carson-Newman College, TN
Cedar Crest College, PA
The College of New Rochelle, NY
College of Notre Dame of Maryland, MD
Corban University, OR
Dallas Baptist University, TX
Dalton State College, GA
Davenport University, MI
Delta State University, MS
Eastern Michigan University, MI
Eastern New Mexico University, NM
Emporia State University, KS
Erskine College, SC
Ferris State University, MI
Flagler College, FL
Georgia Southern University, GA
Gonzaga University, WA
Greenville College, IL
Grove City College, PA
Hamline University, MN
Hawai'i Pacific University, HI
Idaho State University, ID
Illinois Institute of Technology, IL
Johnson & Wales University, CO
Johnson & Wales University, FL
Johnson & Wales University, RI
Johnson & Wales University—Charlotte Campus, NC
Kennesaw State University, GA
Kettering University, MI
Lewis University, IL
Lock Haven University of Pennsylvania, PA
Longwood University, VA
Loyola University Chicago, IL
Massachusetts College of Liberal Arts, MA
Medcenter One College of Nursing, ND
Mercer University, GA
Michigan State University, MI
Mississippi State University, MS
Molloy College, NY

Non-Need Scholarships for Undergraduates
Special Achievements/Activities

Montana State University–Northern, MT
Newman University, KS
Northern Michigan University, MI
Northwestern Oklahoma State University, OK
Northwestern State University of
  Louisiana, LA
Northwood University, MI
Northwood University, Florida Campus, FL
Northwood University, Texas Campus, TX
Notre Dame College, OH
The Ohio State University, OH
Oklahoma State University, OK
Old Dominion University, VA
Olivet College, MI
Oral Roberts University, OK
Pacific University, OR
Patrick Henry College, VA
Peirce College, PA
Portland State University, OR
Ripon College, WI
St. Catherine University, MN
Saint Louis University, MO
Saint Mary's College of California, CA
Salem State College, MA
Schreiner University, TX
Siena College, NY
Sonoma State University, CA
South Dakota State University, SD
Southeastern Louisiana University, LA
Southeast Missouri State University, MO
Southwestern College, KS
State University of New York College at
  Geneseo, NY
State University of New York College of
  Agriculture and Technology at
  Morrisville, NY
Stephens College, MO
Tennessee Wesleyan College, TN
Texas A&M University, TX
Texas A&M University–Texarkana, TX
Texas Christian University, TX
Texas Lutheran University, TX
Texas Tech University, TX
Thomas More College, KY
Towson University, MD
The University of Akron, OH
The University of Alabama at
  Birmingham, AL
University of Evansville, IN
University of Indianapolis, IN
University of Louisville, KY
University of Michigan–Dearborn, MI
University of Mississippi, MS
University of Missouri, MO
University of Missouri–St. Louis, MO
University of Nebraska at Omaha, NE
University of North Dakota, ND
University of South Carolina, SC
The University of Tampa, FL
The University of Texas–Pan American, TX
The University of Toledo, OH
University of Vermont, VT
University of Washington, WA
University of West Georgia, GA
University of Wisconsin–Eau Claire, WI
University of Wisconsin–La Crosse, WI
University of Wisconsin–Stout, WI
Virginia Polytechnic Institute and State
  University, VA
Washington State University, WA
Wayland Baptist University, TX
Webber International University, FL
Wesleyan College, GA

Western Kentucky University, KY
Western Washington University, WA
Wichita State University, KS
Wright State University, OH
Youngstown State University, OH

Religious Involvement

Adrian College, MI
Alaska Bible College, AK
Alaska Pacific University, AK
Albright College, PA
Alma College, MI
Andrews University, MI
Appalachian Bible College, WV
Augsburg College, MN
Austin College, TX
Austin Graduate School of Theology, TX
Averett University, VA
Barton College, NC
Baylor University, TX
Bellarmine University, KY
Belmont Abbey College, NC
Berry College, GA
Bethel College, IN
Bethel University, MN
Bethesda Christian University, CA
Birmingham-Southern College, AL
Blue Mountain College, MS
Brewton-Parker College, GA
Briar Cliff University, IA
Bryan College, TN
Caldwell College, NJ
California Lutheran University, CA
Calvary Bible College and Theological
  Seminary, MO
Calvin College, MI
Campbellsville University, KY
Campbell University, NC
Canisius College, NY
Carroll University, WI
Carthage College, WI
Cedar Crest College, PA
Centenary College of Louisiana, LA
Central College, IA
Cincinnati Christian University, OH
The Citadel, The Military College of South
  Carolina, SC
The College at Brockport, State University of
  New York, NY
The College of New Rochelle, NY
College of Notre Dame of Maryland, MD
The College of Wooster, OH
Concordia University Texas, TX
Corban University, OR
Cornell College, IA
Cornerstone University, MI
Crossroads College, MN
Dallas Baptist University, TX
Davidson College, NC
Defiance College, OH
Drury University, MO
Eastern Michigan University, MI
East Texas Baptist University, TX
Elizabethtown College, PA
Elon University, NC
Endicott College, MA
Evangel University, MO
Fairfield University, CT
Faulkner University, AL
Ferrum College, VA
Flagler College, FL
Franciscan University of Steubenville, OH
Furman University, SC

Gardner-Webb University, NC
George Fox University, OR
Georgetown College, KY
Georgia Southern University, GA
Graceland University, IA
Grace University, NE
Grand View University, IA
Green Mountain College, VT
Greenville College, IL
Grove City College, PA
Guilford College, NC
Harding University, AR
Hawai'i Pacific University, HI
Hendrix College, AR
Hillsdale Free Will Baptist College, OK
Houghton College, NY
Houston Baptist University, TX
Howard Payne University, TX
Huntington University, IN
John Carroll University, OH
Johnson Bible College, TN
Kutztown University of Pennsylvania, PA
Kuyper College, MI
Lakeland College, WI
Lancaster Bible College & Graduate
  School, PA
Lee University, TN
Limestone College, SC
Lindsey Wilson College, KY
Lipscomb University, TN
Malone University, OH
McPherson College, KS
Mercyhurst College, PA
Mid-Atlantic Christian University, NC
Millsaps College, MS
Mississippi College, MS
Molloy College, NY
Moravian College, PA
Morehouse College, GA
Mount Olive College, NC
Mount Vernon Nazarene University, OH
Newberry College, SC
Newman University, KS
North Central College, IL
Northwest Nazarene University, ID
Notre Dame College, OH
Nyack College, NY
Oglethorpe University, GA
Ohio Valley University, WV
Oklahoma Baptist University, OK
Oklahoma City University, OK
Oklahoma Wesleyan University, OK
Olivet Nazarene University, IL
Oral Roberts University, OK
Pacific Union College, CA
Pacific University, OR
Palm Beach Atlantic University, FL
Patrick Henry College, VA
Pfeiffer University, NC
Presbyterian College, SC
Principia College, IL
Rocky Mountain College, MT
Rosemont College, PA
Sacred Heart Major Seminary, MI
Sacred Heart University, CT
Saint Francis University, PA
St. John's University, NY
Saint Louis University, MO
Saint Martin's University, WA
St. Olaf College, MN
San Diego Christian College, CA
Schreiner University, TX
Seton Hill University, PA

Shorter University, GA
Siena College, NY
Silver Lake College, WI
Simpson College, IA
Southern Adventist University, TN
Southwest Baptist University, MO
Southwestern College, KS
Stetson University, FL
Tabor College, KS
Tennessee Wesleyan College, TN
Texas Christian University, TX
Texas Lutheran University, TX
Thomas More College, KY
Transylvania University, KY
Trinity Bible College, ND
Trinity Christian College, IL
Trinity International University, IL
Union University, TN
The University of Alabama at
  Birmingham, AL
University of Great Falls, MT
University of Mary Hardin-Baylor, TX
The University of North Carolina at
  Greensboro, NC
University of Puget Sound, WA
University of St. Francis, IL
University of Saint Francis, IN
University of San Diego, CA
University of South Carolina, SC
University of the Incarnate Word, TX
University of the Pacific, CA
The University of Toledo, OH
The University of Virginia's College at
  Wise, VA
University of West Georgia, GA
University of Wisconsin–Stout, WI
Valley Forge Christian College, PA
Virginia Intermont College, VA
Virginia Polytechnic Institute and State
  University, VA
Virginia Wesleyan College, VA
Washington Bible College, MD
Washington State University, WA
Wayland Baptist University, TX
Wesleyan College, GA
West Virginia Wesleyan College, WV
Whitworth University, WA
William Carey University, MS
William Jewell College, MO
Wofford College, SC
Youngstown State University, OH

Rodeo

Angelo State University, TX
Boise State University, ID
California Polytechnic State University,
  San Luis Obispo, CA
Dickinson State University, ND
Eastern New Mexico University, NM
Idaho State University, ID
Iowa State University of Science and
  Technology, IA
Lewis-Clark State College, ID
Lindenwood University, MO
Michigan State University, MI
Missouri Valley College, MO
Montana State University–Northern, MT
Murray State University, KY
New Mexico State University, NM
Northwestern Oklahoma State University, OK
Oklahoma Panhandle State University, OK
Oklahoma State University, OK
Rogers State University, OK

Sam Houston State University, TX
South Dakota State University, SD
Southeastern Louisiana University, LA
Southeastern Oklahoma State University, OK
Southern Arkansas University–Magnolia, AR
Southwestern Oklahoma State University, OK
Stephen F. Austin State University, TX
Texas A&M University, TX
Texas Tech University, TX
University of Idaho, ID
The University of Montana Western, MT
University of Nevada, Las Vegas, NV
The University of Tennessee at Martin, TN
The University of West Alabama, AL
University of Wyoming, WY
Washington State University, WA

Special Characteristics

Adult Students

Agnes Scott College, GA
Allegheny College, PA
American University, DC
Anderson University, IN
Arkansas State University—Jonesboro, AR
Atlantic Union College, MA
Averett University, VA
Ball State University, IN
Barton College, NC
Bellarmine University, KY
Berry College, GA
Bethel College, IN
Biola University, CA
Birmingham-Southern College, AL
Bloomfield College, NJ
California Baptist University, CA
California Lutheran University, CA
California State University, Chico, CA
Calvin College, MI
Campbellsville University, KY
Carroll University, WI
Cedar Crest College, PA
Coe College, IA
College of Mount St. Joseph, OH
The College of Saint Rose, NY
Concordia University Texas, TX
Dalton State College, GA
Dominican University of California, CA
Dowling College, NY
East Carolina University, NC
East Stroudsburg University of
  Pennsylvania, PA
ECPI College of Technology, VA
ECPI Technical College, VA
Edinboro University of Pennsylvania, PA
Elon University, NC
Evangel University, MO
The Evergreen State College, WA
Faulkner University, AL
Ferris State University, MI
Fitchburg State College, MA
Florida Gulf Coast University, FL
Fordham University, NY
Francis Marion University, SC
Frostburg State University, MD
Gannon University, PA
Georgia College & State University, GA
Grace University, NE
Grand Valley State University, MI
Hampton University, VA
Hillsdale Free Will Baptist College, OK
Hollins University, VA
Indiana University of Pennsylvania, PA

Inter American University of Puerto Rico,
  Barranquitas Campus, PR
Iowa State University of Science and
  Technology, IA
Juniata College, PA
Kent State University, OH
Kentucky State University, KY
Lancaster Bible College & Graduate
  School, PA
Lincoln University, MO
Lipscomb University, TN
Long Island University, C.W. Post
  Campus, NY
Lourdes College, OH
Loyola University Chicago, IL
Marywood University, PA
McPherson College, KS
Medaille College, NY
Mercer University, GA
Meredith College, NC
Mesa State College, CO
Messiah College, PA
Millsaps College, MS
Mississippi State University, MS
Mississippi University for Women, MS
Monmouth University, NJ
Montana State University Billings, MT
Montana State University–Northern, MT
Moravian College, PA
Murray State University, KY
New Mexico State University, NM
North Central College, IL
Northeastern Illinois University, IL
Northern Arizona University, AZ
Northern Illinois University, IL
Northern Kentucky University, KY
Northern State University, SD
Northwestern State University of
  Louisiana, LA
Oakland University, MI
The Ohio State University, OH
Ohio Valley University, WV
Oklahoma State University, OK
Pace University, NY
Piedmont College, GA
Portland State University, OR
Purdue University North Central, IN
Randolph College, VA
The Richard Stockton College of New
  Jersey, NJ
Rogers State University, OK
Russell Sage College, NY
St. Catherine University, MN
St. Edward's University, TX
Saint Francis University, PA
Salem State College, MA
San Diego State University, CA
Seton Hill University, PA
Siena College, NY
Simpson College, IA
Sonoma State University, CA
South Dakota State University, SD
Southeastern Louisiana University, LA
Southern Arkansas University–Magnolia, AR
Spring Arbor University, MI
State University of New York at
  Binghamton, NY
State University of New York College at
  Cortland, NY
State University of New York College at
  Geneseo, NY
State University of New York College at
  Potsdam, NY

Non-Need Scholarships for Undergraduates
Special Characteristics

Stephen F. Austin State University, TX
Texas Christian University, TX
Thomas More College, KY
Towson University, MD
Trinity Christian College, IL
Tusculum College, TN
The University of Akron, OH
The University of Alabama at
  Birmingham, AL
University of Central Missouri, MO
University of Connecticut, CT
University of Hartford, CT
The University of Kansas, KS
University of Kentucky, KY
University of Louisville, KY
University of Maine at Fort Kent, ME
University of Maryland, College Park, MD
University of Mary Washington, VA
University of Massachusetts Boston, MA
University of Massachusetts Dartmouth, MA
University of Memphis, TN
University of Michigan–Dearborn, MI
University of Michigan–Flint, MI
University of Mississippi, MS
University of Missouri, MO
University of Missouri–St. Louis, MO
University of Nebraska at Omaha, NE
University of Nevada, Las Vegas, NV
University of Nevada, Reno, NV
University of New Orleans, LA
The University of North Carolina at
  Asheville, NC
The University of North Carolina at
  Charlotte, NC
The University of North Carolina at
  Greensboro, NC
University of Northern Colorado, CO
University of Pittsburgh at Bradford, PA
University of South Carolina, SC
The University of Tennessee at Martin, TN
The University of Texas at Dallas, TX
The University of Toledo, OH
University of Vermont, VT
University of West Georgia, GA
University of Wisconsin–Eau Claire, WI
University of Wisconsin–Green Bay, WI
University of Wisconsin–La Crosse, WI
University of Wisconsin–Parkside, WI
University of Wisconsin–Stevens Point, WI
University of Wisconsin–Stout, WI
University of Wisconsin–Whitewater, WI
University of Wyoming, WY
Washburn University, KS
Wesleyan College, GA
Western Kentucky University, KY
Western Oregon University, OR
Westminster College, UT
Wichita State University, KS
Widener University, PA
Wilson College, PA
Wittenberg University, OH
Wright State University, OH
Youngstown State University, OH

Children and Siblings of Alumni

Adelphi University, NY
Adrian College, MI
Alaska Pacific University, AK
Albion College, MI
Albright College, PA
Alliant International University, CA
Alma College, MI
American International College, MA

American University, DC
Appalachian Bible College, WV
Arcadia University, PA
Arkansas State University—Jonesboro, AR
Asbury University, KY
Ashland University, OH
Auburn University, AL
Augsburg College, MN
Augustana College, IL
Augustana College, SD
Aurora University, IL
Averett University, VA
Baldwin-Wallace College, OH
Ball State University, IN
Barton College, NC
Bellarmine University, KY
Bemidji State University, MN
Benedictine University, IL
Bethany College, KS
Bethany College, WV
Bethel College, KS
Bethel University, MN
Biola University, CA
Birmingham-Southern College, AL
Bloomfield College, NJ
Blue Mountain College, MS
Boston University, MA
Bowling Green State University, OH
Bradley University, IL
Brescia University, KY
Briar Cliff University, IA
Bryan College, TN
Bryant University, RI
California Baptist University, CA
California Lutheran University, CA
California Polytechnic State University,
  San Luis Obispo, CA
California State Polytechnic University,
  Pomona, CA
California State University, Monterey Bay, CA
Calumet College of Saint Joseph, IN
Calvary Bible College and Theological
  Seminary, MO
Calvin College, MI
Canisius College, NY
Carroll University, WI
Carson-Newman College, TN
Carthage College, WI
The Catholic University of America, DC
Cedar Crest College, PA
Cedarville University, OH
Centenary College, NJ
Central College, IA
Central Michigan University, MI
Centre College, KY
Chapman University, CA
Chatham University, PA
Chestnut Hill College, PA
Christian Brothers University, TN
The Citadel, The Military College of South
  Carolina, SC
Clarke College, IA
Clarkson University, NY
Clearwater Christian College, FL
Cleveland State University, OH
Coe College, IA
Coker College, SC
Coleman University, CA
The College at Brockport, State University of
  New York, NY
College of Mount St. Joseph, OH
The College of Saint Rose, NY
The College of St. Scholastica, MN

Columbia College, MO
Concordia University, MI
Concordia University Chicago, IL
Concordia University, Nebraska, NE
Concordia University Texas, TX
Converse College, SC
Corban University, OR
Cornerstone University, MI
Crown College, MN
Culver-Stockton College, MO
Daemen College, NY
Dakota State University, SD
Delaware Valley College, PA
Delta State University, MS
DePauw University, IN
Dickinson College, PA
Doane College, NE
Dominican University, IL
Dominican University of California, CA
Dordt College, IA
Dowling College, NY
Drake University, IA
Drury University, MO
Duke University, NC
Duquesne University, PA
D'Youville College, NY
East Carolina University, NC
Eastern Kentucky University, KY
Eastern Michigan University, MI
Eastern New Mexico University, NM
East Stroudsburg University of
  Pennsylvania, PA
East Texas Baptist University, TX
ECPI College of Technology, VA
Edinboro University of Pennsylvania, PA
Elmhurst College, IL
Embry-Riddle Aeronautical University, AZ
Emmanuel College, MA
Emporia State University, KS
Endicott College, MA
Erskine College, SC
Eureka College, IL
Evangel University, MO
Fairfield University, CT
Faulkner University, AL
Ferris State University, MI
Fitchburg State College, MA
Florida Institute of Technology, FL
Florida International University, FL
Florida Southern College, FL
Fordham University, NY
Fort Lewis College, CO
Francis Marion University, SC
Franklin College, IN
George Fox University, OR
Georgetown College, KY
Georgia Southern University, GA
Gonzaga University, WA
Gordon College, MA
Graceland University, IA
Grace University, NE
Grand Valley State University, MI
Grand View University, IA
Green Mountain College, VT
Greenville College, IL
Gustavus Adolphus College, MN
Gwynedd-Mercy College, PA
Hanover College, IN
Hartwick College, NY
Henderson State University, AR
Heritage Christian University, AL
Hillsdale Free Will Baptist College, OK
Hofstra University, NY

Hollins University, VA
Hood College, MD
Houghton College, NY
Howard Payne University, TX
Huntingdon College, AL
Huntington University, IN
Idaho State University, ID
Illinois Institute of Technology, IL
Indiana State University, IN
Indiana Wesleyan University, IN
Iona College, NY
Iowa State University of Science and
  Technology, IA
Ithaca College, NY
James Madison University, VA
John Brown University, AR
John Carroll University, OH
Johnson & Wales University, CO
Johnson & Wales University, FL
Johnson & Wales University, RI
Johnson & Wales University—Charlotte
  Campus, NC
Kennesaw State University, GA
Kent State University, OH
Kent State University at Stark, OH
Keuka College, NY
Keystone College, PA
Lake Forest College, IL
Lakeland College, WI
Lancaster Bible College & Graduate
  School, PA
Lasell College, MA
Lawrence University, WI
Lebanon Valley College, PA
Le Moyne College, NY
Lenoir-Rhyne University, NC
LeTourneau University, TX
Lewis-Clark State College, ID
Lewis University, IL
Limestone College, SC
Lincoln University, PA
Lindsey Wilson College, KY
Lipscomb University, TN
Long Island University, Brooklyn
  Campus, NY
Long Island University, C.W. Post
  Campus, NY
Longwood University, VA
Loras College, IA
Louisiana State University and Agricultural
  and Mechanical College, LA
Louisiana Tech University, LA
Luther College, IA
MacMurray College, IL
Malone University, OH
Manchester College, IN
Marietta College, OH
Maryville College, TN
Maryville University of Saint Louis, MO
Marywood University, PA
Massachusetts Maritime Academy, MA
The Master's College and Seminary, CA
Medcenter One College of Nursing, ND
Mercyhurst College, PA
Merrimack College, MA
Methodist University, NC
Michigan State University, MI
Michigan Technological University, MI
Mid-Atlantic Christian University, NC
Mid-Continent University, KY
Midwestern State University, TX
Millikin University, IL
Misericordia University, PA

Mississippi College, MS
Mississippi State University, MS
Mississippi University for Women, MS
Missouri Southern State University, MO
Missouri State University, MO
Missouri University of Science and
  Technology, MO
Missouri Valley College, MO
Molloy College, NY
Monmouth University, NJ
Montana State University, MT
Montana State University Billings, MT
Montana State University–Northern, MT
Montana Tech of The University of
  Montana, MT
Montclair State University, NJ
Moravian College, PA
Morehead State University, KY
Morehouse College, GA
Morningside College, IA
Mount St. Mary's College, CA
Murray State University, KY
Muskingum University, OH
Nazareth College of Rochester, NY
Nebraska Wesleyan University, NE
Newberry College, SC
New England College, NH
Newman University, KS
New Mexico State University, NM
New York Institute of Technology, NY
Nichols College, MA
Northeastern State University, OK
Northern Arizona University, AZ
Northern Kentucky University, KY
Northwest Nazarene University, ID
Northwood University, MI
Northwood University, Florida Campus, FL
Northwood University, Texas Campus, TX
Notre Dame de Namur University, CA
Nyack College, NY
The Ohio State University, OH
Ohio Wesleyan University, OH
Oklahoma Baptist University, OK
Oklahoma State University, OK
Oklahoma Wesleyan University, OK
Olivet College, MI
Oral Roberts University, OK
Ouachita Baptist University, AR
Pacific Lutheran University, WA
Pacific University, OR
Palm Beach Atlantic University, FL
Peirce College, PA
Penn State Abington, PA
Penn State Altoona, PA
Penn State Berks, PA
Penn State Erie, The Behrend College, PA
Penn State Harrisburg, PA
Penn State University Park, PA
Pfeiffer University, NC
Pittsburg State University, KS
Point Park University, PA
Principia College, IL
Randolph-Macon College, VA
Regent University, VA
Rensselaer Polytechnic Institute, NY
Rhode Island College, RI
Ripon College, WI
Rivier College, NH
Roberts Wesleyan College, NY
Rockford College, IL
Rockhurst University, MO
Rocky Mountain College, MT
Rosemont College, PA

Russell Sage College, NY
Sage College of Albany, NY
St. Ambrose University, IA
St. Catherine University, MN
Saint Francis University, PA
St. John Fisher College, NY
St. Joseph's College, Long Island
  Campus, NY
St. Joseph's College, New York, NY
Saint Joseph's University, PA
St. Lawrence University, NY
Saint Martin's University, WA
Saint Mary's College of California, CA
St. Mary's College of Maryland, MD
Saint Mary's University of Minnesota, MN
Saint Paul's College, VA
Saint Vincent College, PA
Salem State College, MA
Salisbury University, MD
San Diego State University, CA
Santa Clara University, CA
Seattle Pacific University, WA
Seattle University, WA
Seton Hill University, PA
Shippensburg University of Pennsylvania, PA
Siena College, NY
Silver Lake College, WI
Simmons College, MA
Simpson College, IA
Slippery Rock University of Pennsylvania, PA
Sonoma State University, CA
Southeastern Louisiana University, LA
Southeastern Oklahoma State University, OK
Southern Adventist University, TN
Southern Arkansas University–Magnolia, AR
Southern Illinois University Carbondale, IL
Southern Nazarene University, OK
Southern Utah University, UT
Southwestern Oklahoma State University, OK
Southwest Minnesota State University, MN
State University of New York at Fredonia, NY
State University of New York College at
  Potsdam, NY
Stephen F. Austin State University, TX
Stetson University, FL
Suffolk University, MA
Susquehanna University, PA
Tabor College, KS
Taylor University, IN
Tennessee Technological University, TN
Tennessee Wesleyan College, TN
Texas Lutheran University, TX
Texas State University–San Marcos, TX
Thiel College, PA
Thomas More College, KY
Trine University, IN
Trinity Bible College, ND
Trinity Christian College, IL
Trinity International University, IL
Truman State University, MO
Union College, KY
Union University, TN
The University of Alabama at
  Birmingham, AL
University of Arkansas, AR
University of Central Missouri, MO
University of Charleston, WV
University of Delaware, DE
University of Dubuque, IA
University of Evansville, IN
University of Houston–Clear Lake, TX
University of Idaho, ID

University of Illinois at Urbana–
Champaign, IL
University of Kentucky, KY
University of La Verne, CA
University of Louisville, KY
University of Mary Hardin-Baylor, TX
University of Mary Washington, VA
University of Massachusetts Amherst, MA
University of Michigan–Dearborn, MI
University of Michigan–Flint, MI
University of Minnesota, Crookston, MN
University of Mississippi, MS
University of Missouri, MO
University of Missouri–St. Louis, MO
University of Mount Union, OH
University of Nebraska at Omaha, NE
University of Nebraska–Lincoln, NE
University of Nevada, Las Vegas, NV
University of Nevada, Reno, NV
University of New Hampshire, NH
University of New Orleans, LA
The University of North Carolina at
Asheville, NC
The University of North Carolina at
Pembroke, NC
University of Northern Colorado, CO
University of Oklahoma, OK
University of Portland, OR
University of Rochester, NY
University of St. Francis, IL
University of South Alabama, AL
University of South Carolina, SC
University of Southern California, CA
University of Southern Mississippi, MS
The University of Tampa, FL
The University of Tennessee, TN
The University of Tennessee at
Chattanooga, TN
University of the Incarnate Word, TX
University of the Ozarks, AR
The University of Toledo, OH
University of Tulsa, OK
University of West Florida, FL
University of West Georgia, GA
University of Wisconsin–Green Bay, WI
University of Wisconsin–La Crosse, WI
University of Wyoming, WY
Ursinus College, PA
Ursuline College, OH
Utah State University, UT
Valparaiso University, IN
Virginia Military Institute, VA
Wake Forest University, NC
Warner Pacific College, OR
Wartburg College, IA
Washburn University, KS
Washington & Jefferson College, PA
Washington State University, WA
Wayland Baptist University, TX
Webber International University, FL
Webster University, MO
Wells College, NY
Wesleyan College, GA
Western State College of Colorado, CO
West Liberty University, WV
Westminster College, MO
Westminster College, PA
Westminster College, UT
West Virginia Wesleyan College, WV
Wheeling Jesuit University, WV
Whitworth University, WA
Willamette University, OR
William Carey University, MS

William Jewell College, MO
Wilson College, PA
Winona State University, MN
Wittenberg University, OH
Wright State University, OH
Xavier University, OH
York College, NE
York College of Pennsylvania, PA
Youngstown State University, OH

Children of Current Students
Alliant International University, CA
Alma College, MI
Augustana College, SD
Bethel College, KS
Bloomfield College, NJ
Blue Mountain College, MS
Bryan College, TN
California State Polytechnic University,
Pomona, CA
Carroll University, WI
Central College, IA
Cincinnati Christian University, OH
The College of New Rochelle, NY
Columbia College, MO
ECPI College of Technology, VA
Elmhurst College, IL
Grace University, NE
Green Mountain College, VT
Huntington University, IN
Johnson Bible College, TN
Lancaster Bible College & Graduate
School, PA
Marymount University, VA
Maryville University of Saint Louis, MO
Marywood University, PA
Misericordia University, PA
Mount Aloysius College, PA
Mount Marty College, SD
Multnomah University, OR
Newman University, KS
Northwest University, WA
Palm Beach Atlantic University, FL
Rivier College, NH
Rockford College, IL
Sacred Heart University, CT
St. Catherine University, MN
Saint Francis University, PA
Trinity Bible College, ND
Union University, TN
The University of Alabama at
Birmingham, AL
University of Great Falls, MT
University of Hartford, CT
University of Michigan–Dearborn, MI
Valley Forge Christian College, PA
Wesleyan College, GA
Wilson College, PA

Children of Educators
Agnes Scott College, GA
Alfred University, NY
Allegheny College, PA
Appalachian Bible College, WV
Aurora University, IL
Austin Peay State University, TN
Bard College, NY
Benedictine College, KS
Bennington College, VT
Bryan College, TN
Calvary Bible College and Theological
Seminary, MO
Campbellsville University, KY

Canisius College, NY
Carthage College, WI
Centenary College of Louisiana, LA
Chowan University, NC
Coe College, IA
Columbia College, MO
Columbus College of Art & Design, OH
Concordia University, Nebraska, NE
Cornell College, IA
Dowling College, NY
East Texas Baptist University, TX
Emmanuel College, MA
Emory & Henry College, VA
Endicott College, MA
Evangel University, MO
Flagler College, FL
Florida College, FL
Grand View University, IA
Hampden-Sydney College, VA
Hardin-Simmons University, TX
Hendrix College, AR
Heritage Christian University, AL
Hillsdale Free Will Baptist College, OK
Jacksonville University, FL
John Brown University, AR
John Carroll University, OH
Johnson Bible College, TN
Judson College, AL
King's College, PA
Lees-McRae College, NC
Lipscomb University, TN
Lycoming College, PA
Mary Baldwin College, VA
Mississippi State University, MS
Moravian College, PA
Mount St. Mary's University, MD
Nebraska Wesleyan University, NE
New England College, NH
New York Institute of Technology, NY
Northern Arizona University, AZ
Northwest Nazarene University, ID
Occidental College, CA
Oklahoma Wesleyan University, OK
Palm Beach Atlantic University, FL
Pfeiffer University, NC
Rockford College, IL
Rosemont College, PA
Russell Sage College, NY
Sage College of Albany, NY
Saint Anselm College, NH
St. Catherine University, MN
Saint Francis University, PA
Saint Mary's College of California, CA
Salem College, NC
Seattle University, WA
Simpson College, IA
Sonoma State University, CA
Southern Illinois University Carbondale, IL
Southwestern College, KS
Tennessee Technological University, TN
Texas Christian University, TX
Union University, TN
Unity College, ME
The University of Alabama at
Birmingham, AL
University of Charleston, WV
University of Dubuque, IA
University of Kentucky, KY
University of Memphis, TN
University of St. Francis, IL
University of St. Thomas, MN
The University of Scranton, PA
The University of Tennessee at Martin, TN

Villanova University, PA
William Carey University, MS
Wright State University, OH

Children of Faculty/Staff

Abilene Christian University, TX
Adelphi University, NY
Adrian College, MI
Agnes Scott College, GA
Alaska Bible College, AK
Alaska Pacific University, AK
Alderson-Broaddus College, WV
Alfred University, NY
Allegheny College, PA
Alliant International University, CA
Alverno College, WI
American International College, MA
American University, DC
Anderson University, IN
Andrews University, MI
Appalachian Bible College, WV
Arkansas State University—Jonesboro, AR
Asbury University, KY
Ashland University, OH
Atlantic Union College, MA
Auburn University, AL
Augustana College, IL
Augustana College, SD
Aurora University, IL
Austin College, TX
Austin Peay State University, TN
Ball State University, IN
Bard College, NY
Bard College at Simon's Rock, MA
Barton College, NC
Baylor University, TX
Becker College, MA
Belhaven University, MS
Bellarmine University, KY
Belmont Abbey College, NC
Belmont University, TN
Bemidji State University, MN
Bennington College, VT
Berklee College of Music, MA
Berry College, GA
Bethany College, WV
Bethany Lutheran College, MN
Bethel College, IN
Bethel College, KS
Bethel University, MN
Bethesda Christian University, CA
Biola University, CA
Birmingham-Southern College, AL
Bloomsburg University of Pennsylvania, PA
Bluefield College, VA
Blue Mountain College, MS
Bluffton University, OH
Bowdoin College, ME
Bowling Green State University, OH
Bradley University, IL
Brenau University, GA
Brescia University, KY
Brevard College, NC
Brewton-Parker College, GA
Bryan College, TN
Buena Vista University, IA
Cabrini College, PA
California Baptist University, CA
California Lutheran University, CA
California State University, Chico, CA
California State University, Stanislaus, CA
Calvary Bible College and Theological
  Seminary, MO

Calvin College, MI
Campbellsville University, KY
Campbell University, NC
Canisius College, NY
Carroll University, WI
Carthage College, WI
Case Western Reserve University, OH
The Catholic University of America, DC
Cedarville University, OH
Centenary College, NJ
Centenary College of Louisiana, LA
Central College, IA
Central Michigan University, MI
Centre College, KY
Chatham University, PA
Chestnut Hill College, PA
Chowan University, NC
Cincinnati Christian University, OH
Clarke College, IA
Clarkson University, NY
Cleary University, MI
Clemson University, SC
Cleveland State University, OH
Coe College, IA
Coker College, SC
College of Mount St. Joseph, OH
The College of New Rochelle, NY
The College of Saint Rose, NY
The College of St. Scholastica, MN
College of the Holy Cross, MA
College of Visual Arts, MN
Colorado State University, CO
Columbia College, MO
Columbia College Chicago, IL
Columbus College of Art & Design, OH
Concordia College, MN
Concordia University, CA
Concordia University, MI
Concordia University Chicago, IL
Concordia University, Nebraska, NE
Concordia University, St. Paul, MN
Concordia University Texas, TX
Converse College, SC
Corban University, OR
Cornell College, IA
Cornerstone University, MI
Covenant College, GA
Creighton University, NE
Crossroads Bible College, IN
Crossroads College, MN
Crown College, MN
Culver-Stockton College, MO
Daemen College, NY
Dallas Baptist University, TX
Dalton State College, GA
Defiance College, OH
Delta State University, MS
DePaul University, IL
DePauw University, IN
Dickinson College, PA
Dickinson State University, ND
Dillard University, LA
Doane College, NE
Dominican College, NY
Dominican University of California, CA
Dordt College, IA
Dowling College, NY
Drury University, MO
Duquesne University, PA
D'Youville College, NY
East Carolina University, NC
Eastern Kentucky University, KY
East Texas Baptist University, TX

Eckerd College, FL
ECPI College of Technology, VA
ECPI Technical College, VA
Edgewood College, WI
Edinboro University of Pennsylvania, PA
Elizabethtown College, PA
Elmira College, NY
Elon University, NC
Embry-Riddle Aeronautical University, AZ
Embry-Riddle Aeronautical University, FL
Embry-Riddle Aeronautical University
  Worldwide, FL
Emmanuel College, MA
Emory & Henry College, VA
Emporia State University, KS
Erskine College, SC
Eureka College, IL
Evangel University, MO
Everest University, FL
Faulkner University, AL
Felician College, NJ
Ferrum College, VA
Flagler College, FL
Florida College, FL
Florida Institute of Technology, FL
Florida Southern College, FL
Fordham University, NY
Fort Lewis College, CO
Framingham State College, MA
Franciscan University of Steubenville, OH
Francis Marion University, SC
Franklin College, IN
Fresno Pacific University, CA
Furman University, SC
Gardner-Webb University, NC
Geneva College, PA
George Fox University, OR
Georgetown College, KY
Georgetown University, DC
Georgia College & State University, GA
Georgian Court University, NJ
Gonzaga University, WA
Grace Bible College, MI
Grace College, IN
Graceland University, IA
Grace University, NE
Grand Valley State University, MI
Grand View University, IA
Greenville College, IL
Guilford College, NC
Hampden-Sydney College, VA
Hampshire College, MA
Hampton University, VA
Hannibal-LaGrange College, MO
Hanover College, IN
Harding University, AR
Hardin-Simmons University, TX
Hartwick College, NY
Heidelberg University, OH
Henderson State University, AR
Hendrix College, AR
Heritage Christian University, AL
Hillsdale Free Will Baptist College, OK
Hollins University, VA
Hood College, MD
Hope International University, CA
Houghton College, NY
Houston Baptist University, TX
Howard Payne University, TX
Huntingdon College, AL
Huntington University, IN
Idaho State University, ID
Illinois College, IL

Non-Need Scholarships for Undergraduates
Special Characteristics

Illinois Institute of Technology, IL
Illinois State University, IL
Illinois Wesleyan University, IL
Indiana State University, IN
Indiana University of Pennsylvania, PA
Indiana Wesleyan University, IN
Iona College, NY
Iowa Wesleyan College, IA
Ithaca College, NY
Jacksonville University, FL
James Madison University, VA
Jamestown College, ND
John Brown University, AR
John Carroll University, OH
The Johns Hopkins University, MD
Johnson & Wales University, CO
Johnson & Wales University, FL
Johnson & Wales University, RI
Johnson & Wales University—Charlotte
  Campus, NC
Johnson Bible College, TN
Johnson C. Smith University, NC
Judson College, AL
Juniata College, PA
Kent State University, OH
Kentucky Mountain Bible College, KY
Kettering University, MI
Keuka College, NY
King College, TN
King's College, PA
Kutztown University of Pennsylvania, PA
Kuyper College, MI
LaGrange College, GA
Lake Erie College, OH
Lakeland College, WI
Lancaster Bible College & Graduate
  School, PA
Lasell College, MA
Lawrence Technological University, MI
Lebanon Valley College, PA
Lees-McRae College, NC
Lee University, TN
Lehigh University, PA
LeMoyne-Owen College, TN
Lenoir-Rhyne University, NC
Lewis & Clark College, OR
Lewis University, IL
Limestone College, SC
Lincoln Memorial University, TN
Lincoln University, MO
Lincoln University, PA
Lindsey Wilson College, KY
Linfield College, OR
Lipscomb University, TN
Long Island University, Brooklyn
  Campus, NY
Long Island University, C.W. Post
  Campus, NY
Louisiana Tech University, LA
Loyola University New Orleans, LA
Lubbock Christian University, TX
Lycoming College, PA
Lynn University, FL
MacMurray College, IL
Maine Maritime Academy, ME
Malone University, OH
Manhattan Christian College, KS
Manhattan College, NY
Marian University, WI
Marquette University, WI
Marshall University, WV
Mary Baldwin College, VA
Marymount University, VA

Maryville College, TN
Maryville University of Saint Louis, MO
Marywood University, PA
Massachusetts College of Pharmacy and
  Health Sciences, MA
Massachusetts Maritime Academy, MA
The Master's College and Seminary, CA
McKendree University, IL
McMurry University, TX
Memphis College of Art, TN
Mercer University, GA
Mercyhurst College, PA
Meredith College, NC
Merrimack College, MA
Messiah College, PA
Methodist University, NC
Miami University, OH
Michigan State University, MI
Mid-Atlantic Christian University, NC
Mid-Continent University, KY
Midwestern State University, TX
Milligan College, TN
Millsaps College, MS
Mills College, CA
Milwaukee Institute of Art and Design, WI
Milwaukee School of Engineering, WI
Minnesota State University Moorhead, MN
Misericordia University, PA
Mississippi College, MS
Mississippi State University, MS
Mississippi University for Women, MS
Missouri Southern State University, MO
Missouri University of Science and
  Technology, MO
Missouri Valley College, MO
Molloy College, NY
Monmouth University, NJ
Montana State University Billings, MT
Montana Tech of The University of
  Montana, MT
Montreat College, NC
Moravian College, PA
Morehouse College, GA
Morningside College, IA
Mount Marty College, SD
Mount Mary College, WI
Mount Olive College, NC
Mount Saint Mary College, NY
Mount St. Mary's University, MD
Mount Vernon Nazarene University, OH
Murray State University, KY
Nazareth College of Rochester, NY
Nebraska Wesleyan University, NE
Newberry College, SC
New England College, NH
Newman University, KS
New Mexico State University, NM
New York Institute of Technology, NY
Niagara University, NY
Nicholls State University, LA
Nichols College, MA
North Central College, IL
Northeastern Illinois University, IL
Northeastern State University, OK
Northern Arizona University, AZ
Northern Illinois University, IL
Northern Kentucky University, KY
Northern Michigan University, MI
North Greenville University, SC
Northwest Christian University, OR
Northwestern College, MN
Northwestern Oklahoma State University, OK

Northwestern State University of
  Louisiana, LA
Northwest Nazarene University, ID
Northwest University, WA
Northwood University, MI
Northwood University, Florida Campus, FL
Northwood University, Texas Campus, TX
Notre Dame de Namur University, CA
Nyack College, NY
Occidental College, CA
Oglethorpe University, GA
Ohio Northern University, OH
The Ohio State University, OH
Ohio University, OH
Ohio University–Chillicothe, OH
Ohio University–Eastern, OH
Ohio University–Lancaster, OH
Ohio University–Southern Campus, OH
Ohio University–Zanesville, OH
Ohio Valley University, WV
Oklahoma Baptist University, OK
Oklahoma Christian University, OK
Oklahoma City University, OK
Oklahoma Panhandle State University, OK
Oklahoma Wesleyan University, OK
Old Dominion University, VA
Olivet College, MI
Olivet Nazarene University, IL
Oral Roberts University, OK
Ouachita Baptist University, AR
Our Lady of the Lake University of
  San Antonio, TX
Pace University, NY
Pacific University, OR
Palm Beach Atlantic University, FL
Patrick Henry College, VA
Peace College, NC
Pfeiffer University, NC
Philadelphia Biblical University, PA
Piedmont Baptist College and Graduate
  School, NC
Piedmont College, GA
Plymouth State University, NH
Point Park University, PA
Presbyterian College, SC
Principia College, IL
Purdue University, IN
Purdue University North Central, IN
Quincy University, IL
Quinnipiac University, CT
Ramapo College of New Jersey, NJ
Randolph College, VA
Randolph-Macon College, VA
Regent University, VA
Regis University, CO
Rensselaer Polytechnic Institute, NY
The Richard Stockton College of New
  Jersey, NJ
Ripon College, WI
Robert Morris University Illinois, IL
Roberts Wesleyan College, NY
Rochester Institute of Technology, NY
Rockford College, IL
Rockhurst University, MO
Rocky Mountain College, MT
Rocky Mountain College of Art + Design, CO
Rosemont College, PA
Russell Sage College, NY
Sacred Heart University, CT
Sage College of Albany, NY
St. Ambrose University, IA
Saint Anselm College, NH
St. Bonaventure University, NY

St. Catherine University, MN
St. Edward's University, TX
Saint Francis University, PA
St. John's College, NM
St. John's University, NY
St. Joseph's College, Long Island
  Campus, NY
St. Joseph's College, New York, NY
Saint Joseph's College of Maine, ME
St. Louis College of Pharmacy, MO
Saint Louis University, MO
Saint Martin's University, WA
Saint Mary's College of California, CA
St. Mary's College of Maryland, MD
Saint Mary's University of Minnesota, MN
St. Norbert College, WI
Saint Paul's College, VA
Saint Xavier University, IL
Salem College, NC
Salem State College, MA
Samford University, AL
San Diego Christian College, CA
San Diego State University, CA
Santa Clara University, CA
Schreiner University, TX
Seattle Pacific University, WA
Seattle University, WA
Seton Hill University, PA
Shenandoah University, VA
Shorter University, GA
Siena College, NY
Simpson College, IA
Skidmore College, NY
Slippery Rock University of Pennsylvania, PA
Sonoma State University, CA
South Dakota State University, SD
Southeastern Bible College, AL
Southeastern Louisiana University, LA
Southeast Missouri State University, MO
Southern Arkansas University–Magnolia, AR
Southern Connecticut State University, CT
Southern Illinois University Carbondale, IL
Southern Illinois University Edwardsville, IL
Southern Nazarene University, OK
Southwestern College, KS
Southwestern University, TX
Spring Arbor University, MI
Spring Hill College, AL
State University of New York at
  Binghamton, NY
State University of New York at New
  Paltz, NY
State University of New York College at
  Potsdam, NY
State University of New York College of
  Agriculture and Technology at
  Morrisville, NY
Stephen F. Austin State University, TX
Stephens College, MO
Stetson University, FL
Stillman College, AL
Stonehill College, MA
Suffolk University, MA
Susquehanna University, PA
Tabor College, KS
Taylor University, IN
Temple University, PA
Tennessee Technological University, TN
Tennessee Wesleyan College, TN
Texas A&M University, TX
Texas Christian University, TX
Texas Lutheran University, TX
Texas Tech University, TX

Thiel College, PA
Thomas More College, KY
Tiffin University, OH
Towson University, MD
Transylvania University, KY
Trevecca Nazarene University, TN
Trine University, IN
Trinity Bible College, ND
Trinity Christian College, IL
Truman State University, MO
Tulane University, LA
Tusculum College, TN
Tuskegee University, AL
Union College, NY
Union University, TN
University of Advancing Technology, AZ
The University of Alabama at
  Birmingham, AL
The University of Arizona, AZ
University of Arkansas, AR
University of Bridgeport, CT
University of Central Missouri, MO
University of Charleston, WV
University of Connecticut, CT
University of Dallas, TX
University of Dayton, OH
University of Delaware, DE
University of Dubuque, IA
University of Evansville, IN
The University of Findlay, OH
University of Florida, FL
University of Great Falls, MT
University of Hartford, CT
University of Idaho, ID
University of Illinois at Urbana–
  Champaign, IL
University of Indianapolis, IN
The University of Kansas, KS
University of Kentucky, KY
University of La Verne, CA
University of Louisiana at Monroe, LA
University of Louisville, KY
University of Maine at Fort Kent, ME
University of Maine at Presque Isle, ME
University of Mary, ND
University of Mary Hardin-Baylor, TX
University of Mary Washington, VA
University of Massachusetts Amherst, MA
University of Massachusetts Boston, MA
University of Massachusetts Dartmouth, MA
University of Memphis, TN
University of Miami, FL
University of Michigan, MI
University of Michigan–Dearborn, MI
University of Minnesota, Crookston, MN
University of Mississippi, MS
University of Missouri, MO
University of Missouri–St. Louis, MO
The University of Montana Western, MT
University of Mount Union, OH
University of Nebraska at Kearney, NE
University of Nebraska at Omaha, NE
University of Nevada, Las Vegas, NV
University of New Hampshire, NH
University of New Hampshire at
  Manchester, NH
University of North Alabama, AL
The University of North Carolina at
  Asheville, NC
The University of North Carolina at Chapel
  Hill, NC
The University of North Carolina at
  Greensboro, NC

The University of North Carolina
  Wilmington, NC
University of North Dakota, ND
University of Northern Colorado, CO
University of Notre Dame, IN
University of Oregon, OR
University of Pittsburgh at Bradford, PA
University of Pittsburgh at Johnstown, PA
University of Portland, OR
University of Puget Sound, WA
University of Rochester, NY
University of Saint Francis, IN
University of St. Thomas, MN
University of San Diego, CA
University of Science and Arts of
  Oklahoma, OK
The University of Scranton, PA
University of South Alabama, AL
University of South Carolina, SC
University of Southern California, CA
University of Southern Indiana, IN
University of Southern Maine, ME
University of Southern Mississippi, MS
The University of Tampa, FL
The University of Tennessee at Martin, TN
The University of Texas at Brownsville, TX
The University of Texas at Tyler, TX
University of the District of Columbia, DC
University of the Incarnate Word, TX
University of the Ozarks, AR
University of the Southwest, NM
The University of Toledo, OH
University of Tulsa, OK
The University of West Alabama, AL
Ursinus College, PA
Ursuline College, OH
Utah State University, UT
Valley City State University, ND
Valley Forge Christian College, PA
Valparaiso University, IN
Vanguard University of Southern
  California, CA
Villanova University, PA
Virginia Intermont College, VA
Virginia Military Institute, VA
Virginia Polytechnic Institute and State
  University, VA
Virginia Wesleyan College, VA
Wabash College, IN
Wagner College, NY
Waldorf College, IA
Warren Wilson College, NC
Wartburg College, IA
Washburn University, KS
Washington & Jefferson College, PA
Washington Bible College, MD
Washington State University, WA
Wayland Baptist University, TX
Waynesburg University, PA
Wayne State College, NE
Wayne State University, MI
Webber International University, FL
Webster University, MO
Wesleyan College, GA
West Chester University of Pennsylvania, PA
Western Illinois University, IL
Western New England College, MA
West Liberty University, WV
Westminster College, MO
Westminster College, UT
Westmont College, CA
West Virginia University, WV
West Virginia Wesleyan College, WV

Non-Need Scholarships for Undergraduates
Special Characteristics

Wheeling Jesuit University, WV
Widener University, PA
Wilkes University, PA
William Carey University, MS
William Jewell College, MO
Williams Baptist College, AR
Wilson College, PA
Winona State University, MN
Winthrop University, SC
Wittenberg University, OH
Wofford College, SC
Wright State University, OH
York College, NE
Youngstown State University, OH

Children of Public Servants
American International College, MA
California State University,
  San Bernardino, CA
Carthage College, WI
College of Staten Island of the City University
  of New York, NY
Dowling College, NY
Framingham State College, MA
Georgia Southern University, GA
Illinois Institute of Technology, IL
Louisiana Tech University, LA
Mercer University, GA
Mississippi State University, MS
Monmouth University, NJ
New Mexico State University, NM
New York Institute of Technology, NY
Northern Arizona University, AZ
Northern Kentucky University, KY
Northwestern State University of
  Louisiana, LA
The Ohio State University, OH
Patrick Henry College, VA
Peirce College, PA
Salem State College, MA
Siena College, NY
Sonoma State University, CA
Southeastern Louisiana University, LA
Southern Illinois University Carbondale, IL
Tennessee Technological University, TN
The University of Alabama at
  Birmingham, AL
University of Delaware, DE
University of Kentucky, KY
University of Memphis, TN
University of Nevada, Las Vegas, NV
University of New Orleans, LA
The University of Texas at Dallas, TX
The University of Toledo, OH
University of Wisconsin–Green Bay, WI
Valdosta State University, GA
Washington State University, WA
Western Washington University, WA
Westminster College, UT

Children of Union Members/Company Employees
Adrian College, MI
Auburn University, AL
Averett University, VA
Calvin College, MI
Central Michigan University, MI
The College of Saint Rose, NY
Cornerstone University, MI
Dowling College, NY
Eastern Washington University, WA
Edinboro University of Pennsylvania, PA
Emmanuel College, MA

Emporia State University, KS
Everest University, FL
Framingham State College, MA
Francis Marion University, SC
Frostburg State University, MD
Grand Valley State University, MI
Hofstra University, NY
Husson University, ME
Illinois State University, IL
Kennesaw State University, GA
Kent State University, OH
Kutztown University of Pennsylvania, PA
Mercer University, GA
Michigan State University, MI
Mid-Continent University, KY
Midwestern State University, TX
Millersville University of Pennsylvania, PA
Millikin University, IL
Montana State University Billings, MT
New Mexico State University, NM
Northern Michigan University, MI
The Ohio State University, OH
The Richard Stockton College of New
  Jersey, NJ
Saint Paul's College, VA
Salem State College, MA
Shorter University, GA
Siena College, NY
Slippery Rock University of Pennsylvania, PA
Sonoma State University, CA
Southwest Minnesota State University, MN
Stephen F. Austin State University, TX
Stephens College, MO
Stonehill College, MA
Texas Christian University, TX
Thomas More College, KY
The University of Alabama, AL
The University of Alabama at
  Birmingham, AL
University of Connecticut, CT
University of Hartford, CT
University of Kentucky, KY
University of Louisville, KY
University of Massachusetts Boston, MA
University of Michigan–Flint, MI
University of Nevada, Las Vegas, NV
The University of North Carolina
  Wilmington, NC
University of Northern Colorado, CO
University of Pittsburgh at Bradford, PA
University of South Carolina, SC
The University of Toledo, OH
University of Wisconsin–La Crosse, WI
University of Wisconsin–Parkside, WI
Western Kentucky University, KY
Western New England College, MA
Western Washington University, WA
West Virginia University, WV
York College of Pennsylvania, PA
Youngstown State University, OH

Children of Workers in Trades
Dowling College, NY
Grand Valley State University, MI
Huntingdon College, AL
Kennesaw State University, GA
Marywood University, PA
Midwestern State University, TX
New Mexico State University, NM
The Ohio State University, OH
San Diego State University, CA
Siena College, NY
Sonoma State University, CA

South Dakota State University, SD
Texas Christian University, TX
The University of Alabama at
  Birmingham, AL
University of Kentucky, KY
University of Michigan, MI
University of Michigan–Dearborn, MI
University of South Carolina, SC
University of Wisconsin–Parkside, WI
West Virginia University, WV
Worcester Polytechnic Institute, MA
Youngstown State University, OH

Children with a Deceased or Disabled Parent
The Baptist College of Florida, FL
California State University,
  San Bernardino, CA
The Citadel, The Military College of South
  Carolina, SC
Clarke College, IA
The College of New Jersey, NJ
College of Staten Island of the City University
  of New York, NY
Dickinson State University, ND
Edinboro University of Pennsylvania, PA
Erskine College, SC
Fordham University, NY
Georgia College & State University, GA
Harding University, AR
Illinois State University, IL
Kent State University, OH
Kentucky State University, KY
Lees-McRae College, NC
Lipscomb University, TN
Louisiana State University and Agricultural
  and Mechanical College, LA
Marian University, WI
Midwestern State University, TX
Millikin University, IL
New Mexico State University, NM
Northeastern State University, OK
Northern Kentucky University, KY
Pace University, NY
Santa Clara University, CA
Seton Hill University, PA
Siena College, NY
Southern Illinois University Carbondale, IL
The University of Alabama at
  Birmingham, AL
University of Hartford, CT
University of Kentucky, KY
University of Louisiana at Monroe, LA
University of Louisville, KY
University of Massachusetts Dartmouth, MA
University of Nevada, Las Vegas, NV
University of New Orleans, LA
University of South Carolina, SC
The University of Texas at Arlington, TX
The University of Virginia's College at
  Wise, VA
Washington State University, WA
Wayne State College, NE
Youngstown State University, OH

Ethnic Background
Abilene Christian University, TX
Adrian College, MI
Alaska Pacific University, AK
Albright College, PA
Alderson-Broaddus College, WV
Alliant International University, CA
American University, DC

Arkansas State University—Jonesboro, AR
Armstrong Atlantic State University, GA
Asbury University, KY
Auburn University, AL
Augustana College, IL
Augustana College, SD
Austin College, TX
Austin Peay State University, TN
Bellarmine University, KY
Benedictine College, KS
Berry College, GA
Bethel College, KS
Bethel University, MN
Biola University, CA
Birmingham-Southern College, AL
Bluefield College, VA
Boise State University, ID
Brescia University, KY
Buena Vista University, IA
Cabrini College, PA
California Lutheran University, CA
California State University, Chico, CA
California State University, Stanislaus, CA
Calvin College, MI
Cedarville University, OH
Centenary College, NJ
Centenary College of Louisiana, LA
Centre College, KY
Clearwater Christian College, FL
Clemson University, SC
Colby College, ME
The College at Brockport, State University of
  New York, NY
College of Saint Benedict, MN
The College of Saint Rose, NY
The College of St. Scholastica, MN
Concordia University, MI
Cornell College, IA
Cornerstone University, MI
Dakota State University, SD
Dickinson State University, ND
DigiPen Institute of Technology, WA
Dominican University of California, CA
Dowling College, NY
Duke University, NC
Duquesne University, PA
East Carolina University, NC
Eastern Michigan University, MI
Eastern New Mexico University, NM
Eastern Washington University, WA
Elmhurst College, IL
Elon University, NC
Emmanuel College, MA
Erskine College, SC
Fairfield University, CT
Ferris State University, MI
Flagler College, FL
Florida Gulf Coast University, FL
Fort Lewis College, CO
Franklin College, IN
Furman University, SC
Gannon University, PA
George Fox University, OR
Grace College, IN
Grace University, NE
Grove City College, PA
Gustavus Adolphus College, MN
Hamline University, MN
Hampden-Sydney College, VA
Hardin-Simmons University, TX
Hawai'i Pacific University, HI
Hope College, MI
Humphreys College, CA

Huntington University, IN
Idaho State University, ID
Illinois Institute of Technology, IL
Indiana University of Pennsylvania, PA
Iowa State University of Science and
  Technology, IA
John Brown University, AR
John Carroll University, OH
Johnson Bible College, TN
Johnson C. Smith University, NC
Juniata College, PA
Kennesaw State University, GA
Kent State University, OH
Kentucky State University, KY
Kenyon College, OH
LaGrange College, GA
Langston University, OK
Lawrence University, WI
Lebanon Valley College, PA
Lenoir-Rhyne University, NC
Lesley University, MA
Lewis-Clark State College, ID
Long Island University, Brooklyn
  Campus, NY
Lourdes College, OH
Macalester College, MN
Manchester College, IN
Marietta College, OH
Maryville University of Saint Louis, MO
Marywood University, PA
McMurry University, TX
Meredith College, NC
Millsaps College, MS
Milwaukee Institute of Art and Design, WI
Mississippi University for Women, MS
Missouri Southern State University, MO
Molloy College, NY
Montana State University Billings, MT
Moravian College, PA
Muskingum University, OH
New England College, NH
New Mexico State University, NM
Northern Illinois University, IL
Northern State University, SD
Northwestern College, MN
Northwest Nazarene University, ID
Oakland University, MI
The Ohio State University, OH
Ohio Valley University, WV
Oklahoma State University, OK
Ouachita Baptist University, AR
Pacific University, OR
Portland State University, OR
Randolph-Macon College, VA
Rensselaer Polytechnic Institute, NY
The Richard Stockton College of New
  Jersey, NJ
Ripon College, WI
Sacred Heart University, CT
St. Catherine University, MN
St. John Fisher College, NY
Shepherd University, WV
Siena College, NY
Simpson College, IA
Slippery Rock University of Pennsylvania, PA
Sonoma State University, CA
South Dakota School of Mines and
  Technology, SD
South Dakota State University, SD
Southwestern College, KS
Southwest Minnesota State University, MN
State University of New York at
  Binghamton, NY

State University of New York at Fredonia, NY
State University of New York at New
  Paltz, NY
State University of New York College at
  Geneseo, NY
State University of New York College at
  Potsdam, NY
Stetson University, FL
Stony Brook University, State University of
  New York, NY
Taylor University, IN
Tennessee Technological University, TN
Texas Christian University, TX
Trinity Christian College, IL
Union University, TN
The University of Alabama at
  Birmingham, AL
The University of Arizona, AZ
University of Arkansas, AR
University of California, San Diego, CA
University of Central Missouri, MO
University of Central Oklahoma, OK
University of Delaware, DE
University of Dubuque, IA
University of Great Falls, MT
University of Hartford, CT
University of Idaho, ID
University of Indianapolis, IN
The University of Kansas, KS
University of Kentucky, KY
University of La Verne, CA
University of Louisville, KY
University of Maine at Presque Isle, ME
University of Mary Hardin-Baylor, TX
University of Michigan–Dearborn, MI
University of Minnesota, Crookston, MN
University of Minnesota, Morris, MN
University of Mississippi, MS
University of Missouri, MO
University of Missouri–Kansas City, MO
University of Missouri–St. Louis, MO
University of Mount Union, OH
University of Nebraska at Kearney, NE
University of Nebraska at Omaha, NE
University of Nebraska–Lincoln, NE
University of Nevada, Las Vegas, NV
University of Nevada, Reno, NV
The University of North Carolina at
  Asheville, NC
The University of North Carolina at
  Greensboro, NC
University of North Dakota, ND
University of Northern Colorado, CO
University of St. Francis, IL
University of South Carolina, SC
University of Southern Mississippi, MS
The University of Tennessee at
  Chattanooga, TN
The University of Tennessee at Martin, TN
The University of Texas at El Paso, TX
The University of Texas at San Antonio, TX
The University of Texas–Pan American, TX
University of the Ozarks, AR
The University of Toledo, OH
University of Vermont, VT
The University of Virginia's College at
  Wise, VA
University of Wisconsin–Eau Claire, WI
University of Wisconsin–Green Bay, WI
University of Wisconsin–La Crosse, WI
University of Wisconsin–Parkside, WI
University of Wisconsin–Stevens Point, WI
University of Wisconsin–Whitewater, WI

Non-Need Scholarships for Undergraduates

Special Characteristics

University of Wyoming, WY
Valley City State University, ND
Wartburg College, IA
Washburn University, KS
Wayland Baptist University, TX
Wayne State College, NE
Webster University, MO
Wesleyan College, GA
Western Carolina University, NC
Western Kentucky University, KY
Western Oregon University, OR
Western Washington University, WA
Westminster College, MO
Westminster College, UT
Westmont College, CA
West Virginia University, WV
Wheaton College, IL
Whitman College, WA
Whitworth University, WA
Widener University, PA
Wittenberg University, OH
Wright State University, OH
Youngstown State University, OH

First-Generation College Students

Abilene Christian University, TX
American International College, MA
American University, DC
Angelo State University, TX
Appalachian State University, NC
Arkansas State University—Jonesboro, AR
Austin College, TX
Averett University, VA
Birmingham-Southern College, AL
Bluefield College, VA
Boise State University, ID
Bowie State University, MD
Brenau University, GA
California Lutheran University, CA
California Maritime Academy, CA
California State University, Chico, CA
California State University,
  San Bernardino, CA
California State University, Stanislaus, CA
Calvin College, MI
Central Michigan University, MI
Centre College, KY
Chowan University, NC
The College at Brockport, State University of
  New York, NY
College of Saint Mary, NE
Colorado State University, CO
Columbia College, MO
Concordia University, CA
Creighton University, NE
Davidson College, NC
DePauw University, IN
Dominican University of California, CA
Dowling College, NY
Eastern New Mexico University, NM
Eastern Washington University, WA
Edinboro University of Pennsylvania, PA
Elon University, NC
Erskine College, SC
The Evergreen State College, WA
Fairfield University, CT
Flagler College, FL
Fort Lewis College, CO
Georgia Southern University, GA
Glenville State College, WV
Graceland University, IA
Guilford College, NC
Gustavus Adolphus College, MN

Idaho State University, ID
Illinois State University, IL
Iowa State University of Science and
  Technology, IA
John Carroll University, OH
Kent State University, OH
Kenyon College, OH
Kutztown University of Pennsylvania, PA
LaGrange College, GA
Lewis-Clark State College, ID
Limestone College, SC
Long Island University, Brooklyn
  Campus, NY
Massachusetts College of Liberal Arts, MA
Meredith College, NC
Mesa State College, CO
Metropolitan State College of Denver, CO
Michigan State University, MI
Midwestern State University, TX
Millsaps College, MS
Minnesota State University Moorhead, MN
Mississippi State University, MS
Monmouth University, NJ
Montana State University Billings, MT
Montreat College, NC
Northern Arizona University, AZ
Oklahoma State University, OK
Ouachita Baptist University, AR
Pacific Lutheran University, WA
Pacific University, OR
The Richard Stockton College of New
  Jersey, NJ
Ripon College, WI
Russell Sage College, NY
Sage College of Albany, NY
St. John Fisher College, NY
Saint Louis University, MO
Salem State College, MA
Salisbury University, MD
San Diego State University, CA
Sonoma State University, CA
South Dakota State University, SD
Southeastern Louisiana University, LA
Southeast Missouri State University, MO
Southern Nazarene University, OK
Southwest Minnesota State University, MN
State University of New York at
  Binghamton, NY
State University of New York at New
  Paltz, NY
Stephen F. Austin State University, TX
Tennessee Technological University, TN
Texas A&M University, TX
Texas A&M University–Corpus Christi, TX
Texas Lutheran University, TX
Texas State University–San Marcos, TX
Texas Tech University, TX
Trinity Christian College, IL
Trinity University, TX
The University of Alabama at
  Birmingham, AL
University of California, San Diego, CA
University of Central Florida, FL
University of Colorado at Boulder, CO
University of Delaware, DE
University of Great Falls, MT
University of Hartford, CT
University of Idaho, ID
University of Illinois at Urbana–
  Champaign, IL
The University of Kansas, KS
University of Kentucky, KY
University of La Verne, CA

University of Massachusetts Boston, MA
University of Massachusetts Dartmouth, MA
University of Michigan–Flint, MI
University of Minnesota, Crookston, MN
University of Mississippi, MS
University of Missouri, MO
The University of Montana Western, MT
University of Nebraska at Kearney, NE
University of Nebraska at Omaha, NE
University of Nevada, Las Vegas, NV
University of Nevada, Reno, NV
University of North Alabama, AL
The University of North Carolina at
  Asheville, NC
University of North Florida, FL
University of St. Francis, IL
University of South Carolina, SC
The University of Texas at Arlington, TX
The University of Texas at Brownsville, TX
The University of Texas at San Antonio, TX
University of Vermont, VT
The University of West Alabama, AL
University of West Florida, FL
University of Wisconsin–Eau Claire, WI
University of Wisconsin–La Crosse, WI
University of Wisconsin–Stout, WI
University of Wyoming, WY
Virginia Intermont College, VA
Virginia Polytechnic Institute and State
  University, VA
Washington State University, WA
Webber International University, FL
Wesleyan College, GA
Westminster College, UT
Whitman College, WA
Wichita State University, KS
William Carey University, MS
Wright State University, OH

Handicapped Students

Appalachian State University, NC
Arkansas State University—Jonesboro, AR
Austin College, TX
Boise State University, ID
Bryan College, TN
California State University, Chico, CA
California State University, Fresno, CA
California State University,
  San Bernardino, CA
Calvin College, MI
Central College, IA
Clear Creek Baptist Bible College, KY
The College of St. Scholastica, MN
College of Staten Island of the City University
  of New York, NY
Columbia College Chicago, IL
Creighton University, NE
Dordt College, IA
East Carolina University, NC
Eastern Washington University, WA
East Stroudsburg University of
  Pennsylvania, PA
Edinboro University of Pennsylvania, PA
Emmanuel College, MA
Emporia State University, KS
Florida Gulf Coast University, FL
Fordham University, NY
Fort Lewis College, CO
Fort Valley State University, GA
Francis Marion University, SC
Gardner-Webb University, NC
Georgia College & State University, GA
Georgia Southern University, GA

Grand Valley State University, MI
Hardin-Simmons University, TX
Hofstra University, NY
Idaho State University, ID
James Madison University, VA
Kennesaw State University, GA
Kent State University, OH
Kutztown University of Pennsylvania, PA
Lock Haven University of Pennsylvania, PA
Louisiana Tech University, LA
Massachusetts College of Liberal Arts, MA
Michigan State University, MI
Mid-Atlantic Christian University, NC
Midwestern State University, TX
Mississippi State University, MS
Murray State University, KY
New Mexico State University, NM
Northern Arizona University, AZ
Northern Kentucky University, KY
Northern State University, SD
The Ohio State University, OH
Oklahoma State University, OK
Old Dominion University, VA
Ouachita Baptist University, AR
Portland State University, OR
Sacred Heart University, CT
Sam Houston State University, TX
San Diego State University, CA
Santa Clara University, CA
Shepherd University, WV
Shippensburg University of Pennsylvania, PA
Sonoma State University, CA
South Dakota State University, SD
Southeastern Louisiana University, LA
Southern Illinois University Carbondale, IL
Southwest Minnesota State University, MN
State University of New York at
  Binghamton, NY
State University of New York at New
  Paltz, NY
State University of New York College at
  Potsdam, NY
Texas Christian University, TX
Texas State University–San Marcos, TX
Texas Tech University, TX
Towson University, MD
The University of Akron, OH
The University of Alabama at
  Birmingham, AL
University of California, San Diego, CA
University of Hartford, CT
University of Idaho, ID
University of Kentucky, KY
University of Mary Hardin-Baylor, TX
University of Massachusetts Amherst, MA
University of Memphis, TN
University of Michigan, MI
University of Michigan–Dearborn, MI
University of Michigan–Flint, MI
University of Mississippi, MS
University of Nebraska at Omaha, NE
University of Nebraska–Lincoln, NE
University of Nevada, Las Vegas, NV
University of New Hampshire, NH
The University of North Carolina at
  Asheville, NC
The University of North Carolina at
  Greensboro, NC
University of North Dakota, ND
University of Northern Colorado, CO
University of South Carolina, SC
The University of Tennessee at Martin, TN
The University of Texas at Arlington, TX

The University of Texas at Dallas, TX
The University of Texas at San Antonio, TX
The University of Toledo, OH
University of West Florida, FL
University of West Georgia, GA
University of Wisconsin–Green Bay, WI
University of Wisconsin–Stout, WI
University of Wisconsin–Whitewater, WI
University of Wyoming, WY
Washington State University, WA
Wesleyan College, GA
Western Carolina University, NC
Western Kentucky University, KY
Western Oregon University, OR
Westminster College, UT
Wheaton College, IL
Wright State University, OH
Youngstown State University, OH

International Students

Adrian College, MI
Agnes Scott College, GA
Alaska Pacific University, AK
Alderson-Broaddus College, WV
Alfred University, NY
Allegheny College, PA
Alliant International University, CA
Alverno College, WI
Anderson University, IN
Andrews University, MI
Appalachian Bible College, WV
Armstrong Atlantic State University, GA
Asbury University, KY
Ashland University, OH
Atlantic Union College, MA
Augsburg College, MN
Augustana College, IL
Augustana College, SD
Austin College, TX
Averett University, VA
Ball State University, IN
Barton College, NC
Belhaven University, MS
Bellarmine University, KY
Bemidji State University, MN
Benedictine College, KS
Benedictine University, IL
Bentley University, MA
Bethany College, KS
Bethany College, WV
Bethel College, IN
Bethel College, KS
Bethel University, MN
Biola University, CA
Bloomfield College, NJ
Bloomsburg University of Pennsylvania, PA
Bluffton University, OH
Boise State University, ID
Bowling Green State University, OH
Brenau University, GA
Brescia University, KY
Brevard College, NC
Brewton-Parker College, GA
Briar Cliff University, IA
Bridgewater College, VA
Bryan College, TN
Buena Vista University, IA
California Baptist University, CA
California Lutheran University, CA
California State University, Chico, CA
Calvin College, MI
Campbellsville University, KY
Canisius College, NY

Carroll University, WI
Centenary College of Louisiana, LA
Central College, IA
Central Michigan University, MI
Chowan University, NC
Cincinnati Christian University, OH
Clarke College, IA
Clarkson University, NY
Clear Creek Baptist Bible College, KY
Coastal Carolina University, SC
Coe College, IA
Coker College, SC
The College at Brockport, State University of
  New York, NY
College of Notre Dame of Maryland, MD
College of Saint Benedict, MN
The College of St. Scholastica, MN
College of Staten Island of the City University
  of New York, NY
Columbia College, MO
Concordia College, MN
Concordia University Chicago, IL
Concordia University, Nebraska, NE
Corban University, OR
Cornell College, IA
Cornerstone University, MI
Covenant College, GA
Crossroads College, MN
Crown College, MN
Culver-Stockton College, MO
Defiance College, OH
DePauw University, IN
Dickinson State University, ND
Dominican University, IL
Dominican University of California, CA
Dordt College, IA
Drake University, IA
Duquesne University, PA
Eastern Michigan University, MI
Eastern New Mexico University, NM
East Stroudsburg University of
  Pennsylvania, PA
East Texas Baptist University, TX
Eckerd College, FL
Edinboro University of Pennsylvania, PA
Elizabethtown College, PA
Elmira College, NY
Elon University, NC
Emmanuel College, MA
Emporia State University, KS
Endicott College, MA
Ferris State University, MI
Ferrum College, VA
Florida Gulf Coast University, FL
Fort Lewis College, CO
Fort Valley State University, GA
Franciscan University of Steubenville, OH
Francis Marion University, SC
Frostburg State University, MD
Furman University, SC
Gannon University, PA
George Fox University, OR
Georgia College & State University, GA
God's Bible School and College, OH
Gonzaga University, WA
Graceland University, IA
Grace University, NE
Grand Valley State University, MI
Green Mountain College, VT
Greenville College, IL
Gustavus Adolphus College, MN
Hamline University, MN
Hampden-Sydney College, VA

Non-Need Scholarships for Undergraduates
Special Characteristics

Hampton University, VA
Hanover College, IN
Harding University, AR
Hartwick College, NY
Harvey Mudd College, CA
Hawai'i Pacific University, HI
Heidelberg University, OH
Henderson State University, AR
Hendrix College, AR
Hollins University, VA
Hood College, MD
Hope International University, CA
Houghton College, NY
Huntingdon College, AL
Huntington University, IN
Idaho State University, ID
Illinois College, IL
Illinois Institute of Technology, IL
Illinois Wesleyan University, IL
Indiana University of Pennsylvania, PA
Iowa State University of Science and
  Technology, IA
Iowa Wesleyan College, IA
Jacksonville University, FL
James Madison University, VA
Jamestown College, ND
John Brown University, AR
Johnson Bible College, TN
Juniata College, PA
Kennesaw State University, GA
Kent State University, OH
Kentucky State University, KY
Keuka College, NY
Keystone College, PA
King's College, PA
Kuyper College, MI
Lancaster Bible College & Graduate
  School, PA
Lawrence University, WI
Lebanon Valley College, PA
Lees-McRae College, NC
Life University, GA
Lincoln University, PA
Lipscomb University, TN
Long Island University, Brooklyn
  Campus, NY
Long Island University, C.W. Post
  Campus, NY
Louisiana Tech University, LA
MacMurray College, IL
Malone University, OH
Manchester College, IN
Mannes College The New School for
  Music, NY
Marymount University, VA
Marywood University, PA
Massachusetts Maritime Academy, MA
The Master's College and Seminary, CA
McMurry University, TX
Mercer University, GA
Meredith College, NC
Merrimack College, MA
Mesa State College, CO
Michigan State University, MI
Mid-Atlantic Christian University, NC
Midwestern State University, TX
Millersville University of Pennsylvania, PA
Millikin University, IL
Mississippi University for Women, MS
Monmouth College, IL
Monmouth University, NJ
Montana State University–Northern, MT
Montclair State University, NJ

Montreat College, NC
Moravian College, PA
Morehead State University, KY
Morningside College, IA
Mount Marty College, SD
Mount Mary College, WI
Mount Vernon Nazarene University, OH
Multnomah University, OR
Murray State University, KY
Nebraska Wesleyan University, NE
Newberry College, SC
New England College, NH
Newman University, KS
New Mexico State University, NM
North Central College, IL
Northern Arizona University, AZ
Northern Illinois University, IL
Northern Michigan University, MI
Northern State University, SD
Northwestern College, MN
Northwestern State University of
  Louisiana, LA
Northwestern University, IL
Northwest Nazarene University, ID
Northwest University, WA
Notre Dame College, OH
Nyack College, NY
Ohio Northern University, OH
Ohio Valley University, WV
Oklahoma Christian University, OK
Oklahoma Wesleyan University, OK
Old Dominion University, VA
Olivet College, MI
Oral Roberts University, OK
Ouachita Baptist University, AR
Pace University, NY
Pacific Lutheran University, WA
Pacific University, OR
Peirce College, PA
Piedmont College, GA
Plymouth State University, NH
Point Park University, PA
Portland State University, OR
Quinnipiac University, CT
Ramapo College of New Jersey, NJ
Randolph College, VA
The Richard Stockton College of New
  Jersey, NJ
Ripon College, WI
Rivier College, NH
Roberts Wesleyan College, NY
Rockford College, IL
Rocky Mountain College, MT
St. Ambrose University, IA
St. Catherine University, MN
Saint Francis University, PA
Saint John's University, MN
Saint Louis University, MO
Saint Mary's University of Minnesota, MN
St. Norbert College, WI
St. Olaf College, MN
San Diego Christian College, CA
Schreiner University, TX
Seattle Pacific University, WA
Seton Hill University, PA
Silver Lake College, WI
Simpson College, IA
Sonoma State University, CA
South Dakota State University, SD
Southeastern Louisiana University, LA
Southeast Missouri State University, MO
Southern Adventist University, TN
Southern Illinois University Carbondale, IL

Southern Nazarene University, OK
Southwestern College, KS
Southwest Minnesota State University, MN
Spring Arbor University, MI
State University of New York at Fredonia, NY
State University of New York at
  Plattsburgh, NY
State University of New York College at
  Oneonta, NY
Stetson University, FL
Tabor College, KS
Taylor University, IN
Tennessee Wesleyan College, TN
Texas A&M University–Corpus Christi, TX
Texas Christian University, TX
Texas Woman's University, TX
Thomas More College, KY
Towson University, MD
Trinity Bible College, ND
Truett-McConnell College, GA
Truman State University, MO
Union University, TN
The University of Akron, OH
The University of Alabama, AL
The University of Arizona, AZ
University of Arkansas, AR
University of Bridgeport, CT
University of Charleston, WV
University of Evansville, IN
University of Great Falls, MT
University of Hartford, CT
University of Idaho, ID
University of Indianapolis, IN
The University of Kansas, KS
University of Kentucky, KY
University of La Verne, CA
University of Louisiana at Monroe, LA
University of Maine at Fort Kent, ME
University of Maine at Presque Isle, ME
University of Mary, ND
University of Mary Hardin-Baylor, TX
University of Miami, FL
University of Michigan, MI
University of Michigan–Dearborn, MI
University of Michigan–Flint, MI
University of Minnesota, Morris, MN
University of Mississippi, MS
University of Missouri, MO
University of Missouri–St. Louis, MO
The University of Montana Western, MT
University of Montevallo, AL
University of Mount Union, OH
University of Nebraska at Kearney, NE
University of Nebraska at Omaha, NE
University of Nebraska–Lincoln, NE
University of Nevada, Las Vegas, NV
University of New Hampshire, NH
University of New Orleans, LA
The University of North Carolina at
  Asheville, NC
The University of North Carolina at Chapel
  Hill, NC
The University of North Carolina at
  Greensboro, NC
University of North Dakota, ND
University of Northern Colorado, CO
University of North Florida, FL
University of Oregon, OR
University of Puget Sound, WA
University of Redlands, CA
University of Rochester, NY
University of Science and Arts of
  Oklahoma, OK

f www.facebook.com/pay4undergrad

University of South Carolina, SC
University of Southern California, CA
The University of Tampa, FL
The University of Texas at Brownsville, TX
The University of Texas at Dallas, TX
The University of Texas at El Paso, TX
The University of Texas–Pan American, TX
University of the Ozarks, AR
The University of Toledo, OH
University of West Georgia, GA
University of Wisconsin–Eau Claire, WI
University of Wisconsin–La Crosse, WI
University of Wisconsin–Parkside, WI
University of Wisconsin–Stevens Point, WI
University of Wisconsin–Stout, WI
University of Wisconsin–Whitewater, WI
University of Wyoming, WY
Ursinus College, PA
Utah State University, UT
Valdosta State University, GA
Valley City State University, ND
Valparaiso University, IN
Wartburg College, IA
Washburn University, KS
Washington Bible College, MD
Washington State University, WA
Wayland Baptist University, TX
Webber International University, FL
Webster University, MO
Wells College, NY
Wesleyan College, GA
Western Illinois University, IL
Western Kentucky University, KY
Western New England College, MA
Western Oregon University, OR
Western Washington University, WA
Westminster College, MO
Westminster College, PA
Westminster College, UT
Westmont College, CA
West Virginia University, WV
West Virginia Wesleyan College, WV
Whitman College, WA
Whitworth University, WA
Wichita State University, KS
Widener University, PA
Willamette University, OR
William Carey University, MS
Williams Baptist College, AR
Wilson College, PA
Wittenberg University, OH
Wright State University, OH
Xavier University, OH
York College of Pennsylvania, PA
Youngstown State University, OH

Local/State Students

Abilene Christian University, TX
Agnes Scott College, GA
Alaska Bible College, AK
Alaska Pacific University, AK
Alliant International University, CA
American University, DC
Angelo State University, TX
Arkansas State University—Jonesboro, AR
Auburn University, AL
Augustana College, SD
Austin College, TX
Averett University, VA
Ball State University, IN
Bard College at Simon's Rock, MA
Barton College, NC
Belhaven University, MS

Bellarmine University, KY
Benedictine College, KS
Berry College, GA
Bethel College, KS
Boise State University, ID
Boston University, MA
Brevard College, NC
Bridgewater State College, MA
Bryan College, TN
Bryant University, RI
California Maritime Academy, CA
California Polytechnic State University,
  San Luis Obispo, CA
California State University, Chico, CA
California State University, Fresno, CA
California State University, Monterey Bay, CA
California State University, Stanislaus, CA
Carthage College, WI
Centenary College, NJ
Centenary College of Louisiana, LA
Central College, IA
Central Michigan University, MI
Chowan University, NC
The Citadel, The Military College of South
  Carolina, SC
Clarke College, IA
Clarkson University, NY
Clemson University, SC
Coastal Carolina University, SC
The College at Brockport, State University of
  New York, NY
Columbia College, MO
Columbus College of Art & Design, OH
Concordia University, Nebraska, NE
Cornell College, IA
Creighton University, NE
Culver-Stockton College, MO
Dakota State University, SD
Dalton State College, GA
Davidson College, NC
DePaul University, IL
DePauw University, IN
DigiPen Institute of Technology, WA
Dordt College, IA
Dowling College, NY
Duke University, NC
Eastern Oregon University, OR
Eastern Washington University, WA
East Stroudsburg University of
  Pennsylvania, PA
East Texas Baptist University, TX
Eckerd College, FL
Edgewood College, WI
Edinboro University of Pennsylvania, PA
Elizabethtown College, PA
Elmira College, NY
Emmanuel College, MA
Endicott College, MA
Faulkner University, AL
Fayetteville State University, NC
Ferris State University, MI
Ferrum College, VA
Fitchburg State College, MA
Flagler College, FL
Florida Gulf Coast University, FL
Florida Southern College, FL
Florida State University, FL
Fort Lewis College, CO
Fort Valley State University, GA
Franciscan University of Steubenville, OH
Frostburg State University, MD
Furman University, SC
Gardner-Webb University, NC

Georgetown College, KY
Georgia College & State University, GA
Graceland University, IA
Grace University, NE
Grand Valley State University, MI
Greenville College, IL
Guilford College, NC
Hamline University, MN
Hardin-Simmons University, TX
Hawai'i Pacific University, HI
Hollins University, VA
Houghton College, NY
Howard Payne University, TX
Huntingdon College, AL
Huntington University, IN
Idaho State University, ID
Indiana University–Purdue University Fort
  Wayne, IN
Iowa State University of Science and
  Technology, IA
James Madison University, VA
Jefferson College of Health Sciences, VA
John Carroll University, OH
The Johns Hopkins University, MD
Johnson & Wales University, CO
Johnson & Wales University, FL
Johnson & Wales University, RI
Johnson & Wales University—Charlotte
  Campus, NC
Juniata College, PA
Kennesaw State University, GA
Kent State University, OH
Kent State University at Stark, OH
Kentucky State University, KY
Kettering University, MI
Kutztown University of Pennsylvania, PA
Lees-McRae College, NC
Lee University, TN
Lenoir-Rhyne University, NC
Lesley University, MA
Limestone College, SC
Lock Haven University of Pennsylvania, PA
Longwood University, VA
Lourdes College, OH
Lynn University, FL
Mansfield University of Pennsylvania, PA
Marist College, NY
Marymount Manhattan College, NY
Marywood University, PA
Massachusetts College of Liberal Arts, MA
McDaniel College, MD
McMurry University, TX
Medcenter One College of Nursing, ND
Mercer University, GA
Mesa State College, CO
Messiah College, PA
Miami University, OH
Michigan State University, MI
Michigan Technological University, MI
Millsaps College, MS
Milwaukee Institute of Art and Design, WI
Mississippi State University, MS
Missouri Southern State University, MO
Missouri State University, MO
Monmouth University, NJ
Montana State University, MT
Montana State University Billings, MT
Montana Tech of The University of
  Montana, MT
Montreat College, NC
Morehead State University, KY
Morehouse College, GA
Murray State University, KY

Non-Need Scholarships for Undergraduates
Special Characteristics

Muskingum University, OH
Newberry College, SC
New England College, NH
New Mexico State University, NM
New York City College of Technology of the
    City University of New York, NY
New York Institute of Technology, NY
Nicholls State University, LA
Northern Arizona University, AZ
Northern Kentucky University, KY
Northern State University, SD
Nyack College, NY
Ohio Valley University, WV
Ohio Wesleyan University, OH
Oklahoma Baptist University, OK
Oklahoma Panhandle State University, OK
Old Dominion University, VA
Ouachita Baptist University, AR
Pacific University, OR
Randolph College, VA
Regis University, CO
The Richard Stockton College of New
    Jersey, NJ
Ripon College, WI
Sacred Heart Major Seminary, MI
Saginaw Valley State University, MI
St. Bonaventure University, NY
St. Catherine University, MN
St. John Fisher College, NY
St. John's University, NY
St. Louis College of Pharmacy, MO
Saint Michael's College, VT
San Diego State University, CA
Schreiner University, TX
Shenandoah University, VA
Shepherd University, WV
Shippensburg University of Pennsylvania, PA
Shorter University, GA
Siena College, NY
Silver Lake College, WI
Slippery Rock University of Pennsylvania, PA
Sonoma State University, CA
Southeastern Bible College, AL
Southeastern Louisiana University, LA
Southern Adventist University, TN
Southern Nazarene University, OK
Southern Utah University, UT
Southwest Baptist University, MO
Southwestern Oklahoma State University, OK
Southwest Minnesota State University, MN
State University of New York at
    Binghamton, NY
State University of New York at Fredonia, NY
State University of New York College at
    Cortland, NY
State University of New York College at
    Geneseo, NY
State University of New York College at
    Oneonta, NY
State University of New York College at
    Potsdam, NY
State University of New York Institute of
    Technology, NY
Stephen F. Austin State University, TX
Sterling College, VT
Stetson University, FL
Sul Ross State University, TX
Tabor College, KS
Tennessee Technological University, TN
Texas A&M University, TX
Texas Christian University, TX
Trinity Christian College, IL
Tulane University, LA

Tusculum College, TN
Tuskegee University, AL
Unity College, ME
University of Advancing Technology, AZ
The University of Akron, OH
The University of Alabama in Huntsville, AL
University of Alaska Fairbanks, AK
University of Bridgeport, CT
University of Colorado at Boulder, CO
University of Connecticut, CT
University of Delaware, DE
University of Georgia, GA
University of Hartford, CT
University of Hawaii at Hilo, HI
University of Idaho, ID
University of Illinois at Urbana–
    Champaign, IL
The University of Kansas, KS
University of Louisville, KY
University of Mary, ND
University of Mary Hardin-Baylor, TX
University of Mary Washington, VA
University of Michigan, MI
University of Michigan–Flint, MI
University of Minnesota, Crookston, MN
University of Minnesota, Twin Cities
    Campus, MN
University of Mississippi, MS
University of Missouri, MO
University of Missouri–St. Louis, MO
University of Nevada, Las Vegas, NV
University of New Hampshire, NH
University of New Orleans, LA
The University of North Carolina at
    Asheville, NC
The University of North Carolina
    Wilmington, NC
University of Northern Colorado, CO
University of Oregon, OR
University of Pittsburgh at Bradford, PA
University of South Carolina, SC
University of Southern Maine, ME
University of Southern Mississippi, MS
The University of Texas at Austin, TX
The University of Texas at Dallas, TX
The University of Texas at El Paso, TX
The University of Texas at San Antonio, TX
The University of Texas–Pan American, TX
The University of Virginia's College at
    Wise, VA
University of West Georgia, GA
University of Wisconsin–Eau Claire, WI
University of Wisconsin–Green Bay, WI
University of Wisconsin–La Crosse, WI
University of Wisconsin–Parkside, WI
University of Wisconsin–Stout, WI
University of Wisconsin–Whitewater, WI
University of Wyoming, WY
Valley Forge Christian College, PA
Vanderbilt University, TN
Virginia Military Institute, VA
Virginia Polytechnic Institute and State
    University, VA
Wake Forest University, NC
Warren Wilson College, NC
Washburn University, KS
Wayland Baptist University, TX
Wayne State College, NE
Webber International University, FL
Western Carolina University, NC
Western Kentucky University, KY
Western New England College, MA
Western Oregon University, OR

Western Washington University, WA
Westminster College, MO
Westminster College, UT
West Virginia University, WV
Wilson College, PA
Winona State University, MN
Wittenberg University, OH
Youngstown State University, OH

Married Students

Alaska Bible College, AK
Appalachian Bible College, WV
Auburn University, AL
Blue Mountain College, MS
California State University, Chico, CA
Cincinnati Christian University, OH
The College at Brockport, State University of
    New York, NY
Crossroads Bible College, IN
Georgia Southern University, GA
Grace University, NE
Johnson Bible College, TN
Lancaster Bible College & Graduate
    School, PA
Mid-Atlantic Christian University, NC
Mid-Continent University, KY
Montana Tech of The University of
    Montana, MT
Newman University, KS
New Mexico State University, NM
Northwest University, WA
Ouachita Baptist University, AR
Sonoma State University, CA
State University of New York at
    Binghamton, NY
Trinity Bible College, ND
The University of Alabama at
    Birmingham, AL
The University of Kansas, KS
University of Nevada, Reno, NV
The University of North Carolina
    Wilmington, NC
Valley Forge Christian College, PA

Members of Minority Groups

Abilene Christian University, TX
Alabama State University, AL
Alaska Pacific University, AK
Alice Lloyd College, KY
Alliant International University, CA
American University, DC
Appalachian State University, NC
Arkansas State University—Jonesboro, AR
Assumption College, MA
Augsburg College, MN
Augustana College, IL
Augustana College, SD
Aurora University, IL
Austin Peay State University, TN
Azusa Pacific University, CA
Baldwin-Wallace College, OH
Ball State University, IN
Bard College at Simon's Rock, MA
Bellarmine University, KY
Beloit College, WI
Benedictine College, KS
Bentley University, MA
Berry College, GA
Bethel College, IN
Bethel University, MN
Bluefield College, VA
Bluffton University, OH
Boise State University, ID

Bowling Green State University, OH
Brescia University, KY
Briar Cliff University, IA
Bridgewater State College, MA
Bryan College, TN
Bryant University, RI
California State Polytechnic University, Pomona, CA
California State University, Chico, CA
California State University, Stanislaus, CA
Calvin College, MI
Cameron University, OK
Carnegie Mellon University, PA
Carson-Newman College, TN
Carthage College, WI
Centenary College of Louisiana, LA
Central College, IA
Central Connecticut State University, CT
Central Michigan University, MI
Cincinnati Christian University, OH
Clarke College, IA
Clarkson University, NY
Clemson University, SC
Coe College, IA
The College at Brockport, State University of New York, NY
College for Creative Studies, MI
The College of New Jersey, NJ
The College of Saint Rose, NY
The College of St. Scholastica, MN
College of Staten Island of the City University of New York, NY
The College of Wooster, OH
Concordia University, Nebraska, NE
Cornell College, IA
Cornerstone University, MI
Covenant College, GA
Creighton University, NE
Crown College, MN
Dakota State University, SD
Dalton State College, GA
Defiance College, OH
DePauw University, IN
Dickinson State University, ND
DigiPen Institute of Technology, WA
Dominican University of California, CA
Dordt College, IA
Dowling College, NY
Drew University, NJ
Duquesne University, PA
Eastern Kentucky University, KY
Eastern Michigan University, MI
Eastern New Mexico University, NM
Eastern Oregon University, OR
East Stroudsburg University of Pennsylvania, PA
Edinboro University of Pennsylvania, PA
Elizabethtown College, PA
Elmhurst College, IL
Elon University, NC
Emporia State University, KS
Erskine College, SC
The Evergreen State College, WA
Fairfield University, CT
Ferris State University, MI
Flagler College, FL
Florida Gulf Coast University, FL
Florida International University, FL
Fort Lewis College, CO
Fort Valley State University, GA
Franklin College, IN
Fresno Pacific University, CA
Gallaudet University, DC

Gannon University, PA
Gardner-Webb University, NC
George Fox University, OR
Georgia College & State University, GA
Georgia Southern University, GA
Gonzaga University, WA
Graceland University, IA
Grace University, NE
Grove City College, PA
Gustavus Adolphus College, MN
Hamline University, MN
Hampden-Sydney College, VA
Hampton University, VA
Hanover College, IN
Hardin-Simmons University, TX
Humphreys College, CA
Idaho State University, ID
Illinois Institute of Technology, IL
Illinois State University, IL
Indiana State University, IN
Iowa State University of Science and Technology, IA
Ithaca College, NY
James Madison University, VA
John Brown University, AR
John Carroll University, OH
Johnson Bible College, TN
Kennesaw State University, GA
Kent State University, OH
Kent State University at Stark, OH
Kettering University, MI
King College, TN
King's College, PA
Kuyper College, MI
Lawrence Technological University, MI
Lehigh University, PA
Le Moyne College, NY
Lenoir-Rhyne University, NC
Lesley University, MA
Lewis-Clark State College, ID
Linfield College, OR
Lipscomb University, TN
Lock Haven University of Pennsylvania, PA
Louisiana Tech University, LA
Lourdes College, OH
Luther College, IA
Manchester College, IN
Marietta College, OH
Maryville College, TN
Maryville University of Saint Louis, MO
Massachusetts College of Liberal Arts, MA
Mercer University, GA
Meredith College, NC
Mesa State College, CO
Miami University, OH
Midwestern State University, TX
Milwaukee Institute of Art and Design, WI
Minnesota State University Moorhead, MN
Misericordia University, PA
Mississippi University for Women, MS
Mississippi Valley State University, MS
Missouri State University, MO
Missouri University of Science and Technology, MO
Monmouth University, NJ
Montana State University, MT
Montana State University Billings, MT
Montana State University–Northern, MT
Morehead State University, KY
Mount St. Mary's University, MD
Mount Vernon Nazarene University, OH
Murray State University, KY
Muskingum University, OH

New Mexico State University, NM
New York City College of Technology of the City University of New York, NY
Nicholls State University, LA
Northern Arizona University, AZ
Northern Illinois University, IL
Northern Kentucky University, KY
Northern Michigan University, MI
Northern State University, SD
Northwest Nazarene University, ID
The Ohio State University, OH
Ohio University, OH
Ohio University–Chillicothe, OH
Ohio University–Eastern, OH
Ohio University–Lancaster, OH
Ohio University–Southern Campus, OH
Ohio University–Zanesville, OH
Ohio Wesleyan University, OH
Old Dominion University, VA
Ouachita Baptist University, AR
Pacific Union College, CA
Point Park University, PA
Polytechnic Institute of NYU, NY
Portland State University, OR
Rensselaer Polytechnic Institute, NY
Rhodes College, TN
The Richard Stockton College of New Jersey, NJ
Rider University, NJ
Ripon College, WI
Rocky Mountain College, MT
Rowan University, NJ
Sacred Heart University, CT
Saginaw Valley State University, MI
St. Ambrose University, IA
St. Bonaventure University, NY
St. John Fisher College, NY
Saint Joseph's University, PA
Saint Louis University, MO
Saint Martin's University, WA
Saint Mary's University of Minnesota, MN
Saint Michael's College, VT
Saint Vincent College, PA
Salem State College, MA
Seattle University, WA
Shepherd University, WV
Simpson College, IA
Slippery Rock University of Pennsylvania, PA
Sonoma State University, CA
South Dakota School of Mines and Technology, SD
South Dakota State University, SD
Southeastern Louisiana University, LA
Southeast Missouri State University, MO
Southern Adventist University, TN
Southern Arkansas University–Magnolia, AR
Southern Illinois University Carbondale, IL
Southern Polytechnic State University, GA
Southern Utah University, UT
Southwestern College, KS
Southwest Minnesota State University, MN
Spring Arbor University, MI
State University of New York at Binghamton, NY
State University of New York at Fredonia, NY
State University of New York at New Paltz, NY
State University of New York College at Cortland, NY
State University of New York College at Geneseo, NY
State University of New York College at Potsdam, NY

Non-Need Scholarships for Undergraduates
Special Characteristics

State University of New York College of
  Agriculture and Technology at
  Morrisville, NY
State University of New York College of
  Environmental Science and Forestry, NY
State University of New York Institute of
  Technology, NY
Stetson University, FL
Stonehill College, MA
Susquehanna University, PA
Tennessee Technological University, TN
Tennessee Wesleyan College, TN
Texas Christian University, TX
Thomas More College, KY
Transylvania University, KY
Trine University, IN
Trinity Christian College, IL
Trinity International University, IL
Union University, TN
Unity College, ME
The University of Akron, OH
The University of Alabama at
  Birmingham, AL
The University of Alabama in Huntsville, AL
University of Alaska Fairbanks, AK
University of California, San Diego, CA
University of Central Missouri, MO
University of Central Oklahoma, OK
University of Delaware, DE
University of Dubuque, IA
University of Evansville, IN
University of Florida, FL
University of Hartford, CT
University of Idaho, ID
The University of Kansas, KS
University of Kentucky, KY
University of Louisville, KY
University of Maine at Fort Kent, ME
University of Mary Hardin-Baylor, TX
University of Massachusetts Dartmouth, MA
University of Memphis, TN
University of Michigan, MI
University of Michigan–Dearborn, MI
University of Michigan–Flint, MI
University of Minnesota, Morris, MN
University of Minnesota, Twin Cities
  Campus, MN
University of Mississippi, MS
University of Missouri, MO
University of Missouri–Kansas City, MO
University of Missouri–St. Louis, MO
The University of Montana Western, MT
University of Mount Union, OH
University of Nebraska at Omaha, NE
University of Nebraska–Lincoln, NE
University of Nevada, Las Vegas, NV
University of New Orleans, LA
The University of North Carolina at
  Asheville, NC
The University of North Carolina at
  Greensboro, NC
University of North Dakota, ND
University of Northern Colorado, CO
University of Northern Iowa, IA
University of North Florida, FL
University of Oklahoma, OK
The University of Scranton, PA
University of South Alabama, AL
University of South Carolina, SC
University of Southern California, CA
University of Southern Indiana, IN
The University of Tennessee at Martin, TN
The University of Texas at Dallas, TX

The University of Texas at El Paso, TX
The University of Texas at San Antonio, TX
University of the Ozarks, AR
The University of Toledo, OH
University of West Florida, FL
University of West Georgia, GA
University of Wisconsin–Eau Claire, WI
University of Wisconsin–Green Bay, WI
University of Wisconsin–La Crosse, WI
University of Wisconsin–Parkside, WI
University of Wisconsin–Stevens Point, WI
University of Wisconsin–Stout, WI
University of Wisconsin–Superior, WI
University of Wisconsin–Whitewater, WI
Valdosta State University, GA
Valley City State University, ND
Vanderbilt University, TN
Villanova University, PA
Virginia Intermont College, VA
Virginia Polytechnic Institute and State
  University, VA
Warner Pacific College, OR
Wartburg College, IA
Wayland Baptist University, TX
Wayne State College, NE
Webster University, MO
Western Carolina University, NC
Western Illinois University, IL
Western Kentucky University, KY
Western New England College, MA
Western Washington University, WA
Westminster College, UT
West Virginia University, WV
Whitworth University, WA
Wichita State University, KS
Willamette University, OR
Williams Baptist College, AR
Winona State University, MN
Wittenberg University, OH
Xavier University, OH
York College of Pennsylvania, PA
Youngstown State University, OH

Out-of-State Students
Abilene Christian University, TX
Alaska Pacific University, AK
Appalachian State University, NC
Arkansas State University—Jonesboro, AR
Auburn University, AL
Aurora University, IL
Averett University, VA
Bellarmine University, KY
Bemidji State University, MN
Benedictine College, KS
Benedictine University, IL
Bethel University, MN
Bloomfield College, NJ
Bluffton University, OH
Boise State University, ID
Brewton-Parker College, GA
Buena Vista University, IA
California Maritime Academy, CA
California State University, Chico, CA
Carnegie Mellon University, PA
Centenary College, NJ
Centenary College of Louisiana, LA
Central College, IA
Central Michigan University, MI
The Citadel, The Military College of South
  Carolina, SC
Cleveland State University, OH
Coastal Carolina University, SC

The College at Brockport, State University of
  New York, NY
The College of New Rochelle, NY
The College of Saint Rose, NY
Concordia University, MI
Concordia University Wisconsin, WI
Cornerstone University, MI
Dalton State College, GA
Davidson College, NC
Defiance College, OH
Delta State University, MS
Dordt College, IA
Eastern Michigan University, MI
Eastern New Mexico University, NM
Edinboro University of Pennsylvania, PA
Emory & Henry College, VA
Erskine College, SC
Flagler College, FL
Florida Gulf Coast University, FL
Florida Southern College, FL
Fort Lewis College, CO
Fort Valley State University, GA
Francis Marion University, SC
Franklin College, IN
Frostburg State University, MD
Gardner-Webb University, NC
George Fox University, OR
Georgetown College, KY
Georgia College & State University, GA
Grace University, NE
Grand Valley State University, MI
Greenville College, IL
Gustavus Adolphus College, MN
Hampden-Sydney College, VA
Hanover College, IN
Hardin-Simmons University, TX
Hawai'i Pacific University, HI
Heidelberg University, OH
Henderson State University, AR
Hollins University, VA
Idaho State University, ID
Iowa State University of Science and
  Technology, IA
James Madison University, VA
Kent State University, OH
Kentucky Wesleyan College, KY
Lewis-Clark State College, ID
Limestone College, SC
Lincoln University, MO
Louisiana Tech University, LA
Lourdes College, OH
Massachusetts College of Liberal Arts, MA
McKendree University, IL
McMurry University, TX
Meredith College, NC
Mesa State College, CO
Miami University, OH
Michigan State University, MI
Misericordia University, PA
Mississippi State University, MS
Mississippi University for Women, MS
Missouri University of Science and
  Technology, MO
Monmouth College, IL
Monmouth University, NJ
Montana State University Billings, MT
Montana State University–Northern, MT
Montana Tech of The University of
  Montana, MT
Morehead State University, KY
Morningside College, IA
Murray State University, KY
New College of Florida, FL

New Jersey Institute of Technology, NJ
New Mexico State University, NM
Nicholls State University, LA
Northeastern State University, OK
Northern Arizona University, AZ
Northern Michigan University, MI
Northwestern State University of
  Louisiana, LA
Northwest Nazarene University, ID
Nyack College, NY
Oakland University, MI
The Ohio State University, OH
Oklahoma Baptist University, OK
Oklahoma Panhandle State University, OK
Oklahoma State University, OK
Ouachita Baptist University, AR
Pacific Lutheran University, WA
Piedmont College, GA
Portland State University, OR
Ramapo College of New Jersey, NJ
Randolph-Macon College, VA
Ripon College, WI
Robert Morris University Illinois, IL
Roberts Wesleyan College, NY
Rockford College, IL
Rogers State University, OK
St. Ambrose University, IA
St. Catherine University, MN
Saint Francis University, PA
Saint Michael's College, VT
San Diego Christian College, CA
Shepherd University, WV
Shorter University, GA
Siena College, NY
Slippery Rock University of Pennsylvania, PA
Sonoma State University, CA
Southeastern Louisiana University, LA
Southeastern Oklahoma State University, OK
Southeast Missouri State University, MO
Southern Adventist University, TN
Southern Arkansas University–Magnolia, AR
Southwestern Oklahoma State University, OK
State University of New York at
  Binghamton, NY
State University of New York at Fredonia, NY
State University of New York at
  Plattsburgh, NY
State University of New York College of
  Agriculture and Technology at
  Morrisville, NY
Tabor College, KS
Tennessee Technological University, TN
Texas Tech University, TX
Thomas More College, KY
Transylvania University, KY
Trinity Christian College, IL
The University of Akron, OH
The University of Alabama, AL
The University of Alabama at
  Birmingham, AL
University of Arkansas, AR
University of Central Missouri, MO
University of Connecticut, CT
University of Dubuque, IA
University of Florida, FL
University of Idaho, ID
University of Indianapolis, IN
The University of Kansas, KS
University of Louisiana at Monroe, LA
University of Louisville, KY
University of Mary Hardin-Baylor, TX
University of Maryland, College Park, MD
University of Michigan, MI

University of Michigan–Dearborn, MI
University of Mississippi, MS
University of Missouri, MO
University of Missouri–Kansas City, MO
University of Missouri–St. Louis, MO
The University of Montana Western, MT
University of Montevallo, AL
University of Nebraska at Kearney, NE
University of Nebraska at Omaha, NE
University of Nebraska–Lincoln, NE
University of Nevada, Las Vegas, NV
University of New Orleans, LA
University of North Alabama, AL
The University of North Carolina at Chapel
  Hill, NC
The University of North Carolina at
  Greensboro, NC
University of Northern Colorado, CO
University of North Florida, FL
University of Pittsburgh at Bradford, PA
University of Science and Arts of
  Oklahoma, OK
University of South Carolina, SC
University of Southern Indiana, IN
University of Southern Maine, ME
University of Southern Mississippi, MS
The University of Tennessee at Martin, TN
The University of Texas at Dallas, TX
The University of Texas at El Paso, TX
The University of Texas at San Antonio, TX
The University of Texas–Pan American, TX
University of Wisconsin–La Crosse, WI
University of Wisconsin–Stevens Point, WI
University of Wisconsin–Stout, WI
University of Wisconsin–Whitewater, WI
University of Wyoming, WY
Virginia Military Institute, VA
Virginia Polytechnic Institute and State
  University, VA
Wartburg College, IA
Washington State University, WA
Wayne State College, NE
Webber International University, FL
Webster University, MO
Wesleyan College, GA
Western Kentucky University, KY
Western New England College, MA
Winona State University, MN
Wright State University, OH
Youngstown State University, OH

Parents of Current Students

Alabama Agricultural and Mechanical
  University, AL
Aurora University, IL
Bloomfield College, NJ
Blue Mountain College, MS
Cincinnati Christian University, OH
The College of New Rochelle, NY
Columbia College, MO
Crossroads College, MN
ECPI College of Technology, VA
Fairfield University, CT
Green Mountain College, VT
Huntington University, IN
Johnson Bible College, TN
Malone University, OH
Maryville University of Saint Louis, MO
Millikin University, IL
Mississippi University for Women, MS
Mount Aloysius College, PA
Mount Marty College, SD
Mount Mary College, WI

New England College, NH
Northwest University, WA
Pace University, NY
Rockford College, IL
St. Joseph's College, Long Island
  Campus, NY
St. Joseph's College, New York, NY
Seton Hill University, PA
State University of New York at Fredonia, NY
Stephens College, MO
Trinity Bible College, ND
The University of Alabama at
  Birmingham, AL
University of Great Falls, MT
University of Hartford, CT
University of the Incarnate Word, TX
Valley Forge Christian College, PA
Wesleyan College, GA

Previous College Experience

Abilene Christian University, TX
American International College, MA
American University, DC
Bellarmine University, KY
Bethel College, KS
Birmingham-Southern College, AL
Boise State University, ID
Brevard College, NC
Carthage College, WI
Cedar Crest College, PA
Centenary College, NJ
Central College, IA
Coker College, SC
The College at Brockport, State University of
  New York, NY
The College of New Rochelle, NY
The College of St. Scholastica, MN
Columbia College, MO
Defiance College, OH
Dowling College, NY
Eastern Michigan University, MI
East Texas Baptist University, TX
ECPI Technical College, VA
Elmira College, NY
Ferris State University, MI
Florida Institute of Technology, FL
Gardner-Webb University, NC
Hawai'i Pacific University, HI
Hendrix College, AR
Hollins University, VA
Huntington University, IN
Idaho State University, ID
Illinois College, IL
Illinois Institute of Technology, IL
Illinois State University, IL
Indiana State University, IN
Lake Forest College, IL
Lancaster Bible College & Graduate
  School, PA
Lees-McRae College, NC
Lewis-Clark State College, ID
Lock Haven University of Pennsylvania, PA
Lourdes College, OH
Manchester College, IN
Manhattanville College, NY
McDaniel College, MD
McMurry University, TX
Memphis College of Art, TN
Meredith College, NC
Misericordia University, PA
Mississippi State University, MS
Molloy College, NY
Monmouth University, NJ

Non-Need Scholarships for Undergraduates
Special Characteristics

Mount Mercy College, IA
New Mexico State University, NM
New York Institute of Technology, NY
Nicholls State University, LA
The Ohio State University, OH
Oklahoma State University, OK
Old Dominion University, VA
Ouachita Baptist University, AR
Pace University, NY
Palm Beach Atlantic University, FL
Point Park University, PA
The Richard Stockton College of New Jersey, NJ
Ripon College, WI
Saint Francis University, PA
Saint Louis University, MO
Shepherd University, WV
Siena College, NY
Slippery Rock University of Pennsylvania, PA
Sonoma State University, CA
Southeast Missouri State University, MO
Southwest Minnesota State University, MN
State University of New York at Fredonia, NY
State University of New York College at Potsdam, NY
State University of New York Institute of Technology, NY
Stephen F. Austin State University, TX
Sterling College, VT
Texas Christian University, TX
The University of Alabama at Birmingham, AL
University of Arkansas, AR
University of Bridgeport, CT
University of Central Missouri, MO
University of Hartford, CT
The University of Kansas, KS
University of Louisville, KY
University of Michigan–Dearborn, MI
University of Mississippi, MS
University of Nevada, Las Vegas, NV
The University of North Carolina Wilmington, NC
University of Oklahoma, OK
University of Science and Arts of Oklahoma, OK
The University of Toledo, OH
University of Wisconsin–Eau Claire, WI
University of Wisconsin–Stout, WI
Warren Wilson College, NC
Western Washington University, WA
York College, NE

Public Servants

College of Staten Island of the City University of New York, NY
Dowling College, NY
Grand Valley State University, MI
Hannibal-LaGrange College, MO
Hardin-Simmons University, TX
Hofstra University, NY
Kentucky State University, KY
New York Institute of Technology, NY
Nicholls State University, LA
Northern Arizona University, AZ
Northwestern State University of Louisiana, LA
Patrick Henry College, VA
Regent University, VA
St. Joseph's College, Long Island Campus, NY
St. Joseph's College, New York, NY
Salem State College, MA

Southern Illinois University Carbondale, IL
Tennessee Technological University, TN
The University of Alabama at Birmingham, AL
University of Kentucky, KY
University of Memphis, TN
University of Michigan–Dearborn, MI
University of New Orleans, LA
The University of Texas at Arlington, TX
The University of Texas at Dallas, TX
The University of Toledo, OH
Washington State University, WA
Westminster College, UT
Youngstown State University, OH

Relatives of Clergy

Abilene Christian University, TX
Albion College, MI
American University, DC
Anderson University, IN
Appalachian Bible College, WV
Arcadia University, PA
Ashland University, OH
Augsburg College, MN
Austin College, TX
Averett University, VA
Barton College, NC
Benedictine University, IL
Bethany College, KS
Bethany College, WV
Bethel College, IN
Bethel College, KS
Bethel University, MN
Bethesda Christian University, CA
Biola University, CA
Birmingham-Southern College, AL
Bluffton University, OH
Boston University, MA
Brevard College, NC
Brewton-Parker College, GA
Bryan College, TN
California Baptist University, CA
California Lutheran University, CA
Calvary Bible College and Theological Seminary, MO
Campbellsville University, KY
Carson-Newman College, TN
Carthage College, WI
Cedar Crest College, PA
Centenary College of Louisiana, LA
Chestnut Hill College, PA
Chowan University, NC
Clarke College, IA
Corban University, OR
Cornell College, IA
Crown College, MN
Dallas Baptist University, TX
Davidson College, NC
DePauw University, IN
Dominican College, NY
Drury University, MO
Duquesne University, PA
Elon University, NC
Erskine College, SC
Evangel University, MO
Faulkner University, AL
Ferrum College, VA
Florida Southern College, FL
Fresno Pacific University, CA
Furman University, SC
Gardner-Webb University, NC
George Fox University, OR
Georgetown College, KY

Gordon College, MA
Grace Bible College, MI
Grace College, IN
Grace University, NE
Green Mountain College, VT
Greenville College, IL
Hamline University, MN
Hannibal-LaGrange College, MO
Harding University, AR
Hardin-Simmons University, TX
Hawai'i Pacific University, HI
Heidelberg University, OH
Hendrix College, AR
High Point University, NC
Hillsdale Free Will Baptist College, OK
Hope International University, CA
Houghton College, NY
Houston Baptist University, TX
Howard Payne University, TX
Huntington University, IN
Indiana Wesleyan University, IN
Jamestown College, ND
John Brown University, AR
Johnson Bible College, TN
Judson College, AL
Kentucky Wesleyan College, KY
King College, TN
King's College, PA
LaGrange College, GA
Lancaster Bible College & Graduate School, PA
Lees-McRae College, NC
Lenoir-Rhyne University, NC
Lindsey Wilson College, KY
Lipscomb University, TN
Lycoming College, PA
Malone University, OH
The Master's College and Seminary, CA
McMurry University, TX
Mercer University, GA
Merrimack College, MA
Methodist University, NC
Mid-Continent University, KY
Millikin University, IL
Millsaps College, MS
Misericordia University, PA
Mississippi College, MS
Montreat College, NC
Moravian College, PA
Mount Vernon Nazarene University, OH
Muskingum University, OH
Nebraska Wesleyan University, NE
Newberry College, SC
Niagara University, NY
North Central College, IL
Northwest Christian University, OR
Northwestern College, MN
Northwest Nazarene University, ID
Northwest University, WA
Nyack College, NY
Ohio Northern University, OH
Ohio Valley University, WV
Oklahoma Baptist University, OK
Oklahoma City University, OK
Oklahoma Wesleyan University, OK
Olivet Nazarene University, IL
Oral Roberts University, OK
Ouachita Baptist University, AR
Pacific Lutheran University, WA
Pacific University, OR
Patrick Henry College, VA
Peace College, NC
Philadelphia Biblical University, PA

Piedmont Baptist College and Graduate
  School, NC
Presbyterian College, SC
Randolph College, VA
Randolph-Macon College, VA
Roberts Wesleyan College, NY
Rosemont College, PA
St. Bonaventure University, NY
St. John's University, NY
Saint Mary's College of California, CA
Salem College, NC
Samford University, AL
San Diego Christian College, CA
Schreiner University, TX
Seattle Pacific University, WA
Shenandoah University, VA
Shorter University, GA
Siena College, NY
Simpson College, IA
Southwest Baptist University, MO
Southwestern University, TX
Spring Arbor University, MI
Stonehill College, MA
Susquehanna University, PA
Tennessee Wesleyan College, TN
Texas Christian University, TX
Thiel College, PA
Transylvania University, KY
Trevecca Nazarene University, TN
Trinity Bible College, ND
Truett-McConnell College, GA
Union University, TN
The University of Alabama at
  Birmingham, AL
University of Dubuque, IA
University of Indianapolis, IN
University of Mary Hardin-Baylor, TX
University of Mount Union, OH
The University of North Carolina at Chapel
  Hill, NC
University of Portland, OR
University of South Carolina, SC
University of the Ozarks, AR
University of Tulsa, OK
Ursuline College, OH
Valley Forge Christian College, PA
Valparaiso University, IN
Virginia Wesleyan College, VA
Washington Bible College, MD
Wayland Baptist University, TX
Wesleyan College, GA
Westminster College, MO
Westminster College, UT
West Virginia Wesleyan College, WV
Whitworth University, WA
William Carey University, MS
Williams Baptist College, AR
Wilson College, PA
Wittenberg University, OH
Wofford College, SC

Religious Affiliation
Abilene Christian University, TX
Adrian College, MI
Agnes Scott College, GA
Alaska Bible College, AK
Alaska Pacific University, AK
Alderson-Broaddus College, WV
American Baptist College of American Baptist
  Theological Seminary, TN
Appalachian Bible College, WV
Arcadia University, PA
Armstrong Atlantic State University, GA

Ashland University, OH
Augustana College, IL
Augustana College, SD
Averett University, VA
Azusa Pacific University, CA
Baldwin-Wallace College, OH
The Baptist College of Florida, FL
Barton College, NC
Bellarmine University, KY
Benedictine College, KS
Bethany College, KS
Bethany College, WV
Bethel College, IN
Bethel College, KS
Bethel University, MN
Birmingham-Southern College, AL
Bluefield College, VA
Blue Mountain College, MS
Bluffton University, OH
Boston University, MA
Brevard College, NC
Brewton-Parker College, GA
Bridgewater College, VA
Buena Vista University, IA
California Lutheran University, CA
Calvary Bible College and Theological
  Seminary, MO
Calvin College, MI
Campbellsville University, KY
Canisius College, NY
Carthage College, WI
The Catholic University of America, DC
Cedar Crest College, PA
Cedarville University, OH
Centenary College, NJ
Centenary College of Louisiana, LA
Central College, IA
Chowan University, NC
Christian Brothers University, TN
Clarke College, IA
Clearwater Christian College, FL
The College at Brockport, State University of
  New York, NY
The College of St. Scholastica, MN
Columbia College, MO
Concordia University, CA
Concordia University, MI
Concordia University Chicago, IL
Concordia University, Nebraska, NE
Concordia University, St. Paul, MN
Concordia University Texas, TX
Cornell College, IA
Covenant College, GA
Creighton University, NE
Crossroads College, MN
Culver-Stockton College, MO
Dallas Baptist University, TX
Defiance College, OH
DePauw University, IN
Dillard University, LA
Doane College, NE
Dominican University, IL
Dordt College, IA
Drury University, MO
Duquesne University, PA
Eastern Michigan University, MI
East Stroudsburg University of
  Pennsylvania, PA
East Texas Baptist University, TX
Eckerd College, FL
Edinboro University of Pennsylvania, PA
Elizabethtown College, PA
Elmhurst College, IL

Emmanuel College, MA
Emory University, GA
Emporia State University, KS
Endicott College, MA
Erskine College, SC
Eureka College, IL
Evangel University, MO
Fairfield University, CT
Faulkner University, AL
Ferrum College, VA
Franciscan University of Steubenville, OH
Franklin College, IN
Fresno Pacific University, CA
Furman University, SC
Gannon University, PA
Geneva College, PA
George Fox University, OR
Georgetown College, KY
Georgia College & State University, GA
Georgian Court University, NJ
Grace College, IN
Graceland University, IA
Green Mountain College, VT
Greenville College, IL
Hampden-Sydney College, VA
Hannibal-LaGrange College, MO
Hanover College, IN
Hardin-Simmons University, TX
Hawai'i Pacific University, HI
Heidelberg University, OH
Hillsdale Free Will Baptist College, OK
Hope International University, CA
Houghton College, NY
Howard Payne University, TX
Huntingdon College, AL
Huntington University, IN
Indiana Wesleyan University, IN
Iona College, NY
Iowa State University of Science and
  Technology, IA
Iowa Wesleyan College, IA
Jamestown College, ND
Jarvis Christian College, TX
Johnson Bible College, TN
Judson College, AL
Kennesaw State University, GA
Kentucky Wesleyan College, KY
LaGrange College, GA
Lakeland College, WI
Lancaster Bible College & Graduate
  School, PA
Lees-McRae College, NC
Lenoir-Rhyne University, NC
Lewis University, IL
Lindsey Wilson College, KY
Loyola University Chicago, IL
Luther College, IA
MacMurray College, IL
Malone University, OH
Manchester College, IN
Marymount University, VA
Maryville College, TN
Marywood University, PA
McKendree University, IL
McMurry University, TX
McPherson College, KS
Medical College of Georgia, GA
Mercer University, GA
Meredith College, NC
Messiah College, PA
Methodist University, NC
Millsaps College, MS
Misericordia University, PA

Non-Need Scholarships for Undergraduates
Special Characteristics

Missouri Southern State University, MO
Molloy College, NY
Montreat College, NC
Moravian College, PA
Morningside College, IA
Mount Aloysius College, PA
Mount Marty College, SD
Mount Olive College, NC
Mount Vernon Nazarene University, OH
Multnomah University, OR
Muskingum University, OH
Newberry College, SC
Northwest Christian University, OR
Northwest Nazarene University, ID
Northwest University, WA
Nyack College, NY
Ohio Northern University, OH
Ohio Valley University, WV
Ohio Wesleyan University, OH
Oklahoma Baptist University, OK
Oklahoma Wesleyan University, OK
Olivet College, MI
Olivet Nazarene University, IL
Ouachita Baptist University, AR
Our Lady of the Lake University of
  San Antonio, TX
Pacific Lutheran University, WA
Pacific Union College, CA
Presbyterian College, SC
Randolph College, VA
Reinhardt University, GA
Rhodes College, TN
Ripon College, WI
Roberts Wesleyan College, NY
Rocky Mountain College, MT
Sacred Heart Major Seminary, MI
Sacred Heart University, CT
St. Ambrose University, IA
St. Bonaventure University, NY
St. Catherine University, MN
St. Edward's University, TX
Saint Francis University, PA
St. John's University, NY
Saint Louis University, MO
Saint Michael's College, VT
Saint Vincent College, PA
San Diego Christian College, CA
Schreiner University, TX
Seattle Pacific University, WA
Seattle University, WA
Shenandoah University, VA
Shorter University, GA
Siena College, NY
Simpson College, IA
Southern Nazarene University, OK
Southwestern College, KS
Southwestern University, TX
Spring Arbor University, MI
State University of New York College at
  Geneseo, NY
Tabor College, KS
Taylor University, IN
Tennessee Wesleyan College, TN
Texas Christian University, TX
Texas Lutheran University, TX
Thiel College, PA
Thomas More College, KY
Transylvania University, KY
Trevecca Nazarene University, TN
Trinity Christian College, IL
Trinity International University, IL
Truett-McConnell College, GA
Union College, KY

Union University, TN
University of Dallas, TX
University of Dayton, OH
University of Dubuque, IA
University of Evansville, IN
University of Great Falls, MT
University of Hartford, CT
University of Indianapolis, IN
University of La Verne, CA
University of Mary, ND
University of Mary Hardin-Baylor, TX
The University of North Carolina at Chapel
  Hill, NC
The University of North Carolina at
  Greensboro, NC
University of Portland, OR
University of St. Francis, IL
University of South Carolina, SC
University of the Ozarks, AR
The University of Toledo, OH
University of Tulsa, OK
Ursuline College, OH
Valparaiso University, IN
Villanova University, PA
Virginia Intermont College, VA
Virginia Wesleyan College, VA
Wake Forest University, NC
Waldorf College, IA
Warner Pacific College, OR
Warren Wilson College, NC
Wartburg College, IA
Washington State University, WA
Wayland Baptist University, TX
Wesleyan College, GA
Western Kentucky University, KY
Westminster College, MO
Westminster College, PA
Westminster College, UT
West Virginia Wesleyan College, WV
Wheeling Jesuit University, WV
Willamette University, OR
William Carey University, MS
Williams Baptist College, AR
Wilson College, PA
Wittenberg University, OH
Youngstown State University, OH

Siblings of Current Students
Albright College, PA
Asbury University, KY
Atlantic Union College, MA
Augsburg College, MN
Augustana College, IL
Augustana College, SD
Aurora University, IL
Baldwin-Wallace College, OH
Barton College, NC
Becker College, MA
Beloit College, WI
Benedictine University, IL
Bethel College, IN
Bethel College, KS
Bethesda Christian University, CA
Blackburn College, IL
Bloomfield College, NJ
Blue Mountain College, MS
Brevard College, NC
Bridgewater College, VA
Bryant University, RI
Buena Vista University, IA
California Baptist University, CA
Calvary Bible College and Theological
  Seminary, MO

Carroll University, WI
Carson-Newman College, TN
Carthage College, WI
The Catholic University of America, DC
Cedar Crest College, PA
Centenary College, NJ
Central College, IA
Chatham University, PA
Cincinnati Christian University, OH
Clarke College, IA
Clearwater Christian College, FL
Coe College, IA
The College of New Rochelle, NY
The College of Saint Rose, NY
The College of St. Scholastica, MN
Columbia College, MO
Concordia University, CA
Concordia University, MI
Corban University, OR
Creighton University, NE
Crossroads Bible College, IN
Crossroads College, MN
Crown College, MN
Daemen College, NY
Doane College, NE
Dominican University, IL
Dowling College, NY
East Texas Baptist University, TX
Elizabethtown College, PA
Elmhurst College, IL
Elmira College, NY
Emmanuel College, MA
Erskine College, SC
Eureka College, IL
Faulkner University, AL
Felician College, NJ
Five Towns College, NY
Florida Institute of Technology, FL
Florida Southern College, FL
Franciscan University of Steubenville, OH
Franklin College, IN
Gonzaga University, WA
Grace University, NE
Green Mountain College, VT
Greenville College, IL
Gustavus Adolphus College, MN
Gwynedd-Mercy College, PA
Hanover College, IN
Harding University, AR
Hardin-Simmons University, TX
Hartwick College, NY
Hillsdale Free Will Baptist College, OK
Hood College, MD
Houghton College, NY
Huntington University, IN
Indiana Wesleyan University, IN
Iona College, NY
Ithaca College, NY
James Madison University, VA
Jamestown College, ND
John Brown University, AR
Johnson Bible College, TN
Johnson C. Smith University, NC
Kettering University, MI
Keuka College, NY
Keystone College, PA
King's College, PA
Lakeland College, WI
Lancaster Bible College & Graduate
  School, PA
Lasell College, MA
Lee University, TN
Lenoir-Rhyne University, NC

Limestone College, SC
Long Island University, C.W. Post
  Campus, NY
Loras College, IA
Lynn University, FL
MacMurray College, IL
Malone University, OH
Marian University, WI
Maryville University of Saint Louis, MO
Marywood University, PA
McDaniel College, MD
Mercer University, GA
Merrimack College, MA
Misericordia University, PA
Molloy College, NY
Monmouth College, IL
Mount Aloysius College, PA
Mount Marty College, SD
Mount Mary College, WI
Mount St. Mary's University, MD
Mount Vernon Nazarene University, OH
Multnomah University, OR
Muskingum University, OH
Nazareth College of Rochester, NY
Nebraska Wesleyan University, NE
Newberry College, SC
New England College, NH
Newman University, KS
Nichols College, MA
Northwest Christian University, OR
Northwestern College, MN
Northwest Nazarene University, ID
Northwest University, WA
Northwood University, MI
Northwood University, Florida Campus, FL
Northwood University, Texas Campus, TX
Oglethorpe University, GA
Ohio Northern University, OH
Oklahoma Wesleyan University, OK
Olivet College, MI
Oral Roberts University, OK
Pacific Union College, CA
Palm Beach Atlantic University, FL
Peace College, NC
Point Park University, PA
Providence College, RI
Quinnipiac University, CT
Randolph-Macon College, VA
Regent University, VA
Ripon College, WI
Rivier College, NH
Roberts Wesleyan College, NY
Rockford College, IL
Rockhurst University, MO
Rocky Mountain College, MT
Rosemont College, PA
Russell Sage College, NY
Sacred Heart University, CT
Sage College of Albany, NY
Saint Anselm College, NH
St. Bonaventure University, NY
St. Catherine University, MN
Saint Francis University, PA
St. Joseph's College, Long Island
  Campus, NY
St. Joseph's College, New York, NY
Saint Joseph's College of Maine, ME
St. Lawrence University, NY
Saint Louis University, MO
Saint Martin's University, WA
Saint Michael's College, VT
San Diego Christian College, CA
Schreiner University, TX

Seton Hill University, PA
Shorter University, GA
Simpson College, IA
Southern Adventist University, TN
Southern Nazarene University, OK
Spring Hill College, AL
Stephens College, MO
Stonehill College, MA
Suffolk University, MA
Thiel College, PA
Thomas More College, KY
Trine University, IN
Trinity Bible College, ND
Truett-McConnell College, GA
Union University, TN
The University of Alabama at
  Birmingham, AL
University of Dallas, TX
University of Dubuque, IA
University of Evansville, IN
University of Great Falls, MT
University of Hartford, CT
University of Mary, ND
University of Michigan–Dearborn, MI
University of St. Francis, IL
The University of Scranton, PA
University of the Ozarks, AR
University of Tulsa, OK
Ursinus College, PA
Ursuline College, OH
Valley Forge Christian College, PA
Wagner College, NY
Wartburg College, IA
Washington Bible College, MD
Webber International University, FL
Wesleyan College, GA
Western New England College, MA
Westminster College, MO
Westminster College, UT
Whitworth University, WA
William Jewell College, MO
Xavier University, OH
York College, NE

Spouses of Current Students

Alaska Bible College, AK
American University, DC
Appalachian Bible College, WV
Augustana College, SD
Aurora University, IL
The Baptist College of Florida, FL
Bethel College, IN
Bethel College, KS
Bethesda Christian University, CA
Bloomfield College, NJ
Blue Mountain College, MS
Boise State University, ID
Bryan College, TN
Calvary Bible College and Theological
  Seminary, MO
Carroll University, WI
Cincinnati Christian University, OH
The College of New Rochelle, NY
The College of St. Scholastica, MN
Columbia College, MO
Crossroads Bible College, IN
Crossroads College, MN
DigiPen Institute of Technology, WA
Elmhurst College, IL
Fresno Pacific University, CA
Georgian Court University, NJ
Grace University, NE
Heritage Christian University, AL

Hillsdale Free Will Baptist College, OK
Hope International University, CA
Huntingdon College, AL
Huntington University, IN
Jamestown College, ND
Johnson Bible College, TN
Lancaster Bible College & Graduate
  School, PA
Lee University, TN
Malone University, OH
Maryville University of Saint Louis, MO
Marywood University, PA
Mid-Atlantic Christian University, NC
Mount Aloysius College, PA
Mount Marty College, SD
Mount Vernon Nazarene University, OH
Newman University, KS
New Mexico State University, NM
Northwest University, WA
Nyack College, NY
Pacific Union College, CA
Palm Beach Atlantic University, FL
Piedmont Baptist College and Graduate
  School, NC
Rocky Mountain College, MT
Russell Sage College, NY
St. Catherine University, MN
Saint Francis University, PA
St. Joseph's College, Long Island
  Campus, NY
St. Joseph's College, New York, NY
Saint Joseph's College of Maine, ME
Southern Adventist University, TN
Trinity Bible College, ND
Truett-McConnell College, GA
Union University, TN
The University of Alabama at
  Birmingham, AL
University of Great Falls, MT
University of Mary, ND
University of Mississippi, MS
University of Southern Indiana, IN
Valley Forge Christian College, PA
Washington Bible College, MD
Wesleyan College, GA
Westminster College, UT

Spouses of Deceased or Disabled Public Servants

College of Staten Island of the City University
  of New York, NY
Eastern Washington University, WA
Francis Marion University, SC
Grand Valley State University, MI
Michigan State University, MI
Mississippi State University, MS
New York Institute of Technology, NY
Northeastern State University, OK
Northern Arizona University, AZ
Northern Kentucky University, KY
Pace University, NY
Southern Illinois University Carbondale, IL
The University of Alabama, AL
The University of Alabama at
  Birmingham, AL
University of Connecticut, CT
University of Kentucky, KY
University of South Carolina, SC
Youngstown State University, OH

Twins

Becker College, MA
Blue Mountain College, MS

Non-Need Scholarships for Undergraduates
Special Characteristics

Calvin College, MI
The Catholic University of America, DC
Central College, IA
Cincinnati Christian University, OH
The College of Saint Rose, NY
Dominican University, IL
Dowling College, NY
East Texas Baptist University, TX
Lake Erie College, OH
Maryville University of Saint Louis, MO
Millikin University, IL
Mount Aloysius College, PA
Ouachita Baptist University, AR
Randolph College, VA
Sacred Heart University, CT
St. Joseph's College, Long Island
  Campus, NY
St. Joseph's College, New York, NY
Simpson College, IA
Union University, TN
The University of Alabama at
  Birmingham, AL
University of Hartford, CT
Virginia Polytechnic Institute and State
  University, VA
Westminster College, MO

Veterans

Agnes Scott College, GA
Alliant International University, CA
Appalachian Bible College, WV
Appalachian State University, NC
Arkansas State University—Jonesboro, AR
Augustana College, SD
Austin Peay State University, TN
Ball State University, IN
Barton College, NC
Benedictine University, IL
Bluefield College, VA
Boise State University, ID
Brown University, RI
California Baptist University, CA
Campbellsville University, KY
The Catholic University of America, DC
Cedarville University, OH
Central College, IA
Central Michigan University, MI
Clarkson University, NY
Cleary University, MI
Coe College, IA
The College at Brockport, State University of
  New York, NY
Columbia College, MO
Concordia University, Nebraska, NE
Concordia University, St. Paul, MN
Concordia University Texas, TX
Culver-Stockton College, MO
Dickinson State University, ND
DigiPen Institute of Technology, WA
Dowling College, NY
Eastern New Mexico University, NM
Eastern Washington University, WA
ECPI College of Technology, VA
ECPI Technical College, VA
Edinboro University of Pennsylvania, PA
Emporia State University, KS
The Evergreen State College, WA
Ferris State University, MI
Framingham State College, MA
Francis Marion University, SC
Frostburg State University, MD
Furman University, SC
Gannon University, PA

Georgian Court University, NJ
Grand Valley State University, MI
Hamline University, MN
Hampton University, VA
Hollins University, VA
Huntingdon College, AL
Huntington University, IN
Illinois Institute of Technology, IL
Indiana State University, IN
Indiana Wesleyan University, IN
Inter American University of Puerto Rico,
  Barranquitas Campus, PR
Jamestown College, ND
John Carroll University, OH
Kentucky State University, KY
Kentucky Wesleyan College, KY
Lake Erie College, OH
Lasell College, MA
Lebanon Valley College, PA
Lees-McRae College, NC
Louisiana Tech University, LA
Marymount University, VA
Maryville University of Saint Louis, MO
Massachusetts Maritime Academy, MA
Metropolitan State College of Denver, CO
Michigan State University, MI
Midwestern State University, TX
Monmouth College, IL
Monmouth University, NJ
Montana State University Billings, MT
Montana State University–Northern, MT
Montana Tech of The University of
  Montana, MT
Montreat College, NC
Mount Olive College, NC
New Mexico State University, NM
New York Institute of Technology, NY
Nicholls State University, LA
Northern Arizona University, AZ
Northern Illinois University, IL
Northern Kentucky University, KY
Northwestern State University of
  Louisiana, LA
Northwest Nazarene University, ID
Oklahoma Baptist University, OK
Oklahoma Panhandle State University, OK
Pace University, NY
Pacific University, OR
Patrick Henry College, VA
Piedmont Baptist College and Graduate
  School, NC
Robert Morris University Illinois, IL
Rochester Institute of Technology, NY
St. Ambrose University, IA
Salem State College, MA
San Diego State University, CA
Seattle Pacific University, WA
Sonoma State University, CA
South Dakota State University, SD
Southeastern Bible College, AL
Southeastern Louisiana University, LA
Southeast Missouri State University, MO
Southern Connecticut State University, CT
Southern Illinois University Carbondale, IL
Southern Nazarene University, OK
Southwest Minnesota State University, MN
Stephens College, MO
Stonehill College, MA
Susquehanna University, PA
Texas A&M University, TX
Texas Christian University, TX
Texas Tech University, TX
Thomas More College, KY

Towson University, MD
Union University, TN
University of Advancing Technology, AZ
The University of Alabama at
  Birmingham, AL
University of Connecticut, CT
University of Idaho, ID
University of Illinois at Urbana–
  Champaign, IL
University of Indianapolis, IN
University of Kentucky, KY
University of Louisville, KY
University of Mary, ND
University of Massachusetts Amherst, MA
University of Massachusetts Boston, MA
University of Massachusetts Dartmouth, MA
University of Michigan–Dearborn, MI
University of Minnesota, Morris, MN
University of Missouri–St. Louis, MO
The University of Montana Western, MT
University of Montevallo, AL
University of Nebraska at Kearney, NE
University of Nevada, Las Vegas, NV
The University of North Carolina at
  Asheville, NC
The University of North Carolina at
  Greensboro, NC
University of Northern Colorado, CO
University of Oregon, OR
University of Pittsburgh at Bradford, PA
University of Puerto Rico at Bayamón, PR
University of Rochester, NY
University of Southern Mississippi, MS
The University of Texas at Dallas, TX
The University of Texas–Pan American, TX
The University of Toledo, OH
The University of Virginia's College at
  Wise, VA
University of Wisconsin–Green Bay, WI
University of Wisconsin–La Crosse, WI
University of Wisconsin–Stevens Point, WI
University of Wisconsin–Stout, WI
University of Wyoming, WY
Washington State University, WA
Wayne State College, NE
Wesleyan College, GA
Western Kentucky University, KY
Western New Mexico University, NM
Western Oregon University, OR
Western Washington University, WA
Westminster College, UT
William Carey University, MS
Wilson College, PA
Youngstown State University, OH

Veterans' Children

Agnes Scott College, GA
Appalachian State University, NC
Arkansas State University—Jonesboro, AR
Benedictine College, KS
Benedictine University, IL
Boise State University, ID
Brevard College, NC
Brown University, RI
The Catholic University of America, DC
Central College, IA
Central Michigan University, MI
Coastal Carolina University, SC
College of Staten Island of the City University
  of New York, NY
Concordia University, Nebraska, NE
Concordia University, St. Paul, MN
Concordia University Texas, TX

Culver-Stockton College, MO
Dickinson State University, ND
DigiPen Institute of Technology, WA
Eastern Washington University, WA
ECPI College of Technology, VA
ECPI Technical College, VA
Edinboro University of Pennsylvania, PA
Emporia State University, KS
The Evergreen State College, WA
Fort Lewis College, CO
Francis Marion University, SC
Frostburg State University, MD
Glenville State College, WV
Grand Valley State University, MI
Hampton University, VA
Huntingdon College, AL
Huntington University, IN
Illinois Institute of Technology, IL
John Carroll University, OH
Kennesaw State University, GA
Lake Erie College, OH
Lasell College, MA
Louisiana Tech University, LA
Michigan State University, MI
Midwestern State University, TX
Montreat College, NC
Mount Olive College, NC
New Mexico State University, NM
Northern Arizona University, AZ

Northern Kentucky University, KY
Northwestern State University of
  Louisiana, LA
Oklahoma Panhandle State University, OK
Old Dominion University, VA
Purdue University North Central, IN
St. Lawrence University, NY
Saint Martin's University, WA
Salem State College, MA
Siena College, NY
South Dakota State University, SD
Southeastern Louisiana University, LA
Southern Nazarene University, OK
Southwest Minnesota State University, MN
Stephens College, MO
Stonehill College, MA
Texas A&M University, TX
Texas Christian University, TX
Texas Tech University, TX
Thomas More College, KY
Union University, TN
University of Advancing Technology, AZ
The University of Alabama at
  Birmingham, AL
University of California, San Diego, CA
University of Kentucky, KY
University of Louisville, KY
University of Maine at Presque Isle, ME
University of Michigan–Dearborn, MI

University of Minnesota, Morris, MN
University of Montevallo, AL
University of Nebraska at Kearney, NE
University of Nebraska at Omaha, NE
University of Nebraska–Lincoln, NE
University of Nevada, Las Vegas, NV
The University of North Carolina at
  Asheville, NC
The University of North Carolina at
  Greensboro, NC
University of North Dakota, ND
University of Oregon, OR
University of Puerto Rico at Bayamón, PR
University of Southern Indiana, IN
The University of Texas at Dallas, TX
The University of Toledo, OH
The University of Virginia's College at
  Wise, VA
University of Wisconsin–La Crosse, WI
University of Wisconsin–Stout, WI
Virginia Commonwealth University, VA
Virginia Polytechnic Institute and State
  University, VA
Washington State University, WA
Wayne State College, NE
Western Illinois University, IL
Westminster College, UT
Youngstown State University, OH

Athletic Grants for Undergraduates

Archery
Texas A&M University, TX | W

Baseball

Abilene Christian University, TX	M
Abraham Baldwin Agricultural College, GA	M
Academy of Art University, CA	M
Adelphi University, NY	M
Alabama Agricultural and Mechanical University, AL	M
Alabama State University, AL	M
Alderson-Broaddus College, WV	M
American International College, MA	M
Angelo State University, TX	M
Appalachian State University, NC	M
Arizona State University, AZ	M
Arkansas State University—Jonesboro, AR	M
Arkansas Tech University, AR	M
Armstrong Atlantic State University, GA	M
Asbury University, KY	M
Ashland University, OH	M
Auburn University, AL	M
Auburn University Montgomery, AL	M
Augustana College, SD	M
Austin Peay State University, TN	M
Azusa Pacific University, CA	M
Ball State University, IN	M
Barry University, FL	M
Barton College, NC	M
Baylor University, TX	M
Belhaven University, MS	M
Bellarmine University, KY	M
Belmont Abbey College, NC	M
Belmont University, TN	M
Bemidji State University, MN	M
Benedictine College, KS	M
Bentley University, MA	M
Bethany College, KS	M
Bethel College, IN	M
Bethune-Cookman University, FL	M
Blessing-Rieman College of Nursing, IL	M,W
Bloomfield College, NJ	M
Bloomsburg University of Pennsylvania, PA	M
Bluefield College, VA	M
Bluefield State College, WV	M
Blue Mountain College, MS	M
Boston College, MA	M
Bowling Green State University, OH	M
Bradley University, IL	M
Brescia University, KY	M
Brevard College, NC	M
Brewton-Parker College, GA	M
Briar Cliff University, IA	M
Brigham Young University, UT	M
Bryan College, TN	M
Bryant University, RI	M
Butler University, IN	M
California Baptist University, CA	M
California Polytechnic State University, San Luis Obispo, CA	M
California State Polytechnic University, Pomona, CA	M
California State University, Chico, CA	M
California State University, Dominguez Hills, CA	M
California State University, Fresno, CA	M
California State University, Fullerton, CA	M
California State University, Monterey Bay, CA	M
California State University, Northridge, CA	M
California State University, Sacramento, CA	M
California State University, San Bernardino, CA	M
Cameron University, OK	M
Campbellsville University, KY	M
Canisius College, NY	M
Carson-Newman College, TN	M
Catawba College, NC	M
Cedarville University, OH	M
Centenary College of Louisiana, LA	M
Central Connecticut State University, CT	M
Central Michigan University, MI	M
Chowan University, NC	M
Christian Brothers University, TN	M
The Citadel, The Military College of South Carolina, SC	M
Clarion University of Pennsylvania, PA	M
Clarke College, IA	M
Cleveland State University, OH	M
Coastal Carolina University, SC	M
Coker College, SC	M
College of Charleston, SC	M
The College of Saint Rose, NY	M
College of the Ozarks, MO	M
The College of William and Mary, VA	M
Colorado School of Mines, CO	M
Columbus State University, GA	M
Concordia University, CA	M
Concordia University, Nebraska, NE	M
Concordia University, St. Paul, MN	M
Concord University, WV	M
Coppin State University, MD	M
Corban University, OR	M
Covenant College, GA	M
Creighton University, NE	M
Culver-Stockton College, MO	M
Dakota State University, SD	M
Dakota Wesleyan University, SD	M
Dallas Baptist University, TX	M
Davidson College, NC	M
Delta State University, MS	M
Dickinson State University, ND	M
Dixie State College of Utah, UT	M
Doane College, NE	M
Dominican College, NY	M
Dordt College, IA	M
Dowling College, NY	M
Drury University, MO	M
Duke University, NC	M
East Carolina University, NC	M
Eastern Michigan University, MI	M
Eastern New Mexico University, NM	M
East Stroudsburg University of Pennsylvania, PA	M
Eckerd College, FL	M
Elon University, NC	M
Embry-Riddle Aeronautical University, FL	M
Emporia State University, KS	M
Erskine College, SC	M
Evangel University, MO	M
Fairfield University, CT	M
Faulkner University, AL	M
Felician College, NJ	M
Flagler College, FL	M
Florida Atlantic University, FL	M
Florida Gulf Coast University, FL	M
Florida Institute of Technology, FL	M
Florida International University, FL	M
Florida Southern College, FL	M
Florida State University, FL	M
Fordham University, NY	M
Francis Marion University, SC	M
Freed-Hardeman University, TN	M
Furman University, SC	M
Gannon University, PA	M
Gardner-Webb University, NC	M
George Mason University, VA	M
Georgetown College, KY	M
Georgetown University, DC	M
The George Washington University, DC	M

Georgia College & State University, GA	M	Lubbock Christian University, TX	M	Ohio Valley University, WV	M
Georgia Institute of Technology, GA	M	Malone University, OH	M	Oklahoma Baptist University, OK	M
Georgia Southern University, GA	M	Manhattan College, NY	M	Oklahoma Christian University, OK	M
Georgia State University, GA	M	Mansfield University of Pennsylvania, PA	M	Oklahoma City University, OK	M
Gonzaga University, WA	M	Marist College, NY	M	Oklahoma Panhandle State University, OK	M
Grace College, IN	M	Marshall University, WV	M	Oklahoma State University, OK	M
Graceland University, IA	M	Maryville University of Saint Louis, MO	M	Oklahoma Wesleyan University, OK	M
Grand Valley State University, MI	M	The Master's College and Seminary, CA	M	Old Dominion University, VA	M
Grand View University, IA	M	McKendree University, IL	M	Oral Roberts University, OK	M
Hannibal-LaGrange College, MO	M	Mercer University, GA	M	Oregon State University, OR	M
Harding University, AR	M	Mercyhurst College, PA	M	Ouachita Baptist University, AR	M
Hawai'i Pacific University, HI	M	Metropolitan State College of Denver, CO	M	Pace University, NY	M
Henderson State University, AR	M	Miami University, OH	M	Palm Beach Atlantic University, FL	M
High Point University, NC	M	Michigan State University, MI	M	Penn State University Park, PA	M
Hofstra University, NY	M	Mid-Continent University, KY	M	Pepperdine University, CA	M
Houston Baptist University, TX	M	Millersville University of Pennsylvania, PA	M	Philadelphia University, PA	M
Huntington University, IN	M	Milligan College, TN	M	Pikeville College, KY	M
Illinois Institute of Technology, IL	M	Minnesota State University Mankato, MN	M	Pittsburg State University, KS	M
Illinois State University, IL	M	Mississippi State University, MS	M	Point Park University, PA	M
Indiana State University, IN	M	Mississippi Valley State University, MS	M	Portland State University, OR	M
Indiana University Bloomington, IN	M	Missouri Southern State University, MO	M	Presbyterian College, SC	M
Indiana University of Pennsylvania, PA	M	Missouri State University, MO	M	Purdue University, IN	M
Indiana University–Purdue University Fort Wayne, IN	M	Missouri University of Science and Technology, MO	M	Purdue University North Central, IN	M
Indiana Wesleyan University, IN	M	Molloy College, NY	M	Queens College of the City University of New York, NY	M
Inter American University of Puerto Rico, Bayamón Campus, PR	M	Monmouth University, NJ	M	Quincy University, IL	M
Inter American University of Puerto Rico, Ponce Campus, PR	M	Morehead State University, KY	M	Quinnipiac University, CT	M
Iona College, NY	M	Morningside College, IA	M	Radford University, VA	M
Iowa Wesleyan College, IA	M	Mount Marty College, SD	M	Reinhardt University, GA	M
Jacksonville State University, AL	M	Mount Mercy College, IA	M	Rider University, NJ	M
Jacksonville University, FL	M	Mount Olive College, NC	M	Robert Morris University Illinois, IL	M
James Madison University, VA	M	Mount St. Mary's University, MD	M	Rockhurst University, MO	M
Jamestown College, ND	M	Mount Vernon Nazarene University, OH	M	Rollins College, FL	M
Kansas State University, KS	M	Murray State University, KY	M	Sacred Heart University, CT	M
Kennesaw State University, GA	M	Newberry College, SC	M	Saginaw Valley State University, MI	M
Kent State University, OH	M	New Jersey Institute of Technology, NJ	M	St. Ambrose University, IA	M
Kentucky State University, KY	M	Newman University, KS	M	St. Andrews Presbyterian College, NC	M
Kentucky Wesleyan College, KY	M	New Mexico State University, NM	M	St. Bonaventure University, NY	M
King College, TN	M	New York Institute of Technology, NY	M	St. Edward's University, TX	M
Kutztown University of Pennsylvania, PA	M	Niagara University, NY	M	St. John's University, NY	M
Lamar University, TX	M	Nicholls State University, LA	M	Saint Joseph's University, PA	M
Lane College, TN	M	Norfolk State University, VA	M	Saint Leo University, FL	M
Lee University, TN	M	North Carolina Agricultural and Technical State University, NC	M	Saint Louis University, MO	M
Lehigh University, PA	M	North Carolina State University, NC	M	Saint Martin's University, WA	M
Le Moyne College, NY	M	Northeastern State University, OK	M	Saint Mary's College of California, CA	M
Lewis-Clark State College, ID	M	Northeastern University, MA	M	St. Mary's University, TX	M
Lewis University, IL	M	Northern Kentucky University, KY	M	Saint Paul's College, VA	M
Limestone College, SC	M	North Greenville University, SC	M	St. Thomas University, FL	M
Lincoln Memorial University, TN	M	Northwestern Oklahoma State University, OK	M	Saint Xavier University, IL	M
Lincoln University, MO	M	Northwestern State University of Louisiana, LA	M	Samford University, AL	M
Lindenwood University, MO	M	Northwest Nazarene University, ID	M	Sam Houston State University, TX	M
Lindsey Wilson College, KY	M	Nova Southeastern University, FL	M	San Diego Christian College, CA	M
Lipscomb University, TN	M	Nyack College, NY	M	San Diego State University, CA	M
Lock Haven University of Pennsylvania, PA	M	Oakland University, MI	M	San Francisco State University, CA	M
Long Island University, Brooklyn Campus, NY	M	The Ohio State University, OH	M	San Jose State University, CA	M
Long Island University, C.W. Post Campus, NY	M	Ohio University, OH	M	Santa Clara University, CA	M
Longwood University, VA	M			Savannah College of Art and Design, GA	M
Louisiana State University and Agricultural and Mechanical College, LA	M			Savannah State University, GA	M
				Seton Hill University, PA	M
Louisiana Tech University, LA	M			Shepherd University, WV	M
				Shippensburg University of Pennsylvania, PA	M
				Shorter University, GA	M
				Siena College, NY	M
				Slippery Rock University of Pennsylvania, PA	M

Athletic Grants for Undergraduates
Baseball

Sonoma State University, CA	M	The University of Arizona, AZ	M	The University of North Carolina at Asheville, NC	M
South Dakota State University, SD	M	University of Arkansas, AR	M	The University of North Carolina at Chapel Hill, NC	M
Southeastern Louisiana University, LA	M	University of Bridgeport, CT	M	The University of North Carolina at Charlotte, NC	M
Southeastern Oklahoma State University, OK	M	University of California, Davis, CA	M		
		University of California, Irvine, CA	M	The University of North Carolina at Greensboro, NC	M
Southeast Missouri State University, MO	M	University of California, Los Angeles, CA	M	The University of North Carolina at Pembroke, NC	M
Southern Arkansas University–Magnolia, AR	M	University of California, Riverside, CA	M	The University of North Carolina Wilmington, NC	M
Southern Connecticut State University, CT	M	University of California, Santa Barbara, CA	M	University of North Dakota, ND	M
Southern Illinois University Carbondale, IL	M	University of Central Florida, FL	M	University of Northern Colorado, CO	M
		University of Central Missouri, MO	M	University of North Florida, FL	M
Southern Illinois University Edwardsville, IL	M	University of Central Oklahoma, OK	M	University of Notre Dame, IN	M
		University of Charleston, WV	M	University of Oklahoma, OK	M
Southern Polytechnic State University, GA	M	University of Cincinnati, OH	M	University of Oregon, OR	M
Southern Utah University, UT	M	University of Connecticut, CT	M	University of Pittsburgh, PA	M
Southwest Baptist University, MO	M	University of Dayton, OH	M	University of Portland, OR	M
Southwestern Oklahoma State University, OK	M	University of Delaware, DE	M	University of Rhode Island, RI	M
		University of Evansville, IN	M	University of Richmond, VA	M
Southwest Minnesota State University, MN	M	The University of Findlay, OH	M	University of St. Francis, IL	M
Spring Arbor University, MI	M	University of Florida, FL	M	University of San Diego, CA	M
Spring Hill College, AL	M	University of Georgia, GA	M	University of Science and Arts of Oklahoma, OK	M
Stanford University, CA	M	University of Hartford, CT	M		
State University of New York at Binghamton, NY	M	University of Hawaii at Hilo, HI	M	University of South Alabama, AL	M
		University of Houston, TX	M	University of South Carolina, SC	M
Stephen F. Austin State University, TX	M	University of Illinois at Chicago, IL	M	University of South Carolina Aiken, SC	M
Stetson University, FL	M	University of Illinois at Springfield, IL	M		
Stonehill College, MA	M	University of Illinois at Urbana–Champaign, IL	M	University of Southern California, CA	M
Stony Brook University, State University of New York, NY	M	University of Indianapolis, IN	M	University of Southern Indiana, IN	M
		The University of Iowa, IA	M	University of Southern Mississippi, MS	M
Tabor College, KS	M	The University of Kansas, KS	M	The University of Tampa, FL	M
Tarleton State University, TX	M	University of Kentucky, KY	M	The University of Tennessee, TN	M
Taylor University, IN	M	University of Louisiana at Monroe, LA	M	The University of Tennessee at Martin, TN	M
Temple University, PA	M	University of Louisville, KY	M		
Tennessee Technological University, TN	M	University of Maine, ME	M	The University of Texas at Arlington, TX	M
		University of Mary, ND	M	The University of Texas at Austin, TX	M
Tennessee Wesleyan College, TN	M	University of Maryland, Baltimore County, MD	M	The University of Texas at Brownsville, TX	M
Texas A&M University, TX	M				
Texas A&M University–Corpus Christi, TX	M	University of Maryland, College Park, MD	M	The University of Texas at San Antonio, TX	M
Texas Christian University, TX	M	University of Massachusetts Amherst, MA	M	The University of Texas of the Permian Basin, TX	M
Texas State University–San Marcos, TX	M	University of Massachusetts Lowell, MA	M	The University of Texas–Pan American, TX	M
Texas Tech University, TX	M	University of Memphis, TN	M	University of the Incarnate Word, TX	M
Tiffin University, OH	M	University of Miami, FL	M	University of the Pacific, CA	M
Towson University, MD	M	University of Michigan, MI	M	University of the Sciences in Philadelphia, PA	M
Trevecca Nazarene University, TN	M	University of Minnesota, Crookston, MN	M		
Trinity Christian College, IL	M	University of Minnesota, Duluth, MN	M	University of the Southwest, NM	M
Troy University, AL	M	University of Minnesota, Twin Cities Campus, MN	M	The University of Toledo, OH	M
Truett-McConnell College, GA	M			University of Virginia, VA	M
Truman State University, MO	M	University of Mississippi, MS	M	The University of Virginia's College at Wise, VA	M
Tulane University, LA	M	University of Missouri, MO	M		
Tusculum College, TN	M	University of Missouri–St. Louis, MO	M	University of Washington, WA	M
Tuskegee University, AL	M	University of Mobile, AL	M	The University of West Alabama, AL	M
Union College, KY	M	University of Montevallo, AL	M	University of West Florida, FL	M
Union University, TN	M	University of Nebraska at Kearney, NE	M	University of West Georgia, GA	M
University at Albany, State University of New York, NY	M	University of Nebraska at Omaha, NE	M	University of Wisconsin–Parkside, WI	M
		University of Nebraska–Lincoln, NE	M	Utah Valley University, UT	M
University at Buffalo, the State University of New York, NY	M	University of Nevada, Las Vegas, NV	M	Valdosta State University, GA	M
The University of Akron, OH	M	University of Nevada, Reno, NV	M	Valley City State University, ND	M
The University of Alabama, AL	M	University of New Haven, CT	M	Valparaiso University, IN	M
The University of Alabama at Birmingham, AL	M	University of New Orleans, LA	M	Vanderbilt University, TN	M
The University of Alabama in Huntsville, AL	M	University of North Alabama, AL	M		

Vanguard University of Southern California, CA	M
Villanova University, PA	M
Virginia Commonwealth University, VA	M
Virginia Intermont College, VA	M
Virginia Military Institute, VA	M
Wagner College, NY	M
Wake Forest University, NC	M
Waldorf College, IA	M
Washburn University, KS	M
Washington State University, WA	M
Wayland Baptist University, TX	M
Wayne State College, NE	M
Wayne State University, MI	M
Webber International University, FL	M
West Chester University of Pennsylvania, PA	M
Western Carolina University, NC	M
Western Illinois University, IL	M
Western Kentucky University, KY	M
Western Oregon University, OR	M
West Liberty University, WV	M
Westmont College, CA	M
West Virginia University, WV	M
West Virginia Wesleyan College, WV	M
Wheeling Jesuit University, WV	M
Wichita State University, KS	M
William Jewell College, MO	M
Winona State University, MN	M
Winthrop University, SC	M
Wofford College, SC	M
Wright State University, OH	M
Xavier University, OH	M
York College, NE	M
Youngstown State University, OH	M

Basketball

Abilene Christian University, TX	M,W
Academy of Art University, CA	M,W
Adams State College, CO	M,W
Adelphi University, NY	M,W
Alabama Agricultural and Mechanical University, AL	M,W
Alabama State University, AL	M,W
Alderson-Broaddus College, WV	M,W
American International College, MA	M,W
American University, DC	M,W
Angelo State University, TX	M,W
Appalachian State University, NC	M,W
Arizona State University, AZ	M,W
Arkansas State University—Jonesboro, AR	M,W
Arkansas Tech University, AR	M,W
Armstrong Atlantic State University, GA	M,W
Asbury University, KY	M,W
Ashland University, OH	M,W
Assumption College, MA	M,W
Auburn University, AL	M,W
Auburn University Montgomery, AL	M,W
Augustana College, SD	M,W
Austin Peay State University, TN	M,W
Azusa Pacific University, CA	M,W
Ball State University, IN	M,W
Barry University, FL	M,W
Barton College, NC	M,W
Baylor University, TX	M,W
Belhaven University, MS	M,W
Bellarmine University, KY	M,W

Belmont Abbey College, NC	M,W
Belmont University, TN	M,W
Bemidji State University, MN	M,W
Benedictine College, KS	M,W
Bentley University, MA	M,W
Bethany College, KS	M,W
Bethel College, IN	M,W
Bethel College, KS	M,W
Bethune-Cookman University, FL	M,W
Black Hills State University, SD	M,W
Blessing-Rieman College of Nursing, IL	M,W
Bloomfield College, NJ	M,W
Bloomsburg University of Pennsylvania, PA	M,W
Bluefield College, VA	M,W
Bluefield State College, WV	M,W
Blue Mountain College, MS	M,W
Boise State University, ID	M,W
Boston College, MA	M,W
Boston University, MA	M,W
Bowie State University, MD	M,W
Bowling Green State University, OH	M,W
Bradley University, IL	M,W
Brenau University, GA	W
Brescia University, KY	M,W
Brevard College, NC	M,W
Brewton-Parker College, GA	M,W
Briar Cliff University, IA	M,W
Brigham Young University, UT	M,W
Bryan College, TN	M,W
Bryant University, RI	M,W
Bucknell University, PA	M,W
Butler University, IN	M,W
California Baptist University, CA	M,W
California Maritime Academy, CA	M,W
California Polytechnic State University, San Luis Obispo, CA	M,W
California State Polytechnic University, Pomona, CA	M,W
California State University, Chico, CA	M,W
California State University, Dominguez Hills, CA	M,W
California State University, Fresno, CA	M,W
California State University, Fullerton, CA	M,W
California State University, Long Beach, CA	M,W
California State University, Monterey Bay, CA	M,W
California State University, Northridge, CA	M,W
California State University, Sacramento, CA	M,W
California State University, San Bernardino, CA	M,W
Cameron University, OK	M,W
Campbellsville University, KY	M,W
Canisius College, NY	M,W
Carson-Newman College, TN	M,W
Catawba College, NC	M,W
Cedarville University, OH	M,W
Centenary College of Louisiana, LA	M,W
Central Connecticut State University, CT	M,W
Central Michigan University, MI	M,W
Chaminade University of Honolulu, HI	M

Chowan University, NC	M,W
Christian Brothers University, TN	M,W
Cincinnati Christian University, OH	M
The Citadel, The Military College of South Carolina, SC	M
Clarion University of Pennsylvania, PA	M,W
Clarke College, IA	M,W
Clemson University, SC	M,W
Cleveland State University, OH	M,W
Coastal Carolina University, SC	M,W
Coker College, SC	M,W
Colgate University, NY	M,W
College of Charleston, SC	M,W
College of Saint Mary, NE	W
The College of Saint Rose, NY	M,W
College of the Holy Cross, MA	M,W
College of the Ozarks, MO	M,W
The College of William and Mary, VA	M,W
Colorado School of Mines, CO	M,W
Colorado State University, CO	M,W
Columbia College, MO	M,W
Columbus State University, GA	M,W
Concordia University, CA	M,W
Concordia University, Nebraska, NE	M,W
Concordia University, St. Paul, MN	M,W
Concord University, WV	M,W
Converse College, SC	W
Coppin State University, MD	M,W
Corban University, OR	M,W
Cornerstone University, MI	M,W
Covenant College, GA	M,W
Creighton University, NE	M,W
Culver-Stockton College, MO	M,W
Daemen College, NY	M,W
Dakota State University, SD	M,W
Dakota Wesleyan University, SD	M,W
Dallas Baptist University, TX	M
Davenport University, MI	M,W
Davidson College, NC	M,W
Delta State University, MS	M,W
DePaul University, IL	M,W
Dickinson State University, ND	M,W
Dillard University, LA	M,W
Dixie State College of Utah, UT	M,W
Doane College, NE	M,W
Dominican College, NY	M,W
Dominican University of California, CA	M,W
Dordt College, IA	M,W
Dowling College, NY	M,W
Drake University, IA	M,W
Drury University, MO	M,W
Duke University, NC	M,W
Duquesne University, PA	M,W
East Carolina University, NC	M,W
Eastern Michigan University, MI	M,W
Eastern New Mexico University, NM	M,W
Eastern Washington University, WA	M,W
East Stroudsburg University of Pennsylvania, PA	M,W
Eckerd College, FL	M,W
Edinboro University of Pennsylvania, PA	M,W
Elon University, NC	M,W
Embry-Riddle Aeronautical University, FL	M
Emporia State University, KS	M,W
Erskine College, SC	M,W

Evangel University, MO	M,W
The Evergreen State College, WA	M,W
Fairfield University, CT	M,W
Fairmont State University, WV	M,W
Faulkner University, AL	M,W
Fayetteville State University, NC	M
Felician College, NJ	M,W
Ferris State University, MI	M,W
Flagler College, FL	M,W
Florida Agricultural and Mechanical University, FL	M,W
Florida Atlantic University, FL	M,W
Florida College, FL	M
Florida Gulf Coast University, FL	M,W
Florida Institute of Technology, FL	M,W
Florida International University, FL	M,W
Florida Southern College, FL	M,W
Florida State University, FL	M,W
Fordham University, NY	M,W
Fort Lewis College, CO	M,W
Fort Valley State University, GA	M,W
Francis Marion University, SC	M,W
Freed-Hardeman University, TN	M,W
Furman University, SC	M,W
Gannon University, PA	M,W
Gardner-Webb University, NC	M,W
George Mason University, VA	M,W
Georgetown College, KY	M,W
Georgetown University, DC	M,W
The George Washington University, DC	M,W
Georgia College & State University, GA	M,W
Georgia Institute of Technology, GA	M,W
Georgian Court University, NJ	W
Georgia Southern University, GA	M,W
Georgia State University, GA	M,W
Glenville State College, WV	M,W
Goldey-Beacom College, DE	M,W
Gonzaga University, WA	M,W
Grace College, IN	M,W
Graceland University, IA	M,W
Grand Valley State University, MI	M,W
Grand View University, IA	M,W
Hampton University, VA	M,W
Hannibal-LaGrange College, MO	M,W
Harding University, AR	M,W
Hawai'i Pacific University, HI	M,W
Henderson State University, AR	M,W
High Point University, NC	M,W
Hofstra University, NY	M,W
Holy Family University, PA	M,W
Houghton College, NY	M,W
Houston Baptist University, TX	M,W
Humboldt State University, CA	M,W
Huntington University, IN	M,W
Idaho State University, ID	M,W
Illinois State University, IL	M,W
Indiana State University, IN	M,W
Indiana University Bloomington, IN	M,W
Indiana University of Pennsylvania, PA	M,W
Indiana University–Purdue University Fort Wayne, IN	M,W
Indiana University–Purdue University Indianapolis, IN	M,W
Indiana University South Bend, IN	M,W
Indiana University Southeast, IN	M,W
Indiana Wesleyan University, IN	M,W

Inter American University of Puerto Rico, Bayamón Campus, PR	M,W
Iona College, NY	M,W
Iowa State University of Science and Technology, IA	M,W
Iowa Wesleyan College, IA	M,W
Jacksonville State University, AL	M,W
Jacksonville University, FL	M,W
James Madison University, VA	M,W
Jamestown College, ND	M,W
John Brown University, AR	M,W
Johnson C. Smith University, NC	M,W
Judson College, AL	W
Kansas State University, KS	M,W
Kennesaw State University, GA	M,W
Kent State University, OH	M,W
Kentucky State University, KY	M,W
Kentucky Wesleyan College, KY	M,W
King College, TN	M,W
Kutztown University of Pennsylvania, PA	M,W
Lake Superior State University, MI	M,W
Lamar University, TX	M,W
Lane College, TN	M,W
Lees-McRae College, NC	M,W
Lee University, TN	M,W
Lehigh University, PA	M,W
Le Moyne College, NY	M,W
Lewis-Clark State College, ID	M,W
Lewis University, IL	M,W
Limestone College, SC	M,W
Lincoln Memorial University, TN	M,W
Lincoln University, MO	M,W
Lindenwood University, MO	M,W
Lindsey Wilson College, KY	M,W
Lipscomb University, TN	M,W
Lock Haven University of Pennsylvania, PA	M,W
Long Island University, Brooklyn Campus, NY	M,W
Long Island University, C.W. Post Campus, NY	M,W
Longwood University, VA	M,W
Louisiana State University and Agricultural and Mechanical College, LA	M,W
Louisiana Tech University, LA	M,W
Loyola University Chicago, IL	M,W
Loyola University Maryland, MD	M,W
Loyola University New Orleans, LA	M,W
Lubbock Christian University, TX	M,W
Malone University, OH	M,W
Manhattan College, NY	M,W
Mansfield University of Pennsylvania, PA	M,W
Marist College, NY	M,W
Marquette University, WI	M,W
Marshall University, WV	M,W
Maryville University of Saint Louis, MO	M,W
The Master's College and Seminary, CA	M,W
McKendree University, IL	M,W
Mercer University, GA	M,W
Mercyhurst College, PA	M,W
Merrimack College, MA	M,W
Metropolitan State College of Denver, CO	M,W
Miami University, OH	M,W

Michigan State University, MI	M,W
Michigan Technological University, MI	M,W
Mid-Continent University, KY	M,W
Midwestern State University, TX	M,W
Millersville University of Pennsylvania, PA	M,W
Milligan College, TN	M,W
Minnesota State University Mankato, MN	M,W
Minnesota State University Moorhead, MN	M,W
Mississippi State University, MS	M,W
Mississippi Valley State University, MS	M,W
Missouri Southern State University, MO	M,W
Missouri State University, MO	M,W
Missouri University of Science and Technology, MO	M,W
Molloy College, NY	M,W
Monmouth University, NJ	M,W
Montana State University, MT	M,W
Montana State University Billings, MT	M,W
Montana Tech of The University of Montana, MT	M,W
Morehead State University, KY	M,W
Morehouse College, GA	M
Morningside College, IA	M,W
Mountain State University, WV	M
Mount Marty College, SD	M,W
Mount Mercy College, IA	M,W
Mount Olive College, NC	M,W
Mount St. Mary's University, MD	M,W
Mount Vernon Nazarene University, OH	M,W
Murray State University, KY	M,W
Newberry College, SC	M,W
New Jersey Institute of Technology, NJ	M,W
Newman University, KS	M,W
New Mexico State University, NM	M,W
New York Institute of Technology, NY	M,W
Niagara University, NY	M,W
Nicholls State University, LA	M,W
Norfolk State University, VA	M,W
North Carolina Agricultural and Technical State University, NC	M,W
North Carolina State University, NC	M,W
Northeastern State University, OK	M,W
Northeastern University, MA	M,W
Northern Arizona University, AZ	M,W
Northern Kentucky University, KY	M,W
Northern Michigan University, MI	M,W
Northern State University, SD	M,W
North Georgia College & State University, GA	M,W
North Greenville University, SC	M,W
Northwest Christian University, OR	M,W
Northwestern Oklahoma State University, OK	M,W
Northwestern State University of Louisiana, LA	M,W
Northwest Nazarene University, ID	M,W
Northwest University, WA	M,W
Notre Dame de Namur University, CA	M,W
Nova Southeastern University, FL	M,W
Nyack College, NY	M,W

Oakland University, MI	M,W	Savannah State University, GA	M,W	Texas Woman's University, TX	W
The Ohio State University, OH	M,W	Seattle Pacific University, WA	M,W	Tiffin University, OH	M,W
Ohio University, OH	M,W	Seattle University, WA	M,W	Towson University, MD	M,W
Ohio Valley University, WV	M,W	Seton Hill University, PA	M,W	Trevecca Nazarene University, TN	M,W
Oklahoma Baptist University, OK	M,W	Shepherd University, WV	M,W	Trinity Christian College, IL	M,W
Oklahoma Christian University, OK	M,W	Shippensburg University of		Troy University, AL	M,W
Oklahoma City University, OK	M,W	Pennsylvania, PA	M,W	Truett-McConnell College, GA	M,W
Oklahoma Panhandle State		Shorter University, GA	M,W	Truman State University, MO	M,W
University, OK	M,W	Siena College, NY	M,W	Tulane University, LA	M,W
Oklahoma State University, OK	M,W	Silver Lake College, WI	M,W	Tusculum College, TN	M,W
Oklahoma Wesleyan University, OK	M,W	Slippery Rock University of		Tuskegee University, AL	M,W
Old Dominion University, VA	M,W	Pennsylvania, PA	M,W	Union College, KY	M,W
Oral Roberts University, OK	M,W	Sonoma State University, CA	M,W	Union University, TN	M,W
Oregon Institute of Technology, OR	M	South Dakota School of Mines and		University at Albany, State University	
Oregon State University, OR	M,W	Technology, SD	M,W	of New York, NY	M,W
Ouachita Baptist University, AR	M,W	South Dakota State University, SD	M,W	University at Buffalo, the State	
Pace University, NY	M,W	Southeastern Louisiana		University of New York, NY	M,W
Palm Beach Atlantic University, FL	M,W	University, LA	M,W	The University of Akron, OH	M,W
Penn State University Park, PA	M,W	Southeastern Oklahoma State		The University of Alabama, AL	M,W
Pepperdine University, CA	M,W	University, OK	M,W	The University of Alabama at	
Philadelphia University, PA	M,W	Southeast Missouri State		Birmingham, AL	M,W
Pikeville College, KY	M,W	University, MO	M,W	The University of Alabama in	
Pittsburg State University, KS	M,W	Southern Arkansas University–		Huntsville, AL	M,W
Point Park University, PA	M,W	Magnolia, AR	M,W	University of Alaska Anchorage, AK	M,W
Portland State University, OR	M,W	Southern Connecticut State		University of Alaska Fairbanks, AK	M,W
Presbyterian College, SC	M,W	University, CT	M,W	The University of Arizona, AZ	M,W
Providence College, RI	M,W	Southern Illinois University		University of Arkansas, AR	M,W
Purdue University, IN	M,W	Carbondale, IL	M,W	University of Bridgeport, CT	M,W
Purdue University Calumet, IN	M,W	Southern Illinois University		University of California, Davis, CA	M,W
Purdue University North Central, IN	M	Edwardsville, IL	M,W	University of California, Irvine, CA	M,W
Queens College of the City University		Southern Methodist University, TX	M,W	University of California,	
of New York, NY	M,W	Southern Polytechnic State		Los Angeles, CA	M,W
Quincy University, IL	M,W	University, GA	M,W	University of California,	
Quinnipiac University, CT	M,W	Southern Utah University, UT	M,W	Riverside, CA	M,W
Radford University, VA	M,W	Southwest Baptist University, MO	M,W	University of California, Santa	
Reinhardt University, GA	M,W	Southwestern College, KS	M,W	Barbara, CA	M,W
Rider University, NJ	M,W	Southwestern Oklahoma State		University of Central Florida, FL	M,W
Robert Morris University, PA	M,W	University, OK	M,W	University of Central Missouri, MO	M,W
Robert Morris University Illinois, IL	M,W	Southwest Minnesota State		University of Central Oklahoma, OK	M,W
Roberts Wesleyan College, NY	M,W	University, MN		University of Charleston, WV	M,W
Rockhurst University, MO	M,W	Spring Arbor University, MI	M,W	University of Cincinnati, OH	M,W
Rocky Mountain College, MT	M,W	Spring Hill College, AL	M,W	University of Colorado at	
Rollins College, FL	M,W	Stanford University, CA	M,W	Boulder, CO	M,W
Sacred Heart University, CT	M,W	State University of New York at		University of Colorado at Colorado	
Saginaw Valley State University, MI	M,W	Binghamton, NY	M,W	Springs, CO	M,W
St. Ambrose University, IA	M,W	Stephen F. Austin State		University of Connecticut, CT	M,W
St. Andrews Presbyterian College, NC	M,W	University, TX	M,W	University of Dayton, OH	M,W
Saint Anselm College, NH	M,W	Stephens College, MO	W	University of Delaware, DE	M,W
St. Bonaventure University, NY	M,W	Stetson University, FL	M,W	University of Denver, CO	M,W
St. Edward's University, TX	M,W	Stonehill College, MA	M,W	University of Evansville, IN	M,W
Saint Francis University, PA	M,W	Stony Brook University, State		The University of Findlay, OH	M,W
St. John's University, NY	M,W	University of New York, NY	M,W	University of Florida, FL	M,W
Saint Joseph's University, PA	M,W	Syracuse University, NY	M,W	University of Georgia, GA	M,W
Saint Leo University, FL	M,W	Tabor College, KS	M,W	University of Great Falls, MT	M,W
Saint Louis University, MO	M,W	Tarleton State University, TX	M,W	University of Hartford, CT	M,W
Saint Martin's University, WA	M,W	Taylor University, IN	M,W	University of Hawaii at Hilo, HI	M
Saint Mary's College of		Temple University, PA	M,W	University of Houston, TX	M,W
California, CA	M,W	Tennessee Technological		University of Idaho, ID	M,W
St. Mary's University, TX	M,W	University, TN	M,W	University of Illinois at Chicago, IL	M,W
Saint Michael's College, VT	M,W	Tennessee Wesleyan College, TN	M,W	University of Illinois at	
Saint Paul's College, VA	M,W	Texas A&M University, TX	M,W	Springfield, IL	M,W
Saint Xavier University, IL	M	Texas A&M University–		University of Illinois at Urbana–	
Samford University, AL	M,W	Commerce, TX	M,W	Champaign, IL	M,W
Sam Houston State University, TX	M,W	Texas A&M University–Corpus		University of Indianapolis, IN	M,W
San Diego Christian College, CA	M,W	Christi, TX	M,W	The University of Iowa, IA	M,W
San Diego State University, CA	M,W	Texas Christian University, TX	M,W	The University of Kansas, KS	M,W
San Francisco State University, CA	M,W	Texas State University–		University of Kentucky, KY	M,W
San Jose State University, CA	M,W	San Marcos, TX	M,W	University of Louisiana at	
Santa Clara University, CA	M,W	Texas Tech University, TX	M,W	Monroe, LA	M,W

University of Louisville, KY	M,W	University of St. Francis, IL	M,W	Warner Pacific College, OR	M,W
University of Maine, ME	M,W	University of St. Thomas, TX	M	Washburn University, KS	M,W
University of Mary, ND	M,W	University of San Diego, CA	M,W	Washington State University, WA	M,W
University of Maryland, Baltimore County, MD	M,W	University of Science and Arts of Oklahoma, OK	M,W	Wayland Baptist University, TX	M,W
University of Maryland, College Park, MD	M,W	University of South Alabama, AL	M,W	Wayne State College, NE	M,W
		University of South Carolina, SC	M,W	Wayne State University, MI	M,W
University of Massachusetts Amherst, MA	M,W	University of South Carolina Aiken, SC	M,W	Webber International University, FL	M,W
University of Massachusetts Lowell, MA	M,W	The University of South Dakota, SD	M,W	West Chester University of Pennsylvania, PA	M,W
University of Memphis, TN	M,W	University of Southern California, CA	M,W	Western Carolina University, NC	M,W
University of Miami, FL	M,W	University of Southern Indiana, IN	M,W	Western Illinois University, IL	M,W
University of Michigan, MI	M,W	University of Southern Mississippi, MS	M,W	Western Kentucky University, KY	M,W
University of Michigan–Dearborn, MI	M,W	The University of Tampa, FL	M,W	Western Oregon University, OR	M,W
University of Minnesota, Crookston, MN	M,W	The University of Tennessee, TN	M,W	Western State College of Colorado, CO	M,W
University of Minnesota, Duluth, MN	M,W	The University of Tennessee at Chattanooga, TN	M,W	Western Washington University, WA	M,W
University of Minnesota, Twin Cities Campus, MN	M,W	The University of Tennessee at Martin, TN	M,W	West Liberty University, WV	M,W
University of Mississippi, MS	M,W	The University of Texas at Arlington, TX	M,W	Westminster College, UT	M,W
University of Missouri, MO	M,W	The University of Texas at Austin, TX	M,W	Westmont College, CA	M,W
University of Missouri–Kansas City, MO	M,W	The University of Texas at El Paso, TX	M,W	West Virginia University, WV	M,W
University of Missouri–St. Louis, MO	M,W	The University of Texas at San Antonio, TX	M,W	West Virginia Wesleyan College, WV	M,W
University of Mobile, AL	M,W	The University of Texas of the Permian Basin, TX	M,W	Wheeling Jesuit University, WV	M,W
The University of Montana Western, MT	M,W	The University of Texas–Pan American, TX	M,W	Wichita State University, KS	M,W
University of Montevallo, AL	M,W	University of the Incarnate Word, TX	M,W	William Jewell College, MO	M,W
University of Nebraska at Kearney, NE	M,W	University of the Pacific, CA	M,W	Winona State University, MN	M,W
University of Nebraska at Omaha, NE	M,W	University of the Sciences in Philadelphia, PA	M,W	Winthrop University, SC	M,W
University of Nebraska–Lincoln, NE	M,W	University of the Southwest, NM	M,W	Wofford College, SC	M,W
University of Nevada, Las Vegas, NV	M,W	The University of Toledo, OH	M,W	Wright State University, OH	M,W
University of Nevada, Reno, NV	M,W	University of Tulsa, OK	M,W	Xavier University, OH	M,W
University of New Hampshire, NH	M,W	University of Vermont, VT	M,W	Xavier University of Louisiana, LA	M,W
University of New Haven, CT	M,W	University of Virginia, VA	M,W	York College, NE	M,W
University of New Orleans, LA	M,W	The University of Virginia's College at Wise, VA	M,W	Youngstown State University, OH	M,W
University of North Alabama, AL	M,W	University of Washington, WA	M,W		
The University of North Carolina at Asheville, NC	M,W	The University of West Alabama, AL	M,W	**Bowling**	
The University of North Carolina at Chapel Hill, NC	M,W	University of West Florida, FL	M,W	Adelphi University, NY	W
The University of North Carolina at Charlotte, NC	M,W	University of West Georgia, GA	M,W	Arkansas State University—Jonesboro, AR	W
The University of North Carolina at Greensboro, NC	M,W	University of Wisconsin–Green Bay, WI	M,W	Bellarmine University, KY	W
The University of North Carolina at Pembroke, NC	M,W	University of Wisconsin–Madison, WI	M,W	Bethune-Cookman University, FL	W
The University of North Carolina Wilmington, NC	M,W	University of Wisconsin–Parkside, WI	M,W	Campbellsville University, KY	M,W
University of North Dakota, ND	M,W	University of Wyoming, WY	M,W	Clarke College, IA	M,W
University of Northern Colorado, CO	M,W	Ursuline College, OH	W	Fayetteville State University, NC	W
University of Northern Iowa, IA	M,W	Utah State University, UT	M,W	Hampton University, VA	W
University of North Florida, FL	M,W	Utah Valley University, UT	M,W	Johnson C. Smith University, NC	W
University of North Texas, TX	M,W	Valdosta State University, GA	M,W	Kutztown University of Pennsylvania, PA	W
University of Notre Dame, IN	M,W	Valley City State University, ND	M,W	Lindenwood University, MO	M,W
University of Oklahoma, OK	M,W	Valparaiso University, IN	M,W	Lindsey Wilson College, KY	M,W
University of Oregon, OR	M,W	Vanderbilt University, TN	M,W	McKendree University, IL	M,W
University of Pittsburgh, PA	M,W	Vanguard University of Southern California, CA	M,W	Newman University, KS	M,W
University of Pittsburgh at Johnstown, PA	M,W	Villanova University, PA	M,W	Pikeville College, KY	M,W
University of Portland, OR	M,W	Virginia Commonwealth University, VA	M,W	Robert Morris University Illinois, IL	M,W
University of Puerto Rico at Bayamón, PR	M,W	Virginia Intermont College, VA	M,W	Sacred Heart University, CT	W
		Virginia Military Institute, VA	M	Saginaw Valley State University, MI	M
University of Puerto Rico, Río Piedras, PR	M,W	Virginia Union University, VA	M,W	St. Ambrose University, IA	M,W
University of Rhode Island, RI	M,W	Wagner College, NY	M,W	Stephen F. Austin State University, TX	W
University of Richmond, VA	M,W	Wake Forest University, NC	M,W	Union College, KY	M,W
		Waldorf College, IA	M,W	University of Nebraska–Lincoln, NE	W
				Ursuline College, OH	W
				Valparaiso University, IN	W
				Vanderbilt University, TN	W
				Webber International University, FL	M,W
				Wichita State University, KS	M,W

Cheerleading

Adelphi University, NY	W
Arkansas Tech University, AR	M,W
Auburn University Montgomery, AL	M,W
Austin Peay State University, TN	M,W
Baylor University, TX	M,W

Benedictine College, KS	M,W
Bethel College, IN	M,W
Brevard College, NC	W
Brewton-Parker College, GA	M,W
Brigham Young University, UT	M,W
California Baptist University, CA	M,W
Campbellsville University, KY	M,W
Catawba College, NC	M,W
College of Charleston, SC	M,W
Culver-Stockton College, MO	M,W
Dakota Wesleyan University, SD	M,W
Delta State University, MS	M,W
Doane College, NE	W
Drake University, IA	M,W
Drury University, MO	M,W
Emporia State University, KS	M,W
Freed-Hardeman University, TN	W
Gardner-Webb University, NC	M,W
George Mason University, VA	M,W
Georgetown College, KY	W
Georgia Institute of Technology, GA	M,W
Grace College, IN	M,W
Hannibal-LaGrange College, MO	M,W
Hawai'i Pacific University, HI	M,W
Hofstra University, NY	M,W
Houston Baptist University, TX	M,W
Indiana Wesleyan University, IN	M,W
Kennesaw State University, GA	W
Kentucky State University, KY	W
King College, TN	M,W
Lewis University, IL	M,W
Lindenwood University, MO	M,W
Lindsey Wilson College, KY	M,W
Manhattan College, NY	M,W
McKendree University, IL	M,W
Metropolitan State College of Denver, CO	M,W
Mid-Continent University, KY	M,W
Midwestern State University, TX	M,W
Mississippi State University, MS	M,W
Montana State University, MT	M,W
Mountain State University, WV	W
Newberry College, SC	W
Northern Arizona University, AZ	M,W
North Greenville University, SC	M,W
Northwestern Oklahoma State University, OK	M,W
Nyack College, NY	M,W
Oklahoma City University, OK	M,W
Oklahoma Panhandle State University, OK	W
Old Dominion University, VA	M,W
Pikeville College, KY	M,W
Pittsburg State University, KS	M,W
Presbyterian College, SC	M,W
Reinhardt University, GA	M,W
Robert Morris University Illinois, IL	M,W
Rocky Mountain College, MT	W
St. Ambrose University, IA	M,W
St. Edward's University, TX	M,W
Savannah State University, GA	M,W
Shorter University, GA	M,W
Southeastern Louisiana University, LA	M,W
Southeast Missouri State University, MO	M,W
Southern Methodist University, TX	M,W
Southwestern College, KS	M,W
Tabor College, KS	M,W
Tarleton State University, TX	M,W

Temple University, PA	M,W
Tennessee Technological University, TN	M,W
Tennessee Wesleyan College, TN	M,W
Texas A&M University–Commerce, TX	M,W
Tiffin University, OH	M,W
Tusculum College, TN	W
Union College, KY	M,W
Union University, TN	W
The University of Alabama, AL	M,W
The University of Alabama in Huntsville, AL	M,W
University of Central Florida, FL	M,W
University of Charleston, WV	W
University of Delaware, DE	M,W
University of Great Falls, MT	M,W
University of Louisiana at Monroe, LA	M,W
University of Maryland, College Park, MD	W
University of Memphis, TN	M,W
University of Michigan, MI	M,W
University of Mississippi, MS	M,W
University of Mobile, AL	W
University of Nevada, Las Vegas, NV	M,W
The University of North Carolina Wilmington, NC	W
University of St. Francis, IL	W
University of Science and Arts of Oklahoma, OK	M,W
University of South Carolina Aiken, SC	M,W
The University of Tennessee, TN	M,W
The University of Texas of the Permian Basin, TX	M,W
University of the Incarnate Word, TX	W
University of West Georgia, GA	M,W
University of Wyoming, WY	M,W
Waldorf College, IA	W
Washburn University, KS	M,W
Wayland Baptist University, TX	M,W
West Chester University of Pennsylvania, PA	W
West Virginia University, WV	M,W
William Jewell College, MO	M,W

Crew

Barry University, FL	W
Boston College, MA	W
Boston University, MA	M,W
California State University, Sacramento, CA	M,W
Clemson University, SC	W
Creighton University, NE	W
Dowling College, NY	M,W
Duke University, NC	W
Duquesne University, PA	W
Eastern Michigan University, MI	W
Fairfield University, CT	M,W
Florida Institute of Technology, FL	W
Fordham University, NY	W
George Mason University, VA	W
The George Washington University, DC	M,W
Indiana University Bloomington, IN	W
Jacksonville University, FL	M,W
Kansas State University, KS	W
Lehigh University, PA	W
Loyola University Maryland, MD	M,W

Marist College, NY	W
Mercyhurst College, PA	M,W
Michigan State University, MI	W
Northeastern University, MA	M,W
Nova Southeastern University, FL	W
Old Dominion University, VA	W
Robert Morris University, PA	W
Robert Morris University Illinois, IL	W
Saint Joseph's University, PA	M,W
San Diego State University, CA	W
Southern Methodist University, TX	W
Stanford University, CA	M,W
Stetson University, FL	W
Syracuse University, NY	M,W
Temple University, PA	M,W
University at Buffalo, the State University of New York, NY	W
The University of Alabama, AL	W
University of California, Davis, CA	W
University of California, Los Angeles, CA	W
University of Charleston, WV	M,W
University of Delaware, DE	W
The University of Iowa, IA	W
The University of Kansas, KS	W
University of Louisville, KY	W
University of Massachusetts Amherst, MA	W
University of Miami, FL	M
The University of North Carolina at Chapel Hill, NC	W
University of Notre Dame, IN	W
University of Oklahoma, OK	W
University of Rhode Island, RI	W
University of San Diego, CA	M,W
University of Southern California, CA	W
The University of Tampa, FL	W
The University of Tennessee, TN	W
The University of Texas at Austin, TX	W
University of Tulsa, OK	W
University of Virginia, VA	W
University of Washington, WA	M,W
Villanova University, PA	W
Washington State University, WA	W
Western Washington University, WA	M,W
West Virginia University, WV	W

Cross-Country Running

Abilene Christian University, TX	M,W
Academy of Art University, CA	M,W
Adams State College, CO	M,W
Adelphi University, NY	M,W
Alabama Agricultural and Mechanical University, AL	M,W
Alabama State University, AL	M,W
Alderson-Broaddus College, WV	M,W
American International College, MA	M,W
American University, DC	M,W
Angelo State University, TX	M,W
Appalachian State University, NC	M,W
Arizona State University, AZ	M,W
Arkansas State University—Jonesboro, AR	M,W
Arkansas Tech University, AR	W
Asbury University, KY	M,W
Ashland University, OH	M,W
Auburn University, AL	M,W
Augustana College, SD	M,W
Austin Peay State University, TN	M,W
Azusa Pacific University, CA	M,W

Ball State University, IN	W	The Citadel, The Military College of		Florida Southern College, FL	M,W
Barton College, NC	M,W	South Carolina, SC	M,W	Florida State University, FL	M,W
Baylor University, TX	M,W	Clarion University of		Fordham University, NY	M,W
Belhaven University, MS	M,W	Pennsylvania, PA	W	Fort Lewis College, CO	M,W
Bellarmine University, KY	M,W	Clarke College, IA	M,W	Francis Marion University, SC	M,W
Belmont Abbey College, NC	M,W	Clemson University, SC	M,W	Furman University, SC	M,W
Belmont University, TN	M,W	Cleveland State University, OH	W	Gannon University, PA	M,W
Benedictine College, KS	M,W	Coastal Carolina University, SC	M,W	Gardner-Webb University, NC	M,W
Bentley University, MA	M,W	Coker College, SC	M,W	George Mason University, VA	M,W
Bethany College, KS	M,W	College of Charleston, SC	M,W	Georgetown College, KY	M,W
Bethel College, IN	M,W	College of Saint Mary, NE	W	Georgetown University, DC	M,W
Bethel College, KS	M,W	The College of William and		The George Washington	
Bethune-Cookman University, FL	M,W	Mary, VA	M,W	University, DC	M,W
Black Hills State University, SD	M,W	Colorado School of Mines, CO	M,W	Georgia College & State	
Bloomfield College, NJ	M,W	Colorado State University, CO	M,W	University, GA	M,W
Bloomsburg University of		Columbus State University, GA	M,W	Georgia Institute of Technology, GA	M,W
Pennsylvania, PA	M,W	Concordia University, CA	M,W	Georgian Court University, NJ	W
Bluefield College, VA	M,W	Concordia University, Nebraska, NE	M,W	Georgia Southern University, GA	W
Bluefield State College, WV	M,W	Concordia University, St. Paul, MN	M,W	Georgia State University, GA	M,W
Blue Mountain College, MS	M,W	Concord University, WV	M,W	Glenville State College, WV	M,W
Boise State University, ID	M,W	Converse College, SC	W	Goldey-Beacom College, DE	M,W
Boston College, MA	M,W	Coppin State University, MD	M,W	Grace College, IN	M,W
Boston University, MA	M,W	Corban University, OR	M,W	Graceland University, IA	M,W
Bowie State University, MD	M,W	Cornerstone University, MI	M,W	Grand Valley State University, MI	M,W
Bowling Green State University, OH	M,W	Covenant College, GA	M,W	Grand View University, IA	M,W
Bradley University, IL	M,W	Creighton University, NE	M,W	Hampton University, VA	M,W
Brenau University, GA	W	Culver-Stockton College, MO	M,W	Hannibal-LaGrange College, MO	M,W
Brescia University, KY	M,W	Daemen College, NY	M,W	Harding University, AR	M,W
Brevard College, NC	M,W	Dakota State University, SD	M,W	Hawai'i Pacific University, HI	M,W
Briar Cliff University, IA	M,W	Dakota Wesleyan University, SD	M,W	Henderson State University, AR	W
Brigham Young University, UT	M,W	Dallas Baptist University, TX	W	High Point University, NC	M,W
Bryan College, TN	M,W	Davenport University, MI	M,W	Hofstra University, NY	M,W
Bucknell University, PA	W	Davidson College, NC	M,W	Holy Family University, PA	M,W
Butler University, IN	M,W	Delta State University, MS	W	Houghton College, NY	M,W
California Baptist University, CA	M,W	DePaul University, IL	M,W	Houston Baptist University, TX	M,W
California Polytechnic State		Dickinson State University, ND	M,W	Humboldt State University, CA	M,W
University, San Luis Obispo, CA	M,W	Dillard University, LA	M,W	Huntington University, IN	M,W
California State Polytechnic		Doane College, NE	M,W	Idaho State University, ID	M,W
University, Pomona, CA	M,W	Dominican College, NY	W	Illinois Institute of Technology, IL	M,W
California State University,		Dordt College, IA	M,W	Illinois State University, IL	M,W
Chico, CA	M,W	Dowling College, NY	M,W	Indiana State University, IN	M,W
California State University,		Drake University, IA	M,W	Indiana University Bloomington, IN	M,W
Dominguez Hills, CA	W	Drury University, MO	M,W	Indiana University of	
California State University,		Duquesne University, PA	M,W	Pennsylvania, PA	M,W
Fresno, CA	M,W	East Carolina University, NC	M,W	Indiana University–Purdue University	
California State University,		Eastern Michigan University, MI	M,W	Fort Wayne, IN	M,W
Fullerton, CA	M,W	Eastern New Mexico University, NM	M,W	Indiana University–Purdue University	
California State University, Long		Eastern Washington University, WA	M,W	Indianapolis, IN	M,W
Beach, CA	M,W	East Stroudsburg University of		Indiana Wesleyan University, IN	M,W
California State University, Monterey		Pennsylvania, PA	M,W	Inter American University of Puerto	
Bay, CA	M,W	Edinboro University of		Rico, Bayamón Campus, PR	M,W
California State University,		Pennsylvania, PA	M,W	Iona College, NY	M,W
Northridge, CA	M,W	Elon University, NC	M,W	Iowa State University of Science and	
California State University,		Embry-Riddle Aeronautical		Technology, IA	M,W
Sacramento, CA	M,W	University, FL	M,W	Iowa Wesleyan College, IA	M,W
Cameron University, OK	M	Emporia State University, KS	M,W	Jacksonville State University, AL	M,W
Campbellsville University, KY	M,W	Erskine College, SC	M,W	Jacksonville University, FL	W
Canisius College, NY	M,W	Evangel University, MO	M,W	James Madison University, VA	W
Carson-Newman College, TN	M,W	The Evergreen State College, WA	M,W	Jamestown College, ND	M,W
Catawba College, NC	M,W	Fairfield University, CT	M,W	Johnson C. Smith University, NC	M,W
Cedarville University, OH	M,W	Felician College, NJ	M,W	Kansas State University, KS	M,W
Centenary College of Louisiana, LA	M,W	Ferris State University, MI	M,W	Kennesaw State University, GA	M,W
Central Connecticut State		Flagler College, FL	M,W	Kent State University, OH	M,W
University, CT	M,W	Florida Agricultural and Mechanical		Kentucky State University, KY	M,W
Central Michigan University, MI	M,W	University, FL	M,W	Kentucky Wesleyan College, KY	M,W
Chaminade University of		Florida College, FL	M,W	King College, TN	M,W
Honolulu, HI	M,W	Florida Gulf Coast University, FL	M,W	Kutztown University of	
Christian Brothers University, TN	M,W	Florida Institute of Technology, FL	M,W	Pennsylvania, PA	M,W
		Florida International University, FL	M,W	Lake Superior State University, MI	M,W

Lamar University, TX	M,W	Mount St. Mary's University, MD	M,W	St. Andrews Presbyterian College, NC	M,W
Lees-McRae College, NC	M,W	Mount Vernon Nazarene		St. Bonaventure University, NY	M,W
Lee University, TN	M,W	University, OH	M,W	Saint Francis University, PA	M,W
Lehigh University, PA	M,W	Murray State University, KY	M,W	St. John's University, NY	W
Le Moyne College, NY	M,W	Newberry College, SC	M,W	Saint Joseph's University, PA	M,W
Lewis-Clark State College, ID	M,W	New Jersey Institute of		Saint Leo University, FL	M,W
Lewis University, IL	M,W	Technology, NJ	M,W	Saint Louis University, MO	M,W
Limestone College, SC	M,W	Newman University, KS	M,W	Saint Martin's University, WA	M,W
Lincoln Memorial University, TN	M,W	New Mexico State University, NM	M,W	Saint Mary's College of	
Lincoln University, MO	W	New York Institute of		California, CA	M,W
Lindenwood University, MO	M,W	Technology, NY	M,W	St. Thomas University, FL	M,W
Lindsey Wilson College, KY	M,W	Niagara University, NY	M,W	Saint Xavier University, IL	W
Lipscomb University, TN	M,W	Nicholls State University, LA	M,W	Samford University, AL	M,W
Lock Haven University of		North Carolina Agricultural and		Sam Houston State University, TX	M,W
Pennsylvania, PA	M,W	Technical State University, NC	M,W	San Diego Christian College, CA	M,W
Long Island University, Brooklyn		North Carolina State University, NC	M,W	San Diego State University, CA	W
Campus, NY	M,W	Northeastern University, MA	M,W	San Francisco State University, CA	M,W
Long Island University, C.W. Post		Northern Arizona University, AZ	M,W	San Jose State University, CA	M,W
Campus, NY	M,W	Northern Kentucky University, KY	M,W	Santa Clara University, CA	M,W
Longwood University, VA	M,W	Northern Michigan University, MI	W	Savannah College of Art and	
Louisiana State University and		Northern State University, SD	M,W	Design, GA	M,W
Agricultural and Mechanical		North Greenville University, SC	M,W	Savannah State University, GA	M,W
College, LA	M,W	Northwest Christian University, OR	M,W	Seattle Pacific University, WA	M,W
Louisiana Tech University, LA	M,W	Northwestern Oklahoma State		Seattle University, WA	M,W
Loyola University Chicago, IL	M,W	University, OK	M,W	Seton Hill University, PA	M,W
Loyola University Maryland, MD	M,W	Northwestern State University of		Shippensburg University of	
Malone University, OH	M,W	Louisiana, LA	M,W	Pennsylvania, PA	M,W
Manhattan College, NY	M,W	Northwest Nazarene University, ID	M,W	Shorter University, GA	M,W
Mansfield University of		Northwest University, WA	M,W	Silver Lake College, WI	M,W
Pennsylvania, PA	M,W	Notre Dame de Namur		Slippery Rock University of	
Marist College, NY	M,W	University, CA	M,W	Pennsylvania, PA	M,W
Marquette University, WI	M,W	Nova Southeastern University, FL	M,W	Sonoma State University, CA	M
Marshall University, WV	M,W	Nyack College, NY	M,W	South Dakota School of Mines and	
Maryville University of Saint		Oakland University, MI	M,W	Technology, SD	M,W
Louis, MO	M,W	The Ohio State University, OH	M,W	South Dakota State University, SD	M,W
The Master's College and		Ohio University, OH	M,W	Southeastern Louisiana	
Seminary, CA	M,W	Ohio Valley University, WV	M,W	University, LA	M,W
McKendree University, IL	M,W	Oklahoma Baptist University, OK	M,W	Southeastern Oklahoma State	
Mercer University, GA	M,W	Oklahoma Christian University, OK	M,W	University, OK	W
Mercyhurst College, PA	M,W	Oklahoma Panhandle State		Southeast Missouri State	
Merrimack College, MA	W	University, OK	M,W	University, MO	M,W
Miami University, OH	M,W	Oklahoma State University, OK	M,W	Southern Arkansas University–	
Michigan State University, MI	M,W	Oklahoma Wesleyan University, OK	M,W	Magnolia, AR	W
Midwestern State University, TX	W	Oral Roberts University, OK	M,W	Southern Connecticut State	
Millersville University of		Oregon Institute of Technology, OR	M,W	University, CT	M,W
Pennsylvania, PA	M,W	Ouachita Baptist University, AR	W	Southern Illinois University	
Milligan College, TN	M,W	Pace University, NY	M,W	Carbondale, IL	M,W
Minnesota State University		Palm Beach Atlantic University, FL	M,W	Southern Illinois University	
Mankato, MN	M,W	Penn State University Park, PA	M,W	Edwardsville, IL	M,W
Mississippi State University, MS	M,W	Pepperdine University, CA	M,W	Southern Methodist University, TX	W
Mississippi Valley State		Pikeville College, KY	M,W	Southwest Baptist University, MO	M,W
University, MS	M,W	Pittsburg State University, KS	M,W	Southwestern College, KS	M,W
Missouri Southern State		Point Park University, PA	M,W	Southwestern Oklahoma State	
University, MO	M,W	Portland State University, OR	M,W	University, OK	W
Missouri State University, MO	W	Presbyterian College, SC	M,W	Spring Arbor University, MI	M,W
Missouri University of Science and		Providence College, RI	M,W	Spring Hill College, AL	M,W
Technology, MO	M,W	Purdue University, IN	M,W	Stanford University, CA	M,W
Molloy College, NY	M,W	Queens College of the City University		State University of New York at	
Monmouth University, NJ	M,W	of New York, NY	M,W	Binghamton, NY	M,W
Montana State University, MT	M,W	Quinnipiac University, CT	M,W	Stephen F. Austin State	
Montana State University		Radford University, VA	M,W	University, TX	M,W
Billings, MT	M,W	Reinhardt University, GA	M,W	Stephens College, MO	W
Morehead State University, KY	M,W	Rider University, NJ	M,W	Stetson University, FL	M,W
Morehouse College, GA	M	Robert Morris University Illinois, IL	M,W	Stonehill College, MA	M,W
Morningside College, IA	M,W	Roberts Wesleyan College, NY	M,W	Stony Brook University, State	
Mountain State University, WV	M,W	Rocky Mountain College, MT	M,W	University of New York, NY	M,W
Mount Marty College, SD	M,W	Sacred Heart University, CT	M,W	Syracuse University, NY	M,W
Mount Mercy College, IA	M,W	Saginaw Valley State University, MI	M,W	Tabor College, KS	M,W
Mount Olive College, NC	M,W	St. Ambrose University, IA	M,W	Tarleton State University, TX	M,W

Taylor University, IN	M,W	The University of Kansas, KS	M,W	University of Southern	
Tennessee Technological		University of Kentucky, KY	M,W	Mississippi, MS	W
University, TN	M,W	University of Louisiana at		The University of Tampa, FL	M,W
Tennessee Wesleyan College, TN	M,W	Monroe, LA	M,W	The University of Tennessee, TN	M,W
Texas A&M University, TX	M,W	University of Louisville, KY	M,W	The University of Tennessee at	
Texas A&M University–		University of Maine, ME	M,W	Chattanooga, TN	M,W
Commerce, TX	M,W	University of Mary, ND	M,W	The University of Tennessee at	
Texas A&M University–Corpus		University of Maryland, Baltimore		Martin, TN	M,W
Christi, TX	M,W	County, MD	M,W	The University of Texas at	
Texas Christian University, TX	M,W	University of Maryland, College		Arlington, TX	M,W
Texas State University–		Park, MD	M,W	The University of Texas at El	
San Marcos, TX	M,W	University of Massachusetts		Paso, TX	M,W
Texas Tech University, TX	M,W	Amherst, MA	M,W	The University of Texas at	
Tiffin University, OH	M,W	University of Massachusetts		San Antonio, TX	M,W
Towson University, MD	M,W	Lowell, MA	M,W	The University of Texas of the	
Trinity Christian College, IL	M,W	University of Memphis, TN	M,W	Permian Basin, TX	M,W
Troy University, AL	M,W	University of Miami, FL	M,W	The University of Texas–Pan	
Truett-McConnell College, GA	M,W	University of Michigan, MI	M,W	American, TX	M,W
Truman State University, MO	M,W	University of Minnesota, Duluth, MN	M,W	University of the Incarnate Word, TX	M,W
Tulane University, LA	M,W	University of Minnesota, Twin Cities		University of the Pacific, CA	W
Tusculum College, TN	M,W	Campus, MN	M,W	University of the Southwest, NM	M,W
Union College, KY	M,W	University of Mississippi, MS	M,W	The University of Toledo, OH	M,W
Union University, TN	W	University of Missouri, MO	M,W	University of Tulsa, OK	M,W
University at Albany, State University		University of Missouri–Kansas		University of Vermont, VT	M,W
of New York, NY	M,W	City, MO	M,W	University of Virginia, VA	M,W
University at Buffalo, the State		University of Mobile, AL	M,W	The University of Virginia's College	
University of New York, NY	M,W	University of Nebraska at		at Wise, VA	M,W
The University of Akron, OH	M,W	Kearney, NE	M,W	University of Washington, WA	M,W
The University of Alabama, AL	M,W	University of Nebraska at Omaha, NE	W	The University of West Alabama, AL	M,W
The University of Alabama at		University of Nebraska–Lincoln, NE	M,W	University of West Florida, FL	M,W
Birmingham, AL	W	University of Nevada, Las Vegas, NV	W	University of West Georgia, GA	M,W
The University of Alabama in		University of Nevada, Reno, NV	W	University of Wisconsin–Green	
Huntsville, AL	M,W	University of New Hampshire, NH	M,W	Bay, WI	M,W
University of Alaska Anchorage, AK	M	University of New Haven, CT	M,W	University of Wisconsin–	
University of Alaska Fairbanks, AK	M,W	University of North Alabama, AL	M,W	Madison, WI	
The University of Arizona, AZ	M,W	The University of North Carolina at		University of Wisconsin–	
University of Arkansas, AR	M,W	Asheville, NC	M,W	Parkside, WI	M,W
University of California, Davis, CA	M,W	The University of North Carolina at		University of Wyoming, WY	M,W
University of California, Irvine, CA	M,W	Chapel Hill, NC	M,W	Ursuline College, OH	W
University of California,		The University of North Carolina at		Utah State University, UT	M,W
Los Angeles, CA	M,W	Charlotte, NC	M,W	Utah Valley University, UT	M,W
University of California,		The University of North Carolina at		Valdosta State University, GA	M,W
Riverside, CA	M,W	Greensboro, NC	M,W	Valparaiso University, IN	M,W
University of California, Santa		The University of North Carolina at		Vanderbilt University, TN	M,W
Barbara, CA	M,W	Pembroke, NC	M,W	Vanguard University of Southern	
University of Central Florida, FL	M,W	The University of North Carolina		California, CA	M,W
University of Central Missouri, MO	M,W	Wilmington, NC	M,W	Villanova University, PA	M,W
University of Central Oklahoma, OK	M,W	University of Northern Colorado, CO	W	Virginia Commonwealth	
University of Charleston, WV	M,W	University of Northern Iowa, IA	M,W	University, VA	M,W
University of Cincinnati, OH	M,W	University of North Florida, FL	M,W	Virginia Military Institute, VA	M,W
University of Colorado at		University of North Texas, TX	M,W	Virginia Union University, VA	M,W
Boulder, CO	M,W	University of Notre Dame, IN	M,W	Wagner College, NY	M,W
University of Colorado at Colorado		University of Oklahoma, OK	M,W	Wake Forest University, NC	M,W
Springs, CO	M,W	University of Oregon, OR	M,W	Warner Pacific College, OR	M,W
University of Connecticut, CT	M,W	University of Pittsburgh, PA	M,W	Washington State University, WA	M,W
University of Dayton, OH	M,W	University of Portland, OR	M,W	Wayland Baptist University, TX	M,W
University of Evansville, IN	M,W	University of Puerto Rico, Río		Wayne State College, NE	M,W
The University of Findlay, OH	M,W	Piedras, PR	M,W	Wayne State University, MI	M,W
University of Florida, FL	M,W	University of Rhode Island, RI	M,W	Webber International University, FL	M,W
University of Georgia, GA	M,W	University of Richmond, VA	W	West Chester University of	
University of Hartford, CT	M,W	University of St. Francis, IL	M,W	Pennsylvania, PA	M,W
University of Hawaii at Hilo, HI	M,W	University of San Diego, CA	M,W	Western Carolina University, NC	M,W
University of Houston, TX	M,W	University of South Alabama, AL	M,W	Western Illinois University, IL	M,W
University of Idaho, ID	M,W	University of South Carolina, SC	W	Western Kentucky University, KY	M,W
University of Illinois at Chicago, IL	M,W	University of South Carolina		Western Oregon University, OR	M,W
University of Illinois at Urbana–		Aiken, SC	W	Western State College of	
Champaign, IL	M,W	The University of South Dakota, SD	M,W	Colorado, CO	M,W
University of Indianapolis, IN	M,W	University of Southern California, CA	W	Western Washington University, WA	M,W
The University of Iowa, IA	M,W	University of Southern Indiana, IN	M,W	West Liberty University, WV	M,W

Westmont College, CA	M,W
West Virginia University, WV	W
West Virginia Wesleyan College, WV	M,W
Wheeling Jesuit University, WV	M,W
Wichita State University, KS	M,W
William Jewell College, MO	M,W
Winona State University, MN	W
Winthrop University, SC	M,W
Wofford College, SC	M,W
Wright State University, OH	M,W
Xavier University, OH	M,W
Youngstown State University, OH	M,W

Equestrian Sports

Auburn University, AL	W
Baylor University, TX	W
California State University, Fresno, CA	W
Murray State University, KY	M,W
Oklahoma Panhandle State University, OK	W
Oklahoma State University, OK	W
St. Andrews Presbyterian College, NC	M,W
Savannah College of Art and Design, GA	M,W
Seton Hill University, PA	M,W
Southern Methodist University, TX	W
Southwestern Oklahoma State University, OK	M,W
Stonehill College, MA	W
Texas A&M University, TX	W
Texas Christian University, TX	W
Tiffin University, OH	M,W
University of Georgia, GA	W
University of Great Falls, MT	M,W
University of Minnesota, Crookston, MN	W
University of South Carolina, SC	W
The University of Tennessee at Martin, TN	W
Virginia Intermont College, VA	M,W

Fencing

Cleveland State University, OH	M,W
New Jersey Institute of Technology, NJ	M,W
The Ohio State University, OH	M,W
Penn State University Park, PA	M,W
Queens College of the City University of New York, NY	W
Sacred Heart University, CT	W
St. John's University, NY	M,W
Stanford University, CA	M,W
Temple University, PA	W
University of Notre Dame, IN	M,W
Wayne State University, MI	M,W

Field Hockey

Adelphi University, NY	W
American International College, MA	W
American University, DC	W
Appalachian State University, NC	W
Ball State University, IN	W
Bellarmine University, KY	W
Bentley University, MA	W
Bloomsburg University of Pennsylvania, PA	W
Boston College, MA	W
Boston University, MA	W
Bryant University, RI	W

Central Michigan University, MI	W
Colgate University, NY	W
College of the Holy Cross, MA	W
The College of William and Mary, VA	M,W
Davidson College, NC	W
Duke University, NC	W
East Stroudsburg University of Pennsylvania, PA	W
Fairfield University, CT	W
Hofstra University, NY	W
Houghton College, NY	W
Indiana University of Pennsylvania, PA	W
James Madison University, VA	W
Kent State University, OH	W
Kutztown University of Pennsylvania, PA	W
Lehigh University, PA	W
Limestone College, SC	W
Lindenwood University, MO	W
Lock Haven University of Pennsylvania, PA	W
Long Island University, C.W. Post Campus, NY	W
Longwood University, VA	W
Mansfield University of Pennsylvania, PA	W
Mercyhurst College, PA	W
Merrimack College, MA	W
Miami University, OH	W
Michigan State University, MI	W
Millersville University of Pennsylvania, PA	W
Missouri State University, MO	W
Monmouth University, NJ	W
Northeastern University, MA	W
The Ohio State University, OH	W
Ohio University, OH	W
Old Dominion University, VA	W
Penn State University Park, PA	W
Philadelphia University, PA	W
Providence College, RI	W
Quinnipiac University, CT	W
Radford University, VA	W
Rider University, NJ	W
Robert Morris University, PA	W
Sacred Heart University, CT	W
Saint Francis University, PA	W
Saint Joseph's University, PA	W
Saint Louis University, MO	W
Seton Hill University, PA	W
Shippensburg University of Pennsylvania, PA	W
Slippery Rock University of Pennsylvania, PA	W
Southern Connecticut State University, CT	W
Stanford University, CA	W
Stonehill College, MA	W
Syracuse University, NY	W
Temple University, PA	W
Towson University, MD	W
University at Albany, State University of New York, NY	W
University of California, Davis, CA	W
University of Connecticut, CT	W
University of Delaware, DE	W
The University of Iowa, IA	W
University of Louisville, KY	W

University of Maine, ME	W
University of Maryland, College Park, MD	W
University of Massachusetts Amherst, MA	W
University of Massachusetts Lowell, MA	W
University of Michigan, MI	W
University of New Hampshire, NH	W
The University of North Carolina at Chapel Hill, NC	W
University of Richmond, VA	W
University of the Pacific, CA	W
University of Vermont, VT	W
University of Virginia, VA	W
Villanova University, PA	W
Virginia Commonwealth University, VA	W
Wake Forest University, NC	W
West Chester University of Pennsylvania, PA	W

Football

Abilene Christian University, TX	M
Adams State College, CO	M
Alabama Agricultural and Mechanical University, AL	M
Alabama State University, AL	M
American International College, MA	M
Angelo State University, TX	M
Appalachian State University, NC	M
Arizona State University, AZ	M
Arkansas State University— Jonesboro, AR	M
Arkansas Tech University, AR	M
Ashland University, OH	M
Auburn University, AL	M
Augustana College, SD	M
Austin Peay State University, TN	M
Azusa Pacific University, CA	M
Ball State University, IN	M
Baylor University, TX	M
Belhaven University, MS	M
Bemidji State University, MN	M
Benedictine College, KS	M
Bentley University, MA	M
Bethany College, KS	M
Bethel College, KS	M
Bethune-Cookman University, FL	M
Black Hills State University, SD	M
Blessing-Rieman College of Nursing, IL	M
Bloomsburg University of Pennsylvania, PA	M
Boise State University, ID	M
Boston College, MA	M
Bowie State University, MD	M
Bowling Green State University, OH	M
Brevard College, NC	M
Briar Cliff University, IA	M
Brigham Young University, UT	M
Bryant University, RI	M
California Polytechnic State University, San Luis Obispo, CA	M
California State University, Fresno, CA	M
California State University, Northridge, CA	M
California State University, Sacramento, CA	M

Athletic Grants for Undergraduates
Football

Campbellsville University, KY	M	Indiana State University, IN	M	Northern State University, SD	M
Carson-Newman College, TN	M	Indiana University Bloomington, IN	M	North Greenville University, SC	M
Catawba College, NC	M	Indiana University of		Northwestern Oklahoma State	
Central Michigan University, MI	M	Pennsylvania, PA	M	University, OK	M
Chowan University, NC	M	Iowa State University of Science and		Northwestern State University of	
The Citadel, The Military College of		Technology, IA	M	Louisiana, LA	M
South Carolina, SC	M	Iowa Wesleyan College, IA	M	The Ohio State University, OH	M
Clarion University of		Jacksonville State University, AL	M	Ohio University, OH	M
Pennsylvania, PA	M	James Madison University, VA	M	Oklahoma Panhandle State	
Clemson University, SC	M	Jamestown College, ND	M	University, OK	M
Coastal Carolina University, SC	M	Johnson C. Smith University, NC	M	Oklahoma State University, OK	M
The College of William and Mary, VA	M	Kansas State University, KS	M	Old Dominion University, VA	M
Colorado School of Mines, CO	M	Kent State University, OH	M	Oregon State University, OR	M
Colorado State University, CO	M	Kentucky State University, KY	M	Ouachita Baptist University, AR	M
Concordia University, Nebraska, NE	M	Kentucky Wesleyan College, KY	M	Penn State University Park, PA	M
Concordia University, St. Paul, MN	M	Kutztown University of		Pikeville College, KY	M
Concord University, WV	M	Pennsylvania, PA	M	Pittsburg State University, KS	M
Culver-Stockton College, MO	M	Lamar University, TX	M	Portland State University, OR	M
Dakota State University, SD	M	Lane College, TN	M	Presbyterian College, SC	M
Dakota Wesleyan University, SD	M	Lincoln University, MO	M	Purdue University, IN	M
Dallas Baptist University, TX	W	Lindenwood University, MO	M	Quincy University, IL	M
Davidson College, NC	M	Lindsey Wilson College, KY	M,W	Robert Morris University, PA	M
Delta State University, MS	M	Lock Haven University of		Rocky Mountain College, MT	M
Dickinson State University, ND	M	Pennsylvania, PA	M	Sacred Heart University, CT	M
Dixie State College of Utah, UT	M	Louisiana State University and		Saginaw Valley State University, MI	M
Doane College, NE	M	Agricultural and Mechanical		St. Ambrose University, IA	M
Dordt College, IA	M	College, LA	M	Saint Paul's College, VA	M
Duke University, NC	M	Louisiana Tech University, LA	M	Saint Xavier University, IL	M
Duquesne University, PA	M	Malone University, OH	M	Samford University, AL	M
East Carolina University, NC	M	Marshall University, WV	M	Sam Houston State University, TX	M
Eastern Michigan University, MI	M	McKendree University, IL	M	San Diego State University, CA	M
Eastern New Mexico University, NM	M	Mercyhurst College, PA	M	San Jose State University, CA	M
Eastern Washington University, WA	M	Miami University, OH	M	Savannah State University, GA	M
East Stroudsburg University of		Michigan State University, MI	M	Seton Hill University, PA	M
Pennsylvania, PA	M	Michigan Technological		Shepherd University, WV	M
Edinboro University of		University, MI	M	Shippensburg University of	
Pennsylvania, PA	M	Midwestern State University, TX	M	Pennsylvania, PA	M
Elon University, NC	M	Millersville University of		Shorter University, GA	M
Emporia State University, KS	M	Pennsylvania, PA	M	Slippery Rock University of	
Evangel University, MO	M	Minnesota State University		Pennsylvania, PA	M
Fairmont State University, WV	M	Mankato, MN	M	South Dakota School of Mines and	
Faulkner University, AL	M	Minnesota State University		Technology, SD	M
Fayetteville State University, NC	M,W	Moorhead, MN	M	South Dakota State University, SD	M
Ferris State University, MI	M	Mississippi State University, MS	M	Southeastern Louisiana University, LA	M
Florida Agricultural and Mechanical		Mississippi Valley State		Southeastern Oklahoma State	
University, FL	M	University, MS	M	University, OK	M
Florida Atlantic University, FL	M	Missouri Southern State		Southeast Missouri State	
Florida International University, FL	M	University, MO	M	University, MO	M
Florida State University, FL	M	Missouri State University, MO	M	Southern Arkansas University–	
Fort Lewis College, CO	M	Missouri University of Science and		Magnolia, AR	M
Fort Valley State University, GA	M	Technology, MO	M	Southern Connecticut State	
Furman University, SC	M	Monmouth University, NJ	M	University, CT	M
Gannon University, PA	M	Montana State University, MT	M	Southern Illinois University	
Gardner-Webb University, NC	M	Montana Tech of The University of		Carbondale, IL	M
Georgetown College, KY	M	Montana, MT	M	Southern Methodist University, TX	M
Georgetown University, DC	M	Morehouse College, GA	M	Southern Utah University, UT	M
Georgia Institute of Technology, GA	M	Morningside College, IA	M	Southwest Baptist University, MO	M
Georgia Southern University, GA	M	Murray State University, KY	M	Southwestern College, KS	M
Georgia State University, GA	M	Newberry College, SC	M	Southwestern Oklahoma State	
Glenville State College, WV	M	New Mexico State University, NM	M	University, OK	M
Graceland University, IA	M	Nicholls State University, LA	M	Southwest Minnesota State	
Grand Valley State University, MI	M	Norfolk State University, VA	M	University, MN	M
Grand View University, IA	M	North Carolina Agricultural and		Stanford University, CA	M
Hampton University, VA	M	Technical State University, NC	M	Stephen F. Austin State University, TX	M
Harding University, AR	M	North Carolina State University, NC	M	Stonehill College, MA	M
Henderson State University, AR	M	Northeastern State University, OK	M	Stony Brook University, State	
Humboldt State University, CA	M	Northeastern University, MA	M	University of New York, NY	M
Idaho State University, ID	M	Northern Arizona University, AZ	M	Syracuse University, NY	M
Illinois State University, IL	M	Northern Michigan University, MI	M	Tabor College, KS	M

Tarleton State University, TX	M
Taylor University, IN	M
Temple University, PA	M
Tennessee Technological University, TN	M
Texas A&M University, TX	M
Texas A&M University–Commerce, TX	M
Texas Christian University, TX	M
Texas State University–San Marcos, TX	M
Texas Tech University, TX	M
Tiffin University, OH	M
Towson University, MD	M
Troy University, AL	M
Truman State University, MO	M
Tulane University, LA	M
Tusculum College, TN	M
Tuskegee University, AL	M
Union College, KY	M
University at Albany, State University of New York, NY	M
University at Buffalo, the State University of New York, NY	M
The University of Akron, OH	M
The University of Alabama, AL	M
The University of Alabama at Birmingham, AL	M
The University of Arizona, AZ	M
University of Arkansas, AR	M
University of California, Davis, CA	M
University of California, Los Angeles, CA	M
University of Central Florida, FL	M
University of Central Missouri, MO	M
University of Central Oklahoma, OK	M
University of Charleston, WV	M
University of Cincinnati, OH	M
University of Colorado at Boulder, CO	M
University of Connecticut, CT	M
University of Delaware, DE	M
The University of Findlay, OH	M
University of Florida, FL	M
University of Georgia, GA	M
University of Houston, TX	M
University of Idaho, ID	M
University of Illinois at Urbana–Champaign, IL	M
University of Indianapolis, IN	M
The University of Iowa, IA	M
The University of Kansas, KS	M
University of Kentucky, KY	M
University of Louisiana at Monroe, LA	M
University of Louisville, KY	M
University of Maine, ME	M
University of Mary, ND	M
University of Maryland, College Park, MD	M
University of Massachusetts Amherst, MA	M
University of Memphis, TN	M
University of Miami, FL	M
University of Michigan, MI	M
University of Minnesota, Crookston, MN	M
University of Minnesota, Duluth, MN	M
University of Minnesota, Twin Cities Campus, MN	M

University of Mississippi, MS	M
University of Missouri, MO	M
The University of Montana Western, MT	M
University of Nebraska at Kearney, NE	M
University of Nebraska at Omaha, NE	M
University of Nebraska–Lincoln, NE	M
University of Nevada, Las Vegas, NV	M
University of Nevada, Reno, NV	M
University of New Hampshire, NH	M
University of New Haven, CT	M
University of North Alabama, AL	M
The University of North Carolina at Chapel Hill, NC	M
The University of North Carolina at Pembroke, NC	M
University of North Dakota, ND	M
University of Northern Colorado, CO	M
University of Northern Iowa, IA	M
University of North Texas, TX	M
University of Notre Dame, IN	M
University of Oklahoma, OK	M
University of Oregon, OR	M
University of Pittsburgh, PA	M
University of Rhode Island, RI	M
University of Richmond, VA	M
University of St. Francis, IL	M
University of South Carolina, SC	M
The University of South Dakota, SD	M
University of Southern California, CA	M
University of Southern Mississippi, MS	M,W
The University of Tennessee, TN	M
The University of Tennessee at Chattanooga, TN	M
The University of Tennessee at Martin, TN	M
The University of Texas at Austin, TX	M
The University of Texas at El Paso, TX	M
University of the Incarnate Word, TX	M
The University of Toledo, OH	M
University of Tulsa, OK	M
University of Virginia, VA	M
The University of Virginia's College at Wise, VA	M
University of Washington, WA	M
The University of West Alabama, AL	M
University of West Georgia, GA	M
University of Wisconsin–Madison, WI	M
University of Wyoming, WY	M
Utah State University, UT	M
Valdosta State University, GA	M
Valley City State University, ND	M
Vanderbilt University, TN	M
Villanova University, PA	M
Virginia Military Institute, VA	M
Virginia Polytechnic Institute and State University, VA	M
Virginia Union University, VA	M
Wagner College, NY	M
Wake Forest University, NC	M
Waldorf College, IA	M
Washburn University, KS	M
Washington State University, WA	M
Wayne State College, NE	M
Wayne State University, MI	M
Webber International University, FL	M

West Chester University of Pennsylvania, PA	M
Western Carolina University, NC	M
Western Illinois University, IL	M
Western Kentucky University, KY	M
Western Oregon University, OR	M
Western State College of Colorado, CO	M
West Liberty University, WV	M
West Virginia University, WV	M
West Virginia Wesleyan College, WV	M
William Jewell College, MO	M
Winona State University, MN	M
Wofford College, SC	M
Youngstown State University, OH	M

Golf

Abilene Christian University, TX	M
Abraham Baldwin Agricultural College, GA	M
Academy of Art University, CA	M,W
Adams State College, CO	M,W
Adelphi University, NY	M
Alabama Agricultural and Mechanical University, AL	M
Alabama State University, AL	M,W
Angelo State University, TX	W
Appalachian State University, NC	M,W
Arizona State University, AZ	M,W
Arkansas State University—Jonesboro, AR	M,W
Arkansas Tech University, AR	M
Armstrong Atlantic State University, GA	M,W
Ashland University, OH	M,W
Auburn University, AL	M,W
Augustana College, SD	W
Austin Peay State University, TN	M,W
Azusa Pacific University, CA	M
Ball State University, IN	M,W
Barry University, FL	M,W
Barton College, NC	M
Baylor University, TX	M,W
Belhaven University, MS	M,W
Bellarmine University, KY	M,W
Belmont Abbey College, NC	M,W
Belmont University, TN	M,W
Benedictine College, KS	M,W
Bethany College, KS	M
Bethel College, IN	M,W
Bethel College, KS	M,W
Bethune-Cookman University, FL	M,W
Bluefield College, VA	M
Bluefield State College, WV	M
Blue Mountain College, MS	M
Boise State University, ID	M,W
Boston College, MA	M,W
Bowling Green State University, OH	M,W
Bradley University, IL	M,W
Brescia University, KY	M,W
Brevard College, NC	M,W
Briar Cliff University, IA	M,W
Brigham Young University, UT	M,W
Bryant University, RI	M
Butler University, IN	M,W
California Baptist University, CA	M,W
California Maritime Academy, CA	M
California Polytechnic State University, San Luis Obispo, CA	M,W
California State University, Chico, CA	M,W

College	
California State University, Fresno, CA	M,W
California State University, Fullerton, CA	M,W
California State University, Monterey Bay, CA	M,W
California State University, Northridge, CA	M
California State University, Sacramento, CA	M
California State University, San Bernardino, CA	M
Cameron University, OK	M,W
Campbellsville University, KY	M,W
Canisius College, NY	M
Carson-Newman College, TN	M
Catawba College, NC	M,W
Cedarville University, OH	M
Centenary College of Louisiana, LA	M,W
Central Connecticut State University, CT	M,W
Chowan University, NC	M
Christian Brothers University, TN	M,W
The Citadel, The Military College of South Carolina, SC	W
Clarion University of Pennsylvania, PA	M
Clarke College, IA	M,W
Clemson University, SC	M
Cleveland State University, OH	M
Coastal Carolina University, SC	M,W
Coker College, SC	M
College of Charleston, SC	M,W
The College of William and Mary, VA	M,W
Colorado State University, CO	M,W
Columbus State University, GA	M
Concordia University, Nebraska, NE	M,W
Concordia University, St. Paul, MN	M,W
Concord University, WV	M
Corban University, OR	M,W
Cornerstone University, MI	M
Covenant College, GA	M,W
Creighton University, NE	M,W
Culver-Stockton College, MO	M,W
Daemen College, NY	M
Dakota Wesleyan University, SD	M,W
Dallas Baptist University, TX	W
Davenport University, MI	M,W
Davidson College, NC	M
Delta State University, MS	M
DePaul University, IL	M
Dickinson State University, ND	M,W
Dixie State College of Utah, UT	M
Doane College, NE	M,W
Dominican College, NY	M
Dominican University of California, CA	M,W
Dordt College, IA	M,W
Dowling College, NY	M
Drake University, IA	M
Drury University, MO	M,W
Duke University, NC	M,W
East Carolina University, NC	M,W
Eastern Michigan University, MI	M,W
Eastern Washington University, WA	W
East Stroudsburg University of Pennsylvania, PA	W
Eckerd College, FL	M
Elon University, NC	M,W
Embry-Riddle Aeronautical University, FL	M,W
Erskine College, SC	M,W
Evangel University, MO	M,W
Fairfield University, CT	M,W
Fairmont State University, WV	M
Faulkner University, AL	M,W
Fayetteville State University, NC	M
Ferris State University, MI	M,W
Flagler College, FL	M,W
Florida Agricultural and Mechanical University, FL	
Florida Atlantic University, FL	M,W
Florida Gulf Coast University, FL	M,W
Florida Institute of Technology, FL	M,W
Florida International University, FL	W
Florida Southern College, FL	M,W
Florida State University, FL	M,W
Fort Lewis College, CO	M
Fort Valley State University, GA	M
Francis Marion University, SC	M
Furman University, SC	M,W
Gannon University, PA	M,W
Gardner-Webb University, NC	M,W
George Mason University, VA	M
Georgetown College, KY	M,W
Georgetown University, DC	M
The George Washington University, DC	M
Georgia College & State University, GA	M
Georgia Institute of Technology, GA	M
Georgia Southern University, GA	M
Georgia State University, GA	M,W
Glenville State College, WV	M,W
Goldey-Beacom College, DE	M
Grace College, IN	M
Graceland University, IA	M,W
Grand Valley State University, MI	M,W
Grand View University, IA	M,W
Hampton University, VA	M,W
Hannibal-LaGrange College, MO	M,W
Harding University, AR	M,W
Hawai'i Pacific University, HI	M
Henderson State University, AR	M,W
High Point University, NC	M
Hofstra University, NY	M,W
Holy Family University, PA	M
Houston Baptist University, TX	M,W
Huntington University, IN	M
Idaho State University, ID	W
Illinois State University, IL	M,W
Indiana State University, IN	W
Indiana University Bloomington, IN	M,W
Indiana University of Pennsylvania, PA	M
Indiana University–Purdue University Fort Wayne, IN	M,W
Indiana University–Purdue University Indianapolis, IN	M
Indiana Wesleyan University, IN	M
Iona College, NY	M
Iowa State University of Science and Technology, IA	M,W
Iowa Wesleyan College, IA	M,W
Jacksonville State University, AL	M,W
Jacksonville University, FL	M,W
James Madison University, VA	M,W
Jamestown College, ND	M,W
John Brown University, AR	M
Johnson C. Smith University, NC	M,W
Kansas State University, KS	M,W
Kennesaw State University, GA	M,W
Kent State University, OH	M,W
Kentucky State University, KY	M
Kentucky Wesleyan College, KY	M,W
King College, TN	M,W
Kutztown University of Pennsylvania, PA	W
Lake Superior State University, MI	M,W
Lamar University, TX	M,W
Lees-McRae College, NC	M
Lee University, TN	M
Lehigh University, PA	M
Le Moyne College, NY	M,W
Lewis-Clark State College, ID	M,W
Lewis University, IL	M,W
Limestone College, SC	M,W
Lincoln Memorial University, TN	M,W
Lincoln University, MO	M,W
Lindenwood University, MO	M,W
Lindsey Wilson College, KY	M,W
Lipscomb University, TN	M,W
Long Island University, Brooklyn Campus, NY	M,W
Longwood University, VA	M,W
Louisiana State University and Agricultural and Mechanical College, LA	M,W
Louisiana Tech University, LA	M
Loyola University Chicago, IL	M,W
Loyola University Maryland, MD	M
Malone University, OH	M,W
Manhattan College, NY	M
Marquette University, WI	M
Marshall University, WV	M,W
Maryville University of Saint Louis, MO	M,W
The Master's College and Seminary, CA	M
McKendree University, IL	M,W
Mercer University, GA	M,W
Mercyhurst College, PA	M,W
Miami University, OH	M
Michigan State University, MI	M,W
Midwestern State University, TX	M,W
Millersville University of Pennsylvania, PA	M
Milligan College, TN	M
Minnesota State University Mankato, MN	M,W
Mississippi State University, MS	M,W
Mississippi Valley State University, MS	M,W
Missouri Southern State University, MO	M
Missouri State University, MO	M,W
Monmouth University, NJ	M,W
Montana State University, MT	W
Montana Tech of The University of Montana, MT	M,W
Morehead State University, KY	M
Morningside College, IA	M,W
Mount Marty College, SD	M,W
Mount Mercy College, IA	M,W
Mount Olive College, NC	M
Mount St. Mary's University, MD	M,W

Mount Vernon Nazarene University, OH	M	St. John's University, NY	M,W
Murray State University, KY	M,W	Saint Joseph's University, PA	M
Newberry College, SC	M,W	Saint Leo University, FL	M,W
Newman University, KS	M,W	Saint Martin's University, WA	M,W
New Mexico State University, NM	M,W	Saint Mary's College of California, CA	M
Niagara University, NY	M,W	St. Mary's University, TX	M
Nicholls State University, LA	M,W	St. Thomas University, FL	M,W
North Carolina State University, NC	M	Saint Xavier University, IL	M
Northeastern State University, OK	M,W	Samford University, AL	M,W
Northern Arizona University, AZ	W	Sam Houston State University, TX	M,W
Northern Kentucky University, KY	M,W	San Diego State University, CA	M,W
Northern Michigan University, MI	M	San Jose State University, CA	M,W
Northern State University, SD	W	Santa Clara University, CA	M,W
North Greenville University, SC	M,W	Savannah College of Art and Design, GA	M,W
Northwest Christian University, OR	M,W	Savannah State University, GA	M,W
Northwestern Oklahoma State University, OK	M,W	Seton Hill University, PA	W
Northwest Nazarene University, ID	M	Shepherd University, WV	M
Notre Dame de Namur University, CA	M	Shorter University, GA	M,W
Nova Southeastern University, FL	M,W	Silver Lake College, WI	M,W
Nyack College, NY	M	South Dakota State University, SD	M,W
Oakland University, MI	M,W	Southeastern Louisiana University, LA	M
The Ohio State University, OH	M,W	Southern Illinois University Carbondale, IL	M,W
Ohio University, OH	M,W	Southern Illinois University Edwardsville, IL	M,W
Ohio Valley University, WV	M,W	Southern Methodist University, TX	M,W
Oklahoma Baptist University, OK	M,W	Southern Utah University, UT	M
Oklahoma Christian University, OK	M	Southwest Baptist University, MO	M
Oklahoma City University, OK	M,W	Southwestern College, KS	M,W
Oklahoma Panhandle State University, OK	M,W	Southwestern Oklahoma State University, OK	M,W
Oklahoma State University, OK	M,W	Southwest Minnesota State University, MN	W
Oklahoma Wesleyan University, OK	M	Spring Arbor University, MI	M
Old Dominion University, VA	M,W	Spring Hill College, AL	M,W
Oral Roberts University, OK	M,W	Stanford University, CA	M,W
Oregon State University, OR	M,W	State University of New York at Binghamton, NY	M
Ouachita Baptist University, AR	M,W	Stephen F. Austin State University, TX	M,W
Our Lady of the Lake University of San Antonio, TX	M,W	Stetson University, FL	M,W
Pace University, NY	M	Tabor College, KS	M,W
Penn State University Park, PA	M,W	Tarleton State University, TX	W
Pepperdine University, CA	M,W	Taylor University, IN	M
Philadelphia University, PA	M	Temple University, PA	M
Pikeville College, KY	M,W	Tennessee Technological University, TN	M,W
Pittsburg State University, KS	M	Tennessee Wesleyan College, TN	M,W
Point Park University, PA	M,W	Texas A&M University, TX	M,W
Portland State University, OR	M,W	Texas A&M University–Commerce, TX	M,W
Presbyterian College, SC	M,W	Texas A&M University–Corpus Christi, TX	W
Purdue University, IN	M,W	Texas Christian University, TX	M,W
Queens College of the City University of New York, NY	M	Texas State University–San Marcos, TX	M,W
Quincy University, IL	M,W	Texas Tech University, TX	M,W
Quinnipiac University, CT	M	Tiffin University, OH	M,W
Radford University, VA	M,W	Towson University, MD	M,W
Reinhardt University, GA	M,W	Trevecca Nazarene University, TN	M,W
Rider University, NJ	M	Troy University, AL	M,W
Robert Morris University, PA	M,W	Truett-McConnell College, GA	M,W
Robert Morris University Illinois, IL	M,W	Truman State University, MO	M,W
Roberts Wesleyan College, NY	M,W	Tulane University, LA	W
Rockhurst University, MO	M,W	Tusculum College, TN	M
Rocky Mountain College, MT	M,W	Tuskegee University, AL	M
Rollins College, FL	M,W	Union College, KY	M,W
Sacred Heart University, CT	M,W		
Saginaw Valley State University, MI	M		
St. Ambrose University, IA	M,W		
St. Andrews Presbyterian College, NC	M,W		
St. Bonaventure University, NY	M		
St. Edward's University, TX	M,W		
Saint Francis University, PA	M,W		

Union University, TN	M
University at Albany, State University of New York, NY	W
The University of Akron, OH	M,W
The University of Alabama, AL	M,W
The University of Alabama at Birmingham, AL	M,W
The University of Arizona, AZ	M,W
University of Arkansas, AR	M,W
University of California, Davis, CA	M,W
University of California, Irvine, CA	M,W
University of California, Los Angeles, CA	M,W
University of California, Riverside, CA	M,W
University of California, Santa Barbara, CA	M
University of Central Florida, FL	M,W
University of Central Missouri, MO	M
University of Central Oklahoma, OK	M,W
University of Charleston, WV	M
University of Cincinnati, OH	M,W
University of Colorado at Boulder, CO	M,W
University of Colorado at Colorado Springs, CO	M
University of Connecticut, CT	M
University of Dayton, OH	M,W
University of Denver, CO	M,W
University of Evansville, IN	M,W
The University of Findlay, OH	M,W
University of Florida, FL	M,W
University of Georgia, GA	M,W
University of Great Falls, MT	M,W
University of Hartford, CT	M,W
University of Hawaii at Hilo, HI	M
University of Houston, TX	M
University of Idaho, ID	M,W
University of Illinois at Springfield, IL	M,W
University of Illinois at Urbana–Champaign, IL	M,W
University of Indianapolis, IN	M,W
The University of Iowa, IA	M,W
The University of Kansas, KS	M,W
University of Kentucky, KY	M,W
University of Louisiana at Monroe, LA	M
University of Louisville, KY	M,W
University of Mary, ND	W
University of Maryland, College Park, MD	M,W
University of Memphis, TN	M,W
University of Miami, FL	W
University of Michigan, MI	M,W
University of Minnesota, Twin Cities Campus, MN	M,W
University of Mississippi, MS	M,W
University of Missouri, MO	M,W
University of Missouri–Kansas City, MO	M,W
University of Missouri–St. Louis, MO	M,W
University of Mobile, AL	M,W
The University of Montana Western, MT	M,W
University of Montevallo, AL	M,W
University of Nebraska at Kearney, NE	M,W
University of Nebraska at Omaha, NE	W

University of Nebraska–Lincoln, NE	M,W
University of Nevada, Las Vegas, NV	M
University of Nevada, Reno, NV	M,W
University of New Haven, CT	M
University of New Orleans, LA	M
University of North Alabama, AL	M
The University of North Carolina at Chapel Hill, NC	M,W
The University of North Carolina at Charlotte, NC	M
The University of North Carolina at Greensboro, NC	M,W
The University of North Carolina at Pembroke, NC	M,W
The University of North Carolina Wilmington, NC	M,W
University of Northern Colorado, CO	M,W
University of Northern Iowa, IA	M,W
University of North Florida, FL	M
University of North Texas, TX	M,W
University of Notre Dame, IN	M,W
University of Oklahoma, OK	M,W
University of Oregon, OR	M,W
University of Portland, OR	M,W
University of Rhode Island, RI	M
University of Richmond, VA	M,W
University of St. Francis, IL	M,W
University of San Diego, CA	M
University of South Carolina, SC	M,W
University of South Carolina Aiken, SC	M
The University of South Dakota, SD	M,W
University of Southern California, CA	M,W
University of Southern Indiana, IN	M,W
University of Southern Mississippi, MS	M,W
The University of Tampa, FL	M
The University of Tennessee, TN	M,W
The University of Tennessee at Chattanooga, TN	M,W
The University of Tennessee at Martin, TN	M
The University of Texas at Arlington, TX	M
The University of Texas at Austin, TX	M,W
The University of Texas at Brownsville, TX	M,W
The University of Texas at El Paso, TX	M
The University of Texas at San Antonio, TX	M
The University of Texas–Pan American, TX	M,W
University of the District of Columbia, DC	M
University of the Incarnate Word, TX	M,W
University of the Pacific, CA	M
University of the Southwest, NM	M,W
The University of Toledo, OH	M,W
University of Tulsa, OK	M,W
University of Virginia, VA	M,W
University of Washington, WA	M,W
University of West Florida, FL	M
University of West Georgia, GA	M,W
University of Wisconsin–Green Bay, WI	M,W
University of Wisconsin–Madison, WI	M,W
University of Wisconsin–Parkside, WI	M
University of Wyoming, WY	M,W

Ursuline College, OH	W
Utah State University, UT	M
Utah Valley University, UT	M,W
Valdosta State University, GA	M
Valparaiso University, IN	M,W
Vanderbilt University, TN	M,W
Virginia Commonwealth University, VA	M
Virginia Intermont College, VA	M
Virginia Military Institute, VA	M
Virginia Polytechnic Institute and State University, VA	M
Virginia Union University, VA	M
Wagner College, NY	M,W
Wake Forest University, NC	M,W
Waldorf College, IA	M,W
Warner Pacific College, OR	M,W
Washburn University, KS	M
Washington State University, WA	M,W
Wayland Baptist University, TX	M,W
Wayne State College, NE	M,W
Wayne State University, MI	M
Webber International University, FL	M,W
West Chester University of Pennsylvania, PA	M,W
Western Carolina University, NC	M,W
Western Illinois University, IL	M
Western Kentucky University, KY	M,W
Western Washington University, WA	M,W
West Liberty University, WV	M,W
West Virginia Wesleyan College, WV	M,W
Wheeling Jesuit University, WV	M,W
Wichita State University, KS	M,W
William Jewell College, MO	M,W
Winona State University, MN	M,W
Winthrop University, SC	M,W
Wofford College, SC	M,W
Wright State University, OH	M
Xavier University, OH	M,W
Youngstown State University, OH	M,W

Gymnastics

Arizona State University, AZ	W
Auburn University, AL	W
Ball State University, IN	W
Boise State University, ID	W
Bowling Green State University, OH	W
Brigham Young University, UT	W
California State University, Fullerton, CA	W
California State University, Sacramento, CA	W
Centenary College of Louisiana, LA	W
Central Michigan University, MI	W
The College of William and Mary, VA	M,W
Eastern Michigan University, MI	W
The George Washington University, DC	W
Illinois State University, IL	W
Iowa State University of Science and Technology, IA	W
Kent State University, OH	W
Louisiana State University and Agricultural and Mechanical College, LA	W
Michigan State University, MI	W
North Carolina State University, NC	W
The Ohio State University, OH	M,W
Oregon State University, OR	W
Penn State University Park, PA	M,W

San Jose State University, CA	W
Seattle Pacific University, WA	W
Southeast Missouri State University, MO	W
Southern Connecticut State University, CT	W
Southern Utah University, UT	W
Stanford University, CA	M,W
Temple University, PA	M,W
Texas Woman's University, TX	W
Towson University, MD	W
The University of Alabama, AL	W
University of Alaska Anchorage, AK	W
The University of Arizona, AZ	W
University of Arkansas, AR	W
University of Bridgeport, CT	W
University of California, Davis, CA	W
University of California, Los Angeles, CA	W
University of California, Santa Barbara, CA	M,W
University of Denver, CO	W
University of Florida, FL	W
University of Georgia, GA	W
University of Illinois at Chicago, IL	M,W
University of Illinois at Urbana–Champaign, IL	M,W
The University of Iowa, IA	M,W
University of Kentucky, KY	W
University of Maryland, College Park, MD	W
University of Michigan, MI	M,W
University of Minnesota, Twin Cities Campus, MN	M,W
University of Missouri, MO	W
University of Nebraska–Lincoln, NE	M,W
University of New Hampshire, NH	W
The University of North Carolina at Chapel Hill, NC	W
University of Oklahoma, OK	M,W
University of Oregon, OR	W
University of Pittsburgh, PA	W
University of Washington, WA	W
Utah State University, UT	W
West Chester University of Pennsylvania, PA	W
West Virginia University, WV	W

Ice Hockey

American International College, MA	M
Bemidji State University, MN	M,W
Bentley University, MA	M
Boston College, MA	M,W
Boston University, MA	M,W
Bowling Green State University, OH	M
Canisius College, NY	M
Clarkson University, NY	M,W
Colgate University, NY	M,W
College of the Holy Cross, MA	M
The Colorado College, CO	M
Davenport University, MI	M
Dordt College, IA	M
Ferris State University, MI	M
Lake Superior State University, MI	M
Mercyhurst College, PA	M,W
Merrimack College, MA	M
Miami University, OH	M
Michigan State University, MI	M
Michigan Technological University, MI	M

Minnesota State University
Mankato, MN | M,W
Niagara University, NY | M,W
Northeastern University, MA | M,W
Northern Michigan University, MI | M
The Ohio State University, OH | M,W
Providence College, RI | M,W
Quinnipiac University, CT | M,W
Rensselaer Polytechnic Institute, NY | M,W
Robert Morris University, PA | M,W
Sacred Heart University, CT | M,W
St. Lawrence University, NY | M,W
Syracuse University, NY | W
The University of Alabama in
Huntsville, AL | M
University of Alaska Anchorage, AK | M
University of Alaska Fairbanks, AK | M
University of Connecticut, CT | M,W
University of Denver, CO | M
University of Maine, ME | M,W
University of Massachusetts
Amherst, MA | M
University of Massachusetts
Lowell, MA | M
University of Michigan, MI | M
University of Minnesota, Duluth, MN | M,W
University of Minnesota, Twin Cities
Campus, MN | M,W
University of Nebraska at Omaha, NE | M
University of New Hampshire, NH | M,W
University of North Dakota, ND | M,W
University of Notre Dame, IN | M
University of Vermont, VT | M,W
University of Wisconsin–Madison, WI | M,W
Wayne State University, MI | W

Lacrosse

Adelphi University, NY | M,W
American International College, MA | M,W
American University, DC | W
Bellarmine University, KY | M
Belmont Abbey College, NC | M,W
Bentley University, MA | M,W
Bloomsburg University of
Pennsylvania, PA | W
Boston College, MA | W
Boston University, MA | W
Bryant University, RI | M,W
Bucknell University, PA | M,W
California State University,
Fresno, CA | W
Canisius College, NY | M,W
Catawba College, NC | M
Central Connecticut State
University, CT | W
Colgate University, NY | M,W
The College of William and Mary, VA | W
Converse College, SC | W
Davenport University, MI | M,W
Davidson College, NC | W
Dominican College, NY | M,W
Dominican University of
California, CA | M
Dowling College, NY | M,W
Duke University, NC | M,W
Duquesne University, PA | W
East Stroudsburg University of
Pennsylvania, PA | W
Edinboro University of
Pennsylvania, PA | W

Erskine College, SC | W
Fairfield University, CT | M,W
Florida Southern College, FL | M
Fort Lewis College, CO | W
Gannon University, PA | W
George Mason University, VA | W
Georgetown University, DC | M,W
Georgian Court University, NJ | W
Hofstra University, NY | M,W
Holy Family University, PA | W
Indiana University of
Pennsylvania, PA | W
Iona College, NY | W
James Madison University, VA | W
The Johns Hopkins University, MD | M,W
Kutztown University of
Pennsylvania, PA | W
Lees-McRae College, NC | M,W
Lehigh University, PA | M,W
Le Moyne College, NY | M,W
Limestone College, SC | M,W
Lindenwood University, MO | M,W
Lock Haven University of
Pennsylvania, PA | W
Long Island University, Brooklyn
Campus, NY | W
Long Island University, C.W. Post
Campus, NY | M,W
Longwood University, VA | W
Manhattan College, NY | M,W
Marist College, NY | M,W
Mercyhurst College, PA | M,W
Merrimack College, MA | W
Millersville University of
Pennsylvania, PA | W
Molloy College, NY | M,W
Monmouth University, NJ | W
Mount St. Mary's University, MD | M,W
New York Institute of Technology, NY | M
Niagara University, NY | W
Notre Dame de Namur University, CA | M
The Ohio State University, OH | M,W
Ohio Valley University, WV | M
Old Dominion University, VA | W
Pace University, NY | M
Penn State University Park, PA | M,W
Philadelphia University, PA | W
Presbyterian College, SC | M,W
Providence College, RI | M
Queens College of the City University
of New York, NY | W
Quinnipiac University, CT | M,W
Robert Morris University, PA | M,W
Sacred Heart University, CT | M,W
St. Andrews Presbyterian
College, NC | M,W
St. Bonaventure University, NY | W
Saint Francis University, PA | W
St. John's University, NY | M
Saint Joseph's University, PA | M,W
Saint Leo University, FL | M
Savannah College of Art and
Design, GA | W
Seton Hill University, PA | M,W
Shepherd University, WV | W
Shippensburg University of
Pennsylvania, PA | W
Slippery Rock University of
Pennsylvania, PA | W

Southern Connecticut State
University, CT | W
Stanford University, CA | W
State University of New York at
Binghamton, NY | M,W
Stonehill College, MA | W
Stony Brook University, State
University of New York, NY | M,W
Syracuse University, NY | M,W
Temple University, PA | W
Tennessee Wesleyan College, TN | M
Tiffin University, OH | W
Towson University, MD | M,W
University at Albany, State University
of New York, NY | M,W
University of Bridgeport, CT | W
University of California, Davis, CA | W
University of Cincinnati, OH | W
University of Delaware, DE | M,W
University of Denver, CO | M,W
University of Florida, FL | W
University of Hartford, CT | M
University of Louisville, KY | W
University of Maryland, Baltimore
County, MD | M,W
University of Maryland, College
Park, MD | M,W
University of Massachusetts
Amherst, MA | M,W
University of Minnesota, Duluth, MN | M
University of New Hampshire, NH | W
University of New Haven, CT | W
The University of North Carolina at
Chapel Hill, NC | M,W
University of Notre Dame, IN | M,W
University of Oregon, OR | W
University of Richmond, VA | W
University of Vermont, VT | M,W
University of Virginia, VA | M,W
Vanderbilt University, TN | W
Villanova University, PA | M,W
Virginia Military Institute, VA | M
Virginia Polytechnic Institute and
State University, VA | W
Wagner College, NY | M,W
West Chester University of
Pennsylvania, PA | W
West Virginia Wesleyan College, WV | W
Wheeling Jesuit University, WV | M

Riflery

Austin Peay State University, TN | W
The Citadel, The Military College of
South Carolina, SC | M,W
Jacksonville State University, AL | M,W
Lindenwood University, MO | M,W
Mercer University, GA | M
Morehead State University, KY | M,W
Murray State University, KY | M,W
North Georgia College & State
University, GA | M,W
Tennessee Technological
University, TN | M,W
Texas Christian University, TX | W
The University of Akron, OH | W
University of Alaska Fairbanks, AK | M,W
University of Kentucky, KY | M,W
University of Memphis, TN | M,W
University of Mississippi, MS | W

Athletic Grants for Undergraduates
Riflery

University of Missouri–Kansas City, MO	M,W
University of Nebraska–Lincoln, NE	W
University of Nevada, Reno, NV	M,W
The University of Tennessee at Martin, TN	M,W
Virginia Military Institute, VA	M,W
West Virginia University, WV	M,W

Rugby

West Chester University of Pennsylvania, PA	W

Sailing

Hampton University, VA	M,W
Robert Morris University Illinois, IL	M,W

Skiing (Cross-Country)

Montana State University, MT	M,W
Northern Michigan University, MI	M,W
University of Alaska Anchorage, AK	M,W
University of Alaska Fairbanks, AK	M,W
University of Colorado at Boulder, CO	M,W
University of Denver, CO	M,W
University of Nevada, Reno, NV	M,W
University of New Hampshire, NH	M,W
University of Vermont, VT	M,W
University of Wisconsin–Green Bay, WI	M,W

Skiing (Downhill)

Montana State University, MT	M,W
Rocky Mountain College, MT	M,W
University of Alaska Anchorage, AK	M,W
University of Colorado at Boulder, CO	M,W
University of Denver, CO	M,W
University of Nevada, Reno, NV	M,W
University of New Hampshire, NH	M,W
University of Vermont, VT	M,W

Soccer

Abilene Christian University, TX	W
Abraham Baldwin Agricultural College, GA	W
Academy of Art University, CA	M,W
Adams State College, CO	M,W
Adelphi University, NY	M,W
Alabama Agricultural and Mechanical University, AL	M
Alabama State University, AL	W
Alderson-Broaddus College, WV	M,W
American International College, MA	M,W
American University, DC	M,W
Angelo State University, TX	W
Appalachian State University, NC	M,W
Arizona State University, AZ	W
Arkansas State University—Jonesboro, AR	W
Asbury University, KY	M,W
Ashland University, OH	M,W
Auburn University, AL	W
Auburn University Montgomery, AL	M,W
Augustana College, SD	W
Austin Peay State University, TN	W
Azusa Pacific University, CA	M,W
Ball State University, IN	W
Barry University, FL	M,W
Barton College, NC	M,W
Baylor University, TX	W

Belhaven University, MS	M,W
Bellarmine University, KY	M,W
Belmont Abbey College, NC	M,W
Belmont University, TN	M,W
Bemidji State University, MN	W
Benedictine College, KS	M,W
Bentley University, MA	M,W
Bethany College, KS	M,W
Bethel College, IN	M,W
Bethel College, KS	M,W
Blessing-Rieman College of Nursing, IL	M,W
Bloomfield College, NJ	M,W
Bloomsburg University of Pennsylvania, PA	M,W
Bluefield College, VA	M,W
Boston College, MA	M,W
Boston University, MA	M,W
Bowling Green State University, OH	M,W
Bradley University, IL	M
Brenau University, GA	W
Brescia University, KY	M,W
Brevard College, NC	M,W
Brewton-Parker College, GA	M,W
Briar Cliff University, IA	M,W
Brigham Young University, UT	W
Bryan College, TN	M,W
Bryant University, RI	M,W
Bucknell University, PA	M,W
Butler University, IN	M,W
California Baptist University, CA	M,W
California Maritime Academy, CA	M
California Polytechnic State University, San Luis Obispo, CA	M,W
California State Polytechnic University, Pomona, CA	M,W
California State University, Chico, CA	M,W
California State University, Dominguez Hills, CA	M,W
California State University, Fresno, CA	W
California State University, Fullerton, CA	M,W
California State University, Long Beach, CA	W
California State University, Monterey Bay, CA	M,W
California State University, Northridge, CA	M
California State University, Sacramento, CA	M,W
California State University, San Bernardino, CA	M,W
Campbellsville University, KY	M,W
Canisius College, NY	M,W
Carson-Newman College, TN	M,W
Catawba College, NC	M,W
Cedarville University, OH	M,W
Centenary College of Louisiana, LA	M,W
Central Connecticut State University, CT	M,W
Central Michigan University, MI	W
Chowan University, NC	M,W
Christian Brothers University, TN	M,W
Cincinnati Christian University, OH	M
The Citadel, The Military College of South Carolina, SC	W
Clarke College, IA	M,W

Clemson University, SC	M,W
Cleveland State University, OH	M
Coastal Carolina University, SC	M,W
Coker College, SC	M,W
Colgate University, NY	M,W
College of Charleston, SC	M,W
College of Saint Mary, NE	W
The College of Saint Rose, NY	M,W
College of the Holy Cross, MA	M,W
The College of William and Mary, VA	M,W
The Colorado College, CO	W
Colorado School of Mines, CO	M,W
Columbia College, MO	M
Columbus State University, GA	W
Concordia University, CA	M,W
Concordia University, Nebraska, NE	M,W
Concordia University, St. Paul, MN	W
Concord University, WV	W
Converse College, SC	W
Corban University, OR	M,W
Cornerstone University, MI	M,W
Covenant College, GA	M,W
Creighton University, NE	M,W
Culver-Stockton College, MO	M,W
Daemen College, NY	M,W
Dallas Baptist University, TX	W
Davenport University, MI	M,W
Davidson College, NC	M,W
Delta State University, MS	M,W
DePaul University, IL	M,W
Dixie State College of Utah, UT	M,W
Doane College, NE	M,W
Dominican College, NY	M,W
Dominican University of California, CA	M,W
Dordt College, IA	M,W
Dowling College, NY	M,W
Drake University, IA	M,W
Drury University, MO	M,W
Duke University, NC	M,W
Duquesne University, PA	M,W
East Carolina University, NC	M,W
Eastern Michigan University, MI	W
Eastern New Mexico University, NM	W
Eastern Washington University, WA	W
East Stroudsburg University of Pennsylvania, PA	M,W
Eckerd College, FL	M,W
Edinboro University of Pennsylvania, PA	W
Elon University, NC	M,W
Embry-Riddle Aeronautical University, FL	M,W
Emporia State University, KS	W
Erskine College, SC	M,W
The Evergreen State College, WA	M,W
Fairfield University, CT	M,W
Faulkner University, AL	M,W
Felician College, NJ	M,W
Ferris State University, MI	M,W
Flagler College, FL	M,W
Florida College, FL	M,W
Florida Gulf Coast University, FL	M,W
Florida Institute of Technology, FL	M,W
Florida International University, FL	M,W
Florida Southern College, FL	M,W
Florida State University, FL	W
Fordham University, NY	M,W

f www.facebook.com/pay4undergrad

College	Grants
Fort Lewis College, CO	M,W
Francis Marion University, SC	M,W
Freed-Hardeman University, TN	M,W
Furman University, SC	M,W
Gannon University, PA	M,W
Gardner-Webb University, NC	M,W
George Mason University, VA	M,W
Georgetown College, KY	M,W
Georgetown University, DC	M,W
The George Washington University, DC	M,W
Georgia College & State University, GA	W
Georgian Court University, NJ	W
Georgia Southern University, GA	M,W
Georgia State University, GA	M,W
Goldey-Beacom College, DE	M,W
Gonzaga University, WA	M,W
Grace College, IN	M,W
Graceland University, IA	M,W
Grand Valley State University, MI	W
Grand View University, IA	M,W
Hannibal-LaGrange College, MO	M,W
Harding University, AR	M,W
Hartwick College, NY	M
Hawai'i Pacific University, HI	M,W
High Point University, NC	M,W
Hofstra University, NY	M,W
Holy Family University, PA	M,W
Houghton College, NY	M,W
Houston Baptist University, TX	M,W
Humboldt State University, CA	M,W
Huntington University, IN	M,W
Idaho State University, ID	W
Illinois Institute of Technology, IL	M,W
Illinois State University, IL	W
Indiana State University, IN	W
Indiana University Bloomington, IN	M,W
Indiana University of Pennsylvania, PA	W
Indiana University–Purdue University Fort Wayne, IN	M,W
Indiana University–Purdue University Indianapolis, IN	M,W
Indiana Wesleyan University, IN	M,W
Iona College, NY	M,W
Iowa State University of Science and Technology, IA	W
Iowa Wesleyan College, IA	M,W
Jacksonville State University, AL	W
Jacksonville University, FL	M,W
James Madison University, VA	M,W
Jamestown College, ND	M,W
John Brown University, AR	M,W
Judson College, AL	W
Kennesaw State University, GA	W
Kent State University, OH	W
Kentucky Wesleyan College, KY	M,W
King College, TN	M,W
Kutztown University of Pennsylvania, PA	W
Lamar University, TX	W
Lees-McRae College, NC	M,W
Lee University, TN	M,W
Lehigh University, PA	M,W
Le Moyne College, NY	M,W
Lewis University, IL	M,W
Limestone College, SC	M,W
Lincoln Memorial University, TN	M,W
Lindenwood University, MO	M,W
Lindsey Wilson College, KY	M,W
Lipscomb University, TN	M,W
Lock Haven University of Pennsylvania, PA	M,W
Long Island University, Brooklyn Campus, NY	M,W
Long Island University, C.W. Post Campus, NY	M,W
Longwood University, VA	M,W
Louisiana State University and Agricultural and Mechanical College, LA	W
Loyola University Chicago, IL	M,W
Loyola University Maryland, MD	M,W
Malone University, OH	M,W
Manhattan College, NY	M,W
Mansfield University of Pennsylvania, PA	W
Marist College, NY	M,W
Marquette University, WI	M,W
Marshall University, WV	M,W
Maryville University of Saint Louis, MO	M,W
The Master's College and Seminary, CA	M,W
McKendree University, IL	M,W
Mercer University, GA	M,W
Mercyhurst College, PA	M,W
Merrimack College, MA	W
Metropolitan State College of Denver, CO	M,W
Miami University, OH	W
Michigan State University, MI	M,W
Mid-Continent University, KY	M
Midwestern State University, TX	M,W
Millersville University of Pennsylvania, PA	M,W
Milligan College, TN	M,W
Minnesota State University Mankato, MN	W
Minnesota State University Moorhead, MN	W
Mississippi State University, MS	W
Missouri Southern State University, MO	M,W
Missouri State University, MO	M,W
Missouri University of Science and Technology, MO	M,W
Molloy College, NY	M,W
Monmouth University, NJ	M,W
Montana State University Billings, MT	M,W
Morehead State University, KY	W
Morningside College, IA	M,W
Mountain State University, WV	M,W
Mount Marty College, SD	M,W
Mount Mercy College, IA	M,W
Mount Olive College, NC	M,W
Mount St. Mary's University, MD	M,W
Mount Vernon Nazarene University, OH	M,W
Murray State University, KY	W
Newberry College, SC	M,W
New Jersey Institute of Technology, NJ	M,W
Newman University, KS	M,W
New York Institute of Technology, NY	M,W
Niagara University, NY	M,W
Nicholls State University, LA	W
North Carolina State University, NC	M,W
Northeastern State University, OK	M,W
Northeastern University, MA	M,W
Northern Arizona University, AZ	W
Northern Kentucky University, KY	M,W
Northern Michigan University, MI	W
Northern State University, SD	W
North Georgia College & State University, GA	M,W
North Greenville University, SC	M,W
Northwest Christian University, OR	M,W
Northwestern Oklahoma State University, OK	W
Northwestern State University of Louisiana, LA	W
Northwest Nazarene University, ID	W
Northwest University, WA	M,W
Notre Dame de Namur University, CA	M,W
Nova Southeastern University, FL	M,W
Nyack College, NY	M,W
Oakland University, MI	M,W
The Ohio State University, OH	M,W
Ohio University, OH	W
Ohio Valley University, WV	M,W
Oklahoma Christian University, OK	M,W
Oklahoma City University, OK	M,W
Oklahoma State University, OK	W
Oklahoma Wesleyan University, OK	M,W
Old Dominion University, VA	M,W
Oral Roberts University, OK	M,W
Oregon State University, OR	W
Ouachita Baptist University, AR	M,W
Our Lady of the Lake University of San Antonio, TX	M,W
Pace University, NY	W
Palm Beach Atlantic University, FL	M,W
Penn State University Park, PA	M,W
Pepperdine University, CA	W
Philadelphia University, PA	M,W
Pikeville College, KY	M,W
Point Park University, PA	M
Portland State University, OR	W
Presbyterian College, SC	M,W
Providence College, RI	M,W
Purdue University, IN	W
Queens College of the City University of New York, NY	M,W
Quincy University, IL	M,W
Quinnipiac University, CT	M,W
Radford University, VA	M,W
Reinhardt University, GA	M,W
Rider University, NJ	M,W
Robert Morris University, PA	M,W
Robert-Morris University Illinois, IL	M,W
Roberts Wesleyan College, NY	M,W
Rockhurst University, MO	M,W
Rocky Mountain College, MT	M,W
Rollins College, FL	M,W
Sacred Heart University, CT	M,W
Saginaw Valley State University, MI	M,W
St. Ambrose University, IA	M,W
St. Andrews Presbyterian College, NC	M,W
St. Bonaventure University, NY	M,W
St. Edward's University, TX	M,W
Saint Francis University, PA	M,W

St. John's University, NY	M,W
Saint Joseph's University, PA	M,W
Saint Leo University, FL	M,W
Saint Louis University, MO	M,W
Saint Martin's University, WA	W
Saint Mary's College of California, CA	M,W
St. Mary's University, TX	M,W
St. Thomas University, FL	M,W
Saint Xavier University, IL	M,W
Samford University, AL	W
Sam Houston State University, TX	W
San Diego Christian College, CA	M,W
San Diego State University, CA	M,W
San Francisco State University, CA	M,W
San Jose State University, CA	M,W
Santa Clara University, CA	M,W
Savannah College of Art and Design, GA	M,W
Seattle Pacific University, WA	M
Seattle University, WA	M,W
Seton Hill University, PA	M,W
Shepherd University, WV	M,W
Shippensburg University of Pennsylvania, PA	M,W
Shorter University, GA	M,W
Siena College, NY	M,W
Slippery Rock University of Pennsylvania, PA	M,W
Sonoma State University, CA	M,W
South Dakota State University, SD	W
Southeastern Louisiana University, LA	W
Southeast Missouri State University, MO	W
Southern Connecticut State University, CT	M,W
Southern Illinois University Edwardsville, IL	M,W
Southern Methodist University, TX	M,W
Southern Polytechnic State University, GA	M
Southwest Baptist University, MO	W
Southwestern College, KS	M,W
Southwestern Oklahoma State University, OK	W
Southwest Minnesota State University, MN	W
Spring Arbor University, MI	M,W
Spring Hill College, AL	M,W
Stanford University, CA	M,W
State University of New York at Binghamton, NY	M,W
Stephen F. Austin State University, TX	W
Stetson University, FL	M,W
Stonehill College, MA	M,W
Stony Brook University, State University of New York, NY	M,W
Syracuse University, NY	M,W
Tabor College, KS	M,W
Taylor University, IN	M,W
Temple University, PA	M,W
Tennessee Technological University, TN	W
Tennessee Wesleyan College, TN	M,W
Texas A&M University, TX	W
Texas A&M University–Commerce, TX	W
Texas Christian University, TX	W
Texas State University–San Marcos, TX	W
Texas Tech University, TX	W
Texas Woman's University, TX	W
Tiffin University, OH	M,W
Towson University, MD	M,W
Trevecca Nazarene University, TN	M,W
Trinity Christian College, IL	M,W
Troy University, AL	W
Truett-McConnell College, GA	M,W
Truman State University, MO	M,W
Tulane University, LA	W
Tusculum College, TN	M,W
Union College, KY	M,W
Union University, TN	M,W
University at Albany, State University of New York, NY	M,W
University at Buffalo, the State University of New York, NY	M,W
The University of Akron, OH	M,W
The University of Alabama, AL	W
The University of Alabama at Birmingham, AL	M,W
The University of Alabama in Huntsville, AL	M,W
The University of Arizona, AZ	W
University of Arkansas, AR	W
University of Bridgeport, CT	M,W
University of California, Davis, CA	M,W
University of California, Irvine, CA	M,W
University of California, Los Angeles, CA	M,W
University of California, Riverside, CA	M,W
University of California, Santa Barbara, CA	M,W
University of Central Florida, FL	M,W
University of Central Missouri, MO	W
University of Central Oklahoma, OK	W
University of Charleston, WV	M,W
University of Cincinnati, OH	M,W
University of Colorado at Boulder, CO	W
University of Colorado at Colorado Springs, CO	M
University of Connecticut, CT	M,W
University of Dayton, OH	M,W
University of Delaware, DE	M,W
University of Denver, CO	M,W
University of Evansville, IN	M,W
The University of Findlay, OH	M,W
University of Florida, FL	W
University of Georgia, GA	W
University of Great Falls, MT	M,W
University of Hartford, CT	M,W
University of Houston, TX	W
University of Idaho, ID	W
University of Illinois at Chicago, IL	M
University of Illinois at Springfield, IL	M,W
University of Illinois at Urbana–Champaign, IL	W
University of Indianapolis, IN	M,W
The University of Iowa, IA	W
The University of Kansas, KS	W
University of Kentucky, KY	M,W
University of Louisiana at Monroe, LA	W
University of Louisville, KY	M,W
University of Maine, ME	W
University of Mary, ND	M,W
University of Maryland, Baltimore County, MD	M,W
University of Maryland, College Park, MD	M,W
University of Massachusetts Amherst, MA	M,W
University of Memphis, TN	M,W
University of Miami, FL	W
University of Michigan, MI	M,W
University of Minnesota, Crookston, MN	W
University of Minnesota, Duluth, MN	W
University of Minnesota, Twin Cities Campus, MN	W
University of Mississippi, MS	W
University of Missouri, MO	W
University of Missouri–Kansas City, MO	M
University of Missouri–St. Louis, MO	M,W
University of Mobile, AL	M,W
University of Montevallo, AL	M,W
University of Nebraska–Lincoln, NE	W
University of Nevada, Las Vegas, NV	M,W
University of Nevada, Reno, NV	W
University of New Hampshire, NH	M,W
University of New Haven, CT	M,W
University of North Alabama, AL	W
The University of North Carolina at Asheville, NC	M,W
The University of North Carolina at Chapel Hill, NC	M,W
The University of North Carolina at Charlotte, NC	M,W
The University of North Carolina at Greensboro, NC	M,W
The University of North Carolina at Pembroke, NC	M,W
The University of North Carolina Wilmington, NC	M,W
University of Northern Colorado, CO	W
University of Northern Iowa, IA	W
University of North Florida, FL	M,W
University of North Texas, TX	W
University of Notre Dame, IN	M,W
University of Oklahoma, OK	W
University of Oregon, OR	W
University of Pittsburgh, PA	M,W
University of Portland, OR	M,W
University of Puerto Rico, Río Piedras, PR	M
University of Rhode Island, RI	M,W
University of Richmond, VA	M,W
University of St. Francis, IL	M,W
University of St. Thomas, TX	M
University of San Diego, CA	M,W
University of Science and Arts of Oklahoma, OK	M,W
University of South Alabama, AL	W
University of South Carolina, SC	M,W
University of South Carolina Aiken, SC	M,W
The University of South Dakota, SD	W
University of Southern California, CA	W
University of Southern Indiana, IN	M,W
University of Southern Mississippi, MS	W
The University of Tampa, FL	M,W
The University of Tennessee, TN	W

The University of Tennessee at Chattanooga, TN	W
The University of Tennessee at Martin, TN	W
The University of Texas at Austin, TX	W
The University of Texas at Brownsville, TX	M,W
The University of Texas of the Permian Basin, TX	M,W
University of the District of Columbia, DC	M
University of the Incarnate Word, TX	M,W
University of the Pacific, CA	W
University of the Southwest, NM	M,W
The University of Toledo, OH	W
University of Tulsa, OK	M,W
University of Vermont, VT	M,W
University of Virginia, VA	M,W
University of Washington, WA	M,W
University of West Florida, FL	M,W
University of West Georgia, GA	W
University of Wisconsin–Green Bay, WI	M,W
University of Wisconsin–Madison, WI	M,W
University of Wisconsin–Parkside, WI	M,W
University of Wyoming, WY	W
Ursuline College, OH	W
Utah State University, UT	W
Utah Valley University, UT	W
Valparaiso University, IN	M,W
Vanderbilt University, TN	W
Vanguard University of Southern California, CA	M,W
Villanova University, PA	M,W
Virginia Commonwealth University, VA	M,W
Virginia Intermont College, VA	M
Virginia Military Institute, VA	M
Virginia Polytechnic Institute and State University, VA	M,W
Wagner College, NY	W
Wake Forest University, NC	M,W
Waldorf College, IA	M,W
Warner Pacific College, OR	M,W
Washburn University, KS	W
Washington State University, WA	W
Wayland Baptist University, TX	M,W
Wayne State College, NE	W
Webber International University, FL	M,W
West Chester University of Pennsylvania, PA	M,W
Western Carolina University, NC	W
Western Illinois University, IL	M,W
Western Oregon University, OR	W
Western Washington University, WA	M,W
Westminster College, UT	M,W
Westmont College, CA	M,W
West Virginia University, WV	M,W
West Virginia Wesleyan College, WV	M,W
Wheeling Jesuit University, WV	M,W
William Jewell College, MO	M,W
Winona State University, MN	W
Winthrop University, SC	M
Wofford College, SC	M,W
Wright State University, OH	M,W
Xavier University, OH	M,W
York College, NE	M,W

Youngstown State University, OH	W

Softball

Abilene Christian University, TX	W
Abraham Baldwin Agricultural College, GA	W
Academy of Art University, CA	W
Adams State College, CO	W
Adelphi University, NY	W
Alabama State University, AL	W
Alderson-Broaddus College, WV	W
American International College, MA	W
Angelo State University, TX	W
Appalachian State University, NC	W
Arizona State University, AZ	W
Arkansas Tech University, AR	W
Armstrong Atlantic State University, GA	W
Asbury University, KY	W
Ashland University, OH	W
Auburn University, AL	W
Auburn University Montgomery, AL	W
Augustana College, SD	W
Austin Peay State University, TN	W
Azusa Pacific University, CA	W
Ball State University, IN	W
Barry University, FL	W
Barton College, NC	W
Baylor University, TX	W
Belhaven University, MS	W
Bellarmine University, KY	W
Belmont Abbey College, NC	W
Belmont University, TN	W
Bemidji State University, MN	W
Benedictine College, KS	W
Bentley University, MA	W
Bethany College, KS	W
Bethel College, IN	W
Bethune-Cookman University, FL	W
Bloomfield College, NJ	W
Bloomsburg University of Pennsylvania, PA	W
Bluefield College, VA	W
Bluefield State College, WV	W
Blue Mountain College, MS	W
Boston College, MA	W
Boston University, MA	W
Bowie State University, MD	W
Bowling Green State University, OH	W
Bradley University, IL	M,W
Brenau University, GA	W
Brescia University, KY	W
Brevard College, NC	W
Brewton-Parker College, GA	W
Briar Cliff University, IA	W
Brigham Young University, UT	W
Bryant University, RI	W
Butler University, IN	W
California Baptist University, CA	W
California Polytechnic State University, San Luis Obispo, CA	W
California State University, Chico, CA	W
California State University, Dominguez Hills, CA	W
California State University, Fresno, CA	W
California State University, Fullerton, CA	W
California State University, Long Beach, CA	W

California State University, Monterey Bay, CA	W
California State University, Northridge, CA	W
California State University, Sacramento, CA	W
California State University, San Bernardino, CA	W
Cameron University, OK	W
Campbellsville University, KY	W
Canisius College, NY	W
Carson-Newman College, TN	W
Catawba College, NC	W
Cedarville University, OH	W
Centenary College of Louisiana, LA	W
Central Connecticut State University, CT	W
Central Michigan University, MI	W
Chaminade University of Honolulu, HI	W
Chowan University, NC	W
Christian Brothers University, TN	W
Clarion University of Pennsylvania, PA	W
Clarke College, IA	W
Cleveland State University, OH	W
Coastal Carolina University, SC	W
Coker College, SC	W
Colgate University, NY	W
College of Charleston, SC	W
College of Saint Mary, NE	W
The College of Saint Rose, NY	W
Colorado School of Mines, CO	W
Colorado State University, CO	W
Columbia College, MO	W
Columbus State University, GA	W
Concordia University, CA	W
Concordia University, Nebraska, NE	W
Concordia University, St. Paul, MN	W
Corban University, OR	W
Cornerstone University, MI	W
Covenant College, GA	W
Creighton University, NE	W
Culver-Stockton College, MO	W
Dakota State University, SD	W
Dakota Wesleyan University, SD	W
Delta State University, MS	W
DePaul University, IL	W
Dickinson State University, ND	W
Dixie State College of Utah, UT	W
Doane College, NE	W
Dominican College, NY	W
Dominican University of California, CA	W
Dordt College, IA	W
Dowling College, NY	W
Drake University, IA	W
Drury University, MO	W
East Carolina University, NC	W
Eastern Michigan University, MI	W
Eastern New Mexico University, NM	W
East Stroudsburg University of Pennsylvania, PA	W
Eckerd College, FL	W
Edinboro University of Pennsylvania, PA	W
Elon University, NC	W
Emporia State University, KS	W
Erskine College, SC	W

Evangel University, MO	W	Kennesaw State University, GA	W	Mount Marty College, SD	W
Fairfield University, CT	W	Kent State University, OH	W	Mount Mercy College, IA	W
Faulkner University, AL	W	Kentucky State University, KY	W	Mount Olive College, NC	W
Fayetteville State University, NC	W	Kentucky Wesleyan College, KY	W	Mount St. Mary's University, MD	W
Felician College, NJ	W	King College, TN	W	Mount Vernon Nazarene	
Ferris State University, MI	W	Kutztown University of		University, OH	W
Flagler College, FL	W	Pennsylvania, PA	W	Murray State University, KY	W
Florida Atlantic University, FL	W	Lake Superior State University, MI	W	Newberry College, SC	W
Florida Gulf Coast University, FL	W	Lees-McRae College, NC	W	Newman University, KS	W
Florida Institute of Technology, FL	W	Lee University, TN	W	New Mexico State University, NM	W
Florida International University, FL	W	Lehigh University, PA	W	New York Institute of Technology, NY	W
Florida Southern College, FL	W	Le Moyne College, NY	W	Niagara University, NY	W
Florida State University, FL	W	Lewis University, IL	W	Nicholls State University, LA	W
Fordham University, NY	W	Limestone College, SC	W	Norfolk State University, VA	M
Fort Lewis College, CO	W	Lincoln Memorial University, TN	W	North Carolina State University, NC	W
Francis Marion University, SC	W	Lincoln University, MO	W	Northeastern State University, OK	W
Freed-Hardeman University, TN	W	Lindenwood University, MO	W	Northern Kentucky University, KY	W
Furman University, SC	W	Lindsey Wilson College, KY	W	Northern State University, SD	W
Gannon University, PA	W	Lipscomb University, TN	W	North Greenville University, SC	W
Gardner-Webb University, NC	W	Lock Haven University of		Northwest Christian University, OR	W
George Mason University, VA	W	Pennsylvania, PA	W	Northwestern Oklahoma State	
Georgetown College, KY	W	Long Island University, Brooklyn		University, OK	W
Georgetown University, DC	W	Campus, NY	W	Northwestern State University of	
Georgia College & State		Long Island University, C.W. Post		Louisiana, LA	W
University, GA	W	Campus, NY	W	Northwest Nazarene University, ID	W
Georgia Institute of Technology, GA	W	Longwood University, VA	W	Notre Dame de Namur University, CA	W
Georgian Court University, NJ	W	Louisiana State University and		Nova Southeastern University, FL	W
Georgia Southern University, GA	W	Agricultural and Mechanical		Nyack College, NY	W
Georgia State University, GA	W	College, LA	W	Oakland University, MI	W
Glenville State College, WV	W	Louisiana Tech University, LA	W	The Ohio State University, OH	W
Goldey-Beacom College, DE	W	Loyola University Chicago, IL	W	Ohio University, OH	W
Grace College, IN	W	Lubbock Christian University, TX	W	Ohio Valley University, WV	W
Graceland University, IA	W	Malone University, OH	W	Oklahoma Baptist University, OK	W
Grand Valley State University, MI	W	Manhattan College, NY	W	Oklahoma Christian University, OK	W
Grand View University, IA	W	Mansfield University of		Oklahoma City University, OK	W
Hampton University, VA	W	Pennsylvania, PA	W	Oklahoma Panhandle State	
Hannibal-LaGrange College, MO	W	Marist College, NY	W	University, OK	W
Hawai'i Pacific University, HI	W	Marshall University, WV	W	Oklahoma State University, OK	W
Henderson State University, AR	W	Maryville University of Saint		Oregon Institute of Technology, OR	W
Hofstra University, NY	W	Louis, MO	W	Oregon State University, OR	W
Holy Family University, PA	W	McKendree University, IL	W	Ouachita Baptist University, AR	W
Houston Baptist University, TX	W	Mercer University, GA	W	Pace University, NY	W
Humboldt State University, CA	W	Mercyhurst College, PA	W	Palm Beach Atlantic University, FL	W
Huntington University, IN	W	Merrimack College, MA	W	Philadelphia University, PA	W
Idaho State University, ID	W	Metropolitan State College of		Pikeville College, KY	W
Illinois State University, IL	W	Denver, CO	W	Pittsburg State University, KS	W
Indiana State University, IN	W	Miami University, OH	W	Point Park University, PA	W
Indiana University Bloomington, IN	W	Michigan State University, MI	W	Portland State University, OR	W
Indiana University of		Mid-Continent University, KY	W	Presbyterian College, SC	W
Pennsylvania, PA	W	Midwestern State University, TX	W	Providence College, RI	W
Indiana University–Purdue University		Millersville University of		Purdue University, IN	W
Fort Wayne, IN	W	Pennsylvania, PA	W	Purdue University North Central, IN	W
Indiana University–Purdue University		Milligan College, TN	W	Queens College of the City University	
Indianapolis, IN	W	Minnesota State University		of New York, NY	W
Indiana Wesleyan University, IN	W	Mankato, MN	W	Quincy University, IL	W
Inter American University of Puerto		Minnesota State University		Quinnipiac University, CT	W
Rico, Bayamón Campus, PR	M,W	Moorhead, MN	W	Radford University, VA	W
Inter American University of Puerto		Mississippi State University, MS	W	Reinhardt University, GA	W
Rico, Ponce Campus, PR	M	Mississippi Valley State		Rider University, NJ	W
Iona College, NY	W	University, MS	W	Robert Morris University, PA	W
Iowa State University of Science and		Missouri Southern State		Robert Morris University Illinois, IL	W
Technology, IA	W	University, MO	W	Rockhurst University, MO	W
Iowa Wesleyan College, IA	W	Missouri State University, MO	W	Rollins College, FL	W
Jacksonville State University, AL	W	Missouri University of Science and		Sacred Heart University, CT	W
Jacksonville University, FL	W	Technology, MO	W	Saginaw Valley State University, MI	W
James Madison University, VA	W	Molloy College, NY	W	St. Ambrose University, IA	W
Jamestown College, ND	W	Monmouth University, NJ	W	St. Andrews Presbyterian College, NC	W
Johnson C. Smith University, NC	W	Morehead State University, KY	W	St. Bonaventure University, NY	W
Judson College, AL	W	Morningside College, IA	W	St. Edward's University, TX	W

Saint Francis University, PA	W	Texas A&M University–Corpus Christi, TX	W	University of Massachusetts Amherst, MA	W
St. John's University, NY	W			University of Michigan, MI	W
Saint Joseph's University, PA	W	Texas State University– San Marcos, TX	W	University of Michigan–Dearborn, MI	W
Saint Leo University, FL	W	Texas Tech University, TX	W	University of Minnesota, Crookston, MN	W
Saint Louis University, MO	W	Texas Woman's University, TX	W	University of Minnesota, Duluth, MN	W
Saint Martin's University, WA	W	Tiffin University, OH	W	University of Minnesota, Twin Cities Campus, MN	W
Saint Mary's College of California, CA	W	Towson University, MD	W	University of Mississippi, MS	W
St. Thomas University, FL	W	Trevecca Nazarene University, TN	W	University of Missouri, MO	W
Saint Xavier University, IL	W	Trinity Christian College, IL	W	University of Missouri–Kansas City, MO	W
Samford University, AL	W	Troy University, AL	W		
Sam Houston State University, TX	M,W	Truett-McConnell College, GA	W	University of Missouri–St. Louis, MO	W
San Diego State University, CA	W	Truman State University, MO	W	University of Mobile, AL	W
San Francisco State University, CA	W	Tusculum College, TN	W	University of Nebraska at Kearney, NE	W
Savannah College of Art and Design, GA	W	Union College, KY	W	University of Nebraska at Omaha, NE	W
		Union University, TN	W	University of Nebraska–Lincoln, NE	W
Savannah State University, GA	W	University at Albany, State University of New York, NY	W	University of Nevada, Las Vegas, NV	W
Seattle University, WA	W			University of Nevada, Reno, NV	W
Seton Hill University, PA	W	University at Buffalo, the State University of New York, NY	W	University of New Haven, CT	W
Shepherd University, WV	W			University of North Alabama, AL	W
Shippensburg University of Pennsylvania, PA	W	The University of Akron, OH	W	The University of North Carolina at Chapel Hill, NC	W
		The University of Alabama, AL	W		
Shorter University, GA	W	The University of Alabama at Birmingham, AL	W	The University of North Carolina at Charlotte, NC	W*
Siena College, NY	W				
Slippery Rock University of Pennsylvania, PA	W	The University of Alabama in Huntsville, AL	W	The University of North Carolina at Greensboro, NC	W
Sonoma State University, CA	W	The University of Arizona, AZ	W	The University of North Carolina at Pembroke, NC	W
South Dakota State University, SD	W	University of Arkansas, AR	W		
Southeastern Louisiana University, LA	W	University of Bridgeport, CT	W	The University of North Carolina Wilmington, NC	W
		University of California, Davis, CA	W		
Southeastern Oklahoma State University, OK	W	University of California, Los Angeles, CA	W	University of North Dakota, ND	W
				University of Northern Colorado, CO	W
Southeast Missouri State University, MO	W	University of California, Riverside, CA	W	University of Northern Iowa, IA	W
				University of North Florida, FL	W
Southern Arkansas University– Magnolia, AR	W	University of California, Santa Barbara, CA	W	University of North Texas, TX	M
		University of Central Missouri, MO	W	University of Notre Dame, IN	W
Southern Connecticut State University, CT	W	University of Central Oklahoma, OK	W	University of Oklahoma, OK	W
		University of Charleston, WV	W	University of Oregon, OR	W
Southern Illinois University Carbondale, IL	W	University of Colorado at Colorado Springs, CO	W	University of Pittsburgh, PA	W
				University of Puerto Rico, Río Piedras, PR	M,W
Southern Illinois University Edwardsville, IL	W	University of Connecticut, CT	W		
		University of Dayton, OH	W	University of Rhode Island, RI	W
Southern Utah University, UT	W	University of Delaware, DE	W	University of St. Francis, IL	W
Southwest Baptist University, MO	W	University of Evansville, IN	W	University of San Diego, CA	W
Southwestern College, KS	W	The University of Findlay, OH	W	University of Science and Arts of Oklahoma, OK	W
Southwestern Oklahoma State University, OK	W	University of Florida, FL	W		
		University of Georgia, GA	W	University of South Carolina, SC	W
Southwest Minnesota State University, MN	W	University of Hartford, CT	W	University of South Carolina Aiken, SC	W
		University of Hawaii at Hilo, HI	W		
Spring Arbor University, MI	W	University of Houston, TX	W	The University of South Dakota, SD	W
Spring Hill College, AL	W	University of Illinois at Chicago, IL	W	University of Southern Indiana, IN	W
Stanford University, CA	W	University of Illinois at Springfield, IL	W	University of Southern Mississippi, MS	W
State University of New York at Binghamton, NY	W	University of Illinois at Urbana– Champaign, IL	W		
				The University of Tampa, FL	W
Stephen F. Austin State University, TX	W	University of Indianapolis, IN	W	The University of Tennessee, TN	W
Stephens College, MO	W	The University of Iowa, IA	W	The University of Tennessee at Chattanooga, TN	W
Stetson University, FL	W	The University of Kansas, KS	W		
Stonehill College, MA	W	University of Kentucky, KY	W	The University of Tennessee at Martin, TN	W
Stony Brook University, State University of New York, NY	W	University of Louisiana at Monroe, LA	W	The University of Texas at Arlington, TX	M
		University of Louisville, KY	W		
Syracuse University, NY	W	University of Maine, ME	W	The University of Texas at Austin, TX	W
Tabor College, KS	W	University of Mary, ND	W	The University of Texas at San Antonio, TX	W
Tarleton State University, TX	W	University of Maryland, Baltimore County, MD	W		
Taylor University, IN	W			The University of Texas of the Permian Basin, TX	W
Temple University, PA	W	University of Maryland, College Park, MD	W		
Tennessee Technological University, TN	W				
Tennessee Wesleyan College, TN	W				
Texas A&M University, TX	W				

University of the Incarnate Word, TX	W	Brenau University, GA	W	Iowa State University of Science and	
University of the Pacific, CA	W	Brigham Young University, UT	M,W	Technology, IA	M,W
University of the Sciences in		Bryant University, RI	M,W	James Madison University, VA	W
Philadelphia, PA	W	Bucknell University, PA	M,W	King College, TN	M,W
University of the Southwest, NM	W	California Baptist University, CA	M,W	Kutztown University of	
The University of Toledo, OH	W	California Polytechnic State		Pennsylvania, PA	W
University of Tulsa, OK	W	University, San Luis Obispo, CA	M,W	Lehigh University, PA	M,W
University of Virginia, VA	W	California State University,		Lewis University, IL	M,W
The University of Virginia's College		Fresno, CA	W	Limestone College, SC	M,W
at Wise, VA	W	California State University,		Lindenwood University, MO	M,W
University of Washington, WA	W	Northridge, CA	M,W	Lindsey Wilson College, KY	M,W
The University of West Alabama, AL	W	California State University,		Lock Haven University of	
University of West Florida, FL	W	San Bernardino, CA	M,W	Pennsylvania, PA	W
University of West Georgia, GA	W	Campbellsville University, KY	W	Long Island University, C.W. Post	
University of Wisconsin–Green		Canisius College, NY	M,W	Campus, NY	W
Bay, WI	W	Catawba College, NC	M,W	Louisiana State University and	
University of Wisconsin–Madison, WI	W	Centenary College of Louisiana, LA	M,W	Agricultural and Mechanical	
University of Wisconsin–Parkside, WI	W	Central Connecticut State		College, LA	M,W
Ursuline College, OH	W	University, CT	W	Loyola University Maryland, MD	M,W
Utah State University, UT	W	Clarion University of		Malone University, OH	M,W
Utah Valley University, UT	W	Pennsylvania, PA	M,W	Manhattan College, NY	W
Valdosta State University, GA	W	Clemson University, SC	M,W	Marist College, NY	M,W
Valley City State University, ND	W	Cleveland State University, OH	M	Marshall University, WV	W
Valparaiso University, IN	W	College of Charleston, SC	M,W	Metropolitan State College of	
Vanguard University of Southern		College of Saint Mary, NE	W	Denver, CO	M,W
California, CA	W	The College of Saint Rose, NY	M,W	Miami University, OH	M,W
Villanova University, PA	W	Colorado State University, CO	W	Michigan State University, MI	M,W
Virginia Intermont College, VA	W	Concordia University, CA	M,W	Millersville University of	
Virginia Union University, VA	W	Converse College, SC	W	Pennsylvania, PA	W
Wagner College, NY	W	Davidson College, NC	M,W	Minnesota State University	
Waldorf College, IA	W	Delta State University, MS	M,W	Mankato, MN	M,W
Washburn University, KS	W	Drury University, MO	M,W	Missouri State University, MO	M,W
Wayne State College, NE	W	Duquesne University, PA	W	Missouri University of Science and	
Wayne State University, MI	W	East Carolina University, NC	M,W	Technology, MO	M
Webber International University, FL	W	Eastern Michigan University, MI	M,W	Morningside College, IA	M,W
West Chester University of		East Stroudsburg University of		Mount St. Mary's University, MD	W
Pennsylvania, PA	W	Pennsylvania, PA	W	New Jersey Institute of	
Western Carolina University, NC	W	Edinboro University of		Technology, NJ	M,W
Western Illinois University, IL	W	Pennsylvania, PA	M,W	New Mexico State University, NM	W
Western Kentucky University, KY	W	Fairfield University, CT	M,W	Niagara University, NY	M,W
Western Oregon University, OR	W	Fairmont State University, WV	M,W	North Carolina Agricultural and	
Western Washington University, WA	W	Florida Agricultural and Mechanical		Technical State University, NC	W
West Liberty University, WV	W	University, FL	M,W	North Carolina State University, NC	M,W
West Virginia Wesleyan College, WV	W	Florida Gulf Coast University, FL	W	Northeastern University, MA	W
Wheeling Jesuit University, WV	W	Florida International University, FL	W	Northern Arizona University, AZ	W
Wichita State University, KS	W	Florida Southern College, FL	M,W	Northern Michigan University, MI	W
William Jewell College, MO	W	Florida State University, FL	M,W	Northern State University, SD	W
Winona State University, MN	W	Fordham University, NY	M,W	Oakland University, MI	M,W
Winthrop University, SC	W	Gannon University, PA	M,W	The Ohio State University, OH	M,W
Wright State University, OH	W	Gardner-Webb University, NC	M,W	Ohio University, OH	W
York College, NE	W	George Mason University, VA	M,W	Old Dominion University, VA	M,W
Youngstown State University, OH	W	The George Washington		Oregon State University, OR	W
		University, DC	M,W	Ouachita Baptist University, AR	M,W
Squash		Georgia Institute of Technology, GA	M,W	Penn State University Park, PA	M,W
University of Great Falls, MT	W	Georgia Southern University, GA	W	Pepperdine University, CA	W
		Grand Valley State University, MI	M,W	Providence College, RI	M,W
Swimming and Diving		Hannibal-LaGrange College, MO	M,W	Purdue University, IN	M,W
Adams State College, CO	W	Henderson State University, AR	M,W	Queens College of the City University	
Adelphi University, NY	M,W	Illinois Institute of Technology, IL	M,W	of New York, NY	M,W
Arizona State University, AZ	M,W	Illinois State University, IL	W	Radford University, VA	W
Asbury University, KY	M,W	Indiana University Bloomington, IN	M,W	Rider University, NJ	M,W
Ashland University, OH	M,W	Indiana University of		Robert Morris University Illinois, IL	W
Auburn University, AL	M,W	Pennsylvania, PA	W	Sacred Heart University, CT	W
Ball State University, IN	M,W	Indiana University–Purdue University		St. Bonaventure University, NY	M,W
Bentley University, MA	M,W	Indianapolis, IN	M,W	Saint Francis University, PA	M,W
Bloomsburg University of		Inter American University of Puerto		Saint Leo University, FL	M,W
Pennsylvania, PA	M,W	Rico, Bayamón Campus, PR	M,W	Saint Louis University, MO	M,W
Boston College, MA	M,W	Iona College, NY	M,W	San Diego State University, CA	W
Boston University, MA	M,W			San Jose State University, CA	W
Bowling Green State University, OH	W				

Savannah College of Art and
  Design, GA   M,W
Seattle University, WA   M,W
Shippensburg University of
  Pennsylvania, PA   M,W
Siena College, NY   W
South Dakota State University, SD   M,W
Southern Connecticut State
  University, CT   M,W
Southern Illinois University
  Carbondale, IL   M,W
Southern Methodist University, TX   M,W
Stanford University, CA   M,W
State University of New York at
  Binghamton, NY
Stephens College, MO   W
Stony Brook University, State
  University of New York, NY   M,W
Syracuse University, NY   M,W
Texas A&M University, TX   M,W
Texas Christian University, TX   M,W
Towson University, MD   M,W
Truman State University, MO   M,W
Tulane University, LA   W
Union College, KY   M,W
University at Buffalo, the State
  University of New York, NY   M,W
The University of Akron, OH   W
The University of Alabama, AL   M,W
The University of Arizona, AZ   M,W
University of Arkansas, AR   W
University of Bridgeport, CT   M,W
University of California, Davis, CA   M,W
University of California,
  Los Angeles, CA   W
University of California, Santa
  Barbara, CA   M,W
University of Charleston, WV   M,W
University of Cincinnati, OH   M,W
University of Connecticut, CT   M,W
University of Delaware, DE   W
University of Denver, CO   M,W
University of Evansville, IN   M,W
The University of Findlay, OH   M,W
University of Florida, FL   M,W
University of Georgia, GA   M,W
University of Houston, TX   W
University of Illinois at Chicago, IL   M,W
University of Illinois at Urbana–
  Champaign, IL   W
University of Indianapolis, IN   M,W
The University of Iowa, IA   M,W
The University of Kansas, KS   W
University of Kentucky, KY   M,W
University of Louisiana at
  Monroe, LA   M,W
University of Louisville, KY   M,W
University of Maine, ME   W
University of Maryland, Baltimore
  County, MD   M,W
University of Maryland, College
  Park, MD   M,W
University of Massachusetts
  Amherst, MA   M,W
University of Massachusetts
  Lowell, MA   M
University of Miami, FL   W
University of Michigan, MI   M,W

University of Minnesota, Twin Cities
  Campus, MN   M,W
University of Missouri, MO   M,W
University of Nebraska at
  Kearney, NE   W
University of Nebraska–Lincoln, NE   W
University of Nevada, Las Vegas, NV   M,W
University of Nevada, Reno, NV   W
University of New Hampshire, NH   W
University of New Orleans, LA   M,W
The University of North Carolina at
  Chapel Hill, NC   M,W
The University of North Carolina
  Wilmington, NC   M,W
University of North Dakota, ND   W
University of Northern Colorado, CO   W
University of Northern Iowa, IA   W
University of North Florida, FL   W
University of North Texas, TX   W
University of Notre Dame, IN   M,W
University of Pittsburgh, PA   M,W
University of Puerto Rico, Río
  Piedras, PR   M,W
University of Rhode Island, RI   W
University of Richmond, VA   W
University of San Diego, CA   W
University of South Carolina, SC   M,W
The University of South Dakota, SD   M,W
University of Southern California, CA   M,W
The University of Tampa, FL   M,W
The University of Tennessee, TN   M,W
The University of Texas at
  Austin, TX   M,W
The University of Texas of the
  Permian Basin, TX   M,W
University of the Incarnate Word, TX   M,W
University of the Pacific, CA   M,W
The University of Toledo, OH   W
University of Vermont, VT   W
University of Virginia, VA   M,W
University of Wisconsin–Green
  Bay, WI   M,W
University of Wisconsin–
  Madison, WI   M,W
University of Wyoming, WY   M,W
Ursuline College, OH   W
Valparaiso University, IN   M,W
Vanguard University of Southern
  California, CA   M,W
Villanova University, PA   W
Virginia Military Institute, VA   M
Virginia Polytechnic Institute and
  State University, VA   M,W
Wagner College, NY   W
Washington State University, WA   W
Wayne State University, MI   M,W
West Chester University of
  Pennsylvania, PA   M,W
Western Illinois University, IL   M,W
Western Kentucky University, KY   M,W
West Virginia University, WV   M,W
West Virginia Wesleyan College, WV   M,W
Wheeling Jesuit University, WV   M,W
Wichita State University, KS   M,W
Wright State University, OH   M,W
Xavier University, OH   M,W
Youngstown State University, OH   W

Table Tennis

Inter American University of Puerto
  Rico, Bayamón Campus, PR   M,W
Lindenwood University, MO   M,W
University of Puerto Rico, Río
  Piedras, PR   M,W

Tennis

Abilene Christian University, TX   M,W
Abraham Baldwin Agricultural
  College, GA   M,W
Academy of Art University, CA   W
Adelphi University, NY   M,W
Alabama State University, AL   M,W
Appalachian State University, NC   M,W
Arizona State University, AZ   W
Arkansas State University—
  Jonesboro, AR   W
Arkansas Tech University, AR   W
Armstrong Atlantic State
  University, GA   M,W
Asbury University, KY   M,W
Auburn University, AL   M,W
Auburn University Montgomery, AL   M,W
Augustana College, SD   M,W
Austin Peay State University, TN   M,W
Azusa Pacific University, CA   M
Ball State University, IN   M,W
Barry University, FL   M,W
Barton College, NC   M,W
Baylor University, TX   M,W
Belhaven University, MS   M,W
Bellarmine University, KY   M,W
Belmont Abbey College, NC   M,W
Belmont University, TN   M,W
Bemidji State University, MN   W
Bentley University, MA   M,W
Bethany College, KS   M,W
Bethel College, IN   M,W
Bethel College, KS   M,W
Bethune-Cookman University, FL   M,W
Bloomfield College, NJ   M
Bloomsburg University of
  Pennsylvania, PA   M,W
Bluefield College, VA   M,W
Bluefield State College, WV   M,W
Boise State University, ID   M,W
Boston College, MA   M,W
Boston University, MA   W
Bowie State University, MD   W
Bowling Green State University, OH   W
Bradley University, IL   M,W
Brenau University, GA   W
Brevard College, NC   M,W
Briar Cliff University, IA   M,W
Brigham Young University, UT   M,W
Bryant University, RI   M,W
Butler University, IN   M,W
California Polytechnic State
  University, San Luis Obispo, CA   M,W
California State Polytechnic
  University, Pomona, CA   M,W
California State University,
  Fresno, CA   M,W
California State University,
  Fullerton, CA   W
California State University, Long
  Beach, CA   W
California State University,
  Northridge, CA   W

California State University, Sacramento, CA	M,W
Cameron University, OK	M,W
Campbellsville University, KY	M,W
Carson-Newman College, TN	M,W
Catawba College, NC	M,W
Cedarville University, OH	M,W
Centenary College of Louisiana, LA	M,W
Chaminade University of Honolulu, HI	M,W
Chowan University, NC	M,W
Christian Brothers University, TN	M,W
The Citadel, The Military College of South Carolina, SC	M
Clarion University of Pennsylvania, PA	W
Clarke College, IA	W
Clemson University, SC	M,W
Cleveland State University, OH	W
Coastal Carolina University, SC	M,W
Coker College, SC	M,W
College of Charleston, SC	M,W
The College of William and Mary, VA	M,W
Colorado State University, CO	W
Columbus State University, GA	M,W
Concordia University, CA	M,W
Concordia University, Nebraska, NE	M,W
Concord University, WV	M,W
Converse College, SC	W
Coppin State University, MD	M,W
Covenant College, GA	M,W
Creighton University, NE	M,W
Dallas Baptist University, TX	W
Davidson College, NC	M,W
Delta State University, MS	M,W
DePaul University, IL	M,W
Dixie State College of Utah, UT	W
Dominican University of California, CA	W
Dowling College, NY	M,W
Drake University, IA	M,W
Drury University, MO	M,W
Duke University, NC	M,W
Duquesne University, PA	M,W
East Carolina University, NC	M,W
Eastern Michigan University, MI	W
Eastern Washington University, WA	M,W
East Stroudsburg University of Pennsylvania, PA	M,W
Eckerd College, FL	M,W
Elon University, NC	M,W
Embry-Riddle Aeronautical University, FL	M,W
Emporia State University, KS	M,W
Erskine College, SC	M,W
Evangel University, MO	M,W
Fairfield University, CT	M,W
Fairmont State University, WV	M,W
Fayetteville State University, NC	W
Ferris State University, MI	M,W
Flagler College, FL	M,W
Florida Agricultural and Mechanical University, FL	M,W
Florida Gulf Coast University, FL	M,W
Florida Institute of Technology, FL	M,W
Florida International University, FL	W
Florida Southern College, FL	M,W
Florida State University, FL	M,W

Fordham University, NY	M,W
Fort Valley State University, GA	M,W
Francis Marion University, SC	M,W
Furman University, SC	M,W
Gardner-Webb University, NC	M,W
George Mason University, VA	M,W
Georgetown College, KY	M,W
Georgetown University, DC	W
The George Washington University, DC	M,W
Georgia College & State University, GA	M,W
Georgia Institute of Technology, GA	M,W
Georgian Court University, NJ	W
Georgia Southern University, GA	M,W
Georgia State University, GA	M,W
Goldey-Beacom College, DE	W
Gonzaga University, WA	M,W
Grace College, IN	M,W
Graceland University, IA	M,W
Grand Valley State University, MI	M,W
Hampton University, VA	M,W
Harding University, AR	M,W
Hawai'i Pacific University, HI	M,W
Henderson State University, AR	M,W
High Point University, NC	M,W
Hofstra University, NY	M,W
Holy Family University, PA	W
Huntington University, IN	M,W
Idaho State University, ID	M,W
Illinois State University, IL	M,W
Indiana University Bloomington, IN	M,W
Indiana University of Pennsylvania, PA	W
Indiana University–Purdue University Fort Wayne, IN	M,W
Indiana University–Purdue University Indianapolis, IN	M,W
Indiana Wesleyan University, IN	M,W
Iowa State University of Science and Technology, IA	W
Jacksonville State University, AL	M,W
Jacksonville University, FL	M,W
James Madison University, VA	M,W
John Brown University, AR	M,W
Johnson C. Smith University, NC	M,W
Judson College, AL	W
Kansas State University, KS	W
Kennesaw State University, GA	W
King College, TN	M,W
Kutztown University of Pennsylvania, PA	M,W
Lake Superior State University, MI	M,W
Lamar University, TX	M,W
Lees-McRae College, NC	M,W
Lee University, TN	M,W
Lehigh University, PA	M,W
Le Moyne College, NY	M,W
Lewis-Clark State College, ID	M,W
Lewis University, IL	M,W
Limestone College, SC	M,W
Lincoln Memorial University, TN	M,W
Lincoln University, MO	W
Lindenwood University, MO	M,W
Lindsey Wilson College, KY	M,W
Lipscomb University, TN	M,W
Long Island University, Brooklyn Campus, NY	W

Long Island University, C.W. Post Campus, NY	W
Longwood University, VA	M,W
Louisiana State University and Agricultural and Mechanical College, LA	M,W
Louisiana Tech University, LA	W
Loyola University Maryland, MD	M,W
Malone University, OH	M,W
Manhattan College, NY	M,W
Marist College, NY	M,W
Marquette University, WI	M,W
Marshall University, WV	W
Maryville University of Saint Louis, MO	M,W
The Master's College and Seminary, CA	W
McKendree University, IL	M,W
Mercer University, GA	M,W
Mercyhurst College, PA	M,W
Merrimack College, MA	W
Metropolitan State College of Denver, CO	M,W
Miami University, OH	W
Michigan State University, MI	M,W
Michigan Technological University, MI	W
Midwestern State University, TX	M,W
Millersville University of Pennsylvania, PA	M,W
Milligan College, TN	M,W
Minnesota State University Mankato, MN	M,W
Mississippi State University, MS	M,W
Mississippi Valley State University, MS	M,W
Missouri Southern State University, MO	W
Molloy College, NY	W
Monmouth University, NJ	M,W
Montana State University, MT	M,W
Montana State University Billings, MT	M,W
Morehead State University, KY	M,W
Morehouse College, GA	M
Morningside College, IA	M,W
Mount Olive College, NC	M,W
Mount St. Mary's University, MD	M,W
Murray State University, KY	M,W
Newberry College, SC	M,W
New Jersey Institute of Technology, NJ	M,W
Newman University, KS	M,W
New Mexico State University, NM	M,W
Niagara University, NY	M,W
Nicholls State University, LA	W
Norfolk State University, VA	M,W
North Carolina Agricultural and Technical State University, NC	M,W
North Carolina State University, NC	M,W
Northeastern State University, OK	W
Northern Arizona University, AZ	M,W
Northern Kentucky University, KY	M,W
Northern State University, SD	W
North Georgia College & State University, GA	M,W
North Greenville University, SC	M,W
Northwestern State University of Louisiana, LA	W

Notre Dame de Namur University, CA	W
Oakland University, MI	W
The Ohio State University, OH	M,W
Oklahoma Baptist University, OK	M,W
Oklahoma Christian University, OK	M,W
Oklahoma State University, OK	M,W
Oklahoma Wesleyan University, OK	M,W
Old Dominion University, VA	M,W
Oral Roberts University, OK	M,W
Ouachita Baptist University, AR	M,W
Our Lady of the Lake University of San Antonio, TX	M,W
Pace University, NY	M,W
Palm Beach Atlantic University, FL	M,W
Penn State University Park, PA	M,W
Pepperdine University, CA	M,W
Philadelphia University, PA	M,W
Pikeville College, KY	M,W
Portland State University, OR	M,W
Presbyterian College, SC	M,W
Providence College, RI	W
Purdue University, IN	M,W
Queens College of the City University of New York, NY	M,W
Quincy University, IL	M,W
Quinnipiac University, CT	M,W
Radford University, VA	M,W
Reinhardt University, GA	M,W
Rider University, NJ	M,W
Robert Morris University, PA	M,W
Robert Morris University Illinois, IL	W
Roberts Wesleyan College, NY	M,W
Rockhurst University, MO	M,W
Rollins College, FL	M,W
Sacred Heart University, CT	M,W
Saginaw Valley State University, MI	W
St. Ambrose University, IA	M,W
St. Andrews Presbyterian College, NC	M,W
St. Bonaventure University, NY	M,W
St. Edward's University, TX	M,W
Saint Francis University, PA	M,W
St. John's University, NY	M,W
Saint Joseph's University, PA	M,W
Saint Leo University, FL	M,W
Saint Louis University, MO	M,W
Saint Mary's College of California, CA	M,W
St. Mary's University, TX	M,W
St. Thomas University, FL	M,W
Samford University, AL	M,W
Sam Houston State University, TX	M,W
San Diego State University, CA	M,W
San Jose State University, CA	W
Santa Clara University, CA	M,W
Savannah College of Art and Design, GA	M,W
Savannah State University, GA	W
Seton Hill University, PA	W
Shepherd University, WV	M,W
Shippensburg University of Pennsylvania, PA	W
Shorter University, GA	M,W
Siena College, NY	M,W
Slippery Rock University of Pennsylvania, PA	W
Sonoma State University, CA	M,W
South Dakota State University, SD	M,W
Southeastern Louisiana University, LA	W

Southeastern Oklahoma State University, OK	M,W
Southeast Missouri State University, MO	W
Southern Arkansas University–Magnolia, AR	W
Southern Illinois University Carbondale, IL	M,W
Southern Illinois University Edwardsville, IL	M,W
Southern Methodist University, TX	M,W
Southern Utah University, UT	W
Southwest Baptist University, MO	M,W
Southwestern College, KS	M,W
Southwest Minnesota State University, MN	W
Spring Arbor University, MI	M,W
Spring Hill College, AL	M,W
Stanford University, CA	M,W
State University of New York at Binghamton, NY	M,W
Stephen F. Austin State University, TX	W
Stephens College, MO	W
Stetson University, FL	M,W
Stonehill College, MA	M,W
Stony Brook University, State University of New York, NY	M,W
Syracuse University, NY	W
Tabor College, KS	M,W
Tarleton State University, TX	W
Taylor University, IN	M,W
Temple University, PA	M,W
Tennessee Technological University, TN	M,W
Tennessee Wesleyan College, TN	M,W
Texas A&M University, TX	M,W
Texas A&M University–Corpus Christi, TX	M,W
Texas Christian University, TX	M,W
Texas State University–San Marcos, TX	W
Texas Tech University, TX	M,W
Tiffin University, OH	M,W
Towson University, MD	M,W
Troy University, AL	M,W
Truman State University, MO	M,W
Tulane University, LA	M,W
Tusculum College, TN	M,W
Tuskegee University, AL	M,W
Union College, KY	M,W
University at Albany, State University of New York, NY	W
University at Buffalo, the State University of New York, NY	M,W
The University of Akron, OH	W
The University of Alabama, AL	M,W
The University of Alabama at Birmingham, AL	M,W
The University of Alabama in Huntsville, AL	M,W
The University of Arizona, AZ	M,W
University of Arkansas, AR	M,W
University of California, Davis, CA	M,W
University of California, Irvine, CA	M,W
University of California, Los Angeles, CA	M,W
University of California, Riverside, CA	M,W

University of California, Santa Barbara, CA	M,W
University of Central Florida, FL	M,W
University of Central Oklahoma, OK	M,W
University of Charleston, WV	M,W
University of Cincinnati, OH	W
University of Colorado at Boulder, CO	W
University of Connecticut, CT	M,W
University of Dayton, OH	M,W
University of Denver, CO	M,W
University of Evansville, IN	W
The University of Findlay, OH	M,W
University of Florida, FL	M,W
University of Georgia, GA	M,W
University of Hartford, CT	M,W
University of Hawaii at Hilo, HI	M,W
University of Houston, TX	W
University of Idaho, ID	M,W
University of Illinois at Chicago, IL	M,W
University of Illinois at Springfield, IL	M,W
University of Illinois at Urbana–Champaign, IL	M,W
University of Indianapolis, IN	M,W
The University of Iowa, IA	M,W
The University of Kansas, KS	W
University of Kentucky, KY	M,W
University of Louisville, KY	M,W
University of Mary, ND	W
University of Maryland, Baltimore County, MD	M,W
University of Maryland, College Park, MD	M,W
University of Massachusetts Amherst, MA	W
University of Massachusetts Lowell, MA	M,W
University of Memphis, TN	M,W
University of Miami, FL	M,W
University of Michigan, MI	M,W
University of Minnesota, Crookston, MN	W
University of Minnesota, Duluth, MN	W
University of Minnesota, Twin Cities Campus, MN	
University of Mississippi, MS	M,W
University of Missouri, MO	W
University of Missouri–Kansas City, MO	M,W
University of Missouri–St. Louis, MO	M,W
University of Mobile, AL	M,W
University of Montevallo, AL	W
University of Nebraska at Kearney, NE	M,W
University of Nebraska–Lincoln, NE	M,W
University of Nevada, Las Vegas, NV	M,W
University of Nevada, Reno, NV	M,W
University of New Haven, CT	W
University of New Orleans, LA	M,W
University of North Alabama, AL	M,W
The University of North Carolina at Asheville, NC	M,W
The University of North Carolina at Chapel Hill, NC	M,W
The University of North Carolina at Charlotte, NC	M,W
The University of North Carolina at Greensboro, NC	M,W

The University of North Carolina at Pembroke, NC — W
The University of North Carolina Wilmington, NC — M,W
University of Northern Colorado, CO — M,W
University of Northern Iowa, IA — W
University of North Florida, FL — M,W
University of Notre Dame, IN — M,W
University of Oklahoma, OK — M,W
University of Oregon, OR — M,W
University of Pittsburgh, PA — W
University of Portland, OR — M,W
University of Puerto Rico at Bayamón, PR — M,W
University of Puerto Rico, Río Piedras, PR — M,W
University of Rhode Island, RI — W
University of Richmond, VA — M,W
University of St. Francis, IL — M,W
University of San Diego, CA — M,W
University of South Alabama, AL — M,W
University of South Carolina, SC — M,W
University of South Carolina Aiken, SC — M,W
The University of South Dakota, SD — W
University of Southern California, CA — M,W
University of Southern Indiana, IN — M,W
University of Southern Mississippi, MS — M,W
The University of Tampa, FL — W
The University of Tennessee, TN — M,W
The University of Tennessee at Chattanooga, TN — M,W
The University of Tennessee at Martin, TN — W
The University of Texas at Arlington, TX — M,W
The University of Texas at Austin, TX — M,W
The University of Texas at El Paso, TX — W
The University of Texas at San Antonio, TX — M,W
The University of Texas–Pan American, TX — M,W
University of the District of Columbia, DC — M,W
University of the Incarnate Word, TX — M,W
University of the Pacific, CA — M,W
University of the Southwest, NM — M,W
The University of Toledo, OH — M,W
University of Tulsa, OK — M,W
University of Virginia, VA — M,W
The University of Virginia's College at Wise, VA — M,W
University of Washington, WA — M,W
University of West Florida, FL — M,W
University of Wisconsin–Green Bay, WI — M,W
University of Wisconsin–Madison, WI — M,W
University of Wyoming, WY — W
Ursuline College, OH — W
Utah State University, UT — M,W
Valdosta State University, GA — M,W
Valparaiso University, IN — M,W
Vanderbilt University, TN — M,W
Vanguard University of Southern California, CA — M,W

Virginia Commonwealth University, VA — M,W
Virginia Military Institute, VA — M
Virginia Polytechnic Institute and State University, VA — M,W
Virginia Union University, VA — M
Wagner College, NY — M,W
Wake Forest University, NC — M,W
Washburn University, KS — M,W
Washington State University, WA — W
Wayne State University, MI — M,W
Webber International University, FL — M,W
West Chester University of Pennsylvania, PA — M,W
Western Carolina University, NC — W
Western Illinois University, IL — M,W
Western Kentucky University, KY — M,W
West Liberty University, WV — M,W
Westmont College, CA — M,W
West Virginia University, WV — W
West Virginia Wesleyan College, WV — M,W
Wichita State University, KS — M,W
William Jewell College, MO — M,W
Winona State University, MN — M,W
Winthrop University, SC — M,W
Wofford College, SC — M,W
Wright State University, OH — M,W
Xavier University, OH — M,W
Xavier University of Louisiana, LA — M,W
Youngstown State University, OH — M,W

Track and Field

Abilene Christian University, TX — M,W
Academy of Art University, CA — M,W
Adams State College, CO — M,W
Adelphi University, NY — M,W
Alabama Agricultural and Mechanical University, AL — M,W
Alabama State University, AL — M,W
Alderson-Broaddus College, WV — M,W
American University, DC — M,W
Angelo State University, TX — M,W
Appalachian State University, NC — M,W
Arizona State University, AZ — M,W
Arkansas State University—Jonesboro, AR — M,W
Ashland University, OH — M,W
Auburn University, AL — M,W
Augustana College, SD — M,W
Austin Peay State University, TN — W
Azusa Pacific University, CA — M,W
Ball State University, IN — W
Baylor University, TX — M,W
Bellarmine University, KY — M,W
Belmont University, TN — M,W
Bemidji State University, MN — M,W
Benedictine College, KS — M,W
Bentley University, MA — M,W
Bethany College, KS — M,W
Bethel College, IN — M,W
Bethel College, KS — M,W
Bethune-Cookman University, FL — M,W
Black Hills State University, SD — M,W
Bloomsburg University of Pennsylvania, PA — M,W
Boise State University, ID — M,W
Boston College, MA — M,W
Boston University, MA — M,W
Bowie State University, MD — M,W
Bowling Green State University, OH — W

Bradley University, IL — W
Brescia University, KY — W
Brevard College, NC — M,W
Briar Cliff University, IA — M,W
Brigham Young University, UT — M,W
Bryant University, RI — M,W
California Polytechnic State University, San Luis Obispo, CA — M,W
California State Polytechnic University, Pomona, CA — M,W
California State University, Chico, CA — M,W
California State University, Dominguez Hills, CA — W
California State University, Fresno, CA — M,W
California State University, Fullerton, CA — M,W
California State University, Long Beach, CA — M,W
California State University, Northridge, CA — M,W
California State University, Sacramento, CA — M,W
Campbellsville University, KY — M,W
Carson-Newman College, TN — M,W
Cedarville University, OH — M,W
Central Connecticut State University, CT — M,W
Central Michigan University, MI — M,W
The Citadel, The Military College of South Carolina, SC — M,W
Clarion University of Pennsylvania, PA — W
Clarke College, IA — M,W
Clemson University, SC — M,W
Cleveland State University, OH — W
Coastal Carolina University, SC — M,W
College of Charleston, SC — W
The College of Saint Rose, NY — M,W
The College of William and Mary, VA — M,W
Colorado School of Mines, CO — M,W
Colorado State University, CO — M,W
Concordia University, CA — M,W
Concordia University, Nebraska, NE — M,W
Concordia University, St. Paul, MN — M,W
Concord University, WV — M,W
Coppin State University, MD — M,W
Corban University, OR — M,W
Cornerstone University, MI — M,W
Culver-Stockton College, MO — M,W
Dakota State University, SD — M,W
Dakota Wesleyan University, SD — M,W
Dallas Baptist University, TX — W
Davenport University, MI — M,W
Davidson College, NC — M,W
DePaul University, IL — M,W
Dickinson State University, ND — M,W
Dillard University, LA — M,W
Doane College, NE — M,W
Dominican College, NY — W
Dordt College, IA — M,W
Drake University, IA — M,W
Duquesne University, PA — M,W
East Carolina University, NC — M,W
Eastern Michigan University, MI — M,W
Eastern New Mexico University, NM — M,W
Eastern Washington University, WA — M,W

East Stroudsburg University of Pennsylvania, PA	M,W	Kutztown University of Pennsylvania, PA	M,W	Northern State University, SD	M,W
Edinboro University of Pennsylvania, PA	M,W	Lake Superior State University, MI	M,W	Northwest Christian University, OR	M,W
Elon University, NC	W	Lamar University, TX	M,W	Northwestern State University of Louisiana, LA	M,W
Embry-Riddle Aeronautical University, FL	M,W	Lees-McRae College, NC	M,W	Northwest Nazarene University, ID	M,W
Emporia State University, KS	M,W	Lehigh University, PA	M,W	Northwest University, WA	M,W
Evangel University, MO	M,W	Lewis University, IL	M,W	The Ohio State University, OH	M,W
The Evergreen State College, WA	M,W	Limestone College, SC	M,W	Ohio University, OH	W
Felician College, NJ	M,W	Lincoln University, MO	M,W	Oklahoma Baptist University, OK	M,W
Ferris State University, MI	M,W	Lindenwood University, MO	M,W	Oklahoma Christian University, OK	M,W
Florida Agricultural and Mechanical University, FL	M,W	Lindsey Wilson College, KY	M,W	Oklahoma City University, OK	M,W
Florida International University, FL	M,W	Lock Haven University of Pennsylvania, PA	M,W	Oklahoma State University, OK	M,W
Florida Southern College, FL	M,W	Long Island University, Brooklyn Campus, NY	M,W	Oklahoma Wesleyan University, OK	M,W
Florida State University, FL	M,W	Louisiana State University and Agricultural and Mechanical College, LA	M,W	Oral Roberts University, OK	M,W
Fordham University, NY	M,W			Oregon Institute of Technology, OR	M,W
Fort Valley State University, GA	M,W	Louisiana Tech University, LA	M,W	Pace University, NY	M,W
Furman University, SC	M,W	Loyola University Chicago, IL	M,W	Penn State University Park, PA	M,W
Gardner-Webb University, NC	M,W	Loyola University Maryland, MD	M,W	Pittsburg State University, KS	M,W
George Mason University, VA	M,W	Malone University, OH	M,W	Portland State University, OR	M,W
Georgetown College, KY	M,W	Manhattan College, NY	M,W	Providence College, RI	M,W
Georgetown University, DC	M,W	Mansfield University of Pennsylvania, PA	M,W	Purdue University, IN	M,W
Georgia Institute of Technology, GA	M,W	Marist College, NY	M,W	Queens College of the City University of New York, NY	M,W
Georgian Court University, NJ	W	Marquette University, WI	M,W	Quinnipiac University, CT	W
Georgia Southern University, GA	W	Marshall University, WV	M,W	Radford University, VA	M,W
Georgia State University, GA	M,W	Maryville University of Saint Louis, MO	M,W	Rider University, NJ	M,W
Glenville State College, WV	M,W			Robert Morris University, PA	M,W
Grace College, IN	M,W	The Master's College and Seminary, CA	M,W	Robert Morris University Illinois, IL	W
Graceland University, IA	M,W	McKendree University, IL	M,W	Roberts Wesleyan College, NY	M,W
Grand Valley State University, MI	M,W	Miami University, OH	M,W	Sacred Heart University, CT	M,W
Grand View University, IA	M,W	Michigan State University, MI	M,W	Saginaw Valley State University, MI	M,W
Hampton University, VA	M,W	Millersville University of Pennsylvania, PA	M,W	St. Ambrose University, IA	M,W
Hannibal-LaGrange College, MO	M,W			Saint Francis University, PA	M,W
Harding University, AR	M,W	Minnesota State University Mankato, MN	M,W	St. John's University, NY	W
High Point University, NC	M,W	Minnesota State University Moorhead, MN	M,W	Saint Joseph's University, PA	M,W
Holy Family University, PA	M,W	Mississippi State University, MS	M,W	Saint Louis University, MO	M,W
Houghton College, NY	M,W	Mississippi Valley State University, MS	M,W	Saint Martin's University, WA	M,W
Houston Baptist University, TX	M,W			Samford University, AL	M,W
Humboldt State University, CA	M,W	Missouri Southern State University, MO	M,W	Sam Houston State University, TX	M,W
Huntington University, IN	M,W	Missouri State University, MO	W	San Diego State University, CA	W
Idaho State University, ID	M,W	Missouri University of Science and Technology, MO	M,W	San Francisco State University, CA	W
Illinois State University, IL	M,W			Santa Clara University, CA	M,W
Indiana State University, IN	M,W	Molloy College, NY	M,W	Savannah State University, GA	M,W
Indiana University Bloomington, IN	M,W	Monmouth University, NJ	M,W	Seattle Pacific University, WA	M,W
Indiana University of Pennsylvania, PA	M,W	Montana State University, MT	M,W	Seattle University, WA	M,W
		Morehead State University, KY	M,W	Seton Hill University, PA	M,W
Indiana University–Purdue University Fort Wayne, IN	W	Morehouse College, GA	M	Shippensburg University of Pennsylvania, PA	M,W
Indiana Wesleyan University, IN	M,W	Morningside College, IA	M,W	Shorter University, GA	M,W
Inter American University of Puerto Rico, Bayamón Campus, PR	M,W	Mountain State University, WV	M,W	Slippery Rock University of Pennsylvania, PA	M,W
		Mount Marty College, SD	M,W		
Inter American University of Puerto Rico, Ponce Campus, PR	M,W	Mount Mercy College, IA	M,W	South Dakota School of Mines and Technology, SD	M,W
Iona College, NY	M,W	Mount St. Mary's University, MD	M,W	South Dakota State University, SD	M,W
Iowa State University of Science and Technology, IA	M,W	Murray State University, KY	M,W	Southeastern Louisiana University, LA	M,W
		New Mexico State University, NM	W		
Iowa Wesleyan College, IA	M,W	Nicholls State University, LA	M,W	Southeast Missouri State University, MO	M,W
Jacksonville University, FL	W	Norfolk State University, VA	M,W		
James Madison University, VA	W	North Carolina Agricultural and Technical State University, NC	M,W	Southern Connecticut State University, CT	M,W
Jamestown College, ND	M,W				
Johnson C. Smith University, NC	M,W	North Carolina State University, NC	M,W	Southern Illinois University Carbondale, IL	M,W
Kansas State University, KS	M,W	Northeastern University, MA	M,W		
Kennesaw State University, GA	M,W	Northern Arizona University, AZ	M,W	Southern Illinois University Edwardsville, IL	M,W
Kent State University, OH	M,W	Northern Michigan University, MI	W	Southern Utah University, UT	M,W
Kentucky State University, KY	M,W			Southwest Baptist University, MO	M,W
King College, TN	M,W			Southwestern College, KS	M,W
				Spring Arbor University, MI	M,W
				Stanford University, CA	M,W

Athletic Grants for Undergraduates
Track and Field

State University of New York at Binghamton, NY — M,W
Stephen F. Austin State University, TX — M,W
Stonehill College, MA — M,W
Stony Brook University, State University of New York, NY — M,W
Syracuse University, NY — M,W
Tabor College, KS — M,W
Tarleton State University, TX — M,W
Taylor University, IN — M,W
Temple University, PA — M,W
Tennessee Technological University, TN — W
Texas A&M University, TX — M,W
Texas A&M University–Commerce, TX — M,W
Texas Christian University, TX — M,W
Texas State University–San Marcos, TX — M,W
Texas Tech University, TX — M,W
Tiffin University, OH — M,W
Towson University, MD — M,W
Trinity Christian College, IL — M,W
Troy University, AL — M,W
Truman State University, MO — M,W
Tulane University, LA — W
Tuskegee University, AL — M,W
Union College, KY — M,W
University at Albany, State University of New York, NY — M,W
University at Buffalo, the State University of New York, NY — M,W
The University of Akron, OH — M,W
The University of Alabama, AL — M,W
The University of Alabama at Birmingham, AL — W
The University of Alabama in Huntsville, AL — M,W
The University of Arizona, AZ — M,W
University of Arkansas, AR — M,W
University of California, Davis, CA — M,W
University of California, Irvine, CA — M,W
University of California, Los Angeles, CA — M,W
University of California, Riverside, CA — M,W
University of California, Santa Barbara, CA — M,W
University of Central Florida, FL — W
University of Central Missouri, MO — M,W
University of Charleston, WV — M,W
University of Cincinnati, OH — M,W
University of Colorado at Boulder, CO — M,W
University of Connecticut, CT — M,W
University of Dayton, OH — W
University of Delaware, DE — W
The University of Findlay, OH — M,W
University of Florida, FL — M,W
University of Georgia, GA — M,W
University of Great Falls, MT — M,W
University of Houston, TX — M,W
University of Idaho, ID — M,W
University of Illinois at Chicago, IL — M,W
University of Illinois at Urbana–Champaign, IL — M,W
University of Indianapolis, IN — M,W
The University of Iowa, IA — M,W

The University of Kansas, KS — M,W
University of Kentucky, KY — M,W
University of Louisiana at Monroe, LA — M,W
University of Louisville, KY — M,W
University of Maine, ME — M,W
University of Mary, ND — M,W
University of Maryland, Baltimore County, MD — M,W
University of Maryland, College Park, MD — M,W
University of Massachusetts Amherst, MA — M,W
University of Massachusetts Lowell, MA — M,W
University of Memphis, TN — M,W
University of Miami, FL — M,W
University of Michigan, MI — M,W
University of Minnesota, Duluth, MN — M,W
University of Minnesota, Twin Cities Campus, MN — M,W
University of Mississippi, MS — M,W
University of Missouri, MO — M,W
University of Missouri–Kansas City, MO — M,W
University of Mobile, AL — M,W
University of Nebraska at Kearney, NE — M,W
University of Nebraska–Lincoln, NE — M,W
University of Nevada, Las Vegas, NV — W
University of Nevada, Reno, NV — W
University of New Hampshire, NH — M,W
University of New Haven, CT — M,W
The University of North Carolina at Asheville, NC — M,W
The University of North Carolina at Chapel Hill, NC — M,W
The University of North Carolina at Charlotte, NC — M,W
The University of North Carolina at Pembroke, NC — M,W
The University of North Carolina Wilmington, NC — M,W
University of North Dakota, ND — M,W
University of Northern Colorado, CO — M,W
University of Northern Iowa, IA — M,W
University of North Florida, FL — M,W
University of North Texas, TX — M,W
University of Notre Dame, IN — M,W
University of Oklahoma, OK — M,W
University of Oregon, OR — M,W
University of Pittsburgh, PA — M,W
University of Portland, OR — M,W
University of Puerto Rico at Bayamón, PR — M,W
University of Puerto Rico, Río Piedras, PR — M,W
University of Rhode Island, RI — M,W
University of Richmond, VA — W
University of St. Francis, IL — M,W
University of San Diego, CA — W
University of South Alabama, AL — M,W
University of South Carolina, SC — M,W
The University of South Dakota, SD — M,W
University of Southern California, CA — M,W
University of Southern Mississippi, MS — M,W
The University of Tennessee, TN — M,W

The University of Tennessee at Chattanooga, TN — M,W
The University of Texas at Arlington, TX — M,W
The University of Texas at Austin, TX — M,W
The University of Texas at El Paso, TX — M,W
The University of Texas at San Antonio, TX — M,W
The University of Texas–Pan American, TX — M,W
University of the District of Columbia, DC — M,W
University of the Incarnate Word, TX — M,W
University of the Southwest, NM — M,W
The University of Toledo, OH — W
University of Tulsa, OK — M,W
University of Vermont, VT — M,W
University of Virginia, VA — M,W
University of Washington, WA — M,W
University of Wisconsin–Madison, WI — M,W
University of Wisconsin–Parkside, WI — M,W
University of Wyoming, WY — M,W
Ursuline College, OH — W
Utah State University, UT — M,W
Utah Valley University, UT — M,W
Valparaiso University, IN — M,W
Vanderbilt University, TN — W
Vanguard University of Southern California, CA — M,W
Villanova University, PA — M,W
Virginia Commonwealth University, VA — M,W
Virginia Military Institute, VA — M,W
Virginia Polytechnic Institute and State University, VA — M,W
Virginia Union University, VA — M,W
Wagner College, NY — M,W
Wake Forest University, NC — M,W
Warner Pacific College, OR — M,W
Washington State University, WA — M,W
Wayland Baptist University, TX — M,W
Wayne State College, NE — M,W
Webber International University, FL — M,W
West Chester University of Pennsylvania, PA — M,W
Western Carolina University, NC — M,W
Western Illinois University, IL — M,W
Western Kentucky University, KY — M,W
Western Oregon University, OR — M,W
Western State College of Colorado, CO — M,W
Western Washington University, WA — M,W
West Liberty University, WV — M,W
Westmont College, CA — M,W
West Virginia University, WV — W
West Virginia Wesleyan College, WV — M,W
Wheeling Jesuit University, WV — M,W
Wichita State University, KS — M,W
William Jewell College, MO — M,W
Winona State University, MN — W
Winthrop University, SC — M,W
Wofford College, SC — M,W
Wright State University, OH — W
Xavier University, OH — M,W
Youngstown State University, OH — M,W

Ultimate Frisbee

Corcoran College of Art and Design, DC	M,W
Ohio University–Zanesville, OH	M,W
St. Louis Christian College, MO	M,W
The University of Texas Medical Branch, TX	M,W

Volleyball

Abilene Christian University, TX	W
Academy of Art University, CA	W
Adams State College, CO	W
Adelphi University, NY	W
Alabama Agricultural and Mechanical University, AL	W
Alabama State University, AL	W
Alderson-Broaddus College, WV	W
American International College, MA	W
American University, DC	W
Angelo State University, TX	W
Appalachian State University, NC	W
Arizona State University, AZ	W
Arkansas State University— Jonesboro, AR	W
Arkansas Tech University, AR	W
Armstrong Atlantic State University, GA	W
Asbury University, KY	W
Ashland University, OH	W
Auburn University, AL	W
Augustana College, SD	W
Austin Peay State University, TN	W
Azusa Pacific University, CA	W
Ball State University, IN	M,W
Barry University, FL	W
Barton College, NC	W
Baylor University, TX	W
Belhaven University, MS	W
Bellarmine University, KY	W
Belmont University, TN	W
Bemidji State University, MN	W
Benedictine College, KS	W
Bentley University, MA	W
Bethany College, KS	W
Bethel College, IN	W
Bethel College, KS	W
Bethune-Cookman University, FL	W
Black Hills State University, SD	W
Blessing-Rieman College of Nursing, IL	M,W
Bloomfield College, NJ	W
Bluefield College, VA	W
Boise State University, ID	W
Boston College, MA	W
Bowie State University, MD	W
Bowling Green State University, OH	W
Bradley University, IL	W
Brenau University, GA	W
Brescia University, KY	W
Brevard College, NC	W
Brewton-Parker College, GA	W
Briar Cliff University, IA	W
Brigham Young University, UT	M,W
Bryan College, TN	W
Bryant University, RI	W
Butler University, IN	W
California Baptist University, CA	M,W
California Maritime Academy, CA	W
California Polytechnic State University, San Luis Obispo, CA	W

California State Polytechnic University, Pomona, CA	W
California State University, Chico, CA	W
California State University, Dominguez Hills, CA	W
California State University, Fresno, CA	W
California State University, Fullerton, CA	W
California State University, Long Beach, CA	M,W
California State University, Monterey Bay, CA	W
California State University, Northridge, CA	M,W
California State University, Sacramento, CA	W
California State University, San Bernardino, CA	W
Cameron University, OK	W
Campbellsville University, KY	W
Canisius College, NY	W
Carson-Newman College, TN	W
Catawba College, NC	W
Cedarville University, OH	W
Centenary College of Louisiana, LA	W
Central Connecticut State University, CT	W
Central Michigan University, MI	W
Chaminade University of Honolulu, HI	W
Chowan University, NC	W
Christian Brothers University, TN	W
The Citadel, The Military College of South Carolina, SC	W
Clarion University of Pennsylvania, PA	W
Clarke College, IA	M,W
Clemson University, SC	W
Cleveland State University, OH	W
Coastal Carolina University, SC	W
Coker College, SC	W
Colgate University, NY	W
College of Charleston, SC	W
College of Saint Mary, NE	W
The College of Saint Rose, NY	W
College of the Ozarks, MO	W
The College of William and Mary, VA	W
Colorado School of Mines, CO	W
Colorado State University, CO	W
Columbia College, MO	W
Concordia University, CA	W
Concordia University, Nebraska, NE	W
Concordia University, St. Paul, MN	W
Concord University, WV	W
Converse College, SC	W
Coppin State University, MD	W
Corban University, OR	W
Corcoran College of Art and Design, DC	M,W
Cornerstone University, MI	W
Covenant College, GA	W
Creighton University, NE	W
Culver-Stockton College, MO	W
Daemen College, NY	W
Dakota State University, SD	W
Dakota Wesleyan University, SD	W
Dallas Baptist University, TX	W
Davenport University, MI	W

Davidson College, NC	W
DePaul University, IL	W
Dickinson State University, ND	W
Dillard University, LA	W
Dixie State College of Utah, UT	W
Doane College, NE	W
Dominican College, NY	W
Dominican University of California, CA	W
Dordt College, IA	W
Dowling College, NY	W
Drake University, IA	W
Drury University, MO	W
Duke University, NC	W
Duquesne University, PA	W
East Carolina University, NC	W
Eastern Michigan University, MI	W
Eastern New Mexico University, NM	W
Eastern Washington University, WA	W
East Stroudsburg University of Pennsylvania, PA	W
Eckerd College, FL	W
Edinboro University of Pennsylvania, PA	W
Elon University, NC	W
Embry-Riddle Aeronautical University, AZ	W
Embry-Riddle Aeronautical University, FL	W
Emporia State University, KS	W
Erskine College, SC	W
Evangel University, MO	W
The Evergreen State College, WA	W
Fairfield University, CT	W
Faulkner University, AL	W
Fayetteville State University, NC	W
Ferris State University, MI	W
Flagler College, FL	W
Florida Agricultural and Mechanical University, FL	W
Florida Atlantic University, FL	W
Florida College, FL	W
Florida Gulf Coast University, FL	W
Florida Institute of Technology, FL	W
Florida International University, FL	W
Florida Southern College, FL	W
Florida State University, FL	W
Fordham University, NY	W
Fort Lewis College, CO	W
Fort Valley State University, GA	W
Francis Marion University, SC	W
Freed-Hardeman University, TN	W
Furman University, SC	W
Gannon University, PA	W
Gardner-Webb University, NC	W
George Mason University, VA	M,W
Georgetown College, KY	W
Georgetown University, DC	W
The George Washington University, DC	W
Georgia Institute of Technology, GA	W
Georgian Court University, NJ	W
Georgia Southern University, GA	W
Georgia State University, GA	W
Glenville State College, WV	W
Goldey-Beacom College, DE	W
Gonzaga University, WA	W
Grace College, IN	W
Graceland University, IA	M,W

Grand Valley State University, MI	W	Louisiana State University and		Northern Arizona University, AZ	W
Grand View University, IA	W	Agricultural and Mechanical		Northern Kentucky University, KY	W
Hampton University, VA	W	College, LA	W	Northern Michigan University, MI	W
Hannibal-LaGrange College, MO	M,W	Louisiana Tech University, LA	W	Northern State University, SD	W
Harding University, AR	W	Loyola University Chicago, IL	M,W	North Greenville University, SC	W
Hawai'i Pacific University, HI	W	Loyola University Maryland, MD	W	Northwest Christian University, OR	W
Henderson State University, AR	W	Lubbock Christian University, TX	W	Northwestern State University of	
High Point University, NC	W	Malone University, OH	W	Louisiana, LA	W
Hofstra University, NY	W	Manhattan College, NY	W	Northwest Nazarene University, ID	W
Holy Family University, PA	W	Marist College, NY	W	Northwest University, WA	W
Houghton College, NY	W	Marquette University, WI	W	Notre Dame de Namur University, CA	W
Houston Baptist University, TX	W	Marshall University, WV	W	Nova Southeastern University, FL	W
Humboldt State University, CA	W	Maryville University of Saint		Nyack College, NY	W
Huntington University, IN	W	Louis, MO	W	Oakland University, MI	W
Idaho State University, ID	W	The Master's College and		The Ohio State University, OH	M,W
Illinois Institute of Technology, IL	W	Seminary, CA	W	Ohio University, OH	W
Illinois State University, IL	W	McKendree University, IL	W	Ohio University–Zanesville, OH	M,W
Indiana State University, IN	W	Mercer University, GA	W	Ohio Valley University, WV	W
Indiana University Bloomington, IN	W	Mercyhurst College, PA	W	Oklahoma Panhandle State	
Indiana University of		Merrimack College, MA	W	University, OK	W
Pennsylvania, PA	W	Metropolitan State College of		Oklahoma Wesleyan University, OK	W
Indiana University–Purdue University		Denver, CO	W	Oral Roberts University, OK	W
Fort Wayne, IN	M,W	Miami University, OH	W	Oregon Institute of Technology, OR	W
Indiana University–Purdue University		Michigan State University, MI	W	Oregon State University, OR	W
Indianapolis, IN	W	Michigan Technological		Ouachita Baptist University, AR	W
Indiana University Southeast, IN	W	University, MI	W	Pace University, NY	W
Indiana Wesleyan University, IN	W	Mid-Continent University, KY	W	Palm Beach Atlantic University, FL	W
Inter American University of Puerto		Midwestern State University, TX	W	Penn State University Park, PA	M,W
Rico, Bayamón Campus, PR	M,W	Millersville University of		Pepperdine University, CA	M,W
Iona College, NY	W	Pennsylvania, PA	W	Philadelphia University, PA	W
Iowa State University of Science and		Milligan College, TN	W	Pikeville College, KY	W
Technology, IA	W	Minnesota State University		Pittsburg State University, KS	W
Iowa Wesleyan College, IA	W	Mankato, MN	W	Point Park University, PA	W
Jacksonville State University, AL	W	Minnesota State University		Portland State University, OR	W
Jacksonville University, FL	W	Moorhead, MN	W	Presbyterian College, SC	W
James Madison University, VA	W	Mississippi State University, MS	W	Providence College, RI	W
Jamestown College, ND	W	Missouri Southern State		Purdue University, IN	W
John Brown University, AR	W	University, MO	W	Purdue University North Central, IN	W
Johnson C. Smith University, NC	W	Missouri State University, MO	W	Queens College of the City University	
Judson College, AL	W	Missouri University of Science and		of New York, NY	W
Kansas State University, KS	W	Technology, MO	W	Quincy University, IL	M,W
Kennesaw State University, GA	W	Molloy College, NY	W	Quinnipiac University, CT	W
Kent State University, OH	W	Montana State University, MT	W	Radford University, VA	W
Kentucky State University, KY	W	Montana State University		Rider University, NJ	W
Kentucky Wesleyan College, KY	W	Billings, MT	W	Robert Morris University, PA	W
King College, TN	W	Montana Tech of The University of		Robert Morris University Illinois, IL	M,W
Kutztown University of		Montana, MT	W	Roberts Wesleyan College, NY	W
Pennsylvania, PA	W	Morehead State University, KY	W	Rockhurst University, MO	W
Lake Superior State University, MI	W	Morningside College, IA	W	Rocky Mountain College, MT	W
Lamar University, TX	W	Mountain State University, WV	W	Rollins College, FL	W
Lees-McRae College, NC	M,W	Mount Marty College, SD	W	Sacred Heart University, CT	M,W
Lee University, TN	W	Mount Mercy College, IA	W	Saginaw Valley State University, MI	W
Lehigh University, PA	W	Mount Olive College, NC	M,W	St. Ambrose University, IA	M,W
Le Moyne College, NY	W	Mount Vernon Nazarene		St. Andrews Presbyterian College, NC	W
Lewis-Clark State College, ID	W	University, OH	W	St. Edward's University, TX	W
Lewis University, IL	M,W	Murray State University, KY	W	Saint Francis University, PA	M,W
Limestone College, SC	M,W	Newberry College, SC	W	St. John's University, NY	W
Lincoln Memorial University, TN	W	New Jersey Institute of		Saint Leo University, FL	W
Lindenwood University, MO	M,W	Technology, NJ	M,W	St. Louis Christian College, MO	M,W
Lindsey Wilson College, KY	W	Newman University, KS	W	Saint Louis University, MO	W
Lipscomb University, TN	W	New Mexico State University, NM	W	Saint Martin's University, WA	W
Lock Haven University of		New York Institute of Technology, NY	W	Saint Mary's College of	
Pennsylvania, PA	W	Niagara University, NY	W	California, CA	W
Long Island University, Brooklyn		Nicholls State University, LA	W	St. Mary's University, TX	W
Campus, NY		Norfolk State University, VA	W	Saint Paul's College, VA	M,W
Long Island University, C.W. Post		North Carolina Agricultural and		St. Thomas University, FL	W
Campus, NY	W	Technical State University, NC	W	Saint Xavier University, IL	W
		North Carolina State University, NC	W	Samford University, AL	W
		Northeastern University, MA	W	Sam Houston State University, TX	W

San Diego Christian College, CA	W	Towson University, MD	W	University of Maryland, College Park, MD	W
San Diego State University, CA	W	Trevecca Nazarene University, TN	W	University of Massachusetts Lowell, MA	W
San Francisco State University, CA	W	Trinity Christian College, IL	W	University of Memphis, TN	W
San Jose State University, CA	W	Troy University, AL	W	University of Miami, FL	W
Santa Clara University, CA	W	Truman State University, MO	W	University of Michigan, MI	W
Savannah College of Art and Design, GA	W	Tulane University, LA	W	University of Michigan–Dearborn, MI	W
Savannah State University, GA	W	Tusculum College, TN	W	University of Minnesota, Crookston, MN	W
Seattle Pacific University, WA	W	Tuskegee University, AL	W	University of Minnesota, Duluth, MN	W
Seton Hill University, PA	W	Union College, KY	W	University of Minnesota, Twin Cities Campus, MN	W
Shepherd University, WV	W	Union University, TN	W	University of Mississippi, MS	W
Shippensburg University of Pennsylvania, PA	W	University at Albany, State University of New York, NY	W	University of Missouri, MO	W
Shorter University, GA	W	University at Buffalo, the State University of New York, NY	W	University of Missouri–Kansas City, MO	W
Siena College, NY	W	The University of Akron, OH	W	University of Missouri–St. Louis, MO	W
Slippery Rock University of Pennsylvania, PA	W	The University of Alabama, AL	W	University of Mobile, AL	W
Sonoma State University, CA	W	The University of Alabama at Birmingham, AL	W	The University of Montana Western, MT	W
South Dakota School of Mines and Technology, SD	W	The University of Alabama in Huntsville, AL	W	University of Montevallo, AL	W
South Dakota State University, SD	W	University of Alaska Anchorage, AK	W	University of Nebraska at Kearney, NE	W
Southeastern Louisiana University, LA	W	University of Alaska Fairbanks, AK	W	University of Nebraska at Omaha, NE	W
Southeastern Oklahoma State University, OK	W	The University of Arizona, AZ	W	University of Nebraska–Lincoln, NE	W
Southeast Missouri State University, MO	W	University of Arkansas, AR	W	University of Nevada, Las Vegas, NV	W
		University of Bridgeport, CT	W	University of Nevada, Reno, NV	W
Southern Arkansas University–Magnolia, AR	W	University of California, Davis, CA	W	University of New Hampshire, NH	W
Southern Connecticut State University, CT	W	University of California, Irvine, CA	M,W	University of New Haven, CT	M,W
Southern Illinois University Carbondale, IL	W	University of California, Los Angeles, CA	M,W	University of New Orleans, LA	W
		University of California, Riverside, CA	W	University of North Alabama, AL	W
Southern Illinois University Edwardsville, IL	W	University of California, Santa Barbara, CA	M,W	The University of North Carolina at Asheville, NC	W
Southern Methodist University, TX	W	University of Central Florida, FL	W	The University of North Carolina at Chapel Hill, NC	W
Southwest Baptist University, MO	W	University of Central Missouri, MO	W	The University of North Carolina at Charlotte, NC	W
Southwestern College, KS	W	University of Central Oklahoma, OK	W	The University of North Carolina at Greensboro, NC	W
Southwest Minnesota State University, MN	W	University of Charleston, WV	W	The University of North Carolina at Pembroke, NC	W
Spring Arbor University, MI	W	University of Cincinnati, OH	W		
Spring Hill College, AL	W	University of Colorado at Boulder, CO	W	The University of North Carolina Wilmington, NC	W
Stanford University, CA	M,W	University of Colorado at Colorado Springs, CO	W	University of North Dakota, ND	W
State University of New York at Binghamton, NY	W	University of Connecticut, CT	W	University of Northern Colorado, CO	W
Stephen F. Austin State University, TX	W	University of Dayton, OH	W	University of Northern Iowa, IA	W
Stephens College, MO	W	University of Delaware, DE	W	University of North Florida, FL	W
Stetson University, FL	W	University of Denver, CO	W	University of North Texas, TX	W
Stonehill College, MA	W	University of Evansville, IN	W	University of Notre Dame, IN	W
Stony Brook University, State University of New York, NY	W	The University of Findlay, OH	W	University of Oklahoma, OK	W
		University of Florida, FL	W	University of Oregon, OR	W
Syracuse University, NY	W	University of Georgia, GA	W	University of Pittsburgh, PA	W
Tabor College, KS	W	University of Great Falls, MT	W	University of Portland, OR	W
Tarleton State University, TX	W	University of Hartford, CT	W	University of Puerto Rico at Bayamón, PR	M,W
Taylor University, IN	W	University of Hawaii at Hilo, HI	W		
Temple University, PA	W	University of Houston, TX	W	University of Puerto Rico, Río Piedras, PR	M,W
Tennessee Technological University, TN	W	University of Idaho, ID	W		
		University of Illinois at Chicago, IL	W	University of Rhode Island, RI	W
Tennessee Wesleyan College, TN	W	University of Illinois at Springfield, IL	W	University of St. Francis, IL	W
Texas A&M University, TX	W	University of Illinois at Urbana–Champaign, IL	W	University of St. Thomas, TX	W
Texas A&M University–Commerce, TX	W	University of Indianapolis, IN	W	University of San Diego, CA	W
		The University of Iowa, IA	W	University of South Alabama, AL	W
Texas A&M University–Corpus Christi, TX	W	The University of Kansas, KS	W	University of South Carolina, SC	W
		University of Kentucky, KY	W	University of South Carolina Aiken, SC	W
Texas Christian University, TX	W	University of Louisiana at Monroe, LA	W		
Texas State University–San Marcos, TX	W	University of Louisville, KY	W	The University of South Dakota, SD	W
Texas Tech University, TX	W	University of Mary, ND	W	University of Southern California, CA	M,W
Texas Woman's University, TX	W	University of Maryland, Baltimore County, MD	W		
Tiffin University, OH	W				

University of Southern Indiana, IN	W
University of Southern Mississippi, MS	W
The University of Tampa, FL	W
The University of Tennessee, TN	W
The University of Tennessee at Chattanooga, TN	W
The University of Tennessee at Martin, TN	W
The University of Texas at Arlington, TX	W
The University of Texas at Austin, TX	W
The University of Texas at Brownsville, TX	W
The University of Texas at El Paso, TX	W
The University of Texas at San Antonio, TX	W
The University of Texas Medical Branch, TX	M,W
The University of Texas of the Permian Basin, TX	W
The University of Texas–Pan American, TX	W
University of the District of Columbia, DC	W
University of the Incarnate Word, TX	W
University of the Pacific, CA	M,W
University of the Sciences in Philadelphia, PA	W
The University of Toledo, OH	W
University of Tulsa, OK	W
University of Virginia, VA	W
The University of Virginia's College at Wise, VA	W
University of Washington, WA	W
The University of West Alabama, AL	W
University of West Georgia, GA	W
University of Wisconsin–Green Bay, WI	W
University of Wisconsin–Madison, WI	W
University of Wisconsin–Parkside, WI	W
University of Wyoming, WY	W
Ursuline College, OH	W
Utah State University, UT	W
Utah Valley University, UT	W
Valdosta State University, GA	W
Valley City State University, ND	W
Valparaiso University, IN	W
Vanguard University of Southern California, CA	W
Villanova University, PA	W
Virginia Commonwealth University, VA	W
Virginia Intermont College, VA	W
Virginia Union University, VA	W
Wake Forest University, NC	W
Waldorf College, IA	W
Warner Pacific College, OR	W
Washburn University, KS	W
Washington State University, WA	W
Wayland Baptist University, TX	W
Wayne State College, NE	W
Wayne State University, MI	W
West Chester University of Pennsylvania, PA	W
Western Carolina University, NC	W
Western Illinois University, IL	W
Western Kentucky University, KY	W

Western Oregon University, OR	W
Western State College of Colorado, CO	W
Western Washington University, WA	W
West Liberty University, WV	W
Westminster College, UT	W
Westmont College, CA	W
West Virginia University, WV	W
West Virginia Wesleyan College, WV	W
Wheeling Jesuit University, WV	W
Wichita State University, KS	W
William Jewell College, MO	W
Winona State University, MN	W
Winthrop University, SC	W
Wofford College, SC	W
Wright State University, OH	W
Xavier University, OH	W
Youngstown State University, OH	W

Water Polo

Arizona State University, AZ	W
California Baptist University, CA	M,W
California State University, Long Beach, CA	M,W
California State University, Monterey Bay, CA	W
Chaminade University of Honolulu, HI	M
Colorado State University, CO	W
Concordia University, CA	M,W
Fordham University, NY	M
Gannon University, PA	M,W
The George Washington University, DC	M
Hartwick College, NY	W
Indiana University Bloomington, IN	W
Iona College, NY	W
Lindenwood University, MO	M,W
Marist College, NY	W
Mercyhurst College, PA	M,W
Pepperdine University, CA	M
Queens College of the City University of New York, NY	M
San Diego State University, CA	W
San Jose State University, CA	W
Santa Clara University, CA	M,W
Siena College, NY	W
Stanford University, CA	M,W
University of California, Davis, CA	M,W
University of California, Irvine, CA	M,W
University of California, Los Angeles, CA	M,W
University of California, Santa Barbara, CA	M,W
University of Maryland, College Park, MD	W
University of Michigan, MI	W
University of Puerto Rico, Río Piedras, PR	M,W
University of Southern California, CA	M,W
University of the Pacific, CA	M,W
Wagner College, NY	W

Weight Lifting

Inter American University of Puerto Rico, Bayamón Campus, PR	M
Inter American University of Puerto Rico, Ponce Campus, PR	M
Lindenwood University, MO	M,W

University of Puerto Rico, Río Piedras, PR	M,W

Wrestling

Adams State College, CO	M
American International College, MA	M
American University, DC	M
Appalachian State University, NC	M
Arizona State University, AZ	M
Ashland University, OH	M
Augustana College, SD	M
Bloomsburg University of Pennsylvania, PA	M
Boise State University, ID	M
Boston University, MA	M
Briar Cliff University, IA	M
Bucknell University, PA	M
California Baptist University, CA	M
California Polytechnic State University, San Luis Obispo, CA	M
California State University, Fullerton, CA	M
Campbellsville University, KY	M
Carson-Newman College, TN	M
Central Michigan University, MI	M
The Citadel, The Military College of South Carolina, SC	M
Clarion University of Pennsylvania, PA	M
Cleveland State University, OH	M
Colorado School of Mines, CO	M
Concordia University, Nebraska, NE	M
Dakota Wesleyan University, SD	M
Davidson College, NC	M
Dickinson State University, ND	M
Eastern Michigan University, MI	M
East Stroudsburg University of Pennsylvania, PA	M
Edinboro University of Pennsylvania, PA	M
Embry-Riddle Aeronautical University, AZ	M
Gannon University, PA	M
Gardner-Webb University, NC	M
George Mason University, VA	M
Hannibal-LaGrange College, MO	M
Hofstra University, NY	M
Indiana University Bloomington, IN	M
Iowa State University of Science and Technology, IA	M
Jamestown College, ND	M,W
Kent State University, OH	M
King College, TN	M
Kutztown University of Pennsylvania, PA	M
Lehigh University, PA	M
Limestone College, SC	M
Lindenwood University, MO	M,W
Lindsey Wilson College, KY	M
Lock Haven University of Pennsylvania, PA	M
McKendree University, IL	M
Mercyhurst College, PA	M
Michigan State University, MI	M
Millersville University of Pennsylvania, PA	M
Minnesota State University Mankato, MN	M
Minnesota State University Moorhead, MN	M

Morningside College, IA	M	Stanford University, CA	M	The University of North Carolina at Greensboro, NC	M
Murray State University, KY	M	State University of New York at Binghamton, NY	M	The University of North Carolina at Pembroke, NC	M
Newberry College, SC	M	Truman State University, MO	M	University of Northern Colorado, CO	M
Newman University, KS	M	University at Buffalo, the State University of New York, NY	M	University of Northern Iowa, IA	M
North Carolina State University, NC	M	University of California, Davis, CA	M	University of Oklahoma, OK	M
Northern State University, SD	M	University of Central Missouri, MO	M	University of Pittsburgh, PA	M
The Ohio State University, OH	M	University of Central Oklahoma, OK	M	University of Pittsburgh at Johnstown, PA	M
Ohio University, OH	M	The University of Findlay, OH	M	University of Puerto Rico at Bayamón, PR	M
Ohio Valley University, WV	M	University of Great Falls, MT	M	University of Puerto Rico, Río Piedras, PR	M,W
Oklahoma City University, OK	M,W	University of Illinois at Urbana–Champaign, IL	M	The University of Tennessee at Chattanooga, TN	M
Oklahoma State University, OK	M	University of Indianapolis, IN	M	University of Virginia, VA	M
Old Dominion University, VA	M	The University of Iowa, IA	M	University of Wisconsin–Madison, WI	M
Oregon State University, OR	M	University of Mary, ND	M	University of Wisconsin–Parkside, WI	M
Ouachita Baptist University, AR	M	University of Maryland, College Park, MD	M	University of Wyoming, WY	M
Penn State University Park, PA	M	University of Michigan, MI	M	Utah Valley University, UT	M
Portland State University, OR	M	University of Minnesota, Twin Cities Campus, MN	M	Virginia Military Institute, VA	M
Purdue University, IN	M	University of Missouri, MO	M	Waldorf College, IA	M
Rider University, NJ	M	University of Nebraska at Kearney, NE	M	Western State College of Colorado, CO	M
Sacred Heart University, CT	M	University of Nebraska at Omaha, NE	M	West Liberty University, WV	M
San Francisco State University, CA	M	University of Nebraska–Lincoln, NE	M	West Virginia University, WV	M
Shippensburg University of Pennsylvania, PA	M	The University of North Carolina at Chapel Hill, NC	M		
South Dakota State University, SD	M				
Southern Illinois University Edwardsville, IL	M				
Southwest Minnesota State University, MN	M				

Co-Op Programs

Alabama Agricultural and Mechanical
  University, AL
Alabama State University, AL
Alfred University, NY
American Jewish University, CA
American University, DC
Andrews University, MI
Antioch University McGregor, OH
Aquinas College, TN
Arcadia University, PA
Arizona State University, AZ
Armstrong Atlantic State University, GA
Atlantic Union College, MA
Auburn University, AL
Auburn University Montgomery, AL
Augsburg College, MN
Augustana College, SD
Austin Peay State University, TN
Averett University, VA
Azusa Pacific University, CA
Ball State University, IN
Barton College, NC
Bastyr University, WA
Bates College, ME
Belmont Abbey College, NC
Belmont University, TN
Bemidji State University, MN
Benedictine College, KS
Berklee College of Music, MA
Berry College, GA
Bethune-Cookman University, FL
Birmingham-Southern College, AL
Blackburn College, IL
Black Hills State University, SD
Bloomsburg University of Pennsylvania, PA
Boise State University, ID
Boston University, MA
Bowie State University, MD
Bowling Green State University, OH
Bradley University, IL
Brewton-Parker College, GA
Brigham Young University, UT
Butler University, IN
Cabrini College, PA
California College of the Arts, CA
California Institute of Technology, CA
California Institute of the Arts, CA
California Lutheran University, CA
California Polytechnic State University,
  San Luis Obispo, CA
California State Polytechnic University,
  Pomona, CA
California State University, Chico, CA
California State University, Dominguez
  Hills, CA
California State University, East Bay, CA
California State University, Fresno, CA
California State University, Fullerton, CA
California State University, Monterey Bay, CA
California State University, Sacramento, CA
California State University,
  San Bernardino, CA

California State University, Stanislaus, CA
Calumet College of Saint Joseph, IN
Canisius College, NY
Carlos Albizu University, PR
Carnegie Mellon University, PA
Case Western Reserve University, OH
The Catholic University of America, DC
Central College, IA
Central Connecticut State University, CT
Chatham University, PA
Chowan University, NC
Christendom College, VA
Cincinnati Christian University, OH
The Citadel, The Military College of South
  Carolina, SC
City College of the City University of New
  York, NY
Clarion University of Pennsylvania, PA
Clarke College, IA
Clarkson University, NY
Cleary University, MI
Clemson University, SC
Cleveland State University, OH
Coastal Carolina University, SC
The College at Brockport, State University of
  New York, NY
College for Creative Studies, MI
College of Charleston, SC
College of Mount St. Joseph, OH
The College of New Rochelle, NY
College of Staten Island of the City University
  of New York, NY
College of the Atlantic, ME
College of the Ozarks, MO
The College of Wooster, OH
Colorado School of Mines, CO
Colorado State University, CO
Columbia College Chicago, IL
Columbus State University, GA
Concordia College, MN
Converse College, SC
Coppin State University, MD
Corban University, OR
Cornell University, NY
Dakota State University, SD
Dakota Wesleyan University, SD
Dalton State College, GA
Davenport University, MI
Defiance College, OH
Delta State University, MS
DePaul University, IL
Dickinson State University, ND
Dillard University, LA
Dixie State College of Utah, UT
Doane College, NE
Dominican College, NY
Dowling College, NY
Drake University, IA
Drury University, MO
East Carolina University, NC
Eastern Michigan University, MI
Eastern New Mexico University, NM

East-West University, IL
Edgewood College, WI
Elmhurst College, IL
Embry-Riddle Aeronautical University, AZ
Embry-Riddle Aeronautical University, FL
Embry-Riddle Aeronautical University
  Worldwide, FL
Emory & Henry College, VA
Emory University, GA
Endicott College, MA
Fairmont State University, WV
Fayetteville State University, NC
Felician College, NJ
Ferris State University, MI
Fisk University, TN
Five Towns College, NY
Florida Agricultural and Mechanical
  University, FL
Florida Atlantic University, FL
Florida Gulf Coast University, FL
Florida Institute of Technology, FL
Florida International University, FL
Florida State University, FL
Fort Lewis College, CO
Franklin College, IN
Freed-Hardeman University, TN
Frostburg State University, MD
Full Sail University, FL
Gannon University, PA
Gardner-Webb University, NC
Geneva College, PA
George Mason University, VA
Georgetown College, KY
The George Washington University, DC
Georgia Institute of Technology, GA
Georgia Southern University, GA
Georgia State University, GA
Glenville State College, WV
Goldey-Beacom College, DE
Gordon College, MA
Grace College, IN
Graceland University, IA
Grand Valley State University, MI
Grand View University, IA
Green Mountain College, VT
Greenville College, IL
Guilford College, NC
Gustavus Adolphus College, MN
Gwynedd-Mercy College, PA
Hampton University, VA
Hanover College, IN
Harding University, AR
Hawai'i Pacific University, HI
Hendrix College, AR
Heritage Christian University, AL
High Point University, NC
Hodges University, FL
Holy Family University, PA
Humboldt State University, CA
Huntingdon College, AL
Husson University, ME
Huston-Tillotson University, TX

Co-Op Programs

Illinois Institute of Technology, IL
Illinois State University, IL
Indiana State University, IN
Indiana University Bloomington, IN
Indiana University East, IN
Indiana University Northwest, IN
Indiana University of Pennsylvania, PA
Indiana University–Purdue University Fort
  Wayne, IN
Indiana University–Purdue University
  Indianapolis, IN
Inter American University of Puerto Rico,
  Bayamón Campus, PR
Inter American University of Puerto Rico,
  Ponce Campus, PR
Iowa State University of Science and
  Technology, IA
Iowa Wesleyan College, IA
Jacksonville State University, AL
Jacksonville University, FL
Jamestown College, ND
Jarvis Christian College, TX
Jefferson College of Health Sciences, VA
John Carroll University, OH
John Jay College of Criminal Justice of the
  City University of New York, NY
Johnson & Wales University, CO
Johnson & Wales University, FL
Johnson & Wales University, RI
Johnson & Wales University—Charlotte
  Campus, NC
Johnson Bible College, TN
Johnson C. Smith University, NC
Kansas State University, KS
Kean University, NJ
Keene State College, NH
Kennesaw State University, GA
Kent State University, OH
Kentucky Mountain Bible College, KY
Kentucky State University, KY
Kentucky Wesleyan College, KY
Kettering University, MI
Keuka College, NY
Keystone College, PA
King College, TN
Kuyper College, MI
Lake Erie College, OH
Lake Superior State University, MI
Lamar University, TX
Lane College, TN
Lasell College, MA
Lawrence Technological University, MI
Lee University, TN
Lehigh University, PA
Lehman College of the City University of
  New York, NY
LeTourneau University, TX
Lewis-Clark State College, ID
Lexington College, IL
Lincoln University, PA
Lindsey Wilson College, KY
Lock Haven University of Pennsylvania, PA
Long Island University, Brooklyn
  Campus, NY
Long Island University, C.W. Post
  Campus, NY
Loras College, IA
Louisiana State University and Agricultural
  and Mechanical College, LA
Loyola University Chicago, IL
Loyola University Maryland, MD
Lynn University, FL
Manhattan College, NY

Marian University, WI
Marist College, NY
Marquette University, WI
Marshall University, WV
Maryville University of Saint Louis, MO
Massachusetts Institute of Technology, MA
Massachusetts Maritime Academy, MA
The Master's College and Seminary, CA
McNally Smith College of Music, MN
Medgar Evers College of the City University
  of New York, NY
Menlo College, CA
Mercer University, GA
Mercyhurst College, PA
Meredith College, NC
Merrimack College, MA
Messiah College, PA
Methodist University, NC
Metropolitan State College of Denver, CO
Miami University, OH
Michigan State University, MI
Michigan Technological University, MI
Millersville University of Pennsylvania, PA
Milligan College, TN
Millikin University, IL
Minneapolis College of Art and Design, MN
Minnesota State University Mankato, MN
Misericordia University, PA
Mississippi College, MS
Mississippi State University, MS
Mississippi Valley State University, MS
Missouri Southern State University, MO
Missouri State University, MO
Missouri University of Science and
  Technology, MO
Molloy College, NY
Monmouth University, NJ
Monroe College, NY
Montana State University Billings, MT
Montana Tech of The University of
  Montana, MT
Montclair State University, NJ
Morehead State University, KY
Morehouse College, GA
Mountain State University, WV
Mount Holyoke College, MA
Mount Ida College, MA
Mount Marty College, SD
Mount Olive College, NC
Mount Saint Mary College, NY
Murray State University, KY
Nazareth College of Rochester, NY
Neumann University, PA
Newberry College, SC
New College of Florida, FL
New England School of Communications, ME
New Jersey City University, NJ
New Jersey Institute of Technology, NJ
Newman University, KS
New Mexico Institute of Mining and
  Technology, NM
New Mexico State University, NM
New York Institute of Technology, NY
Niagara University, NY
Nicholls State University, LA
Nichols College, MA
Norfolk State University, VA
North Carolina Agricultural and Technical
  State University, NC
North Carolina State University, NC
Northeastern Illinois University, IL
Northeastern State University, OK
Northeastern University, MA

Northern Arizona University, AZ
Northern Kentucky University, KY
Northern State University, SD
North Georgia College & State University, GA
North Greenville University, SC
Northwestern Oklahoma State University, OK
Northwestern State University of
  Louisiana, LA
Northwest Nazarene University, ID
Northwest University, WA
Notre Dame de Namur University, CA
Oakland University, MI
Oglethorpe University, GA
Ohio Northern University, OH
The Ohio State University, OH
Ohio University, OH
Oklahoma Baptist University, OK
Oklahoma City University, OK
Oklahoma Wesleyan University, OK
Old Dominion University, VA
Oregon Institute of Technology, OR
Oregon State University, OR
Otis College of Art and Design, CA
Ouachita Baptist University, AR
Our Lady of the Lake University of
  San Antonio, TX
Pace University, NY
Pacific Lutheran University, WA
Pacific Union College, CA
Parsons The New School for Design, NY
Peace College, NC
Peirce College, PA
Penn State Abington, PA
Penn State Altoona, PA
Penn State Berks, PA
Penn State Erie, The Behrend College, PA
Penn State Harrisburg, PA
Penn State University Park, PA
Pennsylvania College of Technology, PA
Piedmont College, GA
Pittsburg State University, KS
Pitzer College, CA
Point Park University, PA
Polytechnic Institute of NYU, NY
Portland State University, OR
Providence College, RI
Purdue University, IN
Purdue University Calumet, IN
Ramapo College of New Jersey, NJ
Reed College, OR
Reinhardt University, GA
Rensselaer Polytechnic Institute, NY
Rhodes College, TN
Rider University, NJ
Robert Morris University, PA
Roberts Wesleyan College, NY
Rochester Institute of Technology, NY
Rockhurst University, MO
Rocky Mountain College of Art + Design, CO
Rogers State University, OK
Rose-Hulman Institute of Technology, IN
Russell Sage College, NY
Rutgers, The State University of New Jersey,
  Camden, NJ
Rutgers, The State University of New Jersey,
  Newark, NJ
Rutgers, The State University of New Jersey,
  New Brunswick, NJ
Sacred Heart University, CT
Sage College of Albany, NY
Saginaw Valley State University, MI
St. Ambrose University, IA

St. Joseph's College, Long Island
    Campus, NY
St. Joseph's College, New York, NY
Saint Joseph's University, PA
Saint Louis University, MO
Saint Martin's University, WA
Saint Mary's College, IN
St. Mary's College of Maryland, MD
St. Mary's University, TX
Saint Mary's University of Minnesota, MN
Saint Paul's College, VA
Saint Vincent College, PA
Saint Xavier University, IL
Samford University, AL
Samuel Merritt University, CA
San Francisco State University, CA
Santa Clara University, CA
Savannah State University, GA
Schreiner University, TX
Shenandoah University, VA
Shepherd University, WV
Shippensburg University of Pennsylvania, PA
Silver Lake College, WI
Simmons College, MA
Simpson College, IA
Sonoma State University, CA
South Dakota School of Mines and
    Technology, SD
South Dakota State University, SD
Southern Connecticut State University, CT
Southern Illinois University Carbondale, IL
Southern Illinois University Edwardsville, IL
Southern Methodist University, TX
Southern Polytechnic State University, GA
Southern Utah University, UT
Southwest Baptist University, MO
State University of New York at New
    Paltz, NY
State University of New York at Oswego, NY
State University of New York at
    Plattsburgh, NY
State University of New York College at
    Cortland, NY
State University of New York College of
    Environmental Science and Forestry, NY
Stephens College, MO
Stevenson University, MD
Stillman College, AL
Suffolk University, MA
Syracuse University, NY
Tabor College, KS
Tarleton State University, TX
Taylor University, IN
Temple University, PA
Tennessee Technological University, TN
Texas A&M University, TX
Texas A&M University–Commerce, TX
Texas A&M University–Corpus Christi, TX
Texas Tech University, TX
Texas Woman's University, TX
Thiel College, PA
Thomas Aquinas College, CA
Thomas More College, KY
Towson University, MD
Trine University, IN
Trinity Christian College, IL
Tulane University, LA
Tuskegee University, AL
Union University, TN
Universidad Adventista de las Antillas, PR
University at Buffalo, the State University of
    New York, NY
University of Advancing Technology, AZ

The University of Akron, OH
The University of Alabama, AL
The University of Alabama at
    Birmingham, AL
The University of Alabama in Huntsville, AL
University of Alaska Anchorage, AK
University of Alaska Fairbanks, AK
The University of Arizona, AZ
University of Arkansas, AR
University of Bridgeport, CT
University of California, San Diego, CA
University of California, Santa Barbara, CA
University of California, Santa Cruz, CA
University of Central Florida, FL
University of Central Missouri, MO
University of Cincinnati, OH
University of Colorado at Boulder, CO
University of Colorado at Colorado
    Springs, CO
University of Colorado Denver, CO
University of Connecticut, CT
University of Dayton, OH
University of Delaware, DE
University of Denver, CO
University of Evansville, IN
The University of Findlay, OH
University of Florida, FL
University of Georgia, GA
University of Great Falls, MT
University of Hartford, CT
University of Houston, TX
University of Houston–Clear Lake, TX
University of Idaho, ID
University of Illinois at Chicago, IL
University of Illinois at Springfield, IL
University of Illinois at Urbana–
    Champaign, IL
University of Indianapolis, IN
The University of Iowa, IA
The University of Kansas, KS
University of Kentucky, KY
University of Louisiana at Monroe, LA
University of Louisville, KY
University of Maine, ME
University of Maine at Fort Kent, ME
University of Maine at Presque Isle, ME
University of Mary, ND
University of Maryland, Baltimore
    County, MD
University of Maryland, College Park, MD
University of Maryland University
    College, MD
University of Mary Washington, VA
University of Massachusetts Amherst, MA
University of Massachusetts Boston, MA
University of Massachusetts Dartmouth, MA
University of Massachusetts Lowell, MA
University of Memphis, TN
University of Michigan, MI
University of Michigan–Dearborn, MI
University of Michigan–Flint, MI
University of Minnesota, Duluth, MN
University of Minnesota, Twin Cities
    Campus, MN
University of Missouri, MO
University of Missouri–Kansas City, MO
University of Missouri–St. Louis, MO
The University of Montana Western, MT
University of Mount Union, OH
University of Nebraska at Kearney, NE
University of Nebraska at Omaha, NE
University of Nebraska–Lincoln, NE
University of Nevada, Las Vegas, NV

University of New Hampshire, NH
University of New Haven, CT
University of New Orleans, LA
University of North Alabama, AL
The University of North Carolina at
    Charlotte, NC
The University of North Carolina at
    Pembroke, NC
The University of North Carolina
    Wilmington, NC
University of North Dakota, ND
University of Northern Colorado, CO
University of Northern Iowa, IA
University of North Florida, FL
University of North Texas, TX
University of Oklahoma, OK
University of Oregon, OR
University of Pittsburgh, PA
University of Pittsburgh at Johnstown, PA
University of Puerto Rico at Bayamón, PR
University of Puerto Rico, Río Piedras, PR
University of Puget Sound, WA
University of Rochester, NY
University of South Alabama, AL
University of South Carolina, SC
University of South Carolina Aiken, SC
The University of South Dakota, SD
University of Southern California, CA
University of Southern Indiana, IN
University of Southern Maine, ME
University of Southern Mississippi, MS
The University of Tampa, FL
The University of Tennessee, TN
The University of Tennessee at
    Chattanooga, TN
The University of Tennessee at Martin, TN
The University of Texas at Arlington, TX
The University of Texas at Austin, TX
The University of Texas at Brownsville, TX
The University of Texas at Dallas, TX
The University of Texas at El Paso, TX
The University of Texas at San Antonio, TX
The University of Texas at Tyler, TX
The University of Texas–Pan American, TX
University of the District of Columbia, DC
University of the Incarnate Word, TX
University of the Ozarks, AR
University of the Pacific, CA
University of the Sciences in Philadelphia, PA
The University of Toledo, OH
University of Vermont, VT
University of Virginia, VA
The University of Virginia's College at
    Wise, VA
University of Washington, WA
University of Washington, Tacoma, WA
University of West Florida, FL
University of West Georgia, GA
University of Wisconsin–Eau Claire, WI
University of Wisconsin–La Crosse, WI
University of Wisconsin–Madison, WI
University of Wisconsin–Stout, WI
University of Wisconsin–Superior, WI
University of Wisconsin–Whitewater, WI
Ursuline College, OH
Utah State University, UT
Utah Valley University, UT
Utica College, NY
Valdosta State University, GA
Valley City State University, ND
Valparaiso University, IN
Vanderbilt University, TN
Vassar College, NY

Co-Op Programs

Vermont Technical College, VT
Victory University, TN
Villa Maria College of Buffalo, NY
Villanova University, PA
Virginia Commonwealth University, VA
Virginia Polytechnic Institute and State
  University, VA
Virginia Union University, VA
Waldorf College, IA
Warner Pacific College, OR
Washburn University, KS
Washington State University, WA
Washington University in St. Louis, MO
Watkins College of Art, Design, & Film, TN
Wayne State College, NE

Wayne State University, MI
Webber International University, FL
Webb Institute, NY
Webster University, MO
Wesleyan College, GA
West Chester University of Pennsylvania, PA
Western Carolina University, NC
Western Connecticut State University, CT
Western Kentucky University, KY
Western Washington University, WA
Westfield State College, MA
Westminster College, MO
Westminster College, UT
Whitman College, WA
Wichita State University, KS

Widener University, PA
Wilkes University, PA
William Jewell College, MO
Wilson College, PA
Winthrop University, SC
Wittenberg University, OH
Worcester Polytechnic Institute, MA
Wright State University, OH
Xavier University, OH
Xavier University of Louisiana, LA
York College, NE
York College of Pennsylvania, PA
Youngstown State University, OH

ROTC Programs

Air Force

Adelphi University, NY*
Agnes Scott College, GA*
Alabama State University, AL
Alaska Pacific University, AK*
Alverno College, WI*
American International College, MA*
American University, DC*
Angelo State University, TX
Arizona State University, AZ
Asbury University, KY*
Assumption College, MA*
Auburn University, AL
Auburn University Montgomery, AL*
Augsburg College, MN*
Augustana College, SD*
Austin Peay State University, TN*
Babson College, MA*
Baldwin-Wallace College, OH*
Barry University, FL*
Baylor University, TX
Belhaven University, MS*
Bellarmine University, KY*
Belmont Abbey College, NC*
Belmont University, TN*
Bentley University, MA*
Bethel College, IN*
Bethel University, MN*
Bethune-Cookman University, FL*
Birmingham-Southern College, AL*
Bloomsburg University of Pennsylvania, PA*
Boston College, MA*
Boston University, MA
Bowling Green State University, OH
Brandeis University, MA*
Bridgewater State College, MA*
Brigham Young University, UT
Bryn Mawr College, PA*
Butler University, IN*
Cabrini College, PA*
California Baptist University, CA*
California Institute of Technology, CA*
California Lutheran University, CA*
California State University, Dominguez
  Hills, CA*
California State University, Fresno, CA
California State University, Northridge, CA*
California State University, Sacramento, CA
California State University,
  San Bernardino, CA
Carnegie Mellon University, PA
Carroll University, WI*
Carson-Newman College, TN*
Case Western Reserve University, OH*
The Catholic University of America, DC*
Cazenovia College, NY*
Cedarville University, OH*
Central Connecticut State University, CT*
Chaminade University of Honolulu, HI*
Chapman University, CA*
Chatham University, PA*
Christian Brothers University, TN*

The Citadel, The Military College of South
  Carolina, SC
City College of the City University of New
  York, NY*
Claremont McKenna College, CA*
Clarkson University, NY
Clark University, MA*
Clearwater Christian College, FL*
Clemson University, SC
Cleveland State University, OH*
The College at Brockport, State University of
  New York, NY*
College of Charleston, SC*
College of Mount St. Joseph, OH*
The College of New Jersey, NJ*
College of Saint Mary, NE*
The College of Saint Rose, NY*
The College of St. Scholastica, MN*
College of the Holy Cross, MA*
Colorado School of Mines, CO
Colorado State University, CO
Columbia College, MO*
Columbia University, School of General
  Studies, NY*
Concordia College, MN*
Concordia University, Nebraska, NE*
Concordia University, St. Paul, MN*
Concordia University Texas, TX*
Corban University, OR*
Cornell University, NY
Creighton University, NE*
Dakota State University, SD*
Dallas Baptist University, TX*
Davidson College, NC*
DePauw University, IN*
Dillard University, LA*
Doane College, NE*
Dowling College, NY*
Drake University, IA*
Duke University, NC
Duquesne University, PA*
East Carolina University, NC
Eastern Michigan University, MI*
Eastern Nazarene College, MA*
East Stroudsburg University of
  Pennsylvania, PA*
Eckerd College, FL*
Elmhurst College, IL*
Elmira College, NY*
Elon University, NC*
Embry-Riddle Aeronautical University, AZ
Embry-Riddle Aeronautical University, FL
Emory University, GA*
Endicott College, MA*
Fairfield University, CT*
Faulkner University, AL*
Fayetteville State University, NC
Florida Agricultural and Mechanical
  University, FL*
Florida Atlantic University, FL*
Florida College, FL*
Florida International University, FL

Florida Southern College, FL*
Florida State University, FL
Fordham University, NY*
Franciscan University of Steubenville, OH*
Gardner-Webb University, NC*
George Fox University, OR*
George Mason University, VA*
Georgetown College, KY*
Georgetown University, DC*
The George Washington University, DC*
Georgia Institute of Technology, GA
Georgia State University, GA*
Goldey-Beacom College, DE*
Gordon College, MA*
Grand View University, IA*
Guilford College, NC*
Hamilton College, NY*
Hamline University, MN*
Harvard University, MA*
Harvey Mudd College, CA
Hawai'i Pacific University, HI*
Heidelberg University, OH*
High Point University, NC*
Houston Baptist University, TX*
Huntingdon College, AL*
Illinois Institute of Technology, IL
Indiana State University, IN
Indiana University Bloomington, IN
Indiana University–Purdue University
  Indianapolis, IN*
Indiana University South Bend, IN*
Iona College, NY*
Iowa State University of Science and
  Technology, IA
Ithaca College, NY*
James Madison University, VA*
John Brown University, AR*
John Jay College of Criminal Justice of the
  City University of New York, NY*
The Johns Hopkins University, MD*
Johnson C. Smith University, NC*
Kansas State University, KS
Kean University, NJ*
Keene State College, NH*
Kennesaw State University, GA
Kent State University, OH
Kent State University at Stark, OH*
Kentucky State University, KY*
Keystone College, PA*
King's College, PA*
La Roche College, PA*
Lawrence Technological University, MI*
Le Moyne College, NY*
Lewis-Clark State College, ID*
Lewis University, IL*
Lincoln University, MO*
Lincoln University, PA*
Linfield College, OR*
Lipscomb University, TN*
Long Island University, C.W. Post
  Campus, NY*

Louisiana State University and Agricultural and Mechanical College, LA
Louisiana Tech University, LA
Lourdes College, OH*
Loyola University Chicago, IL*
Loyola University Maryland, MD*
Loyola University New Orleans, LA*
Lubbock Christian University, TX*
Lynn University, FL*
Macalester College, MN*
Malone University, OH*
Manhattan College, NY
Marquette University, WI
Mary Baldwin College, VA*
Marywood University, PA*
Massachusetts Institute of Technology, MA
McKendree University, IL*
Mercyhurst College, PA*
Meredith College, NC*
Merrimack College, MA*
Methodist University, NC*
Metropolitan State College of Denver, CO*
Miami University, OH
Michigan State University, MI
Michigan Technological University, MI
Midwestern State University, TX*
Milwaukee School of Engineering, WI*
Minnesota State University Moorhead, MN*
Misericordia University, PA*
Mississippi College, MS
Mississippi State University, MS
Mississippi University for Women, MS*
Missouri University of Science and Technology, MO
Molloy College, NY*
Monmouth University, NJ*
Montana State University, MT
Montclair State University, NJ
Morehouse College, GA
Mount Holyoke College, MA*
Mount Mary College, WI*
Mount Olive College, NC*
National University, CA*
Nazareth College of Rochester, NY*
Nebraska Methodist College, NE*
Nebraska Wesleyan University, NE*
New England College, NH*
New Jersey Institute of Technology, NJ
New Mexico State University, NM
New York City College of Technology of the City University of New York, NY*
New York Institute of Technology, NY
New York University, NY*
North Carolina Agricultural and Technical State University, NC
North Carolina State University, NC
North Central College, IL*
Northeastern Illinois University, IL*
Northeastern University, MA*
Northern Arizona University, AZ
Northern Kentucky University, KY*
Northwestern College, MN*
Northwestern State University of Louisiana, LA*
Oakland University, MI*
Occidental College, CA*
Oglethorpe University, GA*
Ohio Northern University, OH*
The Ohio State University, OH
Ohio University, OH
Ohio Valley University, WV*
Oklahoma Baptist University, OK*
Oklahoma Christian University, OK*

Oklahoma City University, OK*
Oklahoma State University, OK
Oral Roberts University, OK*
Oregon State University, OR
Our Lady of the Lake College, LA*
Our Lady of the Lake University of San Antonio, TX*
Pace University, NY*
Peace College, NC*
Penn State Abington, PA*
Penn State Altoona, PA*
Penn State University Park, PA
Pepperdine University, CA*
Philadelphia Biblical University, PA*
Pitzer College, CA*
Plymouth State University, NH*
Point Park University, PA*
Polytechnic Institute of NYU, NY*
Pomona College, CA*
Portland State University, OR*
Purdue University, IN
Quinnipiac University, CT*
Ramapo College of New Jersey, NJ*
Rensselaer Polytechnic Institute, NY
Rhodes College, TN*
Rivier College, NH*
Robert Morris University, PA*
Roberts Wesleyan College, NY*
Rochester Institute of Technology, NY
Rose-Hulman Institute of Technology, IN
Russell Sage College, NY*
Rutgers, The State University of New Jersey, Camden, NJ*
Rutgers, The State University of New Jersey, Newark, NJ
Rutgers, The State University of New Jersey, New Brunswick, NJ
Sage College of Albany, NY*
Saint Anselm College, NH*
St. Catherine University, MN*
St. Edward's University, TX*
St. John Fisher College, NY*
St. Joseph's College, Long Island Campus, NY*
Saint Joseph's University, PA
St. Lawrence University, NY*
Saint Leo University, FL*
St. Louis College of Pharmacy, MO*
Saint Louis University, MO
Saint Martin's University, WA*
Saint Mary's College, IN*
Saint Mary's College of California, CA*
St. Mary's University, TX*
Saint Michael's College, VT*
Saint Vincent College, PA*
Saint Xavier University, IL*
Salem College, NC*
Salem State College, MA*
Salisbury University, MD*
Samford University, AL
Samuel Merritt University, CA*
San Diego Christian College, CA*
San Diego State University, CA
San Francisco State University, CA*
San Jose State University, CA
Santa Clara University, CA*
Scripps College, CA*
Seattle Pacific University, WA*
Seattle University, WA*
Seton Hill University, PA*
Shepherd University, WV*
Siena College, NY*
Skidmore College, NY*

Smith College, MA*
Sonoma State University, CA*
South Dakota State University, SD
Southeastern University, FL*
Southeast Missouri State University, MO
Southern Connecticut State University, CT*
Southern Illinois University Carbondale, IL
Southern Illinois University Edwardsville, IL
Southern Methodist University, TX*
Southern Polytechnic State University, GA*
Spring Arbor University, MI*
Spring Hill College, AL*
Stanford University, CA*
State University of New York at Binghamton, NY*
State University of New York College at Cortland, NY*
State University of New York College at Geneseo, NY*
State University of New York College at Old Westbury, NY*
State University of New York College at Potsdam, NY*
State University of New York College of Environmental Science and Forestry, NY*
State University of New York College of Technology at Canton, NY*
Stephens College, MO*
Stony Brook University, State University of New York, NY*
Swarthmore College, PA*
Syracuse University, NY
Temple University, PA*
Tennessee Technological University, TN*
Tennessee Wesleyan College, TN*
Texas A&M University, TX
Texas Christian University, TX
Texas Lutheran University, TX*
Texas State University–San Marcos, TX
Texas Tech University, TX
Texas Woman's University, TX*
Thomas More College, KY*
Tiffin University, OH*
Towson University, MD*
Transylvania University, KY*
Trine University, IN*
Trinity University, TX*
Troy University, AL
Tufts University, MA*
Tulane University, LA
Tuskegee University, AL
Union College, NY*
University at Albany, State University of New York, NY*
The University of Akron, OH*
The University of Alabama, AL
The University of Alabama at Birmingham, AL*
University of Alaska Anchorage, AK
The University of Arizona, AZ
University of Arkansas, AR
University of California, Berkeley, CA
University of California, Davis, CA
University of California, Irvine, CA*
University of California, Los Angeles, CA
University of California, Riverside, CA*
University of California, Santa Cruz, CA*
University of Central Florida, FL
University of Central Missouri, MO*
University of Chicago, IL*
University of Cincinnati, OH
University of Colorado at Boulder, CO
University of Colorado Denver, CO*

*program is offered at another college's campus

University of Connecticut, CT
University of Dallas, TX*
University of Dayton, OH*
University of Delaware, DE
University of Denver, CO*
The University of Findlay, OH*
University of Florida, FL
University of Georgia, GA
University of Hartford, CT*
University of Hawaii–West Oahu, HI*
University of Houston, TX
University of Houston–Downtown, TX*
University of Idaho, ID*
University of Illinois at Chicago, IL*
University of Illinois at Urbana–
   Champaign, IL
The University of Iowa, IA
The University of Kansas, KS
University of Kentucky, KY
University of Louisville, KY
University of Mary Hardin-Baylor, TX*
University of Maryland, College Park, MD
University of Massachusetts Amherst, MA
University of Massachusetts Boston, MA*
University of Massachusetts Lowell, MA
University of Memphis, TN
University of Miami, FL
University of Michigan, MI
University of Michigan–Dearborn, MI*
University of Michigan–Flint, MI*
University of Minnesota, Crookston, MN*
University of Minnesota, Duluth, MN
University of Minnesota, Twin Cities
   Campus, MN
University of Mississippi, MS
University of Missouri, MO
University of Missouri–Kansas City, MO*
University of Missouri–St. Louis, MO*
University of Mobile, AL*
University of Montevallo, AL*
University of Mount Union, OH*
University of Nebraska at Omaha, NE
University of Nebraska–Lincoln, NE
University of Nebraska Medical Center, NE*
University of Nevada, Las Vegas, NV
University of New Hampshire, NH
University of New Hampshire at
   Manchester, NH*
University of New Haven, CT*
University of New Orleans, LA*
The University of North Carolina at Chapel
   Hill, NC
The University of North Carolina at
   Charlotte, NC
The University of North Carolina at
   Greensboro, NC*
The University of North Carolina at
   Pembroke, NC
University of North Dakota, ND
University of Northern Colorado, CO
University of North Texas, TX
University of Notre Dame, IN
University of Oklahoma, OK
University of Oregon, OR*
University of Pennsylvania, PA*
University of Pittsburgh, PA
University of Pittsburgh at Greensburg, PA*
University of Portland, OR
University of Puerto Rico at Bayamón, PR*
University of Puerto Rico, Río Piedras, PR
University of Redlands, CA*
University of Rochester, NY*
University of St. Thomas, MN

University of St. Thomas, TX*
University of San Diego, CA*
The University of Scranton, PA*
University of South Alabama, AL
University of South Carolina, SC
University of Southern California, CA
University of Southern Maine, ME*
University of Southern Mississippi, MS
The University of Tampa, FL*
The University of Tennessee, TN
The University of Texas at Arlington, TX*
The University of Texas at Austin, TX
The University of Texas at Dallas, TX*
The University of Texas at El Paso, TX
The University of Texas at San Antonio, TX
University of the District of Columbia, DC*
University of the Incarnate Word, TX*
University of the Pacific, CA*
University of the Sciences in
   Philadelphia, PA*
The University of Toledo, OH*
University of Tulsa, OK*
University of Virginia, VA
University of Washington, WA
University of Washington, Tacoma, WA*
The University of West Alabama, AL*
University of West Florida, FL
University of Wisconsin–Madison, WI
University of Wisconsin–Stout, WI*
University of Wisconsin–Superior, WI*
University of Wisconsin–Whitewater, WI
University of Wyoming, WY
Utah State University, UT
Utah Valley University, UT*
Utica College, NY*
Valdosta State University, GA
Valparaiso University, IN*
Vanderbilt University, TN*
Vanguard University of Southern
   California, CA*
Villanova University, PA*
Virginia Military Institute, VA
Virginia Polytechnic Institute and State
   University, VA
Warner Pacific College, OR*
Washburn University, KS*
Washington & Jefferson College, PA*
Washington State University, WA
Washington University in St. Louis, MO*
Wayland Baptist University, TX*
Wayne State University, MI*
Webster University, MO*
Wellesley College, MA*
Wells College, NY*
Wesleyan University, CT*
West Chester University of Pennsylvania, PA*
Western Connecticut State University, CT*
Western Kentucky University, KY*
Western New England College, MA*
Western Oregon University, OR*
Westfield State College, MA*
Westminster College, MO*
Westminster College, UT*
Westmont College, CA*
West Virginia University, WV
Wheaton College, IL*
Widener University, PA*
Wilkes University, PA
Willamette University, OR*
William Paterson University of New
   Jersey, NJ*
Williams College, MA*
Wittenberg University, OH*

Worcester Polytechnic Institute, MA
Worcester State College, MA*
Wright State University, OH
Xavier University, OH*
Xavier University of Louisiana, LA*
Yale University, CT*
York College, NE*
Youngstown State University, OH*

Army

Adelphi University, NY*
Agnes Scott College, GA*
Alabama Agricultural and Mechanical
   University, AL
Alabama State University, AL*
Alfred University, NY*
Alma College, MI*
Alverno College, WI*
American International College, MA*
American University, DC*
Appalachian State University, NC
Arizona State University, AZ
Arkansas State University—Jonesboro, AR
Arkansas Tech University, AR*
Armstrong Atlantic State University, GA
Asbury University, KY*
Assumption College, MA*
Auburn University, AL
Auburn University Montgomery, AL
Augsburg College, MN*
Augustana College, SD*
Aurora University, IL*
Austin Peay State University, TN
Azusa Pacific University, CA*
Babson College, MA*
Baldwin-Wallace College, OH*
Ball State University, IN
Barry University, FL*
Baylor University, TX
Belhaven University, MS*
Bellarmine University, KY*
Belmont Abbey College, NC*
Belmont University, TN*
Benedictine College, KS
Benedictine University, IL*
Bentley University, MA*
Bernard M. Baruch College of the City
   University of New York, NY*
Bethany Lutheran College, MN*
Bethel College, IN*
Bethel University, MN*
Bethune-Cookman University, FL*
Birmingham-Southern College, AL*
Black Hills State University, SD
Bloomfield College, NJ*
Bloomsburg University of Pennsylvania, PA
Boise State University, ID
Boston College, MA*
Boston University, MA
Bowling Green State University, OH
Brandeis University, MA*
Bridgewater State College, MA*
Brigham Young University, UT
Bryant University, RI
Bucknell University, PA
Buena Vista University, IA
Butler University, IN
Cabrini College, PA*
California Baptist University, CA
California Institute of Technology, CA*
California Lutheran University, CA*
California Polytechnic State University,
   San Luis Obispo, CA

ROTC Programs
Army

California State Polytechnic University, Pomona, CA
California State University, Dominguez Hills, CA
California State University, Fresno, CA
California State University, Fullerton, CA
California State University, Long Beach, CA
California State University, Northridge, CA*
California State University, Sacramento, CA*
California State University, San Bernardino, CA
Calvary Bible College and Theological Seminary, MO*
Calvin College, MI*
Cameron University, OK
Campbellsville University, KY*
Canisius College, NY
Carnegie Mellon University, PA
Carroll University, WI*
Carson-Newman College, TN
Case Western Reserve University, OH*
Catawba College, NC*
The Catholic University of America, DC*
Cazenovia College, NY*
Cedar Crest College, PA*
Cedarville University, OH*
Central Connecticut State University, CT*
Central Michigan University, MI
Chaminade University of Honolulu, HI*
Chapman University, CA*
Chatham University, PA*
Christian Brothers University, TN*
Christopher Newport University, VA
The Citadel, The Military College of South Carolina, SC
City College of the City University of New York, NY*
Claremont McKenna College, CA
Clarion University of Pennsylvania, PA*
Clarke College, IA*
Clarkson University, NY
Clark University, MA*
Clearwater Christian College, FL*
Clemson University, SC
Cleveland State University, OH*
Coastal Carolina University, SC
Colby College, ME*
Colgate University, NY*
The College at Brockport, State University of New York, NY
College of Mount St. Joseph, OH*
The College of New Jersey, NJ*
College of Notre Dame of Maryland, MD*
College of Saint Benedict, MN*
College of Saint Mary, NE*
The College of Saint Rose, NY*
College of the Holy Cross, MA*
College of the Ozarks, MO
The College of William and Mary, VA
The Colorado College, CO*
Colorado School of Mines, CO
Colorado State University, CO
Columbia College, MO*
Columbia University, School of General Studies, NY*
Columbus State University, GA
Concordia College, MN*
Concordia University, CA*
Concordia University, Nebraska, NE*
Concordia University, St. Paul, MN*
Concordia University Texas, TX*
Converse College, SC*
Coppin State University, MD

Corban University, OR*
Cornell University, NY
Cornerstone University, MI*
Covenant College, GA*
Creighton University, NE
Crown College, MN*
Curry College, MA*
Daemen College, NY*
Dakota Wesleyan University, SD
Dallas Baptist University, TX*
Dartmouth College, NH*
Davidson College, NC
Delta State University, MS*
Denison University, OH*
DePaul University, IL*
DePauw University, IN*
DeSales University, PA*
Dickinson College, PA
Dillard University, LA*
Dixie State College of Utah, UT
Doane College, NE*
Dowling College, NY*
Drake University, IA
Drury University, MO*
Duke University, NC
Duquesne University, PA
D'Youville College, NY*
East Carolina University, NC
Eastern Michigan University, MI
Eastern Nazarene College, MA*
Eastern Washington University, WA
East Stroudsburg University of Pennsylvania, PA
Eckerd College, FL*
Edgewood College, WI*
Edinboro University of Pennsylvania, PA
Elmhurst College, IL*
Elmira College, NY
Elon University, NC
Embry-Riddle Aeronautical University, AZ
Embry-Riddle Aeronautical University, FL
Emmanuel College, MA*
Emory University, GA*
Endicott College, MA*
Evangel University, MO*
Fairfield University, CT*
Fairmont State University, WV
Faulkner University, AL*
Fayetteville State University, NC*
Ferris State University, MI*
Fisk University, TN*
Fitchburg State College, MA
Florida Agricultural and Mechanical University, FL
Florida Atlantic University, FL
Florida College, FL*
Florida Institute of Technology, FL
Florida International University, FL
Florida Southern College, FL
Florida State University, FL
Fordham University, NY
Fort Valley State University, GA
Franciscan University of Steubenville, OH
Franklin College, IN*
Furman University, SC
Gannon University, PA
Gardner-Webb University, NC
Geneva College, PA*
George Mason University, VA
Georgetown College, KY*
Georgetown University, DC
The George Washington University, DC*
Georgia College & State University, GA*

Georgia Institute of Technology, GA
Georgia Southern University, GA
Georgia State University, GA
Gettysburg College, PA*
Gonzaga University, WA
Gordon College, MA*
Goucher College, MD*
Grace Bible College, MI*
Grand View University, IA*
Grove City College, PA*
Guilford College, NC*
Gustavus Adolphus College, MN*
Hamilton College, NY*
Hamline University, MN*
Hampden-Sydney College, VA*
Hampshire College, MA*
Hampton University, VA
Harvard University, MA*
Harvey Mudd College, CA*
Hawai'i Pacific University, HI*
Heidelberg University, OH*
Henderson State University, AR*
Hendrix College, AR*
High Point University, NC*
Hofstra University, NY
Hood College, MD
Hope College, MI*
Houghton College, NY*
Houston Baptist University, TX*
Huntingdon College, AL*
Husson University, ME
Huston-Tillotson University, TX*
Idaho State University, ID*
Illinois Institute of Technology, IL
Illinois State University, IL
Illinois Wesleyan University, IL*
Indiana State University, IN
Indiana University Bloomington, IN
Indiana University Kokomo, IN*
Indiana University Northwest, IN
Indiana University of Pennsylvania, PA
Indiana University–Purdue University Fort Wayne, IN
Indiana University–Purdue University Indianapolis, IN
Indiana University South Bend, IN*
Indiana University Southeast, IN
Indiana Wesleyan University, IN
Inter American University of Puerto Rico, Bayamón Campus, PR*
Iona College, NY*
Iowa State University of Science and Technology, IA
Ithaca College, NY*
Jacksonville State University, AL
James Madison University, VA
John Brown University, AR*
John Carroll University, OH
The Johns Hopkins University, MD
Johnson & Wales University, RI
Johnson C. Smith University, NC
Judson College, AL*
Kalamazoo College, MI*
Kansas State University, KS
Kean University, NJ*
Kennesaw State University, GA
Kent State University, OH
Kent State University at Stark, OH*
Kentucky State University, KY*
Kentucky Wesleyan College, KY*
Keystone College, PA*
King College, TN*
King's College, PA

*program is offered at another college's campus

Kutztown University of Pennsylvania, PA*
Kuyper College, MI*
Lafayette College, PA*
Lakeview College of Nursing, IL*
La Roche College, PA*
Lebanon Valley College, PA*
Lehigh University, PA
Lehman College of the City University of
  New York, NY*
Le Moyne College, NY*
Lewis-Clark State College, ID*
Lewis University, IL*
Limestone College, SC
Lincoln University, MO
Lincoln University, PA*
Lindenwood University, MO
Lipscomb University, TN*
Lock Haven University of Pennsylvania, PA
Long Island University, C.W. Post
  Campus, NY*
Longwood University, VA
Loras College, IA*
Louisiana State University and Agricultural
  and Mechanical College, LA
Louisiana Tech University, LA*
Lourdes College, OH*
Loyola University Chicago, IL*
Loyola University Maryland, MD
Loyola University New Orleans, LA*
Lubbock Christian University, TX*
Lycoming College, PA*
Macalester College, MN*
Malone University, OH*
Manhattan College, NY*
Mansfield University of Pennsylvania, PA*
Marian University, WI
Marist College, NY
Marquette University, WI
Marshall University, WV
Mary Baldwin College, VA
Marymount University, VA*
Maryville University of Saint Louis, MO*
Marywood University, PA*
Massachusetts Institute of Technology, MA
Massachusetts Maritime Academy, MA*
McDaniel College, MD
McKendree University, IL*
Medaille College, NY*
Menlo College, CA*
Mercer University, GA
Mercyhurst College, PA*
Meredith College, NC*
Methodist University, NC
Metropolitan State College of Denver, CO*
Miami University, OH*
Michigan State University, MI
Michigan Technological University, MI
Mid-Atlantic Christian University, NC*
Middlebury College, VT*
Millersville University of Pennsylvania, PA
Milligan College, TN*
Millsaps College, MS*
Mills College, CA*
Milwaukee School of Engineering, WI*
Minnesota State University Mankato, MN
Minnesota State University Moorhead, MN*
Misericordia University, PA*
Mississippi College, MS
Mississippi State University, MS
Mississippi University for Women, MS*
Mississippi Valley State University, MS
Missouri State University, MO

Missouri University of Science and
  Technology, MO
Molloy College, NY*
Monmouth College, IL
Montana State University, MT
Montana State University Billings, MT
Montclair State University, NJ
Moravian College, PA*
Morehead State University, KY
Morehouse College, GA
Morningside College, IA*
Mount Holyoke College, MA*
Mount Marty College, SD*
Mount Mary College, WI*
Mount Saint Mary College, NY*
Mount St. Mary's University, MD*
Murray State University, KY
National University, CA*
Nazareth College of Rochester, NY*
Nebraska Methodist College, NE*
Nebraska Wesleyan University, NE*
Neumann University, PA*
Newberry College, SC*
New England College, NH*
New England School of
  Communications, ME*
New Jersey Institute of Technology, NJ*
New Mexico State University, NM
New York Institute of Technology, NY
New York University, NY*
Niagara University, NY
Nichols College, MA*
Norfolk State University, VA
North Carolina Agricultural and Technical
  State University, NC
North Carolina State University, NC
North Central College, IL*
Northeastern Illinois University, IL*
Northeastern State University, OK
Northeastern University, MA
Northern Arizona University, AZ
Northern Kentucky University, KY*
Northern Michigan University, MI
North Georgia College & State University, GA
North Greenville University, SC*
Northwestern College, MN*
Northwestern State University of
  Louisiana, LA
Northwest Nazarene University, ID
Northwest University, WA*
Occidental College, CA*
Ohio Northern University, OH*
The Ohio State University, OH
Ohio University, OH
Oklahoma Christian University, OK*
Oklahoma City University, OK*
Oklahoma State University, OK
Old Dominion University, VA
Oregon Health & Science University, OR*
Oregon Institute of Technology, OR*
Oregon State University, OR
Ouachita Baptist University, AR
Our Lady of the Lake College, LA*
Our Lady of the Lake University of
  San Antonio, TX*
Pace University, NY*
Pacific Lutheran University, WA
Palm Beach Atlantic University, FL*
Peace College, NC*
Penn State Abington, PA
Penn State Altoona, PA*
Penn State Berks, PA*
Penn State Erie, The Behrend College, PA

Penn State Harrisburg, PA*
Penn State University Park, PA
Pennsylvania College of Technology, PA*
Pepperdine University, CA*
Pikeville College, KY
Pittsburg State University, KS
Pitzer College, CA*
Plymouth State University, NH*
Point Park University, PA*
Polytechnic Institute of NYU, NY*
Polytechnic University of Puerto Rico, PR*
Pomona College, CA*
Portland State University, OR
Presbyterian College, SC
Princeton University, NJ
Providence College, RI
Purdue University, IN
Queens College of the City University of New
  York, NY*
Quinnipiac University, CT*
Radford University, VA
Randolph-Macon College, VA*
Regent University, VA*
Rensselaer Polytechnic Institute, NY*
Rhode Island College, RI*
Rhodes College, TN*
Rider University, NJ*
Ripon College, WI
Robert Morris University, PA
Robert Morris University Illinois, IL*
Roberts Wesleyan College, NY*
Rochester Institute of Technology, NY
Rockford College, IL*
Rockhurst University, MO*
Rocky Mountain College, MT
Rose-Hulman Institute of Technology, IN
Rosemont College, PA*
Rowan University, NJ*
Russell Sage College, NY*
Rutgers, The State University of New Jersey,
  Camden, NJ*
Rutgers, The State University of New Jersey,
  Newark, NJ
Rutgers, The State University of New Jersey,
  New Brunswick, NJ
Sacred Heart University, CT
Sage College of Albany, NY*
Saint Anselm College, NH*
St. Bonaventure University, NY
St. Catherine University, MN*
St. Edward's University, TX*
Saint Francis University, PA
St. John Fisher College, NY*
Saint John's University, MN
St. John's University, NY
St. Joseph's College, Long Island
  Campus, NY*
Saint Joseph's University, PA*
St. Lawrence University, NY*
Saint Leo University, FL
St. Louis College of Pharmacy, MO*
Saint Louis University, MO*
Saint Martin's University, WA*
Saint Mary's College, IN*
Saint Mary's College of California, CA*
St. Mary's University, TX
Saint Mary's University of Minnesota, MN*
Saint Michael's College, VT*
St. Norbert College, WI
Saint Paul's College, VA*
Saint Vincent College, PA*
Salem College, NC*
Salem State College, MA*

ROTC Programs
Army

Salisbury University, MD
Salve Regina University, RI*
Samford University, AL*
Sam Houston State University, TX
Samuel Merritt University, CA*
San Diego Christian College, CA*
San Diego State University, CA
San Francisco State University, CA*
San Jose State University, CA
Santa Clara University, CA
Savannah College of Art and Design, GA*
Savannah State University, GA
Scripps College, CA*
Seattle Pacific University, WA*
Seattle University, WA
Seton Hill University, PA
Shippensburg University of Pennsylvania, PA
Siena College, NY
Simmons College, MA*
Skidmore College, NY*
Slippery Rock University of Pennsylvania, PA
Smith College, MA*
Sonoma State University, CA*
South Dakota School of Mines and
   Technology, SD
South Dakota State University, SD
Southeastern Louisiana University, LA*
Southeastern University, FL*
Southern Connecticut State University, CT*
Southern Illinois University Carbondale, IL
Southern Illinois University Edwardsville, IL
Southern Methodist University, TX
Southern Polytechnic State University, GA*
Southern Utah University, UT
Southwest Baptist University, MO*
Spring Arbor University, MI
Spring Hill College, AL*
Stanford University, CA*
State University of New York at
   Binghamton, NY*
State University of New York at
   Fredonia, NY*
State University of New York at
   Oswego, NY*
State University of New York at
   Plattsburgh, NY
State University of New York College at
   Cortland, NY*
State University of New York College at
   Geneseo, NY*
State University of New York College at Old
   Westbury, NY*
State University of New York College at
   Potsdam, NY*
State University of New York College of
   Environmental Science and Forestry, NY*
State University of New York College of
   Technology at Canton, NY*
State University of New York Upstate Medical
   University, NY*
Stephen F. Austin State University, TX
Stephens College, MO*
Stetson University, FL*
Stevenson University, MD*
Stillman College, AL*
Stonehill College, MA
Stony Brook University, State University of
   New York, NY*
Suffolk University, MA*
Susquehanna University, PA*
Swarthmore College, PA*
Syracuse University, NY
Tarleton State University, TX

Temple University, PA
Tennessee Technological University, TN
Tennessee Wesleyan College, TN*
Texas A&M University, TX
Texas A&M University–Corpus Christi, TX
Texas Christian University, TX
Texas Lutheran University, TX*
Texas State University–San Marcos, TX
Texas Tech University, TX
Texas Woman's University, TX*
Thomas More College, KY*
Tiffin University, OH*
Towson University, MD*
Transylvania University, KY*
Trevecca Nazarene University, TN*
Trinity College, CT*
Troy University, AL
Truman State University, MO
Tufts University, MA*
Tulane University, LA
Tuskegee University, AL
Union College, KY
Union College, NY*
University at Albany, State University of New
   York, NY
University at Buffalo, the State University of
   New York, NY*
The University of Akron, OH
The University of Alabama, AL
The University of Alabama at
   Birmingham, AL
The University of Alabama in Huntsville, AL*
University of Alaska Anchorage, AK
University of Alaska Fairbanks, AK
The University of Arizona, AZ
University of Arkansas, AR
University of Bridgeport, CT
University of California, Berkeley, CA
University of California, Davis, CA
University of California, Irvine, CA*
University of California, Los Angeles, CA
University of California, Riverside, CA*
University of California, San Diego, CA*
University of California, Santa Barbara, CA
University of California, Santa Cruz, CA*
University of Central Florida, FL
University of Central Missouri, MO
University of Central Oklahoma, OK
University of Charleston, WV
University of Chicago, IL*
University of Cincinnati, OH
University of Colorado at Boulder, CO
University of Colorado at Colorado
   Springs, CO
University of Colorado Denver, CO
University of Connecticut, CT
University of Dallas, TX*
University of Dayton, OH
University of Delaware, DE
University of Denver, CO*
University of Dubuque, IA
The University of Findlay, OH*
University of Florida, FL
University of Georgia, GA
University of Hartford, CT*
University of Hawaii–West Oahu, HI*
University of Houston, TX
University of Houston–Downtown, TX*
University of Idaho, ID
University of Illinois at Chicago, IL
University of Illinois at Urbana–
   Champaign, IL
University of Indianapolis, IN*

The University of Iowa, IA
The University of Kansas, KS
University of Kentucky, KY
University of La Verne, CA*
University of Louisiana at Monroe, LA*
University of Louisville, KY
University of Maine, ME
University of Mary Hardin-Baylor, TX
University of Maryland, Baltimore
   County, MD*
University of Maryland, College Park, MD
University of Massachusetts Amherst, MA
University of Massachusetts Boston, MA*
University of Massachusetts Dartmouth, MA*
University of Memphis, TN
University of Miami, FL
University of Michigan, MI
University of Michigan–Dearborn, MI*
University of Michigan–Flint, MI*
University of Minnesota, Twin Cities
   Campus, MN
University of Mississippi, MS
University of Missouri, MO
University of Missouri–Kansas City, MO
University of Missouri–St. Louis, MO*
University of Mobile, AL*
University of Montevallo, AL*
University of Mount Union, OH*
University of Nebraska at Kearney, NE
University of Nebraska at Omaha, NE*
University of Nebraska–Lincoln, NE
University of Nebraska Medical Center, NE*
University of Nevada, Las Vegas, NV
University of Nevada, Reno, NV
University of New Hampshire, NH
University of New Hampshire at
   Manchester, NH*
University of New Haven, CT
University of New Orleans, LA*
University of North Alabama, AL
The University of North Carolina at Chapel
   Hill, NC
The University of North Carolina at
   Charlotte, NC
The University of North Carolina at
   Greensboro, NC*
The University of North Carolina at
   Pembroke, NC
University of North Dakota, ND
University of Northern Colorado, CO
University of Northern Iowa, IA
University of North Florida, FL
University of North Texas, TX
University of Notre Dame, IN
University of Oklahoma, OK
University of Oregon, OR
University of Pennsylvania, PA*
University of Pittsburgh, PA
University of Pittsburgh at Bradford, PA*
University of Pittsburgh at Greensburg, PA*
University of Portland, OR
University of Puerto Rico at Bayamón, PR
University of Puerto Rico, Río Piedras, PR
University of Puget Sound, WA*
University of Redlands, CA*
University of Rhode Island, RI
University of Richmond, VA
University of Rochester, NY*
University of St. Thomas, MN*
University of St. Thomas, TX*
University of San Diego, CA*
The University of Scranton, PA
University of South Alabama, AL

*program is offered at another college's campus

f www.facebook.com/pay4undergrad

University of South Carolina, SC
The University of South Dakota, SD
University of Southern California, CA
University of Southern Indiana, IN
University of Southern Maine, ME*
University of Southern Mississippi, MS
The University of Tampa, FL
The University of Tennessee, TN
The University of Tennessee at
  Chattanooga, TN
The University of Tennessee at Martin, TN
The University of Texas at Arlington, TX
The University of Texas at Austin, TX
The University of Texas at Dallas, TX*
The University of Texas at El Paso, TX
The University of Texas at San Antonio, TX
The University of Texas Health Science
  Center at Houston, TX*
The University of Texas–Pan American, TX
University of the District of Columbia, DC*
University of the Incarnate Word, TX*
University of the Sciences in
  Philadelphia, PA*
The University of Toledo, OH
University of Vermont, VT
University of Virginia, VA
The University of Virginia's College at
  Wise, VA
University of Washington, WA
University of Washington, Tacoma, WA*
The University of West Alabama, AL*
University of West Florida, FL
University of West Georgia, GA
University of Wisconsin–Eau Claire, WI
University of Wisconsin–Green Bay, WI*
University of Wisconsin–La Crosse, WI
University of Wisconsin–Madison, WI
University of Wisconsin–Parkside, WI*
University of Wisconsin–River Falls, WI
University of Wisconsin–Stevens Point, WI
University of Wisconsin–Stout, WI
University of Wisconsin–Whitewater, WI
University of Wyoming, WY
Ursuline College, OH*
Utah State University, UT
Utah Valley University, UT
Utica College, NY
Valparaiso University, IN*
Vanderbilt University, TN
Vermont Technical College, VT*
Villanova University, PA*
Virginia Commonwealth University, VA*
Virginia Military Institute, VA
Virginia Polytechnic Institute and State
  University, VA
Virginia Union University, VA*
Virginia Wesleyan College, VA*
Wagner College, NY*
Wake Forest University, NC
Washburn University, KS
Washington & Jefferson College, PA*
Washington and Lee University, VA*
Washington State University, WA
Washington University in St. Louis, MO
Wayland Baptist University, TX*
Waynesburg University, PA*
Wayne State College, NE
Webster University, MO*
Wellesley College, MA*
Wells College, NY*
West Chester University of Pennsylvania, PA*
Western Connecticut State University, CT*
Western Illinois University, IL

Western Kentucky University, KY
Western New England College, MA
Western Oregon University, OR
Westfield State College, MA*
Westminster College, MO*
Westminster College, UT*
Westmont College, CA*
West Virginia University, WV
Wheaton College, IL
Wheaton College, MA*
Widener University, PA
Wilkes University, PA*
Willamette University, OR*
William Jewell College, MO*
Wilson College, PA*
Winona State University, MN*
Winthrop University, SC*
Wittenberg University, OH*
Wofford College, SC
Worcester Polytechnic Institute, MA
Worcester State College, MA*
Wright State University, OH
Xavier University, OH
Xavier University of Louisiana, LA*
Yale University, CT*
York College, NE*
York College of Pennsylvania, PA*
Youngstown State University, OH

Naval

Armstrong Atlantic State University, GA*
Auburn University, AL
Augsburg College, MN*
Babson College, MA*
Belmont University, TN*
Boston College, MA*
Boston University, MA
California Maritime Academy, CA*
Carnegie Mellon University, PA
The Catholic University of America, DC*
Chatham University, PA*
Christian Brothers University, TN*
The Citadel, The Military College of South
  Carolina, SC
Clark University, MA*
Clearwater Christian College, FL*
The College at Brockport, State University of
  New York, NY*
The College of Saint Rose, NY*
College of the Holy Cross, MA
Columbia College, MO*
Concordia University, St. Paul, MN*
Cornell University, NY
Duke University, NC
Duquesne University, PA*
Eastern Michigan University, MI*
Embry-Riddle Aeronautical University, FL
Fisk University, TN*
Florida Agricultural and Mechanical
  University, FL
Florida State University, FL*
Fordham University, NY*
Georgetown University, DC*
The George Washington University, DC
Georgia Institute of Technology, GA
Georgia State University, GA*
Guilford College, NC*
Hampton University, VA
Harvard University, MA*
Houston Baptist University, TX*
Husson University, ME*
Huston-Tillotson University, TX*
Illinois Institute of Technology, IL

Indiana University South Bend, IN*
Iowa State University of Science and
  Technology, IA
Jacksonville University, FL
Lewis-Clark State College, ID*
Lincoln University, MO*
Louisiana State University and Agricultural
  and Mechanical College, LA*
Loyola University Chicago, IL*
Loyola University New Orleans, LA*
Macalester College, MN*
Marquette University, WI
Mary Baldwin College, VA*
Massachusetts Institute of Technology, MA
Massachusetts Maritime Academy, MA
Miami University, OH
Milwaukee School of Engineering, WI*
Missouri University of Science and
  Technology, MO*
Molloy College, NY*
Montclair State University, NJ
Morehouse College, GA
New York University, NY*
Norfolk State University, VA
North Carolina State University, NC
Northeastern University, MA*
The Ohio State University, OH
Old Dominion University, VA
Oregon State University, OR
Peace College, NC*
Penn State University Park, PA
Princeton University, NJ*
Purdue University, IN
Queens College of the City University of New
  York, NY*
Rensselaer Polytechnic Institute, NY
Rochester Institute of Technology, NY*
St. John Fisher College, NY*
Saint Joseph's University, PA*
St. Louis College of Pharmacy, MO*
Saint Mary's College, IN*
San Diego State University, CA
San Francisco State University, CA*
Savannah State University, GA
Seattle Pacific University, WA*
Siena College, NY*
Southern Polytechnic State University, GA*
Stanford University, CA*
Stephens College, MO*
Swarthmore College, PA*
Temple University, PA*
Tennessee Wesleyan College, TN*
Texas A&M University, TX
Tufts University, MA*
Tulane University, LA
Union College, NY*
The University of Arizona, AZ
University of California, Berkeley, CA
University of California, Davis, CA*
University of California, Los Angeles, CA
University of California, Santa Cruz, CA*
University of Colorado at Boulder, CO
University of Florida, FL
University of Houston, TX*
University of Idaho, ID
University of Illinois at Chicago, IL*
University of Illinois at Urbana–
  Champaign, IL
The University of Kansas, KS
University of Maine, ME*
University of Maryland, College Park, MD*
University of Massachusetts Boston, MA*
University of Memphis, TN

ROTC Programs
Naval

University of Michigan, MI
University of Michigan–Dearborn, MI*
University of Michigan–Flint, MI*
University of Minnesota, Twin Cities Campus, MN
University of Mississippi, MS
University of Missouri, MO
University of Nebraska–Lincoln, NE
University of New Orleans, LA*
The University of North Carolina at Chapel Hill, NC
University of North Florida, FL*
University of Notre Dame, IN
University of Oklahoma, OK

University of Pennsylvania, PA
University of Pittsburgh, PA*
University of Rochester, NY
University of St. Thomas, MN*
University of San Diego, CA
University of South Carolina, SC
University of Southern California, CA
The University of Tampa, FL
The University of Texas at Austin, TX
University of Virginia, VA
University of Washington, WA
University of Washington, Tacoma, WA*
University of Wisconsin–Madison, WI
Vanderbilt University, TN

Villanova University, PA
Virginia Military Institute, VA
Virginia Polytechnic Institute and State University, VA
Washburn University, KS*
Washington State University, WA*
Westminster College, UT*
Widener University, PA*
Worcester Polytechnic Institute, MA*
Worcester State College, MA*
Xavier University of Louisiana, LA*
York College, NE*

*program is offered at another college's campus

www.facebook.com/pay4undergrad

Tuition Waivers

Adult Students

Alaska Pacific University, AK
Albright College, PA
Appalachian Bible College, WV
Barton College, NC
Bluefield State College, WV
Briar Cliff University, IA
California State University, Stanislaus, CA
The Catholic University of America, DC
Clarke College, IA
Coe College, IA
College of the Atlantic, ME
Concord University, WV
Converse College, SC
Coppin State University, MD
Creighton University, NE
DeSales University, PA
Dickinson State University, ND
Dowling College, NY
Faulkner University, AL
Goucher College, MD
Juniata College, PA
Lane College, TN
Lewis University, IL
Lynchburg College, VA
Marquette University, WI
Medaille College, NY
Mercyhurst College, PA
Messiah College, PA
Nebraska Wesleyan University, NE
New England College, NH
Randolph College, VA
St. Ambrose University, IA
St. Andrews Presbyterian College, NC
Southern Adventist University, TN
Trinity College, CT
University of North Dakota, ND
Utah State University, UT
Webber International University, FL
Wittenberg University, OH

Children of Alumni

Albright College, PA
Appalachian Bible College, WV
Arcadia University, PA
Ashland University, OH
Augsburg College, MN
Baldwin-Wallace College, OH
Barton College, NC
Bethany College, WV
Bethel College, KS
Cabrini College, PA
Calumet College of Saint Joseph, IN
Carthage College, WI
The Catholic University of America, DC
Cedar Crest College, PA
Central Michigan University, MI
Christian Brothers University, TN
Clarke College, IA
Coe College, IA
College of Saint Elizabeth, NJ
Columbia College, MO

Concordia University Chicago, IL
Coppin State University, MD
Crown College, MN
Curry College, MA
Delta State University, MS
Dickinson State University, ND
Dixie State College of Utah, UT
Dominican University, IL
Dowling College, NY
Drake University, IA
Drury University, MO
D'Youville College, NY
Eastern Nazarene College, MA
Erskine College, SC
Florida Southern College, FL
Grand View University, IA
Henderson State University, AR
Hillsdale Free Will Baptist College, OK
Huntingdon College, AL
Kentucky Wesleyan College, KY
Lake Superior State University, MI
Lancaster Bible College & Graduate
   School, PA
Lewis University, IL
Louisiana State University and Agricultural
   and Mechanical College, LA
Louisiana Tech University, LA
MacMurray College, IL
Marymount University, VA
Messiah College, PA
Michigan Technological University, MI
Mid-Atlantic Christian University, NC
Minneapolis College of Art and Design, MN
Mississippi State University, MS
Mississippi Valley State University, MS
Missouri State University, MO
Morehead State University, KY
Morningside College, IA
Murray State University, KY
Nazareth College of Rochester, NY
New England College, NH
Northwestern College, MN
Northwest Nazarene University, ID
Northwood University, Florida Campus, FL
Ohio Northern University, OH
Ohio Wesleyan University, OH
Oklahoma State University, OK
Oral Roberts University, OK
Pacific Lutheran University, WA
Peirce College, PA
Point Park University, PA
Rockhurst University, MO
St. Ambrose University, IA
Saint Louis University, MO
Saint Martin's University, WA
St. Thomas University, FL
South Dakota State University, SD
Southeastern Oklahoma State University, OK
Southern Arkansas University–Magnolia, AR
Texas Lutheran University, TX
Union University, TN
University of Alaska Fairbanks, AK

University of Central Missouri, MO
University of Evansville, IN
The University of Findlay, OH
University of Idaho, ID
University of Mount Union, OH
University of Nebraska at Omaha, NE
University of Nevada, Las Vegas, NV
University of Nevada, Reno, NV
University of Oklahoma, OK
University of St. Francis, IL
University of Saint Francis, IN
The University of South Dakota, SD
University of Southern Mississippi, MS
University of the Ozarks, AR
The University of Toledo, OH
University of Wisconsin–River Falls, WI
University of Wisconsin–Whitewater, WI
University of Wyoming, WY
Utah State University, UT
Valley City State University, ND
Warner Pacific College, OR
Webber International University, FL
Western Kentucky University, KY
Westminster College, MO
William Jewell College, MO
Wittenberg University, OH

Minority Students

Bloomsburg University of Pennsylvania, PA
Concordia College, MN
Concordia University Chicago, IL
Coppin State University, MD
Dickinson State University, ND
Dowling College, NY
Drury University, MO
Edinboro University of Pennsylvania, PA
Fort Lewis College, CO
Geneva College, PA
Illinois State University, IL
Lake Superior State University, MI
Lock Haven University of Pennsylvania, PA
MacMurray College, IL
Massachusetts Maritime Academy, MA
Messiah College, PA
Montana State University, MT
Nazareth College of Rochester, NY
Northern Illinois University, IL
Northwest Nazarene University, ID
Portland State University, OR
St. Ambrose University, IA
St. Thomas University, FL
Shepherd University, WV
Slippery Rock University of Pennsylvania, PA
Southeastern Oklahoma State University, OK
University at Buffalo, the State University of
   New York, NY
University of Evansville, IN
University of Idaho, ID
University of Maine at Presque Isle, ME
University of Minnesota, Morris, MN
University of North Dakota, ND
University of Rhode Island, RI
University of Wisconsin–Eau Claire, WI

Tuition Waivers
Minority Students

University of Wisconsin–La Crosse, WI
Utah State University, UT
Western Washington University, WA
Wittenberg University, OH

Senior Citizens

Adams State College, CO
Albright College, PA
Andrews University, MI
Angelo State University, TX
Appalachian Bible College, WV
Arkansas State University—Jonesboro, AR
Arkansas Tech University, AR
Armstrong Atlantic State University, GA
Asbury University, KY
Ashland University, OH
Atlantic Union College, MA
Augsburg College, MN
Aurora University, IL
Austin Peay State University, TN
Averett University, VA
Barton College, NC
Becker College, MA
Bellarmine University, KY
Belmont Abbey College, NC
Belmont University, TN
Bemidji State University, MN
Benedictine College, KS
Bernard M. Baruch College of the City University of New York, NY
Berry College, GA
Bethel College, KS
Black Hills State University, SD
Bloomfield College, NJ
Bloomsburg University of Pennsylvania, PA
Bluefield College, VA
Bluefield State College, WV
Bob Jones University, SC
Boise State University, ID
Boston University, MA
Bowie State University, MD
Bowling Green State University, OH
Brevard College, NC
Brewton-Parker College, GA
Briar Cliff University, IA
Bridgewater College, VA
Cabrini College, PA
California State University, Chico, CA
California State University, Dominguez Hills, CA
California State University, East Bay, CA
California State University, Fullerton, CA
California State University, Long Beach, CA
California State University, Monterey Bay, CA
California State University, Stanislaus, CA
Calumet College of Saint Joseph, IN
Cameron University, OK
Campbellsville University, KY
Carson-Newman College, TN
Cedarville University, OH
Central Connecticut State University, CT
Central Michigan University, MI
Chestnut Hill College, PA
Chowan University, NC
Christopher Newport University, VA
The Citadel, The Military College of South Carolina, SC
City College of the City University of New York, NY
Clarion University of Pennsylvania, PA
Clarke College, IA
Cleary University, MI
Clemson University, SC

Cleveland State University, OH
Coastal Carolina University, SC
Coe College, IA
The College at Brockport, State University of New York, NY
College of Charleston, SC
College of Mount St. Joseph, OH
The College of New Jersey, NJ
The College of New Rochelle, NY
College of Saint Elizabeth, NJ
College of Saint Mary, NE
The College of St. Scholastica, MN
College of Staten Island of the City University of New York, NY
College of the Atlantic, ME
The College of William and Mary, VA
Columbia College, MO
Columbus State University, GA
Concordia University Chicago, IL
Concord University, WV
Connecticut College, CT
Coppin State University, MD
Covenant College, GA
Culver-Stockton College, MO
Daemen College, NY
Dakota State University, SD
Dakota Wesleyan University, SD
Defiance College, OH
Delta State University, MS
DeSales University, PA
Dickinson College, PA
Dickinson State University, ND
Dixie State College of Utah, UT
Doane College, NE
Dominican College, NY
Dominican University of California, CA
Dordt College, IA
Dowling College, NY
Drake University, IA
Drew University, NJ
Duquesne University, PA
D'Youville College, NY
East Carolina University, NC
Eastern Kentucky University, KY
Eastern New Mexico University, NM
Eastern Oregon University, OR
East Stroudsburg University of Pennsylvania, PA
Elmhurst College, IL
Emporia State University, KS
Faulkner University, AL
Ferrum College, VA
Fitchburg State College, MA
Florida Atlantic University, FL
Florida Gulf Coast University, FL
Florida Institute of Technology, FL
Florida International University, FL
Florida State University, FL
Framingham State College, MA
Francis Marion University, SC
Franklin College, IN
Freed-Hardeman University, TN
Frostburg State University, MD
Gannon University, PA
Gardner-Webb University, NC
George Fox University, OR
George Mason University, VA
Georgia College & State University, GA
Georgia Southern University, GA
Georgia State University, GA
Glenville State College, WV
Goucher College, MD
Grace College, IN

Graceland University, IA
Grand View University, IA
Greenville College, IL
Hanover College, IN
Harding University, AR
Hillsdale Free Will Baptist College, OK
Hofstra University, NY
Holy Family University, PA
Hood College, MD
Howard Payne University, TX
Huntington University, IN
Husson University, ME
Idaho State University, ID
Illinois State University, IL
Indiana State University, IN
Indiana University of Pennsylvania, PA
Indiana University–Purdue University Fort Wayne, IN
Iona College, NY
James Madison University, VA
John Carroll University, OH
John Jay College of Criminal Justice of the City University of New York, NY
Juniata College, PA
Kean University, NJ
Keene State College, NH
Kennesaw State University, GA
Kent State University, OH
Kent State University at Stark, OH
Kentucky Wesleyan College, KY
Keystone College, PA
King College, TN
King's College, PA
Kutztown University of Pennsylvania, PA
Lakeland College, WI
Lake Superior State University, MI
Lancaster Bible College & Graduate School, PA
La Roche College, PA
Lebanon Valley College, PA
Lincoln Memorial University, TN
Lindenwood University, MO
Lindsey Wilson College, KY
Linfield College, OR
Lock Haven University of Pennsylvania, PA
Longwood University, VA
Loras College, IA
Louisiana Tech University, LA
Lourdes College, OH
Loyola University Chicago, IL
Loyola University New Orleans, LA
Lynchburg College, VA
MacMurray College, IL
Malone University, OH
Manhattanville College, NY
Marian University, WI
Marlboro College, VT
Marquette University, WI
Marshall University, WV
Marymount University, VA
Maryville University of Saint Louis, MO
Marywood University, PA
Massachusetts College of Liberal Arts, MA
Massachusetts Maritime Academy, MA
Medaille College, NY
Merrimack College, MA
Messiah College, PA
Methodist University, NC
Metropolitan State College of Denver, CO
Metropolitan State University, MN
Michigan Technological University, MI
Mid-Atlantic Christian University, NC
Midwestern State University, TX

Millersville University of Pennsylvania, PA
Minnesota State University Mankato, MN
Minnesota State University Moorhead, MN
Mississippi State University, MS
Missouri Southern State University, MO
Missouri State University, MO
Monmouth University, NJ
Montana State University, MT
Montana State University Billings, MT
Montclair State University, NJ
Morehead State University, KY
Morningside College, IA
Mountain State University, WV
Mount Mary College, WI
Mount Vernon Nazarene University, OH
Murray State University, KY
Nebraska Wesleyan University, NE
New England College, NH
New Jersey City University, NJ
New Mexico State University, NM
New York Institute of Technology, NY
Niagara University, NY
Nichols College, MA
North Carolina Agricultural and Technical
  State University, NC
North Carolina State University, NC
North Central College, IL
Northeastern Illinois University, IL
Northeastern State University, OK
Northern Illinois University, IL
Northern Kentucky University, KY
Northern Michigan University, MI
North Georgia College & State University, GA
Northwestern State University of
  Louisiana, LA
Notre Dame de Namur University, CA
The Ohio State University, OH
Ohio University–Zanesville, OH
Oklahoma Baptist University, OK
Oklahoma Panhandle State University, OK
Oklahoma Wesleyan University, OK
Old Dominion University, VA
Pace University, NY
Pacific Union College, CA
Peace College, NC
Pikeville College, KY
Plymouth State University, NH
Point Loma Nazarene University, CA
Portland State University, OR
Presbyterian College, SC
Providence College, RI
Purdue University, IN
Purdue University Calumet, IN
Purdue University North Central, IN
Queens College of the City University of New
  York, NY
Quincy University, IL
Radford University, VA
Ramapo College of New Jersey, NJ
Reinhardt University, GA
The Richard Stockton College of New
  Jersey, NJ
Rivier College, NH
Roanoke College, VA
Roberts Wesleyan College, NY
Rockhurst University, MO
Rogers State University, OK
Rosemont College, PA
St. Ambrose University, IA
St. Andrews Presbyterian College, NC
St. Bonaventure University, NY
St. Catherine University, MN
St. John's University, NY

St. Mary's College of Maryland, MD
St. Olaf College, MN
Saint Xavier University, IL
Salem State College, MA
Salisbury University, MD
San Francisco State University, CA
Seattle Pacific University, WA
Shepherd University, WV
Shippensburg University of Pennsylvania, PA
Shorter University, GA
Siena College, NY
Silver Lake College, WI
Skidmore College, NY
Slippery Rock University of Pennsylvania, PA
South Dakota School of Mines and
  Technology, SD
South Dakota State University, SD
Southeastern Louisiana University, LA
Southeastern Oklahoma State University, OK
Southeast Missouri State University, MO
Southern Adventist University, TN
Southern Arkansas University–Magnolia, AR
Southern Connecticut State University, CT
Southern Illinois University Carbondale, IL
Southern Illinois University Edwardsville, IL
Southern Polytechnic State University, GA
Southwestern College, KS
Southwest Minnesota State University, MN
State University of New York College at Old
  Westbury, NY
Stephen F. Austin State University, TX
Sterling College, VT
Suffolk University, MA
Taylor University, IN
Texas A&M University–Commerce, TX
Texas A&M University–Corpus Christi, TX
Texas Tech University, TX
Texas Woman's University, TX
Thiel College, PA
Thomas More College, KY
Tiffin University, OH
Towson University, MD
Trevecca Nazarene University, TN
Trinity Christian College, IL
Truman State University, MO
Union College, KY
Union College, NY
The University of Akron, OH
University of Alaska Fairbanks, AK
University of Arkansas, AR
University of Bridgeport, CT
University of Central Arkansas, AR
University of Central Florida, FL
University of Central Missouri, MO
University of Charleston, WV
University of Colorado at Boulder, CO
University of Connecticut, CT
University of Dayton, OH
University of Delaware, DE
University of Evansville, IN
The University of Findlay, OH
University of Georgia, GA
University of Hartford, CT
University of Houston–Clear Lake, TX
University of Houston–Downtown, TX
University of Idaho, ID
University of Illinois at Chicago, IL
University of Illinois at Springfield, IL
University of Illinois at Urbana–
  Champaign, IL
University of Kentucky, KY
University of Louisville, KY
University of Maine, ME

University of Maine at Presque Isle, ME
University of Mary, ND
University of Maryland, Baltimore
  County, MD
University of Maryland University
  College, MD
University of Mary Washington, VA
University of Massachusetts Amherst, MA
University of Massachusetts Boston, MA
University of Massachusetts Dartmouth, MA
University of Massachusetts Lowell, MA
University of Memphis, TN
University of Michigan–Dearborn, MI
University of Michigan–Flint, MI
University of Minnesota, Crookston, MN
University of Minnesota, Morris, MN
University of Minnesota, Twin Cities
  Campus, MN
University of Missouri, MO
University of Missouri–St. Louis, MO
The University of Montana Western, MT
University of Mount Union, OH
University of Nebraska at Omaha, NE
University of Nevada, Las Vegas, NV
University of Nevada, Reno, NV
University of New Hampshire at
  Manchester, NH
University of New Orleans, LA
University of North Alabama, AL
The University of North Carolina at Chapel
  Hill, NC
University of North Dakota, ND
University of North Florida, FL
University of North Texas, TX
University of Oklahoma, OK
University of Pittsburgh at Greensburg, PA
University of Rhode Island, RI
University of Saint Francis, IN
University of St. Thomas, TX
University of Science and Arts of
  Oklahoma, OK
The University of Scranton, PA
University of South Carolina, SC
The University of South Dakota, SD
University of Southern Mississippi, MS
The University of Tennessee, TN
The University of Tennessee at
  Chattanooga, TN
The University of Tennessee at Martin, TN
The University of Texas at Austin, TX
The University of Texas at Brownsville, TX
The University of Texas at Dallas, TX
The University of Texas at Tyler, TX
The University of Texas of the Permian
  Basin, TX
The University of Texas–Pan American, TX
University of the District of Columbia, DC
University of the Incarnate Word, TX
University of Vermont, VT
University of Virginia, VA
The University of Virginia's College at
  Wise, VA
University of Washington, WA
University of Washington, Tacoma, WA
University of West Florida, FL
University of West Georgia, GA
University of Wisconsin–Green Bay, WI
University of Wisconsin–Parkside, WI
University of Wisconsin–Whitewater, WI
University of Wyoming, WY
Utah State University, UT
Utica College, NY
Valdosta State University, GA

Tuition Waivers
Senior Citizens

Victory University, TN
Villanova University, PA
Virginia Commonwealth University, VA
Virginia Intermont College, VA
Virginia Military Institute, VA
Virginia Wesleyan College, VA
Wartburg College, IA
Washburn University, KS
Washington State University, WA
Wayne State University, MI
Webber International University, FL
Wells College, NY

Wesleyan College, GA
West Chester University of Pennsylvania, PA
Western Connecticut State University, CT
Western Illinois University, IL
Western Kentucky University, KY
Western New England College, MA
Western New Mexico University, NM
Western State College of Colorado, CO
Westfield State College, MA
West Liberty University, WV
West Virginia University, WV
Wichita State University, KS

Widener University, PA
William Paterson University of New Jersey, NJ
Williams Baptist College, AR
Winthrop University, SC
Wittenberg University, OH
Worcester State College, MA
Wright State University, OH
Xavier University, OH
Youngstown State University, OH

Tuition Payment Alternatives

Abilene Christian University, TX	I,P	
Academy of Art University, CA	I	
Adams State College, CO	D,I	
Adelphi University, NY	D,I	
Agnes Scott College, GA	I	
Alabama State University, AL	D	
Alaska Pacific University, AK	D,G,I	
Albright College, PA	I	
Alderson-Broaddus College, WV	I	
Alfred University, NY	D,I,P	
Alice Lloyd College, KY	D	
Allegheny College, PA	I,P	
Alma College, MI	D,I	
American Baptist College of American Baptist Theological Seminary, TN	D	
American Jewish University, CA	I	
American University, DC	I	
Amherst College, MA	D,I	
Anderson University, IN	I	
Anderson University, SC	I	
Andrews University, MI	I	
Angelo State University, TX	I	
Appalachian Bible College, WV	I	
Appalachian State University, NC	I	
Aquinas College, TN	I	
Arcadia University, PA	D,I	
Arizona State University, AZ	I	
Arkansas State University—Jonesboro, AR	I	
Arkansas Tech University, AR	D,I	
Asbury University, KY	I	
Ashland University, OH	I	
Atlantic Union College, MA	G	
Auburn University, AL	I,P	
Augsburg College, MN	I	
Augustana College, IL	I,P	
Augustana College, SD	I	
Aurora University, IL	D,I	
Austin College, TX	I	
Austin Graduate School of Theology, TX	I	
Austin Peay State University, TN	I	
Averett University, VA	I	
Babson College, MA	I	
Baldwin-Wallace College, OH	D,I	
Ball State University, IN	I	
The Baptist College of Florida, FL	I	
Bard College, NY	I,P	
Bard College at Simon's Rock, MA	I	
Barnard College, NY	D,I,P	
Barton College, NC	I	
Bates College, ME	I,P	
Baylor University, TX	I	
Becker College, MA	I	
Belhaven University, MS	I	
Bellarmine University, KY	I	
Belmont Abbey College, NC	D,I	
Belmont University, TN	D,I	
Beloit College, WI	I	

Bemidji State University, MN	I	
Benedictine College, KS	I	
Benedictine University, IL	D,I	
Bennington College, VT	I	
Bentley University, MA	I	
Bernard M. Baruch College of the City University of New York, NY	D,I	
Berry College, GA	I	
Bethany College, KS	I	
Bethany College, WV	I	
Bethany Lutheran College, MN	I	
Bethel College, IN	I	
Bethel College, KS	D,I	
Bethel University, MN	I,P	
Bethune-Cookman University, FL	I	
Biola University, CA	I	
Black Hills State University, SD	D,I	
Blessing-Rieman College of Nursing, IL	I	
Bloomfield College, NJ	D,I	
Bloomsburg University of Pennsylvania, PA	I	
Bluefield College, VA	I	
Bluefield State College, WV	I	
Blue Mountain College, MS	I	
Bluffton University, OH	I	
Bob Jones University, SC	I	
Boise State University, ID	I	
Boston Architectural College, MA	I	
Boston College, MA	I	
Boston University, MA	I,P	
Bowdoin College, ME	D,I	
Bowie State University, MD	D,I	
Bowling Green State University, OH	I	
Brandeis University, MA	I,P	
Brenau University, GA	I	
Brescia University, KY	I	
Brevard College, NC	I	
Brewton-Parker College, GA	I	
Briar Cliff University, IA	D,I	
Bridgewater College, VA	I	
Bridgewater State College, MA	I	
Bryan College, TN	I	
Bryant University, RI	I	
Bryn Mawr College, PA	I,P	
Bucknell University, PA	I,P	
Buena Vista University, IA	G,I	
Burlington College, VT	I	
Butler University, IN	I	
Cabrini College, PA	I	
California Baptist University, CA	I	
California College of the Arts, CA	D,I	
California Institute of the Arts, CA	I	
California Lutheran University, CA	I	
California Maritime Academy, CA	I	
California Polytechnic State University, San Luis Obispo, CA	I	
California State Polytechnic University, Pomona, CA	D,I	

California State University, Chico, CA	D,I	
California State University, Dominguez Hills, CA	I	
California State University, East Bay, CA	I	
California State University, Fresno, CA	I	
California State University, Fullerton, CA	D,I	
California State University, Long Beach, CA	I	
California State University, Monterey Bay, CA	D,I	
California State University, Stanislaus, CA	D,I	
Calumet College of Saint Joseph, IN	I	
Calvary Bible College and Theological Seminary, MO	G	
Calvin College, MI	I,P	
Cambridge College, MA	I	
Cameron University, OK	I	
Campbellsville University, KY	I	
Canisius College, NY	D,I	
Carleton College, MN	I	
Carnegie Mellon University, PA	I	
Carolina Christian College, NC	I	
Carroll University, WI	I	
Carson-Newman College, TN	D,I	
Carthage College, WI	I	
Case Western Reserve University, OH	I	
Catawba College, NC	I	
The Catholic University of America, DC	I,P	
Cazenovia College, NY	I	
Cedar Crest College, PA	D,I	
Cedarville University, OH	I	
Centenary College, NJ	I	
Centenary College of Louisiana, LA	D,I	
Central College, IA	I	
Central Connecticut State University, CT	I	
Central Michigan University, MI	I	
Chaminade University of Honolulu, HI	I	
Chapman University, CA	D,I,P	
Chatham University, PA	I	
Chestnut Hill College, PA	D,I	
Chowan University, NC	D,I	
Christendom College, VA	I	
Christian Brothers University, TN	D,I	
Christopher Newport University, VA	I	
Cincinnati Christian University, OH	I	
City College of the City University of New York, NY	D	
Claremont McKenna College, CA	I,P	
Clarion University of Pennsylvania, PA	I	
Clarke College, IA	D,I	
Clarkson University, NY	I,P	

D = deferred payment system; G = guaranteed tuition rate; I = installment payments; P = prepayment locks in tuition rate

857

Tuition Payment Alternatives

Clark University, MA	I,P	Dartmouth College, NH	I,P	Fisk University, TN	I
Clearwater Christian College, FL	G,I	Davenport University, MI	I	Fitchburg State College, MA	I
Cleary University, MI	D,G,I	Defiance College, OH	I	Five Towns College, NY	I
Clemson University, SC	I	Delta State University, MS	I	Florida Atlantic University, FL	D,I,P
The Cleveland Institute of Art, OH	I	Denison University, OH	I	Florida College, FL	
Cleveland Institute of Music, OH	I	DePaul University, IL	D,I	Florida Institute of Technology, FL	I
Cleveland State University, OH	I	DeSales University, PA	I	Florida Southern College, FL	I
Coastal Carolina University, SC	I	Dickinson College, PA	I	Florida State University, FL	I,P
Coe College, IA	I	Dickinson State University, ND	I	Fort Lewis College, CO	I
Colby College, ME	I	DigiPen Institute of Technology, WA	I	Framingham State College, MA	I,P
Colgate University, NY	D,I,P	Dillard University, LA	I	Franciscan University of	
The College at Brockport, State		Dixie State College of Utah, UT	I	Steubenville, OH	I
University of New York, NY	D,I	Doane College, NE	I	Francis Marion University, SC	I
College for Creative Studies, MI	I	Dominican College, NY	D,I	Franklin & Marshall College, PA	D,I
College of Charleston, SC	I	Dominican University, IL	I	Franklin College, IN	I
College of Mount St. Joseph, OH	D,I	Dominican University of		Franklin W. Olin College of	
The College of New Jersey, NJ	I	California, CA	I	Engineering, MA	I
The College of New Rochelle, NY	I	Dordt College, IA	I	Freed-Hardeman University, TN	I
College of Saint Benedict, MN	I	Dowling College, NY	D,I	Frostburg State University, MD	D,I
College of Saint Elizabeth, NJ	I	Drake University, IA	I	Furman University, SC	I
College of Saint Mary, NE	D,I	Drew University, NJ	D,I,P	Gannon University, PA	D,I
The College of Saint Rose, NY	D	Drury University, MO	D,I,P	Gardner-Webb University, NC	I
The College of St. Scholastica, MN	I	Duke University, NC	D,I,P	Geneva College, PA	I
College of Staten Island of the City		Duquesne University, PA	D,I	George Fox University, OR	I
University of New York, NY	I	D'Youville College, NY	D,I,P	George Mason University, VA	D,I
College of the Atlantic, ME	I	Earlham College, IN	P	Georgetown College, KY	D
College of the Holy Cross, MA	I,P	East Carolina University, NC	D,I	The George Washington	
College of the Humanities and		Eastern Kentucky University, KY	D	University, DC	G,I
Sciences, Harrison Middleton		Eastern Michigan University, MI	I	Georgia College & State	
University, AZ	I	Eastern Nazarene College, MA	I	University, GA	I
College of the Ozarks, MO	I	Eastern New Mexico University, NM	I	Georgian Court University, NJ	I
College of Visual Arts, MN	I	Eastern Oregon University, OR	I	Glenville State College, WV	I
The College of William and Mary, VA	I	Eastern Washington University, WA	I	Goldey-Beacom College, DE	D,I
The College of Wooster, OH	I	East Stroudsburg University of		Gordon College, MA	I
The Colorado College, CO	I	Pennsylvania, PA	I	Goucher College, MD	I,P
Colorado School of Mines, CO	I	East Texas Baptist University, TX	I	Grace Bible College, MI	I
Colorado State University, CO	I	East-West University, IL	I	Grace College, IN	I
Columbia College, MO	D,I	Eckerd College, FL	I	Graceland University, IA	I
Columbia College, PR	I	Edgewood College, WI	I	Grand Valley State University, MI	D,I
Columbia College Chicago, IL	I	Edinboro University of		Grand View University, IA	I
Columbia University, School of		Pennsylvania, PA	I	Green Mountain College, VT	I
General Studies, NY	I,P	Elizabethtown College, PA	I	Grinnell College, IA	I,P
Columbus College of Art &		Elmhurst College, IL	I	Grove City College, PA	I
Design, OH	D,I	Elmira College, NY	I,P	Guilford College, NC	I
Concordia College, MN	I	Elon University, NC	I	Gustavus Adolphus College, MN	G,I,P
Concordia University, CA	I	Embry-Riddle Aeronautical		Gwynedd-Mercy College, PA	I
Concordia University, MI	I	University, AZ	D,I	Hamilton College, NY	I
Concordia University Chicago, IL	I	Embry-Riddle Aeronautical		Hamline University, MN	I
Concordia University, Nebraska, NE	I	University, FL	D,I	Hampden-Sydney College, VA	I
Concordia University, St. Paul, MN	I	Embry-Riddle Aeronautical University		Hampshire College, MA	I
Concordia University Texas, TX	I	Worldwide, FL	D	Hampton University, VA	D
Concordia University Wisconsin, WI	D,G,I	Emerson College, MA	I	Hannibal-LaGrange College, MO	I
Concord University, WV	I	Emmanuel College, MA	I	Hanover College, IN	I
Connecticut College, CT	I	Emory & Henry College, VA	I	Harding University, AR	I,P
Converse College, SC	I	Emory University, GA	I	Hardin-Simmons University, TX	G,I
Coppin State University, MD	D	Emporia State University, KS	D,I	Harrisburg University of Science and	
Corban University, OR	I	Endicott College, MA	I	Technology, PA	D,I
Cornell College, IA	D	Erskine College, SC	I	Hartwick College, NY	I
Cornell University, NY	I	Eugene Lang College The New		Harvard University, MA	I,P
Cornerstone University, MI	I	School for Liberal Arts, NY	I	Harvey Mudd College, CA	I
Covenant College, GA	I	Evangel University, MO	I	Haverford College, PA	I,P
Creighton University, NE	I	The Evergreen State College, WA	I	Hawai'i Pacific University, HI	I
Crossroads Bible College, IN	I	Excelsior College, NY	I	Heidelberg University, OH	I
Crown College, MN	I	Fairfield University, CT	I	Hendrix College, AR	I
Culver-Stockton College, MO	I	Fairmont State University, WV	I	Heritage Christian University, AL	D,I
Curry College, MA	I	Fashion Institute of Technology, NY	I	High Point University, NC	I
Daemen College, NY	D,I	Faulkner University, AL	I	Hillsdale Free Will Baptist	
Dakota State University, SD	D,I	Felician College, NJ	I	College, OK	I
Dallas Baptist University, TX	D,I	Ferrum College, VA	I	Hodges University, FL	I

D = deferred payment system; *G* = guaranteed tuition rate; *I* = installment payments; *P* = prepayment locks in tuition rate

f www.facebook.com/pay4undergrad

Hofstra University, NY	D,I	Kent State University, OH	D,I,P	Macalester College, MN	I
Hollins University, VA	I,P	Kent State University at Stark, OH	I	MacMurray College, IL	I
Holy Family University, PA	D,I	Kentucky State University, KY	I	Maine Maritime Academy, ME	I
Hood College, MD	I	Kentucky Wesleyan College, KY	D,I	Malone University, OH	I
Hope College, MI	I	Kenyon College, OH	I	Manchester College, IN	I
Hope International University, CA	I	Kettering University, MI	I	Manhattan College, NY	D,I
Houghton College, NY	I	Keuka College, NY	I	Manhattanville College, NY	D,I
Houston Baptist University, TX	I	Keystone College, PA	D,I	Mannes College The New School for	
Howard Payne University, TX	G,I	King College, TN	I	Music, NY	I
Humboldt State University, CA	I	The King's College, NY	D,I	Marian University, WI	I
Hunter College of the City University		King's College, PA	D,I	Marietta College, OH	I
of New York, NY	I	Knox College, IL	I	Marist College, NY	I
Huntingdon College, AL	D,G	Kutztown University of		Marlboro College, VT	I
Huntington University, IN	I	Pennsylvania, PA	D,I	Marquette University, WI	I
Husson University, ME	I,P	Kuyper College, MI	I	Marshall University, WV	I
Huston-Tillotson University, TX	D	Lafayette College, PA	I,P	Mary Baldwin College, VA	I
Idaho State University, ID	D	LaGrange College, GA	I	Marylhurst University, OR	I
Illinois College, IL	I	Lake Erie College, OH	I	Marymount Manhattan College, NY	I
Illinois Institute of Technology, IL	I	Lake Forest College, IL	I	Marymount University, VA	I
Illinois State University, IL	G,I	Lakeland College, WI	D,G,I,P	Maryville College, TN	I
Indiana State University, IN	D,I	Lake Superior State University, MI	D,I	Maryville University of Saint	
Indiana University Bloomington, IN	D	Lancaster Bible College & Graduate		Louis, MO	D,I
Indiana University East, IN	D	School, PA	I	Marywood University, PA	D,I
Indiana University Kokomo, IN	D	Lane College, TN	D,I	Massachusetts College of Liberal	
Indiana University Northwest, IN	D,I	La Roche College, PA	I	Arts, MA	I
Indiana University of		Lasell College, MA	I	Massachusetts College of Pharmacy	
Pennsylvania, PA	D,I	Lawrence Technological		and Health Sciences, MA	I
Indiana University–Purdue University		University, MI	I	Massachusetts Institute of	
Fort Wayne, IN	D,I	Lawrence University, WI	I,P	Technology, MA	I
Indiana University–Purdue University		Lebanon Valley College, PA	I,P	Massachusetts Maritime	
Indianapolis, IN	D,I	Lee University, TN	D	Academy, MA	D,G,I
Indiana University South Bend, IN	D	Lehigh University, PA	I,P	The Master's College and	
Indiana University Southeast, IN	D	Lehman College of the City		Seminary, CA	I
Indiana Wesleyan University, IN	I	University of New York, NY	D	McDaniel College, MD	I,P
Inter American University of Puerto		Le Moyne College, NY	D,I	McKendree University, IL	I
Rico, Ponce Campus, PR	D	LeMoyne-Owen College, TN	I	McMurry University, TX	I
Iona College, NY	D,I	Lesley University, MA	I	McNally Smith College of Music, MN	I
Iowa State University of Science and		LeTourneau University, TX	I	McPherson College, KS	I
Technology, IA	D,I	Lewis & Clark College, OR	I	Medaille College, NY	I
Iowa Wesleyan College, IA	D,I	Lewis University, IL	I	Medgar Evers College of the City	
Ithaca College, NY	I	Lexington College, IL	I	University of New York, NY	D,I
Jacksonville State University, AL	I	Life University, GA	I	Memphis College of Art, TN	I
James Madison University, VA	I,P	Limestone College, SC	I	Menlo College, CA	I
Jamestown College, ND	I	Lincoln Memorial University, TN	I	Mercer University, GA	I
Jarvis Christian College, TX	D,I	Lincoln University, MO	I	Mercy College of Northwest	
Jefferson College of Health		Lincoln University, PA	D,I	Ohio, OH	D,I
Sciences, VA	I	Lindenwood University, MO	D,I	Mercyhurst College, PA	I
John Brown University, AR	I	Lindsey Wilson College, KY	I	Merrimack College, MA	G,I
John Carroll University, OH	D,I	Linfield College, OR	I	Messiah College, PA	I
John Jay College of Criminal Justice		Lipscomb University, TN	D,I	Methodist University, NC	I
of the City University of New		Lock Haven University of		Metropolitan State College of	
York, NY	I	Pennsylvania, PA	D,I	Denver, CO	D,I
The Johns Hopkins University, MD	I	Longwood University, VA	I	Metropolitan State University, MN	I
Johnson & Wales University, CO	I	Loras College, IA	I	Miami University, OH	I
Johnson & Wales University, FL	I	Louisiana State University and		Michigan State University, MI	D
Johnson & Wales University, RI	I	Agricultural and Mechanical		Michigan Technological	
Johnson & Wales University—		College, LA	D	University, MI	D,I
Charlotte Campus, NC	I	Louisiana Tech University, LA	D,I	Mid-Atlantic Christian University, NC	D
Johnson Bible College, TN	I	Lourdes College, OH	D,I	Mid-Continent University, KY	D,I
Johnson C. Smith University, NC	I	Loyola University Chicago, IL	D,I	Midwestern State University, TX	I
Jones International University, CO	I	Loyola University Maryland, MD	I	Millersville University of	
Judson College, AL	D,I	Loyola University New Orleans, LA	I	Pennsylvania, PA	I
The Juilliard School, NY	I	Lubbock Christian University, TX	I	Milligan College, TN	I
Juniata College, PA	I	Luther College, IA	I	Millikin University, IL	I
Kalamazoo College, MI	I	Lycoming College, PA	I	Millsaps College, MS	D,I
Kansas State University, KS	D,I	Lyme Academy College of Fine		Mills College, CA	I
Kean University, NJ	I	Arts, CT	I	Milwaukee School of Engineering, WI	I
Keene State College, NH	I	Lynchburg College, VA	I,P	Minneapolis College of Art and	
Kennesaw State University, GA	D	Lynn University, FL	D,I	Design, MN	I

Tuition Payment Alternatives

Minnesota State University Mankato, MN	I	Nicholls State University, LA	D,I	Pepperdine University, CA	I
Minnesota State University Moorhead, MN	I	Nichols College, MA	I	Pfeiffer University, NC	I
Misericordia University, PA	D,I	Norfolk State University, VA	I	Philadelphia Biblical University, PA	I
Mississippi College, MS	D,I	North Carolina State University, NC	I	Philadelphia University, PA	D,I
Mississippi State University, MS	I	North Central College, IL	I	Piedmont Baptist College and Graduate School, NC	I
Mississippi University for Women, MS	I	Northeastern Illinois University, IL	D,G	Piedmont College, GA	I
Mississippi Valley State University, MS	I	Northeastern University, MA	I	Pikeville College, KY	I
Missouri State University, MO	D,I,P	Northern Arizona University, AZ	G,I	Pittsburg State University, KS	I
Missouri University of Science and Technology, MO	I	Northern Illinois University, IL	G,I	Pitzer College, CA	D,I
Molloy College, NY	I	Northern Kentucky University, KY	I	Plymouth State University, NH	I
Monmouth College, IL	I	Northern Michigan University, MI	D,I	Point Loma Nazarene University, CA	I
Monmouth University, NJ	I	Northern State University, SD	I	Point Park University, PA	D,I
Monroe College, NY	I	North Greenville University, SC	I	Polytechnic Institute of NYU, NY	D,G,I,P
Montana State University, MT	D,I	Northwest Christian University, OR	D,I	Polytechnic University of Puerto Rico, PR	D
Montana State University Billings, MT	I	Northwestern College, MN	I	Pomona College, CA	I
Montana Tech of The University of Montana, MT	D,I	Northwestern State University of Louisiana, LA	I	Portland State University, OR	I
Montclair State University, NJ	I	Northwest Nazarene University, ID	I,P	Pratt Institute, NY	D,I
Moody Bible Institute, IL	I	Northwest University, WA	I	Presbyterian College, SC	I
Moravian College, PA	I	Northwood University, MI	I	Prescott College, AZ	D,I
Morehead State University, KY	D,I	Northwood University, Florida Campus, FL	I	Princeton University, NJ	D,I
Morningside College, IA	I	Northwood University, Texas Campus, TX	I	Principia College, IL	I
Mountain State University, WV	I	Notre Dame College, OH	I	Providence College, RI	I
Mount Holyoke College, MA	I,P	Notre Dame de Namur University, CA	I	Purchase College, State University of New York, NY	I
Mount Ida College, MA	I	Nova Southeastern University, FL	D,I	Purdue University, IN	I
Mount Marty College, SD	I	Nyack College, NY	I	Purdue University Calumet, IN	D
Mount Mary College, WI	I	Oakland University, MI	D,I	Purdue University North Central, IN	D,I
Mount Mercy College, IA	I	Oberlin College, OH	I	Queens College of the City University of New York, NY	I
Mount Saint Mary College, NY	I	Occidental College, CA	I,P	Quincy University, IL	I
Mount St. Mary's College, CA	I	Oglethorpe University, GA	I,P	Quinnipiac University, CT	D,I
Mount St. Mary's University, MD	I	Ohio Northern University, OH	I	Radford University, VA	I
Mount Vernon Nazarene University, OH	I	The Ohio State University, OH	I	Ramapo College of New Jersey, NJ	I
Multnomah University, OR	I	Ohio University, OH	I	Randolph College, VA	I
Murray State University, KY	I	Ohio University–Zanesville, OH	I	Randolph-Macon College, VA	I
Naropa University, CO	I	Ohio Valley University, WV	I	Reed College, OR	I
Nazarene Bible College, CO	I	Ohio Wesleyan University, OH	I	Regent University, VA	I
Nazareth College of Rochester, NY	D,I	Oklahoma Baptist University, OK	I	Reinhardt University, GA	I
Nebraska Methodist College, NE	I	Oklahoma Christian University, OK	I	Rensselaer Polytechnic Institute, NY	I
Nebraska Wesleyan University, NE	D,I	Oklahoma City University, OK	D,I	Rhode Island College, RI	I
Neumann University, PA	I	Oklahoma Panhandle State University, OK	G,I	Rhodes College, TN	I
Newberry College, SC	I	Oklahoma State University, OK	I	The Richard Stockton College of New Jersey, NJ	D,I
New College of Florida, FL	D,I	Oklahoma Wesleyan University, OK	D,I	Rider University, NJ	I
New England College, NH	I	Old Dominion University, VA	D,I	Ringling College of Art and Design, FL	I
New England School of Communications, ME	I	Olivet College, MI	I	Ripon College, WI	I
New Jersey City University, NJ	D	Oral Roberts University, OK	I	Rivier College, NH	D,I
New Jersey Institute of Technology, NJ	D,I	Oregon Health & Science University, OR	I	Roanoke College, VA	I
Newman University, KS	I	Oregon State University, OR	D	Robert Morris University, PA	D,I
New Mexico State University, NM	D,I	Otis College of Art and Design, CA	I	Robert Morris University Illinois, IL	I
The New School for General Studies, NY	I	Ouachita Baptist University, AR	D,I	Roberts Wesleyan College, NY	I
The New School for Jazz and Contemporary Music, NY	I	Our Lady of the Lake University of San Antonio, TX	D,I	Rochester Institute of Technology, NY	D,I,P
New York City College of Technology of the City University of New York, NY	D	Pace University, NY	I	Rockford College, IL	I
		Pacific Union College, CA	G,I	Rockhurst University, MO	D,I
New York Institute of Technology, NY	I	Pacific University, OR	D,I	Rocky Mountain College, MT	I
New York School of Interior Design, NY	I	Palm Beach Atlantic University, FL	I	Rocky Mountain College of Art + Design, CO	I
New York University, NY	D,G,I,P	Parsons The New School for Design, NY	I	Rogers State University, OK	I
Niagara University, NY	D,I	Patrick Henry College, VA	I	Rollins College, FL	I
		Peabody Conservatory of The Johns Hopkins University, MD	I	Rose-Hulman Institute of Technology, IN	I,P
		Peace College, NC	I	Rosemont College, PA	I
		Peirce College, PA	I	Rowan University, NJ	D
		Penn State University Park, PA	D,I	Russell Sage College, NY	D,I
		Pennsylvania College of Technology, PA	D	Rutgers, The State University of New Jersey, Camden, NJ	I

D = deferred payment system; G = guaranteed tuition rate; I = installment payments; P = prepayment locks in tuition rate

Rutgers, The State University of New Jersey, Newark, NJ	I
Rutgers, The State University of New Jersey, New Brunswick, NJ	I
Sacred Heart Major Seminary, MI	D,I
Sacred Heart University, CT	I
Sage College of Albany, NY	D,I
Saginaw Valley State University, MI	I
St. Ambrose University, IA	I
St. Andrews Presbyterian College, NC	I
Saint Anthony College of Nursing, IL	D,I
St. Charles Borromeo Seminary, Overbrook, PA	I
St. Edward's University, TX	D,I
Saint Francis Medical Center College of Nursing, IL	I
Saint Francis University, PA	I
St. John Fisher College, NY	D,I
St. John's College, MD	I
Saint John's University, MN	I
St. John's University, NY	D,I
Saint Joseph College, CT	I
Saint Joseph's College of Maine, ME	I
Saint Joseph's University, PA	D,I
St. Lawrence University, NY	I
Saint Leo University, FL	I
St. Louis College of Pharmacy, MO	I
Saint Louis University, MO	I
Saint Martin's University, WA	I
Saint Mary's College, IN	I
Saint Mary's College of California, CA	I
St. Mary's College of Maryland, MD	I
St. Mary's University, TX	I,P
Saint Mary's University of Minnesota, MN	I
Saint Michael's College, VT	I
St. Norbert College, WI	D,I
St. Olaf College, MN	I
Saint Paul's College, VA	D,I
St. Thomas University, FL	I
Saint Xavier University, IL	I
Salem College, NC	I
Salem State College, MA	I
Salisbury University, MD	I
Salve Regina University, RI	I
Sam Houston State University, TX	I
Samuel Merritt University, CA	I
San Diego Christian College, CA	I
San Diego State University, CA	I
San Francisco Conservatory of Music, CA	I
San Francisco State University, CA	I
Santa Clara University, CA	I
Savannah College of Art and Design, GA	I
School of the Museum of Fine Arts, Boston, MA	I
Schreiner University, TX	I
Scripps College, CA	I,P
Seattle Pacific University, WA	D,I
Seton Hill University, PA	D,I
Shenandoah University, VA	I
Shepherd University, WV	I
Shippensburg University of Pennsylvania, PA	I
Shorter University, GA	I
Siena College, NY	I
Silver Lake College, WI	D,I

Simmons College, MA	I
Simpson College, IA	I
Skidmore College, NY	I,P
Slippery Rock University of Pennsylvania, PA	I
Smith College, MA	I,P
South Dakota School of Mines and Technology, SD	D,I
South Dakota State University, SD	D,I
Southeastern Bible College, AL	I
Southeastern Louisiana University, LA	D,I
Southeastern University, FL	I
Southeast Missouri State University, MO	D,I
Southern Adventist University, TN	D,I,P
Southern Arkansas University–Magnolia, AR	I
Southern Connecticut State University, CT	D,I
Southern Illinois University Carbondale, IL	G,I
Southern Illinois University Edwardsville, IL	G,I
Southern Methodist University, TX	I,P
Southern Utah University, UT	I
Southwest Baptist University, MO	I
Southwestern College, KS	I
Southwestern University, TX	I
Southwest Minnesota State University, MN	I
Spring Arbor University, MI	I
Spring Hill College, AL	I
Stanford University, CA	I
State University of New York at Fredonia, NY	I
State University of New York at New Paltz, NY	I
State University of New York at Oswego, NY	I
State University of New York at Plattsburgh, NY	D,I
State University of New York College at Geneseo, NY	D,I
State University of New York College at Old Westbury, NY	I
State University of New York College at Oneonta, NY	I
State University of New York College at Potsdam, NY	I
State University of New York College of Environmental Science and Forestry, NY	D,I
State University of New York College of Technology at Canton, NY	D,I
State University of New York College of Technology at Delhi, NY	I
State University of New York Upstate Medical University, NY	I
Stephen F. Austin State University, TX	I
Stephens College, MO	I
Sterling College, VT	I
Stetson University, FL	I
Stevenson University, MD	D,I
Stillman College, AL	D
Stonehill College, MA	I,P
Stony Brook University, State University of New York, NY	I
Suffolk University, MA	D,I
Susquehanna University, PA	I,P

Swarthmore College, PA	I
Syracuse University, NY	I
Tabor College, KS	I
Tarleton State University, TX	I
Taylor University, IN	I
Temple University, PA	I
Tennessee Technological University, TN	I
Tennessee Wesleyan College, TN	D,I
Texas A&M University, TX	I
Texas A&M University–Commerce, TX	I
Texas A&M University–Corpus Christi, TX	I
Texas Christian University, TX	I,P
Texas College, TX	I
Texas Lutheran University, TX	I
Texas State University–San Marcos, TX	I
Texas Tech University, TX	I
Texas Woman's University, TX	I
Thiel College, PA	I
Thomas Aquinas College, CA	I
Thomas More College, KY	D,I
Tiffin University, OH	I
Towson University, MD	G,I,P
Transylvania University, KY	I
Trevecca Nazarene University, TN	I,P
Trine University, IN	I
Trinity Christian College, IL	I
Trinity College, CT	I
Trinity College of Nursing and Health Sciences, IL	D,I
Trinity University, TX	I
Troy University, AL	I
Truman State University, MO	I
Tufts University, MA	I,P
Tulane University, LA	I,P
Tusculum College, TN	I
Tuskegee University, AL	I
Union College, KY	I
Union College, NY	I
Union University, TN	D,I
Universidad Adventista de las Antillas, PR	G,I,P
University at Albany, State University of New York, NY	I
University at Buffalo, the State University of New York, NY	I
University of Advancing Technology, AZ	I
The University of Akron, OH	I
The University of Alabama, AL	D,I
The University of Alabama in Huntsville, AL	I
University of Alaska Fairbanks, AK	I
University of Arkansas, AR	I
University of Bridgeport, CT	D,I
University of California, Berkeley, CA	I
University of California, Davis, CA	D
University of California, Irvine, CA	I
University of California, Riverside, CA	D
University of California, Santa Barbara, CA	I
University of California, Santa Cruz, CA	D,I
University of Central Arkansas, AR	I
University of Central Florida, FL	D,P

Tuition Payment Alternatives

University of Central Missouri, MO	D,I	University of Mobile, AL	I	The University of Tampa, FL	I
University of Central Oklahoma, OK	D,G,I	The University of Montana Western, MT	D	The University of Tennessee, TN	I
University of Charleston, WV	I	University of Montevallo, AL	I	The University of Tennessee at Chattanooga, TN	D
University of Chicago, IL	I,P	University of Mount Union, OH	I,P	The University of Tennessee at Martin, TN	D
University of Cincinnati, OH	I	University of Nebraska at Kearney, NE	I	The University of Texas at Arlington, TX	I
University of Colorado at Boulder, CO	D	University of Nebraska at Omaha, NE	D,I	The University of Texas at Austin, TX	I
University of Colorado at Colorado Springs, CO	I	University of Nebraska–Lincoln, NE	I	The University of Texas at Brownsville, TX	I
University of Colorado Denver, CO	D,I	University of Nevada, Las Vegas, NV	D	The University of Texas at Dallas, TX	G,I
University of Connecticut, CT	D,I	University of Nevada, Reno, NV	D	The University of Texas at San Antonio, TX	D,I
University of Dallas, TX	I	University of New Hampshire, NH	I	The University of Texas at Tyler, TX	I
University of Dayton, OH	D	University of New Haven, CT	I	The University of Texas Health Science Center at Houston, TX	I
University of Delaware, DE	I	University of New Orleans, LA	D,I	
University of Denver, CO	D	University of North Alabama, AL	I	The University of Texas Medical Branch, TX	I
University of Dubuque, IA	I	The University of North Carolina at Asheville, NC	I	
University of Evansville, IN	I			The University of Texas of the Permian Basin, TX	I
The University of Findlay, OH	I	The University of North Carolina at Chapel Hill, NC	D,I	
University of Georgia, GA	G			The University of Texas–Pan American, TX	I
University of Great Falls, MT	I	The University of North Carolina at Charlotte, NC	I	
University of Hartford, CT	I,P			University of the District of Columbia, DC	D,I
University of Houston, TX	I	The University of North Carolina at Greensboro, NC	I	
University of Houston–Clear Lake, TX	D,I			University of the Incarnate Word, TX	I
		The University of North Carolina at Pembroke, NC	I	University of the Ozarks, AR	I
University of Houston–Downtown, TX	I			University of the Pacific, CA	D
University of Idaho, ID	D,I	University of North Carolina School of the Arts, NC	I	University of the Sciences in Philadelphia, PA	I,P
University of Illinois at Chicago, IL	G,I			
University of Illinois at Springfield, IL	G,I	The University of North Carolina Wilmington, NC	I	University of the Southwest, NM	D
University of Illinois at Urbana–Champaign, IL	G,I	University of North Dakota, ND	D	The University of Toledo, OH	I
		University of Northern Colorado, CO	D	University of Tulsa, OK	I,P
The University of Iowa, IA	I	University of Northern Iowa, IA	I	University of Vermont, VT	D,I
The University of Kansas, KS	G,I	University of North Florida, FL	I	University of Virginia, VA	I
University of Kentucky, KY	I	University of North Texas, TX	I	The University of Virginia's College at Wise, VA	D,I
University of La Verne, CA	D,I	University of Notre Dame, IN	I	
University of Louisville, KY	I	University of Oklahoma, OK	G,I	University of Washington, Tacoma, WA	I
University of Maine, ME	I	University of Oregon, OR	I	
University of Maine at Presque Isle, ME	D,I	University of Pennsylvania, PA	I,P	University of West Florida, FL	D,P
		University of Pittsburgh, PA	D,I	University of Wisconsin–Eau Claire, WI	I
University of Mary, ND	I	University of Pittsburgh at Bradford, PA	I	
University of Mary Hardin-Baylor, TX	I			University of Wisconsin–Green Bay, WI	I
University of Maryland, Baltimore County, MD	I	University of Pittsburgh at Greensburg, PA	I	University of Wisconsin–La Crosse, WI	I
		University of Pittsburgh at Johnstown, PA	I	University of Wisconsin–Parkside, WI	I
University of Maryland, College Park, MD	D,I	University of Portland, OR	D,I	University of Wisconsin–River Falls, WI	I
University of Maryland University College, MD	I	University of Puerto Rico at Bayamón, PR	D,G	
		University of Puerto Rico, Río Piedras, PR	D	University of Wisconsin–Stevens Point, WI	I
University of Mary Washington, VA	I			University of Wisconsin–Stout, WI	I
University of Massachusetts Amherst, MA	I	University of Puget Sound, WA	D,I	University of Wisconsin–Superior, WI	I
		University of Redlands, CA	I	University of Wisconsin–Whitewater, WI	I
University of Massachusetts Boston, MA	I	University of Rhode Island, RI	I	
		University of Richmond, VA	D,I	University of Wyoming, WY	I
University of Massachusetts Dartmouth, MA	I	University of Rochester, NY	I,P	Ursinus College, PA	I
		University of St. Francis, IL	D,I	Ursuline College, OH	I
University of Massachusetts Lowell, MA	I	University of Saint Francis, IN	D,I	Utah State University, UT	D
		University of St. Thomas, TX	D,I	Utah Valley University, UT	D,I
University of Memphis, TN	I	University of San Diego, CA	I	Utica College, NY	D,I
University of Miami, FL	D,I,P	University of Science and Arts of Oklahoma, OK	G,I	Valparaiso University, IN	D,I
University of Michigan, MI	I			Vanderbilt University, TN	I,P
University of Michigan–Dearborn, MI	I	The University of Scranton, PA	I	Vanguard University of Southern California, CA	I
University of Michigan–Flint, MI	I	University of South Alabama, AL	I	
University of Minnesota, Crookston, MN	G,I	University of South Carolina, SC	D,I	Vassar College, NY	I
		The University of South Dakota, SD	D	Vermont Technical College, VT	I
University of Minnesota, Duluth, MN	I	University of Southern California, CA	I,P	Victory University, TN	I
University of Minnesota, Morris, MN	I	University of Southern Indiana, IN	I	Villa Maria College of Buffalo, NY	I
University of Minnesota, Twin Cities Campus, MN	I	University of Southern Mississippi, MS	I	
University of Missouri, MO	I			
University of Missouri–Kansas City, MO	I			
University of Missouri–St. Louis, MO	I			

D = deferred payment system; *G* = guaranteed tuition rate; *I* = installment payments; *P* = prepayment locks in tuition rate

www.facebook.com/pay4undergrad

Villanova University, PA	I	Wells College, NY	I	Wheelock College, MA	I
Virginia Commonwealth University, VA	I	Wesleyan University, CT	I	Whitman College, WA	D
Virginia Intermont College, VA	I	West Chester University of Pennsylvania, PA	I	Wichita State University, KS	I
Virginia Military Institute, VA	I	Western Carolina University, NC	I	Widener University, PA	I
Virginia Union University, VA	D,I	Western Connecticut State University, CT	I	Wilkes University, PA	D,I
Virginia University of Lynchburg, VA	I			Willamette University, OR	I,P
Virginia Wesleyan College, VA	D,I	Western Illinois University, IL	G	William Carey University, MS	D
Wabash College, IN	I,P	Western International University, AZ	D	William Jewell College, MO	I
Waldorf College, IA	D,I	Western Kentucky University, KY	I	William Paterson University of New Jersey, NJ	I
Warner Pacific College, OR	I	Western New England College, MA	I,P	Williams Baptist College, AR	I
Wartburg College, IA	I	Western New Mexico University, NM	I	Williams College, MA	I
Washburn University, KS	I	Western Oregon University, OR	D,G	Wilson College, PA	I
Washington & Jefferson College, PA	D,I	Western State College of Colorado, CO	D,I	Winona State University, MN	I
Washington University in St. Louis, MO	I,P	Western Washington University, WA	I	Winthrop University, SC	I
		Westfield State College, MA	I	Wittenberg University, OH	I
Watkins College of Art, Design, & Film, TN	I	West Liberty University, WV	D,I	Wofford College, SC	I
Wayland Baptist University, TX	I	Westminster College, MO	I	Worcester Polytechnic Institute, MA	D,I
Waynesburg University, PA	I	Westminster College, UT	D,I	Worcester State College, MA	I
Wayne State College, NE	I	West Suburban College of Nursing, IL	I	Xavier University, OH	D,I
Wayne State University, MI	I	West Virginia University, WV	I	Xavier University of Louisiana, LA	I
Webber International University, FL	I	West Virginia Wesleyan College, WV	I	Yale University, CT	I
Webster University, MO	I	Wheaton College, IL	D,I	York College, NE	I
Wellesley College, MA	I,P	Wheaton College, MA	I,P	York College of Pennsylvania, PA	I,P
				Youngstown State University, OH	I

Notes

Notes

Notes

Notes

Notes

Notes

Notes

Notes